THE OXFORD COMPANION TO

edited by

JULIA HARDING AND
JANCIS ROBINSON

EDITED BY

julia HARDING AND jancis ROBINSON

THE OXFORD COMPANION *to*

Assistant Editor
TARA Q THOMAS

Advisory Editor, Viticulture
RICHARD E SMART

Advisory Editor, Oenology
VALÉRIE LAVIGNE

OXFORD
UNIVERSITY PRESS

Great Clarendon Street, Oxford, OX2 6DP,
United Kingdom

Oxford University Press is a department of the University of Oxford.
It furthers the University's objective of excellence in research, scholarship,
and education by publishing worldwide. Oxford is a registered trade mark of
Oxford University Press in the UK and in certain other countries

First Edition published in 1994
Second Edition published in 1999
Third Edition published in 2006
Fourth Edition published in 2015
Fifth Edition published in 2023

Published in the United States of America by Oxford University Press
198 Madison Avenue, New York, NY 10016, United States of America

British Library Cataloguing in Publication Data
Data available

Library of Congress Control Number: 2022951041

ISBN 978-0-19-887131-6

Printed by Sheridan, United States of America

CONTENTS

PREFACE

Editor's preface

A companion is a wonderful thing, and this one is no exception. Its unique combination of depth, breadth, and links between subjects makes it a perfect companion for anyone travelling through the world of wine, for those who are fascinated by it and those who just love it, for pleasure seekers as much as for students.

If you already own a copy, why should you buy this 5th edition of *The Oxford Companion to Wine*? Because the world, and the world of wine, has changed a great deal in the eight years since the 4th edition was published, and every single entry has been reviewed and updated to reflect those changes. The greatest challenge is knowing that even before the ink is dry we will have started a file on possible updates for the 6th edition.

Such changes take us in many directions that are frequently interconnected in the wines we drink. In revised and new entries we have tried to explain advances in scientific and technological understanding that influence the way wine is made and consumed. At the same time, we have recorded the increasingly common and necessary efforts winegrowers around the world are making to care for and regenerate the land in which wine is rooted.

This diversity has taken us to the past and the future, requiring new entries on subjects such as artificial intelligence, biogenic amines, biologicals, blockchain, paper bottles, regenerative viticulture, underwater ageing, and many more. (For a complete list of new entries, see pp. xxiii–xxiv.)

The greatest change we face in wine as in all else is climate change, so it is not surprising that its repercussions are threaded throughout the book and discussed not just in climate-related entries but also in those that describe the regions most affected, either by extremes such as wildfires, drought, and flooding or because of changes in vineyard location or grape varieties planted. Our regional contributors attest to the creeping spread of vineyards to northerly and southerly regions once thought too cool or otherwise unsuitable for viticulture, as well as the ascent to elevations where only mad optimists had previously planted vines (see, for example, the new or expanded entries on Estonia, Finland, Gabon, Latvia, Mexico, Norway, Senegal, Uganda, and Vermont). While the vine has a remarkable ability to adapt, some vineyards have (or may) become too hot, too dry, or too prone to disease to keep producing the style of wine we expect from them, hence our coverage of the growing interest in new wine-grape varieties and the changes in regulations that allow them to be planted.

In addition to bringing the book up to date in every nook and cranny of the wine world, we have taken a scalpel to many of the entries, especially the long geographical ones that covered an entire country, to break them down into more manageable and accessible sections that reflect the names found on wine labels. Along with our scrutiny of all the cross-references that take the reader from entry to entry (for more detail or an explanation of a term), this has made the book easier to navigate and, we hope, even harder to put down, as one entry leads to another across regions and topics. (For a full list of entries grouped by region and topic, see pp. xxix–lii.)

While this edition is only marginally longer overall—the extra 25,000 words taking it to just over one million for the first time—it includes 310 new entries, bringing the total number to 4,489 (including the 335 brief ones that are signposts to other entries). The number of contributors has also expanded, with 109 technical and regional specialists writing for the first time in this edition, bringing the tally of contributors to 267. This has brought an immeasurable increase in depth and accuracy, and we are grateful to every one of them. (See the list of contributors on pp. ix–xix.)

During more than two years of long days and many sleepless nights, what motivated me was not just the impending deadline but also the reminder every time I sipped a delicious wine that this is what the book is all about: an invaluable companion to the liquid in your glass.

When in 1999 I queued up at a bookshop in Bristol to have my copy of the second edition signed by Jancis, my constant inspiration, I had no inkling that just over 20 years later she would pass to me the baton of lead editor for this edition.

I could not have run with it without Jancis's trust in me, built over many years of working and writing together, and her willingness not only to be responsible for reviewing and updating some of the topics but also to guide and advise me when my confidence waned.

Equally, I could not have taken on this weighty responsibility had I not been able to work so closely—albeit physically separated by the Atlantic Ocean—with Tara Q. Thomas, a brilliant assistant editor and great friend who brought not only her editorial skills, global wine knowledge, and diplomacy to this complex task but also her invaluable North American perspective. We may have had to negotiate on many occasions between British and US English to make sure the language of the book is as universally comprehensible as possible, but in every other respect we have seen eye to eye. This has helped to make the book less European and even more truly international—much like wine itself.

The team at OUP, especially Jamie Mortimer, Jo Payne, and Jo Spillane have kept us on the straight and narrow, and we are grateful for their guidance and support.

A few months before I started to climb this wine mountain, I met Deidre Correa, the woman who was to become my wife in September 2022, just a few weeks after I handed in these one million words. Her love, patience, and support have nourished me, both physically and emotionally.

J.E.H.

Founding editor's preface

I have known Julia Harding ever since she turned up on my doorstep in 1998 and said she wanted to work for me. She was then a particularly punctilious copy-editor who had caught the wine bug. I was very impressed by her but sent her away, explaining that I was a control freak who was highly unlikely ever to employ anyone.

In 2001 she joined the wine department of Britain's smartest supermarket group, where she was responsible for what they published about wine. It was during this time that she embarked on the fiendishly difficult Master of Wine programme, culminating in exams with a notoriously low pass rate. In the shortest time possible she passed both theoretical and practical (blind tasting) parts of the exam on her first attempt in 2003 and was chosen as the top student of her year after submitting, and receiving a distinction for, her dissertation in 2004.

At that point I realized I should accept her offer of assisting me like a shot, and so, since 19 December 2005, we have worked side by side, with my admiration for her skills deepening by the day. That 'side by side' is meant in a decidedly 21st-century sense. Although we both live in London, we each work at home and find ourselves in the same room only four or five times a year, most notably at the JancisRobinson.com Christmas dinner. Our communication is mainly by email: many, many emails practically every day.

This communication ground to a near halt for much of 2021 and 2022, however, when I persuaded Julia to take over lead editorship of *The Oxford Companion to Wine* from me. I had been, solo, responsible for the first two editions. And in 2001 Julia had demonstrated her mastery of an *Oxford Companion* manuscript by miraculously condensing the second edition into a *Concise* version. So I knew that when, after completing the fourth edition, I felt my memory was no longer up to marshalling over 4,000 entries totalling almost a million words, Julia was the ideal person to take over as lead editor. She had already proved the most brilliant editor of the viticultural and oenological entries in the third and fourth editions in which she undertook much of the overall editing responsibility anyway.

I was thrilled therefore when she agreed to take on the mammoth task of being in charge of the fifth edition, and I was equally delighted by her choice of assistant editor. Julia and Tara Q. Thomas had already travelled together and bonded over their shared love of Greek wine and high editorial standards. Tara worked for 25 years applying these high standards to the American publication *Wine & Spirits* and agreed to take time off to assist Julia in the two years it takes to put one of these massive reference books together. Tara was responsible for updating all the regional entries (about 40% of the book), while Julia took charge of 50% of the text, including viticulture, oenology, grape varieties, history, packaging, and labelling. I updated the remaining 10% of entries—a very much lighter task that included topics such as people, tasting, and wine and the consumer.

I am hugely grateful to both Julia and Tara for understanding the importance of this book, for maintaining an edifice of great complexity, and, in many instances, giving it a much-needed spring clean. I am confident that this fifth edition is the best yet and am so proud to see the special place it occupies on the shelves of countless wine lovers and wine students the world over. They will not be disappointed this time around. J.R.

CONTRIBUTORS

Advisory Viticulture Editor:

Dr Richard E. Smart

Advisory Oenology Editor:

Dr Valérie Lavigne

Previous Oenology Editors:

Professor A. Dinsmoor Webb, Dr Patrick J. Williams, and Professor Denis Dubourdieu

Contributors are listed in alphabetical order by their initials. MW stands for master of wine, MS for master sommelier, DipWSET for the wset Diploma, CM for Order of Canada, CBE for Commander of the British Empire, OBE for Order of the British Empire, AM for Member of the Order of Australia, and OAM for Medal of the Order of Australia. Unsigned entries are written by the editors Julia Harding, Jancis Robinson, or Tara Q. Thomas. Where several contributors are named at the end of an entry, the initials of the most recent contributor are given last. Initials of contributors to earlier editions are retained unless the entry has been completely rewritten.

A.A. Alberto Antonini studied in Florence, Bordeaux, and at UC davis. A roving consultant winemaker, he has made wine in California, Argentina, Chile, Spain, Portugal, South Africa, Canada, Romania, Armenia, Israel, Uruguay, Australia, and his native Italy.

A.B. Anthony Borneman is a Research Manager at the awri and an Affiliate of the University of Adelaide. He leads research that is focused on applying genomics to understand the genetic basis of biological diversity in winemaking, including grapevines, commercial wine yeast and bacteria, and wild ferments.

A.C. Andrew Corrigan MW is based in Brisbane, Australia, and is manager/part owner of Hidden Creek Winery. President of the Queensland Wine Industry Association, wine consultant, educator, writer, judge, and the author of *Table Talk*, a book about the social aspects of wine, he is also a chartered civil engineer.

A.C.S. Dr Amanda Stewart worked in the wine industry in Oregon and New Zealand before taking up her current post as Associate Professor of Enology and Fermentation at virginia tech, where her research and teaching programmes are focused on wine and cider fermentation.

A.D. Abi Duhr studied oenology at geisenheim university and the University of bordeaux. He lives and works in Luxembourg, where he is owner of Ch Pauqué and runs a wine import company.

A.D.W. The late A. Dinsmoor Webb, Oenology Editor of the first edition of this book, retired in 1982 as Professor Emeritus from UC davis and then continued to write and to act as consultant oenologist worldwide.

A.F. Alice Feiring has written six books on wine and culture and has been a leading authority on natural wine for several decades.

A.H. Alex Hunt MW is a London-based wine merchant with a particular interest in the philosophy and language of tasting, on which he has been extensively published.

A.H.L.R. Anthony Rose, wine correspondent for the British newspapers *The Independent* and *i* (1986–2016), author of *Sake and the Wines of Japan* and *Fizz! Champagne and Sparkling Wines of the World*, and a regular contributor on wine auctions and investment for a wide range of publications. He is a founder member of thewinegang.com.

A.H.P. Alexander Purcell is Emeritus Professor of Entomology at the University of California at Berkeley. His research focused on Pierce's disease and other bacterial diseases of plants spread by insect vectors.

A.J.B. Amanda Barnes is author of the *South America Wine Guide*. She has been based in Argentina since 2009, although she travels frequently on assignments for *Decanter*, *Around the World in 80 Harvests*, and other wine and travel publications.

A.J.D. Anne Duggan is Emeritus Professor of Medieval History at King's College, University of London.

A.J.M. Alex Maltman is Emeritus Professor of Earth Sciences at Aberystwyth University. For nearly 40 years, in addition to teaching and research, he has grown vines and made wine as a hobby and travelled the world's vineyards. He has contributed articles on vineyard geology to both popular magazines and scientific journals and is the author of *Vineyards, Rocks, and Soils: The Wine Lover's Guide to Geology*.

A.L. Anthony Lynch is a California-based importer of French and Italian wines at Kermit Lynch Wine Merchant, the company founded by his father, Kermit Lynch. Raised partially in Provence, he takes a special interest in the wines of the Mediterranean.

A.L.W. Andrew Waterhouse is Professor of Enology and Director of the Robert Mondavi Institute at UC davis, where he previously served as Chair of the Department of Viticulture and Enology. He is a widely published wine chemist, studying phenolics, oxidation, and other topics, and is co-author of *Understanding Wine Chemistry*.

A.M. Angela Muir MW joined John Harvey & Sons in Bristol in 1970 and has since been a consultant for importers and retailers in Britain and France and for producers across Europe and South America. A former trustee of the wset, she has retired to Cyprus.

A.M.R. Arnica Rowan was a professor specializing in sustainable business and is now a private researcher and strategist in the Canadian wine industry.

A.O. Dr Anita Oberholster is a Professor in Cooperative Extension in Enology at the Department of Viticulture and Enology at UC davis. She obtained her first degree in chemistry from stellenbosch university and her PhD in Wine Sciences at the University of adelaide in 2008.

A.P. Dr Andrei Prida, a chemistry graduate of the University of St Petersburg, gained his doctorate from inra Montpellier before postdoctorate studies at UC davis and Miami University. He joined Tonnellerie Seguin Moreau as Head of Research and Development in 2006 and co-ordinates their research in collaboration with the isvv in Bordeaux and other leading institutions.

A.R. Andrés Rosberg is the past president of the Argentine, Pan-American, and International Sommelier Associations. He is a leading wine writer, educator, and judge in his native Argentina.

A.R.P. Andrea Pritzker MW is the founder of Wine inTuition, a wine education and corporate-events business in Sydney, Australia. A certified wset educator, she also works as an independent wine consultant, wine judge, writer, and public speaker.

A.S. Annette Scarfe MW became a Master of Wine in 2012. A wine consultant, she runs tastings and classes for trade and consumers both at home in Singapore and internationally. She also judges at wine competitions across four continents.

A.S.M. Adam Sebag Montefiore worked in the English wine trade before moving to Israel. He has since worked in the Israeli wine industry for 35 years. He is the wine writer for the *Jerusalem Post* and co-author of *The Wine Route of Israel* and *Wines of Israel*.

A.Y. Alder Yarrow is a California-based wine writer, critic, and author of Vinography.com. He is a regular columnist and contributor to JancisRobinson.com, as well as various other wine publications, and the author of the 2014 book *The Essence of Wine*.

B.B. Dr Benjamin Bois is Associate Professor at the Institute of Vine and Wine (IUVV) in dijon. His research at the biogeosciences lab focuses on climate/viticulture relationships. He was president of the Viticulture Commission of the oiv from 2015 to 2018.

B.C. Professor Barry Cunliffe CBE is Emeritus Professor of European Archaeology at the Institute of Archaeology, University of Oxford.

B.C.S. Professor Barry C. Smith is the Director of the Institute of Philosophy at the School of Advanced Study, University of London, and director of The Centre for the Study of the Senses. He has published articles on the multisensory perception of flavour in *Nature*, *Food Quality and Preference*, *Flavour*, and *The World of Fine Wine*. He is editor of *Questions of Taste: The Philosophy of Wine* (2007) and has held visiting positions at the University of California at Berkeley and the École Normale Supérieure in Paris.

B.D. Barry Dick MW studied Food Science at Queens University, Belfast, and Oenology at the University of adelaide. He has made wine in Spain, California, Australia, and the Languedoc and at Château Mouton Rothschild and now acts as the Bulk Sourcing Manager for UK retailer Waitrose.

B.G.C. The late Dr Bryan Coombe was an author, lecturer, and researcher who specialized in grapevine physiology at Waite Agricultural Research Institute, Adelaide. The American Society of Enology and Viticulture awarded him Best Viticulture Paper of the Year 1987 and Best Enology Paper of the Year in 1991.

B.M.W. The late Dr Bernard Watney was initially a physician, but his many interests included wine, wine labels, and corkscrews. He co-wrote *Corkscrews for Collectors*, which has since been translated into French and German.

B.Y.-I. Becca Yeamans-Irwin uses her background in wine science and the environment to dissect, review, and provide commentary on current research in fields in or related to oenology and viticulture at AcademicWino.com. She lives in North Carolina.

C.A. Chloe Ashton is COO of Wine Lister and the auctions and secondary-market correspondent for *The World of Fine Wine* magazine.

C.A.S. Con Simos is a winemaker and Group Manager—Industry Development and Support at the awri. He leads a group of winemakers, viticulturists, and technical specialists who disseminate research results and provide support to the Australian grape and wine sector.

C.B.S. Carlos Borboa Suaréz is a Mexico-based journalist, sommelier, and director of the wine and spirits competition México Selection by Concours Mondial de Bruxelles.

C.C. Dr Christoph Carlen, Master in Agronomy in Plant Production Sciences and PhD in Plant Physiology at the ETH Zurich, is Head of the agroscope Plant Production Systems division and member of the Agroscope board.

C.C.F. Christopher Fielden is a retired British wine merchant and collector of wine books.

C.G. Dr Caroline Gilby MW has a special interest in the wines of Central and Eastern Europe. Her first book, *The Wines of Bulgaria, Romania and Moldova*, won the oiv prize in 2020. She contributes to several major wine reference books, magazines, and websites.

C.H.-C. Curly Haslam-Coates is a Tasmania-based wine educator, writer, and sparkling-wine specialist. As an industry ambassador she encourages others to enter meaningful careers in wine, tourism, and hospitality, with a particularly strong focus on inclusive industry representation and access to education and wine networks.

C.O. Claudio Olla DipWSET is a banker by profession but has been deeply immersed in the wine world for two decades, particularly on his native Sardinia. A wine consultant, wset-accredited educator, and judge, he also contributed to the *World Atlas of Wine* (8th edn, 2019).

C.P. Catherine Petrie MW is a buyer for UK fine-wine merchant Lay & Wheeler. She specializes in Burgundy and the Loire, both regions where she has extensive vineyard and winemaking experience, including two vintages in Sancerre.

C.R.H. Charles R. Hajdamach is one of the UK's top authorities on glass. He lectures internationally and writes extensively on the subject. His books *British Glass 1800–1914* and *20th Century British Glass* remain the standard works on those subjects. In 2000 he was elected a Fellow of the Society of Glass Technology.

C.S.S. Dr Creina Stockley is a clinical pharmacologist actively involved in research into the health effects of wine and wine-derived phenolic compounds, as well as in the preparation of alcohol policy and regulation. Currently Principal of Stockley Health and Regulatory Solutions, she was Health and Regulatory Information Manager at the AWRI from 1991 to 2018. She was also elected President of the OIV Commission IV Safety and Health in 2012, receiving the OIV Merit award in 2019.

C.v.L. Cornelis (Kees) van Leeuwen is Professor of Viticulture at Bordeaux Sciences Agro and the ISVV in Bordeaux. He was the viticulturist at Château CHEVAL BLANC in St-Émilion for 25 years and has written extensively on various aspects of terroir, soil, and wine quality. He is editor in chief of *OENO One*, the open-access journal of vine and wine sciences.

D.A.D. Dr Donald Dibbern is a retired physician specializing in the diagnosis and treatment of allergic diseases and a Fellow of the American Academy of Allergy Asthma and Immunology.

D.A.H. David A. Harvey is a UK wine importer and sometimes writes about wine, including a history of ethical wine farming. He started as a sommelier before working for Frank Cornelissen on Mt Etna in 2004.

D.B. David Bird MW is a Chartered Chemist and a Member of the Institute of Quality Assurance. He has audited wineries throughout Europe and lectures on winemaking techniques. His publications include *Understanding Wine Technology*, now in its fourth edition.

D.Ca. Dario Cantù, plant biologist and Professor of Systems Biology at UC DAVIS since 2012, specializing in grape genomics and grape–microbe interactions.

D.C.G. David Gleave MW is Chairman of Liberty Wines, a London-based wine importer and distributor. He has been extensively involved with Italian wines since 1983, spending three months of every year in Italy.

D.Co. Danilo Costamagna is from Piemonte, Italy, where his grandfather had a small vineyard, but he has lived since 2002 in Norway, where he runs Norsk Vin winery. He has been the head of the Norwegian Grape Growers Association (Foreningen Norske Druedyrkere) since 2020.

D.D. The late Dr Denis Dubourdieu, Advisory Oenology Co-editor of the fourth edition of this book, was a well-travelled winemaker, owner of six Bordeaux wine estates, and renowned Professor of Oenology and research scientist at the University of BORDEAUX who had a particularly significant influence on white winemaking throughout France and abroad.

D.De. Dr Daniel Deckers holds a PhD in Catholic theology, is a senior political editor of the *Frankfurter Allgemeine Zeitung*, teaches as associate scientist at GEISENHEIM UNIVERSITY, and is devoted to the cultural history of German wine.

D.F. Doug Frost MW MS is a Kansas City author who is one of only three people in the world to be both a Master Sommelier and a Master of Wine. He specializes in wines from America's less famous wine-producing states and owns Echolands Winery, based in Walla Walla, Washington.

D.G. Denis Gastin is a widely published Australian-based wine writer, wine judge, and wine educator who has been has been closely monitoring the evolution of the wine industry in Asia for over 30 years.

D.J. Dr Dan Johnson is Pro Vice-Chancellor, Research, Innovation, and Enterprise, at Macquarie University.

D.L.C. Dr Dimitra Capone, an ARC Research Associate with the University of ADELAIDE, has studied many aspects of wine flavour chemistry, including 20 years of experience at the AWRI. She was awarded the 2013 Early Career (Life and Environmental Sciences) SA Science Excellence Award.

D.M. Dave McIntyre is a freelance wine journalist and weekly wine columnist for *The Washington Post.* He was co-founder of a movement called 'Drink Local Wine'.

D.P. Daniel Pambianchi is a winemaking lecturer and consultant and the author of *Modern Home Winemaking* and *Techniques in Home Winemaking.* He is an amateur and professional winemaker, having owned and operated a small commercial winery in Niagara Wine Country in Ontario.

D.P.G. Dr Dylan Grigg runs his own viticulture consultancy in premium wine regions across Australia and overseas. His PhD thesis investigating grapevine age leads him into many old vineyards, including his own.

D.S. David Schildknecht trained in philosophy but has since 1978 worked as restaurateur, retailer, importer, and writer. His coverage of diverse regions has appeared in Stephen Tanzer's *International Wine Cellar*, *Robert Parker Wine Advocate*, and, since 2015, *Vinous.* He is a columnist with *The World of Fine Wine* and Austria's *Vinaria.*

D.V.J. Dirceu Vianna Junior MW is a Brazil-born, London-based wine expert with three decades of experience in the wine industry. He is the founder of Vianna Wine Resources, a wine consulting company, as well as a wine judge, educator, writer, and frequent speaker at global wine events.

E.A.G. Elizabeth Gabay MW has been in the wine trade since 1986. Based in south-eastern France since 2002, she specializes in the wines of southern France and Central Europe and in rosé, on which she published a book in 2018.

E.C. Ed Carr is Group Sparkling Winemaker at Accolade Wines (formerly BRL Hardy), having previously held the same position at Penfolds. In 2018 he received the lifetime achievement award at the Champagne and Sparkling Wine World Championships.

E.C.B. Elaine Chukan Brown is a writer, speaker, and global wine educator specializing in sustainability, diversity, and American wine.

E.J.B. Dr Eveline Bartowsky is R & D Manager and Applied Microbiologist at Lallemand Australia in Adelaide. She is a specialist in malolactic conversion and wine bacteria and fermentation research.

E.L. Ella Lister, investment banker turned wine journalist (*World of Fine Wine*, *Financial Times*, *Decanter*) and entrepreneur, divides her time between London and Paris as she runs the wine department at French newspaper *Le Figaro* while continuing to head up UK-based consulting agency Wine Lister.

E.L.-L. Erica Landin-Löfving is a Swedish-American wine writer and the Chief Sustainability Officer at Vintage Wine Estates in Sonoma, California. She has an MSc in medical biology and has studied ESG (Environmental, Social, and Governance) at Berkeley Law.

E.L.L. ERIN LARKIN made Western Australia her area of expertise when she worked at the *Halliday Wine Companion*. A writer, judge, and presenter based in Perth, she is now the Australian Reviewer for *Robert Parker Wine Advocate*.

E.M. DR EDI MALETIĆ is a Professor at the University of Zagreb, where he is head of the Department of Viticulture and Enology. A specialist in grapevine genetics, he was one of the scientists who discovered the Croatian roots of Zinfandel/Tribidrag.

E.M.C.R. ELLA ROBINSON is Communication Manager at the AWRI.

E.M.G. EVAN GOLDSTEIN MS is a San Francisco–based wine educator and author of the critically acclaimed *Wines of South America: The Essential Guide*.

E.N.H.M. ED MERRISON is a British-born former journalist who has spent the best part of the past 20 years in Australia. A wine judge and Australian Dux of the WSET Diploma based in Victoria's Mornington Peninsula, he makes his living as a wine communicator and educator.

E.P. ERAN PICK MW is Israel's first Master of Wine. A graduate of UC DAVIS, he is general manager and winemaker at Tzora Vineyards.

E.P.-R. The late EDMUND PENNING-ROWSELL was one of the world's most respected wine writers and author of *The Wines of Bordeaux* (see his entry).

E.R. DR EDWARD RAGG MW is co-founder of Dragon Phoenix Wine Consulting, a former Tsinghua University professor, and reviewer of Chinese wines for the *Robert Parker Wine Advocate*. He is co-coordinator of the Institute of Masters of Wine's Australasian programme and a wine educator, wine writer, and published poet.

E.W. DR ERIC WILKES is the General Manager of Affinity Labs, the commercial arm of the AWRI, and has over 25 years of experience in technical research and management within the beverage industries. He specializes in wine chemistry and technical innovation, with a significant interest in environmental concerns.

F.C. FERRAN CENTELLES works for the elBulli-foundation and is the Spanish wine critic for JancisRobinson.com. Voted Best Sommelier in Spain in 2006, he has published three giant wine books.

F.W. FONGYEE WALKER MW is co-founder of Dragon Phoenix Wine Consulting (Beijing) and the first Master of Wine resident in mainland China. She specializes in Mandarin-language wine education and communication, is a frequent contributor to livestreams, podcasts, and media articles, and creates popular television programmes about wine.

G.C. GEOFF COWEY is a Senior Oenologist at the AWRI. A wine scientist, winemaker, wine educator, and wine writer, he manages the AWRI helpdesk, a service which provides advice on technical queries, problems, or knowledge gaps encountered by Australian grape-growers and winemakers.

G.C.P. DR GARY PAVLIS is a professor and agricultural agent at Rutgers University in New Jersey. He has served on the board of directors of the American Wine Society and regularly appears in print, on the radio, and on television educating the public on the intricacies of East Coast winegrowing.

G.K. DR GISELA KREGLINGER is an expert on the theology of wine and teaches at the University of Alabama at Birmingham. She leads wine pilgrimages, holds seminars on wine tasting as a spiritual practice, and is the author of *The Spirituality of Wine* and *The Soul of Wine*. She grew up at a winery in Germany.

G.L.C. DR GLEN CREASY, co-author of the CABI book *Grapes*, is a former lecturer and researcher who is now a viticultural consultant for Sabrosia SAS and part owner of Terre des 2 Sources winery in the Languedoc, France.

G.M. DR GABRIELLA MÉSZÁROS trained as a lawyer and now teaches and writes regularly about wine in Hungary. With her late husband, Dr Gábor Rohály, she published the *Hungarian Wineguide* for 16 years as well as several books on wine and gastronomy. They also founded the first WSET-accredited wine school in Budapest.

G.P. PROFESSOR GARY PICKERING received his doctorate in Wine Science from LINCOLN UNIVERSITY and is currently Professor of Biological Sciences and Psychology at BROCK UNIVERSITY, as well as Adjunct Professor at CHARLES STURT UNIVERSITY. His research includes wine flavour, taste genetics, and climate-change adaptation.

G.R. The late DR GÁBOR ROHÁLY was a physician, a founding member of the Hungarian Wine Academy, and a wine writer who is widely credited with developing Hungary's wine vocabulary.

G.S. GAVIN SACKS is Professor of Food Science at CORNELL UNIVERSITY. His research programme is focused on developing and applying analytical tools for characterizing flavour compounds in wines and grapes, and he is co-author of *Understanding Wine Chemistry*.

G.T. GEOFF TAYLOR worked in the technical/analytical area of the UK wine trade for 25 years until his retirement in 2000. He founded the leading UK wine analysis and consultancy laboratories, now part of Campden BRI, the world's largest independent technical/laboratory-based organization for the food and drink industry.

G.V.I. GIDO VAN IMSCHOOT MS is President of the Flemish Sommelier Association and was European Ambassador of Champagne in 2012. Founder and director of Wine Academy Panta Rhei in Roeselare, he also lectures and has written six books on wine.

G.V.J. DR GREG JONES runs Abacela Vineyards and Winery in the Umpqua Valley, Oregon. After 25 years as a professor and leading research climatologist specializing in natural ecosystems and agriculture, he now conducts applied research for the grape and wine industry in Oregon. He has written widely on wine economics, grapevine phenology, climatological assessments of viticulture, and climate change.

H.A.C. HUGH ANDREW CAILLARD MW, former wine auctioneer, now a multimedia wine expert and historian. His books include *Penfolds: The Rewards of Patience*, *Marqués de Riscal: A Travel Through Time*, and *The Australian Ark* (2023), a three-volume work on the history of Australian wine.

H.B. DR HELEN BETTINSON, former Fellow of Fitzwilliam College, Cambridge, with a particular interest in historical research.

H.G. The late HOWARD G. GOLDBERG wrote for *The New York Times* and was an editor at the paper from 1970 to 2004.

H.G.B. The late BILL BAKER was a wine merchant and wine judge whose distinctive Reid Wines list was famously decorated with unusual vinous quotations and his wit.

H.H. HUON HOOKE is one of Australia's most respected wine writers. Based in Sydney, he makes his living entirely from writing, judging, and educating about wine. A journalist first and wine professional second, he has tertiary qualifications in both fields and has been writing on wine since 1983.

H.H.A. HAMISH AIRD, classicist and former Sub-Warden of Radley College, Oxfordshire, in England.

H.He. Dr Hildegarde Heymann is an author and Distinguished Professor of Sensory Science in the Department of Viticulture and Enology at UC davis. She has worked in all areas of sensory science and has evaluated numerous food and non-food products. Her main areas of expertise are descriptive analysis methodology and multivariate data analyses.

H.J. Hugh Johnson OBE is the world's most successful wine author and was introduced to specialist wine writing by the late André Simon (see entries on both).

H.L. Harriet Lembeck, certified wine and spirits educator based in New York, is a writer and a founder of the Society of Wine Educators.

H.M.W. Dr Hanneke Wilson is the author of *Wine and Words in Classical Antiquity and the Middle Ages*. She is the wine steward of two Oxford colleges, Exeter and Lincoln, and does a little work for wine merchant Haynes Hanson & Clark. She is also the coach of the Oxford University Blind-Tasting Society.

H.-P.H. Hans-Peter Hoehnen qualified at geisenheim university and worked in Australia, New Zealand, and his native Germany until 1997, when he moved to Thailand for three years. He is now a consultant in tropical viticulture and winemaking throughout South East Asia.

H.S. Professor Hans Schultz is President of geisenheim university. He was formerly the Director of the Geisenheim Research Institute and Professor of Viticulture. He has also worked and studied at charles sturt university, at ENSA/inra Montpellier, and at UC davis. Professor Schultz grew up on a wine estate in the Mosel Valley.

I.G.d.C.-A. Dr Iñaki Garcia de Cortazar-Atauri is a Research Engineer at inrae Agroclim. He graduated as an agronomist from the Universidad Publica de Navarra and completed his PhD at INRA. His current research focuses on the interaction between phenology and climate change. He co-ordinates TEMPO, the French National Network of Phenology Observatories, and is a member of the STICS Project team.

I.S. Ilkka Sirén is a wine writer, educator, and occasional wine judge based in Helsinki, Finland. He is a regular contributor to many Finnish wine, food, and lifestyle magazines such as *Viinilehti*, *Maku*, and *Anna*. Internationally, he has written for *Saveur*, *VICE*, and *Wine Enthusiast*, among others.

I.S.-B. Dr Irina Santiago-Brown is a global leader in sustainability in viticulture. Her PhD in grape-growing sustainability was the first in the world, and she developed the Sustainable Australia Winegrowing (SAW) programme. She and her husband Dudley Brown own Inkwell Wines in McLaren Vale, South Australia.

J.A. Dr Jean Aitchison is Emeritus Rupert Murdoch Professor of Language and Communication at the University of Oxford. She gave the Reith Lectures in 1996.

J.A.B. The late Dr Jeremy Black was Director of the British School of Archaeology in Iraq and later a Fellow of Wolfson College, Oxford, and university lecturer in Akkadian. He wrote several studies on Sumerian and Babylonian literature and ancient philology.

J.A.G. Dr Jamie Goode has a PhD in plant biology and for many years worked as a scientific editor. He publishes wineanorak.com and is wine writer for Britain's *Sunday Express*. His books include *Wine Science*, *I Taste Red*, and *Flawless*.

J.A.R. Jamal Awri Rayyis is a NYC-based writer, editor, and educator focused on the intersection of gastronomy, culture, and politics. A pioneer in covering Middle Eastern wine, he is at work on a book on the politics of wine in the Middle East.

J.-B.A. Jean-Baptiste Ancelot, the founder of Wine Explorers, has visited more than 85 countries, documenting their wine industries in his blog as well as in his book *Wine Explorers, le 1er tour du monde du vin* (2019).

J.B.-E. Jenne Baldwin-Eaton, a winemaker in Colorado for 27 years, developed the first Associates of Applied Science Viticulture and Enology programme at Western Colorado Community College, a division of Colorado Mesa University.

J.D. Dr Janet Dorozynski DipWSET has been working in and with the Canadian wine industry for over 20 years. An educator, writer, and wine judge, she writes for publications worldwide and has contributed Canadian content to wset's Global certification courses.

J.E.H. Julia Harding MW, editor of *The Oxford Companion to Wine*, studied modern languages at Cambridge before becoming a freelance book editor. She qualified as a Master of Wine in 2004, winning the Robert Mondavi award for best theory papers and the Tim Derouet Memorial Prize for excellence in all parts of the exam and dissertation. She is Senior Editor at JancisRobinson.com, where she has been a member of the team since 2005. She is cartographic editor of *The World Atlas of Wine* (8th edn, 2019) and co-author of *Wine Grapes* (2012).

J.F.B. Jon Bonné. the former wine editor of the *San Francisco Chronicle*, is author of *The New California Wine*, *The New French Wine*, and *The New Wine Rules*. He has also won three Roederer Awards for wine writing.

J.G. Dr John Gladstones, am, author of *Viticulture and Environment* (1992) and *Terroir and Climate Change* (2011), is former Senior Lecturer in the University of Western Australia Department of Agriculture.

J.H. James Halliday, oam, Australia's most prolific and most respected wine writer, an ex-lawyer who also found time to establish Coldstream Hills winery in the Yarra Valley.

J.H.B. Jullianne Ballou, Associate Director of Strategic Initiatives at UC davis Institute of the Environment, was previously the Warren Winiarski Fellow at the UC Davis Library, where she managed its Wine Writers Collection as well as food and wine collections.

J.H.H. Dr Judith Harvey became a medical practitioner after a distinguished career as a research scientist.

J.J.P. Jeremy Paterson, until retirement Senior Lecturer in Ancient History at the University of Newcastle-upon-Tyne, is a specialist in Roman economic and social history with a particular interest in the Roman wine trade, on which he has published.

J.K. Jeremy Kerswell studied Animal Science at Reading University and worked at several land-based colleges before being appointed Principal of Plumpton College, East Sussex, England, in 2015. He is also part of the Management Advisory Group for WineGB.

J.L. James Lawther MW is a Bordeaux-based wine writer for JancisRobinson.com whose works include *The Heart of Bordeaux* and *The Finest Wines of Bordeaux* as well as contributions to *On Bordeaux* and *Hugh Johnson's Pocket Wine Book*.

J.M.B. The late Michael Broadbent MW was founder of Christie's Wine Department and an author (see broadbent).

J.M.R. Dr Jane Renfrew (Lady Renfrew of Kaimsthorn) is a prehistorian and palaeoethnobotanist and is an Emeritus Fellow of Lucy Cavendish College, University of Cambridge, and a retired Affiliated Lecturer in the Department of Archaeology, University of Cambridge.

J.P. John Platter became a South African wine farmer and wine writer after a career as a foreign correspondent for United Press International. He and his wife Erica founded *Platter's South African Wine Guide*, which became the country's best-selling wine book, a position it has retained since they sold it in 1998. He is also author of *Africa Uncorked* and *My Kind of Wine*.

J.P.H.B. Dr John Barker is widely experienced in the field of wine regulation as a lawyer, consultant, and researcher. He was elected Director General of the OIV in 2023—the first person from the southern hemisphere to take this role. He is a former General Counsel for New Zealand Winegrowers, President of the OIV Law and Economy Commission, and Industry Chair of the WORLD WINE TRADE GROUP.

J.R. Jancis Robinson OBE MW, founding editor of *The Oxford Companion to Wine*, is one of the world's leading authorities on wine. The first person outside the wine trade to have passed the notoriously tough Master of Wine exams, she now writes weekly for the *Financial Times* and daily for JancisRobinson.com, which has members all over the world. Voted the first-ever International Wine Communicator of the Year in 1996, she has won multiple awards and written many books. Most recently she wrote *The 24-Hour Wine Expert* (2017), co-wrote *The World Atlas of Wine* (8th edn, 2019) and *Wine Grapes* (2012), and hosted the BBC Maestro online wine course *An Understanding of Wine*.

J.R.U.-T. Dr José Ramón Úrbez-Torres is a plant pathologist currently working as a Research Scientist for Agriculture and Agri-Food Canada in the Summerland Research and Development Centre in British Columbia. He is also an Adjunct Professor at the University of British Columbia Okanagan and Research Affiliate in the Cool Climate Oenology and Viticulture Institute at BROCK UNIVERSITY. His primary research focus is the etiology, biology, epidemiology, and control of fungal diseases of grapevines and fruit trees, with a special emphasis on grapevine trunk diseases.

J.T. James Tidwell MS is a writer and consultant in Texas. He founded TexSom, the biggest wine-trade education conference in the world, and produces one of the largest wine competitions in the United States. He sits on the Classic Wine Library editorial board and collects rare wine books.

J.T.C.M. Jasper Morris MW is author of the comprehensive book *Inside Burgundy* and runs the website of the same name. Previously he was a noted importer of Burgundy wines, firstly through his company Morris & Verdin Ltd and then with Berry Bros & Rudd.

J.V. Dr José Vouillamoz, Swiss grape geneticist, trained at UC DAVIS, specializing in the study of the origin and parentage of grape varieties through DNA profiling. Co-author with Jancis Robinson and Julia Harding of *Wine Grapes* (2012), he has also authored and co-authored scientific papers and other grape books. He is a member of the Académie Internationale du Vin and the Académie du Vin de Bordeaux.

K.A. Kym Anderson is the George Gollin Professor Emeritus of Economics and foundation Executive Director of the Wine Economics Research Centre at the University of Adelaide and an Honorary Professor of Economics at the Australian National University's Crawford School of Public Policy. His unrivalled global statistical compendia of winegrape plantings, national wine markets, and related e-books are freely available at https://economics.adelaide.edu.au/wine-economics.

K.A.W. Kelli A. White is a sommelier, writer, and educator. Her book *Napa Valley, Then & Now* won both an IACP and a Graphis design award, and her articles have earned her two Roederer Awards. She has contributed to many books, including the *World Atlas of Wine* and *On California*.

K.C. Kirsten Creasy has been a winemaker, educator, researcher, and international consultant for over 30 years. She has recently relocated from New Zealand to the Languedoc, where she is part-owner of Terre des 2 Sources winery.

K.H. Kieran Hirlam is the Project Team Manager for Affinity Labs, the commercial arm of the AWRI. He has worked on specific trials including life cycle analysis and waste transformation opportunities for a broad range of wineries, as well as comparing the impact and influence of alternative packaging.

K.K. Klara Kollárová, DipWSET and Weinakademiker, is a Czech sommelier, wine journalist, and judge.

K.L. Konstantinos Lazarakis MW was the first Greek Master of Wine and is the president of WSPC wine school in Athens, the Buying Director of Aiolos, a fine-wine importer and distributor, and the co-owner of Wine Wonders, a creative design company. He is the author of *The Wines of Greece* (2018).

K.L.B. Dr Karen Block joined the Department of Viticulture and Enology at UC DAVIS in 2011, where she is now the Director of Industry Relations. She received a BS in Chemical Engineering from the University of Michigan and a PhD in Molecular Biology and Pharmacology from the University of Pennsylvania.

K.M. Kristjan Markii, sommelier and wine writer, is president of the Estonian Sommelier Association and lecturer at the Estonian Sommelier School.

K.O. Ken Ohashi MW is a leading Japanese wine and sake consultant and an international judge of wines and sake, running his own Red Bridge Consultancy in Tokyo. He is a Master of Sake.

K.R.P. Dr Kevin R. Pogue is a Professor of Geosciences at Whitman College in Walla Walla, Washington State. Dr Pogue's research focuses on variations in growing conditions related to vineyard topography, climate, and soil chemistry. He has authored the petitions for six AVAS in the Pacific Northwest.

L.B. Larry Brooks studied plant pathology at the University of California at UC DAVIS and has been a winemaker or winemaking consultant in California ever since.

L. & E.S. Lush Susaj lectures in ampelography at the University of Tirana, where he is a professor. He has published widely in both Albania and abroad, as has Dr Elisabeta Susaj, who is a lecturer on genetics and plant breeding at the Agricultural University of Tirana.

L.F.B. Dr Linda Bisson, a microbiologist trained in genetics who specialized in yeast biology. She is a Professor Emeritus of Enology and until her retirement worked as a geneticist in the Agricultural Experiment Station at UC DAVIS.

L.H.-S. Dr Leofranc Holford-Strevens is a classical scholar, author of *Aulus Gellius: An Antonine Scholar and His Achievement*, and editor of the Oxford Classical Text of Gellius. Until his retirement in 2011, he worked for Oxford University Press.

L.M. Linda Murphy is co-author, with Jancis Robinson MW, of *American Wine: The Ultimate Companion to the Wines and Wineries of the United States*, contributor to publications such as *Decanter*, *Sonoma* magazine, and Santa Rosa *Press Democrat* newspaper, and former wine editor of the *San Francisco Chronicle*.

L.T.M. Lucie Morton is an independent viticulturist in the US. She writes, lectures, and consults on ampelography, rootstocks, and vineyard development and is a founding member of the International Council on Grapevine Diseases. She translated *A Practical Ampelography* from Pierre Galet's original and wrote *Winegrowing in Eastern America*.

M.A.S. Dr Mark Sefton was formerly a Principal Research Chemist at the AWRI, where he led the Institute's research programme on the chemistry of volatile grape and wine aroma and flavour compounds, and is now an Adjunct Associate Professor of the University of Adelaide.

M.A.W. Dr Andrew Walker held the Louis P. Martini Endowed Chair at UC DAVIS from 2000 to 2015, when he became the Louise Rossi Endowed Chair in Viticulture. His lab pursues grape breeding and resistance to pests and diseases. He has released five rootstocks with strong nematode resistance and five Pierce's disease-resistant wine-grape cultivars. His teaching includes grapevine identification, vineyard establishment, and pruning.

M.B. Dr Marlize Bekker is a Senior Research Scientist at the AWRI. Her PhD at STELLENBOSCH UNIVERSITY focused on the identification of natural products used in mammalian semiochemical communication. Her main research interests are the formation and fate of undesirable sulfur compounds in wine.

M.C. Professor Dr Monika Christmann is head of the oenology department at GEISENHEIM UNIVERSITY with research and teaching responsibilities. She currently serves as Vice President of the OIV.

M.C.K. Mel Knox is based in California, where he sold wine, taught wine appreciation classes at the University of California, and sold French barrels. He has also been involved in wine production and was awarded the Mérite Agricole by the French government in 2010.

M.C.W. Matt Walls is an award-winning wine writer, author, and broadcaster who contributes to various international publications. He is a contributing editor for *Decanter* and panel chair for the Rhône at the Decanter World Wine Awards. His latest book is *Wines of the Rhône* (2021).

M.D.K. Matthew Dennis Kettmann covers California's Central Coast and southern reaches for *Wine Enthusiast* and is author of *Vines & Vision: The Winemakers of Santa Barbara County*. He is also senior editor for the *Santa Barbara Independent*, where he started his journalism career in 1999.

M.E. Marcel Essling is a Senior Viticulturist with the AWRI and chairs the Agrochemical Reference Group for the Australian wine industry. He belongs to the Wine Industry Technical Advisory Committee and the Market Access Group. In these roles he advises the Australian wine sector on regulatory and technical aspects of agrochemical use in grape production.

M.F. Michael Fridjhon is South Africa's leading wine writer, Visiting Professor of Wine Business at the University of Cape Town's Graduate School of Business, Wine Wizard, and liquor industry specialist.

M.H. Dr Markus Herderich is a food chemist and Group Manager—Research at the AWRI and leads a research group of more than 30 professional scientists. His research interests include oenology, aroma chemistry, analytical chemistry, and metabolomics. He is also an Affiliate Associate Professor at the University of Adelaide and an expert at the OIV.

M.J.D. Maiah Johnson Dunn is a wine writer based in the Finger Lakes region of New York State.

M.J.E. Margaret Emery was the librarian at Roseworthy Agricultural College from 1975 until 1995 and holds a Graduate Diploma in Wine.

M.J.G. Maria Jose Granier has been in Bolivia's wine and singani industry for over a decade. The former president of the Asociación Nacional de Industriales Vitivinícolas (ANIV) and a co-founder of Wines of Bolivia, she currently manages a winery in the Cinti Valley.

M.J.T. Matt Thomson is a winemaker and consultant based in Marlborough, New Zealand. He has an MSc in Biochemistry and has worked 30 vintages in Marlborough and 30 consecutive harvests in Europe. He has consulted in Italy, France, Spain, Hungary, Romania, and Chile.

M.K. Max Kantelia is an electronics engineer turned investor and entrepreneur currently specializing in blockchain, NFT, and metaverse ventures for the music industry and luxury brands.

M.L.-G. Miles Lambert-Gocs researches the wine history and traditions of Eastern Europe, from Slovakia south through Greece.

M.P.K. Dr Mark Krstic is a viticulturist and Managing Director at the AWRI. He is also an Adjunct Professor at Macquarie University and Honorary Senior Fellow at the University of Melbourne.

M.P.L. Martin Lam, food and wine consultant, was the owner, chef, and celebrated wine buyer of Ransome's Dock restaurant in London.

M.R.K. Michael Karam is a British-born Lebanese author of several books on Lebanese wine. He also edited *Tears of Bacchus: A History of Wine in the Arab World*; contributed to *The World Atlas of Wine*, *Hugh Johnson's Pocket Wine Book*, and *The Sotheby's Wine Encyclopedia*; and collaborated on the documentary *Wine and War*.

M.S. Matthew Stubbs MW has 34 years of experience in the wine trade. An advocate for the wines of the Languedoc and Roussillon, he established Vinécole wine school near Carcassonne and lived in the region for 12 years.

M.Ta. Michael Tabone is a wine consultant and the former wine correspondent for the *Sunday Times of Malta*. In 2001 he established Malta's first wine school.

M.Tr. Madeline Triffon MS was the sixth American and the second woman in the world to achieve the Master Sommelier credential in 1987. An American wine specialist and sommelier, she has since mentored many service professionals and is a Chairman Emeritus of the American Chapter of the Court of Master Sommeliers.

M.v.H. Dr Maarten van Helden is a Senior Research Entomologist at the South Australian Research and Development Institute (SARDI). He graduated from Wageningen agricultural university in 1995 and worked as an Associate Professor in plant protection and agro-ecology at Bordeaux Sciences Agro from 1997 to 2016, conducting research on landscape ecology, ecosystem services, and pest management in viticulture.

M.W. Monty Waldin is a wine writer based in the UK. He has written several respected books on both organic and biodynamic wine and gardening. His television series *Chateau Monty* (2008) was the first to document biodynamic wine production from pruning to bottling.

M.W.E.S. Michael Schuster is a wine writer who for many years ran his own wine school in London and has translated the work of Professor Émile Peynaud. He is the author of *Essential Winetasting*.

N.B. Nick Bulleid MW is a freelance winemaking consultant in Australia and New Zealand and was for 13 years a visiting professor at CHARLES STURT UNIVERSITY. He is also a wine writer, wine judge, and wine producer in New South Wales. In 2020 he was appointed a Fellow of the Australian Society of Oenology.

N.F. The late NICHOLAS FAITH was a financial journalist whose numerous specialities included champagne, cognac, and railways.

N.G. NAYAN GOWDA is a wine consultant and itinerant winemaker who has made wine from more than 50 different varieties in eight countries, including Kazakhstan, where he has overseen production at the country's only organic winery.

N.G.W. NIGEL WILSON FBA is Emeritus Fellow and Tutor in Classics at Lincoln College, Oxford. His main work as a classical scholar is as an expert in Greek palaeography and the history of the classical tradition.

N.J.B. The late NICOLAS BELFRAGE MW was the author of four books and countless articles on Italian wine, the region in which he specialized as merchant, importer and agent, and writer.

N.S. NIGEL SOWMAN was awarded a BSc in Viticulture and Oenology by LINCOLN UNIVERSITY in 2000. He returned to Marlborough, New Zealand, to join the newly formed Dog Point vineyard team and has since led the conversion of 270 ha/667 acres of vineyards to organic certification.

O.P.-T. OLGA PINEVICH-TODORIUK is the editor-in-chief of *Drinks+*, the leading Ukrainian wine magazine. She also instigated the Wine Travel Awards, launched in 2021.

O.W. OWEN WHITE is Professor of History at the University of Delaware in the US. He is the author of *The Blood of the Colony: Wine and the Rise and Fall of French Algeria* (2021).

P.A.H. PROFESSOR PAUL A. HENSCHKE is Emeritus Fellow, formerly Principal Research Microbiologist, at the AWRI in Adelaide and is Affiliate Professor at the University of Adelaide. He has more than 40 years' experience in yeast research.

P.A.N. DR PHILIP NORRIE is a medical practitioner and wine producer in New South Wales, Australia, with a particular interest in wine history. He is the inventor of the world's first full-strength resveratrol-enhanced wine.

P.B. DR PAUL BOSS leads the CSIRO High Value Crops Group, which includes most of its grape and wine research. He has been conducting research on grapes and wine since 1994 on topics that include flower and fruit development, secondary metabolism, and the genetics of consumer traits.

P.C. PATRICK COMISKEY is a Senior Correspondent and chief domestic critic for *Wine & Spirits*. For more than a decade he also covered the wine scene for the *Los Angeles Times*. His book *American Rhône: How Maverick Winemakers Changed the Way Americans Drink* was published in October 2016.

P.E.M. PATRICK E. MCGOVERN is the Scientific Director of the Biomolecular Archaeology Project for Cuisine, Fermented Beverages, and Health at the University of Pennsylvania Museum in Philadelphia, where he is also an Adjunct Professor of Anthropology. He has published three books on ancient wine, including *Ancient Wine: The Search for the Origins of Viniculture* and *Uncorking the Past: The Quest for Wine, Beer, and Other Alcoholic Beverages*, together with numerous articles.

P.J.Con. DR PATRICK CONNER received his BS in Horticulture from Purdue University and his PhD in Plant Breeding from CORNELL UNIVERSITY. He is a Professor in the Horticulture Department at the University of Georgia, where he studies the genetics and breeding of pecan trees and Muscadine grapes.

P.J.Cos. DR PETER COSTELLO is a Research Scientist in the Biosciences group at the AWRI. His research has focused on wine lactic acid bacteria, malolactic conversion (MLF), and bacterial spoilage of wine. Recently he has investigated stress tolerances among *Oenococcus oeni* and approaches to improve MLF efficiency.

P.J.W. DR PATRICK WILLIAMS, Oenology Editor of the second edition of this book, was until his retirement the Deputy Director of, and a researcher for 24 years at, the AWRI.

P.K. DR PHILIP KENNEDY is Professor of Middle Eastern and Islamic Studies and Comparative Literature at New York University and the General Editor of *The Library of Arabic Literature* series published by NYU Press.

P.K.C.S. PATRICIA STEFANOWICZ MW is a wine consultant and educator as well as a qualified architect and structural engineer. She is based in the UK and divides her working life between wine and construction project management.

P.L. PETER LIEM is an American wine writer, author of the James Beard Award-winning book *Champagne,* and author of ChampagneGuide.net. He is the co-founder of La Fête du Champagne, one of the world's largest champagne events, and also serves as the regional chair for Champagne at the Decanter World Wine Awards.

P.Le. PASCALINE LEPELTIER MS is a Loire-raised, New York–based sommelier, wine educator, and contributor to *La Revue du Vin de France* writing about the Loire and low-intervention wines. She was awarded the titles of Best French Sommelier and Un des Meilleurs Ouvriers de France in 2018.

P.L.L. PEDER LEHMANN LARSEN is a Danish WSET-educated wine writer, educator, and judge specializing in Danish, Hungarian, and Greek wine.

P.R.D. DR PETER DRY AM is Adjunct Associate Professor, School of Agriculture, Food and Wine, University of Adelaide and former consultant to the AWRI.

P.R.-G. The late PASCAL RIBÉREAU-GAYON was head of the Faculty of Oenology at the University of Bordeaux and one of the most renowned French authorities on making and tasting wine. His father, Jean Ribéreau-Gayon, was also Director of Bordeaux's Institute of Oenology and a descendant of Professor Ulysse Gayon, who worked with Louis Pasteur.

P.S. PAUL STRANG is a musician-cum-lawyer who became a wine writer after buying a house in France in 1961. Twice winner of the Prix Gourmand for books on the wines of France's South West and Languedoc, he was made a Chevalier de l'Ordre du Mérite Agricole for services to French wines in 2020.

P.S.M.C. DR PETER COUSINS is a grape breeder at E & J GALLO, Modesto, California. He has bred and introduced several grape varieties to cultivation, including rootstocks, genetics research varieties, and improved clones. He has collected and studied grape germplasm in nature across North America.

P.T. PATRICIO TAPIA is a journalist based in Santiago with a diploma in oenology and tasting from the University of Bordeaux. Since 1999 he has published *Descorchados,* a guide to South American wines. Tapia also writes regularly for *Wine & Spirits, Adega,* and *Decanter.*

P.T.H.U. TIM UNWIN is Emeritus Professor of Geography and Chairholder of the UNESCO Chair in ICT4D at Royal Holloway, University of London. He is author of *Wine and the Vine* and was one of the founding editors of the *Journal of Wine Research.*

R.B. DR ROGER BROCK is a Senior Lecturer in Classics at the University of Leeds and specialist in Greek history and historiography.

R.D. DR BOB DAMBERGS is a Senior Lecturer in Wine Science at CHARLES STURT UNIVERSITY.

He has been a pioneer in the development of rapid analytical methods such as infrared and UV-visible spectroscopy that are now routinely used within the global wine industry.

R.d.G. Ronald de Groot is founder and editor-in-chief of Dutch wine magazine *Perswijn*, which has been published for over 30 years.

R.D.G. Régis D. Gougeon is Professor of Chemistry and Oenology at IUVV Jules Guyot in dijon, deputy director of research on the physico-chemistry of food and wine, and chairman of the scientific board of the Bourgogne Vigne et Vin cluster, a public-interest group promoting the co-ordination of research, teaching, and transfer across Bourgogne-Franche-Comté.

R.E.G. Rosemary George MW, wine writer, was one of the first women to become a Master of Wine. Her 14 books include three on *Chablis* and, most recently, *The Wines of Roussillon.*

R.E.S. Dr Richard Smart has been Viticulture Editor of every edition of this book and a substantial contributor to it. He is an Australian viticultural scientist, author, and consultant and lecturer in over 40 countries, known particularly for his studies and applications of canopy management, his research on trunk diseases, and his long-standing concern regarding the impact of climate change on the wine sector. He is well known for his oiv-award-winning book *Sunlight into Wine.*

R.E.W. Robert White is Emeritus Professor of Soil Science at the University of Melbourne, Australia. He consults to the wine industry and provides technical advice on soil matters to the awri. His book *Principles and Practice of Soil Science* is a standard textbook for soil science. He has also written *Soils for Fine Wines, Understanding Vineyard Soils,* and *Healthy Soils for Healthy Vines* (with Mark Krstic) and co-edited the four volumes of Earthscan's *Soil Science.*

R.F. Ryoko Fujimoto DipWSET works for a wine and Japanese sake consultancy in Japan. She is also a wine and sake educator, a judge in various international wine competitions, and a contributor to the 8th edition of the *World Atlas of Wine.*

R.F.G. Robert Gorjak was raised in a wine-growing family close to Jeruzalem, Slovenia. He has written five guides to Slovenian wines and is the author of *Slovenia, a Winemaking Country.* With his wife he established Belvin, Slovenia's first wine school.

R.G. Richard Gawel was until 2022 a Research Scientist with the awri. He established ways of describing red wines' mouthfeel and specialized in the chemistry of polysaccharides and phenolics and their effect on white-wine texture.

R.G.V.B. Dr Rob Bramley is a Senior Principal Research Scientist with csiro in Adelaide. Since 1998 he has been at the forefront of research aimed at understanding vineyard variability, the associated development of precision viticulture, and its application to improved understanding of terroir.

R.H. Rosi Hanson is a journalist and author of a book on the recipes and traditions of the French wine harvest.

R.J.M. Richard Mayson, an authority on port, madeira, and Portuguese wines. After working for The Wine Society in the UK, he wrote *Portugal's Wines and Winemakers, Port and the Douro* and *Madeira: The Islands and their Wines.* He is Series Editor for the Infinite Classic Wine Library.

R.J.T. Rachel Triggs worked as a winemaker and wine lawyer prior to joining Wine Australia in 2013. She is a delegate to the oiv and the world wide trade group and is on the boards of the public policy group FIVS and the International Wine Law Association.

R.K.C.T. Dr Reinhard Töpfer has been head of julius-kühn-institut's Institute for Grapevine Breeding Geilweilerhof since 1995 and Honorary Professor at Justus Liebig University, Giessen, since 2014. His expertise is in plant breeding, molecular genetics, and grapevine phenotyping.

R.K.S. Reva K. Singh, a veteran of the Indian magazine industry, is the founder of *Sommelier India Wine Magazine*, India's first print and online publication on wine. In 2009 she founded and was co-chair of the Sommelier India Wine Competition (SIWC).

R.N.H.B. The late Robin Butler was an antiques dealer with a particular interest in wine. He co-wrote *The Book of Wine Antiques* in 1986 and in 2009 wrote *Great British Wine Accessories 1550–1900.*

R.T. Raimonds Tomsons DipWSET was recognized as Best Sommelier of Europe 2017 and Best Sommelier of the World 2023 by the Association de la Sommellerie Internationale. Based in Latvia, he is co-founder of Wine-teach.com, a board member of the Latvian Sommelier Association, and judge at the Decanter World Wine Awards.

R.T. du C. Rémi Teissier du Cros is a forest and wood engineer currently working at Tonnellerie Taransaud, France. Having started his career at the French National Forest Inventory, he now shares his time between research on oak wood and barrels and running the engineering office at the cooperage.

R.Z. Rick Zouad spent many years working as a sommelier in top restaurants in New York City before heading back to his native Morocco, where he is a restaurant and beverage consultant.

S.A. Sarah Ahmed publishes thewinedetective.co.uk and is a recognized authority on the wines of Portugal. A contributor to *The World Atlas of Wine* and columnist for *Revista de Vinhos* and *Decanter,* Ahmed has chaired the judging of Portuguese wines at the Decanter World Wine Awards since 2011.

S.A.S. Dr Simon Schmidt is a Research Manager at the awri. His research interests include understanding the relationship between nutrient availability and yeast fermentation performance, yeast and bacterial stress tolerance, and the role of oxygen in shaping fermentation outcomes.

S.C. Suzie Chung is a Korea-based wine journalist for wine21.com, a wine lecturer and judge, and a wset Level 2 textbook technical editor.

S.C.-J. Samantha Cole-Johnson DipWSET is based in Oregon, where she writes for JancisRobinson.com and teaches wset courses.

S.D.W. The late Dr Steve Wratten was Professor of Ecology at lincoln university in New Zealand as well as being on the staff of the Bio-Protection Research Centre. He was a world leader in biological control of pests.

S.E.A. Susy Atkins is a television presenter and wine writer who is based in Britain but travels widely.

S.F. Professor Sigfredo Fuentes leads the Digital Agriculture, Food and Wine Sciences at the University of Melbourne. His scientific interests include climate change, remote sensing, and the development of new computational tools using artificial intelligence (AI) applications for psychiatry, plant physiology, food, animal, and wine sciences.

S.J.C. Dr Steve Charters MW is Professor of Wine Marketing, School of Wine and Spirits Business, Burgundy Business School, with research interests in the consumer's engagement with wine and the social and cultural context of its production and consumption.

S.J.G. SAM GLAETZER, member of a well-known South Australian winemaking family, has a degree in civil and environmental engineering and a graduate diploma in oenology. He started his career at TREASURY WINE ESTATES before joining CONSTELLATION BRANDS, where he is currently SVP of Global Operations and International Commercial Sales for Wine & Spirits.

S.K.H. SARAH HELLER MW graduated from Yale University with an art degree before embarking on a wine career in Hong Kong. A writer, educator, and visual artist, she received the 2013 WSET Vintner's Cup and was 2022 IWSC Wine Communicator of the Year.

S.N. DR SIMON NORDESTGAARD is a Senior Engineer at the AWRI. His research interests include winery solid–liquid separation techniques and process optimization. He has studied the evolution of many winery technologies and practices from their historical origins through to the current state of the art.

S.P.D.L. SIMON LOFTUS is a retired renowned English wine merchant and award-winning author.

S.P.-T. SOPHIE PARKER-THOMSON MW is a wine-industry consultant and wine producer based in Marlborough, New Zealand. Aside from a brief interlude training as a lawyer, she has spent her life immersed in wine appreciation, education, production, and communication.

S.S. STEPHEN SKELTON MW has grown vines and made wine since 1974. After training in Germany, he returned to Kent, where he made wine until 2000. Since then he has been a vineyard consultant and has written several books on both viticulture and English and Welsh wine.

S.T. DR STEPHEN D. TYERMAN, a Fellow of the Australian Academy of Science, is Emeritus Professor of Viticulture at the University of Adelaide, School of Agriculture, Food and Wine, Senior Editor for *Plant Cell and Environment*, and Associate Editor for the *Australian Journal of Grape and Wine Research*. He is a Clarivate Highly Cited Researcher.

T.C. DR TYLER COLMAN is a wine writer and wine educator. The author of two wine books, *A Year of Wine* and *Wine Politics*, he also blogs at DrVino.com.

T.D.C. TAMLYN CURRIN DipWSET is a wine writer who was born and brought up in Zimbabwe but now lives in the UK and writes for JancisRobinson.com, where she is Sustainability Editor.

T.E.M. DR TIM MARTINSON has been active in grape extension and research at CORNELL UNIVERSITY since completing his PhD in entomology in 1991. Since 2007 he has been statewide Senior Extension Associate at Cornell AgriTech, where he led development of a sustainable practices workbook and directed the USDA-funded Northern Grapes Project. In 2020 he was cited as one of 40 wine industry leaders by *Wine Business Monthly*.

T.H. THOMAS HEATON is a New Zealand food writer and journalist who spent two years in Nepal covering agriculture and the food and beverage industry.

T.H.L. PROFESSOR TERRY LEE OAM was Director of the AWRI in Adelaide before working for E. & J. GALLO in California. He is editor of *The Australian Journal of Grape and Wine Research*.

T.J. The late DR TONY JORDAN OAM started his career as research scientist and lecturer in oenology. He established the Chandon Australia Yarra Valley winery and vineyard for Moët Hennessy, later becoming CEO of the Moët Hennessy Wine Estates Group of Australian and New Zealand wineries, before running his own wine consultancy.

T.K.W. DR TONY WOLF is Professor of Viticulture and has served as viticulturist with VIRGINIA TECH since 1986. His education includes an MS from Pennsylvania State University and a PhD from CORNELL UNIVERSITY, both in viticulture research. He was editor and principal author of the 2008 *Wine Grape Production Guide for Eastern North America*.

T.M.S. TYSON STELZER, wine writer, scientist, and TV host, is the author of 15 books, including *Taming the Screw: A Manual for Winemaking with Screw Caps* and his annual *Champagne Guide*. He is Chief Editor of the *Halliday Wine Companion*.

T.P. PROFESSOR THOMAS PINNEY is a retired Professor of English at Pomona College in Claremont, California, and author of the two-volume *History of Wine in America*.

T.Q.T. TARA Q. THOMAS, assistant editor of *The Oxford Companion to Wine*, is the former Executive Editor of *Wine & Spirits* in New York. She has worked in the wine industry for 25 years as a writer, editor, wine judge, and educator and is now Managing Editor of JancisRobinson.com.

T.R.C. TOM CARSON is the youngest chairman of Australia's National Wine Show and chief winemaker and general manager of Yabby Lake Vineyard, Mornington Peninsula, Victoria.

T.S. The late DR TOM SCOTT was a wine merchant and Honorary Professor in the Institute of Reformation Studies at the University of St Andrews. He specialized in the economic and social history of Germany, 1300–1600.

T.T. TODD TRZASKOS is a lifelong resident of the north-eastern United States, with three decades in Vermont, where he advocates and organizes for local producers and is an avid home winemaker. He is also the author of *Wines of Vermont: A History of Pioneer Fermentation*.

U.C. UMAY ÇEVIKER is a Turkish architect and WSET-educated wine enthusiast with a passion for Türkiye's deep-rooted wine culture. In 2015 he won the Geoffrey Roberts Award for his work with rural vineyards and ancient varieties in Türkiye, and he was a contributor to the eighth edition of *The World Atlas of Wine*.

V.C. DR VÉRONIQUE CHEYNIER, Director of Research at INRAE, has been managing INRA Montpellier's internationally acclaimed research on grape and wine polyphenols for over 30 years. From 2012 to 2016 she was President of Groupe Polyphénols, the international society dedicated to the promotion of research on plant polyphenols.

V. DE LA S. VICTOR DE LA SERNA is a Madrid-based journalist and wine writer, columnist, and former deputy editor for *El Mundo* as well as a wine producer.

V.F. VICENTE FERREIRA is Professor of Analytical Chemistry at the University of Zaragoza and head of the Laboratory for Aroma Analysis and Enology (LAAE). He is a specialist in the chemical analysis of aroma molecules and in the interpretation of sensory perception, specifically in wine.

V.J. DR VLADIMIR JIRANEK is Professor of Oenology and Head of the Department of Wine Science at the University of Adelaide. Through his 30 years' experience he has published extensively on the characterization of wine yeast and bacteria. His work centres on understanding microbial ecology and controlling the impact of microbes on wine quality.

V.K.R. VALENTINA KASPER ROSPUTINSKA is a business innovation executive, WSET Level 3 holder, and co-organizer of Humbuk, natural wine educational pop-ups in Slovakia.

V.L. Dr Valérie Lavigne, Advisory Oenology Editor of this book, has a PhD in Oenology from the University of Bordeaux. She is a Research Associate on secondment from cooper Seguin Moreau to the isvv in Bordeaux. Her research focuses on premature ageing of white and red wines and the aromas of Chardonnay wines. She started as an oenology and viticulture consultant alongside the late Professor Denis Dubourdieu (see above) and now works with Christophe Olivier and Professor Alex Marchal in all of France's main wine regions as well as in Italy, Portugal, Spain, South Africa, Greece, Egypt, Morocco, and Lebanon.

V.P. Dr Vladimír Pukis has a master's degree in linguistics and is the former communications director of Fanagoria winery in Russia. A historian, translator, and ethnologist, he has written several books (in Ukrainian, English, and Russian), including *Wine Lexicon* and *The New Old World: Sketches on the History of Kuban Winemaking*, and contributes to numerous media outlets.

W.B. William Bolter is a Bordeaux-based wine merchant, author, and winemaker who worked for Alexis lichine from 1958 to 1964.

W.G.G. Dr W. Gill Giese Jr is the Viticulture Extension Specialist/Assistant Professor, Department of Plant and Environmental Sciences, New Mexico State University. He has also made wine since 1995, working in several states.

W.J.B. Bill Blatch worked in the Bordeaux wine trade from 1974 until 2012. He is now Senior Consultant in Bordeaux for Christie's and Founder and Senior Partner in Bordeaux Gold, Sauternes specialists.

W.L. Wink Lorch, wine educator, writer, and editor, specializes in the wines of the Jura, Savoie, and French Alps. She has written two award-winning books: *Jura Wine* and *Wines of the French Alps.*

W.M.B. Wojciech Bońkowski MW is the founder of *Ferment*, Poland's only printed wine magazine. He writes for Timatkin.com and *Meininger's Wine Business International*, judges at Decanter World Wine Awards and 50 Great Greek Wines, and has served as President of the Polish Wine Trade Association since 2016.

W.P. Dr Wendy Parr is a New Zealand wine sensory scientist with a PhD in Psychology (Cognition & Psychophysics) and a PhD in Wine Science (Sensory).

W.S. Walter Speller is the Italian correspondent for JancisRobinson.com and a wine writer specializing in Italy. He has contributed to the eighth edition of the *World Atlas of Wine* and to *Decanter* magazine. He divides his time between Padova and his base in London.

W.S.S. Wolfgang Schaefer graduated from geisenheim university before establishing and running a 40-ha viticultural research station in Tanzania in the 1970s. He has since travelled to 78 countries and is a senior consultant on all things related to (sub)tropical viticulture.

W.W. Wayne Wilcox was a Professor of Plant Pathology for 34 years at cornell university in New York State, where he led their grape pathology programme until retiring. He was the senior editor and a major contributing author to the comprehensive *Compendium of Grape Diseases, Pests, and Disorders*, 2nd edition.

X.V. Xeniya Volosnikova is a wine specialist from Kazakhstan now living in Europe while pursuing a dream of becoming her country's first Master of Wine.

Y.S. Young Shi is a Warwick Business School graduate and MW student who divides her time between Shanghai, London, and the world's wine regions. She is a bilingual wine writer, consultant, educator, and wine judge.

ACKNOWLEDGEMENTS

As for the four previous editions, this *Companion* owes most to a host of people around the world who have been extraordinarily generous with their time and knowledge, perhaps because wine is a subject which naturally inspires generosity and enthusiasm.

Dr Richard Smart, Australian viticulturist extraordinaire, went to exceptional lengths as long-standing advisory editor for viticulture to ensure that all the entries related to this multifaceted subject were brought fully up to date. With equal dedication and attention to detail, Bordeaux-based international consultant Dr Valérie Lavigne has assumed the complementary role of advisory editor for oenology, taking on the full weight of this task that she shared in the last edition with her former colleague and mentor the late Professor Denis Dubourdieu.

Nevertheless, when it came to final detailed updates to specific entries, it is remarkable how many specialists came to our aid, not only from the AWRI in Adelaide but also from the University of California at DAVIS and from many other academic and research institutions around the world, including Professor Vicente Ferreira of Zaragoza University and Professor Andrew Sacks of Cornell University, who brought their formidable understanding of, respectively, flavour and sulfur to this edition for the first time. Dr Andrei Prida and Rémi Teissier du Cros ensured even greater precision than before on all things oak- and barrel-related.

Our co-author of *Wine Grapes* Dr José Vouillamoz, as well as considerably revising the entry on his native Switzerland, has updated many of the grape-variety entries based on his unique database of DNA profiles, so that while this volume cannot be as exhaustive as *Wine Grapes*, it is even more up to date in identifying relationships among vine varieties.

Professors Alex Maltman and Robert White made sure the key topics of geology and soil are better defined and described than ever before, and Dr Greg Jones not only substantially revised the entry on climate change but also gave all the main climate-related entries a thorough overhaul. Dr John Barker, recently elected Director General of the OIV, took great pains once again in this edition to clarify and update with lawyerly precision all things regulatory in the EU and beyond.

Patrick McGovern of the University of Pennsylvania Museum has significantly updated his contribution on the origins of what he calls viniculture, and all our other historical entries have been reviewed by their authors to ensure that necessary updates have been made.

We owe an enormous debt to all our regional specialists, many of whom were far more helpful than they need have been, especially those such as Walter Speller, Ferran Centelles, and Sarah Ahmed who reviewed and updated a huge number of entries on Italy, Spain, and Portugal respectively. New to this edition, Carlos Borboa Suárez gave the entry on Mexico a much-needed overhaul, shining a light on a country deserving of much more attention in the wine world. Dirceu Vianna Junior MW did the same for Brazil and in record time. Olga Pinevich-Todoriuk managed to file her entry on Ukraine just before war broke out and updated it later, during the war, nine days after having a baby. And a strong team of US writers, significantly expanded for this edition, made sure the US was better represented than ever before: Alder Yarrow, Elaine Chukan Brown, Kelli White, Matt Kettman, Kevin Pogue, Samantha Cole-Johnson, Maiah Johnson Dunn, Todd Trzakos, Gill Giese, Jenne Baldwin-Eaton, Becca Yeamans-Irwin, Doug Frost MW, Patrick Comiskey, James Tidwell, and Gary Pavlis.

The late Angeliki Tsioli diligently unearthed and distilled the much-amended European wine regulations to produce our unique list of appellations and their permitted grape varieties in Appendix 1. She also gathered from her former employer the OIV their formidable statistics for Appendix 2. Her sudden and premature death in 2022 was a terrible shock, and yet her work on this edition is a testament to her sharp mind, generous heart, patience, and multilingual skills.

There were also many individuals whose initials do not appear at the bottom of any entry but without whose advice or contacts our work would have been very much more difficult. We apologize to anyone whose name we have failed to record—all too easy, alas, when dealing with literally thousands of people during the preparation of this work. Those who made notable contributions to this fifth edition in particular, other than those recorded in the list of contributors, include:

Yves Abautret
Foulques Aulagnon
Niv Benyehuda
Facundo Bonamaizon
Raffaele Boscaini
Philippe Bouin
Iva Boyuklieva
Tamara Brunhart
Ernst Büscher
Tod Cavallo
Karl Chetcuti
Mark Chien
Kerry Damskey
Gearoid Devaney
Frederico Falcão
Gilles Flutet
Leigh Francis
J.M. Gatteron
Jacques Gautier
Giorgios Hadjistilianou
Anthony Hanson MW
Josh Hixson
Anita Jackson
Michael Juergens
Tina Kezeli
Oliver Lea
Jéremie Leduc
Yusif Lezgiyev
Fiona Morrison MW
Antony Moss MW
Mukami Mwarania
María Naranjo Crespo
Signe Nelgen
Richard Neville
Andrew Nielsen
Mike Officer
Sofia Perpera
Steffen Schindler
Harley Smith
Karl Storchmann
Benoît Verdier
Jeanne Vito
John Worontschak
Christian Zechmeister

LIST OF NEW ENTRIES

abv
agglomerate corks
Agroscope
alberese
Alpilles
Alto Piemonte
Amyndeo
Angelica
anti-transpirant
ants
Apalta
appassimento
arboreal viticulture
Arizona
Arkansas
Artémis Domaines
artificial intelligence
aszú
Atlantique
Auckland
Aude
Aveyron
Bagnoli Friularo
Balearic Islands
Ballard Canyon
Bannockburn
barrel ageing
bench
berry cell death
berry shrivel
Biancu Gentile
biogenic amines
biologicals
biotype
blockchain
bottle shock
Brittany
brown marmorated stink bug
bunch closure
Cangas
Canterbury
carbon footprint of wine
Catalanes, Côtes
celebrity wine
Central Otago
Cerasuolo di Vittoria
CERVIM
chalky
Charentais
Chehalem Mountains
Chidiriotiko
chitosan
cleanskin
Clendenen, Jim
Collines Rhodaniennes
Colorado
Comté Tolosan
Contra Costa Country
contrada
Corpinnat
Corrèze
critics, wine
curettage
Della Venezie
dénomination géographique complémentaire
destemmer-crusher
DGB
Dogliani
drones
Dundee Hills
Easter Island
e-commerce
Eola-Amity Hills
epigenetics
espumante
Estonia
Etna
exposure
Fair Play
Familia Torres
Finger Lakes
finish
Finland
Flextank
flint
flysch
foudre
franc de pied
Frankland River
frisante
Friuli Aquileia
Friuli Colli Orientali
Friuli Grave
Gabon
Galotta
Gard
garrigue
geotextiles
Gisborne
glou-glou
Grahm, Randall
Green Valley
growler
haloanisoles
Happy Canyon of Santa Barbara
Harlan
harvest compression
Hautes-Alpes
Hawke's Bay
heatwave
Henkell Freixenet

High Valley
HVE
Île-de-France
Indiana
influencers
Isère
IWCA
Jackson Family Wines
King Valley
Korinthiaki
Kreaca
Kydonitsa
Lacryma Christi
Latvia
Lébrija
legumes
Les Apres
Liliorila
Lithuania
Los Olivos District
low-intervention wine
Macarthur, Sir William
Maratheftiko
marginal climate
Marin
Marlborough
Master Sommelier
Maturana Tinta
Méditerranée
Merwah
método tradicional
MGA
Minnesota
Montagnieu
Moon Mountain District
Moscato di Scanzo
Mount Harlan
MS
Naoussa
Negoska
Nelson
Nerello Cappuccio
New England Australia
New Jersey
New Mexico
NFT
Nizza
noble varieties
NOLO
North Carolina
Northland
North Yuba
no-till
Offida
Ohio
Palacios family
Palestine
Palhete
pálido
Palmento
paper bottles
parcel
partially de-alcoholized wine
Pays d'Oc
pé franco
Pemberton
Pennsylvania
Perlwein
Perruno
pervaporation
Petaluma Gap
pied de cuve
piede franco
piperitone
pithari
polyethylene
Porongurup
Poussard
preservation systems
Puy-de-Dôme
quintal
rachis
Red Hills
regenerative viticulture
Ribbon Ridge
Robe
roble
Romagna Albana
Rosalia
Rosazzo
Ruster Ausbruch
Sable de Camargue
SAFER
St-Guilhem-le-Desert
St-Jean-de-la-Porte
Santa Lucia Highlands
Sta. Rita Hills
Schaumwein
sélection parcellaire
Senegal
Serine
Sezão
Singapore
SLO Coast
Solaris
Sommières
spotted lanternfly
Spurrier, Steven
stabulation
Strohwein
sui lieviti
Szamarodni
talha
tariffs
Thongue, Côtes de
tillage
Togo
traditionelle Flaschengärung
trunk renewal
Tualatin Hills
UGA
Uganda
underwater ageing
unicorn wine
Urgestein
Val de Loire
Vallée du Paradis
Valles de Benavente
Valtiendas
Van Duzer Corridor
Var
Vaucluse
Vermeille, Côte
Vermont
Vidiano
VIFA
vineyard management company
Vinho de Talha
vino de aguja
vino de tea
Vitis amurensis
Vitis riparia
Vitis rupestris
Vitovska
volatile sulfur compounds
Vulkanland Steiermark
Wairarapa
Waitaki
warm-climate viticulture
Weissburgunder
Wente
Whispering Angel
wildfires
Willamette Valley
Winiarski, Warren
World Wine Trade Group
Würzelecht
Yamabudo
Yamhill-Carlton District
Yonne
zero-zero
zymurgy

MAPS OF THE WINE REGIONS

NOTE TO THE READER

Entries are arranged in letter-by-letter alphabetical order up to the first punctuation in the headword, except that names beginning with Mc are ordered as if they were spelt Mac, and St and Ste (French) are arranged as if they were spelt Saint and Sainte. When Château and Châteaux are part of a proper name they appear in full as headwords, but they are abbreviated to Ch and Chx elsewhere. Entries appear under the name of the château and not under C. Place names that start with a definite article are listed under the article (e.g. La Mancha is found under L).

Cross-references are denoted by red small capitals and indicate the entry to which attention is being directed. We have attempted to limit cross-references to other entries likely to amplify or increase understanding of the entry being read. They are not given in all instances where the name of an entry appears in the text.

All wine-producing countries have an entry. The most significant ones also have individual entries for regions within them. Some countries or regions have individual entries for specific appellations, depending on what is on the label and which wines are widely available or especially famous. We have tried to give all the most significant appellations their own entry, as we have the individual people, wine producers, and properties which have played or are playing an important part in the history of wine.

Measurements are given in metric accompanied by the United States equivalent. (See the list of abbreviations.)

The format of this fifth edition is very similar to the fourth, including a complete list of entries by region and topic (see pp. xxix–lii) to provide a specific guide to the scope of this book, and to suggest another way of navigating your way through it. A revealing list of new entries is included on pp. xxiii–xxiv; all new entries are of course included in the thematic listings too.

The appendices include a completely updated list of all significant wine appellations (very rarely found in printed form) together with details of those grape varieties currently specified by them, including many recent changes (an even rarer listing), as well as tables of total vineyard area by country, total wine production, and per capita wine consumption. All have been thoroughly updated to include the most recent OIV statistics available.

Abbreviations

Ch, Chx	Château, Châteaux
ft	feet
gal	US gallon
g/l	grams per litre
ha	hectare
hl	hectolitre
in	inches
l	litre
m	metre

COMPLETE LIST OF ENTRIES BY REGION AND TOPIC

Regions

Africa

Algeria
Breede River Valley
Cape
Cape Agulhas
Cape blend
Cape Verde
Coastal Region
Constantia
DGB
Distell
Durbanville
Elgin
Elim
Ethiopia
Franschhoek
Gabon
Groenekloof
Integrated Production of Wine
jerepigo
Kenya
Klein Karoo
KWV
Lesotho
Madagascar
Malmesbury
Morocco
Muscadel
Namibia
Olifants River
Paarl
Robertson
Senegal
South Africa
Stellenbosch
Stellenbosch University
Swartland
Tanzania
Togo
Tulbagh
Tunisia
Uganda
Walker Bay
Wellington
Western Cape
WIETA
Wine of Origin
Worcester
Zimbabwe

Asia

Asia
Bhutan
Cambodia
Changyu
China

Australia/New Zealand

Austria

France

Germany

Italy

Latin America

North America

Portugal

Spain

Ribera del Guadiana
Ribera del Júcar
Rioja
roble
Rueda
sangría
Sanlúcar de Barrameda
sherry
Sierra de Gredos
Sierra de Salamanca
Sierras de Málaga
solera
Somontano
Spain
Tacoronte-Acentejo
Tarragona
Terra Alta
Tierra del Vino de Zamora
tinaja
tinta
tinto
Toro
Txakoli
Uclés
Utiel-Requena
Valdeorras
Valdepeñas
Valencia
Valle de Güimar
Valle de la Orotava
Valles de Benavente
Valtiendas
Vega Sicilia
vermouth
viña, viñedo
vino de aguja
Vino de Calidad
Vino de la Tierra
Vino de Mesa
Vino de Pago
vino de tea
VORS and VOS
Xérès
Ycoden-Daute-Isora
Yecla

Rest of Europe

Aegean Islands
Agroscope
Albania
Amyndeo
aszú
Belgium
beli
Bikavér
Blandy
Bohemia
Bosnia and Herzegovina
Britain
British wine
Bulgaria
Bull's Blood
Commandaria
Cotnari
Crete
Croatia
Cyprus
Czechia
Denmark
Eger
England
Estonia
Federweisser
Finland
Greece
Hungary
Imperial Tokay
Ireland
Johannisberg
kék
Kosovo
Latvia
Liechtenstein
Lithuania
Low Countries
Luxembourg
malmsey
Malta
Mediterranean
Moldova
Montenegro
Naoussa
Netherlands
North Macedonia
Norway
pithari
Poland
retsina
Romania
Salvagnin
Santorini
Scotland
Serbia
Slovakia
Slovenia
Sopron
Sweden
Switzerland
Szamarodni
Szekszárd
Szepsy, István
Tokaj
Tokay
Türkiye
Ukraine
Villány
Vin des Glaciers
Wales
Yugoslavia

Rest of the World

Afghanistan
Anatolia
Armenia
Azerbaijan
Crimea
Egypt
Georgia
India
Iran
Iraq
Israel
Jordan
Kazakhstan
Kyrgyzstan
Lebanon
Massandra
New Latitude Wines
Pakistan
Palestine
Russia
Soviet Union
Syria
Tahiti
Tajikistan
Turkmenistan
Uzbekistan

Topics

Academe

academe
Adelaide
Agroscope
AWRI
Bordeaux, University of
Brock University
Changins
Charles Sturt University
Conegliano
Cornell University
CSIRO
Davis
Dijon
education, wine
Geisenheim University
INRAE
ISVV
Julius-Kuhn-Institut
Lincoln University
Magarach
Masters of Wine
Master Sommelier
Montpellier, University of
MS
MW
NYSAES
Plumpton College
research
Roseworthy
San Michele all'Adige, Istituto Agrario di
science
Stellenbosch University
symposium
Virginia Tech
Wädenswil
Wagga
WSET

Grape varieties

Abouriou
Acolon
Agiorgitiko
Aglianico
Aïdani
Airén
Alarije
Albalonga
Albana
Albariño
Albarola
Albillo
Aleatico
Alfrocheiro

Zinfandel
Zweigelt

History

Abu Nuwas
agricultural treatises
Amerine, Maynard
amphora
Anatolia
Arab poets
archaeology
Aristophanes
Arnaldus de Villanova
Athenaeus
Baghdad
barbarians
barrel
Becker, Helmut
Bible
Bocksbeutel
British influence on the wine trade
Byblos
Cabinet
Caecuban
Canaan
Carthage
Cato, Marcus
Celts
Charlemagne
Charneco
Chian
claret
classical art, wine in
classical texts
Columella, Lucius Junius Moderatus
containers
Cotnari
crater
crise viticole, la
Cruess, William Vere
Dionysus
doctors
dolium
Domitian
Dutch East India Company
Dutch wine trade
economics of wine
Egypt
Eiximenis, Francisc
Etruscans
Eucharist, wine in the
Factory House
Falernian
flavoured wines
Galen
Gaul
Genoa
Geoponika
German history
glass, history of
gold rushes
Gorbachev, Mikhail
Greece
Guyot, Jules
Hammurabi
Haraszthy, Agoston
Haut-Pays
Henderson, Dr Alexander
Herodotus
Hesiod
hippocras
hock
Homer
Horace
Hundred Years War
Imperial Tokay
Islam
Jefferson, Thomas
jewish heritage in German wine culture
Jullien, André
La Rochelle
libation
Low Countries
lyric poetry
Macarthur, Sir William
Mago
malmsey
Martial
Massic
mead
medicine, wine in
medieval literature
Mediterranean
Mesopotamia
Methuen Treaty
missionaries
monks and monasteries
Mountain
Munson, T. V.
Naples
Oenotria
Omar Khayyám
Opimian
Oporto
origins of viniculture
Osey
palaeoethnobotany and the archaeology of wine
Palladius
Pasteur, Louis
Penning-Rowsell, Edmund
Persia
Petrus de Crescentiis
Peynaud, Émile
Phoenicia
picardan
Pliny
Pompeii
press
Probus, Marcus Aurelius
Prohibition
railways
Redding, Cyrus
religion and wine
resinated wines
Rhenish
rivers
Rome, classical
sack
sacramental wine
Saintsbury, Professor George
salary, wine as
Schoonmaker, Frank
Ségurs
Shaulis, Nelson
Simon, André Louis
Sumer
Surrentine
symposium
Tchelistcheff, André
tent
Theophrastus
tonneau
torna viagem
Varro, Marcus Terentius
Venice
Vila Nova de Gaia
Vínland
Virgil
Vizetelly, Henry
war, effects on wine
Xenophon

Labelling terms

abv
AOC
AOP
Apera
AP number
appellation
appellation contrôlée
artists' labels
Auslese
AVA
BA
Beerenauslese
Bereich
blanc
blanc de blancs
blanc de noirs
British wine
brut
Charta
château
château bottling
Classic
Classico
classification
cleanskin
controlled appellations
crianza
cru
DAC
delimitation, geographical
demi-sec
Denominação de Origem Controlada
Denominación de Origen
Denominación de Origen Calificada
dénomination géographique complémentaire
DO
DOC
DOCa
doce
DOCG
dolce
domaine
DOP
DOQ

Packaging

People/Producers/Brands

Tasting

Vine-growing/Viticulture

Wine and the consumer

Winemaking/Oenology

cork taint
coupage
crush
crushing
crust
cryoextraction
crystals
custom-crush facility
cuve
cuve close
cuvée
deacidification
de-alcoholized wine
débourbage
dégorgement
degree
density
destemmer-crusher
destemming
diacetyl
diammonium phosphate
diatomaceous earth
disgorgement
distillation
distillation, compulsory
DMDC
domaine bottling
dosage
draining
dried-grape wines
Ducellier
échantillon
egg whites
electrodialysis
élevage
enologist
enrichment
enzymes
éraflage
erythorbic acid
esters
estufa
ethanal
ethanol
ethyl acetate
ethyl alcohol
ethyl carbamate
eucalyptus character
evaporation
evaporative perstraction
extract
extraction
faults in wines
fermentation
fermentation in bottle
fermentation vessel
fermented in bottle
fill level
film-forming yeasts
filtration
fining
fixed acids
fizziness
flash détente
flavonoids
flavonols
flavour compounds
flavoured wines
flavourings
flavour precursors
flavour scalping
Flextank
flor
flotation
flying winemakers
foot treading
forests
fortification
fortified wines
foudre
fractional blending
free-run
fruit wines
Fuder
fusel oils
gelatin
geosmin
gluconobacter
glucose
glutathione
glycerol
glycosides
glycosyl-glucose assay
governo
grain
grape composition and wine quality
grape concentrate
grape juice
grape juice composition
grape quality assessment
gravity-fed
gyropalette
haloanisoles
head space
histamine
home winemaking
humidification
hydrogen sulfide
hydrolysis
hydrometer
hygiene
inert gas
infrared spectroscopy
injection
inner staves
ion exchange
IPT
isinglass
isoamyl acetate
isobutyl-methoxypyrazine
laccase
lactic acid
lactic acid bacteria
ladybug taint
lagar
late harvest
lees
lees contact
lees stirring
lie
lightstrike
Limousin
lipids
liqueur wine
low-alcohol wine
low-intervention wine
maceration
macération carbonique
macération pelliculaire
macération préfermentaire
macro-oxygenation
maderization
made-wine
Maillard reaction
malic acid
malolactic conversion
malvidin
manipulation
mannoproteins
marc
maturation of wine
mercaptans
metabisulfite
methanol
méthode ancestrale
méthode champenoise
méthode classique
méthode dioise ancestrale
méthode gaillacoise
méthode traditionnelle
methoxy-dimethylpyrazine
methoxypyrazines
microbes
micro-oxygenation
mistela
monoterpenes
mousseux
moût de raisins partiellement fermenté issu de raisins passerillés
must
must chilling
must weight
mutage
nanofiltration
natamycin
natural alcohol
natural wine
New World
nitrogen
non-alcoholic wine
nouveau
nuclear magnetic resonance
oak
oak ageing
oak chips
oak essences
oak flavour
ochratoxin A
œil-de-perdrix
oenocyanin
oenological tannins
oenologist
oenology
OIV
Old World
orange wine
organic wine
ouillage
oxidation
oxidative winemaking
oxygen
oxygen transmission rate
ozone

Miscellaneous

ABC
adulteration and fraud
authentication
bonded warehouse
bore, wine
CMO
economics of wine
English literature, wine in
EU
fashion
films about wine
garage wines
globalization
harvest traditions
icon wine
information technology
joint venture
labour
law
négociant
New World
numbers and wine
Old World
philosophy and wine
politics and wine
premium wine
provenance
regionality
second wines
Sideways
social media
sustainability
trade, wine
transport of wine
trophy wines
urban wineries
vandalism
wine lake
wine writers
wine writing
world production

A

ABC, acronym for the weary sentiment 'Anything But Chardonnay (or Cabernet)' which encouraged interest in grapes other than the (two most famous) INTERNATIONAL VARIETIES on the part of both producers and consumers. Rhône varieties were the earliest beneficiaries in the 1980s, but by the 2010s INDIGENOUS VARIETIES and ALTERNATIVE VARIETIES, the more obscure the better, were all the rage.

Abel. See HERITAGE CLONES.

Abona, small Spanish DOP covering the semi-desert south of Tenerife in the CANARY ISLANDS. Inland, at Vilaflor, it boasts Europe's highest vineyard, reaching 1,700 m/5,577 ft ELEVATION. Soils are SANDY and CALCAREOUS at its lower levels, with CLAY and well-drained VOLCANIC soils in the higher sites. It produces an increasing number of interesting wines from local grapes such as MALVASIA, LISTÁN, and Baboso Negro (ALFROCHEIRO). V. de la S. & F.C.

Abouriou, early-ripening minor south-western dark-berried vine variety that was still grown on 322 ha/796 acres of France in 2019. It is allowed into Côtes du MARMANDAIS, where Elian Da Ros makes a varietal version. Its wine is relatively high in tannin and low in acidity. DNA PROFILING has suggested a parent–offspring relationship with Magdeleine Noire des Charentes, the obscure mother of Merlot and COT. Known in California as Early Burgundy. J.V.

Robinson, J., et al., *Wine Grapes: A Complete Guide to 1,368 Vine Varieties Including Their Origins and Flavours* (2012).

Abruzzo, mountainous region in central Italy with a significant coastline on the Adriatic Sea to the south of MARCHE and an important producer of wine (see map under ITALY). Abruzzo is fourth among Italy's regions in terms of production, with a total output of 3.4 million hl/87 million gal in 2020. Despite the presence of one of Italy's better red grape varieties, MONTEPULCIANO d'Abruzzo, a climate ranging from MEDITERRANEAN to CONTINENTAL, and largely hilly vineyard sites in the shadow of the 3,000 m/9,843 ft-high Gran Sasso Massif—aspects that help mitigate CLIMATE CHANGE—most of the region's production remains undistinguished.

Abruzzo's best-known varieties, the red Montepulciano and the white TREBBIANO d'Abruzzese, have been underachievers, mainly because of ignorance of site specifics and because YIELDS of more than 100 hl/ha are legal. This is not helped by the facts that until recently the entire region was covered by a single DOC, Abruzzo, and required only 80% of each principal variety (amended to 85% in 2010).

But the region has made convincing attempts at improving quality, helped by falling BULK WINE prices and the VINE-PULL SCHEME of the EU which has seen total vineyard area decline from 36,000 ha/89,000 acres to 32,500 ha in 2020, with just under half of that dedicated to DOC production.

Montepulciano d'Abruzzo was once prized as a blending wine in Italy's north, Germany, and France, but there are an increasing number of more serious examples from single producers, rather than from the omnipresent CO-OPERATIVES. It is generally produced in two styles: young and robustly fruity or structured and ageworthy. The latter are typically aged in large oak casks rather than BARRIQUES as was once fashionable. Most of Abruzzo's whites labelled Trebbiano are made of the bland Trebbiano Toscano rather than Trebbiano d'Abruzzese, which some serious producers prove can turn out complex wines.

The Abruzzo DOC has been divided into five subzones (Alto Tirino, Casauria, Teate, Terre dei Peligni, and Terre dei Vestini), while the tiny DOC Controguerra allows for varietal Chardonnay, Cabernet Sauvigon, and Merlot as well as local varieties. Subject to stricter production rules, several subzones require a VINE DENSITY of at least 4,000 vines/ha compared with DOC Abruzzo's 2,500, the latter due to the TENDONE training method. Two tiny and potentially exciting DOCs, Villamagna and Ortona, share the same tighter rules, but for wines made with a minimum of 95% Montepulciano. The large DOC Cerasuolo d'Abruzzo, requiring a minimum of 85% Montepulciano, can be a source for well-priced *rosato*, with the potential to achieve more, and the tiny Terre Tollesi or Tullum, elevated to DOCG in 2019, excels in white wine made from PECORINO. The region's other DOCG, Montepulciano d'Abruzzo Colline Teramane, has still to prove its worth. In March 2022 new regulations saw the folding of Abruzzo's eight IGTS into a single one called Terre d'Abruzzo; additionally, 'Superiore', stipulating lower yields and higher minimum alcohol, and 'Riserva', stipulating two years of ageing, may appear on labels of Abruzzo DOC and DOCG wines. W.S.

www.vinidabruzzo.it

abscisic acid, or **ABA**, HORMONE that occurs naturally in vines and other plants which regulates growth and physiology. It has been shown to be involved in the control of gene expression, thereby influencing certain characteristics of the vine such as the biosynthesis of ANTHOCYANINS. Its synthesis is encouraged by physiological stresses including short days and WATER STRESS. In the vine, abscisic acid is involved in LEAF FALL, shoot and root growth, bud dormancy, opening of STOMATA, and regulation of grape ripening. The irrigation technique PARTIAL

ROOTZONE DRYING works by manipulating ABA levels. P.R.D. & R.E.S.

Böttcher, C., and Davies, C., 'Hormonal control of grape berry development and ripening', in H. Gerós et al. (eds.), *The Biochemistry of the Grape Berry* (2012).

Keller, M., 'Botany and anatomy', in *The Science of Grapevines* (3rd edn, 2020).

Abu Nuwas (d. 814 CE), half Arab/half Persian, was court poet and close friend of the Abbasid Caliph al-Amīn (reigned 809–813 CE). He was one of the greatest ARAB POETS of classical Arabic/Islamic culture and, despite his eloquence in all the poetic genres, is remembered principally in the Arabic tradition for his wine poems (the *Khamriyyāt*). P.K.

Kennedy, P., *Abu Nuwas: A Genius of Poetry* (2005).

Rowell, A., *Vintage Humour: The Islamic Wine Poetry of Abu Nuwas* (2018).

abv, abbreviation for alcohol by volume. See ALCOHOLIC STRENGTH.

Abymes, CRU just south of CHAMBÉRY whose name may be added to the eastern French appellation SAVOIE. The vineyards border those of APREMONT and the wines are similar: typically light, dry, stony whites made from the local JACQUÈRE grape. W.L.

academe, originally a Greek word for a site of scholastic endeavour, and today a term embracing all that is achieved there. It impinges considerably on the world of wine.

Winemaking was already a sophisticated practical art by the beginning of the 19th century, and Europe's first formal viticultural training school was established in SACHSEN in what is now eastern Germany in 1811–12. In the second half of the century, however, the seminal work of Louis PASTEUR heralded its transition to an applied science worthy of academic study. Vine-growing and winemaking were soon recognized as academic disciplines, and in 1880, coincidentally, both the University of California (now established at DAVIS) and the Institut d'Oenologie at the University of BORDEAUX began teaching and researching VITICULTURE and OENOLOGY. The devastation caused in the mid to late 19th century by FUNGAL DISEASES and the PHYLLOXERA pest may help to explain the coincidence.

During the 20th and early 21st centuries, academic institutions throughout the world have worked in tandem with their local wine industries both to teach the scientific principles of vine-growing and winemaking (increasingly regarded as the single discipline of winegrowing) and to research refinements and solutions. Other academic institutions of importance to wine include ADELAIDE, AGROSCOPE, AWRI, BROCK UNIVERSITY, CHARLES STURT UNIVERSITY, CONEGLIANO, CORNELL UNIVERSITY, DIJON, GEISENHEIM, ISVV, JULIUS-KÜHN-INSTITUT, KLOSTERNEUBURG, LINCOLN UNIVERSITY, MAGARACH, MONTPELLIER, PLUMPTON, SAN MICHELE ALL'ADIGE, STELLENBOSCH, and VIRGINIA TECH. Some of these are government funded, although grants for specific research projects are increasingly sought from industry.

In traditional wine regions, winegrowing was taught by apprenticeship, and apprentices were taught to respect tradition above SCIENCE. Formal academic training has long been the norm in the NEW WORLD, on the other hand. By the late 20th century, however, it was customary for even seventh-generation European wine producers to have received some sort of formal academic training, certainly in their own region and very possibly abroad. This not only reflected a fundamental change of attitude towards the science of wine production on the part of European producers but also played a crucial role in the widespread improvement in wine quality during the 1980s and 1990s. Academe, with its annual crop of graduates, could be said to have spawned FLYING WINEMAKERS. Wine courses today need not be focused on production or tasting, however, with such tertiary qualifications as the wine MBAs available in Bordeaux, Davis, and Sonoma.

Acadie. See L'ACADIE BLANC.

access systems, wine. See PRESERVATION SYSTEMS.

Accolade Wines, global wine group based in Australia, an obvious rival to TREASURY WINE ESTATES. Brands with the longest history are Hardys and Houghton. Other Australian brands include St Hallett, Petaluma, Grant Burge, Banrock Station, House of Arras, and Jam Shed while Echo Falls is a mass-market brand sourced in California. Accolade's Berri Estates in South Australia is the largest grape processor in the southern hemisphere, crushing about 220,000 tonnes of grapes annually. The Park in Bristol, UK—owned by Accolade—is Europe's largest wine packaging and distribution centre in Europe, receiving about 180 million litres of wine a year in BULK, much of it for other companies. Accolade delivers approximately 276 million litres of wine to 130 countries every year.

acetaldehyde, the most common member of the group of chemical compounds known as ALDEHYDES, a natural constituent of nearly all plant material, including grapes. Acetaldehyde is the next to last substance involved in the FERMENTATION pathway (and is therefore a minor constituent of all fermented products). Post-fermentation traces of acetaldehyde remain in all wines.

In pure liquid form, acetaldehyde has a particularly penetrating and unpleasant aroma. Above a certain level it can make the wine smell 'flat', vapid, and OXIDIZED. At slightly higher concentrations, it contributes to the distinctive and characteristic smell of FINO sherry and other FLOR wines. Acetaldehyde binds with SULFUR DIOXIDE. It also adds to ANTHOCYANIN pigments, CATECHINS, and PROANTHOCYANIDINS (condensed TANNINS), and it is thus involved in the formation of PIGMENTED TANNINS and other derived tannins and pigments in wines. When free acetaldehyde is present in an oxidized white wine, it may react with α-ketobutyric acid to form SOTOLON, which is a marker for the premature ageing of white wine aromas (see PREMATURE OXIDATION).

Because it is the first compound formed when OXYGEN reacts with the ETHANOL in wine, winemakers are careful to minimize delicate white wines' exposure to air. (This is not so critical with heavier red wines, possibly because acetaldehyde reacts with tannins and anthocyanins.) Special care must be taken while BOTTLING white wines as this is when the introduction of oxygen can most easily damage the delicate aromas. When a bottle of white wine is only partially emptied, the freshness of its aroma is rapidly lost and replaced by a vapid oxidized smell that is due to, among other reactions, the conversion of ethanol to acetaldehyde. The formation of perceptible acetaldehyde, accompanied by a browning of colour, is a typical sign of OXIDATION. V.C. & V.L.

acetic acid, a simple two-carbon fatty acid which is the main flavour constituent responsible for the aroma and sour taste of VINEGAR. In wine it is the main component of what is called VOLATILE ACIDITY (VA).

Acetic acid is produced by a range of microbial activity including primary FERMENTATION, MALOLACTIC CONVERSION, and other fermentations carried out by spoilage organisms (LACTIC ACID BACTERIA, acetic acid bacteria, and spoilage yeasts including BRETTANOMYCES). If wine is exposed to OXYGEN after fermentation, ACETOBACTER can produce high levels of acetic acid from ETHANOL.

The sensory threshold for acetic acid is about 0.7 g/l. The EU legal limit is 1.07 g/l for dry white and rosé and 1.2 g/l for dry reds. Levels above 1.1–1.2 g/l become unpleasant (sharp, vinegary) and are regarded as a wine FAULT. However, in botrytis-affected white wines, higher levels may be produced because yeast activity is disrupted by the high sugar concentration in the must. In this case, up to 1.47 g/l of acetic acid is permitted. T.J. & V.L.

acetic acid bacteria, a family of genera which includes ACETOBACTER and GLUCONOBACTER.

acetobacter, genus within the family of acetic acid bacteria (AAB) capable of spoiling wine by converting it ultimately into VINEGAR. They are found on all grapes but especially rot-affected grapes. Acetobacter can survive only in OXYGEN and are also one of the very few groups of bacteria which can live in the high-acid (low PH) environment of wine (although see also LACTIC ACID BACTERIA).

Ideal conditions for the growth of acetobacter are temperatures between 30 and 40 °C (86–104 °F), relatively high pH values of between 3.5 and 4, low alcohol concentrations, absence of SULFUR DIOXIDE, and generous supplies of oxygen. For these reasons, safe winemaking favours low storage temperatures, good levels of ACIDITY and alcohol, use of appropriate levels of sulfur dioxide as a disinfectant, and, to minimize oxygen contact, barrels, vats, and tanks kept full at all times, that is with minimum ULLAGE. If this last cannot be avoided, the stored wine is blanketed with CARBON DIOXIDE, NITROGEN, or an INERT GAS mixture. P.J.W.

acid, when used as an adjectival tasting term rather than a chemical noun (see ACIDS), is usually pejorative, a bit like 'tart' or 'sour', and means that the wine has too much ACIDITY.

acid adjustment, euphemism for DEACIDIFICATION or, more usually, ACIDIFICATION.

acidification is the winemaking process of increasing the ACIDITY in a grape must or wine. This is a common practice in warm wine regions (as common as ENRICHMENT, or CHAPTALIZATION, in cool wine regions) and is often the only course open to a winemaker wanting to make a balanced wine from grapes which have been allowed a growing season long enough to develop flavour by reaching full PHYSIOLOGICAL RIPENESS. This is because in warm conditions a large amount of the grape's natural MALIC ACID is degraded during the ripening process. A good level of ACIDS (and therefore low PH) not only increases the apparent freshness and fruitiness of many wines but also protects the wine against attack from BACTERIA and spoilage yeasts such as BRETTANOMYCES, enhances the effectiveness of SULFUR DIOXIDE, and can improve COLOUR (as explained under ACIDITY) as well as increasing a wine's potential to age in bottle.

Acidification is usually sanctioned by local wine regulations within carefully delineated limits in order to prevent stretching of wine by adding sugar and water along with the permitted acid. In TEMPERATE zones such as Bordeaux and Burgundy, acidification is allowed, but with the understandable proviso that no wine may be both acidified and enriched.

The timing of the acid addition varies, but adding acid usually lowers pH so that an addition before or during FERMENTATION results in better microbiological control of subsequent processes and favours the formation of desirable aromas. Fine-tuning of acid levels may take place at the final BLENDING stage, but acid added at this stage can be too obvious.

Regulations vary from country to country, but the most common permitted additives for acidification are, in descending order, TARTARIC ACID, MALIC ACID, LACTIC ACID, and CITRIC ACID. Tartaric is the acid of choice for adding to grape juice before fermentation for several reasons: it is the natural acid of ripe grapes, it is the most effective option, and, unlike both citric and malic acid, which can be attacked by LACTIC ACID BACTERIA, tartaric acid is rarely degraded. Tartaric acid has the disadvantages, however, that it is the most expensive of the four and that significant amounts of the acid may be precipitated as TARTRATES and lost from the wine. If grapes are harvested with high levels of malic acid, tartaric acid may be added so that the wine retains sufficient acidity after MALOLACTIC CONVERSION. Malic acid is used infrequently because of its microbiological instability and its cost. Citric acid, while also being susceptible to microbiological attack, has the merit of being the least expensive and is used widely for inexpensive wines. However, this practice is not permitted in wines made or sold in the EU. It is often chosen for late acid additions because, unlike tartaric acid, it does not affect cold STABILIZATION. Where regulations permit (in the United States, for example), a blend of acids is often used.

EU regulations permit the addition of calcium phosphate (gypsum) to low-acid must destined for fortified wines. In SHERRY country, for example, it is sometimes added in conjunction with tartaric acid.

One of the problems with acidification is that it is difficult to calculate how much acid to add to reach a desired final pH, in part because each wine or must has its own BUFFERING CAPACITY.

See also DEACIDIFICATION. J.A.G. & V.L.

acidity is a general term for the fresh, tart, or sour taste produced by the natural organic ACIDS present in a liquid and one of the primary tastes sensed by tastebuds on the tongue (see TASTING). Wines, together with most other refreshing or appetizing drinks, owe their attractive qualities to a proper balance between this acidic character and the sweet and bitter sensations of other components.

The acidity of the original grape juice has an important influence on wine quality because of its direct influence on COLOUR (see below), its effect on the growth of YEASTS and BACTERIA (harmful and beneficial), and its inherent effects on flavour qualities. It also plays a part in wine AGEING.

Grape juice acidity is highest just at the beginning of RIPENING, at which stage grapes have half as much concentration of acidity as lemons (see also VERJUS).

Acidity is one of the most important components in both grape juice and wine, and it is also easily quantifiable. What is measured, although in different ways in different countries, is usually the TOTAL ACIDITY, which is the sum of the FIXED ACIDS and the VOLATILE ACIDS. To a scientist, acidity is the extent to which a solution is acid, caused by protons (hydrogen ions or H+), which may be present in either free or bound forms. Another way of measuring acidity is to measure the concentration of hydrogen ions (H+) free in solution, using the logarithmic PH scale. Generally the higher the total acidity of a wine, the lower is its pH.

Acidity helps to preserve the colour of red wines because the pH affects the ionization of ANTHOCYANINS, which in turn affects their colour. The lower the pH, the redder (less blue) the colour is and the greater the colour stability. As pH values rise (in less-acid wines), pigments become increasingly blue and the colour becomes less stable with pigments eventually assuming muddy grey forms. Red wines from warmer regions and made without ACIDIFICATION can have colours that are less red (and often with a brownish tinge) than those from colder regions which produce wines with higher acidity.

Excessive acidity—resulting either from excessive concentrations of natural plant acids in less-than-ripe grapes or, more rarely, from over-enthusiastic acidification in the winery—makes wines sharp, tart, and sometimes unpleasant to drink. Too little acidity, on the other hand—the consequence of picking too late, or such heat during ripening that the natural plant acids are largely decomposed—results in wines that are flat, uninteresting, and described typically by wine tasters as 'flabby'.

B.G.C. & P.J.W.

acids, members of a group of chemical compounds which are responsible for the sharp or sour taste of all drinks and foods, including wine. The most important acids contained in grapes are TARTARIC ACID and, usually in slightly lower concentrations, MALIC ACID. Malic acid occurs in many different plants and fruits, but vines are among the very few plants with large concentrations of tartaric acid in their fruit. The principal acid component in most plants is CITRIC ACID, but VITIS VINIFERA vines are also unusual among plants in accumulating only very small amounts of citric acid.

Some other acids involved in the growth of vines accumulate in the berry in very small amounts, and some of these persist into the wine. Other acids found in wines, while possibly present in traces in grapes, are formed mainly during FERMENTATION. Among those present in the largest concentrations are LACTIC ACID, SUCCINIC ACID, ACETIC ACID, and CARBONIC ACID.

Various acids are also occasionally added during winemaking. (See ASCORBIC ACID, SORBIC ACID, and sulfurous acid, which is SULFUR DIOXIDE.)

Acids are important in wine not just because, in moderation, they make it taste refreshing, but also because they prevent the growth of harmful BACTERIA and spoilage yeasts such as BRETTANOMYCES and can keep the wine microbiologically stable. In addition, with higher acidity and therefore likely lower PH, SULFUR DIOXIDE is a more effective antimicrobial substance. Most bacteria, and all of those of greatest danger to people, are incapable of living in distinctly acid solutions such as wines. Two groups of bacteria are major exceptions to this rule, however, the ACETOBACTER and the various LACTIC ACID BACTERIA.

A wine's concentration of acids is called its ACIDITY, which can be measured in various ways. Acidity is closely, if inversely, related to pH. P.J.W. & M.J.T.

OIV, 'International Code of Oenological Practices'. www.oiv.int/en/technical-standards-and-documents/oenological-practices/international-code-of-oenological-practices.

acidulation, winemaking process more commonly known as ACIDIFICATION.

Acolon, GERMAN CROSS of LEMBERGER and DORNFELDER authorized in 2002 and planted mainly in Württemberg and the Pfalz. Plantings totalled 1,432 ha/3,539 acres in 2020.

Aconcagua, wine region of CHILE north of Santiago encompassing the valleys of Aconcagua, CASABLANCA, and SAN ANTONIO.

acrotony. See APICAL DOMINANCE.

additives, as controversial in wine as in any other foodstuff, have long been hidden from wine drinkers since wine was exempt from INGREDIENT LABELLING regulations, although producers had to state on the label if their wines contained SULFITES. Since 2022, all additives used in the production of wines made or sold in the EU have had to be declared on the label or via a QR code. Widely used and perfectly legal additives include YEAST to carry out FERMENTATION, lactic acid bacteria for MALOLACTIC CONVERSION, sugar to increase ALCOHOLIC STRENGTH (see CHAPTALIZATION), acid for ACIDIFICATION, OENOLOGICAL TANNINS for TEXTURE and COLOUR stability, SWEET RESERVE for sweetness, alcohol for FORTIFICATION, ASCORBIC ACID as an ANTIOXIDANT, DIAMMONIUM PHOSPHATE as a yeast nutrient, ENZYMES to improve juice extraction, and SORBIC ACID as a preservative. Specific limits on additions (those on which EU member states have reached agreement) are set out in the OIV's International Code of Oenological Practices. Instances of the use of illegal additives such as FLAVOURINGS and OAK essence may be more common than we think, and prosecutions for ADULTERATION are seemingly rare. Additives should not be confused with PROCESSING AIDS.

See also HUMIDIFICATION, DOSAGE, MICRO-OXYGENATION, and ADULTERATION AND FRAUD.

adega, Portuguese word for cellar or winery.

Adelaide, usual abbreviation in the wine world for the **University of Adelaide**, in South Australia, with which ROSEWORTHY Agricultural College was merged in 1991 into what is now known as the Department of Wine Science, Australia's principal and influential centre of wine education and research (see ACADEME and AUSTRALIAN INFLUENCE).

Most of the teaching in OENOLOGY, VITICULTURE, and wine business studies takes place in the South Australian capital city of Adelaide at the Waite and North Terrace campuses. At the Waite Campus, students undertake their winemaking in the multi-million-dollar Hickinbotham Roseworthy Wine Science Laboratory owned by the University of Adelaide. They also have access to collaborating partners in the Wine Innovation Cluster located on the Waite Campus that includes the Commonwealth Scientific and Industrial Research Organization (CSIRO) Plant Industry, the AWRI, and the South Australian Research and Development Institute (SARDI), all of them having established a considerable international reputation for research in viticulture and oenology. S.T. & V.J.

www.thewaite.org/waite-partners/wine-innovation-cluster

Adelaide Hills, fashionable, relatively high (450–550 m/1,480–1,800 ft), cool wine region in SOUTH AUSTRALIA, part of the MOUNT LOFTY RANGES ZONE with CLARE VALLEY. Lenswood and Piccadilly Valley are officially recognized subregions. The region excels in Chardonnay, Pinot Noir, and Sauvignon Blanc, although SHIRAZ also stands out, both in a fuller style from the lower-elevation west-facing slopes in the north of the region and in a northern Rhône mode (sometimes married with VIOGNIER) from cooler parts. ALTERNATIVE VARIETIES are increasingly grown, the main successes being TEMPRANILLO, NEBBIOLO, PINOT GRIS, and FIANO.

Adelaide Plains, a flat, dry, warm-to-hot region immediately north of Adelaide with one notable winery, Primo Estate (which sources much of its fruit from outside the region). Shiraz makes up just over half of total volume harvested, most of it destined for lower-priced bottlings.

Adelaide Zone, Australian super zone encompassing the MOUNT LOFTY RANGES ZONE, FLEURIEU ZONE, and BAROSSA ZONE, stretching from CLARE VALLEY in the north to the foot of the Fleurieu Peninsula, plus the gaps in between; hence Penfolds Magill Estate is a notable resident. Infrequently used as a GEOGRAPHICAL INDICATION on wine labels.

adulteration and fraud have dogged the wine trade throughout its history. The variability and value of wine have traditionally made it a target for unscrupulous operators, as catalogued in the LITERATURE OF WINE. The long human chain stretching from grower to consumer affords many opportunities for illegal practices. It is important to remember, however, that at various times the law has viewed the same practices differently, sometimes condoning, sometimes condemning them. What we know as adulteration, our ancestors may have classed as a legitimate part of the winemaking process. See also MANIPULATION.

The simplest and most obvious form of adulterating wine is to add water (see HUMIDIFICATION). This is not necessarily fraudulent. In ancient GREECE, for example, no civilized man would dream of drinking undiluted wine, and even today wine made from extremely ripe grapes may achieve better BALANCE if slightly diluted. The practice becomes illegal when done surreptitiously to cheat the consumer or defraud the tax collector.

Another means of stretching wine is to 'cut', or blend, it with spirits or other (usually poorer-quality) wines. BORDEAUX merchants in the 18th century cut fine CLARETS with rough, stronger wine imported from Spain, the Rhône, or the Midi to increase profits, but also because it was genuinely believed that the resulting fuller-bodied concoction was more to the English taste. JULLIEN describes this common practice as *travail à l'anglaise*. Similarly, merchants in 18th-century OPORTO began to adulterate port with brandy. The systematization of this process by the Portuguese government eventually led to an accepted method of 'adulteration', entirely lawful, to produce PORT as we know it today.

Other ways of altering the nature of a wine were perfectly legal. In the past, wines turned sour after a year or two and techniques used to cure or disguise 'sick' wines were commonplace. Classical and medieval recipes suggested adding various substances ranging from milk (perhaps a precursor of FINING with CASEIN) and mustard to ashes, nettles, and LEAD. Although home doctoring was routine, when these techniques were employed by merchants or taverners deliberately to mislead the customer the practice was as illegal as it was ubiquitous. In the 1st century CE, PLINY the Elder bemoaned the fact that 'not even our nobility ever enjoys wines that are genuine'.

It is assumed today that, unless explicitly stated otherwise, wine is the product of naturally fermented grape juice. However, the practice of fabricating wine, as opposed to simply doctoring it, has a long and chequered history, often most prolific and ingenious at times when

true grape wine has been difficult to obtain. In 1709 Joseph Addison wrote in the *Tatler* of the 'fraternity of chymical operators ... who squeeze Bourdeaux out of a sloe and draw Champagne from an apple', apparently a profession of long standing. Even today in CHINA's relatively uncontrolled wine market, it is not uncommon to encounter chemical concoctions sold as wine.

Wines were also fabricated from raisins. In the 1880s and 1890s during the scourge of PHYLLOXERA, a thriving industry manufacturing wine from imported raisins sprang up on the Mediterranean coast. During American PROHIBITION in the 1920s, various methods were contrived to circumvent the law by producing wines at home from raisins, dried grape 'bricks', and tinned GRAPE CONCENTRATE (using techniques common to HOME WINEMAKING today).

One of the most common forms of fraud does not involve any doctoring or fabricating of the wine but merely the renaming of it. Once a region made a name for its wines, others tried to steal it. In Roman times, ordinary wines were passed off as valuable FALERNIAN. From the 19th century, vine-growers have fought for the legal apparatus to protect their names (see AOC), and today producers of some of the most expensive wines go to great lengths to design labels which cannot be counterfeited (see INVESTMENT).

The adulteration or fraudulent sale of wine can be dangerous. The consumer may even be put medically at risk, by the use of lead in ancient times and by METHANOL contamination in the 20th century.

Consumers, growers, and merchants are not alone in trying to prevent adulteration and fraud. Local authorities and (from the last century) governments have fought it. Regulations and legislation have been passed for many reasons: to protect the consumer; to preserve the good name of the local wine; or to facilitate TAXATION.

In medieval London it was illegal for taverners to keep French or Spanish wines in the same cellar as those from Germany to prevent mixing or substitution. A winegrower found selling corrupt wine was forced to drink it, then banned from the trade. German punishments of the time were more severe, ranging from beatings and branding to hanging.

The legal apparatus existing to combat fraud and adulteration today is the culmination of many battles waged by both consumers and trade. In 1820 Frederick Accum published his *Treatise* stating that wine was the commodity most at risk. Thirteen years later Cyrus Redding reported no improvement, and it was not until 1860 that the first British Food and Drug Act was passed.

As for wine-producing countries, the economic distress caused by phylloxera was the main stimulus to legislation. The French government produced a legal definition of wine in 1889, the Germans framed the first GERMAN WINE LAW in 1892 (superseded by the more thorough 1909 version), and the Italians in 1904. The French Appellation Contrôlée system, defining wines by geography rather than simply composition, did not become nationally viable until the 1930s.

Although once rife, adulteration and fraud have been considerably rarer in the wine trade since the adoption of CONTROLLED APPELLATION systems and methods by which to enforce them such as France's Service de la Répression des Fraudes. There have been examples of CONTAMINANTS in wine, both deliberate and accidental, but passing off has become increasingly difficult and, just possibly, less rewarding as wine consumers become ever more sophisticated and more concerned with inherent wine quality than the hierarchy of famous names. Consumers may, with justification, feel that the wine trade has attracted more than its fair share of charlatans because fraud in any field in which expertise is difficult to acquire and viewed with suspicion (such as wine and fine art) attracts more media attention than most other types of commercial fraud.

For details of modern fine wines encountered in fake form, see COUNTERFEIT WINE. H.B. & J.R.

Accum, F., *Treatise on Adulteration of Food and Culinary Poisons* (1820).

Barr, A., *Wine Snobbery: An Insider's Guide to the Booze Business* (1988).

Gibb, R., *Vintage Crime: A Short History of Wine Fraud* (2023).

Johnson, H., *The Story of Wine: From Noah to Now* (2020).

Jullien, A., *Topographie de tous les vignobles connus* (1816).

Loubère, L. A., *The Red and the White: A History of Wine in France and Italy in the Nineteenth Century* (1978).

Redding, C., *A History and Description of Modern Wines* (1833).

Aegean Islands, islands in the Aegean Sea between modern GREECE and TÜRKIYE, populated by Greeks for millennia. In ancient times, some of the best wines came from these islands, with CHIAN wine, from the island of Chios, ranked highly in both ancient Greece and ancient ROME. Wines from Lesbos, Thasos, and Cos also featured strongly. Chian wine was still highly valued in the Middle Ages and traded in quantity by the GENOANS, for example. Today the islands, led by SANTORINI, are home to several important wines and appellations. In addition, several grape varieties such as ASSYRTIKO, MANDILARIA, and LIMNIO are considered quintessentially Aegean. The regional PGI Aegean Sea can be applied to dry and medium-dry wines from any Aegean island (or combination thereof) except for Evvia and Crete, while PGI Cyclades applies only to southern Aegean Islands. K.L.

aeration, the deliberate and controlled exposure of a substance to air, and particularly to its reactive component OXYGEN.

The aeration of wine during WINEMAKING must be carefully controlled, since excessive exposure to oxygen can result in OXIDATION, the possible formation of excess ACETIC ACID, and the loss of aroma compounds. At the beginning of FERMENTATION some aeration is necessary since YEAST needs oxygen for growth. The cellar operation of TOPPING UP can expose the wine to an amount of oxygen that contributes to the BARREL AGEING process. The amount of aeration involved in the cellar techniques of RACKING wine from one container (usually a BARREL) to another, RACK AND RETURN, and PUMPING OVER can also be positively beneficial to a wine's development. Specifically, aeration can often cure wines suffering from REDUCTION and can usually remove malodorous and volatile HYDROGEN SULFIDE and MERCAPTANS.

Often for the same reasons, some aeration before SERVING by pouring the contents of a bottle from a great height or from one container into another can also benefit some wines after AGEING, as can simply swirling the wine in the glass. See also DECANTING and BREATHING.

aerial imagery. See REMOTE SENSING.

Afghanistan, Middle Eastern country in which 96,312 ha/237,992 acres of vines were officially cultivated for TABLE GRAPES and RAISINS in 2020, according to OIV figures. At one time wine may have been made here and shipped along the old Silk Road to India; today, any wine made is kept quite quiet as alcohol is prohibited for its citizens.

Africa. See ALGERIA, CAPE VERDE, EGYPT, ETHIOPIA, GABON, KENYA, LESOTHO, MADAGASCAR, MOROCCO, NAMIBIA, RÉUNION, SENEGAL, SOUTH AFRICA, TANZANIA, TOGO, TUNISIA, UGANDA, and ZIMBABWE.

age in a wine is not necessarily a virtue. See AGEING. See also VINE AGE.

ageing of wine, an important aspect of wine CONNOISSEURSHIP, and one which distinguishes wine from almost every other drink (see BACTERIA). See also BARREL AGEING, CASK AGEING, and ÉLEVAGE.

History

When a fine wine is allowed to age, spectacular changes can occur which increase both its complexity and its monetary value. Ageing is dependent on several factors: the wine must be intrinsically capable of it; it must be correctly stored (in a cool place and out of contact with air; see STORING WINE); and some form of capital INVESTMENT is usually necessary.

Although the BIBLE suggests that Luke understood that old wine was finer than new wine, the Romans (see ancient ROME and, specifically, HORACE) were the first connoisseurs systematically to appreciate fine wines which had been allowed to age, although there is some evidence of wine ageing in ancient GREECE. Certain wines (DRIED-GRAPE WINES, for example) were suitable for ageing because of their high sugar content and were stored in sealed earthenware jars or AMPHORAE. The best, FALERNIAN and SURRENTINE wines, required 15–20 years before they were considered at their best and were sometimes kept for decades.

The Greek physician GALEN (b. 130 CE) noted that an 'aged' wine need not necessarily be old but might simply have the characteristics of age. In other words it was possible, indeed very common, to age wines prematurely by means of heating or smoking them (see ancient ROME). At one time the smoky taste of 'aged' wines became a vogue in itself, though Galen warned that they were not as wholesome as naturally old wines.

After the collapse of the Roman Empire, the appreciation of aged wines disappeared for a millennium. The thin, low-alcohol wines of northern Europe were good for only a few months, after which they turned sour and were sold cheaply. The only wines that could be enjoyed a little longer were the sweeter and more alcoholic wines of the Mediterranean such as MALMSEY and SACK.

By the 16th century, exceptions to this rule could be found in the huge casks of top-quality wine made from RIESLING kept beneath German palaces (see GERMAN HISTORY). These wines were preserved through a combination of sweetness and ACIDITY, the coldness of the cellar, and the cellarmaster's habit of constantly TOPPING UP the cask to avoid OXIDATION.

The real breakthrough came with the introduction in the 17th century of CORKS and glass BOTTLES. The ageing of wine in bottle was pioneered in England by connoisseurs of fine CLARET and PORT. English wine drinkers rediscovered pleasures largely unknown since Roman times.

Other methods of preserving wine were developed or rediscovered: the addition of spirits to a partially fermented wine to produce fortified wines (see FORTIFICATION); the systematic topping up of a SOLERA system to produce wines like SHERRY; and the heating of MADEIRA.

Demand for mature wines transformed the wine trade. Aside from a few wealthy owners, most vine-growers could not afford to keep stocks of past vintages. Only MERCHANTS could do that, and their economic power and hold over the producers increased during the 18th and 19th centuries. This was most demonstrably the case in BORDEAUX, BEAUNE, and OPORTO, where merchants amassed huge stocks, vast fortunes, and powerful reputations. H.B.

Johnson, H., *The Story of Wine: From Noah to Now* (2020).

Younger, W., *Gods, Men and Wine* (1966).

Which wines to age

The ageing of wine is an important element in getting the most from it, but, contrary to popular opinion, only a small subgroup of wines benefit from extended bottle ageing. The great bulk of wine sold today, red as well as white and pink, is designed to be drunk within a year, or at most two, of BOTTLING.

Wines which generally do not improve with time spent in bottle, and which are usually best consumed as soon as possible after bottling, include the following—although this is only the most approximate generalization: wines packaged in any containers other than bottles—BOXES, for example; most basic WINE WITHOUT GEOGRAPHICAL INDICATION in the EU, JUG WINE in the US, and their everyday, commercial equivalents elsewhere; almost all BRANDED wines, with the possible exception of some red bordeaux; most pink wine; all wines released within less than six months of the vintage such as those labelled NOUVEAU.

Fine wines are usually vinified expressly so that they will benefit from ageing in bottle. In the past, this tended to make them unattractive when consumed young, but with more consistent PHYSIOLOGICAL RIPENESS and the evolution in winemaking techniques, including more gentle EXTRACTION, such wines can also be enjoyed in their youth. In some cases the high levels of sugar, acid, and FLAVOUR COMPOUNDS, as in great Rieslings which may not contain much alcohol, can also benefit greatly from bottle ageing. Specific techniques such as MICRO-OXYGENATION may also make wines more approachable without the need for long bottle ageing.

Even among finer wines, different wines mature at different rates, according to individual VINTAGE characteristics, their exact provenance, and how they were made. Such factors as BARREL FERMENTATION for whites and BARREL AGEING for wines of any colour play a part in the likely life cycle of the wine. In general, the lower a wine's PH, the longer it is capable of evolving. Among reds, generally speaking the higher the level of flavour compounds and phenolics, particularly TANNINS, the longer it is capable of being aged. Wines made from Cabernet Sauvignon and Nebbiolo grapes, for example, and many of those made from Syrah/Shiraz, should be aged longer than those based on Merlot—and certainly much longer than the average wine made from Gamay or Grenache. Among white wines, partly because of their higher acidity and FLAVOUR PRECURSORS, the finest Riesling and Loire Chenin Blanc evolve more slowly than wines based on Chardonnay.

In general terms, better-quality wines from the following regions or made from the following grape varieties should benefit from some bottle age, with a *very* approximate number of years in bottle in brackets (of course, it all depends on vintage, winemaker, storage conditions, and many other factors):

WHITES

Almost all wine retailing at under £10/$20: 1–2
Chablis: 3–15
Côte d'Or white burgundy: 3–10
Other wines based on Chardonnay: 2–6
Wines based on Riesling: 3–20
Wines based on Sauvignon Blanc: 1–5
Wines based on Viognier: 1–3
Wines based on Chenin Blanc: 3–15
Skin-fermented whites: 5–10
Botrytized sweet wines: 5–35

REDS

Almost all wine retailing at under £10/$20: 1–3 (although some particularly good red Côtes du Rhône and old-vine Spaniards can provide exceptions)
Bordeaux, Madiran: 5–25
Burgundy: 4–20
northern Rhône: 4–15 (Hermitage longer)
southern Rhône: 3–10
Languedoc, Roussillon: 3–8
Barolo, Barbaresco: 6–25
Brunello di Montalcino: 5–13
Chianti: 4–10
Rioja: 5–20
Ribera del Duero: 3–15
Douro table wines: 4–12
Vintage port: 12–50
Other wines based on Cabernet Sauvignon: 7–17
Other wines based on Pinot Noir: 4–10
Other wines based on Syrah/Shiraz: 4–12
Other wines based on Grenache: 3–8

ICEWINE and all but the finest EISWEIN matures quite rapidly. Most fortified wines and their like, such as VINS DOUX NATURELS and VINS DE LIQUEUR, are bottled when their producers think they are ready to drink. Exceptions to this are the extremely rare bottle-aged SHERRIES, vintage PORT (which is expressly designed for decades of bottle ageing), single-quinta ports, and crusted port.

Producers of most SPARKLING WINES usually claim that their wines are ready to drink on release, but this may not be true when demand exceeds supply. Even if yeast AUTOLYSIS ceases when the wine is disgorged, better-quality young sparkling wines with their high levels of acidity can often improve considerably with an additional year or so in bottle.

Factors affecting ageing

STORING WINE in particular conditions can affect the rate at which wine ages; the lower the TEMPERATURE, the slower the maturation. Conversely, ageing can be hastened by stripping a young wine of its solids (by very heavy FILTRATION or

FINING, for example) and by storing wine in warmer conditions. Thus, a wine stored in a centrally heated Manhattan apartment will mature very much faster than one stored in an unheated warehouse in Scandinavia. In general, the more slowly a wine matures, the greater the complexity of the flavour compounds that go to make up its BOUQUET (see below).

It is also popularly believed that, in general, the smaller the BOTTLE SIZE the faster its contents mature, presumably because of the greater proportion of OXYGEN in the bottle, as a consequence both of the bottling process and of any possible oxygen ingress via the cork seal during ageing. This is one of the reasons LARGE FORMATS carry a premium.

One of the most significant factors affecting ageing is the type of CLOSURE and the amount of oxygen the wine is exposed to. For more details, see OXYGEN TRANSMISSION RATES and TOTAL PACKAGE OXYGEN.

How wine ages

The descriptions below concern only those wines designed specifically to be aged.

Red wines To the untutored taster, older red wines seem to be softer and gentler than harsh, inky young ones. Those who notice such things will also observe a change in colour, typically from deep purple to light brick red. There should also be more SEDIMENT in an old wine than a young one. All these phenomena are related, and are related in particular to the behaviour of phenolics, the compounds of the grape, particularly the skins, including the blue/red ANTHOCYANINS, which together with the astringent but colourless flavonoids form the PIGMENTED TANNINS (tannin-anthocyanin adducts) that are responsible for a red wine's COLOUR and TEXTURE.

Most phenolics are leached out of the grape skins and seeds during RED WINEMAKING. They react with each other, especially under the influence of the small amounts of oxygen dissolved in the wine during such processes as RACKING, TOPPING UP, and, later, bottling, to generate various derivatives including pigmented tannins. There is some evidence that these reactions start during the primary FERMENTATION process, and by about 18 months later the anthocyanins have mostly been converted to derived pigments responsible for the colour of older red wines. A fine red wine ready for bottling, therefore, may contain colourless tannins, a low concentration of anthocyanins, as well as derived pigments including pigmented tannins, and more complex COLLOIDS such as tannin-POLYSACCHARIDES, and tannin-PROTEINS. Reactions and aggregation continue in bottle. When the resulting polymers and particles reach a certain size, they precipitate as dark reddish-brown sediment, leaving wine that is progressively less astringent, some of the red/blue pigments and tannins having been precipitated. Thus, to a certain extent, holding a bottle of wine up to the light to determine how much sediment it has precipitated can give some indication of its maturity (although the amount of sediment deposited is a function not just of time but of storage conditions and the initial composition of the wine, phenolic and protein content for example, and any FINING carried out prior to bottling).

At the same time as these visible changes occur, the impact of the wine on the nose and palate also evolves. A wide range of FLAVOUR PRECURSORS that were attached to glucose detach themselves (through a natural, and time-dependent, process of HYDROLYSIS) and contribute their individual flavour characteristics to the older wine.

Other flavour compounds responsible for the initial primary AROMAS of the grape and those of fermentation (sometimes called secondary aroma, or secondary bouquet) are also interacting, with each other and with other phenolics, so that gradually the smell of the wine is said to be transformed, by a pathway as yet not understood, into a bouquet of tertiary aromas, a very much more subtle array and arrangement of flavours which can be sensed by the nose (see TASTING).

ESTERS are formed from combinations of the increasingly complex array of wine ACIDS with ALCOHOLS. Continued esterification in bottle produces another range of possible aromas, all the more unpredictable since the esters are formed at very different rates.

The rate at which all these things happen is influenced by a host of factors: storage conditions (particularly temperature), the state of the cork or other stopper, the ULLAGE when the wine was bottled, its pH level, and SULFUR DIOXIDE concentration, all of which can inhibit or slow the all-important influence of oxygen.

OENOLOGISTS understand this much about the maturation of ageworthy red wine but are unable to predict with any degree of certainty when such a wine is likely to reach that complex stage called full MATURITY, when it has dispensed with its uncomfortably harsh tannins and acquired maximum complexity of flavour without starting to decay. Part of the joy of wine has long been said to be monitoring the progress of a case of wine, bottle by bottle, but this is strictly a rich person's sport.

White wines If our understanding of red-wine maturation is incomplete, even less is known about the ageing process in white wines. Nevertheless, research has shown the importance of certain grape GLYCOSIDES (and the hydrolysis of these constituents) during white-wine ageing to the development of varietal aroma in the wine. White wines begin life in bottle with a much lower tally of phenolics, although those phenolics strongly influence colour and apparent astringency. White wines become browner with age, presumably because of the slow OXIDATION of their phenolic content.

Ageing potential is indirectly proportional to a white wine's concentration of phenolics. For example, fine Rieslings, which are relatively low in phenolics, can in general age much longer than comparable Chardonnays, which contain more phenolics. However, the concentration of phenolics is also determined by the extent to which they are extracted during PRESSING.

Experienced tasters, however, often note that wines affected by NOBLE ROT have a much greater ability to last than their non-botrytized counterparts. Experience also seems to suggest that white wines which undergo barrel fermentation are capable of lasting longer than those fermented in inert containers and then transferred to barrel for BARREL AGEING. Nevertheless, some unwooded white wines also have a great ageing ability, particularly if they have been aged on their LEES.

Most white wines which can mature over several decades rather than years are notably high in acidity. Few of them undergo MALOLACTIC CONVERSION, with the notable exception of some top white burgundies. Many of the venerable sweet wines which demonstrate exceptional ageing ability today may well have been bottled with higher levels of sulfur dioxide than are acceptable to the modern consumer. See also ATYPICAL AGEING.

Stages of ageing

Maturing fine wines go through a number of perceptibly different stages. Very young wines are usually delicious, full of fruit and vivacity, but slightly simple. At some (unpredictable) time after bottling, anything between a few months and a few years, many fine wines seem to close up, to become surly, to lose their aroma without having gained a bouquet. Their dimensions can be sensed but little else (see TASTING). A variable number of years afterwards, they begin to smell like wine again and to have considerably more palate LENGTH. After this they enter into their most satisfying stage at which the bouquet seems fully developed and astringency has receded, making the mouthfeel attractive, so that the wine is delightful in terms of flavour, texture, length, and all-important BALANCE. (Many serious white Rhône wines are particularly prone to this sort of midlife crisis.) If, however, wine is aged for too long (and no one, alas, can predict when this will be), it enters a stage of decrepitude during which the acidity starts to dominate. This unpredictable journey may help to explain apparently contradictory judgements of the same wine, from WINE WRITERS, wine professionals, and wine consumers alike.

Artificial ageing

This winemaking technique has been practised with varying degrees of enthusiasm according to the demands of the market. Current FASHION dictates that wine should be as 'natural' as possible (and, increasingly, that it should be youthful rather than mature), and so very few table wines are ever subjected to artificial ageing (even if many modern WINEMAKING techniques such as MICRO-OXYGENATION are in fact designed to hasten some natural processes). Wine can be artificially aged by exposing it to oxygen or extremes of temperature, by shaking it to encourage effects of dissolved oxygen, or by exposing it to radiation or ultra-sonic or magnetic waves. The making of MADEIRA and some other RANCIO wines deliberately incorporates exposure to high temperatures, while storing wine in some modern domestic conditions can expose wine to high temperatures rather less deliberately.

This century is seeing considerable experimentation with unusual storage conditions for ageing. Those deliberately storing bottles of wine under water (see UNDERWATER AGEING) have been encouraged by the condition of even century-old champagne dredged up from the Baltic (see record prices in AUCTIONS), while others are seeing what happened when wine is stored at especially high ELEVATIONS or at a variety of TEMPERATURES and HUMIDITIES.

See also MATURITY and STORING WINE.

J.R., V.C. & V.L.

Nevares, I., and del Alamo-Sanza, M., 'Characterization of the oxygen transmission rate of new-ancient natural materials for wine maturation containers', *Foods*, 10/1, (2021), 140.

Ribéreau-Gayon, P., et al., *Traité d'Œnologie 2: Chimie du vin: Stabilisation et traitements* (7th edn, 2017), translated by John Towey as *Handbook of Enology 2: The Chemistry of Wine Stabilization and Treatments* (3rd edn, 2021).

Robinson, J., *Vintage Timecharts* (1989).

agglomerate corks, developed in 1891 by an American businessman, John Smith, occasionally called 'agglo', consist of ground-up cork granules glued together to form a cylinder. These are sold by most cork companies and can perform somewhat similarly to intact cork, though the smallest, poorly made agglos are used on the cheapest bottles. Another inexpensive alternative are colmated corks: one-piece corks in which blemishes and lenticels are filled with a mixture of cork dust and adhesive, then painted.

More recently, companies such as Diam, Amorim, and Cork Supply have offered 'technical' corks, closures made from carefully produced cork particles mixed with an elastic component. The particles are flushed with supercritical CO_2 (in the case of Diam) or undergo other processes to remove TCA (see CORK TAINT), and can have defined OXYGEN TRANSMISSION RATES. Because of this improved performance, technical corks are becoming increasingly popular with winemakers. Diam's Origine uses a plant-based binder and beeswax rather than oil-derived products. Agglomerate corks with discs of natural cork at each end, such as Twin Top from the world's biggest cork supplier Amorim, are also very popular and the standard for SPARKLING WINE. A.L.W.

Agiorgitiko, also known as **Aghiorgitiko** and occasionally St George, most planted and admirably versatile Greek red grape variety native to Nemea in the Peloponnese, whose wines may be made from no other variety. There were 2,185 ha/5,400 acres in Greece in 2021. It blends well with other varieties and can also produce good-quality rosé. The wine produced by Agiorgitiko is fruity but can lack acidity. Grapes grown on the higher vineyards of Nemea can yield fresher, long-lived reds. DNA PROFILING has suggested a parent–offspring relationship with the Greek table grape KORINTHIAKI.

Aglianico, a dark-skinned top-quality southern Italian grape variety long thought to be of Greek origin (the name was said to be a corruption of the word *Ellenico*, Italian for Hellenic), although DNA PROFILING has failed to find a relationship with any known Greek variety. It retained the name Ellenico or Ellenica until the end of the 15th century, when it took its current name. First planted around the Greek colony of Cumae, close to present-day Avellino (home of TAURASI), it is today cultivated in the mountainous centre of Italy's south, in particular in the provinces of Avellino and Benevento in CAMPANIA, and in the provinces of Potenza and Matera in BASILICATA. Scattered plantings of this early-budding vine variety can also be found in CALABRIA, PUGLIA, MOLISE, and on the island of Procida near Naples. DNA profiling has suggested a possible half-sibling relationship with DUREZA and an avuncular relationship with SYRAH. Italy's total plantings were 9,627 ha/23,789 acres in 2015. The vine can ripen so late even this far south that grapes may be picked in November. Attempts to pick it earlier, or to increase yields, invariably lead to a failure to tame its rather ferocious tannins. The grape's best wines are deep in colour with full chocolate and plum aromas, fine-grained tannins, and marked acidity on the palate. Aglianico seems to prefer soils of volcanic origin and achieves its finest results in the two DOCs of Taurasi in Campania and AGLIANICO DEL VULTURE in Basilicata, where elevations are lower and the wines rather softer and earlier-maturing. Its nobility is so obvious that it is now grown in Australia, California, and Argentina.

Robinson, J., et al., *Wine Grapes: A Complete Guide to 1,368 Vine Varieties, Including Their Origins and Flavours* (2012).

Aglianico del Vulture, potentially superior wine, one of only a handful in BASILICATA, based on the tannic and ageworthy AGLIANICO grape planted on the slopes of Mt Vulture, an extinct volcano. The DOC zone consists of close to 570 ha/1,408 acres in the north-west of the zone benefiting from cool nights at an ELEVATION of 450–600 m/1,970 ft. The area was given its own DOC in 1971, while the Superiore and Riserva versions of the wines were elevated to DOCG in 2010. Minimum VINE DENSITY for both DOC and DOCG is a low 3,350 plants/ha, while the high permitted YIELDS of 10 tons/ha for the DOC is lowered to 8 tonnes/ha for the DOCG. Quality-focused producers, however, demand much lower yields from their vines to produce the sturdy, classic red wine with a real propensity for extended cellaring.

Both DOC and DOCG wines must be 100% Aglianico, but styles can differ wildly, with an emphasis on winemaking rather than on the vineyard. The DOC version may not be released on to the market prior to the September following the year of harvest, while the DOCG requires 24 months of ageing, of which 12 must be in oak. French BARRIQUES still feature heavily, but the best wines tend to be aged in large oak casks. Vineyard districts, called CONTRADE, some 70 in total, may feature on labels, but the zone would benefit from more refined geographical DELIMITATION, specifically a much smaller CLASSICO zone to distinguish the HILLSIDES from the many vineyards on the plain. W.S.

www.consorzioaglianico.it

agricultural treatises are the source of much of our evidence for wine in ancient GREECE and ancient ROME. HESIOD was the first Greek to write on agriculture, in the 8th century BCE. CATO, VARRO, COLUMELLA, PLINY, and VIRGIL were all important Roman writers.

agriturismo, late 20th century phenomenon in rural Italy whereby unused or underused farm buildings, a significant proportion of them on wine farms, are converted, typically with state aid, for TOURIST accommodation, thereby exposing many thousands of visitors each year to the practicalities of wine production. Spain has seen a similar *enoturismo* initiative, and farm stays have since become popular worldwide.

agrochemicals, the materials used in agriculture to control pests and diseases. The term includes FUNGICIDES, insecticides, HERBICIDES, bird repellents, plant GROWTH REGULATORS, rodenticides, and soil fumigants and is not limited to synthetic chemicals. A broader definition might also include FERTILIZERS.

Viticulture requires fewer agrochemicals than some other field crops, partly because such a high proportion of vines are grown in warm, dry summer environments in which FUNGAL DISEASES are relatively rare, and also because vines require fewer fertilizers than most other crops (see VINE NUTRITION). However, vines grown in humid, warm summers may require regular SPRAYINGS. Vine-growers, like other farmers, are in general becoming more aware of their use of agrochemicals because of increased environmental concerns (see SUSTAINABILITY) and as alternative approaches become available. Some diseases, notably BOTRYTIS BUNCH ROT, develop tolerance to the repeated use of some chemicals, and so their use is subject to resistance-management strategies. Alternative approaches may take the form of INTEGRATED PEST MANAGEMENT (IPM) programmes, which aim to reduce reliance on agrochemicals through understanding and managing the host–pathogen interaction. The adoption of some form of SUSTAINABLE, ORGANIC, or BIODYNAMIC VITICULTURE restricts the use of agrochemicals to a prescribed list of permitted inputs.

The use of agrochemicals in viticulture is strictly regulated by governments in order to provide better protection for humans and the environment. Advances in analytical methods and an improved awareness of chemical risks has led to the removal of some chemical control options. The products that replace them have to pass stringent registration criteria, including an analysis of the effect the product may have on FERMENTATION. For example, RESIDUES of elemental SULFUR, which is used to protect vines against POWDERY MILDEW, may result in the formation of unpleasant aroma compounds if applied too close to harvest.

Such registrations are therefore lengthy, exacting, and costly. They specify, for example, withholding periods that must elapse between the last application and when the crop is harvested to allow residues of the agrochemical to diminish to suitably low concentrations. To save money, some manufacturers do not register chemicals with all governments, with the result that small and emerging wine industries, like that of the UK, are disadvantaged by having access to only a limited range of products.

When regulations governing agrochemicals are not harmonized across countries, trade barriers may result. For example, the fungicide iprodione was deregistered in 2017 for use on any crop grown in Europe. If it is used elsewhere on products destined for the EU, the official maximum residue limit (MRL) is set at the lower limit of what can be quantified analytically, thus affecting the way fungal diseases are managed worldwide. The *Codex Alimentarius* ('food code' in Latin) was established by the Food and Agricultural Organization (FAO) and the World Health Organization (WHO) to upgrade and simplify international food regulations and to avoid such situations. *Codex* MRLs have been set for some agrochemicals in a range of crops, and several countries accept *Codex* MRLs in the absence of their own.

Although an agrochemical may be present in formulations bearing different proprietary names, it usually has a single common name that is recommended by standards organizations. For example, the fungicide Scala® (from manufacturers Bayer) contains the agrochemical pyrimethanil that is also the active constituent of several other fungicides.

See also RESIDUES. R.E.S. & M.E.

Mollah, M., and MacGregor, A., 'Review of the potential for agrochemicals used in viticulture to impact on the environment' (2002), GWRDC Project CRV 01/04.

Agroscope, the Swiss centre for agricultural research, affiliated to the Federal Office for Agriculture, conducts wide-ranging research, from the vineyard to sensory analysis, at sites in Changins, Pully, Leytron, Cugnasco, and Wädenswil. The challenging landscape of the vineyards and the structure of the industry (see SWITZERLAND) incur high production costs for high-quality wine, making such research essential.

Current priorities include CLONAL SELECTION to safeguard the diversity of INDIGENOUS VARIETIES and the breeding of high-quality DISEASE-RESISTANT VARIETIES such as DIVICO and Divona to drastically reduce the use of AGROCHEMICALS. In order to achieve the maximum potential of the Swiss wine-producing regions, cultivation techniques and farming systems have been developed to ensure the best possible match between soil, climate, and grape variety.

Research in plant protection offers practical solutions for problems caused by pests, diseases, and weeds in the vineyards, including methods of prediction, prevention, and treatment. Agroscope's AgroMeteo platform publishes meteorological information useful for managing phytosanitary problems, while collaboration with companies, institutes, and winegrowers has resulted in the development of natural alternatives and innovative strategies for applying plant-protection products.

Research in oenology and analytical chemistry is focused on improving and adapting winemaking technology, taking into consideration changes brought about by CLIMATE CHANGE and consumer trends. Other priorities include microbiology, oxygen management, and the COLLOIDAL stability of wine. Besides maintaining and improving wine quality, research also addresses questions of food safety and sustainability. C.C.

Ahr, diminutive but increasingly prestigious German wine region of 562 ha/1,389 acres in 2019, specializing in SPÄTBURGUNDER (Pinot Noir) and named after the river which flows east from the hills of the Eifel to join the Rhine near Remagen (see map under GERMANY). The most westerly vineyards hug a circuitous, dramatically rocky stretch of river between Altenahr and Dernau, its steep sides sometimes narrowing to the dimensions of a gorge. Ahr vineyards are variously underlain with BASALT, SLATE, and clay-rich sandstone known as GREYWACKE, whose fast-warming and heat-retentive capabilities, along with shelter from winds and 69% of vine surface exceeding 30° inclination, more than compensates for an unusually northerly location at 50–51° LATITUDE and for ELEVATIONS of up to 300 m/980 ft; indeed, Spätburgunders in excess of 14% natural alcohol are not uncommon. Spätburgunder gained ground steadily here during a German red-wine boom that began in the 1990s, reaching 65% of regional vine surface by 2019. PORTUGIESER, prevalent after the Second World War when Ahr reds were mostly pale, soft, and slightly sweet, is in sharp decline, while FRÜHBURGUNDER retains popularity (with a 6% share). Riesling makes up 9% of vine surface, favouring slate soils, its wines evincing a tropical fruit character reminiscent of those from the MITTELRHEIN.

During the night of July 14–15, 2021, unprecedented rains turned the Ahr into a raging flood that destroyed the region's infrastructure and most of its wine facilities and, in many instances, wine stocks. Prime vineyards remained largely above water, so, thanks to timely helicopter-spraying against fungus and an enormous influx of volunteers from throughout Germany, much of the region's 2021 crop was harvested, then vinified off-site. Infrastructural recovery will take years. It remains to be seen how many of the region's 50-plus estate bottlers—not to mention roughly 1,100 small vine-holders who supply the Ahr's four CO-OPERATIVES (representing in 2019 some three-quarters of its grapes)—will elect to continue growing grapes. D.S.

AI. See ARTIFICIAL INTELLIGENCE.

Aïdani, floral-scented variety grown on SANTORINI and other Greek islands, typically for blending with ASSYRTIKO. DNA PROFILING has shown that Aïdani Mavro is not a dark-skinned mutation. J.V.

air drainage, important topographical and hence climatological consideration in VINEYARD SITE SELECTION. Cold air flows, or 'drains', downhill, and so a continuous slope or HILLSIDE is much less prone to FROST and WINTER FREEZE than a hollow. In regions at risk from these phenomena, zones which accumulate cold air should be avoided as vineyard sites. In general, a vineyard site near the top of a free-standing

hill is ideal since no cold air is imported from above. R.E.S.

air dried. See BARREL MAKING.

Airén is planted at such a low VINE DENSITY in its central Spanish homeland that it is planted on just over 20% of all Spanish vineyard and covers more area than any other white wine variety in the world. Its 2020 total of 204,699 ha/505,822 acres is dramatically reduced from its 2004 total of 305,000 ha/753,350 acres, however, thanks to vigorous VINE-PULL SCHEMES, particularly in LA MANCHA and VALDEPEÑAS, where it has traditionally been blended with dark-skinned Cencibel (TEMPRANILLO) grapes, which are steadily replacing Airén, to produce light red wines. It is increasingly vinified as an inexpensive white wine, however, to yield crisp, neutral, dry white wines for early consumption. In several ways, therefore, Airén is the Spanish equivalent of France's UGNI BLANC. Airén vines are trained into low bushes and have remarkable resistance to the DROUGHTS which plague central Spanish viticulture. The variety is also grown around MADRID.

Aix-en-Provence, Coteaux d'. Mainly dry rosé and some red wines are made from the varied but often spectacularly situated vineyards in this PROVENCE appellation. Stretching from the western frontier with LES BAUX DE PROVENCE as far as east as the Coteaux VAROIS, it includes ELEVATIONS varying from nearly sea level to over 400 m/1,312 ft with considerable TEMPERATURE VARIABILITY. A total of 4,127 ha/10,198 acres of vineyards in 2020 produce serviceable if generally unsophisticated reds and pale pink wines for early consumption. CO-OPERATIVES are relatively important here, but a number of estates such as Chx Calissanne, Revelette, Pigoudet, and Vignelaure are working at promoting a regional and distinctive style from GRENACHE grown at cooler elevations. Cinsaut, Mourvèdre, Counoise, Syrah, Carignan, Cabernet Sauvignon, and small amounts of CALADOC are also allowed. A little white is made from a wide range of grape varieties, mainly VERMENTINO.

ORGANIC VITICULTURE has established a significant hold in this arid, MEDITERRANEAN climate. E.A.G.

Ajaccio. See CORSICA.

Alarije, white grape grown in the EXTREMADURA region of Spain. Called Malvasia Riojana in Rioja and Subirat Parent in Cataluña, it has been shown by DNA PROFILING to be a natural offspring of Gibi and Tortozón. J.V.

Alaska, far north-western state of the United States where Bell's Alaskan Vineyard & Winery in Anchorage successfully makes wine from VITIS VINIFERA planted in the ground but under greenhouse. Because of the cool climate, FRUIT WINES are more common. E.C.B.

Alba, culinary capital of Italy's LANGHE, famous for its red wines and white truffles, and where in the past, before estate bottling became the norm, producers would sell their grapes to bottlers and NÉGOCIANTS on the Piazza Savona immediately after the harvest. Since 2010 it also is the name of a, at least for the moment, rather irrelevant DOC for Nebbiolo-Barbera blends covering all of Roero, Barolo, Barbaresco, and Dogliani. See also ROERO and NEBBIOLO D'ALBA. W.S.

Albalonga, originally described as a 1951 RIESLANER × SILVANER cross but now shown by DNA PROFILING to be Rieslaner × MÜLLER-THURGAU. Grown to a very limited extent in Germany (13 ha/32 acres in 2019), notably in Rheinhessen and the Pfalz, and to an even more limited extent in England. J.V.

Albana, Italian vine made famous by the over-promoted ROMAGNA ALBANA. Now widely planted in the EMILIA-ROMAGNA region, its chief claim to fame is being mentioned in the 13th century by medieval agricultural writer PETRUS DI CRESCENTIIS. Most Albana is late ripening, thin-skinned, and prone to rot, but the **Albana Gentile di Bertinoro** clone has thicker skins than most and results in relatively deep-coloured white wines with marked acidity, which is useful in the best, long-lived sweet versions. Total area planted had declined to 818 ha/2,021 acres by 2020.

Albana di Romagna. See ROMAGNA ALBANA.

Albani, Colli, white wine DOC from the hills south-east of Rome based on MALVASIA Candia (maximum 60%) with up to 50% TREBBIANO (Giallo, Toscano, or Soave) and/or 5–45% of Malvasia di Lazio). Wines can be sparkling or still, dry or sweet. For more information, see CASTELLI ROMANI.

Albania, Mediterranean country situated on the Adriatic coast between MONTENEGRO and GREECE that claims one of Europe's longest histories of vine-growing. French historian Henri Enjalbert considered Albania, the Ionian Islands of Greece, and southern Dalmatia in what is now BOSNIA AND HERZEGOVINA possibly the last European refuge of the vine after the Ice Age. Wine production is believed to have been practised by the inhabitants of Albania in the Bronze Age, and there are written accounts of vines being cultivated in Illyria (as Albania was known in Classical times) as early as the 8th century BCE. Until the Ottoman invasion in the late 15th century, vines were grown in every region, and every parish church had its vineyard. The Ottoman occupation of Albania (1479–1913), the two World Wars, and the isolationist communist regime suppressed the development of the Albanian wine industry, but there is a very considerable level of viticultural potential in this small country, particularly due to its distinctive INDIGENOUS VARIETIES.

Albania is now a parliamentary republic with a population of 2.83 million inhabitants in 2021 and a total land area 28,000 km square, slightly smaller than Belgium. It has a typically MEDITERRANEAN CLIMATE: cool and wet in winter, warm and dry in summer. It is a mountainous country, with only a quarter of its land suitable for agriculture, but over half its population lives off the land, on farms with an average size of 1.14 ha/2.8 acres. Viticulture is an important sector. Nearly half of all the 12,002 ha/29,657 acres of vines are trained on PERGOLAS.

The principal vine-growing regions are Elbasan, just south of the capital Tirana; Fier and Vlorë close to the Adriatic Coast, and Gjirokastër in the far south. French vine varieties such as Merlot, Cabernet Sauvignon, and Chardonnay collectively make up 42% of the vineyard area, but Kallmet, known as KADARKA in Hungary, is locally considered the country's noblest red, valued for its juicy blackberry-vanilla flavours. More attention is also being paid to indigenous varieties such as Cëruja, a high-acid, floral white-wine grape, and Shesh i Zi ('Black Shesh'), a low-yielding variety originating from Shesh, near Tirana, that produces ageworthy, lightly tannic red wines with tart, fragrant plum notes. Viticultural research in Albania is focused on the collection, characterization, and preservation of these and other varieties, including Pulës i Zi, Vlosh, Serina e Zezë, and Debinë e Bardhë, as many can still be found growing wild near pre-Ottoman archaeological sites such as those at Rozafa Castle, Berati town, and Byllis. L.S. & E.S.

Enjalbert, H., *Histoire de la vigne et du vin* (1975).

alberese, a name used in parts of TUSCANY for pale-coloured, marly soils that are more CALCAREOUS and poorer in clay than GALESTRO. Although both albarese and ALBARIZA soils are high in calcium carbonate, they are geologically different. A.J.M.

Albariño, Spanish name of the distinctive, aromatic, high-quality vine grown in Galicia (and as ALVARINHO in the north of Portugal's Vinho Verde region). The grapes' thick skins help them withstand the particularly damp climate and can result in white wines notably high in alcohol, acidity, and flavour. Albariño was one of the first Spanish white grape varieties produced as a VARIETAL and encountered on labels. Most common in Spain in the RÍAS BAIXAS zone, it has become so popular (and expensive) that it represents 96% of all plantings in the DOP. Sometimes oak-matured, and increasingly aged

for several years in stainless-steel tanks before release, it can age better than most light-skinned Spanish grapes however it is made. Occasionally it is blended with LOUREIRA, TREIXADURA, or CAÍÑO BLANCO. Spanish plantings had grown to 5,936 ha (14,668 acres) by 2020. Its wines are so widely exported that it is now also grown in California, Oregon, Washington, Australia (although see also SAVAGNIN), New Zealand, and Uruguay and has been allowed in France since 2010.

Robinson, J., et al., *Wine Grapes: A Complete Guide to 1,368 Vine Varieties Including Their Origins and Flavours* (2012).

albariza, strikingly white soil in the area around JEREZ de la Frontera and SANLUCAR DE BARRAMEDA, ANDALUCIA, south-west Spain, well suited to growing PALOMINO FINO vines.

Soils derived from white siliceous MARL constitute the whole western part of the Guadalquivir river region. Their local names reflect differing proportions of siliceous and CALCAREOUS microfossils, CLAY minerals, and QUARTZ. Albariza consists of 50% or more of calcareous microfossils (including coccolithophores; see CHALK) and clay minerals. Albariza subtypes such as *tosca de barajuelas* have been classified by García del Barrio Ambrosy.

The soil is humus-poor and light in texture, providing healthy aeration and easy root penetration. Its microporosity gives excellent water storage, enhanced by the swelling clay montmorillonite. The slow release of this stored winter moisture is invaluable during Andalucia's arid growing season. A.J.M.

García del Barrio Ambrosy, I., *La Tierra del Vino de Jerez* (1979).

Albarola, neutral white grape disappearing from the Cinqueterre zone of LIGURIA in north-west Italy. Known as Bianchetta Genovese around Genoa.

albedo. See REFLECTION.

alberello, Italian term to describe free-standing BUSH VINES trained according to the GOBELET system.

Albillo, name of several different pale-skinned grape varieties grown and sometimes confused in various parts of Spain, most notably Albillo Mayor in Ribera del Duero and other parts of CASTILLA Y LEÓN, Albillo Real in CASTILLA-LA MANCHA and around MADRID, where some old vines yield honeyed dry wines of real substance, and Albillo de Albacete in MANCHUELA. However, considerable confusion is caused by the use of plain Albillo in Spanish statistics and wine regulations. Both Albillo Mayor and Albillo Real produce wines that are generally low in acidity, full-bodied, and aromatic.

Robinson, J., et al., *Wine Grapes: A Complete Guide to 1,368 Vine Varieties, Including Their Origins and Flavours* (2012).

alcohol, the common name for ETHANOL. The term 'alcohol', which can be applied to any of the ALCOHOLS, derives from the Arabic *al-kuhl*, meaning 'the fine powder used to stain eyelids' (today's kohl), and thus by extension any kind of fine impalpable powder that represents the concentration, or quintessence, of the raw material involved. It was then more widely applied to fluids that represented the essence, or spirit, of something, and thus to any product of distillation.

alcoholic strength, an important measurement of any wine, is its concentration of the intoxicant ethyl alcohol, or ETHANOL. It can be measured in several different ways, the most common being the DEGREE first defined in France by Gay-Lussac in 1884. This was the number of litres of pure ethanol in 100 litres of wine, both measured at 15 °C/59 °F. Later a more precise definition, using 20 °C/68 °F as the reference temperature and some other minor refinements, was adopted in France and by most international organizations. The degree of alcohol is equivalent to its percentage by volume and is sometimes referred to as 'abv', alcohol by volume. In most countries it is mandatory to specify the alcoholic strength of all wines on the label, although it may be written either % or occasionally ° (see also LABELLING INFORMATION).

The alcoholic strength of wine that has not had alcohol added by FORTIFICATION is usually 9–16%, with the great majority of wines being 12.5–14.5% alcohol—considerably higher than as recently as the 1980s thanks not only to CLIMATE CHANGE but also to FASHIONS, a desire for riper PHENOLICS, and the resulting tendency to later picking after extended HANG TIME. A significant proportion of high-quality wine made today in warmer climates is deliberately subjected to some form of ALCOHOL REDUCTION to make it more palatable—high-alcohol wines may taste 'hot' and are likely to be less aromatic because ethanol can mask aromas and flavours—or to satisfy some legal requirement. However, higher-alcohol wines may reduce the perception of TANNINS because alcohol can prevent them from binding with salivary tannins (see ASTRINGENCY).

In Europe, fermented grape juice should usually reach at least 8.5% alcohol (9% in specified warmer zones) before it legally constitutes wine, although exceptions are made for PDO or PGI wines that have traditionally been low in alcohol such as some German wines with PRÄDIKAT and Italian MOSCATO, and EU regulations that came into force in 2023 permit the term DE-ALCOHOLIZED WINE. The technical European legal maximum alcoholic strength for wines that have had no alcohol added is 15%, but derogations are frequently made at this upper limit too (as long as they have not been ENRICHED), not least for Italy's strongest wines such as AMARONE. In the United States, grape-based 'table wine' must legally be between 7 and 14%, while those between 14 and 24% technically qualify as DESSERT WINES.

Since alcohol is the product by FERMENTATION of grape sugar, itself the product of PHOTOSYNTHESIS driven by sunlight, the alcoholic strength of a wine is, very generally, proportional to the proximity of its provenance to the equator and to the precosity of the variety, although many other factors play a part, especially the intentions of the winemaker. High vineyard ELEVATION, poor WEATHER in a particular year, high YIELD, and any RESIDUAL SUGAR are just some of the factors which may decrease alcoholic strength. Severe PRUNING in the vineyard and cellar techniques such as ENRICHMENT, CONCENTRATION, and fortification allow winemakers to manipulate alcoholic strength upwards. Some OLOROSO sherries, for example, can reach alcoholic strengths approaching 24% after EVAPORATION. (See also DRIED-GRAPE WINES.)

There is an important distinction between **actual alcoholic strength**, as defined above, and **potential alcoholic strength**, which refers to what the concentration of alcohol in a wine would be if all the sugars were converted to alcohol. **Total alcoholic strength** is the sum, post fermentation, of the actual alcoholic strength and the potential alcohol of any remaining fermentable sugars. **Natural alcoholic strength** refers to the alcoholic strength of a wine prior to any form of enrichment.

Regulation (EU) No 1308/2013 of the European Parliament and of the Council of 17 December 2013, *Official Journal of the European Union*. eur-lex.europa.eu/eli/reg/2013/1308/2021-12-07.

alcohol reduction typically refers to the removal of alcohol from fully fermented wine using physical separation processes. The aim is to retain all other desirable components, but such techniques are likely to affect the volatile composition of the wine and its sensory profile. The most extreme form is de-alcoholization, resulting in a wine with an ALCOHOLIC STRENGTH of less than 0.5%. Alcohol reduction is used for a number of purposes.

Full-strength wines with excessively high alcohol levels may be adjusted or 'corrected' by a few degrees to improve BALANCE. In some jurisdictions, there is a maximum limit for such adjustments if the product is to be sold as 'wine'. In the EU, for example, the alcoholic strength can be reduced by a maximum of 20% of the original alcohol content and cannot be reduced below 9% (8.5% in the coolest regions). Beyond those limits, from 2023 the product must be sold as a 'wine-based drink', or as DE-ALCOHOLIZED WINE or PARTIALLY DE-ALCOHOLIZED WINE.

Alcohol reduction is carried out using various mechanical methods based on temperature, pressure, and concentration, sometimes in combination. These include the use of a vacuum distillation technique such as the SPINNING-CONE COLUMN, membrane separation techniques such as REVERSE OSMOSIS, ELECTRODIALYSIS, EVAPORATIVE PERSTRACTION, PERVAPORATION, ULTRAFILTRATION, and NANOFILTRATION, as well as the more 'traditional' method of HUMIDIFICATION.

Non-mechanical methods of alcohol reduction such as harvesting earlier or choice of YEAST strain have also shown some success. See LOW-ALCOHOL WINE. J.E.H & J.P.H.B.

AWRI, 'Reducing ethanol levels in wine' (2020). www.awri.com.au/wp-content/uploads/Reducing-ethanol-levels-in-wine.pdf.

OIV, 'International Code of Oenological Practices'. www.oiv.int/en/technical-standards-and-documents/oenological-practices/international-code-of-oenological-practices.

alcohols, those organic chemicals, the simplest members of which consist of carbon, hydrogen, and oxygen atoms arranged so that there is an –OH group present. Many different alcohols are used in commerce and industry, but the most common is ethyl alcohol, or ETHANOL, the alcohol that is the important, and intoxicating, ingredient in wines and spirits. The presence of ethanol in foods and beverages, commonly referred to simply as 'alcohol', is the product of yeast FERMENTATION of natural sugars.

Other alcohols with more than two carbon atoms of ethanol are also the product of fermentation, and these are sometimes called higher alcohols, or FUSEL OIL. The higher alcohols separated from ethanol by DISTILLATION are normally used as solvents in industrial processes. The major constituent of fusel oil is the five-carbon isoamyl alcohol. P.J.W.

aldehydes, a class of chemical compounds midway between the ALCOHOLS and the organic ACIDS in their state of OXIDATION. They are formed during any phase of processing in which an alcoholic beverage is exposed to air. ACETALDEHYDE is the aldehyde of most interest to wine producers. Some aldehydes have quite potent odours, even if they are usually present in only trace concentrations in wines and spirits. As such, aldehydes contribute harmoniously to the overall character.

Those aldehydes containing more than the two carbon atoms of acetaldehyde are in general much more palatable. VANILLIN, for example, is a complex aromatic aldehyde present in the vanilla bean and in many other plants, including some grapes, where it is present as a GLYCOSIDE and is a FLAVOUR PRECURSOR. Vanillin also occurs as a component of the lignin structure of OAK. If new oak casks are used for wine maturation, some of this vanillin is extracted from the wood into the wine (see also OAK FLAVOUR).

One of the most important functions of SULFUR DIOXIDE is to bind with aldehydes, which can make a wine seem flat if present in excess. Once bound, the aldehydes can no longer be tasted, making the wine seem fresher.

See also HERBACEOUS for the part played by **leaf aldehydes**. P.J.W. & M.J.T.

Aleatico, Italian red grape variety with a strong MUSCAT aroma. DNA PROFILING has shown a parent–offspring relationship with the classic MUSCAT BLANC À PETITS GRAINS, hence the Muscat flavour. Aleatico certainly has the potential to produce fine, if somewhat esoteric, fragrant, usually pale red from the Italian 2015 total of just 149 ha/368 acres. Two DOCs enshrine the word 'Aleatico' in the wine lexicon of LAZIO and PUGLIA, but the variety is becoming increasingly rare even if it is still found in TUSCANY, the MARCHE, and UMBRIA. Sweet red Aleatico is one of the few wines to be exported from the Tuscan island of ELBA, and the variety is grown on the island of Corsica. Aleatico is also surprisingly popular in the central Asian republics, notably KAZAKHSTAN and UZBEKISTAN. J.V. & J.E.H.

Alella, town near Barcelona in CATALUÑA (see map under SPAIN) which gives its name to a small Spanish DOP making mainly white wines in increasingly urbanized countryside. To compensate for the loss of agricultural land, the DO was extended northwards in 1989, but by 2021 there were only 227 ha/560 acres of vineyard, a fraction of the area planted in 1956 when Alella was first awarded DO status. The zone used to be known for cask-aged, medium-sweet white wines. Today, it is better known for both sparkling CAVA and dry, still white wine. The chief grape variety is Pansa Blanca, the local name for XARELLO, which is now grown along with CHARDONNAY on granitic sandy soils known as *sauló*. V. de la S. & F.C.

Alenquer, small DOC in a sheltered valley in LISBOA, and seat of boutique modern winemaking using Portuguese and French varieties. Its strength is fuller-bodied red wines.

Alentejo, DOC and VINHO REGIONAL (known as Vinho Regional Alentejano) in southern PORTUGAL corresponding to the province of the same name.

DOC wines, including VINHO DE TALHA, must come from one (or more) of eight subregions which may appear on labels: PORTALEGRE, BORBA, REDONDO, and REGUENGOS de Monsaraz are located in the southern part of the Alentejo, north of the Vidigueira fault (an escarpment); GRANJA-AMARELEJA, VIDIGUEIRA, ÉVORA, and MOURA are located to the south. Many good producers prefer to label wines VR Alentejano, however, while some outside its DOC regions (notably in Beja) must be labelled VR Alentejano, despite their wines' evident high quality.

The sparsely populated Alentejo represents one-third of mainland Portugal, and, in contrast to the north, cereal farms and cork plantations (*latifúndios*) stretch as far as the eye can see. For centuries, the Alentejo's main link with wine was CORK. Around half the world's cork supply is grown in Portugal, nearly all stripped from Alentejo's cork oaks. Southern Portugal bore the brunt of the military-led revolution that rocked the Lisbon establishment in 1974–75 and the economy of the Alentejo was still in disarray in the early 1980s. However, financial assistance from the EU has allowed the CO-OPERATIVE wineries in the towns of Portalegre, Borba, Redondo, Reguengos de Monsaraz, Granja-Amareleja, and Vidigueira to improve wine quality and develop exports. Moreover, it resulted in an increase in the number of ambitious, privately owned estates from 45 to 260 between 1995 and 2010. By 2010 Alentejo not only commanded the biggest share of the domestic market in quality wines (in volume and value) but had also charmed export markets with its generous, fruit-led wines. In 2019, vines were planted on more than 22,000 ha/54,363 acres, and 40% of the vineyards were certified under Wines of Alentejo's pioneering Sustainability Programme (WASP) by 2021.

Large farms offer considerable economies of scale compared with the smallholdings (*minifúndios*) of northern Portugal. This and Alentejo's consistent climate—sunshine hours average over 3,000/annum—hold the key to its bedrock of smooth, easy-going reds. Where summer temperatures frequently exceed 35 °C or even 40 °C/104 °F, conditions can be challenging for top-end wines. Cooler locations such as Portalegre and Borba (elevated), Costa Vicentina (coastal), and Alentejo's water-retentive bands of SCHIST help—especially for white wines, which are a growing strength. So does modern technology: TEMPERATURE CONTROL and IRRIGATION supplements an annual rainfall that rarely totals 600 mm/23 in. Conversely, TALHA wines have put the spotlight on traditional DRY-FARMED grapes. Red wines dominate, making up three-quarters of production—principally blends from ARAGONEZ, TRINCADEIRA, ALICANTE BOUSCHET (which flourishes here), Syrah, and TOURIGA NACIONAL. Several producers make impressive white blends of ANTÃO VAZ, ROUPEIRO, and ARINTO. VERDELHO, ALVARINHO, and VIOGNIER also look promising. S.A.

Mayson, R. J., *The Wines of Portugal* (2020).
www.vinhosdoalentejo.pt

Alexander Valley, California wine region and AVA in northern Sonoma County northeast of Healdsburg and south of Cloverdale. See SONOMA.

Alfrocheiro, one of the most promising red grapes in the DÃO region of Portugal. Its well-constructed blackberry- and strawberry-flavoured wines have such appeal that it can now also be found in the ALENTEJO, TEJO, and BAIRRADA. National plantings in 2020 were 1,198 ha/2,960 acres. It is very susceptible to POWDERY MILDEW and GREY ROT and is not therefore as popular with growers as with winemakers. However, it yields reasonably well, ripens early, and produces deep-coloured wines with good alcohol and acid balance. DNA PROFILING has suggested that Alfrocheiro is the natural parent of at least 20 varieties in the Iberian Peninsula, including CASTELÃO and MENCÍA. Also known as Alfrocheiro Preto, in the Douro it may sometimes be called Tinta Bastardinha, Baboso Negro on the Canary Islands, and Albarín Tinto in Asturias. R.J.M. & J.V.

Algarve, located at the southernmost tip of Portugal and sheltered from northerly winds by the Serra de Monchique, has a long winemaking tradition (of principally FORTIFIED wines). The entire province is designated as a VINHO REGIONAL, with four DOCs, from west to east: Lagos, Portimão, Lagoa, and Tavira. While it shares the high sunshine hours (over 3,000 per year) and warm Mediterranean climate of the ALENTEJO, its northern neighbour, the Algarve does not benefit from the cool respite of pronounced diurnal or seasonal TEMPERATURE VARIABILITY, and vineyard sites must be carefully selected. West of Faro, the land is more exposed to cooler, humid Atlantic influence (Lagos additionally to northern winds); the east is warmer and drier. The Algarve's DOCs used to be centred around local CO-OPERATIVES, but by 2021 only one remained and private investment had grown, allowing for a greater interrogation of individual terroir with both popular Portuguese and French grapes and local grapes Negra Mole (see NEGRAMOLL) and Crato Branco (SÍRIA). Most boutique players focus on domestic sales, but in 1998 the British singer Sir Cliff Richard led the export charge when he established a vineyard and winery near the resort of Albufeira. It was acquired by a Portuguese-French businessman in 2021 following a decade during which Algarve exports quadrupled. Al-Ria in Tavira, founded in 2013 by Lisboa-based Casa Santos Lima, is now the Algarve's biggest producer. Quinta da Aveleda of Vinho Verde has also invested heavily, establishing the Villa Alvor brand in the western Algarve in 2019. S.A.

Algeria was for much of the 20th century one of the world's leading wine producers. Annual output sometimes reached 20 million hl/525 million gal, most of it exported to France, of which it was then a colony. Changes following Algeria's independence in 1962 have reduced production to a figure typically nearer 500,000 hl/13 million gal.

History

As seen in mosaics and Saint Augustine of Hippo's *Confessions*, wine was produced in Algeria in classical times, but viticulture became less evident once ISLAM established itself as the primary form of worship. In the first few decades after French colonization began in 1830, officials typically discouraged viticulture in favour of 'tropical' crops that France did not grow, such as cotton, but such experiments mostly failed. It was not until France's PHYLLOXERA crisis of the 1870s that large-scale wine production in Algeria received official approval and gained momentum. Taking place on lands from which indigenous Algerians had largely been displaced, colonial Algeria's viticulture boom reflected the diverse European origins of its settler population; industry pioneers included colonists of Maltese, Majorcan, and Swiss extraction as well as many regions of France.

Though phylloxera reached Algeria in the 1880s, hitting growers in the east especially hard, by the 1900s Algeria was supplying three-quarters of France's wine imports and was the fourth largest producer in the world. Wealth from the industry, which required extensive vineyard labour as well as work in barrel workshops and ports, had also helped shore up a fragile colonial economy. CO-OPERATIVE wineries were embraced by smaller growers, while bigger producers found influence over the colony's affairs. Muslim Algerians of Arab or Berber ethnicity increasingly performed the basic manual tasks in the vines, though colonial producers often undercut requests for higher wages by using convicts or cheaper labour from neighbouring MOROCCO.

France came to rely on Algerian wine to provide its everyday blended red (and some smarter wines) with strength, colour, and concentration—attributes lacking in the ARAMON then grown so prolifically in the LANGUEDOC. Yet southern French vignerons increasingly perceived Algerian production as unfair competition as the colony's vineyard underwent a major expansion in the 1920s. Colonial representatives in the French parliament successfully resisted the southern wine lobby's attempts to impose a quota on imports, which entered France duty-free as Algeria was considered an integral part of France. Meanwhile the first wine tankers, introduced in the mid 1930s, sparked opposition among port and barrel workers in Algeria and in French receiving ports such as Rouen and Sète, who saw these ships as a threat to their livelihoods. Following the Second World War, tankers would ship most of Algeria's wine across the Mediterranean in steel containers.

Vineyards reached their greatest extent of 400,000 ha/988,400 acres in 1935, and in the final decades of French rule wine often accounted for close to half of Algeria's exports by value. The interruption of maritime traffic to France during the Second World War, however, underlined the industry's dependence on the metropole, while labour disputes revealed a restless Algerian workforce as anti-colonial nationalism spread. During the war for independence that began in 1954, vineyard operations often took place under armed guard as vines became a target of insurgents. French forces sometimes detained Algerian suspects in wine vats, resulting in several instances of mass suffocation. Yet protective measures continued to ensure healthy profits for big producers.

Some wealthier owners had already bought vineyards in choice regions of France before 1962, but a near-total European exodus followed Algeria's independence that year. The eastern plains of CORSICA proved one popular destination for colonists eager to continue large-scale viticulture. Algeria's vineyards were nationalized and passed into a form of collective agriculture, but the sudden loss of expertise and ageing vines hurt production, and political disputes made the French market unreliable. A 1968 deal with the Soviet Union offered an alternative outlet, but the agreement did not reflect production costs. As oil and gas provided new streams of revenue, in 1971 Algeria's government began a major project of uprooting vines. In 1985, the country failed to produce more than one million hl/26.4 million gallons for the first time in a century, while Islamists placed new pressure on growers to abandon viticulture during the country's civil war of the 1990s.

Geography, climate, and industry structure

Algeria's climate is similar to much of southern Spain, with mild winters and hot, dry summers, indeed increasingly so due to CLIMATE CHANGE. In colonial times a high proportion of the wine was produced on plains such as the Mitidja south of Algiers, but the vines that remain—less than 75,000 ha/186,000 acres in 2021—are often in hillier areas in the vicinity of towns such as Aïn Témouchent, Mascara, Mostaganem, Sidi Bel Abbès, and Tlemcen in the west and Médéa in the centre. High-volume, heat-tolerant varieties favoured by colonists such as CARIGNAN, CINSAUT, and ALICANTE BOUSCHET continue to predominate but have been joined by INTERNATIONAL VARIETIES such as Syrah and

Cabernet Sauvignon. The former state wine company, which helped rescue the industry during the civil war, continues to operate as SOTRAVIT (Société de Transformation des Produits Viticoles), but a private company, Grands Crus de l'Ouest, shows more dynamism, producing wine in facilities built in the colonial era. The derelict wineries that are a common sight along the country's roads, however, represent a truer picture of the industry's fall. Once the world's biggest wine exporter, since the 2010s Algeria has become a net importer. O.W.

Alicante, city on Spain's Mediterranean coast long associated with strong, rustic wines which now gives its name to a denominated but shrinking wine zone of 9,100 ha/21,800 acres. This DO extends from the city towards YECLA on the foothills of Spain's central plateau (see map under SPAIN) and allows eight styles of wine including DOBLE PASTA, fortified wines, and a SOLERA-aged wine called FONDILLÓN, a speciality of the region made from very sweet, deliberately overripened grapes. A coastal subzone, the Marina Alta, produces mostly white MUSCAT-based wines. The climate becomes progressively hotter and the landscape more arid away from the coast and YIELDS rarely exceed 20 hl/ha (1.1 ton/acre). The principal grape variety is the red MONASTRELL (Mourvèdre). Other red varieties well suited to the MEDITERRANEAN CLIMATE include GARNACHA and BOBAL. Ninety per cent of the region's wine is produced in CO-OPERATIVES.

Alicante is also a synonym for Garnacha Tintorera, or ALICANTE BOUSCHET, in Spain and is even sometimes used as a synonym for GRENACHE. R.J.M., V. de la S. & F.C.

Alicante Bouschet, often known simply as **Alicante** and sometimes as **Alicante Henri Bouschet**, is the most widely planted of France's red-fleshed TEINTURIER grape varieties although total French plantings had declined to 2,460 ha/6,079 acres by 2018, mainly in the Languedoc and Roussillon.

It was bred between 1865 and 1885 by Henri BOUSCHET from his father's crossing of Petit Bouschet with the popular Grenache, then often known as Alicante, and was an immediate success thanks to its deep-red flesh.

Alicante Bouschet also played a major role in late 19th and early 20th century viticulture as parent of a host of other *teinturiers*, the products almost exclusively of crossings with non-VITIS-VINIFERA varieties. In the second half of the 20th century it profited from its status as the sole *teinturier* to be a *vinifera*, and it is therefore officially sanctioned by the French authorities.

Outside France it is most widely cultivated in Spain, where it is also known as Garnacha Tintorera and where plantings totalled 35,562 ha/87,876 acres in 2020. It is particularly common in CASTILLA-LA MANCHA and GALICIA. The total area planted in Portugal is much smaller (6,458 ha/15,958 acres in 2020), but the variety seems more at home here than in France and can make wines as celebrated as Mouchão in the ALENTEJO.

Alicante is widely grown around the world but nowhere else in any great quantity.

Robinson, J., et al., *Wine Grapes: A Complete Guide to 1,368 Vine Varieties, Including Their Origins and Flavours* (2012).

Aligoté, Burgundy's 'other' white grape variety, may be very much Chardonnay's underdog, but it is clearly a beneficiary of CLIMATE CHANGE. In a fine year, when ripeness can compensate for its characteristic ACIDITY, Aligoté is not short of champions, most notably Les Aligoteurs, an association of producers established in 2018. It is one of the many PINOT × GOUAIS BLANC natural crosses, therefore a sibling of Chardonnay, and was recorded in Burgundy at the end of the 18th century.

The vine is vigorous and its yield varies enormously according to the vineyard site. If grown on Burgundy's best slopes on the poorest soils in warmer years, Aligoté could produce fine dry whites with more nerve than most Chardonnays, but it would not be nearly as profitable.

In the CÔTE D'OR it is far less important than Chardonnay and Pinot Noir, but there was still a total of 1,974 ha/4,878 acres in greater Burgundy in 2018, including 616 ha/1,522 acres in the Côte d'Or. It was largely relegated to the highest and lowest vineyards, where it produced light, early-maturing wines allowed only the Bourgogne Aligoté appellation and traditionally mixed with blackcurrant liqueur as a KIR. However, ambitious producers, treating it with greater respect, are making outstanding wines with long ageing potential. Only the village of Bouzeron in the Côte CHALONNAISE, where some of the finest examples are produced, has its own appellation for Aligoté, in which the maximum yield is only 45 hl/ha (2.5 ton/acre) as opposed to the 60 hl/ha allowed for Bourgogne Aligoté. A little is grown by burgundy enthusiasts in the New World, but it is extraordinarily popular (and rarely tart) in Eastern Europe, where Moldova, Romania, Ukraine, and Bulgaria grow thousands of hectares of it, and it is also a common feature in Russian and Kazakhstani vineyards. J.E.H. & J.V.

Alisos Canyon, young California AVA (2020) of sandy hills just south of the town of Santa Barbara specializing in SYRAH and other Rhône varieties. See SANTA BARBARA.

allergies and intolerances. A key difference between allergy and intolerance is that allergic reactions have an immunological basis, while those due to other mechanisms are classed as intolerances. Intolerance of wine is far more common than true allergy to wine or grapes. The most common **allergens**, substances capable of causing an allergic reaction, are proteinaceous compounds. Among possible allergens in wines are traces of natural PROTEINS not precipitated and removed with the dead yeast cells after FERMENTATION, and traces of proteins from FINING agents used to clarify and stabilize the wine. Pollen-food allergy syndrome affects those severely sensitized to pollens which cross-react with similar proteins in fruit skins, causing oral itching. Grape allergy appears to be largely found around the Mediterranean, associated with specific heat- and acid-stable plant proteins. Even traces of wasp venom found in wine have been reported to cause reactions.

BIOGENIC AMINES, including HISTAMINE, tyramine, and putrescine, are produced chiefly by LACTIC ACID BACTERIA not ordinarily involved in MALOLACTIC CONVERSION. Above individual toxicity thresholds, these compounds can trigger a wide range of wine intolerance symptoms including headache or migraine and are typically at higher concentrations in red wines.

SULFUR DIOXIDE may be a cause of so-called 'white-wine allergy' (strictly speaking an intolerance), and some percentage of asthmatics are particularly sensitive to SULFITES. Although sulfur dioxide is used in both red and white wines, whites typically have both higher sulfite levels and more acidity (which increases its release from solution), resulting in airway irritation and wheezing for those sensitive to this.

Some people, particularly members of certain ethnic groups, experience symptoms such as facial flushing and rapid pulse after consuming even limited amounts of ETHANOL in any form. This alcohol intolerance is due to genetic variations in one or both enzymes involved in the metabolism of alcohol, alcohol dehydrogenase and acetaldehyde dehydrogenase, which together less efficiently process ethanol, resulting in adverse effects of intermediate toxic metabolites.

See also HEALTH and LABELLING INFORMATION.

D.A.D. & S.P.-T.

Decuyper, I. I., et al., 'Adverse reactions to illicit drugs (marijuana, opioids, cocaine) and alcohol', *Journal of Allergy and Clinical Immunology: In Practice*, 9/8 (2021), 3006–14.

Vally, H., and Thompson, P. J., 'Allergic and asthmatic reactions to alcoholic drinks', *Addiction Biology*, 8/1 (2003), 3–11.

Allier is the name of a *département* in central France best known in the world of wine for its OAK, although it is also home to the wines of ST-POURÇAIN.

alluvium, a type of sediment which is deposited by flowing water on floodplains, in riverbeds, in deltas, and in estuaries, often derived from many different and distant sources. Soils formed on alluvial sediments are typically fertile and varied in texture, with particle sizes ranging from CLAY to SILT, SAND, and sometimes GRAVEL or boulders. Variations in DRAINAGE and age can often be seen over a few metres of distance and a few centimetres of depth. Where these soils are stony or sandy, with rapid drainage and generally low water-holding capacity, they are highly valued for viticulture, as in the MÉDOC region of France and Marlborough in NEW ZEALAND. However, vineyards planted on these soils are often variable in VIGOUR, making their management more difficult. **Alluvial fans** are formed when a side stream emerges from the mountains flanking a valley and abruptly slows down, depositing alluvium in a fan-shaped area.
R.E.S. & R.E.W.

almacenista, from the Spanish word *almacén* meaning 'store', is the term for a SHERRY stockholder who sells wine to shippers. In the last decades, as the supply needs of the big houses diminished due to low sales and as the requirements for putting wine directly in the market loosened up, most almacenistas began bottling their wines under their own labels. It has been used as a marketing term by the sherry firm of Lustau, who sells a range of wines under the Almacenista label. J.B.

Almansa, DOP in the eastern corner of CASTILLA-LA MANCHA in central Spain (see map under SPAIN) with 7,200 ha/17,792 acres under vine. It borders the regions JUMILLA and YECLA, which produce similarly strong, sturdy red wines, traditionally used for blending but increasingly sold in bottle, principally from MONASTRELL and GARNACHA TINTORERA grapes, although SYRAH is increasingly planted. The climate is extreme, with temperatures of 40 °C/104 °F in summer and below freezing in winter.
V. de la S. & F.C.

Aloxe-Corton, a small village of charm at the northern end of the Côte de BEAUNE in Burgundy. First references to vineyards in Aloxe date back to 696, while in 775 CHARLEMAGNE ceded vines to the Abbey of St-Andoche at Saulieu. Aloxe is dominated by the hill of Corton, planted on three sides with vineyards including the GRANDS CRUS Corton (almost all red) and Corton-Charlemagne (white).

Corton is the sole grand cru appellation for red wine in the Côte de BEAUNE and covers several vineyards which may be described simply as Corton or as Corton hyphenated with their names. While all Corton wines tend to be dense and closed when young, those from Bressandes are noted for their comparative suppleness and charm; Renardes for rustic, gamey character; Perrières for extra finesse; and Clos du Roi for optimum balance between weight and elegance. Other Corton vineyards are Le Charlemagne, Les Pougets, and Les Languettes, all of which more often produce white Corton-Charlemagne, and Les Chaumes, Les Grèves, Les Fiètres, Les Meix, La Vigne au Saint, and part of Les Paulands and Les Maréchaudes. Further Corton vineyards extend into LADOIX-Serrigny.

Although Corton is planted almost entirely with Pinot Noir vines, a small but increasing amount of white Corton is made, including the HOSPICES DE BEAUNE cuvée Paul Chanson.

The great white wines, however, are those made within the **Corton-Charlemagne** appellation (58 ha/143 acres), which stretches in a narrow band around the top of the hill from Ladoix-Serrigny, through Aloxe-Corton to PERNAND-VERGELESSES, where it descends down the western edge of the hillside. The MESOCLIMATE governing Corton-Charlemagne is fractionally cooler than that of Corton and the soils are different. Whereas red Corton is mainly produced on reddish chalky clay, the soil at the top of the hill and on the western edge is lighter and whiter, its stoniness believed locally to impart a gunflint edge to the wines of Corton-Charlemagne. Chardonnay has entirely replaced the once widely planted Pinot Blanc, Pinot Beurot (see PINOT GRIS), and ALIGOTÉ, though some would favour a return of the latter.

A great Corton may seem ungainly in its sturdiness when young but should have the power to develop into a rich wine with complex, gamey flavours at eight to ten years old. Cortons should, with POMMARD, be the most intense and longest-lived wines of the Côte de Beaune. Corton-Charlemagne also needs time to develop its exceptional character and racy power. Needing a minimum of five years, a good example will be better for a full decade in bottle.

Although more than half the vineyard area is given over to the grands crus, Aloxe-Corton also has its share of PREMIER CRU and village vineyards producing mainly red wines which can be supple and well coloured but mostly do not justify their significant premium over the wines of SAVIGNY-LÈS-BEAUNE. Apart from Les Guérets and Les Vercots, which are adjacent to Les Fichots in the commune of Pernand-Vergelesses, the premiers crus of Aloxe-Corton form a band just below the swathe of grand cru vineyards, extending into Ladoix-Serrigny.

See CÔTE D'OR and map under BURGUNDY.
J.T.C.M.

Chapuis, C., *Aloxe-Corton* (1988), in French.

Alpilles, IGP for still red, rosé, and white wines covering the craggy LIMESTONE slopes of the Alpilles massif near St-Rémy-de-Provence in the Bouches-du-Rhône *département* of France. The IGP has received particular attention in recent years thanks to leading producer Domaine de Trévallon, whose use of a robust amount of Cabernet Sauvignon in their wines makes them ineligible for the local AOC, LES BAUX DE PROVENCE.

Alpine Valleys in Australia's North East Victoria Zone lies immediately east of KING VALLEY and encompasses inter alia the Ovens, Buffalo, Kiewa, and Buckland Valleys. Annual rainfall is surpassed only by parts of TASMANIA. Main varieties are Prosecco (aka GLERA), Chardonnay, and Pinot Noir. See VICTORIA. E.N.H.M.

Alsace, historically much-disputed region now on the eastern border of France, producing a unique style of largely VARIETAL wine, about 90% of which is white. For much of its existence it has been the western German region Elsass. Now separated from Germany by the river RHINE and from the rest of France by the Vosges Mountains, the language and culture of Alsace owe much to both origins but are at the same time unique. Many families speak Alsacien, a dialect particular to the region, quite different from either French or German.

Of all the regions of France, this is the one in which it is still easiest to find villages outwardly much as they were in the Middle Ages, with traditional half-timbered houses and extant fortifications. The hilltops of the lower Vosges are dotted with ruined castles and fortresses, witnesses to past invasions.

Of more than 4,000 grape-growers, about 950 bottle wine, but more than 60% of total production is sold by one of the 20 biggest NÉGOCIANTS and CO-OPERATIVES. Even the large companies are usually family-owned, however.

All still Alsace wines are, by law, bottled in the region of production in tall bottles called *flutes*.

History

For details of the history of the region pre-17th century, see GERMAN HISTORY. Annexed by France in the 17th century, Alsace was reclaimed, with part of Lorraine, by the new German empire in 1871. Shortly after, the twin crises of oïdium (POWDERY MILDEW) and PHYLLOXERA struck. In the aftermath, winegrowers largely abandoned the HILLSIDE sites and planted HYBRIDS on flat, easily accessible land to give large, trouble-free crops.

It was not until after the First World War, when Alsace returned to French rule, that up to one-third of the hillside sites were replanted with VITIS VINIFERA varieties. A setback occurred with the Second World War, when export was impossible, and the area was once more overrun by Germany. Replanting of the better sites gathered momentum in the 1960s and 1970s, when Alsace again started to build up export markets.

Geography and climate

Alsace lies at LATITUDE 47.5–49° N, allowing for a long, cool growing season. The region's vineyards are largely confined to a narrow strip running 100 km/62 miles from north to south along the eastern flank of the Vosges Mountains (see map under GERMANY), spanning the two *départements* of Haut-Rhin and Bas-Rhin. Most large producers are based in the more southerly Haut-Rhin, which is generally associated with better quality, especially for Alsace's characteristic Gewurztraminer (spelt Gewürztraminer in Germany) and Pinot Gris.

Thanks to the protection of the mountains, average annual RAINFALL is one of the lowest in France: 594.4 mm/23.4 in in Colmar, the region's centre. Most vineyards are at an ELEVATION of 175–550 m/574–1,804 ft, above which level much of the mountainside is covered with pine forests. Autumn humidity allows for the production of late-picked VENDANGES TARDIVES and SÉLECTION DE GRAINS NOBLES wines (see below) in good vintages.

Within the wine region, there are at least 20 major soil formations, covering several eras. Higher, steeper slopes of the Vosges have thin topsoil, with subsoils of weathered GNEISS, GRANITE, SANDSTONE, SCHIST, and VOLCANIC sediments. The gentler lower slopes, derived from the Rhine delta bed, have deeper topsoils, over subsoils of CLAY, MARL, LIMESTONE, and sandstone. One of the most important subsoils is the pink *grès de Vosges*, Vosges sandstone, which was used extensively in the construction of churches and cathedrals and which is much in evidence in Strasbourg. The plains at the foot of the Vosges are of ALLUVIAL soils, eroded from the Vosges, and are rich and fertile, generally more suited to the production of crops other than vines.

Winters can be very cold, spring is generally mild, and the summer is warm and sometimes very dry, with heavy HAIL and thunderstorms possible in summer and autumn. In some vintages summer DROUGHT can be a problem, and younger vines planted in the drier, sandy soils can suffer, whereas vineyards on the water-retentive clay soils have an advantage.

As a general rule, the heavier clay and marl soils give a wine with broader flavours and more body and weight, while a lighter limestone or sandy soil gives more elegance and finesse. Flint, schist, shale, and slate soils tend to give wines a characteristic oily, minerally aroma reminiscent of petrol and sometimes described as 'gunflint', especially those made from the Riesling grape.

Vine varieties

At the beginning of the 20th century, the many varieties planted in Alsace were divided into 'noble' and others. Today the region produces seven major VARIETAL wines: RIESLING, Gewurztraminer (Gewürztraminer in German), Pinot Gris, Pinot Noir, Pinot Blanc, Muscat, and Sylvaner. CHASSELAS is also planted but is generally used for blending, and only a handful of producers still bottle it as a varietal wine. AUXERROIS is usually blended with and labelled as Pinot Blanc. There is also a small amount of Chardonnay, forbidden by law but tolerated when labelled as Pinot Blanc or used in the sparkling wine CRÉMANT d'Alsace. Savagnin Rosé is allowed only in KLEVENER DE HEILIGENSTEIN.

Riesling Riesling is Alsace's most esteemed and widely planted variety, accounting for 21% of the area under vine in 2019. It is nearly always presented in a bone-dry style. Young Riesling can display floral aromas, although it is sometimes fairly neutral. With age it takes on complex, gunflint, mineral aromas, with crisp steely acidity and very pure fruit flavours.

Gewurztraminer Gewurztraminer is grown on almost as much land as Riesling but usually represents a smaller percentage of the production; its average yield is the smallest of all the varieties. The largest plantations of Gewurztraminer are in the Haut-Rhin. Its wines are usually dry to off-dry, but its low ACIDITY, combined with high alcohol and GLYCEROL, often gives an impression of sweetness. Gewurztraminer has a distinctive aroma and flavour, floral and spicy, with hints of lychee and grapefruit. Its naturally high sugar levels make it ideal for late-harvest sweet wines, and this is the most frequent variety used in Vendange Tardive wines. Poorly made examples can be blowsy, flat, over-alcoholic, sometimes oily, but the finest can be firm and full-bodied, with notes of bacon fat, leather, and roses.

Pinot Gris Once known as Tokay-Pinot Gris or Tokay d'Alsace, Pinot Gris has been the only permitted name on labels since 2007 according to an agreement between Hungary and the EU. The pink-skinned grape accounted for more than 16% of plantings in 2019. Young Pinot Gris is reminiscent of peaches and apricots, with a hint of smoke, developing biscuity, buttery flavours with age. With its firm backbone of acidity, it can make particularly successful Vendange Tardive wines.

Muscat Alsace grows both MUSCAT BLANC À PETITS GRAINS, known as Muscat d'Alsace, and MUSCAT OTTONEL, which together make up barely 2% of vineyard area. Wines labelled Muscat d'Alsace tend to be a blend of the two and are always dry, with a fresh grapey aroma and flavour. Low in alcohol and acidity, it rarely ages well but makes a charming aperitif. Because of its sensitivity to poor weather at flowering, yields can vary considerably from year to year.

Sylvaner Sylvaner has been losing ground to Riesling, as it is difficult to grow, needs a good site and a warm vintage, yet fetches comparatively little money. By 2019, it accounted for only 5% of Alsace's vineyard area, with higher proportions in the Bas-Rhin than the Haut-Rhin. Good Sylvaner has a slightly bitter, slightly perfumed flavour, with very firm acidity. It has moderate alcohol and is at its best when it is young and fresh.

Pinot Blanc Also labelled Clevner or Klevner, Pinot Blanc is the workhorse of Alsace. As well as forming the base wine for Crémant d'Alsace, Pinot Blanc can produce very good, clean, dry white that is not particularly aromatic but has good acidity, with moderate alcohol. Pinot Blanc and the more common Auxerrois, with which it is frequently blended, accounted for 21% of Alsace's vineyard area in 2019.

Edelzwicker German for 'noble mixture', Edelzwicker indicates a blend of more than one variety, vinified together or separately. Contrary to the name, it is generally one of the cheapest wines in the range, with Chasselas, Pinot Blanc, and Auxerrois common ingredients.

Gentil This term is reserved for AOC Alsace wines comprised of at least half Riesling, Muscat, Pinot Gris, and/or Gewurztraminer, with the make-up Chasselas, Pinot Blanc, and/or Sylvaner. Also, unlike Edelzwicker, each variety must be vinified separately before blending, and the wines must be vintage-dated.

Pinot Noir Pinot Noir represented 11% of the total vineyard area in 2019. It has been deepening in flavour and colour thanks to CLIMATE CHANGE. It is currently the only red grape allowed as a varietal wine in AOC Alsace, though several producers, led by René Muré, are now growing SYRAH, bottling it under the generic VIN DE FRANCE.

See also KLEVENER DE HEILIGENSTEIN.

Viticulture

The varied styles of training in use depend partly on the steepness of the vineyard. Either single GUYOT, with up to 15 buds left on the cane, or double Guyot, with up to eight buds on each cane, may be found, with a VINE DENSITY of 4,400–4,800 vines per ha (1,940 per acre). There are also some CORDON-trained vines, with SPUR PRUNING, generally on older vines. Yield limits vary by variety and denomination.

Vines are generally trained at a height of 60–90 cm/35 in above ground, depending on the site. Vines on the plain are generally trained high to avoid FROSTS, while sloping vineyards can be trained closer to the ground, benefiting to the maximum from the available SUNLIGHT.

The steepest vineyard slopes may be TERRACED, as for example the GRAND CRU sites of Rangen and Kastelberg, or vines may be planted in rows either following the contours of the slope or vertically from top to bottom, depending on the risk of SOIL EROSION. COVER CROPS may be planted to prevent erosion and to give more of a grip to tractors on moderate slopes.

Although MECHANICAL HARVESTING is common on the plains, many vineyards are too steep for machines, and many grapes are still hand-picked. The vintage is always protracted, with varieties ripening at different times. Generally, harvesting starts in mid September and often continues well into November.

A few growers have experimented with late-picked, BOTRYTIZED wines, not merely for the four varieties permitted for the late-harvest wines described below but also with such diverse varieties as Auxerrois and Sylvaner, which can make outstanding wines. One or two growers produce a small quantity of VIN DE PAILLE, from healthy, ripe grapes picked in October and dried on straw over the winter months. There have also been experiments with EISWEIN, from healthy grapes picked in December or even early January.

Winemaking

As in Germany, winemakers measure the sugar content of the grapes, or MUST WEIGHT, in degrees OECHSLE. CHAPTALIZATION, always outlawed for late-harvest wines (see below) and, since 2011, for AOC Alsace Grand Cru, is now relatively rare, even for AOC Alsace, thanks to CLIMATE CHANGE. Indigenous YEASTS are generally sufficient, and few winemakers add yeast cultures, except in an abnormally wet vintage. ACIDIFICATION is not practised.

The number of different varieties, all to be vinified separately, can present a logistical problem. Small operations with one PRESS (usually a bladder press, which gives cleaner juice) will organize picking to allow each variety sufficient time in the press before the next variety is picked.

For white wines, most winemakers prefer to prevent MALOLACTIC CONVERSION by keeping them cool and lightly sulfured, although this is changing, as winemakers have found that it does not seem to alter the quality or keeping ability of the wines. Pinot Noir needs to go through malolactic to soften and STABILIZE the wine and is therefore often kept in an isolated part of the cellar to prevent cross-contamination from LACTIC ACID BACTERIA.

Because over 90% of the wine is white, and because winemakers are emphasizing the primary grape flavours, most wine is vinified and stored in inert containers. Traditional cellars have large oval wood casks, many over 100 years of age, literally built into the cellar. Traditionally the same cask will be used each year for the same varietal. The build-up of TARTRATES forms a glass-like lining to the cask, and there is no likelihood of oak flavours masking the wine's character. If a cask has to be replaced, the new cask will be well washed out to remove as much as possible of the OAK FLAVOUR and will be used for Edelzwicker until all oak flavours have disappeared. A few growers are experimenting with BARREL MATURATION, most widely for Pinot Noir but also occasionally with Pinot Blanc, Pinot Gris, Auxerrois, and even Sylvaner.

The cellars are generally quite cold by the time FERMENTATION is taking place, so many have no cooling system. Winegrowers have found that the BOUQUET and AGEING potential of Riesling, Sylvaner, and Muscat can be enhanced by fermenting at 14–16 °C/61 °F, while Gewurztraminer will take a warmer temperature of up to 21 °C/70 °F. Most wines are bottled within a year of the vintage to retain freshness.

Most Alsace wines are fermented dry. Around the turn of the 21st century some of these supposedly dry wines had perceptible RESIDUAL SUGAR that was difficult to predict from the label, but starting with the 2021 harvest all Alsace wines indicate SWEETNESS on the label, whether in words or an indication on a visual scale. The residual sugar content for *sec* (dry) wines must be less than 4 g/l; *demi-sec* range from 4 to 12 g/l; *moelleux* run from 12 to 45 g/l, and *doux* exceed 45 g/l.

The late-harvest wines

While Alsace winegrowers very occasionally make VIN DE PAILLE and *vin de glace* (see EISWEIN), most late-harvest wines fall into two styles, Vendange Tardive and Sélection de Grains Nobles, defined by law in 1983.

Vendange Tardive, or Vendanges Tardives Late-picked wines have always been produced in Alsace in small quantities in outstanding vintages. To be labelled as Vendange Tardive, a term to which Alsace producers claim exclusive rights in France, a wine must come from a single vintage, from one of the four permitted varieties Riesling, Muscat, Gewurztraminer, or Pinot Gris. The wine must not be ENRICHED in any way, and the minimum sugar concentration at harvest must be 244 g/l (93 °Oechsle) for Riesling or Muscat, and 270 g/l (103 °Oechsle) for Gewurztraminer or Pinot Gris. Picking must take place after a certain date, determined annually by the authorities, who must be informed beforehand of the grower's intention to pick a Vendange Tardive wine and may inspect the vineyard at the time of picking to check the sugar concentration and quantity produced. The wine must also undergo an analysis and tasting after bottling, before the label is granted. Vendange Tardive wines do not have to be BOTRYTIS-affected. The most common variety for Vendange Tardive wines is Gewurztraminer, which can easily attain very high sugar levels. Muscat is the rarest of all and is only possible in occasional vintages. Vendange Tardive wine is not necessarily sweet and may vary from bone dry to medium sweet. Quality varies as widely as sweetness levels.

Sélection de Grains Nobles SGN is a further refinement of Vendange Tardive, where the grapes have reached even higher sugar levels. Wines labelled as Sélection de Grains Nobles, however, nearly always contain a proportion of grapes affected by botrytis, or NOBLE ROT, picked by hand, generally involving several passages through the vineyard. The same four varieties are permitted, with minimum sugar levels of 276 g/l (105 °Oechsle) for Riesling and Muscat, and 306 g/l (117 °Oechsle) for Gewurztraminer and Pinot Gris. The same legislation as for Vendange Tardive governs production (see above). Sélection de Grains Nobles wine is always sweet, although there is a variation in richness and quality, depending on the grape and the grower.

The appellations

Alsace was awarded AOC status in 1962, with the one regional appellation Alsace, or Vin d'Alsace. In 2011 a further two appellations were introduced which may complement the general AOC Alsace:

AOC Alsace communales This denomination is stricter than the regional appellation, and specifies grape variety, VINE DENSITY, PRUNING, VINE TRAINING, and ripeness levels (MUST WEIGHTS). YIELDS for white wines are also lower than those for the general Alsace AOC, at 72 hl/ha as opposed to 80; reds are the same, at 60 hl/ha. The following 13 communes, or inter-communal entities, may be mentioned on the label, alongside 'AOC Alsace': Bergheim, Blienschwiller, Côtes de Barr, Côte de Rouffach, Coteaux du Haut-Koenigsbourg, KLEVENER DE HEILIGENSTEIN, Ottrott, Rodern, St-Hippolyte, Scherwiller, Vallée Noble, Val St-Grégoire, and Wolxheim.

***AOC Alsace* lieux-dits** These are wines which express combinations of grape variety and certain terroirs and have stricter requirements than the AOC communales, including lower yields for white wines (68 hl/ha). Wines from these *lieux-dits* express primary fruit characters of individual grape varieties with nuances specific to the terroir.

Grand Cru	Type of Soil	Commune	Area	Elevation	Aspect	Date
Altenberg de Bergbieten	Marl-limestone-gypsum	67 Bergbieten	29.07 ha	210 to 265 m	south-east	23.11.1983
Altenberg de Bergheim	Marl-limestone	68 Bergheim	35.06 ha	220 to 320 m	south/south-east	23.11.1983
Altenberg de Wolxheim	Marl-limestone	67 Wolxheim	31.20 ha	200 to 250 m	south/south-west	17.12.1992
Brand	Granite	68 Turckheim	57.95 ha	250 to 380 m	south/south-east	23.11.1983
Bruderthal	Marl-limestone	67 Molsheim	18.40 ha	225 to 300 m	south-east	17.12.1992
Eichberg	Marl-limestone	68 Eguisheim	57.62 ha	220 to 340 m	south-east	23.11.1983
Engelberg	Marl-limestone	67 Dahlenheim and Scharrachbergheim	14.80 ha	250 to 300 m	south	17.12.1992
Florimont	Marl-limestone	68 Ingersheim and Katzenthal	21 ha	250 to 280 m	east	17.12.1992
Frankstein	Granite	67 Dambach-La-Ville	56.20 ha	220 to 230 m	east/south-east	17.12.1992
Froehn	Clay-marl	68 Zellenberg	14.60 ha	270 to 300 m	south/south-east	17.12.1992
Furstentum	Limestone	68 Kientzheim and Sigolsheim	30.50 ha	300 to 400 m	south/south-west	17.12.1992
Geisberg	Marl-limestone-sandstone	68 Ribeauvillé	8.53 ha	250 to 320 m	south	23.11.1983
Gloeckelberg	Granite clay	68 Rodern and Saint-Hippolyte	23.40 ha	250 to 360 m	south/south-east	23.11.1983
Goldert	Marl-limestone	68 Gueberschwihr	45.35 ha	230 to 330 m	east	23.11.1983
Hatschbourg	Marl-limestone and loess	68 Hattstatt and Voegtlinshoffen	47.36 ha	210 to 330 m	south/south-east	23.11.1983
Hengst	Marl-limestone-sandstone	68 Wintzenheim	75.78 ha	270 to 360 m	south/south-east	23.11.1983
Kaefferkopf	Granite-limestone and sandstone	68 Ammerschwihr	71.65 ha	240 to 350 m	south/west	14.01.2007
Kanzlerberg	Clay-marl-gypsum	67 Andlau	3.23 ha	250 m	south/south-west	23.11.1983
Kastelberg	Schist	67 Andlau	5.82 ha	240 to 300 m	south-east	23.11.1983
Kessler	Sandy-clay	68 Guebwiller	28.53 ha	300 to 390 m	south-east	23.11.1983
Kirchberg de Barr	Marl-limestone	67 Barr	40.63 ha	210 to 330 m	south-east	23.11.1983
Kirchberg de Ribeauvillé	Marl-limestone-sandstone	68 Ribeauvillé	11.40 ha	270 to 350 m	south/south-west	23.11.1983
Kitterlé	Sandstone-volcanic	68 Guebwiller	25.79 ha	270 to 360 m	south/south-east/ south-west	23.11.1983
Mambourg	Marl-limestone	68 Sigolsheim	61.85 ha	210 to 360 m	south	17.12.1992
Mandelberg	Marl-limestone	68 Mittelwihr and Beblenheim	22 ha	210 to 250 m	south/south-west	17.12.1992
Marckrain	Marl-limestone	68 Bennwihr and Sigolsheim	53.35 ha	200 to 300 m	east/south-east	17.12.1992
Moenchberg	Marl-limestone and colluvial deposits	67 Andlau and Eichoffen	11.83 ha	230 to 260 m	south	23.11.1983
Muenchberg	Sandstone-volcanic-pebbles	67 Nothalten	17.70 ha	250 to 310 m	south	17.12.1992
Ollwiller	Sandy-clay	67 Wuenheim	35.86 ha	260 to 330 m	south-east	23.11.1983
Osterberg	Marl	68 Ribeauvillé	24.60 ha	250 to 320 m	east-south-east	17.12.1992
Pfersigberg	Limestone-sandstone	68 Eguisheim and Wettolsheim	74.55 ha	220 to 330 m	east/south-east	17.12.1992
Pfingstberg	Marl-limestone-sandstone	68 Orschwihr	28.15 ha	270 to 370 m	south-east	17.12.1992
Praelatenberg	Granite-gneiss	67 Kintzheim	18.70 ha	250 to 350 m	east-south-east	17.12.1992
Rangen	Volcanic	68 Thann and Vieux-Thann	22.13 ha	320 to 450 m	south	23.11.1983
Rosacker	Dolomitic limestone	68 Hunawihr	26.18 ha	260 to 330 m	east-south-east	23.11.1983
Saering	Marl-limestone-sandstone	68 Guebwiller	26.75 ha	260 to 300 m	east/south-east	23.11.1983
Schlossberg	Granitic	68 Schlossberg	80.28 ha	230 to 350 m	south	20.11.1975
Schoenenbourg	Marl-sand-gypsum	68 Riquewihr and Zellenberg	53.40 ha	265 to 380 m	south/south-east	17.12.1992
Sommerberg	Granitic	68 Niedermorschwihr and Katzenthal	28.36 ha	260 to 400 m	south	23.11.1983
Sonnenglanz	Marl-limestone	68 Beblenheim	32.80 ha	220 to 270 m	south-east	23.11.1983
Spiegel	Marl-sandstone	68 Bergholtz and Guebwiller	18.26 ha	260 to 315 m	east	23.11.1983
Sporen	Clay-marl-pebbles	68 Riquewihr	23.70 ha	265 to 310 m	south-east	17.12.1992
Steinert	Limestone	68 Pfaffenheim and Westhalten	38,90 ha	250 to 350 m	east	17.12.1992
Steingrubler	Marl-limestone-sandstone	68 Wettolsheim	22.95 ha	280 to 350 m	south-east	17.12.1992
Steinklotz	Limestone	67 Marlenheim	40.60 ha	200 to 300 m	south-south-east	17.12.1992
Vorbourg	Limestone-sandstone	68 Rouffach and Westhalten	73.61 ha	210 to 300 m	south/south-east	17.12.1992
Wiebelsberg	Sand-sandstone	67 Andlau	12.52 ha	200 to 300 m	south/south-east	23.11.1983
Wineck-Schlossberg	Granitic	68 Katzenthal and Ammerschwihr	27.40 ha	280 to 400 m	south/south-east	17.12.1992
Winzenberg	Granitic	67 Blienschwiller	19.20 ha	240 to 320 m	south-south-east	17.12.1992
Zinnkoepflé	Limestone-sandstone	67 Soultzmatt and Westhalten	71.03 ha	250 to 420 m	south/south-east	17.12.1992
Zotzenberg	Marl-limestone	67 Mittelbergheim	36.45 ha	215 to 320 m	east/south	17.12.1992

Alsace Grand Cru The Alsace Grand Cru classification was first defined in 1975 with Schlossberg, a steep, south-facing site above Kayserberg with a history of grape-growing that dates to Roman times. Originally, an Alsace Grand Cru wine had to come from a single named vineyard site, or *lieu-dit*, and a single vintage, and it also had to be made from Riesling, Muscat, Gewurztraminer, or Pinot Gris. Subsequent expansions in 1983, 1992, and 2007 have seen 51 vineyards granted Grand Cru status; blends may also be allowed at the discretion of each Grand Cru's management committee. In 2022, Pinot Noir became eligible for Grand Cru status as well, in the Kirchberg and Hengst vineyards.

The wines from these vineyard sites make up only 4% of Alsace's total production but are the subject of some vigorous debates. Some grand cru sites are of only moderate quality or cover an unreasonably large area, including a number of soils and ASPECTS, some greatly superior to others. Much depends on the attitude of the grower, too: Many growers and co-operatives are producing wines of average quality, cashing in on the grand cru name. Because of this, some winegrowers have eschewed the appellation in favour of their superior brands. Beyer's Riesling Cuvée Particulière, from the Grand Cru Pfersigberg, and Trimbach's Clos Ste-Hune, grown in a parcel within the Rosacker Grand Cru, are prime examples.

Crémant d'Alsace The appellation Crémant d'Alsace was created in 1976 and amended in 2011, formalizing the sparkling wines that had long been made in the region. By 2020 Crémant d'Alsace represented 29% of all AOC wines made in Alsace. Pinot Blanc is by the far the most significant ingredient, although Pinot Gris, Auxerrois, Riesling, and Chardonnay are also used, and Pinot Noir is the only variety allowed for Crémant d'Alsace rosé. As with the late-harvest wines, growers have to identify before the start of harvest which parcels of vines are destined for Crémant d'Alsace production. See also CRÉMANT.

www.vinsalsace.com

Alta Langa. See LANGHE.

Alternaria, vine disease. See BUNCH ROTS.

alternative packaging for wine is slowly becoming more common, for reasons of convenience, economy, and/or SUSTAINABILITY. Glass BOTTLES are still by far the most common, but see also BOXES, CANS, CARTONS, KEGS, PAPER BOTTLES, PLASTIC BOTTLES, and POUCHES.

alternative varieties, Australian name for VINE VARIETIES other than the best-known INTERNATIONAL VARIETIES. They even have their own wine SHOW in Australia.

Altesse, SAVOIE's finest white grape variety, once known as ROUSSETTE, the name of several associated wines in Savoie and BUGEY.

The variety buds early and is therefore frost-prone, but it ripens late. It resists rot well, and the wine produced is relatively exotically perfumed, has good acidity, and is well worth ageing. Total plantings had grown to 424 ha/1,048 acres by 2019.

Robinson, J., et al., *Wine Grapes: A Complete Guide to 1,368 Vine Varieties, Including Their Origins and Flavours* (London, 2012).

altitude, a term commonly used to describe the ELEVATION of a vineyard. While the terms are used interchangeably, altitude—used typically by pilots—actually refers to height above the Earth's surface whereas elevation refers to the height above sea level.

Alto Adige, the alpine and most northerly part of Italy which shares with its neighbour TRENTINO a preponderance of INTERNATIONAL VARIETIES and the absence of a detailed DOC system. With the Austrian Tyrol to the immediate north, its culture is firmly Germanic and its first language is German. Officially known as Südtirol-Alto Adige, and part of Austria until it was annexed by Italy after the First World War, the region owes the Italian part of its name to the River Adige (Etsch), flowing south-east to the Adriatic. At the capital Bolzano the Adige is joined by the Isarco (Eisach) River from the north-east, forming a y-shaped valley on whose slopes viticulture has been practised for millennia. Vineyards are planted at 300–1,000 m/3,280 ft, while the valley floor is reserved for large-scale apple production, which has become so lucrative it has begun to supplant vineyards on lower-lying slopes, too.

Viticulture at dizzying heights is a serious option since the Alps protect Alto Adige from cold winds from the north, while the steepness of the slopes creates excellent ASPECTS for long, slow grape ripening. Due to CLIMATE CHANGE, several producers, notably Franz Haas, campaign for a general allowance for vineyards over 900 m, which, with few exceptions, are outlawed. Marked DIURNAL TEMPERATURE RANGE helps to retain acidity in the grapes, resulting in the fresh, appetizing whites for which the region is especially known. Some districts, notably around the towns of Merano and Bolzano where the dark-skinned LAGREIN and especially Vernatsch (SCHIAVA) are cultivated, even enjoy a sub-MEDITERRANEAN climate.

International grape varieties, introduced in the 19th century under Hapsburg rule, are the norm here. Pinot Grigio, with 662 ha/1,635 acres, is the region's most planted variety, at the cost of Vernatsch (635 ha), closely followed by GEWURZTRAMINER, CHARDONNAY, and PINOT BIANCO. Although KERNER claims only 115 ha/284 acres, it is set to become the next big thing, with a reputation for high-quality white wines.

Over the last 40 years, red wines have lost ground to white wines, which now make up 62% of production. Lagrein, at 486 ha/1,200 acres, has been taken over by Pinot Noir, here called Blauburgunder (494 ha). Its growing popularity has put the spotlight back on Schiava, which once produced pale, early-maturing red wines as a result of overproduction and irrigation but, in the hands of a new generation, now turns out elegant, complex reds, often produced from single vineyards and with WHOLE-BUNCH FERMENTATION.

Nearly two-thirds of Alto Adige production is controlled by CO-OPERATIVES, which process the harvest of hundreds, sometimes thousands, of grape farmers. The power of the co-ops is such that they can dictate the cultivation of certain grape varieties considered marketable. This is the main reason why Alto Adige's INDIGENOUS VARIETIES still receive scant attention. The regulations permit YIELDS up to 14 tonnes/ha, and, although high yields were still the norm in the early 2010s, improvements in the vineyard—primarily reduction of aggressive irrigation and use of fertilizers—has led to increased wine quality. While there has been a move from PERGOLA to lower-yielding GUYOT training systems, many old local varieties remain pergola-trained.

Alto Adige has only three DOCs and no DOCG. Valdadige DOC includes the whole of Alto Adige and neighbouring Trentino. Alto Adige DOC exists for the production of international varieties, while five of its six subregions—Colli di Bolzano, Meranese, Santa Maddalena, Valle Isarco, Valle Venosta—are historic Schiava zones, and the sixth, Terlano, produces exclusively white wines. Lago di CALDARO/Kalterer DOC, south of Bolzano, is exclusively for Schiava.

In a region dedicated to the production of international varietal wines, matching suitable varieties to subzones was never a priority, although there are some exceptions. Bozner Gries, near Bolsano, is locally considered a Lagrein CRU, and Mazzon, near Egna, is considered a Pinot Noir cru, though it is in danger of becoming too hot due to CLIMATE CHANGE. Girlan, its west-facing vineyards immediately south-west of Bolzano, shows increasingly more confidence with Pinot Noir, too. Terlano and VALLE ISARCO have deservedly risen to prominence: the first because of its long-lived Pinot Bianco, the latter because of a handful of small estates producing crystalline wines from vineyards up to 1,000 m. Termeno/Tramin claims to be the cradle of TRAMINER.

In an effort to emphasize the notion of terroir, a list of official *Lagen* or single-vineyard zones, called *menzione geografica aggiuntiva* (MGA) in Italian, has been created, permitting only certain authorized grape varieties. The controversial list more or less reflects the current situation. Producers can still produce any variety they like and bottle it under the plain Alto Adige denomination.

To further strengthen its image as a quality producer, the region has introduced an overarching quality designation, called Gran Alp. Analogous to Gran Selezione in CHIANTI CLASSICO, Gran Alp represents the pinnacle of the quality pyramid of both red and white wines, with more stringent rules on yields and obligatory ageing. But even before it was introduced, its relevance was questioned by the growing number of so-called 'super cuvées', tiny-production, stratospherically priced white wines meant to represent the top of a producer's range as well as of the region as a whole.

See also SANTA MADDALENA. W.S.

www.altoadigewines.com

Alto Piemonte is the area to the north of Barolo and Barbaresco in Italy's PIEMONTE encompassing a string of small historic denominations producing wine based on NEBBIOLO, often called Spanna here. See also BOCA, BRAMATERRA, CALUSO, CAREMA, FARA, GATTINARA, GHEMME, LESSONA, and SIZZANO. W.S.

Alvarelhão, dark-berried vine planted all over northern Portugal, especially in Dão, Douro, Beiras, and to a limited extent Vinho Verde country. In GALICIA it is also known as Brancellao and makes pale aromatic reds for early drinking.

Alvarinho, the Portuguese name of a distinctive white grape variety grown around the town of Moncão in the extreme north-west of Portugal's VINHO VERDE country (and, as ALBARIÑO, in neighbouring GALICIA). The grapes' thick skins help them withstand the particularly damp climate and can result in wines relatively high in alcohol (12–13%), acidity, and flavour. Alvarinho was one of the first Portuguese varieties to appear on the labels of VARIETAL whites and is therefore one of the best known. Portuguese plantings had reached 3,345 ha/8,266 acres by 2020.

Robinson, J., et al., *Wine Grapes: A Complete Guide to 1,368 Vine Varieties, Including Their Origins and Flavours* (2012).

Amador, California county. See SIERRA FOOTHILLS.

Amarone, powerful, red DRIED-GRAPE WINE in the DOC VALPOLICELLA in Italy's north-east. The wine, made of the same grape varieties as Valpolicella, consists of 45–95% CORVINA and/or CORVINONE and 5–30% RONDINELLA. The percentage of Corvinone, more resistant to hydric stress than Corvina, was previously limited to 50% but has been increased as a strategy to mitigate the effect of CLIMATE CHANGE. The blend may also contain up to 25% of other red varieties authorized in the province of Verona, with a maximum of 10% for each variety.

Strictly speaking, Amarone is a *recioto scapata*, literally a RECIOTO that has escaped and fermented to full dryness when the intention was to produce a sweet wine. The yeast, already struggling with the high sugar content in the MUST, would normally stop working because of rising alcohol levels and before all the sugar had been converted. Stylistically, Recioto della Valpolicella and Amarone are similar, but the latter must be dry with no more than 9 g/l RESIDUAL SUGAR (RS) at 14% alcohol, further allowing an additional 0.1 g RS for every 0.10% between 14% and 16%, and 0.15g for every 0.10% above 16%. The pleasant, bitter (*amaro*) aftertaste explains its name. Amarone is a style; its name must be suffixed by 'della Valpolicella' and can be followed by one of the two subzones, CLASSICO or Valpantena, on the label. By law Amarone must be aged for at least two years, four for wines labelled RISERVA.

Amarone has been produced in commercial quantities only since the 1950s. From the 1980s it has been a roaring success, especially in Scandinavia, Germany, and the United States, and production soared from 8.5 to 15 million bottles between 2005 and 2020. The total Valpolicella vineyard area has also increased, from 5,719 ha in 2000 to 8,200 ha/20,263 acres in 2020. Producers are allowed to transform up to 65% of their total grape production into Amarone, regardless of the quality or provenance of the grapes within the Valpolicella zone, which has resulted in wide quality variation. But proposals to restrict Amarone's production to HILLSIDE sites, and/or reducing production on the plains, have not come to fruition.

By law the grapes for Amarone must be dried at least until the first of the December after the vintage. The drying process results in a metabolization of the acids in the grape and a POLYMERIZATION of tannins in the skins, which explains the richness of good Amarone. The wine should be made from selected superior whole bunches, which are dried or raisined in special drying lodges. Traditionally, the drying of grapes was restricted to the Valpolicella hills, above the autumn fog line, where thermal fluctuation warded off the development of BOTRYTIS. Grapes were spread out on mats or wickerwork shelving or strung up from the ceiling or rafters. Today, however, most producers pick the grapes directly into plastic crates and dry them in a temperature- and humidity-controlled warehouse. This technical approach, which ensures minimal handling of the grapes, minimizing the risk of damage and consequent development of rot or mould, has resulted in cleaner, more balanced, but also rather formulaic wines, while encouraging the current industrial-scale production of Amarone.

Traditionally, the wines were aged in large BOTTI, although today BARRIQUE ageing is the norm, resulting in wines with a distinctly international style. In the 2010s the pendulum started to swing back, away from heavy OAK influence and towards lower alcohol and little or no residual sweetness (although reportedly only Bolla produces an Amarone with no residual sugar), while also the first AMPHORA-fermented Amarones have appeared on the market. W.S.

Masnaghetti, A., *Valpolicella: Crus and Valleys* (2014).
Tosi, E., *Amarone Confidential: Everything You Should Know about Valpolicella Wines* (2021).
www.consorziovalpolicella.it

amateur winemaking. See HOME WINEMAKING.

ambient yeast are those that are present in the vineyard and winery, as opposed to inoculated, cultured YEAST.

amelioration, which strictly means 'improvement', is a euphemism for chemical intervention in winemaking with the express purpose of compensating for nature's deficiencies. Thus in cooler wine regions the term is commonly used interchangeably with ENRICHMENT or CHAPTALIZATION. 'Amelioration' is sometimes used more widely, to include both ACIDIFICATION and DEACIDIFICATION, and sometimes for any chemical adjustment to the constituents naturally present in grape juice or wine. See also MANIPULATION.

American hybrids, group of vine HYBRIDS developed in the eastern United States, mainly in the early and mid 19th century and in some cases earlier but also much more recently with cold hardiness in mind. Brianna, for example, was developed in 1983 by the American private breeder Elmer Swenson and involved no fewer than 93 distinct parents from eight different species. The term includes hybrids between native AMERICAN VINE SPECIES of the genus VITIS and a variety of the European vine species VITIS VINIFERA, resulting in such varieties as Black Spanish (JACQUEZ), NORTON, CONCORD, NIAGARA, HERBEMONT, DELAWARE, and Othello. The hybrids' most common parents are the American species VITIS LABRUSCA and *Vitis aestivalis*, along with *vinifera*.

These varieties are used for wine production, for unfermented GRAPE JUICE and jelly, and for TABLE GRAPES. The fruit is typically highly flavoured, and palates accustomed to the taste of *vinifera* varieties find the FOXY character of products made from many American hybrids strong and objectionable.

See UNITED STATES, history, for more background. Following the devastation wreaked by the pest PHYLLOXERA in Europe at the end of the 19th century, the French began experimental hybridizing of *vinifera* with American species, producing the so-called FRENCH HYBRIDS or 'direct producers'. R.E.S. & P.C.

Morton, L. T., *Winegrowing in Eastern America* (1985).

Reisch, B. I., et al., 'Grape', in M. L. Badenes and D. H. Byrne (eds.), *Fruit Breeding* (2012).

Sabbatini, P., and Howell, S. G., '*Vitis* hybrids: history and current status', *Wines & Vines* (January 2014), 135–42.

American vines, loose term for both AMERICAN VINE SPECIES and AMERICAN HYBRIDS.

American vine species, those members of the grapevine genus VITIS which originate in North and South America, including Mexico and the Caribbean. About half the vine species of the world are native to America, but they are poorly suited to WINEMAKING. However, when all efforts to grow European vine species VITIS VINIFERA in North America failed through pest, disease, or climatic extreme (see UNITED STATES, history), wine was made in North America of necessity from these species, detailed below.

After the development of AMERICAN HYBRIDS and the successful cultivation of *vinifera* vines in CALIFORNIA and elsewhere in the Americas, native vines were rarely used for wine. A notable exception is *Vitis rotundifolia*, particularly the SCUPPERNONG and related bronze- and black-fruited varieties used for a sweet, musky wine popular in the southern United States, where they are both grown and cultivated.

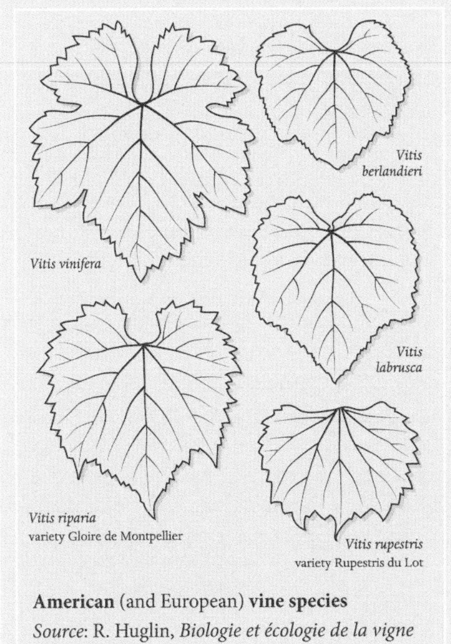

American (and European) **vine species**
Source: R. Huglin, *Biologie et écologie de la vigne*

Vitis vinifera has varied leaf forms among its many varieties, not always with five distinct lobes as shown here.

The most important role for the American species has been to provide the genetic basis for ROOTSTOCKS on to which *vinifera* vines may be grafted (see MUNSON). This became a necessity in most of the world's wine regions by the end of the 19th century to counter the impact of PHYLLOXERA, native to America and to which most American vine species developed resistance or tolerance. The species *Vitis berlandieri*, VITIS RIPARIA, and *Vitis rupestris* are particularly important as sources of protection against phylloxera, and the great majority of the world's vineyards now grow on rootstocks derived from them.

These are some of the more important American vine species (although others are listed under VITIS):

Vitis labrusca Vine species found in the north-eastern United States producing highly aromatic and strongly flavoured berries sometimes described as FOXY. The berries fall easily from the cluster when mature and are called 'slip-skin', in that a berry squeezed between fingers will eject the flesh as a complete ball (non-slip-skin varieties, which are more usual, are squashed when squeezed in this way). Most of the fruit of this species is black, and the leaves are large, thick, and covered on the lower surface with dense white or brown hairs. *Labrusca* is a common parent in American hybrids, including CONCORD and CATAWBA.

Vitis aestivalis Vine species found in the southern and eastern United States which, like *labrusca*, is a common parent in American hybrids. The fruit, typically black, is not strongly aromatic, and the berries adhere to the cluster when mature. This species shows good resistance to DOWNY MILDEW and POWDERY MILDEW and is therefore a common parent in VINE BREEDING programmes. NORTON, which has a reputation for high-quality wine in VIRGINIA, where it was bred, is a hybrid derived from *aestivalis*. Early Spanish settlers of north-eastern MEXICO made wine from WILD VINES of this species as early as 1597.

Vitis riparia This vine species is widely distributed in eastern North America, from Canada to the Gulf of Mexico. The grapes are not strongly aromatic, with black skin and highly acidic juice. *Riparia* is used directly as a rootstock and as a parent of many commercially important rootstocks; the species typically imparts low to moderate vine size to SCIONS and provides protection against phylloxera.

Vitis rupestris Unusual vine species that grows as a small shrub, found typically on gravelly banks of streams or in watercourses in Texas, Oklahoma, Arkansas, and Missouri. The leaves are small and kidney-shaped, and roots tend to grow vertically downwards rather than spreading horizontally. It is a common parent of many commercially important rootstocks because of its phylloxera tolerance or resistance and deep-rooting habit, which can provide protection against drought.

Vitis berlandieri Vine species found on the limestone soils of Texas and Mexico. The grape is black, and its juice is high in sugar and acid without strong flavours. This species is known for being difficult to root from cuttings, but, because of its high phylloxera and lime tolerance or resistance, it is a common parent of many commercially important rootstocks.

Other American species include *Vitis cinerea*, *Vitis vulpina* (*cordifolia*), *Vitis mustangensis*, *Vitis shuttleworthii*, *Vitis acerifolia*, *Vitis californica*, *Vitis arizonica*, *Vitis monticola*, *Vitis palmata*, *Vitis biformis*, and *Vitis tiliifolia*. See VITIS. P.C.

Moore, M. O., 'Vitaceae', in Flora of North America Editorial Committee (eds.), *Flora of North America North of Mexico*, 12 (2016).

Morton, L. T., *Winegrowing in Eastern America* (1985).

Reisch, B. I., et al., 'Grape', in M. L. Badenes and D. H. Byrne (eds.), *Fruit Breeding* (2012).

American Viticultural Area. See AVA.

Amerine, Maynard (1911–98), pre-eminent American OENOLOGIST, teacher, and writer, was trained as a plant physiologist at Berkeley in California before joining the revived Department of Viticulture and Enology at DAVIS in 1935. There he participated in some of the most important branches of its work, including the assessment of VINE VARIETIES for the different regions of California and the re-education of the wine industry to restore and advance the technical knowledge lost during PROHIBITION.

With A.J. WINKLER, Amerine developed the system of classifying wine regions by measuring heat summation (see CLIMATE CLASSIFICATION). The list of his publications extends to nearly 400 items. He served as chairman of his department from 1957 until 1962 and retired from the University in 1974. T.P.

Amigne, rare Swiss white grape variety and a speciality of Vétroz in the Valais used for dry, semi-sweet, and sweet wines. DNA PROFILING has established that Amigne is a likely grandchild of PETIT MESLIER, a rare variety of Champagne. The wine produced is either a powerful dry white with distinctive linden aromas or a sweet (see FLÉTRI) wine with flavours of citrus fruits and bitter almonds. J.V.

amino acids, the basic building blocks of PROTEINS, chemicals essential to all living systems. There are 20 amino acids involved in constructing thousands of proteins of living materials. When these proteins act as catalysts for specific biochemical reactions, they are called ENZYMES.

In ripe grapes, NITROGEN-containing compounds constitute about 1 g/l of juice, of which amino acids make up about half. The most common are proline, arginine, and glutamic acid (see UMAMI). During grape RIPENING, the concentrations of amino acids increase, arginine and proline especially; proline increases more than arginine if the fruit is exposed to light. High concentrations of arginine, resulting from soils with a high nitrogen content, present the danger of production of the carcinogen urethane (ETHYL CARBAMATE) in wine.

YEASTS are able to make most of the amino acids they require, but they will also use intact amino acids from the medium in which they find themselves if they are available. Thus FUSEL OIL is formed in wine as a by-product of the nitrogen metabolism of the yeast cells living in grape juice. After fermentation has finished, yeast proteins break down, secreting smaller peptide units and amino acids into the wine if it is left in the presence of the LEES or dead yeast cells.

Bottle-fermented SPARKLING WINES owe some of their special flavour to the presence of substances associated with yeast breakdown, peptides, and amino acids (see AUTOLYSIS). B.G.C.

Rantz, J. M. (ed.), *Proceedings of the International Symposium on Nitrogen in Grapes and Wine* (1991).

amontillado, Spanish word which etymologically means sherry (or the equivalent wine from other wine regions in ANDALUCÍA) made in the style of MONTILLA. A FINO becomes *amontillado* when the FLOR yeast dies and the wine is exposed to oxygen, becoming amber in hue and richer and nuttier in flavour. This happens if the alcohol exceeds 17%, whether through FORTIFICATION or natural ageing, since the flor yeast cannot work in such an alcoholic environment. A true Amontillado-style sherry is therefore an aged Fino. Cheaper wines created by blending and sweetening used to appear on the market as Amontillado but now must be labelled as Medium. Amontillados are always bone-dry. For more details, see SHERRY. J.B.

ampelography, the science of description and identification of the vine genus VITIS and its cultivated VINE VARIETIES. A volume of vine descriptions is also called an ampelography, the word coming from the Greek *ampelos*, meaning 'vine', and *graphos*, meaning 'description'.

While an awareness of the differences between vine varieties can be seen in the writings of PLINY the Elder, and regional ampelographies emphasizing the aptitudes of various cultivated varieties already existed in medieval Europe, the term 'ampelography' was not coined until 1661, in Philipp Jakob Sachs von Löwenheim's *Ampelographia*, published in Leipzig. The term was not used again until 1807, when Simón de Roxas Clemente y Rubio published a Spanish ampelography.

Some system of distinguishing between grapevine varieties was clearly necessary, since the choice of variety has a fundamental impact on the organoleptic characteristics of a wine and since the same variety often goes by different names in different regions. In addition, when serious vine diseases and pests were introduced to Europe from America (POWDERY MILDEW in 1845, PHYLLOXERA in 1863, DOWNY MILDEW in 1878, and BLACK ROT in 1885), it became essential to identify those species and varieties which showed most resistance to these hazards. Such species were soon used for VINE BREEDING and as ROOTSTOCKS.

Several large regional ampelographies were published near the turn of the century, including Pulliat (1888) and Viala and Vermorel (1901–10) in France; Goethe (1878) in Austria; Rovasenda (1877) and Molon (1906) in Italy; and Hedrick (1908) and MUNSON (1909) in the US.

The most famous modern ampelographer, the late Dr Pierre GALET of MONTPELLIER, began his studies in 1944 by inspecting rootstock plantings, and this led to the publication of a distinguishing key in 1946. These studies were extended to include wine and table grape varieties, and in 1952 his *Précis d'ampélographie pratique* was published, followed by, among other works, *Cépages et vignobles de France*. Galet's comprehensive quantitative description of leaf shape, attained by measuring the lengths and angles of the veins, the ratio of length to width, and the depth of sinuses, is highly objective.

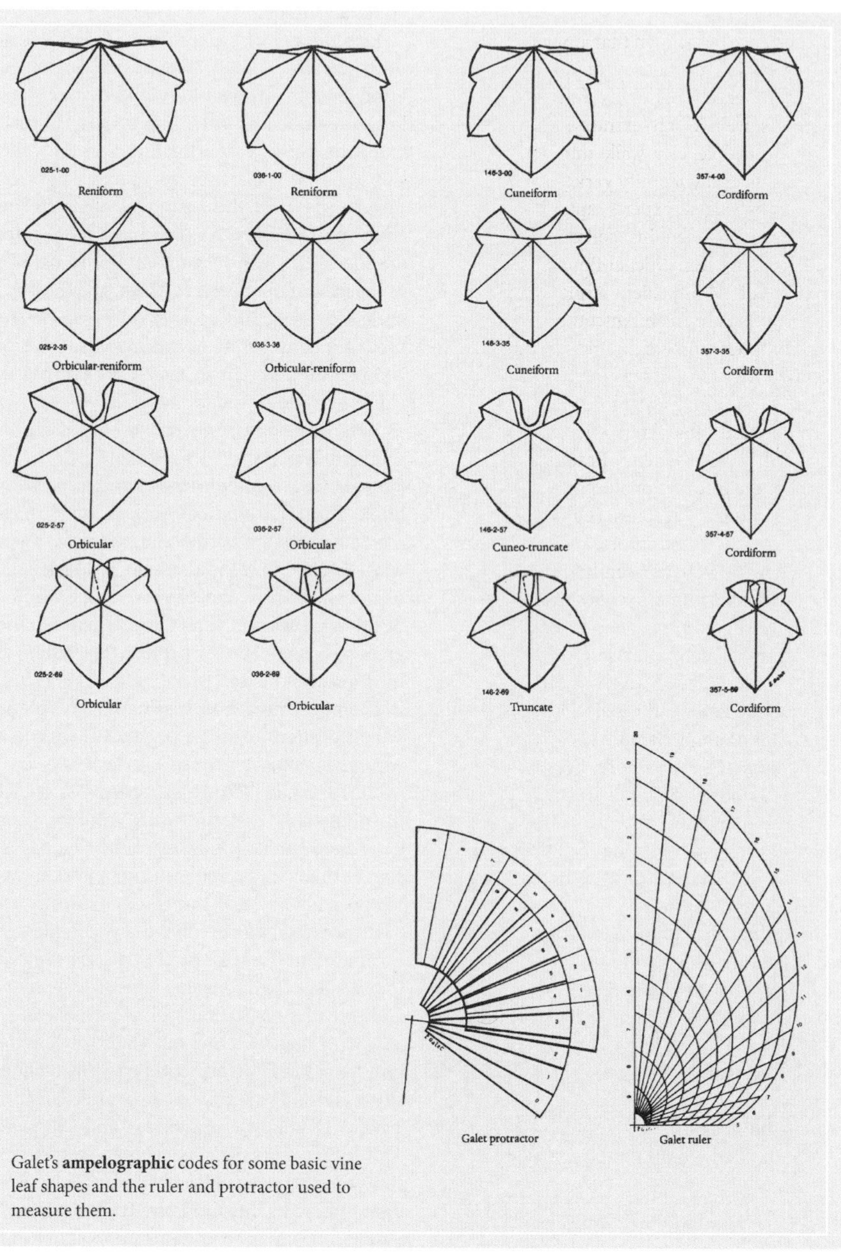

Galet's **ampelographic** codes for some basic vine leaf shapes and the ruler and protractor used to measure them.

Other characteristics have been considered for identification, including the timing of phenological or development stages such as BUDBREAK, fruit maturation, or even LEAF FALL. Such features are known to be controlled by the climate, however, and can be used only in a relative sense for vine varieties in a single region.

The disadvantages of these classification techniques are that, while some characteristics are quite stable, others, such as leaf shape, can vary markedly even on one vine. Major differences can be caused by environmental factors (see EPIGENETICS), but also, and to a lesser degree, by variation between different CLONES, plant age, and the influence of pests and vine DISEASES. There are, however, five characters which are quite stable: sex of the flower; grape skin colour; pulp colour; the taste of berries; and the presence of seeds.

Experience has shown that ampelography is a field of systematic botany requiring very specialized observational skills and interpretative ability, as well as an extraordinary memory. Very few people can walk into any vineyard and unequivocally identify varieties. Some modern acknowledged experts apart from Pierre Galet have included his colleague Paul Truel and successors Jean-Michel Boursiquot, Thierry Lacombe of Montpellier, Anna Schneider of Italy, and the late Allan Antcliff of Australia.

A complex ampelographic procedure was proposed by the Office International de la Vigne et du Vin (OIV) in 1951, based on 65 morphological characters. The International Board of Plant Genetic Resources (IBPGR) and l'Union Internationale pour la Protection des Obtentions Végétales (UPOV) have also produced lists of descriptors, and all three international systems have been harmonized by the introduction of numeric codes. Ampelographic studies have recently been facilitated by the application of computers and electronic data storage and retrieval (e.g. www.vivc.de), but final identification still relies heavily on the judgement of ampelographers.

Attempts were therefore made to develop objective, laboratory-based tests for vine identification, including isozyme analysis and gel electrophoresis of enzyme banding patterns, but DNA PROFILING has proved by far the most successful and effective.

Unfortunately, misnomers are common, especially in the New World, in government collections as well as in commercial nurseries and thus vineyards. Some of the early introductions of vine cuttings to these regions were made before European vine-growers had correctly identified their own varieties. Sometimes name tags on bundles of vine cuttings, all of which look remarkably similar, were simply misplaced or transposed. In other cases, confusion was caused by different synonyms in different European regions. James BUSBY's celebrated vine collection introduced to colonial Australia in 1832, for example, probably contained CINSAUT cuttings under seven different regional synonyms and CHENIN BLANC under three. Paul Truel studied a large collection of French varieties at Domaine de Vassal on the Mediterranean coast (see INRA) in the 1960s and 1970s and found that as many as six distinct varieties grown in different parts of France were a single variety under different names, and there is even more variation in nomenclature between countries. The GRACIANO of Spain, for example, is the same as France's Morrastel, while the Ottavianello of Italy is the same as Cinsaut of France, but more complex examples abound. A labelling error in a Spanish vine collection, perpetuated in France and then again in Australia, led many growers to label their SAVAGNIN BLANC wines as Albariño.

Because its nursery has been able to provide virus-free, high-health vines, the FOUNDATION PLANT SERVICES at the University of California at DAVIS has been an important source of varieties for many NEW WORLD countries. Naming mistakes in this collection were legion and caused inconvenience for both the California wine industry and importers of plant material from Davis. Some examples of such errors cited in California by French ampelographers GALET and Boursiquot, in Australia by Truel, and in New Zealand by Zuur include: Petit Verdot (Gros Manseng), one CLONE of Pinot Noir (Gamay Beaujolais), Négrette (Pinot St George), Valdiguié (Napa Gamay), Melon (Pinot Blanc), Muscadelle (Sauvignon Vert), Tempranillo (Valdepeñas), a clone of Sauvignon Blanc (Sauvagnin Musqué), Trousseau Gris (Grey Riesling), and Touriga (Alvarelhão).

Generally rootstocks are more difficult to differentiate as they do not often fruit, so it is not surprising that problems have also occurred with their naming. In the 1990s, California growers were forced to replace the rootstock AXR1 as it succumbed to phylloxera. This replanting effort was thwarted by finding that the rootstock thought to be SO 4 was in fact 5C Teleki, and Riparia Gloire was mixed with Couderc 1616.

Today ampelographers can rely on the accuracy of DNA PROFILING to identify not only varieties but also CLONES. R.E.S. & J.V.

Roy-Chevrier, J., *Ampélographie rétrospective* (1900).
Galet, P., *Dictionnaire encyclopédique des cépages* (2nd edn, 2015).
Galet, P., and Morton, L. T., *A Practical Ampelography* (1979).
Robinson, J., et al., *Wine Grapes: A Complete Guide to 1,368 Vine Varieties, Including Their Origins and Flavours* (2012).

amphora, Latin word from the Greek for a vessel with two handles. The term is normally used to describe the large pottery containers which were used for the BULK TRANSPORT of many goods and liquids, including wine, in the Mediterranean world throughout classical antiquity (see ancient EGYPT, for example). (See DOLIUM for the vessels used by the Romans for FERMENTATION.) Despite the considerable variety of shape in amphorae, they mainly shared the characteristics of the two handles, a mouth narrow enough to be stoppered, and a bottom which tapered to a point (only a few, notably those of southern France, had flat bottoms). When full, many amphorae were a considerable weight, so the spike on the bottom served as a third handle when lifting and pouring. To carry wine, the inner surface of the porous amphora was sealed with a coating of pine resin (see RESINATED WINES). To stop the mouth, either CORK or a lid of fired clay was pushed down the neck and then secured with a sealing of mortar. Many amphorae were stamped with the name of the potter—not that of the winemaker, as some have suggested—before firing. Modern study of ancient amphorae began after the Second World War, when the use of the aqualung led to the discovery of many wrecks carrying cargoes of amphorae (see CELTS, for example). Scientific study of the clays used, and the detection of tartaric residues as evidence of wine (see ORIGINS OF VINICULTURE), are currently helping to identify the date and origin of the wine. As a result, a much clearer picture of the pattern of trade in goods, such as wine, has emerged. The term 'amphora' also became an expression of capacity, a cubic Roman foot, about 26 1/7 gal, although the actual vessels did not by any means conform to this. Indeed, it is likely that goods, such as wine, were frequently sold wholesale by weight and there were formulae for converting the weight of different goods into capacity. J.J.P.

Demesticha, S., *Per Terram, Per Mare: Seaborne Trade and the Distribution of Roman Amphorae in the Mediterranean* (2015).
University of Southampton, *Roman Amphorae: A Digital Resource* (2014).

Modern usage

Even though the Roman amphora was used exclusively for the transport of wine, the term is now generally used to refer to a vessel used for FERMENTATION (what the Romans called a DOLIUM) and AGEING of wine. Partly inspired by the likes of Gravner and Radikon in FRIULI (see ORANGE WINES), and traditional winemaking techniques in Georgia (see QVEVRI), winemakers have been experimenting with CLAY or, occasionally, CONCRETE 'amphorae' that are typically bigger, more rounded, and handleless. Concrete may provide a less oxidative environment and is easier to use and maintain, but the level of oxygenation depends more on the size of the vessel, the width of the opening, and how it is sealed. Winemakers may design their own

shapes. The more traditional amphora shape, with a narrow base, allows less LEES CONTACT and better SETTLING and results typically in more vibrant wines than those whose shape is closer to that of CONCRETE eggs, which tend to produce richer wines. Amphorae are generally free-standing in a cellar, but some producers bury them, emulating Georgian traditions. Small amphorae with narrow necks are particularly difficult to clean. Ideally the pores of the clay should be very fine, giving a smooth surface that is easier to clean and is less permeable to liquid, although they may also be treated inside, for example with beeswax. Some producers use local clay with the aim of maximizing the possible local footprint on the resulting wine. See also TINAJA, TALHA, and PITHARI.

Amtliche Prüfnummer. See AP NUMBER.

amurensis. See VITIS AMURENSIS.

Amyndeo is the coolest wine region in GREECE, famous for wine from the XINOMAVRO grape. It lies on the north-western slopes of Mount Vermio, on the other side from NAOUSSA, on a plateau at 650 m/2,100 ft in ELEVATION. In the rain shadow of the Vermio, Vitsi, and Voras mountains, the region has cold, snowy winters and relatively dry summers, as well as five lakes that help moderate the temperature. An Amyndeo PDO wine must be a pure Xinomavro, whether red, rosé, or rosé sparkling wine, which has been much in vogue since 2010. The red wines can be full-bodied with admirable COMPLEXITY, especially from centenarian vines in sandy, PHYLLOXERA-free soils. Many international grape varieties have found a welcome home here, too. A blend of Xinomavro, Merlot, and Syrah is becoming a regional speciality, while, in white wines, ASSYRTIKO, CHARDONNAY, MALAGOUSIA, and even several Italian varieties can give impressive results. Nevertheless, these labels qualify only for the regional PGI Florina or PGI Macedonia. The area has been attracting serious investments from producers both inside and outside of the region. K.L.

analysis of grapes, must, and wine is a regular and important part of the WINEMAKING process.

Grapes and must

Traditional analysis of grapes and must is chiefly concerned with just three components: sugar, acid, and PH. For TABLE WINE, for instance, the grapes should ideally contain SUGARS capable of producing wines with an ALCOHOLIC STRENGTH of 10–14% by volume, which means that the grapes should have 18–25% fermentable sugar by weight (see MUST WEIGHT for the various ways in which this can be measured).

The ACIDITY of the grapes or must should also ideally be such that the TOTAL ACIDITY is in the general range of 7–10 g/l expressed as tartaric acid. Some acid is always lost during winemaking, primarily as the alcohol content of the wine increases and the solubility of wine acids decreases. Acidity may be further reduced by MALOLACTIC CONVERSION and cold STABILIZATION. It is therefore necessary to start with more acid in the grapes than is eventually wanted in the wine. However, it should be noted that the production of SUCCINIC ACID during fermentation may occasionally lead to a very slight increase in total acidity.

The chemistry of AGEING is strongly influenced by pH, and, although there is a relationship between pH and total acidity, it is important to measure pH separately. Two samples with the same acidity can have different pH readings because of different POTASSIUM levels and due to differing organic acid profiles.

Sugars are most simply measured by determining the DENSITY of a sample of CLARIFIED grape juice. Measurement of the juice's index of refraction (see REFRACTOMETER) can also provide a close estimate of its sugar content. In establishments with particularly well-equipped laboratories, modern chromatography can provide an extremely accurate sugar measurement. This gives an indication of timing of HARVEST, the POTENTIAL ALCOHOL, and any need for ENRICHMENT, but harvest decisions are often also governed by grape flavour profiles.

In warm wine regions, the accumulation of sugars poses a different problem: in hot, dry weather, sugar synthesis (see PHOTOSYNTHESIS) and acid loss occur so rapidly that picking decisions have to be taken fast, and frequent field analysis may be necessary, normally involving a hand refractometer for sugar.

On arrival at the winery, harvested grapes may also be tested with a probe linked to an autoanalyser. This will typically analyse for sugar content, total acidity, MALIC ACID, pH, and yeast-available NITROGEN. INFRARED SPECTROSCOPY may be used for rapid analysis of ANTHOCYANINS in red grapes.

See SOIL TESTING for the analysis of soils. R.D.

Wine

Analysis of wine involves the measurement of various characteristics which relate to wine quality, stability, and legal requirements, ideally in a well-equipped laboratory. In most specialist wine laboratories, wine analysis also includes a critical tasting to ensure that the wine conforms to type and quality. Wine analysis is also used to help assess blends, estimate shelf life, and ensure that BLENDING and PACKAGING operations have been successfully performed.

Common measurements include those of alcoholic strength, total acidity, VOLATILE ACIDITY, pH, density, RESIDUAL SUGAR, microbiology, and SULFUR DIOXIDE. Laboratories in larger wineries may also be equipped to test for mineral elements such as IRON, COPPER, SODIUM, and potassium. All these parameters either play an important part in assessing quality and stability or are limited by law.

Not all wineries determine all these constituents, and many of the smaller ones have no laboratory at all and have to rely on samples sent to professional analysts.

Wine analysis advanced considerably in the early 21st century with the development of powerful specialist high-tech equipment such as Inductively Coupled Mass Spectrometry (ICPMS), Liquid Chromatography Mass Spectrometry Mass Spectrometry (LCMSMS), and Gas Chromatography Mass Spectrometry Mass Spectrometry (GCMSMS).

ICPMS is a powerful technique which enables the simultaneous measurement of 60 or more different elements (e.g. metals, trace metals) and can be used to help monitor authenticity (see AUTHENTICATION), for example to make sure that wines or batches of allegedly the same wine are, in fact, identical.

Chromatography in very general terms is an analytical technique for separating, then identifying and quantifying the various components and chemicals within liquids such as wine. Of the various types of chromatography, the two most commonly used in wine analysis are complementary: liquid chromatography, generally used to separate non-volatile compounds; and gas chromatography, for separating volatile compounds. The techniques have evolved into very sophisticated analytical tools and can now include a double mass spectrometer: the first confirms the mass of the compound separated; the second breaks down the compound into its components, enabling detection at lower levels, and more certain identification, than previously. Sub-nanogram per litre quantification is now possible. This is important because wine taints such as TCA can be detected by the human nose at nanogram per litre level.

LCMSMS is typically used for SUGARS, TANNINS, PHENOLICS, certain ACIDS, etc.

GCMSMS is typically used for anisoles (TCA, TBA, etc.), BRETTANOMYCES markers such as 4-ethyl phenol, pesticide RESIDUES, aroma profiling for varietals such as Sauvignon Blanc, etc. An additional adaptor, called an odour port or sniff port, can be used to enable simultaneous nosing (smelling) and identification. These are extremely powerful tools available to the modern wine analyst.

Stability prediction tests for TARTRATES, PROTEIN, COLOUR sedimentation, and microbiology are also crucial analyses to ensure a commercially sound and stable product.

Modern analytical methods based on INFRARED SPECTROSCOPY are able to perform rapid multi-parameter analyses, from grape to packed wine, comparing the samples with a pre-established databank. The equipment is therefore an invaluable tool for large-scale wineries and bottling facilities, but for some wine styles, including sparkling wine, it is important to compare the results with those obtained by more traditional methods.

See also NUCLEAR MAGNETIC RESONANCE, and see AUTHENTICATION for the development of non-invasive analysis using spectroscopy. R.D. & G.T.

Reynolds, A.G. (ed.), *Managing Wine Quality 1: Viticulture and Wine Quality* (2nd edn, 2022).

Anatolia, much of modern TÜRKIYE, the land lying between the Black Sea and the Mediterranean. In ancient Asia Minor, grapes were harvested in September and October. In business documents of the Old Assyrian trading colonies in Asia Minor (dating to approximately the 19th century BCE), this season of the year was called *qitip karānim*, or 'grape picking'. The locations of the ancient vine-growing areas are uncertain, but they were probably established in suitably warm, well-watered regions throughout the peninsula, as they are today along major river valleys and along the coasts.

Among the Hittites, the Anatolian civilization in central Turkey in the second millennium BCE, a grape-harvesting festival took place every year. Viticulture was certainly important during the Hittite Old Kingdom (*c.*18th–15th centuries BCE). The king's merit in the eyes of the storm god (who was regarded as the owner of the land) was reflected in the produce of the vineyards and in grain and livestock production. Wine was under the control of royal officials who distributed 'good wine' to certain pensioners (who complained when the quality was not satisfactory). Certain officials during the Old Kingdom bore a title which can be translated as 'wine chief', originally supervisor of the vineyards but later an exalted military rank comparable with general or field marshal.

In Hittite laws (also of the Old Kingdom), the price of grapes was regulated, together with the prices of barley and emmer (a species of wheat). One law makes provisions for damage caused to vines: the offender has to take the damaged vine himself and let the plaintiff take grapes from one of his own good vines at harvest time.

Another law prescribes penalties for the theft of a vine: six shekels of silver for a free man, three if the offender was a slave. Previously the fine was lower, but the offender had been obliged to undergo corporal punishment in addition. Six shekels was also the fine for a free man who damaged another's vine by fire. Viticultural images were used in ritual magic. In an archaic ritual performed during the foundation of a new palace, for example: 'They lay out a vine tendril and say, "Just as the vine puts down roots and sends up tendrils, so may the king and queen put down roots and send up tendrils!"'

Similarly in so-called 'vanishing god' texts we read: 'O Telepinu [a god of agriculture], hold goodness in your mind and heart, just as the grape holds wine in its heart!'

See also ORIGINS OF VINICULTURE and PALAEOETHNOBOTANY. J.A.B.

Gorny, R. L., 'Viticulture and ancient Anatolia', in P. E. McGovern et al. (eds.), *The Origins and Ancient History of Wine* (1995).
Hoffner, H. A., Jr, *Alimenta Hethaeorum: Food Production in Hittite Asia Minor*, American Oriental Series 55 (1974).

Ancellotta, Italian red wine grape valued for its deep colour as a blending ingredient, up to 15% in some types of LAMBRUSCO and up to 60% in REGGIANO. It is also widely used throughout central and northern Italy to add colour to wines deemed too pallid. Total Italian plantings were 1,700 ha/4,201 acres in 2015 with almost all of it in EMILIA-ROMAGNA. It is also grown in Brazil and the Valais in Switzerland.

Ancenis, Coteaux d', small, schistous AOC zone on both sides of the LOIRE between Nantes and Angers producing mainly off-dry whites from Pinot Gris (locally called Malvoisie) and reds and rosés from Gamay.

ancient vine varieties. THEOPHRASTUS (*c.*370–*c.*287 BCE) remarked that there were as many kinds of grapes as there were kinds of soil (*Historia plantarum* 2. 5. 7; also *De causis plantarum* 4. 11. 6). He does not elaborate, but his remark shows how difficult it is to discuss VINE VARIETIES in the classical world. Are varieties that classical authors describe as different really different varieties, or are they examples of the same variety behaving differently in different conditions? Soil is only one factor; climate and winemaking methods are others. We cannot resort to tasting samples or nursery specimens; all we possess are CLASSICAL TEXTS written by authors who were not modern, scientifically trained AMPELOGRAPHERS.

The Greeks did not write systematic treatises on wine, so we must turn to the Latin writers on agriculture and natural history, particularly VIRGIL, PLINY, and COLUMELLA. Virgil's treatment, in *Georgics* 2. 98–108, is the briefest and least systematic of the three, and he does not distinguish different wines, such as Lesbos, from different grape varieties, such as Aminean and Bumastus (the latter primarily a TABLE GRAPE). There are so many varieties, he concludes, that no one knows the number.

Only Democritus knew how many grape varieties existed, Pliny says (14. 20), but his account does not survive. Pliny himself announces that he will give us only the most important vine varieties. Pride of place among the Italian grapes goes to the Aminean, which has five subvarieties, then to the Nomentan, and third comes the Apian, which has two subvarieties and is the preferred grape of Etruria. All other vine varieties, Pliny asserts confidently, are imports from GREECE. Of these, the Graecula, from Chios or Thasos, is as good as the Aminean. Eugenia is good but only when planted in the Colli ALBANI. Elsewhere it does not produce good wine. The same goes for Rhaetic, which grows well in a cool climate, and the Allobrogian, which apparently ripens well in frost. These last three grape varieties produce wines which go lighter with age. The remaining varieties Pliny mentions are ones that he judges to be without distinction as wine grapes.

Columella agrees with Pliny for the most part, but there are differences (3. 2. 7–31). He regards the Aminean as the best grape and puts the Nomentan second. He also recommends the Eugenian and Allobrogian wines, with the same reservation as Pliny, and the Apian. Then he mentions other varieties which are noted for their productivity rather than for their flavour. He does not think highly of the Rhaetic, and he does not rank the Graecula with the Aminean. Vines were still being imported: Columella mentions three grapes which have only lately come to his notice so that he cannot give an opinion on their wines and also another grape which he says is a recent Greek import named Dracontion. Columella's aim is not to give a long and comprehensive list, for that would be impossible (he quotes Virgil's words, *Georgics* 2. 104–6). One should not quibble about names, he concludes, and, knowing that a variety can change out of all recognition if it is planted somewhere new, one should not approve a new grape until it has been tried and tested.

Columella's remarks indicate that farmers were prepared to experiment with new varieties, some of them imported from Greece. Some varieties were probably brought over with the Greek colonists from the 8th century BCE onwards; others were growing in Italy long before they arrived. A Greek name is not a guarantee of Greek origin: some Greek names may be names given to Italian grapes which the Greeks of Sicily and southern Italy used when they started producing wine in their colonies. If so, these names reflect no more than the fact that the Greeks exploited the potential of these grapes commercially before the natives did. H.M.W.

André, J., 'Contribution au vocabulaire de la viticulture: les noms des cépages', *Revue des études latines*, 30 (1952), 126–56.
McGovern, P. E., *Ancient Wine: The Search for the Origins of Viniculture* (2nd edn, 2019).
McGovern, P. E., et al. (eds.), *The Origins and Ancient History of Wine* (New York, 1995).
Tchernia, A., *Le Vin de l'Italie romaine* (1986).

ancient world. See ANATOLIA, ARMENIA, CAMPANIA, CANAAN, CHINA, EGYPT, ETRUSCANS, GREECE, INDIA, IRAN, MESOPOTAMIA, PHOENICIA, ROME, SUMER.

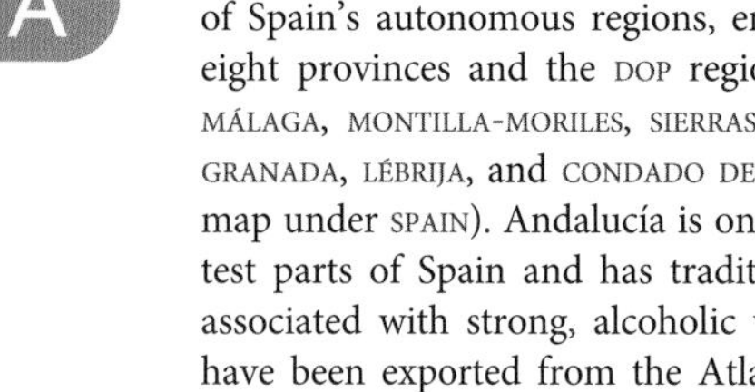

Andalucía, or **Andalusia**, the southernmost of Spain's autonomous regions, encompassing eight provinces and the DOP regions of JEREZ, MÁLAGA, MONTILLA-MORILES, SIERRAS DE MÁLAGA, GRANADA, LÉBRIJA, and CONDADO DE HUELVA (see map under SPAIN). Andalucía is one of the hottest parts of Spain and has traditionally been associated with strong, alcoholic wines which have been exported from the Atlantic port of Cádiz since the PHOENICIANS first established their trading links around 800 BCE (see SPAIN, history). There is evidence of grapes being cultivated during seven centuries of Moorish domination, but wine drinking was seriously punished, and there are doubts whether there was clandestine winemaking. Once the Muslims were expelled from western Andalusia in the mid 13th century, international commerce flourished. By the early 16th century, Andalucía had become one of the most exciting parts of the world, and it would remain so for a few centuries to come. The harbours of Sevilla, Cádiz, and the sherry town of Sanlúcar were key in the expeditions to the New World. It was from Sanlúcar de Barrameda where the first trip around the world took place in 1519, led by the Spanish sailor Juan Sebastián Elcano.

Many wines of Andalucía bear a strong resemblance to each other, and particularly to SHERRY, which has fashioned the region's wine industry. Most are FORTIFIED, although grapes from the arid plateau around Córdoba and Jaén are often so rich in natural sugar that they do not require the addition of spirit to reach an ALCOHOLIC STRENGTH of 14–18%. Until laws were tightened up following the foundation of the Jerez Consejo Regulador in 1934, wines from other parts of Andalucía would frequently find their way into sherry blends.

Since the late 1990s, fine-wine estates have sprouted on the slopes of Sierra Nevada mountains in GRANADA and around Ronda in the province of MÁLAGA. The region also has several VINO DE LA TIERRA appellations. Some of the most compelling wines come from the IGP Vino de la Tierra de Cádiz, which covers a wide range of international and local varieties grown north and east of the port town of Cádiz. Especially exciting are the non-fortified, flor-aged white wines made from PALOMINO FINO, as well as dry red wines made from Tintilla de Rota (GRACIANO). R.J.M. & F.C.

Anderson Valley. Scouts for Louis ROEDERER of Champagne say they hunted in CALIFORNIA until they found somewhere with weather as bleak as Roederer's home in north-eastern France, and that the coast-hugging Anderson Valley in MENDOCINO fitted their requirement perfectly. Anderson's rolling hills are cut through by the Navarro River, and almost all vineyards are planted on some degree of slope. The region has the distinction of being one of California's rare transverse valleys. Running approximately east–west, this orientation allows the cool ocean fog and breezes to penetrate far inland. That said, though Anderson Valley is hardly 1.6 km/10 miles end to end, a steady rise in elevation from 244–396 m/800–1,300 ft combined with a rising wall of hills makes the inland end at Boonville warmer and sunnier than the oft-befogged area between Philo and Navarro, where most of the vines grow.

Redwood logging, sheep, and apples reigned here until grapes came, a little wave of them in the 1970s and a bigger one in the 1980s. In the 1990s, leading producers such as Littorai and William-Selyem drew attention to the region through high-quality single-vineyard bottlings. Though many locals feel the region's true strengths lie in its sparkling wines and aromatic whites, it was the rising popularity of Pinot Noir in post-SIDEWAYS America that resulted in Anderson Valley's growing fame. Today, over 70% of the AVA is planted to Pinot Noir, and nearly all of Mendocino's fine dining and luxury accommodations are located here. While most wineries are small outfits, major players such as Duckhorn have also taken up shop. The result is that Anderson Valley is now better known than the county that claims it. K.W.

Angelica, a historically important type of MISTELA produced during the earliest part of CALIFORNIA's development, named after the city of Los Angeles, where it was a primary product of Mission-period winemaking in the region. It is traditionally made by adding brandy to unfermented or partially fermented grape MUST of the MISSION grape. A.Y.

animals can cause serious damage in the vineyard, most obviously but not exclusively by eating grapes and foliage. Any reductions in foliage can prejudice fruit RIPENING and wine quality, and encourage sunburn.

Most mammals may be kept out by fencing, but fences have to be sunk into the soil for smaller, burrowing animals and be high and cantilevered for animals as large and mobile as kangaroos. Deer, rabbits, rodents, raccoons, and wild boar are some of the most common vineyard animal pests, but baboons can pose a threat in South Africa and ETHIOPIA, as can monkeys in JAPAN, hippos in Ethiopia, elephants in Thailand, bears in Canada, kangaroos and rabbits in Australia, and badgers in the UK, while rattlesnakes can present a danger to vineyard workers. Some vine-growers in New Zealand, on the other hand, deliberately use a combination of electric fencing and sheep to achieve judicious LEAF REMOVAL. Animals of relevance to wine production other than HORSES are referred to in VINE PESTS. See also BIRDS. R.E.S.

Bettiga, L. J., (ed.), *Grape Pest Management* (3rd edn, 2013).

Anjou, major, revitalized, and diverse wine region in the western LOIRE centred on the town of Angers, whose influence once extended all over north-west France. Anjou was the birthplace of Henri II, and its wines were some of France's most highly regarded in the Middle Ages (see LOIRE, history). It was the DUTCH WINE TRADE, however, that developed the sweet white wine production of the region in the 16th and 17th centuries. White grapes, especially CHENIN BLANC, predominated until the 19th century, when the Anjou vignoble reached its peak and PHYLLOXERA arrived. Subsequently a wide variety of grape varieties were planted, yet the evolution of the market over the 20th century led to the predominance of CABERNET FRANC, while Chenin plantings, as well as the total vineyard, with its communal AOC, shrunk by half its peak to 15,484 ha/38,260 acres.

The region's climate is quite mild, being influenced by the Atlantic and protected by the Mauges hills to the south-west. Rainfall is low, with an average of 570 mm/22.4 in. These climatic conditions explain why Anjou offers the largest stylistic diversity of the whole Loire.

Wines claiming the Anjou name predominantly come from the black, metamorphic part of the area, as SAUMUR AOC is usually used for wines on TUFFEAU territory. The terroir of SCHIST with VOLCANIC veins influences wine style, and wines can be rustic when tannins and ripeness development are not handled carefully.

The GROLLEAU vine, mostly used for Rosé d'Anjou, is in retreat, although better vineyard management has resulted in better quality. In the same vein is the most produced AOC of the whole Loire, the rosé Cabernet d'Anjou, made from Cabernet Franc or, seldomly, Cabernet Sauvignon. It can be quite sweet, and usually has high acidity and discernable tannins which can preserve it for decades, yet its long-lasting potential is rarely realized.

Cabernet Franc is increasingly favoured, encouraged by the commercial trove of off-dry rosé as well as by the creation in 1987 of the serious red-wine appellation Anjou-Villages. The best area for such reds immediately south of Angers in the Coteaux de l'Aubance was given its own appellation Anjou-Villages Brissac in 1998. It overlaps the Coteaux de L'AUBANCE AOC. Juicier reds are produced as Anjou Gamay, while Anjou Rouge is the catch-all appellation for lighter, often fresh, red wines, with some peppery PINEAU D'AUNIS added to the blend.

Despite the current enthusiasm for Chenin Blanc, still Anjou Blanc and sweet variations are produced on a modest scale, as are Anjou MOUSSEUX. Anjou Blanc is the most common and for a long time was considered an afterthought. It must contain at least 80% Chenin Blanc, with Chardonnay and Sauvignon Blanc allowed in the blend. An exciting development since the late 1990s has been the emergence of a new, high-quality style of dry Chenin paired with the development of a strong ORGANIC and BIODYNAMIC movement that often revives prime, historic sites to produce healthy grapes picked by hand in TRIES at full maturity. BARREL FERMENTATION and MALOLACTIC CONVERSION are common, and successful, yet a significant proportion of top growers chose to declassify their production in VIN DE FRANCE. Anjou-Coteaux de la Loire near SAVENNIÈRES, once a key area, makes minuscule amounts of sweet Chenin Blanc.

See also the Anjou appellations Coteaux de L'AUBANCE; BONNEZEAUX; Coteaux du LAYON; QUARTS DE CHAUME for sweet wines; and SAVENNIÈRES for dry wines. P.Le.

annual growth cycle. See VINE GROWTH CYCLE.

año, Spanish word for year. Some wines, particularly RIOJA, were once sold without a VINTAGE YEAR but with the number of years' AGEING prior to bottling indicated on the label. **Ano** is the Portuguese word.

Ansonica, alternative name for Sicily's white INZOLIA grape used particularly in the Tuscan Maremma, where it can produce wines of real character.

Antão Vaz, white grape increasingly favoured by winemakers in the ALENTEJO, southern Portugal, especially in the cooler subregion of Vidigueira, where it produces full-bodied VARIETAL wines with notable longevity and is also blended with tarter varieties such as ARINTO. Total 2020 plantings were 1,425 ha/3,521 acres.

anther, the pollen-bearing part of the STAMEN of a flower such as that of the vine. Each of the five anthers of the grape has sacs in which a large number of pollen mother cells develop into pollen grains, about two to three weeks before FLOWERING. The small, dry grains of POLLEN are released, possibly before the CALYPTRA or flower caps have fallen (see POLLINATION). In deliberate VINE BREEDING stamens and caps are removed early, before caps would normally fall, to prevent self-pollination and permit deliberate cross-pollination. B.G.C.

anthesis, another word for FLOWERING.

anthocyanins, members of a complex group of natural phenolic GLYCOSIDES (see also PHENOLICS and FLAVONOIDS) responsible for the colour of black and red grapes. They are also responsible for the colour of red wines, both as wine components and as precursors of PIGMENTED TANNINS and other derived pigments which are formed through reactions of anthocyanins with other wine components. Anthocyanins are common in the plant world and are responsible for the red to blue colours of leaves, fruits, and flowers. The word comes from *anthos*, Greek for 'flower', together with the Greek-derived 'cyan', blue.

The particular anthocyanins found in grapes are limited in number, with mixtures of pigment molecules varying from species to species and from grape variety to grape variety. Indeed, chemical determination of the particular mixture of pigments present in an unidentified grape berry can aid vine identification. Pure VITIS VINIFERA varieties have mostly anthocyanin pigments with only one molecule of glucose (monoglucosides), while many of the AMERICAN VINES used in breeding ROOTSTOCKS and AMERICAN HYBRIDS also have significant amounts of anthocyanins with two molecules of glucose (diglucosides; a fact which greatly aided detection of non-*vinifera* wine in France in the mid 20th century; see University of BORDEAUX).

Anthocyanins have another important characteristic. They are capable of changing form, depending upon the PH, or degree of ACIDITY, of the medium in which they are dissolved, the different forms being red, blue, and colourless. In general, the more acid the grape juice or wine, the greater the degree of ionization of the anthocyanins (giving a higher proportion of the red flavylium cation) and the brighter red the colour; as the acidity decreases, the proportion of colourless and blue forms increases. In mildly acidic conditions, anthocyanins are also bleached by SULFUR DIOXIDE. At wine pH values, grape anthocyanins should be mostly in colourless forms unless the pigments are stabilized by CO-PIGMENTATION or through conversion to derived pigments including pigmented tannins (see below).

The anthocyanin pigments are formed in the grapevine by a sequence of metabolic steps and are first visible when the berry begins to expand. The onset of this stage in the vine's metabolism is called VERAISON and is characterized by rapid growth and accumulation of sugar in the berry together with the first flush of colour in the berries.

The concentration of the pigments in the grape skin increases as the level of sugar increases in the grapes during ripening. The increase is intensified if sunlight falls on the berries—that is, if the berries are in an open CANOPY MICROCLIMATE. Anthocyanin production during ripening is very temperature-dependent and is also strongly influenced by the MACROCLIMATE. During veraison the anthocyanin pigments are formed and sequestered in the berry skins' outer cell layers in all but a few dark-berried grape varieties which have a portion of the pigment present in the pulp of the berry as well as in the skin (see TEINTURIERS).

One important operation during the FERMENTATION of most red wines, therefore, is to transfer the anthocyanin pigments from the skin cells to the wine. Colour transfer is achieved by keeping the skins adequately mixed with the fermenting wine (see MACERATION).

One might reasonably expect that the pigments in the new wine would be identical to those found in the grape skin. This may be the case for a few hours, but once the anthocyanins are mixed with the other phenolics as well as the many products of fermentation, they begin a series of reactions leading to a great diversity of derived pigments and colourless molecules. Derived pigments are classically assimilated to pigmented tannins arising from the addition of tannins to anthocyanins, either directly or through condensation reactions with ALDEHYDES. However, they also include rather small molecules formed by the reaction of anthocyanins with other wine constituents such as ACETALDEHYDE or PYRUVIC ACID, or hydroxycinnamic-acid derivatives. Moreover, most of these reaction products are themselves unstable, and the list of derived pigments found in wine keeps expanding, covering a wide range of colours. Within a few years, only traces of the relatively simple monomeric anthocyanins remain. With wine AGEING, polymers containing anthocyanin molecules may become larger and form aggregates so that some of them exceed their solubility in the wine and are precipitated as SEDIMENT. See AGEING. B.G.C. & V.C.

Cheynier, V., 'Flavonoids in wine', in O. M. Andersen and K. R. Markham (eds.), *Flavonoids: Chemistry, Biochemistry and Applications* (2006), 263–318.

de Freitas, V., and Mateus, N., 'Formation of pyranoanthocyanins in red wines: a new and diverse class of anthocyanin derivatives', *Analytical and Bioanalytical Chemistry*, 401/5 (2011), 1463–73.

Monagas, M., and Bartolome, B., 'Anthocyanins and anthocyanin-derived compounds', in M. V. Moreno-Arribas and C. Polo (eds.), *Wine Chemistry and Biochemistry* (2009).

anthracnose, one of the FUNGAL DISEASES of European origin which affects vines. It is also known as bird's eye rot or black spot. The disease is spread worldwide but is a particular problem in humid regions, as in the eastern UNITED STATES. Before the introduction of DOWNY MILDEW and POWDERY MILDEW, it was the most serious grape fungal disease in Europe, but since BORDEAUX MIXTURE was introduced in 1885 it has been controllable. The disease is caused by the fungus *Elsinoe ampelina*. Small black lesions are produced on the leaves, and this area can die and drop out so that the leaves look as though peppered with gunshot. Small dark-coloured spots are also produced on young shoots, flower cluster stems, and berries. Anthracnose can reduce both the YIELD and quality of the fruit. The disease can be controlled by FUNGICIDES applied early in the growing season. R.E.S.

Antinori, one of Italy's most important wine producers, based in TUSCANY. The modern wine

firm was founded by brothers Lodovico and Piero Antinori in 1895, although the Antinori family can trace their history in the wine trade back to 1385, when Giovanni di Pietro Antinori enrolled in the Vintners Guild of Florence. Like the vast majority of the Florentine nobility, the Antinori were, for centuries, producers of wine on their substantial country properties.

The work of the 19th-century brothers was continued by Piero's son Niccolò, who extended the house's commercial network both in Italy and into foreign markets and purchased the Castello della Sala estate near ORVIETO in Umbria. The house developed a certain reputation for its white wines, sold under the Villa Antinori label, and for its Chianti, made in a soft and fruity style. Although the family fortunes flourished, Antinori was only a medium-sized operation in 1966 when Piero Antinori, the son of Niccolò Antinori, took over.

By the early 1990s, he had increased the annual production fifteen-fold, giving the house a commanding position in Tuscany, based on both the quality of all the firm's wines at various price levels and, above all, the innovative work of Antinori and its OENOLOGIST the late Giacomo Tachis in creating Tignanello, the prototype SUPERTUSCAN; Solaia, which, together with SASSICAIA (initially marketed by the Antinori and whose development was assisted by Tachis), showed the potential for outstanding Cabernet in Tuscany; and Cervaro, a white wine produced at the Castello della Sala based on Chardonnay grapes and, then unusual for Italy, BARREL FERMENTED.

Although it is firmly anchored in Central Italy, where its vineyard holdings were 2,800 ha/6,919 acres in 2019, Antinori has expanded steadily, securing holdings in every important or upcoming Italian wine region: Montenisa in FRANCIACORTA; the historic house of Prunotto in BAROLO; and Tormaresca, a large-scale operation in PUGLIA. In 2021 it bought a majority stake in the Jermann estate in FRIULI and acquired both the Villa di Cigliano near their own modern winery in San Casciano and Tenuta Rubbia al Colle in BOLGHERI, where they also own Guado al Tasso. Further estates in the Antinori portfolio include Pian delle Vigne in MONTALCINO, La Braccesca in MONTEPULCIANO, Tenuta La Farnete in Colli Senesi, and Le Mortelle and Tenuta Monteloro in the MAREMMA.

Internationally Antinori spread its wings quite early on, often through JOINT VENTURES, the most important of which was Antica on Atlas Peak in NAPA Valley in 1993. This was followed in 1995 by Col Solare in a joint venture with Ste. Michelle, in WASHINGTON State. In 2007, again in a joint venture with Ste. Michelle, the legendary Stag's Leap Winery of Napa Valley was acquired. Tuzko Bátaapáti in Hungary had been acquired in a joint venture with Fonterutoli's Lapo Mazzei in 1991. Meridiana on MALTA, producing INTERNATIONAL VARIETIES, was established in 1992, followed by Vitis Metamorfosis, a joint venture with Halewood in ROMANIA, and Haras de Pirque in CHILE's Maipo Valley.

Piero's brother Lodovico Antinori independently created the internationally famous Supertuscans Ornellaia and the all-Merlot Masseto at his own estate near Bolgheri (subsequently owned by the Antinoris' great rivals the FRESCOBALDI). With their sister Ilaria, the brothers have developed the Tenuta di Biserno project at Bibbona just north of Bolgheri with Michel ROLLAND consulting and increasing attention paid to Cabernet Franc. Lodovico, long a fan of Sauvignon Blanc, independently produces one in MARLBOROUGH, New Zealand, with Mount Nelson Estates. W.S.

antioxidants. For their role in protecting must and wine against the effects of OXYGEN during winemaking and wine AGEING, see GLUTATHIONE, SULFUR DIOXIDE, ASCORBIC ACID, NITROGEN, and CARBON DIOXIDE. For their importance in the effects of wine consumption on HEALTH, see FLAVONOIDS and RESVERATROL.

anti-transpirant, a natural film-forming polymer (di-1-*p* menthane) applied to the grapevine CANOPY around VERAISON, known to reduce PHOTOSYNTHESIS and TRANSPIRATION and hence delay berry RIPENING. Trials in Europe, Australia, and New Zealand have shown promising results: lower sugar concentration, lower acidity, enhanced wine flavour, and improved YIELD. This new technique could be useful in the production of lower-alcohol wines and to mitigate the effects of HARVEST COMPRESSION and CLIMATE CHANGE. R.E.S.

Previtali, P., et al., 'A systematic review and meta-analysis of vineyard techniques used to delay ripening', *Horticulture Research* (2022).

ants, more specifically leafcutter ants belonging to the genera *Acromyrmex* and *Atta*, can pose a serious problem in South America, especially in Argentina, where *Acromyrmex* spp. are particularly damaging to young leaves in newer vineyards close to indigenous vegetation and in sandy and stony soils, for example in MENDOZA's Gualtallary subregion. As their name suggests, they cut the leaves and other parts of the vine, taking the spoils to their underground nests to feed the mutualistic fungi that live there. While ants play an essential role in regulating other pests and increasing soil ORGANIC MATTER, they are also capable of defoliating an entire vineyard row in less than a week, and they can severely reduce yields as they are most active between BUDBURST and FLOWERING. They can be controlled with insecticides, but organic alternatives are limited to destroying the nests and distracting the ants with other plants.

AOC stands for *appellation d'origine contrôlée*, often shortened to *appellation contrôlée*, France's famous denomination for its best wines. In 2010, as a result of EU reforms introduced in 2008, this was superseded by *appellation d'origine protegée* (AOP), France's PDO, but many continue to use the term 'AOC'. This much-imitated, prototypical, and inherently protectionist system of designating and controlling the country's all-important geographically based names applies not just to wines but also to spirits such as cognac, armagnac, and calvados, as well as to many foods. It is administered by the INAO, a powerful Paris-based body which also controls the less restrictive denomination *indication géographique protégée* or IGP (formerly VIN DE PAYS). AOP/AOC wines represented approximately 60% of French wine production in 2020, IGP around 30%.

History

France's role as a wine producer had been gravely affected by the viticultural devastation caused by POWDERY MILDEW, DOWNY MILDEW, and PHYLLOXERA in the second half of the 19th century (see FRANCE, history). Fine wines were available in much-reduced quantity, but the LANGUEDOC and ALGERIA had become vast factories for the production of very ordinary wine at very low prices. Laws passed in the first two decades of the 20th century were aimed at bringing an end to the ADULTERATION AND FRAUD that was by then widespread. These were based simply on the principle of geographical DELIMITATION and specified particular areas within which certain wines had to be produced. Bordeaux, Banyuls, and Clairette de Die were among the first; disagreement about exactly which districts should be allowed to produce France's most famous sparkling wine led to riots (see CHAMPAGNE, history).

It rapidly became clear, however, that France's famous wines depended on more than geography. The wrong grape varieties and careless winemaking would not result in a suitable expression of these carefully delimited TERROIRS. By 1923, Baron le Roy, the most influential and well-connected producer of CHÂTEAUNEUF-DU-PAPE, was implementing in his part of the southern Rhône a much more detailed set of rules including not just geographical delimitation but a specification of permitted VINE VARIETIES, PRUNING and vine-TRAINING methods, and minimum ALCOHOLIC STRENGTH.

The French *appellation contrôlée* system evolved into a national reality in the 1930s when economic depression, widespread cultivation of HYBRIDS, and a serious wine surplus increased the incentive for wine merchants to indulge in nefarious blending. The producers of genuine Pommard, for example, had a very real interest in limiting the use of their name to themselves. In 1935 the INAO was created with the express mission of drawing up and enforcing specifications for individual AOCs, which broadly followed the Châteauneuf prototype, and in principle banned hybrids from AOC wine. The great majority of the appellation regulations for France's most famous wines and spirits are therefore dated 1936 or 1937, although they have been continuously revised since.

The legal powers of the INAO, both within France and in its dealings with the EU and beyond, were strengthened substantially in 1990, when it took the conscious decision to try to build the future of French wine on the concept of geographical appellations (eschewing even the mention of vine varieties on the main label) and adopted the specific aim of preserving agricultural activity in certain zones. But in 2004, when France's wine exports were clearly in significant decline and domestic sales stagnant, this policy was dramatically modified to make French wine labels easier to understand and the wines themselves more competitive in the global market. The aim was to raise the average quality of AOC wines and introduce some new regional Vin de Pays categories (most now rebadged as IGP). The INAO continues to wage war on all misused GENERIC wine and spirit names, but, as an increasing number of French wine producers find the detailed AOP/AOC regulations too restrictive, the supremacy of the AOC system is no longer unchallenged orthodoxy.

The regulations' scope

The INAO's detailed regulations for its more than 360 AOP/AOCs are voluminous and constantly revised, covering the following aspects for each appellation. The regulations for the IGP category (with 74 listed in 2020) are similar but generally less restrictive.

Production area All those communes allowed to produce the wine in question are listed, but within each of these communes only certain plots of land are deemed worthy, details of which are lodged with each commune's all-important *mairie* or administrative centre. Vines grown elsewhere within the commune are normally entitled to be sold only as a less specific appellation, an IGP, or VIN DE FRANCE.

Vine varieties The permitted grapes are specified in great detail, along with permitted maximum and minimum proportions in the vineyard (known as the *encépagement*) and in any wine that is a blend (the *assemblage*). Vineyards will generally be inspected to ensure that the correct varieties are planted. Many appellation regulations include half-forgotten but once-significant local varieties. White grape varieties are permitted to a certain extent in some red-wine appellations. See full details in Appendix 1.

Ripeness and alcoholic strength Specific minimum MUST WEIGHTS are generally cited for freshly picked grapes before any CHAPTALIZATION, given in g/l of sugar and as potential NATURAL ALCOHOL. A maximum ALCOHOLIC STRENGTH may also be specified for appellations in which chaptalization is permitted.

Yields Control of YIELDS is a fundamental tenet of the *appellation contrôlée* system even if the maximum yields cited in the regulations were almost routinely increased by about 20% throughout the 1970s and 1980s thanks to a special derogation, now abolished, known as the *plafond limite de classement* or PLC. The regulations now specify a base yield (*rendement*) and a maximum yield (*rendement butoir*), so it is still possible to request a derogation allowing a higher yield if the application can be justified—by the VINTAGE weather conditions, for example.

This section usually includes information on a minimum VINE AGE allowed for AOP/AOC production.

Viticulture This usually specifies a minimum VINE DENSITY, the approved PRUNING regime down to the number of buds, and the permitted vine-TRAINING SYSTEM. In some southern appellations the (limited) extent to which IRRIGATION is allowed may be outlined.

Winemaking This long section may well specify such aspects as compulsory DESTEMMING, or the method of ROSÉ WINEMAKING that must be used (usually by SAIGNÉE), although there is generous use of the vague phrase *usages locaux*.

Pros and cons

France's *appellation d'origine contrôlée* designation is in general a more reliable guide to the country's best wines than, for example, the QUALITÄTSWEIN category of supposedly superior wines in Germany, the liberally applied DOC designation in Italy and Portugal, and its DOP counterpart in Spain (all of the last three modelled on the AOC system). The French system is by no means perfect, however, since it was drawn up not with a clean slate but to legitimize the best current practices. Policing remains a problem, and the Direction Générale de la Concurrence, de la Consommation et de la Répression des Fraudes (DGCCRF) is probably understaffed. Contraventions of the regulations, particularly over-chaptalization, or chaptalization and ACIDIFICATION of the same wine, are difficult to detect (although a complex bureaucracy controls over-production). Misdemeanours are only very rarely publicized, and then usually only as a result of local politics.

A more serious disadvantage of the *appellation contrôlée* system is the extent to which it stifles experimentation. In dramatic contrast to the New World, vine-growers may plant only certain vine varieties. Those wishing to experiment are often restricted to selling the wine not merely as an IGP but as Vin de France.

It is also fanciful to suggest that every wine produced within an appellation inevitably uniquely betrays its geographical provenance. Few blind tasters would unhesitatingly identify a Côtes du MARMANDAIS, for example. And then there are the catch-all appellations such as BORDEAUX AOC, ALSACE, and CHAMPAGNE, whose quality variation is simply frustrating.

The full regulations for every appellation, its *cahier des charges*, can be found online: www.inao.gouv.fr.

AOP stands for *appellation d'origine protegée*. See PDO.

Aosta, or the **Valle d'Aosta (Vallée d'Aoste** to the region's many French speakers), is Italy's smallest region (see map under ITALY). The long, narrow valley formed by the River Dora Baltea as it courses through the mountains of Italy's extreme north-west is Italy's connecting link to France and Switzerland and to the north of Europe beyond. Consequently, wine labels may be written in either Italian or French.

In this rugged alpine landscape, the vineyards, planted on HILLSIDES flanking the Dora Baltea, are frequently TERRACED on dizzyingly steep slopes. In an average year, no more than 19,000 hl/501,926 gal of wine qualifying as DOC is produced from a total of 469 ha/1,158 acres of vines, with 339 ha qualified to produce DOC wines (the balance traded as VINO DA TAVOLA). Despite such minuscule production levels, the region has no fewer than seven subzones suffixing a single overarching DOC, Valle d'Aosta, while a host of INTERNATIONAL and local varieties may appear on labels as single varietals.

At the crossroads between northern and southern Europe, the Valle d'Aosta has found itself with an extremely rich diversity of vine varieties. The three most important local varieties are the red grapes PETIT ROUGE (90 ha/222 acres) and NEBBIOLO (43ha/106 acres) and the white PRIÉ Blanc (38 ha/94 acres), which together account for more than one-third of the region's DOC production. Increasingly important are the ARVINE of Switzerland, called Petite Arvine here, as well as FUMIN. Other native regional and Italian varieties include VIEN DE NUS, Prëmetta, and Moscato di Chambave. French varieties include PINOT NOIR, GAMAY, SYRAH, PINOT GRIS or Malvoisie, PINOT BLANC, and CHARDONNAY.

Production has mainly been in the hands of CO-OPERATIVES, which have a good reputation but have been joined by an association of small producers, Viticulteurs Encaveurs Vallée d'Aoste, aiming at reviving ancient local viticultural practices and favouring INDIGENOUS VARIETIES.

The most interesting wines are the Nebbiolo-based Donnas or Donnaz and the neighbouring

Nebbiolo-based Arnad-Montjovet, as well as the family of fruity Petit Rouge reds such as Enfer d'Arvier, Torrette, and Chambave Rosso. But in the early 21st century its delicate alpine Chardonnay drew attention, as well as the minerally Blanc de Morgex et de La Salle from Prié Blanc grown at ELEVATIONS of up to 1,200 m/3,937 ft. The latter is made from UNGRAFTED vines (PHYLLOXERA does not survive at such high altitude) trained in a low PERGOLA. Thanks to the elevation, the grapes retain acidity well, and fine TRADITIONAL METHOD sparkling wines are made. This acidity is also key to the region's relatively numerous sweet wines. The region's main challenge for the future is to retain its highest-quality steep vineyards when faced with an ageing population. W.S.

www.docvalledaosta.it
Gallino, F., *Vino in Valle* (2013).

aoûtement, French term for CANE RIPENING derived from *août*, French for August, the month in which it generally takes place in the northern hemisphere.

Apalta, warm, sunny DO on the banks of the Tinguirica River in the heart of Chile's COLCHAGUA Valley known especially for old-vine CARMENÈRE planted on GRANITE soils.

Apera, registered in 2012 as the name to replace Sherry for Australian wines previously thus named. At the same time, Fino, Amontillado, and Oloroso were replaced by the more prosaic, but decidedly less Andalucian, Dry, Medium Dry, Medium Sweet, Semi-Sweet, and Sweet.

aperitifs, drinks served before a meal to 'open' (from the Latin *aperire*) the digestive system and stimulate the appetite, of which VERMOUTH and similar drinks are archetypal. Wines commonly served as aperitifs are dry, white, and not too alcoholic: CHAMPAGNE or any dry SPARKLING WINE; FINO and MANZANILLA sherry; MOSEL wines up to SPÄTLESE level of sweetness; less rich ALSACE whites; and MUSCADET, CHABLIS, and virtually any light, dry, still white wine without too much oak or alcohol. Customs vary nationally, however, and the French customarily serve spirits, FORTIFIED WINES, VINS DOUX NATURELS, VINS DE LIQUEUR, and sweet wines such as SAUTERNES before meals. A common all-purpose aperitif, apparently acceptable to French and non-French alike, is the KIR, or *vin blanc cassis*, as well as a blend of white wine and sparkling water sometimes known as a spritzer. The port trade serves white PORT as an aperitif, sherry producers a dry oloroso or fino, too many amateurs a full-bodied Chardonnay.

aphids, small insects of the *Aphidiodae* family that feed by sucking the juices from plants. Several species of aphids attack grapes but seldom cause serious damage in vineyards. See also PHYLLOXERA, often referred to as the grape root aphid.

apical dominance describes plant growth which is greater at the apex of a stem or shoot, suppressing lateral growth further away from the apex, a physiological attribute which helped grapevines survive by climbing in forest habitats in previous millennia (see ARBOREAL VITICULTURE). In viticulture, the term is also used to describe preferential BUDBREAK for the two buds nearest the cut end of the cane, which grow earlier and more strongly than those below. The botanical term 'acrotony' describes a similar phenomenon whereby dormant buds higher up the cane can suppress bursting of lower ones. To encourage fruiting along the entire cane and avoid staggered RIPENING, some viticulturists use an arched cane TRAINING SYSTEM to promote mid-cane budbreak, bending the cane so that the middle section is higher than the base and the apex, but the benefits are not universally acknowledged. Movement of HORMONES in the cane prior to budbreak affects these growth responses. R.E.S.

AP number, written 'A.P. Nr.' on wine labels, short for Amtliche Prüfnummer, adorns the label of every bottle of German QUALITÄTSWEIN. This 10- to 12-digit number is an outward sign that the wine has passed official testing procedures, which involve submitting samples for ANALYSIS and a BLIND TASTING test. Some 95% of wines submitted eventually receive approval. The first digit signifies which of the country's testing stations awarded the AP number. The next code signifies the location of the vineyard. The penultimate pair of digits is the bottler's own code, which supplies the unique identification of a particular lot. If a winegrower has bottled two or more wines of otherwise identical labelling (same site, PRÄDIKAT, and degree of dryness) this number is often referenced as a means of distinguishing them. The final two digits signify the year in which the wine was tested, which for white wines is usually the year following harvest. Austrian Qualitätswein also receives a roughly comparable registration number, known officially as a Staatliche Prüfnummer. D.S.

apoplexy, vine disease. See ESCA.

appassimento, Italian term for the process of drying grapes off the vine, used, for example, in the production of AMARONE and DRIED-GRAPE WINE.

appellation, or **appellation of origin**. See CONTROLLED APPELLATION.

appellation contrôlée, short for *appellation d'origine contrôlée*. See AOC.

apps, wine. See SOCIAL MEDIA.

Apremont, CRU just south of Chambéry whose name may be added to the eastern French appellation SAVOIE. This is Savoie's largest cru and its wines are typically light, dry, floral, or minerally whites made from the local JACQUÈRE grape. W.L.

Apulia, Anglicized form of the Italian region PUGLIA.

Aquileia. See FRIULI AQUILEIA.

Arab poets. The classical period of Arab civilization spawned a rich corpus of BACCHIC poetry which had its roots in pre-Islamic Arabia (530 CE until the emergence of ISLAM). Wine was celebrated as one of a number of standard topics in the composite odes of pre-Islamic poetry. In its treatment, wine was underpinned by the rigid ethical code (*Muruwwa*, approximately *virtus*) that predicated the desert *Weltanschauung* and thus gave voice to exaggerated notions of generosity. It was in this period, when wine was often compared to the saliva of women (to represent a kiss), that the seeds of the erotic register of later Arabic wine poetry were sown. Interestingly one such simile is even contained in the ode composed by Hassān Ibn Thābit, the Prophet's bard, to celebrate the conquest of Mecca shortly before Muhammad's death in 632 CE. Traditional Muslim commentary, basing itself on the Islamic injunction against the consumption of wine, suggests that the simile is interpolated. But this argument is not entirely convincing; for Islam, while criticizing aspects of the culture of poetry, seems to have had little effect in censoring the poetic repertoire.

The essential model provided by this bedouin canon, which constituted the cornerstone of Arabian cultural and tribal identity, was absorbed virtually in its entirety into the nascent Islamic/Arab community; for this reason wine survived as a theme. Soon its treatment came to stand independently from the composite ode; while the descriptive elements of Bacchic verse were based around a core of inherited imagery, a new defiant and anti-religious attitude was introduced that is reflected in a verse by the poet from al-Tā'if, Abū Mihjan al-Thaqafi: 'If I die bury me by the vine, so that its roots may satiate the thirst of my bones.' This solipsistic dirge, showing the poet to have acquired notions of life after death, ignores the new imposing religious eschatology of the nascent Islamic community.

Islam did, of course, have a profound effect on the poets of Bacchism: after a time, usually with the onset of old age, they would repent of their erring in pious Islamic terms. To replace them there was always a new generation of libertines, commonly men of high standing such as governors and even, during the Umayyad period, caliphs. Al-Walīd ibn Yazīd, one of the last Umayyad caliphs (d. 744 CE), was a notorious hedonist (although perhaps maligned by later Abbasid propaganda) whose attitude in some Bacchic fragments is aggressively atheistic: 'Give wine [to drink] . . . for I know there is no Hell-fire!' In this period Bacchism became an urban phenomenon, notably among the libertines of Kufa (modern Iraq), and was eventually to gain a high profile in the Abbasid court circle of Baghdad, particularly during the reign of al-Amīn (reigned 809–13 CE). This son of Hārūn al-Rashīd is famous in literary history as patron and boon companion of the great ABU NUWAS (d. 814 CE).

In his wine poetry, Abu Nuwas synthesized a variety of impulses to produce sometimes complex poems which articulated all the issues relevant to the social dialectic of wine culture in an Islamic society: he expanded both the fantastical and mimetic descriptive repertoire of the *khamriyya*; he fused the Bacchic and erotic registers of poetry to create well-wrought seduction poems that gave voice to a sceptical world view; he structured his poems in such a way as to support the simple rhetoric in defence of wine; finally, with literary sleights of hand, he reconciled the hedonistic ethic with Islamic dogma. It has rightly been said about the finest of these poems that they parallel the impulses and complexity of some English Metaphysical poetry.

From the descriptions of Abu Nuwas and other poets we gain a detailed picture of Bacchic culture: we are familiarized with the wine itself (its provenance, preparation, colour, bouquet, taste, and age—although here a mythological dimension enters into the poet's expression); its effects (physical, psychic, and spiritual); the personages (the boon companion, the pourer, the singing girl, the taverner (Jewish, Christian, or Persian), and the servant girl); the decorum of drinking (generosity, aristocracy, the quest for freedom, the Satanic pact, and, ultimately, belief in divine mercy); and the venues of drinking (the caliphal palace, the tavern, the monastery, gardens, and the vine itself); finally, we learn about the variety of vessels (for drinking: glass, silver and gold cups or goblets, ewers; for storage: jars, tanks or casks, and leather bottles).

After Abu Nuwas, poets who treated wine (throughout the Islamic lands, including al-Andalus in southern Spain) had little new to say; they simply reworked the imagery he had established, while discarding the careful structure of his finest poems. It was only among Sufi mystics that a new, important dimension was added to Bacchic poetry. Foremost among these was Ibn al-Fārid (d. 1235). For these ascetics DRUNKENNESS represented divine intoxication; they simply borrowed the imagery of Bacchic culture to articulate the otherwise ineffable states of mystical experience. Although Abu Nuwas himself was a ribald, Sufi sensitivity is perhaps foreshadowed in some of his most ethereal descriptions of wine:

> [Last night I could not sleep] so give me to drink of the maiden wine who has donned the grey locks of old age whilst still in the womb;
> A wine which [when poured] is replenished with youth . . .
> One preserved for a day when its [seal] is pierced, though it is the confidant of Time itself;
> It has been aged, such that if it were possessed of an eloquent tongue,
> It would sit proudly among people and tell a tale of an ancient time . . .

P.K.

'Khamriyya', *The Encyclopaedia of Islam* (new edn), vol. iv (1978), 998–1009.

Aragón, known as **Aragon** in English. Once a powerful kingdom whose sphere of influence stretched from Spain to NAPLES and SICILY in Italy and Athens in Greece, Aragón is now one of Spain's 17 autonomous regions. In the north-east of the country, it spans the broad valley of the River Ebro which is flanked by mountains on either side (see map under SPAIN). The north is dominated by the Pyrenees, which feed water on to the arid Ebro plain. To the south and east the climate becomes hotter as the land rises towards the central Spanish plateau.

The wines of Aragón used to be strapping potions with natural ALCOHOLIC STRENGTH as high as 17–18%. Red wines, made predominantly from the GARNACHA grape, were mostly sold in bulk for blending. However, four DOP regions designated between 1980 and 1990 changed the profile of Aragón wines. SOMONTANO, in the lush Pyrenean foothills east of the city of Huesca, made the controversial choice to almost entirely forgo INDIGENOUS grape varieties, but south of the Ebro wines from the DOPs of CAMPO DE BORJA, CARIÑENA, and CALATAYUD have benefited from investment in modern wine-making technology, which has revolutionized the style of modern-day Garnacha, sometimes blended with Tempranillo or Syrah. Also promising is the IGP Valdejalón, an enclave just south of Campo de Borja pioneered by Fernando Mora MW at Bodegas Frontonio. Aragón also claims one VINO DE PAGO, Aylés, 47 ha/116 acres just south of Zaragoza. R.J.M. & F.C.

Aragonez, once spelt **Aragónêz**, occasionally spelt **Aragones**, the traditional name for the Spanish red grape variety TEMPRANILLO in Portugal's ALENTEJO region, where it makes concentrated, deep-coloured reds. See under its northern Portuguese name TINTA RORIZ for more information.

Aramon, an offspring of GOUAIS BLANC, is now, happily, a remnant of French viticultural history, a vine variety that burgeoned throughout the LANGUEDOC in the second half of the 19th century (the many who made their fortunes from wine around Béziers were said to live in 'palais d'Aramonie') and was displaced as France's most popular only in the 1960s by CARIGNAN. For decades, particularly after the development of railway links with the populous north of France, Aramon vines were encouraged to spew forth light, everyday wine-for-the-workers that was with good reason called *petit rouge*.

Aramon's great attribute, apart from its prodigious productivity of up to 400 hl/ha (22.8 tons/acre), was its resistance to POWDERY MILDEW, the scourge of what were France's established wine regions in the mid 19th century. The variety was taken up with great enthusiasm and rapidly spread over terrain previously considered too flat and fertile for viticulture. GALET notes that its effects were particularly noticeable in the Hérault, where, between 1849 and 1869, the land under vine more than doubled, to 214,000 ha/528,800 acres.

Unless planted on poor soils and pruned extremely severely, Aramon produces some of the lightest red wine that could be considered red, notably low in alcohol, extract, and character. To render the *rouge* sufficiently *rouge* for the French consumer, Aramon had invariably to be bolstered one of the red-fleshed TEINTURIER grapes, most often ALICANTE BOUSCHET. This gave Aramon a grave disadvantage compared with the deep, alcoholic reds of North Africa, and its popularity began to decline in the mid 20th century, a trend exacerbated by its toll from the 1956 and 1963 frosts. Aramon suffers from the twin disadvantages of budding early and ripening late and is therefore limited to hotter wine regions.

The total French area planted with Aramon shrank from 34,700 ha/85,700 acres in 1988 to 1,266 ha/3,128 acres in 2019.

Aramon Gris and **Aramon Blanc**, lighter-berried mutations, can still (just) be found, particularly in the Hérault.

Galet, P., *Dictionnaire encyclopédique des cépages* (2nd edn, 2015).
Robinson, J., et al., *Wine Grapes: A Complete Guide to 1,368 Vine Varieties Including Their Origins and Flavours* (2012).

Arany Sárfehér, white grape of HUNGARY traditionally grown on the sandy Great Plain for table grapes and sparkling wines. Its 2021 total of 251 ha/620 acres produced light, tart wine.

Arbin, CRU on the steep, warm, south-facing slopes east of Chambéry whose name can be added to the eastern French appellation SAVOIE. Use of the Arbin cru name is restricted to wines from the local MONDEUSE grape, some of the region's finest reds. W.L.

Arbois, the most important appellation in the JURA region in eastern France and named after

Harvesting these 70- to 80-year-old CARIGNAN vines that climb up native trees on the Villalobos estate near the village of Ranguili in Chile's COLCHAGUA Valley is a team effort. The unpruned vines have never been treated with AGROCHEMICALS and YIELDS are extremely low. © Martín Villalobos Encina

the region's main wine town. The scientist Louis PASTEUR was brought up in the town and conducted observations here when invited to turn his attention to wine health. In the 20th century the town was made famous by wine producer Henri Maire, who did much for the revival of the Jura wine region after the Second World War and died in 2003. The wine company he founded still owns over 250 ha/618 acres of Jura's vineyards but left family hands in 2010 and in 2015 was taken over by BOISSET. Jura's largest CO-OPERATIVE, the Fruitière Vinicole d'Arbois, is based in the town. About 35% of Arbois production is red, making it the most important Jura red-wine appellation. The light-coloured POULSARD grape is a speciality of the subappellation of Arbois-Pupillin, where it is named Ploussard, and TROUSSEAU is especially successful in the warmer sites around the village of Montigny-les-Arsures, home to several top vignerons, notably various members of the Tissot family. White wines are often VARIETAL Chardonnay made in unoxidized, Burgundian style, increasingly vineyard-designated. The old synonym *Naturé* is sometimes used for the local SAVAGNIN, to designate fresh, lemony, or so-called 'floral' white wines made from the variety, distinguishing them from the more usual OXIDATIVE styles. The oxidative styles, made from Savagnin on its own or blended with Chardonnay, culminate in the nutty and long-lived Savagnin-only VIN JAUNE. An Arbois 1774 was so much appreciated when tasted in 1994 that other bottles from the same lot have sold for enormous prices, one reaching €57,000 in 2011. VIN DE PAILLE is made under the Arbois appellation, whereas TRADITIONAL METHOD sparkling wine made is sold as CRÉMANT du Jura. See also MACVIN DU JURA.

Wines made from grapes grown within the commune of Pupillin have the right to the subappellation **Arbois-Pupillin**. Pupillin is home to one of the 'fathers' of the natural wine movement in France, retired wine producer Pierre Overnoy, whose estate is run today by Emmanuel Houillon. W.L.

Arbois Blanc is also a synonym for the MENU PINEAU vine variety of the LOIRE.

arboreal viticulture is probably the oldest and most traditional vine-TRAINING SYSTEM, or lack of one. It takes advantage of the natural inclination of the VINE to climb up trees towards direct sunlight without the need for any other support. Managing such vines is challenging, with ladders needed for most vineyard tasks, but recent research into this practice in southern BOLIVIA suggests the method has many advantages: greater biodiversity, including beneficial insects that protect the vine against diseases and other pests (see ECOSYSTEM), protection of the vine from climate extremes such as heat and FROST, and increased soil fertility and carbon sequestration, as well as less SOIL EROSION. Yields are likely to be lower than in a more intensely cultivated modern vineyard, and there may be increased competition for water. Examples of arboreal viticulture are also found in Portugal's Vinho Verde, in Georgia, Chile, Lebanon, in several regions of Italy (where it is known as *alberate*), and in France. In most cases, this looks more like a vineyard with trees to support the vines rather than the more extreme agroforestry seen in Bolivia, with vines co-habiting with trees in the forest.

Oller, P., et al., 'Structure and management of traditional agroforestry vineyards in the high valleys of southern Bolivia', *Agroforestry Systems*, 96 (2022), 375–86.

arbour, an overhead trellis structure used for VINE TRAINING, particularly in southern Italy. See TENDONE.

archaeology has been of great importance in tracing the ORIGINS OF VINICULTURE and plays a part in the ancient history of most wine regions. For a discussion of the techniques available and some of the more significant finds, see PALAEO-ETHNOBOTANY. For some more specific aspects, see also AMPHORAE and the CELTS.

Ardèche, French *département* on the right bank of the RHÔNE, much of which lies between the main concentrations of vineyards which constitute the northern and southern Rhône Valley, and now the name of an IGP for a wide range of generally VARIETAL wines. Chardonnay and Viognier have been particularly successful here for whites, Merlot and Syrah for reds which are typically light- to medium-bodied.

Areni, the characteristic red wine grape of ARMENIA, and also the name of a village on the border with Azerbaijan where the remains of a 4000 BCE winery were identified in 2011. Wines are medium-bodied with real zip, and the best have good ageing potential.

Argaman, ISRAELI 1972 cross of CARIGNAN and the Portuguese SOUSÃO which produces dark, light-bodied reds.

Argentina has been the wine titan of SOUTH AMERICA for much of the 21st century, vying only with CHILE for the largest wine production in the continent. Of the country's 214,798 ha/530,777 acres of vineyard in 2020, 92% grew grapes for wine. Since the 1990s, Argentina has radically shifted to a focus on quality over quantity. Red wine, especially MALBEC, dominates, but white wines have a growing reputation for quality. Considerable investment in new vineyard areas, winemaking technology, RESEARCH, and innovation have all played a part in making Argentina a leader in the NEW WORLD.

History

Unlike North America, where explorers and early settlers found VITIS LABRUSCA growing in abundance, South America depended on the Spanish colonizers for imported European VITIS VINIFERA vines. The vine probably arrived in Argentina by four different routes. The first was directly from Spain in 1541 when vines are thought to have been cultivated, without great success, on the Atlantic coast around the Río de la Plata. A year later, grape seeds were germinated after an expedition from Peru to the current wine regions immediately east of the Andes. Another Peruvian expedition in 1550 imported vines to Argentina, and more vines came from Chile in 1556, just two years after the vine was introduced to Chile's Central Valley. (See SOUTH AMERICA, history, for more details.)

One of the most important grape varieties systematically cultivated for wine in South America was almost certainly the forerunner of Argentina's CRIOLLA CHICA, California's MISSION, and Chile's PAÍS, which were to be the backbone of South American wine production for the next 300 years. Although Argentina was settled from both the east and the west, it was in the foothills of the Andes that the Jesuit MISSIONARIES found the best conditions for vine-growing. The first recorded vineyard was planted at Santiago del Estero in 1557. The city of Mendoza was founded in 1561, and vineyards in the province of San Juan to the north were established on a commercial scale between 1569 and 1589. Soon after that, in 1595, King Felipe II of Spain, who ruled over most of Central and South America, banned the production of wine, except by the Catholic Church. This was intended to protect Spanish wine producers and their exports to Mexico and was therefore not particularly enforced in South America, so secular producers remained, and the wine industry thrived. Contrary to popular belief, this heralded a period of almost 300 years (from the second half of the 16th century to the beginning of the 19th century) of sustained growth, innovation, and a search for wine quality, largely thanks to the powerful MONKS AND MONASTERIES.

Wine soon became the main economic activity, with the wealthiest families of Cuyo and the north-west of Argentina—in what are today the provinces of Mendoza, San Juan, La Rioja, and Salta—engaged in wine production, whether secularly, through family members who were clergy, or both. Export routes to the cities of Buenos Aires, Córdoba, and Santa Fe to the east, to Bolivia to the north, and to Chile to the west were developed from the early 16th century, which created a dynamic proto-bourgeoisie, particularly in the Cuyo region. During this time, the most important grape variety cultivated was CRIOLLA CHICA (also called Uva Negra), and various MUSCATS were also widely grown. TORRONTÉS Riojano, a natural crossing of

Criolla Chica and Muscat of Alexandria, dates from the 18th century. Other natural crossings that appeared in this period and are still widely grown include CEREZA and CRIOLLA GRANDE.

By the skilful use of dams and IRRIGATION channels originally established by the native population, the early settlers were able to produce sufficient wine to meet the needs of a growing population. The 18th century saw major changes. To ensure quality and ageing potential, particularly for wines that had to withstand the journey by cart from Mendoza to Buenos Aires, wines were FORTIFIED or sometimes heated, a precursor of PASTEURIZATION. Some wines were even made, like SHERRY, under FILM-FORMING YEASTS. Wine PRESSES changed from being made of leather and/or oak to being built with bricks, lime, and slate. The first record of FERMENTATION vessels made from OAK instead of the old clay AMPHORAE dates from 1740. The first AMPELOGRAPHIC studies were carried out during the second half of the century, and the government's first winery census took place in 1780. This was a period of dynamic growth, driven by solid institutions, commerce, peace, and the conjunction of a blooming bourgeoisie and the clergy's desire to make the most out of God's creation. By the end of the century, Cuyo was by far Argentina's most important wine region, with about 8,000 people in the cities of Mendoza and San Juan, almost 300 vine growers, and annual wine production of 13 million litres.

Then the wine scene began a decline that lasted nearly 100 years. In 1767 the Jesuits were expelled from Spain, and its colonies and their estates were either abandoned or seized by the Spanish crown. A civil war lasted for much of the early 19th century, and wine was no longer the most important economic activity of the region.

Some good things happened, however, such as the introduction of glass BOTTLES, from 1820. The best example is the well-documented story of General San Martín, the son of a vine-grower and probably Argentina's first wine CONNOISSEUR. After returning from leading a long campaign in Chile and Perú against the Spanish royalists, he went back to Mendoza and organized a dinner with some of the most important people of his time. At this meal, in 1823, he poured one of his favourite wines from Mendoza, and one from a renowned producer of Málaga—transposing the labels before doing so. By the end of the evening, when all attendees had proclaimed the virtues of the bottles with the Málaga label, he had demonstrated two things: that the wines from Mendoza compared well with those of Spain; and that they could age for eight years or more—which was the time his bottles had spent in his underground cellar during his crusade against the Spanish empire.

The second half of the 19th century saw Argentina enjoy a period of relative stability and prosperity built on exports of agricultural and cattle products. Many of those who had fled to Chile returned to Cuyo. Among them was Domingo Faustino Sarmiento, who subsequently became governor of San Juan and then president of Argentina. He campaigned for the creation of an agronomy school, including viticultural research and a vine NURSERY used to gradually improve vineyards, under the direction of a Frenchman exiled in 1851. Under his direction top-quality French varieties, including Malbec, were imported—before the arrival of PHYLLOXERA in Europe, incorporating much of the genetic material that was later lost in Europe. Thus Malbec, Sémillon, Cabernet Sauvignon, and many high-quality varieties were already established in Argentina before a significant wave of European immigrants of the late 1800s and early 1900s further enriched Argentina's viticulture.

In 1885 the RAILWAY between Buenos Aires and Mendoza was completed, lending still greater importance to the vineyards in the foothills of the Andes. The immigrants, many from wine-producing areas of Italy, Spain, and France, brought with them many new vine varieties and their own winegrowing skills. The foundations for Argentina's mammoth domestic wine industry were laid. This had interesting implications. Unlike many New World wine regions where winemaking was restricted to an elite, the origin of Argentina's modern era viticulture was popular and widespread among immigrant families. Even today there are over 23,000 vineyards, with an average size of 9 ha/22 acres. And the immigrants brought their wine-drinking culture with them, which turned Argentina into one of the largest domestic markets in the world. Today, Argentines drink about three-quarters of the national crop.

By the early 20th century, Argentina was the seventh wealthiest developed nation in the world, but the subsequent economic depression and political crisis led to a disastrous drop in the export price of its primary products and then a steep decline in foreign investment. The peso was often devalued. While the landowning classes continued to prosper for some time, or salted away their capital overseas, there was growing unrest among the largely disenfranchised, poorly paid urban masses. When General Juan Domingo Perón came to power in 1943 he appealed directly to the workers with promises of rapid industrialization, better working conditions, and organized, government-controlled unions. For a while Argentina's fortunes revived, but in the mid 1950s Perón and his ambitious and charismatic wife Eva were deposed by the military. From then on a succession of opportunistic military governments led the country into spiralling decline. The urban masses created an unprecedented market for wine so that quantity not quality became the imperative. In the late 1960s and early 1970s, at a time when the UK was drinking approximately 3 litres per capita annually and the Americans even less, the Argentines, despite all their troubles, were quaffing 90 litres of wine per head.

However, over the next two decades, Argentina grew increasingly isolated and suffered from social and political unrest, stifling bureaucracy, corruption, war, and disastrous economic management. Accumulated inflation during the 1980s was over 8,000%, and wine consumption dropped dramatically. A VINE-PULL SCHEME reduced the total vineyard area by one-third, from 314,000 ha in the early 1980s to 205,000 ha/506,350 acres in 1993. A peak of hyperinflation in 1989, however, prompted President Raúl Alfonsín out of office; he was replaced by Carlos Menem, inaugurating a period of political and economic stability not experienced for decades. Under his administration, business confidence in Argentina's future was revitalized, encouraging investment in a wine industry where time had stood still (see also CHILE). Producers began to give serious consideration to the possibilities of exporting.

From the mid 1990s onwards Argentina entered a new wave of high-quality viticulture. Using new CLONES of international varieties and MASS SELECTIONS of some of Argentina's oldest varieties, new vineyards were planted in higher density and with DRIP IRRIGATION. This led not only to a leap in quality but also to an expansion of wine regions, as drip irrigation now made it possible to plant on the rocky, steep slopes of the Andean foothills. The Uco Valley has been at the forefront of this quality boom since the early 2000s. By 2012 Argentina was exporting over US$1 billion (a number which has stabilized at around US$820 million since).

Geography and climate

Argentina's wine regions are widely dispersed—spanning over 3,700 km/2,299 miles from Jujuy in the north to Chubut in Patagonia, and ranging from latitudes 23 to 45° S—but are almost entirely confined to the foothills of the Andes. In this western strip, Argentina's climate is CONTINENTAL, with the four seasons clearly defined. The Cuyo region, where the climate is semi-desert, accounts for 95% of plantings.

Summer temperatures vary from 10 °C/50 °F at night to as much as 40 °C/104 °F during the day. Summers are hot in the regions of San Juan (except for the high-elevation valleys of Pedernal and Calingasta), La Rioja, Catamarca, and the east of Mendoza (Santa Rosa, Rivadavia, San Martín, and Lavalle). In the Calchaquí Valley (Cafayate), upper Mendoza (Luján de Cuyo), Uco Valley (Tupungato, Tunuyán, and San Carlos), and Río Negro, summers are TEMPERATE to warm, making them Regions II and III in the Winkler system of CLIMATE CLASSIFICATION, although the coolest sites in the Uco Valley are

Region I. In winter, temperatures can drop below 0 °C/32 °F with occasional light snowfalls. Heavy winter snow in the high Andes is important as this ensures plentiful supplies of pure water for IRRIGATION.

Rainfall is concentrated in the summer months, which encourages growth, but it seldom exceeds 300 mm/12 in annually, making irrigation essential. Early summer HAIL is the main risk to the vines—as many as 6% of Argentine vineyards are netted against hail—together with FROST. It is customary in Mendoza to own vineyards in different parts of the province to minimize the risk of hail damage. As a result, and even though single-vineyard and TERROIR-driven wines are increasingly important, blends of wines from different parts of the province are also common.

The air is dry and particularly unpolluted. Vine FLOWERING may occasionally be adversely affected by a hot, dry, very strong foehn wind called *zonda*, which blows down from the west mainly in late spring and early summer. The lack of humidity reduces the risk of FUNGAL DISEASES, and vineyards are typically sprayed much less often in Argentina than elsewhere, making ORGANIC VITICULTURE relatively easy although only 6,000 ha/14,826 acres were certified organic by 2019. Full RIPENESS is easily achieved and CHAPTALIZATION is not allowed.

Regions

See map.

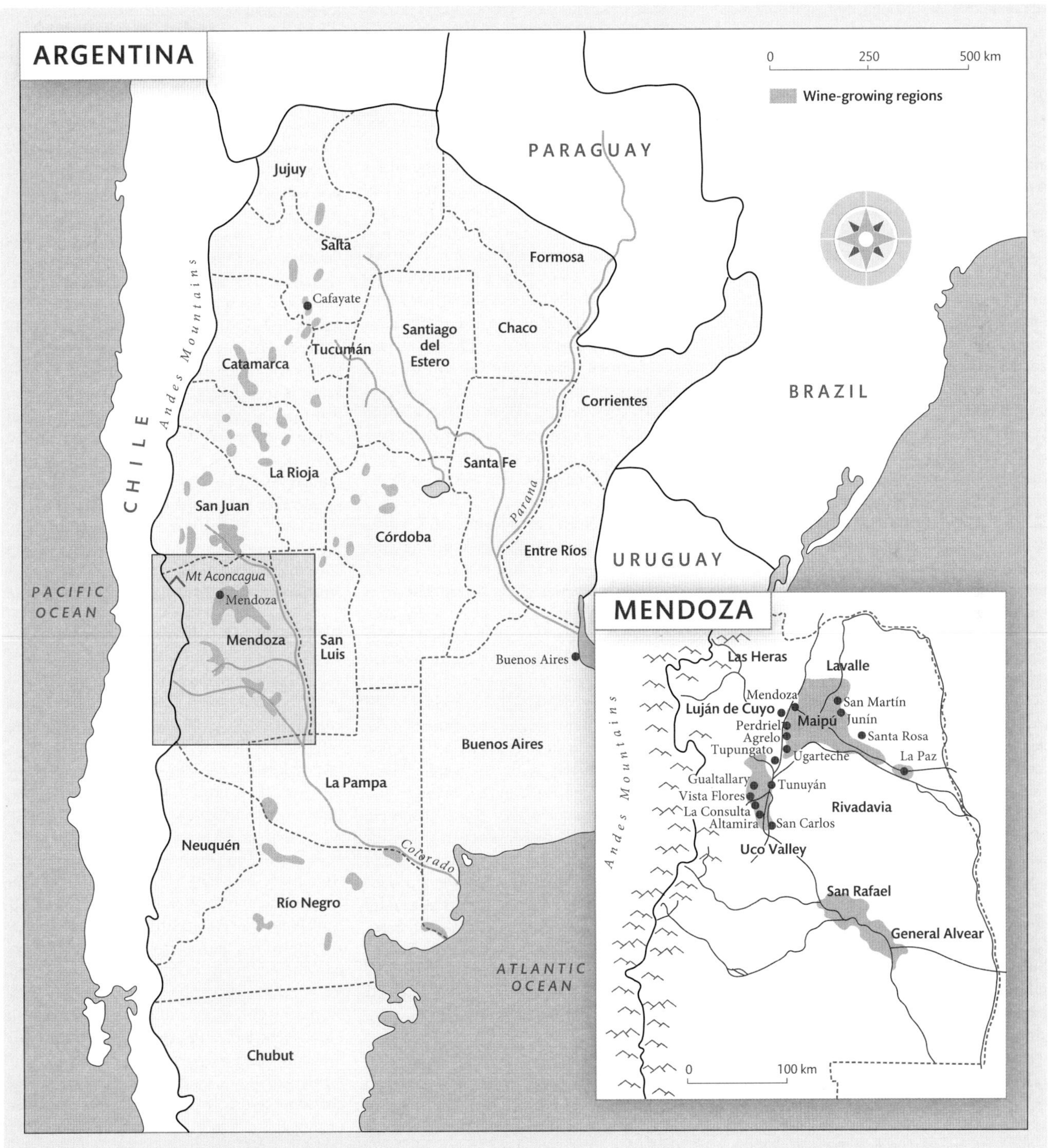

Mendoza In the far west of the country, only a (substantial) mountain range away from Santiago in Chile, this is by far the largest and most important winegrowing province in Argentina, accounting for more than 70% of the country's wine production. The Andes dominate the western skyline, with Mount Aconcagua, at 6,960 m/22,837 ft, the highest mountain in the Americas. With vineyards planted at elevations of 600–1,600 m/1,970 to 5,249 ft, and very varied aspects, soils, and mesoclimates, the region turns out a wide variety of wines, best described by subregion. See MENDOZA for more detail.

San Juan Argentina's second biggest wine-producing region had 44,923 ha/111,007 acres of vineyards in 2020. The capital of the province, San Juan, is 150 km/90 miles north of Mendoza. The climate at these lower elevations and latitudes is much hotter than that of Mendoza, with summer temperatures of 42 °C/107 °F not uncommon and rainfall averaging only 100 mm/4 in per annum.

Long the home of high-yielding pink varieties, especially Cereza, San Juan has gradually moved from quantity to quality production, especially for red grapes such as Malbec and Syrah, San Juan's most planted varieties. Good-value basic reds are also made with Bonarda and Cabernet Sauvignon, but the region is better known for Torrontés and good-value Viognier. It also provides the base for most of Argentina's brandy and VERMOUTHS. The vast majority of San Juan's wine comes from Tulum Valley at an elevation of 650 m/2,132 ft just south of the capital city. Better-quality wines can be found further west at higher elevations, in the Ullum-Zonda Valley at 850 m/2,788 ft and the Pedernal (1,100 m/3,608 ft) and Calingasta (1,500 m/4,921 ft) valleys.

La Rioja Historically the oldest of Argentina's wine-producing provinces, La Rioja is Argentina's third largest region with 7,707 ha/169,044 acres of vineyard in 2020, 20% of which is planted to Torrontés Riojano. La Rioja is little-known abroad, partly because almost the entire production of the province is crushed by the giant CO-OPERATIVE La Riojana. A handful of small-scale producers have started to produce more interesting wines in higher-elevation areas such as Famatina and Chañar Muyo.

Salta, Jujuy, Tucumán, and Catamarca These far north-western provinces are in the Calchaquí Valley, a high valley spanning latitude 24–26° S where vines benefit from more than 300 days of sun per year, as well as lots of wind and ULTRAVIOLET RADIATION. Even the lower vineyards in Salta are at 1,650 m/5,413 ft; the highest, Ayni in Jujuy, sits at 3,329 m/10,921 ft. Because of this elevation, the vines tend towards lower YIELDS and the grapes develop thick skins, the combination producing concentrated, full-bodied, fragrant wines. Promising varieties include Malbec, Cabernet Sauvignon, Bonarda, Syrah, and, particularly, TANNAT, which expresses itself quite differently here compared with those of URUGUAY and MADIRAN. For white wines, Torrontés Riojano is very much at home. Salta has the most vines, with 3,347 ha/8,270 acres of vineyards. Other areas such as Tolombón, Colomé, Molinos, Yacochuya, and Tacuil also have excellent potential.

Río Negro, Neuquén, and Chubut Located in southern Patagonia, these areas are much cooler than the better-known areas to the north and less developed, with 3,397 ha/8,394 acres under vine in 2020 split roughly equally between Río Negro and Neuquén, and just 87 ha in Chubut.

Río Negro has historically been Argentina's principal fruit-growing district, producing apples and pears as well as grapes. The valley is shaped by a river that runs from the west into the Atlantic, forming a green canyon surrounded by arid desert on both sides. Humidity and rainfall are markedly higher than further north. These growing conditions, together with some seriously old vineyards, attracted both Countess Noemi Marone Cinzano and Piero Incisa della Rochetta, from the family that owns SASSICAIA, who respectively established their Noemía (with Hans Vinding-Diers) and Bodega Chacra projects in the province in the early 2000s. Both now practise BIODYNAMIC VITICULTURE, with exciting results.

Unlike Río Negro, the province of Neuquén had no winemaking tradition whatsoever until early this century when the authorities realized that the province was going to run out of its non-renewable mining resources. They constructed an extensive channel that could irrigate about 3,000 ha/7,413 acres of land on which vegetables, orchards, and vineyards have been planted. Bodega del Fin del Mundo led the project, and now several producers make millions of bottles in state-of-the-art wineries, filling them mainly with Sauvignon Blanc, Chardonnay, Pinot Noir, and Malbec.

Chubut, at latitude 42–43° S, was pioneered by the legendary Bernardo Weinert, from the eponymous Mendoza winery, in the late 1990s. Today the province boasts a handful of producers, including Argentine billionaire Alejandro Bulgheroni, who claims the world's southernmost commercial vineyard and winery, Bodega Otronia, with 50 ha planted at 45.33° S. The region's lean, low-alcohol, high-acid, cool-climate wines are redefining Argentine wine.

Buenos Aires, La Pampa, and Córdoba Of these three developing winegrowing areas, only Córdoba, which had 277 ha/684 acres of vines in 2020, has a long tradition of making artisanal wines. La Pampa, a province known more for its cattle, has 279 ha/689 acres planted on the northern border of Patagonia, half of that farmed by Bodega del Desierto, which started planting here in 2001. And Buenos Aires province had 149 ha/368 acres of vineyards planted on slopes near the Atlantic Ocean, where the MARITIME CLIMATE lends itself to Albariño, Pinot Noir, and Sauvignon Blanc.

Vine varieties

Red Malbec is king in Argentina. Accounting for 21% of all plantings and over 60% of Argentina's wine exports in 2020, it has come to seem more at home in Argentina than in its CAHORS homeland. Planted on a total of 45,657 ha/112,821 acres (up from just 9,770 ha in 1996), it tends produces deep-coloured, robust, fruity wines with enough alcohol, weight, and structure to benefit from OAK AGEING, with different expressions in each wine region. The second most planted red wine variety, with 18,153 ha/44,857 acres, is CHARBONO, called Bonarda in Argentina, which is used to make everything from fragrant sparkling rosés to supple red wines. Cabernet Sauvignon is right behind, having grown from less than 2,500 ha in 1990 to 14,129 ha/34,914 acres by 2020; it often appears in prestigious blends with Malbec. Syrah, at 11,797 ha/29,151 acres, is increasingly important, particularly in San Juan, north of Mendoza. A wide range of Italian and Spanish varieties, including TEMPRANILLO, CORVINA, and ANCELLOTA, were presumably brought to the country by the many European immigrants, but it is the French CABERNET FRANC, PETIT VERDOT, and TANNAT that are currently making waves, as well as PINOT NOIR, which seems to have found a home in Patagonia and the high elevations of the Uco Valley.

White Although steadily losing ground, PEDRO GIMÉNEZ (distinct from Spain's PEDRO XIMÉNEZ) is still Argentina's most planted light-skinned grape variety, with 9,587 ha/23,690 acres grown in 2020, particularly in Mendoza and San Juan, where it is used mostly in basic blends. It is also used for making grape concentrate, which Argentina exports in vast quantities, particularly to Japan. Far more interesting is TORRONTÉS Riojano (7,659 ha/18,926 acres), which produces floral, aromatic wine made in a range of styles from dry and crisp to lusciously sweet LATE HARVEST wines. It is planted all over Argentina, but the best usually come from the Calchaquí Valley. Chardonnay, the next most planted white variety with 5,854 ha/14,466 acres, is responsible for both everyday table wines and some of Argentina's most celebrated white wines. Its own so-called Mendoza CLONE was developed at DAVIS in California and is widely planted in Australia and elsewhere. Other white wine grapes, in order of importance, are Moscatel de Alejandría

(MUSCAT OF ALEXANDRIA), Sauvignon Blanc, Chenin Blanc, Torrontés Sanjuanino, and Ugni Blanc, although it is Sémillon that is leading Argentina's white wine revolution, with a good percentage of its 640 ha/1,581 acres being old vines capable of making distinctive, structured white wines. Sparkling wines also make up an important segment of Argentina's white wine production, ranging from easy-drinking TANK METHOD wines, usually made from Chenin Blanc, to rich TRADITIONAL METHOD wines based on Chardonnay.

Pinks Argentina's historically famous pink-skinned varieties are in sharp decline, representing 23% of wine-grape plantings by 2020. CRIOLLA GRANDE, CRIOLLA CHICA, and CEREZA are some of Argentina's oldest varieties and together account for 39,881 ha/98,548 acres. All three are extremely productive varieties and are typically planted in the hotter, flatter, most heavily irrigated vineyards: one bunch on a well-irrigated vineyard can weigh as much as 4 kg/9 lb. MOSCATEL Rosada is also important, with 5,330 ha/13,171 acres. The wine produced from these varieties is usually very deeply coloured white, occasionally pink, often sweet, and sold at the bottom end of the market, in bulk or in litre bottles or cardboard cartons. There is, however, a small Criolla renaissance taking place, with a new generation of winemakers using the varieties to turn out light, juicy, fragrant red wines.

Viticulture

Argentine viticulture has been transformed since the 1990s, with better IRRIGATION techniques, CANOPY MANAGEMENT, methods and timing of HARVEST, incorporation of technology, clonal and MASS SELECTIONS, and studies of the impact of MICROBIAL TERROIR and ULTRAVIOLET RADIATION, for example.

Most vines in Argentina are UNGRAFTED because the biotype of PHYLLOXERA present is a relatively mild one, perhaps because there is a relatively high proportion of SAND in vineyard soils. Some varieties that are vulnerable to NEMATODES, however, tend to be grafted. ANTS can also pose a problem, especially to young vines. Rainfall is so low in most of the country that irrigation is a necessity. Traditionally, water was distributed by an intricate network of canals and ditches that date to the 16th century and then by FLOODING or furrows. In more recent times, the channels of water that flow from the snow-capped peaks of the high Andes have been augmented by deep boreholes. These take water from between 60 and 300 m/984 ft below the surface and can produce as much as 250,000 l/66,000 gal per hour. They are used with the more efficient DRIP IRRIGATION systems that now operate on about 20% of Argentine vineyards. In this unique landscape the cultivated areas resemble green oases in the scorched desert surroundings (as in the irrigated vineyards of Australia but with the majestic Andes as a backdrop). The vast majority of the soils are of alluvial origin, quite poor, and mostly made of sand and stones. Their structure varies from region to region, but a loose greyish sandy texture predominates with substrates of GRAVEL, LIMESTONE, and CLAY. Different forms of CALCAREOUS soils are found in some of the finest terroirs of the Uco Valley, such as Paraje Altamira, Gualtallary, and Vista Flores, as well as Pedernal in San Juan.

Although the immigrants who arrived in the early 20th century brought with them the vertical *espaldera* TRAINING SYSTEM of low training of vines along three wires, the need for greater volume led most vineyard owners to adopt the productive *parral cuyano* trellis system in the 1950s and 1960s (see TENDONE). As in Chile, however, the classic method is increasingly favoured once more in order to facilitate both CANOPY MANAGEMENT and drip irrigation, although Cereza and Criolla Grande vines are still likely to be *parral* trained. By 2020 roughly half of all vines were *parral* trained, and most of the rest were trained with either high or low VSP (see VERTICAL TRELLIS) *espaldera* systems. Over 28% of vineyards were 40 years old or more, and in Salta there is even a vineyard planted in 1862. Only 18% of vines are under 10 years old.

From BUDBREAK to HARVEST takes an average of five months, and the long ripening season normally ensures full maturity. The national institute sets the date of the harvest, which usually begins in mid February and, depending on variety and region, extends until late April. Special permits must be obtained to pick any later than the prescribed end date, mostly for late-harvest wines. MECHANICAL HARVESTERS are slowly becoming more common.

Winemaking and labelling

Since the 1980s Argentina has had an influx of international CONSULTANTS and significant investment and modernization in winemaking technology, giving the country a dynamic winemaking scene. With a diverse network of over 20,000 vine-growers and 800 wineries, Argentina has both boutique and industrial-sized wineries, and winemaking techniques range from artisanal, foot-crushed wines to large-scale productions with state-of-the-art technology. Fermentation vessels are typically stainless steel, concrete, or oak, and both oak-aged and unoaked wines are popular in white and red wines. Argentina also has a booming sparkling-wine industry, both in TANK METHOD and TRADITIONAL METHOD styles. There is also a new wave of PET-NAT and ORANGE WINES emerging from the new generation of winemakers. This generation of winemakers is particularly keen to learn and collaborate, and many work vintages in the northern hemisphere to learn from other wine regions, too.

In terms of labelling, a varietal wine must contain at least 85% of the variety cited, while any variety mentioned on the label must constitute at least 20% of the blend. Wines are classified either IP (Indicación de Procedencia) for table and regional wines, IG (Indicación Geográfica—see GEOGRAPHICAL INDICATION) for *vinifera* wines made from a specific region with certain minimum quality standards, or DOC (Denominación de Origen Controlada) for high-quality wines in which restrictions related to alcohol, winemaking techniques, yields, ageing, and other criteria apply. In 2022, Argentina had two DOCs—Luján de Cuyo and San Rafael—and roughly 100 IGs. A.R. & A.B.

Barnes, A., *The South America Wine Guide* (2021).
Goldstein, E., *Wines of South America* (2014).
Lacoste, P., *Vinos de Capa y Espada* (2013).
www.winesofargentina.org

argilo-calcaire, French term commonly used to describe soil that is a mixture of LIMESTONE (*calcaire*) and CLAY (*argile*).

argols, another word for TARTRATES.

Arinarnoa, 1956 INRA cross of Tannat × Cabernet Sauvignon (although it was originally presented as Merlot × Petit Verdot) of which just over 171 ha/423 acres grew in the Languedoc in 2019, typically producing strong, dark-red wines. It is planted to a very limited extent elsewhere, for example in Uruguay and Brazil. J.E.H. & J.V.

Robinson, J., et al., *Wine Grapes: A Complete Guide to 1,368 Vine Varieties, Including Their Origins and Flavours* (2012).

Arinto, more precisely **Arinto de Bucelas**, historic Portuguese white grape variety most commonly encountered in BUCELAS, in which it must constitute at least 75% of the blend. It is also grown in many other parts of Portugal, notably Tejo and Lisboa. Arinto is respected for its high acidity and citrus flavours and in Bucelas in particular can yield wines which gain interest and complexity with age. As an ingredient in VINHO VERDE it is known as Pedernã. Total plantings in 2020 were 6,351 ha/15,694 acres.

Arinto do Dão is a synonym for MALVASIA Fina in DÃO. **Arinto dos Açores** is an unrelated, high-quality variety indigenous to the Azores. **Arinto Tinto** is a Portuguese synonym for Aragonez, or TEMPRANILLO.

Aristophanes, Greek writer of comedies at the end of the 5th century BCE. In his plays he extols the hard-working peasant farmer in the fields around Athens. One of his characters is a vine-dresser, or early vineyard worker (Trygaios in *The Peace*), and the goddess of peace is called wine-loving and 'giver of grapes'. Aristophanes

criticizes the young for idling and drinking too much. Women also come in for criticism as topers in several of his plays. H.H.A.

Arizona, south-western state in the United States that boasted more than 120 wineries in 2021. The area's winegrowing history dates to the 1600s, when Spanish settlers and missionaries began planting vines in what was then MEXICO. Its modern history began in the south-eastern corner of Arizona in 1976, first in the Sonoita area then moving into nearby Willcox by the 1980s. Both are now federally recognized AVAS. In the 1990s, winegrowing was also established in the Verde Valley at the centre of the state, although as of 2022 its status as an AVA remained pending. As with COLORADO and NEW MEXICO, Arizona's vineyards are grown at high ELEVATION, where the extremes of the state's arid and semi-arid climate are moderated. Even so, the Willcox and Verde Valley areas are considered zone V, or 'very hot' on the Winkler Index (see CLIMATE CLASSIFICATION), while Sonoita counts as Zone IV 'hot.' Summer months bring plenty of sun and warmth, but by autumn monsoon season begins, making early ripening a must. Both WINTER FREEZE and spring FROST are also concerns. Sonoita vineyards sit around 5,000 ft/1,524 m in elevation, while Willcox sites begin at 4,000 ft/1,219 m and climb as high as 7,000 ft/2,134 m. The Verde Valley is comparatively lower, with vineyards at elevations between 3,500 and 5,000 ft/1,067–1,524 m. Incredibly, LIMESTONE can be found throughout all three regions as ancient Arizona once hosted an enormous inland sea. While land is far more available in both Willcox and Sonoita, the two AVAs suffer from less water availability. The Verde Valley benefits from the Verde River, but most land has been given to ranching rights. Though Arizona wine was established originally on Cabernet Sauvignon and Syrah, today the most successful wineries are experimenting with Spanish and Italian varieties. MATARO, GARNACHA, TEMPRANILLO, and MALVASIA do particularly well. PETIT MANSENG made in a dry style has also proven uniquely successful. E.C.B.

Arkansas, southern state of the United States that traces its winemaking history back to the 1880s, when Swiss and German immigrants settled in Altus, a town in a high valley along the Arkansas River, and began making wine from the local CATAWBA and Cynthiana (NORTON) grape varieties. Fifteen years later, a group of Italians settled further north, in Tontitown, in the foothills of the Ozarks, and began producing wine from CONCORD and Cynthiana. The industry grew to include 150 wineries before PROHIBITION, which hit Arkansas particularly hard: even in 2022, 34 of the state's 75 counties are 'dry', prohibiting alcohol sales. Nevertheless, in 2022, the state produced 1,210,910 litres/266,363 gal of wine, placing it 17th in wine production in the US. Winegrowing is focused in the cooler north-western corner of the state, particularly in Altus, now an AVA. There, the sandy soils and a protected position between the Boston and Ouachita mountain ranges allow for the growing of VITIS VINIFERA such as RIESLING, CHARDONNAY, and ZINFANDEL. In the surrounding Arkansas Mountain AVA, WINTER FREEZE can be a risk, putting emphasis on HYBRIDS such as CHAMBOURCIN and Cynthiana, the official state grape, sometimes called the 'Cabernet of the Ozarks'. In the state's southern reaches, heat, humidity, and a risk of PIERCE'S DISEASE make MUSCADINIA the favoured choice. The state's winegrowers are supported by the University of Arkansas's grape breeding programme, focused on creating cold-hardy varieties such as Opportunity, a white grape with RKATSITELI parentage, and Enchantment, a TEINTURIER variety with ALICANTE BOUSCHET parentage.

Arlanza, DOP created in SPAIN in 2008 for land between RIOJA and RIBERA DEL DUERO along the Arlanza River, with 350 ha/865 acres under vine in 2020. Closer in climate to Rioja, it is the source of fresh, fragrant wines from old, often mixed vineyards (see FIELD BLEND).

arm, viticultural term for that part of the vine's woody framework which is more than one year old and from which the CANES and SPURS arise. The location and length of the arms depends on the vine-TRAINING SYSTEM used. Arm is used interchangeably with cordon in some regions, but if both are present, the arm is the shorter and the cordon is the longer. R.E.S.

armazém, Portuguese for 'warehouse' or 'store'. In the towns of Vila Nova de Gaia (see OPORTO) and Funchal (see MADEIRA), *armazéns* (plural form) are the long, low LODGES where PORT and madeira are left to age.

Armenia, relatively small, mountainous, ex-Soviet republic in Transcaucasia with a proven winemaking history dating back at least 6,000 years. Vineyard ELEVATIONS of up to 1,750 m/5,741 ft compensate for its southerly latitude. In 2020, Armenia officially had 15,200 ha/37,560 acres of vineyard and produced 264,000 tonnes/291,010 tons of grapes giving 110,130 hl/2.9 million gal of wine and 391,910 hl of brandy.

History

The Transcaucasian region, including Armenia, is one of the world's oldest centres of viticulture and may be the cradle of grapevine domestication. Ancient Armenia was much bigger than modern Armenia and in classical times included much of eastern TÜRKIYE, AZERBAIJAN, and GEORGIA in the area between the Black Sea and the Caspian Sea. Fossil evidence of the wild vine VITIS VINIFERA subsp. *silvestris* has been identified in the region from the late Pliocene, and carbonized grape pips have been found at several Neolithic sites in the Caucasus. These findings, along with the current populations of wild grapevines and diversity of cultivated material, support this hypothesis.

In 2011, it was announced that the earliest 'winery' in the world had been discovered in the karst Areni-1 cave. Dating back to *c.*4000 BCE, it showed that winemaking was already large-scale, organized, and linked to human ritual. The cave has a rudimentary grape press surrounded by clay wine jars (*karas*) in which traces of grape pigments, alcohol, and grape material have been confirmed by chemical analyses. The atmosphere of the cave has preserved organic material incredibly well, and other finds include a six-millennia-old human brain and a leather shoe from 5,500 years ago. See PALAEOETHNOBOTANY and ORIGINS OF VINICULTURE.

Archaeological evidence has also revealed irrigation canals, wine cellars, wine presses cut into rock, and large *karas* dating to the Iron Age. Argishti I (785–753 BCE), the king of Urartu (an ancient state which is regarded by modern Armenians as a predecessor of their homeland), made his capital Tushpa into a pleasant garden city planted with vineyards. An inscription of his descendant Rusa II (680–639 BCE), who built Teishebaini (today's Karmir Blur) south-west of Yerevan states: 'By command of the god Haldi I have planted these vineyards.' Grape seeds resembling varieties grown today were unearthed during excavations of the Teishebaini fortress from the 8th century BCE. There were also wine cellars, with more than 400 *karas* stamped with the year of production and volume of wine. Discovery of SULFUR close by suggested knowledge of its use in preserving wine. Herodotus (*Histories* 1. 194, see ancient GREECE) described the river trade on the Tigris by Assyrian merchants shipping wine downstream from Armenia.

In 301 CE Armenia became the first nation to adopt Christianity as its official state religion. The Christian faith shaped Armenian culture intimately, and wine became not only an intrinsic part of religious rituals (see EUCHARIST) but also was used for medicinal purposes. The biblical story of Noah is closely linked to Armenia. According to Genesis, Noah made landfall on the slopes of Mt Ararat (in Türkiye today) then planted vines on the foothills in Armenia and made wine. Old manuscripts confirm Armenia's high level of viticultural development, and many regard this period (to 500 CE) as a golden age of winemaking. The next 1,500 years saw waves of invasion and wars that meant wine suffered periods of decline, though it hung on even through the Ottoman period (see ISLAM).

Armenia became part of the Russian Empire in 1828 and saw an increase in grape-growing, winemaking, and distillation for brandy and vodka. Brandy developed particularly strongly in the late 1800s as it was more stable to transport over Armenia's inhospitable mountains. Prior to the First World War, Armenia was the leading brandy producer in the South Caucasus, led by the Yerevan Brandy factory. Vineyards covered 10,800 ha/26,687 acres, providing a living for 100,000 people in holdings typically less than 1 ha. After the First World War, Armenia had a brief period of independence but was invaded by the Soviet army in 1920, becoming the Armenian Soviet Socialist Republic. Private wineries were nationalized and amalgamated into the large Ararat wine trust, followed by establishment of the Hayginkoop agricultural CO-OPERATIVE. Stalin subsequently designated the country as a brandy producer, wine production fell, and vineyards were increasingly planted with neutral and high-yielding grape varieties for distillation.

Modern history

After independence in 1991, Armenia was left impoverished, and winemaking only started to recover in the late 1990s with the first new-era private wineries, often established by returning members of Armenia's considerable diaspora. This accelerated after 2011 with the appearance of genuinely premium quality wines. By 2020, the industry counted 110 registered wineries, but only 40 are serious producers and members of Armenia's Vine & Wine Foundation. Nearly a quarter of production was exported, with the Russian Federation a key market, but quality improvements have gained customers in 34 other countries.

Viticulture and vine varieties

Armenia is a mountainous, largely VOLCANIC landscape with LIMESTONE outcrops, growing vines commercially at 400–1,750 m/1,300–5,580 ft, the elevation moderating the climate, which is dry and CONTINENTAL to dry subtropical. Average annual rainfall is 550 mm/22 in, and summers are dry so IRRIGATION is widespread. Winters are sufficiently severe for 85% of vineyards to need WINTER PROTECTION, and there is risk of spring and autumn FROST. PHYLLOXERA is present only in the Ararat Valley so most of the country's vines are own-rooted (see UNGRAFTED VINE). Trellising is widely used, except for old BUSH VINES in remote areas such as Vayots Dzor that escaped collectivization; such vines can be more than 100 years old. Armenia claims at least 400 indigenous varieties though only 30 or so are used in commercial winemaking. Approximately 20% of the harvest goes for wine, with 70% for brandy and 10% as table grapes. The country has recently set up a nursery project to identify and conserve 350 indigenous varieties with 171 passported accessions planted so far. Area by vine variety is not available until the vineyard register is complete, but important red varieties include the indigenous and highly sought-after ARENI, plus Kakhet, Haghtanak, Sireni, and Karmrahyut. Important white grapes include Voskehat, Kangun, Garan Dmak, Mskhali, Chilar, Lalvari, and Khatun Kharji.

Armenia has five viticultural zones: the Ararat Valley (4,800 ha/11,861 acres), Armavir (5,600 ha), Aragatsotn (1,000 ha), Vayots Dzor (2,000 ha), and Tavush (1,800 ha). The predominantly ethnic Armenian self-declared Republic of Artsakh/Nagorno-Karabakh shrank from 1,380 ha to *c.*700 ha after the 2020 war. C.G.

www.vitis.am
www.vwfa.am

armillaria root rot, worldwide FUNGAL DISEASE which lives in woody plant materials in the soil and attacks a wide range of plants including vines. It is sometimes called the mushroom, oak, or shoestring root rot. It is typically a problem on land where vines have replaced trees, and it is frequently seen in vineyards where oak trees grew previously. Infected vines tend to occur in groups and slowly decline or sometimes die suddenly. The causal fungus, *Armillaria mellea*, produces white fungal mats with a distinct mushroom-like smell under the bark of the vine's lower trunk and roots. The land can be fumigated to ward off this fungus, for which there are no tolerant ROOTSTOCKS.
R.E.S.

Arnaldus de Villanova, sometimes called **Arnaud de Villeneuve**, was a Catalan who died in 1311. He taught MEDICINE at MONTPELLIER, the most important medical school, with Salerno, in medieval Europe. He had an eventful life, attending the sickbeds of popes and kings and engaging in theological controversy. He was an influential physician, and his writings were still reprinted in the 16th century.

Arnaldus is not interested in wine for its own sake: his concern is with the medical proprieties of wine. One of his books, the *Liber de vinis* ('Book on Wines'), deals exclusively with wine as medicine, but references to wine appear throughout his works. The *Liber de vinis* is short: in the 16th-century editions of the complete works, it occupies no more than 10 folio pages. To a modern reader it is bound to appear a strange mixture: GALEN and the Arab philosopher Avicenna; alchemy and astrology; some first-hand observation. Arnaldus' medicine draws heavily on the voluminous writings of Galen (129–99 BCE), physician to the Emperor Marcus Aurelius, but Galen was a far better scientist. Galen wrote in Greek, but knowledge of Greek was rare in the medieval west: some of his works were, however, translated into Arabic and thence into Latin. Through Moorish Spain, Arabic influence on European influence was strong: hence Arnaldus' references to Avicenna and other Arabic authors.

Arnaldus praises wine as a remedy against melancholy and says that it is good for the liver, the urinary tract, and the veins, because it purifies the blood. He recommends it to the old, especially in winter, because it warms the kidneys as well as the entire body, reduces the swelling of haemorrhoids, is beneficial to digestion, gives one a healthy complexion, comforts the mind, and, best of all, slows down the greying of one's hair. Most of his remedies, however, do not involve the drinking of neat or watered wine. He uses wines flavoured with rosemary or borage, recipes which go back to classical antiquity and which were supposed to cure a wide variety of ills; he exploits the antiseptic quality of wine for making poultices and, since the water was not usually reliable, to dissolve other medical substances.

One would not have been safe in Arnaldus' hands. An aside about making wine is spot on, however: the wooden casks in which wine was kept should be clean and free of odours, the grapes should mature properly, and any unripe grapes must be discarded.

He is popularly credited with introducing the first still to France, probably from Salerno, and he was granted a patent for his discovery of MUTAGE (which spawned wines such as those now known as VINS DOUX NATURELS) in 1299 from the powerful king of Majorca. H.M.W.

Lucia, S. P., *A History of Wine as Therapy* (1963).
Sigerist, H. E., *The Earliest Printed Book on Wine* (1943).
Thorndike, L., *A History of Magic and Experiential Science*, 7 vols. (1923–57), ii. 841–61.

Arneis, white grape variety and dry, scented VARIETAL wine of PIEMONTE in north-west Italy. Originally from ROERO, it was traditionally used to soften the red NEBBIOLO grape. Although the wine has a certain history in Piemonte, it seemed on the verge of disappearing in the early 1970s when only two houses, Vietti and Bruno Giacosa, were bottling Arneis. In the 1980s, however, thanks to growing demand for white wine in Piemonte, particularly from houses more renowned for their BAROLO and BARBARESCO, there was an explosion of interest in Arneis, and plantings totalled 1,108 ha/2,738 acres by 2015. This low-yielding variety ripens in the second half of September and gives wines with subtle if interesting perfumes. Modern winemaking has, in the best cases, dealt with the variety's inherently low acidity. The best examples tend to be unoaked and drunk young. It is not planted anywhere else in Italy but is grown to a very limited extent in California, Oregon, Australia, and New Zealand.

Arnsburger, white wine variety developed at GEISENHEIM for sparkling wine and exported

to the island of MADEIRA due to an EU-funded project (with a German consultant). Planted on the north side of the island, the productive, disease-resistant variety is used to make rather tart, unfortified, dry white wine with limited local appeal.

aroma, imprecise tasting term for a relatively simple smell such as that of a grape, fermenting MUST, or young wine. Originally from the Greek word meaning 'spice', it has evolved so that in generally current English it means 'pleasant smell' (as opposed to odours, which may be distinctly nasty). Wine-tasting professionals tend to use the word 'aroma' to distinguish the smells associated with young wines from the more complex aromatic compounds which result from extended BOTTLE AGE, sometimes referred to as BOUQUET. In Australia, the word 'aroma' is often used to refer specifically to VARIETAL characteristics rather than those associated with winemaking or AGEING. Those who distinguish between 'aroma' and 'bouquet' differ as to the point in a wine's life cycle which divides the use of the two terms. For tasters schooled at the University of BORDEAUX, bouquet includes fermentation smells, for example, as well as all those associated with oak ageing and bottle ageing. Others, particularly Burgundians, may refer to grape aromas as primary aromas, fermentation and oak ageing aromas as secondary aromas, and bottle-ageing aromas as either tertiary aromas or bouquet. See also FLAVOUR, AROMA WHEEL, FLAVOUR COMPOUNDS, and ESTER. A.D.W.

aroma compounds. See FLAVOUR COMPOUNDS.

aromatics, informal category of white wines made from particularly aromatic grape varieties, a term commonly used in AUSTRALIA and NEW ZEALAND. Typical examples are VARIETAL Gewürztraminer, Pinot Gris, and Riesling. Other particularly aromatic grape varieties include Sauvignon Blanc and Viognier.

aromatized wines. See FLAVOURED WINES.

aroma wheel, graphical representation of TASTING TERMS used for AROMA, devised at the University of California at DAVIS by Ann C. Noble and others in the early 1980s. Her research into sensory evaluation of wine had

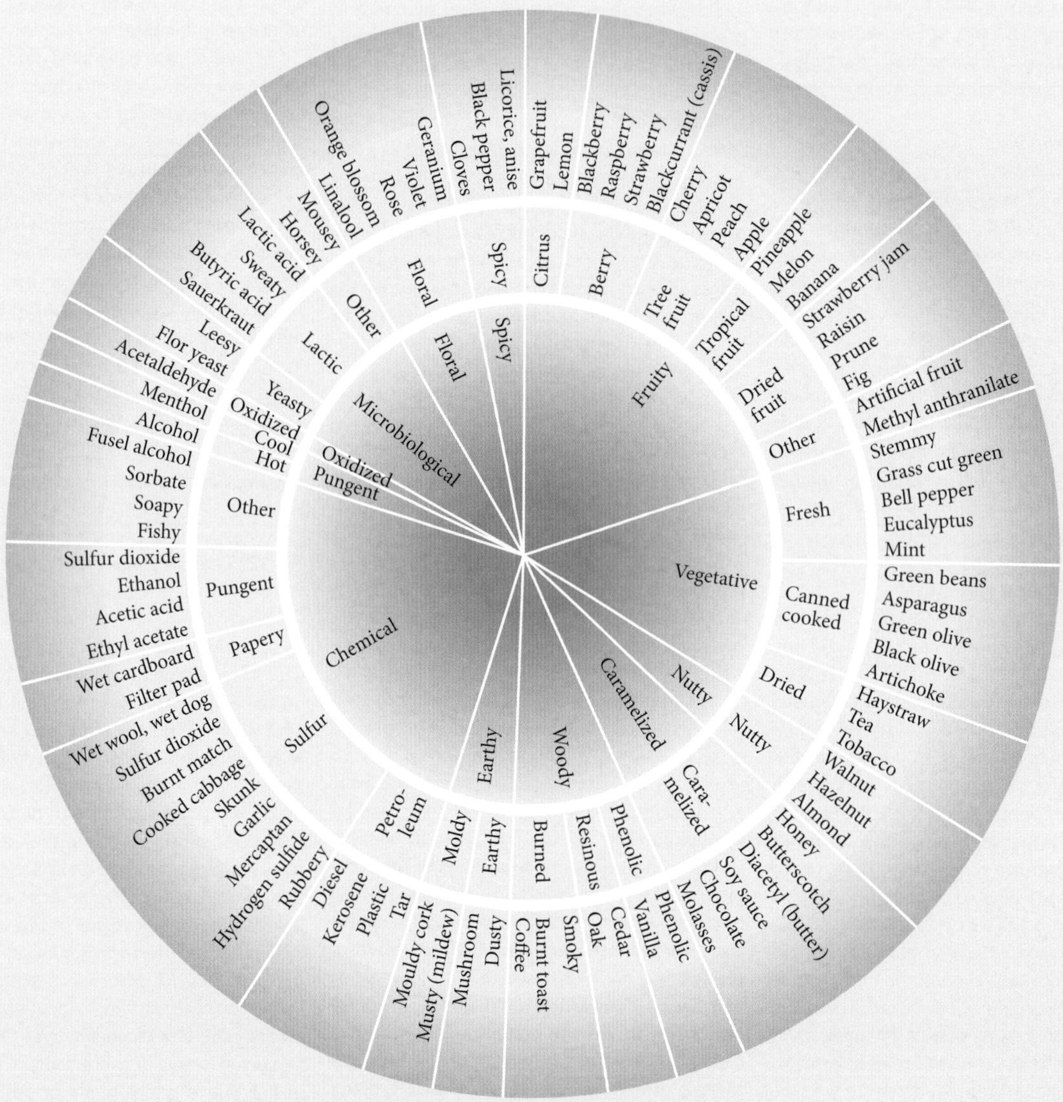

The **aroma wheel** was devised at the University of California at Davis by Professor Ann C. Noble in an attempt to instil some rigour into wine descriptions.
Source: American Journal of Enology & Viticulture, 38/2 (1987). Copyright © Dr Ann C. Noble and *American Journal of Enology & Viticulture*

indicated that there was no general agreement either on terminology or on its application. The aroma wheel was developed to provide a standardized lexicon which can be used widely to describe wine aroma in non-judgemental terms, grouping specific terms which can be defined to provide a basis for communication. In its attempt at clarification and categorization it is used by professionals and provides a good basis on which tasting terms for aroma can be taught to novices, even if, with experience, most individuals tend to develop their own terms, which may be just as precise and descriptive. The aroma wheel does not include terms which describe the physical dimensions of a wine (such as 'full-bodied' or 'tart').

The extensive use of the wine aroma wheel led to the development of an analogous mouthfeel wheel to describe the TEXTURE and MOUTHFEEL sensations of red wines.

Noble, A. C., et al., 'Modification of a standardized system of wine aroma terminology', *American Journal of Enology and Viticulture*, 38/2 (1987).

arrachage, French term for GRUBBING UP vines. The *prime d'arrachage*, payment for participating in the European VINE-PULL SCHEME, made its mark on the southern French landscape from the late 1980s.

Arribes, Spanish DOP in the provinces of Salamanca and Zamora on the border with Portugal, with vineyards flanking the steep, deep canyons of the Duero River. The indigenous dark-skinned JUAN GARCÍA dominates the 337 ha/833 acres of vineyards, although Bruñal (ALFROCHEIRO) is increasingly valued. Whites are made mainly from Malvasía Castellana (DOÑA BLANCA).

arrope, a syrup used for sweetening wine in Spain, especially SHERRY and MÁLAGA, made by boiling down and unfermented grape juice. See GRAPE CONCENTRATE.

Arroyo Grande Valley, California wine region and AVA. See SAN LUIS OBISPO.

Arroyo Seco, California wine region and AVA. See MONTEREY.

Arruda, DOC subregion in central LISBOA in Portugal. Production, focused mostly on BULK reds, is dominated by the CO-OPERATIVE. An ambitious new project by Monte Bluna is revealing the quality potential on Jurassic LIMESTONE at ELEVATION. S.A.

Arrufiac, also known as **Arrufiat**, is a light-skinned, quite tannic grape variety enjoying a modest renaissance in Gascony in SOUTH WEST FRANCE, where there were just 31 ha/77 acres in 2018. An ingredient in PACHERENC DU VIC-BILH and ST-MONT, it was rescued from obscurity in the 1980s by André Dubosc of the Plaimont CO-OPERATIVE. It is typically blended with the MANSENGS, COURBU BLANC, and PETIT COURBU.

Artémis Domaines, the wine division of entrepreneur François Pinault's Groupe Artémis. His first wine acquisition was first growth Ch LATOUR in 1993. This was followed by Domaine René Engel, renamed Domaine d'Eugénie, in VOSNE-ROMANÉE, acquired in 2006; CHÂTEAU-GRILLET in the northern Rhône Valley (2011); Araujo Estate, renamed Eisele Vineyard, in Napa Valley (2013); and Clos de Tart in MOREY-ST-DENIS (2017). In 2022 the group absorbed Champagne Henriot, Champagne Jacquesson, and BOUCHARD PÈRE ET FILS.

artificial intelligence (AI) is being developed and used in four main areas of viticulture and winemaking in order to tackle a wide range of challenges, from CLIMATE CHANGE to COUNTERFEIT WINE. Based on historical developments and recent technological advances, research has been focused on the following potential applications of AI:

- Viticulture management, such as the exploitation and integration of data provided by the tools and techniques of PRECISION VITICULTURE, for example REMOTE SENSING and PROXIMAL SENSING. Applications of AI include the assessment of nutrient and water requirements, early detection and better management of pests and diseases to use resources more efficiently, and bud/grape berry recognition to obtain quality traits and predict yields.
- Estimation of grape composition and prediction of final wine quality, including possible smoke contamination of grapes in the vineyard and SMOKE TAINT in wines due to WILDFIRES.
- Measuring consumer acceptability of wines using biometrics for sensory analysis, including non-invasive physiological assessments such as heart rate, blood pressure, respiration rate, skin-temperature changes, and emotional response from face recognition and AI.
- Counterfeiting and PROVENANCE assessment using digital and non-invasive technology through bottles, such as near-infrared spectroscopy.

These digital technologies based on AI for viticulture and winemaking can also be implemented to develop smart systems (i.e. digital twins, which are a 'virtual model' or a digital counterpart to the viticulturist's/winemaker's decision-making process). These smart systems can be deployed as autonomous tools to invigilate all the processes between vineyard management (based on DRONES and remote sensing), wine production (based on 'electronic noses' and optical sensors), and consumer acceptability (based on biometrics from consumers and emotional response). The aim is to produce targeted wines or maintain styles determined by consumer preference that also maximize use of resources such as nutrients, water, and labour by implementing AI tools throughout the process.

Grape-growers' main concern in the digital era is who owns the data and whether data from their vineyards could be used to improve the viticultural and winemaking practices of competitors. However, this concern is based on the misconception that AI modelling techniques recognize patterns from the actual data. In fact, pattern recognition is created within the AI modelling techniques themselves or the machine, not from the data. Hence data contributes to incorporating site-specific factors which benefit all grape-growers using these technologies. Fuentes and Gago (2022) proposed that agricultural data should be treated as currency using BLOCKCHAIN technology to regulate its usage and management. In fact, it follows the Game Theory principle and therefore benefits the individual grape-growers and the industry as a whole.

AI in viticulture, and in agriculture more generally, could become a turning point in efforts to mitigate and adapt to the challenges posed by climate change, population growth, and reduced arable land on Earth. S.F.

Fuentes, S., et al., 'Novel digital technologies implemented in sensory science and consumer perception', *Current Opinion in Food Science*, 41 (2021), 99–106.

Fuentes, S., and Gago, J., 'Modern approaches to precision and digital viticulture', in J. M. Costa et al., *Improving Sustainable Viticulture and Winemaking Practices* (2022).

Fuentes, S., and Tongson, E., 'Advances and requirements for machine learning and artificial intelligence applications in viticulture', *Wine & Viticulture Journal*, 33/3 (2018), 47–52.

artists' labels, wine LABELS illustrated by works of art, often a different one for each vintage. Baron Philippe de ROTHSCHILD commissioned the Cubist Jean Carlu to design a mould-breaking label for the 1924 vintage of Ch MOUTON-ROTHSCHILD, the first to be CHÂTEAU BOTTLED. He instituted this as an annual custom from the 1945 vintage, with the result that collectors may seek particular labels, thereby adding value to Mouton Rothschild even in lesser or earlier-maturing vintages (of which most bottles tend to have been opened). Since then, vintages of Mouton have enjoyed particular réclame in countries associated with the artist responsible for that year's label. Wine producers all over the world have since emulated this practice, notably Leeuwin Estate of WESTERN AUSTRALIA and Nittardi in CHIANTI CLASSICO, although none to such clever effect.

Mouton Rothschild: Paintings for the Labels (1995).

A

Arvine, also known as **Petite Arvine**, the finest of the INDIGENOUS VARIETIES of the Valais in Switzerland. The wines tend to be nervy with considerable EXTRACT and, often, a vague suggestion of grapefruit and salt. Wines vary in sweetness between dry, mi-FLÉTRI, and downright sweet. Switzerland had 235 ha/581 acres of this grape by 2020.

ascorbic acid, vitamin C, one of the first VITAMINS to be discovered and a winemaking additive used chiefly as an antioxidant. As well as being essential to the human diet, it is involved in plant metabolic processes. The green grape contains significant levels of vitamin C, but much is lost during fruit ripening and winemaking. In a wine context, ascorbic acid (or its isomer erythorbic or iso-ascorbic acid) is of chief importance not to the wine drinker but to the winemaker as a permitted ADDITIVE, within limits, for its ability to prevent OXIDATION by reacting directly with OXYGEN. The EU limit in a finished wine is 250 mg/l.

The chemistry of ascorbic acid in preventing oxidation in white juices and wines is complex, and this has led to confusion about its effectiveness. When used alone as an antioxidant, ascorbic acid reacts very rapidly with oxygen and thus retards oxidation. However, the reaction of ascorbic acid with oxygen produces oxidative products that, in the absence of free SULFUR DIOXIDE, will in turn oxidize wine components. Thus ascorbic acid alone is not a suitable antioxidant in winemaking.

Free sulfur dioxide does not react rapidly with oxygen, thus it is not a good oxygen scavenger and does not fully control wine oxidation. However, the combination of ascorbic acid with free sulfur dioxide is a very effective antioxidant, even in the long term, provided that a level of free sulfur dioxide is maintained in the wine. The ascorbic acid reacts rapidly with any OXYGEN present, and the oxidative products in turn react with the sulfur dioxide and are eliminated.

In combination, ascorbic acid and sulfur dioxide can be used throughout the white winemaking process, from grape crushing and pressing to BOTTLING. In red winemaking, ascorbic acid is not used as some oxidative modification of PHENOLIC compounds, including TANNINS, is usually desirable. P.J.W. & T.J.

aseptic bottling. See STERILE BOTTLING.

Asia. Until the 1990s it was assumed—quite wrongly, as it turned out—that this most populous of continents would never play an important role in the world of wine. This assumption was rapidly disproved in the mid to late 1990s when the world's AUCTION prices were inflated at an unprecedented rate thanks largely to sudden interest from buyers in Hong Kong, Singapore, and Taiwan. Thanks to a boom in the so-called tiger economies, and the much-vaunted HEALTH benefits claimed for red wine, wine-drinking changed from an unusual foreign practice to status symbol in a remarkably short time in countries as varied as Thailand, Taiwan, India, Korea, and—the country with the greatest potential as both consumer and producer—China. Wine-drinking had already infiltrated Japan, and several other Asian countries have embarked on their own domestic wine industries, often based on TABLE GRAPES initially and sometimes bolstered by imported BULK WINE, since the early 1990s. For details of individual countries, see BHUTAN, CAMBODIA, CHINA, HONG KONG, INDIA, INDONESIA, JAPAN, KOREA, MYANMAR, NEPAL, SINGAPORE, SRI LANKA, TAIWAN, THAILAND, and VIETNAM. See also the ex-Soviet Central Asian republics of AZERBAIJAN, KAZAKHSTAN, KYRGYZSTAN, TAJIKISTAN, TURKMENISTAN, and UZBEKISTAN. Countries such as AFGHANISTAN, IRAQ, IRAN, JORDAN, PAKISTAN, and SYRIA devote most of their vineyards to the production of RAISINS but, in Western Asia, ARMENIA, CYPRUS, GEORGIA, ISRAEL, PALESTINE, LEBANON, and TÜRKIYE all have significant wine industries.

Asia Minor. See ANATOLIA.

Asian lady beetle. See LADYBUG TAINT.

aspect, the direction in which a slope faces, also referred to as exposure, an important characteristic of vineyard sites, especially in cool climates. The French equivalent, *exposition*, is often mistakenly used in wine writing in English. For more details, see TOPOGRAPHY.

Aspergillus. See BUNCH ROTS.

aspersion, French for sprinkling and therefore a measure to reduce FROST DAMAGE to vines; see SPRINKLERS.

Aspiran, officially but not popularly known as **Rivairenc**, is a very old dark-skinned grape variety of the LANGUEDOC which once represented about a quarter of all vines in the Hérault *département* but was rarely replanted after PHYLLOXERA because it is not particularly productive. The odd hectare that remains yields limited quantities of light but perfumed red wine, and it is a permitted grape variety in MINERVOIS. Its progeny **Aspiran Bouschet** is almost extinct in France but can be found in Mendoza and Chile. DNA PROFILING has revealed a parent–offspring relationship with CINSAUT.

Asprinio. See GRECO.

Assario, Dão synonym for MALVASIA Fina.

assemblage, French word for the important operation in the production of fine wines of deciding which lots will be assembled to make up the final blend. It plays a crucial role in SPARKLING WINEMAKING when some CUVÉES may be assembled from several hundred different components. Here the complementary nature of each component is of great importance, as is, for all NON-VINTAGE sparkling wines, adherence to a house style.

Assemblage is of almost ritual significance in BORDEAUX, where many CHÂTEAUX make their so-called GRAND VIN carrying the château name by selecting and BLENDING only the best lots. The rejected lots may either be blended to make a SECOND WINE (and occasionally even a third wine) or sold off in bulk to a NÉGOCIANT carrying only the local appellation (Margaux or St-Julien, for example).

This selection process typically takes place between the third and sixth month after the HARVEST (much later in SAUTERNES) and involves the MAÎTRE DE CHAI (winemaker), any OENOLOGIST regularly working for the property, and the proprietor, who must bear the considerable financial sacrifice of exclusions from the *grand vin*, which may sell for three or more times the price of the associated second wine. It is at this stage that the decision is usually taken over whether to incorporate any PRESS WINE.

The normal procedure is to taste samples from each *cuve* or FERMENTATION VESSEL and then simply decide whether it is of sufficiently high quality for the *grand vin*. It has usually been assumed that any blend of wines from the same property is likely to be harmonious. In most other European wine regions, especially BURGUNDY, holdings are often too small to allow this selectivity, although Chave of HERMITAGE in the Rhône, for example, is notable for keeping lots from different PARCELS of vineyard separate until a final assembly just before bottling.

Such a TERROIR-driven approach is slowly becoming more common throughout the wine world, although it is more likely to involve the assembly of blends of various quality levels and character. In this case there may be extensive experiments with small samples of each lot—known as bench blending—before final blends are decided upon. Here the winemaker is concerned not just with each lot's inherent quality but also with its affinity with other components in the blend.

Assyrtiko, top-quality white grape variety grown increasingly widely in GREECE. Its origins lie on the island of SANTORINI, but its ability to retain acidity in a hot climate has encouraged successful experimentation with it elsewhere, notably on the north-eastern mainland around Halkidiki. Its severe mineral profile (see MINERALITY) has made it a successful blending partner for MALAGOUSIA, Sauvignon Blanc, and Sémillon. Its wines can age relatively well. So obvious is its quality that it is Greece's third most planted white wine vine with 2,015 ha/4,979 acres in 2021, and it has even been imported into

Australia, France, South Africa, and California. High demand for the fruit of Santorini's low-yielding vines has led to significant price increases over the last decade.

Asti, town and province in PIEMONTE in north-west Italy whose name appears in local VARIETAL reds made from DOLCETTO, FREISA, GRIGNOLINO, MALVASIA di Casorzo, and, most famously, BARBERA. Unlike its counterpart Barbera d'Alba, made from vines traditionally planted in lesser sites where NEBBIOLO will not ripen, Barbera has always been given supreme vineyard sites in Asti. Barbera d'Asti was elevated to DOCG in 2010, with three superior subzones: Tinella, Colli Astiani or Astiano, and Nizza, the latter elevated to DOCG in 2019. Since 2014 the area has been recognized as a UNESCO World Heritage Site together with the Langhe.

However, Asti is most associated with the playful, aromatic, lightly sparkling wine with modest alcohol levels that was Italy's biggest-selling wine before the ascent of PROSECCO and PINOT GRIGIO. In 1993, along with the superior MOSCATO D'ASTI, Asti Spumante was elevated to DOCG status and renamed Asti, largely to distinguish it from the host of FRIZZANTE or sparkling wines produced in Italy from a wide range of grape varieties of very varying quality.

Both Asti and Moscato d'Asti must be produced from at least 97% Moscato Bianco (MUSCAT BLANC À PETITS GRAINS) in the provinces of Asti, Cuneo, and Alessandria, where vineyards total 9,700 ha/23,969 acres, of which 7,000 ha are on slopes, shared by 4,000 growers spread over 52 communes. Average vineyard size is just 2.45 ha/6 acres. Production has increased from 40 million bottles in the 1970s to 91.5 million bottles in 2020, made possible by a VINE DENSITY of 4,000 vines/ha and a permitted yield of 10 tonnes/ha. Large bottlers and NÉGOCIANT houses have traditionally dominated production, relying on the TANK METHOD. The combination of large-volume production and small-scale viticulture has necessarily made Asti a wine blended from many sources, masking geographical differences in sites. No efforts have been made to distinguish hill sites from lower areas by the creation of a CLASSICO zone. However, an increasing number of producers are bottling their own produce, resulting in more artisanal wines and more wines from SINGLE VINEYARDS and SORÌ (a site with more than 50% inclination). The subzones Santa Vittoria d'Alba and Strevi may appear on Asti labels, and, since 2020, single-vineyard names may appear on all Asti and Moscato d'Asti labels.

Asti comes in several versions, each determined by its alcoholic content, RESIDUAL SUGAR, and intensity of sparkle. Asti differs significantly from Moscato d'Asti: it is more alcoholic (6–9.5% rather than Moscato d'Asti's maximum of 6.5%), and it is fizzier (at least 3 bar of pressure in the bottle rather than Moscato d'Asti's maximum of 2 bar). The best and ripest grapes are normally reserved for Moscato d'Asti.

In 2011 an Asti Spumante Metodo Classico category was introduced, requiring a minimum of 10% alcohol, second fermentation in bottle (see SPARKLING WINEMAKING), and nine months ageing on the lees. In 2017, in response to an international demand for a drier style and to counteract competition from Prosecco, Asti Secco, with 17–32 g/l residual sugar and at least 3 bar of pressure, was created. Since 2020 Asti Spumante may also produce Brut, Extra Brut, Brut Nature, or Pas Dosé versions in addition to the sweeter categories Demi Sec, Secco/Dry, and Extra Dry. W.S.

www.astidocg.info

astringency is a complex of sensations resulting from the shrinking, drawing, or puckering of the tissues of the mouth. Earlier, astringency had been considered as one of the primary TASTE sensations, like sweetness, sourness, and particularly BITTERNESS, with which it has often been confused. It is now recognized as a tactile response not dependent on the taste receptors, however. The word is derived from the Latin *ad stringere*, meaning 'to bind', which presaged the finding that astringent materials could bind to, and precipitate, PROTEINS. The most important astringent materials are TANNINS, and it is these components of a wine that are responsible for the puckery, tactile sensation that is most noticeable in young red wines but can be sensed in a small but increasing proportion of white wines too, particularly those from hard-pressed or SKIN-FERMENTED grapes, most notably in ORANGE WINES. An appropriate degree of astringency contributes very positively to the palatability of a wine, and astringency is central to TEXTURE and MOUTHFEEL. Some of the terms used by tasters to describe the astringency of a wine—for example, 'hard', 'soft', 'green', 'resinous', 'leathery', 'gripping', 'aggressive', 'supple'—are the same as those used to describe the tannins of the wine. The astringent sensation may be modified by ACIDITY, SWEETNESS, PHENOLICS, particularly tannins and PIGMENTED TANNINS, and even serving TEMPERATURE. The effect of these components on apparent astringency has been an area of active research in contemporary OENOLOGY.

Revelett et al. suggest that the 'stickiness' as well as the level of tannins is a factor in how astringent a wine tastes. P.J.W.

Revelett, M. R., et al., 'High-performance liquid chromatography determination of red wine tannin stickiness', *Journal of Agricultural and Food Chemistry*, 62/28 (2014), 6626–31.

Vidal, S., et al., 'Taste and mouth-feel properties of different types of tannin-like polyphenolic compounds and anthocyanins in wine', *Analytica Chemica Acta*, 513 (2004), 57–65.

Aszú, Hungarian term derived from an old form of the word 'dried' and now used solely to denote grapes affected by BOTRYTIS and naturally dried on the vine in TOKAJ. Tokaji Aszú, therefore, means a wine made from shrivelled, botrytized grapes in Tokaj, although the winemaking method is more complicated than that. See TOKAJ for more detail.

ATF, previously known as BATF. See TTB.

Athenaeus (flourished *c.*200 CE) was born in Naucratis, a Greek city in the Nile Delta in Egypt, and wrote in Greek. Nothing is known about his life, and his surviving work, the *Deipnosophistae*, meaning 'The masters of the art of dining', can be dated only from internal evidence. It describes at length how 23 men dine together in ancient ROME and records their conversations; their two most frequent topics are HOMER and wine. Two of the participants are the physician GALEN and the lawyer Ulpian of Tyre; the others are not based on real persons. The work consists of 15 books, but the first two and part of the third survive only in excerpts.

Although wine is the second most frequent topic of the diners' conversation, Athenaeus shows little interest in CONNOISSEURSHIP and none at all in VITICULTURE. Rather than engaging in systematic discussion, Athenaeus assembles curious facts, makes lists, and proposes (often incorrect) etymologies: his enumeration of types of CONTAINERS for wine in Book 11 exemplifies all these tendencies. Most of the wines which he mentions do not belong to his own day (e.g. Coan, Chian, Mendaean, and Thasian). The famous passage attributed to Galen on the wines of Italy (26c–27d) promises to be a discussion of Italian wines in Galen's day, the second half of the 2nd century, but it has none of the rigour and acumen of the great medical writer; in fact, it is almost certainly not by Galen at all. The passage is a series of bald statements, telling us mainly whether a wine is sweet or dry and whether or not it was strong; it does not offer any comparison with wines of earlier periods or different regions. It gives some optimum drinking dates: Alban is best at 15 years old; FALERNIAN needs a minimum of 10 years' ageing, is best after 15 to 20 and, if any older, gives headaches. Falernian can be sweet or dry: we know from other writings (mainly Galen's own) that dry wines were popular in the 2nd century CE, whereas in PLINY's day good wines appear to have been sweet. Athenaeus himself gives us no such historical perspective, however: he is not a historian but a contented collector of snippets. H.M.W.

Brock, R., and Wilson, H., 'Wine in Athenaeus', in D. Braund and J. Wilkins (eds.), *Athenaeus and his World* (2000).

Athiri, vine grown widely in southern Greece with total plantings of 588 ha/1,453 acres in 2021. Its soft, lemony produce is often used for blending, notably with the even higher quality ASSYRTIKO.

Atlantique, one of six massive regional IGPS in France, covering its Atlantic coastal vineyards from the Charente to the northern end of the Lot-et-Garonne *département* and inland to the Massif Central. Over 100 grape varieties are allowed; Bordeaux varieties dominate.

Atlas Peak, CALIFORNIA wine region and AVA in the mountains on the eastern side of NAPA Valley.

atypical ageing (ATA) or **untypical ageing (UTA)**, known as *untypischer Alterungsnote* in Germany, where it was first documented in the late 1980s, is a term used to identify a phenomenon found in white wines worldwide, although varieties such as MÜLLER-THURGAU, KERNER, and BACCHUS seem to be particularly susceptible. It should more accurately be described as a wine FAULT as it is not related to AGEING. Hot, dry conditions immediately before and after VERAISON resulting in extreme WATER STRESS can lead to the development of this aroma/flavour defect. Wines from hot, dry growing seasons and sites are more prone to developing ATA. Vine NITROGEN deficiency may also be a contributing factor, which is why excessive use of certain COVER CROPS that compete with the vines favours the development of this fault. The compound 2-aminoacetophenone (AAP), which is responsible for the FOXY flavour in VITIS LABRUSCA, is also primarily responsible for ATA and is thought to be formed from the precursor indoleacetic acid (IAA) within a few weeks or months of the first addition of SULFITES post-fermentation. Affected wines lose VARIETAL character, develop atypical aromas and flavours described as reminding of naphthalene (mothballs), a wet towel, or old furniture varnish, and may show an increase in bitterness. These characteristics are not exactly the same as those typical of wines suffering from PREMATURE OXIDATION because different aromatic compounds are involved. Methods to minimize the development of ATA include avoiding extreme moisture stress around veraison, ensuring adequate plant nitrogen, and avoiding OVERCROPPING, which could delay maturity. ASCORBIC ACID additions (100–150 mg/l) in conjunction with proper SULFUR DIOXIDE levels in the wine may help to limit the extent of this phenomenon. J.E.H. & V.L.

Schneider, V., 'Atypical aging defect: sensory discrimination, viticultural causes, and enological consequences. A review', *American Journal of Enology and Viticulture*, 65/3 (2014), 277–84.

Aubance, Coteaux de l', small (barely 200 ha/500 acres) but potentially excellent sweet-white-wine appellation in ANJOU on the left bank of the River Loire just south of the town of Angers. It takes its name from the Aubance, a tributary of the Loire. With barely a century of recorded production, it still lives in the shadows of its famous and larger neighbour to the south, the Coteaux du LAYON. If dry white and red Anjou make up the bulk of volume in this zone, as the appellation overlaps the red Anjou-Villages Brissac AOC, the gentle, heat-retaining SLATE hills protected by the Beaulieu and Brissac forest produce vibrant sweet CHENIN BLANC, with more nuanced concentrations than other examples of the area. In exceptional years Coteaux de l'Aubance can be just as noble, if not always as long-lived, as the Loire's more famous sweet whites, and must owe their quality to a succession of TRIES through the vineyard, picking only the ripest grapes. According to the vintage, the wines may be PASSERILLÉS and/or BOTRYTIZED, and, when a higher concentration is reached by pure noble rot, may carry the term SÉLECTION DE GRAINS NOBLES. See also LOIRE, including map. P. Le.

Aubun, rather ordinary black-berried vine variety of the southern Rhône planted on just 282 ha/697 acres in France by 2019. It produces wine not unlike a softer version of CARIGNAN and formed part of James BUSBY's original vine collection taken to Australia, where isolated plantings can still be found, as they can in California.

Auckland is the largest city in NEW ZEALAND, and its greater area is one of the country's oldest wine regions. Located on a fertile isthmus in the north, it is headquarters for some of the largest wine producers (Villa Maria, Delegats). Viticultural plantings have decreased to just over 300 ha/741 acres by 2021 due to increasing urban expansion and the success of wine regions further south. Kumeu, a GEOGRAPHICAL INDICATION (GI) in West Auckland, has a rich wine history and produces some of New Zealand's best Chardonnay. Matakana GI, 70 km/43 miles north of Auckland, and Waiheke Island GI, off the eastern coast, are home to fine Syrah and BORDEAUX BLENDS, with sales bolstered by a thriving metropolitan population. S.P.T.

auctions of wine are the sale of wine by lots by an auctioneer acting as agent for the seller or, in certain instances, as the seller in his or her own right.

History

Auctions have long been an integral part of the wine TRADE. Wine was sold by auction in ancient ROME; in the Middle Ages, before it became commonplace for buyers to visit wine regions, wine shipped in barrel to its final destination (see CONTAINERS) was frequently sold by auction as well as by private contract. In Britain, wine auctions were common at trading ports such as Leith in Edinburgh, Scotland, where the auction room in The Vaults testifies to a once lively auction trade in casks of fine bordeaux. In Germany, the practice of selling wine by auction under the names of village and vintage became well established in the 18th century. The Nassauer'sche Domäne in the Rheingau was among the first to initiate the movement towards establishing conditions of sale by auction in the 1830s.

As wine trading became increasingly competitive with improved transportation and more sophisticated communications, the need for producers to sell their wine by auction diminished. Whereas historically wine auctions were used as a means of selling young or relatively young wine in barrel, today's commercial auction trade relies on bottled wines at all stages of maturity. Once wine was packaged in BOTTLES stoppered with CORKS from the end of the 17th century, it became capable of AGEING and full maturation. With, literally, a new lease of life for fine wine, exceeding decades and, in rare instances, even a century or more, fine wine transcended its previous status as a short-term commodity.

Once wine became capable of being traded across generations, it naturally attracted admirers, collectors, and investors (see INVESTMENT). It became something that, at its finest, could be regarded with the same admiration as a work of art or any other classic auction room collectible. Wine captured in bottle led to a market in older wines whose reputation, based on VINTAGE and name, created a comprehensible and measurable scale of values.

Sales of wine were generally held as part of house sales until wine departments were established in two of the world's leading auction houses, Christie's and Sotheby's. Christie's established its wine department in 1966, when Michael BROADBENT was recruited to build up the department to meet the demands of an increasingly specialized and sophisticated international market. The first auction of the new era was held on 11 October 1966, and the first season achieved sales amounting to £220,634. Not to be outdone, Sotheby's entered the fray in 1970, holding the first auction of its newly formed wine department on 16 September 1970 in Glasgow.

While Christie's and Sotheby's dominated the wine auction scene for many decades, new auction systems and entrants have challenged the status quo. In the late 1970s, The Chicago Wine Company introduced and popularized the 'silent bid' wine auction system in the US.

Archaic laws in New York State prevented the spread of wine auctions in one of the world's most lucrative markets until the late 1980s. Christie's and Sotheby's initially teamed up with local wine merchants until deregulation in the late 1990s. The French auction market was also deregulated in the late 1990s. After all taxes and duties on wine were removed in 2008, HONG KONG rapidly became one of the world's leading wine-auction hubs, frequently recording higher annual revenues than either the United States or Europe.

In 2021 global wine-auction revenues totalled US$582 million, a modest sum compared with the global fine-wine market overall, and dwarfed by the value of saleroom fine-art revenues. Inefficiencies in the auction wine market during the 1980s also led to increased competition from specialist FINE WINE traders, the great majority of them based in the UK. The dot.com boom in the late 1990s spawned electronic wine-auction houses, and online selling in some form has been adopted by most wine-auction companies, including online bidding at live auctions, online-only auctions, and the emergence of online-only auction houses.

Some notable annual auctions

Nevertheless, traditional auctions survive, most notably that of the HOSPICES DE BEAUNE. This former medieval hospice in Burgundy derives a substantial proportion of income for the modern hospital associated with it from the sale of wines produced from vineyards given as bequests over the centuries. At the traditional candle auction, the lots are named after the Hospices' benefactors, each comprising a number of new 228-l/60-gal barrels. Christie's partnered with the Hospices de Beaune between 2005 and 2020, organizing not just the annual sale but also tastings of the wines all over the world. From 2021 and the 161st edition, Sotheby's took over, with their inaugural sale achieving a record total of $15.3 million.

The success of the Hospices de Beaune auction in combining the sale of wines with the glare of publicity has been the role model for a number of latter-day imitators, from LIMOUX to the NAPA Valley.

A number of notable auctions in Germany, largely focused on special lots of Riesling with some Spätburgunder, include those of the VDP's GROSSER RING in the Mosel, VDP Rheingau at KLOSTER EBERBACH, and VDP Nahe-Ahr in Bad Kreuznach. South Africa's Nederburg enhanced its reputation as a wine producer by establishing the Nederburg auction in 1975, at which lots of its top bottlings and those of other producers are offered for sale. The Nederburg sale in turn spawned the annual auction of the Cape Winemakers' Guild, a group of largely independent cellarmasters who started selling small lots of top wines at auction in 1985.

In the United States, distillers Heublein established the first New World wine auction in Chicago in 1969. Since then a combination of strict licensing laws and tax advantages to buyers led to a boom in charity wine auctions in the United States, led by the now famous annual Auction Napa Valley and the Naples Winter Wine Festival in Florida. The prices paid at these charity events are often so inflated by goodwill and/or welcome exhibitionism, however, that they cannot be compared with the United States' thriving commercial auctions as reliable indicators of the market.

The professionals

Christie's is the oldest established wine auctioneer. Wine was a prominent feature in James Christie's first sale on 5 December 1766, which, along with household furniture, jewellery, and firearms, included the sale of 'a large quantity of Madeira and high Flavour'd Claret, late the Property of Noble Personage (Deceas'd)'.

Today's commercial auction scene is dominated by regular sales conducted by a number of professional auction houses, initially London-based. However, in the late 1990s wine auctions elsewhere, particularly in the United States, started to present an increasingly serious challenge to London's hegemony as American cellars became an increasingly lucrative source of supply. In the early 1990s, wine auctions were at long last permitted in New York, but only in association with an established retailer. As a result, Sotheby's established a presence in association with Sherry-Lehmann, holding its first sale in New York on 8 October 1994, while Christie's teamed up with Zachy's. The total value of wine sales in the US overtook the UK total in the mid 1990s.

The introduction of the silent-bid wine auction in the 1980s, followed by the deployment of internet auction technology in the late 1990s, has changed the auction format irrevocably. The vibrant cut and thrust of the live auction room is to a certain extent dwindling as internet trading becomes part of our daily lives.

In 2021, the major wine auctioneers, in declining order of revenues achieved, were Acker Merrall & Condit, Zachys, Sotheby's, Hart Davis Hart, Christie's, Baghera, and Heritage. Other major players were Besch, Bonhams, Steinfels, and Artcurial. Acker Merrall & Condit, Zachys, Sotheby's, and Christie's have become the major players in the all-important Asian wine-auction scene centred on Hong Kong. Asian buyers have also become extremely active in auctions all over the world. Commercial auctions are also held in France, Holland, Belgium, Switzerland, Italy, Singapore, and Australia.

After the bumper years of 2011 and 2012, and the decline in global auction revenues by 16% in 2013, total revenues rose by 5.5% in 2014, possibly affected by increasing concern about PROVENANCE and adverse reaction to the exorbitant en primeur pricing of the 2010 Bordeaux vintage combined with economic uncertainty, particularly in the EU. Auction revenues reached a new peak in 2018, followed by two consecutive years of decline in 2019 (−8%) and 2020 (−12%), the latter decline largely due to pandemic-related restrictions on live sales. This encouraged global auction houses to adopt alternative methods for selling wine during periods of lockdown, such as increased live video-streaming of sales, absentee or online bids, and timed online-only auctions. The average lot price at global live wine auctions in 2020 was $3,694, which nearly doubled in 2021 to $6,991.

Trade structure

Wine auction customers are broadly split between private individuals and the wine trade. Private buyers may have any number of different reasons for buying wine. They may be consumers, collectors, and/or investors (see INVESTMENT). Trade buyers also buy for investment, to fill gaps in a restaurant or merchant's wine list, or as brokers for trade or private clients. Reasons for selling wine vary equally, the traditional three d's of death, debt, and divorce having turned into four, as doctors' orders have also become a factor. Private customers may want or need to sell in order to realize the value of their cellar, or part of it, or to finance further purchases, or as executors selling on behalf of an estate. There is also the phenomenon of single-owner sales, and single-producer sales used for less personal promotion. The wine trade may sell to dispose of surplus or bankrupt stock.

Wines traded

Red bordeaux, or claret, was historically the staple of the wine auction rooms. It is long-lived, enjoys widespread appeal, and it is in relatively plentiful supply. And the relative value of a particular red bordeaux is more readily identifiable than that of any other wine style, the 1855 CLASSIFICATION providing some sort of easily comprehensible framework for evaluating the red bordeaux châteaux most widely traded in the saleroom.

The FIRST GROWTHS—Chx LAFITE, LATOUR, MARGAUX, MOUTON ROTHSCHILD in the Médoc, HAUT-BRION in Pessac-Léognan, CH D'YQUEM in Sauternes, AUSONE and CHEVAL BLANC in St-Émilion, PETRUS, LE PIN and Ch Lafleur of Pomerol—are undisputed members of today's elite. Owing to the classification's rigid composition, a second leading group of properties has emerged, commonly referred to as SUPER SECONDS. Qualification for this group requires not only the strictest commitment to quality but also a record of

consistently high prices which reflects that policy.

Pre-PHYLLOXERA clarets are extremely rare and among the most highly prized bordeaux wines in any sale catalogue. Unique grands formats (large bottles; see LARGE FORMAT) of old vintages, particularly of first growths, are much sought-after by collectors (see BOTTLE SIZE), although perhaps to a lesser degree than in the late 1980s. Specific VINTAGES play an important part, too, with the price of wines from consecutive years often fluctuating by a factor of three according to the reputation of the vintage. The most highly prized pre-war vintages of the 20th century are 1900, 1920, 1926, 1928, and 1929. In the immediate post-war period, the most sought-after trio are 1945, 1947, and 1949. In the latter half of the 20th century and early 21st century, 1953, 1959, 1961, 1982, 1990, 2000, 2005, 2009, 2010, and 2016 rank as the outstanding vintages.

In this century, prices for relatively recent vintages started to outstrip the prices of older vintages. Although the state of the global economy plays a part, much of this has to do with the taste, and the ratings, of influential critics who tend to concentrate on young wines, a practice pioneered by the influential American critic Robert PARKER. There is also a global trend towards drinking wines younger, especially among American and Asian collectors.

Following its meteoric rise in popularity from about 2016 (and the ensuing price increases), burgundy has become the most valuable commodity sold at auction, with Domaine de la ROMANÉE-CONTI, Henri Jayer, Leroy, Rousseau, Leflaive, Comte Georges de Vogüé, Coche-Dury, Domaines Dujac, Roumier, and Jean-Frédéric Mugnier among the most sought-after names. Champagne too has become an auction-room collectible, notably KRUG, ROEDERER Cristal, Dom PÉRIGNON, and Salon. Vintage port is a saleroom regular, although demand for it has been relatively modest, with TAYLOR, FONSECA, GRAHAM, WARRE, DOW, and QUINTA DO NOVAL, the unofficial first growths, as it were, of a group of some 40 or more port houses. Rare MADEIRA makes an occasional appearance at auction.

Auction houses have played a key role in predicting and shaping the success of newer regions for collectible wines, such as Italy and Spain. Among Italy's blue chips, GAJA and certain wines from Giacomo Conterno, Bruno Giacosa, Rocche dei Manzoni, Luciano Sandrone, and Aldo Conterno represent solid collectibles along with the most famous SUPERTUSCANS. From Spain older vintages of VEGA SICILIA, Marqués de Murrieta, Marqués de Riscal, CVNE, and Viña Tondonia from Lopez de Heredia are increasingly seen at auction. The finest wines of the Rhône, notably Hermitage, Côte Rôtie, and Châteauneuf-du-Pape, may be sold at auction, but wines from Germany, Alsace, the Loire, and TOKAJ make only an occasional appearance.

The wines of the NEW WORLD, California and Australia in particular, are making an impact as their track record for ageing becomes more widely accepted and new wines appear on the secondary market. Demand for California wines is particularly strong in the US and is increasing elsewhere. While such older rarities as the 1941 Inglenook Cabernet can fetch very high prices, the focus today is on such CALIFORNIA CULT names as Screaming Eagle, Harlan, Sine Qua Non, Colgin, Araujo (now Eisele), Dominus, Opus One, Shafer, Spottswoode, and Heitz.

It was a wine from Australia, PENFOLDS Grange, that was arguably the first New World wine to be recognized internationally as the equivalent of a Bordeaux FIRST GROWTH. Langton's Classification of Australian Wine, first published in 1990, is a reliable guide to the best-performing Australian wines at auction, now mostly conducted online. In 2022 top Exceptional billing was given to 22 wines, including the saleroom classics Penfolds Grange and Henschke Hill of Grace, Bass Phillip Reserve Pinot Noir, Clonakilla Shiraz-Viognier, Grosset Polish Hill Riesling, Cullen Diana Madeline Cabernet-Merlot, Jim Barry The Armagh Shiraz, Leeuwin Estate Art Series Chardonnay, Wendouree Shiraz, and Wynns John Riddoch Cabernet Sauvignon. While Barossa, McLaren Vale, and Clare Valley Shiraz, as well as Coonawarra and Margaret River Cabernet Sauvignon, enjoy the lion's share of the secondary wine market, there is an increasing interest in Tasmanian Pinot Noir and wines from cooler areas around Melbourne. Penfolds is the leading collectible brand, with rare Grange (vintages 1951 to 1959) and experimental bottlings, including 1962 Bin 60A, achieving the highest prices in the Australian auction market.

Record prices

Red bordeaux has traditionally been the pacesetter for wine auction PRICES. The record of £105,000 for a single bottle of 1787 Ch Lafitte (*sic*) bought for the late Malcolm Forbes at Christie's on 5 December 1985 survived much longer than the wine itself, which turned to vinegar when put on show upright under a bright light (see STORING WINE). It was Lafite again, on this occasion the 1869 vintage, which smashed through the barrier for a standard 75-cl. bottle when three bottles were sold at Sotheby's Hong Kong in October 2010 for HK $1.8 million ($230,000) each. In November 2010, a rare imperial (six-litre bottle) of Ch Cheval Blanc 1947 was sold for £192,000 at Christie's, Geneva, setting a world record for a single bottle, albeit an outsize one.

Since then, burgundy has overtaken bordeaux for record prices. The dizzying rise of Domaine de la Romanée-Conti in the early 21st century has seen records consistently broken by the wines of this exceptional Burgundy producer, while some sales records in recent years have had to be rescinded over allegations of COUNTERFEIT bottles. The most notable bona fide world record for a case of the GRAND CRU Romanée-Conti itself was the $783,619 paid at Sotheby's Hong Kong in November 2013 for 12 bottles of the 1978 vintage. Beyond Domaine de la Romanée-Conti, the world record for the most expensive case of burgundy was won by 12 bottles of Bouchard Père & Fils, La Romanée 1865, sold by Swiss auction house Baghera in April 2021 for $2,142,294.

Beyond bordeaux and burgundy, other rarities have achieved fabulous prices for varying reasons. Thus, individual bottles of the 1907 Heidsieck Champagne salvaged in 1998 from a ship torpedoed by a German submarine during the First World War made up to $275,000 at auctions around the world. The HK$992,000 paid for a special demijohn decanter of 1863 Niepoort port in an Acker Merrall & Condit sale in 2018 is the highest price ever paid for a bottle of FORTIFIED WINE. And in 2000 at Auction Napa Valley, the annual charity fundraiser, an imperial of 1992 Screaming Eagle Cabernet Sauvignon made $500,000 (£297,000).

How to buy and sell at auction

The public forum of the auction room and the intrinsically competitive aspect of bidding for lots often creates an atmosphere of tension and excitement in the saleroom in which it is easy for inexperienced participants to get carried away. The online-only format—which attempts to replicate the live auction environment—differs in that all lots are sold at exactly the same moment. The excitement of an online auction sale is greatest in the last 30 minutes before the auction closes. All the information required about a particular auction is published in the auction catalogue, including details of the lots, estimated prices, conditions of sale, and other general information on such matters as delivery charges, premiums, and other additions to the hammer price such as taxes and duties payable where applicable. Most auctioneers charge a buyer's premium at a house rate that is normally between 10 and 22.5% of the hammer price, as well as a seller's premium which can be negotiated with the auction house and varies according to the amount sold. The internet auction format has taken catalogues one step further, providing potential buyers with instant information regarding vintage conditions, regional information, and tasting notes.

The wines to be sold are in numbered lots. In addition to a number and an estimated price band from lowest to highest, the description of each lot identifies the wine by name, bottle size, and vintage where applicable. Increasing concern about COUNTERFEIT WINES has heightened awareness of the importance of PROVENANCE by both bidders and (most) auctioneers. Given the importance of the condition of the wine, especially older wines, and since wines are not generally available for inspection, the catalogue specifies exact FILL LEVEL, or ULLAGE levels ('mid shoulder' or 'bottom neck', for example, levels illustrated in the catalogue), the condition of the LABEL, whether the wine comes in its original wooden CASE (sometimes abbreviated to 'o.w. c.'), and will generally mention if a cellar is of exceptional pedigree or in previously undisturbed condition. Auction-house policy may vary on inspection and the condition of the wine to be sold. Some auctioneers offer pre-sale tastings of varying degrees of lavishness. Hong Kong has seen extravagant entertainment of potential bidders, usually including examples of the wines to be sold. New York sales often take place in smart restaurants with a meal laid on. Most London sales are arid, workmanlike affairs. Lots which are of particular interest may be supplemented by the auctioneer's tasting notes.

Bidders who are physically present in the saleroom during an auction may bid by raising a hand or by waving a numbered paddle to attract the auctioneer's attention; however, most bids today are conducted via telephone or digitally, through online auction house bidding platforms.

Advance commission bids form a substantial proportion of bids received, and more and more lots are being sold online. Commission, or absentee, bids are treated in exactly the same way as bids in the room. The successful bidders obtain their lot at one increment above the underbidder. In the event of two commission bids of the same amount, it is the one received first that takes precedence.

Unless otherwise stated, bidding is per dozen bottles.

See COOPERAGE for details of French OAK auctions. A.H.L.R., C.A. & E.L.

www.winemarketjournal.com

Aude, IGP encompassing the area between the Côtes CATALANES to the south and the Hérault to the north, the Mediterranean to the east and the more CONTINENTAL CLIMATE of the Malepère massif in the west. A vast, diverse IGP, it is often employed for wines that fall outside the AOC rules of CABARDÈS, CORBIÈRES, Corbières-Boutenac, FITOU, LA CLAPE, LIMOUX, MALEPÈRE, or MINERVOIS.

Aurore, otherwise known as Seibel 5279, a complex FRENCH HYBRID once widely planted in North America and still found occasionally in colder states as well as in Canada. Adaptable and productive, it ripens early but is prone to ROT, and its floral-scented wines are of no great distinction.

Ausbruch, German-language equivalent of the Hungarian ASZÚ, traditionally designating sweet wines made from BOTRYTIZED grapes. Historically best-known among wines so designated is RUSTER AUSBRUCH.

Auslese, a PRÄDIKAT that means literally 'selected harvest' but is officially defined by grape sugar at harvest. In Germany, specific minimum MUST WEIGHTS are laid down for each combination of vine variety and region, ranging from 83 to 100 °OECHSLE. In Austria, the minimum across the board is 21 °KMW (approximately 105 °Oechsle). By German wine law, since 1994 vintage grapes for Auslese should have been picked at least one week after a preliminary picking of less ripe grapes. In practice, an Auslese may well have been picked early in the harvest. At their finest, German wines of Auslese prädikat are long-lived, sweet, often BOTRYTIZED wines, generally from Riesling, and the finest BOTRYTIS frequently occurs early on. In Germany, dry wines are sometimes designated as 'Auslese trocken' (dry Auslese), but with decreasing frequency. Many winegrowers long preferred to use the designation 'Spätlese trocken' even for wine based on must weights far exceeding the minimum for Auslese; and the trend (now official policy within the VDP growers' association) is to dispense entirely with designations of Prädikat for dry wines. In Austria, any wine that is not legally trocken and reflects the relevant minimum must weight is liable to be labelled Auslese. D.S.

Ausone, Château, minuscule but exceptionally fine estate on the edge of the town of ST-ÉMILION. It was named in 1781 after the Roman poet Ausonius, who certainly had a vineyard in the Gironde but probably one facing the River GARONNE rather than in St-Émilion. Recorded in the 1868 Cocks et Féret's *Bordeaux et ses vins* (see LITERATURE OF WINE) as belonging to M. Cantenats, it then passed to a nephew, M. Lafargue, and then to his nephew, Edouard Dubois-Challon, who raised the reputation of the château to the leading position in St-Émilion up to the 1920s, when it was challenged by Ch CHEVAL-BLANC, the only other château to be ranked 'A' in the official CLASSIFICATION of St-Émilion in 1955. From 1939 to the mid 1970s, Ausone was not, with a few exceptional vintages, producing wines of the longevity of their 19th-century predecessors, although there was a marked improvement after the arrival of a new RÉGISSEUR, Pascal Delbeck, in 1976. Until the late 1990s, 50% was owned by Mme Dubois-Challon, widow of Edouard, and 50% by Alain Vauthier, who married Edouard's daughter Cécile, an unsatisfactory arrangement which ended with Vauthier taking control of, and completely renovating, the extraordinary cellars in limestone caves originally excavated to provide stone for building the town. The wine itself has also been dramatically modernized, and the vineyard recuperated.

The estate consists of a mere 7 ha/18 acres—55% Cabernet Franc, 40% Merlot with some Cabernet Sauvignon and Petit Verdot—on the dramatically steep slopes of the Côtes (see ST-ÉMILION) that run along the right bank of the DORDOGNE just below the town. Alain's daughter Pauline makes the wine.

Australia became the world's sixth biggest wine producer in 2005, producing 14.7 million hl/388 million gal of wine in 2004, but by 2013 production had fallen to 12.31 million hl/324 million gal. A significant increase in the demand for Australian wine in China following the China–Australia Free Trade Agreement in 2015 saw Australian wine production peak in 2021 at 15 million hl/396 million gal, making it the fifth largest producer in that year.

Approximately 60% of Australian wine is exported, and in 2022 the UK was the largest export market by value and volume, followed by the US. Notwithstanding, with 40% of Australian wine consumed domestically, the domestic market is highly lucrative.

Australia's vineyard area has remained steady in recent times with a total vineyard area of approximately 145,000 ha/358,300 acres in 2022. As Australia's wine regulatory system does not dictate that specific varieties must be produced in specific viticultural areas, a vast array of wine styles are on offer, from aromatic, dry white table wine through to matured and rich fortified wines. Some of its wines—the unwooded Semillons of the Hunter Valley, the fortified TOPAQUES AND MUSCATS of north-east Victoria—have no direct equivalent elsewhere, but overall the wines manage to be at once distinctively Australian yet fit easily into the world scene.

History

On 24 January two bunches of grapes were cut in the Governor's Garden from cuttings of vines brought three years before from the Cape of Good Hope. The year was 1791, the chronicler Watkin Tench, and the site of the garden is now occupied by the Hotel Inter-Continental in Sydney's Macquarie Street.

Between 1820 and 1840, commercial viticulture was progressively established in NEW SOUTH WALES, TASMANIA, WESTERN AUSTRALIA, VICTORIA, and finally SOUTH AUSTRALIA. It was based upon comprehensive collections of VITIS VINIFERA vines imported from Europe: there are no native vines in Australia, and neither CROSSES nor HYBRIDS have ever taken root. Italian immigrants (in Riverland and Riverina), Silesians (in the Barossa and Clare Valleys), Dalmatians

(in the Swan Valley of Western Australia), and Swiss (Yarra Valley and Geelong in Victoria) all played key roles in the establishment of Australian viticulture.

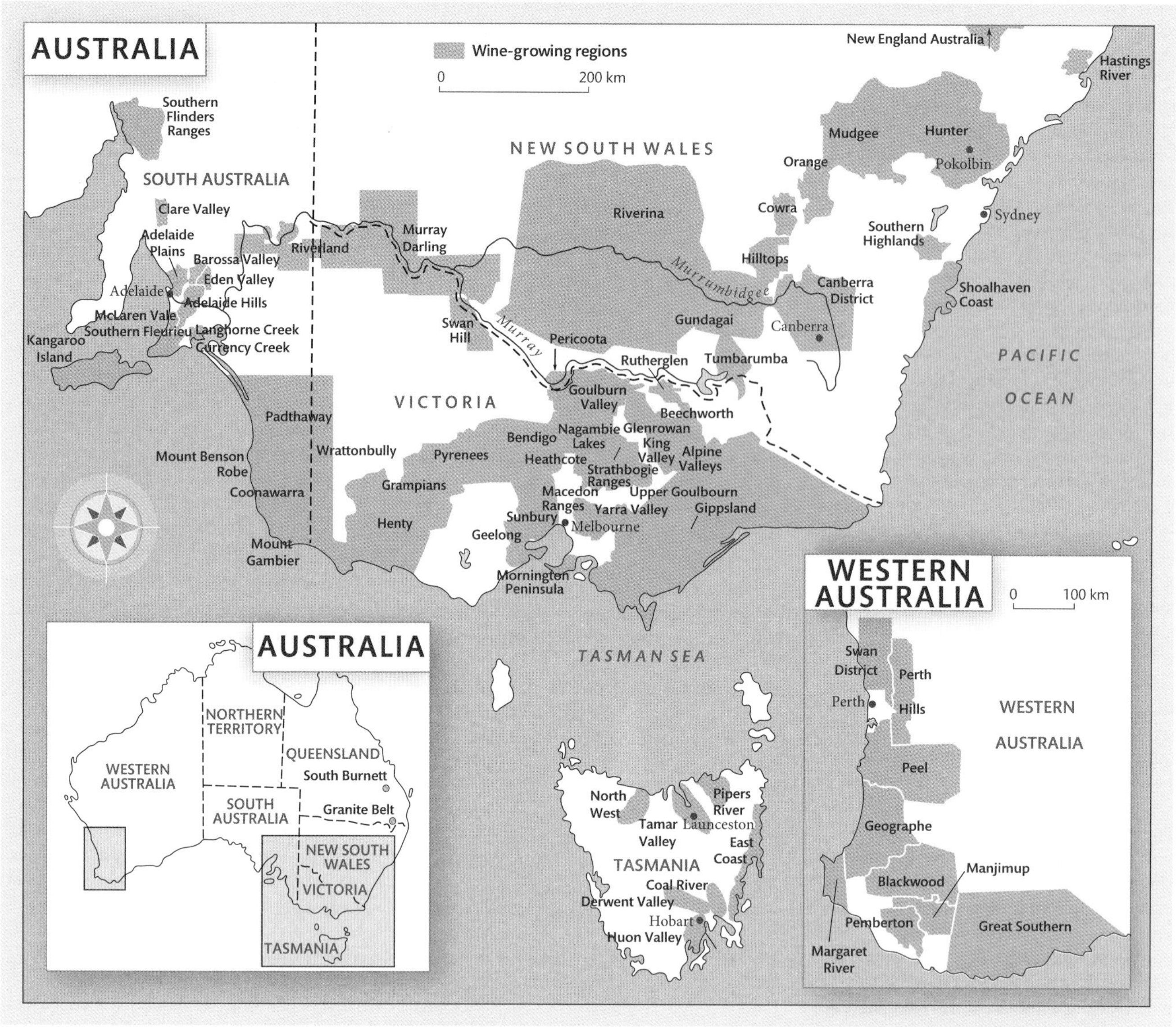

By 1870, South Australia, Victoria, and New South Wales all had substantial industries: that year they produced 8.7 million l/2.3 million gal of wine. Twenty years later Victoria alone was making twice that amount, more than the other two states combined. PHYLLOXERA, first discovered in Victoria (near Geelong) in 1877, and later in New South Wales and Queensland, in 1884 and 1910 respectively, decimated the Australia wine industry, but strict quarantine measures employed in 1874 ensured that South Australia remained phylloxera-free, as have Tasmania and Western Australia.

Australia's production in the early 1900s was dominated by FORTIFIED wine, with the United Kingdom being established as a lucrative export market. From 1927 to 1939, Australia exported more wine to the United Kingdom than did France, mainly because of the Imperial Preference system which created trading advantages within the British Commonwealth. Export controls ensuring the quality, saleability, and merchantability of Australian wine were established at the request of industry in 1930 to ensure the protection of the reputation of Australian wine in overseas markets. Today, wine remains one of the only products for which a bespoke export approval process applies in Australia, with the policy intent being to maintain high quality, authenticity, and integrity.

By 1930, South Australia was producing over 75% of Australia's wine, and the Barossa Valley had become the centre of production, processing not only its own grapes but much of those grown in RIVERLAND.

The industry of today started to take shape in the mid 1950s. Cold fermentation of white wine in STAINLESS STEEL was pioneered (see REFRIGERATION), and the decline in fortified wine production and consumption contrasted with spectacular growth in the consumption of red table wine (up to 1970) and thereafter white table wine. The 1970s witnessed the arrival of the wine cask, Cabernet Sauvignon, and Chardonnay; the phenomenon of the boutique winery; and the re-establishment of viticulture across the cool corner of south-eastern Australia, running east from Coonawarra and Padthaway right through Victoria.

Climate

With a land mass similar to that of the United States, winter snowfields larger than those of Switzerland, and viticulture in every state, it is hazardous to generalize about the Australian climate. However, there are two basic weather patterns, one affecting Western Australia, South Australia, Victoria, and Tasmania (the southern states), the other governing Queensland and New South Wales.

The southern states experience a winter–spring rainfall pattern, with a dry summer and early autumn. Ridges of high pressure, uninterrupted by mountain ranges, sweep across the southern half of the continent from Perth to Melbourne during the vines' growing season; daytime temperatures typically range between 25 and 35 °C/77–95 °F; however, heatwaves can send temperatures up to 48 °C/118 °F, particularly in the warm inland regions. Using the California heat degree system developed by Winkler (see CLIMATE CLASSIFICATION), the climate varies between region I and mid region III, with a preponderance in region II. Because of the lack of summer rainfall, IRRIGATION is considered as important for quality as for quantity.

The other, more northerly, weather system derives from the tropics. It provides a more even rainfall pattern, higher temperatures, and higher humidity. This system defines the subtropical climate for much of the Queensland wine industry and the coastal regions of New South Wales. The Hunter Valley is prone to receive rather too much of its annual rainfall during HARVEST, only to suffer the subsequent dual burden of winter and spring DROUGHT. Its redeeming feature is the humidity and afternoon cloud cover which reduces stress on the vines and mitigates the impact of its region IV heat load.

The Australian harvest is also heavily impacted by the climatic patterns in the Indian and Pacific Oceans, with El Niño conditions typically resulting in hot, dry growing conditions, and La Niña conditions typically providing plenty of rainfall and mild ripening conditions.

Geography

Vine-growing in Australia is concentrated in its south-eastern corner. Just over 2,500 wineries are spread through the states of South Australia, Victoria, New South Wales, Tasmania, and Western Australia and in the Australian Capital Territory. South Australia has the highest production, accounting for just over 50% of the total production, while New South Wales accounts for approximately 30% and Victoria about 17%. Approximately 75% of Australia's total production is in the warm inland regions of Riverland, Murray Darling-Swan Hill, and Riverina. Australia's 20 largest wine producers contribute 70% of overall production.

For more detail, see under the state or territory names, which are, in declining order of production volume: SOUTH AUSTRALIA, NEW SOUTH WALES, VICTORIA, WESTERN AUSTRALIA, TASMANIA, and QUEENSLAND.

Viticulture

The first two decades of the 21st century have seen greater diversity in grape varieties and winemaking practices and a significant adoption of innovative technologies to increase quality and efficiency. SUSTAINABLE VITICULTURE has become increasingly topical, and the Australian wine industry is significantly invested in research and development into best practice biodiversity, soil management, pest and disease management, and water efficiency. There is a move away from FUNGICIDES, PESTICIDES, and HERBICIDES towards more 'natural' grape-growing (see ORGANIC VITICULTURE and BIODYNAMIC VITICULTURE).

New vineyards in premium areas, particularly those in cooler regions, are being established with VINE DENSITIES two or three times greater than traditionally used and with specifically adapted TRELLIS SYSTEMS. The aim is better-quality grapes, at yields which may in fact be greater than those of traditional plantings.

PHYLLOXERA has never entered the states of South Australia, Western Australia, and Tasmania, nor most of New South Wales (including the Hunter Valley), and it is not present in the BULK WINE-producing Riverland. Small parts of Victoria remain affected, but very strict QUARANTINE legislation, actively enforced and respected by viticulturists, prevented any spread from infested areas during the second half of the 20th century, with only one small exception.

In areas where phylloxera is present, it is common for vineyards to be planted on phylloxera-resistant ROOTSTOCKS, but in areas free from the pest most vineyards continue to be planted on their own roots. For example, in South Australia, 76% of vineyards are UNGRAFTED. However, there is a shift towards rootstocks for new plantings, with vine-growers citing drought resistance, salt tolerance, water efficiency, yield, and consistency of fruit set as significant factors for consideration. If a vine-grower wants to change a vine variety, TOP GRAFTING is commonly practised.

Winemaking

The typical medium-sized modern Australian winery is comprehensively equipped with modern winemaking equipment, and most wineries are equipped with laboratories capable of measuring basic analytes, including SULFUR DIOXIDE, sugar, MALIC ACID, PH, TITRATABLE ACIDITY, alcohol, and colour. Most wineries are fitted with powerful REFRIGERATION systems for cooling fermentation in insulated stainless-steel fermenters, as well as a must chiller to cool white grapes immediately after they have been crushed (unless they were machine-harvested at night). The CRUSHER, PRESS, and FILTRATION equipment is usually of French, German, or Italian design and fabrication; and it is highly probable that there will be several large ROTOFERMENTERS supplementing the normal array of FERMENTATION VESSELS, including the Australian-designed Potter fermenters.

Because grapes grown in the warmer regions reach chemical RIPENESS and PHYSIOLOGICAL RIPENESS with relatively low levels of acidity, it is usual for TARTARIC ACID to be added before or during the primary fermentation. In cooler areas, makers of white wines in particular endeavour to harvest the grapes with sufficient natural acidity to preclude, or at least minimize, acid additions. CHAPTALIZATION is prohibited; however, AMELIORATION of high sugar juice and must prior to fermentation is permitted provided the juice or must does not fall below 13.5 °Baumé.

Unlike countries in the EU, Australia does not regulate oenological practices but rather approves ADDITIVES and PROCESSING AIDS for wine and sets maximum limits on the presence of substances such as sulfur dioxide and VOLATILE ACIDITY. Permissions apply to the production of all Australian wine.

The Australian wine industry was built on FORTIFIED WINES, but the most celebrated survivors of this category are the TOPAQUES AND MUSCATS of Rutherglen and Glenrowan.

The twin problems of CORK TAINT and RANDOM OXIDATION have led to the mass migration of winemakers from cork to SCREWCAP. By 2014, 85–90% of bottled wine was sealed with a screwcap.

Vine varieties

In 2022, production of red wine made up 55% of overall production; however, there were strong indications leading into 2023 that the balance is likely to shift towards white wine in future years, with the white grape crush accounting for 45% in 2022.

Approximately 95% of production is attributed to the top ten red and white grape varieties. The following are the country's most widely planted red and white varieties, listed in descending order of volume of wine produced.

Shiraz is Australia's most planted wine-grape variety and is grown in most Australian wine regions. The variety is identical to the SYRAH of France and has a long Australian history. During the 1980s, the familiarity of Shiraz led to its being treated with a thoroughly undeserved degree of contempt. However, the old DRY-FARMED

plantings of the Barossa Valley (producing voluptuously rich, potent wines) and the traditional Hunter Valley wines (which become silky with age) initiated a surge of popularity in both domestic and export markets. In 2022, there were 43,192 ha/106,730 acres of Shiraz, ranking Australia second behind France (60,000 ha) and well ahead of third-placed Spain (20,000 ha). Australia is home to the world's oldest continuously productive Shiraz vines, with some of the oldest plantings believed to date back to 1843.

Cabernet Sauvignon accounts for around 15% of the national CRUSH. Its thick skins and relatively loosely formed bunches provide a natural defence against DOWNY MILDEW and BOTRYTIS, which threaten many regions during the growing season. It is grown in most regions in Australia, though most of the best examples come from the cooler areas of GREAT SOUTHERN, South Australia's LIMESTONE COAST ZONE, MARGARET RIVER, and parts of central and southern VICTORIA. It is commonly blended with Shiraz and/or Merlot.

Merlot has been in Australia since the early 1800s, brought into Australia by John McArthur in 1817 and by James BUSBY in the 1830s; it became especially popular in the 1990s. It now extends some 8,115 ha/20,053 acres, with Langhorne Creek and Coonawarra in South Australia being the largest growing areas outside the warm inland 'river' regions. Merlot is popular for blending, particularly with Cabernet Sauvignon.

Pinot Noir thrives in Australia's cooler viticultural regions, such as Tasmania, Yarra Valley, and the Adelaide Hills. It is just as likely to end up in a classic TRADITIONAL METHOD sparkling wine as in a red table wine.

Petit Verdot first hit the statistical radar in 1999, when 110 ha/272 acres were bearing (and well over twice that were still to come into bearing). It excels in regions with long days and lots of sun, which describes many Australian wine regions. Over two-thirds of all Petit Verdot in Australia is grown in the South Australian RIVERLAND.

Chardonnay is Australia's most widely planted white variety, and second only to Shiraz overall. Australia has approximately 10% of the world's Chardonnay plantings and is the third largest grower of the variety after France and the US. It comes in many expressions—oaked or not, with or without partial or full MALOLACTIC CONVERSION.

Sauvignon Blanc accounts for one in every eight bottles of wine purchased on the Australian domestic off-trade retail market. The variety more than doubled in area from 2001 to 2010, becoming the second largest white wine grape variety after Chardonnay in 2014. It is grown across Australia, from the warmest 'river' regions to the cool climates of the Adelaide Hills and Tasmania, as well as in the maritime climate of Margaret River where it is often found in blends with Semillon.

Pinot Gris/Pinot Grigio is the third largest white variety, with 4,930 ha/12,182 acres in 2022 planted primarily in the warm inland regions and the King Valley.

Semillon (rarely written Sémillon in the New World) is predominantly grown in the RIVERINA. But the best Semillons are 100% VARIETAL, including unoaked versions from the HUNTER VALLEY with an alcohol level of 10.5 to 11%, and those fermented in French oak, with or without a percentage of Sauvignon Blanc, from the Adelaide Hills and Margaret River at more conventional alcohol levels.

Muscat Gordo Blanco (or Muscat of Alexandria, as it is more widely known outside of Australia) is the fifth largest white variety and eighth largest overall. It is almost exclusively grown in the warm inland regions: the Riverland, Riverina, Murray Darling, and Swan Hill. It provides a more positively flavoured wine for cheap 'cask' blends than does SULTANA, and it often goes into lightly sparkling, low-alcohol, slightly sweet wines labelled MOSCATO, which in Australia can be made from any of the Muscat-flavoured varieties.

Another 100 or so varieties are grown, including Grenache and Mourvèdre (often called Mataro), which together with Shiraz often make up the red blends commonly referred to as GSM. In white wines, Riesling deserves special mention: although it has fallen drastically from its peak crush of 46,481 tonnes in 1985, top-quality examples can be had from GREAT SOUTHERN and the Clare (see CROUCHEN) and EDEN VALLEYS. Marsanne has been grown at Tahbilk in the GOULBURN VALLEY for well over 100 years, having been taken there from Yeringberg in the YARRA VALLEY (in turn having come from Switzerland). Much smaller plantings of Roussanne are mainly used to blend with Marsanne. Viognier is exciting a great deal of interest, for dry white wines but especially for the magic it works when CO-FERMENTED with Shiraz. And Verdelho, first imported in 1825 from Madeira by the Australian Agriculture Company, thrives in warm climates and yields well but not prodigiously, producing a popular, easy wine for relatively early drinking.

Increasingly, winemakers are exploring alternative varieties that are suited to dry climatic conditions and resist disease, hence decreasing water and chemical usage. Some varieties, such as ASSYRTIKO and SAPERAVI, are in the infantile stages of exploration by Australian winemakers, while others such as TEMPRANILLO and SANGIOVESE are gaining rapidly in popularity and are expected to become more mainstream in future years, particularly given Australian wine consumers' increasing propensity to drink lighter, more savoury wines and to experiment with different varieties.

Labelling laws

Wine labelling is strictly regulated in Australia in accordance with the Wine Australia Act 2013. Wine Australia maintains a register of GEOGRAPHICAL INDICATIONS (GIs) and other terms afforded protection under the Act such as APERA, the name for what was once called Sherry.

Within the GI scheme, each state is divided into zones: New South Wales and South Australia each have eight, Victoria six, and Western Australia five. There was—and is—no requirement of geographic or climatic particularity, no rules for the drawing of the zone boundaries. Within the zones are regions, which are sometimes further broken down into subregions, each of which must be substantially discrete and have substantial homogeneity in grape-growing attributes in regard to its size. This includes the uniformity of natural characteristics such as rainfall, soil type, geology, and other viticultural characteristics. In total, the country has 114 GIs in 2022.

EU geographical indications and traditional expressions are protected in Australia by virtue of a bilateral agreement between the EU and Australia on trade in wine. That agreement was replicated following the departure of the UK from the EU in the Agreement on Trade in Wine between the Government of Australia and the Government of the United Kingdom of Great Britain and Northern Ireland.

Australia's blending rules require that where a single vintage, variety, or geographical claim is made with respect to a wine, at least 85% of the blend must be comprised of such vintage, variety, or geographical indication. Blending wines of differing vintages, varieties, or origins is allowed. If more than one variety or region are specified, then they are listed in descending order. Thus Cabernet–Shiraz means the wine has more Cabernet Sauvignon grapes than Shiraz; Shiraz–Cabernet the reverse. Wines can claim no more than three GIs.

In accordance with Australia's Label Integrity Program, all parties in the supply chain must keep records verifying vintage, variety, and geographical indication claims. Failure to keep records, make records, or verify label claims with records amounts to an offence that carries a maximum penalty of two years' imprisonment.

Wine trade organization

The Australian wine sector is supported by Wine Australia, a statutory body established by legislation enacted by the federal government to control the export of Australian wine, ensure the truthfulness of Australian wine labels, promote the consumption and sale of Australian wine both domestically and overseas, and invest in grape and wine research and development. Research into improvements in grape and wine quality is led by the Australian Wine Research Institute (see AWRI) and CSIRO. Further, the sector is supported by universities such as CHARLES STURT UNIVERSITY in Wagga Wagga and the University of ADELAIDE where many of the country's most famous winemakers were educated.

Wine is traded freely between Australian states and territories. There are no commercial restrictions on importers, winemakers, distributors, and retailers engaging in trade and commerce directly, and the state and regional wine bodies do not play a regulatory role in the production or sale of wine. The state and territory health authorities are responsible for ensuring compliance with the Australia New Zealand Food Standards Code which sets out the rules pertaining to allergen statements, alcohol, and standard drinks labelling, as well as compositional requirements pertaining to the use of additives and processing aids.

Australia is a member of the OIV and the WORLD WINE TRADE GROUP, both of which provide useful forums for progressing mutual acceptance of oenological processes and harmonization of regulatory practices with a view to facilitating the international wine trade.

One of the particular freedoms of Australia is the BYO restaurant, BYO standing for Bring Your Own. Many restaurants across Australia generously encourage patrons to bring their own wine, including those holding liquor permits, who may charge a CORKAGE fee to offset the reduction in profit margin.

J.H., H.H. & R.J.T.

Allen, M., *The Future Makers* (2010).
Beeston, J., *A Concise History of Australian Wine* (3rd edn, 2001).
Halliday, J., *Australia Wine Companion* (annually).
Major, M. (ed.), *The Australian and New Zealand Wine Industry Directory* (annually).
www.wineaustralia.com
www.wineaustralia.net.au
www.winecompanion.com.au

Australian influence on wine production, marketing, and even distribution is difficult to overestimate. Its VITICULTURISTS (notably the viticulture editor of this *Companion*) pioneered sophisticated CANOPY MANAGEMENT techniques and all sorts of tricks such as niceties of irrigation (see PARTIAL ROOTZONE DRYING) and high-tech SOIL MAPPING. Australia's winemakers travelled the world—especially the northern hemisphere where the HARVEST conveniently takes place during the southern hemisphere lull—quietly infiltrating all manner of wineries with Australian technology, obsession with HYGIENE, and record water usage (see FLYING WINEMAKERS). Graduates of oenology and viticulture courses at Australian universities such as ADELAIDE and CHARLES STURT UNIVERSITY are now dispersed around the world, and the AWRI (Australian Wine Research Institute) is recognized as one of the most important, and practical, forces in ACADEME. It is significant that the world's largest and canniest wine company, E. & J. GALLO of California, deliberately recruited an Australian to lead its wine research department into the new millennium. Australia overtook France to be most important exporter of wine to the UK, one of the world's most significant wine importers, at the beginning of the century; it went on to perform the same trick in the US, but Australian wine was this popular only temporarily with Americans. The spectacular success of YELLOW TAIL tarnished its image so that it came to be dismissively associated with 'critter brands'. Such was Australia's late 20th century success at developing and selling BRANDS to suit the modern international marketplace that for many years it was seen as a model even by such experienced wine exporters as the French. Alliances between Australian companies and global players in the drinks trade have been a notable feature of the GLOBALIZATION of the wine trade (see AUSTRALIA, Wine trade organization).

Australian Wine Research Institute. See AWRI.

Austria produces an average of 2.4 million hl/63 million gal wine a year but is more famous for the quality rather than the quantity of its wines, especially dry and sweet whites, and also reds from the dark-skinned grapes grown on more than one-third of Austria's vineyard area. Average yields are relatively low, around 50 hl/ha (3 tons/acre).

History

Austria is among many places into which CELTIC tribes are thought to have introduced grape-growing, but historical records begin with the ROMANS. That Austria suffered under DOMITIAN's notorious 92 CE edict prohibiting viticultural expansion can only be assumed. But this much is documented: Emperor Probus, in rescinding that edict two centuries later, expressly encouraged new plantings both in Gaul and in Pannonia—the Great Plain that incorporates today's eastern Austria. From his 5th-century base in the Roman garrison town of Mautern, St Severin is said to have sought solitude amid WACHAU vineyards. Control of the subsequently burgeoning vineyards west of Vienna passed largely to a collection of Bavarian ecclesiastical institutions in the wake of Charlemagne's and his son's victories over Avars and Slavs in the late 8th and early 9th century. That ecclesiastical legacy lives on in more than just physical structures that include the Wachau's towering stone terraces of Mediterranean inspiration, begun in the 11th century. Stift Göttweig, a huge winegrowing MONASTERY that dominates the landscape south of Krems, was founded by a bishop of Bavarian Passau in 1083; yet-larger KLOSTERNEUBURG dates from soon afterward; the Freigut Thalern and Schloss Gobelsburg wineries originated with early 12th century Cistercian monasteries; and the Salomon family of Krems-Stein's Undhof have for two centuries been renewing a land-for-wine rental contract with a charitable institution in Passau that first acquired those vineyards around 1200.

An Austrian tradition of small vineyard-holders dispensing their wine—institutionalized eventually as HEURIGER—is often said to have Carolingian origins; and by the Middle Ages, Vienna was notorious for copious production and consumption of wine, for which the Romans named it Vindobona. The evolution of viticulture in what was then westernmost Hungary led to several Neusiedlersee vineyard sites, notably in Jois and RUST, coming under direct royal control, and by the mid 16th century barrels of wine were being branded for those places of origin. Successive waves of Ottoman invasions in the 17th century did not halt the expansion of vineyards. Moreover, many of the 'new settlers' for which the Neusiedlersee is named—waves of Croatians and southern Germans who arrived to repopulate its shores—became winegrowers.

The so-called Biedermeier era of Austrian stability that followed Napoleon saw the emergence not only of a prosperous, wine-drinking middle class but also—thanks especially to efforts by Archduke Johann (1782–1859) in Styria and a series of pioneering agronomists—of vine science and vine nurseries, so that by the mid 19th century the Hapsburg empire had become internationally renowned as a source for viticultural expertise and BUDWOOD. In 1860 a national school of viticulture and winemaking was established at Klosterneuburg. This was also a period of international success for Austrian wine, curtailed by PHYLLOXERA, identified relatively early by Klosterneuburg scientists. Meticulous wine historian Franz Schams identified many of the villages and vineyards that are still considered Austria's best as early as the 1830s, even if they often grew vine varieties different from those found there today. Such was still the case as recently as the mid 20th century, when plantings of GEMISCHTER SATZ (field blends) remained widespread, Silvaner still flourished (under the name 'Österreicher'), while GRÜNER VELTLINER

A

dominated only in selected sectors and Riesling remained a rarity.

The 20th century's world wars visited disaster on Austria, each with different viticultural consequences. Following the collapse of the Austro-Hungarian empire in the wake of the First World War, vast wine regions were shed, including those of Moravia in what is now CZECHIA, FRIULI, CROATIA's Dalmatian Coast, SLOVENIA, SLOVAKIA, and much of today's ROMANIA. The Second World War brought significant physical devastation to Austrian vineyards and the widespread plundering of wine cellars by Soviet occupying troops. In rebuilding Austria's vineyards in the 1950s and 1960s, considerable attention was devoted to efficiency and, where possible, MECHANIZATION (see LENZ MOSER).

After four hard decades of vineyard revival, characterized by the remarkable ascendance of GRÜNER VELTLINER as Austria's national grape, an explosion of ZWEIGELT plantings, and the international re-emergence of the Thermenregion and of the Neusiedlersee's sweet-wine culture, Austria suffered yet another viticultural calamity, this time of its own making. In 1985, dessert wines from the Burgenland region were found to have been laced with diethylene glycol, added by a handful of unscrupulous winegrowers or merchants to imitate the unctuous characteristics imparted by BOTRYTIS. While nobody is known to have been poisoned, the Austrian wine market was devastated. Vinous integrity demanded a completely fresh start. Implementation of stringent quality standards, combined with consumer consciousness of estate bottling and wine purity, led to a rebuilding of Austrian wine culture in ways nobody could have foreseen before the scandal. Through VINEA WACHAU, the Wachau's growers established quality benchmarks that went beyond Austria's new wine laws and set the stage for international prestige. SÜDSTEIERMARK emerged from a century of obscurity to national stardom. And a young Viennese pharmacist named Alois Kracher returned home to transform his family's estate into a beacon of quality, rescuing the reputation of BURGENLAND, the very region from which had emerged the wines that poisoned an industry. By the late 1990s, Austrian wine was enjoying unprecedented export success and prestige that has continued to this day.

Geography, geology, and climate

Austria's vineyards are concentrated in four states: NIEDERÖSTERREICH, WIEN, BURGENLAND, and STEIERMARK (Styria). Along a roughly 100-km/62-mile, almost continuously planted stretch of the Danube's left and occasionally right bank upstream of Vienna and north all the way to the Czech frontier lie those regions of Niederösterreich best known for Grüner Veltliner and Riesling—WACHAU, KAMPTAL, KREMSTAL, TRAISENTAL, WAGRAM, and WEINVIERTEL—which serves as a useful climatic touchstone. Niederösterreich is where Riesling feels at home: cool enough, but dry—like the Vosges rain shadow of ALSACE. Another feature common to most of this sector is wide, regular DIURNAL TEMPERATURE RANGE. Prominent here are soils originating in LOESS and in degraded crystalline rocks to which locals refer as URGESTEIN.

Wien—urban and suburban Vienna—serves as a sort of fulcrum of Austrian winegrowing. Its best-known vineyards, on the city's northwestern edge, are dominated by Grüner Veltliner and GEMISCHTER SATZ but were historically renowned for Riesling. Two smaller concentrations of vines on Vienna's southern fringe feature red grapes as well as white and point towards the conditions that dominate in the adjacent Niederösterreich regions of THERMENREGION and CARNUNTUM, as well as in the four growing regions of Burgenland that hug Austria's border with Hungary. Here, warm air from Hungary's Pannonian Plain dominates the grape-growing season, although winters are often bitterly cold, and precipitation is even lighter than in the wine regions to the west. Most of Austria's red-wine vines (about one-third of the national total) are grown here, and Grüner Veltliner is less important than many other white grapes.

Steiermark (Styria), in Austria's south-eastern reaches, comprises three growing regions, the most important of which is SÜDSTEIERMARK, whose vineyards saturate a sector south of Graz and along a 40-km/25-mile stretch of the Slovenian frontier. Cool and well-watered, the steep hillsides here can support Riesling, but late 20th century choices have led to a dominance of Sauvignon Blanc, Chardonnay, Pinot Blanc (WEISSBURGUNDER), WELSCHRIESLING, and MUSKATELLER.

Vine varieties

Given the huge number of grape varieties grown in Austria and how many are INDIGENOUS or at least little-known elsewhere, an overview is in order (reflecting plantings as of 2021). Among whites, GRÜNER VELTLINER—with roughly a one-third share of plantings nationwide—has become known as Austria's national grape, even though its role in Burgenland is only modest and in Steiermark practically non-existent. (Its thirstiness is also a concern for the future.) Austrian wines from this grape—virtually always dry—capture an otherwise unprecedented range of flavours, including those of lentils, green beans, mange-tout, cress, rhubarb, beetroot, roasted red peppers, tobacco, white and black pepper, citrus zest, iris, and nutmeg. A tactile 'bite' or pleasantly sizzling peppery astringency—referred to by Austrians as *Pfefferl*—is often treated as a varietal signature. Arguably also without precedent is this grape's ability to achieve satisfying ripeness and completeness at levels of POTENTIAL ALCOHOL ranging from as little as 10.5% to as much as 15%. Grüner Veltliner wines can reflect vineyard identity as well as mature impressively in bottle for decades. There can be enormous variation in size and colour of berry; size and shape of cluster; vine VIGOUR; and wine flavour. The painstaking MASS SELECTION undertaken by the Wachau's Franz Pichler in the mid 20th century did much to make possible today's quality, and interest in re-propagating old-vine selections has since increased.

RIESLING by no means takes a back seat to Grüner Veltliner in quality, although it occupies less than 5% of Austria's vineyards. As they do elsewhere, the wines vary considerably in strength and demonstrate an uncanny ability to reflect TERROIR. Most Austrian examples are dry and can tolerate alcohols over 13% rather better than their dry German counterparts, but, after a brief flirtation with strengths of 14% or more, most growers actively seek, through viticultural adaptation and slightly earlier harvest, to keep levels below 13.5%. Austrian Riesling is almost uniformly lower in acidity and tends towards less effusive aromas than its German counterparts, but at its best it offers a crescendo of flavours on the finish. It tends to be leaner in texture than Alsace Riesling and to age a little faster than the best examples of Germany and Alsace or than Austria's best Grüner Veltliner.

WELSCHRIESLING, a traditional mainstay of Austrian viticulture but long in decline, is planted on half again as much land as true Riesling. It is prized commercially for light, bracing examples from Styria and considered a key player in Burgenland's botrytis belt. Some growers, especially in Südsteiermark and Südburgenland, render dry examples with considerable complexity, heralding an increase in respect for this drought-tolerant, acid-retentive variety. Pinot Blanc—here generally called WEISSBURGUNDER—is arguably one of Austria's hidden strengths, capable of subtle and seductive complexity while uniting natural creaminess with refreshing animation. It represents a bit more than 4% of Austrian vineyard, as does Chardonnay. Sauvignon Blanc is treated as a signature grape of Steiermark and is gaining in popularity elsewhere, gradually approaching 4% of total vine surface.

Gelber Muskateller—a variant of MUSCAT BLANC À PETIT GRAINS—has a long tradition throughout Austria and accounts for 3% of plantings. Light, bracing wines in Südsteiermark represent its instance of greatest commercial success. Roter TRAMINER (here typically labelled simply Traminer, as can be both its Gewürz-variant and a rare yellow Austrian strain) and Pinot Gris (here usually called GRAUBURGUNDER) are also grapes of long standing,

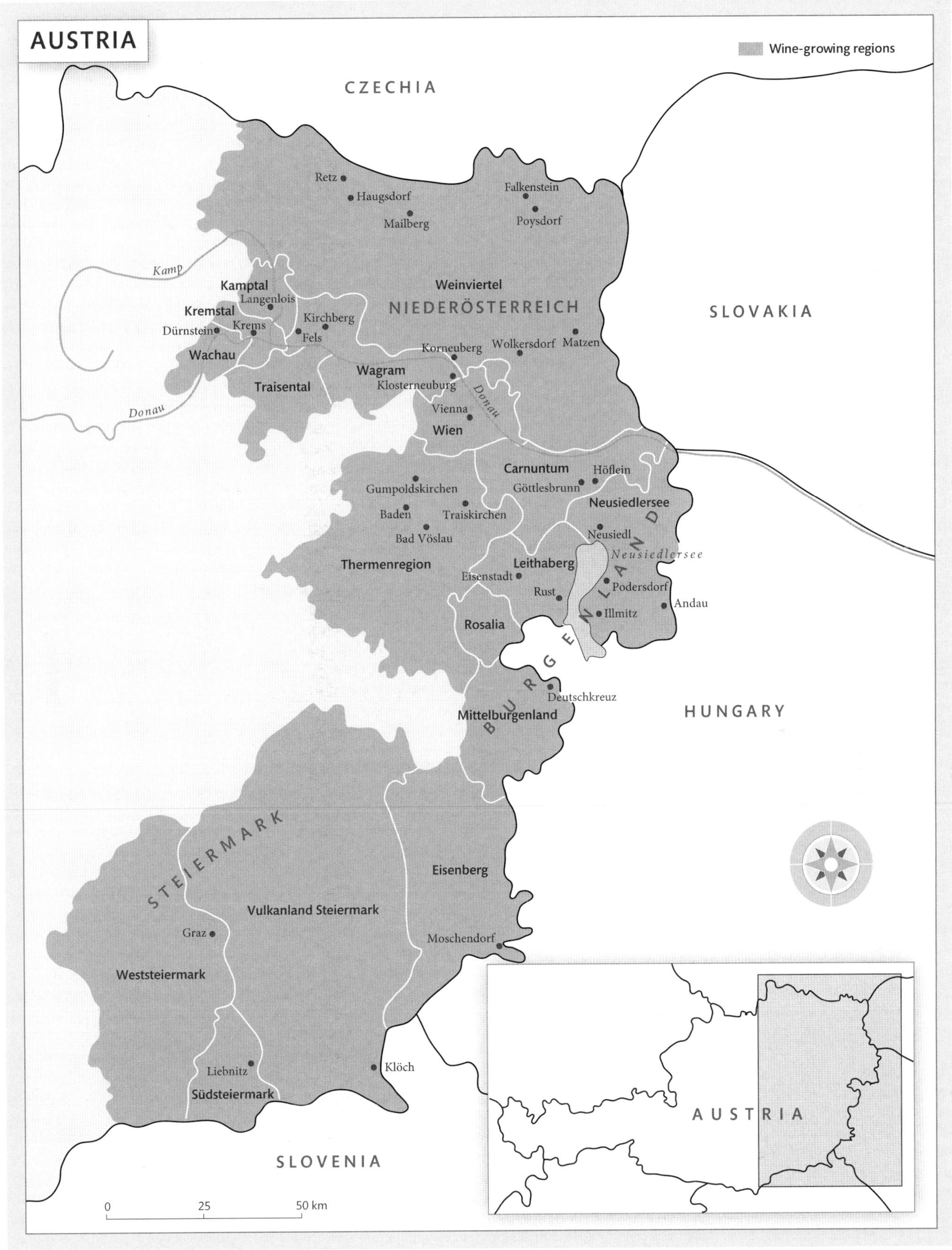
AUSTRIA
Wine-growing regions
CZECHIA
SLOVAKIA
HUNGARY
SLOVENIA
Retz
Haugsdorf
Mailberg
Falkenstein
Poysdorf
Kamp
Kamptal
Langenlois
Kremstal
Krems
Dürnstein
Kirchberg
Fels
Wachau
Weinviertel
NIEDERÖSTERREICH
Wolkersdorf
Matzen
Korneuberg
Wagram
Klosterneuburg
Traisental
Donau
Vienna
Wien
Carnuntum
Höflein
Göttlesbrunn
Gumpoldskirchen
Baden
Traiskirchen
Bad Vöslau
Neusiedlersee
Neusiedl
Thermenregion
Leithaberg
Eisenstadt
Rust
Podersdorf
Illmitz
Andau
Rosalia
BURGENLAND
Deutschkreuz
Mittelburgenland
STEIERMARK
Eisenberg
Vulkanland Steiermark
Graz
Moschendorf
Weststeiermark
Liebnitz
Südsteiermark
Klöch
0
25
50 km
AUSTRIA

albeit each represents well less than 1% of Austrian vine surface. ROTER VELTLINER and NEUBURGER are two highly distinctive indigenous varieties whose wines are capable of remarkable longevity. ROTGIPFLER and ZIERFANDLER are distinctive indigenous varieties associated with the Thermenregion. BOUVIER and SCHEUREBE (here also called Sämling 88) deserve mention for their role in sweet wines from the Neusiedlersee; and FURMINT for its recent revival, particularly in RUST.

Among red wine grapes, ZWEIGELT dominates Austria with a roughly 14% share of the national vineyard and (unlike Grüner Veltliner) has a significant presence in every wine region. Best known for the forward fruitiness of its solo expressions, it also figures in some more ambitious wines, including when blended with other Austrian or Bordeaux varieties. BLAUFRÄNKISCH, while occupying only around 6% of Austrian vineyards (largely in Burgenland), is considered the country's most serious red wine grape. Black fruits, tobacco, resinous herbs, and black pepper are among the characteristics associated with this comparatively high-acid variety, which demonstrates striking ability to reflect its soils and sites of origin. Selections whose grapes are smaller-berried and thicker-skinned than the late 20th century norm are being actively sought and re-propagated, contributing to significant 21st-century improvement.

ST-LAURENT may or may not be an Austrian original, but it is today little known elsewhere, and—given the fragility and finicky temperament it seems to have inherited from Pinot Noir—its dwindling under 1.5% share of acreage signifies an insecure future. At their best, wines from St-Laurent display rich fruit allied to even plusher texture than Pinot Noir (Blauburgunder) which represented just 1.3% of Austria's vine surface. The Bordeaux red varieties are also grown to a limited extent, and, though uncommon, Syrah has some serious proponents in Burgenland and neighbouring Carnuntum. Two once-widespread red-wine varieties, Blauer PORTUGIESER and BLAUBURGER, have dwindled to just over 1% of Austrian vine acreage. Like MÜLLER-THURGAU among white grapes, with its rapidly diminishing share of Austrian acreage, these varieties are largely bereft of grower-champions, though a few strong cases are being made for Portugieser.

Wine labelling

Austria shares much of its wine vocabulary with GERMANY, but a term can vary significantly in both the extent to and meaning with which it is employed in each country. Austrian wine law enshrines the term 'Kabinett' for unchaptalized, dry QUALITÄTSWEIN (Austria's equivalent of PDO) of up to 13% alcohol and from grapes of at least 17 °KMW (84 °OECHSLE). But in practice the term is seldom employed. The term 'Spätlese' imposes a higher minimum MUST weight and may be applied to wine with perceptible RESIDUAL SUGAR. But in practice that term, too, is increasingly absent from Austrian wine labels save in Rust and the Neusiedlersee. With the advent of DAC legislation, the term 'Reserve' has effectively replaced Spätlese in those regions where that term was used for dry wines, while 'Klassik' is often used to refer to wines formerly labelled 'Kabinett'. The official Austrian PRÄDIKATS of Auslese, Beerenauslese, and Trockenbeerenauslese apply to wines of incrementally higher minimum must weights and with noticeable residual sugar. They most often apply in those sectors of Burgenland that specialize in BOTRYTIZED sweet wine, which is also where the more specialized categories of Strohwein (STRAW WINE), EISWEIN, and AUSBRUCH are almost exclusively used. It can be safely assumed that an Austrian wine tastes dry unless it is labelled prominently with one of these so-called Prädikats. The word 'trocken' (signifying less than 9 g/l residual sugar) is therefore seldom displayed with any prominence on Austrian labels.

All Austrian wines meeting the standards set for Qualitätswein wear the *Banderole*, a neck band or capsule top featuring the red and white stripes of the national flag, which serves not only as a guarantee that the wine has met federal production limits and quality controls, including any implied by the terms on its label, but also acts (by means of a long string of tiny digits) to track the wine. Qualitätswein from those regions to which a DAC appellation applies will either be labelled for that DAC or, if they are inapplicable or not submitted for DAC status, be labelled for their state of origin: Niederösterreich, Wien, Burgenland, or Steiermark. The second decade of the 21st century witnessed finalizing of official vineyard names and boundaries as well as aggressive purging from wine labels of allegedly misleading geographical and topographical allusions or fantasy names that might be misconstrued as referencing places. Additionally, beginning in 2016, each authorized vineyard name utilized on a label must be preceded by the word *Ried* (meaning vineyard or site) as well as accompanied by the applicable communal (village) name.

Austrian SEKT (sparkling wine) has its own classification scheme, incorporating an upper tier with protected designation of origin (PDO) further subdivided into categories of Klassik, Reserve, and Grosse Reserve. These last two must be produced by the TRADITIONAL METHOD and spend a minimum of 18 and 30 months respectively on the lees. Reserve Sekt must be labelled for its state of origin, while Grosse Reserve entails a further specification of commune and an option of vineyard designation.

The former Austrian legal category Tafelwein, now simply Wein (see WINE WITHOUT GEOGRAPHICAL INDICATION), is produced in very small volumes, and virtually none is exported. Wines falling into the slightly more elevated official category Landwein, the equivalent of PGI, represent 5–7% of Austrian production. These are labelled for one of three broad geographical areas: Weinland (comprising the states of Niederösterreich, Wien, and Burgenland), Steierland (co-extensive with Steiermark), and Bergland (comprising Austria's five more westerly states). The Bergland designation may take on future significance, because, although little more than 200 ha/490 acres of vines currently qualify, significant pockets of revival are emerging in places where vines last flourished in the Medieval Warm Period, particularly in the state of Kärnten (Carinthia). Meanwhile, Weinland and Steierland are taking on increased prominence due to high-profile growers whose wines are either not submitted or fail to meet the criteria for approval as Qualitätswein. Growers who bottle Landwein relinquish the right to specify its state much less village or vineyard of origin. Some Landwein labels have become notorious for the orthographic contortions and textual circumlocutions employed in attempts to circumvent that limitation. D.S.

Blom, P., *The Wines of Austria* (2nd edn, 2006).
Brook, S., *The Wines of Austria* (2016).
Moser, P., *Falstaff Ultimate Wine Guide Austria* (annually).
Pigott, S., et al., *Wein Spricht Deutsch: Weine, Winzer, Weinlandschaften* (2007).
www.austrianwine.com

authentication. The gripping tale of skulduggery arising from the Christie's 1985 AUCTION of the so-called 'Jefferson Lafite' was the first high-profile case in a subsequent litany of suspected COUNTERFEIT WINES, encouraged by skyrocketing fine-wine PRICES, increased global demand, and the initial complacency of wine producers, auctioneers, and FINE WINE traders. The resulting loss of revenues and the erosion of BRAND values and consumer confidence have highlighted a growing need for the authentication of fine wine in particular. This was emphasized in 2014 when the Indonesian-born fraudster Rudy Kurniawan, also known as Dr Conti, was jailed for 10 years for tricking collectors out of millions of dollars by selling cheap copies of many of the world's most famous wines cooked up in his Los Angeles kitchen.

The need for authentication is not confined to fine wine, however. Wine fraud (see ADULTERATION AND FRAUD) ranges from passing off, such as poor Chinese imitations of PENFOLDS labels under such names as Penfunils and Benfolds, to the sale of fake Chablis, Côtes-du-Rhône, and

BULK WINE mislabelled Pinot Noir for GALLO's Red Bicyclette brand (see SIDEWAYS).

A need to reassure emerging markets, in Asia in particular, has led to a rise in the number of wine appraisal and authentication experts. In the US, Maureen Downey of Chai Consulting advised the FBI investigation into Rudy Kurniawan, while Michael Egan in Bordeaux testified for the prosecution. David Wainwright in Hong Kong and Siobhan Turner MW in the UK are also experienced authenticators. The authority of an expert is important because a certificate of authenticity can itself be a fake or relate to a different bottle.

There has also been much greater exploration by producers and collectors of methods of validating the authenticity of their wines. Anti-counterfeiting measures are limited to a certain extent, however, by a lack of coordinated effort that would result in shared industry standards and solutions such as education, investigation, and law enforcement.

One of the most popular security measures has been the development of the Prooftag Bubble Tag. This device, adopted by several high-profile producers, consists of a translucent polymer with a randomly self-generated constellation of bubbles. The Bubble Tag authenticates a bottle's origins and allows access to information on the producer's website. Its drawback is a tendency to peel off. Other traceability and authentication measures in use or development include proprietary paper with an ultraviolet signature, special and invisible ink, laser and other invisible product markings on bottles and/or labels, holograms with specific pieces of information, microwritings, watermarks, proprietary glass, and DNA codes such as beeswax (whose DNA can be tested and authenticated) under the capsule of DOMAINE DE LA ROMANÉE CONTI's wines.

The more different measures are adopted, the greater the layering and consequently the better the protection against fraud. BLOCKCHAIN is a promising technology but by 2022 was not fully operational for authentication use. Its benefits could be in both the primary and secondary markets—the first acting as a more secure form of some of the available bubble codes, and the latter as a means of guaranteeing the authenticity of a bottle. Research by the University of Adelaide into a technique of molecular fingerprinting of small wine samples using fluorescence spectroscopy is also under way to bolster wine authentication, and Verivin of Oxford have managed optical fingerprinting using Raman spectroscopy of wine in bottles, although in both cases precision is as yet challenging.

No countermeasure though, however advanced, is yet known to be 100% proof against fraud, and so far none can be applied retrospectively to older vintages that are on the secondary market without the benefit of these technologies. A.H.L.R.

Wallace, B., *The Billionaire's Vinegar: The Mystery of the World's Most Expensive Bottle of Wine* (2008).
www.wineberserkers.com/foruminvestdrinks-blog.blogspot.co.uk

autochthonous varieties. See INDIGENOUS VARIETIES.

autolysis, the destruction of the internal structures of cells by their own ENZYMES. In a winemaking context, the term most commonly applies to the action of dead YEAST cells, or LEES, after a second fermentation has taken place during SPARKLING WINEMAKING. Its effects are greatest if wine is left in contact with the lees of a second fermentation in bottle for at least five years, and minimal if LEES CONTACT lasts for less than 18 months. MOUTHFEEL is improved through the release of POLYSACCHARIDES and peptides; OXIDATION is inhibited through the release of GLUTATHIONE and reducing enzymes; and the production of certain MANNOPROTEINS reduces TARTRATE precipitation and improves protein stability. In addition, there is an increase in amino acids, which may be the precursors of those flavour characteristics typically associated with CHAMPAGNE such as acacia, biscuity or bready notes, and other complex aromas from bottle AGEING.

Autolysis also occurs during ageing on lees of still white wines after fermentation. The changes in the chemical composition of such wines are highly desirable.

Alexandre, H., and Guilloux-Benatier, M., 'Yeast autolysis in sparkling wine: a review', *Australian Journal of Grape and Wine Research*, 12/2 (2006) 119–27.

autovinification, method of vinification designed to extract maximum COLOUR from red grapes and used primarily in the production of red PORT. Autovinification, a process involving automatic PUMPING OVER, was developed in ALGERIA in the 1960s, where it was known as the Ducellier system. Faced with a shortage of LABOUR in the 1960s, port producers were forced to abandon the traditional practice of treading grapes by foot in LAGARES. Many isolated QUINTAS had no electricity, and so shippers built central wineries. The power supply was erratic and too weak for sophisticated pumps or presses, so the shippers installed autovinification tanks in order to extract sufficient colour and TANNINS in the short FERMENTATION period prior to FORTIFICATION. Autovinification is a self-perpetuating process induced by the build-up of pressure; no external power source is needed.

Crushed and partially destemmed grapes are pumped into specially constructed autovinification vats (see diagram) which are filled to

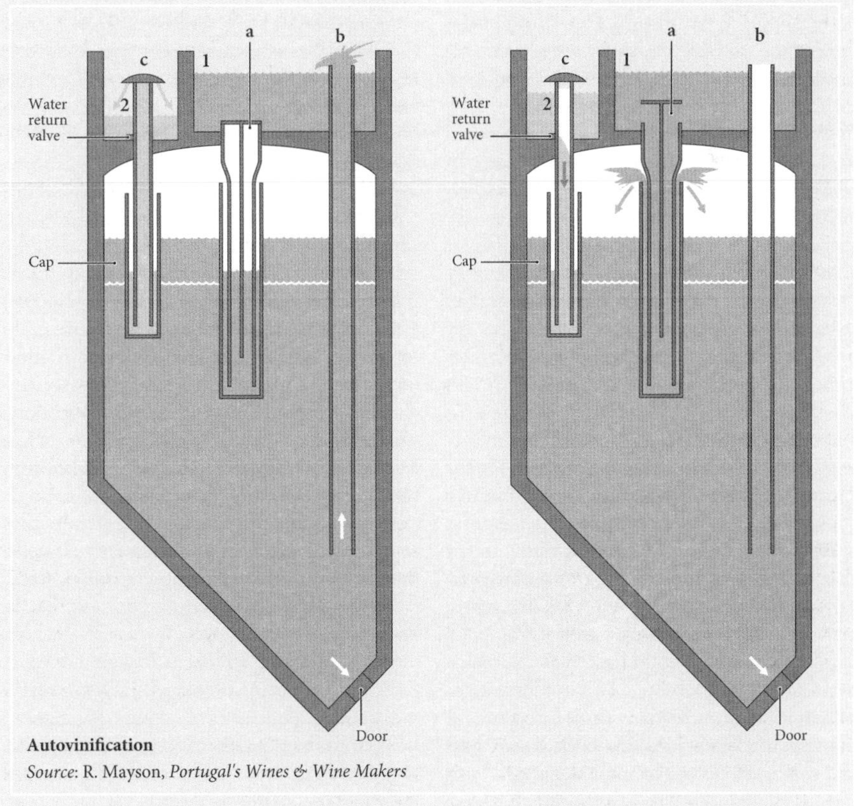

Autovinification
Source: R. Mayson, *Portugal's Wines & Wine Makers*

within about 75 cm/29 in of the top. The vat is closed and the autovinification unit (*a*) is screwed into place. As the fermentation begins, CARBON DIOXIDE is given off and pressure builds up inside the vat. This drives the fermenting must up an escape valve (*b*) which spills out into an open reservoir (1) on top of the vat. Eventually the pressure will also force the water out of a second valve (*c*) into a smaller, separate reservoir (2). When the water has been expelled, the carbon dioxide that has built up in the vat escapes with explosive force through valve (*c*). The fermenting must in reservoir (1) falls back into the vat down the central autovinification unit (*a*), spraying the floating CAP of grape skins, so extracting colour and tannin. At the same moment, the water in reservoir (2) returns to valve (*c*), again sealing in the carbon dioxide, and the process repeats itself. The cycle continues until the winemaker judges that sufficient grape sugar has been fermented to alcohol and sufficient colour extracted, at which time the wine is run off and fortified just as described in PORT winemaking.

At the start of fermentation, when a small amount of carbon dioxide is given off, the autovinification cycle is slow. But when the fermentation is in full swing, the pressure build-up is such that the cycle takes only 10–15 minutes to complete.

Originally autovinification vats were built from epoxy-lined concrete. However, significant modifications have accompanied improvements in both winemaking technology and the power supply to the DOURO Valley, where port is produced. Modern autovinification tanks are made from STAINLESS STEEL and are equipped with REFRIGERATION units to prevent the must from overheating. Some shippers have resorted to traditional pumping over, although this generally provides insufficient EXTRACTION for better-quality port. Other shippers have successfully combined pumping over with autovinification, thereby giving the winemaker greater control over port fermentation than ever before, although lagares, including the new robotic ones, are preferred by many for top-quality ports. R.J.M.

Auvergne, Côtes d', AOC in the Puy-de-Dôme *département*, which is part of the Auverge-Rhône-Alpes region. Nearly midway between Lyon and Limoges, the region features more than 80 volcanic craters, attesting to the VOLCANIC soils that underlie the region's vineyards. From fewer than 300 ha/750 acres of mainly GAMAY, occasionally Pinot Noir, and some Chardonnay vines, light reds and some pinks and whites are made with considerable skill from some of the many small enterprises in the region. Gamay has long been grown here and this was one of the most important wine regions of France in the 19th century, before which Pinot Noir was grown in preference to Gamay. The names of the communes Boudes, Chanturgue, Châteaugay, and Madargue may be appended to Côtes d'Auvergne for reds, Corent for rosés. Most wines are consumed locally; none is expensive.

Auxerre, once an important city in the Yonne *département* of north-east France. Today CHABLIS is the Yonne's most famous and substantial wine appellation, but in the time of CHARLEMAGNE the region centred on Auxerre 20 km/12 miles west had many more vineyards, being a larger centre of population and conveniently situated on a river which leads directly into the Seine and thence to the PARIS basin. It is perhaps not surprising, given its historic importance, that so many vine varieties have the name or synonym AUXERROIS, meaning 'of Auxerre'.

Within the region, IRANCY has had its own appellation for Pinot Noir since 1999, ST-BRIS for its Sauvignon Blanc since 2002, and VÉZELAY for Chardonnay since 2017. There are also regional appellations for light reds made mainly from Pinot Noir and whites from Chardonnay sold as BOURGOGNE with one of these suffixes: Chitry, Côte St-Jacques, Côtes d'Auxerre, Coulanges-la-Vineuse, Épineuil (reds only), and (for whites only) Tonnerre.

Auxerrois is both a synonym for the black-berried MALBEC in CAHORS, where it is the dominant vine variety, and the name of a relatively important white-berried variety in Alsace. And as if that were not confusing enough, **Auxerrois Gris** is a synonym for PINOT GRIS in Alsace, while Chardonnay, before it became so famous, was once known as Auxerrois Blanc in the Moselle—as distinct from **Auxerrois de Laquenexy**, which is the variety today called Auxerrois in north-east France (including Alsace) and LUXEMBOURG.

In 1999, DNA PROFILING at DAVIS showed that this Auxerrois is a progeny of PINOT and GOUAIS BLANC. There are still minuscule plantings of Auxerrois in the Loire, but today it is most important in Alsace, the French Moselle (including Côtes de TOUL), and Luxembourg, where it is most valued, particularly for its low acidity. If yields are suppressed, which they rarely are, the variety can produce excitingly rich wines that are worth ageing until they achieve a bouquet with a honeyed note like that of mature Chablis, the wine which today could be described as 'from AUXERRE' or, in French, *Auxerrois*.

Virtually all of the French 2019 total of 2,543 ha/6,262 acres is in Alsace, where Auxerrois is much more popular than Pinot Blanc even though it is rarely seen on a label. It produces slightly flabby, broad wines which are blended into, or may indeed constitute, many a wine labelled PINOT BLANC. Auxerrois is also a major ingredient in EDELZWICKER.

It is also planted to a limited extent in Germany, the Netherlands, and Canada.

Robinson, J., et al., *Wine Grapes: A Complete Guide to 1,368 Vine Varieties, Including Their Origins and Flavours* (2012).

Auxey-Duresses, a village in Burgundy producing medium-priced red and white wines not dissimilar to neighbouring VOLNAY and MEURSAULT respectively, although more austere in style. The vineyards, which include those of the hamlets of Petit Auxey and Melin, are located on either side of a valley subject to cooler winds than the main Côte de BEAUNE. Pinot Noir vineyards, including such PREMIERS CRUS as Les Duresses and Le Climat de Val, are on the south-east slope of the Montagne du Bourdon. White wines made from Chardonnay account for just above a quarter of the production, covering the slopes adjacent to Meursault. Some vines, atypically for Burgundy, are trained high.

In the past, wines from Auxey-Duresses were likely to have been sold under the names of grander neighbours. It is permissible, though now rare, to label the wines as Côte de Beaune-Villages.

See CÔTE D'OR and map under BURGUNDY.

J.T.C.M.

auxins, one of a number of groups of natural HORMONES present in vines which regulate growth. They are produced in vine parts which are actively growing, such as shoot and root tips. Auxins favour cell growth over cell division but are also involved in inhibiting the growth of LATERAL SHOOTS. Many chemicals have been synthesized which are chemically related and have a similar biological function. For example, the compounds 2,4-D and 2,4,5-T are auxin-like and form the basis of some HERBICIDES, which are used widely in cereal production. Vines, like tomatoes and cotton, are very sensitive to 2,4-D vapours such as can drift over vineyards when neighbouring farmers use aerial spraying, even from considerable distances away. Most vine-growing regions have now enacted laws to protect vineyards from the effects of such hormone spraying. R.E.S.

AVA, the acronym for **American Viticultural Area** and the United States' answer to France's AOC system of permitted geographical designations. The US federal government began developing this system in the early 1980s through its Bureau of Alcohol, Tobacco, and Firearms (BATF; see TTB). AVAs are purely geographical, imposing no restrictions on varieties planted, vineyard practices, or winemaking protocols. The only requirement for their use is that 85% of the grapes in a wine labelled with an AVA come from that region; if the wine is a VARIETAL, the legal minimum of 75% of the named variety must come from the named AVA. (Unlike the AOC/DOC system, however, neither 'AVA' nor 'American Viticultural Area' appears on wine labels.)

Between 1983 and 1991, the BATF approved more than 100 AVAs in the country, more than 60 of those in California, but applications slowed to a trickle in the 1990s as producers were discouraged by the bureaucracy involved without any obvious commercial gain. Yet the 2000s saw a new rush of AVA applications and approvals, as winery marketers realized that Americans were beginning to care about where the grapes were grown and that labels from specific areas commanded more respect (and higher prices) than GENERIC blends. By 2022, there were 266 AVAs in the US, 146 of which were in California.

The TTB website has a complete list of AVAs: www.ttb.gov/appellation

Aveyron, IGP in SOUTH WEST FRANCE. Both inside and outside the AOC areas of MARCILLAC, ENTRAYGUES, and ESTAING, enterprising winemakers are producing original wines, partly from mainstream varieties and partly from local ones such as Négret de Banhars and Rousselet. Jurançon Noir also sometimes appears. Viticulture has reappeared in the west of the *département*, formerly bereft of vines. P.S.

Avesso, meaning 'contrary', a fitting description for this white grape planted in the VINHO VERDE region of northern PORTUGAL, notably in the warmer Baião subregion close to the lower reaches of the River DOURO, where it tends to produce wines of 12–13% alcohol, higher than those made from the other principal grape varieties in the region. It is now being produced as a VARIETAL wine. Plantings totalled 751 ha/1,856 acres in 2020. S.A.

AWRI (Australian Wine Research Institute) is the Australian wine industry's own research, development, and extension organization. Based in Adelaide and established in 1955, its governing board includes members elected by Australian grape and wine producers who pay the Wine Grapes levy. The AWRI's purpose is to support a sustainable and successful grape and wine industry through research, practical solutions, and knowledge transfer.

Research at the AWRI is designed to increase fundamental understanding while remaining responsive to the applied needs of producers and consumers. It has particular research strengths in wine chemistry, sensory science, microbiology, and molecular biology. The AWRI has a strong track record of translating its research results into usable applications and fostering their adoption, as well as at communicating research and practical solutions from around the world. The organization's commercial arm provides specialized grape and wine ANALYSIS, benchmarking, and technical validation services, as well as export certificates and site audits.

The AWRI conducts a wide range of educational seminars and workshops and has published more than 2,200 papers and articles. M.P.K. & E.M.C.R.

AXA, vast insurance group based in France whose wine division **AXA-Millésimes** is very small in the context of the company and very big in the context of fine wine in general and Bordeaux in particular. Claude Bébéar, the company's president and founder, was led to buy the small St-Émilion property Ch Franc-Mayne in 1984 as an indirect result of his friendship with Jean-Michel Cazes of PAUILLAC. Seeing the investment potential of good Bordeaux properties, he founded AXA-Millésimes in 1987, and it was managed by Cazes alongside his own wine holdings, including Ch Lynch Bages until 2000 when Cazes retired and Christian Seely took over. Initial acquisitions included Clos de l'Arlot in NUITS-ST-GEORGES, the CRU BOURGEOIS Ch Pibran, and, also in Pauillac, the second-growth Ch Pichon Baron, a fairytale château which has since been so lavishly refurbished and re-equipped that it regularly challenges the FIRST GROWTHS. In 1992 SAUTERNES first-growth Ch Suduiraut and the Disznókő vineyard in TOKAJ were added, a sweet triumvirate being completed by the acquisition and subsequent restoration of the QUINTA DO NOVAL port business in 1993. In 2018 AXA Millésimes acquired Outpost Vineyard at the summit of Howell Mountain in NAPA Valley, adding the neighbouring Henry Vineyard in 2020. AXA is by no means the only French insurance company to have invested in wine-related real estate, but it is the most wine-minded one.

AXR1, variety of ROOTSTOCK widely used in northern California until, in the late 1980s, it became fatally obvious that it was not resistant to PHYLLOXERA, something French vignerons had known for many decades.

Ayse, sometime spelt Ayze, is an isolated CRU between Bonneville and Chamonix-Mont Blanc whose name may be added to the eastern French appellation SAVOIE. GRINGET is the principal grape variety used for the light white still and TRADITIONAL METHOD sparkling wines. The highly regarded Domaine Belluard accounts for half of production. W.L.

Azal, one of the less aromatic white grapes grown to produce VINHO VERDE and recently showing its mettle in some steely, structured VARIETAL wines with flavours of green apple and grapefruit. Total plantings had fallen to 1,770 ha/4,374 acres by 2020. **Azal Tinto** is unrelated.

azeotrope, from the Greek 'to boil unchanged', a mixture of liquid chemicals which has a boiling point either higher or lower than any one of its components. The principal volatile components of wine tend to form azeotropes of two, three, or more components. Water, ETHANOL, volatile organic ACIDS, ALDEHYDES, ESTERS, acetals, and ketones, many of them powerfully aromatic, are among the azeotrope components in wines. The multiplicity of volatile compounds present in wine and our lack of detailed knowledge of all of the azeotropes possible makes it difficult to predict the composition of distillates (which depend on the varied boiling points of components).

Just as the formation of azeotropic mixtures in a liquid governs the boiling point and composition of the vapour during DISTILLATION, so it governs the composition of the vapours above a liquid in a glass at room temperature. When we smell a wine, our noses are recording the impression created by the azeotropic mixture rather than that of any single component. A.D.W.

Azerbaijan, former Soviet Union state on the Caspian Sea. It also includes the Nakhchevan Autonomous Republic, an enclave surrounded by RUSSIA, GEORGIA, ARMENIA, IRAN, and TÜRKIYE. While the country grows only a fraction of the wine it produced before the fall of communism, vineyard plantings are increasing, with more attention paid to quality instead of quantity.

History

Grape-growing is likely to be one of the oldest branches of Azerbaijan's economy. Archaeology has revealed seeds of cultured grapes, stones for crushing grape berries, and stone fermentation and storage vessels dating back to the seventh millennium BCE at Shomu-Tepe and the second millennium BCE in the settlements of Kültan, Galabaglar, and Galajig.

HERODOTUS, describing a campaign of the Scythian chief Madyas in ANATOLIA in the 7th century BCE, mentioned that viticulture and winemaking were already developed in that region. The Greek geographer Strabo, in the 1st century BCE, reported on grape culture in 'Albania', the old name of part of Azerbaijan.

The Arabian historians and geographers Abulfedy, Masudi, Khaukal, and El Mugaddasi recorded that vineyards existed near the towns of Gianji and Bardy during Arab domination. Viticulture of that region declined in the periods of war and revived in the time of peace. Viticulture was on a commercial scale after 1814 and developed especially fast at the end of the 19th century when two railways were built which provided access to the enormous wine market of RUSSIA.

By the beginning of the 20th century, small viticultural farms were established in the

A

Ganja-Gazakh region as well as much larger enterprises in specialized zones of commercial grape and wine production. In 1940, the total vineyard area was 33,000 ha/81,500 acres, mostly planted by German colonists who began settling in the region in the early 19th century. (In 1941, most all of them were deported to Kazakhstan and Siberia.) The Second World War had reduced this total to 21,000 ha/51,900 acres by 1947, but a subsequent vineyard expansion programme launched in the 1950s resulted in 1.1 million ha planted by the 1970s. Most of these plantings were doomed, however, by a combination of PHYLLOXERA, Mikhail Gorbachev's VINE-PULL SCHEME, and the economic turmoil after independence was declared in 1991. Only 8,000 ha were left in the 1990s. By 2020, plantings were up to 13,422 ha, with 20 wine companies.

See also ORIGINS OF VINICULTURE and PALAEOETHNOBOTANY.

Climate and geography

With its mountainous landscape, Azerbaijan has a very varied climate, from moderately warm with dry winters to cold with abundant rainfall. Annual rainfall in the low and premountainous parts of the country, where grapes are grown, is 250–600 mm/23 in. There are eight unofficial but widely recognized wine regions, with the greatest concentration in the north of the country, from Shirvan (5,343 ha) and Guba-Khachmaz (916 ha) in the north-east to Ganja-Gazagh in the north-west (4,274 ha), with Sheki-Zaqatala (833 ha) in between. Lankaran (4,274 ha) is in the far south-east; Karabakh (171 ha) and Nakhchivan (367 ha) are in the south-west, where temperatures fall low enough to necessitate WINTER PROTECTION for the vines.

Vine varieties

Azerbaijan claims to have more than 400 INDIGENOUS VARIETIES, but only a few are cultivated for wine production. In addition to INTERNATIONAL VARIETIES such as Merlot, Pinot Noir, and Cabernet Sauvignon, the most common local varieties for red wine are MATRASA, SAPERAVI, Tavkveri, Shirvanshahi, and Kindoghy. For white wines, the Georgian grape RKATSITELI makes up about 30% of production, while Bayanshira is the main autochthonous white wine grape. Kahetian MTSVANE is also grown, as well as Chardonnay, Pinot Blanc, and Viognier. In 2018, the government launched a development strategy aimed at expanding the country's vineyards with both indigenous and imported varieties. The country's main export market is the Russian Federation, but sights are set on the US, Netherlands, Ukraine, and China.

www.azerbaijanwine.com

azienda, Italian for a business. An **azienda agricola** is a farm, the equivalent of a French DOMAINE, and the phrase should appear on a wine label only if the grapes were grown and the wine produced on that estate; an **azienda vinicola**, on the other hand, may buy in grapes from elsewhere, while an **azienda vitivinicola** combines both activities.

Azores. New players from the mainland have sparked a winemaking revolution in this archipelago of nine Atlantic islands, an autonomous region of PORTUGAL. In 2004, a VINHO REGIONAL category Açores was created for light red and white wines produced throughout the archipelago from over 50 local, national, and international varieties. Three islands also have their own DOCs with stricter regulations: GRACIOSA, BISCOITOS, and PICO, of which the latter is the most important quantitively and qualitatively.

S.A.

B

BA, common abbreviation, used particularly by English-speakers, for the sweet-wine designation BEERENAUSLESE.

Băbească Neagră, Romania's fourth most planted red wine vine variety, whose name, meaning 'grandmother's black [grape]', compares directly with FETEASCĂ or 'young girl's [grape]'. It has long been grown in the east of the country, but total plantings had fallen to 2,569 ha/6,348 acres by 2021, typically producing light, fruity reds that are considerably less 'serious' than Fetească Neagră.

Babo, alternative name for KMW, the Austrian unit of MUST WEIGHT. See KLOSTERNEUBURG.

Bacchus, common name in ancient ROME for the classical god of wine whom the Greeks called Bacchos or, more usually, DIONYSUS. There was no official Roman festival of Bacchus: the Roman Senate suppressed the **Bacchanalia** in 186 BCE because it saw them not only as a danger to the state but also as a bacchanal in the modern sense, a scene of drunkenness and sexual licence. **Bacchic** poetry is verse with a vinous theme, a speciality of the ARAB POETS. Because the Romans concentrated on the vinous aspect of this much more complex god, and possibly because the word 'Bacchus' is considerably easier to say and spell than 'Dionysus', the Roman name is much more commonly used in modern times and is regarded as a word rich in wine connotations. The word is used emotively around the world to conjure up various conjunctions of wine and pleasure.

Dalby, A., *The Story of Bacchus* (2005).

Bacchus is also the name of one of the most important GERMAN CROSSES. It was bred from a Silvaner × Riesling cross and the lacklustre MÜLLER-THURGAU and in good years can provide growers in Germany with musts notching up the all-important numbers on the OECHSLE scale as well as powerful flavours and character, not unlike Sauvignon Blanc, and is therefore useful for blending with Müller-Thurgau. Unlike the more aristocratic and more popular cross KERNER, however, the wine produced lacks acidity and needs to be fully ripe before it can express its own exuberant flavours.

Bacchus's great allure for growers is that it can be planted on sites on which Riesling is an unreliable ripener and will ripen as early and as productively as Müller-Thurgau. Total plantings in Germany reached a peak of around 3,500 ha/8,650 acres in 1990. This total had fallen to 1,614 ha by 2020, mostly in Franken for straightforward fruity, aromatic wines and in Rheinhessen for BULK WINE blends. Its ability to ripen fully in cool years is a benefit in SAALE-UNSTRUT, as it is in the UK, where Bacchus is valued for its recognizable flavour and is the second most planted white grape, albeit way behind Chardonnay. With the UK's generally lower yields and higher natural acid levels, it does not suffer from the flabbiness of warmer-climate examples and was planted on around 175 ha in 2020.

Baco, François, was, like BOUSCHET, a nurseryman who saw his name live on in the names of some of the most successful of the vine varieties he bred. Baco's specialities were FRENCH HYBRIDS and his most successful was **Baco Blanc**, sometimes called **Baco 22A**, a hybrid of FOLLE BLANCHE and NOAH created in 1898 which was, for much of the 20th century until the late 1970s, the prime ingredient in armagnac—a role now occupied by UGNI BLANC. In 2019 there were 805 ha/1,989 acres in France, mainly in armagnac country.

Baco Noir, or **Baco 1**, resulted from crossing Folle Blanche with a variety of VITIS RIPARIA in 1902; it was at one time widely spread in France but today is best known for its light, fruity, non-FOXY reds in eastern Canada and, to a lesser extent, upstate New York.

bacteria, very small microorganisms which have serious implications in both viticulture and winemaking. Although not common pathogens of the grapevine, BACTERIAL DISEASES are potentially destructive and therefore very important. For beneficial bacteria in the vineyard, see SOIL BIOTA.

In winemaking just two groups of bacteria are important, ACETOBACTER and LACTIC ACID BACTERIA. Since grape juice and wine are both high in ACIDITY, the great majority of bacteria, with the exception of these two groups, are incapable of living in them and, if introduced, do not survive. (Drinks such as cider, perry, orange juice, and beer, which are all much less acid than wine, are subject to many forms of BACTERIAL SPOILAGE to which wine is immune, and therefore they lack wine's AGEING potential.) No known human pathogenic bacteria can survive in wine, however, which is one of the reasons it has been such a safe drink (safer than WATER at some times and in some places) through the ages.

Acetobacter (which do not harm humans) can turn wine, or any other dilute solution containing ETHANOL, into VINEGAR. They require OXYGEN for growth and survival, and they die in its absence (which is why care is taken to exclude oxygen from certain stages of winemaking and all stages of wine preservation—see LEFTOVER WINE).

Lactic acid bacteria produce LACTIC ACID and grow best in environments where there is a very small amount of oxygen. They are important as the agents of MALOLACTIC CONVERSION in wines, by which excess MALIC ACID is decomposed.

R.E.S. & P.J.W.

B

bacterial blight, vine BACTERIAL DISEASE caused by the bacterium *Xanthomonas ampelinus*, so serious that it has led some Greek and French growers to abandon stricken vineyards. It shows its presence by retarding and killing young shoots and is spread by rain, wind, and also pruning tools and increased MECHANIZATION. The disease can be controlled by removing and destroying infected plants and by disinfecting tools, as well as by COPPER sprays. It is present in parts of Europe, South Africa, Australia, and South America that have a MEDITERRANEAN CLIMATE. R.E.S.

www.cabi.org/isc/datasheet/56907

bacterial diseases, group of grapevine diseases caused by BACTERIA, small organisms which do not commonly attack vines but which can be deadly and are difficult to control. Of the bacterial diseases, PIERCE'S DISEASE is the most important, and QUARANTINE authorities around the world are anxious to stop it spreading from America, although it is now present and causing concern in Europe. In parts of North and Central America (southern California, Florida, eastern Texas, and Mexico, for instance), viticulture can be rendered commercially impossible by the natural presence of this disease. Other economically important bacterial diseases are BACTERIAL BLIGHT and CROWN GALL. R.E.S.

Szegedi, E., and Civerolo, E. L., 'Bacterial diseases of grapevine', *International Journal of Horticultural Science*, 17/3 (2011).

Wilcox, W. F., et al., *Compendium of Grape Diseases, Disorders, and Pests* (2nd edn, 2015).

bacterial spoilage, range of wine maladies or FAULTS including gas, haze, cloud, and off-flavours generated by the activity of BACTERIA in wine. These bacteria are either ACETOBACTER or LACTIC ACID BACTERIA. Acetobacter's tendency to transform wine into vinegar can be checked by keeping air away from wine, on the part of both winemaker and wine drinker (see LEFTOVER WINE). Lactic acid bacteria are more varied in their effects, which include a wide range of unpleasant-smelling compounds, depending on the type of bacterium. These are relatively rarely seen today since great care is taken by winemakers (see STABILIZATION and HYGIENE) to guard against spoilage by lactic acid bacteria in the winery and to minimize the risk of bottling a wine with any spoilage bacteria (see FILTRATION, PASTEURIZATION, STERILE BOTTLING), but wines bottled unfined, unfiltered, and with little or no added SULFUR DIOXIDE are more at risk from spoilage (see MOUSY). If lactic acid bacteria do attack a wine in bottle, the results are usually detrimental to the taste and clarity of the wine, and gas is usually produced.

Baden, Germany's longest wine region, stretching over 400 km/250 miles from the border with FRANKEN in the north across the Rhine opposite ALSACE to Lake Constance (the Bodensee) and German-speaking SWITZERLAND in the south (see map under GERMANY). The general and local climate, the varying soils, and the ELEVATION have a marked effect on the wines of Baden's nine districts, or BEREICHE, which had a combined vineyard area of 15,836 ha/39,132 acres in 2019. In this southernmost growing region of Germany, SPÄTBURGUNDER, GRAUBURGUNDER, and Weissburgunder (PINOT BLANC) account for 34, 14, and 10% respectively of the region's vineyard area, making it Germany's Pinot stronghold, and total red wine production hit 40% in 2019. Warm, dry conditions and frequently steep, terraced sites of VOLCANIC origin typically combine to yield wines of naturally abundant alcohol, although, as in many other respects, this huge region harbours considerable diversity, and there are enough cooler sectors for growers so inclined to bottle Pinots that are downright delicate, as well as to support RIESLING. Around 70% of Baden's vine acreage is farmed by growers who belong to one of the region's 80 CO-OPERATIVES (*Winzergenossenschaften*), a number approaching half of Germany's total.

The **Tauberfranken** district covers 610 ha/1,507 acres that intermittently follow the Tauber River until its confluence with the Main at Wertheim. Plantings in this frost-prone area, 70% of them for white wine, have for many years been declining, and hardy MÜLLER-THURGAU represents 45% of all vines, distantly followed by fellow-crossings KERNER and BACCHUS. The wine is similar to that of FRANKEN and is also sold in its neighbour's flagon-shaped BOCKSBEUTEL.

East across the Odenwald, the vineyards of the Bereiche **Badische Bergstrasse** (400 ha/988 acres) and **Kraichgau** (1,250 ha/3,089 acres) run north and south of Heidelberg. The first district is simply a continuation of the HESSISCHE BERGSTRASSE. In both sectors, Müller-Thurgau and Riesling each hover around one-quarter of the hectarage, the latter capable of yielding distinctive, delicate results in GRANITE and SANDSTONE sites along the Bergstrasse.

The extensive **Ortenau, Breisgau**, and **Kaiserstuhl** districts that parallel the Rhine east of the Black Forest between Baden-Baden and Freiburg collectively comprise 53% of Baden vine acreage and are home to Baden's most prestigious estates, although, as elsewhere in this region, grower co-operatives account for a majority of production. Thanks especially to the opportunities afforded by cool sites south of Baden-Baden, Riesling accounts for around 28% of Ortenau vines, and Pinot Noir makes up 42%. Steep porphyry and BASALT sites around Neuweier are especially known for their Riesling. Some 15 km/9 miles south at Waldum, that grape—on weathered GRANITE—vies with Pinot Noir for attention; while a few kilometres closer to Offenburg, the village of Durbach, long a wine-trading centre, gives pride of place to Pinot, although Riesling (known here colloquially as Klingelberger) and Traminer (as Clevner) run close behind in importance and affection. Extending between Offenburg and Freiburg, parts of the Breisgau hug the Black Forest closely enough to benefit from more precipitation than neighbouring districts. Here CALCAREOUS soils promote firm, fruity acidity resulting in Pinot Noir that marries richness with vivacity and whose virtues have become increasingly evident over the past two decades, so that today many of the most intriguing red wines in Germany have Breisgau addresses. Among those villages to have demonstrated outstanding site potential are (from south to north) Mundingen, Köndringen, Malterdingen, Hecklingen, and (in a side valley well into the Black Forest) Münchweier.

West of Breisgau, the primarily VOLCANIC vineyards of the Kaiserstuhl, rearing steeply up from the Rhine, are Baden's most famous and coveted, particularly for Pinots. Northwards from Breisach on the Rhine, Ihringen, Blankenhornsberg, Achkarren, Oberrotweil, and Burkheim harbour the most prestigious Kaiserstuhl vineyards. Largely on the basis of its calcareous LOESS rather than volcanic soils, the 1,033-ha/2,553-acre **Tuniberg** declared its independence from the Kaiserstuhl in 1991, though without having since then achieved significant independent reputation.

Hugging the Rhine in Germany's south-western corner from Freiburg to the Swiss frontier at Basel is the **Markgräflerland**, traditionally best known for its Gutedel (CHASSELAS), whose elegance and soil sensitivity can challenge that of Switzerland's best examples. Like the Breisgau, the Markgräflerland is becoming increasingly recognized for innovative winegrowers and excellent Pinot Noirs, some from the calcareous soils of Istein and Efringen-Kirchen along the Rhine just north of Basel being especially impressive. The **Bodensee** district, most of whose vineyards stretch along the northern shore of the huge eponymous lake, is nearly 100 km/62 miles distant from the Markgräflerland and even further from any other districts of Baden. While known inside Germany more for its tourism than its wines, and hardly known at all outside Germany, this outpost of diverse German viticulture, like its immediate Swiss neighbours around Schaffhausen and Konstanz, can boast some distinctively delicious results, especially with Pinot Noir. D.S.

Baga, red grape found throughout central PORTUGAL but mostly in the BAIRRADA region, where, unusually for Portugal, it accounts for about 80% of dark-skinned varieties and where plantings are increasing again. DNA PROFILING has shown a likely parent–offspring relationship with MALVASIA Fina (under the synonym Arinto do Dão). It is a vigorous variety, resistant to POWDERY MILDEW but ripens late and has a tendency to rot in the damp Atlantic climate of Portugal's western seaboard, threatened by early autumn rains. This small, thin-skinned variety (*baga* means 'berry') produces dark, fairly acidic, tannic wines that can be undrinkably ASTRINGENT if the grapes are underripe. However, well-made wines are full of fruit and capable of long AGEING, and there are a growing number of lighter, more elegant examples. A large amount of Baga ends up as rosé: Sogrape, producers of MATEUS rosé, have a large winery in the Bairrada region. Portuguese plantings totalled 7,133 ha/ 17,626 acres in 2020. J.V. & J.E.H

Baghdad, the capital of modern IRAQ, was founded by the first Abbasid caliph, al-Mansur, in 762 CE. Early in its history the city became the focus of a Bacchic culture (see ARAB POETS), celebrated most eloquently by the poet ABU NUWAS. Although wine was imbibed in the Caliphal court and some outlying districts of the city (al-Karkh, for example), most wine was consumed where it was produced, in the small monasteries and towns that lay outside the city in various parts of Iraq. Their names are preserved in poetry and other sources ('Āna, Hīt, Qutrubbul in the vicinity of the city, for example, and Tīzanabādh further south near Kufa). P.K.

bag-in-box. See BOXES.

Bagnoli Friularo, DOCG in Italy's VENETO on the plain immediately south of Padova dedicated to the production of the red RABOSO, locally known as Friularo. Due to their high natural acidity, the grapes for Bagnoli are dried and then fermented dry or almost dry. The wine resembles AMARONE, if slighter in style. W.S.

Bairrada, evolving DOC wine region in northern Portugal (see map under PORTUGAL). The coastal belt south of OPORTO has been producing wine since Portugal gained independence from the Moors in the 10th century. By the early 1700s, Bairrada's dark, tannic red wines were widely drunk in Britain, masquerading as or blended with PORT from the DOURO Valley to the north. Then in 1756, as part of his measures to protect the authenticity of port (see DELIMITATION), the Marquis of Pombal, Portugal's powerful prime minister, ordered that Bairrada's vineyards should be uprooted.

Despite the foundation in 1887 of the Escola Prática de Viticultura da Bairrada whose efforts to promote and develop the region included producing Portugal's first TRADITIONAL METHOD sparkling wine in 1890, it has taken Bairrada more than two centuries to recover.

For the best part of the 20th century, the merchant bottlers (see NÉGOCIANTS) and CO-OPERATIVES that still dominate production churned out cheap BULK wines for Portugal's African colonies. But this market collapsed in the wake of the 1974 revolution. Bairrada was awarded REGIÃO DEMARCADA (now DOC) status in 1979. Tapping new, more demanding export markets required the merchant bottlers to exert greater control over fruit sourcing and production through the acquisition of vineyards, buying grapes (instead of wine), and investing in winemaking facilities. Most of Bairrada's 2,400 growers own a very small area of vines even today, so most send their grapes either to a merchant or to one of the region's two remaining co-operatives. Around 900 of them alone sell their fruit to SOGRAPE for MATEUS rosé. Bairrada's main quality impetus has come from the handful of dynamic individual winemaking estates that emerged in the 1980s and the successive wave that has reinforced its number. Stalwart supporters of traditional varieties, notably BAGA, have progressively tamed its worst excesses (fearsome tannins and acidity) by optimal VINEYARD SITE SELECTION (warmer, better-drained CALCAREOUS-clay soils are best), trimming this productive grape's yields, and gentler EXTRACTION. Others have taken advantage of DOC rule changes which, from 2003, permitted blending with more approachable, popular varieties such as Touriga Nacional, Cabernet Sauvignon, Merlot, and Pinot Noir. These incomers (sometimes with a dash of white grapes) have successfully fleshed out Baga and have even produced some very promising wines in their own right, especially the Bordeaux varieties, which are well-suited to Bairrada's MARITIME CLIMATE. Keen to reinforce the region's traditional varieties Baga, Maria Gomes, and Bical, from 2009 leading estate Luis Pato began once again to label its top wines Bairrada (as opposed to bottling all as Vinho Regional BEIRAS, now known as Beira Atlântico). In 2020, Baga represented only 40% of red grapes under vine (down from 90%) and 26% of land under vine. However, those who remain committed to producing VARIETAL Baga consistently make some of Portugal's leading reds. With riper, finer tannins and better fruit expression, modern Baga is broachable earlier than in the past and comes in many guises, ranging from easy-drinking GLOU-GLOU to FORTIFIED *vinho licoroso*. White grapes, mostly Maria Gomes (FERNÃO PIRES) and BICAL, once grown primarily by the merchants for TRADITIONAL METHOD sparkling wines, are increasingly valued by Bairrada's leading estates which make some remarkably TERROIR-focused, almost Burgundian whites and, more recently, artisanal traditional-method sparkling wines based on Baga. Sparkling-wine production remains important, representing around 50% of Portugal's output.

The Bussaco Palace Hotel owns a vineyard, Vinha da Mata, in Bairrada from which it has produced an impressively structured Baga-dominated red labelled VM since 2001. However, located on the cusp of Bairrada and Dão, it is best known for Buçaco red and white wines made from grapes sourced from both regions. Once regarded as some of the best table wines in Portugal, older vintages (dating back to the 1940s) are available only to guests dining at the hotel or one of its few associated establishments, apart from those few bottles that occasionally crop up at AUCTION. S.A.

Mayson, R. J., *The Wines of Portugal* (2020).
Woolf, S. J., and Opaz, R., *Foot Trodden: Portugal and the Wines That Time Forgot* (2021).
Ahmed, S., 'Bairrada: the Baga beyond', *The World of Fine Wine*, 40 (2013) 92–9.

Baiyu, Chinese name for RKATSITELI.

balance is essential for quality both in vineyards and in wine.

Vines

Vine balance is a viticultural concept little appreciated by wine consumers yet one which is essential for producing grapes for premium winemaking. A vine is in balance when the amounts of fruit and vegetative growth are appropriate. One index of this is the LEAF TO FRUIT RATIO. Vine balance concerns VIGOUR and it can be managed by the VITICULTURIST, with BALANCED PRUNING and WATER STRESS the principal tools. One of the best measures of vine balance is the ratio of fruit yield to pruning weight, now often called the Ravaz Index after the French researcher who promoted it.

Balanced wine comes from balanced vines, a fact acknowledged even by those who were once critical of high YIELDS in any circumstances. A balanced vine has shoots of moderate vigour (thus medium pruning weight of around 35 g/ 1.23 oz per shoot) and no SHOOT TIP growth during fruit RIPENING. Leaves are of moderate size and number and shoots spaced in such a way as to avoid excess SHADE, with both leaves and fruit well exposed to sunlight. Unbalanced vineyards are either too vigorous (in which case poor ripening results from shading and competition between the ripening grapes and shoot tips for carbohydrates) or not vigorous enough (in which case there is insufficient leaf area for proper ripening). Monitoring shoot-tip growth is seen as an important management tool for vine balance. R.E.S.

Wines

Wine tasters say that a wine has balance, or is well **balanced**, if its ALCOHOLIC STRENGTH, ACIDITY, RESIDUAL SUGAR, TANNINS, and FRUIT complement each other so that no single one

B

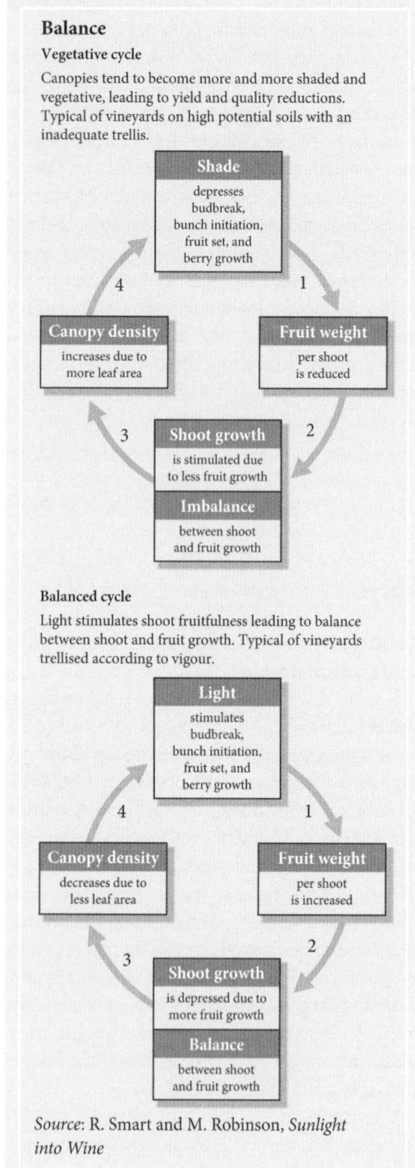

Source: R. Smart and M. Robinson, *Sunlight into Wine*

of them is obtrusive on the PALATE. (Young wines are expected to exhibit more marked tannins than mature ones, however.) This extremely important wine characteristic is unrelated to FLAVOUR, although see also HARMONY.

balanced pruning. The number of buds to be left on the vine at winter PRUNING will determine the vine's growth in the following season and should be assessed in relation to the vine's capacity to support shoot growth. In turn, a balanced pruned vine will produce sufficient shoot growth to ripen the fruit it carries. In practice, an experienced pruner will consider the amount of CANE growth of the last season and the bud number retained the previous year and then adjust the number of buds if the SHOOT growth was excessive or inadequate.

The amount of reserves, or stored CARBOHYDRATES, in the vine roots, TRUNK, and ARMS will determine the growth of developing shoots in the spring. An indication of the amount of vine reserves is the weight or mass of cane prunings removed; the greater the amount of shoot growth in summer, the higher will be the pruning weight and also the stored carbohydrate reserves.

Pruning weights are simply measured by weighing the cane prunings removed at winter pruning. This value is used to judge the appropriate number of buds to retain at winter pruning. For example, one common formula is to retain around 30 buds for each kg/2.2 lb of pruning weight.

If too few buds are left on the vine at winter pruning relative to the stored carbohydrates, then shoots in spring will grow quickly with leaves which are too large and stems which are too thick. The vine will have a high LEAF TO FRUIT RATIO, which may result in poor fruit set (see COULURE). In any event, the leaf-to-fruit imbalance normally leads to a shaded CANOPY MICROCLIMATE and attendant problems of loss of YIELD and quality. Such a situation is common for vines planted too close together on fertile soil.

On the other hand, if too many buds are left at pruning relative to stored carbohydrates, then the resulting large number of shoots will develop only slowly in spring. The leaves will be small and the stems spindly. The danger here is that the leaf area may be too low for the weight of grapes, which will ripen slowly, and wine quality will suffer. This condition is often described as OVERCROPPING.

See also PRUNING. R.E.S.

Smart, R. E., and Robinson, M., *Sunlight into Wine: A Handbook for Winegrape Canopy Management* (1991).

Tassie, E., and Freeman, B. M., 'Pruning', in B. G. Coombe and P. R. Dry (eds.), *Viticulture*, ii: *Practices* (2nd edn, 2006).

Balearic Islands, *Illes Balears* in Catalan and *Islas Baleares* in Spanish, is an archipelago off Spain's east coast and one of its 17 autonomous regions. MALLORCA, the largest island, has the most significant wine industry, with two DOPS, Binissalem and Pla I Llevant, but there are also compelling VINO DE LA TIERRA (VdT) wines made on Formentera, Ibiza, and Menorca. All the islands share the commonalities of a warm MEDITERRANEAN CLIMATE with well over 2,700 sunshine hours yearly and low rainfall (around 400 mm/16 in annually, reaching 650 mm on the north-east coast of Menorca, the most easterly island). Monastrell, Tempranillo, Merlot, and Cabernet Sauvignon dominate plantings on all islands. Syrah is authorized in VdT Menorca and Ibiza wines, while FOGONEU, an indigenous red variety, is authorized for use in VdT Formentera. In white wines, Chardonnay, Malvasia, and Moscatel dominate.

Bali. See INDONESIA.

Ballard Canyon is the smallest AVA in SANTA BARBARA County, with less than one-tenth of its 3,116 ha/7,700 acres planted in 2021 but a strong reputation for Syrah, which makes up more than half its plantings. Cooling Pacific breezes, LIMESTONE and sandy soils, and a DIURNAL TEMPERATURE RANGE of up to 5 °C/9 °F combine for some of California's more elegant styles. M.D.K.

Balling, scale of measuring total dissolved compounds in grape juice and therefore its approximate concentration of grape sugars. It is very similar to the BRIX scale used in the United States. For more details, see MUST WEIGHT.

Bandol, the most serious wine of PROVENCE, typically a deep-flavoured, lush red blend dominated by the MOURVÈDRE grape. Like CHÂTEAUNEUF-DU-PAPE, Bandol produces quintessentially Mediterranean red wines which are easy to appreciate in youth despite their longevity.

The appellation is named after the port from which they were once shipped all over the world. Bandol is now a Mediterranean resort town with little to offer the wine tourist, and the vineyards are on south-facing terraces well inland, locally called *restanques*. As in the smaller appellation of CASSIS along the coast, the vines are protected from the cold north winds but have to fight property developers for their right to continued existence. Around 1,500–1,600 ha/3,700–3,954 acres were cultivated in 2020.

This particularly well-favoured southern corner is one of the few parts of France in which Mourvèdre, the characteristic grape of Bandol, can be relied upon to ripen. Other dark-berried varieties grown include GRENACHE and CINSAUT, much used for the local rosés, together with strictly limited additions of Syrah and Carignan. Despite Bandol's reputation for reds, since the early 2010s the proportion of rosé has risen steadily, accounting for more than 75% by 2020. A small quantity of white Bandol is made from CLAIRETTE blended with Bourboulenc and Ugni Blanc (and no more than 20% Marsanne, Sémillon, Sauvignon Blanc, and/or Vermentino), but little of it escapes the region's fish restaurants.

Winemaking techniques are traditional but evolving. While some producers would like to introduce a red category with no OAK AGEING for a lighter, fresher style, current regulations stipulate that all reds must have at least 18 months in cask. Thanks to the high proportion of Mourvèdre (at least 50%), REDUCTION is a constant threat. Mechanical harvesting is banned. Domaine Tempier is one of the few domaines to have a well-established market outside France, but others such as Pibarnon, Pradeaux, La

Bastide Blanche, and Vannières have a growing overseas presence. E.A.G.

Bannockburn, recognized in 2021, is the only subregional GEOGRAPHICAL INDICATION (GI) in Central Otago, NEW ZEALAND. A warm, dry area on the southern banks of the Kawarau River at the edge of Lake Dunstan in the Cromwell Basin, it is one of the first areas to begin harvesting, often four weeks ahead of the much cooler Gibbston. As elsewhere in Central, vineyards are planted overwhelmingly to Pinot Noir and have thrived in the complex soils that have been modified to a large extent by Bannockburn's strong gold-mining history. S.P.T.

Banyuls and **Banyuls Grand Cru** are the appellations for some of France's finest VINS DOUX NATURELS (VDN), made from vertiginous, terraced, black SCHIST vineyards above the Mediterranean at the southern limit of ROUSSILLON. The dry wines produced in the same vineyards are entitled to the appellation COLLIOURE, Banyuls-sur-Mer and Collioure being two of the four dramatic seaside communes included in these two appellations.

The VDN appellation divides into five colours: Blanc, Rosé, Grenat, Ambré, and Tuilé. For the red VDNs, GRENACHE NOIR must dominate the blend, constituting at least 50% of a Banyuls and 75% Banyuls Grand Cru, which also requires 30 months' OAK AGEING. Also permitted are Grenache Gris, Carignan, Cinsault, Counoise, Mourvèdre, and Syrah. White and Ambré versions rely on GRENACHE BLANC and Gris with MACABEO and TOURBAT and can include small amounts of both Muscats, Marsanne, Roussanne, Vermentino, and Carignan Blanc. Yields are low and the grapes are picked with a high potential alcohol level, often as late as October. Alcohol is added, usually *sur grains*, on the skins, and then the wine is left to age in either a REDUCTIVE or an OXIDATIVE environment, depending on the desired style.

Traditionally Banyuls was an oxidative wine, aged in large old wood casks and often including an initial period of ageing outside in glass BONBONNES. The occasional reminder of the very austere RANCIO style of Banyuls, sometimes matured in a SOLERA system, can occasionally be found in the dustiest cellars. The more recently developed Grenat is a young red wine focused on fresh, heady red-fruit aromas. Banyuls Ambré and Tuilé, and Hors d'Age after five or more years of ageing, demonstrate the extraordinary levels of concentration that can be achieved by Grenache, heat, and time. Such wines are among the few that go well with chocolate, although many a French chef has created savoury dishes, often with a hint of sweetness, to be served expressly with a particular Banyuls. This is a rare appellation, once routinely prescribed medicinally, able to offer 20- and 30-year-old wines as a serious proportion of its total production. See also RIVESALTES and MAURY. R.E.G.

Barbaresco, firmly structured red wine based on the NEBBIOLO grape grown around the village of Barbaresco in the PIEMONTE region in north-west Italy. Long wrongly considered very much the junior of BAROLO in terms of its size and the structure and prestige of its wines, Barbaresco emerged from Barolo's shadow in the 1960s to win recognition of its own striking qualities of elegance and aromatic intensity.

The wine is, in fact, a younger one than Barolo, its name appearing on labels only from 1894 when Domizio Cavazza, professor at the Oenological School of ALBA, founded the Barbaresco CO-OPERATIVE (now the much-admired Cantina di Produttori di Barbaresco). Before that the wines of Barbaresco were often blended with Barolo to add freshness to the latter. Barbaresco did not enjoy Barolo's connection with the House of Savoy and the nobility of the royal court in Turin, and it suffered relative commercial obscurity until the efforts of Giovanni GAJA and Bruno Giacosa in the 1960s demonstrated the full potential of the wine.

The production zone of Barbaresco is north-east and east of the city of Alba and only one-third the size of Barolo, but, as in Barolo, the area under vine has increased dramatically in recent years, from 484 ha in the early 1990s to 733 ha/1,811 acres in 2019. The wine is produced in the townships of Barbaresco, Treiso (formerly part of Barbaresco), and Neive, with a little made in a fragment of Alba. Neive calls itself 'the township of four wines' (the others being MOSCATO, BARBERA, DOLCETTO), and Nebbiolo consolidated its position there only after the Second World War. At the cost of Barbera and Dolcetto, today Neive has 265 ha/654 acres of the more lucrative Nebbiolo, up from 140 ha in 1995. Moscato has remained relatively unaffected by Nebbiolo's rise in popularity, making up half the planted area.

Although soil differences between Barolo and Barbaresco are regularly advanced as a major factor in the style difference, broadly speaking there are more similarities than differences. Barbaresco's soils can roughly be divided into two types. The CALCAREOUS clay of the Tortonion epoch is very similar to that in the Barolo communes of La Morra and Barolo, resulting in a perfumed, FRUIT-DRIVEN style. The second soil type, more compact and resembling somewhat the soils of the Barolo communes Monforte d'Alba and Serralunga d'Alba, is the so-called Sant'Agata fossil MARL, yielding more tannic wines.

Nebbiolo ripens earlier in some parts in Barbaresco than in Barolo, notably in vineyards closest to the River Tanaro, giving rise to the idea of Barbaresco as a lighter style. This is reflected in its ageing requirements: minimum 26 months, with at least 9 months in oak, and 50 months for Barbaresco Riserva, compared with Barolo's 38 months of which 18 are in oak, and 62 months for the Riserva. This has led to the false assumption that Barbaresco is less ageworthy, which in recent past has unfortunately spurred some producers to attempt to emulate Barolo, ignoring Barbaresco's unique style.

Winemaking techniques, which had previously favoured prolonged MACERATION and CASK AGEING, changed in the 1970s and 1980s towards considerably shorter periods in French BARRIQUES in response to modern tastes for rounder, fruitier wines. This was scorned by more traditional winemakers who argued that French oak suppressed Nebbiolo's gentle perfume. Today, an increasing number of Barbaresco producers are returning to long maceration, often up to 40 days, and ageing in large oak casks rather than barrique. If Barbaresco is considered a lighter-bodied wine than Barolo (although these are wines which must have a minimum ALCOHOLIC STRENGTH of 12.5% and easily reach 13.5%), it is not lacking in the TANNINS and ACIDITY that mark the Nebbiolo grape; young Barbaresco is by no means an inevitably pleasurable glass of wine. The work done by the Produttori del Barbaresco, one of Italy's finest co-operatives, and by individual producers such as Angelo Gaja and Bruno Giacosa has helped to establish Barbaresco as a top-quality wine, while a number of smaller producers have begun converting to ORGANIC and BIODYNAMIC VITICULTURE and are using traditional winemaking techniques to produce highly original, long-lived wines with a muscular structure and perfumes of cherry, violets, and, with age, iron, tar, and orange peel.

In Barbaresco as in the rest of Italy, SINGLE-VINEYARD WINES are a relatively recent phenomenon, with the first, Prunotto's Barbaresco Montestefano, appearing in 1961, and there is a less firmly established written record of CRU designation here than in Barolo. Lorenzo Fantini's monograph on Piedmontese viticulture of the late 19th century indicates very few 'choice positions' in Barbaresco (and none whatsoever in Neive). The first attempts to list and rate the finest positions date from the 1960s (Luigi VERONELLI) and the 1970s (Renato Ratti).

NÉGOCIANTS' willingness to pay higher prices for grapes from certain vineyards, however, has established a certain consensus about which are the best: Asili, Montefico, Montestefano, and Rabajà in Barbaresco; Albesani and Gallina in Neive; and Pajorè in Treiso. A certain number of the most famous vineyards—San Lorenzo, Tildin, and Martinenga in Barbaresco, Santo Stefano in Neive—have gained their current prestige from the dedicated work and exacting standards of producers such as Gaja, Giacosa,

B

and Alberto di Gresy. An official list of single vineyards, the so-called MGA (*menzioni geografiche aggiuntive*), was introduced in 2007, long before Barolo did the same in 2010. This list of single vineyards, also referred to as crus, has sensibly retained almost all the historically known vineyards, rarely absorbing them in more famous vineyard names for commercial reasons. W.S.

Masnaghetti, A., *Barbaresco MGA: The Barbaresco Great Vineyard Encyclopedia* (2016).

O'Keefe, K., *Barolo and Barbaresco: The King and Queen of Italian Wine* (2014).

www.langhevini.it

barbarians, uncivilized ancient European people who were introduced to wine by CLASSICAL civilizations (see ROME and GREECE). See also CELTS.

Barbarossa, name used for many, probably unrelated, Italian red grapes, one of which may be identical to the rare **Barbaroux** of Provence.

Robinson, J., et al., *Wine Grapes: A Complete Guide to 1,368 Vine Varieties, Including Their Origins and Flavours* (2012).

Barbera, productive and versatile red grape variety widely planted in northern Italy. Total Italian plantings in 2017 were 18,431 ha/45,544 acres. Recent DNA PROFILING has shown that Barbera is most likely a progeny of Coccalona Nera, an almost extinct, inferior variety from south-eastern Piemonte known as Orsolina in Reggio Emilia and Rohrtraube Blaurot in Germany.

Barbera ripens relatively late, as much as two weeks after DOLCETTO, although in advance of the stately NEBBIOLO. Its chief characteristic is its high level of natural acidity even when fully ripe, which has helped its popularity in hot climates.

Piemonte

Barbera was once known as 'the people's wine' of Piemonte for its versatility and its abundant production. During the 1980s and 1990s, however, a proportion of Barbera underwent a significant metamorphosis as producers, in a parallel development to the Sangiovese-based SUPERTUSCANS, experimented with BARREL AGEING. The prototype was Giacomo Bologna's Bricco dell'Uccellone. New oak and lower yields substantially modifies the character of Barbera, adding a real spiciness to its aroma and a certain quantity of ligneous tannins, which firm up its structure and soften the impact of its acidity. In addition, the extra oxygenation of the wine has helped to curb the variety's natural tendency to REDUCTION. Today Barbera comes in a bewildering range of styles, from the young, cheap, light, and spritzy to powerful, intense, highly priced wines that need extended cellaring, reflecting both variation of producer vision and the extreme heterogeneity of the soils and MESOCLIMATES of the zones where it is planted.

Certain characteristics are constant nonetheless: a deep ruby colour (the wine was frequently used in the past to 'correct' the colour of Nebbiolo grapes grown in BAROLO and BARBARESCO); relatively low levels of TANNINS; and pronounced ACIDITY, which is aggravated by overproduction, Barbera being a variety of exemplary VIGOUR and productivity. The DOC regulations permit generous yields (70 hl/ha in Alba, 63 hl/ha in Asti), relatively low ALCOHOLIC STRENGTH (12% in Alba and Asti, 11.5% in the Monferrato), and high minimum acidity. However, the combination of lower yields and the effects of CLIMATE CHANGE are making it ever harder to keep alcohol levels down and still reach PHYSIOLOGICAL RIPENESS.

ALBA, ASTI, and the MONFERRATO give their names to the three DOC zones of Piemonte, although the zones tend to sprawl across vast extensions of territory: there are 171 townships in the Asti DOC and 215 townships in the Monferrato DOC (with the two zones overlapping to a certain extent). The hills immediately to the north and south of Alba and Monforte d'Alba in the Alba DOC and, in the province of Asti, the area from Nizza Monferrato northwest towards Vinchio, Castelnuovo Calcea, Agliano, Belveglio, and Rocchetta Tanaro are considered classic zones for Barbera. The finest wines tend to come from the DOCG **Barbera d'Asti**. Of the DOCG's three subzones, Nizza, one of the warmest parts of the Asti zone and historically producing the ripest Barbera, was promoted to its own DOCG in 2014. In Asti, Barbera is given the best vineyard sites, whereas in Alba these sites go to Nebbiolo.

An apparently unrelated **Barbera Bianca** is grown on 114 ha/282 acres, mainly in Acqui and Alessandria.

Elsewhere in Italy

Barbera dominates much of Lombardy, especially the vineyards of OLTREPÒ PAVESE, where it makes varietal wines of varying quality and degrees of fizziness, some fine and lively, with the best and most ageworthy coming from Buttafuoco. It is also blended with the softer local CROATINA or BONARDA Piemontese grapes. It is a minor, and decreasing, ingredient in Curtefranca (see FRANCIACORTA) and is found, as elsewhere in Italy, in oceans of basic VINO DA TAVOLA.

Barbera is also much planted immediately south-east of Piemonte in the Colli Piacentini, the hills above Piacenza, of EMILIA-ROMAGNA. Here too it is often blended with Bonarda, particularly in the Val Tidone for the sparkling and occasionally still red Gutturnio DOC. It is also planted in the Colli Bolognesi and Colli di Parma, where it may also produce a VARIETAL wine which rarely has the concentration of Piemonte's best and is regularly fizzy.

The variety was planted in Argentina many years ago and in California and Australia more recently thanks to a FASHION for Italian varieties and its suitability for warm climates. It is also found in Slovenia.

Barbera del Sannio is known in Campania while **Barbera Sarda** is grown on Sardinia, but neither is related to the Barbera of Piemonte.

Bardolino, generally modest but attractive light red wine from the south-eastern shores of Lake Garda in the VENETO region of north-east Italy. As in the other two important Veneto DOCS SOAVE and VALPOLICELLA, the original production zone known as CLASSICO (1,060 ha/2,619 acres encompassing Bardolino, Garda, Lazise, Affia, Costermano, and Cavaion) has been extended to a 1,580-ha zone whose wines are called simply Bardolino. The vineyard area of both zones combined is 2,640 ha, producing some 170,616 hl/4.5 million gallons annually. Like Valpolicella, the wine is made of CORVINA, CORVINONE, and RONDINELLA (Molinara is no longer obligatory), with the possible addition of up to 20% of any authorized variety. Merlot is often used to bolster alcohol levels to the official minimum of 11% (9.5% for straight Bardolino DOC) so that after an additional year of ageing it can be labelled with the DOCG Bardolino Superiore. The rosé version, either still or sparkling, is called Chiaretto, while the NOVELLO indicates wines bottled before 31 December of the vintage year. In general, the determining factor of the wine's general blandness are the high permitted yields of 80 hl/ha. However, in 2021, three official subzones were created—Sommacampagna, La Rocca, Montebaldo—which require lower yields and later releases and forbid CHAPTALIZATION. Increased quality paired with growing demand for rosé has much improved Bardolino Chiaretto, while wineries such as Villa Calicantus and Le Fraghe clearly demonstrate Bardolino's potential. W.S.

www.ilbardolino.com

Barolo, often considered the most powerful and dramatic expression of the NEBBIOLO grape, takes its name from the village of the same name 15 km/9 miles to the south of the town of Alba in the region of PIEMONTE in north-west Italy.

The name Barolo started to appear on labels only in the mid 19th century, coinciding with the introduction of glass BOTTLES in the region around 1844. Before that it had been sold in cask only. Camillo Benzo, Count of Cavour, the architect of Italian unity, played a decisive role in Barolo's fortunes by modernizing his family's estate in Grinzane, with the introduction of a monoculture of vines, an idea that may have been inspired by his frequent travels to France. The French wine merchant Louis Oudart sought to work as his OENOLOGIST, and he is credited with creating the first modern, dry Barolo, although there is no written evidence of his winemaking practices. A decade earlier, Cavour had hired Pier Francesco Staglieno, who introduced fermentation in closed vats, which greatly reduced PREMATURE OXIDATION and levels of VOLATILE ACIDITY in the wines. Staglieno's handbook, published in 1835, already stressed the importance of fermenting wine to complete dryness, which he repeated in correspondence with Cavour on specific casks to be sent to him for consumption.

Giulietta Falletti, Marquise of Barolo, allegedly engaged Oudart for her vast estate extending to La Morra, Barolo, and Serralunga although there are no records to substantiate this. Her wine, which attracted the attention of King Carlo Alberto di Savoia, allegedly inspired him to purchase and develop the estates of the castles of Verduno and Roddi for wine production, while Emanuele, Count of Mirafiori, Vittorio Emanuele II's son by the royal mistress Rosa Vercellana, developed the vineyards around the hunting lodge of Fontanafredda in Serralunga d'Alba. Due to this association with what was then Italy's reigning dynasty, Barolo earned the name 'the wine of kings, the king of wines'.

The core of Barolo has always been the townships of Barolo, La Morra, Castiglione Falletto, Serralunga d'Alba, and Monforte d'Alba, supplemented by outlying areas in a variety of other townships. The Agricultural Commission of Alba added Grinzano, part of Verduno, and a section of Novello in 1909, confirming the previous DELIMITATION work of the Ministry of Agriculture in 1896. This became the official definition of the zone in 1934, not without protests from Barolo and Castiglione Falletto, which considered themselves the true standard-bearers of authentic Barolo. Parts of Diano d'Alba, Roddi, and Cherasco were added in the DOC decree of 1966, then believed to be an error at least on paper, although a new generation of producers show that quality can be achieved. The villages of Roddi and Cherasco have respectively a mere 24.3/60 acres and 2.76 ha planted to Nebbiolo for Barolo.

Most of the Barolo zone falls within the five core townships mentioned above. This sensible demarcation of the zone, disciplined YIELDS (56 hl/ha maximum), and long AGEING requirements (38 months in total with at least 18 months in oak) make this DOCG one of Italy's most strict.

Although in the recent past Barolo was seen as powerful and concentrated, with pronounced TANNINS and ACIDITY, there are significant stylistic differences among the wines of the various zones which tend to roughly reflect the two major soil types conveniently separated by the Alba–Barolo road which runs along the valley floor, dividing La Morra and Barolo to the west from Castiglione Falletto, Monforte d'Alba, and Serralunga d'Alba to the east. The first soil type, calcareous MARLS of the Tortonian epoch which are relatively compact and more fertile, characterize the vineyards of the townships of La Morra and Barolo and, depending on the location of the vineyard, can produce softer, fruitier, aromatic wines. The second soil type, from the Helvetian epoch, with a higher proportion of compressed SANDSTONE, is less compact and less fertile, with the result that the townships of Monforte d'Alba and Serralunga d'Alba yield more intense, structured wines that mature more slowly. The vineyards of Castiglione Falletto are on a spur that divides these two valleys and produce wines that have some of the elegant and more forward character of the wines from Barolo combined with the structure and backbone of those from Serralunga.

All fine Barolo, however, shares certain traits: colour that is never deep (for Nebbiolo, like Pinot Noir, never produces opaque wines), ruby tending relatively rapidly to garnet or brick; and complex and expansive aromas of cherries and plums, evolving with time into dried cherries, rose petals, tar, liquorice, and—according to a few fortunate connoisseurs—the local white truffles. Full flavours are backed by substantial tannins, a dense texture, and lifted but never tart acidity.

One development that has marked contemporary Barolo is ESTATE BOTTLING and the fact that virtually all producers offer at least one SINGLE-VINEYARD WINE. Until 1960 the marketing of the wine was dominated by NÉGOCIANT houses, unsurprising in a production zone where the average property is less than 2 ha/5 acres. Estate bottling represented both an attempt by grape-growers to reap greater economic benefits from their vineyards and a desire to put their name, as well as that of their holdings, before the public. Négociant houses, dealing in large quantities, necessarily blended the wines of different provenances into a house Barolo (just like their counterparts in BURGUNDY). When skilfully done, this did—and still does—accomplish the creation of balanced and harmonious wines which exemplify the general characteristics of Barolo. But certain privileged positions have long enjoyed greater prestige and given more distinctive wines in both the written tradition (from Lorenzo Fantini in the late 19th century to modern writers such as Luigi VERONELLI, Renato Ratti and, more recently, Alessandro Masnaghetti) and in the oral tradition of the zone, opinions made concretely significant by the higher prices paid by négociants for the grapes and wines of certain vineyards. While there is no absolute unanimity, most shortlists of the finest CRUS include Rocche dell'Annunziata, Brunate, and Cerequio in La Morra, spilling over into Barolo; Cannubi and Sarmazza in Barolo; Rocche di Castiglione, Villero, and Monprivato in Castiglione Falletto; Bussia, Ginestra, and previously Santo Stefano di Perno (now included in the unreasonably enlarged Perno, see below) in Monforte d'Alba; and Francia, Lazzarito, Ceretta, Arione, and Vignarionda in Serralunga d'Alba.

The multiplicity of single-vineyard bottlings from the 1980s, in the absence of an official CLASSIFICATION, has had the paradoxical result of focusing attention on and reinforcing confidence in single producers. The situation has, at least partially, been addressed by the introduction of the *Menzione Geografica Aggiuntiva* (MGA), an official list of registered single vineyards throughout the Barolo zone. They are not classified, but they are identified as 'crus', and Masnaghetti has attempted his own unofficial classification. Although most Barolo communes produced a historically faithful list, some, especially Monforte d'Alba, radically pruned the number of its vineyards by including swathes of them within more famous names. Bussia in particular has been unreasonably enlarged since the authorities failed to question this loss of historic vineyards and detail. This ruthless capitalization on famous vineyard names recalls the controversial creation of GROSSLAGE in Germany.

As the world of wine opened up in the 1960s, and as some of the producers in Barolo travelled further than Turin or Rome, they decided that their wines were badly in need of modernizing, triggering a move to TEMPERATURE CONTROL during FERMENTATION, a reduction in the length of MACERATION, a move to PUMPING OVER rather than SUBMERGED CAP in the belief that a lower tannin level and shorter time in barrel were steps in this direction. The leaders of the movement towards a softer style of Barolo were Renato Ratti, Paolo Cordero di Montezemolo, and Elio Altare. The use of ROTOFERMENTERS, allowing for speedy extraction of colour and a swift alcoholic fermentation (generally 7–14 days), as well as shorter ageing periods executed in new French oak barrels, resulted in less tannic, deeper-coloured wines.

The proponents of this new approach were termed 'modernists', while those who retained faith in the old methods were called 'traditionalists'. This rather facile distinction fascinated the wine world in the 1970s and 1980s, but by the beginning of the 21st century the differences between the modernists and traditionalists had come full circle. Some of the modernist versions aged in small French oak developed poorly in bottle, sometimes accompanied by premature oxidation, while the opulence of new-oak aromas tended to obliterate Nebbiolo's fine perfume. The traditionalists have seen their approach vindicated by a growing demand in the international market for their Barolos. Barriques are still in use, but a significant number of producers has returned to ageing in much larger casks, while increasing the total maceration on the skins to 30 and even 60 days in some cases, crucially without resulting in harsh tannins, bitterness, or oxidation. Arguably, better CLONAL SELECTION, lower yields, and higher plant density, combined with increasingly sophisticated knowledge of viticulture, has led to this increase of quality and, with that, an increase in the expression of variety and TERROIR, although CLIMATE CHANGE is putting these quality markers on their head.

An unparalleled series of exceptional vintages in the late 1990s and 2000s—such as 1996, 1997, 1998, 1999, and 2001, as well as the stellar 2010 and 2016—saw demand in the US, German-speaking markets, and the UK grow exponentially and prices escalate. Plantings have increased in response, from 1,714 ha/ 4,285 acres 2004 to 2,208 ha/5,451 acres in 2020. This included Nebbiolo planted in sites that were traditionally reserved for varieties such as DOLCETTO and BARBERA, with most of the production not geared towards Barolo but LANGHE Nebbiolo, which has taken the market by storm as a kind of economy Barolo. Such is its success that other denominations, such as MONFERRATO, recently changed their wine regulations to allow for the variety to appear on labels (to a background of fierce protests from Barolo producers). Meanwhile, Barolo's neighbouring Dogliani DOCG is seeing Dolcetto, its historic grape variety, succumb to Nebbiolo, which guarantees producers a much higher return.

See also BARBARESCO. W.S.

Masnaghetti, A., *Barolo MGA: The Barolo Great Vineyards Encyclopedia* (2015).
O'Keefe, K., *Barolo and Barbaresco* (2014).
Mainardi, G., and Berta, P., *Il vino del Generale: Le Lettere di Paolo Francesco Staglieno, Enologo di Carlo Alberto 1837–1843* (2015).
Staglieno, P., *Istruzione intorno al miglior modo di fare e conservare i vini in Piemonte* (1835).

Baroque, sometimes spelt **Barroque**, is the intensely local grape variety associated with white TURSAN. Although it is now grown almost exclusively in the Landes *département* (46 ha/ 114 acres in 2019), it was at one time known throughout SOUTH WEST FRANCE and was valued by growers in the early 20th century for its resistance to POWDERY MILDEW. The best examples display the unusual combination of high alcohol and fine aroma, something akin to ripe pears.

Barossa Valley, arguably the most famous wine region in AUSTRALIA and the one in which most wine is produced, even if a high proportion of it is shipped in from vineyards outside the valley itself. There is an increasing trend towards planting off the valley floor and on higher ground on the hillsides. On the other side of the coin, the incalculable value of the viticultural bank of Shiraz, Grenache, and Mourvèdre vineyards, up to 170 years old, DRY-FARMED and UNGRAFTED, makes this a heritage area which can be neither duplicated nor replaced. According to Australia's official wine geography, the **Barossa Zone** includes the Barossa Valley and Eden Valley GEOGRAPHICAL INDICATIONS. For more detail, see SOUTH AUSTRALIA.

barrel, cylindrical container traditionally made from WOOD and historically used for the storage and transportation of a wide range of goods. Today, barrels are used almost exclusively in the production of fine wines and spirits and are almost invariably made of OAK, although some have experimented with various combinations of STAINLESS STEEL, clay, CONCRETE, etc. The bulge, or bilge, of barrels means that they can be rolled and spun easily and that, when they are kept horizontal, any sediment naturally collects in one place, from which the wine can easily be separated by RACKING. The average worldwide production for wine and spirits (including cognac and brandy but not bourbon) is one million barrels, with more than half made in France.

Barrels come in many sizes (see BARREL TYPES) and qualities (see BARREL MAKING). The word 'barrel' is conventionally used for a wooden container small enough to be moved, while VATS are larger, permanent containers, sometimes with an open top. COOPERAGE is the collective noun for all wooden containers, whether barrels or vats (as well as the term for the cooper's business or premises), and the word CASK is used for wooden containers of all sizes.

BARREL AGEING is the term used in this *Companion* for ageing a wine in a barrel, while CASK AGEING has been used as a general term for keeping a wine in a larger wooden container. BARREL FERMENTATION is the technique of fermenting wine in barrel.

A barrel is made up of STAVES shaped into a bulging cylinder, with hoops round it, a flat circular head at either end, and at least one hole for a BUNG. See BARREL MAKING for details.

History

Although HERODOTUS refers to palm-wood casks being used to carry Armenian wine to Babylon in Mesopotamia, it is generally accepted that it was the Iron Age communities of northern Europe, notably the CELTS, who developed the wooden barrel for the large-scale transport of goods. Its origins cannot now be recovered, but Julius Caesar encountered barrels during his campaigns in France in the 50s BCE. In the second half of the 1st century CE, PLINY described transport barrels in GAUL in a way that suggests they would have been unfamiliar to his Roman audience. The Latin term *cupa*, which later came to mean 'barrel', at this time normally referred to wood storage tanks, the remains of one of which have been found at POMPEII, near Naples. Barrels or barrel staves have been preserved in waterlogged conditions on sites in Britain (at Silchester) and along the RHINE and the Danube. Famous monuments such as that from Neumagen on the German River MOSEL testify to the use of barrels for the transport of goods. When the Roman army served in northern Europe, it used barrels regularly; they are frequently illustrated in scenes from the columns of Trajan and Marcus Aurelius which commemorated the campaigns of these emperors in the 2nd century CE. There are increasing numbers of archaeological finds of barrels or barrel staves from Roman sites in Britain, along the RHINE, and in Western Europe. The presence of TARTARIC ACID residues in some cases may be evidence for the contents having been wine. (See PALAEOETHNOBOTANY.) The wood used was frequently silver fir.

From the middle of the 3rd century, references in literature and art to the use of barrels in Italy and, to a lesser extent, elsewhere in the Mediterranean are much more frequent. It is possible that the more widespread use of the barrel explains the disappearance of various types of AMPHORAE in this period. It also means that from this period on it is much more difficult to trace trade routes, since wood is much less likely to survive on archaeological sites. From the early medieval period, barrels were the normal means of transporting wine.

See also BARREL MAINTENANCE, BARREL RENEWAL, BARREL STORAGE, GRAIN, INNER STAVES, OAK, OAK FLAVOUR, TOAST, WOOD INFLUENCE, WOOD TYPES.

J.J.P.

Marlière, E., 'Le tonneau en Gaule romaine', *Gallia*, 58 (2001), 181–201.
Sands, R., and Marlière, E., 'Produce, repair, reuse, adapt, recycle: the multiple biographies of a Roman barrel', *European Journal of Archaeology*, 23/3 (2020), 356–80.

barrel ageing, also known as **barrel maturation**, is the winemaking operation of ageing wine in wooden BARRELS to create ideal conditions for the components of the wine to evolve and, in some instances, so that the wood imparts some OAK FLAVOUR to the wine, although the more obvious flavours of oak are today less sought-after than they were in the late 20th century.

Barrels were originally used for the TRANSPORT OF WINE, but winemakers, observing the way wines improved after time in barrel, developed techniques and cellars for deliberate barrel ageing, lasting from a few months for white wines to a year or more for reds.

White wines aged in barrels will often have been BARREL FERMENTED so the main goal is to prolong contact between the wine and the yeast lees (see LEES CONTACT) to enrich the wine with compounds released by yeast AUTOLYSIS. This may also involve LEES STIRRING to increase the exchanges between wine, lees, and wood.

The most obvious advantage of barrel ageing for both red and white wines is that it encourages CLARIFICATION and STABILIZATION of the wine in the most natural, if not necessarily the fastest, way.

When it comes to red wines, the aims are to clarify and stabilize their colour, to refine and soften their tannins giving more volume in the mouth and a longer aftertaste, and to increase the complexity of the aroma and flavour compounds.

The smaller volume of barrels compared with that of larger vats or tanks makes it easier to achieve clarity. Barrels are more sensitive to the ambient temperature in the cellar, and when the temperature drops, salts, particles, and colouring matter (mostly ANTHOCYANINS and FLAVONOLS) precipitate and settle at the bottom of the barrel. The clear wine is separated from the lees and the more turbid wine at the bottom of the barrel by RACKING.

In addition to clarification, other chemical reactions occur during barrel ageing, changing the phenolic structure of the wines. Although some oak flavour may be extracted directly into the wine, one of the more obvious secondary flavour effects of maturing a wine in barrel results from the slow oxygenation of the wine and the oxidation–reduction reactions (see REDOX POTENTIAL) that take place in the barrel. When barrels are filled, stoppered, and rolled, they receive a small but significant amount of OXYGEN. Leaving barrels upright and topping up the evaporated wine weekly can triple the amount of oxygen the wine receives. In the Bordeaux area, the type of BUNG (glass, silicone, polymer, wood, and fabric) and its positioning (on the top or side) are also tools used to regulate the oxygen supply. This uptake of oxygen, however slow or fast, aids in the formation of PIGMENTED TANNINS with colours that are more stable and permanent than those of monomeric anthocyanins.

Oxygenation will also result in smoother, more stable tannins as they form complexes with POLYSACCHARIDES and PROTEINS. If the newly formed phenolic compounds become too large due to POLYMERIZATION, they will precipitate and form sediment. Temperature increases will favour these reactions, and cooling will accelerate precipitation.

MICRO-OXYGENATION in barrel or tank is seen by some winemakers (and accountants) as an attractive alternative to prolonged barrel ageing.

Maturing wine in wood can also add aromatic complexity to a wine thanks to aroma compounds derived from the barrels (see OAK FLAVOUR). WOOD INFLUENCE outlines the factors that govern the process of barrel ageing: size, age, and wood type of the barrel, techniques used in BARREL MAKING, storage conditions, characteristics of the vintage, winemaking techniques, and time. See also TOAST for details of how this plays a part in providing a buffer between the alcohol and the wood's PHENOLICS.

Cellar conditions have a major impact on barrel-aged wine. The temperature in the cellar has an almost immediate impact on the temperature of the wine, which affects the volume of wine in the barrel, directly influencing the internal pressure of the barrel if it is well sealed with a bung. In addition, the relative humidity in the cellar, combined with temperature, has an effect on the wood of the barrel due to the hygroscopic properties of this material (see OAK). Both temperature and relative humidity have an effect on the oxygen supply, the wood aromas, tannin extraction, and even the microbiological balance of the wine.

J.E.H. & R.T. du C.

Ribéreau-Gayon, P., et al., *Traité d'Œnologie 2: Chimie du vin: Stabilisation et traitements* (7th edn, 2017), translated by J. Towey as *Handbook of Enology 2: The Chemistry of Wine Stabilization and Treatments* (3rd edn, 2021).

Roussey, C., et al., 'In-situ monitoring of wine volume, barrel mass, ullage pressure and dissolved oxygen for a better understanding of wine-barrel-cellar interactions', *Journal of Food Engineering*, 291 (2021), 110233.

barrel alternatives, common term for a group of materials and techniques, including the use of OAK CHIPS, BARREL INSERTS, and INNER STAVES (collectively known as oenological oak), sometimes in conjunction with MICRO-OXYGENATION, which are substitutes for BARRELS. Usually offcuts from cooperages or sawmills, toasted in convection ovens or infrared kilns, they save both money and space and have become increasingly sophisticated, offering the winemaker a choice of types of oak as well as different toast levels, but care is needed with the dosage and the length of time the products are in contact with the wine. The shape and size of the pieces influences the composition of the oak and the diffusion of oak compounds into the wine. Since 2006 certain barrel alternatives have been permitted in the EU, although their use is forbidden in some PDO wines. A.P.

barrel fermentation, winemaking technique of fermenting grape juice or must in small BARRELS rather than in a larger FERMENTATION VESSEL. The technique is used principally for white wines because of the difficulty of extracting through a barrel's small bung-hole the mass of skins and seeds which necessarily remains after red wine fermentation, although in the late 1990s fermentation of red wine in barrel, said to improve oak integration and MOUTHFEEL, gained in popularity. In Burgundy, California, and especially Australia, however, some winemakers deliberately put pressed red wines which still retain some unfermented sugars into barrel, thus allowing completion of red wine FERMENTATION in barrel in an attempt to make softer, more approachable wines.

Encouraged by the success of this technique, a few winemakers are taking this further and fermenting small quantities of red grapes entirely in barrels, either by removing the barrel head for an open-top fermentation or by using a specially designed barrel in which the bung-hole in the side of the barrel has been replaced by a porthole in the head, sometimes with a paddle inside to help break up the CAP. If the barrels are stored on a racking system with rollers, barrels can easily be turned to keep the cap mixed with the fermenting must—rather like a mini wooden ROTOFERMENTER. Proponents claim that putting the must into barrel immediately after crushing results in softer tannins, increased stability, and better colour concentration, probably because of the MICRO-OXYGENATION that takes place in barrel.

Barrel fermentation seems particularly well adapted to wine made from CHARDONNAY grapes and some of the finest SWEET WINES. Its advantages are that it offers the possibility of extracting a controlled amount of OAK FLAVOUR into the wine and that, since barrels have a large surface-to-volume ratio, artificial mechanized TEMPERATURE CONTROL may not be needed. It also provides a natural prelude to BARREL AGEING and LEES STIRRING since the lees and the wine are already in the same container.

White wine which is fermented and stored in oak with its yeast solids, or LEES, has a softened, less obvious, and more integrated oak flavour than wine that has been fermented in a larger container before being matured in barrels because the YEAST acts on the highly aromatic oak flavour molecules to transform them biochemically into much less aromatic substances (VANILLIN, for example, is transformed into vanillic acid, which has a higher perception threshold) and because of the adsorption of aromatic compounds on to the yeast cell wall. (The secondary fermentation aromas, however, such as result from ESTERS, fatty acids, and higher alcohols, are substantially unaffected by barrel fermentation.) FINING also removes some oak compounds. Fermentation in barrel also gives large increases in POLYSACCHARIDES, especially MANNOPROTEINS, which add richness and apparent LENGTH of flavour on the palate. The amount of yeast mass in the barrel and the frequency of stirring have a direct and considerable effect on the quantity of polysaccharides formed. The yeast also make and release ENZYMES that could reduce the stability of some aromatic compounds in the wine.

White wines fermented and matured for a few months on their lees in barrel usually have a much lighter colour than those put into barrel after fermentation to mature. Yeast cell walls adsorb certain PHENOLICS, a property that is useful for removing any unwanted colour in champagne, for example, by adding fresh lees.

Stirring up the lees in the barrel also affects oak flavour. If the lees are stirred, they act as an even more effective buffer between the wine and the wood, limiting the extent to which wood TANNINS, and colouring matter, are extracted into the wine. Wines subjected to lees stirring therefore tend to be much paler and less tannic than those whose lees are not stirred. Stirring also minimizes the effects of stratification in the barrel and is a more efficient way to bring wine components in contact with the lees and thereby increase extraction of materials from them.

Fermentation in barrel can also have secondary flavour effects due to temperature, lot size, and precise level of TOAST. The often higher temperature of fermentation in barrel rather than vat causes a change in wine AROMAS, depending on the grape variety. And because each fermentation even of identical juice has a slightly different flavour outcome, the larger number of small-volume lots that are common in barrel fermentation creates more complexity. A 10,000-l/2,642-gal lot would create one fermentation flavour if it were fermented in one tank, for example, but the same lot volume fermented in 70 barrels would produce a much more complex array of flavours.

The disadvantages of barrel fermentation are the relatively small size of the barrel and the time and effort required to clean, fill, and empty it, although the extra degree of complexity gained by the wine is usually worth any extra production costs. The cost of new barrels themselves is such, however, that the technique is restricted to higher-priced wines. With so many fermentations in a non-sterile material, it is always possible that some barrels may be infected with BACTERIA or undesirable yeasts, so extra vigilance is required to eliminate any defective wines.

Fermentation produces a protective blanket of CARBON DIOXIDE on the surface of the wine in the barrel. As fermentation slows and stops, the CO_2 will be displaced by air, allowing uptake of some oxygen from the HEAD SPACE into the wine. The larger ratio of head space to wine volume in barrels, and the permeability of wood to oxygen, will allow more oxygen to enter the wine than would occur if the same volume were in a large tank. However, it is important to keep barrels full (see TOPPING UP) to limit the amount of oxygen exposure so that the wine does not become OXIDIZED or affected by BACTERIAL SPOILAGE. Regular LEES STIRRING will also help to limit oxidation as the lees combine with oxygen.

When barrels are expensive and wine is not, winemakers and winery owners seek ways of economizing on barrel purchases. For alternatives to barrels, see INNER STAVES and OAK CHIPS.

L.F.B., J.E.H. & V.L.

Ribéreau-Gayon, P., et al., 'Making dry white wines in barrels', in P. Ribéreau-Gayon et al., *Handbook of Enology 1: The Microbiology of Wine and Vinifications* (3rd edn, 2021).

barrel inserts, imprecise and expanding term for pieces of wood, usually OAK, added to a barrel too old to impart much OAK FLAVOUR. With larger pieces of wood, the barrel head has to be removed. A food-grade device reminiscent of the tray in an automatic dishwasher is inserted. This holds small oak planks which may be renewed every other year or so. Alternatively, small planks are linked together and attached to the bottom of the BUNG so that they dangle in the wine. For the use of inserts in a tank, see INNER STAVES. See also BARREL RENEWAL and OAK CHIPS.

barrel maintenance. BARRELS are an important investment for a winery, in terms of both their cost and their precious contents. The contents of a barrel may well have a wholesale value of thousands of dollars, while new barrels cost £250 to £1,100 (US$350 to US $1,500) each (for a 225-l barrel), depending on quality and origin. The preparation of new barrels and the maintenance of used ones is therefore an important activity for winemakers and can play a part in determining WOOD INFLUENCE. The costs associated with barrel ageing (buildings and their maintenance, cellar workers, energy, cellar tools and machinery, and loss of wine during handling or through evaporation) can be as much as the purchase price of the barrels.

Preparation for use

Barrels are treated prior to use both to check for leaks and to ensure that the barrel brings the right flavours to the wine. Typically, barrels are simply rinsed or filled with hot or cold water to check for leaks and so that the wood can be rehydrated after shipping and transportation, thus reducing initial leaks. The barrel may be spun and shaken so that, in theory, some of the rough TANNINS are washed out and leaks are revealed. Nowadays more wineries are using steam to check barrels, a method which saves water and time and reduces the risk of introducing microbial organisms such as bacteria into the wood. If a small leak is found, it can usually be plugged with an appropriately sized piece of wood. A leak near the head may indicate that some adjustment is necessary. Occasionally a STAVE may have to be replaced. However, the way the wood has been dried (see BARREL MAKING) has more influence on the tannins than the way the barrels are prepared for use.

In the past, it was not uncommon to treat the barrels with chemicals such as soda ash or ammonium to remove harsh tannins, but this also tended to remove the barrel's TOAST, and most winemakers now prefer to prepare their barrels with water or steam. At some point prior to first use, the exterior of the barrel is often coated with linseed oil or a mildewcide to combat MOULDS, although this is done principally for aesthetic reasons, and linseed is used mainly on larger vats.

Identification

At many wineries a card is attached to the head of the barrel to enable the winemaker to follow the life of each individual barrel. In larger wineries, it is not uncommon to see the sort of barcode used by supermarkets, along with computerized tracking (see INFORMATION TECHNOLOGY). Some coopers now deliver barrels with barcodes, making it easier to identify them and improving their traceability. In smaller wineries, a few letters may suffice. In Burgundy, for example, the chalked letters 'CM/R' might serve to denote 'Chassagne Montrachet, Ruchottes'. And in very small cellars, the single individual in charge may know every barrel so intimately that formal markings are unnecessary. Some wineries are now experimenting with Radio Frequency Identification (RFID) systems.

Cleaning

Barrels must be cleaned between uses and during RACKING, mainly to remove LEES and TARTRATES on the internal surface of the barrel and sometimes also to reduce the population of spoilage microorganisms such as BRETT or ACETOBACTER. Cleaning usually starts by removing tartrates using high-pressure jets of hot water. Harsher chemical treatments with citric acid or potassium carbonate may be needed but are generally avoided.

Steam is preferred for sanitizing the barrel and to remove spoilage microflora because it penetrates the wood, sterilizing not just the surface but also the deeper layers. The process is completed by rinsing the barrel with a solution of SULFUR DIOXIDE or by burning SO_2 inside the barrel.

Alternative techniques such the use of ultrasound, ultraviolet radiation, or dry ice exist but are much less common in practice.

Unused barrels and used empty barrels

Storage of unused empty barrels is problematic for several reasons: wood dehydration may lead to leakages; the oak may adsorb flavours such as TCA; and the wood could be colonized by mould in wet conditions. They are often sheathed in plastic before being shipped long distances to minimize spoilage. The storage of used empty barrels is even more problematic because they contain wine residues which could encourage the growth of harmful microorganisms such as ACETOBACTER and BRETTANOMYCES. To avoid these risks, empty barrels should be rinsed, carefully dried, treated with SULFUR DIOXIDE, and then bunged up every month. Overly long storage is not recommended since it entails excessive use of sulfur dioxide, and sulfuric acid will be formed. Barrels treated in this way must be stored under the same conditions of low temperature and high, but not too high, humidity as full barrels. High-pressure barrel washers can be used in combination with hot water or steam to sanitize barrels with little impact on wood quality, but the steam or water has to penetrate the staves sufficiently.

Most winemakers prefer to avoid the cost and risks associated with the long-term storage of empty barrels by ordering very precise quantities and filling them as soon as possible. See also BARREL RENEWAL and BARREL STORAGE.

J.E.H. & A.P.

Schahinger, G., and Rankine, B., *Cooperage for Winemakers* (rev. edn, 2005).

Jacon, V., *La Barrique: choix, utilisation, manutention* (2003).

barrel making involves far more than mere mechanics and the ability to fashion a watertight container out of nothing but bent wood. As outlined in detail in WOOD INFLUENCE, every stage of barrel manufacture has an impact on wine matured in that barrel. First, the tree is cut down, usually during the autumn or winter when the sap is down. COOPERS usually buy long sections of trunk, ideally from trees that are over 100 years old, and then the process that turns logs into stave wood begins.

Oak selection

Each oak tree is different, with its own sensorial properties, even among trees of the same species (see OAK for those species most important for wine). While the forest itself, often dominated by one species, was once the starting point for selection, in the 1990s research at BORDEAUX UNIVERSITY led to greater emphasis on GRAIN rather than specific forest. However, more recent research by Prida et al. has shown that the two species coexist in the same forest and that intra-specific variability is important for OAK FLAVOUR. Current more sophisticated selection is based on the analysis of individual trees or STAVES, using mainly gas chromatography–mass spectrometry (GC–MS) but also infrared spectrometry, so that a homogeneous lot of trees can be used to make more consistent barrels. This depends on research that elucidates the relationship between oak composition and a wine's sensory profile.

Prida, A., et al., 'Variation in wood volatile compounds in a mixed oak stand: strong species and spatial differentiation in whisky-lactone content', *Annals of Forest Science*, 64/3 (2007), 313–20.

Prida, A., et al., 'Effect of species and ecological conditions on ellagitannin content in oak wood from an even-aged and mixed stand of *Quercus robur* L. and *Quercus petraea* Liebl', *Annals of Forest Science*, 63/4 (2006), 415–24.

Cutting: sawing versus splitting

Logs of appropriate lengths are cut and then split into four lengthwise. The bark and sap wood are cut off so that staves may be cut from radial (rather than tangential) sections of wood.

Because American oak is so much less porous than European, staves of American oak can simply be sawn from each quarter to maximize the yield of each log. This is traditional quarter sawing. The mill worker tosses a quartered bolt on to a conveyor belt. A bandsaw parallel to the conveyor belt lops off a stave, which is sent on its way, while the rest of the log comes back on the conveyor belt to be sawn again.

European oak could well leak if thus sawn, however, and staves have to be cut, or split, much more carefully, minimizing the risk of leakage by following the oak GRAIN. Traditionally, therefore, European oak was split by hand so that the axe blade could follow the grain. Nowadays mechanically operated axes are guided through the wood sections and the resulting staves trimmed, still following the grain. Attempts to saw European oak in order to reduce wastage have largely been abandoned because of the issues with leakage.

In France, wood split by hand from logs for use as staves is known as *merrain* and the men who do this work are known as *merrandiers*. Traditionally this work was done near the forest, but nowadays many cooperages have their own stave-splitting facilities, either near the cooperage or in the forests.

Drying: air versus kiln

After the wood has been split or sawn, it must be dried to approximately 15% relative humidity. The drying process can be achieved either naturally in the open air or artificially using kilns, and the two methods are often combined. French oak has traditionally been air-dried one year for every 10 mm/0.4 in width so that it takes between 18 and 36 months to 'season' wood by drying it, in stacks of potential staves, in the open, preferably on a site far from any industrial activity or any other source of pollution. The optimum length of time varies according to the composition of the oak and the climate. Kiln drying, though quicker, may not give such high-quality results, but it is often used in order to homogenize a pallet of staves after air drying.

Many quality-conscious winemakers will pay a premium for wood dried in the open air, however, and some actually select and buy their own wood in advance of seasoning. Natural drying tends to reduce and modify the structure of the extractable compounds of the wood while heightening its aromatic potential. It has long been thought that, as wood is seasoned outdoors and turns grey, darkening the ground beneath it, harsh tannins are being leached out of the wood. Wine matured in air-dried wood certainly tends to taste less aggressively tannic than the same wine matured in kiln-dried wood. Australian research by Sefton and others, however, indicates that tannin levels in wood do not in fact change during seasoning but that their sensory effect does, with French oak tannins becoming much less noticeable with seasoning and American oak tannins more so.

In the late 1980s, many American cooperages realized that the wine-barrel market called for an entirely different barrel from that traditionally supplied to bourbon producers; they introduced air drying as well as offering barrels labelled with specific geographical origins, just like their French counterparts.

Studies by Nicolas Vivas of the University of BORDEAUX indicate that moulds and enzymes formed on and in the wood during air drying play crucial roles in the flavour of oak and any wine matured in it. Moulds formed on the surface of the wood liberate exocellular ENZYMES, principally heterosidases. They permit the transformation of certain bitter components into molecules which taste more neutral. At the same time, glucose and POLYSACCHARIDES are liberated from the structural elements of the wood.

Vivas has also shown that natural air drying lowers the level of dry EXTRACT, total PHENOLICS, and ellagitannins and raises the level of lactones, vanillins, and eugenols (see OAK FLAVOUR). He cautions that if oak is dried under warm and dry conditions such as those found in much of Australia and California, the results may be similar to those produced in artificial dryers.

Some cooperages maintain that it is not just the duration of the air-drying process that is important but the wood's exposure to rain and the temperature at which the wood is dried. Their wood may therefore be watered to simulate rain, but there has been little scientific analysis of results.

Spillman, P. J., et al., 'The effect of oak wood source, location of seasoning and coopering on

the composition of volatile compounds in oak-matured wines', *Australian Journal of Grape and Wine Research*, 10/3 (2008), 216–26.
Vivas, N., 'Recherches sur la qualité du chêne français de tonnellerie (*Quercus petraea* Liebl., *Quercus robur* L.) et sur les mécanismes d'oxydoréduction des vins rouges au cours de leur élevage en barrique' (PhD thesis, Bordeaux University, 1997).

Assembling

Once the staves are dry enough, they can be assembled into barrels. Barrel making is made possible by the fact that wood can be bent when it has been heated. If the staves are shaped properly, the result will be a barrel. All edges will meet properly, and the barrel will hold liquid without any agent other than the hoops which hold the staves together.

First, the staves are sized and trimmed into oblong lengths that might be called a double taper. Traditionally this work, known as 'dressing' the staves, was done by hand. The stave was 'listed'—that is, given the double taper shape—with a cooper's axe, known as a *doloire* in French. Then the inside of the stave was 'scalloped' with a two-handled hollowing knife to allow for easier bending. Finally the staves were joined on a jointer, known as a *colombe*. Here the staves were given their final shape—rounded at the bilge (the middle) and narrowed at the heads (the ends). Nowadays most of this work is done by machines, saving much time and energy.

Finally, the cooper fits the staves into a frame so that each barrel will have the same circumference. An especially strong and wide stave is chosen for the stave into which the bung-hole will eventually be drilled (see below). Then these staves are arranged around an iron 'raising up' hoop, the result looking like a skirt or a teepee splayed out from the hoop at the top. This job calls for great manual dexterity, although in many American cooperages machines can do much of this work.

Shaping and toasting

Research has shown that the heating process is one of the most important in barrel manufacture, modifying the wood's physical and chemical composition and profoundly influencing any wine stored in the barrel. Heating allows the cooper to shape the barrel. Toasting degrades the wood structure and thereby produces aromatic compounds. There is controversy as to which type of toasting is best, with some suggesting that slower toasting is better for both the flavour and the structure of a wine matured in that barrel. A deep medium toast produces the most desirable character for most woods, but there is variation in effect depending on the geographic origin of the wood, the seasoning of the wood, and the wine style. Ellagitannins from the barrel, which combine with phenolics in the wine to form new and softer tannin compounds and improve colour stability, are reduced by toasting. (See also OAK FLAVOUR and TOAST.)

Various sources of heat can be used to shape the barrel: natural gas, steam and boiling water, or the fire of pieces of oak (*écourtures*). Some cooperages combine techniques and shape the barrel with the aid of boiling water or steam, then finish the barrel with a fire toasting.

Coopers knocking down the hoops and bending the barrels over fire make an exciting spectacle, for a high degree of coordination is required. The would-be barrel is rolled over a cylindrical, vented metal firepot, known as a *chaufferette*, in which small pieces of oak are burned. The coopers walk round the barrel knocking down the temporary iron hoops. They pound the hammer on a hoop driver—a short block of wood with a flat metal end—while watering the wood to keep it from getting too toasted too quickly. After the top of the barrel has been shaped, the coopers wrap cables around the base of the barrel and use a capstan to cinch up the base.

Coopers often categorize the toasting and bending of staves in three stages: the warm-up (*chauffage*), the shaping (*cintrage*), and the toasting afterwards (*bousinage*). It is the last stage which determines the level and depth of toast inside the barrel, which depends crucially on the right combination of humidity and heat.

Natural gas, boiling water, and steam will heat the wood effectively and allow the cooper to bend the staves. Many winemakers prefer this technique as the barrel is easier to clean. Other winemakers prefer barrels shaped over a fire of wood pieces, as the toast on the inside of the barrel provides an interesting 'toasty' flavour to the wine. These winemakers feel that any extra effort in BARREL MAINTENANCE is justified by the special flavour provided by this technique. The amount of time the barrel sits on the fire and the heat of the fire both have a dramatic impact on the appearance of the barrel's interior and on resultant wine flavour. Winemakers can order barrels toasted to their specifications. Some cooperages use an electric ambient heater or a wood fire to toast the heads too, although these are usually left untoasted.

The heads

After the body of the barrel has been formed, then the heads, or barrel-ends, must be made and fitted. Five or six head staves are fitted together with wooden dowels or stainless-steel gudgeons (headless nails). Some cooperages are now using a tongue-and-groove system. Then the head is cut to size, usually round but sometimes slightly oval in shape. Near each end of the body of the barrel, a groove, called the croze, is cut into the inside of the barrel. The head is cut at the edges so that it will fit into the croze.

Formerly all of this work was done by hand, but now virtually all of it is done on machines which have replaced an array of traditional cooper's tools with names (adze, chiv, etc.) to delight the dedicated Scrabble player. Finally the head is fitted into the barrel. To do this the hoops are loosened and the head is inserted into the croze.

Finishing

Before the barrel can be sold or shipped, its outside must be planed so that splinters will not dog cellar work. The barrel is tested for leaks, usually with steam or hot water injected through a small hole drilled in the bung stave. If the barrel passes the test, the small hole is drilled to bung-hole size and cauterized. The temporary iron hoops are removed, and the final ones, usually made of metal and sometimes of chestnut, are fitted.

Developments

The quality of barrels has increased dramatically since the 1990s through mechanization of tasks such as splitting the wood, the chemical analysis of trees to improve oak selection, and the customization of barrels according to the wine that will fill them, as well as the invention of new tools to monitor barrel ageing.

See BARREL INSERTS, BARREL RENEWAL, INNER STAVES, and OAK CHIPS for other ways of imbuing wine with OAK FLAVOUR without having to buy new barrels.

See also BARREL TYPES, OAK, and WOOD INFLUENCE.

M.C.K. & A.P.

Chatonnet, P., 'Origin and processing of oak used in cooperage' and 'Aromatic compounds yielded by oak into wine', in *Le Bois et la qualité des vins et eaux-de-vie* (1992).
Jacon, V., *La Barrique: choix, utilisation, manutention* (2003).
Schahinger, G., and Rankine, B., *Cooperage for Winemakers* (rev. edn, 2005).
Sefton, M. A., 'How does oak barrel maturation contribute to wine flavor?', *Australian and New Zealand Wine Industry Journal* (Feb 1991).
Vivas, N., *Manuel de tonnellerie à l'usage des utilisateurs de futaille* (2nd edn, 2002).

barrel maturation. See BARREL AGEING.

barrel renewal is a way of saving money on expensive barrels that depreciate very quickly. One method involves shaving the interior of the barrel, but BARREL INSERTS, INNER STAVES, and OAK CHIPS are more common alternatives. A cooper removes the barrel head and shaves off all the pigmented wood from inside the barrel with a plane or grouter. In some cases, the barrel is allowed to dry out a bit, and then the

◀ European oak must be cut following the GRAIN to avoid leakage. These 1-metre lengths at the Seguin Moreau STAVE mill near Bordeaux have been scanned to work out the best location for the radial cuts in order to get as many staves as possible out of each precious piece of wood. © Seguin Moreau

cooper retoasts the inside in order to maintain the all-important buffer between the wine and the wood and seal the wood. This system is not perfect because it is difficult to toast wood that has been permeated by alcohol and is therefore not entirely dry. Retoasting seems most effective on relatively young (two- to three-year-old) barrels. Wine aged in shaved and retoasted older barrels rarely has the subtlety of wine matured in new barrels. Another technique involves removing the wine-soaked part of the barrel with dry ice.

barrel storage has both aesthetic and practical ramifications. In most wineries there are visitors to impress, although they tend to find efficient modern reality less impressive than cobwebbed tradition. Some much-visited wineries fill their barrels in full view of the tourists before trucking the wine down the road to a clinical modern barrel warehouse, carefully regulated for both temperature and humidity. In Bordeaux particularly, it is traditional to anoint the band around the middle of the barrel with wine, giving it a neat pink stripe—indeed, in some of today's most immaculate barrel cellars this is the only visible sign that a liquid called wine is involved at all.

Touristic considerations aside, most wineries usually employ one of the following techniques: (1) Barrels are placed on metal pallets and fork-lifted into place. This looks industrial but is easiest on the cellar staff. Barrels can be stored either rolled to the side or with the bung straight up. (2) Barrels are piled one, two, or even three high in neat rows. (3) Barrels are stacked in huge pyramids. These may look good, but the barrels are hard to work and clean as disassembling the stack is a daunting task. (4) A single row of barrels is rolled on to fixed barrel racks. This looks good but is often inefficient in terms of LABOUR costs and use of space. (5) Barrels rest on rollers, supported by a steel framework, making access to each one easier and reducing the need to move the barrels, which can be rotated *in situ* so that LEES STIRRING becomes unnecessary and barrels may be emptied or drained without being removed from the stack.

Storage conditions of full barrels are important (see BARREL MAINTENANCE for unused and empty barrels). If the cellar is too cold, the wine will not develop. If it is too warm, off-flavours and harmful bacteria may develop, and the wine may age too rapidly. If the cellars are too dry, too much wine can evaporate and the barrels themselves can dry out. The ideal temperature is usually around 14–18 °C/57–66 °F, with a relative HUMIDITY over 75%. Below 75%, water evaporates, but above that figure alcohol evaporates. In warm regions, winemakers like to keep the humidity high, but not so high that it becomes impossible to control the growth of moulds.

The winemaker must consider the dew point, that combination of temperature and humidity at which evaporation occurs. Storing empty barrels (and full ones too) at temperatures higher than 18 °C/65 °F invites problems, and storing barrels over 21 °C/70 °F for more than three weeks runs the risk of BACTERIAL BLIGHT and the formation of VOLATILE ACIDS. Constancy of temperature is not as important as it is in a cellar for full bottles, and a winter drop in temperature assists precipitation and therefore CLARIFICATION.

See also TOPPING UP.

barrel types vary considerably, and this list includes some terms used for COOPERAGE, or wooden containers, that are strictly speaking larger than BARRELS.

Before CONCRETE, STAINLESS STEEL, and other inert materials replaced WOOD as the most common material for wine FERMENTATION VESSELS and storage CONTAINERS in the 1960s, each wine region had its own legion of barrel types. Even today such terms as *feuillette*, TONNEAU, and FUDER may be used to measure volumes of wine long after the actual containers themselves have been abandoned. As recently as 1976, Jean Taransaud was able to list four pages of different barrel types used in various French wine regions (see below). By the second decade of this century there was a marked trend away from heavy OAK influence and towards using barrels larger than the traditional sizes listed below, with capacities typically between 300 and 600 l (80 and 160 gal).

France

Barrel types, as most things French, are intensely regionalized. In many cases their capacity has changed over the years.

Bordeaux The **barrique bordelaise**, designated 225 l/59 gal for more than a century, is probably the most famous barrel of all and is used widely outside the region. It is about 95 cm/37 in high, and the staves are only about 20 mm/0.8 in thick (although the export version may be a centimetre or two shorter and have rather thicker staves). The traditional BARRIQUE, sometimes called the 'château' model, has a wooden crossbar at each head and a BUNG at the top and one for RACKING.

The TONNEAU, at 900 l/238 gal equivalent to four barriques, or 100 cases of wine, is much used as a measurement by the Bordeaux trade, even if this large cask is no longer common.

Burgundy Here the standard barrel is the 228-l (60-gal) **pièce**, which is relatively low (88 cm/37 in) and squat, supposedly for practicality, given the narrow doorways and small scale of many Burgundian cellars, and to provide a deeper bilge for the LEES which accumulate in this region where RACKING is generally less frequent than in Bordeaux, for example. The staves are usually notably thicker than those of barriques, about 27 mm. Traditionally these barrels had chestnut hoops or iron hoops painted black, although some domaines have followed the American taste for more workmanlike galvanized hoops, which need no repainting.

The traditional barrel in CHABLIS was the **feuillette**, at 132 l/35 gal about half the size of the *pièce*. This is still the unit in which prices are commonly given, even though the barrel itself is increasingly rare.

Some domaines on the CÔTE D'OR may still have their own size of *feuillette*, holding 114 l/30 gal, or even a **quartaut** holding 57 l/15 gal, used primarily for TOPPING UP or for the produce of a tiny holding in a GRAND CRU.

Cognac The standard cognac barrel now holds 350 l/92 gal, although in 1900 it held only about 275 l/73 gal and only 200 l/53 gal before the French Revolution. Cognac coopers make a wide range of barrels for various wine regions.

Champagne A 205-l/54-gal barrel is traditional here, but those few houses which persist with BARREL FERMENTATION may also buy in Burgundy barrels.

Elsewhere in France A wide range of barrel types is used in the Loire and the Rhône, from small new oak barrels to large wooden vats such as the 600-l/159-gal **demi-muid** used in Châteauneuf-du-Pape. In Alsace, large ovals, or **foudres** of varying capacities, are most common.

Germany

Although Germany formed its own group of daring iconoclasts, the Barrique Forum, in the early 1990s, most of the cooperage used until very recently has been large, old, and typically on the Mosel a **Fuder** holding 1,000 l/264 gal or on the Rhine a **Stück** of 1,200 l/317 gal. A **Halbfuder** and **Halbstück** are half these sizes respectively.

Spain

Spain's most characteristic barrel is the BUTT used for SHERRY. The American oak barrels used in RIOJA, and elsewhere, are 225-l/60 gal **barricas bordelesas** modelled on Bordeaux BARRIQUES. Spanish cooperage can vary considerably in size and shape, however, and new wood has only relatively recently been prized.

Portugal

The PIPE is Portugal's most famous wine measure. Portuguese cooperage, which can vary considerably in size and shape, may be made from French, American, or even Portuguese oak.

Italy

The large **botti**, or wooden casks, traditionally used in Italy are typically made from Slavonian oak and have varying but substantial capacities. The barrique, sometimes called a **carato**, is increasingly common, however, while the small barrels traditionally used for VIN SANTO are **caratelli** holding between 50 and 225 l/13–59 gal. Large upright wooden casks may be called **tini**.

Hungary

Gönci holding 136 l/36 gal are traditional in the production of TOKAJI and are named after the village in which they were usually made.

United States

Before the US became the world's best customer for exported French oak barrels (see COOPERAGE), American winemakers bought 50-gal/190-l American oak barrels produced for the whiskey business. A decline in bourbon sales in the 1980s led to American cooperages tailoring an increasing proportion of their output to wineries' needs, although variations on the *barrique* and *pièce* imported from France are the most desired, and most common, barrels used by American winemakers. Barrels holding 70 gal/265 l—with Burgundy-sized heads and Bordeaux-length staves—have become popular for both aesthetic and practical reasons.

Australia and New Zealand

Barriques of 225 l/59 gal have become the most commonly used barrel, and, if imported from France, are imported whole. **Hogsheads** of 300 l/79 gal and **puncheons** holding 450 or 500 l/118 or 132 gal are regaining popularity. While the latter are too large to manœuvre with ease and do not impart OAK FLAVOUR as fast as some winemakers desire, they are more suitable than *barriques*, for example, for some lighter wines and for the 21st-century trend towards more restrained use of oak. M.C.K. & J.R.

Taransaud, J., *Le Livre de la tonnellerie* (1976).

barrica, Spanish term for a barrel or BARRIQUE. A *barrica bordelesa* is the specific term for a Bordeaux *barrique*, the most common BARREL TYPE used in Spain.

barrique, the most famous of the BARREL TYPES, Bordeaux's relatively tall 225-l/59-gal wooden cask with thinner STAVES than the Burgundian *pièce* and most other barrels.

In the Middle Ages, the commercially acute Bordelais virtually trademarked their distinctive *barrique bordelaise*, carefully designating its dimensions and prohibiting its use outside the region. By the end of the 18th century, it had replaced the unwieldy TONNEAU for transportation as well as storage, and in 1866 it was officially decreed that one must hold 225 l/59 gal, rather than 215–230 l/57–60 gal as previously. Even as recently as this, it was common for some of the most highly regarded wines of Bordeaux to be shipped in *barrique* for bottling, if not by the NÉGOCIANTS of Bordeaux then by wine merchants outside France, particularly in northern Europe.

Today the word *barrique* is often used, particularly outside France, for all manner of wooden BARRELS. In Germany and Italy, for example, the word has been closely and emotively associated with those who employ BARREL MATURATION in small, new OAK rather than traditional CASK AGEING in *botti*, large wooden casks.

Barsac, sweet white-wine appellation in the south-west part of the BORDEAUX region on the left bank of the River GARONNE, just over the climatologically important cool river Ciron from the larger SAUTERNES appellation. All wines produced within Barsac are also entitled to use the appellation Sauternes (though the reverse is not the case). In 2021, 333 ha/750 acres of vineyard were declared. It is traditionally said that the wines of Barsac are slightly lighter than those of Sauternes because of the soil—shallow red SAND over a deep LIMESTONE bedrock on a gentle slope going down to the river, as opposed to Sauternes' rolling hills of gravel over clay. But much depends on individual properties and their vineyard policies. For more details on viticultural and winemaking practices, see SAUTERNES. See also the Barsac properties included in the Sauternes CLASSIFICATION. W.J.B.

Bartons, prominent family in BORDEAUX, originally from Lancashire in the north of England, who joined the Tudor Protestant Ascendancy in Ireland. Unlike most others who joined the BORDEAUX TRADE from abroad, the Bartons maintained their nationality, religion, and family connections. Thomas Barton arrived in Bordeaux in 1722, played a leading part in shipping fine CLARET back to Britain, and died in 1780 a very rich man. His son William (1723–99), with whom he bitterly quarrelled, formed his own company and was prominent in the trade on his own account. His son Hugh (1766–1854) married Anna, daughter of another prosperous merchant, Nathaniel Johnston. The association with Daniel Guestier of a Breton Huguenot family began in 1795, and the NÉGOCIANT Barton & Guestier was formed in 1802.

Highly successful, Hugh Barton bought Ch Langoa in ST-JULIEN in 1821 and acquired in 1826 part of the Léoville vineyard that was to become Ch Léoville-Barton, an even more prominent St-Julien. He died in England, having been succeeded by his son Nathaniel (1799–1867). Barton & Guestier continued to play a leading role in the Bordeaux trade, but PHYLLOXERA, the consequent shortage of authentic bordeaux, and the slump in English demand prior to the First World War led to unprecedented problems. Nathaniel's son Bertram Francis (1830–1904) worked first in the London office but came in 1873 to live in Bordeaux rather than at Langoa. It was his third successor **Ronald Barton** (1902–86) who made Langoa his home. Business was difficult between the world wars, and on the fall of France in 1940 Ronald had hurriedly to leave Langoa, which was soon occupied by the Germans. They did not pillage the cellars as Daniel Guestier told them that the estate belonged to a neutral Irishman, who, however, volunteered for the British army. Although the quality and reputation of second-growth (see CLASSIFICATION) Ch Léoville-Barton and third-growth Ch Langoa-Barton steadily improved, the profitability of Barton & Guestier gradually declined, and in 1954 the American firm of Seagram took half the shares of Barton & Guestier and later acquired complete control.

Ronald Barton's nephew **Anthony Barton** (1930–2022) joined Barton & Guestier in 1951 and subsequently left to form his own merchant business. In 1986 he moved into Langoa and took over complete control of the two classed growths, whose wines are both made at Langoa and have become models of sensibly priced, classic CLARET made for the long term. Anthony's daughter Lilian Barton Sartorius bought Ch Mauvesin Barton in Moulis in 2011. She and her husband Michel, and their children Damien and Mélanie, run these much-admired properties. Damien is especially interested in SUSTAINABILITY. E.P.-R. & J.R.

Barton, A., and Petit-Castelli, C., *La Saga des Bartons* (1991).

Ray, C., *Fide et fortitudine: The Story of a Vineyard: Langoa-Léoville Barton 1821–1971* (1971).

basal buds, or **base buds**, the group of barely visible and compressed buds at the bottom of a SHOOT or CANE. Normally they do not burst unless vines are severely pruned, and they are typically of low FRUITFULNESS. R.E.S.

basalt, a dark-coloured, fine-grained igneous rock (see GEOLOGY) dominated by the two minerals feldspar and pyroxene, though they are usually too fine to be discernible. They weather to provide a good range of potential NUTRIENTS. Dark rocks such as basalt are often said to reradiate warmth at night, but Pogue's study in the Columbia Valley in WASHINGTON and OREGON suggests that the thermal effects operate chiefly during the day.

Basalt is commonly found in association with VOLCANIC materials such as TUFF. In addition to the locations mentioned for them, basalt occurs in many other wine regions, for example VICTORIA (e.g. King Valley and Macedon Ranges) and the HUNTER VALLEY in Australia, the Galilee region of ISRAEL (including the Golan Heights), and in parts of HUNGARY such as Tapolca near Lake Balaton and Somló Hill, where it dominates vineyards. A.J.M.

Pogue, K., 'Influence of basalt on the terroir of the Columbia Valley American Viticultural area' (2010). people.whitman.edu/~pogue/soave.pdf.

Basilicata, a mountainous, virtually landlocked area of southern Italy, is the country's third least populated region. Its name has become synonymous with the extreme poverty in, and abandonment of, much of Italy's deep south, and the countryside has been drained by emigration since the end of the Second World War, while its unspoilt natural beauty still awaits any significant TOURISM boost to the regional economy. Little exists in the way of viticulture either; the region's total vineyard surface declined from 5,567 ha in 2010 to 5,000 ha/12,355 ha in 2020. The Basilicata has only four DOC wines and one DOCG. AGLIANICO DEL VULTURE is qualitatively the most important DOC, with vineyards situated on the slopes of an extinct volcano 56 km/35 miles north of Potenza. The Superiore version was elevated to DOCG status in 2010.

Basilicata's other DOCs include Grottino di Roccanova (a 100% MALVASIA Bianca di Basilicata, with a rather less exciting provision for a SANGIOVESE-based red) and Matera, a hastily and rather generously designated DOC based on Malvasia and the potentially interesting GRECO BIANCO for whites and PRIMITIVO and Sangiovese for reds, while Matera Moro must contain at least 60% Cabernet Sauvignon. The Terre dell'Alta Val d'Agri DOC accommodates mainly INTERNATIONAL VARIETIES, for which demand is waning. W.S.

Belfrage, N., *From Brunello to Zibibbo: The Wines of Tuscany, Central and Southern Italy* (2nd edn, 2003).
www.vinobasilicata.it

Basque country (Euskadi in Basque, País Vasco in Castilian, and Pays Basque in French) produces wines in Spain and France on either side of the western Pyrenees.

Spain
País Vasco or Euskadi is the most ferociously independent of all Spain's 17 autonomous regions. This densely populated, heavily industrialized strip of country facing the Bay of Biscay is not normally associated with wine, even though the important RIOJA region stretches north of the River Ebro into the Basque province of Alava where the Rioja Alavesa subregion is located—home to such important estates as Marqués de Riscal, Contino, Artadi, Martínez Bujanda, Remelluri, and Remírez de Ganuza. The three wholly Basque DOS are the tiny region of **Getariako** TXAKOLINA on the coast 25 km/15 miles west of San Sebastián, the smaller **Bizkaiko Txakolina** around Bilbao, and the newest one, **Arabako Txakolina**.

France
See BÉARN and IROULÉGUY.

Bastardo, Portuguese name for the JURA red wine grape TROUSSEAU. As Bastardo it is a minor variety in the Douro Valley, Dão, and Beiras with total plantings of 591 ha/1,460 acres in 2020. Over the Spanish border in Galicia it is known as Merenzao.

Bâtard-Montrachet, great white GRAND CRU in Burgundy's CÔTE D'OR. For more details, see MONTRACHET.

bâtonnage, French term for the winemaking operation of LEES STIRRING, possibly the most frequently misspelt word in WINE WRITING.

Baumé, scale of measuring total dissolved compounds in grape juice, and therefore its approximate concentration of grape sugars (see MUST WEIGHT). It is used in much of Europe, including France, and in Australia; like other scales used elsewhere (see BRIX and OECHSLE), it can be measured with either a REFRACTOMETER or a HYDROMETER. The Baumé scale is particularly useful in winemaking since the number of degrees Baumé indicates the POTENTIAL ALCOHOL in percentage by volume. (Grape juice of 12 °Baumé, for example, would produce a wine of about 12% alcohol if fermented out to dryness.) The rate of fall in Baumé is one method used to follow the course of an alcoholic FERMENTATION, but it should be noted that its product, ETHANOL, has a low DENSITY and progressively depresses hydrometer readings. B.G.C.

bead, the progress of bubbles in a SPARKLING WINE. A fine bead denotes a steady stream of small bubbles. See also FIZZINESS.

bearer, viticultural term used when pruning for what is effectively the fruiting unit of the vine, the selected long CANES or shorter SPURS bearing the buds that will produce the next season's shoots and crop. See also PRUNING.

Béarn, AOC in SOUTH WEST FRANCE in two distinct sections, around Salies-de-Béarn and near Pau, for white, rosé, and red wines. MADIRAN growers can bottle rosé as Béarn (pink wines not being allowed under the Madiran label), and JURANÇON growers may make a red Béarn (their red wines cannot be sold as Jurançon). Rosés are the main event, but concentrated reds are made, mostly from TANNAT blended primarily with Cabernets Franc and Sauvignon and sometimes with COURBU NOIR, FER, and MANSENG NOIR. The rare, tangy white wines are made mainly from PETIT MANSENG, GROS MANSENG, and the local Raffiat de Moncade. Total vineyard area was 259 ha/650 acres in 2016, and most wines are made by the CO-OPERATIVE at Gan in Jurançon. The region benefits from the Atlantic climate but also enjoys Indian summers. P.S.

Beaujolais, wine region in east-central France, noted at one time for volumes of a fruity wine with wide popular appeal but increasingly for quality wine. For administrative purposes, Beaujolais is often included as part of greater BURGUNDY; this has roots in the politics and commerce of both regions, namely the long-time inclusion by Burgundy NÉGOCIANTS of Beaujolais wines in their line-ups. But Beaujolais is very much a place apart—in terms of climate, topography, soil types, and grape varieties—which has prompted a growing number of producers to frame the two as fully separate entities. Nearly all the region's wine is produced from a single red grape variety, GAMAY Noir à Jus Blanc, much of it by a distinctive winemaking method, CARBONIC MACERATION.

History
As Beaujolais is on the ancient Roman trade route up the RHÔNE and Saône valleys, it is hardly surprising that there are records of Roman vineyards in the region, notably on Mont Brouilly (Brulliacus) and in Morgon. Benedictine MONKS developed vineyards here as early as the 7th century; for much of the medieval period Beaujolais, in wine terms at least, was simply the southern neighbour of the great duchy of Burgundy.

Beaujolais is named after Beaujeu, the town in its western hills founded in the 10th century, and was ruled by the Dukes of Beaujeu before being ceded to the Bourbonnais for a time. The region's viticultural identity was forged in part when Philip the Bold issued an edict against the growing of Gamay in Burgundy proper. Yet Philip's decree would hardly define the fate of either region: Beaujolais also faced discrimination from its northern neighbours in the MÂCONNAIS, who decried Beaujolais wines as 'greatly harmful' for consumption, according to historian Roger Dion. More pointedly, they blocked northbound trade, which in turn would prompt Beaujolais wines to flow south via the Saône to Lyons, defining that city's wine culture. Even so, by the early 18th century, Beaujolais wines were also routinely being shipped to Paris—four million gallons each year, eventually. Indeed, even Philip's bias couldn't keep Gamay out of the CÔTE D'OR, where it flourished through the 19th century. Parisian thirst was only magnified as canal and RAILWAY routes were developed. And Beaujolais in the 1800s was a relatively prosperous place. The best of that era's Beaujolais was reputed on par with Burgundy: JULLIEN ranked Moulin-à-Vent (technically only a sliver of today's AOC) and Chénas on par with the wines of VOSNE-ROMANÉE, Fleurie with the wines of GEVREY-CHAMBERTIN.

A mix of PHYLLOXERA, outsized production, and economic misfortune would unravel much of this. Southern Beaujolais would expand plantings to less suitable, flatter, more fertile land and eventually qualify for no more than basic Beaujolais AOC status, overshadowed by neighbours to the north.

After the Second World War, Beaujolais became associated with fresh, young PRIMEUR wines, shipped to Paris and Lyon where the simple, affordable style became a bistro staple. The wines became a worldwide phenomenon in the 1970s under the name Beaujolais NOUVEAU; at its peak in 1988, Nouveau made up more than 60% of production.

Already, however, a shift was under way towards higher-quality wines, attributed to several prominent producers known as the 'Gang of Four', led by winegrower Marcel Lapierre and mentored by the scientist and négociant Jules Chauvet. This cohort advocated better (typically ORGANIC) farming and minimal SULFUR DIOXIDE, precepts that would influence the NATURAL WINE movement throughout France. In the 2000s, several Burgundian producers acquired land in Beaujolais, including Thibault Liger-Belair and Michel Lafarge, marking a reversal from négociant-dominated trends of the past. These events also reflected shifting economic trends, namely overproduction in the late 1990s and early 2000s, when producers had to resort to compulsory DISTILLATION, plus a flattening of bulk prices paid to growers. That boosted the appeal for growers to make DOMAINE-BOTTLED wines. This increasing interest in TERROIR and quality got another boost with the availability, in the mid 2010s, of precise soil maps for the region's ten CRUS, which engendered a Burgundian level of discussion.

Today, the carefree vibe surrounding Beaujolais continues, amplified by its traditional service in Lyons and in Paris, in a special 46-cl/1 pint bottle known as a *pot*, as well as in sales of BULK WINE for immediate consumption. At the Beaujolais and Villages levels, this is an archetypal lubrication wine, drunk young and *gouleyant*, or gulpable, if served cellar cool. That said, more energy has turned to the crus, particularly Morgon, Moulin-à-Vent, Chénas, and Juliénas, which can improve in bottle for a decade or more. These wines have spiked in both price and quality, rivalling Burgundy at times.

Geography and climate

The total vineyard area of the Beaujolais region is slightly over 13,200 ha/32,600 acres and includes nearly 100 communes, with MÂCONNAIS on its northern boundary (indeed a number of villages service both Beaujolais and Mâcon-Villages AOCs, including ST-VÉRAN and Chaintré). The climate is TEMPERATE and semi-CONTINENTAL, with snow in the foothills of the Massif Central to the immediate west by the time Beaujolais Nouveau is launched and summers sufficiently hot for local houses to be shuttered from summer heat. Counting 1333 degree days (see CLIMATE CLASSIFICATION), the region's heat accumulation lands squarely between that of the Côte d'Or to the north and CÔTE-ROTIE to the south, although, with CLIMATE CHANGE, wines grown in some warmer MESOCLIMATES now routinely exceed 14% alcohol.

In the northern, narrower part of the region, TOPOGRAPHY is varied, the hills ranging from gentle to precipitous. Typically the discussion of Beaujolais soils has begun and ended with GRANITE, but recent soil maps have happily complicated this. The presence of SCHIST, especially in Juliénas and in Morgon, is significant, as is the volcanic soil known as TUFF, plus QUARTZ, SANDSTONE, and more. LIMESTONE appears in the north, at the edge of the Mâconnais, and again in the south, especially in the area known as Pierres Dorées.

And while the southern, flatter sector south of Villefranche is often considered too fertile for the best quality, a formal ranking published in 1893 by the industrialist and ampelographer Victor Vermorel and René Danguy, a prominent professor in Beaune, revealed exceptional LIEUX-DITS in the Bas-Beaujolais, in towns like Jarnioux. The extent to which the region succumbed to a later view as simple peasant wine reflects the deep cultural power of Nouveau, for good or ill.

The appellations

About half of all Beaujolais is sold under the basic appellation Beaujolais, which comes from the Bas Beaujolais plus the flatter land between the hills and the north–south autoroute around Belleville. The second most prolific Beaujolais appellation is Beaujolais-Villages, which must come from the hillier, northern part of the region, its vineyards pushing up into the foothills of the Massif Central. If a Beaujolais-Villages is the produce of just one village or commune, it can append the name of that commune. In the finest sectors of this northern part are the so-called Beaujolais CRUS, ten named communes whose wines had the best historical and commercial reputations.

For more details of individual crus, see, approximately from north to south, ST-AMOUR, JULIÉNAS, CHÉNAS, MOULIN-À-VENT, FLEURIE, CHIROUBLES, MORGON, REGNIÉ, and BROUILLY.

A small but increasing amount of **Beaujolais Blanc** and **Beaujolais-Villages Blanc** is made each year, mainly from Chardonnay grapes. Most is planted on patches of limestone in the north, thus a similarity to MÂCON Blanc, but increasingly growers are adding small amounts throughout the region. A modest amount of refreshing Beaujolais Rosé is made, too, and increasingly growers are harnessing more fertile vineyards to produce sparkling wines, often using a PÉTILLANT NATUREL method.

Basic maximum permitted YIELDS for both Beaujolais and Beaujolais-Villages now stand at 63 hl/ha, those for the Beaujolais crus to 56 hl/ha.

Viticulture

The GOBELET vine-training method is traditional in Beaujolais, somewhat mixed in with single GUYOT in the southern Bas Beaujolais, although even in the north BUSH VINES are often trained using rudimentary means to aid with harvest. For Beaujolais-Villages as well as the crus, PRUNING methods must be much more restrained, either gobelet or *éventail* (see TRAINING SYSTEMS). VINE DENSITY here has long been one of the highest in the world, 9,000–13,000 vines per ha. All picking must be manual because whole bunches are needed for Beaujolais's winemaking technique.

Vine varieties

Gamay Noir à Jus Blanc (so called to distinguish it from the relatively widely planted red-fleshed Gamay TEINTURIERS) accounts for about 98% of the Beaujolais vineyard, which makes Beaujolais the most *monocépagiste* (single-variety) region of any size in France. Virtually all the rest is Chardonnay, along with small amounts of ALIGOTÉ (permitted through vintage 2024) and MELON.

While there has been significant work on CLONAL SELECTION, with more than two dozen clones available today, many quality-minded growers often resort to MASS SELECTION, especially given the proliferation of old-vine material throughout the region.

ROOTSTOCKS used are SO 4, 3309, or (the Beaujolais speciality for granitic soils) Vialla.

Winemaking

Beaujolais is distinguished not just by the Gamay grape but also by its characteristic winemaking method, CARBONIC MACERATION or, more likely, SEMI-CARBONIC MACERATION. This technique has been used so widely in Beaujolais that a misperception has arisen that it originated in Beaujolais, and with Chauvet, when in fact it was pioneered in the mid 1930s by Michel Flanzy, director of the INRAE research station in Narbonne, and others prior to its broad adoption in Beaujolais.

What the region has popularized is a novel hybridization of the technique. Whole bunches arrive at the cellars and are emptied into concrete or stainless-steel FERMENTATION VESSELS generally of 40–300 hl/1,056–7,920 gal capacity. The bottom 10–30% of grapes are crushed by the weight above them and macerate and ferment in the normal way. This proportion increases with time. CARBON DIOXIDE is given off by this fermentation and leaves the upper grapes bathed in the gas so that they undergo intracellular fermentation, yielding the softer, fruitier aspects for which Beaujolais has often been known. This process can be halted after just four days for Nouveau but can continue for up to three weeks for cru wines, the maceration adding structure and density to the wines.

Most wine in the region undergoes MALOLACTIC CONVERSION, except for Nouveau, which typically must undergo STABILIZATION before a hasty bottling. The most long-lived crus receive extended CASK AGEING, often up to a year or more.

While it is tempting to describe carbonic as the region's traditional winemaking, the question of tradition is more complicated. Prior to the 20th century, vinification would largely have followed the same techniques found in Burgundy, and even today Beaujolais winemakers often talk of burgundian vinification—in the style of typical red burgundy. This method not only has endured for decades but also has been further revived by a new cohort of winemakers interested in longevity of their wines, and so it can be easier to think of winemaking on a continuum between the two methods, depending on the producer's preference. The growing tendency towards domaine bottling and away from the négociant trade has only accelerated this, so that the fascination with Beaujolais as a pleasant peasant wine is fading into rear view, as the region relocates its one-time prestige. J.F.B.

Beaumes-de-Venise is a pretty village in the southern RHÔNE that produced such characterful Côtes du Rhône-Villages that in 2005 it was awarded its own AOC for spicy reds based substantially on Grenache and Syrah. In 2020, 22,735 hl/600,595 gal were produced from 680 ha/1,680 acres of vineyards.

The appellation has some excellent high-ELEVATION vineyards, but for centuries it was most famous for its unusually fragrant, sweet VIN DOUX NATUREL, Muscat de Beaumes-de-Venise. In 2020, 5,412 hl/142,970 gal were produced from 312 ha/771 acres of vineyards.

Like the Muscats of the Languedoc (see FRONTIGNAN, LUNEL, MIREVAL, and ST-JEAN-DE-MINERVOIS), this southern Rhône Muscat is made exclusively from the best Muscat variety, MUSCAT BLANC À PETITS GRAINS, and occasionally its darker-berried mutation which contributes colour to the rosé and red versions of the wine. Fermentation is arrested by the addition of alcohol to produce a wine with a minimum of 100g/l RESIDUAL SUGAR and 15% alcohol, yet Beaumes-de-Venise can be more delicate and refreshing than most Languedoc Muscats. Apart from the extremely rare and expensive Hermitage VIN DE PAILLE, the Muscat is the Rhône's only still sweet wine, along with small quantities of RASTEAU Vin Doux Naturel and tiny amounts of sweet CONDRIEU. M.C.W.

Beaune, vinous capital of BURGUNDY giving its name to the Côte de Beaune section of the CÔTE D'OR vineyards. Beaune was founded as a Roman camp by Julius Caesar, became the seat of the dukes of Burgundy until the 13th century, and, although losing political supremacy to Dijon thereafter, has always been the centre of the Burgundian wine industry. In the 18th century, the first merchant houses such as Champy (1720) and Bouchard (1731) were established, and Beaune remains home to such leading NÉGOCIANTS as Louis JADOT, Joseph DROUHIN, Louis LATOUR, and BOUCHARD PÈRE ET FILS.

Beaune wines are mostly red, made from Pinot Noir grapes, although plantings of Chardonnay have increased since the 1990s. There is more SAND in the soil here than in most Côte d'Or villages so the red wines tend to be no more than medium-bodied, best drunk between five and ten years old. While neither as powerful as POMMARD nor as elegant as VOLNAY, Beaune wines are more supple than Corton (see ALOXE-CORTON) and can be a charming introduction to good burgundy.

Before the enforcement of AOC regulations, many local wines were sold as Beaune as a readily marketable label of convenience. Now the town has a good rather than great reputation for its wines, perhaps because there are few outstanding DOMAINES in an appellation dominated by merchants. However, Beaune is blessed with an unusually high proportion, nearly three-quarters, of PREMIER CRU vineyards. Indeed, those of village status are the exception, being limited to small parcels of land clinging to unsuitable upper slopes and some low-lying vineyards with richer soils. Otherwise the vineyards of Beaune form a broad swathe of premiers crus from the border with SAVIGNY-LÈS-BEAUNE to Pommard.

The finest vineyards are regarded as those situated almost directly between the town and the hill above: Les Grèves, Les Bressandes, Les Teurons, and Les Avaux. Beaune-Grèves includes Bouchard's noted Vigne de l'Enfant Jésus vineyard, while Beaune-Vignes Franches includes Louis Jadot's Clos des Ursules.

Other noted premier cru vineyards are Les Marconnets and Clos du Roi, near the border with Savigny, and Clos des Mouches abutting Pommard. Although the red wines from this vineyard are not always memorable, Joseph Drouhin makes a rich, complex, and ageworthy white Clos des Mouches.

Producers with a wide range of Beaune premiers crus (other than the négociants cited above) include Domaine des Croix and Albert Morot.

In 1443 Nicolas Rolin founded the Hôtel Dieu, Beaune's principal tourist attraction. For more details, especially of the famous annual auction, see HOSPICES DE BEAUNE.

See also CÔTE D'OR and map under BURGUNDY. J.T.C.M.

Beaune, Côte de. The Côte de Beaune is the southern half of the escarpment of the CÔTE D'OR, named after the important town and wine centre of Beaune. The greatest white wines of Burgundy and some very fine reds are grown on this stretch. The principal appellations, from north to south, are Corton and Corton-Charlemagne (see ALOXE-CORTON), BEAUNE, POMMARD, VOLNAY, MEURSAULT, PULIGNY-MONTRACHET, and CHASSAGNE-MONTRACHET. See also the separate entry under MONTRACHET.

Red wines from the lesser villages of the Côte may be sold under their own names or as **Côte de Beaune-Villages**. This appellation is available for the wines of AUXEY-DURESSES, Chassagne-Montrachet, CHOREY-LÈS-BEAUNE, LADOIX-Serrigny, Meursault, MONTHÉLIE, PERNAND-VERGELESSES, Puligny-Montrachet, ST-AUBIN, ST-ROMAIN, SANTENAY, and SAVIGNY-LÈS-BEAUNE. See also MARANGES.

Whereas wines labelled Beaune come from the appellation adjoining the town, there is a small group of vineyards on the hill above whose wines are sold under the confusing appellation Côte de Beaune. Of these the best known are Clos des Monsnières and Dessus des Marconnets. Both red and white wines are produced.

See also Côte de NUITS and map under BURGUNDY. J.T.C.M.

Becker, Helmut (1927–89), academic and exceptionally cosmopolitan VITICULTURIST who was chief of the GEISENHEIM Grape Breeding Institute in Germany from 1964 until his death. VINE BREEDING dominated his work. He emphasized the need for deliberate cross-breeding for resistance to DOWNY MILDEW and POWDERY MILDEW. To achieve this end he used not only resistant genes from AMERICAN VINES, as many other vine breeders had, but also those from Asian species of VITIS, in particular *Vitis amurensis*. Under his leadership, the winemaking facilities of the institute were extended and became a model for small-scale winemaking in breeding stations around the world. The products of these micro-vinifications were filed like library books in the research institute's deep, cool cellar, in bottles closed with the CROWN CAPS, of which Becker was a great proponent. Here Professor Becker would regale visitors with tastings of fine, Riesling-like wine made from NEW VARIETIES which were effectively HYBRIDS because of their non-VINIFERA genes and therefore officially outlawed. (Some have since been officially embraced; see DISEASE-RESISTANT VARIETIES.)

He also intensified breeding of ROOTSTOCKS, aiming for complete PHYLLOXERA resistance rather than tolerance. R.E.S.

Beechworth, small but fashionable region in Australia with about two dozen producers in 2022 in the foothills of the Victorian Alps. Several are iconic, notably Giaconda and Castagna, in the North East Victoria Zone. See VICTORIA.

Beerenauslese, literally 'berry selection', refers to sweet Austrian or German wines, usually made from BOTRYTIZED grapes. By German wine law, minimum MUST WEIGHTS are laid down for each combination of vine variety and region and vary from 110 to 128 °OECHSLE. The iconic examples, often prodigiously long-lived, are complex and rich yet exhilarating Rieslings. In Austria, a minimum of 25 °KMW (approximately 127 °Oechsle) is stipulated, and wines bearing this PRÄDIKAT are very common only around the NEUSIEDLERSEE in Burgenland (and then from diverse grapes). D.S.

beetles, insects of the *Coleoptera* order, several of which attack grapevines as well as other horticultural crops and pastures. While particular species of beetles are often specific to a country or region, beetles are a pest to grapevines worldwide. Black beetles (*Heteronychus arator*) attack young vines in spring and can cause ring barking. They are native to South Africa and are also known as African black beetles, but they cause damage in other countries such as Australia, where the elephant weevil (*Orthorhinus cylindrirostris*) tunnels in the vine wood. Japanese beetles (*Popillia japonica*) cause problems by eating vine foliage, especially in the south-eastern US. Apple curculio beetle (*Otiorhyncus cribricollis*), thought to be a native of Europe, and vegetable weevil (*Listorderes costirostris*) also attack young vines in late spring and early summer, causing damage by eating vine leaves and/or young shoots. Beetles of importance in France are *Altica ampelophaga* and *Adoxus vitis*, which eat leaves, and *Otiorhyncus sulcatus*, which eats young shoots and buds. *Rhynchites betuleti* is called *cigarier* in French because it damages PETIOLES so the leaves roll up like cigars. Control of beetles, if necessary, is by application of the appropriate insecticide (see PESTICIDES) or an ORGANIC alternative. See also BORERS. R.E.S. & M.v.H.

Bettiga, L. J. (ed.), *Grape Pest Management* (3rd edn, 2013).

Galet, P., *General Viticulture* (2000).

Beira Interior. Close to the Spanish border in central Portugal, this large, diverse DOC has three subregions: Castel Rodrigo and Pinhel in the north and Cova de Beira to the south. Surrounded by mountains (most vineyards are on plateaus), the region's poor, shallow soils predominantly comprise GRANITE, with areas of SCHIST and veins of QUARTZ. Rising to over 750 m/2,461 ft ELEVATION, northern vineyards experience a harsh CONTINENTAL CLIMATE, producing racy whites from old-vine SÍRIA and Fonte Cal; newcomers Riesling and Chardonnay can be very good too. Due south in the lower, warmer elevations of Cova de Beira, red varieties ripen more consistently. Between the mid 1990s and 2020, a sixfold rise in the number of private producers and restructuring of around one-third of the region's vines (some 5,000 ha/12,356 acres) has significantly increased quality and diversity. Today's TINTA RORIZ, TOURIGA NACIONAL, and TOURIGA FRANCA reds are a world apart from the indifferent RUFETE, MOURISCO, and MARUFO red wines of old. The VINHO REGIONAL designation is Terras da Beira. S.A.

Mayson, R. J., *The Wines of Portugal* (2020).

Beiras, once a VINHO REGIONAL covering most of central Portugal, embracing, from west to east, DOCS BAIRRADA on the Atlantic coast; the rugged, mountainous terrain of DÃO; and BEIRA INTERIOR, and including declassified wine from these areas. It was split into three separate regions in 2009: Beira Atlântico, Terras do Dão, and Terras da Beira.

Belgium, north European country which has traditionally been one of Bordeaux's and Burgundy's best customers but also produces an increasing amount of wine despite its northerly LATITUDE. While the wine industry of LUXEMBOURG to the south-east is older, Belgium has been home to grapevines since the 8th century, in the era of CHARLEMAGNE, when MONKS and noble families tended vines in central and southern Belgium. By the 16th century, viticulture had virtually disappeared due to CLIMATE CHANGE, military devastation, and the increasing influence of Burgundy, but by the 2000s the country's industry began growing quickly in quantity and quality, producing 18,500 hl/488,718 gal of wine in 2020, up from 5,500 hl in 2010.

The country's cool climate favours the production of white wines (about 35% of total production) as well as sparkling (45%).

More than 40 vine varieties are authorized, of which Chardonnay, Pinot Noir, and Pinot Blanc are the most planted. Auxerrois, Pinot Gris, and GERMAN CROSSES such as Regent, Kerner, Johanniter, and Solaris are also common. Most of the country's wineries have less than 3 ha/7.4 acres of vines and produce wine exclusively for local sale although there are now several large wineries specializing in sparkling wine.

Belgium has five PDOS. The first was the **Hageland**, founded in 1997 in the Flemish Brabant region around Leuven; **Haspengouw** followed, its 25 ha/62 acres in East Limburg near the Dutch border. **Heuvelland** is on the other side of the country, in the hills near the French border. **Côtes de Sambres-et-Meuse**, created in 2004, was the first appellation in the southern, French-speaking part of the country; named for the two rivers that cross this southern appellation, it boasted more than 170 growers in 2020. **Maasvallei Limburg**, a 150-km/93-mile strip of sandy gravel that runs from Belgium into the NETHERLANDS, became the first cross-border appellation in Europe upon its approval in 2017.

In addition, there are three SPARKLING WINE appellations: **Vlaamse Mousserende Kwaliteitswijn** covers sparkling wine from the northern, Flemish side of the country; **Crémant de Wallonie** or **Vin Mousseux de Qualité de Wallonie** comes from the French-speaking south. All must be produced by the TRADITIONAL METHOD. For growers eschewing the confines of a CONTROLLED APPELLATION, there are two PGIS—one for Flanders (Vlaamse Landwijn) and one for Wallonia (Vin de Pays de Jardins de Wallonie). Subregions may be mentioned on the label of PDO and PGI wines. G.V.I.

beli, term meaning 'white' or 'light' in many Slavic languages. Beli Pinot is PINOT BLANC, for instance.

Bellet, historic, distinctive, but minute AOC in the far south-east of PROVENCE whose total vineyard area had by 2011 fallen to 50 ha/125 acres. It takes determination to find a bottle outside the Côte d'Azur and even greater determination to find the vineyards themselves, perched in the hills above Nice about 300 m/980 ft above the Mediterranean. Almost equal quantities of all three colours are produced. The scented, full-bodied whites made from the local ROLLE grapes with some Chardonnay and occasionally BOURBOULENC are the appellation's most distinctive wines and reflect well the MESOCLIMATE, which is slightly cooler than much of the rest of Provence. Rosés may be made from BRAQUET while the intriguing FOLLE NOIRE (Fuella) is traditional for red wines, although it is often supplemented by Cinsaut and occasionally Grenache.

bench, a term used particularly in North America to describe a strip of level or gently inclined ground bordered on either side by land sloping in the same direction but with a different gradient. This can arise in a range of circumstances, but viticultural examples, sometimes called **benchlands**, include river terraces (e.g. California's Santa Maria Bench in Santa Barbara and the Russian River benches of Sonoma County), lake terraces (e.g. at Niagara and in the Okanagan Valley in Canada) and the

ALLUVIAL FANS flanking California's Napa Valley (e.g. Oakville and Rutherford benches). A.J.M.

bench blending. See ASSEMBLAGE.

bench grafting, the viticultural operation of GRAFTING vines indoors rather than in the field. This procedure has become widespread since the 1980s, allowing more large-scale production of grafted vines using grafting tools in NURSERIES. It has almost totally replaced manual FIELD GRAFTING. Bench grafting leads to improved productivity and lower unit costs. However, there are claims of increased incidence of TRUNK DISEASE in bench-grafted plants. The procedure is widely used throughout the world and has become an important industry.

Dormant ROOTSTOCK and SCION cuttings (of the chosen variety and CLONE) are gathered from the field after LEAF FALL and stored in special cool stores. After soaking in FUNGICIDE solution, rootstock cuttings are disbudded and scion cuttings are cut into one-node pieces. Using cuttings of similar diameter, a GRAFTING MACHINE cuts the bottom of the scion and the top of the rootstock into a similar shape, the most common being the omega. The scion and rootstock are matched, and the newly grafted cuttings are packed with a moistened, coarse-grained medium in boxes and stacked in humid, warm rooms (28–9 °C/82–4 °F) until the union has CALLUSED (in about two weeks). Once they have hardened, grafts are waxed to reduce water loss then planted out, usually in a field nursery. These plants are grown over the summer and then lifted from the nursery, the roots and shoots trimmed in the field, before delivery to the client in winter, typically in bundles of 50.

Such was the demand for grafted plants in the 1990s that in many countries nurseries sold young grafted plants in the spring and early summer of grafting for immediate planting in the field. Such young plants are called 'green grafts' (although this is not the same as GREEN GRAFTING) and may be about half the price of a dormant, grafted vine which the nursery would sell the following winter. However, good care is essential following spring/summer transplanting of green grafts, especially with regard to water supply and weed control.

In recent years grapevine nurseries have struggled with problems of fungal pathogens in young, grafted plants which can cause poor growth and even the death of the vine (see TRUNK DISEASES). R.E.S.

Bendigo, historic (see GOLD RUSHES), temperate region in Australia's Central Victoria Zone notable for full-bodied, smooth reds. Lack of water for IRRIGATION (a potential problem in dry summers and periodic DROUGHT) limits expansion to fewer than 50 producers. See VICTORIA.

bentonite, FINING agent based on a montmorillonite clay found principally in the state of Wyoming in the western United States, as well as in many other areas of the world. Like most clays, bentonite is a hydrated compound of aluminium and silicon oxides, but it differs in ways that are useful to winemakers. When mixed with water, it swells and assumes a form that has significant powers of adsorption.

Bentonite, so called because it was first discovered in the Fort Benton rock series, is widely used in the NEW WORLD to ensure PROTEIN stability, particularly to remove heat-unstable proteins from white wines, thus taking away the risk of deposits or hazes.

Bentonite fining is sometimes also used in white winemaking for the CLARIFICATION of juice before or during FERMENTATION to limit the instability of proteins post-fermentation and to facilitate rapid bottling. However, bentonite is usually used for fining after fermentation, which can hasten the settling of LEES and thereby reduce the time between RACKINGS. Bentonite is not generally used for red wines because their higher concentration of TANNINS can remove proteins naturally (but see BOTTLE DEPOSIT).

Many wine drinkers prefer a clear white to a hazy one, however strange the idea of a Wyoming clay treatment may seem. Too high a dosage of bentonite can cause loss of flavour resulting from adsorption of flavour molecules on the surface of the fining agent, which is why trials are usually carried out to ensure that the minimum amount is added. V.L. & M.J.T.

Béquignol, productive red-wine vine virtually extinct in its Bordeaux homeland but still grown on 512 ha/1,265 acres in Argentina in 2020, where it is mainly used to add colour. DNA PROFILING has suggested a possible parent–offspring relationship with SAVAGNIN.

Bereich, official term for a German wine-growing district. In some regions such as BADEN, the Bereich names corresponded largely with already familiar designations for well-defined subregions. In other instances, they represent (like the notorious GROSSLAGEN) legal inventions for marketing purposes. Prominent labelling with Bereich names was common for cheaper German wines during the 1970s and 1980s but has since largely disappeared.

Bergerac, extensive AOC in SOUTH WEST FRANCE producing mainly red but also dry and sweet white and rosé wines in the image of BORDEAUX to the immediate west of the region, often at more appealing prices. The greater Bergerac region, named after the principal town at its centre on the River DORDOGNE, is the main appellation of the Dordogne *département* and can boast more beautiful and varied countryside than that of its vinously more glamorous neighbour. Lacking distinctions other than touristic (and gastronomic; Périgord is the home of *foie gras*), it has long been difficult for the wines of Bergerac to escape from the shadow of Bordeaux's more serious wine reputation, but thanks to pioneering producers such as Luc de Conti of Ch les Tour des Gendres and David Fourtout of Vignobles des Verdots, as well as a handful of sweet winemakers, some truly fine wine is being made, sometimes with sophisticated use of OAK.

The climate here is somewhere between MARITIME and CONTINENTAL, but overripeness is a rare characteristic of Bergerac grapes and wines. Soils vary from alluvial silt to CLAY and, on the higher terraces, LIMESTONE. Within the region are smaller districts, generally on higher sites with more obvious potential, which have their own appellations for specific wine types. MONBAZILLAC on the left bank of the river is the best known of these, recognized for the quality of its BOTRYTIZED wine. MONTRAVEL on the right bank makes lightish dry and sweet white wines, as well as a modern, oaked style of red. Both appellations were created in the late 1930s just after the creation of the Bergerac appellation. PÉCHARMANT won its own red-wine appellation in 1946, as did the tiny *moelleux*-wine appellation of ROSETTE. The SAUSSIGNAC sweet-white-wine appellation was created in 1982. To help with their marketing, many producers in these areas choose to sell their wines simply as Bergerac.

The vine was grown in the region in Roman times, but the wines were exported and appreciated in the Middle Ages, when viticulture thrived partly under the influence of MONKS AND MONASTERIES. The history of BORDEAUX outlines why the English were so fond of them and why they were discriminated against by the Bordeaux merchants. After the HUNDRED YEARS WAR, the DUTCH WINE TRADE dominated exports of Bergerac, developing the production of SWEET WINES here from the 16th century and, especially, after Protestant refugees left Périgord for northern Europe after the Revocation of the Edict of Nantes in 1685.

Bergerac was slow to recover from PHYLLOXERA, but the total area planted has grown from a low in the 1990s to 12,000 ha/30,000 acres by 2020. Vines grown are the classic Bordeaux varieties: Cabernets and Merlot for red wines (sometimes with supporting Cot (MALBEC), Mérille, or FER) and Sauvignon, Sémillon, and MUSCADELLE for whites (with occasional help from Chenin). Sémillon is still the most planted light-skinned variety, Merlot the most popular grape for the red wines, which constitute the majority of production.

Most Bergerac reds are very similar to red BORDEAUX AOC. An increasing proportion is sold as longer-lasting, often barrel-aged **Côtes de**

Bergerac, for which ALCOHOLIC STRENGTH tends to be higher.

Some **Bergerac Rosé** is made, generally of Cabernet, but the second most common form of Bergerac is the dry white **Bergerac Sec**, increasingly well-made thanks to the application of some of the techniques employed for better dry white bordeaux. About one-quarter of all white wine is sweet, made mainly from Sémillon, and (beyond Monbazillac, Saussignac, and Montravel) is sold as **Côtes de Bergerac Moelleux**. P.S.

Bergeron, local name for ROUSSANNE in the Savoie appellation of Chignin.

Bergwein, a seldom-encountered official category in AUSTRIA for wine made on slopes steeper than 26% regardless of their region of origin (thus most often applying to the otherwise disparate wines of STYRIA and the WACHAU).

Berlou. See ST-CHINIAN.

berry, botanical term defining a simple edible fruit, derived from a single flower, typically having seeds and a fleshy PULP. Common examples are grapes, currants, cranberries, blueberries, tomatoes, cucumbers, eggplants, and bananas. For more details, see GRAPE. R.E.S.

berry cell death is a recently elucidated phenomenon associated with BERRY SHRIVEL. Cell death in the flesh of the GRAPE berry (mesocarp) occurs late in RIPENING but often before normal HARVEST in several varieties. There is a correlation between the onset of cell death in the mesocarp and the degree of late-season berry shrivel across several varieties, but it is most obvious in Shiraz. For this variety in Australia, for example, it usually begins around 90–100 days after FLOWERING. Elevated temperatures and WATER STRESS accelerate cell death and shrivel in Shiraz. Cell death in the mesocarp likely leads to an imbalance in water gradients that result in a net loss of water from the Shiraz berry, but this does not occur in Chardonnay berries. Cell death is highly correlated with anoxia (lack of oxygen) in the berry, which is thought to be caused by excessive respiratory demand (see RESPIRATION) at high temperatures and a restriction of oxygen diffusion into the berry via lenticels on the berry PEDICEL. The anoxia results in fermentation within the berry and the production of ETHANOL (0.1%, small in wine context but high in a cellular context) that may also be a prelude to cell death. This and the concentration that results from accompanying berry shrivel are likely to affect the flavour profile of wine made from these berries, for example giving a HERBACEOUS character. S.T.

Bonada, M., et al., 'Effect of elevated temperature on the onset and rate of mesocarp cell death in berries of Shiraz and Chardonnay and its relationship with berry shrivel', *Australian Journal of Grape and Wine Research*, 19/1 (2013), 87–94.

Tilbrook, J., and Tyerman, S. D., 'Cell death in grape berries: varietal differences linked to xylem pressure and berry weight loss', *Functional Plant Biology*, 35/3 (2008), 173–84.

Xiao, Z., et al., 'Are berries suffocating to death under high temperatures and water stress?', *Wine & Viticulture Journal*, 34/1 (2019), 42–5.

berry rots. See BUNCH ROTS.

berry shrivel can be linked to SUNBURN, prolonged dehydration, and BUNCHSTEM NECROSIS. Late-season berry shrivel (LSBS) appears to be correlated with what is known as BERRY CELL DEATH. S.T.

Bondada, B., and Keller, M., 'Not all shrivels are created equal: morpho-anatomical and compositional characteristics differ among different shrivel types that develop during ripening of grape (*Vitis vinifera* L.) berries', *American Journal of Plant Sciences*, 3/7 (2012), 879–98.

berry size is considered by many to be a factor in wine quality. It is often said that smaller berries contribute to better wine quality, especially for red wines, since ANTHOCYANINS, PHENOLICS, and FLAVOUR COMPOUNDS are mostly contained in the skins. The higher surface-to-volume ratio of smaller berries potentially results in a higher concentration of these skin compounds in the MUST and hence in the wine. However, there are few scientific studies that confirm this, and berries that are too small, especially if they are the result of MILLERANDAGE or BERRY CELL DEATH, may have a negative effect on wine quality, such as loss of aroma.

Good-quality wine grape varieties typically have small berries, at least compared with both lower-quality varieties and TABLE GRAPES. The average weight of a premium wine grape at full ripeness is 1–2 g, whereas others weigh 3 g or more, up to 10 g/0.35 oz for some table grapes. These values doubtless represent the selection of VINE VARIETIES for their end use.

It is not the case, however, that any vineyard management practice which leads to smaller berries will necessarily improve wine quality. Certainly, WATER STRESS causes small berries, although some of the effects on wine quality may be the result of water stress on VINE PHYSIOLOGY rather than the direct result of small berries. The other simple means of reducing berry size is PRUNING to very many buds in winter, but this is contrary to the principles of BALANCED PRUNING. Such light pruning is associated with smaller berries but also with higher YIELDS and is therefore likely to reduce wine quality, since the vine may struggle to ripen grapes with insufficient leaf area.

Studies in California (with Cabernet Sauvignon) and Australia (with Shiraz and Pinot Noir) have shown that smaller berries do not necessarily make better wine. These studies concluded that it is the vineyard factors which make berries small—water stress in particular—that contribute directly to wine quality, not the smallness of the berries themselves. R.E.S.

Roby, G., et al., 'Berry size and vine water deficits as factors in winegrape composition: Anthocyanins and tannins', *Australian Journal of Grape and Wine Research*, 10 (2004), 100–7.

Walker, R., et al., 'Shiraz berry size in relation to seed number and implications for juice and wine composition', *Australian Journal of Grape and Wine Research*, 11 (2005), 2–8.

Bhutan, Himalayan micro-kingdom with an extremely diverse range of MESOCLIMATES, soils, and ELEVATIONS up to 8,230 m/27,000 ft. In the late 2010s the Bhutan Wine Co. planted Bhutan's first VITIS VINIFERA vineyards, about 16 ha/40 acres in six vineyards at 762–2,682 m/2,500–8,800 ft in elevation. Initial plantings included white varieties Sauvignon Blanc, Chardonnay, Petit Manseng, Chenin Blanc, and Riesling; and red varieties Merlot, Cabernet Sauvignon, Cabernet Franc, Malbec, Pinot Noir, Syrah, Sangiovese, and Tempranillo. The first vintage is slated for 2023, barring any issues with MILDEW, monsoon pressure, and the abundant hungry wildlife that count among local winegrowing challenges.

Biancame, one of the many synonyms of TREBBIANO TOSCANO, used in the Marche, also known as **Bianchello**. J.V.

bianco means 'white' in Italian, and the names of many Italian white wines therefore are Bianco d'/da/di/del Place name. For more details, see under the place name.

Note, however, that **Bianco** is also the name of a small town in CALABRIA where an ancient sweet white DRIED-GRAPE WINE, Greco di Bianco, is still produced today from grapes known locally as GRECO BIANCO.

Bianco d'Alessano, Italian white wine grape of PUGLIA which is frequently blended with VERDECA.

Biancolella, ISCHIAN white wine grape which survives on the island's steep terraces.

Biancu Gentile, rare but increasingly appreciated aromatic Corsican white wine grape planted on 59 ha/146 acres in 2018.

Bible. The subject of wine runs deep in the Bible. The vine is mentioned more often than any other plant, and there are nearly 1,000 references to wine and wine-related themes. Adam planted grains while Noah was the first to plant a vineyard, near Mount Ararat in what is modern-day Türkiye (Gen. 9. 20). Some scholars see here a development of the theme of agriculture in the Bible from grain, a necessity for life, to wine, a culturally highly esteemed

B

beverage. Lamech names his son Noah because he is to bring his people relief from their hard manual labour in a fallen world. This promise seems to have come to fruition when Noah became a winegrower and crafted his first vintage (Gen. 5. 29). From the time of Noah, vineyards, vines, and wine become regular features in the biblical narrative.

Wine as a gift and blessing

The Bible celebrates wine as a gift from God and upholds God as the Creator of all things. Ultimately it is God who causes all plants including the vine to flourish (Gen. 1; Ps. 104). The practice of agriculture and viticulture is therefore understood as a spiritual calling. An important purpose of wine is to gladden people's hearts and bring comfort in times of distress and worry (Ps. 104. 15; 4. 7; Prov. 31. 6–7; Eccles. 8. 15; 10. 19).

In the Song of Solomon, wine is celebrated as a gift from God and its enjoyment is compared with the pleasures of sexual intimacy. The lavish garden imagery harks back to the paradisiacal splendour of the Garden of Eden. It instils a longing in the reader for a restored paradise where people live in perfect harmony with their Creator, each other, and the natural world, enjoying and savouring the fruits of the vine.

Wine takes on a religious role when it becomes part of God's blessing. When Isaac blesses his son Jacob, this blessing includes fruitfulness of the land: '"May God give you of the dew of heaven, of the fatness of the earth, and plenty of grain and wine"' (Gen. 27. 28, 37). When Jacob blesses his son Judah, this blessing goes even further and evokes images of paradise, instilling a longing for flourishing vines and wine flowing in great abundance: '"The sceptre shall not depart from Judah... Binding his foal to the vine and his donkey's colt to the choice vine, he washes his garments in wine and his robe in the blood of grapes"' (Gen. 49. 10–12). Moses also affirmed wine as a blessing from God (Deut. 7. 13). When the Israelites arrived at the border of Canaan, Moses sent out spies to see how fertile the land was. The spies came upon 'the valley of grape clusters' (Hebrew *Eshkol*) during harvest season and brought back on a pole a single cluster of grapes, reporting to Moses that the land showed great abundance (Num. 13). It is this Biblical vision of vineyards and wine that inspired Christian monks and nuns throughout the Middle Ages to plants vineyards as part of their mission, and their impact can still be felt today in many wine regions of the world (see MONKS AND MONASTERIES).

Wine as metaphor

Vineyards and vines were so prominent that they became a metaphor to describe God's relationship with his people. The Psalmist speaks of Israel as a vine that God brought out of Egypt and transplanted into fertile soil (Ps. 80. 8, 14), and God's people are compared to a vineyard (Is. 3. 13–15). God's judgement is compared to a winepress (Joel 3. 13, Lam. 1. 15, Rev. 14. 19–20, 19. 15), and his forgiveness and healing will make Israel 'blossom like the vine' (Hos. 14. 1, 7). In a climactic passage Jesus describes himself as 'the true vine', his Father as 'the vinegrower', and his disciples as his branches, emphasizing the profound union that believers can experience with God (John 15. 1–7).

Wine in cultic practices and celebrations

The Israelites offered up wine as a sacrifice to God. Different sacrifices served different purposes: to solicit God's blessing, to express gratitude, and to receive forgiveness of sin. Offering up the first fruits of their harvest reminded the Israelites that all life, including the fruit of the earth, is a gift from God (Lev. 23. 13; Num. 28. 14; Deut. 14. 22–3; 15. 14).

Wine was served during family and religious celebrations such as the grape harvest, the weaning of a child, marriage feasts, birthdays, the making of covenants, and the enthronement of a king (Gen. 21. 8; 29. 21–2; 40. 20; 2 Sam. 3. 20; 1 Chr. 12. 40).

Wine, drunkenness, and abstinence

Noah is the first person in the Bible to get drunk. The Old Testament portrays drunkenness and the abuse of wine in strictly negative terms and discourages and condemns it (Gen. 9. 20–6; 19. 30–8; Isa. 5. 11–12; Prov. 20. 1).

Some Israelites were to abstain from drinking wine due to their special callings, such as priests serving in the temple (Lev. 10. 9; Ezek. 44. 21) and the Nazirites as part of their special dedication to God (Num. 6. 3–4, 20; Judg. 13. 4, 7, 14). Proverbs discourages kings from drinking wine so they can rule with justice and mercy (Prov. 31. 4–9).

Wine in prophetic speech

When the prophets speak of God's judgement they speak of God withholding his blessings from his unfaithful people, and this includes wine. Israel is even compared to a vineyard from which God has withdrawn his protection because of their oppression of the poor (Isa. 5). To be without wine is a terrible curse and a sign of God's judgement (Deut. 28. 39; Isa. 24. 7; Hosea 9. 2; Amos 4. 9; Mic. 6. 15). When the prophets speak of God's future redemption, they speak of it in terms of vineyard planting, plentiful harvests, and lavish banquets with wine flowing in great abundance (Jer. 31. 5; Isa. 25. 6; Joel 2. 23–4). The prophet Hosea envisions God's redemption as a wedding banquet (Hos. 2. 18–23). The prophet Amos even speaks of a time when '"the mountains shall drip sweet wine, and all the hills shall flow with it"' (Amos 9. 13).

Wine in the New Testament

By the time of the 1st century, when Jesus began his ministry, Jews celebrated the Passover meal with four cups of wine, and wine had become a staple in Jewish culture. Palestinian hills were dotted with wine presses where wine literally flowed down the hills from one basin to another and each village crafted its own vintage. The people lived in expectant hope that God would send an anointed one (messiah) who would deliver them from Roman oppression. And as the prophets foretold, a sure sign of his coming would be joyous feasting and an abundance of choice wine.

The New Testament builds on the Hebrew scriptures and affirms wine as a gift and blessing from God: Jesus' first miracle is to turn water into fine wine at the wedding feast of Cana (John 2), and he offers his disciples a cup of wine in the celebration of the Last Supper (see EUCHARIST). The miracle at Cana is also the first sign given by Jesus that in him the promises of old have been fulfilled. He is the long-awaited messiah. Wine now becomes a symbol of the presence of the messiah who will bring God's deliverance.

Jesus' ministry often took the form of shared meals and the drinking of wine, especially with the marginalized of society—his own people accused him of being a glutton, a drunkard, and a friend of sinners (Matt. 11. 19; Luke 19. 7). The apostle Paul warns against drunkenness (1 Cor. 5. 11; 6. 10; Gal. 5. 21). The New Testament also speaks of the medicinal value of wine (1 Tim. 5. 23; Luke 10. 25–37), and Christians look forward to the second coming of Christ when they will drink wine with Christ in the Father's eternal Kingdom (Matt. 26. 29). G.K.

Kreglinger, G., 'Wine in the Bible', in *The Spirituality of Wine* (2016).

Becker, L., *Rebe, Rausch und Religion: eine kulturgeschichtliche Studie zum Wein in der Bible* (1999).

Bical, Portuguese white grape variety grown mainly in BAIRRADA, as well as in DÃO, where it is called Borrado das Moscas, meaning 'fly droppings'. The wines have good acidity and can be persuaded to display peachy aromas in still VARIETAL versions, although in Bairrada the grapes are often used in blends for sparkling wines. Some capacity for AGEING has been demonstrated, Bical developing an almost RIESLING-like bouquet after a decade in bottle. It was grown on 1,206 ha/2,980 acres in 2020.

Bienvenues-Bâtard-Montrachet, white GRAND CRU in Burgundy's CÔTE D'OR. For more details, see MONTRACHET.

Bierzo, fashionable DOP region in north-west Spain (see map under SPAIN) which administratively forms part of CASTILLA Y LEÓN. However, the River Sil, which bisects it, is a tributary of the Miño (Minho in Portugal), and the wines have more in common with those of GALICIA than those of the DOURO 140 km/88 miles to the south. Sheltered from the climatic excesses of the Atlantic and the central plateau, Bierzo shows promise as a wine region, with tiny plots on steep slopes climbing to 1,000 m/3,280 ft in ELEVATION. The MENCÍA grape is capable of producing balanced, fruity red wines in well-drained soils on the SLATE and GRANITE of this part of Spain. White wines made from GODELLO are also gaining reputation.

In the late 1990s, a group of small, mostly young growers reproduced in Bierzo the same 'miracle' which had happened in PRIORAT one decade earlier—they resurrected a moribund wine region. One of the protagonists, Álvaro PALACIOS, was indeed one of the Priorat pioneers as well. With his nephew Ricardo Pérez Palacios, he reclaimed old vineyards on slate slopes and produced wines with no resemblance to the light reds traditionally produced from fertile valley vineyards. In 2020 the region had 2,349 ha/5,805 acres planted.

In 2017, a new classification scheme was approved for Bierzo wines, allowing mention of smaller geographical units approved by the DOP regulatory board: **Vino de Villa** must come entirely from the named town or district, at yields 20% below that of the DOP Bierzo maximum; **Vino de Paraje** must come from a single recognized place at yields 25% below the DOP maximum. **Vino de Viña Clasificada** designates a wine from a single vineyard or adjacent vineyards at least five years old with yields 30% below the DOP maximum; **Gran Vino de Viña Clasificada** requires that the named vineyard be at least ten years old, with yields 35% below the maximum. R.J.M. & F.C.

Barquín, J., Guitiérrez, L., and de la Serna, V., *The Finest Wines of Rioja and Northwest Spain* (2011).

Biferno, one of only four DOCs in the Italian MOLISE region and arguably its most important.

Big Rivers Zone large catchment area in NEW SOUTH WALES, comprising the Murray Darling, Perricoota, Riverina, and Swan Hill regions.

Bikavér or, on export markets, **Bull's Blood**, is a Hungarian red wine style that may be made in the EGER or SZEKSZÁRD regions. At one time the blend depended heavily on KADARKA, but this demanding local variety was replaced by KÉKFRANKOS, supplemented by Cabernet, Merlot, Syrah, Portugieser, and sometimes Pinot Noir. Both regions are now making serious efforts to produce elegant, fruity Bikavér wines worth ageing that are neither heavy nor aggressively tannic. SINGLE-VINEYARD examples are increasingly found. G.M.

bin, traditional term for a collection of wine bottles, normally stacked horizontally on top of each other, or the process of so storing, or **binning**, them. Thus these bins needed BIN LABELS, and a **bin end** has come to signify a small quantity of wine bottles left over from a larger lot. Some Australian wine companies, notably PENFOLDS, have a tradition of using the word 'bin' in BRAND names.

Binissalem, DOP with 570 ha/1,408 acres of vines on the Mediterranean island of MALLORCA in Spain producing red, white, sparkling, and rosé wines mostly destined for the Balearic holiday resorts. The red wines must contain at least 30% MANTO NEGRO, Binissalem's dominant grape, with up to 30% Gorgollassa; white wines must be at least 50% MOLL or MOSCATEL.

bin labels were necessitated by the practice of binning unlabelled bottles.

The most common form of bin label was made of pottery and was approximately the shape of a coat hanger some 7–13 cm/3–5 in wide. At the apex there was an additional lug, pierced so that it formed a suspension ring. As many were nailed to the cellar masonry, they have often been broken or cracked during removal.

Early English bin labels (dating to the mid 18th century) are delftware (tin-glazed earthenware) with blue or deep magenta calligraphy (upper case) on a white to pale blue ground. Almost all later ones have black lettering on white pottery, although coloured lettering is very rarely seen. European labels came in a variety of forms and often with polychrome decoration; the language of the writing usually provides an obvious clue to the country of origin.

By the 19th century, labels developed rounded shoulders, the earlier ones being angled. Many had a portion of the face left unglazed where more precise details of the bin contents might be written. Home-made labels were sometimes fashioned from wood or slate and would likewise have written information.

In very large cellars and in commercial ones where the bin contents changed frequently, it was established practice to use circular bin labels with numbers that would cross-refer to the cellar records. Many of these, and the coat-hanger variety, are marked with the manufacturer's name (Wedgwood, Copeland, etc.) or the vendor's name (e.g. Farrow & Jackson), almost invariably impressed during manufacture. Bin labels are not much collected in the world of wine antiques, but the most sought-after are delftware examples, those with spelling mistakes, and rarities of name, colour, or form. R.N.H.B.

Bío-Bío, cool, wet subregion of the Southern region of CHILE.

biochar is made by heating organic materials such as wood waste, crop residues, municipal green waste, biosolids or manure to 350–500 °C/660–930 °F in a limited-oxygen environment. This process renders the organic material very resistant to decomposition, which reduces the release of CARBON DIOXIDE from this material into the atmosphere. However, biochar's main contributions to a vineyard soil are to increase the CATION EXCHANGE CAPACITY and the water-holding capacity, especially in sandy soils (see SOIL WATER). It is also said to increase soil biological activity (see SOIL BIOTA), but, because it is an inert material, this effect usually requires the biochar to be co-composted with animal manure to 'activate' it. The Ithaka Institute in Switzerland has developed a European Biochar Certificate, but, because of the variation in commercially available products and their complex interaction with SOIL TYPE, CLIMATE, grape variety and COVER CROP, no firm recommendations can be made for biochar use in vineyards except in relation to carbon storage. Yield responses have been inconsistent. It is usually applied at 8 tonnes per ha or more, so it is an expensive soil amendment if brought in from outside. R.E.W.

Lehmann, J., et al., 'Biochar effects on soil biota: a review', *Soil Biology & Biochemistry*, 43 (2011), 1812–36.

Schmidt, H.-P., et al., 'Biochar and biochar-compost as soil amendments to a vineyard soil: Influences on plant growth, nutrient uptake, plant health and grape quality', *Agriculture Ecosystems and Environment* (2014).

biodiversity. See ECOSYSTEM.

biodynamic viticulture is, depending on your perspective, either an enhanced or an extreme form of ORGANIC VITICULTURE. This controversial practice has produced some impressive results but without the reassurance of conclusive scientific explanation.

Biodynamics is the oldest 'green' farming movement, predating organics by 20 years. It is based on theories described in 1924 by the Austrian philosopher Rudolf Steiner (1861–1925) for agriculture in general. All biodynamic vineyards practise organic viticulture, but biodynamics differs from organics in three ways. The vineyard should become a self-sustaining individual or 'farm organism' (see SUSTAINABLE VITICULTURE and ECOSYSTEM): it should be treated regularly with nine herb- and mineral-based biodynamic 'preparations'; and key tasks such as planting, PRUNING, TILLAGE, PICKING, and BOTTLING should be timed to harness beneficial 'formative forces' exerted by earthly and celestial—planetary, solar, stellar, and especially lunar—rhythms.

France's first biodynamic winegrower, François Bouchet (1932–2005), began using the technique on his 6-ha/15-acre Domaine de Château Gaillard in Touraine in 1962. But France's biodynamic wine movement remained almost non-existent until the late 1980s, when Bouchet began helping leading names such as Domaine Leflaive of PULIGNY-MONTRACHET, Domaine LEROY in Vosne-Romanée, CHAPOUTIER in Hermitage, Huet in Vouvray, and Kreydenweiss in Alsace to convert to biodynamics.

These producers shared a belief that only a less technologically driven form of viticulture would allow wine QUALITY to keep improving; they were emboldened by former INRA soil microbiologist Claude Bourguignon's 1988 declaration that Burgundy's vineyards contained 'less life than Sahara desert sand'. Bourguignon made no claim to understanding how biodynamics works, but his research showed that levels of microbial life in vineyard topsoils (see SOIL BIOTA) were significantly greater on organic and biodynamic plots than on those of conventionally farmed ones. In addition, Bourguignon found significant increases of microbial life on biodynamic vine roots at depths of several metres compared with conventionally and even organically farmed vines; and that the roots were thickest, longest, and most able to penetrate the soil, and to assimilate trace elements (see VINE NUTRITION, MICROBES, and MYCORRHIZA), when grown biodynamically.

The particularity of biodynamics is the use of animal sense organs such as cow horns as sheaths when making six of the nine biodynamic preparations. It is believed that animal organs enable the medicinal properties of the substances encased within—cow manure, ground quartz, oak bark, and the flowers of yarrow, chamomile, and dandelion—to become fully effective throughout the farm, keeping it within what Steiner called 'the realm of the living'. The animal organ sheaths disintegrate naturally or are discarded before the preparation material within is applied. Nevertheless, it is this aspect that convinces non-believers that biodynamics is unscientific and irrational.

The two main biodynamic field sprays are horn manure and horn silica. Only a handful of the former or a few grams of the latter are required per hectare. They are prepared by burying the cow manure or the ground quartz (silica) in a cow horn for six months over winter or summer respectively. Horn manure is sprayed on the soil in the afternoon, in autumn and early spring, to stimulate microbial life in the soil, helping maintain SOIL STRUCTURE and levels of ORGANIC MATTER and encouraging deeper vine roots and TERROIR expression. Horn silica is sprayed over the vines, at sunrise, either side of FLOWERING to regulate plant metabolism and promote stronger, more upright vine growth, to LIGNIFY the wood, and to improve the nutritional and keeping qualities of the wine. One further field spray, the silica-rich common horsetail (*Equisetum arvense*), is sprayed as a fresh tea or fermented liquid manure to encourage fungal spores to remain in the soil rather than affecting the vine. It is a fundamental tenet that all three biodynamic spray preparations are 'dynamized' before application. This involves rhythmically stirring the material in water, first one way and then the other, to create a vortex. When the direction of stirring is changed the water is thought to undergo chaos, allowing beneficial 'formative forces' within the preparation to be transferred to the water and thence to the vineyard when it is sprayed. Organic fertilizer in the form of COMPOST is used to nourish the soil, but biodynamic compost differs from other composts in that the remaining six biodynamic preparations made from yarrow, chamomile, stinging nettle, oak bark, dandelion, and valerian must be inserted into the compost pile, which should be manure-based. The compost preparations are said to infuse the manure with vitalizing living forces whose role is more important to vine growth and form than the actual composted manure. Where specific ingredients are not available, substitutes may be used. For example, *Casuarina stricta* is often substituted for common horsetail in Australia.

Late 20th century MECHANIZATION saw the almost complete disappearance of livestock from vineyards. Biodynamic growers are at the forefront of reversing this trend by acquiring livestock for manure (cows), traction (horses, mules), weed control (sheep), or pest control (chickens to eat cutworms). In this way, vine monocultures begin changing towards the biodynamic ideal of self-sustaining farm organisms, creating a natural equilibrium in which pests and diseases become potentially less potent.

Biodynamic growers see plants as comprising four 'organs'—ROOT, LEAF/SHOOT, FLOWER, and FRUIT—and these are respectively linked to the four elements of earth, water, air, and fire (solar heat). Each plant component is said to be favoured during particular points of the moon's sidereal cycle when the moon passes in front of one of the 12 constellations of the astronomical (rather than astrological) zodiac. Thus, for example, spraying horn manure on the soil for root growth is said to be most effective if the moon is in front of an earth/root constellation such as Bull, Virgin, or Goat. These windows occur every nine days or so but for two or three days only, so only the smallest vineyards, or those with abundant labour, can time all their agricultural work according to the biodynamic calendar. Biodynamicists claim that on conventional vineyards, where neither biodynamic compost nor the field spray preparations are used, the effect of these earthly and celestial rhythms will not be felt, as the soil and the vines will not have been sensitized to them.

Cellar work is also said to benefit from the biodynamic calendar, with, it is claimed, bottling best under Lion if the wine is designed to age (the heat/fruit 'force' will be most concentrated in the wine at this point, so bottling then will capture or seal it).

Where VINE PESTS need to be controlled in biodynamic farming, a number of the pests are collected and burnt, their ashes scattered around the affected area to discourage future infestations.

Biodynamic viticulture alone will not a great wine make: good viticultural and winemaking practices such as CANOPY MANAGEMENT and cellar HYGIENE are also essential. Biodynamic winemaking standards are similar to those used for ORGANIC WINE but impose stricter guidelines regarding ENRICHMENT, NUTRIENT additions, the use of energy-intensive practices (e.g. PASTEURIZATION), MICRO-OXYGENATION, and recyclable PACKAGING.

Between 2013 and 2021, the global biodynamic vineyard doubled to more than 22,000 ha/54,363 acres, according to the American Association of Wine Economists (AAWE). Winegrowers obtain certified biodynamic status either from the German-based Demeter International organization (renamed Biodynamic Federation Demeter International in 2020), the body which de facto controls the Biodynamic (with a capital B) agricultural trademark, or from wine-only bodies such as the France-based Syndicat International des Vignerons en Culture Bio-dynamique (Biodyvin) or the Austria-based respekt-BIODYN. Australian Demeter Bio-Dynamic, privately created and trademarked by consultant Alex Podolinsky, is not a member of Demeter International.

Biodynamic vineyards range in size from a handful of hectares to 600 ha/1,480 acres at Emiliana in Chile, the world's biggest biodynamic wine estate. In 2021, France had the greatest area of certified biodynamic vineyards in the world (10,166 ha/25,121 acres), but as a proportion of total vineyard area Switzerland and Austria top the table with 2.78% and 2.73% respectively.

See also ORGANIC VITICULTURE, ORGANIC WINE, SUSTAINABLE VITICULTURE, REGENERATIVE VITICULTURE, and BIOLOGICALS. M.W.

Storchman, K., and American Association of Wine Economics, *Worldwide Biodynamic Vineyard Area by Country*, 2020/21 (2022).
Waldin, M., *Biodynamic Wine* (2016).

biogenic amines are a diverse group of nitrogenous, low-molecular-weight compounds that are chiefly derived from the decarboxylation of certain AMINO ACIDS by specific microbes. The most commonly known biogenic amines, HISTAMINE, tyramine, and putrescine, all occur in wine and are significant for human health. Produced largely during the winemaking process by LACTIC ACID BACTERIA (LAB), particularly *Pediococcus* and *Lactobacillus* spp., both the amino-acid precursor and LAB are required for biogenic amines (BAs) to accumulate.

If ingested in excessive amounts, BAs can trigger toxicity reactions that mimic allergic response (see ALLERGIES AND INTOLERANCES), with symptoms such as nausea, headache, rhinoconjunctival symptoms, hyper- or hypotension, flushing, rashes, and heart palpitations. ETHANOL inhibits the enzymatic detoxification process, making BAs in alcoholic beverages such as wine and beer more significant. Managing winemaking conditions that control microbial growth, such as total SULFUR DIOXIDE level, PH, and, to a lesser extent, TEMPERATURE, is key to ensuring biogenic-amine concentrations are kept low.

Many countries have informal upper limits on histamine concentrations in wine (ranging from 2 to 10 mg/l), but legal regulation is still a matter of debate. S.P.-T.

biological ageing See FLOR and SHERRY.

biologicals, living or dormant organisms, or by-products of a natural product or process, for example tea made from raw COMPOST, or fermented seaweed. They are used in plant protection through the control of pathogens or as a stimulant for plant and soil health. This is a growing field of research and understanding, with many new products coming on to the market. Theories about such products and processes and how they work have been around for generations, notably as part of BIODYNAMIC VITICULTURE. While many of the early formulations were seen as 'snake oil', there has been real scientific progress towards legitimizing some of them.

Plant protection can happen in three ways:

- by directly attacking the pathogen (typically a fungus, e.g. POWDERY MILDEW or BOTRYTIS)—common formulations use *Trichoderma* spp.
- by outcompeting a pathogen for space on the leaf or berry—common formulations use *Bacillus subtilis* or so-called effective microorganisms (EMs)
- by inducing systemic acquired resistance (SAR), whereby the grapevines' own immune system is activated by enzymes and elicitors that increase the accumulation of PHYTOALEXINS in the vine to protect it from a pathogen.

Biologicals are also used in the control of insect pests, commonly *Bacillus thuringiensis* for moth species. New research is being carried out on the control of MEALYBUGS.

In soil, these products are used to enhance the microbiome, either by adding more of a specific fungi or bacteria (e.g. compost teas, EM) or by feeding and stimulating the existing population (e.g. biodynamic preparations, humic acid, seaweeds, enzymes). This promotes a healthy living soil environment, leading to a healthy plant less susceptible to attack by a pathogen, better equipped to defend itself by SAR, and better equipped to cope with abiotic stresses such as drought/waterlogging and excessive heat/cold. N.S.

biological viticulture, a loose term since all viticulture involves biology, but for more details of the general philosophy implied see ORGANIC VITICULTURE. In France, many ORGANIC WINES are sold as *vins biologiques*. See also BIOLOGICALS.

Biondi-Santi, family synonymous with BRUNELLO DI MONTALCINO and, in 1888, responsible for one of the first wines ever to be so labelled. Before that time Montalcino's fame was based solely on a sweet, often sparkling white based on the MOSCADELLO grape, until Ferruccio Biondi-Santi isolated a particular type of SANGIOVESE on his Il Greppo estate using MASS SELECTION with better resistance to OÏDIUM than Moscadello. It was subsequently called Sangiovese Grosso and officially registered as BBS 11. Ferruccio also increased VINE DENSITY and lowered YIELDS, while eliminating the white grapes that were routinely blended with Sangiovese then.

Tancredi, Ferruccio's son, is credited with founding the first Montalcino CO-OPERATIVE during the crisis years of the 1920s, while focusing on exporting the Bondi-Santi wines. He was soon joined by his son, Franco, who committed himself firmly to Il Greppo's traditional methods which, during the 1980s and 1990s, were challenged by a new generation of Brunello producers preferring to make a more concentrated, richer, and more internationally accessible style by harvesting ultra-ripe grapes, using shorter MACERATION time, and ageing the wines in French BARRIQUES. This modernist approach, which received glowing reviews from the then all-powerful Italian wine guides, was especially successful in the US but made the Biondi-Santi style look outdated and light. However, in 2008 during the scandal described in BRUNELLO DI MONTALCINO, Biondi-Santi rose as the natural defender of Brunello and was subsequently joined by a majority of the region's growers and wine producers who together prevented the proposed change in production rules to allow INTERNATIONAL VARIETIES into Brunello di Montalcino.

With the taste for rich, extracted wines on the wane and a growing international appetite for more locally authentic, TERROIR-driven wines, Biondi-Santi's future looked promising until Jacopo Biondi Santi, who had taken over the estate after the death of his father Franco in 2013, sold the estate to the French EPI conglomerate in 2017. Widespread concerns that the archaic style of wines would be compromised by the new owners have so far proved unfounded. W.S.

Boldrini, M., et al., *This Is My Land: Franco Biondi Santi, Montalcino and Brunello* (2009).

O'Keefe, K., *Franco Biondi Santi: The Gentleman of Brunello* (2005).

biotechnology. See GENETIC MODIFICATION for some examples of viticultural biotechnology.

biotype, a group of CLONES that share similar morphological characteristics. See also PHYLLOXERA for a different use of the term 'biotype'.

birds can be a more serious modern vine pest than PHYLLOXERA in some areas because they are so difficult to control, particularly during grape RIPENING when they feed on grapes. Birds have eaten grapes for about 60 million years as they have co-evolved and in so doing have spread grape seeds in their excreta. This is one reason why grapes are thought to have developed small, black, sugary fruits which attract birds. (Subsequent human selection of MUTATIONS has given us light-skinned grapes.)

For small vineyards in isolated regions, and particularly for early-ripening vine varieties, birds may destroy an entire crop. Unfortunately, the birds begin their destruction as soon as the grapes begin to ripen at VERAISON, so early harvest is not a solution. As well as the potential crop loss, bird pecks provide entry points for BUNCH ROTS. The cost of control measures or damage to the fruit can make some vineyards uneconomic. Birds are often the greatest problem facing vineyards in new viticultural regions, especially if the vineyards are isolated (as in ENGLAND and Long Island in NEW YORK, for example).

The species of birds which attack grapes vary from region to region. The ubiquitous starling is one of the most widespread problem species, but blackbirds, partridges, robins, sparrows, thrushes, and finches are also common. A starling, for example, can eat 60–80 g/2.8 oz of grapes a day. The planting of a vineyard and the consequent provision of an extra food source can actually lead to a population increase of birds. Many growers notice that bird damage depends on the availability of alternative food sources. In the MARGARET RIVER region of Western Australia, for example, silvereye birds do more damage to vineyards when nectar from local eucalyptus trees and saltbush berries is limited. Where vineyards are extensive and the varieties ripen together, damage to individual vineyards is lessened.

B

Many bird-protection devices are based on scaring birds by sight or sound. In time, birds become accustomed to new objects or noises in a vineyard so that, for example, the traditional immobile scarecrow can rapidly lose effectiveness. Other scaring devices include a wide range of auditory contraptions, guns, gas-powered cannon, tape across the vineyards, robotic solar-powered lasers, etc.

NETTING of vineyards is becoming increasingly common. The nets are made of woven string or perforated plastic and can often be reused, and tractor-mounted rollers assist installation and removal. Since the nets provide for virtually 100% effective control yet do not harm birds, they are acceptable to growers and environmentalists alike.

Some local bird populations are affected by eating insects or grapes which contain pesticides used in vineyards, which bird lovers view as an argument against the use of AGROCHEMICALS. R.E.S.

Buchanan, G. A., and Amos, T. G., 'Grape pests', in B. G. Coombe and P. R. Dry (eds.), *Viticulture*, ii: *Practices* (2nd edn, 2006).

McKee, L. J., 'To net or not to net', *Wines & Vines* (March 2010).

bird's eye rot, vine disease. See ANTHRACNOSE.

Biscoitos, DOC on the island of Terceira in the AZORES making small quantities of FORTIFIED WINE and, more recently, TABLE WINE from the VERDELHO grape. Biscoitos is so-called because VOLCANIC stones in the soil resemble biscuits. Between 2014 and 2020, the DOC area under vine increased from 15 to 24 ha/59 acres. S.A.

bisulfite. See SULFUR DIOXIDE.

bitterness, one of the primary tastes (see TASTING) which can be detected via taste buds mainly on the tongue in many wines, even if it is not as common as SWEETNESS and ACIDITY and is often confused with the quite different tactile sensation caused by ASTRINGENCY. Many Italian red wines are relatively bitter, as are some less successful examples of particularly aromatic grape varieties such as Gewürztraminer, typically because of an excess of PHENOLICS. Poorly seasoned OAK can also make a wine taste bitter.

bitter rot, a FUNGAL DISEASE of ripe grapes that is active in warm, humid conditions. It is found only on damaged and almost senescent tissues, but the bitter fruit flavour can be detected in the finished wine. The cause is the fungus *Greeneria uvicola*, and the disease is widespread in the eastern United States, Asia, Australia, and South Africa but not in France or Germany. It is easily controlled by most FUNGICIDES. R.E.S.

black dead arm. See BOTRYOSPHAERIA DIEBACK.

black foot, fungal disease found in young vines in both vineyards and NURSERIES which can lead to the premature decline and death of young vines. Causal agents of this TRUNK DISEASE include more than 20 species of soil-borne fungi in the genera *Campylocarpon*, *'Cylindrocarpon'*, *Cylindrocladiella*, and *Ilyonectria*. *Ilyonectria liriodendra*, *I. macrodidyma*, and *I. torresensis* are known to be the most virulent and widespread. Symptoms include slow growth, poor vigour, chlorotic leaves, brownish-black discoloration of rootstock trunks, roots, graft unions (see GRAFTING), and a reduction in root biomass. Affected young vines usually die during the growing season or in the following winter. Control measures include field rotation, planting clean vines, and avoiding planting in heavy, wet, and poorly drained soils. The most common PHYLLOXERA-resistant ROOTSTOCKS used today are susceptible to black foot. L.T.M. & J.R.U.-T.

Agusti-Brisach, C., and Armengol, J., 'Black-foot disease of grapevine: an update on taxonomy, epidemiology and management strategies', *Phytopathologia Mediterranea*, 52/2 (2013), 245–61.

Gramaje, D., and Armengol, J., 'Fungal trunk pathogens in the grapevine propagation process: potential inoculum sources, detection, identification, and management strategies', *Plant Disease*, 95/9 (2011), 1040–55.

Petit, E., 'Black foot disease', in W. F. Wilcox et al. (eds.), *Compendium of Grape Diseases, Disorders, and Pests* (2nd edn, 2015), 26–8.

black goo, name coined in 1995 by American viticulturist Lucie Morton to describe the symptoms of black spots and tarry ooze in XYLEM vessels produced by *Phaeomoniella chlamydospora* and *Phaeoacremonium* species, fungi that cause premature decline in young vines or PETRI DISEASE in older vines suffering from ESCA. L.T.M.

Morton, L., 'Viticulture and grapevine declines: the lessons of black goo', *Phytopathologia Mediterranea*, 39/1 (2000), 59–67.

black knot, vine disease. See CROWN GALL.

black measles, vine disease. See ESCA.

black rot, FUNGAL DISEASE which is one of the most economically important diseases of vines in the eastern half of the United States and some wetter regions of Europe. The disease is native to North America and was probably introduced to other countries by contaminated cuttings. It was introduced to France, for example, on PHYLLOXERA-tolerant ROOTSTOCKS as early as 1885. The disease is caused by the fungus *Guignardia bidwelli*, which attacks young shoots, leaves, stems, and especially berries. The disease develops only in wet weather; although it occurs across a broad range of temperatures, it is especially problematic in warmer conditions (optimum 28 °C/82 °F). Crop losses can be up to 80%. Control of the disease is based on FUNGICIDES sprayed from spring to VERAISON (crucially during early berry development) and removing infected mummified berries. As might be expected from the origin of the disease, some native American species and their HYBRIDS are relatively tolerant. R.E.S. & W.W.

black spot, vine disease. See ANTHRACNOSE.

Blackwood Valley, relatively young, inland wine region of WESTERN AUSTRALIA.

black xylem decline, a more formal name for the condition BLACK GOO, which affects young GRAFTED VINES. It has been studied for more than 50 years in South Africa and has also caused concern in Europe, Australia, and New Zealand. It was a particular problem in California during the 1980s when unexpected lack of resistance to PHYLLOXERA in the AXR1 ROOTSTOCK forced rapid replanting.

More recently the condition has been associated with a group of fungal diseases known generically as grapevine TRUNK DISEASES, which are spreading globally at an alarming rate. R.E.S.

Blagny, small village in Burgundy's CÔTE D'OR. For more details, see both MEURSAULT and PULIGNY-MONTRACHET.

blanc, **blanche**, masculine and feminine French adjectives meaning 'white' and therefore a common suffix for white wines and light-berried grape variety names.

blanc de blancs, French for 'white of whites', may justifiably be used to describe white wines made from pale-skinned grapes, as the great majority of them are. The term has real significance, however, only when used for white SPARKLING WINES, in the production of which dark-skinned grapes tend to predominate. A blanc de blancs CHAMPAGNE, for example, is, unusually, made exclusively from CHARDONNAY grapes.

Blanc de Morgex, alpine white wine made from the PRIÉ grape, a speciality of the Valle d'AOSTA.

blanc de noirs, French for 'white of blacks', describes a white wine made from dark-skinned grapes by pressing them very gently and running the pale juice off the skins as early as possible. Many such still wines have a slightly pink tinge (see WHITE ZINFANDEL, for example). The term has a specific meaning in the Champagne region, where it is used to describe a CHAMPAGNE made exclusively from PINOT NOIR and PINOT MEUNIER grapes. See also VIN GRIS and BLUSH.

Blanc Fumé is a French synonym for SAUVIGNON BLANC, notably in Pouilly-sur-Loire, centre of the POUILLY-FUMÉ, or **Blanc Fumé de Pouilly**, appellation, many of whose aromatic dry whites do indeed have a smoky, if not exactly smoked, perfume. Thanks to one imaginative American, FUMÉ BLANC is today a much more widely known term (see MONDAVI).

blanco, Spanish for white, as in *vino blanco*, or white wine.

Blandy, a name that is synonymous with MADEIRA, both the island and the wine. The Blandy family has extensive interests on Madeira, including hotels, travel, and property. John Blandy of Dorset came to live on the island in 1808, having been introduced to the island and its wines while working for wine merchant Newton, Gordon, Murdoch. He founded the company in 1811 and his son Charles was astute enough to buy up considerable stocks of mature wine during the outbreak of POWDERY MILDEW in 1852, which contributed to the success of the madeira wine firm Blandy Brothers & Co. in the second half of the 19th century. In 1874, Charles's daughter married a Cossart, of the other important madeira wine firm Cossart Gordon. The tourist showpiece of the madeira wine industry, Blandy's Wine Lodge (the old São Francisco lodge) in Funchal, was once the Blandy family home and offices.

The difficult years of the early 20th century saw the formation of the Madeira Wine Association, which Blandy's joined in the 1920s, eventually acquiring a controlling interest. The group is now known as the Madeira Wine Company, includes all the British madeira firms (Cossart Gordon, Leacock, Rutherford & Miles), and is one of the largest producers on the island. Between 1988 and 2011 the SYMINGTON family had a controlling interest in the Madeira Wine Company, but it is now back in the hands of a Blandy, Chris Blandy, who is actively engaged in reviving the madeira category.

Binney, M., *The Blandys of Madeira (1811–2011)*, (2011).

blanketing, winemaking term for protecting grapes, juice, or wine, particularly from OXYGEN, by applying a gas, usually INERT GAS or sometimes CARBON DIOXIDE.

Blanquette de Limoux. See LIMOUX.

blau or **blauer** is the adjective meaning 'blue' in German, often used for darker-berried vine varieties. Blauburgunder and Blauer Burgunder are PINOT NOIR, for example, while Weissburgunder and Weisser Burgunder are PINOT BLANC.

Blauburger, Austrian red wine grape variety and, like the much more common ZWEIGELT, a cross made in the 1920s by Dr Zweigelt at KLOSTERNEUBURG, in this case of PORTUGIESER and BLAUFRÄNKISCH. Plantings had gone down to 460 ha/1,137 acres in 2022, the majority planted in Lower Austria, where it produces relatively undistinguished light reds although its deep colour makes it a useful ingredient in blends. Hungary has 433 ha, mostly around Eger. There is also a little in Germany.

Blauburgunder, sometimes **Blauer Burgunder**, common name for PINOT NOIR in Austria and Switzerland. In Germany, SPÄTBURGUNDER (occasionally **Blauer Spätburgunder**) is more common.

Blauer Wildbacher, ancient, dark-skinned, perfumed grape variety that is a speciality of WESTSTEIERMARK, where all of the 458 ha/1,132 acres grown in Austria are located. Schilcher wines, marketed as the principal distinction of the region's recently launched DAC, are typically tart, pink and fizzy; but red and sweet variants are becoming common. DNA PROFILING analysis suggests a parent–offspring relationship with GOUAIS BLANC.

Blaufränkisch is the Austrian name for the increasingly respected middle European black grape variety the Germans call LEMBERGER. From pre-medieval times it was common to divide grape varieties into the (superior) 'fränkisch', whose origins lay with the Franks, and the rest. It is today Austria's second most planted dark-berried variety after its progeny ZWEIGELT, producing wines of real character, if notably high acidity, when carefully grown. Its good colour, tannin, and raciness encourage the most ambitious Austrian producers, led by Moric, to treat it like SINGLE-VINEYARD burgundy, and the lavish use of new oak for top bottlings is in decline. For many years it was thought to be the Beaujolais grape GAMAY. Bulgarians still call it Gamé, while Hungarians translate its Austrian name more directly as KÉKFRANKOS. DNA PROFILING has shown that it is a spontaneous GOUAIS BLANC × Blaue Zimmettraube CROSS. Gouais Blanc is known in Austria as Heunisch, and Blaue Zimmettraube is an old dark-skinned variety from lower Styria (today part of SLOVENIA), also called Sbulzìna in FRIULI. The crossing most likely took place in Lower Styria, putting the origin of Blaufränkisch not in Austria but in Slovenia, where 637 ha/1,574 acres of Modra Frankinja are planted.

Its Austrian home is BURGENLAND, where most of its 2,597 ha/6,417 acres are situated. It is grown particularly on the warm shores of the Neusiedlersee, in Mittelburgenland, and at Eisenberg in South Burgenland. As Kékfrankos it grows even more prolifically on the Hungarian side of the lake, notably in SOPRON, whose version has the distinction of having been singled out for mention by Napoleon. Today it is seen both at home and abroad as one of Austria's best local varieties. Blaufränkisch gives varied wine styles with red fruit flavours, firm acidity, and generally good weight, deep colour, and spicy character. The variety called Frankovka in CZECHIA and Serbia is one and the same and here can produce lively, fruity, vigorous wines for early consumption. In SLOVAKIA, as Frankovka or Frankovka Modrá, it is the most important dark-skinned grape, with plantings of 1,260 ha in 2021. In FRIULI in the far north-eastern corner of Italy, the variety is called Franconia and can yield wines with zip and fruit.

The vine buds early and ripens late and can therefore thrive only in a relatively warm climate. However, in the cooler sites of Washington State and on the US east coast, there's a small but growing number of producers who see a promising future for this exciting Austrian emigré.

Blaye, fortified town across the Gironde estuary from Margaux in the BORDEAUX region which has been exporting wine much longer than the famous MÉDOC. It gives its name to a region of scattered vineyards with soils that vary considerably (much more than in neighbouring Côtes de BOURG) but are mainly CLAY and LIMESTONE. At the beginning of the 20th century it produced mainly white wine for distillation into cognac, and even today some of its white wine is distilled. Early 21st century tinkering with nomenclature resulted in most of the wines being sold as **Blaye Côtes de Bordeaux**. Mainly robust, early-maturing, red BORDEAUX BLENDS were produced from 5,543 ha/13,691 acres of vines in 2020 planted predominantly with Merlot. A much smaller number of growers produce reds according to the stricter rules of **Blaye** *tout court*. Around 300 ha/740 acres of Sauvignon Blanc and Sémillon vines are responsible for some particularly successful, lively dry white Blaye Côtes de Bordeaux. J.L.

bleeding. Vines are said to bleed when they lose fluid in spring from pruning cuts. This event can take place over several days and is generally seen following the first few days of warm spring weather. Individual vines can lose up to 5 l/1.3 gal of water. The liquid which drips from the pruning cuts is mostly water, with low concentrations of MINERALS, SUGARS, organic acids, and HORMONES. This is the first visible sign of the start of the new VINE GROWTH CYCLE and corresponds to renewed activity of the root system. Osmotic forces create root pressure, which forces water up through the plant. The term is also used occasionally in winemaking; see SAIGNÉE. R.E.S.

Galet, P., *General Viticulture* (2000).

blend, any product of BLENDING but specifically a wine deliberately made from more than one grape variety as opposed to a VARIETAL wine (which may contain only a small proportion of other varieties).

B

blending different batches of wine is a practice that was once more distrusted than understood. In fact almost all of the world's finest wines are made by blending the contents of different vats and different barrels (see ASSEMBLAGE); CHAMPAGNE, SHERRY, and PORT are examples of wines which are quintessentially blends. It is often the case, as has been proved by the most rigorous of experiments, that a wine blend is superior to any one of its component parts.

Blending earned its dubious reputation before the mid 20th century when wine laws were either non-existent or under-enforced, and 'stretching' a superior wine by blending it with inferior wines was commonplace (see ADULTERATION). Blending of different lots of the same wine as it is commonly practised today to ensure that quality is maximal and consistent was not possible before the days of large blending vats; before then wine was bottled from individual casks or vats, which is one explanation of the much higher degree of BOTTLE VARIATION in older vintages.

Modern blending, important in the production of both fine and everyday wines, may combine wines with different but complementary characteristics: heavily oak-influenced lots aged in new barrels may be muted by blending with less oaky lots of the same wine; wines that have undergone MALOLACTIC CONVERSION may be blended with crisper ones that have not. In the case of ordinary table wines, blending is an important ingredient in smoothing out the difference between one VINTAGE and its successor. Such practices are by no means unknown in the realm of fine-wine production, whether legally sanctioned or not. The wine regulations in many regions permit the addition of a certain proportion of another vintage to a vintage-dated wine or of a certain proportion, generally less than 15%, of wine from a region or even grape variety other than that specified on the label.

In today's competitive and quality-conscious wine market, motivation for blending is more often improvement than deception.

Perhaps the most enthusiastic blenders are the Australians, who regularly blend the produce of two or more different wine regions, possibly many hundreds of miles apart. The philosophical differences between these blenders and the European authorities were resolved by an agreement reached in the mid 1990s allowing the importation of such wines into the EU.

For details of **fractional blending**, see SOLERA. For an alternative approach, in which grape varieties are mixed before fermentation, see CO-FERMENTATION.

blind tasting, form of wine TASTING in which the taster attempts to evaluate and/or identify wines without knowing their identity. Only by blind tasting can a true assessment of a wine's style and quality be made, so subjective is the wine-tasting process. Many professional tastings, those designed to make significant judgements about quality and possibly value, are therefore conducted blind. A comparative tasting, for example, comprises a group of wines of the same approximate age and provenance served blind together in order to evaluate them without prejudicial knowledge of their identity.

Blind tasting with the sole purpose of identification is a particularly masochistic but potentially rewarding exercise, conducted sometimes round the dining table, sometimes in the examination room (as part of a MASTER OF WINE exam, for example). The blind taster generally attempts to identify VINE VARIETY, geographical provenance, and VINTAGE. The first of these should generally be the easiest, but in some cases a wine's geographical provenance can be easier to detect than specific grape variety or blend of varieties. Red bordeaux and white Alsace, for example, tend to express place before grape.

In identifying vintage and general maturity, a wine's COLOUR can be particularly helpful, although, given the extent of vintage variation, a vintage several years from the actual one may well be a better guess than the vintage either side of it. Blind tasting does not usually involve blindfolding the taster (although if this is done, many tasters can even be confused as to whether a wine is red or white, particularly if the wines have similar weight and are made from vine varieties with similar genetic antecedents, as in red and white burgundy). Common practice is to disguise labels or even whole bottles by swathing them in foil, paper, or fabric and identifying them simply by number. A tasting is said to be **single blind** if the tasters know what is being tasted but not which wine is which, whereas in a **double blind** tasting no clues are given.

The OPTIONS GAME was devised by Len EVANS as a way of combining the arcane process of blind tasting with general entertainment. Beginners often make the best blind tasters; experience can confuse.

Burton, N., *The Concise Guide to Wine and Blind Tasting* (3rd edn, 2019).

blockchain, a technology that verifies and records transactions between parties without the need for a central authority. Just as the advent of the internet allowed the transfer of information between multiple parties, blockchain similarly allows the transfer of value and the creation of immutable records of transactions.

Blockchain technology offers a powerful weapon against COUNTERFEIT WINE and ADULTERATION AND FRAUD. A Euromonitor 2018 global study on illicit alcohol suggests that as many as one in four bottles of alcohol may be fake, which can lead to health risks for the consumer and losses in revenue for governments estimated to be $3.6 billion each year.

Implementing the wine supply chain on a blockchain provides a system that can verify the AUTHENTICITY of each batch of wine from the grape-grower to the end consumer, so that at each stage of the supply chain the transaction is recorded as an immutable block in the chain and can be viewed by all participants. These transactions cannot be altered, as any attempt to defraud a transaction record becomes immediately apparent.

The possible applications to the wine supply chain are not limited to the fine-wine trade. The blocks in the chain could also be used to verify the 'ingredients' at each stage, for example any ADDITIVES used in the production process and the TEMPERATURE conditions under which wines are transported. What's needed for this technology to become mainstream is hardware that allows measurement of the critical data points at each stage of the supply chain and the inputting of this data into blockchain platforms.

But while fine-wine producers may be able to absorb or pass on the extra costs to the consumer, more commercial producers will need to find ways to implement it without dramatic price increases per bottle. M.K.

Euromonitor International, 'Size and shape of the global illicit alcohol market' (2018), 12.

bloom on a grape's skin is the whitish covering consisting of waxes and cutin which protects the berry against water loss and helps stop the penetration of spores. 'Blooming' is another term for FLOWERING.

blue fining, largely outmoded though still used winemaking process whereby excess COPPER and IRON are removed from wine by FINING with potassium ferrocyanide. The process works because soluble copper and iron form insoluble compounds with the ferrocyanide ion. A century ago, before STAINLESS STEEL was widely available, winery equipment was often made of iron, copper, or bronze, an alloy of copper and tin. They would be attacked by the ACIDS in wine. Wines containing more than 10 mg/l of iron or 0.25 mg/l of copper could easily form a haze, so blue fining was needed to remove the excess copper and iron dissolved from the equipment after prolonged contact with the metals.

The process was developed by the German chemist Möslinger at the beginning of the 20th century and is still legally used, under strict controls, in many countries. In contemporary winemaking, iron may be introduced from metal grape bins and from BENTONITE fining; vineyard sprays such as BORDEAUX MIXTURE are still a common source of copper. Because of fears that hydrogen cyanide could be formed from potassium ferrocyanide, the use of blue fining is a major regulatory issue for wine treatments internationally and is illegal in many countries. P.J.W.

Blue Nun, the most successful German wine BRAND, and for most of the 20th century a LIEBFRAUMILCH owned by H. Sichel Söhne of Mainz. It was launched with the 1921 vintage in 1923 as a more accessible product than the host of German bottles adorned with Gothic script and long, complicated names. The label initially featured several nuns in brown habits against a bright blue sky. The label, and subsequently the brand, became known as Blue Nun, featuring a single, alluring nun in a blue habit. Long before MATEUS Rosé, Blue Nun became a substantial commercial success as a result of heavy investment in advertising which preyed on the fears of what was then an unsophisticated wine-drinking public. Blue Nun was advertised as the wine you could drink 'right through the meal', thereby solving the awkward problem of FOOD-AND-WINE MATCHING. It began to grow rapidly, mainly in Britain and America, in the 1950s when German wines enjoyed greater prestige than they do today, and Blue Nun commanded about the same price as a second growth (see CLASSIFICATION) red bordeaux. At its zenith, in 1984/5, annual sales in the US alone were 1.25 million cases, with a further 750,000 cases sold elsewhere. Quality was reliably high, despite the quantities needed to satisfy world sales, and blending at the Mainz headquarters was conscientiously undertaken, but sales declined and H. Sichel Söhne and the Blue Nun brand were bought by F. W. Langguth Erben in 1995. An attempt at relaunching the brand, in all three colours, was made in 2014.

Sichel, M. F., *The Secrets of My Life* (2016).

blush wine is made, rather like France's VIN GRIS, by using black-skinned grapes as if to make white wine. The name is said to have been originally coined by Mill Creek winery in California, but the style was promulgated by Bob Trinchero of Sutter Home when he introduced his WHITE ZINFANDEL in 1972. Although that wine was originally dry, it was the slightly sweet version he produced in 1975 that sparked a rage for 'blush' wines in the US in the 1980s. Its success inspired a rash of VARIETALS labelled White Grenache and Merlot Blanc, as well as GENERIC wines. The term is now used around the world, for beverages as diverse as wine, cider, and gin, though it has largely lost its cache and is used mainly for slightly sweet wines sold at the lower end of the market. See also SAIGNÉE.

Boal, often Anglicized to **Bual**, is the MADEIRA name for the MALVASIA Fina grape. Most of the Boal growing to a limited extent on Madeira today (14 ha/35 acres in 2018)—though not nearly as limited as the island's other three traditional varieties—is **Boal Cachudo**. Portugal's Instituto da Vinha e do Vinho (IVV) lists four other Boal Somethings: **Boal Barreiro**, **Boal Branco**, **Boal Espinho**, and **Boal Ratinho**, though only Cachudo and Branco have been shown by DNA PROFILING to be synonyms for Malvasia Fina.

Bobal, a very important Spanish dark-skinned grape variety which produces deep-coloured red wines and even GRAPE CONCENTRATE in south-east Spain, substantially but by no means exclusively for BULK WINE production. In 2019 its plantings totalled 56,184 ha/138,834 acres, making it Spain's third most planted red wine grape after Tempranillo and Garnacha. Its reputation has been growing as producers such as Mustiguillo have managed to fashion velvety reds from high-ELEVATION vineyards in UTIEL-REQUENA. It retains its acidity better than MONASTRELL (which tends to be grown in slightly warmer, more southerly parts of Spain) and is notably lower in alcohol. It is allowed in four DOP areas: Utiel-Requena, VALENCIA, MANCHUELA, and RIBERA DEL JÚCAR. Drought-resistant and always grown as unirrigated bush vines, Bobal is extremely sensitive to springtime cold spells. Young vines may ripen unevenly. Although more rustic than the internationally famous Garnacha and Monastrell, Bobal wines are fresher, with fine colour, a good dark berry component, and an ability to transmit TERROIR.

Bobal Blanco, also known as Tortosí, is still grown to a limited extent in Valencia but is Alcañón and not related to Bobal.

Boca, historically important red-wine DOC in the Novara Hills in northern PIEMONTE, comprising 16.5 ha/40 acres in 2020, up from 12 ha in 2010, divided among 12 producers. Nebbiolo grapes, called SPANNA here, should comprise 70–90% of these intriguing reds. Although marginal in size, Boca produces such good wines, notably Le Piane's, that they are attracting international attention.

Bocksbeutel, bottle in the shape of a flattened flask used in the German wine region of FRANKEN and four communes in the northern Ortenau area of BADEN. The name probably derived from the Low German *Bockesbeutel*, a pouch to carry prayer-books and the like, rather than from any ostensible resemblance to a goat's scrotum (the literal translation). From the early 18th century onwards, the original purpose of the special bottle was to guarantee the authenticity of Würzburger Steinwein. Only after the First World War did it become common throughout Franken. T.S. & D.De.

BOD, biological oxygen demand. See WINERY WASTE.

bodega, Spanish for a wine CELLAR, a WINERY, or a tavern or grocery store selling wine.

body, tasting term for the perceived 'weight'—the sensation of fullness, resulting from DENSITY or VISCOSITY—of a wine on the palate. Wines at either end of the scale are described as **full-bodied** and **light-bodied**.

Next to water, ALCOHOL is the major constituent of wines. It has a much higher viscosity than water and is the major component responsible for the sensation of fullness, or body, as a wine is rinsed around the mouth. ALCOHOLIC STRENGTH is therefore clearly an important factor: the more potent a wine the more full-bodied it is usually said to be.

Sweet wines are not necessarily full-bodied (ASTI, for example, is sweet but very light-bodied, thanks to its low alcohol content).

Contrary to popular conception, GLYCEROL makes only a very minor contribution to density, viscosity, and therefore to body (although it does have a slight effect on apparent sweetness).

Body is not related to wine quality, BALANCE and HARMONY being more important in a wine than whether it is full- or light-bodied.

Amerine, M. A., and Roessler, E. B., *Wines: Their Sensory Evaluation* (2nd edn, 1983).

Bohemia, in the north of CZECHIA, remains better known for the production of beer and GLASSES than for wine even though its winemaking history reaches back to the 9th century. By the 17th century the region boasted 3,500 ha/8,650 acres of vineyards. In 2021, that had dwindled to just 650 ha spread around the cities of Mělník, Litoměřice, and Prague. The production is small and mostly drunk straight from the wineries, save for the sparkling wines of Bohemia Sekt, a substantial business owned by Dr. Oetker. Cooler than MORAVIA and relatively dry, Bohemia specializes in Pinots Noir and Blanc as well as Svatovavřinecké (ST-LAURENT) and Ryzlink Rýnský (RIESLING). K.K.

bois noir. See GRAPEVINE YELLOWS.

Boisset, Burgundy's largest wine producer and one of the world's largest family-owned producers of good-quality wine currently called Boisset, La Famille des Grands Vins, and based in Nuits-St-Georges. It has wineries in Burgundy, the Jura, Beaujolais, the Rhône Valley, and the south of France, as well as in California's Napa Valley, Russian River Valley, Sonoma Valley, and Monterey. It also owns 800 ha/1,977 acres of vines in France and 200 ha in California. Quite a force! Although there's a constantly changing roster of acquisitions and sales of subsidiaries.

It was formed as recently as 1961 by Jean-Claude and Claudine Boisset when Jean-Claude was just 18. The early business was successful enough to acquire NÉGOCIANTS Charles Viénot

B

and Thomas-Bassot in 1982. A portion of the company was floated on the stock market in 1985, and they took over Pierre Ponnelle, Morin Père et Fils, Jaffelin, and Bouchard Ainé & Fils during the next six years. In 1994 the company then diversified into sparkling-wine production via such acquisitions as Charles de Fère and Louis Bouillot Crémants de Bourgogne in 1997 while consolidating its Côte de Beaune holdings by buying Ropiteau Frères, followed in the late 1990s by Mommessin in Beaujolais, J. Moreau & Fils in Chablis, and the fruit liqueur business L'Héritier-Guyot (sold in 2008). Ch Pierreux with 100 ha of vines in Brouilly was acquired in 2002, and Antonin Rodet in Mercurey with its 80-ha domaine was snapped up in 2009.

The company is now styled *négociant-éleveur* with a commitment to ORGANIC and BIODYNAMIC VITICULTURE in its flagship 40-ha/99-acre vineyard holding Domaine de la Vougeraie. The term *viniculteur* was coined to stress Boisset's degree of control of quality in vineyards both owned and bought from.

Having abandoned its JOINT VENTURES in Canada and South America, the company has determinedly expanded into California, building a Franco-American identity from 1992 with the acquisition of Lyeth Estate in the Alexander Valley. This was followed in 2003 by DeLoach in the Russian River Valley, Raymond in the Napa Valley in 2009, and Sonoma's Buena Vista (California's first winery) and Monterey's Lockwood Vineyards in 2011, joining what has come to be known as the Boisset Collection. Also in 2011, Boisset bought négociant Skalli based in Sète in the LANGUEDOC.

In 2012 JCB by Jean-Charles Boisset became the first range of wines from both Burgundy (sparkling and still) and California. (Boisset lives in the Napa Valley with his wife Gina GALLO.) The acquisitions continue: Henri Maire, now Domaine Maire & Fils, and the biggest vineyard holding in the JURA (280 ha) in 2015; creation of the first 'lounge' in Burgundy, La Maison Vougeot in 2016; the substantial Rhône négociant Gabriel Meffre and its 80-ha Domaine de Longue Toque in Gigondas and Vacqueyras in 2018; Alex Gambal in Beaune and the historic Oakville Grocery in Napa in 2019; and in 2021 Louis Bouillot in Burgundy and a winery in Beaucaire now called Les Chais du Sud and designed to ride the wave of Provençal rosé.

Bolgheri, small town in the Tuscan MAREMMA made famous by Marchese Mario Incisa della Rocchetta, who planted Cabernet Sauvignon vines for a house wine as early as the 1940s on his San Guido estate, labelling the resulting wine SASSICAIA. Bizarrely, the DOC created for Bolgheri in 1983 was only for whites and rosé, but it was amended in 1994 to include red wine, and the subzone Sassicaia was created. Prior to this Sassicaia had to be labelled as VINO DA TAVOLA, but due to its high quality it became known as a SUPERTUSCAN, spawning many copies throughout Tuscany. In 2013 Bogheri Sassicaia was created, becoming Italy's only single-estate DOC, evidence that it is this estate more than any other that gives credentials to an area where previously only cattle used to roam.

The success of Sassicaia, Grattamacco (first vintage 1982), and Ornellaia (1985) triggered an investment frenzy in the region, which expanded from 250 ha at the end of the 1990s to more than 1,190 ha/2,940 acres in 2020, with 60 producers.

The DOC's red-wine production is based on Cabernet Sauvignon and Merlot, which until 2011 were presented in blends only, before VARIETAL wines were allowed. Sangiovese and Syrah are also allowed but at no more than 50% of a blend. Most estates produce a classic BORDEAUX BLEND aged in BARRIQUES. The wines are generally of a high quality, but styles can differ due to soil composition and location of the vineyards as much as differences in winemaking. Although once hailed as one of Italy's future fine-wine regions, the lower ELEVATIONS have proved too warm to produce wines of sufficient elegance to mimic Bordeaux, which seems to be the objective of most producers here. However, VERMENTINO, a distinctly Mediterranean white variety, is experiencing an increase in interest.

W.S.

Masnaghetti, A., *Bolgheri: Cellars and Vineyards* (e-book, 2009).

Bolivia in SOUTH AMERICA has a long history of vine-growing and a small but growing modern wine industry. Viticulture was brought to Bolivia from neighbouring PERU in the 16th century by Spanish settlers and Catholic MISSIONARIES. Though the whereabouts of the first vineyards in the country is debated, wines were being produced throughout the region in the late 1500s, sprouting in diverse places like Mizque in present-day Cochabamba, Sutó in present-day Santa Cruz, and Tomina, Pilaya, Paspalla, and Cinti in present-day Chuquisaca. Wine was also made in Tarija, where 71% of the country's vineyards are located today.

PHYLLOXERA and NEMATODES severely hampered Bolivian viticulture in much of the 20th century. Resistant ROOTSTOCKS and good-quality VITIS VINIFERA cuttings were imported in the 1970s in an effort to restore vineyard health. By 2021, the country had 5,000 ha/12,300 acres of vineyard, most of it planted to GRAFTED VINES trained in ESPALIER. IRRIGATION is widely practised throughout the country.

Over 90% of Bolivia's wines come from Tarija, in the far south of the country, close to the Argentine border. At ELEVATIONS of 1,600–2,700 m/5,200–8,800 ft, the climate here is mild CONTINENTAL, with significant DIURNAL TEMPERATURE RANGE and intense levels of ULTRAVIOLET RADIATION. HAIL can be an issue, and many producers have installed nets to protect the vines. RAINFALL can also be challenging, averaging 500 mm/19 in annually, most of it falling during the growing season, encouraging FUNGAL DISEASES. As in all of Bolivia, MUSCAT OF ALEXANDRIA is the most planted variety, as a significant portion of the harvest goes to the production of *singani*, a distillate akin to PISCO, and of which Tarija is the largest producer. However, many producers have converted their vineyards to TANNAT to make red wines, which make up most of Bolivia's production.

The Cinti Valley, about 400 km/249 miles north in the department of Chuquisaca, claims about 8% of Bolivia's land under vine. Most of it is planted to CRIOLLAS, including Negra Criolla (NEGRAMOLL) and Vischoqueña, a red grape unique to Bolivia which gives light-coloured, floral-scented wines with medium tannin structure. The climate is similar to Tarija though Cinti sits at higher elevation (2,200–2,800 m/7,200–8,800 ft) and rainfall averages 300 mm/12 in. The valley is known for its strong *singani* tradition and for ARBOREAL VITICULTURE in which vines are trained around indigenous pink peppercorn (*Schinus molle*) and chañar (*Geoffroea decorticansis*) trees. Many of these vines are very old, and it is thought that this traditional system has helped the vines fend off diseases.

The second largest—and fastest-growing—wine regions are in the east of the country, in the Santa Cruz valleys (16% of total vineyard), near to Santa Cruz de la Sierra, Bolivia's largest city. Vines are planted at 1,600–2,100 m/5,200–6,800 ft) in elevation, and the climate is continental, with about 600 mm/23 in annual rainfall. SYRAH and Tannat are the most popular varieties in this region.

There are also some small vineyards in the La Paz, Potosí, and Cochabamba valleys. The country has a long tradition of *patero* wine, foot-trod and traditionally vinified in clay jars or, more commonly today, plastic vessels.

M.J.G.

Goldstein, E., *South American Wines* (2014).

Bollinger, family-owned Champagne house producing a range of top-quality wines based on Pinot Noir grapes. Bollinger was formed from the de Villermont family's holdings in the village of Aÿ near Épernay, where the company is still based. In 1829, Jacques Joseph Placide Bollinger formed a partnership with Athanase-Louis-Emmanuel de Hennequin, Comte de Villermont, and Paul-Joseph Renaudin, resulting in the house of Champagne Renaudin Bollinger & Cie. In 1837, Jacques Bollinger married de Villermont's daughter Louise Charlotte and became a French citizen. In 1865, the house started to ship low-DOSAGE champagne to Britain, which was unusual for a period in which most champagne reaching the country was sweet. Champagne Bollinger received the Royal Warrant as Official Purveyor of Champagne to Queen Victoria in 1884.

Control of the house eventually passed to Jacques's grandson (also named Jacques), who died young in 1941, leaving his widow Elisabeth 'Lily' Bollinger (1899–1977) in charge. Madame Bollinger oversaw the family vineyards on foot and bicycle for three decades, enduring the 1944 German bombardment of Aÿ while sleeping in the Bollinger cellars. After the Second World War, she increased the house's vineyard holdings, which in 2021 stood at 179 ha/442 acres. By the time of her death, Madame Bollinger had seen sales double to a million bottles a year. She believed that nothing should change the traditional Bollinger style, and to this day the following five rules are obeyed: a majority of grapes from the house's own vineyards, 85% of which are GRAND CRU and PREMIER CRU; Pinot Noir dominance in the blend; BARREL FERMENTATION in over 4,000 old barrels to encourage MICRO-OXYGENATION; reserve wines aged in MAGNUMS; and bottle AGEING for two to four times longer than required even for the non-vintage Special Cuvée. Bollinger RD ('recently disgorged', with marked AUTOLYSIS as a result of being aged for a minimum of 14 years on LEES) was introduced by Madame Bollinger with the 1952 vintage. Rarest of all Bollinger champagnes is the Vieilles Vignes Françaises, a BLANC DE NOIRS produced exclusively from UNGRAFTED Pinot Noir vines that grow in two walled vineyards that were never affected by PHYLLOXERA.

The Bollinger family company, Société Jacques Bollinger, acquired Burgundy producer Chanson in 1999. It also owns a majority stake in the SAUMUR house Langlois-Chateau, as well as a minority stake in the cognac house Delamain. In 2005 the company bought their neighbouring house in Aÿ, Champagne Ayala, one of the original GRANDES MARQUES.

In 2021 Bollinger made its first acquisition outside France: Ponzi Vineyards in Oregon.

See also CHAMPAGNE.

Ray, C., *Bollinger: Tradition of a Champagne Family* (3rd edn, 1988).

Bolognesi, Colli, small DOC zone in the hills of EMILIA-ROMAGNA in north-central Italy. Colli Bolognesi PIGNOLETTO, both still and sparkling, has been elevated to DOCG. See EMILIA-ROMAGNA for more details.

Bolzano, or **Bozen** in German, the main town of ALTO ADIGE in northern Italy. Local light red wines with a minimum of 85% SCHIAVA (Vernatch) may carry the name **Colli di Bolzano** or **Bozner Leiten** as a suffix to the DOC Alto Adige/Südtirol.

Bombino Bianco was planted on 1,138 ha/2,812 acres of southern Italy, mainly in PUGLIA, in 2015. It is distinct from TREBBIANO d'Abruzzo, sometimes called Bombino Bianco di San Severo.

It ripens late and yields extremely high quantities of relatively neutral wine. Some of its synonyms, Pagedebit ('it pays the debts') and Straccia Cambiale ('tear up the invoices') in particular, allude to its profitability to the vine-grower. The dark-berried Puglian **Bombino Nero**, planted on 865 ha, is its natural offspring.

Bonarda, Italian red grape variety, or more accurately the name of three distinct Italian varieties: (1) the Bonarda of the OLTREPÒ PAVESE and Colli PIACENTINI (also planted in southern PUGLIA), which is, in fact, not Bonarda at all but rather the CROATINA grape; (2) the **Bonarda Novarese**, used to soften SPANNA in its range of DOC reds in the Novara and Vercelli hills, which again is not Bonarda but UVA RARA, a variety more widely employed in the Oltrepò Pavese; and (3) the so-called **Bonarda Piemontese**, an aromatic variety which has been virtually abandoned because of its small bunches and low productivity, although it covered 30% of the region's vineyard before the advent of PHYLLOXERA. There are scattered patches around Chieri, near Turin, and further west around Castelnuovo Don Bosco, as well as in Albugnano in Asti.

The only DOC wines in production which bear the name Bonarda are from the Oltrepò Pavese and are, confusingly, made from Croatina.

Bonarda is also the name of the third most widely grown red wine grape variety, after Malbec and Cereza, in ARGENTINA, where total plantings had grown to 18,153 ha/44,857 acres by 2020, which means that Argentina has far more 'Bonarda' planted than Italy, although DNA PROFILING has shown that Argentine Bonarda is unrelated to any of the Italian Bonardas and is in fact identical to California's CHARBONO, which is the Douce Noire of Savoie. The variety makes particularly exuberant, fruity wines for relatively early consumption.

bonbonne, a large glass jar or carboy, also known as a demijohn, typically holding 25 l/6.6 gal, used as a neutral container to store wine, VIN DOUX NATUREL, or brandy, often after a period of wood ageing.

bonded warehouse, one in which no DUTY has been paid on the goods inside it. Prices for wines and, especially, spirits held **in bond** (IB) are therefore considerably lower than those quoted duty paid. It is sensible for any foreigner buying wine to store for possible shipment outside that country to buy it **in bond**. For that reason, many FINE WINE prices are quoted in bond.

Bondola, traditional VITIS VINIFERA grape of SWITZERLAND's Ticino, where it may be an ingredient in the local blend called Nostrano. Largely replaced by Merlot.

Bonnes Mares, red GRAND CRU in Burgundy's CÔTE D'OR. For more details, see CHAMBOLLE-MUSIGNY and MOREY-ST-DENIS.

Bonnezeaux, particularly well-favoured enclave for sweet, BOTRYTIZED white wine made solely from Chenin Blanc near Thouarcé in the ANJOU part of the Loire within the Coteaux du LAYON area on the steep slopes of the right bank of the river. In this respect Bonnezeaux resembles QUARTS DE CHAUME to the north-west, but—perhaps because of its greater extent, 100 ha/247 acres spread across three south-facing hills (Montagne, Beauregard and Fesles) of SCHIST and QUARTZ, and its much more exposed situation—its required ripeness is lower, its acidity brighter while CHAPTALIZATION is allowed, leading to uneven quality and reputation. Yet when the grapes are naturally concentrated by NOBLE ROT, or sometimes by PASSERILLAGE, and picked by mandatory TRIES, Bonnezeaux can live up to its historic fame and turn into a world-class gold nectar able to age for decades. See also LOIRE, including map. P.Le.

books on wine. See LITERATURE OF WINE and WINE WRITING. For references to wine in some more obviously literary works, see ENGLISH LITERATURE, WINE IN.

Borba, DOC subregion in the northern part of the ALENTEJO in southern Portugal. Rising to around 450 m/1,476 ft, the area around Estremoz is home to a cluster of pioneers of modern classic reds based on ARAGONEZ, CASTELÃO, and TRINCADEIRA. S.A.

Bordeaux, important port on the GARONNE River leading to the GIRONDE estuary on the west coast of France. Bordeaux gives its name to a wine region that includes the vineyards of the Gironde *département* and, as such, the wine region that produces more top-quality wine than any other, from a total vineyard area that ballooned in the mid 2000s to about 124,000 ha/306,280 acres but was down to 110,000 ha/271,700 acres by 2020, divided among about 5,500 increasingly impoverished producers as the PRICE gap widened between the most famous wines and the rest. Bordeaux has a higher proportion of large estates than any other French wine region and produces more of the world's FINE wine and TROPHY WINES than anywhere else. The most famous examples represent less than 5% of the region's total production, however, and

B

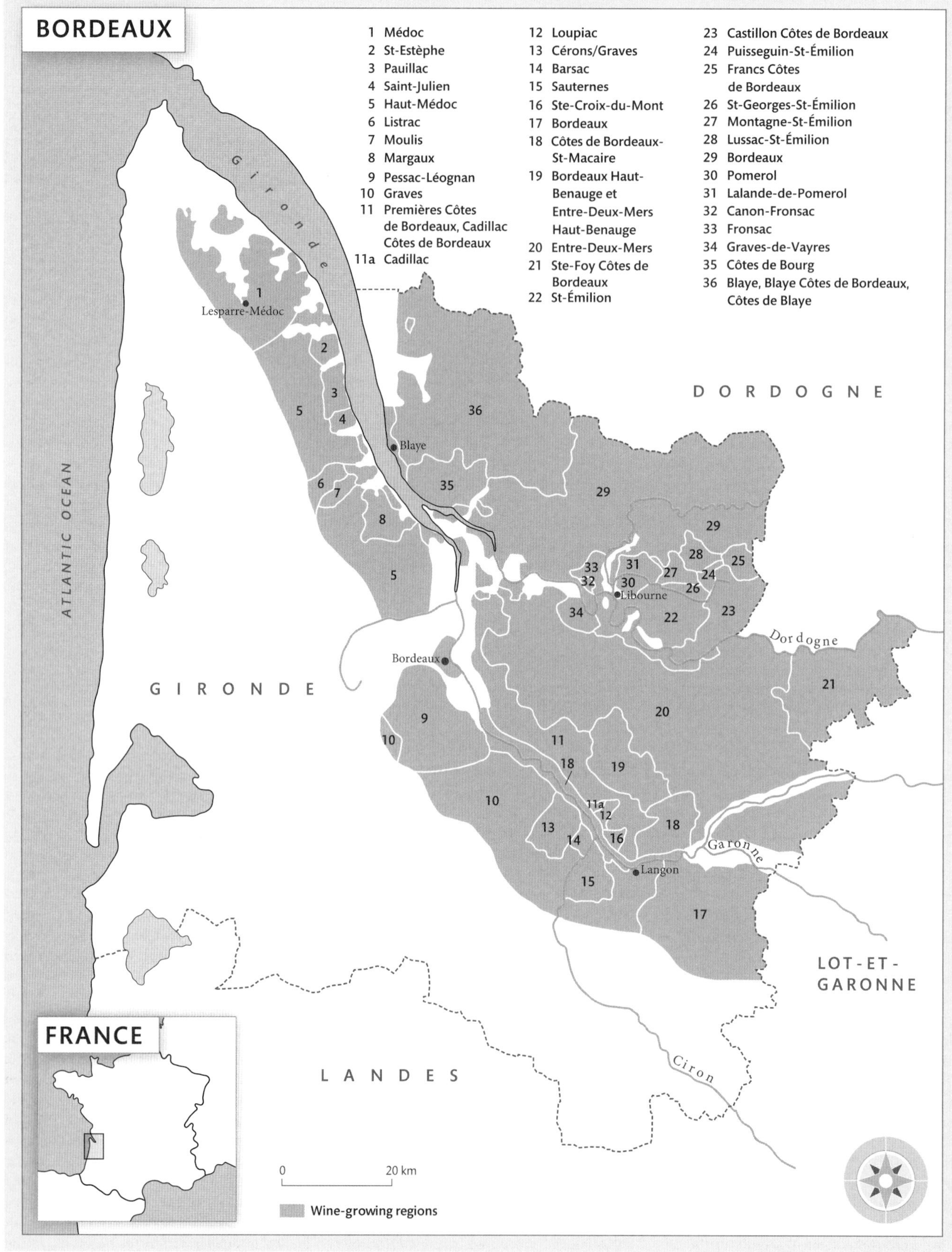
BORDEAUX
1 Médoc
2 St-Estèphe
3 Pauillac
4 Saint-Julien
5 Haut-Médoc
6 Listrac
7 Moulis
8 Margaux
9 Pessac-Léognan
10 Graves
11 Premières Côtes de Bordeaux, Cadillac Côtes de Bordeaux
11a Cadillac
12 Loupiac
13 Cérons/Graves
14 Barsac
15 Sauternes
16 Ste-Croix-du-Mont
17 Bordeaux
18 Côtes de Bordeaux-St-Macaire
19 Bordeaux Haut-Benauge et Entre-Deux-Mers Haut-Benauge
20 Entre-Deux-Mers
21 Ste-Foy Côtes de Bordeaux
22 St-Émilion
23 Castillon Côtes de Bordeaux
24 Puisseguin-St-Émilion
25 Francs Côtes de Bordeaux
26 St-Georges-St-Émilion
27 Montagne-St-Émilion
28 Lussac-St-Émilion
29 Bordeaux
30 Pomerol
31 Lalande-de-Pomerol
32 Canon-Fronsac
33 Fronsac
34 Graves-de-Vayres
35 Côtes de Bourg
36 Blaye, Blaye Côtes de Bordeaux, Côtes de Blaye
Gironde
Lesparre-Médoc
Blaye
DORDOGNE
ATLANTIC OCEAN
Libourne
Bordeaux
Dordogne
GIRONDE
Garonne
Langon
LOT-ET-GARONNE
FRANCE
LANDES
Ciron
0
20 km
Wine-growing regions

Bordeaux's most pressing long-term problem has been selling the other 95% profitably. The best red bordeaux, known by the British as CLARET, are characterized by their subtlety and ability to evolve after years, sometimes decades, of BOTTLE AGEING. The worst can be thin and evanescent. The producers in between suffer because there are simply too many of them to make much impact.

The proportion of bordeaux that is white has fallen from about one-quarter in the 1990s to just over 10%, 1% of which is sweet, in the early 21st century. Small quantities of rosé, light red CLAIRET, and sparkling CRÉMANT are also made. The total quantity of wine produced each year varies considerably according to VINTAGE but currently averages about 4.9 million hl, which represents about one-quarter of France's total AOC wine production. See BORDEAUX AOC for bordeaux wine at its most basic, BORDEAUX, CÔTES DE for a group of right-bank appellations, BORDEAUX TRADE for an account of the workings of the wine trade in Bordeaux, and BORDEAUX, UNIVERSITY OF for details of its important contribution to wine ACADEME.

History to medieval times

The Latin poet Ausonius (*c.*310–393/4 CE) is not only the first author to mention that wine was grown in his native Bordeaux; he was also the region's first known wine-grower. In his poem 'De herediolo' ('On his small inheritance'), dated 379, he tells us that he grows 100 *iugera* (a *iugerum* is approximately two-thirds of an acre or 0.25 ha) of vines. His estate was probably at Bazas, near the river Garonne (although some have suggested St-Émilion). In two of his other poems, 'Mosella' ('On the Moselle') and 'Ordo urbium nobilium' ('The list of distinguished cities'), he describes the banks of the Garonne overgrown with vines. Ch AUSONE is named after him.

Although Ausonius' descriptions indicate that viticulture was well established in Bordeaux in his lifetime, no definite earlier evidence exists. Given that members of the Allobroges tribe were growing wine around Vienne in the RHÔNE Valley in the 1st century CE, the Bituriges may have been doing the same in Bordeaux, but Strabo, author of the *Geography* (completed in 7 BCE), merely says that Bordeaux ('Burdigala' in Latin and in Strabo's Greek) was a place of commerce, and PLINY, writing *c.*77 CE, does not tell us clearly that the Bituriges grew wine (although he does refer to a Biturica vine, which may have been associated with either the Bituriges tribe of Bordeaux or the other to the west of Bourges), so the likelihood is that viticulture spread to Bordeaux after it had come to the Rhône.

We know little about Bordeaux in the centuries following the fall of the Roman Empire. The area was overrun by the Visigoths in the 5th century, and when Clovis defeated the Visigoths in 507 it became part of the Frankish kingdom. CHARLEMAGNE is said to have displayed a temporary interest in FRONSAC. With the economic expansion in Europe which started in the 11th century, demand for wine grew. Initially the new port of LA ROCHELLE, on the Atlantic coast north of Bordeaux, brought wealth to the region in the 12th century; consequently Bordeaux increased both its trade and its production. By 1200 wine was grown in BLAYE, BOURG, the lower DORDOGNE and the Garonne Valley, and in the GRAVES. The Graves was the largest producer, with Ch Pape-Clément its oldest named vineyard. In 1305 Archbishop Bertrand de Goth, who was to become Pope Clement V, presented it to the see of Bordeaux. Throughout the Bordeaux region more red wine was grown than white, but SAUTERNES and CÉRONS probably had white wine, although these white wines cannot have been like the botrytis-affected wines of today, for the deliberate commercial use of NOBLE ROT in Sauternes and Cérons dates from after the Middle Ages. Until the late 17th century the MÉDOC was too marshy to produce much wine and was known mainly for its corn: there were just a few vineyards in what is now called the Bas-Médoc, north of ST-ESTÈPHE. ST-ÉMILION was already a wine-growing district, however. Some of the wine of Bordeaux was neither white nor red but a mixture of white and red grapes fermented together called 'clairet' in Old French, which is the origin of the modern English word CLARET.

Bordeaux's pre-eminence began because of the English connection. In 1152, Eleanor of Aquitaine married Henry Plantagenet, who in 1154 became king of England (and duke of Normandy) as well as acquiring Eleanor's territories, GASCONY and most of western France. To win the favour of the citizens of Bordeaux, King John (1199–1216) granted them numerous privileges. The most important of these was exemption from the Grand Coutume, the export tax imposed on ships sailing from Bordeaux. Also, Gascon merchants were given favoured treatment in London. All this made Gascon wine cheaper for the English than any other imported wine. In the 14th century, most French wine consumed in England was from Gascony, and one-quarter of Bordeaux's wine exports went to England. Against these protective measures La Rochelle could not compete, despite its superior position right on the coast while Bordeaux was 60 miles/100 km upriver. When La Rochelle fell to the French in 1224, it ceased to be a commercial threat to Bordeaux.

Not all the wines sold by the Gascon merchants were from the immediate Bordeaux area. In the HAUT PAYS (Gaillac, Quercy, Nérac, and Bergerac) the climate was more reliable, and its wines were stronger than those of Bordeaux. The Haut Pays wines were more expensive because they were taxed in Bordeaux; and those from the parts of the Haut Pays which had fallen to the French were not allowed into Bordeaux until St Martin's Day, 11 November, or even until Christmas, so that Bordeaux wines dominated the wines available for the fleet which arrived each autumn to deliver the year's new wine to England, Scotland, Ireland, the Low Countries, and the Hanseatic ports.

In 1453, at the end of the HUNDRED YEARS WAR, Gascony reverted to French rule; yet its trade with England soon picked up again, even though it never regained its 14th-century volume. Bordeaux had been a major port before it became a wine-producing area to feed its wine trade. Its winemakers were not patient monks, as they had often been in Burgundy, but opportunistic laymen, whose aim was to cash in on the huge demand for Bordeaux's chief export product, and so they switched from grain to wine. The thin wines of Bordeaux, which before the advent of glass BOTTLES and CORKS did not last from one vintage to the next, cannot have been anything like modern bordeaux. H.M.W.

James, M. K., *Studies in the Medieval Wine Trade* (1971).

Penning-Rowsell, E., *The Wines of Bordeaux* (6th edn, 1989).

Simon, A. L., *The History of the Wine Trade in England*, 3 vols. (1906–9).

Modern history

Trade with Britain continued after the English were expelled, but the DUTCH WINE TRADE gradually became dominant, not so much in wines for their own consumption but in inexpensive white wines for the rest of northern Europe and the Hanseatic states. The Bordeaux merchants had to fight hard to maintain their position in northern Europe, for the Dutch also bought from the Mediterranean countries.

It was the Dutch who drained the marshy MÉDOC in the mid 17th century, thereby creating the basis for the fine wines that made Bordeaux's reputation throughout the world. Before this the best wines were to be found in the well-drained GRAVES near the city, notably Ch HAUT-BRION. Today's leading Médocain estates—Chx LAFITE, LATOUR, and MARGAUX—were probably planted in the last third of the 17th century and reached England, to be offered at auction in the coffee houses of London, only after consignments had been captured at sea in the Anglo-French wars at the beginning of the 18th century.

The simultaneous trade war between Britain and France led to ever-increasing duties on French wines and the Anglo-Portuguese Methuen Treaty of 1703. In return for a Portuguese promise to admit British woollen goods in perpetuity, the British government agreed that duty on French wines should never be less than 50% higher than on the wines of Portugal (and, in fact, Spain). Officially, British wine imports from Bordeaux declined sharply, but smuggling must have been rife, to judge from the prevalence of bordeaux in the household sales conducted by Christie's (see AUCTIONS) after their foundation in 1766. Conditions in both Bordeaux and Britain were ripe for the development of trade in fine CLARET: in the Gironde there was a new affluent bourgeoisie, members of the legal Bordeaux Parlement, with the means to plant and maintain expensive vineyards, while in Britain bordeaux's almost exclusive market was created by a wealthy, landowning aristocracy and, soon, the new industrial middle class.

The necessary link was a Bordeaux merchant class, sufficiently well established to be able to buy, cellar, and export these 'new French clarets'. These merchants came largely from the British Isles and from Germany, which had long been prominent in the inexpensive red bordeaux trade. BARTON & Guestier joined forces in 1725; William, later Nathaniel, Johnston began in 1734; and BROKERS Tastet & Lawton in 1740. These are some of the longer survivors of many more. The German firms of standing appear to have arrived later: Cruse from Danish Schleswig-Holstein, later incorporated into Germany, arrived in 1819; Eschenauer in 1821; and Kressmann in 1858. A substantial French merchant, with its roots in the RHÔNE Valley, was Calvet, which opened a Bordeaux office in 1870. It is also significant that the trade's 'bible' was the creation, in 1850, of an English teacher, Charles Cocks (see FÉRET).

Until well into the second half of the 20th century, most of these firms had their premises in the suburb of Les Chartrons, named after a medieval Carthusian monastery. The Quai des Chartrons, facing the River Garonne, and its side streets was the headquarters of the so-called *aristocratie du bouchon* (aristocracy of the cork).

In 1852, Bordeaux was struck by oidium, or POWDERY MILDEW, the first of a series of vine plagues which were to devastate many other wine regions too. First noted in the sweet wine areas near the Garonne, it spread through the Graves and then into the Médoc. Between 1854 and 1856, all the properties which were rated CLASSED GROWTHS in the 1855 CLASSIFICATION produced a total of only 3,400 TONNEAUX of wine, not much more than half the crop in a prolific year. By 1858 this fungal disease was conquered by spraying with SULFUR, a practice which continues to this day (see below).

Trade with Britain increased as a result of the Anglo-French Treaty of 1860, for in the following year Gladstone, then Chancellor of the Exchequer, reduced duty on French wines to twopence (less than 1p) a bottle. This was a particularly prosperous time for Bordeaux, which had also developed substantial markets in South America and Russia, as well as a small one in North America.

However, the severe onset of PHYLLOXERA in the late 1870s, followed by DOWNY MILDEW in the next decade, proved a serious setback to the trade in everyday GENERIC red and white bordeaux. For the first time ever an import BOND was established in Bordeaux, largely supplied with blending wine from the new vineyards of ALGERIA. On the other hand, excessive FERTILIZATION by important châteaux proprietors to compensate for losses by disease led to large crops of inferior quality and a fall in reputation and price. In 1910, nevertheless, two out of every three bottles of French wine imported into Britain came from the Gironde. They totalled 110,000 hl/2.9 million gal, approximately the same as for BELGIUM, although Germany imported almost twice as much. In 1911, the Gironde *département* was delimited, leading eventually to the establishment of Bordeaux's AOC system in 1936.

A serious slump followed soon after the First World War, with many châteaux changing hands, and this continued in the 1930s. After the First World War, the Russian market had disappeared, the South American one was much reduced, and the US market was closed by PROHIBITION between 1919 and 1933, with hardly time to recover before the Second World War.

At this time the market for fine wines was largely confined to the Médoc and the châteaux in the Graves near to Bordeaux. It was not until after the Second World War—during which Bordeaux, and many large châteaux, were occupied by the German army—that any ST-ÉMILION property other than Ch CHEVAL BLANC was widely known outside France, and the same was true of POMEROL, even Ch PETRUS, although there was a good market for inexpensive St-Émilions in Belgium.

It was not until the end of the 1950s that those châteaux with an international reputation made sufficient profits to begin serious replanting and the installation of modern equipment, notably FERMENTATION VESSELS made of STAINLESS STEEL, although this was an option which many châteaux, including Lafite, Margaux, and MOUTON-ROTHSCHILD, did not take. From the mid 1960s, the United States market became increasingly important, especially for the classed growths. This was particularly marked with the successful 1970 vintage when large American purchases were made as futures, EN PRIMEUR, followed some years later in Britain. Previously, if a vintage was considered likely to be very fine, the BORDEAUX TRADE would sometimes buy SUR SOUCHE, but otherwise a vintage would not be marketed until shortly before or after BOTTLING, either by the château or by the Bordeaux merchants. In 1972, CHÂTEAU BOTTLING became compulsory for the classed growths and was generally applied to the more important properties in the Graves, St-Émilion, and Pomerol. The leading red and white Graves had first been classified in 1953, and the St-Émilions in 1955 (see CLASSIFICATIONS). The Pomerols remain unclassified.

These en primeur campaigns reflected the changed financial situation in Bordeaux (although the generic wines, accounting for up to half the annual crop, continued—and continue—to be sold chiefly within 12 months of the harvest). No longer could most châteaux afford to hold several vintages in stock; nor could the Bordeaux merchants or their customers in France or abroad. For the most part in the 1970s and 1980s, consumers had to bear the financial responsibility of AGEING young red bordeaux and some leading sweet wines.

The 'energy crisis' of 1973, in which Middle East oil producers greatly raised their prices, caused havoc in Bordeaux, where recent vintages had been sold en primeur at excessively high prices. This had applied at all quality levels, and one result was that, in order to meet contracts for generic red bordeaux, the distinguished house of Cruse bought wine from outside the region, involving altered Appellation Contrôlée documents. A sharp fall in prices occurred, as well as subsequent mass disposals of stock by both merchants and leading châteaux. Some of the traditional firms were saved from bankruptcy only by foreign ownership, and the old world of the Chartronnais disappeared forever. Later, classed growth châteaux passed into the financial control of such outsiders as insurance companies (see AXA for example) and multinational corporations.

The succession of fine vintages in the 1980s improved the situation of many châteaux, but competition was so keen on the Bordeaux market that the merchants were unable to build up the financial reserves to tide them over poor years, as they had done in the past. So when Bordeaux was hit first by the heavily FROST-DAMAGED 1991 vintage and then by the diluted 1992, the en primeur trade virtually ceased internationally, and considerable financial problems arose—although the chiefly domestic trade in generic and humble appellation wines continued much as usual.

From the 18th century until 1939, the Bordeaux trade normally called the price tune, and—with the exception of the *belle époque*, from 1858 to 1878—the château owners had to fall into line. For the 30 years from 1961, the leading proprietors then held the whip hand in allocating their new wines to more than 100 Bordeaux merchants. In the early 1990s, when Bordeaux had no great vintages to sell, power was transferred to the consumer. The number of potential purchasers of fine bordeaux grew substantially, however, in the mid 1990s when the exciting 1995 and 1996 vintages were available, in the United States and for the first time in Asia. This, coupled with a widespread economic boom, helped create an unprecedented price spiral in Bordeaux in the 2000s. It faltered temporarily as a result of the invasion of Iraq and financial turmoil in Asia, only to accelerate when the undoubted quality of the 2009 and 2010 vintages coincided with unprecedented, and short-term, interest from investors, many of them without any wine-trade experience, notably but not exclusively from CHINA, a market that had been courted assiduously by the Bordelais. Prices of these vintages subsequently stagnated or fell, and the Bordelais were faced with the combination of a succession of lacklustre vintages and a lack of interest in their wines among many consumers, particularly younger ones. The quality of vintages 2015–20 reignited some interest. E.P.-R., J.R. & J.L.

Geography

The wine districts of Bordeaux hug the Gironde estuary and the Rivers DORDOGNE and GARONNE which flow into it (see map). The largest and most important appellation is BORDEAUX AOC, but there are 65 appellations in all, though many are rarely seen outside the region. The notably flat Bordeaux vineyards are rarely at elevations of more than a few metres above sea level.

Conventionally, in terms of the all-important fine red wines at least, the whole region is split into 'left bank' and 'right bank', or MÉDOC and GRAVES on the west side of the Gironde and St-Émilion and POMEROL on the east side, leaving the vast ENTRE-DEUX-MERS ('between two seas') district in the middle. Within the Haut-Médoc, the superior, higher land closer to Bordeaux, are the world-famous communes, south to north MARGAUX, ST-JULIEN, PAUILLAC, and ST-ESTÈPHE, together with the slightly less illustrious and more inland appellations of LISTRAC and MOULIS. Most of the finest wines of the Graves, on the other hand, have come from an enclave awarded its own appellation in 1987, PESSAC-LÉOGNAN. Pomerol and St-Émilion have their 'satellite' appellations: LALANDE-DE-POMEROL; and Montagne-St-Émilion, Lussac-St-Émilion, St-Georges-St-Émilion, and Puisseguin-St-Émilion (for details of which see ST-ÉMILION). And just west of Pomerol are the historic appellations of FRONSAC and Canon-Fronsac. Other appellations on the right bank of the Gironde are BOURG and BLAYE, grouped as CÔTES de Bordeaux. The GRAVES DE VAYRES enclave near Libourne remains resolutely outside the fold. Although some white wine is made between the two rivers, most of Bordeaux's best white wines are made south of the river Garonne: dry wines from Graves and Pessac-Léognan, and sweet white wines which include some of the finest in the world from SAUTERNES and BARSAC. (See CLIMATE below for a more detailed explanation.) Other, lesser sweet-white appellations in the south-east of the region are CADILLAC, CÉRONS, LOUPIAC, PREMIÈRES CÔTES DE BORDEAUX, STE-CROIX DU MONT, and STE-FOY CÔTES DE BORDEAUX which can also be red.

The most famous vineyards are on particularly well-drained soils, notably GRAVELS in the Médoc and Graves, and more CALCAREOUS terrain in parts of St-Émilion and Ste-Croix-du-Mont. For more details of local soils and conditions, see under these appellation names.

Climate

The mild climate of Bordeaux is tailor-made to produce mild wines, wines that are marked more by subtlety than power. (It is the vine varieties, described below, which endow the wines with longevity.) Unlike the much more CONTINENTAL climate of inland France or the more arid Mediterranean influence in the south of the country, the vineyards of Bordeaux are heavily influenced by their proximity to the Atlantic, here warmed by the Gulf Stream, and this gentle oceanic regulation of the climate extends well inland, thanks to the wide Gironde estuary. Most years the MARITIME CLIMATE protects the vines from WINTER FREEZE (although February 1956 was so cold that many vines were killed) and spring FROST (although April 1991 was so cold that much of that year's growth was frozen to extinction and the crop much reduced). However, CLIMATE CHANGE has led to greater extremes on all fronts (frost, hail, heat, rain).

Spring is generally mild and damp, providing ample supplies of water for the growing season. Bordeaux's climate is hardly marginal, in that most grapes are usually ripened, but the late-ripening Cabernet Sauvignon may not reach full ripeness everywhere every year, and the region's weather is sufficiently unpredictable that the period of the FLOWERING in June is critical, with unsettled weather, especially cold rain and strong winds, seriously prejudicing the quantity of the forthcoming crop. COULURE and MILLERANDAGE are perennial threats, especially to the Merlot crop, although average rainfall in June is markedly lower than in any other month.

Summers are usually warm, with occasional storms but rarely prolonged rainfall. The forests of the Landes to the south protect the wine districts from strong winds off the Atlantic and help to moderate temperatures, which reach an average maximum of 26 °C/79 °F in August, the hottest month. July is usually the driest and sunniest month. Annual average sunshine is well over 2,000 hours. Increasingly, however, during July and August it can be so hot and dry and the vines suffer such WATER STRESS that the ripening process stops altogether. HEAT STRESS may be such that vines have to be picked in August. But generally Bordeaux's grapes ripen steadily, swollen by occasional rainfall, until a harvest between mid September and mid October. Rainfall can vary considerably from vintage to vintage and within the Bordeaux region itself, with the Médoc being wetter overall, with an average annual rainfall of 950 mm/37 in.

Excessive rain is the chief hazard at harvest. In the sweet wine areas, on the other hand, humidity is sought in autumn to encourage the spread of NOBLE ROT. It is no coincidence that Bordeaux's sweet white wine districts are clustered together on either side of the Garonne, about 20 miles upstream of the city, where the river Ciron flows into the Garonne. The waters of the Ciron, shaded for most of its length by the forests of the Landes, are invariably cooler than those of the Garonne and encourage the autumn morning mists which promote the BOTRYTIS fungus. In years when these are followed by warm, dry afternoons, the benevolent form of botrytis, noble rot, forms, and great sweet white wine may be made. In damp years the malevolent form, GREY ROT, simply rots the fruit.

Vine varieties

Bordeaux's most famous, and best travelled, grape variety is that on which the Médoc and Graves depend for their red wines, CABERNET SAUVIGNON. Bordeaux's most planted variety by far, however, is MERLOT, which in 2020 occupied 66% of all red vineyards, three times as much as the later-ripening Cabernet Sauvignon. Merlot predominates not just in the famous right-bank appellations of St-Émilion and Pomerol but more importantly also in the Entre-Deux-Mers (BORDEAUX AOC country) and throughout the right bank, in whose damper, cooler soils Cabernet Sauvignon can be difficult to ripen. CABERNET FRANC, also important on the right bank, where it is often called Bouchet, is the third most planted grape variety. PETIT VERDOT is the only other red grape variety of any importance, playing a minor, but in ripe vintages useful, role in the Médoc. Cot, Pressac, or MALBEC is an ingredient in some right-bank wines and, perhaps thanks to its popularity in ARGENTINA, is increasingly mentioned by producers, as is CARMENÈRE, a red grape variety of historical importance in Bordeaux (mentioned for reasons associated with CHILE).

In addition, in reaction to climatic warming trends, the INAO approved in 2021 four more red varieties for use in a limited and regulated basis for BORDEAUX AOC and Bordeaux Supérieur AOC wines: ARINARNOA, CASTETS, MARSELAN, and TOURIGA NACIONAL. Two white varieties, ALVARINHO and LILIORILA, have also been added to the roster.

In the early 1970s, Bordeaux's single most planted grape variety of either colour was SÉMILLON, but it is now much less important except for sweet wine production. SAUVIGNON BLANC is Sémillon's traditional minor blending partner in sweet white bordeaux but is used increasingly for dry white wines, often unblended, and by 2020 was almost as widely planted as Sémillon. SAUVIGNON GRIS is now also allowed in many dry white bordeaux. The only other white grape variety fully sanctioned by the appellation laws is the Bordeaux and Bergerac speciality MUSCADELLE, but small quantities of UGNI BLANC, COLOMBARD, and Merlot Blanc are also planted and used in white Bordeaux AOC.

In stark contrast to France's other famous fine wine, BURGUNDY, red bordeaux is quintessentially a wine made from a blend of different vine varieties. This is only partly because Merlot and Cabernet are complementary, the flesh of the former filling in the frame of the latter. It is also an insurance policy on the part of growers in an unpredictable climate. Merlot grapes bud, flower, and ripen earlier than Cabernet Sauvignon and are much more susceptible to COULURE, which can seriously affect quantity. Cabernet Sauvignon, on the other hand, ripens so late that a cool, cloudy late summer can seriously affect its quality. Although the ENCÉPAGEMENT, the exact proportions of different vine varieties, varies from château to château, a typical Médoc recipe is 70% Cabernet Sauvignon, 10% Cabernet Franc, and 20% Merlot, while a typical St-Émilion recipe might be closer to 70% Merlot and 30% Cabernet Franc.

Among dry white wines, the recipe is less predictable, although some all-Sauvignon wines are produced. The classic blend for sweet white wines is 80% Sémillon to 20% Sauvignon Blanc. In the wake of the success of Pavillon Blanc de Ch Margaux, an increasing number of white wines have emerged from the red wine country of the Médoc.

Viticulture

With their neat, low rows of densely planted, GUYOT-trained, low-vigour vines, Bordeaux's vineyards are some of the world's most recognizable. Vine TRIMMING is a perennial activity, and VINE DENSITY in less glorious vineyards averages 5,000–6,000 vines per ha, although it is often as high as 10,000 vines per ha/4,000 per acre in the Médoc.

FUNGAL DISEASES thrive in Bordeaux's damp climate, and frequent SPRAYING is a fact of life here. (This may explain why Bordeaux was slow to embrace ORGANIC VITICULTURE, though it has latterly been making up for lost time). The incidence of EUTYPA DIEBACK became a serious preoccupation in the 1980s. BOTRYTIS BUNCH ROT is one of the most common hazards, although in sweet wine districts it is encouraged in its benevolent form as NOBLE ROT. Fertilizers (including manure from specially reared herds at some top properties) and pesticides have played their part in increasing YIELDS. CROP THINNING and selective LEAF REMOVAL during the growing season has been widely employed since the late 1980s—although vignerons are increasingly aware of the hazards of SUNBURN.

The flat, well-drained vineyards submit easily to MECHANIZATION, and, indeed, about 80% of Bordeaux is harvested by MECHANICAL HARVESTING (the top wines, though, are still harvested by hand).

Traditionally the Bordeaux harvest would begin 100 days after the flowering, but the 1990s saw a tendency to leave the grapes on the vine longer to achieve fully ripe PHENOLICS. It has not been uncommon therefore to start picking 110 days or more after the flowering, although a growing trend in the late 2010s was to pick earlier. Grapes for dry white wines and Merlot are in general picked before Cabernet Sauvignon and, especially, grapes for sweet white wines, which may not be picked until November in SAUTERNES.

Bordeaux must be the only region able to command prices high enough to justify hiring HELICOPTERS to agitate cold air during spring FROSTS or to dry grapes during a wet vintage, as Chx MOUTON ROTHSCHILD and PETRUS have been known to do. Since the difficult vintages of the early 1990s, a high proportion of properties have invested in GRAPE SORTING equipment in order to maximize wine quality.

Winemaking

Winemaking techniques in Bordeaux's top estates are regarded as the paradigm by producers of Cabernet and Merlot wines, and of fine sweet white wines, throughout the world. Under the guidance of BORDEAUX University these techniques underwent considerable modernization in the 1970s and are continually being refined. Émile PEYNAUD in particular led the way towards much more approachable, more concentrated red wines, a trend intensified under the influence of consultant Michel ROLLAND. And the way in which dry white bordeaux is made was revolutionized in the 1980s, notably by Denis DUBOURDIEU.

Red wines Classic vinification of red bordeaux requires time and, because of the size of most top estates, considerable space in which to house the wine as it slowly makes itself (see RED WINEMAKING). The process begins in the vat hall or *cuvier*, then moves to a first-year CHAI in which a year's production is stored in barrel, continues in the second-year *chai*, and increasingly necessitates an area for bottle storage.

Grapes are almost invariably DESTEMMED before crushing and fermented in large FERMENTATION VESSELS, known as CUVES in Bordeaux, which may be made of concrete, stainless steel, or even wood, for between five and ten or more days. Some form of TEMPERATURE CONTROL was installed at most properties in the 1970s or early 1980s and is now widespread. Fermentation temperatures are generally slightly higher in Bordeaux than in the NEW WORLD, with 30 °C/86 °F a common maximum during fermentation, although this is trending lower for more gentle EXTRACTION. The concentration of PHENOLICS in ripe Bordeaux Cabernet Sauvignon grapes is such that the precise techniques of extraction are an extremely important aspect of vinification. Much modern research is concentrated on the relative merits of various PUMPING OVER regimes, usually several times a day. The post-fermentation MACERATION is therefore seen as crucial by most winemakers, who allow the newly made wine at least a week and sometimes much longer 'on the skins'.

Some degree of CHAPTALIZATION was long commonplace, and generally well judged, in Bordeaux, although there has been some experimentation with CONCENTRATION techniques, including both osmosis and reverse osmosis, since the early 1990s. AMBIENT YEASTS are common.

After fermentation and maceration, the FREE-RUN wine is racked off the solids into another large vessel, either by PUMP or, in the most meticulously or fortuitously designed properties, by gravity (see WINERY DESIGN). If the free-run wine is drained into a lower tank, the volume of harsher PRESS WINE can be reduced from more than 15% to about 10%, and the wine tastes softer and riper.

After, and increasingly before, MALOLACTIC CONVERSION, the wine is racked into BARRELS made of French OAK, with the typical Bordeaux barrel being called a BARRIQUE. The luxury of new barrels was introduced only in the 1980s, and the proportion of new barrels used even at top estates tends to be lower than in the most lavish New World wineries: rarely more than 60%, and even lower in less ripe vintages. Traditionally, during the first year the wine is racked off its LEES into a fresh barrel every three months or so, as well as being clarified by egg-white FINING. Unless the property is unusually small, the wine is generally moved to a separate second-year *chai*, where it remains until the wine is blended immediately prior to BOTTLING, usually in early summer. The wine then undergoes the all-important period of AGEING in bottle, although this is likely, depending on the state of the market, to take place in the cellars of the BORDEAUX TRADE, the wine merchant, and, most typically, the consumer.

The ASSEMBLAGE is a crucial operation of selection, generally undertaken in the first few months after fermentation, during which it is decided which lots of wine will be blended to form the principal GRAND VIN for that year, which lots will form the SECOND WINE, and which may be sold off at an even lower level, either in BULK or in bottle. In less successful years, less than half of the wine produced on an estate might be selected for the *grand vin*. The actual blending may take place at any time up to bottling, according to the producer's preference. MICRO-OXYGENATION became increasingly popular in the 21st century, being especially useful for preparing early SAMPLES for the all-important annual tastings (see EN PRIMEUR) which determine the reputation of each vintage.

The procedure above is that followed by the CLASSED GROWTHS and those who aspire to that quality level. Most wine which qualifies merely as BORDEAUX AOC is more likely to be fairly ruthlessly filtered than fined and is not given any BARREL MATURATION but is bottled after a few months in tank. Some PETITS CHÂTEAUX may well treat their wines to a stint in barrique, but such barrels are likely to be hand-me-downs from other properties.

For Bordeaux's exclusively red-wine appellations, see MÉDOC, HAUT-MÉDOC, ST-ESTÈPHE, PAUILLAC, ST-JULIEN, MARGAUX, LISTRAC, MOULIS, ST-ÉMILION, POMEROL, FRONSAC, and some of the Côtes de Bordeaux (see BORDEAUX, CÔTES DE).

Dry whites WHITE WINEMAKING is relatively unremarkable in Bordeaux, except that the region was one of the last in France to cling to high doses of SULFUR in finished dry wines (perhaps because of its long history of turning its white grapes into sweet wines, which do need more sulfur), and in the upper echelons of white Graves and Pessac-Léognan BARREL AGEING has one of the longest histories in the world. Bordeaux is also the home of cryomaceration, whereby additional flavour may be imbued by pre-fermentation SKIN CONTACT at low temperatures, known here as *macération pelliculaire*.

For Bordeaux's principal dry white wine appellations, see PESSAC-LÉOGNAN, GRAVES, ENTRE-DEUX-MERS, BLAYE, and BORDEAUX AOC.

Sweet whites Bordeaux's sweet white wine appellations are, in very approximate descending order of quality, SAUTERNES, BARSAC, STE-CROIX-DU-MONT, LOUPIAC, CÉRONS, CADILLAC, PREMIÈRES CÔTES DE BORDEAUX, GRAVES Supérieures, STE-FOY CÔTES DE BORDEAUX, Côtes de Bordeaux ST-MACAIRE, and Bordeaux Supérieur (for which see BORDEAUX AOC).

Basic sweet white bordeaux, often described as *moelleux*, is a simple, sugary wine for which demand is falling. It is typically made by stopping the alcoholic FERMENTATION once it has reached the level of sweetness required. (See RESIDUAL SUGAR.) This is generally achieved by a combination of techniques: chilling, SULFUR DIOXIDE addition, and sterile FILTRATION. Winemakers in Sauternes and Barsac, however, as well as their more ambitious counterparts elsewhere, aim to make very rich BOTRYTIZED wines from grapes at the full limit of ripeness, which may be described as LIQUOREUX. This involves a considerably more painstaking winemaking regime, even more dependent than any other on events in the vineyard, which is described in SAUTERNES. The wine's selling PRICE, which in the 20th century was depressed by the whims of FASHION, may also play a part in determining whether its maker is able or prepared to take the risks involved in trying to maximize ripeness of the grapes. J.R. & J.L.

Brook, S., *The Complete Bordeaux* (4th edn, 2022).
Faith, N., *The Winemasters* (3rd edn, 2005).
Parker, R., *Bordeaux* (4th edn, 2003).
Penning-Rowsell, E., *The Wines of Bordeaux* (6th edn, 1989).

Bordeaux, Côtes de, group of appellations on the right bank of the Garonne that brings together the (mainly red) wines of five smaller regions. The first Côtes de Bordeaux vintage was 2009, and by 2020 the vineyards involved totalled 10,556 ha/26,083 acres. The group comprises CADILLAC CÔTES DE BORDEAUX and CASTILLON Côtes de Bordeaux, which apply specifically to red wines; BLAYE Côtes de Bordeaux for both reds and dry whites; and FRANCS Côtes de Bordeaux and Ste-Foy Côtes de BORDEAUX for reds as well as dry and sweet whites. The appellation **Côtes de Bordeaux** *tout court* applies to any wine made from one or more of these geographically specific appellations, has slightly less strict requirements than them, and is generally used by merchants rather than individuals. These wines tend to have more personality than regular BORDEAUX AOC, the result perhaps of local pride, and can provide some of Bordeaux's better wine values.

Côtes de Bordeaux-ST-MACAIRE applies to white wines made in an enclave across the Garonne from the town of Langon. See also BOURG, GRAVES DE VAYRES, and STE-FOY CÔTES DE BORDEAUX. J.R. & J.L.

Bordeaux, University of, university complex whose Faculté (formerly Institut) d'Oenologie is a centre of oenological ACADEME of world renown. Viticultural research is conducted under the auspices of the Institut National de la Recherche pour l'Agriculture, l'Alimentation et l'Environnement (see INRAE) and Bordeaux Sciences Agro, the agricultural university of Bordeaux.

The institute was founded in 1880 (the same year as the research institute that was to become the University of California at DAVIS) as a mere *station agronomique*, when Ulysse Gayon, the sole Professor of Chemistry at the associated University of Bordeaux, became its director.

Gayon had studied and worked with Louis PASTEUR, the founder of scientific OENOLOGY. He considered the *station*'s function to be the promulgation of sound methods of making and maturing wine. In addition to his contributions to the ANALYSIS of wines, he worked with Alexis Millardet on the development of the copper-based vine treatment designed to combat FUNGAL DISEASES which was to be known as BORDEAUX MIXTURE.

During the 40 years Gayon directed the *station*, its tradition of identifying the practical applications which could be made from research results was established, as was the importance of transmitting information to winemakers in unscientific language.

From 1927 the most significant research in the world on wine and related subjects was carried out at the University of Bordeaux through a collaboration between Jean RIBÉREAU-GAYON, the grandson of Ulysse Gayon, and Émile PEYNAUD, who did not officially join the University until 1949. From 1949, when Jean Ribéreau-Gayon became director of the *station*, the results of basic and extensive research became apparent to winemaker and consumer alike. Chromatography provided legally convincing evidence of the use of HYBRIDS in any wine sample and encouraged their replacement by VITIS VINIFERA vine varieties in the vineyards of Bordeaux and other French winegrowing regions, thereby greatly improving the quality of BORDEAUX AOC and other French wines. At the same time, the understanding of the process of MALOLACTIC CONVERSION gave wine producers the knowledge they needed to control a fundamental step in winemaking and gave them much greater control over the style and quality of the wines they made. Research into the influence of TERROIR on wine style and quality has been conducted at Bordeaux since the early 1960s.

The importance of the education of OENOLOGISTS was officially recognized in 1956 with the creation of an École Supérieure d'Oenologie empowered to award a winemaker's diploma. This became the Institut d'Oenologie in 1963, which was transformed into the Faculté d'Oenologie in 1995. During this period oenology achieved full recognition as a new science, and in 1971 the institute formally became part of the university, its work and educational titles enjoying full academic status. From 1977 to 1997, the work of the institute continued under the direction of Pascal Ribéreau-Gayon, the son of the previous director.

In 2009, the Faculté merged with Bordeaux Sciences Agro and part of INRA to form the ISVV, which encompasses a high level of research and academic training in both oenology and viticulture.

The Faculté is currently engaged in research on subjects which vary from explorations of the nature and effects of different YEASTS to investigations into TANNINS and the characteristics of different families of aroma compounds. The most significant result of research in the 1980s was arguably the dramatic improvement in aroma and subtlety of dry white bordeaux, in which field Denis DUBOURDIEU deserves much credit.

In addition to training oenologists who make wine throughout the world and belong to what is outside France referred to as the 'Bordeaux school' of winemaking, the Faculté supervises doctorates on vinous subjects and is one of only two French organizations to enjoy this privilege, along with SupAgro Montpellier (see INRAE). A prominent feature of the professional training at the Faculté is the importance attached to tasting wines and analysing their characteristics. Since 1949 the Faculté has also given tastings and lectures for growers and cellar workers without scientific training, particularly through the Diplôme Universitaire d'Aptitude à la Dégustation (DUAD), which is one of the world's most in-depth courses in wine TASTING. C.v.L.

Bordeaux AOC. The most important sort of wine produced in Bordeaux, quantitatively if not qualitatively, is that which qualifies for the simple appellation Bordeaux. About half of all the AOC wine produced in the region is on this lowest rung of the ladder of quality. Red Bordeaux AOC was produced from 51,399 ha/ 127,000 acres of vineyard in 2020. Such wine is typically produced outside the more specific commune or regional appellations, although a great deal of red Bordeaux AOC comes from the ENTRE-DEUX-MERS region, whose eponymous appellation applies only to white wine. (A counterpoint to this is the fact that the appellations of the Médoc apply only to red wines, so that even the Médoc's smartest white wines, such as Pavillon Blanc du Ch MARGAUX, are not allowed any appellation grander than Bordeaux AOC. Similarly, dry white wines made from grapes usually grown for SAUTERNES qualify only for Bordeaux AOC.) The other area with the greatest concentration of vineyard dedicated to the production of Bordeaux and Bordeaux Supérieur is that north of Libourne, where Merlot grapes predominate.

The great majority of Bordeaux AOC produced is made, often by CO-OPERATIVES, to be sold for blending anonymously into humble GENERIC wines of very varying quality, but there are also some individual properties, so-called PETITS CHÂTEAUX, which lie outside any grander appellation but which express their own TERROIR and practise CHÂTEAU BOTTLING. Almost 90% of all Bordeaux AOC produced is red, and the white, if sweet, may be labelled **Bordeaux** Moelleux. Made from the same area, **Bordeaux Supérieur** is a generally more concentrated, ambitious wine than Bordeaux AOC with base yields 50 rather than 55 hl/ha that has been aged for at least 10 months. About three times as much Bordeaux AOC Rouge is made as Bordeaux Supérieur, or 'Bord Sup' as the BORDEAUX TRADE call it. Also included in the generic Bordeaux AOC appellation are the relatively rare **Bordeaux Rosé** and slightly deeper-coloured **Bordeaux Clairet** as well as the bottle-fermented sparkling wine CRÉMANT de Bordeaux. **Bordeaux Haut-Benauge** is the name given to the small amount of white wine, both dry and sweet, made in an enclave just across the Garonne from Langon (see also ENTRE-DEUX-MERS).

Most of these wines are designed to be drunk within a year of bottling if white, rosé, or CLAIRET and within two or three years if red. The better examples are unmistakably lighter versions of Bordeaux's grander wines, while the worst can taste like homeless PLONK. With the exception of the best Bordeaux Supérieur reds, few producers can afford to age these wines in OAK, and even fewer of the wines have the concentration to benefit from it, especially since expensive viticultural techniques such as CROP THINNING are hard to justify at this price level, although exceptions are becoming more numerous. Most of the Bordeaux BRANDS are Bordeaux AOC, most notably MOUTON CADET, which started off life with the much grander and more specific appellation of PAUILLAC.

Bordeaux blend, usually a red wine made up of some or all of CABERNET SAUVIGNON, CABERNET FRANC, MERLOT, PETIT VERDOT, and possibly MALBEC and CARMENÈRE. Its white wine counterpart is made from SAUVIGNON BLANC, SÉMILLON, and possibly SAUVIGNON GRIS and MUSCADELLE. See also MERITAGE.

Bordeaux mixture, *bouillie bordelaise* in French, the much-used mixture of lime, copper sulfate, and water first recorded in 1885 by Alexis Millardet, Professor of Botany at BORDEAUX University, as an effective control of DOWNY MILDEW. Use of the mixture was a historic event since it was to become the most important chemical for the control of both FUNGAL DISEASES and BACTERIAL DISEASES for 50 years. There are now alternative FUNGICIDES, many of them containing copper, but it is still used today by very traditional growers in some regions, and it is one of the few preparations permitted in ORGANIC VITICULTURE and BIODYNAMIC VITICULTURE.

There is some debate as to how the treatment was discovered. It was common for Bordeaux vignerons to spray the outside vineyard rows with the blue-staining copper sulfate to deter thieves. No doubt it was noticed that this practice halted the devastation caused by downy mildew which had begun in 1883. Continued use of Bordeaux mixture can lead to accumulation of COPPER in the soil, which can reach toxic levels especially in acidic soils. Some vineyards affected by copper toxicity in the Bordeaux area and elsewhere are much reduced in vigour and production, but the problem can be overcome by adding LIME to the soil. Also, copper sprayed within 14 days of harvest can produce browning, turbidity, and SULFIDE characters in the wine and can result in incomplete FERMENTATIONS. R.E.S.

Delas, J., 'Copper toxicity in viticultural soils', in P. L'Hermite and J. Dehandtschutter (eds.), *Copper in Animal Wastes and Sewage Sludge* (Dordrecht, 1981).

Figiel, R., 'Bouillie bordelaise: the other gift from Bordeaux vineyards', *Practical Winery & Vineyard*, 11/3 (1990), 27–9.

Bordeaux trade. The sheer quantity of wine produced in Bordeaux, the fact that so much requires AGEING, and the historical importance of Bordeaux as a port (see BORDEAUX, history), mean that its wine trade is more stratified than most—even if wine is no longer the city's economically most important commodity.

Bordeaux wines have always been produced by one category of people and sold by another. The wine producers of the region range from world-famous estates with 200 ha/500 acres under vine to owners of 2.5 ha or less, whose grapes are delivered to one of the region's wine CO-OPERATIVES.

The wine merchants, or NÉGOCIANTS, traditionally brought most of the wines they bought into their CHAIS in or around Bordeaux (notably its Quai des Chartrons) to be matured and shipped out to export customers, particularly in Britain and northern Europe, either in barrels or after bottling. They were joined in the early 20th century by merchants in LIBOURNE, who concentrated especially on France and Belgium (see POMEROL).

So great was the quantity of wine to be traded that numbers of middlemen were needed between producers and the merchants, of whom professional brokers, or *courtiers*, such as Tastet & Lawton have become an essential part of Bordeaux's vinous commercial structure. There were 77 of them in 2021. What the merchant supplied originally in addition to the mere buying and selling of wine was technical ability (the cellarmasters' teams were likely to be considerably better technicians than those of the producers) and financing for the grower.

This three-tier way of distributing a large quantity of wine to customers all over the world, known as La Place de Bordeaux, changed considerably after 1945, when even some of the FIRST GROWTHS were still made available to the merchants in BULK, and most of the CLASSED GROWTHS have since 1959 been sold to the merchants on the condition that they are CHÂTEAU BOTTLED.

Since 1945, improvements in winemaking at all levels and, since the 1980s, PRICE increases and inflation levels which have made it impossible for even the biggest merchants to finance large quantities of wine have tended to transform the role of the merchant from principal to broker—certainly for the wines traded EN PRIMEUR. The balance of financial power between the 300 merchants and the 100 or so most significant proprietors, changing over time according to vintage quality and quantity and international demand, in the 21st century shifted in favour of the producers who increasingly became stockholders.

Things are very different at the bottom end of Bordeaux's highly stratified community of wine producers. A huge SURPLUS of AOC Bordeaux and uneconomic selling prices led to demands in 2022 for subsidies to encourage the GRUBBING UP of the region's less glamorous vineyards, even though the wine they produce has improved enormously, partly thanks to CLIMATE CHANGE. Some of this wine finds its way into BRANDS, typically developed by the bigger merchants.

The Bordeaux FINE WINE trade is increasingly involved in selling direct to and STORING WINE for the consumer, having constructed many substantial wine warehouses around the city's fringes. For examples of specific Bordeaux merchants, see BARTON and MOUEIX. W.B. & J.R.

Anson, J., *Inside Bordeaux* (2020).
Brook, S., *The Complete Bordeaux* (4th edn, 2022).
Faith, N., *The Winemasters* (3rd edn, 2005).
Loftus, S., *Anatomy of the Wine Trade* (1985).
Penning-Rowsell, E., *The Wines of Bordeaux* (6th edn, 1989).

Bordo, occasional Romanian name for CABERNET FRANC and sometimes used in north-east Italy for CARMENÈRE.

bore, wine. For some reason, wine bores exist in public consciousness and, it has to be said, in reality in a more vividly pestilential way than art bores, music bores, or even sport bores. Perhaps this is because for most people wine is associated with sensual pleasure rather than analysis and verbal communication, and so their wine-related boredom threshold is low. So far, wine bores are usually men, although women wine bores may be an eventual consequence of greater female financial emancipation. One woman's wine bore can be another person's wine expert, however.

borers, usually BEETLES or their larvae, which bore into the woody parts of plants, sometimes killing them. The branch and twig borer, *Melalqus confertus*, occurs throughout California and parts of Oregon and damages grape CANES. Control is usually by cultural methods, by keeping vines healthy, and by PRUNING off all dying and dead parts and infested wood in winter. Beetle larvae causing problems to vineyards can be quite regionally specific. The fig longicorn (*Dihammus vastator*) beetle larvae causes vine damage only in the Hunter Valley region of Australia, for example. M.J.E.

boron, a MINERAL element required in minute quantities for healthy vine growth and thus called a micronutrient. Boron deficiencies in vines are commonly found in sandy soils where SOIL ACIDITY and RAINFALL are high. Boron is required for the movement of SUGARS and the synthesis of AUXINS in the plant. A major effect of boron deficiency is poor FRUIT SET and MILLERANDAGE caused by the effect of this deficiency on POLLEN tube growth affecting germination, which can result in substantial reductions in YIELD. Bunches on boron-deficient vines often have many small berries, which may lead to uneven ripening (see BERRY SIZE).

Boron toxicity is also possible, sometimes due to over-application of FERTILIZER. Excess boron can, coincidentally, also come from bore water used for IRRIGATION. R.E.S.

Borraçal, synonym for Galicia's CAIÑO Tinto in Portugal's Vinho Verde region, where it makes tart reds.

Borrado das Moscas, the DÃO region's name for the Portuguese variety BICAL.

Bosco, grown on just 42 ha/104 acres of LIGURIA, can make exciting sweet amber wine.

Bosnia and Herzegovina is an independent federal republic since 1992, previously part of YUGOSLAVIA. Located on the western Balkan peninsula with just 12 km/7.5 m of Adriatic coastline and high central mountains, it is divided into the Federation of Bosnia and Herzegovina (FBiH) and Republika Srpska (RP), plus the district of Brčko. Each has its own constitution, and no single administration oversees the wine industry. Viticulture zoning dates to 1984 and identifies six wine districts in two regions: Sjeverna Bosna (Kozaračko, Ukrinsko, Majevičko districts) and Herzegovina (Mostarsko, Lištičko, Jablaničko districts). 'Middle Neretva' is used on export labels to the EU and US for wines from the Mostar area.

Data from the Federal Institute for Statistics for FBiH indicate approximately 4,000 ha/9,884 acres of vineyards in FBiH, producing 42,357 tonnes of grapes in 2020 and 76 registered wine producers. The Ministry for Foreign Trade estimated a further 600 ha/1,483 acres in RP in 2018, producing 5,000 tonnes. Approximately 55% of production is white, led by INDIGENOUS VARIETIES in FBiH but international grapes in RP. Estimates suggest 1,000 growers but only 200 with more than 2 ha. The devastating war between 1992 and 1995 scarred the wine industry, but it is recovering strongly in terms of quality, if not quantity, helped by developing TOURISM.

Herzegovina is by far the most important wine region, especially around Mostar. The CALCAREOUS karst landscape is stony and dry, and summer temperatures can reach 40 °C/104 °F. Plantings are dominated by drought-tolerant indigenous varieties led by ŽILAVKA. It can produce high-quality, aromatic white wine with generous body and good acidity, and that can age well. Records for this variety go back 600 years to the time of Bosnian King Tvrtko. Other local white-wine grapes include Krkošija, Bena, and SMEDEREVKA. Red-wine varieties are dominated by local Blatina, a female variety that requires a cross-pollinator and is usually interplanted and blended with Kambuša (ALICANTE BOUSCHET), Trnjak, Merlot, or occasionally VRANAC. Several producers have revived Trnjak as a varietal wine as it has more depth and structure than Blatina. The cooler, northern Sjeverna Bosna vineyards usually grow INTERNATIONAL VARIETIES including Cabernet Sauvignon, Merlot, and Temjanika (MUSCAT BLANC À PETIT GRAINS). C.G.

www.fao.org
www.wineroute.ba

botanical classification, a system of classifying plants—including vines, but also YEASTS and the organisms responsible for FUNGAL DISEASES of the vine—which shows their relationship one to the other and allows them to be uniquely described and identified. The basic unit of classification is the species; related species are sometimes grouped into genera (plural of genus); related genera into families; and related families into orders. In turn, species can be divided into subspecies, when different types have developed naturally, and into varieties, or occasionally cultivars (a contraction of cultivated variety), when different types have been selected by human hands. VINE VARIETIES can be further divided into three PROLES, according to their geographical origins. Different CLONES of individual varieties have also been selected. The International Code of Nomenclature for algae, fungi, and plants (ICN) regulates the naming of plants and other organisms treated like plants.

Kingdom
Order
Family
Genus
Species
Variety
Prole
Clone

Recent DNA PROFILING has considerably modified the earlier classifications created by botanists; although there are still some controversies, current consensus according to the Angiosperm Phylogeny Group of international systematic botanists is that GRAPEVINES belong to the order Vitales, comprising the Leeaceae family, which consists mostly of shrubs, and the Vitaceae family, which consists of approximately 13–17 genera and about 900 species primarily distributed in tropical regions in Asia, Africa, Australia, the neotropics, and the Pacific islands, with a few genera in temperate regions (*Vitis*, *Parthenocissus*, and *Ampelopsis*).

Most of the plants are climbers and have tendrils opposite leaves on the shoots, the grapevine being representative. Wen et al., using PHYLOGENETIC analyses, list 16 genera in this family, including *Vitis*; the largest genus is *Cissus* with about 300 species, from succulent species such as cacti to the lianas of tropical jungles. *Ampelopsis* and *Parthenocissus* are two more genera closely related to each other and are observably similar to grapevines. Ornamental plants related to the grapevine include the Virginia creeper in the US and Europe, the kangaroo vine in Australia, and Japanese ivy and Crimson Glory in Japan. (A complete list of genera and species and their distribution is given in Wen et al.)

The grapevine genus VITIS, created in 1700 by Tournefort, comprises about 60 species, including VITIS VINIFERA, first studied by Linnaeus in 1735. The full botanical binomial of the most common wine-producing vine species is therefore *Vitis vinifera* L., often abbreviated to *V. vinifera* or (botanically incorrectly) *vinifera* (the first person to describe the species often being listed, usually as initials, after the scientific name). Another convention is the use of Latin, often confected, and italics.

The genus *Vitis*

The *Vitis* genus has traditionally been divided into two distinct sections called *Vitis* (previously *Euvitis*) and MUSCADINIA, and this has been confirmed by DNA classification. The two sections may be differentiated not only on the basis of appearance but also by chromosome number. *Muscadinia* has 40 chromosomes while *Vitis* has only 38. (This is a frustration to VINE BREEDERS, who would welcome ready access to the many pest- and disease-resistant genes of *Muscadinia*.)

Most *Vitis* species are native to North America (see AMERICAN VINE SPECIES) and Asia. The common wine grape species *Vitis vinifera* is native to Europe and the Near East and is commonly divided into two subspecies, the wild *Vitis vinifera* subsp. *silvestris* and the cultivated *Vitis vinifera* subsp. *sativa*. The latter shows great diversity as a result of selection and cultivation by people, and three basic eco-geographic groups of varieties, or proles, were created by Russian ampelographer Negrul in 1938 (*occidentalis*, *pontica*, and *orientalis*), reflecting differences between origin and end use. Each prole contains numerous grape varieties (or cultivars), for example 'Cabernet Sauvignon', which are themselves subdivided into numerous clones. (Botanists put the names of varieties in inverted commas.) See VITIS and VITIS VINIFERA for more details. The full botanical classification of Cabernet Sauvignon might therefore be: order Vitales, family Vitaceae, genus *Vitis*, section *Vitis*, species *vinifera*, proles *occidentalis*, variety 'Cabernet Sauvignon', clone INRA BX 5197. R.E.S. & J.V.

Antcliff, A. J., 'Taxonomy: the grapevine as a member of the plant kingdom', in P. R. Dry and B. G. Coombe (eds.), *Viticulture*, i: *Resources* (2nd edn, 2004).

Wen, J., et al., 'A new phylogenetic tribal classification of the grape family (Vitaceae)', *Journal of Systematics and Evolution*, 56/4 (2018), 262–72.

Zecca, G., et al., 'The timing and the mode of evolution of wild grapes (*Vitis*)', *Molecular Phylogenetics and Evolution* 62/2 (2012), 736–47.

Botryosphaeria dieback, FUNGAL DISEASE affecting the TRUNK and ARMS of the vine caused by a range of 22 species from different genera in the family Botryosphaeriaceae. It is the most widespread TRUNK DISEASE, causing loss of production in both newly planted and mature vineyards. Botryosphaeriaceae fungi primarily infect vines through pruning wounds but can also be found as latent pathogens in NURSERY-propagated material. Virulence depends on the species, but the most characteristic symptoms of the disease are perennial cankers in the wood (typically wedge-shaped) and lack of spring growth. Other symptoms include black or light-brown streaking of the XYLEM vessels, graft failure, cane bleaching, cane dieback, shoot NECROSIS, and bud necrosis. In some grape-growing regions, several Botryosphaeriaceae species are also thought to be involved in causing BUNCH ROTS. Management strategies primarily involve the protection of pruning wounds using either synthetic FUNGICIDES or BIOLOGICALS. More extreme management strategies include CURETTAGE and TRUNK RENEWAL. J.R.U.-T.

Gramaje, D., Úrbez-Torres, J. R., and Sosnowski, M. R., 'Managing grapevine trunk diseases with respect to etiology and epidemiology: current strategies and future prospects', *Plant Disease*, 102/1 (2018), 12–39.

Úrbez-Torres, J. R., 'The status of Botryosphaeriaceae spp. infecting grapevines', *Phytopathologia Mediterranea*, 50 (2011), S5–S45.

botryticine. See NOBLE ROT.

botrytis, without the capital B it botanically deserves, is commonly used as an abbreviation for BOTRYTIS BUNCH ROT, for the fungus that causes it *Botrytis cinerea* Pers, for its benevolent form NOBLE ROT, and occasionally for its malevolent form GREY ROT. Grapes affected by noble rot and the wines produced from them are often called BOTRYTIZED, or **botrytis-affected**.

Elad, Y., et al. (eds.), *Botrytis: Biology, Pathology and Control* (2007).

botrytis bunch rot, vine disease which, of all FUNGAL DISEASES, has the greatest potential effect on wine quality. The disease can also have a disastrous effect on YIELD when the fungus affects almost-ripe grapes. This malevolent form is known as GREY ROT, the most common of the BUNCH ROTS. On the other hand, if it affects ripe, healthy, light-skinned grapes and if weather conditions are favourable, botrytis can develop in a benevolent form called NOBLE ROT, which is responsible for some of the world's finest sweet wines. If it affects red grapes, it always damages PIGMENTS, resulting in wines with a brownish tinge and, often, off-odours associated with rot.

Botrytis rot is a problem especially for vineyards in damp climates. Rainfall near harvest can result in severe disease and thus be a major factor affecting the yield and quality of a particular vintage (as regularly happens in both BURGUNDY and BORDEAUX, for example).

Botrytis spores germinate primarily on wet surfaces. Optimal infection temperatures are 15–25 °C/59–77 °F. The botrytis fungus is most prone to develop within highly succulent, injured, or senescing plant tissues (such as ripening grapes). Berries can become infected soon after their formation, when the fungus attacks withering flower parts and grows into the nascent fruitlet, but natural defences in the expanding green berry then stop any further fungal development. Most of these early infections remain latent and harmless through harvest, but a portion can become active and rot that berry as it becomes ripe, providing a source for rapid disease spread as berries ripen near harvest. An especially common source of initial pre-harvest disease is infected blossom parts that are shed from developing healthy berries but become trapped within the enlarging bunches at BUNCH CLOSURE, providing a platform from which the fungus can later grow directly into the ripening berries at points of contact as they become susceptible near harvest. Initial infections also can develop post-VERAISON when fungal spores, carried by air currents or insects, germinate and infect through the broken berry skin following wounds caused by bird pecks, insect damage, mechanical abrasion, or bursting, when berries within tightly compressed clusters continue to swell with no room to expand, especially when vines takes up water rapidly after rainfall.

Disease spread from these initial sources can be explosive as the fungus grows from one berry to the next in tightly compressed clusters but is much less severe in looser clusters. If the weather turns dry, infected berries tend to dry out, and major changes to the fruit's chemistry can result in grapes suitable for classic BOTRYTIZED wines influenced by noble rot. In continuing wet weather, however, the fungus rapidly spreads as grey rot, and the grape crop can literally rot before the owner's eyes. This explains the urgency of harvest when rot begins to establish itself and weather conditions are conducive to its spread. If the grapes have to be harvested early, the wines are typically lower in alcohol and complexity. Although pre-harvest grey rot is by far the most destructive form of botrytis infection, during prolonged wet springs it can also blight young succulent shoots and emerging flower clusters, which fall off with obvious effects on yield.

Vine varieties, and indeed various CLONES of individual varieties, differ markedly in their susceptibility to botrytis, depending especially on how tightly packed the berries are in the bunch but also on the thickness of the skin and perhaps to some extent on varietal differences in natural defence responses. Varieties with compact bunches of high sugar content are the most susceptible, including Sémillon, Sauvignon Blanc, Muscadelle, Carignan, Pinot Noir, and Merlot. Chardonnay is moderately susceptible and Cabernet Sauvignon quite tolerant.

Modern control measures take two complementary forms: cultural practices and spraying. CANOPY MANAGEMENT practices that avoid excessive leafiness around the bunches, such as LEAF REMOVAL and certain trellis designs, are most useful, providing better exposure to sun and wind to dry the fruit after rain or dew. CROP THINNING can also help. Various practices to reduce FRUIT SET and thus cluster compaction, including pre-bloom leaf removal and applications of plant growth regulators, have been very effective in some situations but have drawbacks that limit widespread adoption. In New Zealand, MACHINE HARVESTERS are used just after fruit set to shake the vine and dislodge infected blossom 'trash' that could otherwise get trapped within bunches and start a pre-harvest epidemic; research shows that this simple practice often reduces disease severity by half.

Chemical control using a FUNGICIDE is the second route and widely practised where the disease is problematic. The number of spray applications required depends on the climate. In some wet regions, up to half a dozen or more may be needed, beginning at FLOWERING and ending before harvest. The last sprays cannot be applied too close to harvest as yeast activity during FERMENTATION may be inhibited by some chemical RESIDUES, quite apart from considerations of potential health risks. Warning systems based on temperature and/or relative humidity have been developed to predict epidemics and help determine the need and timing for sprays. While several categories of fungicides are now used for botrytis control, the fungus has developed resistance to some after only a few years of use, forcing growers to rely increasingly on non-chemical options.

Multiple BIOLOGICAL control products have been marketed recently, with new ones in development. These include specific fungi antagonistic to or competitive with the botrytis fungus; bacteria that produce antifungal compounds; and bacteria, plant extracts, and crushed crustacean shells that purportedly induce natural defence responses by the vine. However, biological controls are variable in their efficacy, and even the best ones must be used in concert with appropriate cultural practices to provide significant benefit.

Botrytis is also a problem for stored TABLE GRAPES and during GRAFTING operations in nurseries.

See GREY ROT and NOBLE ROT for more details of the two different forms of botrytis. For details of how nobly rotten grapes are transformed into wine, see BOTRYTIZED wines. R.E.S. & W.W.

Bettiga, L. J., and Gubler, W. G., 'Bunch rots', in L. J. Bettiga (ed.), *Grape Pest Management* (3rd edn, 2013), 93–103.

Bragato Research Institute, 'Mechanical shaking for rot reduction' (July 2019).

Wilcox, W. F., et al., *Compendium of Grape Diseases, Disorders, and Pests* (2nd edn, 2015).

botrytized, or **botrytis-affected,** wines are those made from white grapes affected by the benevolent form of BOTRYTIS BUNCH ROT, known in English as NOBLE ROT. Distinctively scented in youth, and with considerably more EXTRACT than most wines, they are the most complex and longest lived of all the sweet white table wines. The noble rot smell is often described as honeyed, but it can also have a complex range of aromas including bitter orange, apricot, almond paste, and a certain type of glue.

History

There is no firm evidence that botrytized wines were recognized in antiquity, although Olney points out that a particularly fine ancient Greek wine produced on Chios (see CHIAN) in the 5th century BCE is described as *saprian* by ATHENAEUS, and that the literal translation of this may be 'rotten, putrid'. Noble rot is much more likely to occur in more humid climates than in the MEDITERRANEAN CLIMATE of the Aegean Islands, however, and the extremely unpleasant appearance of grapes infected by noble rot, and the difficulty with which they ferment, must have deterred many early winemakers.

Three important centres of botrytized wine production have their own accounts of the discovery that this particular sort of mouldy grape could be transformed into exceptional wine.

That of the TOKAJ region of north-east Hungary dates from at least 1650 when the priest-cum-winemaker on a particular estate there delayed the HARVEST because of the threat of attack by the Turks. This allowed the development of noble rot; the grapes were vinified separately, as one would expect, and the resulting wine much admired. For diplomatic purposes it was introduced to the French court in the early 18th century, long before French vine-growers had recognized the existence of the noble fungus.

In Germany, the principle of picking selected bunches of grapes (AUSLESE) was understood in the 18th century, but that of the widespread picking of grapes affected by noble rot not until about 1820. In spite of popular beliefs to the contrary, precisely when and where vine-growers first realized the value of noble rot is not certain, although the discovery in Germany is thought to have been in the particularly suitable climate of the Rheingau, which became most famous for botrytized wines. SCHLOSS JOHANNISBERG has certainly promulgated its own claim that in 1775 the traditional harvest messenger—licensed, as usual, to deliver permission to pick from the owner, the distant prince-abbot of Fulda—was delayed, thereby supposedly allowing a noble-rot infection to proceed and resulting in Germany's first botrytized SPÄTLESE.

The sweet wines of Bordeaux and the Loire were much treasured in the Middle Ages, particularly by the DUTCH, but without any specific mention of a special fungus or acknowledgement of any special attribute. The principal French legend concerning the 'discovery' of noble rot—and legend it is widely believed to be—dates from as recently as 1847, at Ch d'YQUEM (although the quality, style, and youthfulness of earlier vintages of Yquem, such as the 1811, suggest that noble rot must have played an important part in wine production there before that date).

The risks and costs involved in making naturally botrytized wine make it necessarily expensive. It has therefore been an economical proposition only when sweet wines are highly valued. Germany's botrytized wines have always been regarded as precious rarities for which a ready market can be found within Germany. France's output of botrytized wines is potentially much greater, but when sweet wines were out of FASHION in the 1960s and 1970s, enthusiasm for producing them inevitably waned, only to be rekindled in the 1980s. In the 21st century, botrytized wines suffer from the more widespread lack of demand for very sweet wines.

Geography and climate

Many conditions have to be met before botrytized wines can be produced. Not only is a MESOCLIMATE which favours misty mornings and warm afternoons in autumn needed, but producers must have the knowledge and the will to sacrifice quantity for nothing more certain than possible quality. Botrytized wines are very much a product of psyche as well as nature.

The district with the potential to produce the greatest quantity of top-quality botrytized wine is SAUTERNES (although it all depends, as everywhere, on the precise WEATHER of the year). The confluence of the Rivers Ciron and GARONNE provide an ideal mesoclimate for the satisfactory development of noble rot. Nearby sweet white wine districts CÉRONS, LOUPIAC, CADILLAC, and STE-CROIX-DU-MONT may also produce small quantities of botrytized wines, although the price fetched by these appellations rarely justifies the additional production costs.

Botrytized wine is also made by the most meticulous producers in MONBAZILLAC and SAUSSIGNAC. With viticultural commitment and skilful vinification, these districts can make botrytized wines to rival all but the very best Sauternes made similarly from Sémillon, Sauvignon, and particularly Muscadelle grapes. One or two fine examples of this style have also emerged from GAILLAC.

On the River Loire, appellations such as Coteaux de l'AUBANCE, Coteaux du LAYON, QUARTS DE CHAUME, BONNEZEAUX, MONTLOUIS, and VOUVRAY can produce botrytized wines in good years, and they are given even greater ageing potential for being made from the acidic Chenin Blanc grape.

Botrytized wines may also be made from such varied grapes as Mâconnais Chardonnays and Alsace Rieslings in exceptional years.

Germany is the other famous source of botrytized wines, usually labelled BEERENAUSLESE or TROCKENBEERENAUSLESE, although the quantities made vary enormously according to vintage. Riesling is the classic grape, although some of the GERMAN CROSSES can be persuaded to rot nobly in an exceptionally suitable year. Noble-rot infections are much more reliable in the BURGENLAND district of Austria, where, thanks to the influence of the NEUSIEDLERSEE, considerable quantities of botrytized Beerenauslesen and Trockenbeerenauslesen are made most years. Over the border in Hungary, TOKAJ is still closely associated with botrytized winemaking, as various parts of ROMANIA, notably COTNARI, once were.

Botrytized winemaking is an embryonic art in Italy, Spain, and most of Portugal, where producers and consumers tend to favour either DRIED-GRAPE WINES or FORTIFIED WINES.

Beyond Europe, botrytized wines are made with increasing frequency. Nederburg Edelkeur was a South African prototype which enjoyed international acclaim in the 1970s. Griffith in NEW SOUTH WALES's Riverina was producing Australian botrytized Pedro Ximénez as early as the late 1950s and is now a centre for the production of relatively early maturing botrytized whites, particularly Semillon. In Australia, New Zealand, South Africa, and particularly California, a host of botrytized Rieslings has emerged.

In California in the late 1950s Myron and Alice Nightingale in the Livermore Valley managed to simulate noble rot by growing spores of the botrytis fungus in a laboratory and spraying them on picked, healthy, ripe grapes before subjecting them to alternately humid and warm conditions for a couple of weeks. The result, Premiere Semillon, was followed by a series of similar wines made at Beringer in the Napa Valley. However, Beringer's Nightingale is now made naturally thanks to a vineyard in Calistoga with a suitable mesoclimate for the development of noble rot. Dolce Winery has also been particularly successful with naturally botrytized wines.

As awareness of noble rot and botrytized wines grows, the number of winemakers anxious to experiment also increases, even if the market is not always rapturous, and they are usually at the mercy of the weather. Even ENGLAND has succeeded in producing botrytized wine.

Vine varieties

Any white grape variety may be infected benevolently by the botrytis fungus; red varieties simply lose their colour and usually develop off-odours. Certain varieties seem particularly sensitive to the fungus and well adapted to the production of botrytized wines, however: Sémillon, Sauvignon Blanc, Chenin Blanc, Riesling, Gewürztraminer, and Furmint are traditional.

Viticulture

The chief viticultural aspect of making botrytized wines is the number of passages or *tries* (see TRI) through the vineyard which may have to be made in order to pick grapes only at the optimum point of botrytis infection, because noble rot is so crucial to quality. See SAUTERNES for a description of the likely routine there. In a year as difficult as 1974 at Ch d'YQUEM (admittedly the most conscientious Sauternes estate), 11 *tries* were made over a ten-week period. In 1990, on the other hand, noble rot spread rapidly and uniformly, and the grapes were picked by early October. In some vintages the spread and quality of botrytis may be so patchy that some estates, for example Yquem, Rieussec, and Suduiraut in 2012, elect not make a GRAND VIN. Hand-picking of these varied but usually disgusting-looking grapes is essential, and the cost of LABOUR is one important element in the price of botrytized wines.

In wet vintages, some producers use modern freeze-concentration techniques known as CRYOEXTRACTION.

Winemaking

If picking botrytized grapes is painstaking, obtaining their juice and persuading it to ferment is at least as difficult because of its composition (see NOBLE ROT). PRESSING is a physically difficult operation, and, contrary to the usual practice, later pressings yield juice superior to the first pressing because it is richer in sugar and the chemical compounds produced by the botrytis fungus. The most dehydrated grapes in the press may not yield juice until they have been pressed twice or three times.

A variety of winemaking methods are used, including the classic method described in SAUTERNES. Fermentation is necessarily extremely slow. The juice seems almost designed to inhibit YEASTS, being so high in sugar and antibiotics such as botryticine. Botrytized musts tend to lack nutrients such as thiamine and ammonia, which is another reason for STUCK FERMENTATIONS. Fermentation may be allowed to stop itself, or SULFUR DIOXIDE addition may be used. Care must be taken that these wines, which often have a RESIDUAL SUGAR level equivalent to about 6% alcoholic strength, do not suffer a SECOND FERMENTATION, and bottling, whether after two winters in new BARRIQUES (as in the top Sauternes properties) or in the following spring (as in the Loire and many German cellars) has to be undertaken with care. Higher levels of sulfur dioxide are needed during vinification and at bottling because the enzyme LACCASE produced by botrytis increases the risk of OXIDATION and is tolerant of high levels of sulfur dioxide. In addition, the chemical composition of botrytized wines means they have significant power to bind sulfur dioxide. This is why EU regulations permit a higher level of total sulfur dioxide for these wines than for all others. The development of *Botrytis cinerea* also results in the production of two POLYSACCHARIDES. One has antifungal properties and inhibits fermentation. The other, a β-glucan, can make FILTRATION much more difficult, especially if crushing, pumping, and pressing are carried out harshly.

Some wines, notably those made from aromatic varieties such as Muscat, are marked by a loss of varietal aroma. This is mainly because botrytis metabolizes the MONOTERPENES such as linalool and geraniol that are responsible for the distinctive aromas of such varieties.

Botrytized wines are capable of extremely long AGEING, for many decades in some cases.

Brook, S., *Liquid Gold: Dessert Wines of the World* (1987).
Nelson, K. E., et al., 'Large-scale production of spores to botrytise grapes for commercial natural sweet wine production', *American Journal of Enology and Viticulture*, 14 (1963), 118–28.
Olney, R., *Yquem* (1985).
Ribéreau-Gayon, P., et al., *Traité d'Œnologie* 1: *Microbiologie du vin: Vinifications* (7th edn, 2017), translated by J. Towey, as *Handbook of Enology* 1: *The Microbiology of Wine and Vinifications* (3rd edn, 2021).

botte, Italian word for a large wooden cask, presumably from the same root as BUTT. The plural is **botti**.

bottle ageing, the process of deliberately maturing a wine after BOTTLING, whether for a few weeks as a conscious effort on the part of the bottler to allow the wine to recover from BOTTLE SHOCK or, in the case of very fine wines, for many years in order to allow the wine to mature.

For more details, see AGEING.

bottle deposit in red wines is a lacquer-like pigmented deposit adhering to the inner bottle surface; it is different from SEDIMENT. This deposition, which may begin in the first few months after bottling, may cover only a small area of the bottle shoulder or may eventually cover the entire glass surface with which the wine is in contact. Wine quality is not affected by bottle deposit, which is unlikely to occur if the wine has been FINED. The deposit is an insoluble complex polymer of PIGMENTED TANNINS and PROTEIN. P.J.W.

bottle fermented, description of some SPARKLING WINES made either by the traditional method or by the transfer method. See SPARKLING WINEMAKING for full details.

bottles, still by far the most common CONTAINERS for finished wine. Glass bottles are inconveniently fragile and relatively heavy, with a CARBON FOOTPRINT higher than any other form of wine PACKAGING, but, importantly for long-term AGEING, they are inert. A standard bottle contains 75 cl/25 fl oz, although see also BOTTLE SIZES.

History

Today it may be taken for granted that wine bottles of different colours and shapes will hold a precise capacity. Nor is it questioned that a paper LABEL will be firmly fixed to the bottle to give a plethora of information, much of it required by law. These, however, are recent developments.

In classical antiquity wine was stored and transported in large, elongated jars called AMPHORAE. They varied considerably in size and quality, but it would certainly be difficult to pour a drinking quantity from such an awkward vessel without using some sort of intermediate container. After the Romans invented glass-blowing, large numbers of flasks and jugs were made, many almost certainly used to serve wine.

Pottery and stoneware jugs were used for centuries in Europe for serving wine, but glass took over as technology to make glass in commercial quantities spread in the 17th century, and by the end of it glass bottles were plentiful, although reserved for the upper classes.

Shape Records from the 11th and 12th centuries show bottles with globular bodies and long necks known as shaft and globe, used for drinking and serving wine. The form developed (see illustration), becoming lower and wider in Britain, while on mainland Europe the flask-shape with an oval cross-section was popular. From *c.*1690 to 1720, the outline of a bottle resembled that of an onion—a wide compressed globular body with a short neck. Larger bottles were made too, whose shape resembled an inflated balloon or bladder. It is thought that all these forms were stored in beds of sand. By the 1720s the 'onion' became taller and the sides flatter—known by collectors as a 'mallet'. Naturally occurring impurities in the constituent ingredients gave glass an olive green hue which varied from pale to almost black and was beneficial to the bottled wine as it excluded light. Most bottles before 1700 had an applied ring of glass just below the rim which gave an anchorage to the string used to hold in a variety of stoppers. These bottles were of substantial weight and thickness too.

Wine drinkers made an important discovery in the 1730s. While it was known that some vintages of wine were better than others even in prehistory, their keeping and consequent maturing qualities were not realized until the introduction of binning, the storing of wine in bottles laid on their sides (see BIN). The effectiveness of CORK as a CLOSURE was thereby enhanced because it was kept wet and expanded by the wine. All this was achieved by the abandoning of onion-, bladder-, and mallet-shaped bottles in favour of cylindrical ones which stack easily. Early cylindrical bottles have short wide bodies with tall necks, but as the century progressed the modern shape evolved. In 1821, Ricketts of Bristol patented a machine for moulding bottles of uniform size and shape, early examples of which are impressed 'patent' on the shoulder of the bottle and the legend 'H Ricketts & Co. Glassworks Bristol' on the base. Thus the modern wine bottle had evolved, all later shapes and colours being decided as a question of aesthetics rather than technical limitation.

Identification From 1636, at the time the English bottle began to appear, it was illegal to sell wine by the bottle. This consumer protection measure was on account of vintners' willingness to take advantage of the varying capacity of blown bottles. From that time and for the next 230 years, wine was sold by the measure and then bottled. Customers who bought regularly had their own bottles and had them marked in order to distinguish them from any others that might be at the vintner's premises waiting to be filled. The usual marking was the attachment at the end of the production process of a disc seal of the same glass as the bottle, upon which was impressed the owner's initials, name, or heraldic device, often accompanied by the date. Innkeepers and taverners had appropriately marked, or 'sealed', bottles too. The seals did not indicate the contents.

Sealed bottles are avidly collected today, the most prized being 17th-century ones, particularly those with dates incorporated in the seal. Named examples are preferred to ones with initials, and earlier ones to later.

Bottles with paper labels indicating the contents, first hand-written and later printed, emerged during the opening years of the 19th century, but in Britain the law prohibiting wine from being sold by the bottle was not relaxed until 1860. Bottles with paper labels printed with pre-1860 vintages are probably relabelled or were intended for non-British markets.

Size Free-blown bottles relied on the skills of the glass-blowers to gather the exact amount of hot glass needed and, with the help of calipers and measuring rods, to create similar size vessels repeatedly and quickly. From about the 1740s, the use of open wooden moulds to shape the glass began the process of standardizing bottle capacities. By 1821, a complete metal bottle mould was patented, and in 1901, in America, Michael J. Owens invented the automatic bottle-blowing machine, which guaranteed the capacity of every bottle.

For a long while a bottle was more or less 1¼ UK pints (70 cl or 25 fl oz) and a magnum was a quart (1.12 l or 40 fl oz). Until the 1970s, when legislation in the EU and elsewhere enforced standardization, bottles varied from about 65 to 85 cl, CHAMPAGNE and BURGUNDY tending to be larger than those for BORDEAUX, while SHERRY bottles were often smaller. R.N.H.B. & C.R.H.

Liefkes, R. (ed.), *Glass* (1997).

Van den Bossche, W., *Antique Glass Bottles: Their History and Evolution (1500–1850)* (2001).

Modern bottles

Choice of LABEL and FOIL are not the only ways in which a wine producer can make a visual statement to a potential customer. Wine bottles are now made in an almost bewildering array of shapes, weights, colours of glass, and design, quite apart from their capacity (see BOTTLE SIZES).

In some regions one specific bottle has been adopted by all but the most anarchic producers, and indeed adoption of a special local, regional, or appellational bottle became particularly fashionable in the 1980s. Examples of special bottles are the heavy, embossed CHÂTEAUNEUF-DU-PAPE bottle (which comes in several rival versions); the BOCKSBEUTEL of FRANKEN; the CHÂTEAU-GRILLET bottle peculiar to a single property; and the long-necked green bottle particular to MUSCADET, although it can sometimes seem that every French appellation has developed its own exclusive bottle.

In general, Italians, with their firm belief in the importance of design, offer the most dazzling range of wine bottles. Some of the particularly artful shapes used for grappa have been adopted by wine producers in Austria and further afield, especially for halves of sweet wine. The problem with some special bottle shapes, however, is that they may well be difficult to store, both on the shelf (many a special bottle is simply too tall for the average supermarket display) and, particularly, in a wine rack designed for standard bottles.

Weight and darkness of glass seem to have been particularly highly valued by Argentines and Italians, although it was once a general rule throughout the wine world that the heavier a bottle, the greater the aspirations of the producer of the wine for its longevity, or at least its price. The weight of a 75-cl bottle can vary between about 345 g and, in extreme cases, more than a kilo. Bottling wine in the lightest, cheapest glass is one way of saving costs, on the bottle itself and on TRANSPORT. Eschewing overweight bottles is one way of saving the planet that is being adopted by more and more enlightened producers around the world. See SUSTAINABILITY.

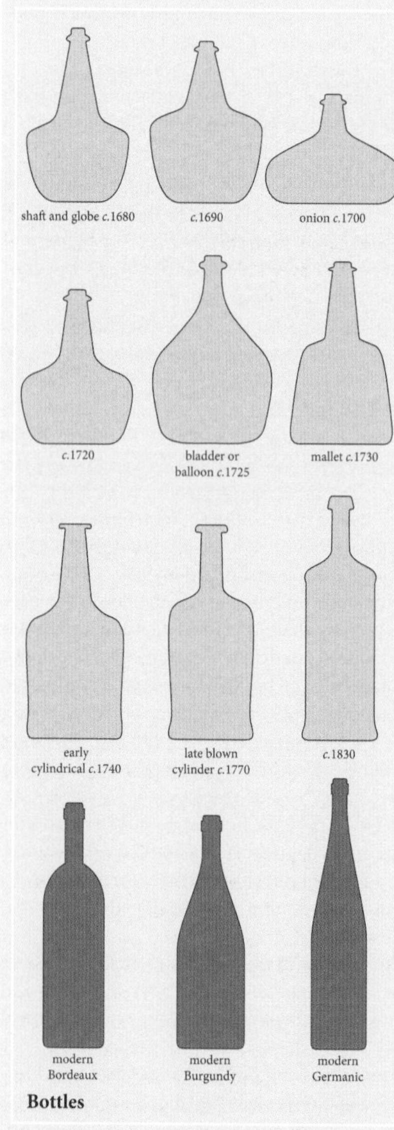

Bottles

Bottle shapes Special designs apart, there are certain standard bottle shapes associated most commonly with certain regions or, increasingly, the styles of wine associated with those regions. Ambitiously made Chardonnays the world over, for example, tend to be put into burgundy bottles. Since the geographical provenance of most wines should be clear from the label, understanding bottle shapes is most useful for the clues they provide as to the intended style of the wine inside them. Some RIOJA producers, for example, put their Garnacha-dominated richer blends into burgundy bottles, while their Tempranillo wines designed for longer ageing are put into bordeaux bottles.

Most champagne and sparkling wines are sold in much the same shape of bottle, moulded to be thick and strong enough to withstand the pressure of up to six atmospheres inside each bottle. Considerable energy and money is expended, however, on designing special bottles for PRESTIGE CUVÉES, Moët & Chandon's Dom PÉRIGNON bottle having set a formidable standard. The precise shape of the lip of a champagne bottle indicates whether the second fermentation took place under a crown cap or under a cork, as it does in some very rare cases.

Bottles vary in the extent to which they have a punt, or inverse indentation, in their base. Most champagne and sparkling wine bottles have a particularly deep indentation because it strengthens the glass, which is under considerable pressure, and, during disgorgement when bottles are inverted, makes it easy for bottles to be lifted by suction during SPARKLING WINEMAKING. Punts are less obviously useful for still wines—although they can make bottles look bigger and more impressive—and deep punts can provide useful purchase for the thumb when SERVING wine from a bottle.

The exact shape and design of the neck and lip of the bottle is determined by what is used to stopper it. Most CLOSURES other than cork need some sort of modification, and the widespread adoption of SCREWCAPS has entailed considerable redesign of bottles. The 1990s saw a marked but mercifully brief FASHION for bottles with a flange but no CAPSULE around the top, which damaged many a CORKSCREW.

Bottle colour Wine keeps best in dark glass—as the Champenois, the most energetic researchers into the effects of bottle choice on wine, have found. ROEDERER Cristal, which has traditionally been sold in clear glass, is always swathed in an orange wrap designed to filter out ULTRAVIOLET RADIATION (see LIGHTSTRIKE for more on this phenomenon). On the other hand, dark glass prevents the consumer from being impressed by the colour of a wine. For this reason, most ROSÉS, not generally designed for AGEING, are sold in clear glass. It is less clear why SAUTERNES and other sweet white bordeaux is sold in clear glass; TRADITION is presumably the explanation. Most wine bottles are, for reasons of both tradition and the orientation of glass furnaces, some shade of green, from pale blueish green to a colour that to all intents and purposes is black. For traditional reasons again, brown glass is used for some Italian wines and for many fortified wines; it was also the traditional way of telling a HOCK or Rhine wine from a MOSEL in green glass. Some German producers use blue-green glass, however, in a nod to Victorian times when blue glass was often used. One of the most distinctive glass colours for wine bottles is the yellow-green used for white burgundy, called *feuille morte* in France and therefore 'dead leaf' in much of the New World. Wines are occasionally marketed in bright blue and bright red bottles.

More clues from the bottle

Most wine bottles are moulded with the mark of their manufacturers, sometimes with their capacity, and all wine sold within Europe from the 1990s should have a lot mark (see LABELLING INFORMATION), a small code stamped on the label, foil, or more usually the bottle, so that each bottle can be traced back to its precise BOTTLING and dispatch.

See also PAPER BOTTLES.

bottle shock, a temporary phenomenon caused by the inevitable agitation of a wine during FILTRATION, BOTTLING, or transportation, resolved quite simply by allowing the wine to rest for a day or two. The term was taken as the title of a 2008 film based very loosely on the late Steven SPURRIER and his JUDGMENT OF PARIS tasting.

bottle sickness, colloquial term used to describe an increasingly rare phenomenon resulting from exposing a wine to too much OXYGEN during bottling, or too little, resulting in REDUCTION and the production of VOLATILE SULFUR COMPOUNDS. High levels of SULFUR DIOXIDE at bottling may also make a wine smell unpleasant. More common is BOTTLE SHOCK.

bottle sizes are standardized in most countries. A bottle containing 75 cl/25 fl oz is now accepted almost universally as the standard wine (but not spirits, which is more usually 70 cl) bottle, with the magnum being 1.5 l, exactly twice the capacity. The standard bottle is about the same size as the first bottles (see BOTTLES, history), whose size may have been determined by the size of container conveniently blown by a (glass-blower's) lungful of air. The bottle has in its time been variously described as a suitable ration of wine for one person at a sitting, one person per day, and two people at a sitting (see CONSUMPTION).

Half-bottles usually contain 37.5 cl and are believed to hasten wine AGEING, partly because they contain more OXYGEN per centilitre of wine

Capacity (l)	Bordeaux	Champagne/ Burgundy
1.5 (2 bottles)	magnum	magnum
2.25 (3 bottles)	Marie-Jeanne	not found
3 (4 bottles)	double magnum	Jéroboam
5 (6 bottles)	Jéroboam*	Réhoboam
6 (8 bottles)	Impériale	Methuselah
9 (12 bottles)	not found	Salmanazar
12 (16 bottles)	not found	Balthazar
15 (20 bottles)	not found	Nebuchadnezzar

* 4.5 litres before 1978

since the bottleneck and ULLAGE are the same as for a full bottle. Most wine bottlers have viewed halves and other bottles smaller than the standard bottle as an unwelcome inconvenience, and BOTTLING technology has been focused on standard bottles, but there continues to be strong demand for half-bottles, particularly in restaurants. There have been various attempts to launch a 50-cl bottle, particularly common for SWEET WINES, and some champagne producers have had notable success with single-serve quarter-bottles.

With the exception of JURA's special 62-cl *clavelin*, the bottle capacities permitted within Europe for still wines are 10 cl, 25 cl, 37.5 cl, 50 cl, 75 cl, and 1, 1.5, 2, 3, 4, 5, 6, 8, 9, and 10 litres (and wine may be served in 18.7-cl bottles, sometimes referred to as 'splits', aboard trains, planes, and the like). Sparkling wine bottles come in 12.5-, 20-, 37.5- and 75-cl and 1.5-, 3-, 4.5-, 6- and 9-litre capacities. The larger-sized bottles, some of them no longer in production, have different names in different regions.

Others including an 18-l Melchior, a 26-l Sovereign, and a 30-l Melchizedek (or Midas) are also known, in theory. Bordeaux collectors particularly treasure larger bottles (often known as 'large formats' or *grands formats*) up to Impériale size, as they favour slow but subtle AGEING. Giant champagne bottles, on the other hand, tend to favour publicity rather than wine quality (sizes larger than a magnum tend to be filled with wine made in smaller bottles).

bottle variation is one of the more tantalizing aspects of wine appreciation. 'There are no great wines, just great bottles', is a popular saying among connoisseurs. It is only to be expected with a product as sensitive to storage conditions as wine (see STORING WINE) that bottles of the same wine will differ—perhaps because one has been exposed to higher temperatures or greater humidity. There can easily be a perceptible difference in quality and character between bottles from the very same CASE. SUBJECTIVITY may play a part, as well as a difference in FILL LEVELS, but it is also possible that the individual wines were subtly different before they went into bottle, or that they were bottled under different conditions or under CORKS of different quality and efficacy. It was not until the 1970s, for example, that it became commonplace for Bordeaux châteaux to ensure that a uniform blend was made before bottling; some of the world's most artisanal producers still bottle by hand from cask to cask. Similarly, wines bottled on two different occasions may find themselves packed in the same case (although modern lot number marking provides more clues in this respect; see LABELLING INFORMATION).

bottling, vital winemaking operation for all wines aside from those packaged in containers other than bottles (see ALTERNATIVE PACKAGING) and those few served straight from a cask or tank as BULK WINE.

Bottling techniques vary greatly according to the size, resources, technical ability, and modernity of the winery, although since the 1960s it has been customary almost everywhere to blend all casks or vats of a given lot of wine together before bottling and to bottle it all at once. (Prior to this there could be considerable BOTTLE VARIATION between different bottlings of even FIRST GROWTHS.)

In the past, bottling lines subjected the wine to considerable AERATION and agitation with a significant impact on wine quality. At one time, high-volume, low-margin wines containing RESIDUAL SUGAR might have been subjected to PASTEURIZATION to ensure microbiological stability, but such methods have been largely replaced by membrane FILTRATION, often in combination with DMDC or SORBIC ACID to further reduce the YEAST population and lessen the risk of refermentation in bottle.

Modern bottling lines use advanced technology to ensure that dissolved OXYGEN is kept to the lowest level possible by constant monitoring and the use of NITROGEN or CARBON DIOXIDE to flush the bottle and exclude oxygen from the HEAD SPACE (see TOTAL PACKAGE OXYGEN). The expensive, high-volume, super-fast bottling lines used for everyday wines often provide the best results because problems with oxygen pick-up tend to be worse at slower speeds, at the start and end of the bottling run, or if there is a stoppage. Oxygen management is likely to be given higher priority in wines not intended for ageing. In this aspect of wine production, big may be beautiful. Nevertheless, last-minute adjustments to wine before bottling, such as FILTRATION or the addition of SULFUR DIOXIDE, may result in the temporary shutting down of the wine (see BOTTLE SHOCK).

Some smaller producers of high-quality wine have the funds to invest in their own high-tech bottling line, but many other small wineries, especially in France, where *mis en bouteille au domaine* has considerable cachet, depend on the services of outside mobile bottling lines, bottling equipment mounted in a truck or lorry which can be brought to the winery for a day or more. Others still follow the ancient tradition of bottling wine from casks or even individual barrels in the cellar, but in general this is a part of the production process that is most often outsourced to specialists.

The specific steps involved in bottling are the preparation of the wine itself (BLENDING, ANALYSIS, and possibly final filtration) together with the preparation of the bottling line (sterilization and the preparation of the filler, corker or capper, labeller, capsuler, and casing machines, as appropriate). High-quality wines suitable for AGEING may not be labelled as soon as they are bottled, because they are stored for some time before being released and the labels may deteriorate in cellar conditions.

Bottling may take place at any time from a few weeks after HARVEST (as with NOUVEAU wines) to when the wine is many years old (as in some of the most traditional Iberian BODEGAS). On smaller wine estates, bottling normally takes place at an otherwise quiet time for cellar staff such as in the spring or early summer.

Place of bottling may be many thousands of miles from where the grapes were originally grown and even from where the wine was made, since BULK TRANSPORT is so very much cheaper than transporting wine in bottle and more environmentally friendly. A 20-foot container will hold approximately 1,100 9-litre cases of bottled wine, but a disposable tank that fits into the same container will hold 24,000 litres of wine. The cost of bottling and bottles being so relatively high in California, Chile, and Australia, for example, some wines destined for sale in the US and Europe are bottled close to the market. According to the OIV, the total volume of wine shipped around the world in bulk (in containers bigger than 10 litres) represented more than 34% of all exported wine in 2020. In Eastern Europe and the former SOVIET UNION in particular, bottling has traditionally taken place much closer to centres of population than to the vineyard. Producers of hand-crafted, top-quality wines, however, usually prefer to conduct the bottling operation themselves since they have greater control over the process and are able to reduce to a minimum the amount of treatment the wine needs prior to shipping. However, for high-volume wines with a limited shelf life in bottle of around 12 months, there is the advantage that the wine is likely to reach the retailers' shelves much sooner after bottling than wine bottled at source. See BOTTLING INFORMATION for the significance of various bottling claims on the label.

While improved technology and QUALITY CONTROL have significantly reduced the risks involved in this mechanical process, the bottled wine can still occasionally develop problems

B

which were not previously apparent. These may be the result of high levels of dissolved oxygen (see TOTAL PACKAGE OXYGEN), incomplete STABILIZATION, the failure of filtration to remove all viable yeast or bacteria, causing post-bottling fermentation, or dilution if water is used to push wine around the winery to the bottling line. Other possible contaminants include those associated with CORK TAINT or SMOKE TAINT. Incorrectly applied labels are not uncommon.

See also BOTTLES. J.R., J.E.H. & B.D.

bottling information. All wine labels must include information about the person who is responsible for the wine in the bottle—usually either the bottler or the importer, sometimes both. Details of the bottler can give useful information about the provenance of a wine.

Common phrases for 'bottled' are *mis en bouteille* in French, *imbottigliato* in Italian, *embotellado* in Spanish, and *engarrafado* in Portuguese. Wines bottled by their producer will state 'bottled by', whereas wines bottled under contract are labelled 'bottled for'.

The bottler's (or importer's) address will also appear on the label, but the presentation must not mislead as to the origin of the wine, for example by highlighting that the wine was bottled in a famous region when the grapes came from somewhere else. For this reason, in the EU the bottler's postcode may sometimes be used instead of the full address, making labels less informative to those not conversant with, for example, French *département* numbers. Italy's stipulation that the bottler's code appear on the CAPSULE, screwcap, or cork is even stricter but is being phased out.

In the EU, PDO or PGI wines may use the name of a 'holding' (e.g. château, domaine, Schloss, Weingut, castello, or casa) only if they are made exclusively from grapes harvested in vineyards exploited by that holding and vinified and bottled entirely at that holding. See CHÂTEAU BOTTLING, DOMAINE BOTTLING, and ERZEUGERABFÜLLUNG.

WINES WITHOUT GEOGRAPHICAL INDICATION may not be described as having been bottled at the domaine or château.

Similar rules apply in other parts of the world. In Chile, for example, *embotellado en origen*, estate-bottled, or its synonyms can be used only for CONTROLLED APPELLATION wines grown, vinified, and bottled on lands owned or held by the producing winery. For US terminology, see ESTATE BOTTLED. J.P.H.B.

Bouchalès is a dark-berried vine variety still grown to a limited extent in Bordeaux and in the Lot-et-Garonne *département*. It is not particularly easy to graft or grow, and total French plantings fell from over 4,000 ha/9,900 acres in 1968 to 68 ha/168 acres by 2018.

Bouchard Père et Fils, one of Beaune's large merchant houses (quite distinct from Bouchard Aîné), and also one of the most important vineyard owners of the CÔTE D'OR with 130 ha/321 acres of vines in more than 100 CLIMATS, three-quarters of them PREMIERS CRUS and GRANDS CRUS. Founded in 1731, it has been based since 1820 in the 15th-century Château de Beaune, a landmark in this medieval wine town with usefully extensive, well-stocked cellars for ageing their top wines, complemented by newer cellars just outside Beaune. The house was established by Michel Bouchard, a Dauphiné textile merchant, and acquired in 1995 by the Henriot family, who added the Chablis firm William Fèvre in 1998. In 2022 the Henriot wine holdings were merged with those of ARTÉMIS DOMAINES.

Bouchet, name for CABERNET FRANC commonly used in St-Émilion and elsewhere on the right bank of the GIRONDE, while Bouchy has been known in MADIRAN.

bouchon is French for CORK, and **bouchonné** describes a faulty, CORKED wine.

bouillie bordelaise. See BORDEAUX MIXTURE.

bouquet, oft-ridiculed tasting term for the smell of a wine, particularly that of a mature or maturing wine. Although its original French meaning was 'small wood' (from the same root as the Italian *bosco* and the English *bosky*), 'bouquet' is a French word for a bunch of flowers which has been used to describe the perfume of a wine since the first half of the 19th century. It is used loosely by many wine tasters to describe any pleasant wine smell or smells but, just as a bouquet (rather than a bunch) of flowers suggests a composition of several varied elements, many wine professionals distinguish between the simple AROMA of the grape and the bouquet of the more complex compounds which evolve as a result of FERMENTATION, ÉLEVAGE, and AGEING. There is little consistency in usage, however, and many authorities differ about the point in a wine's life cycle at which a wine's smell stops being an aroma and becomes a bouquet. See also ESTER, FLAVOUR COMPOUNDS, and FLAVOUR PRECURSORS.

Bourboulenc is an ancient Provençal white grape variety. Ripening late but keeping its acidity well, it is allowed into a wide variety of Provençal and southern Rhône appellations (including CHÂTEAUNEUF-DU-PAPE) but is rarely encountered as a dominant variety other than in the distinctively marine whites of LA CLAPE and an increasing number of other Languedoc whites. France's total area of Bourboulenc was 520 ha/1,285 acres in 2019. Together with Maccabéo (MACABEO), it should constitute more than 50% of the blend for any white MINERVOIS, and it is one of the principal varieties in CORBIÈRES Blanc. Wine produced can be fine, crisp, and aromatic.

Bourg, small town in the BORDEAUX region on the right bank of the River DORDOGNE, just upriver of its confluence with the Garonne, which is surrounded by the **Côtes de Bourg** appellation, also known as **Bourg** and **Bourgeais**. The 3,412 ha/8,428 acres of vineyard that produced Côtes de Bourg in 2020 have a characterful base of CLAY and LIMESTONE with sandy GRAVEL deposits and some MARLS. They are planted substantially with Merlot, and the best reds can be more concentrated and ageworthy than those from the larger BLAYE area to the immediate north; vineyards on the edge of the Gironde estuary are particularly well protected from FROST DAMAGE, thanks to the MARITIME influence. The star of the appellation is Ch Roc de Combes, related to St-Émilion's Ch Tertre-Roteboeuf, on a particularly well-favoured site on the Gironde itself. A little dry white wine is also made.

bourgeon is French for BUD, and *ébourgeonnage* is the viticultural practice of thinning surplus developing buds before FLOWERING, a form of early-season CROP THINNING.

Bourgogne, the French name for both the region of BURGUNDY (La Bourgogne) and burgundy, the wines thereof (*le bourgogne*), which are red, white, and very occasionally rosé. In particular, Bourgogne refers to the most basic, generic category of AOC in Burgundy.

For white wines the generic appellations are BOURGOGNE ALIGOTÉ, **Bourgogne Blanc** (made from Chardonnay grapes), and Coteaux BOURGUIGNONS. For red wines the generic appellations are BOURGOGNE PASSETOUTGRAINS, **Coteaux Bourguignons**, and **Bourgogne Rouge**. The last is usually pure Pinot Noir, although it may technically include the CÉSAR grown in the Yonne *département* and may be made from GAMAY grapes if grown in one of the BEAUJOLAIS crus. A small amount of pink wine is sold as **Bourgogne Rosé**, or **Bourgogne Clairet**. In practice this may be the result of a SAIGNÉE of a red wine from a major vineyard in order to concentrate it.

Bourgogne of whatever colour may be followed by a geographical suffix, either denoting a region (Hautes-Côtes de Nuits, Hautes-Côtes de Beaune, Côte d'Or, Côte Chalonnaise, Côtes d'AUXERRE, Côtes du COUCHOIS); a commune or group of communes (Chitry, Coulanges-la-Vineuse, Épineuil, Tonnerre); or in certain cases a vineyard (Côte St-Jacques at Joigny or La Chapelle Notre-Dame in the Côte d'Or).

Thus it is evident that the scope of 'Bourgogne', be it white, red, or pink, encompasses wide variations in provenance, quality, and style of wine which may not be clear from the label. A Bourgogne Rouge or Bourgogne Blanc made by a grower in one of the major villages of the Côte d'Or (such as MEURSAULT for whites and VOLNAY or CHAMBOLLE-MUSIGNY for reds) is likely to be reliably fashioned in the image of classic CÔTE D'OR burgundy, however, and may well represent excellent value, being generally ready to drink sooner. There is every chance that the wine will be made from vines only just outside the village appellation yet will be sold at half the price.

CRÉMANT de Bourgogne is the generic appellation for sparkling Burgundy, either white or rosé, while the now-rare red version is classified as **Bourgogne Mousseux**.

See also BOURGOGNE ALIGOTÉ, BOURGOGNE PASSETOUTGRAINS, and Coteaux BOURGUIGNONS. J.T.C.M.

Bourgogne, Université de. See DIJON.

Bourgogne Aligoté, a generic appellation in Burgundy for white wines made from the ALIGOTÉ grape, whose production remains stable, despite a recent and sustainable boom in popularity, at around 1,600 ha/3,950 acres. Formerly either refreshingly crisp or disagreeably tart, the latter characteristic providing the basis for *vin blanc cassis*, or KIR, Aligoté has blossomed in recent warmer vintages. Traditionally flourishing in locations such as Chitry in the Yonne, Pernand-Vergelesses in the Côte de Beaune, and BOUZERON (which has its own appellation for Aligoté), Aligoté is now found in ageworthy SINGLE-VINEYARD variations by more enterprising producers. The golden Aligoté Doré is a old selection of the grape, typically found in Bouzeron. J.T.C.M.

Bourgogne Passetoutgrains, red thirst-quencher from Burgundy made from at least 30% Pinot Noir in a blend with Gamay grapes. Often deep in colour and rather savagely animal when young, Passetoutgrains with age can attain greater refinement as the Pinot Noir flavours start to dominate. The best examples come from vineyards in the CÔTE D'OR lying in the plain beyond the main D974 road which divides the finer vineyards from the generic. Only a little more than 200 ha/494 acres remain dedicated to this appellation. J.T.C.M.

Bourgueil, notable red wines made on the north bank of the Loire in the west of the TOURAINE district. Historically related to ANJOU, with which it shares its milder climate, its 1,400 ha/3,400 acres of vineyard experience more oceanic influence than CHINON. Two distinct terroirs shape Bourgueil wines: the lighter, earlier maturing and dominant style comes from the south-facing, alluvial terraces of GRAVEL and SAND in the area closest to the river, while the structured, long-lived bottlings are grown on the TUFFEAU slopes especially in Restigné, Benais, and Bourgueil.

Cabernet Sauvignon is permitted, but CABERNET FRANC is the primary grape. Lean wines are still produced (especially BULK WINES), but quality Bourgueil from the gravel (often made using SEMI-CARBONIC MACERATION) can be explosively juicy with raspberry flavour, while earthier, silkier BARREL-AGED bottlings from the chalk hills can compete with the best CHINON and SAUMUR. In the west, **St-Nicolas-de-Bourgueil**, whose mayor fought in 1937 for it to have its own appellation, generally produces a lighter style, as most of its 1,100 ha/2,700 acres of vines grow on deep, gravelly sand.

A little dry rosé Bourgueil is also made, but the appellation does not, unlike Chinon, encompass white wines. See LOIRE, including map. P. Le.

Bourguignons, Coteaux. This 2013 appellation replaced Bourgogne Grande Ordinaire, applying to minor Burgundy vineyards, growing ALIGOTÉ, Chardonnay, MELON de Bourgogne, Pinot Blanc, and/or Pinot Gris for whites, and Gamay, Pinot Noir, and CÉSAR (in the Yonne) for reds. The key to this is the inclusion of the Gamay grape because the rules for BEAUJOLAIS allow de- or re-classification as Coteaux Bourguignons. J.T.C.M

Bouschet is, like Müller, Scheu, and Seibel, a vine-breeder's surname that lives on in the name of his creations, although in this case there were two Bouschets, a 19th-century father and son whose work, perhaps unfortunately, made the spread of ARAMON possible. In 1824 Louis Bouschet de Bernard combined the productivity of Aramon with the colour expected of a red wine by crossing Aramon with TEINTURIER du Cher and modestly calling the result Petit Bouschet. This expedient CROSS was popular in France throughout the second half of the 19th century and is still, just, to be found in Portugal. Louis's son Henri carried on where his father left off, producing more durably ALICANTE BOUSCHET and GRAND NOIR DE LA CALMETTE as well as a Carignan Bouschet.

Boutenac, subappellation in the north-east of CORBIÈRES.

Bouvier, minor, low-acid white grape variety grown mainly in the Burgenland region of AUSTRIA, where it is particularly used for FEDERWEISSER, as well as for early-bottled wines. It can also be found in Slovenia, Slovakia, and Hungary.

Bouzeron, village in the Côte CHALONNAISE dedicated to the ALIGOTÉ grape. Production is increasing, with 161 ha/393 acres declared in 2018, up from 52 ha in 2012. J.T.C.M.

Bovale, dark-skinned grapes on SARDINIA distinguished as **Bovale Sardo**, a synonym for GRACIANO, and the more common **Bovale Grande**, a synonym for CARIGNAN. Both are used mainly for blending.

boxes, wine. In the late 1960s, an entirely new way of PACKAGING wine was developed in Australia, expressly to provide a significant volume of wine in a package that is not as breakable or heavy as a glass bottle. Subsequent improvements have resulted in a convenient container that is able to preserve wine for up to four to six weeks after opening.

It comprises a collapsible multilayer bag inside a strong cardboard carton (hence bag-in-box, or BIB). Wine is drawn out of a tap designed to minimize the ingress of potentially harmful OXYGEN. Minimizing the oxygen ingress of the bag itself is also critical to the success of the format. There are two main types of bag: in the silver-coloured ones, the oxygen barrier is created by a thin layer of aluminium, usually provided by an aluminium-coated polyester sandwiched between layers of polyethylene via a lamination process; in the clear bags, the barrier is provided by ethylene vinyl alcohol copolymer (EVOH) co-extruded between layers of polyethylene. The main disadvantage of the former is 'flex cracking', which tends to occur during transportation and weakens the oxygen barrier. Both types have significantly reduced OXYGEN TRANSMISSION RATES compared with earlier versions.

This package, known flatteringly as 'cask wine' in Australia (less flatteringly as 'goon bags'), most commonly holds 2.25 or 3 litres of wine. It has grown in popularity in recent years: Sweden, Norway, and Australia all consume 50% or more of their wine from a box. This growth is in part because the improvements to the bags and taps have encouraged winemakers and importers to use this format for higher-quality wine, but also because of its low CARBON FOOTPRINT. A series of life-cycle assessments have identified the BIB format as having the lowest carbon footprint associated with any commonly used wine packaging (more than seven times lower than even lightweight glass bottles). Despite these improvements, bag-in-box wine has a shorter lifespan prior to opening than traditional bottles, typically 9–12 months from filling, although some wines will last longer. For this reason, wines packed in this format are normally those that are considered ready to drink.

Gaia Consulting, 'Update of wine packaging LCA: final report Alko Oy' (2021). www.alko.fi/INTERSHOP/static/WFS/Alko-OnlineShop-Site/-/Alko-OnlineShop/fi_FI/Tavarantoimittajille/Muut/EN/Alko%20wine%20packaging%20LCA%20update_final%20report.pdf.

Brachetto, distinctively aromatic light red grape variety found principally and most successfully round Asti, Roero, and Alessandria in the PIEMONTE region of Italy, although it is also found in Emilia-Romagna. It produces wines, notably **Brachetto d'Acqui** promoted to DOCG status in 1996, that are fizzy, are light in alcohol (usually under 6%), and have both the colour and flavour of roses or strawberries—the light red equivalent of MOSCATO D'ASTI. Occasional dry versions are made in Piemonte. Total Italian plantings in 2015 were 1,692 ha/4,181 acres. Some is planted in Victoria, Australia.

Bragato, Romeo, Dalmatian-born graduate of Italian viticulture studies and employee of the Victorian government in Australia, invited in 1895 to investigate the prospects for viticulture and winemaking in New Zealand. His report was very favourable and became an important document encouraging the development of the industry.

Bragato identified PHYLLOXERA in New Zealand in 1895 and suggested the use of resistant ROOTSTOCKS, but his advice was initially ignored. Offered the position of government viticulturist in 1902, he immediately began importing and distributing these rootstocks (which were to be used again to fight phylloxera outbreaks of the 1980s). He established a research station at Te Kauwhata with experimental vineyards and a training winery, and he also published a handbook, *Viticulture in New Zealand*. Bragato and the fledgling wine industry were, however, not supported by his masters in the Department of Agriculture. In 1908 he lost control of the Te Kauwhata Research Station and in 1909 migrated to Canada in disgust. R.E.S.

Bramaterra, tiny DOC in Italy's Alto PIEMONTE enjoying a renaissance, going from 28 ha in 2014 to 41.5 ha/102 acres in 2020. Wines should contain 50–80% Nebbiolo with CROATINA, UVA RARA, and VESPOLINA. See SPANNA for more detail.

Brancellao, Galician name for the ALVARELHÃO of the Douro.

branco, Portuguese for 'white'. *Vinho branco* is therefore white wine.

brands, interpreted strictly as individual products marketed on the basis of their name and image rather than on their inherent qualities, have a much less dominant position in the market for wine than for drinks such as beer or cola, for instance; thanks to GLOBALIZATION, however, they are growing in importance. The leading industry resource IMPACT Databank calculated that the global market share of the top 25 wine brands in the world, while having grown significantly since the mid 1990s, was still less than 10% by 2020, with three of the top five brands—Franzia (including sangria), Barefoot from GALLO, and all the Robert MONDAVI lines—from California. It is perhaps significant that IMPACT is based in the United States, where distribution is tightly controlled (see THREE-TIER SYSTEM, for example) and where brands account for more than half of all wine sales.

Most sectors of the wine market are relatively fragmented (although the FORTIFIED WINE business is not and has been built on brands), so that brand promotion is difficult to make cost-effective and can leave **branded wines** looking poor value. By far the most common promotion in the 21st century has been based on PRICE and close relationships with the decreasing number of multiple retailers, many of which have been turning away from third-party brands to their own exclusive labels.

Wine brands offer a familiar lifeline to new wine consumers baffled by a multiplicity of unfamiliar, often foreign, proper names. But as wine drinkers become more sophisticated, they learn to decode what initially seems the arcane language of wine names, usually by identifying the major VARIETALS, some of the more important place names, and/or favourite producers. Thus, brands are most sought after in embryonic and fast-growing markets, such as northern Europe and the rest of the English-speaking world between the 1950s and the 1980s, or in Africa and some Asian countries today.

It may be difficult to market branded wines in a competitive market, but it can be even more difficult to maintain consistency of a product as variable as wine. Supplies are strictly limited to an annual batch production process. Wine cannot be manufactured to suit demand, and different vintages impose their own characteristics on the product regardless of consumer taste. A high proportion of all wine drinkers were introduced to wine through brands, and it is to the credit of those brand owners most dedicated to maintaining quality standards whenever the introduction was a happy one.

Notably successful international individual wine brands are relatively few, and they have perforce to be based on wine of which there is no shortage of supply. BLUE NUN, MATEUS rosé, and MOUTON CADET are all examples of brands which in the 20th century achieved annual sales measured in millions of cases. YELLOW TAIL was the miracle brand of the early 21st century.

There are those who argue that the grape varieties CHARDONNAY and PINOT GRIGIO, for example, like the extraordinarily popular PROSECCO, have become brands in their own right, so strong is consumer recognition of the name. Others claim that in certain markets buyers' own brands have become so important, and so cleverly marketed, that, for example, some retailers' names have established themselves as brands. The definition of a wine brand is certainly a loose one. In some respects, the New French CLARETS, named for the estate which produced them, were the first wine brands, emerging in the late 17th century; today, though, the French wine industry blames some of its difficulty in selling everything it produces on its failure to build brands, in conspicuous contrast to the bigger companies in Australia and the US. Certainly any definition which incorporates the notion of relatively elastic supply and some studied promotion would allow that the most successful wine brands of all are the so-called *grande marque* (which translates directly as 'big brand') CHAMPAGNES. In his book, Graham Harding argues that the British created many of these brands in the 19th century.

Harding, G., *Champagne in Britain, 1800–1914* (2021).

Braquet, also called **Brachet**, historic light red grape variety of PROVENCE which is still a valued, if minor, ingredient in the red and pink wines of BELLET near Nice. Yields are low and the vine is relatively delicate, but the wine is truly distinctive. This variety is not related to the much more aromatic Italian BRACHETTO.

Brazil, is the third most important wine producer in South America after Argentina and Chile, although most of its 81,000 ha/200,155 acres of vineyards in 2021 remain planted with non-VITIS VINIFERA varieties. In 2020 there were an estimated 1,200 wineries in Brazil, mostly small family businesses. The country produces a vast variety of wines, with a particular strength in sparkling wines.

History

The first vines were introduced by Portuguese explorers in the state of São Paulo in 1532, but the vines withered in the region's excessive heat and humidity. European settlers followed, planting vines in different areas, eventually finding success in Rio Grande do Sul, in the extreme south, where Brazil shares its border with Argentina and Uruguay.

By the mid 1800s, the industry had turned to high-yielding AMERICAN HYBRIDS such as CONCORD, Isabel (ISABELLA), and NIAGARA to cope with climatic conditions. Hybrids, in fact, still make up most of production: Vinho Fino ('fine wine'), defined as wine produced with *vinifera*, corresponds roughly to 10% of production, and Isabel, brought to Brazil in 1840, is the country's most widely planted variety. Italian immigrants arriving in the late 1870s brought, among other things, grape varieties such as BARBERA, BONARDA, MOSCATO, and TREBBIANO, with mixed results.

The industry entered a new phase in the 1970s when international companies such as Martini & Rossi, MOËT & CHANDON, and Seagram started investing in Brazilian vineyards, bringing new cuttings of *vinifera* varieties including Cabernet Sauvignon, Cabernet Franc, Merlot, Chardonnay, Sémillon, Welschriesling, and Gewürztraminer. These companies also introduced modern winemaking equipment such as automatic TEMPERATURE CONTROL, STAINLESS STEEL, and BARRIQUES.

Competition stepped up in the 1990s, when the Brazilian government reduced import barriers. The increased competition for market share, especially from neighbouring countries CHILE and ARGENTINA, inspired a new round of investments in technology and infrastructure of the wine sector, with lasting effects on wine quality.

Geography and climate

Brazil is a large country, the distance between its north and south equivalent to the distance between London and Baghdad. Grapes are grown in most of its 26 states; however, the most southerly, Rio Grande do Sul (which includes the subregions of Serra Gaúcha, Serra do Sudeste, Campanha, and Campos de Cima da Serra), is responsible for around 90% of total still-wine production and 85% of SPARKLING WINE production.

Colonized mainly by Italian settlers, **Serra Gaúcha** is responsible for the largest proportion of the country's production, most of it made from American and hybrid varieties grown by farmers with average holdings of just 2.5 ha/6 acres. It is here that international companies invested with the objective of capturing a share of the domestic market. This area includes **Vale dos Vinhedos**, Brazil's first DO, created in 2009 and located immediately east of the town of Bento Gonçalves, considered Brazil's wine capital. It also includes Garibaldi, heavily influenced by Italian descendants and traditionally renowned for its sparkling wine. Styles vary from light, off-dry wines made using the TANK METHOD to serious, dry TRADITIONAL METHOD versions.

The undulating topography of Serra Gaúcha permits vineyards to be planted at ELEVATIONS of 300–850 m/984–2,789 ft. Soil is predominantly CLAY over BASALT, and annual average RAINFALL is around 1,700 mm/67 in, of which at least 700 mm falls during the growing season of September to February; hence vineyards were traditionally established using the PERGOLA system to mitigate excess humidity. Modern vineyards are planted using VSP (see VERTICAL TRELLIS). The main red varieties are Merlot, Cabernet Sauvignon, Pinot Noir, Tannat, and Cabernet Franc. Chardonnay, Riesling Itálico (WELSCHRIESLING), many varieties of Moscato, and GLERA are the principal white varieties.

Serra do Sudeste, in the south of the state, is drier and more TEMPERATE, noted for cold winters, dry springs, and warm summers. Its gentle slopes, at 200–500 m/656–1,640 ft in elevation, and granitic soil have demonstrated great potential with many varieties including ALICANTE BOUSCHET, Barbera, Cabernet Franc, Cabernet Sauvignon, Merlot, and Pinot Noir for red wines and Gewürztraminer, Riesling, Moscato, MALVASIA de Cândia, and especially Chardonnay for whites.

Campanha, at LATITUDES 29–31° S, shares a long border with URUGUAY. Unlike in most of the country, seasons here are well defined, with hot summers and winter temperatures dipping to −10 °C/50 °F. Gently undulating plains at 100–300 m/328–984 ft in elevation with sandy soils are suitable for many red varieties such as Cabernet Sauvignon, Cabernet Franc, Merlot, TANNAT, TEROLDEGO, Pinot Noir, MARSELAN, Touriga Nacional, and Tempranillo. White varieties are also cultivated, especially Chardonnay, Sauvignon Blanc, Viognier, Pinot Gris, and Gewürztraminer. Wines tends to be ripe and round, with balanced acidity.

Campos de Cima da Serra is in the north of Rio Grande do Sul, bordering the state of Santa Catarina. Situated on a high plateau at 900–1,100 m/2,953–3,609 ft, the region enjoys a cool climate, with continuous breezes to help protect against FUNGAL DISEASES. The ripening season is long, lasting into early April, whereas harvest in Campanha is typically finished by March. The DIURNAL TEMPERATURE RANGE can be 15 °C/27 °F, ensuring fresh acidity and well-structured wines. Since 2000 there have been several investments, and interesting wines are emerging from varieties such as Cabernet Sauvignon, Cabernet Franc, Merlot, Pinot Noir, Tannat, ANCELLOTA, and Petit Verdot as well as white varieties such as Chardonnay, Sauvignon Blanc, Moscato, Viognier, Glera, and Gewürztraminer.

In the state of Santa Catarina, **Planalto Catarinense** is renowned for being the coldest place in Brazil. Its icy weather has enabled production of the country's first naturally made ICE WINE. Elevations can reach 1,400 m/4,593 ft, hence an association has been created by a group of producers centred at São Joaquim Plateau to promote Vinhos de Altura (High-Altitude Wines). Conditions are especially suited to Sauvignon Blanc and Pinot Noir, while long growing cycles also ensure adequate phenolic ripeness (see PHYSIOLOGICAL RIPENESS) for Cabernet Sauvignon, Merlot, Malbec, Cabernet Franc, Tannat, Syrah, Sangiovese, Nebbiolo, Montepulciano, and Tempranillo.

Vale do Rio São Francisco is the second largest wine-producing area after Rio Grande do Sul (RS). In the north of the country, between the states of Pernambuco and Bahia, it is defined by the São Francisco River, which provides the water for the IRRIGATION that is essential in this semi-arid climate. There is no winter at this latitude; the average temperature is 26 °C/79 °F and the sun shines 300 days a year. Less than 300 mm/12 in of rain falls annually. To encourage vine DORMANCY, producers withhold water. Once the plant is pruned and irrigation re-established, a new growing cycle begins (see TROPICAL VITICULTURE). With such techniques it is possible to harvest individual plots twice each year, which makes grape-growing commercially attractive. Unlike in RS, where most of production is done by smallholders, this region is dominated by a handful of large producers. Red varieties planted include Syrah, Cabernet Sauvignon, Tempranillo, Touriga Nacional, and Alicante Bouschet. White varieties include Moscato, Chardonnay, and Chenin Blanc.

Emerging areas

The state of São Paulo, originally dismissed for being too hot and humid for winegrowing, is today responsible for some of the country's best wines. At its northern end, 200 km/124 miles from São Paulo city, Sauvignon Blanc, Chardonnay, and Viognier have shown potential, and Syrah and Cabernet Franc grown at elevations of 800–1,300 m can be exceptional. To overcome the adverse weather, growers prune twice, forcing the crop to ripen during winter months when conditions are cooler and drier. Over the border, in the state of Minas Gerais, renowned for its coffee plantations, a number of developments have shown serious potential, particularly for Sauvignon Blanc, Chardonnay, Tempranillo, and Syrah. There are also significant projects expanding throughout the states of Paraná, Espirito Santo, Goiás, and Bahia.

As wine quality has improved in the last three decades, Brazilian consumers' interest in wine has followed suit. In 2020, per capita consumption stood at around 2 l/0.5 gal, with the highest consumption in major cities and in the south, where wine is part of the culture due to historical links with Europe. Overall, more than 80% of the still wine consumed in Brazil is imported; by contrast, local producers supply over 80% of sparkling wine sold. Collective work by producers aligned with a clear, consistent message would help Brazilian wines gain more awareness in international markets. D.V.J.

breathing, an operation, believed beneficial by some consumers, involving pulling the cork and letting the open bottle stand for a few hours before it is poured. In fact, in such circumstances the wine can take only the most minimal of 'breaths', and any change is bound to be imperceptible (except possibly in the case of BOTTLE SHOCK). The surface area of wine exposed to the air is so small that the effects of any AERATION as a result of this operation are negligible. See DECANTING for details of effective aeration.

Breede River Valley, important wine region in SOUTH AFRICA.

breeding. See VINE BREEDING.

Breganze, DOC in the VENETO region in north-east Italy, mainly for INTERNATIONAL VARIETIES. Wines of real interest are produced from Bordeaux varieties, but TAI BIANCO, the red MARZEMINO, and the rare Gruaja, probably related to Valpolicella's NEGRARA Veronese, add distinction to the DOC. The local VESPAIOLA, used for the BOTRYTIZED or DRIED-GRAPE sweet white speciality Torcolato, is increasingly produced in a complex dry version called Vespaiolo. There is also a growing number of TRADITIONAL METHOD sparkling wines, which must be made of Pinot Noir only. Maculan put Breganze on the map in the 1980s by focusing on quality instead of quantity: lowering yields, introducing modern winemaking equipment, and using BARRIQUES. Several estates followed his example, but the region receives little attention from the international market. W.S.

Breton, name sometimes used in the middle Loire for the CABERNET FRANC grape. The reference is not to Brittany but to Abbot Breton, who is reputed to have disseminated the vine in the 17th century.

Brettanomyces, sometimes called **brett**, one of the YEAST genera found rarely on grapes but more often in wines, especially those that have undergone BARREL AGEING or CASK AGEING. *Brettanomyces* in its perfect or sporulating form was known as **Dekkera**, but changes to the rules for naming fungi suggest *Brettanomyces* should be used for both sporulating and non-sporulating forms. It is widely considered a spoilage yeast due to the production of off-flavours in wine. There are producers who suggest that at low levels some of the flavours produced by *Brettanomyces* can improve red-wine complexity, but it may not be possible to keep them at this low level. (In some beers, for example Belgium's spontaneously fermented lambic and gueuze beers, *Brettanomyces* and its effects are considered key stylistic attributes.)

The first isolation of *Brettanomyces*, originally designated *Mycotorula intermedia*, in wine was in the 1930s by Krumbholz and Tauschanoff. Although the number of *Brettanomyces* species has expanded and contracted due to changes in methods of identification, of the five species currently recognized, *Brettanomyces bruxellensis* is the only one that has been unequivocally associated with wines worldwide (although there is mounting evidence of hybrids being isolated from wine). This species can grow in both red and white wine, although it is more often associated with red.

A resourceful microbe, *Brettanomyces* can grow either anaerobically or aerobically and utilize a variety of substrates at low levels and under restrictive conditions. The range and quantity of by-products produced by *Brettanomyces* depend on various factors, including levels of substrates, available precursors, and the size of the *Brettanomyces* population in the wine. The most important substrate is RESIDUAL SUGAR, although some OXYGEN is needed to maximize growth.

There are four key by-products of *Brettanomyces* growth which can affect the flavour and aroma of a wine: esterases, volatile fatty acids, tetrahydropyridines, and, arguably the most important, volatile phenols. Two critical volatile phenol compounds have been isolated from *Brettanomyces* activity: 4-ethylphenol (4-EP) and 4-ethylguaiacol (4-EG). 4-EP is often described as introducing an 'animal', 'medicinal', and 'sweaty saddle' flavour to wine. Its presence is an almost certain indicator of a *Brettanomyces* infection, and this is what most diagnostic laboratories test for to verify the presence of *Brettanomyces*. 4-EG in wine has a more appealing smoky, spicy, clove-like aroma. Formation of tetrahydropyridines, which are responsible for MOUSY off-flavour, seems to result from a large population of *Brettanomyces* which is stimulated by exposure of wine to oxygen, for example when the wine is on ULLAGE.

Brettanomyces can create significant levels of volatile phenols in a short period of time and is difficult to manage in the cellar. However, the tools for monitoring *Brettanomyces* have never been more advanced, and winemakers can use microbiological techniques such as selective growth media containing cycloheximide (to inhibit the growth of *Saccharomyces*) and odourless hydroxyphenolic acid precursors (to allow for the production of volatile phenols), DNA-based identification methods, and/or analytical techniques such as gas chromatography–mass spectrometry to monitor volatile-phenol production in high-risk wines.

Brettanomyces strains display variable sensitivity to SULFUR DIOXIDE. Recent research suggests that winery populations are adapting to it but that these more resistant strains can be controlled by maintaining at least 0.625 mg/l molecular sulfur dioxide. Wines are at greatest risk of spoilage if fermentation is sluggish, if the onset of MALOLACTIC CONVERSION is delayed, or if there is insufficient molecular sulfur dioxide present during maturation. HYGIENE is an important factor in controlling the spread of *Brettanomyces* in the cellar. Areas that provide suitable niches for *Brettanomyces* are must lines, dirty crush equipment, barrels, or any tank or transfer line that is not cleaned effectively. There have also been suggestions that the fruit fly (see DROSOPHILA) can carry *Brettanomyces*. Once it is embedded in COOPERAGE, it can be difficult to eliminate from the cellar, and barrels may need to be discarded to significantly reduce the populations. As with other microbes, the cleaner the winery the more control one has over *Brettanomyces*. There are currently only two methods that virtually eliminate *Brettanomyces* at bottling: sterile FILTRATION and dimethyl dicarbonate (see DMDC). A.B.

Chatonnet, P., et al., 'The influence of Brettanomyces/Dekkera sp. yeasts and lactic acid bacteria on the ethylphenol content of red wines', *American Journal of Enology and Viticulture*, 46/4 (1995), 463–8.

Conterno, L., et al., 'Genetic and physiological characterization of *Brettanomyces bruxellensis* strains isolated from wines', *American Journal of Enology and Viticulture*, 57 (2006), 139–47.

Curtin, C., et al., 'Genotype-dependent sulphite tolerance of Australian *Dekkera* (*Brettanomyces*) *bruxellensis* wine isolates', *Letters in Applied Microbiology*, 55 (2012), 56–61.

Romano, A., et al., 'Sensory and analytical re-evaluation of "Brett character"', *Food Chemistry*, 114/1 (2009), 15–19.

Silva, P., et al., 'Studies on the wine spoilage capacity of *Brettanomyces/Dekkera* spp.', *American Journal of Enology and Viticulture*, 55/1 (2004), 65–72.

Snowdon, E. M., et al., 'Mousy off-flavor: a review', *Journal of Agricultural and Food Chemistry*, 54/18 (2006), 6465–74.

bricco, or ***bric*** in the dialect of the north-west Italian region of PIEMONTE, indicates the highest part of an elevation in the landscape or, in particular, a vineyard with a steep gradient at the top of a hill. The term was first used on a wine label by Luciano de Giacomi in 1969 for his Bricco del Drago, a blend of DOLCETTO and NEBBIOLO grapes from Alba, and has been extensively used for the other wines of Piemonte ever since.

Brindisi, Adriatic port and DOC in PUGLIA for robust red wine made mainly from NEGROAMARO grapes and Chardonnay-based whites shipped mainly in BULK.

Britain, or **Great Britain**, has long been one of the most important markets for wine. It regularly imports more wine than any country other than Germany and has shown unusually healthy growth in wine CONSUMPTION since the late 20th century. Its long wine-MERCHANT tradition has made it one of the most discerning, yet open-minded, wine-consuming nations, and London has been an important centre for wine AUCTIONS and FINE WINE trading. Domestic vine-growing in England and Wales has now grown to a scale where most supermarkets and independent wine merchants stock English and Welsh wines, and they can be found on wine lists in many hotels and restaurants. A certain amount of wine is also made from imported GRAPE CONCENTRATE (see MADE-WINE). Historically, Britain's commercial influence helped shape the very existence of such wines as claret, madeira, marsala, port, and sherry (see BRITISH INFLUENCE ON THE WINE TRADE).

See also ENGLAND (especially for history and modern viticulture), SCOTLAND, and WALES.

British Columbia is CANADA's second largest wine region, with 4,478 ha/11,065 acres of vines in the west of the country. European vines are well suited to the various growing areas once believed too cold for VITIS VINIFERA. The province is divided into nine GEOGRAPHICAL INDICATIONS (GIs) with five official sub-GIs. The **Fraser Valley** (40.5 ha/100 acres) near Vancouver and the coastal appellations **Gulf Islands** (46.5 ha) and **Vancouver Island** (112 ha, which includes the **Cowichan Valley** sub-GI) have a cool MARITIME CLIMATE and are largely planted to early-ripening varieties (Pinot Gris, Pinot Noir, Bacchus). Many wineries here buy additional grapes from the dominant appellation **Okanagan Valley** (3,892 ha/9,617 acres) and nearby **Similkameen Valley** (256 ha/633 acres). These latter appellations, comprising 92.5% of British Columbia's vineyards, are 400 km/249 miles east of Vancouver, in the rain shadow of the Coastal Mountain Range. The short growing season is hot and arid, which makes it suited to ORGANIC VITICULTURE. Hot, dry summers have also led to increased risk of WILDFIRES. With the lowest precipitation in southern Canada, IRRIGATION is essential.

Four more GIs were announced in 2018: **Thompson Valley** (36 ha/90 acres), **Shuswap** (40.5 ha), **Lillooet** (20 ha), and the **Kootenays** (34 ha) are small inland regions where vineyards and orchards have grown for decades.

The Okanagan Valley, a superbly scenic glacial trench extending from the 49th parallel north for about 160 km/100 miles, is defined by the vast Okanagan Lake, the largest of the valley's chain of lakes, which tempers the summer heat (see LAKE EFFECT). The southern part of the Okanagan is desert-like and very hot and dry during the growing season. Vineyards throughout the Okanagan are planted on CLAY, GRAVEL, SAND, or LOAM with soil drainage properties depending on site.

The first vines in the Okanagan were planted in 1859 by a French Oblate priest, Charles Pandosy. The earliest attempt at commercial grape-growing was near Salmon Arm in 1907 (in the present-day Shuswap GI) and in 1927 horticulturalist J. W. Hughes planted VITIS LABRUSCA vines in Kelowna and sold grapes to the province's first two wineries.

Plantings of *labrusca* continued over the next 30 years with winter-hardy French and American HYBRIDS introduced in the 1960s. There were also a few experimental plantings with *vinifera*. In 1961 Quail's Gate Winery planted Chasselas, which was mistakenly included in its order of hybrid vines, and in the late 1960s Chenin Blanc and Trebbiano were planted in the south Okanagan Valley. In 1977 the British Columbia government established the Becker Project, hiring Helmut Becker of Germany's GEISENHEIM Grape Breeding Institute to undertake planting trials of Riesling, Pinot Blanc, EHRENFELSER, SCHEUREBE, and GEWÜRZTRAMINER, with many early plantings overseen by Osoyoos Indian Band at their Inkameep Vineyards in the south Okanagan. The positive results spurred more *vinifera* plantings. In the 1970s and 1980s on Vancouver Island there were also government-funded planting trials of almost 100 varieties, including the now widely grown ORTEGA, Pinot Noir, and Pinot Gris.

The 1988 free-trade agreement between Canada and the United States was also a catalyst for quality as it removed the subsidies and protections domestic wines had enjoyed against competing imports. Through federal government assistance, more than two-thirds of *labrusca* and French hybrid vineyards in the Okanagan were pulled out and replaced with *vinifera*.

As the number of wineries grew, the industry formed the British Columbia Wine Institute in 1990 (now known as Wine Growers British Columbia) and adapted the ONTARIO-developed Vintners Quality Alliance (VQA) regulations, which imposed the region's first significant standards of wine quality.

By 2021 British Columbia boasted 288 wineries working with more than 90 grape varieties, with Merlot, Pinot Noir, and Cabernet Sauvignon leading the reds and Pinot Gris, Chardonnay, and Gewürztraminer dominating whites. The appellation rules allow for a wide variety of styles, from sparkling wine to ICEWINE. J.D.

British influence on the wine trade. For centuries, wine consumption in Britain has had significant ramifications in many of the world's most important wine regions. A cool, wet climate has limited the production of wine in ENGLAND, so that British wine drinkers historically had no choice but to look overseas for their supplies. Since they owe no permanent allegiance to any one wine region or wine-producing country, they have traditionally had a broad range from which to choose, although that choice has been dictated by convenience, FASHION, ECONOMICS, and POLITICS as often as by taste.

British influence on the wine trade resulted from more complex circumstances than a simple lack of native wines, however. (Otherwise, British influence on the wine trade would be no greater than, for example, Swedish or Danish—although see DUTCH WINE TRADE.) Britain enjoyed a unique combination of factors: relative prosperity and political power, a worldwide commercial empire supported by a strong navy, and a steadily increasing middle class. These circumstances not only helped to foster an interest in imported wines but also provided the economic clout to acquire them. And at certain times in history, in specific wine regions, the British market was so influential that wine styles evolved, or completely new wines were invented, to satisfy its demands.

The first region fully to devote itself to British needs was SOUTH WEST FRANCE, when it belonged to the English Crown. Indeed it could be argued that for 300 years, from 1152, Britain did have its own extensive vineyards. During this period BORDEAUX was transformed into the most important wine centre in France. Vineyards were planted or extended around the city and far up the rivers Garonne and Dordogne to quench the English thirst. The loss of Bordeaux to the French in 1453 saw a decline in exports to England, but this part of France was by now well established as a commercial wine region.

During the Middle Ages, wine was relatively cheap and plentiful in Britain. Wines from Germany, Portugal, Spain, Italy, Greece, the Mediterranean islands, and the Holy Land could all be found in London taverns, as well as those from France. It was not until the 16th century, however, that British merchants found, in southern Spain, a wine region to compensate for the loss of Bordeaux. Known collectively as SACK, the wines of Andalucía became immensely fashionable in Tudor times despite wars with Spain. Thousands of BUTTS of wine were sent back to England by British merchants settled in Sanlúcar and MÁLAGA. British taste and investment laid the foundations of what was to become the SHERRY industry.

The 17th century brought many problems for wine. The introduction of exotic new beverages such as coffee, chocolate, and teas, as well as the growing popularity of 'hopped' beer, threatened the wine trade. The situation was not eased by the fact that the cost of wine had steadily grown to such a point that only the middle and upper classes could afford it. Crippling customs duties exacerbated the crisis. If the wine trade was to survive in Britain, some drastic changes were needed.

Medieval CLAIRET and Tudor sack had been staple beverages enjoyed by many English. British influence at the end of the 17th century was felt by a different sort of wine producer and encouraged the development of sophisticated superior-quality wines which only a limited clientele could afford. This select English market had particular influence in two areas of France: Bordeaux and CHAMPAGNE.

After the Restoration of Charles II in 1660, all things French were extremely fashionable in London. At this time individual producers in both Champagne and Bordeaux were making efforts to improve the quality of their wines. Champagne was promoted in London by French exiles (although it was English aristocrats who developed the taste for sparkling wine while French connoisseurs decried it as an aberration). Meanwhile a wealthy landowner from Bordeaux, Arnaud de Pontac, succeeded in creating a stir when he opened a restaurant in London, Pontack's Head in Abchurch Street, to sell the wines of his Graves estate of HAUT-BRION.

B

The English aristocracy were delighted by these new styles of French wines, CLARET, and paid through the nose for them. Thus London became the chief market for fine wine and in turn influenced the quality of the wines themselves, for in the wine trade it is export that makes reputations, raises standards, and, above all, provides the driving force for investment. New vineyards were planted in Champagne and in the MÉDOC to exploit these refined English palates and purses.

The next great instance of a British-inspired wine was PORT. The exorbitant cost of champagne and good-quality claret, combined with the supply difficulties that resulted from war with France, caused British merchants to look elsewhere. Political rapprochement with Portugal signalled the possibility of a new, and cheap, source of wine. The British moved into OPORTO, prospected the DOURO Valley for wine and vine-growing potential, and started a boom. Huge quantities of port were sent to Britain from the early 1700s, and as the century progressed the nature of the wine evolved to suit. Originally a rough red table wine, port was soon discovered to be improved by the addition of brandy, which made it even more palatable to the English and considerably more stable for the sea voyage required. A whole new industry was created, and the steep sides of the Douro Valley terraced and planted to victual the English shires.

Similarly, Sicily's MARSALA wine industry was developed by the British when, in the early years of the 19th century, Napoleon set up his Continental System in the hopes that, by depriving his enemies of French wine (among other things), he could cause British morale to collapse.

In 1860, William Gladstone stated that an Englishman's taste in wine 'is not an immutable, but a mutable thing'. He meant that British palates were capable of adapting to whatever was most available or pleasing at any particular period. A host of factors influenced taste, and in turn demand influenced supply. Of all wine-drinking societies, Britain showed these developments most strikingly. Top-quality claret, sparkling champagne, and distinguished vintage port are today sought after all over the world. But ties of tradition and affection remain strong with the British market, a reminder of the fundamental part it played in the evolution of these and many other wines and the wine trade in general.

From the early 1980s, Great Britain was targeted by many of the world's wine producers as one of the few substantial wine markets in which per capita wine consumption was growing. In 2021, according to OIV statistics, only Germany and the US imported more wine than Great Britain, but 56% of German imports were of BULK WINE compared with 32% and 35% for the US and the UK respectively.

The revival of selling wine at AUCTION and the resultant nucleus of FINE WINE traders made London the focus of the fine-wine market until the US and HONG KONG took over. But Britain retains its influence as the chief production centre for the LITERATURE OF WINE and for wine EDUCATION. H.B. & J.R.

Francis, A. D., *The Wine Trade* (1972).

Johnson, H., *The Story of Wine: From Noah to Now* (2020).

Simon, A. L., *The History of the Wine Trade in England* (1906–9).

British wine, a curious alcoholic drink made in the image of WINE from dried grapes, MUST, or GRAPE CONCENTRATE, typically imported into Great Britain. It is known as MADE-WINE, and a decidedly manufactured product it is. It may also contain other fruits or vegetables, honey, sugar, and more. MEAD and ginger wine are also types of British wine.

Most commonly, grape concentrate is imported in bulk throughout the year from wherever happens to be able to supply the best value (Spain is a notable source). The must is reconstituted by adding water and is fermented using selected YEAST strains. Until the 1980s, almost all British wine produced was FORTIFIED, made to resemble sherry or port, or flavoured with ginger or other spices or fruits. Since the early 1980s, British wines of normal TABLE WINE strength have also been made, much to the dismay of the producers of English wine (see ENGLAND), with whose products made from freshly picked grapes there is possible confusion.

Producers of British wine, few and relatively industrial, claim as initial historical precedent a Francis Chamberleyne, who was granted a charter by Charles I in 1635 to make wine from imported raisins. The real catalyst for the establishment of an economically viable British wine trade came when a technique for the concentration of GRAPE JUICE was perfected by Emmanuel Roche of Toulouse, south-west France, who promptly shared it with two Greek brothers Mitzotakis, members of his wife's family, to help them sell a surplus stock of Greek grapes and grape juice in London in 1900. Their Crown Grape Wine Company (worryingly, on the site of a previous VINEGAR plant) eventually became Vine Products, whose premises outside the capital in Kingston-upon-Thames were described in the 1960s as 'the biggest BODEGA in Europe'. This highly profitable concern continued under various owners until 1989.

WSTA, *The Code of Practice of the British Wine Producers' Committee of the Wine and Spirit Trade Association* (2021).

Brittany, or Bretagne in French and Breizh in Breton, may be more known for its apple-based beverages, but winegrowing is increasing in popularity in the 21st century. The peninsula, which juts out into the Atlantic at France's north-western edge, has grown grapes since at least the 5th century but effectively disappeared from wine maps in the 20th century due in part to PHYLLOXERA and then to a Second World War-era prohibition against commercial wine production in the province which lasted until 1 January 2016. Since 2006, the ARVB (Association pour la reconnaissance des vins Breton) has encouraged winegrowing in Brittany; in 2021 a professional group, the ABV (Association des vignerons breton), was launched. By 2022 there were about 40 ha/99 acres of vines in commercial production, with many more in development. The most popularly grown grape varieties in this MARITIME CLIMATE include CHENIN BLANC, CHARDONNAY, PINOT GRIS, and SAVAGNIN, as well as the red grapes GAMAY and PINOT NOIR; there is also experimentation with disease-resistant HYBRIDS and varieties such as ALBARIÑO.

www.vigneronsbretons.bzh

Brix, scale of measuring total dissolved compounds in grape juice and therefore its approximate concentration of grape sugars. It is used in the United States; like other scales used elsewhere (see BAUMÉ and OECHSLE), it can be measured with either a REFRACTOMETER or HYDROMETER. Degrees Brix indicate the percentage of solutes (of which about 90% are sugars in ripe grapes) by weight in the liquid, at a temperature specified for the instrument used. One degree Brix corresponds approximately to 10 g/l sugar.

The **Balling** scale is similar although the specified temperature may differ. For more details, see MUST WEIGHT. B.G.C.

Broadbent, J. Michael (1927–2020), wine taster, writer, and auctioneer known particularly for his experience of fine, old wines. Broadbent trained initially as an architect in London and then joined the late Tommy Layton as a wine-trade trainee in 1952. Three years later he joined Harveys of Bristol, then in its heyday, where he worked for Harry WAUGH and eventually became UK sales director. In 1966, partly as a result of his own personal enterprise in corresponding with the chairman, Broadbent was taken on by Christie's to revive their, and the London, wine AUCTION business. From then until 1992 he ran Christie's wine department and in that capacity traded in and tasted a greater number of fine and rare wines than anyone else in the world.

Naturally didactic, he lectured on wine from the late 1950s and conducted wine tastings all over the world, always emphatically insisting on correct tasting conditions. Never inhibited about airing his elegant wine vocabulary in public, he painstakingly recorded his disciplined impressions of every wine tasted, nearly 120,000 of them in more than 150 notebooks.

It is these notebooks, retyped by his equally hard-working late wife Daphne, which formed the basis for Broadbent's *Great Vintage Wine Book* and the more discursive *Vintage Wine*, unique records of wine-tasting history which stretch back to wines of the early 18th century. Unlike PARKER, his most obvious rival as publisher of personal TASTING NOTES, Broadbent eschewed scoring wines with numbers, preferring to award up to five stars to each wine.

Broadbent's life was marked by competition, particularly with Sotheby's, and ambition. While at Christie's he not only wrote his own classic on the subject of *Wine Tasting*, first published in 1968 and much republished since, but instituted and directed Christie's Wine Publications, which issued many invaluable books—including the *Christie's Wine Review* anthologies—during the 1970s and 1980s. He also wrote a highly personal monthly column for the British magazine *Decanter* from its inception in 1977 until 2013.

Incurably active and apparently indefatigable, he became a MASTER OF WINE in 1960, a freeman of the City of London in 1964, chairman of the Institute of Masters of Wine in 1970, international president of the INTERNATIONAL WINE & FOOD SOCIETY in 1986, master of the City of London's Distillers' Company in 1990, and council chairman of the Wine & Spirit Trades Benevolent Society in 1991; he even stood, unsuccessfully, for sheriff of the City of London in 1993. He was made a Chevalier de l'Ordre du Mérite National in 1979, before he was implicated in the sale of the so-called Jefferson bottles, subsequently shown to be counterfeit. His second marriage, in 2019, was to Valerie Smallwood, the widow of a fellow MW, owner of another fine cellar. His son Bartholomew could be said to have helped establish the United States as the prime market for vintage PORT in the 1990s and continues as a wine importer there.

Broadbent, M., *Vintage Wine* (2002).
Broadbent, M., *Wine Tasting* (various editions 1968–2022).

Brock University is CANADA's leading university for vine- and wine-related ACADEME; it offers North America's only undergraduate and graduate degrees in the study of COOL-CLIMATE VITICULTURE and winemaking. It is home to the Cool Climate Oenology and Viticulture Institute (CCOVI), established in 1996. Students can participate in exchange programmes with Okanagan University College in British Columbia, neighbouring Niagara College, Acadia University in Nova Scotia, and LINCOLN UNIVERSITY in New Zealand. CCOVI graduates make wine in all regions of Canada, as well as in California, Australia, and Germany. The Institute conducts research on grapevine winter injury (see WINTER FREEZE), quality crop improvement through PRECISION VITICULTURE, disease and pest control, particularly SOUR ROT and the Multicoloured Asian Lady Beetle (see LADYBUG TAINT), ICEWINE production and authentication, sparkling wine production, and sensory and consumer perceptions of Ontario wine. CCOVI has created a Grape Preharvest Monitoring Program for berry SAMPLING and analysis, as well as VineAlert, a comparative grapevine-bud cold-hardiness database. Niagara College offers a Winery & Viticulture course as well as a graduate course in Wine Business Management. J.D.

www.brocku.ca/ccovi

brokers, important members of any trade and increasingly important when it comes to wine. Known charmingly as *courtiers* in French, brokers can play a vital role as intermediaries between vine-growers and merchants, or NÉGOCIANTS, discussing, collecting, and exhibiting hundreds of samples, or *échantillons*, and taking a small percentage of any eventual sale.

Another class of brokers, further along the distribution chain, guide those who sell wine through the maze of those who produce it, some of them nursing 'stables' of producers rather in the manner of a literary agent representing a rollcall of authors.

And then, just one or two links away from those who actually pull the cork, there are the FINE WINE brokers, those who sell from a list of glamorous properties and vintages which may, but often do not, belong to them. This last group, many of whom are based in Britain, represents one of the very few sectors of the wine trade that has been highly profitable. Several London firms did extremely well in the 1990s, and especially with the 2009 and 2010 Bordeaux EN PRIMEUR, as the number of wine collectors and investors around the world increased exponentially and ASIA woke up to the delights of fine wine. The sort of wine of interest to fine-wine brokers and traders typically sits in an unbroken CASE in a BONDED WAREHOUSE in Britain while being traded so profitably around the world. The profitability of this business was so obviously attractive to traditional MERCHANTS more used to trading and delivering individual bottles and cases of much less valuable wine that in the early and mid 1990s many of them set up their own broking divisions. Much of these brokers' trade is between their own established customers, a convenient internal market. Towards the turn of the century most of these fine-wine brokers established outposts, often extremely profitable, in HONG KONG.

Brouilly, largest of the BEAUJOLAIS crus, with 1,200 ha/3,000 acres of vineyards producing some of the region's most velvety wines. Vineyards flank the VOLCANIC Mont Brouilly, although **Côte de Brouilly** is an entirely separate appellation including just 315 ha/778 acres on the top portion of the hill. Its wines tend to be more concentrated and longer lived than those of Brouilly. J.F.B.

brown marmorated stink bug is, as the name suggests, an insect winegrowers would not want to crush along with their grapes. This insect (*Halyomorpha halys*) was an accidental introduction from Asia to Pennsylvania in the mid 1990s and is now found in more than 40 states, as well as in Canada, Germany, France, and Italy. The beetle releases two TAINT compounds, tridecane and E-2-decenal, that can affect wine quality. Despite widespread early concern in many parts of the world, the pest has not so far caused substantial problems for wine producers, probably because grapevines are not the insects' preferred food source. R.E.S.

CABI, 'Halyomorpha halys (brown marmorated stink bug)', Invasive Species Compendium. www.cabi.org/isc/datasheet/27377.

Brulhois, AOC in SOUTH WEST FRANCE encompassing 206 ha/510 vineyard acres in the rolling farmland near Agen on both sides of the Garonne. From medieval times Brulhois wines were blended with those of BORDEAUX, but the ravages of PHYLLOXERA in the late 19th century were followed by widespread planting of HYBRIDS. The district's wines made from recently replanted VITIS VINIFERA vines were given VIN DE PAYS status initially before elevation to VDQS in 1984 and to AOC in 2011. The majority are red and must be a blend of at least 70% Cabernet Franc, Merlot, and TANNAT (which must constitute 15–40% of the blend); they can include small amounts of FER, MALBEC, and ABOURIOU. The wines are often described as 'black' and are at their best after five years. Some rosé is also made. There are a handful of independent growers, but most wine is made by one of the two CO-OPERATIVES and consumed locally. P.S.

Brunello, Montalcino name for SANGIOVESE planted there.

Brunello di Montalcino, one of Italy's most prestigious red wines, having been invented as a wine by Ferruccio BIONDI-SANTI, the first to bottle it and give it a distinctive name, in 1865. Conventional descriptions of the birth of the wine stress Biondi-Santi's successful isolation of a superior CLONE of SANGIOVESE, the Sangiovese Grosso or Brunello, an investigation begun by his father Clemente Santi. The 1865 vintage of a wine Clemente had labelled 'brunello' had been a prize-winning entry in the agricultural fair of Montepulciano in 1869, indicating that genetically superior material was available in the zone at an earlier date. (Some records show the wines of Montalcino referred to as Brunello as early as the 14th century; see TUSCANY, history.) Only four vintages—1888, 1891, 1925, and 1945—were declared in the first 57 years of production, contributing an aura of rarity to the wine that translated into high prices and, in Italy at least, incomparable prestige. The Biondi-Santi were the only commercial producers until after the Second World War, and a government report of 1932 named Brunello as an exclusive product of the family, estimating its total annual production at just 200 hl/5,280 gal.

Until the 1960s the region was almost exclusively known for sweet and often sparkling MOSCADELLO. With the arrival of the American company Banfi at the end of the 1970s, Brunello's fortunes took a sharp turn. Banfi's owners, the Italo-American Mariani brothers, who had had huge commercial success with LAMBRUSCO, bought up whole swathes of land in the hotter, southern part of the zone which until then had never been vineyards, planting them with Moscadello for the production of a fizzy sweet white. The plan failed spectacularly, after which the vines were grafted over to Sangiovese and INTERNATIONAL VARIETIES. Banfi started to produce Brunello in great quantity and had such commercial success that soon Brunello turned into an internationally recognized brand with a distinct style. The region, which in the 1960s consisted of 11 producers on a mere 63.5 ha/157 acres, swelled to 2,100 ha/5,189 acres (plus 510 ha/1,260 acres for Rosso di Montalcino) shared by 260 producers by 2020. This dramatic increase was made possible by including land new to viticulture. In 1996 the DOC, Sant'Antimo, was added to the production regulations to allow for the international varieties that inevitably turned up in the wake of the success of SUPERTUSCANS.

The question of Brunello's true identity culminated in a blending scandal in 2008 when Italy's financial police sequestered batches of wines from several producers that were not the mandatory 100% Brunello but rather illegal blends containing international varieties. The scandal, known as Brunellogate (Brunellopoli in Italy), led to a controversial proposal, eventually rejected, to allow the addition of other varieties, highlighting the uncomfortable fact that the official Brunello zone may well include land unsuitable for Brunello vines.

Brunellogate proved a stylistic turning point, as opaque, dark, highly concentrated, oaked wines began to disappear in favour of wines that showed increased transparency and greater stylistic diversity.

MESOCLIMATE, ELEVATION, and clones all play a part in these stylistic differences. The town of Montalcino, 112 km/70 miles south of Florence, enjoys a warmer, drier climate than CHIANTI. Indeed, it is the most arid of all Tuscan DOCG zones, with an annual rainfall of about 700 mm/28 in (compared with over 900 mm in central Chianti Classico). In addition, cool MARITIME breezes from the south-west ensure both excellent ventilation and cool evenings and nights. Sangiovese can reach its maximum ripeness here, giving fuller, more structured wines than anywhere else in Tuscany.

The zone can be split roughly in two: the north, with vineyards at ELEVATIONS up to 500 m on GALESTRO soils; and the warmer south, where there is more CLAY in the soil and where the wines tend to be fuller than the more aromatic wines from the north. Many producers have vineyards in both north and south to give balance to their wines as well as to offset the effects of CLIMATE CHANGE. While winemaking practices may differ from estate to estate, terroir differences put a far greater stylistic stamp on the wines, of which the finest examples manage the tricky balancing act of combining layers of red fruit, bold structure, and elegance.

The DOC regulations of 1960, largely written by Biondi-Santi on the basis of the family's oenological practices, include five to six years' CASK AGEING for the RISERVA and established a model of Brunello as a full-bodied, intense, long-lasting wine, which was confirmed in 1980 by the DOCG rules. The minimum cask-ageing period was lowered to 36 months in 1990 and then to two years in 1998. The once-popular practice of BARRIQUE ageing has been widely supplanted by a return to large oak casks, and a growing number of producers are using CONCRETE, AMPHORAE, and oval casks of Austrian oak.

More attention is being paid to SINGLE-VINEYARD WINES, which are sold at a premium. This growing interest in a hugely profitable aspect of Montalcino's terroir has not broken the region's defiant resistance to producing a detailed map of its vineyards.

The qualitatively heterogeneous Rosso di Montalcino, the 100% Sangiovese DOC wine from either declassified Brunello wine or vineyards unclassified for Brunello production, can be marketed after one year. W.S.

O'Keefe, K., *Brunello di Montalcino: Understanding and Appreciating One of Italy's Greatest Wines* (2012).
www.consorziobrunellodimontalcino.it

brush, the flesh remaining attached to the end of the berry stalk, or stem, after a grape is pulled from the bunch, as occurs during MECHANICAL HARVESTING or DESTEMMING, for example. The brush's size varies between vine varieties, from a barely discernible bit of flesh to a 'tongue' up to 5 mm/0.2 in long. The brush is caused by strong adhesion between the berry and stem, causing tearing of the skin, combined with particular characteristics of the zone of the flesh at the top of the berry. The cells of the brush are rich in TANNINS. The French term is *pinceau*.

The word 'brush' is also used in the US for the total cane growth evident after LEAF FALL. B.G.C.

brut, French word meaning 'crude' or 'raw', adapted by the CHAMPAGNE industry for wines made without (much) added sweetening or DOSAGE. It has come to be used widely for any SPARKLING WINE to indicate one that tastes bone dry. The upper limit for the RESIDUAL SUGAR of a brut champagne has been reduced from 15 to 12 g/l. A wine labelled **extra brut** should contain less than 6 g/l residual sugar. Particularly dry wines may be labelled **brut nature**, with less than 3 g/l residual sugar, and are made without dosage. The word **bruto** may be used in Portugal.

Brynšt, Czech synonym for TRAMINER.

Bual, Anglicized form of BOAL most often used for a style of MADEIRA, richer than SERCIAL and VERDELHO yet not as sweet as that called MALMSEY.

Bucelas, tiny white wine DOC just north of Lisbon, Portugal's capital city (see map under PORTUGAL) and formerly spelt **Bucellas**. At one time it was FORTIFIED, and it is thought to be Shakespeare's Charneco, mentioned in *The Second Part of King Henry IV* and named after one of the local villages. The Duke of Wellington popularized the wine in Britain following the Peninsular Wars, and for a time Bucelas was widely sold and appreciated in Victorian Britain as Portuguese HOCK. Representing at least 75% of DOC wines, ARINTO can make zesty, fruity dry whites in this sub-MEDITERRANEAN CLIMATE thanks to the tempering Atlantic breezes, which funnel up the river Trancão. Oaked, sparkling, and late-harvest styles are produced, too. Nonetheless, as at 2020, there were only 138 ha/341 acres under vine. The acquisition of the region's largest estate by SOGRAPE in 2019 bodes well for future investment. S.A.

bud, a small part of the vine shoot which rests between the leaf stalk or PETIOLE and the shoot stem. In the summer it is covered by green scales, which turn brown in winter. The bud contains three miniature, compressed (primordial) shoots. Normally the best developed of these shoots (from the 'primary' central bud) bursts at BUDBREAK. Grapevine buds are classified as compound and fruitful; their development is complex. B.G.C. & R.E.S.

Budai Zöld, Hungarian white grape grown around Lake Balaton making deeply coloured, full-bodied wine for local consumption.

budbreak, or **budburst**, a stage of annual vine development during which small shoots emerge from vine BUDS. This process begins in the spring of the new growing season and signals the end of DORMANCY, the period of winter sleep. The first sign that dormancy is ending and budbreak imminent is BLEEDING, when the vines begin to drip water from PRUNING cuts. The buds left at winter pruning begin to swell in the few weeks prior to budbreak, and budbreak itself is marked by the first signs of green in the vineyard, as the first young leaves unfold and push through the bud scales.

Budbreak takes place in early spring in cool climates, when the average air temperature is about 10 °C/50 °F. For many northern-hemisphere regions, budbreak occurs in March, and for the southern hemisphere in September. Budbreak is more uniform when winters are cold but not subject to WINTER FREEZE. In warm to hot regions, budbreak is earlier, and in cooler regions it is delayed. In fact in TROPICAL VITICULTURE the vines never achieve proper dormancy, and budbreak can be induced by pruning at any time of the year.

Not all varieties show budbreak at the same temperature. For example, French studies indicate that for the early TABLE GRAPE Pearl of Csaba budbreak occurs at 5.6 °C, MERLOT at 9.4 °C, and UGNI BLANC at 11 °C. Late pruning in winter delays budbreak, and this can be used to reduce the risk of winter FROST and also to delay HARVEST when growth cycles are compressed by CLIMATE CHANGE (see HARVEST COMPRESSION). See also DOUBLE PRUNING.

In temperate regions with warm winters, a few warm days, even in midwinter, can be enough to induce bud swelling, which can lead to budbreak if the warmth persists. One of the very few places around the world to show this problem is the MARGARET RIVER region in Western Australia. Because of the nearby moderating effects of the Indian Ocean, the midwinter (July) mean temperature is a warm 13 °C/55 °F. CHARDONNAY vines are particularly prone to this premature budbreak, with only a few buds breaking on the vine in midwinter and the rest somewhat more erratically later in spring.

For vines which are properly pruned (see BALANCED PRUNING) most of the buds left at winter pruning will burst, and budbreak is near 100%. Budbreak is, however, normally lower for buds in the middle of long CANES. (When vines are left unpruned, as in MINIMAL PRUNING, it is the buds near the ends of canes and higher up the canes which burst preferentially; see APICAL DOMINANCE.) The two buds on either side of the cane just below the pruning cut typically burst. This is because of the flow of HORMONES in the plant and is the reason for pruning to two-bud SPURS. The biggest problem for many vineyards at this time of the year is spring frost, to which the young shoot growth is particularly sensitive. R.E.S.

Huglin, P., and Schneider, C., *Biologie et écologie de la vigne* (2nd edn, 1998).

Iland, P., et al., 'Grapevine growth', in *The Grapevine: From the Science to the Practice of Growing Vines for Wine* (2011).

budding, the viticultural operation of GRAFTING where only a single bud is inserted into the rootstock. The term is also used in the context of BUDBREAK.

budwood, name given to vine CUTTINGS when they are destined for GRAFTING. Depending on the cutting length and bud spacing, four to 12 buds may be taken from each cutting. The budwood is typically put into cold storage to await grafting in the spring.

buffering capacity, the measure of resistance to change in PH by the addition of either acids or bases.

Bugey, Vins du, collective name for the wines of the Ain *département* in the southern Jura Mountains just west of SAVOIE in eastern France, increasingly called just **Bugey**. Vines have been present here since Roman times, and its chequered history has seen it under the rule of the Dukes of Burgundy and the House of Savoy. Under the medieval influence of MONKS AND MONASTERIES the area was considered an important wine producer. The wines were elevated to AOC from VDQS in 2009. In 2020, the region covered roughly 470 ha/1,161 acres in three chief vineyard zones of Cerdon, Belley, and MONTAGNIEU.

In the northern sector, hillside vineyards lie at 400–500 m/1,312–1,640 ft in elevation and produce almost exclusively the sparkling pink **Bugey-Cerdon**. Delicate, medium-sweet, with around 7.5% alcohol, Cerdon is made by the MÉTHODE ANCESTRALE from the Gamay grape and some POULSARD. It accounts for nearly half of Bugey's annual four-million-bottle production. In the southern sector on rolling hills close to the Rhône river other white and pink TRADITIONAL METHOD sparkling wines are important, usually labelled *mousseux* or *pétillant*. The still wines are mainly VARIETAL: Chardonnay dominates whites and traditional-method sparkling wines, and Savoie's ALTESSE performs well as Roussette du Bugey; tiny quantities of ALIGOTÉ and Pinot Gris as well as JACQUÈRE, MONDEUSE BLANCHE, and MOLETTE are also grown. Among reds, Gamay and Pinot Noir are joined by the interesting MONDEUSE NOIRE of Savoie. These were the wines with which the notable gastronome Anthelme Brillat-Savarin grew up, and today attention is being given to the increasing numbers of young, ORGANICALLY run estates. W.L.

Lorch, W., *Wines of the French Alps: Savoie, Bugey and Beyond* (2019).

Bukettraube, or **Buketrebe**, white grape variety, a GERMAN CROSS of SILVANER and TROLLINGER. It is grown almost exclusively but to a limited extent in South Africa (44 ha/109 acres in 2020) for sweet and occasionally BOTRYTIZED dessert wines, with a slightly grapey aroma.

Bulgaria, Eastern European country that has undergone a winemaking revolution from volume production to small, quality-focused estates.

History

The country has a long vinous heritage, with traces of grape-growing found on Neolithic sites and the first written records of wine, plus ornate drinking vessels, linked to ancient Thrace (a territory that includes modern-day Bulgaria). Numerous archaeological finds depict wine consumption, including discoveries at the Thracian temple complex near Starosel dated to the end of the 5th century BCE. PLINY the Elder stated that the first European wine grower was a Thracian named Evmolp. Wine drinking continued with stories linked to Khan Krum, then the country's conversion to Christianity from 864 CE brought new impetus to wine consumption (see EUCHARIST). Ottoman rule from the 15th to the 19th centuries (see ISLAM) suppressed but failed to destroy viticulture, as winemaking survived as a symbol of the Christian community. By liberation in 1878, the country had around 50,000 ha/123,553 acres under vine, and the first law enacted as an independent state was a statute for excise duty on drinks. Unfortunately, PHYLLOXERA arrived soon after, prompting the establishment of Europe's fourth research institute, at Pleven, in 1902.

At the beginning of the 20th century, the first Bulgarian wine CO-OPERATIVES were founded to overcome the problem of fragmented land holdings. After the Second World War, the new communist government, established in 1947, nationalized wine production and quickly set about collectivizing the vineyards. In 1949, the state wine and spirits monopoly Vinprom was set up to control all commercial production and trade.

In 1952, decree number 1058 was enacted, officially promoting viticulture and winegrowing in Bulgaria. Bulgaria had a major role as wine supplier in the Soviet Bloc's planned economy (Comecon), so the industry underwent significant modernization to meet these requirements. Until the early 1960s, INDIGENOUS VARIETIES dominated, especially DIMYAT, PAMID, and MAVRUD, but Comecon demands saw extensive single-variety plots of INTERNATIONAL VARIETIES such as Cabernet Sauvignon, Merlot, and Chardonnay as well as RKATSITELI, MUSCAT OTTONEL, and ALIGOTÉ, often on flatter sites and using higher TRAINING SYSTEMS designed to avoid frost and increase YIELDS. By the 1970s Bulgaria had around 150,000 ha/370,658 acres of wine grapes, chiefly for the SOVIET UNION and Comecon countries. Vinprom controlled 80% of winemaking facilities, with three smaller state-owned 'vine and wine complexes' producing the remainder. All exports went through the state monopoly Vinimpex.

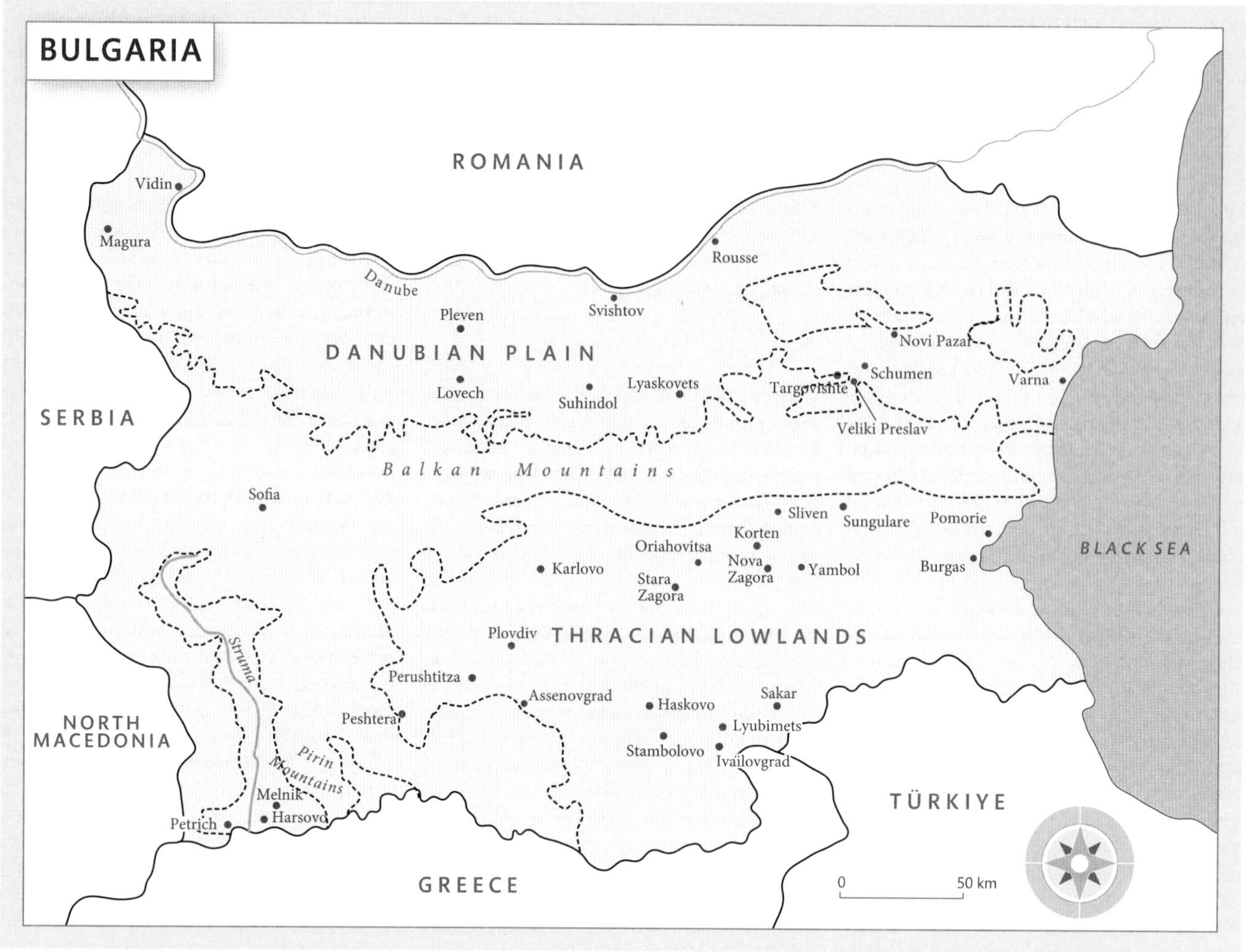

Western expertise came with PepsiCo, the giant American cola manufacturers. In the 1970s they were eager to barter their soft-drink concentrate in Eastern Europe for a saleable product (wine in Bulgaria's case). They established links with California's wine faculty at DAVIS, with Professor Maynard AMERINE, and provided travelling winemakers. This influenced the style of winemaking, for instance vinifying Chardonnay with American oak and full MALOLACTIC CONVERSION. The year 1978 saw the Ordinance of Wines with Controlled Origin; following detailed research, 23 controlled-origin wines were approved between 1982 and 1986. This marked a shift from production of quantity towards quality, and at its peak Bulgaria was the world's fourth largest exporter of bottled wine. It also set the scene for exports of inexpensive but competently made VARIETALS to the west, especially to Britain. This proved to be fortunate timing as demand from the vast Soviet market started to decline, accelerated by GORBACHEV's arrival as Soviet premier. His campaign to curb alcohol consumption in the mid 1980s involved uprooting huge tracts of Bulgarian vineyard. Grape prices were then fixed every year, irrespective of quality, which encouraged the co-operatives to turn their attention away from vines to other crops.

By 1990 the total crop was just 1.8 million hl/ 40 million gal, and this at a time when exports to the West were at record levels.

Post-communism

In 1990, the wine sector was suddenly liberalized as part of the free-market reforms introduced in the wake of the fall of communism in 1989. Throughout the 1990s, the Bulgarian wine industry was in disarray as attempts were made to return land to its pre-1947 owners, though records were often poor and families divided. This process of restitution continued until 2000, with the result that land was handed back in small, fragmented holdings, often to uninterested owners. There was little investment in viticulture due to uncertainties over land ownership. Winemaking also remained separated from grape-growing, and even as recently as the mid 2000s few wineries actually owned vineyards. Yields, already low, declined further, and by the end of the 1990s the Bulgarian wine industry was suffering from a serious fruit shortage. The ensuing fierce competition for grapes encouraged early picking, which in turn led to lean, underripe wines at a time when western consumers expected ripe, fruity wine styles. Bulgaria rapidly lost market share and many wineries found themselves in trading difficulties.

Bulgaria joined the EU in 2007. Undoubtedly, pre-accession EU funding programmes helped to revitalize wine. Subsidies of up to 50% for both winery and vineyard investments brought in substantial foreign capital and enabled some small, individual projects and wine estates—a novelty in Bulgaria at that time. Many wineries took on the huge bureaucratic burden of consolidating landholdings. Today most wineries of any significance own vineyards or source under long-term contracts.

By 2020 there were 282 registered wineries, all privately owned, most by Bulgarians with a handful of foreign investors, and increasingly focused on quality wine. Today Bulgaria has switched from being an exporter to drinking most of its wine at home. By 2019 exports had fallen to 250,212 hl/6,609,902 gal, with the majority (202,915 hl) going to the EU led by Poland, Sweden, and Czechia.

Geography and climate

Bulgaria is a small country just 450 km/280 miles from the western border to the Black Sea and 300 km/200 miles from Romania to the north and Greece and Türkiye to the south. With the exception of the Stara Planina (Balkan mountain range), which runs east to west, and the environs of the capital Sofia, vines are planted all over the country. Vineyards lie mainly at 100–300 m/330–990 ft in ELEVATION, although some north-western vineyards are as high as 600 m/1,967 ft.

The climate is largely CONTINENTAL, moderated by the Black Sea in the east and the Aegean in the south-west. Summers in the south tend to be hot, with temperatures up to 40 °C/104 °F, while the temperature can fall to −25 °C/−13 °F in winter.

The most common climatological hazards are FUNGAL DISEASES caused by humidity. Typical annual rainfall is 470–650 mm/18–26 in, and in non-DROUGHT years rainfall and high temperatures combine to promote rot and both POWDERY MILDEW and DOWNY MILDEW. Increasingly, new vineyards are being planted with IRRIGATION.

Vineyards

As part of EU membership negotiations, Bulgaria negotiated a vineyard area of 153,000 ha/378,071 acres, and indeed official data for 2006 showed an area under vine of 135,760 ha, but this seems never to have been a realistic reflection of what was planted or likely to be planted. By 2020 there were officially 60,162 ha, but less than half was harvested for commercial wine production, producing 735,359 hl/19,426,130 gal of wine. It appears that many small vineyards have simply been abandoned at the same time as wineries have invested in consolidated plots and professional viticulture. There is also still some unofficial grey-market wine and home-distilled grape spirits called *rakia*.

Winemaking

External investment and ongoing EU programmes have been used to fund winery renovations and the installation of STAINLESS STEEL, TEMPERATURE CONTROL, and modern technology across the industry. OAK use is widespread in premium wines, with leading producers usually opting for French oak, although some local oak is appearing now COOPERAGE standards are better. Oak use has also become more subtle, so today's wines are more harmonious. The late 2010s saw considerable dynamism in winemaking, with efforts going into reviving and improving native grape varieties and a diversity of styles appearing, including PET-NAT and ORANGE WINES. Most wineries now have locally trained winemakers who have gained international experience, and Bulgaria has an unusually high proportion of women winemakers, estimated to be close to 50%.

Vine varieties

Bulgaria's commercial plantings are split between 15,791 ha/39,020 acres of red wine grapes and 13,317 ha of white varieties, as of 2020, though the harvest is close to 50:50 as white varieties give higher yields. Red grapes dominate in all regions except the north-east. Bulgaria may have been famous for its Cabernet Sauvignon in the 1980s, but by 2020 Merlot had overtaken it to become the most planted variety at 5,071 ha, followed by Cabernet Sauvignon and PAMID, a local variety fallen out of favour as its light body, low acidity, and low EXTRACT means that it produces only basic wines for early consumption. The most interesting of the red INDIGENOUS VARIETIES is MAVRUD (855 ha), now planted in most southern zones and capable of high quality and ageability. Gamza (KADARKA, 218 ha) is gaining interest in the north. Shiroka Melnishka Loza or broad-leaved MELNIK, which covered 1,580 ha/3,904 acres in 2013, had fallen to 197 ha by 2020. It is very late ripening and can be austere as a red, but its high acidity is proving good for TRADITIONAL METHOD sparkling wines. Confusingly its offspring, the earlier ripening and softer Early Melnik or Melnik 55, is often labelled simply Melnik. The other important local red is RUBIN, a 1944 local cross of Syrah and Nebbiolo that some believe to have potentially higher quality than Mavrud.

In INTERNATIONAL VARIETIES, Syrah has grown strongly to reach 1,032 ha as it suits Bulgarian growing conditions. Cabernet Franc (668 ha) is increasingly impressive as a varietal wine or in blends, while Pinot Noir (516 ha) can produce very good results in cooler spots.

Bulgarian researchers have been enthusiastic developers of crosses, including Buket or Bouquet (Mavrud × Pinot Noir), Evmolpia (Mavrud × Merlot), Melnik 1300 (Saperavi × Shiroka Melnishka Loza), and Ruen (Cabernet × Melnik), as well as a number of lower-quality varieties developed primarily for disease resistance such as dark-skinned Storgozia, a cross of the local Buket with VILLARD Blanc.

White varieties in Bulgaria are led by Muscat Ottonel (3,103 ha), followed by Chardonnay (2,553 ha), which can produce very high-quality wines in Bulgarian conditions. Sauvignon Blanc (1,307 ha) can produce fresh, aromatically true wines in the cool north. The most important local white-wine variety is the FROST-resistant, pink-skinned MISKET Cherven, or Red Misket (1,170 ha). Grown mainly in the Valley of the Roses area, it produces distinctly grapey, short-lived white wines. (Confusingly there are several grapes named Misket—Sandanski, Vrachanski, Varnenski, Kailashki—which are unrelated to each other but which all produce grapey, simple wines.) RKATSITELI once accounted for 40% of Bulgaria's white vines but had fallen to 950 ha by 2020. DIMYAT (791 ha), also known as Smederevka, typically makes ordinary whites, though some more promising oaked and orange versions are starting to appear. Other important whites include Traminer, Ugni Blanc (often used for distillation), Tamianka (MUSCAT BLANC À PETIT GRAINS), Riesling, Viognier, Pinot Gris, and Vermentino. There are a few attempts as well to revive old varieties such as the low-acid Keratsuda in the south-west and Kokorko (Bercebel) in the north.

Regions and quality designations

Winemaking practices were brought into line with EU standards before Bulgaria's accession in 2007. At that point, it established two PGIS that split the country into the northern region of the Danubian or Danube Plain and, in the south, the Thracian Lowlands (sometimes written Thracian Valley). These remain controversial, believed to be the result of lobbying by larger wineries rather than reflecting growing conditions. For instance, it's not hard to see distinct differences between the hot, dry Struma Valley in the south-west and the Black Sea-influenced east coast, though both are officially Thracian Lowlands. PGI wines accounted for over 40% of production in 2019, and in practice these very broad regions allow winemakers considerable freedom to plant a range of varieties and experiment with unusual blends. Increasingly, as producers own or control where they source their fruit, the concept of TERROIR is coming to the fore, in contrast to the historical approach of sourcing grapes all over the country.

The previous era of wine legislation (in the late 1970s) divided the country into five regions: Struma Valley, Black Sea Coast, Danubian Plain, Thracian Valley, and the Sub-Balkan region or Valley of the Roses, based on real science according to sources who worked on it then. And it seems the current authorities agree, with tentative identification of five regions similar to the historic regions in the national wine strategy up to 2025. In 2022 the process of amending legislation appeared to have stalled, but the industry often refers to these five regions.

The current status of PDOS is unhelpful to the industry: 52 are listed and accepted by EU, though most are not used, and they account for less than 1% of production. The rules are strict and bureaucratic, making them almost impossible to use in practice. Two regions, Struma Valley and South Sakar, were in the process of defining new PDOs and seeking EU approval as of 2021. C.G.

Gilby, C., *The Wines of Bulgaria, Romania and Moldova* (2018).
Tanovska, T., and Iontcheva, K., *KATA Catalogue of Bulgarian Wine* 2 (2021).
www.divino.bg
www.bawp.bg

bulk method, alternative name for the TANK METHOD of SPARKLING WINEMAKING.

bulk storage of wine is important in the production and BLENDING of everyday, low-margin commercial wines valued for their affordability and consistency. Large temperature-controlled storage tanks are usually made of stainless steel and may hold as much as 800,000 l/176,000 gal. OXIDATION is always a risk and, if the tank is not completely filled with wine, the HEAD SPACE must be filled with an INERT GAS. Many commercial blends are bottled throughout the year from such tanks, which need to be kept at 12–18 °C/ 54–64 °F. Extremes of heat or cold are likely to have a negative effect on quality. B.D.

bulk transport of wine is the movement of large quantities of wine within a single winery or from one place to another, typically from where it was held in BULK STORAGE to the BOTTLING location, which may not even be in the same hemisphere.

Bulk transport over long distances has increased considerably over the last 20 years in an effort to reduce both financial and environmental costs. Twice as much wine can be transported in the same space in bulk than in bottle, PACKAGING waste is reduced, and locally recycled glass may be used (although bottlers in the producing country suffer the consequences). According to the OIV, 34% of exported wine was moved in bulk in 2020, compared with 30% in 2000. In the same year, 51% of Australia's wine exports were in bulk and 63% of US wine was exported in this way. Other benefits include the better thermal protection offered by a large volume of wine and longer shelf life for wine sold in BOXES. However, local regulations, particularly in Europe, may insist that wine is bottled in the place of production.

Wine is most commonly transported in bulk from one installation to another by road tanker and/or ocean-going tank ships, although rail and barge are not unknown. The two main options used on ships are an ISO tank (a stainless-steel pill-shaped container within a standard ISO frame that can carry up to 26,000 litres/ 6,870 gal) or a Flexitank (a hermetically sealed, collapsible, and flexible single or multilayer polyethylene/polyester bag or bladder, which is fitted into a container and typically holds 24,000 litres). Pipelines are occasionally used to transport wine over short distances, for example between winery sites or to a neighbouring bottling facility.

Whenever wine is moved in bulk, the key considerations are wine quality, wine losses, cost, availability of suitable tanks, environmental impact, the risk to consumers from cross-contamination (especially allergens) unless the tanks are single use, and the safety of winery operators during loading and off-loading.

In terms of wine quality, it is important to guard against OXIDATION and against thermal stress resulting from temperature variation in transit, during layovers, or on the dock. Studies have shown that temperature fluctuations are more likely to occur when wine is transported overland. Flexitanks, because of their flexibility, offer more effective management of ULLAGE levels, a critical factor in controlling the level of dissolved oxygen. Because of this, and because of their global availability and low risk of cross-contamination, they have become the most popular method of shipping a wine in bulk. However, the more solid construction of ISO tanks may offer better thermal protection. Shipping a wine in bulk has placed new demands on the modern winemaker, who must prepare a wine for the rigours of a journey of up to two months, often crossing the equator. Critical factors include the levels of dissolved oxygen and dissolved CARBON DIOXIDE, the latter a good protection in transit and adding freshness to certain wine styles. Ideally the winemaker at the destination should have to make minimal adjustments prior to bottling. B.D.

Tchouakeu Betnga, P. F., et al., 'Effects of transport conditions on the stability and sensory quality of wines', *OENO One* 55/2 (2021).

bulk wine, or wine *en vrac*, as the French call it, is wine that is ready to drink but has not been put into smaller CONTAINERS such as BOTTLES. This may be because it is about to be packaged, because it will be sold to another producer, or because it will be packaged in the country in which it is to be sold. Most of the wine that is sold in bulk is marketed at less than US$10 per bottle and is not meant for long-term ageing. BULK TRANSPORT is by far the cheapest way of moving wine, and it is common for wine to move in bulk between producer and blender or bottler, possibly even between continents and hemispheres.

When SURPLUS PRODUCTION became an increasingly geographically widespread phenomenon in the early 21st century, the bulk-wine market became an important feature of international wine trade, helped considerably by online trading. Today concerns about the cost, both financial and environmental, of transporting wine in bottles has encouraged many large retailers to ship in bulk. (See CARBON FOOTPRINT and SUSTAINABILITY.)

Spain is by far the biggest exporter of bulk wine, at more than one billion litres in 2018, with France its biggest market by far. Way behind Spain at second place was Australia, with just 386 million litres. Italy's main customer for bulk wine is Germany, which imports more than any other country, though in value terms it was overtaken in 2019 by the UK, where the wine is destined for both brands and private labels. China has emerged as a significant buyer of bulk wine, sourced wherever it is cheapest but especially from France and Italy. The country's imposition of punitive trade tariffs on Australia in 2020 put an end to the significant volumes of bulk (and bottled) wine shipped across the Pacific.

Brokers of bulk wine have become increasingly important, and their business is strongly influenced by factors such as the weather during FLOWERING where large quantities of wine are grown, extreme weather events such as HAIL or FROST that can drastically reduce volumes in a particular vintage, currency movements, and FASHIONS in grape varieties (see SIDEWAYS, for example). They follow the bulk markets daily and provide information to their client base.

On a smaller scale, bulk wine may even be sold in measured quantities drawn off from some form of BULK STORAGE. In southern Europe it is still commonplace to take a container, perhaps a BONBONNE or large plastic container, to be filled with bulk wine, which is sold by the litre.

Bullas, DOP of 1,811 ha/4,475 acres just south of JUMILLA in the autonomous region of Murcia in Spain. The region is generally dry and hot, with an annual rainfall of 300 mm/12 in, although the MESOCLIMATE is cooler in the higher ELEVATIONS of the north-west, where vineyards reach 900 m/2,953 ft. Red wines and rosés predominate, primarily from the MONASTRELL grape. F.C.

Bull's Blood, once a wine BRAND named after a historic style of red wine made in HUNGARY, known as BIKAVÉR in Hungarian.

bunch, or cluster, the viticultural term for that part of the grapevine comprising STEM and BERRIES: *grappe* in French, *Traube* in German, *racimo* in Spanish, and *grappolo* in Italian. Before the berries SET, each berry position is occupied by a flower; a bunch develops from the INFLORESCENCE of the vine once the berries have set. In the grapevine the inflorescence grows at the node on the side of the stem opposite to a leaf, an unusual position within the plant kingdom. It is closely related to a TENDRIL, both deriving from the same embryonic organ, the anlage. Depending on the time of development, anlagen produce bunches, tendrils, or SECOND CROP.

Like a tendril, a grape bunch has two arms, called outer and inner. The inner arm develops the bulk of the bunch, while the outer arm may vary in form from a large, well-set 'wing' (as in UGNI BLANC) to a small tendril arm without berries, or it may even abort. Berries on wings sometimes ripen differently from those on the main crop.

Bunches vary hugely in size depending on that year's FRUIT SET and VINE VARIETY, from a few grams to many kilograms. They also vary in shape and tightness depending on the lengthening and flexibility of the STEM and branches and, of course, on setting and BERRY SIZE. B.G.C.

bunch closure, stage in the VINE GROWTH CYCLE between BUDBREAK and VERAISON when the berries begin to touch and the bunch hangs down. It is an indistinct phenological stage but significant for vineyard SPRAYING as it affects penetration of the bunch and hence BOTRYTIS protection. R.E.S.

bunch rots, or **berry rots**, occur in vines all over the world and can be caused by many species of fungi including YEASTS and by BACTERIA. Yield losses can be as high as 80%, and wine made from rotten fruit often smells and tastes tainted, typically mouldy, with a perceptible loss of fruit flavour. Vineyards badly infected with bunch rots themselves have a distinctive and unpleasant smell. Wet weather at HARVEST causes the worst cases of bunch rot, especially if grape skins are broken. The best-known of the bunch rots is BOTRYTIS BUNCH ROT.

Some fungi, such as *Botrytis, Alternaria*, and *Cladosporium*, can infect healthy berries, and these are called 'primary invaders'. 'Secondary invaders' such as *Aspergillus, Rhizopus*, and *Penicillium* gain access to berries split by rain, bird, or insect attack, or diseases such as DOWNY MILDEW and POWDERY MILDEW, ESCA, or WHITE ROT. So-called SOUR ROT is due to a mix of fungi, yeasts, acetic acid bacteria, and fruit fly larvae. Control measures can include SPRAYING, bunch thinning, increasing fruit exposure to wind and sun (see CANOPY MANAGEMENT), and avoiding other pests and diseases which can break berry skins (see also FUNGAL DISEASES). However, once the rot is well established, the grapes are unusable and likely to be left for the birds. R.E.S.

Emmett, R. W., et al., 'Grape diseases and vineyard protection', in B. G. Coombe and P. R. Dry (eds.), *Viticulture*, ii: *Practices* (2nd edn, 2006).

Wilcox, W. F., et al. (eds.), *Compendium of Grape Diseases, Disorders, and Pests* (2nd edn, 2015).

bunchstem. See STEM.

bunchstem necrosis, or **BSN**, physiological condition which causes grape stems to shrivel and die during RIPENING. This condition is also known as waterberry in California, shanking in New Zealand, *Stiellähme* in Germany, and *dessèchement de la rafle* in France. Affected berries do not ripen properly and shrivel on the bunch, although it is rare for all berries to be affected. CABERNET SAUVIGNON vines are particularly prone to this disorder. Affected berries have lower SUGARS, ANTHOCYANINS, and fatty acids but higher ACIDITY. The cause is unknown, but factors associated with the condition are vigorous SHOOT growth, the weather at FLOWERING, and levels of MAGNESIUM, CALCIUM, and ammonium in the plant tissue. Yield can be severely reduced, especially with MECHANICAL HARVESTING, as affected berries fall off. Wines can taste bitter and are poorly coloured. There is no widely accepted control, although magnesium sprays at VERAISON have sometimes reduced the problem. A similar disorder affects INFLORESCENCES at flowering and has been termed **early bunchstem necrosis**, or inflorescence necrosis. R.E.S.

Bondada, B., and Keller, M., 'Not all shrivels are created equal: morpho-anatomical and compositional characteristics differ among different shrivel types that develop during ripening of grape (*Vitis vinifera* L.) berries', *American Journal of Plant Sciences*, 3/7 (2012), 879–98.

bung. A bung, made of glass, plastic, rubber, earthenware, silicone, or wood, is a barrel's stopper, analogous to the cork of a bottle. It is inserted in a **bung-hole**. If a barrel is stored so that the bung is at its highest point (**bung up**), the bung may be left so that gas can escape from the bung-hole. Some bungs incorporate a device that encourages this. If a barrel is stored with the bung at either two or ten o'clock, the position is called **bung over**.

Since OXYGEN tends to enter a barrel around the bung-hole, silicone bungs are sometimes used to keep a particularly tight fit. These also have the advantage of being gentler on the stave in which the bung-hole is drilled, which is weakened and sometimes cracked by the hammering needed on wooden bungs every time the barrel is TOPPED UP.

So-called aseptic bungs, made of plastic or glass, incorporate a container filled with liquid SULFUR DIOXIDE to keep bacteria out of the barrel or cask. Electronic bungs have recently been designed that automatically measure temperature, pressure, oxygen content, and liquid level at regular intervals, helping the winemaker to monitor the barrel without opening it.

Traditionally in Bordeaux and Burgundy, barrels were filled and topped up through the top bung but racked via a RACKING bung on the head of the barrel, but this is now relatively rare. A.P.

Burgenland, topographically heterogeneous Austrian state, home in 2021 to 27% of that country's vine hectarage, best known as its pre-eminent source for red wines (especially from BLAUFRÄNKISCH and ZWEIGELT) as well as for nobly sweet ones (from diverse white and even red grape varieties), and incorporating the DACS of EISENBERG, LEITHABERG, MITTELBURGENLAND, NEUSIEDLERSEE, ROSALIA, and RUSTER AUSBRUCH. (QUALITÄTSWEIN not qualifying or not submitted for DAC labelling will identify Burgenland as its place of origin.) Extending some 160 km/100 miles along the eastern edge of Austria from the outskirts of Bratislava, SLOVAKIA, to a sliver of Austria's border with SLOVENIA, Burgenland was created in 1921 out of the former German West Hungary. (Croatian is the state's second language; see AUSTRIA, history.) D.S.

Burger, white grape variety that was once very important in CALIFORNIA, where it was the state's most planted VITIS VINIFERA variety, having been promoted by one pioneer as greatly superior to the MISSION grape. The total had fallen to 442 ha/1,093 acres by 2020, mainly in the hot SAN JOAQUIN VALLEY, many of the vines planted in the early 1980s.

It is the almost extinct southern French variety Monbadon, probably a natural cross of FOLLE BLANCHE and UGNI BLANC, that was cultivated to a limited extent in the Languedoc until the 1980s. It produces sizeable quantities of neutral wine.

Burgunder, common suffix in German, meaning literally 'of Burgundy', for such grape varieties as SPÄTBURGUNDER, Blauburgunder, Blauer Spätburgunder, or Blauer Burgunder (PINOT NOIR); WEISSBURGUNDER or Weisser Burgunder (Pinot Blanc); and GRAUBURGUNDER or Grauer Burgunder (drier styles of PINOT GRIS).

Burgund Mare means 'big Burgundian' in ROMANIA and is the local name for BLAUFRÄNKISCH.

Burgundy, known as BOURGOGNE in French, province of eastern France famous for its great red and white wines produced mostly from PINOT NOIR and CHARDONNAY grapes respectively. The province includes the viticultural regions of the Côte de Nuits and Côte de Beaune in the *département* of the CÔTE D'OR, the Côte CHALONNAISE and the MÂCONNAIS in the Saône-et-Loire *département*, and CHABLIS and the wines of AUXERRE in the Yonne *département*. In 2018, the total area of Burgundy vineyard was 30,052 ha/74,260 acres, giving an average crop of 1.45 mhl/38.3 million gal of which 60% is white, 29% red, and 11% sparkling.

BEAUJOLAIS in the Rhône *département*, while sometimes being considered part of greater Burgundy, is a distinct region viticulturally, if not administratively, and is treated separately.

B

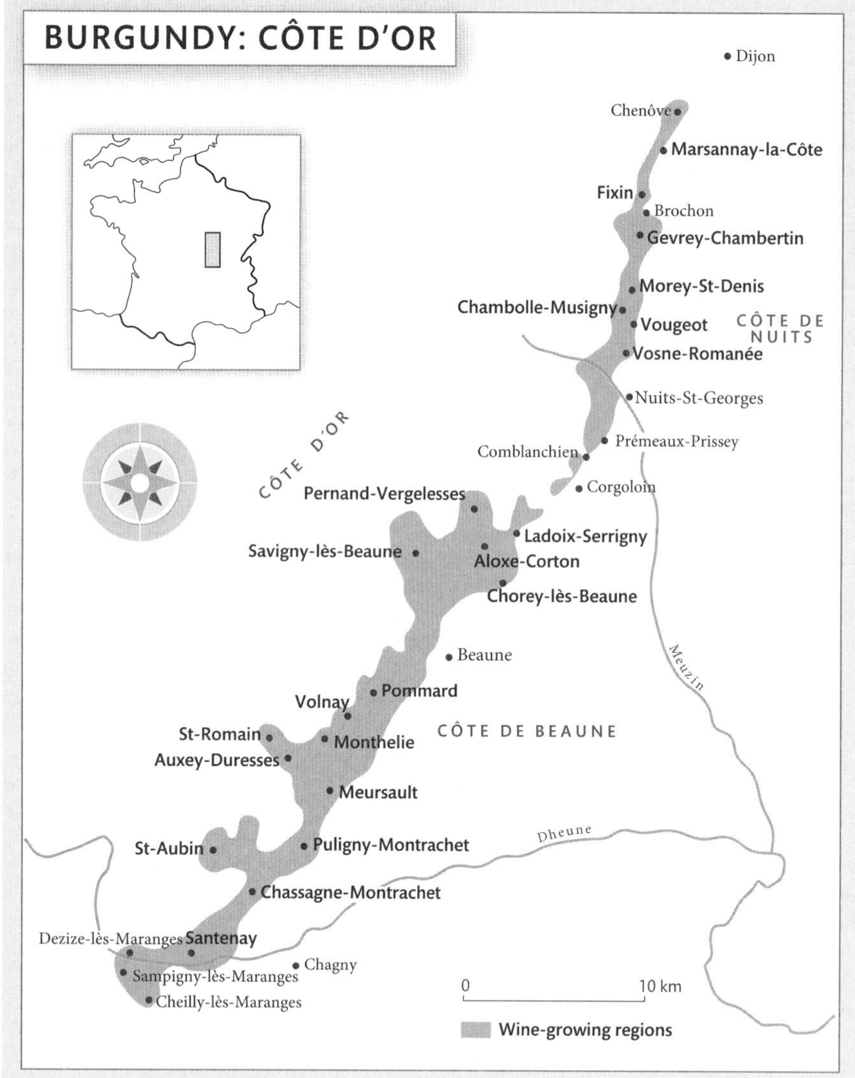

Harvest statistics (five-year average 2015–2019)	
Chablis and Auxerrois	274,471 hl
Côte de Nuits	73,314 hl
Côte de Beaune	161,832 hl
Côte Chalonnaise	77,647 hl
Mâconnais	341,821 hl
Regional appellations	376,407 hl
Crémant	166,241 hl

Ancient history

When the Romans (see ROME, CLASSICAL) conquered Gaul in 51 BCE, they probably found the CELTS inhabiting what is now Burgundy already growing wine, if not yet in substantial quantities. In the early 21st century the remains of a small vineyard dating back to the 1st century CE, apparently for the use of those living in a Roman villa close to Gibriacum (GEVREY-CHAMBERTIN), was unearthed. A tombstone in the village church of Corgoloin depicts what appears to be a Celtic god with a vine in his right hand; other gravestones have carvings of grapes. Also, archaeologists have found no Italian AMPHORAE of the mid 2nd century or later in Burgundy, which may indicate that from then on the region was producing enough wine of its own. From at least the 3rd century onwards, however, wine was transported from Italy in wooden BARRELS instead of amphorae, and wood is far more perishable than pottery.

The earliest literary evidence dates from 312 CE. In a panegyric addressed to Emperor Constantine the Great on the occasion of his visit to Autun (Augustodeunum), the citizens plead poverty. Part of the grim picture their orator paints is abandoned vineyards, the roots of the old vines so thickly intertwined that it would be impossible for a farmer to dig ditches. However old the vines were—and a mere human lifetime's worth of neglect would account for their tangled state—commercial viticulture had clearly been well established by the early 4th century.

As the Roman Empire disintegrated, Burgundy came once more under BARBARIAN rule, by the Franks, the Alamans, and the Vandals. The Burgundians, Scandinavians by origin, founded a kingdom in the RHÔNE Valley, later including Lyons and Dijon, in 456; they were defeated by the Franks under Clovis's sons in 534. The first recorded words in praise of Burgundian wine date from the Merovingian period. Gregory of Tours, who finished his History of the Franks in 591, says that the hills to the west of Dijon produce a noble wine that is like FALERNIAN—the highest praise possible from a Dark Age Latinist. That wine, and the clear water flowing from the springs around the city, are sufficient reasons why in his opinion Dijon should become an episcopal see. In 587 King Guntramn, grandson of Clovis and son of Clotaire, gave a vineyard to the Abbey of St Benignus at Dijon, and in 630 the duke of Lower Burgundy donated vineyards at Gevrey, Vosne, and Beaune to the Abbey of Bèze, near Gevrey. The beginnings of monastic viticulture in Burgundy were in these Merovingian times.

Monastic influence

Nobles, peasants, and monks cultivated the vine under CHARLEMAGNE, when political stability brought prosperity. Medieval Burgundy owes its reputation as a producer of excellent wines largely to the MONKS AND MONASTERIES. The monks had several advantages over lay growers: they had cellars and store rooms in which to mature their wine; and, most importantly, they kept records and had the time and the degree of organization necessary to engage in systematic improvement. The Benedictines of Cluny were the first group of monks to acquire vineyards in Burgundy on a large scale. The foundation in 910 of the Abbey at Cluny in the Mâconnais was the beginning of the Benedictine reform movement. Through benefactions from pious laymen, Cluny came to own all the vineyards around Gevrey by 1273, and in 1232 the duchess of Burgundy granted the Abbey of St-Vivant the vineyards now known as Romanée-Conti, La Romanée, La Tâche, Richebourg, and Romanée-St-Vivant (see also DOMAINE DE LA ROMANÉE-CONTI). It also owned Pommard and vineyards at Auxey and Santenay.

The other group of monks to have a lasting effect on Burgundian viticulture were the Cistercians, an order founded in 1098 which took its name from the site of its first monastery, Cîteaux, east of modern Nuits-St-Georges. Although austerity and asceticism were the aims of the order, in contrast to the luxury and ostentation of the Benedictines, the Cistercians, often through donations, became rich and important landowners.

The Cistercians' first vineyard was given to them by the duke of Burgundy in 1098, not long after their foundation. Soon they were buying vineyards as well: in 1118 the Cistercians of Pontigny on the River Serein purchased, after much haggling, vineyards from the Benedictine monks of St-Martin at Tours from which they produced a white wine, the first CHABLIS. In 1110 the monks of Cîteaux were given land at Vougeot and went on to acquire more land there: it took them until 1336 to acquire enough to form one large vineyard, which they surrounded with a wall, the CLOS DE VOUGEOT. They bought or were given more vineyards all over the CÔTE D'OR and trained their lay brothers to work them: Beaune, Chambolle, Fixin, Pommard, and many more.

Aided by their skilled workforce, the monks had the time, the experience, and the learning necessary to experiment, record, and compare. By observing how different plots of vines produced different wines, the Cistercians discovered the importance of TERROIR and began to acknowledge different CRUS.

In the 12th and 13th centuries, white wine was preferred to red. In an age of murky drinking water, carefully made white wine was valued for its clarity. The wines that were most highly reputed, however, were not those of Burgundy but those of the Île-de-France centred on PARIS, which could easily be transported by RIVERS. Burgundy, on the other hand, was cut off, and its wines, which could only be transported north with much expense and difficulty along bumpy roads, were as yet little known. In medieval French texts, 'vin de Bourgogne' was from Auxerre, whose wines could easily reach Paris along the River Yonne: transport by boat was cheaper, easier, and less harmful to the wine than being carried by horse-drawn cart along bumpy roads. Until the 15th century what we call burgundy was known as 'Beaune'.

Upon his election in 1305 Clement V moved the papal court to Avignon. During this 'Babylonian captivity', which lasted until 1377, the court of the Avignonese popes was famous for its extravagance as well as its corruption, and demand for the wines of Burgundy to the north surged. The wines of 'Beaune' came generally to be regarded as second to none. Urban V (1362–70) went to Rome for three years in 1367 but, exasperated by the political infighting there, returned to Avignon. In a letter, Petrarch made a vain attempt to persuade him to go back to Rome but had to admit that the best burgundy was not to be had south of the Alps. The Babylonian captivity ended with Urban's successor Gregory XI, but the wines of Burgundy retained their high reputation.

The dukes of Burgundy

From a byword for largesse in Avignon, Burgundian wine became a status symbol with the Valois dukes, four generations of whom governed Burgundy from 1363 to 1477. The first duke, Philip the Bold, son of King John of France, took a keen interest in the wine of the region, its most important export. In 1395, he issued a decree declaring the GAMAY grape variety to be harmful to human beings and its planting contrary to Burgundian practice. The first mention of the PINOT NOIR grape, named Noirien, dates only from the 1370s, but in all probability the grape had been in use longer. Modern Gamay has a far higher yield than Pinot Noir, and documentary evidence suggests that the same was true in the 14th century. In the same decree, Philip inveighs against the use of organic FERTILIZERS, presumably because it also increased YIELDS. Philip was trying to maintain quality, while many growers thought that manure and Gamay would make for easy profits. Although Philip the Bold wanted every single Gamay plant uprooted by the next Easter, we find his grandson Philip the Good (1429–67) later still thundering against the inferior vine, which he called a threat to both the wines and the dukes of Burgundy. Fearing for his immortal soul, Philip the Good's rapacious Chancellor Nicolas Rolin built the famous HOSPICES DE BEAUNE in 1443.

But what were these famous wines really like? The white wines of Burgundy were probably made from the grape that also produced the highly reputed white wines of north-eastern France, Fromenteau, which had pale-red berries and white juice and could well be the ancestor of our PINOT GRIS. (The CHARDONNAY of modern white burgundy did not appear in the region until after the Middle Ages.) In the Middle Ages wines were drunk in the year following the vintage, so properly matured burgundy would then have been unknown. H.M.W.

Derlow, R. K., 'The "disloyal grape": the agrarian crisis of late fourteenth century Burgundy', *Agricultural History*, 56 (1982), 426–38.

Dion, R., *Histoire de la vigne et du vin en France* (1959).

Modern burgundy

The duchy of Burgundy was once so proud of having the finest wines and finest court in Christendom that it developed into a state and very nearly a kingdom in its own right. The defeat and death of the over-ambitious Charles the Rash, however, led to its being reincorporated into the kingdom of France. As the monarchy became stronger, the power of the Church declined slowly, so that during the 17th century many of the famous vineyards donated to the Church during the Middle Ages were sold to the increasingly important bourgeoisie in Dijon.

Although transport difficulties (see RIVERS) still hindered burgundy's fame abroad, the famous Pierre Brosse managed to interest Louis XIV in his Mâcon, and the Sun King's physician, Fagon, prescribed old burgundy instead of champagne as the most suitable wine for his monarch's health. Roads began to improve in the 18th century, and the trials and tribulations inherent in road travel diminished, encouraging the start of commercial traffic in Burgundy. The first NÉGOCIANT houses were founded in the 1720s and 1730s, including Champy (1720) and BOUCHARD PÈRE ET FILS (1731), names which have survived to this day.

The earliest major work on the wines of Burgundy, Claude Arnoux's *Dissertation on the Situation of Burgundy*... was published in 1728. It demonstrates the fame of the red wines of the Côte de Nuits and the special reputation of the Œil-de-Perdrix (partridge-eye) pink wines of Volnay, while the existence of white wine in the Côte de Beaune earns only a brief mention.

Most vineyards remained in the hands of Church or nobility until the French Revolution. From 1791 the vineyards were sold off, often divided among several owners. Since then they have further fragmented as a result of the law of equal inheritance among children laid down in the Napoleonic Code. This process has caused much of the difficulty in understanding burgundy: consumers must familiarize themselves not only with a plethora of village and vineyard names but also with the relative merits of possibly dozens of producers of each one.

Burgundy prospered in the early 19th century, although wine PRICES were low even for the fine vineyards. In addition, there was widespread planting of the inferior GAMAY grape to provide wine that was plentiful and cheap, albeit mediocre. Transport conditions continued to improve with the opening of a canal system in Burgundy and, in 1851, the Paris–Dijon railway.

Easy prosperity, however, was first checked by the spread of POWDERY MILDEW in the 1850s and then destroyed by the arrival of PHYLLOXERA in the 1870s. This calamity was finally admitted in the Côte d'Or in 1878 when an infested vineyard in Meursault was surrounded by soldiers. The Burgundians did not find it easy to come to terms with the problem: there were riots in Bouze-lès-Beaune between factions in favour of treating vineyards and those against; a posse of growers in Chenôve actually attacked a team sent in to spray the vines; and American ROOTSTOCKS, the eventual saviours of French vineyards, were banned from the region between 1874 and 1887. Eventually, however, common sense prevailed, and by the 1890s post-phylloxera wines were again on the market. Only the best vineyards were worth replanting after the predations of phylloxera—a silver lining to the disaster.

The Burgundians were well aware of the considerable variation in quality of the wines produced by different plots of land, or *climats*, as they are known in Burgundy. In 1855 Dr Lavalle

B

published his influential *History and Statistics of the Côte d'Or*, which included an informal CLASSIFICATION of the best vineyards. This was formalized in 1861 by the Beaune Committee of Agriculture, which, with Lavalle's assistance, devised three classes. Most of the first class were in due course enfranchised as GRANDS CRUS when the AOC system was introduced in the 1930s.

Most burgundy was sold through the flourishing NÉGOCIANT houses until the years of hardship after the First World War. The economic depression of the 1920s and early 1930s threatened to ruin many small growers. One solution was the CO-OPERATIVE, particularly useful in the Mâconnais, where prices were lower. Another was for proprietors to bottle their own produce, a move which met with opposition from the merchants when growers such as the Marquis d'Angerville, Henri Gouges, and Armand Rousseau pioneered the concept of DOMAINE BOTTLING in the 1930s. Whereas in 1962 wines produced and bottled by growers accounted for only 15% of production, by 1990 nearly half of all Côte d'Or wines were domaine bottled.

Geography and climate

The vineyards of Burgundy are based on LIMESTONE originating in the Jurassic period. This takes the form of undulating CHALK hills in Chablis; a long narrow escarpment running south and a touch west from Dijon to Chagny, the CÔTE D'OR; more isolated limestone outcrops in the Côte Chalonnaise and the Mâconnais; and the vineyards of POUILLY-FUISSÉ beneath the imposing crags of Solutré and Vergisson in the extreme south.

The climate in Burgundy is broadly CONTINENTAL. In contrast to BORDEAUX, Burgundy is a little cooler during the summer, noticeably colder in the winter, and similar in temperature in the spring. Although winters are usually dry, Burgundy tends to suffer from particularly heavy rainfall in May and June and again in October, which may or may not fall after the HARVEST. Spring FROST can be a problem (especially in CHABLIS), while HAIL causes local damage almost every year. Indeed the incidence of hail seems to be on the increase, particularly in the Côte de Beaune, and is perhaps a by-product of CLIMATE CHANGE.

Overall, Burgundy has a shorter and more variable summer than Bordeaux (which is why only early-ripening grape varieties can be grown there), though there are significant climatic differences north to south: among Chardonnay wines, the wines of Chablis, reflecting their northern origin, are tinted green in colour and comparatively austere in flavour; further south, those of the Mâconnais enjoy enough sun to become (relatively) fat and ripe. The temperamental PINOT NOIR vine is less regularly successful. In Auxerrois, historically at the limit of successful ripening, the red wines rarely achieved much depth or body, but they continue to improve in today's climate. Burgundy's greatest reds are produced on the escarpment of the Côte d'Or, especially in the Côte de Nuits.

For more details of Burgundy's special aptitude for wine production, see CLIMATE AND WINE QUALITY.

Viticulture and winemaking

For details, see CÔTE D'OR, CHALONNAISE, and MÂCONNAIS.

Vine varieties

Burgundy has one of the world's least varied ranges of vine varieties. Almost all of the region's best red and white wines are made from Pinot Noir and Chardonnay respectively. According to official 2021 statistics, Chardonnay is grown on 51% of the region's total vineyard area (a proportion swollen by the substantially white wine production of Chablis and the Mâconnais), followed by Pinot Noir (39.5%) and Aligoté (6%), with Gamay, Sauvignon Blanc, and others such as MELON, SACY, and CÉSAR combined comprising 3.5%.

Organization of Burgundian vineyards

The vineyards of Burgundy, especially those of the Côte d'Or, are the most minutely parcellated in the world. This is mainly because the land has been continuously managed and owned by individual smallholders—there was no influx of outside capital with which to establish great estates as in BORDEAUX. But the combination of the Napoleonic Code, with its insistence on equal inheritance for every family member, and the fact that the land has proved so valuable has meant that small family holdings have been divided and subdivided over generations. One vineyard, or *climat*, as it is known here, may therefore be owned by scores of different individual owners, each of them cultivating sometimes just a row or two of vines (see CLOS DE VOUGEOT, for example).

The CLASSIFICATION of the vineyards is according to the potential of the site rather than the fame of the producer. The lowest rung is generic BOURGOGNE in various forms, usually on lower-lying land, then village wines named for the commune they come from. Within most village appellations the better vineyards, with favourable exposure at mid slope, have been designated as PREMIER CRU, while in some locations the very finest vineyards, with characters which transcend the TYPICALITY of their village, have been designated GRAND CRU with appellations of their own.

Organization of trade

Unlike the BORDEAUX TRADE, with its large volume of single appellations and many stratifications of those who sell it, the Burgundian wine trade became polarized between growers and merchants. Because the laws of equal inheritance have been strictly applied in a region of such valuable vineyards, individual growers may for example produce just one barrel of a particular appellation, enough to fill just 25 cases. The market for burgundy was originally built by the merchants, who would buy grapes and wine from many growers before blending and selling the results. Increasingly, individual growers with leading vineyards

Burgundy grands crus
(from north to south)

Commune	Grand cru
Côte de Nuits	
(all for red wine unless otherwise stated)	
Gevrey-Chambertin	Mazis-Chambertin
	Ruchottes-Chambertin
	Chambertin Clos-de-Bèze
	Griotte-Chambertin
	Charmes-Chambertin
	Le Chambertin
	Latricières-Chambertin
	Mazoyères-Chambertin
	Chapelle-Chambertin
Morey-St-Denis	Clos de la Roche
	Clos St-Denis
	Clos des Lambrays
	Clos de Tart
	Bonnes Mares (some)
Chambolle-Musigny	Bonnes Mares (most)
	Le Musigny (some white wine too)
Vougeot	Clos de Vougeot
Flagey-Échezeaux	Grands Échezeaux
	Échezeaux
Vosne-Romanée	Richebourg
	Romanée-St-Vivant
	Romanée-Conti
	La Romanée
	La Grande Rue
	La Tâche
Côte de Beaune	
(all for white wine unless otherwise stated)	
Ladoix-Serrigny	Corton (almost all red)
	Corton-Charlemagne
Aloxe-Corton	Corton (almost all red)
	Corton-Charlemagne
	Charlemagne (scarcely used)
Pernand-Vergelesses	Corton-Charlemagne
	Charlemagne (scarcely used)
Puligny-Montrachet	Chevalier-Montrachet
	Bienvenues-Bâtard-Montrachet
with Chassagne-Montrachet	Le Montrachet
	Bâtard-Montrachet
Chassagne-Montrachet	Criots-Bâtard-Montrachet

have been bottling their own wines. Since the early 1990s, the distinctions between growers and merchants have become increasingly blurred, with many widely admired growers also producing another range of wines made from grapes they did not grow themselves, while most merchants have been increasing their vineyard holdings. For more details, see NÉGOCIANTS.

See also HOSPICES DE BEAUNE and see BOURGOGNE for details of Burgundy's generic appellations. For the names of individual appellations, see BEAUNE, NUITS, CHALONNAISE, and MÂCON. J.T.C.M.

CHABLIS and BEAUJOLAIS are treated separately.

Coates, C., *The Wines of Burgundy* (2008).
Morris, J., *Inside Burgundy* (2nd edn, 2021).
Norman, R. H., and Taylor, C., *The Great Domaines of Burgundy* (3rd edn, 2010).
Pitiot, S., and Servant, J.-C., *The Wines of Burgundy* (12th edn of P. Poupon's original, 2012).
www.bourgogne-wines.com
www.burgundy-report.com
www.insideburgundy.com
www.winehog.org

Busby, James (1801–71), the so-called father of Australia's wine industry, was born in Edinburgh in 1801 and arrived in Sydney with his family in 1824. Prior to his departure, James Busby had travelled to Bordeaux in 1822 to investigate viticulture. During the five-month voyage to New South Wales, he wrote *A Treatise on the Culture of the Vine and the Art of Making Wine*, which was published in 1825. It was the first homegrown manual on winemaking for Australian settlers. While it is now considered one of Australia's most important early books, much of the text is a translation of CHAPTAL's *l'Art de faire le vin* (1807 and 1819). Little of it had any relevance for Australian conditions, and it was not well received.

James Busby took up a government position (aged 23) at the Male Orphan School near Liverpool where he was entrusted to develop and manage the extensive 12,300-acre/4,978-ha estate and to teach viticulture at £100 a year. But the farm closed in 1826, and he then worked as a tax collector. His *A Manual of Plain Directions for Planting and Cultivating Vineyards and for Making Wine in New South Wales*, published in 1830, was much better received. Soon afterwards he 'distributed 20,000 vines to fifty intending growers'. George Wyndham planted 600 cuttings at Dalwood in early September 1830.

Frustrated with the slow grind of the New South Wales colonial government, James Busby returned to Europe, where he embarked on a four-month tour of France and Spain in 1831. His tour was partly sponsored by James and William MACARTHUR, whose Camden Nurseries and Vineyard south of Sydney would become an important source of grapevine and other plant material for the colony. It was during this fateful journey that James Busby assembled the greatest collection of grape varieties to be imported into Australia.

Busby collected 437 varieties from the Montpellier Botanical Gardens and 133 varieties from the French National Collection in the Luxembourg Gardens in Paris. He also sourced 44 cuttings from Syon House near Kew outside London. Those collected in Jerez and Malaga perished on the voyage. The collections were planted in the Sydney Botanical Garden, the Busby family's property Kirkton in the Hunter Valley, and Camden Vineyards.

Busby was praised by the colonial press for donating to Sydney's Botanic Gardens 'vines which have hitherto proved the best adapted for making wine'. Of the Sydney collection, however, the NSW Government Gazette (no. 106) reported in 1834, there were '543 varieties in the whole and only 334 are at present alive'. Lack of funding and poor management led to their demise, and when Busby returned to Sydney in 1840 the collection was non-existent. Although cuttings were distributed to local winegrowers by his brother-in-law William Kelman of Kirkton, James Busby's legacy was secured by Sir William Macarthur, whose thriving plant nursery distributed vines throughout the Australian colonies. Genetic material from the Busby collections survives through Australian vineyards established in the 19th century with, notably, clonal selections of Shiraz and Pinot Noir said to have come from HERMITAGE and CLOS DE VOUGEOT respectively.

Busby's life had entered a new dimension in 1833 with his appointment as the first British Resident at the Bay of Islands in New Zealand. He possessed only nominal power but is commonly credited as an architect of the Treaty of Waitangi proclaimed in 1840. This resulted in New Zealand becoming a formal British possession, thwarting French colonial ambitions in the South Pacific. It also led to James Busby's government position becoming redundant, but he remained in New Zealand and had brought vine cuttings with him in 1833. He planted a small plot of vines at his residence at Waitangi Bay, producing a wine described by French explorer Dumont d'Urville in 1840 as 'a light, white wine, very sparkling and delicious to taste'. In all likelihood it was made primarily from Sweetwater (CHASSELAS) and was the first record of winemaking in New Zealand. A.C.

Caillard, A., *The Australian Ark: A History of Wine 1788 to the Modern Era* (2023).
McIntyre, J., *First Vintage, Wine in Colonial New South Wales* (2012).
Moon, P., *The Rise and Fall of James Busby: His Majesty's British Resident in New Zealand* (2020).

bush vines, an alternative term used mainly in Australia and South Africa to describe GOBELET or HEAD-TRAINED, SPUR-PRUNED vines. The comparison with a bush is apt: the vines are trained to a short trunk, normally free-standing (without a TRELLIS SYSTEM), and are pruned to a few SPURS commonly arranged in a ring on short arms from the trunk. Many of these old, and typically low-vigour, vineyards have been replaced by more productive vines with a trellis system, although those OLD VINES that have survived are increasingly valued.

butt, BARREL TYPE associated particularly with SHERRY production. It is usually made from American oak and has a capacity of 600–650 l/160–170 gal. A *bota chica* or shipping butt holds 500 l and is sometimes used as a unit of measurement. New butts are an inconvenience in the sherry-making process and have to be seasoned by being used for the FERMENTATION of lower-quality wines.

Buzet, Gascon AOC in SOUTH WEST FRANCE up the Garonne river from BORDEAUX. The recent history of the appellation, created in 1973, is inextricably intertwined with the dynamism of the local CO-OPERATIVE, which makes all but a tiny proportion of Buzet. Resistance to a monopoly is led by a handful of independents, among whom the BIODYNAMIC Domaine du Pech stands out.

The region, which extends along the left bank of the Garonne between Agen and Marmande, has known viticulture since Roman times. The fortunes of the district's wines suffered during the HUNDRED YEARS WAR, when the district supported the English crown. Trade was further hampered by the restrictions imposed by the Bordelais on all HAUT-PAYS, or 'high country', wines. PHYLLOXERA seriously affected viticulture in the late 19th century, and a ruling in the early 20th century that the name 'Bordeaux' was restricted to wines produced within the GIRONDE *département* was a further blow to this district in the Lot-et-Garonne, which had habitually supplied BLENDING wines to the Bordeaux merchants.

Buzet's vineyards cover more than 1,900 ha/ 4,695 acres. The GRAVELS and CLAYS of these inland hills are planted with classic red Bordeaux vine varieties Cabernet Sauvignon, Cabernet Franc, and, especially, Merlot; Cot (MALBEC), ABOURIOU, and Petit Verdot are also allowed. Whites rely on MUSCADELLE, Sauvignon, and Sémillon. Long a leader in SUSTAINABLE VITICULTURE, the co-operative also began planting grape varieties such as Tempranillo and Syrah and the recent HYBRIDS Artaban and Vidoc in 2019 in response to CLIMATE CHANGE concerns. P.S.

Byblos, ancient town in LEBANON 40 km/25 miles north of modern Beirut. It had the reputation of being the oldest town in the world and was a PHOENICIAN centre of trading. Its wines were famous in classical times.

B

BYO stands for 'Bring Your Own (Wine)' and is a type of restaurant most common in Australia and New Zealand, where the term was coined. The term is associated with maximum wine-drinking pleasure at minimum cost to the restaurant-goer (in tandem with reduced profit to the restaurateur). New Zealanders claim that the BYO name and concept was born in 1976 when the New Zealand authorities, still notably cautious about the distribution of alcoholic drinks, devised the Bring Your Own licence for restaurants at which diners would be allowed to take their own wine. Australians in the state of Victoria, also famously restrictive in its legislative attitude to alcoholic drinks, maintain that Melbourne had BYO establishments in the 1960s. Wherever its origins, this arrangement has become common for a wide range of restaurants in Australia, New Zealand, and elsewhere, the wine often being bought in a nearby retail establishment. CORKAGE is sometimes but not always charged. The expression in North America is **BYOB**, as in 'Bring Your Own Bottle', most commonly encouraged here and elsewhere either in restaurants too new to have a liquor licence and during quiet periods such as Mondays or when regular customers are on holiday.

Cabardès, LANGUEDOC appellation (since 1999) to the north of Carcassonne which produces red and some rosé wines that testify to its location on the cusp of Atlantic and Mediterranean influences. The grape varieties planted in its 460 ha/1,137 acres of vineyard also represent a Bordeaux/Languedoc cocktail of Cabernet Sauvignon, Cabernet Franc, Merlot, Cot (MALBEC), and some FER Servadou, spiced and fleshed out with the more meridional Syrah, Grenache, and CINSAUT (mainly for rosé). The Bordelais varieties tend to prosper on the western, wetter, deeper soils, while wines produced from the hotter, shallower soils of the eastern Cabardès are more likely to have a high proportion of Mediterranean varieties. Winds almost constantly buffet the small hills punctuated by pines and GARRIGUE and minimize the local wine producers' dependence on AGROCHEMICALS. In contrast to MALEPÈRE, a somewhat similar AOC to the south of Carcassonne, production here is mainly in the hands of a small but committed band of individuals constrained by low financial returns. Winemaking equipment and methods are not always the most sophisticated, but the wines boast an originality and potential for longevity that is unusual for this part of France.

Cabernet is loosely used as an abbreviation for either or both of the black grape varieties CABERNET FRANC and CABERNET SAUVIGNON. In north-east Italy in particular there has been a certain lack of precision about the identity of the Cabernet grown and allowed into the many Cabernet-permitting DOCs, although Cabernet Franc has tended to predominate. Elsewhere, Cabernet is more likely to be an abbreviation for Cabernet Sauvignon. Cabernet is also a popular prefix for recent German and Swiss hybrids such as **Cabernet Blanc**, **Cabernet Carbon**, **Cabernet Carol**, **Cabernet Colonjes**, **Cabernet Cortis**, **Cabernet Dorio**, **Cabernet Dorsa** (the most popular), **Cabernet Jura**, and **Cabernet Mitos**.

Cabernet Blanc, Swiss hybrid bred by Valentin Blattner in 1991 for its DISEASE RESISTANCE. One parent is Cabernet Sauvignon, while the second remains undisclosed but is said to include Riesling and Sylvaner in its genealogy.

Cabernet Franc, fine French black grape variety, much blended with and overshadowed by its progeny the more widely planted CABERNET SAUVIGNON. Only in Anjou-Saumur and Touraine in the Loire Valley, on the right bank of the Gironde in Bordeaux, and in parts of north-east Italy is it quantitatively more important than Cabernet Sauvignon, but Cabernet Franc is sufficiently widely grown to be one of the world's 20 most planted cultivars for wine.

In the vineyard it can be distinguished from Cabernet Sauvignon by its less dramatically indented leaves, but the two share so many characteristics that they had long been thought to be related. In 1997, thanks to DNA PROFILING, it was established that Cabernet Franc was, with the Bordeaux white vine variety SAUVIGNON BLANC, a parent of the noble Cabernet Sauvignon (see CABERNET SAUVIGNON for more details).

There is some evidence that the variety's origins lie in Spanish Basque country, but by the end of the 18th century Cabernet Franc was already documented as producing high-quality wine in the Libournais vineyards of St-Émilion, Pomerol, and Fronsac, where it is often called Bouchet today. Long before this, however, according to Odart, it had already been selected by Cardinal Richelieu, as a well-respected vine of south-west France, to be planted at the Abbaye de St-Nicolas-de-Bourgueil in the Loire by an abbot called Breton, whose name persists as the Loire synonym for Cabernet Franc to this day.

Cabernet Franc is particularly well suited to cool, inland climates such as the middle Loire and the Libournais. It buds and matures more than a week earlier than Cabernet Sauvignon, which makes it more susceptible to COULURE, but it is easier to ripen fully and is much less susceptible to poor weather during harvest. In the Médoc and Graves districts of Bordeaux, where Cabernet Franc constitutes about 10% of a typical vineyard and is always blended with other varieties, it is regarded as a form of insurance against the weather's predations on Cabernet Sauvignon and Merlot grapes. Most Libournais bet on Cabernet Franc in preference to the later, and therefore more difficult to ripen, Cabernet Sauvignon to provide a framework for Merlot, Bordeaux's most-planted variety.

In Bordeaux, plantings of Cabernet Franc and Cabernet Sauvignon were almost equal, at about 10,000 ha/25,000 acres, in the late 1960s, but Cabernet Sauvignon was so often chosen in preference to Cabernet Franc by those replacing unprofitable white-wine vineyards that by 2020 Cabernet Sauvignon covered two-and-a-half times Cabernet Franc's total area in the Gironde of 9,276 ha/22,921 acres.

As a wine, Cabernet Franc tends to be rather lighter in colour and tannins, and therefore earlier maturing, than Cabernet Sauvignon, although CHEVAL BLANC, the world's grandest Cabernet Franc-dominated wine, proves that majestic durability is also possible. Cabernet Franc is, typically, light- to medium-bodied with more immediate fruit than Cabernet Sauvignon and has a marked fragrance, including sometimes some of the HERBACEOUS aromas evident in unripe Cabernet Sauvignon.

Cabernet Franc is still planted all over south-west France, although, in appellations such as BERGERAC and MADIRAN (where Cabernet Franc is known as Bouchy), Cabernet Sauvignon has been gaining ground.

Cabernet Franc was France's sixth most planted black grape variety throughout the 20th century and has now risen to fifth place, with about 35% of its 2019 total of 32,282 ha in the south-west and nearly 30% in the greater Loire Valley. Steadily increasing appreciation (largely within France) of relatively light, early-maturing reds such as SAUMUR-CHAMPIGNY, BOURGUEIL, CHINON, and ANJOU-VILLAGES fuelled demand for Cabernet Franc in the Loire at the expense of Rosé d'Anjou and Chenin Blanc whites. Here Cabernet Franc tends to be the dominant variety in perfumed, fresh red wines that can smell of raspberries and/or pencil shavings.

Cabernet Franc is also well established in Italy, particularly in the north-east (see FRIULI and VENETO in particular), where it has sometimes been encouraged to yield such quantity that wines can be over-herbaceous and where some vines previously thought to be Cabernet Franc have been identified as CARMENÈRE. Some Tuscan and central-Italian producers of Cabernet Sauvignon grow the variety for blending purposes, but in BOLGHERI and the rest of the Maremma it can yield wines of real interest and complexity, as it does at Tenuta di Trinoro in southern Tuscany. In 2015, Italy recorded 5,590 ha/13,813 acres of Cabernet Franc compared with the Cabernet Sauvignon total of 14,220 ha. Elsewhere in Europe, only HUNGARY takes Cabernet Franc particularly seriously—especially in Villány.

Elsewhere, with a few notable exceptions such as Viader in the Napa Valley, Cabernet Franc has generally been grown for the express purpose of blending with Cabernet Sauvignon, following the Bordeaux recipe. California's total plantings of the variety, 3,350 acres/1,356 ha in 2020 concentrated in Napa, Sonoma, and San Luis Obispo, have remained stable for years. The variety has been responsible for some well-balanced, fruity wines in WASHINGTON State, where Cabernet Franc is more resistant to WINTER FREEZE than Merlot, but it has been losing ground to the more fashionable Syrah and the hugely dominant Cabernet Sauvignon, so that there were only 674 acres/273 ha by 2017.

In the cooler northern and eastern wine regions of North America (especially VIRGINIA, the Niagara Peninsula of CANADA, where ICEWINE has been made from it, Pennsylvania, and Long Island in NEW YORK State), Cabernet Franc has emerged as the red VITIS VINIFERA variety of choice, ripening much more reliably than Cabernet Sauvignon and providing much more EXTRACT than do most HYBRIDS.

ARGENTINA's plantings of Cabernet Franc have more than doubled in ten years, reaching 1,352 ha/3,341 acres in 2019, while Chile has 1,685 ha/4,164 acres, some of the best being old vines in MAULE.

In Australia, Cabernet Franc plays a very minor, generally lacklustre, part while most of the best of New Zealand's 91 ha/225 acres (down from 161 ha in 2011) contribute to HAWKE'S BAY blends. Although the likes of Rijk's and Warwick make fine varietal versions, Cabernet Franc is planted on less than 1% of South Africa's vineyards.

As the pendulum swings back from super-concentrated, high-alcohol reds, Cabernet Franc is likely to benefit.

Bowers, J. E., and Meredith, C. P., 'The parentage of a classic wine grape, Cabernet Sauvignon', *Nature Genetics*, 16/1 (1997), 84–7.

Odart, A.-P., *Ampélographie universelle* (1845).

Cabernet Gernischt, Chinese name for CARMENÈRE, probably a misspelling of **Cabernet Gemischt** ('mixed Cabernet').

Cabernet Sauvignon, the world's most renowned, but relatively recent, red wine grape, now the world's most planted grape variety, total plantings having more than doubled between 1990 (when it was the world's eighth most planted variety) and 2016 to nearly 310,671 ha/767,685 acres. From its power base in Bordeaux, where it is almost invariably blended with other grapes, it was taken up in other French wine regions and in much of Europe and beyond, included in BORDEAUX BLENDS or blends with INDIGENOUS VARIETIES, and often used to produce VARIETAL wines, especially in warmer climates. Cabernet Sauvignon is now more widely planted beyond Europe than within it.

Perhaps the most extraordinary aspect of Cabernet Sauvignon is its ability to produce a wine that is so recognizably Cabernet, even if remarkably few wine regions, considering its ubiquity, have so far proved reliable sources of seriously top-quality expressions of this potentially top-quality grape: MÉDOC, PESSAC-LÉOGNAN, NAPA, SONOMA, SANTA CRUZ MOUNTAINS, WASHINGTON State, BOLGHERI, COONAWARRA, MARGARET RIVER, STELLENBOSCH, and part of PENEDÈS spring most readily to mind. What makes Cabernet Sauvignon remarkable to taste is not primarily its exact fruit flavour—which is sometimes likened to blackcurrants or cigar boxes—but its structure and its ability to provide the perfect vehicle for individual vintage characteristics, winemaking and ÉLEVAGE techniques, and, especially, local physical attributes, or TERROIR. Unlike CHARDONNAY, which is almost as widely disseminated, late-ripening Cabernet Sauvignon must be grown in relatively warm climates and can in some years fail to reach full RIPENESS even somewhere as mild as the Médoc.

It is Cabernet Sauvignon's remarkable concentration of PHENOLICS that really sets it apart from most other widely grown vine varieties. It is therefore capable of producing deeply coloured wines worthy of long MACERATION and long-term AGEING. Over the centuries, it has demonstrated a special but by no means exclusive affinity for French OAK. The particular appeal of Cabernet Sauvignon lies much less in primary fruit aromas (with which other varieties such as Gamay and Pinot Noir are more obviously associated) than in the much more subtle flavour compounds that evolve from complex interaction between compounds derived from fruit, fermentation, alcohol, and oak over years in bottle. It is also true, however, that so distinctive is Cabernet Sauvignon that part of the reason it is so widely planted is that, even when irrigated to greedily high yields and hastily vinified without even a glimpse of wood, it can produce a wine with some recognizable relationship to the great Bordeaux growths of the Médoc and Graves on which its reputation has been built.

Cabernet Sauvignon's origins long remained shrouded in mystery, but DNA PROFILING revealed all in 1997. Bowers and Meredith of the University of California at DAVIS showed beyond all reasonable doubt that Cabernet Sauvignon's parents are none other than CABERNET FRANC and the Bordeaux white wine grape SAUVIGNON BLANC, a CROSS that is thought to have happened spontaneously in one of the many vineyards planted with a mixture of different vines in the old days. This neatly explains why Cabernet Sauvignon can smell like either or both of its parents, as well as why Cabernet Franc is mentioned in the literature long before Cabernet Sauvignon.

There are no early references to Cabernet Sauvignon in the LITERATURE OF WINE, and the variety did not start to make any significant impact on the vineyards of Bordeaux until the end of the 18th century, when the great estates were built up and wine with real longevity emerged (see BORDEAUX, history). Baron Hector de Brane, once owner of Ch Mouton, together with his neighbour Armand d'Armailhacq, is credited with its promulgation, if not introduction, in the Médoc.

The distinguishing marks of the Cabernet Sauvignon berry are its small size, its high ratio of pip to pulp (1:12, according to Peynaud, as opposed to 1:25 for Sémillon), and the thickness of its skins, so distinctively blue as opposed to red or even purple. The pips are a major factor in Cabernet Sauvignon's high TANNIN level, while its thick skins account for the depth of colour that is the tell-tale sign of a Cabernet Sauvignon in so many BLIND TASTINGS—as well as the variety's relatively good resistance to ROT.

The vine is susceptible, however, to POWDERY MILDEW, which can be treated quite easily, unlike vine TRUNK DISEASES such as EUTYPA DIEBACK and PHOMOPSIS, which cannot. It is extremely vigorous and should ideally be grafted on to a weak ROOTSTOCK to keep its VIGOUR in check. It both buds and ripens late, one to two weeks after Merlot and Cabernet Franc, the two varieties with which it is typically planted and blended in Bordeaux. Cabernet Sauvignon ripens slowly, which has the advantage that picking dates are less crucial than with other varieties (Syrah, for example); but this has the disadvantage that Cabernet Sauvignon simply cannot be relied upon to ripen in the coolest wine regions, especially when its energy can so easily be diverted into producing dangerously shady leaves, such as in Tasmania or New Zealand, unless CANOPY MANAGEMENT is employed. Cabernet Sauvignon that fails to reach full ripeness can taste eerily like Cabernet Franc (just as unripe Sémillon, coincidentally, resembles Sauvignon Blanc).

Even in the temperate climate of Bordeaux, the flowering of the vine can be dogged by cold weather and the ripening by rain, so that Bordeaux's vine-growers have traditionally hedged their bets by planting a mix of early and late local varieties, typically 75% Cabernet Sauvignon plus a mixture of Merlot, Cabernet Franc, and sometimes a little Petit Verdot in the Médoc and Graves districts. (See CABERNET FRANC for the reasons the Cabernet in St-Émilion and Pomerol is much less likely to be Cabernet Sauvignon.)

A practice that had its origins in judicious fruit farming has proved itself in the blending vat. The plump, fruity, earlier-maturing Merlot is a natural blending partner for the more rigorous Cabernet Sauvignon, while Petit Verdot can add extra spice (if only in the sunniest years) and Cabernet Franc can perfume the blend to a certain extent. Except in warmer wine regions, wines made solely from Cabernet Sauvignon can lack charm and stuffing; the framework is sensational, but tannin and colour alone make poor nourishment. As demonstrated by the increasing popularity of Merlot and Cabernet Franc and even Petit Verdot cuttings, some producers follow the Bordeaux example of blending their Cabernet Sauvignon with other varieties in newer wine regions, even those warm enough to ripen Cabernet fully. In Tuscany, it is sometimes blended with Sangiovese. In Australia and in Provence it is blended with SHIRAZ/SYRAH, with very different results.

Cabernet Sauvignon, with its sophisticated whiff of French glamour, was extraordinarily popular in the NEW WORLD in the last two decades of the 20th century. Indeed, it could fairly be said that one of the first signs of 'modernization' of a wine region was its importation of and experimentation with Cabernet Sauvignon cuttings. Only those regions disbarred for reasons of climate, such as England, Germany, and Luxembourg, have found it difficult to join this particular club.

France

French plantings of Cabernet Sauvignon increased enormously in the 1980s and 1990s but have fallen this century so that in 2019 there were 46,971 ha/116,068 acres, of which about half were in the Bordeaux *département* the Gironde (although within the Gironde Merlot is almost three times as popular). The vine's stronghold is the left bank of the River Gironde, most notably the famously well-drained gravels of the Médoc and Graves CRUS classés, whose selling price can well justify the efficacious luxury of ageing their wine in small, often new, oak barrels. Most of the FIRST GROWTHS are famous for their high proportion of Cabernet Sauvignon. Their wines, although differing in character, are known for their firm structure and longevity.

The vine is also planted over much of SOUTH WEST FRANCE, often as an optional ingredient in its red, and occasionally rosé, wines, although only in BERGERAC and BUZET does it play a substantial part. In more internationally styled wines, however, it may add structure to the Négrette of GAILLAC and FRONTON and to the Tannat of BÉARN, IROULÉGUY, and MADIRAN. It is also used to add substance to the red ST-MONT.

Plantings in the Languedoc and Roussillon have increased substantially since the 1980s, so that the total was 14,810 ha/36,596 acres by 2019, but Syrah and Merlot have proved much more successful, and Grenache and Carignan are also much more widely planted. The most obviously successful southern French Cabernet Sauvignons are those used as ingredients in low-yield blends with Syrah and other Rhône varieties, such as Mas de Daumas Gassac in the Hérault or, further east in Provence, Domaine de Trévallon and Ch Vignelaure. Provence had 2,609 ha of Cabernet Sauvignon in 2019.

Cabernet Sauvignon's only other French territory is the Loire, but Cabernet Franc is more than seven times as widely grown, not least because it is so much easier to ripen.

Outside France

Cabernet Sauvignon is by far the dominant variety for the world's fastest growing wine-producing county CHINA, where, according to the OIV, total plantings have reached 60,000 ha/148,263 acres, far exceeding those of Bordeaux. The variety, incidentally, was also very widely planted in the old Soviet Union, where, according to the most accurate estimates available, there were approximately 30,000 ha/75,000 acres of Cabernet Sauvignon before it was broken up. The variety is still widely planted in RUSSIA, UKRAINE, and MOLDOVA—although in the many wine regions susceptible to WINTER FREEZE, the cold-hardy hybrid CABERNET SEVERNY is popular. Cabernet Sauvignon is also grown in GEORGIA, AZERBAIJAN, KAZAKHSTAN, TAJIKISTAN, and KYRGYZSTAN.

Another country with an extremely important area planted with the world's noblest black grape variety is CHILE, whose grand total of (generally UNGRAFTED) Cabernet Sauvignon grew from about 16,000 ha/39,500 acres to about 42,409 ha between 1997 and 2015, making it the country's most important vine variety even if the total has remained fairly stable while Chile experiments with new varieties. Here the fruit is exceptionally healthy and the wine almost rudely exuberant. Not surprisingly, Cabernet Sauvignon also flourishes in the rest of South America's vineyards: in ARGENTINA, where in terms of quantity it is dwarfed by Malbec, and in BRAZIL, URUGUAY, MEXICO, and BOLIVIA.

Cabernet Sauvignon, even less surprisingly, has been the bedrock of CALIFORNIA CULT wines. Such has been the quality of some of these wines that northern California could fairly be said to have proved itself Cabernet Sauvignon's second home, growing far more in total—38,429 ha/94,960 acres—than its first. Although the dramatic growth in Cabernet plantings has stopped, it is California's most important variety by far, though only just ahead of Chardonnay. In the better, and often extremely carefully tended, sites of northern California, Cabernet Sauvignon can ripen quite well enough to need no grower's insurance or winemaker's additional complexity in terms of other grape varieties, and 100% Cabernet Sauvignon can be a hugely successful recipe. For more detail on the Golden State's Cabernet achievements, see CALIFORNIA.

Cabernet Sauvignon is also one of WASHINGTON State's two major black grape varieties. It definitively overtook Merlot in 2006, and by 2017 plantings totalled 7,530 ha/18,608 acres, double the area devoted to Merlot. Cabernet Sauvignon's vigour and late ripening make it unattractive to growers in damp, cool Oregon, but it has been most successful in other American states including Arizona and TEXAS (where it was by far the most planted variety in 2020). In CANADA, the warmer climate of the Okanagan Valley makes BRITISH COLUMBIA much more suitable than ONTARIO for Cabernet Sauvignon.

If Californians decided early on that the Napa Valley was their Cabernet Sauvignon hotspot, Australians did the same about COONAWARRA and, subsequently, MARGARET RIVER. They, however, have for decades employed a much less reverential policy towards blending their Cabernet. Cabernet–Shiraz blends (a recipe recommended in Provence as long ago as 1865 by Dr GUYOT) have been popular items in the Australian marketplace since the 1960s. The richness and softness of Australian Shiraz is such that it fills in the gaps left by Cabernet Sauvignon even more effectively than can the French Syrah recommended by Dr Guyot. Cabernet Sauvignon and Chardonnay vie for second most planted vine variety, but both lag a long way behind Shiraz. In 2022 there were more than 26,000 ha of Cabernet Sauvignon, mainly in South Australia, particularly Coonawarra.

Cabernet Sauvignon was once important in New Zealand, but by 2022 there were barely more than 200 ha/494 acres, most of them in HAWKE'S BAY. It needs careful CANOPY MANAGEMENT to ripen fully, and Pinot Noir is now firmly the country's signature red.

Cabernet Sauvignon was equally revered in SOUTH AFRICA in the late 20th century, but Shiraz had become far more important by 2020 when total Cabernet Sauvignon vineyards had fallen to 9,916 ha/24,503 acres. Many vines are still plagued by LEAFROLL VIRUS, which can prejudice full ripening.

Cabernet Sauvignon has been an increasingly popular choice for internationally minded wine producers in Spain, where it was planted by the Marqués de Riscal at his Rioja estate in the mid 19th century and could also be found in the vineyards of VEGA SICILIA. It was otherwise virtually unknown on the Iberian peninsula until the 1960s, when it was imported into Penedès by Miguel Torres Jr (see FAMILIA TORRES) and Jean León. It broadened its base in Spain, particularly Cataluña, in the late 20th century—not just for wines dominated by it but for blending, notably with Tempranillo. By 2020 there were 18,651 ha/46,088 acres of Cabernet Sauvignon in Spain, making it the sixth most planted red wine vine, yielding some successful reds and some boring basic varietals, from Penedès to Ronda. In Portugal it is much rarer, planted on 1,626 ha/4,018 acres of vineyard in 2020, mainly around Lisbon and in the Alentejo.

Italy, where Cabernet Sauvignon was introduced, via Piemonte, in the 1820s, now has a very substantial area of Cabernet Sauvignon, 14,240 ha/35,188 acres by 2015, almost triple the total recorded for Cabernet Franc. TUSCANY, SICILY, and the VENETO are the most important regions quantitively. Cabernet Sauvignon played a considerable role in the emergence of SUPERTUSCANS and has been popular as a seasoning in an increasing proportion of not just CHIANTI but a wide range of reds throughout the country. In the early 21st century there was a tendency, arguably regrettable, to amend DOC regulations to allow in a small proportion of INTERNATIONAL VARIETIES, notably Cabernet Sauvignon, even though by this time the demand for INDIGENOUS VARIETIES was growing. Cabernet Sauvignon was long a major ingredient in such Tuscan wines as Solaia, Sassicaia, Venegazzù, and Castello di Rampolla's Sammarco, and it even invaded the NEBBIOLO territory of Piemonte in such bottlings as Darmagi from GAJA.

East of Italy there are many thousands of hectares of Cabernet Sauvignon, which plays a particularly important part in the wine industries of BULGARIA, where its 4,773 ha/11,794 acres in 2020 constituted just over 16% of the country's vines. Russia has even more, with 8,528 ha in 2015, and Ukraine 4,935 ha, but it is also very significant in MOLDOVA, where 4,644 ha were planted, making it the most important dark-skinned variety. ROMANIA had 5,496 ha. The variety can ripen reliably in the warm summers of eastern Europe and, as Bulgaria proved in the 1980s, can provide excellent value if grown and made carefully. Smaller amounts of Cabernet Sauvignon are grown in HUNGARY, AUSTRIA, and GREECE, where it was first planted (in modern times at least) at Domaine Carras.

Perhaps the most tenacious Cabernet Sauvignon grower has been Serge Hochar of Ch Musar in LEBANON, where in the last 20 years it has become, along with Cinsaut, the country's most planted wine grape with around 1,000 ha in 2015. It is also by far the most popular variety in ISRAEL's revitalized wine industry and can make fair, if often expensive, copies of California Cabernet there. There are other, rather less war-torn, pockets of Cabernet Sauvignon vines all over the eastern Mediterranean, notably in TÜRKIYE and CYPRUS, as well as in North Africa. In ASIA, Cabernet Sauvignon is planted by virtually all nascent wine industries and is well established already in JAPAN, where its strong links with the famous châteaux of Bordeaux are particularly prized.

Wherever there are any vine-growers with any grounding in the wines of the world, and where late-ripening grapes are economically viable, they are almost certain to try Cabernet Sauvignon—unless they inhabit one of Bordeaux's great rival regions, Burgundy and the Rhône.

Bowers, J. E., and Meredith, C. P., 'The parentage of a classic wine grape, Cabernet Sauvignon', *Nature Genetics*, 16/1 (1997), 84–7.

Lake, M., *Cabernet* (1977).

Lewin, B., *Claret and Cabs: The Story of Cabernet Sauvignon* (2013).

Cabernet Severny, red wine grape variety specially bred for cold climates at the All-Russia Potapenko Institute in the Rostov region of RUSSIA. It was created by pollination of a HYBRID of DIMYAT (known here as Galan) × VITIS AMURENSIS with a pollen mixture of other hybrid forms involving both the European vine species VITIS VINIFERA and the famously cold-hardy Mongolian vine species *amurensis*. It is grown in Russia and colder parts of Canada.

Cabinet, term of approbation applied to German wines from the 18th century until 1971, when its use was outlawed. A wine labelled Auslese Cabinet, for instance, signified an AUSLESE especially prized by its producer. The term was also used for precious works of art, implying a piece worthy of enshrining in the proprietor's cabinet. It was occasionally spelled with a K. *Kabinettstück* is still used in German in the sense of *pièce de résistance*, and its cachet was borrowed by the 1971 German wine law for the technically defined PRÄDIKAT known as KABINETT. D.S.

Cabrières, village and DÉNOMINATION GÉOGRAPHIQUE COMPLÉMENTAIRE for reds and rosés within the LANGUEDOC AOC inside the CLAIRETTE DU LANGUEDOC zone. The CO-OPERATIVE dominates production, but the launch of Gérard Bertrand's Clos du Temple in 2018, the world's most expensive rosé when it was released, has raised the profile of this obscure region.

Cachapoal, part of the Rapel subregion of the Central Valley in CHILE.

Cadillac, 62-ha/153-acre sweet-white-wine appellation created in 1967 to house the top-quality vineyards of 22 selected villages along the north bank of the GARONNE river, inside the broader PREMIÈRES CÔTES DE BORDEAUX appellation. Strict INAO rules insist on, among other things, the use of only botrytized or raisined grapes (primarily Sémillon and Sauvignon), a minimum pre-fermentation sweetness of one-third more than for the Premières Côtes, and CHÂTEAU BOTTLING. A dozen growers are almost totally dedicated to producing these very sweet wines, nearly but not quite (because of their higher permitted yield of 40 hl/ha) in the generous style of SAUTERNES. Many of the large ENTRE-DEUX-MERS estates who major on dry wine (white and red) also like to try their hand at small cuvées of sweet Cadillac to widen their range. The region takes its name from its principal 13th-century fortified riverside town built during the 100 Years War. In 1801, Lord Lamothe-Cadillac became governor of Louisiana and founded the city of Detroit, whence the automobile brand name. Not to be confused with the red-wine appellation CADILLAC CÔTES DE BORDEAUX. W.J.B.

Cadillac Côtes de Bordeaux, part of the Côtes de BORDEAUX appellation, officially recognized in 2011, for the ambitious reds made on the south-facing slopes along the right bank of the Garonne between Bordeaux and Langon. Merlot with Cabernet Sauvignon and Cabernet Franc are planted on about 1,000 ha/5,000 acres of vineyard dedicated to the production of these often good-value reds. The soils here are very varied, with the *coteaux* rising from the riverbank offering the most valuably gravelly or CALCAREOUS terrain. CLAY predominates on the plateau between the *coteaux* and the ENTRE-DEUX-MERS boundary. The relatively small quantity of sweet white wines produced on this strip of land are called PREMIÈRES CÔTES DE BORDEAUX. There is a recognizable band of seriously ambitious producers here, especially of quite concentrated red wines which may lack the ageing potential of Bordeaux's more famous examples but can offer good value for drinking at three to five years old. J.R & J.L.

Caecuban wine was ranked by the connoisseurs of ancient ROME among the finest wines of Italy for the last century BCE and the first half of the 1st century CE. Caecuban wine was produced on a small vineyard in the low-lying marshy region, south of Terracina, on the west coast of central Italy, between the sea and the Lago di Fondi. The vines were trained up poplars (see ARBOREAL VITICULTURE). Caecuban was a white wine which, following standard Roman practice, was aged for a number of years, during which it deepened to a 'flame' colour. It was described as 'sinewy' and 'packing a punch' by the medical writer Galen. The vineyard was largely destroyed in the middle of the 1st century CE by the ambitious, though abortive, scheme of Emperor Nero to dig a canal to link the bay of Naples with the Tiber. Caecuban never recovered, and the name became simply a generic term for wine with the characteristic colour of the true wine. Small quantities of red wine called Cécubo are produced in the district today. J.J.P.

Pliny the Elder, *Natural History*, 14. 6, translated by H. Rackham (1945).

Cagnina, synonym for TERAN (or Terrano) in Italy's Romagna region.

Cahors, AOC wine region in the Quercy district of SOUTH WEST FRANCE producing exclusively red wine, uniquely in France dependent on the MALBEC or Cot grape (traditionally called here Auxerrois). Cahors is influenced by the Mediterranean as well as by the Atlantic, and, although winters are rather colder than in Bordeaux, the wines tend to be more concentrated. The region's reputation for wines rich in colour and BODY dates from at least the early Middle Ages. The River Lot provided an ideal trade route to the markets of northern Europe via the GARONNE and Bordeaux, and there are records of Cahors being sold in London in the early 13th century.

The wines were appreciated as blending material with the lighter wines of Bordeaux, and in the early 19th century they were famed as the 'black wines of Cahors'. (Such was Cahors's international renown in the 19th century that imitation 'Cahors' was made by at least one of the Russian model wineries in the CRIMEA.) A method to make the wines even blacker had been adopted whereby a portion of the grape juice was boiled to concentrate its colour and fermentable sugars. The produce of this technique was designed specifically for blending rather than drinking.

At this time there were almost 40,000 ha/100,000 acres of vineyards in the greater Cahors region, but PHYLLOXERA reduced it to less than one-tenth of this, resulting in considerable replanting with HYBRIDS. The arrival of the RAILWAYS also gave the populous north ready access to the cheap and plentiful wines of the LANGUEDOC. Cahors fell into decline.

The Caves d'Olt CO-OPERATIVE, established at Parnac in 1947, encouraged a new era of quality winegrowing, increasing the proportion of noble grape varieties and the incidence of good winemaking equipment and technology. The notorious WINTER FREEZE of 1956 all but destroyed the Cahors vignoble and provided an opportunity for almost total reconstruction. An overwhelming majority of the vineyards were replanted with Malbec, a traditional Cahors variety which is nowhere else associated with particularly long-living wines.

In 1971 full AOC status was granted for the region's red wines, the rules stipulating at least 70% Malbec, supplemented by the tannic TANNAT and/or the supple MERLOT. Cahors is exceptional among south-west French appellations in that neither Cabernet vine is allowed in the AOC.

Production in 2020 amounted to 150,000 hl/3,962,581 gal from approximately 3,323 ha/8,211 acres of vines. Within south-west France only BERGERAC makes more wine. Vines may be planted either on the notably thin topsoil of the arid, LIMESTONE plateau, the *causses*, or on the SAND and GRAVEL terraces between the plateau and the river, the *terrasses*. Others come from the *coteaux*, the narrow corridors leading from the one to the other. Modern winemaking skills and techniques tend to blur the distinction between wines from these three sources.

Since its renaissance, Cahors has developed several distinct styles of wine, from fruity and quaffable to velvety, concentrated, and oaked, while a handful of growers continue the old-fashioned traditions (e.g. Clos de Gamot, Clos Triguedina). Wine-making techniques therefore vary accordingly, with variable approaches to MACERATION and BARREL MATURATION, some growers seeking to escape from the success of Malbec in ARGENTINA, others to emulate it.

Cahors is limited to wines made in the Lot *département*. Just over the western boundary in Lot-et-Garonne can be found the IGP Thezac-Péricard, whose wines are similar to but lighter than the Cahors style. Cahors growers seeking escape from AOC rules can produce IGP wines from the Lot, including whites and rosés. P.S.

Caíño Blanco is grown to a very limited extent in north-western Iberia, notably in GALICIA, while **Caíño Tinto** is the Galician name for the rather more common BORRAÇAL.

Cairanne, southern RHÔNE cru, promoted from Côtes du Rhône-Villages to AOC Cairanne in 2015. Only 5% of the wines produced from its 877 ha/2,167 acres of vineyards in 2020 were white; the rest are red, a blend of 40% Grenache plus Syrah or Mourvèdre (or both), possibly with small amounts of a further 16 varieties. Whites must contain at least two of the following: Clairette, Grenache Blanc, or Roussanne (and at least 20% of any that are used). They may also contain Bourboulenc, Marsanne, Piquepoul Blanc, or Viognier. The appellation is spread over the generally south-facing slope of the western flank of a large hill of MARL and pebbles situated between the Aigues and Ouvèze rivers, reaching 350 m/1,148 ft in ELEVATION. (The south-facing slope of the eastern flank is occupied by RASTEAU, an AOC with which Cairanne shares a border.) There is also some flat land at the foot of the hill and a further growing area on the other side of the Aigues. The reds have the characteristic generosity of southern Rhône wines but tend to be less bold and potent than those produced in Rasteau. Whites are typically well balanced, with less body and oak influence than those of CHÂTEAUNEUF-DU-PAPE. M.C.W.

Calabrese, meaning 'of Calabria', is a common synonym for NERO D'AVOLA, while the rare, unrelated **Calabrese di Montenuovo** has been identified as a parent of SANGIOVESE.

Calabria, rugged, mountainous region in southern Italy, is one of the world's oldest wine regions. There were already vines trained on stakes when the first Greek settlers arrived around 400 BCE. This may be why they called this part of Italy Enotria or 'land of the vines': *oinotron* refers to the stake to which the BUSH VINES were tied. Still used in Calabria, they are now officially called *alberello enotrio con palo secco*.

With the arrival of the Romans in Calabria in 300 CE, large-scale agricultural holdings (the so-called *latifundi* worked by slaves) were introduced to the region. Food and wine production became more sophisticated and refined. The system continued for centuries, with slaves replaced by sharecroppers, until in the 1950s it was abolished, replaced by small family farms founded through land donations. A disastrous phase began with the emergence of the *cantine sociale*, CO-OPERATIVES, which encouraged high yields at the cost of quality. Soon more profitable crops such as citrus and kiwi replaced vineyards, which were decimated further by the 2008 EU VINE-PULL SCHEME. In 2019 the total surface was estimated at 10,706 ha/26,455 acres.

By the 2010s a renaissance had begun, spurred on by an interest in Calabria's many INDIGENOUS VARIETIES. Librandi, which conquered the international market in the 1990s with a BARRIQUE-aged blend called Gravello, has been the motor, making up for the absence of any regional academic viticultural department or station with its own extensive clonal research into local varieties such as GAGLIOPPO, the principal red grape of the region and the basis of the Cirò DOC. The Cirò Revolution, a group of producers practising ORGANIC and BIOYDNAMIC VITICULTURE and long MACERATION times, has also been fundamental in forging change. In the tiny neighbouring Melissa DOC, newcomers produce small quantities of boundary-pushing wines fermented in QVEVRI.

Each of Calabria's nine DOCs boasts a host of high-quality, indigenous varieties. In Terre di Cosenza, a very large DOC bordering BASILICATA to the north, the white GRECO BIANCO (unrelated to Campanian Greco), Mantonico, and the red MAGLIOCCO Canino and Dolce take the lead, sometimes in blends with INTERNATIONAL VARIETIES but more and more on their own. Lamezia, on the west coast, shares NERELLO MASCALESE and NERELLO CAPPUCCINO with Sicily's Etna across the Strait of Messina, suggesting an ancient historic link, as does NERO D'AVOLA, here called Calabrese. Around the town of Bianco, the coppery-hued GRECO BIANCO could be a direct descendant of what Greek settlers first found here.

Promising developments come from Vibo Valentia, a Magliocco hotbed without a denomination where seven producers under the banner of Viticoltori Vibonesi are petitioning for a new IGT. Where state subsidies and intervention have failed for decades, private initiative now propels Calabria forwards. W.S.

Librandi, P. (ed.), *Calabria: Valorizzare con Metodi Moderni un'Antica Vocazione Vinicola* (2014).

Gagliardi, G., and Convertini, G., *Il Vino nelle Terre di Cosenza* (2013).

Caladoc, reliable dark-skinned cross of GRENACHE and Cot (MALBEC) created in 1958 by French AMPELOGRAPHER Paul Truel to produce a Grenache-like variety less prone to COULURE. It is a permitted ingredient in Côtes du Rhône and also used to add TANNINS and aroma to some southern French reds. France grew a total of 5,959 ha/14,725 acres by 2019, and there were 2,533 ha in Portugal, mainly in Lisboa, by 2020. It is also grown in Spain, Lebanon, Morocco, and Argentina.

Calatayud, DOP with 3,293 ha/8,137 acres of vines in ARAGÓN in north-east Spain, in arid country on either side of the river Jalón, a tributary of the Ebro (see map under SPAIN). As in much of central Spain, YIELDS rarely rise above 20 hl/ha. Vineyards are planted at 550–1,040 m/1,804–3,412 ft in elevation, where the DIURNAL TEMPERATURE RANGE helps moderate the hot summers; the cierzo, a dry, cold north wind, helps minimize FUNGAL DISEASE pressure. Red grapes make up 92% of plantings, especially GARNACHA, which makes heady, potent red wine, although TEMPRANILLO and SYRAH are also planted. Some crisp white wines are made from VIURA. Most grapes are sold to one of six CO-OPERATIVES, although impressive results come from independent producers such as Escocés Volante, Langa, and Breca. F.C.

calcaire. See LIMESTONE.

calcareous refers to geological materials that are 'limy' (i.e. composed significantly of calcium carbonate, as the mineral calcite), in contrast to siliceous rocks such as GRANITE and SANDSTONE (see GEOLOGY). Calcareous materials include MARL, LIMESTONE (and its subvarieties CHALK and dolomite), and their associated soils.

Calcareous soils abound in the Eastern Mediterranean–Caspian Sea region in which VITIS VINIFERA originated, as well as in the southern European areas through which the vine eventually spread. Consequently they are associated with a number of classic European wines such as CHAMPAGNE, BURGUNDY, BAROLO, and SHERRY.

Most natural caves, some now utilized for wine maturation and storage, are formed in limestone. This is because much natural water contains carbon dioxide dissolved from the air, creating a weak acid that reacts with calcareous materials to form calcium hydrogen carbonate (bicarbonate), which is soluble. This also explains distinctive landscapes such as that of the French *causses*. Similarly, calcareous bedrock is commonly fissured, allowing any deep vine roots to seek water that may be stored there.

Calcareous soils have a higher PH than siliceous soils, typically between 6 and 7, because free hydrogen is removed from water when it is integrated into bicarbonate. This is the pH range in which many nutrients are at their optimum availability (see SOIL ACIDITY, SOIL ALKALINITY). However, above pH 7 many elements become unavailable, so soils excessively high in calcium carbonate are not ideal for viticulture and can cause lime-induced CHLOROSIS. There is a common belief that the raised pH of calcareous soils leads to enhanced acidity in the finished wine, but there is no consistent relationship. A.J.M.

calcium is an essential mineral nutrient (see VINE NUTRITION) and is important in vineyard soils. In the vine, it participates in hormone signalling networks, for example in communicating WATER STRESS; it enhances the structure of cell walls and membranes; and it promotes resistance to microbial attack, such as from GREY ROT and DOWNY MILDEW. Calcium is taken up in soil water by the roots, principally during the period of rapid growth preceding VERAISON. Because it is easily precipitated and can partially block the PHLOEM, after veraison transmission to the fruit declines.

Most rocks yield soils with sufficient calcium for vines. It usually originates from clay minerals or plagioclase feldspar (see GEOLOGY) or from the calcium carbonate that defines the calcareous rocks. Calcium readily displaces sodium from clay surfaces, which increases soil friability, microbial activity, and drainage. (See SOIL TEXTURE and SOIL AND WINE QUALITY.) The drainage encouraged by calcium partly accounts for the suitability of soils in damp northerly European wine regions such as Burgundy and Champagne.

Calcium salts have important effects on soil PH and CATION EXCHANGE CAPACITY. The availability of elements as plant nutrients is broadly correlated with soil pH. Calcium in soils is usually accompanied by a pH of 6–7, at which point many plant nutrients and trace elements are at their most available (see SOIL ACIDITY, SOIL ALKALINITY). The presence of calcium in soils often correlates with the optimum pH for vine growth, which is why liming soils not only tends to improve soil texture but can also increase the availability of nutrients. However, above pH 7, many elements become unavailable, so soils extremely high in calcium carbonate are not ideal for viticulture and cause lime-induced CHLOROSIS. A.J.M.

Caldaro, or **Kaltern** in German, township in ALTO ADIGE, northern Italy. It gives its name to **Lago di Caldaro** or **Kalterersee**, a large DOC zone unreasonably extended into neighbouring TRENTINO for red wines produced from SCHIAVA Grossa, Schiava Gentile, and/or Schiava Grigia. The wines' general lightness owed much to high yields of 14 tons/ha, but a new generation of producers are proving that high quality is possible.

California, highly successful 'wine state' of the United States producing 81% of all US-grown wine, in some years more than 735 million gal/27 million hl in total, and three out of every five bottles sold in the US for a total of $40 billion in 2020, making the state effectively the world's fourth biggest producer of wine. California was also for many years the only source of VITIS VINIFERA wine in the US. California wine, has, since its true commercial beginnings in 1822, experienced several cycles of boom and bust, emerging in the modern era as a powerhouse in the global wine industry, with superior-quality wines anointed by critics as among the best in the world.

History

Franciscan MISSIONARIES planted the first *vinifera* vines with the help of converted, coerced, or conscripted Native Americans in California around 1779 (the native *Vitis californica* and *Vitis girdiana* being unfit for wine). For the next 70 years the Franciscans' MISSION grape remained the basis of California winegrowing, passing from the missions to small growers as the mission lands were secularized under the

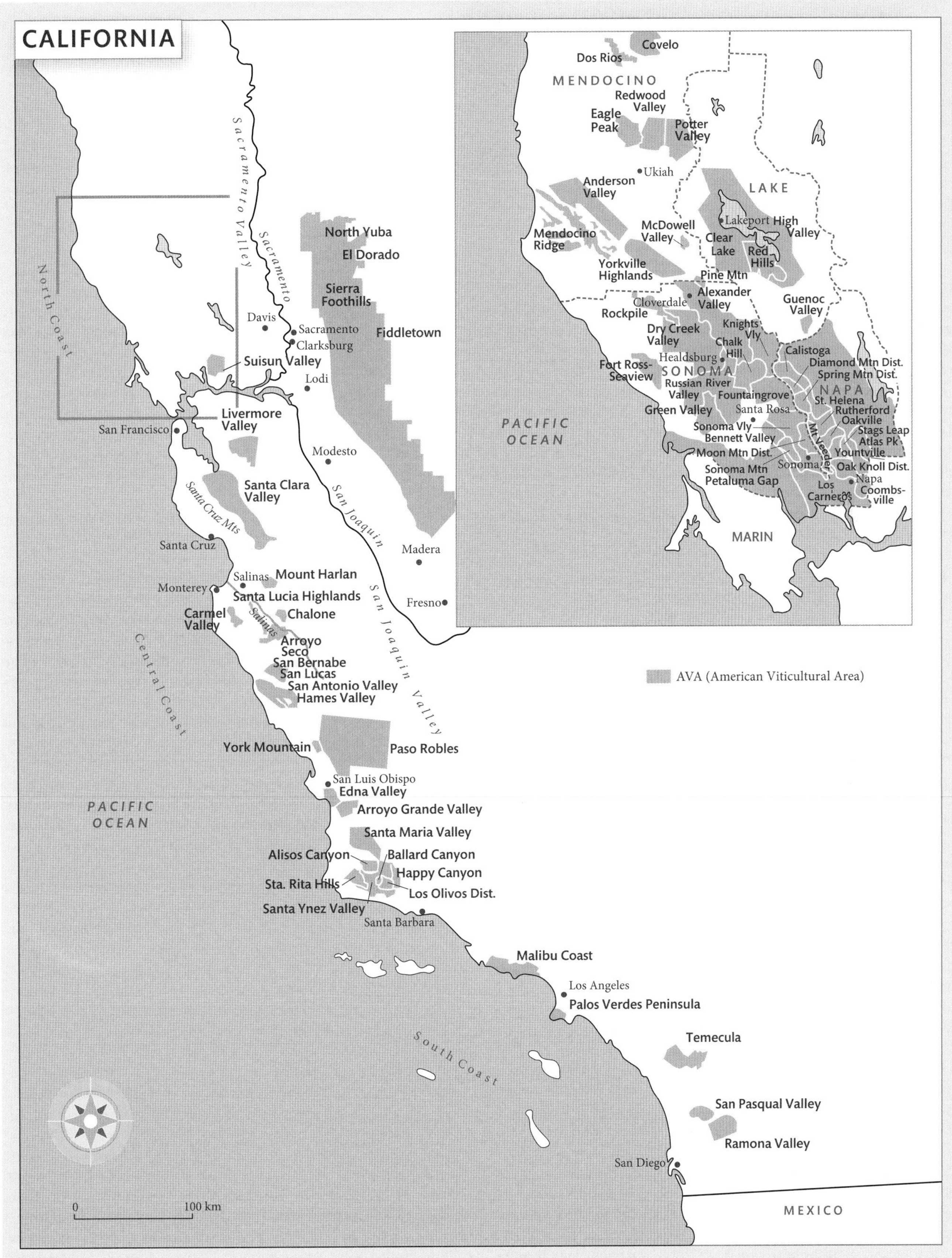
CALIFORNIA
North Coast
Sacramento Valley
Sacramento
North Yuba
El Dorado
Sierra Foothills
Fiddletown
Davis
Sacramento
Clarksburg
Suisun Valley
Lodi
Livermore Valley
San Francisco
Modesto
Santa Clara Valley
Santa Cruz Mts
San Joaquin
Santa Cruz
Madera
Salinas
Mount Harlan
Monterey
Santa Lucia Highlands
Fresno
Carmel Valley
Chalone
Salinas
Arroyo Seco
San Bernabe
San Lucas
San Antonio Valley
Hames Valley
Central Coast
San Joaquin Valley
York Mountain
Paso Robles
San Luis Obispo
Edna Valley
Arroyo Grande Valley
PACIFIC OCEAN
Santa Maria Valley
Alisos Canyon
Ballard Canyon
Happy Canyon
Sta. Rita Hills
Los Olivos Dist.
Santa Ynez Valley
Santa Barbara
Malibu Coast
Los Angeles
Palos Verdes Peninsula
Temecula
South Coast
San Pasqual Valley
Ramona Valley
San Diego
MEXICO
0 100 km
Covelo
Dos Rios
MENDOCINO
Redwood Valley
Eagle Peak
Potter Valley
Ukiah
Anderson Valley
LAKE
Lakeport
High Valley
Mendocino Ridge
McDowell Valley
Clear Lake
Red Hills
Yorkville Highlands
Pine Mtn
Alexander Valley
Guenoc Valley
Cloverdale
Rockpile
Knights Vly
Dry Creek Valley
Chalk Hill
Calistoga
Healdsburg
Diamond Mtn Dist.
Fort Ross-Seaview
SONOMA
Spring Mtn Dist.
Russian River Valley
NAPA
Fountaingrove
St. Helena
Green Valley
Santa Rosa
Rutherford
Oakville
PACIFIC OCEAN
Sonoma Vly
Stags Leap
Bennett Valley
Atlas Pk
Mt Veeder
Moon Mtn Dist.
Yountville
Sonoma
Sonoma Mtn
Oak Knoll Dist.
Petaluma Gap
Napa
Los Carneros
Coombs-ville
MARIN
AVA (American Viticultural Area)

C

newly independent Mexican government beginning in 1834. In 1838, George Yount planted the first vines near the town that now bears his name in Napa. After the US annexation of Alta California in 1847 and the discovery of gold in 1848, winegrowing spread throughout the state. California's fame as a new wine region spread even as far as North Caucasus (see RUSSIA).

Following the GOLD RUSH of 1849, both population and vineyards expanded rapidly in the districts around San Francisco Bay and in Gold Country as demand for many things, alcohol especially, drove a frenzied boom of commercialism. SONOMA Valley had been a centre of winemaking activity since the 1820s thanks to Mariano Vallejo, the Mexicans' military commandant for Alta California, whose wines were good enough to inspire Agoston HARASZTHY to purchase 560 acres in 1857 and begin what would become Buena Vista Winery.

By 1891, Sonoma had 9,180 ha/22,683 acres under vine compared with the NAPA Valley's 18,000 acres, the vast majority of both having been planted by Chinese labourers lately arrived from their work on the transcontinental railroad. The Chinese Exclusion Act of 1882 and the heavy persecution that followed would eventually drive most to leave the region entirely. Accelerated in no small measure by the devastation of Europe's vineyards by PHYLLOXERA, the 1870s and 1880s saw an extraordinary burst of investment in vineyards and wineries, benefiting not just these NORTH COAST counties but also LIVERMORE VALLEY, SANTA CLARA VALLEY, and LODI.

By the end of the 19th century, nearly every region currently producing wine in California had been tried, and production was over 1.1 million hl/30 million gal, largely from the northern part of the state, especially Sonoma, Napa, and Santa Clara counties. The vast central SAN JOAQUIN VALLEY began to be developed for the large-scale production of inexpensive wines in the 1870s, especially in Fresno and Madera counties. The state had officially encouraged winegrowing from the earliest years, recognizing it as one of California's most distinctive contributions to the US economy. A board of State Viticultural Commissioners did useful work from 1880 to 1895, and the wine research and education of the University of California (first at Berkeley and subsequently in DAVIS) began in 1880 and continues today.

Aggressive research and education by E. W. Hilgard and Frederic T. Bioletti at the university produced immediate and significant impacts. By 1881, scholars and growers alike saw clearly that the coastal counties were for finer TABLE WINES, the San Joaquin for everyday table wines. Already California grew more than 300 *vinifera* varieties, with CHASSELAS, ZINFANDEL, BURGER, and of course Mission predominating, even if most of the nearly 800 wineries producing at California's 19th-century peak (about the same number as a century later) sold their wines anonymously in BULK to a handful of blender/bottlers who offered broad ranges of wine types to the trade.

Over-planting, however, and attempts by a few powerful merchants to corner the wine market caused prices of grapes and wine to crash in the 1890s, dropping below production costs. This and the first signs of phylloxera in California caused the first major setbacks for this burgeoning industry, devastating the state's wine production. PROHIBITION, legally in force from 1920 to 1933, challenged the remaining market. It was many decades before some areas recovered their pre-Prohibition status as wine regions, although Napa, Sonoma, and the Central Valley survived by producing and selling SACRAMENTAL and 'medicinal' wines and by shipping grapes and concentrate throughout the country for legal HOME WINEMAKING purposes.

Immediately after the Repeal of Prohibition, the market demanded mostly sweet wines. Relatively few producers attempted to make high-quality table wines from superior varieties. By the end of the Second World War, there were only about 120 producing wineries, most of them bottling their own production. A trade far more familiar with whiskey than wine encouraged the survivors to produce 'full lines', echoing not the old blender/bottlers but importers who were now bringing in broad arrays of wines from Europe sold under GENERIC names. In the THREE-TIER SYSTEM of distribution it may have been the retailers who were most to blame for wanting to keep their domestic orders as simple as their import invoices, reinforced by the general ignorance of the American drinking public. California thus produced wines sold under such generic names as Burgundy and Chablis.

During this time, however, researchers A. J. WINKLER and Maynard AMERINE at Davis were establishing the blueprints for the state's modern understanding of its wine industry, namely by answering the questions of what should be grown where and how to make commercially viable wine at scale. Their work, including Winkler's famous CLIMATE CLASSIFICATION scale, set the stage for California's eventual rise as a global player in wine.

After a period of struggle that lingered beyond the Great Depression and the Second World War, a second grand burst of investment was evident between 1970 and 1985, most obviously in Napa but also in Sonoma. In 1976, the year of the famed JUDGMENT OF PARIS tasting, there were 45 wineries operating in Napa and 47 in Sonoma, and America's annual wine consumption was growing by double digits. That triumph of California wines over their French counterparts in Paris proved to be a watershed moment for the state, putting California wine on the map and sparking significant activity in the domestic market, amplifying America's already growing interest in wine to still greater heights.

New wineries proliferated, production rose, more suitable varieties were extensively planted, higher standards were aimed at, and market demand was swiftly answered, mostly with VARIETAL wines closely tied to their region of origin, a distinct step up from the generic wines that had dominated the state's production since Prohibition.

Although a new strain of phylloxera in the late 1980s slowed things down, growing populations around San Francisco pushed vineyard planting south into MONTEREY, SAN LUIS OBISPO, and SANTA BARBARA counties. Then in the late 1990s a third wave of expansion, in no small part fuelled by the overnight successes of internet and multimedia entrepreneurs in northern California, pushed experimental planting into lesser-known regions as land in the Central Coast, Napa, and Sonoma became increasingly expensive. (See Climate and geography, below, and AVA.) By 2005 the number of wine companies in the state had shot past the late 1980s record of 800 to nearly 1,700, and by 2020 the number of bonded wineries in the state numbered 4,200.

The first wave of commercial California wineries in the 19th century were founded by European immigrants who brought their (primarily) German and French sensibilities and experiences to the industry. These pioneers were followed by a larger population of Anglo-Americans who arrived with the Gold Rush. A later wave of Italian immigrants kept things going during and after Prohibition. In the second half of the 20th century, traditional farming families were joined by an eclectic population of engineers, painters, physicians, pilots, retired industrialists, reformed hippies, and other second careerists who somehow found a calling in wine.

The most ambitious and well-funded of these new players were responsible for the next wave of prestige winery creation in the late 1980s and early 1990s, which found its apotheosis in the so-called CALIFORNIA CULT wines and set the stage for a dramatic and sustained rise in prices for land, grapes, and finished wines. These wineries and their wines also paved the way for a rise in both alcohol levels and extraction (see Winemaking below) as Robert PARKER and other American critics rewarded ripeness and opulence with higher and higher scores. The American palate and pocketbook followed.

The advent of CUSTOM-CRUSH FACILITIES and their associated services, combined with an increasingly flexible market for grape contracts in the early part of the 21st century, dramatically lowered the capital requirements for starting a premium wine label, most importantly eliminating the need to own a vineyard in order to make wine of the highest quality. A significant portion of the new wine companies created since 2010 own no property and make wine in shared facilities. The use of experienced consulting winemakers in conjunction with this estateless approach to production has made it possible for anyone with enough money and determination to launch a wine brand with vineyard-designated wines from well-known sites, made at remarkable levels of quality. So perfected has this model become that it is now impossible to distinguish between fine wines made in this manner and those hailing from landed estates with decades of history.

The market for wine in the United States grows at 1–2% annually, and California continues to supply three-fifths of all domestic requirements, shipping a high of 286 million cases in the generous 2018 vintage. Meanwhile US wine exports, which were negligible after the Second World War, have grown steadily since the mid 1980s, with California supplying 95% of that volume. In 1986, the US exported only 7.3 million gallons/0.275 million hl with a value to the wineries of US$35 million. In 2020, those figures had risen to 100 million gallons/3.7 million hl with a value to the wineries of US$1.36 billion generated from 142 countries. Canada was the biggest importer, followed in order by the UK, EU member countries, Japan, Hong Kong, South Korea, and China.

The considerable costs and legal requirements associated with export and global distribution mean that the majority of California's finest wines never find their way abroad, leaving export sales largely the domain of only the largest or the most persistently dedicated wine brands. T.P., L.M., J.H.B. & A.Y.

Carosso, V., *The California Wine Industry: A Study of the Formative Years* (1951).

Pinney, T., *A History of Wine in America: From the Beginnings to Prohibition* (1989).

Pinney, T., *A History of Wine in America: From Prohibition to the Present* (2005).

Street, R. S., *Beasts of the Field: A Narrative History of California Farmworkers, 1769–1913* (2004).

Sullivan, C., *A Companion to California Wine* (1998).

Climate and geography

Those unfamiliar with California assign it a two-season MEDITERRANEAN CLIMATE. This is but a partial truth that cannot accurately characterize a region with the topographic diversity of America's third largest state. Offshore ocean currents cause an intermittent fog-bank along California's 1,350-km/850-mile-long coast, creating extensive stretches with insufficient sunshine to ripen most grapes. These fogs do not penetrate far inland, because of the 1,000-m/3,300-ft high coastal range, leaving the San Joaquin Valley generally too warm and sunny to grow fine table wines. However, in the sharply convoluted in-between of the Coast Ranges, the jumbled terrain, variable fog, and marine breezes create pockets with growing seasons that echo those of Castellina-in-CHIANTI, ST-ESTÈPHE, BEAUNE, and even Hattenheim in the RHEINGAU. There is no linear pattern. Westerly parts of Santa Barbara County are cooler and foggier than any part of Napa which is some 500 km/300 miles north, while much of Mendocino, nearly 80 miles north of Napa, has hotter summers. Openings to the Pacific Ocean in the Coast Ranges indicate the cool spots, while mountain barriers locate the warmer ones.

While once relatively predictable, precipitation patterns and levels have shown volatility in the wake of widespread CLIMATE CHANGE, with sometimes localized extremes. Frequent DROUGHT effects notwithstanding, total annual RAINFALL north of San Francisco is 615–1,150 mm/24–45 in, while from San Francisco southwards non-drought totals range from 20 inches to the low teens/500 mm to around 330 mm. Occurring in 10- to 20-year cycles during the 19th and early 20th centuries, DROUGHTS are now more frequent and more extreme in California. The state experienced droughts in 1976–7, 1986–92, 2007–9, 2011–19, and again beginning in 2020, which proved to be the driest year since 1924.

Winters in California's grape-growing regions are mild to outright balmy. Damaging WINTER FREEZES are virtually unheard of.

Spring FROSTS, once common, are now less of a factor, though few growers are willing to scrap their costly investments in mitigation, which include SPRINKLERS and WIND MACHINES, huge fans that keep cold air moving in the vineyards. Spring rains sometimes interfere with flowering and fruit set, but rarely disastrously. The near total lack of summer rainfall (between mid June and September) usually makes for a relatively bucolic growing season and easy harvest.

California has been increasingly subject to WILDFIRES near harvest time, whose localized impacts have affected wine grapes to a greater or lesser extent in the 2007, 2008, 2017, 2018, 2020, and 2021 vintages.

It proves difficult to typify soil types in California's vineyards because so much of the state's landforms have been emplaced on the North American tectonic plate and then crumpled together by the Pacific tectonic plate sliding beneath it. Most vineyards have intrusions of several soil types, hence identification and separate vinification of different blocks within vineyards (see PRECISION VITICULTURE) became increasingly valuable tools in the early 21st century for California's most quality-conscious winemakers. As a result, single-vineyard, single-block, and/or single-clone bottlings have proliferated.

The US federal government began holding hearings in 1983 to approve AVA (American Viticultural Area) names for use on labels. That process is ongoing, but it has been widely criticized for outcomes which often seem more marketing-driven or politically expedient than useful to consumers. Before 1983, California's geographical appellations were by and large its counties. Those county names, still much used in practice on wine labels, have been, in descending order of popularity, NAPA, SONOMA, SANTA BARBARA, MENDOCINO, MONTEREY, AMADOR, EL DORADO, LAKE, and SAN LUIS OBISPO. Up to 25% of a wine labelled with the county name may come from elsewhere.

AVAs are purely geographical, imposing no restrictions on varieties planted, vineyard practices, or winemaking protocols. By 2022, California had 144 (out of a national total of 262), with subregions of Napa, Sonoma, and Santa Barbara being the most recognized among wine lovers. More than 20 of the state's AVAs have been added since 2015, with many still so little known that county names often remain more effective at communicating vineyard location. The use of an AVA designation on a wine label requires 85% of its grapes to be grown in the stated AVA.

Individual California AVAs are detailed in this book under the name of the county or larger geographical unit in which they fall, except for CARNEROS, LIVERMORE VALLEY, PASO ROBLES, SAN FRANCISCO BAY, SANTA CLARA VALLEY, SANTA CRUZ MOUNTAINS, and TEMECULA.

Kramer, M., *Making Sense of California Wine* (1992).

Robinson, J., and Murphy, L., *American Wine* (2013).

See www.ttb.gov/wine/american-viticultural-area-ava for more information on AVAs.

Viticulture

After its early reliance on the Chinese, California has historically benefited from particularly adept Mexican LABOUR, but ongoing 21st-century federal crackdowns on illegal immigration and restrictive work-permit policies have made life more difficult for both employers and workers. As demand for skilled vineyard workers has increased, so too have wages, leading many estate wineries, as well as the increasingly popular VINEYARD MANAGEMENT COMPANIES, to move from seasonal to year-round employment. Despite this improvement, many vineyard workers still cannot afford to live in the increasingly expensive regions where they work. Worker safety issues continue to be a topic of concern in the face of summer heat and wildfire smoke.

MECHANICAL HARVESTING has long been common in the CENTRAL VALLEY and in much of MONTEREY, but in light of labour costs NORTH COAST growers at even the highest levels of quality continue to investigate harvesting machines and MECHANICAL PRUNING too.

With the exception of some remaining plots of ancient vines (see HISTORIC VINEYARD SOCIETY), all of California's vineyards have been replanted since the repeal of Prohibition. In the years following that date, California viticultural practices were relatively uniform: head-trained, SPUR PRUNED vines spaced about 8 ft apart in rows about 10 ft/3 m apart. Dry farming was the rule in the North Coast, while flood IRRIGATION was the universal practice in the San Joaquin Valley.

During the 1960s, VINE TRAINING began to move on to wires, with CANE PRUNING for lighter-bearing vine varieties and CORDON for heavier yielders. Overhead sprinkler systems for irrigation became more common, especially in the emerging Central Coast. AXR1 became the ROOTSTOCK of choice because of its vigour and near-universal adaptability, and heavy, dense canopies were the norm. Vine spacing remained at or near 8 ft × 10 ft, or 400–600 vines per acre (1,000–1,500 vines per ha).

Towards the mid 1980s, all of the old rules went by the way, impelled partly by a new mutation of phylloxera, the so-called biotype B; partly by a recurrence of PIERCE'S DISEASE; and, more significantly, by closer observation of the variables caused by California's turbulent geology. It was not uncommon in the early 1990s to see single properties on the North Coast with three or four different vine spacings, ranging between 800 and 2,000 vines per acre, and as many different systems of CANOPY MANAGEMENT. The aim was to take advantage of variations in soil structures and exposures as well as vine varieties.

Since AXR1's resistance to phylloxera had proved disastrously low, rootstock selection was becoming a new art. The 1990s saw a major replanting programme, particularly in Napa and Sonoma, as a direct result of phylloxera and vine disease. The traditional alternative to AXR1 was Rupestris St George, but around 30 rootstocks were being trialled in the mid to late 1990s, with drought-tolerant variations emerging as those favoured by growers throughout the state.

This replanting also took full advantage of the well-developed catalogue of plant material overseen by the UC Davis Foundation Plant Materials Service. Established in 1958 with the goal of distributing virus-free plant material to the state's farmers, FOUNDATION PLANT SERVICES, as it is now known, has developed a catalogue of distinct CLONAL SELECTIONS for most of California's most popular grape varieties, from which nearly all the state's NURSERY stock descends. Most growers in the state choose to replant and propagate these CLONES, though some prefer to source their own cuttings of heritage material from known vineyard sites using MASS SELECTION, believing that genetic diversity trumps being virus-free.

As replanting proceeded, drip IRRIGATION became the norm for many coastal vineyards, with many growers opting for REGULATED DEFICIT IRRIGATION for its ability to both control ripeness and conserve water. DRY FARMING has seen renewed interest in the face of ongoing droughts as has the high-tech-enabled practice of PRECISION VITICULTURE. Growers in the SAN JOAQUIN VALLEY and in other river watersheds such as the RUSSIAN RIVER VALLEY depend upon diversions of water for their irrigation, while most others have wells and/or ponds that fill with winter rains. Those dependent upon river flows or surface catchments can suffer greatly in the midst of drought.

The term SUSTAINABILITY has become nearly ubiquitous in the 21st century, pervading consumer consciousness and purchase decisions. Most major regional marketing bodies and grower associations in California have green initiatives, with many developing certification programmes for their members to drive adoption of sustainable practices across areas such as environmental impact, water conservation, social equity, worker health, and business stewardship. Critics of these programmes suggest they grant certification too easily and need stricter requirements in order to truly make a difference, citing unwillingness to ban chemical FERTILIZERS, soil fumigants, and HERBICIDES such as glyphosate.

ORGANIC VITICULTURE has grown from a cottage industry in the mid 1980s to a full-blown movement. In 2020 an estimated 61,776 ha/ 25,000 acres of California's vineyards were certified organic or in conversion, roughly 4.2% of the state's bearing vineyard acreage, up from 2.1% in 2016. As in many other parts of the world, some growers choose not to seek organic certification, either to avoid the fees required or merely because they wish to leave their options open. BIODYNAMIC VITICULTURE has continued to gain ground as well, with 933 ha certified by Demeter in 2020.

When the focus of winemakers' attention moved from flavour to TEXTURE in the 1990s, grapes tended to be picked at ever-higher BRIX. Since 2000 it became common to see Cabernet Sauvignon destined for higher-priced bottles left on the vine until 27 °Brix and PH levels above 3.7 were achieved. This technique, referred to as extended HANG TIME, was unpopular with growers since desiccation of the berries (see BERRY SHRIVEL) results in reduced tonnage and less income. Ripeness levels in Pinot Noir, Chardonnay, and most other grape varieties also crept upwards from the late 1990s onwards. As with many such trends, a backlash of sorts resulted, with some producers now picking for lower POTENTIAL ALCOHOL levels and higher acidity.

Rising temperatures and increasing drought have driven recent changes in CANOPY MANAGEMENT away from vertical trellising, which some now think provides too much sun exposure, and back to a more traditional CALIFORNIA SPRAWL or even GOBELET in an attempt to provide more shade and slower ripening for fruit.

Winemaking

Without long tradition as either guide or limitation, most California winemakers have consistently looked to achieve the kind of reproducible results their university training exalts. Understanding a process and then controlling it are, thus, the first two goals of the state's typical OENOLOGIST. Of all the steps in winemaking, FERMENTATION has received the most vigorous attention.

Temperature-controlled fermentation began in California in the 1940s. With the advent of STAINLESS STEEL tanks and more integral cooling systems in the 1960s, there came 'designed' fermentation curves for each major grape variety. Ultra-hygienic, precisely controllable stainless-steel tanks and sterile FILTRATION allowed MALOLACTIC CONVERSIONS to be brought under control at the same time. Today it is not at all unusual to have malolactic fermentation induced in one low-PH batch of Chardonnay and deliberately inhibited in another (higher pH) batch, then to blend these components for additional complexity in the resulting wine.

Throughout the modern era, ACIDIFICATION has been the norm across the state, but it is becoming slightly less commonplace as grapes are increasingly sourced from more MARGINAL CLIMATES, where they often have higher natural acidity. DEACIDIFICATION is rarely practised or necessary. CHAPTALIZATION is not permitted, nor ever needed when wines and GRAPE CONCENTRATE from warm inland areas are consistently available for blending.

OAK barrels from French forests came into play as ageing vessels at the beginning of the 1960s; within a decade, BARREL FERMENTATION of white wines was the height of fashion. Chardonnay was and remains foremost among the varieties so fermented. COOPERAGE activity in California surged in the 1990s after studies suggested that treatment and technique were more important than whether the oak was French or American. OAK CHIPS and INNER STAVES are commonly available but used primarily for inexpensive, mass-market wines.

With the exception of some who use oak fermenters, most producers ferment their red wines in tank (see CONTAINERS), almost always in stainless steel, frequently in open-topped vessels which allow manual or mechanical PUNCHING DOWN. The use of CONCRETE vats for fermentation, both rectangular and egg-shaped, has become popular in the 2010s; some are even experimenting with fermentation in buried AMPHORAE. After years of separating MUST from CAP just as the fermentation approached dryness, the vogue of the 1980s was extended MACERATION for as long as 25 days after the end of fermentation. Today a wide variety of maceration techniques, along with MICRO-OXYGENATION, are employed in a quest called TANNIN MANAGEMENT, targeting a soft MOUTHFEEL achieved through a high degree of EXTRACT and ripe tannins.

YEASTS are also much studied. For years, pure strains of specially cultured yeast ruled in California. Towards the end of the 1980s, however, winemakers were increasingly prepared to experiment with AMBIENT YEASTS, and by the turn of the century even large commercial wineries were fermenting as much as one-quarter of their production with naturally occurring ambient yeasts.

Organic winemaking has been defined by the US government for labelling purposes since 2001. However, unlike European regulations, the US does not allow any addition of SULFITES, which would raise the free sulfur dioxide level over 10 parts per million. The production of certified 'organic wine' in California is therefore limited to a small, and somewhat eccentric, segment of the industry. Many more wines go to market with a label claiming 'Certified Organic Grapes' but this number is far fewer than would be expected from the number of vineyards growing grapes without AGROCHEMICALS, in part due to a perceived lack of consumer confidence in wines labelled as organic.

Wine types

In 2020 the state had nearly 344,000 ha/850,000 acres of vines of grape-bearing age. Only 256,975 ha of these produced specifically wine grapes, however, with a significant proportion of grapes being varieties such as THOMPSON SEEDLESS (Sultana), making California one of the world's most important producers of RAISINS.

The majority of California's wine production, largely from the Central Valley and mostly in the hands of a few very large wine companies, is inexpensive table wine sold in supermarkets and liquor stores across the US. California's fine wines make up a relatively small percentage of the state's enormous annual production (Napa and Sonoma combined represent only 10% of the state's annual output) even as their reputation and pricing continue to push into the uppermost echelons of the wine world.

Known for having firmly established the dominance of, and preference for, VARIETAL wines in the American market, California now produces an impressively wide array of wine types and styles, driven primarily by the state's dynamic population of many small, independent wine producers who embrace a spirit of innovation and experimentation. These small wine brands, who increasingly sell their wares directly to consumers online, have enthusiastically expanded their offerings beyond the traditional to include (or sometimes focus entirely on) NATURAL WINE, PET-NAT, SKIN CONTACT and SKIN-FERMENTED white wines, PIQUETTE, VERMOUTH, and even ANGELICA for an increasingly curious and dedicated segment of the wine-drinking public.

After several decades of dominance by a few established domestic pioneers and some European wine companies who began setting up shop in the 1970s (including Louis ROEDERER, Taittinger, Mumm, and HENKELL FREIXENET, among others), the state's traditional sparkling wine category has dramatically expanded, helped in part by the availability of custom-crush facilities capable of handling both TRADITIONAL METHOD and TANK METHOD winemaking as well as new packaging innovations such as aluminium CANS. The 2005 EU–US wine agreement, much to the dismay of the Champenoise, permitted continued use of the designation 'California champagne' for a handful of producers with a previous history of using the term. Apart from these mass-market, very inexpensive bottlings, the vast majority of the state's bubbly wines are labelled as California sparkling wine, with increasing numbers of AVA or even vineyard-specific designations.

In 2000, winemaker Dave Phinney blended a STUCK FERMENTATION of Zinfandel with some Cabernet to produce a faintly sweet blend he called The Prisoner, which quickly rose to be one of the most popular California wines of all time. Following Phinney's lead, wine companies such as GALLO and Trinchero Family Estates developed inexpensive red blends such as Apothic and Ménage à Trois, driving a resurgence of mainstream interest in blended red table wines after many years of VARIETAL dominance, even as the number of individual grape names appearing on California fine-wine labels has skyrocketed.

Vine varieties

California's annual official census of grape varieties tracks more than 110 varieties. According to 2020 data, among red varieties Cabernet Sauvignon is dominant with 32% of working acreage, followed by Pinot Noir at 16%, Zinfandel at 13%, Merlot at 12%, Syrah at 5%, and Petite Sirah at 4%, the last being a key component for many inexpensive red blends.

Among white varieties, Chardonnay reigns supreme at 53%, followed by French Colombard at 10%, Pinot Gris at 10%, Sauvignon Blanc at 9%, Chenin Blanc at 3%, and Riesling and Viognier with roughly 2% of bearing acres apiece.

For decades French Colombard has been a workhorse grape for producers churning out high-volume white and blush wines, thanks to its rather neutral character and tendency towards retaining acidity. Among the red grapes, a similar statement could historically be made about Zinfandel.

More than any other, Zinfandel can lay claim to being California's signature grape variety, not only because of its relative popularity as a wine but because of the crucial role it has played (more than once) in the state's wine history. Conclusively shown in 2003 by Dr Carole Meredith of DAVIS to have originated in CROATIA, the grape arrived in California during the 1850s and flourished in the dry California climate, with key plantings still surviving and producing in Sonoma's Dry Creek Valley, the Russian River Valley, Paso Robles, and Amador County (along with its neighbouring AVAs) in the Sierra Foothills. Its relative hardiness and productivity led it to quickly become among the most popular varieties during the planting boom of the 1880s.

Perhaps the highest concentration of remaining old-vine Zinfandel, including some dating to 1889, can still be found in the expansive LODI AVA, which has long supplied a significant portion of the grapes used in California's most inexpensive wines. This was especially true during Prohibition, when the relatively thick-skinned grape proved suitable for shipping across the country to supply a sudden interest in HOME WINEMAKING. Later, when a stuck fermentation left the 1975 vintage of Sutter Home Winery's rosé a little sweet, the explosive success of the wine they called White Zinfandel spawned many imitators and drove demand for the grape high enough to justify retaining many old plantings.

Even as consumer interests transitioned to drier, more Provençal styles of rosé in the early 2000s, a small number of producers drove a renaissance of premium red Zinfandel wines led by the expensive and hard-to-obtain single-vineyard bottlings of Turley Wine Cellars and the more populist wines of Carlisle or Ravenswood, whose wines were marketed by founder Joel Peterson under the slogan 'No Wimpy Wines'. Interest in Zinfandel among consumers peaked in the early 2000s when the annual ZAP (Zinfandel Advocates and Producers) tastings in San Francisco would draw nearly 10,000 wine lovers eager to taste the work of hundreds of small producers. Peterson and others, including more recently Turley's winemaker Tegan Passalacqua, can be credited with preserving many of the state's oldest vineyards through dedicated demand for dry-farmed, old-vine fruit, as well as through organized efforts at conservation such as the HISTORIC VINEYARD SOCIETY.

Along with the state's justifiably famous Cabernet Sauvignons and Bordeaux-style blends (decreasingly referred to as MERITAGE blends), Chardonnay has also become synonymous with California. In particular, the state has become known for a FRUIT-DRIVEN style characterized by the effects of BARREL FERMENTATION, LEES CONTACT, OAK AGEING, and MALOLACTIC CONVERSION. Popularized by wines such as the best-selling KENDALL-JACKSON's Vintners Reserve, this style of Chardonnay, with its tropical and butterscotch flavours and an occasional dollop of RESIDUAL SUGAR, has become at once the most popular style of wine in America as well as one of the most reviled, spawning the meme ABC—Anything But Chardonnay. Despite this, California winemakers continue to produce a dizzying array of Chardonnay bottlings from an ever-widening range of vineyard sites and MESOCLIMATES, in styles ranging from opulent to austere.

SYRAH, which occupied a mere 5,436 ha/2,200 acres in 1995, grew to more than 46,950 ha by 2013 largely through the success of the state's RHÔNE RANGERS, a group of winemakers championing any and all Rhône varieties. Syrah plantings had by 2020 dropped to 37,066 ha, as winemakers have found it a frustratingly difficult sell to consumers.

Perhaps the single largest trend in California's wine production since the late 1990s has been the rise of PINOT NOIR, which numbered 56,834 ha/23,000 acres in 2004 when the movie SIDEWAYS debuted, and have subsequently grown to 113,668 ha in 2020. The grape's history in California has been tumultuous, going from quite popular after Prohibition to all but dismissed in the 1960s, as winemakers wrestled with both where it should be grown and how it should be made. Other than some commendable work done by producers such as Hanzell, Calera, and Joseph Swan, Pinot Noir would not begin its ascendance until the late 1980s, when the tiny and all but unknown producer Williams Selyem bested all comers at the 1987 California State Fair with their 1985 Rochioli Vineyard bottling from the Russian River Valley.

Interest in the grape was rekindled. In 1991 the average price for a ton of Pinot Noir grapes was $804, but by 2001 the same ton was fetching $1,849. While there were only a few dozen producers of Pinot Noir in 1990, by 2000 there were hundreds. But if American appreciation of Pinot Noir can be said to have been sparked in the 1980s, its obsession most certainly arrived following Hollywood's celebration of the variety in *Sideways*. Since then, sustained demand has been answered with the methodical exploration and planting of cooler, coastal vineyard sites from Santa Barbara to Mendocino, resulting in a dramatic increase in high-quality offerings at many price points. In 2019 the average price per ton of Sonoma Pinot Noir was $3,949. The best California Pinot Noirs now receive ratings from prominent critics commensurate with many of the top examples from Burgundy and hail from multiple regions up and down the coast, suggesting the grape's eminent potential to be among the state's greatest success stories. A.Y.

See also CARNEROS, CENTRAL COAST, CENTRAL VALLEY, LAKE COUNTY, LIVERMORE VALLEY, MENDOCINO, MONTEREY, NAPA, PASO ROBLES, SAN LUIS OBISPO, SANTA BARBARA, SANTA CLARA VALLEY, SANTA CRUZ MOUNTAINS, SIERRA FOOTHILLS, SONOMA, and TEMECULA.

Bonné, J., *The New California Wine* (2013).
Haeger, J. W., *Pacific Pinot Noir* (2008).
Kramer, M., *Matt Kramer's New California Wine: Making Sense of Napa Valley, Sonoma, Central Coast, and Beyond* (2004).
Muscatine, D., et al. (eds.), *The University of California/Sotheby's Book of California Wine* (1984).
www.wineinstitute.org
www.cawg.org

California cult wines, a phrase coined in the 1990s to encompass wines made in CALIFORNIA—typically but not exclusively NAPA Valley Cabernets—for which collectors pay PRICES higher than those of some of Bordeaux's FIRST GROWTHS. They include such names as Araujo, Bryant Family, Colgin, Abreu, Dalla Valle, Grace Family, Harlan Estate, Scarecrow, Schrader, Screaming Eagle, and Sine Qua Non. Their common characteristics include being made in extremely limited quantities by talented consultant OENOLOGISTS currently favoured by FASHION and earning high, often 100-point scores from Robert PARKER's *Wine Advocate*.

California sprawl, term commonly used to describe the CANOPY of a vine trained on a simple TRELLIS SYSTEM, although such systems are not restricted to California. It generally refers to a trellis with a single fruiting wire plus one foliage wire above this, though there are some variations. This results in a sprawling vine without rigorous SHOOT POSITIONING. This inexpensive form of training can lead to a shaded canopy with poor bud FRUITFULNESS and increased vegetative growth. Such vine forms are more typically seen in vineyards in hotter parts of California's CENTRAL VALLEY and are also common in the inland irrigation regions of Australia. See also CANOPY MANAGEMENT.

Calistoga, CALIFORNIA wine region and AVA in northern NAPA Valley.

Callet, MALLORCAN grape of unclear origin, often planted as a FIELD BLEND with its natural parent FOGONEU, the other parent being the obscure Callet Cas Concos. Spanish statistics for 2020 recorded a total of 214 ha/529 acres planted. Callet tends to produce small quantities of light-coloured wine with relatively little alcohol. It is used mainly for rosés and in red blends but is occasionally responsible for elegant, red-fruited varietal wines.

callus, the white, formless tissue that grows from CAMBIUM tissue at cut and wounded surfaces of the grapevine on stems and roots. It is critical for vine GRAFTING since it signifies that the conditions for cell division are favourable and that the underlying graft or bud has united. High humidity, sufficient oxygen supply, and warm temperatures are the major requirements for rapid callus development. In the field, these conditions may be achieved by waxing or by wrapping the tissues tightly with plastic grafting tape. After BENCH GRAFTING, the cuttings are packed with moist material and held in a warm, humid room. (See also TISSUE CULTURE and illustration under GRAFTING.) Callus formation can be inhibited by the presence of TRUNK DISEASES, especially in the ROOTSTOCK cutting. B.G.C.

Hartmann, H. T., et al., *Plant Propagation: Principles and Practices* (8th edn, 2010).

Caluso, town in northern, pre-alpine PIEMONTE famous for a DRIED-GRAPE WINE made of ERBALUCE grapes. Today dry and TRADITIONAL METHOD sparkling versions, often from named vineyards, have triggered a new and much-needed dynamic.

calyptra, or flower cap, of the vine flower consists of the five petals joined together in the form of an inverted cup. The cap separates as a unit and falls from the grape flower at FLOWERING and exposes the STAMENS, which produce pollen, and the stigma, which receives pollen. The rate of capfall is slowed by cold and rain; the duration of capfall in one vine can stretch from a normal 7–10 days to as long as 15–20 days. FRUIT SET is impaired if the caps are retained, and so this very small part of the grapevine can affect YIELD, especially for varieties such as MERLOT. See also FLOWERS, VINE. B.G.C.

Câmara de Lobos, or **Cama de Lobos**, occasionally found on bottles of ancient MADEIRA, is a wine district on the south coast of the island.

Camaralet, obscure, low-yielding vine allowed but hardly grown in BÉARN and JURANÇON in south-west France that can make strongly flavoured white wine.

Camarate, a natural Portuguese ALFROCHEIRO × CAYETANA BLANCA cross making soft, early-drinking reds in BAIRRADA. It is known as MORTÁGUA in ARRUDA.

cambium, a zone of dividing cells in plants such as the grapevine; the inner cells develop into XYLEM and later differentiate into wood, while the outer cells develop into PHLOEM and, later, bark. The matching of cambial zones is important to the success of BUDDING and GRAFTING.

The cork cambium cuts off non-living suberized cells yielding bark, as during vine CANE RIPENING. The cork most readily associated with wine is the CORK derived from the secondary cambium of QUERCUS *suber* and used as CLOSURES. B.G.C.

Cambodia has a single winery, Prasat Phnom Banan, 10 km/6.2 miles from its second largest city, Battambang, in the north-west of the country. It began with vines imported from THAILAND and made its first wine in 2004. The winery produces several thousand bottles of wine, brandy, and grape juice each year, from 10 ha/24 acres of mostly Black Queen and Shiraz vines. D.G.

Campania, region of south-west Italy of which Naples is the capital. In the ancient world, Campania was the home of some of the most renowned wines of Italy, if not of the whole Mediterranean basin: SURRENTINE, MASSIC, and, most famous of all, FALERNIAN.

Despite its southern location, Campania is known for its white wines, as daytime temperatures are largely mitigated by ELEVATION in the mountainous inland (Campania boasts its own ski resorts). Its INDIGENOUS VARIETIES, showcased in Campania's many DOCs and DOCGs, can retain freshness and acidity in a warm climate. On the basis of its soil types the region can be broadly grouped into three parts. The VOLCANIC, sandy soils of DOC Vesuvio and DOC Campi Flegrei (the 'fire fields' named by the Romans, who built thermal baths on the slopes of these extinct volcanoes) are almost in the suburbs of Naples, where the white FALANGHINA and red PIEDIROSSO are planted on their own ROOTSTOCKS as PHYLLOXERA cannot survive there. Once considered workhorse varieties, Falanghina and Piedirosso now receive serious attention, including higher-density vineyards and lower yields. The DOC Vesuvio is based predominantly on Caprettone, Falanghina, and Piedirosso, often from old vines, resulting in white and red Lacryma Christi and now experiencing a qualitative revival.

The second soil type, ALLUVIUM, prevails in the DOC Sannio on the Piana Campania Plain between Naples and Benevento. In the early 2010s, the much smaller DOCs Guardia Sanframondi, Sant'Agata dei Goti (with its own CLONE of the Falanghina as produced by Mustilli), Solopaca, Solopaca Classico, and Taburno (its speciality being AGLIANICO) were all demoted to subzones of Sannio, while a new DOCG, Aglianico del Taburno, was created.

The third soil type is the porous LIMESTONE which typifies the hills of the DOC Irpinia. It was called tufo by the Romans (hence GRECO di Tufo), though incorrectly, as it is not of volcanic origin. Within Irpinia lie the superior DOCGs TAURASI, FIANO di Avellino, and Greco di Tufo, the last two producing Campania's most famous and long-lived whites, typified by peaches and flint, with smoky notes in aged versions. Taurasi is arguably Aglianico's finest and longest-lived expression.

Much of Campania consists of hills and mountains with myriad EXPOSURES and elevations. The higher the elevation, the cooler it is—so cool in fact that the grapes of Fiano di Avellino and Greco di Tufo are not picked before the beginning of October, and the late-ripening Aglianico may be picked even later in Taurasi. With the exception of Mastroberardino, a general focus on quality and ESTATE BOTTLING has been recent (see TAURASI for more details).

The third large Campania DOC, Cilento, lies 50 km/31 miles south of Naples, its coastline dominated by Paestum, one of the largest Greek temple complexes in the world, while its rugged mountainous hinterland is planted with olive trees and vines. Despite its extent, Cilento produces much less wine than Sannio, but its small quantities of Fiano and Aglianico are worth seeking out, especially from such overachievers as Conciliis and Casebianche. North of Cilento the tiny DOC Costa d'Amalfi has low-yielding, PERGOLA-trained vineyards clinging to any available ridge on this stony coast. Whites based on Falanghina and Biancolella and reds based on Piedirosso and Sciasinoso are produced here, while its subzone Tramonti is renowned for its many centenarian vineyards. Aglianico and Piedirosso also feature in the DOC Falerno del Massico to the north, its wines said to have already been appreciated by the Romans (see FALERNIAN). Curiously, a 100% PRIMITIVO is also allowed here. While the demands of TOURISM have replaced the once-renowned viticulture of the island of Capri, Ischia has managed to retain enough vineyards to produce small quantities of complex whites based on the local FORASTERA and BIANCOLELLA and minuscule quantities of red wine based on Guarnaccia (MAGLIOCCO Dolce) and Piedirosso. See ISCHIA for more detail. W.S.

Capalbo, C., *The Food and Wine Guide to Naples and Campania* (2005).
Belfrage, N., *From Brunello to Zibibbo: The Wines of Tuscany, Central and Southern Italy* (2nd edn, 2003).
www.vinocampania.it

Campo de Borja, DOP in the warm, sunny, undulating plains around the town of Borja (after which the Borgia family was named) in Spain's ARAGÓN region (see map under SPAIN). Vineyard ELEVATIONS range from 350 m/1,148 ft in the north-east, along the River Ebro, to 700 m/2,297 ft in the south-west, in the foothills of the Moncayo Mountains. The vast majority of the region's 6,810 ha/16,828 acres of vines are planted to GARNACHA vines, which produce intensely sweet, dark grapes that make heady red wines. The Borsao Borja CO-OPERATIVE has revolutionized the region with its young, intensely fruity reds that have won a large following on export markets. F.C.

Canaan, or the Levant, comprises the coastal and inland areas of the eastern Mediterranean which played an important part in spreading VINICULTURE. The pharaohs of ancient EGYPT were struggling to maintain their control of this area during the 14th century BCE, as we can read in the Amarna letters, an extensive correspondence between the pharaohs and the local puppet rulers and officials of Canaan. 'See that much food and wine—everything in great quantities—is made available for the archers of the king', writes one Egyptian monarch. In the Egyptian *Story of Sinuhe*, Canaan was described as having 'more wine than water'.

Records on cuneiform tablets from the kingdom centre on the city-state of Ugarit (*c.*1500–1200 BCE; modern Ras Shamra near Latakia about 160 km/100 miles north of the vineyards of modern Lebanon) indicate extensive viticulture. A standard formulation in describing properties for real-estate transactions at this date mentions 'a house, together with its [watch-]tower, its olive grove and its vineyard'. However, life was as difficult in this area then as it was in the 1980s, since a complaint addressed by the prefect of Ugarit to a local great king, who was acting as mediator, stated that the people of Siyannu, a neighbouring city, 'have cut down our vines'. The people of Ugarit were obliged to swear not to cut down the vines of Siyannu and, moreover, to swear that they knew nothing of the identity of the perpetrators of such acts in the past. A similar dispute was adjudicated on the same occasion, this time concerning an allegation that wine from Ugarit had been stolen and sold unofficially to dealers at Beirut down the coast.

The southern Levantine wine industry, beginning *c.*4000 BCE, had matured to such a degree that by the time of Scorpion I (*c.*3150 BCE), one of the first rulers of a united Egypt, his tomb at Abydos was stocked with some 4,500 litres of wine imported from southern Canaan. From around 3000 BCE, the Egyptian pharaohs financed the establishment of a royal wine industry in the Nile Delta under the tutelage of Canaanite viniculturists. With the Egyptian winemaking success behind them, the Canaanites on their sea-going 'Byblos ships', made of Cedar of Lebanon, ventured further and further out into the Mediterranean. They and their successors, the Phoenicians, applied a similar formula wherever they went: import wine and other luxury goods, entice the rulers with wine culture by presenting them with speciality wine sets, and then wait until they were asked to help in establishing native industries, including viniculture, by transplanting the domesticated Eurasian VITIS VINIFERA grapevine.

See also ORIGINS OF VINICULTURE and PALAEOETHNOBOTANY. J.A.B. & P.E.M.

McGovern, P. E., *Uncorking the Past: The Quest for Wine, Beer, and Other Alcoholic Beverages* (2009).
McGovern, P. E., *Ancient Wine: The Search for the Origins of Viniculture* (2nd edn, 2019).

C

Canada, has a thriving wine industry, with 12,808 ha/31,650 acres of vineyards in 2021 spread throughout four winegrowing provinces: ONTARIO, BRITISH COLUMBIA, QUEBEC, and NOVA SCOTIA. Given the exigencies of the Canadian climate, grapes are usually grown near large bodies of water that moderate the effects of cold winters and decrease the risk of damaging WINTER FREEZE and spring FROSTS (see LAKE EFFECT). Until the 1970s, the industry depended on winter-hardy North American VITIS LABRUSCA varieties such as CONCORD and NIAGARA, followed by plantings of early-ripening, winter-resistant FRENCH HYBRIDS such as VIDAL BLANC, SEYVAL BLANC, BACO NOIR, and MARÉCHAL FOCH. Since the late 1980s, however, growers have put greater emphasis on VITIS VINIFERA varieties, whose wines enjoy increasing success both at home and abroad.

The Canadian climate is particularly suited to the production of SPARKLING WINES, but it first established a reputation for ICEWINE, of which it is the world's largest producer—not surprising, since sustained temperatures of −8 °C/17.6 °F can be relied upon in most regions each winter.

History

The Canadian wine industry dates from the early 19th century (although see also VÍNLAND). In 1811, a retired German corporal, Johann Schiller, domesticated the *labrusca* vines he found growing along the Credit River west of Toronto and planted a 8-ha/20-acre vineyard. In 1866, the country's first major winery, Vin Villa, was established in Canada's most southerly reaches, on Lake Erie's Pelee Island, by three gentlemen farmers from Kentucky who planted 8 ha of ISABELLA vines. By 1890 there were 41 commercial wineries across the country, 35 in Ontario. As in other wine regions, it was the Church that encouraged the planting of vineyards and fostered the art of winemaking.

PROHIBITION slowed the pace of development as Canadian provinces passed varying laws to limit alcohol sales and consumption between 1916 and 1919. However, Ontario permitted alcohol production for export. As a result, by the time the Ontario Temperance Act was repealed in 1927, 57 wineries were operating in the province.

Most other Canadian provinces ended Prohibition by the late 1920s and created provincially owned retail systems or government MONOPOLIES which control the sale and distribution of beverage alcohol and collect billions of dollars in government revenues. Today, most wine is sold by provincial monopolies such as the Liquor Control Board of Ontario (LCBO), though many smaller wineries rely on CELLAR DOOR sales. Alberta is an exception, with a privatized system since the mid 1990s. British Columbia, Nova Scotia, Manitoba, and Saskatchewan also allow privately owned wine stores to operate alongside government monopoly stores.

This shift in plantings from *labrusca* and hybrids to *vinifera* began after Prohibition, with Brights Winery producing the first Ontario Chardonnay in 1956 and Quail's Gate Winery in the Okanagan Valley planting some Chasselas vines in 1961. The pace picked up in the 1970s and 1980s, with the opening of wineries dedicated to the proposition that *vinifera* vines could be grown on appropriate sites despite the harsh winters and unpredictable springs. This coincided with a shift in public taste towards drier, less alcoholic TABLE WINE, as, until the mid 1970s, most Canadian wines were sweet, highly alcoholic products made from *labrusca* varieties and labelled Sherry or Port, depending on colour. The 1988 free-trade agreement between Canada, the United States, and Mexico was a further catalyst as it removed the protections domestic wines had enjoyed against competing imports and inspired more wineries to focus on *vinifera* varieties.

Since the late 1990s, the number of estate wineries has grown exponentially. Canada is also home to the Cool Climate Oenology and Viticulture Institute (CCOVI) at BROCK UNIVERSITY in the Niagara Peninsula.

Climate

Geographically, the majority of Canadian vineyards are on the same latitude as the LANGUEDOC and CHIANTI, but lower winter temperatures, the freeze–thaw–freeze cycle of early spring, and unpredictable weather at HARVEST mean Canada is ranked as a COOL-CLIMATE wine region.

While some of Canada's wine regions enjoy hotter summers than either Bordeaux or Burgundy, the growing season tends to be shorter. Average sunshine hours during the growing season are 1,485 in the Niagara Peninsula, Ontario; 1,616 in the south of British Columbia's Okanagan Valley; and 1,257 in the Gaspereau Valley in Nova Scotia. Grapes may require CHAPTALIZATION in some years. DROUGHT can be a problem in parts of southern British Columbia, and many producers have installed irrigation systems. Many wineries in Ontario have invested in wind machines to counter cold winter temperatures and spring frosts. Some wineries use GEOTEXTILES for winter protection.

Wine laws

Wine laws are provincially regulated, although wine labelling is governed by the federal Food and Drug Act (1985) and the Safe Food for Canadians Act (2012).

In 1988, Ontario introduced the Vintners Quality Alliance (VQA), a CONTROLLED APPELLATION system similar to but separate from the system introduced in British Columbia in 1990. Each specifies production areas, permitted grape varieties, minimum MUST WEIGHTS, and limits to CHAPTALIZATION, among other details. Varietal wines must be made from at least 85% the stated variety and 95–100% for subappellation wines.

The Nova Scotia Wine Standards Regulations is the legal framework in Nova Scotia, while Quebec has a Protected Geographical Indication (PGI) Vin du Québec governing still and sparkling wine production and another for Quebec ice wine (Vin de glace du Québec).

Any wines that contain imported BULK WINE are not entitled to either a VQA designation or the more general Product of Canada label. These wines, common in Canadian liquor stores, must be labelled as 'International Domestic Blends'.

For more detail on individual regions, see BRITISH COLUMBIA, NOVA SCOTIA, ONTARIO, and QUEBEC. J.D.

Phillips, R., *The Wines of Canada* (2017).
www.winesofcanada.ca

Canaiolo, or **Canaiolo Nero**, red grape variety grown all over central Italy and, perhaps most famously, a permitted ingredient in the controversial recipe for CHIANTI, in which it played a more important part than SANGIOVESE in the 18th century. Plantings declined considerably in the wake of PHYLLOXERA because it was relatively difficult to graft and suffered from poor CLONAL SELECTION, with just over 1,031 ha/2,548 acres remaining in 2015. The decline in popularity of the GOVERNO winemaking trick also hastened its decline, since soft, full-bodied Canaiolo, without either the structure of Sangiovese or the scent of MAMMOLO, was most prized for its resistance to ROT while being dried for *governo* use. However, in the last few years it has become rather fashionable, and Tuscan producers such as Bibi Graetz, Vallone di Cecione, and Le Torre ale Tolfe are making good-quality varietal Canaiolo. Canaiolo is also grown, to an even more limited extent, in LAZIO, LIGURIA, and UMBRIA.

A light-berried **Canaiolo Bianco** is also grown in Umbria, where, in ORVIETO, it is known as DRUPEGGIO, but it has also been declining in popularity.

Canary Islands, or *Islas Canarias* in Spanish, are Spanish islands in the Atlantic Ocean off the coast of Morocco which were famous in Shakespearian England, as witness Sir Toby Belch's call for 'a cup of canary' in *Twelfth Night*. Once known for mediocre wines mainly aimed at tourists, the islands, helped by government subsidies, have developed a reputation for distinctive wines borne from a subtropical climate and VOLCANIC geology quite different from the rest of Spain. The grape varieties grown also set the islands apart, including red varieties NEGRAMOLL and the indigenous LISTÁN NEGRO and white varieties Listán Blanco (PALOMINO FINO),

MALVASÍA, VIJARIEJO, MARMAJUELO, and Gual (which is the same as Madeira's Boal/BUAL). VINE AGE is high. Although construction is encroaching on vineyards, the number of DOPs has ballooned, by the mid 2000s including one for each of the islands of LA PALMA, EL HIERRO, LANZAROTE, and GRAN CANARIA and five for the island of Tenerife (ABONA, TACORONTE-ACENTEJO, VALLE DE GÜÍMAR, VALLE DE LA OROTAVA, and YCODEN-DAUTE-ISORA). Islas Canarias VINO DE CALIDAD was created in 2012 as an umbrella appellation for all the Canary Islands (including Fuerteventura, an island with no DOPs. Its use is voluntary, and it can coexist simultaneously with a more specific DOP. V. de la S. & F.C.

Canberra District, hilly wine region surrounding Canberra, the capital of AUSTRALIA, encompassing around 450 ha/1,112 acres of vineyards in 2020 in the Australian Capital Territory and NEW SOUTH WALES. The climate is largely CONTINENTAL, with warm summers, cold winters, and dramatic DIURNAL TEMPERATURE RANGE, but there is considerable MESOCLIMATE diversity due to variations in ELEVATION, from 300 to 800 m/984–2,625 ft. Most known for Shiraz, the region is also known for Riesling made in a variety of styles and Rhône white varieties including Viognier, Marsanne, and Roussanne. Experimentation is on the rise with small plantings of Grüner Veltliner, Sangiovese, Tempranillo, Graciano, and Malbec. A.R.P.

cane, the stem of a mature grapevine SHOOT after the bark becomes woody (lignified) and tan-coloured, beginning at VERAISON, and starts its overwintering form (see CANE RIPENING and CAMBIUM). After leaves have fallen, the canes of a vine display the total vegetative growth it made during the previous season (called the 'brush' in the US). The number of canes and their weight and average size are important guides to decisions about BALANCED PRUNING and CANOPY MANAGEMENT tactics. The canes are cut at winter PRUNING to reduce the number of buds and to select their position. The cutting may be to SPURS or canes. B.G.C.

cane pruning, a form of winter vine PRUNING in which the BUDS are retained on longer BEARERS called CANES, typically including 6–15 buds. This pruning system usually takes longer to perform by hand than the alternative SPUR PRUNING. Cane pruning is typically used for vines which have fewer FRUITFUL buds at the base of canes, which is the case especially in COOL-CLIMATE wine regions. The tendency in warmer NEW WORLD wine regions is to use spur pruning, which can be equally productive, requires less LABOUR, and can be MECHANIZED. For more details, see GUYOT. See also MECHANICAL PRUNING. R.E.S.

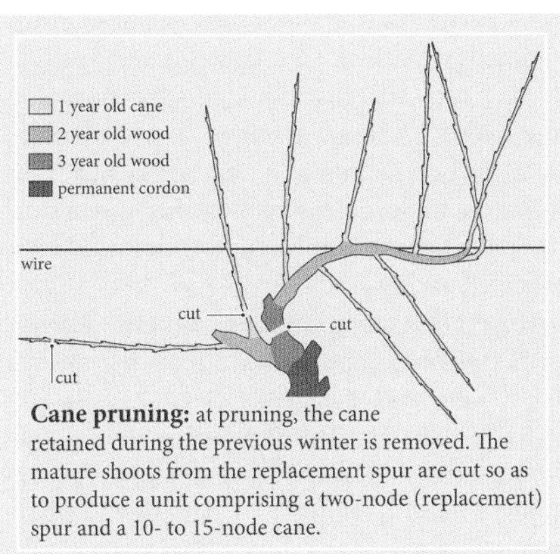

Cane pruning: at pruning, the cane retained during the previous winter is removed. The mature shoots from the replacement spur are cut so as to produce a unit comprising a two-node (replacement) spur and a 10- to 15-node cane.

cane ripening, or lignification, is a viticultural term used to describe a stage in the development of the SHOOT when the stem matures and changes colour from green to yellow and thence to brown. The change involves the formation of corky tissue known as periderm and cellular changes including the accumulation of CARBOHYDRATE reserves, which collectively prepare the stem to withstand the cold of winter. The process begins at the base of the shoot and progresses up towards the tip, as does the dormancy status of its buds. Careful observation shows that the first vineyards to reach this stage, and where it proceeds rapidly, are those which produce the finest wine. This is because early and rapid cane ripening indicates a modicum of WATER STRESS, as well as generous plant levels of carbohydrates, both of which contribute to rapid fruit RIPENING. Cane ripening has therefore been incorporated into vineyard SCORING systems used to predict wine quality.

VERAISON, the change in colour of the grapes, usually occurs at about the same time. R.E.S.

Cangas, a VINO DE CALIDAD and sole appellation in the Asturias autonomous region of north-west Spain. While it extends only 32 ha/79 acres, the potential of the steep slopes, at 400–700 m/1,312–2,297 ft of ELEVATION, is promising, especially for the recovery of the local Albarín Blanco and red grapes Verdejo Tinto, Albarín Tinto, and Carrasquín. F.C.

Cannonau, sometimes spelt **Cannonao**, the Sardinian name for the widely planted red grape variety known in Spain as GARNACHA and in France as GRENACHE (see SARDINIA). A high proportion of the grapes are grown on the east of the island to produce a varietal **Cannonau di Sardegna**, which comes in several forms but most commonly as a full-throttle dryish red. Although the variety has lost ground since the mid 1990s, partly because as a BUSH VINE it is low-yielding and expensive to cultivate, 5,537 ha/13,682 acres of Cannonau were recorded in 2015. Wines from bush vines high up in the province of Nuoro have shown what can be achieved from the island's old Cannonau vines, often more than 80 years old.

Canon-Fronsac, underrated Bordeaux red-wine appellation, the heartland of FRONSAC.

canopy, that part of the vine above the ground, formed by the leaf and shoot system. It includes the trunk, cordon or canes, shoots, leaves, and fruit. It is a term borrowed from forestry, first used for grapevines by Professor Nelson SHAULIS of CORNELL UNIVERSITY. See CANOPY MANAGEMENT.

canopy management, a portfolio of vineyard management techniques used to improve vineyard YIELD and GRAPE COMPOSITION AND WINE QUALITY, as well as to help control some foliar and fruit-affecting VINE DISEASES, especially where vines are of high VIGOUR. Canopy management techniques aim to produce a desirable CANOPY MICROCLIMATE essentially by improving the exposure of leaves and fruit to SUNLIGHT and airflow. The phrase became popular in many parts of the NEW WORLD in the 1980s and early 1990s as part of a growing awareness of the way in which canopy microclimate affects vineyards, but this awareness was not restricted to the New World. Considerable experimental work was also conducted in Europe, and the effects of canopy microclimate are now recognized as partly responsible for the ability of distinguished vineyards to produce great wines (see TERROIR and VITICULTURE).

Some of the underlying principles of canopy management can be traced to early Roman writings. For example, 'BACCHUS loves hills' is partly explained by the fact that low-vigour vines growing on shallower soils on HILLSIDES have open canopies with good fruit and leaf exposure. In modern times, the principles were best formulated by the experimental work of Professor Nelson SHAULIS of Cornell University in New York State. During the 1960s, he showed that increased fruit and leaf exposure to sunlight improved both YIELD and fruit composition. These early studies were also much involved with introducing MECHANICAL HARVESTERS and MECHANICAL PRUNING. Shaulis's work on CONCORD vines influenced researchers from other countries, who extended this work to VITIS VINIFERA vine varieties and also considered effects on wine quality. Studies in Bordeaux by Dr Alain Carbonneau demonstrated wine quality benefits of canopy manipulation in the mid 1970s. Other notable early pioneering studies were by Intrieri in Italy, Kliewer in California, Reynolds in Canada, and Smart in Australia and New Zealand.

Canopy management techniques are essentially aimed at producing an 'open' canopy microclimate, which is characterized by good leaf and fruit exposure to the sun and airflow and therefore not much shade. The benefits of such a microclimate include improvements to wine quality and yield as well as a significant reduction in diseases such as POWDERY MILDEW and BOTRYTIS BUNCH ROT. The ULTRAVIOLET portion of the solar spectrum has been shown to increase PHENOLICS and colour in grapes and wine and also to suppress these diseases. Interest in overcoming the common problems of excessively vigorous vines caused canopy-management techniques to become popular. This was particularly marked in the New World, where a lack of experience to guide site selection and management practices resulted in some vineyards where vines were so leafy and the fruit so shaded that it affected ripeness and wine quality. These problems were exacerbated by the widespread adoption of AGROCHEMICALS developed after the Second World War to control pests, diseases, and weeds, which, along with practices such as FERTILIZATION and especially IRRIGATION, stimulated shoot growth, often excessively. Canopy-management techniques, especially a change in TRELLIS SYSTEM, can offset the negative effects of vines with excess VIGOUR but are not always necessary for low-vigour vineyards such as those found in most of the classic fine-wine regions of Europe.

A common feature of vineyards with a reputation for producing high-quality wines is that they are of moderate to low vigour and have an open canopy. Canopy management techniques can emulate this microclimate. For example, by altering the trellis, it is possible to remove the fruit from the deep shade associated with the depths of the canopy to the outside of the canopy in the sun. Canopy management can also increase yield. In particular, BUDBREAK and FRUITFULNESS are reduced by shade, no doubt an example of adaptive physiology which allowed WILD VINES to fruit only when they had climbed to the top of forest canopies. With increasing global concern about the use of agrochemicals, there is a swing towards using canopy management to help control FUNGAL DISEASES and reduce reliance on sprays (see INTEGRATED PEST MANAGEMENT). Not only is it difficult and wasteful to force sprays to penetrate to the centre of dense canopies, but shaded conditions also encourage diseases such as botrytis bunch rot and powdery mildew.

There is a range of canopy management techniques, the applicability of which varies from vineyard to vineyard. The simplest of these are TRIMMING, which cuts off excessive shoot growth in the summer; SHOOT THINNING, which removes unwanted shoots early in the season; LEAF REMOVAL in the fruit zone, which allows more fruit exposure to sun and wind; and SHOOT POSITIONING, which makes trimming and leaf removal easy and effective. These canopy-management techniques are quite traditional in many parts of the OLD WORLD, and good examples may be seen in the neatly trimmed vineyards in many French regions. PRUNING also affects canopy density, as well as vine BALANCE. These practices may be termed 'Band-Aid viticulture' in the sense that they overcome the problem only in the season during which they are applied and hence need to be reapplied each year.

More permanent solutions require changes to the trellis system, which affects the canopy shape, size, and density. The changes to the trellis usually involve increasing the canopy surface area and decreasing shading. For example, dense canopies in vineyards where rows are as much as 3.5 m/11.5 ft apart can be converted to a trellis system such as GENEVA DOUBLE CURTAIN (GDC), which effectively results in a canopy twice as long as the row. This is achieved by dividing a dense canopy into two less dense canopies, or 'curtains', thereby roughly doubling the canopy surface area. Other popular trellis systems such as the LYRE, SCOTT HENRY, and SMART-DYSON rely on the same principle of increasing the exposed canopy area.

There was initial resistance to the ideas of canopy management, both commercially and among academics, even within the US where the technique was effectively born, although it was eventually taken up there some 20 years behind other regions and seen to be imported from France, Italy, Australia, or New Zealand. This resistance stemmed partly from the fact that Shaulis's initial studies were made with the American grape Concord—even though it was proven quickly enough that VITIS VINIFERA varieties responded in the same way.

There is less scope in the Old World for canopy management, since ROW SPACING is traditionally narrower and trimming and leaf removal are routine. Centuries of trial and error have demonstrated the benefits of open canopies to improve wine quality and reduce vine diseases even if the benefits of canopy management were not always recognized by traditional viticulturists. By the early 1990s, however, there were commercial examples of new trellis systems applied to some more vigorous Old World vineyards in France, Spain, and Italy, and in 2021 Champagne growers voted to change the regulations on VINE DENSITY to allow for bigger vines (*vignes semi-larges* or VSL). Today far more attention is paid to every aspect of the canopy, including height and density.

Contemporary thinking about canopy management suggests the optimal degree of leaf and fruit exposure might vary according to variety and region. There have been instances where excessive fruit exposure has had negative effects on quality. For example, in association with high temperatures it can lead to loss of colour, an effect sometimes called 'berry pinking'; and berries may shrivel if they are exposed to too much heat. See BERRY SHRIVEL and SUNBURN. R.E.S.

Iland, P., et al., 'Climate and the vine', in *The Grapevine: From the Science to the Practice of Growing Vines for Wine* (2011).

Reynolds, A. G., 'Viticultural and vineyard management practices and their effects on grape and wine quality', in A. G. Reynolds (ed.), *Managing Wine Quality 1: Viticulture and Wine Quality* (2nd edn, 2021), 443–539.

Smart, R. E., and Robinson, M., *Sunlight into Wine: A Handbook of Winegrape Canopy Management* (1991).

canopy microclimate, the climate within and immediately around the grapevine CANOPY. This is the third level of climate definition (see also MACROCLIMATE, MESOCLIMATE) and in many ways the one of most relevance to contemporary viticulture because it can be so effectively manipulated, by CANOPY MANAGEMENT, to improve wine quality and YIELD and to reduce VINE DISEASES.

The canopy microclimate at the outside of the canopy is obviously affected by the macroclimate and mesoclimate, but that within the canopy depends on the way the canopy itself alters the climate. For example, if bright SUNLIGHT falls on a dense canopy with few gaps, a leaf facing the sun at midday receives, say, 100 relative units of sunlight. The second leaf in the canopy will receive less than ten units, and the third will receive less than one. So the second leaf in the canopy has a light climate like that of a high-LATITUDE vineyard on an overcast day, while the third layer is just very shaded. In other words, the number of layers of leaves in the canopy has even more effect than vineyard location on canopy microclimate. This drastic reduction in sunlight levels in the canopy is caused by the vine leaves absorbing and reflecting more than 90% of light falling on the upper surface; less than 10% penetrates through to the lower surface.

This simple example illustrates the importance of canopy microclimate and indeed how its effects can override those of regional CLIMATE, CLONE, ROOTSTOCK, and so on. (See VITICULTURE.) A feature of reputable vineyards is that they are typically of low to moderate VIGOUR, and as a result the canopies are not dense and shaded. In many older vineyards (see VINE AGE), leaves and fruit are well exposed to the sun. For vigorous and typically high-yielding vineyards, on the other hand, the canopy interior is a dark, humid, and cool place by day. Not only are the processes of fruit RIPENING slowed, but FUNGAL DISEASES such as BOTRYTIS BUNCH ROT and POWDERY MILDEW are encouraged. Canopy-management techniques can be used to provide high-vigour vineyards with the same canopy microclimate as that of low-vigour vineyards.

Of the various climatological elements such as SUNLIGHT, HUMIDITY, TEMPERATURE, RAINFALL,

EVAPORATION, and WIND, the canopy has greatest effect on sunlight, wind, and evaporation. For sunlight, the values in the centre of a dense canopy can be less than one-tenth of those outside the canopy, while temperature and humidity values are more similar to those outside. Air temperature values are typically slightly cooler in dense canopy interiors, and humidity slightly higher. It is the leaves of the vine canopy that are responsible for creating the distinctive canopy microclimate. They strongly absorb sunlight, lose water as vapour (TRANSPIRATION), and absorb the energy (strictly speaking, momentum) of the wind so that velocity behind just one leaf is very different from that behind one above it. Since evaporation and hence transpiration depend on sunlight, humidity, and wind, it is easy to appreciate that these values will also be reduced below the first leaf layer.

The amount and arrangement of vine leaf area therefore has a significant effect on canopy microclimate. If most leaves and fruit are exposed, the canopy microclimate values will not be too different from those above the canopy. If, on the other hand, the canopy is dense and the majority of leaves and bunches are not visible (and so are shaded), the microclimate values will be very different. A considerable body of research confirms that both wine quality and YIELD are reduced by such shading. A visual impression of the canopy can be definitive in terms of the vineyard's ability to produce good-quality wines and can be the basis of a system of vineyard SCORING used to assess vineyard potential to produce quality wine.

Exposed fruit can produce better wine quality, even in warm to hot climates where HEAT STRESS is anticipated. However, grape bunches exposed to sunlight can reach temperatures 5–10 °C higher than what might already be high air temperatures. Research in Washington State by Spayd and others has carefully separated light and temperature effects. They found a positive benefit of sunlight exposure on the fruit, but this could be negated by high grape temperatures. Exposure to the ULTRAVIOLET part of sunlight improves GRAPE COMPOSITION AND WINE QUALITY. They suggest exposing fruit to the morning rather than afternoon sun, to avoid the problems associated with high temperature such as depression of ANTHOCYANINS. This result reflects the practice common in Bordeaux, for example, of leaf removal on the eastern side of the canopy in the hottest part of the season and then on the western side only later in the season. Extreme exposure to sunlight can also cause SUNBURN. R.E.S.

Smart, R. E., and Robinson, M., *Sunlight into Wine: A Handbook of Winegrape Canopy Management* (1991).

Spayd, S. E., et al., 'Separation of sunlight and temperature effects on the composition of *vitis vinifera* cv. Merlot berries', *American Journal of Enology and Viticulture*, 53 (2002), 171–82.

cans are an increasingly popular form of wine PACKAGING, ideal for smaller formats (e.g. 250, 330, or 350 ml), which has no harmful effect on wine destined for early consumption. The advantages are that cans are lighter and less fragile than BOTTLES, can be infinitely recycled, and have a lower CARBON FOOTPRINT once in use, although their initial manufacture is energy intensive. They also have a lower OXYGEN TRANSMISSION RATE than PLASTIC BOTTLES or POUCHES. However, the material from which they are made is not, unlike GLASS, inert. Cans are lacquered on the inside to give chemical resistance to the acid in the wine. However, if there is the slightest pinhole in the lacquer, the SULFUR DIOXIDE (SO_2) in the wine reacts with the aluminium, producing foul-smelling HYDROGEN SULFIDE. It has also been suggested that free SO_2 may be able to diffuse through the liner, with similar unwanted consequences. Aluminium bottles are now also being used for wine although their performance has not so far been independently trialled.

Allison, R., et al., 'The chemistry of canned wines', Appellation Cornell Research Focus (2020). www.grapesandwine.cals.cornell.edu/sites/grapesandwine.cals.cornell.edu/files/shared/images/Research%20Focus2020-1%20FinalA.pdf.

Canterbury (Waitaha in Māori), around Christchurch on the central east coast of NEW ZEALAND's South Island, represents a collection of small, diverse subregions. Waipara, by far the largest subregion, is a 45-minute drive north of Christchurch and includes both CLAY- and LIMESTONE-based Omihi and GRAVELLY Glasnevin soils. The surrounding hills provide a warmer climate than the rest of Canterbury. Inland from Waipara lies the limestone-rich Waikari subregion.

The VOLCANIC Banks Peninsula and stony Canterbury Plains subregions to the east and west of the city respectively have just a few producers each but are home to the region's first vineyard plantings. New Zealand's first and only university wine school, LINCOLN UNIVERSITY, is based here.

Spring and autumn FROSTS are a constant viticultural challenge, particularly for early-budding Pinot Noir, the region's most planted variety. Sauvignon Blanc takes the number two spot, while Pinot Gris, Riesling, and Chardonnay follow. S.P.T.

cantina, Italian for a cellar, a wine shop (although the word ENOTECA is much more common), and a winery. A *cantina sociale* is a CO-OPERATIVE winery.

cap, the layer of grape solids that floats on the liquid surface during red-wine fermentation and requires careful management. The cap usefully limits the amount of OXYGEN available to the YEAST, thereby encouraging the formation of alcohol, but has to be broken up and SUBMERGED in order to encourage the extraction of the desirable PHENOLICS which add colour, flavour, and longevity to a wine. See MACERATION, PUMPING OVER, RACK AND RETURN, and PUNCHING DOWN.

CAP stands for Common Agricultural Policy, a plank of EU policy which has had long-term effects on world wine production.

Cape, a synecdoche used for SOUTH AFRICA, particularly during the apartheid era.

Cape Agulhas, district in SOUTH AFRICA close to the southernmost tip of the continent.

Cape blend, South African term generally used to describe a red wine in which PINOTAGE is one of the blending components.

Cape Riesling, the old, misleading South African name for CROUCHEN Blanc. From 2010, wine produced from Crouchen Blanc had to be sold as such, or as Cape Riesling, and could no longer be labelled Riesling alone.

Cape Verde, or Cabo Verde, is an archipelago of ten VOLCANIC islands about 600 km/373 miles off the coast of West Africa. There is virtually no rainfall, but, on the island of Fogo, condensation from the huge volcano permits some vine-growing.

capsule, French and occasional English name for the sheath over the top of a cork and bottleneck, otherwise known as a FOIL, just as the **capsule cutter** is more widely known as a FOIL CUTTER. French wine released for sale within France before June 2019 had to have its capsules embossed with a customs seal, known as a **capsule CRD** or *capsule congé*, but this is no longer obligatory. The regulation requiring producers to use a different seal for exported wines was dropped in 2011.

Caramany, GNEISS-dominated enclave within the appellation of Côtes du Roussillon-Villages, encompassing three villages: Caramany itself and neighbouring Cassagnes and Bélesta, with vineyards at an average ELEVATION of 250 m/820 ft. The principal grape varieties grown are Carignan, Grenache, and Syrah, with some LLEDONER PELUT. Wines must contain a minimum of two varieties, with the principal grape making up 40–70% of the blend. R.E.G.

carbohydrates, organic compounds made up of CARBON, OXYGEN, and hydrogen and which include sugars, STARCH, and cellulose. Of particular interest to the wine consumer are the simple sugar molecules GLUCOSE and FRUCTOSE, which together make up the SUGARS in grape juice and which are subsequently fermented into the alcohol which distinguishes wine from grape juice. Sucrose, the sugar molecule made up of glucose and fructose, is manufactured in the leaves of plants, including vines, by PHOTOSYNTHESIS. Sucrose can be converted to all other forms of carbohydrates, such as starch, as a storage compound in the roots and trunks, and cellulose, which is a structural component in all cells. Sucrose is also the basic biochemical building block of plants, and it can be converted to proteins, fats, and organic acids.

Carbohydrate reserves are an important factor in the VINE GROWTH CYCLE. Starch is the principal form of carbohydrate reserve which is stored in the woody vine parts in the autumn. The starch is converted into sugars, which, via RESPIRATION, provide the chemical energy for growing shoots early the following spring. The reason perennial plants, such as vines, can grow to such a large size is the ability to store surplus chemical energy each growing season, which is then available for shoot growth the following season. This allows more rapid growth than for a plant starting out from a seed, which has limited food reserves.

At about VERAISON, when the fruit starts to ripen, the vine begins to replace carbohydrate reserves used earlier that growing season. Sugars are moved into the trunk, arms, and roots, where they are converted to the insoluble storage material starch. As shoots accumulate starch they change colour, from green to brown; this is called CANE RIPENING. Ideally there should be a period of warm, sunny weather after HARVEST during which the leaves can manufacture more sugars to provide the final topping up of starch reserves. However, this ideal state of affairs can be disrupted, for example by large crops of ripening grapes or late-season shoot growth, which slows ripening and limits the amounts of starch formed. Similarly, an autumn FROST which destroys leaves can interrupt the orderly build-up of reserves in the vine. High levels of carbohydrate reserves of sugars and starches make vines better able to withstand WINTER FREEZE, providing them with a sort of biological antifreeze mechanism. Although starch is the main carbohydrate storage compound, there are some other minor compounds such as AMINO ACIDS and carboxylic acids which show the same pattern of autumn accumulation and spring depletion.

Early shoot growth in spring is entirely dependent on these stored reserves, which are mobilized in the woody parts and moved to the developing shoots. If there are too many new shoots growing for the reserves available, individual shoot growth will be checked. The concept of BALANCED PRUNING ensures that the number of buds retained is proportional to the reserves available. The new shoots become independent of these reserves when the majority of leaves reach more than half the final size, and photosynthesis is sufficient to support further growth.

See also OAK FLAVOUR. R.E.S.

Keller, M., 'Partitioning of assimilates', in *The Science of Grapevines* (3rd edn, 2020).

carbon is an essential element that is distributed among the atmosphere (present as CARBON DIOXIDE), plants, animals, and the soil. When plant and animal residues and excreta are returned to the soil, they are colonized by a host of microorganisms, aided by larger soil organisms such as EARTHWORMS, which decompose these residues, releasing carbon dioxide and nutrients and deriving energy for their growth. As the many different carbon compounds in the residues are colonized, and as the organisms multiply and then die, the more resistant compounds and newly synthesized carbon compounds gradually accumulate to form a dark brown to black colloidal material called humus or 'stabilized' ORGANIC MATTER. This cycling of the carbon is important for the nutrition of vines and COVER CROPS, most especially in ORGANIC and BIODYNAMIC VITICULTURE.

See also BIOCHAR. R.E.W.

carbon, activated. See CHARCOAL.

carbonation, the cheapest and least effective method of SPARKLING WINEMAKING, involving the simple pumping of CARBON DIOXIDE into a tank of wine. In EU terminology, carbonated wines are aerated sparkling wines.

carbon dioxide, or CO_2, a naturally occurring atmospheric gas, commonly encountered as the sparkle in soft drinks, beers, and SPARKLING WINES. Its content in the atmosphere is only about 0.042%; yet upon that small amount depends the growth of all living systems, including humans, plants (including vines), yeasts, bacteria, and all fauna dependent on any of these for food. Not least, it is the ultimate raw material of wine and—via a series of biochemical reactions involving the grapevine, yeast cells, and the consumer—results in both assimilation and production of carbon dioxide.

The cycle begins with the combination of carbon dioxide and water into sugars in the vine leaves by PHOTOSYNTHESIS; conversion in the leaves and berries of some of that sugar into a variety of compounds, including those directly or indirectly responsible for ACIDS, COLOUR, and FLAVOUR in the grapes and wine; and, as the final step, transformation of the grape juice into wine by FERMENTATION. Carbon dioxide is released in substantial amounts during fermentation and typically vented to the atmosphere despite the gas's known role in CLIMATE CHANGE. When wine is consumed, the gas returns whence it came with the metabolism of the alcohol and other wine constituents back to carbon dioxide and water, primarily in the liver and exhaled breath of the wine drinker.

Carbon dioxide passes into vine leaves through small pores, or STOMATA. It is absorbed into cells and hence is 'fixed' in the chloroplasts by the action of sunlight.

The carbon-dioxide concentration in the Earth's atmosphere has been rising since the beginning of the Industrial Revolution, largely due to the burning of fossil fuels, and by April 2019 it had reached 420 ppm, the highest level for some 800,000 years. The implications for climate change—with concomitant changes to ecosystems, already observed for vineyards worldwide—are astonishing but quite understandable because of how this gas absorbs the sun's energy. With increasing awareness of climate change and rising atmospheric carbon dioxide levels, it is worth considering the wine industry's role in what may be the Earth's greatest environmental problem. See CARBON FOOTPRINT. R.E.S.

In winemaking

Carbon dioxide can be used throughout the winemaking process to displace OXYGEN from contact with crushed grapes, MUST, or wine, although NITROGEN is generally preferred for must and wine so that they do not become saturated with carbon dioxide. At some wineries, carbon dioxide is deliberately pumped over white grapes as they are received at the winery and pass through the DESTEMMER in order to minimize OXIDATION.

Carbon dioxide also plays an important role in the fermentation of all wines. YEAST metabolizes starches and sugars to produce water and carbon dioxide. In the case of yeast's metabolic activity in six-carbon sugar solutions such as grape juice, the three main by-products are water, ETHANOL, and carbon dioxide. If excess oxygen is available, the yeast obtains more cell-building energy from the sugar by converting it to carbon dioxide and water. With only a moderate oxygen supply, the yeast produces carbon dioxide and the ethanol that distinguishes wine from grape juice.

While wine is fermenting, substantial quantities of carbon dioxide are given off; while not being inherently toxic to humans, carbon dioxide displaces oxygen so that, in a confined space such as a FERMENTATION VESSEL, suffocation is all too possible. Winery workers must exercise particular caution in this respect.

In most still wines, this carbon dioxide is encouraged to dissipate leaving only very small amounts in the finished wine (400–1,200 mg/l depending on the type of wine), although the more protective the winemaking, the more substantial these traces may be, as in, for example, many German and other light, aromatic white wines. (Winemakers may, however, choose to remove carbon dioxide from such wines by SPARGING them with NITROGEN just before bottling.)

In sparkling wines, however, substantial quantities of dissolved carbon dioxide, between two and six atmospheres, are encouraged to remain in the bottle by one of the methods outlined in SPARKLING WINEMAKING. Lesser quantities of carbon dioxide, between one and two atmospheres, may be encouraged in wines such as those labelled PERLANT, PÉTILLANT, or FRIZZANTE by inducing a second but less violent fermentation and preserving the carbon dioxide produced.

In order to enhance the freshness and fruitiness of a wine, some winemakers, especially in hotter regions, pursue a deliberate policy of bottling wine, particularly simple, inexpensive white and rosé wine, with up to one atmosphere of carbon dioxide dissolved in it. This is done by processing the wine at very low temperatures, where carbon dioxide is much more soluble in wine, then bottling it early in order to preserve some of the gas given off during fermentation. The warmer the wine is served, the more obvious is the carbon dioxide to the taster.

While most tasters would be surprised and probably shocked to notice any carbon dioxide in a mature red bordeaux (in which case it could even be taken to be an unwelcome sign of FERMENTATION IN BOTTLE), it is not necessarily a fault in some types of white and rosé wines. Portugal's VINHO VERDE provides many examples of this deliberate wine style, as do many young whites from the MOSEL, and some Italian red wines contain a perceptible level of carbon dioxide, sometimes as a result of the GOVERNO practice of adding dried grapes to provoke a second fermentation.

Carbon dioxide also plays an essential role in CARBONIC MACERATION. R.E.S. & V.L.

Smart, R. E., 'A lump of coal, a bunch of grapes . . .', *Journal of Wine Research*, 21/2–3 (2010), 107–11.

carbon footprint of wine is a key indicator of the SUSTAINABILITY of grape and wine production since it is a measure of the efforts of those in the grape and wine sector to counter CLIMATE CHANGE. A carbon footprint is the total greenhouse gas (GHG) emissions of an organization, individual, service, or product expressed as carbon dioxide equivalents. CARBON DIOXIDE (CO_2), methane (CH_4), nitrous oxide (N_2O), and some fluorinated gases (refrigerants) are the main GHG, and these increase the average temperature of the Earth and the atmosphere by absorption of infrared solar radiation. These gases are emitted naturally but have been significantly increased by human activities such as the use of fossil fuels in electricity and heat generation and in transportation.

Carbon footprints are measured using the method of life-cycle assessment (LCA). LCA studies are typically either 'cradle to grave' (taking into account all impacts from extraction and processing of raw materials through to use, recycling, and disposal) or 'cradle to gate' (considering all impacts until the product leaves the producer's premises). For example, an LCA on a bottle of wine may be performed up to the winery gate or also take into account transport, sale, and disposal of the packaging.

Recent studies in several different countries and wine regions have yielded similar results to that of Abbott and colleagues for the export-dominated Australian grape and wine sector. The authors found that emissions due to grape-growing and winemaking were relatively minor components, at 15% and 17% respectively. Glass manufacture and transport were the hotspots, representing 68% of the average life cycle in the study, highlighting the need for lighter bottles, local sourcing, better recycling, reusable bottles, and ALTERNATIVE PACKAGING.

For grape-growing, diesel and electricity use (generated from fossil fuels) are major contributors to emissions. For wineries, electricity use, largely for refrigeration, is the major contributor. Alternative wind and solar energy sources are now being used by pioneers worldwide. The amount of carbon dioxide captured in vineyards (by vines, COVER CROPS, etc.) is not typically counted as a carbon credit. Perhaps surprisingly, carbon dioxide released to the atmosphere from fermentation is not counted as an emission. These emissions and sinks form part of the short-term carbon cycle and are typically excluded in reporting activities. Dr Damien Martin of Plant and Food Research, New Zealand, has calculated that the activities of the world's wine producers typically lead to a net reduction in atmospheric carbon dioxide of 8 tonnes per ha of vineyard per year. The calculation estimates that for each ha almost ten tonnes are fixed each year by photosynthesis, while each tonne of grapes produces 1.3 tonnes of carbon dioxide during fermentation and a further 0.6 tonnes treating WINERY WASTE. R.E.S., E.W. & K.H.

Abbott, T., et al., 'Assessing the environmental credentials of Australian wine', *Wine and Viticulture Journal*, 31/1 (2016), 35–7.

Ferrara, C., and De Feo, G., 'Life cycle assessment application to the wine sector: a critical review', *Sustainability*, 10/2 (2018), 395, 1–16.

Smart, R., et al., 'Towards Australian grape and wine industry carbon neutrality . . . the possible dream', *Grapegrower and Winemaker*, 680 (2020), 100–5.

carbonic acid is the acid formed when CARBON DIOXIDE is dissolved in water, H_2CO_3.

carbonic maceration, red winemaking process in which the first phase of fermentation is conducted in a completely anaerobic atmosphere, which transforms a small amount of MALIC ACID and SUGAR IN GRAPES into ETHANOL, along with traces of many flavourful aromatic compounds, without the intervention of YEASTS. This occurs only if the SKINS remain intact, unbroken by DESTEMMING or CRUSHING.

Other WHOLE-BUNCH FERMENTATION techniques such as SEMI-CARBONIC MACERATION, or the inclusion in the fermenter of a percentage of whole bunches or whole berries as well as crushed grapes, result in some carbonic maceration occurring within the whole berries but with lesser amounts of the distinctive flavours in the wines. Wines made in this way are typically light-bodied, brightly coloured, and fruity, for early consumption, most famously but by no means exclusively in the Beaujolais region of France.

Louis PASTEUR observed in 1872 that grape berries held in air differed in flavour from those held in a CARBON DIOXIDE atmosphere. Michel Flanzy published a study on carbonic maceration in 1935 and reported that wine produced in this way was much brighter-coloured, less tannic, and more distinctively perfumed, as described below. The aromas can override varietal fruit character but can also add aroma to wines with low fruit intensity.

For full carbonic maceration, intact whole bunches of grapes are placed in a closed fermentation vessel and an anaerobic atmosphere is created, generally obtained by using CARBON DIOXIDE to exclude OXYGEN. A modified version, patented by Stephen Hickinbotham in 1986, involves whole grape bunches placed into a plastic bag supported by a pallet box, into which a small quantity of dry ice in an insulated container has already been placed. The plastic bag is then sealed and sometimes fitted with a one-way valve, to allow carbon dioxide to escape while preventing entry of air.

Carbon dioxide is absorbed by the grape berries, filling the berry to around 50% of its volume. This causes grapes to change from aerobic respiration to fermentative anaerobic metabolism. Intracellular fermentation takes place within the intact berry. Carbonic-maceration character and structure occur best if grapes are kept at temperatures around 30–32 °C/86–90 °F for five to eight days. At lower temperatures over a period of up to three weeks, more subtle and short-term aromas are produced, but the intensity of the characters can vary depending on grape variety or wine style. To complete fermentation, the fruit is destemmed, crushed, and fermented with yeast under normal winemaking conditions, either with the skins or off the skins after PRESSING.

During the anaerobic phase, intracellular reactions involving the enzyme malic dehydrogenase metabolize malic acid into ethanol, SUCCINIC ACID, and aminobutyric acid but

C

without producing any LACTIC ACID. This results in a decrease in TOTAL ACIDITY and an increase in PH of about 0.25 units. The grape alcohol dehydrogenase enzyme transforms SUGAR IN GRAPES into ethanol and carbon dioxide. Only 0.5–2.2% of ethanol is produced, possibly because at this concentration the ethanol begins to disrupt the cell membrane integrity. The quantity of carbon dioxide produced during the first 24 hours is approximately the same as that absorbed. GLYCEROL and shikimic acid are produced, with shikimic acid degrading to cinnamic acids, then converting to aroma compounds associated with carbonic maceration: benzaldehyde (cherry, kirsch, almond), vinylbenzene (styrene, plastic), and ethyl cinnamate (cinnamon, strawberry, honey). Other ENZYMES can produce volatile aromas that may contribute to carbonic-maceration flavour, including ethyl and methyl vanillate (vanilla), ethyl 9-decenoate (sweet, fruity, quince), and 1-octanol (almond/buttery). Carbonic maceration wines often exhibit lower primary fruit flavours because some fruity ESTERS form only in an oxygen-rich environment during crushing. During carbonic maceration, ethanol acts as a solvent, and ANTHOCYANINS diffuse from the skin into the PULP, turning the flesh pink. Any TANNINS extracted into the pulp at low alcohol concentrations would more likely be from the skin than from the seeds, which could lead to a perception of softer tannins in the wine.

Under commercial winemaking conditions, it is almost impossible to produce a wine that depends wholly on carbonic maceration for the first phase of fermentation. See SEMI-CARBONIC MACERATION and WHOLE-BUNCH FERMENTATION for more common alternatives.

Although Beaujolais is the most famous wine region where carbonic maceration or semi-carbonic maceration is widespread, the techniques are also used for the Beaujolais grape Gamay in other parts of France, in some red burgundy, in Pinot Noir and Shiraz in the NEW WORLD using variations of whole-bunch fermentation, and in the eastern US to decrease naturally high levels of malic acid. It has also been turned to positive use in the southern Rhône, and it assists in making commercial reds from the sometimes tough Carignan grape for early drinking in the Languedoc and Roussillon in southern France—although there is an increasing tendency to blend carbonic-maceration wines with traditionally made wines. G.C.

Flanzy, M., 'Nouvelle méthode de vinification', *Comptes rendus des séances de l'Académie d'agriculture de France*, 21 (1935), 935–8.

Tesniere, C., and Flanzy, C., 'Carbonic maceration wines: characteristics and winemaking process'. *Advances in Food and Nutrition Research*, 63 (2011), 1–15.

Carcavelos, tiny DOC within Portugal's Lisboa region, renowned in its heyday for FORTIFIED WINES. However, its vineyards, planted on CALCAREOUS soils, have almost been obliterated by the westward expansion of the capital city Lisbon along the Tagus estuary (see map under PORTUGAL). A cynic's view of Carcavelos is that it was created by the Marquis of Pombal, Portugal's autocratic 18th-century prime minister, because he had to do something with the grapes from his country residence at nearby Oeiras. He even flouted his own regulations and permitted Carcavelos to be blended with PORT. Thanks to Pombal, Carcavelos enjoyed a brief period of popularity in Britain in the early 19th century (and see AUCTIONS for evidence of its renown even earlier). More recently, a 21st-century partnership between the Municipality of Oeiras and the Ministry of Agriculture kick-started production under the Villa Oeiras brand and has inspired followers (including the Municipality of Cascais). In consequence, while remaining miniscule, the land under vine is increasing. Just 12 ha/30 acres were in production in 2021; new plantings will take full advantage of the 25 ha currently authorized for DOC production.

Carcavelos is predominantly made from white grapes, which must comprise at least 75% Galego Dourado, Ratinho, and ARINTO. Rarer red examples must comprise at least 75% CASTELÃO and Preto Martinho. Most wines are also non-vintage blends but, since 2004, COLHEITA styles have emerged.

Carcavelos is usually fermented dry and fortified with GRAPE SPIRIT to 15–22% alcohol; the spirit is typically sourced from Portugal's brandy heartland, Lisboa's Lourinhã region. A small amount of *vinho abafado* (fermenting grape must preserved by the addition of alcohol) is added after FERMENTATION to sweeten the wine. Regulations introduced in March 2021 provide for a range of sweetness levels based on RESIDUAL SUGAR: Seco (≤65 g/l), Meio-doce (65–130 g/l), and Doce (≥130 g/l). The wines must be aged for at least two years in wood. Longer CASK AGEING gives the wine a nutty character akin to a tawny port, but, given the proximity of the Atlantic, Carcavelos is lighter-bodied and fresher, with saline notes.

R.J.M. & S.A.

Cardinal, red TABLE GRAPE, a CROSS, grown for wine production in Vietnam, Thailand, and Sri Lanka. *Cardinal* is also a (Burgundian) name for a red wine mixed with CASSIS.

Carema, alpine red-wine zone of PIEMONTE in north-west Italy, bordering on the Valle d'AOSTA, is the northernmost zone of Piemonte in which the great NEBBIOLO, here called PICUTENER, is cultivated (although see also VALTELLINA). Viticulture is not an easy task in this mountainous region, and the PERGOLA-trained vineyards on the slopes of a morainic amphitheatre have been wrested from steep gradients by means of TERRACES at 350–700 m/1,150–2,300 ft.

The wine itself has a recognizable Nebbiolo character, with higher ACIDITY and less BODY than the wines of the Langhe or than the group described in SPANNA, making for perfumed and impressively long-lived wines. Carema's total vineyard area was just 17 ha/42 acres in 2020, supplying a growing number of young producers banded together under the Giovani Vignaioli Canavese name. Ferrando, founded in 1890, saved the DOC from obscurity thanks to its legendary Carema Etichetta Nera, a 100% Nebbiolo aged for three years in cask and produced in only the best vintages. The minimum ageing period for DOC wines is two years, in oak or chestnut. The umbrella DOC Canavese includes Carema as well as almost all of CALUSO. W.S.

www.caremavini.it

Carignan, known as **Cariñena**, **Samsó**, and **Mazuelo** in Spain, **Carignane** in the US, and **Carignano** in Italy (**Bovale Grande** on Sardinia), late-ripening black grape variety which was once so widely planted in the LANGUEDOC and ROUSSILLON that it was France's most planted vine for much of the last century. Thanks to EU bribes, it had fallen to being the sixth most planted red wine grape in France by 2019, when plantings totalled 31,273 ha/77,277 acres.

Nowadays Carignan seems a very odd choice indeed, although presumably it seemed obvious to many *pieds noirs* returning in the mid 20th century from ALGERIA, where the wine industry depended at one time on its 140,000 ha/350,000 acres of Carignan. In much of southern France, its wine is high in everything—acidity, tannins, colour, bitterness—except finesse and charm. This gives it the double inconvenience of being unsuitable for early consumption yet unworthy of maturation. The astringency of basic red from the Languedoc has owed much to Carignan's ubiquity, although blending with Cinsaut or Grenache helped considerably, and CARBONIC MACERATION helped disguise, if not exactly compensate for, Carignan's lack of youthful charm. The vine is not even particularly easy to grow. It is extremely sensitive to POWDERY MILDEW, quite sensitive to DOWNY MILDEW, prone to rot, and prey to infestation by grapevine MOTHS. Its diffusion was presumably beneficial to the AGROCHEMICAL industry. Its bunches keep such a tenacious hold on the vine that it does not adapt well to MECHANICAL HARVESTING and is mainly grown as BUSH VINES.

There must have been some attribute which led to the almost exclusive dissemination of Carignan throughout the Midi in the 1950s and 1960s, and there was: YIELD. The vine can quite easily be persuaded to produce almost 200 hl/ha (11 tons/acre), ideal for a thirsty but not discriminating post-Second World War market. It also buds late, which gave it extra allure as a substitute for the much lighter ARAMON, previously France's number one vine, which had been badly affected by the frosts of 1956 and 1963. It ripens late, too, however, limiting its cultivation to Mediterranean wine regions. The regulations for the Languedoc and Roussillon appellations have been forced to embrace the ubiquitous Carignan, but it is hard to argue that, for example, Minervois or Corbières are improved by their optional Carignan component. Those wines that depend most heavily on varieties such as Syrah, Grenache, and Mourvèdre and least on Carignan are almost invariably the most successful—with the exception of some wines made with care from well-sited old BUSH VINES, which can make concentrated marvels such as those of Domaine of the Bee in Roussillon, Bertrand Bergé, and Domaine Jones in Fitou.

The fuller-bodied white MUTATION **Carignan Blanc** can still be found in some vineyards of the Languedoc and, in particular, Roussillon.

Although the vine (like Grenache) may have originated in Spain in the province of Aragón, it is not widely planted there today. **Cariñena** is not even the principal grape variety in the wine that carries its most obvious Spanish synonym CARIÑENA. It is grown chiefly in Cataluña and also plays a major part in the wines of PRIORAT (where it is also known as Samsó and where some of the finest Carignan-dominant wines in the world are to be found), COSTERS DEL SEGRE, PENEDÈS, TARRAGONA, and TERRA ALTA, so that Spain had total plantings of 5,658 ha/13,981 acres in 2020.

Because of its late-ripening habits, Carignan can thrive only in relatively hot climates. It has been grown in ISRAEL since 1870 and is still widely planted there as a workhorse grape, occasionally producing quality wines from old bush vines. In Italy, there were still 1,684 ha/4,161 acres in 2015: as Carignano in Lazio and most commonly on Sardinia (perhaps as a result of that island's long dominance by Aragón), where it makes strong, rich, velvety reds and rosés, notably some seriously exciting Carignano del Sulcis. A recent survey on Sicily, based on DNA PROFILING, established that around 70% of NERELLO CAPPUCCIO vines are in fact Carignano. It is also grown on Cyprus, in Türkiye, and in Croatia.

The vine, gaining a vowel as **Carignane**, has been important in the Americas. Although it is rarely seen as a VARIETAL, there were still about 893 ha/2,206 acres in California's hotter regions in 2020, for the vine's productivity and vigour are valued by growers, if not consumers. Old bush vines produce the best wines and are highly prized. Likewise, Chile's old-vine Carignan is enjoying something of a revival with the support of the Vignadores de Carignan organization. It is also grown (to a much lesser extent) in Mexico, Argentina, and Uruguay. Occasional bottlings of savoury old-vine Carignan have surfaced in South Africa.

Cariñena, town in north-east Spain which lends its name to both a DOP and a vine variety, widely grown in southern France as CARIGNAN. Although it is thought to have originated in the area, the vine (officially known as Mazuelo in Spain) has been widely abandoned here in favour of GARNACHA, which seems better suited to the arid growing conditions in this, the largest of the four DOP zones of the ARAGÓN region (see map under SPAIN), with 14,300 ha/35,336 acres planted. But Cariñena, like so many other Spanish regions, is trying to break with the viticultural and winemaking flaws of the past. Tempranillo and Cabernet Sauvignon have also been planted, and the local red wine rarity Vidadillo rediscovered. Among the white vine varieties that cover one-fifth of Cariñena's total vineyard area, MACABEO and GARNACHA BLANCA have been joined by PARELLADA from Penedès. The CO-OPERATIVES, led by San Valero and Grandes Vinos y Viñedos, have been fully modernized. V. de la S. & F.C.

Carmel Valley, California AVA with a handful of small wineries and 121 ha/300 acres of vineyards draped across steep slopes in the drainage area of the Carmel River, 16–19 km/10–12 miles inland from Carmel Bay. Several wineries throughout the state source fruit from the region, particularly Cabernet Sauvignon and Merlot, which make up more than 70% of plantings. Despite sitting within Monterey County, Carmel Valley does not fall within the bounds of the Monterey AVA and instead sits within the larger CENTRAL COAST AVA. A.Y.

Carmenère is a very minor dark-skinned grape variety in Bordeaux today but was, according to viticulturist Joseph Daurel, widely cultivated in the Médoc in the early 18th century and, with its parent CABERNET FRANC, established the reputations of its best properties. Daurel reports that the vine is vigorous and used to produce exceptionally good wine but was abandoned because of its susceptibility to COULURE and resultant low yields. It yields small quantities of exceptionally deep-coloured, full-bodied wines that can taste decidedly HERBACEOUS if the grapes are not completely ripe. The PAUILLAC-classed growth Ch Clerc Milon usually includes a small percentage in its ASSEMBLAGE, and the odd VARIETAL emerged in Bordeaux in the early 2000s.

Its new power base is CHILE, where plantings had reached 10,836 ha/26,776 acres by 2020, particularly as a result of correct VINE IDENTIFICATION rather than new plantings. It was discovered in 1994 that a substantial proportion of the vines previously believed to be Merlot are in fact this historic variety, presumably imported directly from Bordeaux in the late 19th century. It ripens even later than Cabernet Sauvignon and if yields are limited—by grafting on to low-vigour ROOTSTOCKS, for example—has the potential to make very respectable wines, combining some of the charm of Merlot with the structure of Cabernet Sauvignon, although for many winemakers it is best as an ingredient in a BORDEAUX BLEND.

Correct identification also grew the official total of Carmenère plantings in Italy from 45 to 1,000 ha between the censuses of 2000 and 2010. Most of these were previously thought to be CABERNET FRANC in northern and north-eastern Italy. Much is used for blending, but the likes of San Leonardo in TRENTINO and Ca'del Bosco in LOMBARDY make a sturdy varietal **Carmenero**. Even more recently, DNA PROFILING showed that the variety known as CABERNET GERNISCHT in CHINA is in fact Carmenère.

Daurel, J., *Les Raisins de cuve de la Gironde et du sud-ouest de la France* (1892).

Carmignano, historic central Italian red wine made 16 km/10 miles north-west of Florence in a zone noted since the Middle Ages as one of TUSCANY's finest for red-wine production. The vineyards are located on a series of low hills at 50–200 m/160–650 ft of ELEVATION, unusually low for the SANGIOVESE grape which forms the base of the blend, giving wines with lower ACIDITY and softer TANNINS than those of CHIANTI CLASSICO.

The wines were first given legal status by Cosimo III de'Medici—himself a major proprietor in the Carmignano zone at the villa of Artimino—who included them in his selection of four areas of superior wine production in an edict of 1716 which prohibited other wines from using the names of the selected areas. The grand-ducal wines were sent regularly to Queen Anne of England, who apparently appreciated their quality. The wines were also praised by Giovanni Cosimo Villifranchi (1773) and Cosimo Ridolfi (1831).

The report of the Dalmasso Commission in 1932 (see ITALY and TUSCANY) assigned Carmignano to the nearby zone of Chianti Montalbano, where cooler temperatures, higher elevations, and, crucially, higher yields result in Chianti wines of lighter body and higher acidity more suitable for early drinking. Independent status was restored in 1975, however, with the granting of a DOC for Carmignano, the only Tuscan DOC to require the inclusion of CABERNET SAUVIGNON and/or Cabernet Franc (up to 20%) in a Sangiovese-based blend years before their use became common in the so-called SUPERTUSCANS and long before the production rules of Chianti and Chianti Classico were loosened to allow INTERNATIONAL VARIETIES in the blends. It was awarded DOCG status in 1990. A provision for up to 10% white wine grapes remains, reflecting historic viticultural practices but no longer used by any quality-conscious producers.

The alleged tradition of Cabernet Sauvignon in the zone was of major assistance in detaching it from Chianti Montalbano. The vineyards of Ugo Contini-Bonacossi of Villa di Capezzana, who was instrumental in obtaining the DOC for the region and was the zone's major producer, were grafted with cuttings from Ch LAFITE in the 1970s. He claimed to be reviving a local tradition begun by the Medici. This view is supported by the zone's CONSORZIO, which maintains that Cabernet Sauvignon vines were planted here as early as the 16th century at the request of Catherine de Medici, then Queen of France, although supporting evidence is lacking.

The wine must be aged for at least eight months in oak or chestnut casks (12 for Riserva) and released after 1 June in the second year following the harvest. Although in the past many Carmignano wines were aged, at least partially, in French BARRIQUES, many producers have returned to ageing the wines in large oak casks, while Fattoria di Bacchereto uses clay AMPHORAE.

The DOC for younger wines and for rosé is Barco Reale di Carmignano (referring to the 'royal park', as distinguished in the Medici edict of 1716). The rosé, often obtained by SAIGNÉE, has a long history here as Vin Ruspo, a reference to peasants drawing off, or 'robbing', the pale juice from the cask at the beginning of fermentation. VIN SANTO di Carmignano has its own DOC. W.S.

Belfrage, N., *Brunello to Zibibbo: The Wines of Tuscany, Central and Southern Italy* (2003).
www.consorziovinicarmignano.it

Carmine, California CROSS whose antecedents include Carignan, Cabernet Sauvignon, and Merlot. It has an intense Cabernet flavour and is planted to a limited extent in the US. Mainly blended.

Carnelian, like CARMINE, a black grape CROSS developed from Carignan, Cabernet Sauvigon, and Garnacha in and specifically for California by Dr H. P. Olmo of DAVIS. It was supposed to be a hot-climate Cabernet, but too many of the Grenache characteristics predominate to make it easy to pick. Its California influence is limited and restricted to the SAN JOAQUIN VALLEY, where total plantings fell to 66 ha/164 acres by 2020. It is also grown to a limited extent but with surprising success in Western Australia, where it was originally thought to be SANGIOVESE.

Carneros, also known as **Los Carneros** ('the rams' in Spanish), a moderately cool, windy AVA in California that sprawls across the last, low hills of the Mayacamas Range before it slips beneath San Francisco Bay. The larger part of the AVA lies within SONOMA County; grapes from that portion can also use the Sonoma Valley AVA. The smaller segment, in NAPA County, is equally entitled to use the Napa Valley AVA. The region is one of the state's older wine districts: Agoston HARASZTHY planted grapes in it before 1870. A property originally called Stanly Ranch was famous as a vineyard by 1880. However, persistent fog and wind as well as challenges with sourcing water made vine-growing difficult and, when PHYLLOXERA struck hard in the 1880s, there began a swift slide into a long night.

The move back to Carneros began to gain momentum in the 1970s, then picked up in the mid 1980s, partly on the strength of some impressive Pinot Noirs and as much or more because of traditionally made SPARKLING WINES of Chardonnay and Pinot Noir. Those remain the predominant varieties in the region's 3,237 ha/8,000 acres of vines, though also successful are COOL-CLIMATE Cabernet Sauvignon, Merlot, and Syrah in the northern part of the Napa side and Vermentino on the Sonoma side. L.M. & E.C.B.

Carnuntum, Austrian winegrowing region immediately east of Vienna, named after a Roman city whose ruins grace the Danube's shoreline. Its 831-ha/2,053-acre vine surface in 2021 features nearly every grape variety planted in Austria. Considering its GEOLOGICAL and MESOCLIMATIC diversity, it is likely that the region will continue to produce a wide variety of wine styles. But its most ambitious growers have discovered some highly distinctive combinations of variety and site, as witness the reputation of Gerhard Markowitsch (in Carnuntum's best-known wine village, Göttelsbrunn) as one of Austria's top Pinot Noir producers; or the revival, spearheaded by Dorli Muhr and Dirk van der Niepoort, of BLAUFRÄNKISCH on the once-renowned Spitzerberg, a LIMESTONE-rich remnant of the Carpathians that sits a mere 15 km/9 miles from SLOVAKIA's capital Bratislava and nearly touches the northern tip of BURGENLAND. As of the 2019 vintage, a Carnuntum DAC allows Blaufränkisch and ZWEIGELT for reds, CHARDONNAY, WEISSBURGUNDER, and GRÜNER VELTLINER for whites, as well as cuvées of which the aforementioned varieties comprise at least two-thirds. D.S.

carotenoids, important class of plant PIGMENTS whose red, orange, and yellow colours complement the green of chlorophyll and the blue and red of ANTHOCYANINS. They are derived from the chloroplasts in green grapes. Carotenoids are TERPENOIDS with 40 carbons and belong to the LIPID group of organic compounds. They include two main groups—xanthophylls and carotenes—which are prominent in grapes and provide the skin colour of so-called white grapes, as well as being associated with vine leaf colours in autumn; carotenes also form a substrate for synthesis of many FLAVOUR COMPOUNDS and FLAVOUR PRECURSORS. Carotenoids serve as accessory pigments in the process of PHOTOSYNTHESIS. B.G.C.

Carricante, white wine grape speciality of ETNA on Sicily and dominant grape in the blend for Etna Bianco. Wines are crisp with citrus notes, and the best can age well. Plantings totalled just 710 ha/1,754 acres in 2020.

Carso, or **Carso-Kras**, small DOC consisting of just 53 ha/131 acres of vineyards in FRIULI in north-east Italy, on a GRAVELLY plateau between Gorizia and Trieste and bordering Slovenia. A smaller subzone, called Terrano Classico, is situated immediately around the city of Trieste. The DOC produces mainly dark, tannic reds high in acidity made from the Terrano grape (see TERAN), which responds well to BARREL MATURATION. Terrano is often confused with REFOSCO DAL PENDUCOLO ROSSO, which is also allowed in the Carso DOC, in addition to INTERNATIONAL VARIETIES such as Chardonnay, Sauvignon Blanc, GLERA, and Cabernet Sauvignon.

Kras is also a PDO in SLOVENIA. W.S.

Belfrage, N., *Barolo to Valpolicella: The Wines of Northern Italy* (2nd edn, 2003).
Robinson, J., et al., *Wine Grapes: A Complete Guide to 1,368 Vine Varieties, Including Their Origins and Flavours* (2012).

Cartagène is the traditional, strong, sweet aperitif of the LANGUEDOC in southern France, made, rather like a VIN DE LIQUEUR, by adding grape spirit to barely fermenting grape juice.

Cartaxo, DOP subregion of TEJO in central southern Portugal.

Carthage, ancient city on the north coast of Africa just east of modern Tunis which played a part in wine history as a result of the maritime expansion of the PHOENICIANS who settled there in the late 9th century BCE. A famous passage of the historian Diodorus (20. 8) paints a vivid picture of the country estates of the Carthaginian elite of the late 4th century BCE, flourishing on the fertile soils around Carthage with a mix of farming, which included viticulture. However, at no period did Carthaginian wine figure prominently in trade. It was eclipsed by North Africa's importance as a producer of corn and olive oil, most particularly in the period when it was part of the Roman Empire. Still, there can be little doubt that Carthage's elite shared the same interest in viticulture as the rest of the Mediterranean world.

It was for them that a large work, written in Punic, of 28 books on agriculture was produced by a certain Mago. Little is known of the writer or of his date; but his work fits most easily into the great explosion of handbooks on agriculture written in the Hellenistic period, particularly in the 3rd and 2nd centuries BCE. Like these other works, Mago's treatise is lost; our knowledge of its contents is entirely derived from references to it and quotations from it in the later writers. Of these the largest number are about vines, although it would be dangerous to infer from this very fragmentary selection that viticulture had particular prominence in his work. While Mago's work probably contained much that was taken from the earlier AGRICULTURAL TREATISES produced in the Greek world, it was not without information based on personal observation. As COLUMELLA (*De re rustica* 3. 12. 5–6) noted, Mago's advice to plant vines on north-facing slopes is particularly appropriate to Africa (see TOPOGRAPHY). Large extracts from Mago were translated into Greek and incorporated in a treatise on agriculture by Cassius Dionysius of Utica, near Carthage (VARRO, *De re rustica* 1. 1. 10). More surprisingly a decree of the senate ordered a translation of Mago into Latin (Columella, *De re rustica* 1. 1. 13). The most likely occasion for this must be in connection with one of the schemes for Roman settlement in North Africa in the period after Rome's destruction of Carthage in 146 BCE. Columella was to call Mago 'the father of country matters', probably primarily because his work in its Latin version gave Romans convenient access to the vast literature on agriculture from the Hellenistic world.

The most famous Carthaginian of all is commemorated in the name of the CO-OPERATIVE and principal producer of CHÂTILLON-EN-DIOIS in the foothills of the French Alps, the Cellier Hannibal. J.J.P.

Greene, J. A., 'Beginnings of Phoenician/Punic wine production', in P. E. McGovern, et al. (eds.), *The Origins and Ancient History of Wine* (1995).

Prados Martínez, F., 'Wine production in the Phoenician and Punic world. Notes about wine culture and consumption through the archaeological and literary sources', *Gerión. Revista de Historia Antigua*, 29/1 (2012), 9–35.

Cartizze. See PROSECCO.

cartons, method of PACKAGING wine in what are effectively cardboard 'bricks', sometimes known as tetrapacks, that has been particularly popular for everyday wines in Latin American countries such as CHILE. They are becoming more popular elsewhere in the light of concerns about SUSTAINABILITY. Cartons are light, made of renewable materials, exceedingly space-efficient, non-breakable, and relatively easy to recycle. Their CARBON FOOTPRINT is reckoned to be lower than that of any type of wine packaging. They also offer producers a much larger LABELLING area than BOTTLES. They are made mainly from paperboard, with polyethylene and aluminium, often with a resealable plastic closure, and, before opening, can keep wine fresh for between 18 months and two years.

Alko, 'Update of wine packaging LCA: final report Alko Oy' (2021). www.alko.fi/INTERSHOP/static/WFS/Alko-OnlineShop-Site/-/Alko-OnlineShop/fi_FI/Tavarantoimittajille/Muut/EN/Alko%20wine%20packaging%20LCA%20update_final%20report.pdf.

Casablanca, relatively cool wine valley in the Aconcagua region of CHILE.

casa vinicola, or AZIENDA vinicola, on the label of an Italian wine indicates a producer who buys in grapes or wine, like a French NÉGOCIANT.

case. Beer and milk may be sold in crates, but, contrary to popular usage, wine is sold in cases of 6 or 12, the basic trading units in the fine-wine trade and much of the wholesale wine trade. As wine PRICES have risen, an increasing proportion of fine wine has been offered in six-bottle cases, which have long been favoured by the German wine trade, but a 12-bottle case requires less overall packaging and is therefore more SUSTAINABLE. Most cases are made of cardboard outers, with cardboard vertical or papier mâché horizontal dividers. Wine merchants truly dedicated to the mail-order business ensure that they use only particularly strong cases designed to minimize breakage.

Many FINE WINES designed for prolonged AGEING are dispatched from their producers in heavy wooden cases, however, usually made of rough pine, branded with the name, and often the logo, of the producer on the **case ends** (which can be attractive enough for future use as decoration or table mats). These cases are usually nailed down and can be opened only with a chisel or screwdriver and hammer, often breaking the wooden lid. Wine sold in unopened cases is presumed, in the fine-wine market, to be worth sufficient premium that they are usually designated 'o.w.c.', or 'original wooden cases', in AUCTION catalogues.

A **split case** may be one that is torn but may also be one that contains six bottles of each of two different wines, or four bottles of each of three different wines. One bottle of each of 12 different wines becomes a **mixed case**.

casein, the principal milk PROTEIN, is used by winemakers as a FINING agent particularly useful for removing brown colours from white wines. It is also used to a lesser extent in the general CLARIFICATION of young wines. Precipitated from milk by the addition of ACIDS, casein is chiefly used in the form of sodium or potassium caseinate. When this salt is added to cloudy wine, it reacts with some of the wine acid, forming a curd which adsorbs and precipitates most of the very small particles, including the PIGMENTS causing discoloration. In many countries, the use of casein must be declared on the label. See LABELLING INFORMATION. A.D.W.

Casella Family Brands, Australia's biggest family-owned wine producer whose empire has been built on the phenomenal success in the US of YELLOW TAIL. The previous generation, Sicilian immigrants, settled in the small RIVERINA town of Yenda and started a small wine business in 1969. By 2022 the current version owned such historic producers as Peter Lehmann of Barossa Valley, Brands Laira of Coonawarra, Morris of Rutherglen, and Bailey's of Glenrowan. In 2022 they sold off 7,258 ha/17,935 acres of vineyard in New South Wales and South Australia to concentrate on making and selling wine.

cask, wooden container for wine, often used interchangeably with the word BARREL, a cylindrical container small enough to be rolled. The term is also used less precisely, however, for wooden containers of any size—whether larger, immobile containers such as the oval *Fuder* or *foudre* common in Germany and Alsace or the *botte* of Italy—and also including quite large, immovable containers which may or may not be open-topped.

In the 1970s, the Australian wine industry neatly, if misleadingly, coined the term **cask wine** for wine packaged in a bag packed inside a cardboard BOX, a wine type unlikely to have been either made or aged in wood of any sort (although OAK CHIPS may well have played a part in some).

cask ageing, winemaking practice of AGEING a wine after fermentation in a large wooden container sometimes too old to impart any obvious OAK FLAVOUR. It may well, however, exert some WOOD INFLUENCE and help considerably to achieve natural CLARIFICATION and STABILIZATION. White wines subjected to cask ageing for several months include some of the great white wines of the LOIRE, GERMANY, and ALSACE. Red wines subjected to cask ageing, sometimes for several years, include many of the traditional wines of the RHÔNE, ITALY, SPAIN, PORTUGAL, and GREECE.

The alternatives, and possible supplements, to cask ageing are BARREL AGEING, ageing in inert CONTAINERS such as stainless-steel tanks (with or without the use of INNER STAVES or OAK CHIPS), BOTTLING almost immediately after FERMENTATION as in NOUVEAU wines, and AGEING in bottle.

casse, historic wine FAULT involving spoilage by an excess of IRON, COPPER, or PROTEIN or by TARTARIC ACID precipitation.

cassis is French for blackcurrant and is used often as a tasting note for red wines, particularly red wines based on Cabernet Sauvignon grapes. Dry white wine mixed with some blackcurrant liqueur is known as both a *vin blanc cassis* and KIR (while red wine mixed with blackcurrant liqueur is sometimes called a *cardinal*).

C

Cassis, small, mainly white-wine appellation in PROVENCE. The encroachment of Greater Marseilles on this old fishing village keeps total plantings to just under 265 ha/654 acres in this sheltered amphitheatre, protected from the mistral by the Cap Canaille, one of the highest cliffs in France.

Three-quarters of the wine is full, dry, and herby white, made mainly from CLAIRETTE and MARSANNE, plus some Ugni Blanc or Sauvignon Blanc for freshness. A little rosé and even less red are also made, mainly from MOURVÈDRE (which ripens easily here, as in nearby BANDOL), GRENACHE, and CINSAUT. Little Cassis is allowed to escape by the annual influx of summer visitors, however.

Castel, France's, probably Europe's, biggest wine company and the world's third largest, was founded in Bordeaux by nine Castel brothers and sisters in 1949 and is still family-owned. As well as owning dozens of Bordeaux châteaux and selling prodigious quantities of wine, Castel is an important distributor of beer and WATER in France and North Africa. Castel acquired BARTON & Guestier, the Bordeaux NÉGOCIANT, and bought the Nicolas retail chain in 1988, their chief rival Société des Vins de France in 1992, Domaines Virginie in the Languedoc in 1999, the British retail chain Oddbins in 2002 (which it subsequently sold off), and the Burgundy négociant Patriarche in 2011. It is also involved in a JOINT VENTURE for the production of Chinese wine and distribution of French wines in CHINA with CHANGYU and, together with SUNTORY of Japan, owns a Bordeaux négociant and a substantial share of Ch Beaumont and the CLASSED GROWTH Ch Beychevelle.

Castelão, usefully versatile but declining Portuguese red wine grape, with total plantings of 8,934 ha/22,076 acres in 2020, down from more than 14,000 ha in 2000. It makes varied but generally fruity, sometimes surprisingly long-lived, reds all over southern Portugal. It is known variously as Periquita in Setúbal, João de Santarém in Oeste, and Castelão Francês in many regions. DNA PROFILING has shown that Castelão is a natural cross of ALFROCHEIRO and CAYETANA BLANCA.

Castel del Monte, DOC named after the imposing 13th-century octagonal fortress in PUGLIA in the far south-east of Italy, associated with red wine from the NERO DI TROIA grape, although it may also be 100% AGLIANICO or either of the two CABERNETS. Pink versions are also increasingly produced. The same flexible production rules are applied to the white, which was traditionally based on BOMBINO BIANCO, but varietal CHARDONNAY and SAUVIGNON BLANC are also allowed. Confusingly, three parallel DOCGS were created in the early 2010s—Castel del Monte Bombino Nero DOCG, Castel del Monte Nero di Troia Riserva DOCG, and Castel del Monte Rosso Riserva DOCG (minimum 65% Nero di Troia)—though none has the track record for quality this level implies.

W.S.

Castelli Romani, extensive but potentially outstanding DOC for the wines of the VOLCANIC hills south-east of Rome in the region of LAZIO (see map under ITALY). Eleven DOCs fall completely within the zone, the most illustrious being FRASCATI.

Since the creation of DOC Frascati in 1966, white varieties have become dominant in the region—mainly MALVASIA di Candia and the superior Malvasia Puntinata. A variety of strains of TREBBIANO is also grown—mainly the insipid Toscano but also Verde and Giallo.

The red CESANESE—both Cesanese di Affile and the slightly more common Cesanese Comune—has begun to make a hesitant comeback, inspired in part by Camillo Mancini's 1888 monograph 'Lazio Viticolo e Vinicolo', in which he hails Cesanese as one of Italy's most outstanding varieties. This recently rediscovered monograph has given a new generation of ORGANIC and BIODYNAMIC producers the inspiration and conviction to revive the region's reputation.

Other potentially interesting DOCs are Cori (based on the local Bellone for whites and Nero Buono for reds), Colli Lanuvini (whites based on Malvasia and reds on Merlot and Sangiovese), and the DOC Roma, which allows Malvasia in blends and varietal bottlings and also in the archaic Romanella (a MÉTHODE ANCESTRALE sparkling wine still surviving thanks to current interest in PÉTILLANT NATUREL wines), as well as reds based on MONTEPULCIANO blended with Cesanese, Cabernet Sauvignon and Franc, and/or Syrah.

Once regarded as avant-garde due to their large-scale production of IGT Lazio wines made from international varieties, Colli Romani producers have begun to increase their range with local varieties, while Viognier—partly or wholly BARREL-FERMENTED—can be convincing, if expensive. But few of these wines, self-consciously detached from the history and traditions of the zone, have provided a key to resolving the area's viticultural problems, which are exacerbated by high vineyard land PRICES, given that the hills are such an attractive place to live for Romans who want to distance themselves from the congestion of the city.

W.S.

Mancini, C., *Il Lazio Viticolo e Vinicolo* (1888).

Castets, almost extinct vine, probably selected from an escaped seedling in a forest in the Aveyron, SOUTH WEST FRANCE. It was, unexpectedly, a parent of several NEW VARIETIES bred in SLOVAKIA in the 1970s.

Castilla, **Castile** in English, old central Spanish kingdom divided by mountains into CASTILLA Y LEÓN, or Old Castile, in the north and CASTILLA-LA MANCHA, or New Castile, in the south. When a wine label refers solely to 'Castilla', it references the VINO DE LA TIERRA indication covering all the municipalities of the autonomous region of Castilla-La Mancha.

F.C.

Castilla-La Mancha, known as **Castile-La Mancha** in English (historically, Castilla la Nueva or New Castile), the lower, southern half of the plateau that makes up central Spain (see map under SPAIN). At ELEVATIONS of 400–1,000 m/1,300–3,500 ft, this is Spain at its most extreme. Winters are long and cold with temperatures often falling below 0 °C/32 °F for days on end. In summer the thermometer regularly rises above 35 °C, even 40 °C/104 °F, and little if any rain falls between May and September. The vast expanse of country which turns green in the spring quickly darkens to burnt ochre in July and August as all but the deepest riverbeds dry up completely. The locals say that they suffer 'nine months of winter and three months of hell'. Despite these fierce conditions, Castilla-La Mancha claims nearly half the total vineyard hectarage of Spain, with drip IRRIGATION having amply compensated for the widespread VINE PULL since 2000. Around 458,300 ha/1,132,484 acres of vineyard yield about 20 million hl/530 million gal of wine (averaging yields of 43 hl/ha, or 2.6 tons/acre). One of Castilla-La Mancha's nine DOP regions, LA MANCHA itself, is planted mainly with the robust white-wine vine AIRÉN.

Despite determined uprooting, there are still an estimated 200,000 ha of DROUGHT-resistant Airén in the zone of La Mancha alone (less than half of them producing DOP wine), making it one of the world's most widely planted vine varieties—although Cencibel (alias TEMPRANILLO) has been catching up fast. By 2020 there were 71,000 ha of Cencibel in Castilla-La Mancha, and it dominates in the VALDEPEÑAS, MONDÉJAR, and UCLÉS DOPs as well. To the east, the variety joins Syrah and such INDIGENOUS VARIETIES as BOBAL, GARNACHA, and MONASTRELL in the Ribera del Júcar and MANCHUELA DOPs. North-west of Toledo, Garnacha produces sturdy reds in MÉNTRIDA. In the far east, Monastrell and Garnacha Tintorera (ALICANTE BOUSCHET) predominate in the ALMANSA DOP.

Today more attention is being paid to local varieties Tinto Velasco (2,000 ha in Spain) and Moravia Dulce (1,900 ha; see MARUFO) as red grapes suited to the region's ever-warmer climate (see CLIMATE CHANGE). The region also grows possibly Spain's most fragrant renditions of MACABEO. ALBILLO Real (not to be confused with Albillo Mayor from RIBERA DEL DUERO) is gaining a reputation for aromatic, rounded white wines.

Another development that contrasts strongly with centuries of BULK WINE production has been a blossoming of distinguished single-estate wines (see VINO DE PAGO) that have vastly outgrown clichés about La Mancha wines, all of them inspired by the pioneering efforts of the Marqués de Griñón at his Dominio de Valdepusa. Also, many of the most interesting wines are not labelled by DOP but instead with the more generic PGI Vino de la Tierra Castilla or even Vino de España. V. de la S. & F.C.

Castilla y León, **Castile and León** in English, is the largest of the 17 autonomous regions of Spain. This northern part of Spain's central plateau, at 880–1,000 m/2,900–3,300 ft of ELEVATION, takes up about one-fifth of the entire country. Centred on its capital, the university city of Valladolid, most of Castilla y León is thinly populated table land almost encircled by mountains. It is separated from the hub of Spain (MADRID and CASTILLA-LA MANCHA) by the central mountain range which rises to over 2,000 m near Ávila and Segovia (see map under SPAIN). To the north, the Cordillera Cantabrica, which peaks at over 2,600 m, deflects the maritime influence of the Bay of Biscay.

The climate here is harsh. Short, hot summers are followed by long, cold winters when temperatures can drop to −10 °C/14 °F. Under often clear skies, temperatures drop quickly after sunset, and even in summer nights are cool. FROST is a threat until mid May. Rain falls mainly in winter and amounts to 400–500 mm/15–19 in a year. Much of the land is poor and unable to support anything other than sheep. However, the river Duero (known as DOURO in Portugal), which cuts a broad valley in the rather featureless plain, provides a natural water source. Grain, sugar beets, and vines are grown along its length.

A regional variant of the red TEMPRANILLO vine, variously called Tinta del País, Tinto Fino, Tinto Aragonés, and Tinta de Toro, is the chief good-quality grape variety in five of the region's 13 DOPs: the well-known RIBERA DEL DUERO, as well as ARLANZA, LEÓN, TIERRA DEL VINO DE ZAMORA, and TORO.

The largest of these is RIBERA DEL DUERO, which extends for about 100 km/60 miles either side of the river and is internationally known for its red wines. Downstream of Ribera del Duero, RUEDA has established itself as Spain's leading white-wine region since the 1990s, while neighbouring TORO, straddling the Duero near the Portuguese border, gained worldwide recognition a decade later. Tierra del Vino de Zamora neighbours Toro and produces a lighter version of it. CIGALES, north of Valladolid, specializes in rosé wine. BIERZO, abutting GALICIA in the north-west, makes fragrant, characterful reds from the MENCÍA grape. León, halfway between Bierzo and Ribera, produces an early-drinking Tinta del País. CEBREROS, part of the Sierra de Gredos neighbouring MADRID, is focusing on delicate high-elevation GARNACHA. To the west is ARRIBES with wines based on the local JUAN GARCÍA.

A category of growing importance is the umbrella IGP Vino de la Tierra de Castilla y León (not to be confused with the Vino de la Tierra de Castilla, which refers to wines from the CASTILLA-LA MANCHA region). Vino de la Tierra de Castilla y León is the appellation preferred by top wineries that were not included in Ribera del Duero when the boundaries were drawn, such as Abadia Retuerta (in Sardón del Duero) or Mauro (in Tudela del Duero), whose wines resemble the best Ribera del Duero.

V. de la S. & F.C.

Castillon. Named after the town of Castillon-la-Bataille, the battle referred to being that which brought an end to the HUNDRED YEARS WAR, **Castillon Côtes de Bordeaux** is a dynamic, well-priced red-wine appellation, part of the Côtes de BORDEAUX group, effectively an eastern extension of ST-ÉMILION in Bordeaux. With 1,958 ha/4,836 acres of vineyard in 2020 on mixed soils of CLAY, LIMESTONE, and some SANDSTONE with SILT, sand, and stones on the alluvial terrace above the river DORDOGNE, it is much bigger than its northern neighbour FRANCS but produces similarly sturdy red wines based on Merlot grapes with generally better structure than regular red BORDEAUX AOC. Vineyards closest to the river tend to produce more supple wine than those at higher ELEVATIONS such as Ch d'Aiguilhe, one of the more important producers. The region, whose land is still relatively affordable, has benefited from the application of expertise from grander RIGHT BANK appellations.

Catalanes, Côtes, is the IGP which covers all the vineyards of ROUSSILLON in France except for the four villages of the appellations of BANYULS and COLLIOURE, for which the IGP is Côte VERMEILLE. Côtes Catalanes will be made by wine growers who do not have quite the right grape varieties in the correct proportions for the appellation—or by those who reject its constraints. The particular interest of Côtes Catalanes is the white wine, often a single-varietal MACABEO or GRENACHE GRIS, in preference to a blended appellation Côtes du Roussillon. Among the red wines, varietal CARIGNAN from OLD VINES demonstrates the significant improvement in the quality of this once-maligned grape variety, contributing to the rise in its reputation.

R.E.G.

Cataluña, **Catalonia** in English, Catalunya in Catalan, a proud and industrious region on the Mediterranean coast which encompasses part of southern France (see ROUSSILLON) and part of north-east Spain (see maps under FRANCE and SPAIN), some of whose inhabitants do not consider themselves either French or Spanish or, even if they do, think of themselves as Catalan first. Cataluña is one of Spain's 17 autonomous regions, with Barcelona its capital.

Barcelona and its densely populated hinterland is a hive of enterprise and industry, and it is therefore no coincidence that Cataluña was at the vanguard of Spain's 20th-century winemaking revolution. The region began to stir in the early 1870s when José Raventos began making sparkling wine by the TRADITIONAL METHOD in the town of Sant Sadurni d'Anoia. He founded the giant Codorníu firm, and his foresight generated the CAVA industry, which earned its own Denominación de Origen (see DOP) in 1986.

In addition to most of Spain's Cava, Cataluña produces an eclectic range of wines from traditional, powerful reds to cool-fermented dry whites.

Much of the credit for the transformation of Cataluña's wine industry in the late 20th century must go to the late Don Miguel Torres Carbó and his son Miguel A. Torres (see FAMILIA TORRES), who imported INTERNATIONAL VARIETIES to plant alongside INDIGENOUS VARIETIES such as GARNACHA, MONASTRELL, and TEMPRANILLO (called Ull de Llebre in Catalan), and the Cava grapes, PARELLADA, MACABEO, and XARELLO.

The climate in Cataluña is strongly influenced by the Mediterranean. The coastal belt is warm and equable with moderate rainfall, but conditions become progressively more arid and extreme further inland. There are ten DOP regions—ALELLA, EMPORDÀ, CONCA DE BARBERÁ, COSTERS DEL SEGRE, MONTSANT, PENEDÈS, PLA DE BAGES, PRIORAT, TARRAGONA, and TERRA ALTA—plus the catch-all DOP CATALUNYA. Of these, Penedès is the most important in terms of quantity, although the late 20th century transformation of Priorat resulted in some of Spain's highest wine prices.

Cataluña has long been an important centre of CORK production and is a particularly important source of corks for sparkling wines.

V. de la S. & F.C.

Catalunya, Catalan name for the region of CATALUÑA and controversial DOP created in the early 21st century for blends made from anywhere in the region. Big bottlers such as FAMILIA TORRES were the chief proponents and are the chief beneficiaries.

Catarratto, Sicilian grape variety that is Italy's second most widely planted white grape after TREBBIANO Toscano and is grown on 29,528 ha/72,965 acres on the island as of 2020. Also known as **Catarratto Bianco Lucido** (sometimes simply Lucido) and **Catarratto Bianco Comune**, probably two CLONES of the same variety, Catarratto has been revealed by DNA PROFILING to be a natural Mantonico Bianco × GARGANEGA cross. It is planted almost exclusively in the far western province of Trapani and was in the past much used for the production of MARSALA. Today there is an increasing number of varietal wines or blends with INTERNATIONAL VARIETIES. The variety is specified in the regulations of ten DOC zones and seven IGTS. Any SURPLUS is likely to be distilled or transformed into GRAPE CONCENTRATE. See SICILY for more details.

Catawba, deep-pink-skinned, late-ripening AMERICAN HYBRID of an American species and SÉMILLON. It was extremely popular in the 19th century and is still grown to a certain extent, particularly in NEW YORK State and OHIO. Identified in North Carolina in 1802 even before CONCORD, it produces white and pink, still and sparkling, rather FOXY wines ranging from dry to very sweet.

catechin and its isomer **epicatechin** are PHENOLIC compounds (see also FLAVONOIDS) found mainly in grape seeds but also in stems, berry skins, and, in lower amounts, flesh. They contribute to bitterness in wines and are the constitutive units of TANNINS (see also PROANTHOCYANIDINS), which are responsible for ASTRINGENCY and increasing the stability of ANTHOCYANINS (see CO-PIGMENTATION and PIGMENTED TANNINS), leading to longer-lived COLOUR in wines. Because of the increased SKIN CONTACT involved during RED WINEMAKING, catechin concentrations are usually higher in red wines than in whites, but they are involved in browning reactions in both. Catechin may play a role in protecting vine parts from microbial attack as a pre-existing chemical barrier, but it is also produced by vines in response to DOWNY MILDEW infection.

Catechin, epicatechin, and other flavanol monomers such as gallocatechin and epigallocatechin are often referred to as **catechins**. Like other flavonoids, catechins are antioxidant compounds that may contribute to the HEALTH benefits of moderate wine consumption, particularly with regard to blood pressure. Catechins and related compounds may have a greater effect than that of RESVERATROL and related stilbenes, which are present in wine in much lower concentrations. Also, unlike resveratrol, these compounds are widely present in other fruits and vegetables, cocoa, and beverages such as teas.

The concentrations of catechins vary with vine variety, with PINOT NOIR, then MERLOT, notably high among well-known red wine grapes, and SYRAH lowest. As with resveratrol, cool, damp climates seem to stimulate more catechin synthesis than do hot, dry ones.

V.C. & G.L.C.

Goldberg, D. M., et al., 'Catechin and epicatechin concentrations of red wines: regional and cultivar-related differences', *American Journal of Enology and Viticulture*, 49 (1998), 23–34.

Mangels, D. R., and Mohler, E. R., 'Catechins as potential mediators of cardiovascular health', *Arteriosclerosis, Thrombosis, and Vascular Biology*, 37/5 (2017), 757–63.

cation exchange is a process by which cations (positively charged ions) in solution in a soil exchange with other cations that are held on negatively charged CLAY particles and ORGANIC MATTER. These cations are called exchangeable cations. The quantity of cations, expressed as moles of charge per kilogram of soil, defines the CATION EXCHANGE CAPACITY. Cation exchange can result in concentrations of exchangeable ALUMINIUM in very acid soils (soil PH less than 5) that are potentially harmful to vine roots. Conversely, in soils with high concentrations of soluble salts, the exchange of SODIUM for CALCIUM cations can lead to very high pH soils (greater than pH 9) when the salts are leached out. The structure of such soils is potentially unstable, with the consequence that drainage is impeded and waterlogging can occur. See also ION EXCHANGE. R.E.W.

White, R. E., *Understanding Vineyard Soils* (2nd edn, 2015).

cation exchange capacity (CEC), the amount of positively charged ions a soil can hold, is a significant factor in the degree to which SOIL NUTRIENTS are available to the vine. CEC is determined by SOIL TEXTURE, the amount of ORGANIC MATTER in the soil, and the amount and type of CLAY. Sandy soil has a low CEC. Fine-textured soil such as clay, with a high level of organic matter, tends to have a high CEC.

Cato, Marcus (234–149 BCE), Roman statesman advanced as a writer on agricultural and viticulture matters, known as 'Cato the Elder' or 'Cato the Censor' to distinguish him from his great-grandson. He grew up on his father's farm near Reate, north-east of Rome, then fought against CARTHAGE in the Second Punic War and afterwards had a distinguished political career. He became known as a strict moralist, castigating the 'new' extravagance, ostentation, and luxury and advocating a return to the 'old' virtues of austerity, honesty, and hard work. He wrote books on many subjects and published his speeches. PLINY the Elder praises him for the breadth of his learning (*Natural History* 25. 4), and COLUMELLA (*De re rustica* 1. 1. 12) and Cicero (*Brutus* 16. 61) honour him as the father of Latin prose. His only surviving work, *De agri cultura* ('Concerning the cultivation of the land'), also known as *De re rustica* ('Concerning country matters'), is important not only because it is the first lengthy prose work in Latin. *De agri cultura* is not divided into books or arranged systematically in any other way: Cato's remarks on viticulture and winemaking are scattered throughout the treatise. The advice he gives is of a severely practical kind. His prime concern is making farming, including winegrowing, profitable through hard work and careful management. For instance, he stresses that the grapes should always be thoroughly ripe when harvested or one's wine will lose its good reputation. And in the making and storing of wine he was aware of the importance of HYGIENE to prevent the wine turning to VINEGAR. After the vintage, the wine jars should be wiped twice a day, each with its own broom. After 30 days, when FERMENTATION is complete, the jars should be sealed, or the wine can be drawn off its LEES if desired as an alternative to LEES CONTACT. The type of estate he has in mind produces chiefly wine and olive oil: hence his extensive section on the construction of presses. H.M.W.

Astin, A. E., *Cato the Censor* (1978).

Thielscher, P., *Des Marcus Catos Belehrung über die Landwirtschaft* (1963).

caudalie, French term for a unit of sensory measurement equal to one second's LENGTH of a wine's impact on the palate after swallowing or spitting.

Cava, Spanish SPARKLING WINES made using the traditional method of SPARKLING WINEMAKING. The term 'Cava' was adopted by the Spanish in 1970 when they agreed to abandon the use of the potentially misleading term 'Champaña'. The word originates in CATALUÑA, which produces most but not all Cava, and where it means 'cellar'. It was here in the town of Sant Sadurní d'Anoia that José Raventós, head of the family firm of Cordoníu, made the first bottles of TRADITIONAL METHOD sparkling wine after a visit to France in 1872. Early growth in the industry coincided with the arrival of PHYLLOXERA, which first appeared in Catalan vineyards in the 1880s. Vineyards that had once made sturdy red wines were uprooted and replanted with MACABEO, PARELLADA, and XARELLO, the triad of grape varieties which is the mainstay of the Cava industry to this day. In 1889, the Raventos family were joined by Pedro Ferrer, who founded the firm of FREIXENET. Codorníu and Freixenet are now two of the largest sparkling wine producers in the world, with their own winery outposts in CALIFORNIA.

Unlike any other Spanish DOP, the Cava *denominación* is not restricted to a single delimited area. However, since Spain joined the EU in 1986, the EU authorities have insisted that Cava should be made from grapes grown in prescribed regions. As a result, the use of the term 'Cava' is restricted to sparkling wines from a list of municipalities in Catalonia, VALENCIA, ARAGÓN, EXTREMADURA, NAVARRA, RIOJA, and the BASQUE country. However, 95% of all Cava is made in Cataluña, mostly in and around the town of Sant Sadurní d'Anoia. Total production amounts to over 250 million bottles yearly, compared with 300 million bottles of CHAMPAGNE.

The light, aromatic Macabeo (the Viura of Rioja) comprises about half of the blend for a typical Cava, its late BUDBREAK making it a popular choice for vineyards prone to spring FROSTS. The productive and indigenous Xarello vine, which thrives at relatively low ELEVATIONS, is the second most important, and its aromas of fennel and apples are one of Cava's distinguishing features. Parellada performs better above 300 m/900 ft, where it produces finer wines relatively low in BODY. Subirat Parent (ALARIJE) is also used. CHARDONNAY was officially authorized for Cava in 1986; PINOT NOIR was accepted in 1998. The dark-skinned varieties GARNACHA, MONASTRELL, and TREPAT are also permitted, Trepat only in rosé.

To qualify for the DOP, Cava must be made according to the local adaptation of the TRADITIONAL METHOD. The wine must spend at least nine months on its lees before DISGORGEMENT, and attain an ALCOHOLIC STRENGTH of 10.8–12.8% by volume. YIELDS, set at a maximum of 1 hl of must per 150 kg of grapes, are higher than those allowed in Champagne. Most REMUAGE is now carried out automatically in a *girasol* or GYROPALETTE, a Spanish invention which can handle hundreds of bottles at a time.

The perceived mass-market image of Cava has led to a growing disenchantment among better-quality producers. By 2014 a number of them in Penedès—including Albet i Noya, Mas Comptal, Loxarel, and Colet—had left the appellation to join the PENEDÈS DOP.

In January 2019, another group of producers, unhappy with Cava's image and rules against citing subzones on wine labels, withdrew from the DOP to produce quality sparkling wines under their own brand, CORPINNAT. The DOP Cava responded in 2021 with new regulations, including, most notably, extended ageing periods for Cava Reserva (18 months), Gran Reserva (30 months), and Cava Paraje Calificado, a sort of SINGLE-VINEYARD Cava (36 months). To qualify for these superior categories, wines must be sourced from vineyards at least ten years old.

Most importantly, a number of zones and subzones were approved, although it seems too late to draw Corpinnat producers back into the fold. The zones are: **Comtats de Barcelona** (near Barcelona, with subzones Valls d'Anoia Foix, Serra de Mar, Conca del Gaià, Serra de Prades, Pla de Ponent); **Valle del Ebro** (north-central Spain, with subzones Alto Ebro, Valle del Cierzo); **Viñedos de Almendralejo** in Extremadura; and **Levante**, in Valencia's eastern highlands. V. de la S. & F.C.

www.cava.wine

cave, French for a CELLAR or winemaking establishment and as close as the French language comes to an equivalent of a WINERY. A **caviste** is French for a specialist wine retailer. See also CHAI.

cave co-opérative, French for one of France's 600 wine CO-OPERATIVES. They vinify nearly 50% of all AOC wine and 69% of IGP.

www.lacooperationagricole.coop

Cayetana Blanca, high-yielding Spanish white grape variety travelling under many aliases, including Pardina and Jaén Blanco in Spain and Mourisco Branco in Portugal. Official 2020 Spanish vine statistics still distinguished between Cayetana and Pardina, but plantings totalled 34,579 ha/85,447 acres. It produces low-acid, neutral-flavoured wines which oxidize easily. It is particularly popular, as Pardina, in the EXTREMADURA region, especially in Badajoz province on the border with Portugal, where much of its produce is distilled into Brandy de Jerez. In Rioja it may be known as Cagazal, and Baladí is another synonym. The variety is closely related to many other Iberian varieties. There were 844 ha/2,086 acres of Mourisco Branco in Portugal in 2020, mostly in Beiras.

Robinson, J., et al., *Wine Grapes: A Complete Guide to 1,368 Vine Varieties, Including Their Origins and Flavours* (2012).

Cayuga White, AMERICAN HYBRID with SEYVAL genes released in 1972 from Geneva in New York (see CORNELL). It is grown in the north-east of the United States and makes fruity white wines.

Cebreros, DOP recognized in 2019 in Ávila in CASTILLA Y LEÓN in west-central Spain, little-known despite its outstanding feature, very old GARNACHA vineyards on steep SLATE slopes rising up to 1,200 m/3,937 ft in ELEVATION. White wines are made from ALBILLO. F.C.

CEC. See CATION EXCHANGE CAPACITY.

celebrity wine. The second decade of the 21st century saw a rash of wines and champagnes launched on the basis of their relationship with a famous (and sometimes not-so-famous) actor, singer, broadcaster, chef, or sports personality. The wines are rarely top-notch, and presumably their prices factor in a commission for said sponsor, but the wine industry has in general welcomed the phenomenon on the basis that these products probably attract some newcomers to the habit of buying and drinking wine.

cell, the structural unit of living organisms, the smallest unit capable of independent existence. YEAST and BACTERIA are examples of single cells, while one grapevine has billions of cells. Each plant cell consists of a protoplast surrounded by a cell wall, but it can be differentiated into a host of forms. A cell in the flesh of a ripe grape berry, for example, can be 0.5 mm/0.02 in in length with a thin, wavy cell wall lined by an equally thin cytoplasm surrounding the vacuole, a 'sea' of water with dissolved sugars, acids, and hundreds of other solutes, otherwise known as grape juice. Other cells within the berry can be entirely different. A PHLOEM element aligns end to end with others to form a tube through which elaborated sap moves in a network throughout the plant. Adjacent fibre cells in the XYLEM are long and slim with thick walls hardened by the wood polymer, lignin. The complex functioning of the leaf provides other examples of cell forms: STOMATAL cells function to allow carbon dioxide in and oxygen and water vapour out; others function as the 'CARBOHYDRATE factory'; and cells in its dense network of veins are designed to move water and minerals up from the roots (in the xylem) and to move sugars and other elaborated organic nutrients out to the rest of the plant (in the phloem).

Despite this diversity, all cells of a plant have the same genetic information in their nuclei and, with some exceptions, may be separated and cultured as single protoplasts. By TISSUE CULTURE methods, these can then be used for the regeneration of another plant like the parent. The genetic material in each cell will therefore be 'tuned' for its differentiation and functioning by the dictate of its neighbours in that tissue and by its reaction to signals received from other tissues and organs. B.G.C.

Taiz, L., et al., *Plant Physiology and Development* (6th edn, 2018).

cellar, widely used word that is roughly the English counterpart to CAVE, CANTINA, and BODEGA in French, Italian, and Spanish respectively, terms which can be applied to both wine shops and winemaking premises (see WINERY), but the English term is used mainly to refer to a winery or, in its domestic sense (see below), to a collection of wine and the place in which it is stored prior to opening.

Location

Traditional underground cellars have the great advantages of being secure, dark, at a constant low temperature without recourse to external energy sources, slightly damp, and rarely disturbed. As outlined in STORING WINE, these constitute ideal conditions. Few modern dwellings have anywhere that enjoys all these advantages, and to recreate them it may be necessary to spend lavishly on specialist help in constructing or adapting quarters with low lighting levels

C

and specially controlled temperature and humidity (and as few visitors as the expender of all this money and effort can bear). Another option is the use of refrigerated cabinets that can be programmed to maintain certain temperature and humidity levels, but they are expensive and guzzle energy relative to their capacity. Less expensive options include insulating a small room or large cupboard, insulating a space under some stairs, using a dark corner of a distant spare room or a closet against an outside wall, or converting (or building) a secure outhouse (although care must be taken that the TEMPERATURE never falls so low as to freeze the wine and push the corks out). It is important that any makeshift cellar is far from any heat source, even a hot-water pipe and, especially, a boiler, although a constant medium temperature is less harmful than violent temperature swings. Those living on ground level can even excavate, and depend on a trapdoor.

Accessibility is an advantage or disadvantage depending on the cellar owner's personality and attitude towards the cellar. Paying for professional storage may be the only realistic option for some, but in this case cellar records (see below) are essential.

Design

Wine can be stored in the unopened CASES in which it is bought, but this is practical only for wines years away from being ready to drink and requires steady and sturdy shelves. A system which incorporates cases without lids on individual runners is particularly space-efficient. Wine racks take up more room but allow bottles to be kept horizontal and corks damp (not strictly necessary for bottles with SCREWCAPS or SPARKLING WINE) and retrieved individually. Racks with slots for individual bottles offer the best access for very mixed cellars, but larger compartments, or BINS, can be used for larger quantities of bottles of the same wine.

It of course makes sense to keep the wines nearest MATURITY in the most accessible positions and vice versa (which dictates how wines may be kept in double-depth racks). There will be a slight temperature variation between the top and bottom of the cellar. Light levels are also likely to be higher at the top than the bottom, so there are at least two reasons why the fullest, least-fragile, slowest-maturing wines such as vintage port should be stored at the top and bottles as sensitive as, say, those containing sparkling wines should be stored close to floor level.

Contents

There is little point in devoting space and capital to storing wine unless it is difficult or expensive to replace (such as an EN PRIMEUR rarity) or will positively improve as a result of AGEING. There is no such thing as an 'ideal cellar', and an individual's ideal depends entirely on his or her tastes and consumption patterns.

Records

Cellar records are not necessary, but they can add to the pleasure of wine collectors with a love of order and memorabilia. (The other school enjoys the twin elements of chaos and serendipity in plundering their wine cellars.) Traditional cellar records have a good-sized page for each case of wine acquired, stating price, supplier, and date of purchase. Below this a dated tasting note for each bottle tasted can be inserted, together perhaps with details of the circumstances in which it was opened. (Those using professional wine storage need, for obvious reasons, to keep full details of where and since when the wine has been stored.)

INFORMATION TECHNOLOGY can offer other (often much more sophisticated and flexible) possibilities for cellar record-keeping. CELLARTRACKER and its imitators store personal cellar records online.

See also STORING WINE.

Gold, R., *How and Why to Build a Wine Cellar* (4th edn, 2007).
Sims, P., *The Home Wine Cellar* (2004).

cellar door has a very specific meaning originating in Australia, where it denotes the physical interface between a winery and its visiting customers. See TOURISM.

cellar rat, colloquial term for a relatively junior WINERY worker, especially itinerant ones following in the footsteps of FLYING WINEMAKERS.

CellarTracker, website that houses the world's largest collection of TASTING NOTES, more than nine million by late 2021. This fully searchable database is free to use (a donation is optional) and is made up of contributions from 750,000 (mainly amateur) users all over the globe. It was set up in 2003 by Eric LeVine, then employed by Microsoft, as a personal cellar-management tool, but the social and knowledge-sharing implications rapidly became apparent, especially for following the AGEING of specific, generally quite fine, wines. The site is also integrated with those of a host of WINE WRITERS.

www.cellartracker.com

cellar work, general term for all the processing steps requiring human intervention or monitoring in WINEMAKING. In the narrower sense of what cellar workers actually do—apart from overseeing grape reception, DESTEMMING, CRUSHING, FERMENTATION, CLARIFICATION, FILTRATION, BLENDING, STABILIZATION, and BOTTLING—it generally entails operating PUMPS, adding FINING agents and other additions or PROCESSING AIDS, and almost constant cleaning (see HYGIENE). Cellars in which small barrels are used for both fermentation and maturation involve the most physical work, including filling, RACKING and moving barrels, TOPPING UP, and possibly STIRRING. See also ÉLEVAGE.

Celts, peoples who inhabited western Europe before the rise of ancient ROME. Many of them were introduced to wine by the Romans, when some were already skilled COOPERS.

The first clear evidence that wine drinking with its attendant rituals was penetrating the courts of the prehistoric BARBARIAN elites in western central Europe (eastern France, southern Germany, and Switzerland) appears in the archaeological record in the 6th century BCE.

Griffon-headed cauldrons, CRATERS, jugs and strainers, and fine painted Attic cups, all of which would have been used at a Greek SYMPOSIUM, were shipped to Mediterranean ports such as Massilia (Marseilles). From there they were transported along the navigable RIVERS into the hinterland to be used in the complex systems of gift exchange which bound these peoples to the Greek and Etruscan traders of the south. Along with these trappings of civilization came wine. How much of it, if any, was at this stage Greek or Italian is difficult to tell. What is certain is that the large ceramic AMPHORAE in which the wine was transported inland were manufactured along the coast of southern France in the vicinity of Marseilles, suggesting, but not proving, that most of the wine consumed was locally manufactured.

The courts of the elite, places such as Mont Lassois on the main south–north trade route between Burgundy and Paris (where the celebrated Vix crater, a bronze vase 1.64 m/5.4 ft high and clearly made in ancient GREECE, was found), and Heuneburg in Germany, lasted for a comparatively short time. They were flourishing in the 530s and 520s BCE but had ceased to exist by the end of the next century as the old social order collapsed in a turmoil of unrest caused by migrating bands of Celts who were to thrust deep into Italy, Greece, and Türkiye.

By the end of the 3rd century BCE, a new order was beginning to emerge in the western Mediterranean. Rome was growing rapidly in power and had won a decisive victory over the CARTHAGINIANS in Spain, but their military involvement was to last for almost two centuries before the peninsula could be regarded as fully conquered. This meant a continuous movement of military detachments, supplies, and officials using the ports and the roads in southern France linking Italy and Spain. Inevitably the cities and the native tribes of Provence and Languedoc got used to this traffic and no doubt profited from it; so too did Roman entrepreneurs keen to exploit the new markets being opened up. For them the love of wine which the Celtic tribes of the interior so evidently possessed was a heaven-sent opportunity to offload, with profit, the considerable wine surpluses being generated by the large estates of northern and western Italy. As one contemporary writer somewhat incredulously remarked of the Celts of GAUL, 'They will give you a slave for an amphora of wine thus exchanging the cup-bearer for the cup.' While this does not necessarily imply the actual exchange rate, it shows which surpluses the two societies were prepared to exchange with each other for mutual benefit.

In the Celtic world it was important for those aspiring to power to host elaborate feasts to entertain their followers and others. The more exotic the commodities offered, the greater the status of the host. Wine from the south was in considerable demand and was avidly consumed. The drunken Celt who took his wine undiluted—something no civilized man would have done—was several times remarked upon by contemporary writers.

Wine was usually transported by sea in large ceramic amphorae made in distinctive styles and fabrics which can be quite closely dated and assigned to specific localities of manufacture. This means that it is possible to study the developing wine trade in some detail, and, since several of the estates produced amphorae with their own identifying stamps, individual marketing strategies can be identified. By studying the relative proportions of Italic and local amphorae in the successive levels of settlement sites in southern France, it is possible to show that throughout the 2nd century BCE, when Provence and Languedoc were finally annexed by Rome, there is little trace in the archaeological record that local wine was drunk at all. In parallel with this, the number of shipwrecks containing amphorae found off the southern French coast increases noticeably, presumably reflecting the corresponding increase in the volume of trade.

Once offloaded at ports such as Massilia and Narbo (Narbonne), the amphorae were transported inland by road or river. En route a *portorium* (or transport tax) was charged at each settlement through which the wine passed, trebling the price charged by the time it eventually reached the native consumers. From the borders of Provincia of ancient Rome, modern Provence, the wine penetrated the territory of the neighbouring tribes. At two locations, one just outside Toulouse and the other at Chalon-sur-Saône, substantial quantities of discarded Italian amphorae have been found. No precise count can now be made, but estimates in the tens of thousands are unlikely to be far from the truth. These must surely be major trans-shipment points where wine was decanted into skins or BARRELS (for which the Celts of the CAHORS region were particularly famed) for the more arduous journeys by cart into the wild interior. Not all wine was decanted, however. Considerable numbers of amphorae have been recovered from major native *oppida* (towns) at Montmerlhe, Essalois, Jœuvres, and Mont-Beuvray between 20 and 100 km (12–62 miles) beyond the frontier. From here much of it passed into the hands of the local nobility to be consumed with relish in their lavish feasts.

The volume of wine imported into Gaul at this time is difficult to estimate in detail, but a conservative assessment suggests that it may have reached 100,000 hl/2.6 million gal a year. When it is remembered that the largest trading system operating in pre-industrial Europe—the Gascon wine trade to Britain and Flanders in the 14th century (see BORDEAUX)—was 750,000 hl/20 million gal a year, the intensity of the Roman operation can be appreciated.

By the end of the 2nd century BCE Italian wine was reaching all parts of France, mainly along the navigable rivers, but some, still in its amphorae, was being reloaded on to ships in the GIRONDE estuary to be transported along the Atlantic coast of France to Brittany. There much of it was consumed, but a small quantity was carried by Breton sailors on the last leg of its journey via Guernsey to the British port on Hengistbury Head, overlooking Christchurch harbour, constituting the earliest attested importation of wine to ENGLAND, or Britain. One wonders whether after such a journey it was even barely drinkable. B.C.

Cunliffe, B., *Greeks, Romans & Barbarians: Spheres of Interaction* (1988).

Tchernia, A., *Le Vin de l'Italie romaine* (1986).

Tchernia, A., 'Italian Wine in Gaul at the end of the Republic', in P. Garnsey et al. (eds.), *Trade in the Ancient Economy* (1983).

Cencibel, synonym for the Spanish black grape variety TEMPRANILLO, especially in central and southern Spain, notably in LA MANCHA and VALDEPEÑAS, where it is the principal dark-skinned variety.

Central Coast, one of CALIFORNIA's umbrella AVAS, this sprawling wine region technically encompasses nearly all of the land from San Francisco to Los Angeles, inland from the coast almost to the CENTRAL VALLEY. In practice, the important and unique viticultural areas referenced by the name are concentrated in its midsection, the counties of MONTEREY, SAN LUIS OBISPO, and SANTA BARBARA.

Central Otago grows NEW ZEALAND's most southerly grapevines, some of them cultivated beyond the 45th parallel. It is New Zealand's only wine region with a CONTINENTAL CLIMATE and has greater diurnal and seasonal TEMPERATURE VARIABILITY than any other. The region is as dependent on Pinot Noir as Marlborough is for Sauvignon Blanc, representing 80% of the region's vines and 1,626 ha/4,018 acres planted. Pinot Gris is a distant second followed by Riesling.

Gibbston was, with Wanaka, one of the original areas to be planted with vines, as recently as the early 1980s. Gibbston is the coolest subregion and typically the last to be harvested. Alongside BANNOCKBURN in the Cromwell basin, it is regarded as the most prestigious subregion, though there are promising signs from the basin's Lowburn and Bendigo areas, producing some of the ripest styles. Central Otago's often voluptuous and intensely fruity Pinot Noir has helped put New Zealand red wine on the world map. S.P.T.

Central Ranges Zone, broad Australian zone in NEW SOUTH WALES along the western slopes of the Great Dividing Range comprising the Cowra, Orange, and Mudgee regions.

Central Valley, refers in CALIFORNIA to a broad, fertile, sunny valley that grows more than half the fruits, vegetables, and nuts in the United States. Stretching about 80 km/50 miles across and 725 km/450 miles long, it is divided into the SACRAMENTO VALLEY in the north, which produces small quantities of wine, and the hot, vast SAN JOAQUIN VALLEY in the south, which supplies the majority of the state's BULK WINE (and TABLE GRAPES and RAISINS). The Sacramento River from the north and the San Joaquin River from the south drain into the Central Valley Delta, which includes such AVAS as CLARKSBURG and, on slightly higher ground, LODI.

CHILE also has a Central Valley which includes the subregions (from north to south) Maipo, Rapel, Curicó, and Maule and which is used as an appellation for wines grown in more than one region.

Central Victoria Zone comprises the wine regions Bendigo, Goulburn Valley, Heathcote, Strathbogie Ranges, and Upper Goulburn in the Australian state of VICTORIA.

centrifugation, winemaking operation of CLARIFICATION using a **centrifuge**, typically employed in large wineries to quickly clarify wines or to clarify white grape juice before FERMENTATION. The equipment is expensive to buy and run, but the separation force induced by rotation of the centrifuge bowl at around 4,800 rpm is up to 6,000 times greater than that experienced during gravity SETTLING, considerably reducing the time taken to clarify the liquid. When used on juice, in which the difference in DENSITY between the solids and the liquid is smaller than in wine, it is often coupled with FLOTATION to improve the throughput.

A stack of *c.*250 conical discs in the centrifuge divides the feed into many thin layers so particles need to fall only a short distance before they hit a disc and slide down into the periphery of the bowl. Solids are further compacted there and then periodically discharged. Horizontal decanter centrifuges, which are able to process materials with a high solids content such as lees, are sometimes used, but the separation forces and product clarity are typically lower than with disc-stack centrifuges. S.N.

Centurian, CALIFORNIA vine cross with the same parentage as CARNELIAN but released three years later in 1975. The state's total acreage had fallen to 37 ha/92 acres by 2020, all in the central SAN JOAQUIN VALLEY. It has viticultural advantages over Carnelian but no organoleptic distinction.

cépage, French for VINE VARIETY. A VARIETAL wine, one that is sold by the name of the principal grape variety from which it is made, is known as a **vin de cépage** within France, a term which has had some pejorative sense in comparison with a geographically named wine which qualifies as AOC. High-quality vine varieties such as Syrah (as opposed to such traditional varieties as Carignan and Alicante Bouschet) are described as **cépages améliorateurs**, or 'improving varieties', in the south of France.

Cerasuolo di Vittoria is SICILY's only DOCG and takes its name from a town in the province of Ragusa in the south of the island. Grapes are grown on red sandy soils with a high ferrous content (see IRON). NERO D'AVOLA (up to 70%) with FRAPPATO (maximum 50%) form the blend of this wine for which the yield has sensibly been capped at 52 hl/ha. Wines that are released after 31 March in the second year following the harvest may be called Classico. In 2014 the DOC Vittoria was created, to allow for varietal bottlings of the increasingly popular Frappato, as well as Nero d'Avola and the white INZOLIA. W.S.

Cerceal, or **Cerceal Branco**, white Portuguese grape variety with high acidity found mainly in the DOURO, DÃO, and BAIRRADA. Not the same as the SERCIAL of MADEIRA.

Cercial is the BAIRRADA synonym for Cerceal Branco, also known as **Cercial do Douro**.

Cerdon. See BUGEY.

Cereza, quantitively very significant pink-skinned grape variety in ARGENTINA, where it is second only to Malbec in the total area planted: 26,195 ha/64,729 acres in 2020. A CROSS between CRIOLLA CHICA and MUSCAT OF ALEXANDRIA, and taking its name from the Spanish word for 'cherry', it produces mainly white and some rosé wine of extremely mediocre quality for early consumption within Argentina, typically sold in cardboard packs, as well as being used for GRAPE CONCENTRATE.

Cérons, historic (see BORDEAUX, history) but struggling sweet-white-wine appellation on the left bank of the GARONNE. Just north of BARSAC and SAUTERNES, it produces wines which rarely demonstrate either the finesse of the first or the concentration of the second of these two more famous appellations, possibly partly because much more generous YIELDS are allowed but also because selling prices make sacrifices for quality difficult. In effect, Cérons is a buffer zone between Barsac and the GRAVES, and its dry whites and reds are entitled to the Graves appellation. CLAY is slightly more common here than in Barsac and Sauternes, and the generally flatter land may also play a part in reducing the likelihood of BOTRYTIS. Only 20 ha/49 acres produced sweet whites in 2020. J.R. & J.L.

certified planting material, BUDWOOD, CUTTINGS, and GRAFTED VINES which have normally been through a form of quality assurance to ensure trueness to type, freedom from known VIRUS DISEASES and BACTERIAL DISEASES, and typically designated clonal origin. Various bodies, often government controlled, offer such certification programmes around the world. See CLONE, CLONAL SELECTION, and VINE IMPROVEMENT.

CERVIM, the Centro di Ricerca, Studi, Salvaguardia, Coordinamento e Valorizzazione per la Viticoltura Montana, is an organization created in 1987 under the auspices of the OIV to encourage the preservation of mountain winegrowing. Based in the Valle d'AOSTA of northern Italy, the group includes members in Austria, France, Germany, Greece, Portugal, Slovenia, Switzerland, and Spain, as well as one winery in PERU, in 2022. CERVIM members may use the trademark Cervim-Heroic Viticulture for wines grown at ELEVATIONS of at least 500 m/1,640 ft, gradients exceeding 30%, or on terraces, steep slopes, or small islands (such as Tenerife in the CANARY ISLANDS). Members also benefit from the group's research projects such as SCORPION, aimed at developing autonomous ROBOTS capable of precision PESTICIDE spraying in steep terrain as well as administering ULTRAVIOLET RADIATION treatments to replace AGROCHEMICALS.

www.cervim.org

Cesanese, the red grape variety of LAZIO. The superior **Cesanese di Affile** clone (once a minor ingredient in the cult wine Trinoro of southern Tuscany and now planted at Passopisciaro, its sister property on ETNA) is very slightly more common than **Cesanese Comune**, which has larger berries and is also known as Bonvino Nero. Total plantings of both were only 446 ha/1,102 acres in 2015.

César, minor vine speciality of the far north of Burgundy, where it can contribute backbone to such light, soft reds as IRANCY. DNA PROFILING at DAVIS suggested it is a progeny of PINOT and Argant.

Chablis is the uniquely steely, dry, ageworthy white wine of the most northern vineyards of BURGUNDY in north-east France, made, like all fine white Burgundy, from Chardonnay grapes. Paradoxically, however, in the NEW WORLD, particularly in North America in whose vineyards a wine as austere as Chablis is virtually impossible to produce, the name Chablis has been borrowed as a GENERIC name for the most basic white wine. Happily that practice is now almost insignificant. The true Chablis appellation has increased considerably since the early 1990s and in 2020 included a total of 5,771 ha/14,260 acres of Chardonnay vineyard around the town of Chablis and 19 other villages and hamlets in the Yonne *département*, near the city of AUXERRE. Created in 1938, the Chablis appellation comprises four ranks, of which the top is GRAND CRU Chablis, with seven named vineyards. Then come the PREMIERS CRUS, including 79 vineyard names, many of which are rarely used; then Chablis, by far the most common and infuriatingly variable appellation; and finally Petit Chablis, the lowliest. The best vineyard sites are on the south-west-facing slopes of the valley of the Serein, the small river that flows through Chablis to join the Yonne.

Chablis is quite separate from the rest of Burgundy, divided from the CÔTE D'OR by the hills of the Morvan, so that BEAUNE, for example, is over 100 km/62 miles to the south. In fact, the vineyards of Chablis are much closer to CHAMPAGNE and its southernmost vineyards in the Aube *département* than to the rest of Burgundy, and until early in this century it was not unusual for wine from Chablis to find its way into the champagne makers' cellars in Reims and Épernay.

History

Although it was the Romans who introduced vines to Chablis, as to so many other parts of FRANCE, it was the medieval church, notably the Cistercian MONKS of the nearby abbey of Pontigny, who firmly established viticulture as an essential part of the rural economy, possibly even introducing the Chardonnay vine. (See BURGUNDY, history.)

Towards the end of the 19th century, the Yonne as a whole was a flourishing wine region, with some 40,000 ha/98,842 acres of vines. Vineyards lined the banks of the river Yonne, as far as Joigny and Sens. The best known of these Yonne wines was Chablis, and the name was used to describe the ample quantities of dry white wine then being transported with great convenience along the rivers Yonne and Seine to satisfy the thirsty Parisian market.

Three factors combined were responsible for the sharp decline in the vineyard area at the end

of the 19th century. POWDERY MILDEW appeared in Chablis in 1886, though a cure had already been found; likewise for PHYLLOXERA, which first reached Chablis in 1887. However, many growers were reluctant to replant their vineyards, for the opening of the Paris–Lyons–Marseilles RAILWAY in 1856 considerably reduced their share of the Paris market. Thanks to the railways, Chablis lost its advantage of proximity to the capital and was simply unable to compete with the cheap wines of the MIDI, which could now be transported easily to the capital. Consequently the vineyard area gradually declined until it reached a mere 500 ha in the mid 1950s, before the fortunes of the appellation revived.

Climate

Climate has always played an important role in determining the success and quality of Chablis. Essentially the climate is semi-CONTINENTAL, with no maritime influence, so that the winters are long and hard and the summers often, but not always, fairly hot. There is all the climatic uncertainty, and therefore vintage variation, both in quality and quantity, of a vineyard far from the equator.

One key factor in determining how much wine will be produced is the possibility of spring FROSTS, which can damage young vine shoots. Depending on how advanced the vegetation is, the vineyards are vulnerable from the end of March until well into May. Since the end of the 1950s, after a decade of vintages particularly badly affected by frost, various methods of protection evolved. Heaters, or SMUDGE POTS, may be lit in the vineyards; they are expensive but efficient. The alternative technique of using SPRINKLERS to spray the vines with water from the moment the temperature drops to freezing point has also been increasingly practised. Electric cables, cleaner than smudge pots, may also be laid to raise ambient temperatures while taking advantage of France's reduced night tariffs. Such measures can be sufficiently effective to make the difference in some years between a crop of reasonable quantity and virtually no crop at all. It is now perfectly possible to make a viable living from vines in Chablis, whereas in the 1950s growers needed both eternal optimism and another crop, so polyculture was common.

Vineyard expansion

It was the development of effective frost protection in the early 1960s that encouraged today's increase in the vineyard area of Chablis, which has not been without controversy. The seven CLIMATS of Chablis Grand Cru total slightly over 100 ha/247 acres and are all on one slope facing south-west just outside the town. They are Les Clos, Blanchots, Bougros, Vaudésir, Valmur, Preuses, and Grenouilles. There is also, in true Burgundian fashion, an anomaly. The tiny vineyard of La Moutonne is partly in Vaudésir and partly in Preuses, but, for some illogical and doubtless bureaucratic reason, an official INAO decree confirming its status as a grand cru has never been issued, even though its wines certainly demonstrate that it qualifies.

Much of the dispute over the vineyard expansion has centred on the premiers crus. By the early 21st century there were 79 in all, totalling 778 ha/1,922 acres in 2020. Some are often seen on labels, while others are much more obscure, and some such as Vaudevey came into existence only with the expansion of the appellation. Their protagonists argue that they are on slopes that were planted before the phylloxera crisis and that their TERROIR closely resembles that of the long-established premiers crus. Some of the lesser-known vineyards may use a better-known umbrella name, so that for example L'Homme Mort may be sold as Fourchaume, as follows, with umbrella names followed by their associated premiers crus:

Mont de Milieu
Montée de Tonnerre: *Chapelot, Pied d'Aloue, Côte de Bréchain*
Fourchaume: *Vaupulent, Côte de Fontenay, L'Homme Mort, Vaulorent*
Vaillons: *Châtains, Séchet, Beugnons, Les Lys, Mélinots, Roncières, Les Epinottes*
Montmains: *Forêt, Butteaux*
Côte de Léchet
Beauroy: *Troesme, Côte de Savant*
Vauligneau
Vaudevey: *Vaux Ragons*
Vaucoupin
Vosgros: *Vaugiraut*
Les Fourneaux: *Morein, Côte de Prés Girots*
Côte de Vaubarousse
Berdiot
Chaume de Talvat
Côte de Jouan
Les Beauregards: *Côte de Cuissy*

By 2020 some 3,702 ha/9,148 acres of vineyard was planted for AOC Chablis, 12% more than ten years previously and considerably more than was originally envisaged when the appellation was granted, much of the arable land having been given over to vines. By 2020, 1,189 ha of a permitted 1,800 ha of Petit Chablis had been planted.

Notwithstanding the area's northern location and unusual climate, the unique flavour of Chablis wine is commonly claimed to be due to the soil. There remains no explanation of why this might be. The soil is often described as 'Kimmeridgian' though the term actually refers to bedrock, not the soil, and merely indicates the time at which it formed—during the Kimmeridgian age, a subdivision of the Jurassic period, 152–157 million years ago. Kimmeridgian LIMESTONES and MARLS, some with conspicuous fossils, underlie many of the vineyards. This includes the grand cru sites, which are all on the south-west-facing, optimal mid-slope locations (but see COLLUVIUM), whereas the more exposed sites at the top of the slopes yield Petit Chablis wines. They are underlain by a generally similar but younger bedrock usually referred to in a wine context as Portlandian, also a time term though one technically now obsolete (Tithonian is correct). The geology at Kimmeridge and at Portland in Dorset, south-west England, from where the names derive, is quite different from that at Chablis.

Viticultural practices in Chablis are very similar to those in the rest of Burgundy, apart from the overriding need to protect the vines from frost.

The use of oak

In the cellar, as elsewhere in France, winemaking techniques improved enormously in the late 20th century, so that there is a better understanding of such elements as MALOLACTIC CONVERSION and the need for TEMPERATURE CONTROL during fermentation. The most interesting and controversial aspect of vinification in Chablis is the use of OAK, Chablis being the one fine wine area where Chardonnay is not automatically oaked.

Those who want the purest flavour of Chablis, with the firm streak of acidity and the mineral quality that the French describe as *goût de pierre à fusil*, or gunflint, tend to favour STAINLESS STEEL. Domaine Louis Michel is generally considered to be the epitome of this style, although others who employ it successfully, but not necessarily exclusively, include Jean Durup, Domaine de Chantemerle, and Maison Régnard.

Other producers believe that oak barrels allow for a gentle oxygenation of the wine that adds an extra dimension of complexity to its flavour. Producers such as Domaine Vincent Dauvissat and Domaine Raveneau may ferment their wine in vats and then, once the alcoholic FERMENTATION is finished, move the wine into oak for a few months' BARREL MATURATION. Others, such as Domaine Jean Collet and Domaine Jean-Paul et Benoît Droin, ferment in barrel. The proportion of new barrels in a cellar in Chablis can vary. Some producers buy very few each year, wishing to avoid the marked vanilla flavours that new wood can impart, while Domaine William Fèvre, for example, depends on sister company BOUCHARD of Beaune for used barrels. While the 228-l Burgundy barrel is traditional, producers are increasingly moving towards larger barrels such as 500–600-l *demi-muids* or 50-hl *foudres*. Generally only grand cru and premier cru Chablis is matured in wood. Paradoxically it is not unknown for a Chablis that has seen no wood to take on, as it matures, a certain firm nuttiness that suggests some ageing in oak.

The Chablis market

Surprisingly, perhaps, until the early 1980s Chablis was hardly appreciated in France itself as most of it was sold on the export market, usually through the large NÉGOCIANTS of Burgundy, based mainly in Beaune. Currently nearly one-third of all Chablis is vinified by the local CO-OPERATIVE, La Chablisienne, which works well for its appellation. The trend, as elsewhere, has been for an increasing number of producers who originally sold their wine in bulk to négociants to bottle and sell their wine themselves. Some of them have even started their own négociant businesses.

Chablis has always been affected by significant variations in the size of the vintage, and prices have fluctuated accordingly (much more dramatically, for example, than in the more regulated but climatically similar Champagne market). However, some of the commercial instability has disappeared with the growth in the vineyard area so that there is more Chablis available to satisfy world demand. Generally Chablis is a more prosperous appellation than it was in the 1970s, for with the possibility of frost protection the growers are much more certain of making a viable living from their vines than ever before.

Chablis remains one of the great white wines of the world. It is sometimes overshadowed by the greater opulence of a fine Meursault or Corton-Charlemagne, but it has an individuality of its own that sets it apart from the great white burgundies of the Côte d'Or. There is a unique streak of steely acidity, a firm flintiness, and a mineral quality that is not found elsewhere in Burgundy. Like all great white burgundy, it benefits from, but all too rarely receives, BOTTLE AGEING. A premier cru will be at its best at ten years, while a grand cru could easily benefit from 15 or more years of maturation. A 1947 Côte de Léchet, not one of the best premiers crus but from a great vintage, was still showing a remarkable depth of flavour with the characteristic *goût de pierre à fusil* when it was 40 years old. R.E.G. & A.J.M.

Bro, L., and Moreau, M., *Chablis, Porte d'Or de la Bourgogne* (1998).
Cannard, H., *Les Vignobles de Chablis et de l'Yonne* (1999).
Fèvre, W., *Le Vrai Chablis et les autres* (1978).
George, R., *The Wines of Chablis and The Grand Auxerrois* (2019).

Chacolí. Castilian spelling of the Basque wine TXAKOLI.

chai, French, and particularly Bordelais, term for a place where wine and occasionally brandy is stored, typically in BARREL. Thus a smart Bordeaux CHÂTEAU will have (perhaps) the château building itself with no direct winemaking function, a cuverie (see CUVE) in which fermentation takes place, a first-year *chai* in which the most recent vintage's crop undergoes BARREL AGEING, and a second-year *chai* to which it is moved at some point before the year's end in order to make way for the next year's crop. The NEW WORLD counterpart to the *chai* is sometimes called the barrel hall. See also CAVE.

chalk, a white, highly porous sedimentary rock (35–40% voids) made up of calcium carbonate, usually with impurities of clay and silica. Pale-coloured crumbly rocks and soils are often loosely called chalk, especially if they are CALCAREOUS. However, true chalk, which is relatively rare under vineyards, is dominated by the fossilized remains of coccolithophores, a marine alga that flourished during late Cretaceous times in the still, sunlit, warm ocean waters in what was to become northern Europe. The resulting sea-floor sediment eventually hardened to give the strikingly white rocks and soils that underlie vineyards in southern ENGLAND and parts of northern France. In CHAMPAGNE, the better vineyards are mostly on CLAYS, with only the longer roots reaching the underlying chalk.

As chalk weathers it releases CALCIUM and bicarbonate ions so that only the impurities remain to form a thin soil. Chalk-derived SOILS are valued in viticulture because of their excellent STRUCTURE and free DRAINAGE. However, the underlying chalk has the capacity to store substantial amounts of water. Because vine ROOTS can usually penetrate into the chalk bedrock, a moderated moisture supply is assured regardless of short-term fluctuations in RAINFALL. Most chalk soils are of low FERTILITY, resulting in restricted vine VIGOUR and naturally good CANOPY MICROCLIMATE.

See also ALBARIZA; and see DEACIDIFICATION for the use of chalk in winemaking, and CHALKY as a tasting term. R.E.W. & A.J.M.

Chalk Hill, California wine region and AVA north of Santa Rosa and south-east of Healdsburg. See SONOMA.

chalky, a TASTING TERM typically used metaphorically to describe a wine's TEXTURE, usually dry and finely grained like chalk dust. For some tasters it is an aspect of MINERALITY.

Chalone, small California wine region and AVA in the mountains east of the Salinas Valley. Chalone's reputation was made by the winery of the same name set high in the Gavilan Mountains, notably with Chardonnay, Pinot Blanc, and Pinot Noir. Although Chalone looks directly down to the Arroyo Seco AVA, it remains worlds apart in climate (being above the fog) and soils, which are a unique mix of crystal-laden CALCAREOUS rock and decomposed GRANITE. Despite sitting within Monterey County, Chalone does not fall within the bounds of the MONTEREY AVA and instead sits within the larger CENTRAL COAST AVA. A.Y.

Chalonnaise, Côte, red and white wine-producing region in the Saône-et-Loire *département* of BURGUNDY between the CÔTE D'OR and the Mâconnais. The Côte Chalonnaise takes its name from the town of Chalon-sur-Saône, which had been an important CELTIC trading centre in ancient GAUL. As well as generic BOURGOGNE Côte Chalonnaise, mostly red from the Pinot Noir grape, there are five village appellations: MERCUREY and GIVRY produce mostly Pinot Noir with small quantities of white wine; MONTAGNY is exclusively a white-wine appellation growing the Chardonnay grape; RULLY offers both red and white wines and is a centre for the sparkling wine industry in a small way; while BOUZERON uniquely has its own appellation exclusively for the ALIGOTÉ grape.

Although the soils in the Côte Chalonnaise are similar to those of the Côte d'Or, being based on LIMESTONE with a complex admixture of other elements, the vineyards are more scattered since there is no regular escarpment to provide continuity of suitable slopes.

Viticultural practices are broadly similar to those in the Côte d'Or. Vinification is sometimes carried out in barrels, although only the best producers use any new OAK. Bottling normally takes place in the summer before the new vintage.

Maximum yields for Mercurey are the same as those for VILLAGE WINES in the Côte d'Or, whereas the other appellations of the Côte Chalonnaise may produce a little more. Although cheerfully fruity while young, few wines from this region have enough body to age well. J.T.C.M.

Chambertin, **Chambertin-Clos de Bèze**, **Chapelle-Chambertin**, **Charmes-Chambertin**, **Griotte(s)-Chambertin**, **Latricières-Chambertin**, **Mazis-Chambertin**, **Mazoyères-Chambertin**, and **Ruchottes-Chambertin**, great red GRANDS CRUS in Burgundy's CÔTE D'OR. For more details, see GEVREY-CHAMBERTIN.

Chambolle-Musigny, village and appellation of particular charm in the Côte de Nuits district of Burgundy producing red wines from Pinot Noir grapes. A fine Chambolle-Musigny has a rich, velvety elegance which rivals the finesse of Vosne-Romanée or the power of Gevrey-Chambertin. There are two GRAND CRU vineyards, Le Musigny and Bonnes Mares (in part), and some fine PREMIERS CRUS, including the exceptional Les Amoureuses.

Le **Musigny** ranks with Romanée-Conti, La Tâche, Richebourg, Chambertin, and Chambertin-Clos de Bèze as one of the pinnacles of great burgundy (see DOMAINE DE LA ROMANÉE-CONTI, VOSNE-ROMANÉE, and GEVREY-CHAMBERTIN for details of these). The vineyard lies between the scrubland at the top of the slope and the upper part of CLOS DE VOUGEOT, on a slope of 8–10% which drains particularly well through the oolitic LIMESTONE. The soil is more CHALK than CLAY, covered by a fine SILT, a combination which leads to the exceptional grace and power of Le Musigny, an iron fist in a velvet glove.

Of the 10.7 ha/26 acres of Le Musigny which is split between Musigny, Petits Musigny, and La Combe d'Orveau, seven are owned by Domaine Comte de Vogüé. De Vogüé also produce a small amount of Musigny Blanc (previously declassified to Bourgogne Blanc while the vines were young).

Adjacent to Le Musigny lies the premier cru Les Amoureuses, whose reputation and price suggest that this vineyard is worthy of elevation to grand cru. If a little less powerful than Le Musigny itself, the wines of Les Amoureuses demonstrate a very similar style. The next most sought-after premier cru, and the largest, is Les Charmes, although CLIMATE CHANGE has had the effect of shunting quality up the hillside to Les Cras and Les Fuées.

The other grand cru of Chambolle Musigny is **Bonnes Mares**, situated to the north of the village and overflowing into MOREY-ST-DENIS. The wines show more sturdiness than silkiness, are less graceful than Le Musigny, but have evident power and structure. Bonnes Mares is noted for its ageing capacity. Ownership is spread over more than 30 proprietors, the largest being again de Vogüé. Other notable producers based in Chambolle-Musigny include Domaines Barthod, Roumier, and Mugnier.

See also CÔTE D'OR, and map under BURGUNDY.

J.T.C.M.

Chambourcin is a dark-berried FRENCH HYBRID commercially available only since 1963 and popular in the 1970s, particularly around the mouth of the Loire. In 2019 France still grew a total of 498 ha/1,231 acres, mostly in the Loire Valley. This extremely vigorous, productive vine tolerates wet weather well, shows good resistance to DOWNY MILDEW, and produces better-quality wine than most hybrids, being deep coloured and full of relatively aromatic flavour. Its winter hardiness finds it well distributed, if not exactly common, in the US. It was successfully planted by Cassegrain in the warm, damp climate of Hastings Valley in NEW SOUTH WALES in Australia, a culture unfettered by anti-hybrid prejudice, and has since spread up and down Australia's east coast, including Queensland, with outbreaks elsewhere.

chambré, French word also used in English to describe a wine that has been deliberately warmed to room TEMPERATURE before serving (from *chambre*, 'room'). Most rooms nowadays are rather warmer than the ideal serving temperatures for most wines, however.

Champagne, name derived from the Latin term *campania*, originally used to describe the rolling open countryside just north of Rome (see CAMPANIA). In the early Middle Ages, it was applied to a province in north-east France (see map under FRANCE). It is now divided into the so-called 'Champagne pouilleuse', the once-barren but now cereal-growing CALCAREOUS plains east of Reims, and the 'Champagne viticole' (capital letters indicate the geographical descriptions, lower case is used for the wine).

Champagne, with its champagne towns Reims and Épernay, was the first region to make SPARKLING WINE in any quantity, and historically the name champagne became synonymous with the finest, although Champagne is now responsible for less than one bottle in 12 of total world production of all sparkling wine. In common with other French regions making fine wines, notably Burgundy and Bordeaux, champagne has formed the model for other aspiring winemakers, especially in Australia and the west coast of the United States, employing the same grapes and the same SPARKLING WINEMAKING method as the French originals (known now as the TRADITIONAL METHOD).

History

Champagne was at the crossroads of two major trade routes, north–south between Flanders and Switzerland and east–west from Paris to the Rhine. Its position made it prosperous but also ensured that it has been fought over many times in the course of the past 1,500 years. One of the most important battles in history was fought at Châlons-sur-Marne (now Châlons-en-Champagne) in 455 CE, when Attila the Hun was finally repulsed. Subsequent battles included a savage civil war, the Fronde in the middle of the 17th century. As late as 1914 the famous 'Taxis de la Marne' brought French reinforcements from Paris to repulse the German invaders, who had (briefly) occupied Épernay and reached the outskirts of Reims. But successive conflicts merely interrupted the progress of the vineyard.

Although there are numerous legends concerning earlier vineyards, the first serious mention is at the time of St Rémi at the end of the 5th century CE. For nearly eight centuries after Clovis, first king of the Francs, was baptized in Reims in 496, the city's position as the spiritual centre of France naturally boosted its fame.

Vines had already been planted around the city, mainly by the numerous local abbeys and by the local nobility. But until the 17th century there was no generic 'vin de Champagne'. Since the 9th century, wines from the MONTAGNE DE REIMS south of the city had been known as *vins de la montagne*, those from the Marne Valley as *vins de la rivière*, or river wines. A number of villages, notably Bouzy and Verzenay on the Montagne and Aÿ and Épernay in the Marne Valley, were already being singled out for the quality of their wines. The wine trade was centred on Reims and Châlons-sur-Marne, and the wines had the great advantage of immediate access to the Marne, which joined the Seine just east of PARIS (see RIVERS).

But the wines did not sparkle: they were light, pinkish still wines made from the Pinot Noir grape. In the last half of the 17th century, winemaking greatly improved under the auspices of leading clerical winemakers, led by Dom PÉRIGNON, who transformed the Abbey of Hautvillers, above Épernay, into the region's leading centre of viticultural progress. The wines' fame grew greatly in the second half of the 17th century when they were introduced to the Court of Versailles, notably by the Marquis de Sillery, a large landowner in the region, and by the Marquis de St-Évremond, who introduced champagne to London society after he was banished to Britain in 1662.

In the cold winters normal in the region, the wines had a tendency to stop FERMENTATION and then to start refermenting in the spring. For a long time this was considered something of a nuisance, as the resulting release of CARBON DIOXIDE was often strong enough to break the flimsy bottles normal at the time. The development of stronger BOTTLES by British glassmakers permitted drinkers to enjoy the resulting sparkle. Indeed it was the café society of London, encouraged by St-Évremond, which probably first enjoyed true 'sparkling champagne' (see contemporary references in ENGLISH LITERATURE).

The habit was taken up by the licentious court round the duke of Orléans, who became regent of France after the death of Louis XIV in 1715, but serious winemakers (and their clients) continued to believe that sparkling champagne was inferior to the still wines of the region. Moreover even the stronger bottles could not reliably withstand the pressure generated by the SECOND FERMENTATION. So, throughout the 18th century, only a few thousand bottles were produced every year, and up to half of them would break.

The champagne business we know today was born in the first 40 years of the 19th century. The first notable step was taken by Madame (VEUVE) CLICQUOT. One of her employees developed the system of PUPITRES to assist in the REMUAGE process. CORKS were improved, and a corking machine developed. Understanding, and then mastering, the second fermentation took longer. The scientist and minister CHAPTAL had understood that 'sparkling wines owe their tendency to sparkle only to the fact that they have been enclosed in a bottle before they have completed their fermentation'. But it took a young pharmacist from Châlons-sur-Marne, Jean-Baptiste François, to enable winemakers to measure the precise quantity of sugar required to induce a second fermentation in the bottle without inducing an explosive force.

C

François died in 1838, shortly after he had published his formulae. But within a generation Champagne had become the home of the world's first 'wine industry', one dominated by a number of internationally famous BRAND names. Most of these were those of young entrepreneurs from the Rhineland, such as Messrs KRUG, BOLLINGER, and ROEDERER, who showed greater commercial nous than the local merchants, only a few of whom, apart from Madame Clicquot and Monsieur MOËT, survived.

But for over half a century, until well into the 1950s, Champagne suffered from a number of problems which clouded its earlier successes. The important Russian market collapsed in 1917, and two World Wars, separated by the slump, closed the export markets on which the region depended so heavily. The arrival of PHYLLOXERA in Champagne in 1890 intensified competition from other sparkling wines, from Germany as well as from other areas of France, and intensified the fraudulent habits of some of the region's more unscrupulous merchants, who were wont to import juice and wine for bottling and sale as champagne.

The mood darkened further in 1911, when the first attempts to define the region entitled to produce champagne were introduced. The initial plan's exclusion of the Aube, a region 112 km/70 miles south-east of Épernay, incited Aube farmers to riot; this is turn led some members of the French government to suppress the delimitation entirely, which provoked the infamous April 1911 riots in the Marne. In the end the delimitation was retained, and eventually the Aube was included as a separate 'second zone', although it was included in the main appellation when the boundaries were finally fixed in 1927.

The events of 1911 shook the whole winemaking community, and 25 years later the resulting desire for common action resulted in the combined group of growers and merchants known as the Commission de Châlons, set up in 1935 under the impetus of the remarkable Robert-Jean de Vogüé, head of Moët, and Maurice Doyard, who was able to rally the growers. At a time when growers were virtually giving away their grapes, the Commission provided them with some stability. Six years later, the desire for joint action led to the formation of the CIVC, the Comité Interprofessionnel du Vin de Champagne, the pioneering attempt, much copied elsewhere, to provide winemaking regions with an organization that would represent all the interests involved.

For 60 years from 1950, the region enjoyed unprecedented prosperity, with sales peaking in 2007 at almost 340 million bottles. Traditional export markets, such as Britain, the United States, Belgium, Japan, and Switzerland, took increasing quantities. Nevertheless the French market has long consumed more champagne than all export markets and accounts for roughly half of total sales by volume. Traditional brands have been less dominant in the domestic market than outside France, where they account for nearly 90% of sales. In recent decades, however, grower champagnes have increasingly gained prominence in export markets around the world, influencing consumer perception despite representing a small fraction of market share.

In the domestic market, nearly half of total sales are made by individual GROWERS, CO-OPERATIVES, and co-operative unions. The first co-operatives in Champagne were founded just before the First World War and grew rapidly in the early 1960s. Today there are 140 co-operatives, some of whom press grapes and make base wines to supply négociant houses, with others making champagnes that can either be sold under their own brands or returned to members for sale under their own label, which is signified by the letters RC before the grower's code on the label. The largest co-operative unions, each of which represents thousands of growers, have become major forces, both in supplying buyers' own brands and promoting brands of their own.

The competition from the co-operatives added to the pressure on the (usually family-owned) MERCHANTS. In the 1960s and 1970s, Moët & Chandon absorbed Mercier and Ruinart, the latter the oldest firm in the region; that union became the basis for LVMH, today by far the dominant grouping in Champagne. The growers' increasing power was reflected in a rapid rise of grape prices during the 1980s, and while the prices had up until then been dictated by the CIVC, in 1990 the market was freed and buyers allowed to negotiate pricing directly with growers.

Geography and climate

The region permitted to call its wines 'champagne' was strictly defined by law in 1927. It sprawls from Charly-sur-Marne a mere 50 km/30 miles east of Paris along the Vallée de la Marne subregion to the Montagne de Reims subregion and south from Épernay along the Côte des Blancs and its southern extension, the Côte de Sézanne. A separate subregion is the Côte des Bar in the Aube, 112 km south-east of Épernay. While there was a proposal in 2007 to add 45 new communes to the appellation, this has not taken place. In 2020, the appellation comprised roughly 34,300 ha/84,750 acres, up from the 1993 total of 27,500 ha: 66% in the Marne; 10% in the Aisne; and 23% in the Aube. Only one-tenth of the vines are owned by merchants, who can now add to their holdings only under very strict conditions. The remainder is owned by about 16,000 growers (far fewer than there used to be), many of whom own less than a hectare of vines.

Much of the appellation—and Champagne is now the only major French region to have just one appellation—and all the better CRUS are on the slopes of the hills typical of the region. The vines' roots dig deep into CALCAREOUS depths, providing ideal conditions of DRAINAGE and HUMIDITY: while most of the appellation lies on a bedrock of chalk from the Late Cretaceous, the Aube's Côte des Bar is on Kimmeridgian MARL and LIMESTONE, like its neighbour Chablis. The Champagne vineyard's exposure to the cold northern winter inevitably makes grape-growing a precarious operation, with the quality of the wines varying from year to year. As a result, champagne is traditionally a wine blended not only from a number of villages and grape varieties but also from several vintages. The poverty of the soil requires constant addition of FERTILIZER, either the *cendres noirs*, the natural compost found on the region's hilltops, or, until it was outlawed in the late 1990s, finely ground (and curiously multicoloured) household rubbish from Reims or even Paris.

The different qualities of grapes from the region's 319 widely spread crus led to the establishment in 1911 of a scale of prices according to the status of each commune, called the *échelle des crus*. Since 1990 these prices have no longer been controlled, but in general grapes from the 17 grand cru communes continue to fetch higher prices than those from the 42 communes called premiers crus.

Vine varieties

In the past, a number of grape varieties were planted in Champagne. But today almost the whole vineyard is planted with three: Pinot Noir, Pinot Meunier, and Chardonnay. Pinot Noir, which accounts for just over one-third of the total acreage, is no longer as dominant as it was but still accounts for 38% of all plantings and often provides both structure and complexity to a blend. It thrives most notably on the slopes around the Montagne de Reims, but it's also the primary grape variety of the Aube's Côte des Bar, in the south. Chardonnay, planted on 30% of the total vineyard, has been traditionally grown on the east-facing slopes of the Côte des Blancs but has proved suitable in many other subregions, especially the Côte de Sézanne. In Champagne it grows vigorously and buds early, thus making it susceptible to spring FROSTS. It imparts a certain austerity and elegance to young champagnes, but it is long lived and matures to a fine fruitiness. The remaining 32% is planted with PINOT MEUNIER, a variety much more important in Champagne than anywhere else, particularly in the Marne Valley. It provides many champagnes with an early-maturing richness and fruitiness. Four other grape varieties—Pinot Blanc, Pinot Gris, Arbane, and PETIT MESLIER—are also authorized in the appellation, but all together account for less than 0.3% of total plantings.

Thanks to new CLONES and viticultural methods, the YIELD of grapes has grown greatly: from an average of 3,670 kg/ha in the 1940s to a fixed base of 10,400 kg/ha today, which can be revised upwards or downwards depending on the quality of the year. The first limit was set in 1935. Nowadays, the Comité Champagne sets the yield each year, usually well below the maximum limit set by EU regulations, which is 15,500 kg/ha. Since 1992, 160 (rather than the earlier limit of 150) kg of grapes are required to produce 102 l of juice, which means that the maximum permitted yield is 65 hl/ha.

VINE DENSITY is notably high, and vines are often replanted after 25–30 years. The grapes are usually picked in September, on dates now fixed per grape variety village by village but which are in general becoming earlier as a result of CLIMATE CHANGE. (ACID levels have also been falling.) They cannot be harvested unless they contain that year's fixed minimum level of POTENTIAL ALCOHOL. But since the level can be as low as 8%, sugar may be added (see CHAPTALIZATION) to boost the alcohol level to 11% after the alcoholic fermentation, and the second fermentation supplements the final ALCOHOLIC STRENGTH by up to another 1.5%. Most champagne is about 12.5% alcohol.

Winemaking

The pressing of the grapes is difficult, since the juice of what is to be a white wine must not be tainted by the skin of the mainly black grapes used. The traditional champagne PRESS is a vertical basket press, holding 4,000 kg/8,800 lb of grapes, a quantity known as a *marc* and a standard unit of measurement in the region. These presses are also called Coquard presses after the name of the manufacturer. A number of other types of press have since been introduced, although the traditional press is valued for the quality of its pressing and is still in widespread use.

Since 1990, all pressing centres have had to comply with certain minimum standards. Traditionally 2,666 l/704 gal were extracted from every *marc*: the first 2,050 l were the *cuvée*, the next 410 l the *premières tailles*, while the final 206 l were the *deuxièmes tailles*. The total yield has now been reduced by 115 l to 2,550 l per 4,000 kg (or 102 l per 160 kg, as the INAO regulations express it) and the *deuxièmes tailles* abolished.

The juice is allowed to settle for 12–48 hours, at a low temperature. A small but increasing number of producers ferment the juice in OAK, but the overwhelming majority of the grapes are fermented in STAINLESS STEEL vats holding 50–1,200 hl (1,320–31,700 gal). The fermentation TEMPERATURE also varies, between 12 and 25 °C/54–77 °F. Most winemakers use a YEAST strain specially developed by the CIVC.

The resulting base wines are called *vins clairs*, and most, but by no means all, undergo MALOLACTIC CONVERSION immediately after the first fermentation. Traditionally champagne has been made from wines from a number of vineyards, and a major part of the work of a *chef de cave* in a champagne house is the art of blending, but many growers (and a few firms) make wines from a single commune or vineyard. Major firms often use wines from up to 200 communes for their blend. They also use 10–50% of *vins de réserve* from earlier vintages, generally stored in stainless steel or concrete vats. Before the wine is bottled, a measured dose of bottling liquor (*liqueur de tirage*), a mixture of wine, sugar, and specially developed yeasts, is added to the wine. The bottles are then capped, usually with a plastic-lined crown cap. Following TIRAGE, LEES CONTACT, RIDDLING, and DISGORGEMENT, a sweetening DOSAGE is usually added before final corking. A few champagnes are sold without any added sugar at all; most are BRUT.

For more information, see in SPARKLING WINEMAKING, traditional method.

Styles of champagne

Champagne comes in myriad styles. The broadest style category is by the colour of the grapes used: while most champagnes blend white and black varieties, BLANC DE BLANCS is made exclusively from the Chardonnay grape, while BLANC DE NOIRS is made exclusively from black grapes.

This century has seen a FASHION for **rosé champagne** made either by adding a small proportion of red wine to the blend or, less usually, by letting the juice remain in contact with the grape skins for a short time during fermentation.

Most champagnes are multi-vintage blends, with no age statement on the label, though most producers also make single-vintage champagnes. Historically made three or four times in every decade, vintage cuvées are often made more frequently now, partially due to the warming climate but also as a stylistic choice. While there is nothing intrinsically superior about a champagne from a single vintage, in practice these are often made from a special selection of grapes. All the major firms have also now followed the example of Dom Pérignon (originally made by Moët & Chandon) and Roederer with its Cristal bottling and produce 'luxury', 'de luxe', or PRESTIGE CUVÉES to show their house styles at their best. These are usually, but not always, also vintage-dated.

Champagne producers also label their sparkling wines by sweetness level. By far the most common style is Brut, with a maximum permitted RESIDUAL SUGAR of 12 g/l. Wines with residual sugar less than 6 g/l may be called Extra Brut, while those without any added dosage at all, and with residual sugar under 3 g/l, may be called Brut Nature, Non Dosé, or Zéro Dosage. These bone-dry wines have become more common as warmer vintages have increased grape maturity, but some champagne specialists believe some dosage is essential for a well-balanced champagne and are concerned that undosed champagnes cannot benefit from the effects of any MAILLARD REACTION. For a listing of the full range of sweetness levels allowed, see DOSAGE.

Champagne labels also include a code printed next to the registered number of the bottler that indicates the type of company that issued the wine:

NM: négociant-manipulant, one of the big houses/firms/négociants
RM: récoltant-manipulant, a grower who makes his or her own wine
CM: coopérative de manipulation, one of the co-operatives
RC: récoltant-coopérateur, grower selling wine made by a co-op
MA: marque d'acheteur, buyer's own brand
SR: société de récoltant, a small family company (rare)
R: récoltant, very small-scale growers (very rare).

Some producers also include a disgorgement date on the back label, as many houses disgorge their wines several times a year or even more frequently, and the flavours can change the longer the wines sit on the lees. A few houses release late-disgorged versions of certain cuvées, such as Bollinger's R.D. (meaning 'recently disgorged') or Jacquesson's D.T. (meaning 'dégorgement tardif'), to highlight the character derived from extra time on the lees.

The small proportion of still wines made in the region are sold under the appellations Coteaux CHAMPENOIS and the rare pink ROSÉ DES RICEYS. RATAFIA de Champagne is a local fortified apéritif. N.F., J.R. & P.L.

Faith, N., *The Story of Champagne* (1988).
Juhlin, R., *4000 Champagnes* (2005).
Liem, P., *Champagne* (2017).
Stevenson, T., and Avellan, E., *Christie's World Encyclopedia of Champagne & Sparkling Wine* (4th edn, 2019).
www.champagne.fr

champagne method. See TRADITIONAL METHOD.

Champenois, Coteaux, appellation used for the relatively rare still wines of CHAMPAGNE in northern France, covering the same geographical area as the sparkling-wine appellation. For every one bottle of still white Coteaux Champenois produced, perhaps 20 of still red Coteaux Champenois are produced (in a good vintage) and 16,000 bottles of sparkling champagne. The wines of this cool region are generally high in acidity and light in body, although the best are becoming richer and more complex as a result of both CLIMATE CHANGE and improved winemaking and viticultural techniques. The village of Bouzy on the MONTAGNE DE REIMS has a particular reputation for its red Coteaux Champenois, partly perhaps because of the appeal of the name Bouzy Rouge, as do Aÿ, Cumières, and Ambonnay. These red wines are typically produced only in the ripest vintages, usually from Pinot Noir but sometimes Pinot Meunier. Due to their lower yields and specialized production, they tend to be priced similarly to the region's sparkling wines.

See also ROSÉ DES RICEYS. P.L.

Chamusca, DOP subregion of TEJO in central southern Portugal.

Chancellor, productive but minor red FRENCH HYBRID developed from two SEIBEL parents. It was long known as Seibel 7053 but was named Chancellor in NEW YORK in 1970. Encountered occasionally in the US.

Changins, federal viticultural research station near Nyon on Lake Geneva, western SWITZERLAND, established in the late 19th century and now part of AGROSCOPE.

Changyu. Changyu Pioneer Wine Co. is China's oldest and largest wine producer and, according to one independent analysis of 2010 turnover, was the world's fourth biggest wine company. It was founded in Yantai, Shandong province, in 1892 by Zhang Bishi, an officer in the Qing government. He introduced VITIS VINIFERA varieties from Europe in 1896. The winemaker then was Maximilian, son of Baron Auguste Wilhelm von Babo, founder of the pioneering viticultural college KLOSTERNEUBERG.

In the 1950s, Premier Zhou Enlai presented Changyu brandy as a diplomatic gift to the Geneva Conference delegates, recorded as 'diplomacy of Gold Medal brandy'. Chairman Mao instructed Changyu to develop its wine production 'so the people may enjoy a bit more wine'. Today it claims to have a total of 20,000 ha/49,400 acres of vineyard potential and an overall production capacity of 200,000 tonnes, much of it focused on basic and mid-market lines.

As for its premium production facilities, in 2002 the company formed a JOINT VENTURE with the French CASTEL group in Yantai to establish Chateau Changyu Castel winery, signalling a new era for Chinese wine in which the word CHÂTEAU takes on the special significance of a dedicated wine estate with TOURISM potential. The primary grape variety is CABERNET GERNISCHT. In 2006, Changyu and Aurora Icewine Co. of Canada built the Golden Icewine Valley in Liaoning Province, capable, it is claimed, of producing half of the world's ICEWINE. Its vineyard holdings of about 333 ha/820 acres are dominated by VIDAL. Thanks to the LAKE EFFECT, winters are cold but not too dry. In 2007 the company used investments from the US, Italy, and Portugal, as well as China, to establish Chateau Changyu AFIP Global north-east of Beijing, with 200 ha of vineyard dedicated principally to upmarket varietal Cabernet Sauvignon and Chardonnay. Chateau Changyu Baron Balboa was built in the extravagant image of a 19th-century French château in Xinjiang in the far west of China with 333 ha of vineyards and a NURSERY planned. Chateau Changyu Moser XV is a joint venture with LENZ MOSER of Austria in Ningxia, while Chateau Changyu Rena in Shaanxi is Tuscan-inspired and has what is claimed to be the largest underground wine cellar in Asia.

Construction of two more production facilities started in the mid 2010s in Yantai: Chateau Tinlot, named after former OIV chairman Robert Tinlot; and Chateau Koya, dedicated to brandy production (Changyu acquired a cognac house in 2013). They also acquired Kilikanoon Wines in Australia, Viña Indómita in Chile, Marqués del Atrio in Spain, and Ch Mirefleurs in Bordeaux. In 2020, with Tencent, Changyu developed the first national BLOCKCHAIN traceability platform that connects consumer verification with anti-counterfeiting measures (see AUTHENTICATION). Changyu claim to have lifted thousands of farmers out of poverty thanks to their grape contracts. Y.S.

Chapoutier, family-owned merchant-grower based at Tain-l'Hermitage in France's northern RHÔNE. One of the Rhône Valley's great names, established in 1808 and with 32 ha/80 acres of precious HERMITAGE vineyard, it languished somewhat in the late 20th century. During the 1980s, when Chapoutier's peers (GUIGAL and Jaboulet, for example) and numerous small growers were catching the imagination of the wine world with the improving quality of their wines, Chapoutier wines stood out precisely because they seemed unexceptional by comparison. This situation changed dramatically in 1990 when Max Chapoutier's son Michel took over the running of the company, with outspoken passion and an early devotion to BIODYNAMIC VITICULTURE and a real determination to express TERROIR. In 1996, the firm became the first wine producer to have labels in Braille. But what really distinguishes the company is its combination of high-quality wines, often vineyard-designated, and almost restless vineyard acquisition, not just in the Rhône Valley but then Roussillon, Australia, Alsace, and Portugal.

By 2021 Chapoutier owned 1,242 ha/3,069 acres of land, of which about 500 ha/1,235 acres are planted with vines producing 10.7 million bottles. Currently working in this family business are Michel, Corinne, Mathilde, and Maxime Chapoutier.

Walls, M., *Wines of the Rhône* (2021).

Chaptal, Jean-Antoine (1756–1832), French chemist, statesman, and polymath who rose from humble beginnings to be appointed Minister of the Interior under Napoleon. He was the son of an apothecary and studied chemistry at the University of MONTPELLIER, where a Chair of Chemistry was founded for him in 1781. In 1798 he was elected a member of the Chemistry Section of the Institut de France and was a leading figure of early 19th century industrialization in France, becoming first President of the Société d'encouragement pour l'industrie nationale and one of the main organizers of the Paris Expositions in 1801, 1802, and 1806. He is best known in wine circles for his *l'Art de faire le vin* (1807) and his support for the concept of increasing the ALCOHOLIC STRENGTH of wine by adding sugar to the must, the procedure now known as CHAPTALIZATION. After the French Revolution of 1789, there was a considerable increase in the amount of poor-quality wine made in France. This provided the incentive for Chaptal to compile his famous *Traité théorique et pratique sur la culture de la vigne* (1801). As a practical scientist Chaptal was particularly concerned at the declining reputation of French wines, increasing ADULTERATION AND FRAUD in the wine trade, and ignorance on the part of many French wine producers about the scientific advances that could help them. He firmly believed that it was perfectly natural, and desirable, to add sugar to MUST in order to improve it. Although he encouraged farmers to use GRAPE CONCENTRATE, he recognized that sugar from cane or beet was also capable of having a similar effect. Chaptal's treatise synthesizing beneficial winemaking techniques current at the beginning of the 19th century marked a turning point in the history of wine technology. It was translated into Italian, Spanish, German, and Hungarian. Two American versions appeared, and James BUSBY published a translation in Australia in 1825. P.T.H.U.

Blouin, D., and Emptoz, G., 'La Société d'encouragement pour l'industrie nationale et la Conservatoire des arts et métiers (1801–1811)', *Artefact: Techniques, Histoire et Sciences Humaines*, 10 (2019), 75–95.

Chaptal, J. A., *Traité théorique et pratique sur la culture de la vigne* (1801).

Gough, J. B., 'Winecraft and chemistry in 18th century France: Chaptal and the invention of chaptalization', *Technology and Culture*, 39 (1998), 74–104.

chaptalization, common winemaking practice, named after its French promulgator Jean-Antoine CHAPTAL, whereby the final ALCOHOLIC STRENGTH of a wine is increased by the addition of sugar to the grape juice or MUST, before and/or during FERMENTATION, although if it is added before the higher sugar level will make it harder for the YEAST to multiply.

Contrary to popular belief, Chaptal did not invent the process, which had been the subject of common experiment, not least by the innovative French chemist Pierre-Joseph Macquer.

Although the practice is still commonplace in northern Europe, potential alcoholic strength is increasingly raised by adding products other than beet or cane sugar (particularly grape products of which there is often a surplus in many wine regions). See ENRICHMENT for more details.

In 1993, the EU, concerned about its wine SURPLUS, officially announced its disapproval of chaptalization and its intention to curb the practice because it tended to encourage higher YIELDS. Although this announcement made little difference to winemaking practices, chaptalization, once routine in northern Europe, is becoming less common, partly because grapes tend to be picked later and riper, perhaps partly because of CLIMATE CHANGE.

Producers of Pinot Noir, most notably in Burgundy but also in Oregon and elsewhere, often add sugar during alcoholic fermentation, particularly towards the end, even if some might not readily confess to it. The aim is not primarily to increase the final alcohol level but to extend the fermentation and thereby improve the flavour and texture of the wine. It is said that earlier picking followed by this fractional chaptalization (which is less disruptive to yeast metabolism) often produces better results than fruit picked later with higher sugar levels.

Gough, J. B., 'Winecraft and chemistry in 18th century France: Chaptal and the invention of chaptalization', *Technology and Culture*, 39 (1998), 74–104.

Regulation (EU) No 1308/2013 of the European Parliament and of the Council of 17 December 2013.

char, term sometimes used of barrels. See TOAST.

Charbono, the California name for the virtually extinct DOUCE NOIRE of the Savoie region in the French Alps, also known as Corbeau and Charbonneau. Charbono clings to existence on 30 ha/74 acres on the North Coast, especially in the Napa Valley. As varietal wine it can be difficult to distinguish from Barbera grown under similar circumstances. DNA PROFILING has shown it is identical to the BONARDA of Argentina.

Robinson, J., et al., *Wine Grapes: A Complete Guide to 1,368 Vine Varieties, Including Their Origins and Flavours* (2012).

charcoal, or **oenological charcoal**, adsorbent material occasionally used in wine processing to remove COLOUR and off-flavours caused by BOTRYTIS, SOUR ROT, and SMOKE TAINT. Charcoal is obtained by the dry distillation of wood or other carbon-rich animal and plant materials. The sort of charcoal most frequently used in winemaking is generally known as activated carbon, which has been processed to increase its surface area and its capacity for adsorption.

In winemaking it is used mainly to adsorb the colloidal pigment polymers responsible for amber or brown colours in white wines, for example in the manufacture of Pale Cream SHERRY, or to lighten the colour of MUST destined for rosé wines. Off-flavours in wine are occasionally removed using a grade of oenological charcoal with a smaller pore size, transforming an unsaleable wine into a neutral one for use in a basic blend. However, this may have an extremely negative effect on the quality of the wine by removing positive colour, flavour, and aroma compounds.

AWRI, 'Treating smoke-affected grape juice with activated carbon'. www.awri.com.au/wp-content/uploads/2021/02/Treating-smoke-affected-grape-juice-with-activated-carbon.pdf.

Chardonel, cunningly named vine CROSS of SEYVAL BLANC and CHARDONNAY made at New York State's Geneva experimental station (see CORNELL) in 1953. Originally tested in eastern US under the name GW9, it was named and released only in 1990. The variety is more resistant to WINTER FREEZE, POWDERY MILDEW, and BOTRYTIS than Chardonnay and is planted to a limited extent in cooler American states. Wines may resemble either Seyval Blanc or Chardonnay.

Chardonnay, a name so familiar to wine lovers around the world that many do not realize that it is the name of a white grape variety. In its Burgundian homeland, Chardonnay has long been the sole vine responsible for all of the finest white BURGUNDY. As such, in a region devoted to geographical labelling, its name was known only to vine-growers. All this changed with the advent of VARIETAL labelling in the late 20th century, when Chardonnay virtually became a BRAND. It is perhaps fitting that a variety so governed by the whims of FASHION should have seen considerable stylistic changes in the sorts of wine sought by its legion of fans. Until the mid 1990s, rich, oaky varietals were the height of modishness, but this has been followed by a trend towards leaner, more appetizing, and definitely less oak-dominated Chardonnays.

Chardonnay-mania reached a peak in the late 1980s, and the variety was subsequently planted so widely that a glut was assured in the late 1990s. The reaction to this glut led to a shortage of Chardonnay in the early 21st century in Australia, for example. There is hardly a country in which wine is produced that does not at least try to produce commercially acceptable Chardonnay in marketable quantities. During a single decade, the 1980s, the world's total area planted with Chardonnay vines quadrupled, to nearly 100,000 ha/247,000 acres—and by the mid 2000s it had surpassed 174,000 ha/430,000 acres. According to an OIV report in 2017, total global plantings were 210,000 ha, although the rate of increase had definitely slowed, thanks to what has been called the 'Bridget Jones effect', by which Chardonnay came to be associated with mass-market demand (see ABC). So popular is Chardonnay that synonyms are rarely used (although some Austrians in Styria persist with their name Morillon). The wine's relatively high level of alcohol, which can often taste slightly sweet, probably played a part in this popularity, as for a time did the obvious appeal of the OAK so often used in making Chardonnay. But it is not just wine drinkers who appreciate the broad, easy-to-appreciate if difficult-to-describe charms of golden Chardonnay. (The AWRI's initiative, analysing the component parts of each major variety's flavour, found Chardonnay a particularly nebulous target, identifying flavour compounds also found in, among other things, raspberries, vanilla, tropical fruits, peaches, tomatoes, tobacco, tea, and rose petals.)

Vine-growers appreciate the ease with which, in a wide range of climates, they can coax relatively high yields from this vine, whose natural VIGOUR may need to be curbed by either dense planting, low-vigour ROOTSTOCKS or CANOPY MANAGEMENT. Wine quality is severely prejudiced, however, at yields above 80 hl/ha (4.5 tons/acre), and yields of 30 hl/ha or lower are usually needed for seriously fine wine. Growers' only major reservation is that it buds quite early, just after Pinot Noir, which regularly puts the coolest vineyards—those of Chablis, CHAMPAGNE, and Chile's CASABLANCA Valley, for example—at risk from spring FROSTS. It can suffer from COULURE and occasionally MILLERANDAGE, and the grapes' relatively thin skins can encourage rot if there is rain at harvest time, but it can thrive in climates as diverse as those of CHABLIS in northern France and Australia's hot RIVERLAND. Picking time is critical for, unlike Cabernet Sauvignon, Chardonnay can quickly lose its crucial acidity in the latter stages of ripening.

Winemakers love Chardonnay for its reliably high ripeness levels and its malleability. It will happily respond to a far wider range of winemaking techniques than most white varieties. The Mosel or Vouvray winemaking recipe of a long, cool fermentation followed by early bottling can be applied to Chardonnay. Or it can be treated to BARREL FERMENTATION and/or BARREL MATURATION, some of the highest-quality fruit being able to stand up to new oak. It accommodates each individual winemaker's policy on the second, softening MALOLACTIC CONVERSION and LEES STIRRING without demur. Chardonnay is also a vital ingredient in most of the world's best SPARKLING WINE, not just in Champagne,

C

demonstrating its ability to age in bottle even when picked early. And, picked late, it has even been known to produce some creditable BOTRYTIZED wines, notably in the Mâconnais, Romania, and New Zealand. Chardonnay blends happily with other less fashionable, cheaper varieties such as Chenin Blanc, Sémillon, or Colombard to meet demand or PRICE POINTS at the lower end of the market. But perhaps this is because its own character is, unlike that of the other ultra-fashionable white, Sauvignon Blanc, not too pronounced. Chardonnay from young or over-productive vines can taste almost aqueous. Basic Chardonnay may be vaguely fruity (apples or melons), but, at its best, Chardonnay, like Pinot Noir, is merely a vehicle for the character of the vineyard in which it is grown (see TERROIR). As in many other ambitious wines fashioned in the image of top white burgundy, its 'flavour' has sometimes been that of the oak in which it was matured or the relics of the winemaking techniques used (see above). When the vineyard site is right, yields not too high, acid not too low, and winemaking skilled, Chardonnay can produce thrilling, savoury, dry, full-bodied wines that will continue to improve in bottle for one, two, or, exceptionally, more decades but—unlike Riesling and the best, nobly rotten Chenin Blanc and Sémillon—it is not a variety capable of making whites for the very long term, and white burgundies, in particular, have shown a tendency to PREMATURE OXIDATION.

Chardonnay's origins were long considered obscure, but DNA PROFILING finally provided the answer to this mystery. Along with a host of other varieties common in north-eastern France, it is the progeny of Pinot Noir and GOUAIS BLANC (see PINOT).

There is a rare but distinct pink-berried mutation, **Chardonnay Rose**, as well as a headily perfumed **Chardonnay Blanc Musqué** version, sometimes used in blends. Some of the 31 official French CLONES of Chardonnay have a similarly grapey perfume, notably 77 and 809, which have been quite widely planted and can add a rather incongruously aromatic note to blends with other clones of the variety. The arguably over-enthusiastic application of CLONAL SELECTION techniques in Burgundy means that growers can now choose from a wide range of Chardonnay clones specially selected for their productivity, particularly 75, 78, 121, 124, 125, and 277. Those seeking quality rather than quantity are more likely to choose 76, 95, and 96. Many New World wine regions began their love affair with Chardonnay on clones such as the Mendoza clone, only to find it rekindled by the introduction of better clones from Burgundy, sometimes known as Dijon clones. In California, the Wente HERITAGE CLONE is held in high regard.

In France the total area planted with Chardonnay—44,151 ha/109,099 acres in 2019—has long been second only in rankings of pale-skinned varieties to the Cognac and Armagnac grape Ugni Blanc. Chardonnay is significant in every single French wine region except for Alsace and Bordeaux and is particularly so in greater Burgundy, the Languedoc, and Champagne, where Chardonnay constitutes about one-third of the vineyard area. Chablis is quintessential Chardonnay country, and plantings totalled more than 6,000 ha by 2019. In the Burgundian heartland, the CÔTE D'OR, Chardonnay plantings had increased to 2,572 ha by 2019 at the expense of ALIGOTÉ but were outnumbered two-and-a-half times by those of Pinot Noir, whereas in the Côte CHALONNAISE and the MÂCONNAIS to the south Chardonnay is twice as common overall as Pinot Noir, Mâcon Blanc being by far the most common (and affordable) incarnation of white burgundy. Although the regulations allow Aligoté into Beaujolais Blanc and Pinot Blanc into white wines labelled Bourgogne and Mâcon, most of these less expensive white burgundies are in practice made predominantly from Chardonnay. To the initial horror of the INAO, there has been an increasing trend towards slipping the word 'Chardonnay' on to white burgundy labels to increase their appeal to non-French consumers.

In the Languedoc, Chardonnay was first planted to add international appeal to the lemony wines of LIMOUX. By 2000 there were nearly 9,000 ha of Chardonnay in the Languedoc, a total that had grown to 16,610 ha by 2019, more than 7,000 of them in the hot Hérault *département*, although this is essentially red-wine country.

Chardonnay is grown in virtually all European wine-producing countries and makes copies of white burgundy of varying qualities, even if much of Spain south of Cataluña (where it plays a part in CAVA) is too hot, and Portugal wisely tends to concentrate on its INDIGENOUS VARIETIES. Even Germany, Rieslingland, now grows Chardonnay on 2,377 ha of vineyard, and it is an important ingredient in the sparkling wine production of ENGLAND.

Italy has a long history of Chardonnay cultivation, especially on its subalpine slopes in the north. Total plantings across the country in 2015 were 19,769 ha/48,850 acres. For decades, Italians were casual about distinguishing between their Pinot Bianco (PINOT BLANC, also known as Weissburgunder in the Italian Tyrol) and their Chardonnay (traditionally called Gelber, or Golden, Weissburgunder in the Italian Tyrol). Alto Adige Chardonnay was the first Italian Chardonnay accorded DOC status, in 1984, although the vine has since been working its magic on producers all over Italy from Puglia to Piemonte and, of course, Aosta towards the French border. Nowadays much of Italy's Chardonnay is produced, often without much distinction, in Friuli, Trentino, and, to a more limited extent, the Veneto, where much of it is used as ballast for GARGANEGA. Some fine examples are produced in favoured sites in both Friuli and Trentino, but a considerable proportion is siphoned off to become SPUMANTE, as it is in Lombardy, where it can add finesse to some fine fizz. Chardonnay gained ground rapidly in Italy in the 1990s, being planted in Tuscan spots where Sangiovese is difficult to ripen. Piemonte, cooler than Tuscany, has, not unsurprisingly, had more overall success with the variety. See under these geographical names for more details of Italian Chardonnays.

Much less dramatic Chardonnay is also produced in Switzerland, particularly in Geneva, the Valais, and Bündner Herrschaft (see map under SWITZERLAND). In AUSTRIA, where the variety is also known as Morillon in STYRIA, Chardonnays include relatively rich, oak-matured versions; lean, aromatic styles modelled on their finest Rieslings; and sweet, BOTRYTIZED wines. The variety is planted throughout Eastern Europe but, with the notable exception of some fine, artisanal Slovenian examples, yields and temperatures are often too high for real distinction.

Few would have believed in 1980, when California had just 7,200 ha/18,000 acres of Chardonnay, that by 1988 the state's total plantings would for a while overtake France's (rapidly increasing) total. In the 21st century, France more than caught up, even though Chardonnay remains California's most-planted variety with a 2020 total of 36,699 ha/90,684 acres. Thanks to the red-wine boom, the rate of new plantings reached a peak in the mid 1990s. See under CALIFORNIA for more detail of the state's evolving styles of Chardonnay.

Chardonnay has been embraced with equal fervour throughout the rest of North America, from British Columbia in CANADA to Long Island in NEW YORK, although it is usually more restrained in character than the once stereotypical rich California style. In 1990, Chardonnay overtook Riesling to become the most planted variety of any hue in WASHINGTON State, but red wine is now far more important, and the 2017 Chardonnay total of 3,149 ha/7,782 acres makes it only the most-planted white wine grape. Chardonnay is also increasingly well regarded in Oregon (where plantings totalled 1,039 ha/2,568 acres in 2019 and the introduction of Dijon clones has had a profound effect on quality) as well as Virginia and Texas. The scale of America's romance with Chardonnay in general and oak-aged Chardonnay in particular was reflected in the international COOPERAGE business in the 1990s.

Various South American countries have been seeking out cooler spots to imbue their

Chardonnay with real verve and concentration. CHILE's Pacific-influenced regions, most notably the Casablanca Valley and San Antonio/Leyda, and the high-elevation vineyards of Argentina's Uco Valley are the most obvious examples. Their best wines combine fruit purity and accessibility. In ARGENTINA, where the variety has shown impressive finesse, Chardonnay overtook Ugni Blanc, Chenin Blanc, Sémillon, and Sauvignonasse in the 1990s to become the country's second most planted white wine grape after Torrontés. Total Argentine plantings were 5,853 ha by 2020. Chile has even more, 10,919 ha in 2020, and Chardonnay was the country's most planted white wine grape for the first decade of this century, but Sauvignon Blanc is now way ahead. The Australian wine industry's all-important export trade was long centred on its particularly user-friendly and frequently adapted style of Chardonnay. Rich fruit flavours, often disciplined by added acid and flavoured by OAK CHIPS, were available at carefully judged price points. Such was the strength of demand for AUSTRALIAN Chardonnay in the late 1980s that the area of Chardonnay vines increased more than fivefold during the decade so that in 1990, Chardonnay, with its 4,300 ha/10,600 acres, became Australia's most-planted white wine grape variety (although 1,300 ha were too young to bear fruit). Plantings peaked in 2007 with more than 32,000 ha, but reaction to a glut left total Chardonnay plantings at 21,442 ha in 2015, slightly less than those of Cabernet Sauvignon, Australia's second most popular variety after Shiraz. The style of typical Australian Chardonnay changed more rapidly than any other nation's with steeliness, almost austerity, now seen as virtues. Nevertheless, the average life expectancy of typical Australian (and many other non-European) Chardonnay is short, but glorious exceptions abound in cooler spots such as the Adelaide Hills, Victoria, and Tasmania and can give fine white burgundy a run for its money.

NEW ZEALAND's love affair with Chardonnay was relatively short. Only in the last decade of the 20th century did Chardonnay plantings outnumber those of the Sauvignon Blanc that has now been anointed queen of Kiwi vines. By 2022 total plantings of Chardonnay, just over 3,000 ha/7,413 acres, had fallen to less than one-eighth those of Sauvignon Blanc, even though the naturally high acidity of New Zealand wines suits Chardonnay so well. Chardonnay has had a chequered history in South Africa. Planting material in the late 1970s and early 1980s was frequently smuggled rather than submitted for QUARANTINE, and at one time significant quantities of AUXERROIS contaminated the authenticity of 'Chardonnay' vineyards. For a while Chardonnay was the country's third most planted white wine grape, albeit a long way behind Chenin Blanc and Colombard, but in 2006 Sauvignon Blanc, as in New Zealand, overtook Chardonnay, whose plantings in 2020 were just 6,587 ha.

Although Chardonnay can thrive in relatively hot climates (such as Australia's irrigation zones), it has to be picked before acids plummet (sometimes before the grapes have developed much real character, although this is usually caused by excessively high yields), and it does require relatively sophisticated techniques, including TEMPERATURE CONTROL, in the cellar. This is why it is not especially well suited to hot Mediterranean wine regions, and well-balanced Chardonnays with real interest from the likes of Greece, Israel, and Lebanon tend to be exceptions.

Charentais, IGP for TABLE WINES made in the Cognac region of France, following the river Charente to the Atlantic. A MARITIME CLIMATE keeps average annual temperatures at a cool 13 °C/55 °F and provides plenty of HUMIDITY; annual precipitation averages 800–1,200 mm/31–47 in. LIMESTONE soils dominate. White wines are made mainly from SAUVIGNON BLANC and CHARDONNAY; UGNI BLANC and COLOMBARD are widely grown but mainly for distillation or PINEAU DES CHARENTES. Reds and rosés rely on Bordeaux varieties and pinot noir. Four subregions are allowed on wine labels: Charente-Maritime, Île de Ré, Île de Olérin, and St-Sornin.

Charlemagne, king of the Franks 768–814, crowned Holy Roman Emperor in 800, the man who ushered in civilization, order, and prosperity after the long Dark Ages, ruling a Christian kingdom based at Aachen (Aix-la-Chapelle) which included virtually all of France, Belgium, Germany, and Switzerland.

Charlemagne's name is associated by modern wine drinkers with one of the greatest white burgundies, Corton-Charlemagne (whose vineyards include a plot known as Le Charlemagne), produced on land he gave to the Abbey of Saulieu in 775 (see ALOXE-CORTON for more detail). Charlemagne's secretary and biographer Einhard tells us, however, that Charlemagne was a moderate man: he never drank more than three cups of wine with dinner, and he hated to see people drunk (*Life of Charlemagne*, ch. 24). Only a temperate man is truly interested in wine: when he renamed the 12 months of the year in his native language, he called October 'windume-manoth', the month of the wine harvest (Einhard, ch. 28).

This Old Frankisch name reflects the growing importance of wine in the Carolingian era, for under Charlemagne and his heirs more and more vines began to be grown. Viticulture had of course been long established in a large part of Charlemagne's empire. The Greek colonists had introduced winegrowing to Massilia (now Marseilles) from 600 BCE onwards. When the Romans, under Julius Caesar, conquered Gaul in 51 BCE, they gradually expanded the small-scale viticulture of the Gauls, who had drunk mainly beer. The Roman settlers planted their first vineyards in southern Gaul, and by the 2nd century wine was grown extensively in most of Gaul. The Romans also planted vines in the MOSELLE Valley, on the left bank of the Rhine, and in the areas we now know as ALSACE, the PFALZ, and RHEINHESSEN.

The spread of Christianity was one reason for the expansion of viticulture that took place during Charlemagne's reign and continued for another two centuries afterwards. The Church needed a daily supply of wine to celebrate the EUCHARIST. Also, monasteries, many of which were new foundations, needed wine for the monks and their guests (see MONKS AND MONASTERIES), and vineyards were planted all over northern France and even southern Belgium.

The Rule of St Benedict permitted a modest daily ration of wine, more on holy days and feast days; important guests who stayed at the monastery had to be suitably entertained, for they might one day repay the monks generously for their hospitality. Monasteries usually had their own vineyards, and often these had been donated by local landowners who hoped for a place in heaven. Bishops also wanted wine, not just for the day-to-day running of their households but also as a status symbol to put themselves on a par with the nobility of the district. Bishops, like monks, had their own vineyards, and some bishops may even have moved their sees to be nearer vineyards: at least, this may explain why the bishopric of Langres moved south to Dijon (at the north of the CÔTE D'OR), that of Tongres to Liège in modern Belgium, and that of St-Quentin to Noyon north of Paris. Thus Christianity fostered the production of two grades of wine, wine for daily consumption and a superior kind that was designed to impress prestigious guests.

In 816, the Council of Aachen added a third category of ecclesiastical viticulture. The Council prescribed that a college of canons, living under monastic rule, should be attached to every cathedral and that the canons should grow wine. Often they tended vineyards adjacent to those of their bishops; collegiate churches could be founded elsewhere in the diocese as well, and they also acquired their own vineyards.

Unlike education, viticulture was not the preserve of the Church, however: laymen also grew wine. The factor that decided where they established their new vineyards was not TERROIR but ease of transport. If the enterprise was to be commercially viable, the area had to be near a navigable RIVER or within easy reach, by road, of a major town or city. This is why so much wine was grown around PARIS, AUXERRE, and in

CHAMPAGNE, despite the fact that it was too cold there for the vine to yield ripe and abundant fruit. If the summer had not been hot, there was nothing for it but to drink thin, acidic wine until the following autumn, unless one could afford to buy better wine from elsewhere. An interesting document from the last decade of the 8th century deals with the management of vineyards in secular ownership. It is known as the 'Capitulare de villis', or 'Concerning estates' (a capitulary being a collection of ordinances). Linguistic evidence and local references show that it was drawn up for Aquitaine, which was administered by Charlemagne's son Louis the Pious before he succeeded his father. The list of plants and herbs which it says must be grown in the estate's market garden owes more to the library than to real horticulture, but the advice it gives on winegrowing is sound and practical. Not only should the king's inspectors claim the portion of the vintage that is the royal household's due, but they should also oversee hygienic procedures in the vineyard. WINE PRESSES should be clean, and grapes should not be trodden with the feet. Wine that is to be sent to the palace should be put into proper wooden BARRELS instead of leather wineskins. An inventory of the entire estate should be drawn up each Christmas, including the wine it has produced that autumn and any older wine left over.

The 'Capitulare de villis' has no connection with Charlemagne himself, and there is no solid evidence that he initiated the planting of any vineyard, although parts of France and the RHEINGAU were first planted in his day. Viticulture flourished not because of a *dirigiste* policy but because political unity had brought prosperity. External threats, most importantly from the Moors and the Magyars, could not be prevented and had to be dealt with, but, within the frontiers of the Holy Roman Empire, peace reigned, and viticulture was so successful that there was a surplus of wine. Landowners had to resort to the right of 'banvin', by which none of their tenants was allowed to sell wine until the lord had sold his own. In the south, wine was part of everyday life; in the north it was more of a luxury item, but it could still be obtained readily.

How different things were in England! When the English scholar Alcuin, friend of Charlemagne and tutor to his court at Aachen, went back to his native country for a visit, he complained bitterly in a letter, dated 790, to a Frankish ex-pupil. The wine has run out, and his stomach aches with sour beer: please send wine. Beer has its uses, but it is not a civilized drink. In the 8th century, the Frankish kingdom was a better place for a wine drinker to be than Anglo-Saxon England.

See also GERMAN HISTORY. H.M.W.

Bassermann-Jordan, F., *Geschichte des Weinbaus*, 3 vols., i (1907).

Dion, R., *Histoire de la vigne et du vin en France* (1959; rpt 1977).

Duby, G., *Historie de la France rurale*, 4 vols., i (1975).

Einhard and Notker the Stammerer, *Two Lives of Charlemagne*, tr. Lewis Thorpe (1969).

Latouche, R., *The Birth of Western Economy* (1961).

Charles Sturt University, one of Australia's foremost research and teaching institutions for grape-growers and winemakers. Courses started in 1976 within the Riverina College of Advanced Education, Wagga Wagga, New South Wales (NSW), to satisfy the need within the rapidly growing wine industry for a teaching institution in addition to ROSEWORTHY. In 1989, the College combined with other regional teaching institutions in NSW to form Charles Sturt University (CSU). The School of Agricultural and Wine Sciences offers Bachelor of Wine Science, Bachelor of Viticulture, and Bachelor of Wine Business degrees in either viticulture or wine science over six years part-time by online studies, with on-campus residential schools and workplace learning. Initially a controversial option for the wine industry, online is now a widely accepted means of learning, allowing students to continue in their current profession while studying. There is also a Bachelor of General Studies (Science), which may be exited earlier at Diploma or Associate Bachelor stages for the student to transfer to the above or other courses. CSU also offers postgraduate studies leading to Doctor of Philosophy and Master of Philosophy qualifications.

In 1997, CSU formed an alliance with the NSW Government's Department of Primary Industries and the NSW Wine Industry Association to form the National Wine and Grape Industry Centre, which undertakes industry-focused research and extension services to assist the wine industry in applying best practice.

N.B.

Charmat, see TANK METHOD.

Charneco, Portuguese white wine, probably fortified, popular in England in the 16th and 17th centuries and mentioned by Shakespeare in *The Second Part of Henry VI*. It is probably the forerunner of BUCELAS. R.J.M.

Charta (pronounced 'karta'), an association of RHEINGAU wine producers founded in 1984 and the designation given to one or two special Riesling bottlings made annually by each member in accordance with the association's standards for YIELDS, MUST WEIGHTS, and permissible vineyards of origin. (Paradoxically, these may not be labelled with the names of specific vineyards.) Charta Rieslings must be finished TROCKEN or HALBTROCKEN—a stricture intended as homage to tradition—and pass three BLIND TASTING tests, after which they are bottled in tall flute-shaped bottles embossed and labelled with a double Romanesque arch. (Some estates use this as an opportunity to commission Charta-dedicated ARTISTS' LABELS.) The qualitative impetus behind this association and its wines is often rightly associated with the subsequent emergence of ERSTES GEWÄCHS and GROSSES GEWÄCHS as quality wine categories, although the number of participating growers has fallen steadily in recent years from a high of nearly 50.

D.S.

Chasan, light-skinned, early-budding CROSS of Palomino Fino (known in France as LISTÁN) and Pinot (originally said to be Chardonnay) made under INRA auspices by French AMPELOGRAPHER Paul Truel. It is planted on a limited scale in the Midi, particularly in the Aude *département*, and France's total plantings were just 428 ha/1,058 acres by 2018.

Chassagne-Montrachet, village in the Côte de Beaune district of Burgundy's CÔTE D'OR more famed for its white wines from the Chardonnay grape than for its equally plentiful red wines from Pinot Noir. Until the mid 1980s, the village produced more red wine than white, but the significant premium for white Chassagne led to considerable planting of Chardonnay, even on relatively unsuitable soils. The five-year average (2015–19) of production saw 3,670 hl of red and 10,148 hl of white Chasssagne-Montrachet, including PREMIERS CRUS.

The better soil for Pinot Noir, limestone MARL with a red gravel content, lies mainly on the south side of the village towards Santenay and incorporates most of the village appellation, although the PREMIERS CRUS La Boudriotte, Morgeot, and especially Clos St-Jean make excellent red wines. Red Chassagne-Montrachet tends to be somewhat hard and earthy when young, mellowing with age but rarely achieving the delicacy of truly fine red burgundy.

The fame of Chassagne rests with the white wines at village, premier cru, and especially GRAND CRU level. Chassagne shares the Le Montrachet and Bâtard-Montrachet vineyards with neighbouring Puligny and enjoys sole possession of a third grand cru, Criots-Bâtard-Montrachet (see MONTRACHET for more details). Among the premiers crus, the most exciting are En Cailleret, Grande Montagne, La Romanée, Grandes Ruchottes, Blanchot Dessus, and Vide-Bourse. Suitable white-wine soil tends to have more oolitic LIMESTONE and less marl in its make-up.

The white wines of Chassagne are noted for their steely power, less rounded than MEURSAULT when young, sometimes similar to PULIGNY-MONTRACHET if less floral. Good vintages from good producers such as Ramonet and the extended Colin, Gagnard, and Morey clans should age from five to ten years.

See map under BURGUNDY. J.T.C.M.

Chasselas, even if by no means the most revered white grape variety, is widely planted under dozens of names around the world and has a particularly long, intriguing history. DNA PROFILING suggests its origins lie in French SWITZERLAND, where it certainly produces its finest wines today, often called Fendant, its common synonym in the Valais. Chasselas is still Switzerland's most planted white wine grape and is particularly common in the canton of Vaud, where more than 60% of the 2020 total of 3,606 ha/8,911 acres are grown. Individual villages all over French Switzerland but particularly on the northern bank of Lac Léman have won acclaim for their TERROIR-specific interpretations of what can be a relatively neutral grape.

In France, it is rather despised, not least because, as Chasselas Doré, it is France's most common TABLE GRAPE. Total French plantings had declined to just over 500 ha by 2019. It is rapidly disappearing from Alsace, where it is regarded as the lowest of the low and is generally sold as EDELZWICKER or under some proprietary name that excludes mention of any grape variety. Planted in the area responsible for Pouilly-Fumé, it makes the distinctly inferior white labelled Pouilly-sur-Loire and, as might be expected, approaches respectability only as it nears Switzerland, in SAVOIE. Here it is the main grape grown in the *département* of Haute-Savoie on the south side of Lake Geneva in the Vin de Savoie CRUS of CRÉPY, MARIGNAN, Marin, and Ripaille.

The variety's long history has enabled it to spread far and wide. In Germany, where it is known as Weisser GUTEDEL and is grown on 1,105 ha/2,731 acres, mainly in BADEN, it has been known since the 16th century. It is no longer nearly as important in central Europe as it once was but can still be found in Hungary, Romania, Russia, and Serbia. Outside Europe it is most important in Chile.

château may be French for 'castle' but in wine parlance it usually means a vine-growing, winemaking estate, to include the vineyards, the cellars, often the wine itself, and any building or buildings on the property, which can range from the non-existent (as in the case of Ch Léoville-BARTON, for example, which is made in the cellars of Ch Langoa-Barton), through the most rudimentary shack, to the sumptuous classical edifice called Ch MARGAUX. The term is most commonly used in BORDEAUX, where the 18th edition of the FÉRET guide lists more than 14,000 châteaux, although common use of the term developed only in the second half of the 19th century, when the owners of the great estates could afford to build grand lodgings to go with them. Only five of the original 79 properties in the Médoc, Graves, and Sauternes listed in the famous 1855 CLASSIFICATION, for example, were described as châteaux then. Bordeaux proprietors soon learnt the value of a Château prefix and have long adopted the policy of renaming properties almost at will, in particular suffixing their own surname as, for example, Ch Prieuré-LICHINE and Chx Mouton- and Lafite-ROTHSCHILD. The word 'château' is by no means uncommon outside Bordeaux, however, mainly within but sometimes outside FRANCE (where it tends to lose its circumflex). According to current French law, the word 'château' may be used only of a specified plot, or collection of plots, of land, which means that it is perfectly possible for CO-OPERATIVES, for example, to produce a wine labelled as Château Quelquechose (see CHÂTEAU BOTTLING). Some producers make a range of wines carrying the name of the property but reserve the word 'château' for their top bottlings.

château bottling, the relatively recent practice of BOTTLING the produce of a CHÂTEAU on that property. Such a wine is said to be **château bottled**, or *mis(e) en bouteille au château* in French, an expression used throughout France but particularly in BORDEAUX. (Its counterpart in BURGUNDY is DOMAINE BOTTLED, while in the NEW WORLD the term ESTATE BOTTLED is often used.)

Initially all wine was sold in BULK, and subsequently it was up to the MERCHANTS, whether in the region of consumption or production, to put the wine into bottle. Even as recently as the mid 20th century, the great majority of wine left the property on which it was produced in BARRELS. ADULTERATION AND FRAUD was therefore all too easy among less scrupulous merchants and particularly tempting in the wake of the world wine shortages which followed POWDERY MILDEW and PHYLLOXERA at the end of the 19th century.

It was the young Baron Philippe de ROTHSCHILD who did most to promote château bottling when he took over Ch MOUTON ROTHSCHILD in the early 1920s. He succeeded in persuading all the first growths (and Ch Mouton Rothschild of course) of the wisdom of bottling all of their principal output, the so-called GRAND VIN, on their own territory. This involved a certain amount of investment, but the resulting reliability and cachet more than compensated.

Good bottling lines require a level of investment that is unrealistic for many a small wine property, however, so contract bottlers and mobile bottling lines are much in demand, and producers may not be able to bottle at the precise time they would prefer. Others still bottle by hand, some with scant regard for HYGIENE and consistency. Such considerations mean that bottling at source is not necessarily superior to careful BULK TRANSPORT of the wine to a top-quality bottling plant.

Château-Chalon, extraordinary wine made in the JURA region of eastern France with its own small appellation named after the hilltop village where it is produced. In the 17th century or even earlier, the abbesses from the Abbey of Château-Chalon may have been the first in the region to make a VIN JAUNE style of wine, historically named 'Vin de Garde'. Unlike other Jura appellations, Château-Chalon must be a *vin jaune* and thus must be made exclusively from SAVAGNIN grapes grown on the local grey MARL. (Other wines produced by local growers are entitled to the Côtes du Jura appellation.) In 1952 the appellation was the first in France to instigate vineyard inspections pre-harvest before the vintage is approved. The noble decision was made not to bottle any wine under the appellation in 1974, 1980, 1984, and 2001. Like all *vin jaune*, the wine must be kept for at least six years and three months before bottling, most of this time spent in partially filled, untouched casks under *voile*, the local benevolent FILM-FORMING YEAST. The resulting wine is exceptionally spicy and mineral-rich, pale to deep golden, and long lasting. It must be bottled in a special *clavelin* bottle containing 62 cl, supposedly the amount of wine that remains from a litre of wine kept in a cask in Ch-Chalon for six years. The result is a wine that shares some flavour characteristics with SHERRY but has more finesse, working well as a gastronomic partner (especially with the local Comté cheese and poultry of Bresse, also AOC products) and as a candidate for extended BOTTLE AGEING. It is said to develop 'curry' flavours in bottle, thanks to the compound SOTOLON. With only 55 ha/136 acres planted, production volumes vary wildly, from zero to, in a good year, around 1,600 hl/42,267 gal.

W.L.

Château-Grillet, one of France's smallest wine appellations and one of the few with a single owner (see also DOMAINE DE LA ROMANÉE-CONTI). Château-Grillet's few hectares of vineyard represent an enclave within the CONDRIEU zone between the communes of Vérin and St-Michel-sur-Rhône in the north of the northern Rhône. A virtual amphitheatre carved out of the granite shelters the narrow terraces of VIOGNIER vines from the north winds. Already appreciated by Thomas JEFFERSON in the late 18th century, Château-Grillet has always been in single ownership. Until it was bought by François Pinault, owner of Ch LATOUR, in 2011, it belonged to the Neyret-Gachet family and descendants. Annual production was barely 2,000 cases of Château-Grillet's distinctive fluted brown bottle, one of the last to grow from 70 to 75 cl. Between the 1970s and the 2010s, the wine maintained its high price more by its rarity than because it was obviously one of France's finest wines.

The new team in charge of the original 3.5-ha/8.6-acre estate make a second wine, sold as Côtes du Rhône, and are refining the

style, which is less headily perfumed than the best Condrieu and always dry. Since converting the estate to BIODYNAMIC VITICULTURE and refurbishing the winery, quality has become more reliable. The result is a restrained, taut wine which may improve in bottle for a decade or even two. The latest addition to the range is Condrieu La Carthery, produced from a few rows of vines that border the Château-Grillet growing area at the top of the amphitheatre.
M.C.W.

Châteaumeillant, small, isolated AOC in central France around the town of Châteaumeillant between ST-POURÇAIN and TOURAINE (see map under FRANCE). Mainly GAMAY with some Pinot Noir and a little Pinot Gris produce red and VIN GRIS from 83 ha/205 acres of sandy CLAY soils over SANDSTONE, SCHIST, and GNEISS. One CO-OPERATIVE dominates production.

Châteauneuf-du-Pape, the oldest, largest, and most qualitative of all the CRUS of the southern RHÔNE, producing mainly powerful, potent, full-bodied red wines and a much smaller volume of full-bodied, opulent whites.

The first written references to wine produced here date back to 1157, but it is with the arrival of the popes that winemaking takes on a greater significance. The wine takes its name, which means 'Pope's new castle', from the relocation of the papal court to Avignon in the 14th century and in particular from the construction of summer quarters just north of the city in a village once known as Calcernier for its limestone quarry. It is now called Châteauneuf-du-Pape. The Gascon Pope Clément V (after whom Ch Pape-Clément in PESSAC-LÉOGNAN is named) arrived at Avignon in 1309 and is supposed to have ordered the planting of vines, but it was his successor John XXII who is credited with developing a papal vineyard in Châteauneuf-du-Pape.

By the end of the 18th century, wines were being exported to Europe and the United States, and the name of Châteauneuf-du-Pape began to be recognized internationally. Its reputation steadily grew with the establishment of several large private estates until the arrival of PHYLLOXERA in 1866, which ravaged the vineyards.

Reconstruction of the vineyards was financially devastating, and the Châteauneuf-du-Pape vignerons were just some of those affected by the ADULTERATION AND FRAUD that were rife in the early 20th century. By 1923, the most energetic and well connected of their number, Baron Pierre Le Roy de Boiseaumarié (1890–1967) of Ch Fortia, had successfully drawn up a set of rules for the production of Châteauneuf-du-Pape, with the co-operation of his peers, which was the prototype for the entire AOC system. Thus France's first appellation was granted on 14 May 1936. Among what have now become the usual regulations, it involved the first geographical DELIMITATION of the original production zone. Another notable feature was the minimum specified ALCOHOLIC STRENGTH, 12.5%, which must be achieved without the aid of external sugar addition, or CHAPTALIZATION. Hand-picking and TRIAGE of picked grapes was mandated, and rosé production was disallowed.

Perhaps it is because of the antiquity of Châteauneuf-du-Pape's wine regulations that so many VINE VARIETIES are permitted by the appellation. Today 18 varieties are authorized, and any permitted grapes can be used for reds or whites, in any proportion. That said, GRENACHE makes up about 80% of red varieties planted in Châteauneuf-du-Pape, with yields officially restricted to just 35 hl/ha (2 tons/acre). It can produce wines which combine concentration and structure with the usual sweet fruit of Grenache, although it is particularly prone to COULURE.

MOURVÈDRE is an increasingly popular ingredient, although it needs the warmest MESOCLIMATES to ripen fully, while SYRAH from the northern Rhône has also been planted by producers who admire its TANNINS and structure. CINSAUT is also grown but to a declining extent. Of the other permitted dark-skinned varieties, MUSCARDIN, VACCARÈSE, PICQUEPOUL Noir, TERRET Noir, and COUNOISE, only the last is grown to any significant extent, and it has its admirers. For white Châteauneuf-du-Pape, the most common varieties are Grenache Blanc, CLAIRETTE, BOURBOULENC, and ROUSSANNE. Clairette Rose and Piquepoul Blanc are also grown. Piquepoul Gris, Grenache Gris, and Picardan are very rare.

The appellation covers around 3,200 ha/7,907 acres of relatively flat vineyards at varying ELEVATIONS and ASPECTS above the river in Châteauneuf-du-Pape and the neighbouring communes of Bédarrides, Courthézon, Orange, and Sorgues. The highest point is 128 m/420 ft above sea level. The terrain is traditionally characterized by large pebbles, or *galets roulés*, some of them several inches across, which cover many of the more photographed vineyards, supposedly retaining heat and speeding the RIPENING process of the traditionally low-trained BUSH VINES. Soils in Châteauneuf-du-Pape are more varied than this, however (see soil map in Johnson and Robinson, 2019), and those at the celebrated Ch Rayas, for example, are predominantly sandy without a GALET in sight. Other main soil types are a compacted red SANDSTONE locally known as *grès rouge* and LIMESTONE. Most wines are blends from different subzones, particularly the classic blends some estates call their Tradition bottlings, though highly priced Special Cuvées have proliferated since the late 1980s, some of which are SINGLE-VINEYARD WINES. The size and diversity of the TERROIR and the number of producers make for a stylistically varied appellation.

Red wines are typically fermented in large old oak *foudres* or CONCRETE tanks, and they can be matured in these vessels or in smaller oak BARRELS. New oak tends to be reserved for Syrah or Mourvèdre rather than Grenache. The challenge of growing Grenache in this hot, Mediterranean climate is that sugar levels can rise quickly, leading to alcohol levels that can reach 17%. However, when the alcohol is balanced with adequate acidity, tannins, and concentration of fruit, the wines can be powerful, long-lived, and impressively complex. An increasingly popular way of achieving this is WHOLE-BUNCH FERMENTATION. Though many red Châteauneufs are drunk young, the most qualitative wines tend to show their best after 10 years in bottle. Today there are over 300 producers.

At just 8% of production, white Châteauneuf-du-Pape is a relative rarity, and it may be made according to a wide range of formulae. The wines are almost always full-bodied, and most should be drunk young, although some, such as the white wines of Ch de Beaucastel, Clos des Papes, and Domaine de Beaurenard, can develop for 25 years or more in bottle and sit alongside the finest white wines of France. See also RHÔNE.
M.C.W.

Johnson, H., and Robinson, J., *The World Atlas of Wine* (8th edn, 2019).

Châtillon-en-Diois, small appellation for still, dry wines in the cooler eastern half of the Diois growing area in the Drôme Valley, between the northern and southern RHÔNE. Reds and rosés must be at last 75% GAMAY, with optional Pinot Noir or Syrah; whites are from Chardonnay and/or ALIGOTÉ. The local sparkling wine, CLAIRETTE DE DIE, is much more common.
M.C.W.

Chaume, hillside hamlet surrounded by 60 ha/150 acres of praised CHENIN BLANC vineyards dedicated to sweet wines. From 2014, it became the only PREMIER CRU of the LOIRE under the Premier Cru Coteaux du LAYON Chaume AOC. See also QUARTS DE CHAUME.

Chautagne, CRU in the upper Rhône Valley north of Chambéry whose name may be added to the French appellation SAVOIE. Production is dominated by the CO-OPERATIVE, and it is best known for its red wines, in particular from Gamay but also from Pinot Noir or the local MONDEUSE.
W.L.

Chaves, westernmost DOC subregion of TRÁS-OS-MONTES in north-east Portugal, with predominantly GRANITIC soils and relatively high amounts of rain and humidity.
S.A.

Chehalem Mountains, wine region and AVA within the WILLAMETTE VALLEY of Oregon.

Chelois, Seibel FRENCH HYBRID planted to a very limited extent in the north-eastern US but starting to attract attention in NEW YORK's Finger Lakes.

Chelva, leading Spanish TABLE GRAPE also grown for RIBERA DEL GUADIANA in Extremadura, western Spain. Also known as Montúa. Spain's plantings totalled 4,832 ha/11,940 acres in 2020.

Chenanson, productive CROSS of GRENACHE Noir and Jurançon Noir planted on about 450 ha/1,112 acres in southern France in 2019, presumably popular because it is more productive and deeper-coloured than Grenache.

Chénas, the smallest of the ten BEAUJOLAIS crus, in the far north of the region and often in the shadow of MOULIN-À-VENT, not because of quality but because the latter appellation appropriated many of the commune's best LIEUX-DITS. From just 230 ha/570 acres divided between the villages of Chénas and La Chapelle de Guinchay, the wines can be hard to find, but they merge the best qualities of Moulin-à-Vent and FLEURIE. J.F.B.

Chenin or **Chenin Blanc**, in its native region often called Pineau or Pineau de la Loire, is probably the world's most versatile grape variety, capable of producing some of the finest, longest-living sweet whites and a wide range of fine dry whites. It is also responsible for a considerable volume of sparkling wine; in SOUTH AFRICA, where it is by far the most planted variety, it is even used as the base for a wide range of FORTIFIED WINES and spirits. Although in its most common high-yield, NEW WORLD form its distinctive flavour reminiscent of honey and damp straw is usually lost, it retains the naturally high acidity that dogs it in some of the Loire's less ripe vintages but can be so useful in hot climates.

South Africa, with a 2020 total of 17,147 ha/42,371 acres, has almost twice as much Chenin planted as France's 2019 total of 10,362 ha/25,605 acres, which has remained unchanged for the last two decades. On the Cape, Chenin is prized for its acidity, productivity, and good resistance to disease and wind. The vine may have been one of the original collection imported in 1655 by Jan van Riebeeck. A dedicated band of Chenin Blanc specialists has emerged in South Africa, focusing on the best sites and on restoring to high-quality production old vineyard blocks.

In the 1980s, CALIFORNIA also had more Chenin planted than France, but total plantings had fallen to about 1,726 ha/4,265 acres by 2020. In stark contrast to South Africa and the Loire, California has very few champions of the variety, and most of it is used as the usually anonymous base for everyday commercial blends of reasonably crisp white of varying degrees of sweetness, often blended with the much more widely planted FRENCH COLOMBARD. Both of these workhorse varieties are planted primarily in the hot, dry Central Valley, a setting that might be described as the antithesis of Chenin's Loire homeland. (It also presumably helps extend quantities of, and add acidity to, cheaper wines labelled Chardonnay.) Chappellet's Chenin can be worth AGEING, and in Clarksburg at the north end of the Central Valley it can take on a distinctive melony, musky flavour. In New Zealand it has almost disappeared, and Millton is virtually the only producer to understand the variety. Australia grew just over 415 ha in 2022 and treated it largely with disdain as low-cost (high-yielding) blending material, usually extending Chardonnay, Sémillon, and Sauvignon Blanc. Plantings had fallen to about 1,744 ha in Argentina by 2020 and to under 40 ha in Chile.

The variety was exported to Israel to establish vineyards there at the end of the 19th century.

If Chenin appears to lead a double life—biddable workhorse in the New World, superstar in ANJOU-Saumur and TOURAINE—it seems clear that the explanation lies in a combination of climate, soil, and yield. In California's Central Valley, the vine is often expected to yield 10 tons per acre (175 hl/ha), while even the most basic Anjou Blanc should not be produced from vines that yield more than 45 hl/ha. It is hardly surprising that Chenin's character seems diluted outside the Loire, where it has been known for centuries under various names such as Plant d'Anjou and Pineau de la Loire. Unpublished DNA PROFILING at INRAE suggests that Chenin is a natural cross between SAVAGNIN and SAUVIGNONASSE. It is also a half-sibling of VERDELHO and SAUVIGNON BLANC as well as a parent of Meslier St-François.

The vine is vigorous and has a tendency to bud early and ripen late, both of which are highly inconvenient attributes in the cool Loire Valley (though hardly noticeable characteristics in the hotter vineyards of the New World). CLONES that minimize these inconveniences have been selected, and 14 are now officially sanctioned in France. It is prone to BOTRYTIS BUNCH ROT—usefully so for LATE HARVEST styles.

About one-third of all France's, which means the middle Loire's, Chenin was abandoned in the 1970s, often in favour of Cabernet Franc in Anjou-Saumur and Touraine and to make way for the temporarily more fashionable Gamay and Sauvignon de Touraine in the east of the middle Loire. It is today most planted in the heart of Anjou-Saumur and Touraine, as well it might be to judge from the superlative quality of the best wines of such appellations as ANJOU, BONNEZEAUX, Coteaux de l'AUBANCE, Coteaux du LAYON, JASNIÈRES, MONTLOUIS, QUARTS DE CHAUME, SAUMUR, SAVENNIÈRES (the grape's one definitively dry appellation), VOUVRAY, and CRÉMANT de Loire.

In most of the best Loire Chenins and certainly all of the great sweet wines, Chenin is unblended, but up to 20% of Chardonnay or Sauvignon is allowed into an Anjou, and even more catholic blends are allowed into whites labelled Val de Loire. If middle-Loire white has any character at all it is that of Chenin, increasingly valued as the region's signature grape, in contrast to the widely planted Sauvignon Blanc and Chardonnay. While basic Loire Chenin exhibits simply vaguely floral aromas and refreshingly high acidity (together with too much SULFUR DIOXIDE if made in one of the more old-fashioned cellars), the best have a physically thrilling concentration of honeyed flavour, whether the wine is made sweet (MOELLEUX), dry/*sec* (an increasingly popular style, often incorporating some BARREL AGEING), or *demi-sec*, together with Chenin's characteristically vibrant acidity level.

It is undoubtedly this acid, emphasized by a conscious distaste for MALOLACTIC CONVERSION and concentrated in some years by BOTRYTIS, that helps preserve the finest Chenins for decades after their relatively early bottling. (In all of these respects, together with lateness of ripening and a wide range of sweetness levels that are customary, Chenin is France's answer to Germany's RIESLING.)

Chenin with its high acidity is a useful base for a wide range of sparkling wines, most importantly Saumur Mousseux but also Crémant de Loire and even some rich sparkling Vouvrays, which, like their still counterparts, can age beautifully. Treasured for its reliably high acidity and useful perfume, it is also an ingredient, with Mauzac and Chardonnay, in the sparkling wines of LIMOUX.

Cheval Blanc, Château, very fine BORDEAUX property in ST-ÉMILION. In 1832, Henriette Ducasse married Libourne négociant Jean Laussac-Fourcaud, bringing with her 12 ha/30 acres of land including part of the narrow GRAVEL ridge that runs through Figeac and neighbouring vineyards and reaches PETRUS just over the border in POMEROL. This became Ch Cheval Blanc, which, in the International London and Paris Exhibitions in 1862 and 1867, won the medals still prominent on its labels. In 1892, Albert reversed the order of his double surname, and it remained in the Fourcaud-Laussac family until 1998 when it was sold to Bernard Arnault, chairman of LVMH, and Belgian businessman Albert Frère. Pierre, one of the LURTONS, has been general manager since 1991.

The estate has 39 ha of vines: 51% Cabernet Franc, 47% Merlot, and 2% Cabernet Sauvignon. A total of 53 very different plots have been identified and, since an ultra-modern CHAI was built in 2011, have been picked and vinified separately. Average production is about 7,000 dozen bottles a year. Le Petit Cheval is the second wine. The high percentage of CABERNET

FRANC, a variety felicitously originally favoured by Jean Laussac-Fourcaud which has proved particularly well-suited to the CLAY soils of Cheval Blanc, gives the wines a deep colour and a rich, concentrated blackcurrant bouquet and flavour. Merlot is mostly planted on plots with more gravel. Although excellent wines were made towards the end of the 19th century and before the First World War, the property's international reputation was made with the 1921, which had enormous concentration and sweetness. Other very successful wines were made in the 1920s and even in 1934 and 1937, but its more modern fame was achieved with the rich, porty 1947—quite different from the style aimed at today. A Sancerre-like dry white wine, Le Petit Cheval Blanc, is grown on part of what was Ch La Tour du Pin Figeac, acquired in 2006.

Chevalier-Montrachet, great white GRAND CRU in Burgundy's CÔTE D'OR. For more details, see MONTRACHET.

Cheverny in the middle LOIRE was promoted to full AOC status in 1993 and produces a wide range of wines from its 532 ha/1,315 acres in the north-east corner of TOURAINE near Blois (see LOIRE map). Light reds and rosés may be made from Pinot Noir and Gamay with a minimum of 15% Cabernet Franc or Côt (MALBEC). But most Cheverny is based on Sauvignon Blanc, typically blended with a little Chardonnay, Chenin Blanc, and/or MENU PINEAU, and can offer a good-value northern riposte to SANCERRE and POUILLY-FUMÉ. Wines made from the local ROMORANTIN grape have their own 48-ha appellation **Cour Cheverny**.

Chian wine, from the island of **Chios**, was highly prized in both ancient and medieval times. See AEGEAN ISLANDS and DRIED-GRAPE WINES for more details.

Chianti, the name of a specific geographical area between Florence and Siena in the central Italian region of TUSCANY, associated with tangy, dry red wines of varied quality. The Chianti zone is first identified in documents of the second half of the 13th century which named the high hills between Baliaccia and Monte Luco 'the Chianti mountains' but without reference to the actual wine (although see TUSCANY, history). In the 18th century the name was applied to the townships of Castellina, Radda, Gaiole, and Greve (including Panzano) that formed the nucleus of the medieval League of Chianti under Florentine jurisdiction. These townships became one of the very first wine regions anywhere to be officially demarcated, in an edict drawn up in 1716 by Cosimo III, Grand Duke of Tuscany to protect authenticity and combat fraud. In the 1930s the Italian government's Dalmasso commission enlarged this historic zone to capitalize on the Chianti name (see CHIANTI CLASSICO).

The legally oenological Chianti extends over 15,500 ha/38,285 acres and includes eight subzones that can appear on wine labels: Colli Fiorentini, CHIANTI RUFINA, Montalbano, Colli Senesi, Colline Pisane, Colli Aretini, Montespertoli, and Terre di Vinci; other parts of this extended region may produce wine labelled simply Chianti. There are quality-oriented producers outside the Chianti Classico heartland, but much of the wine that qualifies for the basic Chianti appellation lacks distinction.

Production regulations for Chianti and its seven subzones have always been less strict than for Chianti Classico. SANGIOVESE, the main variety in the wines, may represent as little as 70% of the blend compared with the minimum 80% for Chianti Classico, and white wine grapes may comprise up to 10% of the blend, except in Chianti Colli Senesi. (In 2022 proposals to lower the minimum of Sangiovese to 60% of the blend had been sent to Rome for approval.) Maximum permitted YIELDS at 9 ton/ha (8 for Colli Senesi) are higher than Chianti Classico's 7.5 ton/ha, while the minimum alcohol of 10.5% (11% for Colli Arentini, Colli Fiorentini, Colline Pisane, Montalbano, and Montespertoli; 11.5% for Colli Senesi; 12% for Riserva) indicates a tolerance for less ripe fruit compared with Chianti Classico's 11.5% minimum.

Large volumes of Chianti are bought by bottlers furnishing large retailers at the lowest possible price, a practice which has done little to incentivize investments and increase overall quality. In what is widely considered a concession to the Chinese market especially, in 2019 the CONSORZIO increased the allowed RESIDUAL SUGAR from 4 to 9 g/l. The very irregular quality of wine labelled simply Chianti has always had a detrimental effect on Chianti Classico's reputation, especially when the latter shifted its focus from quantity to quality from 1984 onwards when all of Chianti was elevated to DOCG status. Chianti has applied to use the GRAN SELEZIONE category, a further slap in the face of Chianti Classico, which originally created it to set its top wines apart from Chianti proper. As Gran Selezione is part of Italy's legal framework, Chianti Classico seems powerless to claim the category exclusively for its own use. W.S.

Nesto, B., and Di Savino, F., *Chianti Classico: The Search for Tuscany's Noblest Wine* (2016).

www.consorziovinochianti.it

Chianti Classico, the heartland of the CHIANTI zone, was given its fundamental geographical DELIMITATION by the Medici Grand Duke Cosimo III in an edict of 1716, one of the first examples of such legislation, and was defined as the townships of Radda, Gaiole, and Castellina in addition to the township of Greve (including Panzano).

In 1924 the 'Consortium for the defence of Chianti wine and its symbol of origin' was founded to fight the cheap imitations seeking to take advantage of the growing international demand for Chianti Classico. At the request of the CONSORZIO in 1932 a government committee, known as the Commissione Dalmasso, was sent to the region to demarcate the original, CLASSICO zone; much to the frustration of the Consorzio, the commission enlarged the zone with six additional subzones. The new enlarged region was what is now more or less Chianti proper, defended by the commission on the basis of presumed common oenological practices rather than suitability or historical evidence. To integrate such a large and diverse area, the production regulations set up by the Dalmasso commission were decidedly flexible, with regulations requiring only 50–80% Sangiovese, the region's most important red variety, while allowing the inclusion of the white Malvasia and Trebbiano, believed to have been traditionally interplanted with red varieties in the area's vineyards.

Little is known of the precise varietal composition of the wines before the 19th century, although the work of Cosimo Villifranchi (1773) suggests that the wine was a blend dominated by CANAIOLO with smaller amounts of Sangiovese, MAMMOLO, and MARZEMINO. Modern Chianti can be said to have been invented by Baron Bettino RICASOLI, who, in a letter in 1872, synthesized decades of experimentation and recommended that the wine be based on Sangiovese ('for bouquet and vigour') with the addition of Canaiolo to soften the wine. Malvasia was suggested as appropriate for wines to be drunk young, although its use was discouraged for wines intended for AGEING.

By the 1960s the old sharecropping system was officially abolished, leading to an exodus of workers looking for paid work in the growing industrial cities in the north. Mixed agricultural estates were transformed into a monoculture, without much attention paid to VINEYARD SITE SELECTION for the many newly planted vineyards. The government promoted high-yielding CLONES of Sangiovese as well as the white Trebbiano, believing that a focus on quantity rather than quality would help to improve the economic state of the region. The DOC regulations of 1967, guided by the 'Ricasoli formula', therefore required 10–30% of the white grapes Trebbiano and Malvasia. Because of the resulting low quality and the fact that 100% Sangiovese wines were now outlawed, several quality-oriented producers decided to opt out of the DOC system and produce instead, often using new winemaking techniques such as BARREL MATURATION, wines labelled VINO DA TAVOLA which gained swift recognition (see SUPERTUSCANS). This presented the Consorzio with an embarrassing and absurd situation.

From the beginning of the 1980s the Consorzio finally understood that, for Chianti Classico's quality—and price—to increase, it needed to focus on improving the output from its vineyards. By then most vineyards, planted in the 1960s and exhausted from excessive yields, had to be replanted. The Consorzio launched Chianti Classico 2000, an in-depth study into clones, ELEVATIONS, and soil compositions, the results of which were freely divulged to the producers. At the same time, many investors from outside the region arrived, attracted by the low land prices. Many of these incomers had little prior knowledge of winegrowing and relied heavily on consultant OENOLOGISTS. Overall wine quality improved considerably. INTERNATIONAL VARIETIES were often added to make the wines more appealing to international palates.

At last, in 1996, Chianti Classico became autonomous, was granted its own DOCG, and was therefore no longer a subzone of Chianti. The suffix Classico was to be restricted to the original 7,000-ha/17,500-acre zone, with stricter regulations such as lower yields and a minimum 80% Sangiovese. Most Chianti Classicos made today are 100% Sangiovese, or Sangiovese with local varieties, as the focus has shifted away from international varieties and BARRIQUE ageing.

Despite many a marketing campaign aimed at distancing itself from generic Chianti, the Consorzio of Chianti Classico has still to make the difference clear to the general public. The region is already subdivided into nine communes (Greve in Chianti, San Casciano in Val di Pesa, Tavarnelle Val di Pesa, Barberino Val d'Elsa, Castellina in Chianti, Poggibonsi, Radda in Chianti, Gaiole in Chianti, and Castelnuovo Berardenga), but the Consorzio refused to condone subzone naming on labels. Instead, in 2014 the Consorzio added GRAN SELEZIONE to the top of the denomination pyramid, which consists of Chianti Classico as its base and Chianti Classico RISERVA (with a mandatory 24 months of ageing) above it. While relentlessly promoted by the Consorzio, to its frustration Chianti has also requested the use of the category, which, as it is part of Italy's legal framework, cannot be claimed exclusively by Chianti Classico.

However, in 2021 the Consorzio finally announced the introduction of UGAS (*unità geografiche aggiuntive*), naming 11 communes or subzones allowed to appear on labels as a suffix to Chianti Classico. The communes are: Castellina, Castelnuovo Berardenga, Gaiole, Greve, Lamole, Montefioralle, Panzano, Radda, San Casciano, San Donato in Poggio, and Vagliali. However, going against the grain, the Consorzio still sees Gran Selezione as the ultimate relevance and restricts UGAs to communal wines only. W.S.

Nesto, B., and Di Savino, F., *Chianti Classico: The Search for Tuscany's Noblest Wine* (2016).
Masnaghetti, A., and De Cristofaro, P., *Chianti Classico: The Atlas of the Vineyards and UGAs* (2022).
Consorzio Vino Chianti Classico, *Progetto di Ricerca e Sperimentazione. Chianti Classico 2000* (1996).
www.chianticlassico.com

Chianti Rufina, north-eastern and smallest of the seven subzones that form CHIANTI. Rufina was first identified as an area of superior production in Cosimo III de' Medici's grand-ducal edict of 1716, which names the zone Pomino, a village within Rufina, after the famous estate of the Albizi family. Pomino, now owned substantially by FRESCOBALDI, has its own DOC for blends of INTERNATIONAL VARIETIES, but the delimited zone of the DOC of 1967 followed to a substantial extent the territory first delimited by Cosimo III, with an extension to the west of the confluence of the Sieve and Arno rivers.

The vineyard soils of Rufina are similar to those of CHIANTI CLASSICO, consisting of GALESTRO, ALBERESE, and LIMESTONE at ELEVATIONS of 200–700 m/655–2,300 ft. It is said that these higher elevations are responsible for the wines' trademark acidity and longevity, but relatively few modern Rufina wines demonstrate these qualities. Only a fraction of the region's growers bottle wine; most sell their grapes to NÉGOCIANTS or bottlers, who often sell the result as Chianti rather than Chianti Rufina since it entails less bureaucracy.

All this obscures the fact that the best of Rufina can truly be outstanding (as evidenced by the wines of Selvapiana), if producers eschew high yields and the inclusion of 30% of international varieties (and up to 10% white varieties) in what is a historic Sangiovese-based wine. Rufina's potential at least equals that of Chianti Classico, but the region has been slow to emulate the latter's continued efforts to improve overall quality. Realizing this, in 2018 the Rufina Consorzio presented research that identified the best vineyards of 19 producers. Beginning with the 2017 harvest, these vineyards can appear on labels of wines made from 100% Sangiovese from these plots after ageing 36 months, 24 of which must be in large oak casks. W.S.

www.chiantirufina.com

Chiavennasca, synonym for the noble NEBBIOLO vine and grape in VALTELLINA.

Chidiriotiko, dark-skinned grape variety planted on the Greek island of Lesbos.

Chignin, CRU near Chambéry whose name can be added to the eastern French appellation SAVOIE. Most Chignin is a scented dry white made from the local JACQUÈRE grape variety, although the name may be used for VARIETAL reds, too. Chignin-Bergeron is technically a separate CRU with a slightly smaller geographic area, based on rich, dry white wines from ROUSSANNE, Bergeron being a local name for the grape. W.L.

Chile. With a particularly varied climate and topography, this long, narrow South American country on the Pacific Ocean was long associated with reliable, inexpensive wines, but the current generation of winemakers has proved that it can produce more than bargains. The Spanish may have introduced viticulture, but since the 19th century France has had the greatest influence on the Chilean wine industry, primarily with Bordeaux varieties such as Cabernet Sauvignon, Merlot, and CARMENÈRE. However, in Chile's climate and soils, each of them has achieved a local identity very different from that of Bordeaux. In addition to these varieties, the 21st century has also seen the rediscovery of varieties such as PAÍS (aka Listán Prieto), CARIGNAN, and CINSAUT which have contributed to the diversity of Chilean wine today.

Chile has been one of the world's most energetic wine exporters since the 1990s. In 2021, vineyards covered 210,000 ha/518,921 acres, and total wine production was about 13.4 million hl/354 million gal, nearly 70% of which was destined for export.

History

The VITIS VINIFERA vine, and deliberate cultivation of it for wine, was brought to the Americas by the Spanish (see SOUTH AMERICA, history). Cortés imported vine cuttings, or more probably seeds, directly from Spain to Mexico where the first successful American vintage was produced, but it is not clear whether the vines first cultivated in the mid 16th century at Cuzco in PERU, the progenitors of the Chilean wine industry, came from Mexico or directly from Europe. It is generally agreed, however, that Spanish settlers brought the vine to Chile some time in the 1550s, the vine probably arriving in the Central Valley with Juan Jufre and Diego Garcia de Cáceres in 1554. This was partly so that the early Spanish settlers could celebrate the EUCHARIST with its produce. Specific grape varieties mentioned by the Jesuit priest Alonso Ovalle include Moscatel, Torontel, Albilho, Mollar, and 'the common black grape' (presumably related to PAÍS).

Some early vineyards were ransacked by native peoples, notably in the far south of the country, but the capital Santiago has been associated with continuous wine production for more than four centuries. In the 17th century, Spain attempted to protect its export trade of wine to South America by banning new plantings of vineyards there, but with little success. Indeed, in 1678 the Chilean governor recommended not only that the ban be lifted but also

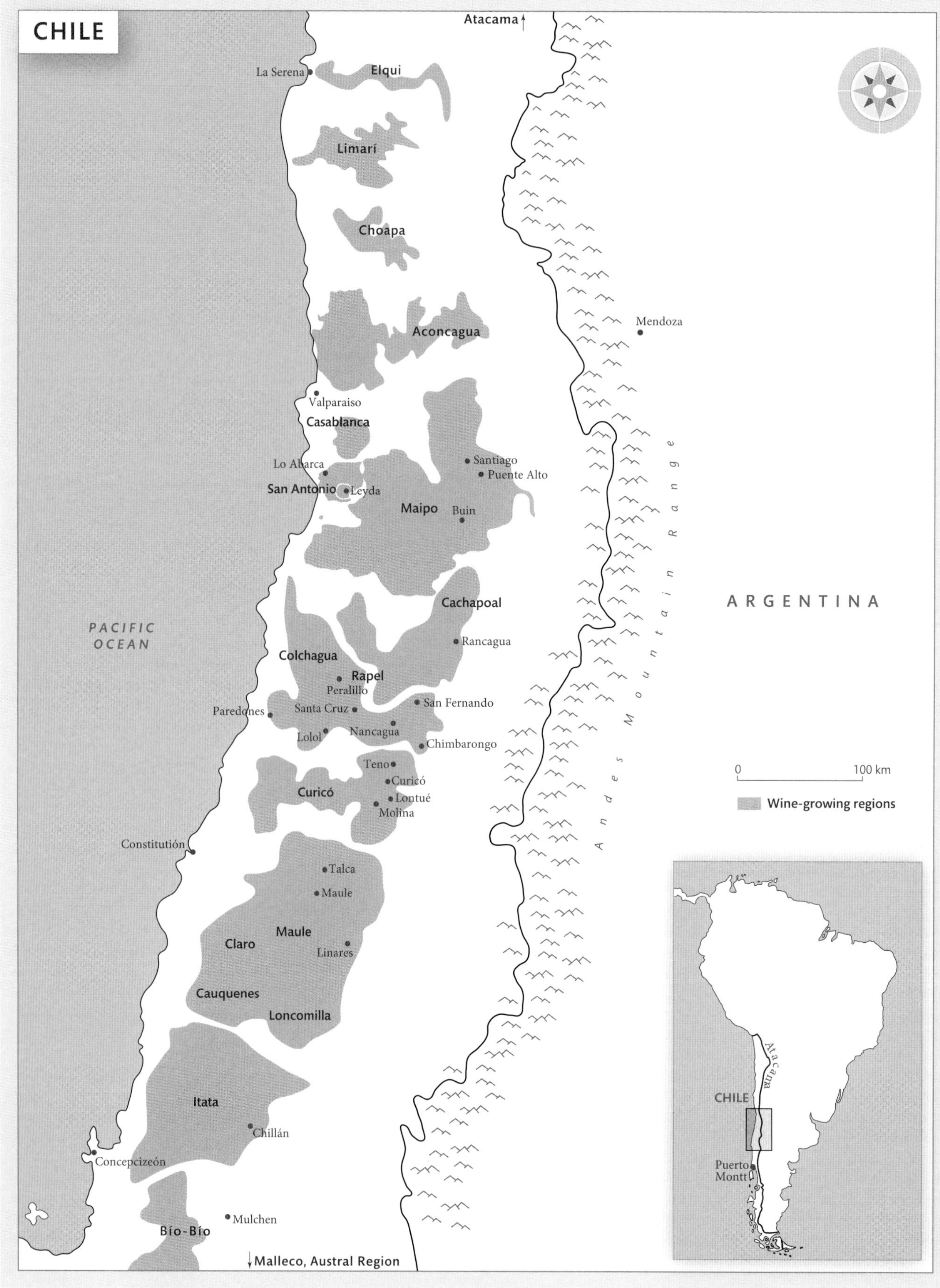
CHILE
Atacama
La Serena
Elqui
Limarí
Choapa
Aconcagua
Mendoza
Valparaiso
Casablanca
Lo Abarca
San Antonio
Leyda
Santiago
Puente Alto
Maipo
Buin
Andes Mountain Range
Cachapoal
Rancagua
ARGENTINA
PACIFIC OCEAN
Colchagua
Rapel
Peralillo
Paredones
Santa Cruz
San Fernando
Lolol
Nancagua
Chimbarongo
Teno
Curicó
Curicó
Lontué
Molina
0 100 km
Wine-growing regions
Constitución
Talca
Maule
Maule
Claro
Linares
Cauquenes
Loncomilla
Itata
Chillán
Concepcizeón
Mulchen
Bío-Bío
Malleco, Austral Region
Atacama
CHILE
Puerto Montt

that vineyards should be actively encouraged. In the 18th century, Chile was known for the quantity and affordability of its wines, much to the dismay of some Spanish wine producers.

At that time, and into the early 19th century, the wines were fairly primitive by modern standards, commonly sweetened with boiled, concentrated MUST, for example. It was Chile's great good fortune that an energetic Frenchman, Claudio Gay, persuaded the Chilean government to set up the Quinta Normal, an experimental nursery for all manner of exotic botanical specimens, including European vines, as early as 1830. This meant that Chile had its own collection of *vinifera* cuttings safely banked in viticultural isolation before the onset of the world's late 19th century vineyard scourges of POWDERY MILDEW and PHYLLOXERA, although it was private enterprise which, as so often, provided the spur to the nation's wine industry.

Now independent of Spanish domination, wealthy Chileans began to travel and experience a wider world, which included the fine wines of Europe. One of these was Silvestre Ochagavía Echazarreta, who in 1851 imported a range of vine varieties. These cuttings were to form the basis of Chile's modern wine industry. A class of gentlemen farmers was emerging in Chile, some of whom had made their fortunes as a result of Chile's rich mineral deposits. Owning a vine-growing country estate on the fertile land outside Santiago, preferably run by one of the many French refugees from phylloxera, was a sign of success in 19th-century Chile.

It was not long before Chile could boast the world's only healthy wine industry, both viticulturally and financially, run effectively by ten rich families (several of them of Basque origin) and their descendants. The industry, still (as today) substantially in private hands, was so profitable, and per capita wine consumption so high, that it was increasingly energetically taxed and constricted as the 20th century wore on. Restrictions on both planting vineyards and alcohol consumption placed a brake on the industry; by the early 1980s, wine prices had plummeted and about half of Chile's vineyards had been pulled up. It was not until the return of free trade and democracy in the 1980s that the industry began to recover. Between 1987 and 1993, more than 10,000 ha/25,000 acres of vineyard were planted with INTERNATIONAL VARIETIES, significant investments were made in winemaking technology, and the focus of the wine industry switched from quantity for the domestic market to quality for export markets.

Today, Chile's wine-related activity continues to be concentrated among just four companies—CONCHA Y TORO, Santa Rita, Santa Carolina, and San Pedro—which account for approximately 80% of the country's total production. Yet, over the last two decades, investors from other fields of commerce have more recently entered the fray via the likes of Ventisquero, Matetic, and Casas del Bosque. Foreign investment has also come from California (KENDALL-JACKSON, MONDAVI), France (Chx MOUTON ROTHSCHILD, Lafite-ROTHSCHILD, and others), and Spain (FAMILIA TORRES). In addition, a number of smaller, independent producers have emerged, some banding together to form producers' groups such as MOVI (Movimiento de Viñateros Independientes) and Chanchos Deslenguados. Some of Chile's most diverse and exciting wines today come from members of these organizations.

Geography and climate

Chile extends nearly 4,300 km/2,670 miles north to south. It is also very narrow (at its narrowest it is barely 95 km/59 miles wide). Squeezed between the Pacific Ocean and the Andes (80% of Chile is mountainous), land suitable for viticulture is limited, although quite varied. Of the 136,288 ha/336,774 acres planted in 2018, nearly 74% was dedicated to red wine grapes.

Although Chile's vineyards stretch from latitude 23 to 46° S, the great majority of Chilean wine is produced in latitudes 32–38° S. A northern hemisphere counterpart to these latitudes would be North Africa and southern Spain, but in Chile temperatures are considerably mitigated by the influence of the Pacific and its cold Humboldt current.

Until the 1980s, Chile's finest wines (primarily Cabernet Sauvignon) came from sectors close to the Andean foothills in the Maipo Valley, while the simple, keenly priced VARIETAL wines for which Chile was best known abroad were grown on the fertile, well-irrigated lands of the Central Valley. This 1,000-km-long plateau nestles between two mountain ranges: a relatively low coastal range, with peaks reaching 300–800 m/1,000–2,600 ft; and the Andes, which can reach elevations of 6,000 m here. The valley is dissected by many rivers which carry torrents of melted snow from the Andes to the Pacific during the growing season: IRRIGATION made easy.

Although there are distinct variations between individual regions and subregions (see below), the climate in the Central Valley is generally MEDITERRANEAN, with warm, dry summers and annual rainfall averaging 300–800 mm/12–31 in restricted to the winter, thanks to the effect of the Pacific high-pressure area. Rainfall in the Central Valley tends to increase both in the south and east, on the slopes of the Andes. On the valley's western edge, summer temperatures average 15–18 °C/59–64 °F and may rise to 30 °C/86 °F, with clear skies, strong sunlight, and relatively low humidity of just 55–60%. On the valley's eastern edge, however, because of cold air drainage from the Andes at night, there is a much wider DIURNAL TEMPERATURE RANGE, contributing to particularly good levels of ACIDITY and COLOUR in grapes.

Since the early 1980s, more attention has been paid to developing viticulture in cooler wine zones such as Casablanca Valley, established in 1982. The San Antonio and Limarí Valley regions, developed in the latter half of the 1990s, are the most obvious examples of more daring viticulture in less reliable climates. Projects that bear particular mention include the Flaño family's Viñedos de Alcohuaz winery, at 2,000 m/6,652 ft ELEVATION in the Elqui Valley, and Casa Marín, trailblazers in Lo Abarca, just 4 km/2.5 miles from the cold Pacific Ocean in the San Antonio Valley.

Southern regions such as Bío-Bío and Malleco are also being developed for serious wine production. In carefully selected sites in places such as Mulchén and Traiguén, vines can yield good white wines and some exciting reds, especially Pinot Noir, although FROST and excessive rain may prejudice quality south of Temuco. Meanwhile traditional and historic zones such as Itata have been rediscovered by wineries from the central zone such as De Martino and Miguel Torres, who are crafting wines from the region's old Cinsault, País, and Moscatel de Alejandría vines.

Regions and soils

Traditionally, Chile's wine regions were divided from north to south following administrative and provincial divisions rather than according to likely TERROIR effects. This system is slowly being modified. A first step was the 2013 geographical divisions of the wine valleys into Andes, Entre Cordilleras (between mountain ranges), and Costa (coastal). This transversal division from east to west aims to reflect the impact of the effects of the Andes as well as the Pacific—both cooling influences—in contrast to the valleys, where the climate tends to be warmer. Dozens of exceptions are already evident, but this general division is at least a first step towards recognizing the influence of Chile's mountainous topography and the Pacific Ocean on the character of its wines.

From north to south the main wine regions, with their most significant subregions, are as follows (see map):

Coquimbo: Elqui, Limarí, Choapa
Aconcagua: Aconcagua, Casablanca, San Antonio (including Leyda)
Central Valley: Maipo, Rapel (including Cachapoal, Colchagua), Curicó (including Teno, Lontué), Maule (including Claro, Loncomilla, Tutuven and its subregion Cauquenes)
Southern region: Itata, Bío-Bío, Malleco
Austral region: Cautin, Osorno

In general, Chile's vineyards are planted on flat, fertile land where water is readily available either naturally or through irrigation, so that vine

C

root systems are relatively shallow. ALLUVIAL soils predominate in Aconcagua and are also present to the south in Maipo, although here there are LOAMS and occasionally CLAY soils too. In both the Maipo region and the Cachapoal district of northern Rapel, there are mixtures of loam, clay, and SAND, some of which may be subject to SOIL EROSION on slopes. Soils are similar in southern Rapel and Maule, while VOLCANIC soils extend from south of Curicó to the Bío-Bío region, interrupted only by sand and sandy loam around Linares. Some parts of Cachapoal, Colchagua, and the Southern region suffer from relatively poor drainage, can be quite swampy, and may need no irrigation.

Coquimbo Coquimbo, 500 km/311 miles north of the capital Santiago, primarily comprises the Limarí and Elqui Valleys (as well as the little-developed Choapa Valley) and was historically focused on TABLE GRAPES and Chile's own CONTROLLED APPELLATION grape spirit pisco, to which nearly 9,172 ha/22,664 acres of vineyards were dedicated in 2018. Another 3,147 ha/7,776 acres of vineyards are dedicated to wine production, mostly in Limarí and Elqui. There is intense SUNLIGHT throughout the year and less than 100 mm/4 in of annual rainfall. Although some fine wines have emerged, water shortages are threatening the region's survival, a factor that historically dissuaded vine growers from planting here. It wasn't until the mid 1990s that Viña Francisco de Aguirre started to produce exciting table wines in the Limarí Valley, 20 km from the Pacific coast where Viña Tabalí had been established by the early 2000s. The cooling ocean influence plays an important part in delaying ripening in both Limarí and Elqui, which, in combination with rocky soils of clay and LIMESTONE, yields some of the region's best wines.

Aconcagua Named after the river which bisects it, Aconcagua is made up of three distinct zones. The interior of Aconcagua is one of Chile's hottest, driest wine regions, with summer temperatures often above 30 °C/86 °F. Soils are mainly alluvial, and the region produces some good red wines. To the west is the intermediate region, a much gentler climate cooled by coastal breezes. This is home to the Aconcagua vineyards responsible for such Chilean classics as Don Maximiano from Viña Errázuriz and Seña, grown closer to the coast. A third area is on the hillsides of the coastal range in Manzanar, strongly influenced by cold breezes off the Pacific Ocean. With clay and stony soils and gently rolling hills, this new area is part of the westward expansion taking place in several Chilean valleys and already producing exceptional Chardonnay and Pinot Noir.

Casablanca and San Antonio Although both zones are coastal and, politically speaking, belong to the Aconcagua Valley, Casablanca and San Antonio—the two largest sources of cold-climate whites in Chile—are different in various aspects. Casablanca's vineyards are cooled to Winkler Region I (see CLIMATE CLASSIFICATION) by cool morning fogs, the result of the Pacific's icy Humboldt current (which has a similar effect thousands of miles up the coast in California). Frequent cloud cover slows ripening and reduces the average number of clear days per year to 180, as opposed to 240–300 in the interior. Spring FROSTS are a real hazard, but specialist grape-growers and most of the big companies have planted varieties such as Sauvignon Blanc, Chardonnay, and Pinot Noir extensively since the region's beginnings in the early 1980s. As the region runs from east to west, temperatures rise with distance from the ocean, and there can be more than a month's difference in harvest dates between eastern Casablanca (also known as Upper or Alto Casablanca) and the western zone (Lower or Bajo Casablanca). Soils vary enormously, although they generally tend to be sandy in Alto Casablanca and become increasingly GRANITIC with a higher clay content with proximity to the coast.

Planting began in San Antonio in the late 1990s. Climate, soils, and topography are quite similar to Bajo Casablanca. The landscape typically features rolling hills, clay, and granitic soils; like nearly all of Chile's coastline, it is cooled by coastal breezes. San Antonio Valley and its most planted area, Leyda, runs north–south, parallel to the coast, with an average direct distance from vineyard to ocean of 15 km/9 miles. Sauvignon Blanc is the valley's flagship variety, and promising Pinot Noir, Chardonnay, and sparkling wine is also made.

Maipo The most famous wine region in Chile, surrounding the capital Santiago, is not one of the largest. In 2018, some 11,584 ha/28,624 acres of vines were recorded, with a clear predominance of red over white grapes. Cabernet Sauvignon and Chardonnay were the most widely planted, although Merlot, Carmenère, and Sauvignon Blanc are also important. Annual rainfall averages just 300 mm/12 in, most of it falling in the winter. IRRIGATION is common, although the water can be quite saline around the Maipo river from which the region takes its name. Maipo is famous for producing Chile's most lauded Cabernet Sauvignon, especially towards the foot of the Andes Mountains, in areas such as Macul, Pirque, and Puente Alto.

Rapel About 150 km south of Santiago, Rapel had more than 45,142,000 ha/111,548 acres of vineyards in 2018 and is divided into two subzones: Cachapoal to the north and Colchagua to the south. Both are transversal valleys running from the Andes to the Pacific Ocean, which results in pronounced differences in the wines depending on their proximity to the cooling influence of the Andes (Alto Cachapoal and Alto Colchagua). Some of Chile's finest red wines come from the Andean foothills here, especially in individual zones such as Apalta, where French-owned winery Casa Lapostolle and Viña Montes have helped develop the region's reputation for fine Merlot, Carmenère, and Syrah. Cabernet Sauvignon, Carmenère, and Merlot are the most planted grape varieties, and the region has become especially known for full-flavoured red wines. Wineries such as Santa Emiliana, Santa Rita, Undurraga, and Viña Montes all made considerable vineyard investments in Colchagua in the 1990s. The latest trend in Rapel, specifically in Colchagua, has been to take maximum advantage of its transversal characteristics by exploiting coastal zones such as Lolol and especially Paredones (just 15 km/9.3 miles from the Pacific), which produces Pinot Noir and Sauvignon Blanc to rival those of Casablanca and San Antonio.

Curicó Formed by the subregions Lontué and Teno, Curicó Valley was put on the international map when Miguel Torres (see FAMILIA TORRES) arrived there in 1979. By 2018, the valley had 19,653 ha/485,563 acres planted. Curicó has two MESOCLIMATES. Towards the east, around Molina and north of the Claro river, the climate is cooled by Andean breezes. To the west, the coastal range minimizes the ocean influence, and the climate is warmer, sometimes notably hot and dry. Even though the valley does not have any particular speciality, the wide range of varieties planted are generally good quality.

Maule The largest wine region in Chile's Central Valley, Maule covers some 34,155 ha/84,398 acres according to official records (although there are some doubts about the efficiency of filing vineyard statistics in this region of smallholders). In its wide territory, the climate can vary from very warm in the central plains to cloudy and cool towards the coast. The PAÍS vine variety used to dominate plantings, especially in the rain-fed areas, and it has been the traditional raw material for the historic *pipeño*, a peasant wine designed to quench thirst. A new generation of producers has rescued this variety, using it to craft wines of great freshness and juiciness, often labelled Secano Interior. Maule also has more CARIGNAN planted than any other valley, and the variety is now undergoing a revival among Chilean producers. The grapes from old vines in DRY-FARMED coastal zones provide the raw material for members of VIGNO (Vignadores del Carignan/Carignan Vintners), an association that aims to promote this long-forgotten variety, planted on the smooth granite slopes of the valley, in old *secano* (unirrigated) vineyards. Maule also has more than half of Chile's 800 ha/1,976 acres of SÉMILLON, once the most widely planted variety in the country (before Sauvignon Blanc and Chardonnay arrived in the late 1980s) and today undergoing a lively revitalization thanks to wineries such as J. Bouchon, Roberto Henríquez, and Carmen.

Southern region Southern Chile had 12,837 ha/31,720 acres of vines in 2018, split evenly between red and white grapes. Formed by Itata, Bío-Bío, and the newer Malleco subregion, this region is more open than Maipo and Rapel, lacking the protection of a high coastal range, so rainfall is higher and average temperature and sunshine hours are lower. By far the most common vine variety is PAÍS, planted on a total of 4,130 ha/10,205 acres and now the object of a strong revival led by small producers such as French winemaker Louis-Antoine Luyt as well as large wineries such as Concha y Toro. With more than 842 ha/2,080 acres planted, CINSAUT is the region's rising star, especially in the DRY-FARMED zones of Itata, where it produces both simple, thirst-quenching wines as well as complex reds offering a sense of place. The most widely planted white-wine grape is Moscatel de Alejandría (MUSCAT OF ALEXANDRIA), with 3,962 ha/9,790 acres. Little by little, it is being taken more seriously by wineries such as De Martino who vinify it carefully with fine results. However, research in the early 1990s in the Chillán area suggested that, with drip irrigation and appropriate training systems such as the LYRE, good-quality wine from the best-known INTERNATIONAL VARIETIES could be made here. The proof of that lies in the Mulchén and Negrete areas where wineries such as Cono Sur produce crisp Riesling and ripe Pinot Noir. And Malleco, a region 650 km/403 miles south of the capital first planted during the mid 1990s by Felipe de Solminiach, partner in Viña Aquitania, is now home to a small but solid community of producers. Chardonnay and Pinot Noir excel in its cool clay and granite soils.

Austral Region Located about 925 km/574 miles south of Santiago, this is Chile's southernmost wine region. Formed by the valleys of Osorno and Cautín, it is cool and rainy, with only 28 ha/68 acres of vines planted in its VOLCANIC soils, but wineries from the north such as Casa Silva and Miguel Torres, together with smaller projects such as Coteaux de Trumao and Trapi del Bueno, are finding success with varieties such as Chardonnay, Sauvignon Blanc, and Pinot Noir.

Viticulture

IRRIGATION is essential in nearly all Chilean vineyards and, as in Argentina, is made possible by the melting snows of the Andes, diverted along a series of canals and channels as well as through the use of deep wells that exploit groundwater. DRIP IRRIGATION was introduced only in the early 1990s. As a result of this ready and plentiful water supply, most vineyards have good access to water during the growing season. On the slopes of the coastal range in the west of southern regions, rainfall is often sufficient, as it is in most of the Southern region. FERTILIZERS are widely employed, but their use is regulated to avoid an excess of VIGOUR. Drip irrigation allows FERTIGATION in some of the more viticulturally developed areas.

Average YIELDS in Chile are about 70 hl/ha (4 tons/acre). Over-irrigated, high-yielding vines can experience difficulties in RIPENING. This is particularly true of varieties which ripen relatively late, such as Cabernet Sauvignon and Chile's speciality CARMENÈRE, or of high TRAINING SYSTEMS. There is a predictably rich cultural diversity of training and trellis systems in Chile. Some vines, particularly those dedicated to TABLE GRAPES, are trained in variations on the TENDONE system in the high, arbour-like *parrón* trellis which encourages shade (like the *parral* of ARGENTINA). The standard Spanish practice of growing unstaked vines as free-standing BUSH VINES has been common since the Spanish conquest but is today usually restricted to País, Carignan, and Moscatel vines, notably from Maule Valley to the south. The Bordeaux post-PHYLLOXERA immigrants introduced row trellising to Chile at the end of the 19th century, and this has evolved in two distinct ways. Low, narrow rows of vines that are traditional in Europe tend to be double GUYOT pruned or SPUR PRUNED cordons, depending on variety, and used mainly to produce better-quality wines. More common for basic wine production are more widely spaced vines (sometimes with cross-pieces, described as Californian), which permit the increasingly common phenomenon of vineyard MECHANIZATION. In the 1990s, most new plantings were in long narrow rows 2–2.5 m/6.5–8 ft apart, with vines planted 1.2–1.5 m apart. Australian CANOPY MANAGEMENT techniques were introduced in some vineyards in the early 1990s.

HARVEST of wine grapes begins at the end of February for such early-maturing varieties as Chardonnay, continues through to the end of April for Cabernet Sauvignon, and can last well into May for Carmenère.

No Chilean vine-growers feel they need to study ROOTSTOCKS, since the country is free of phylloxera and the consequent need for grafting. Some FIELD GRAFTING has been undertaken, however, in the rush to increase the proportion of fashionable grape varieties planted. And such is the prevalence of NEMATODES in Chilean vineyards, because of *vinifera*'s low resistance to them relative to American vine species, that some authorities suggest using American rootstocks to combat this problem. Chile's vines are by no means free of VIRUS DISEASES: POWDERY MILDEW and BOTRYTIS BUNCH ROT are annual and potentially extremely costly vine diseases, with VERTICILLIUM WILT another serious vine health hazard. DOWNY MILDEW infections occurred in some areas for the first time during the heavily EL NIÑO-influenced 1997–8 growing season. The absence of summer rains means that SPRAYING is generally much less frequent than in many other wine regions, however. ORGANIC VITICULTURE has been becoming more prevalent.

Vine varieties

VINE IDENTIFICATION arrived relatively late in Chile. Conscious of its unique status as a wine-producing country yet unravaged by phylloxera, Chile imposes a particularly strict QUARANTINE on imported plant material, which has helped to maintain certain aspects of its viticultural isolation. The quality and identity of the vines grown was the most dramatic example of this. Most vines called Sauvignon by the Chileans, for example, were almost certainly Sauvignon Vert, SAUVIGNONASSE (or Friulano), and occasionally Sauvignon Gris, rather than the more familiar Sauvignon Blanc. Only a small but increasing proportion of Sauvignon Blanc, almost exclusively based on CLONES developed in California, had been planted by the early 1990s, and even by the mid 2000s official statistics claiming 7,400 ha/18,300 acres of Sauvignon Blanc and just 200 ha of Sauvignon Vert probably did not reflect the true proportions of these two varieties. Thanks to the new plantations and more fastidious differentiation between Sauvignons Blanc and Vert, official statistics for 2018 suggest there are 15,222 ha/37,614 acres of Sauvignon Blanc versus 448 ha/1,107 acres of Sauvignon Vert.

Similarly, vines called Merlot are usually in fact a mixture, and sometimes a FIELD BLEND, of Merlot and the old Bordeaux variety CARMENÈRE, first identified as such in Chile in 1994. The vine identification required to distinguish Merlot from Carmenère is continuing, and since the mid 1990s the word 'Carmenère' has increasingly appeared on wine labels both as a varietal wine and, perhaps more suitably, an ingredient in a blend.

Until the 1990s, the most commonly planted grape variety was the dark-skinned PAÍS, identical to the CRIOLLA CHICA of Argentina and the MISSION of California, a direct descendant of Listán Prieto cuttings imported by the Spanish colonists. Although the variety is currently undergoing a revival, plantings have been declining since the 1980s, when there were some 30,000 ha planted; by 2018 there were just 10,319 ha/25,498 acres, the great majority planted in the southern Maule and Bío-Bío regions.

Today Cabernet Sauvignon is the most important variety in Chile by quite a margin, with

40,204 ha/99,346 acres planted, followed by Sauvignon Blanc, Merlot, and Chardonnay. MUSCAT OF ALEXANDRIA counts just over 4,368 ha, about half the total planted in the mid 2000s. The early years of this century saw a dramatic increase in plantings of Syrah, which totalled 7,528 by 2018, and Pinot Noir with a total of 4,045 ha (60% as much as is planted on the CÔTE D'OR).

Such new plant material as is allowed in has come mainly from DAVIS, as well as from European nurseries. The idea of clonal material, absent in the Chilean viticultural scene until the early 1990s, is now common when it comes to new vineyard plantations.

Winemaking

Chile has undergone possibly the most dramatic technological revolution in the wine world. Wineries were for decades underfunded as the domestic market could be satisfied with often oxidized white wines and faded reds made with the most traditional of equipment. All wines were made from grapes trucked, often in very high temperatures with scant regard for OXIDATION, to wineries equipped with little in the way of TEMPERATURE CONTROL; they were made exclusively in vats made either of CONCRETE or the coarse local *raulí* (evergreen beech) WOOD, usually coopered many decades previously. In the late 1980s, however, the wine industry made a commitment to the long-term future of Chile as a wine exporter and began to invest in the equipment necessary for that goal. Outside investors assisted the influx of both equipment and expertise, and since then the wineries of Chile were invaded, at a pace usually determined by the enterprise's size and cash flow, by pneumatic PRESSES, OAK BARRELS, STAINLESS STEEL, and modern filters. Today one is likely to find a fair share of ceramic eggs, terracotta AMPHORAE, and other earthenware vessels in addition to concrete and steel tanks, a nod to current trends in low-intervention winemaking.

J.R. & P.T.

Goldstein, E., *Wines of South America* (2014).
Tapia, P., *Descorchados, The South American Wine Guide* (annual).
www.winesofchile.org

China, vast Asian country with its own indigenous vine species (see VITIS) but a relatively short modern tradition of growing VITIS VINIFERA grapes to make wine. In recent decades, China's development as a wine-producing nation has evolved alongside the country's rapid modernization, holding the world's third largest vineyard area (after SPAIN and FRANCE), albeit mostly planted to TABLE GRAPES. As consumption growth has slowed in recent years, the domestic industry has become increasingly focused on quality production in a bid to target a minority of more engaged consumers.

Ancient history

Various grape species have long been grown in China, including *Vitis amurensis* (see below). Geological fossils show that *Vitis romanetii Roman du Caill. ex Planch.* existed in Linqu county, Shandong province, 26 million years ago, while the earliest chemically attested instance to date of grapes being used in a fermented beverage was during the seventh millennium BCE at the Neolithic site of Jiahu, Henan. The earliest written record of grapes in China is in the poem *Qi Yue* in the *Odes of Bin* from the *Classic of Poetry* (*Shijing*), dating back to the Shang Dynasty (*c.*1600 BCE–*c.*1000 BCE):

> In the sixth month partake of plums and grapes; in the seventh, cook vegetables and pulses; in the eighth, knock the jujube harvest down; in the tenth, reap rice and ferment the wine for spring, for the benefit of the elders.

The introduction of *vinifera* to China can be dated to the 4th century BCE. In *On Ancient Central Asian Tracks: Brief Narrative of Three Expeditions in Innermost Asia and Northwestern China*, Marc Aurel Stein describes the tidy plots of vineyard sites outside the courtyards of houses in the ancient city of Niya (1st–3rd century CE), 150 km/93 miles north of the modern Minfeng county, in the Shan Shan prefecture of Xinjiang. A 1959 archaeological investigation of Niya excavated relics from an ancient tomb (carbon-14 dated to 2,295±75 years old) decorated with patterns of grape bunches as well as dried grapes in containers. It appears, therefore, that there was viticulture here dating back to the 3rd to 1st centuries BCE. Archaeological expeditions in southern TURKMENISTAN and UZBEKISTAN, which unearthed grapes as well as text descriptions and decorations of grapes from a 4th-century BCE residential site, also suggest that *vinifera* may well have been introduced to China from Central Asia along the Silk Road.

Two notable old varieties of *vinifera*, both TABLE GRAPES, are the dark-skinned Dragon's Eye (*Longyan*) and pale Mare's Teat (*Manai*), the former long grown along the path of the Great Wall and, for even longer, also in far western China. Their import to and successful cultivation within China demonstrates that viticulture prospered in many such western parts of the territory. Wine was also made from the native grapes of the *Vitis thunbergii* species, found naturally in the provinces of Shandong and Jiangxi, from the *Vitis heyneana* of Guangxi province, *Vitis davidii* of Jiangxi and Hunan provinces, and *Vitis amurensis* from north-eastern China (Liaoning province).

References to grape-derived alcohol in ancient sources are rare and often found as an 'exotic' beverage, as can be seen from this Tang Dynasty (618-907 CE) poem set in the western Chinese borderlands:

> Wonderous wine in the moon-glowing cup,
> I desire to drink, but am urged onwards by the *pipa*
>
> Please do not mock me for battle-field drunkenness, for up to now how many have returned safely from war?

This poem, unlike many, clearly states that the wine is produced from grapes. Indeed, a challenge in understanding the history of (grape) wine is that Chinese does not distinguish between alcohols from different sources: the relevant character 'jiu' literally means alcohol in any form, so it is difficult to distinguish wine from beer or spirits. In fact, most references to 'wine' in literature and the arts refer to grain-based alcohol, either distilled (*baijiu*) or an oxidized rice wine (*huangjiu*). Thus, it is hard to clearly state which classical references refer to wine from grapes and which to alcoholic drinks in general.

See also ORIGINS OF VINICULTURE and PALAEOETHNOBOTANY.

McGovern, P. E., 'Fermented beverages of pre- and proto-historic China', *Proceedings of the National Academy of Sciences USA*, 101/51 (2004), 17593–8.

Modern history

China is usually considered a NEW WORLD country mainly because its modern wine industry traces its roots to as recently as the late 19th century. At this time, the development of the modern Chinese wine industry began to emerge under the influence of foreign settlements, particularly Catholic missionaries. In 1892, Zhang Bishi, a native of Guangdong, who had been stationed in southern Asian countries in service of the Qing government, returned to China and established the CHANGYU winery in Yantai, the longest continually existent winery in China to date. Zhang introduced over 100 *vinifera* varieties from Europe and apparently employed the then Austrian consul as his winemaker. Shang Yi winery was set up by French Catholics in 1910 in the suburbs of Beijing mainly to supply wine for Mass, becoming known as the Beijing Winery. Other early wineries include Yi Hua winery (in Shanxi) established by Chinese nationals in 1921, and the Chang Bai Shan and Tung Hua (Tonghua) wineries in Jilin, set up and managed by the Japanese during the Japanese Occupation.

In 1949, the wineries were expanded by the new Communist government and, for reasons of economy, resulted in the blending of grape wine with other juices, water, colouring agents, and fermented cereals. The industry remained highly unsophisticated until after 1978 when China opened again to the outside world.

After 1979 foreign investment was encouraged, and the following year Cognac giant Rémy Martin set up the first JOINT VENTURE winery—the Sino-French Joint Venture Winery (Dynasty)—with the Tianjin Agriculture Bureau.

◀ Tiansai Skyline of the Gobi, a grape oasis in the desert at the foot of the Tianshan Mountains in Xinjiang's Yanqi Basin in north-west CHINA, was established in 2010. Thanks to IRRIGATION from mountain snowmelt, they have pioneered varieties such as MARSELAN and MALBEC and are highly regarded for their CHARDONNAY. © NYSH Productions

C

Xinjiang's first Western-style winery, Lou Lan, was established by the state in the 1970s (although is now in private hands). In 1988, the state-owned enterprise China National Cereals, Oils, Foodstuffs Import & Export Corporation (COFCO) started making Great Wall–branded wines in Hebei. Both Dynasty and Great Wall applied modern winemaking techniques to produce simple, medium-dry white table wines from the local Dragon's Eye, MUSCAT OF HAMBURG, and other local table grapes. China's first 'château-style' wine estate to plant and produce VARIETAL and vintage-dated wines, Huadong, was started by Englishman Michael Parry just outside Qingdao in 1985 and bore the appellation Tsingtao. In 1987 Pernod Ricard set up the Dragon Seal winery on Beijing's outskirts. All such ventures relied on imported vinification equipment, European vine cuttings, and foreign OENOLOGISTS, with other Chinese wineries following their lead.

Beginning in the mid-to-late 1990s, the Chinese government, motivated by HEALTH concerns and concern for grain supplies, encouraged the development of fruit-based alcohol rather than traditional grain-based drinks, while wine consumers switched from favouring white to red wine. *Baijiu* (white spirits) producers began to make or bottle wines. Between 1996 and 2004, more than 100 new wineries, state-owned and private, were established. Even high-ELEVATION Yunnan turned to wine production with the Shangrila Wine Company planting vineyards in the late 1990s.

In recent years, regions have exploded with projects, with some of the largest, such as the CITIC Guoan group (Niya brand, previously Vini Suntime), setting up in Xinjiang and Ningxia. At the same time, smaller Chinese family-owned wineries have been emerging from behind the behemoths to take their place on the world stage: these include Silver Heights in Ningxia (2007), Tiansai Skyline of the Gobi in Xinjiang (2010), and Longting in Shandong (2013).

In addition, foreign companies have continued to establish JOINT VENTURE projects including Pernod Ricard's Helan Mountain, LVMH's Domaine Chandon (Ningxia) and Ao Yun (Yunnan), and DBR Lafite's Domaine de Long Dai (Shandong), bringing further international expertise to China's vineyards and wineries.

Geography and climate

The vast majority of the ~783,000 ha/1,934,835 acres of Chinese vineyards (2021) are planted with TABLE GRAPES and RAISINS. Most viticultural areas are in a band at latitude 33–40° N across the north of the country stretching from the largest area in Xinjiang (over 20% of vineyard area) to Ningxia, Gansu, Shanxi, Hebei, and Shandong. The extreme north (Liaoning province) is devoted to ICE WINE production, and the most southerly vineyards are in high-elevation Yunnan.

Overall, China's climate is not highly amenable to wine production: winters can be extremely arid and cold, while in the summer and autumn the monsoon rains bring high humidity resulting in FUNGAL DISEASES and ROT. This ripening period-specific humidity affects nearly all of China's vineyard areas, though effects are greatly reduced in the desert-like conditions of China's far west (Xinjiang).

European styles of VINE TRAINING can be seen only where WINTER PROTECTION is unnecessary for vines. Historically, the most important of these areas was Shandong (19,500 ha/48,185 acres in 2021) protected from winter extremes by its MARITIME CLIMATE, although this can also bring heavy rainfall and disease pressure during ripening. In the far south in Yunnan province, the Shangri-la area—close to Tibet and shared between Yunnan and Sichuan provinces—has a long, frost-free season in its steep valleys located at elevations of 1,600–2,900 m/5,249–9,514 ft. above the Mekong river. At such low latitudes (27–28 °N), the high elevation moderates temperatures and valley winds reduce fungal disease pressure.

For all other areas, vines require winter protection due not only to extremely low temperatures but also to the desiccating winds that sweep across northern China. In the far west, Xinjiang has the lowest natural rainfall (around 80 mm/3 in); but irrigation water is available through the Tianshan snow-capped mountains and Bositeng Lake. This huge province is generally divided into northern and southern areas, with varying elevations of over 1,000 m to the sub-sea-level area of Turpan (155 m/500 ft below). The naturally dry environment, high summer temperatures, along with plentiful sunshine and flat plains (mainly sandy LOAM over GRANITE) mean that vines are relatively disease-free and require only minimal SPRAYING. Much of the wine produced in its 33,500 ha/82,780 acres (2021) is sold in BULK.

To the east of Xinjiang lie Ningxia and Gansu, with similar monsoon-influenced CONTINENTAL CLIMATES featuring very arid winters and hot, potentially moist, summers with relatively limited rainfall (290 mm/11 in). Both have high sunshine hours and are cooler than Xinjiang but have similarly short growing seasons with winter burial needing to be completed by mid November.

Ningxia, particularly the subregion of Donglu, Helan Mountain, has been massively developed in recent years with the support of local government. There are around 34,000 ha/84,015 acres of vineyard with plans to expand to 66,000 ha/163,089 acres by 2025, all irrigated by the Yellow River, located on plains of gravelly and sandy soils (the region lies directly east of the Tengri desert). Gansu is much smaller: accounting for just 2,000 ha/4,942 acres (2021) of vineyard area for wine with a shorter frost-free period relative to Ningxia.

Moving towards the east, Shanxi (2,500 ha/6,177 acres) and Hebei (7,000 ha) experience less severe winters, requiring less extreme winter protection but encountering greater disease pressure from more marked monsoonal influence. Finally, in Liaoning (700 ha/1,729 acres) to the far north, winter protection is essential against the frigid temperatures, and cold-hardy cultivars are preferred.

Grape varieties

The modern era of selecting and breeding table and wine grapes (see VINE BREEDING) started in China in the 1950s, with one key aim being to breed red wine varieties with cold resistance. The highly cold-resistant Mongolian species VITIS AMURENSIS has been widely used in crossings with *vinifera* to create varieties which can survive below −20 °C/−4 °F. For example, the cold-resistant Beichun, Beihong, and Beimei varieties were bred in Beijing in 1954 by crossing MUSCAT OF HAMBURG with *amurensis*. Other crosses were also created by organizations such as the Shandong Grape Experiment Station and the Zhengzhou Fruit Research Institute, including: Meichun, Meiyu, Meinong, Hongzhilu (all Merlot × Petit Verdot crosses), Quanbai (Riesling × Petit Verdot), Quanyu (Riesling × Muscat of Hamburg), as well as Yan 73, and Yan 74 (Alicante Bouchet × Muscat of Hamburg), which are found in limited qualities to this day.

However, most commercially cultivated wine grapes today are standard INTERNATIONAL VARIETIES. The original stocks from the wineries established at the turn of the 20th century continued to be cultivated, including Cabernet Gernischt, confirmed by DNA PROFILING to be CARMENÈRE. During the 1950s and 1960s, Soviet bloc consultants brought in varieties such as RKATSITELI and SAPERAVI, which are mainly found in Xinjiang. Since the late 1970s, many cuttings have been brought in from the US and Europe, but lack of quality control and expertise resulted in widespread problems with FANLEAF DEGENERATION and other viruses. China's first vine NURSERY was established in the north of the Shandong Peninsula in the early 2000s as a joint venture between COFCO and the French nursery Arrive and was rapidly followed by others. However, the selection of varieties was relatively narrow until the 2000s when both government agencies such as the Ningxia Grape Development Bureau and private wineries began to import a wider range including AGLIANICO, TEMPRANILLO, MALBEC, and MARSELAN.

Black varieties account for over 80% of wine grape plantings. With Cabernet Sauvignon at 60,000 ha/148,263 acres, the next three main varieties, Merlot, Carmenère and CABERNET

FRANC, account for only 18,000 ha/44,478 acres in total. Other black varieties include SYRAH, PINOT NOIR, SAPERAVI, PETIT VERDOT, CARIGNAN, and a small percentage of the above-mentioned Chinese varieties with a growing area of Marselan, favoured due to its disease resistance, high YIELD, and plentiful PHENOLICS. Malbec is also expressing great potential in Xinjiang, where conditions are comparable to ARGENTINA. Of white varieties, CHARDONNAY and Riesling (principally WELSCHRIESLING but also some true RIESLING) account for 6,000 ha/14,826 acres, with PETIT MANSENG, also notable for high disease resistance, emerging as a Shandong potential star.

Viticulture

Traditionally grapes were supplied on contract, grown on intensively subdivided lands with farmers making final decisions, thus accounting for the high proportion of table grapes, which are less risky and achieve higher prices due to the demand and respect for quality fruit in the domestic market. The traditional viticultural practices of fan trellis systems (see TRAINING SYSTEMS), dense foliage, high YIELDS, heavy IRRIGATION, peanut/bean inter-row plantings, and early picking to avoid disease (combined with grape prices being determined by weight) all hindered quality grape production. Thus, in the modern era, wineries are actively negotiating land leases to be able to manage their vineyards directly. However, the rural workforce is increasingly ageing as young Chinese move to cities, making LABOUR shortages and costs an issue in some regions. Vineyard development is also hindered by the limited lease-span (30 years) given on agricultural land (in China all land is owned by the state), making long-term investment a challenge.

WINTER PROTECTION is essential in most regions and accounts for about one-third of viticultural costs (providing increased pressure for mechanization throughout China). It is achieved mainly through earth-burial as GEOTEXTILES are hard to anchor in the high winds and do not combat desiccation well. Vines are also generally unearthed very late in the season (even after BUDBREAK in some cases) due to the dangers of desiccation from dry spring winds. As the vine ages, burial also becomes more problematic as trunks need to be bent down to assist burial, which can result in damage. Plant material is divided between ungrafted and GRAFTED because winter burial of young vines can also result in graft damage. Thus, many newly established vineyards still plant ungrafted materials, as PHYLLOXERA is not widespread. Winter protection also means that Chinese vineyards have unique TRAINING SYSTEMS to facilitate this practice, with all the traditional fan systems lacking a unified fruit zone (resulting in uneven ripeness). Modern vineyards have established *changzi* training (slanting trunk with renewed CORDON) to overcome this problem.

IRRIGATION is widespread, traditionally done by flooding but now with most areas converted to drip for conservation and SUSTAINABILITY. Most disease pressure is related to the monsoonal rain influence and dense canopies. ANTHRACNOSE, POWDERY MILDEW, DOWNY MILDEW, DEAD ARM, and WHITE ROT are commonplace. Some wineries are attempting ORGANIC VITICULTURE but the majority rely on modern FUNGICIDES. Harvest and spraying dates are also difficult to manage under the traditional farmer-co-operation model, giving another reason for wineries to move to the CHÂTEAU model.

Winemaking and wine styles

Despite the popularity of the medium-dry white styles of the 1980s and 1990s, since 2000 China has wholeheartedly embraced dry red, Bordelais winemaking, due in part to perception of the health benefits and to the influence of Bordeaux as the then main choice of overseas training for Chinese oenologists. Heavy extraction and use of excessive new oak, along with a lack of knowledge of international styles, resulted in many clumsy wines in the early 2000s. Owing to high levels of warmth and sunlight, high alcohol levels also present a challenge and can co-exist with unripe tannins and greenness (due to traditional fan training systems and lack of harvest timing control). But breakthrough success emerged when Helanqingxue Winery's Jiabeilan 2009 Grand Reserve achieved a Decanter Trophy in 2011, spurring many into a quality direction. The investment of multinationals such as LVMH (Chandon and Ao Yun) and Pernod Ricard has also added more international expertise; and recent years have seen Chinese students returning from overseas (US, Australia, Germany) bringing greater experience of global styles, resulting in the emergence of sparkling wines, medium-dry rosés, lighter reds, and more focus on whites. NATURAL WINES have also begun to appear with some experimenting with fermentation in traditional Chinese ceramic pots.

In 2021, China's wine industry received arguably its greatest boost when the government promulgated plans to triple the current vineyard area in Ningxia by 2035 and to increase wine production value to more than US$30 billion (more than seven times its current size). However, perhaps the greatest challenges for Chinese wine production lie in convincing domestic consumers, who have become increasingly enamoured of imported wines, to return to Chinese wine while courting international consumers to experiment with this new country of origin. E.R. & F.W.

Chinon, the largest red-wine appellation of the LOIRE by volume located around the royal city of CHINON in the TOURAINE district in which a small amount of rosé and in-demand dry white CHENIN BLANC are also produced. CABERNET FRANC, locally called Breton, is the main grape variety, and if CABERNET SAUVIGNON is allowed up to 10%, its presence is anecdotal while Chenin plantings are on the rise. Chinon's vineyards stretch south of the Loire on both banks of the Vienne over 2,400 ha/5,900 acres after expanding its western boundaries from Candes-St-Martin to Seuilly just east of SAUMUR-CHAMPIGNY in 2016 (Chinon had fallen to a few hundred hectares in the 1950s). Yet the majority of the wines are made on the right bank with Cravant-les-Coteaux as the main producing commune. Protected by forests to the east and west and by small hills called *puys*, Chinon enjoys one of the warmest climates of Touraine, and its wines tend to be more concentrated than those of its neighbours. Two main styles of wines are made from three distinct soil types. Lighter reds, close in style to St-Nicolas-de-Bourgueil, come from the *varennes*, a local name for the ALLUVIAL terraces of the Loire and the Vienne, with elegant examples produced in Panzoult. The more structured, barrel-aged CABERNET FRANC wines are made on the steep yellow and white TUFFEAU slopes (like in BOURGUEIL) and the sandy LIMESTONE plateaus covered with FLINTY clay (knowns as *perruches*), with Beaumont-en-Véron, Chinon, and Cravant as lauded areas. Single vineyards already praised by the region's most famous son, the early 16th century writer Rabelais, appear frequently on wine labels. Once considered little more than light refreshment, Chinon wines have become more satisfying with improved viticulture to reach ideal maturity. The top wines of growers such as Baudry or Philippe Alliet can be cellared a decade or more, and, although a good proportion of wine ends up in merchants' blends of variable quality, an ambitious generation is taking root in the area. See LOIRE, including map. P. Le.

chip budding, a popular method for the BUDDING of vines, with a long history. It is known as the yema bud in Europe and California. During the first growing season of the ROOTSTOCK, a piece is cut from its original wood and a matching chip piece with a bud is cut from a SCION cutting. The chip is inserted in the stock with CAMBIUM zones matching, then wrapped tightly with budding tape (see illustration). Chip budding, which may take place at any time of year, may also be used for TOP GRAFTING.

See also FIELD GRAFTING. B.G.C.

Chiroubles, highest ELEVATION of the BEAUJOLAIS crus, producing wines that can be refreshing but also rustic. The soils continue the mix of sandy and denser GRANITE in neighbouring FLEURIE and MORGON but wines can be strident or tart when young. Total vineyard area is a modest 301 ha/743 acres. J.F.B.

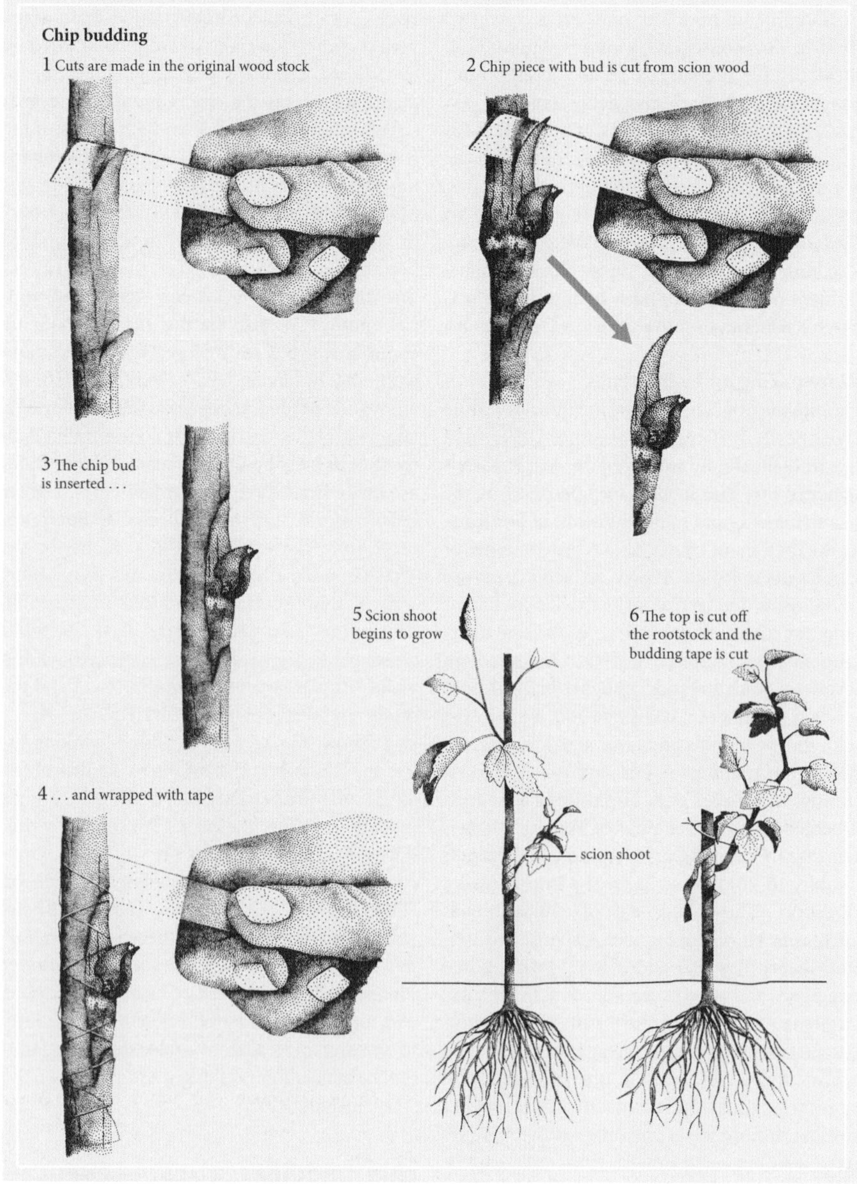

chitosan, a natural POLYSACCHARIDE derived from **chitins**, the principal components of the cell walls of fungi and plants and found in the skeletons of insects and the shells of crustaceans. While chitosan's mode of action is not fully understood, it is promoted as a versatile PROCESSING AID, especially for its antimicrobial properties, for example in relation to BRETT, LACTIC ACID BACTERIA, and ACETOBACTER. Only chitosan derived from the fungus *Aspergillus niger* has been authorized by the OIV and the EU for use in winemaking. It has also been found to be effective as an antioxidant, as an adjunct in CLARIFICATION, and to remove COPPER from wine. In the vineyard, trials suggest spraying vines with chitosan may increase PHENOLIC compounds in grapes.

Castro Marín, A., et al., 'Relevance and perspectives of the use of chitosan in winemaking: a review', *Critical Reviews in Food Science and Nutrition*, 61/20 (2021), 3450–64.

Chitry, commune near AUXERRE whose name may be appended to that of BOURGOGNE.

chloroanisoles. See HALOANISOLES.

chlorosis, vine disorder in which parts or all of the foliage turn yellow due to lack of chlorophyll. The most common and extreme chlorosis is that which is visible in spring and early summer and is caused by IRON deficiency, which is common in CALCAREOUS soils. Lime-induced chlorosis became a problem in parts of France as an indirect consequence of the PHYLLOXERA invasion at the end of the 19th century, since AMERICAN VINE SPECIES sourced initially in the eastern US and used as phylloxera-resistant ROOTSTOCKS were more prone to iron deficiency than were the original VITIS VINIFERA root systems. This problem, known in French as *chlorose calcaire*, has been largely overcome now by the selection of lime-tolerant rootstocks suitable for calcareous soils, such as 41 B or the newer Fercal. In Burgundy and Champagne, where soils tend to be high in limestone, it has been difficult to find rootstocks with sufficient lime tolerance for healthy vine growth. This sensitivity of early post-phylloxera rootstocks to lime-induced chlorosis may provide part of the explanation for an apparent drop in quality in post-phylloxera wines, according to some historical authorities.

Chlorosis is a common symptom of deficiencies of other nutrients such as NITROGEN, SULFUR, and MAGNESIUM. It can also be caused by some VINE DISEASES. The effect may be general, as for FANLEAF DEGENERATION virus, or more localized, as in, for example, the so-called oil spot on leaves due to DOWNY MILDEW infection. R.E.S.

Chorey-lès-Beaune, village near (*lès* in old French) BEAUNE in Burgundy producing red wines from Pinot Noir grapes. Chorey lies in the plain below the main D974 road, as do most of the appellation's vineyards. There are no vineyards of PREMIER CRU status, and much of the wine is sold as Côte de Beaune-Villages. The best-known producer based here is Domaine Tollot-Beaut. A good Chorey is similar to a village SAVIGNY-LÈS-BEAUNE or a lesser ALOXE-CORTON. A tiny quantity of white Chorey-lès-Beaune is made from Chardonnay.

See also CÔTE D'OR and map under BURGUNDY. J.T.C.M.

Christianity and wine. See EUCHARIST, RELIGION, BIBLE, MONKS AND MONASTERIES, and MISSIONARIES.

Cienna, NEW VARIETY bred in Australia from the Spanish SUMOLL and CABERNET SAUVIGNON and released, with its sister variety Tyrian, in 2000. Both varieties have good sugar-to-acid ratios, low PH, good colour and flavour, and adequate yields. Cienna is very tannic.

Cigales, DOP in northern Spain, north of Valladolid in CASTILLA Y LEÓN (see map under SPAIN), higher and cooler than TORO, with impressive average VINE AGE. This DOP has traditionally produced dry rosé wines made from Tinto del Pais (TEMPRANILLO) and some GARNACHA grapes, but an increasing number of dry reds show real potential. Since 2011, regulations allow the production of white wines based on VERDEJO, as well as sparkling and sweet wines. F.C.

Ciliegiolo, widely dispersed Italian red grape variety of Tuscan origin named after its supposed cherry-like flavour and colour. It has been declining in extent, although it can make some excellent VARIETAL wines, particularly Sassotondo's Maremma examples, and can be a usefully soft blending partner for SANGIOVESE, particularly in CHIANTI. DNA PROFILING revealed that Ciliegiolo is a progeny of Sangiovese and Muscat Rouge de Madeère (or Moscato Violetto). Plantings totalled 897 ha/2,216 acres in 2015.

cincturing, viticultural practice that involves removing, with a knife or special tool, a ring (3–8 mm/0.1–0.3 in wide) of conducting tissue (PHLOEM) around a TRUNK, CANE, or SHOOT, normally to improve FRUIT SET. Also called girdling or ringing in English and *incision annulaire* in French, the technique is more widely used for TABLE GRAPES than for wine production, which can rarely justify the necessary LABOUR cost. Cincturing stops both the upwards and downwards flow of nutrients and plant hormones, until the wound heals over. R.E.S.

cineole. See EUCALYPTUS CHARACTER.

Cinsaut, sometimes written **Cinsault**, is a red grape variety known for centuries in the Languedoc region of southern France that has much in common with GRENACHE. Although it has good drought resistance and its best wines by far come from vines that yield less than 40 hl/ha (2.3 tons/acre), it can all too easily be persuaded to yield generously and unremarkably. The wines it produces tend to be light, soft, and, in extreme youth, aromatic and charmingly cherry-fruited. Although prone to ROT, it is particularly well adapted for rosé production and is widely planted throughout southern France, especially in the Hérault and Var *départements* in the Languedoc and Provence respectively. It differs from Grenache by virtue of its long history, its shorter growing season, and its easier adaptation to MECHANICAL HARVESTING.

There was a threefold increase in French plantings in the 1970s, when Cinsaut was officially sanctioned as an 'improving' grape variety with which to replace ARAMON and ALICANTE BOUSCHET, mainly in the Aude and Hérault *départements*. Since then, the economic realities of quality's supremacy over quantity have slowed Cinsaut's fortunes, and Languedoc producers have been much more likely to plant a variety with as much character and cachet as Syrah, Merlot, Mourvèdre, or Cabernet Sauvignon. Cinsaut is used almost exclusively to add suppleness, perfume, and immediate fruit to blends (typically compensating for the ubiquitous but curmudgeonly CARIGNAN), although all-Cinsaut rosés are increasingly common.

It is an approved but hardly venerated ingredient in the CHÂTEAUNEUF-DU-PAPE cocktail and is often found further east in Provence, as well as on CORSICA, where it is mostly blended, with only 247 ha/610 acres remaining in 2019.

Total French plantings of Cinsaut fell throughout the 1980s to less than 50,000 ha/123,500 acres (still more vineyard than Cabernet Sauvignon) and by 2019 were only 19,885 ha/49,137 acres. The variety was most important in the 1950s and early 1960s when ALGERIA, then constitutionally part of France, was an important wine producer and depended particularly heavily on its healthily productive 60,000 ha of Cinsaut. Since Algerian wine was then used primarily for blending in France, notoriously for adding body to less reputable burgundies, some of this North African Cinsaut may still be found in a few older bottles of 'burgundy'. It is still common in MOROCCO and has long played an important part in the wine industry of LEBANON, where it formed the backbone of the wine industry for 160 years and is now experiencing a resurgence in popularity.

Cinsaut has in its time played a major part in South as well as North Africa (which makes it all the stranger that South Africa has had little ROSÉ culture). Having been imported from southern France in the mid 19th century, it was South Africa's most important red-wine vine until the mid 1960s and was overtaken by Cabernet Sauvignon as the Cape's most planted red grape variety only in 1993. In 2020, it was South Africa's sixth most planted red wine grape with 1,701 ha/4,203 acres in total, its old vines increasingly treasured. Cinsaut was once known carelessly as Hermitage in South Africa (although there is no Cinsaut in the northern Rhône). Thus South Africa's own grape variety speciality, a cross of Pinot Noir with Cinsaut, was named PINOTAGE, now much more respected in South Africa than Cinsaut.

In both France and Australia (where its fortunes waned rapidly in the 1970s and 1980s), Cinsaut has occasionally been sold as a table grape under the name Oeillade even though it is not related to OEILLADE NOIRE. In southern Italy, it is known as Ottavianello and is planted around Brindisi, producing light, unremarkable red wines. Cinsaut can also be found in Türkiye.

Cirò, with Terre di Cosenza, currently the only DOC of any quantitative significance in the southern Italian region of CALABRIA.

citric acid, a common plant acid, abundant in some fleshy fruits such as lemons but rare in grapes. The grape is unusual among fruits in that its major acid is TARTARIC ACID (and MALIC ACID), rather than citric acid, whose concentration in the juice of most grape varieties is only about one-twentieth that of tartaric acid.

Citric acid is also one of the ACIDS used in winemaking for the purposes of ACIDIFICATION. It is inexpensive but unsubtle and is used almost exclusively for inexpensive wines. It is always added after rather than before fermentation, since it can be converted to ACETIC ACID by the yeast. It is produced commercially by fermenting SUCROSE solutions; very small amounts are recovered from processing citrus fruits. It is also used extensively after cleaning with caustic soda. In the EU it is not permitted for ACIDIFICATION, but it can be used to prevent CASSE if BLUE FINING is not possible. See also DIACETYL. B.G.C. & A.D.W.

CIVC. Thanks to the **Comité Interprofessionnel du Vin de Champagne**, CHAMPAGNE is one of the most thoroughly organized wine regions in the world. The CIVC was established in 1941 as a co-operative organization grouping champagne GROWERS, CO-OPERATIVES, shippers, and houses under its auspices. Growers/co-operatives on the one hand and merchants/champagne houses on the other each have a president to represent them. The CIVC is charged with organizing and controlling the production, distribution, and promotion of the wines of Champagne, as well as undertaking fundamental research for the region. Until 1990 it set a price for the grapes and still intervenes, as in pandemic-struck 2020 for instance, to regulate the size of the harvest and decide whether any of it should be 'blocked', or retained as juice rather than vinified and sold. The CIVC is financed by a levy on production and a tax on champagne sales.

The CIVC is also responsible for tenaciously defending the Champenois's exclusive right to use the word 'champagne'. A landmark victory was won in the English courts in 1960, and since then the name has achieved legal protection in most major markets, although not in the United States for established brands. The CIVC has fought a number of battles to ensure that the name Champagne is not used for other products, including a cigarette and a brand of perfume. N.F. & J.R.

Clairet, dark-pink wine style that is a speciality of the BORDEAUX region, recalling the sort of red wines that were shipped in such quantity in the Middle Ages from Bordeaux to ENGLAND and which originally inspired the English word CLARET. Dark-skinned grapes are fermented in contact with the skins for about 24 hours before fermentation of this lightly coloured wine continues to dryness. Bordeaux Clairet should be drunk as young as possible.

Clairette is a much-used name for southern French white grape varieties. **Clairette Ronde**, for example, is the Languedoc name for the ubiquitous UGNI BLANC, and various Clairettes serve as synonyms for the much finer BOURBOULENC.

True **Clairette Blanche**, however, is a very old Languedoc variety grown on a total of 2,254 ha/5,570 acres of French vineyard in 2019, being allowed into a wide range of southern Rhône, Provençal, and Languedoc appellations, even lending its name to three (see below). Clairette is a traditional variety well suited to poor, dry soils. Its small, thick-skinned grapes ripen relatively late but can ripen dangerously fast at the end of the growing season. In the southern Rhône, it is particularly popular for adding aroma and acidity to a blend, not least with the fatter GRENACHE BLANC. Clairette is widely distributed throughout the eastern Midi, especially in the Gard, where it produces CLAIRETTE DE BELLEGARDE, and in the Hérault for CLAIRETTE DU LANGUEDOC, two of the Languedoc's earliest CONTROLLED APPELLATIONS, presumably because these white wines were so unlike the typical produce of the Midi. Its other stronghold is the Drôme *département* since Clairette is the main ingredient in CLAIRETTE DE DIE and CRÉMANT DE DIE.

Partly because it was an ingredient in PICARDAN, the variety spread far and wide, including to southern RUSSIA, in the 19th and early 20th centuries. At one time there were sizeable plantings in Algeria. It is known as Clairette Blanche in South Africa, where it was once as widely planted as in France. Some old plantings can still be found.

Clairette de Bellegarde, very small AOC which can be used exclusively by the commune of Bellegarde that lies at the heart of the larger AOC COSTIÈRES DE NÎMES. The wines, which must be made of 100% CLAIRETTE Blanche, are soft, with low acidity, yet can have impressive longevity. In 2020, just 180 hl/4,755 gal were bottled under the appellation. M.C.W.

Clairette de Die, the most important appellation in the Diois region centred around the town of Die near the river Drôme, a tributary of the Rhône between Valence and Montélimar. According to PLINY, wine has been made here since Roman times. Die's gently fizzing wines may predate those of Champagne.

Two different sorts of sparkling Clairette de Die are made. **Clairette de Die Brut** is a dry sparkling white wine made from 100% CLAIRETTE by the transfer method (see SPARKLING WINEMAKING) and has an alcoholic strength of 11–12%. It makes up about 5% of production. The other 95% is **Clairette de Die Méthode Ancestrale**, a gently sparkling, grapey white wine made from at least 75% MUSCAT BLANC À PETITS GRAINS, the rest Clairette, by the *méthode dioise ancestrale*. It is bottled with at least 35 g/l RESIDUAL SUGAR (though 50–55 g/l is more common) and 7–9% alcohol.

The Diois also produces CRÉMANT de Die, a TRADITIONAL METHOD dry sparkling wine.

Three-quarters of the sparkling wines made under these sparkling Diois appellations are made by local CO-OPERATIVE Jaillance.

Local still wines may qualify as CHÂTILLON-EN-DIOIS. Whites may also qualify as Coteaux de DIE. M.C.W.

Clairette du Languedoc is a slightly more important appellation than CLAIRETTE DE BELLEGARDE, again exclusively from the CLAIRETTE grape. One of the named subappellations of the southern French LANGUEDOC AOC, it lies north-east of Pézenas. The appellation has suffered an extremely confused image as, despite its relatively small production (100 ha/247 acres in 2020), it is allowed a wide array of wine styles, from an ultra-modern, early-picked, yellowish-green, dry white wine for early drinking to a deep brown RANCIO, sweet VIN DE LIQUEUR. M.S.

Clare Riesling. See CROUCHEN.

claret, English (not American) term generally used to describe red wines from the BORDEAUX region, or red bordeaux. 'Claret' has also been used as a GENERIC term for a vaguely identified class of red table wines supposedly drier, and possibly higher in TANNINS, than those wines sold as generic burgundy (although, in the history of Australian wine SHOWS, it has been known for the same wine to win both claret and burgundy classes).

History

In medieval France, most red wine was the result of a short FERMENTATION, usually of no more than one or two days. The short period of contact with the grape skins meant that the resultant wines were pale in colour and were probably very similar to the rosés of today. Such wines exported from Bordeaux were known as *vinum clarum, vin clar*, or CLAIRET, and it is from the last of these that the English term 'claret' is derived. Other much darker wines were also made by pressing the remaining skins, effectively the same as modern PRESS WINE, and these were known as *vinum rubeum purum, bin vermelh*, or *pinpin*.

Although the term *clairet* was widely used during the medieval period in France, the word 'claret' does not appear to have been used at all extensively in England until the 16th century. In the second half of the 17th century, a new type of wine, of much higher quality and deeper colour, began to be produced in the GRAVES and on the sands and gravels of the MÉDOC to the north-west of Bordeaux. These wines, the provenance of specific properties, where close attention was paid to grape selection, improved methods of vinification, and the use of new oak BARRELS, became known by the beginning of the 18th century as New French Clarets, and the earliest and most famous of them were HAUT-BRION, LAFITE, LATOUR, and MARGAUX (see BORDEAUX, history). P.T.H.U.

Higounet, C. (ed.), L'Histoire de Bordeaux (1963) 8 vols.

Marquette, J., 'La Vinification dans les domaines de l'archevêque de Bordeaux à la fin du Moyen Âge', in A. Huetz de Lemps (ed.), *Géographie historique des vignobles*, i (1978).

Pijassou, R., *Un grand vignoble de qualité: le Médoc* (1980).

clarete is a historic Iberian term for a wine somewhere between a rosé and a light red. It is etymologically, though not oenologically, related to CLARET. In PORTUGAL a niche revival of the style has led to regulation: since 2017 *clarete* can be used only to label very light-coloured red wines made exclusively from red grapes with an ALCOHOLIC STRENGTH which is no more than 2.5% above the minimum legal requirement. In Spain, *clarete* remains a blend of white and red grapes and is seeing a renaissance in CIGALES and RIBERA DEL DUERO. S.A. & F.C.

claret jugs. See DECANTERS.

Clare Valley, wine region in SOUTH AUSTRALIA with a strongly CONTINENTAL CLIMATE and warm summer days and cool nights. This combined with differences in soil, ELEVATION, degree of slope, and ASPECT enables the region to produce some of Australia's finest Riesling as well as excellent Shiraz, Cabernet Sauvignon, and Malbec. While wines are sturdy and powerful, alcohol levels are generally lower than those of the Barossa Valley or McLaren Vale.

clarification is the progressive removal of solid particles of matter from MUST or wine and should not be confused with STABILIZATION. At the must stage, it involves the removal of particles of grape skins, stems, seeds, and pulp and is carried out only when making white or rosé wines. If they are not removed, there is a risk of OXIDATION and off-flavours in the finished wine. Red wines are not commonly clarified before fermentation because the skins are fermented with the juice (see RED WINEMAKING).

Clarification can usually be accomplished by simply holding the liquid in a storage tank until the larger particles settle (see SETTLING) and then pumping, or RACKING, the clear upper layer from the compact layer of solids at the bottom of the tank. The clarified must is then warmed to start the fermentation. Pectin-splitting ENZYMES are sometimes added to aid the settling of the solids.

Settling is too slow for a large winery, so recourse is made to mechanical methods such as CENTRIFUGATION, but a centrifuge is an expensive piece of equipment, using a large amount of electricity, and is therefore not suitable for smaller wineries. FLOTATION, another mechanical method of clarification, is cheaper and quicker and used by larger wineries but works really well only on must.

The degree of clarification of must is important because some of the solid particles act as nutrient for the yeasts during FERMENTATION due to the amino acids, minerals, and vitamins adsorbed on their surface. Too much clarification can result in a fermentation that is difficult to start. The style of the wine may also influence the degree of clarification. With Chardonnays, for example, it may be desirable to have a relatively high proportion of grape solids which produce various characters during fermentation. Winemakers may wish to eliminate most grape solids from the juice of more aromatic varieties in order to accentuate varietal fruit flavours.

After the completion of fermentation, another clarification takes place to rid the new wine of all colours of the products of fermentation, also known as the gross LEES. These are mainly the yeast cells, both dead and viable, plus cellular matter from the grape. When treating wine that has been fermented in barrels and then racked and returned to fresh barrels, the residual cloudy matter that gathers in the bottom of the barrels is known as the fine lees. This is highly valued by winemakers because it is the source of added complexity to the maturing wine.

Settling of the solids at this stage of the process is comparatively rapid because there is a greater difference in density between wine and its particulate matter than between sugar-laden must and grape solids. The wine can be racked off comparatively easily but will still be hazy, so further treatment will be needed. A large winery will probably use a centrifuge, but smaller establishments will use a series of FILTRATIONS.

Further treatment, known as STABILIZATION, is usually necessary. D.B.

Clarksburg, California wine region and AVA covering 37,630 ha/92,985 acres along the Sacramento–San Joaquin River Delta. The delta channels cool Pacific air that helps moderate the warm inland temperatures, allowing varieties such as CHENIN BLANC to thrive; other high-acid whites such as ALBARIÑO and VERMENTINO are being established there as well. Much of the AVA is composed of deep-soiled islands surrounded by marshlands and river tributaries, so most vineyards achieve sizeable yields. E.C.B.

classed growth is a vineyard, estate, or château included in a wine CLASSIFICATION. The term is used almost exclusively in BORDEAUX for those châteaux included in the 1855 classification of the Médoc and Sauternes, the 1955 classification of Graves, and sometimes for those properties included in the regularly revised St-Émilion classification. The term is a direct translation of the French 'CRU classé'.

Classic, official German wine designation introduced in 2000, though little used outside Germany, for dry-tasting wines (maximum 15 g/l RESIDUAL SUGAR) vinified from traditional grape varieties, harvested at at least 12% POTENTIAL ALCOHOL (11.5% in the Mosel). It is not to be confused with the term KLASSIK as used (principally) in AUSTRIA.

classical art, wine in. Wine was so deeply embedded in the culture of the classical world that it is inevitable that it would figure prominently in the art of that world. The vessels used for mixing and drinking wine (see CRATER, for example) were frequently decorated with scenes which played on the association with wine. Most notably, the fine Attic Black and Red Figure pottery of the 6th and 5th centuries BCE sometimes contains rural scenes of men harvesting grapes and treading them, as well as scenes from the *komos* (revels) and the SYMPOSIUM, in which the craters and cups are depicted in use. Sometimes it is possible to suspect an ironic commentary taking place. A famous Red Figure cup by the so-called Dokimasia painter has scenes of revelry around the outside with the awkward spaces under the handles filled by men crouched or crawling, the worse for drink, while inside the cup an old man is depicted being sick. Another playful irony is that nearly all these scenes can be found translated to another world, in which men are replaced by satyrs, uninhibited by the conventions of human society and presided over by the god DIONYSUS. Not surprisingly, Dionysus achieves a greater prominence in the art of the world of drinking than his place in the pantheon would suggest as his due. Feasting and banquets with wine also form the subject of some of the most memorable frescos from the tombs of the ETRUSCANS, where, for example, the Tomb of the Leopards at Tarquinia beautifully illustrates the funeral meal held near the tomb in honour of the dead.

Scenes of the vintage and the pressing of the grapes, with the role of humans frequently played by *amorini*, cupids, are found in great numbers at all periods throughout the Roman world, in paintings, sculptured reliefs, sarcophagi, decorated glass, and ivory plaques. Part of the explanation for the popularity of the themes, particularly on sarcophagi, is the obvious mystical symbolism of the vine and wine. Scenes of country life, including vines and the vintage, play a significant part in Roman painting from the 1st century BCE onwards and are most elaborately and impressively illustrated in mosaic. The vintage and tasks connected with viticulture, such as pruning and the cleaning and pitching of DOLIA, are often found in mosaics which illustrate the seasons or the tasks of the rural calendar. As a genre, these had a long history, which went back to the Hellenistic period in mosaic and may be connected with illustrated manuscript calendars. Fine examples in mosaic come from GAUL (St-Romain-en-Gal) and North Africa (the Maison des Mois at El Djem). From the 3rd century CE the elite of North Africa adorned their houses with mosaics which reflected the work of their estates. One of the most remarkable examples of realism in classical art must be the mosaic of the Labours of the Fields from Cherchel in Algeria, with men hoeing between TRELLISED vines.

The potential of the vine and wine as mystical symbols also explains why this was one of the themes of classical art which was most easily taken over by Christianity. A key monument is the church of Santa Costanza on the Via Nomentana in the north of Rome, a work of such rare beauty as to justify on its own a visit to that city. Santa Costanza was the mausoleum of Constantina, the daughter of Constantine, the first Christian emperor. Her huge porphyry sarcophagus has cherubs engaged in the vintage, a theme which is taken up by the remarkable mosaics which run round the ceiling of the ambulatory. The themes are traditional. Nothing is specifically Christian in these mosaics, but they are given a Christian connotation by the other, more overtly Christian, mosaics which would have adorned the dome. J.J.P.

Dunbabin, K. M. D., *The Mosaics of Roman North Africa* (1978).

Isler-Kerovi, C., *Dionysos in Archaic Greece: An Understanding Through Images* (2007).

Lissarrague, F., *The Aesthetics of the Greek Banquet: Images of Wine and Ritual* (1990).

classical texts. The vine and the olive are the plants that characterize Mediterranean civilization. To grow them is the sign of a settled, not a nomadic, existence. Their products can be used as part of the daily routine: olive oil for cooking and washing, wine for drinking, or to mark a special occasion in the life of a community, when people would anoint their heads with fragrant oil and drink the best wine. In wine-producing countries, wine can be an ordinary drink or a luxury item: classical literature reflects both.

This starts with HOMER (the end of the 8th century BCE) and HESIOD (*c.*700 BCE), the earliest Greek authors. Wine is mentioned frequently in the grander context. In Hesiod's *Works and Days*, the cultivation of the vine is part of the order of nature as laid down by the gods: the secular and the religious were not distinct spheres. HERODOTUS' *Histories* (5th century BCE) have many observations on wine and its uses among foreign nations. The Greeks had no books on agriculture, but THEOPHRASTUS (*c.*370–*c.*287 BCE) could be called the first systematic botanist. A very late Greek author, ATHENAEUS (*fl.* 200 CE), is a good source of information on the wines of his day.

Among the Romans, VIRGIL (70–19 BCE), HORACE (65–8 BCE), and MARTIAL (*c.*30–103/4 CE) are the poets who display a particular interest in wine: Virgil chiefly in the *Georgics*, Horace throughout his poems, and Martial in many of his epigrams on the mores of his time. PLINY the Elder (23/4–79 CE) devoted an entire book of his *Natural History* to all aspects of wine. Other prose writers wrote treatises on agriculture: CATO (234–149 BCE), VARRO (116–27 BCE), COLUMELLA (1st century CE), and the derivative PALLADIUS (4th century CE). H.M.W.

classical vine varieties. See ANCIENT VINE VARIETIES.

classical wines. See GREECE and ROME for general comments, as well as CAECUBAN, FALERNIAN, MASSIC, OPIMIAN, and SURRENTINE wines specifically.

classical world. See ancient GREECE and ancient ROME.

Classico, Italian term appended to the names of various DOC or DOCG wines to indicate that they have been produced in the historic zone, that which, at least in theory, offers the ideal conditions of soil and climate and gave the wine its name.

The name of the wine *without* the adjective Classico is usually applied to a significant expansion of the original production zone into areas which generally, but not always, cultivate the same grape varieties but in different, and usually less satisfactory, conditions, frequently with more lenient production requirements. The origins of this practice, which occurred well before the establishment of the DOC system in the 1960s and has often been driven by economic motives, lie in the regulation of the use of the name CHIANTI established by the Dalmasso Commission in the 1930s (see CHIANTI CLASSICO). This precedent was widely followed as the various DOCs came into being between 1963, when the law regulating the demarcation of Italy's wine regions was passed, and 1975; since then a number of Italy's historically important wines are now produced in both a Classico and a regular version. These include BARDOLINO, CALDARO, CHIANTI, CIRÒ, Garda, ORVIETO, SANTA MADDALENA, SOAVE, TERLANO, VALPOLICELLA, and VERDICCHIO.

The practice, not dissimilar to the creation of Germany's notorious GROSSLAGEN, reflects a permanent tension in Italy's DOC system. Often the most quality-conscious producers keen for promotion to DOCG status lobby for it to be restricted to the original Classico zone but find themselves opposed by big companies with holdings throughout the enlarged zone. However, in some cases, Classico zones themselves are seen to be underperforming.

classification of various wine estates and vineyards is in general a relatively recent phenomenon, dictated by the increasingly sophisticated wine market of the last 150 years or so. It has to a certain extent been superseded by the even more recent phenomenon of SCORING individual wines.

There were earlier instances of classifying individual vineyards, however. The vineyards of JURANÇON in south-west France were officially evaluated as early as the 14th century. Tax collectors in GATTINARA did the same in the 16th century. In 1644, the council of Würzburg in FRANKEN rigorously ranked the city's vineyards according to the quality of wine they produced (see GERMAN HISTORY). The first mention of a classification of TOKAJ vineyards dates from 1700, although the classes were not ratified until 1737 (and the vineyards probably not officially mapped until 1786 under Emperor Joseph II).

Bordeaux

BORDEAUX, with its plethora of fine, long-lasting wine from well-established estates and its well-organized market, is the wine region which has been most subject to classification of individual châteaux. The most famous wine classification in the world is that drawn up in 1855 of what became known as the CLASSED GROWTHS of the MÉDOC, and one GRAVES (see over). In response to a request from Napoleon III's 1855 Exposition Universelle in Paris (possibly so that dignitaries there should effectively know what to be impressed by), the Bordeaux BROKERS formalized their own and the market's ranking with a five-class classification of 60 of the leading Médoc châteaux plus the particularly famous and historic Graves, HAUT-BRION; and a two-class classification of SAUTERNES and BARSAC. This classification merely codified the market's view of relative quality as expressed by the prices fetched by individual estates' wines. (It also formalized previous informal lists of those wines widely regarded as the best by the likes of Thomas JEFFERSON, Wilhelm Franck, Alexander HENDERSON, and Cyrus REDDING.) The brokers issued the 1855 classification through the Bordeaux Chamber of Commerce and were careful to explain that it was based on a century's experience. Within each of their classes, from FIRST GROWTHS, or PREMIERS CRUS, down to fifth growths, or cinquièmes CRUS, the brokers listed châteaux in descending order of average price fetched. Thus, it is widely believed, LAFITE, the 'premier des premiers', headed the list because it commanded prices in excess even of LATOUR, MARGAUX, and Haut-Brion (although others have argued that the first growths were simply listed in alphabetical order). In the original classification, the term CHÂTEAU was rarely used.

The 1855 classification has endured remarkably well considering the many and various changes to the management and precise extent of individual properties since it was compiled, with only Chx MOUTON ROTHSCHILD and Léoville-BARTON in the same hands. Ch Dubignon-Talbot has not produced wine since the arrival of PHYLLOXERA in the late 19th century. Edmund PENNING-ROWSELL notes that Palmer's low ranking may have been influenced by the fact that the property was in receivership in 1855 and that Cantemerle, a property relatively new to the Bordeaux market, was added to the bottom of the list in a different hand. The only official revision of this much-discussed list took place in 1973, when, after much lobbying on the part of Baron Philippe de ROTHSCHILD, Ch Mouton-Rothschild made the all-important leap from top of the second growths to become a first growth (although see also SUPER SECOND). It could be argued that such a classification contains an element of self-preservation in that highly classified properties are thereby able to command prices which sustain the investment needed to maintain their status, although the history of Ch Margaux in the 1960s and 1970s demonstrates that other factors may affect this hypothesis, and in the 1980s and 1990s many Bordeaux proprietors, for example Ch Léoville Las Cases, were driven by competition and ambition to invest, and in some cases price, at a level above that suggested by their official ranking.

The 1855 classification of Sauternes and Barsac is also printed on p. 182. Reflecting price and the *réclame* then attached to sweet wines, it elevated Ch d'YQUEM to premier cru supérieur, a rank higher even than any of the red wine first growths, and listed 11 châteaux as first growths and 14 as seconds.

Other than Haut-Brion's inclusion in the 1855 Médoc classification, the wines of the Graves district were not officially classified until 1953. This one-class list, slightly augmented in 1959, appears on p. 182. It avoided some possible controversy by employing a democratically alphabetical order. It should be said, however, that there is a wide differential between the prices commanded by Ch Haut-Brion and its close rival Ch La Mission-Haut-Brion, for example, and those fetched by Chx Bouscaut and de Fieuzal. The Graves district was subsequently divided into Graves and PESSAC-LÉOGNAN.

The classification of ST-ÉMILION, formally drawn up in 1955, is most frequently reviewed and amended and therefore most controversial. Modifications were published in 1969, 1985, 1996, 2006, 2012, and 2022 (see pp. 181–2 for this latest version). The updated rules published in 2018 focus on the vineyard boundaries (which cannot be extended between reclassifications), a tasting of the ten previous vintages (15 for the highest ranking), prices, the reputation and distribution of the wines and the estate's efforts at promotion (including tourism), and technical aspects. The top tier comprises the premiers grands crus classés, subdivided into A and B, then the much bigger tier, the

C

Bordeaux

The Official Classification of Médoc and Graves of 1855

	Commune	Appellation		Commune	Appellation
First Growths (Premiers Crus)					
Ch Lafite-Rothschild	Pauillac	Pauillac	Ch Haut-Brion*	Pessac	Graves, now Pessac-Léognan
Ch Margaux	Margaux	Margaux			
Ch Latour	Pauillac	Pauillac	Ch Mouton Rothschild**	Pauillac	Pauillac
Second Growths (Deuxièmes Crus)					
Ch Rauzan-Ségla	Margaux	Margaux	Ch Brane-Cantenac	Cantenac	Margaux
Ch Rauzan-Gassies	Margaux	Margaux	Ch Pichon Baron	Pauillac	Pauillac
Ch Léoville Las Cases	St-Julien	St-Julien			
Ch Léoville-Poyferré	St-Julien	St-Julien	Ch Pichon-Longueville, Comtesse de Lalande	Pauillac	Pauillac
Ch Léoville-Barton	St-Julien	St-Julien			
Ch Durfort-Vivens	Margaux	Margaux	Ch Ducru-Beaucaillou	St-Julien	St-Julien
Ch Gruaud-Larose	St-Julien	St-Julien	Ch Cos d'Estournel	St-Estèphe	St-Estèphe
Ch Lascombes	Margaux	Margaux	Ch Montrose	St-Estèphe	St-Estèphe
Third Growths (Troisièmes Crus)					
Ch Kirwan	Cantenac	Margaux	Ch Cantenac-Brown	Cantenac	Margaux
Ch d'Issan	Cantenac	Margaux	Ch Palmer	Cantenac	Margaux
Ch Lagrange	St-Julien	St-Julien	Ch La Lagune	Ludon	Haut-Médoc
Ch Langoa-Barton	St-Julien	St-Julien	Ch Desmirail	Margaux	Margaux
Ch Giscours	Labarde	Margaux	Ch Calon-Ségur	St-Estèphe	St-Estèphe
Ch Malescot St-Exupéry	Margaux	Margaux	Ch Ferrière	Margaux	Margaux
Ch Boyd-Cantenac	Cantenac	Margaux	Ch Marquis d'Alesme Becker	Margaux	Margaux
Fourth Growths (Quatrièmes Crus)					
Ch St-Pierre	St-Julien	St-Julien	Ch La Tour-Carnet	St-Laurent	Haut-Médoc
Ch Talbot	St-Julien	St-Julien	Ch Lafon-Rochet	St-Estèphe	St-Estèphe
Ch Branaire-Ducru	St-Julien	St-Julien	Ch Beychevelle	St-Julien	St-Julien
Ch Duhart-Milon	Pauillac	Pauillac	Ch Prieuré-Lichine	Cantenac	Margaux
Ch Pouget	Cantenac	Margaux	Ch Marquis-de-Terme	Margaux	Margaux
Fifth Growths (Cinquièmes Crus)					
Ch Pontet-Canet	Pauillac	Pauillac	Ch du Tertre	Arsac	Margaux
Ch Batailley	Pauillac	Pauillac	Ch Haut-Bages-Liberal	Pauillac	Pauillac
Ch Haut-Batailley	Pauillac	Pauillac	Ch Pédesclaux	Pauillac	Pauillac
Ch Grand-Puy-Lacoste	Pauillac	Pauillac	Ch Belgrave	St-Laurent	Haut-Médoc
Ch Grand-Puy-Ducasse	Pauillac	Pauillac	Ch de Camensac	St-Laurent	Haut-Médoc
Ch Lynch-Bages	Pauillac	Pauillac	Ch Cos-Labory	St-Estèphe	St-Estèphe
Ch Lynch-Moussas	Pauillac	Pauillac	Ch Clerc-Milon	Pauillac	Pauillac
Ch Dauzac	Labarde	Margaux	Ch Croizet-Bages	Pauillac	Pauillac
Ch d'Armailhac***	Pauillac	Pauillac	Ch Cantemerle	Macau	Haut-Médoc

* This wine, although a Graves, was universally recognized and classified as one of the original four first growths.
** This wine was decreed a first growth in 1973.
*** Previously Ch d'Armailhaq, Ch Mouton-Baron-Philippe, and Ch Mouton-Baronne-Philippe.

The Official Classification of St-Émilion of 1955 (Reclassified 2022)

Premiers Grands Crus Classés

A. Ch Pavie Ch Figeac

B. Ch Beau-Séjour Bécot Ch Beauséjour (Héritiers Duffau-Lagarrosse) Ch Bélair-Monange Ch Canon Ch Canon La Gaffelière Clos Fourtet Ch Larcisse-Ducasse La Mondotte Ch Pavie Macquin Ch Troplong Mondot Ch Trottevieille Ch Valandraud

C

Grands Crus Classés

Ch Badette	Clos St-Martin	Ch Fonroque	Ch La Marzelle	Ch Moulin du Cadet
Ch Balestard La Tonnelle	Clos de Sarpe	Ch Franc Mayne	Ch Laniote	Ch Péby Faugères
Ch Barde-Haut	Ch Corbin	Ch Grand Corbin	Ch Larmande	Ch Petit Faurie de Soutard
Ch Bellefont-Belcier	Ch Corbin Michotte	Ch Grand Corbin-Despagne	Ch Laroque	Ch de Pressac
Ch Bellevue	Ch Côte de Baleau	Ch Grand Mayne	Ch Laroze	Ch Ripeau
Ch Berliquet	Couvent des Jacobins	Ch Gaudet	Ch Lassègue	Ch Rochebelle
Ch Boutisse	Ch Croix de Labrie	Ch Haute-Sarpe	Ch La Serre	Ch Rol Valentin
Ch Cadet-Bon	Ch Dassault	Ch Jean Faure	Ch La Tour Figeac	Ch St-Georges-Côte-Pavie
Ch Cap de Mourlin	Ch Destieux	Ch La Commanderie	Ch Le Châtelet	Ch Sansonnet
Ch Chauvin	Ch Faugères	Ch La Confession	Ch Le Prieuré	Ch Soutard
Clos Badon Thunevin	Ch de Ferrand	Ch La Couspaude	Ch Mangot	Ch Tour Baladoz
Clos Dubrueil	Ch Fleur Cardinale	Ch La Croizille	Ch Monbousquet	Ch Tour St-Christophe
Clos des Jacobins	Ch Fombrauge	Ch La Dominique	Ch Montlabert	Ch Villemaurine
Clos de l'Oratoire	Ch Fonplégade	Ch La Fleur Morange	Ch Montlisse	Ch Yon-Figeac
Clos St-Julien				

The Official Classification of Sauternes-Barsac of 1855

Superior First Growth (Premier Cru Supérieur)

Ch d'Yquem	Sauternes

First Growths (Premiers Crus)

	Commune		Commune
Ch La Tour-Blanche	Bommes	Ch Climens	Barsac
Ch Lafaurie-Peyraguey	Bommes	Ch Guiraud	Sauternes
Ch Clos Haut-Peyraguey	Bommes	Ch Rieussec	Fargues
Ch de Rayne-Vigneau	Bommes	Ch Rabaud-Promis	Bommes
Ch Suduiraut	Preignac	Ch Sigalas-Rabaud	Bommes
Ch Coutet	Barsac		

Second Growths (Deuxièmes Crus)

	Commune		Commune
Ch de Myrat	Barsac	Ch Naïrac	Barsac
Ch Doisy Daëne	Barsac	Ch Caillou	Barsac
Ch Doisy-Dubroca	Barsac	Ch Suau	Barsac
Ch Doisy-Védrines	Barsac	Ch de Malle	Preignac
Ch d'Arche	Sauternes	Ch Romer du Hayot	Fargues
Ch Filhot	Sauternes	Ch Lamothe-Despujois	Sauternes
Ch Broustet	Barsac	Ch Lamothe-Guignard	Sauternes

The Official Classification of Graves of 1959

Classified Red Wines of Graves

	Commune		Commune
Ch Bouscaut	Cadaujac	Ch Malartic-Lagravière	Léognan
Ch Carbonnieux	Léognan	Ch La Mission Haut-Brion	Talence
Domaine de Chevalier	Léognan	Ch Olivier	Léognan
Ch de Fieuzal	Léognan	Ch Pape Clément	Pessac
Ch Haut-Bailly	Léognan	Ch Smith Haut Lafitte	Martillac
Ch Haut-Brion	Pessac	Ch La Tour Haut-Brion	Talence
Ch Latour-Martillac	Martillac		

Classified White Wines of Graves

	Commune		Commune
Ch Bouscaut	Cadaujac	Ch Latour-Martillac	Martillac
Ch Carbonnieux	Léognan	Ch Laville Haut-Brion*	Talence
Domaine de Chevalier	Léognan	Ch Malartic-Lagravière	Léognan
Ch Couhins	Villenave d'Ornon	Ch Olivier	Léognan
Ch Couhins-Lurton	Villenave d'Ornon		

* Since 2009, this wine has been produced under its original name, Ch La Mission Haut-Brion.

grands crus classés. The 2006 classification was disputed and suspended in the spring of 2007, and then reinstated in 2009. The 2012 classification, which was conducted by a commission of recognized wine experts from outside Bordeaux nominated by the INAO, also resulted in several legal disputes. In 2021, two of the then four grands crus classés A, Chx Ausone and Cheval Blanc, withdrew because they did not agree with the judging criteria. A third, Ch Angélus, left in early 2022, and others have followed. The deceptively grandiose rank of GRAND CRU (minus the classé) is awarded annually to scores of individual wines as part of the AOC system and is therefore separate from this decadal classification.

POMEROL is the only important fine-wine district of Bordeaux never to have been classified, although its star PETRUS is conventionally included with Chx Lafite, Latour, Margaux, Haut-Brion, Mouton-Rothschild, Cheval Blanc, and Ausone as an honorary first growth.

There have been regular attempts to revise and assimilate the various classifications of Bordeaux, most notably that drawn up by Alexis LICHINE in 1959. Most serious writers on bordeaux make their own revisions, more or less confirmed by the market.

See also CRU BOURGEOIS for those MÉDOC properties classified as just below the status of a fifth growth.

Burgundy

Burgundians were also well aware of the considerable variation in quality of the wines produced by different plots of land, or CLIMATS, as they are known in Burgundy. In 1855, Dr Lavalle published his influential *History and Statistics of the Côte d'Or*, which included an informal classification of the best vineyards. This was formalized in 1861 by the Beaune Committee of Agriculture, which, with Lavalle's assistance, devised three classes. Most *climats* included in the first class eventually became grands crus when the AOC system was introduced in the 1930s. See under BURGUNDY for a full list of Burgundian grands crus, and see under individual village names for details of their premiers crus.

Elsewhere

Few other regions of France have anything approaching an official classification, although see ALSACE for a list of those vineyards accorded grand-cru status, CHABLIS for details of crus in this northern outpost of Burgundy, and CHAMPAGNE for some details of the classification of individual villages there.

There have been attempts, typically by WINE WRITERS or producers' associations, to produce classifications of the best vineyards, or best wines, of many countries, notably Germany (see GROSSE LAGE) and Italy (see VERONELLI), but these have generally been too controversial to be widely adopted. With the exception of the DOURO, where individual vineyards have been classified for the quality of port they produce, the wine regions of Portugal and Spain are in too great a state of flux to submit satisfactorily to classification, like those of eastern Europe and the rest of the Mediterranean. See also VINO DE PAGO.

In the New World, Australia prefers to classify not vineyards but individual wines, often much blended between areas, by awarding them medals and trophies in their famous SHOWS. Langton's Classification of Australian Wine, produced periodically, distinguishes wines on the basis of track record and reputation at AUCTION. In North America, on the other hand, it seems that classification may never appeal to the democratic California wine industry. See also CLIMATE CLASSIFICATION.

Langton's Classification of Australian Wine VII. www.langtons.com.au/classification.

Markham, D., *1855: A History of the Bordeaux Classification* (1998).

Anson, J., *Inside Bordeaux* (2020).

Gotti, L., and Pitiot, S., *Les Vins de Bourgogne* (16th edn, updated 2020).

clay refers to a particular type of MINERAL found in some rock types and in soil. It is also a generic description of sediment or soil that is made up of small, plate-like particles. Soils described as 'clays' have a high content of clay minerals but may also contain fine particles of calcium carbonate (in soils formed on LIMESTONE) and QUARTZ (in soils that have been weathering over a long period of time). Because of their negative charges and large surface areas, clay minerals hold large amounts of exchangeable cations (see CATION EXCHANGE).

Clay-sized particles interact with soil ORGANIC MATTER to form the basic building blocks of SOIL STRUCTURE. Different clay minerals predispose to variations in the stability of a soil's structure. For example, kaolinite clays tend to support stable structures, whereas montmorillonite clays (also known as smectite), which show marked swelling when wet and shrinkage on drying, may cause structural instability, especially if sodium cations are present. Such instability in subsoils can result in poor DRAINAGE and waterlogging, which is detrimental to healthy vines. Mica-type clays can hold significant amounts of POTASSIUM cations within their structures, which is slowly released on exchange with other cations in the soil water. Vine uptake of this potassium may adversely affect grape and wine quality. Clay can be important in vineyard subsoils because of its water-holding capacity, as in parts of POMEROL, for example. R.E.W.

For clay FERMENTATION VESSELS, see AMPHORA, QVEVRI, TALHA, TINAJA, and PITHARI.

cleanliness, an important quality in wine (a wine should not have any off-odours) and in wineries, for which see HYGIENE.

cleanskin, a term used in Australia and New Zealand to describe a wine sold without any indication of the producer's identity, particularly useful in a time of glut.

cleft grafting, a popular method for changing VINE VARIETY in the vineyard (see TOP GRAFTING). The severing of the TRUNK may be at ground level or just below the head; the latter is preferred because DESUCKERING is simpler, less vine training is required, and the extra wood of the trunk aids the rapid establishment of the new vine. The trunk is cut horizontally in early spring and the stump split across the middle to about 5 cm/2 in depth. SCION pieces of one or two nodes are prepared from dormant CANES with a long-tapered wedge. After the trunk is split and spread, the pieces are inserted one on each side so that CAMBIUMS of ROOTSTOCK and scion are matched to facilitate their bonding. The wounds are sealed with grafting mastic, then with paint. NOTCH GRAFTING is an alternative. See diagram. B.G.C.

Clendenen, Jim (1953–2021), founded Au Bon Climat winery in SANTA MARIA VALLEY in a shed by Bien Nacido vineyard in the 1980s and stuck admirably to the lessons he had learnt in Burgundy, even when they resulted in Pinot Noirs and Chardonnays much leaner than were then in FASHION. They contrasted markedly with the man himself, in terms of both restraint and, alas, longevity.

Clevner, name used for various forms of PINOT. In SWITZERLAND it is often applied to PINOT NOIR or Blauburgunder grown in the canton of Zurich. In ALSACE Clevner or Klevner are usually synonyms for PINOT BLANC, but see also KLEVENER DE HEILIGENSTEIN.

climat, French, particularly Burgundian, term for a specific vineyard site defined by, as the name suggests, all of its climatological as well as geographical characteristics, otherwise known as TERROIR. Thus the Burgundian grower uses the word *climat* interchangeably with 'vineyard'. A *climat* is generally but not always smaller than a specific appellation. The term *climat* may for example be used to refer to a grand cru such as Richebourg. To further complicate matters, most appellations have over the centuries been subdivided into small parcels, each with its own traditional name, known by local geographers as a LIEU-DIT.

climate, long-term WEATHER pattern of an area, an extremely important variable in the winemaking equation. For more details, see MACROCLIMATE in particular but also CLIMATE CLASSIFICATION,

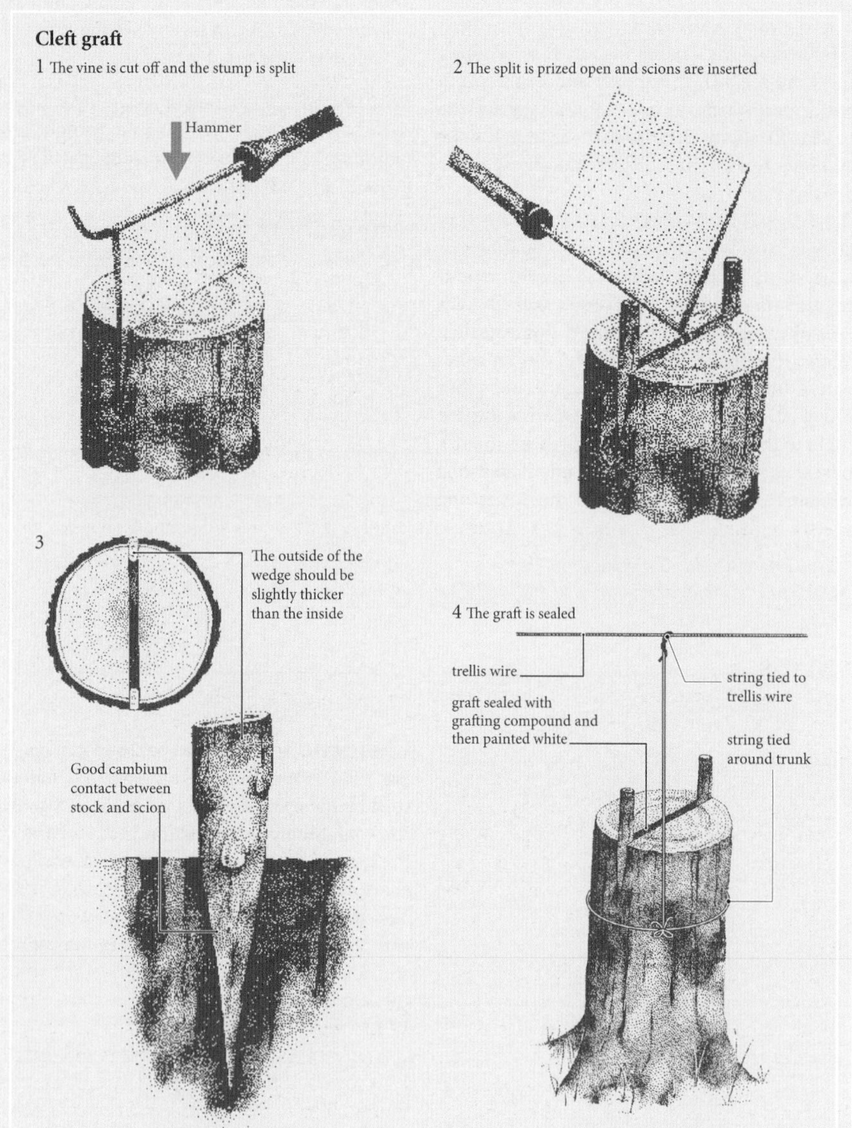

Source: B.G. Coombe and P.R. Dry (eds.), *Viticulture*, ii: *Practices*

CLIMATE CHANGE, CONTINENTALITY, COOL-CLIMATE VITICULTURE, LATITUDE, MEDITERRANEAN CLIMATE, RAINFALL, SUNLIGHT, TEMPERATE, TEMPERATURE, TEMPERATURE VARIABILITY, WARM-CLIMATE VITICULTURE, and, importantly, CLIMATE AND WINE QUALITY. For details of climate on a smaller scale, see MESOCLIMATE and MICROCLIMATE.

climate and wine quality. Climate influences both the QUALITY and styles of wine that a region can produce best. At the extremes, a climate can be so unsuitable for grape-growing that to produce good wines regularly is impossible or, at best, uneconomic. Cooler climates are best suited to producing light, delicate, and aromatic wines, while very hot climates are most suitable for FORTIFIED WINE production.

Temperature

Average mean TEMPERATURE during RIPENING strongly influences potential wine style. Defining grape maturity as that appropriate to making dry TABLE WINES, mean temperatures averaging above about 21 °C/70 °F in the final month to maturity lead to a rapid loss of MALIC ACID from the grapes and to lower TOTAL ACIDITY and generally higher PH in the juice. Conversely, an average mean temperature below about 15 °C/59 °F in the final month minimizes acid loss to the point that acid levels may be too high. There is also often a risk that the grapes will not ripen fully at all.

Average conditions during ripening cannot be estimated directly from raw climatic statistics because they depend in part on when ripening occurs. That, in turn, depends on the heat requirements of individual VINE VARIETIES to reach maturity. Some are early maturing and have a relatively low total heat requirement. These will ripen successfully in cool climates, and in hot climates ripen very early. Late-maturing varieties need a long, warm growing season and a high heat total to ripen at all. Jones classifies the main wine-grape varieties into four maturity groups (see CLIMATE CLASSIFICATION).

Beyond that, individual grape varieties differ in their optimum ripening temperatures for quality. Many of the early-maturing varieties are best when ripened under relatively cool conditions. The berries of some of them are very sensitive to heat, particularly red-wine varieties such as Pinot Noir. Such varieties nevertheless need warmth during ripening to give enough colour and body for red wines, a contradiction which explains their limited and specialized climatic adaptations. Other equally early-maturing varieties, usually for white wine, can tolerate considerable heat during ripening and can give good quality across a wide range of climates. Chardonnay, Verdelho, and to a lesser extent Sauvignon Blanc are good examples. Late-maturing varieties such as Grenache, Mourvèdre, Carignan, and Muscat of Alexandria need not only high heat totals to reach maturity but also moderately high temperatures during ripening for maximum wine quality.

Temperature variability

Whereas potential wine style depends broadly on average mean temperature during ripening, quality appears to be related at least as much to short-term temperature variability from day to day and week to week. See TEMPERATURE VARIABILITY and DIURNAL TEMPERATURE RANGE.

Sunlight

Contrary to common perception, cool viticultural climates are probably more limited by their low temperatures than by lack of SUNLIGHT. Sunlight duration acts mainly by controlling sugar in grapes and therefore potential wine alcohol content at a given stage of physiological ripening. In practice, however, the relative contributions of sunlight and temperature are hard to distinguish because low temperatures and low sunlight hours tend to go together. Poor seasons in cool climates are usually both cloudier and colder.

Paradoxically, sunlight duration appears to limit wine style and (sometimes) quality as much in warm as in cool climates, even though their sunlight hours over the season are usually greater. The explanation lies in rates of RESPIRATION. Vines respire more sugar at high temperatures for their normal metabolism but do not photosynthesize any faster; they therefore need more sunlight hours to generate a sugar surplus for ripening the fruit. It is why, for instance,

Australia's often cloudy Hunter Valley produces only table wines despite being very warm; and why mild to warm, but cloudy, regions of northern New Zealand such as Auckland produce predominantly light table wines. Similar factors appear to apply through much of central and northern Italy.

Regions with unlimited sunlight hours and high sunlight intensity are nevertheless not necessarily at an advantage because they commonly suffer from excessive TEMPERATURE VARIABILITY, low relative humidities, and WATER STRESS (see below). But in the absence of these adverse factors, ample sunlight does appear to be universally beneficial. A strong and constant sugar flow to the ripening berries assures not only their sweetness and sufficient alcohol in the wine but also that colour, flavour, and aroma compounds are not limited by a lack of sugar substrate for their formation.

Timing of the sunlight is important. Studies such as that of Gadille in Burgundy show that the most critical period for quality is around the start of ripening (August in most European viticultural regions). Good conditions then assure an ample reserve of sugar in the vine, both for early conversion in the leaves and berries into flavour and aroma compounds, or their precursors, and so that sugar and flavour ripening of the berries can continue unabated under the cooler and less sunny conditions normally encountered later. (See also ULTRAVIOLET RADIATION.)

Rainfall

The general implications of rain for viticulture are discussed under RAINFALL.

For wine quality, the biggest impacts of too much or too little rainfall occur during ripening. Most agree that any severe WATER STRESS at that stage is deleterious. On the other hand, heavy rain during the ripening period, especially if accompanied by lack of sunshine, commonly results in incomplete ripening and thus a poor vintage. Heavy rain close to maturity is especially damaging because it can cause berry splitting and subsequent fungal infection of the bunches (see BOTRYTIS BUNCH ROT). This occurs most typically in certain varieties with tight bunches, such as Chenin Blanc and Zinfandel, and where the vines were under drought stress prior to the rain.

Relative humidity and evaporation

Strong evaporative demands place the vines under water stress, which, in extreme cases, can cause leaf loss and substantial collapse of vine metabolism. Obvious fruit damage often follows through excessive exposure to the overhead sun. Milder water stress can still reduce PHOTOSYNTHESIS and sugar production in the leaves and hence reduce both quantity and fruit quality. Mechanisms are discussed more fully under EVAPORATION and HUMIDITY.

Wind

The effects of WIND STRESS are largely on vine health and yield, via reduced disease incidence on the one hand and closure of the leaf STOMATA and especially direct physical damage on the other. Dry winds may also reduce wine quality through increased evaporation, as explained above.

At the same time, the daily alternating land and sea breezes of the summer months that occur with some regularity in coastal regions of the dry continents markedly benefit both vine physiological functioning and wine quality. They are especially important in Australia and on the west coast of the United States, and they are doubly advantageous: dry land winds at night and in the early morning reduce the risk of FUNGAL DISEASES; then mild, humid afternoon sea breezes reduce stresses on the vines and greatly improve day conditions for photosynthesis and ripening. The same applies on a reduced scale around inland lakes and rivers. See TOPOGRAPHY and TERROIR.

Summary

Two climatic types appear to offer the best compromises for both viticulture and wine quality. The first is that boasting cool-to-mild growing-season temperatures and uniform-to-predominantly-summer rainfall, such as is found in western and central Europe. Within that context, the best vineyard sites have specialized MESOCLIMATES with more than usual sunshine, warmth, and length of frost-free period.

The second broad climatic type is the winter-wet/summer-dry MEDITERRANEAN CLIMATES, where summer heat is regularly moderated by afternoon sea breezes or high DIURNAL TEMPERATURE RANGE, and irrigation can be supplied in late summer if needed and permitted. Advantages over the uniform and summer-rainfall climates include more reliable summer sunshine and less risk of excessive rain and humidity during the ripening period.

For more detail, see TEMPERATURE, TEMPERATURE VARIABILITY, SUNLIGHT, RAINFALL, HUMIDITY, and WIND. See also COOL-CLIMATE VITICULTURE and CLIMATE CHANGE. R.E.S. & G.V.J.

Becker, N., 'Site climate effects on development, fruit maturation and harvest quality', in R. E. Smart et al. (eds.), *Proceedings of the Second International Symposium for Cool Climate Viticulture and Oenology: 11–15 January 1988, Auckland, New Zealand* (1988).

Gadille, R., *Le Vignoble de la Côte Bourguignonne* (1967).

Gladstones, J., *Viticulture and Environment* (1992).

Huglin, P., and Schneider, C., *Biologie et écologie de la vigne* (2nd edn, 1998).

Jones, G. V., et al., 'Climate, grapes, and wine: structure and suitability in a variable and changing climate', in P. Dougherty (ed.), *The Geography of Wine: Regions, Terroir, and Techniques* (2012), 109–33.

climate change. Growing grapes for wine is a climatically sensitive endeavour, with narrow geographical zones providing the best production and quality characteristics. Winegrowing is therefore at greater risk from climate change than more broadly grown agricultural crops.

WEATHER and climate present three distinct spatial/temporal scales of risks and challenges to viticulture and wine production: first, individual weather events, which are mostly short term and localized (e.g. HAIL, WINTER FREEZES, FROST, excessive heat or heavy rain); second, climate variability, which is measured on seasonal to decadal timescales and typically regionalized (e.g. DROUGHT or wet periods, warm or cold periods); and third, climate change, which is recognized as long term and regional to global in scale (e.g. warming, cooling, changes in moisture regimes). In addition, one factor often influences and/or changes another—climate variability can change the frequency of individual weather events, and climate change can alter the nature of climate variability.

Historically climate change has been brought about by both internal and external natural processes such as volcanic events, ocean/snow/ice dynamics, solar variation, and meteoroid impacts. However, it is becoming increasingly evident that contemporary and future climate changes have become greatly influenced by human behaviour, through changes in atmospheric composition, deforestation, desertification, urbanization, and ocean acidification, which together alter the Earth's surface and atmosphere and the way each holds and distributes heat. Probably the greatest concern for future climate change comes from increasing fossil-fuel consumption and rising CARBON DIOXIDE (CO_2) levels in the atmosphere. To study climate change, scientists use empirical methods (based on observations and/or proxy data, such as tree rings), dynamic methods (based on complex three-dimensional, mathematical models of our Earth–atmosphere system), or a combination of the two. Models are also used to better understand the magnitude of human influences on global climates through attribution science, a field of research that is largely used in climate studies. Attribution research attempts to test whether—and by how much—human-induced climate change may be responsible for changes in temperature and precipitation along with extreme weather events.

Historical and contemporary climate changes

The grapevine is one of the oldest cultivated plants and, along with the process of making wine, has resulted in a rich geographical and

Changes in the global temperature relative to 1850–1900, from the 2021 Intergovernmental Panel on Climate Change (IPCC) Summary for Policymakers

(a) Change in global surface temperature (decadal average) as **reconstructed** from palaeoclimate archives (1–2000) and directly **observed** (1850–2020), both relative to 1850–1900 and decadally averaged. The vertical bar on the left shows the estimated temperature (very likely range) during the warmest multi-century period in at least the last 100,000 years, which occurred around 6,500 years ago during the current interglacial period (Holocene). The shading with white diagonal lines shows the very likely ranges for the temperature reconstructions.

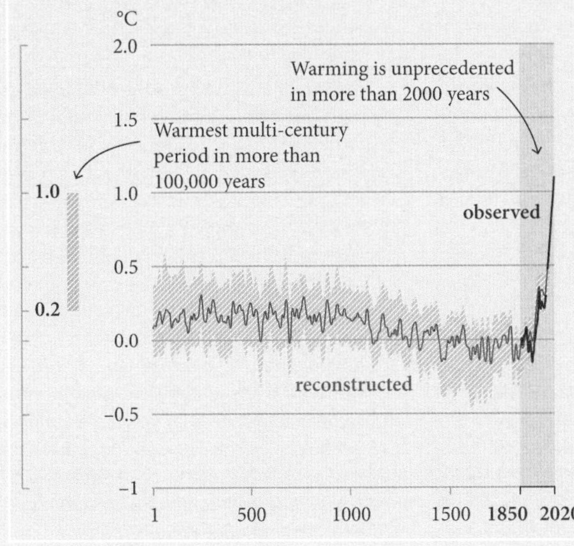

(b) Changes in global surface temperature (annual average) as **observed** and simulated using **human & natural** and **only natural** factors (both 1850–2020). Graph lines show the multi-model average, and shading shows the very likely range of simulations.

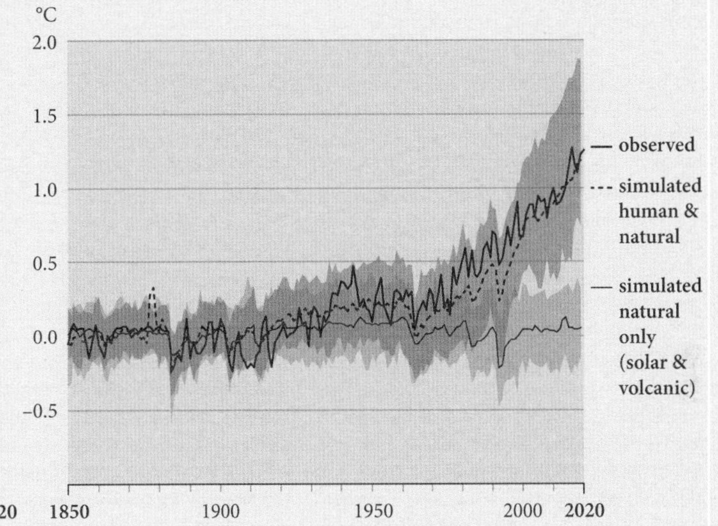

cultural history (see ORIGINS OF VINICULTURE). This history has shown that wine-growing regions developed throughout Eurasia when the climate was most conducive. In addition, records of dates of harvest and yield for European viticulture have been kept for nearly a thousand years, revealing large swings in growing-season temperatures and productivity. For example, Pfister's historical research describes how during the medieval Little Optimum, roughly 900–1300 CE, average temperatures were up to 1 °C/1.8 °F warmer, with vineyards planted as far north as the coastal zones of the Baltic Sea and southern England. Recorded harvest dates for northern Europe from the High Middle Ages (12th and 13th centuries) show that fruit was ripening in early September, as compared with late September to mid October during the late 20th century, and that growing-season temperatures were roughly 1.7 °C/3 °F warmer. However, during the Little Ice Age (14th to late 19th centuries), temperature declines were dramatic, resulting in northern vineyards being abandoned and growing seasons so short that harvesting ripe grapes even in southern Europe was difficult. Labbé and colleagues examined grape-harvest dates in Burgundy from 1354 to 2018, finding that outstanding hot and dry years that were outliers in the past have since 1988 become the norm, with many years since 2000 the warmest on record. The research also shows that harvest dates from 1988 to 2018 were 13 days earlier than the average of the previous 600-plus years: mid September instead of late September to early October. Data from 2014 to 2021 show this trend continuing, with harvest dates earlier than mid September, as early as 20 August in the extremely warm 2020 vintage.

Today our understanding of climate change and the potential effects on VITICULTURE and wine production has become increasingly important as changing levels of greenhouse gases and alterations in Earth surface characteristics bring about changes in the Earth's radiation balance, atmospheric circulation, and hydrologic cycle. In its latest report, the Intergovernmental Panel on Climate Change (IPCC) stated that warming of the climate system is unequivocal and that, since the middle of the 20th century, many of the observed changes are unprecedented over decades to millennia. Each of the last four decades has been successively warmer than any decade that preceded it since 1850. Global surface temperatures were 0.95–1.2 °C/1.71–2.16 °F higher in 2011–2020 than in 1850–1900. However, temperature changes have not been globally uniform, and the warming trends have been found to be asymmetric with respect to seasonal and diurnal cycles, with greatest warming occurring during the winter and spring and at night (resulting in a smaller DIURNAL TEMPERATURE RANGE).

Averaged globally, the eleven warmest years on record have all occurred since 2005. Other climate-related observations include: the Greenland and Antarctic ice sheets losing mass over the last few decades; glaciers on average continuing to shrink worldwide; decreases in snow-cover extent in the northern hemisphere and floating ice in the Arctic Ocean; global mean sea level rising on average 20 cm over the past century; and worldwide precipitation over land having increased by 5–10%. Furthermore, changes in many extreme weather and climate events have been observed in every region across the globe, including changes in the frequency, severity, and even geography of HEATWAVES, heavy precipitation, droughts, extreme fire events (see WILDFIRES), hail, and tropical cyclones. The IPCC has indicated that extreme-event occurrences are increasingly attributed to human influences on the climate system.

Contemporary research shows that the impact of climate change on viticulture and wine has been widespread. Numerous effects on

◀ The frequency and severity of WILDFIRES such as the 2004 Geysers Fire in SONOMA County's Mayacamas Mountains are increasingly attributed to CLIMATE CHANGE. This fire appears to have burnt out when it reached DRIP-IRRIGATED vineyards owned by JACKSON FAMILY WINES near the top of the forested ridgeline. 4,947 ha/12,225 acres were charred in five days. © George Rose

plant growth, fruit characteristics, and pest and disease issues (see below) have been observed in wine regions globally, with indications that they are likely to continue in the future. Many studies around the world have documented changes in average climate conditions that have produced warmer and longer growing and DORMANT periods. Growing-season temperatures in many of the best wine-producing regions in the world increased 1.43 °C/2.57 °F during 1900–2017. Trends between day and night temperatures vary by region, with some seeing much more significant warming at night and others seeing more heat-stress events through higher daytime temperatures. In addition to warmer growing seasons with greater heat accumulation, many of the world's wine regions have experienced a decline in FROST frequency and shifts in the timing of frosts. However, cold extremes still occur, and warmer spring temperatures leading to early BUDBREAK can lead to severe FROST DAMAGE, as in much of Europe in 2017 and 2021, for example. Furthermore, warmer winters and lack of winter DORMANCY disrupt the vine's internal clock, ultimately affecting vine growth and productivity the next year.

Grapevine PHENOLOGICAL timing has shown strong relationships with the observed warming in wine regions, with trends ranging from 5 to 30 days earlier over numerous CULTIVARS and locations (Jones et al. 2012, Cameron et al. 2021). Changes are greatest for the timing of VERAISON and harvest, and interval lengths between the main phenological events have also shortened, with the length of time from BUDBREAK to FLOWERING, flowering to veraison, or veraison to harvest dates shortening by two weeks or more. An analysis over all locations and cultivars shows that grapevine phenology has been responding by roughly 5–10 days per 1 °C/1.8 °F of warming over the last 30–50 years. With this earlier and more rapid plant growth, the potential for changes to ripening profiles and wine styles is evident. Many regions have seen trends towards higher sugar and lower acidity levels that are significantly correlated with increases in temperatures. As a result of these changes in GRAPE COMPOSITION, combined with changing consumer preferences (see HANG TIME, for example), higher alcohol levels have been observed in many regions. Furthermore, research in some regions shows that harvests that occur earlier in the summer, in a warmer part of the growing season, will result in hotter fruit being harvested, typically leading to loss of flavour and aroma compounds, as well as the potential for greater BERRY SHRIVEL unless irrigation is increased (Webb et al.). See HARVEST COMPRESSION.

Research on climate change effects on pest and disease pressure indicates that we are likely to see increases in populations and severity but also shifts to new areas further towards the poles, with warmer winters and warmer night temperatures (discussed below).

Soil interactions with climate, pests, and disease also strongly influence YIELD and wine quality. Numerous studies have shown that SOIL EROSION, degradation, and SALINITY are likely to be major indirect effects of climate change on viticulture and wine production. Climate change is expected to lead to a more vigorous hydrological cycle, including more total rainfall and more frequent high-intensity rainfall events. Furthermore, a changing climate and societal demands on water will increase the pressure to restrict irrigation, ultimately increasing rootzone salinity with a greater impact on wine quality over time.

In addition, researchers have found that increases in carbon dioxide will cause more vegetative growth (see VIGOUR) in grapevines and the need for increased water-use efficiency, although the increased growth is likely to come at the expense of grape quality. However, while we understand some of the issues surrounding the impact of CO_2 on growing grapes, research is only now starting to explain more fully how increasing CO_2 concentrations along with warmer temperatures and changes in available water relate to vine growth, phenological timing and phase lengths, yield formation, fruit ripening and composition, and, most importantly, wine quality. Finally, an important indirect effect of increased CO_2 for the wine industry has also been identified: changes in the texture of OAK wood may alter its suitability for wine barrel production.

Future predicted climate changes

Current climate modelling—using predictions based on a range of future CO_2 emissions, which are the largest contributors to total increases in temperatures—projects that the globally averaged surface temperature will likely increase 1–5.7 °C/1.8–10.3 °F by 2081–2100 relative to what was seen globally during the 1850–1900 period. The projected warming will likely continue to exhibit interannual-to-decadal variability and will not be regionally uniform, with variation in the rate of warming and whether the warming comes from greater increases in daytime or night-time temperatures. Research suggests that wine-region growing-season temperatures will increase by approximately 2 °C/3.6 °F by 2050, with increased seasonal TEMPERATURE VARIABILITY. However, the warming rates in wine regions are likely to vary: locations in the northern hemisphere are expected to warm more than those in the southern hemisphere. In addition, regions at higher LATITUDES or inland are expected to warm more than those in coastal zones (Jones & Schultz). Both observations and models also suggest that in most viticultural locations in Australia and California, for example, this projected warming is likely to lead to a decrease in rainfall and/or snowpacks in the surrounding mountains, leading to greater WATER STRESS and reductions in water resources in the future.

Global studies have shown broad shifts to higher latitudes, with COOL-CLIMATE VITICULTURE found further north in Europe and North America today (Jones & Schultz). Similar poleward shifts have been seen and are projected in the southern hemisphere, although this is likely to affect only small areas of New Zealand, Tasmania, and the southern regions of Argentina and Chile, due to landmass limitations. Regional research by Moriondo and colleagues on spatial modelling of suitable zones for viticulture in Europe and the western US shows latitudinal, coastal, and elevation shifts from historic wine regions. Similar results have been found elsewhere, with estimations that potential viticultural area could expand in some regions while contracting in others.

Future climate change of the magnitudes predicted will have numerous effects on society and natural ECOSYSTEMS. Likewise, it presents numerous potential influences on, and challenges to, the wine industry, including additional changes in the timing of grapevine phenology, likely to result in a disruption of balanced composition and flavour in grapes and wine. In addition, the changes are not likely to be uniform across all regions and varieties but are likely to be related to climatic thresholds for optimum growth and quality. Furthermore, the warming will clearly force decisions on the mix of varieties grown and the wine styles produced in particular regions: those that currently have a cool climate will have a greater choice of viable varieties, while in many of today's warmer regions the future climates will be challenging for optimum grape growth and wine production from most varieties (Santos et al. 2021a). Current and future adaptations to changes in climate are many; they include better understanding of the cultivar limits to climate conditions, changes in vineyard management strategies (see PRECISION VITICULTURE), winemaking refinements, developments in soil–rootstock compatibility, and continued plant breeding and genetic research (Santos et al. 2021b).

While the Earth's climate is always changing, strong regional identities have developed in terms of cultivars and wine styles. Therefore, any future climate change has the potential to influence cultural change. To prepare for the future, the wine industry will most certainly need to help mitigate future changes in climate and integrate planning and adaptation strategies to adjust to those changes that the IPCC says may be irreversible due to past and future greenhouse-gas emissions. H.S. & G.V.J.

Cameron, W., et al., 'A comparison of the effect of temperature on grapevine phenology between vineyards', *OENO One*, 55/2 (2021), 301–20.

IPCC, 'Summary for policymakers', in *Climate Change 2021: The Physical Science Basis*. www.ipcc.ch/report/sixth-assessment-report-working-group-i/.

Jones, G. V., et al., 'Climate change and global wine quality', *Climatic Change*, 73 (2005), 319–43.

Jones, G. V., et al., 'Climate, grapes, and wine: structure and suitability in a variable and changing climate', in P. Dougherty (ed.), *The Geography of Wine: Regions, Terroir, and Techniques* (2012), 109–33.

Jones, G. V., and Schultz, H. R., 'Climate change and emerging cool climate wine regions', *Wine & Viticulture Journal* (2016).

Jones, G. V., 'The state of the climate', *Proceedings of the 21st GiESCO International Meeting: A Multidisciplinary Vision towards Sustainable Viticulture* (2019), 32–43.

Labbé, T., et al., 'The longest homogeneous series of grape harvest dates, Beaune 1354–2018, and its significance for the understanding of past and present climate', *Climate of the Past*, 15/4 (2019), 1485–1501.

Moriondo, M., et al., 'Projected shifts of wine regions in response to climate change', *Climatic Change*, 119/3-4 (2013), 825–39.

Pfister, C., 'Variations in the spring-summer climate of central Europe from the High Middle Ages to 1850', in Schultz, H. R., and Jones, G. V., 'Climate induced historic and future changes in viticulture', *Journal of Wine Research*, 21/2 (2010) 137–45.

Santos, J. A., et al., 'Long-term adaptation of European viticulture to climate change: an overview from the H2020 Clim4Vitis action', *IVES Technical Reviews Vine and Wine* (2021a).

Santos, J. A., et al., 'Short-term adaptation of European viticulture to climate change: an overview from the H2020 Clim4Vitis action', *IVES Technical Reviews Vine and Wine* (2021b).

Webb, L. B., et al., 'Observed trends in winegrape maturity in Australia', *Global Change Biology*, 17/8 (2011), 2707–19.

The effect of climate change on vineyard pests and diseases

Over the last few decades, climate change has correlated with the migration of some vineyard pests and diseases. In France, for example, the FLAVESCENCE DORÉE phytoplasma and the associated LEAFHOPPER vector *Scaphoideus titanus* were first described in Armagnac in 1956. The disease has been found in Bordeaux (1994) and has been increasing in the area ever since. The vector still seems to be moving further north, to Saumur-Champigny (2006) and then Burgundy and Champagne in 2012. The related phytoplasma disease *bois noir* (see GRAPEVINE YELLOWS) now occurs in southern Germany. The European grapevine MOTH (*Lobesia botrana*), originating from the warmer Mediterranean areas, also seems to be travelling northwards, replacing the cool-climate vine moth (*Eupoecilia ambiguella*) in some areas of the Loire Valley. This northwards insect migration is generally considered to be due to the impact of warming on insect distribution, which is known to be one of the first biological indicators of climate change.

Some vineyards in the southern hemisphere are facing warmer and drier weather conditions, which, in theory, should not favour increases in disease development. In both hemispheres, however, trends towards higher temperatures are combined with more irregular and more intense rainfall. Generally, warmer and wetter conditions increase fungal disease pressure by encouraging more infection cycles. In European vineyards, DOWNY and POWDERY MILDEWS and BOTRYTIS BUNCH ROT are now considered more aggressive. By the mid 2010s powdery mildew was a more common phenomenon in Champagne than ever before, perhaps because of warmer temperatures. BLACK ROT, even though it was introduced more than a century ago from the US, has been spreading in many European countries, from Germany to Hungary and even to places with warm, dry climates such as Portugal and central Italy. More generations of grapevine moths, mites, and leafhoppers are generally observed with higher temperatures, and additional late-season flights of insects such as European grapevine moths have been regularly observed in PHEROMONE traps in warm years in the Bordeaux region, even if without an increase in actual damage by the mid 2010s.

Pathologists studying grapevine pests and diseases face a similar dilemma. Are recent changes in the distribution or impact truly part of longer-term effects brought about by climate change, or are they due to changes in, for example, vineyard management, PESTICIDE use, or global transport, or are they a genuine movement into a new ecological niche for a species?

Climate modelling is also allowing scientists to assess how climate change might influence pest and disease occurrence in the future. For example, Salinari et al. simulated likely future downy-mildew attacks in Acqui Terme in north-west Italy for the decades around 2030, 2050, and 2080. The modelling predicted an increase in temperature and a decrease in precipitation; the former outweighed the latter in terms of influence and was sufficient to predict increased disease pressure and more severe epidemics. Two more sprayings would be required early in the season. However, pests and diseases may also change over the longer term. Fungi, for example, are able to adapt themselves not only to climate change but also to the types of AGROCHEMICALS used for their control. This is another challenge in situations with higher disease pressure, where more sprays are required to ensure sufficient control. Unfortunately, more reliance on chemical applications can favour development of resistant fungal strains. The grapevine as host plant has also to be considered in terms of its sensitivity to pests and diseases in a changing climate. Whether climate change will make grapevines more sensitive or more resistant to pests and diseases is a difficult question since both pest/disease and the vine are affected by either higher temperatures and/or increased carbon dioxide concentration (Pugliese et al., Reineke and Selim). Crossing resistant cultivars (see DISEASE-RESISTANT VARIETIES) with sensitive VITIS VINIFERA varieties that have high qualitative traits could be a key factor in successfully adapting to changing vineyard climates. G.V.J. & B.B.

Pugliese, M., et al., 'Effects of elevated CO2 and temperature on interactions of grapevine and powdery mildew: first results under phytotron conditions', *Journal of Plant Diseases and Protection*, 117 (2010), 9–14.

Reineke, A., and Selim, M., 'Elevated atmospheric CO2 concentrations alter grapevine (*Vitis vinifera*) systemic transcriptional response to European grapevine moth (*Lobesia botrana*) herbivory'. *Scientific Reports*, 9 (2006), 2995.

Salinari F., et al., 'Downy mildew (*Plasmopara viticola*) epidemics on grapevine under climate change', *Global Change Biology*, 12/7 (2006), 1299–307.

climate classification, the description and grouping of climates for viticultural purposes.

History

Climate classification is a way of categorizing the world's climates based on a region's biome (i.e. the dominant collection of plants and animals that occupy the habitats of that region). The most familiar classification scheme is probably the one devised by Köppen used in geography and ecology.

Specialized classification systems have been developed for viticulture. The first scientific study of viticultural climates was that of the French researcher A. P. de Candolle in the mid 19th century, a time when reliable climatic data were just starting to become available. De Candolle observed that BUDBREAK in European vineyards corresponded closely with the dates on which average mean temperature reached 10 °C/50 °F. He proposed that useful heat for vine growth and RIPENING could be measured by the amount that actual mean temperatures exceed 10 °C. Therefore, a summation of the excesses for all growing-season days would give a measure of the total plant-usable heat.

Numerous applications of the heat-summation concept have been developed for viticulture. The first extensive practical use of de Candolle's method was in 1944 in California, where AMERINE and WINKLER classified observations of temperatures above 10 °C/50 °F (growing degree days, GDD) in the state over a fixed vine-growth and ripening season, from 1 April to 31 October, into five classes, which they called regions. These regions broadly correlated with those geographical areas in California with cool to warm to hot climates for general grape-ripening capabilities and wine styles (see table). Subsequent research by Jones and colleagues examining temperature conditions in western US vineyards and in New Zealand identified the need to update this classification by creating additional classes at both the lower and upper ends since the original classification did not encompass today's cool and hot limits.

Although successful in California, the Winkler Index (WI), is not fully accepted elsewhere. It works well in California partly because temperatures there are quite closely correlated with other climatic factors possibly related to viticulture and wine quality: directly with total SUNLIGHT, and inversely with HUMIDITY (see also CLIMATE AND WINE QUALITY). Temperature alone thus gives a reasonably adequate index of all the relevant climatic variables, but it also, more importantly, is the prime driver of vine PHENOLOGY.

The Huglin Index, developed in Europe, uses a similar formula but gives more weight to maximum temperatures, making an adjustment for longer day lengths found at higher latitudes and usefully differentiating coastal from inland areas. It thus reveals CONTINENTALITY and LATITUDE differences.

Tonietto and Carbonneau used the Huglin Index along with a dryness index, which corresponds to the potential water balance of the soil, and a cool-night index, developed as an indicator of night-time temperature conditions during maturation. The authors combined the three indices into the Multicriteria Climatic Classification System that represents the variability of some viticultural climates worldwide.

In Australia, Smart and Dry developed a classification that involves five separate climate elements: temperature, sunlight, rainfall, evaporation, and humidity. They preferred to use the simple statistic of average mean temperature for January (MJT; July in the northern hemisphere) as a usable index of summer heat. It is complemented by an index of continentality (the difference between mean summer and winter temperatures) to show the amplitude of swings in temperatures through the year, together with indices of sunlight, humidity, and water relations. The resulting five-variable classification gives a reasonable overview of viticultural climates and has been used for VINEYARD SITE SELECTION and regional comparison.

Also in Australia, Gladstones developed the Biologically Effective Degree Days (BEDD) index. In essence it is a method of predicting an average ripening date for any defined grape maturity type in any environment. It employs growing-season temperature summations over a 10 °C/50 °F base but with refinements that entail (1) imposing an upper limit (19 °C/66.2 °F) on the monthly average mean temperatures, beyond which no further increases are credited; (2) a correction factor proportional to the average day length of each month (long days giving greater biological effectiveness for a given greater mean temperature; see LATITUDE); (3) a correction for each month's average daily temperature range (a narrow range resulting in greater effectiveness, for a given mean). These considerations in the BEDD provide a predicted ripening date that forms the basis for evaluating or comparing environments as to their likely grape-variety adaptations and potential wine quality.

Other systems based on temperature have been simpler. Prescott in Australia found that the average mean temperature of the warmest month gave essentially as good a climatic indication as the seasonal temperature summation. Jones used average growing-season temperature (GST) for the seven-month growing season (see COOL-CLIMATE VITICULTURE), which classifies cool, intermediate, warm, and hot climates for viticulture and wine production. The GST index is very strongly correlated with growing degree days and is being increasingly recognized and used in wine-region climate classifications. G.V.J.

Amerine, M. A., and Winkler, A. J., 'Composition and quality of musts and wines of California grapes', *Hilgardia*, 15 (1944), 493–575.

Anderson, J. D., et al., 'Analysis of viticulture region climate and structure and suitability in New Zealand', *Journal International des Sciences de la Vigne et du Vin*, 46/3 (2012), 149–65.

Gladstones, J., *Viticulture and Environment* (1992).

Jones, G. V., et al., 'Spatial analysis of climate in winegrape growing regions in the western United States', *American Journal of Enology and Viticulture*, 61/3 (2010), 313–26.

Huglin, P., 'Nouveau mode d'évaluation des possibilités héliothermiques d'un milieu viticole', *Comptes Rendus de l'Académie d'Agriculture de France* (1978), 1117–26.

Prescott, J. A., 'The climatology of the vine (*Vitis vinifera*). 3. A comparison of France and Australia on the basis of the warmest month', *Transactions of the Royal Society of South Australia*, 93 (1969), 7–15.

Smart, R. E., and Dry, P. R., 'A climatic classification for Australian viticultural regions', *Australian Grapegrower and Winemaker*, 196 (1980), 8, 10, 16.

The wine regions mentioned in the rightmost column include examples from the coolest to the warmest in each of Winkler's categories. The location of the weather station (in brackets) may not be within the vineyards. There will be some wine-producing regions that are split across two Winkler regions; for example, parts of Bordeaux are in Region III.

Class/Region	C° units	F° units	General ripening capability and wine style	Region (weather station location)
Too cool	<850	<1500	Most varieties could not ripen consistently.	
Region Ia	850–1111	1500–2000	Only very early-ripening varieties achieve high quality, mostly hybrid grape varieties and some *Vitis vinifera*.	Nova Scotia (Kentville), Sussex (Eastbourne), Champagne (Reims)
Region Ib	1111–1389	2000–2500	Only early-ripening varieties achieve high quality, some hybrid grape varieties but mostly *Vitis vinifera*.	Rhine Valley (Geisenheim), Marlborough (Blenheim), Burgundy (Dijon)
Region II	1389–1667	2500–3000	Early and mid-season table-wine varieties will produce good-quality wines.	Coonawarra (Coonawarra), Piemonte (Turin), Bordeaux (Mérignac)
Region III	1667–1944	3000–3500	Favourable for high production of standard- to good-quality table wines.	Rioja (Logroño), Sonoma Valley (Sonoma), Margaret River (Margaret River)
Region IV	1944–2222	3500–4000	Favourable for high production but acceptable table-wine quality at best.	Napa Valley (St Helena), southern Rhône (Avignon), Stellenbosch (Nietvoorbij)
Region V	2222–2700	4000–4900	Typically only suitable for extremely high production; fair-quality table wine or table-grape varieties destined for early-season consumption are grown.	Madeira (Funchal), Patras (Patras), Jerez (Jerez de la Frontera)
Too hot	>2700	>4900	Likely more suited to table grapes and raisins.	

Tonietto, J., and Carbonneau, A., 'A multicriteria climatic classification system for grape-growing regions worldwide', *Agricultural and Forest Meteorology*, 124 (2004), (1–2): 81–97.

climate effects on vine diseases. The climate has a major effect on VINE DISEASES, and this interaction can be a major factor determining where grapes are grown. The most commercially important are FUNGAL DISEASES, and these are normally encouraged by warm, humid, and rainy conditions. Most of the world's viticulture is therefore carried out in regions with dry summers and less attendant risk of disease, for example the Mediterranean area. However, as the risk of fungal disease decreases, the likelihood of DROUGHT increases; in those parts of Europe where irrigation is generally prohibited (such as southern France), the effects of drought can be substantial. Some regions such as California, Chile, and Western Australia can be so dry during summer that DOWNY MILDEW, one of the worst vine fungal diseases, is generally not present.

Sometimes climate effects on vine disease are subtle and difficult to discern. For example, the phytoplasma disease FLAVESCENCE DORÉE is known to occur in epidemics, with severity varying markedly from year to year. This is thought to result from climate-induced natural variations in population levels of the insect vector. While the insect population swings are dramatic, the weather perturbations responsible are typically so slight as to be barely distinguishable from the average. RAINFALL (and sometimes dew) has a major effect on diseases, especially those caused by fungi. Water is important for spore germination and dispersal by splashing, as for DOWNY MILDEW and DEAD ARM, and so a rainy spring can cause epidemics of these diseases. Rain near the time of harvest causes grape berries to split, allowing many BUNCH ROT fungi and bacteria to gain entry and ruin the fruit. Many fungi spores such as those of BOTRYTIS BUNCH ROT and downy mildew germinate in high humidity. The fungal disease POWDERY MILDEW develops in the shade of dense vine canopies and is also encouraged by overcast weather. Rainfall during winter makes PRUNING wounds susceptible to invasion by TRUNK DISEASE fungi. In years of low rainfall and drought conditions, the presence of root-damaging pests such as PHYLLOXERA and NEMATODES are more evident.

TEMPERATURE is a major factor in disease development and spread, with temperatures of 20–27 °C/68–81 °F favouring the germination of powdery-mildew spores. Freezing winter temperatures can cause vine trunks to split, allowing the entry of the CROWN GALL bacterium.

WIND is important in spreading diseases: for example, BACTERIAL BLIGHT is spread in wet, windy weather. Otherwise wind generally helps reduce disease by drying leaves and fruit after rain and dew.

Climate effects on disease have a significant effect on wine quality, and there is no more important example than that of botrytis bunch rot. Intermittent rainy, humid, and warm weather near the time of harvest causes anguish to grape-grower and winemaker alike, because of the risk of losing both yield and quality. Yet, following infection, a change to dry weather can encourage the formation of NOBLE ROT. Costs of grape production are higher when the weather induces disease because of the need for treatments and possible crop loss. R.E.S.

Wilcox, W. F., et al., *Compendium of Grape Diseases, Disorders, and Pests* (2nd edn, 2015).

Clinton, dark-skinned *Vitis riparia* × *Vitis labrusca* AMERICAN HYBRID. It is planted in Brazil, and its wine has a pronounced FOXY flavour. It has also been known in Italian SWITZERLAND.

clonal selection, one of the two principal means of improving a vine variety (the other being the elimination of VIRUS DISEASES). Clonal selection is the practice of selecting a single superior plant in the vineyard and then taking cuttings from this vine for PROPAGATION. The selection is generally made with a particular attribute such as YIELD or fruit RIPENESS in mind. Clonal selection contrasts with MASS SELECTION, where a group of superior vines is selected.

Grapevines, in common with many other perennial crops, are produced by vegetative propagation—that is, by using cuttings which are genetically identical. (This contrasts with agricultural field crops, which are multiplied by seeds that are different one from another—although sexual reproduction leading to the production of seedlings is the means by which NEW VARIETIES are created.) In vegetative propagation, each bud from a so-called 'mother vine' essentially gives rise to a plant of the same CLONE (except for those very rare cases in which a bud MUTATION has taken place).

Clonal selection for vines was first demonstrated in 1926 in Germany, where it has been most widely practised. Other European countries have also developed clonal-selection initiatives, but the practice is less well developed in some countries of the NEW WORLD.

Clonal selection depends on the fact that adjacent vines in a vineyard of the same variety may be different, sometimes discernibly different. More often the differences can be established only after some years of careful measurement. Differences on a vine-to-vine scale would not normally be expected from soil variation. There are two possible explanations: a difference in genetic make-up between the vines due to mutations, or a difference in the incidence of diseases in the vines.

It is important to be able to tell the difference because some diseases are 'graft transmissible' (i.e. they are carried from one vine generation to the next in CUTTINGS; see below). The most common and commercially important transmissible disease agents are VIRUSES. Such disease agents are transmitted by careless selection of the BUDWOOD or ROOTSTOCK material used at GRAFTING (and thus a human influence). However, diseases caused by viruses, VIROIDS, FUNGI or PHYTOPLASMA are sometimes transmitted by NEMATODES or INSECTS.

There has been disagreement among viticultural scientists working in this area as to whether genetic difference or virus diseases are more significant in causing vine-to-vine differences. Professor Helmut BECKER, an acknowledged authority on clonal selection based at GEISENHEIM in Germany, argued for the genetic difference principle, while the virologists led by Austin Goheen of the University of California at DAVIS believed that virus infection was the more important. Most viticulturists would now agree that both influences are important.

Whether the vine-to-vine difference in the field is due to mutation or to a disease, the effects can be passed on to myriad new vines obtained by vegetative propagation. This is the basis of the viticultural technique of clonal selection.

The process of clonal selection is necessarily long and requires considerable investment of resources. To make reliable field selections requires several years of records (up to nine are used in Germany) followed by comparative trials of many different clones of the one variety for evaluation. After waiting three years for the first harvest, five to ten more years are necessary to monitor yields and fruit ripeness. Clonal selection should also involve making trial wine to assure trueness to VARIETAL type. Selected clones may not therefore be released until 15 or more years after the initial selection in the field. And, given the possibilities of both mutation and the spread of viruses by natural means, clonal selection should be an ongoing process. There has already been a release of second-generation clones in Germany; fields originally planted to one clone have been selected again for 'clones of clones'.

There is no doubt that clonal selection has played an important part in improving both yield and wine quality from modern vineyards. When grafting became popular in the 1880s to overcome phylloxera, virus diseases were inadvertently spread. Many vineyards planted as late as the 1960s contained off-types, rogue vines (i.e. not the intended variety), and virus diseases. As more healthy and true-to-type planting material becomes available as a result of clonal selection, then these problems disappear. Most reputable nurseries worldwide will provide only plants propagated from clonally selected rootstocks and scions.

Mechanisms for clonal selection and propagation vary from country to country. Generally the studies are conducted by government-funded scientists (although it is not unusual for a leading Bordeaux château, for example, to be doing its own clonal selection from vines naturally adapted to that property). In France, the extent to which planting material was infected by viruses up to the mid 1940s led to the formation of the Institut des Vins de Consommation Courante (IVCC). This organization and its affiliates tested selected clones and supplied CERTIFIED PLANTING MATERIAL. France AgriMer now oversees the certification process, although the research is generally carried out by the Institut Français de la Vigne et du Vin (IFV). In Germany, certification was introduced voluntarily after the First World War, and the scheme later became law. The EU adopted guidelines for propagation material in the early 1990s. In Australia, South Africa, and New Zealand, there are well-established VINE IMPROVEMENT programmes utilizing clonal selection as well as virus elimination. In California, the programme is conducted by the FOUNDATION PLANT SERVICES at the University of California at Davis. In South Africa, there is a Vine Improvement Association, and a number of organizations specialize in heat treatment to eliminate viruses (see THERMOTHERAPY).

For many vine varieties, the differences in appearance and performance between clones with the same virus status is small. This suggests that genetic differences are generally minor and that the mutation rate is low. Some varieties, such as Pinot Noir, show extreme variation between clones, which indicates that it is a very old variety that has had time to accumulate many mutations. While varieties have for some time been distinguishable by DNA PROFILING, it is only very recently that genome testing has been able to distinguish clones (see CLONE).

It is difficult to understand the effect of clonal selection on commercial wine quality since so many vineyards are planted with mixed clones. While most Old World countries have a wide range of clones available, sometimes (because of limited importations) a New World country might have only a few for any one variety. An extreme example is Sauvignon Blanc in New Zealand, where all commercial plantings up until the early 1990s can be traced to a single clone imported from the United States. Some producers and researchers are critical of the limited availability of only improved clones from nurseries. They argue that either MASS SELECTION or a range of clones produces better, more characterful wine than a single virus-free, moderate- to high-yielding clone. Unfortunately, some clones were released on the basis of purely viticultural evaluation, which has fuelled suspicion about their effect on wine quality.

French Wine and Vine Institute, 'What is clonal selection?' www.vignevin.com/en/article/what-is-clonal-selection.

Roach, M. J., et al., 'Population sequencing reveals clonal diversity and ancestral inbreeding in the grapevine cultivar Chardonnay', *PLOS Genetics*, 14/11 (2018).

R.E.S.

clone in a viticultural context is a single vine or a population of vines all derived by VEGETATIVE PROPAGATION from cuttings or BUDS from a single 'mother vine' developed by deliberate CLONAL SELECTION.

Vine nurseries may sell a range of different clones of each vine variety, each with different attributes and characteristics and individually identified by numbers and/or names. In Germany, for example, there is a formal process of clonal evaluation and a systematic numbering system. Normally government agencies are involved in selection, evaluation, and distribution to nurseries, and often the availability of clones and their acceptance varies regionally. Some clones are so outstanding that they become internationally distributed. Clones of Riesling from GEISENHEIM in Germany are examples of this. In the 1990s, there was considerable interest in Burgundian (sometimes called Dijon) clones; see particularly CHARDONNAY and PINOT NOIR.

After decades of unsuccessful research, DNA studies have been able to distinguish clones by comparing the complete genome of a variety. This was achieved in 2017 for Nebbiolo (98 clones) and in 2021 for Cot/Malbec (14 clones), opening the door for genomics-based CLONAL SELECTION.

Though rarely used, the term **subclone** refers to a clone obtained by induced or spontaneous mutation of an existing clone or one that is the result of EPIGENETIC changes in the vineyard.

R.E.S & J.V.

Galet, P., *Dictionnaire encyclopédique des cépages* (2nd edn, 2015).

Keller, M., *The Science of Grapevines* (3rd edn, 2020).

Mullins, M. G., et al., *Biology of the Grapevine* (1992).

clos is French for 'enclosure'; any vineyard described as a *clos* should be enclosed, generally by a wall. This is a particularly common term in Burgundy but is also used elsewhere. Similarly, the term *cuve close* refers to the sealed tank which gives its name to a bulk method of SPARKLING WINEMAKING. The first new-wave producers of PRIORAT adopted this term for their single-vineyard wines.

Clos de la Roche, leading red GRAND CRU in Burgundy's CÔTE D'OR. For more details, see MOREY-ST-DENIS.

Clos de Tart, Clos des Lambrays, and **Clos St-Denis,** red GRANDS CRUS in Burgundy's CÔTE D'OR. For more details, see MOREY-ST-DENIS.

Clos de Vougeot, also known as **Clos Vougeot**, famous walled vineyard in BURGUNDY created originally by the monks (see MONKS AND MONASTERIES) of Cîteaux. Between the 12th and early 14th centuries the Cistercians purchased or received as donations the land, much of which needed clearing and planting, which subsequently became known as the Clos de Vougeot. By 1336, the 50-ha/120-acre plot was complete and enclosed by stone walls on all sides.

The Cistercians maintained ownership until the French Revolution, when all clerical estates were dispossessed, although Dom Goblet, the monk responsible for the vineyards and the wine, had a sufficiently fine reputation to retain his job in the short term. In due course, Clos de Vougeot was sold on to Julien-Jules Ouvrard in 1818, the year before he bought DOMAINE DE LA ROMANÉE-CONTI, and remained in single ownership until 1889. Since then ownership has fragmented so that today there are over 80 proprietors.

A small chapel and rudimentary buildings, damaged during the religious wars, were rebuilt and enlarged in 1551, becoming the current Ch du Clos de Vougeot, a major tourist attraction. It is also home to the CONFRÉRIE des Chevaliers du Tastevin, a brotherhood which organizes copious feasts and the tastings for the Tastevinage. For this, producers submit wines to a jury; those selected are entitled to use the 'tasteviné' label, which should enable the wine to be sold more easily or at a higher price.

For more historical detail, see BURGUNDY, history. The vineyard and wines of Clos de Vougeot are described under VOUGEOT.

J.T.C.M.

closures for wine containers are necessary to avoid excessive contact with OXYGEN and have changed remarkably little until recent times. CORKS are still the principal closures used for wine BOTTLES, just as they were more than two centuries ago when bottles became strong enough to allow for a closure. Closures need to offer a reliable seal, present an inert surface to the wine, have an OXYGEN TRANSMISSION RATE comparable to that of cork, be easy to remove, and be available at a relatively low cost (<$0.50 each). Alternative closures have become increasingly common since the mid 1980s, thanks primarily to a rise in the incidence of CORK TAINT.

Historical context

Cork was known in ancient EGYPT and GREECE, where it was used alongside other materials to provide AMPHORAE with a wide variety of airtight stoppers. Roman authors such as CATO, writing in the 2nd century BCE, refer to the need to seal jars with cork and pitch when the fermentation was complete. However, this use of cork does not appear to have continued into the early medieval period, possibly because the main potential supply of European cork was in southern Iberia, which had been conquered by the Moors in the 8th century. Medieval illuminations illustrate barrels generally sealed by wooden stoppers, with cloth frequently placed between the barrel and the stopper to provide a more airtight seal. Pitch and wax were also sometimes used to give additional protection. In the long period during which wine was mainly stored in and served from the BARREL, the most common stopper was some form of BUNG.

With the development of stronger glass bottles during the 17th century, it was necessary to devise new methods of stoppering. Glass stoppers, ground to fit individual bottles and tied to them with thread, were therefore introduced and survived well into the 19th century. Indeed, as they are found in DECANTERS, they remain in use to this day, now also used for bottled wine (see below). However, such stoppers are expensive, and gradually from the beginning of the 17th century cork became the most frequent substance used to seal bottles. The use of corks also required the invention of another piece of equipment, the CORKSCREW or, as it was first called, the bottlescrew. The earliest corks were not pressed completely into the bottles and so could be pulled out without excessive difficulty. However, by the end of the 17th century the introduction of corkscrews enabled corks to be fully inserted into the necks of bottles. P.T.H.U.

Pecci, A., et al., 'Use and reuse of amphorae. Wine residues in Dressel 2–4 amphorae from Oplontis Villa B (Torre Annunziata, Italy)', *Journal of Archaeological Science: Reports*, 121 (2017), 515–21.

Simon, A. L., *Bottlescrew Days: Wine Drinking in England during the 18th Century* (1926).

Modern closures

Modern technology, prompted by an increasing awareness of the extent of CORK TAINT and bottle-to-bottle variability, offers a range of alternatives to the traditional cork. These include synthetic closures (see below), SCREWCAPS, CROWN CAPS (largely for sparkling wine), and AGGLOMERATE CORKS. However, few have a proven track record for long-term AGEING, and there is still considerable attachment on the part of many wine drinkers to the ritual of pulling a cork, so premium wines meant for ageing are still closed with a cork in most markets.

The alternatives capitalize on the frustration with the variable performance of natural cork as well as cork taint. At additional cost, cork producers now offer analysis of each cork sold, to eliminate any taint. However, so far there is no method to evaluate the OXYGEN TRANSMISSION RATE of each cork before its use. It should be noted that all closures have variability due to inherent differences in the closure (natural corks are, not surprisingly, the most variable), the bottle, and the sealing process. There is currently a range of novel closures, such as ProCork (a natural cork sealed at both ends with a barrier membrane to protect the wine from oxygen and taint) and glass stoppers such as Vinolok. Others have come and gone.

Synthetic closures

Also known as 'plastic corks', these have appealed to producers on the basis of cost and reliability. They satisfy the wine drinker's need to wrestle with a CORKSCREW while alleviating the risk of CORK TAINT, but they have the disadvantage of not being biodegradable, and some are difficult to extract from, and reinsert into, the neck of the bottle. The better synthetic closures now available are made by an extrusion process with a separate smooth plastic sleeve. Nomacorc, the dominant brand of synthetic corks, has released a series of closures offering different oxygen transmission rates to suit different wine styles. Another concern surrounds the capacity of synthetic closures to 'scalp' flavour by absorbing volatile components from the wine (see FLAVOUR SCALPING). Natural corks also do this but to a lesser extent. More research is needed on the possibility of contamination by non-volitile components that could affect taste of a wine. Synthetic closures are cheaper than most natural corks and have the advantage that, unlike screwcaps, they do not require producers to adopt new bottles and BOTTLING lines.

See also CAPSULES. A.L.W.

cloudiness. See SUNLIGHT.

cloudy wine. See FAULTS and STABILIZATION.

Cloudy Bay, seminal winery in the Marlborough region of NEW ZEALAND, the brainchild of David Hohnen of Cape Mentelle in WESTERN AUSTRALIA. Its debut release in export markets of a moodily labelled varietal Sauvignon Blanc in 1985 created a reputation for Marlborough Sauvignon and a cult following for Cloudy Bay almost overnight, even though the grapes were bought in and that vintage's wine made under contract at another winery. The enterprise, based in its own premises since 1986, became a distant offshoot of the VEUVE CLICQUOT, and hence LVMH, empire in 1990. It also produces Marlborough Chardonnay and Pinot Noir, a sparkling wine Pelorus, and, since the 2010 vintage, a Pinot Noir from Central Otago.

cluster, alternative, viticultural term for a BUNCH of grapes.

CMO, abbreviation for the EU's common market organization, its regulatory framework for wine.

Coal River Valley, the second largest wine-growing region in TASMANIA, located just north-east of Hobart.

Coastal Region, a conveniently extensive wine region in SOUTH AFRICA, home to several of the country's most important wine districts and wards, including CONSTANTIA, Darling, FRANSCHHOEK, PAARL, STELLENBOSCH, SWARTLAND, TULBAGH, and WELLINGTON. The name appears on labels of a substantial proportion of South African wines.

cochylis, better known as the vine moth. See MOTHS.

Cockburn, PORT house which became the brand leader in the important British market with the launch in 1969 of its Special Reserve ruby. This premium ruby transformed the market, which had hitherto been split between basic ruby port sold in pubs and vintage port for the wealthy. Consequent demand for Douro grapes led to new plantings, the first significant economic growth for the valley's farmers since the 1920s. Cockburn's were wine merchants in Leith, Edinburgh, in the 18th century. In 1815 Robert and John Cockburn set up a port company in Portugal and by 1870 were the second biggest exporter. In 1847, the brothers Henry and John Smithes joined the company, which became Cockburn Smithes & Co. John Smithes married Eleanor Cobb and both the Smithes and Cobb families remained in the firm for generations. Their grandson, John Smithes (1910–99), was a pioneer in the 1930s, experimenting with CLONAL SELECTION at Quinta do Tua and identifying TOURIGA NACIONAL as one of the best grapes. The last family member Peter Cobb joined Cockburn's in 1960 and retired in 1999. In 1962, Cockburn's became part of Harveys of Bristol and subsequently part of the Allied-Domecq conglomerate, which sold it to the American whiskey distillers Beam in 2005. The next year Beam sold Cockburn's vineyards and stocks of wine to the SYMINGTONS, who acquired the brand in 2010. Cockburn had a fine reputation, commanding high prices, for their vintage ports in the mid 20th century, but had some unconventional views on vintage port; it declared the lighter 1967 rather than 1966 against the popular vote but decided against declaring 1977 and 1980 before releasing a 1983. Cockburn's have long sourced wines in the higher reaches of the DOURO, owning Quinta do Vale Coelho since the 1890s and purchasing in 1978 Quinta do Ataide, where they made some of the first batch plantings of Touriga Nacional. Ataide has 171 ha/423 acres of vineyard including a 2.25-ha experimental plot with 53 INDIGENOUS VARIETIES. In 1989 Cockburns acquired Quinta dos Canais, a 272-ha property on the north bank of the Douro, which had long provided the backbone of Cockburn vintage port, Ataide is now largely used for the production of unfortified Douro wine and the Symingtons are hard at work rebuilding Cockburn's reputation as a producer of vintage port. R.J.M.

Cocks et Féret. See FÉRET.

Cococciola, white-wine variety of PUGLIA and ABRUZZO, where it is blended with TREBBIANO. There were 1,671 ha/1,678 acres in 2015.

Coda di Volpe Bianca, ancient, full-bodied white grape grown near Naples in CAMPANIA. Plantings had fallen to 77 ha/190 acres by 2015.

Códega, Douro synonym for SÍRIA, Portugal's widely planted white wine grape.

Códega de Larinho, particularly soft, tropical-fruited white wine grape most common in the DOURO and TRÁS-OS-MONTES regions of northern Portugal. There were 942 ha/2,328 acres planted in 2020.

co-fermentation, the simultaneous fermentation of two or more varieties in the same vessel, is said to lift a wine's floral aromas, enhance its TEXTURE, and improve the brilliance and intensity of the colour.

The technique has its origins in Europe, most notably in the CÔTE RÔTIE appellation in the northern Rhône. Here, the red variety SYRAH is co-fermented with the white variety VIOGNIER. Up to 20% Viognier is permitted, but 5–10% is more usual. This practice found increased favour in Australia and other parts of the NEW WORLD from the 2000s. Co-fermentation does not have to be a combination of red and white grapes—in the United States, for example, co-fermentation may originally have been a natural consequence of FIELD BLENDS such as ZINFANDEL and PETITE SIRAH. Another notable historical example is found in the CHIANTI region of Italy, where the primary red grape, Sangiovese, was traditionally fermented with small amounts of the red variety Canaiolo Nero and the white varieties Trebbiano and Malvasia, although this practice has become uncommon.

Research by Dr Roger Boulton, Professor of Enology and Chemical Engineering at DAVIS, indicates that red varieties may contain low levels of co-factors (sometimes known confusingly as co-pigments), which are said to aid CO-PIGMENTATION and thus the formation of deeper and more stable colour in red wines. The addition of a variety with higher levels of co-factors may aid co-pigmentation, and co-fermentation may originally have been adopted because it was seen to increase colour stability and intensity.

When Syrah, or Shiraz, and Viognier are co-fermented, there are many different techniques used to add the Viognier: whole fruit at the crusher; whole grapes, or pressed skins and grapes or just juice added to the crushed Shiraz must.

Differing harvest dates may put constraints on co-fermentation but these can be overcome by modern REFRIGERATION techniques. Further research is needed to ascertain the best combinations of varieties and the best proportions. Too many white grapes might simply dilute the colour of a red wine. T.R.C. & J.E.H.

Boulton, R., 'The copigmentation of anthocyanins and its role in the color of red wine: a critical review', *American Journal of Enology and Viticulture*, 52/2 (2001), 67–87.

co-inoculation. See MALOLACTIC CONVERSION and YEAST.

Colares, exceptional but now minuscule DOC wine region in Sintra on the west coast of Portugal, just north of the capital Lisbon (see map under PORTUGAL). These vineyards were spared from the PHYLLOXERA pest in the 19th century thanks to their SANDY composition but have struggled to survive today's commercial pressures. Located on a narrow strip of sand dunes on the clifftops above the Atlantic, with roots anchored in the CLAY below, 50% of the UNGRAFTED VINES are RAMISCO. Made principally from MALVASIA de Colares, which is genetically distinct from other known Malvasia grapes, white Colares is distinctly salty and mineral, sometimes like a FINO sherry, while Ramisco can be reminiscent of a particularly austere PINOT NOIR.

The region was badly hit by the collapse of the Brazilian market in 1930, and a year later the Lisbon government created the Adega Regional, a CO-OPERATIVE winery, which all growers were eventually obliged to join for their wine to be entitled to the Colares denomination. In 1990, the EU forced the government to abolish the Adega Regional's monopoly. As at 2021, the DOC comprised just 15 ha/37 acres of vineyard (down from over 1,800 ha in the 1930s). Ramisco and Malvasia de Colares are also being planted in Sintra's CALCAREOUS soils; the resulting wines (classified IGP Lisboa) show increasing promise, if not the same structure or intensity as Colares DOC. R.J.M. & S.A.

Mayson, R. J., *The Wines of Portugal* (2020).
Woolf, S. J., and Opaz, R., *Foot Trodden: Portugal and the Wines That Time Forgot* (2021).

Colchagua, part of the Rapel subregion of the Central Valley of CHILE. CARMENÈRE excels in its warm climate and GRANITE soils.

cold soak, MACERATION technique particularly popular for Pinot Noir.

colheita, Portuguese word meaning 'crop' or HARVEST and, by extension, VINTAGE. It also signifies a style of PORT or MADEIRA from a single year aged in wood for at least seven or five years respectively before bottling. These wines may also be labelled 'Single Harvest'. R.J.M.

collage, French term for FINING.

collar rot, one of the FUNGAL DISEASES of the vine which particularly attacks young vines growing in cool, moist soil, caused by the *Pythium* fungus. The vines are weakened and may die. Vines grafted on to Rupestris St George ROOTSTOCKS are most susceptible. Control is achieved by removing soil from the base of the trunk and reducing soil moisture. R.E.S.

collecting wine became a popular hobby in the 1980s. Americans in particular have tended to call anyone who buys FINE WINE a **collector** rather than a wine enthusiast, connoisseur, or *amateur* (the French term), suggesting that the thrill lies in acquisition and possession rather than in consumption. Ever since the development of cylindrical BOTTLES in the 1730s, when it first became possible to maintain a personal CELLAR, there have been individuals whose purchasing patterns amounted to building up a specific **collection** of certain wines. The rapid economic growth of the late 1970s and 1980s, however, together with a succession of good vintages to be bought EN PRIMEUR and the emergence of a truly international consumer wine press (see Robert PARKER, for example), resulted in the emergence of a significant group of serious wine collectors around the globe (notably in the United States, Germany, and Asia). They communicate and trade with each other through the AUCTION houses, fine-wine merchants, and the specialist BROKERS, but the collecting instinct seems weaker in those born after 1990, or even 1980.

colli, singular *colle*, is Italian for 'hills', and its use in a wine name indicates that the wine is produced on slopes of a certain ELEVATION (it is an almost direct equivalent of France's CÔTE, Côtes, and Coteaux). Accordingly, articles about Colli Somewhere are listed not under Colli but under S for Somewhere.

Elevation is obviously in the eye of the beholder, however, and the word *colli* is used to describe both mere knolls and near-mountainous viticulture at elevations of over 500 m/1,600 ft. *Colli* and its variations can be found not only as the title of various DOCs but also as a part of their descriptive apparatus: CHIANTI, for example, is produced in the Colli Senesi and the Colline Pisane (Chianti dei Colli Senesi, Chianti delle Colline Pisane). The absence of the word does not imply that a given wine is produced in the flatlands; much of Italy's finest wine—BARBARESCO, BAROLO, BRUNELLO DI MONTALCINO, VINO NOBILE DI MONTEPULCIANO—is produced from HILLSIDE VINEYARDS without that fact being indicated in the wine's name. Vineyards in

VALTELLINA often reach more than 700 m; ETNA's vineyards can reach over 1,000 m.

Collines Rhodaniennes, IGP which loosely follows the northern RHÔNE growing area. Around two-thirds of production is red, mostly Syrah. Around one-third is white, commonly made with Viognier. Only a very small amount of rosé is produced. Soils are predominantly GRANITIC. The wines of SEYSSUEL, close to the city of Vienne, are of particular interest. M.C.W.

Collio, or **Collio Goriziano**, is a qualitatively important, predominantly white wine DOC zone on the north-eastern border of Italy with Slovenia.

Collio, a corruption of COLLI, Italian for 'hills', is in the province of Gorizia. Half of what was once a single wine zone was annexed in 1918 by Italy, with the border running straight through vineyards. The other half is now known as Goriška Brda (see SLOVENIA). Before the Second World War, Collio extended much further eastward, and some of these sites are among the very finest of the entire zone. However, plans to create a supranational Collio/Brda denomination has yet to come to fruition as has the joint application in 2017 for UNESCO World Heritage Site status.

Within the region of FRIULI, Collio is the fourth biggest DOC in terms of area planted and volume of production after FRIULI GRAVE, ISONZO, and FRIULI COLLI ORIENTALI, but its fragrant and lively whites, which account for 85% of total production, have created an image of quality for Friuli throughout the world. Collio's red wines, overwhelmingly from MERLOT and CABERNETS SAUVIGNON and FRANC, tend to resemble LOIRE reds, at times with a similar vegetal quality and a certain lightness of body and texture.

The territory itself extends across the hills from the Judrio river in the west—the former boundary between Austria and Italy and now Collio's boundary with the climatologically similar Colli Orientali—to the Slovenian border in the east. Vines are planted on a CALCAREOUS marl alternating with layers of SANDSTONE called 'FLYSCH of Cormons' after an important township in the heart of the zone.

After two World Wars had ravaged the zone, it was rebuilt on viticulture, which became even more important at the beginning of the 1960s when the sharecropping system was abolished and many growers seized the chance to buy vineyards. Pinot Grigio became the inevitable cash cow and was planted widely. Other international, mainly white, varieties, notably Sauvignon Blanc and Chardonnay, as well the red Bordeaux varieties followed suit, and the early adoption of modern vinification techniques, particularly TEMPERATURE CONTROLLED fermentation, resulted in what were then Italy's cleanest, most modern wines.

With an international market awash in modern VARIETAL whites, today Collio struggles to maintain its former pole position. However, in the past Collio was a white wine made from local varieties, predominantly RIBOLLA Gialla with FRIULANO and MALVASIA Istriana, and labelled Collio without the suffix BIANCO. Today 12 varieties are allowed in the blend, while an additional 12 white and four red varieties can be suffixed to Collio on varietally labelled wines.

The rediscovery of a 1767 document which includes a CLASSIFICATION of Collio's vineyards into nine categories has sparked interest in Collio's subzones, though they remain theoretical so far. Plans to introduce a new DOC category, Collio Classico, for the classic blend of Ribolla Gialla, Friulano, and Malvasia Istriana have led to nothing, while a young generation who could forge change are hampered by high vineyard prices.

A beacon of hope remains in Josko Gravner, who came full circle in his career, having embraced stainless steel and international varieties only to then reject them in favour of Ribolla Gialla, SKIN-FERMENTED as was the historical practice, in QVEVRI. While Gravner is considered by many a radical, his minimalism and devotion to Ribolla puts into sharp contrast those paying only lip service to the variety that is intrinsic to Collio. W.S.

Capalbo, C., *Collio: Fine Wine and Foods from Italy's North-East* (2009).
Cosma, S., 'Dotato d'eccellentissimi vini, è il contado di Goritia . . . ', *Viticoltura nel Goriziano* (1992).
Brozzoni, G. (ed.), *Ribolla Gialla Oslavia. The Book* (2011).
www.consorziocolliocarso.it

Colli Orientali del Friuli. See FRIULI COLLI ORIENTALI.

Collioure, one of the prettiest seaside villages on the Mediterranean coast just north of the Franco-Spanish border, is also an AOC for heady, deep, usually red table wines whose aromas of ripe fruits and spice reflect the fact that Collioure comes from exactly the same area as BANYULS. The characteristics of the vintage determine what proportion of the grapes become Collioure rather than Banyuls, with cooler vintages resulting in more Collioure. And with the decline in the popularity of VIN DOUX NATUREL, most estates now focus on Collioure. The BUSH VINES are mainly planted on steep SCHIST terraces, making any MECHANIZATION well-nigh impossible. Yields are inevitably tiny. GRENACHE NOIR is the principal grape variety for the red and rosé wine, with Syrah, Carignan, and Mourvèdre. There is also a tiny amount of COUNOISE, not found elsewhere in Roussillon. The full-bodied whites are made mainly from Grenaches Blanc and Gris. R.E.G.

colloid, substance consisting of ultramicroscopic particles suspended in another substance. Wine colloids are very finely divided solids in particles with diameters ranging from about five nanometres to one micrometre. These are principally large organic molecules, most of which are polymers made of POLYSACCHARIDES including PECTINS and of smaller molecules such as PHENOLICS, PIGMENTED TANNINS, and TANNINS (see POLYMERIZATION). They do not contribute to a wine's VISCOSITY. When FINING and FILTRATION are successfully accomplished, less than 20% of colloids are removed so that wine quality is not affected. D.D. & V.L.

colluvium is material that has moved downslope under the influence of gravity, whereas ALLUVIUM is transported by RIVERS. The difference is significant for viticulture given that HILLSIDE VINEYARDS—usually characterized by a thin veneer of rock fragments commonly derived from the bedrock that caps the hill—are generally considered superior to those on plains and valley floors, where alluvium dominates. The grand cru vineyards of CHABLIS, for example, are sited mid-slope on the famous Kimmeridgian bedrock, but a substantial proportion of the colluvium that coats the slopes consists of fragments of the younger Portlandian hilltop limestone.

Studies by Wittendal have suggested that the majority of the grand cru vineyards in Burgundy's CÔTE D'OR are on colluvium. Colluvial sediment can comprise any geological material: for example, VOLCANIC bedrock in Coombsville, NAPA Valley; SCHIST and GNEISS in Central Otago, NEW ZEALAND; and GRANITE on the slopes flanking the Curicó Valley in central Chile. A.J.M.

Wittendal, F., 'Great Burgundy wines: a principal components analysis of "La Côte" vineyards', paper prepared for the 11th Œnometrics Conference 2004, Dijon, France. citeseerx.ist.psu.edu/viewdoc/download?doi=10.1.1.184.8571&rep=rep1&type=pdf.

Colombard is a natural cross of CHENIN BLANC × GOUAIS BLANC. This widely planted Charentais white grape variety was traditionally blended with UGNI BLANC and FOLLE BLANCHE, but considered inferior to both, as an ingredient in cognac. As Colombard's star waned in France, almost half of total plantings being pulled up in the 1970s, it waxed quite spectacularly in California, where, as **French Colombard**, it became the state's most planted variety of all, providing generous quantities of reasonably neutral but reliably crisp base wine for commercial, often quite sweet, white blends to service the prevailing FASHION for white wine.

Its disadvantages of being prone to rot and POWDERY MILDEW are much lesser inconveniences in the hot, dry Central Valley, where almost all of California's Colombard is planted. And Colombard's disadvantages for the distillers of Charentes—that its wine is more alcoholic and less acid than that of the other cognac varieties—are positive advantages for consumers of the wine in its undistilled state.

The annual rate of planting of French Colombard in California slowed to a standstill towards the end of the 1980s and then picked up briefly in the early 2000s, but by 2020 total plantings were 6,950 ha/17,173 acres (whereas Chardonnay's total was more than 90,000 acres).

It would take some sorcery to transform Colombard into an exciting wine, but pleasantly lively innocuousness is well within reach for those equipped with STAINLESS STEEL and TEMPERATURE CONTROL. In a nice example of transatlantic switchback, the producers of the Armagnac region set about duplicating California's modern winemaking transformation of the dull Colombard grape on their own varieties surplus to brandy production, thus creating the hugely successful Vin de Pays des Côtes de Gascogne. Colombard plantings have been steadily growing in France. It is the most planted variety in the Gers *département* where more than half of France's 2019 total of 11,500 ha/28,417 acres was concentrated, although it is grown all over SOUTH WEST FRANCE.

It is even more widely planted, as Colombar, in SOUTH AFRICA, where it was once important to the local brandy industry, and is now also popular for cheap, commercial off-dry white. Total Cape plantings have remained steady, with 10,507 ha/25,963 acres recorded in 2020, making it the country's second most important wine grape, just ahead of Cabernet Sauvignon. As in Australia, it provides usefully crisp blending material with Chenin Blanc and the much more fashionable Sauvignon Blanc. Australia's total plantings had fallen to 1,386 ha in 2022, mainly in the irrigated inland regions.

Colombia, South American country with a tropical climate and a relatively short history of viticulture. Colombia long depended on imported wines and spirits from Spain and developed a taste for sweet FORTIFIED WINES such as MÁLAGA. The initial output of the first vines planted here in the 1920s and 1930s was therefore directed towards this style of wine, as well as to the production of TABLE GRAPES. When wine imports from non–South American countries were punitively taxed in the mid 1980s, however, consumers became accustomed to the dry table wines of Chile and Argentina, and Colombia began to produce small quantities of dry wines from VITIS VINIFERA vines. The main grape-growing zone is in Boyacá department north-east of the capital Bogotá, where wineries such as Marqués de Puntalarga and Viñedo Ain Karim have set up shop. Annual precipitation in Boyacá is about 1,360 mm/53.5 in, with significant rainfall throughout the year. DOWNY MILDEW is the principal hazard, and vines have to be defoliated by hand in order to provide a short period of DORMANCY (see TROPICAL VITICULTURE). The country had 4,292 ha/10,060 acres of grapevines in 2020 according to the OIV, up from 2,591 ha/6,400 acres of vines in 2013.

E.M.G.

Goldstein, E., *Wines of South America* (2014).

Colorado, a state in the midwest United States split by the Rockies, a mountain range that runs along the Great Divide. The wine industry is concentrated on the western slope, the mountainous terrain offering multiple high-desert MESOCLIMATES and the highest-ELEVATION vineyards in the US.

Most plantings of grapes and fruit trees in the western slope followed the construction of the Grand Valley Canal in 1883, which brought irrigation water to an area that may see maximum precipitation of 30 cm/12 in annually. While grape-growing thrived on a small scale up until PROHIBITION, Colorado's first modern commercial winery, Ivancie Cellars in Denver, was not established until 1968. At this time, VITIS VINIFERA varieties were introduced into the Grand Valley, marking the birth of a wine region in Colorado.

By 2021, Colorado had 160 wineries, two AVAs, and 324 ha/800 acres of vineyards. Soils on the western slope range from Cretaceous Mancos SHALE and Gyproc Mesa CLAY to sandy LOAM. *Vinifera* makes up 80% of the state's plantings; with an increase in climatic challenges in the 2010s, HYBRIDS now make up 20% of the state's vineyards.

The Grand Valley AVA extends along the bottom of the steep north-west flank of the Grand Mesa, the largest flat-top mountain in the world. At 1,219–1,494 m/4,000–4,900 ft, it boasts 3800 F° growing degree days (GDD; see CLIMATE CLASSIFICATION) supporting 202 ha/500 acres of varieties in 2020, including, in decreasing order of acreage, Cabernet Sauvignon, Riesling, Merlot, Cabernet Franc, and Chardonnay.

The West Elks AVA, on the broader south-western side of the Grand Mesa in Paonia, is even higher, at 1,676–2,134 m/5,500–7,000 ft, with 2400 F° GDD. Its 40 ha/100 acres are planted mainly to Riesling, Pinot Noir, Chardonnay, and Gewürztraminer.

The state's vineyards face unique weather challenges, including late spring and early fall FROSTS and unpredictable WINTER FREEZE events. PHYLLOXERA, discovered in 2015/16, is slow-spreading, as the short growing season limits the pest's population cycle; confirmed positive acreage was near 5% in 2022. Summers bring intense ULTRAVIOLET RADIATION and triple-digit Fahrenheit temperatures, causing sugar levels to shoot up quickly while other ripening parameters such as colour, flavour, and PHENOLICS lag behind. Yet over the past 50 years advances in technology, training, education, and information sharing have resulted in dramatic improvements in the quality and recognition of Colorado's wines.

J.B.E.

Colorino, rare, deep-coloured dark grape variety used traditionally to add colour to blends in CHIANTI and VINO NOBILE DI MONTELPULCIANO. Four different varieties of Colorino can be distinguished. They are capable of adding TANNINS and colour to Sangiovese without the aromatic impact of Cabernet Sauvignon, once considered essential because of perceived demand for a certain style.

colour of wines. Wines are classified as red, white, rosé, or ORANGE but can vary widely in colour within these broad categories, sometimes with little obvious distinction between a light red and a dark rosé.

Red wines

Red wines derive their colour from the natural organic red/blue ANTHOCYANIN pigments, of which there are varying concentrations in the skins of darker-skinned grapes (only TEINTURIER grape varieties have red pulp). These concentrations depend on the VINE VARIETY, the RIPENESS of the grape, viticultural practices, and the environmental conditions such as soil and weather, all of which may affect YIELD. The amount of anthocyanins leached into the resulting wine depends on many factors including BERRY SIZE, homogeneity of berry ripeness, and length and temperature of the MACERATION of skins and new wine, together with the extent to which techniques to encourage EXTRACTION such as PUMPING OVER and PUNCHING DOWN are used. All these factors influence the intensity of colour in a young red wine.

Although the actual hue of a young red wine is influenced partly by the grape variety (Cabernet Sauvignon grape skins, for example, are blue-black, while those of Grenache are much more crimson), this is much less so than one might expect. A more important influence is the acidity of the grape juice. In low PH solutions, anthocyanins exist in bright-red-coloured forms, while as pH rises they change to a more colourless form. In general, therefore, the more acid the grape juice, the brighter the colour—although very high-acid grapes may be unripe and deficient in available anthocyanins.

The anthocyanins as they occur in the grape are responsible for the colour of a red wine only in its very early life. In a red wine more than a few weeks old, the colour is due increasingly to products formed from anthocyanins, including PIGMENTED TANNINS, which are polymeric species resulting from reactions of anthocyanins with tannins. Pigmented tannins and other derived pigments have a wide range of colours, from orange to purple, but the purple species tend to be less stable so that brick-red pigments gradually become predominant.

Red wines which undergo BARREL AGEING also tend to have more stable colour than those which do not, because small amounts of OXYGEN promote the formation of the wine's pigmented tannins. During AGEING, reactions of the phenolics and anthocyanins continue, forming an ever-increasing diversity of larger pigmented tannins. The larger ones aggregate and precipitate as SEDIMENT, depleting the wine of pigment.

The bleaching effect of SULFUR DIOXIDE on grape anthocyanins also means that red wines with a high level of free sulfur dioxide tend to be paler than they would be with a lower level. However, most of the red pigments generated in wine by anthocyanin reactions are resistant to sulfite bleaching so that this effect decreases as the wine ages. Also, if red wines are bottled with high sulfur-dioxide levels, the normal chemical interactions among the phenolics and other wine constituents to generate BOUQUET are disrupted.

The colour of a young red wine can vary from blackish purple (as in a vintage PORT, for example) through many hues of crimson to ruby. With age, red wines take on brick and then amber hues, lightening with time. The colour at the rim of a glassful of wine can give the most telling indication of the hue and therefore age of a wine, while looking straight down through a glassful of wine from above can clearly reveal the intensity of colour (see TASTING).

During the 1990s, winemakers tended to make ever-deeper-coloured red wines. This trend was encouraged by the increasing importance of large comparative tastings in JUDGING WINE. Because many (though by no means all) of the world's best red wines are deeply coloured (particularly those based on Cabernet Sauvignon and Syrah grapes, for example), there was a tendency among wine judges to favour deeply coloured wines. This led to a considerable increase in the number of red wines which owe their deep colour to over-EXTRACTION and/or colour added in the form of OENOCYANIN, TEINTURIER wines, or proprietary colouring agents such as California's Mega Purple made from RUBIRED grapes, which offer concentrated anthocyanins without tannins and often a little extra sweetness. However, the taste for deeply coloured wine has started to recede in the 21st century in line with a growing appreciation of lighter and fresher red wines.

See also RED WINEMAKING and RED WINES for more information, including names for red wines in languages other than English.

White wines

Although red wines are red, white wines are not white. Very occasionally they are colourless, but they usually range from pale green through straw, pale copper, and deep gold to amber.

The stems, skins, and pulp of the light-skinned grapes used for making white wines contain a large and complex mixture of PHENOLICS similar to those found in dark-skinned grapes but not the red/blue-coloured ANTHOCYANINS. The absorption of light by these white-wine phenolics occurs mainly in the ultraviolet range but extends into the visible range sufficiently to cause a light yellow colour in the wines we call 'white'. After CRUSHING of the grapes, these phenolics are exposed to oxygen and to the acids and other constituents of the grape juice, which causes a number of enzymatic and chemical reactions (including OXIDATION and POLYMERIZATION) which result in changes of colour from light yellow to amber and eventually to brown. To minimize extraction of phenolic compounds into the must and subsequent oxidative browning, white wines are usually made with minimum SKIN CONTACT. Although most white wines are made from light-skinned grapes, white wines may be made from dark-skinned grape varieties (see BLANC DE NOIRS) using minimum skin contact and/or CHARCOAL treatments.

Different 'white' grape varieties contain a slightly different array of phenolics, which results in differently coloured wines. Palomino and Pinot Blanc, for example, are particularly prone to oxidation and browning, while Riesling has traces of non-phenolic compounds which can cause a greenish tinge to the basic yellow.

Must browning is due to enzymatic oxidation and is highly dependent on the phenolic content (especially hydroxycinnamic acids) of the juice. During fermentation, yeast cells can absorb some of the brown polymerized materials which are then removed with the LEES. (Much the same phenomenon allows the use of quite distinctly pale-pink base wines from Pinots Noir and Meunier in the blend for BOTTLE FERMENTED sparkling wines which, after DISGORGEMENT, are white.) Some varieties used for white wines such as Gewürztraminer and Pinot Gris have greyish pink to purple skins and tend to result in deeply coloured wines with a strong pinkish yellow hue.

Careful protection from oxidation in pre-fermentation stages (for instance by addition of SULFUR DIOXIDE or ASCORBIC ACID) reduces must browning but maintains a rather high level of phenolics in the wine, especially if some skin contact has led to extraction of CATECHINS or PROANTHOCYANIDINS. This may result in increased browning susceptibility of the wine and, under some circumstances, may produce a pink tinge to the basic yellow.

With age, small amounts of oxygen act on phenolic compounds to brown them and apparently deepen a white wine's colour. With extreme AGEING of many decades, a very old white wine can be the same medium-intensity amber colour as a red wine of the same age.

White wine colour is also affected by the wine's levels of pH and sulfur dioxide; low pH and high sulfur dioxide concentration has a bleaching effect—as has hydrogen peroxide, which is occasionally used to make wine look paler.

Wines made from grapes affected by NOBLE ROT tend to have a particularly deep golden colour. Those which have been given extended skin contact tend to brown relatively early, while young white wines subjected to BARREL FERMENTATION and LEES CONTACT tend to be markedly paler than those fermented in STAINLESS STEEL and then transferred to cask for barrel ageing because darker pigments are absorbed by the lees.

During the 1990s, white wines in general became paler, as unintended oxidation became rarer, barrel fermentation more common, and barrel ageing more skilfully handled. See also WHITE WINEMAKING, WHITE WINES, and ORANGE WINE.

Rosé wines

These wines, which vary enormously in hue and intensity, owe their combination of pink colour and white-wine characteristics either to a very short SKIN CONTACT with dark-skinned grapes, or, for some everyday wines and pink sparkling wines, to the BLENDING of red and white wines. The proportions of anthocyanins, hydroxycinnamic acids, and tannins in the wine, depending on the grape variety and winemaking process, influence the pigment composition and thus the colour. In addition, wines that are pale bluish pink are likely to be the results of PROTECTIVE techniques, while those with an orange tinge may well have been exposed to some (possibly deliberate) oxidation. While a blindfolded taster can in some circumstances find it difficult to distinguish between low-tannin red wines and fuller-bodied white wines, it can be almost impossible on the basis of taste alone to distinguish a rosé wine from a white one.

See also ROSÉ WINEMAKING, ROSÉ WINES, and AGEING. J.R. & V.C.

Columella, Lucius Junius Moderatus, important, but long uncredited, source of information on wine production in ancient ROME. Little is known about his life except that he was born in Gades (Cádiz near JEREZ) and that he was an officer in the Roman army in Syria. He composed his treatise on farming, *De re rustica*, in 60–5 CE. It is divided into 12 books, all in prose except the tenth, on gardens. This book was written in hexameter verse as an addition to VIRGIL's *Georgics*, which Columella admired. Columella's work shows by far the best grasp of technical detail of all the surviving Roman treatises on farming, and this is particularly clear in his treatment of VITICULTURE. Books 3 and 4, the most important of the treatise, deal with vine-growing, but much practical

C

advice on winemaking is also contained in Book 12, which outlines the duties of the bailiff's wife. He discusses what grape variety to use in which type of soil; yield in relation to labour and capital outlay (he assumes that a well-managed vineyard will yield at least 20, and possibly 30, AMPHORAE *per iugerum*, approximately 20 hl/ha (1.1 tons/acre)); planting; propagating; pruning; training and dressing; grafting (Books 3–4); the vintage; and winemaking (Book 12). Half of an earlier, shorter work called *De arboribus* ('On trees') also survives; it has a section on vines which is much briefer than the corresponding sections of *De re rustica*. H.M.W.

Martin, R., *Recherches sur les agronomes latins* (1971).
White, K. D., *Roman Farming* (1970).

Comité Interprofessionnel, body representing all interests concerned with the production of a certain wine and the French counterpart to the CONSORZIO of Italy and Spain's CONSEJO REGULADOR. The model for all such organizations was the CIVC of Champagne.

Commandaria, a deep amber sweet wine produced from partially dried grapes from the island of Cyprus with flavours of orange peel, walnut, and raisins and an alcohol content usually around 15%.

The Mediterranean island was known for sweet wines, called Nama, long before the Knights Hospitallers (or Knights of St John) made Cyprus their headquarters in 1281. Like all religious orders, the Knights acquired land on a large scale and grew wine. Their organization was strictly hierarchical, divided into priorates, then bailiwicks, and lastly commanderies. A commandery was a manor or group of manors under the authority of a commendator. Each commandery had its vineyard or vineyards, and the wine shipped from them became known as Commandaria. (See the history of CYPRUS.)

In 1993, Commandaria became the first Cypriot wine to be granted full legal protection covering both its geographical origin and production techniques. Now a PDO, Commandaria must be produced within a strictly defined region comprising 14 wine-producing villages in the Troodos foothills about 30 km/20 miles north of Limassol, from the red grape variety MAVRO and/or the white XYNISTERI, grown as BUSH VINES, and planted at a low VINE DENSITY of 2,000–2,750 vines per hectare. The demarcated area includes only vineyards planted at 400–900 m/1,312–2,953 ft in ELEVATION; those on the north-western side are mainly planted in CALCAREOUS soils, while those on the steeper, higher north-eastern side are largely VOLCANIC. (Both grape varieties are usually used, but a few lighter, subtler versions of Commandaria are made from white grapes only.) Total area planted as of 2022 was 424 ha/1,048 acres.

The grapes are picked very ripe to overripe, with minimum MUST WEIGHTS of 13 °Baumé for Xynisteri and 14 for Mavro, then sun-dried for about two weeks, on mats on the ground or on racks above ground, to a concentration of at least 21 or 23 °Baumé respectively. After fermentation, the wine must have an alcoholic strength of at least 10% without FORTIFICATION and no more than 1.5 g/l VOLATILE ACIDITY. At that point, the wine may but need not be fortified by the addition of grape spirit at 95–96% or with grape distillate at around 70% alcohol to a maximum of 20% actual alcohol. Its total POTENTIAL ALCOHOL must be at least 22.5%.

The wine must be aged for at least two years in wood, although in practice ageing is at least five years. Mainstream producers use a SOLERA-like system called *mana* in which older barrels are topped up with younger wines, although recently single-vintage Commandarias have appeared as part of the revival of the island's long wine heritage.

Although even within Cyprus it is of very limited commercial importance, Commandaria is one of the world's classic sweet wines.

See also DRIED-GRAPE WINES. C.G. & A.M.

Vrontis, D., and Thrassou, A., 'The renaissance of Commandaria: a strategic branding prescriptive analysis', *Journal for Global Business Advancement*, 4/4 (2011), 302–16.

Commanderie, common French term for a CONFRÉRIE.

commune, French for 'village' or 'parish'. The Italian counterpart is a **comune**.

competitions, wine. Well-run reputable wine competitions can be extremely lucrative for the organizers and can play an important part in marketing, which is why some wine labels are adorned with MEDALS and the like, and some retailers' lists and shelves are dotted with lists of awards. Care should be taken when studying these claims to ensure that the competition was a recent and respected one and that the successful wine was exactly the same bottling as the one on offer. Three of the most ambitious and successful international wine competitions have their roots in the UK: the International Wine and Spirit Competition, the International Wine Challenge, and the Decanter World Wine Awards. They attract thousands of entries from around the world, and most of their garlanded wines are of genuinely superior quality. Most wine competitions in wine-producing countries are national rather than international. Some of France's most important are associated with agricultural shows, especially those of Paris and Mâcon. Some of the more respected of the many wine competitions held regularly in the US are Dan Berger's International Wine Competition, the Critics Challenge International Wine Competition, the Indy International in Indiana, the Long Beach Grand Cru, the Los Angeles International Wine Competition, the Pacific Rim International, the San Diego International Wine & Spirits Challenge, the San Francisco International Wine Competition, the San Francisco Chronicle Wine Competition, the Sunset International Wine Competition, the TEXSOM International Wine Awards, and the New York Wine Classic for NEW YORK wines only. The explosion of interest in wine in CHINA has been accompanied by a rash of wine competitions there. It should be remembered, however, that few of the world's most revered producers enter such competitions, and certainly none of those wines that are available in only very limited quantities ever do. It is difficult to imagine there will ever be a wine competition which will identify the best, rather than the best of those who have something to gain by entering.

In Australia they are known as wine SHOWS. For more details of how competitions and wine shows work, see JUDGING WINE.

Completer, ancient white grape variety grown in Graubünden in eastern Switzerland. The wine produced—distinctive, pungent, acidic, and full-bodied—is a speciality of Bündner Herrschaft. DNA PROFILING at DAVIS showed in 2004 that Completer is one of the parents of LAFNETSCHA. Subsequently, a few vines of Completer discovered among Lafnetscha vines supported this parentage and the unanticipated presence of Completer in the Valais. J.V.

Complexa, Portuguese red-wine variety bred from CASTELÃO, Tintinha, and MUSCAT OF HAMBURG in the 1960s and introduced to MADEIRA as an experimental, deeper-coloured, softer alternative to TINTA NEGRA.

complexity, a TASTING TERM of approval when applied to FLAVOUR in wine, and a characteristic commonly viewed as a central component of wine QUALITY. Complex wines possess multiple flavours as well as flavour diversity. The term implies coherence: chaotic or jarring flavours are not considered complex. The term can also be used, typically when describing older wines, to suggest intricate subtlety, requiring sustained mental effort to grasp, as with a complex puzzle. A.H.

compost, the name given to the product of microbial action on organic wastes under controlled conditions in piles or windrows. Compost can be created from WINERY WASTE, typically POMACE, and it may be mixed, for example, with animal manures and sometimes with municipal garden waste, which encourages microbial action and resultant high temperatures. The compost must be turned regularly to maintain aerobic conditions and be kept at a temperature of 55 °C/131 °F for at least three days to destroy pathogens and weed seeds. Compost is applied to vineyard soils and, being rich in ORGANIC MATTER and NUTRIENTS, improves water storage and vine growth. However, compost-making and distribution requires handling large quantities of material, and for this reason most vine-growers around the world use manufactured FERTILIZERS as a source of nutrients, and may incorporate mown COVER CROPS or prunings into the soil as a source of organic matter. The use of compost and other organic soil amendments is an integral part of ORGANIC and BIODYNAMIC VITICULTURE. R.E.S.

computers. See INFORMATION TECHNOLOGY.

Comté Tolosan, a wide-ranging IGP covering the whole of SOUTH WEST FRANCE. This is a haven for those wishing to avoid the rules or boundaries of the AOCs. The wines range from the superb (Ch Cabidos) to the unmentionable. P.S.

Conca de Barberá, DOP of 3,800 ha/9,390 acres of vines in Spanish CATALUÑA, sandwiched in between PENEDÈS, COSTERS DEL SEGRE, and TARRAGONA (see map under SPAIN). At around 500 m/1,600 ft in ELEVATION, this DOP experiences cold winters, and hot summer days are tempered by cool winds from the sea. Miguel Torres of Penedès (see FAMILIA TORRES) recognized the grape-growing potential of the LIMESTONE country around the Castillo de Milmanda and makes two of his most ambitious SINGLE-VINEYARD WINES there: the white Milmanda and the red Grans Muralles. At one time, most of Conca de Barberá's grapes were used to produce CAVA, but today more still wines are made, particularly some interesting rosé and red wines from the local TREPAT vine. V. de la S. & F.C.

concentrated grape must. See GRAPE CONCENTRATE.

concentration, umbrella term for any winemaking operation which serves to remove volatile substances, mainly water, from grape juice, must or wine. Its most common application has been in the production of GRAPE CONCENTRATE. However, a range of concentration techniques is used on grapes, juice, and MUST to produce more concentrated wines, often only on a certain portion of the grapes or liquid. The traditional SAIGNÉE method entails the bleeding of free-run juice from the must after a short pre-fermentation MACERATION period. More complex techniques are described below.

One component in a mixture can be concentrated using differences in boiling points, in freezing points, or in molecular size. The usual technique for making grape concentrate is to use differences in boiling points in a low-pressure, low-temperature evaporator. While very effective in concentrating sugar, this technique has the disadvantage of also removing volatile FLAVOUR COMPOUNDS.

A more recent technique, used since 1989 in some parts of France as an alternative to ENRICHMENT, involves evaporating grape must under vacuum. The water in the must evaporates at temperatures of about 20 °C/68 °F, no hotter than fermentation temperatures and therefore involving no dangerous loss of flavour. In practice, to achieve an acceptable rate of evaporation temperatures much higher have to be used, which can have a negative effect on the flavour of the final wine (see FLASH DÉTENTE). The equipment needed (known in French as a *concentrateur sous vide*) is relatively expensive but has the advantage of being able to handle unclarified grape must. Increasingly, though, vacuum concentrators are being superseded by REVERSE OSMOSIS machines.

Freeze concentration uses differences in freezing points to make a range of sweet wines of varying qualities. The EISWEIN of Germany and Austria and the ICEWINE of Canada and elsewhere is made by picking frozen grapes from the vine, crushing them, and filtering the must without allowing the mixture to thaw so that water is removed in the form of ice. Ice crystals are collected on the filter along with the more usual grape solids (skins, etc.), and the result is grape juice with a lower concentration of water but a higher concentration of SUGARS, ACIDS, and other SOLUBLE SOLIDS.

Natural freezing on the vine is replicated by producers in such different regions as SAUTERNES (where it is called CRYOEXTRACTION) and NEW ZEALAND. Grapes, musts or juice can be frozen by using special chillers, dry ice (the solid form of carbon dioxide) or liquid nitrogen. This technique can also be used selectively, not just for sweet white wines but also on grapes destined to make dry white wines, not all of which are fully ripe. Since just-ripe grapes freeze at 0 °C/32 °F but fully ripe grapes freeze only at −6 °C or below, the mixture of grapes is chilled before crushing to an intermediate temperature so that it yields only the ripest juice (although it will yield nothing if there are no ripe grapes in the first place). The technique can only be practised on individual batches of grapes, however, so is relatively labour-intensive.

One final method of concentrating grape must is also the oldest: desiccation. See DRIED-GRAPE WINES.

Because in general these methods remove only water from the grapes, juice or must, all other components are concentrated. An increased concentration of fermentable SUGARS results in a wine with a higher ALCOHOLIC STRENGTH. Increased concentrations of PHENOLICS in many cases result in red wines with more BODY, potential for AGEING, and possibly more flavour. Increased ACIDITY, however, can result in wines that are aggressively tart, especially in less ripe years or in cooler wine regions. In some cases, particularly in cooler areas, musts which have been concentrated may have to be further subjected to DEACIDIFICATION, although in TEMPERATE climates TOTAL ACIDITY is usually only very slightly raised once TARTRATES have been precipitated.

Concentration is also used as a TASTING TERM. A.O.

OIV, 'International Code of Oenological Practices'. www.oiv.int/en/technical-standards-and-documents/oenological-practices/international-code-of-oenological-practices.

Concha y Toro. The dominant wine producer in Latin America was founded in Pirque, CHILE, in 1883 by Don Melchor Concha y Toro, a prominent businessman and politician. Its 2021 total of 11,624 ha/28,723 acres made it one of the world's leading vineyard owners. Since the mid 20th century, efforts have been focused on modernization and developing export markets.

The Casillero del Diablo ('the Devil's Cellar') BRAND is one of the world's most successful, with global sales of over six million cases annually (2.6 million of which are in the UK).

In 1993 the company founded Cono Sur winery to provide more innovative styles of wine, specializing in Pinot Noir. It was an early espouser of SUSTAINABILITY, a policy now applied throughout the group. Other significant winery projects followed, including Bodega Trivento in Mendoza in 1996 (now the fourth largest winery in Argentina) and vineyards in the cool Limari Valley in northern Chile. In 2011 Concha y Toro acquired Fetzer and Bonterra in Mendocino, California, thereby extending its vineyard holdings outside South America for the first time. In 2021 the company achieved B Corp certification across its entire group of wineries.

Concha y Toro is distinguished by the quality of its winemakers, wines, and management at virtually all price levels. Its top wines include Don Melchor Cabernet Sauvignon, Carmín de Peumo Carmenère, and the Terrunyo wine range. Since 1997, Concha y Toro has had a JOINT VENTURE, Almaviva in Puente Alto, with the Rothschilds of Ch MOUTON ROTHSCHILD.

Since the 1980s the company has been led by Eduardo Guilisasti, whose family have a majority shareholding (27.8%) of Viña Concha y Toro Family of Wineries, as it is now known. His siblings Rafael, Pablo, and Isabel are also closely involved in the running of the business.

Concord, the most widely planted vine variety grown in the eastern United States, notably in NEW YORK State, where there were more than 7,642 ha/18,883 acres in 2011. It started life as a chance seedling of an American vine species with the American hybrid CATAWBA. The pronounced FOXY flavour of its juice—synonymous with 'grape' flavour in the US—makes its wine an acquired taste for those raised on the produce of VITIS VINIFERA vines. It was named after Concord, Massachusetts, by Ephraim W. Bull, who introduced it, having planted the seeds of a WILD VINE there in 1843. It is particularly important for the production of GRAPE JUICE and grape jelly, but 5–10% of it is used to produce a wide range of wines, some KOSHER, often with some considerable RESIDUAL SUGAR. Viticulturally, the vine is extremely well adapted to the low temperatures of New York and is both productive and vigorous. It is planted in many eastern states of the US and widely in Washington State, where most of its grapes go into juice and GRAPE CONCENTRATE. Concord is also widely found in Brazil.

Huber, F., et al., 'A view into American grapevine history: Vitis vinifera cv. 'Semillon' is an ancestor of 'Catawba' and 'Concord'', *Vitis*, 55/2 (2016), 53–6.

concrete, popular since the 19th century for the construction of large FERMENTATION VESSELS and tanks for storage and AGEING, though upstaged by the introduction of shiny STAINLESS STEEL vats from the 1970s onwards. Nevertheless, concrete's greater thermal inertia, longevity, cost-effectiveness, and overall influence on wine QUALITY are still appreciated by many top producers, including Bordeaux's PETRUS, and the material is experiencing a renaissance. Traditionally lined with epoxy resin to prevent direct contact between the concrete and the wine and to make cleaning easier, especially the removal of TARTRATE crystals, concrete tanks do have the potential disadvantage of allowing very little OXYGEN exchange, which is important in the evolution of TANNINS. Some producers therefore prefer unlined concrete for its greater oxygen ingress. Since the early 2000s, so-called **concrete eggs** have been gaining in popularity among a small group of producers around the world because the shape not only offers a high level of contact between the wine and the LEES but also appears to encourage convection currents that improve fermentation kinetics. They range in size from around 500 to 1,500 litres (130–400 gal) and are usually unlined but treated with tartaric acid solution before use. Early adopters include Michel CHAPOUTIER, South Africa's Eben Sadie, and Alfred Tesseron at Ch Pontet-Canet.

Condado de Huelva, Spanish DOP of 2,900 ha/7,166 acres of vines in ANDALUCÍA, close to the city of Huelva between the JEREZ region and the border with Portugal (see map under SPAIN). Nowadays few of its wines, which have typically been FORTIFIED and made in the image of its neighbour SHERRY, are exported, but the region has a long history (see SPAIN, history). In 'The Pardoner's Tale', Chaucer refers to the wines of Lepe, a small town just outside the modern Condado de Huelva DOP and a notorious source of blending wine; by the early 16th century the wines of Huelva were being exported to northern Europe and the emerging colonies in South America. From the 17th century, however, much of Huelva's production was sold to Jerez, where it was blended anonymously into sherry SOLERAS. Huelva became a DOP in its own right in 1964. The principal grape is the rather neutral ZALEMA along with a little PALOMINO (15% of the vineyard area).

Most wines here are white and dry, but there are several specialties that speak to the closeness of Jerez. Condado PÁLIDO is a pale, dry, FORTIFIED WINE matured in a solera under a blanket of FLOR, therefore not unlike FINO sherry. Condado Viejo is a RANCIO style of wine aged in a solera and resembling a somewhat rustic Jerez OLOROSO. Vinos de Licor are MISTELA-like fortified sweet wines. Vino Naranja, literally 'orange wine', is Spain's only aromatized wine (through maceration with orange peel) with an appellation of origin (and bears no relation, therefore, to ORANGE WINE). V. de la S. & F.C.

Condrieu, small AOC in the far north of the northern RHÔNE that is likely to be the original source of VIOGNIER, its sole grape variety. This appellation encompasses seven right-bank communes (which happen to span three *départements*: the Rhône, Loire, and Ardèche) just south of the red-wine appellation CÔTE RÔTIE where the river turns a bend and the best vineyards are exposed to the south and south-east (see map under RHÔNE). The vine has probably been cultivated here for two millennia, since nearby Vienne was an important Roman city, although the total Condrieu vineyard fell to fewer than 10 ha/25 acres in the mid 1960s, when the wine was virtually unknown outside local restaurants and other fruit crops were much more profitable.

When the appellation was established in 1940, there were just three communes (Condrieu, Vérin, and St-Michel-sur-Rhône), but in 1967 the appellation was extended further south to include a succession of remote parcels of land dotted along the communes of Chavanay, Malleval, St-Pierre-de-Boeuf, and Limony. In 1986, another revision removed all vineyards over 300 m/984 feet in ELEVATION to include only the best exposed slopes. The vineyards of Condrieu now stretch across 14 km/8.7 miles north to south, covering 209 ha/516 acres in 2020. It is climatically similar to Côte Rôtie, with cold winters and with summers whose warmth is concentrated by the sloping vineyards and captured by the dark GRANITIC soils.

At one time Condrieu was a sweet or medium-sweet wine, but today almost all is made dry, and the wines are always full-bodied. Vinification methods are variable, with differing opinions on such fundamentals as the desirability of MALOLACTIC CONVERSION, LEES STIRRING, and use of OAK.

The ageability of Condrieu is a contentious topic. Most believe it is at its best in the first few years after bottling, when its floral perfume is at its most exuberant. After eight to ten years, the wines take on a more nutty, honeyed aroma, and those from the best sites are sustained by an inner salinity, which provides structure even if they are low in acidity.

France's only other all-Viognier appellation, CHÂTEAU-GRILLET, is an enclave within the Condrieu zone. M.C.W.

Conegliano, town in the VENETO region of north-east Italy that was home to Italy's first school of OENOLOGY, founded by Antonio Carpenè and Giovanni Battista Cerletti in 1876 as the Scuola di Viticoltura ed Enologia di Conegliano. Renamed the Scuola Enologica G. B. Cerletti, the school's influence extends all over Italy as it has trained many of Italy's producers and OENOLOGISTS. Along with Valdobbiadene, the town is also the centre of PROSECCO production.

Over more than a century, the University of Padua's agricultural department developed its research and training programmes in viticulture and oenology at Conegliano. Today its campus brings together the Centro Interdipartimentale per la Ricerca in Viticoltura ed Enologia (CIRVE); the Scuola Enologica G. B. Cerletti; the Centro Regionale per la Viticoltura, Enologia e Distillati; and the Centro di Ricerca per la Viticoltura di Conegliano (CRA-VIT), established in 1923 and now with further units around Italy.

Since 1967, CRA-VIT's work at Conegliano has focused on viticulture, with four central units concerned with AMPELOGRAPHY and VINE IMPROVEMENT, biology and protection, PROPAGATION, and cultivation techniques. It is the main experimental viticultural station in the Veneto with a 9-ha/22-acre nursery for an ampelographical collection of VINE VARIETIES established in 1951 and home to the Italian national register for grape cultivars. Another 20 ha were added in 1963, accommodating a total of over 2,000 varieties. The station is responsible for CLONAL SELECTION and ROOTSTOCK research.

One of CRA-VIT's first directors was Professor Dalmasso, whose Dalmasso Commission made a significant report on the state of the Italian wine industry (see ITALY). His successor Professor Manzoni produced many crosses (see INCROCIO Manzoni) still cultivated today. In 1933, Conegliano became involved in combating ADULTERATION AND FRAUD in the Veneto and then also, from 1965, in FRIULI. In 1986 the adulteration and fraud service became independent. W.S.

Conegliano-Valdobbiadene, DOCG for PROSECCO from the original production zone on the hills between these two towns in Italy's VENETO. **Colli di Conegliano** covers the same area but is the DOCG for the production of still white wines based on Manzoni Bianco (see INCROCIO), reds of Cabernets Sauvignon and Franc, and two rare PASSITO wines, Refrontolo and Torchiato di Fregona.

confréries, French 'brotherhoods' or associations, dedicated in particular to advancing the cause of various foods and drinks throughout France. More than 150 of them, most of them founded in the second half of the 20th century, are devoted to such various products as macarons, jams, olives, and local shellfish. A high proportion of them, almost half, are based on specific wines and other alcoholic drinks. One of the most famous is the Confrérie des Chevaliers de Tastevin in Burgundy (see CLOS DE VOUGEOT). The Commanderie du Bontemps du MÉDOC et des Graves, founded in Bordeaux in 1949 by the energetic Henri Martin, is also well known and is the LEFT BANK answer to the oldest of these *confréries*, the Jurade de ST-ÉMILION. The latter dates from the late 12th century, when the town councillors of this ancient town were given particular powers and responsibilities by the English crown which then governed it (see BORDEAUX, history); it was reconstituted in 1947. These *confréries* are devoted to an annual programme of pageantry, feasting, robe-wearing, and the *intronisation* (enthronement) of honorary converts to the cause.

connoisseurship of wine is a (disappearing) art in search of a less emotive name. The word **connoisseur** in English, like its counterpart *connaisseur* in French, conjures up a frightening vision of an elderly male so steeped in wine, wine knowledge, and wine prejudices as to be completely unapproachable. Much more attractive and widely acceptable terms are those which convey not just knowledge but an element of relish, such as 'wine lover', 'wine enthusiast', or the common and attractive French term *amateur du vin*. None of these terms, incidentally, has any connotation of gender.

Whatever the drawbacks of the term, connoisseurship or wine expertise is an art that can give pleasure, and it involves less an arid grasp of the precise ENCÉPAGEMENT of each vineyard and the fermentation regimes for each vintage than an intelligent appreciation of how wines are likely to taste in a given environment, at a certain stage in their evolution, before or after other wines, and, importantly, with different foods. This is what consumers rather than producers are for. Experience can contribute to connoisseurship, but only if the consumer tastes with humility, attention, and an open mind. Mentors are useful, but some newcomers to wine have an instinctive grasp of connoisseurship. A true connoisseur meets each wine halfway and tries to show it in the best possible light, in stark contrast to professional wine JUDGING. Some wine drinkers seem determined to judge rather than enjoy wine. See wine TASTING, AGEING, SERVING, and FOOD-AND-WINE MATCHING. A connoisseur is not necessarily a wine BORE; and while deep pockets help, they are not a prerequisite.

Consejo Regulador, Spanish term meaning 'regulating council' (see COMITÉ INTERPROFESSIONNEL). Spanish wine law is administered through a network of *Consejos Reguladores* representing each DOP. They comprise vine-growers, wine producers, and merchants who between them decide on the ground rules for their region. These days some producers, especially the younger generation, are leaving the DOP system in search of more freedom or because they do not feel represented by it. F.C.

Consorzio, Italian word for a consortium or association of winegrowers, NÉGOCIANTS, and CO-OPERATIVES representing the interests of a single wine region or DOC/DOCG. However, since the 2008 reforms of the EU wine market, the consorzio role has changed drastically. QUALITY CONTROL, which used to be the consorzio's concern, is now in the hands of a neutral third party, and consorzios are now concerned more with promotion and marketing, while several have added to this the ambitious task of routing COUNTERFEIT wines in the international market. If at least 60% of production is controlled by consorzio members, a mandatory levy, referred to as *erga omnes*, can be imposed on any producer wishing to use the relevant DOC or DOCG name on labels, whether they are a member or not. Its counterpart in France is the COMITÉ INTERPROFESSIONNEL; in Spain the CONSEJO REGULADOR. W.S.

Constantia, legendary 18th- and 19th-century dessert wines from the Cape, SOUTH AFRICA, then a Dutch colony. Their fame was never matched by any other New World wines, and at their height they commanded more prestige, sold at more fabulous prices, and enjoyed more crowned patronage than the most celebrated wines of Europe (with the possible exception of Hungarian TOKAJI). Constantia was even ordered by Napoleon from his exile on St Helena.

The Cape wines were grown on a subdivision of the 750-ha/1,850-acre Constantia Estate just outside Cape Town, founded in 1685 by an early Dutch governor, Simon van der Stel. However, it was Constantia's subsequent owners who achieved acclaim and prosperity, principally Hendrik Cloete, who purchased and restored one of the subdivisions in 1778. Quality and fame gradually diminished in the late 19th century, partly as a result of the Cape's declining importance to the British wine market and partly because Constantia's higher labour costs, especially after the abolition of slavery in 1834, and the lower yields associated with its cool climate made wine production economically marginal. By 1885 Cloete's estate was bankrupt, and under the name of Groot Constantia it has been state-owned ever since. In 1975, its management passed into the hands of a control board and in 1993 into a trust. In recent times Groot Constantia has made sound, increasingly impressive, conventional wines. A neighbouring privately owned estate, Klein (Little) Constantia, an 1823 deduction from Groot Constantia, was the first to take up the challenge of recreating the legend. It replanted vineyards with Muscat of Frontignan (MUSCAT BLANC À PETITS GRAINS) in the early 1980s and now produces a white dessert wine known as Vin de Constance to local and international acclaim.

The sweet wines of Constantia, both red and white (the latter the more expensive), were made principally from this small-berried Muscat and its dark-berried mutation, probably including the lesser MUSCAT OF ALEXANDRIA, the dark red PONTAC, and CHENIN BLANC. Records show that slightly under 50% of Constantia wine in the early 19th century was sold without any varietal claim. Analyses of recently opened bottles (still perfumed with a tang of citrus and smoky richness) reveal they were probably unfortified although high in alcohol, apparently confirming records that the grapes were left on the vines long after ripeness to achieve shrivelled, but not BOTRYTIZED, concentration (see DRIED-GRAPE WINES for more details of the technique). Other stories suggest the wines may have been FORTIFIED by shippers for protection on the long, rough, and hot journey across the equator to Europe.

Today Constantia is a demarcated wine ward in Cape Town's southern suburbs, on the slim peninsula pointing into the south Atlantic, cooled by the sea for relatively slow summer ripening with average daily temperatures of 18–21 °C/64–70 °F and very wet but moderate winters (average annual rainfall over 1,000 mm/39 in). Rich, loamy Table Mountain SANDSTONE and decomposed GRANITE soils nurture vigorous growth, and even shy-bearing classic vines require ruthless TRIMMING and CROP THINNING. Here a handful of vineyards have, since the mid 1980s, once again been producing classic wines from land once part of the historic estate developed by Governor van der Stel.

See also SOUTH AFRICA, history. J.P. & M.F.

Burman, J., *Wine of Constantia* (1979).
James, T., *Wines of the New South Africa: Tradition and Revolution* (2013).
Johnson, H., 'Groot Constantia', in *The Story of Wine* (1989).

Constellation Brands, holding company of Constellation Wines, is a leading international producer and marketer of virtually all forms of alcoholic beverage, and it has certainly done its bit for the mergers and acquisitions sector. Thanks to consistent acquisition, it became the world's largest wine business in 2004. In 2006 it acquired Canada's biggest wine company Vincor, only to sell it in 2016. In 2011 it had refocused on its American roots and sold off to what would become ACCOLADE all of the Australian, South African, and UK interests it had so recently acquired. In 2021, in an effort to concentrate on what it regards as its premium brands—including Robert MONDAVI and The Prisoner in California, Ruffino in Italy, and Kim Crawford in New Zealand—the company sold off about 30 brands to E. & J. GALLO and in 2022 despatched more to the WINE GROUP.

consultants are used with increasing frequency in wine production. Consultant VITICULTURISTS are particularly useful since those who operate on an international scale can impart knowledge gleaned from a wide variety of different vine-growing environments, although strictly local specialists such as David Abreu in northern California can forge an international reputation. Like viticulturists, the more energetic consultant OENOLOGISTS can use their expertise in both hemispheres, although their work is necessarily limited by the timing of HARVEST. One of the first internationally famous consultant oenologists was Professor Émile PEYNAUD. Today his best-known successor from Bordeaux is Michel ROLLAND, although dozens of other highly respected consultants operate in Bordeaux alone, and there are now hundreds of winemakers who travel the globe and offer, if not consultancy, then hard graft (see FLYING WINEMAKERS). Consultants play an increasingly important role in wine production everywhere but have long been particularly important in Bordeaux, California, and Italy, where today specialist, often local, consultants are preferred for their intimate knowledge of each TERROIR. Examples include Sangiovese expert Castelli, while Simonit & Sirch are agronomist consultants specializing in a specific type of PRUNING.

Many restaurateurs and hoteliers, most airlines, and even some wine retailers employ consultants in their wine selection. Some well-heeled collectors also take INVESTMENT advice from consultants.

consumption of wine throughout the world fell from a peak of around 285 million hl/7,500 million gal a year in the years 1976–80 to about 225 million hl in the early 2000s, then peaked at about 255 million hl in 2007 only to fall in the wake of the global financial crisis to under 240 million hl in 2014. The next peak was about 247 million hl in 2017, but total consumption in 2020 was less than 235 million hl, largely thanks to pandemic-related restrictions. Total WORLD PRODUCTION continues to be considerably more than this, resulting in a global wine SURPLUS that is most acute in Europe, the most important producer and consumer of wine if regarded as a continent. But on a national level, by 2014 the US had decisively pulled ahead of France to become the world's biggest consumer of wine. The main reason for the drop in global consumption has long been sharp falls in average wine consumption by France and Italy, traditionally the world's two most important producers and consumers of wine, but since 2017 consumption in China—quite recently the world's fifth most important wine market—also declined considerably. The countries in which most wine is estimated to have been consumed in 2021 were, in declining order, the US, France, Italy, Germany, UK, Spain, China, Russia, Argentina, and Australia.

National annual per capita wine consumption figures in litres according to the OIV are to be found in Appendix 2.

containers for wine are used at four main stages in a wine's life: during the FERMENTATION that creates it; during its MATURATION; for its TRANSPORT; and for SERVING it. Moreover, while wine containers have changed throughout history, they have also varied through space, with each winemaking region becoming characterized by vessels of different dimensions.

Historical context

Many different materials were used for drinking and serving wine in the ancient world, particularly in CHINA. In prehistoric times in the eastern Mediterranean and the Caucasus, wine was generally put in earthenware jars, such as the Georgian QVEVRI, or sometimes into wooden containers, soon after the grapes had been trodden or pressed. This basic fermentation technology remained the norm until the 20th century, when VATS or tanks of CONCRETE and STAINLESS STEEL were introduced. The basic receptacles used for storing and transporting wine in classical antiquity were pottery AMPHORAE, which varied greatly in size and shape but which could be sealed, thus preventing the potentially harmful access of OXYGEN. Larger pottery vessels for storing wine in the Roman world were known as DOLIA. During the 1st century BCE, experiments were also undertaken in transporting wine in these *dolia*, anchored amidships, but their use did not persist. By the end of the 2nd century CE, amphorae production declined in Italy, although it continued in other parts of the eastern and southern Mediterranean, and most wine began to be transported long-distance in wooden BARRELS. For short distances, numerous other vessels, in particular animal skins, were also used, especially in Iberia.

Throughout the medieval period, wooden barrels served as almost the only vessels used for maturing and transporting wine, and their sizes came to reflect local custom and requirements. The standard barrel size in England, for example, the BUTT or PIPE, was fixed by statute in the 15th century at 126 imperial gallons (572.8 l). However, in southern Italy at the same time their wooden *botti* held about 454 l, while in Bruges the butt had a capacity of about 910 l; in Spain it varied from 454 to 477 litres. Meanwhile, it had been discovered in Germany that wines from good vintages with a high sugar content kept in larger barrels, providing they were not subjected to RACKING, lasted longer. This led to the construction of huge wooden tuns, containing thousands of litres, among the most famous of which were the Strasbourg Tun of 1472 and the Heidelberg Tuns of 1591 and 1663.

For serving wine, small jugs made of pottery were generally used during the medieval period. However, from the 16th century onwards, glass BOTTLES became more frequent for this purpose, and by the second half of the 17th century these bottles began to be used to store and mature wines. Bottle shapes evolved so as to allow extended AGEING, and thus were born both VINTAGE wines and CONNOISSEURSHIP. Moreover, the use of bottles enabled completely new types of wine, such as CHAMPAGNE, the New French CLARETS, and vintage PORT, to be produced from the 17th century onwards. P.T.H.U.

McGovern, P. E., *Ancient Wine: The Search for the Origins of Viticulture* (2019).

Peacock, D. P. S., and Williams, D. F., *Amphorae and the Roman Economy: An Introductory Guide* (1986).

Unwin, P. T. H., *Wine and the Vine: An Historical Geography of Viticulture and the Wine Trade* (1992).

Modern times

For details of containers used for fermentation, see FERMENTATION VESSELS, which may be either open topped or closed and may have a capacity as big as 300 hl/7,925 gal. Wines are matured prior to bottling in closed containers (to avoid OXIDATION), either in tanks made from materials such as STAINLESS STEEL, CONCRETE, or POLYETHYLENE or in some form of COOPERAGE, from small, new barrels to large, old casks, or in clay AMPHORAE, QVEVRI, TINAJAS, TALHAS, and PITHARI, or concrete eggs, or even glass BONBONNES or globes. Wine may be blended in even larger tanks holding up to 15,000 hl. Wine is transported either in BULK, usually in food-grade 250-hl stainless steel tankers or disposable 'flexitanks', or in bottle. When transport containers are used for shipping wine in bottle, care is taken by some fine-wine merchants and some fine-wine producers that the wine is shipped only in reefers, or temperature-controlled containers, and sometimes only during cooler times of year. This is particularly important for wines which have undergone a minimum of FILTRATION and vital for NATURAL WINES. For more details, see TRANSPORT.

The most common container for wine on its final journey to the GLASS, occasionally via a DECANTER, is the bottle, but see PACKAGING for the increasing number of alternatives.

contaminants, potentially harmful substances found in wine as a result of air or water pollution (see SMOKE TAINT, for example); vineyard treatment RESIDUES; poor winery HYGIENE; contaminated pallets, packaging materials or transport containers; ignorance; or ADULTERATION AND FRAUD. They are often difficult to identify and very potent, with extremely low perception thresholds, although the ability to detect them is not universal even among professional tasters. A contaminant becomes a TAINT only once it can be smelt or tasted.

Ignorance is possibly the most forgivable reason for contamination since the scope of what is regarded as, and can be measured as, a contaminant grows wider with the rapid progress of science and measuring techniques. LEAD, for example, which was deliberately added to wines by the Romans, is now known to be a serious neural toxin. ETHYL CARBAMATE, on the other hand, has been regarded as a contaminant only since the late 1980s. And it was only in the 1990s that the contaminating effect of some apparently innocuous treatments of wooden beams in some winemaking establishments became apparent (see TRIBROMOANISOLE).

Nowadays, contamination as a result of poor winery hygiene is extremely rare, although it may be caused by products such as chlorine sanitizers that are designed to clean the winery but which form chlorophenols when they come into contact with phenols in rubber, resin, or plastic fittings, resulting in plastic or medicinal off-flavours in contaminated wine. A leak of brine from a refrigerant unit is another possible hazard. Research by Chatonnet et al. detected levels of phthalate contamination that exceeded the EU's specific migration limits for alcoholic drinks in 11% of the French wines tested, thought to be due mainly to the epoxy-resin coatings inside older vats.

Pollution is difficult to guard against. Wine producers are increasingly wary of some AGROCHEMICALS, however. Orthene, a fungicide used widely in the early 1980s with no ill effects apparent during winemaking, produced a range of wines with an extremely unpleasant smell after several years' BOTTLE AGE. Many German wines made in the early to mid 1980s, particularly the 1983s, exhibited this particular contamination. The ST-ESTÈPHE property Ch Phélan-Ségur destroyed its entire 1984 and 1985 production because of Orthene contamination. Even after a particular product has been banned, it may still contaminate the environment. Chlorophenols, for example, are active ingredients in wood preservatives, fungicides, and biocides that have been used over many years and form HALOANISOLES. American authorities in particular have regularly applied stringent tests to imported wines for traces of suspected contaminants, such as procymidone from agrochemical residues. Other potential contaminants from the vineyard include hydraulic oil leaked from mechanical harvesters or spray drift from PESTICIDES.

The wine trade, like every other commercial activity, has its villains, but they are increasingly rare. Fortunately, very few of the substances which the least scrupulous producers are tempted to add illegally to wine (SORBITOL, for example) are harmful—with the notable and horrifying exception of lethal doses of METHANOL added to one Italian producer's wines in 1987.

See also ADULTERATION, which sometimes involves the deliberate addition of contaminants.

J.R. & J.E.H.

Chatonnet, P., et al., 'Contamination of wines and spirits by phthalates: types of contaminants present, contamination sources and means of prevention', *Food Additives & Contaminants: Part A*, 31/9 (2014), 1605–15.

continental climate is one with a high degree of continentality, defined as the climatic effect that results from locations being insulated from the influences of oceanic or large bodies of water (see LAKE EFFECT). This is typically measured as the difference between the average temperature of its hottest month and that of its coldest month. Climates with a wide annual range are called continental; those with a narrow range, MARITIME.

LATITUDE influences continentality. In the tropics, annual temperature swings are usually small even in continental interiors. The larger land masses of the northern hemisphere have the greatest continentality (see RUSSIA and CANADA, for example), while in the middle latitudes of the southern hemisphere (30–60° south of the equator) the effect of continentality is smaller, as continental areas are not as large at higher latitudes (see SOUTH AMERICA and SOUTH AFRICA, for example). Mountain ranges also influence continentality, acting as a topographic barrier affecting airflow and creating a rain shadow of warmer and drier zones on the leeward side of the mountains.

Wine regions with continental climates are more variable, typically experiencing colder winters, greater spring FROST risk, and hotter summers, often with higher humidity and precipitation, than those located closer to the coast or to a large body of water. Common measures used in viticulture that capture aspects of continental climates are the mean temperature of the warmest month (January/July, depending on the hemisphere, hence MJT), the Huglin Index (see CLIMATE CLASSIFICATION), and seasonal or DIURNAL TEMPERATURE RANGE. For the effects on ripening, see CLIMATE AND WINE QUALITY.

See also MEDITERRANEAN CLIMATE. G.V.J.

continuous method, SPARKLING WINEMAKING process developed in the USSR and at one time used in Portugal. It has now been largely phased out in Russia in favour of the TANK METHOD.

Contra Costa Country, once-prolific wine-growing region situated at the juncture of SAN FRANCISCO BAY and Suisun Bay where generally hot weather is moderated by afternoon breezes. The region is home to more than 405 ha/1,000 acres of vineyards planted in generally SANDY soils, several of them dating to the 19th century. The oldest and highest-quality CARIGNAN, MOURVÈDRE, and ZINFANDEL fruit is generally owned or consistently purchased by several dozen wineries located elsewhere in the North Coast, though the AVA hosts several smaller wineries in and around the town of Brentwood. A.Y.

contract winemaking. See CUSTOM-CRUSH FACILITY.

contrada, plural *contrade*, signifies a district, quarter, or a hamlet in Italian. *Contrade* are common throughout the whole of Italy but nowadays and in a wine context are almost exclusively associated with Etna; the term is widely but incorrectly understood to stand for 'single vineyard'. See ETNA for more detail.

W.S.

controlled appellations, or appellations of origin, a method of LABELLING wine and regulating quality that is modelled on France's AOC system. Controlled appellations such as the EU's protected designations of origin (PDO) are distinguished within the broader category of GEOGRAPHICAL INDICATIONS by the inclusion of strict rules governing viticultural and winemaking practices that reinforce a close link between the inherent characteristics of the wine and its place of origin. Typical controls will include restrictions on YIELD, grape varieties, and vine-management techniques. The restrictions of the controlled-appellation model make them less common outside Europe; even within Europe, controlled appellations are criticized on the grounds that they limit innovation and tend to maintain traditional practices unquestioningly. (See Appendix 1 for a complete list of controlled appellations for which particular grape varieties are specified, with their permitted grapes.)

In 2021, the OIV published the following definition of appellation of origin: 'Any denomination recognised and protected by the competent authorities in the country of origin, consisting of or containing the name of a geographical area, or another denomination known as referring to such area, which serves to designate a wine or spirit beverage as originating in that geographical area, where the quality or characteristics of the wine or spirit beverage are due exclusively or essentially to the geographical environment, including natural and human factors, and which has given the wine or spirit beverage its reputation.'

In the United States, all geographical DELIMITATIONS (including AVAs) are legally known as 'appellations of origin', although they do not include rules on viticultural and winemaking practices. J.P.H.B.

cooking with wine. Good wine used in the kitchen adds depth and dimension to a dish in the way that spices, herbs, vinegars, and stocks can. The recipes of Apicius, the most famous Roman chef, show that wine was commonly used in his sauces, and it has found a place in the kitchen ever since.

Wine is an essential ingredient in many dishes and can be used in every stage of cooking, from marinating raw ingredients to providing the final finish to a dessert. It is all the more curious, therefore, that so little research has been done into exactly what happens to wine during cooking, particularly as a result of the application of heat.

The boiling point of ETHANOL is 78 °C/172 °F, considerably lower than that of water, so any wine used in cooking becomes progressively less alcoholic if heated to above 78 °C for any length of time. As a sauce is 'reduced' with wine, the other components in the wine such as RESIDUAL SUGAR, ACIDITY, and FLAVOUR COMPOUNDS become more or less marked.

The most common ways in which wine is used in the kitchen are listed below.

Deglazing: pouring wine (or another liquid such as stock) into a pan in which something has been roasted or sautéed in order to dissolve the remnants of that operation in the liquid to make a sauce. Wine adds body and depth to the sauce, as in *beurre blanc*, for example.

Marinade: a method of imparting extra flavour, and/or tenderizing, which takes the form of cooked and uncooked marinades in which the wine may be combined with other ingredients to add savouriness, sweetness, and acidity and to intensify flavour.

Stocks: wine is often used instead of, or as well as, water, to provide the essential base for soups, stews, and sauces or when cooking dishes such as risotto.

Court-bouillon: a method of cooking fish, shellfish or white meat in which herbs and spices are infused in white wine and water in which the food is subsequently poached.

Sauces: many of the so-called 'small sauces' based on the mother sauces of classic cuisine use wine to deglaze, to reduce, and to add liquid, flavour, acidity and/or sweetness. Examples include *bordelaise* using red wine, *périgueux* using madeira, and *sauce Robert* using white wine.

Stews and casseroles: wine, preferably from the same area as the dish, is an integral part of many regional stews and casseroles in wine-producing regions, for example *boeuf bourguignon*.

Jellies: poached foie gras set in a Gewurztraminer jelly is an Alsace speciality. Sweet jellies can be made from Sauternes or any other sweet wine.

Desserts: wine has a surprisingly wide range of applications for sweet foods and pâtisserie. Red wine is used for poaching pears and macerating strawberries (a speciality of Bordeaux), while wines such as MARSALA and SHERRY are used in, respectively, zabaglione and English trifle. In Italy, strong, usually sweet wines, typically VIN SANTO, are served with dry biscuits which are moistened in them.

There is much debate about the necessary quality of **cooking wine**, some regarding the saucepan or stockpot as the ideal repository for any wine considered too nasty to drink, others insisting that only the finest wine will do. At one extreme, if using a faulty (e.g. CORKED) wine, the fault will show in the finished dish, but on the other hand the full range of volatile FLAVOUR COMPOUNDS of a great wine will not survive the application of any fierce or prolonged heat.

Empirical research suggests that wines which are very tannic, well-aged or relatively fruitless on the palate are the least suitable for cooking. Wines with soft TANNINS (if red), good acidity, and plenty of ripe fruit are the all-round best choices. FORTIFIED WINES and sweet wines are some of the most reliable options, bringing more flavour and depth to dishes than most other wine styles.

Ultimately, however, the choice of wine depends on several factors, all of which have an impact on the different molecular components of wine. The length of cooking time and the intensity of heat have the greatest impact on flavour and structure, whether to denature or accentuate, and accompanying ingredients also interact with the wine chemically and/or sensorially (cream softens acid, acid counteracts sweetness, strong proteins such as those in beef flank counterbalance tannins). Important, too, is the role the wine serves, whether tenderizing or bringing flavour, texture, richness, sweetness, acidity, or bitterness.

As contradictory opinions indicate, however, it is clear that much more research is needed in this area before we can separate myth from science. M.P.L. & T.D.C.

Percival, F., 'Coq au what? Cooking with wine', *The World of Fine Wine*, 30 (2010).

Poussier, L., and Poussier, O., *Desserts and Wines* (2004).

McGee, H., *On Food and Cooking* (2004).

cool-climate viticulture and WARM-CLIMATE VITICULTURE are indefinite terms as the transition between different viticultural climates is an approximation. The term 'cold-climate viticulture' is typically used to refer to those wine regions that experience WINTER FREEZE and where WINTER PROTECTION of vines is essential. Hot-climate viticulture produces mainly TABLE GRAPES and RAISINS; it cannot, in general, produce high-quality wine grapes of any kind. In between are a range of climates suited to successfully growing wine grapes that have been defined in various CLIMATE CLASSIFICATION indices. For example, cool climates are defined by Regions Ia, Ib, and II on the Winkler Index, the very cool and cool classes on the Huglin Index, and within 13–15 °C on the growing-season average-temperature index.

The distinguishing characteristic of cool viticultural climates is that they will regularly ripen only early-maturing grape varieties such as CHASSELAS, MÜLLER-THURGAU, GEWÜRZTRAMINER, CHARDONNAY, PINOT NOIR, and GAMAY; and only in especially warm MESOCLIMATES can varieties such as RIESLING, and some red varieties considered early to mid season, be ripened. Ripening also tends to take place under cool to mild conditions due to shorter growing seasons. This combination of climate and variety leads to wines which, at their best, are fresh, delicate, and aromatic. Most are white or only pale red, because full development of ANTHOCYANIN pigments and TANNINS in the grape skins generally needs greater warmth.

Major areas of cool-climate viticulture would certainly include the northern half of France (the LOIRE, CHAMPAGNE, CHABLIS, BURGUNDY, and BEAUJOLAIS); LUXEMBOURG, GERMANY, SWITZERLAND, DENMARK, and AUSTRIA; in the US, the Lower Columbia Valley of WASHINGTON, the Willamette Valley of OREGON, and the coolest coastal strip of northern CALIFORNIA; the most southern vineyards of CHILE; some elevated vineyards of SOUTH AFRICA; the South Island and southern North Island of NEW ZEALAND; and in Australia, the whole of TASMANIA, small areas of the higher Adelaide hills in SOUTH AUSTRALIA, and southern VICTORIA. Note that ENGLAND and WALES are examples of MARITIME climates with very cool summers, inhibiting RIPENING for many varieties, and may be referred to as very cool climates.

See also CLIMATE AND WINE QUALITY.

R.E.S. & G.V.J.

Gladstones, J., *Viticulture and Environment* (1992).

Jackson, D., and Schuster, D., *The Production of Grapes and Wine in Cool Climates* (rev. edn, 1998).

Coonawarra, wine region in the Limestone Coast Zone of SOUTH AUSTRALIA popularly revered for Cabernet Sauvignon, grown on its famous strip of TERRA ROSSA soil. Its cool MEDITERRANEAN climate is very similar to that of Bordeaux; it is slightly warmer and has less growing season rainfall, but Cabernet Sauvignon is normally picked in the second half of April (or, in Bordeaux terms, the second half of October). The name means 'honeysuckle' in the language of the Bindjali First Nations people.

cooperage is a collective noun for wooden containers but has been more traditionally used for both the activities and workplace of **coopers**, those who make and repair small BARRELS and larger wooden VATS. At one time all wine or spirit producers of any size would have had their own small cooperage, but today the craft is perpetuated mainly by specialist cooperage businesses. The French term is *tonnellerie*.

History

Until relatively recently, coopers played an important role not only in the wine business but also in myriad aspects of daily life. Almost all containers—buckets, barrels, tanks—were made by coopers from various woods (see BARRELS, history). Barrels were made to hold salted fish, flour, gunpowder, oil, turpentine, salt, sugar, butter, and many other household commodities since they retain liquids safely, keep the elements out, and are easy to manœuvre.

Coopers' guilds were already established by the end of the 9th century; during the Middle Ages, laws relating to apprenticeships and guild memberships were codified throughout Europe (with nepotism already playing its part). At the end of the 18th century, there were approximately 8,000 coopers in Paris alone. It is still possible to meet coopers who are the last in a line of craftspeople dating back to the 17th century. Such skilled workers, who can probably make barrels with handtools alone, may well have served traditional apprenticeships that often involve extensive work in different regions of their own countries as well as abroad.

As Europeans colonized the New World, they inevitably took their coopering skills with them. John Alden, one of the more famous early North American colonists of Plymouth, Massachusetts, was a master cooper, and by 1648 there were enough coopers to form a guild in this New England colony. America's important export trade of STAVES and logs to Europe began slightly later in the 17th century, when the Spanish controlled large parts of what is now the United States.

During the 19th century, coopering remained an important craft, but the advent of metal (and later plastic) containers ultimately reduced coopering to an adjunct of the drinks business. More than one million barrels were made for salted herring in Britain in 1913, for example, but by 1953 the number had dropped to around one-tenth of this figure, and now this business is virtually extinct.

American PROHIBITION had a dramatic impact on the sale of fine wines and spirits and, in turn, on the cooperage business—particularly in the United States but also in the British Isles, where only those coopers working on beer barrels were unaffected. Before the Second World War, most beer barrels were made of wood and many breweries had their own cooperages, but by the early 1960s wooden barrels had been replaced by metal ones. In much of the wine industry, too, wood was replaced by concrete, stainless steel, and other neutral materials, particularly for larger tanks (see CONTAINERS).

Cooperage today

As wooden barrels are expensive to buy, use, and maintain, they tend to be used only for products whose sale price can justify such a major investment or, in the case of older containers, by those who have inherited them.

Cooperages are found wherever there is a wine or spirits business that needs barrels, notably in America, Scotland, and France but also in Italy, Spain, Portugal, Ireland, eastern Europe, Germany, Australia, and South Africa. They make new vats and barrels (see BARREL MAKING) and/or repair or maintain older barrels and vats (see BARREL MAINTENANCE and BARREL RENEWAL).

There are no serious industry analysts of the contemporary cooperage business, such as there are in the automotive or electronics industries, since it is effectively just a small part of the timber industry. Nor is there any official regulatory or inspection body as there is in the wine trade. Consequently, statistics related to the cooperage industry are little more than educated guesses. Naturally all coopers maintain that their oak is the best wood, entirely hand split and seasoned in the open air, and that their competitors cut corners. In the absence of facts, winemakers have to rely on results rather than rhetoric.

United States The great majority of wooden barrels traded today are made in the American Midwest for the ageing of bourbon whiskey, primarily by two cooperages. No one really knows how many American oak barrels are used in winemaking, but it is likely that more than 100,000 go directly to wineries in the United States alone, and, according to the Associated Cooperage Industries of America, the production rate for both bourbon and wine is increasing.

Nearly all American logs come from privately held forests in the eastern half of the US, notably in Minnesota, Wisconsin, Kentucky, Arkansas, Tennessee, the Virginias, the Carolinas, and Missouri. These logs are purchased by stave-mill operators, some of whom also run cooperages. Cooperage use accounts for about 3% of all American white oak harvested every year. Most American oak is used for furniture, construction, veneer, and pulp.

The logs are cut into appropriate lengths, quarter-sawn, planed, and then sold to cooperages. Customers for American oak staves are found not only in bourbon country but in cooperages in California, Australia, and even Spain, where American oak has until recently been used almost exclusively for wine maturation, most notably in RIOJA and JEREZ, for the historical reasons outlined.

For whiskey to be called bourbon, it must, according to American government regulations that are a blessing to the cooperage business, be aged in a 'new, charred white oak barrel', so large quantities of used whiskey barrels are commercially available, many of them relatively new. Over two million used bourbon barrels are sold each year to Spain, Scotland, Ireland, Japan, Thailand, India, Puerto Rico, Canada, and Taiwan, as well as to producers of other North American spirits. Most of them are used to mature spirits: various brandies, rums, and whiskies. The Scotch whisky industry is a particularly important consumer of American oak, at any one time using approximately 13 million casks in total. In some cases American oak barrels are sent to Jerez en route to Scotland, where some distillers still prefer to use casks infused with sherry flavours as was the norm in the 19th century, when sherry was shipped in cask to British wine merchants, who would then pass on these casks to the Scotch whisky industry. Now that sherry is no longer shipped in cask, some Scotch whisky distillers in Scotland have their barrels 'broken in' in Jerez with sherry.

France The French cooperage business is much smaller than its American counterpart but is much more important to the wine business. According to the Fédération Française de la Tonnellerie, around 658,000 French oak barrels were produced in 2019, two-thirds of which were exported. The domestic market for these barrels is primarily in BORDEAUX, BURGUNDY, and Cognac, where most French cooperages are located. More than 40% of the exported barrels go to the United States. The balance is shipped to 30 other countries, most notably Italy, Spain, Australia, New Zealand, South Africa, Chile, Argentina, and Germany. As well as selling to Bordeaux, Burgundy, Cognac, and Armagnac, French cooperages are also developing new 'export' markets selling to ambitious winemakers in French regions that had abandoned new barrels. The RHÔNE, LANGUEDOC, ROUSSILLON, and SOUTH WEST FRANCE, as well as the LOIRE, have all become important purchasers.

In France about one-third of all forests are owned by local or national government. However, the sale of over 80% of all lots, carefully delineated groups of trees, is administered by the Office National des Forêts (ONF). In September and October, wood auctions are held all over France, but for the buyer of oak destined to be turned into barrels and vats the most important auctions are held in Nevers, Châteauroux, and Moulins.

A potential buyer bids on the trees in a delineated section, which should be at least 100 and preferably well over 120—sometimes 160—years old before providing suitable wood for casks. Buyers have the right to go into the forest, measure the trees, and even bore into them 30 cm/12 in to see how straight is the GRAIN. They must decide how much of each type of wood there is, how it can be used, and, of course, how much they should bid.

As not every tree in an auction lot can be used for STAVES, French cooperages usually work with wood brokers who have other customers. The most valuable part of a tree is that with the tightest and straightest grains, which can be used for panelling. The furniture and construction industries are important customers.

French barrels cost at least double those made of American oak. French logs are much more expensive because they must be hand split rather than machine sawn and demand more expensive drying methods. (see BARREL MAKING). French cooperages also tend to be smaller and less automated than their American counterparts. But the special qualities of French oak ensure that it is the most sought after by modern winemakers and able to command a considerable premium.

As the use of French oak has become more widespread, staves are now shipped all over the world, notably to Australia, Italy, South America, South Africa, America, Spain, and Portugal, where they may be made up into barrels in local cooperages.

No system of AOC limits the period of time French oak barrels may be used for any wine or spirit. Consequently the sale of used French oak barrels is not as organized as that for American barrels. In Burgundy, producers often use most of their new barrels for their grandest appellations, and lesser appellations get proportionately fewer new barrels. In Bordeaux, one proprietor will often own several châteaux and will treat his or her most prestigious property to the luxury of new oak before passing the barrels down the chain to a lowlier property. Alternatively, used barrels are sold to wineries unable to command the sort of price that can support expensive new barrels or where winemakers do not want the taste of new oak. In the New World, used barrels are often traded between wineries. Relatively young ones, especially those used for white wine, are highly valued, but barrels more than ten years old are usually sold to be cut in half for flower planters.

Hungary There are two major cooperages in Hungary, both affiliated to French cooperages, and many smaller ones.

Italy In Italy, a relatively small but lively cooperage industry makes barrels and vats primarily with oak imported from France and Slavonia (eastern Croatia).

Spain Barrels have been important to the Spanish wine and sherry industries for centuries, and the cooper's craft is sustained there. In Jerez, new barrels are spurned for the maturation of fine SHERRY and will probably be used at least three times for FERMENTATION before being used to mature a top-quality OLOROSO. The older a cask, the more expensive it is, and some bodegas boast casks (or butts, as they are usually called here) that are more than 200 years old.

Portugal The demands of the PORT industry, and a ready supply of Portuguese oak, have kept the cooper's craft alive in northern Portugal, such that French coopers have even imported Portuguese barrel makers.

Australia Distance from most of the world's established coopers has inspired the establishment of several cooperages in South Australia.

M.C.K.

Jacon, V., *La Barrique: choix, utilisation, manutention* (2003).

Margot, P., *Chêne-Merrandier-Tonnelier-Copeaux & Cie* (2014).

Vivas, N., *Manuel de tonnellerie à l'usage des utilisateurs de futaille* (2nd edn, 2002).

co-operatives, ventures owned jointly by a number of members and controlled by them democratically, are extremely important as wine producers. They have the advantage for their members of pooling winemaking and marketing resources and costs, giving them negotiating power, and helping to ensure the sustainability of their members' vineyards. Like individual producers, co-operatives in Europe may be eligible for EU subsidies, for example for investment in buildings and equipment. In most countries they also enjoy the commercial advantage of being able to describe their wines as bottled by the producer, using such reassuring phrases as MIS(E) EN BOUTEILLE *à la propriété* and ERZEUGERABFÜLLUNG more usually associated with much smaller, individually managed wine enterprises. The better co-operatives are becoming increasingly skilled not just at winemaking but also at marketing specific bottlings that look and taste every bit as distinctive as the individually produced competition. Co-operatives have traditionally been at their strongest in areas where wine's selling price is relatively low and where the average size of individual holdings is small, although co-operatives are also quite significant in CHAMPAGNE and there are several in the MÉDOC, for example; and in regions such as Italy's ALTO ADIGE, co-operatives are among the most well-known and highly respected winegrowers. The majority of wine co-operatives were formed in the early 1930s in the immediate aftermath of the Depression. In recent years, there has been notable consolidation, with smaller co-operatives joining together for economies of scale.

France

France's *caves coopératives* (often referred to locally simply as *la cave*) are declining in number and influence, but in 2021 the national total of 570 were still responsible for nearly 60% of all wine produced in France and an annual turnover of €5.2 billion. The average number of members, or *adhérents*, of each co-operative is also declining as holdings are amalgamated, and members have been encouraged to grub up less suitable vineyards by the EU VINE-PULL SCHEME. Co-operatives are a particularly strong force in the LANGUEDOC and ROUSSILLON, in CHAMPAGNE, and in PROVENCE. Co-ops' speciality is IGP wine—they produce more than 60% of the French total (compared with 30% of PDO wine)—but those which have established a reputation for particularly sound AOC wines sold outside their own region include Union CHAMPAGNE, Nicolas Feuillatte, La Chablisienne of CHABLIS, the co-operative at Tain l'HERMITAGE, the Plaimont co-operative organization in GASCONY, and a number of ALSACE co-operatives, notably those of Turckheim and Wolfberger. The average quality of wine made in French co-ops has improved since the early 1990s and France's CRISE VITICOLE, enabling their members to survive when they could not have done so in isolation and today helping them to promote and participate in local WINE TOURISM.

Germany

In GERMANY, wine co-operatives have played an increasingly significant role since 1868, when the first one was formally established in the AHR. As outlined in GERMAN HISTORY, co-operatives offered smallholders the chance to compete in the newly quality-conscious German wine market of the late 19th and early 20th centuries. German has several words for co-operative: *Winzergenossenschaft, Winzerverein, Winzervereinigung, Weingärtnergenossenschaft* or *Weinbauernverband*.

Nearly two in every three German vine-growers today belong to the local co-operative, but, because their vineyards are often a small, part-time activity, together they represent around one-third of the total German area under vine. Two of the 13 wine regions of Germany have a central co-operative cellar which is fed grapes, wine, or must by more localized co-operatives. By 2021, the number of co-operatives in Germany had fallen to 141, of which 84 made wine on the premises. However, the vineyard area processed by the co-ops remains stable.

The co-operative movement is particularly strong and successful in the most southerly region of BADEN, where about 70% of all wine produced is sold under the auspices of the giant central Badischer Winzerkeller at Breisach. This vast enterprise is larger than any winery in France. The Baden co-operatives (71 in total) have been particularly active in transcending the co-operative image of quantity over quality by developing superior, small-volume bottlings of distinctive wines. Co-operatives are also extremely important in the WÜRTTEMBERG region, where there are 34, their central cellar being the Württembergische Weingärtner-Zentralgenossenschaft at Möglingen. They are also important in Germany's four smallest regions, SAALE-UNSTRUT, AHR, HESSISCHE BERGSTRASSE, and SACHSEN. In the MOSEL region, Moselland in Bernkastel processes about 22% of the region's output but also handles winemaking and marketing for three co-operatives in the Pfalz, Rheinhessen, and Nahe. In the RHEINGAU, the role of co-operative cellars is very much less significant.

Italy

In Italy, the *cantina sociale* is no less important, accounting for about 60% of the country's production. There are nearly 500 co-operatives comprising 148,000 members. EU policies have favoured co-operatives in the past, but, as EU subsidies dwindle, the quality of the wine and the ability to run the co-operative on a commercial basis become increasingly important. One of the most respected Italian co-operatives, in the far north-west, is the Produttori del BARBARESCO, whose origins are 19th-century. The influence of the *cantina sociale* (*Kellereigenossenschaft* in German) is particularly strong in TRENTINO, where 15 co-operatives are responsible for most of the region's production, and in the much smaller ALTO ADIGE, where 12 co-operatives are responsible for 70% of wines produced. There they have the highest revenue per hectare of vines in any Italian province, sell mainly to hotels and restaurants, and are critically important to many other industries, particularly tourism. Girlan, Cantina Terlano, Colterenzio, Kurtatsch, and Cantina Produttori Valle Isarco are all impressive. In the VENETO, co-operatives have also traditionally been responsible for the bulk of production, particularly in Verona, where a large number of producers of Soave and Valpolicella either buy from or supplement their production through purchases from the local co-op.

The co-operative Riunite of EMILIA-ROMAGNA was famous in the early 1980s for engulfing the United States and other markets in a tidal wave of LAMBRUSCO. It is still Italy's leading co-operative by turnover. Castelli del Grevepesa is one of TUSCANY's better co-operatives. Further south, quantity, and not always quality, is the chief characteristic of the co-operatives that proliferate practically wherever the vine is grown, although Cantina di Taburno with Luigi Moio as CONSULTANT is a leading light. The Copertino co-operative in PUGLIA makes a good job of its eponymous red. The islands SARDINIA and SICILY were once dominated by co-operatives, of which Settesoli in Sicily and Santadi in Sardinia are models of quality. Settesoli has cooperated in the local research institute in CLONAL SELECTION, variety and soil matching, and the conservation of almost extinct INDIGENOUS VARIETIES—all of which have helped to improve and increase wine quality in Sicily.

Spain and Portugal

As in Italy, co-operatives are extremely important in Iberia, where grapes are so often grown alongside other crops. Approximately 60% of each vintage is delivered to one of Spain's 572 wine co-operatives (some of which are groups of co-ops), and 35% of Portugal's crop is received by its 75 co-ops (see PORTUGAL, history).

Although the movement began in the early years of the 20th century, it substantially increased in importance in the 1950s, when the wine market was relatively depressed. One of the earliest wine co-operatives was in Olite in NAVARRA, where the movement was particularly powerful, at one time absorbing as much as 90% of grape production. It wasn't until the 1980s that many Iberian co-operatives even began to consider bottling wine, so much of their produce was sold off either for DISTILLATION or as BULK WINE. Today this figure varies from region to region, but in Galicia, for example, the co-operatives bottle almost their entire production, as they do in Rioja. Co-ops are also very important in Castilla-La Mancha, where they number more than 200 and vary in quality. In most regions, particularly in the north, the trend is towards more bottled wine and better quality. Successful small or mid-sized co-ops include Martín Códax in RÍAS BAIXAS, the Capçanes, Masroig, and Falset co-ops in MONTSANT, Viticultors del PRIORAT, Cooperativa Virgen de la Asunción in RIBERA DEL DUERO, Cuatro Rayas in RUEDA, Mazas Cooperativa in TORO, and Sonsierra Cooperative in RIOJA; larger operations producing quality wines include Cooperativas San Alejandro in CALATAYUD and Grandes Vinos and San Valero in CARIÑENA. In the fortified wine regions of JEREZ, much of the rest of ANDALUCÍA, and the DOURO, co-operatives are less important than the long-standing links between vine-growers and individual wine producers.

Rapid growth of Portugal's export market and the private sector during the 21st century spurred co-operatives to adapt and survive (or fail, as some have, most recently in Portalegre). Higher standards of viticulture, with corresponding increases in grape prices for members, better viniculture (including the recruitment of talented consultant winemakers, e.g. Anselmo Mendes at Biscoitos), and marketing have resulted in a broader base of quality. Leading examples include the co-operatives of Monção (VINHO VERDE), Penalva (DÃO), Cantanhede (BAIRRADA), Pegões (PENÍNSULA DE SETÚBAL), Borba (ALENTEJO), Adega de COLARES, and Pico and Biscoitos in the AZORES (whose survival ensured the future of these islands' traditional varieties).

Rest of the world

Practically wherever wine is made, co-operatives thrive, though there are now very few in Eastern Europe since the privatization of the state co-operatives. Notable examples include Klet Brda and Klet Krško in Slovenia, and there are a few in Croatia, for example PZ Svirče.

Co-operatives have played a particularly important role in the development of the wine industry in the United States (where the last one closed in 2000), South Africa, and Argentina. In 20th-century South Africa, most growers were members of co-ops, whereas in 2020 there were 45 so-called producer cellars, where resources are pooled, but only a handful of those are regulated as co-operatives. In South America, there are still large and successful co-operatives in both Argentina and Brazil, with smaller ones in southern Chile. In Australia, pressure placed on growers by legal and fiscal constraints, as well as the power of the big BRANDS, make it virtually impossible, or at least uneconomic, to run a co-operative.

Copertino, DOC for rosé and robust red wine made mainly from NEGROAMARO grapes on relatively flat terrain in PUGLIA.

co-pigmentation, a mechanism of colour stabilization, involving the interaction of ANTHOCYANIN pigments with another molecule (co-pigment).

In aqueous media, anthocyanins are present under different forms in equilibrium, including red and violet pigment species and colourless hydrated forms. The latter predominate at mildly acidic PH values such as encountered in plant cell VACUOLES and in wine. However, the anthocyanin pigmented forms stack vertically with other species present in the solution (co-pigments) to form complexes from which water is excluded. This results in enhanced colour intensity due to a shift of the balance from the colourless hydrated forms towards the dehydrated pigment forms involved in these stable complexes. The role of co-pigmentation in wine colour can be estimated by comparing red colour intensity before and after disruption of co-pigmentation complexes by dilution in a wine-like buffer. Co-pigmentation has been reported to account for 30 to 50% of the colour of young red wines, on the basis of such measurements. V.C.

Boulton, R., 'The copigmentation of anthocyanins and its role in the color of red wine: a critical review', *American Journal of Enology and Viticulture*, 52/2 (2001), 67–87.

Escribano-Bailon, M. T., and Santos-Buelga, C., 'Anthocyanin copigmentation: evaluation, mechanisms and implications for the colour of red wines', *Current Organic Chemistry*, 16/6 (2012), 715–23.

copita, special tulip-shaped glass in which SHERRY has customarily been served in Spain, supposedly designed to maximize the AROMA, though some producers prefer a regular wine GLASS.

copper, a micronutrient required in very small concentrations for healthy vine growth (see VINE NUTRITION). Copper is toxic to plants except in very dilute concentrations. Reports of copper deficiencies in vineyards are rare, probably because of the very small requirements by the vines but also because of the widespread use of FUNGICIDES containing copper. In acid soils, the copper from fungicide sprays can actually reach toxic levels, and some parts of the MÉDOC have been affected by copper toxicity. After the annual application of several kg of copper per ha, as in BORDEAUX MIXTURE, for about a century, the level of copper in the soil can be toxic and vine growth severely stunted. Generous applications of ORGANIC MATTER make the copper less available to the vines, as does the addition of lime, which will help to neutralize the toxic effect of copper by raising the soil PH.

Since brass fittings and pumps are now rarely used in wineries, the problem of copper CASSE has been virtually eliminated. However, this has caused an increase in SULFIDES in wines, as these would have been removed by the copper added to the wines every time a brass fitting was used. Winemakers now need to consider a small, controlled addition of copper to remove them. Tight-sealing corks or screwcaps will highlight the issue if left untreated. THIOLS are vulnerable to removal by copper, but only if the copper is added in excess. The insoluble copper sulfate is usually then removed through SETTLING or FILTRATION. R.E.S. & M.J.T.

AWRI, 'Removal of volatile sulfur compounds'. www.awri.com.au/industry_support/winemaking_resources/storage-and-packaging/pre-packaging-preparation/removal-volatile-sulfur-compounds.

Coravin. See PRESERVATION SYSTEMS.

Corbeau. See CHARBONO.

Corbières, largest appellation by volume (averaging 550,000 hl/14,529,463 gal annually) in the LANGUEDOC region of southern France, producing some excitingly dense, herby red wines, a small amount of rosé, and a little increasingly well-made white wine from 10,600 ha/26,193 acres of vineyard in 2016. The terrain here in the Pyrenean foothills (see map under LANGUEDOC) is extremely varied and so hilly that it is difficult to generalize about soil types and TOPOGRAPHY. In recognition of this, the appellation was in the 1990s subdivided into 11 so-called TERROIRS, although not without a certain amount of local dissent. The basic distinctions in this southernmost corner of the Aude *département* are between coastal zones influenced by the Mediterranean, the northern strip on the Montagne d'Alaric (some of which has more in common with MINERVOIS), the westernmost vineyards, which are cooled both by Atlantic influence and by ELEVATION, and the rugged, mountainous terrain in the south and centre in which the FITOU appellation forms two enclaves.

Vineyards in the south-west of the appellation are as high as 450 m/1,500 ft above sea level, and HARVEST may not take place until well into October; those in the coastal Sigean area can vary enormously in elevation, but the high average temperatures and very low annual rainfall are partly compensated for by the marine influence. One of the most admired terroirs is that of Boutenac in the hills south of Lézignan, which has particularly poor soils on a LIMESTONE base in what is known locally as Corbières' 'golden triangle'. In 2005, **Corbières Boutenac** was granted its own subappellation for wines that, unusually, must contain 30–50% Carignan and satisfy certain minimum ageing periods.

In AOC Corbières, SYRAH, MOURVÈDRE, GRENACHE NOIR, and LLEDONER PELUT must represent at least half the blend in all red wines, and the once-dominant CARIGNAN may not make up more than half. Some producers particularly value the spice and concentration of wine from old vines, which in Corbières effectively means old Carignan. Warmer parts of Corbières can ripen Mourvèdre on a regular basis. Plantings of CINSAUT, useful along with Syrah for rosé, are more limited here than in neighbouring Minervois. PIQUEPOUL NOIR, TERRET, and GRENACHE GRIS are also allowed in red and rosé Corbières, with some of the white wine grapes allowed in the rosé. White Corbières, a rare but often refreshing dry wine, is made principally from BOURBOULENC, MACABEO, GRENACHE BLANC, MARSANNE, ROUSSANNE, and VERMENTINO, providing an interesting aromatic palette for the increasing number of producers prepared to experiment with superior white winemaking. M.S.

cordon, part of the vine's woody framework, arising from the top of the trunk and on which arms are borne (see diagram under PRUNING). Cordons can be at any angle but are generally trained along horizontal WIRES or, as in some TENDONE trellises, shallowly sloped wires. The most common arrangement is a bilateral cordon in which two horizontal cordons are arranged in opposite directions from the top of the trunk, but any number of arrangements are possible. The unilateral cordon is common in some parts of Europe. Because of ease of management and MECHANIZATION, SPUR PRUNING using horizontal cordons is being increasingly adopted in New World viticulture. Usually the cordon is trained to its permanent position and remains there, unless it is destroyed by TRUNK DISEASES. See vine-TRAINING SYSTEMS. B.G.C. & R.E.S.

cordon de Royat, an old form of CORDON TRAINING used in France for wine grapes since the end of the 19th century (see illustration below). The system was proposed by Lefebvre, director of the French agricultural school of Royat. The classic form is a unilateral CORDON on a short trunk (about 30–50 cm/12–20 in), the term 'unilateral' meaning that the cordon is trained only to one side of the trunk and extends mostly from one vine to another. The vines are normally SPUR PRUNED to two-bud spurs. The number of spurs is limited for each variety under AOC laws and set out in the *cahiers des charges*. R.E.S.

cordon training, a form of VINE TRAINING in which the trunk terminates in a CORDON, and the vine is then typically subjected to SPUR PRUNING. The alternative is HEAD TRAINING, where the vines are usually subjected to CANE PRUNING. The cordon is normally horizontal and can be unilateral (trained only to one side of the trunk) or bilateral (to both sides). See also CORDON DE ROYAT and PRUNING. R.E.S.

corkage, charge customarily levied in a restaurant for each bottle of wine brought in and consumed on the premises rather than bought from the restaurant's own selection (although see also BYO). The term is derived from the fact that the number of corks pulled represents the number of bottles consumed. There is considerable variation in the amount charged and the grace with which the practice is accepted.

corked, pejorative tasting term for a wine spoiled by a cork stopper contaminated with

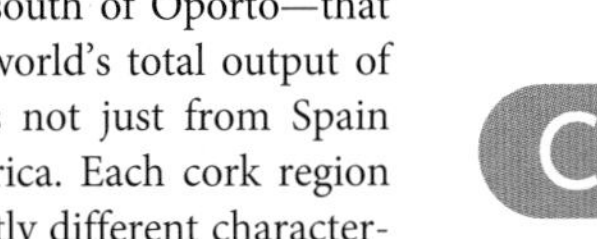

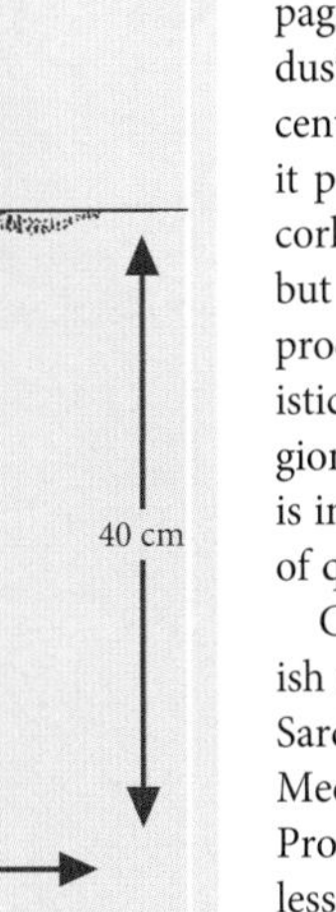

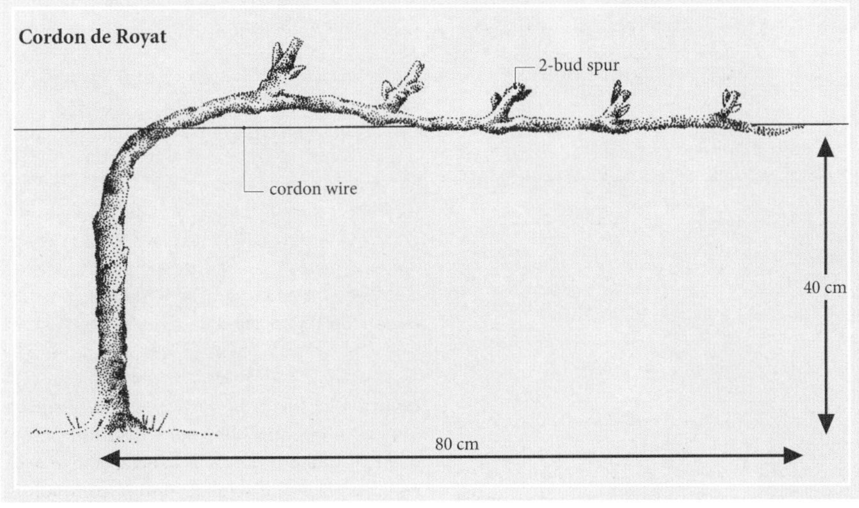

CORK TAINT. A wine spoiled by cork taint may also be described as **corky**, and the condition is known as **corkiness**. This is one of the most serious wine FAULTS as in most cases it irrevocably imbues the wine with such a powerfully off-putting smell that it cannot be drunk with any enjoyment. The unpleasantly, almost mould-like, chemical smell of TCA may also be present in smaller doses that may initially be noticed only by noses particularly sensitive to it or particularly familiar with the wine, but the odour usually intensifies with aeration, and it is difficult for tasters to enjoy a wine once their attention has been drawn to TCA's existence. Even a low level of taint often results in a slight dulling effect on the BOUQUET and palate, and levels well below the threshold of most drinkers' awareness have been shown to suppress fruit characters significantly.

The problem of corkiness was perceived by the wine industry to have increased from the 1980s, which soured relations between the wine and the cork industries and led to a marked increase in the use of alternative CLOSURES, particularly SCREWCAPS. However, cork producers are investing in new methods that have significantly reduced the incidence of cork taint, giving wine producers renewed confidence in the use of cork as a closure.

It is commonly but erroneously believed that a wine with small fragments of cork floating in it is 'corked'. This may be a SERVING fault but is certainly not a wine fault.

Taber, G., *To Cork or Not to Cork* (2007).

corks, wine-bottle stoppers, without which the appreciation of fine wine, and in particular AGEING, might never have evolved. Cork's unique combination of qualities has made it by far the most popular stopper for wine. In the late 20th century the science of wine production bounded ahead of the science of cork production, to the detriment of relations between the two industries (see CORKED wine), but cork producers have started to catch up in the 21st century.

History

See CLOSURES.

The cork tree

The cork tree, *Quercus suber*, is a relatively young species of OAK and is unusual in that its bark is so thick and resistant that it can be stripped from the trunk and large branches without hurting the tree.

It grows in sandy soils free of chalk and prefers annual rainfalls of 400–800 mm/15–30 in, temperatures which never fall below −5 °C/23 °F, and an ELEVATION of 100–300 m/330–1,000 ft. This effectively restricts cork oaks to the coast of the western Mediterranean, particularly Spain, North Africa, and much of Portugal, where cork plays a significant role in the economy. The cork industry was born in Cataluña but was disrupted by the Spanish Civil War. The commercial stability of Algeria, which still grows more than 10% of the world's cork (though much less than Morocco's 18%), was called into question in the 1960s, so that Portugal is now the centre of the world's cork business, and cork is an important contributor to the Portuguese economy. Portugal's cork forests, centred on the Alentejo, are today the most extensive, their 736,000 ha/1.82 million acres representing 34% of the world's 2.2 million ha of cork trees, significantly assisted in the late 1980s by EU grants.

Spain has the next largest total area planted with cork oaks, about 574,000 ha, mostly in the south and west of the country, from which a high proportion of the cork is shipped across the border for processing in Portugal's more temperate climate (although, in the north-east, Cataluña is still an important supplier of corks, especially to France and particularly to Champagne). So entrenched is the modern cork industry in Portugal—many of the processing centres are located just south of Oporto—that it produces 49% of the world's total output of cork, helped by imports not just from Spain but also from North Africa. Each cork region produces cork with slightly different characteristics. One of Portugal's most prized cork regions is Evora. Although forestry management is important, the most significant determinants of quality occur at the processing stage.

Cork trees, if not a cork industry, also flourish along the west coast of Italy, on Sicily, and Sardinia, as well as on Corsica and along the Mediterranean coast of France, particularly in Provence, and in Algeria, Tunisia, and to a lesser extent California, but little is made of these plantations commercially.

The bark of the cork tree is sufficiently thick to yield commercially useful cork from its 25th year, and cork trees are regularly stripped during the summer months, no more than every nine years by Portuguese law. On average, modern husbandry means that each hectare of cork forest yields 230 kg/500 lbs of cork; the older the tree, the more cork it will yield. Although the average life expectancy of a cork tree is about 170 years, there is one tree in the Montijo region south-east of Portugal's capital Lisbon estimated to be about 240 years old which has yielded 1,200 kg of cork from a single stripping. Cork farming, an activity often administered by the state, is an even longer-term undertaking than growing vines, which have an active wine-producing life of around 30 years on average (but see OLD VINES).

The bark micro-structure is unique in that it consists of very small, closely packed, usually 14-sided cells which have undergone a process known as suberinization. This renders it light, elastic, inert, and relatively impermeable to gases and most liquids except particularly strong acids or bases. These qualities and its low conductivity make cork a useful and versatile commodity as an insulator, particularly for the automotive and construction industries, but the principal use for cork is still cork stoppers and, in particular, wine corks.

Cork processing

Modern cork processing follows traditional methods, albeit helped by increasingly sophisticated technology. The strips of cork bark yielded by the annual stripping are stacked and left outside for seasoning (just as oak is in BARREL MAKING) for at least six months. Good drainage and airflow are important at this stage to minimize the risk of TCA development. Still in large strips, the cork is then boiled for about 90 minutes, both to make it more flexible and in an effort to kill off any moulds and other contaminants. This water needs constant replacing

C

It took four craftsmen two hours to harvest this impressive but still relatively young CORK oak in Estremadura near PORTUGAL's border with Spain. Trees like this, which are never felled, may be harvested dozens of times over their possible 250-year lifespan. © Amorim

or processing to prevent contamination of subsequent batches. The planks are then left to rest in the warehouse of the cork-processing plant for two to three days before being sorted by hand and cut into strips as wide as the length of the final cork stopper. Corks are then punched out of these strips, usually by hand-operated punches but using an increasing degree of mechanization. Machines are more efficient and are now able to scrutinize each strip for impurities. Maximizing yield is a significant factor since only about 40% of all the commercially viable cork harvested is suitable for stoppers. The balance is used for AGGLOMERATE CORKS or other products.

Corks are deliberately punched at right angles to the growth of the cork tree, so that any lenticels (occasional knots in the wood) remain transverse and so that the risk of possible leakage due to lenticels is minimized. The ends of the cork stoppers are then polished to present a smooth surface to the wine.

Various treatments then follow. Bleaching by immersing the corks in a bath of chlorine solution had the twin aims of cosmetic appeal (whitening) and hygiene, but after the discovery that chlorine increases the likelihood of TCA formation and therefore the incidence of CORK TAINT, it was largely superseded by hydrogen peroxide. After complaints from the wine industry in the late 20th century, the major cork producers switched to other sanitizing treatments, with hygiene the main aim, and invested substantially in quality control to reduce TCA incidence. Today cork buyers can request, at additional cost, an analysis of each cork in order to remove any TCA-tainted samples, effectively eliminating the cork-taint problem. (The most fastidious buyers, such as Barbaresco's GAJA, work with several suppliers to spread any risk and also test every batch of corks independently.)

Corks are graded on visual quality (the fewer the markings the higher the grade), branded with the name of the wine producer, and often coated with paraffin, a silicon-based product, or occasionally beeswax to make them easier to extract and reinsert and to ease their passage through BOTTLING equipment.

Finally, corks are sealed into large plastic bags, typically with SULFUR DIOXIDE as a disinfectant, although irradiation and simple holes for aeration are used as respectively more and less sophisticated alternatives. Subsequent storage conditions are critical to minimize mould growth and TCA contamination: ideal is a ventilated, odour-free environment at a temperature of 15–20 °C/59–68 °F in a relative humidity of 50–70%.

The range available

Although the first cork stoppers were tapered, the development of CORKSCREWS made tightly fitting cylindrical corks the norm. Modern corks are available in varying lengths, from 25 to as much as 60 mm (1–2.3 in), according to the AGEING aspirations, or extravagant exhibitionism, of the wine producer. The longer the cork, the longer it is likely to remain an intact and viable stopper (see RECORKING) and, in principle, the lower the OXYGEN TRANSMISSION RATE. However, there is a limit to the length at which cork effectiveness can continue to increase, since most bottlenecks allow only 50–55 mm of cork length to make contact with the glass. There is much less variation in diameter, however, with 24 mm being the norm for a bottleneck with an internal diameter of 18.5 mm, although corks 23 and 26 mm wide are not unknown, depending on the diameter of the necks of BOTTLES used.

The quality of the cork material itself also determines the price and potential life of the stopper. Until the 21st century, the ranking was based solely on visual imperfections. Today, grading includes specific cleaning programmes and fault-testing protocols, as well as assessments of beauty and length. The longest, finest one-piece TCA-tested cork with a guarantee can cost 25–50 times as much as the cheapest, shortest AGGLOMERATE CORK.

T-stopper corks with plastic or wooden tops attached to a natural or agglomerate cork are used for some wines, particularly FORTIFIED WINES and some SWEET WINES, as well as for many spirits.

Corks for SPARKLING WINES—commonly known, with scant regard for appellation laws, as champagne corks—have to be made to very particular specifications. Initially cylindrical, they are much wider than normal corks, about 30 mm, and have to be (half-)driven into the bottleneck, forcing them into a mushroom shape. Champagne corks are held in place, against the force of the pressure of undissolved gas inside the bottle, by a wire muzzle. Because such corks are too wide to be punched whole from the bark of most cork oaks, and to moderate the cost of such a large cork, champagne corks are usually made from cork agglomerate with one, two, or occasionally three discs of natural cork stuck on to the end which goes into the bottleneck and is in contact with the wine.

Clues from the cork

In general, as corks age they will absorb some wine and lose their resilience and ultimately their capacity to seal against the bottleneck; the narrower and more misshapen a cork extracted from a bottle appears, therefore, the longer it has been there. This is a particularly useful clue to the likely age of a non-vintage sparkling wine, or at least to the time that has elapsed since DISGORGEMENT. It can also provide a clue to the likely age of any other wine which has lost its label or, perhaps in the case of vintage PORT, never had one (although see also RECORKING).

Most fine-wine corks are emblazoned with the name of the wine producer, the cork manufacturer's logo or code, and, sometimes, the vintage. If the vintage year is branded on the ends of a cork, it means the producer opted for fire or laser branding; this is more expensive than the ink that is forbidden on cork ends. Different countries adopt different conventions. On some French corks, for example, you might see MIS EN BOUTEILLE *à la propriété*.

A short agglomerate cork, or a low-grade colmated cork, suggests that the bottler had little regard for the ageing ability of this wine, while a particularly long, one-piece, TCA-tested, unbleached natural cork is indicative at least of ambition or optimism.

If a cork has crystals on the end that has been in contact with the wine (white in the case of a white wine and dyed dark red by a red wine), these are harmless TARTRATES. If a cork seems damp or mouldy at either end, this is not necessarily a sign of any wine fault. Some wine waiters are taught to smell the cork and present it to the customer as an essential part of wine service (see SERVING WINE), but the state of a cork is no sure guide to the state of the wine it stoppered.

For alternatives to corks, see CLOSURES, CROWN CAPS, SCREWCAPS, AGGLOMERATE CORKS, and SYNTHETIC CLOSURES. A.L.W.

Taber, G., *To Cork or Not to Cork* (2007).

corkscrews, wide range of devices for extracting CORKS from the necks of wine BOTTLES.

It might be thought that cork extraction would prove an easy matter with any simple screw device, given the relatively soft, resilient nature of the stopper. However, there have been many hundreds of inventions since the middle of the 18th century with the aim of producing a better, more efficient corkscrew, and as yet none has been accepted as the perfect instrument. In particular, no corkscrew has yet been shown to be infallible with old PORT corks, so PORT TONGS are sometimes employed instead. The extraction operation can vary considerably. Corks vary in length and can also, as they accommodate to the shape of the bottleneck, vary in shape. Furthermore, cork undergoes ageing in old bottles and may partially disintegrate on extraction. The necks of old port bottles, for example, usually have a slightly bulbous form, so that the lower part of the cylindrical cork is weakened where it ballooned out and became cone shaped. Italian wine bottles tend to be narrow at the neck, tightly compressing corks and making them relatively difficult to penetrate.

History

The free-blown, onion-shaped wine bottles (see BOTTLES, history) of the 17th century did

C

not have a standard size of neck. Under these circumstances, tapered corks made a satisfactory stopper, especially as a portion remained proud of the bottle top, facilitating manual removal. The mould-made cylindrical glass bottle which evolved from about 1740 could be BINNED horizontally to keep the cork moist and at the same time to save space. This necessitated a driven cylindrical cork of standard diameter, and the removal of such a cork required a special tool.

Simple corkscrews leave the operator to do the work of screwing the worm (the curly metal bit) into the cork and pulling it out unassisted. Various modifications of handle, shaft, and worm can increase the efficiency of these manœuvres: the handle should be formed to give a good pulling grip; the shaft can be fitted with a metal disc, or button, to obtain more complete contact with the cork; and the worm should be a steel helix 5.7 cm/2.2 in long, be of good open pitch, and have an outer diameter of between 0.8 and 1 cm.

Although it is possible that simple corkscrews were in use by the mid 17th century in England, the earliest extant examples date from the 1690s.

Mechanical corkscrews are designed to reduce the amount of physical effort required during the three manœuvres of piercing, pulling, and disposing of the cork. Mechanical handheld corkscrews can never be used with the rapidity of an efficient wall- or bar-mounted mechanical instrument, although the modern handheld **Lever Pull**, really a miniature bar-screw in concept, can be used at remarkable speed.

National characteristics

Until fairly recently, the best corkscrews from the points of view of function, design, and quality of workmanship were made in wine-neutral Britain. The two-lever Italian corkscrew with a gimlet-like worm overcame the erstwhile problem of their short, tight corks.

The Germans rarely used anything other than the centre worm and often combined this with an inventive use of springs and ball bearings. In 1882, Karl Wienke of Rostock, Mecklenburg, conceived of using a knife-like handle as a lever. Known affectionately as the **waiter's friend**, it is still the essential tool of a SOMMELIER worldwide. The development of an articulated lever makes this model even easier to use as the cork is extracted in two stages, keeping it more upright and less likely to break.

The French were keen on nickel plating, contrasting with the bronzed finish of English pieces, as well demonstrated by the lazy tongs models of both countries.

Americans printed the wooden handles with advertisements and became largely preoccupied with self-pullers and other models which used the frame of the corkscrew as a fulcrum and derived from the French *à cage* principle. **Screwpull**, invented in the 1970s by Herbert Allen, is the culmination of applying this principle using strong modern plastics and a teflon-coated helix. Many other manufacturers today use teflon-coated worms, copying the Screwpull principles.

A two-pronged extractor became jokingly known as the **butler's friend**, as it enabled the cork to be extracted and replaced without evident damage and, possibly, the wine to be replaced with one less fine. A more recent development has been The Durand, incorporating a traditional helix within a butler's friend (also known as an Ah-So) and designed especially for old bottles with fragile corks.

B.M.W. & R.N.H.B.

Bibliographical note: Literally dozens of books about corkscrews have been published, with Donald Bull, Ron Maclean, and Ferd Peters particularly prolific authors of them.

cork taint in a wine is often characterized as an off-putting, mouldy, wet-cardboard or wet-dog character. It suppresses fruit and shortens the length of finish of the wine. In its most subtle form, cork taint has a slight dulling effect on the aroma and flavour. At its extreme, it renders a wine quite unapproachable.

Although research results vary, between 3 and 5% of all wines sealed under cork display a musty taint. This is caused by a number of potent organic compounds, the most significant of which is 2,4,6-trichloroanisole or TCA. These taint compounds are metabolic products of fungi naturally present in cork or which have grown in the cork at various processing stages. Initially the occurrence of this taint was ascribed to the washing of cork planks by chlorine-containing bleaches; these have since been replaced by peroxide, but cork taint has remained a problem. It seems that the structure of cork, which is permeated by fine pores (lenticels) to facilitate gas exchange, will always harbour fungi with the potential to produce taint compounds. A study by Duncan, Gibson, and Obradovic has demonstrated the presence of TCA in the bark of cork trees in a Portuguese cork forest. See HALOANISOLES.

Only tiny amounts of TCA are needed to cause a taint problem since its aroma detection threshold in wine is about 3–4 ng/l. Over the past two decades, the major international cork producers have modified their production processes, from storage of the raw material through to the final sorting of the corks. Autoclaving the bark reduced the quantity of TCA by about 85% and is practised by all of the large companies. However, each company has developed proprietary methods that use a combination of pressure and temperature to drive the TCA out of the corks once they have been punched out. Such methods involve, for example, ozone, vacuum steam, dry steam or extraction using an ethanol bath.

AGGLOMERATE CORKS have also come a long way in reducing levels of TCA. Several of the larger producers guarantee theirs corks to be TCA-free. The greatest changes have been in the sorting and storing procedures of the raw bark as well as fine-tuning the supercritical CO_2 extraction of the TCA and using better-quality plant-based binders to stick the granules together. Some companies are using head-space ionization technology to screen individual corks for volatile TCA so as to eliminate batches with high levels prior to final processing. In many cases, the level of TCA in agglomerate corks is lower than those in the punched corks.

Many cork producers are reporting an increase in sales of natural corks as a result of these improvements. Research has identified the potential contribution of chemicals other than TCA to taint in wine. These include other chloroanisoles such as tetrachloroanisole (TECA) and PCA, as well as alternatives to chloroanisoles. MDMP (see METHOXY-DIMETHYLPYRAZINE) has been identified as a key compound responsible for a 'fungal must' taint in wines that is possibly second only to TCA. TBA (see TRIBROMOANISOLE) also creates musty aromas in wine but is caused by contamination from the winery environment. This tallies with the observation that 'cork taint' can come from sources other than the cork—most notably from wooden structures in wineries that have been chemically treated—though the taint may still be transferred to the wine via the secondary contamination of the cork. But despite a few fairly high-profile instances of winery contamination, it seems that the cork is the culprit in the vast majority of cases.

J.A.G. & K.C.

Chatonnet, P., et al., 'Identification and responsibility of 2,4,6-tribromoanisole in musty, corked odors in wine', *Journal of Agricultural and Food Chemistry*, 52 (2004), 1255–62.

Duncan, B. C., et al., '2,4,6-trichloroanisole and cork production', *Australian and New Zealand Wine Industry Journal*, 12/2 (1997), 180–4.

Gonález-Centeno, M. R., et al., 'Use of a plastic film to eliminate the cork taint of a contaminated wine: improvement of organoleptic quality', *IVES Technical Reviews* (2020). ives-technicalreviews.eu/article/view/4540.

Prak, S., et al., 'Fungal strains isolated from cork stoppers and the formation of 2,4,6-trichloroanisole involved in the cork taint of wine', *Food Microbiology*, 24 (2007), 271–80.

corky bark, virus-like disease and one of the few which can kill vines. It is one of a complex of diseases known as RUGOSE WOOD. Symptoms of the disease resemble those of LEAFROLL VIRUS, in that leaves turn red or yellow and roll

downwards in the autumn. Vines infected with corky bark retain their leaves after they would naturally have fallen. It can be transmitted to healthy grapevines by the longtailed mealybug *Pseudococcus longispinus*, which may be regulated by the use of PHEROMONES. There is no control for infected vineyards, and vine removal is the only solution if many vines are infected.
R.E.S.

Cornalin, ancient and almost extinct variety from AOSTA that was shown by DNA PROFILING to be identical to HUMAGNE ROUGE in the Swiss Valais. It is therefore an offspring of ROUGE DU PAYS, confusingly renamed Cornalin in the Valais in 1972. J.V.

Cornas, small but dynamic appellation located at the southern end of the Northern RHÔNE making robust red wines that can rival the best of HERMITAGE and CÔTE RÔTIE. The most favourable vineyards are planted on a rumpled, steep, largely east-facing slope that overlooks the village of Cornas, with some notable exceptions such as Reynards facing south. Much of the vineyard land is terraced, with vines grown on STAKES known as *échalas*. Soils are a SANDY, decomposed GRANITE, planted entirely to Syrah. This is a hot MESOCLIMATE, although more recent plantings have taken advantage of the fresher temperatures on the plateau west of the slope, which rises to 400 m/1,312 ft in ELEVATION.

Until the late 1990s, Cornas had a reputation for making particularly rustic wines, often with an 'animal' side that was probably caused by BRETTANOMYCES. Brett is no longer more of a problem here than it is anywhere else in the Rhône, but the wines have retained a certain wildness of character, with an intense tannic structure. The wines are not as reliably ageworthy as those of HERMITAGE, but some examples can endure 20 to 30 years in bottle. In 2020, 5,243 hl/138,505 gal were made from 155 ha/383 acres, so only marginally more than Hermitage, but Cornas has more land left to plant. M.C.W.

Cornell University has conducted viticultural research at Cornell AgriTech (formerly the New York State Agricultural Experiment Station) in Geneva, NY, since the 1880s. VINE breeders have released 57 varieties of juice, table, and wine grapes since 1906. As part of the breeding programme, DISEASE-RESISTANT and winter-hardy AMERICAN VINE SPECIES are crossed with VITIS VINIFERA as well as with Asian species of the VITIS genus. Two USDA-ARS units are housed at AgriTech: the Plant Genetic Resources Unit (PGRU) and the Grape Genetics Research Unit (GGRU). The PGRU makes over 1,300 genotypes of cold-hardy *Vitis* germplasm available for grape breeders. Scientists from the GGRU apply genomics and DNA sequencing to identify useful DNA markers (2,000, covering 99% of the genome) to accelerate VINE BREEDING.

The principles of sunlight utilization in grapevine canopies were elucidated by Dr Nelson SHAULIS leading to modern CANOPY MANAGEMENT such as shoot positioning and the GENEVA DOUBLE CURTAIN training system. The modern mechanical grape harvester was also developed by Shaulis, E. S. Shepardson, and grower Roy Orton. (See MECHANICAL HARVESTING.)

Oenology studies at Cornell began in the 1960s. CAYUGA WHITE, Cornell's first wine grape variety, was released in 1972. More recent releases include CHARDONEL (1990), TRAMINETTE (1996), Valvin Muscat, Noiret, Corot Noir (2006), and Aromella and Arandell (2013). Studies in microbiology, fermentation, flavour chemistry, and wine production are ongoing. Cornell's plant pathologists, grape physiologists, entomologists, extension specialists, and others develop technologies to enhance the quality and TERROIR of New York's grapes and wines and to sustainably control diseases and pests.

Cornell recently instituted undergraduate and one-year master's degrees in OENOLOGY and VITICULTURE, with teaching at Geneva and on the main campus in Ithaca. T.E.M.

Cornifesto, minor dark grape in the DOURO, making light reds and PORTS. A natural ALFROCHEIRO × CAYETANA BLANCA cross.

Corpinnat, a collective EU brand of Catalan sparkling wine registered in 2017 by some of the best former producers of CAVA in reaction to what they considered an erosion of Cava's reputation and standards. Corpinnat wines must come from within a tightly delimited area in PENEDÈS and are subject to stricter regulations such as mandatory hand-harvesting, ORGANIC VITICULTURE, and stringent YIELD limits. Wines must be vinified on the winery premises and age at least 18 months. There were 11 members as of 2022. F.C.

Corrèze, small AOC in SOUTH WEST FRANCE around Brive-la-Gaillarde, yielding a range of white and red wines as well as VINS DE PAILLE. Whites depend on CHENIN BLANC; reds are mainly Cabernet Franc, with Merlot and Cabernet Sauvignon. Wine bearing the DÉNOMINATION GÉOGRAPHIQUE COMPLÉMENTAIRE **Coteaux de la Vézère** must be entirely Franc grown on the SLATE soils of south Corrèze. P.S.

Corse is the French name for CORSICA.

Corsica, or Corse in French, is a mountainous Mediterranean island with distinctive, characterful wines. Measuring about 180 km/112 miles long and 80 km wide, it comprises a chain of abrupt mountains rising dramatically above a perimeter of capes, gulfs, and sandy beaches. The island produces many styles of wine, all products of long hours of Mediterranean sunshine, salty breezes, and poor, rocky soils surrounded by the island's signature aromatic shrubland, the *maquis*. Average annual production is 375,500 hl/9.9 million gal with nearly two-thirds of production leaving the island—about 45% to mainland France and 20% exported to Germany, Belgium, and the US.

C

History

Corsican wine is intimately tied to the island's turbulent history of invasions and occupations, a result of its strategic location in the Mediterranean. Viticulture can be traced back to Phocaean settlement in 565 BCE at modern-day Aléria, on the east coast. The Greeks and then Romans significantly developed viticulture all over the island. Under Genoese rule from the 13th to 18th centuries, Corsican wine took on newfound economic importance, enjoying strong commercial ties with the Italian mainland. It is during this period that grapes such as Sangiovese—known on the island as NIELLUCCIU—are thought to have been introduced to Corsica. After the Genoese signed over the island to France in 1768—one year before the birth of Corsica's most famous son, Napoleon, to a wine-growing family in Ajaccio—viticulture continued to prosper, with local wines being exported around the world.

The wine industry was revolutionized in the 1960s with the repatriation of many French *pieds noirs* from ALGERIA. The returning colonists engaged in widespread planting of high-yielding imported grape varieties and introduced modern techniques aimed at increasing production. Total vineyard area grew fourfold to over 30,000 ha/74,132 acres, producing 2 million hl/53 million gal. This rapid industrialization damaged Corsican wine's image and dealt a major blow to small-scale, traditionally minded farmers.

The 1980s marked a turning point, as EU subsidies led to a campaign of mass uprooting in response to the European WINE LAKE crisis. Coupled with a Corsican cultural movement that placed newfound focus on the island's viticultural heritage, Corsican vineyards began to be restructured with an emphasis on quality. By 2020, vineyards accounted for 5,782 ha/14,287 acres, and varieties once introduced for BULK WINE have been replaced by nobler vines, coinciding with renewed interest in Corsica's wealth of indigenous cultivars.

Geography and climate

With more than 100 peaks over 2,000 m/6,560 ft in elevation, Corsica is essentially a large mountain range sitting in the sea. Its array of valleys and hillsides with varying ELEVATIONS and EXPOSURES to wind and maritime influence results in many diverse MESOCLIMATES. The island is among France's sunniest regions, averaging 2,470–2,885 hours of sunshine annually. Although some parts of the island see significant rainfall, summers are very dry. Colder air from the sea and mountains tempers hot summer days, keeping nights relatively cool and ensuring decent diurnal temperature range. Wind is extremely influential, with the Cap Corse and Bonifacio averaging only 16 windless days per year. In addition to local sea and land breezes, important winds include the violent mistral from Provence; the libeccio from Gibraltar; the dry, cold tramontane from the Alps; the cool gregale from the Appenines; and the warm sirocco blowing in from the Sahara.

Corsica has four principal soil types: granite across the west and south; schist in the north-east including the Cap Corse, the mountainous finger of land pointing France-wards; pockets of limestone in Patrimonio and on the island's southern tip around Bonifacio; and alluvial soils on the flatter east coast.

Viticulture

Vines are typically cultivated in the craggy foothills between mountains and the sea. As in southern France, gobelet training is traditional, but other systems such as cordon de Royat and single Guyot have become more widespread with mechanization. The most common rootstock is 110R, chosen for its resistance to drought. The frequent winds help to ward off disease, the main viticultural concerns being summer drought, downy mildew, powdery mildew, and flavescence dorée. For AOC wines, irrigation is prohibited, and vine density must be at least 4,000 vines per ha (1,600 per acre). in 2021, 22% of vineyards were farmed organically (see organic viticulture), and biodynamic viticulture has also taken a foothold.

Vine varieties

Nielluccìu (sangiovese), Sciaccarellu (mammolo), and Vermentinu (vermentino) are the most important Corsican varieties, representing nearly 60% of all plantings.

Niellucciu, probably introduced during the period of Genoese occupation, is the most planted variety, accounting for 27% of vineyard area or 1,552 ha/3,835 acres in 2020, much of it in the north of the island, where it thrives on the calcareous-clay soils of Patrimonio. Niellucciu-based reds are dark and powerful, showing notes of black fruit, licorice, spices, and a savory gaminess. Their firm acidity and grippy tannins provide good ageing potential. It is increasingly used to make bright, crisp rosés as well.

Sciaccarellu (961 ha/2,375 acres) has an affinity for southern Corsica's granite soils, yielding lively, floral reds low in tannin and high in alcohol, with an extravagant perfume of smashed berries, pepper, and wild herbs. It also produces delicate, fresh rosés.

In Corsica, Vermentinu (854 ha/2,110 acres) asserts its status as one of the Mediterranean's finest white grapes. Grown all over the island, it produces fruit-driven quaffers as well as complex, full-bodied wines with the capacity for bottle age. These gently floral, dry whites often show hints of lemon, pear, tropical fruits, fresh herbs, honey, and almond, with a subtle bitterness and mouthwatering salinity that make up for their relatively low acidity.

Southern French varieties such as grenache, cinsaut, and carignan are well adapted to the climate and can still be found planted alongside their Corsican counterparts, while international varieties are increasingly rare. Muscat blanc à petits grains (278 ha/687 acres) has long been grown in Corsica, yielding delicately perfumed sweet—and occasionally dry—wines, especially in the north-east.

Recent years have seen the resurgence of Corsica's numerous indigenous varieties. The CRVI (Centre de Recherche Viticole Insulaire) is engaged in much research and experimentation with these heirloom varieties, some of which have shown real potential in the face of climate change. Biancu gentile, Genovese, Riminese, Codivarta, barbarossa, Carcaghjolu Neru, Minustellu, Morescone, and aleatico—to name just a few—are increasingly used.

Vinification

Almost 70% of all Corsican wine is made by co-operatives, which, like some of the smaller wineries, took advantage of EU grants available for the installation of modern stainless steel tanks and refrigeration equipment, crucial in Corsica's hot climate. Rosés, usually made by direct press, are typically fermented cold in tank with malolactic conversion blocked. The same is true for white wines, although some growers are using methods such as barrel fermentation, full malolactic conversion, and skin contact to create deeper, more textural whites. Global demand for rosé has led pink wine to reach 70% of production in 2020, much of it produced by co-ops, followed by red (17%) and white (13%).

Red winemaking is relatively traditional; fermentation takes place in steel or concrete tanks, with higher-end cuvées often barrel-aged. Some growers are experimenting with alternative vessels including concrete eggs, amphorae, and acacia casks. Additionally, there is a growing contingent of domaines using low-intervention techniques associated with natural wine such as ambient yeast fermentation, minimal sulfur dioxide additions, and bottling without filtration.

Regions

Corsica has nine AOCs: the regional appellation Corse; two cru appellations, Patrimonio and Ajaccio; five village appellations prefixed with 'Corse-' (Calvi, Coteaux du Cap Corse, Figari, Porto Vecchio, Sartène); and one Vin Doux Naturel AOC, Muscat du Cap Corse. AOC wines represent 32% of total production, while Île de Beauté, the island's one IGP, accounts for 63%, with the remaining 5% labelled as Vin de France.

Patrimonio is Corsica's first appellation, awarded AOC status in 1968. Patrimonio forms a large amphitheatre of vineyards between the base of the Cap Corse and the Gulf of St-Florent. Just over 400 ha/988 acres of vines are shared between 39 domaines on a matrix of schist and fossil-studded limestone and clay, with occasional incursions of granite. Starring Niellucciu (minimum 90%), the deeply coloured and full-blooded reds make up over 40% of production. Rosés, accounting for one-third of production, are bright, chiselled, herb-scented thirst-quenchers. Patrimonio's whites (100% Vermentinu) are medium- to full-bodied with floral aromas, fleshy fruit, and a fresh mineral backbone. With age, they veer towards notes of petrol, gunflint, and honey. While most producers still use stainless steel or concrete, more and more are experimenting with wood and other vessels with encouraging results. The appellation was France's first to ban the use of synthetic herbicides.

Ajaccio, Corsica's second cru appellation, stretches from its capital city of Ajaccio, on the west coast, to remote inland hillsides to the north and south. Its 17 producers farm a total of 248 ha/613 acres on sandy decomposed granite. Sciaccarellu is the leading grape variety, giving fragrant, crunchy reds scented of wild myrtle and smashed berries. Delicate, floral rosés and whites are also produced. Domaine Abbatucci, a pioneer in biodynamic viticulture on the island, has played a crucial role in the preservation of Corsica's indigenous grapes with its nursery of heirloom varieties dating back to the 1960s.

Corse. This generic AOC is the dominant one on the island, primarily comprising wines from the 'Plaine Orientale', an alluvial zone stretching along the eastern coast from Bastia to Solenzara. Many of the larger estates were established here in the 1960s, its richer, flatter soils being more conducive to mechanization. Rosé dominates, at more than 75% of production. The 1,462 ha/3,613 acres are shared between 22 producers and all four of Corsica's co-ops.

Corse-Coteaux du Cap Corse is a mountainous peninsula in the island's north-east historically renowned for fortified Muscat and Rappu (a rare sweet red made from aleatico). However, its rugged schist soils are also conducive to fine white wines. Five domaines here share just 32 ha/79 acres.

C

Corse-Calvi encompasses 262 ha/647 acres and 11 producers in the north-west. Its granite terroirs range from coastal hillsides to inland plateaus surrounded by mountains, cut off from the Mediterranean's influence. The diversity of wine styles echoes this variety, although the area is notable for citrusy, herbaceous Vermentinu and powerful reds made mostly from Niellucciu, Sciaccarellu, and Grenache.

Corse-Figari comes from 143 ha/353 acres of vines and nine producers in the south-west of the island. Over half of production is red in this particularly hot, rugged, windswept region where granite soils yield robust, spicy wines.

Corse-Porto Vecchio comprises 90 ha/222 vineyard acres and four producers in the far south-east.

Corse-Sartène encompasses 245 ha/605 acres of vineyard and eight domaines in the granitic rolling hills around the eponymous village between Ajaccio and Figari. It is renowned primarily for full-bodied Sciaccarellu-based reds.

Muscat du Cap Corse is a distinctive VIN DOUX NATUREL made by 28 producers from just 39 ha/96 acres of MUSCAT BLANC À PETITS GRAINS grown on the Cap Corse and within the Patrimonio appellation. The grapes ferment partway until MUTAGE with a neutral grape spirit. The resulting wines must be 15–18% alcohol, with at least 90 g/l RESIDUAL SUGAR. Their sun-soaked flavours and delicate scents of maquis herbs, wildflower honey, and candied citrus shine with local desserts and cheeses. A.L.

www.vinsdecorse.com

Cortese, Italian white grape variety most closely associated with south-east PIEMONTE, in the province of Alessandria, where it was first recorded in the early 17th century. No relatives have so far been identified. Total plantings were 2,405 ha/5,943 acres by 2015, and it is the basis of no fewer than nine DOCS. Its most highly regarded wine is GAVI, produced initially to serve the fish restaurants of Genoa and the Ligurian coast. The Cortese dell'Alto Monferrato a few miles west, like the Cortese grown on the Colli Tortonese, rarely achieves the ripeness or winemaking proficiency of Gavi. At its best, the wine is clean and fresh. The use of oak is usually misguided.

Corton and **Corton-Charlemagne**, respectively the great red and white GRANDS CRUS in and around ALOXE-CORTON in Burgundy's CÔTE D'OR.

Coruche, subregion of TEJO in central, southern Portugal.

Corvina, or **Corvina Veronese**, the dominant and best grape variety of VALPOLICELLA and BARDOLINO in north-east Italy, producing fruity red wines with a characteristic sour-cherry twist on the finish. Wines from the better Valpolicella producers who reduced yields in the 1980s and 1990s demonstrated that lack of BODY was not an inherent characteristic of Corvina. Since then, it has enjoyed great success as the best variety for AMARONE. Producers such as Allegrini have also illustrated that wines made solely or predominantly from Corvina such as La Poja can be serious, barrel-aged reds. Corvina, sometimes called Cruina, has traditionally been confused with CORVINONE. DNA PROFILING at SAN MICHELE ALL'ADIGE in 2005 supported a parent–offspring relationship with RONDINELLA. Presumably fuelled by the popularity of Amarone, Italy's total plantings of Corvina Veronese increased substantially in the early 21st century to reach 6,222 ha/15,375 acres by 2015.

Corvinone, red grape variety grown mainly in the VALPOLICELLA zone. It is so similar to CORVINA that it was long mistaken as merely a different CLONE of Corvina, although DNA PROFILING has established that it is a distinct variety. It is now highly regarded as a grape for such DRIED-GRAPE WINES as AMARONE and RECIOTO as its loose bunches and large berries make it particularly suited to DRYING. Total plantings had grown to nearly 1,140 ha/2,817 acres by 2015.

cosecha is Spanish for VINTAGE YEAR.

Costa Rica in Central America has one commercial winery and vineyard, an Israeli-Californian-Costa Rican venture started in 2011. By 2022, 20 ha/49 acres of INTERNATIONAL VARIETIES were planted in the hills above Copey at an ELEVATION of 2,400 m/7,874 ft.

Costers del Segre, DOP in north-east Spain in semi-DESERT near the Catalan city of Lerida (see map under SPAIN) and in the lusher mountains bordering the Priorat DOP to the east. The climate is severe, with winter temperatures dipping below freezing in winter and exceeding 35 °C/95 °F in high summer. RAINFALL barely reaches 400 mm/15 in per year. The River Segre, a tributary of the Ebro after which this fragmented DOP is named, is little more than a seasonal stream.

The history of Costers del Segre was initially the history of one estate: Raimat, which covers 3,200 ha/7,900 acres of arid country 15 km/9 miles north-west of Lerida. When Manuel Raventós, owner of CAVA producer Codorníu, first visited the property in 1914, he found infertile salt plains abandoned by farmers. An IRRIGATION artery, the Canal de Aragón y Cataluña, has since transformed the estate into an oasis, but it took over 50 years of planting cattle fodder, pine trees, and cereals before the soil was fit for vines. Today the Raimat vineyard covers 2,000 ha, which amounts to one-third of the Costers del Segre DOP. Cabernet Sauvignon, Merlot, Pinot Noir, and Chardonnay flourish alongside INDIGENOUS VARIETIES such as Tempranillo, Parellada, and Macabeo.

Of the region's seven subzones—Artesa de Segre, Urgell, Garrigues, Pallars, Raimat, Segrià, and Valls del Riu Corb—Pallars is the most prominent, thanks to pioneer producer Castell d'Encús as well as to ELEVATIONS reaching above 1,100 m/3,609 ft, where the cooler temperatures are seen as an advantage in the face of CLIMATE CHANGE and have even encouraged some producers to plant PINOT NOIR. V. de la S. & F.C.

Costières de Nîmes. Situated in the far south-west of the RHÔNE Valley, this appellation was considered part of the Languedoc by French authorities until 1989, when it was passed to the Rhône. In 2020, 2,844 ha/7,028 acres of vineyard produced 153,380 hl/4,051,871 gal of wine, 43% red, 48% rosé, and 9% white. The growing area can be roughly split into two sections: a northern part whose dominant wind is the mistral, and a southern area, closer to the sea, which is more affected by the dewy marin wind. These sea breezes help to temper afternoon temperatures, making the southern section the cooler of the two; more white varieties are planted here as a result. Soils in both areas are mainly the rounded stones known as *galets roulés* and CLAY. Wines of all colours must be a blend. Grenache is widely planted, but Syrah is the most popular grape for red wines, with Grenache Blanc and Roussanne for whites. M.C.W.

Cot, or **Côt**, is an important French synonym for the black grape variety of French origin also known as MALBEC and, in CAHORS, Auxerrois.

Côte means 'slope' or 'hill' in French. *Côtes* is the plural, while *Coteau* (*Coteaux* in plural) means much the same thing but possibly on a smaller scale. Since French vine-growers are great believers in the viticultural merits of hillsides, all of these make suitable wine names. Thus, any index of French wine names contains long lists of Côte, Côtes, and Coteaux de, du, de la, and des various place names, suggesting, often with reason, that the wine comes from the slopes above these places. Some of these prefixes are eventually dropped, however. Côtes de Buzet, for example, was renamed plain BUZET in the late 1980s, and Côtes du Ventoux has become VENTOUX.

For this reason—and to save readers having to remember whether a wine is, for example, a Coteaux de Somewhere or a Coteaux du Somewhere—such an entry would be listed under S for Somewhere, rather than under Coteaux. Their Côte and Côtes counterparts are listed similarly. The only exceptions to this are names in which the Côte, Côtes, or Coteaux are integral. They follow this entry.

Côte des Blancs, area of CHAMPAGNE on east-facing slopes south of Épernay noted for the quality of its Chardonnay grapes.

C

Côte d'Or, the heart of the BURGUNDY wine region in eastern France in the form of an escarpment supporting a narrow band of vineyards for nearly 50 km/30 miles southwards (and a touch west) from Dijon, capital of the *département* of the same name (see map under BURGUNDY). The name 'Côte d'Or' apparently translates directly as 'golden slope', evoking its autumnal aspect, but some think it may be an abbreviation of 'Côte d'Orient', a reference to the fact that the escarpment on which the vines flourish faces east. Viticulturally it is divided into two sectors: the Côte de NUITS, in which great red wines are made from the Pinot Noir vine; and the Côte de BEAUNE, where the reds are joined by the finest white wines made from Chardonnay.

The Côte d'Or represents the fault line separating the hills of the Morvan from the plain of the Saône, which, in the Jurassic period 195–135 million years BCE, was an inland sea. The predominant rock is Jurassic LIMESTONE, which favours both Chardonnay and Pinot Noir vine varieties. However, the escarpment features many differing forms of limestone and other rocks. Oolitic limestone, which originated as a precipitation around marine debris of carbonate of lime from the seawater, is usefully porous and provides good DRAINAGE compared with marlstone, which is made up of clay, sand, gravel, and marl, the result of decomposition of older mountains such as the Ardennes.

The escarpment is also broken up by streams—the Vouge in Vougeot, the Meuzin in Nuits-St-Georges, the Rhoin in Savigny, the Dheune and Avant-Dheune further south—running down from the hills eventually to join the Saône, as well as by dry valleys (*combes*) such as the Combe de Lavaux in Gevrey-Chambertin. These breaks vary the orientation of the vineyards: thus Clos-St-Jacques is exposed more to the south than to the east, while much of Corton-Charlemagne actually faces south-west. The streams also affect the composition of the soil by bringing down alluvial deposits.

A cross-section of the Côte reveals topsoil too sparse on the hilltop and too fertile in the plain to produce wine of any quality. The vineyard area begins to the west of the Dijon–Lyons railway line, but only the most basic wines made from ALIGOTÉ and GAMAY are produced here. Approaching the main Dijon–Chagny road, the D974, the vineyards are still on flat, fertile land, but Pinot Noir and Chardonnay are planted to produce BOURGOGNE Rouge and Bourgogne Blanc. These in turn give way to village APPELLATION vineyards; as the ground starts to slope upwards, drainage improves, and the soil is less fertile.

Where the slope becomes more pronounced and clay gives way to stonier topsoil, the vineyards are designated PREMIERS CRUS, reflecting the potential quality of the wines from land which drains well and enjoys greater exposure to the sun. The finest of these vineyards, in certain villages only, are classified as GRANDS CRUS (listed under BURGUNDY). The premier and grand cru vineyards are mainly at elevations of 250–300 m/800–1,000 ft above sea level. Near the top of the slope, where the soil is almost too poor, there is usually a narrow band of village appellation vineyards providing fine but light wines.

Viticultural practices are relatively constant for both major grape varieties throughout the Côte d'Or. VINE DENSITY is notably high—about 10,000 vines per ha (4,000 per acre)—and vines are trained and pruned chiefly according to the single GUYOT system (although CORDON DE ROYAT is increasingly employed to restrict vigour in younger vines and those on over-productive ROOTSTOCKS). Harvesting is still mostly manual, especially for Pinot Noir. Yields are usually restricted at village level to 50 hl/ha (3 tons/acre) for red wines and 57 hl/ha (3.5 tons/acre) for white, reduced by 2 hl/ha for premiers crus.

There are no set rules for the production of great red burgundy, and every domaine or NÉGOCIANT house revels in its own idiosyncrasies. Principal options include DESTEMMING of the grapes (wholly, partly, or not at all); length of MACERATION period; fermentation TEMPERATURE; length of BARREL AGEING; type of OAK barrels used; and RACKING, FINING, and/or FILTRATION regimes. The better wines of the Côte d'Or are all matured for at least a year, more often 18 months, in 228-l/59-gal oak BARRELS, a proportion of which are usually new.

The qualities of great red burgundy are not easy to judge young, especially since the wine tends to be less deeply coloured than equivalent wines from Bordeaux or the Rhône. When young, a fine burgundy should show a bouquet of soft red fruit, ranging from cherries to plums depending on the vineyard and vigneron; complexity comes with maturity, the fresh fruit components giving way to more evolved aromas, often redolent of truffles or undergrowth (*sous-bois*, according to French palates).

Some wines are weighty, others intensely elegant, but all should have concentration. Style depends in part on the character of the village: GEVREY-CHAMBERTIN, VOUGEOT, NUITS-ST-GEORGES, CORTON, and POMMARD tend to produce robust, long-lived wines; CHAMBOLLE-MUSIGNY, VOSNE-ROMANÉE, and VOLNAY epitomize finesse and elegance. Within each village, different vineyards display their individual characteristics according to the exact SOIL STRUCTURE, ELEVATION, and TOPOGRAPHY.

Differences in annual WEATHER patterns are crucial in determining quality in the region. Burgundy is at a climatic crossroads, experiencing Atlantic, Mediterranean, and Baltic weather systems. A cool breeze from the north (*la bise*) is ideal to temper anticyclonic conditions in the summer; a southern wind brings heat but also danger; HAIL often results when the warm wind swings round to the west, the wettest direction. This has become an increasing problem in recent years with Volnay badly hailed in 2004, 2008, 2012, 2013, and 2014. Since then, FROST has become a greater scourge, with damage in 2017 and 2019 and more serious episodes in 2016 and 2021.

There is probably greater vintage variation in Burgundy than in any other wine region. In some VINTAGES—2004, 2008, and 2011 for instance, more rarely since—Pinot Noir grapes struggled to ripen fully, although growers who conscientiously restrict yields often produce excellent wines. The 1996 vintage, which produced fine wines for ageing, was unusual in that September sunshine ripened the grapes fully, judging by the sugar levels, yet cool nights maintained the acidity at levels normally associated with an unripe year. In other years, excessive rainfall can either swell the crop to produce dilute wines, as in 1982, 1992, 2000, and to some extent 2017 (red) and 2018 (white), or encourage ROT (as in 1986 and 1994). Most difficult to judge are the hot vintages in which the fruit in the wine is either supported or, sometimes, overwhelmed by TANNINS (as in 1976 and 1983) or can appear ultra-ripe (2003, 2009, and 2018–20). Balance may be best achieved in those vintages where ripeness is only just attained, as in 2002 and 2010. However, the greatest vintages of the past 50 years have been 1978, 1985, 1990, 1999, 2005, and 2015.

Great white burgundy is produced in the Côte de Beaune, notably in the villages of MEURSAULT, PULIGNY-MONTRACHET, and CHASSAGNE-MONTRACHET, along with a small enclave further north yielding the grand cru Corton-Charlemagne (see ALOXE-CORTON). The soils suited to Chardonnay production tend to be paler in colour than the iron-rich, redder soils on which the Pinot Noir thrives (see SOIL COLOUR). The Chardonnay vine is hardier than the Pinot, the grapes ripen more easily, and the wines require less delicate handling. It is easier to make good white burgundy than good red, but very little great white burgundy is made.

The grapes are pressed (usually without SKIN CONTACT), left to settle, then fermented in oak casks for up to a year (see BARREL FERMENTATION), although those with suitable cellars prefer to keep the wine for a second winter in wood, usually racking the wine into older barrels while retaining the fine LEES. Others keep the wine for six months in tank. In the early months some producers like to stir the lees to nourish the wine (see LEES STIRRING).

Fine white burgundy, when young, is more likely to show the character of the oak in which it has been vinified than the grapes from which it came. Hallmarks of quality are fullness of BODY, balance of ACIDITY, and persistence of flavour. Only after two or more years of bottle age will a fine Meursault or Puligny-Montrachet start to show the quality of the fruit. This will deepen with age and, although vegetal tones may appear, they should not overwhelm the natural elegance of the wine. A village appellation wine should be at its best from three to eight years old, a premier cru from five to ten years, while a grand cru worthy of its status needs a full decade of BOTTLE AGEING (but see also PREMATURE OXIDATION).

For more detail, see under names of individual villages or appellations. See BEAUNE, CÔTE DE and NUITS, CÔTE DE for a full list of the villages in each. To most of the villages and towns in the Côte d'Or was appended the name of their most famous vineyard, typically in the late 19th century. Thus, for example, Vosne became Vosne-Romanée and Puligny became Puligny-Montrachet. J.T.C.M.

Coates, C., *The Wines of Burgundy* (2008).
Morris, J., *Inside Burgundy* (2nd edn, 2021).
Norman, R., and Taylor C., *The Great Domaines of Burgundy* (3rd edn, 2010).
Pitiot, S., and Landrieu-Lussigny, M., *Climats et lieux-dits des Grands Vignobles de Bourgogne* (2012).

Côte Rôtie, one of the most prestigious appellations of the Northern RHÔNE, considered by many to be the equal of HERMITAGE, though very different in style. The name translates as 'roasted slope' but has been until recently a MARGINAL CLIMATE for ripening Syrah, the dominant vine variety. Situated at the northern limit of the northern Rhône growing area close to the village of Ampuis, the appellation comprises a series of steep, terraced hillsides that rise up from the river Rhône to an ELEVATION of around 325 m/1,066 ft. Due to the course of the river, these dramatic vineyards typically face east, south-east, and south, enjoying beneficial exposure to the sun.

This red-only appellation is divided into 73 LIEUX-DITS over three communes. Two of the most well known are the Côte Blonde and the Côte Brune immediately to its north-east. These names derive from the two main soil types in the appellation: Blonde refers to pale yellow GNEISS, Brune to dark brown SCHIST. Somewhat confusingly, since gneiss predominates from Côte Blonde southwards, the entire half of the appellation is sometimes referred to as 'the Côte Blonde'; conversely, it is schist that dominates from Côte Brune northwards, so this side of the appellation is sometimes referred to as 'the Côte Brune'. The gneiss soils contain less CLAY, are relatively free-draining, and produce a lighter-structured, more fragrant style of wine. The heavier schistous soils typically produce a more full-bodied, rounded, structured style of Syrah that is usually somewhat longer-lived. In the far south of the appellation there is also some GRANITE; other minor soil types include pebbly ALLUVIUM and pockets of LOESS. Some vines are trained on wires, but most are trained on one or two stakes known as *échalas* (see TRAINING SYSTEMS).

One peculiarity of the appellation is that up to 20% VIOGNIER is allowed in the wine, although this must be co-planted with the Syrah and CO-FERMENTED. In practice more than 10% is rare, as it can dominate the finished wine. Viognier is more commonly grown towards the south of the appellation, close to neighbouring CONDRIEU. It can add aromatic lift, alcohol, and texture to the red wines. Pure Syrah wines tend to age a little longer—typically up to ten years, the best 20–30 or more.

Vines have been grown here since Romans were settled nearby, as mentioned by PLINY the Elder, among others. After PHYLLOXERA, the appellation was slow to be replanted and until the 1970s was rather moribund. Attention was drawn to the appellation thanks to the meticulous work of Marcel GUIGAL, whose company continues to be a driving force. In 2020, 330 ha/815 acres of vineyards produced 11,467 hl/ 302,926 gal of wine that was bottled under the appellation. M.C.W.

Cotnari, appellation (DOC in Romania) most noted internationally for once-famous sweet white wine produced in hilly countryside in the north-eastern Moldovan Hills (see ROMANIA for geographical details). First documented in the 15th century, it once rivalled Hungarian TOKAJI as an elixir of FASHION sought after in the courts of northern Europe.

Cotnari wines are almost all produced by the large former state winery Cotnari SC or its premium off-shoot Casa de Vinuri Cotnari, owned by the second generation of the same families. Both are very protective of the Cotnari name, so it has been difficult for other producers to gain a foothold here. Cotnari wines remain very popular in Romania.

The DOC allows wine to be made from any of four local white grape varieties plus red FETEASCĂ Neagră and pink-skinned Busuioacă de Bohotin. The wines are often vinified from dry to semi-sweet, as single varieties, or as a traditional blend containing a minimum of 30% GRASĂ (which provides the body and sugar). TĂMÂIOASĂ Românească provides its 'frankincense' aromas (and sugar without losing acidity in the Cotnari MESOCLIMATE), Francuşă gives acidity (it must make up at least 30% in a blend, although it can suffer from poor FRUIT SET), and Fetească Albă the aroma. Occasionally, Grasă ripens to very high sugar levels and may be affected by NOBLE ROT. Such wines can be long-lived and impressive—and are released occasionally as 'collection' wines. C.G.

Couchois, Bourgogne, Côtes du, appellation created in 2000 for red wines made from Pinot Noir grown around the town of Couches north-west of the Côte Chalonnaise. See BOURGOGNE.

Couderc Noir, a FRENCH HYBRID of a dark-berried VITIS RUPESTRIS × *Vitis lincecumii* cross and VITIS VINIFERA, is one of several productive but undistinguished hybrids that proliferated in the MIDI in the early 20th century). Although not as popular as VILLARD once was, Couderc Noir was so widely planted that France's total area of Cabernet Sauvignon did not overtake that of Couderc Noir until well into the 1970s. By 2019 total plantings were just 142 ha/351 acres. The wine produced can be aggressively non-*vinifera* in taste.

Coulanges-la-Vineuse, commune near AUXERRE whose name may be appended to that of red, white, and rosé BOURGOGNE.

coulure, French term, also commonly used by English speakers, for one form of poor FRUIT SET in the grapevine. Excessive shedding of OVARIES and young berries results in relatively few berries per bunch, either during or soon after FLOWERING. To a great extent, coulure is a natural and necessary phenomenon, since the vine cannot possibly ripen the crop if all the flowers remained as berries. However, for some varieties in some years, coulure can be excessive and YIELD drastically reduced. This can have a disastrous effect on grape-growers' incomes and can also affect grape supply and wine prices in certain years. GRENACHE vines are particularly susceptible to coulure, as are MALBEC, CABERNET SAUVIGNON, and MERLOT.

Coulure is caused by an imbalance in the levels of CARBOHYDRATES in vine tissue. Weather conditions around flowering which reduce PHOTOSYNTHESIS—such as periods of cloudy, cold, and wet weather—will cause coulure and can have devastating effects on yield for some varieties. Coulure also happens where the total leaf area, and thus photosynthesis, is limited. Low carbohydrate levels can also be due to competition between INFLORESCENCES and vigorous shoot growth, combined with warm temperatures, which favour RESPIRATION. Very fertile soils, excessive application of FERTILIZERS, especially those high in NITROGEN, vigorous ROOTSTOCKS, and PRUNING too severely (see BALANCED PRUNING) can also cause coulure.

There is little growers can do to prevent coulure. It is not always possible to grow varieties which are not susceptible, as particular varieties may be required by local regulations or for a certain style or blend. CLONAL SELECTION can be effective in reducing susceptibility for varieties such as Merlot and Malbec. Topping shoots (see TRIMMING) during flowering can reduce coulure by temporarily stopping competition for carbohydrates between actively growing SHOOT TIPS and INFLORESCENCES. Later pruning may also help because a delayed BUDBREAK will increase the possibility of warmer weather at flowering. Some chemical GROWTH REGULATORS can reduce coulure by inhibiting shoot growth. A Coulure Index (CI) was defined for the first time in 2009—the higher the numerical value, the greater the expression of the condition. R.E.S. & P.R.D.

Collins, C., and Dry, P. R., 'Response of fruitset and other yield components to shoot topping and 2-chlorethyltrimethyl-ammonium chloride application', *Australian Journal of Grape and Wine Research*, 15 (2009), 256–67.

Illand, P., et al., 'Flowering and fruitset', in *The Grapevine: From the Science to the Practice of Growing Vines for Wine* (2011).

Counoise is one of the more rarefied varietal ingredients in red CHÂTEAUNEUF-DU-PAPE, easily confused in the vineyard with the much lesser southern Rhône variety AUBUN, with which it may sometimes be mingled in older vineyards. It is authorized as a supplementary ingredient for most red-wine appellations around the southern Rhône, including LANGUEDOC AOC, but, although VARIETAL southern French versions are made, it is not widely grown outside Châteauneuf-du-Pape. Total French plantings increased in the 1980s to around 900 ha/2,200 acres but in 2019 were only 322 ha.

As a vine, it leafs and ripens late and yields conservatively. As a wine, it is not particularly deeply coloured or alcoholic but adds lift, a peppery note, and lively acidity to a blend. Enthusiasts such as the Perrin family of Ch de Beaucastel typically use about 5% of Counoise in their red Châteauneuf-du-Pape and have disseminated it around California's Central Coast and beyond via their Tablas Creek vine NURSERY there.

counterfeit wine has, alas, become more common as FINE WINE has become more valuable. Wine of all sorts has been subject to ADULTERATION AND FRAUD for centuries, but the escalation in prices of the most sought-after names, the rapid increase in the number of (often inexperienced) COLLECTORS, and the fact that a fine wine may be consumed many years after it was bought combined, in the late 20th and early 21st centuries, to provide irresistible opportunities for fraudsters in general and counterfeiters in particular.

In less developed markets, poor-quality wine may be packaged in a poor copy of a famous wine's BOTTLE, LABEL, and CAPSULE; but usually more sophisticated methods are called for, leading to a new breed of wine CONSULTANT who is expert in, inter alia, precise label design and typeface evolution for the most valuable wines (see AUTHENTICATION). Wines that have been particularly popular with counterfeiters are, of course, the rarest, which means that the likes of PETRUS, DOMAINE DE LA ROMANÉE-CONTI, and Henri Jayer burgundies have appeared at auction unfeasibly often, just as vintages 1961 and 1945 of fine bordeaux have. A favourite recipe for fake top-vintage Petrus, for example, has been a mixture of off-vintage Petrus with particularly ripe California red. Printers are necessary accomplices for counterfeiters.

The most common counterfeits have included Chx Cheval Blanc 1921 and 1947, Lafite 1787 and 1870, Lafleur 1947 and 1950, Latour à Pomerol 1961, Margaux 1900, and Petrus 1921 and 1947. Among other counterfeits, there have been discoveries of fake 1990 Penfolds Grange and of 1994 and 1995 SASSICAIA, but even mid-priced wines such as Rioja and MOUTON CADET have been victims.

Wine AUCTIONS provide the perfect arena for such frauds, but counterfeit wines have also been sold by retailers and privately. This has led to an increase in interest in each bottle's precise PROVENANCE and calls for some sort of system akin to motor vehicles' logbooks, perhaps using BLOCKCHAIN technology.

Producers of most wines targeted by fraudsters have been taking anti-counterfeit measures such as special invisible marks on various aspects of packaging of this century's vintages, but mature fine wine should be bought only from the most impeccable of sources. Premiums for wines direct from château, domaine, or estate have risen.

Wallace, B., *The Billionaire's Vinegar* (2008).

Steinberger, M., 'A Vintage Crime', *Vanity Fair* (July 2012).

country wines. See HOME WINEMAKING.

coupage, French and EU term for BLENDING. It means literally 'cutting' and retains a slightly pejorative overtone, tending to be reserved for wine blending at its least glamorous, while the French word ASSEMBLAGE is more commonly used for blending different lots of a fine wine. EU regulations prohibit the *coupage* of all sorts of different wines, including EU with non-EU wines, or WINE WITHOUT GEOGRAPHICAL INDICATION with PDO and PGI wines.

Courbu Blanc, Basque speciality often blended with PETIT MANSENG and GROS MANSENG, distinct from PETIT COURBU. See also HONDARRABI. **Courbu Noir** is an almost extinct speciality of BÉARN.

courses, wine. See EDUCATION.

court-noué, common French term for FANLEAF DEGENERATION, a virus disease of the vine.

Cova de Beira, large subregion within BEIRA INTERIOR in central Portugal. Wines bearing the name are rarely seen on export markets.

cover crop, a crop of plants other than vines established in the vineyard, typically between the rows, generally to benefit the vineyard soil by increasing ORGANIC MATTER but also for biodiversity (see ECOSYSTEM). Sometimes known as a sward. Cover crops may be sown, or volunteer plants or WEEDS encouraged to grow, as an alternative to bare soil created by TILLAGE. They are normally grown over the summer or winter and mown during the vine-growing season, primarily to avoid water competition, or they may be removed by tillage. Typical sown cover crops are grasses and legumes. The grasses used may be native to the area or specially introduced species such as perennial rye grass, fescue, or bent grasses, although often cereals such as barley or oats are used for autumn sowing. Legumes sown as cover crops to fix atmospheric NITROGEN into the soil include clovers, medics, peas, vetches, and beans. Occasionally, deep-rooted cover crops such as chicory (*Chicorium intybus*) are sown to compete for soil water with over-vigorous vines, especially in deep, fertile soils in high-rainfall areas. Cover-crop management is more difficult in high-density, narrow-spaced vineyards (see VINE DENSITY).

The most common reason for sowing cover crops is to increase the organic matter in the soil and hence improve its structure and water-holding capacity. This is achieved with species such as cereals and grasses that grow quickly and produce plenty of bulk, which can then be incorporated into the soil by shallow tilling. Cover crops with a deep tap root (such as radish and chicory) or which are hollow-stemmed (such as oats) maintain soil structure by facilitating water infiltration. When a cover crop is slashed, the residues left on the soil surface reduce the amount of EVAPORATION from the topsoil.

Cover crops are also commonly sown to stop SOIL EROSION in areas with storms and are especially useful in sloping vineyards. The roots of the cover crop bind the soil and resist the flowing water. Tall cover crops are also used in newly established vineyards to combat high winds, which can cause damage to young plants. Cover crops also help reduce SOIL COMPACTION.

Another important use of cover crops is to compete with the vines, especially when they are too vigorous, and to encourage earlier RIPENING and improve wine quality. Slight WATER STRESS hastens the ripening process, so cover crops, which compete with the vines for water and nutrients (especially nitrogen), can help to generate this stress in areas of high summer rainfall. Nitrogen from legume cover crops and plenty of soil moisture can lead to excessive vine VIGOUR. Some mowers throw the cover crop clippings under the vines, thus forming a MULCH to reduce evaporation.

Apparently weedy vineyards should not necessarily be dismissed as untidy; they may represent a deliberate ploy to improve wine quality. Deep-rooting crops such as mustard, lucerne (alfalfa), and chicory can be particularly useful to use up subsoil water which more shallow-rooted grasses cannot reach.

Cover crops should be grown with caution. In spring, they make the vineyard more prone to FROST than if the soil is bare. The cover crop may play host to insects which spread diseases such as FLAVESCENCE DORÉE. If the cover crop is not mown or cultivated in summer it can use excessive amounts of water or nutrients, and the vines can suffer as a result. Because of competition with vines for nitrogen, the use of cover crops can also cause STUCK FERMENTATIONS (although ORGANIC growers claim the reverse is the case). These effects can be offset by close mowing or by killing the cover crop by tilling or HERBICIDES. Cover crops reduce the problems caused by dust from traffic on bare soil alleyways in the vineyard; dust can encourage MITES.

In arid Central Otago, New Zealand, where animal manure is scarce, cover crops sown to supply nitrogen to the vines have been maintained by the installation of a shallow DRIP IRRIGATION line in the mid row. R.E.S. & R.E.W.

Nicholas, P. R., et al., 'Cover crops', in P. Nicholas (ed.), *Soil, Irrigation and Nutrition* (e-book, 2004).

Smart, R., 'Making organic vineyards sustainable: the Amisfield approach', *Wine Business Monthly*, Feb (2019), 160–5.

Wheeler, S. J., et al., 'Vineyard floor management improves wine quality in highly vigorous *Vitis vinifera* "Cabernet Sauvignon" in New Zealand', *New Zealand Journal of Crop and Horticultural Science* 33 (2005), 317–28.

Cowra, southernmost region in Australia's Central Ranges Zone in NEW SOUTH WALES, with 932 ha/2,303 acres of vineyards planted in 2020. Warm and dry with cool nights, the region is best known for generous styles of Chardonnay. Reds including Shiraz, Cabernet Sauvignon, and Grenache are also produced. A.R.P.

crater, big, deep bowl with a wide mouth used in ancient GREECE for mixing wine, most often with water. The crater was characteristically 12–18 in (30–45 cm) high and could be either painted pottery or made of bronze. The most remarkable example is the huge bronze crater, over 5 ft/1.5 m high and probably of Spartan manufacture, which was found at Vix in France (see CELTS). J.J.P.

Crato Branco, Algarve synonym for Portugal's SÍRIA grape.

Cream, the sweetest, darkest style of SHERRY (with the exception of PX, which is even sweeter and darker), created expressly for the sweet-toothed British market by Harveys of Bristol. Bristol Milk was a style of sweet sherry sold successfully in the early 19th century by both Averys and Harveys. The story goes that a lady visitor to the cellars in 1882, on tasting Harveys' new, as-yet-unnamed BRAND of sweet sherry, observed, 'If that is Milk, then this is Cream.' Harveys Bristol Cream was thus named, and it became the most successful branded sherry in the world. This sweet style of sherry is eschewed by the Spaniards, for it is essentially the product of BLENDING not necessarily very distinguished sherries with sweetening and colouring wines. **Pale Cream** was another highly successful sherry style launched, with huge initial success, by Croft in the 1970s. Most Pale Cream is essentially sweetened FINO, though it may occasionally be the same as Cream but with the colour removed, by CHARCOAL or other treatments. Cream sherries generally have a RESIDUAL SUGAR content that is equivalent to 4.5–6.5 °BAUMÉ.

Crémant, term used as France's shorthand for the country's finest dry sparkling wines made outside Champagne using the traditional method of SPARKLING WINEMAKING. The term was adopted in the late 1980s, when the expression *méthode champenoise* was outlawed by the EU (and replaced by MÉTHODE TRADITIONNELLE). The principal provenances of modern Crémants are Alsace, Bourgogne (Burgundy), Loire, and Limoux. The best sparkling wines of LUXEMBOURG are also called Crémant. Crémant de Saumur and Crémant de Vouvray were the first non-champagne sparkling wines to use the term, and in the mid 1970s the Crémant de Loire appellation was born, soon followed by Alsace and Bourgogne. Bordeaux and Limoux joined the official Crémant appellations, created under INAO authority, in 1990 and were followed by Die in 1993, Jura in 1995, and Savoie in 2014.

Although grape varieties and TERROIRS vary from region to region, certain strict sparkling winemaking rules are imposed, including WHOLE-BUNCH PRESSING; a maximum yield of 100 l per 150 kg of grapes (the same as CHAMPAGNE prior to 1993); a maximum SULFUR DIOXIDE content of 150 mg/l; and a minimum of 12 months between initial bottling and release.

Crémant d'Alsace

Sparkling winemaking using the TRADITIONAL METHOD in Alsace dates from the late 19th century and in the 1980s became an important commercial activity, representing almost a quarter of the region's output. Only the grape varieties Pinots Blanc, Noir, and Gris, together with the related Auxerrois, and Riesling and such Chardonnay as is planted in Alsace, may be used (i.e. no Gewurztraminer or Chasselas), and any rosé must be made entirely of Pinot Noir. Maximum yields are 80 hl/ha (4.5 tons/acre). The wines are well made, tend to have a particularly fine mousse, high acidity, and to be relatively light in BODY. Only if substantial proportions of Riesling are used do they acquire strong flavour. Production is in the hands of nearly 500 small-scale producers whose blending capability is usually limited. A total of 3,940 ha/9,736 acres were devoted to the wine in 2019.

Crémant de Bordeaux

A small and declining amount of sparkling wine has been made in the BORDEAUX region since the end of the 19th century. Today production is controlled by a handful of companies which have not established a clear style or identity for the white and pink wines.

Crémant de Bourgogne

This appellation, created in 1975, replaced that of Bourgogne Mousseux (now used exclusively for sparkling red burgundy), under which name sparkling burgundy of all colours enjoyed considerable commercial success in the 1950s and 1960s. As of 2021, the appellation is open solely to white and rosé wines made from any grape varieties grown in BURGUNDY, although Gamay may not constitute more than 30% of the blend. RULLY in the Côte Chalonnaise and AUXERRE in the far north of Burgundy are the principal sources of Crémant de Bourgogne (CÔTE D'OR grapes being in general worth considerably more when sold as still wine), and there can be considerable stylistic differences between their produce. Crémant from southern Burgundy can be full and soft, a good-value alternative to bigger styles of champagne, while Crémant made in the north is usually lighter and crisper.

Crémant de Die

Crémant de Die is a dry sparkling wine made by the TRADITIONAL METHOD from at least 55% CLAIRETTE grapes with no more than 10% of the Muscat Blanc that is grown for another of the region's three sparkling wines (see CLAIRETTE DE DIE for more details), and the balance ALIGOTÉ.

Crémant du Jura

Created in 1995, this appellation represents more than 25% of Jura wine production. The wines may be white or rosé from any of the authorized JURA grape varieties, although the white must be at least 70% Chardonnay, Pinot Noir, and Trousseau, and the rosé at least half Poulsard, Trousseau, or Pinot Noir. In practice,

C

few white Crémants du Jura are made from anything other than Chardonnay, although some interesting white blends with Savagnin are available. All but the largest producers have their base wine made sparkling by one of two specialist companies who then return the finished wines to individual producers to market. Whereas the larger Jura wineries tend to make excellent-value Brut or Demi-Sec versions, since the mid 2010s several organic producers have made high-quality Brut Zéro or Nature Crémant du Jura.

Crémant de Limoux
This appellation represents the increasing champenization of the ancient sparkling wines of LIMOUX in a particularly cool, high corner of the southern Languedoc. In 1990, Blanquette de Limoux became an appellation reserved for sparkling wines made principally from the MAUZAC grape grown traditionally in the region. Crémant de Limoux, in contrast, focuses on Chardonnay and Chenin Blanc, with no more than 20% Mauzac allowed. The rosé version must contain at least 15% Pinot Noir. In 2018, a total of 823 ha/2,034 acres were devoted to the wine, a very high proportion of which is made by the CO-OPERATIVE.

Crémant de Loire
Crémant de Loire was created in 1975 and encompasses the Anjou, Saumur, and Touraine regions. Most of the middle Loire's wide palette of grape varieties may be used to produce Crémant, with the sensible exception of Sauvignon Blanc, whose aroma has yet to prove itself an attractive sparkling wine ingredient. GROLLEAU grapes may not represent much of any blend, and in practice CHENIN BLANC is the most common dominant component, clearly distinguishing the flavour of most Crémant de Loire from Crémants made from Pinots and Chardonnay to the east. Levels of winemaking are generally high among the nearly 200 producers (including several important co-operatives and NÉGOCIANTS).

Crémant de Luxembourg
Luxembourg has a long tradition of sparkling winemaking, and its particularly acid wines were at one time valued as base wines for SEKT. The Crémant de Luxembourg appellation was created in 1991, following the INAO rules laid down for French wines. Permitted grape varieties are Elbling, Pinot Blanc, Rivaner (Müller-Thurgau), Sylvaner, Auxerrois, Chardonnay, Pinot Gris, Gewürztraminer, Muscat Ottonel, and Riesling for white wines, Pinot Noir for rosé.

Crémant de Savoie
This appellation was introduced in 2014, replacing SAVOIE *mousseux* and *pétillant*. Blends should be composed of at least 60% JACQUÈRE and the local ALTESSE, with a minimum of 40% Jacquère (Altesse is optional), supplemented by other permitted Savoie white grapes such as Chasselas or Chardonnay and up to 20% red grapes. SEYSSEL and AYSE have their own appellations for TRADITIONAL METHOD sparkling wines. In 2020 these three sparkling appellations combined accounted for just 5% of Savoie wine production.

Crépy, CRU (formerly a small appellation in its own right) within the eastern French region of SAVOIE above the south shore of Lake Geneva producing generally dull, light, dry white wines from the CHASSELAS grape.

Crete, large island in the south-east of GREECE famous for the Minoan civilization (*c.*2000–1400 BCE). Its wines were most famous in the Middle Ages when the island was known as Candia. In modern times, Crete spent most of the 20th century producing wines to be consumed on the island, but the new millennium witnessed a paradigm shift, with more quality-minded producers who have saved a number of rare but superb varieties from oblivion along the way.

Most vineyards are on the north of the island, protected from hot winds from North Africa by the island's mountain ranges, the tallest of which reach 2,456 m/8,058 ft. The island's most important viticultural centre is the area south of the port city of Heraklion, which includes the PDOs Archanes, Dafnes, and Peza, although ambitious producers are also found around Chania in the west and Sitia in the east. The mountainous landscape gives rise to diverse soils and MESOCLIMATES, which in turn support a plethora of local grape varieties. The pale red LIATIKO, the third most important black grape on the island, ripens very early, sometimes as early as July; its high sugar content and low tannin levels make it particularly prized for sweet DRIED-GRAPE WINES. Robust red wines are made from the tannic, deep-coloured Mandilari (MANDILARIA), often augmented with the less-tannic and most widely planted red variety KOTSIFALI.

The island's most important local white grape is VILANA, which makes soft, floral white wines, blended with Thrapsathiri for PDO Sitia. Potentially more exciting but far rarer is VIDIANO, a white grape originating in Rethymno making full-bodied whites. There are many other rare vine varieties such as Dafni, Plyto, and even a single plant of Samos Muscat Noir that has been rescued from extinction by observant growers.

Crete also boasts two PDOs dedicated to wines made in a style that harkens back to the wines traded by the Venetians in the Middle Ages: PDO Malvasia Handakas-Candia and PDO Malvasia Sitia. Both are blends of sun-dried grapes, in both fortified and non-fortified variations. Confusingly, the grape variety Malvasia may make up only a small amount of the blend; the bulk must be made up of Assyrtiko, Thrapsathiri, and Liatiko, with Vidiano in Handakas-Candia and Athiri in Sitia. Also allowed is a small amount of MUSCAT BLANC À PETITS GRAINS.

See also MALVASIA, MALMSEY. K.L.

crianza, Spanish term used both to describe the process of AGEING a wine and also for the youngest officially recognized category of a wood-matured wine. A crianza red wine may not be sold until its third (second for whites and rosés) year, and it must have spent a minimum of six months in cask. Crianza white and rosé must be aged for at least 18 months, including six months in wood. In RIOJA and other regions such as RIBERA DEL DUERO, where the term is most commonly used, the wine must have spent at least 12 months in oak BARRICAS. An increasingly frequent, albeit unofficial, category now is **semi-crianza**, or *roble* (meaning OAK), for wine aged in cask for less time than the crianza minimum. With the term JOVEN fully accepted for fruity young wines without cask ageing, the slightly derogatory description *sin crianza* had all but disappeared by the late 1990s.

Crimea, important wine-producing peninsula off southern UKRAINE surrounded by the Black Sea. After decades of being controlled by and selling most of its wines in Ukraine, the region was annexed by RUSSIA in 2014.

Grapes were grown here from at least the 4th century BCE. Archaeological evidence includes stone fences, remnants of viticultural plots and wineries, and wine AMPHORAE in the Tauric settlement of Uch-Bash near Inkerman. There have also been wine-related finds in the ancient town of Myrmecium in the east of the Kerch Peninsula. The unearthed tomb of a Scythian chief dated 500 BCE was arranged with an amphora of CHIAN wine at its head.

By the 19th century, Crimea's wines were well regarded among the Russian aristocrats who came to vacation along its south coast. Cyrus REDDING noted in 1833 that 'the Crimea wines are thought the best in the empire'. The wine-loving Count Mikhail Vorontsov, governor-general of that part of Russia which then included the Tauric province, began to build the Alupka Palace and associated winery in the 1820s; it still produces FORTIFIED WINES in quantity. He also laid the foundations for the MAGARACH Institute for wine research. Vorontsov imported a wide range of European grape varieties, as did his successor as principal Crimean wine innovator, Prince Lev Golitsyn. In 1882 Golitsyn established the Novyi Svit (New World) winery, which, inter alia, produced pre-revolutionary Russia's 'Shampanskoye' and continues to make sparkling wine today.

Since then, vineyard plantings have fluctuated wildly, reaching their zenith in 1959 with 152,500 ha/376,836 acres. In 2020 just 18,067 ha remained, spread throughout three wine-making regions: the interior Steppe; the South Coast, specializing in strong, sweet wines made like VINS DOUX NATURELS as well as Kagor (a name inspired by CAHORS), a deep-coloured wine made from MUST heated before fermentation, with MASSANDRA the dominant winery; and the West Coast, associated with dry varietals produced by small, new-wave operations such as Oleg Repin and Uppa, a winery from sommelier Pavel Shvets.

In addition to international varieties, Crimea's vineyards feature many crosses, such as Bastardo Magarachsky, a cross between BASTARDO and SAPERAVI. There is also renewed interest in INDIGENOUS VARIETIES, particularly Kokur, used primarily for dry, still, and sparkling white wines. O.P.-T.

Criolla Chica is the Argentine name for the Listán Prieto of Spain, the PAÍS of Chile, the MISSION of California, and the Negra Corriente of PERU. It was thought to be descended from the seeds of grapes (presumably well raisined after their voyage under sail across the Atlantic) imported by the Spanish conquistadores possibly as early as the 16th century (see SOUTH AMERICA), but it was in fact introduced as CUTTINGS. Criolla Chica was planted on just 338 ha/835 acres in 2020 and is therefore much less common in Argentina than the other pink-skinned grape varieties CRIOLLA GRANDE and CEREZA. Its wine is generally paler but of a slightly better quality.

Criolla Grande, the fourth most planted vine variety in Argentina after MALBEC, CEREZA, and BONARDA, is a spontaneous Listán Prieto (CRIOLLA CHICA) × MUSCAT OF ALEXANDRIA cross. Although the area planted with this coarse, pink-skinned grape has declined substantially, there were still 13,348 ha/32,984 acres in 2020. Almost all Criolla Grande is in Mendoza province. Criolla Grande is a low-quality CRIOLLA and is lighter-skinned than CRIOLLA CHICA. The two Criollas, along with Cereza and Moscatel Rosada, form the basis of Argentina's declining trade in basic deep-coloured white or pale pink wine sold very cheaply in litre bottles or cardboard cartons.

Criollas, generic name for vine varieties that have been common in SOUTH AMERICA, particularly ARGENTINA, since the arrival of the conquistadores. They include CEREZA, CRIOLLA CHICA, CRIOLLA GRANDE, various local Moscatels, PEDRO GIMÉNEZ, and various TORRONTÉS.

Criots-Bâtard-Montrachet, great white GRAND CRU in Burgundy's CÔTE D'OR. For more details, see MONTRACHET.

crise viticole, la, widely used phrase for France's wine crisis of 1907 (see LANGUEDOC) and also that of the early 21st century resulting from plummeting wine sales both at home and abroad. Sales stagnation affected not just the Languedoc, with its huge volumes of surplus VIN DE TABLE and VIN DE PAYS and its notoriously militant vignerons, but also AOC wines, notably MUSCADET and to a lesser extent BEAUJOLAIS and the less favoured parts of BORDEAUX.

critics, wine A subgroup of WINE WRITERS who see the assessment of specific wines, often SCORING them, as their principal role.

Crljenak Kaštelanski, 'the red wine grape of Kaštela', a region north of Split in Croatia. It has turned out to be ZINFANDEL and is being planted once more by Croatians. See also TRIBIDRAG.

Croatia, or Hrvatska, is one of the most successful wine producers of the former YUGOSLAVIA on the Balkan peninsula. In recent years Croatia has become hugely popular as a tourist destination with close to 21 million foreign visitors in 2019, vastly outnumbering its resident population of 4.1 million and creating a ready-made market for its wines.

History

Viticulture in this region dates to the ancient Greeks and possibly earlier with the Illyrians. The UNESCO-listed Stari Grad plain on the island of Hvar may be the world's oldest continuously cultivated viticultural site, dating to the 4th century BCE, with its original layout of geometric parcels, or *chora*, divided by stone walls. Grape-growing increased in importance under ROMAN occupation. The land was part of the Ottoman empire from the 15th century and was subsequently part of the Habsburg empire when grape-growing flourished until the arrival of PHYLLOXERA. Under 20th-century socialist rule, wine production became centred on large, collectivized state wineries.

The break-up of Yugoslavia and the brutal wars of independence that followed in the early 1990s had a significant effect on viticulture. In 2020, there were still around 17,000 uncleared landmines in the country. After a late start as an independent nation (compared with neighbours such as SLOVENIA and HUNGARY), Croatia has accelerated the development of a fascinating wine industry based on private wine producers, although it has suffered from the common Balkan problem of fragmented land holdings. In 2020, the country had 26,864 wine entities in its register, with 1,575 wine producers, though only 145 had over 10 ha/25 acres.

Geography and vine varieties

Falling within the latitudes of 46–42° N, Croatia stretches 1,880 km/1,170 miles along the Adriatic coast, with 1,244 islands adding a further 4,398 km of coastline. Within this are 18,759 ha/46,354 acres of vineyard in 2020, spread among 18 PDOs in two categories—*Vrhunsko Vino* (premium quality wines, 11.9% of 2019 harvest) and *Kvalitetno Vino* (quality wines, 72% of 2019 harvest)—plus table wines (*Stolno Vino*). The unusually wide range of climatic influences plus a plethora of grape varieties—Croatia claims to grow around 200 varieties, around 40 identified as indigenous—gives rise to an impressive diversity of wines.

The coastal regions of **Istria and Kvarner** have a mild climate, with MEDITERRANEAN influences meeting the cold air flowing down from the Alps, and share both climate and cultural influences with both north-east Italy and Slovenia. Iron-rich red soils are widespread. White wines dominate, particularly those made from MALVAZIJA ISTARSKA, Croatia's second most planted variety (1,626 ha in 2020). Most often vinified without oak in a fresh, fruity style, it also responds well to being picked later and vinified, often with extended SKIN CONTACT, in barrels of acacia or oak. Reds are less important in this region, with the most characteristic being TERAN (Terrano), a firm, high-acid variety grown on 237 ha in 2020. The name was the subject of dispute with Slovenia, which has registered 'Teran' as a protected term, but is now allowed provided 'Hrvatska Istra' is clearly specified on the label. Merlot produces some fine wines and is sometimes blended with Teran. The island of Krk's speciality is the delicate white Žlahtina grape. There are three PDOs: Primorska Hrvatska/ Hrvatsko Primorje, Hrvatska Istra, and Muškat Momjanski.

Dalmatia stretches south from Zadar to the country's southern border with MONTENEGRO and includes the important wine-growing islands of Korčula, Hvar, Vis, and Brač. Its often steep and rocky vineyards enjoy sunny summers and are noted for their treasure trove of INDIGENOUS VARIETIES. They produce some of the country's most full-bodied reds, frequently over 15% alcohol. This is the only Croatian region where reds predominate, especially PLAVAC MALI (Croatia's third most planted grape with 1,427 ha/3,526 acres in 2020). This is the grape responsible for Dingač, the first protected designation in Croatia in 1965, from the seaside terraces of the Pelješac Peninsula. CRLJENAK KAŠTELANSKI, rescued from just nine vines at Kaštela near Split in 2002, was shown by DNA PROFILING to be ZINFANDEL (aka Tribidrag) and also a parent of Plavac Mali, along with Dobričić. It has since been planted much more widely. Babić (314 ha) is another good-quality red wine grape grown on famously stony coastal vineyards near Šibenik and the UNESCO-listed hillsides of Primošten. POŠIP (330 ha) is Dalmatia's most important white wine grape and is producing increasingly exciting wines, especially from

Korčula, Hvar, and Brač. Other interesting pale-skinned Dalmatian varieties include Grk, Debit, Vugava, Bogdanuša, Gegić, and Maraština. A traditional sweet wine from dried grapes called Prošek is made on islands such as Hvar and Brač but is subject to legal action in 2021 from Italy's PROSECCO producers, who cite consumer confusion. Dalamatia's PDOs are: Sjeverna Dalmacija, Dalmatinska zagora, Srednja i Južna Dalmacija, Dingač, and Ponikve.

The inland zone of **Slavonia and Croatian Danube** is the home of Croatia's most important wine grape Graševina (WELSCHRIESLING, planted on 4,525 ha/11,181 acres). This relatively flat region of plains with a few low hills reaches as far north-east as the foothills of the Fruška Gora Range. White grapes predominate, and the long, warm autumns encourage the production of sweet, late-harvest whites. Graševina is often a workhorse grape but arguably reaches its peak around the historic town of Kutjevo and the Golden Valley area, while Traminac (GEWÜRZTRAMINER) can also be notable, especially around Ilok. More recent arrivals of INTERNATIONAL VARIETIES such as Chardonnay and Sauvignon Blanc are proving successful. Reds are led by Frankovka (BLAUFRÄNKISCH), but some promising wines have now been made from Pinot Crni (Pinot Noir), Merlot, and Cabernet Sauvignon. Slavonia is also famous for its OAK, particularly beloved of Italian producers for their large oak casks (*botti*). PDOS are: Istocna Kontinentalna Hrvatska, Hrvatsko Podunavlje, and Slavonija.

The **Croatian Upland** region surrounding the capital Zagreb is the coolest zone, with small family vineyards dotted across green hillsides. International white grapes predominate, and some fresh, zesty Sauvignons, crisp Rieslings, and decent Pinot Gris and Pinot Noir, especially in Plešivica, have been produced. Also made are some impressive ICE WINES, increasingly good sparkling wines, and several NATURAL and ORANGE WINES. FURMINT under its local name of Pušipel is impressing in Zagorje-Međimurje in the north, in both still and sparkling versions. It also appears as Moslavac in Moslavina, where the native variety Škrlet is also found for fresh, fruity wines. PDOs are: Zapadna Kontinentalna Hrvatska, Moslavina, Prigorje-Bilogora, Plešivica, Pokuplje, and Zagorje-Međimurje E.M. & C.G.

www.vinacroatia.hr/en/
www.total-croatia-wine.com

Croatina, red grape variety from the borders of the PIEMONTE and LOMBARDY regions of northern Italy. The vine buds and ripens late but yields good quantities of fruity wine with a certain bite, designed to be drunk relatively young. Its common synonym is Bonarda, under which name it is used to make an appetizing VARIETAL red in the OLTREPÒ PAVESE zone of south-west Lombardia. The variety is quite distinct from BONARDA Piemontese. Total plantings of Croatina were 2,678 ha/6,617 acres in 2015.

Croft, port shipper with a particularly long history. Its precursor Phayre and Bradley was established in 1678 and a tercentenary celebrated in 1978, but the head of the FLADGATE PARTNERSHIP, which acquired Croft in 2021, claims even earlier beginnings. The first Croft, from York, became a partner in 1736, and from 1769 the company was known as Croft and Co. In 1911 the firm was taken over by Gilbey's, and the majority shareholding eventually passed into the hands of the multinational corporation that became Diageo. Port shipper Morgan Brothers was acquired in 1952.

Croft expanded into the SHERRY business in the difficult era of the early 1970s, invading Jerez with energy and one novel idea: an entirely new style of sherry, Pale CREAM, which could offer the beguiling combination of a pale, sophisticated appearance with the reassuring sweetness of a cream. It was such an enormous and much-imitated success that a series of ultra-modern bodegas known as Rancho Croft was needed. Croft's Jerez adventure ended in 2001, when Diageo sold the bodegas to GONZÁLEZ BYASS for €54 million. Some of its best old SOLERAS were acquired by a new, quality-minded company, Tradición.

crop thinning, viticultural practice, known as *éclaircissage* or *vendange verte* (green harvest) in French, which is widely claimed to improve wine quality by encouraging fruit RIPENING. Some bunches are removed from the vine, and those remaining should in theory ripen more quickly with the benefit of improved LEAF TO FRUIT RATIO. Crop thinning is usually carried out by hand and is therefore expensive. MECHANICAL HARVESTERS are occasionally used to thin crops, removing individual berries or parts of bunches.

The YIELD is reduced more or less proportionately to the bunches removed (although the remaining berries may be slightly enlarged), which means that only those growers able to guarantee top prices for their produce can afford the operation. The technique became common in the early 1990s among the better wine producers in Bordeaux, where it had been practised at PETRUS since 1973.

Crop thinning is normally carried out at the start of VERAISON, when it is obvious which bunches are slow to ripen. This is also referred to as colour thinning. It is cheaper if done earlier, but there is a risk that the remaining bunches will become too tight due to larger berries and so be prone to BOTRYTIS BUNCH ROT. Later bunch removal has more impact on yield, and earlier removal on fruit ripening. Crop thinning is common for varieties with large bunches, such as Merlot, and for Pinot Noir, again especially for CLONES with large bunches.

Thinning is also appropriate when it is obvious that the vintage will be late, decreasing the chance of ripening a large crop, and when yield estimates suggest there is going to be more crop than can probably be ripened, especially in cool climates.

The theory of crop thinning is that the remaining fruit ripens earlier and so has better levels of SUGARS and ANTHOCYANINS for red varieties. However, many studies have shown that these benefits are limited and that crop levels need to be greatly reduced for a small change in GRAPE COMPOSITION. For many vineyards where the yield is in BALANCE with shoot growth and the leaves and fruit are well exposed, there will be little benefit from crop thinning. Some viticulturists believe that thinning may bring more psychological benefit to the grower than physiological benefit to the vine and that thinning is best done on the day of harvest. R.E.S.

Reeve, A., et al. 'Vineyard floor management and cluster thinning inconsistently affect "Pinot Noir" crop load, berry composition, and wine quality', *Hortscience*, 53/3 (2018), 318–28.
Reynier, A., *Manuel de viticulture* (12th edn, 2016).

cross, the result of breeding a new variety by **crossing** two VINE VARIETIES, or the natural (i.e. spontaneous) crossing of two varieties in the field without human intervention. If the varieties are of the same species, usually the European VITIS VINIFERA species, then the result may also be known as an **intraspecific cross**—MÜLLER-THURGAU would be one example. Crosses of the same species are different from HYBRIDS, sometimes called **interspecific crosses**, which contain the genes of more than one species of the VITIS genus.

cross-flow filtration. See FILTRATION.

Crouchen, or **Cruchen**, white grape variety producing neutral wines in both South Africa and Australia. It originated in the western Pyrenees of France but is no longer grown there in any quantity, thanks to its sensitivity to FUNGAL DISEASES. There are records of its shipment to the Clare Valley in SOUTH AUSTRALIA in 1850, and it was long confused with Sémillon, which Australians were wont to call Riesling. It was therefore known principally as Clare Riesling in Australia until 1976, when AMPELOGRAPHER Paul Truel identified it as this relatively obscure French variety. Just 33 ha/82 acres remained in 2022. The South Africans finally started to name their Crouchen correctly rather than calling it Cape Riesling just as it virtually disappeared from their vineyard statistics, with a 2020 total of 159 ha.

crown caps, small metal caps used on beer and soda bottles, have proved to be a very reliable closure for long-term wine-bottle storage (see Helmut BECKER) and provide an extremely cheap and efficient closure for any sort of liquid. Many wine drinkers find their association with what they regard as less sophisticated drinks unacceptable, particularly in a restaurant, but they have been enjoying a modest renaissance with the PET-NAT category. The crown cap is also used nearly universally for closing SPARKLING WINE bottles during the TIRAGE process; DISGORGING is much more difficult if a cork has to be extracted. Some sparkling wines have been released under crown seal in Australia and California, to minimize the possibility of CORK TAINT.

crown gall, BACTERIAL DISEASE which occurs on over 600 plant species, including vines, particularly when grown where winters are so cold that vines can be damaged (see WINTER FREEZE). High incidence of the disease can make vineyards uneconomic. The debilitating effects of crown gall following freeze injury is an important limitation to the commercial cultivation of all VITIS VINIFERA varieties in regions or sites subject to very cold winter temperatures. The disease is much less common in cold-tolerant species and HYBRIDS.

Crown gall, also known as black knot, is caused mainly by *Agrobacterium vitis* (occasionally by *Agrobacterium tumefaciens*, the predominant causal agent in other crops). The major symptom is the growth of fleshy galls (tumours) on the lower trunk which can girdle the trunk and cause portions of the vine above to die. The bacterium lives inside nearly all vines and so is routinely spread via propagation and if infected stock is planted, but it causes disease only after injury occurs. Control is difficult. Research in the early 1990s showed that hot-water treatment of dormant CUTTINGS (50 °C/122 °F for 30 minutes) reduces levels of the bacterium, and TISSUE CULTURE can provide total elimination, allowing production of nursery stock free of *Agrobacterium*. Avoiding the pathogen in new plants can significantly reduce the impact of sub-lethal winter-freeze injury to trunks. In the north-eastern United States, growers train the vines with up to five trunks so that there is always a young healthy trunk to replace dead or dying ones, a technique that also helps to manage TRUNK DISEASES. See TRAINING SYSTEMS. W.W.

Wilcox, W. F., et al., *Compendium of Grape Diseases, Disorders, and Pests* (2nd edn, 2015).

Crozes-Hermitage, the northern RHÔNE'S largest appellation, regularly producing more than 13 times as much wine as the much more distinguished vineyards of HERMITAGE which it surrounds, and around 25% more than the similarly priced, and similarly extended, appellation of ST-JOSEPH across the river. Like both these appellations, Crozes-Hermitage is usually red and made exclusively of the SYRAH grape, although just over one-tenth of production is full-bodied dry white wine made from the MARSANNE grape supplemented by ROUSSANNE. Up to 15% of white grapes may be added to red Crozes at FERMENTATION, though in practice this is extremely rare.

The appellation was originally granted to the village of Crozes to the north of Hermitage in 1937, then it was extended in 1952 to include a further ten communes. The terroir is far from homogeneous, however. The cooler, GRANITIC hillsides to the north of Hermitage (at Gervans, Érôme, and Serves-sur-Rhône) typically produce a lean, fresh style of wine. The Syrah grown on the successive flat GRAVEL and CLAY terraces to the south and east of Hermitage (at Chanos-Curson, Beaumont-Monteux, Pont-de-l'Isère, and La Roche-de-Glun) is relatively rich and generous. The communes of Mercurol and Larnage, with its white kaolin clay, were historically better known for whites and today produce fine examples of both colours. Total vineyard area in production expanded by about one-quarter between 1990 and 2005; by 2020 wine was produced by 1,818 ha/4,492 acres. Around half of this is produced by the high-quality CO-OPERATIVE Cave de Tain. The appellation's best reds can be kept for five years or more (and in good years can happily survive for ten or more), but the average Crozes, red or white, is usually at its best drunk young. M.C.W.

cru, French term for a vineyard, usually reserved for those officially recognized as of superior quality. Such recognition was already known in ancient ROME. In English the word is often translated as 'growth' (*crû* is the past particle of *croître*, 'to grow'). PREMIERS CRUS, for example, are called FIRST GROWTHS in BORDEAUX, according to one of their official CLASSIFICATIONS. A cru that has been 'classified' is a **cru classé**, or CLASSED GROWTH. In Bordeaux, the term 'cru' is applied to an estate and its vineyards. In BURGUNDY'S vineyard hierarchy, on the other hand, it is applied to a vineyard, with 'premier cru' being the level below GRAND CRU. The latter can have a very specific meaning, notably in ALSACE.

The ten top-ranked communes in BEAUJOLAIS are called crus, and their produce is cru beaujolais. The term 'cru' also refers to a DÉNOMINATION GÉOGRAPHIQUE COMPLÉMENTAIRE and may precede the name of the DGC on the label.

In SWITZERLAND, the first two vineyards to be officially awarded grand cru status were the neighbouring Dézaley and Calamin in Vaud.

The term has been enthusiastically adopted in Italy, most recently to refer to superior vineyards that have achieved the status of MGA. The local dialect for a site of the highest quality in PIEMONTE is SORÌ.

cru artisan was recognized by the EU in 1994 as a 'traditional expression' reserved for AOC wines from a particular category of wine estates in the Médoc, Haut-Médoc, Margaux, Moulis, Listrac, St-Julien, Pauillac, and St-Estèphe. A cru artisan is more humble, and generally much smaller, than a CRU BOURGEOIS.

cru bourgeois, a category of red-wine properties, or CRUS, designated bourgeois, or a social stratum below the supposedly aristocratic crus classés, in the MÉDOC region of Bordeaux. While the crus classés represent about 25% of the Médoc's total wine production from 60 estates, the crus bourgeois, from a possible total of more than 250 generally much smaller estates, represent a further 30% or so. The properties can vary, however, from simple smallholdings to others such as Ch Larose-Trintaudon, the largest estate in the Médoc, or Ch Lilian Ladouys of St-Estèphe, which totals 80 ha/198 acres.

The description 'cru bourgeois' has been used orally for several centuries and appeared in an early edition of Cocks et FÉRET in the mid 19th century, but the First World War and then the dire state of the international wine market at the end of the 1920s called for a new impetus. A first CLASSIFICATION of the crus bourgeois of the Médoc was drawn up in 1932, and one can only imagine the difficulties of bestowing this supposed commercial advantage, ranked into three classes, on a few hundred Médoc wine farmers. Thirty years later, when the Syndicate of Crus Bourgeois set about revitalizing itself, it was discovered that, of the 444 members registered in 1932, more than 300 had been absorbed into other estates or converted their land from viticulture to another crop such as pines instead. The lack of official recognition by the Minister of Agriculture when the list was first drawn up in 1932 was a constant source of difficulty and potential abuse of the title, but the designation 'Cru Bourgeois' was officially recognized in the EU labelling laws of 1979 on condition that its use be codified by the French government.

In 2003 there was an ill-fated attempt to draw up a permanent classification of crus bourgeois properties, but from 2008 cru bourgeois became not an official designation of estates but a self-regulated accolade awarded annually to particular wines on the basis of BLIND TASTING by a professional panel and announced each September two years after the harvest. In 2020 the focus reverted once again to estates, with the introduction of a five-year classification awarded on the basis of a blind tasting of five vintages renewable every five years. Additionally, as of 2025, all crus bourgeois wineries must be farmed under SUSTAINABLE VITICULTURE, achieving at least HVE Level 2 status, with Level 3 reserved for Supérieur and Exceptionnel properties. Thus the number of crus bourgeois varies. In general this category can offer some of Bordeaux's best-value and most accessible wines. They are made mainly from Cabernet Sauvignon grapes but often contain a high proportion of Merlot, usually supplemented by some Cabernet Franc. Some BARREL MATURATION is usually involved in the making of the most highly priced crus bourgeois, even if only a small proportion of new OAK is lavished on this wine category. However, viticulture and winemaking at the best crus bourgeois can be very similar to that practised by the crus classés (even if the selling prices are much lower). The wines are generally ready to drink between four and eight years old, but the best may be aged up to 15 years. J.R. & J.L.

Cruess, William Vere (1886–1968), biochemist, teacher, and author, was the link between work in wine research and teaching of the pre-PROHIBITION and post-Repeal eras in CALIFORNIA and thus had a central role in the restoration of the California wine industry. Professor of Food Technology at the University of California at Berkeley, Cruess had researched FERMENTATION before Prohibition. In the 'dry years' he studied such things as the production of grape syrup and other VINE PRODUCTS. Immediately upon Repeal he undertook to re-establish viticultural and oenological research at the University of California and did so with remarkable speed and efficiency. His *Principles and Practices of Wine Making* (1934) was the first work for the guidance of commercial winemaking published after Repeal.

Cruet, CRU east of the vermouth town of Chambéry whose name may be added to the eastern French appellation SAVOIE for white wines from the JACQUÈRE variety. Cruet is dominated by the region's largest CO-OPERATIVE. W.L.

crush, mainly American term for the whole HARVEST season, named after one of the first processes in the winery (CRUSHING) rather than what happens in the vineyard.

crusher-destemmer. See DESTEMMER-CRUSHER.

crushing, winemaking operation of breaking open the grape berry so that the juice is more readily available to the YEAST for FERMENTATION. It increases the initial speed of EXTRACTION of colour and flavour components from the skin, and in white-wine production it increases the speed of juice DRAINING but releases juice with higher solids levels compared with WHOLE-BUNCH PRESSING.

Crushing was traditionally done by foot, but this is relatively inefficient and expensive. However, it is said to be more gentle than mechanical crushing and is prized in regions such as the DOURO. It can also useful in small-scale winemaking. Modern crushers generally use intermeshed counter-rotating rollers spaced just far enough apart to pass grape seeds (which can exude bitter TANNINS if smashed). Typically, crusher rollers are attached as an extra stage on destemmers (see DESTEMMING). In practice, the destemmer itself may also result in some degree of grape crushing, as do pumps that might be used to move grapes to a PRESS or fermentation tank. Machine harvesting may also result in a small degree of crushing. S.N.

Nordestgaard, S., 'Gentle or intense grape crushing?', *Australian and New Zealand Grapegrower and Winemaker*, 639 (2017), 77–82.

crust, name for the SEDIMENT that forms in bottle-aged PORT. **Crusted port** is a style of port created by British shippers in order to provide some of the qualities of vintage port in a shorter time and therefore at a lower price.

cryoextraction, or freeze CONCENTRATION (*cryo* referring to very low temperatures), the winemaking practice of freezing grapes prior to PRESSING first proposed by French OENOLOGIST Serge Chauvet. It replicates the process of leaving grapes to freeze on the vine that is essential to the production of ICE WINE and may be used to reduce dilution, for example to concentrate the juice from BOTRYTIZED grapes in wet vintages when natural conditions do not allow this to happen on the vine. Freshly picked grapes are held overnight at sub-zero temperatures, −5 or −8 °C/15 °F, and then pressed immediately. The freezing point of grape must depends on its concentration of sugars, so only the less concentrated grapes freeze. Pressing the grapes straight out of the cold room therefore yields only the juice of the non-frozen, ripest grapes, whose chemical composition remains unchanged. The colder the grapes are kept, the less juice is obtained, but it will be the most concentrated from the ripest grapes. In the late 1980s a few SAUTERNES properties experimented with the technique, and it is still used at some CLASSED GROWTHS. Cold rooms at a temperature of around −2 °C may also be used for so-called 'supraextraction', an alternative to MACERATION. Freezing and then thawing the skins releases more FLAVOUR PRECURSORS. V.L. & A.O.

crystals in a bottle of white wine, on the underside of a cork, or on the inside of a vat are harmless deposits. See TARTRATES for a full explanation.

Cserszegi Fűszeres, IRSAI OLIVÉR × TRAMINER cross developed in Hungary in 1960 and widely planted there for basic grapey wines. Plantings totalled 3,999 ha/10,102 acres in 2021, mainly in Kunság.

CSIRO **(Commonwealth Scientific and Industrial Research Organization)**, founded in 1926, is Australia's national science agency and one of the world's largest and most diverse research institutions. Its charter covers research into areas of economic, environmental, and social benefit to AUSTRALIA. Early grapevine research focused on solving immediate problems relating to the adaptation of northern-hemisphere practices, irrigation, and pest and disease control to the new Australian viticultural frontiers.

After the Second World War, CSIRO's viticultural research broadened to include nematology (see NEMATODES), IRRIGATION, hydrology, and basic VINE PHYSIOLOGY. In the 1960s, there was an even greater shift in emphasis to viticultural research. A new laboratory was opened on the Waite Campus in ADELAIDE to accommodate a group of plant physiologists. As well as conducting seminal research into topics including plant hormones, FLOWERING, and FRUIT SET, more applied research stimulated changes in industry practices, such as the introduction of the complementary management techniques of MINIMAL PRUNING and MECHANICAL HARVESTING.

CSIRO holds Australia's largest collection of grapevine germplasm at Irymple, Victoria, which includes around 680 varieties and many non-VITIS VINIFERA species. VINE BREEDING and selection has yielded a number of new varieties such as TARRANGO, TAMINGA, TYRIAN, CIENNA, and Mystique as well as successful table grapes and RAISINS.

In the 1990s, CSIRO extended its research to encompass computer modelling of vine growth, water and nutrient application, YIELD estimation, DNA PROFILING to identify varieties, and PRECISION VITICULTURE. GENETIC MODIFICATION is an increasingly important avenue of research in viticulture worldwide, and CSIRO achieved the transformation of SULTANA and a range of wine grape varieties in the late 1990s. The genes controlling the production of colour, TANNINS, and FLAVONOLS in berries were also identified.

New CSIRO wine-grape research initiatives include a focus on disease resistance, RIPENING, abiotic stress, and flavour and aroma development in berries, this last aimed at understanding the management and genetics of grape flavour and aroma and links to final wine style.

Results of CSIRO research have given Australian viticulturists access to improved varieties, ROOTSTOCKS resistant to salt and nematodes, and water and nutrient management strategies suited to intra-vineyard variation and different environments. P.B.

Cuba. Attempts have been made to establish commercial vineyards on this tropical Caribbean island since Spanish colonists arrived in the 1500s, but most Cuban wines today rely on imported bulk wine or home-grown fruit.

cultivar, term developed by professional botanists to mean a group of plants sharing common characteristics persisting under cultivation that have either been selected or otherwise genetically manipulated by humans. According to the rules of plant taxonomy, 'cultivar' would be a more appropriate term than VARIETY, but it does not have a wide following outside professional botanists and horticulturists, except in South Africa where it is widely and generally used. It has a major deficiency in that it has no adjectival form and, therefore, no counterpart to VARIETAL.

cultivation. See TILLAGE.

curettage, *curettage* in French, also known as vine surgery or dendrosurgery, the surgical removal of dead wood to prolong the life of vines affected by TRUNK DISEASES.

Cholet, C., et al., 'Plant resilience and physiological modifications induced by curettage of Esca-diseased grapevines', *OENO One*, 55/1 (2021).

currants, small, dark, dried grapes (see RAISINS) made from the Greek vine variety KORINTHIAKI, called **Zante Currant** in Australia and Black Corinth in California.

Currency Creek, a cool MARITIME region in the Fleurieu Zone of SOUTH AUSTRALIA producing BORDEAUX BLENDS (white and red) and Shiraz from 1,032 ha/2,550 acres of vines in 2022.

Curtefranca. See FRANCIACORTA.

custom-crush facility, American term for a winery specializing in vinifying grapes on behalf of many different vine-growers, typically those without their own winemaking equipment. The various wines are kept separate and marketed by the growers under their own labels. Such operations have played an important part in establishing ambitious new wine producers, as in CALIFORNIA and Long Island in NEW YORK, and indeed whole new wine regions such as Marlborough and Central Otago in NEW ZEALAND, where new or small-scale growers can ill afford to build their own wineries.

Custoza, or **Bianco di Custoza**, an increasingly ambitious dry white wine produced in the VENETO region of north-east Italy in a wide stretch of territory extending south-west from the city of Verona partially overlapping the BARDOLINO DOC zone on the shores of Lake Garda and immediately south of the lake. The vineyard area planted increased from 1,200 ha in 2011 to 1,400 ha/3,459 acres in 2020, reflecting the wines' growing market value. The blend historically consists of Fernanda (CORTESE), GARGANEGA, and Trebbianello (a local strain of FRIULANO), with Trebbiano Toscano a minor ingredient. The result can be captivating, with Cortese adding perfume and precision, Friulano weight, and Garganega depth. Research in SOIL composition and MESOCLIMATES has resulted in the identification of ten subzones in the DOC, which has led to greater attention in matching varieties to soils. This, in combination with lower yields and modest prices, makes Custoza one of Italy's best-value white wines. W.S.

www.custoza.wine

cut cane, viticultural technique designed to increase the sugar concentration in almost-ripe grapes. The term originated in Australia, where the technique is typically used to produce sweet wines, but it is apparently also used very occasionally for dry red wines in Italy, where it is referred to as *taglio del tralcio*. By cutting the canes almost at the time of HARVEST, water supply to the fruit is halted, and so the berries start to shrivel (as in the production of DRIED-GRAPE WINES). Sugar concentration is elevated as water is lost through the berry skin, and ACIDITY may also be increased. The technique, resulting in grapes known as PASSERILLÉS in French, was developed to avert rain spoilage of grapes intended for drying. R.E.S.

cuttings, cut lengths of CANES used for vine PROPAGATION. Cuttings are the basis of propagation for commercial grape production, whether as own-rooted plants (see ROOTLINGS) or as SCION varieties for GRAFTED VINES. Both methods are representative of asexual or vegetative propagation, and the progeny are considered as CLONES of the source vines. In commerce, cuttings are cut from dormant vines in lengths of 30–45 cm/12–18 in. Once made, the cuttings are kept cool and moist and planted in a nursery in spring for roots to form at the base and a shoot to grow from the top bud. The plant is now called a rootling. It is typically lifted from the nursery in autumn and planted in its vineyard position the following spring. B.G.C.

cutworms, the larvae of several species of MOTHS, are a serious pest for all sorts of crops worldwide, including grapevines. They hide in the soil or under the vine's bark during the day and emerge to feed and cause damage at night, particularly to the buds. Young vines are particularly prone to damage. Cultural practices, natural enemies, and climatic factors may keep cutworms to tolerable levels, but there are no really effective insecticides.

University of California Agriculture & Natural Resources, UC IPM Pest Management Guidelines: cutworms. www2.ipm.ucanr.edu/agriculture/grape/Cutworms/.

cuve is the French word for a vat or tank. Thus a *cuverie* is the vat hall, typically where fermentation takes place. *Cuves* may be made of any material—wood, concrete or, most likely, stainless steel—and come in many different shapes and sizes. See FERMENTATION VESSEL.

cuve close, French for 'sealed tank'. See TANK METHOD.

cuvée, French wine term derived from CUVE, with many meanings in different contexts. In general terms it can be used to mean any containerful, or even any lot, of wine, and therefore wine labels often carry relatively meaningless descriptions incorporating the word *cuvée*. *Tête de cuvée*, on the other hand, is occasionally used for the top bottling of a French wine producer.

In CHAMPAGNE and in relation to other traditional-method sparkling wines, *cuvée* is a name for the first and best juice to flow from the press (see SPARKLING WINEMAKING). The blend of base wines assembled for second fermentation in bottle is also known as the *cuvée*. Thus the term is often used in many champagne and sparkling wine names.

Elsewhere, *cuvée* may be used to describe any ambitious blend, particularly of different vine varieties. German speakers often use the term to refer to any sort of blend, preferring it to German *Verschnitt*.

Cyprus, eastern Mediterranean island about 800 km/500 miles east of GREECE and 75 km south of TÜRKIYE. Most wine production is concentrated in the southern Greek part of the island. The few wineries that do exist in the northern Turkish-controlled zone are of little commercial significance. Despite the island's importance in the ancient wine trade (see below), Cyprus wine languished in terms of quality for most of the 20th century. Investment from the 1990s led to an improvement in production techniques and resulting wines; EU membership in 2004 stimulated even greater changes and restructuring of the industry. However, production dwindled to just 7,613 ha/18,812 acres by 2020. Of these, 583 ha/1,440 acres were new plantings.

History

Wine cultivation and production in Cyprus are believed to date back 5,500–6,000 years. Archaeological evidence including residue from stone press bases and vats confirm winemaking in Cyprus in the Early Bronze Age (2,100–2,000 BCE). Because of its position in the eastern Mediterranean, the island has changed hands many times. In antiquity, domination by various foreign powers alternated with brief periods of independence. In 58 BCE Cyprus became part of the Roman province of Cilicia in Asia Minor. In 668 CE Cyprus was occupied by Arabs; when they were finally expelled in 965, Cyprus became an advance base of the Greek navy. In 1191, during the Third CRUSADE, Richard I, king of England, conquered Cyprus and sold it to the Templars, who soon gave it back to him, whereupon he presented it to the rejected king of Jerusalem, Guy de Lusignan. Guy de Lusignan imposed a feudal system on Cyprus and governed the island as a separate kingdom, which it remained until it became a colony of then-powerful VENICE in 1489.

The Crusaders and Venetian expansionism made the island part of the Latin West, which soon became fond of its wines. The earliest record of Cyprus wine being drunk in the West is dated 1178 when Count Baldwin of Guines offered it to the Archbishop of Reims. The Old French poem *La Bataille des vins* (see MEDIEVAL LITERATURE) awards the palm to *chypre*, Cyprus wine, because it is stronger and sweeter than any wine in western Europe (FORTIFICATION and MUTAGE were as yet unknown). We do not know when the wines of Cyprus first reached the English market, but in the 13th and 14th centuries they, along with other sweet wines from the East and from Italy (see ENGLAND), fetched higher prices than the wines of GASCONY and LA ROCHELLE. The Venetians shipped them from Cyprus to Venice in their galleys, and from Venice they distributed them all over Europe.

The modern Cypriot dessert wine, Commandaria, harks back to the Crusades, when the Knights Hospitallers moved their headquarters from Acre to Cyprus, where each 'commandery' (manor) made wine. For more details, see COMMANDARIA. H.M.W. & A.M.

Dion, R., *Histoire de la vigne et du vin en France* (1959).

Hadjisavvas, S., *The Archeology of Wine in Cyprus* (2020).

Simon, A. L., *The History of the Wine Trade in England*, 3 vols. (1906–9).

Modern history

Ottoman rule (1571–1878) brought a steep decline in both wine production and the importance of the wine industry, which remained underdeveloped until the middle of the 19th century. The first of the modern wineries, Haggipavlu, was founded in 1844. British administration of the island (1878–1960) saw a revitalization of the industry.

After the Second World War, most of the island's wine exports fell into four categories: large volumes of very basic wine for Eastern Bloc countries; wine intended for industrial uses such as VERMOUTH, SANGRÍA, or, in German-speaking countries, *Glühwein*; GRAPE CONCENTRATE sent to Japan, Central and Eastern Europe, and the United Kingdom, where it was reconstituted and made into BRITISH WINE; and Cyprus FORTIFIED WINE.

This was Cyprus 'sherry'-style wine, medium and medium-sweet, fortified and exported in millions of cases, mainly to Britain. From the 1980s the style died out as fresh white wine became technically possible. Cyprus lost over 70% of its vineyard land in the 1980s and 1990s. Entry into the EU in 2004 put an end to government grape price subsidies, and vineyard land further contracted.

By 2020 the downward trend was beginning to reverse. The big four wineries—KEO, ETKO (Haggipavlu family), SODAP (a CO-OPERATIVE, also known as Kamenterena Winery), and LOEL—had dominated production for decades, but a new generation of winegrowers were busy either buying and replanting vineyards or developing relationships with small landowners in a pursuit of quality- rather than quantity-driven production. In 2020, the Department of Agriculture recorded 3,800 ha/9,390 acres of vines and 116 registered wineries, up from 52 wineries in 2014.

Climate and geography

At latitude 35° N, Cyprus has a typically MEDITERRANEAN climate, with mild winters, hot summers, and precipitation mainly confined to the winter months. However, the island's central mountain massif rises to over 1,700 m/5,577 ft in ELEVATION. Summer temperatures can vary more than 12 °C/54 °F between low- and high-elevation vineyards. Harvest extends from mid July into early November depending on grape type and site elevation.

Rainfall is low, at 500 mm/19 in per annum at lower elevations and 900 mm/35 in for the higher. DRIP IRRIGATION is permitted but rare because of limited water availability and very fragmented, small vineyard holdings.

Most wine vineyards are on the south- and west-facing slopes of the Troodos Mountains, the best at elevations of 500–1,500 m/1,650–4,950 ft. To bring the industry in line with the EU, a CONTROLLED APPELLATION scheme has been developed, with PDOs for Commandaria, Laona Akama, Pitsilia, Vouni Panayia-Ambelitis, Krasochoria Lemesou, Krasochoria Lemesou-Afames, and Krasochoria Lemesou-Laona, although the scheme has so far been little used except for Commandaria. More common are the four PGI regions: Pafos/Paphos, on the western side of the island; Lemesos (Limassol in anglicized form) to its east, stretching from the southern coast up into the Troodos Mountains and encompassing the Commandaria PDO; Larnaca further east along the coast; and Lefkosia, inland and encompassing PDO Pitsilia, where vines grow at elevations as high as 1,450 m/4,757 ft.

Pitsilia and the northern half of Commandaria have igneous soil and subsoil. Elsewhere soils are of sedimentary LIMESTONE with a particularly high active LIME content.

Climatic hazards are restricted to HAIL and, in higher-elevation vineyards, spring and autumn FROST. The lack of humidity means that DOWNY MILDEW is unknown, but growers regularly spray against POWDERY MILDEW. BOTRYTIS is found only in grape bunches that have previously been attacked by eudemis MOTHS or other INSECTS. Almost all vines are GOBELET trained, except for some non-indigenous varieties supported by TRELLIS SYSTEMS.

Vine varieties

Cyprus has never been invaded by PHYLLOXERA, and its UNGRAFTED VINES are protected by strict QUARANTINE, slowing the introduction of INTERNATIONAL VARIETIES. Save for SYRAH—which, as elsewhere around the Mediterranean, is really at home here—and white varieties Chardonnay, Sémillon, and Sauvignon Blanc, the focus is on native varieties. PALOMINO and MUSCAT OF ALEXANDRIA (called Malaga here), once popular for use in fortified wines, have declined steeply in hectarage. Only Viognier, ASSYRTIKO, and one or two other Greek varieties have arrived recently.

Since 2004, production of the island's largest-production varieties, MAVRO and XYNISTERI, has nosedived, as winegrowers change emphasis from quantity to quality and as well as abandon low-elevation vineyards in preference for cooler altitudes in the face of CLIMATE CHANGE.

Today Xynisteri is the most common white variety in Cypriot vineyards, accounting for 27.5% of the total annual production in 2022, marking the success of white wine sales for summer drinking for the tourist trade. Rosés do well, too.

Although Cyprus does produce serious, long-lived dry red wines, these are only just becoming appreciated. Mavro remains the dominant red wine grape, but more attention to matching grape varieties to MESOCLIMATE has instigated a rediscovery of ancient varieties: MARATHEFTIKO (called Vamvakada in Pitsilia), a feminine variety that needs to be co-planted with a pollinator but has great colour, fine-grained tannins, and black- and red-cherry flavour, now produces nearly a half-million tonnes per year, and the deeper, darker, wilder Lefkada is also increasing in volumes. Yiannoudi, a newly rediscovered sister grape to Maratheftiko, has made its way into commercial production in the last decade. Rediscovered white grapes including Spourtiko (light, apple-y, low alcohol), Promara (riper, more pronounced apple and pear flavours), Morokanella/Kanella (warmer, more floral), and its cousin Vassilisa (similar but more delicate) are just creeping on to the market.

See also COMMANDARIA. C.G. & A.M.

www.cypruswinemuseum.com

www.winesofcyprus.co.uk

cytokinins, natural HORMONES in vines produced in the root tips and affecting the growth of other parts of the plant. Cytokinins favour cell multiplication and affect growth and development of SHOOTS and INFLORESCENCES. Fewer cytokinins are produced in dry soils as well as in cold and wet soils, and this appears to be critical for BUDBREAK and early shoot growth.

Czechia officially split from SLOVAKIA in 1993, taking less than one-third of the productive vineyard area, just over 40% of wine production, and around two-thirds of the wine consumption of the original Czechoslovakia. In 2018, the republic counted 18,200 ha/44,500 acres of vines, which fulfils only 60% of the local demand, so very little Czech wine is exported.

About two-fifths of the country's vineyards lie on gentle slopes, usually topped by forests, while the rest are on undulating plains which slope towards the Danube Basin. The republic and its vineyards divide into two distinct regions: the tiny vineyards of PDO BOHEMIA on the banks of the River Labe (Germany's Elbe) in the north; and the larger PDO MORAVIA to the south along the Austrian and Slovakian borders.

In terms of GEOLOGY, both regions are very varied. In BOHEMIA vines are traditionally planted on the warm slopes of the main rivers Labe and Vltava. In Prague the subsoil is mostly Silurian and Devonian LIMESTONE with various VOLCANIC components; Mělník and Roudnice are mostly on 'opuka', limestone marl, while in the north around Litoměřice the soil is predominantly alkaline BASALT. Moravia´s most notable terroir is the GRANITE of Brno Massif in Dolní Kounice and the Jurassic limestone of the Pálava Hills. The lower reaches where most vineyards are situated tend towards CLAY and SAND, but the major influences are the relatively low ELEVATION (100–250 m/330–820 ft above sea level) and the CONTINENTAL CLIMATE. Rainfall in Moravia is relatively low, on average 510 mm/20 in annually, which has encouraged the adoption of ORGANIC VITICULTURE. A trend in NATURAL WINE has become significant, too, led by Milan Nestarec.

Because of their position north of the Danube, most of the slopes face south and are protected by higher land in the north. The vines are trained like those of Germany and Austria, mostly using the Rhinehessen pruning system. Nearly 65% is planted to white grapes, particularly Veltlínské Zelené (GRÜNER VELTLINER), MÜLLER-THURGAU, Ryzlink Rýnský (RIESLING), Rulandské Bílé (PINOT BLANC), Ryzlink Vlašský (WELSCHRIESLING), and Rulandské šedé (PINOT GRIS). The aromatic variety Pálava (MÜLLER-THURGAU x Traminer) is on the rise and very promising in both dry and sweet wines. Also notable are wines from Sylvánské zelené (SILVANER), Neuburské (NEUBURGER), and Moravian Muscat (Muscat Ottonel x Prachtraube). Plantings of HYBRIDS such as SOLARIS, Hibernal, and Johanniter have grown, too, especially for organic growers. The country has the world's largest area of Svatovavřinecké (ST-LAURENT) at 1,012 ha/2,500 acres, but the most planted red variety is Frankovka (BLAUFRÄNKISCH), followed by ZWEIGELTREBE, PINOT NOIR, and Modrý Portugal (PORTUGIESER). There are many other interesting dark-skinned varieties, including Czech crossings such as André, Alibernet, Cabernet Moravia, and Neronet.

Wine laws in Czechia are modelled on German wine laws, using as a basis RIPENESS, here measured in °NM (normalized MUST WEIGHT measurement) similar to the KMW scale of Austria although 1 °CNM denotes 1 kg of sugar per 100 l of grape must while 1 °KMW denotes 1 kg of sugar in 100 kg of must. CHAPTALIZATION is allowed and sometimes practised, although less so given CLIMATE CHANGE. In addition to PDO and PGI classifications, Czech wines may also be classified by VOC (*Víno originální certifikace*), an appellation system based on place and grape varieties. Of the 13 VOCs, the most noteworthy are VOC Znojmo, the oldest, focusing on Sauvignon Blanc, Grüner Veltliner, and Riesling; VOC Pálava (in Mikulov) for Welshriesling on limestone; and VOC Modré Hory (in Velké Pavlovice) for St. Laurent, Bläufrankish, and Blauer Portugieser.

SPARKLING WINE, ICE WINE, and STRAW WINE are also Czech specialities. K.K.

D

DAC, Districtus Austria Controllatus, denotes AUSTRIAN appellations of origin established and regulated by grower-dominated regional wine committees and intended to define and promote a typical style and flavour profile (or multiple profiles, including specified grape varieties) for each of Austria's growing regions. With the approval of the Thermenregion DAC in 2023, all 17 of Austria's winegrowing regions have DACs, listed here alphabetically with each one's inaugural vintage:

CARNUNTUM (2019)
EISENBERG (2009)
KAMPTAL (2008)
KREMSTAL (2007)
LEITHABERG (2008)
MITTELBURGENLAND (2005)
NEUSIEDLERSEE (2011, revised and much expanded from 2020)
ROSALIA (2017)
RUSTER AUSBRUCH (2020)
SÜDSTEIERMARK (2018)
THERMENREGION (2023)
TRAISENTAL (2006)
VULKANLAND STEIERMARK (2018)
WACHAU (2020)
WAGRAM (2002)
WEINVIERTEL (2002)
WESTSTEIERMARK (2018)
Wiener Gemischter Satz (2013; see WIEN)

A potential revision of the DAC governing Wien to encompass that region's wines from Grüner Veltliner and Riesling is under discussion.

The capital letters DAC appear on labels in immediate conjunction with the relevant name. In some instances, a separate DAC Reserve tier is legislated. D.S.

Dão, REGIÃO DEMARCADA since 1908, this DOC in north-central Portugal produces some of the country's most elegant, mineral wines (see map under PORTUGAL). Locked in on three sides by granite mountains and sheltered from the Atlantic, Dão benefits from long, warm summers and abundant winter rainfall (which supports the pine forests whose resin notes can be detected in mature Dão wines, especially reds, but also those made from ENCRUZADO). GRANITIC sandy soils are well drained (sometimes too well drained—WATER STRESS can prejudice ripening in the lead-up to harvest). Small and scattered, the vineyards (which cumulatively occupy just 3.5% of the DOC's footprint) are stocked with a wealth of INDIGENOUS VARIETIES, including Portugal's flagship red grape TOURIGA NACIONAL which is thought to have originated here. For much of the second half of the 20th century, however, the wines rarely lived up to expectations, a consequence of heavy-handed government intervention since the 1940s.

In an attempt to impose some form of organization on the highly fragmented, largely subsistence economy in the north of Portugal, the Salazar government introduced a programme of co-operativization. Ten CO-OPERATIVES were built in Dão between 1954 and 1971, and the authorities gave them the exclusive right to buy grapes. Private firms were effectively restricted to purchasing ready-made wine. Wines became ever more standardized and, as co-operatives were poorly equipped and paid scant attention to HYGIENE, standards fell. This monopolistic legislation was felt to be incompatible with Portugal's membership of the EU, and the law institutionalizing Dão's co-operatives was overturned in 1989. Some enterprising initiatives followed, led by SOGRAPE, which built a modern winery in the heart of the region, and an influential band of single estates whose ever-rising numbers have consolidated Dão's revival of fortunes. A 21st-century wave of newcomers counts notable Douro producers and NATURAL WINE enthusiasts among its number. Just five co-operatives remain.

About 80% of Dão wines are red, thanks to the modern era's introduction of planting varietally blocked vineyards (traditional vineyards comprised FIELD BLENDS). Touriga Nacional, Tinta Roriz (TEMPRANILLO), Jaen (MENCÍA), and ALFROCHEIRO Preto have become the mainstay of the region's leading wines, although efforts are underway to revive some of its more obscure varieties. Although tannins are accentuated by the high acidity in the region's wines, modern reds are much less austere and tannic than in the past when many wines suffered from excessive MACERATION with stalks and protracted ageing in old CASKS or CONCRETE tanks. New French OAK and overripeness can mar TERROIR expression, but the pendulum (in some quarters at least) is swinging back in favour of greater restraint.

White wines improved markedly in the early 21st century, becoming fruitier without sacrificing varietal complexity or the region's hallmark freshness. Encruzado is without doubt the jewel in the crown, making ageworthy VARIETAL wines that may be crisp and fragrant or more Burgundian if BARREL FERMENTATION is employed. Encruzado may also be blended with less structured varieties such as MALVASIA Fina and BICAL, known here as Borrado das Moscas. The VINHO REGIONAL is Terras do Dão. S.A.

Mayson, R. J., *The Wines of Portugal* (2020).
Woolf, S. J., Opaz, R., *Foot Trodden: Portugal and the Wines That Time Forgot* (2021).
www.cvrdao.pt

DAP. See DIAMMONIUM PHOSPHATE.

Davis, the usual abbreviation in the wine world for the influential wine-related faculties of the University of California at Davis, a small city 70 miles north-east of San Francisco in California's Central Valley. Although the university is known throughout the world as a centre for research and instruction in agriculture, it began as the home of the University Farm established in 1906.

Until the late 19th century, grape-growing and winemaking in California had been relatively haphazard, with numerous problems generally unrecognized. An act of the state legislature in 1880 directed the nascent University of California to start research and teaching in VITICULTURE and OENOLOGY. The fact that Berkeley, the original site of the university, was too cold and foggy for grape-growing encouraged the establishment of the farm in the warm, inland climate of Davis.

The then Professor of Agriculture, Eugene Hilgard, soon recognized that grafting VITIS VINIFERA SCIONS on to hybrid ROOTSTOCKS was the only practical solution to the world's PHYLLOXERA epidemic. He also recognized the importance of matching vine variety to soil and climate for fine-wine production. Hilgard established early co-operation between ACADEME and practitioners.

PROHIBITION brought a temporary hiatus in Davis's wine-related activities, though the study of viticulture continued. The department moved to Davis shortly after the end of Prohibition; in 1959 UC Davis was declared an independent general campus, no longer a branch of UC Berkeley. The university hired a powerful group of academics, including the late Albert J. WINKLER, famous for his DEGREE DAY/heat-summation method of CLIMATE CLASSIFICATION; Harold P. Olmo, breeder of NEW VARIETIES; and well-known oenologist Maynard A. AMERINE. The department was and still is responsible for the development of assays and technologies routinely employed in wineries internationally, along with a curriculum used throughout the world.

Current research efforts are dedicated to understanding the impact of viticultural practices such as REGULATED DEFICIT IRRIGATION, YIELD, clonal variation, and SITE SELECTION on wine composition and perceived quality. In addition, novel molecular and genetic technologies have been developed and applied for the improvement of both scion and rootstock varieties with the aim of producing vines less susceptible to pests and diseases and increasing understanding of grape berry maturation and flavour and aroma development. Genomics technologies have been used to further understand the YEAST and bacterial fermentations of wine, to profile the presence and persistence of both wild and spoilage flora, and to map winery and vineyard microbes (see SOIL BIOTA) and their impact on grape and wine quality. The department is similarly engaged in profiling the key chemical components responsible for wine aroma and flavour, as well as linking the development and evolution of these components to vineyard practices, using consumers and professionals for sensory evaluation. The department is also playing an important role in defining the bioactive compounds of wines responsible for the health benefits of moderate consumption (see HEALTH). Sophisticated tools for the ANALYSIS of wine chemistry, aroma, flavour, and ageability are also being pioneered and applied to the investigation of wine composition. Consumer-preference profiling is being exploited to better understand the phenomenon of preference. Work on vine-variety identification using DNA PROFILING continues along with the breeding of new varieties resistant to various pests and diseases and those that are DROUGHT- and salt-tolerant, as well as researching solutions to help the industry survive recent and potential future WILDFIRES.

The department's new facilities, opened in 2008, have ushered in a new era of teaching, research, and SUSTAINABILITY. The teaching and research winery, opened in 2013, is the most advanced and sustainable in the world. The Davis campus also houses the FOUNDATION PLANT SERVICES.

Davis continues to be one of the principal centres for teaching and research in viticulture and oenology, and it has trained numerous winemakers from around the world. It has become synonymous with a scientific approach to wine production and understanding wine quality as opposed to one informed solely by TRADITION and observation. K.L.B.

day-night temperature difference. See DIURNAL TEMPERATURE RANGE.

deacidification, winemaking process of decreasing the excessive ACIDITY of MUST, grape juice or wine made in cold wine regions or, in particularly cool years, in TEMPERATE wine regions. A number of techniques have been developed and are usually strictly governed by local regulations.

MALOLACTIC CONVERSION is a way of lowering acidity biologically, but it is difficult to persuade LACTIC ACID BACTERIA to work in very acid conditions.

Winemakers may choose not to use biological methods for reducing acidity because malolactic conversion can introduce other flavours and reduce the fruitiness of a wine. There are other forms of deacidification which rely on chemical processes, notably adding compounds to must, juice or wine that will eliminate acidity as CARBON DIOXIDE and insoluble solids that can be filtered or settle out. Potassium bicarbonate and calcium carbonate are commonly used. In some very cool regions, where grapes have higher MALIC ACID levels, the addition of calcium carbonate can lead to an imbalance in the proportion of malic acid to TARTARIC ACID. Double-salt deacidification resolves this by reducing both the malic and tartaric acids in the juice. Other methods include REVERSE OSMOSIS and ELECTRODIALYSIS.

Deacidifications are most effective after fermentation, partly because alcohol decreases the solubility of cream of tartar, thereby reducing some of the must acidity, and fermentation itself produces a better mix of flavour by-products in the more acid solution.

Deacidification is not the commonplace procedure that ACIDIFICATION is in warmer regions. It is practised in northern Germany, Luxembourg, Burgundy, the United Kingdom, Canada, New York State, Tasmania, and New Zealand's South Island in certain years but is becoming less common as a result of CLIMATE CHANGE. M.J.T.

dead arm or **dying arm**, common names for several fungal diseases in vine wood that cause cankers and dieback. See TRUNK DISEASES, EUTYPA DIEBACK, PHOMOPSIS, and BOTRYOSPHAERIA DIEBACK.

dead fruit. See OVERRIPENESS.

de-alcoholization. See ALCOHOL REDUCTION.

de-alcoholized wine, one that has undergone ALCOHOL REDUCTION, or de-alcoholization, to produce a wine with an ALCOHOLIC STRENGTH below 0.5% in an attempt to provide a drink that tastes like wine but has none of the negative implications for HEALTH and has fewer calories than regular wine. Such wines fall within the increasingly popular NOLO category. The process of removing alcohol from wine makes it less microbiologically stable and FILTRATION more difficult. There has been a lively debate in some traditional wine-producing countries over whether such products should be entitled to use the word 'wine' in their name. The EU resolved this by creating a formal legal category for 'de-alcoholized wine' in 2021, taking effect in 2023. The same term is regulated in the US, with 'alcohol-removed' an accepted alternative. Other countries may use different terminology, for example NON-ALCOHOLIC WINE or 'alcohol-free wine'. See also PARTIALLY DE-ALCOHOLIZED WINE. J.E.H & J.P.H.B.

Schneider, I., and Marzolph, F., 'Alcohol-free wine presents challenges in filtration and quality assurance', *Wine Industry Advisor* (June 2022).

Debina, the sprightly white grape variety that is solely responsible for the lightly sparkling white wines of Zítsa in Epirus high in north-west GREECE near the Albanian border but also used to produce still whites and ORANGE WINES. At these ELEVATIONS (600–700 m/1,968–2,297 ft) acidity levels remain high.

débourbage, French term for SETTLING out solids from MUST.

decanters, vessels, usually glass and stoppered, into which wine is poured during DECANTING.

The decanter as we know it today has changed form very little in the last 250 years, in that it is a handleless clear glass bottle with a capacity of about a litre and, normally, a stopper. Stopperless decanters are known as carafes. The shape and the decoration have changed in line with fashion and as technology has allowed. Since the capacity is noticeably more than that of a standard 75-cl/27-fl oz bottle, it allows the wine to 'breathe' and develop (see AERATION).

History

The decanter's origins lie with the Roman serving bottle, which was typically square. Some Roman glass bottles may have been used for serving wine, but the Romans also used silver. After the collapse of the Roman Empire, glass production went into a sharp decline until the revival of the glass trade in Renaissance Italy. By the 16th century, Venice had emerged as the principal centre of glass-making.

While the glass trade was expanding, other developments were afoot. Popular throughout northern Europe during the 16th and early 17th centuries were bulbous earthenware jugs with flat, small handles and short, narrow necks.

A more sophisticated finish, sometimes employed, was a salt glaze which produced a textured surface not unlike orange peel. In addition, Chinese porcelain jugs were being imported for the most sophisticated of tastes, while some preferred their wine served in carved rock crystal. Whether the jug was salt glaze, tigerware, porcelain, or crystal, all the better-quality pieces were given silver or silver-gilt mounts. For the grandest, gold was used.

Throughout the medieval period and well beyond, pouring vessels were also made in bronze and silver, but these media often gave way to glass once a centre of production became established in a country. The new glass serving vessels represented the latest in fashion and technology and were quickly adopted by society. For almost a century, England—which was an important wine market—relied on imports until George Ravenscroft and others started producing glass using lead oxide as a flux in the 1670s. This, together with his flint glass, allowed the production of usable jugs and glasses. His developments gave Britain a lead that lasted for about 100 years.

Contemporary with the jug, decanters were also made which took the same form as bottles but with a much greater sophistication of material, decoration, and workmanship.

With the exception of very early decanter jugs, decanters first acquired stoppers in the 1730s.

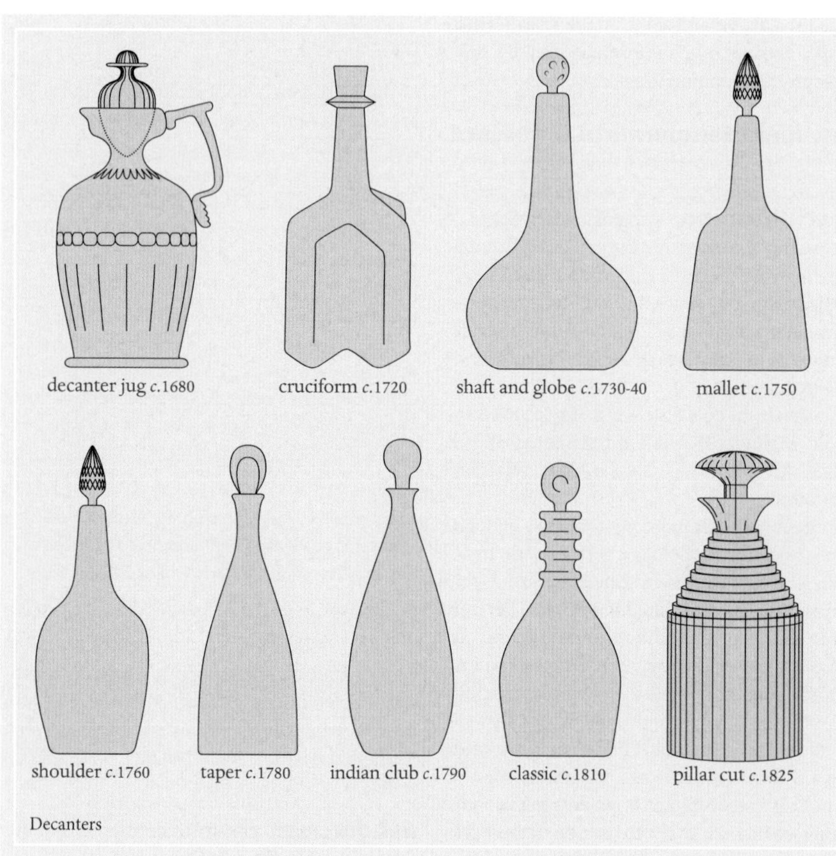

Decanters

In the early 19th century, the introduction of steam-driven cutting tools and better lighting from oil lamps produced a fashion for profusely cut decanters, although plain ones continued to be made too. From the 1820s a wide variety of shapes and patterns gained favour at the expense of a well-defined progression of design, and many of these are now considered desirable antiques.

The 1840s saw the return of the 'shaft and globe' shape that had been popular a century before. This form continued in fashion until the 20th century, gradually changing in proportion and weight of cutting. The 1870s saw acid-etched decoration of machine precision and other applications of mechanical and chemical technology which enabled decanters to be made in a variety of complex patterns. Some decanters from this time were raised on a foot, a new idea that remained popular for the remainder of the century.

Decanters were not the only vessels from which wine was served. Jugs were made in silver throughout the 18th century. Glass CLARET jugs were made during the 19th century and followed the pattern of decanters, the only difference being the addition of a handle and a modified rim to form a pouring lip.

Claret jugs of glass mounted with silver, silver plate, or gilt became popular from about 1835. One favoured design, incorporating a globular body with a wide neck, closely imitated the jugs of the late 16th century.

The Arts and Crafts movement influenced some designs for claret jugs, as did art nouveau and late 19th century interest in Japanese forms. Novelty jugs would also be made in the form of a duck, walrus, seal, or some other animal, with the body in glass and the head in silver or silver plate. All these forms were prevalent in the closing 30 years of the 19th century.

While it is not possible to describe every sort of decanter, there is one type which should not pass unmentioned. It has a conical body, giving it a very wide base, and it usually has neck rings. Many are plain but some have cut decoration. Plain or decorated with cutting, all are considerably heavier than their standard counterparts. Originally called 'rodneys', today they are known as ship's decanters. R.N.H.B.

Butler, R., *Great British Wine Accessories 1550–1900* (2009).

McConnell, A., *The Decanter: An Illustrated History of Glass from 1650* (2004).

Modern decanters

Any container—a simple jug, for example—can be used as a vessel for wine, so long as it is made of an inert material and can hold at least the contents of a bottle while, ideally, leaving a considerable surface area in contact with air. Some decanters, notably one designed in the late 1980s by the Ch LATOUR management, are shaped so that a bottle exactly fills them to their maximum width, thereby maximizing the potential for AERATION. Some decanters are designed specifically for magnums, or double-sized bottles. Others have handles, all manner of different shapes, engravings, shadings, or designs, including one to ensure circulation with a semi-spherical base that cannot be laid to rest other than in a special cradle by the host's elbow (see PASSING THE PORT). Wine need not be served from clear glass, or even glass at all, but most wine's COLOUR (whites as much as reds) can give great aesthetic and anticipatory pleasure.

See LEAD for details of the limited extent to which this toxic element may be leached from different sorts of decanters.

decanting, optional and controversial step in SERVING wine, involving pouring wine out of its bottle into another container called a DECANTER.

Reasons for decanting

The most obvious reason for decanting a wine is to separate it from any SEDIMENT that has formed in the bottle which not only looks unappetizing in the glass but usually tastes bitter and/or ASTRINGENT. Before winemakers mastered the art of CLARIFICATION, this was necessary for all wines. Today such a justification of the decanting process effectively limits it to those wines outlined in AGEING as capable of development in bottle, in most of which some solids are precipitated as part of the maturation process. Vintage and crusted PORTS in particular always throw a heavy deposit (since they are bottled so early in their evolution), as do red wines made with no or minimal FILTRATION. It is rare for inexpensive, everyday TABLE WINES to throw a deposit, and most large retailers insist on a level of filtration that makes a deposit unlikely (although not unknown in older, higher-quality reds). To check whether a wine bottle contains any sediment, stand it upright for an hour or more and then carefully hold it up to the light for inspection at the base (although some BOTTLES are too dark for this exercise to be effective).

Another traditional but disputed reason for decanting is to promote AERATION and therefore encourage the development of the wine's BOUQUET. Authorities as scientifically respectable as the late Professor Émile PEYNAUD argued that this is oenologically indefensible: that the action of OXYGEN dissolved in a sound wine when ready to serve is usually detrimental and that the longer it is prolonged (i.e. the longer before serving a wine is decanted), the more diffuse its aroma and the less marked its sensory attributes. His advice was to decant only wines with a sediment and then only just before serving. If they need aeration because of some wine FAULT such as REDUCTION or MERCAPTANS, then the taster can simply aerate the wine by agitating it in the glass. Peynaud's argument was that from the moment the wine is fully exposed to air (which happens when it is poured, but not to any significant extent during so-called BREATHING) some of its sensory impressions may be lost, and so decanting immediately before serving gives the taster maximum control.

It is certainly wise advice to decant fully mature wines only just before serving, since some are so fragile that they can withstand oxygen for only a few minutes before succumbing to OXIDATION. And it is also true that the aeration process of an individual glass of wine can be controlled by the person drinking out of it. However, there are certain types of young wines, ultra-traditional BAROLO most obviously, which may not have been included in Professor Peynaud's experiments with decanting regimes but which can be so concentrated and tannic in youth that to lose some of their initial sensory impressions is a positive benefit.

There is also the very practical fact that many hosts find it more convenient to decant before a meal is served rather than in the middle of it. There are also people who enjoy the sight of (perhaps both red and white) wine in a decanter so much that they are prepared to sacrifice the potential reduction in gustatory impact.

How to decant

Some authorities argue that bottles that have been stored horizontally should be disturbed as little as possible before being decanted, so it is best to transfer them to either a DECANTING CRADLE or a (much more expensive) decanting machine. The alternative and more common method involves standing the bottle upright for as long as possible before opening, certainly a few hours for wines which have a great deal of sediment, to allow the sediment to fall through the wine to the base of the bottle. Whichever method is used, ensure that the decanter looks and smells absolutely clean, and find a strong light source against which the bottle can be held (a candle, flashlight, desk light, or unshaded table lamp will do). After opening the bottle as gently as possible and wiping the lip of the bottle clean to avoid any possible contamination, particularly if the CAPSULE is old enough to contain LEAD, steadily pour the contents of the bottle into the decanter watching the lower shoulder of the bottle with the light source behind it. The sediment should eventually collect in the shoulder, and the pouring action can be halted as soon as any sediment starts to spill into the bottleneck.

To extract maximum volume of liquid from a bottle with sediment, or if there is no time to let all the sediment fall to the bottom of the bottle, or if a cork collapses into fragments in the bottle during extraction, the wine can be filtered into the decanter through clean fabric such as muslin, a paper coffee filter, or a special inert wine filter.

Peynaud, É., *Le Goût du Vin* (1983), translated by M. Schuster as *The Taste of Wine* (2nd edn, 1996).

decanting cradles, bottle carriers, usually made of wicker or metal, which keep the bottle at a perpetually inclined angle with the bottleneck only slightly higher than the base of the bottle, so that the SEDIMENT does not have to fall through the wine to the base of the bottle between STORING horizontally and pouring.

Special **decanting machines** have also been constructed, designed to pour wine gently out of a bottle held horizontally so that the deposit hardly moves at all.

De Chaunac (Seibel 9549), early-ripening, productive, disease-resistant, dark-skinned FRENCH HYBRID grown for a wide range of wine styles in NEW YORK's Finger Lakes region and in Ontario in CANADA.

defoliation, loss of leaves of a vine, can be caused by various agents. If extensive and badly timed, it adversely affects fruit RIPENING and wine quality, although the precise effects depend on the time of the year. Defoliation is, of course, a natural process and happens at the end of each growing season in the autumn. Normally it is caused by the first FROST, but it may also be through mechanical damage or merely senescence due to shorter days and lower temperatures. By this time the vines have lost most of the green colour from their leaves and are no longer effective at PHOTOSYNTHESIS. Providing the vine's reserves of CARBOHYDRATES are topped up by late-season photosynthesis, there is no negative effect of defoliation.

However, defoliation can occur at any time of the growing season due to climate, disease, or pests. Frosts at any time in the growing season can partially or totally defoliate vines, as can HAIL. A mild hailstorm may simply tear some leaves, but a severe hailstorm will rip off all the leaves and cut green shoots back to their thick basal stubs. FUNGAL DISEASES such as DOWNY MILDEW can also cause defoliation if left unchecked. Similarly, insect pests such as the WESTERN GRAPELEAF SKELETONIZER and GRASSHOPPERS, as well as grazing ANIMALS, can defoliate entire vines.

The vine responds to defoliation by producing new leaves on lateral shoots. However, this new growth will depend on stored carbohydrate reserves of the vine for a month or so, and so will weaken the vine until the new leaves are able to produce carbohydrates by photosynthesis and build up reserves again. While vigorous vines may be able to recover from a single defoliation, repeated defoliation can weaken the vine perhaps to the point of death.

Defoliation will have an impact on fruit growth and ripening. A low LEAF TO FRUIT RATIO causes a reduction in levels of fruit sugars (see SUGAR IN GRAPES) as well as in PHENOLICS, with an adverse effect on colour and flavour of the resultant wine. However, the vine can compensate for a lower-than-ideal leaf area by automatically increasing the rate of photosynthesis, so that practices such as LEAF REMOVAL and TRIMMING do not normally cause negative effects. Good-quality wine can be made only from vines with a sufficient area of healthy leaves exposed to sunlight. R.E.S.

dégorgement, French term for the DISGORGEMENT operations at the end of the traditional method of SPARKLING WINEMAKING.

degree, the ALCOHOLIC STRENGTH of a wine, identical to the wine's percentage of ETHANOL by volume. This was traditionally regarded as the most vital statistic of all for everyday French VIN DE TABLE, whose price was generally quoted per *degré/hecto*, as though its only important characteristics were its potency and volume—perhaps with some justification since, at this quality level, wines with low alcohol levels tended to have been over-produced and to be low in fruit and concentration.

degree days, unit devised to measure the TEMPERATURE component of climate. See CLIMATE CLASSIFICATION for more details.

dehydration, winemaking process used in the production of DRIED-GRAPE WINES—and a frequent consequence of extended HANG TIME. The dehydration process transforms grapes into RAISINS and has to be arrested before completion if appetizing wines are to be made from the results.

See also BERRY SHRIVEL.

Dekkera. See BRETTANOMYCES.

Delaware, dark-pink-skinned VITIS LABRUSCA × *Vitis aestivalis* vine variety that is quite popular in NEW YORK and, for reasons that are now obscure, also planted in JAPAN and KOREA. Its early ripening is presumably an advantage in Japan's damp autumns. The wine is not as markedly FOXY as that of its great New York rival CONCORD. It was first propagated in Delaware, Ohio, in 1849.

délestage. See RACK AND RETURN.

delimitation, geographical. The central purpose of geographical delimitation of a wine area, typically into a CONTROLLED APPELLATION, is to establish a distinctive identity for the wines produced within it and provide a means whereby the provenance of those wines can be guaranteed. It is based primarily upon the assumption that different environments give rise to wines of different character (see TERROIR), but it is also increasingly used as a means to market wines from specific places.

Since classical antiquity, wines from certain regions tended to be called after the area of their production, with many gaining particularly high reputations (FALERNIAN, for example, in ancient Rome), but the first legal vineyard delimitation may well have been that of CHIANTI, Pomino, and CARMIGNANO in 1716 by Cosimo III de' Medici, Grand Duke of Tuscany, in a document which further states that penalties will be incurred if any wine makes a false claim to be from those demarcated regions. The DOURO Valley of northern Portugal was famously first delimited in 1756, associated with the establishment of the Companhia Geral da Agricultura das Vinhas do Alto Douro. During the 18th century, there had been many disputes over the sources and qualities of wines exported from Oporto (see PORT), as well as conflicts between foreign wine shippers and the Portuguese growers; the formation of the Companhia Geral, with its strictly defined areas of operation, was designed to remedy the situation. At the heart of this legislation was the establishment of a specific area in the upper Douro Valley from which farmers were able to obtain higher prices for their wines compared with those produced elsewhere.

During the 18th century in other parts of Europe, CLASSIFICATIONS of the different qualities of wine were becoming increasingly common. Thomas JEFFERSON, for example, commented on the various categories of wines from Bordeaux and Burgundy in 1787. In the 19th century, more formal classifications emerged, with the most famous of these being the classification of the wines of the MÉDOC and Lavalle's classification of the wines of the CÔTE D'OR, both of which date from 1855. By the early 20th century, in the wake of the devastation caused by POWDERY MILDEW and PHYLLOXERA, there were two fundamental problems facing the wine industry: ADULTERATION AND FRAUD. Many wines contained a range of ADDITIVES designed to mask their flavour; and wine purporting to come from a respected source frequently contained wines from elsewhere. In order to overcome these problems, groups of growers, such as those in Chablis and Bordeaux, decided to form their own associations to guarantee the origin of their wines. National governments then began to concern themselves more formally with the geographical delimitation of areas of wine production, with the French taking a first step in 1905 towards the creation of a national system of wine control based on the delimitation of areas of origin. Through further laws, most notably those of 1919 and 1927, this eventually culminated in 1935 in the law creating the *appellations d'origine contrôlées* (see AOC).

Numerous systems were also developed in other countries. In GERMANY, for example, the German wine law of 1930 included the use of vineyard names, although the perceived quality of Germany's wines was long based not primarily on geography but on MUST WEIGHTS.

Italian wine laws also include an element of geographical delimitation, as represented in the creation of the *denominazione di origine controllata* (DOC) system in 1963 and more recently in the 1992 legislation with its specific reference to Indicazione Geografica Tipica (IGT).

The precise practical methods of geographical demarcation vary from country to country but are usually based on the compilation of a detailed vineyard register and include varying degrees of political intrigue (see, for example, ROMAGNA ALBANA). Producers wishing to gain a certain status must satisfy regional and national committees as to the quality, origin, and distinction of their wines. One of the most rigorous systems of geographical delimitation is that adopted in France under INAO auspices, which requires that commissions of inquiry examine the relationships between such factors as GEOLOGY, SOILS, TOPOGRAPHY, DRAINAGE, slope, ASPECT, and wine quality. In BURGUNDY, for example, the geological origin of the soils is a determining factor in differentiating the GRAND CRU vineyards.

The central feature of geographical delimitation as it applies to wine is not just that it is intended to lead to improvements in wine quality, thus enabling the wines to be sold at a higher price, but also that it is a legislative procedure whereby a privileged monopolistic position is created for producers within a demarcated area. Whether a given vineyard falls within or outside the legal boundary of a delimited wine region can have important commercial consequences, which is why the much more recent demarcation of America's AVAS, South Africa's WINE OF ORIGIN, and some of AUSTRALIA'S even newer GIs (see GEOGRAPHICAL INDICATION)—many of them based more on political than geographical boundaries—can be such a contentious process.

The creation of geographically delimited areas remains highly controversial.

P.T.H.U. & J.R.

Meloni, G., and Swinnen, J., 'Trade and terroir. The political economy of the world's first geographical indications', *Food Policy*, 81 (2018), 1–20.

Pomerol, C. (ed.), *The Wines and Winelands of France: Geological Journeys* (1989).

Unwin, T., *Wine and the Vine: An Historical Geography of Viticulture and the Wine Trade* (1991).

Delle Venezie, with over 28,000 ha/69,189 acres, is Europe's, and probably the world's, largest denomination devoted to a single grape variety, PINOT GRIGIO. In 2020, 45% of the variety's total global production came from this area alone. With 200 million bottles produced annually, the majority sold abroad, Pinot Grigio delle Venezie has come to stand for a style: fresh, easy, often neutral, and low-priced.

Before its elevation to DOC in 2017, delle Venezie was an IGT allowing for a host of single varieties from the area encompassing FRIULI Venezia Giulia, VENETO, and TRENTINO. Subsequently the IGT was renamed Trevenezie and strictly excluded Pinot Grigio, which became the sole permitted variety of the DOC covering the same area.

The impetus for the change is the loose production regulations of IGTs, which allows for little control, opening up the potential for fraud, such as wines labelled as Pinot Grigio but with little or none of the variety in the bottle. The Delle Venezie DOC was created to increase overall quality, stop prices declining, and create an identity for the variety in Italy's north-west, where it has traditionally been grown.

The recently founded Consorzio delle Venezie tries to draw attention to the fact that Pinot Grigio is not a white but a red variety, traditionally and historically fermented on the skins, resulting in a wine with a light pink-copper hue, called *ramato*, or coppery. With the rise in popularity of so-called NATURAL WINES, this archaic style might become fashionable. W.S.

demi-muid. See BARREL TYPES.

demi-sec, French term meaning 'medium dry' (see SWEETNESS). In practice, the term is used particularly for Chenin Blanc wines in ANJOU-Saumur and TOURAINE. See DOSAGE for official EU sugar levels in SPARKLING WINES.

Denmark. With its far northern LATITUDE, Denmark has a very MARGINAL CLIMATE for winegrowing. CLIMATE CHANGE has helped in the development of a wine industry, as have NEW VARIETIES (HYBRIDS or DISEASE-RESISTANT VARIETIES) such as SOLARIS and Rondo. The country's first commercial vintage was 2001, a year after gaining EU recognition; by 2020 there were around 100 commercial producers, many very small-scale, farming roughly 125 ha/309 acres of vines. Wine is produced in most parts of Denmark and from the country's four PGIs: Jutland, Funen, Zealand, and Bornholm. The country's largest producer, Dyrehøj Vingård, is located in Røsnæs, in the north-western corner of Zealand, where the climate is drier and sunnier than the Danish average. In 2018 Denmark was granted its first (and Europe's most northerly) Protected Designation of Origin (PDO), Dons in East Jutland, for sparkling wines only; Skærsøgaard is its first winery.

A recent speciality of Denmark is fruit wines. Frederiksdal on Lolland are well known for their cherry wines, and Andersen Winery in East Jutland produces sparkling wines from apples, rhubarb, and other fruits.

For the Australian wine region called Denmark, see WESTERN AUSTRALIA. P.L.L.

www.vinavl.dk

Klitgaard J., *Danske Vingaarde (Danish Vineyards)* (2009).

Denominação de Origem Controlada, the name of a CONTROLLED APPELLATION in PORTUGAL, which replaced the earlier Região Demarcarda when Portuguese wine laws were revised for EU entry. For more details, see DOC.

Denominación de Origen, Spanish CONTROLLED APPELLATION. See DO.

Denominación de Origen Calificada, Spain's superior CONTROLLED APPELLATION. See DOCA.

dénomination géographique complémentaire (DGC), meaning 'complementary geographical denomination', bureaucratic French term for a 'subappellation' or a noted subzone within a CONTROLLED APPELLATION, typically a COMMUNE, whose name can be appended to that of an AOC on a wine label, for example Ayze (Savoie Ayze) or Lugny (Mâcon Lugny).

See also CRU and MGA.

Denominazione di Origine Controllata. See DOC.

Denominazione di Origine Controllata e Garantita. See DOCG.

density, a measurement of the concentration of matter in units of mass per unit volume. In wine it is usually expressed as g/cc, and occasionally as g/ml, at 20 °C/68 °F (which must be specified since wine's mass per unit volume decreases as its temperature increases). Wine is an interesting mixture because it contains dissolved solids (SUGARS, ACIDS, PHENOLICS, and MINERAL salts) which increase its density above that of pure water, but it also contains ALCOHOL, which is less dense than water. The result is that very dry wines can have densities near 0.9 g/cc while very sweet wines that are low in alcohol (such as some Italian MOSCATO, for example) can have densities around 1.03 g/cc.

A term closely related to density, and used in technical wine ANALYSIS, is **specific gravity**. The specific gravity is the ratio of the weight or mass of a volume of a liquid to the weight of an equal volume of water. It is thus a pure or unitless number which differs only slightly from density, according to temperature (since the density of water is only exactly 1 g/cc at a temperature of 3.98 °C).

Wine densities are also frequently reported in terms of one of the traditional scales used for measuring the sugar-solution concentrations (see BALLING, BAUMÉ, BRIX, OECHSLE), which also measure wine density but in units other than g/cc. These scales all use different units (see MUST WEIGHT for equivalencies), with Oechsle bearing the most obvious relationship to specific gravity: a MUST with the specific gravity of 1.070, for example, is said to measure 70 °Oechsle. Density is usually measured with a HYDROMETER or mustimeter; while a range of alternative electronic density meters are available, hydrometers are the instrumental standard for this measurement. A.D.W.

deposit. See BOTTLE DEPOSIT and SEDIMENT.

Derenoncourt, Stéphane (1963–), influential, self-taught, now international winemaking CONSULTANT based on Bordeaux's right bank. Originally from the far north of France, he first picked grapes in Fronsac in 1982 and continued as a lowly vineyard worker. He did not make wine until 1990, at Ch Pavie Macquin, and claims that his winemaking philosophy is informed by his experiences in the vineyard, by expressing TERROIR, and by Burgundian sensibilities.

In 1999 with his wife Christine he acquired Domaine de l'A, an estate in CASTILLON. With a team of eight qualified oenologists he advises around 140 estates from vine to wine. About 60 of these estates are on Bordeaux's RIGHT BANK, 30 on the LEFT BANK, and 25 elsewhere in France. Others are in Spain, Portugal, Italy, Austria, Greece, Turkey, Ukraine, Morocco, Lebanon, Syria, Virginia, and California (Inglenook).

derived pigments. See ANTHOCYANINS.

desert, an arid, treeless region. True deserts are not conducive to growing grapes for wine, even where IRRIGATION water is available. Low HUMIDITY and extreme temperature ranges place stresses on the vine which usually preclude good grape quality. With irrigation they can still be very suitable for TABLE GRAPES, especially early-maturing varieties, and for RAISINS, but wine grapes seldom rise above mediocre quality. See CLIMATE AND WINE QUALITY.

Some near-desert regions used extensively for viticulture include the SAN JOAQUIN VALLEY of California; the southern reaches of the Okanagan Valley in BRITISH COLUMBIA; ARGENTINA's Mendoza region; the Bekaa Valley of LEBANON; parts of ISRAEL; AZERBAIJAN on the west coast of the Caspian Sea; parts of northern CHINA; the lower Murray Valley of SOUTH AUSTRALIA and VICTORIA; and the Little Karoo of SOUTH AFRICA. J.G.

dessert wines usually mean SWEET WINES, but according to American regulations any wine between 14 and 24% alcohol is designated a dessert wine, even if dry and unfortified, and attracts a higher tax rate.

DGB, major South African wine producer formed in 1990 by the merger of Douglas Green of Paarl and Union Wines. Important brands include Boschendal, Bellingham, Franschhoek Cellars, and The Old Road Wine Co. Operating only in the bottled wine sector, it accounts for 10% of South African packaged wine exports and 12% share by value of local bottled wine sales. The DGB sourcing model is a combination of three owned vineyards, one rented farm, and 59 managed contract estates totalling 400 selected vineyard blocks. M.F.

destalking. See DESTEMMING.

destemmer-crusher, common combination of winemaking equipment which carries out the operations of both DESTEMMING and CRUSHING, in that order. Historically, crusher-rollers sometimes preceded the destemmer and 'crusher-destemmer' was a better description, but that configuration is now rare (except in small-scale winemaking). S.N.

destemming, the winemaking operation of removing the STEMS, or stalks, from bunches of grapes. It usually takes place immediately before CRUSHING. Grape stems contain TANNINS, which can be leached into the wine during FERMENTATION, making the wine taste HERBACEOUS and/or ASTRINGENT, depending on the variety and how ripe the stems are. Destemming saves space in fermenters and presses, but the inclusion of stems can help dissipate the heat of fermentation and make pressing easier by providing structure to the press cake.

While most grapes are now destemmed, this was not the case historically, and there remain high-profile exceptions to destemming, such as WHOLE-BUNCH PRESSING in CHAMPAGNE, black grapes used for CARBONIC MACERATION in BEAUJOLAIS, and WHOLE-BUNCH FERMENTATION in BURGUNDY and parts of the RHÔNE. Destemming also very slightly increases the resultant colour and ALCOHOLIC STRENGTH because stems, if included, may adsorb pigments and absorb alcohol.

Destemming machines, or **destemmers**, most commonly employ a rotating shaft with paddles that convey and remove the stems from the grapes inside a perforated cylinder. The cylinder has holes that allow grapes but not most stems to fall through; it usually also rotates, just at a slower speed than the paddles. Some newer destemmers work by shaking the grapes from the stems rather than by rotary movement, which can be a more gentle process. Destemmers with oscillating cups rather than a rotating shaft are particularly effective in excluding the stems. Often the destemmer is accompanied by a set of crusher rollers (that can be bypassed if desired), and the combined device is known as a DESTEMMER-CRUSHER.

Destemming can now also often be performed on machine harvesters. MECHANICAL HARVESTING has always resulted in partial destemming as some grapes are shaken from the vine without their stems, but the complete destemming of grapes on machine-harvesters is a newer phenomenon. It is sometimes accompanied by an on-harvester mechanical SORTING system.

A very few producers destem by hand, thereby keeping the berries whole. The gentler handling is very time-consuming, but proponents believe it results in improved wine quality. S.N.

desuckering, the common viticultural practice of removing unwanted young shoots, known as suckers or WATER SHOOTS, that grow from latent buds. On the vine TRUNK, suckers grow mostly on the lower part, from either the ROOTSTOCK or SCION, and in the HEAD of the vine. Varieties differ in their production of water shoots; GEWÜRZTRAMINER, for example, produces many. The operation is carried out in spring, several weeks after BUDBREAK, when the water shoots are 10–15 cm/4–6 in long. The work is relatively tiresome, as for many vineyards the shoots can be near the ground, although shoots can be removed from trunks mechanically by mounting on the front of a tractor a rotating cylinder with rubber straps attached. HERBICIDES are also used. If the vine is thought to be infected with TRUNK DISEASE, some suckers should be retained as part of the process of TRUNK RENEWAL.

When desuckering is carried out on CORDON-trained vines, it may be termed SHOOT THINNING. R.E.S.

Deutsche means 'German', thus **Deutscher** Wein is what appears on the labels of Germany's WINE WITHOUT GEOGRAPHICAL INDICATION (once called Tafelwein); **Deutscher Sekt** is a SEKT or sparkling wine made in Germany from German fruit; and the **Deutsche Weinstrasse** is a famous wine route through Germany's PFALZ region.

dew, water which condenses on objects, such as leaves, when the air in immediate contact with them is cooled below dew point, the temperature at which the air becomes fully saturated by its current content of water vapour (see HUMIDITY). Dew contributes little directly to the water supply of the vine. However, the latent heat of vaporization that is released during condensation plays a positive role by slowing night-time temperature drop. The risk of FROST is appreciably reduced when the air contains enough water vapour to result in dew.

Dew has a major (mostly unfavourable) impact on the incidence of VINE DISEASES. It provides the necessary conditions for spore germination and the establishment of several fungal-disease organisms, most notably those for DOWNY MILDEW, BLACK ROT, and the malevolent form of botrytis bunch rot, GREY ROT, even in the absence of wetting rain.

See CLIMATE AND WINE QUALITY and TOPOGRAPHY. J.G.

DGC. See DÉNOMINATION GÉOGRAPHIQUE COMPLÉMENTAIRE.

diacetyl, a product of MALOLACTIC CONVERSION with a powerful butterscotch or butter aroma. The ability to detect diacetyl depends on its concentration and the wine type and style. The perception threshold varies from 0.2 mg/l for Chardonnay to 0.9 mg/l for Pinot Noir to 2.8 mg/l for Cabernet Sauvignon. At low concentrations, it may be perceived as nutty or toasty and add desirable complexity. In excess, as was once common in NEW WORLD Chardonnays, it is perceived as distractingly obvious butteriness, masking fruit flavours. The amount of diacetyl produced depends on the bacterial strain and the rate of progress of the malolactic conversion as well as temperature, oxygen availability, the wine's pH, SULFUR DIOXIDE content, and, importantly, CITRIC ACID concentrations. P.J.W.

Bartowsky, E. J., and Henschke, P. A., 'The "buttery" attribute of wine—diacetyl—desirability, spoilage and beyond', *International Journal of Food Microbiology*, 96 (2004), 235–52.

Diageo, the world's largest alcoholic drinks company, is now very, very much more interested in spirits than wine—and in BRANDS above all else. Its London fine-wine merchant Justerini & Brooks is somewhat anomalous but earns a Royal Warrant.

diammonium phosphate, or **DAP**, common YEAST nutrient added during FERMENTATION. Research has shown that it not only encourages fermentation but that appropriate addition may also result in the production of complex compounds and ESTERS that make wines taste more fruity and floral. The current EU limit is 1 g/l, and 0.3 g/l for the second fermentation of SPARKLING WINE.

Torrea, D., et al., 'Comparison of inorganic and organic nitrogen supplementation of grape juice—effect on volatile composition and aroma profile of a Chardonnay wine fermented with *Saccharomyces cerevisiae* yeast', *Food Chemistry*, 127 (2011), 1072–83.

Diamond Mountain, California AVA on the north-western edge of the NAPA Valley.

diatomaceous earth (DE), once widely used in FILTRATION, is a naturally occurring, highly porous, chalky textured sedimentary rock made mainly of silica and consisting of fossilized remains of diatoms, a type of hard-shelled algae. It is also known as Kieselguhr. Because of increasing concerns about potential health hazards and safe disposal of used DE, it is now frequently replaced by cross-flow filtration.

Die, town between the RHÔNE Valley and the Alps (see map under FRANCE) whose name features in the **Clairette de Die** and **Crémant de Die** sparkling-wine appellations and **Coteaux de Die**, a light, still, dry white wine made from

CLAIRETTE grapes. According to PLINY, the local tribe in Roman times, the Voconces, made a sparkling sweet wine and practised an early form of TEMPERATURE CONTROL by plunging barrels full of fermenting must into the river. Most wines are sparkling, and many of them are sweet and grapey. For more information, see CLAIRETTE DE DIE, CRÉMANT, and CHÂTILLON-EN-DIOIS.

diet, wine as part of. Some medical research suggests that wine may be drunk for dietary reasons. Wine contains various VITAMINS and MINERALS but in such small concentrations that, for them to make any sufficient contribution to the human diet, excessive amounts of ALCOHOL would also have to be ingested. 'Moderate' wine consumption has been shown to have a beneficial effect for several medical conditions, however, and wine consumption clearly plays a part in the much-vaunted **Mediterranean diet** (see HEALTH).

No wine is 'slimming', but dry DE-ALCOHOLIZED WINE is usually lower in calories than most.

In Mediterranean countries, before there was a ready supply of safe drinking WATER it was natural to drink wine because it was abundant and relatively cheap. But wine forms part of our diet for reasons beyond necessity or ease of access.

The concept of maintaining good health through diet can be traced back to ancient GREECE and the Greek Hippocrates, in particular, although wine was included in the dietary laws of Moses 1,000 years earlier.

As late as the 1860s, doctors were still matching wines to lifestyles, as they would be termed today. For example, Dr Robert Druitt suggested CLARET 'for children, for literary persons, and for all those whose occupations are chiefly carried on indoors'. The fuller-bodied wines of BURGUNDY, the MIDI, and GREECE he considered better suited to manual workers. H.B. & J.R.

Corder, R., *The Red Wine Diet* (2007).
Johnson, H., *The Story of Wine: From Noah to Now* (2020).
Newman, C., *The White Wine Diet* (2004).

Dijon, capital of BURGUNDY and the focus of the region's vinous ACADEME, the Institut Universitaire de la Vigne et du Vin (IUVV) Jules Guyot in the Université de Bourgogne. In 1856 the scholar Claude Ladrey, friend of Louis PASTEUR, started a course in Dijon that applied chemistry to VITICULTURE and OENOLOGY. In 1901, the institute was founded, awarding its first higher diploma in oenological studies in 1909. Endowed with an experimental vineyard in MARSANNAY (3.6 ha/9 acres) since 1917, the institute is now internationally recognized for teaching and research in both viticulture and oenology.

Dijon offers the fifth-year Diplôme National d'Oenologue; two master's degrees (Vine, Wine, Terroir and Fermentation Processes for the Food Industry); three bachelor's degrees (Vine Science, Marketing of Wine and Oenotourism, and Strategic Management of the Vitivinicultural Operation); and three university diplomas in continuing education (Practical Oenology, Wine, Culture and Oenotourism, and Learn and Understand Wine Tasting). Research concentrates on five main areas: grapevine immunity, the impact of CLIMATE CHANGE, microbiology, physical chemistry, and sensory analysis. The UNESCO chair of Culture and Traditions of Wine and the Burgundy Vine and Wine cluster are hosted at the IUVV Jules Guyot. Humanities and Social Sciences also contribute to the research advances in vitculture and wine at the university.

Certain CLONES of CHARDONNAY and PINOT NOIR clones such as 115 and 777, imported from Burgundy, are sometimes known as **Dijon clones**. R.D.G.

iuvv.u-bourgogne.fr

Dimyat, also spelt **Dimiat**, BULGARIA's widely planted white INDIGENOUS VARIETY whose total area stood at 7,914 ha/9,556 acres in 2021, a considerable increase over the previous decade. It is grown mainly in the east and south of Bulgaria, where it is regarded as a producer of perfumed everyday whites of varying levels of sweetness but usefully dependable quality. The vines yield copper-coloured grapes in great quantity. The wines should be consumed young and cool. DNA PROFILING has shown Dimyat to be the offspring of GOUAIS BLANC and Coarnă Albă and to be a parent of CABERNET SEVERNY and others. It is the same as Serbia's SMEDEREVKA.

dining clubs, private societies of like-minded individuals who meet over meals. A high proportion of what are called dining clubs are in fact wining clubs, devoted to the consumption and discussion of fine wines. See also SAINTSBURY.

Dionysus, the classical god of wine, for whom 'Bacchus' was the more common name among the Romans. However, grapes and vines are not his only attributes, and neither is wine the only aspect of his cult.

Although some scholars have argued that wine is a secondary element in his cult and that the god Dionysus was a late importation from the East, he is a wine god, an Olympian, and an important influence on ancient GREECE. The earliest festival known to be devoted to Dionysus, the three-day feast of the Anthesteria, is a wine festival. It gives its name to the spring month of Anthesterion and celebrates the broaching of the new wine (the wine of the most recent vintage, which was always kept until the next spring). Clay tablets dating from the late Bronze Age (*c.*1200 BCE) connect Dionysus with wine and thus provide further evidence for the early cult of Dionysus as a wine god.

Dionysus has been taken to be a non-Greek because he is a god of epiphanies. He appears suddenly, from outside, to strike people with madness, most famously represented in Euripides' tragedy *The Bacchae* (probably written shortly after 408 BCE), about Dionysiac frenzy. Although the play praises Dionysus for his gift of wine which lessens the cares of mortals, the madness that he brings is not the result of excessive consumption of wine.

The essence of the cult of Dionysus is the surrender of personal identity. Hence one of Dionysus' symbols is the mask, and he is often depicted in vase paintings of drinking ceremonies as a mask set up on a column draped in cloth. His other attributes are the thyrsus, a tall stick with a bunch of ivy leaves on top—ivy because it is evergreen and produces its berries in the winter, when the mountain ritual takes place and the vine is bare. He is also depicted with grapes or a wine cup; often he takes on an effeminate appearance with long flowing locks. He is frequently equated (especially by HERODOTUS in the 5th century BCE) with the Egyptian god Osiris.

One well-known myth about Dionysus concerns the invention of wine. Dionysus discloses the secret of winemaking to the peasant Icarius and his daughter Erigone, with whom he had lodged as a guest, in return for their hospitality. Obedient to the god's command to teach the art to other people, Icarius shares his wine with a group of shepherds. At first they enjoy this delicious new drink, but as the unaccustomed wine overwhelms them they begin to suspect Icarius of having poisoned them. So they turn on him and batter him to death with their clubs. For a time his body cannot be found, but eventually Icarius' faithful dog Moera leads Erigone to the spot where he lies buried. Erigone hangs herself in despair. However, in death they receive their due rewards: Icarius becomes the star Boötes, his daughter the constellation Virgo, and Moera becomes Canis, or Sirius, the dog star. Boötes, also known in Greek as 'the grape-gatherer', rises in the autumn, at the time of the vintage, and in the warm climate of Greece the vintage may well have taken place some time before the autumnal equinox, still under the constellation of Virgo. It is also interesting to note that PLINY the Elder recommends the rising of the dog star, 2 August, as the day when wine jars should receive their inside coating of RESIN to make them airtight in readiness for the vintage.

Dionysus is a god who strives against reason, calm, and order. As such he is a god of the people, dangerous and subversive to those in authority. His cult attracts further suspicion because it is surrounded by secrecy.

D

Gradually Dionysiac orgies appear to have become orgies in the modern sense, and among the Romans the cult of Dionysus was a disreputable affair. Livy gives a lurid account of the banning of the Bacchanalia, but it should not be forgotten that Livy was a historian of conservative tendencies, an admirer of Augustus, who lamented what he considered to be the recent slide into luxury and immorality. Bacchus certainly played little part in the official religion of ancient ROME; he was too dangerous a god. Among the Romans he survives in a sanitized version: jolly Bacchus the wine god, giver of wine and bringer of joy, who makes sorrow bearable. Satyrs and nymphs gambol about him harmlessly, and Silenus is a cheerful old soak. This is the Bacchus that survived into the Renaissance, familiar from the pictures of Titian and his contemporaries. The Romans reduced the complex god of the Greeks to little more than wine personified. H.M.W.

Burkert, W., *Griechische Religion der archaischen und klassischen Epoche* (1977), translated by J. Raffan as *Greek Religion* (1985).

Carpenter, T. H., *Dionysian Imagery in Archaic Greek Art* (1986).

Dalby, A., *Bacchus. A Biography* (2003).

Seaford, R., *Dionysus* (2006).

Wilson, H., *Wine and Words in Classical Antiquity and the Middle Ages* (2003).

direct producer, term used for a group of vines, also known as FRENCH HYBRIDS, bred from the late 19th century onwards in an effort to combine the pest and disease resistance of AMERICAN VINE SPECIES with the desirable fruit characters of the European VITIS VINIFERA species. They are called direct producers, and sometimes hybrid direct producers, or HDPs, because, unlike *vinifera* VINE VARIETIES, they do not need GRAFTING on to PHYLLOXERA-tolerant ROOTSTOCKS. They are not all sufficiently phylloxera-tolerant, however, and added soil stresses such as DROUGHT or WEEDS can see them weakened by phylloxera. R.E.S.

direct shipping, cause célèbre in the US, which banned shipping of wine direct from winery to consumer until a seminal Supreme Court decision in 2005 liberalized direct shipments into some states yet allowed others to keep their borders closed to wine shipments from out of state. See UNITED STATES, regulations, for more detail of this bypassing of the notorious THREE-TIER SYSTEM.

disease-resistant varieties, semantically expedient term for grapevines introduced by the German Bundessortenamt (Plant Variety Rights Office) in 1995 that were bred specifically to produce wines that taste like those made from VITIS VINIFERA yet meet consumer demands for reductions in AGROCHEMICAL use by incorporating some non-*vinifera* genes for resistance to various common VINE DISEASES. The term replaces the previously pejorative terms 'HYBRIDS' or 'interspecific hybrids' for some of their most promising results of VINE BREEDING and acknowledges the substantial progress achieved in recent decades. The German term is *Pilzwiderstandsfähige Rebsorten*, often abbreviated to PiWi.

There had been substantial bias against such new varieties, especially those including genes from AMERICAN VINE SPECIES, because of historical associations with poor wine quality and FOXY flavours. The bureaucratic hurdle of the EU's former ban on non-*vinifera* vines for QUALITY WINE (designed initially to exclude the earlier AMERICAN HYBRIDS and FRENCH HYBRIDS, though lifted in 2021) was bypassed by classifying these new disease-resistant varieties as *Vitis vinifera* subspecies *vinifera*.

PHOENIX, the product of BACCHUS and VILLARD Blanc, was the first variety so registered (in 1992), and other German-bred varieties such as REGENT, Merzling, RONDO, Bronner, Johanniter, Prinzipal, Saphira, and SOLARIS have followed, all registered as *Vitis vinifera*. Thanks to this creative taxonomy, which is based on morphological characteristics, these disease-resistant varieties can be grown for quality-wine production, though they still have to be registered for such in any given EU region. The Swiss are very proud of their new variety DIVICO. Five new PIERCE'S DISEASE-resistant varieties (whites Ambulo Blanc and Caminante Blanc and reds Camminare Noir, Errante Noir, and Paseante Noir) were released from the UC DAVIS grape-breeding programme in 2019. INRAE's ResDur programme in France has resulted in the release of several new varieties resistant to POWDERY MILDEW and DOWNY MILDEW (see NEW VARIETIES). R.K.C.T. & M.A.W.

Basler, P., and Scherz, R., *PIWI-Rebsorten: Pilzwiderstandsfähige Rebsorten* (2011).

CDFA, *Pierce's Disease Research Symposium Proceedings*, www.cdfa.ca.gov/pdcp/research.html.

Schneider, C., et al., 'INRA-ResDur: the French grapevine breeding programme for durable resistance to downy and powdery mildew', *Acta Horticulturae*, 1248 (2019), 207–14.

diseases, vine. See VINE DISEASES and individual diseases.

disgorgement, or **dégorgement** in French, an integral stage in the TRADITIONAL METHOD of sparkling winemaking entailing the removal of a pellet of frozen sediment from the neck of each bottle. For more detail and alternative techniques, see SPARKLING WINEMAKING.

Distell, dominant wine and spirits producer in the SOUTH AFRICAN market and the ninth largest wine company by volume in the world, acquired by brewers Heineken in 2021. Formed in 2000 from the merger of Stellenbosch Farmers Winery and Distillers Corporation, it focuses on such commercial brands as Chateau Libertas, Grand Mousseux, and Tassenberg and had reduced its vineyard holdings to 620 ha/ 1,532 acres by 2021.

It enjoys 40% by value of the country's domestic wine business and over 80% of the domestic brandy trade but only around 17% of wine exports. M.F.

distillation, the separation of the constituents of a liquid mixture by partial vaporization of the mixture and the separate recovery of the vapour and the residue. When applied to wine (or any other fermented liquid), the result is a considerably stronger alcoholic liquid: brandy in the case of wine and other fermented fruit juices; calvados in the case of certain apples from northern France; and whisky in the case of fermented barley.

distillation, compulsory. In an effort to curb, and dispose of, SURPLUS wine production, the EU authorities instituted a system in 1982 whereby any wine produced over a certain limit should theoretically be compulsorily bought, at a standard and not-too-attractive price, and distilled into industrial ALCOHOL (resulting, perhaps inevitably, in an alcohol surplus). Average annual quantities distilled under this scheme in the 1980s were well over 30 million hl/790 million gal, or about one-fifth of total European production. In 1993 the European Commission admitted that the scheme had done little to curb over-production; it announced stricter measures designed to offer less financial support to over-producers and to curb abuse of the system. Between 1993 and 1996, the amount distilled was reduced to about 10% of production, but the Commission decided to crack down. In 1998 it introduced a 'crisis distillation' measure which was intended to deal only with exceptional cases of market disturbance and serious quality problems but continued to play an important part in the European wine market. Following further reforms of the common market organization (CMO) for wine in 1999, distillation was 'no longer an obligatory measure in the event of serious wine market crises', and it could be applied to QUALITY WINE. An EU report published in 2002 concluded that distillation was not an efficient way of eliminating structural surpluses and suggested alternative measures such as paying growers a premium for CROP THINNING. Compulsory distillation was finally phased out in 2013 as a result of the wide-ranging 2008 reforms to the CMO. However, in 2014 Spain decided to distil 4 million hl (106 million gallons) to try to balance its own surplus.

The arrival of COVID-19 in 2020 and the associated closures and restrictions imposed on the hospitality sector to restrict its spread represented a grave threat to the EU wine sector. In order to preserve producers' incomes and avoid a massive surplus of unsold wine, the EU introduced support measures including allowing member states to once again fund crisis distillation—a measure that was enthusiastically taken up by some members. J.E.H & J.P.H.B.

diurnal temperature range, or **diurnal temperature variation**, the range in temperatures from the high during the day to the low during the night, also called thermal amplitude or diurnal swing. It is mainly influenced by the HUMIDITY of a region: lower humidity produces higher daytime temperatures and lower night-time temperatures, while regions with higher humidity see lower daytime temperatures and higher night-time temperatures. Regions at higher ELEVATIONS also experience greater diurnal temperature ranges. A high diurnal temperature range is often considered most important during RIPENING because moderately high daytime temperatures foster sugar development, while cool nights slow down maturation, preserve aromas, and retain ACIDITY in the grapes, resulting in greater freshness in the wines.

See also TEMPERATURE VARIABILITY. J.V.G.

Divico, red grapevine HYBRID created at CHANGINS by Jean-Laurent Spring from GAMARET and Bronner, released in 2013 and spreading quickly in Switzerland (66 ha/163 acres in 2020) thanks in part to its resistance to the major FUNGAL DISEASES. Wines typically have fine tannins, aromas of blueberries, and a slightly bitter finish. J.V.

divided canopy, group of vine-TRAINING SYSTEMS which involve separation of a leaf CANOPY into two or more subcanopies, sometimes called curtains. The expression was popularized by Professor Nelson SHAULIS in the 1960s and 1970s as part of his pioneering promotion of CANOPY MANAGEMENT. One of the most important divided-canopy training systems is the GENEVA DOUBLE CURTAIN developed by Shaulis. The LYRE, SCOTT HENRY, and SMART-DYSON are more recent developments. The advantage of canopy division is that it increases the surface area of the canopy that is exposed to SUNLIGHT, while reducing canopy SHADE. Both yield and wine quality can increase as a result. R.E.S.

DMDC (dimethyl dicarbonate), often known by its US trade name Velcorin, is a sterilant used to eliminate the risk of microbial spoilage. For red wines, it is particularly useful in preventing BRETTANOMYCES growth in bottle. For other wines with some RESIDUAL SUGAR, it is used more generally for microbial stability. DMDC is short-lived in wine and works by deactivating ENZYMES in the spoilage microorganism to rapidly kill cells, even at low concentrations (<50 mg/l for *Brettanomyces* in wine). Any remaining DMDC breaks down in the wine within 1–2 days, to produce small amounts of CARBON DIOXIDE and METHANOL. This PROCESSING AID is currently approved in the United States, South Africa, Australia, and New Zealand for use in the production of dry wines and in the EU for wines with at least 5 g/l residual sugar. The maximum limit in the EU, the US, and Australia, also recommended by the OIV, is 200 mg/l. While it was originally developed for commercial wines, it has been accepted more widely for higher-quality wines. J.E.H. & A.B.

DNA profiling, also known as **DNA typing**, **DNA fingerprinting**, or **DNA testing**, allows the unequivocal identification of any living individual. This technique was developed in 1985 in forensic science to confound criminals; it was first applied to grape CULTIVARS in 1993 by Australian researchers. Since a grape variety is made of CLONES reproduced asexually by VEGETATIVE PROPAGATION, it is genetically comparable to a human individual. The identification technique is based on small pieces of variable DNA called molecular markers, the most successful using repetitive pieces of DNA called **microsatellites**. They exist in any living organism, and their length varies from one individual to another. Analysis of 8 to 12 microsatellites is enough to obtain a unique 'genetic identity card', looking like a supermarket barcode, for every variety. This technique, for which data exchanges between laboratories is relatively easy, allowed, for example, identification of the enigmatic PETITE SIRAH in California and solved the long-standing mystery of ZINFANDEL's identity.

DNA profiling technique complements classical AMPELOGRAPHY and offers the advantage of unambiguously identifying grape varieties (as well as ROOTSTOCKS) from any part of the plant, (except seeds, which are already progenies), independently of the factors potentially influencing the vine's morphology that can mislead ampelographers, such as environmental conditions (e.g. DROUGHT), the development stage (e.g. woody canes used for trading, often impossible to identify visually) or sanitary state (e.g. viruses). There are between 5,000 and 10,000 grape cultivars in the world, for which about 24,000 names have been recorded; thus the same grape often has several names (synonyms) in different regions. Inversely, the same name can be used for several distinct varieties (homonyms). DNA profiling can be very helpful in correcting misnomers and detecting synonyms (e.g. Zinfandel and Primitivo) and homonyms (e.g. the REFOSCO group), and thus it is useful in managing important ampelographic collections. The development of affordable whole-genome sequencing and SNV (single-nucleotide variation) genotyping techniques allowed the discrimination of clones (in this case of Nebbiolo) for the first time in 2017, opening the door for future research.

Microsatellites follow the laws of heredity: half of them come from the mother and half of them come from the father. Much like paternity testing in humans, by looking at a high number of microsatellites (30 to 50) it is possible with DNA profiling to reconstruct the parentage of a variety when both parents are still available. Researchers Carole Meredith and John Bowers at DAVIS were the first to uncover an unexpected parentage in 1997 when they surprised the whole wine world by announcing that CABERNET SAUVIGNON is the result of a (probably spontaneous) CROSS between Cabernet Franc and Sauvignon Blanc. Later on, in collaboration with Jean-Michel Boursiquot at MONTPELLIER, they revealed additional unexpected parentages such as those of CHARDONNAY and GAMAY (both in 1999) and SYRAH (in 2000). Many additional parentages have since been discovered by these and other scientists around the world, including those of SANGIOVESE, MERLOT, and TEMPRANILLO.

DNA profiling has also been used to correctly ascertain the varietal identity of fresh and dried grapes as well as the varietal origin of FREE-RUN juice.

Through DNA profiling, parent–offspring pairs can also be determined when one parent is missing, though it is impossible to infer the direction of the relationship. Pedigree reconstruction makes available unprecedented information about history and migrations of grape cultivars, providing a better understanding of the genetic events that led to today's range of cultivars. The largest pedigree that appears in Robinson, Harding, and Vouillamoz's *Wine Grapes* groups no fewer than 156 European wine grape varieties that are linked by parent–offspring relationships.

However, the 'holy grail' of reconstructing the exhaustive genealogical tree of all existing cultivars will almost certainly never be attained, since many parents have disappeared because of FROST, pests (e.g. PHYLLOXERA), or lack of interest. J.V.

Bowers, J. E., and Meredith, C. P., 'The parentage of a classic wine grape, Cabernet Sauvignon', *Nature Genetics*, 16/1 (1997), 84–7.

Robinson, J., et al., *Wine Grapes: A Complete Guide to 1,368 Vine Varieties, Including Their Origins and Flavours* (2012).

Thomas, M. R., et al., 'Repetitive DNA of grapevine: classes present and sequences suitable for cultivar identification', *Theoretical and Applied Genetics*, 86 (1993), 173–80.

Sefc, K. M., et al., 'Microsatellite markers for grapevine: tools for cultivar identification and pedigree reconstruction', in K. A. Roubelakis-Angelakis (ed.), *Grapevine Molecular Physiology and Biotechnology* (2nd edn, 2009), 565–96.

DO stands for Denominación de Origen, the name of Spain's PDO denomination, which is now widely called DOP, Denominación de Origen Protegida.

doble pasta, dark, full-bodied Spanish wine produced by running off a proportion of fermenting must after two days and adding more crushed grapes to refill the vat. The ratio of skin to pulp is effectively doubled, producing wines with a deep, black colour and very high levels of TANNIN. Doble pasta wines have traditionally been made in JUMILLA, YECLA, UTIEL-REQUENA, MANCHUELA, and ALICANTE, where they are used for blending, but they are being superseded by GRAPE CONCENTRATE. R.J.M.

DOC, initials which stand for Denominação de Origem Controlada in PORTUGAL and Denominazione di Origine Controllata in ITALY, those countries' PDO denomination for superior wines.

A DOC system has also been in operation in ROMANIA since 1975.

Denominação de Origem Controlada

In Portugal, DOC stands for Denominação de Origem Controlada. An alternative term, Denominação de Origem Protegida (DOP), is also available, having been introduced after the EU wine market reforms of 2008. On joining the EU in 1986, Portugal undertook revision of its wine laws to bring them into line with those of other European countries, most notably France. Each of the regions which had already been designated a REGIÃO DEMARCADA (RD) in earlier legislation (BUCELAS, CARCAVELOS, COLARES, DÃO, MADEIRA, SETÚBAL, VINHO VERDE, BAIRRADA, and DOURO) were subsequently designated as DOCs. The system equates roughly with the French AOC and sets out permitted grape varieties, maximum yields, periods of ageing in BULK and bottle, and analytical standards for specified types of wine. Samples must be submitted to the local body controlling that region's wine industry, who grant numbered seals of origin to producers whose wines have satisfied the regulations.

See VINHO REGIONAL (VR) for the denomination below DOC/DOP.

Denominazione di Origine Controllata

Italy's PDO denomination has had a chequered history. Italian wine was first regulated systematically in 1963 in an effort to bring Italy's wine laws into line with those of fellow EU founding nation France. A few of Italy's most famous wines had already been given legal recognition and protection in the 1930s, but this new system was designed to be much more comprehensive and modelled on France's AOC. This meant that individual production zones were DELIMITED; permitted VINE VARIETIES specified, often with specific percentages; levels of ALCOHOL, TOTAL ACIDITY, and EXTRACT were established; and limits, often very generously, placed on YIELDS. Viticultural and winemaking practices were regulated, albeit often in the haziest of terms: 'in conformity with existing practices' or 'so as to not change the nature of the wine' are frequent phrases in the DOC rules. As in the case of the French archetype, this system was set up to protect wine regions against COUNTERFEIT products and imitations, but it has often seemed more concerned with enshrining in law existing practice than in optimizing QUALITY IN WINE, a consequence of forcing Italy's radically different situation into a foreign model.

Towards the end of the 1970s, ambitious producers, particularly those in the CHIANTI CLASSICO zone, became disillusioned with DOC rules which required them to include white wine grapes in their red wines and began to label their best wines with the lowest category VINO DA TAVOLA (see SUPERTUSCANS). See also DOCG, a category designed to be superior to DOC.

In an attempt to correct this confusing situation, the DOC system was overhauled in 1992. Its main innovations were to allow DOC zones to be broken down into subzones, townships, hamlets, microzones, individual estates, and vineyards and to give the entire structure a vertical and hierarchical basis; the smaller the geographical unit, the stricter the production limits and criteria. Producers wishing to use a single-vineyard name for their DOC and DOCG wines had to register their vineyard and define its extent with the authorities, a reform aimed at curbing the multiplication of invented single-vineyard names (following the Italian FASHION for individual CRUS) with no real territorial basis. While many of these reforms were sensible and well-intentioned, the excessively generous yields of most DOCs were rarely curbed.

The perceived lack of flexibility in permitted grape varieties was also reversed when all but a handful of DOC regulations expanded to allow a broad range of grape varieties, almost always INTERNATIONAL VARIETIES. Perversely, this altered some of Italy's most distinctive wines beyond recognition (see BRUNELLO DI MONTALCINO, for example). This liberalization and GLOBALIZATION came at a time when interest in INDIGENOUS VARIETIES and authentic, TERROIR-driven Italian wine began to grow rapidly.

In the past the failure of the DOC system was evidenced by the fact that by the 1990s DOC wine represented only one-third of the potential production of vineyards designated DOC. While in the last decade Italian wine production overall has declined, 45% of all Italian wine was DOC in 2020, and there were 331 DOCs, 76 DOCGs, and 118 IGTs. The introduction of the EU reforms to the common market organization (CMO) for wine, which came into force in 2008, required all EU member states to register all denominations by the end of 2011; after that date, any changes would need to be approved by the EU rather than by individual member states. This prompted Italy to rush to create and elevate DOCs, resulting in some that exist on paper only or were created purely out of commercial opportunism, such as DOCs Venezia (see VENICE) and ROMA. W.S.

Belfrage, N., *Life Beyond Lambrusco: Understanding Italian Fine Wine* (1985), 44–51.

DOCa, Denominación de Origen Calificada, is a step up from DO/DOP in SPAIN, reserved for regions complying with certain conditions including above-average grape prices and stringent quality controls. RIOJA was the first Spanish region to be awarded DOCa status, in 1991, followed by PRIORAT in 2000.

doce, Portuguese for 'sweet'. See SWEETNESS and, for official EU sugar levels, DOSAGE.

DOCG stands for Denominazione di Origine Controllata e Garantita, a legal category established in ITALY in 1963 for its highest-quality wines, at the same time as its DOC was created as an Italian version of the French AOC system. The express purpose of this category was to identify and reward the finest Italian wines, which were to be 'guaranteed' (the G) and not merely 'controlled'. The 'guarantee' consists of a laboratory analysis of, among other aspects, the wine's minimum extract, as well as a panel tasting.

If the DOC system did not enjoy general credibility because it was eventually applied liberally and with little rigour, the DOCG title, in contrast, was conferred with admirable parsimony in its first years of existence. It was not even used until 1980; by 1992, when the DOC system was overhauled by law 164, only 11 wines had been deemed worthy of receiving the honour. The first five DOCGs to be conferred were BAROLO, BARBARESCO, CHIANTI, BRUNELLO DI MONTALCINO, and VINO NOBILE DI MONTEPULCIANO, the last of which was the first to be elevated, after having applied as early as 1969. The awarding of DOCG status to ROMAGNA ALBANA in 1986, however, was widely regarded as political in inspiration—a violation of both the letter and spirit of law 930 and, as such, a threat to the viability of the DOCG category itself. It met with such criticism that it was hoped the backlash would have prevented repetition of such an episode.

The authorities nevertheless found themselves in a similar situation with the approval of DOCG for SOAVE, which, while merited in part of the zone, turned into a series of political compromises rather than a coherent attempt to define that which represents the best of Soave. By 2021 there were 76 DOCG wines, many created since the EU reforms of 2008. Several of the new DOCGs make sense, such as Amarone della Valpolicella, but many are likely to create confusion or trigger incredulity, notably elevations of Superiore or Riserva versions within an existing DOC, such as Bardolino Superiore and Verdicchio dei Castelli di Jesi Riserva, since these suffixes have so far proved unable to guarantee superior quality. In the past, the greatest successes of DOCG have been to decrease YIELDS and promote an image of quality, but the all-too-frequent cases in which the elevation has not involved stricter production rules has diluted their significance. W.S.

doctors of medicine through the ages have displayed an uncommon affection for wine, and not just because of wine's uses as a MEDICINE and beneficial effects on HEALTH. Doctors have long been enthusiastic wine consumers (see Alexander HENDERSON, for example), collectors, and, more recently, producers. There are numerous examples of vineyard owners who combine viticulture with practising medicine. Docteur Peste's slice of the CORTON vineyard is sold each year in the HOSPICES DE BEAUNE auction, itself a medical charity, for example. The MOSEL in Germany has an example of what might be called double-doctoring, in that the producer Dr Thanisch owns a portion of the world-famous Doctor, or Doktor, vineyard of Bernkastel.

Particularly strong medical connections can be traced in the history of AUSTRALIAN wine. During the transport of convicts and subsequent migrant trade of the 19th century, doctors became accustomed to using wine as medicine, and many established their own vineyards on settling in Australia. More than 160 such cases can be cited, including the founders of what were long Australia's three largest wine companies—Hardys, Lindemans, and Penfolds—as well as those of labels such as Angove, Houghton, Stanley, and Minchinbury. Australia was founded in the rum age, developed in the beer age, and is now maturing in the wine age.

See also LITERATURE OF WINE. J.R. & P.A.N.

Norrie, P. A., 'Australia's three leading wine doctors', *Journal of Medical Biography*, 3 (1995), 218–24.

Dogliani, DOCG immediately south of BAROLO in Italy's Piemonte region devoted to DOLCETTO, but under threat of being largely replaced with the much more profitable NEBBIOLO for the production of LANGHE Nebbiolo. W.S.

dolce, Italian for 'sweet'. See SWEETNESS and, for official EU sugar levels, DOSAGE.

Dolceacqua, or **Rossese di Dolceacqua**, wine from the north-western coast of Italy. For more details, see ROSSESE and LIGURIA.

Dolcetto, an early-ripening, deep-coloured, low-acid red grape variety cultivated almost exclusively in the provinces of Cuneo and Alessandria in the north-west Italian region of PIEMONTE. The wines produced are soft, round, fruity, and fragrant with flavours of liquorice and almonds. Most are designed to be drunk in their first two or three years, although well-made bottles of Dolcetto d'Alba and Dolcetto d'Ovada can easily last at least five years. Dolcetto therefore plays an important role in the economy of various estates, providing a product which can be marketed early while the wines based on BARBERA or, particularly, NEBBIOLO grapes demand extended ageing in cask and bottle. Unlike Barbera, Dolcetto is rarely blended with other varieties, chiefly because it is so rarely planted outside VARIETALLY-minded Piemonte.

As a precocious ripener, ripening up to four weeks before the majestic Nebbiolo, Dolcetto also permits growers to exploit either higher or less favourably exposed vineyard sites and thus maximize the return on their holdings. In the precious BAROLO and BARBARESCO zones, for example, Dolcetto is rarely planted on a south-facing site unless the vineyard is too high to ripen Nebbiolo reliably. And in the zones of Dogliani, Diano d'Alba, and Ovada, Dolcetto is planted where other varieties may not ripen at all. There is a consensus among growers in the Dolcetto d'Alba DOC, source of much of the finest Dolcetto, that the variety prefers the characteristic white MARLS of the right bank of the Tanaro and cannot give maximum results in heavier soils.

The grape is relatively easy to cultivate, apart from its susceptibility to FUNGAL DISEASES and a tendency to drop its bunches in the cold mornings of late September; but it is far from easy to vinify. While low in ACIDITY, relative to Barbera at least, and therefore *dolce* (sweet) to the Piemontese palate, Dolcetto ('little sweet one') does have significant TANNINS, which producers have learned to soften with shorter fermentations. So rich are the skins of Dolcetto in ANTHOCYANINS that even the shortest fermentation rarely compromises the deep ruby and purple tones of the wine. Like Barbera, it is prone to REDUCTION. Because it is generally vinified early and fast (to make way for Barbera and Nebbiolo in the winery), most Dolcetto is made to be drunk early without ceremony, but Dolcetto d'Ovada DOCG has been associated with fine, elegant Dolcettos that are worth ageing, while Dogliani or Dolcetto di Dogliani DOCG produces truly exceptional, ageworthy, and complex wines radically different from the many uninspiring but cheaper Dolcettos.

There are seven Dolcetto DOCs in Piemonte: Acqui, ALBA, ASTI (where little is planted, GRIGNOLINO being the young wine of choice), Diano d'Alba, Dogliani, Langhe Monregalesi, and Ovada. Alba, Ovada, and Dogliani are quantitatively the most significant, while the Langhe Monregalesi is a barely extant curiosity.

Ormeasco is LIGURIA's version of Dolcetto and is therefore the southernmost extent of Dolcetto territory in Italy. It grows just on the Ligurian side of the mountains that separate Piemonte from Liguria. In 2015, there were 4,381 ha/ 10,826 acres of Dolcetto planted in Italy. In 2020, DNA PROFILING suggested that Dolcetto was a Dolcetto Bianco × Moissan CROSS.

A fashion for Italian wine and food has spread Dolcetto to the US, Australia, and New Zealand.

Robinson, J., et al., *Wine Grapes: A Complete Guide to 1,368 Vine Varieties, Including Their Origins and Flavours* (2012).

Dôle. See SWITZERLAND.

dolium, a large earthenware vessel used in the ancient Roman period. Sometimes with a capacity of several thousand litres, they were often wholly or partly buried in the floor of a barn to create a stable temperature environment for FERMENTATION and provide storage for the wine until it was transferred to AMPHORAE (see also QVEVRI). Recently, at least ten Roman wrecks have been discovered in the western Mediterranean in which the cargo space was largely taken up by a number of *dolia*, thus creating the ancient equivalent of a tanker for the transport of BULK WINE. All these ships probably originated at Minturnae, the port on the west coast of Italy which was the outlet for MASSIC and FALERNIAN. This 1st-century CE experiment seems to have been short-lived, probably because of the inherent instability of such ships. J.J.P.

Hesnard, A., 'Entrepôts et navire à dolia: l'invention du transport de vin en vrac', in Meeks, D., and Garcia, D. (eds.), *Techniques et Économies Antique et Médiévales: Le Temps de l'Innovation* (1997), 130–1.

domaine, French word for an estate, typically a vine-growing and winemaking estate in BURGUNDY.

domaine bottling, the relatively recent practice of BOTTLING the produce of a DOMAINE on the property which produced it (although bottling at least in the region of production was advocated as early as 1728; see LITERATURE OF WINE). Such wines are described as **domaine bottled**, or *mis(e) en bouteille au domaine* in French. It is the BURGUNDY equivalent of Bordeaux's CHÂTEAU BOTTLING. Domaine bottling began in the economic crisis years of the early 1930s. but it was not until energetic foreign wine MERCHANTS such as Frank SCHOONMAKER and Alexis LICHINE visited Burgundy in the second half of the 20th century that the better individual producers were encouraged, and in many cases subsidized, to bottle their own production, typically with the help of mobile BOTTLING lines. The movement gathered pace in the 1980s and 1990s and is now seen as standard. However, many domaines also now produce some NÉGOCIANT bottlings, and most of the classic négociants are concentrating more on wines from their own vineyards, so that in either case the small print of BOTTLING INFORMATION may provide the only clue to the original provenance of the grapes: if the label states *mis (e) en bouteille au domaine*, then the wine is made from fruit grown in their own vineyards. Otherwise the label is more likely to note *mis(e) en bouteille par*... followed by the producer's name.

See also ESTATE BOTTLED.

Domaine de la Romanée-Conti, the most prestigious wine estate in Burgundy, based in Vosne-Romanée. 'The Domaine', as it is frequently called, is co-owned by the de Villaine and LEROY families and produces mainly GRAND CRU wines: two whites, Le MONTRACHET and Corton-Charlemagne, and seven reds, Romanée-Conti and La Tâche (both MONOPOLES of the domaine), Richebourg, Romanée-St-Vivant, Échezeaux, Grands Échezeaux, and Corton. For more details of individual wines, see VOSNE-ROMANÉE, ÉCHEZEAUX, and ALOXE-CORTON. The Domaine is the exception to the law according to which no estate in Burgundy may be named after a specific vineyard. Its wines are notable for their richness, subtlety, and longevity.

History

What is now Romanée-Conti was identified by the monks of St-Vivant as Le Cloux des Cinq Journaux in 1512 and sold off, as Le Cros de Cloux, in 1584 to Claude Cousin. His nephew and heir Germain Danton sold again to Jacques Vénot in 1621. Vénot's daughter married a Croonembourg, whose family retained the vineyard, now known as La Romanée (first mentioned in 1651), for four generations until it was sold to the Prince de Conti in 1760. The title Romanée-Conti was not used, however, until after dispossession by the revolutionaries and its sale by auction in 1794.

Romanée-Conti was bought by Julien Ouvard in 1819 and sold by his heirs to Jacques-Marie Duvault-Blochet 50 years later. Duvault-Blochet's eventual heirs were the de Villaine family. In 1911, Edmond Guidon de Villaine became director of what was now known as the Domaine de la Romanée-Conti, selling a half-share in 1942 to his friend Henri Leroy.

Over the years, Duvault-Blochet built up major vineyard ownership including part of Échezeaux, Grands Échezeaux, Richebourg, and the section of La Tâche known as Les Gaudichots. In 1933, the rest of La Tâche was bought from the Liger-Belair family, making a monopoly, and a small holding of Le Montrachet (0.67 ha/1.6 acres) was added in three slices between 1963 and 1980. The Domaine entered into a long-term contract to farm and produce the wines of Domaine Marey-Monge's holding of Romanée-St-Vivant before eventually buying the land in 1988. This was financed by temporarily selling part of their Échezeaux vineyards and a slice of Grands Échezeaux, although they continued to farm the land and bottle the wines. From 2009 the Domaine has also made a Corton, having leased three vineyards there from the estate of Prince Florent de Mérode. The produce of further vineyards owned by the Domaine in Vosne-Romanée and Bâtard-Montrachet is sold in BULK or kept for domestic consumption. In 2018 the Domaine was offered and accepted to lease four large PARCELS of Corton-Charlemagne, the first vintage being 2019.

Today the Domaine continues to be owned jointly by the de Villaine and Leroy/Roch families. Perrine Fenal, daughter of Lalou Bize-LEROY, represents the latter; Bertrand de Villaine, who took over as co-director from his uncle Aubert de Villaine in 2022, the former. J.T.C.M.

Meadows, A., *The Pearl of the Côte* (2010).
Olney, R., *Romanée-Conti* (1991).

domestic wine production. See HOME WINEMAKING.

Domina, modern red CROSS of PORTUGIESER × SPÄTBURGUNDER (Pinot Noir) that combines the productivity of the first with the ripeness, tannins, and colour of the second, if not its finesse and fruit. The total vineyard area in Germany, mainly Franken, was 354 ha/875 acres in 2020.

Domitian, Roman emperor (81–96 CE) who, in the words of the eulogy by the contemporary poet Statius (*Silvae* 4. 3. 11–12), restored 'to chaste Ceres the acres which had so long been denied her and lands made sober'. By a famous edict, possibly from 92 CE, Domitian banned the planting of new vineyards in Italy and ordered the destruction of at least half of the vineyards in the provinces (Suetonius, *Domitian* 7). He may also have sought to ban the planting within cities of small vineyards, of the sort which have been found at POMPEII. His purpose was not, as some have supposed, an attempt to protect the price of Italian wine at a time of general overproduction; rather, it was a heavy-handed attempt to divert investment into the production of cereals, the supply of which was a perennial problem for the large cities of the Roman Empire. There was no way that Domitian could enforce such a ban, and, following the protests which we know came from Asia, he did not persist with the measure. Hence the much later efforts of the Emperor Probus (276–82 CE) to encourage the planting of vineyards should not be taken as a sign that the ban lasted for centuries, as has often been thought. J.J.P.

Dom Pérignon. See PÉRIGNON, DOM.

Doña Blanca, also known as **Valenciana**, Cigüente, Malvasía Castellana, and Moza Fresca, variety grown in north-west Spain, particularly in Monterrei, Bierzo, and to a much lesser extent Valdeorras, where it is known as Valenciana. DNA PROFILING has shown that it is identical to the Portuguese variety SÍRIA. In 2020 there were 1,947 ha/4,811 acres planted in Spain.

Dona Branca, soft, northern Portuguese white wine grape planted on 24 ha/59 acres in 2020.

Donnaz, or **Donnas**, red wine based on NEBBIOLO grapes made in Italy's Valle d'AOSTA.

DOP, or **Denominación de Origen Protegida**, previously known as DO (which is still widely used), the mainstay of Spain's wine quality control system and equivalent to PDO. The EU's denomination reforms implemented in Spain in 2010 have been followed by some of the more recent Spanish appellations, but both DO and DOP are permitted on labels.

Each region awarded DO/DOP status is governed by a CONSEJO REGULADOR made up of representatives of the regional government (or the Ministry of Agriculture in the three multiregional appellations Rioja, Jumilla, and Cava), vinegrowers, winemakers, and merchants who earn their livelihoods in the region. These regional governments decide on the boundaries of the region, permitted VINE VARIETIES, maximum YIELDS, limits of ALCOHOLIC STRENGTH, and any other limitations pertaining to the zone. Back labels or neck seals are granted by the Consejo to certify that a wine meets the standards laid out in the DOP regulations. A superior category, Denominación de Origen Calificada (see DOCA), was created in 1991.

Spanish wine law has been subject to some criticism as the list of regions promoted to DOP status continues to lengthen (see also PORTUGAL). By 2022 there were 101 DOPs, including the 24 VINOS DE PAGO (no fewer than 11 DOPs in the CANARY ISLANDS alone). The system has most often helped the newer, lesser-known DOPs improve quality levels to no small degree, but some older, well-known Consejos Reguladores continue to uphold certain local quirks, which may sometimes stifle enterprise and initiative among growers and winemakers, as INAO has been known to do in France.

See also the additional Spanish denomination VINO DE CALIDAD. V. de la S. & F.C.

In Portugal DOP stands for Denominação de Origem Protegida, a term which may eventually replace DOC.

DOQ, or **Denominaciò d'Origen Qualificada**, the Catalan equivalent of DOCA.

Dordogne, river in SOUTH WEST FRANCE which rises on the Massif Central south-west of Clermont-Ferrand, flows through the Corrèze *département* (whence the merchants of LIBOURNE came), flows through BERGERAC and related appellations, and runs into the GIRONDE to form the more northerly of the two 'seas' referred to in the name of ENTRE-DEUX-MERS, with ST-ÉMILION, POMEROL, FRONSAC, and finally BOURG on its right bank.

dormancy, sleep, the normal state of vines in winter. Grapevine BUDS have three defined stages of dormancy: conditional, organic, and enforced. Dormancy nominally starts with autumn LEAF FALL, although buds are in a state of organic dormancy from VERAISON onwards. PRUNING is carried out when the vines are dormant, and buds and CUTTINGS taken from the vines at this time are used in PROPAGATION. The first sign that enforced dormancy is ending and BUDBREAK is imminent is BLEEDING, when the vines begin to drip water from pruning cuts.

R.E.S.

Illand, P., et al., 'Climate and the vine', in *The Grapevine: From the Science to the Practice of Growing Vines for Wine* (2011).

Dornfelder, the most popular German CROSS, bred in 1956 by August Herold, who had unwisely already assigned his name to one of its parents, the lesser HEROLDREBE, and so Dornfelder owes its name to the 19th-century founder of the Württemberg viticultural school. A HELFENSTEINER × Heroldrebe cross, Dornfelder incorporates every important red-wine vine grown in Germany somewhere in its genealogy and happily seems to have inherited many more of their good points than their bad.

The wine is notable for its depth of colour (useful in a country where pigments are at a premium), its good acidity, and, in some cases, its ability to benefit from BARRIQUE ageing and even to develop in bottle. Producing wines that are velvety textured, slightly floral, and sometimes with just a hint of sweetness, Dornfelder is easier to grow than Spätburgunder, has much better resistance to ROT than Portugieser, stronger stalks than Trollinger, better ripeness levels than either, earlier ripening than Lemberger (Blaufränkisch), and a YIELD that can easily reach 120 hl/ha (6.8 tons/acre) (although quality-conscious producers are careful to restrict productivity). It is hardly surprising that it continues to do well in most German wine regions, especially Rheinhessen and the Pfalz, where results are particularly appetizing. Germany's total plantings stood at 7,332 ha/18,118 acres in 2020 but appear to be slowing.

dosage, the final addition to a SPARKLING WINE which may top up a bottle in the case of TRADITIONAL METHOD wines and also determines the sweetness, or RESIDUAL SUGAR, of the finished wine. In French this addition is called the *liqueur d'expédition*, in Spanish *licor de expedición*, and in Italian *sciroppo di dosaggio*. In traditional-method wines, it usually comprises a mixture of wine and sugar syrup. Champagne is naturally so high in ACIDITY that even wines with relatively high residual sugar can taste bone dry. BOTTLE AGE or extended AUTOLYSIS are excellent substitutes for dosage, however, and, in general, the older the wine, the lower the necessary dosage to produce a BALANCED wine, and vice versa. The 21st century has seen a fashion for champagnes made with no, or zero, dosage. The table below gives the legal classification of sweetness levels for sparkling wine and champagne within the EU. This information must be included on the label.

EU classification of sweetness levels for champagne and sparkling wine

RS g/l	Example descriptions
< 3 with no sugar added after the second fermentation	brut nature/naturherb/bruto natural/pas dosé/zéro dosage
0–6	extra brut/extra herb/extra bruto
< 12	brut/herb/bruto
12–17	extra dry/extra trocken/extra seco/extra sec
17–32	sec/trocken/secco or asciutto/dry/seco
32–50	demi-sec/halbtrocken/abboccato/medium dry/semi seco
> 50	doux/mild/dolce/sweet/dulce

double pruning, a time-consuming viticultural technique in which the vines are pruned twice, which alters the timing of vine development (see PHENOLOGY). Double pruning may be carried out for one of two reasons: to delay BUDBREAK and hence reduce FROST hazard in COOL CLIMATES; or to delay harvest and hence potentially increase wine quality in hot regions.

Early winter pruning encourages earlier budbreak, increasing the risk of frost injury in cool, frost-prone climates, but if an initial pruning is light, leaving many buds, budbreak of basal buds is delayed and a second, more complete, pruning can then be done after the danger of frost has passed.

Double pruning in hot climates entails pruning the vines normally in winter and then again in early summer just after FLOWERING. This delays fruit ripening from the heat of midsummer to the cooler conditions of autumn. It reduces yields but can substantially improve wine quality.

R.E.S.

Douce Noire, what CHARBONO is called in its Savoie home.

Douro, Portuguese DOC named after the river which rises as the Duero in Spain (see RIBERA DEL DUERO) before turning south to form the frontier with PORTUGAL, then weaving west, where it cleaves through the GRANITE mountains of northern Portugal before finally slipping past Oporto into the Atlantic swell (see maps under PORTUGAL and SPAIN).

First demarcated in 1756, making it one of the world's oldest delimited wine regions (see DELIMITATION and PORTUGAL, history), the Douro Valley's since-modified irregular outline corresponds closely with an outcrop of pre-Cambrian SCHIST, which is hemmed in by GRANITE. For over two centuries, the demarcation applied only to the FORTIFIED wine PORT, which usurped the position of 'blackstrap' table wines that dominated Douro production until the latter part of the 18th century. That changed in 1979, when the DOC was extended to include unfortified TABLE WINE. The first glimmer of the region's true potential for table wines appeared decades earlier, when port shippers FERREIRA launched Barca Velha 1952, a red wine from the Douro Superior, upstream of the port heartland. Making TABLE WINES did not take hold, however, until the 1990s, following Portugal's accession to the EU. This provided invaluable funds for research and new equipment. It also led to the demise of the port shippers' de facto monopoly over exports, enabling estates to make and sell their own wine. In the spirit of Barca Velha, early efforts focused on ambitious, upmarket reds. But this century has seen the emergence of many a mid-priced and even entry-level Douro table wine as the number of port shippers and independent wine farms (*quintas*) making table wine has mushroomed. While quality is correspondingly more variable, the Douro still produces some of Portugal's most consistent red wines. Today production sometimes exceeds that of port and is expected to grow.

The Douro's unfortified wines can be made from a single variety or, more typically, a blend of as many as 50 of the region's 100-plus approved INDIGENOUS VARIETIES, which are similar to those used for port. Should winemakers stray from the approved list (a miniscule amount of well-known French varieties are planted), wines are labelled Vinho Regional DURIENSE. The region's varietal versatility reflects the sheer diversity of the world's largest mountain vineyard (as of 2020, of about 250,000 ha/617,763 acres, 43,708 ha/108,005 acres were under vine).

Divided into three subregions (the westernmost Baixo or Lower Corgo, Cima or Upper Corgo, and the Douro Superior/Upper Douro, which reaches the Spanish border), in general terms it is progressively warmer and drier towards the east. However, since the steep, schistous slopes extend from around 150 m/492 ft to a substantially cooler 900 m/2,953 ft in ELEVATION and face every which way (the Douro DOC tracks not only a 100-km/62-mile stretch of the River Douro but also the valleys of its tributaries), there is many an exception. The first decade of this century saw a sharper focus on taut, mineral white wines sourced from elevated sites and the 'Altos' (peripheral highlands), some located on GRANITE soils, including the Planalto (i.e. plateau) de Alijó, which is a key source of fortified MOSCATEL do Douro (a DOC) and one of Portugal's premier ESPUMANTE brands, Vértice). Earlier picking, the use of older and larger oak barrels, and elevation also result in greater freshness and restraint among the better reds. The quest for individuation and concerns about CLIMATE CHANGE have led some to question 1970s viticultural studies whose outcome was a shift away from the tradition of field blends towards varietally homogeneous plantings of the supposedly superior red-wine varieties TOURIGA NACIONAL, TINTA RORIZ, TOURIGA FRANCA, TINTA BARROCA, and TINTO CÃO—five were even mandatory for new vineyards planted under the 1982 Trás-os-Montes Integrated Rural Development Project (which encouraged the restructuring of over 3,700 ha of abandoned vineyards). In the 2020s, traditional red-wine varieties that are returning to favour on account of their freshness or lighter body include TINTA FRANCISCA, Donzelinho Tinto, Touriga Brasileira, Folgasão, Tinta Amarela (TRINCADEIRA), Cornifesto, SOUSÃO, RUFETE, BASTARDO, and Malvasia Preta. For whites (mostly from old field blends), key varieties include RABIGATO, CÓDEGA DO LARINHO, VIOSINHO, GOUVEIO, MALVASIA Fina, Donzelinho Branco, and ARINTO. In 2017, ALVARINHO was accorded Douro DOC status. S.A.

Mayson, R. J., *The Wines of Portugal* (2020).
Woolf, S. J., and Opaz, R., *Foot Trodden: Portugal and the Wines That Time Forgot* (2021).
de Almeida, J. N., 'Vine, wine and life: a portrait of the Douro Region in recent times', in Fundação Francisco Girão, *Francisco Girão: An Innovator in Viticulture in the North of Portugal* (Volume II, 2011).
www.ivdp.pt

Douro bake, traditional expression for the character imparted to wines, especially PORT, matured in the hot, dry climate of the DOURO Valley (rather than the much cooler, damper atmosphere of VILA NOVA DE GAIA, where port has traditionally been matured by the shippers). Some wines matured in the Douro seem to develop faster with greater evaporation, losing colour, browning, and sometimes acquiring a slightly sweet, caramelized flavour—although poor and sometimes unhygienic storage conditions often have a greater impact on wine quality than does the climate. Many reputable shippers successfully age large stocks of port in the Douro, usually in air-conditioned lodges. R.J.M.

doux, French for 'sweet'. See SWEETNESS and, for official EU sugar levels, DOSAGE.

Dow, important port shipper. See SYMINGTONS.

downy mildew, one of the most economically significant diseases affecting vines, often called peronospora in parts of Europe, and *mildiou* in France. It is a particular problem in regions with warm, humid springs and summers such as many wine regions in northern Europe. Typically (and in this book) referred to as a FUNGAL DISEASE, downy mildew is not in fact caused by a fungus but by *Plasmopara viticola*, a related organism termed a peronosporomycete. This organism is indigenous to eastern North America, and so some species of native AMERICAN VINES such as *Vitis cordifolia, Vitis rupestris,* and *Vitis rotundifolia* are relatively resistant. Commercially important varieties of VITIS VINIFERA, however, are highly susceptible.

The disease caused havoc in the vineyards of Europe when it was accidentally introduced before 1878, probably on American vines imported as grafting stock to combat PHYLLOXERA. By 1882 the disease had spread throughout France. The famous BORDEAUX MIXTURE was first used as a preventive spray to control this disease.

Downy mildew is now widespread around the world, but a few areas with low spring and summer rainfall are essentially free of it, including Afghanistan, northern Chile, Egypt, and Western Australia. It has occurred spasmodically in California and southern Chile.

The disease attacks all green parts of the vine, and young leaves are particularly susceptible. Severely affected leaves will drop off, reducing PHOTOSYNTHESIS and thus delaying fruit RIPENING. Levels of fruit SUGARS, vine reserves of CARBOHYDRATES, and ANTHOCYANINS are typically depressed. BUDBREAK and early SHOOT growth can be delayed the following spring. Severe infections result in pale, puny reds and weak whites.

The symptoms of the disease are described quite aptly by the name. Leaves show patches of dense, white cottony growth on the undersurface. The earliest stage is the so-called 'oil spot', easily seen on the upper leaf surface when it is held up against the light. PETIOLES, TENDRILS, young INFLORESCENCES, and developing berries are also affected. The organism spends the winter in fallen leaves and can sometimes survive in the buds. Spores germinate in the spring when temperatures reach 11 °C/52 °F, and they are spread to the vine by rainsplash from the soil. Spores are further spread and germinated with high humidity (95–100% relative humidity), warm temperatures (18–22 °C), and moisture. The most severe epidemics of the disease occur with frequent rainstorms and warm weather. The low yields of French vintages such as 1886, 1910, 1915, 1930, 1932, 1948, 1957, 1969, and 2021, produced after wet growing seasons, were probably at least partly due to downy mildew.

There are two principal protection approaches. The first and most common is to use protective sprays which are often based on COPPER. However, the protection lasts for only ten days or so, especially when the shoots are growing rapidly in early spring. Curative fungicides which act against established infections became available in the early 1990s, but these are more expensive. A modern approach is to install a VINEYARD WEATHER STATION which can predict outbreaks by measuring the weather and facilitate more timely SPRAYING.

An alternative but generally less popular approach to the control of this disease is to plant DISEASE-RESISTANT VARIETIES. European vine breeders, especially at GEISENHEIM and Geilweilerhof in Germany, have been particularly successful in developing varieties which require no, or less, spraying against downy mildew, with native American vines contributing the resistant genes. Increased environmental awareness will encourage their use, but there is consumer resistance to NEW VARIETIES. R.E.S.

Goode, J., *Wine Science: The Application of Science in Wine* (3rd edn, 2021).
Wilcox, W. F., et al., *Compendium of Grape Diseases, Disorders, and Pests* (2nd edn, 2015).

drainage, free movement of water through the SOIL PROFILE or across the land surface; or alternatively, the removal of surplus water by artificial means. The importance of good soil drainage for viticulture and wine quality cannot be overstated. For a detailed discussion, see Seguin. See also TERROIR and SOIL AND WINE QUALITY.

All good vineyard soils are well drained, whether naturally or by artificial drainage. Permanent waterlogging or prolonged waterlogging after the start of spring growth is lethal to vine roots. Even marginal waterlogging can be harmful, causing restriction of root and soil microbial activity and the consequent starvation of the vine for nutrients and root-produced growth substances (see CYTOKININ). Soils that are cold and wet at the time of FLOWERING are a major factor in poor berry setting, or COULURE. However, if waterlogging is temporary and the soil dries out at or just after flowering, with mild WATER STRESS before VERAISON, it is still possible to produce fine wines, especially on ALLUVIAL soils when SAND or GRAVEL is layered over finer sediment. Such waterlogging may reduce root depth but will not necessarily affect eventual wine quality.

Waterlogging confined to the SUBSOIL can still be a serious disadvantage, through killing or inactivation of the deeper roots. This can result in a vine with only a shallow effective root system, readily subject both to later DROUGHT (after the surface moisture has evaporated or been used) and to excessive water uptake following rains during ripening. Seguin argues that such irregularity in the supply of SOIL WATER can be seriously detrimental to wine quality. Subsoils that are regularly waterlogged can be identified by their bleached, blue-grey colour (see SOIL COLOUR), while well-drained subsoils are usually yellow, brown or reddish, and mottled subsoils indicate intermittent waterlogging.

As a broad rule, light-textured and stony soils drain freely, while tight or heavy CLAY soils (see SOIL TEXTURE) restrict drainage. Subsoils composed of the latter type can result in water tables 'perched' on top of them. These develop most commonly on gradients, where seepage of water down the slope through the surface soil is interrupted by barriers of rock or of clay reaching or approaching the surface.

However, even heavy soils and subsoils can drain adequately if they have good crumb structure (see SOIL STRUCTURE). This depends on their chemical nature, including sufficient contents of CALCIUM and, in the upper layers, ORGANIC MATTER. Unstructured soils can easily pack down to form impermeable hardpans below the surface when subjected to trampling or wheeled traffic (see SOIL COMPACTION). Vineyards are commonly RIPPED before planting to facilitate drainage (see RIPPING).

Several other management factors can influence soil drainage. Deeply tap-rooted COVER CROPS, such as mustard or lupins, can help to create and maintain vertical channels which allow water to infiltrate freely into the deeper soil layers. The maintenance of an organic surface MULCH, whether applied or originating naturally from cover crops, attains the same effect through encouraging EARTHWORM activity. These useful creatures also help to distribute surface organic matter and nutrients through the soil profile. Finally, the application of LIME or gypsum can help on some acid soils, by improving their crumb structure and permeability.

Artificial drainage, where required, can be of several types according to situation and need. Webber and Jones describe them in detail. All forms of artificial soil drainage are expensive, but, on otherwise valuable land for producing high-value grapes, they can be essential. Drainage did, after all, transform the Médoc from a marsh to one of the world's most admired wine regions (see BORDEAUX, history).

J.G. & C.v.L.

Seguin, G., ' "Terroirs" and pedology of wine growing', *Experientia*, 42 (1986), 861–72.

Webber, R. T. J., and Jones, L. D., 'Drainage and soil salinity', in B. G. Coombe and P. R. Dry (eds.), *Viticulture*, ii: *Practices* (2nd edn, 2006).

draining. In WHITE WINEMAKING the operation usually takes place just after CRUSHING, although some winemakers choose to move crushed fruit straight to the PRESS. Any juice run off without pressing is called drainings. The FREE-RUN juice is drained off the grape skins in a **draining tank** or **draining vat**, many of which incorporate special design features to assist the separation of liquids from solids. Similarly, in red-wine fermentation, the red wine run off the skins may also be called drainings.

DRC, famous initials in the world of fine wine, standing for the DOMAINE DE LA ROMANÉE-CONTI.

dried grapes. See RAISINS.

dried-grape wines, varied and growing category of generally intense, complex, often sweet wines made from partially raisined grapes. The production technique, involving either leaving the grapes to raisin on the vine or picking and then drying them by various methods, is associated with most of the celebrated wines of antiquity. This early CONCENTRATION technique continues one of the oldest traditions in the gastronomic world.

In the classical world this winemaking style may well have evolved because of problems of wine conservation, particularly for wines traded and consumed outside their area of origin, semi-dried grapes naturally resulting in sweeter, stronger, and therefore more stable wines. (BOTRYTIZED wines and the technique of FORTIFICATION were developed many centuries later.) The dried-grape tradition has proved particularly resilient close to its origins, notably in Italy.

Ancient history

The technique of twisting the stems of grape bunches to deprive them of sap and leaving them to raisin on the vine may have originated in CRETE, but vinification techniques for dried grapes were perfected in ancient GREECE. The ancient Greeks also learned from other inhabitants of the eastern Mediterranean, particularly the Hittites of Anatolia. The first description of how to make wine from dried grapes is provided by HESIOD, in the 8th century BCE. His *Works and Days* describes how grapes should be dried in the sun 'for ten days and nights' and then in the shade for a further five, before fermenting the wine in jars.

Such methods were responsible for the famous wines of the islands (Chios, Lesbos, and Thasos) which were so highly prized by HOMER and succeeding writers. These wines were often noted as being at their best after many years' maturation, when they had 'lost their teeth': clear evidence of the longevity which only dried-grape wines could provide before the invention of stoppered bottles. Sealed AMPHORAE may have been relatively airtight containers, but long journeys in Mediterranean heat demanded exceptionally robust wines.

Coincidental with the rise of the Greek city states was the emergence of the most adventurous traders of the Mediterranean, those of PHOENICIA. They exported the wines of Lebanon (and the winemaking practices of CANAAN) along the littorals of North Africa and to Spain, Sardinia, and Sicily. One of their colonies was CARTHAGE, founded in 814 BCE, where in about 500 BCE Mago wrote his seminal work on agriculture, now known only in the extensive quotations which survive in the works of succeeding classical authors, notably the Roman COLUMELLA. Redding quotes Mago in the following passage, which summarizes the Graeco-Roman understanding of dried-grape vinification:

> Let the bunches of grapes quite ripe, and scorched or shrivelled in the sun, when the bad and faulty ones are picked out, be spread upon a frame resting on stakes or forks and covered with a layer of reeds. Place them in the sun but protect them from the dew at night. When they are dry (sufficiently shrivelled) pluck the grapes from the stalks, throw them into a cask and make the first must. If they have been well drained, put them, at the end of six days, into a vessel, and press them for the first wine. A second time let them be pounded (or trodden) and pressed, adding cold must to the pressing. This second wine is to be placed in a pitched vessel, lest it become sour. After it has remained twenty or thirty days, and fermented, rack it into another vessel and stopping it close immediately, cover it with a skin.

Other writers in ancient ROME such as CATO, PLINY, HORACE, and VIRGIL add other details (such as storing these wines in the rafters, as with modern Tuscan VIN SANTO), but in general they repeat the principles laid down by their Mediterranean forebears.

The Romans, like the Greeks, planted vineyards wherever they went—in Spain, France, Germany, and central Europe, perhaps even in England. Only in the last would the climate have been too austere for the production of *passum* (PASSITO) wines; elsewhere the practice became embedded in the complex strata of vinicultural history, a rich seam of vinous tradition to be mined in later centuries, after the long upheavals which followed the collapse of the Roman Empire.

Evolution since the Middle Ages

Italy The *vinum reticum* of Verona praised by Pliny was presumably the ancestor of today's RECIOTO and AMARONE. It was relatively common for wines to be made from grapes dried on the vine cut off from the flow of sap by having their stems twisted, or *torcolato*. (This Venetian word is found in the name of a modern white Recioto made in Veneto's BREGANZE from partially dried VESPAIOLA grapes, alluding to the way the grapes are twisted around ropes to dry or are basket-pressed. Similarly, the Italian equivalent *torchiato* is heard in today's Torchiato di Fregona, a sweet wine made in Treviso.) The dried-grape tradition was presumably enhanced in 1204 when Venice conquered Crete, the stronghold of this classical heritage. The result seems to have been a revival of dried-grape winemaking throughout the growing Venetian empire, not just in Veneto but on the islands and coast of what is now SLOVENIA and CROATIA.

In early 14th century PIEMONTE, such wines were in great demand; they are mentioned again in the mid 17th century, but the tradition survives only as a curiosity today. In TUSCANY, however, VIN SANTO survives as an apparently unbroken tradition, practised by most of the best estates. Versions exist in other parts of Italy, notably in TRENTINO. Other survivals include the VERDUZZO of Ramandolo, the generally overrated PICOLIT of FRIULI, the remarkable Rosenmuskateller of TRENTINO-ALTO ADIGE, SFORZATO or Sfursat of VALTELLINA, ALBANA passito from Romagna, and SAGRANTINO passito from Umbria. In the south and islands, examples of this renascent tradition include a range of wines based on raisined MOSCATO, ALEATICO, MALVASIA, and Nasco grapes, not to mention Vecchio Samperi, the rare unfortified wine in the style of MARSALA from de Bartoli. Perhaps the best-known example of passito wine in southern Italy today is Vallone's Amarone-like Graticciaia, dried not three months under the winery roof but about ten days under the Puglian sun, still hot immediately after the grape harvest. And the island of Pantelleria is famous for a wine made from dried Moscato grapes.

Elsewhere It is clear from REDDING that dried-grape wines were much more common in early 19th century France than today. He mentions the VIN DE PAILLE of Alsace, two types from Argentat in the Corrèze (way upriver of modern BERGERAC), one of them slightly sparkling, and what sounds like a magnificent example from the SCIACCARELLU grape made at Sartène in CORSICA. He also makes clear that MUSCAT DE RIVESALTES was then a true raisin wine, often the result of twisting grape stems on the vine, and not, as now, a fortified blend. In contemporary France, the tradition survives only in the *vins de paille* of Hermitage and the Jura, made as curiosities by a small number of producers in each region, in quantities so tiny that they rarely reach the market.

In Spain, the classical traditions continued in muted form through the Muslim occupation and were revived thereafter. The most notable surviving derivatives are the Andalusian specialities SHERRY, MONTILLA, and MÁLAGA, whose richer styles have always been made with semi-dried grapes, but these are not pure dried-grape wines because most (although not Telmo Rodriguez' Molino Réal Málaga) are now fortified. Elsewhere in Spain the tradition is almost extinct.

Surprisingly few dried-grape wines can be found in Greece today. The rich wines of Sámos date from the replanting of the island's vineyards in the 16th century, but those of SANTORINI are descendants of the classical prototypes, as is the COMMANDARIA of Cyprus.

There are records of straw wine (*Strohwein*) being made in FRANKEN in Germany; a rich red dried-grape wine just over the border in Switzerland from Italy's VALTELLINA; a 'green' wine of remarkable strength produced near Cotnar on the borders of Moldova and Romania (see COTNARI); and of course the rather special case of TOKAJI in Hungary. The last survives, as does *Strohwein* in Austria, Switzerland, and Germany, although the term *Strohwein* is protected in the first two and thus prohibited in the third; most of the others have vanished. The only notable additions to the once splendid roll-call of wines from the old Austro-Hungarian empire are a few straw wines and reed wines from AUSTRIA.

Redding mentions Shahoni, the 'royal grape' of the province of Cashbin in Persia, claiming that 'the grapes are kept over the winter, and remain on the vine a good deal of the time in linen bags', and also lists from Argentina a 'sweet wine, resembling Malaga, made at Mendoza at the foot of the Andes, on their eastern side' as well as the famous CONSTANTIA from South Africa, now revived. In modern times there have also been experiments with dried-grape wines in California and Australia (see CUT CANE). S.P.D.L.

Modern production techniques

Grapes with maximum EXTRACT and SUGARS are required, which normally entails restricting YIELDS. Such grapes may be picked either before, at, or after full RIPENESS. Twisting the stalk was once practised in the Veneto, but most growers now prefer to dry their grapes off the vine.

Those who pick slightly before full maturation claim there is less risk of ROT, thicker skins, enhanced resistance during drying, and higher acidity, all of which favour aroma, freshness, balance, and longevity—and concentrate the grapes which remain on the vine.

Only the ripest, healthiest grapes are generally picked, which today means a pre-selection by experienced pickers. Healthy grapes are vital since any incipient mould or rot soon spreads during the drying process. Skins must remain intact, to which end the grapes may well be laid in small trays for transport to the winery. The bunches should be *spargolo*, loose rather than compact, so that air circulates around the individual berries during the all-important drying process.

Sun drying is still practised in places such as the Sicilian island of PANTELLERIA off Tunisia, in southern PUGLIA, and on the Greek island of SANTORINI. The process can be many times faster than drying under cover, but this can result in excessive colour, caramelized flavours, and loss of aroma, bypassing some of the microbiological transformations which are the essence of fine dried-grape wine.

Most grape drying for commercial purposes happens in a winery loft, where windows may be opened to let in plenty of air (essential against the development of rot and mould). Bunches are hung up vertically (on hooks or on long strings) or are laid out horizontally on neutral, bone-dry materials. Straw is rarely used because of its attractions for mice. Wire mesh, nylon nets, and wooden or plastic fruit boxes were 20th-century developments; more traditional cane and rush mats and bamboo racks remain popular in much of Italy. Today, in zones where dried grapes constitute an important factor in the local wine economy, purpose-built grape-drying plants have been created complete with temperature control and wind machines.

The duration of the drying process is dictated by the grape variety, the type of wine required, and microclimatic conditions during drying. Sugar-rich Greek grape varieties such as MUSCAT, ALEATICO, and MALVASIA require less time than more northern varieties. Three weeks may suffice for a Muscat, whereas a Veronese variety such as GARGANEGA for a white RECIOTO or CORVINA, CORVINONE or RONDINELLA for a red Recioto or Amarone will need three to four months—in some cases, for Recioto, even up to six months. Ideal conditions include considerable currents of dry air, and humidity is such a problem in some valley sites that drying facilities are being moved to higher elevations. Excessive heat is generally regarded as negative, as is excessive cold.

The main effect of drying grapes is loss of water and the consequent concentration of sugars. The relationship between water loss and sugar gain is relatively direct so that a water loss of one-third from grapes picked at 12 °BAUMÉ would result in a wine of 16% alcohol (if all the sugar were fermented out). Depending on the wine style desired, the loss of grape weight by evaporation varies between 10 and 60%, with the norm for a PASSITO wine being 35–40%, so the potential alcohol is raised by just over one-third.

Other components behave less predictably. The TOTAL ACIDITY in grapes undergoing a 40% dehydration rises not by 40% but by around

25%. These and other organic substances go through various transformations, resulting in the loss or development of certain aromas in the process. The longer the drying period, the greater the biological change of organic substances and resultant wine quality.

NOBLE ROT may develop on the grapes during dehydration, but it is not desired by most practitioners, particularly those making the drier styles of dried-grape wines such as Amarone. A further problem is insect infestation, particularly of bees, wasps, and hornets.

Crushing or pressing should ideally be as gentle as possible. Gravity may be used to clarify white must; in the case of red wines, stems may be totally or only partially removed.

The MUST of raisined grapes is so concentrated that it slows FERMENTATION, an effect accentuated in cooler climates, especially where the long drying period may mean that the grapes are crushed in midwinter and the ambient temperature is naturally low. In Italy, fermentation may therefore safely take place in wood and may need to be started by heating or by adding specially cultured local YEAST. In traditional areas, the right yeasts have been in the atmosphere for centuries. *Saccharomyces uvarum* begins the job in Valpolicella, according to Masi, while *Saccharomyces bayanus* is able to work at higher temperatures and at the ALCOHOLIC STRENGTH of 16% or more that is necessary for many Amarones.

Some producers allow the fermentation to stop and start for months or even, as in the case of the late Giuseppe Quintarelli, two to three years, allowing Nature to decide how sweet the final wine will be. Most, however, use RACKING and, increasingly, REFRIGERATION to stop fermentation.

The wine is then generally racked off its LEES and the lees sometimes used to enrich normal VALPOLICELLA, the process called RIPASSO. In Tuscany, the so-called GOVERNO process is employed.

Dried-grape wines tend to be particularly high in VOLATILE ACIDS, a direct result of high sugar levels (accentuated if any BOTRYTIZED grapes have been included). The ACETIC ACID of such a wine may well exceed legal levels, sometimes entailing unacceptably high SULFUR DIOXIDE additions. Many argue that high levels of volatile acidity are essential to the quality of such wines, and some maintain that false 'passito' wines can be exposed precisely by improbably low levels of acetic acid.

Dried-grape wines may be divided into two categories: those in which the fresh primary AROMAS are retained; and those in which primary aromas are sacrificed to the development of a more complex ones. The former include most wines based on aromatic varieties such as Muscat, Brachetto, Aleatico, and Riesling, as well as sweet whites where the emphasis is on fruit, such as Recioto di Soave. These are subjected as far as possible to PROTECTIVE WINEMAKING techniques.

Vin de paille and Vin Santo, with their RANCIO character, are the most notable examples of the OXIDATIVE style. Amarone and Recioto della Valpolicella of the traditional type are also treated oxidatively, the aim being to incorporate in the final tasting experience an evolution of aromas due in some measure to exposure to oxygen. Traditional Amarone and Recioto are, typically, the result of prolonged maceration, deliberately frequent racking, and ageing for years in large, old barrels. Strong, dry Valpolicella Amarone is a notable example, as is Vin Santo with the rancio character encouraged by traditionalists. Since the 1980s, there has been a movement away from such classic styles, however, and modernist Amarone and Recioto producers are aiming for more FRUIT-DRIVEN wines.

Italy produces more dried-grape wine than anywhere else, not least because of the dramatic increase in Amarone production, but experimentation with the technique has spread to Australia, South America, North America, and much of Europe. N.J.B.

Belfrage, N., and Loftus, S., 'Dried grapes: the classic wines of Antiquity', *Journal of Wine Research*, 4/3 (1993), 205–25.

Masi, Grupo Technico, *Amarone and Recioto; Historical and Technical Notes* (private communication, 1990).

Paronetto, L. (ed.), *Appassimento and Amarone: The Essence of the Venetian Art of Winemaking* (2014).

Redding, C., *The History and Description of Modern Wines* (1833).

Tachis, G., *Il Libro del Vin Santo* (1988).

drinking, the activity for which wine was designed, now threatened by rising average ALCOHOLIC STRENGTH. TASTING is different.

drinking vessels. Before the development of glass-making enabled the production of GLASSES (the most common modern wine-drinking vessels), a wide variety of drinking vessels were used for wine. Pottery cups were commonplace, and goblets made of a variety of metals, but even earlier than this wine was sucked through a reed, either from a bowl such as a CRATER or possibly from a hollowed-out gourd or similar vessel provided by Nature. See ancient EGYPT, INDIA, and ARMENIA.

Modern history

The majority of drinking vessels are glass, but—despite its use for thousands of years—glass has not always been available (see GLASS, HISTORY OF). In such times, the principal alternative was silver. There are other occasions when glass was too fragile for a particular environment. Clear drinking glasses were an expensive commodity, beyond the means of most people in the 18th century, but then so was wine—at least in countries where wine was not produced.

Silver was most commonly used for wine-drinking vessels until the Venetian glass industry burgeoned in the 16th century. Although glass became preferred, trade in it was limited; except for exceptional grand occasions and settings, in each country wine was usually consumed from indigenous vessels.

The social history of drinking and eating habits and customs has inevitably played an important part in the history of drinking vessels. FASHIONS change and, for example, the favoured shape for champagne has evolved over the last century from a saucer via a plain tall narrow glass flute to a tulip or regular wine-glass shape. The first introduction of suites of glasses in limited sizes was in the late 18th century, but the designated use for each size can only be conjectural.

It is often observed that many 18th-century drinking glasses are small, but they have to be considered in context. They were not placed on the table for the diner to quaff at will. Rather, they were brought by the footman to each diner when requested and were taken after each draught to await another request. It may be speculated that the larger goblets were used by gentlemen after the servants had been dismissed towards the end of the meal.

By the mid 19th century, service *à la russe* had become fashionable, with its place settings of cutlery and glasses with which a diner today would be familiar. The 'new' arrangement dispensed with the need for a footman for each diner, and it was the cause of the widespread use of long sets of glasses, with each diner having up to six glasses for different wines, not to mention tumblers and finger bowls.

Glass Drinking vessels in both silver and glass were made by the Romans. The glass-making craft went into decline after the collapse of the Roman Empire; although glass was made in small quantities, it was not until the Renaissance that glass-making gained a prominent place in the decorative arts in VENICE. By the 16th century, Venice was producing fine and elegant drinking glasses. The soda glass was almost colourless and very thin. The often-decorated baluster stems had elements of very narrow section.

Draconian attempts to prevent the secrets of glass-making from leaving Venice were put in place in order that the city should retain its supremacy. However, a few of those with the knowledge did leave, and small factories sprang up all over Europe in consequence. To raise revenue, the English monarch granted glass-making monopolies on payment of a fee, and in 1574 Elizabeth I let a lapsed monopoly fall to Giacomo Verzelini. A few of his glasses, closely

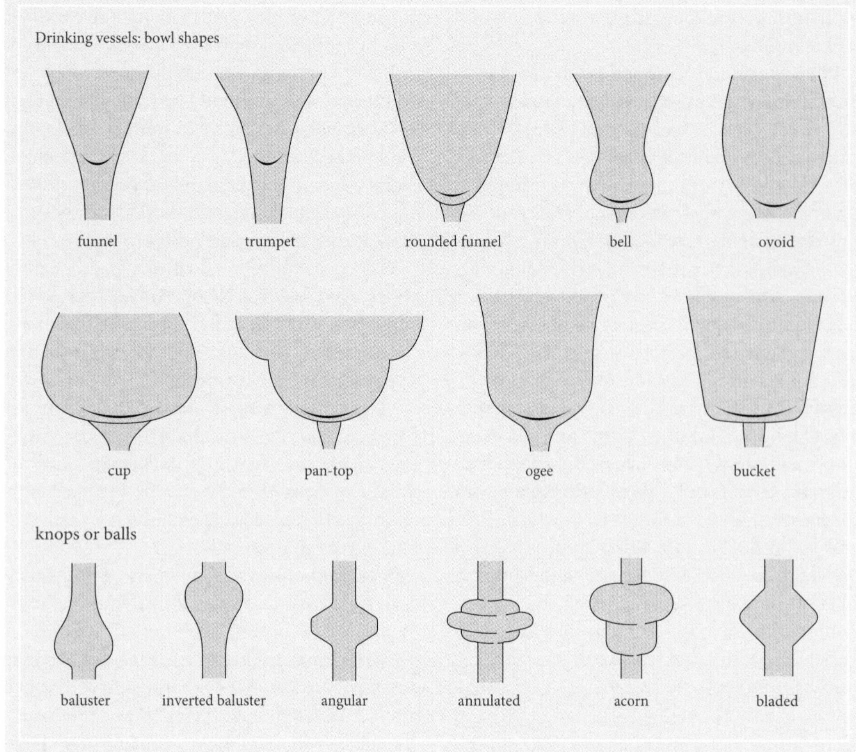

following Venetian models, sometimes dated and usually engraved, survive. England and subsequently Britain became the dominant production centre.

In the early 17th century, wood-fired furnaces were outlawed in England, hence the setting up of glass houses in coal-producing areas—Newcastle, Stourbridge, and Bristol. As described in DECANTERS, a major advance in glass technology was made in the 1670s by George Ravenscroft with the introduction of lead and flint glass, and it was this which enabled British glass-makers to hold world supremacy for the ensuing hundred years. However, drinking glasses were still being made in Italy and in large numbers in what is now Germany and the Netherlands throughout the 17th century.

The earliest lead glass was frequently unstable and soon after manufacture developed crizzling: a myriad of short cracks within the glass that gave it a milky effect. Ravenscroft and others in England soon improved the recipe and technique, enabling them to produce glasses of a rich weight and colour, quite unlike the light, pale products of Venice. The soda glass of Venice lent itself to thin and elegant shapes, often embellished with lattice designs in opaque white glass within the form or with coloured elements. The English lead glass, by contrast, was heavy and with a grey tint, capable of being drawn into bold plastic forms.

The drinking glass can be divided into three parts: the bowl, stem, and foot. Made separately, the parts were put together during the final stages of production. The bowl can take a variety of shapes, each with a name recognized in the large glass-collecting fraternity. Trumpet, ovoid, bell, and bucket are obvious shapes, but rounded funnel, ogee, cup, and pan-top are also illustrated above.

The stem of a wine glass is perhaps the element offering most opportunity for decorative treatment. The stem may be straight or with swellings called knops. The early examples were generally heavily knopped, the main element of the stem often of baluster outline but with other swellings above, below, or both. The knops, like the bowls, have names such as acorn, bladed, baluster, annulated, and ball, all of which are more or less self-descriptive (see diagram).

Beneath the stem is the foot. Most wine glasses have a foot of a flattish conical section, some raising the stem 5 mm/0.25 in or more away from the table, others by three times as much. Most glasses before the mid 18th century have an additional feature called a folded foot. Long before English glass became pre-eminent it was realized that if, when the foot was made, the rim was folded underneath itself, a much sturdier glass was the result. Some glasses have a domed or tiered foot rather than a conical one.

During the 1670s and 1680s, wine glasses followed the Venetian forms, some of which had changed little over 100 years. By the 1690s, the particular qualities of lead glass began to be appreciated and resulted in the manufacture of glasses of substantial weight and a solid form quite distinct from the Venetian tradition. Over the next 20 years, designs were refined to what many consider the zenith of glass-making, characterized by bold, pure, unadorned form. Many glasses were lightened by air bubbles or tears being blown within the stem and occasionally at the base of the bowl, but the form remained substantial. These glasses are referred to as heavy balusters.

The heavy balusters became lighter as time progressed, partly perhaps because of taxation on the weight of glass. The bold designs became more fussy, with increased numbers of elements in the stem, and the stem itself became thinner. The heavy balusters had given way to light balusters and balustroids by the 1730s and 1740s. Some glasses had stems moulded of polygonal section; these are known as Silesian stems. During the 1740s and 1750s many glasses had stems that had inserted in them a series of small bubbles. When twisted and stretched these formed helices of air within the stem, or air twists. By this time, too, it was becoming fashionable for the stems to be straight sided, and folded feet were at the end of their span.

A popular form in the 1760s was the result of twisting opaque white or coloured glass into the stem, instead of air bubbles.

The next phase of glass-making was the facet stem—quite simply the cutting of the stem with shield, diamond, or hexagonal facets. Traditionally air twists have been dated to the 1750s, opaque twists to the 1760s, and facet stems to the 1770s. It seems far more likely in view of the general shape and proportion of these styles that they were made more or less concurrently; whatever the truth, it marked the end of the golden age for British glass collectors. Facet stems continued to be made to the end of the century, with the stems becoming shorter and the overall proportion degenerating.

During the 18th century, there were forms of embellishment other than pure shape. Wheel-engraving produced fine decoration in the 1730s and 1740s, sometimes being delicate bands of flowers and scrolls around the rim, while glasses engraved with Jacobite and Williamite symbolism had their enthusiastic followers. In the 1760s, the enamelled decoration of William and Mary Beilby of Newcastle enjoyed royal and other esteemed patronage, while in the following decade the gilt decoration of James Giles drew its admirers, as did the stipple engraving of David Wolff.

The 19th century saw the fast decline of design, with many drinking glasses cut to match the cut decanters of the period. At this time, too, the idea of having glasses in different sizes and shapes for different drinks was becoming widespread, although this idea was not unknown in the 1780s. By the mid century, glasses could be ordered in large suites with sizes from goblet to liqueur matching the decanters, claret jugs, and finger bowls. Decoration was either cut or acid-etched and in a variety of patterned styles.

The 20th century saw an interest in antiques, and a large quantity of glass was made, much of it in the Georgian style. For the amateur it can be difficult to distinguish between a Georgian decanter of, say, 1815 and a copy made 100 years later. Wine glasses with green and cranberry-coloured bowls on clear stems also became popular at this time.

Silver During the 16th century and before, glass was a very highly prized commodity, and wine would normally have been consumed from silver or silver-gilt goblets. Early wine cups—often with a cover—were invariably heavily decorated and were considered status symbols. Many that remain are so large that their use must have been communal. Smaller cups for individual use date back to the Middle Ages, but by the 1570s a standard pattern of a wide, shallow bowl on a baluster stem emerged. The making of silver drinking cups appears to have almost stopped by about the 1650s, probably due to the impact of Venetian glass and the subsequent burgeoning of glass-making in England.

There was a revival of silver drinking goblets in the 1780s which lasted for some 25 years. These were usually quite large, having ovoid bowls often made in prevailing styles during the 19th century in small numbers.

Other materials Drinking vessels were made in a variety of other media. Before long-distance maritime trade became frequent, ostrich eggs and coconuts were particularly prized for their exotic rarity and were mounted in silver as cups. At a more basic level, the horns of various animals were used for drinking, and wood was lathe-turned into cups and goblets. Antique cups of pottery and earthenware are also occasionally found. R.N.H.B.

Bickerton, L. M., *18th Century Drinking Glasses, An Illustrated History* (1987).

Butler, R., *Great British Wine Accessories 1550–1900* (2009).

Seddon, G. B., *The Jacobites and Their Drinking Glasses* (1995).

drip irrigation, a form of IRRIGATION in which water is applied literally as drops to each vine from a pressure-reducing plastic device (the dripper) attached to a plastic pipe suspended about 40 cm/10 in above the ground from posts along each vine row. The technique was developed in Israel and Australia in the 1960s and has been widely adopted wherever irrigation is permitted. Drip irrigation has transformed viticulture. Unlike flood irrigation, it allows irrigation of vineyards on undulating land and uses a limited water supply to maximum advantage. The technique requires extensive filtration of irrigation water, and soluble FERTILIZERS can be added directly to it, a process known as FERTIGATION.

Refinements include pressure-compensated drippers to manage a range of TOPOGRAPHIES, burying irrigation lines, or connecting the dripper to a buried emitter, techniques which usefully reduce evaporation from the wet soil surface. Research into the benefits of above- or below-ground systems in Australia and New Zealand has shown contradictory results, but a buried drip system placed mid row allows LEGUMES to be grown and managed by mowing, a convenient source of NITROGEN for organic vineyards (see COVER CROPS). R.E.S.

Nicholson, T., 'Going underground', *New Zealand Winegrower* (2017). www.ruralnewsgroup.co.nz/wine-grower/wg-industry/going-underground.

Wine Australia, 'Surface irrigation remains the best option' (2016). www.wineaustralia.com/news/articles/surface-irrigation-remains-the-best-option.

drones, or **unmanned aerial vehicles (UAVs)**, are proving useful and versatile in the vineyard, for example for measuring vine VIGOUR, temperature, and wind conditions; SPRAYING; potentially monitoring pests and diseases; and deterring BIRDS. They are less expensive than helicopters and conventional aircraft, and they can get much closer to the vines. See also REMOTE SENSING and ROBOTS.

drosophila, an insect pest of grapevines. The names 'fruit fly', 'Mediterranean fruit fly', 'vinegar fly', and 'pomace fly' are all applied to various species of *Drosophila*, in particular *Drosophila melanogaster*. *Drosophila* feed and reproduce in fermenting fruits and can frequently be found in the domestic fruit bowl. The major damage they cause in grapes, with a drastic reduction in wine quality, is the spread of bunch rots, especially SOUR ROT. *Drosophila* multiply rapidly—with a period of only six to eight days for the egg-to-egg reproductive cycle in hot climates—which explains why this fly has been used so much for the study of genetics. They are also a common problem in wineries during vintage, when insects can contaminate wine by spreading harmful bacteria, particularly ACETIC ACID BACTERIA. Maggots may develop in overripe fruit. Control is difficult and includes the destruction of breeding places, such as piles of rejected fruit and pomace.

While *Drosophila melanogaster* is an inconvenience, the Spotted Wing Drosophila (*Drosophila suzukii*) is an acknowledged pest which is causing concern in many vineyard and fruit-growing regions. This small insect has been known in Japan as a pest of soft-skinned fruits such as strawberries, cherries, and grapes since the early 1900s. It was first noted in North America on California strawberries in 2008 and has now spread north to Oregon and British Columbia, south to Mexico, and as far east as Quebec by 2013. The insect was first reported in Spain in 2008, and by 2012 had been reported in 11 countries, causing severe problems in several European regions in 2014. The main cause for concern is that the female has a strong, serrated ovipositor, enabling her to lay eggs in ripening fruit. Eggs hatch in a day, and maggots feed inside the fruit with no visible sign of their presence from the outside, making it difficult to eliminate the grapes from the harvest. R.E.S.

www.cabi.org/isc/datasheet/19938 for *D. melanogaster*

www.cabi.org/isc/datasheet/109283 for *D. suzukii*

drought, a severe and prolonged deficit of RAINFALL, compared with that normally received. Its implications for viticulture depend on the region and its normal climate. In cool and wet viticultural regions, drought years often produce the best vintages, especially of red wines. This is because excessive vegetative growth, or excess VIGOUR, is arrested; YIELDS are limited; BERRY SIZE may remain small with purported benefits for wine quality; and sunshine and warmth are greater than average. Such effects are well known in Europe and New Zealand.

However, severe WATER STRESS reduces yield and negatively affects the vine's ability to ripen grapes. It is almost always detrimental to wine quality, especially if it occurs during ripening.

Most dry viticultural climates are regularly warm and sunny enough, and drought is nearly always detrimental: whether directly, in the case of DRY-FARMED vineyards, or indirectly via a lack and/or reduced quality of IRRIGATION water. California suffered a periodic drought from 2011 to 2017 and again in 2020, with more than half of California suffering 'extreme drought' in 2021, causing stresses on underground water reserves and leading to devastating WILDFIRES. Australia also suffered drought and irrigation water restrictions, as well as bushfires, earlier in the 21st century and again in 2017–19. These phenomena are increasingly associated with CLIMATE CHANGE. Drought in such climates reduces growth and yield, and if very severe they can disrupt the ripening process more or less completely. In desert regions, drought is the norm, and commercial viticulture may survive only if sufficient irrigation is available.

See also CLIMATE AND WINE QUALITY.

R.E.S. & J.E.H.

Drouhin, Joseph, one of the most respected grower-merchants in Burgundy. Founded in 1880, the firm is based above historic cellars in the city of Beaune, dating from the 13th century. Joseph's son Maurice, who took over control of the firm in 1918, built up its reputation for quality and acquired a number of important vineyard holdings, starting with the Clos des Mouches (see BEAUNE). After the Second World War, exports of Joseph Drouhin wines increased considerably.

Robert Drouhin took over control of the house in 1957 and made many significant vineyard acquisitions, particularly on the Côte de NUITS, including Musigny, Griotte-Chambertin, Bonnes Mares, and Grands Échezeaux. An outpost in CHABLIS was established as long ago as 1968, with holdings in several GRANDS CRUS and PREMIERS CRUS. In 2020 the firm's holdings (all organically cultivated, with biodynamic practices) totalled 79.92 ha/197.49 acres. Drouhin also vinifies and distributes wines from the Laguiche family domaines, including Le Montrachet.

At 12,500 plants per ha its VINE DENSITY is one of the highest in Burgundy (where the average is 10,000). Drouhin was one of the first firms to investigate and embrace the fundamentals of modern winemaking, although many traditional techniques are also used. The clean, rigorous wines are never among Burgundy's richest but are serious expressions of each appellation. Today the firm is run by Robert's children Philippe, Véronique, Laurent, and Frédéric, together with Véronique's eldest daughter Laurène.

Somewhat ironically in view of Maurice's stated aim that Joseph Drouhin should concentrate on burgundy exclusively, Robert Drouhin was the first Burgundian to make a significant investment in a wine region outside France. **Domaine Drouhin Oregon**, established in 1987, owns 100 ha/250 acres of vines in production in Oregon's Dundee Hills. Roserock vineyard in the Eola-Amity Hills was acquired in 2013. These Oregon wines are vinified by Véronique Drouhin.

drunkenness and its history is inextricably entwined with that of wine, since one of the chief reasons wine has been cherished, and prohibited, is its property to intoxicate. Excessive wine drinking has therefore always had moral or religious connotations, beginning with the 'shameful' intoxication of Noah after the Flood (see BIBLE).

Varying definitions of what constitutes excessive drinking have prevailed at different times and in different societies, with opinions sometimes diverging within that same society. It is also important to note that drinking has always accompanied festivity and ritual and that societies have developed rules to contain it. The fear that these rules may be violated and society threatened is therefore apparent at almost every stage in the history of drunkenness.

Wine drinking is first documented in the ancient civilizations of the Middle East; the same is true of drunkenness (see SUMER and ancient EGYPT). An early Mesopotamian tablet describes a man drunk from strong wine: 'he forgets his words and his speech becomes confused, his mind wanders and his eyes have a set expression'. The suggested hangover cure includes liquorice, beans, and wine, to be administered before sunrise and before he has been kissed. The request of an Egyptian woman living in the 17th Dynasty may have been typical: 'Give me 18 cups of wine, behold I should love drunkenness.' Other races were quick to point the finger of over-indulgence at the Egyptians.

Sources show that drunkenness was both tolerated and at times denounced in these ancient civilizations. Although wine played a part in all their religions, the voice of disapproval most frequently heard was clerical. The ancient Jews also displayed a somewhat equivocal attitude towards wine drinking. The Old Testament contains many warnings against drunkenness alongside mentions of the positive benefits of temperate wine drinking. Some Jewish religious sects, such as the Nazarenes, chose to abstain altogether.

Society in ancient GREECE also showed a marked ambiguity in attitudes towards wine drinking. On the one hand, strict guidelines were laid down to curb any excess. Plato advised no wine before the age of 18 and moderation until 30. The all-male drinking party known as the SYMPOSIUM was, when properly observed, a strictly controlled ritual of drinking combined with poetry, entertainment, and debate. The aim was pleasant intoxication without loss of reason. See HERODOTUS for some more details.

On the other hand, some Greek wine drinkers drank specifically to lose their reason. The worshippers of the wine god DIONYSUS deliberately became intoxicated; indeed this was, in their eyes, a fundamental point of their religion. The authorities took fright at their wild behaviour, identifying drunkenness with a breakdown in social order. Despite attempts to ban the cult, its popularity continued into the Roman era, but attitudes towards drunkenness shifted somewhat afterwards. The Christian Church, while hallowing wine as a sacrament (see EUCHARIST), sought to dissociate itself from the riotous habits and heavy drinking of earlier religions. Behaviour reminiscent of the Dionysiac cult was met with excommunication. When St Bernard developed the Cistercian order in Burgundy he originally intended abstinence for his brethren; this was soon dropped. Monks earned a reputation for excessive drinking in the Middle Ages, but this reflected their dominance in winegrowing as much as in wine consumption (see MONKS AND MONASTERIES).

There were periods in ancient INDIA when drunkenness was considered a desirable state. Drunkards in the Middle East faced a formidable obstacle, however, in Muhammad's total prohibition on wine (see ISLAM). Wine drinking did not cease because of it but had to be covert. Drinking among the upper classes of Persian society, for example, took place at secret parties reminiscent of Greek symposia, with their strictly ritualized etiquette and emphasis on poetry and discussion (see ARAB POETS).

Meanwhile in Europe the scope for drunkenness was considerably increased with the discovery of DISTILLATION in the 12th century. Intoxication reached new heights as demand for this new liquor spread across the continent. The Dutch and Germans gained reputations throughout Europe for their drunkenness. In 17th-century Holland, drinking hours were applied to keep drinking in check. In Britain, too, drunkenness on the streets was increasingly blamed on spirits. By the 18th century wine was relatively expensive, and only the middle and upper classes could afford this route to drunkenness.

The Victorians were not the first to confront the problem of drunkenness, but they put it on a new footing. Alcoholism was defined as a disease in the mid 19th century and came to be identified with degeneracy of race. In Britain, wine was not seen as the main culprit—indeed it was seen by many, including Prime Minister Gladstone, as the remedy against drunkenness. The new catchword was 'temperance', and, while in the minds of some this meant the encouragement of moderate wine drinking to combat the medical and social ills of addiction to spirits, to a growing band of (often religiously inspired) campaigners it denoted complete abstinence. The governments of Britain and the United States adopted differing interpretations. Gladstone lowered the duty on light TABLE WINES to improve the health and morals of the British, while American states gradually voted themselves 'dry', culminating in full-blown PROHIBITION, which came into force in 1920. See also HANGOVER. H.B.

Lucia, S. P. (ed.), *Alcohol and Civilization* (1963).
Sournia, A., *Histoire de l'alcoolisme* (1986), translated by N. Hindley as *A History of Alcoholism* (1990).
Vickers, M., *Greek Symposia* (1978).

Drupeggio, name for the high-acid CANAIOLO Bianco that adds interest, with Trebbiano grapes, to Grechetto, Malvasia, and Verdello, in the ORVIETO wine of central Italy. Total plantings had fallen to 81 ha/200 acres by 2015.

dry, adjective often applied to wines, usually to describe those in which there is no perceptible SWEETNESS. Such wines may have as much as 10 g/l of RESIDUAL SUGAR, or even more in wines with particularly high ACIDITY (which tends to counterbalance sweetness), but in general the level is under 2 g/l. In this sense, virtually all but the most commercial red wines are dry, while white, rosé, sparkling, and fortified wines can vary considerably between **bone dry**, **dry**, **medium dry**, medium sweet, and sweet.

Some wines, particularly reds, are said to have a 'dry finish' if they are especially ASTRINGENT.

For the technical definition of 'dry' as laid down in EU labelling regulations, see SWEETNESS.

Dry Creek Valley, California wine region and AVA north-west of Healdsburg. See SONOMA.

dry extract. See EXTRACT.

dry-farmed vineyards rely entirely on natural RAINFALL and are sometimes referred to as rain-fed.

There can be little doubt that some European areas with both moderate rainfall and MEDITERRANEAN CLIMATES, now practising dry farming, could in many circumstances improve their YIELD and wine quality if limited IRRIGATION were allowed. Excessive WATER STRESS causes loss of PHOTOSYNTHESIS and eventually of the leaves themselves, and it can seriously prejudice normal RIPENING.

On the other hand, even in NEW WORLD regions where irrigation is widely practised, dry-farmed vineyards are often prized for the quality of their fruit, for which some wineries will pay a premium, thereby allowing such vineyards to remain economical. As WATER shortages become more prevalent with CLIMATE CHANGE, dry-farmed vines are likely to become more common, at least in regions of moderate rainfall, as will the use of irrigation. J.G. & R.E.S.

dry-grown. See DRY-FARMED.

dryland viticulture. See DRY-FARMED.

Dubourdieu, a father and son of particular importance in the history of white winemaking in BORDEAUX. The father Pierre (1923–2021), owner—with son Denis—of Ch Doisy-Daëne in BARSAC, produced the first dry white wine in the SAUTERNES area, and it is still made today. He was also instrumental in helping the Vaslin company improve the action of their grape PRESSES, and he was clearly an inspiration to his son Denis, co-oenology editor of the 4th edition of this book, with whom he worked on many experiments.

Denis Dubourdieu (1949–2016) was a research scientist at BORDEAUX University and owner and winemaker at Ch Reynon in CADILLAC CÔTES DE BORDEAUX, Clos Floridène and Ch Haura in the Graves, and Ch Doisy-Daëne and Ch Cantegril in Barsac. In 2014 he bought Ch Doisy-Dubroca, a small classified estate next to Doisy-Daëne. He was also, with his associates Dr Valérie Lavigne and Christophe Olivier, an international CONSULTANT in OENOLOGY.

He and his research team have been a significant influence on white winemaking, not just in Bordeaux but throughout France and abroad. His early areas of research were into the nature of *Botrytis cinerea* and in particular NOBLE ROT; earlier picking dates to enhance the AROMA of wines made from aromatic white grape varieties; and the influence of fermentation TEMPERATURES and selected YEAST on white wines. Later he investigated FLAVOUR COMPOUNDS in grape pulp and skins, identification of which can assist in the matching of vine varieties to soils and in aspects of vinification strategy such as picking dates, fermentation temperatures, and—a favourite research area of his—the extent of pre-fermentation maceration (see SKIN CONTACT). In particular, he elucidated the chemical nature of the varietal aromas of SAUVIGNON BLANC wines and their odourless precursors located in the grapes; he also demonstrated for the first time that yeast metabolism is involved in the transformation of FLAVOUR PRECURSORS into wine aromas. He also clarified the significant REDUCTIVE and FINING properties of yeast LEES during BARREL FERMENTATION and BARREL AGEING, rationalizing the ancient practice of BÂTONNAGE and also explaining why white wines fermented and aged in barrel are less oaky, oxidized, and astringent than those put into barrel only after fermentation and without lees. Denis Dubourdieu and co-researchers also studied the aroma compounds associated with oak BARRELS; they identified furan-methanthiol as the molecule responsible for the 'toasty' flavour of wines aged in oak. They also extensively investigated various off-odours in wines: those associated with REDUCTION, OXIDATION (including PREMATURE OXIDATION); GRASSY aromas due to ISOBUTYL-METHOXYPYRAZINES; and the ethylphenols associated with BRETTANOMYCES contamination. Most importantly for wine enthusiasts, his explanations of many of the phenomena of vinification have helped winemakers exploit them on a practical level.

Dubourdieu, D., 'Vinification des vins blancs secs en barriques', *Le Bois et la qualité des vins et eaux-de-vie* (1992).

Ribéreau-Gayon, P., et al., *Traité d'Œnologie* 1: *Microbiologie du vin: Vinifications* (7th edn, 2017), translated by J. Towey as *Handbook of Enology* 1: *The Microbiology of Wine and Vinifications* (3rd edn, 2021).

Ribéreau-Gayon, P., et al., *Traité d'Œnologie 2: Chimie du vin: Stabilisation et traitements* (7th edn, 2017), translated by J. Towey as *Handbook of Enology 2: The Chemistry of Wine Stabilization and Treatments* (3rd edn, 2021).

Ducellier, name associated with a special fermentation vat designed to extract, without electricity, maximum colour and TANNINS even in short fermentation periods. The system was devised for winemaking in ALGERIA but is now most commonly used to make PORT. See AUTOVINIFICATION.

Duché d'Uzès. In 2020, this region west of the central Côtes du RHÔNE growing area encompassed 317 ha/783 acres. Given its size, relatively little wine is currently bottled under the AOC. The production is 55% red, 16% rosé, and 29% white. Red wines are majority Syrah with Grenache; rosés are majority Grenache with Syrah; whites are majority Viognier with Grenache Blanc. M.C.W.

dulce, Spanish for 'sweet'. See SWEETNESS and, for official EU sugar levels, DOSAGE.

Dundee Hills is a wine region and AVA in the WILLAMETTE VALLEY of Oregon. It is often referred to as 'the Red Hills of Dundee' for its ruddy-coloured VOLCANIC clay soils.

Dunkelfelder, dark-skinned GERMAN CROSS notable mainly for the depth of its colour, a useful commodity in Germany's blending vats. Originally said to be a Blauer Portugieser × Teinturier cross, DNA PROFILING has shown it to be Madeleine Angevine × TEINTURIER. It is popular with growers if not consumers. German plantings totalled 206 ha/509 acres in 2019, mostly in the Pfalz. It is also grown to a limited extent in Switzerland and England. J.V.

Duras is perhaps the oldest vine variety still used in the once-famous red wines of GAILLAC. Its presence distinguishes them from the complex mosaic of other blending permutations that comprise the reds of SOUTH WEST FRANCE. It is not grown in the Côtes de Duras, nor anywhere else in any significant amount outside the Tarn *département*, where Gaillac is the chief appellation. In the Tarn, however, like its blending partner FER, it steadily gained ground thanks to Gaillac's powerful internal lobby against incoming INTERNATIONAL VARIETIES. But total plantings have started to decline once again, down from a peak of more than 1,000 ha/2,471 acres in 2008 to 781 ha/1,930 acres in 2019. The wine is deeply coloured, full-bodied, and lively. VARIETAL Duras wines produced in Gaillac show particularly good structure and acidity, eloquently demonstrating a marriage of CÉPAGE to TERROIR well worth defending. DNA PROFILING has shown that it is a natural CROSS of TRESSOT × SAVAGNIN.

Duras, Côtes de, red and white wine AOC (since 1937) of SOUTH WEST FRANCE, bounded by Côtes du MARMANDAIS to the south, BERGERAC to the north, and ENTRE-DEUX-MERS to the west. The town of Duras, with its impressive castle, marks the eastern extremity of the Entre-Deux-Mers plateau, and the 1,943 ha/4,857 acres of vines are planted either on LIMESTONE hilltops or on slightly more sheltered limestone and CLAY slopes.

The vine varieties are essentially those of BORDEAUX, and a specifically Duras character in the red wines is difficult to discern (although winemaking techniques such as BARREL MATURATION are increasingly employed). White Côtes de Duras can display originality, however, in fresh, dry Sauvignons and the sweet or MOELLEUX wines usually produced from Sémillon and MUSCADELLE.

The district has become a hotbed of ORGANIC and BIODYNAMIC VITICULTURE among the smaller producers, while the energetic CO-OPERATIVE of Landerrout-Duras is responsible for about half of the region's wines. P.S.

Durbanville, an important ward in the Coastal Region in SOUTH AFRICA, part of the Tygerberg district.

Durella, tart, white grape of the VENETO producing both sparkling and sweet wines.

Dureza, scarcely cultivated Ardèche dark-berried vine variety famous chiefly as a parent of Syrah, with MONDEUSE BLANCHE, and as a possible half-sibling of AGLIANICO.

Duriense, Portuguese VINHO REGIONAL whose boundaries correspond to the DOURO region, but producers may use a much wider range of grape varieties. As a result, a handful of credible examples of Pinot Noir, Syrah, Petit Verdot, Malbec, Sauvignon Blanc, Riesling, and Chardonnay bear witness to the Duriense's great diversity of TERROIR. S.A.

Durif is a well-travelled black grape variety, revealed in 1999 as probably a CROSS of PELOURSIN with SYRAH, propagated by a Dr Durif in south-eastern France in the 1880s. Today it has almost disappeared from France, but it is still cultivated in both North and South America as the dominant proportion of all vines called PETITE SIRAH.

As Durif, it was long grown in Australia's RUTHERGLEN, making a prodigiously inky, alcoholic wine of surprising quality. In the late 1990s and early 2000s, it was enthusiastically planted by RIVERINA growers who valued the way it retains deep colour and strong flavour even when heavily cropped. They were responsible for over half the national total of 625 ha/ 1,544 acres in 2015.

dusting, a vineyard practice designed to apply AGROCHEMICALS in dry powder form. Typical of such operations is the application of finely ground elemental SULFUR dust to control the fungal disease POWDERY MILDEW. Most vineyard agrochemicals are applied by SPRAYING, using a liquid formulation with water as the carrier. R.E.S.

Dutch East India Company, powerful trading organization which played a seminal part in the wine history of SOUTH AFRICA. Founded in March 1602 by the amalgamation of four Holland and two Zeeland companies which had been set up between 1596 and 1602 to conduct trade in East Asia, the General United Chartered East-India Company in the United Netherlands (Vereenigde Oost-Indische Compagnie: VOC) dominated European trade with the Orient for the rest of the 17th century, with counters and outposts strung out along the extended sea routes which linked the Netherlands with southern Africa, India, Ceylon, Sumatra, Java, Borneo, and Japan. Apart from its participation in the bulk transport of FORTIFIED WINES such as MADEIRA and spirits to the ends of its seaborne empire, it played a vital part in the Dutch penetration of southern Africa and in the establishment of viticulture on the Cape of Good Hope. See SOUTH AFRICA, history. A.J.D.

Dutchess, white AMERICAN HYBRID based on VITIS LABRUSCA, *Vitis aestivalis*, and VITIS VINIFERA grown with limited success in New York State. Created in 1868 by Andrew Jackson Caywood in Poughkeepsie, New York.

Dutch wine trade, a major influence on the history of international trade in wine. By the middle years of the 17th century, the Dutch republic had achieved a dominant position in the world trade in wines and spirits (and much else besides)—greater, even, than that of ENGLAND, whose Navigation Acts of the 1650s were directed specifically at Dutch freight. John Locke recorded in 1678 that the Dutch conducted more trade through BORDEAUX than England. Amsterdam, Rotterdam, and Dordrecht were world emporia. Its geographical position, at the estuaries of three great RIVERS, Schelde (Scheldt), Maas (Meuse), and Rhine, made it a natural point of convergence for river-based traffic; its wealthy bourgeoisie created a consumer demand distributed throughout the region, in addition to that of the nobility; and, lastly, its relative proximity to long-established and highly productive winegrowing areas enabled it to become a major conduit for the highly prized wines of the Rhineland and Alsace (see GERMAN HISTORY).

The RHINE (and its distributaries Waal and Lek) was virtually a wine highway, linking Cologne with Dordrecht and Rotterdam. Moreover, Middelburg in Zeeland, on the island of Walcheren at the estuary of the Schelde, had been the principal port of call for a centuries-old and highly lucrative seaborne traffic which linked the Atlantic seaboard with Scandinavia and the lands of the Baltic; formerly the principal staple (official market) for the whole of the Netherlands and earlier still the out-port serving the Flemish and Brabançon cities of Bruges, Ghent, and Antwerp, it had been secured for the independent Netherlands after the rising against Spain in 1568.

Hanseatic League

Although merchants from the region had been handling wine from very early times, it was not until the late 13th century that the Dutch, principally Hollanders and Zeelanders, entered the thriving maritime commerce which linked the countries of the Atlantic seaboard with the Baltic, as associates of the German Hansa (the Hanseatic League). This powerful alliance of about 80 merchant towns had by that time established a virtual monopoly of Baltic and Scandinavian trade by organizing large fleets of merchant vessels to transport basic commodities in bulk. From 1237 they began to acquire rights in English markets; and from 1252 they acquired trading privileges in Flanders, with reduced customs in Bruges and its out-port Damme.

Thus they gained access to the Atlantic trade and the estuaries of the 'wine rivers' of Europe: Adour, Lot-Tarn-GARONNE, LOIRE, Seine, Schelde (Scheldt), Maas (Meuse), and Rhine-MOSEL, to which would later be added the Guadalquivir, for SHERRY, and the DOURO for PORT, or at least their prototypes. French wines, chiefly from Gascony and Poitou, French salt from the bay of Bourgneuf, English wool, and Flemish cloth constituted the major commodities traded for the produce of the northern lands. This was the commerce which enriched the cities of Ghent, Bruges, Ypres, Antwerp, and many others. Wine consumption was a mark of wealth in northern lands. At a time when a wage-earning man might have to spend one-third of his income on bread, noble households devoted more than one-third of their expenditure to wine, although cheap wine was readily available in taverns and inns, where it had to compete with locally brewed beer and ale.

Zeelanders and Hollanders played an increasing role in the transportation of wines from Bordeaux and LA ROCHELLE to England, Flanders, and the Baltic from the last quarter of the 13th century onwards, gradually supplanting the Flemings and Brabançons, and they were joined in the course of the 14th century by mariners and traders from Dordrecht, Zierikzee, and Middelburg. In the first quarter of the 14th century, wine represented respectively 31% and 25% of imports into England and the Low Countries (Flanders, Zeeland), although this very high proportion was never equalled again. Much of this wine was re-exported: Gascon wine from England; Poitevin, Loire, and Rhine wines from Flanders and Zeeland.

The Dutch dominated the Bourgneuf salt trade during the 15th century, acquired a large share in the export of CLAIRET from Bordeaux and of the cheaper, white Poitevin wines from La Rochelle, and established a direct trade between Bourgneuf and the Baltic, carrying principally salt and wine and returning to the Low Countries with fish, furs, and grain. The chief commercial centre was the thriving port of Middelburg, recognized by the Habsburg government in 1523 as the official French-wine staple for the whole of the Netherlands, where merchant ships of all countries transported their wares.

After England's loss of Gascony in 1453, before which wine was exported from Bordeaux to England and then re-exported by licence, the Dutch secured the lion's share of the direct trade out of Bordeaux so that Hanseatic and Dutch vessels shipped huge quantities of wine to Middelburg. The western French wines of Poitou, Saintonge, and Aunis were transported in Dutch and Breton ships. Expensive sweet Mediterranean wines (from the Peloponnese, Crete, Cyprus, and Rhodes) were carried by ships from GENOA and VENICE. Some Rhine wines also found their way to Middelburg, but the bulk of these highly favoured wines travelled down the Rhine by barge to Dordrecht. From Middelburg and Dordrecht wines could radiate by sea or pass by river to Antwerp and thence to the rest of the region and beyond. The Dutch employed fleets of full-rigged ships of relatively large tonnage (up to 200 tons), which enabled them to undercut the freight charges of their competitors by a significant margin.

Expansion outside Europe

During the 16th century, three major changes, economic, religious, and political, contributed to the further expansion of Dutch commerce. The first was the fragmentation of the Hanseatic League itself, of which the Dutch were major beneficiaries and agents, enabling them to establish a virtual monopoly of Scandinavian and Baltic trade. The second, and much more dramatic, event was the undermining of Antwerp's commercial dominance by Spanish attempts to retain control of the Netherlands during the last third of the 16th century. The third was the declaration of independence from Spain made in 1581 by the seven northern provinces (Holland, Zeeland, Utrecht, Gelderland, Groningen, Friesland, and Overijssel). Although the United Provinces did not secure final international recognition until the treaty of Westphalia in 1648, they were from the 1580s a formidable maritime force, opposed to Spanish hegemony on religious and political grounds. After Antwerp's capture by Spanish forces in 1585, the United Provinces blocked the entry to the River Schelde and so cut the principal artery which linked Antwerp to Middelburg and the North Sea. The Dutch economy was thus for the first time decisively detached from the rest of the Netherlands in terms of capital, shipping, and the expertise of refugee Jews, who had earlier fled Spain and Portugal and migrated north with their commercial knowledge and connections to Amsterdam, which grew to become the major commercial, maritime, and banking centre of the Western world for the next century or so. Amsterdam, in north Holland, became heir to the Hanseatic League's Baltic trade and to Antwerp's international banking and commerce.

By the end of the 16th century, the Dutch fleet equalled the combined commercial fleets of Spain and Portugal and far outstripped those of France and England. It was thus able to take advantage of Iberian colonial expansion in the Americas and participate in South East Asian commercial colonialism. The DUTCH EAST INDIA COMPANY was founded in 1602; the West India Company in 1621. These major enterprises, which transformed the Netherlands into a colonial power and a major competitor of the English, French, and Portuguese, were driven not by wine but by the desire to control as much as possible of the commerce of the New World and Asia: sugar, tobacco, calico, spices, and their manufactured products. But the handling of wine remained a significant part of the commercial interests of the independent Netherlands, whose fleets competed for markets around the globe. Wine, brandy, and vinegar constituted nearly 40% of Dutch imports from France in 1645; most of the 224 ships which loaded wine at Bordeaux in 1682 were Dutch; and wines, fortified wines, and spirits were carried to the furthest corners of their trading empire, to North America, Surinam, the Caribbean islands, South Africa, Ceylon, and the Malay archipelago (Sumatra, Java, Borneo).

Influence on wine styles

Dutch interest in the transport of and trade in wines helped shape the evolution of wine production according to the dictates of changing taste and the requirements of the long-distance transportation of a perishable product by sea. Until the end of the 17th century, most wines could not survive from one vintage to the next, and many were spoiled and undrinkable within six months of the vintage, partly because they were transported in large oak casks, 'tuns' of 900 l weighing 1,000 kg, inclusive of the wood, which constituted the units of freight. Even before the creation of overseas colonies, wine destined for the Baltic had to overwinter at some convenient point. The grape harvest occurred too late in the year to permit immediate transportation to the northern lands, since the Baltic and White Seas often became impassable from November onwards. To overcome these disadvantages the Dutch popularized *mistelles*, wines fortified by the addition of brandy to stop fermentation and prolong the life of the wine, and *vins pourris*, made from overripened grapes. They also introduced the French to the stabilizing effects of SULFUR candles (known in French as *allumettes hollandaises* for many years) and encouraged the production of distilled liquors, based on both grain and grape. Amsterdam and Rotterdam became the principal international markets for wines and brandy in the 17th century, sustained by regular and reliable supplies, bulk storage, and an international network of merchants. One effect was the increase in planting white grape varieties in western France, to satisfy the tastes of the Dutch market.

At the same time, they practised BLENDING wines from different areas to increase the bulk of more popular varieties, to improve the taste or increase the BODY of inferior wines, or simply to make them conform to the changing palates of consumers. From the 15th century, for example, the English came to prefer stronger and sweeter wines than formerly. Thus the weak *clairet* of Gascony was 'strengthened' by blending with CAHORS or Portuguese wines. When in the 16th century the English developed a liking for SACK, the white wines of southern Spain (exported through Seville and Cádiz), and when at about the same time the CANARY ISLANDS and MADEIRA began producing sweet wines (malmseys and madeiras) from the MALVASIA grape (introduced from Crete), the Dutch entered that trade too, making significant inroads into the rapidly growing trade in Portuguese wines (via Lisbon, Lamego, and Oporto). And, of course, it was the Dutch who had the technical skills with which to drain the marshes of the MÉDOC in the mid 17th century, thereby enabling production of what were to be recognized as some of the finest red wines in the world.

Dutch prominence in the wine trade in the 16th and 17th centuries was merely one aspect of their general primacy in all aspects of international commerce during that period. They were principally merchants and shippers, controlling all aspects of trade, purchase, transport, storage, and sale to local merchants and retailers. Their purchasing power enabled them often to dictate advantageous terms to the producers and the large tonnage of their ships enabled them to transport their wares at relatively low cost. Such was their access to the wine-producing areas of Europe that they were able to circumvent the English embargo on all French wines during the Anglo-French war of 1690–6 by passing them off as Spanish, Portuguese, or even Rhenish and by transporting them in the appropriate casks.

By the 1690s, however, this dominance was being seriously undermined by an aggressive trade war with England, culminating in the Franco-Dutch war of 1692–4, in which Holland's commercial enemies conspired with France against her. A combination of protectionist legislation in England, widespread piracy, the successful French invasion of 1692, and the rapid rise of English seaborne trade (especially from Bristol and London) marked the end of the Dutch supremacy, though not of Dutch involvement in the world trade in wines and spirits.

The Dutch also played the crucial role in dictating the style of modern MUSCADET. A.J.D.

Craeybeckx, J., *Un grand commerce d'importation: les vins de France aux anciens Pays-Bas (xiii–xvi siècle)*, École Pratique des Hautes Études, section VI, Centre des Recherches Historiques (1958).
Israel, J. I., *Dutch Primacy in World Trade 1585–1740* (1989).
James, M. K., *Studies in the Medieval Wine Trade* (1971).

duty is levied on wine importation and movement into circulation from BOND in many countries at an extremely variable level. In general, countries in which viticulture is an economically (and therefore politically) important activity, such as France and Italy, tend to have extremely low duties on wine, while countries such as the UK which produce little or no wine, and/or those with restrictive policies on the sale of alcoholic drinks, such as Scandinavian countries, tend to have high duties. Wine duty may be a flat rate per litre, with fixed or sometimes variable rates according to style and ALCOHOLIC STRENGTH, as in the UK, or calculated ad valorem as in China and much of Asia. In HONG KONG, customs officials used to be issued with a set of current prices for all commonly encountered wines, but in 2008 the territory transformed itself into Asia's, or at least China's, wine hub by slashing wine duty to zero. For some historical background, see TAXATION.

E

Early Burgundy, California name for a grape once grown there in some quantity and eventually identified as the ABOURIOU of SOUTH WEST FRANCE. The same name has also been used in California for Blauer PORTUGIESER.

Early Muscat, bred in California as a TABLE GRAPE but has been successful on a very small scale as a wine grape in Oregon.

earthworms, segmented ANIMALS which have an important role in improving soil conditions for plant growth. Their burrowing improves soil mixing and aeration, and their feeding breaks down and redistributes ORGANIC MATTER, facilitating NUTRIENT uptake by the vine. Because a high level of mixing of organic matter is associated with SOIL FERTILITY, an abundance of earthworms is generally considered beneficial by many growers, especially those involved in ORGANIC VITICULTURE. Earthworms are encouraged by MULCHES, which reduce soil surface temperature, provide organic matter, and help retain moisture. They are discouraged by bare, HERBICIDE-treated soils, and their species diversity and biomass are reduced by TILLAGE and by copper-containing FUNGICIDES. See also SOIL BIOTA. R.E.S.

Easter Island, or Isla de Pascua in Spanish, is the most remote place for viticulture in CHILE. Distant about 3,700 km/2,299 miles from the mainland, this far-flung Pacific island is thought to have been first planted to vines around 1860 by French missionaries. They sited them on the slopes of the Rano Kau volcano to protect them from the WIND, the main viticultural challenge here, but they ultimately abandoned their efforts. At the beginning of the 2020s, two projects were under way to revive the island's viticulture, one by winemaker Fernando Almeda and the other by businessman José Mingo, both working in conjunction with locals. In addition to 4 ha/10 acres planted with Chardonnay, Pinot Noir, Garnacha, and other varieties, both projects were reproducing plants from abandoned vines whose varietal identity is still unknown. The first wines from these young vines were expected in 2022. P.T.

eating grapes. See TABLE GRAPES.

échantillon, French for 'sample'. See SAMPLING.

Échezeaux, GRAND CRU of the village of Flagey-Échezeaux in Burgundy's Côte de Nuits, producing red wines from Pinot Noir grapes. While wines of VILLAGE or PREMIER CRU status in Flagey-Échezeaux are sold under the name of neighbouring VOSNE-ROMANÉE, the majority of the commune's vineyard land is shared between the two grands crus Échezeaux and Grands Échezeaux.

Échezeaux is perhaps fortunate to be rated grand cru in its entirety (36 ha/89 acres), as many of its wines are relatively light. The vineyard is made up of 11 LIEUX-DITS ranging from Les Treux, which has a deep CLAY soil with indifferent DRAINAGE, to Les Échezeaux du Dessus, where the soil is shallower and chalkier and the wine correspondingly finer. It is not the equal, however, of neighbouring Grands Échezeaux (8 ha), which also abuts CLOS DE VOUGEOT.

There are 21 owners of Grands Échezeaux and over 80 of Échezeaux. Proprietors of both include DOMAINE DE LA ROMANÉE-CONTI, Domaine d'Eugénie, Domaine Lamarche, and Domaine Mongeard-Mugneret.

See also CÔTE D'OR and map under BURGUNDY. J.T.C.M.

ecological viticulture. See ORGANIC, BIODYNAMIC, and REGENERATIVE VITICULTURE, BIOLOGICALS, and SUSTAINABILITY.

e-commerce, selling wine online rather than in a store or via a printed catalogue, has been around for almost as long as the internet, but it suddenly became more prevalent around the world when so many wine consumers around the world were confined to their homes by the coronavirus pandemic. Wine merchants unfamiliar with existing platforms found themselves leaning heavily on younger, junior members of staff more familiar with INFORMATION TECHNOLOGY.

economics of wine, a field of study that aims to improve our understanding of what affects the demand for and supply of different types of wines and wine grapes and, thereby, the prices, quantities, and qualities of wines sold in regional and national markets and traded internationally. This area of study has grown considerably in recent years, for several reasons. One is the increasing GLOBALIZATION of wine. Another is that wine growers have shown, perhaps more clearly than any other farmers, the possibilities for adding value to their primary product, particularly by differentiating it according to its TERROIR or, for those growers who also venture into winemaking, via wine marketing investments. Wine producers are increasingly investigating which specific attributes of wine appeal to consumers in order to better target production and marketing efforts domestically and abroad. Some producers and buyers also benefit from INVESTMENT IN WINE. The demand for the best vintages of iconic wines as a way of storing wealth has grown along with affluence, including in newly wealthy countries such as China.

The basic point that excess supply can depress prices was well understood at the time of DOMITIAN's command in the 1st century CE to pull up half of the Roman Empire's vines planted outside Italy in the hope of holding back collapsing Italian wine and grape PRICES. For centuries, Spanish royalty also sought to restrict vine plantings in their Latin American colonies. More recently, Jean Milhau argued in his 1935 book, *Étude économétrique du prix du vin en France*, that wide variations in producer prices and incomes were due to huge swings in harvest volumes while CONSUMPTION remained insensitive (inelastic) to price. He argued that prices could be stabilized within certain limits by regulating the volumes released from the wineries' stocks and by distilling SURPLUSES. That idea became the cornerstone of France's wine policy in 1935, which also created a separate market organization for quality wines (see INAO). After the Second World War, integration of (initially six) European economies led to a single market and a common wine policy by 1970 (see EU). That policy soon involved compulsory DISTILLATION to support producer prices in an attempt to stem the flow of cheaper wines from Italy into France and appease social unrest in the LANGUEDOC—the so-called 'wine wars' of the 1970s. Its long-lasting effects included driving YIELDS up and quality down.

The study of wine demand initially focused on estimating the responsiveness of consumers to changes in price (relative to other beverages), taxes, and income. It then broadened to studying the many other aspects of wine that appeal to buyers such as regional reputations, varieties, brands, styles, closures, production methods, and vintages. Economists, most notably Orley Ashenfelter of Princeton University, have contributed to the reputation of VINTAGES by using econometric analysis to forecast the future value of each vintage's iconic wines, based on RAINFALL and TEMPERATURE data during the growing season. When Ashenfelter forecast in 1991 that the 1989 and 1990 vintages were likely to be outstanding for red bordeaux, many professional wine writers and judges at the time disagreed, but now there is almost unanimous agreement that they were exceptionally good years. More recently, economists have drawn on behavioural studies and neurosciences to explore, for example, the impact of price information on the consumer's perception of wine quality. Some studies suggest that blind tasters often prefer cheaper wine if they are unaware of its price but, if told it is expensive, their perception of a wine's quality is raised, according to brain scans.

Even though international trade in wine has grown in significance only during the past three decades, economists have cited wine for two centuries in their teaching of international trade theory. This is because wine was used by English economist David Ricardo when in 1817 he introduced the compelling notion of comparative advantage to explain the benefits of free trade between textile-exporting England and wine-exporting Portugal following the METHUEN TREATY.

There is both an American and a European Association of Wine Economists (www.wine-economics.org and www.euawe.com respectively), each of which has an annual conference. The *Journal of Wine Economics* has been published commercially since 2006 (currently four issues per year published by Cambridge University Press), and wine economics is recognized by ACADEME at, for example, the ISVV in Bordeaux, the Free University of Bozen-Bolzano, UC DAVIS, the University of ADELAIDE, and STELLENBOSCH University. K.A.

Alonso Ugaglia, A., et al. (eds.), *The Palgrave Handbook of Wine Industry Economics* (2019).
Anderson, K., *The International Economics of Wine* (2020).
Ashenfelter, O., et al. (eds.), *Handbook of the Economics of Wine*, vols. 1 and 2 (2018).
Castriota, S., *Wine Economics* (2020).

ecosystem, vineyard, the plant and animal communities which interact with each other and with their environment—TEMPERATURE, WIND, RAINFALL, and SOIL NUTRIENTS—in and around the vineyard. A vineyard is a living, functioning ecosystem. Because of the perennial nature of vineyards, the diversity of organisms and their interactions is more complex than in annual cropping systems. Complex interactions can stabilize in an ecosystem through ecosystem services (ES) such as BIOLOGICAL control of pests, diseases, and weeds, reduction of SOIL EROSION and SOIL COMPACTION, carbon capture from the atmosphere, nutrient provision to the plants, etc.

However, agricultural practices can severely reduce these free services, with the result that high levels of artificial inputs such as PESTICIDES, FERTILIZERS, and deep RIPPING are needed. Vineyards typically have high pesticide inputs (see AGROCHEMICALS), which is costly to the business and to the environment as many of these compounds have detrimental 'off-target' effects on flora and fauna above and below ground. These effects can extend beyond the vineyard through run-off and drift.

Compared with other cropping systems, viticulture, especially wine grapes, is an excellent model for developing sustainable systems as the aim is to produce a reasonable amount of grapes that taste good and are then vinified. Leaf damage, some loss of grapes, some cosmetic damage to the berries, and even an occasional insect in the harvest do not pose a threat to wine quality.

SUSTAINABLE VITICULTURE schemes usually start by using (collective) monitoring, for example insect traps and weather stations, and recording systems to track inputs of water, energy, and fertilizers. Modelling disease risks based on these data can be used to decrease pesticide use and reduce costs. Some of these schemes—including Greening Waipara in New Zealand, the Saumur-Champigny biodiversity project, and the EU-funded BioDiVine project in St-Émilion and other European wine regions—also attempt to improve ES and functional biodiversity (i.e. biodiversity that is useful to the grower) to minimize inputs and their impact on the environment.

These projects involve growing plants, usually native species, either between or under vineyard rows, or the creation of hedgerows and shelterbelts alongside vineyards, aiming at improving regulation of pests and diseases by natural enemies. Such plantings can provide these natural predators with SNAP—shelter, nectar, alternative food, and pollen, their key requirements. For example, parasitic wasps are a very important group of biological control agents. Having flowers in the vineyard can increase these insects' longevity there from three to 30 days because of the sugars and amino acids that floral nectars contain. The more traditional inter-row grasses that are used for vineyard COVER CROPS do not offer much SNAP as they produce no nectar.

This illustrates that a mix of different plants can have multiple functions, so that improving one ES service (grasses reducing erosion and compaction) can negatively affect another (lack of nectar for beneficial insects). Agroecology research is needed to determine whether creating biodiversity by growing specific plants, for example annual exotic flowering plants such as alyssum, buckwheat, and tansey, is more efficient than letting nature establish a more natural biodiverse vegetation by means of slightly adapted and cheaper management, for example reduced mowing, mowing alternate rows, use of roller crimpers on the cover crops, or fewer HERBICIDES.

A less expected but clearly welcome result from so-called 'landscape and biodiversity' projects is that growers gain a great deal of personal and communal satisfaction from this positive approach to biodiversity and readily communicate their experiences. Moreover, it makes the landscape more visually attractive for wine TOURISM, and social and economic aspects are an integral part of SUSTAINABILITY. S.D.W. & M.v.H.

Gurr, G. M., et al. (eds.), *Biodiversity and Insect Pests: Key Issues for Sustainable Management* (2012). bioprotection.org.nz/research/programme/greening-waipara.
Stefanucci, S., et al., 'Functional biodiversity in the vineyard' (2018). www.oiv.int/public/medias/6367/functional-biodiversity-in-the-vineyard-oiv-expertise-docume.pdf.
Wratten, S., et al. (eds.), *Ecosystem Services in Agricultural and Urban Landscapes* (2013).

Ecuador bottles a considerable quantity of wine, but the extent of its vineyards is considerably more limited. TROPICAL VITICULTURE, enforced DORMANCY, and the considerable application of FUNGICIDES are essential here on the equator where it rains most days. The limited plantings of INTERNATIONAL VARIETIES are mainly at ELEVATIONS of over 2,500 m/8,000 ft near the capital Quito or on the coast in the hinterland of Guayaquil and anchored by the Dos Hemisferios winery. Tungurahua province, a valley near Ambato, south of Quito, now has a few small winery operations among the fruit orchards, and Viña del Guayacán in Loja is the first winery in the south of Ecuador producing premium small-batch wines. E.M.G.

Goldstein, E., *Wines of South America* (2014).

edel means 'noble' in German, and thus **Edelfäule** is German for NOBLE ROT, and EDELZWICKER is the name chosen to add lustre to a not particularly noble blend in ALSACE. Similarly, Gutedel is the German synonym for the not particularly noble CHASSELAS grape.

Edelzwicker, Alsace term, originally German, for what is usually a relatively basic blend. See ALSACE.

Eden Valley, wine region (High Eden is a subregion) abutting SOUTH AUSTRALIA's Barossa Valley, with high ELEVATION and a fine reputation for limey, long-lived RIESLING and elegant, medium-bodied Shiraz (Henschke's Hill of Grace, for example).

Edna Valley, California wine region and AVA on the ocean side of the coastal mountains. See SAN LUIS OBISPO.

education, wine. Education plays an important part in the production, sale, and enjoyment of a product as complex and, in many countries, as foreign as wine. Detailed knowledge of wine involves an appreciation of history, geography (inevitably including a host of foreign names), science, and technology, quite apart from the development of practical tasting skills.

Education for wine-producing professionals is discussed under ACADEME and is, naturally, concentrated in the world's wine regions. Some universities, such as BORDEAUX, offer courses, especially in tasting, that are open to wine merchants and the general public. There is even more overlap between wine-trade education, courses designed specifically for the wholesale and retail trade, and consumer education; the most enthusiastic wine consumers may well want to know more about wine than the less academically inclined wine traders. The Institute of MASTERS OF WINE, for example, the leading international wine-trade educational body which opened its notoriously stiff series of trade examinations to those unconnected with the wine trade in the early 1990s, admitted its first Master of Wine (MW) without any connection with the wine trade, a Hollywood lawyer, in 1993.

While trade education is usually undertaken by this sort of professional body (the leading international organization is the London-based WSET), consumer education may be undertaken by a wide range of lecturers and wine merchants. This can take the form of TASTINGS so informal as to constitute a party, tutored tastings, BLIND TASTINGS, or some form of wine TOURISM. This century has seen an explosion of interest in wine courses, especially in the US where many of those who run them belong to the Society of Wine Educators, in the UK with its Association of Wine Educators, and in Asia.

Other forms of wine education include both print and online articles (see WINE WRITERS), books (see LITERATURE OF WINE), various forms of audio-visual instruction such as television and radio programmes and online wine courses, aspects of SOCIAL MEDIA, and software (see INFORMATION TECHNOLOGY). Interactive wine tasting is a way of combining the practical with the theoretical.

Eger, town in north-east HUNGARY whose wines have been exported since the 13th century, although various Turkish incursions interrupted this trade. Eger's most famous siege was during the 16th-century Ottoman occupation when, according to legend, the defenders of Eger were so dramatically fortified by a red liquid which stained their beards and armour that the Turks retreated, believing their opponents to have drunk BIKAVÉR, or Bull's Blood. But the truth is that Bikavér production and bottling started only at the beginning of the 20th century.

The town gives its name to a PDO on the foothills of the volcanic Bükk Mountains where rainfall is low and spring tends to come late. This is one of Hungary's cooler wine-producing areas, and therefore the wines have good aromas and acidity. The geological make-up is diverse, with CALCAREOUS sections alternating with patches of LOESS, ALLUVIAL SOILS, and extensive VOLCANIC rocks, especially TUFF. The southern slope of the Nagy-Eged Hill is one of Hungary's most valuable vineyard sites, and the highest at 536 m/1,759 ft. Pajdos, Síkhegy, and Grőber are very distinctive too.

Grown on over 200 ha/500 acres, KÉKFRANKOS (Blaufränkisch) dominates Eger's vineyards, though KADARKA, the renowned grape of Eger's halcyon days, is being rediscovered, and Pinot Noir and Shiraz are also planted. As for white wines, Eger, like Balatonfüred-Csopak and Somló, produces some of the finest Olaszrizlings (WELSCHRIESLING) in all Hungary. Other fine whites are made from Chardonnay, LEÁNYKA, KIRÁLYLEÁNYKA, and HÁRSLEVELŰ. G.R. & G.M.

egg whites play a surprisingly important part in the production of fine red wines. Their particular albumin content makes them highly desirable FINING agents for red wines because they act relatively gently, adsorbing harsh and bitter TANNINS in preference to the softer tannins and STABILIZING the colour of red wines prior to bottling. Five egg whites are usually sufficient to fine excess COLLOIDS from a 225-l/59-gal barrel of young red wine. The separation of yolks from egg whites can form an important part of CELLAR WORK in some seasons (and egg yolks can be a significant waste product of winemaking).

Egiodola, tannic French 1954 vine CROSS of FER SERVADOU with ABOURIOU whose total French plantings had fallen to 177 ha/437 acres by 2019. There are limited plantings in Brazil.

égrappage, French term for DESTEMMING grapes meaning literally 'debunching'.

Egypt, North African country which makes small quantities of wine from its 78,852 ha/194,848 acres of vineyard in 2020, about 99.5% of which is devoted to producing TABLE GRAPES. The ancient Egyptians provide us with some of the oldest depictions of winemaking techniques, however.

Ancient Egypt

Remains of grapes have been found in late Predynastic sites (*c*.3300–3000 BCE), but the vine is not part of the country's native flora and was probably introduced from CANAAN in Predynastic times, despite HERODOTUS' false claim (*Histories* 2. 77) that there were no vines in Egypt. The southern Levantine industry had matured to such a degree that by the time of Scorpion I (*c*.3150 BCE), one of the first rulers of a united Egypt, his tomb at Abydos was stocked with some 4,500 l/1,900 gal of imported wine from southern Canaan. The wine was laced with terebinth tree resin, to which fresh fruit (grapes and figs) and a variety of herbs (including thyme and savory) had been added. Beginning around 3000 BCE, the Egyptian pharaohs financed the establishment of a royal wine industry in the Nile Delta.

The best grapes were considered to come from the Nile Delta; by the time of the New Kingdom (*c*.1550–1050 BCE), viniculture had been introduced to the oases of the western desert and the middle Nile. Vines—irrigated, and manured with bird droppings—were grown in walled gardens, sometimes among other fruits such as olives, and trained over pergolas (see TENDONE).

As in ancient GREECE and ancient ROME, there were two distinct winemaking operations: treading, or CRUSHING, to yield some FREE-RUN juice; and PRESSING the remainder with a sack-press. When harvested, grapes were trodden by foot by labourers who could hang on to overhead supports or suspended ropes. The vat was deliberately shielded from the heat, and an offering of the must was made to the goddess Renenutet. Tomb paintings illustrate wine production amply, although the precise details are not always clear. After treading, the pressing was often carried out in a special sack-press with a pole fixed in a loop at either end of what was effectively a giant jelly bag. This was then twisted by several workers in opposite directions, and the liquid was collected in a vessel beneath. The liquid flowing out of the sack-press is always depicted as red. In Old Kingdom times (*c.*2686–2181 BCE) the wine was transferred to large jars, later called AMPHORAE.

In scenes dating from the New Kingdom, MUST flows from the trough along a small conduit into a receptacle. In the sack-press apparently only the skins would have been pressed. Probably the FREE-RUN juice and the PRESS WINE were fermented together. Depictions show only the transfer of the must from the press into amphorae. In one illustration the contents of the press are transferred to large fermentation vats, then pressed in the sack-press and transferred into amphorae.

The actual alcoholic fermentation took place in the amphorae, from which the ancient Egyptians would then deliberately exclude air, just like many modern winemakers. The filled amphorae were covered with cloth or leather lids, smeared with Nile mud, and then sealed. Small holes to allow the continuing escape of CARBON DIOXIDE were later blocked up.

White wine is likely attested in the Scorpion I tomb, based on the yellowishness of the residue, and in some of the amphorae in the Tutankhamun tomb, based on chemical analyses. Egyptian wines were generally RESINATED WINES, from the beginning of the royal winemaking industry to the end of the Pharaonic period. Wine was also drunk for medicinal purposes, when it was sometimes flavoured with Levantine and Egyptian herbs, *kyphi* (a mixture of raisins, honey tree resins, herbs, and other plants), and sometimes other less pleasant ingredients such as asses' hair and the dung of various animals and birds.

Wine trade organization It is clear from the seals on amphorae and from the titles of certain officials that the manufacture and delivery of wine were already organized at royal level in the earliest periods. Wine is often shown in scenes on wall paintings. Lists from the Fifth Dynasty distinguish five types of wine according to origin. 'Wine from Asia' and Canaan is also mentioned, and Canaanite wine amphorae are found in the New Kingdom. Inscriptions on amphorae of that period usually indicate year, vineyard site, owner, and chief winemaker (rather more information than is given on most modern wine labels). Most but not all centres of wine production lay on the western arm of the Nile Delta.

Wine drinking Wine was drunk by gods, kings, and nobles, especially at feasts, and was rated only slightly behind beer, which was the most common beverage of ancient Egypt. Amphorae, often painted with vine leaves, are depicted on tables or resting on stands. The wine was sieved as it was poured out. Servants would fill small beakers for serving, sometimes carrying a second small jug (possibly containing water to dilute the wine, but more likely a herbal concoction). The wine was drunk from bowls or goblets (which sometimes rested on stands). The king Akhenaten and his family are shown drinking at the royal capital Tell-el-Amarna (14th century BCE). Priests received wine as part of their daily rations, likewise army officers and foreign mercenaries; but the workers of Amarna received none, an indication of its value. By contrast, the workers who had built the pyramids received a daily allotment of two 'bottles' or about 4–5 l/1–1.3 gal of beer.

Religion and wine Wine is said to be the drink of gods, and also of the dead (along with beer and milk). Thus it was important in cult worship and is frequently mentioned in lists of offerings, sometimes several sorts together. It was frequently offered as nourishment to deities by the king or private persons, also symbolizing purification. LIBATIONS of wine and water were made at temples and tombs throughout the country.

The goddess Hathor, 'the mistress of DRUNKENNESS', was the Egyptian equivalent of the Sumerian beer goddess Ninkasi. She was closely associated with a lesser goddess 'who makes beer', Menqet. One festival to honour Hathor, appropriately designated the 'the Drunkenness of Hathor', at her temple in Dendera, recalled the story of how the goddess had gone on a rampage to destroy a rebellious humanity in her form as the lioness goddess, Sekhmet. Just in time, Re diverted her from her mission by filling the inundated fields with 'red beer', which Hathor interpreted as a sign that she had accomplished her task. She then over-indulged and forgot to carry out the devastation of humankind. The yearly celebration at Dendera coincided with the inundation of the Nile during the summer, when reddish iron-rich soils were washed down from the Atbara River in Sudan, giving the waters the appearance of 'red beer'. By drinking alcoholic beverages at the festival—both wine and beer—and celebrating with music and dance, humanity shared in Hathor's transformation into her more benign form as the feline Bastet.

Classical authors identified Osiris as the benefactor who bestowed wine on humankind, comparing him in this respect to the Greek god DIONYSUS. The grape certainly became a symbol of the dying and rising god. Vines depicted in tomb paintings symbolized the deceased's hope for resurrection. Other texts refer to wine as the perspiration of Re or as the eyes of the god Horus. His pupils are said to be grapes through which wine flows. In the later periods the term 'Green Eye of Horus' was used to refer to wine.

See also ORIGINS OF VINICULTURE and PALAEOETHNOBOTANY. J.A.B. & P.E.M.

James, T. G. H., 'The earliest history of wine in Egypt', in P. E. McGovern et al. (eds), *The Origins and Ancient History of Wine* (1995).

Lesko, L. H., 'Egyptian wine production during the New Kingdom', in P. E. McGovern et al. (eds), *The Origins and Ancient History of Wine* (1995).

See articles 'Wein', 'Weinkrug', 'Weinopfer', and 'Weintrauben', in *Lexikon der Ägyptologie* (1975–86), cols. 1169–92 (the standard scholarly reference work on the subject).

Modern wine production

The production and sale of wine in Egypt was state-controlled from 1963 until its privatization in 1998. Today, brewers Heineken own the leading and thoroughly modern Egyptian wine producer Gianaclis, and in 2021 there were two others. SULTANA (called Banati locally) and a range of INTERNATIONAL VARIETIES are grown on trellises, mainly in the north of the country, although VINE AGE is low and DROUGHT and heat remain challenges. Satellite technology is harnessed to apply DRIP IRRIGATION with precision. Grapes are picked between late June and early August and are generally chilled before transport to sophisticated wineries equipped with STAINLESS STEEL. French oak BARRIQUES are used for some wines, but most are drunk young.

Ehrenfelser is one of the more FROST-resistant better GERMAN CROSSES, developed at GEISENHEIM in 1929. Although it was said to be a RIESLING × SILVANER cross, DNA PROFILING has shown that it is Riesling × Knipperlé. It is not nearly as versatile in terms of site as KERNER, which became a more obvious choice as a flexible Riesling substitute. Total German plantings of Ehrenfelser had fallen to 36 ha/90 acres by 2019, mainly in the Pfalz and Rheinhessen.

Einzellage, literally 'individual site' in the wine regions of GERMANY. Almost all of Germany's vineyards are officially registered as one of approximately 2,600 **Einzellagen**, which can vary in size from a fraction of a hectare to more than 200 ha/494 acres, the average being about 38 ha. Only wines of the category QUALITÄTSWEIN are allowed to be labelled with an Einzellage. Names of Einzellagen must be preceded on labels by the name of the village in which they are located; thus a wine from the Mandelring vineyard in the village of Haardt is called Haardter Mandelring.

An Einzellage should not be confused with a Grosslage, which follows the same formula of 'town+vineyard name' but is in reality a collection of many sites in the vicinity of—but by no means always clustered around—the town in question. See GROSSLAGE. D.S.

Eisacktaler, German for Valle Isarco, one of six subzones of the DOC of ALTO ADIGE producing pure, dry white wines as well as a red wine, suffixed with Klausner Laitacher, based on SCHIAVA, LAGREIN, and/or PINOT NERO.

Eisenberg, tiny wine village in Austria's SÜDBURGENLAND adjacent to and named for a high hill dominated by iron-rich SCHIST; its twin over the Hungarian border, Vaskereztes, shares the same etymology. Since 2008 Eisenberg has lent its name to an official DAC for BLAUFRÄNKISCH wines grown throughout the region. Those additionally labelled Reserve must be raised in cask or small barrels, must reach 13% alcohol, and cannot be marketed until the second calendar year following their harvest. D.S.

Eisheiligen, Germany's Ice Saints, including the saints Pancras, Servatius, Boniface, and Sophie, or *Kalte Sophie*, whose commemoration days fall between 11 and 15 May. After 15 May, the risk of spring FROST in the vineyards is deemed past.

Eiswein designates German wines produced from grapes frozen on the vine and pressed while still frozen. The deliberate picking of Eiswein with any significant frequency seems to have originated in the 1960s, and from the 1980s the practice became routine at most top estates, excepting those farming vineyards not prone to deep FROST. Freezing concentrates not just the SUGAR in the grapes but also ACIDITY and EXTRACT, and Riesling Eiswein is routinely the highest in acid (as well as some of the highest-priced) of any German wines. For best results, a frost of at least −8 °C/18 °F is required, for which grapes are generally harvested between five and eight o'clock in the morning of the first sufficiently cold November or December days. Eiswein picked in January or even February is increasingly common, if seldom as high in quality. Such wines are still labelled for the calendar year of the growing season. Before 1971, Eiswein was frequently labelled for the date of picking or nearest Saint's Day (Nikolauswein, for example, designated a wine harvested on 6 December), but such information is currently not permitted on the label. Since 1982, Eiswein has had its own PRÄDIKAT with the minimum MUST WEIGHT of a BEERENAUSLESE, namely 110–128 °OECHSLE depending on the region and variety; in AUSTRIA the minimum is 25 °KMW (approximately 127 °Oechsle). The harvesting of Eiswein has become much more routine as a result of the widespread use of semi-permeable PLASTIC SHEETING that hugs the vines to protect grapes from birds and rain while waiting for a suitably deep frost. (Protection from wild boar is another matter, and more potential Eiswein is lost to these marauders than to any other cause.) While the classic concept of Eiswein for most growers is a wine from BOTRYTIS-free grapes, this is not a legal requirement, and the use of film sometimes traps humidity, thereby promoting botrytis. If the harvest does not achieve the requisite ripeness or the character deemed appropriate to Eiswein by the individual winegrower, the wine usually ends up being bottled as an AUSLESE or subsumed into another wine, even though these practices are technically legally questionable.

See also ICEWINE in Canada. D.S.

Eiximenis, Francisc (*c.*1340–*c.*1409), Catalan Franciscan friar and author of *Lo Crestià* ('The Christian'), an encyclopedia of the Christian life. Thirteen books were planned but only four were finished. It is aimed at a popular, not a learned, audience, and hence it is written not in Latin but in the vernacular, Catalan. As a result it had little to no influence on other European authors of the Middle Ages (see LITERATURE OF WINE).

Its third book, *Lo terç del Crestià*, dated 1384, is concerned with sin. The section on gluttony deals with DRUNKENNESS (chs. 350–9) and the etiquette of wine drinking (chs. 362–7, 393–5). Eiximenis is aware of the medical properties of wine, but his interest is in the moral aspects of drinking. Drunkenness, he says, leads to every conceivable vice, but, taken in moderation, wine is a good thing. All other nations, except perhaps the Italians, drink too much: only the Catalans have the art of sensible drinking. This means three cups at dinner, three at supper: one should never have more than four, and there is to be no drinking between meals. Although he disapproves of the fastidious habits of connoisseurs, he does tell where the best wines are to be found. They are the strong, sweet wines of the Mediterranean, particularly MALMSEY (Malvasia), the Cretan Candia, and Picapoll from MALLORCA. He ranks Italian wines above French wines and insists that strong wines (these do not include the wines of France) should be mixed with water, the stronger the wine the more water. H.M.W.

Gracia, Jorge J. E., 'Rules and regulations for drinking wine in Francisc Eiximenis' *Terç del Crestià* (1384)', *Traditio*, 32/1 (1976), 369–85.

Gracia, Jorge J. E., 'Francisc Eiximenis' *Terç del Crestià*: edition and study of sources, chs. 359–436' (PhD thesis, University of Toronto, 1971).

Elba, Mediterranean island off TUSCANY, where emigration and the booming tourist industry have drastically reduced the role of wine in the overall economic picture. The entire island is covered by one DOC, called Elba, with 107 ha/264 acres in production in 2020, three-quarters of it white wine. The one DOCG is a sweet DRIED-GRAPE WINE, the red PASSITO-style ALEATICO. W.S.

Elbling, ancient, and some would say outdated, light-skinned vine variety cultivated in the Mosel Valley since the Roman era. At one time it was effectively the only variety planted in LUXEMBOURG and dominated the extensive vineyards of medieval Germany (see GERMAN HISTORY). Today it is increasingly unpopular in Luxembourg (5% of the country's vineyard in 2020) and in Germany, where only 475 ha/1,174 acres remains, most of it in the upper reaches of the MOSEL above Trier, in which CHALK dominates SLATE and Riesling has difficulty ripening. Much of the Elbling grown here is used for SEKT. While the vine is distinguished for its antiquity and productivity, its wines are distinguished by their often searing acidity and their relatively low alcohol. DNA PROFILING in Austria suggested a parent–offspring relationship with GOUAIS BLANC.

El Dorado, California county and AVA. See SIERRA FOOTHILLS.

electrical resistance tomography. See PROXIMAL SENSING.

electrodialysis, a sophisticated, electrically driven membrane FILTRATION process which allows the removal of selected ions (electrically charged molecules), has been used since the 1960s to desalinate water and was adapted for use in the STABILIZATION of wine by INRA in the 1990s. In this context it is used to remove potassium, TARTRATES, and bitartrates. Despite the relatively high capital costs of the technology, it is gaining acceptance in the wine industry because it uses 80% less energy than cold stabilization, it is much faster, and its total running costs are up to 40% lower. The volume of water used to extract the tartrate salt has been significantly reduced by the use of REVERSE OSMOSIS, and there are said to be no adverse effects on wine quality. No further filtration is required to remove the potassium-bitartrate crystals before bottling, although the wine does have to be filtered prior to electrodialysis to avoid clogging the membranes. One of the greatest advantages of this process is that it allows great control over what and how much is removed from the wine.

Electrodialysis may also be used to remove calcium (another potential source of instability), to remove sodium chloride (see SALINITY), and to lower the PH of a wine without ACIDIFICATION.

Electrodialysis is more selective than ION EXCHANGE and is widely used in the EU and most other wine-producing countries that regulate winemaking processes—but only for tartrate stabilization. There are a number of units in wineries in Italy, France, Germany, and Spain, with others in South Africa and the US. Mobile

Apu Winery, named after a sacred mountain god, planted this experimental PINOT NOIR vineyard in the Curahuasi Valley in PERU in 2019 at an ELEVATION of 3,300 m/10,827 ft in the Andes Mountains. By PRUNING in January, the vines are better able to withstand the effects of the rainy season from November to March. © Apu Winery

units are in use in the EU, the US, Chile, Argentina, Australia, and New Zealand.

OIV, 'International Code of Oenological Practices'. www.oiv.int/en/technical-standards-and-documents/oenological-practices/international-code-of-oenological-practices.

Wollan, D., 'Membrane and other techniques for the management of wine composition', in A. G. Reynolds (ed.), *Managing Wine Quality 2: Oenology and Wine Quality* (2nd edn, 2021), 183–212.

electromagnetic induction. See PROXIMAL SENSING.

élevage, French word that describes an important aspect of winemaking but has no direct equivalent in English. *Élevage* means literally 'rearing', 'breeding', or 'raising' and is commonly applied to livestock, or humans, as in *bien élevé* for 'well brought up'. When applied to wines, it means the series of cellar operations that take place between FERMENTATION and BOTTLING, suggesting that the winemaker's role is rather like that of a loving parent who guides, disciplines, and civilizes the raw young wine that emerges from the FERMENTATION VESSEL. The word AGEING is often used as an alternative, although this may refer to both pre- and post-bottling.

For details of the various stages of *élevage*, see RED WINEMAKING, WHITE WINEMAKING, and BARREL AGEING.

elevation, the height above mean sea level of a location such as a vineyard, often mistakenly referred to as altitude. Local elevation of vineyards above valley floors or flat land determines their air drainage and TEMPERATURE relations, including liability to FROST. (See also TOPOGRAPHY, MESOCLIMATE, and CLIMATE AND WINE QUALITY).

The elevation of a vineyard can have important effects on its climate and therefore on its viticultural potential. Other things being equal, temperature falls by about 0.6 °C/1.1 °F per 100 m/330 ft greater height. However, the influence of elevation on climate varies depending on whether the area is on the windward or leeward side of the mountainous area. Windward zones will typically be cooler and wetter with height, while leeward zones, known as rainshadows, will typically be warmer and drier. Good examples of this effect are found in ALSACE, eastern WASHINGTON, RIOJA, and MENDOZA. Planting vineyards at higher elevations is commonly considered a means of avoiding the impact of increasing temperatures related to CLIMATE CHANGE. For example, FAMILIA TORRES and Castell D'Encus in Cataluña have developed vineyards in the nearby Pyrenees, while Prager have been planting much higher land than previous generations in the WACHAU, and Bisol's Vigna 1350 project is high up in the Dolomites. Others seeking the benefits of elevation include Franz Haas and Alois Lageder in Italy's ALTO ADIGE and Gaia in Nemea, GREECE.

With the increased market emphasis on fresher styles of wine, ever-higher vineyard sites have also been sought in the warmer wine regions. Examples include the ADELAIDE HILLS, the Central Ranges of NEW SOUTH WALES, and VICTORIA in Australia; La Carrera in the Uco Valley and other high-elevation plantings in ARGENTINA; the foothills of the Andes in CHILE; and California's SIERRA FOOTHILLS.

The lower temperatures at higher elevations retard both vine BUDBREAK, reducing the risk of late frost, and, in particular, RIPENING, so that nights are cooler during the ripening period, leading to higher acid concentration. Effects on GRAPE COMPOSITION AND WINE QUALITY have been widely studied, for example in relation to TEMPRANILLO in Rioja. Such research is useful for predicting the impact of climate change on wine quality.

Elevated vineyards also experience more ULTRAVIOLET RADIATION, which is likely to increase quality because of stimulation of PHENOLIC synthesis.

Most of the world's highest established vineyards are in Latin America, but they are being challenged by new plantings in the Himalayas. Three of the world's highest commercial vineyards are Swiss-born Donald Hess's plantings in the northern province of Salta, Argentina. Colomé, near Molinos, is at 2,200–2,300 m/7,218–7,546 ft; El Arenal, Payogasta, is at 2,400–2,500 m/7,874–8,200 ft; Altura Máxima, also near Payogasta, is at 3,111 m/10,207 ft). Even higher is the Pinot Noir vineyard planted by Apu Winery in 2019 at 3,300 m/10, 827 ft in Curahuasi, Peru, and those in Uquía, in Quebrada de Humahuaca, Jujuy, north of Salta, at 3,329 m. BOLIVIA has vines up to 2,640 m in the Cotagaita Valley. The highest vineyards in the US are in Fremont, Colorado (2,103–2,133 m/6,900–7,000 ft), and Mora, New Mexico (2,332 m/7,650 ft).

In the Himalayas in Asia, there are small commercial vineyards up to 2,900 m/9514 ft in the south-west of CHINA. The world's highest vineyard is said to be in Lhasa, Tibet Autonomous Region of China, at 3,563 m/11,690 ft. The highest European vineyard is probably in Vilaflor on the island of Tenerife, at 1,700 m/5,577 ft. On mainland Europe, there are vines at 1,368 m/4,488 ft at Barranco Oscuro in GRANADA and up to 1,090 m/3,576 ft and 1,250 m/4,100 ft in SWITZERLAND and AOSTA respectively.See also DIURNAL TEMPERATURE RANGE. R.E.S., J.E.H. & G.V.J.

Arias, L. A., 'Climate change effects on grapevine physiology and biochemistry: benefits and challenges of high altitude as an adaptation strategy', *Frontiers in Plant Science* (2022).

Iland, P., et al., 'Climate and the vine', in *The Grapevine: From the Science to the Practice of Growing Vines for Wine* (2011).

Ramos, M., and Martinez de Toda, F., 'Variability in the potential effects of climate change on phenology and on grape composition of Tempranillo in three zones of the Rioja DOCa (Spain)', *European Journal of Agronomy*, 115/2 (2020).

Elgin, predominantly white-wine district in the Cape South Coast region of SOUTH AFRICA. Its cool, high vineyards in apple-orchard country east of Cape Town are a source of fine Chardonnay and Sauvignon Blanc, as well as some successful Pinot Noir and Shiraz.

El Hierro, Spanish DOP covering the whole of the eponymous island in the CANARY ISLANDS, with just 200 ha/494 acres of vineyards. Of the 13 varieties allowed in the DOP, the dominant grape is the white VIJARIEGO, but some reds and rosés are also made. V. de la S.

Elim, very cool ward in SOUTH AFRICA's Cape Agulhas district on the southernmost tip of Africa within the Cape South Coast region. While initially lack of CRUSH facilities, low temperatures, and baboons were threats to its survival, the community of passionate pioneering producers are now safely established.

ELISA, acronym for 'enzyme-linked immunosorbent assay', a serological test which can also be used to detect vine pathogens. First used in plant pathology in the mid 1970s, the technique is now used routinely to determine the presence of a wide range of vine pathogens, and test kits are available commercially. R.E.S.

Golino, D., et al., 'Laboratory testing for grapevine diseases', in L. J. Bettiga (ed.), *Grape Pest Management* (3rd edn, 2013), 61–8.

ellagitannins. See OAK FLAVOUR and PIGMENTED TANNINS.

El Niño, one phase of anomalous sea surface temperatures (SSTs) in the tropical Pacific that, together with the opposite phase La Niña, are the result of the 'southern oscillation' from west to east across the equatorial waters of the Pacific. The El Niño–Southern Oscillation (ENSO) is one of the planet's largest climate variability mechanisms resulting from atmospheric and oceanic interactions. It affects wine-region climates in North America, Australia and New Zealand, South Africa, South America, and Europe. Oscillations between La Niña (cold SSTs) and El Niño (warm SSTs) influence variations in precipitation and temperatures in many regions, especially those around the Pacific Ocean basin. However, the effect of ENSO on climate variability varies tremendously in magnitude with each event and can have very different impacts depending on the location of the wine region; it is also often coupled with other more influential regional mechanisms. For example, El Niño events in 1982–3 resulted in a very wet winter in California while leading to drier and hotter conditions in Australia. G.V.J.

Elqui, valley in the northern Coquimbo region of CHILE historically important for the production of PISCO but increasingly known for its wine, especially those varieties coming from its higher ELEVATIONS.

embotellado is Spanish for 'bottled'.

Emerald Riesling, one of the earliest of the vine varieties developed at the University of California (see DAVIS) by Dr H. P. Olmo to emerge in VARIETAL (white) wine. It has been shown by DNA PROFILING to be a CROSS of Malvasia Aromatica di Parma and GRENACHE and had its heyday in the late 1960s and early 1970s before slumping towards oblivion. It is planted to a very limited extent in SOUTH AFRICA and ISRAEL. J.V.

Emilia, western part of EMILIA-ROMAGNA.

Emilia-Romagna, Italian wine region which stretches across north-central Italy from the eastern Adriatic coast to include vast tracts of inland Emilia in the west, which is quite distinct from coastal Romagna in the east (see map under ITALY).

There are four very individual areas, each producing distinct wines: the hills around Piacenza in the north-west bordering LOMBARDY; the plain in central Emilia around Parma, Reggio nell'Emilia, and Modena; the hills around Bologna; and the hills in Romagna between Imola and Rimini bordering TUSCANY to the south-east.

The Colli Piacentini, geologically and climatically similar to the contiguous OLTREPÒ PAVESE of Lombardy, is divided into three subregions—Monterosso Val d'Arda, Valnure, and Trebbianino Val Trebbia—which may appear on labels. Many of its FRIZZANTE or lightly sparkling whites from MALVASIA Candia, the rare ORTRUGO, or Trebbiano, or reds from BARBERA and CROATINA (which after it has obtained its sparkle becomes Bonarda for reasons unknown) are made by the TANK METHOD in industrial volumes, although complex, TRADITIONAL METHOD versions are slowly gaining ground. The area's most interesting other developments come from the subzone of Riverargo-Vigolzone, with complex varietal PINOT NOIR and BARBERA, CABERNET blends, and Malvasia di Candia often labelled as IGT Emilia. The DOC Gutturnio, once a suffix to Colli Piacentini and with a CLASSICO subzone as its heart, produces sparkling red wine based on Barbera and Croatina, but it is the still red that has untapped potential. In the little-known Val Tidone, Gaetano Solenghi is one of the very few who still makes spectacular, ageworthy PASSITO wines from Malvasia Candia.

The flat Emilia plain is often associated with LAMBRUSCO. Since the 1970s this light, frothy, and often slightly sweet red has been a huge export success. Its industrial-sized production once completely dominated Lambrusco's image, but the trend is now in favour of the artisanal, dry, and often bottle-fermented versions produced by a new generation. (See LAMBRUSCO for more detail.)

The Colli Bolognesi, the hills immediately south-west of Bologna, are dominated by Cabernet Sauvignon, Merlot, and Chardonnay. The good results achieved here can be traced back to the pioneering but now defunct estate Terre Rosse, whose founder Enrico Vallania planted these varieties in the 1960s, aiming at making long-lived wine without any use of OAK. The local white Pignoletto (see GRECHETTO), producing fresh, lively, and often lightly sparkling whites, now has its own Colli Bolognesi Pignoletto DOCG, although most Pignoletto ends up in the tanks of large bottlers and CO-OPERATIVES.

The Romagna hills, covered by the enormous DOC Romagna, are home to some of both the best and the worst of the region's output. Total production is dominated by co-ops turning out industrial quantities of insipid SANGIOVESE and TREBBIANO. The image of ROMAGNA SANGIOVESE has suffered particularly from this indifference, but a growing group of quality-focused producers have become instrumental in changing its tarnished reputation. (See ROMAGNA SANGIOVESE for more details.) ROMAGNA ALBANA, grown in the same extensive area as Romagna Sangiovese and elevated to DOCG in 1986 to considerable scepticism, is beginning to prove its worth with fine PASSITO and BOTRYTIZED versions as well as some serious barrel- or amphora-fermented dry wines, often from single vineyards. W.S.

www.consorziovinidiromagna.it
www.tutelalambrusco.it

Empordà, DOP in the extreme north-east corner of Spanish CATALUÑA separated from ROUSSILLON only by the French border (see maps under SPAIN and FRANCE). The zone has a long history of wine production, though it was nearly extinguished when PHYLLOXERA swept through the vineyards in the 1900s. Many of the TERRACES that climb the low foothills of the Pyrenees were never replanted. The climate is MEDITERRANEAN, with strong WINDS such as the tramontana that can protect the vineyards from FROST and VINE DISEASES but also stress the vines. Empordà used to produce RANCIO wines (*vi ranci*), sometimes called Garnatxa, the Catalan name for the GARNACHA grape. This vine variety and Cariñena (CARIGNAN) still account for 80% of production, although for a long time they were mostly turned into BULK WINE for the local market. Inspired by the quality-conscious Castillo de Perelada estate, however, smaller producers such as and Espelt, Terra Remota, and Roig Parals have significantly changed the perception of a region that used to be known as Empordà-Costa Brava. V. de la S. & F.C.

Enantio, 1980s name for vine grown in TRENTINO to produce deep-red wine, still sometimes referred to as Lambrusco a Foglia Frastagliata, 'toothed leafed Lambrusco', which is unrelated to any other LAMBRUSCO. Recent DNA PROFILING at SAN MICHELE ALL'ADIGE revealed a likely parent–offspring relationship with NEGRARA Trentina, and it seems to be closely related to TEROLDEGO and LAGREIN too. There were 178 ha/440 acres planted in Italy in 2015.

encépagement, widely used French term for the mix of *cépages*, or VINE VARIETIES, planted on a particular property. These proportions (typically for a MÉDOC estate, for example, Cabernet Sauvignon 60%, Cabernet Franc 20%, and Merlot 20%) do not necessarily correspond to the proportions of each grape variety in a given wine, partly because different varieties vary generally in terms of productivity, but also because factors such as FLOWERING and FROST may dramatically influence the YIELD from each variety in a given growing season.

Encostas d'Aire, DOC within LISBOA on the slopes of the Serra d'Aire in western Portugal. In 2005, two subregions were accorded DOC status: Alcobaça and Medieval de Ourém. The former revolves around terroir (LIMESTONE-based soils) and (predominantly white) varieties; the latter, revived by a handful of producers (and spearheaded by Quinta do Montalto), enshrines ancestral viticultural and oenological practices inherited from 12th-century Cistercian MONKS. Vines must be trained low and grown at relatively high density (minimum 4,000 vines/ha; 6,000 vines/ha is recommended). The permitted grape varieties, FERNÃO PIRES (80%) and TRINCADEIRA (20%), start fermentation separately (the latter on skins) and are blended towards the end of fermentation; Fernão Pires lends herbal lift and freshness, while Trincadeira contributes colour, red fruits, spice, and tannic grip to these intriguing garnet-hued wines. S.A.

Woolf, S. J., and Opaz, R., *Foot Trodden: Portugal and the Wines That Time Forgot* (2021).

Encruzado, fine Portuguese white grape variety most commonly planted in DÃO but also found in the PENÍNSULA DE SETÚBAL. It can yield well-balanced, full-bodied VARIETAL wines capable of AGEING and well-suited to BARREL FERMENTATION. Total Dão plantings in 2020 were 639 ha/1,579 acres.

engarrafado, Portuguese for 'bottled'.

England, the largest and warmest country in Great BRITAIN and the only one which produces wine in any quantity, albeit on a small scale relative to most European wine-producing countries.

History

Perhaps the Romans introduced viticulture to England, but, whether they did or not, they cannot be held responsible for introducing the grapevine itself, because archaeologists have found prehistoric remains of the pollen of VITIS VINIFERA vines at Marks Tey in Essex, as well as seed at Hoxne in Suffolk (see PALAEOETHNOBOTANY).

Both these finds go back to the Hoxnian Interglacial (i.e. the period between the Second and Third Ice Ages), when summers were warmer than they are now. Grape seeds dating from the Hoxnian have also been found in the NETHERLANDS, north GERMANY, DENMARK, and POLAND. Since the British Isles were still part of continental Europe at the time (they did not become separated until after the Fourth Ice Age), this shows that *vinifera* had spread to regions of northern Europe which are now too cold for grapes. The seeds and pollen found in East Anglia are not accompanied by remains of cereals or other signs of agriculture. A more recent find at a Roman site at Wollaston in the Nene Valley near Wellingborough in the south Midlands is of what appear to be planting holes together with grape pollen, suggesting that this was the site of a vineyard.

Seeds have been found at Roman sites in London, Bermondsey, Silchester in Hampshire, and Gloucester, and stalks at a Roman villa near Boxmoor in Hertfordshire, but all without any evidence of cultivation, so these may be the remains of imported raisins. And even if grapes were grown in England, we cannot prove that they were made into wine. Wine was certainly imported from Italy, even before the Roman invasion of 43 CE: remains of AMPHORAE testify to that. (See CELTS for evidence that a small quantity of wine was carried to Hampshire at the end of the 2nd century BCE.) The earliest wine drinkers in Britain were the Belgae, a Celtic tribe that had invaded Britain in two waves, the first in 75 BCE and the second in 20 BCE, after the Romans had put down the Belgic rebellion in Gaul. The British Belgae kept in close contact with their kinsmen in Gaul, who were prodigious drinkers of Italian wine. In the reign of Cymbeline (Cunobelin), 10–40 CE, galleys came up the River Colne to Camulodunum (one mile from Colchester in Essex).

Wine consumption probably increased after the Roman invasion of Britain, for remains of amphorae and pottery drinking cups are common finds on the sites of Roman towns and country houses. Recent finds show that amphorae were manufactured at Brockley Hill, Middlesex, which appears to have been an important pottery centre, and also at other London sites. They are of a type that, according to archaeological evidence from southern France, were used as containers for locally produced wine; the London amphorae were probably the work of immigrant potters from France. The amphorae all date from 70–100 CE: perhaps this short period could be explained by the edict issued by the Roman emperor DOMITIAN, which, by reducing the number of vineyards in the provinces, put a stop to the Romano-British wine industry. Remains of imported amphorae are rare after 300 CE, but it seems unlikely that the Romano-British were now producing enough wine to meet their own needs. In any case, from the 3rd century onwards wine began increasingly to be transported not in amphorae but in wooden BARRELS, which are perishable, so one would not expect to find many amphorae dating from the 4th century CE and certainly no wooden casks.

Our earliest conclusive evidence for wine-growing in Britain, then, must be Bede's *Ecclesiastical History*, which he finished in 731. It opens with a general description of Britain and Ireland, including geography, climate, agriculture, animals, nations, and languages. 'Britain', Bede says, 'is rich in grain and timber; it has good pasturage for cattle and draught animals, and wines are cultivated in various localities' (Book 1, ch. 1). Unfortunately, that is all he tells us about Anglo-Saxon viticulture—although in any case Bede has been shown to be a less than reliable source of information on viticulture in Ireland. As well as growing their own, the Anglo-Saxons certainly bought wine from the Franks. In the 8th and 9th centuries, Southampton was one of the largest ports of northern Europe and well placed for trade with northern France, especially Rouen (see PARIS). In return for animal hides, the merchants of Southampton obtained gold, silver, glassware, and wine. However, as Viking pirates began to capture more and more ships, overseas trade was disrupted, and if imported wine was available at all it must have been a rare luxury item.

The Anglo-Saxons' daily drink was beer, but they needed wine for the EUCHARIST: supply being erratic, it made sense for monasteries to have their own vineyards, as some had probably been doing since Bede's day (see MONKS AND MONASTERIES). A charter, dated 955, of King Edwy, great-grandson of King Alfred, grants a vineyard at Pethanesburgh, Somerset, to the monks of Glastonbury Abbey. But not all vineyards were owned by monks. The Laws of King Alfred regard viticulture as important enough to make it an offence for anyone to destroy a vineyard; no mention is made of monasteries here. An 11th-century document lists looking after the vineyard as one of the duties of the manager of a secular estate, and out of the 38 vineyards named in Domesday Book, only 12 were monastic. More importantly, if the figure is accurate—and William the Conqueror's surveyors did their work thoroughly—38 vineyards cannot possibly have produced a plentiful supply of wine for the whole of England. (According to the Bayeux Tapestry's depiction of William's invasion of England in 1066, he judged it as important to take wine with him as he did arms.)

Wine continued to be grown in England during the 12th and 13th centuries. There were vineyards as far north as south Yorkshire, and the praise lavished on the wines of Gloucestershire by the 12th-century chronicler William of Malmesbury demonstrates that English wine was no thin, sour plonk. Worcestershire, too, was renowned for its wine. This golden age of English viticulture was the result of a long period of warm summer weather, which started in the mid 11th century (see CLIMATE CHANGE). It ended abruptly in the 14th century, when the ocean currents changed and summers became wet and cloudy. Moreover, when on his marriage to Eleanor of Aquitaine Henry II acquired Gascony, and when King John (1199–1216) granted the citizens of BORDEAUX numerous privileges in order to win their favour, Gascon wine became cheaper to buy for the English than any other wine, imported or home-produced. Around 1,300 commercial vineyards were grubbed up all over England, and grapes made way for more profitable crops: this is how the Vale of Evesham, still famous for its plums and apples, came to be planted with fruit trees. Monastic viticulture continued for longer, but between 1348 and 1370 the Black Death carried off one-third or more of the population, lay and ecclesiastic alike. Not only did many monks die, but the ensuing shortage of labour deprived the monasteries of their unsalaried workforce, the lay brothers. English viticulture did not cease altogether, but it was no longer commercially viable, even for the monks.

But with a wine-drinking Norman aristocracy, domestic production could never have satisfied demand. Via Rouen, then governed by the king of England, who was also duke of Normandy (until John lost Normandy), the English had ready access to the wines of the Île-de-France (see PARIS), which in 1200 were the most expensive on the English market, although people bought more of the wines of Poitou (see LA ROCHELLE) and Anjou (see LOIRE), probably with reason, for they must have been less acidic. With the rise of Bordeaux, this changed, and until the end of the HUNDRED YEARS WAR the English bought more wine from Gascony than from anywhere else, with wine being second only to wool in importance for English trade at this time. Wine was shipped to England, principally to the port of Southampton, twice a year from Bordeaux, in the autumn and in the spring. Even if the vintage had been early, the new wine did not usually reach England before November; the wines that arrived in the spring were the wines 'of rack', so-called because they were not racked off their LEES until the spring. The wines 'of rack', an early form of SUR LIE, fetched higher prices. Since there was nothing better in which to keep the wine than wooden casks, OXIDATION was the norm, and wine did not keep from one year to the next. The wine of the previous year was therefore sold off cheaply at AUCTION as soon as the new vintage appeared on the market in England. White wine was more expensive than red.

E

French wines were not the only wines to be drunk in 14th-century London. From the 1350s onwards, sweet wines from southern Europe began to be introduced (see VENICE, NAPLES, and GENOA), and they became the most expensive available. The most highly prized of these was 'vernage', the Italian VERNACCIA. Another favourite was 'malvesye', or MALMSEY, supplied mainly by Cyprus and Crete. Because of their additional strength and sweetness, these wines lasted longer than the thinner, drier wines that the English had been used to and were greatly prized. The wines of Alsace and the Rhine were highly valued because they were so brilliantly clear. Spanish wine, which was higher in alcohol than other wines, was regarded mainly as cheaper heady plonk, and better, more expensive, wines were often cut with it (see SPAIN, history).

Attempts were made to protect the consumer from ADULTERATION AND FRAUD, but their frequency suggests that they were not always successful. In 1321, a proclamation was made that in London all wines should be graded 'good' or 'ordinary' and the casks marked; everyone would have the right to see the wine drawn, and maximum prices were fixed. Merchants and innkeepers refused to cooperate and were promptly fined. The marking of casks was probably abandoned, but the right to see one's wine being drawn is reiterated from one writ and proclamation to the next, and one even says that taverners should keep red wines and white in different cellars: a note of desperation is clearly creeping in. A London proclamation of 1371 makes clear what the unfortunate drinker was subjected to: overcharging, adulteration, and wine that was off. It makes one grateful for clearly labelled, tamper-free modern packaging: the glass BOTTLE and modern CLOSURES have improved the wine drinker's life almost beyond imagination. H.M.W.

Dion, R., *Histoire de la vigne et du vin en France* (1959).
Dion, R., *Studies in the Medieval Wine Trade* (1971).
Simon, A. L., *The History of the Wine Trade in England*, 3 vols. (1906–9).
Turner, M., *Chaucer, A European Life* (2019).

Modern English wine

The revival of viticulture in the British Isles—mainly in England but also in Wales (and even Scotland)—that began in the mid 20th century has matured into a small but significant industry with a planted area in 2021 of 3,750 ha/9,266 acres. Average annual production from 2016 to 2020 was 8.7 million bottles, including a record 13.11 million in 2018. While initially English wines were often light and acidic, CLIMATE CHANGE has led to a revolution in the VINE VARIETIES grown and in QUALITY IN WINE. This is especially true of the BOTTLE-FERMENTED sparkling wines which are increasingly being compared to champagne. English and Welsh wine is subject to EU winemaking regulations (although post-Brexit these are being slowly amended to be tailored to UK conditions) and is made strictly from freshly picked, UK-grown grapes.

The revival of viticulture began in 1945 when Raymond Barrington Brock started what became the Oxted Viticultural Research Station, a privately funded experimental NURSERY where, over the next 25 years, Brock trialled 600 vine varieties. Buoyed by the success of some of Brock's trials, the first commercial vineyard, all 0.4 ha/1 acre of it, was planted at Hambledon in Hampshire by Major-General Sir Guy Salisbury-Jones in March 1952. More vineyards followed, slowly at first, but as wines were produced from these early vineyards more pioneers took up the cause, and by the mid 1960s there were over 40 vineyards spread across the south of England and Wales. The hot summer of 1976 provided the spur for many new growers to enter the industry, and the area under vine rose to a high point of 1,065 ha/ 2,632 acres in 1993, after which it declined as competition increased and consumer demand for the still wines then typically based on GERMAN CROSSES waned. This decline continued until 2003 heralded an era of much warmer summers, as well as considerable success in tastings and the marketplace of SPARKLING WINES made from the champagne varieties Chardonnay, Pinot Noir, and Pinot Meunier. Together they spurred a new wave of planting.

The biggest change in UK vineyards has been in the range of vine varieties grown. Varieties such as MÜLLER-THURGAU, REICHENSTEINER, MADELEINE × ANGEVINE 7672, HUXELREBE, SCHÖNBURGER, and BACCHUS, plus the French-American hybrid SEYVAL BLANC (which together accounted for 74% of the UK area under vine in 1980), have been widely replaced by Chardonnay and Pinot Noir, which were planted on about half of all English vineyard by 2014 and are almost exclusively used for sparkling wines. For still white wines, Bacchus is the most widely grown with around 9%, followed by Seyval Blanc with 4%. Reichensteiner and SOLARIS each claim 2%. Red-wine varieties, excluding Pinot Noir and Meunier, account for only 0.15% of the planted area. Red and rosé wines account for around 15% of production.

Almost 85% of England's 800 officially recorded vineyards (of 0.10 ha or more) and 191 wineries are located in the southern counties. East Anglia accounts for a further 11% of vineyard. The best are in the traditional fruit-growing regions of the UK on sheltered sites below 100 m/330 ft ELEVATION. To many people's surprise, vineyards are planted in almost every county of England, and Yorkshire boasts 15 wine producers. However, the chances of achieving commercial viability lessen the further north a vineyard is situated, with YIELDS and quality in some of the more challenging regions considerably lower than in the warmer southern counties.

Although much of the south of the UK and some of the western regions have a climate that is softened by the Gulf Stream, the MARITIME CLIMATE brings summer gales and high summer RAINFALL which can disrupt FLOWERING so that yields are dramatically reduced. In 2012, for example, spectacularly bad weather during pollination reduced the total UK crop by about two-thirds, with some large producers picking not a single grape. Official average yields are very low, around 25 hl/ha between 2011 and 2020, but well-sited, well-managed vineyards can expect to average 50–60 hl/ha.

Harvesting usually takes place between the end of September and the end of October, depending on variety and region, but in 2013 the latest grape harvest ever recorded in the UK saw some growers still picking Chardonnay on 20 November. Natural MUST WEIGHTS tend to be low by global standards, with most grapes achieving 7–9% POTENTIAL ALCOHOL, although with certain varieties and in warmer years, such as 2020, 13–14% has been recorded. Levels of natural acidity tend to be high, with PH around 2.9 to 3.2 and TOTAL ACIDITY (expressed as tartaric acid) between 8 and 15 g/l. Under current winemaking regulations, ENRICHMENT is allowed by up to 3% every year and 3.5% in 'abnormal' years. ACIDIFICATION is not permitted (nor often needed), except in sparkling wines post-DISGORGEMENT where 1 g/l may be added for STABILIZATION purposes (as in Champagne and other EU regions where sparkling wine is made).

The UK has its own CONTROLLED APPELLATION system, set up under EU regulations with four distinct categories. Those qualifying as PDO are known as Quality Wines; PGI wines are called Regional Wines; Varietal Wines are WINES WITHOUT GEOGRAPHICAL INDICATION labelled varietally which have gone through a certification process; and those which carry neither grape variety nor vintage are labelled simply UK Wine.

England and Wales are increasingly recognized as legitimate wine-producing regions, with wines regularly winning trophies and gold medals in UK and international wine

COMPETITIONS. Where once the industry was populated by amateurs and retirees, today's modern vineyards are staffed by well-trained and experienced viticulturists and winemakers, many trained at PLUMPTON. Some vineyards are even into the second and third generations of the same family. While many smaller vineyards rely on TOURISM and local sales, more and more UK wines are stocked by bigger retailers and quite smart restaurants. Some vineyards even export their wines. See also IRELAND. S.S.

Skelton, S. P., *Wine Growing in Great Britain* (2nd edn, 2020).
Skelton, S. P., *The Wines of Great Britain* (2019)
www.winegb.co.uk

English literature, wine in. References to specific wines in English literature are relatively common and provide a useful record of FASHIONS in wine styles and the history of wine imports to the British Isles from the time of Chaucer to the present day. Literary references to wine drinking are legion, presumably because it encouraged conversation—civilized, bawdy, or sometimes nonsensical. Generic 'wine' is mentioned too often to report, and more detailed and revealing references specifying wine type or provenance are scarce in English literature before the 17th century.

The first English writer to demonstrate a serious interest in wine was Geoffrey Chaucer (1345–1400), himself the son and grandson of a vintner. *The Canterbury Tales* are dotted with references to specific wines (see CONDADO DE HUELVA, for example). The Prologue details contemporary eating and drinking habits, while the 60-year-old knight in 'The Merchant's Tale' drank spiced wine in the form of 'ypocras, clarree, and vernage' (see VERNACCIA) for 'courage' in the bedchamber.

BORDEAUX was England's chief medieval wine supplier, and it dominates wine references in the literature until long after Aquitaine was ceded to France. William Shakespeare's (1564–1616) 'good familiar creature' in *Othello* would undoubtedly have been bordeaux, although 'sherris SACK' was Falstaff's favoured drink in *1 Henry IV*, and Sir Toby Belch's call for 'a cup of CANARY' in *Twelfth Night* also demonstrates the increasing importance of Spanish wines. Shakespeare's contemporaries Robert Herrick, John Webster, and Robert Burton certainly refer to wine, but only Burton (1577–1640) mentions the evocative names of Alicant, Rumney, and Brown Bastard (respectively, wines from ALICANTE, sweet wines made in the Greek style, and a sweet blend from Portugal, presumably based on BASTARDO grapes).

The life of Samuel Pepys (1633–1703) seems to have been a succession of drinks if his diary provides an accurate record, with references to TENT, Canary, Rhenish (wine from the RHINE), and English wine from vineyards around London (see ENGLAND). Pepys also famously provides the first reference to New French CLARETS, in particular that of 'Ho Bryan' (HAUT-BRION). Pepys mentions champagne, as does the comic playwright Sir George Etherege (?1634–91), who qualifies the reference with 'sparkling'. These, together with a brief note from Dean Swift (1667–1745), are the earliest mentions of what must have been a very new product (see CHAMPAGNE, history). Edward Ravenscroft (*fl.* 1671–97), the relatively obscure author of a rollicking farce *The London Cuckolds* (1682), is very forthcoming, with sack and PORT mentioned almost as many times as pretty women. John Gay (1685–1732) even published in 1708 a rather indifferent poem entitled 'Wine' which mentions the mysterious drink 'Golorence'.

In the 18th century, the number of references to wine by English dramatists, novelists, and poets rises dramatically. R. B. Sheridan (1751–1816) insists about claret in *School for Scandal* that 'women give headaches, this don't', and champagne appears more than once in his *Paris Sketchbook.* David Garrick (1716–79) provides one of the first mentions of burgundy in English: 'rich Burgundy with a ruby tint'. As today, however, opinions about the relative merits of various wine regions are divided. The observation of Tobias Smollett (1721–77) in his *Travels through France and Italy* that 'the Wine known as Burgundy is so weak and thin' is a useful indication of the general derision of any wine region other than Bordeaux.

Samuel Johnson (1709–84) and Parson Woodforde (1740–1803) both give disquieting insight into the prodigious quantity of food and drink which then customarily appeared at table. Boswell reports Johnson's observation that 'few people had intellectual resources sufficient to forgo the pleasures of wine. They could not otherwise contrive how to fill the interval between lunch and dinner.' And during travels in Germany, 'I drank too much Moselle, imagining it to be a mere diuretic.' The next day he 'was uneasy from the Moselle'. There is a disparaging reference to Florence wine, which 'neither pleases the taste nor exhilarates the Spirits'.

Jane Austen (1775–1817) admits to some of her characters drinking wine, although only in appropriate quantities of course. Among very few references to specific wines, the treasured South African CONSTANTIA is considered a suitable restorative for a young lady in *Sense and Sensibility.* Keats refers to claret frequently in correspondence, but his most famous vinous reference is in 'Ode to a Nightingale' ('O, for a draught of vintage!' etc.). George Crabbe (1754–1832), whose works illustrate his somewhat grim sense of humour, describes the sorts and conditions of men who drink various wines in 'Champagne the courtier drinks the spleen to chase, the Colonel Burgundy, Port His Grace...' Crabbe's approver Lord Byron (1788–1824) is entertaining on the subject of wine and DRUNKENNESS, recommending 'hock and soda-water' as a hangover remedy. He also turned wines into verbs, as in 'We clareted and champagned till two' in a letter to Thomas Moore. In his *Don Juan* VI. 607–8, one of the most misquoted pieces of literature (often confused with Keats), Byron eventually declares, 'If Britain mourn her bleakness we can tell her, the very best of vineyards is the cellar', an admirable sentiment.

The 19th-century writers indicate the increasing range of wines imported to the British Isles as well as the widening appreciation and understanding of them. In *Melincourt*, Thomas Love Peacock (1785–1866) describes wine as both 'a hierarchical and episcopal fluid' and 'the elixir of life', and further references appear in *Crotchet Castle.* Peacock was clearly a burgundy aficionado, daring to suggest that 'an aged Burgundy runs an ageless Port'. George Meredith (1828–1909), who married the widowed daughter of Peacock, shares his interest in burgundy; precise references to Musigny and Romanée appear in *The Egoist* and *One of our Conquerors.* R. S. Surtees (1805–64), the master of comic fox-hunting novels, brings port, champagne, and 'tolerable St Julien doing duty for Ch Margaux' into such pieces as *Handley Cross* and *Mr Sponge's Sporting Tour.* He sagely advises against the excesses of the previous century: 'no side dishes, no liqueurs, only two or three wines'.

At a somewhat more elevated level, William Thackeray (1811–63) names Beaune and Chambertin and also refers to claret, sherry, and madeira, also commenting, 'if there is to be Champagne have no stint of it ... save on your hocks, sauternes, and moselles, which count for nothing'. This last quotation is from *Pendennis*, in which appears the character Captain Shandon, heavily based on William Maginn (1793–1842), who wrote under the pseudonym Sir Morgan O'Doherty, Bt. As a regular contributor to *Blackwoods Edinburgh Magazine* Maginn wrote many wonderful 'Maxims', many of which refer to or include wine and food: they are well worth searching out, as is the 'Spectator ab extra' of A. H. Clough (1819–61), an entire poem devoted to food and drink of which the first stanza has particular appeal for this writer:

> Pass the bottle and damn the expense
> I've heard it said by a man of sense
> That the labouring classes could scarce live a day
> If people like us didn't eat, drink and pay.

Henry James (1843–1916) is particularly descriptive about Burgundy and its vineyard in *A Little Tour of France.* Robert Louis Stevenson (1850–94) also enthuses over Burgundy in

Travels with a Donkey in the Cévennes. His ill health led to frequent foreign journeys even as far afield as California: *The Silverado Squatters* is the first literary work to include reference to the vineyards there.

Other serious 19th-century writers who regularly included comments on wine are Robert Browning (1812–89), who clearly enjoyed Chablis; Charles Dickens (1812–70), whose novels, as one might imagine, mention punch more often than wine; and, most amusingly, Saki, or H. H. Munro (1870–1916), who delights in his many comments on wines and the manners of those who serve it, such as 'the conscious air of defiance that a waiter adopts in announcing that the cheapest Claret on the list is no more'. Finally, Edward Fitzgerald (1809–83), the erudite translator of the 11th-century ARAB POEM *The Rubáiyát of Omar Khayyám*, must be cited, as one particular passage has cut wine merchants to the quick ever since publication: 'I often wonder what the Vintners buy, one half so precious as the goods they sell.'

The 20th century sees further geographical extension of the wine regions mentioned in English literature, as well as a greater awareness of the variety and quality of the products available. Hilaire Belloc (1870–1953) wrote much in praise of all sorts of drink, notably 'Advice', which is full of vinous references, and his 'Heroic Poem in Praise of Wine', which expresses the sentiment 'Dead Lucre: burnt Ambition: Wine is best'. The *Forsyte Saga* of John Galsworthy (1867–1933) abounds with references to hock, especially Steinberger. Aldous Huxley offers the somewhat jaded assessment that 'Champagne has the taste of an apple peeled with a steel knife', while Eric Newby in *Love and War in the Apennines* also paints a grim picture of the wine 'the Italians call *vini lavatori*'. But the balance is redressed by P. G. Wodehouse, whose characters' 'form' can often be restored by various vinous substances. Evelyn Waugh's diaries and letters inform us of his own serious wine-drinking habits, although only *Brideshead Revisited* among his works contains many specific wine references. He wrote a monograph *Wine in Peace and War* for wine merchants Saccone & Speed and was paid, according to his son Auberon, at the rate of a dozen bottles of champagne per thousand words. More recent novelists whose work displays a deep understanding of wine include Sybille Bedford and Dick Francis, who in one of his novels treats good wine extensively. Wine is one of several alcoholic drinks to figure largely in Kingsley Amis's work.

Are spy stories literature? Ian Fleming's James Bond has rather common tastes in champagne, and more than once Fleming mentions a vintage of Taittinger or Dom Pérignon which was never made. This usefully illustrates the way in which wine, mentioned by authors throughout the history of literature, is used more for illustrative purposes than anything else. In ingested form, however, wine has probably offered writers more inspiration than opium, and their references to it have helped us better understand the chronology of importation and imbibing of wine through the ages. See also MEDIEVAL LITERATURE. H.G.B.

One wine-soaked novel I would like to have discussed with the late Bill Baker, who wrote the article above, is Paul Torday's successor to *Salmon Fishing in the Yemen*. The hero of *The Irresistible Inheritance of Wilberforce* drinks himself, knowledgeably, to death. Novelist Anthony Quinn reminds me that in Thomas Harris's *The Silence of the Lambs*, Hannibal Lecter boasts of eating a victim's liver with fava beans and a 'big Amarone', changed rather weedily in the movie, this former film critic notes, to a 'nice Chianti'. J.R.

enologist is the American and South African spelling of OENOLOGIST, just as **enology** is the alternative spelling of OENOLOGY, the study of wine and, especially, winemaking.

enoteca, term used frequently in Italy for a wine shop with a significant range of high-quality wines, while quite a few still offer the local wine or wines as *vino sfuso*, or in BULK, which are poured straight from the cask into demijohns brought along by customers. It contrasts with a *bottiglieria*, a shop with a more pedestrian selection, and a *vineria*, run by a *vinaio*, more of a tavern, in which wine is sold by the glass as well as by the bottle. Various **enoteche** in Italy offer tasting facilities, and some serve food to accompany the wines—from the mere appetite-stimulating to the most ambitious cuisine. The word comes from the same root as OENOTRIA, the ancient Greeks' name for Italy, and *theke*, Greek for a case or receptacle.

Enotria, corruption of the ancient Greek name for what is now Italy. See OENOTRIA.

enoturismo. See AGRITURISMO.

en primeur, wine trade term, French in origin, for wine sold as futures before being bottled. It comes from the word PRIMEUR. En primeur sales are a relatively recent speciality, but not exclusivity, of CLASSED GROWTHS by the BORDEAUX TRADE (see BORDEAUX, history). Cask SAMPLES of wines have customarily been shown in the spring following the vintage. Thousands of trade and media representatives descend on Bordeaux each spring for carefully organized programmes of tastings. Sales are solicited, through BROKERS and then NÉGOCIANTS, as soon as proprietors decide to announce their opening PRICE, and market reaction is keenly monitored by interested parties. A particular property often releases only a certain proportion, or *tranche*, of its total production, depending on its need for cash and reading of the market.

This form of early sale has long been available to the wine trade but was undertaken by wine consumers only from the late 20th century. It has been most popular in times of frenetic demand such as in the very early 1970s (when some wine was even sold *sur souche*, or on the vine before the grapes were picked) and since the 1980s, when a succession of good VINTAGES coincided with widespread economic prosperity and the accessibility of early VINTAGE ASSESSMENTS from the wine trade and press. The consumer pays the opening price as soon as the offer is made and then, up to two years later, having paid the additional shipping costs and DUTY, takes delivery of the wine after it has been bottled and shipped. The theory is that, by buying wine early, the consumer not only secures sought-after wines but also pays less. This is by no means invariably the case, however, as outlined in INVESTMENT IN WINE.

En primeur purchases have many disadvantages in periods of economic recession. Not only may prices stagnate or even fall, but there is a much higher risk that one of the many commercial concerns in the chain between wine producer and wine consumer will fail, leaving the consumer with the possibility of having paid for the wine without any certainty of receiving it. There is also the important fact that en primeur purchases inevitably mean investing in an embryonic product. A third party's assessment of a single cask sample taken when it is just six months old is a poor justification for financial outlay on a liquid that is bottled only a year later (and is particularly hazardous for a wine as notoriously transient as red BURGUNDY), unless the wine market is extremely buoyant.

Buying en primeur may make financial sense only for the most unanimously lauded vintages and the most sought-after wines, and then only in a rising market, although it can of course give a great deal of pleasure to those with a strong wine-COLLECTING instinct.

en rama, literally 'raw', a condition of fino or manzanilla SHERRY whereby, unlike mass-market BRANDS, it is only very lightly filtered before being bottled and sold.

enrichment (*enrichissement* in French, *Anreicherung* in German, *arricchimento* in Italian, *enriquecimiento* in Spanish), winemaking operation whereby the fermentable sugars of grape juice or MUST are supplemented in order to increase the ALCOHOLIC STRENGTH of the resultant wine. This is traditionally and habitually done to compensate for natural underripeness in cool regions or after particularly cool summers in warmer regions. The original process, generally called CHAPTALIZATION after its French promulgator CHAPTAL, involves adding sugar, whereas the wider term 'enrichment' encompasses the addition of sugar, concentrated grape must (see GRAPE CONCENTRATE), and rectified concentrated grape must (RCGM) and is the term favoured in official EU terminology. While it is impossible to know the extent to which enrichment is used around the world, a report in 2012 suggested that in Europe an average of 55 million hl (1,453 million gal) of wine was enriched every year, corresponding to 30% of total EU wine production. It seems unlikely that it is still at this level.

Enrichment is the winemaking counterpoint to ACIDIFICATION, which is the norm in hot wine regions. Most regions' wine regulations set limits for these processes; most of them, as in Burgundy, for example, forbid the enrichment and acidification of the same batch of wine.

Geography

Enrichment is the norm in climates which cannot be relied upon to bring grapes to full ripeness every season: for example, throughout northern Europe, in the north-eastern wine regions of the United States, throughout CANADA, in BRAZIL, in JAPAN, and in much of NEW ZEALAND, especially for red wines.

At the coolest limits of vine cultivation it is a prerequisite of wine production. Within the EU, permission to chaptalize and the maximum permitted increase in ALCOHOLIC STRENGTH depend on the EU climatic zone in which an area falls. A country's own regulations may also forbid the practice unless permission has been specifically granted because of the vintage conditions.

The poorest summers in ENGLAND and LUXEMBOURG, for example, the so-called Zone A of the EU, yield grape sugar levels in some varieties that have difficulty reaching the legal minimum NATURAL ALCOHOL level of 5%. Here musts may be enriched to a maximum increase in alcoholic strength of 3% (3.5% in particularly unripe years).

Winemakers in Europe's Zone C1, which includes Burgundy, for example, may enrich their musts by up to 1.5%.

In Bordeaux, also in Zone C1, chaptalization has also been the norm historically; thanks to CLIMATE CHANGE and the development of alternative techniques for juice CONCENTRATION, however, the practice of enrichment is becoming a choice rather than a necessity except perhaps in difficult vintages such as 2021.

Enrichment is also much relied upon, especially for more commercial wines, in Eastern Europe, Switzerland, Austria, and Germany. Indeed the major distinction between Germany's better-quality wine (classified as wine with PRÄDIKAT) and ordinary QUALITÄTSWEIN was long that Prädikatsweine could not be enriched by added sugar (although they could include SÜSSRESERVE of comparable ripeness added for sweetening purposes after fermentation). Similarly in AUSTRIA, sugar may not be added to wines of Kabinett quality or above. See PRÄDIKAT for the current situation.

In southern France, notably the Languedoc, Roussillon, the southern Rhône, Provence, and Corsica, and throughout the rest of the south of the EU, chaptalization is expressly forbidden, but enrichment using concentrated must of various sorts is often permitted and even encouraged, depending on the quality level of the wine and the characteristics of the VINTAGE. This sort of enrichment by adding concentrated must is commonplace in northern Italy and has provided an end use for vast quantities of otherwise SURPLUS wine made in southern Italy (see Materials below).

Winemakers prohibited from practising enrichment tend to scorn the practice as artificial and manipulative (just as those in cooler regions, prohibited from adding acid, are wary of the practice of ACIDIFICATION).

There are wine regions, however—such as TASMANIA, the recently planted vineyards on the southern tip of SOUTH AFRICA, and even some of the higher vineyards of northern Italy—in which chaptalization is prohibited, to the detriment of wine quality in some seasons, simply because they belong to a political unit whose other wine regions are too hot to need it.

Materials

SUCROSE is the usual enrichment material used. In northern Europe this has normally been refined sugar beet or, occasionally, cane sugar.

In an effort to help drain Europe's WINE LAKE, however, EU authorities tried to encourage the use of high-strength grape-sugar syrups made from SURPLUS wine, especially in Italy and southern France (see GRAPE CONCENTRATE and RECTIFIED GRAPE MUST for more details), but compulsory DISTILLATION and other market reforms have been more effective at reducing the surplus. Enrichment using grape concentrate is also permitted in Australia, but sugar may be added only to induce the second fermentation for sparkling wines.

Technique

The enrichment material may be added before and/or during FERMENTATION. Both sugar and acid tend to inhibit yeast growth, however. Adding the enriching sugar when fermentation is already fully under way avoids the delay which could ensue if it were added to the unfermented juice or must. It is also favoured as a way of extending the fermentation by some winemakers, especially in Burgundy.

About 1.8 kg/4 lb of sugar is needed to raise the alcoholic strength of 1 hl of wine by 1% (slightly less for less dense white and rosé wine musts), which means that stacks of sugar sacks can be a regular sight in many large and not-so-large French wine cellars.

When conducted properly, enrichment increases the volume of the wine negligibly, has no tasteable effect on the wine, and merely compensates for Nature's deficiencies in a particular growing season. Enriched wines certainly should not taste sweet, since all of the fermentable SUGARS should have been fermented into ALCOHOL; the wine should merely have more BODY and better BALANCE than it would otherwise have.

The non-winemaking observer may wonder, however, why in an age in which many consumers wish to curb their consumption of alcohol, when alcohol levels are rising, and there is a global wine surplus, the wine industry deliberately increases the alcohol content of so many of its products, in many cases to compensate for overcropped vines (see YIELD).

In recent years, concentration techniques such as vacuum evaporation and REVERSE OSMOSIS have become popular ways to enrich musts by removing water. In many ways, these subtractive techniques may be less 'unnatural' and open to abuse than additive techniques such as chaptalization. See also MANIPULATION.

Entraygues-Le Fel, AOC on the right bank of the upper Lot in SOUTH WEST FRANCE focused on the SCHIST hillsides of Le Fel and the GRANITE of Entraygues. Half the production is in red wine, and some rosé is made, the wines based on FER grapes (here called Mansois) although several local oddities are also allowed, including Négret de Banhars. The rarer whites are mainly CHENIN BLANC. With ten or so producers and no CO-OPERATIVE, quality is impressively high. P.S.

Entre-Deux-Mers, large area of the BORDEAUX wine region between the Rivers DORDOGNE and GARONNE; hence a name which means 'between two seas'. A high proportion of the vineyard land in this pretty, green region (which has much in common with BERGERAC to its immediate east) produces light, often slightly austere red wine made from MERLOT and CABERNET grapes and sold as BORDEAUX AOC. Indeed, since vine-growers converted their white-wine vineyards to red varieties in the 1960s and 1970s, the Entre-Deux-Mers district has become the chief source of red Bordeaux AC. The Entre-Deux-Mers region contains several other appellations, some of them enclaves such as GRAVES DE VAYRES, STE-FOY CÔTES DE BORDEAUX, and Côtes de Bordeaux St-Macaire. Haut-Benauge is another whose dry white wines have their own appellation, **Entre-Deux-Mers Haut-Benauge**. The PREMIÈRES CÔTES DE BORDEAUX and its sweet-white winemaking enclave lie between the Entre-Deux-Mers appellation and the river Garonne, in the same territory as produces red CADILLAC CÔTES DE BORDEAUX. Wines sold as Entre-Deux-Mers are dry whites made mainly from SAUVIGNON BLANC together with SÉMILLON, MUSCADELLE, and SAUVIGNON GRIS grapes. After Bordeaux AC, this is the biggest dry-white-wine appellation in the Bordeaux region, on a vineyard area that totalled 1,617 ha/ 3,994 acres in 2020. CLAY and SANDY clay predominate although there are pockets of LIMESTONE, especially just across the Dordogne from ST-ÉMILION. This is one of the few French wine districts to have adopted the LENZ MOSER system of high vine TRELLISING to any great extent. Most Entre-Deux-Mers should be drunk as young as possible and without great ceremony. J.R. & J.L.

Eola-Amity Hills, wine region and AVA within the WILLAMETTE VALLEY of Oregon.

enzymes, proteins present in all biological systems that act as catalysts by inducing or accelerating specific biochemical reactions. Enzymes, named using the suffix -'ase', are characterized by both the specificity of the chemical group or substrate they act on and the reaction which they catalyse. Endogenous enzymes are those that the organism itself produces, whereas exogenous enzymes are those that are prepared commercially.

Endogenous enzyme activities of the vine are central to the biological processes by which grape berries develop and ripen. Wine is the enzymatic transformation or FERMENTATION of grape juice by thousands of endogenous enzymes originating from the grape juice, YEAST cells, and other microorganisms.

BOTRYTIS also produces the enzyme laccase, which promotes very rapid OXIDATION and browning of juice and young wine exposed to oxygen. At the end of fermentation, exposure to any oxygen has to be avoided until the combination of higher ALCOHOLIC STRENGTH, TANNINS, and added SULFUR DIOXIDE reduce the laccase activity, thereby making the wine stable to enzymatic oxidation. Alternatively, heat treatment of the wine can be used to inactivate (denature) the enzyme.

Winemakers influence the outcome of enzymatic reactions (via PH, TEMPERATURE, SULFUR DIOXIDE levels, and choice of yeast and bacteria) to produce specific wine styles.

As not all endogenous enzymes are efficient under winemaking conditions, since the 1970s winemakers have increasingly used exogenous enzymes to speed up or improve some processes. Enzyme research is active and the range of exogenous enzymes available is increasing. They are produced mainly from natural fungi, *Aspergillus niger* and Tricoderma species. Examples of these enzymes and their uses are described below.

Pectinases (polygalacturonase, pectin lysase, and pectin methyl esterase), also known as pectolictic enzymes, often in combination with cellulase and hemicellulase, can be used to break down PECTINS in cell walls to enhance juice extraction in white wines (see PRESSING) and colour EXTRACTION in reds during fermentation. Pectinases also reduce juice viscosity and thereby accelerate CLARIFICATION by breaking down pectin molecules in the juice.

Glycosidases release AROMA compounds (especially in varieties high in MONOTERPENES such as Muscat, Riesling, and Gewürztraminer) bound to sugars in an odourless GLYCOSIDE form thereby increasing the aromatic intensity of the wine. This process also occurs naturally but very slowly.

Glucanases are used to accelerate AUTOLYSIS in wines aged on yeast LEES. The enzyme breaks down the cell walls releasing MANNOPROTEINS into the wine. Glucanases are also used in wines affected by BOTRYTIS BUNCH ROT, which can have high levels of glucans (polysaccharides of glucose), which makes FILTRATION more difficult. Beta-glucanase breaks down these molecules, making the wine easier to filter.

Lysozyme, an enzyme isolated from egg whites, attacks the cell walls of LACTIC ACID BACTERIA and is used to inhibit MALOLACTIC CONVERSION. T.J. & V.L.

IFV, 'Enzymes in oenology: production, regulation, applications' (2019). www.vignevin.com/wp-content/uploads/2019/03/CI_ENZYMES_ANG_VF2.pdf.

epicatechin. See CATECHIN.

epigenetics refers to a range of heritable and reversible molecular processes that may change gene function but do not alter the underlying DNA sequence. These complex and interrelated processes play fundamental roles that are critical to gene regulation, contributing to plant growth, development, and response to environmental cues. Epigenetic regulation may be mediated by a number of processes known as markers. One such marker widely studied in plants is DNA methylation (i.e. the addition or removal of methyl groups (CH_3) on the cytosine base of genomic DNA).

It is becoming increasingly clear that these markers are critical in plant reproduction and particularly in a plant's response to its environment. DNA methylation plays an important role in phenotypic plasticity, which is the ability of an individual organism to change its observable traits in response to a change in its environment, including various types of stress and inputs. In some species, this provides a selective advantage. DNA methylation patterns have been identified in response to DROUGHT and salt tolerance and have also been used in differentiating grapevine CLONES that are genetically very similar (see DNA PROFILING).

In grapevines, epigenetic sensitivity to both environment and vine management has been shown to exist. In one study of 22 Shiraz vineyards in Australia's Barossa region, epigenetic profiles showed relationships based on location and PRUNING method even though the vines in those vineyards were genetically very similar. Comparable results were found with Malbec in MENDOZA. DNA methylation patterns have also been shown to differ with VINE AGE and PROPAGATION method.

While genetics is the main factor shaping diversity in the visible traits of grapevines and their fruit, epigenetics is likely providing an additional layer of variability that could influence grape development, such as TANNIN accumulation, and vines' adaptation to their environment. D.P.G.

Xie, H., et al., 'Global DNA methylation patterns can play a role in defining terroir in grapevine (*Vitis vinifera* cv. Shiraz)', *Frontiers in Plant Science* (2017).

Épineuil, red-wine commune near AUXERRE whose name may be appended to that of BOURGOGNE.

éraflage, French term for DESTEMMING grapes.

Erbaluce, ancient but minor white wine grape speciality of Caluso in the north of the PIEMONTE region of north-west Italy. Dry Erbaluce used to be relatively light-bodied and acidic because it was picked too early, but serious, long-lived examples can now be found, along with TRADITIONAL METHOD sparkling wines. Erbaluce's most famous, if rare, manifestation is the golden sweet Caluso PASSITO. Total Italian plantings were 316 ha/781 acres in 2015.

erinose mite. The grapevine is the only known host in the plant kingdom to the grape erineum mite, *Colomerus vitis*, sometimes called grape leaf blister mite. The mite is widely distributed but usually causes only minor damage in commercial vineyards. The damage first appears as pinkish or reddish swellings or galls on the upper surfaces of the leaves. Beneath the gall, the concave portion of the leaf is lined with a felty mass of plant hairs or 'erinea'. This is one of the most unsightly grape-pest problems, yet it has negligible effects on vine performance. Control is usually by preventive applications of SULFUR dust, and, as this is often applied to control POWDERY MILDEW, these mites are often incidentally controlled. M.J.E.

Ermitage, alternative and historic name for HERMITAGE in the northern Rhône. Occasional synonym for MARSANNE.

erosion. See SOIL EROSION.

Erste Lage, literally 'first[-class] site', is an expression that has entered German and Austrian wine discourse in recent years with numerous distinctive meanings best explained in historical context. While Germany's VDP growers' association professed an ongoing interest in vineyard CLASSIFICATION from the 1980s, this was always in the context of delimiting a premium class of dry wines, for which the name ERSTES GEWÄCHS was long entertained. Following the RHEINGAU growers' 1999 success in gaining legal recognition by the state of Hessen for the designation Erstes Gewächs, the VDP nationally adopted the name GROSSES GEWÄCHS for an almost identically conceived category, applying it by implication to those vineyard sites classified as worthy of generating a wine so designated. In 2003, the Mosel regional VDP, most of whose members placed emphasis on residually sweet Riesling, adopted Erste Lage for wines from top-ranked sites that failed the test of legal dryness imposed on Grosse Gewächse. In 2006, the VDP adopted Erste Lage as 'the unifying overarching concept in all regions for wines of the uppermost category', thus making Grosses Gewächs a name for legally dry (TROCKEN) wine from an Erste Lage.

In 2012, the VDP elected to make GROSSE LAGE the apex of its classificatory pyramid and to add a PREMIER CRU level, for which the term 'Erste Lage' was repurposed. A German wine law of 2021 recognizes the terms 'Erstes Gewächs' and 'Grosses Gewächs', specifying minimal POTENTIAL ALCOHOL, maximum YIELD, and earliest possible release dates for each category. However, what wines should be accorded Erstes or Grosses Gewächs status and how a corresponding vineyard classification would be determined has been left for regional committees to determine.

As of 2021, the regional VDPs of the AHR and THE MOSEL have not made use of the Erste Lage category, while the VDP RHEINHESSEN has recognized a classificatory tier known as 'Aus Ersten Lagen', but without according Erste Lage status to any specific, named vineyards.

In AUSTRIA, inspired in part by the VDP's classificatory efforts, the TRADITIONSWEINGÜTER ÖSTERREICH unveiled in 2010 their own evolving classification of Erste Lage sites, signified on labels by a logo intentionally patterned after that utilized by the VDP, featuring a prominent Arabic number 1. An eventual upgrade of certain sites to the status of GROSSE LAGE is envisioned. However, Austrian wine law currently recognizes no vineyard classifications. D.S.

Erstes Gewächs designates dry (TROCKEN) wines from a limited number of ostensibly top sites in GERMANY'S RHEINGAU and HESSISCHE BERGSTRASSE. Quality-conscious Rheingau growers introduced this term in the 1990s to refer to their top dry wines from classic grape varieties, and their lobbying resulted in the 1999 recognition of this category by the German state of Hessen and its being permitted on labels. This legal monopolization by Hessen prompted the VDP growers' association to instead promote the term GROSSES GEWÄCHS, utilizing it in a very similar way, albeit without any state or national legal recognition. In 2013 it was agreed within the VDP that, to avoid confusion about the association's prestige category of dry wine, its Rheingau members would henceforth use the term 'Grosses Gewächs' to denote 'grand cru' wines and 'Erstes Gewächs' for a 'premier cru' level. A 2021 German wine law established Erstes Gewächs as a category of dry wine and set parameters for YIELD, minimum POTENTIAL ALCOHOL, and release date, leaving further specifications (such as a classification of vineyards) to the regional Schutzgemeinschaften ('protective associations') tasked with 'product specification' for PGI and PDO wines. See also ERSTE LAGE. D.S.

erythorbic acid, alternative antioxidant to ASCORBIC ACID.

Erzeugerabfüllung, German word meaning 'producer bottling'. As in France (see MIS EN BOUTEILLE), the term may be used by CO-OPERATIVES as well as estates. The terms GUTSABFÜLLUNG and 'Schlossabfüllung' are officially defined in slightly more restrictive terms and are nowadays seldom used. D.S.

esca, FUNGAL DISEASE believed to be as old as vine cultivation. Although the causal agents are found in most of the world's wine regions, it is most severe in vineyards located in warmer and drier MEDITERRANEAN CLIMATES, for example in France, Italy, Portugal, Spain, and California. Esca affects mature vines (usually more than ten years old) and is characterized by white-rot symptoms in the wood. It is considered to be a complex of diseases that start with cuttings used in PROPAGATION (see TRUNK DISEASES). The Greek word *yska* signified both rotten grape wood and the spongy Basidiomycete fungal bodies.

The fungi *Phaeomoniella chlamydospora* and *Phaeoacremonium minimum* are known to be the main pathogens associated with esca. However, up to 24 other species of *Phaeoacremonium* and several *Cadophora* species have been reported in vines showing symptoms of esca. Additionally, esca is the only trunk disease in which Basidiomycete species play a role, with species in the genera *Fomitiporia*, *Fomitiporella*, *Inonotus*, *Inocutis*, and *Phellinus* regarded as the causal agents of the white rot.

The first symptoms—shoot tip and tendril dieback—are observed in mid spring, followed later in the season by tiger-striping of the leaves, which eventually turn reddish in red varieties and chlorotic in white ones. A third symptom, grey- to dark-brown speckling on the berry skin (hence the name 'black measles'), is economically worse for TABLE GRAPE growers than for winegrowers. The last symptom, apoplexy, is characterized by a sudden wilting of the vine, including shrivelling of the fruit and fallen leaves. Vines affected by apoplexy may appear completely healthy the following season. Internal wood symptoms include light- to dark-brown and black streaking similar to that observed in vines with PETRI DISEASE. In older vines, a white rot characterized by a yellowish spongy mass of wood can be observed in the centre of the TRUNK and/or CORDONS.

Although there is currently no cure for the esca complex, research has shown that stress avoidance and the protection of PRUNING wounds using FUNGICIDES can significantly reduce the incidence and severity of the disease. ORGANIC growers are also trialling BIOLOGICAL controls that incorporate various strains of the non-pathogenic *Trichoderma* fungus to combat esca and other trunk diseases. More extreme management strategies include CURETTAGE and TRUNK RENEWAL. L.T.M. & J.R.U.-T.

Gramaje, D., et al., 'Managing grapevine trunk diseases with respect to etiology and epidemiology: current strategies and future prospects', *Plant Disease*, 102/1 (2018), 12–39.

Gubler, W. D., et al., 'Esca, Petri, and grapevine leaf stripe disease', in W. F. Wilcox et al. (eds.), *Compendium of Grape Diseases, Disorders, and Pests* (2nd edn, 2015), 52–7.

Esgana Cão, synonym for the Portuguese white grape variety known on the island of Madeira as SERCIAL. Its full name on the mainland means 'dog strangler', presumably a reference to its notably high acidity. It can, occasionally, be found as an ingredient in VINHO VERDE and BUCELAS.

Espadeiro, minor grape variety producing mainly crisp pink wines in Portugal's VINHO VERDE country. It can produce quite heavily and rarely reaches high sugar levels.

espalier, a relatively unusual TRAINING SYSTEM, more desirable for aesthetic than commercial reasons, for vines or other fruit trees, by which the plant is trained to grow in a single plane to form a flat shape, for example against a wall (see diagram below). Espalier training leaves a trunk and one or two arms with several canes which are trained in the same plane with a trellis or wire for support. Different vines are trained to different heights in the French Espalier de Thoméry. R.E.S.

espumante, Portuguese term for sparkling wine with a pressure of not less than 3 bar.

espumoso, Spanish for 'sparkling'. TRADITIONAL METHOD Spanish sparkling wine that is exported is most often labelled CAVA.

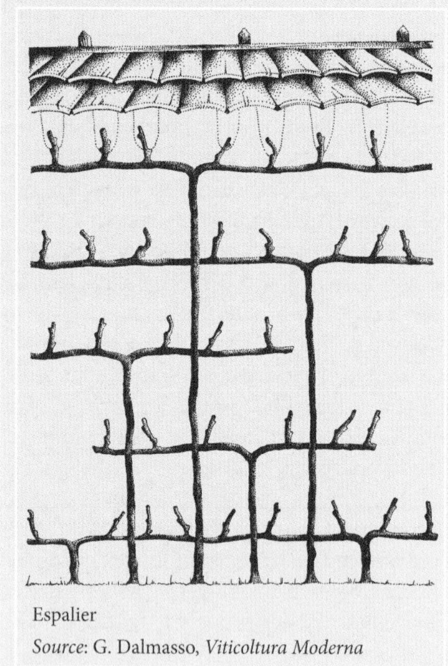

Espalier
Source: G. Dalmasso, *Viticoltura Moderna*

Esquitxagos, misleadingly interesting synonym for VALENCIA's bland white wine grape MERSEGUERA.

Estaing, miniature AOC on the banks of the Lot in the Aveyron *département* in SOUTH WEST FRANCE. Reds are based on FER and GAMAY grapes and the rarer whites on CHENIN BLANC, although the Cabernets and several local varieties are also allowed. A CO-OPERATIVE dominates production.

estate bottled, term used on labels which has a very specific legal meaning in the US, where an estate-bottled wine must be made and bottled at the winery using grapes from vineyards the winery owns or controls; both vineyards and winery must be in the AVA specified on the label. This is the American counterpart of CHÂTEAU BOTTLED or DOMAINE BOTTLED. **Estate grown** is not (yet) legally defined but indicates that the grapes come from vineyards owned or controlled by the producer.

estate wine, term in common parlance, but not in federal law, in the US that suggests loosely that the wine came entirely from grapes farmed on the winery's own property. 'Estate wine' may be casually construed to be exactly synonymous with ESTATE BOTTLED, which has legal status, but technically it is not.

In South Africa, 'estate wine' is a specific term for a wine that was grown, made, and bottled on a single geographical unit registered with the Wine and Spirit Board. Many German producers refer to their most basic bottling of Riesling as their Estate Riesling, *Gutsriesling* in German.

esters, compounds formed by reaction of ACIDS with ALCOHOLS. The two most common forms of esters in wine are FERMENTATION esters, commonly found in the aroma of young white wine, and esters that are chemically formed during AGEING.

The fresh, fruity aroma of young wines derives in large part from the presence of the mixture of esters produced during fermentation, which is why it is usually called fermentation AROMA. The precise nature of esters formed during fermentation is strongly influenced by the fermentation temperature, as well as the YEAST strain and other factors. For more details, see TEMPERATURE.

Since wines contain much more ETHANOL than any other alcohol, and since the most common ester-forming volatile organic acid is ACETIC ACID, it is not surprising that the most common ester in wine is ETHYL ACETATE, but many more combinations are possible from among the acids and alcohols present; this helps to explain why wines differ so greatly in their aroma and, after years in bottle, BOUQUET. (See also ISOAMYL ACETATE.)

A number of esters that do not have a particularly marked odour are also present in wines. Among these are those resulting from reaction of the ethyl alcohol produced by fermentation with TARTARIC, MALIC, SUCCINIC, and other acids of the grape and wine, and such a process lowers the acidity and can mellow a wine.

When an acid reacts with an alcohol, water is produced in addition to the ester. This reaction is assisted or catalysed by the hydrogen ion, a substance plentiful in acid (low PH) solutions such as wines. Hydrogen ions not only catalyse the formation of esters from acids and alcohols but also function as catalysts for the splitting of esters into their acid and alcohol segments. The result of these two tendencies, formation and splitting, is that wines contain mixtures of the four participants in the reactions: organic acids, alcohols, the several esters from the possible combinations, and water. The relative amounts of the four participants in the two reactions is governed by their concentrations and the reaction rates for formation and splitting. Given enough time, a state will be reached in which the net formation of esters just balances the splitting of them. This is known as the equilibrium state. In practice, the equilibrium state in wines is not reached but merely approached, because the formation rates for some esters are extremely slow under wine storage conditions.
P.J.W. & V.L.

Waterhouse, A. L., et al., *Understanding Wine Chemistry* (2016).

Estonia, Baltic country south of FINLAND with a rich tradition for fruit wines, mostly made from apples and/or rhubarb but increasingly including grapes. Owing to the location, between latitudes 57.5 and 59.7° N, the climate is challenging, with an average temperature of only 5–7 °C/41–45 °F, dropping as low as −35 °C/−31 °F in wintertime. Spring FROST is common and autumn starts early, leaving only a short vegetation period. In colder spots, grapes are often growing in greenhouses, or vines are covered with GEOTEXTILES. In warmer plots, vines grow on open land. Climate warming has helped but has also brought diseases common in central Europe such as POWDERY MILDEW and DOWNY MILDEW. Both TABLE GRAPES and wine grapes are allowed for wine production, but the most common and best varieties for wine are the cold-hardy, early-ripening SOLARIS and RONDO. Other notable varieties are REGENT, Hasanski Sladki, and Zilga, but many more varieties grow in the gardens of hobby growers. By 2022, the country had more than two dozen commercial wineries, about half of them producing grape wines. However, in late 2021 the EU officially recognized Estonia as a wine-producing country, opening up funding and research opportunities for local growers and producers, so this number is expected to rise quickly.
K.M.

www.aiandusliit.ee/veinitee.com/

Estremadura, old name for the DOP known since 2009 as LISBOA.

estufa, Portuguese word meaning 'hothouse' or 'stove', also applied to the tanks used to heat wine on the island of MADEIRA, thereby accelerating its development and maturation. The heating process itself is called **estufagem**. *Estufas* simulate the effects of the long tropical sea voyages in the 18th and 19th centuries when madeira (and SETÚBAL) was, at first accidentally and then deliberately, stowed in the hold of a ship to age prematurely as a result of the temperature changes involved in a round trip, or *torna viagem*, across the tropics.
R.J.M.

ethanal, synonym for ACETALDEHYDE.

ethanol, common name for ethyl alcohol, the most potable of the ALCOHOLS and an important, intoxicating constituent of wine and all other alcoholic drinks. Ethanol, often called simply 'alcohol', is colourless and odourless but can have considerable impact on how a liquid tastes.

Ethanol is the most potent component of wine (and the most obvious of those that distinguish it from GRAPE JUICE), but it is probably the least discussed by wine consumers (unless in the context of HANGOVERS). For although ethanol does not have a taste, it has an effect, not just on the human nervous system but also on how a wine tastes. The ethanol content in a perfectly BALANCED wine should be unfathomable, but wines that are slightly too high in alcohol may 'burn' or taste 'hot', especially in the aftertaste. White wines high in ethanol (over

13%) may have a slightly bitter aftertaste. Ethanol contributes to VISCOSITY, and some argue that wines described as full-bodied, or having considerable BODY, are high in ethanol while wines that are low in viscosity and body are low in ethanol. However, this is an oversimplification because many different compounds contribute to a wine's body and MOUTHFEEL. See ALCOHOLIC STRENGTH for ways in which the ethanol level may be manipulated.

Ethanol is produced in two ways, the most traditional and natural of which is by the fermentation by YEAST of solutions that contain SUGARS, such as that involved in wine production. It is required in huge volumes by industry, however, as a solvent for perfumes and as a raw material for the synthesis of products such as drugs, plastics, lacquers, polishes, plasticizers, and cosmetics. Most of the ethanol used by industry, other than that produced by distilling the European wine SURPLUS, is produced in factories by hydrating ethylene, a component of petroleum.

See ALCOHOLIC STRENGTH for the varied concentrations of ethanol to be found in different wines, HEALTH for the effects of alcohol consumption in the form of wine, and REDUCED-ALCOHOL WINES. V.L.

Ethiopia in north-east Africa can produce quite respectable red wine and some white from vines grown at relatively high ELEVATIONS. The Awash winery in Addis Ababa, based on vineyards established by the Italian troops who occupied part of the country from 1936 to 1941, has been joined by a CASTEL project with 162 ha/400 acres of vines planted 2007–9 near Ziway, 160 km/100 miles south of the capital. It sells VARIETALS made from INTERNATIONAL VARIETIES under the brand names Rift Valley and Acacia from vineyards surrounded by a wide trench designed to deter pythons, hippopotamuses, and hyenas.

ethyl acetate (EA) is an organic aroma compound (ESTER) that can give a wine fruity aromatic qualities at low levels but is considered a FAULT at high levels when the aroma resembles that of nail-polish remover.

There is no legal limit for the level of ethyl acetate in wine, and it is not regularly monitored in the winery. The sensory detection threshold is around 12 mg/l, with healthy wines reaching levels of about 60 mg/l. Wines with over 150 mg/l EA are generally considered faulty.

EA is produced by both yeast and bacteria. YEAST naturally produce EA when fermentation by-products react with ETHANOL. This ester can be re-used by the yeast or it can be excreted into the wine. EA levels after fermentation can vary widely depending on the choice of yeast. Non-*Saccharomyces* species tend to produce higher levels of EA.

ACETIC ACID BACTERIA can also form EA by reacting with ethanol, and this is why EA is intrinsically linked to VOLATILE ACIDITY in wine. The presence of EA in a wine can enhance the perception of VA. However, when VA is measured in a wine, the ethyl acetate level is not measured as it is not a volatile acid. K.C.

ethyl alcohol, scientific name for ETHANOL, the alcohol most commonly encountered in wine and other alcoholic drinks.

ethyl carbamate is a naturally occurring component of all fermented foods and beverages. In the case of the YEAST *Saccharomyces cerevisiae*, ethyl carbamate is formed by the reaction between ETHANOL and urea, which in turn is produced by the degradation of the AMINO ACID arginine, one of the main NITROGEN sources in grape juice and MUSTS. In the late 1980s, ethyl carbamate was added to the growing list of compounds suspected of human carcinogenicity on the basis of animal tests.

Most wine types contain ethyl carbamate concentrations well below the limit suggested by US authorities of 15 μg/l per litre (60 μg/l in fortified wines). High-alcohol sweet wines which have been heated during production (such as MADEIRA) are likely to be the wines with the highest levels of ethyl carbamate. The level may also be influenced by the yeast strain, by MALOLACTIC CONVERSION, and by high temperatures during MACERATION and storage.

Ribéreau-Gayon, P., et al., *Traité d'Œnologie 2: Chimie du vin: Stabilisation et traitements* (7th edn, 2017), translated by J. Towey as *Handbook of Enology 2: The Chemistry of Wine Stabilization and Treatments* (3rd edn, 2021).

ethylphenol. See BRETTANOMYCES.

Etna is Europe's largest still-active volcano on the east coast of SICILY near the city of Catania; the DOC of the same name produces high-quality reds, rosés, and sparkling wines based on NERELLO MASCALESE and whites from CARRICANTE. Viticulture has been practised for centuries if not millennia on Etna's black VOLCANIC soils, and vineyards and their position have largely been determined and at times obliterated by lava streams.

Until the beginning of the 20th century, the wines from Etna were in high demand in the north of Europe, especially for blending purposes. Huge volumes of grapes were vinified in palmenti (see PALMENTO), north-facing, naturally cool, gravity-fed cellars built into the slope. At nearby Riposto, casks filled with wines were rolled through the shallows of the sea to be lifted on to ships, the wine destined for France, among other countries, as blending material.

At the end of the 19th century, the Murgo estate was already producing large quantities of TRADITIONAL METHOD sparkling wine, while on Etna's still little-known west side the barons of Spitaleri di Muglia experimented with French varieties as well as Italian varieties Nerello Mascalese, NERO D'AVOLA, GUARNACCIA, Mantonico, CARRICANTE, and NEBBIOLO on steep, terraced vineyards at 800 m/2,625 ft in ELEVATION and higher.

Etna's vineyards survived PHYLLOXERA because the pest cannot thrive in the volcanic soils, but many of its vineyards, especially those in high, hard-to-reach places, were abandoned. Others were pulled up, the high-density centenarian vineyards replanted with straight rows of vines trained on WIRES. Local agronomist Salvo Foti has been instrumental in preserving the traditional planting practice called *quinconce,* consisting of a square grid of 13 vines.

The Etna DOC was established in 1968, covering vineyards on the north and east side of the volcano and four towns in the south—Belpasso, Paternò, S. Maria di Licodia, and Biancavila—but Etna started its ascendance only in the early 2000s when Andrea Franchetti and Marc De Grazia independently bought land on Etna's north side, where vineyards can be found up to 1,000 m/3,281 ft and higher. Both first dabbled in INTERNATIONAL VARIETIES, but once they turned their attention to INDIGENOUS VARIETIES Etna began to see an enormous rise in popularity, resulting in huge investments and an influx of newcomers all keen to explore its cool volcanic terraces. Between 2011 and 2020 Etna more than doubled the number of producers (from 176 to 383) and area planted (from 5,682 ha to 11,183 ha/27,634 acres).

Today the Etna DOC forms a sickle shape around Etna's peak, leaving only the west side, where there was little viticulture post-phylloxera, outside of the DOC, even though its grapes are regularly sold to producers on the north side. Etna Superiore applies only to the commune of Milo, the undisputed CRU of long-lived, complex white Carricante. The whole denomination is divided into CONTRADE, districts named after the hamlets, which have conveniently provided the first step towards a cru system. W.S.

Foti, S., *Etna: I Vini del Vulcano* (2020).
Spencer, B. N., *The New Wines of Mount Etna: An Insider's Guide to the History and Rebirth of a Wine Region* (2020).

Étoile, L'. See L'ÉTOILE.

Étraire de l'Adui, or **Étraire de la Duï**, is a historic and increasingly rare grape variety grown before PHYLLOXERA on the fringes of the south-east Rhône Valley and Savoie. It is related to PERSAN.

Etruscans. The origins of viticulture in TUSCANY are as problematic as the origins of the Etruscan peoples who flourished in central north Italy from the 8th century BCE until being absorbed by the Romans from the 3rd century onwards. However, at its height, Etruscan society was heavily influenced by the culture of the Greek colonies of southern Italy. They imported fine Greek pottery for use in the SYMPOSIUM and made their own copies. The dinner and drinking party was a favourite theme in the lavish paintings which adorned their tombs. Indeed, the Etruscans became a byword among Greek and Roman moralists for luxurious living and then-eccentric customs, such as allowing wives to participate in banquets. There are literary references to Etruscan wine from the late 3rd century BCE, but much earlier, from the late 7th century, the wine was exported in a distinctive type of AMPHORA well beyond Italy to southern France. Indeed, it is likely that this early trade played a role in introducing wine and viticulture to GAUL. Various wines are attested throughout the region in the classical period, although none was universally recognized as of the highest class. See ORIGINS OF VINICULTURE. J.J.P.

Bouloumie, B., 'Le Vin etrusque', *Quaderni della scuola di specializzazione in viticoltura e enologia* (Turin), 7 (1983), 165–88.

Cerchiai, C., *L'alimentazione nel mondo antico: gli Etruschi* (1987).

McGovern, P. E., et al., 'The beginning of viniculture in France', *Proceedings of the National Academy of Sciences of the United States of America*, 110/25 (2013), 10147–52.

EU stands for European Union, previously known as the **European Community**, a group of 27 advanced Western industrialized countries co-operating on both economic and political fronts. Twenty-four of the 27 members produce wine (of which seven only in marginal quantities), making the Union the world's leading wine economy, producing 165 million hl/ 4,360 million gal in 2020 and accounting for 45% of the world's winegrowing areas, 65% of production, 60% of global consumption, and 70% of exports (including intra-EU trade).

The area under vine in the EU stood at 3.3 million ha/8.2 million acres in 2021, down from almost 3.5 million ha in 2013 and almost 4 million ha in 1987. This represents just over 45% of the total global vineyard area (these OIV statistics include vines used to produce RAISINS and TABLE GRAPES, and these two categories represent a higher proportion of total vineyard area in Asia than in Europe). According to official EU data, of the 3.2 million ha of vines planted for wine production in the EU, on average 1.2 million ha produce grapes for PDO wines, 1.5 million ha for PGI wines, and nearly 0.4 million ha for WINE WITHOUT GEOGRAPHICAL INDICATION. Spain has the most extensive area under vine in Europe (940,086 ha planted for wine in 2021) and, indeed, the world; Italy, however, produces more wine than Spain, which used to have the lowest-yielding vines in the EU (see SPAIN for how this has changed).

The main EU wine-producing countries are, in descending order of wine production: Italy, Spain, France, Germany, Portugal, Romania, Hungary, Austria, Greece, Bulgaria, Croatia, Slovenia, Czechia, Slovakia, Cyprus, and Malta. (BELGIUM, DENMARK, ESTONIA, LITHUANIA, the NETHERLANDS, POLAND, IRELAND, and SWEDEN also produce a small amount of wine.) In 2020, total EU production of wine was around 165 million hl/4,360 million gal (world production in 2020 was approximately 260 million hl, according to OIV statistics).

The EU is an important net exporter of wine, and exports to non-EU countries were worth nearly €14 billion in 2020–21, representing 28.4 million hl/750 million gal, or over 17% of production. Italy is the biggest exporter in the EU (and the world) by volume, with exports of 20.8 million hl worth €6.2 billion. Spain follows closely behind in terms of volume with 20.2 million hl, albeit with lower earnings of €2.6 billion. France sits in third place in volume terms (13.6 million hl) but leads Europe and the world in terms of value (€8.7 billion). The US is the biggest market, taking 25.2% of EU exports by volume and 28.6% by value. Since Brexit, the UK has become the second most important export destination (rather than an internal market), taking 13% of EU exports by volume and 11.4% by value.

EU member states are also significant importers of wine both from other EU countries and from outside the Union. Germany, the world's second largest importer behind the UK, imported 14.1 million hl in 2020 worth €2.5 billion—57% of which was BULK WINE. France, the Netherlands, Belgium, Portugal, and Sweden are also significant wine importers. In 2020–21, the four top external sources for EU imports were South Africa, Chile, Australia, and the US, representing more than 60% of wine imports from outside the EU. Wine imported into the EU, known as 'third-country wine', must conform to European wine law and may not be blended with wine made within the EU.

The EU wine sector is subject to an overarching regulatory framework called the 'common market organization' (CMO), which is part of Europe's common agricultural policy (CAP). The wine CMO includes rules on the free movement of wine between member states, winemaking practices, labelling, and trade with 'third countries' outside the common market. Its defining feature, until 2008, was the segregation of the wine sector into QUALITY WINE, which was regulated to manage 'quality', and TABLE WINE, which was granted subsidies to control production and the market. This essentially political and cultural divide was imported from France's wine law, reflecting that country's efforts to manage production in the poorer Midi while protecting the more privileged producers of well-known wine regions.

From the very first wine CMO in 1970, it was evident that accommodating the more liberal rules (and cheaper wines) that existed in Italy and the stricter regime prevailing in France within a single market would be a significant challenge. Blockades and violent protests through the 1970s and early 1980s, fuelled by rampant overproduction of table wine and nationalistic sentiment, testified to the difficulty of the task. The accession of Spain, Portugal, and Greece in the mid 1980s multiplied the complexity of the problems.

The wine CMO went through several iterations over the years, resulting in a proliferation of subsidies and controls, such as DISTILLATION, GRUBBING UP of vines, PLANTING RIGHTS, and price supports, ostensibly intended to bring supply and demand in the wine sector into balance. These largely failed because policymakers were torn between maintaining the incomes of the poorer producers of WINES WITHOUT GEOGRAPHICAL INDICATION and realigning the wine sector with the demands of the modern wine market. Usually the political imperative to prop up the poorer producers won out, resulting in a ballooning budget.

By the mid 2000s, a rethink of the wine CMO had become both essential and politically achievable. The sharp decline of traditional table wine, soaring production of wines with a geographical indication, the accession of new EU member states, budget constraints, and competition from the NEW WORLD were all factors.

The reform introduced in 2008 took the radical step of dissolving the quality-wine and table-wine categories. In their place a new hierarchy was created: protected denominations of origin (PDOs—covering AOC, DOC, DO, etc.); Protected Geographical Indications (or PGIs—covering VIN DE PAYS, IGT, Landwein, Vino de la Tierra, etc.); and wines without geographical indication. The last were granted permission to use grape-variety names on the label, thereby allowing the creation of a new class of VARIETAL wines. Each member state has its own precise terminology based on these overarching categories. The new hierarchy brought wine into alignment with the PDO/PGI system for other foods in the EU. Winemaking rules were linked to OIV recommendations as a means of benchmarking them internationally. Labelling was also simplified and liberalized to some extent.

The 2008 reform also transformed the regime for support measures, making them available to all categories of wine (not just wines without geographical indication) for a more targeted range of purposes, with a total budget of around

€1.2 billion per year. In the first years of the reform, a key focus of support measures was, as before, to balance supply and demand, with grubbing-up measures contributing to a reduction in the total EU vineyard of 370,000 ha (10%), an exercise considerably more successful in some countries than others.

A further change in 2013 ended certain support measures, notably the notorious 'crisis distillation' (in pre-reform times, every year was a crisis year)—although emergency COVID relief saw a resurrection of this measure in 2021. In recent years, the focus of support measures has shifted towards 'investments in enterprises', 'restructuring and conversion' (largely making vineyards and wineries suitable for PDO/PGI production), and 'promotion' (i.e. offshore marketing).

The CAP reform adopted in 2021 for implementation in 2023 places more emphasis on environmental and social SUSTAINABILITY in agriculture—in line with the so-called 'European Green Deal' strategy. The range of financial measures to support 'green' initiatives and economic resilience to CLIMATE CHANGE is increased. Certain rules have also been modernized, allowing the use of DISEASE-RESISTANT VARIETIES in PDO wines, creating new categories for DE-ALCOHOLIZED WINE and PARTIALLY DE-ALCOHOLIZED WINE, and introducing mandatory INGREDIENT LABELLING and energy labelling for wine.

Alongside the wine CMO, the EU has negotiated a series of agreements with several non-EU wine-producing countries, including Australia (1998, 2008), Canada (2003), Chile (2002), South Africa (2002), Switzerland (2002), the US (1984, 2005), and the UK (2020). These agreements cover concerns such as reciprocal arrangements regarding oenological practices, the reciprocal protection and control of wine denominations (which in some cases implies the phasing out of GENERICS), trade facilitation, dispute-resolution procedures, and in some cases tariff quotas. On the EU side, these agreements form a key part of a long-term strategy to secure protection for their GEOGRAPHICAL INDICATIONS, while for non-EU countries the incentive has been to improve their ability to compete in the EU market.

See also WORLD WINE TRADE GROUP.

J.E.H. & J.P.H.B.

www.ec.europa.eu/info/food-farming-fisheries/plants-and-plant-products/plant-products/wine_en

eucalyptus character refers to an aroma and flavour found in red wine, most commonly in Australia and California and also in Chile, described variously as 'eucalypt', 'camphor', or 'minty'. For some winemakers this characteristic is a selling point, whereas others prefer to avoid it or at least to limit its presence as far as possible. In 2010 the AWRI assessed consumer response to eucalypt flavour in red wines and found that, even at very low levels, most consumers reacted to the flavour, and more consumers preferred wines with the 'minty' flavour than disliked it.

Most species of Eucalyptus, which are native to Australia but are now grown on every continent, contain essential oils in their leaves and, depending on the species, the main component of the oil is a volatile compound called 1,8-cineole, commonly known as eucalyptol. It is present in a wide range of foods, beverages, and therapeutic products. Research on California Merlot has determined that 1,8-cineole can be perceived even at very low concentrations such as 1.1 µg/l and can be recognized at 3.2 µg/l.

While the compound may be found in wines made from grapes grown with no Eucalyptus trees nearby, research has indicated that Eucalyptus trees growing close to vineyards are the primary source of the flavour in wine and that only negligible levels found in wine are from grape-derived FLAVOUR PRECURSORS.

In one study, grapes harvested from rows further than 25 m (80 ft) from Eucalyptus trees gave wines with very low levels of 1,8-cineole while those grown closer to the Eucalyptus trees contained significantly higher amounts. The compound is at its highest levels in the skin of the grape berry and is extracted during fermentation on skins. While the absorption of the compound by grape berries is important, it is much less a factor than the presence of Eucalyptus leaves or bark in harvested grapes. MECHANICAL HARVESTING of rows close to Eucalyptus trees will, more than likely, produce bins of grapes containing numerous Eucalyptus leaves, and these have a very significant effect on eventual levels of 1,8-cineole in wine. Even during hand harvesting, Eucalyptus leaves can be trapped within the grape bunches. The key to managing 1,8-cineole levels in wine is therefore to control the amount of MOG (material other than grapes).

A further study showed that the compound could also be found at relatively high levels in Bordeaux Cabernet Sauvignon wines made from vineyards in which was found an invasive plant (*Artemisia verlotiorum*) that contains 1,8-cineole as a major constituent. It is possible that other regionally specific vegetation could also influence wine flavour.

M.P.K. & D.L.C.

Capone, D. L., et al., 'Vineyard and fermentation studies to elucidate the origin of 1,8-cineole in Australian red wine', *Journal of Agricultural and Food Chemistry*, 60 (2012), 2281–7.

Farina, L., et al., 'Terpene compounds as possible precursors of 1,8-cineole in red grapes and wines', *Journal of Agricultural and Food Chemistry*, 53 (2005), 1633–6.

Herve, E., et al., 'Eucalyptol in wines showing a "eucalyptus" aroma', in A. Lonvaud et al. (eds.), *Actualités Oenologiques: VIIème Symposium International d'Oenologie, Bordeaux* (2003), 598–600.

Poitou, X., et al., '1,8-Cineole in French red wines: evidence for a contribution related to its various origins', *Journal of Agricultural and Food Chemistry*, 65 (2017), 383–93.

Eucharist, wine in the. The significance of wine in the sacrament of the Eucharist (also called the Lord's Supper or Holy Communion) derives from wine representing the blood of Christ in this most sacred celebration of the Christian church.

According to the New Testament, Christ instituted this ritual when he celebrated the Jewish Passover with his disciples, transforming it into the Last Supper. As he gave bread and wine to his disciples, he commanded them to 'do this in remembrance of me'. Christ singled out one of the four cups of wine consumed during the Passover meal and said: 'This cup is the new covenant in my blood. Do this, as often as you drink it, in remembrance of me.' The Eucharist then commemorates Christ's death on the cross: the wine represents the blood that he shed, while the bread represents his broken and crushed body.

In the Gospel of Matthew, Christ elaborates on and extends the mysterious meaning of this ritual:

> 'While they were eating, Jesus took a loaf of bread, and after blessing it he broke it, gave it to the disciples and said, "Take, eat; this is my body." Then he took a cup, and after giving thanks he gave it to them, saying, "Drink from it, all of you; for this is my blood of the covenant, which is poured out for many for the forgiveness of sin. I tell you, I will never again drink of this fruit of the vine until that day when I drink it new with you in my Father's kingdom."' (Matt. 26. 26–9)

In the Eucharist Christians remember the death of Jesus Christ to atone for the sins of the world and to heal and restore humanity's fractured relationships with God, each other, and the created world at large. Christians also believe that, through Christ's death and resurrection, death has lost its finality; and Christ invites believers to receive eternal life (1 Cor. 15. 51–7).

For Christians this act of remembrance is no mere recalling of a historical event or a theological idea. Rather it is an active participation in the reality of Christ's redeeming presence in the world that harks back to his death and looks forward to his second coming (Isa. 25. 8, Rev. 21. 1–5). Christ will invite believers to the great wedding feast between God and his people in his Father's kingdom where His followers will savour wine in perfect and harmonious communion with the triune God of love and grace: Father, Son, and Holy Spirit. For Christians, drinking wine from the Eucharistic cup is therefore a most sacred experience of God's redemption.

The Jewish Scriptures foreshadow this as they speak of God's redemption as a great banquet and wedding feast where wine will flow in abundance (Amos 9. 14–15, Isa. 25. 6, Hos. 2. 18–23). The prophet Amos even speaks of a time when 'the mountains shall drip sweet wine, and all the hills shall flow with it' (Amos 9. 13). The imagery used here inspires a yearning for a restored paradise.

When Jesus performs his first miracle at the wedding feast of Cana, transforming water reserved for the Jewish rite of purification into an abundance of choice wine, he gives his first sign that in him the promises of old are being fulfilled (John 2). No longer are scapegoats, temple sacrifices or ritual cleansings needed for believers to draw near to God. Christ's death on the cross is the ultimate sacrifice and the saving bridge between God and humanity.

In the celebration of the Eucharist, Christians ingest this great mystery. As they eat consecrated bread and drink consecrated wine, they are reunited with God and each other into one spiritual family where love and forgiveness flow freely, like the choice wine at the wedding feast of Cana.

The celebration of the Eucharist then is the church's principal act of faithfulness as believers enter into the redemptive death of Christ only to be raised up into new and eternal life, united in Christ as God's beloved family that remains rooted in Christ, the only true vine (John 15).

Eucharist literally means 'thanksgiving' and harks back to its first celebration, where Jesus prayed the traditional Jewish prayer of thanksgiving over the bread and wine. It also expresses gratitude for the gift of God's salvation, forgiveness, and healing.

It is this positive understanding of wine in the Eucharist and in the BIBLE more generally (there are nearly one thousand wine and wine-related references in the Bible) that inspired monks and nuns to plant vineyards throughout Europe and beyond. See MONKS AND MONASTERIES.

Controversy

The celebration of the Eucharist has caused confusion, disputes, and controversy since its inception. The idea of drinking blood was condemned as an abomination in Jewish faith and culture, as blood was considered the centre of life and belonged to God alone. Early followers of Christ were misunderstood when they 'ate' the body of Christ and 'drank' Christ's blood in the form of bread and wine.

In the early church Christians celebrated the Lord's Supper in their homes, and it quickly became an expression of their status in society: some celebrated it as a lavish feast and got drunk on too much wine, while others were poor and left the Lord's Supper hungry. Rather than bringing Christians together into one family where resources were freely shared, it solidified their economic status and differences. The apostle Paul wrote a fierce letter against such divisive practice (1 Cor. 11).

During the Protestant Reformation in the 16th century, many disputes emerged surrounding the celebration of the Eucharist. The Reformers, including Martin Luther and John Calvin, reintroduced the drinking of wine in the Eucharist to all believers (over time it had been restricted to priests only). Controversies emerged as to how Christ was present in the celebration of the Eucharist and how often it should be celebrated: daily, weekly or even less frequently. Both Martin Luther and John Calvin emphasized the importance of the weekly celebration of the Lord's Supper. Other Protestant traditions confined it to the margins of their religious life.

The question of Christ's presence in the elements of bread and wine also became a topic of heated discussion during the Reformation. Orthodox and Catholic Christians have held to a strong understanding of Christ's presence in the elements of bread and wine. Martin Luther followed suit by calling this great mystery the 'real presence' of Christ in bread and wine. John Calvin believed that Christ's body and blood are spiritually present in the bread and wine, and Ulrich Zwingli argued that bread and wine have a mere symbolic function. Despite all these differences there was a shared belief that Christ is present in the celebration of the Eucharist more generally speaking. Today we see a renewed effort to emphasize and celebrate the shared beliefs rather than the philosophically dense arguments.

From at least the 2nd century the idea that wine had to be used in the celebration of the Eucharist was challenged by some in the church. Great theologians such as Martin Luther, John Calvin, and John Knox fiercely defended the presence of wine in the Eucharist. They not only had their own wine cellars but were often paid in wine for their preaching ministries. It was only in the 19th century that this began to change when a Methodist minister, Thomas Welch, discovered how to pasteurize grape juice and keep it from fermenting into wine. The widespread use and abuse of distilled spirits in the 19th century led to the temperance movement, which led to PROHIBITION in the United States. Many Protestant churches in Britain and the US banned the use of wine in the Lord's Supper and continue to do so. The Orthodox, Catholic, Lutheran, Anglican, and Episcopalian churches have kept using wine in the Eucharist but many now offer grape juice for those who live in recovery or suffer from alcohol addiction.

See also RELIGION and MONKS AND MONASTERIES.

G.K.

Kreglinger, G., 'Wine in the Lord's Supper: Christ present in wine', in *The Spirituality of Wine* (2016).
Jeremias, J., *The Eucharistic Words of Jesus* (1966).
Macy, G., *The Banquet's Wisdom: A Short History of the Theologies of the Lord's Supper* (2005).

eudemis, better known as the European grapevine moth. See MOTHS.

eugenol. See OAK FLAVOUR.

European Union. See EU.

European vines, much-used description for varieties of the common vine species VITIS VINIFERA, as opposed to AMERICAN VINE SPECIES and Asian vine species.

Euskadi. See BASQUE.

Eutypa dieback, one of the most destructive FUNGAL DISEASES included in the TRUNK DISEASE complex that can lead to the replanting of whole vineyards. Originally known as dying arm, it is called *eutypiose* in France. Distribution is worldwide, over a wide range of climates, but with the highest incidence in regions with more than 300 mm/12 in rainfall a year. Today it is the most common trunk disease in South Australia (where it was first discovered in 1957), in south-west France, and in the North Coast and Sacramento regions of California. Studies conducted in the late 1990s estimated that California growers spend over $260 million a year in strategies to control the disease. Loss of net income caused by Eutypa dieback is estimated at $20 million a year in Australia for Shiraz alone.

Eutypa is caused by the diatrypaceous fungus *Eutypa lata*, which also attacks many other plants, especially apricots. Although recent studies have identified up to 11 other Diatrypaceae fungi associated with the disease, *E. lata* is the only one known to cause the foliar symptoms that characterize this disease and allow its identification in the field. Symptoms rarely show in vineyards less than eight years old, but this can be several years after infection has occurred. *E. lata* spores are released during or shortly after rain and can be spread up to 100 km/60 miles by wind. Infection in grapevines occurs mainly via PRUNING wounds in mild temperatures.

Eutypa dieback can be easily diagnosed in the spring: young shoots are stunted and yellow with small, misshapen, cupped leaves caused by toxins and/or secondary metabolites produced by the fungus in the infected trunks cordons. Symptoms in the wood include wedge-shaped cankers which are indistinguishable from those seen in vines affected by BOTRYOSPHAERIA DIEBACK and PHOMOPSIS dieback. No VITIS VINIFERA variety is immune, but some such as Cabernet Sauvignon, Sauvignon Blanc, Grenache, and Syrah are more susceptible.

Removing infected ARMS and TRUNKS, commonly known as vine surgery, may allow the vine to thrive, but once the infection begins downward movement in the trunk, TRUNK RENEWAL may be necessary. Painting or spraying the fresh pruning wound with approved FUNGICIDES is very effective in preventing infection. This disease can have drastic effects on yield, as old vineyards degenerate long after the onset of the initial infection. Given the commercial interest in wine made from old vines (see VINE AGE), this disease is particularly regrettable. R.E.S. & J.R.U.-T.

Gramaje, D., et al., 'Managing grapevine trunk diseases with respect to etiology and epidemiology: current strategies and future prospects', *Plant Disease*, 102/1 (2018), 12–39.

Rolshausen, P. E., et al., 'Eutypa dieback', in W. F. Wilcox et al. (eds.), *Compendium of Grape Diseases, Disorders, and Pests* (2nd edn, 2015), 57–61.

Euvitis, considered by many botanists to be one of two sections of the genus VITIS (see BOTANICAL CLASSIFICATION), the other being MUSCADINIA. These two are considered to be two separate genera by others, since *Euvitis* and *Muscadinia* vines differ in chromosome number and in appearance. All of the commercially important wine, table, and raisins belong to the genus *Euvitis*. R.E.S. & J.V.

Wan, Y., et al., 'A phylogenetic analysis of the grape genus (*Vitis* L.) reveals broad reticulation and concurrent diversification during neogene and quaternary climate change', *BMC Evolutionary Biology*, 13/141 (2013).

EU wine is wine at its most basically European, a blend of WINES WITHOUT GEOGRAPHICAL INDICATION from more than one country in the EU, sometimes referred to as Euroblends. They must be labelled 'Blend of wines from different countries of the European Union' or 'European Union Wine'. The constituents of such wines tend to vary with the vagaries of the bottom layer of the European wine market.

Evans, Len (1930–2006), promoter, taster, judge, consumer, teacher, and maker of wine who did more to advance the cause of wine in Australia than any other individual. Born in Felixstowe, England, he was an architect manqué, like his friend the late Michael BROADBENT, but in Evans's case the distraction was professional golf rather than wine. He emigrated to New Zealand in 1953 and arrived in Sydney, Australia, two years later, where his stepping stone into what was to become a lifetime's immersion in wine was working in a new hotel. His energetic enthusiasm for wine was such that by 1965 he was the first National Promotions Executive for the Australian Wine Board. Evans was one of the few to see that the future lay in table wine rather than in the sweet FORTIFIED drinks in which Australia then specialized. A natural performer and publicist, Evans caused such a stir that Australians were apparently convinced that real men could indeed drink table wine, and it become increasingly important to Australia's social life and economy.

By 1969 he was writing books and articles on wine, had left the Wine Board, and was starting up the Rothbury Estate in the HUNTER VALLEY and establishing his own restaurant-cum-dining club at Bulletin Place by Sydney Harbour. He collected people, preferably famous, with as much enthusiasm as seriously fine wine, but distinguished himself in his practical relish of both. He did not just transform BLIND TASTING into a competitive sport but even oversaw the creation of a game predicated on it, the OPTIONS GAME, which was subsequently put to work raising substantial sums for charity under Evans's direction.

In the late 1970s, it seemed as though Evans, by now an intimate of the great and the good of the wine world, was about to take it over. Financed by a tax lawyer friend Peter Fox, he acquired properties in GRAVES, SAUTERNES, and the NAPA Valley, with plans to staff them using an early version of the FLYING WINEMAKER concept. His exceptional tasting skills had also been recognized by his numerous invitations to judge at Australia's important wine COMPETITIONS and by his appointment as chairman of judges (the first of many) at the Royal Sydney Show.

In 1981, Peter Fox was killed in a crash and the Evans Wine Company was thrown into turmoil. From the remains, Rothbury survived, as did the Petaluma winery in the ADELAIDE HILLS, with which Evans was involved from the start. Evans attempted to rusticate himself at his much embellished mud hut 'Loggerheads' overlooking Rothbury.

From then he continued to write, broadcast, and keep tables or halls full of people entertained, while reminding them that wine is for drinking. His crucial part in educating those with clear potential in the Australian wine industry is commemorated by the Len Evans Tutorial, an annual orgy of blind tasting. He was awarded an Order of the British Empire as well as numerous wine industry distinctions and was made a Chevalier de l'Ordre du Mérite Agricole in 1994.

Oliver, J., *Evans on Earth* (1992).

evaporation, conversion of water (or other liquids) from the liquid to the gaseous or vapour state, brought about by the input and absorption of heat energy. It has important implications for both growing vines and maturing wines. High evaporation is favoured by high SUNLIGHT, high WIND speed, and low HUMIDITY.

Viticulture

There are three sorts of evaporation in the vineyard. First, there is evaporation from the soil, which is especially significant while the soil surface is wet. Then there is evaporation from the vine leaves, and lastly from other parts of the vine (bunches wet from rain, for example), which can have important disease implications.

The power of the atmosphere to evaporate water is related inversely to its humidity and directly to its temperature. Climate records of evaporation, or potential evaporation, have been sparse but are improving. Comparisons are further confused by the fact that different countries use different instruments for measurement of evaporation. Nevertheless, broad averages for regions can be estimated with fair accuracy, and these allow calculation of IRRIGATION requirements, for example.

Evaporation from the soil reduces the amount of water available to the vine and so can encourage WATER STRESS.

Evaporation out of grapevine leaves (a process known as TRANSPIRATION) takes place mainly through pores, or STOMATA, which form openings on the underside of the waxy leaf surface. It is regulated by opening and closing of the stomata, with partial closure taking place at night. Transpiration is increased by direct exposure to sunlight, which provides the energy needed for evaporation. The combined water loss from a vineyard is the sum of the evaporation from the soil and transpiration from the vines (and possibly any associated COVER CROP or weeds) and is called evapotranspiration.

Inadequate evaporation from wet leaves and bunches is a factor in FUNGAL DISEASE infection. Vine-growers in many climates deliberately trim vines and remove leaves from the vicinity of the bunches, partly to allow in more light but partly also to encourage air flow and evaporation and thus avoid diseases such as BOTRYTIS BUNCH ROT (see CANOPY MANAGEMENT). J.G. & R.E.S.

Wine maturation

Evaporation also causes a loss of liquid stored in BARRELS, other wooden containers, and porous vessels such as AMPHORAE. For a 225-l barrel, liquid loss varies from 1 to 9% per year. In new barrels, evaporation is very low for the first 40–60 days as the liquid impregnates the staves. Thereafter, the rate of evaporation is influenced by the conditions in the cellar and various cellar operations such as RACKING or TOPPING UP. When the cellar temperature is high and the relative humidity low, evaporation is high. Conversely, evaporation is low with high relative humidity and a low temperature. Wine subjected to BARREL AGEING in a high-humidity storage cellar will decrease in ALCOHOLIC STRENGTH, whereas that stored in a dry cellar will increase. This is why, in the low-humidity SHERRY bodegas of JEREZ, it is common practice to sprinkle water on the earth floors to raise the relative humidity and therefore prevent the alcoholic strength of the wine under FLOR film yeast from increasing to the point at which the yeast would be killed.

The way the barrels or containers are used can also affect evaporation. For example, the use of a glass or aseptic BUNG or overly frequent topping up exerts a positive pressure on the inner surface of the barrel, and this pressure pushes the wine into the stave or vessel wall, favouring evaporation. On the other hand, a barrel tightly sealed with a silicon bung or with a bung on the side will create a negative pressure, retaining the wine and diminishing evaporation.

Evaporation makes regular topping up of a barrel necessary. The space left by evaporation is called the ULLAGE.

Moutounet, M., et al., 'Gaseous exchange in wines stored in barrels', *Journal des Sciences et Techniques de la Tonnellerie* (France) (1998).

Roussey, C., et al., 'In-situ monitoring of wine volume, barrel mass, ullage pressure and dissolved oxygen for a better understanding of wine-barrel-cellar interactions', *Journal of Food Engineering*, 291 (2021), 110233.

evaporative perstraction is a relatively novel membrane technique used as a means of ALCOHOL REDUCTION. It lowers the alcohol content of wine by a process in which the wine and a stripping solution (usually water) pass through a microporous, hydrophobic hollow fibre membrane contactor on opposite sides. In essence it is the transfer of alcohol through a porous membrane between two phases that are moving in opposing directions.

Wollan, D., 'Membrane and other techniques for the management of wine composition', in A. G. Reynolds (ed.), *Managing Wine Quality 2: Oenology and Wine Quality* (2nd edn, 2021), 183–212.

evapotranspiration, total loss of water from a vineyard. See EVAPORATION and TRANSPIRATION.

Évora, UNESCO World Heritage Site, capital, and high-quality DOC subregion of the ALENTEJO in southern Portugal.

ex cellar(s), professional way of buying direct from wine producers and the price they quote, which excludes TRANSPORT and DUTY in the importing country and any retailer's margin. This price will invariably be less than one quoted to a tourist or consumer at the CELLAR DOOR.

excoriose, vine disease. See PHOMOPSIS.

exposure. Sometimes used to refer to the ASPECT of a slope. The English word 'exposition' is a commonly misused direct translation of the French term *exposition*.

extra brut. See DOSAGE.

extract, or **dry extract**, or **total dry extract (TDE)**, the sum of the non-volatile solids of a wine: the SUGARS, non-volatile ACIDS, MINERALS, PHENOLICS, GLYCEROL, glycols, nitrogenous compounds, and traces of other substances such as PROTEINS, PECTINS, and gums. Sometimes sugars are deliberately excluded to give sugar-free extract. Wines' extract, including sugars, usually starts at 17–30 g/l but can vary considerably depending on the wine's SWEETNESS, COLOUR (red wines usually having a higher extract than whites, thanks to their greater PHENOLIC content), and age, since some extract is precipitated as SEDIMENT over the years. Cooler and wetter years, with higher levels of acidity in the grapes, are likely to produce wines with higher levels of dry extract, and BOTRYTIS is also likely to increase its concentration.

Historically, extract was determined by the simple but time-consuming expedient of evaporating a measured quantity of wine and weighing the residue, but this method is imprecise and has generally been replaced by using what is known as the Tabarié formula, techniques involving the measurement of ALCOHOLIC STRENGTH, the DENSITY, and the RESIDUAL SUGAR (if sugar-free extract is required).

To be high in extract, a wine does not necessarily have to be high in alcohol or BODY. Many fine German wines are high in extract and yet are low in alcohol and are light-bodied, especially Rieslings made from low-yielding vines. Dry extract helps a wine to age well, but there is otherwise no correlation between high extract and high QUALITY IN WINE.

Ribéreau-Gayon, P., et al., *Traité d'Œnologie 2: Chimie du vin: Stabilisation et traitements* (7th edn, 2017), translated by J. Towey as *Handbook of Enology 2: The Chemistry of Wine Stabilization and Treatments* (3rd edn, 2021), 81–98.

extraction in a wine context usually refers to the extraction of desirable PHENOLICS from grape solids before, during, and after FERMENTATION, although **over-extraction** is a common fault when colour is associated with quality so that phenolics dominate the wine, often making wines heavy and tannic. Such wines lack FRUIT and BALANCE. See MACERATION for more details.

Extremadura, one of the 17 autonomous regions in SPAIN and, perhaps surprisingly, the country's fourth most important wine region. Sheep are reputed to outnumber people in this semi-arid upland area between CASTILLA-LA MANCHA and PORTUGAL (see map under SPAIN). CORK is an important crop here, but most of the wine made here is sold in bulk for DISTILLATION and ends up as brandy de Jerez.

A single DOP covers most of the region's wine areas: RIBERA DEL GUADIANA. Cencibel (TEMPRANILLO), GARNACHA, GRACIANO, and, increasingly, Cabernet Sauvignon and Syrah dominate among red grape varieties, and PARDINA among white ones. But the region was still underperforming in 2021, except for Bodegas Habla, which bottles its wines under the PGI Vino de la Tierra Extremadura. V. de la S. & F.C.

Ezerjó, white grape variety planted on about 369 ha/912 acres of vineyard in Hungary in 2021 but scarcely known elsewhere. Most of the wine produced is relatively anodyne, but Móri Ezerjó produced from the vineyards near the town of Mór enjoys a certain following as a light, crisp, refreshing drink. It also produces strong, sweet wines, BOTRYTIZED in good vintages. Ezerjó means 'a thousand boons'.

Faberrebe, or **Faber**, waning, early-ripening German vine cross bred by Georg Scheu at Alzey in Rheinhessen in the early 20th century. Most of its 228 ha/563 acres in 2020 were in the Rheinhessen. A little is also grown in England.

Factory House, handsome Georgian monument in OPORTO, standing on land granted in 1806 in perpetuity 'from this day and forever to the consul of the British nation and his corporation and their successors', is a testament to the historic role of the British in the port wine trade. The only surviving example of any Factory House, it is possibly the only actual building constructed as a meeting place for a 'factory', a body of traders or 'factors' buying and selling any commodity in a foreign country. The Portuguese were probably the first to establish such a factory, which they called a *feitoria*, in one of their earliest West African settlements. The first British factory was established by the East India Company near Bombay in 1613. By the beginning of the 18th century, British factories had been established in all major Portuguese ports, including of course Oporto, from which wine was an important export (see PORTUGAL). The Factory House, probably the first and only permanent meeting place for the Oporto factory, was begun in 1786 and finished, under the supervision of the consul John Whitehead, four years later. The cost of the land and the building was paid by the 'Outward Fund', voluntarily levied by the British shippers on their own exports of port.

The British factory's enjoyment of their grand, and determinedly exclusive, new clubhouse was cut short by the French invasion of Portugal in 1807. The official reopening of the Factory House took place at a dinner based on the number 11 on 11 November 1811. In the previous year, George III and the Prince Regent of Portugal had signed a commercial treaty that stipulated that there should be no more British factories in Portugal. The factory itself was therefore abolished and replaced by the British Association in Oporto as British port traders trickled back to enjoy a period of unparalleled prosperity.

The British Association is made up exclusively of members drawn from the British port shippers. By the early 21st century, the remaining British-owned port companies accounted for less than one-third of all sales by volume but were still firmly entrenched in Oporto, as evinced by the city's Cricket and Lawn Tennis Club, the oldest British school in Europe, and an Anglican church.

The Factory House continues to be maintained for the exclusive use of the remaining British port shippers, although at such traditional Wednesday lunches as still take place there are often more Portuguese (directors of the British companies and their friends) than British around the table.

Delaforce, J., *The Factory House at Oporto* (1983).

Fair Play, California wine region and AVA in the El Dorado County area of the SIERRA FOOTHILLS. The region's vineyards sit at 2,000–3,000 feet in ELEVATION, and ZINFANDEL is the main grape variety, with Rhône varieties growing in importance.

fake wine. See COUNTERFEIT WINE and ADULTERATION AND FRAUD.

Falanghina. **Falanghina Beneventana** of Benevento province is the less common of Campania's two distinct Falaghinas, while the leafy-smelling **Falanghina Flegrea** of Campi Flegrei is Campania's signature white wine grape, which may have provided a basis for the classical FALERNIAN and is now the base for Falerno del Massico and Sannio DOCs. It produces attractive, unoaked, fragrant wines of real interest. Modern fermentation enabled producers to preserve its aromas, which gave it a new lease of life from the mid 1990s. There were 3,643 ha/9,002 acres of the latter in 2015, and 323 ha/798 acres of the former.

Falernian, or **Falernum**, was the most famous and most highly prized wine of Italy in the Roman period ('Do not try to compete with Falernian cellars', advised VIRGIL, *Georgics* 2.96). It was produced on the southern slopes of Monte Massico, the range of hills which runs down to the west coast of Italy in northern CAMPANIA. With a precision which was unusual for the Romans, three distinct zones, or CRUS, were distinguished: Caucinian on the hilltops, Faustian on the slopes (probably in the region of present-day Falciano), and Falernian proper at the edge of the plain. Recent archaeological survey has revealed numerous Roman farms in this region, and part of a vineyard of Roman date has been excavated. The vines were trained up trees (see ARBOREAL VITICULTURE) and also on trellises on poles of willow.

Falernian was a white wine of at least two types, one relatively dry, the other sweeter. As with other Roman fine wines such as CAECUBAN and MASSIC, it was normal to age it considerably. It was considered drinkable between 10 and 20 years. Its distinctive colour, deep amber, was probably the result of MADERIZATION, which may also explain the references to 'dark' Falernian in one source. The frequent descriptions of the wine's 'strength' and 'heat' suggest a high ALCOHOLIC STRENGTH. One curious claim was that it was the only wine which could be set alight! Despite the concern of PLINY in the second half of the 1st century CE that the reputation of Falernian was being endangered by a commitment to quantity rather than quality, the wine remained in the front rank until at least the 4th century CE.

The contemporary revival is Falerno del Massico, produced in white, blended red, and all-PRIMITIVO versions in modern CAMPANIA. See also ATHENAEUS. J.J.P.

Familia Torres, one of Spain's leading family-owned producers of premium wine and Spanish brandy, based in PENEDÈS, near Barcelona. The present company was founded in Vilafranca del Penedès in 1870 by Miguel and Jaime Torres with the fruits of Jaime's investments in shipping and other commercial enterprises in Cuba. Miguel's son Juan expanded the business within Spain and left a thriving family business to his son, another Miguel, in 1932. After confiscation, disruption, and even winery destruction during the Spanish Civil War, Miguel rebuilt the business and as early as the 1940s decided to concentrate on selling wine in bottle rather than in BULK.

Perhaps the most significant development in the history of Torres came in 1959 when Miguel's son Miguel A. Torres went to study in DIJON. This resulted in experimental plantings of INTERNATIONAL VARIETIES imported from France and Germany. Torres also introduced vine TRELLIS SYSTEMS, a modern laboratory, TEMPERATURE CONTROLLED stainless-steel fermentation, and the bottling of red wines after just 18 months' BARREL AGEING in cool cellars hewn out of the hillside. All of these techniques, and a host of other innovations, were then unknown elsewhere in Spain.

Vindication of Miguel A. Torres's achievements came in 1979, when, in a well-publicized, international follow-up to the JUDGMENT OF PARIS, Torres Gran Coronas Black Label 1970 was voted winner of the top Cabernet class. In 1980 he spent a sabbatical year at MONTPELLIER and has since introduced higher VINE DENSITIES, MECHANICAL PRUNING, and a programme to recuperate Catalan INDIGENOUS VARIETIES. About 75% of all Spanish wine produced by Torres is exported.

On the death of his father in 1991, Miguel A. Torres became president of the company. He has also been one of Spain's most prolific wine writers and was one of the first wine producers in the world to take CLIMATE CHANGE seriously. With the Torres & Earth plan started in 2008, a CO_2 reduction of 34% per bottle was achieved by 2020. Torres owns about 1,300 ha/3,210 acres of vineyard in Penedès, PRIORAT, and other areas of Spain, 400 ha in Chile (established in 1978 near Curicó), and 32 ha in California. His sister Marimar owns and manages Marimar Estate in SONOMA County's Russian River Valley. In 1999—a decade earlier than most of its peers—Torres founded its own distribution company in Shanghai, which today is one of the leading wine distributors in China. Since September 2012, Miguel A.'s son, another Miguel, has been general manager of Torres, while Miguel A.'s daughter Mireia directs the Innovation and Knowledge department, the Jean Leon winery which Torres acquired in 1994, and the Familia Torres Foundation. The fifth generation's most recent winemaking projects include Mas de la Rosa (DOQ Priorat), Purgatori (DO COSTERS DEL SEGRE), and a DO Penedès made from the local Forcada variety. The current generation has converted most of the Familia Torres vineyards to ORGANIC viticulture and is pioneering in Spain the evolution towards REGENERATIVE VITICULTURE. They aim to become a net zero emissions winery by 2040.

fanleaf degeneration, sometimes called **fanleaf virus**, one of the oldest known VIRUS DISEASES affecting vines. Records of it date back some 200 years in Europe, and there are indications that it may have existed in the Mediterranean and Near East since grape culture began. Rather than being a single disease, it is in fact a complex of related diseases which include forms known as yellow mosaic and vein banding. Shoot growth is typically malformed, leaves are distorted and asymmetric, and teeth along the edge are elongated. Shoots show abnormal branching with double nodes (see FASCIATION), short internodes, and zigzag growth. Leaves on infected plants look fanlike—hence the name. Bunches are smaller than normal, with poor FRUIT SET and many SHOT BERRIES. Sensitive varieties such as Cabernet Sauvignon can lose up to 80% of potential yield and have a shortened productive life.

The disease can be detected by INDEXING using varieties of other species of VITIS such as Rupestris St George, or with other plants such as *Chenopodium*, or more recently by serological tests using ELISA. The virus is spread by infected planting material, and this reached widespread proportions in the late 1880s with the adoption of grafting vines on to ROOTSTOCKS resistant to PHYLLOXERA. A second means of spread was discovered in California in 1958. The NEMATODE *Xiphinema index* spreads the disease within a vineyard by feeding on the roots of infected plants and then healthy ones. Thus the symptoms of the disease spread slowly around an original infected plant.

There is no control for an infected vineyard, and it must be removed. The virus particle can survive in root fragments for over six years. Nematode populations were reduced by FUMIGATION, now often prohibited. The most successful method is to plant virus-free vines in a nematode-free soil. Fanleaf-free planting material is readily created by THERMOTHERAPY or TISSUE CULTURE. (See also NEPOVIRUSES.) R.E.S.

Bettiga, L. J., (ed.), *Grape Pest Management* (3rd edn, 2013).

Wilcox, W. F., et al., *Compendium of Grape Diseases, Disorders, and Pests* (2nd edn, 2015).

Fara, red wine DOC on the brink of extinction, covering in 2020 just 8 ha/20 acres in the Novara Hills of eastern PIEMONTE in north-west Italy. The wines are made from 50–70% NEBBIOLO, here called SPANNA.

Far North Zone in SOUTH AUSTRALIA has a single region, Southern Flinders Ranges.

fasciation, a growth abnormality, of SHOOTS in particular, in which the stem is broadened and flattened as though there were several shoots fused side by side. It is relatively rare in grapevines, although some varieties seem to be prone. The cause is unknown, but it is a common symptom of FANLEAF DEGENERATION infection. B.G.C.

fashion has played a part in wine consumption, and therefore eventually wine production, for at least two millennia. The wine drinkers of ancient ROME favoured white wines, preferably old and sweet (see FALERNIAN, for example). Indeed, throughout much of the modern age, sweet, heady wines have been prized above all others. In the early Middle Ages, the wine drinkers of northern Europe had to drink the thin, tart, sometimes spiced ferments of local vineyards because TRANSPORT was so rudimentary, and RHINE wines were considered the height of fashion. But when these consumers were introduced to such syrupy Mediterranean potions as the wines of CYPRUS and MALMSEY, wines traded energetically by the merchants of, for instance, VENICE, a fashion for this richer style of wine was established. By the 16th century, for example, light, white ALSACE wine was regarded as unfashionable by the German wine drinker (see GERMAN HISTORY), who was, as now, beginning to favour red wines. Many fashions were restricted to one particular district or region, particularly before the age of modern communications. It is clear that the wines favoured by the French court in the medieval period, for example, were considerably influenced by fashion and, possibly, more pragmatically political considerations (see MEDIEVAL LITERATURE and ST-POURÇAIN).

Towards the end of the Middle Ages, fashion seems to have begun to favour not just RESIDUAL SUGAR but ALCOHOLIC STRENGTH too. Such wines as SACK and TENT from southern Spain were valued for their potency, although by the end of the 17th century seafaring and exploration brought a new range of drinks to the trendsetters of northern Europe which were very much more fashionable than any form of wine.

A new age demanded new products, and the most durable of these were the so-called New French Clarets (see CLARET and BORDEAUX, history), whose initial success was largely due to fashion. In the 18th century, however, no wines were more fashionable than a clutch of what a modern salesperson might call 'speciality items': Hungarian TOKAJI, South African CONSTANTIA, and Moldavian COTNARI. These were available in necessarily very limited quantities, but the wine styles created during or soon after this period illustrate the wine qualities regarded as fashionable then: PORT, MADEIRA, MÁLAGA, and MARSALA are all remarkable for their colour, alcohol, and usually sweetness.

By the 19th century, much more detailed evidence of the wines then considered most fashionable is available, not just in the form of CLASSIFICATIONS and a number of books specifically comparing different wines (see LITERATURE OF WINE) but also in the form of price lists—for wine PRICES have reflected fashions in wine throughout history. It would surprise the modern wine drinker, for example, to see the high prices fetched by German wines compared with the classified growths of Bordeaux from the late 19th to the mid 20th centuries. The late 19th century was also a time when CHAMPAGNE was considered exceptionally modish in northern Europe, notably in St Petersburg.

In the 1920s and 1930s, wine in almost any form was extremely unfashionable. This was the age of the cocktail on one side of the Atlantic and of PROHIBITION on the other. These phenomena, together with the marked decline of traditional markets and a worldwide economic depression, threatened many small-scale vine-growers with penury (this was the era during which so many wine CO-OPERATIVES were established).

It was not until well after the Second World War, when some measure of real economic recovery and stability had returned, that wine slowly re-established itself as a fashionable drink (although it had long been a drink of necessity in wine-producing areas). As foreign travel became an economic possibility for the majority of northern Europeans, consumers in non-producing countries began to link wine with a way of life they associated with leisure, the exotic, and warmer, wine-producing countries.

By the late 1970s, wine CONNOISSEURSHIP itself was beginning to be fashionable, and the economic boom of the 1980s provided the means for a new generation of collectors. This led inevitably to a fashion for marathon 'horizontal' and 'vertical' TASTINGS of scores of bottles at a time. Buying wine EN PRIMEUR was particularly fashionable in this decade of superlative VINTAGES.

What has been most remarkable about fashions in wine consumption in the late 20th and early 21st centuries, however, has been how rapidly wine production has reacted to them and in some cases created them (see NATURAL WINE, ORANGE WINE, ROSÉ WINES, MOSCATO, PINOT NOIR, MERLOT, PET-NAT, REDUCED-ALCOHOL WINE, and wine BOXES among others). The speed of producer reaction is doubtless related to the development of wine criticism in media more immediate than books (see WINE WRITING).

Perhaps the most significant fashion of the 1970s and 1980s was for VARIETAL wines, especially but by no means exclusively in the NEW WORLD. This led to a dramatic increase in the area planted with INTERNATIONAL VARIETIES—Chardonnay, Cabernet Sauvignon, briefly Merlot, and subsequently, thanks to a single film SIDEWAYS, Pinot Noir, in particular. From about the 1980s winemakers reacted quickly to successive fashions for and then against obviously OAKY wines, both white and red.

The 1990s saw an even more significant development, however: a dramatic shift in consumer taste away from white wines to red. Just when a high proportion of northern CALIFORNIA's post-PHYLLOXERA replantings and AUSTRALIA's ambitious new plantings were assigned to the then-fashionable Chardonnay, it became clear that the wine drinker of the 1990s, particularly the new army of ASIAN wine consumers, would in fact much prefer red—partly for heavily touted perceived HEALTH benefits.

Towards the end of the last century, the phenomenon known as Parkerization (see PARKER, Robert M.) resulted in a marked increase in average ALCOHOLIC STRENGTH and depth of colour in reds. By the second decade of this century, however, there was a very obvious retreat from this style in most wine regions.

The fashion for international vine varieties was replaced in the early 21st century by one for INDIGENOUS VARIETIES and ALTERNATIVE VARIETIES. Rapid changes of varietal fashion are inconvenient for a plant that takes three years to produce a commercial crop, but there is always TOP GRAFTING. Other 21st-century preoccupations include minimizing ADDITIVES and ALCOHOL as well as ORGANIC and BIODYNAMIC wines.

Fashion being as fickle as it is, this is one of the most frequently updated entries in this *Companion*.

fats. See LIPIDS.

fattoria, Italian for 'farm', also used for a wine estate. A *fattoria* is generally bigger than a PODERE, which is often a small farm carved out of a larger property and designed to be just large enough to be managed by one sharecropper/tenant plus family.

Faugères, progressive appellation in the LANGUEDOC region in southern France. A total of 1,780 ha/4,400 acres of vineyard, mainly at relatively high ELEVATIONS (250–400 m/820–1,312 ft) on schistous foothills of the Cévennes, look down on the plains around Béziers. The AOC Faugères vineyards are planted with quintessentially Mediterranean grape varieties that produce big yet elegant reds due to the elevation and SCHIST soils. Average yields are low, around 30 hl/ha, and 40% of the vineyard is certified ORGANIC with another 10% in conversion in 2021. The ubiquitous CARIGNAN, which by 2014 was limited to 40% of any blend, is being replaced by Syrah, Grenache (or its relative LLEDONER PELUT), and Mourvèdre, while Cinsaut is still grown for fruit and rosés. The white wines, only 4% of the production, are also hauntingly impressive and are based on ROUSSANNE, GRENACHE BLANC, MARSANNE, and VERMENTINO. Further plans are afoot to include more environmental measures in the AOC regulations for what is one of the Languedoc's distinctive and most consistent appellations. M.S.

George, R., *The Wines of Faugères* (2016).

faults in wines vary, of course, according to the taste of the consumer. Some diners will quite wrongly 'send back' a wine (see SERVING WINE and SOMMELIER) simply because they find it is not to their taste. Taste varies not only according to individuals but also according to nationality. Italians are generally more tolerant of BITTERNESS, Americans of SWEETNESS, Germans of SULFUR DIOXIDE, the French of TANNINS, and the British of decrepitude (see MATURITY) in their wines, while Australians tend to be particularly sensitive to MERCAPTANS and most Americans view HERBACEOUSNESS as a fault rather than a characteristic. To winemakers, however, wine faults are specific departures from an acceptable norm, the least quantifiable of which may be a lack of TYPICALITY. However, with the rapid growth of the NATURAL WINE movement, many winemakers and consumers are revising their opinions of what constitutes a fault. The reduced use of sulfur dioxide as a microbial inhibitor, the growing preference for SPONTANEOUS FERMENTATION and high-solids fermentation, and reduced FILTRATION create wines that walk a fine line between complex and intriguing or faulty and undrinkable.

Visible faults

Faults in a wine's appearance are generally either hazes, clouds, or precipitates in the bottle. STABILIZATION is designed to avoid all these hazards. Haze and cloud in bottled wines can have a variety of causes, of which the most common today is the growth of YEAST or BACTERIA. Mycoderma is a yeast-related fault which forms a film on the wine's surface (and so may be visible to winemakers, if not to wine consumers). Clouds from heat-unstable PROTEINS and from heavy-metal contamination do occur but they are much less frequent than they were in the era of copper and brass pipes and taps.

Precipitates, especially crystalline ones, are found from time to time and are usually the harmless result of excess potassium or calcium TARTRATES finally coming out of solution. Tartrate stabilization usually prevents this, but calcium tartrate may not form until several months after bottling, so it is very difficult to determine if a wine is calcium-tartrate stable. From white wines, these may form as needle-like colourless or white crystals on the end of the cork in contact with the wine or in the bottom of the bottle, where they look misleadingly like fragments of glass. From red wine, tartrate crystals are usually dyed red or brown from the adsorbed PHENOLICS. See SEDIMENT.

Visible bubbles in a supposedly still wine are frequently viewed as a fault. Some wines, particularly off-dry whites, are deliberately bottled with a trace of CARBON DIOXIDE gas to make them taste more refreshing. Bubbles in a bottle of older wine, particularly a red wine, usually indicate unintentional FERMENTATION IN BOTTLE, however, and are definitely a fault.

While most consumers would agree that cloudy wines are faulty (although see NATURAL WINE), there is much less agreement about COLOUR. Some wine judges in COMPETITIONS automatically disqualify rosé wines with a hint of amber, even though it is difficult to make a blueish-pink wine out of the GRENACHE grape variety, for example—and wines of all sorts and hues turn amber with age.

OXIDATION, which can brown wines prematurely, is a fault in young table wines but is best confirmed by the nose.

Smellable faults

Some wines smell so stale and unpleasant that the taster is unwilling even to taste them. The most likely explanation for this is a mouldy cork causing CORK TAINT. Such a wine is said to be CORKED, but a wine served with small pieces of cork floating in it indicates a fault in the SERVICE of the wine rather than a fault in the wine. Contact with fragments of sound cork does not harm wine.

Other off-odours can vary considerably. Oxidized wines (see above) smell flat and aldehydic (see ALDEHYDES). VINEGARY wines indicate the presence of ACETIC ACID due to microbiological activity by bacteria and yeast. ETHYL ACETATE, HYDROGEN SULFIDE, MERCAPTANS, excess SULFUR DIOXIDE, and the smellable compounds generated by some bacteria can all be reasons for judging a wine faulty. (See also REDUCTION.) The picture is complicated, however, by the fact that we all vary in our sensitivities to most of these compounds (see TASTING and LADYBUG TAINT), and some of them may be more acceptable in some sorts of wine than others. Acetaldehyde, for example, is the principal odorant of FINO sherries but definitely indicates over-oxidation in white wines and makes red wines taste vapid and flat. Although the average palate should not detect acetic acid on a fault-free wine, there are some much-admired, full-bodied red wines (such as some PORT, PENFOLDS Grange, and VEGA SICILIA) whose VOLATILITY was historically much higher than the norm. Many fine German winemakers at one time deliberately used relatively high concentrations of sulfur dioxide to preserve some of their best wines for a long life in bottle.

A wine may not smell clean because of the influence of one or several CONTAMINANTS such as agrochemical RESIDUES. If it smells of geranium leaves, there has probably been some bacterial degradation of SORBIC ACID, although this can easily be controlled by adding sulfur dioxide with the sorbic acid.

A wine may smell MOULDY either because of BACTERIAL SPOILAGE or because it has taken on the smell of a less-than-clean container.

Another much-discussed microbiological fault, which can cause a wine to smell mousy or animal/medicinal, has been attributed to the action of yeasts of the BRETTANOMYCES genus, closely related to Dekkera. More detailed studies on the causes of mousy off-flavour in wine have indicated that LACTIC ACID BACTERIA, including particular strains of *Lactobacillus* and to a lesser extent *Oenococcus* and *Pediococcus*, are capable of producing the off-flavour compounds responsible for this most unpleasant fault. It cannot normally be smelled in wine unless it is alkalinized or rubbed in the palm of the hand (an action which neutralizes wine acidity). This mousy flavour is volatile only at neutral or high PH, which explains why it is not immediately apparent but builds up in the back of the mouth once a wine has been swallowed or expectorated, as the palate slowly returns to neutral pH through the buffering action of saliva.

See also GEOSMIN, GERANIUM, MOULDY, TRIBROMOANISOLE, METHOXY-DIMETHYLPYRAZINE, and ISOBUTYL-METHOXYPYRAZINE.

Tasteable faults

Most faults are already obvious to the nose and need only confirmation on the palate (which is why in a restaurant it is, strictly speaking, necessary only to smell a sample of wine offered by the waiter). Some contaminations, notably from metal, are easier to taste than smell, however, and a wine that is excessively tannic or bitter (see BALANCE) will not display this fault to the eye or nose. See also CONTAMINANTS. K.C.

Bird, D., and Quillé, N., *Understanding Wine Technology* (4th edn, 2021).

Goode, J., *Flawless: Understanding Faults in Wine* (2018).

Favorita, local synonym for the VERMENTINO cultivated near ALBA, both on the left bank of the Tanaro in the ROERO zone and slightly less successfully on the right bank in the LANGHE Hills. Gagliardo was one of the first to champion the variety in Roero, in 1974.

Federspiel, the middle in terms of MUST WEIGHT and alcohol among the three categories of dry white wine in Austria's WACHAU region—specifically from unchaptalized grapes of minimum 83 °OECHSLE/17 °KMW and harbouring 11–12.5% finished alcohol by volume. The name originates from falconry. See also STEINFEDER and SMARAGD. D.S.

Federweisser, German term for young wine popularly consumed before bottling—generally cloudy and often still fermenting—and typically referred to in Austria as Sturm or HEURIGER. Confusingly, the term 'Federweisser' is used in German-speaking Switzerland to refer collectively to white wines made from black grapes.

feinherb, a traditional term of approbation permitted on German wine labels since 2000 that is neither amenable to intelligible literal translation nor legally defined. Many growers use it as a substitute for HALBTROCKEN, a concept whose appeal to German consumers fell significantly towards the end of the last century. It remains widely used for wines of overt, albeit modest, sweetness. D.S.

Fendant, Valais name for the most planted white wine grape in SWITZERLAND, the productive CHASSELAS.

Fer, alias **Fer Servadou** (and many other aliases), is a characterful, tannic black grape variety traditionally encouraged in a wide range of the sturdy red wines of SOUTH WEST FRANCE. In MADIRAN, where it is often called Pinenc, it is a distinctly minor ingredient, alongside Tannat and the two Cabernets. In GAILLAC, where it is known as Braucol, it has overtaken DURAS to become the dominant variety. It is technically allowed into wines as far north as Bergerac, but today it is particularly important to the red wines of the Aveyron *département*, ENTRAYGUES, ESTAING, and the defiantly smoky, rustic MARCILLAC. The iron-hardness of the name refers to the vine's wood rather than the resulting wine, although it is well coloured, concentrated, and interestingly scented. Fer has also been invited to join the already crowded party of varieties permitted in CABARDÈS.

French plantings had grown to 1,570 ha/3,880 acres by 2019, and DNA PROFILING has shown it to be a progenitor of CARMENÈRE.

Féret, sometimes known as *Cocks et Féret*, important directory of Bordeaux châteaux which was first published in 1846 as *Bordeaux, its Wines and the Claret Country* by the Englishman Charles Cocks, who died in 1854 (*see* LITERATURE OF WINE). A French version followed in 1850, with the emphasis on classifying wines in order of merit, also published in Bordeaux by Féret. It played a significant part in establishing the 1855 CLASSIFICATION and continues to be updated, expanded, and published by members of the Féret family to this day. It has always provided a useful historical record of the evolution of different properties' and districts' reputations. (The 1868 edition, for example, ranked PETRUS as a mere CRU BOURGEOIS.) As a sign of the times, the 20th edition of what is now known simply as *Bordeaux et ses vins* was published in 2023, in e-book format, in French, English, and, significantly, Mandarin.

www.feret.com

Cocks, C., and Féret, C., *Bordeaux and its Wines* (20th edn, 2023).

Mustacich, S., 'The Book that Defined Bordeaux', WineSpectator.com (2013). www.winespectator.com/webfeature/show/id/48495.

fermentation, as it applies to wine, is the process of converting SUGAR to ETHANOL (ethyl alcohol) and CARBON DIOXIDE effected by the anaerobic (oxygen-free) metabolism of YEAST. It comes from the Latin word *fervere*, to 'boil'; any mass containing sugar that has been infused with yeast certainly looks as though it were boiling, as it exudes carbon-dioxide bubbles.

History

Before yeast's metabolic processes were properly understood, the word 'fermentation' was also used to describe a much wider range of chemical changes that resulted in the appearance of boiling and in some of which carbon dioxide evolved. These have included the leavening of bread, the production of cheese, and the tumultuous reactions of acids with alkalis. Today such changes involving the intervention of yeast or BACTERIA in aerobic processes are not usually considered true fermentations.

By the middle of the 19th century, understandings of science were such that opinions were divided about the nature of 'organized ferments' as opposed to 'unorganized ferments' in fermentation. Thanks to Louis PASTEUR, we now know that it is the organized ferments and their agents yeasts and bacteria that are primarily responsible for alcoholic fermentation. They act through their internal ENZYMES (enzymes were responsible for Pasteur's unorganized ferments), which, functioning as catalysts, mediate the series of reactions involved in the conversion of sugar into alcohol and carbon dioxide.

The net change during fermentation of one glucose molecule giving two alcohol and two carbon dioxide molecules expressed as a chemical equation is:

$$C_6H_{12}O_6 \rightarrow 2C_2H_5OH + 2CO_2$$

Many years and the research talents of several scientists—notably Embden, Meyerhof, and Parnas—have elucidated the successive steps in the apparently simple conversion of sugars to the metabolic end products, alcohol and carbon dioxide.

The complex process

The first steps in the process attach phosphate groups to the sugars. Next comes a series of steps in which the six-carbon sugar is split into two three-carbon pieces, one of which is then rearranged into the structure of the other. After some further rearrangements, this three-carbon molecule loses its terminal carboxylic carbon atom in the form of carbon dioxide gas. The residual part is the two-carbon compound ACETALDEHYDE, which goes next to alcohol if oxygen is lacking, or into another multi-step series of reactions eventually yielding energy, water, and more carbon dioxide if generous amounts of oxygen are available.

The net change when oxygen is present in excess is one glucose plus six oxygen molecules giving six carbon dioxide and six water molecules, as shown by this chemical equation:

$$C_6H_{12}O_6 + 6O_2 \rightarrow 6CO_2 + 6H_2O$$

Ideally for the yeast, therefore, the process should be carried out with generous quantities of oxygen available, for then much more cell-building energy is produced. For the winemaker, however, it is important that this process can be modified by limitation of the oxygen supply because then alcohol, rather than water, is produced along with carbon dioxide. Without the alcohol there would be no wine.

(It is interesting that this same series of steps in decomposition of sugar is employed by people during muscular activity, another form of fermentation. In human beings and other mammals, the three-carbon compound pyruvate is converted to LACTIC ACID and supplies energy for muscular action.)

A number of intermediate compounds are involved. The biochemical reactions converting one compound into its successor in this series are not 100% efficient, with the result that small amounts of certain of the intermediate compounds accumulate in the wine. These compounds and the products of their reaction with other substances in the mixture contribute to what is known as fermentation, or secondary, AROMAS. Included among these compounds are acetaldehyde, ETHYL ACETATE, and numerous other ESTERS and FUSEL OIL.

Physical chemistry tells us that the reaction of six-carbon sugar to ethanol and carbon dioxide yields generous amounts of energy. A significant portion of this energy is captured during the process and used by the yeast for its own purposes. Another major portion of the energy, however, is not captured but appears as waste heat. Unless this waste heat is removed from the fermenting mass, its temperature will rise, reaching levels which damage or kill the yeast cells and stop the reaction, resulting in a STUCK FERMENTATION which can be very difficult to restart. Heat removal is not a major problem when fermentations are conducted in a small FERMENTATION VESSEL because the greater ratio of surface to volume furnishes sufficient radiation and conduction surfaces from which the heat can be dissipated. In a large container, however, the amount of heat liberated is so large that it cannot all be radiated or conducted away and some REFRIGERATION system is needed.

Monitoring fermentation

Progress of a fermentation can be monitored in several ways. The most obvious is by simply observing activity in the fermentation vessel: as long as carbon dioxide is vigorously given off, the yeast are still working. Laboratory fermentations are sometimes followed by weighing the fermentation vessel at frequent intervals, thus obtaining a record of the weight of carbon dioxide gas lost and therefore, by calculation, the amount of sugar remaining. Chemical analyses of the unfermented sugar remaining, or of the alcohol produced, are accurate measures of the course of fermentation but are seldom used as they are complex and time-consuming. The technique most commonly used in the cellar is a measurement of the DENSITY of a sample of fermenting juice.

Density can be determined quickly and with reasonable accuracy by floating a calibrated HYDROMETER in the juice. Although most hydrometers are calibrated to read the remaining sugar's percentage in weight, it must be remembered that this calibration is for a sugar in water solution. When alcohol, less dense than water, is added to the solution during fermentation, the hydrometer reading no longer gives a true reading of the sugar remaining. Indeed, when all of the fermentable sugar has been converted into alcohol, these hydrometers will give the apparently ridiculous reading of less than no sugar. The problem of deciding when the fermentation is complete matters because the presence of small amounts of sugar renders the wine susceptible to bacterial attack and necessitates different treatment after fermentation. Today there are quick, simple paper strips or pills which can reliably detect the presence of even very small amounts of fermentable sugars. Handheld density meters are increasingly common; these are faster, and data can be downloaded directly to a computer. Larger producers may have tanks that monitor fermentation using in-line densitometers or pressure sensors, with readings automatically fed into the computer system. (See also ARTIFICIAL INTELLIGENCE.)

Factors affecting fermentation

The time required for complete fermentation of white grape juice or crushed red grapes varies greatly. The TEMPERATURE maintained in the fermenting mass is the principal factor affecting duration of fermentation (as well as resultant character of the wine), more even than the initial sugar concentration (see MUST WEIGHT), YEAST type, the aeration of the MUST, and the quantity of micronutrients in the juice, especially NITROGEN. In general, red-wine fermentations are complete within four to seven, days but white wines, which are frequently fermented at much lower temperatures, may sometimes require longer, possibly two to three weeks, or occasionally months (see DRIED-GRAPE WINES, for instance).

Other factors which influence the course of a fermentation include agrochemical RESIDUES and various chemical additions such as too high a concentration of SULFUR DIOXIDE. In the most commercially minded wineries, fermentations may be deliberately hastened so that a single fermentation vessel may be used twice or even three or more times a season.

In the making of certain styles of wine, such as PORT, VIN DOUX NATUREL, and other VINS DE LIQUEUR, the fermentation may be arrested deliberately by the addition of alcohol, usually grape spirit. For sweet wines such as SAUTERNES, fermentation may be stopped by the addition of SULFUR DIOXIDE.

The above is an outline of the most usual sorts of fermentation, but there are many variants, including BARREL FERMENTATION, CARBONIC MACERATION, ROSÉ WINEMAKING, and, quite distinct from the primary or alcoholic fermentation, FERMENTATION IN BOTTLE, MALOLACTIC CONVERSION, and SECOND FERMENTATION.

See also MACERATION, the process that inevitably accompanies red-wine fermentation, and also RED WINEMAKING, WHITE WINEMAKING, and SPARKLING WINEMAKING. A.D.W.

Halliday, J., and Johnson, H., *The Art and Science of Wine* (1992).

Ribéreau-Gayon, P., et al., *Traité d'Œnologie* 1: *Microbiologie du vin: Vinifications* (7th edn, 2017), translated by J. Towey, as *Handbook of Enology* 1: *The Microbiology of Wine and Vinifications* (3rd edn, 2021).

fermentation in bottle plays an important part in SPARKLING WINEMAKING. In most still wines, however, it is one of the wine FAULTS most feared by winemakers in wines that have not been appropriately filtered (see FILTRATION). It usually results from the presence of some RESIDUAL SUGAR together with live cells of either YEAST or BACTERIA under conditions which favour their growth. (High ALCOHOLIC STRENGTH and high levels of SULFUR DIOXIDE inhibit the growth of such microorganisms.) It is also possible that a completely dry wine will appear to start fermenting in bottle if it contains a high concentration of MALIC ACID since live LACTIC ACID BACTERIA may metabolize the malic acid causing a MALOLACTIC CONVERSION in bottle.

The implications of a fermentation in bottle for the wine consumer can range from an inconsequential level of carbon dioxide in the wine to the generation of such large quantities of the gas that it explodes. This latter, potentially dangerous, occurrence is most likely if the wine contains significant amounts of fermentable sugar and is kept at warm room temperatures. If the fermentation is bacterial rather than by yeast, gas is usually produced, together with off-flavours, cloud, or haze (see BACTERIAL SPOILAGE).

A low level of gas in a wine, particularly a young white wine, is by no means necessarily a sign of unwanted fermentation in bottle. Many winemakers deliberately retain (from fermentation) or incorporate a low level of CARBON DIOXIDE to enliven some wines. A.D.W.

fermentation vessel. The container in which FERMENTATION (or MACERATION, in the case of red wines) takes place can vary enormously in size, material, and design: from a small plastic bucket (in the case of some HOME WINEMAKING) to an oak BARREL (in the case of white wines and a very few red wines undergoing BARREL FERMENTATION) to a CONCRETE or POLYETHYLENE tank or egg to what is effectively a vast, computerized STAINLESS STEEL tower (for high-volume everyday wines). Stainless steel has the advantage that both cleaning and TEMPERATURE CONTROL are much easier than for wooden or concrete fermentation vessels; most modern white and rosé wines, and many reds, are fermented in stainless-steel tanks. Polyethylene tanks are lighter and much cheaper than stainless steel and are also easy to clean.

Wooden fermentation vessels are still used by many winemakers, however. Traditional wine producers in Germany, Alsace, and the Loire may well use large, old, wooden CASKS which offer natural STABILIZATION and CLARIFICATION. Scrupulous attention needs to be paid to cellar HYGIENE to avoid contamination of the wine by microorganisms.

Red wine may be fermented either in large wooden casks or open-topped wooden vats. An open top requires constant surveillance since BACTERIA in the presence of oxygen can attack the floating CAP of skins, which will dry out and fail to achieve proper MACERATION without PUMPING OVER or PUNCHING DOWN. The cap may alternatively be kept SUBMERGED with a headboard or some other design feature.

Wooden fermentation vessels are treasured by some traditionalists for red-wine maceration, however, as they retain heat especially well, which favours the extraction process, and tend to have a much higher diameter-to-height ratio than some stainless-steel tanks, which favours the contact between wine and solids.

Modern stainless-steel tanks—and design modifications of them such as various autovinifiers (see AUTOVINIFICATION), computer-controlled fermentation vessels, self-draining vessels, and Vinomatic automatic vinifiers—are closed at the top and automatically offer a high degree of hygiene. Tronconic vats (shaped like a truncated cone), whatever they are made of, are better for punching down.

Concrete vats, both lined and unlined, are also widely and increasingly used for fermentation, even at highly respected FIRST GROWTHS in Bordeaux, where stainless steel is regarded as more sensitive to temperature variation. Unlined concrete also allows MICRO-OXYGENATION.

Clay, the original material for fermentation vessels, is making a comeback. See AMPHORA, QVEVRI, TALHA, TINAJA, and PITHARI.

fermented in bottle, legitimate description of a SPARKLING WINE made by the traditional, transversage, or transfer methods described in SPARKLING WINEMAKING. Only traditional-method wines could claim to be **fermented in *this* bottle**, however.

Fernão Pires, Portugal's most planted white wine grape, grown throughout central and southern PORTUGAL. Adaptable, it is not only productive but also manages to make distinctively scented, reasonably crisp wines and is now being taken more seriously in TEJO and LISBOA. Known in BAIRRADA as Maria Gomes, Fernão Pires was still planted on a total of 11,717 ha/28,953 acres of Portugal in 2020 and to a very limited extent in South Africa, Australia, and California.

Ferreira, one of the leading Portuguese port shippers, established in 1751. Dona Antónia Adelaide Ferreira, the *grande dame* of the DOURO Valley, was perhaps one of the most dedicated personalities in the PORT industry in the latter half of the 19th century. Born in 1811 in Régua, Dona Antónia devoted her life to the Douro, ruling her vast property portfolio of more than 20 estates as a benevolent dictator. She invested much of her considerable fortune in planting and improving her properties throughout this harsh terrain. The father of her first husband, António Bernardo Ferreira, founded one of the largest and most stately quintas in the Douro, the Quinta do Vesúvio, which the family owned until its sale in 1989 to the SYMINGTONS. Until 1987, Ferreira was owned by descendants of Dona Antónia, but the company is now part of the extensive SOGRAPE portfolio, with Quinta do Porto the estate most closely associated with Ferreira. In the 1980s, the properties were the subject of considerable research and investment, with the company pioneering the vertical system of planting whereby vine rows are aligned uphill rather than along contours. Ferreira is the leading brand of port in Portugal and pioneered the production of high-quality dry red wines in the Douro, of which their famous Barca Velha was the prototype in 1952.

fertigation, the viticultural practice of mixing soluble FERTILIZERS with IRRIGATION water for direct application to grapevine roots. The technique is most often used with DRIP IRRIGATION systems, for which each vine has a water outlet. Fertilizers are placed in a tank through which the irrigation water passes, and so the vine is fed with appropriate amounts of water and nutrients as the irrigation season proceeds. Some nutrients such as NITROGEN are readily available in a soluble form (urea); others such as PHOSPHORUS require a relatively expensive formulation to render them immediately soluble. Some vineyard additions such as gypsum and lime are quite insoluble and also require special formulations. R.E.S.

fertility, viticultural term for the FRUITFULNESS of buds or shoots and also of vineyard soils. See SOIL FERTILITY.

fertilizers. Vines, in common with other plants, may require additions of fertilizers to overcome a deficiency in the soil of a particular nutrient (see SOIL NUTRIENTS). However, grapevines do not require such fertile soils as many other crops. Indeed, the vineyards most highly regarded in terms of the quality of wine they produce are generally grown on relatively infertile soils. While a modicum of nutrient stress may enhance quality, this is not to suggest that the fewer the soil nutrients the greater the wine quality. For example, a severe NITROGEN deficiency will limit shoot, root, and leaf growth as well as fruit yield while also causing a STUCK FERMENTATION, potentially contributing to poor wine quality. Typically, a vineyard producing wine will receive less fertilizer than one producing TABLE GRAPES.

Fertilizers are commercial formulations rich in plant nutrients. They are typically manufactured (for example, superphosphate) but may be a mined natural product (for example, rock phosphate). COMPOST is not commonly used in large commercial vineyards because of its lack of cost-effectiveness. More commonly, compost made from a combination of plant materials and animal manures (mainly that of poultry, sheep, or pig) is used in smaller vineyards, where its use is encouraged for ecological benefits (see ORGANIC VITICULTURE and BIODYNAMIC VITICULTURE). Animal manures are also used alone, but, unless they are readily and cheaply available (for example from cattle deliberately kept on the estate or sheep grazing in the vineyard), their use is restricted because of the relatively high cost of applying sufficient nutrients in this form.

The mineral elements most likely to be deficient in vineyards are nitrogen, POTASSIUM, PHOSPHORUS, ZINC, BORON, IRON, MANGANESE, and MAGNESIUM. The fertilizers commonly used to overcome some of these deficiencies are therefore urea, calcium or ammonium nitrate, potassium chloride or potassium sulfate, superphosphate, zinc sulfate, boric acid or borate, and magnesium sulfate. Fertilizers supplying the macronutrients (see SOIL NUTRIENTS) nitrogen, phosphorus, and potassium are normally applied in amounts giving up to 50, 15, and 25 kg of nitrogen, phosphorus, and potassium, respectively, per ha per year. They can be spread on the ground under vine or applied through an irrigation dripline by FERTIGATION. The micronutrients (see SOIL NUTRIENTS) are required in small amounts only, typically less than 5 kg per ha, applied every four to five years. Thus fertilizers compensating for deficiencies of the micronutrients zinc, manganese, boron, iron, and MOLYBDENUM can be either mixed with other fertilizers and applied to the ground or else sprayed on to the leaves as foliar fertilizers.

The efficiency of fertilization varies with the type of fertilizer and the soil. For example, phosphate fertilizers are not readily available to plants grown in acid soils high in iron and aluminium oxides, so liming (see LIME) might increase growth because it makes phosphorus more available to the vine. Similarly, with high rainfall or irrigation, the nitrate form of nitrogen is leached so easily that it is lost to the vine roots unless they are very deep. The nitrate may end up contaminating nearby streams and groundwater, as has been reported in many countries, making fertilizer use in viticulture (and other forms of agriculture) the subject of scrutiny by those concerned with SUSTAINABILITY.

Fertilizer use can affect wine quality. Too much nitrogen can stimulate vine growth to such an extent that RIPENING is prejudiced, and the resultant wines may be thin, pale, and HERBACEOUS. Excessive use of potassium may also detrimentally increase wine PH and affect the colour stability of red wines. R.E.S. & R.E.W.

Christensen, L. P., and Smart, D. R. (eds.), *Proceedings of the Soil Environment and Vine Mineral Nutrition Symposium* (2005).

White, R. E., *Understanding Vineyard Soils* (2nd edn, 2015).

Fetească, Fetiaska, or **Feteaska** means 'maiden' and is associated with three important Eastern European vine varieties. The 'royal' **Fetească Regală**, thought to be a CROSS of 'white' Fetească Albă and Francușă, was (just) the most planted variety in 2021 in ROMANIA where it produces crisp, scented whites from 12,289 ha/30,367 acres of vineyard. It is also found in HUNGARY under the name Királyleányka. Romanian plantings of **Fetească Albă**, which almost certainly originated in the historic region of Moldavia (including today's Republic of MOLDOVA and the Romanian region of Moldova) and is often used for sparkling wines, totalled 12,076 ha/29,840 acres in 2021. It is known in Hungary as Leányka. In Moldova, where the two are often blended, Albă is more widely planted than Regală, and in UKRAINE statistics do not distinguish between the two. The dark-skinned **Fetească Neagră**, whose red wines show potential when well vinified and yields are severely restricted, was much less common and planted on just over 3,100 ha/7,660 acres in Romania; it is also grown in Ukraine. DNA PROFILING suggests that the dark-skinned Fetească is a particularly old variety and may not be related to either of the light-skinned ones. J.V.

Fiano, strongly flavoured classical vine responsible for CAMPANIA's **Fiano di Avellino** DOCG in southern Italy. Wines made from this variety are assertive but lack the aromatic lift of **Fiano Aromatico**, or MINUTOLO. It is also planted in PUGLIA, MOLISE, and increasingly SICILY. Italian vineyard statistics do not distinguish between the two Fianos but show a total of 2,087 ha/5,157 acres. Total Australian plantings had reached 380 ha/939 acres by 2022.

Fiddletown, California wine region and higher of the two AVAS in the Amador County area of the SIERRA FOOTHILLS.

Fié, occasionally written **Fiét** or **Fiers**, old Loire synonym for SAUVIGNON GRIS. This CLONE has largely been abandoned because of its remarkably low yield, but producers such as Jacky Preys of Touraine pride themselves on their richer versions of Sauvignon made from particularly OLD VINES.

Fiefs Vendéens, small, scattered, Atlantic-influenced AOC zone south of the MUSCADET zone in the LOIRE, qualified by one of the communes Brem, Chantonnay, Mareuil, Pissotte, or Vix, each with its own ENCÉPAGEMENT. Most wines are summery GAMAY-based rosé, yet a few growers like Thierry Michon produce profound white from CHENIN BLANC and red from CABERNET FRANC, NÉGRETTE, or Pinot Noir. P.Le.

field blend, refers to a vineyard that is planted to a mixture of varieties and also to wines from these vineyards. Rare today, this was once a common-sense form of insurance since weather or disease does not affect all varieties in the same way. Such plantings are often found in older vineyards, especially in parts of SPAIN, PORTUGAL, ROUSSILLON, CALIFORNIA, and SOUTH AFRICA. Varieties in field blends are often complementary; for example, a high-acid variety randomly planted among a low-acid variety may improve wine quality when harvested and fermented as one, and this diversity is seen as a means by which to increase COMPLEXITY and BALANCE. Not to be confused with CO-FERMENTATION. See also GEMISCHTER SATZ. J.E.H. & D.P.G.

field grafting, viticultural operation of planting ROOTSTOCK rootlings in their vineyard position and inserting SCION buds. It was common for replanting on PHYLLOXERA-tolerant rootstocks until the 1980s, when BENCH GRAFTING became more common, providing cheaper plants. Many types of bud insertion

F

may be used, but CHIP BUDDING is common. The success rate is highest in warm to hot climates but can be erratic, and careful attention to watering, nutrition, and the tending of each vine is needed. This method is therefore most suitable for small vineyards with good soils and a well-trained workforce. It may also be used to change varieties on vine trunks infected with TRUNK DISEASE, but care must be taken to insert buds at least 30 cm/12 in below any trunk staining.

(See TOP GRAFTING for details of the viticultural operation of changing VINE VARIETY in an established vineyard.) B.G.C. & R.E.S.

F

fifth growth. See the CLASSIFICATION of Bordeaux.

fill level, an aspect of individual bottles of wine which can be closely related to the condition of the wine. The lower the fill level when a wine is bottled, the more the space between the top of the wine and the bottom of the cork (the so-called HEAD SPACE or ULLAGE) in which OXYGEN may be trapped in the bottle and may hasten the AGEING process. Most bottlers try to ensure that there is minimal ullage space in the bottle immediately after BOTTLING, a depth of 5–10 mm/0.2–0.4 in to allow for expansion if ambient temperature ever exceeds the usual bottling temperature of 20 °C. On modern bottling lines, the bottle may be flushed with INERT GAS before and after filling in order to limit as far as possible the oxygen in the head space (see TOTAL PACKAGE OXYGEN). Subsequent reductions in temperature cause a reduction in the wine's volume, thereby apparently lowering the fill level.

For wines designed for early consumption, this is unlikely to make much difference, but fill levels are important indicators of the condition of a fine and, especially, mature wine, so that fill levels should always be specified by the AUCTION houses and other fine-wine traders. The lower the fill level, the more likely a harmful level of OXIDATION and therefore the lower should be the selling price. Some sorts of wine, for example vintage PORT and SAUTERNES, seem more resilient to low fill levels than others.

During long-term AGEING, some wine is likely to be absorbed by the CORK, resulting in a drop in fill level of perhaps 7 mm after ten years. (To reduce this absorption effect, Ch MOUTON-ROTHSCHILD adopted a policy of using shorter corks from the 1991 vintage.) Other reasons for a low fill level include poor control during bottling, wine being bottled at too high a temperature, and a faulty cork. In any event, it is always wise policy to pick bottles with the highest fill levels off the shelf and to drink bottles of wine from the same case from lowest to highest fill level, since the wine in bottles with the lowest fill level is likely to be the most evolved.

Note that the fill level in wine GLASSES should ideally be less than half the height of the glass and never more than two-thirds, in order to provide somewhere for the AROMA to collect. V.L.

film-forming yeasts, sometimes called **film yeasts**, or mycoderma, comprise a group of grape- and wine-associated species of YEASTS which require OXYGEN for their characteristic growth and metabolism. For this reason they appear on the surface of wine in barrels or vats that are not kept completely filled. Some, such as FLOR, being strains of *Saccharomyces cerevisiae* and genetically closely related to wine fermentation strains, can add desirable oxidative aromas and flavours, whereas other species, often referred to as 'non-*Saccharomyces* yeasts', produce off-flavours, while others have a relatively neutral sensory impact.

Film-forming yeasts are widely dispersed in vineyard regions and are among the types encountered in spontaneous or non-inoculated fermentations. When sugar is present, they are producers of alcohol and carbon dioxide but have low alcohol tolerance. Thus, while they are active in the early stages of SPONTANEOUS FERMENTATIONS when traces of oxygen remain, they become dominated by the more alcohol-tolerant *Saccharomyces* species, which finish the sugar conversion. After fermentation, exposure of the wine to oxygen can stimulate film formation. These yeast species typically form more ESTERS, predominantly ETHYL ACETATE, and ALDEHYDES, and sometimes ACETIC ACID, than do *Saccharomyces*, consequently producing an undesirable, OXIDIZED flavour profile.

Initially, small islands of a thin film form on the surface of wines in tanks or barrels that are not completely full and, if left unchecked, can develop into a creamy to grey, dense biomass, referred to in flor wine production as 'velum' (*voile* in French, as in *vin de voile*). These yeasts require oxygen for film formation and thus act as a signal to the winemaker that a more frequent TOPPING UP regime is required. If wine has to be kept under ULLAGE, then maintaining a HEAD SPACE of inert gas and an adequate concentration of sulfur dioxide in the wine will usually prevent film formation. For white wines, the ACETALDEHYDE produced is a negative factor, but for red wines short exposure to a film of *Candida vini* (see below) does little damage.

Film-forming strains of *Saccharomyces* yeasts perform a vital function in the production of wines such as flor SHERRY, VIN JAUNE, and some TOKAJI.

Modern molecular methods, including whole-genome sequencing, are being used to redefine yeast genetic relationships, which has had implications for naming conventions. Previously the commonly encountered film-forming non-*Saccharomyces* species were said to belong to the genera *Pichia* and *Candida*, representing spore-forming (teleomorphic) and non-spore-forming (anamorphic) yeasts respectively. Such a generalization is no longer possible. However, it remains the case that teleomorphic and anamorphic forms of the same yeast can be known by different names. For example, the film-forming yeast species previously known as *Candida mycoderma* (anamorph), commonly observed on the surface of stored wine, is now known as *Candida vini* and also by the name of its teleomorph form *Kregervanrija fluxuum* (formerly *Pichia fluxuum*). Similarly, *Candida pelliculosa* (anamorph) is also known as *Wickerhamomyces anomalus* (previously *Pichia anomala*, teleomorph). Efforts are being made to resolve which names will take precedence. P.A.H. & S.A.S.

Daniel, H.-M., et al., 'On the reclassification of species assigned to Candida and other anamorphic ascomycetous yeast genera based on phylogenetic circumscription', *Antonie Van Leeuwenhoek*, 106/1 (2014), 67–84.

Fugelsang, K. C., and Edwards, C. G., *Wine Microbiology—Practical Applications and Procedures* (2007).

Sponholz, W.-R., 'Wine spoilage by microorganisms', in G. H. Fleet (ed.), *Wine Microbiology and Biotechnology* (1993), 395–420.

films about wine. As wine has become more deeply embedded in popular culture, not least in the US, so films about wine have proliferated in the 21st century, but wine features strongly in at least three in the 20th century. Perhaps the earliest of the modern era was Hitchcock's *Notorious*, a 1946 spy thriller whose plot turns on the whereabouts of the key to a wine CELLAR. Food was perhaps more important than wine in the 1987 classic *Babette's Feast*, but her one sumptuous blow-out meal served to her austere Danish employers included SHERRY, 1860 VEUVE CLICQUOT champagne, an 1846 CLOS DE VOUGEOT, and a cognac. There is no doubt about wine's role in the 1996 thriller *Blood and Wine*, which stars Jack Nicholson as a Florida wine merchant who turns to crime. The 1998 remake of *The Parent Trap* set male parent Dennis Quaid on a Napa Valley wine estate.

By far the most powerful mainstream film about wine ever was SIDEWAYS, the 2004 comedy set in CENTRAL COAST wine country. Its success spawned many other film treatments in which wine is more or less deeply embedded, but the most high-profile was *Bottle Shock*, a 2008 comedy drama based extremely approximately on Steven SPURRIER and the JUDGMENT OF PARIS taste-off between California and France.

At almost the same time as *Sideways* was released came the first of a series of documentary films about wine. Ex-sommelier Jonathan Nossiter's *Mondovino* was a passionate if somewhat tendentious complaint about growing GLOBALIZATION in wine. In 2012, *Somm* documented four young Americans' real-life quest for the MASTER SOMMELIER qualification involving BLIND TASTING tests deliberately made gruelling; this was followed up by two more films in the *Somm* series. Soon afterwards came *Red Obsession*, a high-quality Australian documentary about the Chinese love affair with red wine, bordeaux in particular. The same team made the popular *Blind Ambition*, released in 2021 and 2022, about four Zimbabwean refugees who became top sommeliers in South Africa. The 2016 documentary *Sour Grapes* about COUNTERFEITER Rudy Kurniawan made quite an impact.

In 2020 Netflix's drama *Uncorked* about a young man's quest to become a Master Sommelier joined a swelling corpus of wine-themed movies.

filtration, the process that removes particulate matter from a liquid. At the end of fermentation, wine contains a vast amount of solids, including yeast cells, bacteria, grape cellulose, proteins, and pectins. All of these have to be progressively removed in order to produce a clear wine that is ready to be bottled. The first stage consists simply of settling under gravity to remove the gross matter. In a large winery, this might be accelerated by the use of CENTRIFUGATION or FLOTATION. This is followed by filtration.

There are two principal categories of filtration: depth filtration and surface or absolute filtration. **Depth filtration** involves the use of a relatively thick layer of a finely divided material such as DIATOMACEOUS EARTH, or pads made of cellulose fibres. As the cloudy wine passes through the layer, small particles are trapped in the tortuous channels and clear liquid passes through. This form of filtration is useful for removing large quantities of solid matter because the thickness of the filtration layer presents a large volume of medium in which the particles are trapped. The ROTARY VACUUM FILTER is the extreme example of depth filtration because it can be used to separate wine from the thick deposits at the bottom of a fermentation tank. A sheet filter fitted with thick pads of cellulose fibres is used for removing fine particles in preparation for the final filtration prior to bottling. The risk involved in using depth filtration is that, by increasing the pressure or flow-rate beyond the specified maximum, particles can be forced through the filter to the clean side.

Surface filtration, typically carried out before bottling, depends on a thin but strong film of plastic polymer material with uniform-sized holes which are smaller than the particles being removed from the wine. It is thus impossible for particles to cross the filter, hence the alternative term 'absolute filtration'. The shortcoming here is that, if presented with too much particulate matter, the filter will become blocked. Tangential or cross-flow filtration is an ingenious development of surface filtration where the liquid flows parallel to the filter surface and keeps the filter membrane clear, avoiding clogging. The commonest form of surface filter, as used in many wineries, is the membrane filter, which consists of a set of membrane cartridges within a simple cylindrical housing. These are manufactured in a variety of pore sizes, from 5 to 0.45μ.

The use of the 0.45μ membrane is often incorrectly referred to as 'sterile filtration'. It is not totally sterile as in the production of intravenous liquids, but merely devoid of yeasts and bacteria that could cause degradation of the bottled wine at some time in the future. A more accurate term would be 'aseptic filtration'.

Filtration of wine is somewhat controversial in that it is recognized that minimum intervention is often the best approach since every time wine is handled, processed, or even moved, there can be a slight loss of quality. The best approach is to let time do the job by SETTLING. However, this is a slow process which often has to be accelerated, particularly for large-scale production. Correctly applied, filtration is perfectly satisfactory for the production of high-quality wine. D.B.

finca, Spanish for 'estate'. **Finca Élez** is a Spanish VINO DE PAGO created especially for the high-elevation estate of Manuel Manzaneque.

fine wine is a nebulous term, used by the AUCTION houses (and, less accurately, some pubs in Britain) to describe the sort of wines they sell, which roughly coincide with those described in INVESTMENT. For example, within Bordeaux, a wine would generally have to be of CLASSED GROWTH level or equivalent to qualify as 'fine'.

The extent to which this category of wine coincides with the best wine the world produces has declined slowly but steadily since the 1970s. Buying from, selling to, and in many cases in direct competition with the auction houses are the **fine-wine traders** who specialize in servicing the needs of COLLECTORS and the like. See BROKERS for more details.

See also PHILOSOPHY AND WINE.

Finger Lakes, a hotbed of cool-climate wines in upstate NEW YORK and birthplace of the state's VITIS VINIFERA revolution. The AVA, established in 1982, is defined by 11 long, deep, skinny lakes carved by Ice Age glaciers that left behind diverse soil deposits of LIMESTONE, SHALE, GRAVEL, and silt. The region particularly excels with RIESLING but also supports an exceptionally rich array of grape varieties, from *vinifera* to native AMERICAN VINE SPECIES and French and American HYBRIDS. It also boasts an especially creative, energetic wine industry, with 144 wineries in 2021 producing everything from PET-NATS and PIQUETTES to TRADITIONAL METHOD sparkling wines and barrel-aged reds. For more details, see NEW YORK. M.J.D.

www.newyorkwines.org
www.fingerlakeswinealliance.com

fining, winemaking process with the aim of CLARIFICATION and STABILIZATION of a wine whereby a **fining agent**, one of a range of special materials, is added to coagulate or adsorb and precipitate quickly the COLLOIDS suspended in it. Fining (*collage*, or 'sticking', in French) is important because, by encouraging these microscopic particles to fall out of the wine, the wine is less likely to become hazy or cloudy after bottling.

Most young wines, if left long enough under good conditions, would eventually reach the same state of clarity as fining can achieve within months, but fining saves money for the producer and therefore eventually the consumer. Fining is most effective in removing molecules of colloidal size, which include polymerized TANNINS, PIGMENTED TANNINS, other PHENOLICS that can cause browning in young white wines, and heat-unstable PROTEINS. (Other reasons for clouds, hazes, and deposits in bottled wines include TARTRATES and BACTERIA. See STABILIZATION for details of other methods of removing them.)

Over the centuries, a wide range of fining agents has doubtless been essayed, but scientific and technical advances have eliminated those (such as dried blood powder) that are dangerous to health and those (such as various gums) that are less than fully effective in improving the wine. Many fining agents, deriving variously from EGG WHITES, milk, fish bladders, and American BENTONITE clay deposits, may strike consumers as curious winemaking tools, but it should be recognized that only insignificant traces, at most, of the fining agent remain in the treated wine. Nevertheless, in many countries, including the EU, Australia, New Zealand, and Canada, the use of any fining agent that is considered an 'allergenic substance' must be declared on the label if such a substance is above the detection limit in the finished wine (see LABELLING INFORMATION), and therefore many winemakers are dropping the use of animal-derived proteinaceous fining agents. In 2012 the OIV halved the detection limit for potentially allergenic proteinaceous fining agents set out in its oenological code. It is, however, important to distinguish between ADDITIVES such as OENOLOGICAL TANNINS, which are intended to change the flavour or structure of the wine, and PROCESSING AIDS such as bentonite, which are used to improve stability and/or clarity.

Today two general classes of fining agents are used: powdered mineral or plastic materials that are insoluble (including PVPP); and protein-based organic compounds in liquid form. Bentonite, an unusual form of clay, is particularly effective in adsorbing certain proteins and, to a limited extent, bacteria. SILICA functions similarly but somewhat less effectively. Kaolin, another type of clay, is even less effective than silica. Activated carbon (CHARCOAL) has been used to remove brown colours and is also effective in removing some off-odours. Potassium ferrocyanide may still be used as a fining agent for removing copper and iron (see BLUE FINING).

Organic compounds used as fining agents include proteins such as the CASEIN from milk, albumin from egg whites, ISINGLASS from the swim bladders of fish, and GELATIN from waste meat, which form insoluble complexes with the unstable pigments and tannins. There is a tendency to move away from animal-based products in the interests of VEGETARIANS AND VEGANS; it is possible to obtain vegetable gelatin, and proteinaceous fining agents derived from peas and potatoes have been developed.

Everyday wines, both white and red, are normally fined earlier and to a greater extent than fine wines. Fining trials are always carried out to ensure the minimum effective amount of fining agent is added. Given the extra time accorded the making of fine wines, many of the potentially unstable components polymerize earlier and deposit without human assistance. In general, white wines need fining to preserve their lighter colour and to prevent heat-unstable proteins forming a cloud, while red wines need it to stabilize their colour and for a reduction of astringent and bitter tannins. The fining operation removes components that are soluble but potentially subject to polymerization and cloud or that may precipitate with time.

See also FILTRATION, which cannot remove these soluble substances and acts only on particulates. J.E.H. & D.B.

Finland has been growing grapes for over 100 years. Finland's countryside manor houses used to supply grapes such as Frankenthaler (TROLLINGER) to the Russian Imperial House. Greenhouses were used to ensure ripening. During the Finnish Civil War and its aftermath, much grape-growing knowledge was forgotten. In the 1970s, hardy Baltic varieties such as Zilga began to appear in the backyards of many grape-growing hobbyists; today, HYBRIDS and DISEASE-RESISTANT VARIETIES such as RONDO and SOLARIS are also common, and some VITIS VINIFERA vines are planted as far north as Vaasa. Most grape-growing happens in the south and south-west of the country and in the Åland Islands in the Baltic Sea. However, when Finland joined the EU in 1995 it forfeited the status of a wine-producing country in exchange for farm subsidies. Hence, grape wine is sold as 'an alcoholic beverage made from fermented grapes'. This favours wines made from fruits and berries other than grapes, a long-standing Finnish tradition also protected by Finland's alcohol MONOPOLY, which prohibits CELLAR DOOR sales of grape wines. I.S.

finish, TASTING TERM for the impression a wine gives at the end of the TASTING process. If the sensations provoked by the wine are prolonged, the wine is said to have a long or persistent finish. If not, the wine may be described as short. A long finish, or aftertaste, is, along with BALANCE, a sign of quality in a wine—so long as it is pleasant. But a finish that is too BITTER or TANNIC may be the result of a FAULT.

fino, Spanish word with two related meanings in the sherry-making process. Without its initial capital, *fino* refers to a type of wine that is the counterpoint to the richer, darker *oloroso* (see SHERRY). Fino with an initial capital refers to a style of wine, the commercial result of filtering and bottling a *fino*, the palest, lightest, and driest sherry style (along with MANZANILLA), and quintessentially the product of the *fino* type of sherry preserved and influenced by the film-forming yeast FLOR. Fino de Jerez is by far the most common, but Fino may be made in several sherry towns, including Chiclana, Chipiona, and Trebujena, as well as in MONTILLA-MORILES and CONDADO DE HUELVA. Most Fino has an alcoholic strength of 15% and is bone dry. A freshly opened bottle of true, dry, light Fino is one of the most appetizing wines in the world. For more details, see SHERRY. V. de la S. & J.B.

first growth is a direct translation of the French PREMIER CRU, but its meaning tends to be limited to those BORDEAUX wine properties judged in the top rank according to the various CLASSIFICATIONS: Chx LAFITE, LATOUR, MARGAUX, HAUT-BRION, MOUTON ROTHSCHILD, and d'YQUEM, together often with the unclassified but generally acknowledged star of POMEROL, PETRUS. Just below these red bordeaux in terms of status are the so-called SUPER SECONDS.

Fitou, rugged and remote red-wine appellation on 2,200 ha/5,434 acres of LANGUEDOC vineyard in two enclaves within the CORBIÈRES zone where it meets ROUSSILLON (see map under LANGUEDOC). When the boundaries of this, the first dry red wine appellation of Languedoc, were drawn up in 1948, local politics prevailed, and Fitou has remained with a great tract of Corbières bisecting it. The clay-limestone soils of Fitou Maritime (coastal Fitou) are quite different from the arguably potentially more interesting SCHISTS of Fitou Montagneux (mountainous Fitou), 40 minutes' drive inland—the purity in the wines of Domaine Bertrand-Bergé argue convincingly for the virtues of a mountain climate. The low-yielding vines on the infertile soils of these Pyrenean foothills are capable of great expression, but the appellation underperformed in the 1970s and 1980s. The region is even more in the grip of CO-OPERATIVES than the Corbières, with the Mont Tauch co-operative in Tuchan responsible for over half of all production. In the last decade, however, new dynamic estates have reinvigorated this appellation and shown what a mix of OLD VINES and fabulous TERROIR can achieve.

The traditional varieties Carignan and Grenache must make up 60% of the final blend with a minimum of 20% of each (this is one of the few appellations that demands a minimum Carignan component). A minimum of 10% of Syrah (better suited to Fitou Montagneux) and/or Mourvèdre (which thrives in Fitou Maritime) must be also included in the blend.

The two territories demarcated for Fitou may also produce RIVESALTES and MUSCAT DE RIVESALTES. M.S.

fixed acids, those organic ACIDS of wines whose volatilities are so low that they cannot be separated from wine by DISTILLATION. The two main fixed acids of wine are TARTARIC ACID and MALIC ACID, but several other non-volatile acids are present in small amounts. Unfortunately, the distinction between fixed and volatile acids is not precise because there are some acids which have intermediate volatilities. Among these are LACTIC ACID and SUCCINIC ACID, both found in wine. The fixed acids are important in wines because they are the acids that give wine its refreshing tartness, as well as its natural resistance to bacterial attack. VOLATILE ACIDS, on the other hand, are more obviously odorous than fixed acids and generally produce fruity or, when present in excess, vinegary aromas. TOTAL ACIDITY, a standard wine measurement, is the sum of the fixed acids and volatile acids. A.D.W.

Fixin, appellation abutting Gevrey-Chambertin in the Côte de Nuits district of Burgundy, producing red wines of a similar style to its neighbour, though currently of lesser fame. Fixin wines have a similar sturdiness to Gevrey but have less powerful fruit and fragrance.

There are seven PREMIER CRU vineyards: Les Arvelets and Les Hervelets (partly interchangeable, as wine grown in the former may be labelled the latter), Clos de la Perrière, Clos Napoléon, Clos du Chapître, Le Clos, and Le Meix Bas. Dr Lavalle, writing in 1855, noted Le Chapître, Les Arvelets, and Clos Napoléon but singled out Clos de la Perrière for special praise since at that time the Marquis de Montmort sold it at the same price as his CHAMBERTIN.

Fixin Blanc is also made, though rare, as the AOC included just 5.29 ha/13 acres of Chardonnay in 2018.

See also CÔTE D'OR and map under BURGUNDY. J.T.C.M.

fizziness is the bubbling that occurs in a SPARKLING WINE when the bottle is opened and the wine is poured into a glass. In a sealed bottle the cork maintains a pressure of up to 6 atmospheres, and there is equilibrium between the dissolved CARBON DIOXIDE and the carbon dioxide in the HEAD SPACE. When the bottle is opened and the wine is poured into a glass, the pressure above the wine is reduced to ambient pressure of about 1 atmosphere, and the wine is said to be supersaturated with carbon dioxide.

In this state, carbon dioxide does not suddenly rush from the wine as bubbles. Carbon dioxide is lost by individual molecules diffusing through the surface and by bubble formation at so-called nucleation sites, which are located on particles stuck to the glass or floating in the wine, and often from imperfections (rough spots) in the glass surface. Photographic research by Liger-Belair shows these sites are largely hollow cylindrical cellulose fibres from paper or cloth used to dry the glass. (Conversely resdidual chemicals from detergents or rinse aids may supress the formation of bubbles.)

Carbon dioxide molecules diffuse into minute gas pockets in the nucleation sites, forming a bubble, and when the bubble grows big enough, buoyancy causes it to lift off and rise to the surface of the wine. This process is then repeated so a stream of bubbles is seen emerging from each site. As the bubbles rise, carbon dioxide from the supersaturated wine continues to diffuse into them and thus they get bigger.

Bubbles reaching the surface of the wine can clearly be seen to have different diameters. This is because different nucleation sites have different shapes and sizes and because the nucleation sites are at different distances from the surface, so the bubble diameters grow by different amounts as they rise. The loss of carbon dioxide is very slow: a bottle or glass of gently bubbling fizz takes many hours to go flat.

It is often observed that the bubbles in old cellared bottles of CHAMPAGNE are smaller and slower (lazier) moving to the surface. This is simply because the bottle has, over the years, slowly lost pressure and thus the degree of supersaturation with carbon dioxide is less, resulting in slower bubble growth, both at the nucleation sites and on the way to the surface.

Most fully sparkling wines such as champagne are sold with a pressure of 5–6 atmospheres, about three times that inside a car tyre, which is the pressure which a normal champagne cork and bottle can withstand without undue risk. Such wines may be described as *mousseux* or CRÉMANT in French, *espumoso* in Spanish, *espumante* in Portuguese, SPUMANTE in Italian, and SEKT in German. Fizziness in champagne seems to be decreasing in the 21st century, perhaps due to the greater use of reserve wines.

Many wines are somewhere between still and this level of pressure, however. Wines with a gentle but definite sparkle may be described as PÉTILLANT or PERLANT in French, FRIZZANTE in Italian, SPRITZIG in German, *vino de aguja/vi d'agulla* (literally, needle wine) in Spanish/Catalan, and *frisante* in Portuguese, although many variations in nomenclature exist. European wine law defines a sparkling wine as any wine with an excess pressure of not less than 3 atmospheres (for quality sparkling wine, for example one with a PDO, it is 3.5), while a semi-sparkling wine has a pressure of 1–2.5 atmospheres. The amount of pressure can be controlled by the winemaker by varying the amount of sugar added at the second fermentation or TIRAGE stage or, in the case of CARBONATION, simply by controlling the amount of gas dissolved in the wine.

Some wines sold as still wines may fizz very gently, however. This could be a sign of a FAULT but is more likely to be a deliberate winemaking feature. See CARBON DIOXIDE for more details.

J.R., T.J. & E.C.

Jordan, A. D., and Napper, D. H., 'Some aspects of the physical chemistry of bubble and foam phenomena in sparkling wine', *Proceedings of the Sixth Australian Wine Industry Technical Conference* (1986).

Liger-Belair, G., *Uncorked: The Science of Champagne* (rev. edn, 2013).

Fladgate Partnership, The, was formed in 2001 when Taylor Fonseca Vinhos S.A. (see TAYLOR'S and FONSECA) purchased CROFT and Delaforce (subsequently sold). The group, whose name was inspired by Taylor's full name—Taylor, Fladgate & Yeatman—remains family owned and is run by descendants of the Yeatman family. In 2022 it had 781 ha/1,931 acres of properties in the DOURO Valley with over 1.6 million vines.

Taylor's vintage PORT is consistently one of the most admired and longest lived, and its Quinta de Vargellas single-QUINTA bottling can often be almost as concentrated. Vargellas, Taylor's best-known property in the remote eastern reaches of the Douro, was acquired in 1893 when it was still suffering from the ravages of PHYLLOXERA. This acquisition marked the start of Taylor's now considerable landowning and farming activities. Quinta de Terra Feita in the Pinhão Valley, which had been supplying port to Taylor's since the 1890s, was bought in 1974. In 1990 Terra Feita de Cima was added, followed in 1993 by São Xisto next door to Vargellas, which was further extended in 1999. Quinta do Junco was acquired in 1998. In the late 20th century Taylor's popularized the filtered LBV (late-bottled vintage) style of port. In the early 21st century it pioneered the release of special, small-volume releases of luxury ports.

In 1948 Taylor, Fladgate, & Yeatman acquired Fonseca and have continued to build on the firm's reputation for excellent, dramatic vintage ports. Quinta do Cruzeiro in the Pinhão Valley had been supplying wine for Fonseca since the 19th century and was acquired in 1973. Five years later the company bought Quinta do Panascal in the Távora Valley, which is a key ingredient in Fonseca vintage port as well as producing single-quinta vintage ports. Quinta de Santo António was replanted in the 2000s, and farming is entirely ORGANIC. Fonseca's best-known wine is probably the superior ruby reserve port Bin 27. Vintage ports from earlier-maturing years are sold under the name Guimaraens and are blended from the same properties as produce Fonseca vintage port.

With Croft came the 109-ha/269-acre Quinta da Roêda near Pinhão, and in 2008 the brand was used to launch rosé port, Croft Pink, on an unsuspecting world.

In 2013 The Fladgate Partnership purchased shipper Wiese & Krohn and its impressive stocks of mature tawnies. Eschewing Douro table wines, its focus is premium port, with a global market share of more than 33% of this category. The company has also ventured into wine-related hotels, first in the Douro with The Vintage House hotel and, since 2010, with the Yeatman in Vila Nova da Gaia overlooking Oporto. This was followed in 2020 by an ambitious cultural centre nearby, the World of Wine, or WOW. In 2020 and 2021 quintas Bragão, Arruda, and Vedejosa were added to the portfolio.

flash détente, also known as flash EXTRACTION, is a variation on THERMOVINIFICATION typically used to increase the speed/extent of extraction of colour from grape skins, treat mouldy grapes, and remove GREEN aromas. It can also be used to increase the intensity and complexity of high-quality well-ripened grapes from warm vintages. MUST is heated to around 85 °C/185 °F for a few minutes then introduced into a vacuum chamber. Under the partial vacuum, the boiling point of the must is lower than at atmospheric pressure, so some liquid vaporizes instantly. This weakens the skin cell walls and enhances extractability of POLYSACCHARIDES and TANNINS during maceration. The instant evaporation has the effect of cooling the remaining must down to around 30 °C. The vapour is condensed and this condensate, often rich in green aromas, can be kept separate or added back as desired, sometimes after treatment with activated carbon (see CHARCOAL). *Flash détente* is a useful technique, but it may accentuate harsh tannins when applied to underripe grapes. A gentler 'half' flash process is now also commonly used. In this variant, a weaker vacuum is used that cools the must to around 50 °C. ENZYMES are added and a warm maceration performed for several hours, sometimes during the filling of a large membrane press. This helps further improve and speed up extraction of sufficient polysaccharides and tannins. At 50 °C the added enzymes are around their optimum activity, but there is no risk of OXIDATION from LACCASE since this is denatured by the short time at 85 °C. *Flash détente* (in this context *détente* means 'release') systems are installed in France and to varying extents in other winemaking regions around the world. S.N.

flavescence dorée, a PHYTOPLASMA disease of the vine and the most serious and widespread of the diseases known generically as GRAPEVINE YELLOWS. The disease has the potential to threaten many of the world's vineyards and is becoming ever more widespread due to CLIMATE CHANGE. It is transmitted in the field by *Scaphoideus titanus*, an insect originally native to the eastern United States and Canada and apparently introduced to Europe after the Second World War, but it may also be introduced to the vineyard via infected plant material from NURSERIES.

Flavescence dorée was the first recorded phytoplasma grapevine disease, appearing in the Armagnac region in south-west France on the vine variety BACO 22A in 1949. It spread rapidly throughout France towards the end of the 20th century. Affecting only isolated vineyards in Armagnac and the Languedoc in 1982, by 1987 it had spread to Cognac, throughout the Languedoc and to the northern and southern Rhône. By 1992 it had reached the Loire Valley, Bordeaux, and the Côtes du Rhône, arriving in the Mâconnais in 2014 and spreading to the Côte d'Or from there. It was recorded in the Jura and the Swiss Valais in 2016.

For symptoms and variants, see GRAPEVINE YELLOWS. R.E.S.

CABI, 'Grapevine flavescence doree phytoplamsa', Invasive Species Compendium. www.cabi.org/isc/datasheet/26184.

flavonoids, a large group of PHENOLIC compounds that includes ANTHOCYANINS, CATECHINS, and the FLAVONOLS. More than 9,000 flavonoids from a wide variety of plant sources have been described. In wine, they contribute to COLOUR, ASTRINGENCY, TEXTURE, and possibly BITTERNESS, although this last is less well documented. Up to 90% of the phenolic content in red wine is made up of flavonoids; in white wines the proportion may be lower because of less EXTRACTION from the skins, stems, and seeds. The antioxidant and cancer chemopreventive capacity of many flavonoids may contribute to the HEALTH benefits of moderate wine consumption. G.L.C.

flavonols, a group of PHENOLIC yellow PIGMENTS belonging to the FLAVONOID family found mostly as GLYCOSIDES such as glucosides and glucuronides. QUERCETIN glycosides, the most common flavonols in grapes, are abundant in vine leaves and present in skins and stems. Their concentration can be enhanced in grapes (and therefore in wine too) by exposing the berry cluster to the sun (see CANOPY MANAGEMENT). Indeed, Price and colleagues argue that the quercetin level in grape berries can be used as an index of the sun exposure they have experienced. Like CATECHIN, quercetin may enhance PIGMENT stability in young wines through CO-PIGMENTATION and has antioxidant properties similar to those of RESVERATROL (see HEALTH). The release of flavonol aglycones from the corresponding glycosides may also result in a hazy wine as these molecules are poorly soluble in wine. B.G.C., P.J.W. & V.C.

Price, S. F., et al., 'Cluster sun exposure and quercetin in Pinot Noir grapes and wine', *American Journal of Enology and Viticulture*, 46 (1995), 187–94.

flavour, arguably a wine's most important distinguishing mark. As outlined in TASTING, most of what is commonly described as wine's flavour is in fact its AROMA (or alternatively, in the case of older wines, its BOUQUET). This, the 'smell' of a wine, may be its greatest sensory characteristic but is also the most difficult of its attributes to measure and describe. A wine's flavour could, in its widest sense, be said to be the overall sensory impression of both aroma (as sensed both by the nose and from the mouth) and the taste components and may therefore incorporate the other, more measurable, aspects of ACIDITY, SWEETNESS, BITTERNESS, occasional saltiness, ALCOHOLIC STRENGTH, FIZZINESS, and ASTRINGENCY. It has, further, been proposed that the definition of flavour be enlarged to include not just how a wine smells, tastes, and feels (including, for example, the burning sensation associated with particularly alcoholic wines) but also individual tasters' psychological predetermination, the all-important factor of SUBJECTIVISM including personal preferences, expectations, and ALLERGIES AND INTOLERANCES determined by individuals' cultural, regional, psychological, and physical influences. (See PHILOSOPHY AND WINE.) In this *Companion*, however, the word 'flavour' is used interchangeably with 'aroma'. See also FLAVOUR COMPOUNDS and FLAVOUR PRECURSORS.

flavour compounds are, strictly speaking, all those substances in wines that can be smelled or tasted (see TASTING). However, the term is most often used in a narrower sense, synonymously with 'aroma compounds', to refer to those volatile molecules detected by the olfactory system. In this sense, flavour compounds are directly responsible for wine aromas and also for in-mouth aroma perceptions but not for those that are related to taste, touch, or chemesthesis (sensations felt when chemical compounds activate the trigeminal nerve—e.g. the cooling effect of menthol). Flavour compounds are also key determinants of the persistence of white-wine flavour (see LONG).

Volatile molecules in wine can be described as flavours only if they are present at concentrations above or close to their odour thresholds. Of the more than 1,000 volatile molecules found in wines, only about 80 can genuinely be considered to be wine flavours.

These flavours are present in a vast range of concentrations, from nanograms per litre (parts per trillion), typically 1–10 ng/l, to more than 100 g/l for ethanol. This wide range and the difficulty involved in analysing the most diluted compounds makes a comprehensive analysis of all relevant flavour compounds in wine complicated and expensive, requiring highly trained technicians and no less than three separate analyses using sophisticated analytical instruments.

In order to relate the flavour chemicals in wine to flavour perceptions, it is essential to understand that the olfactory system is not a chemical analyser but rather a communication system in which some messages (flavour perceptions) are associated with individual flavours, while other messages are carried out by groups of similar flavour compounds, referred to as aroma vectors. It has been estimated that the 80 wine flavour compounds can be grouped into 35 aroma vectors, which in turn can be classified into 10 aromatic categories. The most complex aroma vector is that of fruity ESTERS, which includes up to 14 fruity-smelling ethyl esters that are responsible for the backbone of a wine's fruit flavours.

Eleven aroma vectors are by-products of fermentation, while 17 come from the grape and seven others come from oak wood or from OXIDATION. Some grape-related aroma vectors take a long time to develop because they are present in the grape as odourless FLAVOUR PRECURSORS. Some of these precursors will, after long AGEING periods, be converted into wine flavours by spontaneous, but tremendously slow, natural chemical reactions. This is one key explanation for the fact that the best wines require several years of ageing to develop their flavour fully. It also explains the subtleties of the connection between grape and wine flavours. The specific aroma of wines made from different grape varieties should be attributed not to the presence of specific aroma vectors but to the proportions of a number of vectors. Nevertheless, some aroma vectors are indeed represented more in wines from specific varieties, such as some TERPENES in wine made from Muscat, cis-rose oxide (another terpene) in Gewürztraminer, or 4-methyl-4-mercaptopentan-2-one (4MMP) in Sauvignon Blanc (see THIOLS).

The role that a particular aroma vector plays in a wine depends on its concentration and on the presence of other vectors that are 'competing' or 'potential partners'. A dominant vector which is clearly identified in the wine may be referred to as a flavour impact compound.

Where an aroma compound is not dominant, it may still be identifiable or it may blend synergistically with other odours to produce a new one, usually of higher intensity. Some compounds, such as β-damascenone, are particularly notable as blenders. At normal levels (1–4 ug/l), β-damascenone acts mainly as a fruit enhancer; at higher levels (5–12 ug/l) it adds a ripe fruit character; and only at very high levels (>20 ug/l), usually found in DRIED-GRAPE WINES, it becomes an impact flavour compound.

Below are some of the most important grape-derived flavour compounds that have been identified so far.

Monoterpenes: linalool and geraniol (citrus-floral aroma) are particularly explicit in Muscat wines but add subtle floral notes to other white varieties such as Riesling and Albariño. Cis-rose oxide (rose) is particularly noticeable in Gewürztraminer. PIPERITONE, p-menthane lactones, and neomenthyl acetate (mint) have recently been identified as key contributors to freshness in aged Bordeaux wines. ROTUNDONE (pepper) is responsible for these notes in Syrah, Graciano, Duras, and many other reds.

Carotenoid-derived (norisoprenoids): r-damascenone (ripe plum), particularly evident in wines made from sun-dried grapes such as Pedro Ximenez but ubiquitous in all wines. While d-ionone (violets) is seldom identifiable, it contributes to berry notes and has recently been shown to be significant in Pinot Noir. TDN (kerosene) is explicit in some old Rieslings but also found in most aged wines.

Polyfunctional thiols: 4-methyl-4-mercaptopentan-2-one (4MMP, box-tree, blackcurrant, passion fruit), 3-mercaptohexanol (3MH, grapefruit, passion fruit), and 3-mercaptohexyl acetate (3MHA, passion fruit, sweaty). These compounds are clearly perceptible in Sauvignon Blanc but are essential for the freshness of many other white and rosé wines and for the perception of blueberry and blackberry notes in reds.

Others: ethyl cinnamate and ethyl dihydrocinnamate (white flowers); dimethyl sulfide (truffle; but see SULFIDES); volatile phenols such as guaiacol, eugenol, and isoeugenol (spicy, carnation; but see BRETTANOMYCES); vanillins such as vanillin, acetovanillone, and methyl vanillate (vanilla, nutmeg); furaneol (sugar cotton/candyfloss); alkyl-2-methoxypyrazines (bell pepper).

See PHENOLICS and AGEING. V.F.

Ferreira, V., et al., 'Wine aroma vectors and sensory attributes', in A. Reynolds (ed.), *Managing Wine Quality, 2: Viticulture and Wine Quality* (2nd edn, 2021).

Ferreira, V., and Lopez, R., 'The actual and potential aroma of winemaking grapes', *Biomolecules*, 9/12 (2019), 818.

Ferreira, V., et al., 'A new classification of perceptual interactions between odorants to interpret complex aroma aystems. Application to model wine aroma', *Foods*, 10/7 (2021), 1627.

Tomasino, E., and Bolman, S., 'The potential effect of β-ionone and i-damascenone on sensory perception of Pinot Noir aroma', *Molecules*, 26 (2021), 1288.

flavoured wines, somewhat amorphous category of wines whose basic wine grape flavour is modified by the addition of other flavouring materials. VERMOUTH is a flavoured FORTIFIED wine, while the Greek RETSINA is perhaps the most strikingly flavoured unfortified wine.

History

Flavoured fermented fruit drinks predate pure grape wine. They were infused with herbs and spices in many ancient cultures for use as medical tonics, and resins were added to both flavour and stabilize such drinks.

Evidence of flavoured wines from the Neolithic era has been found from Asia to the Middle East. For example, in the Henan province of north-central China, pottery shards dated 6200–5600 BCE were found to contain dried residue of grape or hawthorn wine flavoured with sweet mead and bitter rice malt. Analysis has shown that a wine made in the Zagros Mountains in Iran *c.*5400–5000 BCE was preserved with terebinth (see ORIGINS OF VINICULTURE). Ancient Egyptians worshipped their god Ra with wine infused with honey, juniper, myrrh, and other aromatic herbs; complex samples have been analysed from 3150 BCE. One of the most stimulating examples of flavoured wines from a *c.*2500 BCE Iranian archaeological site was found to contain poppy, ephedra, and marijuana.

Descriptions and recipes abound in ancient texts from MESOPOTAMIA to ROME and GREECE. PLINY listed as wine flavourings virtually everything from figs and carob to artemesia. Herbs and honey not only covered off-flavours and also gave appeal to light-bodied wines (see GERMAN HISTORY). There have long been local specialities of wines flavoured with herbs, spices, flowers, or nuts.

In Europe throughout the 17th century, 'hippocras', red or white wine infused with sugar, honey, and exotic spices, was widely popular for its flavour and supposed aphrodisiac properties. The name refers to the *manicum hippocraticum* (Hippocrates' sleeve), the muslin bag through which the infused wine was strained. In south Central Europe, wine flavoured with spices imported from the east and south, and indigenous European herbs such as artemisia, evolved into the VERMOUTHS we know today.

Pliny the Elder, *Natural History*, translated by H. Rackham (1945), Book 14.

Younger, W., *Gods, Men and Wine* (1966).

Modern variations

Although high-quality modern craft VERMOUTHS can be found today, most non-fortified commercially available flavoured wines are dilute, low in alcohol, and with very fruity flavours, not unlike fizzy drinks. Such products should be distinguished from FRUIT WINES, whose alcohol derives from the sugars of the (non-grape) fruit itself.

Ford, A., *Vermouth: A Spirited Revival, with 40 Modern Cocktails* (2019). A.M.R.

flavourings are available to wine producers but are entirely illegal. Of the three sorts of flavourings used in the food and beverage industry—natural, nature-identical, and artificial—the last can be discounted because they are easily detectable, and natural and nature-identical flavourings are readily available, no more expensive, and still relatively difficult to detect. Natural and nature-identical flavourings which can add or increase the characteristics of grape varieties such as CABERNET SAUVIGNON and SAUVIGNON BLANC are available. Modern analytical techniques (see ANALYSIS) are able to detect additions at very low levels, and there have been a number of successful prosecutions. Since these flavourings are so intense, they can be effective at concentrations as low as 0.001% and the addition of, for example, 100 ml/3.6 fl oz of essence to a 100-hl/2,640-gal vat is an operation which could be performed easily and discreetly. G.T.

flavour precursors are odourless and hydrophilic forms of flavour molecules or of molecules that can eventually and spontaneously yield flavour molecules. They include GLYCOSIDES (sugar derivatives) and cysteinyl derivatives (derivatives of cysteine or GLUTATHIONE). These flavourless compounds occur naturally in grapes (and many other fruits) as products of the normal metabolic activity of the fruit, and they are both numerous and more abundant than the free FLAVOUR COMPOUNDS. Their importance to wine comes from their ability to release and so augment, or keep constant during AGEING, the level of flavour compounds, some positive, some less so. They are essential for wine longevity as they constitute a pool of additional potential flavour molecules. Some precursors could also contribute to the persistence of flavour in the mouth, since some enzymes present in saliva can promote the release of the aroma while the wine is in the mouth.

In the case of glycosides, the release is by spontaneous HYDROLYSIS. Such hydrolysis can produce the aroma molecule directly, as with many linalool precursors (see MONOTERPENES), or can produce a molecule that is transformed by other spontaneous but slow natural chemical processes into the aroma molecule, for example β-damascenone or TDN. In these last two instances, the flavour takes much longer to be produced.

In the case of cysteinyl precursors, most of the release is carried out by YEASTS during fermentation, although they transform only a small fraction of the precursors. Most recent evidence supports the idea that the remaining precursors help, by slow spontaneous hydrolysis, to maintain a high level of the aroma molecule, which in this case is an unstable polyfunctional THIOL. V.F.

Ferreira, V., and Lopez, R., 'The actual and potential aroma of winemaking grapes', *Biomolecules*, 9/12 (2019), 818.

flavour scalping refers to the partial absorption from wine of some aroma and FLAVOUR COMPOUNDS by wine bottle CLOSURES and other types of packaging material (such as the bladders used in wine BOXES) during storage. This process mostly affects wine components that are the least soluble in water. Various flavour-scalping studies of sensorially relevant compounds in wine, some looking at changes in the same wines over several years, have shown that some compounds are not significantly scalped by any closures, while other compounds can be scalped by up to 98% depending on the closure type. The extent of absorption is a function of time in the bottle or other package and the sorptive capacity of the closure, with some SYNTHETIC CLOSURES having a much greater sorptive capacity than natural bark CORKS or technical closures made of processed cork bark. SCREWCAPS have little or no sorptive capacity. Bottles sealed with a particular closure will exhibit little bottle-to-bottle variation in this phenomenon. Flavour scalping does not necessarily diminish wine quality since some wine components can have an unfavourable impact on wine aroma; it does not affect all wines equally and, indeed, will not affect many wines at all. M.A.S., D.J. & D.L.C.

Capone, D., et al., 'Flavour "scalping" by wine bottle closures', *Australian and New Zealand Wine Industry Journal*, 18/5 (2003), 16–20.

flétri, French term, from *flétrir*, meaning 'to wither', used to describe grapes which have been dried, or partially dried (*mi-flétri*), before fermentation to increase the sugar content. It is used most commonly in SWITZERLAND and occasionally in the Valle d'AOSTA. See also DRIED-GRAPE WINES.

fleuraison, or **floraison**, French terms for FLOWERING.

Fleurie, arguably the most prominent of the BEAUJOLAIS crus after MORGON. Its 827 ha/2,043 acres contain some of the region's most historically reputed LIEUX-DITS, including Poncié and Chapelle des Bois, with some soils composed of sandy pink GRANITE, but also rougher, altered granite and CLAY in spots, especially towards MOULIN-À-VENT in the north-west, where wines can be quite meaty and full-bodied. It is farmed by several of the region's most esteemed names, including Dutraive and Métras—all of which has made the wines increasingly dear. J.F.B.

Fleurieu Zone in SOUTH AUSTRALIA encompasses the regions of Currency Creek, Kangaroo Island, Langhorne Creek, McLaren Vale, and Southern Fleurieu.

Flextank, trademarked brand of POLYETHYLENE tank. A flexitank, on the other hand, is a container used in the BULK TRANSPORT of wine.

flight, name for a series of different but related servings of wine, served in a bar or restaurant by the GLASS or as part of a TASTING. Australians tend to call them brackets.

flint, an ultra-fine-grained silica (silicon dioxide) rock found especially in association with CHALK that occurs sporadically across northern and central Europe as far east as Kazakhstan, as well as in parts of North America and South Australia. It originated on ancient sea floors as gelatinous masses of siliceous algae, which with time hardened into bands and lumps. Flint is seen today, usually as tough pebbles in the soil, in some vineyards in ENGLAND, CHAMPAGNE, and parts of the LOIRE such as SANCERRE and Pouilly-sur-Loire. Flint pebbles enhance soil DRAINAGE and, being inert, restrict nutrient availability (see VINE NUTRITION), though they can damage farm machinery.

Flint (*silex* in French) is tasteless and odourless but nevertheless is a popular metaphorical tasting term, especially for cool-climate white wines, perhaps an allusion to flint breaking to give points and edges or to the distinctive smell created by striking two pieces of flint together. That odour is due to the vaporization of polysulphane compounds arising from minuscule impurities in the flint. Use of the term 'gunflint' (*pierre à fusil*) alludes to the smell of steel sparking as it strikes the natural flint once used in firearms. A.J.M.

Maltman, A. J., 'The striking story of flint', *The World of Fine Wine*, 65 (2019), 146–53.

Floc de Gascogne is the Armagnac region's answer to the PINEAU DES CHARENTES of Cognac. This strong, sweet red and white VIN DE LIQUEUR, awarded AOC status in 1990, is made by arresting the fermentation of local grape juice at an early stage by adding young armagnac, which in this case must have been produced by the same enterprise. The resulting liquid, of which about 17% is alcohol, is aged for at least nine months (although not necessarily in wood, as for Pineau). It is usually drunk as an aperitif but is also much used by Gascony's famously resourceful chefs.

flooding in wine regions is a common occurrence since many are located close to creeks and rivers. Boundaries for wine regions are often established based upon the drainage areas of the dominant rivers, with many vineyards planted on river terraces, on ALLUVIAL FANS, on hillsides, or alongside creeks. Flooding in wine regions can occur at any time of year with heavy winter rains the most common cause, although spring floods due to snowmelt and summer floods due to intense thunderstorms also occur in many wine regions.

The extent of flood damage in any area varies depending on the amount, intensity, duration, and area affected by precipitation. Vineyard damage from flooding occurs mostly from the physical impact of water movement, for example destruction of TRELLIS SYSTEMS, uprooting vines, or completely eroding vineyard blocks. Vineyards may also be compromised by prolonged waterlogging of the soil. Late-winter or early-spring flooding can drastically reduce the oxygen available to the vines roots, limiting their ability to take up nutrients or water and exacerbating the competition for oxygen between root and soil microorganisms. Flooding may also disrupt FLOWERING or increase disease pressure due to rain and high humidity.

Some mitigation of flood damage is possible, for example by planting above flood-prone areas, creating water pathways around vineyard blocks or installing drainage zones where water tables rise quickly. However, heavy rainfall events have become on average more intense and more frequent due to CLIMATE CHANGE, contributing to a global increase of flooding events of about 65% over the last 25 years. G.V.J.

flood irrigation. See IRRIGATION.

flor, or **flor yeasts**, are benevolent FILM-FORMING YEASTS which are able to form a veil (*voile* in French), velum, or film of yeast cells which floats on the surface of a wine. Flor yeasts are typified by those native to the JEREZ region of southern Spain which produce Fino and Manzanilla SHERRY. These yeasts have been assigned many names by different microbiologists over the years, including *Saccharomyces bayanus, S. beticus, S. capensis, S. cheriensis, S. fermentati, S. montuliensis*, and *S. rouxii*. However, they are now considered to be synonyms of *S. cerevisiae*.

Flor yeasts are all capable of fermenting sugar in an anaerobic phase of their metabolism. In Jerez they are the active sugar-fermenting yeast. When all fermentable sugar has been consumed, these yeasts have the capacity to switch to another metabolic phase in which they use alcohol and oxygen from the atmosphere to produce a waxy or fatty coating on the cells' exterior which permits them to float on the wine's surface. The flor yeasts begin to form as small white curds on the surface of the wine, typically in the spring after fermentation as the ambient temperature begins to rise. These increase in size until the surface is completely covered by a thin white film which gradually thickens and browns. They also produce ACETALDEHYDE and other products which characterize the aroma of film or flor sherries. This process is known as biological ageing.

Many studies have shown that these desirable yeasts will form films only in the narrow ALCOHOLIC STRENGTH range of 14.5 to 16%. Below 14.5 the usual result is VINEGAR; above 16% the yeast struggles and dies, resulting in an *oloroso* style of sherry. Film sherry cannot be made in STAINLESS STEEL tanks because the yeast uses so much alcohol that the wine becomes watery and eventually acetifies. In wooden barrels such as the BUTTS of Jerez, in the area's low-humidity cellars, there is enough preferential EVAPORATION of water through the wood that the water loss just balances the alcohol used by the yeast, the end result being sherry.

Flor yeasts have been studied in detail by Fornachon in Australia, by Niehaus in South Africa, and by CRUESS in California, all regions hospitable to the flor yeast strains and the PALOMINO grape used for sherry, and where wines similar to sherry have been produced (although see also CYPRUS).

Flor or a similar film-forming yeast has been observed on wines in many and varied parts of the world, both ancient and modern.

Flor wines are made in MONTILLA, RUEDA, and Huelva (see CONDADO DE HUELVA) in Spain and in the ALGARVE in southern Portugal, where flor is also used to make a rather crude aperitif wine. See also JURA, whose VIN JAUNE is very similar to sherry, and TOKAJI in Hungary. Similar wines are also made in ROMANIA and, by Plageoles, in GAILLAC. P.A.H.

Flora, CALIFORNIA aromatic white vine CROSS. Perhaps the most delicately aromatic of Dr H. P. Olmo's DAVIS creations (see also CARNELIAN, EMERALD RIESLING, RUBY CABERNET, and SYMPHONY), Flora is grown to a very limited extent in California, Australia, and New Zealand.

flotation, a technique of juice CLARIFICATION based on the tendency of grape solids to attach to rising bubbles. The solids rise to the top of a vessel, with the clear juice then removed from underneath. Gas, usually NITROGEN, is dissolved in juice under pressure, and this pressure is then released, creating very small bubbles as the gas comes out of solution. Adjuvants such as BENTONITE and proteins are usually added to improve flocculation of grape solids and bubbles. Gelatin was previously the most common protein used for the process, but vegan alternatives are increasingly common, including pea and potato proteins and fungi-derived CHITOSAN. Flotation is a faster and more energy-efficient method of juice clarification than cold settling. If air is used as the flotation gas instead of nitrogen, hyperoxidation (see OXIDATION) can be performed at the same time.

Flotation has its origins in minerals processing, but the techniques used in winery flotation are mainly from the water industry. Modern winery flotation began in Italy around 1990 with continuous wastewater-clarification-style systems with large, specialized separation tanks. Compact systems that work by recirculation of juice in a winery's existing tank and are better suited to smaller wineries have since been developed. Flotation has also been used in Australia since around 1980 as a secondary juice clarification stage after juice CENTRIFUGATION, in which case adjuvants are not as important since larger denser solids have already been removed. S.N.

flower cap of the vine is known as the CALYPTRA.

flowering, important event in the VINE GROWTH CYCLE, the process preceding the fertilization of vine flowers and their subsequent development into berries. The sequence of events includes the opening of individual flowers, with the CALYPTRA (fused cap of petals) being shed, POLLEN being liberated, and ovules becoming fertilized. Fertilization leads to BERRIES being set (see FRUIT SET), the stage following flowering.

Compared with many other plants, the vine has unattractive small green flowers, and the flowering process in the vineyard is so notably unspectacular that it is likely to be missed by the casual observer. The vine-grower, however, is aware that this process is particularly important in the chain of events that leads up to HARVEST; with some varieties and some weather conditions, a poor flowering can mean financial disaster for the vineyard owner.

Flowering, or bloom, takes place about 6–13 weeks after BUDBREAK, the period being shorter for warm climates and early varieties. The vine flower usually contains both male parts (STAMENS) and female parts (a pistil-containing OVARY). The flowering process begins as the cap falls away, exposing the stamens. POLLINATION is the process whereby pollen grains are shed and land on the moistened stigma surface where they germinate. They then penetrate the style and fertilize the ovary, leading to fruit set and the creation of a berry. The fertilized ovaries form seeds, with up to four per berry. The wall of the flower tissue enlarges to form the SKIN and PULP of the grape berry. See diagram.

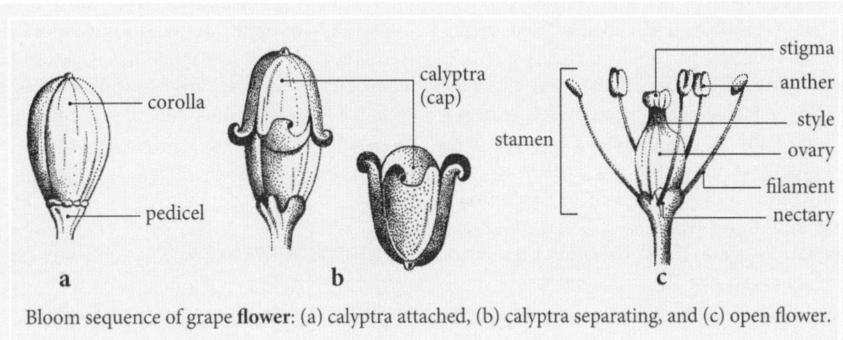

Bloom sequence of grape **flower**: (a) calyptra attached, (b) calyptra separating, and (c) open flower.

Most wine grape varieties have perfect, or hermaphroditic, flowers (that is, with well-developed and functional male and female parts). Some varieties such as CURRANT, SULTANA, and Perlette, more suitable for RAISINS and TABLE GRAPES, have non-functional or defective female parts. Berries from such varieties are typically seedless or have small, poorly developed seeds; they therefore tend to be small because of a lack of HORMONES produced by normal seeds.

Cold, wet, and windy weather at flowering has a bad effect on flowering and fruit set and—in countries such as ENGLAND where grapevines are grown at the cool limit of viticulture—is a major cause of poor YIELDS. Studies in Europe (in CHAMPAGNE, for example) have shown that regional vineyard yield can be correlated with the concentration of pollen in the lower atmosphere, which in turn can also be correlated with weather conditions. Many studies have shown that the vine flower is probably self-pollinated, with insects and wind making little contribution; even flowers surrounded by a bag tend to set perfectly (although cross-pollination between flowers is possible). However, grape flowers do release a pungent, reputedly aphrodisiac, odour, from odour glands at the base of the pistil, which is known to attract insects. R.E.S.

Keller, M., 'Phenology and growth cycle', in *The Science of Grapevines* (3rd edn, 2020).

flowers, vine. The grapevine flower is not showy and has little attraction for birds, but it has the normal complement of sepals and petals surrounding the sexual parts: the male in the stamens and the female in the pistil. Flowers are grouped together on an inflorescence (see BUNCH). The five petals are locked together to form a cap or CALYPTRA, and at FLOWERING they fall off, usually as a unit joined at the base; this is called 'capfall', an important PHENOLOGICAL stage. Once the caps are off, the STAMENS expand to their full length and the inflorescence begins to look fluffy. A wet, glistening coating covers the stigma at the top of the pistil when it is ready to receive large numbers of POLLEN grains lodged on this surface.

Different species and varieties of grapevine have one of three types of flower. The most common, and most FRUITFUL, are those with bisexual or hermaphrodite flowers, whose pistil and stamens are both functional. Some vine varieties (such as MADELEINE ANGEVINE and MARATHEFTIKO) may have female or pistillate flowers, with a well-developed, functional pistil but with reflexed stamens which contain usually sterile pollen; with cross-pollination, using fertile pollen, these varieties become fruitful. And other varieties, particularly ROOTSTOCKS, may have male or staminate flowers (with functional stamens but no pistil) and therefore do not bear fruit. Most species of VITIS, in their native habitats, have male and female flowers on separate vines, which ensures cross-pollination and hence genetic diversity among the seedling progeny (see SEXUAL PROPAGATION). Commercial VINE VARIETIES are almost invariably bisexual and self-fruitful, and genetic diversity is avoided by VEGETATIVE PROPAGATION.

Flowering occurs in late spring when shoots have developed 17–20 visible INTERNODES. This is a crucial stage in the reproductive development of the grape since a host of mishaps may lead to unsuccessful pollination or failure to develop into a berry (see FRUIT SET). B.G.C.

Keller, M., 'Phenology and growth cycle', in *The Science of Grapevines* (3rd edn, 2020).

flowers in vineyards may be deliberately planted at row ends or even between rows as COVER CROPS. Rose bushes at row ends are commonplace in the Médoc and, increasingly, elsewhere, either for aesthetic reasons or because they may act as early indicators of a POWDERY MILDEW attack. Flowers may also be planted between the rows as a pollen source to attract insects considered beneficial to vineyard ECOSYSTEMS.

Flurbereinigung refers to the wholesale restructuring to which most of Germany's vineyards have been subjected since the 1950s, involving improved accessibility, grading, consolidation of growers' highly fragmented holdings, and of course replanting. Without this restructuring, many vineyards would long since have been abandoned as not economically viable to till. But the process—which must be agreed to by a majority of landholders who share its costs with the state—is often contentious. Owners of vineyards marginally located or extremely difficult to access are offered the opportunity of opting out, and some vineyards have been deemed too steep and rocky to be amenable to restructuring. It is largely as a result of these two situations that ancient terraces and vines, some UNGRAFTED, remain in certain sites, especially along the SAAR and MOSEL. D.S.

flying winemakers, term coined by English wine merchant Tony LAITHWAITE for a team of young Australian winemakers he hired to work the 1987 vintage in French CO-OPERATIVE wineries. The idea was to apply Australian hard work and technological expertise to inexpensive grapes, thereby producing a unique range of wines for his mail-order wine business. The original scheme depended on the fact that AUSTRALIA has a substantial number of highly trained winemakers (see ACADEME) who are relatively idle during HARVEST time in the northern hemisphere, where most of the world's wine is made. This sort of bought-in OENOLOGY initially worked best in areas with a considerable quantity of relatively inexpensive grapes but whose technical potential was yet to be realized. It thus excluded the classic wine regions and much of the NEW WORLD but decisively included southern France, much of Italy (especially Puglia and Sicily), and Iberia, Eastern Europe, some of the more open-minded South African wineries, and South America. The concept was such a success that it was much imitated and developed into a phenomenon with a long-term impact on winemaking techniques and wine styles all over the world (see GLOBALIZATION) in the 1990s, although the marked increase in local oenological training and skills has made the phenomenon less common.

By the late 1990s, several teams of itinerant winemakers had developed from permanent bases in both France and Britain. But in general hundreds of career flying winemakers have been replaced by much smaller numbers of recent oenology graduates who combine travelling with work experience in cellars and vineyards around the world before finding their vocational location or returning home. INFORMATION TECHNOLOGY has enabled virtual winemaking from a distance of several time zones and many thousands of miles. By the 21st century, the winemaker who had only ever made wine in a single location was almost the exception.

flysch, Alpine sedimentary rocks, typically a disordered combination of SANDSTONE and SHALE, formed under the sea from the detritus of the infant Alps as they rose rapidly and were vigorously eroded. Soils derived from flysch are quite varied, with some coarse and gravelly, some sandy, and some that are quite CALCAREOUS (see MARL), and they go by a host of different local names such as *opok*, *opoka*, *opoc*, *poca*, or *ponca*.

Foch, common North American name for the MARÉCHAL FOCH vine.

Fogoneu, minor red wine grape of the BALEARIC ISLANDS of Mallorca, where it is usually blended with CALLET and MANTO NEGRO, and Formentera.

foil, alternative name for the CAPSULE which covers the cork and neck of a wine bottle. The term is most commonly used for bottles of sparkling wine because in this case it is almost invariably made of metal foil, whereas the 'foil' covering tops of bottles of still wine may be made from a wide range of materials. Traditionally LEAD or lead alloys were used, but in Europe these were found to be a major source of soil contamination in disposal sites, and lead contamination of wine was traced to this source, so the use of lead foils has been phased out and was prohibited in the US and the EU in 1993. Older bottles with lead foils should be wiped carefully around the bottleneck between pulling the cork and serving. Various plastics, tin, and aluminium are also used. Of the two most common types, one is made from polyvinyl chloride (PVC) with an aluminium top and is heat-shrunk on to the bottle (alternatives made from more environmentally friendly polyethylene terephthalate (PET) are also available); the other is a polylaminate consisting of layers of polyethylene and aluminium which is spun into place. The foil is there largely for aesthetic reasons, since the CLOSURE should provide an airtight seal, and only a faulty one will allow any seepage of wine. The length and design of a foil is another purely aesthetic matter, although some clear identification on the top of the foil can be very useful in a CELLAR full of bottles on wine racks. In an effort to minimize packaging and waste, some producers have simply abandoned the foil, although within the EU this is not an option for those who make sparkling wines. Others have rediscovered the wax seal, which is thought to protect the cork and reduce the risk of seepage or oxygen ingress, as well as having aesthetic appeal.

foil cutter, gadget for SERVING wine which helps cut the FOIL neatly just below the lip of the bottle, with the twin advantages of avoiding unsightly and possibly dangerous torn metal edges and ensuring no likelihood of the wine's being poured over a foil which might taint it. Some foil cutters are blades incorporated into CORKSCREWS; others are separate prongs with small circular blades which cut the foil when rotated. Life without a foil cutter is quite feasible; living without one after being introduced to it is not.

Folgasão, vine of disputed origin producing promising whites from 41 ha/101 acres in 2020, mainly in Terras de Cister in northern Portugal.

Folle Blanche, white grape variety, a natural GOUAIS BLANC progeny, once grown in profusion along the Atlantic seaboard of western France, providing very acidic but otherwise neutral base wine for distillation by the largely DUTCH WINE TRADE. It never regained its position after PHYLLOXERA ravaged the vineyards of Europe in the late 19th century, and France's total plantings of Folle Blanche continue to decline: from 12,104 ha/29,910 acres in 1968 to 945 ha/2,335 acres in 2019, mainly for GROS PLANT production. It has also been grown to a very limited extent in California and possibly in northern Spain.

Folle Noire, occasional synonym for various French dark-berried grape varieties including JURANÇON and Fuella Nera. Unrelated to FOLLE BLANCHE. See BELLET.

Fondillón, strong, semi-sweet RANCIO wine from ALICANTE made from overripened dark-skinned MONASTRELL grapes and matured like an *oloroso* SHERRY. The wine is not fortified but naturally achieves 16% minimum alcohol; it is allowed a maximum 45 g/l RESIDUAL SUGAR. Both SOLERA and static ageing are performed, with a minimum mean age of 10 years. F.C.

Fonseca, common Portuguese surname associated with two important but unrelated wine producers in PORTUGAL.

Fonseca is a highly respected PORT shipper, now part of the FLADGATE PARTNERSHIP. It was founded by the Fonseca and Monteiro families in 1815 and acquired by Manoel Pedro Guimaraens in 1863. With the exception of the 1955 produced by Dorothy Guimaraens, every single Fonseca vintage port between 1896 and 1991 was made either by Frank Guimaraens or his great-nephew Bruce. Bruce's son, Australian-trained fifth-generation David Guimaraens, continues the good work. Fonseca Guimaraens, as it was then known, was acquired by Taylor, Fladgate, and Yeatman in 1949, but the two houses maintain separate identities and styles of port within the group now known as the Fladgate Partnership, under which entry more detail can be found.

José Maria da Fonseca is a family company based in the south of the country at Azeitão in Arrábida on the SETÚBAL peninsula. Originally a producer of rich, fortified Setúbal, it is now more important as a producer of a wide range of unfortified Portuguese wines, notably under the name Periquita, designed for the international market.

food, wine as. See DIET.

food-and-wine matching may be an extremely complex, detailed subject, a set of rules embedded in one's national culture, or an activity only for gastro-bores, according to one's point of view.

For some of the most fanatical wine enthusiasts, food is an obstacle between palate and wine glass, whose flavours can get in the way of a decent wine-tasting session. For others, food without wine and wine without food is inconceivable, and the whole is greater than the sum of the parts.

It is perfectly physically possible to drink any sort of wine with any sort of food. But as anyone who has brushed their teeth with toothpaste and directly afterwards taken a sip of wine will attest, specific FLAVOUR COMPOUNDS can have a profound effect on each other and our perception of them. It is also recognized that certain foods have very specific effects on wine.

The following should be read in conjunction with the article on TASTING.

Traditional approaches are based on the premise that food-and-wine matching is an art, not a science, and can be broadly traced back to three roots.

French *gastronomie* led the way in establishing conscious and specific choices for food-and-wine pairings, particularly with the birth of *haute cuisine*. Escoffier, the highly influential French chef born in the mid 19th century, could be described as the father of food-and-wine pairing, but it was French-born wine merchant, gourmet, and prolific author André SIMON who turned it into a pursuit, famously saying, 'Food without wine is a corpse; wine without food is a ghost. United and well matched, they are as body and soul: living partners.'

Some regions, especially in Europe, have deeply entwined relationships between their local culinary traditions and their locally produced wines which have been embedded in the culture for centuries. This has informed a 'local wine with local food' mantra that inspires pairings such as Loire goat's cheese with Pouilly-Fumé, or lamb chops with rioja.

Two other old and long-held adages, 'white wine with fish and red wine with meat' and (attributed to British wine merchants) 'buy on apple, sell on cheese', formed the foundation for wine-pairing 'rules' which governed thinking for much of the 20th century. The first was based on a valid principle of matching the weight, power, and flavour intensity of the food with the weight, power, and intensity of the wine; however, it is a generalization that ignores many other factors. The second was also based on sound fact: that sweet, high-acid foods can make wine taste thin and tart, while oily, salty foods such as cheese coat the mouth and can flatter or even mask tartness or thinness in a wine.

But, as Hanni points out, wine-and-food matching is an ongoing process of sensory adaptation. If a sensory message to the brain is constantly repeated (such as the taste of sourness in food), then it will suppress our sensitivity to the source of stimulation, making the wine that follows taste less sour.

Current interest in food-and-wine pairings can probably be traced to the United States, where it became a subject of intense scrutiny in the 1980s as wine producers, under pressure from so-called neo-Prohibitionists, sought to distance wine from drinks consumed principally for their alcohol content by putting it firmly on the dining table. The increasingly important role of professional SOMMELIER has contributed to a certain reverence for the subject. It has also led to a reactionary school of thought which insists that there is no such thing as food-and-wine matching—that you can and should drink any wine with any food, and the only thing that matters is that the wine suits your mood and your preferences.

One of the biggest changes over the last three decades has been a surge in wine-related scientific research in how we taste and smell and in the molecules and compounds that create flavours and TEXTURES. Spearheaded by neuroscientists such as Gordon M. Shepherd, bioengineers and food chemists such as Bernard Lahouisse and François Benzi, sommeliers such as François Chartier and the late Juli Soler, and chefs such as Ferran Adrià and Heston Blumenthal, the art of food-and-wine pairing has turned into a science.

Although it has long been known that there are certain foods which have very specific effects on wine, scientists are discovering that there are others which stimulate physiological and chemical changes in the sensory receptors of the mouth and the brain and change the way we perceive flavour and texture. For example, chemical compounds such as capsaicin in chilli and allicin in raw garlic stimulate the receptors in our mouth that detect heat and pain, which is why chilli and raw garlic 'burn'. When these receptors are activated, wine feels colder, tannins feel more ASTRINGENT, and we are less able to perceive fruit in wine. Sweetness and carbon-dioxide bubbles provide sensory distraction from the pain, which is why sparkling wines and off-dry wines are often recommended as good companions for spicy food.

Research also shows that flavour molecules are subject to synthetic processing—in other words, they interact with each other. Not only are there synergies and reactions between flavour molecules that can result in a totally different flavours, but the matrix of water, air, alcohol, fat, and protein through which we taste and process them by chewing, sipping, and swallowing profoundly affects perception, as does temperature. Aromas and other matrix molecules work like building blocks – they can enhance, amplify, transform, depress or cancel out other aromatic molecules. All this points to evidence that bringing food and wine together in the mouth, or even consuming them one after another, can trigger changes in flavour, texture, and perception that can alter the overall tasting experience. This helps us to understand why some combinations are so much better or worse than others. Ongoing studies by Lahousse, Coucquyt, and Chartier, among others, are exploring the synergies of flavour compounds not only to understand the science behind why classic pairings such as Cabernet Sauvignon with lamb work so well but also to create new, creative pairings by linking foods and wines that contain the same or similar molecular compound components and therefore result in flavour tonality when put together. For example, the nutty-, caramel-, curry-smelling SOTOLON found in VIN JAUNE, SHERRY, and SAUTERNES is also in fenugreek seeds (used in many curries), soy sauce, dried mushrooms, and maple syrup. Chartier suggests pairing curry with Sauternes.

Perfect matches, however, are unlikely for several reasons. We all have individual odour-perception thresholds, and studies show that of our 400 olfactory receptors, approximately one-third of them differ from person to person. In addition, our gender, age, state of health, and cultural conditioning also affect the way we taste. One person's perfect pairing may not suit the next person. More recently, scientists and psychologists have become interested in our multisensory experience of tasting, some suggesting that how well a dish goes with a wine might be as much affected by our senses of hearing, touch, and sight as by taste and smell. Playing different music, for example, may affect the way we experience how well a wine goes with a meal.

When it comes to specific combinations of food and wine, as well as general guidelines, it is useful to be aware of what Moore refers to as 'game-changer' ingredients. As well as chilli and garlic mentioned above, she includes lemon and vinegar for their piercing acidity, which can distort the taste of low-acid wines. If vinegar or lemon dominate the dish, choose a wine with high acidity. Herbs and spices can also alter the synergy of an ingredient or a dish with wine, depending on the intensity of the herb/spice and the amount used in a dish. Eugenol in cinnamon, clove, and nutmeg; piperine in black pepper; zingerone in ginger; allyl isothiocyanate in mustard, wasabi and horseradish; and sanshool in Sichuan pepper all stimulate the trigeminal nerve one way or another and in high-enough concentration may affect the perception of wine drunk at the same time.

Globe artichokes contain a substance called cynarin which is thought to inhibit the sweet receptors of the mouth. A mouthful of liquid such as water or wine removes the inhibition and makes the liquid taste metallically sweet. Suggested pairings are white wines with some astringency (such as SKIN-FERMENTED or ORANGE WINES) or bitterness.

A broad framework for food-and-wine pairing is more useful than rules or specifics. In fact, many clichéd wine–food suggestions are unhelpful. For example, a recommended pairing of Gewürztraminer with Asian food ignores the staggering breadth of Asian cuisine – and surely stems from the linguistic, not gastronomic, fact that Gewürz means 'spice'. However, a few simple principles can be relied on, as follows.

Salt reduces the impact of acidity, so salty food tends to be better with high-acid wines than low-acid wines.

Salt accentuates the flavours in sweet things (e.g. salted caramel), so salty foods such a cheeses can be very good with sweet wines.

Acidity in food has the impact of making a wine taste less acidic, so pairing a high-acid dish with a low-acid wine, even a balanced one, can make the wine taste flabby and flat. High-acid wines are best with foods strongly influenced by vinegar or sharp citrus.

Sweet food can make wines taste bitter and sour. Pair sweet foods with a wine that is a little sweeter than the food. Savoury dishes with a touch of sweetness, such as Moroccan pastilla, are often best paired with off-dry wines such as a Kabinett Riesling.

Humans are more sensitive to bitterness than to any other taste, and it is thought that there are five or six different types of bitter. Very bitter foods, such as chicory or some olive oils, can make a smooth, fruity wine taste too sweet. But in the kitchen, bitter ingredients are often balanced out in a dish by acidity, sweetness, fat or salt—so the same principle can be applied by pairing a primarily bitter dish with wines that are either bitter themselves (Italian wines often have bitterness), acidic, salty (such as coastal-vineyard Albariño), a little sweet (off-dry Riesling), or richly textured from lees or tannins.

Umami, that deeply savoury taste found in ingredients such as parmesan, yeast, soy sauce, dashi, anchovies, and tomatoes, tends to be complemented by sweetness, bright flavours, acidity, bitterness, and more umami—think of how well a rich, sweet, acidic tomato sauce goes with fresh basil, olives, capers, and chicken or meatballs. Umami therefore goes well with many wine styles: fruity, acidic, herbal, bitter, dry, savoury or sweet.

There is a theory that fat is the sixth sense of taste, and it is understood that we taste wine differently when paired with fatty foods. But fat is complicated because fatty foods not only activate the fatty-acid receptors on our tongues but also usually come with salt or sweetness (activating those receptors), plus they have the textural impact of coating our mouths. In addition, there are flavour compounds that are more fat-soluble, so fat can change the flavour of a wine in our mouths. It is widely accepted that fatty foods are best paired with wines that have good acidity or texture (tannins).

A final rule of thumb is the use of bridging ingredients. Roast lamb with a tart, green sauce of lemon and fresh herbs would be fine with an ASSYRTIKO instead of a red wine. Salmon rubbed with Creole spices and grilled could be served with a fruity Merlot; poaching it and dressing it with hollandaise sauce and paired white burgundy would be perfect; and salmon yakitori calls for a fruity Pinot Noir or a fino sherry.

T.C.

Chartier, F., *Taste Buds and Molecules* (2010).
Coucquyt, P., et al., *The Art & Science of Foodpairing* (2020).
Goode, J., *I Taste Red* (2016).
Hanni, T., *The Cause and Effect of Wine and Food* (1991).
Moore, V., *The Wine Dine Dictionary* (2017).
Shepherd, G. M., *Neurogastronomy* (2013).
Shepherd, G. M., *Neuroenology* (2017).
www.matchingfoodandwine.com

foot treading, traditional method of CRUSHING only rarely found outside Portugal's DOURO Valley, where it is still used for the production of some of the finest ports. CHAPOUTIER of Hermitage and some BURGUNDY producers also use feet for breaking up the CAP of their top red unfortified wines.

Forastera, simple white wine grape from the island of ISCHIA near Naples.

Forcallat Tinta, blending grape grown on 360 ha/890 acres of CASTILLA-LA MANCHA, VALENCIA, and Murcia, making curious-smelling, light-coloured red wine.

forests, by supplying wood of a certain sort, have an important impact on the character and flavour of wine made using COOPERAGE made from that wood. See WOOD TYPES and OAK.

Forez, Côtes du. A range of GRANITIC and VOLCANIC hills between the upper reaches of the Loire River and Lyons in eastern France give their name to light, vigorous red and rosé wines made, like BEAUJOLAIS, from the GAMAY grape. The wines, designed for early drinking, may taste reminiscent of those of the Côte ROANNAISE to the north, although the region's higher elevation makes for a slightly less dependable climate. Full AOC status was granted to Côtes du Forez in 2000. Wines made outside the AOC regulations can take the IGP Urfé. Plantings had fallen to below 100 ha/250 acres by the early 2010s, but a new generation of winegrowers brought it up to 150 ha by 2020.

fortification, the practice of adding spirits, usually **grape spirit**, to wine to ensure microbiological stability, thereby adding

ALCOHOLIC STRENGTH and precluding any further FERMENTATION.

The principle behind this addition of alcohol is that most BACTERIA and strains of YEAST are rendered impotent, unable to react with sugar or other wine constituents, in solutions containing more than 16–18% alcohol, depending on the strain of yeast.

The stage at which spirit is added has enormous implications for the style of fortified wine produced. The earlier it is added in the fermentation process, the sweeter the resulting wine will be. VINS DE LIQUEUR such as PINEAU DES CHARENTES, for example, are simply blends of sweet, unfermented, or hardly fermented grape juice with grape spirit, known as *mistelles* in France (see MISTELA). An even stronger charge of alcohol is added before fermentation to a significant proportion of the rich grape juice used in the production of Australia's TOPAQUE AND MUSCAT. For most port-style wines (including the sweeter styles of MADEIRA) and for all VINS DOUX NATURELS, fortification takes place during fermentation. Much of the natural grape sugar is retained by arresting fermentation before its completion, thereby boosting alcoholic strength to a pre-ordained level: usually 18–20% in PORT but 15–16% in most vins doux naturels. In the making of SHERRY, similar wines such as MONTILLA, and the drier styles of MADEIRA, spirit is added to dry, fully fermented wine only at the end of fermentation. Any sweetness in such wines is usually due to a pre-bottling addition of sweetening agent, often itself a mixture of grape juice and spirit (see MISTELA, PX).

The spirit used for fortification comes from a variety of sources and could be based on grapes, sugar beet, cane sugar, agricultural by-products or even petroleum. Local regulations specify the types of spirit allowed for a given fortified wine, and only grape spirit is allowed for fortified wines of any quality. Carbon dating usefully allows the immediate detection of petroleum-based spirit in any wine, however.

The method of DISTILLATION of the spirit plays a part possibly even more important than its source. The most neutral spirits are the products of a continuous still, which contain a minimum of flavour congeners (the impurities which contribute to the character of a spirit) and tend to be used in the fortification of wines that are designed for early consumption and deliberately exhibit the characteristics of the base wine (the MUSCATS of southern France, for example). Spirits produced by pot-still distillation on the other hand are much more violently flavoured and are rarely used to fortify wines.

A.D.W. & J.E.H.

fortified wines are those which have been subject to FORTIFICATION and therefore include SHERRY, PORT, MADEIRA, VERMOUTH, MÁLAGA, MONTILLA-MORILES, MARSALA, TOPAQUE AND MUSCAT, VINS DOUX NATURELS, and several strictly local specialities. Liquids such as VINS DE LIQUEUR (see also MISTELA) made by adding spirit to grape juice rather than wine are not, strictly, fortified wines. Practically all warm wine regions (see AUSTRALIA, CALIFORNIA, CYPRUS, and SOUTH AFRICA, for example) make some sort of fortified wine, often in the image of port and sherry even if they are not allowed to use those protected names within Europe. It is an almost invariable rule that anywhere hot enough to produce good fortified wine is too hot to provide the ideal climate for its consumption. See also LIQUEUR WINE.

Fort Ross-Seaview, California AVA in the Sonoma Coastal Mountains. See SONOMA.

foudre, French for FUDER, commonly encountered in ALSACE.

Foundation Plant Services (**FPS**), a self-supporting service department of the University of California at DAVIS which produces, tests, maintains, and distributes disease-tested plant propagation material. It also provides plant importation, quarantine, and testing services.

fourth growth. See the CLASSIFICATION of Bordeaux.

foxy, usually pejorative tasting term for the highly distinctive flavour of many wines, particularly red wines, made from AMERICAN VINES and AMERICAN HYBRIDS, vine varieties developed from both American and European species of the VITIS genus, particularly *Vitis labrusca*. (Wines made from many other hybrids—SEYVAL and NORTON, for example—are completely free of **foxiness**.) The CONCORD grape, widely planted in NEW YORK State, is one of the most heavily scented, reeking of something closer to animal fur than fruit, flowers, or any other aroma associated with fine wine, although the candy-like aroma is, incidentally, quite close to that of the tiny wild strawberry or *fraise des bois*. The compound chiefly responsibe for this aroma in NIAGARA grapes is 2-aminoacetophenone, while methyl anthranilate does the job in Concords. Earlier harvesting or long CASK AGEING reduces some of Concord's foxy characteristics.

H.L. & B.G.C.

fractional blending, prosaic English name for the labour-intensive SOLERA system of maintaining consistency of a blended wine, particularly SHERRY, over many years.

franc de pied, French for UNGRAFTED.

France, the country that produces more fine wine than any other, and in which wine is so firmly embedded in the culture that such French people as are interested in wine have a quasi-spiritual relationship with it. In 2021, France held on to its claim of largest wine consumer in the EU (and second largest in the world, after the United States), although per capita wine consumption has fallen, from over 100 l a year in 1977 to under 50 l by the early 21st century, thanks to social changes and increased restrictions on advertising alcohol and on drunk driving. By the end of the 20th century, France's wine export market was also facing stiff competition from other wine-producing countries, although while third in export volume worldwide in 2021, it remains number one in terms of value, pulling in a record high of €15.5 billion according to FEVS, the Federation of French Wine and Spirits Exporters.

France is second only to Spain in land under vine, although the total area planted with vines has shrunk considerably since the late 1970s (see EU and its VINE-PULL SCHEME) down from 1.23 million ha/3.04 million acres to just under 800,000 ha (including vines dedicated to brandies and TABLE GRAPES) by the early 2010s, where it has held fairly steady since. Average annual wine production fell from 65 million hl in the late 1980s to under 50 million hl in the 2010s; in 2021, total production was 37.6 million hl, although that particular year was one of the smallest harvests since 2000, 14% lower than its previous five-year average.

There are few wine producers anywhere who would not freely admit that they have been influenced by the great wines of BORDEAUX, BURGUNDY, CHAMPAGNE, or the RHÔNE (see map). Other qualitatively significant wine regions, perhaps better appreciated within France than abroad, include ALSACE (for historical details of which see GERMAN HISTORY), BEAUJOLAIS, CHABLIS, JURA, LOIRE, PROVENCE, SAVOIE, and SOUTH WEST FRANCE. France's most important wine region by far in terms of quantity has long been the LANGUEDOC, plus ROUSSILLON to the immediate south, but vine-pull schemes have shrunk the regions' vineyard area and much improved the average quality of wine produced there. The Mediterranean island of CORSICA is also under French jurisdiction, although it shares many characteristics with the Italian island of SARDINIA.

Although the first instance of geographical DELIMITATION was in Portugal's DOURO Valley, France is the birthplace of the widespread application of the notion that geography, or TERROIR, is fundamental in shaping the character and quality of a wine. This resulted in the early 20th century in the much-copied AOC, or *Appellation Contrôlée* system. Its governing body is INAO. AOC wines are sold under the geographical name of the appellation rather than by vine variety, in contrast to the substantially VARIETAL wines of the NEW WORLD. AOC wines, considered within the EU's PDO category, represent an increasing proportion of all French wines, about 58% by 2018; IGPs make up another 34%. The rest is either distilled into cognac, armagnac, or other brandies or sold as VIN DE FRANCE. This category, created in 2009, includes very basic wines as well as an increasing number of high-quality wines deliberately made outside the restrictions of AOC and IGP rules. This is also the fate of wines rejected by AOC tasting panels.

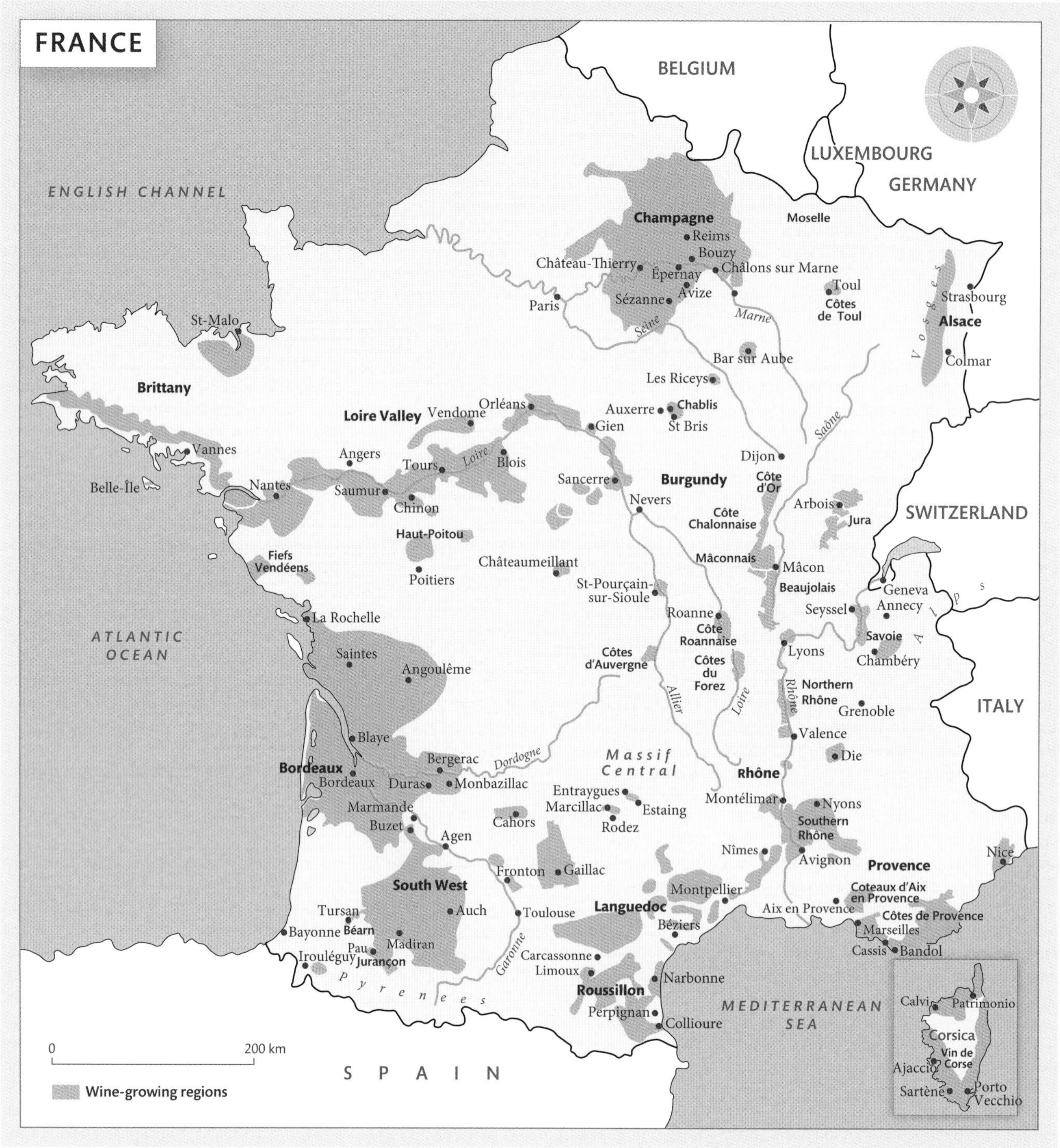

Curiously, and perhaps because wine is so deeply entrenched in French history and culture, wine CONNOISSEURSHIP and to a certain extent the wine TRADE are not as evolved in France as, for example, in Australia, Belgium, Great Britain, Switzerland, and the United States. Although things are slowly changing, the average French citizen has bought and drunk little other than the wine produced closest to him or her, whether geographically or by virtue of family or friendship. This has tended to stifle the development of wine retailing, although the number of specialist wine MERCHANTS, known here as *cavistes*, has increased significantly since the early 1980s. As might be expected in a country associated with so many forms of gastronomic excellence, wine appreciation in France is closely tethered to the table. Wine is rarely drunk without food, and France's chefs and SOMMELIERS have been regarded as the rightful repositories of wine knowledge.

Although France is the world's principal wine exporter, it is also a major wine importer. Wine has been imported ever since Massilia was settled by the Greeks (see below), but it was the development of the Languedoc as a virtual factory for particularly light red wines at the end of the 19th and the beginning of the 20th centuries that meant vast quantities of strong, deep-coloured red wines had to be imported for BLENDING, from North African colonies initially and subsequently from southern Italy and Spain.

France is so important as a role model to the world of wine that many terms used internationally are French in origin (BLANC DE BLANCS and VERAISON are just two examples). France is recognized the world over as a centre of wine research and ACADEME and has benefited ever since the time of Colbert in the late 17th century from the country's ability to identify and solve potential problems on a national level (see OAK). The OENOLOGICAL and viticultural faculties of the universities of BORDEAUX and MONTPELLIER have long enjoyed international prestige, and considerable viticultural research emanates from INRAE stations.

One of France's great commercial strengths in recent years has been that it is the world's prime source of oak for top-quality wine and brandy COOPERAGE. France is the world's leading exporter of wine BARRELS.

History

Around 600 BCE, Greek immigrants arrived from Phocaea in ANATOLIA and founded Massalia (Marseilles) as a Greek city (see ancient GREECE). One of the colonists' importations was viticulture, although in 2013 Patrick McGovern found evidence that they were probably preceded by Etruscans (see ORIGINS OF VINICULTURE). In the 2nd century BCE, the settlement, now known as Massilia, had become vital to the Romans, by then a major power (see ancient ROME), if they were to safeguard their trading route with Saguntum (modern Sagunto, near Valencia in Spain). When Massilia was attacked first by the Ligurians and then by the Celtic tribes of the Allobroges and the Arverni (of modern AUVERGNE), self-interest made the Romans take on the defence of the city. As a result they gained a new province, named at first Provincia (modern PROVENCE) and later, with the foundation of the Roman city of Narbo (modern Narbonne) in 118 BCE, Gallia Narbonensis. Massilia remained Greek until 49 BCE.

In the eyes of the Greek colonists, vines grew where olives and figs grew: the commercial exploitation of the three together had long been characteristic of Mediterranean agriculture, so it did not occur to a Mediterranean people that the vine could be cultivated further north than the olive and the fig. The wines of Massilia were available in Rome, but they were cheap and nasty. Even before Caesar's conquest of Gaul in 51 BCE, the Gauls had consumed Italian wine in prodigious quantities, as the evidence from AMPHORAE found in France shows. The Greek geographer Strabo, who finished his *Geography* in 7 BCE, said that Massilia and Narbo produced the same fruits as Italy but that the rest of Gaul was too far north for the olive, the fig, and the vine (4. 2. 1). His statement may have been too sweeping, however, and in the 1st century CE good wine certainly did come from Gaul. PLINY tells us in his *Natural History* that in Vienna (modern Vienne in the RHÔNE Valley) the Allobroges produced RESINATED WINES which were a source of national pride and for which they charged high prices (14. 57). For more details, see GAUL.

Thus the first French wine of note was a Rhône wine. Yet at the same time or earlier the inhabitants of Gallia Narbonensis may themselves have taken the vine beyond the familiar territory of the olive and the fig, to GAILLAC in modern SOUTH WEST FRANCE. Archaeological evidence shows that in the second half of the reign of the Emperor Augustus (he was Imperator from 27 BCE to 14 CE), amphorae were being made in large numbers in workshops near Gaillac and near Béziers in the LANGUEDOC. This suggests that they were needed for wine that was grown there and not imported. The RIVERS Tarn and GARONNE would have provided convenient transport to the Atlantic coast, where BORDEAUX was already a trading post. Since these wines are not mentioned by any classical author, they probably did not reach Rome, unlike the wines of Vienne.

Gaillac and Vienne are beyond the northern limit for olive trees, but they do sustain another tree that is considered characteristic of Mediterranean vegetation: the evergreen oak, QUERCUS *ilex*. Where the evergreen oak grows, the climate is hot enough to produce a good grape harvest every year without fail. Yet viticulture advanced further north, away from the evergreen oak, to where the success of the vintage was no longer guaranteed. Bordeaux and BURGUNDY were next in line; by the 3rd century CE, wine was grown in both regions, despite the possibility of cold, wet summers when the grapes might not ripen fully. Yet even if the harvest failed occasionally, the demand for wine was such that the expansion of viticulture made economic sense.

The Romans had regarded the CELTS as drunks and, hence, a source of great profit—immoderate fools who drank wine unmixed with water until they fell into a stupor. But when the drunken Celts started growing their own wine, its reputation was soon to surpass that of the Italian wines that they had once imported. After Bordeaux and Burgundy came the LOIRE and the Île-de-France (the PARIS basin including CHAMPAGNE). By the 6th century CE, even the west of BRITTANY had vines, and wine was grown further north than it is now, well north of Paris.

As the Roman Empire disintegrated, Gaul ceased to be a Roman province and was overrun by Germanic invaders. The Visigoths, the Burgundians, and the Franks established kingdoms in Gaul; eventually, Aquitaine and Burgundy were subjected to Frankish rule. Under the Romans, the Gauls had been governed from the south; the Franks had come from the north, and Clovis, the first of the Merovingian kings (481–511), established Paris as the capital city of a kingdom that hardly extended further than the Île-de-France. Under CHARLEMAGNE and his heirs, the royal court's principal seats were Aachen (Aix-la-Chapelle) and Paris. Hence political power, and the wealth that went with it, were concentrated in the north. In the Mediterranean, wine was part of everyday life, but in Paris and Aachen, on the northernmost limits of viticulture, wine was a luxury item, and from a luxury item it became a status symbol. Also, because Gaul was largely Christian by the 6th century, the Church's requirements added impetus to northern viticulture (see EUCHARIST). Monasteries and churches needed wine; local magnates, both lay and spiritual, wanted good wine.

McGovern, P. E., 'The beginning of viniculture in France', *The Proceedings of the National Academy of Sciences USA*, 110/25 (2013), 10147–52.

Monastic influence

Monasteries had their own vineyards (see MONKS AND MONASTERIES and BURGUNDY), and so, often, did cathedrals. From the Carolingian era onwards, lay viticulture generally used the system of 'complant', which meant that a winegrower would approach an owner of uncultivated land with an offer to plant it. Since it takes about five years for new vines to start yielding a decent quantity of fruit, the grower would be given that length of time to work the vineyard; after that, half the land would revert to the owner, while the vines on the other half would become the possession of the grower, on condition that part of the harvest, or sometimes a monetary payment, be given every year in perpetuity. The Loire wine QUARTS DE CHAUME, for instance, owes its name to the complant mode of ownership and production: the *quart*, or fourth, refers to the share the vigneron owed the landowner (in 1440, the Abbey of Ronceray d'Angers); and *chaume* refers to an uncultivated plot that is to be planted with vines. As labour grew more expensive, the conditions became more favourable to the grower: in the course of the 13th century, the owner would often no longer reclaim half of the property, but the grower, and the grower's children and children's children after, would continue to make their annual payments in wine or money. The system made it possible for wild country to be colonized and cultivated at no expense to the landowner: in this way, the new winegrowing region of Poitou (see LA ROCHELLE) was planted so efficiently in the 12th and 13th centuries. The advantage to growers was that they were not serfs, tied to the land, but free, entitled to a large share of what they produced. It was therefore in their interest to make wine for which they could get a good price; nevertheless the owner exercised ultimate control, for the decisions of how and with what grapes to plant the vineyard was the owner's, as was the right to terminate the contract and evict the vigneron if the wine was not good enough.

In the Middle Ages, wine was France's chief export product, and the reasons why certain nations drink some wines in preference to others go back to this period. The English drink CLARET because BORDEAUX was at one time governed by the English crown and later remained the largest supplier of wine to England. The Scots drink claret because of the Auld Alliance with France against England. The Flemish and the Dutch have traditionally bought wines of Burgundy because Flanders and the southern part of the Netherlands were part of the dukedom of Burgundy and Burgundy's trade routes were mostly overland to the north. But transporting wooden BARRELS of wine along bumpy roads was difficult and expensive: whether a region exported a large share of its wine or produced wine mainly for its own consumption depended on its proximity to navigable RIVERS rather than on the quality of its wines. Apart from its trade with the north, which did not develop until the 15th century, Burgundy did not export much wine, whereas regions accessible by water, such as the LOIRE, the Île-de-France around PARIS, and GASCONY, did. The chief ports were LA ROCHELLE, Rouen, and Bordeaux respectively, with Bordeaux serving both the Bordeaux area and the HAUT-PAYS.

The ships used to transport wine before the 12th century were longboats like the Viking ships. But in the 12th century, the new ports of La Rochelle and Gravelines (on the English Channel near St-Omer), as well as the new Flemish ports of Nieuwpoort (near Ypres) and Damme (near Bruges), adopted a new type of ship, the cog. The cog was a broadly built ship, with a roundish prow and stern, more manœuvrable than the old kind and specifically designed for carrying freight. Its capacity was far larger than that of the old longboat, and soon all other ports started using it as a more efficient way of transporting wine. The cog doubled up as a warship if need arose.

The unit in which wine was measured, the TONNEAU, derived from Bordeaux. A tonneau, or wooden barrel, could hold 252 old wine gallons, or 900 l/238 US gal. A Paris tonneau was 800 l, but, because of the prominence of Gascon merchants in London and English merchants in Bordeaux, the Bordeaux measure became the standard. Many cogs could hold as many as 200 tonneaux; in practice, a barrel containing 900 l was too heavy to handle, and casks half or one-quarter the size were used. Such was the importance of the medieval wine trade that—from being the space occupied by a tun of wine—a tonneau, or ton in English, became the unit used for measuring the carrying capacity of any ship, whatever its load. H.M.W.

Dion, R., *Histoire de la vigne et du vin en France* (1959).

Duby, G. (ed.), *Histoire de la France rurale*, tome 1 (1975).

Lachiver, M., *Vins, vignes, vignerons* (1988).

Modern history

The social turmoil of the French Revolution at the end of the 18th century made few important changes to the patterns of wine production (although it did engender an entirely new class of consumers and new styles of *restauration* for them). Until the middle of the 19th century, the vine was cultivated much more widely in France than it is today, and such now-abandoned areas as, for example, the Côtes d'AUVERGNE on the Massif Central, Paris, and the MOSELLE were flourishing wine regions. As communications improved, the patterns of the wine trade changed, although Bordeaux continued to operate with a certain degree of autonomy, thanks to its geographical position and long-established trading links with northern Europe, first ENGLAND and then the DUTCH WINE TRADE. The 17th and 18th centuries saw an explosion of interest in wine production in the Gironde, and by the mid 19th century, when the world's most famous wine CLASSIFICATION was formalized at a magnificent exhibition in Paris, the great CHÂTEAUX of the MÉDOC were enjoying a period of prosperity that would not be rivalled until the 1980s. Wine continued to be important to the Burgundian economy, and French wine was recognized throughout the civilized world as one of the cornerstones of civilization itself. CHAPTAL had devised ways of improving overall wine quality (for ADULTERATION AND FRAUD was rife in the immediate aftermath of the Revolution), and France was beginning to produce its own wine experts such as the widely travelled and independently minded JULLIEN. A historian might say that a catastrophe to end this golden age was inevitable.

In fact there was a series of catastrophes, all viticultural, which had devastating effects on both the quantity and quality of wine produced. Oidium, or POWDERY MILDEW, was the first of a succession of disastrous imports from North America, presumably the result of the 19th-century passion for collecting botanical specimens. Unlike European vines, most American vines are resistant to this FUNGAL DISEASE, and so it was not until it had been imported to Europe that its effects—of reducing quantity, quality, and colour—were noted, in 1852. The 1854 vintage in France was the smallest for more than 60 years. French vineyards were just returning to health, thanks to the development of SULFUR dusting, when another curious vine condition was noted: inexplicable debilitation and, eventually, death. The cause was a tiny aphid-like insect, PHYLLOXERA, which was to ravage the vineyards of the world but affected southern France first, causing the greatest commercial havoc there while a remedy was sought. Since phylloxera affects only the roots of vines, the only effective solution was eventually found to be to graft European vines on to resistant American ROOTSTOCKS. But the renewed importation of North American plant material seems to have brought with it two more deadly American fungal diseases: DOWNY MILDEW, whose effects on wine quality and quantity were first noted in 1878 and lasted until well into the 20th century; and BLACK ROT, which was evident from the mid 1880s.

It is hardly surprising therefore that French vignerons saw their salvation in planting HYBRIDS, vines with at least some genes from AMERICAN VINE SPECIES to provide a defence against these completely new and unforeseen hazards to one of France's greatest glories. First, after considerable debate, American hybrids were planted, followed by, in the early 20th century, so-called FRENCH HYBRIDS, the results of which tasted more like the European VITIS VINIFERA vines' produce.

There was such a crisis in wine quality in the late 19th century that the great scientist PASTEUR was asked to look into the matter, and the result was a giant step forward for the science of winemaking, in which France has long been at the forefront of research (see University of BORDEAUX in particular).

By the turn of the century, the plains of the LANGUEDOC had been transformed into a great factory producing light red for drinkers in northern France, now commercially accessible thanks to the development of the RAILWAYS. These light wines were given weight, alcohol, and colour by the produce of new vineyards in ALGERIA.

Two World Wars left France's wine business in serious need of reorganization. Vigorous efforts were made to uproot hybrids, and a thorough programme of research dedicated to the concept of wine quality was initiated both in universities (see ACADEME) and in specialized research institutes. In the second half of the 20th century France became the world's most thoroughly and harmoniously organized wine producer, with the development of the powers of the INAO and increasing emphasis on the importance of the AOC system for which it is responsible.

In the 21st century, however, the number of vignerons who feel limited by the dictates of the AOC system has grown considerably, as has the number of wines sold simply as a VIN DE FRANCE, many of them classed as NATURAL WINES.

Geography and climate

France does not have the monopoly on fine wine production, but its geographical position is such that it can produce wine from an exceptionally wide range of grape varieties with a good balance of sugar and acidity, although CLIMATE CHANGE is evident throughout the country. With wine regions lying between LATITUDES 42 and 49.5° N, France can provide the two most suitable environments identified in CLIMATE AND WINE QUALITY for growing grapes. In the south, the MEDITERRANEAN CLIMATE can be depended upon to ripen grapes fully, but not so fast that they do not have time to develop an interesting array of FLAVOUR COMPOUNDS and PHENOLICS. In the west, relatively high latitudes are tempered by the influence of the Atlantic's Gulf Stream. In the east, centuries of viticultural tradition have established what seem to be potentially perfect marriages between grape variety and particularly favoured terroir in the more CONTINENTAL climate of Burgundy, Alsace, and Champagne, France's most northerly wine region where, over the centuries, the ideal wine style has evolved to take advantage of the area's climate and special geology.

France also has a wide variety of SOIL TYPES, much charted and revered (although see GEOLOGY and SOIL AND WINE QUALITY for a discussion of the limited extent to which they may affect wine quality).

Vine-growing in modern France is concentrated in the south, but there are vineyards in all regions other than the most mountainous and the coolest, which excludes most of the Massif Central, the high-elevation mass in the middle of the country, much of the alpine region on the south-east, and the flat north-western sector closest to Great Britain. See map.

Vine varieties

France conducts a full agricultural census only every decade or so. The most recent was conducted in 2020, accounting for 364 varieties.

CARIGNAN was France's most planted vine variety for many decades, thanks to its ubiquity across Languedoc and Roussillon, but by the turn of the century Merlot had assumed this role, accounting for 114,785 ha/283,640 acres by 2020. Second most planted was the white grape UGNI BLANC, grown chiefly for distillation into brandy, with 92,514 ha, while red grapes GRENACHE and Syrah came in third and fourth, with 87,745 ha and 67,040 ha consecutively. Cabernet Sauvignon continued a long downward trend, falling from 53,400 ha in 2000 to 46,971 in 2020, just a little ahead of Chardonnay at 44,141 ha. Carignan now takes a distant eighth place, with 31,273 ha, even behind Cabernet Franc (32,282 ha) and Sauvignon Blanc (31,773 ha).

The HYBRIDS, so widely planted in the mid 20th century, are all but a distant memory, though climate change concerns have increased openness to NEW VARIETIES such as Arinarnoa and Marselan, crosses which were authorized for Bordeaux vineyards in 2021. (See also VIFA.)

More attention is also being paid to France's treasury of traditional INDIGENOUS VARIETIES, either imported as a result of shifting political power (many of France's most planted red varieties were originally Spanish) or those still to be found in limited quantity in SOUTH WEST FRANCE. They are less numerous than in ITALY, but that probably reflects France's national efficiency and centralism.

Viticulture

Most vineyards in France are immediately recognizably French. With its generally reliable rainfall and supply of soil water, northern France has the highest VINE DENSITY in the world, with up to 13,000 plants per ha, and the vines are typically planted in neat, low-trained rows, often using GUYOT systems of pruning and training (typically dictated by the detail of AOC regulations). French vignerons have in general had centuries to match cultural practices to local conditions, although in the early 20th century many less suitable terrains were planted in an extension of classic zones. IRRIGATION is usually unnecessary in northern and western France and is strictly, if sometimes only theoretically, controlled in the south. The relatively humid climate of western France means, however, that frequent SPRAYING against FUNGAL DISEASES is often necessary. In the early 1990s, concern was increasingly expressed at the use of AGROCHEMICALS in many French wine regions, particularly Burgundy, where ORGANIC VITICULTURE and BIODYNAMIC VITICULTURE is increasingly common. Other common viticultural hazards are FROST in the north, HAIL in Burgundy, and DROUGHT in the south, with both of the last two on the increase. Crop levels can vary considerably since the weather during FLOWERING is by no means predictably fine; WINTER FREEZE has been known to kill a substantial proportion of vines, as in 1956; and spring frosts can seriously affect total national production, as in 1991 and 2021.

French viticultural research is of a high level and coordinated nationally under the auspices of INRAE, which has stations all over the country. Many of the world's vine-growers regard French NURSERIES as their prime source of planting material, and there has been considerable work on CLONAL SELECTION.

France's vine-growers are probably the most regulated and restricted in the world, however. For all wines other than the basic VSIG, dates of HARVEST are limited by regional annual decree, and YIELDS are minutely regulated. A low yield is generally regarded as the safest prerequisite for wine quality, but in the 1980s the maximum basic yield allowed by AOC regulations was routinely increased by a so-called *plafond limite de classement*, or PLC, supplement often as high as 20%. Yields are now set annually. Since the late 1980s, CROP THINNING has been the norm for many quality-conscious producers. The 1990s saw the introduction of GRAPE SORTING tables to increase wine QUALITY. MECHANIZATION was introduced to lowlier appellations in the late 1980s and 1990s. PRECISION VITICULTURE techniques are in use at the better, larger properties.

Winemaking

In many wine regions, TRADITION has long been as important as SCIENCE in determining winemaking techniques, although France's winemakers can and do draw on many centres of OENOLOGICAL academe for instruction and research (see ACADEME for a list of those described in further detail in this *Companion*).

Techniques vary enormously in France's hundreds of thousands of *caves*, but in general—and in sharp contrast to the New World—PROTECTIVE JUICE HANDLING and an obsession with winery HYGIENE are relatively rare. Mastery of MALOLACTIC CONVERSION and OAK AGEING, on the other hand, have long been taken for granted.

Part of French winemakers' easy relationship with BARREL MATURATION comes from the fact that France is the centre of the world's wine COOPERAGE industry.

France is also the birthplace of CHAPTALIZATION, and a high proportion of its wines have depended on some degree of ENRICHMENT, although CLIMATE CHANGE suggests that France may need to introduce more widespread ACIDIFICATION too, forbidden for wines that have been chaptalized. Another winemaking practice once regarded as quintessentially foreign in France, the use of OAK CHIPS, is now tolerated for IGP and VSIG wines. Further up the quality ladder there is some experimentation with CONCENTRATION techniques.

Less than one-quarter of all wine consumed in France is white, and in the hot summers of the south of France rosé is more likely to be consumed than white, as a sort of red for high temperatures.

Wine quality categories

Of the average French harvest, wines from the most revered quality wine category AOC represent the most significant proportion, while the most basic wine for immediate consumption, that classified as Vin de France, or VSIG, is made in ever-decreasing quantity. In between these two categories lies the category of IGP wines. The remaining proportion of an average year's French wine production is designed for DISTILLATION into brandy such as cognac and armagnac.

For details of the history, climate, geography, vine varieties planted, and wines produced, see under regional, or even more geographically specific, names, including PARIS. For individual regions, see also ALSACE, BEAUJOLAIS, BORDEAUX, BUGEY, BURGUNDY, CHABLIS, CHAMPAGNE, CORSICA, JURA, LANGUEDOC, LOIRE, PROVENCE, RÉUNION, RHÔNE, ROUSSILLON, SAVOIE, and SOUTH WEST FRANCE. See also VIN and immediately following entries, as well as CRÉMANT for some of France's better-quality sparkling wines.

Bettane, M., and Desseauve, T., *Le Classement* (annually).
Jefford, A., *The New France* (2002).
Johnson, H., *The Story of Wine* (1989).
Johnson, H., and Robinson, J., *The World Atlas of Wine* (8th edn, 2019).
Le Guide Hachette des Vins (annually).
www.vins-france.com
www.inao.gouv.fr

Franciacorta, wine region in the hills immediately east of Brescia, with a relatively short history of producing TRADITIONAL METHOD sparkling wine from Chardonnay and Pinot Noir with some Pinot Bianco. Its name is a corruption of the medieval Francae Curtes, 'Curtes' meaning 'communes' and 'Francae' meaning 'exempt of taxes', referring to the region's privileged position at the time.

Spread over 19 villages, the area is also demarcated as DOC Curtefranca (formerly known as Terre di Franciacorta) for still white and red wines made from INTERNATIONAL VARIETIES. In the 1980s and 1990s these answers to Bordeaux and Burgundy, often treated to lavish amounts of new OAK, sold well, but this international style has largely lost its economic relevance. Franciacorta's history begins in 1961 with the release of the first traditional-method sparkling wine ever to be produced in the region, by the house of Guido Berlucchi.

Franciacorta modelled itself in both style and nomenclature closely on CHAMPAGNE, a strategy that has become an obstacle given the competition on the international stage and is not made any easier by the Prosecco's enormous success and much lower price point. Encouraged by the largest Franciacorta players, grape-growers began planting vines in the plains, which has led to overproduction and lower grape prices. The area under vine has grown from 800 ha/ 2,000 acres in the late 20th century to 2,900 ha/ 7,166 acres in 2020, producing 16 million bottles of sparkling wine annually.

CLIMATE CHANGE is perceived by the region as another challenge, with a recent solution being the legal inclusion of Erbamat, a neutral, low-alcohol, high-acidity variety. There is also a trend in zero-DOSAGE wines, made with no added sugar, mostly pioneered by producers working in ORGANIC or BIODYNAMIC VITICULTURE.

Franciacorta comes in various styles, almost all mimicking Champagne, if a little stricter in its ageing requirement of 18 months on the LEES for non-vintage wines. Rosé and Satèn, a Franciacorta bottled at lower pressure and hence creamier in texture, must age for 24 months; vintage Franciacorta at least 30; and the rarely seen Riserva for 60 months. W.S.

www.franciacorta.net

Franconia, English name for the German wine region FRANKEN, and a local name for the BLAUFRÄNKISCH grape variety in FRIULI in northern Italy.

Francs, village which gives its name to the small Francs Côtes de Bordeaux appellation on the RIGHT BANK between ST-ÉMILION and BERGERAC. The original settlement took its name from a detachment of Franks sent there by Clovis after defeating the Visigoths (see FRANCE, history). The wines have considerably more personality than regular BORDEAUX AOC, and the area's revival in the 1980s owed much to the Belgian Thienpont family (also associated with LE PIN and Vieux Château Certan). In 2020, 395 ha/976 acres of vineyard were producing sturdy Merlot-based reds on high clay-limestone slopes, many of which enjoy a favourable west/southwest exposure. Tiny amounts of Sémillon-based white, both dry and sweet, were also made in memory of a style once traditional for this area. For more detail, see BORDEAUX. J.R. & J.L.

Franken, known in English as **Franconia**, distinctive wine region in central GERMANY, with a total of 6,124 ha/15,133 acres of vineyard in 2019. Severe winters and autumns as well as spring FROSTS are among the challenges that result in some of Germany's most variable YIELDS, but this has not deterred a near tripling of total vineyard area since the 1960s. The features for which Franken wine is best known are arguably neither its grapes nor its distinctive soils and wines but rather the fact that nearly all of it is marketed in squat, flattened BOCKSBEUTEL bottles at prices most German growers can only dream of; as well, most is consumed within the region itself.

While representing just under one-quarter of planted surface (as does MÜLLER-THURGAU), SILVANER—introduced here 350 years ago as 'Österreicher'—is nonetheless rightly considered Franken's flagship grape, yielding robust, ageworthy, and minerally complex results. RIESLING and PINOT NOIR (though confined to one western sector) also excel. Several of the many vine crosses prominent in mid 20th century Germany—notably BACCHUS, KERNER, SCHEUREBE, and RIESLANER—are, like Müller-Thurgau, more successful than usual in Franken, whose soils high in active LIME seem to tame these grapes' less appetizing characteristics. The traditional field blend of diverse, multicoloured varieties called Altfränkischer Satz, or Frentsch, is undergoing a promising revival. Dry wines have dominated in this region since the 1970s, when Germany's Riesling-centric growing regions were only moving in that direction. Nobly sweet elixirs are relatively rare but can be stunningly complex and long-lived, like their Riesling relatives in other parts of Germany.

South of the city of Aschaffenburg along the right bank of the Main, Franken's westernmost vineyards, collectively known as the Mainviereck, feature dramatically steep SANDSTONE terraces whose late 20th and early 21st century revival has resulted in some of Germany's most impressive Pinot Noirs (as well as distinctive Riesling), notably from the Schlossberg and Centgrafenberg vineyards of Klingenberg and Bürgstadt respectively. Some 25 km/16 miles east but still along the Main, vineyards around Marktheidenfeld mark the transition from Triassic sandstone to fossiliferous MUSCHELKALK, Riesling sharing space with Silvaner. Vineyards dominate the eastern half of a huge northerly bow inscribed by the Main, as well as a plunge to the south that embraces the city of Würzburg, whose Stein, Innere Leiste, and Pfülben vineyards are among Franken's most celebrated sources of Silvaner and (in rather austere renditions) Riesling. Eastern viticultural Franconia includes numerous smaller outposts, but many vineyards are near the Main. Eschendorf, not far west of Würzburg, is especially notable for its Lump vineyard, where Muschelkalk intersects with the distinctive Triassic MARL known as Keuper, a geological formation that dominates vineyards in the Steigerwald of Franken's southeast whose best-known wine village and site are, respectively, Iphofen with its Julius-Echter-Berg. D.S.

Frankland River GEOGRAPHICAL INDICATION within the Great Southern in WESTERN AUSTRALIA that stands out for top-quality Shiraz, Cabernet, and Grenache as well as dry RIESLING.

Frankovka, or **Frankovka Modrá**, Slovak synonym for the red BLAUFRÄNKISCH grape.

Franschhoek, or **Franschhoek Valley**, wine district in the Coastal Region of SOUTH AFRICA and home to many historic cellars. Established in the late 17th century to accommodate the influx of French Huguenots (the name means 'French Corner'), it is an important TOURISM centre within easy driving distance of Cape Town.

Fransdruif, or just **Frans**, traditional Afrikaans name, meaning 'French grape', for the PALOMINO FINO grape in South Africa.

Frappato, increasingly celebrated—and planted—Sicilian red grape variety which can add fruit and floral freshness to NERO D'AVOLA and NERELLO MASCALESE in the south-east of the island, notably CERASUOLO DI VITTORIA DOCG, but can also make juicy VARIETAL wines. Probably a descendant of SANGIOVESE, it was grown on a total of 965 ha/2,385 acres in 2020.

Frascati, LAZIO's most famous DOC. Named after the town of Frascati immediately east from Rome, the wine was for centuries based on the local MALVASIA del Lazio (a cross between MUSCAT OF ALEXANDRIA and SCHIAVA Grossa) locally called Malvasia Puntinata, or the rather neutral Malvasia Bianca Candia. The official production rules, however, do not distinguish between the two and allow up to 30% of the high-yielding TREBBIANO Toscana, which has diluted the wine's character to that of a rather neutral white for everyday drinking, of which most is absorbed by Rome and its many tourists.

Rome's expanding suburbs have slowly crept up on Frascati's vineyards, causing a continuing decline in producing area, to 901 ha/2,226 acres in 2018. The once exceptionally high average yield of 112 hl/ha at the beginning of the century has dropped to 58 hl/ha but without a dramatic increase in quality.

In 2011, in an effort to improve the situation, the entire zone was elevated to DOCG for Frascati Superiore, for which the production regulations demand lower YIELDS (11 tonnes/ha rather than the 14 tonnes/ha for plain Frascati) and with a higher minimum alcohol, implying a wine made from riper grapes with more extract. The traditional sweet version of Frascati, **Cannellino di Frascati**, was also elevated to DOCG level, with the stipulation that the grapes must be late-harvested. They may also undergo partial drying, and the minimum RESIDUAL SUGAR must be at least 35g/l.

While Frascati's production is dominated by large operations, some of them regularly produce at least one superior bottling based on a higher percentage of Malvasia Puntinata, often complemented by the local Bellone grape. Examples such as the Superiore version from Casal Pilozzo express much more faithfully the original Frascati characteristics but have difficulty in finding a market willing to pay the premium. There are now some left-field examples as well, such as the SKIN-FERMENTED blends of Malvasia del Lazio and Bellone from Ribelà.

W.S.

Belfrage, N., *Brunello to Zibibbo. The Wines of Tuscany, Central and Southern Italy* (2003).
Canuto, F., and De Santis, L., *Frascati* (2002).
www.consorziofrascati.it

fraud, wine. See ADULTERATION AND FRAUD.

free-run is the name used by winemakers for the juice or wine that will drain without PRESSING from a mass of freshly crushed grapes or from a FERMENTATION VESSEL. Depending on the type of vessel used for DRAINING and the winemaking process, it constitutes 60–85% of the total juice available and is generally superior to, and much lower in TANNINS than, juice or wine whose extraction depends on pressing. Most modern white wine is made from grapes that pass through a DESTEMMER-CRUSHER before going into a draining tank with a perforated bottom through which the free-run juice passes to the fermentation vessel. Many winemakers boast of using only free-run juice in the production of fine white wines, but PRESS WINE, the wine produced by pressing what is left, may be useful as a BLENDING element.

In RED WINEMAKING, the free-run wine is that which, after SETTLING, is drained or RACKED away from the skins. In some wineries, free-run red wine is also recovered from specially designed transfer conveyors. Whatever remains goes into the press to yield press wine, which can be even more useful for its tannin concentration when making up blends of red wines.

freeze. See WINTER FREEZE.

freeze concentration. See CONCENTRATION.

Freisa, or **Freisa Piccola**, is a distinctive, wild-strawberry-flavoured red grape variety indigenous to the PIEMONTE region of north-west Italy and, more specifically, to the provinces of Asti, Alessandria, and Cuneo in scattered vineyards which reach almost to the gates of the city of Turin.

The vine has been known in Piemonte for centuries. DNA PROFILING has shown that Freisa has a parent–offspring relationship with NEBBIOLO. Freisa musts can be quite high in both ACIDITY and TANNINS like Nebbiolo, although its wines are coarser in terms of the tannins and flavours.

The wine exists as a VARIETAL in a range of styles but traditionally appears as a slightly frothy wine from a SECOND FERMENTATION, which retains some unfermented RESIDUAL SUGAR to balance the slight bitterness from the LEES. The frizzante or sparkling version of Freisa, with its decisively purple colour and aromas of raspberries and violets, is reminiscent of good LAMBRUSCO, if much more tannic and tart.

It is DOC in both dry and sweet (*amabile*) styles in the following areas: the larger Freisa d'ASTI and the minuscule Freisa di Chieri, the LANGHE, the MONFERRATO, and the rare Pinerolese. Its popularity has declined rapidly in recent years in its native Piemonte.

Modern technology, in the form of pressurized tanks, now permits producers better control of both the residual sugar level and the amount of CARBON DIOXIDE in the wine, and this type of Freisa, which does not undergo a second fermentation in the bottle, tends to be distinctively drier and almost imperceptibly fizzy. Today producers such as Aldo Vajra and Coppo make a more ageworthy, completely dry, and completely still type of Freisa aged in BARRIQUE, and a handful make a Freisa Nebbiolata, in which the wine is refermented on the skins of Nebbiolo used for BAROLO. Tannins abound in this style.

By 2015, total Italian plantings had fallen to 514 ha/1,270 acres. It is also known in California.

Freixenet. See HENKELL FREIXENET.

French-American hybrids. See FRENCH HYBRIDS.

French Colombard, common California name for one of the state's most planted grape varieties, the French white COLOMBARD.

French hybrids, group of vine HYBRIDS bred in France in the late 19th and early 20th centuries, usually by crossing or hybridizing AMERICAN VINE SPECIES with a European VITIS VINIFERA variety (see VINE BREEDING). These are also known as direct producers, hybrid direct producers, HDPs, or, in French, *hybrides producteurs directs*. One early response to the invasion of PHYLLOXERA in Europe was to plant American varieties, since most had phylloxera tolerance. In Europe they proved to be both hardy and resistant to a wide range of FUNGAL DISEASES, but, because of the strange, often FOXY, flavour of the wine they produced, it has been illegal to plant the likes of ISABELLA, NOAH, Othello, Black Spanish (JACQUEZ), and HERBEMONT in France since 1934.

The aim of the early hybridizers was to combine the pest and disease resistance of the American species with the accepted wine quality of the European wine species *vinifera*. (See DISEASE-RESISTANT VARIETIES for current breeding techniques with similar aims and promising results.) A group of French breeders such as François BACO, Castel, Georges COUDERC, Ferdinand Gaillard, Ganzin, Millardet, Oberlin, Albert SEIBEL, Bertille SEYVE, and Victor VILLARD, as well as, more recently, Joanny Burdin, Galibert, Eugene Kuhlmann, Pierre Landot, Ravat, Jean-François Seyve's sons Joannes and Bertille (who married Villard's daughter and developed the important SEYVE–VILLARD series of hybrids), and Jean-Louis VIDAL, produced thousands of new hybrid varieties with such aims in mind. They used AMERICAN HYBRIDS as parents as well as American vine species. *Vitis aestivalis*, *Vitis rupestris*, *Vitis riparia*, and *Vitis berlandieri* were common parents because of their excellent disease and pest resistance and a reduction in the strong fruit flavour associated with *Vitis labrusca*. Some of the ROOTSTOCKS used today were bred by these hybridizers, particularly Castel, Couderc, Ganzin, and Millardet. Active hybridizers in other countries included the Italians Bruni, Paulsen, Pirovani, and Prosperi.

These hybrids were widely favoured because of disease resistance and high productivity, so by 1958 about 400,000 ha/988,000 acres of French hybrids were planted in France, or about one-third of the total vineyard area. Wine quality was, however, often inferior, especially from the earlier French hybrids. With continued crossing and back crossing, the objectionable features in the taste of the wine could be reduced (see diagram for NEW VARIETIES). French planting regulations since 1955 have deliberately discouraged vine varieties associated with poor wine quality, however, both hybrids and *vinifera*. With the exception of Baco 22A (also known as Baco Blanc), which may be used for armagnac, hybrids have been systematically phased out of French wine and brandy production, even though 20 older hybrids—including Villard Noir, CHAMBOURCIN, and PLANTET for red wines and Villard Blanc for white wines—are still authorized for wine in France, if only for WINE WITHOUT GEOGRAPHICAL INDICATION. There is currently renewed interest in these hybrids due to their disease resistance.

The French hybrids have been planted outside France and have made significant contributions at some time or other to the wine industries of the eastern UNITED STATES (see NEW YORK in particular), CANADA, ENGLAND, and New Zealand, where French hybrids were planted in the majority of vineyards into the 1960s and used for FORTIFIED WINES. From the 1960s onwards, in almost all of these regions these hybrids have been systematically replaced by *vinifera* varieties for reasons of wine quality, although in some sites in Canada and New York subject to WINTER FREEZE only a hybrid such as Vidal will survive (and has produced some fine ICE WINE), while Seyval Blanc is still grown to a limited extent in England. R.E.S. & J.E.H.

Galet, P., and Morton, L. T., *A Practical Ampelography: Grapevine Identification* (1979).

Sabbatini, P., and Howell, S. G., 'Vitis hybrids: history and current status', *Wines & Vines* (January 2014), 135–42.

French paradox, term coined in the United States in 1991 to express the infuriating fact that the French seem to eat and drink themselves silly with no apparent ill effects on their coronary health. Immediately after this thesis was aired on prime-time television in the United States, with red wine consumption cited as a possible factor in reducing the risk of heart disease, US sales of red wine quadrupled, and GALLO had to put their leading branded GENERIC Hearty Burgundy on allocation. For more details, see HEALTH. A similar association between red wine consumption and health benefits has played an important part in the wine boom in ASIA.

Frescobaldi, one of Florence's most prominent noble families since the 13th century, are among the largest landholders in TUSCANY with a wide range of agricultural activities. The Frescobaldi holdings can be divided into three distinct blocks: the first, Tenuta di Castiglioni to the south-west of Florence, where the family started to produce wines as early as the 1300s; the second, to the east of Florence, which produces classic CHIANTI RUFINA from the Nipozzano estate and the wines of Pomino; and the third Castelgiocondo, in MONTALCINO, whose acquisition in 1989 made Frescobaldi the largest potential producer of Brunello. By 2022 Frescobaldi's substantial holdings in Montalcino also included the independently run Tenuta Luce della Vite producing a Brunello as well as Luce, a SUPERTUSCAN blend of Sangiovese and Merlot.

In 2000 Frescobaldi ventured outside Tuscany when it acquired the Conti Attems estate in FRIULI. In 2004 they acquired control of the Ornellaia estate in BOLGHERI, their first foray into what had been an Antinori fief. In 2018 a separate cellar was built for Masseto, the luxurious Merlot made on the estate that is sold exclusively through the Place de Bordeaux. Also in the Maremma, Frescobaldi now produce INTERNATIONAL VARIETALS on their Tenuta dell'Amiraglia and in 2014 finally became owners of a CHIANTI CLASSICO property when they acquired Tenuta Perano in Gaiole-in-Chianti. Gorgona, a blend of Vermentino and Inzolia produced on the eponymous Tuscan island, is a social project in collaboration with the Gorgona Penal Institute. W.S.

fresh grapes. See TABLE GRAPES.

frisante, Portuguese term for a semi-sparkling wine with a pressure of 1–2.5 bar.

Friulano, name adopted for SAUVIGNONASSE in the early 21st century in FRIULI for the region's leading white wine variety once known, to the fury of Hungarians, as Tocai Friulano. Total plantings have been slowly declining but were 2,503 ha/6,185 acres in 2015, in all major DOC zones (FRIULI COLLI ORIENTALI, COLLIO, FRIULI GRAVE, FRIULI AQUILEIA, and ISONZO). Buttrio, Manzano, and Rosazzo in the Colli Orientali, and the areas between Cormons and Brazzano, between Brazzano and Dolegna, and Capriva di Friuli in the Collio DOC, are classic subzones. The wine itself is light in colour and body, is floral in aroma, and has pronounced green-almond notes. It is designed to be drunk young.

Friuli, or **Friuli-Venezia Giulia**, the north-easternmost region of Italy, borders on Austria to the north and SLOVENIA to the east and has long been a confluence of three distinct peoples and cultures: Italian, Germanic, and Slavic. (See map under ITALY.) Despite endorsements of local wines by the usual succession of popes, emperors, princes, and princelings, Friuli's history of distinctive wines remained largely hidden until the late 1960s, when the introduction of both German winemaking philosophy and TEMPERATURE CONTROL—innovations usually credited to producer Mario Schiopetto—gave Italy's first fresh, fruity, internationally styled white wines. This created a FASHION which has waned as Friuli's wines made from INTERNATIONAL VARIETIES became less distinctive and as interest in INDIGENOUS VARIETIES waxes. This style of (predominantly white) WINEMAKING is one of the characteristic features of the region's production; the other is the large number of wines produced by each single estate.

Friuli's geographical position on land successively disputed by Romans, Byzantines, Venetians, and Habsburgs ensured that a large number of varieties would be available for planting. The white FRIULANO, RIBOLLA Gialla, MALVASIA di Istria, VERDUZZO, and PICOLIT and red REFOSCO DAL PENDUNCOLO ROSSO, REFOSCO Nostrano, SCHIOPPETTINO, PIGNOLO, and the acidic Tazzelenghe are considered indigenous (although see ROBOLA, for example). RIESLING, WELSCHRIESLING (here called Riesling Italico), TRAMINER, MÜLLER-THURGAU, and BLAUFRÄNKISCH (locally called Franconia) are imports from Austria. The French varieties PINOT BIANCO, PINOT GRIGIO, CHARDONNAY, SAUVIGNON, CABERNET, MERLOT, PINOT NERO, and CARMENÈRE were introduced during the 19th-century Habsburg domination (and greatly expanded during the replanting of Friuli's vineyards after the ravages of PHYLLOXERA), which lasted until 1918 in the case of the province of Gorizia.

The result has been a multiplicity of single VARIETAL wines in each of its four DOCGs and 12 DOCS. If the proliferation of DOC wines with varietal names attached to specific zones has created some confusion among consumers, the geography of Friuli's DOC structure is fairly easy to understand. Udine marks the northern border beyond which low temperatures make viticulture an impractical proposition in most cases. To the south of Udine exist two distinct bands of grape-growing territory: the two hillside DOCs of FRIULI COLLI ORIENTALI and COLLIO with calcareous MARL soils; and the ALLUVIAL plain with plentiful quantities of sand, pebbles, and rocks deposited by the various rivers—the Tagliamento, the Natisone, the Judrio, the Isonzo—which criss-cross the plain. These flatlands are divided into five DOCs, moving from west to east: LISON-PRAMAGGIORE (shared with Veneto), Latisana, FRIULI GRAVE, FRIULI AQUILEIA, and ISONZO. The HILLSIDE VINEYARDS give wines of greater personality. Isonzo, which borders Collio, stands out among the DOCs of the plain, its best wines able to challenge those of the hillsides.

Since 2018 the overarching DOC Friuli Venezia Giulia, previously an IGT covering the entire region, has been approved. Yields of 14 tonnes/ha seems overgenerous, suggesting the DOC's aim is to enable declassification of wines within the DOC system rather than resorting to the lower and more anonymous IGT. Additionally, this new umbrella DOC has managed to legally reserve the category 'Ribolla Spumante' exclusively for Friuli, prohibiting other regions, such as Veneto, to use the variety for varietally labelled sparkling wines. Since 2011 the DOC PROSECCO also covers the whole of Friuli (as well as that of neighbouring Veneto).

For more details, see CARSO, COLLIO, FRIULI AQUILEIA, FRIULI COLLI ORIENTALI, FRIULI GRAVE, ISONZO, and LISON-PRAMAGGIORE. W.S.

Zanfi, A., *Friuli: Terre, Uomini, Vino* (2004).
www.winesfriuliveneziagiulia.it

Friuli Aquileia, DOC within FRIULI in north-eastern Italy comprising 16 communes in whole or part on a plain south of Udine. The white must consist of at least 50% FRIULANO, while the Rosso must contain at least 50% REFOSCO dal Peduncolo Rosso. The balance in both can be any authorized variety, most of which are INTERNATIONAL VARIETIES, which dominate the production in the greater region. W.S.

Friuli Colli Orientali, formerly Colli Orientali del Friuli, literally the eastern hills (*colli*) of the FRIULI region in north-east Italy, comprising more than 2,000 ha/4,942 acres of vineyard.

The territory of the DOC begins to the east of the city of Udine near the SLOVENIAN border and continues to the border of the province of Udine. The dividing line between the Colli Orientali and the COLLIO DOC is neither geological nor climatic but simply historical: Udine and its province became part of Italy in 1866, while the neighbouring area of Collio, in the province of Gorizia, was not reunified with the rest of Italy until the end of the First World War. The contiguous zones in fact have the same sort of soil: the so-called 'FLYSCH of Cormons', with alternating layers of calcareous marls and sandstone.

Wine has a documented history here, as in most parts of Italy, since the days of the Roman Empire, but the zone first began to attract significant attention in the 1970s, when cold fermentation techniques began to produce here (and in the Collio DOC) significant quantities of fresh, fruity, and aromatic white wines, predominantly based on INTERNATIONAL VARIETIES, especially Pinot Grigio, Chardonnay, and Sauvignon Blanc, pioneering efforts for Italy.

Significant development of red wines came in the 1980s as producers began planting Merlot, Cabernet Sauvignon, Cabernet Franc, and Pinot Noir, the wines frequently aged in small oak barrels. A certain number of these reds were released as an ambitiously priced VINO DA TAVOLA, because individual producers wanted to either distance the wines from their allegedly more facile antecedents, make an unorthodox blend of varieties, or copy the success of the highly priced SUPERTUSCANS. In the last decade the market has begun to turn away from these brawny styles, and the region's red wines have become less concentrated, less oak-driven, and more elegant.

White wines, particularly from Chardonnay or Pinot Bianco, are also moving away from BARREL FERMENTATION and BARRIQUE ageing towards fresher styles, while a range of SKIN-FERMENTED white wines, including the historical, copper-hued Pinot Grigio Ramato, have begun to attract attention.

Although international varietal wines, especially whites, still prevail, producers have begun to focus on INDIGENOUS VARIETIES and the specific TERROIRS of the subzones where historically they were cultivated: Cialla for RIBOLLA Gialla, VERDUZZO, REFOSCO DAL PENDUNCOLO ROSSO, and SCHIOPPETTINO; Rosazzo for Ribolla Gialla and PIGNOLO; Prepotto for Schioppettino; and Faedis for a scented local grape known as Refosco Nostrano. The red Schioppettino, saved from extinction in the 1970s, is now cultivated by 20 producers who have founded an association dedicated to its promotion.

Friuli Colli Orientali has not one but two historic sweet wines, either LATE HARVEST or DRIED-GRAPE WINES: DOCG Colli Orientali del Friuli Picolit includes the subzone Cialla, while DOCG Ramandolo applies to Verduzzo and more or less covers the same area as DOC Friuli Colli Orientali. Both wines can be complex and long-lived. W.S.

www.colliorientali.com

Friuli Grave, formerly Grave del Friuli, vast DOC zone in the FRIULI region of north-east Italy which sprawls across the southern portion of the provinces of Pordenone and Udine. This is flatland whose GRAVEL- and SAND-based soil has been deposited over the millennia by the many rivers and streams that cross the territory before adding their waters to the Adriatic. It owes its name to the same etymological root as the gravelly GRAVES region of Bordeaux in France. The DOC, with 2,000 ha/4,942 acres of vineyard producing 300,000 hl annually, is responsible for more than 50% of Friuli's output and is so large that it is more akin to an IGT than anything else. Exceptionally high permitted yields (91 hl/ha) make it difficult to see how the DOC contributes to good-quality wine production. Almost all INTERNATIONAL VARIETIES are grown here, with piercingly herbaceous Sauvignon Blanc once the DOC's flagship but now encountering fierce international competition. That is not to say that the DOC is unsuitable for the production of high-quality wines, but its formidable size precludes generalizations. W.S.

frizzante, Italian wine term for semi-sparkling wine (as opposed to SPUMANTE, which is used for fully sparkling wines). *Frizzante* wines, which can be dry, semi-sweet or sweet, generally owe their bubbles to a partial second fermentation in tank, a sort of interrupted TANK METHOD process (although see also PROSECCO COL FONDO). A wine labelled *frizzante* must have between 1 and 2.5 bar pressure, and *spumante* at least 3 bar. Often undervalued because of the production method, *frizzante* wines are economically very important, with 400 million bottles produced in Italy in 2020.

Fromenteau, name for several grape varieties, used as a synonym for both the ROUSSANNE of the Rhône and SAVAGNIN of the Jura. **Fromenteau Gris** is a synonym for PINOT GRIS.

Fronsac, small but once famed red-wine appellation in the Bordeaux region just west of the town of Libourne on the RIGHT BANK of the River DORDOGNE (see map under BORDEAUX). The wooded low hills of Fronsac, along with **Canon-Fronsac**, the even smaller and more famous appellation to the immediate south, constitute Bordeaux's prettiest countryside, and the region's elevation, unusual so close to the Gironde estuary, gave it great strategic importance. Fronsac was the site of a Roman temple and then of a fortress built by CHARLEMAGNE, who is locally supposed to have taken a particular interest in this wine. The wine benefited further in the mid 17th century when the Duc de Richelieu, also Duc de Fronsac and a man of considerable influence, replaced the fortress with a villa in which he entertained frequently. According to Enjalbert, the first great right-bank wines were produced, around 1730, in Canon-Fronsac. Even well into the 19th century, the wines of Fronsac were much more famous than those of POMEROL on the other side of Libourne.

The low-lying land beside the river and any alluvial soils further inland from the Dordogne and its tributary the Isle are entitled to only the BORDEAUX AOC, while the Fronsac and Canon-Fronsac appellations are concentrated on the higher land where LIMESTONE predominates and SANDSTONE is also characteristic. Merlot and Cabernet Franc (Bouchet) are the dominant grape varieties, densely planted on the land entitled to the Fronsac appellation and the more restricted area, mainly around the villages of St-Michel-de-Fronsac and Fronsac itself, which are entitled to the supposedly superior Canon-Fronsac appellation. The region with its cool soils performs particularly well in hot vintages.

Wines made in the 1960s and 1970s were often both austere and slightly rustic. The 1980s saw considerable refinement of techniques and investment in winemaking equipment, notably some new barrels, so that Fronsac added suppleness to its density. It does not have the lush character of Pomerol but can offer a keenly priced alternative to more famous red bordeaux, with the juicy fruit of a St-Émilion and the ageing potential of a Médoc. Even the commercial muscle of the MOUEIX family, who owned Chx Canon-Moueix, La Dauphine, and Canon de Brem, as well as distributing several others, from the 1980s until the early 21st century, failed to win the region the success it probably deserves. The largest and most picturesque property on the entire right bank is Ch de la Rivière. In 2020 Fronsac had 774 ha/1,912 acres in production, and Canon-Fronsac 224 ha/553 acres, with red wine grapes only. J.R. & J.L.

Enjalbert, H., *Les Grands Vins de St-Émilion, Pomerol et Fronsac* (1983), translated by H. Coleman as *Great Bordeaux Wines* (1985).

Frontenac, relatively recent dark-skinned HYBRID, also known as **Frontenac Noir**, grown for PORT-style wines in the Upper Plains and Midwest of the United States. Its high acidity generally requires some RESIDUAL SUGAR. The MUTATION **Frontenac Gris** has produced some white wine, but the more recent mutation **Frontenac Blanc** may well prove more popular. Both Noir and Blanc are gaining ground in QUEBEC.

Frontignac, Australian synonym for MUSCAT BLANC À PETITS GRAINS.

Frontignan is the name of the wine long called Muscat de Frontignan, the most important of the Languedoc's four Muscats. Now a distinctly unglamorous town on the semi-industrial lagoon between Montpellier and Sète, Frontignan was famous for the quality of its MUSCAT for centuries. It was probably one of France's earliest vineyard sites, being close to the salt marshes around Narbonne. PLINY the Younger singled out this particular 'bees' wine' for mention in his letters. ARNALDUS DE VILLANOVA, who is credited with the discovery of the process by which most Muscat de Frontignan is made today (see VIN DOUX NATUREL), claimed that his daily ration of the wine, as advised by the then all-powerful Aragón monarch, made him feel years younger. It was popular in both Paris and London in the 17th and 18th centuries, doubtless with wider appeal then than the dry reds of south-west France that were also shipped north. 'Frontiniac' was specifically praised by the philosopher John Locke in 1676, while both Voltaire and, even further afield, Thomas JEFFERSON were well-documented and enthusiastic purchasers. In the 18th and 19th centuries, Frontignan clearly made red as well as white wines which were compared with those of that other favourite of our sweet-toothed ancestors, CONSTANTIA. See also LANGUEDOC, history, for details of a claimed link between Frontignan and Ch d'YQUEM.

Muscat de Frontignan, despite being one of the first AOCs, and certainly the first VIN DOUX NATUREL appellation, to be officially recognized, fell into decline for much of the 20th century. Only the rather lighter MUSCAT DE BEAUMES-DE-VENISE somehow escaped the malaise that affected the market for France's sweeter wines until the 1980s, when the winemakers of Frontignan awoke as if from a deep sleep and started to produce a much higher proportion of more delicate, more refreshing, yet more characterful golden Muscats (although some dark, turgid, raisiny Frontignan can still be found). As in all Languedoc Muscats (see LUNEL, MIREVAL, and ST-JEAN-DE-MINERVOIS), only the finest Muscat variety, MUSCAT BLANC À PETITS GRAINS, should be used, and the final wine must be at least 15% alcohol with a sugar content of at least 110 g/l. Cheaper Muscats made well outside the region but marketed vigorously to tourists do nothing for the image of this once-great appellation. CO-OPERATIVES dominate output, but much of the credit for revitalizing winemaking in Frontignan can go to Ch de la Peyrade, whose seaside vineyards may not be the Mediterranean's most picturesque but are reliably warm enough to maximize Muscat Blanc's potential.

A small proportion of Muscat de Frontignan is fortified so early it qualifies as a VIN DE LIQUEUR.

Muscat de Frontignan is also a common synonym for Muscat Blanc à Petits Grains in South Africa.

Fronton, red and rosé AOC of 2,400 ha/6,000 acres of vineyards in SOUTH WEST FRANCE just 30 km/19 miles north of Toulouse. The wines, often called 'the Beaujolais de Toulouse', are distinguished by local grape variety NÉGRETTE, which makes subtle reds with notes of wildflowers and sometimes liquorice. It must constitute at least 50% of a grower's vineyard, with Syrah and the Cabernets being the most important of the many other permitted varieties. Oak ageing tends to mask the grape's character, while ORGANIC production (as at Ch Plaisance) enhances it. The CO-OPERATIVE is an important producer. Rosé production is on the increase, but there is no white Fronton as yet, though some growers bottle whites as COMTÉ TOLOSAN. P.S.

frost, the ice crystals formed by freezing of water vapour on objects which have cooled below 0 °C/32 °F. Such frosts are known as white frosts, or hoar frosts. Black frosts cause freezing and extensive killing of plant tissue itself, without any necessary hoar formation. Frost is a major viticultural problem as it can damage and kill shoots and fruit, in spring and autumn. FROST PROTECTION is expensive and not always effective; see also FROST DAMAGE.

Frost frequencies are, in many studies, imputed arbitrarily from weather records. Temperatures as recorded in the standard Stevenson screen used by meteorologists, at 1.25 m/4.1 ft above the ground, are always higher than at ground level. A screen temperature of 2.2 °C/36 °F is normally assumed to indicate a light ground frost, and one of 0 °C a heavy ground frost. Temperatures at vine height of −1 °C or lower after BUDBREAK in spring will usually cause serious injury to the young shoots. Even 'light' frosts can often cause damage somewhere in the vineyard, because their incidence tends to be patchy, depending on TOPOGRAPHY. Geiger covers this aspect in detail.

Two main types of frost are distinguished: radiation and advection. Radiation frost occurs typically on still, dry, cloudless nights. Without cloud, mist, or much water vapour to absorb and trap heat radiated from the ground and plant tissues, heat escapes freely to space, and rapid surface cooling results. Air in immediate contact with these surfaces then becomes cooled. The coldest air, being densest, remains or collects close to the ground and in depressions. Lowest air temperatures in the early morning on flat land are at 5–15 cm/2–5 in above ground, rising with height to a relatively warm 'inversion' layer, commonly some 15–30 m/49–100 ft above, beyond which temperatures gradually fall again with elevation. This pool of cold, dense air close to the ground is stable unless dispersed by wind or unless it can flow away by gravity to still lower regions (see TOPOGRAPHY).

Advective frosts result from such flows of already chilled air from elsewhere. They can originate locally, following valleys or other natural courses of AIR DRAINAGE, or arrive from up to several hundreds or perhaps thousands of kilometres away. J.G.

Geiger, R., Aron, R. H., and Todhunter, P., *The Climate near the Ground* (7th edn, 2009).

McCarthy, M. G., et al., 'Soil management and frost control', in B. G. Coombe and P. R. Dry (eds.), *Viticulture*, ii: *Practices* (2nd edn, 2006).

frost damage occurs in vineyards mostly in spring but also in autumn and occasionally summer, when the air temperature drops below freezing (see also FROST). Ice forms in the plant tissue of buds which have begun to break, young shoots, leaves, and INFLORESCENCES, which may subsequently turn brown and die. The vine can respond by growing more shoots from BASAL BUDS, but these are typically less fruitful, and so the crop is reduced and delayed.

Frost in the autumn causes DEFOLIATION, which is a problem if the fruit is not ripe and the vine's reserves of CARBOHYDRATES have not been restored. Frost has much more impact on YIELD than on wine QUALITY, although if SPRINKLER irrigation is used before harvest to ward off autumn frost, the additional water in the soil can have serious consequences for RIPENING.

FROST PROTECTION can be difficult and expensive, but frost is so destructive that vineyard owners are often forced to adopt extreme measures.

Typically cool-climate regions are more prone to spring frost. For example, in 1991 frost damage was so great in western France that total French wine production, which averaged nearly 55 million hl in 1991–2000, was less than 43 million hl/1,135 million gal. Equally bad were the severe spring frosts of 2021, which contributed to even lower yields of 36 million hl, 18% down on the five-year average.

However, spring frost damage to vines is by no means confined to cool viticultural climates. That is because the VINE GROWTH CYCLE is adapted to the general course of temperatures experienced, with spring budbreak delayed in cool climates until the average mean temperature reaches about 10 °C/50 °F, as described under CLIMATE CLASSIFICATION. More damaging can be short-term TEMPERATURE VARIABILITY, such that an early spring warm enough to induce budbreak may frequently be followed by a return to killing frosts after growth has started, as occurred in north and central Italy as well as in France in 2021. The early growing season was advanced by unseasonably warm weather (24–27 °C/75–80 °F in north-east France at the end of March) followed by arctic cold temperatures in early April, with clear nights and temperatures below −9 °C/16 °F recorded in some vineyards. Paradoxically, such events can occur in otherwise hot vineyard regions, such as the high plains of TEXAS, which were also severely hit in 2021. This is because the early spring is often hot, which encourages early budbreak, but this may be followed by cold of arctic origin which can severely damage vines.

Note the distinction between frost and WINTER FREEZE, a related but different vine injury.

R.E.S. & J.E.H.

frost protection. The first way to avoid FROST, which can so easily destroy the grapes for one year, is to plant on slopes from which surface-chilled air can drain away freely (see AIR DRAINAGE). Free-standing and projecting hills offer the best protection because they have no external sources of chilled air and so what slips away must be replaced from the warmer atmosphere above (see TOPOGRAPHY). This is the most effective form of frost protection, but it is generally an option only when developing vineyards in new regions that allow such VINEYARD SITE SELECTION.

Planting on frost-prone sites is normally confined to grape varieties with naturally late BUDBREAK, such as (where the growing season is long enough) CABERNET SAUVIGNON, CARIGNAN, MOURVÈDRE, CLAIRETTE, and TREBBIANO. RIESLING, SYLVANER, MÜLLER-THURGAU, and SAUVIGNON BLANC are classed as having mid-season budbreak. Unfortunately some of the prime-quality varieties grown in COOL CLIMATES, such as PINOT NOIR and CHARDONNAY, burst early and are very vulnerable to spring frosts (see CHABLIS, for instance). The selection of individual sites with minimal frost risk is crucial for such varieties. Some HYBRIDS are more cold-hardy. The risk in any situation can be reduced to a small extent by late PRUNING, but this can delay the effective time of budbreak by only up to about a week.

Another method, employed on flat land subject to radiation frosts, is to use high TRELLIS SYSTEMS so that the main vine growth stands above the coldest air layer that settles close to the ground on still nights. In practice, however, there is little difference in frost sensitivity of commercial trellis systems, and this method offers limited benefit. COVER CROPS between the rows also needs to be cultivated or rolled by the time of budbreak, so as to lower the effective cooling surface. If the soil is compacted, it most readily absorbs day heat to depth and reradiates it continuously through the night. STONES AND ROCKS in the soil surface assist in this.

Stationary WIND MACHINES are often employed to break up the sedentary lower cold-air layer and mix in warm upper air; these have become part of the vineyard landscape in NAPA and SONOMA Valleys and in ONTARIO, for example. They are expensive to install and use a lot of fuel, but in the long run they are less expensive than HELICOPTERS, which are widely used for the same purpose in NEW ZEALAND and can cover a much wider area but have to be hired by the hour. There is also a mobile fan machine that gathers cold air and blasts it vertically upwards, mixing it with the warmer air. Fog-creating machines have also been used to mix the inversion layer and to minimize frost damage.

Small oil burners, often referred to as smudge pots, can also create limited local heating which may help to promote convectional mixing of upper and lower air. They have lost favour because of the numbers of pots required, not to mention fuel, smoke, lost sleep, and the general inconvenience of operating them in the cold darkness of the early morning. French *bougies antigel* (anti-frost 'candles'), usually filled with paraffin (often candle-factory waste) or with stearin as a greener alternative, are increasingly popular but still labour-intensive.

Burning straw bales—so that the smoke prevents the sun from burning the buds or shoots after frost—was used in Burgundy after the severe frosts of 2017 and 2018, for example, but the practice is prohibited or strictly controlled.

In vineyards with sprinkler IRRIGATION, the SPRINKLERS can be turned on when temperatures fall to danger levels. (In vineyards where irrigation is not permitted, Chablis for example, water has to be taken from a nearby river or reservoir.) This aspersion technique both warms the vines and soil directly and (if the soil was previously dry) improves its heat conductivity so that more warmth comes up from below. The release of latent heat as the water freezes on the vines protects the vine tissue from injury. However, the additional water in the vineyard may be unwelcome. The use of heated vineyard wires has shown good results, but installation is expensive. Other forms of equipment, such as static or trailer-mounted gas-heated blowers, have not so far been widely adopted. Trials with various vine treatments, such as CHITOSAN or essential oils, have so far been inconclusive.

R.E.S. & J.E.H.

www.wine-searcher.com/m/2021/04/the-complete-guide-to-fighting-frost

fructose is, with GLUCOSE, one of the two principal SUGARS of the grape and sweet wines. It is a six-carbon atom sugar, or a hexose. Common table sugar, SUCROSE, is made up of one molecule of fructose and one of glucose.

The grapevine leaf in the presence of sunlight, water, and carbon dioxide makes sucrose by a complicated series of steps called collectively PHOTOSYNTHESIS. The sucrose is transferred in the plant sap from the leaf to the grape berry. There the sucrose is split into fructose and glucose, the forms in which it is stored in the berry. The vine is unusual among fruiting plants in the extent to which it is capable of concentrating the two sugars, fructose and glucose, in its berries; sugars routinely represent 18–25% of grape juice weight, while 12% is the norm in apple and pear juice.

Fructose accumulates in the grape berry along with glucose but at lower concentrations during the early stages. However, at RIPENESS, and especially when grapes are overripe, fructose levels often exceed those of glucose. The glucose–fructose ratio is thus an indicator of grape ripening (roughly 1:5 at veraison but less than 1 at full ripeness). This is important because fructose is remarkable in that it has between 1.3 and 1.8 times the sweetening power of either glucose or sucrose (which has led to its manufacture in large quantities for use in so-called diet foods).

During FERMENTATION of grape juice, both fructose and glucose are consumed. Furthermore, in the acid and enzymic environment of grape juice, any sucrose present is split into its constituent parts, fructose and glucose, and will consequently be fermented. With selected strains of wine YEASTS, nearly all the fructose and glucose are converted to alcohol and carbon dioxide, leaving the wine with only traces of fermentable sugars. A.D.W. & B.G.C.

früh is German for 'early'. Thus, for example, Früher Roter Malvasier is early red MALVASIA.

Frühburgunder, or **Blauer Frühburgunder**, increasingly highly regarded, small-berried MUTATION of SPÄTBURGUNDER (Pinot Noir) which ripens a good two weeks earlier. By 2020, total German plantings stood at 233 ha/576 acres, most notably on the steep slate slopes of the AHR Valley and on the red sandstone soils around Bürgstadt in FRANKEN, where low-yielding examples exhibit intense fruit. Also known as Pinot Noir Précoce.

Frühroter Veltliner, 'early-ripening, red-skinned VELTLINER', is a pink-skinned grape variety most commonly encountered in Austria, sometimes under the name Malvasier, where plantings, mainly in the WEINVIERTEL district of Lower Austria, had fallen to 253 ha/625 acres by 2021. The wine produced is often less distinguished than that made from Austria's most common grape variety GRÜNER VELTLINER, being notably lower in acidity in many cases. Yields are also generally lower. DNA PROFILING in Austria showed that Frühroter Veltliner is not related to Grüner Veltliner at all but is a spontaneous CROSS between ROTER VELTLINER and SILVANER.

In Germany, it has been known in Rheinhessen, as **Frühroter Malvasier** or occasionally Roter Malvasier; in Hungary as Korai Piros Veltelini. It is slightly less rare in Czechia (under the name Veltlínské Červené Rané) and Slovakia (as Veltlínske Červené Skoré). In France's Savoie, it is known confusing as both Velteliner Rouge Précoce and Malvoisie, the latter also used for PINOT GRIS.

fruit. To a VITICULTURIST, 'fruit' is a synonym for GRAPE, the former used more commonly than 'grapes' in English-speaking countries. To an OENOLOGIST or wine taster, fruit is a perceptible element essential to a young wine. Young wines should taste fruity, although not necessarily of grapes or any particular grape variety. During bottle AGEING, the fruity FLAVOUR COMPOUNDS in a good wine evolve into more complex elements, sometimes described as BOUQUET; in a less good wine, the fruit simply dissipates to leave a non-fruity wine sometimes described as 'hollow'. The word **fruity** is sometimes used in wine descriptions concocted for marketing purposes as a euphemism for 'sweet'. See also RIPENING.

fruit-driven, a TASTING TERM used to convey the fact that a wine has a dominance of grape-derived fruit flavour rather than being dominated by flavours that originate from processes or treatments which the wine has undergone such as BARREL FERMENTATION, BARREL AGEING, LEES CONTACT, MALOLACTIC CONVERSION, or, in the case of a sparkling wine, the influence of yeast AUTOLYSIS.

fruit fly. See DROSOPHILA and MEDITERRANEAN FRUIT FLY.

fruitfulness, viticultural term describing the average number of bunches of grapes per shoot. It can also be used to describe the potential productivity of buds. A shoot of low fruitfulness will have zero or one bunch only, while a **fruitful** one may have two or three or, very rarely, four. Some varieties are known to be very fruitful, common examples being the so-called FRENCH HYBRIDS, no doubt due to their part-American parentage. At the other end of the fruitfulness spectrum is SULTANA, which has notoriously low fertility of buds at the base of canes. Most of the commercially important wine grape varieties fall between these two extremes, and two bunches per shoot is most common. Where fruitfulness is low, the vine-grower must prune to CANES as opposed to SPURS, as shoots which arise from short spurs will typically be of lower fruitfulness, arising as they do from BASAL BUDS.

Potential fruitfulness is determined at about the time the vines flower, as the buds are developing on the growing shoot. This process is known as INITIATION and is encouraged by warm, sunny weather and an open CANOPY that allows the sunlight to penetrate to the developing buds and adjacent leaves. By late summer it is usually possible to estimate the potential number of bunches which will be produced the following year by dissection and microscopic examination of the buds. The vine-grower anxiously assesses fruitfulness just as soon as the small bunches are evident on the developing shoots in spring. Normally, the higher the bunch number the higher is the potential yield of that season, although of course there are many other critical stages, especially FRUIT SET, before the harvest is brought in. R.E.S.

Iland, P., et al., Flowering and fruit set', in *The Grapevine: From the Science to the Practice of Growing Vines for Wine* (2011).

fruit set, an important and delicate stage of the vine's development after FLOWERING which marks the transition from flower to grape berry. The setting period of about a week is a critical one for the vine-grower, since it is a major determinant of the size of the crop, yet the grower can do little to change the course of events. Only 'set' or fertilized flowers grow into the berries from which wine is made; the others fail to grow and eventually fall off. Fruit set occurs immediately after flowering and is the result of successful POLLINATION achieving fertilization of the ovules and the development of seeds. The GRAPE SEED contains an embryo, formed by the union of the sperm cells from the POLLEN and the egg cell of the OVARY. Most wine grape varieties contain up to four seeds. The more seeds there are, the larger is the berry.

Only about 30% of flowers become berries, although the range can be from almost zero to 60%. Those flowers that do not set fall from the bunch in a process called 'shatter'. It is not clear whether fruit set is more influenced by organic nutrition (CARBOHYDRATE supply) or by HORMONES, but the crucial role played by the weather during this period is beyond dispute.

At one extreme, and common in hot DRY-FARMED regions, high temperatures and winds, low humidity, and attendant WATER STRESS can reduce fruit set. On the other hand, cold, cloudy, and rainy weather at flowering commonly reduces fruit set, and such conditions can cause widespread yield losses. Strategies to improve fruit set include using BALANCED PRUNING to avoid rapid shoot growth, ensuring balanced VINE NUTRITION (particularly NITROGEN, BORON, and ZINC) and water supply, topping shoots during flowering (see TRIMMING), or the application of certain chemical GROWTH REGULATORS such as CCC (2-chloroethyltrimethyl-ammonium chloride) before flowering. CINCTURING vine trunks at flowering is labour-intensive and likely to be used only for TABLE GRAPES.

A new process known as Thermal Plant Treatment (TPT) has demonstrated significant improvement in fruit set in California and Oregon. Gas-fuelled heater-blowers mounted on a trailer direct a transient air blast of 150 °C/300 °F into the canopy during fruit set. This has led to an increase of around 25% in berries per bunch across several trial sites.

Fruit set can be said to have been poor when fruit yield is lower than normal as a consequence of COULURE, which leaves few berries per bunch, MILLERANDAGE, which leaves a high proportion of seedless berries and 'live green ovaries' (LGOs) per bunch, or both. B.G.C., P.R.D. & R.E.S.

Iland, P., et al., 'Flowering and fruit set', in *The Grapevine: From the Science to the Practice of Growing Vines for Wine* (2011).

Parker Wong, D., 'Flash heat treatment shown to benefit vines and wine', *Vineyard & Winery Management* (May–June 2015), 56–60.

fruit wines, made by the FERMENTATION of fruits other than grapes, include cider and perry but not beer or sake, since these last derive their fermentable sugars from hydrolized starch. Drinks made from tree fruits and berries are particularly common in cool-climate regions of North America, the UK, France, and northern Europe.

Berries contain so little fermentable sugar that sugar-cane-derived SUCROSE or other tree fruits or grapes may be added (a form of ENRICHMENT) to obtain sufficient ALCOHOL for stability (see STABILIZATION). Fruit ACIDS split the sucrose into fermentable GLUCOSE and FRUCTOSE, as does a natural ENZYME found in YEASTS.

In most cases, acid levels are so high that it is necessary to dilute the crushed fruit to reduce tartness in the resulting wine, although some tree fruits require acid additions for balance. Citrus fruits have high levels of CITRIC ACID; MALIC ACID dominates the acid mix in apples and other tree fruit. (Grapes are distinguished by their high levels of TARTARIC ACID, which is more resistant to attack by BACTERIA.)

Lack of yeast NUTRIENTS can be a problem in persuading fruits other than grapes to ferment. Commercial preparations of deactivated yeast, nitrogen, phosphorus, and potassium to make up the fruit's natural deficiencies are commonly available to those who practise HOME WINEMAKING.

Top-quality cider, made from fresh, bitter or bittersweet apples, fermented using AMBIENT YEAST, with no added sugar or acid, is enjoying a revival, particularly in cooler parts of North America and northern Europe. So-called co-ferments in which grapes are fermented with other fruits and flowers, but which may not be labelled as wine, are also gaining in popularity. Ciderkin is a PIQUETTE made from apple must.

With the exception of craft cider, few fruit wines improve with AGEING. Primary fruit flavours fade rapidly, and most are best consumed within a year of bottling. A.D.W.

Fuder, German word for a large wooden BARREL, typically one with a capacity of 1,000 l/264 gal used in the MOSEL region. (The STÜCK is more commonly used in RHINE regions.) A **Halbfuder** contains 500 l and was traditionally used for transporting wine from the Mosel. The French equivalent is *foudre*.

full. A wine is described as full, or **full-bodied**, if it is high, but not excessively high, in ALCOHOL and VISCOSITY. See BODY for more details.

Fumé Blanc is the curious descendant of the Loire synonym BLANC FUMÉ for the white grape variety SAUVIGNON BLANC. In the early 1970s, California's famous ideas man Robert MONDAVI had one of his most famous inspirations, that of renaming the then unfashionable Sauvignon Blanc as Fumé Blanc, thereby imbuing it with some of the glamour of imported French Pouilly-Fumé. He also gave it some OAK AGEING and a dark green bordeaux-shaped BOTTLE (both entirely alien to Pouilly-Fumé). This formula proved a runaway success, and Fumé Blanc became the highly successful name of a wine type in America, Israel, and elsewhere, even though there was little agreement about what defined it. By the 21st century, the name was waning in popularity.

fumigation, the viticultural practice of fumigating vineyard soils with the aim of killing soil-borne VINE PESTS or VINE DISEASES. Less common than in the past, it is usually carried out before planting. The earliest example of viticultural fumigation was the use of carbon bisulfide in France to combat PHYLLOXERA in the 1880s. Approximately 68,000 ha/167,960 acres were treated, requiring the painstaking insertion of about 30,000 holes per ha (12,000 per acre). Phylloxera is now controlled by GRAFTING, and today fumigation is used primarily to control the NEMATODE vector *Xiphenema index* of the virus disease FANLEAF DEGENERATION, but also for ARMILLARIA ROOT ROT, CROWN GALL, and occasionally squirrels and gophers.

Fumigation is difficult since it requires deep injection of a volatile chemical or gas which will permeate every pore to kill effectively. The exercise is most effective if the soil is porous and not too wet. Newly fumigated vineyards in environmentally conscious areas such as California are covered with a large plastic sheet to prevent the fumigant being lost to the atmosphere. Some fumigants were banned in the early 1990s since they were found to contaminate groundwater, and the use of ozone-depleting methyl bromide was banned in the EU in 2010. Where possible, resistant ROOTSTOCKS are a better alternative, as well as the application of post-planting PESTICIDES. R.E.S. & J.E.H.

Fumin, renascent dark-berried vine speciality of the Valle d'AOSTA whose firm produce, from 25 ha/62 acres in 2015, is usually blended.

funds, wine. Wine funds aggregate investors' funds with a view to creating a professionally managed, balanced portfolio of FINE WINES. The first credible wine funds were the UK-based operations The Wine Investment Fund and the (now defunct) Vintage Wine Fund, which opened for business in January 2003.

Wine investment funds emerged as a result of the steady growth in the value of fine wine and with it the new respectability of fine wine as a part of SWAG, the tangible asset class that comprises silver, wine, art, and gold. The prestige conferred by fine-wine ownership and the thrill of the chase have contributed to the phenomenon of wine investment in general and the wine investment funds in particular.

In parallel with art funds, the mid 2000s saw a glut of wine funds, and by 2014 there were more than a dozen such operations across Europe, the US, and Asia with estimated investments under management of between £150 and £200 million.

Wine funds were originally aimed at professional investors and high-net-worth individuals. While certain professional businesses have now been active for many years, other funds have been hampered by low liquidity, growing too fast in a relatively small market, questionable valuation standards, and poor portfolio selection.

Wine funds necessarily rely on a continuing rise in overall fine-wine prices in order to provide returns to their investors. It was of considerable concern to wine funds and their investors when the Bordeaux bubble burst in mid 2011, following an unprecedented pricing surge for the region's successful 2009 and 2010 vintages. Many businesses running purely as wine funds did not survive. Fund managers taking a long-term view, creating diverse portfolios, and paying particular attention to PROVENANCE are presumably the ones most likely to succeed today. A.H.L.R., C.A. & E.L.

Lister, E., 'Liquid Assets', *World of Fine Wine*, 32, 33, 34.

fungal diseases, very large group of vine diseases which are caused by small, mostly microscopic, and filament-shaped organisms. Since fungi lack chlorophyll they need to live on other organisms to obtain nourishment. Fungal diseases have been of major significance in affecting grape production over centuries, with important consequences for both quantity and quality. Today they receive little public attention since they can successfully be controlled by a wide range of AGROCHEMICALS. In fact the famous fungicide BORDEAUX MIXTURE was used commercially to control DOWNY MILDEW in 1885 and for 50 years was the most important control of other fungal and bacterial plant diseases. Fungal-disease epidemics are commonly related to weather conditions; examples are downy mildew and BOTRYTIS BUNCH ROT, both of which are favoured by warm, wet or humid weather, while POWDERY MILDEW is favoured by overcast, cool weather.

Many of the economically important fungal diseases originated in America, and therefore common varieties of the European VITIS VINIFERA species have no resistance. Thus, when powdery mildew was introduced in 1847 and then downy mildew in 1878, French *vinifera* vineyards were devastated. Fungal diseases can attack shoots and leaves but also developing bunches and ripe fruit. Some fungi such as *Armillaria* and *Verticillium* attack roots. Of more recent concern are a group of fungi which cause TRUNK DISEASES. They spread in vineyards and are also common contaminants of young vines propagated in grapevine NURSERIES.

Botrytis is the fungus with which wine consumers are probably most familiar. In its benevolent form (see NOBLE ROT), it contributes to a high proportion of the most famous SWEET WINES. The more common malevolent form (see GREY ROT) causes substantial yield and quality losses, on the other hand.

Common fungal diseases are ANTHRACNOSE, ARMILLARIA ROOT ROT, BLACK ROT, BOTRYTIS BUNCH ROT, BUNCH ROTS, COLLAR ROT, DEAD ARM, DOWNY MILDEW, ESCA, EUTYPA DIEBACK, POWDERY

F

MILDEW, TEXAS ROOT ROT, VERTICILLIUM WILT, and WHITE ROT. Other groups of vine diseases include BACTERIAL DISEASES, PHYTOPLASMA diseases, and VIRUS DISEASES. R.E.S.

Emmett, R. W., et al., 'Grape diseases and vineyard protection', in B. G. Coombe and P. R. Dry (eds.), *Viticulture*, ii: *Practices* (2nd edn, 2006).

Wilcox, W. F., et al. (eds.), *Compendium of Grape Diseases, Disorders, and Pests* (2nd edn, 2015).

fungi, a group of small and often microscopic multicellular or filamentous organisms which derive their energy living as saprophytes on dead plant or animal tissue or as pathogens on living tissue. Fungi include YEASTS important in fermentation and many organisms causing vine FUNGAL DISEASES.

fungicide, type of PESTICIDE that is effective against FUNGAL DISEASES in vineyards. The first of the modern fungicides used for any crop was the BORDEAUX MIXTURE used on grapevines against DOWNY MILDEW in 1885. Fungicides are applied by SPRAYING at times which are deemed effective to prevent fungal development or control existing disease. Fungicides are thus classified as protectants or eradicants, depending on the timing of application. Protectant fungicides are applied before the fungus infects the vines, and they prevent infection by inhibiting fungal development on the plant surface.

Eradicant fungicides are effective when applied after the infection has occurred. They can either inhibit or kill fungi present on or in the vine, thus preventing these fungi from further disease development. A typical characteristic of eradicants is their ability to penetrate plant tissues, most being systemic. Some eradicant fungicides can be applied one week or more after infection and still be effective.

Systemic fungicides have the ability to infiltrate and move within plants. Movement may be relatively localized, such as from one side of a leaf to the other (translaminar), or extensive, via the vine's vascular system. Contact fungicides are not absorbed by plant tissue: they act on the surface, and so good coverage of the target is critical. Examples include SULFUR and COPPER formulations. Copper ions are toxic to zoospores of downy mildew and prevent infection on the surface of plant tissue.

Mixtures of active ingredients may be used in formulations for different purposes and may take advantage of synergistic effects: copper oxychloride and zineb mixtures, for example, or to create mixtures of protectant and eradicant fungicides, as for copper oxychloride and metalaxyl. Some fungicides may be used against more than one fungal pathogen: azoxystrobin is effective against both downy mildew and BOTRYTIS BUNCH ROT, for instance, whereas others have a narrow range of action.

It is important to keep levels of fungicide RESIDUES below limits specified for toxicological reasons. For wine grapes, there is an additional consideration: residues of some fungicides will inhibit yeast activity, thus affecting fermentation and resultant wine quality.

As with other pesticides, the potential for development of resistance to fungicides varies according to the type of fungicide. Fungicides can be grouped according to their mode of action as either multi-site or single-site inhibitors. Multi-site inhibitors are toxic in more than one way, and the chance of developing resistant strains by mutation is therefore low. This group includes protectant fungicides which have been widely used in viticulture for decades without any significant decrease in efficacy. Single-site inhibitors have more specific toxicity; because they inhibit only one or a few steps in fungal metabolism, the chance of resistant strains arising is much greater. Many of the newer fungicides fall into this group. Strategies that delay or prevent the development of resistant strains include restrained use, the use of mixtures of multi- and single-site inhibitor fungicides, and alternation of single-site inhibitors during the season. Over time, resistance to fungicides used for POWDERY MILDEW and BOTRYTIS BUNCH ROT has developed.

Some 'natural' substances have been tested and proven to be effective against fungal pathogens. Activated potassium bicarbonate, paraffinic oil, and milk or whey have been researched for powdery mildew control. In some cases commercially available products have been developed. Species of *Aureobasidium*, *Bacillus*, and *Trichoderma* have been found to compete with fungal pathogens such as downy mildew and BOTRYTIS and reduce infection levels. Other compounds, it is suspected, elicit plant disease resistance mechanisms; if applied ahead of infection, they can reduce damage by fungal disease. See also AGROCHEMICALS. P.R.D. & M.E.

McGrath, M. T., 'What are fungicides', *Plant Health Instructor* (APS, updated 2016).

Fungicide Resistance Action Committee, www.frac.info

Russell, P. E., 'A century of fungicide evolution', *Journal of Agricultural Science*, 143 (2005), 11–25.

furfurals. See OAK FLAVOUR.

Furmint, fine, fiery white TOKAJ grape variety grown most widely in Hungary; in Štajerska Slovenija (Styrian Slovenia) just over the Slovakian border from Tokaj and in Croatia under the name Pušipel (sometimes, Moslavac); and in Romania. It is also being revived in Austria for both dry and sweet wines, particularly in Rust (see RUSTER AUSBRUCH), where it dominated until the early 20th century and was reintroduced from Tokaj by Robert Wenzel in the 1980s. DNA PROFILING has shown that it has a parent–offspring relationship with GOUAIS BLANC; the other parent is thought to be the totally obscure Alba Imputotato frrom Romania. Furmint is also a parent of HÁRSLEVELŰ.

Helpfully for the great sweet wine that is Tokaji, the grapes are particularly sensitive to NOBLE ROT, yet the wine is characterized by very high acidity, which endows the wine with long ageing potential, high sugar levels, and rich, fiery flavours. In Tokaji it is usually blended with up to half as much of the more aromatic grape variety Hárslevelű, and some Sárga Muskotály (MUSCAT BLANC À PETITS GRAINS) is also sometimes included in the blend.

Furmint can easily produce wines with an ALCOHOLIC STRENGTH of 14% or higher, and sturdy, characterful dry Furmint can age extremely well, in addition to being delicious in youth. Although most of Hungary's 3,605 ha/8,908 acres of Furmint are in Tokaj, in Somló it can also make impressively concentrated dry wines. The vine buds early, but ripening slows towards the end of the season, and in some years the BOTRYTIZED (*aszú*) grapes may not be picked until well into November.

The vine has been known in Tokaj since at least the late 16th century, and it is still grown to a limited extent in South Africa, where it was imported in tandem with Hárslevelű.

fusel oil, or **fusel oil alcohols**, a general collective term for the complex and varied mixtures of natural organic chemicals, largely higher alcohols, that are separable as wine is distilled into brandy. It can be removed by efficient distillation, but varying amounts are retained in brandies for its contribution to the flavour. It is predominantly a by-product of the nitrogen metabolism of the YEAST during fermentation and of only minor importance to the wine drinker since it represents such a small proportion of wine aroma.

futures. In wine, wine bought before it is bottled and therefore long before it can be delivered. See EN PRIMEUR and INVESTMENT.

FYROM. See NORTH MACEDONIA.

G

Gabon, Central African country on the Atlantic coast where viticulture dates back to 2003 with the creation of the Domaine d'Assiami, the one and only vineyard in the country. Imagined by former President Omar Bongo Ondimba in his native region after his meeting with Dominique Auroy, French founder of a TAHITI vineyard, the estate saw its first vines planted in 2008 on the SANDY soils of the Batéké plateau, in the village of Assiami in the south-east of the country. Located just 300 km/186 miles south of the equator, the region has a TROPICAL CLIMATE, hot and humid, with an average of 1,900 mm/75 inches of rain per year, most of it falling March–April and October–November. In order to achieve optimal grape quality, the vines are managed to draw out the ripening phase between June and September, when rainfall is typically less than 150 mm/6 in. J.-B.A.

Gaglioppo, predominant red grape variety in CALABRIA in the far south of Italy whose mid-ruby, quite tannic wines can be hauntingly scented, sometimes of roses. DNA PROFILING has shown it to be a natural CROSS of SANGIOVESE and Mantonico Bianco and therefore a sibling of NERELLO MASCALESE. It thrives in dry conditions and is occasionally found further north. Italy's total plantings of the variety stood at 4,626 ha/ 11,431 acres in 2015.

Gaillac, dynamic, variegated AOC in SOUTH WEST FRANCE that is also of considerable historic importance. As outlined in the history of FRANCE, archaeological evidence suggests that Gaillac may have been one of the first viticultural centres of ancient GAUL, with wine production well established in the early years of the 1st century CE.

Gaillac certainly seems to have been producing wine long before BORDEAUX, the port through which its wines would have been shipped after being transported down the rivers Tarn and GARONNE. BARBARIAN invasions then curbed wine production until it was revived by MONKS at the Abbey of St-Michel-de-Gaillac in the 10th century. Gaillac wines were highly prized both locally and in northern Europe, especially ENGLAND, in the Middle Ages. Its export trade was thwarted, however, by the protectionist measures imposed by the merchants of Bordeaux.

The Albigensian Crusade and the religious wars of the 12th–13th centuries inevitably disrupted trade, although there is evidence that the English were once more buying Gaillac with enthusiasm in the 16th century, and the region, along with LIMOUX, was already associated with SPARKLING WINE production in 1680.

The powerful, deeply coloured red wines of Gaillac continued to be prized by blenders in the early 19th century when ADULTERATION AND FRAUD were rife, but the arrival of PHYLLOXERA towards the end of the century drove many local farmers to exploit crops other than the vine.

In modern times, around 60% of Gaillac's annual production of 155,000 hl/4,094,667 gal is red wine, with 30% white—including dry, sparkling, and sweet wines—and the rest rosé. Gaillac wines are made on both sides of the river Tarn. On the north bank, there is a subsidiary area called Gaillac Premières Côtes, where some of the best wines are made and where the production rules are stricter. Further north is the Cordes plateau, its CHALKY soils the source of many of Gaillac's best dry whites.

The most distinctive local white grape variety is white- or pink-skinned MAUZAC, whose wines have a strong apple-peel aroma and sometimes a certain astringency. LEN DE L'EL is another increasingly popular local variety, and MUSCADELLE is the third principal grape. The three together must make up at least half of any dry white Gaillac. Sauvignon Blanc is also allowed, although iconoclasts such as Robert Plageoles happily ignore it, opting instead to produce a range of idiosyncratic wines such as a *vin de voile* aged under FILM-FORMING YEAST and a *vin* DOUX from ONDENC, an old variety now making a comeback and a reminder that, until the 1960s, dry white wine was not made in Gaillac.

Gaillac also produces a slightly fizzy white called Perlé, and sparkling wines are made here by the *méthode gaillacoise*, a close relation of the *méthode ancestrale* (see SPARKLING WINEMAKING). These range in style from dry to sweet.

Gaillac reds can have the structure of a good bordeaux but more spicy flavours, substantially based on the spicy DURAS and full-bodied FER (called Braucol locally), sometimes supplemented by Syrah as well as other local varieties. The relatively recent arrival GAMAY was planted in the 1960s to provide Gaillac vignerons with income from PRIMEUR wines. The AOC regulations of Gaillac hint at thousands of hours of local political manœuvre. There is a clear division between the aspirations of the most innovative independent growers and the forces of mass production driven by the local CO-OPERATIVES and NÉGOCIANTS. P.S.

Gaja, one of the most renowned producers of high-quality, estate-bottled wines in PIEMONTE, traces its origins to 1856 when the Gaja family opened a tavern in their home town of BARBARESCO and began serving their own wines to accompany the food. By the end of the 19th century, the wines were already being bottled and supplied to the Italian army in Abyssinia, a highly unusual development in their home district of the Langhe, where a tradition of bottled wine assumed real significance only from the 1960s. The firm became an important force after the Second World War under the direction of Giovanni Gaja, who began an important series of vineyard purchases in what is now the Barbaresco DOCG zone, a strategy that has given the house a total vineyard area of 101 ha/249 acres, dwarfing all other family-owned Barbaresco houses, and an excellent selection of superior vineyard sites.

Gaja wines gained worldwide recognition under Giovanni's son Angelo Gaja, who took over in the late 1960s. Trained at the oenological school of Alba and at MONTPELLIER, an indefatigable traveller in the world's major viticultural areas, and a tireless and charismatic champion of his native region and its wines, he gave a new international perspective to the wines, pioneering small BARREL AGEING of both Barbaresco and BARBERA and introducing INTERNATIONAL VARIETIES to the vineyards of Piemonte (his Cabernet Sauvignon is called Darmagi, Piemontese for 'what a shame', supposedly his father's reaction). He also acquired land in nearby BAROLO, with the 1988 Barolo Sperss marking a return to the zone from which the Gaja family made a wine from purchased grapes until 1961.

In the 1990s Gaja expanded his horizons even further, purchasing the Pieve di Santa Restituta estate in Montalcino, where the first BRUNELLO DI MONTALCINO produced under his supervision was made in 1993 and, more recently, the development of the Ca' Marcanda estate in BOLGHERI on the Tuscan coast.

In 1999 Gaja announced that he was renouncing the name he had made so famous and selling all the wine previously sold as Barbaresco DOCG, including his fabulously expensive single-vineyard Sorì San Lorenzo, Sorì Tildin, and Costa Russi bottlings, as DOC Langhe Nebbiolo, the catch-all appellation for declassified Barolo and Barbaresco and for wines containing up to 15% 'foreign' varieties such as Cabernet Sauvignon, Merlot, and Syrah. But now that Gaja's daughter Gaia, with her brother Giovanni and sister Rosella, is at the helm, the Barbaresco denomination has been restored on labels, with further geographical precision expected. In 2017 Gaja founded IDDA, a JOINT VENTURE with Alberto Graci on Etna's little-known but promising south-west flank rather than in the overcrowded north. W.S.

Steinberg, E., *The Vines of San Lorenzo* (1992).

Galen, Greek physician whose work in the 2nd century CE was influential in Greece, Rome, and beyond. He identified the antiseptic properties of wine. See ATHENAEUS and MEDICINE.

Galen, *Selected Works*, translated by P. N. Singer (1997).

galestro, the local name for soils of finely splitting scaly CLAY (*argille scagliose*) and MARLY clay that characterize many of the best vineyards in CHIANTI CLASSICO as well as in parts of MONTALCINO. The region's bedrock consists of an intricate arrangement of marls, CALCAREOUS marls, fine SANDSTONES, and scaly clay. The resulting soils are in places flaky and lustrous, well drained yet moist. A.J.M.

galet, or **galet roulé**, is a French term for a pebble, cobble, or even a boulder (see GEOLOGY) that is well rounded due to abrasion through continual rolling in fast-moving water.

The celebrated river-worn galets of CHÂTEAUNEUF-DU-PAPE and other parts of the southern Rhône are composed of strikingly white QUARTZITE. Although it is probably the underlying CLAYS and SANDS that are more significant for vine growth, these *galets* are so iconic that the name is now applied to rounded rock fragments in other vineyard regions, irrespective of their composition. In the Boutenac area of CORBIÈRES, for example, the *galets* are formed from a brown-stained quartzite; in California's ARROYO SECO, *galets* are a mixture of rock types; and Walla Walla, WASHINGTON, has old river channels filled with *galets* of dark BASALT. A.J.M.

Galet, Pierre (1921–2019), father of modern AMPELOGRAPHY based in MONTPELLIER. Galet's working life was devoted to the science of describing and identifying VINE VARIETIES on the basis of minute botanical observation—an expertise he perfected while hiding from the German occupation in the international VITIS collection in the grounds of the Department of Viticulture at the University of Montpellier. From 1946 to 1989, Galet was part of an elite teaching group that included Jean Branas, Denis Boubals, and François Champagnol at ENSA (now Montpellier Institut Agro), regarded as a centre of viticultural ACADEME. He taught thousands, including Paul Truel, whose own work was of worldwide significance, and Jean-Michel Boursiquot, who has succeeded him. Other acolytes include Lucie Morton (US), Umberto Camargo (Brazil), Erika Maul Dettweiler (Germany), and Anna Schneider (Italy).

Galet began by self-publishing a prodigious body of work which he continually updated. His foundational four-volume *Cépages et vignobles de France* came out between 1956 and 1964. Volume 1 was devoted entirely to American *Vitis* species, ROOTSTOCKS, and French-American HYBRIDS; Volumes 2 and 3 to VITIS VINIFERA wine grapes and Volume 4 to *vinifera* TABLE GRAPES. In 1988, when Volume 1 had become a rare book, he published Tome 1: *Les Vignes américaines*, 553 pages with colour illustrations. This was followed by Tome II: *L'Ampélographie française*, 400 pages devoted to *vinifera* wine grapes. His original Volume 4 on table grapes remains available but not renewed. Ever-active, at age 95 Galet oversaw an astonishing compilation of his ampelographic writing in *Dictionnaire encyclopédique des cépages*, illustrating and characterizing almost 10,000 grape varieties.

Beyond ampelography were Galet's two volumes of *Maladies et parasites de la vigne* (1977 and 1988). His textbook on general viticulture *Précis de viticulture*, first published in 1970 with the final 7th edition in 2000, was an essential reference. In 1983 he was lauded by the OIV for the entirety of his published work and awarded the Officier de l'Ordre du Mérite Agricole in 2013.

Outside the classroom, Galet's authoritative vine identification, which predated genetic sequencing, helped settle legal disputes and informed wine regions around the world as to which grape varieties they were growing under which names. He travelled to vineyards throughout the Americas, North Africa, Cyprus, Afghanistan, Nepal, Thailand, and South Korea (Truel inspected the vineyards of Australia and Portugal). For those who learn his methods, grape leaves become the face of the grape variety—recognizable wherever they may be. This creates a special and intimate relationship with vines growing freely up a tree or constrained to a trellis before their fruit makes its way to the table or glass. L.T.M.

Galet, P., *Dictionnaire encyclopédique des cépages et de leurs synonymes* (2015).

Morton, L., 'A tribute to Pierre Galet, master ampelographer and mentor', *Wine Business Monthly* (September 2019).

Galicia, Spain's Atlantic north-west and one of the country's 17 autonomous regions encompassing the DO wine regions of RÍAS BAIXAS, RIBEIRO, RIBEIRA SACRA, MONTERREI, and VALDEORRAS. Separated by mountains from CASTILLA Y LEÓN, Galicia has developed in isolation from the rest of Spain, the region being geographically and culturally closer to northern Portugal than to Madrid (see map under SPAIN). The locals speak Gallego, a close relative of Portuguese. The wines also used to share an affinity with the light, acidic VINHO VERDE produced south of the Miño (Minho in Portuguese), the river that divides this part of Spain from Portugal, but they have become fuller and more substantial with the recovery of INDIGENOUS VARIETIES and the use of modern winemaking techniques.

Wines were exported from Galicia as early as the 14th century, but northern European merchants quickly moved on in search of fuller-bodied wines from the DOURO in northern Portugal. The progressive fragmentation of agricultural holdings left the region with a subsistence economy, and since the 19th century the countryside has suffered from depopulation as people move away to find work. Many of the magnificent TERRACES in the PORT vineyards of the Douro were constructed by itinerant labour from Galicia. Since Spain joined the EU in 1986, however, Galicia has benefited from a massive injection of funds which has transformed its wine industry.

Climatically, Galicia is a transition region from the wet Atlantic coast to the typicial Mediterranean conditions of the Peninsula. On the coast, RAINFALL averaging more than 1,300 mm/ 50 in a year is compensated for by an annual average of over 2,000 hours of sunshine. Vines flourish in these humid conditions, and YIELDS of over 100 hl/ha (5.7 tons/acre) are unequalled anywhere else in Spain. Most of the vineyards are towards the south in the provinces of Orense and Pontevedra and also in Lugo to the east. Rías Baixas, with its prized ALBARIÑO grape, was the engine of Galician rebirth, and its vibrant, dense wines can command high prices. But success has also meant, in the case of some producers, excessive yields and an abusive reliance on such techniques as the use of selected YEASTS. On the Miño river, wines are often blends of Albariño, LOUREIRA, and CAÍÑO BLANCO.

Inland, the Ribeiro DO is making impressive progress. Local whites are complex blends dominated by TREIXADURA and TORRONTÉS, while reds from native varieties are making a remarkable comeback. In the inland Valdeorras and Ribeira Sacra DOs, light reds from the MENCÍA grape are prevalent, but the appley, white GODELLO grape is their main asset. The youngest DO, MONTERREI, has historic significance. It, too, has joined Galicia's dramatic improvement in wine quality. V. de la S. & F.C.

Barquín, J., Guitiérrez, L., and de la Serna, V., *The Finest Wines of Rioja and Northwest Spain* (2011).

gallic acid, a measurement of TANNIN.

Gallo Winery, E. & J., based in Modesto, CALIFORNIA, is the largest winemaking operation in the world and is still family-owned and family-operated. Gallo was developed by the brothers Ernest (1909–2007) and Julio (1910–93) from the vineyards of their father, who shipped grapes for HOME WINEMAKING during PROHIBITION. On the eve of Repeal in 1933, the brothers obtained a licence to manufacture and store wine, and on the demise of Prohibition at the end of that year they began the rapid expansion of their business. Their father and uncle had been associated with the wine business, and winemaking in some form went on in the CENTRAL VALLEY, where the Gallos lived and grew grapes, throughout Prohibition.

Nevertheless, Ernest Gallo's success in establishing a national distribution network—first, while still in his teens, as a grape broker, and then for wine—stands as an extraordinary feat, particularly in view of the business milieu of the era, still dominated by the thuggish outlaw element nurtured by Prohibition.

Julio's special charge was production. By 1935, just two years after Repeal, the winery was producing 350,000 gal/13,300 hl of wine, and in 1936 the brothers built a new facility with a capacity of 1.5 million gal. The new winery's design showed their concern for the highest level of technical efficiency, as its capacity showed their determination in pursuing new and larger markets. In common with most large California wineries, the Gallos at first sold largely in BULK to bottlers; in 1937 they began to promote their own label and to devise their own marketing methods. The development of the firm thereafter was as a completely self-contained enterprise: it either owned its own vineyards or signed growers to long-term contracts; built its own glass factory; maintained its own sales force; acquired control over distributorships; and operated its own research department, its own print shop, and its own transport company. All this continues today. The company is quite remarkably powerful—and quite remarkably secretive.

By 1950 Gallo had the largest wine-production capacity in the United States, and by 1967 it held first position in sales. Moreover, Gallo's sales and marketing operation was long considered the academy for such functions in America. At one time, almost all the top wine sales executives in the US had at least a short stint with Gallo on their résumés. In the 1950s and 1960s, Gallo so revolutionized concepts of wine retailing in America that it was said that Gallo salespeople knew more about a store's inventory than its owner. No wonder Gallo has been accused of having a domineering influence over the rest of the industry, particularly, through its sheer size, in the councils of the trade organization the (California) Wine Institute.

Known from the beginning for sound, inexpensive wines of every kind, including FLAVOURED WINES, wine coolers, FRUIT WINES, brandy, and bulk-process SPARKLING WINES, Gallo inevitably became synonymous with basic JUG WINE.

From 1977, however, Gallo made a determined effort to associate its name with better-quality wines, VARIETALS sold in bottles stoppered with a CORK. By the early 1980s, Gallo was already the largest purchaser of grapes in the Napa Valley. By the end of the 1980s, Gallo had become the largest vineyard owner in Sonoma County. After years of buying grapes and wine from the North Coast, Ernest and Julio signalled their faith in Sonoma County by buying Frei Brothers in Healdsburg in 1977. Gallo have since added MacMurray Estate Vineyards, J Vineyards & Winery, Asti Winery, Laguna Ranch, Del Rio Vineyard, and Two Rock Vineyard in the Russian River Valley; Frei Ranch, Chiotti Vineyard, and Stefani Vineyard in the Dry Creek Valley; Barrelli Creek Vineyard in the Alexander Valley; and the legendary Monte Rosso Vineyard in the Sonoma Valley.

In the 1990s, Gallo began acquiring properties in the Central Coast, including the Olson Ranch in Monterey County and Sunnybrook Ranch in San Luis Obispo County.

Between 2012 and 2017, Gallo purchased Talbott Winery and Sleepy Hollow Vineyard in the Santa Lucia Highlands; Rancho Real and the renowned Sierra Madre Vineyard in Santa Barbara County; Snows Lake Vineyard in Lake County; Ledgewood Creek Vineyard in Solano County just east of the Napa Valley; and Cypress Ranch, a portion of the Palisades Vineyard, and the famous 1,300-acre Stagecoach Vineyard in the Napa Valley.

In 2002, Gallo acquired the highly regarded Louis M. Martini Winery, the first time the company had ever purchased a BRAND, soon to be joined by the Mirassou brand. In 2005, Gallo acquired the Barefoot Cellars brand, which has grown to be the largest-selling wine brand in the world. William Hill Estate Winery and the Canyon Road brand were purchased in 2007, along with Edna Valley Vineyard in 2011. The next year Courtside Cellars in San Miguel was added, along with its first acquisition in Washington State, Columbia Winery. Gallo continued to expand its premium portfolio so that by 2020 it also owned Asti Winery, The Ranch Winery, Orin Swift Cellars, Locations, Pahlmeyer, and Jayson by Pahlmeyer.

In 2021 Gallo announced the acquisition of more than 30 brands from CONSTELLATION BRANDS, including Black Box, a bag-in-BOX operation; Clos du Bois, Estancia, Franciscan, Mark West, Ravenswood, Taylor, Vendange, and Wild Horse in California; Hogue in Washington State; and Arbor Mist flavoured wines and Manischewitz KOSHER wine in New York State, adding five new wineries. The Nobilo New Zealand Sauvignon Blanc brand was also acquired in a separate transaction with Constellation, and Denner Vineyards in Paso Robles was bought by Gallo in late 2022.

Gallo began importing Italian wine in 1996, which it sold under the name Ecco Domani. Gallo currently imports wine from Argentina, Chile, France, Italy, Spain, New Zealand, and Spain. Maze Row Wine Merchant is its premium wine import arm.

Today Gallo is the largest exporter of California wines, and it currently has offices in the UK, Germany, Poland, Hong Kong, Japan, Canada, and Mexico.

Gallo, E. and J., *Our Story* (1994).
Hawkes, E., *Blood and Wine: The Unauthorized Story of the Gallo Wine Empire* (1993).

Galotta, red grape CROSS bred in Switzerland by André Jaquinet at CHANGINS from ANCELLOTTA and GAMAY, producing deeply coloured, tannic,

G

full-bodied wines often used in blends. Authorized in 2009, there were 57 ha/141 acres planted by 2020.

Gamaret, red grape CROSS bred in Switzerland by André Jaquinet at CHANGINS from GAMAY and REICHENSTEINER. The variety has good rot resistance and makes quite powerful, structured wines. Total Swiss plantings had reached nearly 439 ha/1,085 acres by 2020. It is more popular than fellow cross GARANOIR, is authorized in Beaujolais, and is occasionally found in Italy.

Gamay, or **Gamay Noir**, ancient Burgundian red grape variety solely responsible for the distinctive, evolving, and no longer unfashionable wines of BEAUJOLAIS. GALET cites 30 different Gamays, many quite unrelated to the Beaujolais archetype, many of them particular CLONAL SELECTIONS of it, and many more of them red-fleshed TEINTURIERS once widely used to add colour to vapid blends. Red-fleshed versions can still be found, particularly in the Mâconnais and Touraine, and France grew 115 ha/284 acres of **Gamay Teinturier de Bouze** in 2019. The 'real' Gamay is officially known as **Gamay Noir à Jus Blanc** to draw attention to its noble pale flesh, and it is a natural offspring of Pinot and Gouais Blanc (see PINOT).

The introduction of Gamay to the vineyards of the CÔTE D'OR in the late 14th century was viewed as scandalous by those whose livelihood did not personally depend on rearing productive vines, and great efforts were made to retain PINOT NOIR at the expense of the less noble newcomer.

The vine is a precocious one, budding, flowering, and ripening early, which makes it prone to spring FROSTS but means that it can flourish in regions as cool as much of the Loire. It can easily produce too generously, and the traditional GOBELET method of training is designed to match this aptitude to the GRANITIC soils of the better Beaujolais vineyards.

Although today an increasing proportion of Beaujolais, particularly from the CRUS, is vinified like red burgundy with full BARREL AGEING and is expected to age for several years in bottle, Gamay juice long tended to be vinified in a hurry, not least because of strong market pressure in the 1970s and 1980s for Beaujolais NOUVEAU. As a wine, Gamay tends to be paler and bluer than most other reds, with relatively high acidity and a simple but vivacious aroma of freshly picked red fruits, often overlaid in the Nouveau era by the less subtle smells associated with rapid CARBONIC MACERATION such as bananas, boiled sweets, and acetone. In the Mâconnais and Switzerland, it is often blended with Pinot Noir, endowing the nobler grape with some precocity but often blurring the very distinct attributes of each.

Gamay and Beaujolais are entirely interdependent. Few wine regions are so determinedly *monocépagiste* as Beaujolais: in 2019 all but 800 ha of the Rhône *département*'s 14,832 ha/36,651 acres of vines were Gamay Noir. Vinification techniques vary, but most common are local variants on SEMI-CARBONIC MACERATION. Similar, often lighter and arguably truer, wines are made from the Gamay grown in the small wine regions of central France, particularly those around Lyons and in the upper reaches of the Loire such as CHÂTEAUMEILLANT, Coteaux du LYONNAIS, Coteaux du GIENNOIS, Côtes d'AUVERGNE, Côtes du FOREZ, Côte ROANNAISE, and ST-POURÇAIN.

Outside Beaujolais, perhaps because its wines were so long unfashionable, the Gamay vine has been losing ground. In the Côte Chalonnaise and the Mâconnais between Beaujolais and the Côte d'Or, Gamay was displaced as principal grape variety by Chardonnay during the 1980s, and Pinot Noir plantings had surpassed those of Gamay by the 21st century. The generally unexciting quality of Gamays made here is expected to continue this trend. Gamay took up just 117 ha of the Côte d'Or's valuable vineyard in 2019.

Gamay is widely planted in SAVOIE, grown especially in the CRU of Chautagne. It is also grown all over the Loire, especially in the Loir-et-Cher *département* upstream of Tours, but is not glorified by any of the Loire's greatest appellations. Gamay de Touraine can provide a light, sometimes acid, but usually cheaper alternative to Beaujolais, but it is most widely grown west of Touraine, alongside Sauvignon, for such light, lesser-known names as CHEVERNY and Coteaux du VENDÔMOIS. Considerable plantings in the south-west, greater Loire, and the Mâconnais brought France's total area of Gamay Noir up to 23,187 ha/57,296 acres in 2019.

Outside France, the most notable attempts to develop this under-appreciated variety have been in North America, with the first plantings in the 1970s. In 2020, Ontario boasted 172 ha/425 acres, British Columbia 76 ha/189 acres, and Oregon 55 ha/136 acres, the last two showing growth in recent years. Oregon even hosts an annual 'I Love Gamay' festival. While California has plantings of Gamay Noir, the variety referred to as **Napa Gamay** is actually VALDIGUIÉ.

Gamay is also grown in small quantities in New Zealand, Australia, South Africa, and Italy, and it is often confused with BLAUFRÄNKISCH (to which it may well be related) throughout eastern Europe. It plays a relatively important role in the vineyards of TÜRKIYE, SERBIA, and KOSOVO.

Beyond Beaujolais, it is chiefly valued by the Swiss, who grow it widely and often blend it with Pinot Noir to produce Dôle (*see* SWITZERLAND).

Galet, P., *Dictionnaire encyclopédique des cépages* (2nd edn, 2015).

Robinson, J., et al., *Wine Grapes: A Complete Guide to 1,368 Vine Varieties, Including Their Origins and Flavours* (2012).

Gamay del Trasimeno. See GRENACHE NOIR.

Gambellara, dry white wine from the VENETO region of north-east Italy. Based on GARGANEGA grapes (a minimum of 80%, with 20% of TREBBIANO di Soave or Trebbiano Toscano), it is produced in the townships of Gambellara, Montebello Vicentino, Montorso, and Zermeghedo, only a short distance from SOAVE but in the neighbouring province of Vicenza. Gambellara covers only about 600 ha compared with Soave's 6,991 ha/17,275 acres in 2020 but with generally more Garganega and lower yields from its VOLCANIC soils. Since the enlargement of the PROSECCO zone, much of the Garganega planted on the plains south of the town of Gambellara has been replaced with GLERA, so HILLSIDE VINEYARDS represent a healthy 60% of the Gambellara total.

Soil research conducted at the beginning of the century identified six subzones—Faldeo, Taibane, Monti di Mezzo, San Marco, Creari, and Selva—which have begun to appear on labels. Much of Gambellara's output has lacked ambition, but perceptions are changing with estates such as the biodynamic La Biancara Estate, with its SKIN-FERMENTED wines, even if some of the wines are labelled IGT rather than Gambellara, not least because of a quality-control system unwilling to recognize the wines as typical.

The DOC Gambellara zone is elevated to DOCG for the sweet RECIOTO di Gambellara, which has a long history in the region, while Gambellara CLASSICO is not a smaller, historic subzone but a wine with higher alcohol and from (marginally) lower yields. Gambellara VIN SANTO is a PASSITO wine made from grape bunches dried for at least 60 days. W.S.

Gamé, Bulgarian name for BLAUFRÄNKISCH.

www.consorziogambellara.com

Gamza, name for KADARKA in BULGARIA.

garage wines, unofficial, late 20th century term for wines made with ambition in such small quantity that a garage would suffice as winery. Their makers were known as **garagistes**. Although the term came to be used globally, the phenomenon was first observed on Bordeaux's RIGHT BANK, with miniature wine estates producing ultra-modern, deep-coloured, early-maturing, often sweet, oaky, flattering reds, typically in quantities of a few hundred cases, apparently aimed to catch the eye of then-omnipotent wine critic Robert PARKER. LE PIN in Pomerol was the archetype and is the only one to have experienced sustained demand.

Echikson, W., *Noble Rot: A Bordeaux Wine Revolution* (2004).

Garanoir, red grapevine CROSS created at CHANGINS by André Jaquinet from GAMAY and REICHENSTEINER. It makes less concentrated, softer, fruitier wines than its sister cross GAMARET and was planted on 230 ha/568 acres in Switzerland in 2020.

Gard, IGP for the *département* which stretches from the coast of Nîmes inland to the Cevennes Mountains. The smaller IGPs Cévennes and Coteaux du Pont du Gard as well as the AOCS of COSTIÈRES DE NÎMES, TAVEL, and LIRAC sit within it. Mediterranean varieties mix with INTERNATIONAL VARIETIES, often appearing in varietally labelled wines.

Garganega, vigorous, productive (often over-productive), late-ripening white grape variety of the VENETO region in north-east Italy. Its most famous incarnation is SOAVE, in which it may constitute anything from 70 to 100% of the blend, often sharpened up by the addition of TREBBIANO di Soave (VERDICCHIO) but increasingly plumped up by CHARDONNAY and other imports. In the Soave CLASSICO zone, with yields kept well in check and where it is allowed to ripen fully, it can produce the fine, delicate whites redolent of lemon and almonds which give Soave a good name. Naturally high in acid, it can give balanced yet steely wines that have an alluring, delicate spiciness. The vine is also responsible for GAMBELLARA. Other wines in which it plays a major part include Bianco di CUSTOZA, Colli Berici, and Colli Euganei, and it is also grown to a more limited extent in both FRIULI and UMBRIA. In 2007, DNA PROFILING revealed that Garganega is identical to Sicily's GRECANICO DORATO. Italian vineyard statistics reported 8,522 ha/21,058 acres of Garganega in 2015 (but the over 4,000 ha of Grecanico Dorato are listed separately). Garganega also seems to be a parent of a wide range of Italian varieties. It is also grown in Australia.

Robinson, J., et al., *Wine Grapes: A Complete Guide to 1,368 Vine Varieties, Including Their Origins and Flavours* (2012).

Garnacha is the Spanish, and therefore original, name for the increasingly fashionable grape known in France and elsewhere as GRENACHE. Its most common and noblest form is the dark-berried and light-fleshed **Garnacha Tinta** (**Garnaxa** in Catalan). As this variety, ubiquitous in much of Spain, has been re-evaluated from weed to asset (spurred on initially by PRIORAT's success and more recently by the finesse of wines from the Sierra de GREDOS, northern NAVARRA, and RIOJA Oriental), VARIETAL versions have become more common, as have blends with the firmer TEMPRANILLO, and the word 'Garnacha' is increasingly seen on wine labels.

Even after extensive GRUBBING UP in the 1980s and 1990s, when the variety was under-appreciated, in 2004 a total of 82,300 ha/203,300 acres made Garnacha Tinta Spain's second most planted red wine grape after Tempranillo. By 2020 Spain's Garnacha Tinta total had fallen to 58,764 ha/145,209 acres, very slightly more than the BOBAL total and little more than one-quarter of the Tempranillo total. It is grown particularly in Aragon and Castilla-La Mancha, being an important variety in such wine regions as Rioja, Navarra, Empordà-Costa-Brava, Campo de Borja, Cariñena, Costers del Segre, the Gredos Mountains, Madrid, La Mancha, Méntrida, Penedès, Priorat, Somontano, Tarragona, Terra Alta, Utiel-Requena, and Valdeorras. In Rioja it provides stuffing and immediate charm when blended with the more austere Tempranillo. The cooler, higher vineyards of Rioja Alta are reserved for Tempranillo, while Garnacha is the most common grape variety of the warm eastern Rioja Oriental region, where the vines can enjoy a long ripening season. The juiciness apparent in these early-maturing riojas can be tasted in a host of other Spanish reds and, especially, rosados. Garnacha has been adopted with particular enthusiasm in Navarra, where it has been the dominant grape variety and dictates a lighter, more obviously fruity style of red and rosado than in Rioja. In many other areas, Garnacha is typically DRY-FARMED as an old BUSH VINE (average vine age is high) so that the wines can be quite concentrated and tannic.

Perhaps the most distinctive, and certainly the most expensive, Spanish wines based on Garnacha Tinta (sometimes incorporating some **Garnacha Peluda**, more commonly known as LLEDONER PELUT) are from Cataluña's Priorat, making concentrated wine in which the produce of old Garnacha vines is often blended with Carignan grapes, and from the Gredos Mountains.

Garnacha Blanca is the light-berried GRENACHE BLANC, of which in 2020 there were about 2,972 ha/7,344 acres in Spain, where it plays a role in full-bodied, north-eastern whites such as those of Alella, Priorat, Tarragona, Rioja, and Navarra. Old-vine Garnacha Blanca is particularly important in Cataluñya's TERRA ALTA.

Garnacha Tintorera, Spanish synonym for the red-fleshed ALICANTE BOUSCHET, Tintorera being Spanish for 'dyer' or TEINTURIER. Also known as Negral. Spain grew 35,562 ha/87,876 acres of this variety in 2020.

Almost three-quarters is in CASTILLA-LA MANCHA, where its deep colour is presumably much appreciated.

Garonne, river that rises south of Toulouse in SOUTH WEST FRANCE and flows north-west towards the Atlantic and on which the city of BORDEAUX is situated. The confluence of the Garonne and the DORDOGNE, between MARGAUX and BOURG, marks the southern end of the GIRONDE estuary. The Garonne was an important trade route through south-west GAUL in the era of ancient ROME and continued to play a vital role in the medieval wine trade, where there was particular commercial rivalry between the wines produced upriver in the HAUT-PAYS, either on the Garonne or on its tributaries the Lot and the Tarn, and those produced in Bordeaux's immediate vicinity.

Today the Garonne links, travelling north-west down river, FRONTON, LAVILLEDIEU, BRULHOIS, BUZET, Côtes du MARMANDAIS, CADILLAC CÔTES DE BORDEAUX, GRAVES, and Bordeaux's sweet-white-wine areas SAUTERNES and BARSAC.

G

garrafeira, word used by winemakers, wine bottlers, and wine collectors in PORTUGAL meaning a 'private wine cellar' or 'reserve'. The term was once widely used on wine labels to denote a red wine from an exceptional year that has been aged for at least 30 months before sale, including at least 12 months in bottle. White and rosé garrafeira wines, which are now fairly rare, must be aged for at least 12 months, including at least six months in bottle, to qualify. The law additionally states that the term can be used only for DOC or VINHO REGIONAL wines with outstanding organoleptic characteristics. Traditionally most garrafeiras were blends of wines from different parts of the country, labelled with the name of the merchant who bottled them. Under legislation introduced in the early 1990s, all garrafeiras must display their region of origin. See also PORT. R.M. & S.A.

Garrido, minor speciality of the CONDADO DE HUELVA region in southern Spain.

garrigue, French word for Mediterranean scrubland that is sometimes borrowed as a TASTING TERM for wines with aromas reminiscent of wild herbs.

Garrut is a Catalan synonym for Monastrell or MOURVÈDRE.

Gascony, proud region in SOUTH WEST FRANCE which today comprises armagnac country and such wines as MADIRAN and TURSAN. In the Middle Ages it was incorporated into Aquitaine and was therefore, like BORDEAUX, under English rule for nearly 300 years from the middle of the 12th century. The IGP **Côtes de Gascogne** and the overlapping IGP **Gers** were launched in the 1970s by the Grassa family (owners of Domaine du Tariquet, the largest single estate in the south-west) and the CO-OPERATIVE Producteurs Plaimont, largely in response to the decreasing sales of armagnac. The white wines, based mostly on COLOMBARD and UGNI BLANC grapes, have become extremely popular for their vivacity, freshness, and boiled-sweet character, and they have spawned a host of independent growers. There are also Merlot-based reds and rosés, generally less interesting. P.S.

Gattinara, small but historically important wine region in the hills between the towns of Vercelli and Novara in the ALTO PIEMONTE producing red wines based on NEBBIOLO, called Spanna here. Its vineyards, already classified in the 16th century, encompassed only 111 ha/274 acres in 2020. In the 19th century, these hills were far more widely planted with Nebbiolo than the LANGHE, and the wines were more highly prized than either BAROLO or BARBARESCO. The long decline of viticulture here was halted when Gattinara was awarded DOCG status in 1990. In 2004 an overarching DOC, Coste della Sesia, including the Lessona and Gattinara zones, was created to safeguard its wine production. Although production regulations faithfully reflect the historical practice of blending in the local UVA RARA and/or VESPOLINA grapes (maximum 10%), used in the past to compensate for unripe Nebbiolo grapes in cool vintages, practically all Gattinara is now made of 100% Nebbiolo, a sign of improved viticulture, lower yields, and, possibly, CLIMATE CHANGE. Gattinara is a seriously ageworthy wine with mandatory ageing of 35 months (47 months for Riserva), and SINGLE-VINEYARD WINES are the rule rather than the exception. The region received a further boost in 2019 when Roberto Conterno of Barolo's Giacomo Conterno estate took a majority stake in the historic Nervi estate. Conterno's move will undoubtedly be followed by other investors in the near future. W.S.

Gaul, part of western Europe closely approximating to modern France which existed before the rise of classical ROME. The elites of the CELTIC communities beyond the Alps were large-scale consumers of wine long before they were producers. The accoutrements of the Greek and Roman dinner party are frequently found amid the grave goods of Celtic chieftains. Their passion for wine was even claimed as the motive for the Gallic invasions of the Mediterranean world from the 4th century BCE onwards (see e.g. Livy, 5. 33). The import of wine from Etruria (see ETRUSCANS) and the arrival of Greek settlers at Massilia (Marseilles) in the late 7th century BCE stimulated viticulture in southern Gaul. From them the Gauls 'got used to living by the rule of law, and to pruning the vine, and planting the olive' (Justin, 43. 4. 1). The widespread ready market in Gaul for wine, as well as the slaves who were offered in exchange, was a major stimulus for exports from Italy, particularly in the last century BCE (Diodorus, 5. 26). But the real impetus for the creation of local vineyards came with the arrival of Roman settlers from the end of the 2nd century BCE. By the end of the 1st century BCE southern France and the RHÔNE Valley (Gallia Narbonensis) were planted with all the fruit that Mediterranean visitors expected. But beyond the Cévennes was a world where 'no vine, olive, or fruit grew', as the great scholar VARRO (*De re rustica*, 1. 7. 8) noticed while on campaign there. The reasons for this were part sociological and part ecological. Some tribes banned the drinking of wine and even massacred traders, in the belief that consumption undermined their manliness and was the explanation of their defeats by Julius Caesar's armies. More significant was the need for vines which were resistant to FROST. The 1st century CE was a time of considerable development in the south, including wines from Baeterrae (Béziers) and around Vienne (see CÔTE RÔTIE), where the Allobrogica vine was noted for producing a wine with a natural resinated taste. Wines from this region competed in the markets of Italy and the western Mediterranean, as the finds of the distinctive local AMPHORAE confirm. Elsewhere in Gaul it is more difficult to trace the introduction of viticulture. The GARONNE was an important trade route from an early date; so it is highly likely that the BORDEAUX region was developed in the 1st century CE. On the other hand, the first references to vineyards in BURGUNDY, on the MOSELLE, and in the area of PARIS belong to the 4th century CE. However, recent archaeological finds suggest that viticulture may have developed considerably earlier in many regions than the inadequate literary sources suggest. The scale of production should not be exaggerated. Viticulture in regions such as the Moselle continued after the end of the Roman Empire. However, the modern map of wine production in France owes less to the Romans than to the Christian Church in the post-Roman period (see CHARLEMAGNE and MONKS AND MONASTERIES). J.J.P.

Brun, J.-P., *Archéologie du vin et de l'huile en Gaule romaine* (2005).

Dion, R., *Histoire de la vigne et du vin en France des origines au XIXe siècle* (1959).

Gavi, or **Cortese di Gavi**, is a renowned Italian dry white DOCG zone of 1,511 ha/3,733 acres and the most interesting expression of the CORTESE grape in PIEMONTE (but see also CUSTOZA). It is produced in 11 communes (Bosio, Carrosio, Capriata d'Orba, Francavilla Bisio, Gavi, Novi Ligure, Parodi, Pasturana, San Cristoforo, Serravalle Scrivia, and Tassarolo) in the south-east of the province of Alessandria. Although the name of each commune (and even single vineyards) may appear on labels, stylistic differences are not always evident, and most wines are blends of more than one commune. The best Gavi are elegant, with aromatic white fruit, mineral notes, and a long, tangy, citric finish. In the past the wines tended to be rather neutral, caused by excessively high maximum yields, which have recently been reduced to 60 hl/ha, and lower yet for single-vineyard wines. For a white wine best known in its still form, Gavi comes in a surprisingly wide range of styles: FRIZZANTE, SPUMANTE, and METODO CLASSICO (with a minimum required LEES CONTACT of 18 months), as well as MÉTHODE ANCESTRALE. Although there are several BARRIQUE-aged examples, most producers stick to the conventional temperature-controlled fermentation in stainless steel. More interesting Gavi tends to come from producers who focus on ORGANIC and BIODYNAMIC practices and ferment the wine with AMBIENT YEAST.

Thanks partly to the high quality achieved by the pioneering La Scolca estate in Rovereto di Gavi, the wine enjoyed great commercial success in the 1960s and early 1970s. Increasing competition in its category from TRENTINO, ALTO ADIGE, and FRIULI has subsequently put Gavi under a certain commercial pressure, but the trend towards INDIGENOUS VARIETIES in combination with its inimitable style, appreciated by an international market looking for lighter wines, works in Gavi's favour. W.S.

www.consorziogavi.com

GDC, vine-TRAINING SYSTEM. See GENEVA DOUBLE CURTAIN.

Geelong, wine region in the Port Phillip Zone of the Australian state of VICTORIA. Its cool, dry climate lends itself to complex, intense Pinot Noir and Chardonnay. Shiraz also does well. Most of the 45 producers are small, both family-owned and -operated.

Geilweilerhof. See JULIUS-KÜHN-INSTITUT.

Geisenheim University, former research institute for viticulture, horticulture, beverage technology, and landscape architecture, since 2013 known properly as **Hochschule Geisenheim University**. Founded in 1872 by Eduard von Lade to improve the science of growing fruit, particularly apples, it has continued a tradition of combining education with applied research. In 1876 Professor Müller joined Geisenheim as a biologist and in 1882 bred the variety MÜLLER-THURGAU, which later became one of the most planted in Germany.

Today research in VITICULTURE and OENOLOGY focuses on environmental stress effects on grapevine physiology and fruit maturation, with particular emphasis on the possible effects of CLIMATE CHANGE on viticulture and on biotic stresses such as VINE DISEASES; quantifying greenhouse-gas emissions from viticultural soils; studying the effects of elevated CARBON DIOXIDE on all aspects related to grapevine development and fruit quality; the development of new biological and technological strategies to minimize the use of PESTICIDES in both ORGANIC and conventional viticulture; molecular and physiological studies of PESTS and diseases; secondary metabolites formed during fruit development, focusing on FLAVOUR PRECURSORS and PHENOLICS and their dynamics during fruit processing and winemaking; WATER STRESS and the use of new technologies to guide irrigation for grapes and horticultural crops; molecular and traditional genetics, including VINE BREEDING for DISEASE RESISTANCE, CLONAL SELECTION for improved quality and vine health, plant regeneration *in vitro*, research on the adaptation of ROOTSTOCKS to different soil and climate conditions, the genetics of PHYLLOXERA resistance and of YEAST and BACTERIA, and the detection of GENETICALLY MODIFIED organisms; all aspects of wine microbiology; steep-slope viticulture (see HILLSIDE VINEYARDS) and the development of new technologies for MECHANIZATION such as REMOTE SENSING, GLOBAL NAVIGATION SATELLITE SYSTEMS in machine guidance, efficient SOIL WATER management, as well as an economic evaluation of vineyard management under these conditions; new technologies in juice and wine production related to SUSTAINABILITY and consumer expectations; the replacement of wine ADDITIVES by new membrane technologies; and alcohol and acid management in the vineyard and winery. Other areas of activity include identifying and describing objective analytical and sensorial parameters for wine QUALITY as well as optimizing CLOSURES and PACKAGING for wines. Other studies focus on wine ECONOMICS and market research, including studies on consumer preferences, the dynamics of the global wine market, success factors in marketing, enterprise management, and economic analyses of different segments of the wine industry. M.C.

www.hs-geisenheim.de
www.facebook.com/hsgeisenheim

gelatin, the gel familiar in jelly and jello, used by winemakers as a FINING agent. This animal product is particularly useful for precipitating excess TANNINS as large insoluble molecules which can be removed by FILTRATION. Gelatin is deliberately avoided by those making VEGETARIAN AND VEGAN WINES.

Gelber Muskateller. See MUSKATELLER.

gemischter Satz, German term for an interplanting or FIELD BLEND of multiple grape varieties and, by implication, for a wine made from the CO-FERMENTATION of fruit from such plantings. Once common, such plantings are now rare throughout the German-speaking world. In Vienna, although a distinct minority, they are the basis for that urban growing region's DAC known as Wiener Gemischter Satz. See WIEN.

generic wine, one named after a wine type (and usually borrowed from a European place name), as opposed to a VARIETAL, which is named after the grape variety from which the wine was made. Such wines have been particularly common in Australia and the United States. Early CALIFORNIA wineries borrowed European place names shamelessly. Before PROHIBITION one could buy not just St-Julien and Margaux made in the state but even wines named after particular châteaux. After Prohibition, stricter laws limited such borrowings; towards the end of the 1980s, Red Table Wine, White Table Wine, and Rosé began to replace place names on many of the more reputable labels. An EU–US trade agreement implemented in 2006 limited the use of so-called semi-generics to BRANDS that existed before the agreement was signed, but Chablis, Burgundy, and other borrowed names remain in widespread use by a number of large-volume producers, giants GALLO foremost among them. The generic term must be preceded by the place of origin, for example California Chablis or American Champagne. However, the agreement did nothing to demand even the faintest approximations of the original in terms of grape varieties or style. Chablis could and can be just as sickly sweet as Rhine, and both can be made from THOMPSON SEEDLESS or any other white grape. Burgundy, Chianti, and Claret could all come from the same tank and probably have done.

While generic names can still be found on many wine labels, particularly in non-exporting or developing wine regions, bilateral trade agreements between the EU and other wine-producing countries have continued to limit the use of generic names. Thus, for example, the Australian company PENFOLDS had to change the name of their most famous wine from Penfolds Grange Hermitage to Penfolds Grange. No third-country wine entering the EU may carry a geographical name recognized as a European wine name.

Outside Europe, CHAMPAGNE, or its local-language equivalent, is still occasionally used as a generic name for SPARKLING WINE, although not usually for the best-quality products, and the CIVC are particularly active in trying to prevent this.

generoso is a Spanish and Portuguese term for a FORTIFIED WINE.

genetic modification, sometimes called **genetic manipulation** or **genetic engineering**, a modern approach to breeding which involves transfer of genes between organisms. This technology has applications in both VITICULTURE and OENOLOGY, and the techniques used are extremely useful for the study of other aspects of vine biology and for more wide-ranging YEAST research.

A proposed benefit of genetic modification is the ability to insert foreign genes, responsible for a particular desirable characteristic, into the genetic material of traditional VINE VARIETIES such as Cabernet Sauvignon, without altering the genes responsible for their other characteristics. There are hopes of introducing resistance to FUNGAL DISEASES and VIRUS DISEASES as well as to INSECT PESTS by the use of this technique, as well as improving berry RIPENING and quality. Whether such genetically modified vines can retain the same variety name remains to be legally tested. Research groups around the world have produced genetically modified vines; since the late 1990s and early 2000s, field trials have been in progress in Germany, Italy, Australia, and the US with the aim of improving fruit quality and disease resistance. Many governments have introduced strict testing procedures for genetically modified organisms, and consumer resistance in parts of Europe has been considerable. It is expected that the commercial availability of genetically modified vines will depend on market acceptance of wines derived from these plants.

See also TISSUE CULTURE and INTERNATIONAL GRAPE GENOME PROGRAM.

Biotechnology's powerful array of tools has, arguably, seen its widest expression in the modification of the DNA of YEAST. It is the precision with which this can be done in yeast that has driven progress in this area. In its most basic form, a gene which codes for a protein having a particular property can be added, replaced, or removed to change that property. In this way, a genetically modified (GM) yeast can acquire new characteristics, such as the release of enhanced varietal flavour, by introducing a gene that liberates a TERPENOID or THIOL aroma compound from grape-derived precursors, or it can be freed of an undesirable property, such as excess HYDROGEN SULFIDE production. An extension of GM, synthetic biology, allows for more complex engineering to be performed, including the expression of complex biosynthetic pathways from other organisms. This can include providing yeast with the ability to produce plant-derived compounds such as terpenes, ANTHOCYANINS, and VANILLIN. Genetically complex properties—such as fermentation robustness or temperature profile, for which relevant genes have not yet been identified—cannot yet be modified at the gene level in a targeted way.

GM yeast tend to arouse the same concerns as do any other GM products. They have been approved for use in wine production in only a few countries, including the US and Canada. Early examples include the GM wine yeast ML01, produced in Canada. It has two new genes which enable it to consume malic acid, negating the need for the bacterial MALOLACTIC CONVERSION. This yeast is used to improve the taste and colour stability of wine as well as to avoid the production of undesirable compounds (HISTAMINES). Newer strains, capable of making various monoterpenes, raspberry-ketone or LACTIC ACID during wine or beer production, are now being generated in the US, where specific labelling is not required for wine produced using GM yeast, provided that the yeast has been removed and is no longer detectable (see PROCESSING AIDS).

While GM yeast are still not widely approved for use in winemaking, this technology also facilitates an understanding of the genetic basis for many important winemaking properties of yeast and can therefore greatly assist yeast modification by conventional breeding techniques. The development of non-GM yeast in which hydrogen sulfide production has been eliminated is a good example of the benefit of this GM technology. P.A.H. & A.B.

Cebollero, E., et al., 'Transgenic wine yeast technology comes of age: is it time for transgenic wine?', *Biotechnology Letters*, 29/2 (2007), 191–200.

Perl, A., and Eshdat, Y., 'Grape', in E. C. Pua and R. R. Davey (eds.), *Biotechnology in Agriculture and Forestry 60: Transgenic Crops V* (2007), 189–208.

Schuller, D., and Casal, M., 'The use of genetically modified *Saccharomyces cerevisiae* strains in the wine industry', *Applied Microbiology and Biotechnology*, 68/3 (2005), 292–304.

Vivier, M. A., and Pretorius, I. S., 'Genetic improvement of grapevine: tailoring grape varieties for the third millennium—a review', *South African Journal of Oenology & Viticulture*, 21/1 (2000).

Geneva double curtain, often abbreviated to **GDC**, a vine-TRAINING SYSTEM whereby the CANOPY is divided into two pendent curtains, trained downwards from high CORDONS or CANES. The system was developed by Professor Nelson SHAULIS of the Geneva Experiment Station in upstate New York in the early 1960s. The vines are planted in about 3-m/10-ft rows and the TRUNK divided at about 1.5 m height to form two parallel CORDONS about 1.3 m apart. The foliage is trained downwards from these cordons, forming the so-called double curtains. This training system was one of the first examples of a DIVIDED CANOPY developed in the NEW WORLD; by reducing shade, it increases both yield and grape quality (see CANOPY MICROCLIMATE). While initially developed for the American variety CONCORD, the system has been applied to VITIS VINIFERA wine grapes, especially in Italy. It was one of a number of TRELLIS SYSTEMS advocated as part of CANOPY MANAGEMENT improvement in the 1990s. The GDC system is particularly useful for high-VIGOUR vineyards with wide row spacing. While most wine-grape varieties have more erect shoots than the American vines GDC was developed with, it has been found suitable for use in many vineyards, and some notable increases in yield and wine quality have resulted from use of the system. R.E.S.

Smart, R. E., and Robinson, M., *Sunlight into Wine: A Handbook for Winegrape Canopy Management* (1991).

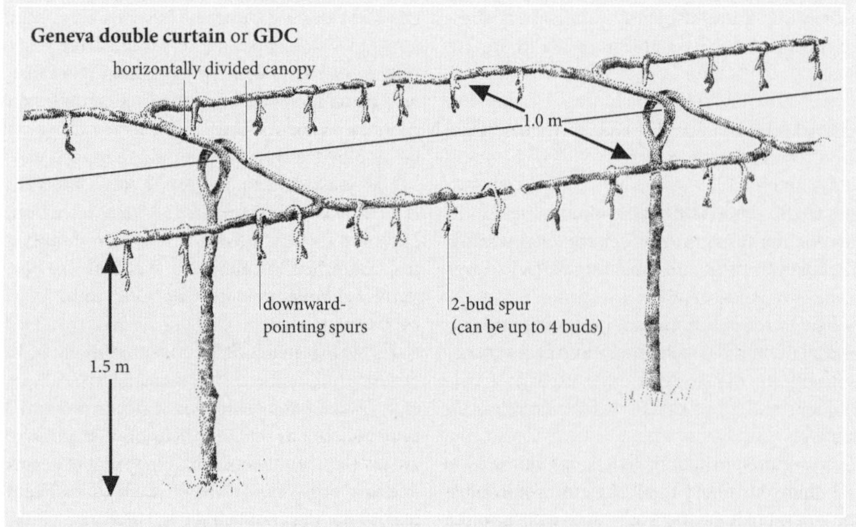

Genoa, north-west Italian port and the principal city of the LIGURIA region. After the fall of ancient ROME and the BARBARIAN invasions, Genoa was occupied by the Lombards, a Germanic tribe, in 642. Under the Lombards, the region disintegrated economically, and the old Roman highways across the Apennines and along the coast were not maintained. It took Genoa until the early 11th century to recover fully from the effects of Lombard rule.

Genoa was therefore initially at a grave disadvantage compared with the city that was to become its deadly rival, VENICE. The Genoese navy had fought to protect its ships from Saracen sea power in the two centuries before the Crusades, together with Amalfi, Pisa, and Venice, and Genoa had established trading posts in the Byzantine empire, although it was nowhere near as successful in this as Venice. Nevertheless, Genoa's rise, like Venice's, was at first based on its eastern trade, and by the time of the Crusades it was battling with Venice, and occasionally Pisa, for economic control of the eastern Mediterranean. The Latin kings of Jerusalem were dependent on Venetian, Genoese, and Pisan naval power for their protection, and so they granted these cities trading areas in their ports. Whereas Venice continued to trade mostly with Constantinople and the Near East, Genoa's interests centred largely on Palestine and Syria. Along with sugar, glass, and textiles, it shipped wine from vineyards there, many of which had been planted by Christian settlers, to Italy, where these strong, sweet wines were accounted a luxury and bought by rich merchants for their own consumption.

Along with luxury goods acquired in the East, Genoa also began to export cheap bulky goods such as grain, salt, oil, alum (for dying woollen cloth), and wine to western and northern Europe. The overland route was prohibitively expensive, and so from the 13th century onwards Genoa organized regular sailings to Bruges and Southampton in galleys, which used their oars to get into and out of ports swiftly, regardless of the prevailing winds. The voyage still took several months, and only strong, sweet wines such as VERNACCIA ('vernage'), produced mainly in Liguria, and the MALMSEYS of the Aegean had any chance of arriving in drinkable condition. The Venetians did not follow the Genoese galleys until 40 years later. In the late 14th century, Genoa abandoned its galleys in favour of the much larger cogs, which had a capacity of 700 to 800 tons and could travel from Genoa to Southampton with only one stop on the way, at Cádiz (see SPAIN).

See also NAPLES and ITALY. H.M.W.

Lopez, R. S., 'The trade of mediaeval Europe: the South', *The Cambridge Economic History of Europe*, 7 vols. ii: *Trade and Industry in the Middle Ages* (1987).

Melis, F., 'Produzione e commercio dei vini italiani nei secoli XIII–XVIII', *Annales cisalpines d'histoire sociale*, 1/3 (1972), 107–33.

Geographe, moderately cool, gently hilly wine region in WESTERN AUSTRALIA with 790 ha/ 1,952 acres of vines in 2020.

geographical delimitation and **geographical designation**. See DELIMITATION, GEOGRAPHICAL.

geographical indication (GI) is a catch-all term that is intended to accommodate the various approaches to the labelling of geographical DELIMITATIONS across the globe. It encompasses those straightforward systems typical of NEW WORLD countries that control only the origin of the grapes, as well as the

European CONTROLLED APPELLATION model that also regulates conditions of production such as variety and yield.

In 2021, the OIV published the following definition: 'Any denomination protected by the competent authorities of the country of origin, which identifies a wine or spirit beverage as originating in a specific geographical area, where a given quality, reputation or other characteristic of the wine or spirit beverage is essentially attributable to its geographical origin.'

GIs can vary greatly in size and consequently in the promise of specificity that they convey. South Eastern Australia and France's Pays d'Oc are immense, covering many thousands of hectares, whereas the smallest, such as the Burgundy grands crus, cover just a few hectares. But in every case they should be more than a mere indication of source. They must signify a link between a place and the characteristics of the wines that are produced there.

Geographical indications were recognized as a special form of intellectual property in 1994 through the WTO's Agreement on Trade Related Aspects of Intellectual Property. The agreement defines a GI as 'an indication that identifies a good as originating in the territory of a country, or a region or locality in that territory, where a given quality, or reputation, or other characteristic, of the good is essentially attributable to its geographical origin'. This definition applies not only to wine but to all products.

Every one of the 159 member countries of the WTO is required to provide a means for the legal protection of GIs against misuse. Wines and spirits have a higher level of protection than other products, but it would be fair to say that each country interprets its obligations differently, resulting in a diverse range of approaches to GI protection as well as a reasonable amount of controversy.

Many countries have incorporated the term 'geographical indication' directly into their legislation, including Australia and China. The EU created the Protected Geographical Indication (PGI) category for wines in 2008, although this is seen as a lower guarantee of typicality than the more strictly controlled Protected Designation of Origin (PDO) category. J.P.H.B.

Gangjee, D. S. (ed.), *Research Handbook on Intellectual Property and Geographical Indications* (2016).

geographical information system (GIS), database which can store, analyse, and display in map form geographically related data such as soil type, climate, ELEVATION, and crop history. GIS is an essential tool in PRECISION VITICULTURE. R.G.V.B.

geology is the scientific study of the solid Earth, although the term has also come to refer to the materials and processes involved with it. Vineyard geology, therefore, means the ground in which the vines are rooted. The loose earth on the surface is derived from bedrock. Such earth is called SOIL if it has incorporated moisture and ORGANIC MATTER and can therefore support plant life. Because grapevines can thrive in strikingly stony soil and even root into bedrock, the distinction in vineyards between rock and soil is unusually blurred.

Many of the world's vineyards are located on sediment that is now distant from its source, while in others the soil is derived from the local bedrock, which may be visible as outcrops protruding through the loose material. All exposed bedrock is under constant chemical and physical attack (weathering), breaking it down into the fragments generally called stones (see STONES AND ROCKS). Smoothed pieces a few centimetres or so across are referred to as pebbles or, if larger, cobbles. As the material is further fragmented, it becomes SAND, SILT, and CLAY. Loose material on hillsides tends to slip down the slope due to gravity (see COLLUVIUM). The world's largest vineyards are on flat plains, carved by rivers over millennia and now covered by ALLUVIUM. All these fragmented products and the bedrock itself are composed of minerals.

Minerals

In geology, minerals are natural, inorganic solids in which the constituent atoms have an ordered, systematic structure. (In the nutrient sense, minerals are soluble single elements; see VINE NUTRITION.) The two most abundant elements in the outer part of the Earth are oxygen (46%) and silicon (28%); consequently the most common minerals are various silicates, in which the two elements are rigidly bonded together, alone in the case of QUARTZ (silicon dioxide) but usually with a number of other elements.

Some minerals relevant to vineyard geology are not silicates but are composed of a single element, such as CARBON (the mineral graphite), largely responsible for the colour of rocks such as dark SHALES; and SULFUR, found in VOLCANIC areas. Non-silicate compounds include the oxides (e.g. hematite, the iron oxide contributing to the distinctive red colour of TERRA ROSSA) and sulfates such as gypsum. Especially important are the carbonates, particularly calcium carbonate (the mineral calcite). Materials dominated by calcite, such as LIMESTONE and MARL, are described as CALCAREOUS.

The silicate minerals are complex and numerous, including the family of mica minerals such as silvery muscovite and shiny black biotite; iron-calcium-magnesium minerals such as pyroxene and amphibole; serpentine, a magnesium silicate unusual in that it can be inimical to grapevines; feldspar, a large group of important rock-forming minerals; and quartz, often referred to as silica. This last can assume a wide variety of forms, including the grey, rather opaque form known as FLINT.

CLAY is used to denote a particularly fine grain size in soils, but it is also the name of a family of flaky silicate minerals found in rocks and soils that are especially varied and intricate.

Rocks

Fundamental though minerals are, more noticeable in many vineyard soils are the larger stony pieces: the rigid, solid aggregates of minerals termed 'rock'. Rocks are classified into three groups according to their origin.

Igneous rocks solidified from a melt. Lava chills at the Earth's surface to form rocks such as BASALT, often with associated volcanic products such as TUFF. Molten material at depth tries to move upwards, progressively cooling until the mass finally solidifies while still deep underground, forming a plutonic igneous rock which may eventually be exposed at the surface by erosion of the overlying rocks. GRANITE is the most widespread plutonic igneous rock in vineyards.

Sedimentary rocks come about because of the weathering of outcrops into loose particles, in geology called 'sediment'. Over time, it tends to be moved across the land surface and out to sea, but at any stage the sediment may be stationary long enough for the grains to become naturally bonded together into a coherent mass, a sedimentary rock. The particle sizes that constitute SANDSTONE, siltstone, and claystone correspond to the grain-size terms for soils described above. Conglomerates have reasonably smooth pebble-sized fragments; in breccia the fragments are angular. Claystone is often referred to as mudstone, especially if it incorporates silt-sized fragments. Shale is a variety of mudstone which tends to splinter along uneven weaknesses, giving a rock that is soft and easily eroded. From the Latin for 'clay' (*argilla*) comes the adjective 'argillaceous', in French *argilo-*, added to rock names where there is a significant clay content. In warm, shallow seawater, accumulations of dead organisms made of calcite and chemical precipitates of calcium carbonate become hardened into limestone, including subvarieties CHALK and dolomite, the latter rich in magnesium. Some clay content gives an argillaceous limestone; even more, a marl or even a calcareous claystone. A certain cachet is often attached to calcareous materials in vineyards but largely for circumstantial rather than scientific reasons.

Metamorphic rocks are formed when rocks deeper underground experience greater pressure and are progressively warmed, slowly undergoing a variety of chemical and physical changes. At any stage, the changes may cease and a combination of uplift and erosion may lead to the material being excavated and visible at the surface. The metamorphic processes can imbue the rock with a planar aspect and a tendency to split. Where it is not possible to discern the individual minerals responsible for this, the rock is known as a SLATE. If the minerals are visible—though then the clean-splitting property is less marked—it is called a SCHIST. If the secondary planes consist of bands of different minerals, it is termed a GNEISS. Marble is the metamorphic equivalent of limestone; QUARTZITE is metamorphosed quartz-rich sandstone.

Geological time and fossils

Vineyard descriptions often mention periods of geological time. A famous example is the controversy over whether true CHABLIS can be produced from Portlandian as well as Kimmeridgian soils. These two terms refer to intervals of geological time rather than to the actual nature of the material, what geologists call its lithology. For viticulture, it is really the lithology and its properties that are relevant, not the remote geological time period in which the bedrock happened to form. However, the age of the overlying soil, typically hugely younger than its parent bedrock, is relevant in that it influences SOIL DEPTH and SOIL FERTILITY.

Fossilized seashells catch the eye in a number of the world's vineyards (see MUSCHELKALK, for example), and microfossils, visible only under the microscope, are essential constituents of important vineyard soils such as CHALK and ALBARIZA. Nearly all fossils are the result of durable geological minerals (most commonly calcite and quartz) replacing and replicating the shape of the original organism. Consequently, despite much mythology, fossils bring nothing different to the nutrition of the vines or the composition of the resulting wine.

Role of vineyard geology

Fundamentally, it is the interplay between erosion and variously arranged bedrock of differing toughness that governs the lie of the land and all that stems from that (see, for example, ELEVATION, HILLSIDE VINEYARD, and TOPOGRAPHY). More directly, the intensity and spatial orientation of planes of weakness in bedrock influence water and vine-root penetration, and its propensity for weathering helps determine the SOIL DEPTH. SOIL COLOUR affects the thermal and ULTRAVIOLET RADIATION behaviour of soil and therefore vine performance.

However, much research indicates that the chief physical effect of geology is its influence on how easily water is stored and transmitted in soil (see DRAINAGE). Two properties are fundamental: porosity expresses what proportion of the substance is space, available for water storage; permeability represents how well water can flow through the material. A good vineyard soil balances the two (see SOIL WATER and SOIL STRUCTURE). In bedrock, water flows partly by using interconnected pores between the constituent mineral particles and partly along the cracks and fissures which exist to some extent in all solid rock.

The other dominant role of geology is its provision of SOIL NUTRIENTS or MINERAL nutrients essential for vine growth. Most are needed only in very small quantities, and the majority of rocks possess ample supplies. However, their availability to vine roots is another matter, because the elements are tightly bonded in the physical soil framework and somehow have to become loosened, dissolved, and transported. In fact, it has been estimated that although a typical vineyard sited on GRANITE will contain abundant potassium, as little as 2% might actually be available to the vines. MYCORRHIZAL fungi and other microorganisms may be involved, but usually chemical weathering acts to generate clay minerals which, thanks to their CATION EXCHANGE CAPACITY, can release elements into water in the soil so that the roots can absorb them (see VINE NUTRITION and VINE PHYSIOLOGY). However, the weathering processes are too slow to yield a fresh supply of nutrients each year; in practice, much of the nutrient supply comes from recycled decayed material in the form of ORGANIC MATTER. Thus stones and bedrock have relatively little direct role in nutrient supply. The vine roots do not distinguish the origin of their nutrients: a complex geology does not lead to complex wines.

Geology and wine flavour

Before modern science, winemakers thought, understandably, that vines and hence wine were made entirely of matter derived from the soil, laying the basis for the European tradition of a special alliance between soil and wine that continues today (see TERROIR). Despite discoveries such as the pre-eminent roles of PHOTOSYNTHESIS and microbial FERMENTATION, it still seems *de rigueur* in winery descriptions to at least mention the vineyard geology and, often, to extol some special virtue. For some enthusiasts, the Earth–wine relationship approaches the mystical, an intimacy unparalleled in any other agricultural product.

In practice, in much of the world the geological factors outlined above tend to be overridden by artificial manipulation: earth moving, RIPPING, DRAINAGE installation, COVER CROPS, and the rest. Two particularly conspicuous interventions are IRRIGATION and the application of FERTILIZERS: WATER STRESS is engineered; nutritional imbalances are routinely corrected.

The extent to which the natural vineyard geology affects wine flavour is unclear. Claims that wines made identically from adjacent sites taste different simply because the geology differs are hard to evaluate because other natural factors will vary along with the geology, particularly concerning MESOCLIMATE, CANOPY MICROCLIMATE, and soil microbiology. Similarly, because its properties interact with a whole matrix of other factors, a soil that is superb in one place may well perform differently elsewhere. Wines of comparable character can come from very different soils, and statements that certain types of geology are always best for a particular grape variety lack consistency, as do assertions about which soils give what qualities to wine. Some wine attributes are given names that sound geological, such as 'mineral', 'earthy', or 'flinty', but they have no literal connection with the soils. Vineyard minerals and rocks are practically insoluble and do not volatilize—prerequisites for giving taste and odour.

Scientifically, geology is clearly important for vine performance and can therefore influence the character and flavour of the finished wine. But its role is indirect, subtle, and complex. Anecdotes notwithstanding, vineyard geology cannot—in any direct, literal way—be tasted in wine. A.J.M.

Maltman, A., *Vineyards, Rocks, and Soils: The Wine Lover's Guide to Geology* (2018).

van Leeuwen, C., and de Rességuier, L., 'Major soil-related factors in terroir expression and vineyard siting', *Elements*, 14/3 (2018), 159–65.

Geoponika, a compilation of advice on agriculture put together about 950 CE at the behest of the scholarly Byzantine Emperor Constantine VII Porphyrogenitus, as part of a grand scheme of digests of knowledge. It was heavily based on a compilation of some three centuries earlier by Cassianus Bassus from Bithynia, who in turn used a collection made by Vindonius Anatolius of Beirut in the 4th century CE. Of the 20 books, the largest section, Books 4–8, consists of a long list of precepts on viticulture and winemaking. The work was much used in the Middle Ages and was translated into Arabic, Syriac, and Armenian. In 1157 Burgundio of Pisa translated the books on viticulture into Latin. J.J.P.

Dalby, A., *Geoponika: Farm Work. A Modern Translation of the Roman and Byzantine Farming Handbook* (2011).

Georgia, independent state between the Black Sea and southern slopes of the High Caucasus. One of the world's great and historic centres of both wild and cultivated vines, it contains the autonomous republics of Apkhazeti and Adjara as well as the former autonomous district of South Ossetia.

History

Wine is integral to the culture of Georgia, a small country whose history is a succession of struggles for independence from such empires as the Assyrian, Roman, Persian, Byzantine,

Arabian, Osmanli, and Russian—and, latterly, that of the Soviet Union. Throughout all these struggles, Georgia has retained a strong identity, including its own language, customs, Christian religion, and a national reverence for wine that has persisted for more than 8,000 years and which is kept alive in Georgia's famous *supra*, a feast punctuated by traditional dancing, singing, and toasts, lubricated with jugfuls of wine and moderated by the *tamada* or toastmaster. Archaeology provides ample evidence that viticulture was long an important occupation of the Georgian people and wine drinking an integral part of their culture. Wine residue, grape seeds, special knives for vine pruning, stone presses, pottery, silver and gold vessels for wine, and jewellery depicting grape bunches and leaves dating back to 6000–5000 BCE have all been unearthed in the Shulaveris-Gora Neolithic site in Lower Kartli and other sites in Georgia. Rich ornaments of fruited vines are found on the walls of ancient churches in Samtavisi, Ikalto, Zarzma, Gelati, Nikortsminda, and Vardzia. According to Apollonius of Rhodes (3rd century BCE), the Argonauts, having arrived in the capital of Kolkhida-Aia (nowadays Kutaisi) centuries earlier, saw twining vines and a fountain of wine in the shade of the trees.

Georgian legends and folklore bear witness to that people's love of the grapevine. Georgia adopted Christianity in the 4th century, and the first cross was made of vines to show that the Christian faith and the vine were the most sacred treasures of the nation.

The Middle Ages was Georgia's golden age of wine. For many centuries, viticulture was of great agricultural and economic importance to the country. In the second half of the 19th century, vineyards covered 71,200 ha/176,000 acres, but FUNGAL DISEASES and PHYLLOXERA reduced the total vineyard area to 37,400 ha by the beginning of the 20th century. In order to restore the vineyards, the country had to import phylloxera-resistant ROOTSTOCKS.

The 20th century was the era of Soviet winemaking; during this time, a number of Georgian TERROIRS were identified and developed, but quality was routinely, and efficiently, sacrificed for the vast quantities required by the Soviet market. GORBACHEV's anti-alcohol campaign of 1985–7 dramatically reduced the market for Georgian wine, although it mainly affected the state vineyards since no Georgian farmers would be willing to pull out their own vines. In 1990, as the Soviet Union was disintegrating, the total area of the vineyards was 115,599 ha/285,500 acres, down from a peak of 134,300 ha in 1976. Viticultural investment was sorely needed. By 2004, the total was 37,419 ha; in 2021 it reached 50,000 ha.

See also ORIGINS OF VINICULTURE and PALAEOETHNOBOTANY. P.T.H.U.

Viticulture and vine varieties

Vines in Georgia (unlike those in RUSSIA) do not need WINTER PROTECTION, and new vineyards are planted to GRAFTED VINES. Vineyards mostly use TRELLIS SYSTEMS and various TRAINING SYSTEMS such as CORDON, GUYOT, traditional Georgian systems, and PERGOLAS.

WILD VINES are widely distributed in Georgia, where *Vitis vinifera* subsp. *silvestris* can still be seen. By both natural and artificial selection, they have given rise to more than 500 identifiable INDIGENOUS VARIETIES and CLONES. The two most widely planted are the indigenous RKATSITELI and SAPERAVI. Although INTERNATIONAL VARIETIES are also appreciated, around 95% of Georgian wine is made from indigenous varieties, including the light-skinned Chinuri, Goruli Mtsvane, Khikhvi, Kisi, Krakhuna, Mtsvane Kakhuri, Tsitska, and Tsolikouri; and the dark-skinned Aladasturi, Aleksandrouli, Avasirkhva, Asuretuli Shavi, Chkhaveri, Mujuretuli, Ojaleshi, Otskhanuri Sapere, Saperavi, Shavkapito, Tavkveri, and Usakhelouri. Many of these Georgian varieties were ignored during the Soviet era because of their low YIELDS but are now being more widely planted and are valued for quality potential and for their distinctiveness. However, one of the difficulties Georgia currently faces in exporting wines is that foreign consumers are unfamiliar with the names and flavours of these traditional Georgian grape varieties. The ancient and uniquely Georgian tradition of fermenting, storing, and ageing wines in clay QVEVRI buried underground has never been lost and, in fact, has seen a noticeable revival in the 2000s. This winemaking method was inscribed on the UNESCO Representative List of the Intangible Cultural Heritage of Humanity in 2013, and in 2020 the OIV General Assembly adopted a definition of white wine with maceration, a special category applicable in particular to wines made in qvevri. Even though qvevri-makers are a dying breed, qvevri wines have begun to attract international attention, particularly among proponents of NATURAL WINE.

Climate and geography

Georgia's TOPOGRAPHY and GEOLOGY are complex. Mountains of the High Caucasus in the north account for about 30% of its total area. The peculiarities of the relief determine a great diversity in the country's soil and climatic conditions, which, in turn, influence grape culture. The climate varies from moderate to subtropical. In the east, annual rainfall is 300–800 mm/12–32 in; the west sees 1,000–2,800 mm/40–110 in. HAIL is a perennial threat.

Georgia has ten viticultural regions: Kakheti and Kartli in south-eastern Georgia; Meskheti in the south; Imereti in the centre; Racha and Lechkhumi in the north; and Adjara, Guria, Samegrelo, and Apkhazeti near the Black Sea. These encompass 25 CONTROLLED APPELLATIONS, 18 of which were recognized by the EU in 2021, with others still awaiting final approval.

Kakheti has always been the most important wine region in the country. It is home to almost 70% of Georgia's vineyard, produces about 80% of its wine, and comprises the richest agricultural land in the south-east of the country in the Alazani and Iori valleys. The climate here is generally moderate, in parts subtropical, with wide variations in annual precipitation depending on location. Cinnamonic forest soils (reddish with high mineral content and enriched with CLAY) and CALCAREOUS soils, some of them ALLUVIAL, are found in the region.

In terms of MESOCLIMATIC conditions and types of wines produced, Kakheti can be subdivided into three main subregions and 19 appellations (e.g. Tsinandali, Mukuzani, Kvareli, Manavi, Napareuli, and Kindzmarauli). The principal grape varieties are Saperavi for reds and Rkatsiteli, Mtsvane Kakhuri, Khikhvi, and Kisi for whites. Alongside more modern technologies, these regions produce the traditional Kakhetian wines, made distinctively tannic and flavourful by FERMENTATION in special clay qvevri followed by an extended MACERATION of up to six months, very much as wines were made thousands of years BCE. Kindzmarauli's speciality is semi-sweet reds. It is in this region that Georgians and incomers have invested most of their hopes for the future of Georgian wine.

Kartli is the heart of Georgia; it inspired the original name for the country, Sakartvelo, and occupies a vast territory in the Mtkvari Valley, including the Mukhrani Lowlands and Gori. These wines are the country's most European, and the region produces the fruit for 15% of Georgia's sparkling wines and brandy production. The zone is moderately warm, with hot and dry summers; vineyards must be irrigated because of the low rainfall (350–500 mm/19 in per year). Main grape varieties are Chinuri and Goruli Mtsvane for whites and Shavkapito and Tavkveri for reds. The capital of Georgia, Tbilisi, where wineries making mainly sparkling wines and brandy are located, is in this zone. Tbilisi's oldest winery, founded in 1897, has a unique collection of ancient wines.

Imereti, the second largest of Georgia's wine regions, is in the eastern part of west Georgia, in the basins and gullies of Rioni Kvirila and other rivers. The most important grape varieties are Tsitska, Tsolikouri, and Krakhuna for whites and sparkling wines and Aladasturi and Otskhanuri Sapere for reds. The one appellation is Sviri. In addition to using modern winemaking methods, Imereti also uses a very particular technique, similar to Kakheti's except that grape skins are added to the clay jars (here called *churi*) during fermentation, a little like Italy's GOVERNO, and this is followed by a maceration of six to eight weeks.

Racha and Lechkhumi comprise Georgia's smallest wine region but one of the country's most important winemaking centres. Vineyards are mainly in the Rioni and Tskhenistskali valleys. Moderate rainfall (1,000–1,300 mm/40–50 in a year), southerly exposure, and the assortment of local vine varieties such as Tsulukidzis Tetra and Tsolikouri for whites and Aleksandrouli, Mujuretuli, Usakhelouri, and Orbeluri Ojaleshi for reds encourage grapes with a sugar content as high as 30%. The region is famous for its natural semi-sweet wines such as the reds of the Khvanchkara and Usakhelouri appellations. Demand for these wines on some markets is so high that Aleksandrouli, Mujuretuli, and Usakhelouri grapes fetch some of the highest prices in the country. Producing high-quality wines from these grapes is a growing trend.

Meskheti, one of Georgia's most ancient winemaking regions, is the origin of some of the oldest Georgian grape varieties. Although viticulture is challenging here, with vineyards traditionally terraced high on the slopes along the Mtkvari river at 900–1,300 m/2,950–4,265 ft, where it is very dry and IRRIGATION is needed, the region is experiencing a revival and a remarkable growth of new plantings.

Towards the Black Sea, the regions of Apkhazeti, Adjara, Guria, and Samegrelo are all known for both semi-sweet and dry wines. Guria, in the south-west, is humid and subtropical. Vines are mainly in the Supsa and Gubazouli valleys and mostly still trained using the traditional methods known as *maghlari* (up trees; see ARBOREAL VITICULTURE) or *olikhnari* (up low trees or tall poles); the main varieties are Chkhaveri, Jani, Mtevandidi, and Skhilatubani. Samegrelo, the ancient region of Colchis, is also humid and subtropical, with long summers and cold winters. Ojaleshi is the main variety, with its own PDO Salkhino Ojaleshi introduced in 2020; Chergvali, Cheshi, Chvitiluri, and others are also grown, all mostly *maghlari* trained. Apkhazeti, a historic winemaking region in north-western Georgia, is planted mainly with Avasirkhva, Amlakhu, and Kachichi. Adjara, which has many climatic microzones, has seen a revival of viticulture and winemaking in recent years. The local varieties are Brola, Khopaturi, and Mekrenchkhi.

The future for Georgia

Georgia has an enviably strong wine and hospitality culture, national belief in its wines, a wide range of high-quality INDIGENOUS VARIETIES, a unique tradition of fermenting wines in qvevri, and no shortage of historically established TERROIRS. The Georgian government and private sector's changing vision for the future of Georgian winemaking pressured exporters to improve quality and to look further afield to markets such as western Europe, the US, Japan, China, and Hong Kong; by 2022 Georgian wine was being exported to over 60 countries. Although annual per capita consumption is around 20 l/5 gal, exports are crucial since much of the domestic demand is satisfied by HOME WINEMAKING. Around one-quarter of the 400,000–450,000 tons of grapes harvested annually in Georgia are used for 'family wine'. Imported wines represent just 3% of the total domestic market.

Foreigners have invested in the Georgian wine industry since the mid 1990s, and government support programmes have attracted new investments in vineyards, wineries, winemaker training, and regulatory oversight. Georgia continues to pursue its course of moving closer to Europe and promoting its wines more effectively around the world through the Georgian Wine Association and the Georgian National Wine Agency.

www.gwa.ge

geosmin, a compound with a strong earthy or muddy aroma that is a by-product of soil bacteria and fungi, particularly *Penicillium expansum*, and is usually associated with wine FAULTS. Found in red and white wines made with ROTTEN grapes, it is also present in some wines with CORK TAINT. The same aroma arises when rain falls on dry earth. See also MICROBIAL TERROIR.

La Guerche. S., et al., 'Origin of (-)-geosmin on grapes: on the complementary action of two fungi, botrytis cinerea and penicillium expansum', *Antonie van Leeuwenhoek*, 88/2 (2005), 131–9.

geotextiles, permeable fabrics used as an alternative to burying vines for WINTER PROTECTION, particularly in CANADA. Trials have shown that this method results in less damage to the vines and the soil and better YIELDS.

Willwerth, J., et al., 'Best management practices for reducing winter injury in grapevines', Brock University, Cool Climate Oenology & Viticulture Institute (2014). www.brocku.ca/webfm/Best_Practices_Manual__Winter_Injury_Sept_14_(5).pdf.

geranium, pejorative TASTING TERM for the smell of crushed geranium leaves that is given off by wines in which LACTIC ACID BACTERIA have reacted with the fungistat (a chemical that prevents fungi from growing) SORBIC ACID. This geranium smell, which occurs in very varied concentrations and for which the compound 2-ethoxyhexa-3,5-diene is responsible, first appeared in wines during the 1970s, when sorbic acid use became common. Its formation can be prevented by adding SULFUR DIOXIDE at the same time as the sorbic acid to prevent the growth and activity of the lactic acid bacteria responsible. A.D.W.

German crosses, an important group of VINE VARIETIES that are the result of VINE BREEDING, an activity that was particularly vigorous in the first half of the 20th century but which continues to this day, most notably at Geilweilerhof, GEISENHEIM, and the research institutes of Freiburg and Weinsburg.

The man who bred Germany's first commercially successful modern cross was in fact Swiss, Dr Hermann Müller (see MÜLLER-THURGAU), whose eponymous vine variety was to become the most planted in Germany in the second half of the 20th century, almost 100 years after it was developed. A succession of new crosses followed in the 20th century, notably from research institutes at Alzey, Freiburg, Geilweilerhof, Geisenheim, Weinsberg, and Würzburg, producing a large number of NEW VARIETIES usually designed to achieve the high MUST WEIGHTS encouraged by the German wine law of the time. The most successful white wine varieties, in descending order of area planted in Germany at the beginning of the 21st century, are KERNER, BACCHUS, SCHEUREBE, FABERREBE, HUXELREBE, ORTEGA, MORIO-MUSKAT, REICHENSTEINER, EHRENFELSER, SIEGERREBE, OPTIMA, and Regner. Others include PERLE, NOBLING, WÜRZER, KANZLER, SCHÖNBURGER, FREISAMER, Findling, RIESLANER, Juwel, ALBALONGA, and, more popular in England than Germany, PHOENIX. Few of these crosses make distinctive, attractive, and characterful wines, although Kerner, Ehrenfelser and, particularly, Scheurebe and Rieslaner can make fine wines if sufficiently ripe. More typically, the vines have been planted to yield good quantities of wines with high must weight.

Successful German crosses for red wine include DORNFELDER, HEROLDREBE, and HELFENSTEINER, bred by Dr August Herold in the 1950s, as well as a host of others bred usually for their COLOUR, such as REGENT, DOMINA, or red-fleshed TEINTURIERS, including Deckrot, DUNKELFELDER, and Dacapo. RONDO has proved popular in England.

See also DISEASE-RESISTANT VARIETIES.

R.K.C.T.

German history. This article encompasses the history of wine production not just in GERMANY but also in ALSACE.

The origins of viticulture to 800 CE

Although the WILD VINE *Vitis vinifera silvestris* may be traced back to prehistoric times on the upper Rhine, the cultivated, wine-yielding vine species VITIS VINIFERA—and with it viticulture in

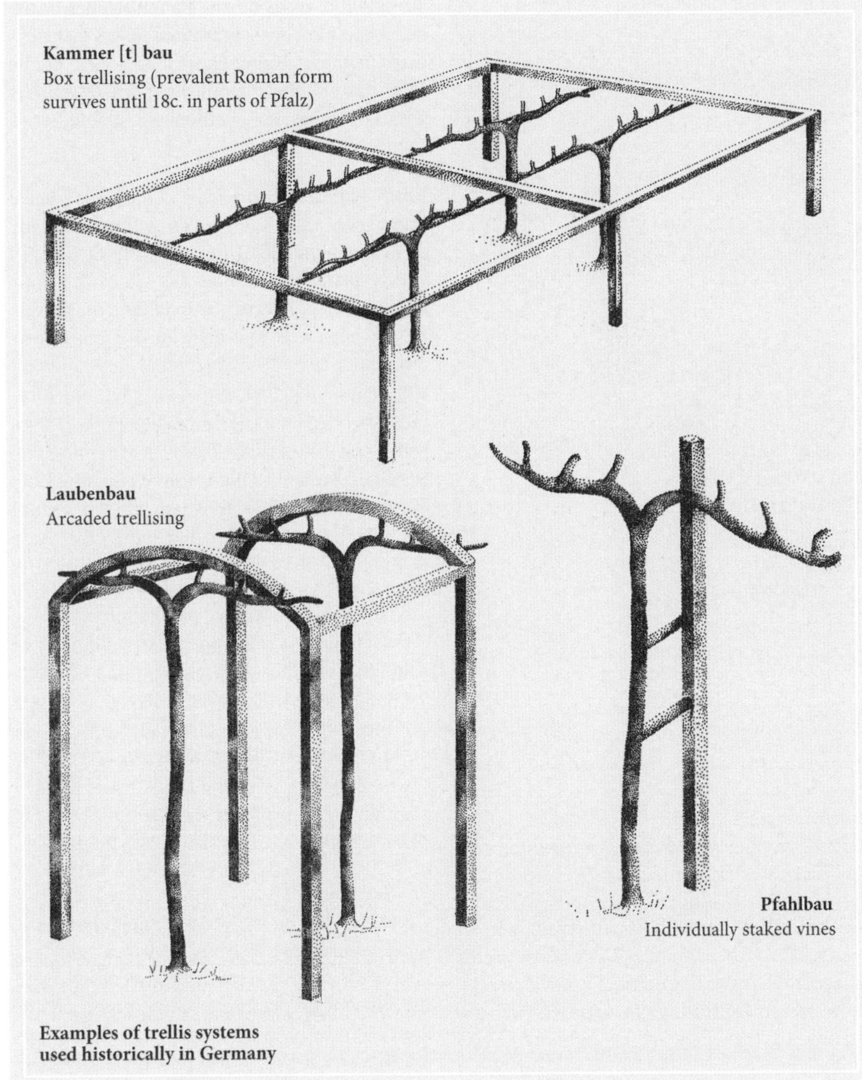

Examples of trellis systems used historically in Germany

Germany—almost certainly owe their origins to the Romans (see ancient ROME).

Although archaeological discoveries have unearthed curved pruning knives near the sites of Roman garrisons on the left bank of the Rhine which can be dated to the 1st century CE, we cannot be sure they were used for vines. Emperor PROBUS (276–82) is traditionally regarded as the founder of viticulture in Germany, but firm literary evidence only occurs with the tract *Mosella*, written around 370 by the Roman author Ausonius of Bordeaux, who lyrically describes the steep vineyards on the banks of the river.

Continuity of viticulture is suggested by the use of typically Roman forms of TRELLIS SYSTEMS on low and high frames (*Kammer(t)*-, and *Lauben*- or *Rahmenbau*), which survived in parts of the Palatinate as late as the 18th century. Evidence of winegrowing under the Merovingians can be seen in the pious donations of their kings: Dagobert I (622–88) gave vineyards at Ladenburg on the Neckar (in what is now the most northerly, Oberrhein district of BADEN) to the church of St Peter in Worms. This grant is especially significant, since it offers one of the earliest pointers to vines on the right bank of the Rhine.

Until the era of CHARLEMAGNE, nevertheless, winegrowing was concentrated west of the Rhine: from Alsace down river into the Palatinate (the modern German wine regions of PFALZ and RHEINHESSEN) and thence downstream along the middle Rhine as far as Koblenz. Winegrowing extended up three left-bank tributaries: the NAHE Valley down to Bingen, where winegrowing is securely documented from 750; the Mosel (with its own tributaries, the SAAR and RUWER), where the tradition of Roman viticulture was vigorously maintained by monastic foundations such as St Maximin and St Martin in Trier; and the most northerly European winegrowing district, the AHR Valley south of Bonn, where vines had been planted on sheltered slopes from at least the 3rd century CE.

East of the Rhine, in the districts beyond the frontier of Roman occupation, the spread of viticulture went hand in hand with the missions of Christian monks such as St Kilian in Franken and St Columban in Bavaria.

Apart from the existence of red wines, cited by the north Italian poet Venantius Fortunatus around 570, next to nothing is known about grape varieties and the quality of wine in this period. T.S.

Scott, T., 'Medieval viticulture in the German-speaking lands', *German History*, 20 (2002), 95–115.

Viticulture's importance in the Middle Ages

From the foundation of the Carolingian empire, the history of German wine can be traced with greater confidence. CHARLEMAGNE's numerous capitularies (law codes, relating particularly to landholding) contain instructions to his officials to plant vines. His true significance, however, lay in the support he gave to the spread of Christianity, for churches and convents were the principal cultivators and consumers of quality wine (see MONKS AND MONASTERIES).

Many vineyards still famous today originate in monastic settlements of the High Middle Ages. In the RHEINGAU, Archbishop Ruthard of Mainz (1088–1109) founded a Benedictine abbey on the slopes above Geisenheim, the Johannisberg, later known as SCHLOSS JOHANNISBERG. In 1135, his successor, Archbishop Adalbert, gave the Steinberg vineyard above Hattenheim to the Cistercians, whose KLOSTER EBERBACH remains the informal headquarters of the German wine trade to the present. On the river MOSEL, Archbishop Baldwin of Trier founded the Carthusian priory of St Alban in 1335, which was endowed with vineyards at Eitelsbach on the Ruwer, the Karthäuser Hofberg. In FRANKEN (Franconia), too, the bishops of Würzburg actively encouraged viticulture along the river Main.

Elsewhere, secular princes played a leading part, especially in the Palatinate, where the count-electors had promoted Bacharach on the Rhine as the entrepôt for wine from their many territories on both banks of the river.

Although viticulture was dominated by the Church and the aristocracy, bourgeois ownership of vineyards was common, too, either corporately by city councils or by individual merchants and investors.

The rapid expansion of viticulture after the millennium, which came to a halt only in the 16th century, can largely be attributed to the recovery in population and the rise of towns as centres of consumption and exchange: 'a wine landscape is an urban landscape' ran the medieval tag. But the spread of vineyards into the higher valleys, often far from urban centres,

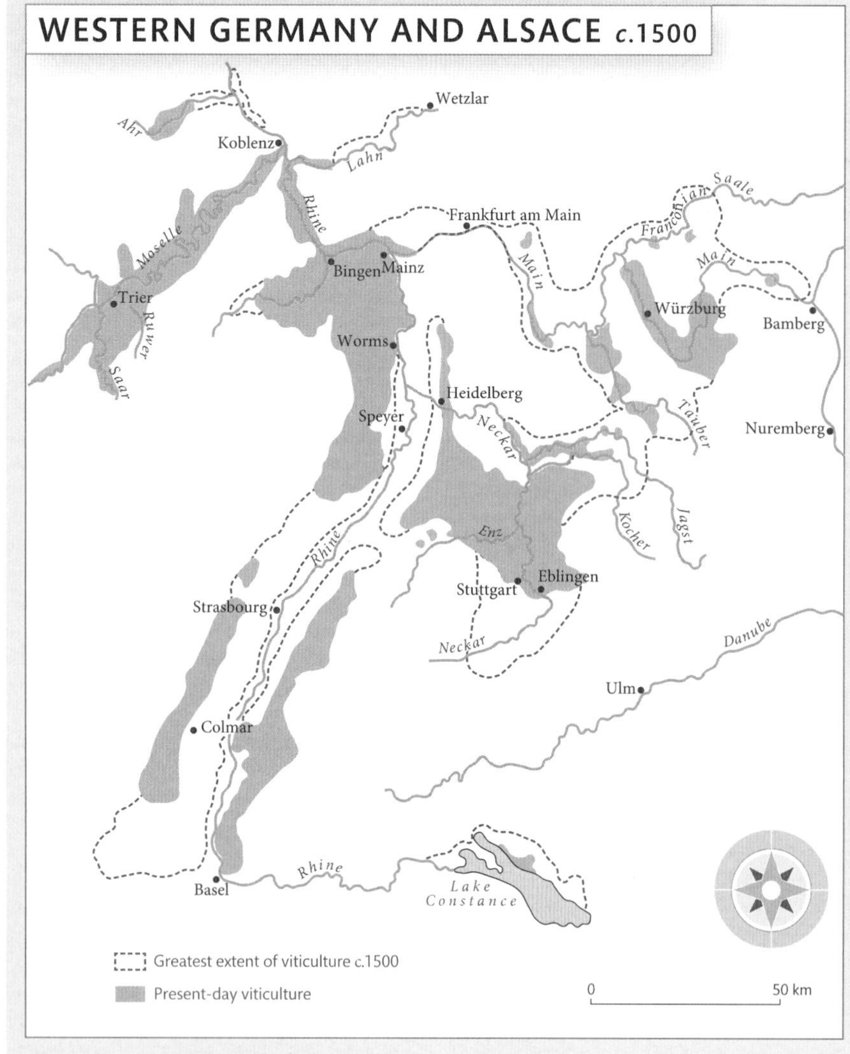

can only be explained by the foundation of the new ascetic religious orders, Cistercians and Carthusians, who established their houses from the 12th century at a deliberate distance from civilization. In Alsace, for example, vineyards followed convents into the remote valleys of the Vosges. Apart from the heartlands of medieval viticulture in Alsace, the Palatinate, and the Mosel Valley, all of which witnessed the further intake of land for vineyards up to 1500, winegrowing had spread by 1300 to the Rheingau, and throughout BADEN (with vineyards on Lake Constance from the 8th century), WÜRTTEMBERG, and Franken.

By 1500, even the rolling uplands of Swabia and the heavily afforested valleys of northern Franken had been cleared for vines. There viticulture reached its greatest extent in the 15th century, covering perhaps four times the area under vines today (see map of Western Germany and Alsace *c.*1500).

In eastern Germany, the Ottonian emperors promoted viticulture in their Saxon dynastic lands from the late 9th century. Vines were planted on the Elbe around Dresden and Meissen, and on the Saale and Unstrut, especially around Freyburg (see SAALE-UNSTRUT). Even in Brandenburg around Berlin and Jessen, east of Wittenberg up to Torgau, vines were grown on a commercial basis from the 14th to the 16th centuries. In the eastern part of the empire, Kloster Pforte near Naumburg played a similar role to that of Kloster Eberbach in the Rheingau.

The sites chosen for planting were by no means those on which wines still thrive today. Low-lying level sites were preferred; in Alsace, acknowledged as producing the best wines of medieval Germany, vineyards stretched across the plains from the Ried down to Mulhouse. From the 10th century, vines were at last being planted on slopes in TERRACES, with low walls to prevent SOIL EROSION. The famous slopes of the Rheingau were initially planted in the 11th century: first the Rüdesheimer Berg, then in the 12th century the Johannisberg and Steinberg, with the slopes of Rauenthal not planted until the 13th.

Vine varieties Workaday wine was made everywhere from the ELBLING grape, by far the commonest medieval variety, with RÄUSCHLING widely planted in Baden. SILVANER, which arrived in Franconia only in 1659, was extensively grown, but rarely as a high-quality grape in its own right; until the 20th century, it was generally planted together with Traminer and Riesling (see GEMISCHTER SATZ). Of the better grapes, MUSCAT (red and white) was grown on the Rhine and in Alsace, TRAMINER chiefly in the latter. RIESLING is first documented at Rüsselsheim on the river Main just east of the modern Rheingau in 1435, though a century earlier a vineyard in Kinzheim in Alsace was known as 'zu dem Russelinge'. The variant orthography of these early references, however, makes it difficult to determine whether the Riesling or the Räuschling grape is meant. There is every likelihood that Riesling had been established and recognized as a high-quality grape much earlier than the sources suggest, for in 1477 Duke René of Lorraine, in praising the red and white wines of Alsace, mentioned in particular its Riesling.

In the Middle Ages, many Alsace wines were fortified (see FORTIFICATION) or spiced (see FLAVOURED WINES) in order to compete with the fuller-bodied Mediterranean wines such as SACK and MALMSEY. Red wine was made from the Blauburgunder (PINOT NOIR) grape on the upper Rhine in Alsace and throughout Germany where it was spread by Cistercian MONKS from the 12th century (Affental had already acquired a reputation by 1330). In Württemberg, by contrast, where much of the production, then as now, consisted of light red wines, the TROLLINGER grape already predominated. The Ahr Valley may have been planted with red grapes, but those cannot have included Pinot Noir, which was not introduced there until the 18th century. T.S.

Scott, T., 'Medieval viticulture in the German-speaking lands', *German History*, 20 (2002), 95–115.

The wine trade in the Middle Ages

Although the quantity of wine harvested in medieval Germany never approached that of France, Italy, or the Iberian peninsula, production on the left bank of the Rhine always exceeded local consumption, so that commerce in wine became an economic necessity. Until the rise of towns, the wine trade was largely in the hands of the Church. Because the best vineyards lay along the Rhine and its tributaries, shipments of wine could pass easily down one of the great arteries of European trade to northern

Germany, the Low Countries, Scandinavia, and England. Ease of transport, however, was offset by the numerous tolls which local lords levied on cargoes shipped down the Rhine.

Cologne and Frankfurt dominated Germany's medieval wine trade, a point tellingly illustrated by the decision of Kloster Eberbach, the important abbey in the rural depths of the Rheingau, to acquire its own cellars in Cologne in 1162 and in Frankfurt 50 years later. But their pattern of trade differed.

Throughout the Middle Ages, Cologne's trade with the Baltic, Scandinavia, and England was far more extensive than Frankfurt's. The city's wine trade reached its peak in the late 14th and early 15th centuries. Cologne continued to play a major role in the export of the best German wines, but its trading area was increasingly exposed to the rise of beer as the everyday drink of northern Germany. It was Frankfurt's merchants who increasingly specialized in Alsace wines, although their popularity was challenged during the 15th century by wines from the Palatinate and the Rheingau.

Although German wines were firmly established in northern Europe during the Middle Ages, there were limits to their share of the market. In the southern Low Countries 'Rhine wine' was consumed, but it had to compete with the heavier wines of Burgundy, Auxerre, and also Bordeaux. In England, too, German wines faced a stiff challenge from France, as the trade with Gascony flourished from the 12th century. But German wine was not confined to northern markets. Alsace wines were extensively exported to southern Germany, Switzerland, and central Europe. T.S.

Scott, T., 'Medieval viticulture in the German-speaking lands', *German History*, 20 (2002), 95–115.

Crisis and decline, 1500–1650

The Thirty Years War, which ravaged Germany in the early 17th century, left few viticultural regions unscathed, with the exception of Württemberg, thanks to ducal intervention and support. But the real problem arose from the loss of manpower through the casualties of war. The decline in exports of ALSACE wines is symptomatic of the difficulties. Wine consumption was dictated by FASHION, and by 1500 taste was moving away from the often spiced (see FLAVOURED WINES) white wines of Alsace towards those of the PALATINATE and the RHEINGAU, as well as to the lighter wines of FRANKEN. At the same time, demand for heavier red wines was increasing, so that Alsace found itself having to plant more PINOT NOIR vines together with 'Lampersch' (a red wine variety from Lombardia in Italy) to compete with imports from France and the Mediterranean.

The excessive expansion of vineyards up to 1500 brought about a slump in the land market by 1540, with a consequent collapse in the price of wine, much of it in any case of dismal quality, having been grown on sites quite unsuitable for viticulture.

It is no coincidence that the widespread agrarian rebellion of 1525 known as the German Peasants' War was concentrated in the winegrowing areas, where the peasantry had been exposed to the fluctuations of the market, demands by lords for higher taxes on its crop, and the need to subdivide holdings into unprofitably small PARCELS by the laws of partible inheritance (see BURGUNDY, history), and yet peasants were compelled to cling to their foothold in commercialized viticulture for want of alternative employment.

Throughout the century, viticulture retreated from the cooler, more remote valleys; poor-quality vineyards in the plains were abandoned in favour of slopes with better exposure and drainage. As the century wore on, the demand for grain for bread and brewing swelled, so that corn prices outstripped wine prices, and much land reverted to tillage. Nevertheless, on the eve of the Thirty Years War, around 350,000 ha/865,000 acres of land in Germany were still under vines, over four times the extent of viticulture today. The 16th century also saw greater emphasis on better-quality white varieties.

A first classification Although the use of individual site names to distinguish quality (as opposed merely to identifying different vineyards) was largely unknown before 1800, there is one striking instance of ranking by quality in this period. In 1644 the council of Würzburg in FRANKEN classified the city's vineyards into four groups. T.S.

Bibliographical note: There is no reliable survey in English. Readers of German may consult Bassermann-Jordan, F. von, *Geschichte des Weinbaus*, 3 vols. in 2 (2nd edn, 1923; repr. 1991).

Weinhold, R., *Winzerarbeit an Elbe, Saale und Unstrut: eine historisch-ethnographische Untersuchung der Produktivkräfte des Weinbaus auf dem Gebiet der DDR* (1973).

Schröder, K. H., *Weinbau und Siedlung in Württemberg*, Forschungen zur deutschen Landeskunde, 73 (1953).

Schmitt, S., 'Mittelalterlicher Weinbau am Neckar', in Christhard Schrenk and Hubert Weckbach (eds), *Weinwirtschaft im Mittelalter* (1997), 93–121.

Militzer, K., 'Handel und Vertrieb rheinischer und elsässischer Weine über Köln im Spätmittelalter', in A. Gerlich (pub.), *Weinbau, Weinhandel und Weinkultur* (1994).

Recovery and improvement, 1650–1800

The recovery of German viticulture after the depredations of the Thirty Years War was slow and painful. Only FRANKEN (Franconia), which had been the scene of fierce fighting in the 1630s, experienced a swift recuperation in vineyards and wine prices in the 1650s. In the PALATINATE, viticulture was not fully restored until the 1710s. There many growers, despairing of making a decent living, emigrated to America in the early 18th century. The region was further afflicted by the wars of Louis XIV of France from 1674 to 1700, as indeed were districts on the left bank of the Rhine as a whole, including the MOSEL.

The vineyards of BADEN and WÜRTTEMBERG, which had suffered least the previous century, may have declined by as much as 80% by the end of the 18th century. In ALSACE, however, the loss of a workforce was partly compensated for by policies to encourage immigration from France, Lorraine, and Switzerland.

Efforts to improve viticulture from the late 17th century onwards pursued a double strategy: to encourage the planting of better-quality grape varieties, often on selected new sites, while at the same time prohibiting the clearing of land for vines where only poor quality could be expected. In what is now the MOSEL, for instance, the Abbey of St Maximin had been replanting at Grünhaus on the RUWER since 1695; as many as 100,000 new cuttings, it has been reckoned, were put down. But at the other end of the scale, more land was constantly being taken in by small growers, so that the prince-archbishops of Trier issued an edict in 1720 banning the clearing of forest for new vineyards.

In 1750, another decree enjoined the production of natural, unsugared (*naturrein*) wines, and in 1786 the last archbishop-elector, Clemens Wenceslas (r. 1768–1801), a keen champion of viticulture, ordered that inferior grapes be grubbed up and replaced with the RIESLING vine. At Bingen, the archbishop of Mainz decreed in 1697 that the famous Scharlachberg ('scarlet slope', perhaps because it once grew red wines) be planted exclusively with Riesling.

Likewise in the Rheingau, Constantine, prince-abbot of the ancient Benedictine abbey of Fulda, which had acquired the site and castle of Johannisberg (see SCHLOSS JOHANNISBERG), ordered the replanting of the vineyards with Riesling and 'Orléans' vines in the 1760s. In this period, the sources begin to distinguish the quality of Rhine wines according to village or, on occasion, site.

Vine varieties In Alsace, improvement owed nothing to the French crown, everything to local initiatives by institutions such as the Jesuit College at Sélestat, which began to plant Riesling in 1756 in place of lesser vines. Alsace saw the development of two new varieties in the 18th century. In 1756 Johann Michael Ortlieb of Riquewihr pioneered an early-ripening clone of RÄUSCHLING, the Kleiner (small) Räuschling (also known as Ortlieber or, in Alsace, as KNIPPERLÉ). In 1740 the mayor of Heiligenstein by Barr, Erhard Wantz, introduced a new variety under the name of KLEVENER.

In much of southern Germany, Silvaner was displacing ELBLING, but the real innovation was the development of PINOT GRIS by Johann Seger Ruland in Speyer around 1711. Although it spread quickly, the Ruländer suffered a rapid decline because its early ripening meant that its harvest could not be held back until the later-maturing Riesling, so that peasant growers preferred to let it rot rather than gather it early only to have to deliver up a fine wine as a tithe to their feudal lords. Not until tithing was abolished in the wake of the French Revolution did Ruländer establish its rightful place among German wines of distinction.

The 17th and 18th centuries also saw the first attempts to make specially selected or late-picked wines. Use of the term CABINET to indicate a wine of reserve quality is first encountered at Schloss Vollrads in the Rheingau in 1716, then at Kloster Eberbach in the Rheingau in 1739. The picking of individual ripe berries off the stalks (*Abrappen*) was also deployed, particularly with Traminer grapes, to make what were in effect AUSLESEN, although the wines were relatively short lived. Nevertheless, the potential of picking grapes affected by NOBLE ROT was well recognized by the early 18th century.

Despite these advances, the period up to 1800 was a troubled one for German wine in export markets. Cologne and Frankfurt maintained their leading role in overseas trade, and the 18th century witnessed the first wine AUCTIONS of quality wines. Cologne's merchants were proud of their adherence to the oenological equivalent of the brewing purity laws (*Reinheitsgebot*), which forbade blending Rhine wines with those from the south, especially France and Italy. Yet their stranglehold on the market in Rhenish wines was challenged in the 1670s when English merchants began to buy at source. T.S.

Bibliographical note: There is no reliable survey in English. For readers of German, Bassermann-Jordan, cited above, remains an indispensable guide, but some information may be gleaned from O. W. Loeb and T. Prittie, *Moselle* (1972).

The rise of modern viticulture, 1800–1900

The French Revolution and its aftermath wrought profound changes in German viticulture. During the Revolution itself, the PALATINATE was invaded and occupied, although in the succeeding Napoleonic Wars it was barely affected. The whole of Germany on the left bank of the Rhine was ceded to France, which proceeded to reorganize the region's administration into four departments.

On the MOSEL, these political upheavals led to around one-fifth of the vineyards, many of them owned by the Church, changing hands, and once the estates of the empire had agreed upon the abolition of all ecclesiastical principalities at the diet of Regensburg in 1803, another 25% came under new ownership.

Although after the fall of Napoleon the Church regained some of its estates, a new and substantial class of peasant and bourgeois vineyard proprietors had been created. On the right bank of the Rhine in the RHEINGAU, Johannisberg (see SCHLOSS JOHANNISBERG) passed through several hands, including Napoleon's general Marshal Kellermann, before it fell to Austria at the Congress of Vienna in 1815 and was bestowed upon Prince Metternich, then foreign minister. On the Main, the estates of the prince-bishops of Würzburg in FRANKEN, or Franconia, were acquired after a short interlude by the Bavarian crown in 1816.

In ALSACE, however, the repercussions of the Revolution were quite different. Once it had become part of the French customs area, growers hastened to increase production in order to capitalize upon a huge internal market. The result was the renewed planting of inferior vine varieties on low-lying sites. Moreover, the imposition by France of tolls on foreign wines hurt Alsace in particular, since it elicited reprisals from Baden, Württemberg, and Switzerland, all still important customers for Alsace wines.

At the Congress of Vienna, the political map of Germany was redrawn. The Mosel became part of the Prussian Rheinprovinz; RHEINHESSEN (west of the Rhine) was absorbed into the grand duchy of Hesse-Darmstadt together with the Bergstrasse; the Rheingau fell to the dukes of Nassau; and what remained of the Palatinate, the Pfalz proper, was reunited with Bavaria. From 1805/6 Saxony (see SACHSEN) and WÜRTTEMBERG had been elevated to kingdoms, BADEN to a grand duchy. The regulation of customs dues between these independent states became a matter of urgent necessity.

When Bavaria and Württemberg joined Prussia to create the general customs union (*Zollverein*) of 1834, followed by Baden and Hesse-Darmstadt the next year, all the major winegrowing districts were in open competition with each other. As a result, the better wines prevailed and the market in lesser wines collapsed, although at least the *Zollverein* enabled German wines to compete on more favourable terms in the domestic market with French wines, especially those from BORDEAUX, which had begun to reach the north German cities in huge quantities in the 1820s. Baden and Württemberg were the worst hit by the new competition. In Baden the tithe was abolished in 1833, but the area under cultivation constantly receded, and many winegrowers emigrated to ALGERIA or VENEZUELA.

The development of the transport network, above all the RAILWAYS, allowed rapid and easy distribution of the better wines from the more favoured regions, so that Württemberg's production declined by 40% in the 19th century. Franken, too, suffered because of Bavaria's link with the Palatinate and the loss of workers to the emerging industry; the area under vines shrank by 60% between 1850 and 1900.

Only the foundation of the German empire in 1871 put an end to all internal customs barriers. Yet the reabsorption of Alsace and Lorraine in that year brought little relief to winegrowers there. Alsace may have constituted 26% of German vineyards, yielding 39% of production after 1871, but its wines were threatened by imports of cheap wines from France, sweetened wines from across the Rhine, and preferential trade treaties signed by Germany with Austria and Italy in 1891 and with Spain in 1893.

Quality in the ascendant Quality of production became the central concern of German vine-growers and administrators after 1800. The beginnings of quality DELIMITATION can be traced to the 1830s. Wine ordinances in the German states began to prescribe that grapes of different levels of ripeness should be harvested separately. Their measurement was greatly facilitated by systems for weighing the must to achieve a specific MUST WEIGHT, refined in the 1830s by the Pforzheim physicist Ferdinand OECHSLE, whose system is still in use today.

Growers' associations for the improvement of wines and viticulture were founded in many German territories. The state authorities, moreover, played a vital role by establishing schools of viticultural research and teaching. Württemberg was the pioneer in 1860 with its academy at Weinsberg, followed by Prussia's establishment of the institute at GEISENHEIM in 1872, after it had annexed the Rheingau from Nassau in 1866. The Hessian wine academy at Oppenheim dates from 1885; in 1899 citizens of Neustadt an der Weinstrasse founded a wine school to serve the Palatinate; Mosel (Trier) and the Nahe (Kreuznach) acquired a Prussian academy in 1893. These endeavours were underpinned by the creation of state domaines. The earliest was set up by Baden at Meersburg on Lake Constance in 1802, followed shortly thereafter by the Bavarian state domaine in Würzburg and the Herzogl. Nassauische domaine at Kloster Eberbach from its abbatial estates throughout the Rheingau. After its acquisition of Nassau, the domaine was owned by Prussia. At the end of the century, Prussia established further state domaines: in 1896 on the Saar/Moselle with estates at Ockfen, then extended to Avelsbach and Serrig, and on the Nahe at Niederhausen in 1902.

The emphasis on quality, however, placed the smaller peasant growers in a quandary. Without the capital to invest in better vines and winemaking equipment, they were left with inferior grape varieties on poorer sites in a shrinking market. The only solution, albeit imperfect, was to seek safety in numbers by banding together in CO-OPERATIVES. The first such growers' union was formally established on the River AHR in 1869.

Towards the end of the century, viticulture fell victim to Germany's late industrialization, which sucked LABOUR into the cities. In terms of marketing, the German wine trade was torn between the lure of the controlled addition of sugar—pioneered by the chemist Ludwig Gall (the German counterpart to Jean CHAPTAL in France), which helped to make thin, sour wines from sun-starved soils saleable (see CHAPTALIZATION) —and the reputation which attached to untreated, *naturrein* wines. The first national Wine Laws of 1892 and 1901 had permitted controlled sugaring, but the wine law of 1909 restricted sugaring to 20% of the undiluted wine. In 1910, four groups of natural-wine auctioneers formed the Verein Deutscher Naturweinversteiger (VDNV), today known as the VDP.

One answer was to turn the more acidic vintages into sparkling wine, known in German as SEKT. With some good vintages in the 1860s, Sekt had become a highly popular drink in Germany by the late 19th century.

The true threat to German viticulture, however, lay in VINE PESTS and VINE DISEASES—DOWNY MILDEW in particular and PHYLLOXERA (*Reblaus* in German), which first appeared in Germany in 1874 in Bonn-Annaberg and Karlsruhe before being found in vineyards in the Ahr Valley in 1881. T.S.

The 20th-century wine industry

The first half of the 20th century was a period of deep recession in the German wine industry. The area under vines shrank still further, from around 90,000 ha/220,000 acres in 1914 to less than 50,000 ha/123,000 acres in 1945. Both World Wars placed severe strains on Germany's domestic economy and caused considerable dislocation in its export markets. Exports had reached a peak of 190,000 hl/5 million gal by 1914, but in the aftermath of the First World War the situation was bleak.

The major growing regions on the left bank of the Rhine were occupied by France until 1930. In the PFALZ region, moreover, the activities of separatist groups severely disrupted civilian life up to 1924, which hit the wine industry in particular. A series of bad vintages from 1922 until 1932, in combination with the raging inflation and the economic hardship of the Weimar period, ruined many wine merchants and growers, especially the smaller proprietors. A flood of imports from France and Luxembourg, as specified by the Versailles Treaty, undercut the prices which German producers could charge; many growers faced bankruptcy, and by 1928 exports had collapsed to no more than 39,000 hl/1 million gal per annum.

The Nazi era helped to revive domestic consumption of German wine, but the National Socialist policy of subordinating all private associations to state control (*Gleichschaltung*) meant, for the wine industry, that all independent professional bodies except the VDNV were abolished and replaced by a single Union of Viticulture under one president, thereby destroying the enterprise and initiative of individual growers and regional wine associations. The end of the Second World War heralded the return of some of the consequences of the First. German growers faced a shortage of labour but an abundance of cheap imports from France and Algeria. In their zone of occupation in the Pfalz and Moselle, the French requisitioned wine and blocked its movement on a grand scale.

The parlous state of exports in the 1930s persuaded some merchants, principally those trading to the United Kingdom, to try to increase sales by marketing BRANDS, which could contain more than one grape variety, were sourced from more than one region of production, and were usually sweetened. This is the origin of LIEBFRAUMILCH.

Undoubtedly the most significant step forward for German viticulture in the first half of the century was the wine law of 1930, which went far towards rectifying the deficiencies of the 1909 law. It provided a clear definition of what constituted a natural, as opposed to a CHAPTALIZED, wine and also forbade the blending of red and white and of German and foreign wines.

Viticulture Between 1950 and 1990 German viticulture underwent a dramatic transformation. The area under vine once again expanded steadily and in the modern era measures well over 100,000 ha/250,000 acres. But the most startling development was the increase in YIELDS. At the beginning of the century the average of 20 hl/ha (1.1 tons/acre) was no more than what might have been expected of an abundant vintage in any preceding century. By 1950 that had doubled to 40 hl/ha, and by the 1980s it frequently exceeded 100 hl/ha (5.7 tons/acre), although today's more discriminating growers are cropping less heavily.

From the 1950s there was a radical restructuring of German vineyards, known as FLURBEREINIGUNG. The number of individual sites has been substantially pruned, and since the German wine law of 1971 a new vineyard register has been compiled and average wine quality has improved immensely. T.S.

See also JEWISH HERITAGE IN GERMAN WINE CULTURE, and see GERMANY for more on the modern wine scene.

Hallgarten, S. F., *German Wine* (1976).
Langenbach, A., *German Wines and Vines* (1962).
Loeb, O. W., and Prittie, T., *Moselle* (1972).
Pigott, S., *The Mosel and Rheingau, Including the Ahr, Nahe and Pfalz* (1997).

Germany, major wine producer in Europe with both wines and problems quite unlike those of anywhere else. Grape-growing in Germany is a small but culturally conspicuous part of the country's farming industry. Germany's annual wine production of 7–8 million hl/185–211 million gal has made it Europe's fourth biggest wine producer for many years, albeit distant behind France, Italy, and Spain. Unlike France and Italy, however, Germany makes about as much wine as it consumes, while also being the largest importer of wine in the EU. Regrettably German wine law has scarcely helped the country's wine reputation, and the majority of German wine is still sold in BULK, often on price rather than quality. These unfortunate factors notwithstanding, the profile of German wine—in particular that of Riesling—has risen significantly in prestige at home and abroad since the 1990s. What's more, while nearly all of Germany's growing regions can still be considered COOL-CLIMATE and capable of producing wines with incomparable finesse, the struggle to ripen grapes sufficiently that dominated viticulture here for centuries has eased dramatically thanks to CLIMATE CHANGE as well as viticultural and attitudinal changes.

History

See GERMAN HISTORY.

Geography and climate

Over the centuries, the German vineyard has expanded and contracted. See GERMAN HISTORY and map there. Many of Germany's best vineyards are on the steepest slopes, quite unsuited to anything other than the vine. Overlooking the rivers RHINE, Neckar, Main, NAHE, AHR, and MOSEL and its tributaries, their high cost of cultivation is justified only by the quality of the wine they can produce. In the steep vineyards, three times as many labour hours are spent tending the vine as is the case on flat or gently sloping terrain, where the natural position of the vine-grower is on the seat of a tractor.

Several other factors limit MECHANIZATION in the vineyards, among which are the tradition of selective harvest and the smallness of the holdings, although that has been somewhat mitigated by the wholesale vineyard reorganization known as FLURBEREINIGUNG. Vine-growing in Germany was once the work of peasants, controlled by the Church and the nobility. In 2020, roughly half of Germans who grow wine grapes do so part time with average holdings of slightly

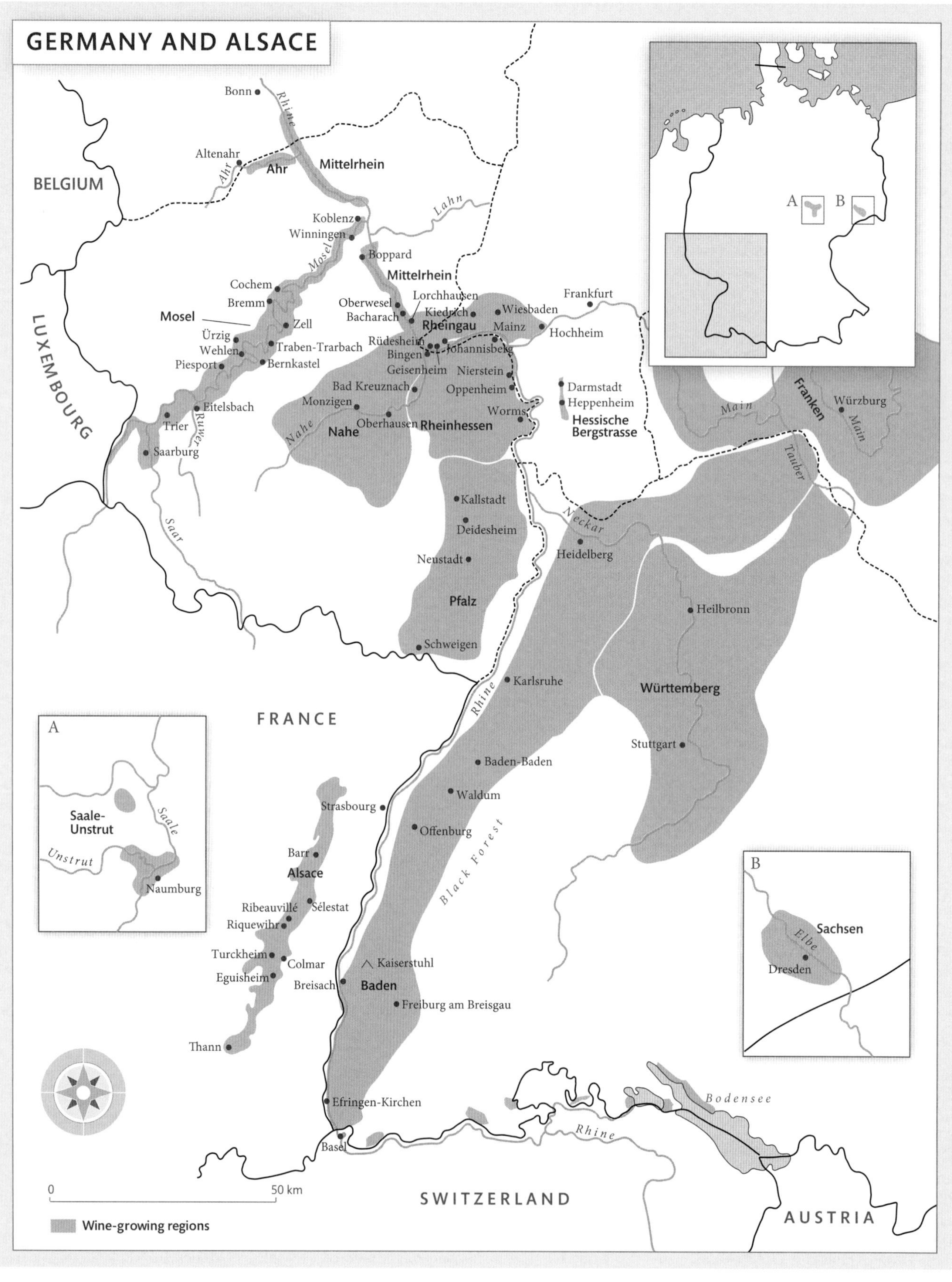
GERMANY AND ALSACE
BELGIUM
LUXEMBOURG
FRANCE
SWITZERLAND
AUSTRIA
Bonn
Rhine
Altenahr
Ahr
Mittelrhein
Koblenz
Lahn
Winningen
Mosel
Boppard
Mittelrhein
Cochem
Bremm
Mosel
Zell
Ürzig
Wehlen
Traben-Trarbach
Piesport
Bernkastel
Eitelsbach
Trier
Ruwer
Saarburg
Saar
Oberwesel
Bacharach
Lorchhausen
Kiedrich
Wiesbaden
Rheingau
Mainz
Frankfurt
Hochheim
Rüdesheim
Bingen
Johannisberg
Geisenheim
Nierstein
Oppenheim
Bad Kreuznach
Monzigen
Worms
Nahe
Oberhausen
Rheinhessen
Darmstadt
Heppenheim
Hessische Bergstrasse
Main
Franken
Würzburg
Tauber
Neckar
Kallstadt
Deidesheim
Neustadt
Heidelberg
Pfalz
Heilbronn
Schweigen
Karlsruhe
Württemberg
Stuttgart
Baden-Baden
Waldum
Offenburg
Black Forest
Strasbourg
Barr
Alsace
Ribeauvillé
Sélestat
Riquewihr
Turckheim
Colmar
Eguisheim
Kaiserstuhl
Breisach
Baden
Freiburg am Breisgau
Thann
Efringen-Kirchen
Basel
Rhine
Bodensee
A
Saale-Unstrut
Saale
Unstrut
Naumburg
B
Sachsen
Elbe
Dresden
0
50 km
Wine-growing regions

under 2 ha/5 acres, selling their fruit to merchants or more likely participating in a CO-OPERATIVE (*Winzergenossenschaft*), the category responsible for around 30% of German wine production. Since the late 20th century, picking at larger estates has generally been done by temporary workers from eastern and southern Europe, among whom Poles and later Romanians have been pre-eminent.

For more geographical detail, see map of Germany and Alsace in this entry; see also entries under the names of individual wine regions which are, in declining area of total vineyard, RHEINHESSEN, PFALZ, BADEN, MOSEL, WÜRTTEMBERG, FRANKEN, NAHE, RHEINGAU, MITTELRHEIN, SAALE-UNSTRUT, AHR, HESSISCHE BERGSTRASSE, and SACHSEN. Most German wine labels carry the name of the region in which the wine was produced.

Viticulture

The vine-growing regions of the EU are divided into climatically different zones. In Germany, Baden shares Zone B with several French regions including Alsace, Champagne, and the Loire Valley. Although the remaining German regions are all in cooler Zone A, their MACROCLIMATES and MESOCLIMATES are perhaps the most varied of all the world's vineyards. Mesoclimatic variations within a single site or EINZELLAGE can result in simultaneous pickings of the same variety which exhibit significant differences in potential alcohol and flavour. According to research at GEISENHEIM, the average alcohol content of wine of the same vineyard can vary from one vintage to another by over 6%. The degree of LATITUDE, topographical features such as a favourable exposure to the sun, shelter from frequent cold winds or damaging FROSTS, and the ELEVATION are some of the factors which dramatically influence the quality of German viticulture.

Some 5–7% of Germany's vines are individually supported by POSTS, particularly in the Mosel, where relatively tight spacing between vines on steep slopes is the norm. But this method is in decline as old vineyards continue to be subjected to *Flurbereinigung* and workers with the requisite skills disappear. Elsewhere, vines are trained on WIRES in rows, often with wide spacing, although an international 21st-century FASHION for tight spacing is influencing German replanting.

Some 4–5% of all vines—particularly in the Mosel, where some villages and vineyards never succumbed to PHYLLOXERA—are UNGRAFTED. But this proportion is also in decline, as is average VINE AGE due to ongoing *Flurbereinigung*. And incidences of phylloxera led to bans on ungrafted plantings. Although German research stations, most notably Geisenheim, have for nearly a century been famous for their clonal selections, which dominate Germany's vineyards, many growers are increasingly enthusiastic about MASS SELECTIONS.

Among growers whose aim is to produce top-quality fruit, PRUNING is usually to 6–8 buds per square metre, depending on the variety. To produce a more concentrated must, excess bunches of grapes are removed in the months following the FLOWERING in June and often again in late summer (see CROP THINNING). The aim in VINE TRAINING in recent decades has been not just to harvest healthy, ripe grapes but also to delay or reduce sugar accumulation (whereas, for most of the 20th century, high must weights were the principal goal) and sometimes to reduce costs by facilitating MECHANICAL PRUNING and MECHANICAL HARVESTING. Machines are increasingly used even at prestigious estates, sometimes employed for speed after human hands have cost-intensively performed a 'negative Auslese' to remove rotten or otherwise imperfect fruit. Training and pruning regimens are undergoing considerable rethinking in climatically altered scenarios where even SUNBURN has become a significant problem. (In another sign of the times, the German wine law was amended in 2021 to allow IRRIGATION in years of DROUGHT or excessive heat.) Among the many factors insufficiently emphasized in the 1971 German wine law was YIELD: Germany's average yields have long been the highest of any significant wine-producing country, generally well over 70 and sometimes over 100 hl/ha. But considerable attention is given to that factor in 2021 legislation, prompted in part by yield reduction having been a major theme of the VDP growers' association.

Ripeness can vary significantly from one bunch to another on the same vine as well as within the cluster, not to mention the presence or absence of BOTRYTIS. Riesling growers in some regions of Germany, notably the Rheingau, have for two centuries responded with selective picking of individual clusters or even berries, and in the course of the late 20th century this became nearly universal practice among quality-conscious German Riesling growers, with at least a portion of most vintage's crop, resulting in sweet wines with a PRÄDIKAT level of AUSLESE and above, but often also ensuring entirely healthy fruit for the dry (TROCKEN) wines that make up the majority of production. However, some influential growers make a point of practising block picking for some wines, showcasing the sort of complexity that comes from bunches and berries in diverse states of ripeness and botrytis influence. Prior to the late 20th century, block-picking was the norm.

While Germans exhibit a high level of support for SUSTAINABLE and ORGANIC VITICULTURE, vines' disease sensitivity, difficulty of vineyard access, and precipitation patterns in German wine regions have slowed the spread of organic viticulture compared with the situation in neighbouring Austria and France. In the Mosel, for example, PESTICIDES or HERBICIDES sprayed from helicopters are the only effective means of reaching vines on ultra-steep, rocky slopes. Such sprays easily drift into neighbouring vineyards, a deterrent to going organic. Under such circumstances, there is no point in a small landholder attempting to work organically, as the sprays will inevitably drift into his or her vineyards. But the 21st century has seen organic and BIODYNAMIC VITICULTURE making significant inroads in Germany, even on the Mosel.

Winemaking

While Germany has been a leader in winemaking technology as well as viticultural research, a movement towards minimal intervention and rediscovering traditional methods is a significant part of today's German wine scene. The resulting tension is reflected in the practices of most cellars. Sophisticated PRESSES, typically operating at two atmospheres or less, are sometimes essentially programmed to re-enact the regimen of ancient basket presses, and not a few strong young German growers have rehabilitated antique specimens of the latter. CENTRIFUGES, FILTERS, FINING agents, and ENZYMES are employed by many estates to ensure ultra-clean juices that are then fermented with carefully selected YEAST cultures. But the virtues of minimal gravity settling, retention of solid matter, and SPONTANEOUS FERMENTATION (which in the Mosel never went entirely out of fashion) are being affirmed by a growing share of winegrowers. Early RACKING, CLARIFICATION, and BOTTLING of young white wines is still the norm, but the role of LEES CONTACT as well as lighter FINING and FILTRATION and later bottling in enhancing flavour and stability are taken increasingly seriously by many winegrowers. CHARCOAL-fining to remove off-aromas and flavours in vintages featuring GREY ROT and other fungal infections is still common but is increasingly seen as a last resort. Sensitivity to levels of SULFUR DIOXIDE, albeit lagging, has tracked international trends.

Extremely varied weather this century has forced German growers to practise, most unusually, ACIDIFICATION (initially in 2003) and to rediscover DEACIDIFICATION techniques. Resort to CHAPTALIZATION is nowadays rare within the ranks of Germany's top growers—hard as that is for any grower born before 1960 to imagine. Many other techniques that have become prevalent elsewhere remain illegal in Germany, notably CRYOEXTRACTION (EISWEIN may not be made using a freezer), REVERSE OSMOSIS, and other post-harvest means of must CONCENTRATION.

Since the 1980s, dry wine has come to dominate the so-called fine-wine market inside Germany, especially in restaurants and among consumers of premium-priced bottlings, where

TROCKEN came to be viewed as an imprimatur of drinkability, not to mention social respectability. But many German winegrowers remain committed to making wines with some sweetness, especially from Riesling, albeit very differently than of old. Addition of SÜSSRESERVE, the usual means of rendering or fine-tuning sweet wine during the 1970s and 1980s, has almost completely given way to practices such as arresting fermentation through a combination of low temperatures, adding SULFUR DIOXIDE, and STERILE BOTTLING. The results of stopped fermentation are chemically and organoleptically different from those of adding Süssreserve. Only the latter allowed growers to experiment in order to determine optimum BALANCE and achieve a desired RESIDUAL SUGAR level. At least as common today as taking measures to guarantee a certain level of residual sugar are measures taken to reduce residual sugar in a wine whose fermentation has stopped above the legal limit for a dry wine (see TROCKEN): supplementary inoculation with cultured yeast, warming to restart fermentation, and BLENDING. Riesling especially, if left to its own fermentative devices, has a habit of coming to rest HALBTROCKEN, half- (or medium) dry, a state that most contemporary German growers seem somehow to find ideologically repugnant and many German consumers seem to spurn.

BARREL MATURATION in casks of varying sizes is frequently practised with Riesling, not to mention with red wines. Use of the traditional 1,200-litre *Stückfass*, 2,400-l *Doppelstück*, and 1,000-l Mosel FUDER never died out and are today increasingly employed, especially by top estates. And as elsewhere, 300- and 600-litre and even larger casks as well as CONCRETE vessels are increasingly supplementing or replacing the classic 228-litre Burgundian PIÈCE for Pinots of both colours.

Vine varieties

The 1971 German wine law, with its focus on quality designations defined solely by must weight, discounted the significance of grape variety and significantly disadvantaged Riesling in the marketplace. But today the importance of grape variety and the qualitative pre-eminence of Riesling among Germany's white wine grapes (like Pinot Noir among those for red) is undisputed. Covering in 2020 just over 23% of German vineyard surface, Riesling boasts more than double the surface area of Müller-Thurgau, the next most planted white variety. SILVANER, while traditionally important, now registers just 4.5% of German vineyard surface, having been overtaken by GRAUBURGUNDER (Pinot Gris) and WEISSBURGUNDER (Pinot Blanc) at 7.1% and 5.7% respectively. Chardonnay, at 2.3%, recently edged out Kerner, one of numerous CROSSES (others include Bacchus, Huxelrebe, and Ortega) that rose to prominence after the Second World War but have since drastically declined in surface area. Among CROSSES, acid-retentive and distinctively aromatic SCHEUREBE has a special claim to excellence, though in terms of surface area it has recently been overtaken by Sauvignon Blanc. Among varieties with ancient legacies albeit 1% or less of nationwide surface are TRAMINER, GUTEDEL (Chasselas, important in Baden's Markgräflerland), and ELBLING (dominant in the Upper Mosel), while acid-retentive RIESLANER retains eloquent partisans in the Pfalz and its native Franken.

Plantings of red-wine varieties have increased dramatically since the 1990s, SPÄTBURGUNDER (Pinot Noir) having by 2020 overtaken Müller-Thurgau to become, with an 11.3% share, Germany's second most widely planted grape. Dornfelder, a cross responsible for much of Germany's red-wine boom, increased its share of surface more than fourfold between 1995 and 2020, to 7.1%. Among traditional black grapes, PORTUGIESER has slipped to 2.5%, while TROLLINGER, Lemberger (aka BLAUFRÄNKISCH) and SCHWARZRIESLING range from 1.8 to 2% each thanks to their prominence in Württemberg. Tiny shares also accrue to FRÜHBURGUNDER and ST-LAURENT, thanks primarily to partisans in the Ahr and Pfalz respectively, as well as—predictably, given their French notoriety—to Cabernet Sauvignon, Merlot, and Syrah.

Wine labelling

The overwhelming majority of German wine is officially QUALITÄTSWEIN. A portion of this, the amount varying according to quality of vintage and subject to long-term labelling trends, is bottled unchaptalized and bears a so-called PRÄDIKAT, of which there are six: KABINETT, SPÄTLESE, AUSLESE, BEERENAUSLESE, TROCKENBEERENAUSLESE, and EISWEIN, each pegged to a minimum MUST WEIGHT. A long-term trend is towards omitting these Prädikat designations for dry wines. Whereas a Beerenauslese, Trockenbeerenauslese, or Eiswein is almost inevitably bottled with a high level of RESIDUAL SUGAR, designation of a wine as Kabinett, Spätlese, or Auslese bears no direct relation to the sweetness of the finished wine. Among wines not labelled as trocken (dry), FEINHERB, or halbtrocken (medium dry; see SWEETNESS for the official EU classification of such terms), an Auslese will generally, though not always, taste noticeably sweeter than a Spätlese, which will in turn taste sweeter than a Kabinett. All German Qualitätswein carries an AP NUMBER on its label, certifying its having passed analytical and sensory examinations.

The tradition of picking parcel by parcel and often selectively within parcels, combined with what many Germans would claim is a national passion for minutiae, can make for dozens of different bottlings at a given wine estate. And German Riesling is arguably capable of more stylistic diversity than any other combination of place and variety. The resulting multiplicity of bottlings, combined with the divided ownership of individual sites, has made it very difficult for vineyard names to have any widely recognized associations of flavour, bouquet, or style. The German wine law has in recent decades added new layers of terminology while adapting but not jettisoning the old. An obvious example is the wine law promulgated in 2021, designed to bring German regulations into conformity with EU categories and principles under the rubric of narrower geographical specifications equalling higher promised quality, yet without displacing the existing Prädikat hierarchy. What the rubric amounts to in practice could perhaps be better expressed as: 'The higher the level of official prestige and of purported quality, the narrower the permitted degree of geographical specificity with which a wine may be labelled.' Qualitätswein falls into the categories of generic (Gutswein); communal or village designated (Ortswein); and site-specific (Lagenwein), though a producer could choose to bottle all of his or her wines under vineyard names or, for that matter, to market entirely under fantasy names. Any authorized vineyard name must be preceded on labels by the corresponding communal or village name. Authorized names include those of an official EINZELLAGE or of a *Gewann* (the smallest cadastral unit) that has been registered for label usage by a grower with holdings in that *Gewann*. Many producers are enthusiastic about the opportunity for adding geographical specificity—as of 2021, more than 300 such *Gewann* names had been registered in Rheinland-Pfalz (incorporating Mosel, Nahe, Ahr, Mittelrhein, Rheinhessen, and Pfalz). *Gewann* designation often permits the singling-out of a core vineyard whose name was co-opted for an Einzellage—e.g. Im Pitterberg (*Gewann*) as opposed to Pittersberg (Einzellage)—and can correct for the extreme heterogeneity of many a sprawling Einzellage.

A CLASSIFICATION of German estates similar to the 1855 one of the Médoc and Graves had prominent proponents among journalists and growers in the late 1980s. From the mid 1990s, momentum gathered for a system of classifying vineyards, with the sites at the apex of a qualitative pyramid being designated an ERSTES GEWÄCHS (first growth) or GROSSES GEWÄCHS (great growth), categories which entered German wine law in 2021 by analogy to 'premier cru' and 'grand cru', albeit without much specificity or any classification of vineyards (in contrast with what the VDP producers' organization has established for its members). It can scarcely be argued that this development, or the proliferation of vineyard designations, will alleviate Germany's perennial dilemma of hard-to-decipher wine labels and consumer confusion.

The 21st century has experienced a diminution of what had been a vicious cycle of overproduction and depressed prices from nugatory flatlands, and an increase in interest in excellent, steep vineyard land. The international reputation of Germany's revered Riesling is higher than at any time in almost a century. Unprecedented levels of technological sophistication are meeting their equal in quality aspirations, responsibility to the environment, and rediscovery of ancient viticultural wisdom. And a reaction appears to have set in both against the stylistic straitjacket of German consumers' and opinion-makers' fanaticism for legally dry wine and against the threat of global gustatory uniformity, promising German wines and winegrowers an opportunity to flourish with that dazzling stylistic diversity of which they, and especially the Riesling grape in their soils, are uniquely capable.

See also AHR, BADEN, FRANKEN, HESSISCHE BERGSTRASSE, MITTELRHEIN, MOSEL, NAHE, PFALZ, RHEINGAU, RHEINHESSEN, SAALE-UNSTRUT, SACHSEN, and WÜRTTEMBERG. D.S.

Braatz, D., et al., *Wine Atlas of Germany* (2014).
Pigott, S., *Wein Spricht Deutsch: Weine, Winzer, Weinlandschaften* (2007).
Reinhardt, S., *The Finest Wines of Germany* (2012).
www.winesofgermany.co.uk
www.deutscheweine.de

Gevrey-Chambertin, small town in the Côte de Nuits producing some of Burgundy's most famous red wines from Pinot Noir grapes. The area allowed the appellation was sharply reduced in the late 1990s to exclude some less favoured land towards the plain; but with about 400 ha/1,000 acres under vine—including an overflow of vineyards into neighbouring Brochon, which does not have its own AOC, as well as 80 ha/198 acres of GRANDS CRUS—this is still the largest viticultural source in the Côte d'Or. In 1847, Gevrey annexed the name of its finest vineyard, Chambertin, somewhat tediously dubbed 'the king of wines and wine of kings' (although it was in fact the Emperor Napoleon's favourite wine).

Gevrey-Chambertin wines are typically deeper in colour and firmer than their rivals from Vosne-Romanée and Chambolle-Musigny. Good examples may take time to develop into perhaps the richest and most complete wines of the Côte d'Or. Given the ease with which the village name sells, there used to be plenty of under-achievers in Gevrey-Chambertin, especially at grand cru level, but the quality of wines today from producers such as Denis Bachelet, Pierre Damoy, Claude Dugat, Dugat-Py, Duroché, Sylvie Esmonin, Fourrier, Harmand-Geoffroy, Heresztyn, Henri Magnien, Denis Mortet, Rossignol-Trapet, Joseph Roty, the exceptional Armand Rousseau, and Trapet is reassuring.

In all, Gevrey boasts nine grands crus, the pick of which are Chambertin and Chambertin-Clos de Bèze. The latter, comprising 15.4 ha/38 acres, may equally be sold as Le Chambertin. It is hard to differentiate between the two qualitatively, although Clos de Bèze is slightly further up the hill than Chambertin, with a less deep soil, giving wines which are fractionally less powerful but full of sensual charm.

Le Chambertin, 12.9 ha (plus the 15.4 of Clos de Bèze), is the flagship: if not quite as sumptuous as Musigny or Richebourg, nor as divinely elegant as La Tâche or Romanée-St-Vivant, Chambertin is matched only by Romanée-Conti (see VOSNE-ROMANÉE) for its completeness and its intensity.

Two other grand cru vineyards, Mazis-Chambertin and Latricières-Chambertin, lie on the same level as Chambertin and Clos de Bèze; one, Ruchottes-Chambertin, is to be found a little higher up the slope, while Charmes-Chambertin, Mazoyères-Chambertin, Griotte-Chambertin, and Chapelle-Chambertin are further downhill.

Mazis-Chambertin (12.59 ha), also written Mazy-, is usually regarded as being next in quality to Chambertin and Clos de Bèze, especially in the upper part, Les Mazis-Haut. The flavours are just as intense, the structure perhaps just a little less firm. Latricières (6.94 ha) is less powerful, although the wines are explosively fruity when young, with an entrancingly silky texture, especially when a sunny vintage warms up the cool CLAY soil. Ruchottes (3.50 ha), thanks to a particularly thin CALCAREOUS soil, is lighter in colour, angular in style, but again impressively intense in a fine, lacy style.

Griotte-Chambertin (5.48 ha), which possibly owes its name to the grill-pan shape of the vineyard rather than the griottes cherry aromas which the wine seems to have, and Chapelle-Chambertin (5.39 ha) are also a touch lighter in style. Charmes-Chambertin covers 31.6 ha if Mazoyères-Chambertin is included, which is usually the case. Together this constitutes the largest grand cru in the village; as with Clos de Vougeot and Échezeaux, its size precludes homogeneous quality. Some of the vineyard, such as the part stretching down to the main road, the D974, should perhaps not be classified as grand cru, although a good Charmes is one of Gevrey-Chambertin's most seductive, fragrant wines when young.

Some of the grands crus are matched, if not surpassed, by the best of the premier cru vineyards, especially those with an ideal south-eastern ASPECT such as Les Cazetiers and Clos St-Jacques. Indeed, Domaine Armand Rousseau, the most famous name in Gevrey thanks to the eponymous Armand's pioneering DOMAINE BOTTLING in the 1930s, charges significantly more for Clos St-Jacques than for several grands crus in an impressive range of wines.

See also CÔTE D'OR and map under BURGUNDY. J.T.C.M.

Gewürztraminer, often written **Gewurztraminer**, is the aromatic variant of the pink-skinned SAVAGNIN, shown by DNA PROFILING to be identical to TRAMINER, and is responsible for some of the most distinctively perfumed, full-bodied white wines of all. Gewürztraminer may not be easy to spell but is blissfully easy to recognize—indeed many wine drinkers find it is the first, possibly only, grape variety they are able to recognize from the wine's heady aroma alone. Deeply coloured, opulently aromatic, and broader than almost any other white wine, Gewürztraminer's faults are only in having too much of everything. It is easy to tire of its weight and its exotic flavour of lychees and heavily scented roses, although ALSACE's finest Gewurztraminers are extremely serious wines, with an occasional savoury note reminiscent of bacon fat in some of the most complex examples, capable of at least medium-term AGEING.

Gewürztraminer is the name adopted in the late 19th century for the dark-pink-berried aromatic or MUSQUÉ mutation of Traminer (and adopted as its official name, without the umlaut, in Alsace in 1973). Although much has been read into the direct German translation of *Gewürz* as 'spice', in this context it simply suggests 'perfume'. Traminer Musqué, Traminer Parfumé, and Traminer Aromatique were all at one time French synonyms for Gewürztraminer. It is also known as Roter Traminer in German and Traminer or Termeno Aromatico, Traminer Rosé, or Rosso in Italy. Its long history in Alsace means that it is occasionally known as some sort of KLEVNER, particularly in this case Rotclevner.

Gewürztraminer has become by far the most planted variant of Traminer. The grapes are certainly notable at harvest for their variegated but incontrovertibly pink colour, which is translated into deep golden wines, sometimes with a slight coppery tinge. Gewürztraminers also attain higher alcohol levels than most white wines, with over 14% being common, and acidities can correspondingly be precariously low. MALOLACTIC CONVERSION is almost invariably suppressed for Gewürztraminer, and steps must be taken to avoid OXIDATION.

If all goes well, the result is deep-golden, full-bodied wines with a substantial spine and concentrated heady aromas whose acidity level will preserve them while those aromas unfurl. In a lesser year or too hot a climate, the result is either an early-picked, neutral wine or an oppressively oily, flabby one that can easily taste bitter.

Viticulturally, Gewürztraminer is not exactly a dream to grow. Relative to the varieties with which it is commonly planted, it has small bunches and is not particularly productive. Its early budding leaves it prey to spring FROSTS, and it is particularly prone to VIRUS DISEASES, although the viticultural station at Colmar has developed eight virus-free CLONES, certified between 1971 and 2003.

The finest examples still come almost exclusively from Alsace, but the number of interesting examples made elsewhere has been growing.

Germany relegates its Roter Traminer to a very minor rank, well behind Riesling, with 1,119 ha/2,765 acres in total in 2021, including some plantings of the non-aromatic sort, which is very occasionally bottled separately. The variety needs relatively warm sites to avoid spring frost damage and to assure good FRUIT SET so that in northern Germany Riesling is usually a more profitable choice for growers. More than half of Germany's Roter Traminer is planted in the Pfalz and Baden, where it can produce wines of discernible character, but they can tend to flab. At Rhodt in the Pfalz, a Roter Traminer vineyard said to be more than 400 years old styles itself the world's oldest.

There were 263 ha/650 acres of Traminer planted in Austria in 2021 (the name is used to refer to pink and aromatic MUTATIONS as well), but here too it has been largely consigned to the non-modish wilderness, even though some examples—dry or slightly sweet wines from Styria and BOTRYTIZED sweet wines from Burgenland—can exhibit an exciting blend of race and aroma and can develop for many years in bottle.

The variety is grown, in no great quantity but usually distinctively, throughout Eastern Europe: called Tramini in Hungary, Dišeči Traminec in Slovenia, and Traminer or Traminer Roz in Romania. Most of the vines are the aromatic mutation and demonstrate some of Gewürztraminer's distinctive perfume but often in dilute form, typically overlaying a relatively sweet, lightish white. Hungarians are particularly proud of their Tramini grown on the shores of Lake Balaton. It is grown by the Romanians in Transylvania, by the Bulgarians in the south and east, and also, as Traminer, in Russia, Moldova, and Ukraine, where it is sometimes used to perfume sparkling wine.

It is grown in small quantities in Switzerland and in ever smaller quantity in Luxembourg. In Iberia, Torres grow it in the High PENEDÈS for their Viña Esmeralda, and it is essentially a mountain grape even in Italy, where about 1,121 ha/2,770 acres of Traminer Aromatico are still grown, particularly in Alto Adige. The less scented and less interesting Traminer is also grown to a limited extent.

Outside of Europe, Gewürztraminer presents a challenge. Many wine regions are simply too warm to produce wine with sufficient acidity, unless the grapes are picked so early (see HARVEST, timing), as in some of Australia's irrigated vineyards, that they have developed little Gewürztraminer character. Australia's Traminer/Gewürztraminer made a modest recovery in the decade to 2013 but has since declined to 679 ha/1,678 acres. It has become popular as a perfumed ingredient in newer wine styles such as PÉTILLANT NATUREL and SKIN-FERMENTED whites.

The variety has been more obviously successful in the cooler climate of NEW ZEALAND, although even here total plantings were 193 ha/477 acres in 2021, despite some lively examples from Gisborne on the east coast of the North Island. This, incidentally, was one of the earliest identifications of varietal/geographical matching in the southern hemisphere.

Another happy home for Gewürztraminer is in the Pacific Northwest of America, particularly in Washington and Oregon, although the variety has lost ground to Riesling in Washington and to Pinot Gris in Oregon. Washington had 164 ha/405 acres in 2017 (down from a high of 775 acres in 2011) and could demonstrate some appetizing life in several well-vinified examples, even if too many were too sweet. In Oregon, the 61 ha/150 acres in the ground in 2020 are used to make a range of styles from dry to sweet, white to ORANGE, with some contributing to multi-varietal blends, although rot can be a problem in this wetter climate.

Gewürztraminer remains a relatively minor variety in California, however, whose 1,643 ha/589 acres, almost half of them in Monterey, too often bring forth oil rather than aroma (see CALIFORNIA for more on the wines). There are a few hectares of Traminer in Argentina and some increasingly convincing bottlings from Chile, particularly from cooler, southern vineyards, but generally South America relies on TORRONTÉS and MOSCATEL to provide aromatic whites. Limited plantings in South Africa have so far yielded sweetish wines but some of the right aromas.

It seems likely that serious Gewürztraminer will remain an Alsace speciality for some years yet.

Galet, P., *Dictionnaire encyclopédique des cépages* (2nd edn, 2015).

Robinson, J., et al., *Wine Grapes: A Complete Guide to 1,368 Vine Varieties, Including Their Origins and Flavours* (2012).

Ghemme, ancient, tiny red-wine zone high up in the subalpine Novara Hills in the Alto PIEMONTE region of north-west Italy. Its promotion to DOCG in 1997 was intended to rescue its minuscule vineyard surface, which was up to 83 ha/205 acres in 2020. Like GATTINARA across the river Seisa in the Vercelli Hills and LESSONA and BRAMATERRA, Ghemme is made from the NEBBIOLO grape (minimum 85%) with the possible addition of UVA RARA (locally known as Bonarda Novarese) and/or VESPOLINA. For more details, see SPANNA, the local name for Nebbiolo.

GI. See GEOGRAPHICAL INDICATION.

gibberellins, naturally occurring plant HORMONES which regulate vine growth as for other plants. Isolated in 1941 from a rice fungus, they have been much studied since. In the vine they are formed in growing tissue in the leaves, roots, and berries. Many thousands of hectares of seedless varieties, notably Thompson Seedless (SULTANA), are treated by spraying with gibberellins during FLOWERING and shortly afterwards, resulting in larger berries suitable as TABLE GRAPES. Since the first trials at GEISENHEIM and Oppenheim in Germany, the application of gibberellic acid to seeded grapes in the middle or at the end of full bloom has been included in the Plant Protection Act in several countries. The technique causes berry shatter (see FRUIT SET) and results in a substantial reduction in both BOTRYTIS BUNCH ROT infection and the development of SOUR ROT. Careful calculation of the dose is required since some varieties can respond with reduced fruitfulness the year following the application. R.E.S. & H.S.

Giennois, Coteaux du, small AOC which extends on both banks of the Loire from just north of POUILLY-FUMÉ in the upper Loire to the town of Gien. Although the zone is quite extensive and encompasses both CALCAREOUS and FLINT soils, it comprised just 195 ha/482 acres in 2019. Most of the wines are crisp, pale whites made exclusively from Sauvignon Blanc, mostly harvested by machine, but some light reds and rosés are also made from a blend of Gamay and Pinot Noir. Joseph Balland-Chapuis is one of the most dedicated producers in this region, where spring FROSTS are a perennial threat.

See also LOIRE, including map.

Gigondas, the first Côtes du Rhône-Villages to be promoted to CRU in the southern RHÔNE, in 1971, named for a particularly pretty village perched within the Dentelles de Montmirail, the dramatic LIMESTONE formations visible from many neighbouring appellations. The grape varieties are similar to those grown in Châteauneuf-du-Pape, but the TERROIR is very different. A proportion of the vineyard is grown at high ELEVATION, up to 500 m/1,640 ft, while the rest tumbles down slopes facing west and north-west past the village and into the flatter land below. The effects of elevation and EXPOSURE help bring freshness to the wines, as do the CALCAREOUS soils. Thanks to the action of the Nîmes Fault, soils are particularly complex here, even for the southern Rhône, with large amounts of limestone and MARL and a band of Miocene sand and SANDSTONE underneath the village.

In 2021, wines were made from 1,225 ha/3,033 acres of vineyards, 99% red, 1% rosé. Wines must be at least half GRENACHE and must include some SYRAH and/or MOURVÈDRE; a further list of secondary grapes can make up no more than 10% of the blend (although in 2022 a move was under way to increase the allowed maximum for the more DROUGHT-resistant CINSAUT to 20%). White wines must be labelled Côtes du Rhône Blanc, but there may soon be AOC Gigondas Blanc, based on CLAIRETTE. Vines have been cultivated here since Roman times, and the village might take its name from the Latin word *jucundus*, meaning 'joyful'. The style of red wine here is concentrated and generous, with a welcome freshness. Though drinkable on release, they typically show their best after ten years in bottle. M.C.W.

Gingin. See HERITAGE CLONES.

Gippsland, vast, relatively cool Australian zone of coast and rolling hills stretching from just beyond the eastern fringe of Melbourne to the state of VICTORIA's eastern border with NEW SOUTH WALES. Some very good Pinot Noir and Chardonnay are produced, but the zone's size and scattered nature of its less than 200 ha/490 acres of vineyards renders generalizations meaningless.

girasol. See GYROPALETTE.

girdling, making an incision round a vine trunk, cane, or shoot, usually to improve FRUIT SET. For more details, see CINCTURING.

Girò, red grape used for dry, sweet, and FORTIFIED WINES on SARDINIA. It is unrelated to the aromatic, pink-skinned **Giró Blanc** grown on Mallorca.

Gironde, the estuary which separates the MÉDOC from BLAYE and the south-western extreme of cognac country and gives its name to the *département* that contains the city of Bordeaux and the Bordeaux wine region. The rivers DORDOGNE and GARONNE flow into the Gironde (see map under BORDEAUX).

GIS. See GEOGRAPHICAL INFORMATION SYSTEM.

Gisborne, (Tairawhiti in Māori) in the North Island of NEW ZEALAND, is the first city to see the sun each day due to its easterly location. Its climate is warm, temperate, and very maritime. Viticultural challenges emanate from easterly low-pressure systems during late summer and early autumn which bring rainfall, humidity, and the odd tropical cyclone. BOTRYTIS BUNCH ROT is a challenge and arguably a feature of the region's wines, with rich, honeyed aromatics across all varieties.

In recent times plantings have declined due to competition from the lucrative kiwi-fruit industry, but the Gisborne GEOGRAPHICAL INDICATION remains important for both BULK WINE as well as for boutique players who produce an array of mostly white wines. Chardonnay takes podium position with 620 ha/1,532 acres, producing opulent wines with flavours of ripe pineapple and melon. Pinot Gris varies in style and sweetness, typically displaying ripe pear and spice characters, while the little GEWÜRZTRAMINER planted is distinctive for its intense aromatics and oily texture. Millton Vineyards, a leader in BIODYNAMIC VITICULTURE, is a flagship producer. S.P.-T.

Givry, famous as the preferred wine of King Henri IV, produces mostly red wine in the Côte CHALONNAISE district of Burgundy. White wine constitutes only one-fifth of total production but is often particularly interesting with a soft bouquet reminiscent of liquorice. The reds have more structure and ability to age than those of neighbouring RULLY but less depth than Mercurey. Nearly half the 303 ha/749 acres of productive vineyard area in 2018 is designated PREMIER CRU, but the vineyards which most merit the higher rank are those on the hillside between Clos Salomon and the Cellier aux Moines. J.T.C.M.

glass, history of. For more than 3,000 years, glass has played a unique role in the history of wine, in terms of both serving (GLASSES, DRINKING VESSELS, and DECANTERS) and storage (BOTTLES).

Glass vessels were known in the ancient world (first appearing in EGYPT *c*.1500 BCE) and became common during Roman times, when the techniques of glass-blowing spread throughout the Roman Empire. Wine was sometimes drunk from glass tumblers, and surviving examples show astonishingly intricate craftsmanship. Glass bottles were used as decanters for carrying wine to the table, but not for storage because they were too fragile.

Glass-making continued after the collapse of Roman power. By the time of the Renaissance, VENICE had become the centre of luxury production. Venetian glassware was exported throughout the known world, and Italian craftsmen settled across Europe setting up new workshops. In Tudor England, aristocrats preferred Venetian-style glasses to silver (which was considered too common), but glass was so expensive that several diners were expected to share each beaker.

The problem with glass was that it was too light and therefore too fragile to withstand either transport or storage. The most common CONTAINERS for wine were BARRELS for bulk and leather, tin, or stoneware bottles for everyday use.

A turning point in the history of glass (and the history of wine) came early in 1615, when a timber shortage led to the introduction of coal-fired furnaces in England. Hotter furnaces and open-topped clay pots made possible the production of bottles that were not only darker and heavier but also stronger. At first these dark, onion-shaped bottles were used mainly as decanters and for personal use, but by the beginning of the 18th century they were used for the long-distance transport of wine. Initially the French had to rely on English imports, but by 1790 there were five factories around Bordeaux (still an important centre of glass production) producing 400,000 English-style bottles.

This development was revolutionary because it made possible the AGEING of wine. The necessary corollary was the CORK, whose use became common at this time. The advantages of ageing in bottle were most noticeable in PORT, a staple drink in Georgian England. As the practice of BINNING wine became more common, the shape of wine bottles evolved towards the taller cylindrical shape (*c*.1760) we know today.

Meanwhile a revolution in drinking glasses had emanated from the two southern English workshops of George Ravenscroft, who in 1675 had discovered how to make LEAD crystal. This gave rise to a whole new style of English glassware quite distinct from intricate Venetian fashions. Increasingly, different glasses were designed and produced to be used specifically for certain wines, and by the end of the 18th century the concept of a uniformly decorated glass service was well established throughout Europe. H.B. & C.R.H.

Charleston, R. J., *English Glass and the Glass Used in England, c.400–1940* (1984).

Tait, H. (ed.), *5000 Years of Glass* (new edn, 2012).

glass, wine by the. In an increasing proportion of the world's restaurants and bars, particularly in the United States, wine is served by the glass, sometimes matched to specific dishes on a menu. This is especially useful for those who want to drink less than a half or full bottle, want to taste as many different wines as possible in a FLIGHT of different small servings, or want to practise focused FOOD-AND-WINE MATCHING in a group that has ordered a wide range of different dishes. When carefully administered, with a high level of professional service and due attention to LEFTOVERS in opened bottles, possibly using special storage systems involving INERT GAS, this is an admirable service to the consumer. See also PRESERVATION SYSTEMS.

glasses, not just the final CONTAINER for wine but an important instrument for communicating it to the human senses (see TASTING). Wine can be drunk from any DRINKING VESSEL, but clean (and only clean) GLASS has the advantage of being completely inert and, if it is clear, of allowing the taster the pleasure (or in the case of

BLIND TASTING the clues) afforded by the wine's appearance: colour, clarity, and so on.

For this reason, wine professionals and keen amateurs prefer completely plain, uncoloured, unengraved, uncut glass, preferably as thin as is practicable to allow the palate to commune as closely as possible with the liquid. Thin-rimmed glasses are particularly highly valued.

The ideal wine glass also has a stem—indeed, Americans call wine glasses 'stemware'—so that the wine taster can hold the glass without necessarily affecting the wine's TEMPERATURE (a critical element in wine tasting). The stem also enables a glass to be rotated easily (although it takes a certain knack); rotation, as explained in TASTING, is essential for maximizing AROMA or BOUQUET. This rotation process also means that the ideal wine glass narrows towards the rim, to minimize the chance of spillage during rotation and to encourage the volatile FLAVOUR COMPOUNDS to collect in the space between the surface of the wine and the rim of the glass.

Individuals have their own aesthetic preferences, but any glass which fits the above criteria will serve as a wine glass, including some relatively inexpensive examples. There is a sensual thrill to be had, however, in really thin crystal. This is usually expensive, although central Europe, and BOHEMIA in particular, has a long tradition of producing fine glasses at good prices.

For many households, a single wine glass shape and size will do, traditionally supplemented by smaller glasses for FORTIFIED WINES and an elongated one for SPARKLING WINES. Purists, however, use slightly different glasses for different sorts of wine, conventionally (although not particularly logically) a smaller glass for white wines.

In this respect there is no greater purist than Georg Riedel, an Austrian glass-maker who is unusual for his wine CONNOISSEURSHIP. His family business makes different glasses for specific wines, supposedly based on analysing how taste characteristics are optimized on the nose and palate by minute variations in glass design. Those determined to take full advantage of all Riedel permutations may need to give up a room or two to accommodate the necessary number of glasses, however, and in practice most people content themselves with just two or three possible glass types, often chosen as much on appearance as on efficacy.

Over the centuries, various specific glasses have come to be associated with different wine types.

CHAMPAGNE and other sparkling wines were long drunk in a flat, saucer-like glass called a **coupe**, but this was abandoned in favour of the tall **flute**, which preserves the wine's MOUSSE though suppresses the aroma. Because of this, an increasing number of sparkling wine producers prefer a shape more closely resembling a regular wine glass.

In Spain, SHERRY has traditionally been served in the COPITA, and it tastes infinitely better in a part-filled glass in this elongated tulip shape than it does brimming over a cut-glass thimble sometimes favoured elsewhere. But some of the more fastidious sherry producers also prefer (a smaller pour in) a regular wine glass, as do some PORT producers.

The ideal port glass is not so very different from the copita, although it is usually rather bigger in order to allow maximum appreciation of the complex bouquet of a vintage port.

BURGUNDY, particularly red burgundy, has come to be served in glass balloons, sometimes so large they resemble fishbowls. The idea, apart from lusty exhibitionism, is that a good burgundy can offer such a rich panoply of aromas that they should be given every chance to escape the wine and titillate the taster. Most wine connoisseurs use the shape on a reduced scale.

The wines of ALSACE and GERMANY are sometimes served in particular forms of glass such as the **Rohmer**, often with green or brown glass stems, mainly for traditional reasons.

See also SERVING WINE.

glassy-winged sharpshooter, LEAFHOPPER insect (*Homalodisca vitripennis*) of great significance in some southern California wine regions since the 1990s as it is a vector of PIERCE'S DISEASE. It is able to fly longer distances than other leafhoppers and feed on both soft and hardwood stems, allowing the disease to spread more rapidly. It has been detected in Australia but has not become established and poses no immediate threat to vineyards as the Pierce's disease bacterium is not present.

R.E.S. & M.A.W.

Glenrowan, warm, historic Australian wine region in the North East Victoria Zone (see VICTORIA), famous for Ned Kelly, FORTIFIED WINES, and full-bodied reds from its 13 growers in 2022. See TOPAQUE AND MUSCAT.

Glera. The PROSECCO grape was renamed Glera in 2009 so that Prosecco could attain (greatly expanded) geographically protected status. Total plantings in Italy, almost exclusively in the Veneto, had reached 19,730 ha/48,754 acres by 2015. Recent DNA PROFILING revealed that Glera is a natural offspring of the obscure and no longer cultivated Austrian variety Vulpea.

J.V.

globalization of the world's wine markets continues to accelerate. There was always some trade in wine between Mediterranean countries, and a degree of trade expansion in the five decades prior to the First World War, but until the late 20th century intercontinental interactions involved little more than the exporting of CUTTINGS and traditional production expertise. Most wine was consumed in the country of production, and those countries were mostly in Europe. But since the 1980s, with the fall in TRANSPORT and communication costs and the rise of E-COMMERCE, the wine industry has embraced new modes of internationalization. They include a greater export focus by the main producers, mergers and acquisitions of what are becoming multinational wine companies (see below), the not-unrelated growth of supermarket chains operating internationally as wine retailers, and the increase in OENOLOGISTS and VITICULTURISTS employed in multiple countries and, often, in both the northern and southern hemispheres.

Globalization has brought significant changes in demand. Gradual deregulation of wine retailing in Britain and elsewhere from the 1970s allowed rapidly expanding supermarket chains to compete with traditional sellers of wine and attract new consumers. Those chains responded to new consumers' preferences by sourcing robust, fruity wines that are more approachable and affordable than FINE WINE but better than traditional basic European wine. For national advertising to be profitable for those chains, and for wineries (and in some cases the supermarket chains themselves) seeking to build BRANDS, large quantities of homogeneous wine are needed year after year. New World producers were initially more adept at responding to this new demand, and one of the consequences was *la* CRISE VITICOLE.

The share of global wine production volume exported, which had previously been well below 15% and mostly Mediterranean or intra-European, grew dramatically from the late 1980s and by 2015 had reached 40%. Meanwhile the NEW WORLD's share of global wine exports has risen from 3% in the late 1980s to almost one-third (if sparkling wine is excluded). Recognizing their poor performance, Europe's producers began belatedly in the mid 2000s to adapt their practices to compete. The world's three leading wine-exporting countries, Italy, Spain, and France, as a group now export about 40% of their production volume, up from just 20% a generation ago. Between 2002 and 2015 the share of wine that is exported from the New World in BULK rose from less than 15% to more than 50%. Bottling in the country of destination can reduce both transport costs and wine's CARBON FOOTPRINT. It also reflects the growth of supermarkets' own brands, as well as their demands for prompt delivery of those and other branded wines. The new bulk container shipping technology offers greater opportunities to blend wines from any region of the world and so may add to the commoditization of the most popular wine category.

The dramatic expansion in international wine trade is part of a general tendency for global trade to grow faster than production, fuelled in part by the lowering of trade restrictions and the freeing up of markets for foreign currency exchange. This greater openness means winemakers and hence grape-growers are far more exposed now than pre-1990 to exchange-rate volatility and also to greater import competition in their domestic market as consumers seek an ever-broader range of wine varieties, qualities, and styles. Wide fluctuations in exchange rates after the global financial crisis of 2008 substantially altered national shares in key markets, as did CHINA's emergence as a significant player in global wine markets.

Greater openness and international travel also alter tastes and preferences. This has been very clear in the EU, where shares of beer, spirits, and wine in national alcohol consumption have gradually converged. But nowhere has the emergence of wine consumption been more striking than in ASIA, albeit from a low base. Between 2001 and 2017, Chinese wine imports grew from 30 to 750 million litres. Initially they were of low- to medium-quality (often bulk) wines, but more recently they have been of wines that are more expensive than average wine imports elsewhere. Further large increases in wine consumption and probably imports are expected as China's middle class grows, since Chinese per capita consumption of grape wine is still around 1 litre per year (less than 3% of China's total alcohol consumption). **Mergers and acquisitions** accelerated from the mid 1980s when Louis Vuitton bonded with Moët-Hennessy to form LVMH. At about the same time, UK-based Grand Metropolitan (now DIAGEO) invested in California wineries, and Paris-based Pernod Ricard added Jacob's Creek to its portfolio of brands via Orlando Wyndham in Australia. Global drinks company interest rests mainly with sparkling wines, brandies, and vermouths, however, which have lent themselves much more easily to global branding than weather-dependent still wines produced just once a year. Pernod had entered the mass market before, only to leave it to wine-focused operators such as CONSTELLATION BRANDS, GALLO, and CASTEL; Diageo did the same in the mid 1990s. Pernod Ricard signalled a return to the fray by acquiring Montana (renamed Brancott Estate) and other significant wine brands when Allied Domecq broke up in 2005.

A second phase of international consolidation drew Australian producers closer to the American market with the merger of California's Beringer with the Mildara Blass subsidiary of Australian brewers Foster's in 2001 and with the acquisition of Hardys of Australia by Constellation in 2003. Foster's subsequently separated its wine business from beer to form Treasury Wine Estates, and Constellation sold their Australian arm, now called Accolade, to a private-equity firm in 2011. When in late 2020 China imposed punitive tariffs on imports of Australian wine, Treasury sourced non-Australian wine for their Australian brands that had been so lucrative in China.

Companies such as ANTINORI, Gallo, and MONDAVI have also been involved in a changing roster of JOINT VENTURES and acquistions which have helped to globalize wine. A more recent development has been Chinese investment in vineyards and wineries, often for distribution reasons, particularly in France.

The emergence of large international wine companies and brands, built on economies of scale, and the ease with which technology and know-how can now be transferred have led to significant shifts of wine-grape production from western Europe to the globe's cheapest vine-growing regions. But globalization is bound by TERROIR and the need for companies to offer differentiated wines of place—one of the main reasons the largest wine companies have a much smaller global market share than do the largest beer, spirits, and soft-drink companies. See also BRANDS. K.A.

Anderson, K., and Nelgen, S., *Global Wine Markets, 1860 to 2016: A Statistical Compendium* (2017), available as a free e-book at www.adelaide.edu.au/press/titles/global-wine-markets.

Anderson, K., and Pinilla, V. (eds.), *Wine Globalization: A New Comparative History* (2018).

Simpson, J., *Creating Wine: The Emergence of a World Industry, 1840–1914* (2011).

global navigation satellite system (GNSS), the collective name for the various satellite-based navigation systems (including the original US-owned global positioning system or GPS) which allow detailed mapping of specific vineyard features to a positional accuracy of 1 m/3 ft or less through the use of differential corrections. Differential GNSS (dGNSS or, more commonly, dGPS) is an essential component of PRECISION VITICULTURE. R.G.V.B.

global warming. See CLIMATE CHANGE.

glou-glou, term for a wine, usually red, that is especially easy to drink—*glou* is French for 'glug'. Such wines are typically fairly light in colour and BODY, are low in TANNINS and ALCOHOL, have relatively high ACIDITY, and have an emphasis on the wine's FRUIT. They are often part of the NATURAL WINE movement, and many are made with WHOLE-BUNCH FERMENTATION and little if any SULFUR DIOXIDE or other ADDITIONS. Often served lightly chilled, they may also be called *vins de soif*.

Ayscough, A., 'A brief history of glou-glou' (2018). www.wine.sprudge.com/2018/01/30/a-brief-history-of-glou-glou.

gluconobacter, a genus within the acetic acid bacteria family associated more with grapes than wine because of its high sugar tolerance. Like ACETOBACTER species, gluconobacter species are capable of spoiling wine by converting it into vinegar.

glucose is with fructose one of the two principal SUGARS of the grape and of sweet wines. Like fructose, it is a six-carbon-atom sugar, or a hexose.

The two major sugars that accumulate in grapes occur in about equal amounts; at the beginning of RIPENING, glucose exceeds fructose (up to fivefold), but in wines made with over-ripe grapes there is less glucose than fructose at the end of FERMENTATION. Glucose also serves a very important function as the major sugar used by the vine for forming GLYCOSIDES (see also FLAVOUR PRECURSORS). Common table sugar, sucrose, is made up of one molecule of glucose and one of fructose. See FRUCTOSE for details of the unusual relationship between these sugars and the grape. B.G.C. & A.D.W.

glutathione, or **glutathion**, sulfur-containing compound (tripeptide) found in grape juice and an important antioxidant which has been shown to play a significant part in the AGEING of wines and in protecting them from PREMATURE OXIDATION. It also has an important role in the formation of some precursors of VOLATILE SULFUR COMPOUNDS and in stabilizing the THIOLS which characterize the aroma of Sauvignon Blanc and possibly some other white grape varieties.

Glutathione also plays a major role in GRAPE COMPOSITION AND WINE QUALITY: higher levels of glutathione lead to higher levels of FLAVOUR PRECURSORS and lower levels of PHENOLICS. V.L.

glycerol, or **glycerine**, member of the chemical class of polyols and a minor product of alcoholic fermentation. The name derives from the Greek word for 'sweet', and glycerol does indeed taste slightly sweet, as well as oily and heavy. It is present in most wines in concentrations ranging from about 4–6 g/l, although BOTRYTIZED wines may have concentrations of around 10 g/l.

While glycerol does have a slight effect on the apparent sweetness of a wine, contrary to popular conception it makes only a very minor contribution to a wine's apparent VISCOSITY and bears no relation to the TEARS observed on the inside of many a wine glass. Whereas sensory tests have demonstrated that glycerol imparts sweetness at a threshold of about 5.2 g/l in white wine, a level of more than 28 g/l would be needed before any difference in viscosity were noted. A.D.W. & T.H.L.

glycolysis. See YEAST.

glycosidase. See ENZYMES.

glycosides are naturally occurring molecules made up of two parts joined by a glycosidic linkage; one of the parts is a sugar, frequently GLUCOSE, and the other may be a non-sugar, called an aglycone. Common aglycones are phenolic compounds, for example ANTHOCYANINS, although TERPENOIDS and a number of other compound types are found **glycosylated** in many plant tissues, including fruits. Glycosides present in wines come from the grape, and here the sugar is usually glucose, although it too may be connected to a second, non-glucose sugar residue. Formation of a glycoside changes the physical and chemical properties of molecules that are glycosylated. Glycosides are usually more water soluble and invariably much less volatile than the aglycones from which they were derived. It is still not clear why they form in plants, but glycosylation is presumed to aid detoxification and the transport of aglycones, or to make plant tissues rigid. Plants and fruits often have a higher concentration of glycosides than of aglycones. The sensory properties of flavour-active aglycones are profoundly diminished by glycosylation, and such glycosides, known as FLAVOUR PRECURSORS, are a reserve of FLAVOUR and contributors to VARIETAL flavour expression of some grape varieties such as MUSCAT (as opposed to aspects of flavour that arise from vinification) and BOUQUET in wines. Following the recognition of glycosides as flavour precursors, a development in the mid 1990s was the determination of this class of compound in grapes and wines through measures of glycosyl-glucose. See also INFRARED SPECTROSCOPY. P.J.W.

glycosyl-glucose assay, or **G-G assay**, an experimental measure of grape and wine composition, developed in the mid 1990s, based on the recognition of the role of GLYCOSIDES as FLAVOUR PRECURSORS of varietal wine flavour. The assay as applied to a grape, juice, or wine sample involves (*a*) isolation of the glycosides, (*b*) their complete hydrolysis to yield glucose, and (*c*) quantification of the glucose. The G-G assay has been applied to both light- and dark-skinned grape varieties, at early stages of berry development through to harvest; to MUSTS and juices during fermentation; and to wines before, during, and after AGEING. The assay is particularly important for white varieties, where there are few alternative ways of analysing secondary metabolites. With red varieties, most of the glycosides are ANTHOCYANINS. The assay allows the viticulturist and oenologist to relate the glycoside component of grape composition, obtained before harvest, to the glycoside concentration of a wine, irrespective of its style, years after its vinification. It has revealed the decrease in G-G in wines with ageing as glycoside HYDROLYSIS progresses, the range in glycoside concentration in juices of the same varieties grown in different regions, and the different rates of increase in glycoside concentration in fruit grown under different conditions. In the late 1990s, the assay was advocated as a valuable new tool to viticulturists wishing to investigate the influence of vine-growing practices on grape composition. As such it holds promise of an objective measure of fruit composition pertinent to wine quality. However, the assay is relatively complex and time consuming, requiring specialized skill. For this reason there has been little uptake by commercial wineries, and new methods utilizing INFRARED SPECTROSCOPY that offer rapid analysis of G-G in grapes are more popular. R.D.

Boido, E., et al., 'Characterization of glycosylated aroma compounds in Tannat grapes and feasibility of the near infrared spectroscopy application for their prediction', *Food Analytical Methods*, 6 (2013), 100–11.

Salinas, M. R., et al., 'Analysis of red grape glycosidic aroma precursors by glycosyl glucose quantification', *Talanta*, 89 (2012), 396–400.

GM and **GMO**. See GENETIC MODIFICATION.

GM 6494-5. See RONDO.

gneiss, a dense, tough, coarse-grained rock (pronounced 'nice') in which distinct bands have developed, distinguishing it from other metamorphic rocks. These irregular bands, typically of paler feldspar and QUARTZ alternating with darker biotite or amphibole, range in thickness over a few millimetres to centimetres with an irregularity that distinguishes the appearance of gneiss from the layers seen in some sedimentary rocks (see GEOLOGY). It is resistant to weathering and usually yields thin, rather acid soils. It occurs, for example, in AUSTRIA's Kamptal and Wachau regions, in MUSCADET, ROUSSILLON, and CÔTE RÔTIE in France, in parts of the US state of VIRGINIA, and in CANADA's Okanagan Valley. A.J.M.

GNSS. See GLOBAL NAVIGATION SATELLITE SYSTEM.

gobelet, or **goblet**, a form of vine-TRAINING SYSTEM, used since Roman times, whereby the SPURS are arranged on short ARMS in an approximate circle at the top of a short TRUNK, making the vine look something like a goblet drinking vessel. The vines are free-standing (apart from a small supporting STAKE when young), and the system is best suited to low-VIGOUR vineyards in drier climates. This is a form of HEAD TRAINING and is generally subject to SPUR PRUNING. The trunk is short, typically 30–50 cm/12–19 in, and the foliage is unsupported by WIRES.

The gobelet is widespread in France, from Beaujolais southwards, although it is now less common than it was because it is generally more economical to train vines on trellis systems rather than have them free-standing. The traditional spacing was 1.5 by 1.5 m (5 ft), but the distance has been increased to allow tractor access. With low-vigour vineyards the foliage can be relatively erect, but shoots may trail on the ground in high-vigour vineyards, and there can be substantial SHADE. Grape yield and quality may suffer as a result. The system is used widely in many Mediterranean countries. In Italy, the system is called *alberelli a vaso*, in Spain *en vaso*, and in Portugal *en taça*. In many NEW WORLD countries such as Australia and South Africa, the traditional, low-vigour gobelet-trained vines are often called BUSH VINES; in California, viticulturists tend to refer to them as head-trained, spur-pruned vines. Many have been replaced by vines with some form of trellising to accommodate the improved VIGOUR of newer vineyards, even if OLD VINES are increasingly valued by some winegrowers. R.E.S.

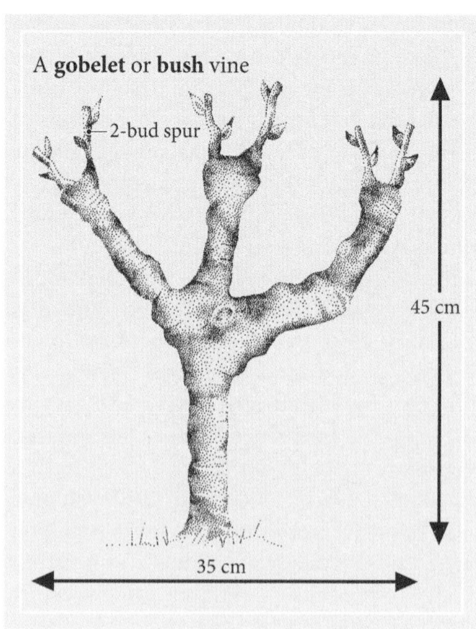

A **gobelet** or **bush** vine

Galet, P., *General Viticulture* (2000).

goblets. See DRINKING VESSELS.

Godello, fine white grape variety native to north-west Spain and northern Portugal rescued from near extinction in the 1980s and grown on more than 1,400 ha/3,459 acres of north-west Spanish vineyard by 2020. As Godello it is responsible for well-structured, tense dry whites in VALDEORRAS. DNA PROFILING shows it to be identical to a Portuguese variety known as Gouveio in the Douro and also in Dão (where it used to be known as Verdelho do Dão), and it is therefore a sibling of VERDEJO, their parents being SAVAGNIN and Castellana Blanca. Total plantings in Portugal were 1,045 ha/2,582 acres in 2020, rather more than of the distinct GOUVEIO REAL.

Goldburger, bland Austrian gold-skinned CROSS of WELSCHRIESLING and Orangetraube. Just 39 ha/96 acres of this vine remained in

2020, almost all of them in BURGENLAND, mainly used for sweet wines.

Goldkapsel, unregulated term of approbation referring to German Rieslings. Use of gold capsules to signify superior quality was a response, initially and still primarily in the MOSEL, to the 1971 German wine law's prohibition on labels of traditional terms such as CABINET, *feine*, *feinste*, or *hochfeinste*. Because the band of permissible MUST WEIGHT for AUSLESE is especially broad and Auslesen are the products of selective picking, usually in very small volumes, there is ample room for gradations. Some growers even designated really fine examples ***lange* Goldkapsel** (long gold capsule), and the abbreviations GKA and LGKA became established. From the 1990s the designations spread to wines of all possible PRÄDIKATS including, at some estates, dry wines, the standards employed being entirely estate-specific. Wines referred to in this way on price lists sometimes lack a physical gold capsule, and in recent years some growers have snuck the tiny letters GKA or LGKA on to a label without the authorities finding grounds to object. D.S.

Goldmuskateller, German name for the golden-berried MOSCATO Giallo grape speciality in ALTO ADIGE.

gold rushes have played a significant role in the development of NEW WORLD wine production through their influence both on demand for alcoholic beverages and on LABOUR supply. In CALIFORNIA, commercial viticulture had emerged during the 1830s, and with the discovery of gold in 1848 there was a massive increase in demand for all types of alcohol in the gold-mining counties of Amador, Calaveras, El Dorado, Nevada, Placer, and Tuolumne. However, by the 1850s, once the first flush of gold fever was over, a number of the immigrants, seeking to profit from the rising price of wine, turned to grape-growing and winemaking as a more reliable source of income. By 1857 it is estimated that there were some 1.5 million vines in California, and only three years later, after the enactment of legislation in 1859 which exempted vineyards from taxation, this total had risen to some 6 million.

Viticulture had been introduced into Australia on the establishment of the new colony in New South Wales in 1788. Its subsequent spread followed the increasing pace of colonization and settlement, with new vines being planted almost as soon as each new colony was founded. During the first half of the 19th century, however, despite the activities of proponents such as James BUSBY, winemaking remained a minority interest. The gold rush of 1851 changed this by attracting numerous immigrants to VICTORIA, with large numbers coming from France, Switzerland, Italy, and Germany, countries which had long traditions of viticulture and winemaking. Many, failing to make a success of prospecting, turned to farming, and in particular to viticulture, with the result that the pattern of vineyards in Victoria closely reflected the scattered distribution of the gold. In particular, during the 1870s and 1880s, the gold-mining areas of Ballarat, Bendigo, Great Western (now Grampians), and the Murray river all became important wine regions.

In New Zealand, the Otago gold rush of the 1860s likewise led to the gold mines, now long since abandoned, that are still a feature of wine country in this part of New Zealand. In 1864, for example, the Frenchman John Désiré Feraud used some of the fortune he made from a gold claim at Frenchman's Point to plant a vineyard on the Dunstan Flats. His wines won prizes in Sydney and Melbourne in the late 1870s and early 1880s. P.T.H.U.

Fountain, J., and Thompson, C., 'Wine tourist's perception of winescape in Central Otago, New Zealand', in M. Sigala and R.N.S. Robinson (eds.), *Wine Tourism Destination Management and Marketing* (2019).

Halliday, J., *The Australian Wine Compendium* (1985).

Sullivan, C. L., *A Companion to California Wine* (1998).

González Byass, the largest producer of SHERRY, still run by the family that founded the house. In 1835, 23-year-old Manuel María González Angel set up business as a shipper in JEREZ in southern Spain. Within months he had joined forces with D. Juan Dubosc to make their first large shipment to London: 48 hogsheads and a quarter cask, sent to Robert Blake Byass, who was to become their UK agent. The FINO brand Tío Pepe was born in the mid 1800s, named after Manuel's uncle José Angel y Vargas (*tío* being Spanish for 'uncle'), who helped his nephew establish the SOLERA. In 1855, Robert Blake Byass became a shareholder in the business, and in 1870 his sons and the sons of the founder entered the firm that became González Byass & Co.

In the mid 1980s, González Byass started to expand outside Jerez and now owns Bodegas Beronia (Rioja and Rueda), Cavas Vilarnau (Barcelona), Finca Constancia (Vino de la Tierra de Castilla), Finca Moncloa (Vino de la Tierra de Cádiz), Viñas del Vero (Somontano), Pazo de Lusco (Rías Baixas), and Dominio Fournier (Ribera del Duero). In 2016 the company expanded outside Spain to include Viñedos Veramonte and Neyen Apalta Estate in Chile. This was followed by the acquisition of Pedro Domecq (Mexico), and by 2022 the company owned a total of 2,143 ha/5.295 acres of vineyard in Spain, Chile, and Mexico.

Fifth-generation Mauricio González Gordon has been at the helm since 2006 during a period of change and expansion which has also included the development of a premium spirits portfolio, built on the success of its range of Jerez brandies, including the renowned Lepanto.

González Gordon, M., *Sherry: The Noble Wine* (3rd edn, 1990).

Gorbachev, Mikhail (1931–2022), last President of the Soviet Union (1985–91) and significant in the history of wine because of his 1985–8 national campaign against alcohol abuse. Measures were energetically directed not just against vodka consumption but also against the production and importation of wine. The immediate domestic effect was that the total vineyard area in the SOVIET UNION fell by one-third between 1980 and 1990.

The anti-alcohol campaign had equally dramatic consequences in countries from which the Soviet Union had been importing huge quantities of wine; see for example, BULGARIA, ROMANIA, HUNGARY, GEORGIA, and CYPRUS. These countries suddenly had to find new customers for an important proportion of their annual grape harvest—customers who would certainly be more demanding than their Soviet predecessors—or simply abandon vines and wine production to a significant degree.

Gordo, or **Muscat Gordo Blanco**, originally Spanish synonyms for MUSCAT OF ALEXANDRIA since adopted by Australia.

Gouais Blanc, genetically important, light-skinned grape variety commonly planted in central and north-eastern France in the Middle Ages which produced rather ordinary, acid wine, while the more highly valued Pinots were planted on more favoured sites. DNA PROFILING has shown that Gouais Blanc and Pinot had a great number of important progeny in northern France (see PINOT). Following that discovery, researchers became more interested in this ancient variety and realized that, besides its numerous synonyms in France, Gouais Blanc is also identical to Belina Drobna, Štajerska Belina, and Heunisch Weiss or Weisser Heunisch in Eastern Europe, as well as to Liseiret and Preveiral in Italy. Moreover, more than 60 additional possible parent–offspring relationships have been suggested between Gouais Blanc and French or European varieties, including RIESLING, BLAUFRÄNKISCH, and FURMINT. Gouais Blanc has been called a 'key variety' for grape diversity in Europe by some researchers, and some others have even nicknamed it the 'Casanova of grapes'. Despite its relative scarcity in France, in 2021 it was added to the official catalogue of varieties permitted there. VARIETAL Gouais Blanc is produced by Josef-Marie Chanton of Visp in Switzerland's Valais under the name Gwäss, by Georg Breuer in the

RHEINGAU, and some is also grown in Australia, where it has been known as Best's No 4. J.V.

Goulburn Valley, long-established temperate wine region with some two dozen producers in Australia's Central Victoria Zone. Nagambie Lakes is a subregion with Tahbilk and Mitchelton its leading wineries. See VICTORIA.

goût, French noun for TASTE in all its senses. Some wines, particularly old CHAMPAGNES, are described as suiting the **goût anglais**, or English taste (supposedly for wine necrophiliacs). Sweet champagne was described as satisfying the **goût russe** in the days of the imperial court. (The late 19th century Champenois defined champagne sweetened to satisfy the *goût russe* as one with 273–330 g/l of RESIDUAL SUGAR, as opposed to the *goût anglais* of 22–66 g/l.)

A wine made from fruit adversely affected by HAIL, for example, might be described in French as having a **goût de grêle**. Another much discussed and loosely applied TASTING TERM is **goût de terroir**, sometimes used about those aspects of flavour deemed to derive from the TERROIR rather than from the grape variety but sometimes erroneously and pejoratively used as a synonym for the term 'earthy'.

Gouveio Real, minor pale-skinned vine variety of which 110 ha/272 acres remained in northern Portugal in 2020, mainly in the Douro, where it makes full-bodied whites. It is distinct from **Gouveio**, a Portuguese synonym for the GODELLO of north-west Spain.

governo, also known as *governo all'uso toscano*, since it is most closely associated with TUSCANY, is a winemaking technique once widely used in the various CHIANTI production zones and occasionally in UMBRIA and the MARCHE. The technique consisted of setting aside and drying grapes from the September and October harvest, pressing them in mid to late November, and introducing the resulting unfermented grape juice into young wines which had just completed their alcoholic FERMENTATION, thereby restarting a slow fermentation. This practice led to a slight increase in the ALCOHOLIC STRENGTH of the wines and an increase in the level of CARBON DIOXIDE in the wine, some of which inevitably remained in young Chianti, bottled and marketed in the spring after the harvest. One of the precise purposes of the *governo* was to make the wines marketable at an earlier date by accelerating the malolactic conversion. Occasionally a second addition (*rigoverno*) is made in spring, producing a deeply coloured, fragrant wine with low acidity.

Today *governo* is much less widely used as producers have striven to transform Chianti's image from a quaffing wine to a serious candidate for AGEING, although producers of NATURAL WINE as well as researchers at the universities of Pisa and Tuscia are showing renewed interest in this ancient method. The technique was also used in the VERDICCHIO production zone in the Marche, to add fizz and a slight sweetness—from the high sugar content of the dried grapes—to counteract Verdicchio's occasionally bitter finish. It has virtually disappeared there now. W.S.

GPS. See GLOBAL NAVIGATION SATELLITE SYSTEM.

Graciano, sometimes called **Graciana**, is a richly perfumed black grape variety once widely grown in Rioja in northern Spain. It had fallen from favour because of its inconveniently low yields, thereby depriving modern Rioja of an important flavour ingredient with considerable freshness, but by 2020 plantings had grown to 2,570 ha/6,351 acres, from which some increasingly interesting VARIETAL bottlings are made in Rioja and Navarra, and there were experimental plantings as far afield as Toledo. This is Portugal's TINTA MIÚDA, France's Morrastel, the Tintilla de Rota grape of Jerez, and BOVALE Sardo, Muristellu, and Cagnulari on Sardinia.

The vine buds very late and is prone to DOWNY MILDEW but can produce wine of great character and EXTRACT, albeit notably acidic in youth. As Morrastel, it was popular in the Languedoc and Roussillon until the mid 19th century, when Henri BOUSCHET stepped in to provide growers with a more productive, more disease-resistant, but wildly inferior CROSS of Morrastel with Petit Bouschet, Morrastel-Bouschet, which in time replaced virtually all of the original Morrastel in French vineyards. True Morrastel, or Graciano, is still grown in southern France in minute quantities.

The variety known as Xeres in California, which has also been planted on a similarly limited scale in Australia, is probably Graciano, as is Graciana, the variety of which there are small plantings in Mendoza, Argentina.

Robinson, J., et al., *Wine Grapes: A Complete Guide to 1,368 Vine Varieties, Including Their Origins and Flavours* (2012).

Graciosa, island in the AZORES and DOC for its dry white wine made from VERDELHO (mostly), Arinto dos Açores, and Terrantez do Pico. With just 14.3 ha/35.3 acres in 2021, small quantities are made. The CO-OPERATIVE also makes LICOROSO (fortified) and *espumante* (sparkling) styles. S.A.

grafted vine, a vine consisting of a SCION grafted to a ROOTSTOCK, typically produced by a grapevine NURSERY or a vine grafter (see FIELD GRAFTING). The vines may be sold by the nursery as a growing plant soon after GRAFTING, with limited root and shoot growth and ready for planting in early summer, or, more conventionally, as a dormant one-year-old vine. The latter are grown in a field nursery for around six months, then removed, trimmed of shoots and roots, and bundled and cool-stored. They are prepared for despatch for planting the following spring.

Most countries in the world have PHYLLOXERA infestation, and therefore grafted vines are common. Countries such as Chile, where phylloxera is not present, or Australia, where phylloxera is largely contained by QUARANTINE, may use UNGRAFTED VINES, which are not resistant to phylloxera but grow satisfactorily in most situations and are cheaper. R.E.S.

grafting, the connection of two pieces of living plant tissue so that they unite and grow as one plant, has been a particularly important element in growing vines since the end of the 19th century, when it was discovered that grafting on to resistant ROOTSTOCKS was the only effective weapon against PHYLLOXERA.

History

The grafting of vines as a means of PROPAGATION was well known in ancient ROME, and it is referred to as early as the 2nd century BCE by CATO in his treatise *De agri cultura*. Knowledge of grafting survived through the medieval period, but it was in the 19th century that it came into particular prominence as the only method of satisfactorily ensuring the continued production of wine in the face of the threat posed by phylloxera. European varieties of VITIS VINIFERA had little resistance to phylloxera. It was only through the grafting of *vinifera* cuttings on to American species of VITIS, which had sufficient phylloxera resistance, that traditional European grape varieties could continue to be cultivated, and thus wine with the commercially acceptable taste thereof could still be made. Early experiments to counter phylloxera had generally centred on chemical treatments or flooding, but during the 1870s, those, such as Laliman, who had been advocating the use of AMERICAN VINE SPECIES as rootstocks gained increasing support. Eventually, at the 1881 International Phylloxera Congress in Bordeaux, it became generally accepted that grafting of French scions on to American rootstock was the best solution, and this led to much experimentation to identify the best rootstocks for particular soil types. On a regional scale, however, widespread adoption of grafting awaited the efforts of people such as Gustave Foëx, director of the agricultural school at MONTPELLIER, who in 1882 produced a small booklet recommending the use of American vines, written in a clear style specifically designed for the small wine producers of the Languedoc. Traditionally grafting was done by hand in the field (FIELD GRAFTING). Today, however, most grafting in Europe is done by machines which join together SCION and rootstock, usually in an omega-shaped cut (see BENCH GRAFTING). In

Two types of machine **grafting** used for bench grafts
Source: R. J. Weaver, *Grape Growing*

California and to a lesser extent South Africa, field grafting is still common.

P.T.H.U. & R.E.S.

Foëx, G., *Instruction sur l'emploi des vignes américaines à la reconstruction du vignoble de l'Hérault* (1882).

Gale, G., *Dying on the Vine: How Phylloxera Transformed Wine* (2011).

Laliman, L., *Études sur les divers travaux phylloxériques et les vignes américaines* (1879).

Modern viticultural practices

Vines are grafted or budded to take advantage of the desirable properties of the rootstock variety. Foremost is resistance or tolerance to soil-borne pests and diseases, especially phylloxera and NEMATODES. Other properties are tolerance to soil SALINITY, to high LIME levels, and to soil waterlogging or DROUGHT, as well as an ability to modify VIGOUR or to hasten or delay RIPENING. If conducted in the vineyard, as FIELD GRAFTING, the practice offers a method of changing a VINE VARIETY. If conducted indoors, before planting, it is called BENCH GRAFTING, which may in warm climates be complemented by NURSERY grafting.

The uniting of the scion with the rootstock is achieved by a slow growth process: a mass of undifferentiated cells, the CALLUS, develops at each cut edge of the respective CAMBIUMS (zones of dividing cells), so it is important to position the two cambiums opposite each other and close together. Thereafter, the scion piece is part of the whole plant vascular system.

A number of factors determine success or failure in grafting, in addition to the skill involved in cutting and matching of cambiums. The first is that the graft needs specific environmental conditions such as warm temperatures (24–30 °C/75–86 °F) and high humidities (90–100%) around the union. The second is the compatibility of the scion/stock combination. The third, and probably the most serious, is that some rootstocks are difficult to root (see ROOTLING), which can affect the overall success of grafting. It has been shown that grafting success is reduced if the scion or rootstock is infected by any of the fungi involved in TRUNK DISEASES.

Particular forms of graft include CLEFT GRAFTING, NOTCH GRAFTING, and WHIP GRAFT. See also GRAFTED VINE and GREEN GRAFTING.

B.G.C. & R.E.S.

grafting machine, a device used in GRAFTING by making cuts through the vine ROOTSTOCK and SCION pieces with mirror-image shapes that permit snug fitting. Shapes used include castellate and omega. Grafting machines are an essential part of the factory-like methods used for BENCH GRAFTING, but innovative growers have used modified machines for NURSERY grafting and FIELD GRAFTING. B.G.C.

Graham, important port shipper. See SYMINGTONS.

Grahm, Randall (1953–), California winegrower arguably more famous for his words than for his wines. After a stint at DAVIS he founded Bonny Doon winery in the SANTA CRUZ MOUNTAINS intending to make great Pinot Noir. He never did. But his debut, 1984 vintage of a Rhône blend Le Cigare Volant, sowed the seeds for the entire RHÔNE RANGERS movement in California.

For someone with such a quirky—nay, goofy—image (his winemaking experiments included macerating rocks in his wines to achieve MINERALITY), he proved exceptionally good at creating popular wine BRANDS. He successfully sold his Big House and Cardinal Zin brands in 2006 and Pacific Rim in 2010 before selling Bonny Doon Vineyard in its entirety in 2019 in order to concentrate on a 400-acre property near San Juan Bautista he calls Popelouchum. His lofty plan there is to breed no fewer than 10,000 new grape varieties from seed 'and perhaps produce a true *vin de terroir* in the New World', he has written.

His wines may not have thrilled connoisseurs, but his words did. His exceptionally erudite and playful newsletters did consistently and were eventually compiled into the book cited below. Journalists know that he can be relied upon for a quote more entertaining than anyone else's.

Grahm, R., *Been Doon So Long: A Randall Grahm Vinthology* (2009).

grain is visible on the end of a barrel STAVE at the bevelled edge, which is also known as the chime. Since staves are split along the radial plane, it can be seen across the width of the stave end. Each light and then dark alternation represents a one-year growth ring for the oak tree. The average width of each annual growth ring is called the grain by COOPERS and barrel users.

Every year, the tree forms a new growth ring in the CAMBIUM layer under the bark. Seen under a microscope, a ring can be broken down as a succession of spring wood (or early wood) and summer wood (late wood). Vessels in spring wood are more numerous and wider than in summer wood. Summer wood therefore has a higher density of fibres and parenchyma and fewer vessels.

Grain can be measured in two ways: either by the number of growth rings per centimetre/inch or by the average width of these rings. Grain is generally considered tight if there are 4–5 rings per cm or if the rings are narrower than 2–3 mm.

Many factors affect grain size. In addition to the work of the forester, who selects and raises the trees in each plot year after year, thereby regulating tree growth and therefore grain, different soil and climate conditions in oak forests produce different types of grain. Trees growing in dry areas, with a high population density and on poor soil, tend to have tight grains. But grain also varies through the life of the same tree. The older the tree, the more slowly its diameter grows and the tighter its grain. Similarly, the grain at the foot of a tree will be wider than at the top.

It is acknowledged that grain is wider for *Quercus robur* and tighter for *Quercus petraea* (see OAK). This is due to the effect of differences in the ecological behaviour of each species. In general, *Quercus robur* requires more water and light and hence exhibits faster growth and wider grains where it tends to be grown. *Quercus*

G

petraea, which better withstands dry soils and a lack of light, tends to be located on top of hills. But these species frequently co-exist in the same forest plots, in which case individuals of either species will rarely show significant differences in grain size. These species are sold together by forest managers. Sorting by grain, coopers tend to find a larger percentage of *Quercus robur* with wide grain than with tight grain, although this empirical approach is in no way systematic. *Quercus alba*, or American white oak, shows a wide range of ring widths, depending on the growing conditions, but because it is dense and has a high number of tyloses (see OAK) the grain may have little influence on wine during BARREL AGEING. Nevertheless, some coopers do grade white oak according to grain size.

Contrary to popular belief, tight grain is more porous than wide grain. Indeed, a slowing down in oak growth primarily affects summer wood, and the proportion of early wood in the ring (the large vessels) is greater. Tight grain therefore has more spring wood per centimetre and thus has more void than wide grain, which has more summer wood and therefore more fibre and parenchyma. This explains why there are differences in wines aged in barrels with wide grain compared with those aged in ones with tight grain. However, it is important to distinguish between total porosity (the void in the wood) and active porosity, which is connected to the exterior environment and allows OXYGEN diffusion. Studies show that active porosity varies significantly with no direct relationship to grain. Barrel permeability is therefore more complex and less influenced by grain than by other anatomical factors of wood, particularly the number of tyloses, which block the vessels (see OAK), or by coopering practices such as assembling the staves and the intensity of TOASTING.

Comparisons of barrels made from tight-grain versus wide-grain French oak showed that tight grain released more aromatic compounds (e.g. eugenol, whisky lactones) over time than wide grain, and wide grain released more wood TANNINS (ellagitannins). It was also observed that the release of various compounds from the wood differed from one grain type to another. Since porosity is higher for tight grain, it is easier for the wood to interact with wine, which releases the most accessible compounds in the wood more quickly.

See also WOOD INFLUENCE.

Pracomtal, G. de, et al., 'Types of oak grain, wine élevage in barrel', *Practical Winery & Vineyard* (Jul 2014), 64–9. R.T. du C.

Grampians, temperate wine region in Australia's Western Victoria Zone, somewhat cooled by ELEVATION and Southern Ocean influences, producing smooth, medium-bodied Shiraz and Cabernet Sauvignon. Great Western, the historic heart of the region and home to 1860s-founded Best's and Seppelt, is now a subregion of Grampians. See VICTORIA.

Granada, province and DOP in ANDALUCÍA between the high Sierra Nevada mountain range and the Mediterranean with an old viticultural tradition and 300 ha/741 acres of vines in 2020. Average vineyard ELEVATION is 1,200 m/3,937 ft, including some of continental Europe's highest vineyards. The elevation and humidity provide a much cooler growing environment than the LATITUDE would suggest. There is one VINO DE LA TIERRA, Cumbres del Guadalfeo, 79 ha in the south of the DOP. INTERNATIONAL VARIETIES dominate, although Moscatel de Alejandría (MUSCAT OF ALEXANDRIA) and GARNACHA often appear in blends. F.C.

Gran Canaria, CANARY ISLAND with its own DO and 245 ha/605 acres of vines planted up to 1,300 m/4,265 ft in ELEVATION in VOLCANIC soils. LISTÁN Bianco dominates plantings, with MARMAJUELO and MALVASIA; reds are mainly made from LISTÁN NEGRO.

grand cru means literally 'great growth' in French. In Burgundy's CÔTE D'OR a grand cru is one of 33 particularly favoured vineyards (see BURGUNDY for list), a decided notch above PREMIER CRU. In CHABLIS and ALSACE, grand cru is a separate, elevated AOC accorded to specific vineyards listed in the relevant entries. In Bordeaux, the words 'grand cru' usually apply to a specific property or château and depend on the region in which it is located (see CLASSIFICATION). See also QUARTS DE CHAUME and CHAMPAGNE, geography and climate.

Grande Rue, La, red burgundy GRAND CRU vineyard in VOSNE-ROMANÉE.

grandes marques, obsolete, self-imposed term for some of the major houses or BRANDS of CHAMPAGNE. The original Syndicat des Grandes Marques was founded in 1882 but was disbanded in 1997. The term means literally 'big brand' in French and is still used informally.

grand format. See LARGE FORMAT.

Grand Noir de la Calmette hardly deserves a name that suggests it is the great black grape variety of the BOUSCHET experimental vine-breeding station, Domaine de la Calmette. Bred from Petit Bouschet and the common ARAMON, it has a very high yield and, from its TEINTURIER parent, red flesh (although not as red as Alicante Bouschet's). Often known simply as **Grand Noir**, it was widely planted in France until the 1920s and is now almost extinct there. See also GRAN NEGRO.

Grand Roussillon, little-used VIN DOUX NATUREL appellation in ROUSSILLON used effectively for declassified RIVESALTES. It may be any of the three colours and also comes in RANCIO form.

Grands Échezeaux, red GRAND CRU in Burgundy's CÔTE D'OR. For more details, see ÉCHEZEAUX.

grand vin, name current in BORDEAUX for the main wine produced by a CHÂTEAU (as opposed to a SECOND WINE or *second vin*).

granite, a coarse-grained, pale-coloured igneous rock of plutonic origin (see GEOLOGY). Feldspars are the dominant constituent, especially potassium feldspar, with lesser amounts of QUARTZ and minerals such as mica and amphibole. The potassium feldspar tends to weather to kaolinite (see CLAY) and release POTASSIUM, which can affect juice ACIDITY. In parts of the northern RHÔNE and South Africa's WESTERN CAPE, the granite bedrock has weathered into kaolinite (china clay) to the extent it is mined for pottery. Granite soils tend to be acid, poorly fertile, and, because the quartz grains resist weathering, sandy and well-drained. Granite is widespread in vineyards: examples include DÃO, the Granite Belt of QUEENSLAND, parts of BEAUJOLAIS, coastal CHILE, and the SIERRA FOOTHILLS. A.J.M.

Granite Belt, wine region and GEOGRAPHICAL INDICATION in the extreme south of QUEENSLAND, Australia, about three hours' drive south-west of Brisbane, on the border with NEW SOUTH WALES, with more than 305 ha/754 acres of vineyards. On the tableland of the Great Dividing Range at ELEVATIONS of 700–1,000 m/2,297–3,281 ft, the region experiences warm days and cold nights. Here humidity and summer rainfall are less of an issue than spring FROST. Although the region is dominated by GRANITE and coarse SANDS from weathered granite (indeed granite boulders are readily visible across the district and in nearby Girraween National Park), the terrain is diverse, from the arid, windy, rocky landscape of the Eukey Road high country to the deeper, wetter soil of the Ballandean area, the flat, exposed Summit, Severnlea with deeper soil and wind protection, and sunny Pyramids Road.

The Granite Belt Strange Bird marketing initiative has encouraged planting of Spanish and Italian grape varieties, and warm-climate ALTERNATIVE VARIETIES are expected to be increasingly important. In the colder, rocky subregions, a 'Syrah' style of Shiraz, with spicy red-berry aromas, complexity from WHOLE-BUNCH FERMENTATION, and limited oak influence, is a common premium style. A.C.

Granja-Amareleja, subregion of the southern part of the ALENTEJO adjacent to the Spanish border in one of the most arid parts of southern Portugal. Ungrafted MORETO vines thrive on the SANDY left bank of the Guadiana river; the red grape is a traditional component of VINHO DE TALHA. S.A.

Gran Negro, or **Grão Negro**, local name for GRAND NOIR DE LA CALMETTE in Galicia, particularly in Valdeorras, where there were still 545 ha/1,347 acres in 2020. It was introduced here after the PHYLLOXERA invasion. As **Grão Negro** it is also grown in southern Portugal.

Gran Reserva, Spanish term for a wine supposedly from an outstanding VINTAGE which has been subject to lengthy BARREL AGEING, the exact period varying from DO to DO, before release. Rioja produces the great majority of all Gran Reservas. For much of the 20th century, Gran Reservas represented Spain's finest and most expensive wines, but many of the country's most celebrated winemakers are nowadays concerned to preserve more FRUIT in their top bottlings and do not necessarily equate quality with time spent in wood.

See also RESERVA.

Gran Selezione, controversial category of supposedly superior CHIANTI CLASSICO introduced in 2014.

grape, the berry or fruit of the grapevine, or VINE, whose juice is the essential ingredient for making WINE. A grape is *raisin* in French, *uva* in Italian and Spanish, and *Rebe* in German. The grapes produced by commercial viticulture are sold either as TABLE GRAPES or RAISINS, or they are crushed and processed into wine or GRAPE JUICE, GRAPE CONCENTRATE, or RECTIFIED GRAPE MUST. Wine production is, however, the most important use, accounting for some 80% of the world's grape production. The solids, including stems, skins, seeds, and pulp, left after these juicing processes are called grape POMACE. There are usually less than 100 grapes to a BUNCH for wine-grape varieties, and berries are individually relatively small.

The form and appearance of grape berries varies hugely between VINE VARIETIES. Their shape varies from flattened through to spherical and oval through to elongated and finger-like; colour from green to yellow, pink, crimson, dark blue, and black; and size from as small as a pea (as in CURRANT, for example) to the huge, egg-like berries of some recently bred table-grape varieties which may weigh as much as 15 g/0.5 oz each. The majority of wine grapes, however, are spherical to short oval, 1–2 g in weight, and are coloured yellow (called 'white' by vine-growers) or very dark purple (called 'black' or 'red').

Grape berries are borne on the end of a short stalk called the PEDICEL, which is in turn attached to the RACHIS or STEM. The peduncle is the stem where it connects to the SHOOT. At the end of the berry opposite the pedicel is a small stub of dead tissue which is the remnant of the style and stigma (see FLOWER). Some varieties, for example Riesling, have corky lenticels scattered over the skin. When cut open, the grape is seen to have two units (carpels) side by side, each enclosing a space (a locule) in which are the seeds. When the berry enlarges, the space becomes compressed by encroaching flesh. The significant parts of a berry are the flesh, skin, and seeds. The pericarp tissue is formed from the wall of a ripened ovary, which creates three layers as it grows and develops. These are the endocarp, surrounding the seed, the middle juicy part called the mesocarp, and the outer layer (i.e. the skin) called the exocarp.

Flesh or pulp

The mesocarp (i.e. the flesh or pulp) is the bulk of the PERICARP. The pulp contains the juice in the VACUOLES of pericarp cells. A section across the flesh (see diagram) shows that there are about 40 large parenchyma cells from beneath the skin to the single cell layer that is the inner lining. A central core of vascular strands connects to a mesh of veins that encircles the outer edge of the flesh like a chicken-wire cage and provides the vascular connection with the rest of the vine; the veins contain the XYLEM, which transports water and minerals from the roots, and PHLOEM, which is the all-important pathway for sugar from the leaves. Another zone with a different texture is the so-called BRUSH, which is the lighter-coloured part of the flesh near the junction with the pedicel.

The pulp and the juice are the most important part of the grape to the winemaker and to the wine drinker, for they contain the main components of the finished wine. Because the juice of all grapes (apart from the specialist TEINTURIER varieties) is a pale grey, white wine can be made from grapes of all colours, so long as the juice is not left in contact with dark skins. Red wines can be made only by leaching colour from such skins, while pink wines can be made either from short contact with dark skins or more prolonged contact with pink or red skins.

Skin

The grape's exocarp or skin is the tough, enveloping layer around the grape that holds it together. The outside layer, or BLOOM, forms the grape's typically whitish surface. It consists of wax plates and cutin, both of which resist water diffusion and hence water loss from the berry. They also impede penetration of fungal spore growths and other biological infections. The fatty acids and sterols from the bloom supply important nutrients for the growth of YEAST during FERMENTATION.

Below the wax and cutin are the cell layers that form the skin; the first is the true epidermis, and below this are about seven cell layers

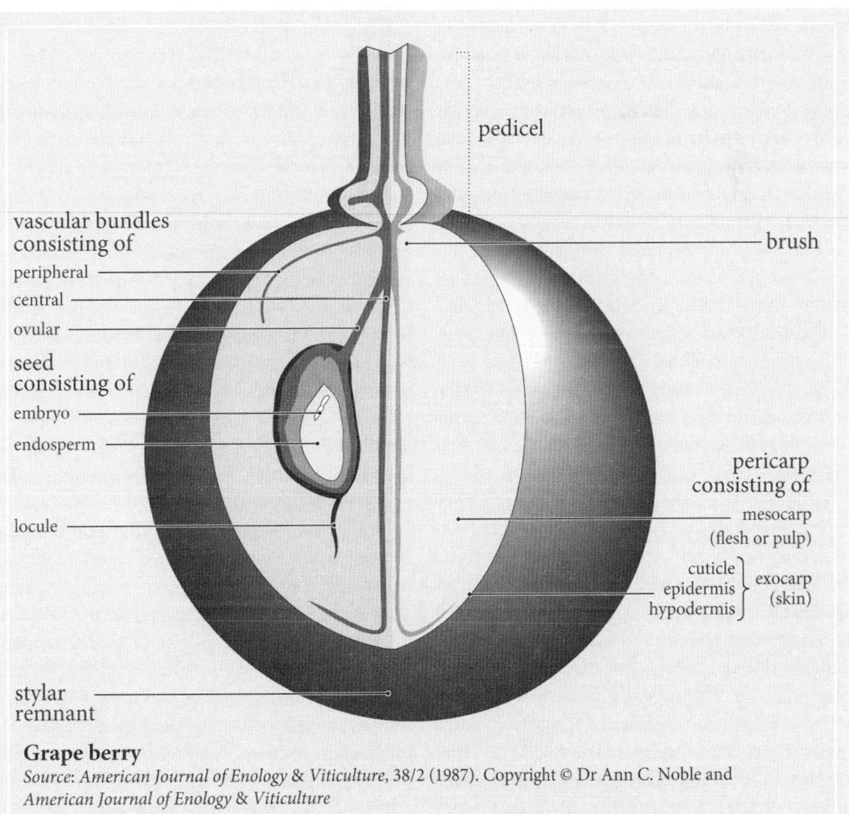

Grape berry
Source: American Journal of Enology & Viticulture, 38/2 (1987). Copyright © Dr Ann C. Noble and *American Journal of Enology & Viticulture*

forming the hypodermis, in which are concentrated most of the berry PIGMENTS, yellow CAROTENOIDS, and xanthophylls, and the red and blue ANTHOCYANINS important in the making of red wine. As well as some TANNINS, a significant amount of a grape's FLAVOUR COMPOUNDS are also associated with the skin layers.

There are other differences in the chemical composition of skin compared with the underlying flesh: besides phenolics, they are rich in POTASSIUM. Skins constitute 5–12% by weight of a mature grape berry, depending on the vine variety. The thickness of grape skin can vary from about 3 to 8 µm.

G

Seeds

Seeds of grapes vary in size and shape between varieties; for example, those in MUSCAT BLANC À PETITS GRAINS are about 5 mm long, while those in the table grape Waltham Cross are nearly 10 mm. Their number per berry, typically one or two, tends to be a characteristic for each variety. Four is possible since each carpel bears two ovules. However, some abnoraml Alphonse Lavallée (Ribier) berries with double the number of carpels may have eight seeds. Often, incompletely developed seed structures, called stenospermic (thin-seeded), occur alongside fully developed seeds. The greater the number and amount of seed development, the larger the berry; this relationship is mostly a reflection of differences in amount of cell division in the pericarp mediated by the plant hormone GIBBERELLIN.

Seeds are only of minor importance in winemaking although if they are crushed, bitter tannins are released. Unlike the stems, they are not easily separated from the berry, but in WHITE WINEMAKING the contact time between juice and seeds and the absorption of tannins from the seeds is minimal. In RED WINEMAKING, on the other hand, the prolonged contact between the seeds and an increasingly alcoholic solution means that tannins are very likely to be dissolved. Grape seeds have served as a source of edible or industrial oil.

See also GRAPE COMPOSITION AND WINE QUALITY and RIPENING. (For other parts of the vine plant, see VINE MORPHOLOGY.) B.G.C. & R.E.S.

Coombe, B. G., 'Research on development and ripening of the grape berry', *American Journal of Enology & Viticulture*, 43 (1992), 101–10.

grape composition and wine quality. Grape composition is the essential basis of wine quality, and knowledge of grape composition is critical for those winemakers interested in making the appropriate wine style, although the significant impact of winemaking practices cannot be denied. The concentrations of component chemical groups play a part. Grape SUGARS, for example (see MUST WEIGHT), determine the possible potential ALCOHOLIC STRENGTH of the wine. ACIDS and nitrogenous compounds (see NITROGEN) affect the course of FERMENTATION and exert their own effects on flavour. POTASSIUM salts have effects on PH and thus on microbiological activity and oxidative STABILITY. PHENOLICS contribute to levels of COLOUR and TANNINS. A multitude of volatile compounds alter aroma (see ACIDITY, AMINO ACIDS, FLAVOUR COMPOUNDS, and SUGARS).

Grape composition is constantly changing during RIPENING. A central factor in grape ripening is the steady increase in sugar concentration after sugar accumulation has been triggered at VERAISON. Another feature is that acidity declines, due mainly to the RESPIRATION of malate but also to dilution by berry growth and the formation of salts, especially with potassium, which increases concurrently with sugar. Colour and tannins increase in skins early during ripening. Less is known about the timing of the increase in aroma compounds and FLAVOUR PRECURSORS because until recently they have been difficult to measure, but in some varieties intensity appears to develop late in the ripening process, after sugar concentration has levelled (see GRAPE QUALITY ASSESSMENT). Wine quality depends on the integration of these chemical groups in such a way that there is a balance between components, coupled with an intensity of VARIETAL character. R.D. & R.E.S.

Boss, P. K., 'Towards the prediction [sic] wine outcomes from grape compositional measures', *Proceedings of the ASVO Workshop on Assessing Grape Quality* (2011).

grape concentrate is what is left when the volatile elements are removed from fresh grape juice. Rarely used to produce really fine wine, it can provide a useful supply of grape SOLUBLE SOLIDS for use long after the HARVEST. Grape concentrate is the main ingredient, for example, in so-called MADE-WINES produced without the benefit of freshly picked grapes (see BRITISH WINE and HOME WINEMAKING). Grape concentrate can also be used in BLENDING to soften and sweeten dry wines of everyday commercial standard made in cooler regions. It was once widely used in Germany, for example (see SÜSSRESERVE). For more details of grape concentrate used for sweetening purposes, see SWEET RESERVE.

Grape concentrate is also in some circumstances used for ENRICHMENT, increasing the eventual alcohol content of a wine (it is a permitted pre-fermentation ADDITIVE in Australia, for instance, although sugar is not). It is also used to sweeten some other fruit juices and foodstuffs. Concentrate is also used to produce a small category of high-intensity red and purple colourants, used to enhance colour and add body to wines.

Historically, winemakers made a form of grape concentrate by simply boiling grape juice until the volume was reduced by at least one-half. This resulted in a liquid with a strong cooked, caramel flavour, however, and such an additive is used exclusively for sweet, dark, strong wines such as rich SHERRY, MÁLAGA, and MARSALA. In Spain it is known as *arrope*.

Today the caramelizing effect is avoided by CONCENTRATION of the grape juice under very low temperatures in vacuum evaporators. Modern low-pressure concentrators are expensive and therefore tend to be operated by specialists who may use them to concentrate other fruit juices at other times of year. Most grape juice is subject to CLARIFICATION and is reduced in TARTRATES before concentration so that the solids precipitated are minimal when water is removed. See also RECTIFIED GRAPE MUST.

Red grape concentrate may be made by first heating the grapes to extract PIGMENTS into the juice before concentration. A.D.W.

grape juice is a sweet, clear, non-alcoholic liquid. Winemakers generally use the term to refer to liquid from grapes at any stage after DRAINING or PRESSING up to the point when FERMENTATION occurs. It is thus quite different from MUST, though the term 'must' is often used for both. If grape juice is preserved by holding it at temperatures so low that any YEAST or BACTERIA are inhibited, it can be used in commercial winemaking to soften or sweeten new, dry wines. However, since the development of efficient juice concentrators, it has generally been supplanted in winemaking by GRAPE CONCENTRATE, which can be stored much more cheaply, is inherently stable against microbiological attack, and dilutes the wine much less.

A certain amount of grape juice is bottled and sold as a drink, but since it so readily ferments it needs to be protected from yeast contamination. This is usually done by PASTEURIZATION and/or ULTRAFILTRATION and heavy additions of SULFUR DIOXIDE. Many VITIS VINIFERA varieties lose their pleasant, fresh taste after pasteurization, and the American grape-juice industry uses the non-*vinifera* CONCORD variety. It is very difficult to distinguish VARIETAL character in most grape juices, other than such conspicuous flavours as those associated with MUSCAT and Concord grapes. Wine drinkers generally find grape juice bears disappointingly little relation to wine.

grape juice composition. The relative proportions of the compounds that make up grape juice are constantly changing as the berries ripen, so the time of HARVEST greatly affects composition. Most of the sugary solution that results when grapes are squeezed or crushed derives from the contents of the VACUOLES of the cells of the PULP, although heavy CRUSHING and PRESSING add further solution from vacuoles of the skin and vascular strands, thereby mixing many different compounds into the must. Thus the composition of the juice that issues when berries are crushed changes with the pressure and time of crushing; the first, FREE-RUN juice has fewest suspended solids and skin extracts; further pressing yields juice with more PHENOLICS and POTASSIUM salts, and hence lower TOTAL ACIDITY.

Fermentation of juice with the skins, as in red winemaking and SKIN-FERMENTED whites, yields still more FLAVOUR COMPOUNDS and PIGMENTS that are enriched in the cells of the skin. See GRAPE.

See also ACIDITY, AMINO ACIDS, ANTHOCYANINS, ASCORBIC ACID, CAROTENOIDS, CITRIC ACID, FLAVOUR PRECURSORS, FRUCTOSE, GLUCOSE, GLYCOSIDES, LIPIDS, MALIC ACID, MINERALS, PECTINS, PROTEINS, SOLUBLE SOLIDS, STARCH, SUCROSE, TANNINS, TERPENOIDS, VARIETAL character, VITAMINS, and the all-important SUGAR IN GRAPES. B.G.C.

grape quality assessment is needed by winemakers for long-term strategic planning and, in the short term, for the planning of each vintage, especially in fixing HARVEST dates.

Assessment is often a matter of combined judgement by grape-growers and winemakers, using experience of the performance of previous vintages as the main guide, supplemented by visual inspection, tasting of berries, and by measurements of GRAPE COMPOSITION (see SAMPLING and ANALYSIS). Previous experience with the variety, the region, and the vineyard contribute to such assessments. Ultimately it is a trade-off between continuing improvements in grape composition and any deterioration in the quality of the berries.

All commercial wineries measure at least the sugar content of the juice (see MUST WEIGHT) since this determines the POTENTIAL ALCOHOL of the wine, which is important for BODY and BALANCE; and in some regions ENRICHMENT may be prohibited or limited. If the sugar level becomes too high, it is very difficult to reduce the alcohol legally except through BLENDING. In some regions, sugar content is sufficient to indicate forthcoming wine quality, especially in cool regions (unless, of course, major catastrophes such as disease or extreme weather intervene). In warm to hot regions, sugar alone is an unreliable guide to quality.

Most wineries will also measure the ACIDITY and the PH of the maturing grapes, bearing in mind that ACIDIFICATION is not permitted in some regions.

To be able to monitor other changes in grape composition during RIPENING requires specialized fruit-sampling techniques, expensive analytical equipment, and trained personnel, beyond the means of small and even many large wineries.

Research by Deloire has shown that measuring grams of sugar per berry allows the easy determination of when sugar accumulation in the berry has stopped, thereby making it possible to predict optimal harvest dates for any given wine style. Studies by Antalick et al. have demonstrated the commercial usefulness of this approach although the differences in berry development make such approaches less precise.

Another recent proposal has been to assess white grape skin colour as a guide to harvest date and aroma dominance (Deloire 2013).

The importance of aroma and so-called 'aromatic maturity' is increasingly recognized, as discussed by van Leeuwen et al., but it is difficult to measure. Valuable information can be obtained by collecting and storing juice samples at intervals during grape development and running comparative 'sniffing tests' using gas chromatotography-olfactometry, but these are costly and difficult because of their subjective nature. INFRARED SPECTROSCOPY can be used to measure many different grape constituents, including red grape colour, expressed as the concentration of total ANTHOCYANINS. This is quicker and simpler than the GLYCOSYL-GLUCOSE ASSAY, an experimental technique developed in the mid 1990s.

Many other characteristics of the harvest contribute to the assessment of its quality, including the amount and type of berry ROT, the presence of broken skins due to heavy RAINFALL, HAIL, or physical damage. The extent of BERRY SHRIVEL, SUNBURN, evenness of ripening, and BERRY SIZE are other important factors. Mechanically harvested fruit will also be assessed for contamination with material other than grapes (MOG).

See also ANTHOCYANINS, FLAVOUR COMPOUNDS, FLAVOUR PRECURSORS, GRAPE COMPOSITION AND WINE QUALITY, PHENOLICS, SUGARS.

R.D., R.E.S. & M.J.T.

Deloire, A., 'Predicting harvest date using berry sugar accumulation', *Practical Winery & Vineyard* (May 2013), 58–61.

Deloire, A., 'New method to determine optimal ripeness for white wine styles', *Practical Winery & Vineyard* (Winter 2013), 75–9.

van Leeuwen, C., et al., 'Aromatic maturity is a cornerstone of terroir expression in red wine', *OENO One* (June 2022).

grape sorting (*triage* in French) is the sorting of grapes according to quality prior to winemaking, typically involving the removal of unripe, overripe/shrivelled or diseased grapes, leaves, stem fragments, PETIOLES, or any other undesirable components from harvested grapes. Sorting may begin in the vineyards at harvest if the pickers are trained to do so, but grapes may also be sorted by hand on a vibrating table or conveyor belt known as a sorting table (*table de tri* in French) when they arrive at the winery. This is a labour-intensive and therefore expensive process.

Many automated sorting systems have been developed since the early 2000s. These machines use various separation techniques and combinations of techniques, including image analysis (optical sorting), vibrating screens, roller screens, air-knives that blow light material away, and density baths in which ripe grapes sink while unripe grapes float. While hand-sorting can be performed before and/or after DESTEMMING, automated sorting equipment generally works on destemmed grapes—although some vibrating bunch conveyors with screens may perform a degree of sorting. New styles of shaking destemmer often have an integrated roller sorting system, and this has enabled more wineries to implement some level of sorting.

There is also a growing trend to integrate automated destemming and sorting systems with MECHANICAL HARVESTERS. The current on-harvester sorting systems can require the use of slower harvesting speeds in high-yielding vineyards, making them less practical, but there are ongoing developments and compromises that will make sorting on harvesters even more common. S.N.

grape varieties. This term is often used interchangeably with 'vine varieties', since different varieties of vine have predictably different grapes or berries. The effect of grape varieties on wine quality is discussed under VINE VARIETIES. Different varieties of vine produce grapes with very different and distinct characteristics, as outlined in this book under thenames of individual varieties. Wines made predominantly from a single grape variety, usually specified on the label, are called VARIETAL wines.

See TABLE GRAPES and RAISINS for examples of these specialized varieties.

grapevine, an alternative name for the plant on which most of the world's wine trade depends. It is known by most wine producers and consumers as the VINE, although botanically there are many other plant species which are vines. See also BOTANICAL CLASSIFICATION.

grapevine Pinot Gris virus. See VIRUS DISEASES.

grapevine red blotch virus, or **grapevine red blotch disease**, a new circular DNA geminivirus first described by scientists at CORNELL and UC DAVIS in 2012 and now recognized as a serious problem in the US. Two strains have been identified. The virus is known to seriously impair the RIPENING potential of the fruit in infected vines. Symptoms include red blotchy leaves in red-wine varieties and yellow leaves in whites, although infected symptomless vines have also been seen.

The origin of this emerging disease is unknown, but the primary source to growers is infected plant material that was previously certified free of known viral pathogens. In addition, the virus is spread from sick to healthy vines via insect vectors, including a treehopper.

By the end of 2014, the presence of this virus had been recorded in NURSERY plants in California. Nurseries in the US, as well as their clients, are now testing for red blotch in the hope of eliminating it from the plant-material stream.

It has spread throughout the US and is also reported in Mexico, India, Italy, Korea, Switzerland, Argentina, Canada, and France, linked to imported plant material originating from California. In California and Oregon, this virus has been found in *Vitis californica* and in VITIS RIPARIA as well as in naturalized hybrids of these with VITIS VINIFERA, often in riparian habitats. L.T.M.

CABI, 'Grapevine red blotch virus', Invasive Species Compendium. www.cabi.org/isc/datasheet/120353.

Cieniewicz, E., et al., 'Prevalence and genetic diversity of grabloviruses in free-living *Vitis* spp', *Plant Disease*, 102/11 (2018), 2308–16.

Morton, L., 'On the trail of Red Blotch virus: view from the East', *Wine Business Monthly* (Feb 2013), 132–9.

grapevine yellows, generic term for a group of related PHYTOPLASMA diseases of grapevines which pose a serious threat to vineyards in many wine regions of the world because there is no known control. The best-known is FLAVESCENCE DORÉE. Variants, which have been shown by a form of DNA PROFILING called polymerase chain reaction to be related, include *bois noir* in north-eastern France, Bordeaux, and Switzerland, *Vergilbungskrankeit* in Germany, leaf curl and berry shrivel in New York State, and Australian grapevine yellows. A similar disease has been described in Romania, Israel, Chile, Italy, and, more recently, Slovenia, Croatia, Hungary, and Spain. These diseases can kill young vines and makes old vines uneconomical. They are spread by infected plants from the NURSERY and further spread by insects called LEAFHOPPERS, to which many common vineyard WEEDS and COVER CROPS are alternative hosts. The diseases occur sporadically in epidemics, and varieties vary in their sensitivity.

The first sign of grapevine yellows can be delayed BUDBREAK and very slow SHOOT growth until FLOWERING. Later, shoots on infected vines stop growing while leaves yellow and curl downwards. Later in the season, shoots droop as though made of rubber. When affected early in the season, bunches fall off. Otherwise, the berries shrivel and taste bitter. Symptoms seem to vary from year to year, and crop levels fluctuate. During epidemics, as for example in the PROSECCO region in northern Italy in 1995, yields of some vineyards dropped to one-tenth of a normal crop. The Australian experience is that vineyards with well-established infections yield at about half the rate of healthy vineyards.

Different species of leafhopper seem to be associated with the spread of different forms of grapevine yellows. Flavescence dorée is transmitted in the field by *Scaphoideus titanus*. *Vergilbungskrankheit* and *bois noir* are spread by the leafhopper *Hyalesthes obsoletus*, and in Australia the vector for some strains of the phytoplasma is *Zeoliarus atkinsonii*.

Other plants can furthermore act as reservoirs of the disease in that insects spread the disease to and from them and grapevines. These so-called host plants include many broadleaf weeds and cover crops such as nettles, mallow, chicory, dandelion, thistles, bindweed, deadly nightshade, and many clovers. The infection spreads rapidly when the appropriate insect vector and host plants are also present in or around the vineyards, which is becoming more common as vineyard TILLAGE is practised less frequently. Disease epidemics in France and Italy have been associated with the natural fluctuations in leafhopper populations, and this is probably the case everywhere.

There is no effective control of grapevine yellows diseases. Insecticide sprays (see PESTICIDES) can reduce the leafhopper populations—especially of *Scaphoideus*—and reduce the spread of the disease. The removal of broad-leaf cover crops and weeds reduces insect levels and opportunities for feeding on host plants. However, if the vineyards are small and are surrounded by native vegetation, this can be impractical. The spread of these diseases by infected planting material can be reduced if young plants are treated by hot water before they leave the nursery (typically 50 °C/120 °F for 30–45 minutes when fully dormant). This will kill phytoplasma as well as some other diseases, but regrettably not all nurseries follow this practice.

Chardonnay and Riesling are among the most susceptible VITIS VINIFERA varieties, followed by Grenache, Tannat, Pinot Noir, and Pinot Gris. Some AMERICAN VINE SPECIES are tolerant. Grapevine yellows diseases may eventually be as destructive to the world's viticulture as was PHYLLOXERA, because they are widespread, they are spreading even further due to CLIMATE CHANGE effects on insect distribution, and they cannot be controlled with resistant ROOTSTOCKS. Wine quality does not appear to be affected, but the supply of grapes, especially of Chardonnay and other sensitive varieties, can be. R.E.S.

Wilcox, W. F., et al., *Compendium of Grape Diseases, Disorders, and Pests* (2nd edn, 2015).

Grasă, or **Grasă de Cotnari**, the 'fat' white grape of COTNARI in ROMANIA, where it is grown exclusively. Total plantings stood at 549 ha/1,357 acres in 2021. It can reach extremely high MUST WEIGHTS—in 1958, Grasă grapes in Cotnari reached a sugar concentration of 520 g/l—but needs the balancing acidity of grapes such as Tămâioasă Românească in a blend. The vine is usefully sensitive to NOBLE ROT and may be the same as Hungary's Kövérszőlő.

Graševina, Croatian name for the republic's most planted vine variety, WELSCHRIESLING, whose origins may well be Croatian.

grasshoppers, insects of the families *Acrididae* and *Tettigoniidae* which can feed on the vine. Reductions in vineyard leaf area impair grape RIPENING, with potentially severe effects on wine quality. In California, for example, the devastating grasshopper (*Melanoplus devastator* Scudder) is particularly harmful to vineyards, causing damage by defoliation, usually in mid to late summer. In eastern Australia, the Australian plague locust (*Chortoicetes terminifera*) can be a major pest. Dense swarms can descend very quickly on vineyard areas, especially when pastures dry out. Control where necessary is usually by insecticides (see PESTICIDES). M.J.E.

Buchanan, G. A., and Amos, T. G., 'Grape pests', in B. G. Coombe and P. R. Dry (eds.), *Viticulture*, ii: *Practices* (2nd edn, 2006).

grassy, TASTING TERM usually used synonymously with HERBACEOUS.

Grau, German for 'grey' or *gris*.

Grauburgunder, or **Grauer Burgunder**, German synonym for PINOT GRIS used for the increasingly popular dry wines made from this grape in Germany. (Sweeter wines are sometimes labelled RULÄNDER.) Its success in producing spicy, full-bodied dry wine accounts for the marked increase in total area planted with the variety in Germany: its 7,356 ha/18,177 acres by 2020, an increase of 90% since 2000, make it the country's fourth most planted white wine grape and considerably more popular than WEISSBURGUNDER (Pinot Blanc). Only Italy grows more of this grape variety (see PINOT GRIGIO) than Germany. It needs a good site with deep, heavy soils to maximize the impressive level of EXTRACT of which it is capable. It is a particularly popular speciality of the warm BADEN region, although there are around 2,000 ha in both RHEINHESSEN and the PFALZ, too.

Grave del Friuli. See FRIULI GRAVE.

gravel consists of rock fragments greater than 2 mm/0.08 in in diameter, referred to as pebbles if they have been worn smooth by running water. Known in French as *graves*, gravel is key to the names of the two appellations below, for example. Gravelly soils are the most distinctive soil type of Bordeaux's LEFT BANK wine region. During the Ice Ages, beginning some 2 million years ago, glaciers moved slowly to the Atlantic coast from the Massif Central and the Pyrenees, following the course of the Garonne and Gironde rivers and pushing back the high right bank. When the glaciers melted and retreated, their vigorous outwash streams spread gravel far and wide. The vineyards of the GRAVES are characterized by their gravelly surface, and gravel is nowhere so prevalent as at Ch HAUT-BRION, where in places it is 16–20 m/50–65 ft deep. Such soils offer excellent DRAINAGE, imposing on the vine the moderate WATER STRESS favoured for wine quality. See VINE PHYSIOLOGY and SOIL AND WINE QUALITY.

Gravel soils are also highly prized for quality wine production on the plateau of ST-ÉMILION, in CHÂTEAUNEUF-DU-PAPE, in FRIULI GRAVE, and in the Gimblett Gravels region of HAWKE'S BAY and MARLBOROUGH in New Zealand. Such soils are also widespread in the Ningxia region of CHINA, near the Helan Mountains. Chx Haut-Brion and La Mission-Haut-Brion are now viticultural oases in the southern suburbs of Bordeaux, indicating that the land is more valuable for housing than for vines. R.E.S. & R.E.W.

Anson, J., *Inside Bordeaux* (2021).

White, R. E., and Krstic, M. P., *Healthy Soils for Healthy Vines* (2019).

Graves, French for 'gravelly terrain', and a term at one time used for many of Bordeaux's wine districts, but now the name of one large region extending 50 km/30 miles south-east of the city along the left bank of the river GARONNE (see map under BORDEAUX). Graves is Bordeaux's only region famous for both red and white wines, although its aristocratic, mineral-scented, Cabernet-dominated red wines are made in much greater quantity than its dry whites. In the early 1990s, about 1,800 ha/4,500 acres were planted with red wine grapes, while about 950 ha produced dry white Graves. By 2020 the areas were 2,613 and 659 ha respectively. **Graves Supérieures** is an AOC for sweet wines, to which 136 ha were dedicated in 2020, producing wines very similar to, but generally slightly drier and coarser than, those from the enclave entitled to the CÉRONS appellation.

The Graves, and in particular the outskirts of Bordeaux, the Grabas de Burdeus, is the birthplace of CLARET. In the Middle Ages, much of the light CLAIRET dispatched in such quantity to England was grown in these vineyards within easy distance of the quayside; the Médoc was largely marshland (see BORDEAUX, history). Ch Pape-Clément is Bordeaux's first named château, while HAUT-BRION was the first New French Claret noted in London, by Samuel Pepys, in 1663. Thomas JEFFERSON noted that late 18th century 'Grave' wines were considered the finest Bordeaux had to offer. It was presumably this historic fame which had Ch Haut-Brion, Graves's most famous property, included with the finest Médoc châteaux in the famous CLASSIFICATION in 1855.

For centuries Graves encompassed all the vineyards south of the border with the MÉDOC in a great sweep around the city and upstream along the Garonne as far as Langon, with the exception of the enclaves for sweet-white-wine appellations BARSAC, CÉRONS, and SAUTERNES. In 1987, the appellation of PESSAC-LÉOGNAN was formed, a northern slice of the original Graves appellation which includes all its most famous properties, as well as the southern suburbs of Bordeaux itself.

The creation of this new premium appellation had the effect of somewhat declassifying the historic name Graves, although some excellent wines are conscientiously made within the modern Graves appellation on the varied GRAVEL terraces which have been deposited there over ALLUVIAL deposits with the occasional sandy outcrop over the millennia. The reds, which can taste like country cousins of their more urbane neighbours in Pessac-Léognan, can often be good value and mature earlier than their Médoc counterparts. It is in this area that some serious barrel-fermented, or at least oak-aged, dry whites are made, from Sauvignon and Sémillon grapes in varying proportions. J.R. & J.L.

Graves de Vayres, a small BORDEAUX district, named after the historic town of Vayres, which has nothing to do with GRAVES but is just across the river DORDOGNE from the town of Libourne. From a total of 337 ha/832 acres in 2020 of, not surprisingly, gravelly soil, with patches of SAND, the appellation produces light red wines made substantially from Merlot grapes, although many of them are sold under the simple BORDEAUX AOC. White wines are usually dry, often based on Sémillon, occasionally given BARREL MATURATION, and were produced from just 64 ha in 2020.

gravity-fed, describes a WINERY that is constructed on different levels, often into a hillside, or uses lifts, so that grapes, MUST, juice or wine are moved by gravity rather than by PUMPS in the belief that wine quality is improved by more gentle handling.

Great Southern, high-quality, COOL-CLIMATE wine region encompassing 2,545 ha/6,289 acres of vines in the extreme south-west of Australia, including subregions Albany, Denmark, Frankland River, Mount Barker, and Porongurup. See WESTERN AUSTRALIA for more detail.

Great Western. See GRAMPIANS.

Grecanico Dorato, white grape variety grown on Sicily shown by DNA PROFILING in 2007 to be the GARGANEGA of the Veneto. The wines currently made may not be maximizing its full potential.

Grechetto, strictly **Grechetto di Orvieto**, sometimes **Greghetto**, characterful central Italian white grape variety most closely associated with UMBRIA. It is an ingredient in ORVIETO and in the whites of TORGIANO and the Colli Martani DOC, typically blended with Trebbiano Toscano and Verdello. The grapes' thick skins provide good resistance to DOWNY MILDEW. **Grechetto Gentile** is a synonym for PIGNOLETTO, and DNA PROFILING suggests a parent–offspring relationship between the two Grechettos. Several DOC regulations specify simply 'Grechetto'. There were 1,824 ha/4,507 acres of Grechetto di Orvieto in Italy in 2015 (and 1,174 ha of Pignoletto).

Greco, or **Greco di Tufo** (which has its own DOCG for the zone around the village of Tufo), is a late-ripening Campanian white wine grape that has been shown by DNA PROFILING to be identical to Asprinio, under which name it often appears as a lightly sparkling wine. The variety also grows in northern Puglia, Lazio, and Tuscany and is genetically distinct from GRECO BIANCO. Wines tend to be dry and assertive, with more BODY than aroma. J.V.

Greco Bianco is a CALABRIAN vine variety best known for its sweet whites made from semi-dried grapes grown around the town of Bianco on the south coast. There were 2,050 ha/5,066 acres planted in Italy in 2015. It is not related to the Campanian GRECO (di Tufo) nor to **Greco Bianco di Gerace**, which has been shown by DNA PROFILING to be identical to MALVASIA di Lipari.

At least four other varieties have a synonym that begins 'Greco Bianco'. The popularity of the name shows how widely Greek origins were assumed. J.V.

Greco Nero, name for at least five dark-berried CALABRIAN vine varieties.

Greece, renascent Mediterranean wine producer with a particularly rich history of wine made in classical times from the 7th century BCE and on in the Roman era (see ancient ROME). Early Greek colonization led to the vine being taken to all parts of the Mediterranean. In modern Greece, vineyards covered around 109,000 ha/269,345 acres in 2021, with only about 61,000 ha producing grapes for wine. RAISINS and TABLE GRAPES are important to the agricultural economy. About 60% of annual wine production of 2.5–3 million hl/79,251,600 million gal is of white wine. More than 85% of Greek wine is consumed within the country, though the financial turmoil of the early 2010s encouraged many top wineries to invest in exports.

Ancient Greece

Origins Wine was important in Greek society from the earliest times, forming part of the Greek cultural identity. The ancient Greeks were aware that other societies, such as the Babylonians in MESOPOTAMIA and the inhabitants of ancient EGYPT, made and drank wine, but for them it was a luxury, and they normally drank beer (a drink disparaged by Greek writers as inferior and fit only for foreigners) or else 'wine' made from dates or lotus. Complete ignorance of viticulture was the mark of savages; so too was the drinking of undiluted wine, which was associated with northern BARBARIANS such as the Scythians (in modern CRIMEA).

There is evidence of winemaking in Neolithic Greece (at Dikili Tash *c.*4300 BCE), and the vine was widely cultivated by the early Bronze Age. Wine was clearly a significant element in the culture of Minoan CRETE before 2000 BCE: remains of grapes and of installations for wine production (treading floors and spouted vats) have been found by archaeologists at palaces and villas, and some of the large storage jars found in the palace complexes surely contained wine rather than olive oil; an ideogram for 'wine' has been identified in the early script Linear A, and artistic evidence suggests the use of wine in ritual contexts. Given the links between Crete and Egypt in this period, the Minoans might be expected to have been influenced by their neighbours and to have exported to supply the demand there and elsewhere in the Near East, though much trade was evidently more local. In turn, Crete will have influenced contemporary Thíra (modern SANTORINI), where vines and grapes are depicted on painted pottery.

Mycenae There is no doubt of the importance of wine in Mycenaean culture (*c.*1600–1150 BCE), which followed and developed on the mainland from Minoan culture: evidence from Mycenae, Tiryns, and Sparta includes grape pips and residues of wine, as well as the seal of a jar bearing the impression of vine leaves, while the palaces have revealed many storage jars, including a complete cellar at Pílos which contained at least 35 large jars, some labelled as containing wine. The evidence of the Linear B script, preserved on clay tablets fired hard in the destruction of the palaces, confirms that wine was important: the palace records contain many references to it and include words for 'wine', 'vineyard', and, apparently, 'wine merchant', not to mention allusions to the god DIONYSUS. Finds of Mycenaean pottery abroad imply that they were exporting wine and oil to Syria, Palestine, Egypt, Cyprus, Sicily, and southern Italy, while the discovery of a few small CANAANITE jars (the earliest AMPHORAE) at Mycenae may suggest that connoisseurs were also importing foreign wines; certainly wine appears to have been a luxury item largely restricted to the elite.

Early Greek literature In the poetry of HOMER and HESIOD, the earliest Greek literature, wine is an essential part of life. It is naturally drunk by Greek and Trojan heroes at their feasts, but it is also used in the rituals of sacrifice, prayer, and burial, to solemnize agreements, and for therapeutic purposes; it is also the human drink, whereas gods drink nectar. A depiction of the vintage, in an enclosed vineyard, is part of the encapsulation of human life on the shield which Hephaestus makes for Achilles (*Iliad* 18. 561 ff.). Wine is the touchstone of civilization: even the Cyclopes in the *Odyssey* drink it, but without cultivating the vine, unlike the pleasure-loving Phaeacians, and, when offered the fine wine of Maron, Polyphemus swigs it neat until he falls into a stupor. Homer implies that the vine was widespread in Greece in his time, describing several places as 'rich in vines' (including Phrygia; in this as in other respects the Trojans are as civilized as the Greeks), and he gives us our earliest reference to specific wines, Pramnian and Ismarian, while Hesiod mentions Bibline. Advice on viticulture forms part of Hesiod's *Works and Days*: he mentions pruning and the harvest, including drying the grapes before vinification to make early forms of DRIED-GRAPE WINES.

The extent of viticulture In the classical period, vines were grown throughout Greece, and, through colonization, the Greeks carried viticulture to Sicily and southern Italy (which the Greeks called OENOTRIA, 'land of trained vines'), southern France, and the Black Sea. Some producers operated on a large scale, with extensive estates: we can infer the existence of vineyards of 8–10 ha and 30 ha/74 acres on the island of Thásos in the northern Aegean in the late 5th century BCE and of one of about 12 ha in Attica in the middle of the 4th century, and Diodorus records a cellar at Acragas in Sicily with a storage capacity of 12,000 hl/317,000 gal and a vat holding 400 hl/10,500 gal (*Library of History* 13. 83). Viticulture was also probably part of the normal system of polyculture, which in Greece was founded on grain, vines, and olives.

Trade Viticulture was important to the economy of many cities, as is shown by the number of states whose coinage bears wine-related designs. Greek wine was traded within Greece—with Athens, the largest and richest city, offering the best market—and exported throughout the Mediterranean world, especially to Egypt, the Black Sea, Scythia, and Etruria (modern TUSCANY). Soon the colonial cities began to produce and export their own wine. (See CELTS for archaeological evidence of the geographical extent to which Greek wine and drinking rituals were adopted.) Amphorae from Marseilles are found along the southern coast of France and up the RHÔNE Valley, while in the CRIMEA archaeology has revealed extensive estates, their vineyards protected from the prevailing winds by low walls and planted with indigenous vines which were gradually domesticated, rather than with imported varieties.

The scale of the Greek wine trade can be inferred from the widespread finds of amphorae and the seals which indicate their origin. The richest evidence is from the island of Thasos, which took elaborate precautions to regulate its wine trade, both to maximize tax revenues and to prevent fraud which would damage its reputation; amphorae were required to be of standard sizes and were sealed with the name of an annual magistrate, which acted as a guarantee of authenticity; other states, notably Rhodes, also used this system. Thasos also protected its commerce by forbidding citizens to import foreign wine.

Viticultural practices No vine grown today can be confidently traced back to any ancient Greek variety, although we know the names of 50 or more, some of which were cultivated in Italy in Roman times, and names such as GRECO, GRECHETTO, and AGLIANICO (i.e. Helleniko) reflect popular traditions of continuity (although DNA PROFILING suggests that these are more romance than reality). Roman writers noted that the YIELDS of Greek varieties were low, although their quality was good. In the 4th century BCE, the botanically expert THEOPHRASTUS was aware of the need to match varieties to soil type and MESOCLIMATE and recommended PROPAGATION by cuttings or suckering. A variety of vine-training systems was used: often vines were supported by forked props or trained up trees (see ARBOREAL VITICULTURE), but a few varieties naturally formed bushes, and sometimes plants were simply left to trail on the ground; training on trees meant climbing up, or using trestles, to pick the grapes. PRUNING was known to have an important effect on YIELDS and quality, and land leases sometimes specify that the lessors be allowed to oversee it towards the end of a lease, as well as regulating the use of manure as FERTILIZER.

Vinification The HARVEST was early by European standards: Hesiod recommends early September. Vase paintings suggest that, in many cases, PRESSING took place near the vineyard: the grapes were trodden inside a handled wicker basket which stood in a wooden trough with low legs, from which the juice ran through a spout into an earthenware vat sunk in a hole in the ground; sometimes a sieve was placed over the mouth of the vat. As pickers brought grapes in, they were added to the basket, while the treader held on to the basket handles or a ring or rope overhead (or a convenient vine) to keep his balance and worked at CRUSHING in time to a flute. There are also scenes of treading in the vat itself, in which case the skins and pips will not have been strained out, and the wine will have taken colour from the skins, an early form of PUNCHING DOWN. In either case, the vats will then have been covered and the juice taken for FERMENTATION in larger-capacity *pithoi* (see PITHARI); these could be 3 m/10 ft high, with a mouth measuring 1 metre across. Larger, more specialized establishments had permanent stone treading floors rather than wooden ones, but otherwise the process was the same; although the beam PRESS was normally used for olives, there is little evidence for its use in wine production in classical Greece, and the screw press probably appeared only in Roman republican times. Small-scale producers may well have employed more primitive forms of pressing, such as torsion in a fabric container, but no evidence for these survives.

References to the drying of grapes in Hesiod and the *Odyssey* (see DRIED-GRAPE WINES) suggest that this was the early norm, but in later times practices varied: a Lesbian wine, Protropon, was made from FREE-RUN juice, while in other cases grapes were deliberately harvested unripe to produce a wine with high ACIDITY (Omphakias); fresh MUST itself was sometimes drunk, as was boiled must. Finally, the solids left after treading could be moistened with water and trodden again to yield a low-quality PIQUETTE called Deuterias or Stemphulites.

Although wine was often transferred from the fermentation vessels once fermentation was over, it is clear that it had not been subjected to proper RACKING or FINING since a sieve or strainer through which to pour the wine is a standard feature of the SYMPOSIUM; although Theophrastus may refer to the addition of gypsum, which was later used for the purposes of both CLARIFICATION and ACIDIFICATION, he describes this as an Italian practice. References to 'strained wine' suggest that it was unusual, and the straining may have been done at the point of sale rather than during production.

Common additives The basic wine could be 'improved' by various additives: the use of a small percentage of seawater or brine seems to have begun in the 4th century BCE, apparently as a flavouring, although it probably also had preservative qualities, and the technique was associated with particular areas of production, notably the island of Kos, and marked a shift in taste during antiquity. We also hear of the addition of aromatic herbs, to produce a sort of VERMOUTH, and of perfume being added both in production and by the consumer, as well as of the use of boiled must and, on Thasos, the addition of a mixture of dough and honey to produce a special CUVÉE for consumption on state occasions. BLENDING of different wines was also practised: Theophrastus gives one example, a mixture of hard but aromatic wine from Heraclea with soft Erythraean (a salted wine) which lacks BOUQUET, and says that there are many other blends known to experts (see TASTING, ancient history). There is some evidence, mainly in the Bronze Age, for the deliberate addition of pine or terebinth resin, but it is likely that storage (see below) was normally a more significant cause of such flavours.

Containers for wine Finished wine was normally stored in AMPHORAE lined with resin or pitch (see RESINATED WINES) to limit porosity, which will have affected the taste to some extent, and pitch was also used to secure the stopper, which was usually of pottery, although the use of cork was known. Amphorae of the classical period held 20–75 l/5–20 gal, depending on their origin, and added 5–15 kg/11–33 lbs to the total load. These commercial amphorae are, of course, to be distinguished from the much smaller painted pots, also called amphorae, used to present the wine when it was drunk. In the *Odyssey* (2. 340 ff.), Telemachus had wine drawn off from the big *pithoi* in which it had been ageing into amphorae for his journey abroad. Homer also refers quite frequently to wine kept in wineskins, but in classical times skin bags were probably mainly filled for rapid consumption; despite being lighter and, perhaps, less fragile, they will have flavoured the wine, being usually made from the skin of a sheep or goat.

Selling wine In Athens, wine was bought mainly from wine sellers for immediate consumption: after the purchaser had sampled the wine, the required amount was ladled or siphoned from the amphora into a jug or small amphora which the purchaser usually provided; wealthier customers, however, and those holding parties will have bought an amphora at a time. Evidence on price is scanty, but for imported wine of good quality, such as Chian or Mendean, in Athens in the 4th century BCE a *chous* of about 3.25 l cost between one-quarter of a drachma and 2 drachmas (a drachma being a day's wage for a craftsman). Of course, these were luxury wines, with prices to match. One Athenian, urged to improve his morals by the Areopagus, the Council of Elders, cited drinking Chian, along with keeping a mistress, as evidence of a life of blameless hedonism appropriate to a gentleman. See also MERCHANTS, ancient history.

Specific wines Some idea of the leading wines of classical Greece can be obtained from references in literature, particularly lyric poetry and the Athenian comic poets; these make it clear that in Athens, at least, there was a degree of CONNOISSEURSHIP, different poets singing the praises of different wines while disparaging their rivals. The most frequently praised wines are those of Thasos, Lesvos, Mende, and Khios (especially one called Ariousian), while those of Ismaros (in Thrace), Naxos, Peparethos (modern Skopelos), Acanthos, and, from the 4th century, Kos were also admired.

This makes it clear that, although other areas had their admirers, the regions which produced the best wines were, by general consent, the AEGEAN ISLANDS, particularly to the east, and Chalkidike (modern Halkidiki, see below) and Thrace on the northern mainland.

Two other much-praised wines, Pramnian and Bibline, are problematic. Pramnian, whose name goes back to Homer, is associated with a number of places—Lesvos, Smyrna, and the island of Ikaros (modern Ikaria, in the Dodecanese)—and indeed, according to ATHENAEUS, some considered it a generic name for dark wine, or long-lived wine. However, there was also a vine variety called Pramnian, and it seems most likely that Pramnian, which perhaps originated on Ikaria, came to be used as the name of wine of the style of the original, 'neither sweet nor rich, but dry, hard and unusually strong', whether or not made from the original vine.

In the case of Bibline, the problem is a confusion of names, since there was also Bybline wine, from Byblos in PHOENICIA, which is highly praised for fragrance by the 4th century BCE gastronome Archestratus. Bibline, however, took its name from a region in Thrace, where it originated, and came from a vine called Bibline, which was apparently subsequently introduced elsewhere. Since scribes were prone to confuse the two, allusions cannot always be reliably attributed to one or the other, but both evidently had excellent reputations. On these interpretations, both Pramnian and Bibline will also fall within the top zone outlined above. In all cases, wines are praised in terms of their origins; we never hear of particular estates or producers as being superior.

What was Greek wine like? First, it could be of three colours, white, black or red, and tawny, the last being less frequently mentioned; Homer's wine is always dark. Greeks were sensitive to aromas and often speak of wines being fragrant; more specifically, they refer to wine as 'smelling of flowers', an expression often almost equivalent to our BOUQUET, although the way in which the comic poet Hermippus talks of a mature wine 'smelling of violets, roses and hyacinth' shows that it was not always metaphorical; the same passage attributes a scent of apples to Thasian wine. The sweetest wines were said to lack bouquet, which could, according to Theophrastus, be supplied by blending, spicing, or perfuming.

In taste, wine is often praised as sweet, honeyed, ripe, and soft, and this must have appealed to the Greek palate, to judge from the production of PASSITO, or dried-grape wine, and even sweet wine further concentrated by boiling. Given the likely ripeness of the grapes, the limitations of natural YEASTS, and, perhaps, the risk of STUCK FERMENTATION without TEMPERATURE CONTROL, sweetness must have been the most frequent outcome and is often assumed by Greek writers: Aristotle distinguishes among heavy drinkers between drunkards and the sweet-toothed. However, this was not always the case. As noted earlier, grapes were sometimes picked unripe, and some varieties, like Pramnian, were naturally more austere; one vine was allegedly called 'smoky' (*Kapnios oenos*) because the wine was so sharp as to bring tears to the eyes, like smoke. Medical writers discussing the qualities of wines class them as dry or sweet white; and dry, sweet, or medium red/black—there was obviously a wide range of styles.

Wine ageing Given the vagaries of vinification, much Greek wine will not have lasted long, succumbing either to OXIDATION, which medical and scientific writers discussed as a form of decomposition, or to spoilage, the risk of which was noted by Aristotle. It is not surprising that the people of Thasos traded in VINEGAR as well as wine and that sour wine was a regular cheap drink, especially since the risk of oxidation must have increased as a large jar was emptied.

Nevertheless, some wines clearly aged, since old wine was highly regarded by the Greeks: 'praise old wine, but the flowers of new songs', said the poet Pindar, and comic poets noted that women preferred old wine but young men. The old wine praised by Hermippus (above) was described as *sapros*: literally, 'rotten' or 'decomposed', but obviously referring in the case of wine to the production of secondary flavours through AGEING; older wine was also described as having 'lost its bite'. We never find discussion of particular VINTAGES (unlike Roman wines and specific vintages such as OPIMIAN wine mentioned by Roman writers), and there is little reliable evidence as to how long good wine might keep. Theocritus speaks of drinking four-year-old wine, perhaps from Kos, in the early 3rd century BCE, and in the same era Peparethian wine was regarded as a slow developer in requiring six years to reach maturity, while the elder PLINY (in the 1st century CE) considered all foreign wines middle-aged at seven years old; comparisons with the wines of ancient ROME, which evidently matured more slowly, might allow one to guess that few Greek wines lasted more than ten years, a good age for a wine in the heroic age (*Odyssey* 3. 390–2) but not a very long time by modern standards, especially given that the CONTAINERS were very much larger than modern ones, so that the rate of development should have been proportionately reduced.

The uses of wine Wine had many uses for the Greeks. It was of course important as a food and drink (it was doubtless often safer than water), and the SYMPOSIUM, which centred around the drinking of wine, was one of the most important Greek social forms. Wine was almost always drunk diluted with water: the ratio varied, normally ranging between 2 : 3 and 1 : 3, which would give a range in ALCOHOLIC STRENGTH of about 3–6% and generally at the lower end of this range (roughly the same as British draught beer). This dilution should be viewed under the light that ancient Greeks consumed every pour of wine in one sip, since the kylix, a round-bottomed drinking vessel, would spill the wine if set down. Weaker mixtures are disparaged in comedy (and even 1 : 3 called for a good wine), but 1 : 1 was considered by some dangerous to the HEALTH, and the regular drinking of unmixed wine a habit confined to barbarians. The mixed wine was also normally cooled, sometimes in special pottery coolers; the very rich added snow.

The medical uses of wine were numerous and much discussed by medical writers. Its advantages as a pick-me-up, tonic, and analgesic were obvious, and by experience it became clear that certain wines were nourishing, diuretic, good for the digestion, and so on, but the qualities of different types were also discussed in terms of the four essential qualities (hot, cold, wet, dry) in order to decide how they should be used to correct imbalances in the bodily humours.

There are occasional references to procedures for making wine-based medicines, either by adding drugs to the wine or by treating the vines with an appropriate agent. Certain wines also had the reputation of producing medical side-effects: those of Troizen (just across the Saronic Gulf from Athens), for example, were said to render the drinker sterile. The Greeks were also well aware of the hazards of consuming wine to excess, and Athenaeus mentions popular remedies for a HANGOVER.

After social aspects, however, the most important aspect of wine was its place in religion. A LIBATION (*sponde*) of wine was offered as a sort of first fruit whenever wine was drunk (at the symposium different gods were invoked for each bowlful), and drink offerings were part of the formula for prayers; hence treaties and truces were referred to as *spondai*, because they were sanctified by prayers and libations. Wine was used to quench the burning offerings on the altar at a sacrifice and was one of the liquids poured on the ground as an offering to the dead.

More than this, however, wine was directly associated with a particular divinity: Dionysus was the patron god and the symbol of wine, as Demeter was of cereals, and one of the 12 major divinities (a further indication of the basic importance of wine to the Greeks). R.B.

Wine festivals

For the Athenian of the 5th century BCE, festival days in honour of the gods at set times of year gave the sort of relaxation now provided by weekends. Many of them were associated with wine drinking, vine-growing, and the HARVEST. The most important of these, the Anthesteria, in honour of Dionysus, celebrated the opening of wine jars in February to test the new wine. It included processions and ritual wine-drinking contests and was probably closest to the modern idea of a wine festival. Nonetheless, at the heart of the festival was the serious business of the dedication of the new wine to Dionysus.

Other festivals included the Oschophoria, a vintage celebration in September which seems to have been restricted to aristocratic families: two young men led a procession carrying vine branches with the grapes still on them (*oschoi*) in honour of Dionysus. The Apatouria in the same month was the festival when young males were registered in their *phratries*, or clans, and there was much associated pouring of wine. The last day of this festival was called Epibda and came to mean 'the morning after'. Strangely, there does not seem to have been a particularly important festival at the time of the grape harvest. At the Dionysia celebrated in the countryside around Athens, a jar of wine and a vine headed the procession.

The great festivals of Athens, the Panathenaia and the City Dionysia, were less dominated by the vine (perhaps because they were held further from the vineyards), but there is no doubt that wine was enjoyed at them. H.H.A.

Bibliographical note: There is no modern book in English specifically on Greek wine, and works on ancient wine (cited under ancient ROME) tend to pass rapidly on to Rome, where the evidence is much fuller; however, Roman sources are not necessarily reliable evidence for Greek practice 500 years earlier. Of the ancient sources, ATHENAEUS' *Deipnosophistae* collects much classical literary material (especially Books 1–2, 25e–40f), and Theophrastus' *Enquiry into Plants and On the Causes of Plants* (especially 3. 11–16) contains a lot of botanical lore; all are accessible in translation in the Loeb Classical Library. On Athenaeus, see Brock, R., and Wilson, H., 'Athenaeus on Greek wine', in D. Braund and J. Wilkins (eds.), *Athenaeus and His World* (2000), 455–65, 587–8 with further general bibliography. On the Minoan and Mycenaean periods see Pratt, C. E., *Oil, Wine and the Cultural Economy of Ancient Greece* (2021). Grace, V., *Amphoras and the Ancient Wine Trade* (2nd edn, 1979), is a good general introduction to AMPHORAE; see also Koehler, C., in P. E. McGovern, et al. (eds.), *The Origins and Ancient History of Wine* (1995), ch. 20. Sparkes, B. A., 'Treading the Grapes', *Bulletin Antieke Beschaving*, 51 (1976), 47–64, collects and discusses the pictorial evidence for the vintage. Wilson, H., *Wine and Words in Classical Antiquity and the Middle Ages* (2003), is mainly concerned with the literary, social, and religious uses of wine but also deals with AGEING; Boulay, T. 'Wine appreciation in ancient Greece' in J. Wilkins & R. Naudeau (eds.), *A Companion to Food in the Ancient World* (2015), 273–82 is stimulating, though based substantially on late sources. On festivals, see Parker, R., *Polytheism and Society at Athens* (2005), ch.14.

Medieval history

In the medieval Greece that was part of the Byzantine empire, wine was grown by private individuals and by monasteries (see MONKS AND MONASTERIES). Monasteries were foremost among the great landowners because, as in western Europe, they received donations and bequests from the laity. In the 8th and 9th centuries, agriculture was exceptionally profitable; its chief products were wine, fruits, cotton, and medicinal herbs. As in antiquity, the best wines came from the AEGEAN ISLANDS, Chios first of all, and Thasos and Crete. The wines of THRACE and ANATOLIA (Cappadocia in particular) were ranked second to these. Evidence from shipwrecks shows that wine was still transported in amphorae in the 7th century, whereas wooden BARRELS were commonly used in western Europe from the 3rd century CE. After the 7th century, the Greeks, too, started using wooden casks, which are lighter and easier to handle than amphorae.

In the 12th century, Constantinople (on the site of modern Istanbul) was the centre of the Byzantine empire's wine trade. Wines were shipped to Constantinople from the Aegean Islands, from Thebes, and also from near Monemvasia, a port on the southern Peloponnese, which gave its name to MALVASIA and its English corruption MALMSEY. Monasteries were exempted from customs duties and were therefore at an advantage compared with private growers and traders: the monasteries of Patmos and Mount Athos, for instance, made large profits from selling their wines in Constantinople.

But the private growers and wine merchants of Greece faced a much greater problem than unfair competition from monks. In 1082, the Emperor Alexius I Comnenus had granted VENICE trading facilities at Constantinople and in 32 towns without payment of taxes of any kind. As a result so much money disappeared to the west that Byzantium was economically ruined. Wine producers and wine merchants suffered badly. With no duties to pay, the Venetians were able to sell wine much more cheaply than any Greek could. Often this was imported Italian wine, but most of the wine came from Crete, known then as Candia, which was a colony of Venice (and remained so until the mid 17th century). Worse still, many taverns in Constantinople were owned by Venetians so, in Constantinople at least, they controlled the retail trade as well.

It took until the middle of the 14th century for the Byzantine government at least to try to protect the empire's own trade. The Venetians agreed in 1361 to accept a distinction between wholesale and retail trade and to impose a tax of their own, with the proceeds of course going to Venice, on taverns run by Venetians. In the 15th century, tax was finally levied on wine imported by Venetians, but by then it was too late, for Byzantium's wine trade was no longer viable. Crete and CYPRUS, under Venetian ownership, continued to produce the strong, sweet wines that were capable of surviving the long sea voyage to western Europe, but the harbour of Monemvasia, close to Byzantium's own supply of Malvasia wines, was now too small to take the larger ships that the west had increasingly come to adopt. From the late 14th century onwards, it lost out to Cyprus and Crete as a port, and the south-west Peloponnese declined as a producer of export-quality wine. All trade in Greek wine ceased in the late 15th century, when, after the fall of Byzantium, the Ottoman Turks occupied the Peloponnesian shore and drove out its inhabitants. H.M.W.

Kazhdan, A. P. (ed.), *The Oxford Dictionary of Byzantium*, 3 vols. (1988).

Lambert-Gócs, M., *The Wines of Greece* (1990).

Nicol, D. M., *Byzantium and Venice* (1988).

Modern history

The centuries of domination by the Ottoman Turks were to blight Greek viticulture and winemaking until well into the 20th century. Winemaking was not normally forbidden to the Christian population, but communication difficulties resulted in a localized peasant industry viewed by the Turkish rulers as a useful means of raising revenue through TAXATION. Thus, while France, for example, was developing fine-wine regions and their markets, Greece remained in what might be termed the vinous Dark Ages.

The battle for independence was prolonged and tortuous, and the exhausted and impoverished modern Greek state, founded in 1830, had preoccupations more important than the creation of a fine-wine industry. It was not until well after the two World Wars and the subsequent bitter civil war that Greece began to modernize its fragmented wine industry. Two kinds of aristocracy are needed to produce fine wine: one able to afford quality-oriented viticulture and production and another able to afford buying high-quality wine. Greece had neither.

The Vine Institute of Athens, which experiments with winemaking techniques and advises winemakers, was founded in 1937, and some major wine companies were established in the late 19th century, but they were chiefly concerned with DISTILLATION and, later, BULK WINE sales. CO-OPERATIVES were established mainly in the 1930s, providing much-needed stability to vine-growers. Only in the 1960s was any significant proportion of Greek wine sold in bottle rather than directly from the barrel.

The 1960s, however, saw considerable investment in modern technology, and the 1970s ushered in Greece's first generation of trained OENOLOGISTS. The 1980s signalled a new era for Greek wines. A number of oenologists moved out of the large companies to start their own projects, while other Greeks established small, quality-oriented estates. By the early 21st century the mavericks of the 1980s had commercially successful mid-sized wineries, and an increasing number of small ventures appeared across the country.

Geography and climate

At latitudes of 34–42° N, Greek vineyards are commonly but mistakenly thought to be some of the world's warmest. In fact, the diverse TOPOGRAPHY and the mountainous landscape create mild or even cool MESOCLIMATES, though largely unsuspected by summer tourists enjoying the Greek sun in a coastal resort.

The climate is generally predictably MEDITERRANEAN, although there can be considerable variation between the CONTINENTAL-influenced vineyards in the mountains of Epirus and Macedonia, where grapes may not even reach full RIPENESS, and the intense heat of Patras, Crete or Rhodes, where harvest may start in July. ELEVATION plays a major role, too: while vines can be found growing on flat land near sea level, such as at Ankhialos, high-elevation vineyards are increasingly sought-after.

Most vineyards are sufficiently close to the sea for maritime breezes to moderate temperatures, but lack of water, particularly on the islands and in the south, is a major challenge. The first three months of the year are generally the wet months, and many wine areas have no rain at all for six months, which can make the establishment of young vines extremely difficult. IRRIGATION is considered an annual necessity in many areas.

As the country experiences much seismic activity, it is rare to find an area with a single prevailing soil profile. However, the soils devoted to vines or olives are generally of low fertility, since the few high-fertility regions tend to be devoted to more lucrative or essential crops. Subsoils on the mainland tend to be LIMESTONE, while on the islands they are mainly

VOLCANIC. CLAY, LOAM, SCHIST, and MARL are all found, as well as sandy clay and CHALK.

Viticulture

The Greek land-tenure system means that much of the vineyard area is in the hands of smallholders. Little by little, the large companies which buy in many grapes have been working more closely with these vine-growers and promulgating more modern viticultural techniques. Grape PRICES were long determined by sugar levels, which too often resulted in dangerously low levels of ACIDITY, but these problems have been largely resolved by the big commercial concerns and the more modern co-operatives. The more ambitious of the small estates now practise thoroughly modern viticultural techniques.

Traditionally most vines were left to grow as BUSH VINES, but almost all new vineyards have been designed with TRELLIS SYSTEMS on wires. However, in certain areas, unique trellis and pruning systems have been adapted, after centuries of trial and error, to local conditions. Pre-eminent examples are the basket-trained vines (see TRAINING SYSTEMS) on the windy sites of SANTORINI, *aplotaries* on Paros (see APLOTARIA), where vine canes are left to grow on the ground, or even the vines trained around olive trees in Messinia. CORDON systems of pruning and training are more common than GUYOT.

Viticultural CONSULTANTS have been instrumental in improving Greek vineyards. Vine VIRUS DISEASES are common in some vineyards and certain grape varieties. The most common ROOTSTOCKS are 110 R or 41 B, which offer much-needed DROUGHT resistance.

Vine varieties

Greece remains a largely unexplored source of ancient INDIGENOUS VARIETIES, of which more than 300 have been identified. Many of them are used solely for the TABLE GRAPE or dried-fruit industries, however, and others are used in tiny quantities on a purely local basis. There is still considerable work to be undertaken in VINE IDENTIFICATION, not just in rediscovering classical varieties but in discovering the relationships between Greek varieties and those grown in neighbouring countries such as Italy and Albania. The success of varieties such as MALAGOUSIA (virtually unheard of in 1993 but currently responsible for top-quality wines from no fewer than 150 producers), VIDIANO, Limniona, KYDONITSA, and many more suggests it will take decades for Greek viticulture to fully capitalize on the potential of its native grapes. There is also a growing interest in Greek varieties from other countries such as Australia, South Africa, Italy, and the US, inspired in part by CLIMATE CHANGE concerns that have winegrowers searching for more drought- and heat-resilient varieties.

Greek wine-grape varieties can offer unique characters and flavours. The mild climate and the tradition of consuming wine with food has favoured varieties that are relatively low in alcohol and based more on acidity and freshness than softness and body. Many varieties are grown in regions where attaining full ripeness is difficult, resulting in wines with distinctively COOL-CLIMATE characteristics. Many grapes are very specific to place, as well. For example, Debina is a speciality of Epirus, and Xinomavro of Macedonia, but Greek vine-growers are increasingly experimenting with varieties such as ASSYRTIKO and AGIORGITIKO in areas far from their traditional homes.

The most important white wine grapes in Greece are Assyrtiko, RODITIS, ROBOLA, SAVATIANO, MOSCHOFILERO, VILANA, DEBINA, and both MUSCAT BLANC À PETITS GRAINS and MUSCAT OF ALEXANDRIA. The Greek port of Monemvasia also gave its name to the MALVASIA grape. Among Greek red grape varieties, the most important to the modern Greek wine industry have been Agiorgitiko, LIMNIO, MANDILARIA, and XINOMAVRO. See regional details below for more local grape varieties.

In addition to these native varieties, INTERNATIONAL VARIETIES make up around 10% of total plantings. These include Chardonnay and Sauvignon Blanc among whites and Cabernets Sauvignon and Franc, Merlot, Grenache Noir, Cinsaut, and Syrah among red grape varieties. These appear sometimes in VARIETAL versions but more often in blends with Greek varieties.

Winemaking

While Greece was behind the curve in modernizing its wineries, with refrigeration and stainless-steel tanks coming into widespread use only in the 1980s, today winemaking technology is as modern as anywhere, although the trend is a return to traditional methods such as fermentation using AMBIENT YEASTS and reduced SULFUR DIOXIDE additions.

Better-quality red wines have traditionally been matured in large, old casks. After a couple of decades of over-using French, mainly new, BARRIQUES for the BARREL MATURATION of reds and even some whites, the pendulum is swinging back to more subtle oaking or even the use of CONCRETE vessels or clay AMPHORAE.

Wine laws

Greek wine laws were drawn up in the early 1970s and refined in the early 1980s as Greece prepared to join the EU. Since 2009 the top quality category is designated PDO or Protected Designation of Origin, of which there were 33 in 2021. The words Réserve or Grande Réserve indicate PDO wines with extended AGEING.

Protected Geographical Indication wines (PGI), which constitute the next tier and of which there were 120 in 2021, may be made in a wide variety of specified areas, nearly always from a range of vine varieties that includes both Greek and foreign grape varieties. The term 'Kava' is sometimes used to indicate high-quality PGI wines made only in small quantities and subjected to prolonged ageing.

The large category of WINE WITHOUT GEOGRAPHICAL INDICATION, known now simply as 'Wine from Greece' but formerly as table wine, includes some of Greece's most successful GENERIC brands as well as some more interesting wines made outside appellation regulations.

Wine regions

Wine is made all over Greece, often on a very small scale. The following includes those quality wine regions which have established their own identity within Greece and sometimes abroad; see map.

Northern Greece The regions of Macedonia and Thrace are noted mainly for their red wines, although wines of all hues are made there today. Xinomavro is arguably the most important grape variety with no less than four PDOs dedicated to it. The wines of NAOUSSA and AMYNDEO must be pure Xinomavro; to the north-east, in the slightly warmer PDO Goumenissa, it is blended with NEGOSKA grapes. Rapsani also favours Xinomavro but belongs to Thessaly in Central Greece (see below).

Côtes de Meliton on the slopes of Mount Meliton on the Halkidiki peninsula is the appellation specially created by Domaine Carras, a wine estate developed with the well-publicized assistance of Professor Émile PEYNAUD of Bordeaux. Its wines are made with a mixture of Greek and international vine varieties, notably Cabernet Sauvignon. The estate also pioneered the rediscovered elegant indigenous white variety MALAGOUSIA.

Since at least 1990, the coastal area of Kavala and its landlocked neighbour Drama have been enormously influential in introducing a particularly modern style of Greek wine, with exceptional red BORDEAUX BLENDS and Assyrtiko/Sauvignon Blanc white blends.

Thrace, famous for its wines in antiquity, is slowly reclaiming its past glory, mainly around Mount Ismaros and in Avdira, using the local MAVROUDI red grape, as well as blends of Greek and international varieties.

In the mountains of Epirus, not far from the town of Ioánnina and near the border with ALBANIA lies PDO Zitsa, which is most famous for lightly sparkling white wines from the local DEBINA grape, which is able to achieve full flavour ripeness at only 11% alcohol. To the immediate south-west, in the mountains around Ioánnina, are Greece's highest vineyards at Metsovo: the PGI starts at 500 m and soars to 1,200 m/4,000 ft. Cabernet Sauvignon and the local Vlahiko dominate reds; Debina and GEWÜRZTRAMINER provide fresh white wines.

Central Greece Thessaly, on the north-east coast of Central Greece, was not particularly important for quality wine production in past decades, but its combination of steep SCHIST slopes, ELEVATIONS reaching 900 m/3,000 ft, and OLD VINES yield small quantities of ageworthy reds. Rapsani is its most important PDO, produced on the foothills of Mount Olympus from Xinomavro (here grown at its most southerly point) blended with Krassato and Stavroto grapes and given CASK AGEING.

Further south-west, Messanikola is Greece's smallest PDO, 95 ha/234 acres focused on red wines made from the grape of the same name. High-quality wines are also being made in Tyrnavos (especially reds made from the indigenous Limniona) and the high elevations of Meteora.

Attica, together with Viotia, form the most important vine-growing area of Greece. Mainly planted with SAVATIANO, the region was once looked down on for its role in producing low-quality RETSINA, but in the 2010s the tables turned: by focusing on old vines and high-elevation areas, producers have proved Savatiano's potential for producing high-quality and even ageworthy white wines.

Other areas such as the island of Evvia, and Atalanti in Fthiotida, have produced excellent wines since at least the 2000s from a wide range of grape varieties, from Syrah and Cabernet Sauvignon to Assyrtiko, Agiorgitiko, and indigenous varieties Mavrokoundoura and Asprokoundoura.

Peloponnese This large southern peninsula has the greatest number of Greek wine PDOs, as well as some interesting PGI wines. On the plateau of Mantinia in Arcadia, at elevations of about 600 m/2,000 ft, the pink-skinned

Moschofilero grape produces fresh, dry, aromatic, slightly spicy, sometimes sparkling whites; with extended SKIN CONTACT, it can also yield interesting rosés. In Nemea, not far from the Corinth Canal that separates the Peloponnese from mainland Greece, the Agiorgitiko grape is grown on MARL and deep red soil. It can produce fruity, simple, dry or sweet red wines in the region's lower elevations; at 450–900 m/1,476–3,000 ft, the wines become more structured and intense, capable of AGEING. As in Naoussa, the 2000s saw a trend in new French BARRIQUES, but gentler oaking is becoming the norm. Since the late 1990s, Nemea has seen more investment in high-tech wineries than any other Greek region, resulting in some outstanding bottlings. Leading vineyards have been replanted with a higher VINE DENSITY.

The vineyards around Patras on the north coast are responsible for four PDOs. The Patras PDO is for dry white wines made from Roditis grapes grown on the slopes around the town. Muscat of Patras is a strong, sweet VIN DOUX NATUREL-style dessert wine from Muscat Blanc à Petits Grains grapes, as is Rion of Patras, which is almost extinct owing to the encroachment of buildings on the vineyard area. Mavrodaphne of Patras is a popular appellation for sweet reds, made from at least 51% Mavrodaphne and supplemented by the locally grown Korinthiaki (Corinth or CURRANT). Fermentation is arrested when ALCOHOLIC STRENGTH has reached about 4% (as in making PORT), and the wine, like tawny port, is then aged in wood. Examples aged 10–12 years in cask can be delicious. Wines falling outside of the PDO regulations may be bottled under the PGI Achaia.

In the far south-east of the peninsula is the medieval city of Monemvasia, which lends its name to the PDO Monemvassia-Malvasia, a barrel-aged sweet white wine made from several varieties of sun-dried grapes, including Monemvassia (at least 51%), Assyrtiko, and the rare Kydonitsa. Other significant viticultural areas include Ilia in the western Peloponnese, where REFOSCO has been grown by Mercouri for more than a century, and Messinia in the south-west, where, interestingly, Cabernet Sauvignon excels.

The islands Of the Ionian Islands off Greece's west coast, Kefalonia is best known for its wine, particularly the powerful, dry white ROBOLA. Vines here were individually trained on high, stony land, and mainly UNGRAFTED, leading Venetians to call Robola a *vino di sasso*, or wine of stone. Some dry, unfortified red wines from MAVRODAPHNE are also made, possibly the finest examples of this genre. Rarer are Mavrodaphne and Muscat dessert wines similar to those of Patras.

The Cyclades may be best known for the structured whites of SANTORINI, but wine is made on several of its islands. The PDO Paros red is a powerful, quite tannic wine made from a curious blend of the deeply coloured MANDILARIA lightened by the addition of half as much of the white grape called Monemvassia (see MALVASIA). PDO Malvasia of Paros is a sweet white, from sun-dried Monemvassia and a small percentage of Assyrtiko. Vines are trained along the ground using the APLOTARIA system as protection against the strong winds. Strong winds are also a characteristic of SANTORINI as well as Tinos, the home of a small group of top-quality producers working with Assyrtiko, Mavrotragano, and local varieties such as Potamisi. Small amounts of wines are also made on Mykonos, Naxos, Serifos, and Syros.

Of the Dodecanese islands, Rhodes has been an important producer of wine since classical times. Today PDO Rhodes includes dry whites based on ATHIRI and rosés and reds based on MANDILARIA, here known as Amorgiano. Sparkling wines, for decades a local tradition, now have their own PDO, including white and red versions. Only grapes grown on the higher reaches of the north or north-eastern slopes qualify for appellation wines. The PDO Muscat of Rhodes applies to both late-harvest and fortified sweet Muscat wines. Some wines are also made on the island of Kos.

The AEGEAN ISLANDS claim two of Greece's most famous sweet Muscat wines. On Samos, Muscat Blanc à Petits Grains is grown up to 800 m/2,600 ft above sea level, often on TERRACES on the island's steep hillsides, and the vintage can last a full two months, depending on vineyard ELEVATION. Muscat of Samos comes in several forms: Samos Doux is a MISTELA, while Samos Vin Doux Naturel is made by stopping the fermentation slightly later. Anthemis is an outstanding barrel-aged example. Potentially finest of all, however, is Samos Nectar, an unfortified wine made from sun-dried grapes capable of being fermented into a wine of 14% alcohol, which is then given three years in cask. Old vintages of the top bottlings can be sublime and great value for money. France is the single largest market, importing in BULK more than half of the island's annual production.

Limnos was the original home of the LIMNIO grape, which is still grown there, producing the PDO Limnos (also spelt Lemnos) red wine. But the island is more famous for Muscat wines, both dry and sweet. The PDO Muscat of Limnos, a sweet wine made from Muscat of Alexandria, is widely admired, being surprisingly delicate in both LATE HARVEST and VIN DE LIQUEUR forms.

The last of the appellation wines of commercial importance come from Crete, an island so large and diverse it is covered in detail under CRETE.

See also AEGEAN ISLANDS, RETSINA, and SANTORINI. K.L.

Lazarakis, K., *The Wines of Greece* (2018).
winesofgreece.org

green, tasting term often used for a wine made from grapes that did not reach full RIPENESS; as popular taste has evolved towards wines with higher acidity, however, it is no longer necessarily pejorative and may be used for wines that remind the taster of green vegetation.

green grafting, viticultural term for BUDDING and GRAFTING in the vineyard or nursery using green stem tissue. Green grafting offers less flexibility in timing than CHIP BUDDING and T-BUDDING because the ROOTSTOCK shoots must be green, and so it must take place in late spring or early summer. As with T-budding, the SCION pieces to be inserted may be from stored winter cuttings or the current season's green shoots. B.G.C.

green harvest. See CROP THINNING.

greenhouse effect. See CLIMATE CHANGE.

Green Valley of Russian River Valley is a cool, foggy California AVA in SONOMA best known for Pinot Noir and sparkling wines.

Grenache Blanc, the white-berried form of GRENACHE NOIR, was once important in France but now ranks eleventh among white grape varieties. However, there has been a modest revival in the last 15 years and the variety was grown on a total of 5,896 ha/14,569 acres of France in 2019, throughout the Languedoc and Roussillon, where it produces full-bodied whites that vary from fat and soft to nervy, floral, terroir-driven cellar candidates. In unfortified wines it is typically blended with the likes of Grenache Gris, Clairette, Bourboulenc, Marsanne, Roussanne, Viognier, Macabeo, and Rolle, adding supple fruit if not necessarily longevity. It need not necessarily be consigned to the blending vat, however. If carefully pruned and vinified, it can produce richly flavoured, full-bodied VARIETALS that share some characteristics with Marsanne and can be worthy of ageing in small oak barrels. It is also an ingredient in white Châteauneuf-du-Pape and is a significant ingredient in Roussillon's VINS DOUX NATURELS. The variety is also found in varietal form in California and occasionally in South Africa.

See GARNACHA BLANCA for details of the variety in Spain.

Grenache Gris, the least significant of the three Grenaches is a pink-skinned MUTATION of GRENACHE NOIR and is most important in Roussillon, where two-thirds of France's 2,190 ha/5,412 acres in 2019 were grown. It is more perfumed than GRENACHE BLANC and can add interest to unfortified wines. A small amount of Garnacha Roja is grown in northern Spain.

Grenache Noir, increasingly fashionable vine variety that in the late 20th century was the world's second most widely planted, sprawling all over Spain and southern France, but by 2016 had slumped to eighth place, thanks largely to the EU VINE PULL SCHEME. It probably owes its early dispersal around the western Mediterranean to the strength and extent of the ARAGÓN kingdom. As GARNACHA, it probably originated in Spain in the northern province of Aragón before colonizing extensive vineyard land both north and south of the Pyrenees, notably in Roussillon, which was ruled by Spain, and more particularly by the kingdom of Aragón, for four centuries until 1659. From here Grenache presumably made its way east and was certainly well established in the southern Rhône by the 19th century. Although Grenache was not planted in Rioja before PHYLLOXERA struck in 1901, this productive, resistant variety then practically replaced native vines in what is now Rioja Oriental and made significant inroads in Alta and Alavesa. Grenache is undoubtedly, however, the same grape variety as Sardinia's CANNONAU, which the Sardinians claim as their own, advancing the theory that the variety made its way from this island off Italy (where it is also known as Granaccia or Tai Rosso and, confusingly, as Gamay del Trasimeno in Umbria) to Spain when Sardinia was under Aragón rule, from 1297 until 1713.

Whatever its origins, Grenache has been uprooted to such an extent in Spain (see GARNACHA) that France has the world's largest Grenache presence, 84,745 ha/209,409 acres in 2019—more than any variety other than Merlot. For a vine that covers so much terrain, until recently its name has been rarely encountered by the wine drinker, much of it being blended with other varieties with more colour and backbone. Grenache produces essentially very fruity, rich, sweet-tasting wine, with varying degrees of tannin depending on the degree of WATER STRESS.

With its strong wood and upright growth, Grenache Noir is well suited to traditional BUSH VINE viticulture in hot, dry, windy vineyards. It buds early, can be prone to COULURE, and ripens relatively late (after Cabernet Sauvignon). In regions allowing a relatively long growing cycle, it can achieve heady sugar levels and indeed does not achieve full PHYSIOLOGICAL RIPENESS without them. The wine produced is, typically, paler than most reds (although low yields tend to concentrate the pigments, and tannins, in Spain and some Châteauneuf-du-Pape vineyards), with a tendency to oxidize early, a certain rusticity, and more than a hint of sweetness. If the vine is irrigated, as it has tended to be in the NEW WORLD, it may lose even these taste characteristics. If, however, as by the most punctilious Châteauneuf-du-Pape producers, it is pruned severely on the poorest of soils and allowed to reach full maturity of both vine and grape, it can result in excitingly dense reds that demand several decades' cellaring. The rediscovery of Rhône reds in the late 1980s (see RHÔNE RANGERS, for example) encouraged some New World producers to invest more effort in their own Grenache, even though its sturdy trunk has made it less widely popular in the modern era of MECHANICAL HARVESTING.

See GARNACHA for details of the variety in Spain.

In France, the majority of Grenache is planted in the southern RHÔNE Valley. Here seas of Côtes du Rhône of varying degrees of distinction are produced alongside smaller quantities of CHÂTEAUNEUF-DU-PAPE, GIGONDAS, and the like. Although blending has been the watchword here, notably with the more structured Syrah, older vintages of such monoliths as the famously concentrated Châteauneuf-du-Pape Ch Rayas show what can be done by Grenache and determination alone. The variety's kingdom spreads north to the Drôme *département*, where it also dominates, on nearly 7,000 ha. Grenache is responsible for much of southern France's fruitiest, fullest rosé, most obviously and traditionally in TAVEL and in neighbouring LIRAC but also much further eastwards into Provence proper, where Grenache is strongly identified with its significant rosé production. In the Languedoc and Roussillon, Grenache plays a generally unsung supporting role, together with its downy-leaved close relative LLEDONER PELUT, which is also habitually cited in the AOC regulations for red wines. In Roussillon, Grenaches of all three colours (see also GRENACHE BLANC and GRENACHE GRIS) are valued not only for their dry wines but as the vital ingredient in the region's distinctive VINS DOUX NATURELS.

Grenache Noir is being uprooted on Corsica in favour of local varieties, but on SARDINIA, as Cannonau, it still plays a dominant role in the island's reds and dessert wines. The vine is also grown around the Mediterranean, for example in Croatia.

Grenache's ability to withstand DROUGHT and heat made it a popular choice with New World growers when FASHION had little effect on market forces. Extensive historic acreage in the central San Joaquin Valley, and some in Mendocino, constituted the majority of the 1,780 ha/4,399 acres that remained in California in 2020. The wine typically made from these OLD VINES—cheap, sweet, gimmicky Grenache Rosé or 'White Grenache'—had done little for Grenache's image in California, but the state's RHÔNE RANGERS have rejuvenated the variety's image with new plant material imported straight from the Rhône Valley in their Central Coast vineyards. Grenache has benefited from Washington State's love affair with Rhône wines although only 86 ha/212 acres were recorded there in 2017, less than one-twentieth as much as Syrah.

Grenache was Australia's most planted black grape variety until the mid 1960s. Shiraz (Syrah) overtook it in the late 1970s, but it was not until the early 1990s that Australia's Cabernet Sauvignon output overtook that of Grenache. By 2022 the total area planted with Grenache in Australia had fallen to 1,801 ha/4,450 acres, high-yielding vines in Riverland having been pulled out while more cosseted vines have been planted in McLaren Vale and the Barossa Valley, and old-vine Grenache is increasingly treasured. VARIETAL Grenache has been less popular in Australia than GSM blends and has not featured much in South America.

Robinson, J., et al., *Wine Grapes, A Complete guide to 1,368 Vine Varieties, Including Their Origins and Flavours* (2012).

G

grès, French term for SANDSTONE.

Grés de Montpellier, named CRU within the LANGUEDOC AOC in southern France created in 2003 for red wines made mainly from Syrah and Mourvèdre with Grenache Noir. The region encompasses 46 communes a broad sweep of hinterland of the city of Montpellier, generally cooled by breezes from the nearby Mediterranean.

grey rot, sometimes known as **grey mould** and sometimes just **bunch rot**, the malevolent form of BOTRYTIS BUNCH ROT and one of the most harmful of the FUNGAL DISEASES that attack vines. In this undesirable bunch-rot form, the *Botrytis cinerea* fungus rapidly spreads throughout the berry flesh and the skin breaks down. Other fungi and bacteria then also invade the berry and the grapes become rotten. Badly infected fruit develops off-flavours, ACIDITY is significantly reduced, and PHENOLICS are oxidized by LACCASE; badly infected vineyards themselves have a characteristic mouldy and often vinegary smell. Wines produced from such fruit smell mouldy, and red wines look pale and grey-brown. Research in Champagne has shown that botrytis can have a negative effect on the foaming properties of champagne. When the *Botrytis cinerea* fungus attacks healthy, ripe, white wine grapes and the weather conditions are favourable, it results in so-called NOBLE ROT, which can produce some of the world's finest sweet wines.

greywacke, pronounced 'graywacky', from the German *Grauwacke*, is a tough, dark-grey SANDSTONE, with a high CLAY content. Most sedimentary rocks (see GEOLOGY) show a fairly uniform grain size, whereas greywacke, formed in turbid deep-sea water, shows characteristically jumbled grain sizes, with thick accumulations of coarse material (typically of QUARTZ, feldspar, and rock fragments) closely intermixed with fine clay. On land it weathers slowly, giving stony, free-draining soils.

Greywacke is found in South Africa's Western Cape, in California's RUSSIAN RIVER VALLEY, and in Germany's MOSEL, AHR, and MITTELRHEIN, but perhaps most famously it is found in NEW

ZEALAND, where it constitutes much of the bedrock spine of both islands. Detritus derived from it dominates the GRAVELS of regions such as Hawke's Bay, Marlborough, and Waipara. A.J.M.

Grignan-les-Adhémar, name adopted in 2010 for an extensive appellation on the northern fringes of the southern RHÔNE for mainly red wines. (Its original name, Coteaux du Tricastin, was abandoned because it was too readily associated with a nearby nuclear power plant.) In 2020, wines were produced from 1,270 ha/3,138 acres of vineyards; 74% red, 16% rosé, 10% white. Although the climate here is definitively MEDITERRANEAN, the higher vineyards and more exposed terrain produce slightly lighter wines than those of the Côtes du Rhône, which they resemble. Grenache and Syrah are the principal varieties for reds and rosés, Grenache Blanc and Viognier for whites. M.C.W.

G

Grignolino, ancient grape variety of the PIEMONTE region in north-west Italy already documented in 1249 as Berbexinis (the synonym Berbesino is still used). Native of the MONFERRATO hills between Asti and Casale and vinified almost invariably as a pale red VARIETAL wine with an almost alpine scent and a tangy ACIDITY, it has naturally high TANNINS thanks to having three-to-four times more seeds (*grignole* means 'pips' in the Monferrato dialect) than most varieties. But these tannins were seen as a disadvantage and avoided by short MACERATION times, thus stripping the wine of its ageing potential and depth and creating the misconception that it must be drunk young.

The growing appreciation for Nebbiolo and its tannic structure has helped Grignolino's fortunes, as has the foundation in 2016 of Monferace, a private association of 12 Grignolino producers who choose to adhere to strict production rules requiring 100% Grignolino and ageing for at least 40 months, including 24 in CASK. This harks back to the variety's historic reputation as an ageworthy wine and aims to eradicate the early-drinking image.

Grignolino has its own DOC areas, Grignolino Monferrato Casalese (270 ha/667 acres) and Grignolino d'Asti (308 ha), slightly overlapping with the DOCG of ASTI, and is allowed in a further five DOCs. Total plantings in Italy in 2021 were 645 ha/1,593 acres, compared with 743 ha in 2011, practically all in Piemonte. W.S.

Grillet, Château. See CHÂTEAU-GRILLET.

Grillo, Sicily's second most planted white grape variety, was once used as the base for the best MARSALA. Grown as BUSH VINES, it produced potent, full-bodied base wines that were supplemented by a proportion of the more aromatic INZOLIA. DNA PROFILING established that Grillo is a natural CROSS of Sicily's CATARRATTO with MUSCAT OF ALEXANDRIA and that Rossese Bianco of Liguria is identical to Grillo. At its best, it gives full-bodied wines of real interest, although they lack the aromatic intensity that has made Inzolia's transformation from FORTIFIED WINE to dry white wine variety so much easier. Plantings have grown substantially and had reached 8,444 ha/20,866 acres on the island by 2020. See SICILY for more details.

Gringet, not, as was long thought, a synonym for SAVAGNIN but a distinct variety used mainly for full-bodied, floral, still and sparkling wines in AYSE in SAVOIE.

Groenekloof, cool, predominantly white-wine ward in the Darling district in SOUTH AFRICA.

Grolleau Noir, sometimes known as **Groslot** and one of the numerous natural progenies of GOUAIS BLANC, is the everyday red grape variety of TOURAINE. It produces extremely high yields of relatively thin, acid wine, and it is to the benefit of wine drinkers that it is so systematically being replaced with Gamay and, more recently, Cabernet Franc. It was once much more important, but total French plantings have been steady this century at around 2,000 ha/4,942 acres. The status of the variety is such that it is allowed into the rosé but not red versions of AOC wines such as SAUMUR and Touraine. It has played a major part only in Rosé d'Anjou, in which it is commonly blended with Gamay, which ripens just before it. Plantings of the pink-skinned mutation **Grolleau Gris**, in much the same part of France, totalled 573 ha/1,416 acres in 2019.

Groppello Gentile, red grape variety grown to a limited extent on about 78 ha/193 acres, mainly in the Italian wine region of LOMBARDY. It is the most important of the Groppellos.

Groslot is a common synonym for the Loire's red vine variety GROLLEAU.

Gros Manseng, assertive and increasingly popular Basque white grape grown on about 3,965 ha/79,798 acres of SOUTH WEST FRANCE in 2019 to produce drier versions of Jurançon and various Béarn wines, as well as being one of the more characterful ingredients in Gascon dry whites. It is known as Iskiriota Zuri Handia over the border in Spain's Basque country (see TXAKOLI). DNA PROFILING established a parent–offspring relationship with the rarer, thinner-skinned PETIT MANSENG. It yields more generously and produces discernibly less elegant, less rich, but still powerful wine. Unlike the smaller-berried Petit Manseng, it is not sensitive to COULURE. Gros Manseng, unlike Petit Manseng, is rarely used for sweet wines. J.E.H. & J.V.

Gros Plant du Pays Nantais is an AOC overlapping that of MUSCADET. The wines are from FOLLE BLANCHE, called Gros Plant here, with the rare Colombard and Montils permitted. The area comprises a wide, ocean-influenced arc south-east of the city of Nantes, with the well-drained igneous and metamorphic hillsides of Grandlieu and Vallet the best for taming Gros Plant's VIGOUR. Tart by nature, the variety can make bracingly acidic, austere wines when overcropped, but quality winegrowers can produce examples that combine ripeness and salty freshness, building TEXTURE and aromatic complexity with LEES CONTACT. The Folle Blanche vine was introduced to this region by the DUTCH WINE TRADE for DISTILLATION purposes and outnumbered the MELON vine until the ravages of PHYLLOXERA in the late 19th century. Gros Plant was promoted from VDQS to AOC in 2011. The decreasing production represents one-tenth of the Muscadet output, with a large proportion enjoyed locally. P. Le.

Gros Rhin, Swiss synonym for SILVANER, to distinguish it from Petit Rhin, or Riesling.

Grosse Lage, term adopted in 2012 by Germany's VDP for those vineyards classified by its members as their best and hence capable of generating a GROSSES GEWÄCHS. Prior to that, the term ERSTE LAGE was used for such vineyards, but it is now used for an ostensibly lesser tier of vineyards (effectively the PREMIERS CRUS, with Grosse Lagen being the GRANDS CRUS). D.S.

Grosser Ring, the Mosel branch of the VDP growers' association in GERMANY. Founded in 1908 in Trier, where its annual September AUCTIONS are still a prestigious feature of the country's wine calendar as well as an indicator of vintage quality and market health, the group comprises around 30 growers. D.S.

Grosses Gewächs (pronounced 'guh-*vex*') is a prestige dry wine category devised by the VDP growers' association in GERMANY and in use (though no longer exclusively by its members) since 2002. Within the VDP, wines so designated originate in vineyard sites classified by the VDP as a GROSSE LAGE. Such a site is typically an EINZELLAGE, but increasingly many producers make use of a provision permitting the registration of any cadastral site name for labelling purposes. Grosse Gewächse (plural) must be cropped at YIELDS of no more than 50 hl/ha, be hand-harvested, at no less than the MUST WEIGHT required for SPÄTLESE (though CHAPTALIZATION is permitted, and the wines are nowadays labelled without PRÄDIKAT), and be subjected to sensory review. Grosses Gewächs wines are typically bottled in glass embossed with a logo featuring a grape cluster and the numeral 1 and (since vintage 2007) are labelled with the initials GG. In imitation of Burgundian GRAND CRU practice,

VDP members typically promote Grosse Gewächse without reference to their commune (village) of origin, with the result that some names—Herrenberg, for example—can be found on wines from several different sites. A 2021 German wine law recognizes Grosses Gewächs (together with an effectively PREMIER CRU counterpart, ERSTES GEWÄCHS) and sets parameters for yield, minimum ALCOHOLIC STRENGTH, and release date. D.S.

Grosslage designates a collective vineyard site as delimited by Austrian or German wine law (and under no circumstances should it be confused with the superior class of single-vineyard sites defined by the VDP as GROSSE LAGEN). Generally co-opting a traditional place name with cachet (but sometimes made up), Germany's Grosslage designations must be conjoined to the name of a particular wine village but typically cover vineyards (each officially known as an EINZELLAGE) in far-flung and far less prestigious villages, the thinly disguised intent being, by means of the German labelling template village+vineyard, to trade on the prestige earned by sites outside the Grosslage. Thus, Niersteiner Gutes Domtal refers to vast acreage spread across 15 disparate villages and 32 Einzellagen of which only one—obscure—falls within the communal limits of the Rheinhessen's justly famous wine village Nierstein. Another notorious example is Piesporter Michelsberg in the Mosel. By the 1990s, use of Grosslage designations had greatly diminished. A very few German Grosslage names—most notably Bernkasteler Badstube—remain widely used even by the most quality-conscious growers because they incorporate sites within the designated village that are high quality but lesser known. However, a 2021 revision to the German wine law stipulates that from 2026 any Grosslage designation—or any newly minted collective site designations—must be preceded by the word 'Region' and eliminate reference to commune (village); for example, no longer Piesporter Michelsberg but Region Michelsberg. However, this change was still being hotly disputed in 2022.

The word 'Grosslage' remains an officially recognized term in Austria but is not used on labels. D.S.

Gros Verdot, an unusual Bordeaux variety without the concentration or interest of PETIT VERDOT. It is grown to a limited extent in California and possibly also in South America.

grower, the all-important producer of the raw material for winemaking. These individuals may be called grape-growers, more precisely vine-growers, possibly even winegrowers (or wine-growers) if they also vinify. Terms in other languages include *vigneron* and *viticulteur* in French and *vignaiolo* in Italian. Wine producers who grow their own grapes and vinify them into wine but on a limited scale are often referred to somewhat carelessly and often inaccurately as **small growers**. A significant proportion of all vine-growers produce only grapes, however, which they sell to CO-OPERATIVES, merchant-bottlers (see NÉGOCIANT), or larger wine operations.

growler, a resealable jug commonly used in the United States for the sale of beer and kombucha; more recently, growlers are sometimes used for wine, for off-site consumption. While Europeans have long been allowed to bring refillable vessels to a winery to have them filled with wine, the practice has been complicated in the US by the arcane rules of the TTB and remains rare. Growlers are gaining traction in other countries such as Argentina, which began allowing the sale of wine in growlers in 2021 as a more environmentally friendly option to bottled wine, saving on glass, labels, and transportation.

growth cycle. See VINE GROWTH CYCLE.

growth regulators, synthetic substances which act on vines like HORMONES to regulate their growth and development. A synthetic AUXIN, 4-CPA, has for example been used to improve FRUIT SET. Synthetic GIBBERELLINS have been used to increase berry size, especially for the seedless SULTANA, and a synthetic ethylene-releasing compound termed 'ethephon' can be used to hasten grape maturity and enhance coloration in particularly cool climates. More recently applied to viticulture, hydrogen cyanamide encourages early and complete BUDBREAK, which can be useful for TROPICAL VITICULTURE. These chemicals are mostly used for TABLE GRAPES, and their application to both table grapes and wine grapes is regulated by rules governing the use of AGROCHEMICALS. R.E.S.

grubbing up vines is known as *arrachage* in France, where it became a common practice as part of the EU's various VINE-PULL SCHEMES aimed at reducing the European WINE LAKE, notably in the 1980s and 1990s. Outside Europe the practice is generally referred to as 'ripping out'.

The more traditional reason for grubbing up a vineyard is that the VINE AGE is so high and the average YIELD so low that the vineyard is no longer economic (although the prestige associated with OLD VINES may retard this process). Weak demand for wine grapes, signalled by wineries failing to renew contracts with growers and/or continued periods of low prices, sometimes below production costs, may also lead to vineyard removal.

A vineyard may be grubbed up because its owner wishes to change VINE VARIETY or CLONE, although this may be achieved by TOP GRAFTING, or field grafting on to the existing TRUNKS and root systems. Vineyards are normally grubbed up when invaded by a pest as deadly as PHYLLOXERA (as thousands of acres were in northern California in the late 1980s), and a disease such as LEAFROLL VIRUS, ESCA, or GRAPEVINE YELLOWS may damage production to such an extent that grubbing up is the only option. In the early 2010s, TRUNK DISEASE infection had become a major reason for vineyard removal in California and around the world, as the proportion of dead and missing vines increases with age.

If the vineyard is to be replanted, care must be taken that the soil is free of pests and diseases. FUMIGATION may be necessary; see also NEMATODES.

Grumello, one of five subzones of VALTELLINA in the far north of Italy.

Grüner Veltliner. The most commonly planted vine variety in AUSTRIA is grown elsewhere in Eastern Europe and is increasingly respected worldwide. This well-adapted variety was planted on 14,612 ha/36,107 acres of Austria in 2020, almost 50% of the country's white wine grape area, and is particularly dominant in Lower Austria. DNA PROFILING in Austria has shown that Grüner Veltliner is a spontaneous CROSS between SAVAGNIN and the obscure St Georgener from Eisenstadt but is not genetically related to ROTER VELTLINER or FRÜHROTER VELTLINER.

The vine can be productive and is relatively hardy but ripens too late for much of northern Europe. Yields of 100 hl/ha (5.7 tons/acre) are possible in the least distinguished vineyards and the resulting wine is inoffensive if unexciting. However, at its best, arguably in the Wachau, Kamptal, Kremstal, Weinviertel, and Wagram and in the hands of some of the most ambitious growers in Vienna, Grüner Veltliner can produce wines which combine perfume and substance. The wine is typically dry, full-bodied, peppery, or spicy, and with time in bottle it can start to taste positively Burgundian. Grüner Veltliner can produce a variety of wine styles, from base wines for Austrian SEKT, simple wines served at HEURIGER, popular medium-bodied peppery wines to very opulent, concentrated wines. Grüner Veltliner may be regarded as Austria's biggest asset and adorns restaurant wine lists around the globe. It can be difficult for non-German speakers to pronounce so is often abbreviated to 'Gruner' or 'GV'.

The variety has long been grown just over Lower Austria's northern border in CZECHIA—where it is known as Veltlin or Veltlínské Zelené and is the country's most widely planted variety—and in the Sopron vineyards of HUNGARY as Zöldveltelini. It is also known in Germany's Rheinhessen and Pfalz regions and is proving successful and versatile in Australia, New Zealand, and North America.

GSM on a wine label indicates the popular, southern-Rhône-inspired blend of Grenache, Syrah/Shiraz, and Mourvèdre. GSM is particularly common in Australia but also made in California and Washington State.

GST. See CLIMATE CLASSIFICATION.

guaiacol. See BRETTANOMYCES, FLAVOUR COMPOUNDS, OAK FLAVOUR, and SMOKE TAINT.

Guarnaccia, Calabrian synonym used for CODA DI VOLPE BIANCA. Guarnaccia Nera is a Campanian synonym for MAGLIOCCO Dolce.

Guenoc Valley, California AVA. See LAKE COUNTY.

Guigal, family-owned merchant-grower based at Ampuis, CÔTE RÔTIE, in the northern Rhône. Although established as recently as 1946 by Étienne Guigal, Maison Guigal is the most famous of any of the Rhône Valley's merchants or growers with collectors and investors. This is very largely due to the efforts of its manager since 1961, Étienne's only son Marcel, a man of exceptional modesty and a gifted, meticulous winemaker. Marcel's son Philippe, OENOLOGIST and chief winemaker, joined the estate in 1997 and is a worthy successor. Guigal owns more than 150 ha/370 acres, of which slightly more than 30 ha/75 acres is prime vineyard in Côte Rôtie. It was the wines made from three of its best PARCELS, extravagantly praised by influential American wine writer Robert PARKER in the early to mid 1980s, that first drew international attention to Guigal. It would be fair to say that the quality of Guigal's top wines, along with Parker's persistent enthusiasm for them among many other Rhône wines, spearheaded a resurgence of interest in the whole region.

Guigal's so-called 'LaLa' wines (La Mouline, La Landonne, and La Turque) are dark, dense, mouth-fillingly rich and oaky expressions of the SYRAH grape (supplemented by up to 11% of co-planted VIOGNIER in the case of La Mouline, 7% for La Turque); they are made from low yields of very ripe, late-picked fruit aged for three-and-a-half years in 100% new OAK and bottled without FINING or FILTRATION. They are particularly impressive when young and their quality is beyond question, but opinions are divided about their style; Côte Rôtie purists seek transparency. Reputation and rarity combined (only 400–700 cases of each are made each year) have also made them extremely expensive and therefore game for criticism, fair or not. From the 1990s offerings have included the more plentiful Côte Rôtie Ch d'Ampuis, La Doriane, a special CONDRIEU, and, from the 2001 vintage, Ermitage Ex Voto.

In 1984 Guigal bought and revitalized the firm of Vidal Fleury, the company where Étienne Guigal worked at the age of 14 (from 1923 until 1940) before founding his own. The former Jean-Louis Grippat and de Vallouit estates were absorbed by Guigal in 2001 followed by the Bonserine estate in 2006. In 2017 the Guigal family moved into the southern Rhône with the purchase of Ch de Nalys's well-situated 77 ha/190 acres of vines, although they had long (meticulously) sourced wine in the south for their NÉGOCIANT bottlings such as their great-value Côtes-du-Rhône. M.W.E.S. & J.R.

Gumpoldskirchen, wine centre in the THERMENREGION district of Austria famous for white wines made from ZIERFANDLER (or Spätrot) and ROTGIPFLER grapes.

Gundagai, small, hilly wine region in southern NEW SOUTH WALES comprising low-lying warm areas and cooler vineyard sites at higher ELEVATIONS in the foothills of the Australian Alps. It is known for ripe, vibrant Shiraz, full-flavoured Cabernet Sauvignon, and diverse styles of Chardonnay. A.R.P.

Gutedel, meaning 'good and noble' in German, is not the most obvious synonym for CHASSELAS but is still used in Germany, particularly in the Markgräflerland, southern BADEN, which—along with neighbouring areas of Alsace and Switzerland—is sometimes referred to as the Gutedel Triangle on account of this variety's ubiquity and continued popularity. The wines, generally juicy and straightforward, may have notes of almond and hay in the better examples, and particularly old vines in CALCAREOUS sites can evince both distinction and MINERALITY. A dark-berried form, **Roter Gutedel**, is also known in Baden.

Gutsabfüllung. See ERZEUGERABFÜLLUNG.

guttation, botanical term applied to vines losing water through small pores at the leaf margin, due to root pressure. It can be seen early in the morning for vines in wet soil under cool conditions. See also BLEEDING.

Gutturnio, red wine from EMILIA-ROMAGNA in Italy, overwhelmingly produced as FRIZZANTE (8.5 million bottles in 2020) but potentially more interesting in its still form.

Guyot, Jules, respected 19th-century French scientist with a particular interest in viticulture and winemaking whose name lives on in the system of CANE PRUNING which had been in use in France for a long time but which he promulgated in the 1860s. His practical treatises on growing vines and making wine were translated into English in the second half of the 19th century and are enthusiastically followed by vignerons around the world.

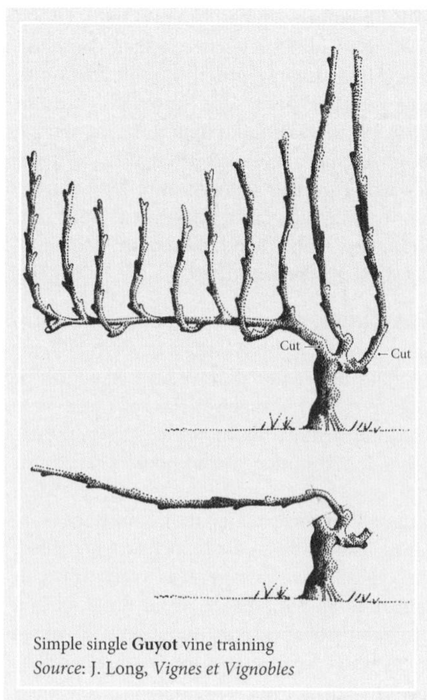

Simple single **Guyot** vine training
Source: J. Long, *Vignes et Vignobles*

The basic principle of Guyot pruning is to leave six- to ten-bud CANES and for each a single two-bud SPUR at the base; shoots from this spur form the cane the following year (see PRUNING). The **Guyot simple** form, also known as single Guyot, has one cane and one spur. **Guyot double**, or double Guyot, the most common vine-TRAINING SYSTEM in Bordeaux, has two canes and two spurs, and the canes are trained to each side. Sometimes the canes are arched, as in the Jura. Galet lists regional variations of the Guyot. See PRUNING for more details. R.E.S.

Galet, P., *General Viticulture* (2000).

gyropalette, or **girasol**, special metal crate holding many dozen inverted bottles of TRADITIONAL METHOD sparkling wine in a remote-controlled, movable frame. This is the mechanized form of RIDDLING and was developed in CATALUÑA in the 1970s. They are now widely used in CHAMPAGNE, ITALY, and elsewhere. *Girasol* is Spanish for 'sunflower', which also turns during a 24-hour period.

For more details, see SPARKLING WINEMAKING.

H

HACCP. See QUALITY ASSURANCE.

hail, frozen raindrops or ice bodies built up by accretion, typically falling in thunderstorms. To the normal ill effects of heavy summer RAINFALL is added direct physical damage to the vines and fruit. Impact on the vines ranges from ripping and stripping of the leaves to bruising and breaking of the young stems—effects which can carry over to the following season. Damage to young bunches may destroy or at least reduce the crop, although compensatory growth of the remaining berries may minimize the effects on final YIELD. Hail damage while berries are ripening, on the other hand, is invariably more serious. Smashed berries are prone to ROT and ferment on the vine, rendering even undamaged parts of the bunches unusable. BURGUNDY is particularly and apparently increasingly prone to hail damage, as is Mendoza in ARGENTINA. Hail is said to cost French agriculture more than €500 million a year.

Hailstorms characteristically follow irregular but well-defined pathways through an area, sometimes devastating parts of a vineyard but leaving other parts untouched. Local TOPOGRAPHY may result in a tendency for the storms to follow preferred pathways, but largely their incidence and route is unpredictable. Various prevention techniques have been tried, including seeding the clouds with silver iodide or dry ice, from planes or cannon, and using hail cannon that generate shock waves intended to disrupt the formation of hail. Covering the vines with netting is another laborious and expensive option which reduces the impact of hailstones but may also reduce the amount of SUNLIGHT reaching the vines—desirable only in the hottest wine regions. The technologies can hardly be described as proven, but they have found supporters among vine-growers understandably desperate to protect their hard-won crops. Insurance against hail is rarely cost-effective.

J.E.H. & R.E.S.

hail disease. See WHITE ROT.

halbtrocken designates German wines that have 5–18 g/l of RESIDUAL SUGAR depending on the TOTAL ACIDITY. Levels above 12 g/l are permitted—governed by the formula: maximum residual sugar equals total g/l of acidity plus 10—up to an absolute limit of 18. Halbtrocken wines falling within 12–18 g/l are almost entirely from acid-endowed RIESLING.

Among the top German producers in the 21st century there has been a tendency to bottle fewer wines that fit the criteria for halbtrocken, as well as labelling those that do as FEINHERB or without any reference to degree of SWEETNESS. In Austria, any wine is officially halbtrocken (and then labelled as such, albeit in tiny print) if it exceeds the maximum residual sugar set for TROCKEN (which varies with total acidity) but does not exceed 12 g/l. D.S.

haloanisoles, group of related compounds including chloroanisoles such as trichloroanisole (TCA) and 2,3,4,6-tetrachloroanisole (TECA) as well as bromoanisoles such as tribromoanisoles (TBA) responsible for the musty odour of CORK TAINT and some instances of winery contamination. TCA was the first identified and is the most prevalent contributor to the problem.

The formation of chloroanisoles in cork bark is not yet fully elucidated, but the first step occurs when chlorine reacts with phenol to produce compounds such as trichlorophenol (TCP). This may occur for several reasons, including formation during chlorine bleaching of cork bark (no longer used in the production of CORKS) or perhaps even direct biosynthesis in cork tissue before the bark has been removed from the tree. In addition, there is the direct application of organochlorine biocides such as chlorophenol fungicides used on cork trees in the forests. Although these fungicides have been banned in Europe since 1995, chlorophenols are very stable and still present in groundwater.

If this first step remains unclear, the final step is well understood: the chlorophenols are degraded by fungi in the presence of moisture, a reaction catalyzed by the enzyme methylase, yielding the haloanisoles.

Research has not yet provided a definitive understanding of the important origins of chlorophenols in cork bark, so the presence of chloroanisoles remains a problem in cork production. In addition, similar precursor phenols are present in all wood-related material found in a typical winery, including corks, BARRELS, wooden pallets, structural wood, and wood-treatment products.

See TCA, TBA, and TECA. J.E.H. & A.L.W.

Hammurabi (end of 18th century BCE), king of BABYLONIA, responsible for uniting MESOPOTAMIA with its capital Babylon. His law code survives on baked clay tablets and contains the earliest references to wine shops and wine sellers.

Hanepoot, traditional Afrikaans name for South Africa's most planted Muscat vine variety, MUSCAT OF ALEXANDRIA.

hangover, one of wine's least welcome effects, normally following some DRUNKENNESS or certainly excessive consumption. Drinking wine with or after food and drinking at least as much WATER as wine can lessen the likelihood of a hangover. Homeopathic prophylactics include milk thistle extract (silymarin) and nux vomica. There is no evidence that wine hangovers are different from those caused by any other form of ALCOHOL, although inexpensive wine, non-organic wine, wine consumed with grain-based alcholic drinks, and bottle-aged PORT have all been accused of increasing the risk of hangover. The only indisputably effective control is moderation.

hang time, American expression that has come to be associated with the controversial practice of postponing the harvest beyond traditional ripeness. This can result in partly shrivelled and dehydrated berries that yield overripe flavours and such high ALCOHOLIC STRENGTH that MUSTS may need dilution with water. Proponents of long hang time argue that wines made from such grapes have better aroma and flavour and softer TANNINS. The practice appears to have become less popular in the second decade of the 21st century than it was in the last decade of the 20th. Very ripe, dehydrated grapes shrivel as a result of BERRY CELL DEATH and weigh less than those picked at conventional ripeness, generally resulting in lower payments for growers paid by weight. See also BERRY SHRIVEL and RIPENING.
R.E.S.

Happy Canyon of Santa Barbara, warmest, easternmost AVA of SANTA BARBARA, south of the San Rafael Mountains and northwest of Lake Cachuma. A protected valley with clay, loam, and some sandy soils and dramatic DIURNAL TEMPERATURE RANGE, it is planted mainly to Bordeaux and Rhône varieties. The name comes from the region's popularity with moonshiners during PROHIBITION. M.D.K.

Haraszthy, Agoston (1812–69), early CALIFORNIA winegrower and promoter, frequently but wrongly identified as the 'father of California wine'. Born in Austro-Hungary, he went to the United States in 1842 and to California in 1849, where he engaged in multifarious activities, including politics, horticulture, and gold-refining. In 1856, he bought a SONOMA County vineyard and established the Buena Vista winery, still extant today. In 1861, as a member of the state commission on viticulture, he travelled to Europe and sent back many thousands of vine cuttings to California. His account of this trip and of his work as a winegrower in California—*Grape Culture, Wines, and Wine-Making* (1862)—first brought California as a wine state to the attention of the nation and is Haraszthy's main claim to importance in the history of wine in America.

After losing control of the Buena Vista winery he migrated to Nicaragua, where he died in mysterious circumstances. In the years after his death it came to be believed that Haraszthy was the first to show the possibilities of winegrowing in California, the first to introduce superior grape varieties into the state, and in particular the first to introduce the ZINFANDEL vine. None of these is true, but the story has become legendary and difficult to dislodge.
T.P.

McGinty, B., *Strong Wine: the Life and Legend of Agoston Haraszthy* (1998).
Pinney, T., *A History of Wine in America* (1989).

hard, TASTING TERM applied to wine that is high in astringent TANNINS and apparently lacking in FRUIT. See TEXTURE.

Harlan, name synonymous with quality, ambition, and the long term in the NAPA Valley. H. William (Bill) Harlan scouted for land there from the early 1970s, put Meadowood country club and resort on the wine map as the site of the famous wine AUCTION from 1981, founded Merryvale Vineyards soon after, and then acquired land on the west side of the valley that would in 1987 produce the first vintage of the meticulously managed Harlan Estate. The first vintage to be released commercially was 1990, in 1996, when Merryvale was sold and BOND, a group of single-vineyard wines from around the valley, was founded. Since then Harlan Estate, usually 75% Cabernet Sauvignon, has been established as a peer, certainly in terms of PRICE, of Bordeaux's FIRST GROWTHS. Next up was a decidedly upmarket members' club Napa Valley Reserve with its own winery next to Meadowood and the acquisition of the sprawling site for Promontory, also in the foothills of the Mayacamas Mountains, managed by Bill's son Will, who took over as managing director of Harlan Estate, BOND, and The Mascot, Harlan's SECOND WINE, in 2021.

harmony, TASTING TERM for a component of wine QUALITY related to BALANCE, but encompassing FLAVOUR as well as structure. A wine is harmonious if all its aromatic and structural elements are in proportion, with no individual element being too prominent, and if they complement each other to form a coherent whole. For example, a wine with herbaceous, barely ripe aromas but, in contrast, full BODY and low ACID on the palate might be said to lack harmony. A.H.

Harriague, name for TANNAT in Uruguay, inspired by a Basque viticultural pioneer there.

Hárslevelű, white grape variety, whose name means 'linden leaf', most widely grown in the Tokaj region of Hungary where it produces elegant, spicy, aromatic dry white wines with good ageing potential. It also brings perfume to FURMINT, the variety that has been shown by DNA PROFILING to be its parent and with which it is often blended in the famous dessert wine TOKAJI. It can also make very good sparkling wine.

Hárslevelű is widely planted elsewhere in Hungary, to a national total of 1,445 ha/3,571 acres in 2021, and produces a varied range of VARIETAL wines. Good Hárslevelű is typically full-bodied yet fresh, with a honey-sweet character when very ripe. In Somló, it produces a leaner and less aromatic wine. The wines labelled Debrő Hárslevelű, an appellation in the Eger region, are usually bottled with some RESIDUAL SUGAR. Dry and sweet wines are produced around Villány-Siklós.

The variety is also grown over the border from Hungary's Tokaj region in SLOVAKIA, in Austria's Burgenland, and in South Africa.

harvest, the process of picking ripe grapes from the vine and transferring them to the winery (or field pressing station), as well as its occasionally festive, if frenetic, duration.

This transition period in the winemaking cycle from vineyard to cellar is also known as VINTAGE or crush in much of the NEW WORLD, RÉCOLTE or *vendange* in France, *vendemmia* in Italy, *Ernte* in Germany, COSECHA in Spain, *vindima* in the DOURO, and *colheita* in the rest of Portugal.

Timing

A critical aspect of harvest is its timing, choosing a point during the grape RIPENING process when the balance between its natural accumulation of SUGARS and its decreasing amount of natural plant ACIDS is optimal (see SAMPLING). In all but the rare ideal vintages, it is a compromise involving multiple factors: target alcohol level, ideal flavour/aroma profiles, tannin profile (for red wines), acidity, PH, disease levels, health of the vines, and the weather forecast. However, logistical considerations to do with the harvesting operation, or the capacity to receive and process grapes, may constrain these decisions.

Typically this is a frenzied period, especially in hotter climates where warm, dry weather can rapidly accelerate ripening, causing different varieties to ripen at the same time. In cooler climates, an orderly harvest can be disrupted by humid and wet weather and possible ROT, by heavy RAINFALL making vineyard access difficult, by HAIL damage, or even by FROST. ACIDIFICATION and ENRICHMENT are respectively the most common rescue operations in the case of grapes picked slightly after or before ideal maturity if they are permitted by local wine regulations. MICRO-OXYGENATION may also help reduce the HERBACEOUSNESS resulting from slightly unripe fruit.

Timing of the harvest is additionally complicated by the fact that the fruit in different parts of a single vineyard may vary in ripeness, and the picking may need to be done in several stages (see PRECISION VITICULTURE).

Although the timing of harvest depends on fruit RIPENESS, it also depends on the region, the grape variety, and the type of wine required (Pinot Noir grapes destined for sparkling white wine are invariably picked much earlier than they would be for a still red wine, for example). Harvest can theoretically take place somewhere in the world in every month of the year but typically takes place in autumn (see VINE GROWTH CYCLE): September and October in the northern hemisphere and March and April in the southern hemisphere. In very hot climates, harvest may start earlier in the summer, while at the coolest limits of vine cultivation grapes may be picked when all the leaves have fallen from the vine and there is snow on the ground. Some German EISWEIN is not picked until the January following the official year of harvest (which it must by law carry on the label, no matter when it was picked).

The effects of CLIMATE CHANGE are increasingly seen in earlier harvest dates and HARVEST COMPRESSION. In Australia, for example, picking in the HUNTER VALLEY can start in December and in 2020 the Champagne harvest began in mid August. Most wine regions around the world are on average harvesting around two to three weeks earlier than they were 30 years ago.

Manual harvesting

The traditional method of harvesting, by hand, consists of cutting the STEM of individual bunches and putting the bunches into a suitable container. This method, as opposed to MECHANICAL HARVESTING, can be employed regardless of terrain, row spacing (see VINE DENSITY), and precise vine-TRAINING SYSTEM. It also allows pickers to select individual bunches according to their ripeness and to eliminate unhealthy fruit affected by ROT or DISEASE. Very occasionally pickers may be instructed to leave unripe fruit on the vine, although this is not always easy to determine by the time of harvest.

Occasionally individual berries are harvested, in the case of bunches affected by BOTRYTIS, an operation that is possible only with a very high LABOUR input. This is most famously practised at Ch d'YQUEM and other properties in Sauternes as well as in other vineyards specializing in botrytized sweet wines in SOUTH WEST FRANCE, Austria, Germany (see AUSLESE, BEERENAUSLESE, and TROCKENBEERENAUSLESE), and Hungary, but the technique may also be employed in the production of (necessarily expensive) dry wines when the vineyard has been attacked by less noble rot.

The cost of manual harvesting increases dramatically when yields are low, for particularly widely spaced vines, or on particularly steep vineyards as in the MOSEL.

The efficiency of hand-picking depends on vineyard conditions. If the fruit is at a convenient height and the crop heavy, an experienced picker can harvest up to 2 tonnes/4,400 lbs a day. Output is reduced by worker fatigue or when the fruit is at a less convenient height—close to the ground as in traditional Bordeaux vineyards, for example, or trained on the overhead TRELLIS SYSTEMS of southern Italy, northern Portugal, Argentina, and Chile. Light crops are also particularly expensive to pick by hand, where bunches are small because of the grape variety (GEWÜRZTRAMINER, for example) or because of poor fruit set (see COULURE). In such circumstances, even an experienced picker may have less than 500 kg/1,100 lb to show for a day's work.

Manual harvesting requires little equipment. The stems are cut by small secateurs or hooked-tip knives. The fruit is put into a small container holding perhaps 5 or 10 kg of fruit. This was traditionally (and still is in parts of Europe) a wooden trug, cane basket, or leather hod strapped on to the pickers' backs, but nowadays it is most likely to be an unromantic but lighter and easier-to-clean plastic container which may be emptied at intervals into a larger container for transport to the winery, or field pressing station, typically by tractor. These larger containers, often called 'gondolas' in the New World and holding between 500 kg and 2 tonnes, are passed down the row before being towed to the winery. In many vineyards, the fruit is simply emptied into the back of a trailer, although the shallower the depth of fruit, the less damage it will suffer, and so containers full of grapes are increasingly stacked on trailers for transport to the grape reception area.

The harvest workforce varies from region to region. In much of Europe, picking teams include both experienced locals and casual workers, often students and itinerant workers, even members of the family. Iberia traditionally supplied picking teams that would systematically work their way northwards through Europe from region to region as they successively reached ripeness. Similarly, Australian vineyards of the 1950s and 1960s were traditionally picked by the large numbers of itinerants who moved between the sugar-cane fields of northern Australia and the vineyards of the south. But increased mechanization in the sugar-cane industry has necessitated increased mechanization of the Australian wine industry. In the western United States, the typical grape-picker is Mexican. Wine farms in South Africa enjoy access to relatively inexpensive labour, although since 1994 regulatory protection for rural employees has been strengthened. When in the late 1980s the Iron Curtain was torn down and EU membership raised wages in Spain and Portugal, eastern Europe became an important source of itinerant labour for vineyard owners in northern Europe.

However, finding and employing seasonal workers has become more difficult, due partly to increasing prosperity in these countries and partly to bureaucracy and restrictions on freedom of movement; in Burgundy, for example, some producers are following the example of their counterparts in the New World and turning to companies set up to manage and hire out harvest crews. While this is more expensive, it means a domaine can employ pickers on the days they are needed rather than right through harvest.

Providing this annual influx of workers with accommodation, sustenance, and, often, transport is an increasingly onerous task each harvest. It is said that in many wine regions mechanical harvesting is the direct result of protest by the spouses and children of vineyard owners, to whom much of this annual workload has traditionally fallen.

See also MECHANICAL HARVESTING.

R.E.S. & J.E.H.

Coombe, B. G., and Dry, P. R. (eds.), *Viticulture*, ii: *Practices* (2nd edn, 2006).

Loftus, S., *Puligny-Montrachet: Journal of a Village in Burgundy* (1992).

harvest compression is a feature of many vineyard regions around the world, especially with the pronounced climate warming of the last three decades (see CLIMATE CHANGE). In warm to hot regions in particular, HARVEST starts earlier and is over more quickly. This is a consequence of more varieties having more similar maturity dates, making the task of harvest scheduling more difficult. These problems are exacerbated in the winery, with more fruit being processed in shorter periods, creating pressure on the allocation of appropriate FERMENTATION VESSELS. Detailed phenology studies in Australia have shown that advancement in maturity is related more to earlier VERAISON than to accelerated ripening. R.E.S.

Cameron, W., et al, 'Is advancement of grapevine maturity explained by an increase in the rate of ripening or advancement of veraison?', *Australian Journal of Grape and Wine Research*, 27/3 (2021), 1–14.

Labbé, T., et al., 'The longest homogeneous series of grape harvest dates, Beaune 1354–2018, and its significance for the understanding of past and present climate', *Climate of the Past*, 15 (2019), 1485–1501.

Petrie, P., and Sadras, P., 'Quantifying the advancement and compression of vintage', *Australian and New Zealand Grapegrower & Winemaker*, 628 (2016), 40–1.

harvest traditions celebrate the culmination of a year's hard work in the vineyard and, in areas which have not yet succumbed to MECHANIZATION, encourage the pickers in their back-breaking task.

France

Harvest traditions are at their strongest in France. The church plays a role in many European villages, where a symbolic bunch of grapes is blessed before the harvest and a thanksgiving service held at the end (see also RELIGION). (New World producers such as Robert MONDAVI of California have emulated this tradition.)

Vineyard owners and other members of their families try to be present for the harvest even if they usually work in a distant city. At the end of the harvest a certain amount of horseplay almost inevitably accompanies the picking of the last rows, and one or two pickers end up being thrown into the sticky mass of grapes (a tradition endangered by the increasing use of shallow plastic containers to transport grapes to the cellar).

Traditionally the tractor pulling the final load is decorated with flowers before it drives, horn blaring, to the cellar. On some estates the pickers still offer a bouquet of flowers to the owner and speeches are made. Large or small, almost all estates celebrate the end of harvest with a party, and some regions have their own name for this: *la* PAULÉE in BURGUNDY, *la gerbebaude* in BORDEAUX, and *le cochelet* in CHAMPAGNE.

Most harvest traditions are gastronomic, however, and the major events in a picker's day are the three meals which punctuate it (or four if the *casse-croute*, a second breakfast normally taken in the vines, is counted). In France, the kitchens during the harvest are usually run by women who are part of a family team, helped by other local women who may work in the vines during the rest of the year. For 11 months they cook only for their families and friends, but for one month they must turn themselves into restaurateurs of a special kind. Working in often rudimentary kitchens, they must feed demanding pickers both well and economically. Soups, rabbit dishes, and dishes such as *pot-au-feu*, *coq au vin*, and *blanquettes* are often requested by pickers nostalgic for an era when long, slow cooking was the norm. A harvest would not be a harvest in Burgundy without a *bœuf bourguignon*, for example, and in Bordeaux the bonfires of *sarments*, or vine shoots, on which are grilled steaks and sausages may be kept blazing to form the focus of informal dancing and singing after dinner.

The harvest cook's work is regularly interrupted to administer first aid, and when the cook's long day ends, she (and it is still usually she) is likely to be kept awake by pickers at play. Small wonder that there is something of a revolt among the younger generation of vine-growers' spouses, who may anyway have full-time jobs elsewhere. Caterers are increasingly used, and high unemployment has in some cases substituted, for students in search of a good time, local people who would rather increase their earnings by forgoing lunch. Bureaucratic regulations are creating increasingly onerous paperwork; stricter standards may soon be enforced in respect of the lodgings provided for pickers. These developments are contributing substantially to the substitution of MECHANICAL HARVESTERS for human pickers and, therefore, to the death of harvest traditions.

The menus for each day, handwritten in notebooks every year, enlivened by anecdotal remarks, may, together with the photograph albums kept on many estates, eventually be the only record of harvest traditions. R.H.

Rest of Europe

Harvest traditions are most likely to survive where vineyards are picked by approximately the same people each year, which is why few survive in Italy and Germany, where grapes are increasingly picked by immigrants with no tradition of grape-picking in their families. As mechanization invades a wine region, so harvest traditions retreat, presumably until revived as a public-relations exercise. This means that harvest traditions are more likely to survive where LABOUR costs are relatively low.

A prime example of this has been the DOURO Valley, where PORT is made, although even here rural labour shortages are having an effect. Even in the early 21st century, however, it was still just possible to associate a genuine sense of folk tradition and celebration with the harvest, as some local pickers invade the QUINTAS at which they and their families have traditionally worked every autumn for decades. The increasingly depopulated TRÁS-OS-MONTES region has supplied many of the teams, or *rogas*, of pickers who brought noise, chatter, and traffic to a region marked by its silence the rest of the year.

At a few properties in the Douro, pickers' feet were still expected to provide a more bucolic, gentler, and more effective alternative to the mechanical CRUSHER, or robotic lagar (see FOOT TREADING). Members of the *roga*, or sometimes only its male members, are expected not only to pick the grapes but to make the wine as well. Donning shorts, and with their arms around each others' shoulders, they march methodically backwards and forwards across the granite LAGARES, often thigh-high in sticky purple grapes, to a chant or beat of a drum. Once a floating CAP of skins has visibly been separated from the juice beneath, *liberdade* (liberty) is declared and the march evolves into dancing, traditionally to the sound of an accordion but nowadays, more often than not, to recorded music from a stereo system. Traditionally the leader of the *roga* would present the owner of the farm or winery, the *patrão*, with a decorated vine branch at a final celebratory vintage feast.

New World

Such traditions as have evolved around the harvest, or crush, in the New World tend to be the direct result of having large numbers of people—often from very different backgrounds, doing work unfamiliar to many of them—come together in the open air. The weather conditions, especially the temperature and sunshine, have greatest effect on worker comfort and, thereby, on the development of traditions. In many parts of the New World, harvest can be a time of heavy physical work for moderately low pay under trying conditions. Where the weather is hot, the harvest can start very early in the morning, and meal breaks are short as there is often little opportunity to relax in a hot, dusty, vineyard with little available shade.

Many of the social aspects of harvest are changing with use of the mechanical harvester. One harvester and operator can pick as much in three shifts during the 24 hours as could hundreds of human pickers during the day.

Hanson, R., *Recipes from the French Wine Harvest* (1995).

Hastings River, a warm and humid wine region on the north coast of NEW SOUTH WALES about 400 km/250 miles up the coast from Sydney, has a history of viticulture dating back to 1837, though production restarted only in 1980 after a significant decline. With average annual rainfall of 944 mm/37 in, disease pressure is significant, making mildew-resistant hybrid CHAMBOURCIN an important red variety. In the driest years, Chardonnay, Sémillon, Verdelho, and Cabernet–Merlot blends can be successful. A.R.P.

Haut, French for 'high'. See the rest of the name if there is no relevant entry under H.

Haut-Brion, Château, the most famous property in the GRAVES district in BORDEAUX producing both red and white wines; today, after years of fierce competition, it is run in tandem with Ch La MISSION HAUT-BRION. Manuscripts from the beginning of the 15th century mention extensive vineyards around the LIEU-DIT Aubrion. In 1521 Ch Haut-Brion became the first Bordeaux wine to be named after its TERROIR rather than its owner or parish, and thus it could claim to be the world's first luxury wine BRAND. Jean de Pontac was one of the most important owners of Haut-Brion: as early as 1525, he defined the vineyard as it is today, and he built the château in 1549. His great-nephew Arnaud III de Pontac, Président of the Bordeaux Parliament, invented the 'New French Claret Haut-Brion', a new type of red wine benefiting from ageing, which laid the foundations of great bordeaux. In 1660, the cellar records of the British King Charles II mention that no fewer than 169 bottles of the 'wine of Hobriono' (*sic*) were served at the royal table. The wine was praised by Samuel Pepys, the London diarist, who recorded on 10 April 1663 that he 'drank a sort of French wine called Ho Bryan that hath a good and most particular taste I never met with'. In 1666, the son of Arnaud III de Pontac, François-Auguste, opened a tavern in London called Pontack's Head which soon became 'the most fashionable place in all of London' where luminaries such as Locke, Swift, Defoe, Dryden, and the members of the Royal Society came to dine or buy Haut-Brion.

Thomas JEFFERSON also praised it on his visit to Bordeaux in 1787 as American minister in France. In 1801, Charles-Maurice de Talleyrand Périgord, Minister of Foreign Affairs to Emperor Napoleon I, bought Ch Haut-Brion and used its wines and the talent of the famous chef Antonin Carême, 'king of chefs and chef of kings', to diplomatic ends. In 1855, on the occasion of the Exposition Universelle held in Paris, Ch Haut-Brion was listed as one of four first growths in the famous CLASSIFICATION of Bordeaux wines.

After a further series of not very successful owners in a very difficult time, the château was bought in 1935 by Clarence Dillon, an American banker. Today the property is run by his grandson Prince Robert of Luxembourg, President and CEO since 2008, with his mother, the Duchesse de Mouchy. In 2004, Jean-Philippe Delmas became deputy managing director when his innovative father, Jean-Bernard, retired.

The 49.9 ha/123.3 acres of vineyard are planted with just 42% Cabernet Sauvignon, 46% Merlot, 11% Cabernet Franc, and 1% Petit Verdot. The SECOND WINE was renamed Le Clarence de Haut-Brion (from Ch Bahans-Haut-Brion) in 2007 in honour of Clarence Dillon. About 500 cases of the property's rare dry white Ch Haut-Brion Blanc are produced from a 2.9 ha vineyard planted with 52% Sémillon and 48% Sauvignon Blanc. About 1,000 cases of a second white wine, La Clarté de Haut-Brion, common to both Chx Haut-Brion and La Mission Haut-Brion, are also produced.

In early summer 2011 family-owned Domaine Clarence Dillon purchased Ch Tertre Daugay in St-Émilion and renamed it Ch Quintus. Two years later the neighbouring property, Ch L'Arrosée, was also acquired with the intention of restoring the united properties to their former glory. In 2021 Ch Grand-Pontet was added to Ch Quintus, and a visitor centre and wine shop were opened at Ch Haut-Brion in Bordeaux.

Hautes-Alpes, a rugged region and IGP extending 130 ha/321 acres in the southern foothills of the French Alps. The high ELEVATION (600–1,300 m/2,000–4,265 ft) makes it cooler than neighbouring PROVENCE yet drier than SAVOIE to its other side. While the IGP allows a great number of grape varieties, it is perhaps best known as the homeland of Mollard, a grape making light, fresh reds that was saved from extinction by Marc Allemand, who has been making a varietal example since 1984.

Hautes-Côtes de Beaune and **Hautes-Côtes de Nuits**, sometimes known collectively as the **Hautes-Côtes**, vineyards dispersed in the hills above the escarpment of the Côte d'Or in Burgundy. Most of the production is red wine from Pinot Noir, with some white wine made from Chardonnay or occasionally Pinot Blanc or Pinot Gris, but at ELEVATIONS reaching 500 m/1,640 ft the grapes do not ripen easily. This is also suitable ground for BOURGOGNE ALIGOTÉ, especially as the blackcurrant bushes needed for the production of CASSIS can often be seen growing alongside.

Forty-seven communes are included in the Hautes-Côtes appellations. The most prolific villages include Meloisey, Nantoux, and Échevronne above the Côte de Beaune; and Villars-Fontaine, Magny-lès-Villars, and Marey-lès-Fussey above the Côte de Nuits. There is a good CO-OPERATIVE for the Hautes-Côtes wines located just outside Beaune. Many leading growers in the Côte de Nuits such as the Gros family now also offer affordable wines from the Hautes-Côtes.

See also CÔTE D'OR and map under BURGUNDY.

J.T.C.M.

Haut-Médoc, the higher, southern part of the Médoc district of Bordeaux which includes the world-famous communes of MARGAUX, PAUILLAC, ST-ESTÈPHE, and ST-JULIEN, as well as the less glamorous LISTRAC and MOULIS. The Haut-Médoc AOC applies only to red wines made within its 4,682 ha/11,569 acres. For more details, see MÉDOC.

Haut-Pays, French term meaning 'high country' which was used in the Middle Ages to describe the area upstream of BORDEAUX which produced wine (and had done so for longer than Bordeaux, since at the beginning of the Christian era winemaking spread north-west from Narbonne towards the Atlantic). This included GAILLAC, BERGERAC, Quercy (modern CAHORS), and Nérac (BUZET). The more dependable climate here often produced wines stronger than the light, thin wines then made in the Bordeaux region itself and were seen as a serious commercial threat. The port of Bordeaux penalized them by taxing them heavily and barring them from the port until the region had exported its own wines. See also HUNDRED YEARS WAR.

Haut-Poitou, AOC zone almost due south of SAUMUR in which 90 ha/222 acres of vines on calcareous clay produce crisp red, white, and rosé wines. Whites are mainly Sauvignon Blanc, although up to 40% FIÉ (Sauvignon Gris) is permitted. Reds and rosés are mainly Cabernet Franc with various Gamays and Pinot Noir allowed to make up the rest; Merlot is allowed in red wines. The CO-OPERATIVE at Neuville dominates production.

Hawaii, chain of islands in the Pacific and one of the 50 United States. Owing to the humidity, which encourages FUNGAL DISEASES, the state produces mainly FRUIT WINES, including a pineapple sparkling wine. However, fast-draining VOLCANIC soils and temperate higher ELEVATIONS allow vine-growers some success with CROSSES such as SYMPHONY, as well as VITIS VINIFERA such as Grenache, Syrah, and Malbec. In 2021 the state was awarded its first AVA, Ulupalakua, 29 ha/70 acres ranging from 475 m/1,560 ft to 564 m/1,850 ft in ELEVATION on the south-west slopes of Mount Haleakala on Maui.

Hawke's Bay, first planted by Catholic missionaries in 1851, is the second-largest wine region in NEW ZEALAND, with 4,643 ha/11,473 acres under vine in 2021.

Situated on the east coast of the North Island, it vies with both Marlborough and Nelson each year in the battle for the country's highest sunshine hours. With its temperate MARITIME CLIMATE, the region's growing season accumulates more degree days (see CLIMATE CLASSIFICATION) than any other main winegrowing region, which is why it is one of the few regions that hangs its hat on red Bordeaux blends as well as rich, textural expressions of Chardonnay.

Its complex soils can be simplified down to two main types: CLAYS and GRAVELS. From the 1980s, pockets of less fertile and more free-draining soils across the region's river plains were sought out for viticulture. More recently the cooler inland LIMESTONE-based hills of Central Hawke's Bay have shown potential for Sauvignon Blanc, Pinot Noir, and Pinot Gris.

The subregions of Hawke's Bay can largely be grouped by soil type and MESOCLIMATE. Coastal areas such as Bay View in the northern Esk Valley area and Te Awanga to the south benefit from the cool maritime conditions allowing a long growing season for Chardonnay and Pinot Noir. The free-draining alluvial gravels and stony terraces across the region's four river valleys and plains accommodate the earliest viticultural areas of Meeanee and Taradale as well as premium areas such as Bridge Pa and the country's only trademarked subregion, the Gimblett Gravels. The latter is an 800-ha/1,977-acre area of gravel soils on an ancient riverbed comprising 90% red varieties—primarily Merlot with some Syrah and Cabernet Sauvignon. Its eponymous association of producers formed in 2001 and collaboratively promotes their wines.

While Cabernet Sauvignon has been an important part of Hawke's Bay's history, plantings have declined in recent times to just under 200 ha, from a peak of over 500 ha 20 years ago. It can be challenging to ripen but was lauded as a star performer in the warmer years of 2013, 2014, 2019, and 2020.

Chardonnay and Merlot are the most planted Hawke's Bay varieties with 1,049 ha and 981 ha respectively, while Sauvignon Blanc comes close behind at 886 ha. Historically the top Hawke's Bay reds were Bordeaux-style blends; however, Syrah is now challenging their exalted status. There is arguably still no consistent style, with producers pursuing both perfumed northern RHÔNE-esque examples with little oak influence as well as richer, riper iterations closer to Australian Shiraz. Hawke's Bay Chardonnay tends towards ripe stone fruit and sometimes tropical nuances thanks to the plenitude of the Mendoza CLONE, while Sauvignon Blanc is a softer, fleshier wine than its Marlborough counterpart. It often has a nectarine or stone-fruit character, a useful indicator of regional identity. S.P.-T.

head, or crown, of a vine is the top of the TRUNK where CORDONS branch, or where some SPURS are retained to produce new CANES in cane pruning.

head space, that space in a container holding a liquid that is not taken up by that liquid. In wine containers it is often called the ULLAGE, or ullage space. In large, modern wineries, the head space of stainless-steel tanks is often deliberately filled by an INERT GAS as a preservative measure. Similarly, many BOTTLING lines use inert gas to exclude oxygen from the head space.

head training, a form of VINE TRAINING whereby the trunk has a definite head, or roughly circular knob, consisting of old wood rather than arms of a CORDON. **Head-trained** vines may be subject to CANE PRUNING or SPUR PRUNING (see GOBELET). The head may be anywhere between 40 cm/1.25 ft and 1 m/3.3 ft from the ground. The GUYOT system is a common cane-pruned form of head training. R.E.S.

health, effects of wine consumption on. Until the 18th century, wine played a central role in medical practice, not least because it was safer to drink than most available water, as outlined in MEDICINE. But wine of course contains ALCOHOL, and it and its primary breakdown product ACETALDEHYDE are toxic to the body's tissues. Its contribution to damage to the liver, pancreas, and brain, and to accidents, is well known. Less well known is that the incidence of certain cancers, wasting of nerves and muscles, blood disorders, infections, psoriasis, raised blood pressure, strokes, and infertility increases with heavy consumption. Alcohol consumption during pregnancy can affect the developing foetus, stunting its growth and causing birth defects and behavioural and intellectual problems (termed 'foetal alcohol spectrum disorder'). This has resulted in a proliferation of health warning labels on wine bottles in many countries (see LABELLING).

Since the early 1990s, however, a substantial and increasing body of research has shown that modest consumers have lower mortality than heavy consumers or non-drinkers, suggesting that alcohol consumption (and perhaps especially wine consumption) can have a net beneficial effect on health. The clinical, experimental, and medical evidence to date continues to be so convincing that the link between moderate consumption and reduced risk of heart disease is acknowledged by the World Health Organization in its commentaries on alcohol. Moderate consumption is very generally considered to be 20–30 g/0.7–1 oz alcohol per day for men and 10–20 g/0.35–0.7 oz alcohol per day for women.

Coronary heart disease

The most beneficial effect of wine is its contribution to reduced mortality from coronary heart disease, the western world's major killer. This develops when plaques of cholesterol build up in the arteries supplying the heart muscle. These furred-up arteries cannot supply the heart muscle with enough oxygen, resulting in the pain of angina. Heart attacks happen when blood clots block these narrowed arteries completely, cutting off the oxygen supply. Heavy drinkers develop increased cholesterol levels as well as raised blood pressure, weakened heart muscle, and a susceptibility to potentially fatal abnormal heart rhythms. Given this record, it was not just the temperance movement which believed that moderate consumption must surely be doing some harm. Yet there is now a mass of evidence that those who drink moderately are less likely to develop coronary heart disease and to die from it than either those who drink heavily or those who have never drunk alcohol. Furthermore, it is the alcohol in alcoholic drinks which has been identified as the single most important ingredient in prevention of coronary heart disease.

Alcohol, it seems, moderates the level of inflammatory blood chemicals called cytokines which adversely affect blood cholesterol and blood-clotting proteins. Blood carries LDL (low-density lipoprotein) cholesterol, which forms the plaques which block arteries, and HDL (high-density lipoprotein) cholesterol, which mops them up. Moderate alcohol consumption improves the balance between the harmful and beneficial forms of cholesterol. Blood clots are formed by platelets—small shards of old cells which float harmlessly in the blood until they are chemically triggered to stick together in a tangle of threads of fibrin protein. Alcohol has two anticoagulant effects which make blood less likely to clot in the wrong place. It makes the platelets slightly less sticky, and it reduces the level of fibrin available to form a clot. An added benefit for moderate consumers, and particularly moderate wine consumers, is increased vascular elasticity, enabling a more rapid flow of blood through the arteries and lowering risk of heart and blood pressure problems.

The anticoagulant effect of alcohol lasts less than 24 hours. This may explain why the risk of a heart attack is reduced during the day following a couple of drinks. The traditional wine drinker's glass or two with the evening meal provides a steady, safe level of alcohol. In contrast, the beer or spirit drinker's Saturday night binge leaves him or her temporarily over-anticoagulated (and at increased risk of a stroke due to bleeding) until he or she has metabolized the alcohol, then at increased risk of heart attack until the next night out. Binge drinking of wine carries the same health risk as any other alcoholic drink taken to excess.

Alcohol is not the only compound of cardiovascular significance in wine. Red wine, much more than white, is rich in PHENOLICS, which have antioxidant, anti-blood-clotting, and anti-inflammatory properties. There are hundreds of phenolic compounds in wine, but attention has focused on RESVERATROL. Like alcohol, resveratrol modulates the breakdown of LDL cholesterol in the laboratory and so may help to reduce the formation of plaques in the body. Heart attacks are not the only problem caused by furred-up arteries. They cause peripheral vascular disease, which leads to angina-type pain in the leg muscles when their activity exceeds the ability of the arteries to the legs to provide oxygen. Most strokes are caused by blockages of blood vessels, so it is not surprising that moderate alcohol consumption reduces the risk of strokes. However, the anticoagulant effects of alcohol, which are beneficial if the stroke is caused by a blood clot, are likely to make the stroke worse if it is due to bleeding into the brain.

A growing number of studies conclude that the way alcohol is consumed—the pattern of drinking—is key to potential health benefits. Studies show that regular moderate consumption, predominantly with meals, significantly reduces the risk of a heart attack.

It is therefore likely that it is the combination of alcohol, its phenolic compounds, and the usual consumption pattern of wine (versus that of other alcoholic drinks) that makes wine the most beneficial alcoholic beverage for cardiovascular health. These factors may explain the FRENCH PARADOX. See also FLAVONOLS.

Cancers

Awareness of the influence of lifestyle on cancer risks has stimulated research into the relationship between drinking and cancers. Alcohol consumption increases the risk of cancers of all parts of the digestive tract except the stomach. The link becomes progressively weaker from mouth to rectum. The risk is tripled for cancer of the mouth and throat, and doubled for cancer of the oesophagus. The mucosal surfaces of these organs come into direct contact with imbibed alcohol, and it has been suggested that the risk of developing these cancers is less if the alcohol is consumed with food.

Food and drink passes from the oesophagus to the stomach, and there is good news about alcohol and stomach cancer. Ulcer sufferers were traditionally advised to avoid alcohol lest it irritate the lining of the stomach. However, gastritis, peptic ulcers, and stomach cancer are now known to be strongly associated with infection by the bacterium *Helicobacter pylori*, and a short course of treatment designed to eradicate *H. pylori* is saving many former sufferers a lifetime of treatment and abstinence. Furthermore, studies have shown that moderate wine and beer drinkers are significantly less likely to be infected with *H. pylori* than non-drinkers, possibly due to the anti-microbial effects of alcohol. If moderate consumers are less likely to have *H. pylori* infection, they should have fewer ulcers, a deduction supported by evidence from the US. Recent studies suggest that regular moderate consumption may reduce the chances of infection with *H. pylori* more than occasional consumption of heavier amounts of alcohol. St Paul's advice to 'use a little wine for thy stomach's sake' proves to have been wise.

Drinking alcohol is associated with a modest increase of the risk of cancer of the bowel (colon and rectum). As with cancers of the upper digestive tract, the risk is greater with high consumption of alcohol.

Studies of the incidence of breast cancer show that even the moderate consumption of alcohol is associated with an increase in risk. Four to five drinks per day increase the risk by 50% compared with only one drink per day.

Preliminary studies suggest that moderate alcohol consumption may offer some protection from cancer of the prostate and the kidney and non-Hodgkin's lymphoma, but more evidence is needed to confirm this.

Respiratory problems

SULFITES are produced naturally by FERMENTATION and so occur at low levels (10–50 mg/l) in all wines. Small amounts are also routinely added to most wines as a preservative. Asthmatics who are sensitive to sulfites may experience respiratory problems after drinking wine with concentrations of sulfur dioxide above 45 mg/l. So in most countries, wines containing more than 10 mg/l are labelled accordingly. BIOGENIC AMINES such as HISTAMINE are generally present in low concentrations in wine, but they can contribute to respiratory problems in histamine-allergic or sensitive individuals (see ALLERGIES AND INTOLERANCES), especially if they consume wine together with foods high in histamine such as some cheeses. Wine also contains salicylates that can trigger respiratory problems in salicylate-allergic individuals.

Headaches

Biogenic amines in wine, such as histamine and tyramine, can trigger migraines for some migraine sufferers. Red wine generally contains more biogenic amines that white. It has also been suggested that PHENOLIC compounds could be a trigger. In the test tube phenolics liberate serotonin (5-hydroxytryptamine) from cells; this is the chemical messenger that plays a part in the initiation of migraine.

Additionally, the alcohol in wine and its breakdown product, ACETALDEHYDE, act on the brain. The pain of headaches is referred via pain receptors to the surface of the head from deep structures such as the brain and its related tissues. The headache experienced after consuming alcohol is generally related to blood alcohol concentration (BAC). Alcohol and acetaldehyde readily diffuse from the blood into the fluids of the brain and spinal cord where they directly irritate the brain's cells and tissues, causing pain at the front surface of the head. The more wine consumed, the higher the BAC, the more the brain will be irritated, and the more severe the headache.

Dementia

The intoxified brain does not function well (whatever its owner may temporarily believe), and the deleterious effect on intellectual function of long-term assault with heavy alcohol is well known. It comes as a pleasant relief to find that moderate wine consumers have improved cognitive function compared with both heavy wine consumers and non-drinkers, and they are less likely to develop dementias such as Alzheimer's disease. Studies suggest that RESVERATROL may additionally be 'dementia-protective' by increasing the brain's blood flow as well as directly benefiting the cells and tissues of the brain.

Musculo-skeletal problems

Excessively heavy drinkers are prone to fracture their bones such as the hips and vertebrae; a consequence of the effects of too much alcohol on their bone density and structure in addition to an increased rate of falls. Alcohol has been shown to have directly damaging effects on cellular bone formation as well as indirectly affecting the pancreas and cytokine and endocrine systems, which also influence cellular bone formation. However, studies show an association between moderate consumption of alcohol, and in particular wine, and improvement in bone density. Men and post-menopausal women at risk of osteoporosis may find one or two glasses of wine a day beneficial rather than harmful.

Rheumatoid arthritis has been shown to be less common in those who take moderate alcohol in any form, potentially from alcohol's anti-inflammatory actions, although any improvement in sufferers' symptoms may be due to the pleasure of a glass of wine rather than its physiological effects.

Diabetes mellitus

Although diabetics are obliged to watch carefully what they eat and drink, alcohol taken with a meal does not substantially alter their blood sugar level and is therefore an appropriate element in a diabetic's diet. As the World Health Organization acknowledges, moderate consumers of alcohol, and particularly wine drinkers, have a significantly lower risk of developing Type-2 diabetes mellitus than heavy drinkers and non-drinkers. Type-2 diabetes is the form of diabetes which typically develops in middle age and is usually treatable with diet and tablets. Type-2 diabetes is due not so much to lack of insulin but to decreased response to it. Research shows that moderate drinkers are more sensitive to insulin than non-drinkers, probably because alcohol moderates the effect of the cytokines, which appear to contribute to the development of Type-2 diabetes.

Gastrointestinal problems

As already described, alcohol is associated with an increase in the incidence of all gastrointestinal cancers except those of the stomach. But wine is more active against the bacteria that cause travellers' diarrhoea than bismuth, another traditional and distinctly less palatable remedy. More encouraging news: moderate drinkers are at reduced risk of developing gallstones.

Sensible drinking

Health authorities in many countries have disseminated 'low risk' or 'sensible drinking levels'; these suggested maxima for personal consumption of alcohol are usually expressed in 'units', or STANDARD DRINKS, of alcohol, though there is wide variation between what constitutes a unit and how many of them may safely be consumed.

These limits are at best only a rough guide as individuals' reactions to alcohol must always be taken into consideration when assessing recommended consumption levels. Sex, age, build, genetic make-up, state of health, drinking with or without food, and drug intake all affect the way alcohol is metabolized. For instance, women, regardless of their weight or size, absorb relatively more alcohol glass for glass than men because of differences in levels of stomach enzymes, their lower body water content meaning that alcohol is more concentrated in their tissues. They also break down alcohol relatively more slowly than men because of differences in levels of liver enzymes and, if they are also taking the contraceptive pill and/or other breakdown competing medications, they eliminate alcohol more slowly. This may explain why women who drink in excess of the recommended daily units experience significantly greater risks of poor health outcomes than men who do likewise. Additionally, women's tissues are more susceptible to the damaging effects of alcohol. Conversely, it appears that the relationship between moderate consumption and better general health is stronger for women.

Aside from any specific health benefits, it emerges that self-reported health—a good predictor of all-cause mortality—is best for moderate consumers, and especially for moderate wine consumers. Indeed, in 2011 the US Center for Disease Control and Prevention proposed that moderate alcohol consumption was one of four healthy lifestyle behaviours related to a lower mortality risk, along with not smoking, eating a healthy diet, and physical activity. The mortality risk for those who also consumed alcohol was significantly lower than for those exhibiting only the three other behaviours. This observation has subsequently been seen in many more countries. And there is a benefit that the studies of mortality cannot identify. A final word which won't appear in studies of mortality: the healthy can enjoy a drink, but for those whose lives are restricted by chronic disease a glass of wine may be one of the few pleasures left. That is a substantial health benefit. J.H.H. & C.S.S.

Baglietto, L., et al., 'Average volume of alcohol consumed, type of beverage, drinking pattern and the risk of death from all causes', *Alcohol and Alcoholism*, 41/6 (2006), 664–1.

Chiva-Blanch, G., et al., 'Effects of wine, alcohol and polyphenols on cardiovascular disease risk factors: evidence from human studies', *Alcohol and Alcoholism*, 48/3 (2013), 270–7.

Ford, E. S., et al., 'Low-risk lifestyle behaviors and all-cause mortality: Findings from the National Health and Nutrition Examination Survey III Mortality Study', *American Journal of Public Health*, 101/10 (2011), 1922–9.

Jani, B. D., et al., 'Association between patterns of alcohol consumption (beverage type, frequency and consumption with food) and risk of adverse health outcomes: a prospective cohort study', *BMC Medicine*, 19/8 (2021).

Koch, M., et al., 'Alcohol consumption and risk of dementia and cognitive decline among older adults with or without mild cognitive impairment', *JAMA Network Open*, 2/9 (2019).

Ma, H., et al., 'Alcohol consumption levels as compared with drinking habits in predicting all-cause mortality and cause-specific mortality in current drinkers', *Mayo Clinic Proceedings*, 96/7 (2021).

Neuenschwander M., et al., 'Role of diet in type 2 diabetes incidence: umbrella review of meta-analyses of prospective observational studies', *BMJ*, 366 (2019).

Rehm, J., et al., 'Alcohol use and dementia: a systematic scoping review', *Alzheimer's Research & Therapy*, 11 (2019).

Simons, L. A., et al., 'Lifestyle factors and risk of dementia: Dubbo Study of the elderly', *Medical Journal of Australia*, 184/2 (2006), 68–70.

Stockley, C. S., 'Is it merely a myth that alcoholic beverages such as red wine can be cardioprotective?', *Journal of Science of Food and Agriculture*, 92/9 (2012), 1815–21.

Heathcote, temperate Australian wine region in the Central Victoria Zone, cooled somewhat by the Mount Camel Range. This expanding region continues to diversify beyond the rich, earthy Shiraz upon which its reputation is built and which lured the likes of northern Rhône growers Alain Graillot and CHAPOUTIER. See VICTORIA.

heat stress affects vines when air temperatures are high. Very high daytime temperatures, of more than 40 °C/104 °F, cause the vine to 'shut down', or virtually cease PHOTOSYNTHESIS, as the ENZYMES responsible can no longer work. High temperatures also lead to WATER STRESS, especially when accompanied by bright sunshine, low humidity, and strong, dry winds. High temperatures cause fast RESPIRATION in vines, and this leads to, for example, low levels of MALIC ACID in mature fruit in hot regions. VARIETAL character and red COLOUR in grapes are also depressed by high temperatures. Australian research into the physiological impact of CLIMATE CHANGE has shown that, in a biochemical sense, sugar and ANTHOCYANIN accumulation in ripening berries is 'decoupled' by elevated temperatures. Some researchers claim that even more moderate daytime temperatures, in excess of only 25 °C, can depress colour formation and varietal flavour expression. R.E.S.

Sadras, V. O., and Maran, M. A., 'Elevated temperature decouples anthocyanins and sugars in berries of Shiraz and Cabernet Franc', *Australian Journal of Grape and Wine Research*, 18 (2012), 115–22.

Spayd, S. E., et al., 'Separation of sunlight and temperature effects on the composition of *vitis vinifera* cv. Merlot berries', *American Journal of Enology and Viticulture*, 53 (2002), 171–82.

heat summation, a computation involving addition of mean temperatures over the growing season that forms part of many systems of CLIMATE CLASSIFICATION.

heat-treated vines, vines which have undergone **heat treatment**, or THERMOTHERAPY, to eliminate virus disease. Not to be confused with HOT-WATER TREATMENT.

heatwave, a period of two or more consecutive days of abnormally hot weather. Such conditions can have severe and adverse effects on grapevines and field workers. For the former, WATER STRESS dominates the plant's physiology: leaves wilt and STOMATA close as the vine is unable to take up sufficient water to meet TRANSPIRATION needs. Leaves and fruit experience high and damaging temperatures, especially if also exposed to direct SUNLIGHT. Where possible and permitted, the grower should provide adequate water by irrigation when a heatwave is imminent. See also SUNBURN. R.E.S.

hectare, common agricultural measurement of area equivalent to 100 ares, 10,000 sq m, or 2.47 acres.

hedging. See TRIMMING.

Heida, Swiss-German synonym for SAVAGNIN BLANC and a speciality of Visperterminen.

Helfensteiner is famous principally as a parent of DORNFELDER, the more successful German red-wine CROSS. The cross of FRÜHBURGUNDER × TROLLINGER has all but disappeared, even from WÜRTTEMBERG.

helicopters are more expensive than fixed-wing aircraft, which limits their application to viticulture. Their manœuvrability is a bonus, however. They are particularly useful for crop SPRAYING, and the turbulence created by the rotors helps the spray to penetrate, although there may be complications where individual landholdings are small. They are commonly used as airborne WIND MACHINES in New Zealand and very occasionally in Europe to stir up cold, dense air just above the vineyard surface with warmer air above to prevent spring FROST DAMAGE. It is not uncommon, for instance, to have helicopters on standby when the risk of frost is high. On occasion they have been used in an attempt to dry excess moisture off vine leaves and bunches immediately after heavy RAINFALL at HARVEST.

Hemel-en-Aarde. See WALKER BAY.

hen and chicken. See MILLERANDAGE.

Henderson, Dr Alexander (1780–1863), Scotsman who qualified as a doctor and then moved to London and contributed to a wide range of publications, including the *Encyclopaedia Britannica*. After visiting the wine regions of France, Germany, and Italy, he wrote *The History of Ancient and Modern Wines*, which was published in 1824 (eight years after JULLIEN but nine years before REDDING). Some of the most useful aspects of his book reflect some aspects of his medical training: his observations on the art of wine TASTING.

Henkell Freixenet, world's biggest producer of sparkling wine since the German-based company Henkell acquired Freixenet, the largest producer of TRADITIONAL METHOD sparkling wine and most significant exporter of CAVA from Spain. Freixenet has four production centres in San Sadurní d'Anoia—Freixenet SA, Segura Viudas SA, Castellblanch SA, and Torrelavit SA—as well as wineries in a number of DOP regions around Spain: Solar Viejo in Rioja, Morlanda in Priorat, Garbó in Montsant,

Valdubón in Ribera del Duero, and Vionta in Rías Baixas. The combined production of Cava alone is now more than 140 million bottles per year. Best-known brands are the medium-dry Carta Nevada, launched in 1941, and Cordon Negro, a brut Cava in a distinctive, frosted black bottle. Freixenet's overseas interests include the Bordeaux NÉGOCIANT Yvon Mau, Henri Abelé in Champagne, the Wingara Wine Group and Katnook Estate in Australia, Gloria Ferrer in the CARNEROS district of California, Finca Doña Dolores, a sparkling wine estate in MEXICO, and Finca Ferrer in the Uco Valley of Mendoza in Argentina.

Henriques, Justino. See JUSTINO'S.

Henty, particularly cool Australian wine region in the Western Victoria Zone (see VICTORIA) with only about a dozen wineries. Pioneered as a source for sparkling wine grapes, it also produces fine TABLE WINES, especially Riesling from the likes of Crawford River.

herbaceous, TASTING TERM for the leafy or grassy aroma of crushed green leaves or freshly cut grass. **Herbaceousness** is generally considered a defect only when present in excess (although American tasters tend to be much less tolerant of it than, for example, the British). Wines made from the produce of SAUVIGNON BLANC, SÉMILLON, CABERNET SAUVIGNON, CABERNET FRANC, or MERLOT vines which failed to ripen fully are often excessively herbaceous. In general, the younger the vines, the greater their VIGOUR; and the earlier the grapes are picked, the more pronounced the herbaceousness. One cause of vegetative herbaceous aromas, particularly in wines of Sauvignon Blanc and Cabernet Sauvignon, is the presence of METHOXYPYRAZINES originating from the grape; see also FLAVOUR COMPOUNDS. Another source of herbaceousness is six-carbon-atom leaf aldehydes.

Numerous investigations have shown that they, and the corresponding six-carbon-atom ALCOHOLS, derive from linoleic and linolenic, which are both fatty acids found in plant leaves and in the fruit. These decompose rapidly once the grape berry is crushed to yield hexanal, hexenal, and the related unsaturated alcohols, all six-carbon-atom compounds which can react further during FERMENTATION to produce a wide range of flavour compounds which are responsible for the aroma called herbaceous. Another reason a wine may taste herbaceous is from vine leaves inadvertently crushed with the grapes (see MOG). Early MECHANICAL HARVESTERS were particularly prone to do this, and the grapes were often so mangled that it was impossible to separate the wet leaves from them. Wines made from such a blend would also not surprisingly be high in leaf aldehydes and taste distinctly leafy or herbaceous, a problem accentuated when such mechanical harvesters are used on relatively young vineyards. More sophisticated machine harvesters have reduced leaf contamination considerably. P.J.W.

Herbemont, dark-skinned *Vitis aestivalis* × *Vitis cinerea* HYBRID grown in Brazil because of its resistance to FUNGAL DISEASES.

herbicides, AGROCHEMICALS applied to vineyards to control the growth of WEEDS. They may be either pre-emergent (or residual) or post-emergent (knockdown). The latter group comprises two types, contact and systemic herbicides. Residual herbicides act against germinating seedlings of the weeds, while post-emergent herbicides damage growing weeds. Typically, herbicides are applied only to the strip of ground directly under the vine, and weeds or COVER CROPS growing between the rows are controlled by TILLAGE or mowing. Herbicides are used even between rows in some vineyard regions, though there can be risks of soil erosion or loss of water infiltration without the ORGANIC MATTER produced by plant growth in this zone.

In areas of winter rainfall, a contact or systemic spray is typically applied in late autumn to early winter, followed by a pre-emergent herbicide in the early spring. In regions with summer rainfall, or for irrigated areas, further contact or systemic sprays may be needed to control weeds that grow during the growing season. Most herbicides used in vineyards are low-hazard chemicals which present no danger to the operator (see AGROCHEMICALS). Many of the knockdown chemicals are inactivated by soil and so leave no soil RESIDUES.

Continued use of some herbicides leads to resistance by some weed species, so-called 'escape' weeds, which were previously suppressed by the herbicide. Although herbicides are relatively inexpensive, their use can cause high soil surface temperatures, preventing vine root growth near the surface, and loss of organic matter, so that there may be fewer EARTHWORMS and a loss of soil biodiversity. Some herbicides can even damage vines, either by wetting vine leaves inadvertently or when herbicides are leached into the rootzone, as can happen with young vines, sandy soils, and irrigation.

Concern about environmental pollution as a result of herbicide use has been growing, and vine-growers are more frequently substituting undervine ploughing for herbicide use—helped by the increasing sophistication of machinery for this type of tillage (see WEED CONTROL). Glyphosate, one of the most controversial herbicides, has been widely used in vineyards for many years but is being banned for some uses in some regions, for example inter-row use in France from 2022. Alternative control methods such as the use of electric currents, heat or hot foam are not yet proven. R.E.S.

heritage clones, term used particularly in parts of the New World with a relatively long history of vine-growing, such as California and Australia, for CUTTINGS from particularly historic vines. Examples in Australia are those from century-old UNGRAFTED VINES which may be traced back to early imports into the colony from pre-PHYLLOXERA Europe. They are typically virus-free, having been exported from Europe before the introduction of the GRAFTING that is known to spread VIRUS DISEASE. In California such selections as Calera, Mt. Eden, Swan Pinot Noir, and Rudd and Wente Chardonnay CLONES are regarded as part of the state's viticultural heritage. The Abel Pinot Noir clone, said to have been imported illegally from DOMAINE DE LA ROMANÉE-CONTI in Burgundy, was planted in New Zealand in the 1970s, having been confiscated by Malcolm Abel, who happened to be both a customs officer and a winemaker. In Western Australia, the complex history of the revered Gingin Chardonnay clone, imported into Australia in 1957 from an old block at DAVIS, has only recently been elucidated thanks to the identification of clonal genetic markers.

Roach, M. J., et al., 'Origin of Chardonnay clones with historical significance in Australia and California', *Australian Journal of Grape and Wine Research*, 26/4 (2020).

heritage varieties. See INDIGENOUS VARIETIES.

Hermitage, the most famous northern RHÔNE appellation of all, producing extremely limited quantities of seriously long-lived reds and about one-third as much full-bodied dry white wine, which some believe is even more distinguished. Although the appellation is only the size of a large Bordeaux estate, Hermitage was one of France's most famous wines in the 18th and 19th centuries when the name alone was sufficient to justify prices higher than any wine other than a FIRST GROWTH bordeaux (which were sometimes strengthened by the addition of some Hermitage until the mid 19th century). The origin of the name 'Hermitage' is not so much shrouded in mystery as obscured by many conflicting legends, most of them concerning a hermit, *ermite* in French. Not least of the puzzles is how and when Ermitage acquired its H (dropped for some modern bottlings, notably by CHAPOUTIER), although there was no shortage of English-speaking enthusiasts of the wine in the 18th century (including Thomas JEFFERSON). The first recorded mention of Hermitage in English was in Thomas Shadwell's 1680 play *The Woman-Captain*, 'Vin de Bon, Vin Celestine, and Hermitage, and all the Wines upon the fruitful Rhône'. These wines were also a great favourite with the Russian imperial court, but the economic upheavals of the first half of the 20th century affected Hermitage as much as any Rhône appellation. While the surrounding appellation CROZES-HERMITAGE has, like most of the Rhône Valley, seen considerable changes and extension over the last 50 years, Hermitage is a constant, give or take a winemaking tweak or two.

There are 138 ha/341 acres of vines on the hill of Hermitage, which almost pushes the town of Tain l'Hermitage below into the Rhône (see map under RHÔNE). The hill itself is built around a section of granite that was once shorn from the Massif Central by the Rhône, which now constitutes around 25% of its mass (its western flank) on to which other types of rock have fused and bonded during successive geological ages. This steep, south-facing slope exists thanks to a brief kink in the river when the Rhône flows briefly west to east. SOIL EROSION is a frequent problem here, and TERRACES are necessary in the steepest sections.

It is not surprising that such a celebrated vineyard has long been divided into various LIEUX-DITS, all with their own soil types and reputations for wine types. There are 20 officially recognized, the most famous of which are at the western granitic end of the hill. Les Bessards has a topsoil of sandy gravel on GRANITE and produces some of the most linear and intense wines. Le Méal produces richer wines from a soil with more LIMESTONE and bigger stones towards the top of the slope, where L'Hermite is crowned with a small stone chapel owned by Paul Jaboulet Aîné and has more SAND and fine LOESS over granite. CLAY and large stones predominate in the lower *lieux-dits* of Les Gréffieux and Les Dionnières. Other famous CLIMATS include Les Beaumes, Maison Blanche, Péléat, Les Murets, and Les Rocoules. Although white and red grapes are planted all over the hill, some of the finest white Hermitage comes from higher vineyards.

Producers such as Jean-Louis Chave, the modest master of Hermitage, delight in blending the produce of holdings all over the hill to produce a complex, well-balanced expression of each vintage. Other producers such as Chapoutier and Ferraton prefer to bottle *lieux-dits* separately in order to illustrate their individual characters.

Unlike CÔTE RÔTIE upriver, red Hermitage is in practice made from pure Syrah (although the AOC regulations permit the addition of up to 15% white grapes). The wine is typically very deeply coloured, full-bodied, and concentrated, with a robust tannic structure. They usually start to show their best at around 20 years after vintage, and the best can age for 50 years or more.

White Hermitage, made from the MARSANNE and/or ROUSSANNE, is typically very full in BODY, and some of the more serious examples such as Chave's and Chapoutier L'Ermite or De l'Orée are among the world's longest-living dry white wines. Both red and white are typically matured in small and medium-sized oak barrels, usually with at least some new oak, and whites typically undergo MALOLACTIC CONVERSION.

In very ripe years, a few producers, notably Jean-Louis Chave, Paul Jaboulet Aîné, and Cave de Tain, still make tiny amounts of sweet white VIN DE PAILLE.

Hermitage has also been used as a synonym for SHIRAZ in Australia, where, for example, PENFOLDS Grange was originally called Penfolds Grange Hermitage. Hermitage was also the historic South African synonym for CINSAUT and is sometimes used in Switzerland for Marsanne.

M.C.W.

Herodotus, prolific ancient Greek writer. The *Histories* of Herodotus (490/480–425 BCE), a native of Halicarnassus in Asia Minor, are not a history in the modern sense: the Greek word *historia* means 'an investigation'. Herodotus' main subject is the conflict between the Greeks and the Persians, and as such his book is history; but it is also an investigation into the geography and anthropology of the east in Herodotus' own day, for as a young man he had travelled widely in the Greek-speaking world and in Egypt and Africa.

Forming part of Herodotus' descriptions of the customs of foreign nations are some intriguing observations about wine and DRUNKENNESS. He says that the Assyrians use palm-wood casks to transport wine, in boats built in Armenia, down the Euphrates (1. 194). In fact, Herodotus' curiosity concerns the construction of the boats: their cargo is mentioned in an aside and he expresses no surprise at the Assyrians' use of palm-wood BARRELS instead of AMPHORAE. He has just told us that the date palm supplies the people with food, honey, and wine and that Assyria is the world's largest producer of grain. The country does not grow vines (1. 193) but, as we know from other sources, Babylon imported wine from ARMENIA. This is probably what the casks contained: with date palms growing all around, transporting fermented date juice would not have made sense. See also MESOPOTAMIA.

All of Book 2 and the beginning of Book 3 are taken up with Herodotus' description of Egypt before he goes on to relate the Persian conquest of that country. He states that the Egyptians have no wine made of grapes but drink one made from barley (2. 81). This cannot be true, for we know that the vine was grown there in the 5th century BCE. Egyptian wine may have been too scarce, however, for Herodotus to have come across it on his travels. Egypt certainly imported wine from Greece and PHOENICIA, as Herodotus mentions (3. 8). He says that it came in earthenware jars and that, when the wine had been finished, the mayor of the town had to collect the empty jars and send them to Memphis, where they would be filled with water and sent to the Syrian desert. This system was devised by the Persians immediately after they had conquered Egypt so that they could reach Egypt through the Syrian desert without risking death through thirst.

When the Persians have subjugated the Egyptians, the king, the megalomaniac Cambyses, marches against the Ethiopians. The expedition is a disaster, and the Ethiopians recognize the Persians' superiority in one respect only: they have wine, and that is the reason for their longevity (3. 23). But Cambyses is too fond of it, and when he is told so by a court official he wrongly deduces that the Persians regard this as the cause of his madness (3. 35), which, along with his cruelty, seems to have been congenital (3. 38). Wine can cause madness, though: Cleomenes, king of Sparta, went mad and died as a result of drinking wine unmixed with WATER, a nasty habit he had picked up from those notorious drunkards the Scythians (6. 85). Only a barbarian would drink unmixed wine. The Persians are all great drinkers of wine, and their frequent drunkenness explains one of the strangest of their customs. The sensible part is that any decision they take when they are drunk they reconsider when they are sober. But the opposite also holds: any decision taken when they are sober has to be reconsidered when they are drunk (1. 135). Far from regarding drunkenness as undesirable and immoderate behaviour, the Persians, if Herodotus is to be trusted, viewed it as an altered state of consciousness that is as valuable as sobriety. H.M.W.

Herodotus, *The Histories*, trans. Aubrey de Sélincourt, rev. A. R. Burn (1972).

Wilson, H., *Wine and Words in Classical Antiquity and the Middle Ages* (2003).

Heroldrebe is the marginal dark-berried GERMAN CROSS to which the prolific breeder August Herold put his name. This PORTUGIESER × LEMBERGER cross yields regularly and prolifically, about 140 hl/ha (8 tons/acre), but ripens so late that it is suitable only for Germany's warmer regions, particularly the Pfalz. Total plantings had fallen to 90 ha/222 acres by 2020. It spawned DORNFELDER.

Herzegovina. See BOSNIA AND HERZEGOVINA.

Hesiod (*c*.700 BCE), the earliest agricultural writer of ancient GREECE, wrote *Works and Days*. Most of this is homely advice for the farmer: 'Be sparing of the middle of the cask, but when you open it, and at the end drink all you want; it's not worth saving dregs.' He is the first writer to tell of simple rustic pleasures: 'I love a shady rock and Bibline wine [from BYBLOS], a cake of cheese, and goat's milk, and some meat of heifers pastured in the woods, uncalved, of first-born kids. Then I may sit in the shade and drink the shining wine, and eat my fill, and turn my face to meet the fresh west wind, and pour three times an offering from the spring which always flows, unmuddied, streaming down, and make my fourth LIBATION one of wine.' Hesiod gives the time for the grape HARVEST as 'when Orion and the dog star [Sirius] move into the mid sky'. H.H.A.

Hessische Bergstrasse. The northern vineyards on the western slopes of Germany's Odenwald constitute Germany's smallest official wine region, comprising 463 ha/1,100 acres. As of 2019, 40% was planted with RIESLING and can yield impressive dry wines. The largest and most prestigious estate is the Hessische Staatsweingüter (known nowadays for their fabled headquarters as KLOSTER EBERBACH) while a majority of the region's growers deliver their crops to the CO-OPERATIVE in Heppenheim known as Bergsträsser Winzer. D.S.

Heuriger, derived from the word for 'today' but signifying by implication 'this season', or 'the latest', is an AUSTRIAN institution whose social dimensions extend far beyond the only weeks-old wine so described. Emperor Josef II in 1784 formally established the right of Austrian winegrowers to dispense their young wines by the glass (along with a rudimentary repast) at establishments whose function was signified by the hanging of bush-like bundles of evergreens over the door, for which reason such an establishment is still referred to within Austria as a *Buschenschank*. The still-cloudy, often only partially fermented young wine is variously known as Staubiger ('dusty one'), FEDERWEISSER, or Sturm ('storm'). Groups of Heurigen with their rows of tiny press houses at the edge of a village or its vineyards are prevalent throughout the former Hapsburg Empire, and within Austria many of these still double as dispensaries. Many top Austrian wine estates dispense tavern-style year-round, at least on weekends, out of economic necessity. The Heurigen of Austria's thirsty capital Vienna (WIEN) and of the adjacent THERMENREGION are especially numerous and seasonally frenetic. D.S.

higher alcohols. See FUSEL OIL.

High Valley. California AVA. See LAKE COUNTY.

hillside vineyards. Even in ancient ROME it was said *Bacchus amat colles*, or BACCHUS loves the hills, suggesting that hillside vineyards have long been regarded as a source of high-quality wine.

This is partly because hillside soils are typically shallow, so that vineyard VIGOUR is relatively low, a factor commonly associated with higher wine quality. Over millennia, topsoil tends to be washed down the hillsides and accumulates on the valley floors. Vines planted there will typically be more vigorous, as the soils are deeper and the roots will be able to reach more water and nutrients.

Hillside vineyards: the warmth received by direct radiation on the vineyard depends on the elevation of the sun combined with the inclination of the vineyard towards the sun. The elevation of the sun controls the thickness of the atmosphere (an absorbing medium) through which the radiation passes. The inclination of the vineyard is independent of this variation.

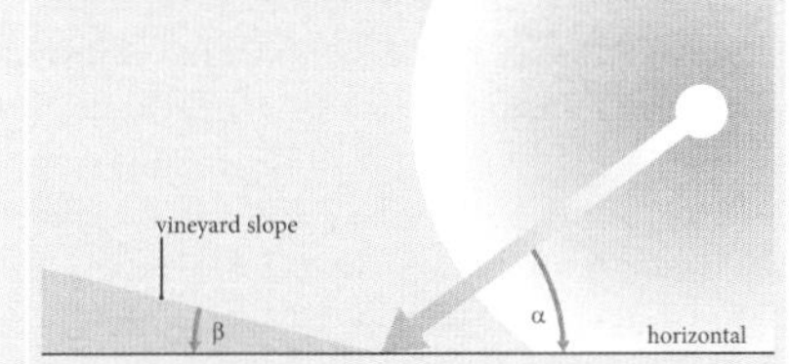

$I = k \sin\alpha + q \sin\beta$

Where I = Intensity of radiation received in vineyard
k and q = constants
α = angular elevation of sun
β = angle of inclination of the vineyard to the horizontal along a meridian

Vines may also be planted on hillsides for reasons of MESOCLIMATE. Hillsides are less prone to FROST because cold air can drain freely away at night (see AIR DRAINAGE and TOPOGRAPHY). If the slopes face the equator, they receive more sunshine during the day and are warmer. In hotter regions, vineyards may be planted on hillsides to take advantage of cooler temperatures at higher ELEVATIONS.

Hillside vineyard sites have their drawbacks, including SOIL EROSION, and in California's NAPA Valley there are strict regulations to avoid erosion. Working on steep slopes is particularly tiring: productivity is affected, and the costs are higher. In most vineyards of the world, rows run up and down the slopes. Where the slopes are too steep for tractors, as in the CÔTE RÔTIE, parts of the MOSEL Valley, and SWITZERLAND, everything must be done by hand or by machines winched down into the vineyards. Where rows run across the slopes, the vineyard is normally laid out in TERRACES, as in Portugal's DOURO Valley or France's hill of HERMITAGE, to both protect against erosion and facilitate mechanization. R.E.S.

Hilltops, moderately cool, high-ELEVATION wine region situated at 450 m/1,476 ft in the south-western slopes of the Great Dividing Range in NEW SOUTH WALES. With red wine grapes covering 80% of its 591 ha/1,460 acres in 2020, Hilltops is best known for fragrant, elegant, spicy Shiraz and classic, well-structured Cabernet Sauvignon. A host of other red varieties including Nebbiolo, Barbera, Corvina, Sangiovese, Grenache, and Tempranillo are also gaining traction. A.R.P.

hippocras, popular medieval FLAVOURED WINE.

histamine, a small organic nitrogenous molecule responsible for ALLERGIC and allergy-like reactions, is thought to play a central role in certain people's reactions to wine. A better-known example involving this mechanism is scombroidosis, a type of food poisoning due to fish spoilage. Histamine in wine is chiefly produced by the decarboxylation of histidine (an amino acid) to histamine by certain microbes, particularly some strains of LACTIC ACID BACTERIA such as *Pediococcus* and *Lactobacillus*.

Wine ANALYSIS has demonstrated that typical histamine concentration in wine is <5 mg/l in whites and <10 mg/l in reds, though some styles, such as wines with no added (or late-added) SULFUR DIOXIDE, may contain higher concentrations. Low levels or reduced function of diamine oxidase, the enzyme which breaks down histamine, in some individuals may result in intolerance of wine containing even these levels of histamine. Ethanol itself inhibits amine metabolism, thus higher alcohol content might worsen this effect. See also BIOGENIC AMINES and ALLERGIES AND INTOLERANCES. D.A.D.

Maintz, L., and Novak, N., 'Histamine and histamine intolerance', *American Journal of Clinical Nutrition*, 85/5 (2007), 1185–96.
Parker-Thomson, S., 'What is the relationship between the use of sulphur dioxide and biogenic amine levels in wine?', *Institute Masters of Wine* (2021). www.mastersofwine.org/wp-content/uploads/2021/02/Sophie-Parker-Thomson-MW-What-is-the-Relationship-Between-the-Use-of-Sulphur-Dioxide-and-Biogenic-Amine-Levels-in-Wine.pdf

Historic Vineyard Society was formed in CALIFORNIA in 2011 to preserve the state's rich heritage of old vines by carefully assembling a registry of those 50 years old and older. In 2022, the non-profit organization listed 159 vineyards, including many dating to the late 1800s, such as Bechthold in LODI and Bedrock in SONOMA.

Hochgewächs, an ancient but little-used approbation for German wines meeting higher standards than the minima set for QUALITÄTSWEIN but not qualifying for a PRÄDIKAT.

Hochschule Geisenheim University. See GEISENHEIM UNIVERSITY.

hock, traditional generic English term for (white) Rhenish wines, from the RHINE regions of GERMANY, sometimes for the wines of Germany in general. In 20th-century Britain it typically referred to a simple QUALITÄTSWEIN, and it was by no means uncommon for the same wine to be offered as Hock to a gentlemen's club and LIEBFRAUMILCH to a supermarket buyer.

The term is a contraction of 'hockamore', an English rendering of the adjective

'Hochheimer', denoting wines from the important wine centre of Hochheim on the river Main just west of Frankfurt (see RHEINGAU).

The earliest firm reference in English occurs in Thomas D'Urfey's play *Madam Fickle; or, The Witty False One* in 1676: 'Here's a glass of excellent old Hock.' The *Oxford English Dictionary* gives a first reference in 1625 in John Fletcher's play *The Chances*, but this depends on a corrupt reading of 'hock' for 'hollock', a light red wine. However, it is likely that the term was already current in England by the 17th century, for its use is closely linked to the growth in popularity of Rhenish and Main wines, which began to supplant the wines of ALSACE in export markets after 1500 (see GERMAN HISTORY).

At the outset, 'hock' appears to have described only wines from the middle Rhine: in an address to the Royal Society in 1680, Anthony van Leeuwenhoeck, the inventor of the microscope, spoke of 'vinum Mosellanicum, vinum Rijncoviense and vinum Rhenanum, quod vulgo hogmer dicitur' (called 'hogmer' in the vernacular). In 1703, Johann Valentin Kauppers in his *De natura . . . vini Rhenani* could still distinguish between 'Rhine wines' and wines from the Rheingau, but in the course of the 18th century hock became the general designation of German wines sold in Britain. T.S.

Holland. See NETHERLANDS.

Homer, writer(s) in ancient GREECE of the epic poems the *Iliad* and the *Odyssey*. Homeric poems are usually dated to the 8th century BCE, and wine features regularly in both. See also CLASSICAL TEXTS.

home winemaking, small-scale domestic activity indulged in for fun, to save money, or both. Because such wine attracts no DUTY, it is especially popular in countries with high excise duties. Some countries with no or limited viticulture such as Britain have a long tradition of making FRUIT WINES and wines based on plants, flowers, or even root vegetables. The term 'country wines' is used to cover wines made from anything but grapes.

Home winemaking became popular in the United States during PROHIBITION, when making an annual allowance of 100 gal/3.75 hl of wine per adult, up to a maximum of 200 gal/7.5 hl per household (a limit that still applies in the US), was the only legal way the average American household could procure alcoholic drink. Technology was primitive, and tales of exploding bottles were common, but the pursuit was so popular that vineyard acreage in California doubled between 1919 and 1926.

After Repeal, home winemaking continued, mostly in the hands of European immigrants with strong winemaking traditions. However, by the early 1990s the growth in home winemaking had slowed, with fewer than half a million Americans making roughly 2.5 million cases of wine a year, mainly from grapes grown in California and shipped by rail to the rest of the country but also from juice or GRAPE CONCENTRATE. Today, home winemakers have access to juice and grapes grown not only in California but also in Oregon and New York State, for example, as well as from other major grape-growing countries such as Italy, Chile, Argentina, and South Africa. In Great Britain the hobby peaked in the late 1980s, with grape concentrate the usual raw material, producing MADE-WINE, which lacks the fresh fruitiness of wine made from the juice of freshly picked grapes.

It was Canada that popularized home winemaking. Kits based on canned grape-juice concentrate had been introduced in the 1950s, but a new type of kit made by Canada's Brew King, using a combination of concentrates and flash-PASTEURIZED fresh grape juice and including much of the necessary equipment, encouraged many new recruits.

In addition, the introduction in the Canadian provinces of Ontario and British Columbia of 'wine on premise' shops, and of *centres de vinification* in Quebec, where customers could vinify an unlimited amount of wine for personal use, free of any tax, led to a huge increase in home-made wine.

Today the world's major wine-kit manufacturers are all based in Canada but distribute throughout the world. D.P.

homoclime, or 'analogue climate', is a geographical term meaning 'similar climate'. It remains a common approach to VINEYARD SITE SELECTION in the NEW WORLD to search for homoclimes of established wine regions, implicitly assuming that CLIMATE is the primary determinant of wine quality. Homoclimes can be found with digitized maps and GEOGRAPHICAL INFORMATION SYSTEMS, using temperature and rainfall data but also considering SUNLIGHT, HUMIDITY, and EVAPORATION. For example, Tamar Ridge Vineyards used this approach to identify new vineyard regions in Tasmania with the same climate as that of New Zealand's MARLBOROUGH region. R.E.S.

Hondarrabi Beltza, rare Spanish BASQUE red wine grape related to Cabernet Franc and grown to produce red and rosé TXAKOLI. The pale-skinned grapes making white Txakoli are called **Hondarrabi Zuri**, of which Spain's total plantings had grown to 741 ha/1,831 acres by 2020. But these vines are probably a mix of COURBU BLANC, CROUCHEN, and, according to one reference sample for DNA PROFILING, the American hybrid NOAH. Hondarrabi is also spelt Hondarribi or Ondarrabi.

Hong Kong has been the hub of ASIAN wine markets since 2008, when duty on wine was slashed to zero with this very intention. Duties on wine imported to the rest of CHINA are substantial and therefore many Chinese wine collectors continue to buy and store their FINE WINES in this special administrative region. The number of wine STORAGE FACILITIES, wine MERCHANTS, wine AUCTIONS, and wine trade fairs in Hong Kong subsequently soared. By the second decade of the 21st century, auction totals in Hong Kong had overtaken those in Europe and the United States (though the latter has since reclaimed the lead), and virtually every fine-wine trader had a Hong Kong outpost. Reliable statistics are not available but, on top of official re-exports of several million litres annually, a considerable quantity of fine wine is thought to cross the border into China from Hong Kong. Beyond fine wine, the city is a significant regional base for wine competitions, wine media, and wine education, to the extent that the WSET chose Hong Kong for its first international office in 2016. A few URBAN WINERIES vinifying imported grapes opened in the region in the late 2000s and early 2010s but have since closed down. S.K.H.

Horace (Quintus Horatius Flaccus) (65–8 BCE), the Latin poet, did not write a systematic guide to viticulture, although wine does figure prominently in his work and reflects his Epicurean philosophy of enjoying its pleasures in moderation. He tells us that at the Sabine farm which his patron Maecenas gave him he does not grow wine (*Epistles* 1. 14), but as a token of his gratitude he serves Maecenas the local wine, laid down by the poet himself in the year that his patron had recovered from a serious illness (*Odes* 1. 20). This matching of the wine to the guest and the occasion is a constant feature of Horace's invitation poems and other poems about drinking: see also *Odes* 1. 9 and 4. 2 (simple wines for intimate occasions), 3. 21 (a wine from the year of the poet's birth for an honoured guest), 1. 37 (a grand old CAECUBAN to celebrate the defeat of the monstrous Cleopatra), 3. 14 (a wine that goes back to the Social War, 91–88 BCE, to celebrate Augustus' return), and 3. 28 (Caecuban of Bibulus' consular year, 59 BCE, in honour of Neptune).

Horace cannot afford the very best wine, old FALERNIAN; to spend a feast day drinking that would be the greatest happiness (*Odes* 2. 3). Note that to Horace good wine is always old wine: the Romans (and the Greeks) preferred old wine to the wine of the current vintage. *Epistles* 1. 19 is Horace's contribution to the debate about poetic inspiration. Callimachus (*c.*310/05–*c.*240 BCE) first raised the question of whether water, symbol of the purity of poetic labour, or wine, which brings poetic frenzy, is the better drink for a poet. On the authority of

Cratinus (*c*.520–*c*.423 BCE), Horace sides with the wine drinkers, for were not Homer and Ennius (see ancient GREECE), the fathers of Greek and Latin epic respectively, wine bibbers? 'Laudibus arguitur vini vinosus Homerus', Horace asserts: 'in his praises of wine, wine-bibbing Homer betrays himself.' To the modern reader, Horace seems to have more in common with today's civilized wine enthusiast than does any other classical writer. H.M.W.

Commager, S., 'The function of wine in Horace's Odes', *Transactions of the American Philological Association*, 88 (1957), 68–80.
Griffin, J., *Latin Literature and Roman Life* (1985).
Wilson, H., *Wine and Words in Classical Antiquity and the Middle Ages* (2003).

horizontal trellis. See TENDONE and TRAINING SYSTEM.

hormones, natural substances present in trace concentrations in vines and other plants which move from one organ or part of the plant to another to regulate growth and development. Synthetic GROWTH REGULATORS may have similar chemical structures and a similar mode of action. Three groups of hormones promote growth: AUXINS, GIBBERELLINS, and CYTOKININS. Two groups inhibit growth: ABSCISIC ACID and ethylene. R.E.S.

horses are making a return to vineyards as an alternative to TRACTORS in response to concerns about SOIL COMPACTION. See also BIODYNAMIC VITICULTURE, TILLAGE, LABOUR, and SUSTAINABLE VITICULTURE.

Hospices de Beaune, charity auction which has taken place in BEAUNE annually since 1859 on the third Sunday in November, a key feature of the Burgundian calendar. The beneficiaries are the combined charitable organizations of the Hôtel Dieu, founded in 1443 by Nicolas Rolin, chancellor of the duchy of Burgundy, and the Hôpital de la Charité.

The produce of vineyard holdings donated by benefactors over the centuries is auctioned at prices usually well in excess of current commercial values. Nevertheless, the results serve as some indication of the trend in bulk wine prices for the new vintage.

The cuvées sold are named to commemorate original benefactors such as Nicolas Rolin and his wife Guigone de Salins or more recent ones such as de Bahèzre de Lanlay, an inspector of aerial telegraphs. The Hospices de Beaune also provides the occasion for 'Les Trois Glorieuses', the three great feasts held over the weekend at CLOS DE VOUGEOT on Saturday night, in Beaune on Sunday night, and in MEURSAULT for the extended lunchtime bottle party that is the Paulée de Meursault on Monday.

The Hospices de Nuits also holds a charity wine auction; see NUITS-ST-GEORGES.

See also AUCTIONS. J.T.C.M.

hot bottling. See PASTEURIZATION.

hot-water treatment is used by QUARANTINE authorities and vine NURSERIES to sterilize dormant grapevine CUTTINGS or nursery plants. These are immersed in hot water at around 50 °C/122 °F, or slightly warmer, for a few minutes to destroy surface contaminants and for up to 30 minutes for internal diseases such as FUNGI and PHYTOPLASMA. Hot-water treatment is also used to control CROWN GALL bacteria, NEMATODES, and PHYLLOXERA and other insects. The process is used in nurseries to control TRUNK DISEASES. There should be no damage to the plants if the temperature is accurately regulated and storage protocols followed. Not to be confused with THERMOTHERAPY. R.E.S.

Howell Mountain, CALIFORNIA wine region and AVA defined by ELEVATION. See NAPA Valley.

Hrvatska. See CROATIA.

Hugel, one of the best-known and oldest wine producers in ALSACE, having been established in 1639. The family business is run today by the 12th and 13th generations. The Hugels, based in Riquewihr, make fine wines from their own 30 ha/74 acres of vineyard around the village planted mainly with Riesling and Gewurztraminer, together with a little Pinot Gris and Pinot Noir. Their Estate (once Tradition) range can be excitingly full and the Grossi Laüe (once Jubilee) range masterful. The Hugel family also pioneered the resurrection of Alsace's late-harvest wines and were instrumental in drawing up the rigorous requirements for these VENDANGES TARDIVES and SÉLECTION DE GRAINS NOBLES wines. They are arch exponents of these styles themselves and produce them, along with the Grossi Laüe range, exclusively from their own GRAND CRU and Pflostig vineyards. The Hugel family, of which three family members work in the Riquewihr wine business, have long been champions of maximizing quality in Alsace's finest wines but do not recognize the Alsace Grand Cru appellation, which they feel is no guarantee of quality. The Hugels buy in grapes, never wine, for their basic range of bottlings from about 55 ha/135 acres of vineyard under contract from more than 60 growers. Marc Hugel and his nephew Marc-André are in charge of winemaking.

Humagne Blanche, Swiss Valais white grape which, unexpectedly, is not related to HUMAGNE ROUGE. The wine produced is elegant, though less expressive than ARVINE. DNA PROFILING has shown that Humagne Blanche is the parent of LAFNETSCHA and that it is also found in south-west France as MIOUSAT. J.V.

Humagne Rouge, relatively rare red wine grape of the Swiss Valais region whose wines are wild and rustic, with unusual aromas of dried vine leaves and relatively soft TANNINS. DNA PROFILING at CHANGINS and Aosta showed that this variety is identical to CORNALIN of the Valle d'AOSTA and confirmed that it is not related to HUMAGNE BLANCHE. J.V.

humidification, euphemism for the (usually illegal but increasingly common) winemaking operation of adding water to reduce ALCOHOLIC STRENGTH. Lack of regulation and transparency concerning the amount of water that is allowed for the purposes of incorporating any oenological substances, for example ADDITIVES and PROCESSING AIDS, makes this an even more grey area.

humidity, or moisture content, of the atmosphere has considerable implications both for vine growth and for STORING barrels and wine, whether in bulk or bottle. Humidity is normally measured as per cent relative humidity (% RH): the amount of water vapour a given volume of air holds, as a percentage of the maximum it could hold at the same temperature. The latter amount increases with temperature, so the RH of air containing a constant amount of water vapour falls as temperature rises, and vice versa. Humidity can also be expressed as saturation deficit, which is a direct measure of the evaporative power of the atmosphere. Actual EVAPORATION is further influenced by WIND and SUNLIGHT.

Relative humidity follows a regular daily cycle, normally being highest in the early morning, when temperature is lowest, and lowest in the early to mid afternoon, when temperature is highest. High humidity is conducive to the spread of FUNGAL DISEASES, especially when combined with high temperatures after rainfall, for example. High morning humidity creates DEW, which is also important for some diseases. The afternoon humidity, together with sunshine, temperature, and wind, dominates in determining evaporation rate and therefore the likelihood of WATER STRESS. The contrast between morning and afternoon RH tends to be greatest inland and least near coasts.

Gladstones argues that high humidity levels, critically those in the afternoon, are conducive to high wine quality, but it is difficult to separate this influence from that of lower temperatures.

Viticultural regions of the world with high afternoon RH during the fruiting period, and lower daytime temperature, include those mentioned in COOL-CLIMATE VITICULTURE. See WARM-CLIMATE VITICULTURE for wine regions where there is also an inverse general relationship between afternoon summer temperatures and RH.

Typical areas of intermediate humidity include the southern Rhône Valley of France; most inland areas of Portugal producing table wine, such as Dão, and of Spain; Bulgaria; intermediate and warmer parts of the coastal valleys of California, such as the Napa and Santa Clara Valleys; Stellenbosch and Paarl in South Africa; the Western Australian west coast and hills; Barossa, Adelaide Hills, Langhorne Creek, and Coonawarra in South Australia; Grampians and other parts of the Great Dividing Range in Victoria; and the Hunter Valley and, marginally, Mudgee in New South Wales.

For details of humidity and barrels, see EVAPORATION. For details of humidity and wine storage, see STORING WINE. R.E.S.

humus. See ORGANIC MATTER.

Hundred Years War. The sporadic fighting between the kings of England and France known as the Hundred Years War (1337–1453) changed both the political map of Europe and the nature and volume of the medieval wine trade. Both crowns claimed ownership of the wine regions of western France, which, through the wealthy port of BORDEAUX, supplied England with almost all its wine.

The hostilities had a marked effect on the wine trade. First, the large and commercially successful vineyards of the HAUT PAYS, or 'high country', upstream from Bordeaux (GAILLAC, BERGERAC, BUZET, CAHORS) were for the most part under French control. This increased English reliance on the lesser vineyards of Bordeaux and its environs, encouraging their expansion.

Second, the ships carrying wine back to England faced the risk of greater piracy. Convoys organized for their protection proved expensive. Reduced supplies and greater freight costs led to a dramatic rise in the price of wine in England.

After Bordeaux's surrender at CASTILLON in 1453, England remained a major market for its wines, although the overall volume of this trade was not to reach the pre-war peak for many centuries. English merchants became more willing to look beyond western France for their wine imports, while Bordeaux attracted a wider clientele of merchants from northern Europe.

See also BORDEAUX, history. H.B.

Dion, R., *Histoire de la vigne et du vin en France* (1959).

James, M. K., *Studies in the Medieval Wine Trade* (1971).

Renouard, Y., *Études d'histoire médiévale* (1968).

Hungary, central European wine-producing country with a distinctive range of vine varieties and wines. Hungary usually produces less wine than its eastern neighbour ROMANIA but considerably more than, for example, AUSTRIA and BULGARIA. Some 64,000 ha/158,147 acres were devoted to vines in 2021, and almost 70% of them produced white wines. Total Hungarian wine production has been decreasing and is now usually below 4 million hl/105 million gal a year, of which about one-fifth is exported.

History

Vine-growing and winemaking have been practised in what is now modern Hungary since at least Roman times, when it was part of the Roman province of Pannonia. The Magyar tribes who arrived here at the end of the 9th century found flourishing vineyards and familiarity with winemaking techniques. Under Bela IV (1235–70), the king who rebuilt Hungary after the Mongol invasion of 1241, wine production was given such priority that immigrants from areas with particular expertise in vine-growing and winemaking were invited to rebuild the devastated areas, and by the end of his reign wines from the towns of SOPRON and

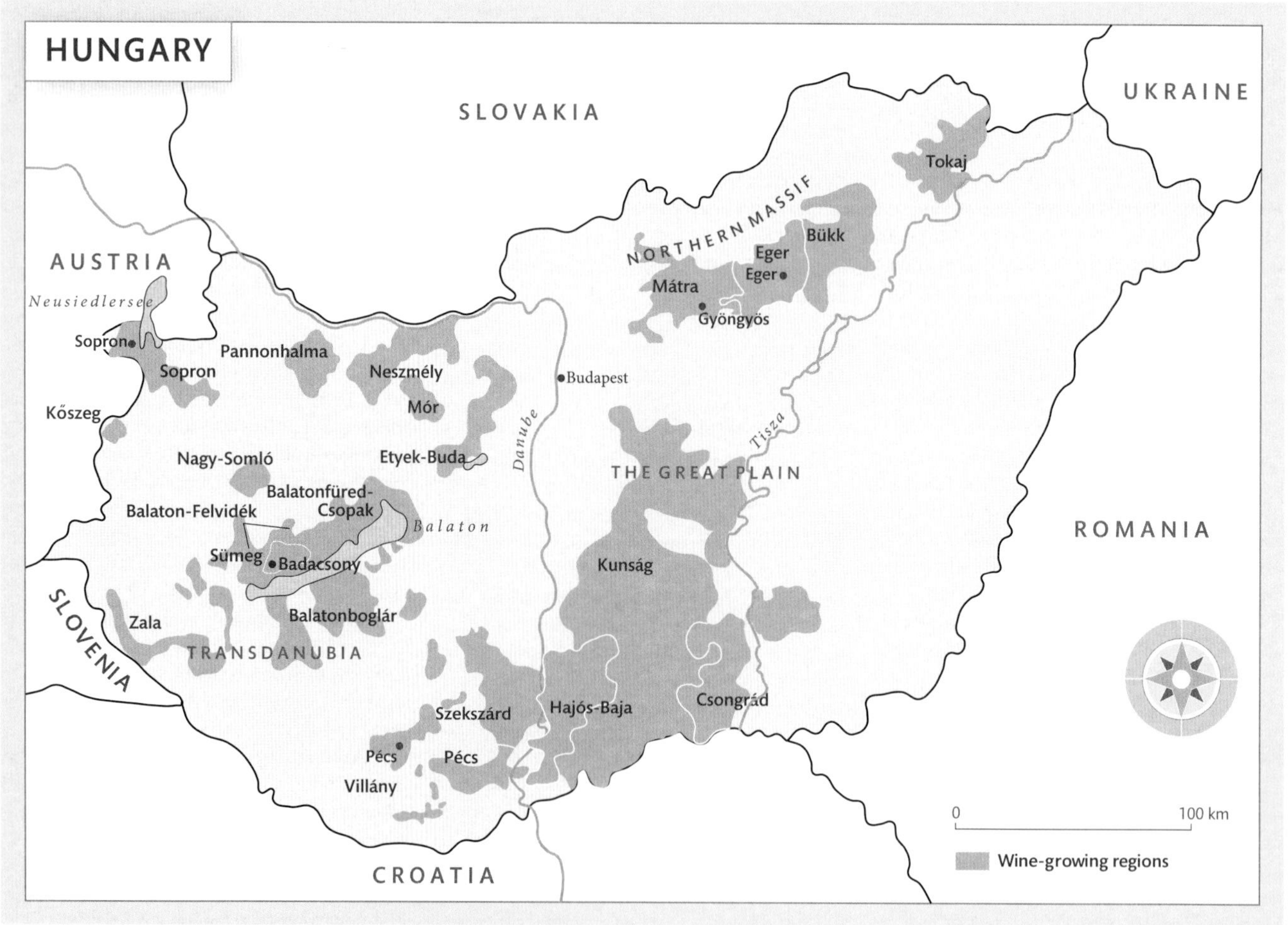

EGER were being exported in relatively large quantities. Hungary's most famous wine, TOKAJI, is first mentioned in records in the late 15th century, although it was almost certainly dry at this time.

Following the defeat and death of Louis II at the battle of Mohács in 1529, much of the country was under Muslim rule for a century and a half, during which wine production survived but did not thrive (see ISLAM).

The most important development in the 17th century was the emergence of sweet, rich Tokaji Aszú. As early as 1641, a Vine Law for the entire Tokaj-Hegyalja district was drawn up which regulated VINEYARD SITE SELECTION, the construction of TERRACES, IRRIGATION, manuring, and harvesting. By 1570, NOBLE ROT was recognized, and the laws for Aszú formulated. For more details, see TOKAJ.

In 1686 the city of Buda was liberated from the Turks, followed within the next few years by the rest of Hungary, which then became part of the vast Habsburg empire. In 1711 a bid for independence led by Ferenc Rákóczi failed, but it had the effect of spreading the fame of Tokaj wines to the court of the French king, Louis XIV, to whom Rákóczi had sent sample bottles as gifts. This was the beginning of Tokaj's formidable international reputation.

The vineyards of Tokaj were some of the first to be submitted to CLASSIFICATION, in 1700; the first national vineyard classification anywhere, a five-level rating, was undertaken in Hungary in 1707–8 as part of general appraisal of the country's resources.

PHYLLOXERA struck Hungary in the 1870s, devastating the southern vineyards at Pancsova initially and eventually spreading to the Northern Massif and Tokaj-Hegyalja. Replanting on phylloxera-resistant ROOTSTOCKS began in 1881, but scientific proof that phylloxera could not thrive in sandy soils had just been published, encouraging the planting of new vineyards in the Great Plain, between the Danube and Tisza rivers, where vines were also discovered to be helpful for stabilizing the shifting sands.

Zsigmond Teleki (1854–1910) bred the famous 5 BB Teleki rootstock which proved perfectly suited to producing high-quality grapes even when planted in the desolate, intensely CALCAREOUS hillsides of Villány. When Teleki died in 1910, his sons Andor and Sándor continued the NURSERY business with great success, maintaining subsidiaries in six countries, until the Second World War. Ironically, Franz Kober in Oppenheim eventually collected most of the recognition by subjecting Teleki's CLONES to further selection, and indeed the rootstock is more commonly known today as 5 BB Kober. Móricz Preysz (1829–77) was the pioneer of PASTEURIZATION, publishing his work on the technique, then needed to stabilize Tokaji, in 1861, two years before Louis PASTEUR developed pasteurization.

In 1947, the National Association of Hungarian Vine-Growers, Wine Trades, and Wine-Growing Communities was forced to suspend its activities when the communist state monopoly took control. An era of state farms and state wineries followed, during which all wine exports were funnelled through the state-controlled trading company Monimpex. Half of all production was at one point handled by just two wineries designed to export huge quantities of very ordinary wine to the SOVIET UNION. Unlike the similarly organized BULGARIAN wine industry, that of Hungary suffered a period of stagnation and generally low technology that stultified the development of Hungarian wine until the return of a free-market economy and private enterprise in the late 1980s. However, because a considerable proportion of Hungarian vines had remained in private hands in the communist era, Hungary was able to adapt production to the more stringent requirements of Western importers more quickly than other ex-Comecon countries.

In the post-communist division of vinicultural spoils, there was no shortage of Western interest in the unique Tokaji wines, and the influx of foreign winemakers, western European capital, and EU finance enabled much-needed investment in modern winery equipment, resulting in a marked improvement in wine quality. And the early 21st century saw a marked increase in the number of ambitious, quality-focused wineries—many Hungarian-owned—with improved VINEYARD site selections and plant material, respect for TERROIR, and better winemaking, especially for dry white wines. The best winegrowers have come to realize that their high-acid wines do not require the same barrel regimes as wines from warmer regions and have drastically reduced the amount of new wood used in the winemaking process, switching out the once-popular 225-l barrels for larger formats. So-called NATURAL WINES are also on the rise.

Geography and climate

Hungary, which lies between latitudes 45° and 50° N, is landlocked, but the River Danube (called Duna in Hungary) flows through it from north to south, dividing it in almost equal halves. To the west lies Transdanubia, which includes Central Europe's largest lake, Balaton. Here, complex soils of BASALT with CLAY and sandstone dominate. Other soils include LIMESTONE and SLATE, particularly around Balatonfüred. (See map.) East of the Danube is the Great Plain, an area of mainly SAND and LOESS, except in the volcanic hills of the Northern Massif north-east of the capital Budapest. In the extreme north-east, bordering SLOVAKIA, is the Tokaj (formerly Tokaj-Hegyalja) region.

See below and separate entries for EGER, SZEKSZÁRD, TOKAJ, and VILLÁNY for details of individual wine regions.

Hungary's climate is essentially CONTINENTAL and Central European, involving cold winters and warm summers. The sun shines for an average of about 2,600 hours a year, and annual rainfall averages 500–800 mm/20–31 in.

Wine regions

Hungarian law in the 21st century established 22 wine regions. In 2009, in keeping with the EU reforms of CONTROLLED APPELLATION terminology, these were replaced by 36 PDOs (*Oltalom alatt álló eredet megjelöléssel* in Hungarian, or OEM) and 13 PGIs (*Oltalom alatt álló földrajzi jelzéssel*, or OFJ). The following PDOs may be considered pre-eminent: Badacsony, Balatonboglár, EGER, Etyek-Buda, Somló, SOPRON, SZEKSZÁRD, TOKAJ, and VILLÁNY. Names such as Mátra, Neszmély, and Pannonhalma may also be familiar from export labels. The wine regions fall into three major geographical groups, as outlined below.

Transdanubia The wine regions in this western part of Hungary, between the Austrian border and the Danube, are strongly influenced by the waters of Lake Balaton, Lake Fertö (called NEUSIEDLERSEE in Austria), and the Danube itself. Wines from this area may be labelled by the PGI **Dunántúl** and its variations Dél-, Észak-, and Nyugat-dunántúl (South, North, and West Dunántúl).

Traditionally the northern side of Lake Balaton was the vine-growing area, with the famous Badacsony Hill on the volcanic slopes at the south-west end. The surface area of water in the lake has a considerable ameliorating effect on the MESOCLIMATE (see TOPOGRAPHY) and the wines tend to be full and powerful. This is home to the ancient KÉKNYELŰ grape variety, and it also grows fine Pinot Gris (Szürkebarát) and Olaszrizling (WELSCHRIESLING). **Balatonfüred-Csopak** also lies on the northern shore, on sandstone, slate, and marl, and is known for its Olaszrizling, a speciality upheld by the Csopak Kódex, an independent association devoted to maintaining its reputation through strict regulations for viticulture and vinification.

On the slopes of an extinct volcano north-west of Lake Balaton is the small PDO region of **Nagy-Somló** and the even smaller PDO **Somló**, whose wood-aged, blended wines once enjoyed a reputation similar to those of Tokaj. JUHFARK is prized here, along with Furmint, but Olaszrizling, Hárslevelű, and Traminer have been in the ascendant. Somló has been attracting increasing investment as its potential for elegant, ageworthy wines with a distinctive mineral character becomes evident.

Sümeg is just 40 km/25 miles south-west, in the Balaton Highlands (Balaton-Felvidék), and grows a wide variety of grape varieties in its heavy calcareous clay soils. What sets the PDO apart is its focus on natural winemaking, requiring extremely low yields and vine-growing without any AGROCHEMICALS as well as LOW-INTERVENTION WINEMAKING.

On the south shore of the lake is **Balatonboglár**, where the fertile soils include SAND and LOESS. Important grapes grown here are Olaszrizling, KIRÁLYLEÁNYKA, Zöldveltelini, IRSAI OLIVÉR, Chardonnay, Muscat, Merlot, and Pinot Noir. Base wines for excellent sparkling wines are also produced here.

Sopron, the most westerly wine region of northern Transdanubia and effectively a continuation of NEUSIEDLERSEE, Austria's most revered source of sweet white wine, is dominated by ambitious growers of Austro-German extraction. Today Sopron is mainly devoted to red wines made from Kékfrankos (BLAUFRÄNKISCH), Cabernet Sauvignon, Cabernet Franc, Merlot, Pinot Noir, and Syrah, which can be particularly elegant when grown on the SCHIST soils here.

Further south, in the southernmost end of the Alps, is the PDO **Kőszeg**, where Kékfrankos excels, just as it does just across the border from Austria's MITTELBURGENLAND.

In the north are two increasingly important white wine areas: **Neszmély** and **Mór**, between Sopron and Budapest, which are best known for crisp but well-balanced Olaszrizling and Sauvignon Blanc, tart EZERJÓ, LEÁNYKA, and aromatic GEWÜRZTRAMINER. Some thrilling red wines from Kékfrankos and Pinot Noir are also produced. Etyek stands out for its TRADITIONAL METHOD sparkling wine, bottled under the PDO **Etyeki Pezsgő** and made in white and rosé versions from Chardonnay and Pinots Blanc, Noir, or Gris grown in the region's LIMESTONE soils.

Southern Transdanubia has three important wine regions. **Villány** is most famous for the saddle of land in the Villány Hills which manages to produce highly prized reds even in difficult years. Cabernet Franc is most successful here, although Kékfrankos, Merlot, Syrah, and Zweigelt are also good.

Szekszárd has traditionally been associated with KADARKA, which it has managed to ripen more healthily than most regions, owing to its long, warm summers, but plantings total barely 100 ha/250 acres. This native red variety has been supplanted by vigorous Merlot and Cabernet, but Szekszárd producers tend to achieve a higher average quality with their Kadarka, Kékfrankos, and BIKAVÉR wines. The cooler area around Bátaszék, 15 km/9 miles to the south, can produce some particularly good Sauvignon Blanc and Grüner Veltliner. ANTINORI own a winery in Tolna, the neighbouring region.

Pécs, Hungary's warmest wine region, is at constant risk of DROUGHT. A wide range of white and red vine varieties is cultivated here.

The Northern Massif This range of hills running north-east from Budapest along the border with Slovakia contains four wine regions: **Mátra**, EGER, **Bükk**, and TOKAJ.

In the foothills of the Mátra Mountains, the soils are mainly VOLCANIC, and most of the wine produced is white, mainly from Olaszrizling, Muscat, and Királyleányka. The region also produces some elegant, fruity reds, especially from Kékfrankos and Pinot Noir. Quality is growing rapidly here, with an influx of talented young winemakers.

Just east of the Mátra foothills, in the foothills of the Bükk Mountains, is the wine region named after the historic town of EGER. Spring often comes late here and rainfall is low. Some white wines are made, principally from local varieties such as Olaszrizling, Leányka, Királyleányka, and Irsai Olivér. Some of the region's finest white wines are bottled as Egri Csillag ('Star of Eger'), a blend of at least four local varieties. Yet the region's reputation is for age-worthy red wine, notably Egri Bikavér, once known on export markets as Bull's Blood. At one time the blend depended heavily on Kadarka, but as elsewhere this challenging native variety was replaced by Kékfrankos and Zweigelt, supplemented by Cabernet, Merlot, and Syrah.

North-east of Eger lies the **Bükk** region. With the mountains at its back, the region's 1,011 ha/2,498 acres of vines are largely protected from the cold north winds as well as rain. The diverse soils support a range of varieties, generally favouring whites—Leányka, Chardonnay, and CSERSZEGI FŰSZERES—with some fruity, elegant reds made from Kékfrankos and Zweigelt.

Tokaj is even further north-east, into the foothills of the Zemplén Mountains. See TOKAJ for more detail.

The Great Plain This vast, flat expanse (known as Alföld in Hungary) south of Budapest and between the Danube and Hungary's second river, the Tisza, accounts for nearly half the country's vineyards. The plain was heavily planted after the PHYLLOXERA invasion because of phylloxera's intolerance of sandy soils and because vines were better at stabilizing the soil than the fruit trees planted earlier.

MECHANIZATION is easy on this flat land, but the DROUGHT in summer and FROST in both late spring and autumn are a perennial threat, and the combination of sandy soil and high summer temperatures means that soil temperatures can be very high indeed.

INDIGENOUS and INTERNATIONAL VARIETIES of Olaszrizling, Rajnai Rizling (RIESLING), Kékfrankos, Kadarka, Cserszegi Fűszeres, and Ezerjó are planted here. The Great Plain encompasses the PGI **Duna-Tisza Közi** and the PDOs **Csongrád**, **Hajós-Baja**, and **Kunság**, but wine quality is generally indifferent. The more recent PDO **Duna** may be used for wines from those three more specific and well-established regions.

Vine varieties

Wine labelling is mostly VARIETAL. Hungary had a particularly rich selection of INDIGENOUS VARIETIES, many of which were largely abandoned after PHYLLOXERA invaded in the late 19th century. A potentially exciting selection of localized white grape varieties can still be found, such as KÉKNYELŰ, found almost exclusively in Badacsony on the north shore of Lake Balaton, and JUHFARK, known mainly in Somló.

Indigenous varieties which are relatively widely planted include EZERJÓ, a light speciality of the Mór region west of Budapest; FURMINT, the most characteristic ingredient of Tokaji; and HÁRSLEVELŰ, which is usually a lesser Tokaji ingredient and is also widely grown throughout Hungary. The indigenous Leányka and Királyleányka are used for light-bodied aromatic wines. Efforts are being made to replant old Hungarian grapes such as Bakator, BUDAI ZÖLD, Szerémi Zöld, KÖVIDINKA, and Sárfehér. Newer crosses such as the Muscat-like IRSAI OLIVÉR and the grapey cross CSERSZEGI FŰSZERES are now being more widely planted for their own intrinsic character and quality. Other light-berried crosses include ZÉTA, ZENGŐ, ZEFIR, and ZENIT. Hungary's most characteristic red grape variety is KADARKA, although Csókaszőlő is making a comeback, and PORTUGIESER (once known as Kékoportó) can also make some appetizing wines here.

A range of central European vine varieties is grown: Olaszrizling (WELSCHRIESLING), Zöldveltelini (Austria's GRÜNER VELTLINER), Cirfandli (Austria's ZIERFANDLER, a speciality of Pécs); and, for red-wine production, KÉKFRANKOS (along with Nagyburgundi, the Hungarian name for BLAUFRÄNKISCH), and Austria's ZWEIGELT.

A wide range of vine varieties have been imported into Hungary from western Europe, however, including Chardonnay, Sauvignon Blanc, Riesling (generally called Rajnai Rizling or Rheinriesling), Gewürztraminer (Tramini), Muscat Ottonel and Yellow Muscat, the deeper-hued Muscat Blanc à Petits Grains (both of which are sometimes called Sárga Muskotály), and Pinot Gris, whose distinctively Hungarian synonym is Szürkebarát. Red-wine varieties imported from the West include Merlot and, to a much lesser extent, Cabernet Sauvignon and Cabernet Franc, as well as a smaller amount of Pinot Noir and Syrah.

See also EGER, SZEKSZÁRD, TOKAJ, and VILLÁNY.

G.R. & G.M.

Liddell, A., *The Wines of Hungary* (2003).
Mészáros, G., Ambrus, L., and Rohály, G., *Terra benedicta* (2019).

Hunter Valley Zone, historic warm, humid NEW SOUTH WALES wine zone two hours north of Sydney in which **Hunter** is a region and Broke Fordwich, Pokolbin, and Upper Hunter are subregions. The region is best known for its distinctive, long-lived dry SÉMILLON wines.

Chardonnay and Shiraz are also well-regarded.

Huxelrebe is an early 21st century German vine CROSS that enjoys some popularity both in Germany and, on a much smaller scale, in ENGLAND. Although like SCHEUREBE and FABERREBE it was actually bred by Georg Scheu at Alzey, this cross takes its name from its chief propagator, nurseryman Fritz Huxel. It was bred in 1927 from ELBLING (not Chasselas as the breeder originally indicated) and Courtillier Musqué, as confirmed by DNA PROFILING. The cross is capable of producing enormous quantities of rather ordinary wine—so enormous in fact that the vines can collapse under the strain of the grapes. If pruned carefully, however, and planted on an average to good site, it can easily reach Auslese MUST WEIGHTS even in an ordinary year and produce a fulsome if not exactly subtle wine redolent of honey, musk, and raisins for reasonably early consumption. In England, its ripeness is a useful counterbalance to naturally high acidity. In Germany, it is grown almost exclusively in Rheinhessen and the Pfalz; although it continues to lose ground, there were still 396 ha/979 acres in 2019. Gysler and Seehof manage to spin gold from it.

HVE, abbreviation for *Haute Valeur Environnementale*, a French certification system for SUSTAINABLE VITICULTURE.

hybrids, in common viticultural terms, the offspring of two varieties of different species, as distinct from a CROSS between two varieties of the same species, which is also known as an intraspecific cross. (See VITIS for details of the various species of the vine genus.) EU authorities prefer the somewhat cumbersome term 'interspecific cross' to the word 'hybrid', which has pejorative connotations within Europe.

Hybrids can occur naturally by cross-pollination, as happened, for example, in early American viticulture (see AMERICAN HYBRIDS). More commonly, however, hybrids have been deliberately produced by people (see NEW VARIETIES and VINE BREEDING) to combine in the progeny some of the desirable characteristics of the parents. This viticultural activity was particularly important in the late 19th century, when European, and especially French, breeders tried to combine the desirable wine quality of European VITIS VINIFERA varieties with AMERICAN VINE SPECIES' resistance to introduced American pests and diseases, especially PHYLLOXERA, which was devastating European vineyards (see FRENCH HYBRIDS).

Grafting European vines on to American ROOTSTOCKS proved the eventual solution to phylloxera, and many of today's commercially important rootstocks are hybrids. Early rootstocks were often pure varieties of a single American vine species chosen for their resistance to phylloxera. It was subsequently found, however, that hybrid rootstocks with combinations of genes from several American vine species allowing tolerance of various soil conditions and diseases were more successful in the nursery.

Different species of *Vitis* contain genes with natural tolerance or resistance to winter cold, lime-induced CHLOROSIS, SALINITY, DOWNY MILDEW, POWDERY MILDEW, BOTRYTIS BUNCH ROT, CROWN GALL, PIERCE'S DISEASE, NEMATODES, WINTER FREEZE injury, and phylloxera. It is logical, therefore, to explore the possibilities of new hybrid varieties for wine production in an age of increasing concern about the AGROCHEMICALS which are used to control some of these. Vine breeders such as those at Geilweilerhof, DAVIS, and MONTPELLIER have proved that new hybrids, now called DISEASE-RESISTANT VARIETIES, may, without recourse to agrochemicals, produce good wine with no recognizably non-*vinifera* characteristics which, in controlled tests, cannot be distinguished from that of their pure *vinifera* counterparts. As a result, EU authorities allow hybrids such as RONDO, REGENT, PHOENIX, and ORION, as well as the more recent French hybrids Artaban, Vidoc, Floréal, Voltis, Coliris, Lilaro, Sirano, Selenor, and Opalor, into wines with GEOGRAPHICAL INDICATION.

The pedigree of many modern hybrids can involve seven or eight generations of crosses so that their ancestry is typically complex and includes *vinifera*, American varieties, possibly Asian varieties, and also early released French hybrids. R.E.S & J.E.H.

Mullins, M. G., et al., *Biology of the Grapevine* (1992).

hydrogen sulfide, or H_2S, is the foul-smelling gas, reminiscent of rotten eggs, which even at very low concentrations (parts per billion) is easily recognized in wine because it is highly volatile and has a very low sensory detection threshold. Although it can form at any stage of wine production, hydrogen sulfide is produced most commonly during alcoholic FERMENTATION. Hydrogen sulfide production during fermentation is associated with a deficiency in the amount of NITROGEN (often referred to as yeast-assimilable/available nitrogen, or YAN) in the grape must or juice. The nitrogen content of grapes is highly variable and depends on many factors, including grape variety, soil type and NUTRIENT status, climate, and vineyard management practices, such as type and amount of nutrient application, IRRIGATION, and use of COVER CROPS. Nitrogen-deficient grape musts are often supplemented with nitrogen, typically in the form of DIAMMONIUM PHOSPHATE (DAP), which usually suppresses the appearance of hydrogen sulfide, although not all yeast strains respond equally well to DAP.

Because grape must does not have sufficient sulfur-containing AMINO ACIDS, which are essential for yeast protein synthesis and cell growth, yeast use inorganic sulfur sources—sulfate and, when added, sulfite—present in the must. The inorganic sulfur is metabolically reduced to hydrogen sulfide, which is immediately incorporated into a nitrogen precursor molecule (*o*-acetylhomoserine) to synthesize the sulfur amino acids cysteine and methionine. However, if a deficiency of nitrogen occurs, the cell is unable to synthesize the nitrogen precursor molecule and, consequently, hydrogen sulfide escapes into the wine. The addition of nitrogen (i.e. DAP) decreases the accumulation of hydrogen sulfide in the wine, not by stopping its formation in the yeast cell but by allowing the yeast to make the amino acid precursor. Novel strains of wine yeast that are not capable of producing significant amounts of hydrogen sulfide have recently been developed, for example at both the AWRI and at DAVIS using conventional breeding and selection techniques.

Residual sulfur in the must from vineyard fungicide can easily be reduced to hydrogen sulfide by the highly REDUCTIVE conditions generated by fermenting yeast. Decreasing or eliminating sulfur residues by ceasing sulfur applications to the fruit zone soon after VERAISON can help. (Elemental sulfur is used to control powdery mildew, which is no longer an issue on the grapes once they reach 12 °BRIX, but it may still be necessary to spray the foliage.)

When present at low levels, hydrogen sulfide may add complexity to wine aroma (see VOLATILE SULFUR COMPOUNDS), but at concentrations above its odour threshold, hydrogen sulfide imparts the smell of rotten eggs, which is considered a FAULT. Fortunately, hydrogen sulfide is very volatile and can usually be removed by the SPARGING action of CARBON DIOXIDE produced during fermentation. However, hydrogen sulfide formed or released towards the end of fermentation, or after fermentation is completed, is of concern to the winemaker. If allowed to remain in the wine, it can react with other wine components to form MERCAPTANS, disulfides (see SULFIDES), which have pungent garlic, onion, or rubber aromas, and polysulfanes, which may act as latent sources of hydrogen sulfide in wines post-bottling.

Hydrogen sulfide can usually be removed from the new wine by a small addition of copper sulfate, and it is also effectively eliminated during RACKING, where it is carried along with released carbon dioxide. Unfortunately, copper sulfate may react not only with off-flavours but also with desirable varietal aromas. In the case of robust wines (especially reds), sulfur compounds can also be removed by AERATION thanks to two mechanisms. Firstly, the oxygen uptake by the yeast allows them to make cell-wall sterols, which improves the ability of the yeast to absorb nitrogen from the must. Secondly, the various techniques of PUMPING OVER, RACK AND RETURN or direct introduction of air to the tank all serve to blow off any hydrogen sulfide that may have formed. This practical strategy has been shown to suppress the formation of hydrogen sulfide in red ferments with the added benefit of enhancing positive red-fruit attributes.

If a winemaker notices that a fermentation has produced high levels of hydrogen sulfide, they will usually rack the wine from the yeast lees early as the lees will continue to release hydrogen sulfide during ÉLEVAGE.

Finally, the type of CLOSURE and PACKAGING can also influence the development of sulfidic odours. Closure selection affects oxygen ingress, which may protect against hydrogen sulfide formation. Similarly, packaging material can either protect against the formation of hydrogen sulfide or be directly involved in the formation of sulfidic odours. For example, REDUCTIVE faults associated with hydrogen sulfide have been reported in some canned wines, which may be due to the reaction of SO_2 with the aluminium. M.B. & M.J.T

Allison, R., et al, 'The chemistry of canned wines', Research Focus 2020-1, Cornell University, Department of Food Science (2020).

Kreitman, G. Y., et al., 'Loss and formation of malodorous volatile sulfhydryl compounds during wine storage', *Critical Reviews in Food Science and Nutrition*, 59/11 (2019), 1728–52.

Rauhut, D., 'Usage and formation of sulphur compounds', in H. König et al. (eds.), *Biology of Microorganisms on Grapes, in Musts and in Wine* (2009).

Siebert, T. E., et al., 'Hydrogen sulfide: aroma detection threshold study in white and red wines', *AWRI Technical Review*, 183 (2009), 14–16.

Ugliano, M., 'Oxygen contribution to wine aroma evolution during bottle aging', *Journal of Agricultural and Food Chemistry*, 61/26 (2013), 6125–36.

Ugliano, M., et al., 'Effect of nitrogen supplementation and *Saccharomyces* species on hydrogen sulfide and other volatile sulfur compounds in shiraz fermentation and wine', *Journal of Agricultural and Food Chemistry*, 57/11 (2009), 4948–55.

Viviers, M. Z., et al., 'Effects of five metals on the evolution of hydrogen sulfide, methanethiol, and dimethyl sulfide during anaerobic storage of Chardonnay and Shiraz wines', *Journal of Agricultural and Food Chemistry*, 61/50 (2013), 12385–96.

hydrolysis, a chemical reaction with, or involving, water and often catalysed by the hydrogen ions of acids. Hydrolysis is the reaction whereby an ESTER is split into its acid and alcohol components and GLYCOSIDES into their sugar and aglycone parts. The reaction is of great importance to the AGEING of wine when slow hydrolysis affects the FLAVOUR PRECURSORS, releasing aroma-active aglycones from their flavourless glycosides. P.J.W.

hydrometer, an instrument used for measuring the SOLUBLE SOLIDS, sugar content, or MUST WEIGHT of juice and wine before and/or during fermentation, consisting of a closed glass tube with a bulbous base, weighted so that it floats upright. The floating depth is inversely proportional to the DENSITY of the solution and is read by matching the bottom of the meniscus against a scale within the stem. This scale may be calibrated as for BAUMÉ, BRIX/Balling, OECHSLE, or % alcohol by volume (see ALCOHOLIC STRENGTH). As with all such density measurements, correction for the temperature of the solution is necessary. B.G.C.

hygiene, an essential discipline in modern cellar management, involving cleanliness of winemaking premises and equipment and a great deal of WATER.

History

Winery hygiene was clearly already regarded as important in ancient ROME, as suggested by writers such as CATO and references in classical literature to SULFUR.

At the heart of the transformation from traditional mouldy cellars to their spotlessly clean modern counterparts has been a desire by winemakers to obtain much greater control over the processes of vinification and the maturation of wine, primarily through an emphasis on hygiene. While the pace of scientific research on the microbiology and biochemistry of winemaking has quickened appreciably since 1945, its origins lie in the middle of the 19th century with the experimental work of Louis PASTEUR. Until then, the precise reasons why pressed grapes would ferment into wine—and then become unpalatable if left open to the air for any length of time—were unknown. Practical experience had convinced Roman winemakers of the need to use chemicals such as sulfur to help prevent spoilage, and by the late 15th century in Germany it was recognized that wine kept in large barrels that were subjected to regular TOPPING UP would last longer than wine kept in small barrels which were left on ULLAGE. However, it was Pasteur who first reported in western Europe that wine deteriorated mainly as a result of the actions of microorganisms and that these could be killed by heating the wine in the absence of oxygen (although see HUNGARY, history).

Much of the impetus for the changes in winery hygiene in the late 20th century came from the New World, in particular from institutions such as the Department of Viticulture and Enology at the University of California, DAVIS, where the driving mentality during the 1950s and 1960s was towards the eradication of poor-quality wine. This, it was argued, could best be achieved through tight control of the FERMENTATION process, excluding the chance interference of a range of microorganisms. More recently, innovative research at the AWRI has also played a significant part in advancing the importance of winery hygiene. Above all, greater hygiene has enabled the adverse effects of ACETOBACTER and other spoilage microorganisms such as BRETTANOMCYES to be avoided. P.T.H.U.

Current practice

Hygiene is regarded as vital by modern winemakers (although it is still ignored by some of the more traditional ones, several of whom somehow manage to produce top-quality wine). Old cellars, while usually more picturesque, are almost impossible to keep clean and free of BACTERIA and YEASTS.

Most modern wineries, on the other hand, are designed with sanitation and hygiene in mind. STAINLESS STEEL and POLYETHYLENE tanks can be easily cleaned and sanitized; hard floors are designed to drain dry; and all equipment is sited and mounted so that it can be cleaned thoroughly around, above, and below the unit. Vast quantities of water are used, together with non-foaming detergents and sterilizing agents, by carefully trained staff. Research at Stanford University into the use of hydrogels could be a promising alternative that reduces water consumption and loss of wine when pipes and hoses are cleaned. In many wineries, all places where finished wine is exposed to the atmosphere are in separate, aseptic rooms, and care is taken particularly during BOTTLING, to its limit in STERILE BOTTLING. See also BARREL MAINTENANCE and WINERY WASTE.

Some local winemaking traditions supposedly rely on cellar moulds (see TOKAJ in Hungary, for example).

Hygiene, or sanitation, is also important where the grapes are received, as overripe and damaged fruit can easily attract insects, particularly DROSOPHILA and other fruit flies. Piles of POMACE and stems should also be distanced from the winery as these can become a breeding ground for insects. A.D.W.

Mitham, P., 'Clean wineries for quality wines', *Wines & Vines* (Nov 2013), 34–9.

Rieger, T., 'Microbial monitoring and winery sanitation practices for quality control', *Wine Business Monthly* (Oct 2015).

Yu, A. C., et al., 'Scalable manufacturing of biomimetic moldable hydrogels for industrial applications', *Proceedings of the National Academy of Sciences of the United States of America*, 113/50 (2016).

hyperoxidation. See OXIDATION.

I

IBMP, or **2-isobutyl-3-methoxypyrazine**. See ISOBUTYL-METHOXYPYRAZINE.

ice wine, direct Anglicization of the German EISWEIN, sweet wine made from ripe, healthy grapes picked when frozen on the vine and pressed so that water crystals remain in the PRESS and the sugar content of the resulting wine is increased. This sort of true ice wine is a speciality of CANADA, where it is written ICEWINE. It is also increasingly made elsewhere, including AUSTRIA, CHINA, LUXEMBOURG, OREGON, and MICHIGAN. The term has also been used in other English-speaking wine-producing countries for wines made by artificial freeze CONCENTRATION, or CRYOEXTRACTION.

Icewine is CANADA's version of EISWEIN. While Canada is the world's largest producer of ice wine, it comprises less than 5% of the country's total wine production by volume. It is made predominantly in ONTARIO, as well as in BRITISH COLUMBIA, QUEBEC, and NOVA SCOTIA. In 2014, a Government of Canada standard of identity was created stipulating that only wine made exclusively from grapes naturally frozen on the vine can be called 'icewine', 'ice wine' or 'ice-wine', whether made in or imported into Canada. The word 'Icewine', one word with a capital I, is trademarked by Wine Growers Canada, a national trade association. Grapes for VQA Icewine in Ontario and British Columbia must be harvested and pressed in a continuous process while the air temperature is −8 °C/17.6 °F or lower (compared to −7°C/19.5 °F for German Eiswein) with an average minimum sugar level of all grapes used in the final blend not less than 35 °Brix (around 154 °Oechsle, considerably higher than the minimum in Germany and Austria). Residual sugar at bottling must be at least 100 g/l in Ontario and British Columbia. Wineries must be registered with the delegated provincial authority and indicate their intention to make Icewine prior to harvest and advise when they have harvested. All Icewine must be VARIETAL and made from VITIS VINIFERA grapes or the French hybrid VIDAL, grown and pressed within a recognized Viticultural Area. Canadian wineries were the first to make sparkling Icewine and Icewine from red wine grapes. J.D.

Schreiner, J., *Icewine: The Complete Story* (2002).

icon wine, an expression favoured by marketing people for highly priced, often heavily oaked, wine. Icons are generally regarded as ultra-premium wines, which cost more than super-premium wines, which are in turn more expensive than premium wines. The rest is all but undrinkable.

Idaho, a Pacific Northwest state of the United States with a distinctly CONTINENTAL CLIMATE and three large AVAS. Most of the state's 65 wineries are found in the south-western part of the state where the Snake River Valley AVA and, within it, Eagle Foothills AVA lie on VOLCANIC ash and SANDY loam over ancient deposits from the long-extinct Lake Idaho. Much of Idaho's wine country is described as 'high desert', though the vineyards of Eagle Foothills, at about 762–1,067 m/2,500–3,500 ft in ELEVATION, particularly benefit from proximity to Prospect Peak and the airflow from the hills around it. Those GRANITIC slopes also add pebbly material to the vineyards.

A newer, lower-elevation AVA to the north, Lewis-Clark Valley, is engendering enthusiasm for its VITIS VINIFERA wines, including Bordeaux and Rhône varieties. The AVA shares many characteristics with the Walla Walla Valley AVA of OREGON and WASHINGTON, just 160 km/99 miles west—not only its LOESS soils but also that it drapes across the state line; about one-quarter of the AVA is in Washington State. D.F.

IFOAM, International Federation of Organic Agriculture Movements. See ORGANIC VITICULTURE.

IGP, short for *indication géographique protégée*, France's PGI category, which has replaced the old VIN DE PAYS and represents about 30% of all wine produced in France. Regulations for an IGP wine are much less strict than for an AOC wine. To qualify as an IGP, a wine must come from a specified area, be made of certain specified grape varieties (usually a much longer list than for an AOC wine), reach a certain minimum ALCOHOLIC STRENGTH, and be submitted to a tasting panel. Each IGP has its own specification, known as a *cahier des charges* (available on the INAO website, along with a map).

French wine producers who farm vineyards within an area that qualifies as an AOC have a choice between making an AOC/AOP (PDO) wine or an IGP wine, or even a wine without geographical indication (VSIG) that will be labelled VIN DE FRANCE, either because yields are too high to qualify for an AOC, or because the grape or mix of varieties used is not permitted by the AOC regulations, or because the tasting panel judges that the style does not conform to that outlined in the *cahier des charges*. In general, IGP wines may be produced from grapes which yield up to 90 hl/ha (5 tons/acre), while 50 hl/ha or so is a more likely maximum YIELD permitted by AOC regulations.

Some of France's 76 IGPs (as of 2022) are regional, for example Pays d'Oc (for wines from the LANGUEDOC and ROUSSILLON) or Val de LOIRE; some are departmental, named after one of France's *départements*, such as Aude, Gard, or

Gers. Some are more locally specific, named after some historical or geographical phenomenon such as Cité de Carcassonne and Alpilles. Some IGP names represent strokes of genius. The image of Corsica is transformed in the name Île de Beauté. Le Pays Cathare recalls the colourful history of this part of the western Languedoc, while one of Roussillon's most popular IGPs rightly emphasizes the region's ethnic origins in Côtes Catalanes. The most important single IGP by far is Pays d'Oc, France's prime source of VARIETAL wine. About 85% of all IGPs are grown in the Languedoc, Roussillon, Provence, or the southern Rhône. This category has also provided a useful way of selling the surplus produce of vines grown in regions specializing in brandy production. Crisp, dry white IGP Côtes de Gascogne has been the commercial saviour of vignerons in Armagnac country since the early 1980s, while the Cognac counterpart is now named Charentais.

IGT, or **IGP**, stands for Indicazione Geografica Tipica/Indicazione Geografia Protetta, corresponding to the EU denomination PGI. Either IGT or IGP may appear on labels. This category of wines was created in ITALY by law 164 in 1992 as an approximate equivalent of the French VIN DE PAYS. It officially enabled producers to give more information on the labels of their myriad esteemed, and often extremely expensive, wines than selling them as a VINO DA TAVOLA. IGT was created as the basis of a quality pyramid with DOC in the middle and DOCG at the top. Many producers are unable or unwilling to opt for any denomination higher than IGT, either because they produce wines from vine varieties and/or use winemaking techniques not permitted by the local DOC regulations, or because the quality control system, which must establish a wine's TYPICALITY, is unable or unwilling to adapt to changes in viticulture and winemaking resulting in different styles. Wines produced and bottled without SULFUR DIOXIDE, unfiltered wines, and SKIN-FERMENTED white wines fall victim to this. Particularly popular IGTs include Trevenezie, Puglia, Terre Siciliane, Toscana, and Veneto. W.S.

Île de Beauté is a nickname for CORSICA as well as the IGP zone covering the entire island. Many producers opt for this denomination—or forgo appellations completely, choosing the VIN DE FRANCE designation—to have more freedom, especially as most Corsican INDIGENOUS VARIETIES are not permitted by AOC regulations. The same goes for the recent revival of the historical LIMESTONE terroir of Bonifacio, spearheaded by Clos Canarelli from nearby Figari. Not yet recognized by any of Corsica's AOCs, these wines must be labelled as IGP or Vin de France. A.L.

Île-de-France. IGP approved in 2020 for still red, white, and rosé wines produced in and around PARIS. Five subregions may appear on wine labels: Paris, Guérard, Coteaux de Provins, Coteaux de Suresnes-Mont-Valérien, and Coteaux de Blunay.

imbottigliato is Italian for 'bottled'.

impériale. See BOTTLE SIZES.

Imperial Tokay, historical name used for wine produced on the vineyard properties of the Austrian Habsburg emperors in the TOKAJ-Hegyalja region of Hungary, especially during the 19th century. The Habsburg holdings were concentrated in the village of Tarcal, particularly the highly respected Szarvas vineyard that had been confiscated from the rebellious Prince Ferenc Rákóczi II in 1711. The term became widely known in western Europe following the creation of the Austro-Hungarian Monarchy in 1867. However, Imperial Tokay was usually misunderstood as either necessarily far superior to all other Tokaji wines or an alternative term for Eszencia. M.L.-G.

INAO, the **Institut National de l'Origine et de la Qualité** (formerly the Institut National des Appellations d'Origine), is the public organization in charge of recognizing, granting, administering, regulating, and protecting the French *appellations contrôlées*, or AOC, now known as *appellation d'origine protégée* or AOP (see PDO), and the other official *signes* such as IGP that identify quality and origin for agricultural products, including not just wines and spirits but also other alcoholic drinks, dairy products, olive oil, meat, honey, fruit and vegetables, etc. In 2020 there were more than 360 AOC/AOPs for wine (including the 51 separate ALSACE grand cru appellations) and 75 IGPs for wine, as well as 50 AOPs for dairy products and 45 for meat, poultry, olive oil, etc.

Now that IGP wines also come under the INAO umbrella, the INAO supervises more than 90% of French wine production. Nearly 75,000 vine-growers therefore are bound by its rules and depend on its protection—as well as its efforts to continue France's reliance on geographically based wine names rather than VARIETAL wines, known in French as *vins de cépage*. The headquarters are in Paris, but its decision-making structure operates through regional committees of wine professionals.

The INAO was founded in 1935; because France's leading role in the world of wine was undisputed for much of the 20th century, it provided a role model for the administration of more embryonic GEOGRAPHICAL INDICATION schemes being developed in other countries. During the 1980s, however, increasing competition on the domestic and export markets encouraged a re-examination of the role of the INAO. The result was an even stronger INAO, given additional powers in 1990, dedicated to defending and promoting the notion of controlled, geographically determined appellations for products that owe their characteristics to their place of origin and a prescribed mode of production. It is empowered to protect them against imitation both in France and abroad, convinced that France's viticultural future depends on its ability to trade on its uniquely well-established wine names.

Any group of wine producers can apply to the INAO to establish an AOP or an IGP. They have to prepare a dossier by giving reasons for the request, proof of the traditional use of the name of the proposed appellation, full details of the terroir and how it affects production, and economic details concerning added value, markets, sales, prices, and comparative prices of similar products. Once an application has been agreed by the INAO, it has to be approved by the EU and published in the *Journal Officiel de l'Union Européenne*.

The INAO is also concerned about the sustainability of AOPs and IGPs, reviewing regulations relating to methods of production, defending appellations against the effects of urbanization, and supporting them in anticipating and adapting to CLIMATE CHANGE (see, for example, VIFA) as well as in finding ways to reduce inputs such as fertilizers, irrigation, pesticides, and herbicides.

incrocio, Italian for 'vine CROSS'. A wine made from **Incrocio Manzoni** grapes, for example, is made from one of Signor Manzoni's many crosses of one VITIS VINIFERA variety with another. His Incrocio Manzoni 6.0.13, Riesling × Pinot Blanc, often known simply as Manzoni Bianco, is the most widely planted with 339 ha/838 acres in 2015, throughout Italy but especially in the south. Incrocio Manzoni 2.15 is Prosecco (now GLERA) × Cabernet Sauvignon. Incrocio Terzi No 1 is a Barbera × Cabernet Franc cross grown in Lombardy.

indexing, method of testing vines for VIRUS DISEASES, PHYTOPLASMA diseases, and their like by GRAFTING buds from an indicator vine—one which shows typical symptoms of the disease—on to the vines being tested. Cabernet Franc, for example, is used as an indicator vine variety to test for LEAFROLL VIRUS. Indexing tests have been replaced by serological methods; see ELISA. R.E.S.

India, large Asian country where wine consumption, production, and quality are increasing steadily. A growing middle class should maintain this trend, despite high taxes, licensing fees, discriminatory inter-state policies, and several dry states.

History

The vine was probably introduced into north-west India from Persia during the Indus civilization in the fourth millennium BCE, but wine may not have been made from its fruit for many centuries. The gradual invasion of Aryan tribes from central Asia during the second millennium BCE produced the Vedic period (*c.*2000–800 BCE), a blossoming of culture in north-west India. The Aryans enjoyed gambling, music, and intoxicating drink, and in the four Vedas, the world's oldest religious texts, two drinks are mentioned: *soma*, a milky drink ceremoniously prepared immediately before a sacrifice and probably containing hallucinatory hemp; and *sura*, a potent secular drink made from either barley or paddy (rice) fermented with honey.

While praising the fierce and hard-drinking Aryan warrior god Indra, the Vedas clearly condemn the effects of drinking. Later, Hindu, Buddhist, and Jain texts reveal similar dichotomies. Kautilya, chief minister under the Mauryan King Chandragupta (ruled *c.*324–300 BCE), was the author of the Arthasastra, a remarkable text on statecraft in which he condemns alcohol and yet chronicles the king's drinking bouts and mentions *madhu* (wine) of various varieties and qualities. This is the first documentation of wine made from grapes in India.

Down the centuries, wine has maintained its status in India as a drink of the Kshatriya caste of aristocrats and warriors rather than of the masses, who have preferred more potent alcohol prepared from the staple local agricultural cereal crops.

The contradictory attitudes towards intoxicating drinks continue into modern times. The Muslim (see ISLAM) Mughal emperors' royal vineyards were in the Deccan; the alcoholic emperor Jehangir (who ruled 1605–27) would drink himself insensible on double- and triple-distilled wine (brandy), violating the Qur'ān's command not to lose one's sensibilities through intoxication.

Secular independent India's Constitution, adopted on 26 January 1950, recommends total PROHIBITION of alcohol among its aims (in deference to Mahatma Gandhi, the father of the nation) but remains a state subject. Only a few states such as Gujarat, Tamil Nadu, Andhra Pradesh, and Haryana ever enforced, variously, limited or total prohibition. Today Gujarat (Mahatma Gandhi's home state) is the only major state that still has prohibition.

Although the orthodox of all faiths may abstain, Indians everywhere (except Gujarat) are free to consume wine and other alcohol if they choose.

Indian viticulture was encouraged in the 19th century as the Victorian British upper classes enjoyed drinking wine. Vineyards were established in Kashmīr, Bārāmati, Surat, and Golkonda. A number of Indian wines were exhibited at the Great Calcutta Exhibition of 1884 and elicited favourable comment. But in the 1890s, Indian vineyards, like their European counterparts, succumbed to PHYLLOXERA.

Since Independence in 1947, wine production has increased very slowly as it requires long-term investment and, ideally, a strong local market. Goa continued to produce low-quality fortified wines made in the image of PORT, an industry initiated by Portuguese colonists in the 16th century.

Until the 1990s, the small Indian wine industry went virtually unnoticed outside the country, partly because of the quality of the wine, made by rudimentary village operations, excepting a large winery and distillery established in Hyderābād and Bangalore in 1966 by the Shaw Wallace group, producing Golconda and Bosca wines.

Viticulture

India's 111,000 ha/274,287 acres of vineyards produce around 3.5 million tons of grapes a year, of which less than 2.5% are used as TABLE GRAPES and RAISINS. Established vineyards of mainly table grapes are found in the temperate north-west and as far south as the state of Tamil Nadu. Two-thirds of the country's area under vine, however, is in the south-central states of Mahārāshtra (86,000 ha/212,510 acres), Karnataka (18,100 ha/44,726 acres), and Tamil Nadu (2,700 ha/6,672 acres). In Mahārāshtra, cultivation is concentrated around Pune, Nāshik, Bārāmati, Sangali, and Sholhāpur on the west of the Deccan Plateau, about 300 km/180 miles in length and 60 km in width, 135 km inland from Mumbai. The remainder of southern India's plantings are near Bangalore and around Hyderābād.

Plantings range from ELEVATIONS of 300 m/984 ft on the Deccan in Mahārāshtra to over 500 m in Karnataka and a few at 800 m on the slopes of Sahyadri. With India's hot summer and heavy monsoon, temperatures in growing areas range from 8 °C/46 °F in winter to 45 °C/113 °F in summer, 625–1,500 mm/25–60 in of rain falling between June and August depending on the region. There is little unseasonal rain. Humidity levels are high, particularly during the monsoon, moderated only by afternoon winds. Eastern regions suffer most from humidity and extreme heat.

Over half the total vineyard area is planted to SULTANA, although INTERNATIONAL VARIETIES are increasingly planted by the leading wine companies. Indigenous TABLE GRAPES such as Anab-e-shahi are grown along with Bangalore Blue (ISABELLA) and Bangalore Purple, which are the major varieties in Tamil Nadu, Telengana, and Karnataka along with some Gulabi (MUSCAT OF HAMBURG) and small amounts of Perlette. These varieties account for less than 10% of Indian grapes, however.

Vines are trained high on wire and bamboo with wide ROW SPACING to retain SOIL WATER, prevent SUNBURN, and maximize aeration of the vines, minimizing the risk of FUNGAL DISEASES. Since the early 1980s, DRIP IRRIGATION has been used throughout the growing season. Pruning takes place in April and October with harvest (always manual in India) in February and March. Average YIELDS are 32 tons/ha. In warmer regions, particularly Andhra, Karnataka, and Tamil Nadu, two harvests a year are possible. See TROPICAL VITICULTURE.

The contemporary wine industry

The current renaissance of Indian viticulture began with pioneers Chateau Indage (known later as Indage Vintners) in 1984 near Pune in Mahārāshtra and Grover Vineyards in 1988 north of Bangalore in Karnataka, both of which set themselves the goal of exporting. Indage produced an impressively elegant sparkling wine for the international market. A short-sighted and aggressive overseas expansion programme and diversification in 2007/08 resulted in its collapse soon afterwards. Grover Vineyards trialled 33 vine varieties initially and settled principally on Cabernet Sauvignon and Clairette, which grow on PERGOLAS. Its first wine was released in 1992. With French oenologist Michel ROLLAND as its wine CONSULTANT, Grover's quality and reputation grew steadily. The company, merged with Nāshik-based Vallée de Vin (whose main brand is Zampa) to form Grover Zampa Vineyards in 2012, has grown considerably with new acquisitions.

Sula Vineyards, founded by former Silicon Valley engineer Rajeev Samant, set up its winery in Nāshik in Mahārāshtra in 1999 with the help of Californian wine consultant Kerry Damskey. Sula produced India's first varietal Chenin Blanc, Sauvignon Blanc, Riesling, and Zinfandel. In 2005 Sula overtook Grover to become India's largest wine producer following the demise of Indage Vintners. Today Sula's market share is around 70%, with sales of around 11 million bottles in 2020. The company also imports and distributes wine and has spearheaded wine TOURISM in India.

India's wine industry has also attracted significant outside investment: DIAGEO is a major shareholder in Four Seasons; LVMH launched Chandon India in 2014; Jean-Charles BOISSET is a partner in J'Noon, and Fratelli Wines is India's first Indo-Italian collaboration.

KRSMA Estates, a boutique winery near the UNESCO heritage site of Hampi in Karnataka, became India's first winery to be voted among the World's 50 Best Vineyards in 2020.

R.K.S.

Csizmadia-Honigh, P., *The Wines of India: A Concise Guide* (2015).

Chandra, A., 'Six of the Best', *Sommelier India Wine Magazine*, 16/4 (2020), 40–45.

Sharma, G., 'Nashik on the Move', *Sommelier India Wine Magazine*, 16/3 (2020), 40–45.
www.karnatakawineboard.com

Indiana, midwestern state in the UNITED STATES with more than 120 vineyards and wineries, many residing within the Indiana Uplands AVA, an area of 1,530 square miles (396,268 ha) next to the massive Ohio River Valley AVA (6,733,969 ha/16,640,000 acres) in 2022. Indiana Uplands wineries include Oliver Winery, established more than half a century ago and among the Midwest's largest wineries. Most Indiana wines are based upon fruits, HYBRIDS, and AMERICAN VINE SPECIES though a significant amount of VITIS VINIFERA-based wines are produced as well. The state was the site of some early vinous efforts by Swiss vineyardists, particularly Jean Jacques Dufour, author of *The American Vine-Dresser's Guide* (1826), which remained the dominant treatise far into the 19th century. D.F.

indicator. See INDEXING.

indigenous varieties, VINE VARIETIES that are intensely local to a particular area and have a relatively long tradition of being grown there. Researchers in SWITZERLAND and GASCONY were some of the first to rescue near-extinct local varieties in the 1980s, but they have been followed by a host of others in the early 21st century, particularly but not exclusively in Italy. A discernible FASHION for indigenous varieties emerged as a reaction to an earlier one for INTERNATIONAL VARIETIES.

Indonesia had six wineries by 2022, all on the resort island of Bali, and around 400 ha/988 acres of grapevines. The industry pioneer, Hatten Wines, is by far the largest winemaking enterprise, turning out 1.3 million bottles a year. It began making wines from locally grown grapes in 1994, operating from an old rice wine factory at Sanur Beach in the south-east of the island, but its vineyards are in the Buleleng region in the island's north-west (latitude 8° S). Here, ELEVATION provides some modest respite from the relentless TROPICAL heat and humidity, but climatic conditions are such that the vines crop almost continuously.

Indonesia's original vineyards were planted by European settlers with the French VITIS VINIFERA varieties Alphonse Lavallée (Ribier) and Belgia. Both remain the major varieties, grown on overhead PERGOLAS to better manage the humidity, and are now used extensively for winemaking. Probolinggo Biru, a white-berried variety likely introduced from India, is being cultivated by Hatten for sparkling wines. Hatten also grow Syrah, MALVASIA NERA, SOLARIS, CHENIN BLANC, COLOMBARD, and Swiss HYBRIDS Muscat Bleu and Cabernet Blanc, PRUNING twice to force DORMANCY, allowing just one harvest per year (see TROPICAL VITICULTURE). Sababay, Bali's second largest producer, supplements domestically grown grapes with imported concentrates for its wines. Using imported grapes or MUST is popular because it allows consumers access to 'imported' wine without the onerous taxes. D.G.

inert gas, a gas used to protect wine from OXIDATION, including CARBON DIOXIDE, NITROGEN, and argon. Of these, the only truly inert gas is argon. Carbon dioxide is ideal for removing oxygen from storage vessels because it is heavier than air. Inert gas mixtures are often used because carbon dioxide dissolves in wine, possibly giving a higher-than-desirable residual concentration of this gas. Argon, like nitrogen, has a very low solubility in wine, and inert gas mixtures of either or both of these two with carbon dioxide can, with modern metering equipment, be selected to leave a residual level of dissolved carbon dioxide that is optimal for the style of wine under storage. Inert gases are also used to flush the oxygen from hoses and pumps, as well as during BOTTLING. D.B.

Inferno, one of five subzones of the VALTELLINA Superiore DOCG in the far north of Italy.

inflorescence, the structure that bears the flowers (see BUNCH for more details). At FLOWERING, the grape flower becomes a BERRY and the inflorescence a bunch.

influencers have an increasing effect on FASHION and sales of wine, thanks to their presence in SOCIAL MEDIA. As in other spheres, some write what they are paid to while others have much higher ethical standards and enrich WINE WRITING (and imagery) in general. For newcomers, social media is the obvious gateway to a wine-related career.

information technology (IT) has revolutionized the world of wine as much as any other. Computers are now used throughout the production process. In the vineyard they can schedule and control IRRIGATION, for example, or measure weather and predict and even control SPRAYING regimes. They can assist VINEYARD SITE SELECTION by analysing and mapping data on CLIMATE, SOIL, VIGOUR, and TOPOGRAPHY. By monitoring, for example, WATER STRESS or FERTILIZATION needs in different parts of a vineyard, IT and ARTIFICIAL INTELLIGENCE can help control wine quality (see QUALITY IN WINE) and BERRY SIZE and in the long term can contribute towards SUSTAINABILITY. In the winery, IT can weigh and SAMPLE grapes, sort them (see GRAPE SORTING) sort control CRUSHING and PRESSING operations, ensure the most vigilant TEMPERATURE CONTROL, and eventually oversee BOTTLING.

Thanks to information technology, wine ANALYSIS is today much more sophisticated than could have been imagined even a decade ago, and there have even been attempts to mechanize the process of TASTING. During fermentation, IT-integrated tanks provide temperature and wine composition data for each tank, not just in the winery but for a CONSULTANT who may be thousands of miles away. During ÉLEVAGE, the content and history of individual tanks, barrels, and pallets can also be tracked.

Information technology has greatly assisted such techniques as DNA PROFILING in vine-variety identification and the possible new technique of 'fingerprinting' a vineyard by analysis of its MINERALS.

Those who sell wine, whether to consumers or in BULK to the trade, can use information technology to administer all aspects of TRANSPORT, STORAGE, stock control, and retailing, as well as being able to present their wares directly to potential customers via the internet—which can be an advantage when selling a commodity as tightly regulated, heavy, and fragile as bottles of wine (see E-COMMERCE). The internet has spawned a new generation of independent, often very small, online wine merchants, and has greatly widened the appeal of wine AUCTIONS.

As well as offering wine consumers a new market place, for both buying and selling, and a new medium for wine information, opinion, and EDUCATION via myriad websites, blogs, and online posts, the internet has provided them with an unprecedented forum for discussion, not just about the wines themselves but also about WINE WRITERS, a new sort of consumer power, even if one that tends to attract wine BORES. Platforms such as Twitter, Facebook, and Instagram (see SOCIAL MEDIA) are spreading the diversity of wine to a much less specialized, more democratic readership, encouraging the discovery of wines from a broader range of countries and sources. These tools have helped wine producers, retailers, and regions to find new routes to the consumer.

Those who keep and wish to share detailed cellar records and TASTING NOTES have reason to be grateful for the flexibility and sorting ability of IT (see CELLARTRACKER). And price-comparison websites such as Wine-Searcher.com have revolutionized wine retailing and encouraged fair PRICING on a global scale.

As online technologies develop, the international wine market is being revolutionized. For example, our mobile phones can now provide us with more information than we could have dreamt of simply by being pointed at a wine label or QR code. Microchips inserted in cases of wine provide fine-wine lovers with myriad data on shipping TEMPERATURES. They are expected to play an increasing part in fighting COUNTERFEIT WINE and much else besides.

infrared spectroscopy is fast becoming a routine ANALYSIS method in wine laboratories.

This ground-breaking technique relies on the fact that all organic compounds have a unique spectral fingerprint in the Near Infrared (NIR) and Mid Infrared (MIR) regions of the electromagnetic spectrum. In the past it has been difficult to interpret these fingerprints on grape or wine samples, but by the 2010s the availability of cheap instrumentation, computing power, and software development meant that it had become a standard method of analysis in food and agriculture, including the wine industry.

The critical advantages of IR spectroscopy are that very little sample preparation is required, no dangerous laboratory chemicals are needed, multiple analyses can be tested simultaneously, and, once the methods have been developed and programmed into the instrument, very little user training is required. NIR is less sensitive than MIR, but the lower absorbance makes it more penetrating, capable of analysis of grape must, whole grapes, grapevine tissue, and soil. The penetrating power of NIR can also be utilized to analyse packaged wine non-destructively, by scanning through the bottle. MIR is more sensitive and is better suited to the analysis of clarified grape juice and wine.

IR spectroscopy may be used to analyse, for example, SUGAR, PH, ACIDITY, moisture content, TANNINS, ANTHOCYANINS, and GLYCOSYL-GLUCOSE. Grapes can also be analysed for negative quality indicators, such as fungal spoilage by BOTRYTIS and POWDERY MILDEW. Water potential of grapevine leaves is used as an indicator of WATER STRESS and can be analysed non-destructively by IR spectroscopy to aid IRRIGATION scheduling. Grapevine wood (see CANE and TRUNK) can be analysed for starch and sugar, to determine over-wintering vine storage reserves. Wines can be analysed for most routine measures such as DENSITY, ALCOHOL, pH, total acidity, sugar, VOLATILE ACIDITY, anthocyanins, tannins, and organic ACIDS. In addition to quantitative methods, with appropriate software qualitative methods such as classification of growing region and grape variety can be performed with the IR fingerprint, allowing the possibility of rapid wine AUTHENTICATION. IR spectroscopy can also be used to uncover ADULTERATION of wine. R.D.

Gishen, M., et al., 'The analysis of grapes, wine, and other alcoholic beverages by infrared spectroscopy', in E. C. Y. Li-Chan et al. (eds.), *Applications of Vibrational Spectroscopy in Food Science* (2010), 539–56.

ingredient labelling. Since detailed specification on labels of ingredients in foodstuffs is mandatory in most major markets, the EU has proposed that wine should also be subject to this requirement, and the US looks set to follow. By 2021 the EU producers' association, the CEEV, had made considerable progress towards this development, which will be mandatory for all wine sold in the EU by the end of 2023. Since all ingredients (not PROCESSING AIDS as defined by the OIV) will have to be listed, as well as nutritional information, in the language of each country in which the wine is sold, this could be extremely difficult on traditional printed LABELS. Even some of the most lauded wines in the world may have to cite yeast (unless AMBIENT), sugar (if CHAPTALIZED), and TARTARIC ACID (if acidified), together with any other ADDITIVES. Mindful of this, the CEEV has developed a global platform for digital U-labels, an alternative to printed labels whereby all this can be communicated by a QR code on the bottle, with automatic translations. Producers of NATURAL WINE presumably welcome any public airing of the wide array of additives used by their more industrial rivals, but smartphones may become an essential accessory for curious wine drinkers. See also LABELLING INFORMATION.

initiation, botanical term for the start of the vine's fruiting when the first signs of bunches are evident as small pieces of tissue in the developing bud. These buds are themselves developing beside the leaf stalk on the shoots as they grow in spring. Initiation starts simultaneously with the FLOWERING stage of the growing season. Warm, sunny weather conditions at this time favour initiation, with one, two, occasionally three, or very rarely four bunches per bud initiated. When this bud bursts the following year, it will be termed FRUITFUL. Cold, cloudy weather depresses fruit bud initiation, and varieties vary in fruitfulness.

Part of the annual variation in vineyard YIELD is thus due to weather conditions affecting initiation during the year previous to the crop being harvested. The time when the vines are flowering is the most critical period for bunch initiation. Warm sunny weather encourages both the flowering of the year's crop and, in the buds developing in the leaf axil on the developing shoot, the initiation of next year's crop. R.E.S.

Keller, M., 'Phenology and growth cycle', in *The Science of Grapevines* (3rd edn, 2020).

injection, alternative name for CARBONATION, the cheapest and least effective method of SPARKLING WINEMAKING involving the simple pumping of CARBON DIOXIDE into a tank of wine.

inner staves, or **inserts**, planks of wood, usually OAK (exclusively oak in the EU), placed in a stainless-steel tank and held in position by a metal framework, are a way of imparting oak flavour and other attributes such as STRUCTURE, roundness, and LENGTH to wine more cheaply than by fermenting or ageing in BARRELS since the staves are easily replaced. Tank staves are sometimes used in conjunction with MICRO-OXYGENATION to mimic the use of barrels for fermentation or maturation without the cost of barrels, a barrel cellar, and barrel cellar workers. Staves may also be used in oxygen-permeable tanks made of food-grade POLYETHYLENE. See also BARREL INSERTS.

INRAE (l'Institut National de la Recherche pour l'Agriculture, l'Alimentation et l'Environnement). The National Research Institute for Agriculture, Food and the Environment was created in 2020 by merging **INRA**, the National Research Institute for Agricultural Research, and IRSTEA, the National Research Institute of Science and Technology for the Environment and Agriculture. It is under the control of both the Ministry for Scientific Research and the Ministry of Agriculture.

INRAE brings together a community of 12,000 people, with just over 200 research units and around 40 experimental units in 18 centres across France, three of which specialize in grapevines and wine. A world leader in agricultural and food sciences, plant and animal sciences, and ecological and environmental research, the institute's ambition is to be a key player in responding to major global challenges such as population growth, CLIMATE CHANGE, the scarcity of resources, and the decline in biodiversity by building solutions that promote both yield and quality as well as sustainable management of resources and ecosystems.

INRAE Bordeaux, part of the ISVV, specializes in grapevine ecophysiology, genetics, ROOTSTOCKS, pest and diseases, OENOLOGY, and experimental economics.

INRAE Montpellier focuses on ecophysiology and 3D plant modelling, taking into account WATER and HEAT STRESS; genetic diversity; oenology; PRECISION VITICULTURE; water management; viticulture systems under Mediterranean conditions; and the socio-economics and institutional management of the wine industry. The Montpellier Pôle Vigne-Vin brings together the various research and technology departments involved in the vine and wine industry in Montpellier and the Institut des Hautes Études de la Vigne et du Vin to disseminate technological innovation and to train agronomists and oenologists.

At Colmar, research focuses on genetic breeding, berry composition, and FUNGAL and VIRUS DISEASES. Researchers have identified innovative solutions that meet the challenges of SUSTAINABLE VITICULTURE, including new varieties resistant to DOWNY MILDEW and POWDERY MILDEW.

INRA's most significant contributions to advances in viticulture since its foundation in 1946 include the introduction of CLONAL SELECTION in France to help combat virus diseases and thus improve quality and YIELDS; the development of LOW-INPUT VITICULTURE (often referred to as *lutte raisonnée*), establishing the best use of fertilizers on high-quality vineyards, reducing the use of FUNGICIDES, and breeding DISEASE-RESISTANT VARIETIES; and understanding the influence on wine quality of different vine-TRAINING SYSTEMS and the condition of grapes at HARVEST. Other research priorities have included grape RIPENING, the organoleptic properties of PHENOLIC compounds, wine stability, biology of wine YEASTS, and control of FERMENTATIONS.

IRSTEA's historical contributions are related to water management (developing IRRIGATION systems, for example) and, in collaboration with Montpellier SupAgro, precision viticulture.

INRA's collection of 7,000 VITIS VINIFERA varieties and HYBRIDS, held at the Domaine de Vassal on the Mediterranean coast, is now managed by INRAE and known as the Centre de Ressources Biologiques de la Vigne (CRB-Vigne). It works in partnership with the Institut Français de la Vigne et du Vin (IFV) and other professional bodies and has been a centre for the analysis, preservation, and management of biodiversity, especially with regard to pest and disease resistance and wine quality. The sandy soils are free of both PHYLLOXERA and the nematode *Xiphinema index*. Some NEW VARIETIES, MARSELAN, for example, have also been developed here; thanks to the work of AMPELOGRAPHERS such as Paul Truel and, later, Jean-Michel Boursiquot and Thierry Lacombe, Domaine de Vassal is a worldwide focus for vine identification. Work began in 2014 to move the collection to INRAE's experimental unit Pech Rouge near Narbonne. J.E.H. & I.G.d.C.-A.

www.inrae.fr/en

insecticides. See PESTICIDES.

insect pests. A wide variety of insects attack grapevines. Injury may occur as a result of direct feeding action, where reductions in leaf amount or leaf health can delay RIPENING with serious implications for wine quality, or as a result of carrying (vectoring) a particular VIRUS DISEASE or PHYTOPLASMA disease.

Alternatively the vine root system can be attacked, which leads to development of WATER STRESS and restricted VINE NUTRITION. While minor stress may enhance wine quality (see VINE PHYSIOLOGY), the more likely outcome of root damage by insects such as PHYLLOXERA (the most destructive of all insect pests) is severe stress or vine death. Insect pests such as phylloxera attack only grapevines, while many others attack a range of different plants.

Different insect pests attack grapes and vines in different parts of the world and in different districts, and what may be an important pest in one area may be unimportant or non-existent in another. The most important in European vineyards are the BEETLES *écrivain* and *cigarier*, the MOTHS cochylis, eudemis, and eulia, and MITES. The MEDITERRANEAN FRUIT FLY can be a pest in some areas of Australia but is not present in the United States, while LEAFHOPPERS are serious pests in California but not Australia. Other insects, such as CUTWORM and GRASSHOPPERS, are general agricultural pests worldwide.

Insect pests which affect only the appearance of grapes concern growers of TABLE GRAPES but not growers of wine grapes, who are more likely to be concerned with effects on YIELD or wine quality. Grape RIPENING can be seriously delayed, for example, when the WESTERN GRAPELEAF SKELETONIZER reduces leaf area and thus reduces PHOTOSYNTHESIS; vineyards can be destroyed as young plantings by cutworms or when mature by MARGARODES and phylloxera. Perhaps more insidiously, insects such as the fruit fly (see DROSOPHILA) can carry spores associated with BUNCH ROTS, and the MEALYBUG can transmit LEAFROLL virus. Leafhoppers spread the serious GRAPEVINE YELLOWS and PIERCE'S DISEASE and make such disease notoriously difficult to control. The larvae of some insect BORERS, such as the fig longicorn borer (*Acalolepta vastator*) in the Hunter Valley, can live inside grapevines and cause damage to the trunk.

Over recent decades, insects have also been found to cause wine taints when they are present on the fruit at harvesting and crushing. See LADYBUG TAINT and BROWN MARMORATED STINK BUG.

In general, insect pests are relatively easy to control in vineyards, although insecticides (see PESTICIDES) are among the more dangerous AGROCHEMICALS for operators to apply. Modern approaches to viticulture are more environmentally aware than previously, and so persistent chemicals such as DDT are no longer used, and INTEGRATED PEST MANAGEMENT, designed to reduce insecticide use, is becoming increasingly common, as are ORGANIC and BIODYNAMIC VITICULTURE. For example, predatory mites are encouraged, to control levels of damaging mites.

See also entries for the specific pests ANTS, APHIDS, BEETLES, BORERS, BROWN MARMORATED STINK BUG, CUTWORMS, DROSOPHILA, ERINOSE MITE, GRASSHOPPERS, LEAFHOPPERS, LOCUSTS, MARGARODES, MEALYBUGS, MITES, MOTHS, PHYLLOXERA, SCALE, SPOTTED LANTERNFLY, THRIPS, and WESTERN GRAPELEAF SKELETONIZER. R.E.S.

Bettiga, L. J., (ed.), *Grape Pest Management* (3rd edn, 2013).

Buchanan, G. A., and Amos, T. G., 'Grape pests', in B. G. Coombe and P. R. Dry (eds.), *Viticulture*, ii: *Practices* (2nd edn, 2006).

integrated pest management, or **IPM**, a term which dates back to the mid 1970s in Europe. Initially developed for INSECT PESTS, IPM now encompasses the control of diseases, weeds, and physiological vine disorders and has the potential to increase economic returns for the grower and improve environmental and human safety by reducing, limiting or even eliminating the use of AGROCHEMICALS.

IPM is considered by conventional growers as a form of SUSTAINABLE VITICULTURE, but most IPM management systems differ from ORGANIC VITICULTURE because they tolerate the use of industrially synthesized products such as HERBICIDES, PESTICIDES, and FERTILIZERS. However, IPM aims to stop the regular, calendar-based spraying of chemicals in a potentially wasteful manner and instead to apply such treatments in a more accurately timed way and targeted to specific threats.

Thus IPM takes account of the environment, particularly weather phenomena recorded in VINEYARD WEATHER STATIONS, the occurrence and life cycles of pests, and the incidence of natural enemies and alternative host plants. It requires a knowledge of the biology of the pest and, monitoring of the occurrences of the pest and any natural predators. All this information is integrated into a decision-making process, often involving computer applications based on disease modelling and, increasingly, using ARTIFICIAL INTELLIGENCE.

A number of VINE PESTS and diseases have been studied under the aegis of IPM philosophy. For example, the European grapevine MOTHS *Lobesia botrana* and *Eupoecilia ambiguella* can cause extensive damage, and studies have shown that their population levels can be limited naturally by VIRUS DISEASES and protozoan diseases. Similarly, MITES which damage vines can be controlled by other species of predatory mites, but sometimes the latter's beneficial effect can actually be limited by the application of pesticides, in particular some FUNGICIDES. Indeed, the increased use of some agrochemicals has altered the balance of predator to pest mites. M.W. & R.E.S.

Grandperrin, T., 'From industrial pesticides to Integrated Pest Management: a new trend in vineyard practices', *The Wine Industry Advisor* (2020). www.wineindustryadvisor.com/2020/11/06/new-trends-vineyard-practices.

University of California Agriculture & Natural Resources, UC IPM: grape. www2.ipm.ucanr.edu/agriculture/grape.

integrated production, or **IP**, European system of viticulture, developed in the 1970s, aimed at reducing environmental degradation in vineyards while at the same time maintaining economic viability of viticulture. It is similar in philosophy to SUSTAINABLE VITICULTURE. As the name suggests, it has its roots in INTEGRATED PEST MANAGEMENT, or IPM.

South Africa's INTEGRATED PRODUCTION OF WINE (IPW) is a voluntary scheme established in 1998 and emphasizes the importance of balancing the needs of the natural habitat with those of winegrowers. See also ORGANIC and BIODYNAMIC VITICULTURE.

Integrated Production of Wine (IPW) in SOUTH AFRICA is a voluntary environmental SUSTAINABILITY scheme established in 1998. The scheme's criteria are based on international standards and were drafted taking account of International Federation of Wines and Spirits (FIVS) and the OIV's guidelines for sustainable viti-viniculture. For grape production these include SOIL PREPARATION, VINE NUTRITION, IRRIGATION, CANOPY MANAGEMENT, GROWTH REGULATORS, INTEGRATED PEST MANAGEMENT, and handling of AGROCHEMICALS. Only grapes that qualify for IPW may be used for IPW wines. The cellar and wine-production guidelines cover issues such as SULFUR DIOXIDE levels as well as WINERY WASTE management. The production practices of members and aspirant members of the scheme are evaluated and audited by the Wine and Spirit Board. Wines which have achieved an appropriate level of IPW compliance are marketed with an IPW certification seal. The World Wildlife Fund (WWF) Biodiversity & Wine Initiative operates with the IPW certification scheme and aims to minimize the loss of natural habitat by working with producers who commit to set aside protected areas for long-term conservation. M.F.

International Grape Genome Program (IGGP), a framework for multinational collaborative grapevine research, with an emphasis on grapevine genomics. This project fosters efforts to characterize grape genes responsible for resistance to pests and diseases, vine growth, and fruit quality. These efforts result in the identification of genetic markers capable of expediting and optimizing classical VINE BREEDING. They also lead to the identification of grape genes that could be used to genetically modify and improve grapevines while having limited impact on variety integrity, a process known as cisgenics. See GENETIC MODIFICATION and PIERCE'S DISEASE.

www.vitaceae.org

international varieties, loose term for those VINE VARIETIES with an international reputation for their VARIETAL wines. They are planted in almost every major wine region in which they stand a chance of ripening. Foremost among them are the red-wine variety CABERNET SAUVIGNON and the white-wine variety CHARDONNAY (which many consumers take to be either a place or, more usually, a BRAND). Other strong candidates as international varieties are MERLOT, PINOT NOIR, and, especially, SYRAH/SHIRAZ among reds and SAUVIGNON BLANC, RIESLING, MUSCAT, GEWÜRZTRAMINER, VIOGNIER, PINOT BLANC, and PINOT GRIS among whites. As winemakers and wine consumers constantly search for new excitement, the list of possibilities grows longer. MOURVÈDRE, TEMPRANILLO, SANGIOVESE, and NEBBIOLO could already be said to have joined this elite with all manner of others in the wings. But the second decade of this century, as part of a reaction to GLOBALIZATION, saw a certain backlash against international varieties in favour of INDIGENOUS VARIETIES and ALTERNATIVE VARIETIES.

International Wine & Food Society (IWFS), the oldest and most cosmopolitan of the gastronomic societies for consumers rather than professionals. Initially simply the Wine & Food Society, it was founded in London in 1933 by André SIMON and like-minded friends. Its aim, other than providing a readership for a journal *Wine and Food* which Simon planned to edit, was to promote the highest quality of raw materials and an appreciation of how they could best be served and consumed. An early motto was 'Not much, but the best'. Launched in full economic depression (partly as a reaction to the culinary decline which resulted from it), the society attracted its fair share of criticism initially and might well have withered had not the Repeal of PROHIBITION opened up North America to the proselytizing of M. Simon. Soon there were branches all over the United States, where it is most important today, although the IWFS remains based in London. André Simon and his early colleague A. J. A. Symons launched the first pocket VINTAGE CHART in 1935, and it is annually revised by a special committee of the IWFS to this day, providing useful income through sales to publishers of diaries and the like. The journal, abandoned in 2000, was at one stage edited by Hugh JOHNSON.

internet. See INFORMATION TECHNOLOGY.

internode, the part of the stem between NODES. The internode length varies between different VINE VARIETIES and with growing conditions. It is shorter with weak shoots, low temperatures, WATER STRESS, mineral deficiencies (especially of NITROGEN), and the position along the shoot (with the nodes closest together at the base and the tip). Shoots on vigorous vines have long internodes and are large in diameter. Measured lengths vary from about 1 mm to 350 mm/13.6 in, but commercially used cuttings usually have internode lengths between 50 and 150 mm. B.G.C.

interspecific hybrid denotes the result of sexually crossing more than one grapevine species, while a CROSS of varieties of the same species is **intraspecific**. See HYBRID and VITIS for some background.

intolerance of wine. See ALLERGIES AND INTOLERANCES.

invecchiato, Italian for 'aged', although *affinato* is more frequently used.

invertase, a very important ENZYME in the grape berry for converting the larger molecule SUCROSE to its constituent molecules of GLUCOSE and FRUCTOSE in the ripening fruit so that sugar develops (see SUGAR IN GRAPES). The name 'invertase' comes from the so-called 'invert' sugars of glucose and fructose. The reaction of this enzyme differs from that of other enzymes in that it is not reversible. This is one of the most widespread enzymes in the plant kingdom and, indeed, one of the most efficient. It can metabolize 1 million times its own weight of sucrose with no loss of activity. The enzyme is located in the VACUOLE of berry cells, where it functions readily in the acidic environment. R.E.S.

investment in wine is the acquisition of wine for gain, whether as a means of making money, financing consumption, or a combination of the two.

The principal object of wine investment is to make a profit on wine which has increased in value as it matures. The essential premise on which wine investment is based is that demand for the wine in question exceeds supply, a premise that is often hard to gauge with accuracy, although it can help to secure wines of limited availability or high FASHION that may not appear again on the market.

Buying 'earliest, cheapest, lowest' is usually available to those in the know or with solid contacts. Indeed, historically the wine trade itself, with its inside knowledge, has been known to 'take a position' on a vintage, buying grapes on a speculative hunch. This practice, known as buying *sur souches* (i.e. while the grapes are still on the vine) was referred to in Roman times by PLINY the Younger (8. 2) and became part of the folklore of the BORDEAUX TRADE, as discussed below.

Speculation and buying for consumption need not be mutually exclusive. Indeed, spreading the risk by buying mixed portfolios of wine with both disposal and consumption in mind makes sound sense and is normally advised by companies dealing in wine investment. In times of economic uncertainty, a tangible asset such as wine can bring with it comfort and prestige, and with a life expectancy for tax purposes of less than 50 years, it does not generally attract capital gains tax in the UK, unlike in the US, where the higher, collectible capital gains tax is charged when collectors sell wine. There may, however, be circumstances in which even UK tax officials would regard wine investment as a business and tax it accordingly. Vintage PORT, in particular, with a life expectancy of 50 years or more, is liable not to be regarded as a wasting asset for tax purposes.

The popularity of wine as an investment has led to the creation of a number of investment schemes, or wine FUNDS, based in the UK, some of which are regulated by the Financial Services Authority (FSA), unlike those of wine merchants whose main aim is to move stock.

Since 2012, the FSA has attempted to tighten the rules to prevent consumers from being sold risky investments.

But wine investment is inevitably a gamble, especially for anyone under the mistaken impression that making money from it is simply a question of holding on long enough to one's stock. Speculation in wine tends to be especially risky because wine is subject to the unpredictable fluctuations of market forces. Buyers' and sellers' markets come and go, and wine PRICES are as liable to go down as up. BORDEAUX, for reasons discussed below, has been the principal medium of wine investment. The name Bordeaux is virtually synonymous with wine investment, and its turbulent past bears witness to fortunes made and unmade in the name of wine.

In more recent years, the wine-investment scene has embraced a wider portfolio of wine regions, notably Burgundy, as well as Champagne, Italy, Spain, and California. It has also attracted unscrupulous individuals who have manipulated secondary wine market data and extrapolated media reports to build a case for wine investment. Because fine wine is held in distant warehouses for many years, it is the perfect vehicle for unscrupulous traders. Promises of high returns have often not been fulfilled because of fat broker margins, high storage costs, weakening currency-exchange markets, company failure, and shady dealings. COUNTERFEIT WINE accounts for a small proportion of the fine and rare wine market, but in periods of high speculation and expectations some fraudsters have attempted to circulate wines of questionable provenance, especially in emerging and particularly buoyant markets.

Bordeaux: cyclical history

The first great boom in Bordeaux resulted from a period of prosperity which coincided with shortages caused by POWDERY MILDEW in the 1850s. The canny merchant Hermann Cruse had struck the first speculative blow already, when in 1848 he had bought up vast quantities of the 1847 vintage, only to release his hoard at undisclosed prices following Napoleon III's imperial accession. British Chancellor of the Exchequer (later to be Prime Minister) Gladstone's reduction of duty on French wine following the 1860 Anglo-French Commercial Treaty and the Single Bottle Act of 1861 (which paved the way for the off-licence and thus a retail trade in alcoholic drinks) further fuelled demand for red bordeaux.

Following the fine vintages of 1864 and 1865, prices doubled. Two successive lean years then led to speculative buying of the hard and slow-maturing 1868 vintage, *sur souches*. Chx Lafite and Margaux offered their 1868 to the Bordeaux market, achieving record prices which were not to be surpassed for another 58 years. But this was already the beginning of the end of the first golden era of wine. The Bordeaux merchant Edouard Kressmann mirrored Hermann Cruse's earlier coup with his successful speculative purchase of the fine 1870 vintage harvested during the Franco-Prussian War. The 1875 vintage marked the end of this flamboyant period, however, as the imminent plagues of DOWNY MILDEW and PHYLLOXERA cast a blight over the vineyards of Bordeaux (see BORDEAUX, history).

History was to repeat itself nearly a century later. During the post-war period of economic regeneration, the turning point came in 1959, when, following two devaluations of the French franc, the Americans first decisively entered the market for fine Bordeaux wines. The 1959 vintage was hailed as the vintage of the century, a term which has subsequently come to be applied ad nauseam to almost any vintage of note (usually revealing more about the ability of the Bordelais to feed speculation than about the quality of the vintage at issue). The clamour increased for the small but spectacular vintage of 1961. Between 1958 and 1961, the prices of the FIRST GROWTHS, on which most of the speculative activity was focused, more than quadrupled. By 1961, they had widened the gap between themselves and the other CLASSED GROWTHS to such an extent that their reputation as blue-chip investment wines became even more firmly established.

Towards the end of the decade, the devaluation of the French franc in 1969 and the rivalry between Chx LAFITE and MOUTON ROTHSCHILD contributed to a fresh climate of speculation that was to grip Bordeaux in the early 1970s. An opening-price battle between the first growths heralded the start of a boom, underpinned by a widespread feeling that demand would outstrip supply for the foreseeable future. A flood of foreign investment capital washed into Bordeaux to lap up the 1970 and 1971 vintages. Extortionate prices were asked—and paid—for the 1972 vintage, even though it turned out to be lean and mean.

A market develops

As inflation soared, red bordeaux became a wine investor's primary haven. The AUCTION houses Christie's and Sotheby's, whose new wine departments were established in, respectively, 1966 and 1970, provided the ideal forum for acquisitions and disposals. During the same period, numerous investment schemes were established to attract corporate finance, while wine merchants such as Justerini & Brooks set up their own schemes to cater for the speculative appetites of consumers.

Rising oil prices and the collapse of American financial hegemony already signalled impending disaster by the spring of 1973. Tastings of the 1972 vintage coincided with the prospect of a large 1973 vintage, which turned out to be unexceptional in quality. Circumstances were aggravated by a scandal in which the Bordeaux house of Cruse was charged with—and subsequently convicted of—fraud. By 1975 Chx Lafite and Mouton Rothschild had buried the hatchet and offered surplus stocks through Christie's.

Speculation fever was rekindled by the *annus mirabilis* of 1982, when an exceptional red Bordeaux vintage coincided with a relatively weak French franc and a strong American dollar. Opening prices of the first growths, FF170, were more than double those of the 1980s. The fashion for buying EN PRIMEUR, boosted by the superb 1982 vintage, created a new wave of populist investment fervour. The momentum for this new form of speculative buying was buoyed by a succession of fine vintages during the 1980s and by, for the first time, accessible press comment on the relative merits of individual, if embryonic, wine samples (see WINE WRITING). The 100-point SCORING system, introduced by the American critic Robert PARKER, brought fresh impetus to invest and an independent basis for assessing fine wine.

In the early to mid 1990s, despite particularly fine crops in 1985, 1986, 1989, and 1990, the market took a downward turn. The unfulfilled promise of increasing consumption was further aggravated by an embarrassing surplus of fine bordeaux. Following two successive great vintages in 2009 and 2010, with an influx of interest from Asia and exorbitant prices to match, three consecutive vintages of average quality called into question the entire future of the en primeur market and the Place de Bordeaux as the principal incubators of the secondary market. Confidence was also dented by the proliferation of unscrupulous peddlars of wine investment schemes (some of whom owned very little wine and knew even less about it, but were adept at cold calling) and some widely publicized counterfeit wines. In the subsequent decade, prices of fine bordeaux failed to recover their 2011 peak. The en primeur campaign for the 2019 vintage—held when global pandemic restrictions precluded tastings in Bordeaux—created an opportunity to reset release prices downwards. That most 2019s came to market cheaper than any vintages physically available incited a resurgence in demand for the region's wines.

The electronic trading platform Liv-ex doubles as an independent monitor of market activity and prices. Its expanded indices show a growing spread of investment-grade wines from outside Bordeaux, in particular from Burgundy, Champagne, the Rhône, Italy, and the New World. Bordeaux's share of the secondary market decreased steadily from 2011, plummeting from 65% in 2011 to 30% in 2021 and conceding ground to Burgundy, in particular the

DOMAINE DE LA ROMANÉE-CONTI, as an investment vehicle.

How to minimize the risks

The lessons of the recent past are that, in order to fulfil the promise of any investment, timing, knowledge, and skill (not to mention a measure of luck) are all essential preconditions for would-be investors, whether individuals or companies. Timing requires knowledge both of market conditions and of the potential of a wine for maturing. The finer the wine, generally speaking, the longer it takes to reach its peak and the longer it remains on a plateau of maturity. One of the best ways to acquire such knowledge is to keep abreast of the pronouncements of the most influential wine critics, but anyone buying for investment would be well-advised to read a range of expert opinions on any particular wine or vintage and keep track of price indices such as those published by winemarketjournal.com.

At the same time, investors need to be aware of less immediately obvious features of wine investment such as the importance of optimum storage conditions (see STORING WINE), the costs of storage, insurance, and reselling involved, disposal options, length of holding time, and ownership issues such as obtaining evidence, insofar as possible, to one's title to the goods. The better the guarantee of storage in ideal conditions, the higher the likely PROVENANCE. At the commercial auction houses, the vendor can expect to receive the current auction market price on disposal. At the same time, vendors should be aware of the requirement to pay a vendor's premium or, if a disposal is effected through a specialist wine BROKER or FINE WINE trader, commission on the disposal.

Investors need also to take full account of the buying options. If the conditions are right, the simplest and most attractive method of purchasing has been buying en primeur, or futures, but this no longer offers the returns it once did. Indeed, it may well have run its course.

Wine may also be bought at auction, in which case issues of provenance and storage conditions are paramount. For both reasons, any such purchase should be made at a commercial auction house holding regular, professionally run sales. And wine should ideally be bought in complete, original CASES offered in BOND, to avoid the additional expenses of paying duty and tax. As demand has increased since the 1990s, prices have risen to encourage investors other than the traditional wine lover, and investment wine today is increasingly formalized through brokers and wine FUNDS.

Suitable wines for investment

The factors that make wine a worthwhile investment are numerous and complex. For one thing, political and economic auguries, specific market conditions, and likely future trends need all to be taken into account. Purchasing is usually best done in a buyer's market when conditions allow investors to take advantage of low prices such as during the glut at the end of the 1980s or those of the pandemic-affected 2019 en primeur campaign. The emergence of new secondary fine-wine markets such as those in ASIA can also promote capital growth in wine.

Wine purchased for investment must be available at a price attractive enough to give purchasers, after a reasonable period of holding on to stock, a return on their initial outlay that is at least comparable with other forms of investment. It follows that the type and format of wine chosen must be intrinsically capable of increasing sufficiently in value over a period of time. Generally speaking, investment wines should be capable of ageing for a good 20 years or longer so that investors are able to hold on to the wines and sell when the market is right (although the fine-wine market today seems to prefer young wines to old). Investment wines must either have an established reputation or, where the investor is in a position to evaluate likely trends, be lesser-known wines with the potential to gain in value. Investment-grade wines should come from a good, preferably great, vintage and should be capable of being easily traded. Account should be taken of the fact that magnums and LARGE FORMAT bottles may attract a premium on disposal.

Only a handful of wines fulfil these limited but strict criteria. Beyond wines with established reputations, the market for investment becomes too highly specialized for any but the best-informed insiders to dabble in with any degree of confidence or measure of success. When in doubt, *caveat emptor*, buyer beware, is always the best maxim.

See also AUCTIONS, EN PRIMEUR, and PRICE.

A.H.L.R., C.A. & E.L.

Faith, N., *The Winemasters* (2nd edn, 1999).
Lewin, B., *What Price Bordeaux?* (2009).
www.worldoffinewine.com
www.liv-ex.com

Inzolia, sometimes spelt **Insolia**, white grape variety grown mainly on SICILY and to a much more limited extent in TUSCANY, where it is known as Ansonica. There were 4,563 ha/11,275 acres planted on Sicily in 2020. Its genetic roots seem to be in western Sicily, where it was valued as a relatively aromatic ingredient, with Grillo, in top-quality MARSALA. Today it is more often encountered as a VARIETAL, or blended with the much more common CATARRATTO, in dry white table wines. The best examples on Sicily show a certain nuttiness; the worst could do with more acid and more flavour. Tuscany's best Ansonica bottlings tend to be fuller bodied and more characterful.

ion exchange, chemical process used, for example, to soften water. Ion-exchange resins are available in two forms, cationic and anionic, making it a very versatile treatment that can be used for the removal of excess POTASSIUM from must or wine, reducing the possibility of TARTRATES and changing the ACIDITY. Using a cationic resin, the potassium (K+) in the wine is exchanged for sodium (Na+) from the resin, producing sodium bitartrate, which is more soluble than potassium bitartrate. This results in an undesirable increase in the sodium content of the wine. However, the resin can be charged with a mixture of hydrogen (H+), the source of acidity, and sodium, giving a useful result of tartrate stability combined with an increase in acidity. Alternatively, an anionic exchange resin could be used in its hydroxyl (OH−) form, where the OH− ion is exchanged for the tartrate ion. Its use is permitted in most winemaking countries but is strictly regulated.

Bird, D., and Quillé, N., *Understanding Wine Technology* (4th edn, 2021).
OIV, 'International Code of Oenological Practices'. www.oiv.int/en/technical-standards-and-documents/oenological-practices/international-code-of-oenological-practices.

IPT, or **indice de polyphénols totaux**, common French measurement of total PHENOLICS, including TANNINS and ANTHOCYANINS.

IPW. See INTEGRATED PRODUCTION OF WINE.

Iran, large country in the Near East once known as PERSIA, under which heading details of Iran's important vinous history are to be found. Alcoholic drinks of all sorts are officially prohibited in modern Iran (see ISLAM), but HOME WINEMAKING is not unknown. According to OIV statistics, total vineyard area was 158,000 ha/390,430 acres in 2021. The country is an important producer of RAISINS.

Irancy, small Burgundy AOC near AUXERRE created in 1999 for structured reds from Pinot Noir with up to 10% of the local CÉSAR or Pinot Gris grapes. Nowadays SINGLE-VINEYARD WINES (Palotte, Mazelots, etc.) are featured.

Iraq, Middle Eastern country in which only 6,309 ha/15,590 acres of vines remained in 2020, grown chiefly for RAISINS and TABLE GRAPES, according to OIV statistics. In ancient times it was part of MESOPOTAMIA, where there was a thriving trade in wine. See also BAGHDAD for evidence of early medieval viticulture, as well as ISLAM for an explanation of Iraq's modern relationship with wine.

Ireland may well have been a more faithful customer of GASCON wines than was England. Several Irishmen have played a part in the history of Bordeaux wine: the BARTONS provide one example, and the Lynch of PAUILLAC's Ch Lynch-Bages another.

There have been several attempts over the last 50 years at establishing commercial vineyards in the Republic of Ireland, but none has really succeeded. The climate, while mild, is just too wet and windy. In recent years, a few vineyards have been planted using new PiWi hybrids (see DISEASE-RESISTANT VARIETIES), which may prove more successful. S.S.

iron, an element essential for healthy vine growth in low concentrations, therefore known as a micronutrient (see VINE NUTRITION). Normally enough iron is taken up from the soil to meet a vine's needs, but iron deficiency is not uncommon. For example, lime-induced CHLOROSIS is a well-known disorder of vines growing on alkaline or CALCAREOUS soils. Leaves turn yellow, particularly between the veins, because iron is unavailable for the manufacture of chlorophyll. In alkaline and calcareous soils, iron occurs in insoluble compounds, which makes it unavailable to the vine roots. Soils can be analysed for their tendency to induce iron deficiency (see LIME, ACTIVE).

The problem cannot be solved simply by adding a fertilizer such as iron sulfate because the iron will be made unavailable by the SOIL ALKALINITY. However, iron sulfate can be applied as a foliar spray. Alternatively, iron may be added to the soil as a chelate, where iron is bound in an organic complex that prevents it from being precipitated in an insoluble form. UNGRAFTED VINES are reasonably lime-tolerant. However, if tolerance of PHYLLOXERA or NEMATODES is required, then ROOTSTOCKS with a *Vitis berlandieri* parent are preferred. R.E.W.

AWRI, 'Trace elements' (2020). www.awri.com.au/wp-content/uploads/4_nutrition_trace_elements.pdf.

Irouléguy. AOC since 1970, this Basque vineyard at the foot of the Pyrenees in SOUTH WEST FRANCE owes much of its fame to being on one of the main routes for pilgrims crossing to St-Jacques. Its presence on the French side of the mountains is due to the work of the abbots of Roncevaux in Spain. The Treaty of the Pyrenees ceded all land on the French side to France, so the church moved the vineyard today called Irouléguy (a small local village) to France and gradually abandoned it to local farmers.

The Basque language is alive and well here and features on its bottles. The contents are largely red, based on TANNAT (not more than 50% allowed), the balance being either or both of the Cabernets. They are sturdy wines but not so powerful as the Tannat-based wines of MADIRAN. Rosé is becoming more important, and there are a few whites based on PETIT COURBU and both Gros and PETIT MANSENG. Wines which do not comply with the rules or are made outside the AOC boundaries may be marketed as IGP Pyrénées-Atlantiques.

The appellation's 200 ha/494 acres of vines are grown largely on steep terraces, notably those at Ispoure just behind the town of St-Jean-Pied-de-Port. Yields are therefore low. The soil is mostly SANDSTONE, with just a few hectares based on CLAY. The area is protected from the north winds and enjoys more sunshine than most others. There is an energetic CO-OPERATIVE and a dozen or so independent growers including the much-respected Michel Rieus-peyroux (Maison Arretxea). P.S.

irrigation, the application of water to growing plants such as vines, effectively a simulation of RAINFALL, which can be essential in drier regions. Few vineyard practices are more maligned, or misunderstood, than irrigation.

Opponents tend to think of irrigation as appropriate only for maximizing yield for TABLE GRAPES, RAISINS, and BULK WINES in hot, arid regions, using furrow or sprinkler distribution. That is some of the background for the view that only DRY-FARMED VINES can produce outstanding wines and that irrigation inevitably reduces quality or the expression of TERROIR.

Widespread adoption of DRIP IRRIGATION since the 1960s has blurred the distinction. Early trials were carried out in ISRAEL and AUSTRALIA. Since then it has replaced furrow and sprinkler irrigation in arid regions and is extensively used in MEDITERRANEAN CLIMATES, which are regularly dry during the summer growth and ripening periods, and also in climates with more uniform rainfall but which nevertheless periodically suffer from dry periods. The capacity to avoid severe WATER STRESS improves grape and wine quality, provided that irrigation does not excessively stimulate vine growth and yield. See also SOIL AND WINE QUALITY; SOIL WATER.

Irrigation is one of the oldest agricultural and viticultural techniques and was clearly practised, for example, in ancient EGYPT and in ancient ARMENIA too. The need for irrigation depends entirely on CLIMATE. Where EVAPORATION is high and rainfall low, vines invariably suffer water stress and may die. Many of the world's vineyards are in Mediterranean climates, where the rain falls mostly over the winter and the summers are dry and hot. The degree of water stress in the vineyard during the summer depends on winter rain storage in the soil. Soils such as sand and gravel hold only limited amounts of water, silts and clays much more. Vines with only shallow roots because of restricting soil conditions also experience water stress. On the other hand, some soils are able to store so much water from winter rainfall that vines can grow through the summer without significant water stress. Typically these are deep loamy or silt soils and are commonly found on valley floors. Some of the deeper soils of California's Napa Valley are representative, and these may be found side by side with shallower soils where there is a need to irrigate.

While a modicum of water stress is desirable to encourage fruit RIPENING and enhance wine quality, excessive water stress has serious implications. In these circumstances, irrigation applied in a restricted fashion can actually improve quality (see PARTIAL ROOTZONE DRYING and REGULATED DEFICIT IRRIGATION).

It is easy to understand irrigation's notoriety, however. When vines have access to generous supplies of water, whether from rainfall, irrigation or soil-stored water, they grow rapidly, producing long shoots, large leaves, and much lateral growth with big berries; and where YIELD is increased, then ripening is delayed. Such vineyards typically have shaded CANOPIES. All of these are features of vineyards which produce poor-quality wine grapes. Yield is also greatly increased: depending on the severity of the water stress, irrigation may improve yield by 300% or more. In SPAIN, for example, increased use of irrigation in the late 1980s, often in association with the planting of higher-yielding CLONES, led to a marked increase in production despite significant EU-subsidized GRUBBING UP.

Irrigation is widely practised in the NEW WORLD but less frequently in the Old (although irrigation is commonplace in some of the oldest vineyards in the world in the Near East and central Asia). At one time it was in principle banned in much of the EU other than for young vines, but it is now much more widely permitted, sometimes, as in Austria, with the proviso that it is used to improve quality rather than to increase yields, although how or whether this is actually controlled is another matter. Restrictions do still apply in parts of France in the period just prior to harvest, with special derogations in times of DROUGHT, but such restrictions are typically applied locally rather than nationally. While some still believe that irrigation is intrinsically inimical to wine quality, and there are many examples of intentional over-irrigation, some of those who deliberately install irrigation systems in southern Europe are motivated by the desire to make better wine. The modern view is that excessive water stress can be as damaging to quality as can excessive irrigation and that in drier regions carefully controlled irrigation can be a useful technique for maximizing yield and/or quality. Indeed, because of CLIMATE CHANGE, some famous Old World wine regions may need to turn to irrigation in the future.

The mechanics

Soils vary in their ability to store water. The field capacity is the maximum amount of water a thoroughly wetted soil will retain after normal drainage. The driest moisture content at which vines can extract water from the soil is called the permanent wilting point. Between these two limits is the soil's available water capacity. The ability to store water is highest for clay and silt soils and lowest for coarse sands and gravels. The latter soils are preferred for fine-wine production as there is less likelihood of excessive water supplies to the vine following rainfall.

The irrigation strategy employed by a vine-grower depends on his or her ambitions for quality and yield. Irrigation amount is measured as a depth of water applied: for unrestricted irrigation in a very hot climate, up to 800 mm/31 in of water can be applied during the growing season. Smaller quantities of water, say 200–300 mm/8–12 in, are more typically applied in cooler regions which are generally more humid, so there is less EVAPORATION.

There are several ways of deciding when to irrigate. In desert regions where the climate is relatively constant, such as much of Argentina, California, and inland Australia, irrigation is generally done by the calendar. The interval between irrigations can be longer in the early spring and late autumn, but the vineyards are irrigated most frequently in midsummer, when evaporation is highest. VINEYARD WEATHER STATIONS, either communal or located in the vineyards, are used to measure EVAPOTRANSPIRATION. In areas with more rainfall, and especially where it is irregular, irrigation has to be much more carefully timed according to measurements of either the soil moisture or, less frequently, the plant WATER STRESS.

Soil moisture can be measured in several ways. Instruments used to measure moisture at selected depths in the rootzone include tensiometers, gypsum blocks, and neutron moisture meters. More recently, capacitance probes and time domain reflectometry (TDR) have been employed. Data may be recorded in the field or transmitted by telemetry to the viticulturist's computer.

Plant stress can be assessed by the experienced viticulturist observing stress symptoms such as drooping shoot tips, tendrils, and leaves. Leaf temperature can also be measured, as can plant water potential, by using a so-called PRESSURE BOMB, which is common in California. However, values are much affected by sampling and time of day.

Methods of irrigation vary considerably. The ancient method, still used in some desert areas for bulk wine production, is **flood irrigation**. For this to work, the vineyard floor must be flat and the rows not too long. Furrow irrigation (see ARGENTINA) is very similar but allows greater control. More recent developments have been **sprinkler** irrigation, where sprinklers are typically about 20 m/65 ft apart and span several rows, and DRIP IRRIGATION. R.E.S.

Iland, P., et al., 'Water, soil and the vine', in *The Grapevine: From the Science to the Practice of Growing Vines for Wine* (2011).

Irsai Olivér, aromatic Hungarian white vine CROSS of Pozsony Fehér × Csabagyöngye originally developed in the 1930s as a TABLE GRAPE. It is gaining ground in Hungary, with 2,376 ha/5,871 acres in 2021. It ripens extremely early and reliably (although it is prone to POWDERY MILDEW) and produces extremely light, intensely aromatic wines strongly reminiscent of MUSCAT. Also grown in Slovakia and Czechia.

Isabella, sometimes **Isabel** or **Isabelle**, widely distributed AMERICAN HYBRID of VITIS LABRUSCA × PETIT MESLIER. It is said to have been named after a southern belle, Isabella Gibbs, and to have been developed in South Carolina in 1816. It can withstand tropical and semi-tropical conditions and has been planted widely, notably in MOLDOVA, BRAZIL, where it is by a substantial margin the most common vine variety, and INDIA, where it is known as Bangalore Blue. In New York State, it was one of the first hybrids to be planted after PHYLLOXERA's late 19th century devastation, but it has largely been replaced by CONCORD. New plantings were banned in France in 1934. The vine is high yielding, but the wines are very obviously FOXY.

Ischia, island and tourist destination in the Bay of Naples in the Italian region of CAMPANIA (see map under ITALY) which has managed to preserve a small part of the vineyards which once covered a significant part of the island. The DOC Ischia wine, produced from 103 ha/254 acres of vineyards in 2020, is most commonly a white blend based on 45–70% FORASTERA grapes, with BIANCOLELLA. Reds are typically a blend of GUARNACCIA and PIEDIROSSO (locally known as Per'e Palummo). The latter, on its own, may be either a dry red or a sweet DRIED-GRAPE WINE. While these red wine grapes are widespread in Campania, Forastera and Biancolella are almost exclusively grown on Ischia on steep, terraced vineyards, often accessible only by boat or monorail. W.S.

Isère, IGP in the Rhône-Alpes region of south-east France, on the border with Italy. White wines dominate in this cool, damp, and windy region, making up about 65% of production, particularly from Chardonnay, ALTESSE, and JACQUÈRE. The subappellation Grésivaudan applies to wines from the foothills of the Chartreuse, Belledonne, and Vercors mountain ranges; Balmes Dauphiné designates wines from a cooler area around 50 km/31 miles south-east of Lyons.

For the vine-training system, see TRAINING SYSTEMS.

isinglass, a particularly pure PROTEIN obtained from the bladders of sturgeon and other freshwater fish that has been used for FINING wine for centuries. As early as 1660, King Charles II of England regulated the use of isinglass by merchant VINTNERS.

Like GELATIN, isinglass reacts with the excess TANNINS in harsh young red wines. Although expensive and difficult to prepare, isinglass is also occasionally used in the CLARIFICATION of white wines. However, there is a noticeable trend away from the use of animal-derived products for fining, mainly in the interests of VEGETARIANS AND VEGANS, and isinglass is now rarely used, especially on red wines. If used, it does not need to be declared on the label as it is not present in the final wine.

Islam, the Muslim religion founded by the Prophet Muhammad (spelt variously Mohammed, Mohamet, etc.) in the 7th century CE, has had, and continues to have, a most profound effect on the history of wine. The consumption of any alcoholic drink was prohibited by Muhammad, so wine is neither officially consumed nor enthusiastically produced in most of the Near and Middle East, some of North Africa, and parts of Asia. Wine is therefore no longer made in much of the land most closely associated with the ORIGINS OF VINICULTURE, and the rise of Islamic fundamentalism in the late 20th century represents a considerable constraint on the world's wine consumption.

Muhammad's prohibition

Wine (in Arabic *khamr*) was not prohibited from the outset of the Prophet Muhammad's preaching (between 610 and 632). Islam, both dogma and practice, emerged initially as the product of continuous revelation (the Qur'ān, often spelt Koran) during the Prophet's lifetime and his responses to the vicissitudes of the early Islamic community (these are recorded in the *hadīth* literature and constitute the second most substantive source of Islamic law). There are four verses in the Qur'ān which refer to wine; the first is quite positive (Sura 16, verse 69): 'We give you the fruit of the palm and the vine from which you derive intoxicants and wholesome food.' The following two verses are cautionary but are not considered by Muslim jurists to enjoin abstinence from alcohol (Sura 2, verse 216, and Sura 4, verse 46): 'They will ask you concerning wine and gambling. Answer, in both there is great sin and also some things of use unto men, but their sinfulness is greater than their use.' 'Believers do not approach your prayers when you are drunk, but wait till you can grasp the meaning of your words; nor when you are polluted—unless you are travelling the road—until you have washed yourself.'

There is consensus among medieval Muslim jurists, however, that the fourth verse, which came in response to disturbances in the community, was tantamount to an injunction (although it is not couched in the same language as the prohibition on other dietary items, such as pork)

(Sura 5, verse 92): 'Believers, wine and games of chance, idols and divining arrows are abominations devised by Satan. Avoid them so that you may prosper. Satan seeks to stir up enmity and hatred among you by means of wine and gambling and to keep you from the Remembrance of Allah and from your prayers.'

Although this verse was understood universally to articulate prohibition, there was dissension when it came to establishing the precise nature of forbidden wine. *Khamr*, the word used in the Qur'ānic verses, is the Arabic generic term for wine. There were, however, many types of fermented beverages known to pre-Islamic and later Arabs. The second caliph, 'Umar ibn al-Khattāb, is reported in the *hadīth* literature to have settled the question: 'Wine has been prohibited by the Qur'ān; it comes from five kinds of fruits: from grapes, from dates, from honey, from wheat and from barley; wine is what obscures the intellect.' The issue remained whether beverages prepared in a way different from wine were prohibited. For example *tilā'* appears to have been allowed by 'Umar; this was a kind of syrup made from grape juice which was cooked until two-thirds of it evaporated. However, the same source relates that 'Umar punished a man who became drunk on this concoction.

Another tradition quotes the Prophet stipulating the kinds of vessels in which fruit juice beverages could be made or stored: '. . . I forbid four things: *dubbā'* [a gourd], *hantam* [glazed wine jars], *muzaffat* [a vessel smeared with pitch] and *naqīr*.' When asked about the nature of *naqīr* he answered: 'It is a palmtrunk which you hollow out; then you pour small dates into it and upon them water. When the process of fermentation has finished, you drink it with the effect that a man hits his cousin with the sword.' The community was, therefore, enjoined to store fruit beverages in leather skins that prevented fermentation.

Nabīdh, date wine, is the drink about which there has been the most controversy. Several traditions state that this beverage was among the drinks prepared by Muhammad's wives and drunk by him: 'Aisha said: 'We used to prepare *nabīdh* . . . in a skin; we took a handful of dates or a handful of raisins, cast it into the skin and poured water upon it. The *nabīdh* we prepared in this way in the morning was drunk by him in the evening; and when we prepared it in the evening he drank it the next morning.' Despite this, three of the four Sunni schools of law as well as the Shiah prohibit *nabīdh*. The Hanafi school allows it when used in moderation, although intoxication is still prohibited.

Most jurists now consider discussions about types of wine to be secondary casuistry. What is deemed crucial, on the basis of *hadīth*, is that any beverage which intoxicates should not be consumed.

Despite the Qur'ānic injunction, even those types of wine recognized to be *harām* continued to be imbibed in many periods of Islamic history; this is best reflected in the rich tradition of Bacchic poetry which had its roots in pre-Islamic Arabia but flowered as a poetic genre in the early Abbasid period (see ARAB POETS). This canon of literature is largely mimetic and most certainly reflects the drinking habits of a significant sector of the Islamic community, notably—in some cases—the caliph and his entourage.

The wines consumed

Both Arabic poetry and other sources such as agricultural works tell us much about wine as a product. Although wine was produced in al-Tā'if in the Hijaz (156 km/97 miles south-east of Mecca) from pre-Islamic times, it was imported mainly by Jewish and Christian merchants from SYRIA and MESOPOTAMIA. With the expansion of Islam, Arabs were introduced to finer wines grown mostly in the Christian monasteries of Iraq. 'Ana in upper Mesopotamia is only one of many areas that were known for viticulture. It was in the taverns around monasteries and in the monasteries themselves that most wine was consumed, as well as in some of the outlying towns of Baghdad, districts of Baghdad itself (especially al-Karkh), and not infrequently the caliphal court at the very heart of the Islamic community.

The most lauded of beverages were four types of wine—white, yellow, red, and black—made from both red and white grapes, from a variety of vine varieties whose names are preserved in medieval agricultural books (Heine gives details of 21 of them, including KIŠMIŠ). In poetry, the date wine *nabīdh* was despised (cf. above). Grape wine was always mixed with water before drinking (one-third wine to two-thirds water, about the same dilution as in ancient GREECE). The poets were fascinated by the bubbles which this mixing produced; although wine was celebrated as an ancient product ('It has aged since the time of Adam'), it may be that it was often very young and thus still fermenting when consumed. There were three classes of age: young wine, which was less than a year old, low in alcohol, and had little bouquet; middle-aged, which was a year old; and old wine, which one source claims was usually sour. P.K.

Heine, P., *Weinstudien, Untersuchungen zu Anbau, Produktion und Konsum des Weins im arabisch-islamischen Mittelalter* (1982).

'Khamr', *The Encyclopaedia of Islam*, vol. iv (new edn, 1978).

Kueny, K., *The Rhetoric of Sobriety: Wine in Early Islam* (2001).

Effect of Islam on wine history

In the Middle Ages, Muslim conquest by no means outlawed wine production, however. Muhammad's caliph successors were based in Damascus and, subsequently, in BAGHDAD, which had its own local wine industry. Wine production continued in Moorish Spain (the Alhambra built by the Moors in 14th-century Granada has its Puerta del Vino), Portugal, North Africa, Sicily, Sardinia, Corsica, Greece, Crete, and other eastern Mediterranean islands, usually under the heavily taxed auspices of Jews or Christians, even though they were ruled by Muslims. The Ottoman Turks made repeated raids on various eastern European wine regions in the Middle Ages and, if the TOKAJ legend is based on fact, could therefore be said to have been indirectly responsible for the discovery of BOTRYTIZED WINES. For some more details, see SPAIN, GREECE, and CYPRUS.

It is because of the dissemination of Muslim techniques associated with alchemy that the art of DISTILLATION is said to have spread through western Europe. Indeed the word ALCOHOL itself is of Arab origin.

isoamyl acetate is an ESTER present in all fermented beverages. At higher concentrations, it is sometimes associated with banana-like aromas, and it is often found in cool-fermented white wines and red wines that have undergone CARBONIC MACERATION. Some yeast strains are selected for their ability to produce high levels of esters, especially isoamyl acetate, during fermentation.

isoamyl alcohol. See ALCOHOLS.

isobutyl-methoxypyrazine, more properly, **2-isobutyl-3-methoxypyrazine**, or **IBMP**, smells of green or bell peppers and grass and is found in all green matter. The perception threshold in red and white wines is 615 ng/l, and the concentration is higher in unripe grapes and in fruit with low sun exposure because it is very sensitive to ULTRAVIOLET RADIATION. It is more often found in late-ripening varieties such as Cabernets Sauvignon and Franc and Carmenère. IBMP is very common in Sauvignon Blanc, where it is not generally considered a fault. Wines with high levels of IBMP may be described as HERBACEOUS.

Isonzo del Friuli, or **Friuli Isonzo**, relatively small DOC in the extreme north-east of Italy in the FRIULI region overlapping with the COLLIO zone. The Rive di Giare, the plain to the south of the Collio hills formed by the Isonzo river on its way to the Adriatic, is, from a geological point of view, split in two. The left bank of the Isonzo is like FRIULI GRAVE: a mixture of gravel and soil formed by fluvial and glacial deposits. The Rive Alte, the right bank, inland towards FRIULI COLLI ORIENTALI, is less fertile red gravel and said to produce Isonzo's best wines. The DOC's production rules allow each sub-zone to be mentioned on labels, but in reality they are rarely seen.

The zone included just over 681 ha/1,682 acres of DOC vineyard in 2020. As in the rest of Friuli, most wines are VARIETAL. The whites are generally fresh, simple, and fruity, while the reds are soft and forward, both colours often determined by the very high yields of 12–13 tonnes/ha allowed. Practically all white wine grapes may also be used to produce a late-harvest or a sweet DRIED-GRAPE WINE, while rosés may be varietal or a blend of white and red wine. All colours can come in SPUMANTE versions, too. While Isonzo's wines are generally clean and solid, the region lacks a clear identity because of the stress on INTERNATIONAL VARIETIES and a lack of an individual CONSORZIO since 2015. W.S.

isopropyl-methoxypyrazine (IPMP). See METHOXYPYRAZINES.

Israel, state on the eastern shore of the Mediterranean, bordering LEBANON to the north, SYRIA and JORDAN to the east, and EGYPT to the south. Some of its 7,989 ha/19,741 acres of grapevines also extend into the disputed territory of the West Bank (see PALESTINE).

History

Historically the land of milk and honey (see CANAAN), this region has a long and illustrious relationship with wine. It was both necessary for religious ritual, particularly in Judaism and Christianity (see RELIGION AND WINE), and it was a mainstay of the economy. The region is rich in archaeological evidence of wine's importance in culture and trade, including a 3,800-year-old Canaanite palace at Tel Kabri in Galilee (the largest Canaanite wine cellar found to date) as well as a 1,500-year-old wine complex at the ancient port city of Yavne (the largest Byzantine winery), where annual production is estimated to have been 2 million litres. Over centuries, the Canaanites, Israelites, Greeks, Romans, Nabateans, Byzantines, and Crusaders all left their mark in winemaking in the Holy Land. (See also PALAEOETHNOBOTANY.)

The Ottoman period, *c.*14–early 20th centuries, decimated the region's commercial wine industry, but Jews and Christians always made wine, for their own use. There were also wineries mainly making sacramental wines in the Old City of Jerusalem from the mid 19th century; by the late 1800s, the Templars, and MONKS AND MONASTERIES such as Cremisan and Latroun, were also producing wine.

Beginning in 1882, Baron Edmond de ROTHSCHILD, owner of Ch Lafite in Bordeaux, began providing funds and French expertise for what would become the basis of the modern Israeli wine industry. He planted vineyards, built two large wineries with underground cellars, and founded the Société Coopérative des Grandes Caves in 1906, which traded as Carmel and dominated Israeli wine for over 100 years. In the 1980s, the Golan Heights Winery was founded, bringing expertise from California, cutting-edge technology, and an understanding of the importance of high-ELEVATION vineyards. Its success spurred a boom in small wineries, led by Domaine du Castel and Margalit Winery, that saw the number of wineries blossom from 12 in 1990 to more than 350 by 2022.

Geography and climate

Israel shows a wide diversity of soils and MESOCLIMATES, stretching 424 km/263 miles north to south along the eastern shore of the Mediterranean Sea. While Israel's Ministry of Agriculture recognizes five broad regions, the Israeli Professional Enology & Viticulture Organization (IPEVO) have produced a map (2019) with 15 regions defined by topography, climate, and soils. The most important of these are as follows:

Golan Heights, a volcanic plateau in the north-east which rises to 1,200 m/3,937 ft in elevation, with soils of TUFF and BASALT. Winter temperatures can dip to freezing, and rainfall can be as much as 1,100 mm/39 in annually.

Galilee, of which the Upper Galilee, bordering LEBANON, is the main vine-growing area. The soils are shallow TERRA ROSSA on LIMESTONE with some VOLCANIC soil, and the higher vineyards sit at 400m/1,312ft–800m/2,624 ft in elevation.

Coastal Plain, south of Haifa and south-east of Tel Aviv, including Zichron-Hanadiv Valley, with deeper RENDZINA soils and more Mediterranean influence.

Judea, in the centre of the country, including the Judean Foothills, rolling hills up to 400 m/1,312 ft of elevation with white chalky soils.

Judean Hills, rising towards Jerusalem, where old terraces are cut into very shallow terra rossa soils over limestone bedrock. Elevations range from 400 m/1,312 ft to 900 m/2,952 ft.

Shomron Hills, north of Jerusalem, a high-elevation (up to 800 m/2,624 ft) region with shallow soils on limestone bedrock.

Negev, in the south, including Mitzpe Ramon at 800 m/2,624 ft in elevation, a DESERT climate with LOESS soils and a broad DIURNAL TEMPERATURE RANGE.

The central mountainous region that runs down the spine of the country includes the West Bank, the territory in dispute since 1967 that is partially under the auspices of the Palestinian Authority. Both Israeli and Palestinian wineries operate there.

Viticulture

Historically, vineyards were concentrated in the warm, deep-soiled, low-elevation coastal regions. Over the years, winegrowers have been moving north and east in search of cooler, higher elevations. The main concentration of vineyards is now in the Galilee and Golan Heights in the north and the Judean Foothills and Judean Hills in the centre of the country. Average temperatures for July–August can range from 18 to 30 °C/65–86 °F. A major problem during flowering may be the *hamsin* (hot winds), when temperatures soar.

Most vineyards are spur-pruned on VSP training systems (see VERTICAL TRELLIS), although some new plantings of Grenache and Mourvèdre and some old-vine Carignan and Petite Sirah are BUSH VINES. DRIP IRRIGATION, pioneered by the Israelis in the 1960s, is widely used, although a growing number of vineyards on the valley floor are DRY-FARMED. CANOPY MANAGEMENT is used to maximize the phenolic ripeness at harvest. Sugar accumulation is not a problem, but there is a need to retain acidity and balance through deficit irrigation and ULTRAVIOLET RADIATION control. Nets are sometimes used to protect the fruit from SUNBURN.

The majority of the harvest is from August to October, but it can begin in late July with white grapes in the warmer regions.

Grape varieties

In the 1900s, the workhorse grape varieties were CARIGNAN, which predates Rothschild's arrival, and Alicante. Today, the dominant varieties for quality red wines are Cabernet Sauvignon, Merlot, Syrah, and PETIT VERDOT; whites are made from Sauvignon Blanc and Chardonnay. Increased attention is being paid to Mediterranean grape varieties such as Grenache, Mourvèdre, Roussanne, Marsanne, and Viognier, as well as 'adopted' varieties such as Carignan, PETITE SIRAH, and Colombard. Muscat of Alexandria is mainly used for lightly sweet, frizzante MOSCATO. Once most wines were marketed under VARIETAL names, but Rhône-style blends are increasingly popular.

Some crosses are grown, such as MARSELAN and Argaman, an Israeli cross of Carignan and SOUSÃO. There is also increased interest in Holy Land INDIGENOUS VARIETIES such as Dabouki, Marawi/Hamdani, Jandali (whites), and Bittuni (red), which were preserved through the Ottoman Empire period mainly by Palestinian growers in the Hebron region.

After decades of LEAFROLL VIRUS problems, new CLONAL SELECTIONS are being sought from South Africa, and the Golan Heights Winery has its own propagation block and nursery.

See also KOSHER (although by no means is all Israel's wine kosher). A.S.M. & E.P.

Heskett, R., and Butler, J., *Divine Vintage: Following the Wine Trail from Genesis to the Modern Age* (2012).

Sacks, E., and Montefiore, A., *The Wine Route of Israel* (2015).

Sacks, E., and Montefiore, A., *Wines of Israel* (2020).
Saslove, R., and Haran, G., *Wine Journey, An Israeli Adventure* (2021).
www.wines-israel.com
www.winesofisrael.com

Istria. See CROATIA.

ISVV, the Institut des Sciences de la Vigne et du Vin de Bordeaux, brings together under one roof in Villenave d'Ornon, a southern suburb of Bordeaux, the grape and wine research teams and students of several academic institutions, including BORDEAUX University, Bordeaux Sciences Agro, and INRAE Bordeaux. The first director, until his death in 2016, was Denis DUBOURDIEU. The current director is Philippe Darriet.

Italian Riesling, or **Italian Rizling**, sometimes **Italianski Rizling**, occasional synonyms for RIESLING ITALICO. See WELSCHRIESLING.

Italy, with FRANCE one of the world's two mammoth wine producers, sometimes producing as much as 47 million hl/1,033 million gal a year. Italy has more land under vine than any other country other than France and SPAIN, although, thanks to the European VINE-PULL SCHEME, the total has been reduced from close to 1.4 million ha/3.4 million acres in the early 1990s to 718,000 ha/1,774,217 acres by 2021. The country remains the second largest wine market in the EU and third worldwide (after the United States and France), with an estimated consumption of 24.2 million hl in 2021, and only Spain exports more wine. A significant but declining proportion of the wine exported from Italy has been inexpensive wine for BLENDING in and possible re-export from France and Germany, but a good 78% of exports are now in bottle, and Italy's top wines are sought after around the world, especially in the US and German-speaking markets.

Italy cultivates the vine virtually everywhere in the peninsula, from the Alps in the north to islands that are closer to the coast of North Africa than to the Italian mainland (see map). Viticulture traditionally impinged on the national consciousness, on the national imagination, and on daily life in a way that is hardly conceivable to those not accustomed to the Mediterranean way of life and its dietary trinity of bread, olive oil, and wine. It was unthinkable for Italians to sit down and eat without wine on the table until about the late 1980s, since when per capita wine consumption, as in France and Spain, has been plummeting.

To consider the history of wine in Italy is to consider the history of Italy itself, however; wine and Italian civilization are virtually synonymous. The ancient Greek name for much of Italy already acknowledged the importance of viticulture to the peninsula: OENOTRIA, or 'land of trained vines'.

Italy, Magna Graecia, and Roman Italy

The pastoral past of the tribes of Italy may be reflected in the use of milk in LIBATIONS rather than wine (see PLINY, *Natural History*, 14. 88), but viticulture and wine will have made an early impact as part of GREEK and ETRUSCAN culture (see ORIGINS OF VINICULTURE for more details). SICILY may have played a key role in the development of viticulture on the mainland. The Sicilian Murgentina grape, which flourished in volcanic soils, was successfully transplanted near POMPEII on the slopes of Vesuvius, where it was called locally the Pompeian grape. This in turn was introduced further north around Clusium (Chiusi) in Etruria, where it proved particularly prolific. Again, the Eugenia, the high-quality grape from Tauromenium (Taormina in Sicily), successfully found a home in the Colli ALBANI south of Rome but failed elsewhere.

Incidental mentions by historians suggest that by the time that Hannibal invaded Italy in the late 3rd century BCE, vines could be found throughout the peninsula, from beyond the Po Valley, down the Adriatic coast, and in CAMPANIA; but little wine was of particular note before the middle of the 2nd century BCE according to Pliny (*Natural History*, 14. 87). It was Pliny, too, who in a key passage (*Natural History*, 14. 94 ff.) made a particularly acute observation. He noted that OPIMIAN wine of the year when Opimius was consul (121 BCE) was accepted as one of the greatest VINTAGES, but that this applied generally to wine in that year, not to any particular CRUS. An edict of the censors of 89 BCE imposing a price limit on costly wines refers only to wine made from the Aminnean grape (see ANCIENT VINE VARIETIES), not to any estates.

The creation of the grands crus of Roman Italy belongs to the 1st centuries BCE and CE. This fact is more or less confirmed by ARCHAEOLOGY. The expansion of villas connected with wine production and overseas trade, as evidenced by their AMPHORAE, may have begun in the late 3rd or 2nd centuries, but the real growth is later. Three factors were involved in this development. First there was the exceptional growth of the city of ROME, which created a huge market for wine. Second, the opening up of trade routes to GAUL and SPAIN stimulated the growth of vineyards in the areas immediately behind ports; and finally there was the interest of the Roman aristocracy with an ever-increasing level of wealth to invest. So it is no accident that the areas in which the great wines of Roman Italy developed were LAZIO and Campania, regions within easy reach of the Roman market and where the Roman elites had their country homes. In the Colli Albani, the mainly sweet wines of Alba itself were highly prized, as were those of Velletri. The Emperor Augustus gave a boost to the wines of Setia (Sezze) by favouring them above all others. Beyond Terracina, CAECUBAN, produced in the marshes around the Lago di Fondi, was in the very front rank of wines. The wines from the slopes of Monte Massico, particularly the various types of FALERNIAN, long remained the most favoured. In northern and central Campania, the wines of Cales, along with Gauranum (from Monte Barbaro, overlooking the northern end of the bay of Naples) had reputations which were close to that of Falernian. Then on the bay of Naples itself were the noted vineyards of Pompeii and the Sorrento peninsula. The very light white wine of this region, SURRENTINUM, made from the Aminean Germana Minor grape, enjoyed very high status in the 1st century CE, although it did not win universal approval ('high-quality vinegar' was the view of the Emperor Tiberius).

Few wines outside Lazio and Campania ever approached the status of these wines, and none exceeded it. To the north and west, Etruria (TUSCANY) had a great variety of wines, but only those of Luni and Genoa in Liguria made much impact. In Magna Graecia (southern Italy), several areas produced wines of some note, including Tarentine (from Taranto). The Adriatic coast of Italy presents an interesting test case. It would be difficult to guess at the importance of the wines of this area simply from the rather limited literary evidence. But the evidence of amphorae shows that PUGLIA and ancient Calabria and, perhaps, areas further up the east coast exported wine to all the countries round the Adriatic and to the Greek world from the 2nd century. Brindisi certainly was the focus for a flourishing export trade. Further north, Hadrianum, the wine of Atri, and the adjoining Praetuttian vineyards (roughly the northern area of Montepulciano d'ABRUZZO) achieved a high reputation in the 1st century CE. A significant development is to be associated with the time of the first Roman emperor, Augustus (31 BCE–14 CE); this was the increasing prominence of northern wines from the Po Valley and beyond. The distinctive type of amphora which carried the wines of this region was sometimes stamped with the names of those who rose to prominence in the entourage of Augustus and had estates in the region. These amphorae doubtless carried Praetuttian, the wines of Ancona, of Ravenna, and of the towns along the Via Aemilia. VIRGIL, Augustus' court poet, reflected the emperor's liking for the wines of Verona (see VENETO), made from the Rhaetic grape (although, because of its distance from the sea, it is unlikely this area's wines achieved more than a passing prominence). Augustus' wife Livia did her bit to promote the wines of the FRIULI region, by publicly ascribing her longevity to an exclusive diet of the wine of Pucinum, beyond Aquileia.

Archaeology has combined with history to give us this picture of viticulture in Roman Italy, which differs in significant ways from the current scene. It should always be

ITALY
SWITZERLAND
AUSTRIA
HUNGARY
SLOVENIA
CROATIA
BOSNIA AND HERZEGOVINA
FRANCE
TUNISIA
Alps
Alps
TRENTINO-ALTO ADIGE
Bolzano
Trento
FRIULI
Udine
Gorizia
Trieste
VALLE D'AOSTA
LOMBARDIA
Novara
Vercelli
Milan
Pavia
VENETO
Verona
Venice
Turin
Asti
Alba
PIEMONTE
Piacenza
Po
EMILIA-ROMAGNA
Bologna
LIGURIA
Genoa
SAN MARINO
LIGURIAN SEA
Florence
Apennines
TOSCANA
Bolgheri
Siena
Montalcino
Perugia
UMBRIA
Orvieto
MARCHE
Ancona
ADRIATIC SEA
Elba
CORSICA
LAZIO
Rome
Frascati
ABRUZZO
MOLISE
Naples
Ischia
CAMPANIA
Capri
Bari
PUGLIA
BASILICATA
Taranto
SARDEGNA
Oristano
Cagliari
TYRRHENIAN SEA
CALABRIA
Lipari
Palermo
Marsala
SICILIA
MEDITERRANEAN SEA
Pantelleria
0
200 km

remembered that, as now, there would be an enormous consumption of undistinguished, local wines which never travelled and are rarely to be identified in the historical record. J.J.P.

Pliny the Elder, *Natural History*, translated by H. Rackham (1945), Book 14.
Tchernia, A., *Le Vin de l'Italie romaine* (1986).

Medieval history

The fall of the Roman Empire did not put an end to viticulture in Italy, but barbarization and economic collapse meant the disappearance of the market for fine wines. With Goths, then Lombards, in Rome and most of the north, and the remains of the empire administered precariously from Ravenna, Falernian and Caecuban had become distant memories. Yet the Italian diet remained based on bread, olives, and wine, and so wine continued to be grown.

The Dark Ages were a period of economic stagnation; except for the importation of luxury goods from the Near East, trade was local. We know little about the wine that was grown until the 11th century, when population, production, and exchange increased, and Italy, particularly northern Italy, became politically and economically the most important part of Europe (see GENOA and VENICE). Between the 11th and the 14th centuries, the population of Italy grew from 7 to 9 million inhabitants. People of all social classes migrated to the towns, including members of the nobility. As a result, urban communes came to govern the countryside. South of Tuscany, however, the aristocracy lived near the land; the feudal system, with its lack of distinction between trade and agriculture, persisted.

One of the reasons for the strength of the Italian economy was that it had monopolized the trade in luxury items. These included the strong, sweet wines of Crete, Cyprus, and other parts of the Aegean (see MALMSEY) but also goods produced in Italy itself, such as high-quality wool and silk (from Lucca and Florence). When it became possible to transfer credit throughout the Mediterranean and western Europe (instead of having to carry and exchange actual coins), Florence became the banking capital of Europe. The Florentine house of ANTINORI is a good example of several of these developments. The Antinoris were, and still are, a noble Tuscan family that moved from the country to the city; having made their money in banking, they diversified into selling wine and also used their capital to buy up land to grow their own wine.

The rich merchants of the cities became a new market for fine wines. Good wine became a sign of affluence and a source of profit: it is no coincidence that the merchant dynasties of Bardi and FRESCOBALDI should have gone into winegrowing, buying up land for the purpose. All over Italy, the usual way to improve land was to deforest it and plant it with vines. When there was enough moisture, the vines were raised on trees, stakes, or trellises (see TENDONE), in the Roman way, to increase yields by exposing the grapes to the sun. Thus sown and planted crops could be raised in the same fields. In the drier regions, particularly in the south (with the exception of CAMPANIA), the vines were left to grow unsupported, as BUSH VINES, or left to trail on the ground in vineyards or at least in separate plots.

Vine-growing as well as winemaking in medieval Italy were much as they had been in the days of the classical AGRICULTURAL TREATISES, and in one crucial respect things were worse: since AMPHORAE and other impermeable earthenware vessels were no longer available, wine was kept in wooden BARRELS, which were hard to clean and not airtight. Unless a wine contained high proportions of two natural preservatives, sugar and alcohol, it would not last out the year.

The Roman VINE VARIETIES seem to have disappeared. In his treatise on agriculture (*c.*1304) PETRUS DE CRESCENTIIS, who had read the classical authorities and often repeats their advice, does not mention any of the famous Roman grape varieties. He lists some 37 contemporary Italian varieties, but he makes no attempt to relate those to the grapes encountered by his classical predecessors. The list he gives is mostly concerned with the northern half of Italy and, especially, his own city of Bologna. The list is not a great help to the modern scholar, because his descriptions are too brief for identification and many of the names are unrecognizable (although see below). None of Petrus' 17 red wine varieties has a familiar name, and Petrus does not devote much space to them. Like most medieval drinkers, he preferred white wines to red.

From the 13th century onwards, wine was medieval Italy's most profitable cash crop. Sharecropping was traditional throughout the country, with the landowner taking half the wine or more if production was high. Sometimes a contract was drawn up for a longer period at a fixed rent. Smallholders survived in the highlands but in Tuscany and the northern plain they could not afford to stay on the better land. Peasants occasionally retailed their wine, but usually the landowners regulated sales to the towns. Consumption was high (the figure for Florence, *c.*1338, is a gallon a week for every man, woman, and child, but estimates for Milan and Venice are much higher); yet production more than met demand, particularly in Campania.

Italy is mountainous and has few navigable RIVERS, which made internal transport costly and difficult before the coming of the RAILWAYS. Also, because Italy was not a political unity, there were obstacles in the form of tolls, duties, and differences in coinage, weights, and measures. Transport by sea was cheap and export to other countries no more laborious than much internal trade, so merchants in northern Italy or near the sea readily turned to foreign markets. The northern districts sold wine in Switzerland and Germany, the Marche exported to the Levant via Venice, which enjoyed tax privileges in Constantinople, and Genoese ships took the wines of Liguria to Spain, Flanders, and England. Nevertheless, the volume of Italy's international wine trade was merely the surplus production of a fertile vine-growing country. The Italians could afford not to deprive themselves of any of the wine they wanted to drink and still make money out of what remained.

See also GENOA, NAPLES, VENICE, and TUSCANY. H.M.W.

Jones, P., 'Italy', in *The Cambridge Economic History of Europe*, 7 vols., i: *The Agrarian Life of the Middle Ages* (1966).
Marescalchi, A., and Dalmasso, G. (eds.), *Storia della vite e del vino in Italia*, 3 vols. (1993).

Modern history

That the revival of Europe's trade in the early Middle Ages began in the Mediterranean is by now universally accepted. It is therefore no surprise that specific references to what were to become some of Italy's most important grapes and wines can be found as early as the late 13th and early 14th centuries. The country's chronicles, both civic and monastic, of the 14th and 15th centuries abound with descriptions of the leading wines of their day—at times identified by grape variety, at times identified by their production zone. Many of them coincide, at least nominally, with the current wines of these same zones.

English records seem to indicate that wines such as Vernaccia, Trebbiano, and Greco were all known as such at this time. Sante Lancerio, cellarmaster to Pope Paul III, recounted the wines of his day in an account of papal travels in 1536, describing, criticizing, and praising the prominent products of his epoch, among which we find Aglianico, Aleatico, and Greco from the south, Vino Nobile di Montepulciano, Trebbiano di Romagna, Sangiovese di Romagna from the centre, and Cinqueterre from the north. And in Andrea Bacci's work we find a full-fledged treatise on Italy's wines, an attempt to deal with and describe the country's viticultural production in a national context, a surprising phenomenon inasmuch as Italy was far from being a nation in the modern sense in the late 16th century.

But it was precisely at this time—in the 17th and then the 18th centuries—that the development of Italian viticulture and wines began to diverge from that of its neighbours. This critical period, which saw the rise of wine in BOTTLES stoppered with CORK, left Italy virtually untouched. Old bottles from this period are non-existent. Although some of Tuscany's leading

NÉGOCIANT houses trace their history back to the Middle Ages (see ANTINORI and FRESCOBALDI), they, and the few Piedmontese houses which have existed since the late 18th century, sold bulk rather than either bottled wine or estate wines until relatively recently.

Any overall evaluation of the quality of Italian wine in the 18th century is impossible, but signs of deterioration exist. The 'Florence' wines so greatly appreciated in the late 17th and early 18th centuries by Lady Sandwich, Swift, and Bolingbroke are described as 'disagreeably rough' by Sir Edward Barry in 1775, and there is good reason not to dismiss his words as a mere subjective reaction. Pietro Leopoldo, grand duke of Tuscany, during an inspection tour of his realm in 1773, reported a significant loss of viticultural commerce with England due to the lessened quality of the wines of Chianti. And many of Italy's wines, including many of its most famous ones, did not assume their current form until quite recently: Barolo and Barbaresco were allegedly sweet wines until the middle and end of the 19th century, respectively (although this may well have been simply because the wines did not routinely ferment to complete dryness); Chianti did not become a predominantly Sangiovese wine until the late 19th century; Brunello di Montalcino did not even exist as a wine until the end of the 19th century (see BIONDI-SANTI, who were bottling wine by then); Orvieto and Cinqueterre were predominantly sweet wines until the modern epoch; and the best-known wines of central Italy such as Orvieto, Verdicchio, Frascati, and the other white wines of the Castelli Romani were regularly SKIN-FERMENTED until the 1970s. The INTERNATIONAL VARIETIES which today play so important a role in the viticulture of Italy's north-east—Trentino-Alto Adige, Veneto, and Friuli—began to assume a significant role only after the replanting of the country's vineyards in the wake of PHYLLOXERA in the early 20th century. The crisp and refreshing white wines of Friuli are entirely a post-Second World War phenomenon; Sicily's first dry table wines were created only in 1824, by Duke Edoardo di Salaparuta.

The reasons for this period of stagnation, which in Italian historical literature is often called the period of Italy's *decadenza*, are not difficult to determine. The country experienced an extended domination by foreign powers, first by the Spanish Habsburgs both in the north and the south, then by Spanish Bourbons in the south and Austrian Habsburgs in the north. Meanwhile the increased influence—both temporal and spiritual—of Counter-Reformation Catholicism effectively removed the country's destiny from its own hands. Even more significant was the general shift of trade and commerce from south to north, from the Mediterranean to the Atlantic, which transformed Italy's geographical position for the first time in two millennia from that of a central to that of a peripheral power. Italy was on the fringes of a Europe in which the most prosperous and progressive areas, the northern markets, were increasingly dominated by the fine wines of France and Germany.

The unification of Italy in 1861 and a slow but steady period of economic growth did much to reverse the decline of the previous two-and-a-half centuries. It was the economic boom after the Second World War which created a class of consumers with both an interest in wine and the means to purchase it, which gave Italian wine producers confidence in their own capacities and their own products. Although a keen importer of champagne, the Italian wine market has been understandably preoccupied by Italian wine and in the late 20th century came to be shaped by a handful of annual wine guides. While many encouraged INTERNATIONAL VARIETIES at the expense of Italy's rich heritage of INDIGENOUS VARIETIES and for many years encouraged the use of French BARRIQUES—not to mention favouring particular consultant OENOLOGISTS—this century has seen a return to a focus on Italy's unique grape varieties and TERROIRS.

Major developments in the recent history of Italian wine are described under DOC, DOCG, and IGT.

Geography and climate

Generalizations about a peninsula 1,200 km/750 miles long extending through about 10° LATITUDE are not easy. The dominant geographical feature of the 'boot' is the Apennines, which begin close to the border with France and then form the central ridge down the peninsula to the 'toe' in Calabria. In the far north are the Alps; in Sicily, the Madonie form yet another chain of central mountains, while Etna rises to 3,350 m/10,990 ft. Italian agriculture has traditionally been organized vertically, with the richer soils of the valley floors used for grain and vegetable cultivation and cattle grazing and with the hills reserved for vine and olive cultivation. Good-quality viticulture is almost entirely a HILLSIDE phenomenon in Italy; there are no Italian equivalents of the *vignoble* of Bordeaux, and the Friuli Grave and other flat viticultural areas of Friuli do not produce wine at the same quality level as the higher nearby districts of Collio and Colli Orientali.

A significant number of the country's most admired wines come from CALCAREOUS soils. Piemonte, Tuscany, the hillside zones of Friuli, and the Salento in Puglia all provide examples of this. The other dominant soil type is VOLCANIC, present in such zones as Soave and Colli Euganei in the Veneto, the Castelli Romani south-west of Rome, the coast of Naples (Campi Flegrei, Ischia), the interior of Campania and Basilicata, and Sicily.

ELEVATION, ASPECT, WIND, TOPOGRAPHY, SOIL composition, and proximity to the sea all affect climate. That Cabernet Sauvignon can be grown at latitude 46.30° N (north of Bordeaux) is due to the narrow, heat-trapping alpine valleys of Alto Adige. Umbria is generally cooler than Tuscany albeit further south; a wide span of central Italy—Umbria, the Marche, Lazio—is more renowned for white wines than for reds, while Piemonte, in the far north, is principally a producer of powerful red wines. Even Sicily confirms the rule that, in Italy, geography is not destiny: the island produces as much white wine as red.

While the climate of far northern Italy may be CONTINENTAL, that of central and southern Italy is MEDITERRANEAN. Italy's indigenous red grape varieties—with the exception of Dolcetto—are almost invariably later ripeners. Nebbiolo, Barbera, Refosco, Corvina, Sangiovese, Sagrantino, Aglianico, Negroamaro, Nerello Mascalese, and Nero d'Avola all require sustained heat throughout the summer and early autumn to ripen properly and lose their tannic and acidic asperity, and successful ripening is therefore far from automatic. Poor VINTAGES are by no means a strange phenomenon in Italy, although increased viticultural knowledge, strict grape selection, and CLIMATE CHANGE resulting in warmer growing seasons and notably earlier harvests have made completely disastrous vintages a thing of the past.

Viticulture

Two features distinguish Italian viticulture: first, the late development of vineyards as such and a significant presence until relatively recently of polyculture in grape-growing areas; second, the long-standing dominance of vine-TRAINING SYSTEMS created expressly for high YIELDS and easy MECHANIZATION, such as GUYOT.

Polyculture, a common phenomenon throughout Europe at one time, lasted into the modern epoch in Italy. Grain and vegetables such as potatoes were planted between rows of vines and central Italy was dominated by a type of mixed culture in which vines, planted amid olive groves and rows of grains, were trained up trees to prevent the grapes from being eaten by the animals allowed to roam freely in the fields (see ARBOREAL VITICULTURE). Modern vineyards, planted exclusively with vines in regular rows, did exist, particularly in Italy's north-west, but viticulture in general was merely part of a general system of agriculture, one cash crop among many. It is no surprise, therefore, that when Italy's vineyards were replanted in the 1960s and 1970s, frequently with the assistance of EU funds, vineyards were generally adapted to the new exigencies of mechanization and productivity. Whereas in France the practicalities of mechanization were adapted to the existing low-trained vines and high VINE DENSITY, Italian vineyards were redesigned when they were replanted to make them compatible with the TRACTORS and other machines which were then becoming generally available. The result was spacings of up to 3 m/10 ft between the rows and high training systems. This low-density viticulture, with an average of 2,500–3,300 vines per ha, coupled with the generous YIELDS due to high-yielding CLONES, had as their inevitable result the very high yields per vine, often as much as 5 kg/11 lb of grapes, and a reduction in vine longevity.

The higher training systems, especially PERGOLA, while offering improved protection against HAIL and FUNGAL DISEASES, were until recently thought to reduce the amounts of reradiated heat and result in less ripe grapes with higher acidity, rougher tannins, and lower levels of EXTRACT. Recent research has shown that there is no marked difference in grape quality between Guyot and pergola-trained vines if yields are kept low; likewise, experiments with planting densities in central Italy have shown improved results at 7,500–10,000 vines per hectare and little if any improvement at higher densities, and so the 1980s fascination with ever-higher-density plantings is waning. Expansive vine-training systems such as TENDONE have found new favour, especially with old vines and ancient clones, and in ABRUZZO, for example, are producing some of the region's best wines. The ALBARELLO (bush vine) system once standard in the south may be LABOUR-intensive but tends to result in high-quality wine. More extreme horizontal systems such as Sylvoz, Casarsa, and other particularly productive CORDON systems are no longer popular. Meanwhile, in reaction to the environmental toll of vine moncultures, a new generation of BIODYNAMIC VITICULTURISTS have re-introduced polyculture in some places.

CLONAL SELECTION aimed at identifying and reproducing qualitatively superior clones of indigenous vine varieties and the most appropriate ROOTSTOCKS to graft them on to has been a relatively recent activity, although important research programmes were conducted specifically for Sangiovese, Nebbiolo, and some other indigenous varieties in the 1990s. The popularity of Kober 5 BB and other over-productive rootstocks, a feature of the planting period from 1965 to 1980, is unlikely to be repeated.

Winemaking

If Italian viticulture has tended to follow its own course, with little attention paid to the practices of other countries, the same cannot be said of its OENOLOGY and winemaking practices. Indeed, substantial investments in cellar equipment have made Italian winemaking facilities some of the most modern in Europe, and Italians make equipment such as BOTTLING lines that is some of the best, and most exported, in the world.

CHAPTALIZATION is forbidden, but ENRICHMENT with concentrated grape must is permitted in some areas and within certain limits.

Wooden FERMENTATION VESSELS, once vigorously abandoned in favour of STAINLESS STEEL, have been gradually making a comeback, especially tronconic ones, while CONCRETE vats and tanks are again widely used for both FERMENTATION and storage. TEMPERATURE CONTROL is widely accepted for the production of both red and white wines, and the PUNCHING DOWN of the cap of red wines has become as widespread as regular PUMPING OVER during fermentation, while there is a noticeable trend towards using the traditional *cappello sommerso* or SUBMERGED CAP technique, especially in Barolo and Barbaresco. The lengthy fermentations and MACERATIONS of the past, sometimes up to six weeks, were shortened, substantially so by most producers aiming for faster maturing and easier to sell wines, slightly less so by avant-garde producers seeking the highest quality. A new generation, however, combines both ancient and modern techniques in an ongoing investigation into what leads to original wines.

WHITE WINEMAKING techniques changed drastically in the 1970s and 1980s, with the introduction of cool fermentations, FILTRATION, and CENTRIFUGES. The most fundamental change of all was to end the practice of SKIN-FERMENTED white wines, once common in Friuli and throughout central Italy. Gains in lightness and freshness were obvious but were achieved at the price of a certain standardization. Producing white wines of more character without sacrificing the newly achieved crispness and cleanliness is the current challenge for Italian white winemaking and there has been a return in some quarters to fermenting white wines on the skins.

Fermentation may have evolved considerably in the second half of the 20th century, but ÉLEVAGE underwent more profound modifications during the same period. Large casks, usually oval rather than upright, were long the preferred containers for CASK AGEING red wine in Italian cellars; long ageing periods, particularly for what were considered the grandest wines, were an almost unvarying rule; used barrels were generally preferred to new ones (although this may often have been for financial rather than qualitative reasons). Many of Italy's most renowned red wines have tannins which need a considerable time in cask to soften and round, and periods of two years in cask are by no means uncommon. In hot vintages many producers prefer to bottle their wines immediately after the mandatory oak ageing, to preserve freshness and halt premature ageing of their wines.

OAK has generally been the preferred wood for casks, much of it from Slavonia or elsewhere in central Europe. In the south of Italy, in areas such as Basilicata and Sicily, where chestnut forests abound and there are no local oak sources, the traditional chestnut cooperage has been gradually replaced by oak casks to achieve a more international style and to avoid the bitterness which old chestnut casks can impart, although many producers are experimenting with a return to chestnut.

The 1980s and 1990s saw Italian cellars invaded en masse by new French BARRIQUES, with Sangiovese and Barbera the first varieties to be widely aged in new small oak barrels. This century there is a marked return to larger, older casks (with considerations of HYGIENE paramount) in order to avoid dominating the flavours of Italy's indigenous grape varieties with those of oak. There is also a move towards eliminating any added wood flavour by using vessels such as AMPHORAE and QVEVRI, for fermentation as well as ageing.

Vine varieties

Italy boasts many hundreds of INDIGENOUS VARIETIES, and this is increasingly celebrated by a new wave of growers keen to rediscover local specialities. In 2020 the most planted variety was SANGIOVESE, with 55,100 ha/136,096 acres, down from 86,000 ha in 1990. The second most planted variety was GLERA, the variety responsible for Prosecco, with 34,154 ha, closely followed by Pinot Grigio (31,360 ha), CATARRATTO (29,575 ha), MONTEPULCIANO (27,000 ha), Merlot (27,000 ha), and Chardonnay (23,000 ha), its total presumably boosted by its popularity with producers of sparkling wines.

Large-scale plantings of INTERNATIONAL VARIETIES—principally French, although there is also some Riesling and Gewürztraminer—were initially confined to the country's north-east (which, in many cases, was under either direct Austrian rule or strong Austrian influence until 1919). They are planted in an arc stretching from Franciacorta in the eastern part of Lombardia through Trentino-Alto Adige, the northern part of the Veneto (the provinces of Vicenza and Treviso), and Friuli. Subsequent plantings of international varieties tended to follow international FASHION: various members of the Pinot family in the 1970s; Chardonnay, Sauvignon Blanc, and Cabernet in the 1980s; Syrah and Viognier in the 1990s. Central Italy, with only the late-ripening Sangiovese an important red grape, has seen considerable plantings of Cabernet, Merlot, and Syrah, especially on the Tuscan coast. But overall the fashion is waning, even if some producers and producer associations still seem to view the inclusion of some of them in official regulations as a passport to commercial success.

Organization of trade

Italy's wine trade resembles those of its European neighbours in terms of a division of labour between individual properties, commercial and NÉGOCIANT houses, and CO-OPERATIVE wineries. What distinguishes Italy is the overwhelming importance of the last two categories, a dominance which is the direct result of the extreme fractioning of vineyard property with individual holdings averaging just 1.8 ha/4.45 acres. Intermediaries for the marketing of the wines, be they négociants or co-operatives, are thus indispensable links in the distribution chain which connects growers to consumers. Private estates of a certain size are an important reality in Tuscany, Puglia, Sicily, and, to a lesser extent, in Friuli, while the development of a significant number of prestigious small 'domaines' in the finest zones of Piemonte might be considered a riposte to BURGUNDY.

Large commercial houses were a relatively late development in Italy, virtually all of them having been founded after the unification of the country in 1861 and thus being a century younger than comparable houses in France, Spain, and Portugal. This is because Italy was not a country prior to its unification, and the movement of merchandise across the borders of the many small states which existed in the peninsula was costly and cumbersome. REDDING cites 'a vexatious system of imposts' as a major cause of Italian viticultural backwardness in the 19th century. There was very little in the way of a national market and little knowledge of even the finest products outside their specific production zones. Even today, négociant houses are a major presence only in Piemonte, Tuscany, the Veneto, and Sicily, while co-operative wineries play a significant role in virtually all Italian regions.

Co-operatives, several founded as early as the end of the 19th century, became the dominant force in the production and distribution of Italian wine in the late 20th century, a logical development considering the political dominance of the Christian Democratic party in the country's various governments and the favour shown to co-operative movements in the social doctrine of the Roman Catholic church. Income maintenance has been as significant a concern as the products themselves; this objective has entailed large volumes, which, thanks to ample subsidies, could be marketed at low prices. Quality has not always been the strong point of the resulting wines, although individual co-operatives, particularly in the north, have always been conscious of the need to create products that would please consumer palates. Italy enjoyed particular success in the 1970s and 1980s with its exports of the Riunite co-ops' LAMBRUSCO. This sweet foaming red has been joined by Pinot Grigio and Prosecco as the commercial ballast of Italy's wine exports.

As EU and national subsidies are reduced, Italian wines, like any other European wine, will have to respond more readily to free-market economics. While the total volume of wine produced has declined considerably, consumption within Italy has declined even faster, and Italy now exports around 70% of its wine, making full use of EU marketing incentives to help sell its wines in third markets.

There can be few doubts that Italy's new prosperity and the worldwide popularity of Italian food have changed prospects and possibilities for Italian wine. And there can be even fewer doubts that admirers and enthusiasts of Italian wine have never had such an embarrassment of riches as at the beginning of the third millennium CE.

For details of individual regions, see ABRUZZO, ALTO ADIGE, BASILICATA, CALABRIA, CAMPANIA, EMILIA-ROMAGNA, FRIULI, LAZIO, LIGURIA, LOMBARDIA, MARCHE, MOLISE, PIEMONTE, PUGLIA, SARDINIA, SICILY, TRENTINO, TUSCANY, UMBRIA, Valle d'AOSTA, and VENETO.

For details of terms to be found on Italian wine labels, see CLASSICO, DOC, DOCG, IGT, and RISERVA. A wine that fails to qualify as any of these is a WINE WITHOUT GEOGRAPHICAL INDICATION and is labelled simply VINO or Vino d'Italia.

W.S.

Anderson, B., *Wine Atlas of Italy* (1990).
Belfrage, N., *From Barolo to Valpolicella: The Wines of Northern Italy* (2nd edn, 2003).
Belfrage, N., *From Brunello to Zibibbo: The Wines of Southern Italy* (2nd edn, 2003).
Fabrizio, G., et al., *Gambero Rosso Vini d'Italia* (2014).
Giavedoni, F., and Gily, M. (eds.), *Guida ai Vitigni d'Italia. Storia e Charatteristiche di 600 Varietà Autoctone* (2011).
Johnson, H., and Robinson, J., *The World Atlas of Wine* (8th edn, 2019).
Robinson, J., et al., *Wine Grapes: A Complete Guide to 1,368 Vine Varieties, Including Their Origins and Flavours* (2012).
Soldati, M., *Vino al Vino* (7th edn, 2010).
Masnaghetti, A. (ed.), *Enogea: Newsletter Bimestrale Indipendente* (bi-monthly newsletter about Italian wine).
dati-censimentoagricoltura.istat.it

Itata, subregion in southern CHILE rediscovered by De Martino winery in 2011, when it began to vinify wines from the region's old vines of Cinsault (see CINSAUT). Now the region is increasingly also known for old PAÍS and MUSCATEL, which grow on hills facing the sea in the Cordillera de la Costa. P.T.

IVDP, Instituto do Vinho do Douro e do Porto, which governs the production of both PORT and DOURO wine.

IWCA. Founded in 2019 by JACKSON FAMILY WINES and FAMILIA TORRES, International Wineries for Climate Action is a growing group of wine producers committed to continuing to reduce the wine industry's CARBON FOOTPRINT to zero by sharing knowledge and by regular audits.

J

Jackson Family Wines, growing international empire of high-quality, environmentally aware wine estates spun out of KENDALL-JACKSON of Sonoma, California.

In 1986, Jess Jackson and his second wife Barbara Banke acquired 1,000 acres/400 ha in SANTA BARBARA County based on the historic Tepusquet Vineyard and founded Cambria Winery and Vineyard, with Banke the listed owner. Stonestreet in ALEXANDER VALLEY followed three years later, and in 1991 a partnership was formed with a STAVE mill in the Vosges to assure OAK quality. Today this operation has grown into Merrain International.

By the mid 1990s, they were making wine in Chile and Italy and had bought what would be Hartford Family Winery in the Russian River Valley, Gauer Estate in the Alexander Valley, and another high vineyard on Howell Mountain. They continued to expand into mountain vineyards, especially those benefiting from Pacific influence.

In the early years of this century they acquired wine estates in Australia and St-Émilion.

Jess Jackson died in 2011 at age 81 after a long bout with cancer. Barbara Banke has since taken charge and has only increased the company's (including Kendall-Jackson's) commitment to SUSTAINABILITY, including the establishment of the Jess S. Jackson sustainable winery at DAVIS. With FAMILIA TORRES, the company founded International Wineries for Climate Action (IWCA), an attempt to decarbonize the wine sector, in 2019. Under Banke, and presumably with CLIMATE CHANGE in mind, the company has moved determinedly into Oregon and in early 2022 owned 40 wineries in California, Oregon, Australia, Chile, France, Italy, and South Africa, each allowed an unusual degree of autonomy and totalling a landholding of 15,000 ha/37,000 acres, of which about one-third is planted to vines.

Jacquère is the most planted white grape variety in SAVOIE, where it produces high yields of lightly scented, essentially alpine dry white. It is one of the numerous natural progenies of GOUAIS BLANC. Plantings were a steady 920 ha/2,273 acres in 2019. Late ripening and relatively hardy, it has also been successfully grown for IGP blends in the northern Rhône.

Jacquez, also known as Black Spanish, dark-skinned American hybrid grown in TEXAS thanks to its resistance to PIERCE'S DISEASE and in Brazil for everyday wines and juice.

Jadot, Louis, merchant-grower based in BEAUNE, selling Burgundy and, from 2013, operating in OREGON, where they founded Résonance. They own 132 ha/326 acres of vineyards in the CÔTE D'OR, 75 ha/185 acres in BEAUJOLAIS, and 18 ha/44 acres in Fuissé in the MÂCONNAIS. The company has been owned by the Kopf family since 1985. Founded in 1859 by the eponymous Louis Jadot, the company was run from 1962 to 1992 by André Gagey, who joined the firm as an assistant in 1954. When Louis-Alain Jadot, last of the family line, died prematurely in 1968, Gagey was asked by the family to become general manager. He was succeeded by his son Pierre-Henry, whose son Thibault now works for the company. Jadot's success has been very much due to the combined talents of André Gagey and winemaker Jacques Lardière, who retired in 2013 to be succeeded by Frédéric Barnier. Both red and white NÉGOCIANT wines, made from bought-in fruit, are thoroughly reliable, but the firm's reputation is based on the high quality of its domaine wines. Jadot's holdings have continued to increase, not least in Beaujolais, notably Ch des Jacques in the 1990s and Domaine Ferret in 2008.

Jaen, **Jaen Tinto**, and **Jaen du Dão**, synonym for Galicia's MENCÍA red wine grape in Portugal's DÃO region, where it ripens early to produce deeply coloured wines that are notable for their modest acidity. Occasionally seen as a VARIETAL, it is normally stiffened with Touriga Nacional and Alfrocheiro. The vine was planted on a total of 3,249 ha/8,028 acres in northern Portugal in 2020. Jaén Blanco is a synonym for CAYETANA BLANCA.

Jahrgang, German for VINTAGE (as in the year rather than the HARVEST process, for which the word is *Ernte*).

Jakot, Slovenian name for the FRIULANO vine variety, the old name Tokaj spelt backwards.

Japan. More known for its sake and shochu, Japan also has a winemaking history of nearly 150 years, even though wine drinking has only recently become common. Though per capita consumption remains small compared with that of Europe and the United States, wine is produced in most prefectures, with 331 wineries and total production of 82,319 kl in 2020, and is forecast to grow further thanks to increased technical and financial support from both public and private sectors.

History

The exact origins of grape cultivation in Japan are unclear, obscured by several competing legends, but are believed to date as far back as the 8th century. It is thought that grapes had been cultivated only as TABLE GRAPES until the 15th century, when Portuguese MISSIONARIES brought red wine as gifts for the feudal lords of Kyushu in southern Japan in 1545. Others who followed continued the practice so that the locals acquired a taste for wine and began to import it regularly.

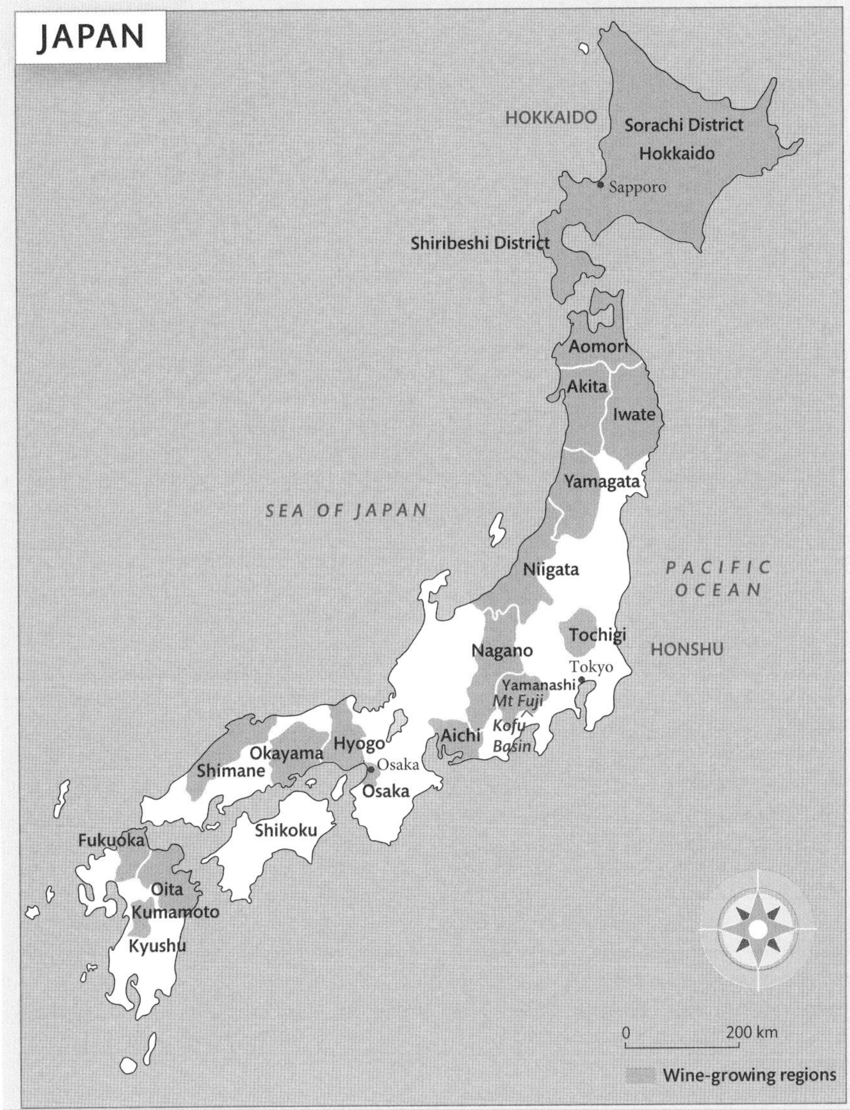

Until recently, it was believed that Japanese winemaking first began in the 19th century, when winemaking was encouraged by the Meiji government. However, newly discovered historical documents suggest a period of winemaking around 1627; the history is now being reconsidered.

In 1874, commercial winemaking began in Yamanashi Prefecture, and in 1877 the first privately owned winery was established in Katsunuma, in the centre of the prefecture. The winery sent two employees to France to study viticulture and oenology; their efforts convinced local authorities to permit the import of European VITIS VINIFERA and AMERICAN VINES as the basis for a new industry.

In 1893, Zenbei Kawakami, often credited as the 'father of Japanese wine', established a vineyard in Niigata and began developing HYBRID varieties suited to Japan's climate. Of the 22 varieties he developed, MUSCAT BAILEY A became one of the signature red wine grapes of Japan. Hybrids dominated the wine industry until the 1980s, when Japan's first 'wine boom' saw per capita consumption double during the 1980s, and an increased exposure to imported wine spurred a movement towards *vinifera* varieties.

Japanese wineries also focused on investment in modern winemaking equipment and on training their winemakers in the methods used in the major wine-producing nations (Suntory even went so far as to buy the ST-JULIEN classed growth Ch Lagrange, and the 1980s saw several substantial Japanese investments in the German, California, and Australian wine industries).

Since 2000, the growing demand for wines has spurred local authorities and regional wine associations to set voluntary standards in terms of varieties, viticulture, and winemaking, with an emphasis on Japan-grown wines. In recent years, the National Tax Agency Japan, the Ministry of Agriculture, Forestry and Fisheries (MAFF), and local municipal governments, among other official bodies, have been endeavouring to promote the wine sector.

Geography and climate

Japan is a long, narrow archipelago stretching from latitudes 26° to 44° N, with about 75% of the land surface covered by mountains. It is surrounded by the Pacific Ocean, the Sea of Okhotsk, and the East China Sea, sitting at the intersection of warm and cold currents. As the vineyards are widely spread out, the array of MESOCLIMATES is diverse, from subtropical to subarctic.

As of 2022 there were five GEOGRAPHICAL INDICATIONS (GIs) registered for wine: Yamanashi, Nagano, Yamagata, Hokkaido, and Osaka. The first three, all on the main island Honshu, account for almost 71% of the country's total production. Because of the subtropical, MARITIME CLIMATE and high level of precipitation, with the rainy season and typhoons complicating the growing season and prolonged rainfalls at harvest, an overhead PERGOLA trellising system known as *Tana-jitate* is traditionally used to allow ventilation as a defence against FUNGAL DISEASES.

Yamanashi Prefecture, west of Tokyo, boasts the largest area under vine, with 3,800 ha/9,390 acres (including TABLE GRAPES). The vineyards and wineries are concentrated around the Kofu basin centred on Katsunuma, surrounded by high mountains that provide protection from moist winds. The vineyards are mainly located on slopes at 300–550 m/984–1,805 ft in ELEVATION, with good DRAINAGE and fresh breezes. The high DIURNAL TEMPERATURE RANGE and long hours of sunshine during the growing season help the grapes to achieve PHYSIOLOGICAL RIPENESS. The region produces 96% of the country's Koshu grapes and 62% of Muscat Bailey A.

Nagano Prefecture, inland and west of Yamanashi, ranks second in production of Japanese wine. Surrounded by the Japanese Alps, more than 80% of its farmland is above 500 m/1,640 ft in elevation. Similar to Yamanashi, Nagano Prefecture has relatively low rainfall with a climate suited to fruit-growing. Nagano is the largest producer of Merlot, Concord, and Niagara grape varieties in Japan. Kikyogahara, the birthplace of winemaking in Nagano, is known for its Merlot. Syrah grown in Ueda has attracted much attention in recent years. And Chardonnay from Chikuma River basin, produced in various styles according to elevation and soil, is also highly valued. This last area is particularly booming, boasting nearly half of the wineries in Nagano, thanks to local programmes offering training and support for new producers.

Hokkaido, Japan's northernmost island at latitudes 42–45° N, is rarely influenced by tropical cyclones and typhoons, but it is very cold, classified as Region I according to the Winkler Index (see CLIMATE CLASSIFICATION). Yet the region is drawing increased attention from winemakers looking for alternatives in the face of CLIMATE CHANGE. In addition to many new small-scale wineries, there are several large producers, and the region has attracted some prominent outside talent: Étienne de Montille from Burgundy has invested in Hakodate, and Italian consultant Riccardo Cotarella is working in Yoichi. A CUSTOM-CRUSH FACILITY in Iwamizawa also plays an important role in encouraging the local wine industry.

The centre of wine production in Hokkaido is the Shiribeshi district in the south-west and the Sorachi district in the centre. The Shiribeshi district—the larger of the two—rarely feels any influence from the cold currents of the Pacific Ocean, so there is little risk of frost damage or WINTER FREEZE and grape yield is stable. In Yoichi and Niki, government subsidies are used to support wine tourism projects as well as winery improvements.

Throughout the prefecture, grape varieties with high cold tolerance dominate, particularly white varieties KERNER and NIAGARA. In red grape varieties, Zweigeltrebe (ZWEIGELT) has the largest area under vine, and Pinot Noir is increasing. Less cold-hardy vines are pruned before snowfall and then buried under soil or snow for WINTER PROTECTION.

Japanese vineyard soils are in general very acid (see PH, SOILS).

Vine varieties

In Japan, the demand for table grapes is high, and so the majority of its 16,700 ha/41,267 acres of vineyard in 2020 is planted to Kyoho, Delaware, Pione, Shine Muscat, and other table grapes. Some table grapes are also used for wine.

The most significant Japanese variety is KOSHU. This is the descendant of the vines carried along the Silk Road to Japan 800 to 1,200 years ago and, in the public eye at least, is virtually synonymous with the industry of Katsunuma.

Koshu has survived as an important variety because it has adapted to the difficult growing conditions in Yamanashi Prefecture and because it is supported by long tradition. Also used as a table grape, it has high VIGOUR and a low rate of sugar accumulation. Koshu also contains a specific precursor which forms a THIOL compound, 3-mercaptohexanol, that gives an aroma of grapefruit, as found in Sauvignon Blanc. The grape lends itself to diverse wine styles, from still white wines to sparkling, dessert, and ORANGE wines. NIAGARA and DELAWARE are also popular for white wines, and ALBARIÑO cultivated along the coast of Niigata is attracting attention.

The major red grape varieties used for wine are Muscat Bailey A, CONCORD, and Merlot. Highly tolerant of wet, cool climates, Muscat Bailey A has a characteristic strawberry flavour and modest tannins that makes it amenable to a wide range of wine styles, from sparkling and rosé to reds in both early-drinking and ageable styles.

An indigenous variety, YAMABUDO, has also been gaining attention. This red variety belongs to *Vitis coignetiae*, an indigenous Asian vine species, and was registered for wine use with the OIV in 2020.

Industry organization

Until 2015, domestically produced wine or wines bottled from imported wines and/or fermented from concentrated must were permitted to be called 'domestic wine'. In 2015, Japan's National Tax Agency introduced new labelling standards, stipulating that only wine made 100% from grapes grown in Japan can be labelled as 'Japan wine'. These wines may also be labelled by GEOGRAPHICAL INDICATION, grape variety, and vintage. In 2020, the production of 'Japan wine' was about 20% of total wine production and forecast to increase.

However, the rapid rise in the number of wineries intent on producing wine from domestically grown grapes has led to a shortage of vine cuttings as well as grapes. In addition, as wine grapes trade at a lower price than table grapes in Japan, fewer growers produce wine grapes, and the number is dwindling. In response, the number of wineries who own their own vineyards is gradually increasing. Large wineries continue to dominate production, but 85% of Japan's wineries are small-scale, producing less than 100,000 l/26,417 gal. K.O. & R.F.

Jasnières, white-wine appellation of just 75 ha/185 acres in 2020 dedicated to CHENIN BLANC and sheltered within the Coteaux du LOIR district in the northern Loire. Shared by the communes of Lhomme and Ruillé-sur-Loir, the vineyards cover a steep south-facing slope protected from the north winds by the Bercé forest (a favourite of coopers). Declared 'the best white wine in the world' three times by food critic Curnonsky, Jasnières failed to live up to its fame and almost disappeared in the 1950s, but growers such as Joël Gigou followed by outsiders such as Eric Nicolas have resurrected the appellation and its potential. Locals see Jasnières as 'the SAVENNIÈRES of Touraine' because of the austere profile of the dry wines in their youth but the region's complex geology of FLINT, CLAYS, and mica SCHIST over Turonian LIMESTONE allows for a broader expression of style resembling a steelier VOUVRAY. Rare, notable NOBLE ROT wines are also made. See also LOIRE, including map. P. Le.

Jefferson, Thomas (1743–1826), third president of the United States, a wine lover whose interest in wine and hopes for American winegrowing typified the early Republic. As a VIRGINIA farmer, Jefferson grew grapes from all sources, native (see VITIS, AMERICAN VINE SPECIES) and VITIS VINIFERA, at his estate Monticello for 50 years with uniform lack of success: no Monticello wine ever materialized, but the hope never died. His vineyard at Monticello has been restored to the form it had in 1807.

As ambassador to France (1784–9), Jefferson made himself expert in wine, travelling to all the major French wine regions as well as to those of Germany and Italy. He tasted, discussed, and bought widely, and he acted also as agent and adviser for his friends in the selection and purchase of wines. The record of this activity contained in his papers is a small encyclopedia of pre-Revolutionary wine and wine production. As president (1801–9), Jefferson was celebrated for the variety and excellence of his cellar at the White House in Washington, which abounded in CHAMBERTIN, MARGAUX, HERMITAGE, YQUEM, and TOKAY.

At all times, Jefferson was eager to assist the many efforts to solve the riddle of successful winegrowing in America: he gave land next to his Virginia estate to support Philip Mazzei's Italian Vineyard Society, an ambitious effort to grow wine by importing Italian vines and vineyard workers; he encouraged such neighbours as James Madison and James Monroe in their viticultural experiments; and it was during his administration that land on the river Ohio in Indiana was granted to Swiss-born Jean Jacques Dufour for the enterprise that resulted in the first successful commercial wine production in the United States.

By such assistance, and by minimizing wine TAXATION, Jefferson hoped to make the US a wine-drinking country. He could be extravagant in his optimism: a wine from the native Alexander grape he called equal to Chambertin; a sweet SCUPPERNONG from North Carolina he thought would be 'distinguished on the best tables of Europe'. The US, he affirmed, could 'make as great a variety of wines as are made in Europe, not exactly of the same kind, but doubtless as good', even though his own experience contradicted the proposition.

Jefferson's personal pleasure in wine was clear: 'Good wine is a daily necessity for me', he wrote. He also saw wine as an element in his vision of a nation of independent yeomen: 'no nation is drunken where wine is cheap', hence wine should be the nation's drink. T.P.

Bottles of late 18th century wines such as Ch LAFITE, supposedly ordered and even initialled by Jefferson, fetched record-breaking prices at AUCTION in the late 20th century but were subsequently shown to be COUNTERFEIT.

de Treville Lawrence, R. (ed.), *Jefferson and Wine* (2nd edn, 1989).
Gabler, J. M., *Passions: The Wines and Travels of Thomas Jefferson* (1995).

jerepigo, or **jerepiko**, unfermented dessert 'wines' in South Africa, the Cape's version of MISTELLE produced by adding alcohol to grape juice, generally from inland regions, before fermentation. Many are made from MUSCADEL, which name on the label may legally serve to indicate style as well as variety. Initially about 17% alcohol, many are now closer to a more recent lower limit of 15%, often with intense ripe fig and MUSCAT flavours. These traditional, warming wines, both red and white, once popular in South African winters but now sold in ever-declining volumes, probably derive their name from JEROPIGA.

Jerez, or **Jerez de la Frontera**, city in ANDALUCÍA, south-west Spain, that is the centre of the sherry industry. Jerez is also the name of the DOP which produces sherry. In Spain the wine is known as *vino de Jerez* (or simply *Jerez*), and 'sherry' is an English corruption of the Spanish word (while in France the town and drink are known respectively as Xérès and *xérès*). The town owes its full name to the fact that in the Middle Ages it was on the frontier between Christian and Moorish Spain. For more details on the wine, see SHERRY.

jeroboam. See BOTTLE SIZES.

jeropiga, Portuguese term for grape must prevented from fermenting by the addition of grape spirit. *Jeropiga* is often used to sweeten FORTIFIED WINES. (*Vinho abafado*, on the other hand, is partially fermented before spirit is added; see CARCAVELOS.)

jetting. See SPARKLING WINEMAKING.

Jewish heritage in German wine culture. By their Christian names, they could not be distinguished from their colleagues in Prussia or elsewhere in Germany. But by their family names, many of the late 19th century champions of the wine trade in Germany could be easily identified as Jewish: the sons of Hermann SICHEL, who spread from the old Rhenish wine capital Mainz throughout Europe and conquered the New World; Leo Levitta, who was raised in Rüdesheim on the Rhine; Julius Langenbach, a citizen of Worms, the town that centuries ago hosted one of the largest Jewish communities north of the Alps; and Sigmund Loeb, who had deserted the windy Hunsrück only to become one of the most renowned wine merchants of Trier and president of the Moselle Trade Association. In the last quarter of the 19th century, some excellent vintages, peace in notoriously war-torn Europe, and the free-trade spirit during the first wave of GLOBALIZATION helped propel Jews to the forefront of the German wine trade. Their centuries-old mercantile skills helped, as did the European aristocracy and nouveau-riche bourgeoisie's desire to acquire what were then regarded as the world's finest wines, as well as a thirst among emigrant communities throughout the Americas for wine from their German homeland.

Although Jews formed a significant part of the national and international German wine trade, there is no evidence that they endured particular scrutiny during the anti-semitic stirrings at the end of the 19th century. There was certainly some unease when Jewish brokers and merchants formed quasi-monopolistic structures, such as those in Franken and the southern Pfalz. But according to the few sources available, there was neither stigma nor bias towards Jews by government officials in the prosecution of wine ADULTERATION AND FRAUD. And during the First World War, German Jews turned out to be as patriotic as everybody else. Sigmund Loeb's only son Otto Wolfgang was not the only one to fight in France.

When the war was over, the main export markets for German wine were off limits. The victorious UK despised the symbols of German prepotency, PROHIBITION had closed the US market, and Russia was torn apart by the Bolshevist revolution. In the 1920s, most parts of Western Europe stumbled from one political and economic crisis into another. The German wine market was close to collapsing and, as a result, so was the business of brokers and merchants. Once again, the Jews drew on their skills and their international networks. Alfred Fromm moved from Franken to Bingen across the Rhine from the Rheingau where he set up a new export business; the Sichels created the famous BLUE NUN—one of the first BRANDS in wine history. When Hitler was elected in 1933, some 60% of German wine was traded by Jewish agents and merchants, which was the main reason the Nazis held back from cracking down immediately on the Jewish wine community. The other reason: by exporting high-value wine, Jewish merchants delivered the precious foreign currency that the Nazis needed for the German war machine.

Only after the Olympic games in 1936 in Berlin, by which time non-Jewish wine marketing had consolidated, did the Nazis crack down on Jewish brokers, merchants, and retailers. Families such as the Levittas split up, with some members heading into exile; Sigmund Loeb's son, Otto Wolfgang, had already founded a subsidiary in London, O. W. Loeb, and managed to introduce opera lovers at the Glyndebourne Festival to Moselle wines; the Sichels eventually escaped to London and the US.

The 'Reichskristallnacht' in November 1938 marked the beginning of the final extinction of Jewish entrepreneurship in Germany. Those who had not left Germany were forced to sell their businesses or lost permission to do so. Although there are no detailed records, it seems that quite a number of merchants survived the Holocaust, thanks to their international contacts. However, the brokers whose work was based on their local networks were murdered or gassed. Ludwig Levitta, one of the finest palates of his time, was deported with his wife and son to Theresienstadt and perished at Auschwitz in 1943.

Despite the Holocaust, most of the exiled Jews did not hesitate to engage in the German wine trade again and to restore the reputation of German wine in the UK and the US. Alfred Langenbach (d. 1964) published *The Wines of Germany*, the first comprehensive survey of German wines ever published in the English language (1951). Fritz Hallgarten (d. 1991) documented his experiences in his memoir *Rhineland-Wineland* (1951), and Otto W. Loeb (d. 1974) drew on his and his father's unique knowledge for his book *Moselle* (1971).

By that time, Loeb's efforts to initiate hundreds of members of Cambridge University Wine & Food Society into the mysteries of German Riesling and the wines of California had borne plenty of fruit—Hugh JOHNSON was one of the best and brightest of his adepts. Alfred Fromm (d. 1998) had joined Franz W. Sichel in influencing the reorientation of the California wine industry towards quality wine. Even with Peter Max F. Sichel (b. 1922) no longer active in the wine world from his base in New York and O. W. Loeb of London now under different ownership, the Jewish heritage of German wine cultural is still alive and, one hopes, will never be forgotten. D.De.

João de Santarém, name used for the widely planted CASTELÃO red wine grape in parts of the TEJO region of Portugal.

Johannisberg, Valais name for SILVANER grapes in SWITZERLAND.

Johnson, Hugh (1939–), world's best-selling wine author. Johnson's passion for wine began when he was at Cambridge University, where he read English. One of the great stylists of the LITERATURE OF WINE, on graduation he was immediately taken on as a feature writer for Condé Nast magazines. As a result of his close friendship with André SIMON, the founder of the International Wine & Food Society, he became general secretary of the society and succeeded the legendary gastronome as editor of its journal. At the same time he became wine correspondent of the *Sunday Times* and embarked on his first book *Wine*, whose publication in 1966 established him as one of the foremost English gastronomic writers of the time. More than 750,000 copies have been printed, in seven languages. He revised it in 1974.

His next book was even more successful, even though it allowed only limited scope for Johnson's matchless prose. *The World Atlas of Wine* represented the first serious attempt to map the world's wine regions and first appeared in 1971. More than 4.5 million copies in a total of 20 languages have been sold of this and subsequent editions in 1977, 1985, 1994, 2001, 2007, 2013, and 2019, the last four co-written with Jancis Robinson.

Pausing only to edit *Queen* magazine 1968–70, he then wrote a best-selling book on trees, *The International Book of Trees*, inspired by his acquisition of an Elizabethan house in Essex. In 1977 he went on to devise and write an annual wine guide, *The Pocket Wine Book*, which has sold more than 12 million copies in a dozen languages, between its first edition and 2023.

The more expansive *Hugh Johnson's Wine Companion* followed in 1983 and was revised in 1987, 1991, 1997, and 2003 with Stephen Brook. It sold widely in the US as *Hugh Johnson's Modern Encyclopedia of Wine*, in France, and in Germany as *Der Grosse Johnson*. This prolific output, encouraged by Johnson's publishers Mitchell Beazley, was supplemented in 1979 by *The Principles of Gardening*, another bestseller, and a succession of co-authored and less serious wine books (including even a 'pop-up' version).

Johnson's most distinctive work, however, did not appear until 1989. *The Story of Wine* is a *tour de force*, a sweep through the history of wine in which Johnson's literary skills and breadth of vision are headily combined. The book, updated and republished in 2020 as *The Story of Wine: From Noah to Now*, was written to coincide with an ambitiously international 13-part television series, *Vintage: A History of Wine*, written and presented by Johnson. In 1992, he co-authored *The Art and Science of Wine* with Australian James Halliday. *A Life Uncorked* (2005), republished in 2022 as *The Life and Wines of Hugh Johnson*, is his most reflective and autobiographical work.

Between 1986 and 2000 Johnson sold the Hugh Johnson Collection, glassware and other wine accessories, with notable success in Japan, where he was a consultant to Jardines Wines and Spirits. He also served (1986–2001) on the administrative council of first growth Ch LATOUR and has been president of the *Sunday Times* Wine Club run by LAITHWAITE's since its inception in 1973. In 1990, Johnson co-founded The Royal TOKAJI Wine Company, a reflection of his interest in wine history. Other activities include regular journalism on gardening. For 25 years from 1975 he was editorial director of the *Journal of the Royal Horticultural Society* and since 1975 has written a gardening column, now a blog, under the pseudonym Tradescant (www.tradsdiary.com), anthologized in 1992, 2009, and 2021. In 2005 and 2007 respectively, none too hastily one might argue, the French made him a Chevalier de l'Ordre National du Mérite and the British an OBE.

Johnson is one of the most vocal opponents of SCORING wine, and his writing has been characterized more by a sensual and historical enthusiasm for wine in all its variety than by the critical analysis of individual wines.

Johnson, H., *The Life and Wines of Hugh Johnson* (2022).

joint venture, common phenomenon in the late 20th century whereby two enterprises with very different strengths combine to produce a wine or wines. The modern prototype was that announced in 1979 between Baron Philippe de ROTHSCHILD of Bordeaux and Robert MONDAVI of California to produce Opus One, the luxuriously priced Napa Valley Cabernet Sauvignon, combining Mondavi's knowledge of and holdings in the Napa Valley with the prestige and winemaking expertise associated with Baron Philippe's first growth Pauillac Ch MOUTON ROTHSCHILD. Most joint ventures are designed to justify a premium over the other wines made *in situ* by virtue of a much-heralded connection with a glamorous outsider, but they are also evidence of the GLOBALIZATION of wine. Joint ventures are particularly well suited to new wine regions such as those in CHINA and INDIA, for example, where the winemaking expertise of an established wine producer blends well with an enterprise which can offer local knowledge and contacts.

Jongieux, CRU in the upper Rhône Valley west of Aix-les-Bains whose name may be added to the French appellation SAVOIE. Vineyards produce a range of still varietal wines from MONDEUSE, PINOT NOIR, or GAMAY for reds and, more commonly, JACQUÈRE for whites. Above Jongieux village is a steep vineyard slope, reserved for the separate Marestel cru, which may append its name to ROUSSETTE de Savoie. W.L.

Jordan, Middle Eastern country on the eastern bank of the Jordan River with a viticultural tradition reaching back to at least 3500 BCE (see ORIGINS OF VINICULTURE). In 2021, however, of its 8,792 ha/21,726 acres of vineyard only 280 ha were dedicated to wine production, of which Zumot, an ORGANIC producer, owns nearly 200 ha. These are located in Jordan's north, in Sama as-Sirhan, at 630 m/2,133 ft in ELEVATION. Here the broad DIURNAL TEMPERATURE RANGE makes it possible to ripen grapes into October. While the climate is generally arid, humidity can reach 80% on summer mornings. Vine rows are oriented east–west to take advantage of the west wind, which keeps grape bunches aerated and reduces FUNGAL DISEASES. Vines depend on DRIP IRRIGATION, the water sourced from deep underground. A mixture of CLAY and LIMESTONE soils allows for moisture retention as well as good drainage; BASALT and GRANITE also appear. Of the 38 varieties Zumot has trialled since 2000, Cabernet Sauvignon excels; Syrah, Petite Sirah, Carmenère, Malbec, Viognier, Gewürztraminer, Sauvignon Blanc, Petit Manseng, and Chardonnay are also promising. However, the prevailing culture and high alcohol taxes ensure that wine remains a niche market, mainly appreciated by tourists; Jordanians themselves generally prefer arak, their aniseed-flavoured spirit.

joven, Spanish for 'young', sometimes used to indicate wines destined for early consumption.

Juan García, crisp, lively, local dark-skinned vine speciality of the ARRIBES zone in Castilla y León, on the border with Portugal, where it is usually mixed in the vineyard with other, lesser vines. In 2020 there was a total of 626 ha/1,547 acres in Spain. On rocky hillside sites, it can produce highly perfumed, relatively light reds. A natural cross of CAYETANA BLANCA and ALFROCHEIRO, it is also known as Mouráton.

Juan Ibáñez, synonym for the MORISTEL red wine grape in northern Spain.

judging wine, an activity that most wine drinkers undertake every time they open a new bottle, but also a serious business on which the commercial future of some wine producers may to a certain extent depend. For details of domestic, amateur wine judging, see TASTING.

The judging process at a more professional level can vary from a gathering of a few friends, a few bottles, and much hot air to a COMPETITION in which wines have been carefully categorized by wine type, style, and possibly price and are tasted BLIND, in ideal conditions, without any consultation until a possible final discussion of controversial wines. Back-up bottles are always needed in case of CORKED bottles and to verify whether any other FAULT is confined to a single bottle. SCORING systems vary but typically involve awarding a specific allocation of points for various different aspects such as appearance, NOSE, PALATE, perhaps TYPICALITY, and overall quality. MEDALS and trophies are often awarded as a result. Wine SHOWS are particularly important in Australia.

For the results of professional wine judging on an individual or small-group basis, see WINE WRITING.

Judgment of Paris, famous blind tasting comparing hand-picked California and French wines organized in Paris in 1976 by British wine writer, then Parisian caviste, Steven SPURRIER. Much to the fury and embarrassment of the renowned French tasters, California surprised everyone by winning hands down. The French claimed that this was simply because NEW WORLD wines mature faster, but a repeat tasting held 30 years later simultaneously in London and Napa had much the same result. The tasting made the reputations of producers such as Stag's Leap Wine Cellars and Mayacamas.

Taber, G., *Judgment of Paris: California vs. France and the Historic 1976 Paris Tasting that Revolutionized Wine* (2005).

jug wine, term used in the US for the most basic sort of wine, a counterpart to VIN ordinaire or PLONK. After PROHIBITION was repealed in 1933, most inexpensive California GENERIC table wine was bottled in half-gallon and gallon (1.9- and 3.9-l) glass jugs or flagons with SCREWCAPS to satisfy a demand largely made up of thirsty immigrant labourers from the Mediterranean and Eastern Europe. As this market segment has aged and died without direct replacement, jug wines have waned.

Juhfark, distinctive white grape variety once widely grown in Hungary whose total plantings had fallen to 160 ha/395 acres by 2021. After the PHYLLOXERA invasion it never regained its importance and is today found almost exclusively in the Somló region, where it produces tart wine which ages well. The vine, whose name means 'ewe's tail', is inconveniently sensitive to both frost and DOWNY MILDEW.

Juliénas, one of the ten BEAUJOLAIS crus, home to important LIEUX-DITS, including Les Mouilles and Les Capitans, which yield stoic and long-lived wines, particularly from higher elevations among its 564 ha/1,393 acres. J.F.B.

Julius-Kühn-Institut, viticultural research station at Siebeldingen in the Pfalz region of GERMANY known to insiders as Geilweilerhof and specializing in breeding vine varieties which combine resistance to FUNGAL DISEASES with superior wine quality. As early as 1926, Peter Morio and later Professor Husfeld were working on combining the desirable characteristics found in Asian and AMERICAN VINE SPECIES with the wine quality produced by VITIS VINIFERA varieties. Much of the focus of research is on improving VINE BREEDING efficiency, with particular reference to pest and disease resistance, frost and drought resistance, as well as important wine constituents (particularly aroma and PHENOLIC compounds), the genetic resources of *Vitis*, grape genomic research, biotechnology, and the development of sensor-based phenotyping technology. The most famous varieties from Geilweilerhof are MORIO-MUSKAT, BACCHUS, OPTIMA, and DOMINA. In the early 1990s, the successful breeding work of Professor Alleweldt led to the release of the first DISEASE-RESISTANT VARIETIES such as PHOENIX (1992) and REGENT (1994). By 2004, Regent was planted on more than 2,000 ha/5,000 acres in Germany, representing a breakthrough in the acceptance of NEW VARIETIES. Other new cultivars with both good disease resistance and potential wine quality were released later: Villaris, Felicia, Calardis Blanc, and Calardis Musqué (white); and Calandro and Reberger (black). Geilweilerhof provides three grapevine databases on its website, and the journal *Vitis* has been published since 1957. See also GEISENHEIM.

Since 2008 the station has also housed a plant protection department of the JKI, which focuses on the causal agents and control of diseases and pests of viticulture and fruit crops and advises the German government on these issues. M.C. & R.K.C.T.

www.julius-kuehn.de/en/zr
www.julius-kuehn.de/en/ow

Jullien, André (1766–1832), seminal wine writer, Parisian wine merchant, and one of the first explorers of the *world* of wine, venturing even as far as 'Chinese Tartary' in order to discover and assess all international wine regions and their produce. His was an extraordinary outlook, and it must have been a demanding journey, in an era when his peers barely ventured beyond the threshold of their wine shops. He had clearly read the contemporary LITERATURE OF WINE, which, until that point, concerned itself almost entirely with the details of how to grow vines and how to make wine (see CHAPTAL, for example). His aim was to discover and categorize the characteristics of as many different CRUS as he could find, travelling throughout eastern Europe, along the Silk Road to Asia, as well as discovering the vineyards of Africa. There can be few WINE WRITERS today who are as well travelled. The result was the publication in Paris in 1816 of *Topographie de tous les vignobles connus*, a substantial volume full of useful detail which includes the most comprehensive wine CLASSIFICATION (into five classes according to quality) ever undertaken. Much of it was translated into English and published, in abridged form, as 'a manual and guide to all importers and purchasers in the choice of wines' in London in 1824. In effect, Jullien's work set the style for a high proportion of modern WINE WRITING.

For more details of Jullien's classification, see the LITERATURE OF WINE.

Jumilla, DOP in the north of Murcia in central, southern Spain (see map under SPAIN) producing mainly red wines. The climate is arid, with just 300 mm/11.7 in of RAINFALL in a year. The principal grape variety is the red MONASTRELL, which ripens in the summer temperatures of around 40 °C/104 °F to produce high-alcohol wines.

About half of the region's much-reduced total area of 21,620 ha/53,424 acres of vines lies in Castilla-La Mancha and the rest in the region of Murcia. For this reason, Jumilla is one of the three DOPs in Spain regulated by the Agriculture Ministry and not by regional authorities.

Much of the wine from Jumilla was traditionally produced by the DOBLE PASTA method and used for blending with lighter wines from other parts of Spain. The vast San Isidro CO-OPERATIVE dominates the region's production, although since the mid 1980s a number of smaller, private producers have been striving, with some success, to tame Monastrell. Jumilla's recognition on international markets, notably thanks to the wines of Casa Castillo and El Nido, is not matched in Spain so that most of the best wines are exported. F.C.

Jura, small eastern French wine region between Burgundy and Switzerland that produces an extremely wide range of wines relative to its extent, including such unusual wine types as VIN JAUNE, VIN DE PAILLE, and MACVIN DU JURA, as well as a certain amount of MARC du Jura. Since the late 2000s the region has caught the imagination of sommeliers and wine amateurs worldwide.

Although this was once an important wine region, with nearly 20,000 ha/49,400 acres of vines in the early 19th century, in 2019 there were only about 2,072 ha of vineyards planted out of a possible 11,000 ha for the appellation. The climate here is even more CONTINENTAL than in Burgundy and winters can be very cold. There is significantly higher rainfall too. Most vineyards are on west-facing slopes at ELEVATIONS of 250–450 m/820–1,476 ft on the foothills of the Jura Mountains east of the Bresse plain. The chief town is Lons-le-Saunier, although ARBOIS is deemed to be the wine region's capital. Although it has a certain symmetry with the CÔTE D'OR on the other side of the Saône, the geology is quite different with various colours of CLAY-rich MARL from the Triassic and Early Jurassic geological epochs. To eliminate use of chemical herbicides, today most vineyards are ploughed at least every other row with the other grassed down. Vines were often traditionally trained with bended canes but most today are in double GUYOT, relatively high off the ground. The ORGANIC and the NATURAL WINE movements are important in Jura: in 2020, it counted as the French wine region with the highest proportion of certified BIODYNAMIC area under vine at approximately 8%, while total certified organic vineyards account for close to 20% of the region.

Five grape varieties are of importance in modern Jura (although more than 40 played a role at the end of the 19th century). Chardonnay, which has been grown in the Jura since the Middle Ages, accounted for 43% of total plantings in 2019. Its consistent ripening and YIELD make it popular with growers who use it to make dry white wines of several distinct styles as well as for CRÉMANT du Jura and Macvin. Since better TERROIR selections and different winemaking techniques have been adopted, some Chardonnays now rival those from the Côte d'Or. More unusual are those made in an oxidative style with or without the influence of FLOR-like yeast called the *voile*, or veil. The most extensively planted red grape POULSARD, often called Ploussard, grown particularly in Arbois-Pupillin, makes very pale reds or occasionally deep-coloured rosés, sometimes with an orange tint. A variety prone to REDUCTION, since the 2010s it has been increasingly vinified and bottled with no added SULFUR DIOXIDE, sometimes using CARBONIC MACERATION, making it much sought-after internationally among lovers of natural wine. Poulsard is also used for *vin de paille*. Another local red wine grape variety, TROUSSEAU, needs the additional warmth of gravelly soils to ripen and is grown chiefly near Arbois, where some producers are capable of fashioning it into deep-flavoured, long-lived reds. Pinot Noir may be used as a VARIETAL wine or in a red blend or CRÉMANT, as well as for rosé or red Macvin du Jura.

Jura's most distinctive grape variety, however, is the white SAVAGNIN, also called Naturé, genetically identical to TRAMINER and hence GEWÜRZTRAMINER. In the 21st century the versatile Savagnin has been used for an increasing range of white-wine styles including ORANGE (or macerated whites), although it is especially known as the sole permitted variety for the extraordinary, nutty, long-lived *vin jaune*, sold in the distinctive 62-cl *clavelin* squat bottle. (Other Jura wines may be sold in another specially shaped bottle with the word 'Jura' stamped on the shoulder.) See VIN JAUNE and CHÂTEAU-CHALON, which specializes in this unusual wine.

See also the more varied appellation ARBOIS, which makes red, pink, and white still wine along with *vin jaune* and *vin de paille*.

Côtes du Jura, the region's second most important appellation after Arbois, includes an extended but scattered vineyard area stretching around 80 km/50 miles from north to south. The area includes vineyards north of Arbois, near the historic salt-production and spa town of Salins-les-Bains; the densest plantings are south of Pupillin towards Lons-le-Saunier, especially around the Comté cheese-capital of Poligny, and villages including Passenans, Darbonnay, and Arlay (home to the historic vineyards of Ch d'Arlay that can trace Pinot Noir plantings back to the 13th century but today are best known for long-lived, peaty *vin jaune* and complex *vin de paille*). South of Lons-le-Saunier Chardonnay predominates in the area known as the Sud Revermont, long known for sparkling wines and oxidative styles. The grapes here often ripen a week earlier than further north, and the area is more prone to spring FROST DAMAGE. With land cheaper than around Arbois, several renowned organic producers, led by Domaine Ganevat, have given new life to villages such as Gevingey, Ste-Agnès, and Rotalier. In some areas, alongside marls, there are more limestone outcrops, and wines can be close in style to top barrel-aged Mâconnais. Jura's largest producer and négociant, La Maison du Vigneron, part of Les Grands Chais de France, owns and buys mainly from Côtes du Jura vineyards; its winery is east of Lons-le-Saunier with a large facility for making Crémant du Jura and a vast *vin jaune* barrel cellar. This appellation is also used for wines from vineyards in L'Étoile and Château-Chalon that do not fit those appellations' criteria.

The appellation L'ÉTOILE is reserved for white wines only, including *vin jaune* and *vin de paille*. Crémant du Jura, sparkling wines which are generally white and occasionally rosé, and white, rosé or red Macvin may be produced anywhere in the region.

Winemaking techniques are generally traditional, with almost no use of new oak barrels but much use of older barrels, small and large, although many reds are matured only in tank. Both Chardonnay and Savagnin white wines are increasingly made conventionally, in which case they may be described as OUILLÉ (topped up); however, the tradition also continues of making them OXIDATIVELY, as in the case of *vin jaune*.

The wines are distinctive; whereas they were for many years drunk almost entirely within the greater Franche-Comté region which encompasses Jura, by 2020 exports reached 18% in some years. With marked acidity and mineral characteristics, they make particularly good candidates for FOOD-AND-WINE MATCHING. W.L.

Lorch, W., *Jura Wine* (2014).

Jurançon is the name, closely associated with SOUTH WEST FRANCE, of a distinguished white wine both dry (Jurançon Sec) and sweet (labelled simply Jurançon); of a relatively important, if undistinguished, dark-berried vine variety; and of an entirely unimportant light-berried vine.

The wine

This fashionable, tangy, distinctive white wine has been celebrated and fiercely protected since the Middle Ages, and Jurançon was one of France's earliest AOCS. In the 14th century, the princes of BÉARN and the parliament of NAVARRA introduced the concept of a CRU by identifying and valuing specific favoured vineyard sites. Locals claim this as France's first attempt at vineyard CLASSIFICATION, just as they claim the drop of Jurançon with which the infant Henri IV's lips were rubbed at his baptism in 1553 was responsible for most of his subsequent achievements. The Dutch were great enthusiasts for this wine, and there was also a flourishing export trade across the Atlantic until PHYLLOXERA almost destroyed the wine. Jurançon's reputation was further advanced in the early 20th century by the enthusiasm of the French writer Colette.

Historically Jurançon wines were exclusively sweet, but a dry style was introduced in the 1970s so that today there are two distinct AOCs: Jurançon Sec and Jurançon. Any wine bearing the name of Jurançon *tout court* is and has to be sweet.

In 2023 vines were grown on about 1,400 ha/3,460 acres of vineyards in this hilly, relatively cool corner of southern France near Pau at the relatively high average ELEVATION of 300 m/984 ft. Spring FROSTS are such a threat that many vines are ESPALIER-trained, but the Atlantic influence ensures sufficient RAINFALL. Although there are four distinct areas of production with widely different TERROIRS, a hint of honey is never far away in Jurançons of every style. The wines from the lower-lying Monein district are typically fuller in body than those from the higher-lying Chapelle de Rousse. The former is partly on CLAY, with pebbles (*galets*) on the higher ground. The latter is characterized by a mixture called 'poudingue', a cement-like crushed CHALK mixed with *galets*.

The principal grape varieties are PETIT MANSENG and GROS MANSENG, but the dry version may include up to 50% of local varieties PETIT COURBU, COURBU, Camaralet de Lasseube, and Lauzet.

Gros Manseng is chiefly responsible for Jurançon Sec, for which yields of 60 hl/ha (3.4 tons/acre) are allowed. Petit Manseng, with its small, thick-skinned berries, is ideal for the production of Jurançon's real speciality, long-living, sweet Jurançon made from grapes partially dried on the vine (see PASSERILLÉ) at a maximum yield of 40 hl/ha but often much less. If several TRIES are made through the vineyard (two are mandatory), the results may be bottled separately. These MOELLEUX wines, whose green tinge seems to deepen with age, serve well as APERITIFS and with a wide range of foods. There are also sweeter wines labelled VENDANGES TARDIVES, made only from Petit and Gros Manseng and harvested as late as December. OAK is used to increasing effect, particularly in the LATE HARVEST style.

There is a high-quality CO-OPERATIVE at Gan, where two-thirds of all Jurançon Sec is made, largely from members in the Monein region. There is also an increasing number (65 in 2023) of independent producers.

Red and rosé wines made in Jurançon must be sold as BÉARN.

The vine varieties

A red wine grape called Jurançon was once commonly grown all over south-west France, but today it is rather despised and rare. A white version is even rarer, confined to the making of armagnac. Neither has today anything to do with the wines of Jurançon. P.S.

Justino's, the largest single shipper of MADEIRA, bottling under a variety of names including Cruz, the largest single BRAND of Madeira (and PORT) in France. Established in Funchal in 1870 and taken in hand by a new owner in 1981, Justino's operates from modern industrial premises outside the city. The company was formerly known as Justino Henriques but was renamed to avoid confusion with Henriques & Henriques, which is also now controlled by the French import and distribution group La Martiniquaise. Quality has improved considerably, TINTA NEGRA is taken seriously, and a range of TABLE WINES is also made for the local market.

K

Kabinett, one of six so-called PRÄDIKATS applying to German wine that has not been CHAPTALIZED and reaches—depending on growing region and grape variety—MUST WEIGHTS of 70–82 °OECHSLE. As such, Kabinett designates the lightest end of the Prädikat spectrum, and Mosel Kabinetts that have RESIDUAL SUGAR are often as low as 7 or 8% alcohol. Widespread use of the term 'Kabinett', like the pegging of quality designations to minimum must weights itself, is a product of the 1971 German wine law. The name was chosen for its association with the English word CABINET, widely used in Germany prior to 1971 as a general term of approbation for wines in all styles. Kabinett still has resonance in the German marketplace even for wines from regions such as BADEN and the PFALZ, where dry Kabinetts may significantly exceed 13% alcohol and where among reputed producers most vintages since 1987 have involved no chaptalization. The VDP prohibits utilization of this and other Prädikat designations for legally dry (TROCKEN) wines.

Austrian wine law enshrines the term 'Kabinett' for unchaptalized, dry Qualitätswein of up to 13% alcohol and from grapes of at least 17 °KMW (84 °Oechsle), but the term is little used, particularly since the advent of DAC status for much of NIEDERÖSTERREICH, whereby 'Reserve' on labels of Riesling or Grüner Veltliner effectively replaces 'Spätlese trocken' and non-Reserve DAC bottlings are those that would formerly have been labelled 'Kabinett'. D.S.

Kadarka, Eastern European late-ripening red wine grape of uncertain origin but considered indigenous in Bulgaria (under the name Gamza), Romania (as Cadarča), and Albania (as Kallmet), widely planted across the Carpathian Basin before the arrival of PHYLLOXERA. In Hungary, the variety grew on a total of just 274 ha/677 acres in 2021 and has been substantially replaced by the viticulturally sturdier KÉKFRANKOS, and by PORTUGIESER in Villány. Kadarka, ideally trained as BUSH VINES, can produce wines that are light ruby in colour, finely structured, and with a delicate aroma only if yields are curbed. The best examples are found mainly around Szekszárd, Eger, and Hajós and in southern Slovakia and Serbia. Bulgaria's 218 ha/539 acres of Gamza are planted mainly in the north, where it can produce wines of interest from long growing seasons if yields are restricted.

Kalecik Karası, vine variety that makes particularly fruity reds north-east of Ankara in TÜRKIYE where there are 7,044 ha/17,406 acres.

Kalterer or **Kalterersee**, German for the DOC in TRENTINO and ALTO ADIGE known in Italian as Caldaro or Lago di Caldaro, based on SCHIAVA grapes.

Kamptal, named for the river Kamp that traverses it, is an AUSTRIAN winegrowing region immediately north-east of the KREMSTAL. Centred on the town of Langenlois and incorporating the nearby villages of Gobelsburg, Kammern, Legenfeld, and Zöbing, its diminutive perimeter is deceptive since an extremely high density of vineyards comprising 3,582 ha/8,851 acres (in 2021) represent 8% of Austrian vine acreage, third in regional size after the WEINVIERTEL and NEUSIEDLERSEE. Like the nearby WACHAU (of which it was once loosely considered part), the Kamptal features a wide DIURNAL TEMPERATURE RANGE but slightly less rain and greater vulnerability to FROST. It shares the Wachau's prominence of soils derived from LOESS and GNEISS but boasts even greater geological diversity, as witness the Permian SANDSTONE that defines its best-known vineyard landmark, the massive, terraced Heiligenstein, arguably among the top 20 sites for RIESLING worldwide. The nearby Gaisberg is this region's other renowned vineyard for Riesling, which by 2021 had grown to 10% of Kamptal acreage, while in between those two the gently sloping, loess-dominated Lamm is the region's most famous site for GRÜNER VELTLINER, which is planted on 55% of all Kamptal vineyard. Successful flirtations with other varieties are numerous, especially Chardonnay, Pinot Blanc (WEISSBURGUNDER), Sauvignon Blanc, Pinot Noir, ST-LAURENT, and ZWEIGELT. Known also for its density of ambitious, environmentally conscious growers, the Kamptal has benefited from winegrower Willi Bründlmayer's status as a long-standing unofficial ambassador for Austrian wine as well as from the chairmanship of Austria's TRADITIONSWEINGÜTER by Michael Moosbrugger, a Bründlmayer protegé who has had responsibility for the 850-year-old monastic estate of Schloss Gobelsburg since 1996.

Kamptal DAC is the official Austrian DAC appellation for Kamptal Grüner Veltliner and Riesling wines. A DAC Reserve category specifies higher minimum potential alcohol and later release. QUALITÄTSWEIN that does not qualify as Kamptal DAC must be labelled with its state of origin, NIEDERÖSTERREICH. This applies in particular to the 35% of Kamptal wines made from grapes other than Grüner Veltliner or Riesling. D.S.

Kangaroo Island, cool, maritime region 13 km/8 miles off the coast of SOUTH AUSTRALIA with just 144 ha/356 acres of vines in 2022. With 40% of the island subject to environmental conservation, the island is especially known for its concentration of endemic flora and fauna. R.J.T.

Kanzler, MÜLLER-THURGAU × SILVANER cross bred at Alzey in 1927 of which only 25 ha/62 acres remained in 2020 because it does not yield well.

Kazakhstan, independent central Asian, former Soviet republic. The largest land-locked country in the world, south of Russia and bordering China, it has an extreme CONTINENTAL climate, with summer temperatures exceeding 30 °C/86 °F and winter temperatures averaging −20 °C/−4 °F.

Evidence of grape culture in Kazakhstan dates back to the 7th century CE. The country's most ancient viticultural areas are around Turkestan in South Kazakhstan (where the grapevine was imported from the Samarkand and the Fergana regions of UZBEKISTAN) and the Panfilov area of the Almaty region (where grapevines are popularly believed to have come from CHINA's western Xinjiang province).

At the end of the 19th century, grapes were grown on a small scale by private farms. The development of commercial grape culture began in the 1930s, when the first fruit- and winegrowing state farms such as Issyk in the Almaty region, Uch-Bulak in the Zhambyl region, and Juvaly and Kaplanbek in South Kazakhstan were established. Viticulture developed rapidly after 1957, the land under vine expanding from 4,997 ha in 1958 to about 28,000 ha/69,190 acres prior to Mikhail GORBACHEV's anti-alcohol campaign in 1985. Most vineyards dedicated to wine production were subsequently pulled out and replaced with other crops or abandoned. More vineyards were lost after Kazakhstan declared independence from the Soviet Union in 1991 and vineyards belonging to the state farms were allocated among locals who often lacked the resources to care for the vines.

The 21st century has seen an increased investment from foreign and domestic sources in both vineyards and wineries. There has been a small but steady influx of viticultural and winemaking consultants from the UK, Australia, France, and Italy who have worked with local producers to improve quality. As with other parts of the former Soviet Union, there has been a move to produce fresher, more international styles and a move away from the sweet, heavy wines of the past. By 2021, the Kazakhstan's Bureau of National Statistics reported a total vineyard area of 13,240 ha/32,716 acres producing over 195,000 hl/5.5 million gals of wine.

As less than 4% of Kazakhstan offers favourable soil and climatic conditions for commercial grape culture, most vineyards are located in the warmer south and south-east of the country, principally in the Almaty, Zhambyl, South Kazakhstan, and Kyzylorda regions. Even here winters can be very cold, and most vineyards need WINTER PROTECTION. The exception is the Turkestan area, where mild winters allow vines to be GUYOT-trained with no winter protection.

The annual rainfall is 700–1,000 mm/27–39 in in the Trans-Ili and Talas Alatau but is as little as 100–150 mm/4–6 in in some areas of the Aktobe region in the west. IRRIGATION is the norm. PHYLLOXERA has never been detected, but most vines are GRAFTED for predictability in results and security of harvest volumes. Most vineyards are planted on flat areas, but some climb to 600–800 m/1,969–2,625 ft in ELEVATION in the foothills of Tian Shan mountain range.

There is currently no GEOGRAPHICAL INDICATION system in Kazakhstan and no official list of grape varieties permitted/recommended for winemaking. Popular wine varieties include Georgian ones such as RKATSITELI and SAPERAVI as well as local varieties Bayanshira, Kuljinski, and Maiski Cherny and CROSSES such as Rubinovy Magaracha. There is increasing interest in INTERNATIONAL VARIETIES, especially Cabernet Sauvignon, Merlot, Sauvignon Blanc, and Chardonnay but also Riesling, Pinot Noir, Aligoté, Aleatico, Cabernet Franc, and Gewürztraminer.

X.V.

kegs, increasingly popular form of wine PACKAGING that keeps large volumes of wine fresh for six weeks or more after they have been broached and is therefore particularly well suited to wine-by-the-glass offerings. The reusable stainless-steel kegs similar to those used for beer are filled directly with wine. INERT GAS propels the wine out of a tap and fills the keg to prevent OXIDATION. The alternative is the single-use PET kegs with an alufoil bag inside, not unlike those used in wine BOXES. The wine is propelled by compressed air pumped into the keg around the bag, thus preventing oxygen ingress. The former are much heavier to transport but can be reused or recycled. The latter are much lighter but not as straightforward to recycle. Both have a lower CARBON FOOTPRINT than glass bottles and take up less storage space. Kegs have been adopted with enthusiasm in America, initially in California and New York as part of a direct relationship between wineries and local bars and restaurants, and are increasingly popular in the UK, Ireland, Sweden, Denmark, Norway, and Australia. Some retailers particularly concerned with SUSTAINABILITY encourage their customers to fill their own containers from kegs.

Alko, 'Update of wine packaging LCA: final report Alko Oy' (2021). www.alko.fi/INTERSHOP/static/WFS/Alko-OnlineShop-Site/-/Alko-OnlineShop/fi_FI/Tavarantoimittajille/Muut/EN/Alko%20wine%20packaging%20LCA%20update_final%20report.pdf.

kék means 'blue' in Hungarian and, as such, can be a direct equivalent of BLAU in German or even NOIR in French.

Kékfrankos, Hungarian name for the increasingly fashionable red grape variety known in Austria as BLAUFRÄNKISCH (of which it is a direct translation) and grown on 7,542 ha/18,637 acres of Hungary in 2021, mainly around Szekszárd, Mátra, Eger, Villány, and, most successfully, in Sopron near the Austrian border, where it is responsible for some of Hungary's finest reds. It makes more straightforward wines and rosé in the Danube region. Many young producers have started to make concentrated, fruity bottlings, as well as NATURAL WINES.

Kéknyelű, revered but very rare white grape variety grown in Hungary, notably in Badacsony on the north shore of Lake Balaton, and named after its 'blue' stalk. Yields are very low; wines are crisp and perfumed. There were just 48 ha/119 acres planted in 2021.

Kékoportó, unofficial name for the PORTUGIESER grape in Hungary. Most of the 779 ha/1,925 acres planted in 2021 were in Villány, where it can occasionally produce concentrated wines, but it is also found in Eger, Kunság, and Szekszárd.

Keller is the German word for a cellar, even a small domestic cellar, while **Kellerei** refers to NÉGOCIANT facilities with a significant above-ground presence. A German wine specifying a Keller rather than a WEINGUT on the label is usually the produce of a merchant rather than an estate. In ALTO ADIGE, the Italian Tyrol, **Kellereigenossenschaft** is a common name for one of the many wine CO-OPERATIVES. **Kellermeister** is German for 'cellarmaster', similar to MAÎTRE DE CHAI in France.

Kendall-Jackson, original brand name of the winery and vineyard empire begun by attorney Jess Jackson in Lake County, California, in 1974. In many ways, Jess Jackson exemplifies the entrepreneurial nature of the CALIFORNIA wine industry as well as the go-go climate of the 1980s. He entered the wine industry almost accidentally when he purchased a small pear and walnut ranch as a weekend retreat. He planted grapes but had trouble selling them for a decent return, so he began to investigate converting them to wine.

Happily disregarding the California industry's movement towards vineyard designations, he concentrated instead on blending from various regions to achieve certain taste characteristics. To say this strategy worked would be a grave understatement, and K-J Vintner's Reserve Chardonnay is still America's most popular Chardonnay. Its hallmarks initially were refreshingly strong ACIDITY, creamy oak vanillins (see OAK FLAVOUR), exotic pineapple fruit flavour, and softness and immediate drinkability from just-perceptible RESIDUAL SUGAR. Classically inclined SHOW judges put up token resistance to the residual sugar, but consumers had no such reservations.

Speculation is that a dollop of Muscat-based SWEET RESERVE is the mystery ingredient driving this successful recipe. Verification is not available because Jackson went to court in

K

1992 to prevent his winemaker Jed Steele from revealing what he claimed were 'trade secrets', on his departure from K-J. Despite a noteworthy historical precedent in the California wine industry of shared information, Jackson prevailed.

Today the famous mass-market Chardonnay undergoes BARREL FERMENTATION with LEES stirred monthly. Kendall-Jackson sells a wide range of other California VARIETALS from a base in Sonoma that doubles as a tourist destination. See also JACKSON FAMILY WINES.

Kenya, African country virtually on the equator, with a very limited production of wines. VITIS VINIFERA came to the highlands of Maua with Italian missionaries in the early 1900s; BARBERA is still grown in home gardens around the area. Kenya's largest commercial wine producer, however, is in the Rift Valley north-west of Nairobi, where Rift Valley Winery began planting vines in 1992. Its Shiraz, Merlot, and Sauvignon Blanc, bottled under the Leleshwa brand, benefit from quick-draining VOLCANIC soils and ELEVATIONS over 1,900 m/6,235 ft, where the DIURNAL TEMPERATURE RANGE can be 6–32 °C/11–58 °F. Another vine-grower, Mukami Mwarania, has started a vineyard nearby with Barbera cuttings from Maua. The equatorial warmth allows for multiple harvests, though some producers revert to one growing season June–September (see TROPICAL VITICULTURE). In addition to climatic challenges, animals including giraffes and antelopes can wreak havoc in a vineyard.

Kerner, the most successful GERMAN CROSS, which, because of its Riesling-like wines, is still planted on 2,257 ha/5,577 acres of Germany, mainly in the Pfalz and Rheinhessen. It is also relatively popular in Württemberg, where it was bred from a red parent TROLLINGER (Schiava Grossa) × RIESLING. The large white berries produce wines commendably close to Riesling in flavour except for their own leafy, sometimes candied and mawkish, aroma and slightly coarser texture. It is a cross which does not need to be subsumed in the blending vat but can produce respectable VARIETAL wines, up to quite high PRÄDIKAT levels, on its own account. Kerner is popular with growers as well as wine drinkers because of its late budding and therefore good FROST resistance. The 112 ha/277 acres of Kerner planted in Italy's Alto Adige in 2020 produce some of the region's most widely admired wines. It is also planted in Switzerland, England, Canada, and quite successfully in JAPAN.

Kevedinka. See KÖVIDINKA.

King Valley, Australian wine region in North East VICTORIA. ELEVATION of up to 800 m/2,625 ft is key to its versatility and COOL-CLIMATE credentials. Brown Brothers traces its roots back to the 1880s, but this former tobacco-farming area's big swing to wine came in the latter stages of the 20th century. Descendants of Italian migrants have championed SANGIOVESE, PINOT GRIGIO, GLERA (known in Australia as Prosecco and now by far King Valley's most prevalent variety), and others, while Chardonnay and Pinot Noir remain important.

kir, alternative name for a *vin blanc-cassis*, dry white wine and blackcurrant liqueur, named after a hero of the Burgundian resistance movement during the Second World War, Canon Kir, who was also mayor of Dijon. The typical base wine is the relatively acid BOURGOGNE ALIGOTÉ and to most palates a dash of crème de cassis is all that is needed. A **kir royal** is made with sparkling rather than still white wine.

Királyleányka, meaning 'princess', is identical to FETEASCĂ Regală in Romania, making lightly perfumed, crisp whites. Much of Hungary's 2021 total plantings of 949 ha/2,345 acres is in the north of the country, particularly in Balatonboglár. It may be an offspring of FETEASCĂ Albă, known as LEÁNYKA in Hungary.

Kisi, GEORGIAN vine variety making headily perfumed, well-structured whites planted on 317 ha/783 acres of vineyard in its Kakheti homeland in 2019.

Kişmiş, **Kišmiš**, **Kismis**, **Kishmish**, Middle Eastern synonyms for the common SULTANA.

Klassik, when noted with an uppercase 'K' on an AUSTRIAN label (or price list), generally refers to unoaked, fruit-forward wines. The most established such category is Steierische Klassik, used for wines grown in the state of STEIERMARK and associated especially with the crisp, dry wines of SÜDSTEIERMARK that are intended for early drinking. The term 'Klassik' is also used—though generally without appearing on the relevant labels—for the lighter, non-Reserve of two categories of wine within many of Austria's DACS, and as of 2015 it designates a specific category of Austrian SEKT with a PDO. The name is also sometimes colloquially employed in Germany for the least expensive or simplest bottlings, as some French growers use the term *Tradition* to denote their basic bottling even though the word rarely appears on labels. Klassik is not to be confused with the specific category of German wine known as CLASSIC. D.S.

Klein Karoo, inland semi-desert ostrich- and sheep-farming region that is also an official wine region in SOUTH AFRICA also known as Little Karoo. The town of Calitzdorp is widely regarded as the PORT-style wine capital of South Africa.

Klevener de Heiligenstein is an ALSACE oddity, a vine speciality of the village of Heiligenstein in the Bas-Rhin planted in 1740 by its mayor Erhard Wantz. It is a locally adapted SAVAGNIN ROSE, occasionally known as **Clevner de Heiligenstein**, grown within five neighbouring communes of Heiligenstein to produce a dry wine, less scented than Gewurztraminer, with less alcohol and a little more acidity. In good vintages it can age well. In 2011 it was recognized as one of 14 DÉNOMINATIONS GÉOGRAPHIQUES COMPLÉMENTAIRES that may be specified within the Alsace appellation. See also GERMAN HISTORY.

Klevner, like CLEVNER, is, and more particularly was, used fairly indiscriminately in Alsace and other German-speaking wine regions for various vine varieties, notably but not exclusively for various forms of PINOT. References to Klevner in Alsace in the mid 16th century are common.

Kloster Eberbach, monastery in the RHEINGAU region of Germany with a tradition of viticulture; now seen as the cultural wine centre of the Rheingau. Kloster Eberbach was founded in 1135 by Bernard of Clairvaux. Throughout the Middle Ages, Cistercian monks produced wine at the monastery and made its name as one of the most important wine estates of its time. Through viticultural enterprise, the monastery became extremely powerful, owning a fleet of ships which sailed the Rhine. Kloster Eberbach nowadays lends its name to the vast Hessian State Domaine or Hessische Staatsweingüter, whose incomparable Cabinetkeller boasts abundant stocks of wines from the 19th century. Close to the adjacent MONOPOLE Steinberg vineyard is a lavishly appointed 21st-century production facility where SCREWCAPS were pioneered in Germany.

See also MONKS AND MONASTERIES.

S.E.A. & D.S.

Klosterneuburg, small city on the right bank of the Danube just west of Vienna in AUSTRIA whose Augustinian monastery (*Stift*) has been a major vineyard owner since the Middle Ages. Since 1860 it has housed Austria's centre for viticultural and oenological research (see ACADEME), also giving its name to Austria's standard measurement of MUST WEIGHT, commonly referred to by its abbreviation KMW. While the vineyard holdings of Stift Klosterneuburg include substantial tracts in the nearby growing regions of WIEN, THERMENREGION, and CARNUNTUM, its home vineyards long held the official status of a GROSSLAGE within the otherwise left bank region of WAGRAM. This status left neither party satisfied, but the Wagram DAC created in 2002 retains Klosterneuburg, while treating it as just one among 27 recognized communes. D.S.

KMW, or **Klosterneuburger Mostwage**, named for its origins at KLOSTERNEUBURG, is AUSTRIA's traditional unit of measurement for MUST WEIGHT, equivalent to approximately 5 °OECHSLE.

Knights Valley, inland California wine region and AVA between the northern end of Napa Valley and the southern end of Alexander Valley. See SONOMA.

Korea, rugged, mountainous peninsula on the Asian mainland, between China and Japan, encompassing the Korean Peninsula and more than 3,300 islands. Since 1945, the country has been split in two parts, North (the Democratic People's Republic of Korea) and South (the Republic of Korea).

While the country claims 13,294 ha/32,850 acres of vines in 2021, the vast majority are TABLE GRAPES. Grape wine gained a foothold only after Christian missionaries arriving in the late 1880s began to grow vines and make wine. The first commercial wine made from grapes grown in Korea was Sunry Port Wine, released in 1969. Produced by the Hankuk Suntory Co. in co-operation with Suntory Japan, it was made from mountain grapes grown in Daejeon, in central South Korea. Wine did not take off, though, until Doosan Majuang, first released in 1977, gained the Vatican's approval as a SACRAMENTAL WINE. Wine consumption in Korea has since soared, but the market is still almost entirely reliant on imports as the climate makes grape-growing challenging, especially for VITIS VINIFERA. Summers are hot and humid, with temperatures often reaching 30 °C/86 °F in August, and average annual rainfall is 600–1,500 mm/24–59 in, with 40% of it falling in June–September. Winters are dry and windy, with temperatures below freezing. In addition, wine producers that plant *vinifera* do not benefit from the government support that is given when local grape varieties are used. Consequently, only small amounts of *vinifera* are cultivated, mostly Chardonnay, Muscat of Alexandria, and Riesling. More popular are VITIS LABRUSCA varieties such as Campbell Early, the most commonly cultivated variety, and VITIS AMURENSIS such as Sanmeoru. Many HYBRIDS are also grown, especially MUSCAT BAILEY A. Korean hybrids such Cheongsoo, Cheonghyang, and Cheongporang are gaining popularity, producing white wines with a refreshing character. Most wine grapes in South Korea are grown in Yeongcheon in the south-east, where the ALLUVIAL sandy soils, TEMPERATE climate, marked DIURNAL TEMPERATURE RANGE, and lower-than-average rainfall allows grapes to reach PHYSIOLOGICAL RIPENESS, attaining 24 °BRIX in some years. Yeongdong in west-central South Korea has also developed a small wine industry, its one corporate winery and 42 farm wineries attracted by the region's relatively low rainfall, abundant sunshine, and well-draining GRAVEL, SAND, and LIMESTONE soils. S.C.

Korinthiaki, dark-skinned variety from Greece mainly used for CURRANTS but also an important constituent (up to 49%) in MAVRODAPHNE of Patras. It takes its name from a corruption of the word 'Corinth'. Very occasionally used for winemaking in California and Australia.

kosher (meaning 'pure'). To the Jewish people, there is no communal, religious, or family event without wine. The vine was one of the seven fruits blessed in the Bible, and there is even a special blessing devoted to wine: 'Blessed are You, Lord our God . . . who creates the fruit of the vine.'

Adhering to the Jewish dietary laws (kashrut) is essential for all Orthodox Jews. Kosher wine laws were established in ancient times, so an observant Jew could avoid drinking *Yayin Nesech*, a wine used for idol worship, and *Stam Yeinam*, wine made by non-Jews.

For a wine to be considered kosher, only religious Jews may handle the product and touch the winemaking equipment from the time the grapes arrive at the winery. Only kosher substances may be used in the process. Examples of FINING agents not permitted include (animal-derived) gelatin, (dairy-derived) casein, and isinglass (because it comes from a non-kosher fish). Kosher wine is suitable for VEGETARIANS and, if egg whites are not used for fining, also for vegans.

There are also additional agricultural laws, which are observed only in Israel.

1. *Orlah*. For the first three years, fruit from the vine may not be used for winemaking.
2. *Kilai Ha'Kerem* (cross-breeding). Growing other fruits between the vines is prohibited.
3. *Shmittah*. Every seventh year, the fields should be left fallow. However, because of economic realities, often the land is symbolically sold to a non-Jew for the duration of this sabbatical year.
4. *Trumot and Ma'asarot*. Just over 1% of the production is poured away in remembrance of a tithe once paid in the time of the Holy Temple in Jerusalem.

Today, *Shmittah* and *Trumot and Ma'asarot* remain mainly symbolic.

'Kosher for Passover' means the wine and barrels have not come into contact with bread, grain, or products made with leavened dough. Most kosher wines are also 'Kosher for Passover'. The agricultural laws date back to the Bible and the laws of kashrut to Talmudic times.

Kosher regulations have no bearing on wine quality; standard winemaking procedures are followed in the HARVESTING, FERMENTATION, MATURATION, BLENDING, and BOTTLING. The kosher certification is irrelevant to quality.

Kosher wines were mainly sweet until Carmel in Israel began producing dry kosher wines, but the 1980s saw a major improvement in kosher wine quality led by the Golan Heights Winery in Israel, Hagafen and Herzog in California, and Royal Wine worldwide. In Israel especially, the change was pronounced as wineries began focusing on INTERNATIONAL VARIETIES in the vineyard, implementing cutting-edge technology in the winery, and employing internationally trained winemakers. (See ISRAEL for more detail.) The kosher winemaking industry was changed forever, being geared to quality.

There are, however, two categories of wine that damage the image of kosher wines. *Kiddush* wines are sacramental wines, usually red and sweet, made for use in religious rituals by traditionalists. Manischewitz and Palwin are two well-known examples.

Mevushal wines are kosher wines that have been PASTEURIZED to 80 °C/175 °F, using flash pasteurization or FLASH DÉTENTE. This is an extra requirement by some kosher caterers and kosher restaurants, particularly in the US. It is of interest mainly to the strictly religious as it permits the wine to remain kosher even if served by a non-observant waiter. Most kosher wines, and those of the finest quality, are not *mevushal*.

The largest market for kosher wine is Israel (though there are many non-kosher Israeli wineries), followed by the US and France. In Israel and California there are wineries devoted to making kosher wines, and many well-known wineries make kosher cuvées, such as Ch Léoville-Poyferré and Ch Pontet-Canet in BORDEAUX and Mayacamas Vineyards in NAPA. Today, kosher wines are made in almost all wine-producing countries. A.S.M.

Rogov, D., *Rogov's Guide to Kosher Wines* (2011).

Koshu, best-known INDIGENOUS VARIETY in JAPAN. The pink-skinned grape is grown both for the table and for wine, and more wine is produced from this variety than from any other in Japan. Its thick skins withstand Japan's humid summers relatively well. Most Koshu is PERGOLA-trained with SPUR PRUNING, while ambitious producers such as Grace have started to train it low on double GUYOT, reducing yields and producing some of the most concentrated examples of Koshu. Koshu wine can rarely be accused of an excess of flavour, but it can be a fine accompaniment to sashimi. Still, sparkling, sweet, and oaked versions are made. DNA PROFILING by Goto-Yamamoto in 2015 suggested that Koshu is a natural HYBRID between an as-yet-unidentified variety of VITIS VINIFERA and an unknown variety, which is itself a hybrid between an individual of *Vitis davidii* and another unidentified variety of *vinifera*.

Goto-Yamamoto, N., et al., 'Genetic analysis of East Asian grape cultivars suggests hybridization with wild Vitis', *PLOS ONE*, 10/10 (2015).
www.koshuofjapan.com

Kosovo, or Kosova (spelling preferred by the majority ethnic ALBANIAN population), is a territory south of SERBIA. It declared its independence in 2008 and is recognized as a state by around 100 countries, crucially not including Serbia. This leaves its wine industry covered by two sets of legislation—its own and Serbia's. The climate is mild CONTINENTAL, with Mediterranean influences, enjoying 276 sunny days per year on average and sufficient rainfall throughout the year to avoid IRRIGATION (Dukagjini averages 770 mm/30 in). Vineyards are typically at ELEVATIONS of 300–600 m/985–1,969 ft, surrounded by spectacular mountains.

As with the rest of the Balkans, wine history goes back at least 2,000 years. In the 1950s, the YUGOSLAV regime imposed high-volume wine production in the region via four large-scale state wineries. Most of the wine was blended with the exception of the light, medium-sweet red Amselfelder sold to Germany in volumes of 32 million litres/8.5 million gal in the 1980s. Kosovan vineyards then totalled about 9,000 ha/22,200 acres. Vineyard area fell to under 4,000 ha after the collapse of Yugoslavia and war in the late 1990s.

Today's industry is completely private and being modernized to align with EU standards, with new legislation on wine quality and zoning, as well as work going on to define PGIs and PDOs and to conserve local varieties. In 2021 there were 3,483 ha/8,607 acres on the vineyard register, while wine production was 92,979 hl/2,456,245 gal in 2020. Kosovo has designated two wine regions, Dukagjini and Kosovo Region. Dukagjini is further divided into north and south subregions. (Note that Serbian law recognizes two regions of North and South Metohija.) The south has five vineyard zones: Rahovec, Suhareka, Prizren, and the smaller Gjakova and Malisheva. The north has three small zones: Peja, Istog, and Klina. Kosovo grows more red wine grapes (1,653 ha) than white (872 ha) with the remainder as TABLE GRAPES. Local grapes are most important, led by Vranç/VRANAC (500 ha) and Prokupë/PROKUPAC (345 ha); Pinot Noir, Zhameta/ŽAMETOVKA, and Gamé/GAMAY are also grown. SMEDEREVKA (373 ha) dominates white plantings, followed by WELSCHRIESLING, Chardonnay, Riesling, and Prokup e Bardhë. The domestic market remains small, with annual consumption of just 2.5 litres per capita, so exports account for over 70% of production, largely to Croatia, Serbia, and Albania. C.G.

skkv.rks-gov.net

Kotsifali. Generous, spicy, if soft wines are produced from this red-grape speciality of the Greek island of CRETE, where it is the most common dark-skinned variety. It is best blended with something more tannic such as MANDILARIA. Total plantings in Greece were 1,246 ha/3,079 in 2021.

Kövérszőlő, one of the oldest and rarest grape varieties in TOKAJ and possibly the same as GRASĂ in Cotnari, Romania. There were 43 ha/106 acres in north-west Hungary in 2021.

Kövidinka, common pink-skinned Hungarian variety known as Ružica in Croatia and North Macedonia and as Kevedinka in Serbia.

krater. See CRATER.

Kratošija, relatively important grape in MONTENEGRO that is the same as ZINFANDEL.

Kreaca, white grape variety grown in SERBIA and, under the name Creață, in neighbouring parts of Romania. Its produce tends to be somewhat heavy. Also known as Banat Riesling or Banat Rizling.

Kremstal, wine region whose 2,256 ha/5,575 acres of vines in 2021 represent 5% of AUSTRIA's vineyards and characterized by considerable geological and mesoclimatic diversity. Long considered part of the WACHAU, the towering rocky terraced vineyards on the region's western edge—in particular those of the Krems-Stein suburb—segue seamlessly into those of today's official Wachau. These include two of Austria's greatest RIESLING vineyards, the (Steiner) Hund and Pfaffenberg, as well as the estimable Kögl and Wachtberg that are closer to the city of Krems proper. The valley of the diminutive river Krems incorporates only 7 km/4.3 miles of vineyards that are dominated by LOESS close to Krems city limits, rising to magnificent rocky steepness upstream around Senftenberg, whose Ehrenfels, Hochäcker, and Pellingen vineyards are home to Riesling (10.8% of total Kremstal vineyard) and GRÜNER VELTLINER. The eastern and north-eastern fringes of Krems are dominated by mounds of loess, anticipating the soil and exposure of the neighbouring WAGRAM. Grüner Veltliner (59% of total Kremstal vineyard) overwhelmingly dominates in this sector, which includes wine villages Gedersdorf, Gneixendorf, Rohrendorf, and Stratzing. The Kremstal also incorporates extensive vineyards on the Danube's right bank, where SAND and GRAVEL from the Danube, which meandered around numerous islands until late 20th century dredging, vie with loess for vine roots' attention, and the varietal mix extends even to Cabernet Sauvignon and Merlot. Heading east from Mautern (in the Wachau), the villages of Furth, Palt, Oberfucha, and Tiefenfucha are dominated by the massive mountaintop Göttweig monastery—itself an important vineyard owner—while further downstream Hollenburg hugs the Danube's shoreline and shares its 'Hollenberg' conglomerate with the neighbouring TRAISENTAL.

Kremstal DAC is the appellation applying to this region's Grüner Veltliner and Riesling. Non-DAC QUALITÄTSWEIN grown here is labelled NIEDERÖSTERREICH. A February 2022 revision officially organizes Kremstal DAC wines into the categories of regional (Gebietswein), communal (Ortswein), and vineyard-designated (Riedenwein) while condensing potential communes of origin approved for labelling to just nine. D.S.

Krug, small but important Champagne house founded in Reims in 1843 by Johann-Joseph Krug, who was born in Mainz, Germany, in 1800 and had come to work in Champagne. From 1824 he was known as Joseph. By 1866 the firm occupied its current modest cellars, around whose courtyard the Krug family lived until 2014. Joseph Krug's vision was to craft the very best champagne he could every year, regardless of variations in climate, and so he created his Champagne n°1. Krug does not make an ordinary NON-VINTAGE champagne but specializes exclusively in PRESTIGE CUVÉES, of which the multi-vintage Grande Cuvée, modelled on Champagne n°1, is the flagship, having replaced the rather fuller-bodied Private Cuvée in 1979. Krug Grande Cuvée, sold at a similar price to Krug vintage-dated bottlings, was first made with a blend of 60–70 wines from five to six different years, but today the blend includes even more wines from even more years.

Krug is known for its plot-by-plot approach to champagne creation whereby each plot of vines is vinified and kept separately until the final blending decisions are made. Every year, the *chef de cave* tastes 400 wines—250 wines of the year and 150 reserve wines—each made from a single plot. In 1971 Krug acquired and replanted the CLOS du Mesnil, a walled vineyard of 1.84 ha/4.5 acres. Its Chardonnay grapes provide one of Champagne's few SINGLE-VINEYARD WINES, of which the 1979 vintage was the first. The 0.68 ha/1.7 acres of Clos d'Ambonnay planted exclusively with Pinot Noir is responsible for an even more expensive wine launched with the 1995 vintage. Small quantities of Krug vintage champagnes are aged on the LEES in the cellars for around 20 years and are then DISGORGED and presented as Krug Collection. In 2011, acknowledging the considerable variation between the Krug Grande Cuvées produced each year, Krug introduced the Krug iD, back-label codes identifying when each cuvée was disgorged and giving full details and composition of each bottle of Krug. Krug has been owned by LVMH since 1999, although sixth-generation Olivier Krug is director of the house, part of the tasting committee, and represents the house in Champagne and abroad.

Arlott, J., *Krug: House of Champagne* (1976).
Fountain, N., *Krug: A Journey Through History* (2011).

Krug, Charles (1825–92), German-born American wine producer, came to San Francisco in 1852 as a newspaper editor. After vineyard ventures in San Mateo and SONOMA, Krug settled in the NAPA Valley in 1860, founding a winery near St Helena in 1861. Krug was not the first Napa Valley winemaker, but he soon became the most eminent of his day and inevitably came to be called the 'father of Napa wine'. His success came in part because he understood public relations and because he developed his own sales organization. The winery he founded was acquired by the MONDAVI family in 1943 and is still notable among Napa Valley establishments, although Robert Mondavi left to set up on his own in 1965 after an acrimonious dispute with his brother Peter, whose family still run the enterprise. T.P.

Kuč. See TRBLJAN.

kvevri. See QVEVRI.

KWV, the South African Co-operative Wine Growers' Association, or Ko-operatiewe Wijnbouwers Vereniging van Zuid-Afrika, was a statutory body established in 1918 after years of glut and grower bankruptcy, to fix production quotas and to minimize extreme swings between surplus and shortage. Over time, and as a result of the close ties between successive white governments and the influential grape-farming lobby, it became the dominant force in the South African wine industry. In 1998 it was relieved of its statutory authority and converted from CO-OPERATIVE to a company. It is now a moderate-sized player in the domestic and export market, producing increasingly impressive wines in its premium ranges, as well as aged brandies which enjoy international renown. M.F.

Fridjhon, M., and Murray, A., *Conspiracy of Giants* (1986).
James, T., *Wines of the New South Africa: Tradition and Revolution* (2013).
South African Wine Industry Directory (annually).

Kydonitsa, meaning 'little quince' and often marked by the aroma of that fruit, is a recently rescued and promising light-skinned vine variety from Lakonia in the southern Peloponnese that is increasingly appreciated in GREECE, with new plantings from Nemea to Macedonia.

Kyrgyzstan, mountainous central Asian republic on the border between KAZAKHSTAN and China that had a strong wine industry until Mikhail GORBACHEV's anti-alcohol campaign in 1985 resulted in widespread GRUBBING UP of vineyards. In 2020, the country had just 5,202 ha/12,854 acres of vineyard, according to OIV statistics, most of it in TABLE GRAPES and RAISINS.

L

labelling information. The amount of information required on wine LABELS seems to increase dramatically each year, encouraging some producers to use QR codes to provide consumers with a wealth of non-mandatory information. From 2022, the EU's new U label allows producers to provide the list of ingredients (see INGREDIENT LABELLING) and the nutritional declaration digitally or in print.

In the past, approaches to wine labelling differed significantly between countries, but the demands of international trade have led to a gradual convergence in the types of information required on a label (if not necessarily the underlying philosophies). The following basic items of information are now mandatory in virtually every country in some form or another.

Wine designation: usually this will be a self-explanatory term such as 'wine' or 'sparkling wine'. Wines made within the EU must, where applicable, indicate their status as a PDO or PGI and/or the name of the relevant PDO or PGI. In the US, the 'class and type' designation may be a generic term such as TABLE WINE (for wines between 7% and 14% alcohol) or a grape-variety name.

Country of origin: most wine-producing countries take this to refer to the origin of the grapes.

Name and address of importer, producer, or bottler: this is usually provided in a fairly straightforward fashion, although, within Europe, there are controls on the size of an address which happens to incorporate the name of a CONTROLLED APPELLATION on the label of a WINE WITHOUT GEOGRAPHICAL INDICATION, or even a PGI wine, so some sort of postal code is sometimes substituted.

Volume of wine: usually expressed in millilitres (ml or mL) or, in Europe, centilitres (cl or cL). See BOTTLE SIZES and BOXES.

Alcoholic strength: stated as a percentage of alcohol by volume (often abbreviated to 'alc. x% vol' or 'x% vol'). Tolerances can differ considerably, from the +/− 0.5% alcohol variance permitted in the EU and China to +/− 1.5% in the US, Australia, and New Zealand. However, for wines that are made to be exported to a range of countries, winemakers tend to stay within the strictest tolerances. See ALCOHOLIC STRENGTH. In some jurisdictions, STANDARD DRINKS information is also required.

Lot marking: packaged wine must be marked with a lot number unique to an individual batch or bottling so that it can be traced in the event of any complaint or recall. In Europe, the mark is an L followed by a coded date of packaging.

Allergen information: in most countries it is now obligatory to state on the label that a wine contains SULFITES if it contains more than 10 mg/l of SULFUR DIOXIDE. Sulfur dioxide is used to a certain extent in the making of virtually all wine and is a by-product of FERMENTATION, therefore virtually all wine contains this level of sulfites.

In most countries it is also now required to include a reference to the presence of egg or milk residues if the wine has been FINED with EGG WHITES, milk, or CASEIN and if these are present above detection limits (0.25 mg/l) in the finished wine, even though there is scant evidence of any health issues associated with the tiny concentrations found in wine as a result of such processing. See also VEGETARIAN AND VEGAN WINES.

Health-related information: health 'warnings' of various sorts are becoming more common on wine labels. Increasingly these are required by law, such as the US Surgeon General's warning and the mandatory pregnancy advisory messages and pictograms in France, South Africa, Australia, and New Zealand. In other countries such as the UK, these initiatives are voluntarily adopted by producers.

INGREDIENT LABELLING and energy labelling have recently been mandated by the EU and are under consideration in other countries as well.

The following items of information are generally optional but, if used, are subject to certain rules. Note that exporting producers must comply not only with the rules in their own country but also with those in the market to which they are exporting.

Geographical reference: typically, all but the most basic wines, or the most experimental, are distinguished by some form of geographical label reference that is more specific than the country of origin. In most cases this will be a GEOGRAPHICAL INDICATION (GI) of some sort, possibly accompanied by the name of a smaller area such as a vineyard name. The minimum permitted proportion of the blend that must be sourced from the named area often depends on the type of GI and ranges from 75% (US, Chile) to 80% (China), 85% (NZ, Australia, US AVAS, European PGIS), or 100% (Argentina, South Africa, European PDOS). In some jurisdictions, including the US and Australia, it is permitted to have more than one geographical indication on the label, but the regulations are varied and complex.

Vintage year: the year in which the grapes were harvested, although in rare cases (e.g. Canadian ICEWINE harvested in the new year) the vintage may in fact be the year in which most of the growing took place. The minimum content of wine sourced from the vintage ranges from 75% (Chile) to 80% (China), 85% (Australia, NZ, South Africa, US, European PGIs), or 95% (AVAs, Argentina, South Africa, European PDOs). See VINTAGE YEAR and NON-VINTAGE.

Varietal information: within many countries, including the EU, Argentina, Australia, New

Zealand, Switzerland, South Africa, and Uruguay, if a single variety is specified on a label of wine then it must comprise at least 85% of the wine. For other countries, such as the US, China, Chile, and Brazil, the minimum content for a wine labelled as a single VARIETAL is 75%. If more than one variety is mentioned on the label, in many countries (e.g. the US, Europe, South Africa, and Chile) together they must comprise 100%. The varieties must typically be listed in descending order.

Bottling information: the relationship between the source of the grapes and the producer or bottler is indicated by exactly how this is expressed. See BOTTLING INFORMATION for more details.

On a CHAMPAGNE label, the code printed next to the registered number of the bottler tells you the type of business responsible for the wine.

Environmental labelling: labels indicating the status of a wine as ORGANIC, BIODYNAMIC, SUSTAINABLE, or similar are now common. Such claims are usually validated by accreditation to a particular programme or standard, some national, some international.

See also SWEETNESS and FIZZINESS. J.P.H.B.

labels, the principal means by which a wine producer or bottler can communicate with a potential customer and consumer (although see also BOTTLES, CASE, FOIL).

Wine labels are a relatively recent development, which awaited the widespread sale of bottled wine and use of glues strong enough to stick to glass, in about 1860. Before then wines were sold unlabelled and stacked in BINS, and served in decanters, so BIN LABELS and decanter labels are the precursors of today's wine-bottle label. For many years, wines were identified by branded CORKS rather than by paper labels, a habit that persisted longest for vintage PORT.

Every wine in commercial circulation has to have a main label, as its passport quite apart from its function as a sales aid. Many wines also have a **neck label**, typically carrying the VINTAGE YEAR, so that the producer need not have new main labels printed for each new vintage, although labelling requirements can change so rapidly that in practice this sometimes seems necessary (see LABELLING INFORMATION). As wine consumers have become ever more sophisticated and curious, however, an increasing proportion of bottles carry a **back label** giving additional background information. This can vary from a genuinely useful outline of grape varieties used, vintage conditions, approximate SWEETNESS level, and serving advice to a collection of fine-sounding words involving the 'finest' grape varieties picked at 'perfect ripeness' in 'optimum conditions' and vinified according to the 'highest standards' but containing no genuine information whatsoever. Now that the amount of mandatory information required on wine labels is so considerable, some design-conscious bottlers try to beat the system by conveying all of this detail on what is obviously meant to be the back label, while applying to a second label (which the retailer, but not the labelling inspector, is meant to treat as the main label) a dramatic design statement without all the clutter of the mandatory information.

Labels matter to lawyers and officials, and they matter enormously to the retail wine trade, in which they communicate far more effectively with many consumers than any recommendation or award, but they are relatively unimportant to wine sales from a website or catalogue or in the hotel and restaurant industry. The Italians have been as innovative in label design as in that of bottles, and some modern designs can be arresting, effective, innovative, and sometimes all three. ARTISTS' LABELS have a certain following. Producers of established wines have usually inherited a label and rarely do anything more than slightly modify it. The fact that the label of PETRUS would win no design award seems to do little to hinder sales. The label design of wine BRANDS, however, is an extremely important factor in their success.

Labels are usually, but not always, applied straight after BOTTLING as part of the same mechanized process. Some very small-scale producers still apply their labels by hand with pots of glue. Producers of champagne and other sparkling wines take particular care to use strong, water-resistant adhesive in applying their labels since their bottles are likely to spend their last hours in public circulation immersed in a bucket of water.

Wine labels have such a fascination of their own (and can help recollection of the circumstances of a wine's consumption) that wine-**label collecting** is a recognized activity. Some of those who practise it call themselves vintitulists.

labour. Viticulture, unlike winemaking, has long required a substantial input of labour. The Romans used slaves, while MONKS AND MONASTERIES played an important part in medieval vine-growing. A peasant class was long necessary to maintain viticulture in Europe, and increasingly vineyard labour was paid for by leasing part of the vineyard to the labourer, sharecropping or, in French, MÉTAYAGE. Conscription or coercion of workers, for example Native Americans by Francisan missionaries or Chinese labourers in CALIFORNIA at the end of the 19th century, is rarely mentioned. The close association between vine-growing and people began to alter towards the end of the 20th century, however, mainly because of changes in technology.

There are three levels of labour input to viticulture: people alone, people plus draught animals, and people plus machines, including ROBOTS. In ancient vineyards, all work was done by people: WEED CONTROL, PRUNING, TRIMMING, DESUCKERING, LAYERING, and HARVESTING. The labour input was high, and vineyards on the plains required between 70 and 80 person-days per hectare per year. This means that any one person might tend about 3 ha/7 acres, with due allowance for using other labour at times of peak demand such as harvesting and pruning. The YIELD from such vineyards was not high compared with modern standards. A generous 33.5 hl/ha (2 tons/acre) meant that one person's labour might produce a maximum of about 15 tonnes of grapes. For HILLSIDE VINEYARDS, one person might tend only about 100 sq m of vineyard, although this was not necessarily full-time work, with a likely output of tens of kilograms of grapes per person per year. Such vineyards relying totally on manual labour are increasingly rare, as the price of labour has increased much more than the price of wine.

Intensive labour input continued for many vineyards up until the mid to late 19th century, when the invasion of POWDERY MILDEW, DOWNY MILDEW, and PHYLLOXERA led to the need for SPRAYING and the use of ROOTSTOCKS. Previously many vineyards had been planted haphazardly without rows and with high VINE DENSITY, almost like a field of wheat. Unhealthy vines were replaced by layering from adjacent vines. With the need to spray, and also for TILLING, draught animals became more common, not only horses but also mules, oxen, and even dairy cows. In France's Auvergne, for example, cows provided meat, milk, and labour. Vines then needed to be planted in rows to make easy the passage of the animal, and there were typically many fewer plants per hectare because of the cost of GRAFTING plants on rootstocks. One horse was able to work 7 ha, and one person was needed for every 3 ha. A typical family farm consisted of about 7 ha of vines, one horse with two drivers, and one labourer.

After the Second World War, the pattern of viticulture changed in France and elsewhere with the widespread introduction of MECHANIZATION. This was no simple matter, as there were conflicts between generations of farmers about replacing horses with TRACTORS, as well as substantial changes in the support services in rural villages. Mechanics and fuel sellers replaced blacksmiths and fodder merchants. In the end, economic necessity determined the future; one person and a tractor was now able to tend 30 ha of vineyards, although with manual labour including pruning, trimming, and harvesting, 1 ha still required 43 days' work throughout the year. Growers outside Europe were generally quicker to switch to tractors.

In the 1960s, the mechanization revolution intensified. Under-vine tilling had been largely replaced by HERBICIDES, and then there was the introduction of MECHANICAL HARVESTING in the late 1960s, followed by that of MECHANICAL PRUNING in the 1980s. Some sprays were even applied from the air, using aeroplanes or HELICOPTERS (and, more recently, DRONES). There are some large corporate vineyards in south-eastern Australia where the total annual labour input is less than 50 person-hours per hectare: all operations are carried out mechanically including harvesting and pruning; spray units treat multiple rows at once; and weed control is by herbicides. On large estates with this degree of mechanization, one worker is required for each 30 ha, and the output can be more than 400 tonnes of wine grapes. This figure, compared with less than 15 tonnes per person about a century earlier, demonstrates how labour productivity has increased through mechanization. However, mechanization can compromise quality. For example, if simple mechanical pruning is not followed up by hand to regulate the number of buds retained, the principles of BALANCED PRUNING may be violated.

Australian examples are relevant because of the acute rural labour shortage there and in New Zealand, although Asian and Pacific-island immigrants, as well as working students, were providing some solutions in the first decades of the 21st century. The wine industries of South America have never known a labour shortage. The same is true of South Africa, even after the abolition of the *dop* system, which continued long after it was outlawed. It encouraged workers to receive a portion of their wages in wine, thus keeping them in thrall to their employers. In California and elsewhere on the west coast of the US, Mexico has provided an exceptionally skilled viticultural labour force. At one time they were typically seasonal workers, but now they are more likely to be immigrants, sometimes the second or third generation of their family to be working in the vineyards (see CALIFORNIA).

Future developments are not obvious. With improved INFORMATION TECHNOLOGY, there is renewed interest in developing robots for mechanical pruning, for example, but the variability of vineyards, of terrain, and of the weather make the task of robot development and use more difficult than for the factory floor.

It seems likely, however, that an increasing proportion of vineyard tasks will be mechanized, even in countries where labour resources are not necessarily limiting or expensive, since mechanization is seen to offer benefits of timeliness as well as of economics. However, where the slopes are too steep for mechanized tilling, or where there is a wish to avoid SOIL COMPACTION, a small number of producers have returned to using ploughs pulled by draught animals such as horses.

Once the grapes have been delivered to the winery, winemaking requires relatively little labour. A WINEMAKER is required to make decisions and, increasingly, programme a computer which may control such operations as TEMPERATURE CONTROL and RACKING wine from one container to another (see INFORMATION TECHNOLOGY).

Only CAP MANAGEMENT, BARREL AGEING, and, particularly, LEES STIRRING require much manual labour (see CELLAR WORK). Otherwise, emptying vessels and cleaning are the chief manual operations. R.E.S. & J.R.

labrusca. See VITIS LABRUSCA.

L'Acadie Blanc, winter-hardy grape variety speciality of NOVA SCOTIA, also planted in Quebec. Named after the French term for Nova Scotia, it is a cross of Cascade (a complex HYBRID created by SEIBEL) and SEYVE-VILLARD 14–287 made in 1953 at Vineland Research, Ontario (now part of Guelph University). It ripens early, has good disease resistance, and is particularly suitable for regions with very short growing seasons.

laccase, a powerful oxidative ENZYME particularly associated with BOTRYTIS BUNCH ROT which turns grape MUST brown.

La Clape used to be a subappellation within the LANGUEDOC in southern France but was awarded its own AOC in 2015. Once an island off the busy Roman port of Narbo (Narbonne), La Clape is today a quintessentially Mediterranean coastal mountain just south of Narbonne boasting one of France's highest average annual totals of sunshine. On the CLAY and LIMESTONE southern slopes of the rocky massif, the climate is heavily influenced by the sea. Vineyard ELEVATIONS can vary by as much as 200 m/980 ft, and the winds, particularly the tramontane, are ever present. La Clape is particularly well suited to growing BOURBOULENC, which must represent at least 40% of the grapes used in the production of La Clape's iodine-scented white wines; it must be blended with GRENACHE BLANC, and a host of other white grapes are allowed. However, most wine produced from the appellation's 807 ha/1,994 acres of vineyard in 2020 is full-blooded red, based on Grenache blended with Mourvèdre and/or Syrah and heavily scented by GARRIGUE. M.S.

Lacrima di Morro d'Alba, fast-maturing, wild-strawberry-scented red grape speciality of Morro d'Alba in the MARCHE. There were 252 ha/623 acres in Italy in 2015.

La Crosse, promising, cold-hardy, light-skinned complex American HYBRID released in 1983 and widely dispersed in the Midwest.

Lacryma Christi, is a blended white wine (CODA DI VOLPE with up to 20% FALANGHINA and/or GRECO) or red wine (PIEDIROSSO with maximum 20% AGLIANICO) from the Vesuvio DOC in CAMPANIA. Until recently the wines were considered mediocre, but the efforts of a new generation, often custodians of old-vine PERGOLA vineyards rooted in VOLCANIC black sand, have resulted in greater quality. W.S.

lactic acid, one of the milder ACIDS in wine, present in much lower concentrations than either MALIC ACID or TARTARIC ACID. Lactic acid, named after *lactis*, Latin for 'milk', is most frequently encountered as the principal acid in yoghurt, sour milk, and sauerkraut. Lactic acid is a common participant in both plant and animal metabolic processes. It is the end-product of intense muscular activity in animals (see ACIDS); a by-product of the alcoholic FERMENTATION process in wines and beers; and the end-product of the metabolic action of the many LACTIC ACID BACTERIA.

In wine, lactic acid can be produced by bacteria both from traces of sugar and from malic acid. The function of MALOLACTIC CONVERSION, which a high proportion of red wines and some white wines undergo, is to transform harsh malic acid into the much milder lactic acid. A.D.W.

lactic acid bacteria, or **LAB**, an abbreviation of **lactic-acid-producing bacteria**, are some of the few BACTERIA that can survive in such an acidic solution as wine. They all produce LACTIC ACID. Those of importance to winemaking can be subdivided into the three genera: *Oenococcus* (of which the best-known species is *Oenococcus oeni*, formerly called *Leuconostoc oenos*), *Lactobacillus*, and *Pediococcus*.

Lactic acid bacteria are recognized for their ability to conduct MALOLACTIC CONVERSION, which converts harsher malic acid into milder lactic acid.

LAB naturally occur throughout the vinification process from grapes to wine. They can become so deeply embedded in the fibres of wooden VATS and BARRELS that they are not easily removed by conventional cleaning practices. Typically proliferating after the completion of FERMENTATION, they improve the sensory properties of wines with excess malic acid and contribute to their microbial stability. A winery may rely on spontaneous malolactic conversion or deliberately introduce lactic acid bacteria in order to have greater control over the process. *Oenococcus oeni* is the LAB species most tolerant to low PH (< 3.5) and ETHANOL and is generally preferred as it produces wines with favourable sensory properties.

Unfortunately, however, many strains of lactic acid bacteria, especially *Lactobacillus* and *Pediococcus* spp., can potentially cause wine spoilage (e.g. MOUSY off-flavours, over-production of DIACETYL, and turbidity). This is most likely to happen after the completion of malolactic conversion, when traces of sugar remain as nutrients in the wine, when wine pH is above the growth threshold for *Lactobacillus* and *Pediococcus* spp. (> pH 3.4–3.5), and when SULFUR DIOXIDE concentration is insufficient. Some species of LAB can also produce BIOGENIC AMINES, notably HISTAMINE, tyramine, and putrescine. These amines can range in concentration from 0 to 10 mg/l in white wine and 0–30 mg/l in red wine. Very few strains of *Oenococcus oeni*, for example, have been shown to produce histamine and putrescine, and those that do are not selected as malolactic starter cultures. A range of other viticultural and winemaking factors can also affect the concentration of biogenic amines in wine.

See also ALLERGIES.

Fortunately, however, lactic acid bacteria are very sensitive to sulfur dioxide and are much easier to control than ACETOBACTER. Lactic acid bacteria grow best in very weakly acidic solutions and in the presence of ETHANOL in a temperature range of 15–30 °C/59–86 °F, although they are intolerant of high concentrations of ethanol. Bacteriologists regard them as 'fastidious' in that they require a wide range of micronutrients.

Their effect on new or young wine can therefore be limited by sulfur dioxide, low temperatures, and frequent RACKING so as to eliminate the possibility of providing micronutrients from the YEAST decomposition products in the LEES. P.J.C.

Bartowsky, E. J., 'Bacterial spoilage of wine and approaches to minimize it', *Letters in Applied Microbiology*, 48 (2009), 149–56.

Costantini, A., et al., 'An overview on biogenic amines in wine', *Beverages* 5 (2019), 19.

Franqués, J., et al., 'Presence of *Oenococcus oeni* and other lactic acid bacteria in grapes and wines from Priorat (Catalonia, Spain)', *LWT—Food Science and Technology*, 81 (2017), 326–34.

Moreno-Arribas, M. V., et al., 'Biogenic amines and the winemaking process', in A. Reynolds (ed.), *Managing Wine Quality 2: Oenology and Wine Quality* (2nd edn, 2021), 595–618.

lactones. See OAK FLAVOUR.

Ladoix, the appellation from the village of **Ladoix-Serrigny** in the Côte de Beaune district of Burgundy's CÔTE D'OR, producing about 70% red wines from Pinot Noir grapes, sometimes sold as Côte de Beaune-Villages (see BEAUNE, CÔTE DE). White wines are growing in popularity, especially those grown towards the top of the slope. Unusually in Burgundy, some of the PREMIERS CRUS are designated for red wine only (e.g. Les Joyeuses) or white wines only (e.g. Les Gréchons), while bizarrely a small number of premier cru vineyards located in Ladoix such as Les Moutottes are sold under the name Aloxe-Corton. Furthermore, 6 ha of Corton-Charlemagne and 22 ha (out of 160) of Le Corton, including part of Le Rognet and Les Vergennes, are actually sited in Ladoix (see ALOXE-CORTON for more details).

See also CÔTE D'OR, and map under BURGUNDY. J.T.C.M.

ladybirds. See LADYBUG TAINT.

ladybug taint, also known as **lady beetle** or **ladybird taint**, is an off-flavour found in both grape juice and wine that contributes undesirable peanut and green aromas and flavours, and possibly excessive bitterness. Two lady beetle species that migrate to vineyards during autumn—the seven-spot ladybird/ladybug (*Coccinella septempunctata*) from Europe and particularly the multicoloured Asian lady beetle (or harlequin ladybird, *Harmonia axyridis*)—are responsible. Both were originally introduced to North America to control aphids, but *Harmonia axyridis* is very invasive and is now also established in Europe, England, South America, South Africa, and New Zealand. It is unlikely that the beetles directly harm or taint the grapes. Instead, they cause contamination after they are inadvertently harvested with the fruit and are incorporated in the MUST. The compounds responsible are alkyl-methoxypyrazines—components of the insects' haemolymph—and are difficult to remove from affected juice and wine, although juice settling and must-heating prior to fermentation can help. While not always openly acknowledged, ladybug taint is a problem in some wines and vintages across many of the world's wine regions, including the US, France, Germany, and Canada. The first major widely reported incidence of ladybug taint in northern North America was in 2001, while the 2004 and 2011 vintages in Burgundy were probably the first two to be widely discussed in this context. G.P.

Pickering, G. J., and Botezatu, A., 'A review of ladybug taint in wine: origins, prevention, and remediation', *Molecules*, 26/14 (2021), 4341.

Pickering, G. J., et al., 'Influence of *Harmonia axyridis* on the sensory properties of white and red wine', *American Journal of Enology and Viticulture*, 55/2 (2004), 153–9.

Pickering, G. J., et al., 'Prevalence and management of alkyl-methoxypyrazines in a changing climate: viticultural and oenological considerations', *Biomolecules*, 11/10 (2021), 1521.

Lafite, Château, subsequently **Ch Lafite-Rothschild**, FIRST GROWTH in the MÉDOC region of BORDEAUX. The vineyard, to the north of the small town of PAUILLAC and adjoining Ch MOUTON ROTHSCHILD, was probably planted in the first third of the 17th century. Inherited in 1716 by the SÉGURS, who also owned Ch LATOUR, it was sold in 1784 to Pierre de Pichard, an extremely rich president of the Bordeaux Parlement who perished on the scaffold. The estate was confiscated and sold as public property in 1797 to a Dutch consortium which in 1803 resold it to a Dutch grain merchant and supplier to Napoleon's armies, Ignace-Joseph Vanlerberghe. When he fell on hard times, he resold it to his former wife in order to avoid its falling into a creditor's hands. Perhaps for the same reason, or to avoid splitting it up under French inheritance laws, in 1821 she apparently sold it to a London banker, Sir Samuel Scott, for 1 million francs. He and then his son were the nominal owners for over 40 years. But when the real proprietor Aimé Vanlerberghe died without issue in 1866, the family decided to sell it and pay the fines owed because of the concealment. In 1868, after a stiff contest with a Bordeaux syndicate, it was knocked down to Baron James de ROTHSCHILD of the Paris bank, for 4.4 million francs, including part of the Carruades vineyard. Baron James died in the same year, and the château has remained in the family ever since. Baron Eric de Rothschild took over direction of the property from his uncle Baron Élie in 1974, handing over to his daughter Saskia in 2018. In the famous 1855 CLASSIFICATION, Lafite was placed first of the PREMIERS CRUS, although there is controversy as to whether the order was alphabetical or by rank. Yet, as Christie's AUCTIONS in the 1960s and 1970s of 19th-century British country mansion cellars showed, in Britain Lafite was nearly always the favoured first growth.

The château itself is a 16th-century manor. The vineyard, one of the largest in the Haut-Médoc, had grown to 112 ha/276 acres by 2014: 72% Cabernet Sauvignon, 25% Merlot, 2% Cabernet Franc, and 1% Petit Verdot. Annual production varies, even more so since the estate was certified ORGANIC in 2021. About one-third of the crop goes into the GRAND VIN most years and the rest into the SECOND WINE, called Carruades de Lafite but not restricted to wine produced on the plateau in the vineyard known as Les Carruades, but this also varies. See ROTHSCHILDS AND WINE for other wine investments made by the owners of Ch Lafite. E.P.-R. & J.R.

de Rothschild, S., *Château Lafite: The Almanac* (2020).

Lafnetscha, rare Swiss Valais white grape often mistaken for COMPLETER. In fact, DNA PROFILING at DAVIS showed in 2004 that Lafnetscha is an offspring of HUMAGNE BLANCHE of the Valais and Completer of Graubünden. J.V.

Lafões, relatively undeveloped Portuguese DOC within the Vinho Regional Terras do DÃO and bordering VINHO VERDE. Sometimes referred to as *verdascos*, the light, dry white wines are not dissimilar to old-school Vinho Verde. Red wines—the mainstay of production—are light, acidic, and relatively rustic. S.A.

L

lagar, term used in PORTUGAL for a low-sided stone trough where grapes are trodden and fermented. Modern examples are made from stainless steel, but most have been replaced by conventional fermentation vats except in the DOURO Valley, where some of top ports continue to be foot-trodden in *lagares*. See PORT for more detail.

Lagoa, DOC in the ALGARVE in southern Portugal centred on the region's sole remaining CO-OPERATIVE winery.

La Gomera, rugged, mountainous CANARY ISLAND with its own small DO and 120 ha/300 acres of terraced vines planted at ELEVATIONS of 300–600 m/984–1,968 ft. White wines dominate here, mostly made from FORASTERA.

Lagorthi, name for VERDECA in Greece, where it is admired for its aromatic whites but is all too rare.

Lagos, westernmost DOC in Portugal's ALGARVE, exposed to northern winds and ocean on two sides, hence cooler and more humid than inland areas. S.A.

Lagrein, well-connected red INDIGENOUS VARIETY grown on 486 ha/1,200 acres in ALTO ADIGE in 2020 and on 215 ha in TRENTINO. Although often over-produced, it can produce **Lagrein Scuro** or **Lagrein Dunkel**, somewhat tannic reds of real character, as well as fragrant yet sturdy rosé called **Lagrein Rosato** or **Lagrein Kretzer**. Lagrein can be slightly bitter on the finish, and its presence, valued for both TANNINS and colour, can at times be detected in blends. DNA PROFILING has established that Lagrein is a natural CROSS between TEROLDEGO from Trentino and SCHIAVA Gentile from Alto Adige, a great-grandchild of Pinot, and a cousin of Syrah. J.V.

Lairén, very old minor southern Spanish white grape variety also known as Malvar and often mistaken for AIRÉN.

Laithwaite's, the world's biggest family-owned wine retailer and Britain's biggest wine company. It was founded as Bordeaux Direct in 1969 by Tony Laithwaite, a geography student who worked on a modest wine farm in CASTILLON, fell in love with wine, and began driving it back to the UK to sell from a railway arch in Windsor. His wife Barbara came on board the next year and steered the company with awesome efficiency until 1991. A key milestone was launching the Direct *Sunday Times* Wine Club in 1973, with Hugh JOHNSON as president. This feet-first introduction to the logistics of selling wine by mail order was enabled by Laithwaite's whimsical charm and lateral thinking; he has always prided himself on operating outside the wine-trade mainstream.

Never to be seen at the usual round of trade tastings, Laithwaite travelled the world instead and claims responsibility for introducing the British to the wines of Bulgaria, Romania, Moldova, Czechoslovakia, Australia, New Zealand, the Languedoc, Chile, Portugal ('the post-MATEUS new era'), and even England. Laithwaite's, Barbara Laithwaite, and one of their three sons now have, separately, their own English vineyards.

It was Tony Laithwaite who coined the expression FLYING WINEMAKER and in the 1980s made full use of putting southern-hemisphere winemakers to work in some of Europe's more primitive CO-OPERATIVE cellars. This fitted perfectly with the Laithwaite *modus operandi* of selling exclusive labels at high margins to customers who delighted in apparently buying them from their personal, compulsively literate friend Tony Laithwaite, a relationship which seemed to survive his short-term addition to the *Sunday Times* Rich List. By the 1990s the great majority of British direct wine sales, via whichever society or special offer, were fulfilled from Laithwaite's state-of-the art warehouse in the Berkshire countryside. They at last gained a major toehold in the traditional wine trade by acquiring the historic Averys of Bristol between 2002 and 2006 and sell and store considerable quantities of FINE WINE as well their trademark quirkier offerings.

The Laithwaites had long before acquired and replanted the CASTILLON vineyard on which Tony Laithwaite did his apprenticeship, and in 2007 they opened their own substantial winery, the Chai au Quai, nearby. In 2003, to capitalize on the number of highly trained, under-funded, and, often, under-employed OENOLOGY graduates in South Australia, Laithwaite's opened the RedHeads Studio in McLaren Vale, a CELLAR RATS' playpen from which the company was able to buy the cream of the crop.

But the real game-changer came in 2006 when Laithwaite's acquired two businesses in the US, one in Connecticut and one in Illinois, which gave the firm a base from which to invade the growing American wine market. Today they operate the *Wall Street Journal*'s wine club as well as Laithwaite's in the US.

The next year they expanded into direct wine sales in Australia, where they operate the wine club of *The Australian* newspaper and Virgin Wines. In 2014 they franchised wine merchants in Taiwan and Hong Kong. By 2020 revenues were £360 million.

Laithwaite, T., *Direct: My Story* (2019).

Lake County, smallest viticultural district among CALIFORNIA'S NORTH COAST counties. In this inland district east of MENDOCINO County and north of NAPA County, a vigorous but short-lived 19th-century industry died out with PROHIBITION, leaving scant historic guidance to the growers who restored vineyards to the region during the 1970s. The region boasts a unique climate: it is entirely high ELEVATION, with most vineyards planted above 457 m/1,500 ft, and this exposes the vines to more sunshine but also more ULTRAVIOLET RADIATION, which is thought to thicken the grape skins. Summers are hot but the winters can be cold and harsh, which is why much of the county's 3,845 ha/9,500 acres of vines are grown close to the moderating influence of Clear Lake, the largest lake entirely within California.

Of the seven sub-AVAS in 2022, two particularly stand out. **Red Hills AVA** rises above the lake's southern shores, its VOLCANIC and sometimes obsidian-laced soils adept at producing tannic, mineral-inflected Cabernet Sauvignon. Napa's Andy Beckstoffer is a vocal proponent of the region's potential and famously gave away several vintages of Cabernet fruit to top California producers in an attempt to spread the word.

High Valley AVA, north-east of Clear Lake, is a transverse valley with high, steep walls known for its wild weather and fast winds that cool down the grapevines and slow ripening. Sauvignon Blanc and Tempranillo are the early favourites, but Cabernet Sauvignon boasts significant plants as well. K.A.W.

lake effect, the year-round influence on vineyards from nearby large lakes, permits vine-growing in areas such as the north-east United States and Ontario in Canada despite their high LATITUDES, even if CLIMATE CHANGE has made this influence less predictable. In winter, the large lakes provide moisture to the prevailing westerly winds, which creates a deep snow cover, protecting vines from WINTER FREEZE even in very low temperatures, and the lake may eventually freeze, depending on its size. In early spring, the westerly winds blow across the very cold or frozen lake and become cooler, retarding BUDBREAK until the danger of FROST has passed. In summer the lake warms up. By autumn/fall, the westerly winds are warmed as they blow across the lake. The warm breezes on the vines lengthen the growing season by delaying the first frost. In other parts of the world, however, lakes and large inland seas also moderate climate through temperature effects alone. See MARITIME CLIMATE. H.L.

Lalande-de-Pomerol, Bordeaux appellation very much in the shadow of POMEROL, the great red-wine district to its immediate north. It includes the communes of Lalande-de-Pomerol and Néac and produces lush, Merlot-dominated wines which can offer a suggestion of the concentration available in a bottle of fine Pomerol but at a fraction of the price. Including about 1,100 ha/2,700 acres of vineyards, the Lalande-de-Pomerol appellation is much bigger than that of Pomerol, and its soils are composed of CLAY, SAND, and some well-drained GRAVELS in the south where it is divided from the Pomerol appellation only by the Barbanne river. At one time, the Barbanne separated that part of France which said *oc* for 'yes' (see LANGUEDOC) from that part which said *oil* and spoke the *langue d'oil*. J.R. & J.L.

La Livinière. This commune in the hilly far north of MINERVOIS in the LANGUEDOC successfully campaigned, hard and justifiably, for a special subappellation in 1999; in 2023 it was awaiting approval for standalone AOC status. Its 445 ha/1,100 acres extend over the rocky LIMESTONE plateau of Le Petit Causse, the vineyards climbing to 400 m/1,312 ft in ELEVATION, where the cool temperatures help to retain acidity and verve in the wines. Those wines are red, full-bodied, and structured blends of at least 40% SYRAH and/or MOURVÈDRE, with GRENACHE and LLEDONER PELUT, and smaller amounts of CARIGNAN, CINSAUT, PIQUEPOUL Noir, Rivairenc (ASPIRAN), and TERRET Noir allowed.

La Mancha. Europe's largest single demarcated wine region, in CASTILLA-LA MANCHA in the heart of Spain (see map under SPAIN). By 2012 the vineyards of the DOP La Mancha had shrunk to 160,000 ha/385,000 acres and have held steady since. Most of the area is arid table land stretching from the satellite towns south of Madrid to the hills beyond VALDEPEÑAS nearly 200 km/125 miles south. The Moors christened it Manxa, meaning 'parched earth', an apt description of the growing conditions. RAINFALL is unreliable, with annual totals averaging 300–400 mm/12–16 in. Summers are hot with temperatures rising over 40 °C/104 °F, while winters are bitterly cold with prolonged FROSTS. Looking on the bright side, FUNGAL DISEASES are almost unknown in La Mancha's dry growing season.

The doughty AIRÉN vine seems to be well suited to these extreme conditions and is therefore popular among La Mancha's 14,100 smallholders as of 2021. The variety covers about 200,000 ha/494,210 acres in the Castilla-La-Mancha autonomous region, nearly three-quarters of which is unirrigated BUSH VINES. It forms the basis of many of the region's fresh, inexpensive, if rather neutral dry white wines, sometimes blended with VERDEJO, SAUVIGNON BLANC, or CHARDONNAY.

Red wines rely mainly on Cencibel (TEMPRANILLO) grapes, alone or in blends with SYRAH, GARNACHA, CABERNET SAUVIGNON, MERLOT, and others. That said, the 2010s saw a rise in interest in local varieties such as Malvar (LAIRÉN), Tinto Velasco, Moravia Dulce (MARUFO), and Garnacha Tintorera (ALICANTE BOUSCHET). A large part of the annual harvest is also distilled into industrial alcohol or sent to JEREZ to make brandy de Jerez.

Most of the region's most interesting wines are not labelled DO La Mancha, as many producers prefer to use more generic IGPS such as Vino de la Tierra Castilla or even the simple Vino de España. V. de la S. & F.C.

Lambrusco, central Italian VARIETAL wine based on the eponymous red grape variety, or rather varieties, that was enormously popular with the mass market in the US and northern Europe in the 1980s. So successful was it that special white, pink, and 'light' versions were created, the colour and alcohol often being deliberately removed. Lambrusco's enormous commercial success has made it the most scorned and least understood of all Italian wine styles, although its industrial image is now challenged by a new generation of artisanal, dry versions.

Lambrusco also refers to a grape variety with several forms grown principally in the three central provinces of EMILIA—Modena, Parma, and Reggio nell'Emilia—although significant plantings can be found across the river Po in the province of Mantova, and occasional plantings can be found as far afield as PIEMONTE, TRENTINO, and even BASILICATA.

The 2010 Italian vine-variety census distinguished between one Lambrusca and no fewer than 11 forms of Lambrusco, of which the most planted were **Lambrusco Salamino** (a national total of 5,003 ha/12,357 acres), **Lambrusco Grasparossa** (2,726 ha), **Lambrusco Maestri** (2,223 ha), **Lambrusco di Sorbara** (1,606 ha), and **Lambrusco Marani** (1,394 ha). (See also ENANTIO.) Lesser amounts of **Lambrusco Viadanese**, **Lambrusca di Alessandria** (known as Nebbiolo de Baja in MEXICO), **Lambrusco Oliva**, **Lambrusco Montericco**, **Lambrusco Barghi**, Lambrusco Benedetti, and Lambrusco del Pellegrino are also grown.

The total production of Lambrusco in 2020 was a staggering 160 million bottles, with only one-fourth produced under DOC rules, the majority labelled IGT Emilia. Efforts to increase the quality of Lambrusco have led to a change in production rules so that for IGT Emilia, the SECOND FERMENTATION for Lambrusco must be within Emilia. While most Lambrusco found on export markets is medium sweet or sweet, the traditional wine is dry and much favoured by Italians themselves, the pronounced ACIDITY and FIZZINESS being thought to help digest Emilia's hearty cuisine.

Most Lambrusco today is a fairly anonymous, standardized product made in industrial quantities by CO-OPERATIVES or large commercial wineries using the BULK METHOD together with heavy FILTRATION, STABILIZATION, and, frequently, PASTEURIZATION. This approach has tended to obscure the distinctive qualities of the different vine varieties and zones. However, five Lambrusco DOCs were created based on terroir and varietal differences, and an increasing number of artisan producers can be found in each. The first four are exclusive to the province of Modena.

DOC Modena encompasses the whole of Modena province, with some 9,000 ha/22,240 acres planted to any Lambrusco and 5,000 ha/12,355 acres registered as DOC. The two largest producers, Chiarlo and Cavicchioli, produce 40 million bottles between them annually.

DOC Lambrusco Salamino di Santa Croce is the northernmost DOC on an extensive plain of ALLUVIAL sediment, SAND, and SILT. The high-yielding vines result in simple, violet-scented, fruity wines with medium tannins, although wines such as Luciano Saetti's SINGLE-VINEYARD Lambrusco proves that quality can be obtained here.

DOC Lambrusco di Sorbara overlaps with Lambrusco Salamino di Santa Croce and produces pale, rosé-like wines which tend to be dry and lively. Elegant wines come from potassium-rich sandy soils, while heavier wines come from clay-dominated soils.

DOC Lambrusco Grasparossa di Castelvetro is the furthest south. This early-budding, early-ripening, and least-vigorous Lambrusco is planted on undulating foothills around Castelvetro on sandy soils containing silt and marl. Considered the finest DOC of Lambrusco, its wines are rich in aroma, colour, extract, and tannin and may contain a little RESIDUAL SUGAR in compensation.

DOC Lambrusco Mantovano applies to the typically dry sparkling wines made in Lombardia.

Lambrusco is one of the suffixes of the DOC REGGIANO in EMILIA-ROMAGNA. Within this large area lies DOC Colli di Scandiano e Canossa, where Lambrusco Grasparossa is planted on HILLSIDES only, and yields are 16 tonnes/ha as opposed to the 18 tonnes/ha allowed in DOC Reggiano. T.D.C. & W.S.

Favaro, C., Everyone Calls It Lambrusco (2017).
Robinson, J., et al., *Wine Grapes: A Complete Guide to 1,368 Vine Varieties, Including Their Origins and Flavours* (2012).

La Méjanelle, small CRU (50 ha/124 acres) within the LANGUEDOC AOC in southern France, just east of MONTPELLIER. Unlike the rest of the AOC, this is a historic zone of individual estates, most notably Ch de Flaugergues. Syrah, Grenache, and Mourvèdre dominate in these particularly MEDITERRANEAN vineyards, even as the city continues to expand.

Landot, or **Landot 4511**, cold-hardy FRENCH HYBRID making soft red wine in the north-eastern United States.

Landwein, PGI category of dry Austrian or German wine. In GERMANY, Landwein must

L

have an ALCOHOLIC STRENGTH of at least 0.5% more than the minimum level for German WINE WITHOUT GEOGRAPHICAL INDICATION. Austria's much higher minimum is 14 °KMW (68 ° OECHSLE), reflecting the warmer climate. Especially in Austria, this once rarely seen category has become the default for a number of experimental-minded and NATURAL WINE producers who do not aspire to, or whose wines fail to achieve approval as, QUALITÄTSWEIN. D.S.

Langhe, plural of **Langa**, name given to the hills to the north and south of the city of Alba in the province of Cuneo in PIEMONTE on the right bank of the river Tanaro. The soils, composed of clay MARLS, are the classic ones for the NEBBIOLO grape and produce the Langhe's most famous wines BAROLO and BARBARESCO, although they can also yield BARBERA, DOLCETTO, and MOSCATO of excellent quality. The hills gradually rise to the south of Monforte d'Alba, creating a climatic limit to the cultivation of Nebbiolo, and to the south of Dogliani up to 600 m/1,970 ft. The highest part of the area is increasingly important for the production of TRADITIONAL METHOD sparkling wines based on Chardonnay and Pinot Noir under the DOCG Alta Langa.

Langhe is also the name of a regional DOC, overlapping with the DOCG ROERO on the left bank of the Tanaro (and therefore not part of the Langhe geographically). Langhe DOC was originally created in 1994 to allow for the production of INTERNATIONAL VARIETIES, either as VARIETAL bottlings or blends often aged in BARRIQUES and commanding high prices but which could only be labelled as VINO DA TAVOLA. Today Langhe DOC allows for 13 varieties, including non-traditional grape varieties such as Chardonnay, Sauvignon Blanc, and Riesling, as well as local ones such as ARNEIS and NAS'CETTA. (The latter obtained its own subzone, Novello, in 2010. It must comprise 100% of this variety rather than the 85% allowed under the Langhe DOC.)

Most Barolo and Barbaresco producers bottle a Nebbiolo for relatively early drinking and label it Langhe Nebbiolo because, perversely, the DOC Nebbiolo d'Alba is almost entirely confined to the left bank of the Tanaro, coinciding with Roero, and includes only tiny parts of the classic Barolo communes. This is also done because international demand for this wine, seen as an economically priced alternative to Barolo and Barbaresco, has inspired frantic plantings of Nebbiolo throughout the region, raising fears of future overproduction and devaluation. Its success is such that Nebbiolo threatens to replace Dolcetto, the main variety in the Dogliani DOCG, which lies within the Langhe. W.S.

Arnulfo, C., *Langhe e Roero. From the Soil to the Glass* (2012).
www.langhevini.it

Langhorne Creek, largely flat, productive wine region in SOUTH AUSTRALIA cooled by Lake Alexandrina and the nearby Southern Ocean. It has an unusual ability to produce large yields of medium-bodied red wines which achieve sensory ripeness in its TEMPERATE climate. There were 6,069 ha/14,997 acres of vineyards in 2022; Verdelho and Malbec are specialities.

language of wine. Wine-talk is a problem: 'When trying to talk about wine in depth, one rapidly comes up against the limitations of our means of expression . . . We need to be able to describe the indescribable. We tasters feel to some extent betrayed by language', comments Émile PEYNAUD.

Wine-talk is triply disadvantaged: first, people TASTE and smell wine differently from each other; second, a partially obscure conventional vocabulary has arisen: the wine flavour described as gooseberry, for example, does not taste very much like gooseberries (quite apart from the difficulties caused by the fact that gooseberries are known in only a limited number of cultures); third, the need to impress customers in a cut-throat market has led to ear-catching and sometimes bizarre descriptions: 'a fascinating old, old smell of unswept floorboards', 'old tarpaulin fringed with lace', 'Wham bam thankyou ma'am red, all rich, gooey, almost treacly fruit-dark plums and prunes awash with liquorice and chocolate and cream'.

In many ways, wine descriptions are in their linguistic infancy, parallel to the days when linguistic sounds could be described only by comparison to other sounds: in the 16th century, English *a* was described as like 'the balling of the sheepe when she feedeth', for example. Phonetics now has an International Phonetic Alphabet, with agreed parameters, but this is still far from true of wine terminology.

Descriptive terms should be distinguished from expressive or evaluative ones, it is sometimes argued. Yet even this proves to be difficult for wine: even the most straightforward descriptions are bizarre by the standards of 'normal' usage. An English speaker asked to describe the colours red and white is likely to mention blood versus snow, yet a red wine is typically reddish-purple and a white one pale straw, each with a range that goes beyond the usual boundaries for red and white. Other wine colour terms are equally odd: black, as in Greek MAVRODAPHNE 'black-daphne' or the old 'black wine' of CAHORS, refers simply to a hue darker than is usual for wines.

Yet colours illustrate one useful way in which wine terms can be partially analysed, by looking at the internal structure of the wine vocabulary. Red and white are opposites on a scale with rosé in the middle. Such antonyms are an anchor-point in descriptions. Possibly for this reason, the terms 'sweet' versus 'dry' are the first technical terms to be widely understood and are now regularly found in supermarket classifications, even though, outside a wine context, the average person would oppose sweet to sour, and dry to wet.

Technically, antonyms such as 'sweet' versus 'dry' are gradable, in that 'sweet' means 'sweet in relation to a norm', even though the norm is far from clear. Further opposites/scales have not generally caught on, though some recur in descriptions, as 'young' vs 'mature', 'light' vs 'heavy', 'crisp' (nicely acidic) vs 'flabby'—though a basic problem is that a word such as 'flabby' tends to be used as a general derogatory term, so is also found in opposition to terms such as 'hearty', 'sturdy', 'meaty', which indicate a wine with BODY.

Synonyms are also useful in understanding vocabulary structure, and words for wines with 'body' abound—'beefy', 'big', 'broad', 'chunky', 'powerful', 'robust'—though none has yet won out over others.

As the above examples show, most wine descriptions involve adjectives, though ones with a somewhat specialized interpretation. Adjectives depend for their meaning on the words to which they are attached: an old wine will be younger than an old house, but possibly older than an old friend, who may well not be aged. Many wine adjectives consist of a noun plus ending -y, as 'buttery', CHALKY, 'chocolatey', 'earthy', 'FLINTY', 'flowery', 'fruity', 'grapey', 'herby', 'meaty', 'nutty', 'oaky', 'peppery', 'silky', 'spicy', 'sugary', and 'velvety'.

Readers of wine columns sometimes get the misleading impression that 'anything goes'. Yet the majority of wine-flavour descriptions cover a fairly narrow range, mostly of other food words, as 'appley', 'gamey', 'grapefruity', 'minty', 'peachy', 'plummy'—though these are often 'code' terms, in that a wine described as 'grapefruity' or 'minty' does not (to the uninitiated) taste very much like either. Terms that move outside these food flavours relate easily only to a small portion of wine qualities, as with the power terms listed above for wines with body. A further set relate perceived smoothness to fabrics, so wines may be 'velvety', 'silky', 'satiny'—though even here, the range of fabrics is limited: a wine may be soft, though is not normally woolly. Shape and TEXTURE terms tend to be applied to wines with a high degree of ACIDITY, as 'angular', 'austere', 'flinty', 'steely'. The AROMA (nose) is perhaps the aspect of wine that has caused the greatest controversy in recent years and seems to be hardest to convey: 'cat's pee', 'pencil shavings', 'sweaty saddles', and 'tobacco' had relatively little attention paid to them, yet fury erupted when a serious critic referred to a wine as smelling of hamster cages. Any successful metaphor must achieve cultural resonance and avoid cognitive dissonance: it must fit in with existing traditions and preconceptions or risk being rejected.

Yet in many cases, wine descriptions are unclear only out of context or when single words are used. Humans often think about word meanings in terms of 'prototypes' or typical examples. Prototypes are bundles of characteristics: so a robin, a prototypical bird, has a red breast, is fairly small, has wings, slender legs, and so on. Similarly, a bunch of features characterize particular wines, some of them accurate, some evocative: a Sauvignon Blanc, for example, popularly referred to as 'cat's pee on a gooseberry bush', is spoken of as being 'acidic', 'clean', 'refreshing'. However, increasingly wines are acquiring shorthand labels for these bundles of characteristics: some Chardonnays, such as those produced in MEURSAULT, were once, before a more austere style predominated in the village, labelled 'buttery' for a fairly rich white wine—a description that was accepted even by those who love Meursault wines but dislike butter. A rioja is recognized and labelled 'oaky', even by those who have no idea why this tag is used.

All of this suggests that wine knowledge is becoming increasingly sophisticated. A future hope is that a more sophisticated classification system of the vocabulary of wine can match the knowledge of its drinkers.

See AROMA WHEEL, TASTING, TASTING NOTES, TASTING TERMS, TASTING-NOTES LANGUAGE, and PHILOSOPHY OF WINE. J.A.

Lehrer, A., *Wine and Conversation* (2nd edn, 2009).
Peynaud, É., *Le Goût du Vin* (1983), translated by M. Schuster as *The Taste of Wine* (2nd edn, 1996).

Languedoc, France's best-value, most fluid wine region, certainly its most important in terms of volume of wine produced and in terms of the significance of viticulture to the region's economy. The Languedoc takes its name from a time when its inhabitants spoke Occitan, the language in which *oc* (rather than *oil*) is the word for 'yes', hence *langue d'oc*. It comprises the three central-southern *départements* of the Aude, Hérault, and Gard, a sea of little other than vines just inland from the beaches of the Mediterranean (see map and FRANCE).

For administrative purposes, the Languedoc is considered part of the Occitanie region, although prior to 2016 it was often bracketed with the region to its immediate south, as in **Languedoc and Roussillon**. Between them at the turn of the century a total of 31,541 vignerons cultivated 241,537 ha/596,596 acres of vineyard, one-quarter of all French vines. (It had represented one-third a decade earlier.) But strenuous EU-inspired VINE-PULL SCHEMES aimed at reducing Europe's wine SURPLUS were specifically targeted at France's deep south with considerable success. By 2018, Languedoc's vineyards covered 62,900 ha/155,429 acres of vines.

Despite its quantitative importance, Languedoc produces only about one-eighth of France's AOC wines. For many years, the Languedoc's only appellation was Fitou, but in 1985 Corbières, Minervois, and the catch-all appellation Coteaux du Languedoc (now LANGUEDOC) were elevated from VDQS to AOC status; by 2021, there were 23 AOCs and 20 IGPS.

A high proportion of the vast area included in these AOC zones is dedicated to non-appellation wine, however, either because the ENCÉPAGEMENT is outside the appellation specifications or because the vigneron continues to be more interested in quantity than quality. In addition, some important producers, dissatisfied with the detail of the appellation laws, routinely ignore the AOC system and put their effort into making high-quality IGP wines instead. The Languedoc remains by far the principal producer of VSIG and produces nearly 60% of France's intermediate IGP, much of it labelled regionally and, typically, VARIETALLY, as Pays d'Oc.

About 18% of the Languedoc's AOC wine output was white in 2018. The best Languedoc whites, after a decidedly OAK-dominated phase, have become increasingly fine and interesting.

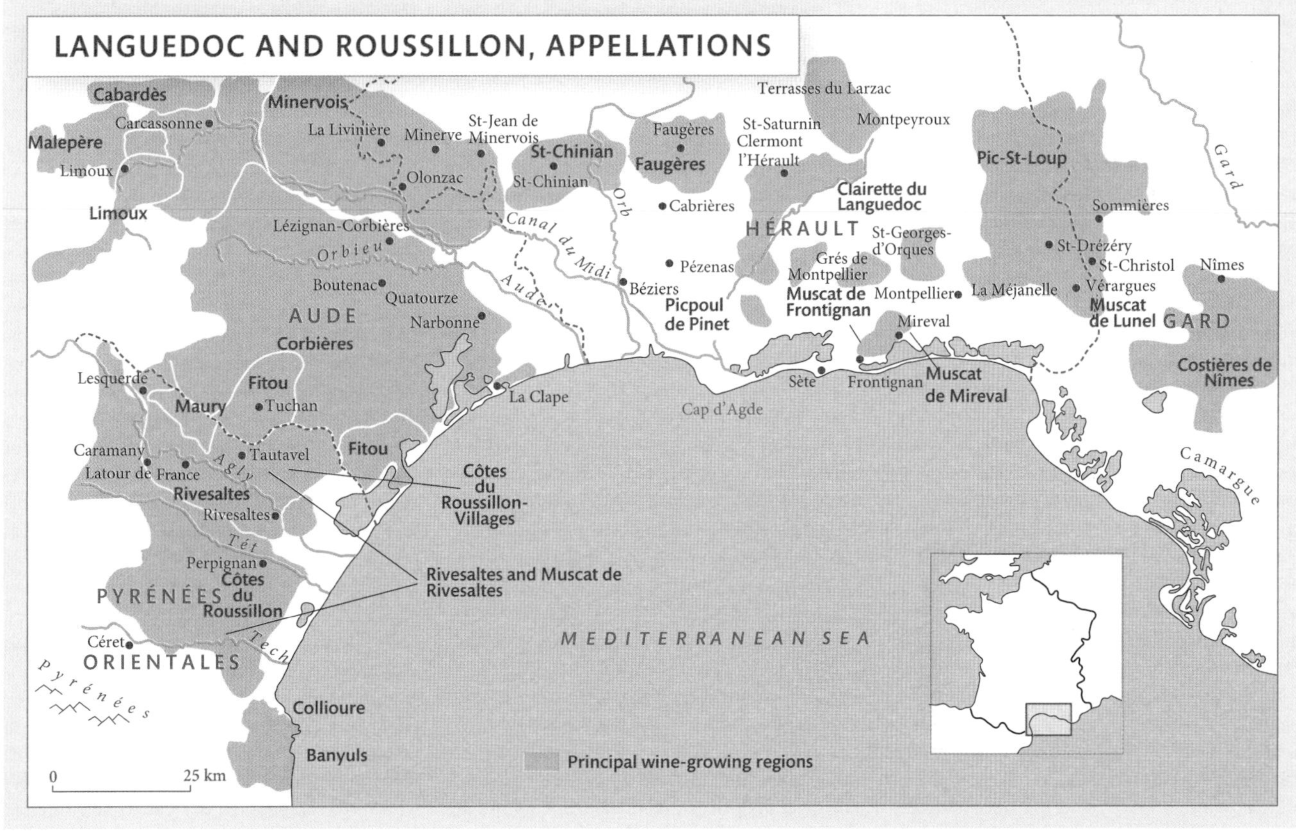

Almost as much rosé wine is made, and it, too, has been taken more seriously in the last decade, much of it being made in a lighter PROVENCE style. A substantial quantity of VIN DOUX NATUREL is made (see MUSCAT), and LIMOUX is the Languedoc's centre of SPARKLING WINEMAKING. The Languedoc is still principally a source of red wine, however, a typical representative being no longer a thin, pale remnant of the region's past as a BULK WINE supplier but a dense, exciting, increasingly supple ambassador of some of France's wildest countryside.

History

Vines were planted as early as 125 BCE on the hills near the Roman colony of Narbo, modern Narbonne, which today produce Corbières, Minervois, and Languedoc AOC. Narbonne was then an important Roman port, protected by what was then the island of LA CLAPE. Cargoes would be taken upriver as far as Carcassonne and then transported overland to join the GARONNE and thence to the Roman legions in Aquitaine. The hinterland of Narbonne and Béziers came to produce so much wine that it was exported to ancient ROME, although the edict of DOMITIAN was designed to put a stop to this.

It was not until the Middle Ages, under the auspices of the Languedoc's MONKS AND MONASTERIES, that viticulture once again thrived (although today only the Abbaye de Valmagne and Abbaye de Fontfroide retain their wine-producing roles). Already the University of MONTPELLIER was established, and ARNALDUS DE VILLANOVA oversaw several important developments for wine and spirit production there. The development of greatest potential significance for the Languedoc and its wines was the late 17th century construction of the Canal du Midi, which connected the Mediterranean with the Atlantic. The Bordelais were by now so experienced at protectionism, however (see HAUT-PAYS, for example), that the wine producers of the Languedoc failed to benefit substantially from this new distribution network until the end of the 18th century.

Much more profitable were the efforts of the DUTCH WINE TRADE in the late 17th century to develop northern European markets for *picardan*, a sweet white wine made from CLAIRETTE and PICQUEPOUL grapes that was well known in Holland by 1680, and subsequently for eaux-de-vie. The port of Sète was established in 1666 and became particularly important for exports to ENGLAND and the NETHERLANDS, Narbonne having long since silted up. Sweet wines were also produced, notably a DRIED-GRAPE WINE made from Muscat grown at FRONTIGNAN, whose inhabitants insist that it was as a result of a visit by a Marquis de Lur-Saluces to Frontignan after the great frost of 1709 that Ch d'YQUEM became a sweet wine property, and that their straight-sided bottle was adopted for bordeaux.

By the mid 19th century, the vineyards of the Languedoc could be divided into the HILLSIDE VINEYARDS, vines planted on GRAVELLY terraces at mid ELEVATION (roughly approximating to the majority of modern Languedoc appellations), and vines, mainly ARAMON and TERRET grapes, planted on the plains for DISTILLATION into brandy.

In 1855, the Languedoc's fortunes were to change forever as a result of its first RAILWAY connection, via Lyons, with the important centres of population in the north. A link via Bordeaux was opened the next year. From 1850 to 1869, average annual wine production nearly quadrupled in the Hérault *département*. The arrival of PHYLLOXERA could hardly have been worse timed, but, thanks to feverish experimentation and the eventual adoption of GRAFTING, as well as HYBRIDS and some of the new BOUSCHET crosses, the Languedoc vineyard was the first to be reconstituted after the devastations of this American pest. By the end of the 19th century, the Languedoc became France's principal wine supplier, producing 44% of France's entire wine production, from 23% of the country's total *vignoble*.

This superficial success was at some cost, however. Dr GUYOT had in 1867 warned against the over-industrialization of the Languedoc wine trade and the increasing influence of VINE VARIETIES and practices designed to produce quantity rather than quality. By the turn of the century, the plains of the Languedoc, the Hérault particularly, were being milked of thin, light, pale red that needed blending with the much more robust produce of new colonial vineyards in ALGERIA to yield a commercially acceptable drink. France had sown the seeds of its (continued) dependence on wine imports. Such was the extent of commercial interference in the French table-wine market, including widespread ADULTERATION AND FRAUD, that prices plummeted, and France's social crisis of 1907 provoked what were merely the first in a long series of wine-related riots.

Since then the vignerons of the Languedoc, typically but by no means always members of one of the region's hundreds of CO-OPERATIVES, many of them formed in the 1930s and most now part of a larger group, have been some of the world's most politicized. Their sheer number has given them political power, but the fall in demand for basic VIN DE TABLE and difficulty in selling even the keenly priced VIN DE PAYS, which took its place as the Languedoc's principal product, led to increasing frustration among growers.

Land here is relatively inexpensive, which has drawn a wide range of investors, both producers with an established record in a more famous wine region and complete outsiders.

Geography and climate

The great majority of the Languedoc's vines are or were planted on the flat, low-lying plain, particularly in the southern Hérault and Gard. In the northern Hérault and western Aude, however, vines may be planted several hundred metres above sea level, in the foothills of the Cévennes and the Corbières Pyrenean foothills, sometimes at quite an angle. Soils are very varied and can include GRAVELS, LIMESTONE, SCHIST, and VOLCANIC stones.

The climate in all but the far western limits of the Languedoc (where Atlantic influence is apparent) is definitively MEDITERRANEAN, and one of the major viticultural hazards is DROUGHT. Annual rainfall is often as little as 400 mm/15.6 in by the coast. July and August temperatures often exceed 30 °C/86 °F; such rain as does fall tends to arrive in the form of localized deluges. WIND is common throughout the growing season, with the tramontane bringing cool air from the mountains.

Viticulture

The Languedoc is a mosaic of predominantly privately owned vineyards. The size of the average holding is small and usually much divided between parcels inherited from various different branches of the family. BUSH VINES still predominate, although an increasing proportion of vines, especially the newer INTERNATIONAL VARIETIES, are being trained on WIRES. IRRIGATION is theoretically permitted only within strictly specified limits, and in practice only the best and the worst producers tend to have any form of available irrigation system. The flatter, larger vineyards lend themselves to MECHANICAL HARVESTING, but their parcellation, and ripping out, has slowed the inevitable invasion. The region is by no means free of FUNGAL DISEASES, and some sprayings are usually necessary.

Vine varieties

The dominant late 20th century vine variety CARIGNAN has been definitively routed by the VINE-PULL SCHEME of the EU, and in 2015 was only the third most planted variety in the Languedoc after Syrah and then Grenache Noir. Merlot, grown mainly for IGP wines, covers almost as much ground as Carignan, with Cabernet Sauvignon some way behind. Most red-wine appellations in the Languedoc specify various combinations of Syrah, Grenache, and Mourvèdre, with declining proportions of Carignan and most often, usually as minor blending ingredients, CINSAUT (especially good for rosés and fruity reds) and the Grenache relative LLEDONER PELUT.

By far the most planted white wine grape, though even less common than Cabernet Sauvignon, is Chardonnay, used for both varietal IGP wines and the still and sparkling wines of LIMOUX. Sauvignon Blanc is the next most planted and Viognier the fourth most popular white wine grape, further signs of how important INTERNATIONAL VARIETIES are to white-wine production here. Each white-wine appellation has a different cocktail of preferred ingredients from a palette of traditional pale-skinned Languedoc varieties, including BOURBOULENC, CLAIRETTE, GRENACHE BLANC, MACABEO, PIQUEPOUL, and VERMENTINO, although ROUSSANNE and MARSANNE are also specified occasionally.

Winemaking

While many traditional producers still work with modest materials and means and CO-OPERATIVES still dominate production, winery techniques and equipment have improved significantly in the last decade in the Languedoc. As many new incumbents have taken over family domaines and outside investors have arrived in the region, so the move to adopt new materials and techniques has gathered pace. STAINLESS STEEL has gained a significant foothold in the winery; likewise CONCRETE *cuves*, which fell out of favour in the 1990s, have been refurbished or newly installed as the enthusiasm for this medium has returned. It is now also common to see oak BARRELS, often new, of various sizes from BARRIQUES to demi-muids (see BARREL TYPES) in cellars as producers experiment with BARREL AGEING. CARBONIC MACERATION is still common for Carignan, but Syrah, Grenache, and Mourvèdre are vinified in everything from concrete egg to clay AMPHORA. The increased interest in white and rosé production has also led to more sophisticated TEMPERATURE CONTROL from reception to maturation. BARREL FERMENTATION and BARREL AGEING for these styles is now also more commonplace.

For more specific information, see the individual appellations CABARDÈS, CLAIRETTE DU LANGUEDOC, CORBIÈRES, FAUGÈRES, FITOU, LANGUEDOC AOC, LIMOUX, MALEPÈRE, MINERVOIS, PICPOUL DE PINET, and ST-CHINIAN, and also the vin de liqueur CARTAGÈNE, and various MUSCAT vins doux naturels. M.S.

Clavel, J., and Baillaud, R., *Histoire et avenir des vins en Languedoc* (1985).
www.languedoc-wines.com

Languedoc AOC was established in 2007 to create a generic appellation for the whole of this region in southern France. It replaced the former Coteaux du Languedoc, which covered several areas from Nîmes to Narbonne. Languedoc AOC, somewhat confusingly, extends across the whole of both Languedoc and Roussillon, covering all four *départements* of the Gard, Hérault, Aude, and Pyrénées-Orientales. It can be used for red, white, and rosé wines and allows producers to blend across regions under an appellation designation. It provides an alternative to the other cross-regional option of IGP Pays d'Oc but stipulates lower yields (max 50 hl/ha) and that the wines must be a blend of at least two varieties.

Although much of the zone qualifies for the basic Languedoc appellation, a number of subappellations, CRUS, or specific 'named terroirs' (see DÉNOMINATION GÉOGRAPHIQUE COMPLÉMENTAIRE) are allowed to append their own name to that of the appellation on labels. These include CABRIÈRES, GRÉS DE MONTPELLIER, LA MÉJANELLE, MONTPEYROUX, PÉZENAS, QUATOURZE, ST-CHRISTOL, ST-DRÉZÉRY, ST-GEORGES-D'ORQUES, ST-SATURNIN, and SOMMIÈRES. M.S.

www.languedoc-wines.com

Lanzarote, Spanish DOP including the whole of this relatively flat island in the CANARY ISLANDS. There were still 1,837 ha/4,539 acres of vineyards in 2020, clearly dominated by the white MALVASIA Volcánica grape variety, as on LA PALMA. In reds, LISTÁN NEGRO dominates. Lanzarote's vines are often planted in individual shallow indentations in the black VOLCANIC soil and protected from the strong Atlantic winds by stone walls. The El Grifo winery, founded in 1775, has been a pioneer in the development of modern dry Malvasía, and the overall quality of the other producers, led by Los Bermejos and Mozaga, has advanced significantly.
V. de la S. & F.C.

La Palma, Spanish DOP that includes the entire eponymous island in the CANARY ISLANDS. The vineyard surface of the VOLCANIC island had by 2019 dropped to 537 ha/1,327 acres, planted at 200–1,400 m/656–4,600 ft in ELEVATION. A large range of grape varieties are cultivated, dominated by NEGRAMOLL and LISTÁN blanco, but La Palma's most distinguished wine is traditional sweet MALVASIA, almost forgotten in recent years but whose reputation, as Canary SACK, goes back to Elizabethan England. Its most traditional wine is *vino de tea*, a spicy, resinous wine aged up to six months in barrels made from the Canary pine (*Pinus canariensis*).
V. de la S. & F.C.

large format, BOTTLE SIZE larger than the standard 75-cl size and of particular interest to collectors and investors (provided it is filled with FINE WINE).

La Rochelle, port on the Atlantic coast about 160 km/100 miles north of BORDEAUX in the *département* of Charente-Maritime. In the Middle Ages, La Rochelle was a New Town, having been founded in 1130, in an age of economic expansion. The climate at La Rochelle is hot and dry enough for the winning of sea salt, and salt was initially the basis of La Rochelle's economy. Merchants came from the north to buy salt, but they also wanted wine, and it was in response to that demand that the people of La Rochelle turned to viticulture. Because of its favourable climate, Poitou was a more reliable producer than the Seine basin (see PARIS), Reims (see CHAMPAGNE), BURGUNDY, or the RHINE. Hence the English and the Flemish turned more readily to the wines of Poitou, all the more so because these wines were less acidic than those of Reims and Paris. La Rochelle also exported its wines to Normandy, Scotland, Ireland, and even Denmark and Norway. In 1199, Poitou was the wine the royal household bought most of, with the wines of ANJOU and the Île-de-France coming second and third. But in 1224, when La Rochelle fell to the French, it had to cede its position as leading wine supplier to Bordeaux, although the wines of La Rochelle remained popular with the English in the 14th and 15th centuries.

The grape varieties were probably those of Burgundy and the Paris region: MORILLON, which was an early form of PINOT NOIR; and Fromenteau, thought to be the ancestor of PINOT GRIS. In documents of the 13th and 14th centuries, a third variety appears: called Chemère, Chemière, Chenère, or Chenère Blanche, it is likely to have been the parent of CHENIN BLANC. In accordance with medieval preference, most of the wines that Poitou made were white.

See also DUTCH WINE TRADE and HAUT-POITOU.
H.M.W.

Dion, R., *Histoire de la vigne et du vin en France* (1959).

L

Laški Rizling, the name current in SLOVENIA, SERBIA, and some other parts of the former Yugoslavia for the white grape variety known in Austria as WELSCHRIESLING (under which name more details and more of its many synonyms appear). It is the most widely planted variety in Slovenia, cultivated most successfully in the country's higher vineyards (just over the border from the spirited Welschrieslings of STYRIA) and in Serbia's Fruška Gora, where it can produce equally crisp and delicately aromatic wines, often under the historical name Grašac. Few of these superior examples have been exported, however, whereas for decades in the second half of the 20th century a Slovenian BRAND, Lutomer Riesling (renamed Lutomer Laški Rizling after German lobbying), was the best-selling white wine in the UK, its heavily sweetened style conveying little of the intrinsic character of the variety.

La Tâche, great red GRAND CRU in Burgundy's CÔTE D'OR. For more details, see VOSNE-ROMANÉE and DOMAINE DE LA ROMANÉE-CONTI.

late harvest, a general term used to describe grapes that have been harvested later than is normal for dry wines in order to make a SWEET WINE, generally without the aid of NOBLE ROT. They are usually left on the vine so that the berries are rich in sugar (see MUST WEIGHT) or, even longer, so that the fruit starts to desiccate, resulting in DRIED-GRAPE WINES. See VENDANGES TARDIVES for a highly regulated French example of a late-harvest wine.

lateral shoot, sometimes called simply a **lateral**, secondary shoot that grows from the axil of a leaf on the main shoot. Its origin on grapevines is linked with the complex development of the BUD. At most nodes, especially on weak vines, the lateral shoot is short (less than 20 mm/0.8 in), fails to become woody, and drops off in autumn leaving a prominent scar at the side of the bud. But on more vigorous shoots, especially at the middle nodes or at the end where vigorous shoots have been topped or trimmed, the lateral shoot grows in the same way as a primary shoot, producing hardened permanent wood. Sometimes, lateral shoots are fruitful (see SECOND CROP). Laterals that develop on secondary shoots are called tertiaries; quaternaries have even been seen on extremely vigorous vines. B.G.C.

Latin America. See SOUTH AMERICA and MEXICO.

latitude, angular distance north or south of the equator, measured in degrees (°) and minutes (′). The main northern-hemisphere viticultural regions extend between 32° and 51° N, and most of those in the southern hemisphere between 28° and 42° S. Those closer to the poles are cooler, and near the equator warmer. Viticulture is spreading polewards and is likely to continue to do so due to CLIMATE CHANGE. Whereas ten years ago 52° N in ENGLAND (and Ireland) was around the northern limit, vines are now planted in NORWAY and SWEDEN, up to 61° N. The extension in the southern hemisphere is limited by the general size of landmasses, with Chiloé Island, CHILE, at 43° S; Sarmiento, ARGENTINA, just under 46°; and vineyards in Central Otago, NEW ZEALAND, at just over 46°. Some vines are also cultivated for wine production in tropical lowlands and highlands or irrigated desert conditions as close to the equator as 8–9° (e.g. lowlands such as the Pernambuco region in north-east BRAZIL). See TROPICAL VITICULTURE.

Comparisons between hemispheres based purely on latitude are misleading. Northern-hemisphere vineyards are on average warmer during the growing season at given latitudes, a fact largely related to their greater CONTINENTALITY. But even over the whole year, the northern hemisphere is on average warmer than the southern hemisphere at similar latitudes, partly because of the greater land mass and its disposition around the North Pole and partly (in the case of western Europe) because of warming by the Gulf Stream.

Comparisons between vineyard regions based on latitude can also be misleading, since TEMPERATURE, which is influenced more by distance from the sea and ELEVATION than by latitude, has a greater impact than latitude on VINE PHYSIOLOGY, PHENOLOGY, and wine style. See CLIMATE AND WINE QUALITY, HUMIDITY, TEMPERATURE VARIABILITY, DIURNAL TEMPERATURE RANGE, and map under WORLD PRODUCTION. R.E.S & G.V.J.

Jones, G. V., et al., 'Climate, grapes, and wine: structure and suitability in a variable and changing climate', in P. Dougherty (ed.), *The Geography of Wine: Regions, Terroir, and Techniques* (2012), 109–33.

Latium, Anglicized version of the Italian wine region LAZIO.

Latour, Château, famously long-lived FIRST GROWTH in the MÉDOC region of BORDEAUX. The originally square tower from which the château takes its name was one of a defensive line against ocean-going pirates. Vines were already planted here in the late 14th century, and at least one-quarter of the land was vineyard by 1600. At the end of the 17th century, a number of smallholdings were accumulated into one ownership under the de Mullet family. The New French Clarets they produced made their first publicized appearances in AUCTIONS in London coffee houses early in the 18th century. Owned from 1677 by the Clauzel family, it passed by marriage to the powerful SÉGURS, who also owned LAFITE, MOUTON, and Calon-Ségur. On the death in 1755 of the Marquis Nicolas-Alexandre de Ségur, 'Le Prince des Vignes', his properties passed to his four daughters, three of whom in 1760 acquired Latour. Their male descendants owned the château, which in 1842 became a private company, until its purchase by the British Pearson family in 1963, with 25% acquired by Harveys of Bristol and a diminishing minority remaining in the hands of the French families. The property was greatly improved, with STAINLESS STEEL tanks controversially installed as FERMENTATION VESSELS in time for the 1964 vintage, partly on the advice of director Harry WAUGH. In 1989, the estate was sold to multinational corporation Allied-Lyons, already owners of Harveys, for the equivalent of £110 million. In 1993, Allied-Lyons sold their 94% share of the property to French businessman François Pinault (who acquired the London AUCTION house of Christie's in 1998), when Latour was valued at £86 million. See ARTÉMIS DOMAINES.

Thanks to 21st-century expansion, the estate comprised 96.5 ha/238 acres of vineyard by 2022 with 75% Cabernet Sauvignon vines, 24% Merlot (increased from 15% in the 1980s), and a very small amount of Cabernet Franc and Petit Verdot, with an average annual production of about 25,000 cases (less than it once was) of the three wines made there. In 1966 a SECOND WINE, Les Forts de Latour, made from the produce of young vines and from three plots on the other side of the St-Julien–Pauillac road, was introduced as a permanent fixture. A third wine is also bottled and sold as Pauillac. Latour's wines generally require much longer to develop than those of the other first growths, and they often have greater longevity. Latour is also known for its ability to produce good wines in lesser vintages.

It also possesses better archives, back to the 14th century, than any other wine estate in Bordeaux and so has spawned an unusual and useful array of monographs.

Since 2008, HORSES have worked the vineyards, and the estate was certified ORGANIC in 2018 with L'Enclos, a key walled vineyard, farmed BIODYNAMICALLY. In 2012 Latour's director Frédéric Engerer decided to withdraw from the annual Bordeaux EN PRIMEUR market, the first major Bordeaux château to do so, with a view to releasing wines only as they are ready to drink.

Faith, N., *Latour* (1991).
Higounet, C. (ed.), *La Seigneurie et le vignoble de Château Latour* (1974).
Penning-Rowsell, E., *Château Latour: A History of a Great Vineyard 1331–1992* (1993).

Latour, Louis, one of Burgundy's most commercially astute, and oldest, merchants. Jean Latour first planted vines in Aloxe-Corton, then called simply Aloxe, in 1768; his family had grown vines on the plain to the east of Beaune since the 16th century. Jean's son was the first in a long line of Louis Latours and enlarged the domaine considerably. It was not until the late 19th century that the family added wine brokering to their vine-growing activities.

With an eye to the developing export markets, the third Louis Latour bought the Lamarosse family's NÉGOCIANT business in Beaune's historic Rue des Tonneliers in 1867; this was so successful that in 1891 he was able to buy Ch Corton-Grancey in Aloxe-Corton, one of the earliest purpose-built GRAVITY-FED wineries in the world. With this acquisition came one of the most handsome, and most photographed, houses in the Côte d'Or and some notable vineyards around the hill of Corton to add to the Latour family holdings, which already included some Chambertin, Romanée-St-Vivant, Les Quatre Journaux; and Chevalier-Montrachet, Les Demoiselles. (Today Domaine Louis Latour enjoys the largest single holding of GRAND CRU vineyards on the CÔTE D'OR.) It was the third Louis Latour who is reputed to have realized the hill of Corton's potential for great white wine when he replanted some of the hill now designated Corton-Charlemagne with Chardonnay vines after PHYLLOXERA had laid waste to vineyards originally planted with Pinot Noir and Aligoté.

Innovations of succeeding Louis Latours include a succession of 'new' and increasingly daring white wines. What was then known as Grand Pouilly (and subsequently became

◀ Slinde Vineyard on the northern side of the Sognefjord in western NORWAY is one of Europe's most northerly, at a LATITUDE of 61.2° N. Planted by Bjørn and Halldis Bergum in 2014, these south-facing SOLARIS vines benefit from the mild winters and high SUNLIGHT intensity of the country's deepest and longest fjord. © Bjørn Bergum

known as Pouilly-Fuissé) was introduced to the United States in the 1930s, immediately after the Repeal of PROHIBITION. A wine known as MÂCON-Lugny was introduced as a respectable alternative to Côte d'Or white wines in close co-operation with the Lugny CO-OPERATIVE. Louis Latour also pioneered the planting of Chardonnay vines in the relatively unknown ARDÈCHE in the early 1980s. The firm has 350 ha/965 acres of vines under contract to local growers, whose produce is vinified at Latour's winery in Alba. In the late 1980s, Louis Latour bought land in the Var *département* in PROVENCE, planting the Beurot selection of Pinot Noir to produce gentle red wines sold as Pinot Noir, Domaine de Valmoissine. Louis Latour acquired Chablis producer Simonnet-Febvre in 2003 and Beaujolais producer Henry Fessy in 2008. Continuing their development of Pinot Noir and Chardonnay grown in fringe areas, they more recently acquired land in the Terres Dorées in BEAUJOLAIS and in Auxois midway between Chablis and Dijon.

The house enjoys a solid reputation for its white wines but has in the past incited controversy over its endorsement of PASTEURIZATION of even its finest red wines. They use and sell barrels from their own cooperage.

L

Latour-de-France, small village on brown SCHIST that once guarded the border between France and Spain, and whose name may be a suffix to the appellation Côtes du ROUSSILLON-Villages. It covers Cassagnes, Montner, Estagel, and Planèzes as well as Latour-de-France itself. Wines must be a blend of at least two varieties, with Syrah and Mourvèdre accounting for at least 30% (together or separately) and Grenache Noir, Carignan Noir, and Lladoner Pelut allowed. The main variety should not be more than 70% of the blend. The village is also known for an energetic band of producers of NATURAL WINES.

Latvia, former Soviet republic on the Baltic Sea bordered by LITHUANIA to the south, ESTONIA to the north, and RUSSIA and Belarus to the east. Winegrowing in this far northern country dates to the 14th century, when German crusaders planted vines on a hill in Sabile, a town in what was then Livonia, but died out with the Livonian War in the late 1500s. Several more starts were made, including in the early 1930s, when growing wine grapes in greenhouses became a trend, but the country's modern industry started only in the 21st century, with the restoration of the Sabile vineyard and the start of a GARAGE winemaking movement led by the country's most prominent winegrower Martins Barkans at Abavas. While Latvia has a rich tradition of fruit wines, VITIS VINIFERA is challenging to grow in the climate, with its cold winters, short summers, and wet autumns. Therefore the majority of the estimated 30 ha/74 acres of vines in 2022 are cold-hardy HYBRIDS such as Zilga, a Latvian CROSS, as well as ZWEIGELT, BACCHUS, and RONDO for red wines and SOLARIS and Muscaris (Solaris × Muscat) for whites. Stylistically most wines are semi-sweet, as they were in Soviet times, but the taste for dry wines is growing, as is interest in NATURAL WINE.
R.T.

law is of fundamental importance to the wine sector. It is what requires wine to be made from fresh grapes without the addition of colouring or flavouring. It is what turns a distinctive TERROIR into a CONTROLLED APPELLATIONS. It dictates who can grow, produce, and sell what, where, and how—and of course how much tax they must pay (see TAXATION). It controls what can and cannot be said on labels and in advertising. It is the forum where every major crisis, issue or contest of ideas in wine is eventually played out, from PHYLLOXERA to PROHIBITION to pregnancy warning labels (see LABELLING INFORMATION).

Different countries approach the regulation of wine in different ways according to their histories, legal systems, and the relative importance of wine in their economies. The 27 EU countries share an overarching wine regulation strongly influenced by France's wine laws. It is comparatively prescriptive in approach but also provides the basis for systematic financial support that is not enjoyed by most other wine countries. Elsewhere, wine laws vary considerably but are typically more flexible than those of the EU.

The oldest known set of wine laws are part of the code of Babylonian king HAMMURABI (d. 1750 BCE). Two perennial wine-law questions—ADULTERATION AND FRAUD and public order—are addressed, although the punishments are somewhat stricter than for equivalent infractions today. Law 109, for example, states: 'If a wine merchant has collected a riotous assembly in her house and has not seized those rioters and driven them to the palace, that wine merchant shall be put to death.' Throughout subsequent millennia, where there has been trade in wine there have been laws regulating production, preventing adulteration, controlling consumption, and levying taxes according to the mores of the times.

The modern wine sector has evolved in lockstep with modern wine law. The phylloxera crisis of the mid 19th century precipitated the development of national wine laws within Europe. To address the problem of COUNTERFEIT WINES in the wake of grape shortages, France created a formal legal definition for wine in 1889. It prohibited any product from presenting itself as wine unless it was 'the exclusive product of the fermentation of fresh grapes or the juice of fresh grapes'. Without this protection, wine could have followed another path to become a largely manufactured product.

While there are many older precedents, the legal notion of a nationally regulated system of geographical DELIMITATION for wine is also comparatively modern. France's AOC system was fully formed only in 1935. It established a link we now take for granted between the government, winegrowers, and the place of production. The idea of geographical distinctiveness, of TERROIR, is now virtually inseparable from the system of laws that define and control the places where wine is grown, even if these laws and the ideas they embody differ quite significantly around the world.

Many other factors have influenced the laws governing wine and thus the direction of the wine sector—perhaps none more so than PROHIBITION in the US. The current laws governing the US wine sector are a direct legacy of Prohibition, and some of the country's most successful wine producers today emerged in its aftermath.

Today, law remains a major factor in the development of the wine sector. Concerns about harmful consumption of alcohol have given rise to laws requiring minimum pricing, tax increases, and warning labels in many countries. Lawmakers wrestle with questions thrown up by winemaking techniques never contemplated in past centuries. Debate surrounds the issue of whether or not NATURAL WINE should be legally defined. Governments grapple with the implications of new technological tools such as BLOCKCHAIN that have the potential to transform legal compliance and traceability. There is no doubt that the law will continue to play a major role in mediating the technological and social forces that shape wine in the future. J.P.H.B.

layering, known as *marcottage* in French, is an ancient method of vine PROPAGATION which involves taking a long CANE from one vine and training it down to the soil, then burying a section to normal planting depth but with the end bent up and emerging in a desired position. This is a useful method of filling empty spaces in established vineyards but only if resistant ROOTSTOCKS are not required. Thus layering may be used only in areas without PHYLLOXERA, NEMATODES, and other soil-borne pathogens (such as BOLLINGER's Vieilles Vignes vineyard, the Greek island of SANTORINI, COLARES in Portugal, and much of Australia and Chile). The foster vine may be left connected to the parent or may be separated after it has reached normal size.
B.G.C.

laying down wine is an English expression for holding wine as it undergoes AGEING. Thus most people lay down wine in their (however notional) CELLARS. Considerable quantities of red bordeaux are **laid down** by collectors all over the globe, for example.

Layon, Coteaux du, 1,400 ha/3,400 acres of CHENIN BLANC making generally medium-sweet white (much richer from the best independent vignerons) in the ANJOU district of the LOIRE. TERROIR means everything here, for Coteaux du Layon should be an intense wine made ideally from several *tries* (see TRI) through the vineyard, selecting BOTRYTIZED grapes or, more frequently with CLIMATE CHANGE, those that have begun to raisin on the vine. Yields vary enormously according to the conditions of the vintage but are officially limited to 35 hl/ha for the generic appellation and 30 hl/ha for wines labelled Coteaux du Layon plus the name of one of the villages Beaulieu (-sur-Layon), Faye (d'Anjou), Rablay (-sur-Layon), Rochefort (-sur-Loire), St-Aubin (de Luigné), and St-Lambert (du Lattay), and 25 hl/ha for CHAUME. The stretch that includes the seven village CRUS is spread along both sides of the Layon river for about 20 km/12 miles with most of the best vineyards located on the south-west-facing slopes of the right bank in an extremely narrow strip of sometimes terraced vineyards. Two small areas within this zone produce wines of such quality that they have earned their own appellations, BONNEZEAUX and QUARTS DE CHAUME. On the left bank, flatter, sandier hills also enjoy the botrytis-inducing MESOCLIMATE yet produce lighter expressions. Producers such as Claude Papin of Ch Pierre Bise vinify grapes grown on SLATE, SCHIST, CLAY, and SANDSTONE separately to demonstrate the variation in style and potential longevity. Wines may be sold as DEMI-SEC, MOELLEUX, and, sweetest of all, LIQUOREUX.

After a period in the late 1990s when maximum possible sugar levels were sought at all costs, top growers today such as Philippe Delesvaux, Dom de Juchepie, Emmanuel Ogereau, or Patrick Baudouin tend to pick at 18–23% POTENTIAL ALCOHOL, producing wines with RESIDUAL SUGAR of around 100 g/l, perhaps up to 200 g/l from the finest *tries*, which are sweet but balanced by the naturally high acidity of Chenin Blanc. In favourable vintages, some superb, long-lived wine is produced in this appellation, with the most concentrated, NOBLE ROT-affected wines designated SÉLECTION DE GRAINS NOBLES. Yet a substantial quantity of ordinary just-sweet wine is sold under the name Coteaux du Layon.

See also LOIRE, including map. P. Le.

Lazio, known as Latium in English, is the ancient homeland of the Latins (see ITALY, history), the seat of Italy's government and administration in the capital, Rome (see map under ITALY), and the IGT Lazio covering the entire region. After a decade of decline, Lazio's total vineyard area was 18,323 ha/42,000 acres in 2020 but is now showing signs of recovery. With only 3% of its wine exported and average vineyard holdings of 1.4 ha/3.5 acres, Lazio remains largely a supplier to an undiscerning local market.

Most of Lazio's 27 DOCs are dedicated to the production of white wines, with a provision for reds based on Sangiovese, Montepulciano, and Merlot. These undistinguished DOCs, in combination with a notable absence of viticultural and oenological research centres and a general lack of interest in INDIGENOUS VARIETIES, make for a lacklustre picture. This overshadows the fact that a large part of Lazio's vineyards are on VOLCANIC soils, with the potential to produce high-quality wines.

But there are signs of a renaissance, especially in the triangle of Piglio, Affile, and Olevano Romano, the epicentre of the red CESANESE, which can produce characterful, structured reds. Before PHYLLOXERA struck, this variety was once at least as important in the CASTELLI ROMANI as its whites, while nowadays the historic FRASCATI is shockingly underperforming in this DOC. The same can be said of Est!Est!!Est!!!, which in spite of its name is an insipid drink.

The Cori DOC is one of very few to remain faithful to the local varieties, the white Bellone and the red Nero Buono di Cori grape, while the DOC Aleatico di Gradoli, a sweet DRIED-GRAPE WINE, is on the brink of extinction.

The IGT Lazio has long been the resort for wines made of INTERNATIONAL VARIETIES but did little to increase Lazio's visibility and identity. In a twist of fate, this IGT now offers refuge to a new generation making original wines from indigenous varieties but, perversely, refused under the DOC system as 'atypical'. W.S.

www.vininelazio.com

Le. For anything prefixed 'Le', see under the next letter of the name.

lead, one of the familiar and widely dispersed heavy metals, which occurs naturally in trace amounts in all plants, therefore in grapes and, usually in microgram per litre quantities only, in wines. This ubiquitous element, which has no known biological function in plants or animals, is now known to be a neural toxin of particular danger to children. This has resulted in the reformulation of many products, particularly petroleum products, so as to exclude lead.

History

Lead has been associated with wine since the time of ancient ROME. The Romans recognized that lead not only prevented wines from turning sour (and rescued those that already had) but also made them taste sweeter (see PLINY). What they did not know, however, is that, even when taken in only very small quantities over a long period, lead is a poison.

Its dangers were understood from the end of the 17th century when a German doctor, Eberhard Gockel of Ulm in Württemberg, noticed that the symptoms suffered by some of his wine-drinking patients matched those observed in lead miners. Gradually legislation was passed in Europe banning the use of lead in wine, but the practice continued. At last, in 1820, the campaigner Frederick Accum complained that 'the merchant or dealer who practises this dangerous sophistication, adds the crime of murder to that of fraud'.

Poisoning could result not only from the wilful addition of lead to wine. The Romans heated grape juice in lead vessels in order to produce *sapa*, a sweet concentrate used as a wine additive and in cooking, and even in the 19th century wine BOTTLES were cleaned with lead shot, thereby contaminating the wine.

H.B.

Viticultural aspects

Grapes containing lead may produce wine containing lead. However, two principal sources of lead in grapes are now prohibited: leaded fuels that resulted in exhaust particles settling on both grapes and soil in roadside vineyards; and the insecticide lead arsenate, which had previously contaminated many vineyard soils, especially those with high SOIL ACIDITY. R.E.S.

Lead in modern wine

Most of the traces of lead from grapes are precipitated out with the LEES during winemaking. However, as analytical methods have improved, microgram quantities per litre are likely to be found in most wines.

The equipment used in modern wineries should not result in any lead contamination. The few wines which contained lead in milligram per litre concentrations derived it principally from capsules or FOILS which contained lead, or from lead-crystal DECANTERS. Modern bottles are made of lead-free glass, and lead foils were banned in the US in 1996 and were no longer in use elsewhere by the end of the 20th century. On older wines made before the ban, seepage of wine around the cork can corrode the foil; if the lip of the bottle is not thoroughly cleaned before pouring, the wine may be contaminated by some of the lead salt.

Lengthy storage of wines in lead-crystal decanters provides time for the wine acids to leach some lead from the glass, but keeping a wine in a lead-crystal glass or decanter for the usual period of no more than a few hours is too short for dangerous amounts of lead contamination. One study found a lead concentration of around 5 mg/l in PORT left in a lead-crystal decanter for four months, so that 10 l of it would have to be consumed in a short time for a potentially toxic human intake of lead.

Analyses of thousands of representative samples of wine suggest that the lead content of wines is decreasing in general but in the early 1990s ranged from 0 to 1.26 mg/l, with the average lead content being 0.13 mg/l, values well below any legal maximum. An Australian study found that there was minimal uptake of lead from wine when it was consumed with food. H.B., R.E.S. & J.E.H.

Accum, F., *Treatise on Adulteration of Food, and Culinary Poisons* (1820).
Eisinger, J., 'Early consumer protection legislation: a 17th century law prohibiting lead adulteration of wines', *Interdisciplinary Science Reviews*, 16/1 (1991), 61–8.
Gulson, B. L., et al., 'Contribution of lead in wine to the total dietary intake of lead in humans with and without a meal: a pilot study', *Journal of Wine Research*, 9/1 (1998), 5–14.
Pliny the Elder, *Natural History*, translated by H. Rackham (1945), Book 14.

leaf (*feuille* in French, *Blatt* in German, *foglia* in Italian, *hoja* in Spanish). Vine leaves range in size up to that of a dinner plate but are normally the area of a human hand (100–200 cm^2). Their individual area correlates with shoot VIGOUR and also varies with vine variety (Merlot has large leaves, for example, while Gewürztraminer has small leaves). The vine is a leafy plant with sometimes many hectares of total leaf area per hectare of vineyard. A proportion of these leaves will be shaded and therefore not PHOTOSYNTHETIC. The total leaf and shoot system of a vine is known as the CANOPY.

The green, flat zone of the leaf connected to the stem by the PETIOLE is known as the leaf blade, or lamina. The lamina of a grape leaf expands to nearly its full area in six or more weeks, growing to a shape and form characteristic for each VINE VARIETY. The arrangement of the five lobes, the shape of the 'teeth' at the edge of the leaf, the size and shape of the sinuses, and especially the angle and lengths of the main veins are features that are measured (ampelometry) for vine variety identification by AMPELOGRAPHERS.

Leaf colour is responsive to VINE NUTRITION, becoming yellow all over with deficiencies of nitrogen and SULFUR, or patterned with yellow or red and/or dead zones with most other deficiencies. Similarly, yellow and dead areas on leaves occur with some virus infections and as a result of HERBICIDE contamination, although usually in different patterns. With the onset of autumn, leaf colour changes naturally from green to yellow or red, depending on the vine species and the presence of certain VIRUS DISEASES. See LEAFROLL VIRUS, for example. B.G.C.

leaf aldehydes make wines taste HERBACEOUS.

leaf fall, the process which occurs naturally in autumn, often after the first FROST, which marks the end of the VINE GROWTH CYCLE. Ideally this is some time after HARVEST, so that the vine has been able to build up its reserves of the CARBOHYDRATES important for growth the following spring. See also DEFOLIATION. R.E.S.

leafhoppers, members of the insect family Cicadellidae which can cause both direct and sometimes serious indirect damage to vineyards. In California, both the grape leafhopper, *Erythroneura elegantula*, and the closely related and biologically similar variegated grape leafhopper, *Erythroneura variabilis*, cause damage to grapes. They begin to feed on grapevine foliage as soon as it appears in spring, by sucking out the contents of leaf cells. As injury progresses, heavily damaged leaves lose their green colour and PHOTOSYNTHESIS is much reduced. TABLE GRAPES are spoilt by spots of leafhopper excrement. The damage caused is in direct proportion to the numbers, so when there are 20 or fewer leafhopper nymphs per leaf, no control is required. If there are more, insecticides are used, but leafhoppers also have a number of natural enemies, the most important being a tiny wasp, *Anagrus epos*.

Some other leafhopper pests do not cause direct damage but spread important grape diseases. PIERCE'S DISEASE of the Americas is spread by so-called sharpshooter leafhoppers (subfamily Cicadellinae). The bacteria that cause Pierce's disease inhabit the XYLEM of the plants, and xylem sap-feeders can transmit the bacteria from plant to plant. FLAVESCENCE DORÉE is caused by a PHYTOPLASMA that inhabits the PHLOEM and appears to be transmitted exclusively by the leafhopper *Scaphoideus littoralis*. A.H.P. & R.E.S.

Bettiga, L. J. (ed.), *Grape Pest Management* (3rd edn, 2013).

leaf removal, vineyard practice aimed at helping to control BOTRYTIS BUNCH ROT and other BUNCH ROTS and at improving GRAPE COMPOSITION and therefore wine quality. Typically the leaves are removed around the bunches to increase exposure to the sun and wind. The bunches dry out more quickly after dew and rain so that moulds are less likely to develop. Further, increased exposure to SUNLIGHT, especially to ULTRAVIOLET RADIATION, helps the berries produce more of the PHENOLICS and FLAVOUR COMPOUNDS important in wine quality. The optimal time is when berries are pea-sized, according to studies by Deloire. Grape SUGARS are also increased and MALIC ACID and METHOXYPYRAZINES are reduced, all of which contribute to improved wine quality. Leaf removal is also used to improve the colour of black and red TABLE GRAPES.

In Europe it is common to remove leaves nearer to the time of harvest, primarily to reduce the risk of botrytis bunch rot. Studies by Poni in Italy have shown that removal of lower, mature leaves on the shoot by the time of flowering reduces fruit set or berries per bunch. As a result, the bunches are looser, with less berry-to-berry contact, and are therefore less prone to botrytis bunch rot. Sugar and ANTHOCYANIN levels were also found to be higher. The leaves adjacent to the bunches are important suppliers of CARBOHYDRATES by photosynthesis, so removal may have negative effects on bunch development and RIPENING.

Excessive leaf removal in warm to hot climates can have negative effects on fruit composition (see SUNBURN) because the bunches are heated by the sun to temperatures up to 15 °C/27 °F above air temperature, and consideration must also be given to the increasing incidence of HEATWAVES. The alternative is to do less removal on the western side of the canopy to avoid exposure when daily temperatures are at their highest in the afternoon.

Traditionally leaf removal has been done by hand, requiring about 50 hours of LABOUR per hectare (2.5 acres), but machines which take less than five hours per hectare to remove leaves by suction and/or cutting have been developed, and manual leaf removal can often be excessive unless labour is well supervised.

Decreasing dependence on AGROCHEMICALS in the vineyard has led to renewed interest in leaf removal. As well as making the fruit less prone to FUNGAL DISEASES by improving aeration, leaf removal can also increase the effectiveness of such chemicals as may be applied to protect the fruit. R.E.S.

Deloire, A., et al., 'Berry primary and secondary metabolites in response to sunlight and temperature in the grapevine fruit zone', *IVES Technical Reviews* (2020).
Poni, S. L., et al., 'Effects of early defoliation on shoot photosynthesis, yield components, and grape composition', *American Journal of Enology and Viticulture*, 57/4 (2006), 397–407.
Smart, R. E., and Robinson, M., *Sunlight into Wine* (1991).

leafrollers. See MOTHS.

leafroll virus, virus disease that is widespread in all countries where grapes are grown. The disease is now thought to be due to a complex of ten different filamentous viruses referred to as grapevine leafroll associated viruses (GLRaVs). Of all the VIRUS DISEASES of vines, it can have the most serious effects on wine quality. These dramatic effects are not understood by the many appreciative TOURISTS in wine regions who marvel at the attractive autumnal red colours of vineyards. Few realize that these colours often indicate the presence of a serious disease, although other factors may also contribute to autumnal colours. Leafroll virus causes YIELD to be reduced by as much as 50%. Wine quality is also affected because of delayed RIPENING. Thus wines from infected vines are lower in alcohol, colour, flavour, and body. The disease does not kill vines, so they are infrequently removed, yet removal is the only known treatment.

Characteristic symptoms are downwards and backwards rolling of the leaf blade in autumn. The area between the leaf veins turns red for black-fruited varieties and, less obviously, yellow for white-fruited varieties. Some varieties such as Cabernet Franc and Chardonnay show the classic symptoms; others such as Riesling and most ROOTSTOCKS show no symptoms at all. Infected vines may be stunted, but this is hardly sufficient for diagnosis.

Leafroll probably originated in the Near East along with VITIS VINIFERA and was carried along with grape CUTTINGS. The disease is spread chiefly by humans, using cuttings or buds from infected vines. Cuttings for BUDWOOD are taken when the vines are dormant and no leaves are present to show symptoms, making it impossible to distinguish healthy from infected plants. Once infected planting material is used, then the new vineyard is immediately infected and will perform at below its potential for its lifetime.

As GRAFTING on to PHYLLOXERA-resistant rootstocks has become more commonplace, this virus disease, like many others, has become more widespread because grafting increases the chances of using infected material. Thus, many OLD WORLD vineyards planted early in the 1900s show the virus. Some tasters believed that grafting to phylloxera-resistant rootstocks from the 1880s onwards led directly to a decline in wine quality. In fact this supposed drop in quality may have been an effect of the increased spread of leafroll virus due to grafting.

Of recent concern are reports of the natural spread of GLRaV, especially strain 3, beginning in South Africa in 1985 and subsequently to Spain, Italy, Australia, California, and New Zealand. This strain can have significant effects on YIELD and GRAPE composition. MEALYBUGS and soft scale have been shown to be vectors. Successful management programmes have been introduced in South Africa, New Zealand, and California involving removing affected vines, control of vectors, and replanting with disease-free vines. Since disease symptoms are harder to detect on white wine grape varieties, CHIP BUDDING a dark-skinned grape variety (preferably Cabernet Franc) on the trunk of the white vine can reveal the virus.

Because there is no control for this disease, growers should ensure that they plant only material that is tested free of the virus. The University of California at DAVIS led the world in developing a 'clean stock' programme, now known as FOUNDATION PLANT SERVICES, with the result that vineyards planted in California since the early 1960s are generally virus free. In addition, this virus-tested planting stock has been exported; for example, many of the vineyards of Australia and New Zealand are planted with such material. The virus is detected by INDEXING, or by using faster and more reliable methods such as immunoassays (see ELISA) or nucleic acid-based RT-PCR. Healthy planting material is produced by eliminating viruses using THERMOTHERAPY or heat treatment or, more reliably, by TISSUE CULTURE. Propagation is recommended from these 'clean' mother plants. R.E.S.

Almeida, R. P. P., et al., 'Ecology and management of grapevine leafroll disease', *Frontiers in Microbiology*, 4 (2013).

Bettiga, L. J., (ed.), *Grape Pest Management* (3rd edn, 2013).

Cieniewicz, E., and Fuchs, M. F., 'Grape leafroll disease', Cornell University IPM factsheet. www.ecommons.cornell.edu/handle/1813/43103.

leaf to fruit ratio, viticultural measurement which indicates the capacity of a vine to ripen grapes. The ratio of vine leaf area to fruit (grape) weight determines just how well a vine can mature grapes and how suitable they will be for winemaking. Although it is less understood and discussed, it can have an even more important effect on wine quality than YIELD, although it is the latter that is highly regulated in most European CONTROLLED APPELLATIONS and frequently discussed by OENOLOGISTS and WINE WRITERS.

This ratio indicates the vine's ability to manufacture compounds important for grape RIPENING. If most leaves are exposed to the sun, then the leaf area is generally proportional to the ability of the vine to make SUGARS by PHOTOSYNTHESIS. Against this should be set the weight of grapes to be ripened.

A low value of leaf to fruit ratio, for example 5 sq cm per g grape weight, indicates that the fruit will ripen sluggishly, and so levels of SUGAR IN GRAPES will increase slowly along with PHENOLICS and FLAVOUR, but PH will be relatively high for the corresponding sugar level. The other extreme of, say, 30 sq cm per g grape weight suggests a very leafy vine with a small crop of grapes, but one which will ripen quickly and completely and so produce better wine quality than for the low leaf to fruit ratio. Such low yields, however, may be uneconomic, and so most vine-growers would aim to manage their vineyards with a sufficient but not excessive leaf to fruit ratio (see vine BALANCE). A value of between 10 and 15 sq cm per g grape weight is considered adequate for ripening of most vine varieties, although higher values are considered necessary by some for PINOT NOIR and perhaps MERLOT. Also, high leaf to fruit ratios must be carefully managed in the vineyard in order to avoid any negative effects on wine quality due to canopy SHADE. R.E.S.

Kliewer, W. M., and Dokoozlian, N. K., 'Leaf area/crop weight ratios of grapevines: influence on fruit composition and wine quality', *American Journal of Enology and Viticulture*, 56/2 (2005), 170–81.

Martínez de Toda, F., and Balda, P., 'Delaying berry ripening through manipulating leaf area to fruit ratio', *Vitis* 52/4 (2013), 171–6.

leafy, tasting term usually used synonymously with HERBACEOUS.

Leányka, meaning 'maiden', widely planted Hungarian white wine grape identified by DNA PROFILING as Romania's FETEASCĂ Albă. Varietal Leányka has long been produced in EGER and neighbouring Bükk and Mátra. Total plantings were a declining 604 ha/1,493 acres in 2020. It may be a parent of KIRÁLYLEÁNYKA (see FETEASCĂ Regală). For more details, see HUNGARY.

Lebanon, one of the oldest sites of wine production, incorporating some of the ancient eastern Mediterranean land of CANAAN and, subsequently, most of PHOENICIA, whose people were arguably the first to treat wine as a tradable commodity (see ORIGINS OF VINICULTURE). In Baalbek—the ancient Greek, and then Roman, city in the Bekaa Valley which is the vine-growing centre of Lebanon—is the temple of BACCHUS, built in the middle of the 2nd century.

In the Middle Ages, the rich wines of Tyre and Sidon were particularly treasured in Europe and were traded by the merchants of VENICE, to whom these ports belonged for much of the 13th century. In 1517, what is now Lebanon was absorbed into the Ottoman Empire and winemaking was forbidden, except for religious purposes, allowing Lebanon's Christians, mainly Maronites and Greek and Armenian Orthodox, to perpetuate a tradition of viniculture. In 1857, the Jesuit missionaries of Ksara introduced new vine varieties—mainly CINSAUT and CARIGNAN with some Grenache and Ugni Blanc—and production methods from French-governed Algeria, laying the foundations of the modern Lebanese wine industry.

The French administration that governed Lebanon between the wars created unprecedented demand for wine, while Lebanon's post-independence role as a cosmopolitan financial hub allowed the new wine culture to take hold. It lasted until 1975 when the country descended into a 15-year civil war. Although just two harvests were lost to the fighting, only Ch Musar, which recognized the need to penetrate new markets if it was to survive, genuinely thrived during this turbulent period, establishing an enduring fan base in the UK.

With peace came growth. The success of Ch Kefraya, which began producing wine in 1978 after decades of supplying grapes to other producers, and the popularity of NEW WORLD wines galvanized Lebanon's few established wineries and inspired a new generation, many of whom were producers of arak, the aniseed-flavoured eau-de-vie that is the country's national drink,

L

to exploit the potential of the Bekaa Valley's formidable TERROIR.

In the quarter-century since the mid 1990s, the number of wineries has increased from five to nearly 50. In 2020, total production was estimated to be 9 million bottles from 2,000 ha/ 5,000 acres of vines dedicated to wine production. In 2013, a National Wine Institute, a public/private body, was officially established with a view, inter alia, to creating a system inspired by France's AOC. In its first eight years it achieved next to nothing, but the election of a new board at the end of 2021 offered some hope that the institute might be given the funding and the latitude to execute its mandate. Meanwhile, the Union Vinicole du Liban (UVL), a loose association of leading producers, remains a credible and effective organization.

The Bekaa Valley is the epicentre of the wine industry. The majority of the vineyards are in the Western Bekaa, Zahlé, and more recently the drier regions of Baalbek and Hermel. More a plateau than a valley, and sitting at an ELEVATION of around 1,000 m/3,280 ft between the Lebanon and Anti-Lebanon mountain ranges, the Bekaa enjoys dry summers, cool nights, and consistent rainfall so that the grapes rarely ripen before the middle of September. Minimal vineyard treatments are needed, and almost half of all vines for wine production are trained on WIRES, although the sprawling and vigorous GOBELET form is still widely used, offering SHADE in a region with little risk of POWDERY MILDEW. Average yields are around 5 tonnes/ha.

Other regions are emerging. Home to eight producers, the northern district of Batroun has a MESOCLIMATE that allows it to produce wines at an elevation which would be otherwise too low in a hot country like Lebanon: its hills and valleys create a wind corridor, funnelling cooling clouds from the Mediterranean on an almost daily basis in summer. The vineyards of the west, sea-facing Mount Lebanon, the Chouf, and Jezzine in south Lebanon have different TERROIRS and have contributed to expanding Lebanon's variety of styles, often by planting varieties such as ALBARIÑO, TOURIGA NACIONAL, and SAPERAVI, not found in the Bekaa.

French influence on the country is still apparent in the grape varieties most commonly planted and the wines made. Ch Musar remains Lebanon's most celebrated producer, its top wine a gamey blend of Cabernet Sauvignon, Carignan, and Cinsaut. It has been both fêted as a work of genius and dismissed as an anachronism, flawed with excessive VOLATILE ACIDITY and hype, but its fans are legion. Influenced by a close relationship with the BARTONS of Bordeaux in the early 1960s, the Hochars introduced DESTEMMING and BARREL AGEING in new French OAK.

But styles are changing. Faouzi Issa at Domaine des Tourelles has led a movement to champion Lebanon's so-called heritage varieties, Cinsault and Carignan, as well as OBEIDEH and MERWAH. At Ch Kefraya, whose Cabernet–Syrah blend Comte de M 1996 convinced the outside world that there was more to Lebanese wine than Ch Musar, there is now Saperavi made in AMPHORA, as well as a blend of Assouad Karech and Asmi Assouad, two local varieties 'rediscovered' by Kefraya's winemaker Fabrice Guiberteau.

Even Ch Ksara, Lebanon's biggest producer, responsible for more than one-third of all the wine sold in Lebanon, has been gradually shedding its reputation for classic French blends such as its 'Chateau' wine, a MÉDOC tribute act that debuted in 1921, introducing VARIETAL bottlings of Merwah and OLD VINE Carignan.

In total, around 40 varieties are grown in Lebanon, including a parcel of the little-known French variety ARINARNOA and the local white-wine variety Meksassi.

High-elevation Lebanese whites, once an afterthought, are now being taken seriously. In addition to Chardonnay, Sauvignon Blanc, and to a lesser extent Viognier, the increasingly popular INDIGENOUS VARIETIES Obeideh and Merwah (or Merweh) are demanding long-overdue respect in both varietal wines and blends.

Both Sept, a microwinery from the tiny village of Nehla in the Batroun region, and the equally bijou Vertical 33, perched on an east-facing mountain overlooking the Bekaa Valley, have championed indigenous and 'heritage' grape varieties, while Sept's owner, Maher Harb, made an even more avant-garde statement with Lebanon's first SKIN-FERMENTED Obeideh. M.R.K.

Heskett, R., and Butler, J., *Divine Vintage: Following the Wine Trail from Genesis to the Modern Age* (2012).

Karam, M. (ed) *Tears of Bacchus: A History of Winemaking in the Arab World* (2020).

www.winesoflebanon.co.uk

Lébrija, a VINO DE CALIDAD in Andalucía in southern Spain promoted by the González Palacio family. While their vineyard is in the JEREZ cultivation area, it does not fall within the ageing area, so they cannot use terms such as MANZANILLA even though the wines are made in the image of SHERRY. F.C.

lees, old English word for the dregs or sediment that settles at the bottom of a container such as a FERMENTATION VESSEL. Wine lees are made up of dead YEAST cells, the cell membranes of pulp, stem and skin fragments, and insoluble salts and macromolecules that are deposited during the making and ageing of wine. A distinction is sometimes made between **fine lees** and **gross lees**, the latter comprising mainly the yeast cells, both dead and viable, plus cellular matter from the grape.

In the production of everyday wines, clear wine is separated from the lees as soon as possible after FERMENTATION and quickly clarified and stabilized (see CLARIFICATION and STABILIZATION). Some wines, especially white, may be deliberately left on their lees for some months in order to benefit from lees AUTOLYSIS. This is called LEES CONTACT.

Fine wines left on lees for a considerable time usually require much less drastic processing than more ordinary wines that were separated early from the lees, because autolysis releases MANNOPROTEINS from the lees, and these naturally stabilize wines by inhibiting the crystallization of TARTRATES and encouraging the precipitation of PROTEINS.

Deposits of FINING agents used in clarification such as BENTONITE and CASEIN are also referred to as lees. They are usually simply settled to permit the recovery of as much wine as possible but in some large wineries are processed by ROTARY DRUM VACUUM FILTRATION to salvage a bit more wine with a strong lees flavour.

Once the maximum amount of good wine has been recovered, usually by RACKING after prolonged SETTLING, the lees may be used to remove any unwanted colour from wines such as champagne. The lees are also valuable for their potassium acid tartrate (cream of tartar) and small amounts of alcohol. Other methods of lees disposal need to ensure they minimize the environmental impact of organic WINERY WASTE. V.L.

lees contact, increasingly popular and currently fashionable winemaking practice known to the ancient Romans (see CATO) whereby newly fermented wine is deliberately left in contact with the LEES. This period of lees contact may take place in any container, from a bottle (as in the making of any BOTTLE FERMENTED sparkling wine where yeast AUTOLYSIS produces desirable flavour compounds) to a large tank or vat—although a small oak BARREL is the most common location for lees contact. It may take place for anything between a few weeks and, in the special case of some sparkling wines, several years (see SPARKLING WINEMAKING). Most commonly, however, lees contact is prolonged for less than a year after the completion of FERMENTATION.

Lees contact encourages MALOLACTIC CONVERSION because the LACTIC ACID BACTERIA necessary for malolactic conversion feed on micronutrients in the lees. This has the effect of adding complexity to the resultant wine's flavour. Many producers, particularly those of white BURGUNDY and other wines based on CHARDONNAY grapes, try to increase the influence of the lees on flavour by LEES STIRRING. Both lees contact and lees stirring also enhance the structure and MOUTHFEEL of a wine since some molecules released from the dead yeast cells by autolysis can significantly reduce astringency and increase body.

The results of lees ageing on Chardonnay in barrel have been summarized by Gambetta et al.: yeast lees contribute to floral and fruity aromas, but overall they reduce the ESTER content of the wine and release polysaccharides (mainly MANNOPROTEINS) into the wine; the lees adsorb both positive ester-derived aromas but also negative off-odours (MERCAPTANS); they attenuate the impact of wood from the barrel; and they create an overall REDUCTIVE environment that protects the wine from OXIDATION. Lees contact also naturally improves the PROTEIN and TARTRATE stability of wines.

White wines made with deliberate lees contact are sometimes described as SUR LIE, a description commonly used to differentiate one type of MUSCADET from another, although in this case small barrels rarely play a part in the process. Lees contact even in BULK STORAGE is increasingly used as a way of increasing and stabilizing flavour in everyday white wines.

Red wines, with their more robust flavours, gain less obvious benefit from lees contact not least because the lees include much more vegetal matter and fewer yeast cells. Neverthless, there is a growing trend to leave red wine on the lees even though it increases the risk of BRETTANOMYCES. Ageing red wines on lees has been shown to reduce BITTERNESS and ASTRINGENCY and give roundness and more BODY to red wines (Del Barrio-Galán et al., 2011)—more so than ageing in barrel alone (Fernández et al., 2011). This is due at least in part to the adsorption of condensed TANNINS to yeast lees (Mazauric and Salmon, 2006) or to yeast POLYSACCHARIDES. Ageing on lees has also been shown to improve the colour stability of red wines (Escot et al., 2001).

Wines left in contact with lees in large stainless-steel tanks after fermentation are very likely to develop HYDROGEN SULFIDE, disulfide, or mercaptan odours. This is why it is important to rack new wine from its gross lees (see LEES), so that the lees level does not become too thick, or to keep the wine separate from the lees for a month, during which time they lose their ability to generate VOLATILE SULFUR COMPOUNDS. V.L.

Del Barrio-Galán, R., et al., 'Techniques for improving or replacing aging on lees of oak aged red wines: the effects on polysaccharides and the phenolic composition', *Food Chemistry*, 127/2 (2011), 528–40.

Escot, S., et al., 'Release of polysaccharides by yeast and the influence of released polysaccharides on color stability and wine astringency', *Australian Journal of Grape and Wine Research*, 7/3 (2001), 153–9.

Fernández, O., et al., 'Effect of the presence of lysated lees on polysaccharides, color and main phenolic compounds of red wine during barrel ageing', *Food Research International*, 44/1 (2011), 84–91.

Gambetta, J. M., et al., 'Factors influencing the aroma composition of Chardonnay wines', *Journal of Agricultural Food Chemistry*, 62/28 (2014), 6512–34.

Lavigne-Cruège, V., and Dubourdieu, D., 'Demonstration and interpretation of the yeast lees ability to adsorb certain volatile thiols contained in wine', *Journal International des Sciences de la Vigne et du Vin*, 30/4 (1996).

Mazauric, J. P., and Salmon, J. M., 'Interactions between yeast lees and wine polyphenols during simulation of wine aging: II. Analysis of desorbed polyphenol compounds from yeast lees', *Journal of Agricultural and Food Chemistry* 54/11 (2006), 3876–81.

lees stirring, *bâtonnage* in French, is the winemaking operation of mixing up the LEES in a barrel, cask, tank, or vat with the wine resting on them. It is an optional addition to the process of LEES CONTACT and is often employed, particularly for whites which have undergone BARREL FERMENTATION. As the French name suggests, such stirring is usually done with a stick, although some racking systems allow the barrel itself to be rotated *in situ*.

Lees stirring is done partly to avoid the development of malodorous sulfur compounds by homogenizing the REDOX POTENTIAL in the upper and lower parts of the barrel. This prevents the formation of HYDROGEN SULFIDE in the lees (see LEES CONTACT).

Stirring up the lees in the barrel also affects OAK FLAVOUR, however. If the lees are stirred, they act as a buffer between the wine and the wood because their cell walls adsorb compounds extracted from the wood such as TANNINS and PIGMENTS. Wines subjected to lees stirring therefore tend to be much paler and less tannic than those whose lees are not stirred.

Regular lees stirring also stimulates the release of MANNOPROTEINS, thereby improving the stability of the wine. Some producers believe that the technique makes the wine heavier and that over-zealous stirring may increase the risk of PREMATURE OXIDATION, but stirring actually helps the lees consume any dissolved oxygen in the wine, reducing the risk of oxidation. V.L.

left bank, an expression for the BORDEAUX wine regions that are on the left bank of the rivers GARONNE and GIRONDE. It includes all the MÉDOC appellations, including MARGAUX, PAUILLAC, ST-ESTEPHE, and ST-JULIEN, as well as GRAVES, CÉRONS, SAUTERNES, BARSAC, and PESSAC-LÉOGNAN. The most obvious characteristic shared by the red wines of these appellations, as distinct from RIGHT BANK appellations, is that the dominant grape variety is Cabernet Sauvignon rather than Merlot and Cabernet Franc.

leftover wine in an opened container such as a half-empty bottle is prey to OXIDATION, and steps must be taken in order to prevent it turning to VINEGAR—which could happen within hours or even minutes for a very old wine, within two or three days for most young table wines and most bottle-matured PORT, within a few weeks for a robust wood-matured port such as a tawny, or OLOROSO sherry, or within months, possibly years, for most MADEIRA.

Because OXYGEN is the villain in this piece, the easiest way to avoid spoilage of leftover wine is to decant it into a smaller container, perhaps a half-bottle, which approximates as closely as possible to the volume of wine left. There are also patent devices for filling the ULLAGE in a bottle or decanter with INERT GAS, by pumping or spraying, or an attempt can be made to create a vacuum with a pump device. Some drop small, inert objects such as spheres of glass into an opened bottle to restore the fill level to the bottleneck. Leftover wine, no matter what the container or colour, is best stored cool to slow the reactions involved in its deterioration.

The most satisfactory way of disposing of wine leftovers is surely to drink them, and the leftovers of some wines, particularly concentrated young red wines, can taste better, and certainly softer, after a day or even two on ullage (see AERATION and DECANTING).

Leftover wine can also be used quite satisfactorily as COOKING wine or to make vinegar.

legno riccio, Italian name for the RUGOSE WOOD complex of vine VIRUS DISEASES.

legs, outmoded tasting term and alternative name for the TEARS left on the inside of a glass by some wines.

legumes, a common component of vineyard COVER CROPS due to their ability to fix atmospheric NITROGEN into the soil. Legumes are members of the Leguminosae family and include clovers, trefoils, lucerne, lupins, and medics. R.E.S.

Leithaberg, wine region in AUSTRIA covering 2,878 ha/7,112 acres in 2021. It is named for the predominantly LIMESTONE and SCHIST Leitha Hills (the Leithagebirge) that, prior to the creation of BURGENLAND, formed the Austro-Hungarian border and that extend to the western and northern fringes of the NEUSIEDLERSEE. The Leithaberg DAC applies to wines from what was formerly known as the Neusiedlersee-Hügelland growing region, including red and dry whites grown in Rust (which has its own DAC, RUSTER AUSBRUCH, for sweet wine). Leithaberg DAC reds must be at least 85% BLAUFRÄNKISCH—a grape variety that represented 21% of the region's vineyard surface area in 2021—together with any combination of Pinot Noir,

ST-LAURENT, and/or ZWEIGELT. They must be OAK-AGED and not released before September of the second year following harvest. Whites may comprise any combination of Pinot Blanc, Chardonnay, GRÜNER VELTLINER, and/or NEUBURGER. The region's non-DAC wines are labelled for their state of origin, Burgenland.

Burgenland's state capital, Eisenstadt, and several of its hillside suburbs—Müllendorf, Grosshöflein, and St Georgen in particular—are home to outstanding reds and whites which benefit from CALCAREOUS soils and prevailing breezes. East of Eisenstadt, Schützen-am-Gebirge reflects a transition to soils based on weathered GNEISS and mica SCHIST, outstanding for Blaufränkisch but also supportive of white varieties, which dominate the next village north, Donnerskirchen, where even RIESLING flourishes on an especially high stretch of hills. Closer to the Neusiedlersee and running north–south, Breitenbrunn, Purbach, and Oggau also distinguish themselves. Although Rust is famous for sweet whites, it is also where modern appreciation of VARIETAL Blaufränkisch arguably began, with Ernst 'ET' Triebaumer's 1986 Mariental bottling. Möbisch, on Lake Neusiedl immediately south of Rust, St Margarethen, Siegendorf, and Zagersdorf—more or less midway between the lake and the Leitha range—are worth noting for reds from Blaufränkisch and St-Laurent as well as for both dry and sweet whites. D.S.

Lemberger, also known as **Blauer Lemberger** and occasionally **Limberger**, is the German name for the black grape variety much more widely grown in Austria as BLAUFRÄNKISCH and in Hungary as KÉKFRANKOS. Germany has very much less of the variety planted, but like all red varieties it has steadily become more popular so that by 2020 there were 11,940 ha/4,794 acres in all, mostly in Württemberg, where it is so successful that it may carry the GROSSES GEWÄCHS designation.

Lemberger once had a limited following in WASHINGTON State, but plantings had fallen to 22 ha/54 acres in 2017.

Len de l'El, also spelled **Len de l'Elh**, a primary but not necessarily major ingredient in the white wines, especially the sweet ones, of GAILLAC. Its name is local dialect for *loin de l'œil*, or 'far from sight'. This vigorous vine needs a well-ventilated, well-drained site if it is to escape ROT in lesser years. All but three of France's 626 ha/1,547 acres in 2019 were in Gaillac country.

length or persistence of flavour is an important indicator of wine quality. See the tasting term LONG.

Lenz Moser, a TRAINING SYSTEM developed in Austria in the 1920s by Dr Lenz Moser III. It employs wider rows (about 3.5 m/11.5 ft) and higher trunks (1.3 m) than had previously been the norm, thereby reducing VINE DENSITY. Lenz Moser's ideas influenced Professor Nelson SHAULIS, who developed the GENEVA DOUBLE CURTAIN.

The Lenz Moser system found favour in parts of Europe in the mid 20th century because it decreases LABOUR and therefore production costs, without any need for special machinery. French and German studies found reductions in fruit quality, however, probably because of SHADE in the fruit zone, and it is now less common even in Austria. It is also known as high culture, or *Hochkultur* in German. The name is probably more familiar as that of one of the biggest wine producers in Austria, with operations as far afield as China. R.E.S.

León, promising DOP created in 2008, encompassing some 1,465 ha/3,515 acres of vineyards south of the BIERZO appellation in north-west SPAIN on well-drained, LIMESTONE-based ALLUVIAL terraces. This is the birthplace of the red PRIETO PICUDO grape and shares with Asturias the white Albarín, so that its wines are quite different from those of its neighbours that are dominated by Tempranillo and Mencía. V. de la S. & F.C.

Léon Millot, minor French HYBRID producing small quantities of dark-red wine in northern Europe and North America, where its early ripening is valued.

Le Pin. This micro-estate in POMEROL originally consisted of just one hectare of vines on a gentle, south-facing slope of GRAVEL and SAND, with deep CLAY subsoils. It was bought for a million French francs in 1979 by three members of the Thienpont family, Belgian NÉGOCIANTS who also own nearby Vieux Château Certan in Pomerol and properties in the FRANCS Côte de Bordeaux. The vineyard had previously been farmed by a grower in Lalande-de-Pomerol *en* MÉTAYAGE, and its produce had for years been vinified there and sold as Le Pin, but not as a CHÂTEAU BOTTLED wine. When the Thienponts bought it, one-third of the vines were only a year old. The first commercial vintage was 1979, and until the mid 1980s the wine was quite a hard sell. Jacques Thienpont, who commuted between Belgium and Bordeaux, managed to buy out his two co-investors in 1988 and, by adding a further 1.5 ha in three contiguous plots, now owns and manages the grand total of about 2.5 ha/6 acres, all Merlot. The wine was always distinctive, deep, and luscious with an almost Burgundian richness, absolutely in tune with the FASHION for early-maturing, sensual wines. Le Pin was the first red bordeaux to have its MALOLACTIC CONVERSION completed in 100% new oak barrels (no great investment when the total production of the property averaged 600 cases). Demand for this rarity escalated towards the end of the 1980s, and the price of the fashionable 1982 vintage reached a peak of £2,500 a bottle in 1997, just before the ASIAN boom began to falter. Le Pin's success inspired the rash of new, small, luxury RIGHT BANK estates (see GARAGE WINES). In 2011 a new winery designed by Belgian architects Robbrecht en Daem was inaugurated. In 2010 Jacques Thienpont bought 8 ha/20 acres of ST-ÉMILION grand cru vineyard, the former Ch Haut-Plantey, renamed L'If (the French word for a yew tree, another conifer). The cellars are located next door to Ch Troplong Mondot (incidentally also owned by the Thienpont family between 1921 and 1933). A third estate, L'Hêtre (French for 'beech tree') in CASTILLON, was added to the portfolio in 2016.

Leroy, famous name in French wine, not just because **Baron le Roy** of CHÂTEAUNEUF-DU-PAPE was instrumental in the development of the AOC system, but also in the CÔTE D'OR. The NÉGOCIANT house **Maison Leroy** was founded in the small village of Auxey-Duresses in 1868, and its extensive warehouses there still house substantial stocks of fine, mature burgundy. Henri Leroy joined the family firm in 1919 and made his fortune exporting fortified wine from the Charentes to Germany between the two World Wars. This enabled him to buy a half-share in the world-famous DOMAINE DE LA ROMANÉE-CONTI (DRC), a holding inherited equally by his two daughters Pauline Roch-Leroy and **Lalou Bize-Leroy** on his death in 1980.

Lalou, a prodigious taster, avid rock climber, and glamorous dresser, had been co-director of the Domaine since 1974 and contributed considerably to its winemaking policy of quality above all. She also ran Maison Leroy, but Burgundy's steady move towards DOMAINE BOTTLING made her job of buying the finest raw materials for her négociant skills of ÉLEVAGE increasingly difficult. In 1988, helped by an £8 million investment from her Japanese importers Takashimaya, she succeeded in buying the Domaine Noëllat of VOSNE-ROMANÉE, an already fine canvas on which to paint her vision of the perfect domaine, soon renamed **Domaine Leroy**. This domaine now comprises 22 ha/54 acres of some of the Côte d'Or's finest vineyards, including a total of nearly 7 ha in nine different GRANDS CRUS.

This effectively entailed setting up in competition with DRC, since the Domaine Leroy is based in the same village and, like DRC, has holdings in the grand crus ROMANÉE-ST-VIVANT and RICHEBOURG. Unfettered by the commercial considerations of the dozen or so shareholders in DRC, Lalou was able to institute fully BIODYNAMIC VITICULTURE, almost uneconomically low YIELDS, and every possible winemaking luxury. The wines, which come from a much broader range of (mainly red-wine) appellations than those of DRC, are extremely concentrated, expressing as definitively as possible their exact geographical provenance.

Lalou also owns the Domaine d'Auvenay, another biodynamically farmed enterprise founded in 1988, with total holdings of around 4 ha in 80 PARCELS, including small plots in five different grands crus.

A sales company, **Société Leroy**, enjoyed the exclusive distribution rights to DRC wines, some of the most highly priced in the world, in all markets except the US and UK until a bitter dispute in 1992 which ousted Lalou from co-directorship of DRC. Today, only Domaine Leroy prices rival those of DRC.

Lalou's daughter Perrine Fenal is now co-director of the Domaine de la Romanée-Conti.

Les Aspres became part of Côtes du ROUSSILLON-Villages in 2017. Covering 19 villages in the Eastern Pyrenees, the AOC is devoted exclusively to red wines blended from at least three of the four allowed grape varieties (Syrah, Mourvèdre, Grenache, Carignan) and aged at least 12 months. R.E.G.

Les Baux de Provence. A spectacular and famous small hilltop settlement in the far west of PROVENCE dominated by Michelin-starred restaurants and their customers' cars gives its name to a local AOC created in 1995 and substantially amended since. The AOC's 232 ha/573 acres sit mainly on LIMESTONE rubble from the craggy Alpilles chain, and it is slightly warmer and wetter than much of the Coteaux d' AIX-EN-PROVENCE AOC, from which it was ceded. Red wines are made from Grenache, Syrah, and Mourvèdre, which must together make up at least 60% of the blend, together with Cinsaut, Counoise, Carignan, and Cabernet Sauvignon (the last of which must represent no more than 20% of the total, thus forcing the respected Domaine de Trévallon to use the IGP denomination ALPILLES). Cinsaut takes the place of Mourvèdre in the rosés, which make up about two-fifths of the appellation. Clairette, Grenache Blanc, and Vermentino are the principal grapes for the white version although Marsanne, Roussanne, Bourboulenc, and Ugni Blanc may be included in the blend. The region prides itself on its high percentage of winegrowers practising ORGANIC and BIODYNAMIC VITICULTURE, even having (unsuccessfully) petitioned the INAO to require organic viticulture in the appellation regulations. The mistral wind helps to keep the vines healthy. E.A.G.

Lesotho. One hectare (2.5 acres) of mainly Chenin Blanc with some Pinotage was planted in 2008 in this land-locked country surrounded by SOUTH AFRICA at an ELEVATION of 1,791 m/5,876 ft some 25 km/15.5 miles east of Maseru, with guidance from the South African winery Groot Parys 1,100 km/685 miles to the south. Challenges include spring HAIL, summer rain, and scarcity of electricity and water, but by 2022 the Thamea family had doubled the size of the vineyard and was distributing wines under the Sani Wines label. Other Lesotho wineries import South African fruit for their wines.

Lesquerde, far western communal appellation of Côtes du ROUSSILLON-Villages in a mountain enclave dominated by GRANITE. Carignan, Grenache, and Syrah provide the backbone of these concentrated reds. R.E.G.

Lessona, tiny historical and increasingly important red wine DOC in the Vercelli Hills in the subalpine north of the PIEMONTE region of north-west Italy. On just 17 ha/42 acres a growing number of producers make a wine from NEBBIOLO grapes (here called SPANNA), optionally softened with some UVA RARA or VESPOLINA from vineyards on yellow SANDS of marine origin. The Sella estate was established way back in 1671. In 1999 Paolo De Marchi, former owner of Isole e Olena in Chianti Classico, revitalized his family estate, Villa Sperino, inspiring others to follow, including a new generation of winegrowers who have started buying land here. W.S.

L'Étoile, small appellation in the JURA region of eastern France which specializes in traditional, OXIDATIVE white wines aged in non-topped-up barrels. These are often pure Chardonnay but may be Chardonnay blended with the local SAVAGNIN grape. From the 2010s there has been an increasing number of *ouillé* (topped-up) Chardonnays from these fossil-laden MARL soils. It also produces VIN DE PAILLE, CRÉMANT du Jura, and the extraordinarily nutty VIN JAUNE. W.L.

Leyda, subvalley of San Antonio Valley in CHILE that began to be planted in the late 1990s and is now a reliable source of Sauvignon Blanc, Pinot Noir, and Chardonnay grown under the influence of cool Pacific Ocean breezes. P.T.

Liatiko, ancient Cretan vine that is this Greek island's third most planted, producing relatively soft, light red, usually blended with the stronger MANDILARIA and KOTSIFALI to make sweet wines (exported in great quantity by Venetian merchants in medieval times), and dry reds, sometimes blended with SYRAH. VARIETAL wines are typically pale and quickly lose their colour intensity with age. There were around 400 ha/988 acres on the island in 2021.

libation, the pouring out of wine (and occasionally other liquids: water, oil, milk, honey) as a religious act is found widely in human societies. The practice of offering a libation to a god was universal in the Greek and Roman world and was an essential element in animal sacrifice. Whenever wine was drunk in formal gatherings, such as SYMPOSIA, a libation was poured while a prayer was said to invoke a chosen god. Libations also regularly accompanied prayers and sacrifices on all sorts of occasions. The origins of the practice are to be found in the offering of the first fruits to gods; but libation should also be seen in the context of the way in which social intercourse between humans (and by analogy between humans and gods) was maintained by the mutual exchange of gifts. Libations poured on the ground were also specifically seen as a gift for the dead. 'The souls are nourished by libations', as Lucian says. J.J.P.

Burkert, W., *Greek Religion* (1985).

Libourne, small port on the RIGHT BANK of the Dordogne in the Bordeaux region. It is now the commercial centre for the right-bank appellations, although it was established in the 13th century, much later than ST-ÉMILION's port Pierrefitte, and was at the time considered a parvenu in comparison with FRONSAC. In modern history, its wine trade is much more recent than the Chartronnais of the BORDEAUX TRADE in the great city across the Garonne, and its more modest traders concentrated initially on selling in northern mainland Europe rather than in the British Isles. Of merchants based here on the banks of the river Dordogne, J. P. MOUEIX is the most important. For more details, see POMEROL, the wine region on the eastern outskirts of the town.

The wines from St-Émilion, Pomerol, and especially Fronsac are sometimes referred to collectively as **Libournais**.

Lichine, Alexis (1913–89), was born in Russia but, unlike André TCHELISTCHEFF, another Russian who was to shape the American wine industry, he and his family left before the Revolution, and he was educated in France.

After the Repeal of PROHIBITION, Lichine sold wines, first in a shop in New York and subsequently for the gifted American wine importer Frank SCHOONMAKER. After the Second World War, in which he served with distinction, he returned to finding French and German wines from individual estates and selling them in an America where wine was all but unknown.

His success in doing this was considerable and came from a flair for seeing and recounting the romantic side of wine and winemaking, as well as appreciating the pleasures wine can bring.

During the 1950s, he became a major figure in the French wine world, setting up his own company, Alexis Lichine & Co., to sell only CHÂTEAU BOTTLED and DOMAINE BOTTLED wines, for the most part from major properties. He sold this company to British brewers Bass-Charrington in 1964 and gradually left the commercial world to make wine and write books. For more detail, see the LITERATURE OF WINE.

Lichine assembled a group of investors to buy and renovate the MARGAUX second-growth Ch Lascombes in 1952 and ran the property with great success before selling it, again to Bass-Charrington, in 1971. He also bought in 1951 the fourth-growth Ch Prieuré at Cantenac just outside Margaux. He officially renamed this property, based on an old Benedictine priory, Ch Prieuré-Lichine in 1953, and it was at this property, typically one of the first to welcome passing visitors, that he died in 1989. His son Sacha ran the property until its sale in 1999 and then created the hugely successful brand WHISPERING ANGEL, a ground-breaking Provençal rosé. W.B. & J.R.

licoroso, Portuguese sweet FORTIFIED WINE (as opposed to a GENEROSO, which may be dry).

lie or **lies**, French for LEES.

Liebfraumilch, quintessentially mild, slightly sweet white wine from GERMANY's RHEINHESSEN, PFALZ, NAHE, or (rarely) RHEINGAU regions known almost exclusively in export markets where it weaned many a potential wine drinker off soft drinks. In its heyday in the 1980s, it accounted for an extraordinary, some would say horrifying, 60% of all German wine exported. These wines were generally dominated by SILVANER, MÜLLER-THURGAU, or KERNER grapes, but the **Liebfrauenstift-Kirchstück** (Our Lady's Cloister) in Worms from which the name Liebfraumilch was derived continues to be a source of good RIESLING.

lieblich appears (albeit usually in small print) on labels of Austrian wines with 19–45 g/l RESIDUAL SUGAR. In Germany, the term is seldom seen on labels, but it often used informally to describe German wines sweeter than those labelled TROCKEN, HALBTROCKEN, or FEINHERB.

L

Liechtenstein, principality between SWITZERLAND and AUSTRIA with about 20 ha/49 acres of vines in 2021. The majority of its vineyards are concentrated on the capital Vaduz, above and at some distance from the river RHINE, where the climate is strongly influenced by warming föhn winds. There are about a hundred vine-growers and just four commercial wine producers, of which the biggest is Hofkellerei des Fürsten von Liechtenstein, run in tandem with the Hofkellerei Wilfersdorf in Austria's WEINVIERTEL. Viticulture is mainly focused on white wines from Chardonnay, Pinot Blanc, and Riesling, with some reds from Merlot, Pinot Noir, and ZWEIGELT.

Ospelt, M. and Müller, W., *Weintradition Liechtenstein* (2004).

lieu-dit (plural **lieux-dits**), French term used quite generally to refer to the local, traditional name of a small area of land, usually defined by TOPOGRAPHY or history. Such locally given names are also used more specifically, especially in ALSACE, Burgundy, and the RHÔNE, to refer to a plot of land or vineyard within a larger appellation. In Burgundy, these names are used on labels for vineyards below PREMIER CRU in rank, for example Les Tillets in the commune of Meursault.

lifted, tasting term for a wine with a high but not excessive level of VOLATILE ACIDITY. Such a wine may also be said have **lift** conferred on it.

light. A wine is described by wine tasters as light, or **light-bodied**, if it is low in ALCOHOL and VISCOSITY. See BODY for more details. Wines are sometimes also described as light as opposed to FORTIFIED.

light brown apple moth. See MOTHS.

lightning, a climatic phenomenon, an electric discharge from the atmosphere under storm conditions, which may strike a vineyard and, by travelling along a wire, damage vines around the point of contact. Most vines recover after a lightning strike, however.

lightstrike, known as *goût de lumière* in French, is the damaging effect that light at short wavelengths in the ultraviolet and blue end of the spectrum can have on wine, as well as products such as beer and milk. The light provokes a chemical reaction with riboflavin and AMINO ACIDS in the wine, resulting in malodorous sulfur-related compounds such as dimethyl disulfide (DMDS) and methanethiol (see MERCAPTANS), which smell variously of cardboard, garlic, and cooked cabbage. White wines in clear bottles exposed to artificial light, particularly fluorescent light, even for a relatively short period of time, are the most likely to be affected, although bright daylight is equally damaging. Sodium lighting is often used in cellars in Champagne for this reason. Green glass is better than clear but not as good as amber, and red wines are less likely to be affected because PHENOLICS, especially TANNINS, help to protect the wine. Coating or sleeving the bottle is another solution but again adds to the production costs. Some champagne producers such as Roederer protect their best bottles by wrapping them in amber-coloured cellophane. Reducing the intensity and changing the direction of shop lighting would be a cheaper solution but harder to control. Research by the CIVC has concluded that amber-coloured LED lights exclude those wavelengths that cause lightstrike.

Carlin, S., et al., 'Flint glass bottles cause white wine aroma identity degradation', *Proceedings of the National Academy of Sciences of the United States of America*, 119/29 (2022).

Fracassetti, D., et al., 'Light-struck taste in white wine: protective role of glutathione, sulfur dioxide and hydrolysable tannins', *Molecules*, 26/17 (2021), 5297.

Maujean, A., et al., 'Contribution à l'étude des « goûts de lumière » dans le vin de champagne. II. Influence de la lumière sur le potentiel d'oxydoréduction. Corrélation avec la teneur en thiols du vin', *OENO One*, 12/4 (1978), 277–90.

lignification, botanical term for the process in which SHOOTS or STEMS become woody. See also CANE RIPENING.

Liguria. The crescent-shaped strip that runs along Italy's Mediterranean coast from the French border to the edge of Tuscany is Italy's third-smallest wine-producing region after the Valle d'Aosta and Molise. See map under ITALY, and see GENOA, VERNACCIA, and ITALY for some historical detail. The extremely rugged terrain—the Apennines descend virtually all the way to the sea—combined with the minute size of individual properties makes agriculture in general and viticulture in particular a marginal activity, and the greater economic possibilities offered by the thriving tourist industry and commercial flower-, vegetable-, and olive-growing have steadily depleted the workforce from the region's vineyards ever since the Second World War. However, Liguria's total vineyard area, 1,615 ha/3,990 acres, has been stable in recent years, with more than half of it dedicated to the production of DOC wine.

A crossroads of trade and traffic between Italy, France, and Spain, Liguria has long cultivated myriad vine varieties, and a census of the province of Imperia in 1970 revealed no fewer than 123. Many of these have since been abandoned, although renewed interest in INDIGENOUS VARIETIES has saved several from extinction, notably the white Scimiscià, which in 2003 was officially included in the national register. The region is concentrating its efforts on the white wine grapes VERMENTINO (PIGATO) and BOSCO and the red varieties ROSSESE, SANGIOVESE, and DOLCETTO (the last of these called Ormeasco in Liguria). Ormeasco, Pigato, Rossese, and Vermentino each have their own overarching DOC within the Riviera Ligure di Ponente zone, a wide stretch of territory between Genoa and the French border, which has been divided in five subzones: Albenga, Finale, Quiliano, Riviera dei Fiori, and Taggia.

Liguria's most renowned wine, the white Cinqueterre, is perhaps most famous for its vertigo-inducing vineyards perched on TERRACES sculpted into cliffsides high above the Ligurian Sea. The wine itself, made from Vermentino plus Albarola and/or Bosco, occasionally rises above thirst-quenching level. The rare Sciacchetrà, a sweet Cinqueterre made from PASSITO grapes, is enjoying a modest comeback.

Production of Vermentino is concentrated in Castelnuovo Magra, to the south of La Spezia in the Colli di Luni DOC zone, and in Diano Castello and Imperia in the province of Imperia. The name Pigato is traditional in Ranzo and Pieve di Teco, north of the city of Imperia. Ormeasco (DOLCETTO) is produced almost exclusively in Pornassio and Pieve di Teco. The Rossese grape, sometimes called 'Italy's Pinot Noir', has its own DOC near Ventimiglia, Rossese di Dolceacqua or simply Dolceacqua. The wine, combining aromas of blackcurrants and roses with power and delicacy, is produced on steep vineyards clinging to the coast, fighting a losing battle against greenhouses for vegetables. This admired but tiny DOC is divided among 14 villages, each with their own CRU vineyards at 400 m/1,312 ft ELEVATION, sometimes higher. A new generation, determined to save the steep vineyards from being abandoned, is focusing on the production of high-quality wines which seem ripe for elevation to DOCG status. W.S.

Liliorila, a 1956 BAROQUE × CHARDONNAY cross recently authorized in Bordeaux, within certain limits (see VIFA), because of its potential resilience to CLIMATE CHANGE.

Lima, large DOC subregion of VINHO VERDE in north-west Portugal on the Lima River, best known for particularly floral VARIETAL wines made from the LOUREIRO grape. Single-estate examples, typically from inland areas, are among Vinho Verde's best. S.A.

Limarí, valley in the northern region of Coquimbo in CHILE increasingly known for Chardonnay and Pinot Noir.

lime, in the forms of slaked lime (calcium hydroxide) or ground limestone (calcium carbonate), can be added to soils to neutralize SOIL ACIDITY. Because limestone is very insoluble, it should be thoroughly incorporated through TILLAGE to be fully effective. **Liming** is therefore most appropriately used, if needed, before vine PLANTING. It is relatively easy to change the topsoil PH but very difficult in effect to change it in the subsoil (below 50cm/20 in). The CALCIUM in lime or LIMESTONE also helps to give the soil a stable and friable structure (see SOIL STRUCTURE). Gypsum (calcium sulfate), which is more soluble than lime, can be used to supply calcium in soils where acidity does not need to be corrected. One common problem of over-liming is lime-induced CHLOROSIS (IRON is involved in photosynthesis and deficiency results in yellowing of leaves). R.E.W.

lime, active, refers to calcium carbonate that is more available to the vine than LIMESTONE rock because it is finely divided (less than 0.02 mm diameter) and therefore more soluble. Its presence in the soil is not necessarily due to underlying limestone, which is generally hard and insoluble, and may be the result of soil-forming processes in a low-rainfall environment. There is no direct relationship between the amount of active lime in the soil and wine quality. However, active lime raises a soil's PH above 7 and may enhance the vine's root development. Too much may lead to lime-induced CHLOROSIS. See also LIME and SOIL ALKALINITY. J.E.H. & R.E.W.

Baize, D., 'Total and "active" calcium carbonate', *Soil Science Analyses. A Guide to Current Use* (1993).
White, R. E., *Soils for Fine Wines* (2003).

limestone, constituted principally of the MINERAL calcite (calcium carbonate), is the most common CALCAREOUS rock. Increasing proportions of CLAY give argillaceous limestone (see ARGILO-CALCAIRE) and MARL; dolomitic limestone or dolomite is calcium-magnesium carbonate. CHALK is a special subvariety of limestone. Most limestones formed in warm, sunlit shallow seas (resembling the Bahamas today) and can be rich in fossils (see GEOLOGY), the accumulated debris of calcareous organisms such as plankton, corals and clams. **Pedogenic limestone**, however, forms *in situ* in relatively arid areas such as Central Otago and Mendoza when carbon dioxide dissolved in soil water encounters calcium released by weathering of parent rocks.

Common limestones differ from chalk in being hard and not readily penetrated by plant roots, except through cracks. Unless mineral material is brought in by wind or water, the depth of soil formed on limestone depends on the impurities (clay, SILT, and SAND) in the limestone because the dissolution of calcite produces only calcium and bicarbonate ions. Limestones tend to yield stony soils with a PH around neutral, invariably well drained but also with good water storage. Depending on impurities, the colour ranges from almost white to darker greys and other colours. Some limestone soils, such as the Mediterranean TERRA ROSSA, are red-brown in colour; these are moderately alkaline and have a good clay-loam texture and structure.

Some limestone soils overlie substantial reserves of ground water, generally of high quality for IRRIGATION. The longer roots of well-established vines may reach this water, if it is not too deep. Deep RIPPING to shatter the hard limestone may be carried out before PLANTING, typically to 1 m/3 ft depth, but any slabs of limestone brought to the surface may need to be removed. Limestone-derived soils are in general valued most highly in COOL-CLIMATE viticultural regions. The great wines of BURGUNDY come from vines grown on the slopes of the CÔTE D'OR escarpment, where various Jurassic limestones predominate.

The red limestone-derived terra rossa of Coonawarra in SOUTH AUSTRALIA similarly produces some of Australia's best red wines from Cabernet Sauvignon and Shiraz, both vine varieties being close to the cool limit for their reliable ripening.

In warm climates, however, such as in the south of France and the Riverland of South Australia, limestone soils are not regarded as superior or even necessarily as suitable for viticulture (see SOIL AND WINE QUALITY). The high pH of purer limestones can prompt nutritional difficulties, root growth can be restricted, and most of the North American ROOTSTOCKS on to which vines are grafted in order to combat phylloxera perform poorly on limestone. R.E.W. & A.J.M.

Limestone Coast Zone, moderately cool, high-quality wine area in SOUTH AUSTRALIA encompassing the traditional lands of the Buandig, Bindjali, and Ngarrindjeri people. The zone includes the Coonawarra, Mount Benson, Mount Gambier, Padthaway, Robe, and Wrattonbully wine regions. The districts of Bordertown and Penola in the upper south-east of the region are candidates for official recognition, too. Bordertown, the furthest north, is the warmest area, producing robust Shiraz and Cabernet Sauvignon, for example. Mount Gambier, to the extreme south, is the coolest, best suited to Pinot Noir and Chardonnay.

Limnio, dark grape variety native to the island of Límnos in GREECE, where it can still be found. It has also transferred successfully to Halkidikí in north-east Greece, where, sometimes blended with Cabernet, it produces a full-bodied wine with a good level of ACIDITY and some herbal aromas. **Limniona**, a promising dark-skinned variety recently resurrected on mainland Greece, is unrelated, according to DNA PROFILING.

Limousin, old French province centred on the town of Limoges, and a term encountered most frequently in the wine world as a name for the region's OAK.

Limoux, small town and appellation in the eastern Pyrenean foothills in southern France. For centuries it has been devoted to the production of white wines that would sparkle naturally after a second fermentation during the spring. They became known as **Blanquette de Limoux**, *blanquette* meaning simply 'white' in Occitan. Locals claim that fermentation in bottle was developed here long before it was consciously practised in CHAMPAGNE, dating the production of cork-stoppered sparkling wines at the Abbey of St-Hilaire from 1531 (Limoux is just north of CATALUÑA, a natural home of the CORK oak), although Stevenson casts doubt on both the date and claims that the wine was sparkling.

The region's vineyards are so much higher, cooler, and further from Mediterranean influence than any other Languedoc appellation (even MALEPÈRE to its immediate north) that many are Atlantic-influenced even though they are just inland from the CORBIÈRES hills. Within the region there are several distinct zones differing in ELEVATION, soil types, and the influence of the Atlantic or Mediterranean.

The grape used traditionally was MAUZAC, called locally Blanquette, but increasing amounts of CHARDONNAY and, to a lesser extent, CHENIN BLANC have been planted so that in the 1980s the Limoux vineyards were much valued as one of southern France's very few sources of Chardonnay grapes from mature vines. Still wines made from them were then in great demand, especially for export markets. This international success was cleverly capitalized upon by Toques et Clochers, an annual charity AUCTION of Chardonnay barrel samples, inspired by the famous HOSPICES DE BEAUNE auction but embellished by the involvement of some of France's most famous chefs. These often lean, oak-aged Chardonnays regularly fetched prices far in excess of their then classification as VINS DE PAYS so the Limoux appellation was thoroughly overhauled in 1993. It now encompasses still whites made mainly from Chardonnay (although Chenin Blanc and Mauzac may be included, or may be the main or sole variety), with, unusually, compulsory BARREL FERMENTATION and BARREL AGEING.

In 2004, a red wine Limoux appellation was added, with Merlot compulsorily making up at least 50% of the blend and Côt (MALBEC), Syrah, and Grenache constituting at least 30%. Cabernet Sauvignon and Cabernet Franc may play a part—truly an Atlantic and Mediterranean blend. Such (relatively light) wines used to be sold as the IGP Haute Vallée de l'Aude, a name now more commonly encountered on the region's most promising red wine grape, Pinot Noir.

But Limoux is essentially a sparkling wine town. Blanquette de Limoux is the region's most famous product, a fruity sparkling wine made up of at least 90% Mauzac, although Chardonnay and/or Chenin Blanc may play a minor part. The **Crémant de Limoux** appellation was devised in 1990 for more complex TRADITIONAL METHOD sparkling wines. In 2006, a rosé style was permitted using up to 15% Pinot Noir in the blend. See CRÉMANT for more details.

Limoux's distinctly marginal speciality is Blanquette Méthode Ancestrale (see SPARKLING WINEMAKING), a sweeter, often slightly cloudy, less fizzy sparkling wine made exclusively from Mauzac grown on 65 ha/160 acres in 2012 and left to ferment a second time in bottle without subsequent disgorgement of the resultant sediment. Like the GAILLAC Mousseux made from Mauzac by the *méthode gaillacoise* with similar regard for tradition, these hand-crafted wines are low in alcohol, are high in Mauzac's old-apple-peel flavours, and can taste remarkably like a superior sweet cider.

Limoux's sparkling wine business is dominated by the dynamic local CO-OPERATIVE, which sells a range of bottlings under such names as Aimery and Sieur d'Arques, but there are also some fine individual estates in the pretty hills here.

Stevenson, T., *How The English Invented Champagne* (2014).

Lincoln University New Zealand's specialist land-based university with research and teaching focused on agricultural science. The VITICULTURE and OENOLOGY programme, established in 1989, offers undergraduate and postgraduate studies. Teaching programmes emphasize the integration of grape-growing and winemaking from vine to glass. The university has its own vineyard and is home to the Centre for Viticulture and Oenology, a research hub that brings together scholars and scholarship related to viticulture and wine production. COOL-CLIMATE grape varieties important to New Zealand's wine industry, namely Sauvignon Blanc and Pinot Noir, receive particular attention. Current research areas include: grapevine physiology and berry composition; SUSTAINABLE grape production; oenology, including FERMENTATION processes and wine chemistry and composition; sensory science related to how wines are perceived, appreciated, and consumed; and wine marketing and TOURISM. W.V.P.

www.lincoln.ac.nz

lipids, a group of chemicals that includes oils, fats, and waxes. Lipids are distinctive in plants because, despite the plant's watery environment, they are not soluble in water, and this is the basis of their important roles. They make up the membranes of plant CELLS which keep apart entirely different zones of metabolic activity, often with large differences in ACIDITY on either side of the membrane. They make energy-rich reserves of food as in seeds, grapeseed oil being a good example. Also they coat the surface of the plant with a water-impermeable layer of waxy cutin which stops desiccation. A host of other compounds have lipid-like structures, including important plant pigments such as chlorophyll and CAROTENOIDS. The sediment in MUST contains a significant amount of lipids that play an important role in FERMENTATION. If CLARIFICATION of the must is too severe (so that the turbidity is less than 150 NTU), the risk of sluggish fermentation is higher than in more turbid juices with higher levels of solids. B.G.C. & D.D.

Liqueur Muscat, old name for the very special sort of STICKIE made in AUSTRALIA from Brown MUSCAT grapes. For more, see TOPAQUE.

liqueur wine is the official EU term for FORTIFIED WINES that have an ALCOHOLIC STRENGTH of not less than 15% and not more than 22%. See also VIN DE LIQUEUR.

liquoreux, French term meaning 'syrupy sweet', used for very rich, often BOTRYTIZED, wines that are markedly sweeter than MOELLEUX wines.

liquoroso, Italian for a strong, usually sweet, FORTIFIED WINE.

Lirac, large appellation on the west bank of the Southern RHÔNE producing wine from 818 ha/2,021 acres of vineyards in 2020. It includes three communes other than Lirac, of which Roquemaure was an important 16th-century port from which wines would be shipped as far north as England and Holland (see RIVERS). In the 18th century, Roquemaure was a much more important wine centre than CHÂTEAUNEUF-DU-PAPE. Lirac is now the only southern Rhône AOC apart from VACQUEYRAS to make wine in all three colours. For reds and rosés, the majority of the blend must be composed of Grenache, Syrah, Mourvèdre, and/or Cinsaut, with a long list of secondary varieties that can also be included. For whites (10% of production), the majority of the blend must comprise Bourboulenc, Clairette, Grenache Blanc, and/or Roussanne. In all three colours, the wines are unmistakably southern Rhône but often have a distinct finesse to their shape and texture. The terrain is a patchwork of soils, with vines grown on SAND, CLAY, GALETS, and LIMESTONE.

See map under RHÔNE. M.C.W.

Lisboa, VINHO REGIONAL in western Portugal sometimes known colloquially as Oeste (West) and known until 2009 as Estremadura. Although it incorporates no fewer than nine DOCS—ALENQUER, ARRUDA, BUCELAS, CARCAVELOS, COLARES, ENCOSTAS D'AIRE, Lourinhã (exclusively for brandy or aguardente), ÓBIDOS, and Torres Vedras—as of 2021 all but 3% of wine from this sizeable coastal strip is classified as Vinho Regional (VR). A growth spurt of certified wine (as opposed to VINHO or the returnable 5 l/1.3 gal flagons known as *garrafoes*, once the mainstay of taverns and restaurants all over the Portuguese-speaking world) has shifted the emphasis from quantity to quality. The region's ten remaining CO-OPERATIVES now represent only around one-fifth of VR sales following a rising tide of privately owned producers. Exposure to Atlantic westerlies can be challenging for volume red winemaking, sometimes resulting in thin reds with clumsy RESIDUAL SUGAR levels. However, fast-improving contemporary commodity wines have leveraged the capital's popularity as a TOURISM destination to great effect. While Bucelas, Carcavelos, and Colares, historically the most distinguished wine regions, are now too small to be qualitatively significant, all are experiencing a revival of interest from producers and consumers alike. Exciting Atlantic VR wines from Sintra are in growth, some even made from Colares's rare signature grapes, RAMISCO and MALVASIA de Colares. Elsewhere across this extensive VR, hitherto uncelebrated pockets of excellence are steadily emerging, typically defined by Lisboa's propitious CLAY and LIMESTONE soils, ELEVATION (up to 500 m/1,640 ft), or coastal locations. Recently introduced promising varieties include TOURIGA NACIONAL and TINTA RORIZ (Tempranillo), together with such INTERNATIONAL VARIETIES as Syrah, Cabernet Sauvignon, Grenache, Pinot Noir, Sauvignon Blanc, Riesling, and Viognier. Local grapes such as ARINTO, FERNÃO PIRES, VITAL, MOSCATEL, Jampal, CASTELÃO, and TINTA MIÚDA are being re-explored, too, and, in the right hands and right places, are producing exciting wines. S.A.

Mayson, R. J., *The Wines of Portugal* (2020).
Woolf, S. J., and Opaz, R., *Foot Trodden: Portugal and the Wines That Time Forgot* (2021).

Lison-Pramaggiore, DOC mainly in the VENETO region of north-east Italy created in 1986 by the fusion of two previous DOCs, the Cabernet di Pramaggiore and Tocai di Lison. The DOC Lison was created in 1971 for the production of Tocai Bianco and Tocai Rosso, now officially known as Tai Bianco (identical to FRIULANO) and Tai Rosso (the same as GRENACHE) after Hungary successfully claimed ownership of the Tocai name. It was joined in 1972 by Pramaggiore to accommodate Merlot. With the unification of the two DOCs in 1985 a raft of new varieties such as Pinot Bianco, Chardonnay, Pinot Grigio, Sauvignon Blanc, and Friuli's Refosco was allowed, with Malbec added in 2000. As a result of the EU viticultural reforms of the late 2000s, the entire Lison part of the DOC was, questionably, elevated to DOCG status, allowing Tai Bianco and Tai Rosso only. The Lison Classico DOCG denotes wines from the original heartland of the zone.

The vineyards themselves are in the wide plain created by the Piave River as it descends from the hills of Conegliano and Montello towards the Adriatic and, as such, can be considered an eastward continuation of the PIAVE DOC zone, extending into the Pordenone province of FRIULI. Total vineyard surface in 2020 was 172 ha/425 acres. The wines are fresh and pleasurable, if not memorable, with Cabernet (predominantly Franc) regularly giving the most interesting results. Cooler vintages, together with the high percentage of Cabernet Franc and high yields in the vineyards (90 hl/ha), tend to bring out a HERBACEOUSNESS which may be more appealing to local markets than to international ones. W.S.

www.lison-pramaggiore.it

Listán, synonym for PALOMINO FINO, the white grape variety that can produce superb SHERRY around JEREZ. As Listán, or **Listán Blanco**, some of its most interesting wines are those grown on the VOLCANIC soils of the CANARY ISLANDS, where it can produce unfortified wines of much greater tension, individuality, and distinction than most of those on the Spanish mainland. The rebirth of Canary wines in the 1990s thus gave this much-maligned variety a new lease on life. The Spanish vine census of 2020 cites the total area of 'Listán Blanco de Canarias' as 1,580 ha/3,904 acres. **Listán de Huelva** is a distinct but minor Andalucian pale-skinned variety while the dark-skinned, well-travelled PAÍS of Chile is known in Spain as **Listán Prieto**.

Listán Negro, recently appreciated INDIGENOUS VARIETY, also known as Almuñeco, which dominates wine production on the island of Tenerife in the CANARY ISLANDS, planted on 1,511 ha/3,734 acres in 2020. CARBONIC MACERATION has managed to coax exceptional aromas out of this medium-bodied wine.

Listrac, or **Listrac-Médoc**, one of the six communal appellations of the Haut-Médoc district of BORDEAUX. In relation to the other five (MARGAUX, ST-JULIEN, PAUILLAC, ST-ESTÈPHE, and even MOULIS, with which it is often compared), Listrac seems the least well favoured. It is, just, the furthest of them all from the Gironde estuary, and the vineyards (354 ha/874 acres declared in 2020) are planted on mainly clay-limestone on a gentle rise which, at an ELEVATION of about 40 m/131 ft, constitutes some of the highest land in the MÉDOC. Although the Merlot grape is increasingly planted, the wines can be relatively austere in youth. The most cosseted property is probably the late Baron Edmond de ROTHSCHILD's Ch Clarke, and the trio Fourcas-Borie, Fourcas-Dupré, and Fourcas-Hosten (also well-pampered) are generally reliable. J.R. & J.L.

literature of wine. The literature that concerns wine specifically, as opposed to references to wine in more general writing (for which see ENGLISH LITERATURE), is a complicated tapestry of texts and books that has been woven from a broad variety of strands from classical times to the present day. Most writers concern themselves with how and where grapes are grown, how and where wine is made, and how individual wines taste, but their methods vary considerably, and there are works on wine which are also works on travel, history, medicine, agricultural matters, and gastronomy.

Early works and agriculture

Many early works are richer in references to the effects of drinking wine (see DRUNKENNESS) than to the wine itself. CLASSICAL TEXTS constitute the earliest known literature of wine (although see also ancient MESOPOTAMIA). While Mago of CARTHAGE clearly inspired many subsequent writers, his text does not survive, and the first known classical writers to concentrate on wine and winemaking were probably CATO (234–149 BCE) and VARRO (116–27 BCE). Cato, particularly, was keen on the profit motive in winemaking, and his instructions appear mainly to have been aimed at quantity rather than quality, even suggesting, at one point, how Coan wine (from Kós, one of the AEGEAN ISLANDS) could be faked from Italian grapes.

Much more modern in his outlook towards the production of wine was COLUMELLA (2 BCE–65 CE), whose family, based near Cádiz in southern Spain, may well have owned vineyards. His *De re rustica* gives detailed advice on such matters as CLONAL SELECTION, the planting of vineyards, and the need for wines to be as NATURAL as possible: 'The wine is clearly the best which can solely give pleasure by its own nature.' PLINY the Elder (23–79 CE) was the last great classical writer on wine and winemaking, although he was clearly influenced by Varro. The works of all these three, and the more derivative PALLADIUS in particular, were translated and used as textbooks throughout Europe until the end of the 16th century.

In these books, viticulture was treated merely as a part—albeit a major part—of the broader subject of agriculture. This tradition was continued by such writers as PETRUS DE CRESCENTIIS (1230–1310), an Italian lawyer who was forced to leave his own country and spent 30 years in exile in Spain and France. One volume of his monumental *Liber ruralium commodorum* dealt specifically with winegrowing and winemaking. The work was translated into French on the instructions of Charles V.

The first French writer to attempt to classify wines in any way was Charles Étienne (1504–64). His *Vinetum . . .* first appeared in Lyons in 1536. This was subsequently translated into French and incorporated in *L'Agriculture et maison rustique des maistres Charles Étienne et Jean Liebault* (1564) (Liebault was Étienne's son-in-law). This was a bestseller and was translated into English by Richard Surflet in 1606. It was followed in due course by the *Nouvelle Maison rustique* by Louis Liger of AUXERRE, which appeared in many editions throughout the 18th and early 19th centuries. While this book deals with a broad selection of rural topics, the section on wine is particularly fascinating with its details of the then-popular wines of Orléans, Burgundy, and Champagne. The characteristics are also given of 50 different VINE VARIETIES grown in France both for table grapes and for winemaking, of which 'morillon noir' is today's PINOT NOIR and 'gamet' is today's GAMAY. More than 15 varieties of MUSCAT are mentioned, but CABERNET SAUVIGNON is notably absent (in the late 1990s DNA PROFILING explained why).

In some ways, an English equivalent was Philip Miller's *Gardeners' Dictionary*, which first appeared in 1731. Here, under the headings 'Vitis' and 'Wine', are detailed articles on such subjects as grape varieties, Burgundy, Champagne, and English vineyards, although he says of these last, 'There have of late years been but very few vineyards in England, tho' they were formerly very common.'

As wine was the everyday drink throughout much of Europe, in parallel with the books on the agricultural aspects of wine there were others devoted, perhaps only in part, to its keeping and serving. In England the anonymously written *Mystery of Vintners* appeared in 1692, and *L'Art d'améliorer et de conserver les vins* (1781) was first published in Paris, under the title *Dissertation sur les vins*, in 1772. Further editions came out in Liège and Turin soon afterwards. The information they gave was often plagiarized and adapted to appear in such general books as *The Laboratory, or School of Arts* (1799).

Wine as medicine

The role of wine in the world of MEDICINE had been important from the earliest of times. It was used widely as a medium for the infusion of medicinal herbs, and many wine-based remedies were given in such books as *The Secrets of Alexis of Piedmont*, which appeared in a number of languages from 1555 onwards.

Indeed the first book specifically on wines in English, *A New Book of Wines* (1568), was written by William Turner, who studied medicine at Cambridge. He warned of the danger of drinking the sweet, heavy wines of the Mediterranean as opposed to the healthy, light wines of the Rhine.

This medicinal tradition was adapted by the wine merchant Duncan McBride in his *Choice of Wines* . . . (1793), which included general discussion about the wines that were available at the time and their potential application for various medical conditions.

A much later sequel is *Wine is the Best Medicine* (1974, updated 1992) by the Frenchman Dr E. A. Maury. This had a more rational approach to the subject, with a variety of individual French wines being recommended for everything from flatulence to cystitis.

DOCTORS have always had a major role to play in English wine literature. Sir Edward Barry was a Bath physician whose *History of Classical Wines* appeared in 1775. He was criticized for relying too closely on the work of the 16th-century papal medical adviser Barrius, but he also includes an appendix on modern wines and viticulture in England.

Doctors were also responsible for the first two 'modern' books to deal with wine in depth. While the title of *A Practical Treatise on Brewing, Distilling and Rectification*, by R. Shannon MD (1805), might put off the oenophile, there is 'A Copious Appendix on . . . Foreign Wines, Brandies and Vinegars'.

Dr Alexander HENDERSON's *The History of Ancient and Modern Wines* (1824) is perhaps the first book in English to attempt to give descriptions of a broad range of wines, based upon his own travels to France, Germany, and Italy. It is also the first book to try to analyse the science of TASTING.

The golden age

In the number of wines it talks about, Henderson's book is overwhelmed by what must be the most remarkable book on wine ever published, the *Topographie de tous les vignobles connus* (1816) by André JULLIEN, a Parisian wine merchant who was born in Burgundy. In this are rated all the wines, not just of France but of all known wine regions of the time, including California, South America, South Africa's Cape, and 'Chinese Tartary'! He forecasts (or perhaps helps to shape) the 1855 CLASSIFICATION in Bordeaux by rating as first-class wines Lafitte (*sic*), Latour, Ch-Margaux, and Haut-Brion.

Outside Europe, his favourites all seem to be dessert wines, including TOKAJI, CONSTANTIA, COMMANDARIA, and COTNARI. Both his first-hand experience and his reading must have been gargantuan for him to compile such a work of reference. He followed this up with another classic, *Manuel du Sommelier* (1822). Cavoleau's *Oenologie française* was a similar work to the *Topographie*, coming from the same publisher 11 years later though limited to French wines.

The 19th century was a golden age for wine writing in Britain. Cyrus REDDING (1785–1870), a journalist whose interest in wine was stimulated during five years based in Paris, wrote *A History and Description of Modern Wines* (1833) as a result of first-hand observation of the ADULTERATION AND FRAUD which were then prevalent in the wine trade.

Many books were written by wine merchants, often criticizing the practices of their colleagues or vaunting their own specialities (a common thread through modern wine writing). Perhaps the most enjoyable to read is Thomas Shaw, whose *Wine, the Vine and the Cellar* (1863) is an agreeable blend of reminiscences, knowledge, and simple advice. He was convinced even then that 'in wine tasting and wine talk there is an enormous amount of humbug'. Another of his campaigns was against excessive DUTIES on wine, and this led to the famous Gladstone budget in 1862 in which they were considerably reduced.

Charles Tovey was a wine merchant in Bristol in south-west England, and in the introduction to *Wine and Wine Countries* (1862) he says that 'there can be no question that the Wine Trade is losing its position by the introduction into it of unscrupulous traders'. He drew heavily upon his 50 years' experience in denouncing and describing their deceits.

This same theme was continued by his London colleague James L. Denman, who wrote copiously on wine adulteration. His more particular interest, however, both commercial and literary, was the wines of Greece.

Another doctor to write on wines was John Thudichum, who had come to London from Germany, where his father had written technical books on wine. One of his particular hobby horses was the adding of gypsum to SHERRY, but his credibility within the trade was compromised by extensive research that he had carried out in Jerez, trying to produce AMONTILLADO by purely chemical means. His *Treatise on Wines* (1872), written with another doctor, A. Dupré, does, however, give a clear picture of viticulture and vinification at that time. Somerville & Ross's *In the Vine Country* (originally serialised 1890–1 and republished to great acclaim in 2021) is that rare thing, a pre-1960 book on wine by women.

Specialist books

While all these books give a general idea of the wines of Europe and, in some cases, the world, some specialist books on individual regions had also begun to appear. One of the first of these was published in London as early as 1728. This was the *Dissertation sur la situation de Bourgogne* by the French tutor to the son of a Mr Freeman. Arnoux, in this brief book, describes the various wines of Burgundy and how they are made. He also makes a plea for them to be imported into England in bottle rather than in cask. This book must have met with some success, for it was soon translated into English and was subsequently used by Philip Miller in his *Gardeners' Dictionary* and by Robert Shannon.

It was more than a century until the next two classic books on the vineyards of Burgundy appeared, and coincidentally they did so in the same year, 1831. Morelot's *Statistique de la vigne dans le département de la Côte d'Or* is largely what its title suggests, although the second half of the book deals with both viticulture and vinification in the region. The *Histoire et statistique de la vigne et des grands vins de la Côte d'Or* by Lavalle is a more readable book, for it gives many historical details concerning Burgundy and its wines, as well as more information about the characteristics of the wines from the various villages and ownership of the vineyards.

In Bordeaux, the first book of significance was the *Variétés bordelaises* of Abbé Beaurein (1784–5), which noted that the English were at last showing interest in the wines of the Médoc. The first major book dealing solely with the wines of Bordeaux, however, was the *Traité sur les vins du Médoc* of William Franck (1824), which ran into several editions. In many ways this was the forerunner of Charles Cocks's book *Bordeaux, its Wines and the Claret Country* (1846), which was translated into French four years later and became the classic reference work on Bordeaux wines, known after its original authors as 'Cocks et FÉRET'. An interesting independent view of the region is also given by the Paris merchant Charles Pierre de Saint in *Le Vin de Bordeaux* (1855).

Writing on Portuguese wines was dominated by the English. In 1787 John CROFT wrote *A Treatise of the Wines of Portugal*, and this was followed by the many works of James Forrester (1809–61), who, from his position in the trade, took a strong stance against the many adulterations that were taking place.

The 19th century saw the rapid expansion of vineyards in the NEW WORLD, and guidance was sought in Europe as to how to make the finest wines. From this came two interesting works. The first was the *Journal of a Tour through some of the Vineyards of Spain and France* by James BUSBY, which was published in Sydney in 1833. This is a fascinating account of a three-month trip, mainly by stagecoach, to find the right vine varieties for planting in Australia. The interpretation of what he learned appeared in two further books. The journey, almost 30 years later, by Agoston HARASZTHY, one of the pioneers of California viticulture, was largely by train. Perhaps because of his origins, he spent more of his time in the various states of Germany and none at all in France. His *Grape*

Culture, Wines and Wine-Making, a journal of this tour, appeared in New York in 1862 and did much to establish the reputations of both Haraszthy and California wine.

A third, and earlier, New World traveller to have recorded his memories of vineyard visiting is Thomas JEFFERSON, later to become president of the United States. During his five years as minister to France (1784–9), he took advantage of his situation by visiting many of the vineyards of Europe, and his diaries leave a fascinating picture of a layman's perception of the world of wine as it then was.

One final wine writer of Victorian times was the journalist and publisher Henry VIZETELLY. His books on champagne, port, and sherry are notable for their many illustrations. These works, with their beautiful engravings, many used by modern publishers, are the forebears of the lavishly illustrated wine books published today.

Technical literature

Parallel with this growth in books on the vineyard regions and their wines, there was a considerable body of work on VITICULTURE and WINEMAKING. In France at the end of the 18th century, the Burgundian Béguillet and Parisian Maupin both wrote detailed works which were widely read.

In England, William Speechly, gardener to the Duke of Portland, wrote a *Treatise on the Culture of the Vine* (1790), which went into three editions. This dealt with both hothouse and open-air vines in ENGLAND and discusses some of the vineyards which were then planted there and the wines they produced.

Three French writers of the 19th century whose names live on in the world of wine are Jean-Antoine CHAPTAL (1756–1832), Dr Jules GUYOT (1807–72), and Louis PASTEUR (1822–95). Chaptal was the essential polymath, rising from humble beginnings to become Minister of the Interior under Napoleon. In 1799 he wrote the article on wine for the monumental *Dictionnaire d'agriculture* of the Abbé Rozier, but he is better known for his *L'Art de faire le vin* (1807) and for his support for the concept of increasing the alcohol strength of wine by adding sugar to the must, the procedure now known as CHAPTALIZATION.

Jules Guyot was instructed under the Second Empire to carry out a survey of the vineyards of France and to make recommendations as to how viticulture might be improved. His three works on viticulture in north and central France (1860), the east (1863), and the west (1866) give a vital picture of France before the arrival of PHYLLOXERA. His name lives on as a method of VINE TRAINING. It is largely to him that we owe the parade-ground look of today's vineyards in place of the unruly appearance of vines subjected to the traditional practice of LAYERING.

Louis Pasteur's *Études sur le vin* (1866) deals with the question of vinification and particularly the advantages of the heat treatment, or PASTEURIZATION, of wine. His is also the first detailed work on the role that YEASTS have to play in FERMENTATION. Another important work on the techniques of vinification was *Le Vin* (1867), by the Burgundian Comte de Vergnette-Lamotte.

Over ten years from 1901, MONTPELLIER professor of viticulture Pierre Viala, backed by industrialist Victor Vermorel, produced his unsurpassed seven-volume *Ampélographie*, a guide to 5,200 grape varieties, with the 627 most important considered in detail and 500 of them beautifully illustrated in colour by Jules Troncy and Alexis Kreÿder.

Modern wine writing

The 20th century saw a great resurgence in wine writing, particularly in Britain. Much of the credit has been laid at the door of Professor George SAINTSBURY, whose erudite miscellany of vinous reminiscences, *Notes on a Cellar-Book* (1920), was published when he was 75 years old. (It was reprinted twice within four months and has run through many editions since.)

Influential writers during this period included H. Warner Allen, a wine-loving journalist who wrote *A History of Wine* (1961), as well as Maurice Healy and Stephen Gwynn.

André SIMON (1877–1970) was extraordinarily prolific. His early writings were largely on the history of the wine trade, and he was, all his life, passionately interested in wine books, compiling a number of bibliographies on food and drink (see below). As a member of the wine trade, he introduced a degree of accuracy to his work that is missing from some of the 'gentlemen' wine writers cited above. In all he wrote more than 100 works in which his knowledge is matched by his readability.

Subsequent wine writing in Britain continued this parallel, with works coming from writers who took to wine and wine professionals who took to writing.

From the British wine trade have come such as Tommy Layton, a prolific writer on the wines of the Loire, Alsace, Spain, and Italy; his one-time office boy Michael BROADBENT, whose *Great Vintage Wine Book* and *Vintage Wine* are unrivalled collections of tasting notes on thousands of wines going back to the 17th century; Clive Coates MW on the wines of Burgundy and Bordeaux; both Anthony Hanson MW and Jasper Morris MW on Burgundy; the late John Radford on Spanish wines; Gerald Asher, long based in the United States; the late Steven Spurrier; and many others.

Representing the world of the professional writer were the biographer and founder of the Good Food Club, Raymond Postgate, whose *The Plain Man's Guide to Wine* proved so successful that it went through 16 editions in 26 years; Edmund PENNING-ROWSELL, whose frequently revised book on the wines of Bordeaux was a masterpiece of research; the polished journalist Cyril Ray; and John Arlott, another journalist (and cricket commentator) whose enjoyment of wine and the pleasure it brings shone through his writing.

The late 20th century saw something new in the world of wine books: writers deliberately writing for their customer, the reader, rather than for their own pleasure, their work often embellished with ambitious illustration. Oz Clarke, Jamie Goode, and Tom Stevenson have been particularly prolific, Andrew Jefford regrettably less so. But the most successful and innovative of these have undoubtedly been Hugh JOHNSON and Jancis Robinson. Even more popular than the former's *Wine* and *The Story of Wine* is his *World Atlas of Wine*, which first appeared in 1971 and has sold more than 4.5 million copies. From the 5th edition, this has been co-authored by Jancis Robinson. She has written widely herself, notably producing *Wine Grapes*, with Julia Harding and José Vouillamoz, and editing the first four editions of *The Oxford Companion to Wine*.

In the rest of Europe, much of the wine literature was originally written in English, although the Dutch writer Hubrecht Duijker achieved a broad international readership. Few French writers are read outside France, although each region has had its specialized writers such as Pierre Poupon, Pierre Forgeot, and Jean-François Bazin on Burgundy, René Pijassou and Bernard Ginestet on Bordeaux. An exception, for the technically minded, is Pierre GALET's work on AMPELOGRAPHY, a worthy successor to Pierre Viala's earlier volumes. The works of Émile PEYNAUD on winemaking and wine TASTING have also been widely read outside France. In Spain, José Peñín led the growing number of writers on wine, as VERONELLI did in Italy.

In the United States, wine writing became a boom industry in the late 20th century. This was led by Alexis LICHINE, who before the Second World War joined the wine trade with Frank SCHOONMAKER, himself a successful writer on wine.

Other effective American wine authors have included Karen MacNeil, Ed McCarthy, and Mary Ewing Mulligan MW (whose books in the 'for Dummies' series have been particularly successful), Kevin Zraly, and—the most powerful wine writer of all—Robert PARKER, who wrote several popular books and wine guides, most notably on Bordeaux and the Rhône. Kermit Lynch and Terry Theise are perhaps the most accomplished writers to have emerged from the US wine trade.

Wine writing in Australia was led by Len EVANS, followed by the even more prolific James Halliday. These vineyard owners have been followed by a host of career wine writers such as Max Allen and Peter Forrestal. In New Zealand, the field has been led by Bob Campbell MW and Michael Cooper.

It is easy to chart through wine literature the change in public perception of wine, from élitist to populist, a move encouraged by wider travel and higher disposable incomes. Annual pocket books are supplemented by specialist buyer's guides such as Bettane & Desseauve's on French wines, Peñín's on Spain, Gambero Rosso on Italy, Platter's on South Africa, and many, many more. Increasingly popular are wine-travel guides which cover specific regions and, along with recommended producers to visit, include maps, travel advice, and recommendations for places to stay, eat, shop, and explore. Other writers, such as Alice Feiring, create an almost evangelistic narrative for particular styles of wine.

The increasing interest in wine seen from the late 20th century has led to a corresponding increase in the range of wine books available and—perhaps more significantly—in the media by which wine writing is disseminated.

The biggest and most dramatic change has been the move from print to digital. Online magazines, newsletters, interactive consumer-driven apps such as Vivino and Instagram, blogs, websites, and self-published e-books mean that wine writing is no longer the exclusive domain of print publishers or wine experts. They may be self-published and/or print on demand, such as the works of Jamie Goode, Ben Lewin MW, Neal Martin, Allen Meadows (aka Burghound), and Stephen Skelton MW.

Subscription websites are seen to guarantee journalistic integrity, but consumers are used to, comfortable with, and influenced by short reads interspersed by pop-up advertising and advertorial. Opinion has proliferated, and not all of it is based on knowledge. Content on many wine websites is not fact-checked by editors.

The 21st-century style of wine writing has, in parallel, shifted from formal and didactic to casual, chatty, inclusive, multi-sensory, and interactive. Online wine writing can be immediately corrected, updated, adapted to trends, and tailored to SEO (search-engine optimization). Apps such as Twitter and Instagram encourage brevity. Visual cues such as charts and photographs are now a powerful part of the narrative. 'Story-telling' as a communication tool is recognized as a welcome alternative to pedantically presented information.

The ever-evolving literature of wine is infinite, and, as appreciation of wine spreads around the world, so will demand for words on wine. See also LANGUAGE OF WINE, MEDIEVAL LITERATURE, WINE WRITING, and INFORMATION TECHNOLOGY.

C.F. & T.D.C.

Useful bibliographies:

Amerine, M. A., and Borg, A. E., *A Bibliography on Grapes, Wines, Other Alcoholic Beverages and Temperance: Works Published in the United States before 1901* (1996).

Gabler, J. M., *Wine into Words: A History and Bibliography of Wine Books in the English Language* (2nd edn, 2004).

Simon, A., *Bibliotheca vinaria* (1913, and facsimile: 1979).

Vicaire, G., *Bibliographie gastronomique* (1890, and facsimile: 1978).

Lithuania is an emerging winegrowing country despite its climate, which is nearly too cold for growing VITIS VINIFERA. The short vegetative period is framed by FROSTS in mid May and the end of September, and winter temperatures can drop to −28 °C/−18 °F. Until as recently as 2007, most plantings were cold-resistant non-certified HYBRIDS created in the mid 20th century by local breeder Antanas Gailiunas.

However, since 2018 the country has seen a major increase in grape-growing and winemaking, with an estimated 50 ha/124 acres of vines planted by 2022. SOLARIS is now the most popular white grape variety, followed by St Pepin, Adalmiina, FRONTENAC Blanc, Muscaris, and Johanniter. There are also small plots of RIESLING, most planted close to the Baltic Sea or in the warmer centre of Lithuania.

RONDO was the first red wine grape variety planted by enthusiasts in the beginning of 21st century, but because of its low resistance to FUNGAL DISEASES it soon conceded to REGENT. The cold-hardy MARÉCHAL FOCH, FRONTENAC, LÉON MILLOT, and MARQUETTE are gaining in popularity, and some experiment with FRÜHBURGUNDER. Wasps and birds are the main threats to these early-ripening grapes. GEOTEXTILES are sometimes used to protect against WINTER FREEZE. Most plantings measure less than 3 ha/7 acres, and production facilities are modern but very small, often used for both grape- and fruit-wine production. This may soon change: with EU approval in December 2021 of Lithuania as a winegrowing country, forecasters are predicting a 30–40% increase in vineyard hectarage annually.

A.S.

little leaf, a symptom of ZINC deficiency of vines. An associated symptom is a PETIOLAR sinus that is wider than normal.

Livermore Valley, California wine region and AVA spanning Alameda and Contra Costa counties, east of San Francisco Bay. As Livermore's western hills screen out nearly all the sea fogs common on the bay itself, it is quite warm and frequently windy, as evinced by the turbines blanketing the hills of Altamont Pass at the eastern edge of the valley.

Planted first in 1846 by Robert Livermore, who lent his name to the region, Livermore boomed in the 1880s, when Carl H. Wente, James Concannon, and Charles Wetmore established a thriving wine region long before NAPA or SONOMA came on the scene. Just before the onset of PROHIBITION, it hosted more than 2,428 ha/6,000 acres of vines and 50 wineries. Livermore was the first region to produce varietally labelled Chardonnay and Sauvignon Blanc, and most of the Chardonnay planted in the state can be traced back to the region's original Wente HERITAGE CLONE.

Well-drained, stonier-than-GRAVES soils, created by an ancient riverbed, are particularly suited to BORDEAUX varieties, but Livermore's wines command little attention compared to those from Napa or even Sonoma's Alexander Valley. (The exception, perhaps, is Steven Kent Winery, whose top bottlings command Napa-like prices.) The region's primary reds are mid-priced wines made from Zinfandel and Petite Sirah; in whites, Chardonnay continues to be widely planted.

For 40 years vine acreage has been under severe pressure from urbanization, but scions of Wente Vineyards have crafted a land-use compromise with the political authorities: 10 acres of land are set aside for open space or agricultural uses whenever permits are issued for an acre of home or business development.

L.M. & A.Y.

Robinson, J., and Murphy, L., *American Wine* (2013).

Lledoner Pelut or **Lladoner Pelut**, the downy-leaved variant of GRENACHE also known as GRENACHE Poilu or Velu in the south of France and GARNACHA Peluda or Lledoner Pelut in Spain. Both vine and wine closely resemble Grenache Noir except that it is less susceptible to COULURE and therefore yields more consistently and, usefully, reaches PHYSIOLOGICAL RIPENESS at lower sugar levels. It is officially and widely sanctioned in the Languedoc and Roussillon, often being specified in AOC regulations alongside Grenache. But by 2019 France's total had fallen to 284 ha/702 acres, largely in Roussillon, while Spain grew 538 ha/1,329 acres in 2020, mainly in Castilla-La Mancha and to a lesser extent in Cataluña. VARIETAL versions are rare.

Robinson, J., et al., *Wine Grapes: A Complete Guide to 1,368 Vine Varieties, Including Their Origins and Flavours* (2012).

loam, the ideal soil for the growth of most plants, consisting of balanced proportions of clay, silt, and sand (see SOIL TEXTURE). With enough ORGANIC MATTER, loams have a friable, crumby structure (see SOIL STRUCTURE). These desirable characteristics are enhanced where CALCIUM is prominent among the ions bonded to the clay particles and organic matter. A good LOAM has a high capacity to store water and plant nutrients but, unlike stiff CLAY, is not compact enough to impede the free DRAINAGE of water. Rich, loamy soils can encourage excessive VIGOUR in vines, however, particularly in cool to mild climates with ample RAINFALL, so loams (which exist in almost all regions) are not always ideal for viticulture. J.G. & R.E.W.

locusts can damage vines. See GRASSHOPPERS for more detail.

lodge, term used by British shippers of PORT and MADEIRA for a building where wine is stored and matured, especially in Vila Nova de Gaia in OPORTO and more recently in Funchal, Madeira. It is derived from the Portuguese word *loja* meaning 'shop' or 'warehouse'. The Portuguese themselves tend to use the term ARMAZÉM. R.J.M.

Lodi, town in the CENTRAL VALLEY of California that also gives its name to a sizeable AVA. Cooler than either the northern or southern halves of the valley, this prolific farming region was populated from the late 19th century largely by German smallholders who formed CO-OPERATIVES to sell their grapes to large marketing companies such as CONSTELLATION BRANDS, Sebastiani, and JFJ Bronco in the late 1970s and early 1980s. The deep, rich-soiled valley floor was built up by ALLUVIAL deposits from rivers running out of the Sierra Nevada, then pooling before running out to the Pacific Ocean through the Central Valley delta and San Francisco Bay. Lodi is inland from, less watery than, and thus warmer than the CLARKSBURG AVA to the northwest, but it is much less warm than Madera, Fresno, and other districts further south in the SAN JOAQUIN VALLEY.

The AVA sits 145 km/90 miles east of the San Francisco Bay and surrounds the Mokelumne and Cosumnes rivers, extending into the Sacramento–San Joaquin Delta to the west and towards the SIERRA FOOTHILLS in the east. Daily winds known locally as 'Delta Breezes' keep Lodi cooler than the rest of the Central Valley, particularly at the western end, which is the windiest and lowest in ELEVATION and has the deepest soils. Moving north and east, elevations climb, temperatures increase slightly, and soils become rockier.

The diverse growing conditions have inspired the creation of seven sub-AVAs: Alta Mesa, Borden Ranch, Clements Hills, Cosumnes River, Jahant, Mokelumne River, and Sloughhouse. They also allow Lodi to grow more than 125 grape varieties, the most in the state. The AVA has always been most famous for ZINFANDEL, but Cabernet Sauvignon is its most-planted variety. Old-vine FIELD BLENDS with Zinfandel, CARIGNAN, and ALICANTE BOUSCHET remain important, and Lodi claims what appears to be the oldest Cinsaut vineyard in the world, Bechthold, planted in 1886. In white-wine varieties, Chardonnay dominates. The AVA also has a sizeable collection of German, Austrian, and Iberian varieties. E.C.B.

www.lodiwine.com

loess, an accumulation of CLAY and SILT particles that have been deposited by the wind. Loess is typically pale-coloured, unstratified, and loosely cemented by calcium carbonate. Favoured for viticulture because it is porous, permeable, readily warmed, and easily penetrated by roots, it is common in WASHINGTON state and TOKAJ and is found in some vineyards in AUSTRIA, GERMANY, and CHINA. A.J.M.

Loir, Coteaux du, northerly AOC of the greater LOIRE region on the confusingly named Loir tributary about 40 km/25 miles north of Tours in the Sarthe *département*. Viticulture dates to the Middle Ages here, but in 2019 there were just 70 ha/173 acres planted, excluding JASNIÈRES, which sits within it. All three colours of wine are made, with PINEAU D'AUNIS making up at least 65% of the reds and rosés. Cabernet Franc may stiffen reds and GROLLEAU is allowed into its light, dry rosés. Gamay and Côt (MALBEC) are allowed in both. The region's dry white wines, made entirely from Chenin Blanc, tend to be light and fresh.

See also LOIRE, including map.

Loire, France's most famous river and name of one of its most varied wine regions, which produces France's third biggest volume of wine after BORDEAUX and the RHÔNE. Loire wines are greatly appreciated locally and in Paris, but—with the famous exceptions of SANCERRE and POUILLY-FUMÉ—are still widely underrated outside France. This may be partly because the Loire's best red wines are often distinguished by their freshness and delicacy rather than by their weight and longevity and partly because so many of its finest white wines are made solely from Chenin Blanc, a grape variety associated with some rather ordinary wine outside the middle Loire.

History

We know little about the early history of viticulture in the Loire valley, but recent archaeological discoveries suggest that it was extant at least in the upper Loire in the 1st century CE (see GAUL), and it was certainly well established by the 5th century. In a letter to a friend, probably prepared for publication *c.*469, Sidonius Apollinaris (*c.*430–*c.*480), who was born in Lyons but spent a large part of his life in the Auvergne, praises the country of the Arverni (the Auvergne) for its landscape, its fertile fields, and its vineyards. In 475, ROME was forced to cede the Auvergne to the Visigoths, but the depredations of the barbarians left vine-growing safe.

In the next century, Gregory of Tours (*c.*539–94) makes frequent mention, in his *History of the Franks*, of viticulture in the Loire region. As bishop of Tours, he took a great interest in the wine of his diocese (modern TOURAINE). He tells us that, in 591, drought was followed by rain so that the grain harvest was ruined but the vines yielded abundantly. He also tells in detail of the Bretons' often successful attempts to seize the vineyards and/or grapes of the Nantes region (modern MUSCADET) in the 6th century.

The wines of the Loire continued to be held in high regard, and not only by the Bretons, who gave up plundering and bought the wines they wanted. The inhabitants of west Brittany had grown some wine themselves, but in the 13th century they quit viticulture in favour of growing grain and instead purchased their wines from Nantes. Like Nantes, Touraine produced wine of export quality, and by the end of the 11th century the wine of SANCERRE was already well reputed. In the 12th century it was exported to Flanders and sold via Orléans.

From the late 11th century onwards, the aspiring bourgeoisie of the newly rich Flemish cities wanted more and more of its chief status symbol, which was wine (see DUTCH WINE TRADE). With its excellent river connections, the Loire region was especially well placed to meet this growing demand. Some of its wine was shipped to Flanders, or further north, or to England: some of it was carried to PARIS by river to be consumed there or sold on. Angers in particular grew rich on the Flemish guildsmen's desire for social advancement, and vines were planted even just outside its city walls. The count of ANJOU granted Angers the monopoly of carrying wine on the rivers Maine and Loire as far as the Breton port of Ingrandes; in addition, merchants could not buy their wines direct from the vineyards but had to buy them at Angers. These two privileges put the producers of SAUMUR at a disadvantage. The wines of Saumur were not fashionable in France, and Saumur was badly placed for overseas trade. In England in the late 12th century, before the rise of BORDEAUX, Anjou was the only wine to rival Poitou, shipped from LA ROCHELLE, in popularity. Anjou remained highly esteemed in England throughout the Middle Ages.

In France itself, the Loire wine that was most prized was one that has now all but disappeared from public regard: ST-POURÇAIN, made on the river Sioule in the Loire Basin. King Louis IX served it at a banquet in Saumur to celebrate his brother Alphonse's 21st birthday. St-Pourçain fetched high prices during the 14th century and was a favourite with the papal court at Avignon. The wines of the COTEAUX DU LAYON did not become famous until the 15th century.

For more historical detail, see entries under individual wine names. H.M.W.

Dion, R., *Histoire de la vigne et du vin en France* (1959).

Geography and climate

So long is the extent of the viticultural Loire that generalizations are impossible. The Loire's vineyards vary from the CONTINENTAL climate which produces Sancerre and Pouilly-Fumé to the Muscadet region on the Atlantic coast. Loire wine regions represent today, however, the north-western limit of vine cultivation in Europe (with the exception of ENGLAND's vineyards). Spring FROST can be a serious problem, as it was in 1991, when it destroyed up to 90% of the crop in some of the Loire's wine regions; 2016, 2017, and 2019 were also frost-challenged. The character of Loire wines can vary considerably from VINTAGE to vintage, since in a cool summer the grapes may struggle to reach full RIPENESS, while a particularly hot year such as 1989, 1990, 1997, 2003, 2005, 2009, 2011, and 2018 may result in some exceptional sweet white wines, some of them BOTRYTIZED in the middle Loire, but can rob the Loire's dry white Sauvignons of their nerve and leave some MUSCADET dangerously limp.

The region is sufficiently far from the equator, however, that few of its red wines can be accused of being tannic, and the naturally high acidity associated with these latitudes, and some of its grape varieties, make much of the Loire's produce an ideal base wine for SPARKLING WINES.

Viticulture

The Loire is essentially a region of increasingly consolidated family holdings; the average holding has increased from 10 to 25 ha/25–62 acres in recent years, and many farmers have abandoned their other crops to concentrate on viticulture. In the middle Loire, RAINFALL is relatively low, but SPRAYING against FUNGAL DISEASES is still frequent elsewhere. VINE DENSITY is relatively high, between 4,000 and 5,000 plants per ha (1,600–2,000 per acre) on average, with up to 10,000 plants per ha in some Sancerre vineyards. Excess VIGOUR was a problem in the late 1980s and early 1990s and resulted in HERBACEOUS flavours in many of the red wines, although CANOPY MANAGEMENT has generally resolved this. COVER CROPS have long been the norm, and CROP THINNING was introduced in the early 1990s. MECHANICAL HARVESTING is relatively common but cannot be used for the sweet white wines of the middle Loire, where successive *tries* (see TRI) through the vineyards are needed to select only the ripest grapes.

Winemaking

White winemakers of the Loire traditionally followed very similar principles to their counterparts in Germany, assiduously avoiding MALOLACTIC CONVERSION and any new OAK influence, preferring instead to ferment and store wines in inert containers and to bottle wines early, possibly after some LEES CONTACT in the case of Muscadet. For years, Loire reds suffered from a lack of EXTRACTION.

The result of the particularly competitive wine market of the 1980s and a drop in demand for sweet wines in the late 1990s, however, was to stimulate a rash of experimentation in cellars along the length of the Loire. BARREL AGEING and in some cases BARREL FERMENTATION were introduced for both reds and whites (see ANJOU, specifically). Some producers encouraged their white wines to go through malolactic conversion, while red winemakers worked hard to extract greater colour and TANNINS from their red wine musts with prolonged SKIN CONTACT, TEMPERATURE CONTROL, and PUMPING OVER regimes. (It should be said that, in many a Loire autumn and winter, temperature control is just as likely to include heating the MUST as cooling it.) Skin contact prior to fermentation was also introduced for some white wines, especially Sauvignons.

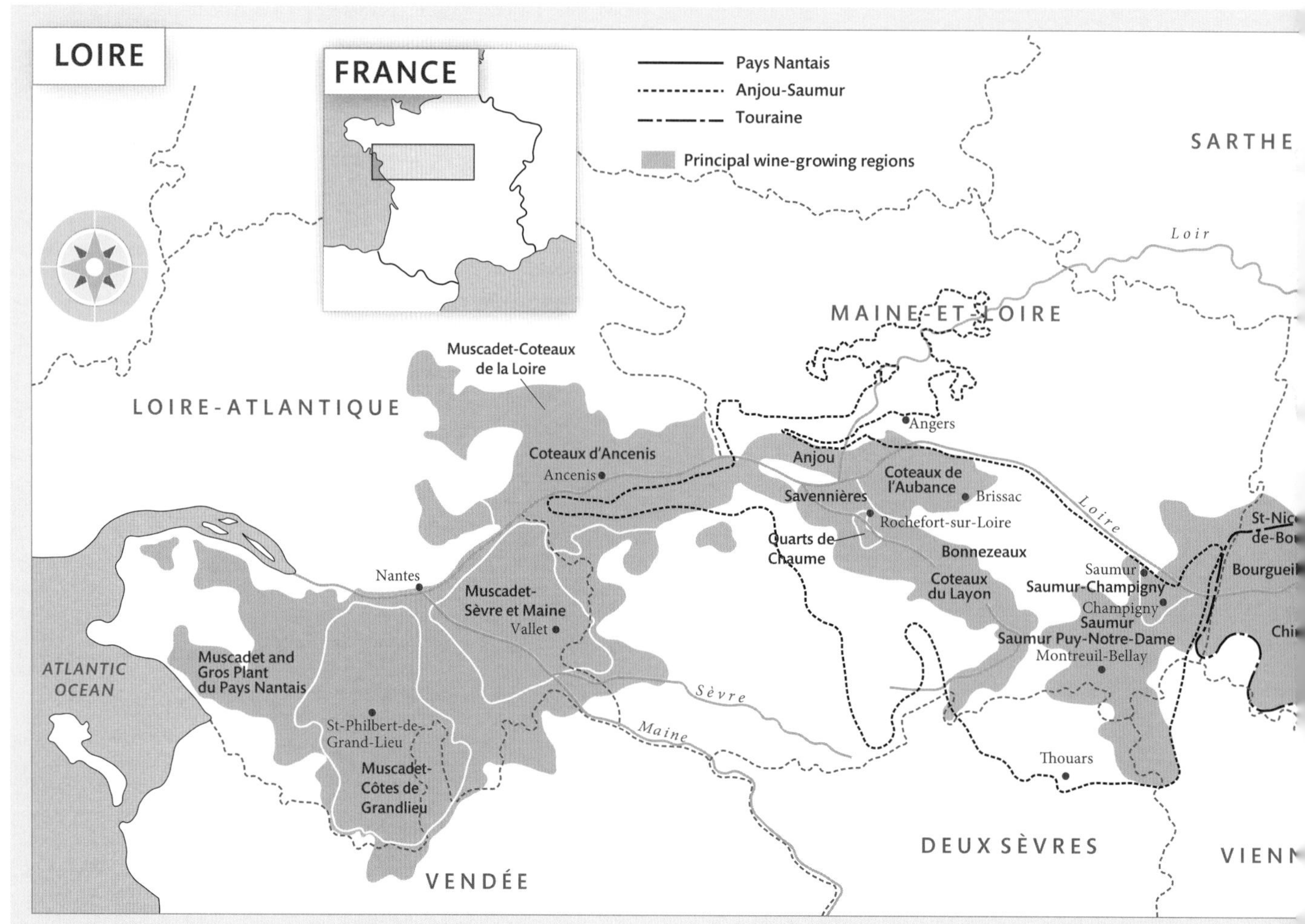

CHAPTALIZATION has been the norm in the Loire for both reds and whites, except in exceptionally hot vintages.

Vine varieties

At the mouth of the Loire, MELON de Bourgogne and FOLLE BLANCHE predominate. The upper Loire is, in the early 21st century anyway, the terrain of Sauvignon Blanc for white wines and Pinot Noir for reds and rosés. Most of the most successful sites in the middle Loire have proved themselves suitable for either CABERNET FRANC or CHENIN BLANC, but in the thousands of hectares of vineyard planted around them, there is a greater diversity of vine varieties than anywhere else in France, including a mix of CABERNET SAUVIGNON, MALBEC, GAMAY, PINOT MEUNIER, PINOT GRIS, CHARDONNAY, and of course seas of Sauvignon and Pinot Noir. This is usually explained in terms of spheres of Bordeaux and Burgundy influence, but it indicates that, outside its most famous appellations, the regions of the Loire have been searching for their own wine identities. The vineyards of the Loire were particularly badly hit by PHYLLOXERA. The heavily CALCAREOUS soils in many regions meant that CHLOROSIS was a common problem when vines were replanted GRAFTED on to resistant ROOTSTOCKS. The Loire, with its relatively cool climate, persisted with a higher proportion of HYBRIDS longer than any other French wine region. The limits on the role of Chardonnay and Cabernet Sauvignon included in the rules of so many Loire appellations show that the authorities at least are aware of the danger of the Loire losing its own identity, and there are signs of a revival of some varieties that are exclusive to the Loire such as PINEAU D'AUNIS, MENU PINEAU, ROMORANTIN, and Meslier-St-François, although the distinctly ordinary GROLLEAU is in retreat.

Wines produced

Of all French wine regions, the Loire produces the greatest diversity of wine styles: from still through all types of sparkling wine, including the generic CRÉMANT de Loire; from bone dry and searingly tart to unctuous LIQUOREUX (although still with a high degree of acidity); and all hues from water white to deep purple. Rosés are a speciality of the Loire, whether the various VINS GRIS made well upstream, the famous Rosé d'Anjou, various pink Cabernets, or the generic ROSÉ DE LOIRE. The most common IGP wine produced in the Loire is known as Val de Loire.

Travelling upstream, the major districts, with each appellation for which there is a separate entry, are as follows (see map):

Pays Nantais: MUSCADET; GROS PLANT DU PAYS NANTAIS; Coteaux d'ANCENIS; FIEFS VENDÉENS.

Anjou-Saumur: ANJOU; SAVENNIÈRES; Coteaux du LAYON; QUARTS DE CHAUME; BONNEZEAUX; Coteaux de l'AUBANCE; SAUMUR.

Touraine: TOURAINE; CHINON; BOURGUEIL; VOUVRAY; MONTLOUIS; CHEVERNY; VALENÇAY.

Upper Loire: REUILLY; QUINCY; MENETOU-SALON; SANCERRE; POUILLY-FUMÉ.

Northern outposts: Coteaux du LOIR; JASNIÈRES; Coteaux du VENDÔMOIS.

On the bend: ORLÉANS; Coteaux du GIENNOIS.

Southern outposts: HAUT-POITOU; CHÂTEAUMEILLANT; ST-POURÇAIN; Côtes d'AUVERGNE; Côte ROANNAISE; Côtes du FOREZ (although some of these are very far from the Loire and its climatic influence).

J.R. & C.P.

www.loirevalleywine.com
jimsloire.blogspot.co.uk
www.vins-centre-loire.com

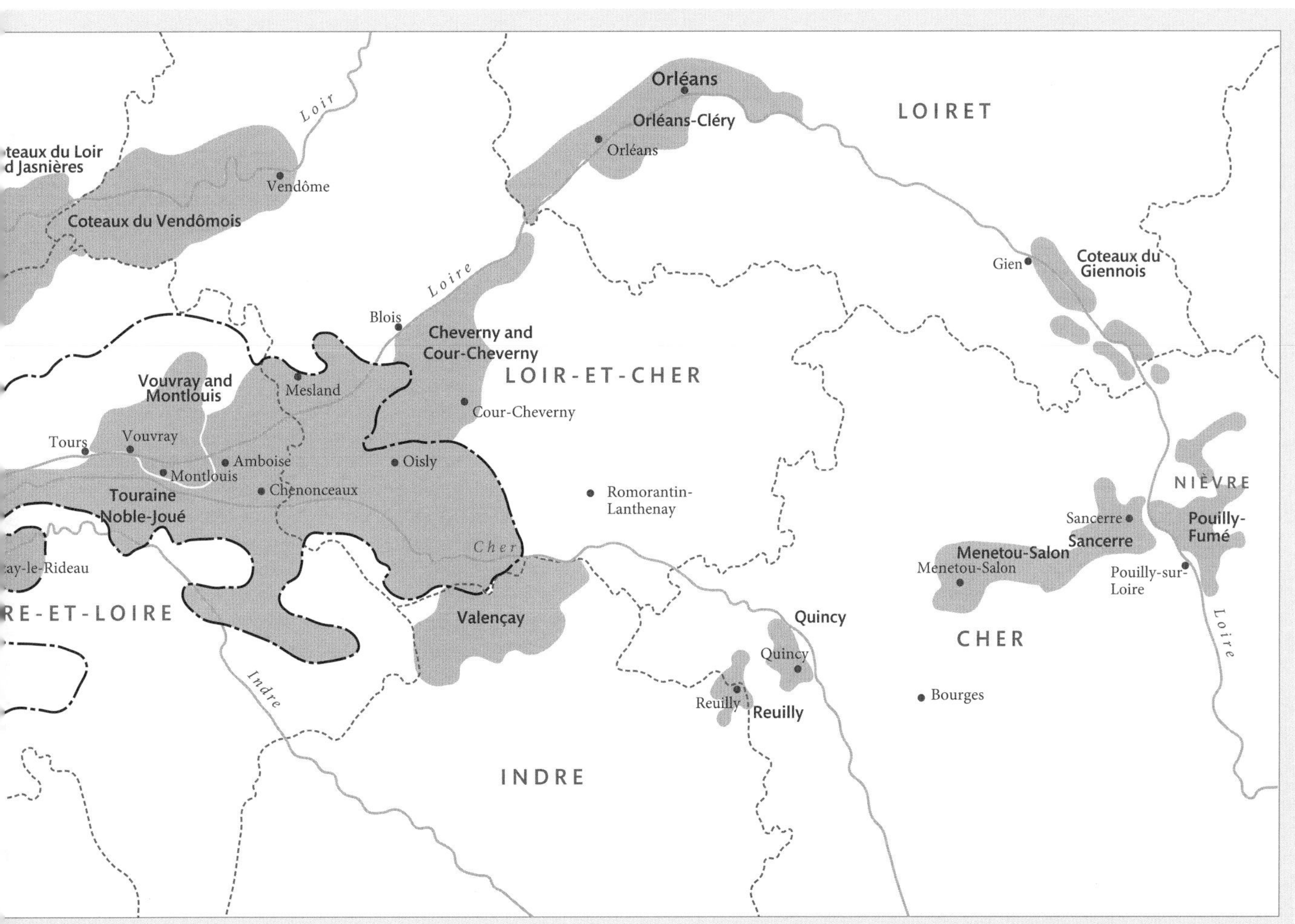

Lombardy, known as **Lombardia** in Italian, is the fourth-largest and, with over 10 million inhabitants, most populous region of Italy; it was the driving force behind the country's post-Second World War economic boom, the dynamo which has given Milan and its hinterland one of Europe's highest standards of living.

Lombardy's principal centres of viticulture are in the hills, divided among no fewer than 21 DOCs and five DOCGs which cater mainly for the many local palates. Currently the five most important areas, each producing very distinct styles of wine, are FRANCIACORTA, LUGANA, OLTREPÒ PAVESE, VALTELLINA, and LAMBRUSCO Mantovano, which is a continuation of the Lambrusco cultivation area in Emilia-Romagna.

One of Lombardy's truly indigenous varieties, GROPELLO, cultivated immediately southwest of Lake Garda, was awarded its own Valtènesi DOC in 2011 but in 2016 demoted to a subzone of the large Riviera del Garda DOC (with a provision for a ludicrous minimum of 30% Gropello), which, together with Lugana DOC, falls entirely within the Garda DOC shared with the Veneto. Its demotion suggests the Valtènesi DOC needs the association with Lake Garda for marketing reasons. W.S.

L

long, much-derided tasting term for wines whose impact on the PALATE is particularly persistent. A wine that is long is usually of high quality. On the basis of studies in other food systems, it is assumed that wine COLLOIDS have a role to play in lengthening the palate of a wine. This occurs through the interaction of various FLAVOUR COMPOUNDS with particular colloids resulting in some or all of the wine's flavour compounds being retained in the mouth, along with the associated polymers, after the wine has been swallowed. Delayed release of the flavour compounds then accounts for the persistent or long palate of the wine. See also TASTING and CAUDALIE. P.J.W.

Longyan, red-skinned grape grown in CHINA whose name means 'dragon's eyes'.

Los Carneros. See CARNEROS, California wine region and AVA.

Los Olivos District, largest sub-AVA of SANTA YNEZ VALLEY, a broad, flat ALLUVIAL terrace planted mainly to Bordeaux varieties, plus some SYRAH.

lot marking. See LABELLING INFORMATION.

Loupiac, small, sweet-white-wine appellation of 264 ha/652 acres nestling between CADILLAC and STE-CROIX-DU-MONT on the right bank of the River Garonne in BORDEAUX. Slightly smaller than Ste-Croix-du-Mont and eight times smaller than BARSAC, its vineyards are situated on multifaceted exposures of clay-limestone and occasionally clay-gravel, bordering and above the wooded valleys created by streams running down to the Garonne, often dominated, as in the Médoc, by 'Folies': impressive neo-classical châteaux built as secondary residences by the 18th-century Bordeaux bourgeoisie. The wines are made primarily from SÉMILLON grapes, plus some Sauvignon Blanc and MUSCADELLE, by law harvested manually, over several passes (see TRI) when the grapes are overripened, either affected by NOBLE ROT or raisined. The minimum required pre-fermentation sweetness is one-third less than in Cadillac, accounting for a lighter style of wine, reputed locally as 'delicate and nervous'. W.J.B.

Loureiro, fine, 'laurel-scented', ancient MINHO white grape variety that is the most planted in this VINHO VERDE country in northern Portugal and the second most widely planted white variety in Portugal, which recorded 6,302 ha/15,573 acres in 2020. It is known as **Loureira** or **Loureira Blanca** over the border in GALICIA in north-west Spain. Often blended with TRAJADURA (Treixadura in Spain), it can also be found as a particularly aromatic VARIETAL wine. It can yield quite productively in the north of the Vinho Verde region and produces its best quality, usually quite low in alcohol, around Braga, Ponte de Lima, and the coast.

low-alcohol wine. Used informally, this term refers to wines with a lower than normal ALCOHOLIC STRENGTH. This may be achieved through work in the vineyard such as reducing the leaf area (CANOPY MANAGEMENT) or harvesting earlier, through the choice of YEAST strain or by BLENDING different lots of wine. Certain commercial YEAST strains and some non-*Saccharomyces* yeast (e.g. *Metschnikowia pulcherrima*) have been shown to reduce alcohol levels by between 0.2% and 1%, although the latter will not complete fermentation on its own. Higher fermentation temperatures and open-top fermenters may also decrease alcohol levels.

The most common way to produce a low-alcohol wine is to arrest FERMENTATION by refrigeration, resulting in a sweet, low-alcohol, often lightly sparkling drink. This is a particularly common technique in Italy and is conducted at all sorts of quality levels (see MOSCATO D'ASTI or LAMBRUSCO, for example).

Many countries restrict the term 'low alcohol' to wines that have been subjected to ALCOHOL REDUCTION and have a very low maximum alcoholic strength, for example 1.2% in the EU and UK or 1.15% in Australia and New Zealand. Such wines are increasingly popular as part of the fashion for NOLO wines. Owing to their reduced alcoholic strength, such wines are usually excluded from DUTY, reducing their price.

See also ALCOHOL REDUCTION and DE-ALCOHOLIZED WINE. J.E.H. & J.P.H.B.

Prezman, F., et al., 'Reducing alcohol content in wines by combining canopy management practices and biological techniques', XIIth International Terroir Congress, Zaragoza (2018).

Puškaš, V. S., et al., 'The aptitude of commercial yeast strains for lowering the ethanol content of wine', *Food Science and Nutrition*, 8/3 (2020), 1489–98.

Low Countries, historical region of north-west Europe including the NETHERLANDS, BELGIUM, and LUXEMBOURG which once played an important part in the wine and spirit trade. See DUTCH WINE TRADE.

Lower Austria. See NIEDERÖSTERREICH.

Lower Murray Zone, in SOUTH AUSTRALIA, has a single but very important region, the RIVERLAND.

low-input viticulture, or **low-intervention viticulture**, alternatives to so-called conventional viticulture which aim to minimize inputs to the vineyard. This may be of AGROCHEMICALS, with the aim of improving the environment (see ORGANIC and BIODYNAMIC VITICULTURE), or of inputs such as LABOUR, with the aim of improving the vineyard's profitability. This latter approach was popular in Australia in the 1990s, although the philosophy is more appropriate to the production of BULK rather than FINE WINE. Reducing agrochemical input may in practice increase the labour input.

low-intervention wine is an alternative, rather more descriptive, term for NATURAL WINE.

Luberon is a sort of buffer state between the RHÔNE and PROVENCE, or more precisely between the VENTOUX appellation and that of Coteaux d'AIX-EN-PROVENCE (although French officialdom places it firmly in the Rhône). The appellation, created in 1988, produces significant quantities of wine from around 3,300 ha/8,154 acres of vines, mainly medium-bodied rosés and lightish reds based on Grenache and Syrah (at least 60% of the blend), with smaller amounts of Mourvédre, Carignan, Cinsault, and Marselan allowed. Those who try hard can produce herb-scented reds with some concentration and AGEING potential. As temperatures get rather cool at night (and in winter), the region can produce some of the crisper, more interesting white wines of the southern Rhône and even some successful Pinot Noir in the cooler spots. White wines are made from Grenache Blanc, Clairette, Bourboulenc, Vermentino, and possibly some Marsanne and Roussanne, with the proportion of Ugni Blanc limited to 50% and Viognier to 10%. Rosés may incorporate up to 20% of white grapes and have particular allure when drunk locally to the sound of cicadas. E.A.G.

Lugana, dry white Italian wine based on the grape known as Turbiana or Trebbiano di Lugana and the same as Trebbiano di Soave (VERDICCHIO), produced south and south-west of Lake Garda in the province of Brescia, straddling the provinces of Lombardy and Veneto.

From 2011 to 2020, the region saw plantings grow from 1,100 ha/2,718 acres to over 2,500 ha. Responsible for this growth is Lugana's exponential success in Germany, which takes as much as 40% of its total production. Owing to this unexpected commercial boom, and because bottling outside of the DOC is allowed, counterfeit wines began to appear, which the CONSORZIO has tried to counteract by making an official banderole applied to the neck of the bottle mandatory. At the same time, the success has inspired investment interest by outside producers.

The DOC can be divided in two parts, of which the first is a narrow band of strikingly white clay-limestone soils on the south shore of Lake Garda known locally known as *menadel.* The second, south of the Strada Provinciale 11, in the hills near San Martino della Battaglia, has sandier soils yielding less expressive wines. Differences of TERROIR are often obscured by high yields, while ageworthy versions of Lugana were not uncommon in the past, as evidenced by Ca' Lojera's version which is aged for five years and has inspired the official creation of a Riserva category. W.S.

www.consorziolugana.it

Lunel is the centre of the **Muscat de Lunel** appellation for sweet, golden VIN DOUX NATUREL made from MUSCAT BLANC À PETITS GRAINS grapes grown on potentially interesting infertile inland soils between Montpellier and Nîmes. Yields are low and vinification techniques improving, although many local vine-growers have been more interested in developing lower-alcohol, dry Muscats or wines that qualify as LANGUEDOC AOC. A single CO-OPERATIVE is responsible for almost all the wine produced, which, as any geographer might suspect, tastes like a cross between the Muscats of FRONTIGNAN and those of ST-JEAN-DE-MINERVOIS. Lunel's historical claim to fame is less convincing than Frontignan's: its Muscat was dispatched to console Napoléon on the island of St Helena. The town does call itself the Cité du Muscat, however.

Lunel is also the occasional Hungarian name for a yellow-berried form of Muscat Blanc à Petits Grains grown in the TOKAJ region.

Lurtons, ramified family of property owners and winemakers in BORDEAUX, owning more wine estates in the Bordeaux region than any other single family. The original Lurton property is the modest Ch Bonnet in the ENTRE-DEUX-MERS, supplemented by Ch Brane-Cantenac in MARGAUX in 1925. André (1924–2019) built up an empire mainly in the GRAVES while his younger brother Lucien (1925–2023) built up an impressive empire of CLASSED GROWTHS (among them Chx Brane-Cantenac, Durfort-Vivens, and Desmirail in Margaux, Bouscaut in Pessac-Léognan, and Doisy-Dubroca and Climens in Barsac) before passing them on in 1992 to his ten children.

André's son Jacques has succeeded his father, while his brother François produces wine in France, Spain, and South America.

In 1991 Pierre Lurton (son of Dominique, André and Lucien's younger brother) became the estate manager at Ch CHEVAL BLANC, the St-Émilion first growth, and, later, Ch d'YQUEM for LVMH.

Lussac-St-Émilion, large satellite appellation of ST-ÉMILION in Bordeaux with 1,414 ha/3,493 acres in 2020 making robust reds on a GRAVEL plateau in the west and cooler CLAY soils in the north.

lutte raisonnée, literally 'reasoned struggle', is a French term that describes an approach to viticulture which tries to minimize the application of AGROCHEMICALS so that they are used only when absolutely necessary and not as a matter of routine. See also INTEGRATED PEST MANAGEMENT and SUSTAINABLE VITICULTURE.

Luxembourg, or **Luxemburg**, was long the EU's smallest and coolest-climate wine producer before being rivalled in both respects by ENGLAND, BELGIUM, the NETHERLANDS, and DENMARK. The rarely exported wines produced are relatively dry and, depending on grape variety, reminiscent of those of Alsace or England in style. With the exception of an increasing number of light reds and rosés made from Pinot Noir and ST-LAURENT vines, the wines made on the western, Luxembourg bank of the river MOSELLE are white. In 2020 there were 1,236 ha/3,054 acres of exceptionally productive vineyard.

History

The German MOSEL, below Trier, and the Luxembourg Moselle above it had to surmount the same problems—COOL CLIMATE and political change—for centuries, but since the First World War the two regions have adopted different solutions. After the war, during which the Grand Duchy remained neutral, Luxembourg was required to break the free-tariff agreement that had been made with Prussia in 1842. Thus a ready market for Luxembourg's sharp whites made from the ELBLING grape evaporated, and Germany looked elsewhere for base wines for SEKT and suitable blending material for the Rheinpfalz's flabbiest wines. The Champagne house Mercier opened up an offshoot in Luxembourg in the late 19th century. A new economic agreement with Belgium signed in 1921 did little to soak up the surplus; Belgian taste is for the richness of POMEROL, the vinous antithesis of Elbling. Thus Elbling has been replaced by softer varieties.

Geography and climate

Luxembourg's vineyards are in two of the Grand Duchy's eastern cantons, Remich and Grevenmacher. On the ALLUVIAL plain of Remich, the heavier soils tend to produce less aromatic, heavier, earlier-maturing wines from such villages as Remich, Wintrange, and Schengen. Parts of the narrower valley of Grevenmacher to the north have been reshaped by terracing, as in the Mosel across the German border, but yields are lower, CALCAREOUS soils predominate, and wines such as the village of Ahn's fine Rieslings are particularly slow maturing. Luxembourg suffers a wide range of cool-climate-related problems such as spring FROSTS, HAIL, and COULURE, so that yields can vary substantially.

Viticulture and vine varieties

Most Luxembourg still wines are VARIETAL wines and labelled as such. Rivaner is the name used here for the MÜLLER-THURGAU that so effectively replaced Elbling in the 20th century that by the early 1980s it was planted on half of the Grand Duchy's total vineyard, being relatively easy to ripen whatever the local conditions. Its ability to yield obligingly high quantities was so abused by many growers, however, that it became synonymous with mediocrity and declined considerably to 276 ha/682 acres by 2020, about one-fifth of the country's vineyard. Much of it was replaced by Pinot Gris (195 ha/482 acres), highly regarded for its low acidity and its ripening potential. Pinot Blanc (165 ha/408 acres) and Pinot Noir (128 ha/316 acres) have also been enthusiastically planted, chiefly for CRÉMANT sparkling wine. Pinot Blanc's close relative AUXERROIS enjoys higher status in Luxembourg than anywhere else in the world (and certainly higher than in Alsace, where ten times as much is planted). Its low acidity is a positive attribute this far from the equator; when yields are curbed, BARREL-AGED Luxembourg Auxerrois can produce smoky, full-bodied wines worth AGEING. Total plantings in 2020 were 193 ha/477 acres. Although some Chardonnay and Gewürztraminer is planted, the only other significant variety is Riesling (164 ha/405 acres), whose stately ageing curve put many Luxembourg wine drinkers off for years, but a new generation of producers seems to have understood the need to pick Riesling later and achieve more consumer-friendly flavours.

Prior to the 2000s, CHAPTALIZATION was often a necessity, but CLIMATE CHANGE has made it less so. Still, the wines can be marked by relatively high acidity, and DEACIDIFICATION may be practised by some producers. An increasing number of wineries have moved to ORGANIC VITICULTURE, inspired by research led by the Stëftung Hëllef fir d'Natur (Foundation Help for Nature) as well as the success of Domaine Sunnen-Hoffmann, the country's first certified estate (2001). Today some 18 producers have taken partly or totally the same direction.

Appellations

There is just one Appellation Protégé (AOP), Luxembourg's answer to the AOC system of France: Moselle Luxembourgeoise is allowed for practically all wines, both still and sparkling, although they all must be submitted for analysis and tasting. Superior wines (excluding Pinot Noir and Elbling) may also be ranked a Grands Premiers Crus and Premiers Crus if yields do not exceed 75 hl/ha and 85 hl/ha respectively. (The maximum yield allowed for the French MOSELLE is 60 hl/ha.) Furthermore, the use of the terms 'Côtes de', 'Coteaux de,' and 'Lieu-Dit' are also regulated. Wines labeled 'Côtes de' have maximum permitted yields of 100 hl/ha (115 for Elbling and Rivaner); those labelled 'Coteaux de' and 'Lieu-Dit' must be manually harvested at less than 75 hl/ha within specifically delineated areas.

Since 1993, there has been some limited experimentation with ICE WINES and other sweet wines, with official regulation in 2001. Pinots Blanc and Gris and Riesling picked at −7 °C/19 °F with a MUST WEIGHT of at least 120 °Oechsle may be labelled *vin de glace*. The same regulations allow Auxerrois, Pinot Blanc, Pinot Gris, and Gewürztraminer with 105 °Oechsle and Riesling with 95 °Oechsle to be sold as VENDANGES TARDIVES, while the appellation VIN DE PAILLE may be used for Auxerrois, Pinot Blanc, Pinot Gris, and Gewürztraminer with at least 130 °Oechsle.

More than one-quarter of Luxembourg's total AOP wine production is in sparkling wines, both MOUSSEUX and especially TRADITIONAL METHOD. For more details, see CRÉMANT de Luxembourg.

Industry organization

As in the German Mosel, the average vine-holding is extremely small—4.77 ha/12 acres in 2020—although it is gradually increasing as more of the smallest holdings are sold to larger landowners. The number of growers more than halved during the 20 years up to 2020 to 268. Just 30% of vines are grown by independent domaines which make wine themselves. Several wine CO-OPERATIVES together function as Vinsmoselle and represent 52% of the Grand Duchy's wine production. A.D.

aop.lu/luxembourg

LVMH, scrupulously even-handed acronym for Moët Hennessy-Louis Vuitton, the French luxury goods conglomerate which has a dominant interest in the CHAMPAGNE industry, not least through its subsidiaries, which include MOËT & CHANDON, KRUG, VEUVE CLICQUOT, and Ruinart, and a leading position in Cognac through Hennessy. For more details of LVMH's champagne interests, see MOËT & CHANDON. Since the late 1950s the company has developed a substantial position in the premium SPARKLING WINE market through the creation and development of the Chandon brand in Argentina, Brazil, the US, Australia, China, and India.

LVMH's still-wine assets include CLOUDY BAY, Cape Mentelle in WESTERN AUSTRALIA, Terrazas de los Andes in MENDOZA, Numanthia in TORO, and Newton in the NAPA Valley, where the company bought a controlling stake in Colgin in 2017. In 2019 it acquired Ch Galoupet in PROVENCE and, subsequently, a controlling stake in the producer of the leading rosé brand, also in Provence, WHISPERING ANGEL. In 1998 LVMH acquired a substantial stake in Ch d'YQUEM, while its chief executive Bernard Arnault became co-owner of Ch CHEVAL BLANC. Another jewel in the crown is the GRAND CRU Clos des Lambrays in MOREY-ST-DENIS, bought for an eye-watering sum in 2014. Ao Yun is an ambitious, small-production Cabernet blend made at ELEVATION in Yunnan, the result of a four-year search for China's most propitious red-wine-producing area.

www.lvmh.com

Lyonnais, Coteaux du, light white, pink, but mainly red wines made chiefly from about 280 ha/692 acres of vines in the hills both north and south-west of the city of Lyons, considered part of greater Burgundy by French wine authorities, and drunk mainly by its inhabitants. The red wines, all GAMAY, can be every bit as good as nearby BEAUJOLAIS, although the appellation was granted only in 1984. A small amount of white wine is also made, from Chardonnay and ALIGOTÉ. The CO-OPERATIVE at Sain-Bel vinifies three-quarters of production.

lyre, a vine-TRAINING SYSTEM whereby the CANOPY is divided horizontally into two curtains of upward-pointing SHOOTS, resembling a lyre in shape (see illustration). The system was developed in Bordeaux in the early 1980s by Dr Alain Carbonneau (see MONTPELLIER). Carbonneau was much influenced by the pioneering studies of Nelson SHAULIS in CANOPY MANAGEMENT. The lyre system improves the CANOPY MICROCLIMATE and leads to improvement in YIELD and wine quality because of better leaf and fruit exposure to SUNLIGHT. Either SPUR PRUNING or CANE PRUNING can be used. Further use of this system has been delayed by the unavailability of suitable MECHANICAL HARVESTERS. The system has been adopted in NEW WORLD vineyards in particular, especially in California, and to a lesser extent in Australia, New Zealand, Chile, and Uruguay, but it has also been implemented in some vineyards in Beaujolais.

Cross-section of **lyre**-trained vines during the growing season.

Vine training to the **lyre** system showing spur pruning (cane pruning can also be used).
Source: R. Smart and M. Robinson, *Sunlight into Wine*

The lyre system is essentially an inverted GENEVA DOUBLE CURTAIN, with the two adjacent curtains of foliage trained upwards rather than downwards. Both systems are used to reduce the shading of dense canopies (see SHADE). The lyre system is typically recommended for medium-VIGOUR vines, whereas the GDC can harness higher vine vigour. The lyre system has shown substantial improvements in wine quality where it has been evaluated. R.E.S.

Coombe, B. G., and Dry, P. R. (eds.), *Viticulture*, ii: *Practices* (2nd edn, 2006).
Smart, R. E., and Robinson, M., *Sunlight into Wine: A Handbook for Winegrape Canopy Management* (1991).

lyric poetry. There are many references to wine in the lyric poets of ancient GREECE. Archilochos, writing in the middle of the 7th century BCE, describes the comfort brought by wine on a long sea journey:

Along the rowers' benches bring your cup
And lift the lids of the big wine jars up
And drain the good red wine: we can't, 'tis clear
Be sober all the time we're watching here.

Fifty years later, Alkaios of Lesbos (who knew and admired the poetess Sappho) has many references to wine, often in vigorous verse: 'Wet your lungs with wine; for the dog star is coming round, and everything is thirsty with heat.' In an early variant of not waiting for the sun to be over the yard-arm, he writes: 'Drink! Why wait for the lamps? The day is almost done!'

The curmudgeonly Theognis, writing at the same time, probably from Megara on the isthmus of Corinth, extols the value of wine and the dangers of DRUNKENNESS: 'Stand by ready to pour for those who want to drink. We cannot have a party every night. Still because I am moderate in my use of honeyed wine, I reach my house before I think of soothing sleep, and I make clear how divine a beverage for man is wine.' H.H.A.

M

Macabeo is northern Spain's second most planted white grape variety (considerably after AIRÉN), whose total had grown to 55,073 ha/136,088 acres by 2020. Around the early 19th century it spread to southern France, where, as **Maccabéo** or **Macabeu**, it was still planted on 1,714 ha/4,235 acres in 2019, mainly in ROUSSILLON. It buds and ripens too late to be grown much further north but is quite productive.

It is grown in most Spanish regions apart from Galicia and the far south with the greatest areas in CASTILLA-LA MANCHA, where it makes relatively bland dry whites, and in CATALUÑA, where it is an ingredient in CAVA, generally blended with Xarello and Parellada. Around 2,000–3,000 ha remain in each of ARAGÓN and RIOJA, where, as Viura, it replaced Malvasia Fina and Garnacha Blanca after PHYLLOXERA. Average VINE AGE is high in Rioja and can be matched by wine QUALITY if yields are restricted.

In early-picked form, in Roussillon it is either a fairly characterless white or a useful ingredient in rosé. However, in both Roussillon and Rioja it can also make fine BARREL-AGED and ageworthy whites. In the LANGUEDOC, in the white wines of Minervois and Corbières, it may be blended with BOURBOULENC, GRENACHE BLANC, and a host of other southern white varieties.

Robinson, J., et al., *Wine Grapes: A Complete Guide to 1,368 Vine Varieties, Including Their Origins and Flavours* (2012).

Macarthur, Sir William (1800–82), was the most influential wine pioneer in the Australian colonies during the 19th century. Although James BUSBY is regarded as the father of the Australian wine industry, he did little to nurture it, having left New South Wales in 1833 for New Zealand. William Macarthur on the other hand fostered viticulture and winemaking throughout his lifetime through patronage, philanthropy, and grand agricultural visions for Australia.

William Macarthur was the youngest son of wealthy pastoralists John and Elizabeth Macarthur, who played an important role in developing the colony's wool and wine industries. In 1808 William and his brother James accompanied John Macarthur to England, where they were educated until 1815, when they travelled with their father to France, witnessing Napoleon Bonaparte's triumphant return to Paris. After a brief period in Switzerland during the lead-up to the Battle of Waterloo, they journeyed through the south of France and sourced grapevine CUTTINGS. After their return to Australia in 1817, the cuttings and other plant material including 'olive, fig and caper' were planted at the Macarthur's Camden Park estate, prime agricultural land south of Sydney. But it became evident once the cuttings bore fruit that a mix-up by the London nurseryman entrusted to look after the cuttings resulted in only a few new varieties being introduced into New South Wales.

A letter in 1824 from the 24-year-old William Macarthur mentions 'the first vintage at Camden is ready to be pressed and a few bottles will be sent to England'. The following year more grape varieties were imported into New South Wales. According to James Busby, John Macarthur was the first to introduce the Burgundy Grape (Pinot Noir), Miller's Burgundy (PINOT MEUNIER), VERDELHO, Sweetwater (CHASSELAS), and three types of MUSCADELLE. But it was William Macarthur who initiated and managed the importation of vine cuttings.

On learning of Busby's plan to return to Europe, James and William Macarthur partially sponsored his seminal journey through Spain and France in 1830. On his return to New South Wales in 1831, duplicate cuttings of Busby's 'great vine importation' were planted at Camden Park. In 1834 the Busby Collection planted in Sydney's Botanical Garden was appraised by Francis Forbes, Alexander McLeay, Sir John Jamison, and William Macarthur at the behest of Governor Major General Sir Richard Bourke. Almost certainly this led to Camden Nurseries importing 'a collection of the best sorts cultivated in the Medoc' in 1837. This included the first importation of Cabernet Sauvignon. William Macarthur also claims to have brought in the first Riesling cuttings to Australia in 1838 (with the assistance of German vineyard workers from the famed Marcobrunn vineyard in the Rheingau who were employed to supervise the vineyards at Camden).

By the 1840s, Camden Park was the colony's most significant nursery of colonial vines, ornamental trees, and plant material. It supplied cuttings to Thomas Shepherd's Darling Nurseries at Darlington, Bailey's Gardens in Adelaide, and John Pascoe Fawkner and John James Rule near Melbourne. Macarthur also sold vine cuttings directly to landed farmers, including the Ryrie, Angas, Gilbert, and Reynell families. In addition, Camden Park was a renowned breeding stud of thoroughbred horses.

Wealthy, enlightened, curious, and generous in nature, William Macarthur was by far the most influential wine man of his day. 'Letters on the culture of the vine, fermentation, and the management of wine in the cellar, by Maro' (a pseudonym he used) were regularly published by newspapers (and then compiled into a book in 1844), distilling the progress of winemaking in New South Wales and inspiring settlers to grow grapes and make wine. In 1850 William Macarthur established the New South Wales Vineyard Association, which played an important role in developing a colonial wine industry.

William Macarthur's interests and achievements were much wider than viticulture and would eventually lead to a knighthood (the first Australian-born colonialist to receive this honour) and to being appointed a Chevalier of the Légion d'Honneur by Napoleon III. His practical expertise in mixed farming, economic botany, agricultural science, and winemaking helped shape the progress of colonial agriculture and the Australian wine industry during the mid-to-late 19th century. The destruction of Camden Vineyards by PHYLLOXERA around 1885 just three years after his death marked the end of an era. H.A.C.

Macedon Ranges, fashionable Australian wine region in VICTORIA's Port Phillip Zone, with sparkling wines, Chardonnay, and Pinot Noir performing well on account of its ELEVATION-derived cool climate.

Maceratino, increasingly rare white grape grown on 39 ha/96 acres of the MARCHE in 2015. Possibly related to VERDICCHIO.

maceration, ancient word for steeping a material in liquid with or without a kneading action to separate the softened parts of the material from the harder ones. This important process in RED WINEMAKING involves extraction of the PHENOLICS (TANNINS, colouring materials, or ANTHOCYANINS, FLAVOUR PRECURSORS, and non-glycosylated FLAVOUR COMPOUNDS) from the grape skins, seeds, and stem fragments into the juice or new wine. Maceration is governed by TEMPERATURE, by contact between the solids and liquid and the degree of agitation, by time, and by the composition of the extracting liquid, in this case the grape juice as it becomes wine. Although some everyday red wines are made simply by a rapid fermentation lasting just two or three days, many winemakers encourage an additional post-fermentation maceration, particularly for long-lived wines such as red BORDEAUX. If fermentation is slow to start, possibly due to the low temperature of the grapes and/or the use of AMBIENT YEAST, the winemaker may take advantage of or even encourage the pre-fermentation maceration that results.

The maceration process should never extract all of the phenolics from red grapes, only the best part. This is why the winemaker's choices regarding the intensity, method, and duration of extraction are critical. The speed at which the anthocyanins are released from the skins depends on the vintage and the variety, starting during the aqueous phase before the tannins are released. The extraction of tannins increases as the alcohol level rises. Reactions progressively occur among the compounds newly released, leading to the formation of PIGMENTED TANNINS. Winemakers must use trial and error, often over many years, to decide which are the optimum maceration conditions for each grape variety and season. Rapid laboratory analyses can help to estimate colour and tannins (and Ferré has shown in his *Traité d'œnologie bourguignonne* that extraction reaches a maximum of 80% of the grapes' available colouring matter on the sixth day of maceration), but the winemaker's eye and palate often prove surer guides.

Both heat and alcohol encourage the extraction of compounds, which is fortunate since both are produced by fermentation. As fermentation continues, heat is produced and the increasingly alcoholic liquid becomes a better and better solvent for the organic compounds to be extracted.

During fermentation, the bubbles of CARBON DIOXIDE gas generated tend to make the grape skins float to the surface in the FERMENTATION VESSEL to form a layer known as a CAP. For generations, winemaking ingenuity has been harnessed to devise methods of breaking up and submerging the cap to keep the skins and liquid in contact. This is relatively simple with small batches of fermenting grapes (see PUNCHING DOWN). With larger batches, a system of either grids or coarse mesh screens must be devised to keep the cap SUBMERGED, or liquid from the bottom of the tank must be pumped to the top and sprayed over the skins (see PUMPING OVER and RACK AND RETURN).

Several proprietary systems have been devised to extract the desirable organic compounds from the grape skins into the fermenting wine. Some of these use a quick high-temperature phase to disrupt the cells containing anthocyanins and liberate the desirable organic compounds (see THERMOVINIFICATION and FLASH DÉTENTE); others use mechanical stirrers or rotating tanks (see ROTOFERMENTERS) which keep the skins and liquid in contact; or some form of AUTOVINIFICATION. The use of pulsed electric fields has been found to make the cell membranes in the skins more permeable without the need to heat the must. Nanofiltration is another method that avoids the use of heat and has been successfully tested in Bordeaux. Trials in New Zealand found that cutting up the grape skins prior to fermentation increased the speed of extraction. In general, heat and mechanical agitation systems are used for ordinary wines, while the more sensitive techniques of punching down or pumping over are preferred for finer wines, although care must be taken that any pumps used are relatively gentle. In squat tanks there is greater extraction than in tall ones because of the greater relative area of skin-to-juice contact.

Along with temperature, liquid composition, and intimacy of contact, the fourth factor influencing colour, tannin, and flavour extraction is time of contact, an aspect, albeit less than perfectly understood, over which winemakers can have total control (provided they have access to sufficient vat space). In general the longer the solids and liquids are in contact, the greater the degree of extraction, but it depends on the frequency of pumping over or punching down. It has been shown, however, that the extraction of the desirable compounds slows down considerably after the new wine approaches 10% alcohol and is at its height during the earlier phases of fermentation. The total maceration time varies according to the phenolic content of the skins (itself a function of grape variety and weather) and according to the desired style of wine. In red winemaking, maceration usually lasts at least as long as fermentation does, but it may be prolonged for a further week, sometimes longer. Punching down and pumping over are usually avoided during this later phase so as not to extract more astringent tannins. Care must also be taken to avoid the increased risk of high levels of VOLATILE ACIDITY, by protecting the cap with INERT GAS. Maintaining the temperature of the wine at 28–30 °C/82–86 °F during any post-fermentation maceration will improve the texture of the tannins.

Some wine producers favour a pre-fermentation **cold maceration** of red grapes rather than maceration of skins in an alcoholic liquid. This optional winemaking operation involves the maceration of grape skins with juice while the mass is held at a low temperature with the aims of extracting colour and producing more intense fruit aromas. A quite different red winemaking technique is CARBONIC MACERATION, practised particularly in BEAUJOLAIS and for other red wines designed for early consumption.

See also BARREL FERMENTATION for an outline of a red winemaking option which dispenses with post-fermentation maceration altogether.

In WHITE WINEMAKING, maceration is usually actively discouraged by separating the juice from the skins as soon as possible in order to avoid extraction of tannins, since no colouring matter is required and the resultant ASTRINGENCY is generally viewed as a fault in white wines. However, some winemakers deliberately allow a certain period of SKIN CONTACT for white grapes before they are crushed, and in the late 1980s this technique (known as **macération pelliculaire** in French) was encouraged by Denis DUBOURDIEU among others in order to produce more flavourful dry white wines. Sauvignon and Gros Manseng grapes, for example, are held for 4–8 hours at about 18 °C/64 °F, resulting in juice higher in flavour compounds and flavour precursors, tannins, POTASSIUM salts, and POLYSACCHARIDES, and wines with more BODY and a slightly higher PH. Fermenting white wine on the skins has become increasingly popular, particularly but not exclusively in tandem with the use of clay fermentation vessels such as AMPHORAE, TINAJAS, TALHAS, PITHARI, and QVEVRI. See SKIN-FERMENTED and ORANGE WINE. The OIV has recently added 'white wine with maceration' to the list of 'special wines' in its International Code of Oenological Practices.

Maceration is also important in the production of fruit-flavoured spirits such as the *crème de cassis* used in making a *vin blanc cassis* or KIR, which is the aromatic and deeply coloured product of blackcurrants macerated in alcohol. V.L.

OIV, 'International Code of Oenological Practices'. www.oiv.int/en/technical-standards-and-documents/oenological-practices/international-code-of-oenological-practices.

macération carbonique, French term for CARBONIC MACERATION.

macération pelliculaire, French term for the pre-fermentation maceration of white grapes described in MACERATION and known in English as SKIN CONTACT.

macération préfermentaire, French term for pre-fermentation MACERATION. In Beaujolais, the term *macération préfermentaire à chaud* (*MPC* or *thermo*) refers to a technique involving heating just-picked grapes to about 65 °C/150 °F then chilling them back down to about 25 °C after 12 hours. The first part of fermentation is carried out on the GRAPE skins, but fermentation is completed after pressing (see THERMOVINIFICATION).

McLaren Vale, intensively planted, historic SOUTH AUSTRALIAN wine region especially noted for rich reds. These have a distinctive and often useful dash of dark chocolate in their make-up and are typically high in alcohol. An eclectic collection of winemakers makes for a vibrant cellar door scene, and many producers experiment with alternative Mediterranean varieties and innovative winemaking styles. Notwithstanding, the bulk of production is dominated by Shiraz, Cabernet Sauvignon, and Grenache. R.J.T.

Mâcon, important commercial centre on the River Saône and capital of the **Mâconnais** dynamic district of BURGUNDY which produces considerable quantities of white wine and some red. Unlike in the Côte d'Or to the north (see map under FRANCE), vineyards on the rolling LIMESTONE hills of the Mâconnais are interspersed with land dedicated to livestock and arable farming. Côte d'Or producers as renowned as Leflaive and Lafon have invested in this southerly region.

The climate and ambience of the region differ from the Côte d'Or however: southern tiles are used for roofs, cicadas can be heard in summer, and the vineyards benefit from more sun, less rain, and little risk of frost. BEAUJOLAIS is to the immediate south of the Mâconnais.

Viticultural practices are broadly similar to those in the CÔTE D'OR, except for the widespread use of LYRE training systems, although yields may be a little higher, up to a permitted 66–70 hl/ha for whites and 58–64 hl/ha for reds, depending on the exact denomination. Vinification is sometimes carried out in barrels, although only the best producers use new OAK. Bottling normally takes place in the summer before the next vintage.

The appellations of Mâconnais, in approximately ascending order of quality, are, for white wines made from Chardonnay: **Mâcon**; **Mâcon-Villages** or **Mâcon** followed by a particular village name (for more details of which, see MÂCON-VILLAGES); ST-VÉRAN; Pouilly-Vinzelles, Pouilly-Loché, and POUILLY-FUISSÉ. Red-wine appellations are **Mâcon** and **Mâcon** followed by a particular village name. Almost all these red wines are made from the GAMAY grape since, although Pinot Noir is permitted, such wines may be sold as BOURGOGNE Rouge at a higher price than Mâcon fetches.

In 1998, the villages of Viré and Clessé, including the hamlet of Quintaine, were given their own appellation, VIRÉ-CLESSÉ. J.T.C.M.

Mâcon-Villages, appellation covering the great majority of the white wines of MÂCON. The wines may be sold either as Mâcon-Villages or as Mâcon followed by the name of the particular village. Viré and Lugny have been the best known by virtue of their CO-OPERATIVES. The full list of 27 villages or groups of villages with the right to the appellation is: Azé, Bray, Burgy, Bussières, Chaintré, Chardonnay (whence the grape may have taken its name), Charnay-lès-Mâcon, Cruzille, Davayé, Fuissé, Igé, Loché, Lugny, Mancey, Milly-Lamartine, Montbellet, Péronne, Pierreclos, Prissé, La Roche-Vineuse, Serrières (reds only), St-Gengoux-le-National, Solutré-Pouilly, Uchizy (whites only), Vergisson, Verzé, and Vinzelles.

Most Mâconnais wines are vinified in STAINLESS STEEL or glass-lined CONCRETE vats for early bottling and consumption within a year or two of the vintage. A handful of growers are producing significantly finer wines through low yields followed by BARREL FERMENTATION and BARREL AGEING. J.T.C.M.

macroclimate, also called regional climate, means a climate broadly representing an area or region on a scale of tens to hundreds of kilometres. Unlike the more precise terms MICROCLIMATE and MESOCLIMATE, 'macroclimate' approximates to what is normally meant by the word 'climate'. It is usually based on data from a long-established and topgraphically representative weather station within the region.

Macroclimatic data have to be used with caution when applied to viticulture. Informed adjustments are nearly always needed for differences in ELEVATION, slope, and ASPECT before reasonable estimates can be made for the mesoclimates of actual vineyards. This is especially so in cool regions, where small differences in local temperature can make differences in timing and completeness of RIPENING. R.E.S.

Dry, P. R., and Smart, R. E., 'Vineyard site selection', in P. R. Dry and B. G. Coombe (eds.), *Viticulture*, i: *Resources* (2nd edn, 2004).

macro-oxygenation, an umbrella term for the deliberate exposure of wine to OXYGEN that contrasts with MICRO-OXYGENATION, including the very specific technique of that name. See AERATION, PUMPING OVER, RACK AND RETURN, RACKING, BARREL FERMENTATION, and BARREL AGEING. See also TOTAL PACKAGE OXYGEN.

Macvin du Jura, powerful VIN DE LIQUEUR made in the JURA in eastern France by blending hardly fermented grape juice with MARC du Jura. This somewhat sweet but curiously earthy drink should be served cool as an APERITIF or with ice cream dishes. A version involving spices and heated must was made as early as the 14th century. Macvin white, rosé, or red was awarded its own AOC, the 400th created by the INAO, in 1991. W.L.

Madagascar, large tropical island off the east African coast which was a French colony between 1896 and 1960 and has a wine industry that has since been run largely by Chinese immigrants. The island had about 2,704 ha/6,682 acres of vines in 2020 according to OIV figures. Due to heat and humidity, mainly HYBRID vines are grown in the central Hauts-Plateaux area at ELEVATIONS of 750–1,350 m/2,361–4,429 ft. Swiss settlers encouraged the Betsileo farmers to apply their expertise growing rice on high terraces to viticulture in the 1960s. The hundreds of vinegrowers, with just a few hectares of vineyard each, are centred on Fianarantsoa and Ambalavo.

Madeira, Atlantic island belonging to Portugal, nearly 1,000 km/625 miles from the Portuguese mainland and 750 km/466 miles off the coast of North Africa, now a DOP for FORTIFIED wines. (The island's unfortified wines take either the DOP Madeirense or the IGP Terras Madeirenses; see MADEIRENSE.) Fortified madeira makes up nearly 94% of the island's production and is probably the world's most resilient and longest-lived wine.

History

Like PORT, madeira seems to have begun as an unfortified wine. There are few early records, but Madeira's strategic position in the middle of the Atlantic put the island at an advantage, and its capital Funchal became a natural port of call for ships en route to Africa, Asia, and South America. Madeira's wine industry was well established by the end of the 16th century (less than 200 years after the discovery of the island). However, the early madeira wines were unstable, and many deteriorated long before they reached their destination. Alcohol (probably distilled from cane sugar) was therefore added to some wines to help them survive a long sea voyage, although FORTIFICATION did not become general practice until the mid 18th century.

In the second half of the 17th century, ships en route to India (including many of the DUTCH EAST INDIA COMPANY fleet) called regularly at Funchal to pick up casks of wine termed *pipas* or PIPES. It was soon found that madeira somehow tasted better after pitching and rolling across the tropics in the hull of a ship. With this came a fashion for *vinho da roda*, wines that had benefited from a round trip, as opposed to *vinho canteiro*, wine which matured on the island, called after the trestles (*canteiros*) on which the pipes rested in the warehouse (ARMAZÉM). Wines continued to undergo long tropical sea journeys to induce this special flavour until the 1900s. Over the preceding century most shippers turned to using ESTUFAS, rooms or tanks in which the wine could be artificially heated to simulate the rapid maturation brought about by a long sea journey—although the finest madeiras continue to be aged naturally on *canteiros* (see below).

With the colonization of North America in the 17th century, Madeira established an important export market. By the end of the 18th century, the new North American colonies were buying one-quarter of all the wine produced on the island. Madeira was held in such high esteem that it was used to toast the Declaration of Independence in 1776. Colonial troops returning to Britain opened up a new market for madeira there, and the drink became popular with Portuguese settlers in Africa and in Brazil as well. Demand began to outstrip supply. Then, in 1851, the first of a series of crises struck Madeira's wine industry. Oidium or POWDERY MILDEW reached the island (in the same year as it was first identified in BORDEAUX) and quickly spread through the dense vineyards, almost wiping out production in just three years.

The industry revived after it was found that oidium could be controlled by dusting the vine leaves with SULFUR, but shortly afterwards PHYLLOXERA struck, leaving the island's wine-based economy in ruins. From the mid 1870s, vines all over the island were replaced by sugar cane. Wine shippers abandoned Madeira, and many vineyards were never replanted.

Phylloxera-resistant AMERICAN VINE SPECIES were introduced a decade or so later, but many farmers, seeking a rapid return to prosperity, cultivated VITIS *labrusca*, *riparia*, *rupestris*, and hybrid vines rather than using them merely as ROOTSTOCKS on to which Madeira's traditional VITIS VINIFERA varieties could be grafted.

Madeira's wine industry returned to normal levels of production at the beginning of the 20th century, and shipments to traditional markets were restored. But the island's economy was dealt another blow by the Russian Revolution in 1917 and then by PROHIBITION in the United States. Many firms were forced to close, but a number chose to form the Madeira Wine Association, renamed as the Madeira Wine Company in 1981.

Although at the end of the 17th century there were about 30 wine shippers operating on Madeira, by the mid 2010s there were just six exporters, of which JUSTINO'S (Justino Henriques) is now the largest wine producer on the island, although the best known is probably the Madeira Wine Company comprising BLANDY, Cossart Gordon, Leacock, and Rutherford & Miles among more than 20 brand names. In 1988, the SYMINGTON family of OPORTO took control of the company and thoroughly overhauled the winemaking practices and equipment. In 2011 they sold back their stake to the Blandy family.

France, Germany, and the Benelux countries are the largest markets for modern madeira, although most of the wine destined for these countries is of very basic quality and bought for cooking rather than drinking. The United States, Japan, and the United Kingdom are the main markets for better-quality madeira.

Viticulture

Madeira is a difficult place to grow grapes. Nearly all the island's vineyards are planted on tiny step-like terraces called *poios*, carved from the red or grey BASALT bedrock. Although most of the newer vineyards are CORDON-trained, most vineyards are planted on low trellises (known as *latada*) similar to those of the VINHO VERDE region on the Portuguese mainland. These serve to raise the CANOPY above the ground, making the grapes less vulnerable to the FUNGAL DISEASES that thrive in this damp, subtropical climate. With a mean annual temperature of 19 °C/66 °F and high rainfall, powdery mildew and BOTRYTIS BUNCH ROT are constant threats.

Viticulture at this latitude is only made possible by ELEVATION. Madeira rises to over 1,800 m/5,900 ft, and the mountains are almost perpetually covered in cloud as moisture in the warm oceanic air is forced to condense. Annual rainfall on the island's summit reaches nearly 3,000 mm/117 in, over three times the total in the island's capital Funchal on the south coast. The network of IRRIGATION channels called *levadas* now extends to over 2,000 km/1,200 miles, supplying the 1,700 growers farming 420 ha/1,038 acres of piecemeal VINIFERA vineyard authorized to produce both DOP Madeira and Madeirense wines. MECHANIZATION is rendered impossible by both the terracing and the small size of the vineyard plots. As a result, cultivation costs are high; many vineyards on the south of the island have fallen prey to property speculation, while others on the north side, mostly planted with American hybrids, have been abandoned.

Vine varieties

The most planted variety by far is the red-skinned Tinta Negra or NEGRAMOLL (formerly known on the island as Tinta Negra Mole) which has been the principal *vinifera* variety on the island since phylloxera arrived at the end of the 19th century. It was long denigrated, somewhat unfairly in view of its versatility, but is now officially 'recommended'. It is sometimes blended with the more recently introduced red-skinned COMPLEXA grape. Plantings of the traditional varieties SERCIAL, VERDELHO, BUAL, MALVASIA, and TERRANTEZ are slowly increasing once again since their rout as a result of phylloxera. Other varieties planted are principally disease-resistant AMERICAN HYBRIDS such as Cunningham and Jacquet, although they are no longer permitted as ingredients in madeira and should be used exclusively in the production of the island's rustic table wine. Small quantities of ARNSBURGER and Cabernet Sauvignon are planted on the north side of the island for the production of unfortified wine. Listrão (PALOMINO) is planted on the nearby island of Porto Santo where a small quantity of FORTIFIED WINE is made, mostly for the local market.

Winemaking

Methods of production vary enormously according to the market and the price that the wine commands. Production revolves around the use of the ESTUFA system and its natural alternatives.

The *estufagem* process has been much improved in recent years with concrete tanks having been largely replaced by stainless steel (*cubas de calor*) ranging in size from 20,000 to 50,000 l/5,280–13,200 gal and widely used for large-volume production. Hot water circulates through a jacket around the tank, heating the wine to a maximum temperature of 55 °C/130 °F for at least 90 days. The process is carefully monitored by the wine industry's controlling body IVBAM (Instituto do Vinho, do Bordado e do Artesanato da Madeira) which also represents Madeira's other traditional industries, embroidery and handicrafts.

A second type of *estufagem* (once used exclusively by the Madeira Wine Company) takes place in 600-l/158-gal wooden casks or lodge pipes which are stored in warm rooms (*armazens de calor*) heated by the nearby tanks or by steam-filled hot water pipes. Temperatures would usually range between 30 and 40 °C, and the wines developed over a longer period, usually six months to a year.

Some of the smaller shippers and stockholders (*partidistas*) refuse to resort to the *estufa* to age their wines. These madeiras are left to age naturally in 600-l pipes stowed under the eaves of *armazéns* in Funchal, heated only by the sun. These *vinhos de canteiro* often mature in cask for 20 years, although some may remain in this state for a century or more before bottling and are usually destined for vintage lots.

One of Madeira's most pressing problems was a lack of good-quality base wine caused by a shortage of grapes from *vinifera* varieties. The white Sercial, Verdelho, Malvasia, and Terrantez varieties are challenging to grow and still in relatively short supply. Most madeira is therefore made from the versatile and more productive Tinta Negra.

Traditionally, shippers bought unfermented MUST direct from the growers, who trod the grapes by foot in LAGARES. Today few winemakers use *lagares*, and the main shippers buy grapes rather than must, from farmers all over the island. Most firms ferment in 25,000-l/6,600-gal vats made from stainless steel, but a few still use lined concrete or even ferment small quantities of wine in cask. Tinta Negra is usually pressed and fermented on its own; Malvasia and Bual are traditionally fermented on their skins, while Sercial and Verdelho musts are separated from the grape skins before fermentation.

Higher-quality wines (usually those made with a high percentage of the more expensive noble grapes) are made by arresting the fermentation with 95%-strength grape spirit to produce a wine with an ALCOHOLIC STRENGTH of 17–18%. Wines made from Malvasia and Bual are fortified early in the FERMENTATION process, leaving up to 7 °Baumé (see MUST WEIGHT for conversions into other measurement scales) of RESIDUAL SUGAR in the wine. Verdelho and Sercial are fermented until they are practically dry, although they may be sweetened at a later stage with either *vinho surdo* or *abafado*. *Surdo* is an intensely sweet MISTELA fortified to an alcoholic strength of 20%, often before fermentation has begun, while *abafado* is a drier wine arrested at a later stage.

In the past, producers of the cheapest wines would ferment all wines dry, leaving the fortification until after the wines have passed through the *estufa*. This saved on the cost of valuable alcohol, a few degrees of which are lost through evaporation during *estufagem*. The wines are sweetened after fortification according to style and often darkened with caramel.

The wines' age is counted from the point at which *estufagem* has been completed. Until 2002 the most basic wines were generally shipped in BULK (*granel*), but this practice has been suspended. Only so-called 'denatured' wines (usually adjusted with salt and pepper) are now permitted to be shipped in bulk.

Styles of madeira

The quality of even the most basic madeira improved greatly in the late 1990s and early 2000s. Inexpensive wines are now much fresher and cleaner, even if they are not as incisive as cask-aged examples. Finer wines are distinguished by their high-toned RANCIO aromas and searing ACIDITY. Madeira varies in colour from pale gold to deep mahogany, with a yellow-green tinge appearing on the rim of well-aged examples.

Standard blends Madeira's wines were traditionally named after the principal grape varieties grown on the island: Sercial, Verdelho, Bual (or Boal), and Malvasia (or MALMSEY), these names denoting increasingly sweet styles of madeira. But since phylloxera destroyed many of Madeira's best vineyards at the end of the 19th century, much of the island's wine has in reality been made from either AMERICAN HYBRIDS or the local *vinifera* variety Tinta Negra. The use of American hybrids has technically been illegal since 1979. From the beginning of 1993, Madeira has been made to conform to the EU requirement that a VARIETAL wine must contain at least 85% of wine made from the specified grape variety. Insufficient quantities of the traditional varieties resulted in renaming most standard blends simply 'Dry', 'Medium Dry', 'Medium Sweet', 'Medium Rich', and 'Rich' or 'Sweet'. Since 2015 wines made from Tinta Negra may be labelled as such, qualified with the sweetness designations above.

Sercial is usually grown in the coolest vineyards, at heights of up to 800 m/2,640 ft or close to sea level on the north side of the island. Many growers erroneously believed that the variety is related to Germany's RIESLING, but it is in fact the same as the ESGANA CÃO (meaning dog strangler) which grows on the Portuguese mainland, the grapes exhibiting the same ferocious levels of ACIDITY. At high ELEVATION, Sercial ripens with difficulty to make a 10% base wine which is dry, tart, and astringent when young. With fortification and ten or more years' ageing in cask, a good Sercial wine develops high-toned, almond-like aromas with a nervy character and a searing dry finish. The Sercial wines range in RESIDUAL SUGAR from 0.5 to 1.5 °Baumé. Sercial is also now used to make some interesting dry, unfortified wines.

Verdelho, which also tends to be planted on the cooler north side of the island, ripens more easily than Sercial and therefore lends itself to producing a medium-dry wine with Baumé readings of 1.5–2.5° after fortification. With age, the wines develop an extraordinary smoky complexity while retaining their characteristic tang of acidity. Verdelho is the main grape on the island for dry, unfortified white wines.

Bual, or Boal in Portuguese, is grown in warmer locations on the south side of Madeira. It achieves higher sugar levels than either Sercial or Verdelho and, after fortification to arrest the fermentation, Bual wines range from 2.5 to 3.5 °Baumé. These dark, medium-rich, raisiny wines retain their acidic verve with age. Bual is known by the name MALVASIA Fina in mainland Portugal, and this is now its official name.

Malmsey The MALVASIA grapes which produce malmsey are usually grown in the warmest locations at low elevations on the south coast, especially around Câmara de Lobos. Varieties include Malvasia Cândida, its pink-skinned mutation Malvasia Cândida Roxa, and Malvasia Babosa. Of these, Malvasia Cândida is the most highly prized and ripens to produce the very sweetest madeira wines, gaining richness and concentration with time in cask. The most widely planted Malvasia is a more productive variety known as Malvasia Branca de São Jorge. Sugar readings in a malmsey range between 3.5 and 6.5 °Baumé, but the wines are rarely cloying as the sweetness is balanced by characteristically high levels of acidity. Like all high-quality madeira made from traditional varieties, malmseys are some of the most resilient in the world and will keep in cask and bottle for a century or more.

Historic styles Madeira's unparalleled ability to age means that styles of wine long abandoned by the island's wine shippers may still be found and enjoyed. **Rainwater** is a pale, off-dry or medium-dry style of madeira bottled before it is ten years old and named after wine which was supposedly diluted by rain during shipment to the United States. Still made in small quantities, Rainwater madeira is defined as being dry to medium dry (1–2.5 °Baumé) with an alcohol level of 18%. Two other styles of madeira based on the TERRANTEZ and BASTARDO grapes are rarely made since both varieties are almost extinct on the island, although Terrantez has made a modest comeback and is much sought after. Intensely sweet wines made from three types of Moscatel (MUSCAT), usually produced for blending, are occasionally bottled on their own.

Qualities of madeira

A generally accepted hierarchy (from the youngest and most basic to the oldest and most distinguished) parallels the different styles of madeira as follows. Age designations do not refer to an exact, minimum, or average age but are effectively an indication of style.

Bulk wine (*granel*) accounted for over 20% of total sales in 2019. Since 2002, only denatured wines (usually spiced with salt and pepper for culinary use) may be exported in bulk.

Corrente, more commonly known as 'three year old', are blended wines, bottled after *estufagem* and ageing in tank, rarely in wood. All are based on the red Tinta Negra and Complexa grapes. The law stipulates that madeira wine may not be bottled before 31 October of the second year of the harvest. This puts the minimum age of bottled madeira at two to three years.

Five Year Old madeira is a blended five-year-old wine, some or all of which will have undergone *estufagem* in tank. A proportion of the blend is likely to have been aged in cask. Most are made from Tinta Negra and Complexa grapes, but some are made exclusively from the more sought-after traditional varieties (see above). They may be labelled Reserva/Reserve and Velho/Old.

Ten Year Old denotes a wine in which the youngest component in the blend will be around ten years old, having aged in cask, usually without recourse to *estufagem*. These wines are mostly varietal and are labelled accordingly. They may be designated 'Reserva Especial'/'Special Reserve' or 'Reserva Velha'/'Old Reserve'.

Fifteen Year Old denotes a blended, 15-year-old wine which may be designated Reserva Extra/Extra Reserve.

Twenty Year Old, Thirty Year Old, Forty Year Old, Fifty Year Old, and Over Fifty Years Old are officially permitted designations but rarely used, as a wine from a single year with 20 years of age qualifies as a vintage or *frasqueira* madeira. However, since the redefinition of solera (see below), some shippers have begun bottling small quantities of exceptional wine with these designations.

Solera wines were made using the SOLERA system more commonly associated with SHERRY, but, having been much abused, it was temporarily prohibited for madeira by EU law—although some very good old bottlings of 19th-century soleras can still be found. The legislation introduced in 1998 requires that the solera be based on a wine from a single year, of which not more than 10% can be withdrawn in any one year. This must be replenished with a wine of similar quality, the maximum number of additions being ten, after which all the wine in the solera must be bottled at the same time. This definition has not found favour with the madeira shippers; as of 2021, no solera wines were being bottled.

Colheita or 'Harvest' wines are from a single year, or harvest, bottled after ageing at least five years in cask. These are effectively early-bottled *frasqueira* or 'vintage' wines which share the individuality if not the concentration or the complexity of a wine aged for a minimum of 20 years (see below).

Frasqueira (Vintage) is the official term which denotes 'vintage' madeira: wine from a single year which, unlike vintage PORT, must age in cask for a minimum of 20 years. Most wines spend considerably longer in wood than this and sometimes pass their later years in 20-l/5-gal glass carboys, or *garrafões*, before bottling. The wines are extremely resistant to OXIDATION, and vintage madeira—especially Sercial with its very high level of acidity—is capable of many decades' bottle AGEING. Shippers carrying stocks of old vintages are so confident of madeira's ability to withstand oxidation that they keep the bottles standing upright so that there is no risk of CORK TAINT spoiling the wine.

Serving madeira

Madeira is probably the most robust wine in the world. Little can harm the wine after it has gone through the *estufa* or been aged for 20 or more years in cask. Most shippers storing bottles upright RECORK their most venerable vintages, say, once every 20 years. All wines tend to throw a deposit (see SEDIMENT) with age, but madeira throws less than most. DECANTING is recommended for all older madeiras, simply to allow any BOTTLE SHOCK to dissipate. A wine that has been in bottle for many years will benefit from being decanted a day before serving. Drier Sercial and Verdelho styles benefit from being served 'cellar cool' rather than iced. Sweeter Buals and Malmseys should be served at room temperature. Once opened, a bottle of madeira can last for months, even years, on ULLAGE.

R.J.M.

Cossart, N., and Berk, E., *Madeira, The Island Vineyard* (2011).
Liddell, A., *Madeira: The Mid-Atlantic Wine* (2014).
Mayson, R., *Madeira, the Islands and Their Wines* (2015).
www.vinhomadeira.com

Madeira Wine Company. See BLANDY.

Madeirense, DOP created in 1999 for the non-FORTIFIED wines of the island of MADEIRA and Porto Santo (the small, arid island around 70 km/43 miles from Madeira itself). A VINHO REGIONAL designation, Terras Madeirenses, was created in 2004 and is much less frequently used. In 2000 a government-sponsored winery, São Vicente, began encouraging growers to vinify wines from a wide range of permitted varieties—those for Madeira but also mainland, French, and German varieties. The Madeira Wine Company (see BLANDY) led the charge for Madeira shippers with its Atlantis brand, launched in 1992. Vintages can be challenging and quantities fluctuate, however with greater experience, mainland dry-winemaking input, and a trickle of new players (including more shippers), quality is on the rise. Aromatic and salty, with vibrant acidity and tropical fruit, VERDELHO is most promising for whites and featured in the island's first ESPUMANTE in 2014, together with a splash of Sercial. TINTA NEGRA is a solid bet for rosé wines. Attempts at producing Cabernet Sauvignon, Merlot, and Syrah in the humid, TEMPERATE climate seem misconceived. Porto Santo's lead variety is Listrão (Spain's PALOMINO FINO); Caracol is exciting interest too. Two producers were commercializing light wines as of 2022 (Companhia de Vinhos dos Profetas e dos Villões and JUSTINO'S), while Barbusano is making a blend of Verdelho from its Madeira vineyards and Caracol from Porto Santo.

S.A.

Mayson, R. J., *The Wines of Portugal* (2020).

Madeleine Angevine, early-ripening CROSS most common as a TABLE GRAPE but the parent of several wine grapes, including the confusingly named **Madeleine × Angevine 7672**, first sent to the UK from Alzey Research Institute in Germany in 1957 and now officially renamed Alzey 7672 to avoid mistaken identity. It is responsible for some light, grapey wines in England and has also been planted in WASHINGTON State, Sweden, and Denmark.

maderization, occasionally **madeirization,** is the process by which a wine is made to taste like MADEIRA, involving mild OXIDATION over a long period and, usually, heat. Such a wine is said to be **maderized**. Although this tasting term is occasionally applied pejoratively to mean that a wine is OXIDIZED, it should properly be applied only to wines with a high enough ALCOHOLIC STRENGTH to inhibit the action of ACETOBACTER, which would otherwise transform the wine into VINEGAR. Very few maderized wines are made today by simply ageing the wine at cellar temperature; the oxidation process is instead hastened by heating or 'baking' the wine as on the island of Madeira. Oxidation reactions, like most organic chemical reactions, can be roughly doubled in speed by a temperature rise of 10 °C/18 °F. For example, a wine requiring ten years at a cellar temperature of 20 °C to develop a maderized character could manifest approximately the same character after about two-and-a-half years at 40 °C or 15 months at 50 °C. Maderized wines are normally amber to brown in colour and have a distinctive cooked or mildly caramelized flavour. Wines processed at excessively high temperatures may taste burnt and harsh. Most such wines are FORTIFIED and sweetened before being marketed. Madeira and similar maderized wines were particularly popular in the 18th and early 19th centuries but have since fallen out of FASHION. See also RANCIO wines.

A.D.W.

made-wine, somewhat inelegant and loosely defined name for wine made not from freshly picked grapes, which is a prerequisite for any liquid referred to as WINE, but from reconstituted GRAPE CONCENTRATE, sometimes also from other fruits. The advantages for producers are that it can be made throughout the year and that grapes can be sourced wherever they happen to be cheapest. BRITISH WINE is one popular rendition, but made-wines are also found in Japan and and Eastern Europe, for example. The produce of many HOME WINEMAKERS is made-wine.

Madiran, dynamic distinctive red-wine appellation in SOUTH WEST FRANCE which has gently remodelled its concentrated, traditionally tannic wines, GASCONY's signature red.

There are said to have been vineyards here in Gallo-Roman times, and certainly the wines of Madiran were appreciated in the Middle Ages by pilgrims en route for Santiago de Compostela. About 1,190 ha/2,941 acres south of the greater Armagnac region produce Madiran. Soils are mainly CLAY and LIMESTONE with so-called *grebb*, or *grip*, granules and pebbles strengthened with IRON and MANGANESE oxide from Pyrenean glacial ALLUVIAL deposits. The climate in Madiran is softened, and often moistened, by the Atlantic to the west, but autumn is usually dry.

The traditional grape variety is TANNAT, its very name hinting at the naturally astringent character of its high level of TANNINS. The AOC regulations require that Tannat comprises 60–80% of the vineyard, and many top cuvées depending heavily, even exclusively on Tannat. Any balance should be Cabernet Sauvignon, Cabernet Franc, and/or FER. The wine traditionally needed long bottle AGEING, but some of Madiran's most dynamic winemakers have been experimenting with ways of softening the impact of Tannat (DESTEMMING is mandatory), including hand-picking only the ripest grapes, gentle handling, new oak, and MICRO-OXYGENATION to produce wines which have density, potential for ageing, but more charm in youth. Madiran can taste like a CLASSED GROWTH bordeaux given the sort of Gascon twist needed to cope with *magret de canard*. The leader of the appellation has been Alain Brumont, who produces both Montus and Bouscassé.

From the same area comes white PACHERENC DU VIC-BILH. Some producers use Tannat to make a sticky, near-black VIN DE LIQUEUR not unlike BANYULS and a good match for chocolate.

Madrid, Vinos de. The DOP Vinos de Madrid forms a semicircle around the southern suburbs of the Spanish capital Madrid, with 8,400 ha/20,757 acres of vines and 51 wineries in 2020. It is made up of four subzones: Arganda (the largest, in the south-east); Navalcarnero (the smallest, in south-central), San Martín de Valdeiglesias (west); and El Molar in the higher elevations to the north. White wines are made mainly from Malvar (LAIRÉN) and AIRÉN; ALBILLO Real is traditional in San Martín. For red wines, GARNACHA dominates, while Tinto Fino (TEMPRANILLO, also called Tinto Madrid here) rules in Arganda. Some INTERNATIONAL VARIETIES are also allowed. A handful of producers have shown real potential, particularly those in the western part of the region (see SIERRA DE GREDOS).

V. de la S. & F.C.

Magarach, wine and vine research institute at Yalta in CRIMEA, founded in 1828, more than 50 years before DAVIS or the Institute of Oenology at the University of BORDEAUX and now known as the All-Russian National Research Institute Viticulture and Winemaking 'Magarach' RAS. Although its activities have been unusually wide-ranging, the institute has been particularly distinguished in developing HYBRID varieties and special vinification techniques.

The extent of its three experimental vineyards has been reduced from nearly 2,000 ha/5,000 acres to around 600 ha/1,482 acres, and they include a vine collection with more than 4,000 varieties from 41 countries. Some of the most successful of the 30 vine varieties designed to combine quantity with quality are **Rubinovy Magaracha** (CABERNET SAUVIGNON × SAPERAVI), Bastardo Magarachsky (BASTARDO × Saperavi), and Magarach Early or Ranniy Magaracha. A newer generation of DISEASE-RESISTANT VARIETIES has since been developed with specific resistances to various PESTS and DISEASES. Since 1893 the institute has collected 1,135 strains of microorganisms for winemaking.

At one time much of Magarach's effort was directed towards producing convincing copies of various classic wine styles (Magarach Malmsey, for example). The institute's own cellar harbours nearly 40,000 sample bottles, some of them containing wine from the mid 19th century.

Specific research avenues tend to have a particularly practical aspect, involving hundreds of patents. New vine varieties created by the institute grow in RUSSIA, MOLDOVA, KAZAKHSTAN, AZERBAIJAN, and elsewhere.

Magliocco. CALABRIA in southern Italy was home to a total of 674 ha/1,665 acres of dark-berried Magliocco vines in 2015: **Magliocco Canino**, a late-ripening likely relative of Sangiovese, and the more tannic and more common **Magliocco Dolce**. Librandi have made efforts to revive it as a VARIETAL, but it is also often blended with GAGLIOPPO.

magnesium, mineral element essential for healthy vine growth. It is a component of chlorophyll, and so CHLOROSIS is a common symptom of magnesium deficiency. The most conspicuous symptom is discoloration between the main veins of the leaf, which becomes particularly noticeable around VERAISON. This zone is yellow for white varieties, red for dark fruit varieties. This deficiency can be severe in some situations, reducing YIELDS and slowing fruit RIPENING. Magnesium deficiency may be associated with BUNCHSTEM NECROSIS, in which the bunch stems and berries shrivel before ripening. Maturity is affected and wine quality suffers.

Soils high in POTASSIUM encourage magnesium deficiency. Similarly, some ROOTSTOCKS such as SO 4 and Fercal are incapable of taking up sufficient magnesium and tend to show deficiency symptoms. Magnesium deficiency is overcome by applying fertilizers to the soil or by using foliar sprays. R.E.S. & R.E.W.

White, R. E., *Understanding Vineyard Soils* (2nd edn, 2015).

magnum, large bottle containing 1.5 l/54 fl oz, or the equivalent of two bottles. It is widely regarded as being the ideal size for AGEING fine wine, being large enough to slow the ageing process but not so big as to be unwieldy or unthinkably expensive (unlike some other LARGE FORMATS). Magnums generally command a premium.

Mago, influential classical writer on agricultural, including viticultural, matters. See CARTHAGE and PHOENICIA for more details.

Maillard reaction. Named after French chemist Louis-Camille Maillard, this chemical reaction between REDUCING SUGARS and AMINO ACIDS or PROTEINS is commonly seen in the browning of untreated foods and in the taste of toast and seared meat. In wine, Maillard-reaction products are important in complex aromas of bottle-aged CHAMPAGNE and in the nutty, port-like, and bacon flavours of wine made from DRIED-GRAPE WINES. See also RANCIO.

Maipo, subregion in the north of the Central Valley in CHILE where the country's first vines imported from France were planted in the mid 19th century. It now boasts some of the country's most characterful Cabernet Sauvignon, especially from areas such as Macul, Pirque, and Puente Alto, close to the foot of the Andes and bathed by cool mountain breezes. P.T.

maître de chai, term often used in France, particularly in Bordeaux, for the cellarmaster, as opposed to the RÉGISSEUR, who might manage the whole estate, or certainly the vineyards. It means literally 'master of the CHAI'. As SCIENCE and ACADEME invade winemaking, the winemaking decisions are increasingly made by an OENOLOGIST.

Málaga, city and Mediterranean port in ANDALUCÍA, southern Spain (see map under SPAIN), which lends its name to three DOPS that cover the same geographical area: Málaga for sweet and FORTIFIED WINES; Sierras de Málaga for still wines; and Pasas de Málaga for the region's tasty traditional RAISINS.

Since the 1960s, Málaga has become more famous as the tourist gateway to the Costa del Sol, but its wine industry has a long and distinguished history dating back to antiquity. The Moors continued to make wine, calling it *xarab al Malaqui*, or Málaga syrup, probably to remove any reference to alcohol but also evoking the extraordinary sweetness of the grapes growing in the hills above the city. In the 17th and 18th centuries, Málaga, often spelt **Malaga**, was exported worldwide, and by the mid 19th century there were over 100,000 ha/247,000 acres of vineyard, making Málaga Spain's second-largest wine region. (See, for example, the part it played in the history of ARGENTINE wine.) Exports of Mountain, as the wine became known in Great Britain and North America, totalled 30,000–40,000 BUTTS (as much as 220,000 hl/5.8 million gal) a year.

In the mid 19th century, Málaga was dealt a double blow, first by POWDERY MILDEW and then, in 1876, by the arrival of PHYLLOXERA, which was devastating to the local economy. The terraced vineyards, then covered with Muscat grapes, to the north and east of the city were abandoned, and many families emigrated to South America. Málaga never really recovered until the 1960s, when tourism became Málaga's major industry. From a peak immediately prior to the arrival of phylloxera of 113,000 ha/279,000 acres, the region's vineyard area was only 1,200 ha in the early 21st century. Where there were once over 100 BODEGAS near the port in the centre of the city, the number of producers had risen from two in the late 1990s to 14 by 2003 and 45 by 2021.

This rugged region runs 150 km/90 miles east to west and 60 km/40 miles north to south and is almost completely mountainous, with vineyards planted up to 1,000 m/3,280 ft in ELEVATION. There are five zones. The coastal area, or Costa Occidental, comprises La Axarquía (a region of steep, SLATE-covered slopes that recall those of PRIORAT), Montes, and Manilva and has a MEDITERRANEAN CLIMATE. Further inland, the Norte and Serranía de Ronda areas experience a more extreme CONTINENTAL CLIMATE.

The principal grape variety nowadays is Moscatel de Alejandría (MUSCAT OF ALEXANDRIA), closely followed by PEDRO XIMÉNEZ, which now may be imported from MONTILLA-MORILES to the north, although according to regulations it may not exceed 10% of the volume. In the cooler mountain zone immediately north of the city, Moscatel is also used in the production of dry wines.

Traditionally, Malága was a DRIED-GRAPE WINE made by leaving the grapes in the sun on grass mats for seven to 20 days to concentrate the natural sugars. Today the wines are made using a number of different methods. Often the sweetness is obtained by arresting the fermentation with grape spirit (as for MISTELA or VIN DOUX NATRUREL), and the wine is called *vino dulce natural.*

A *vino naturalmente dulce* is made from LATE HARVEST or slightly sun-dried Moscatel in which the fermentation has stopped naturally or has been stopped by lowering the fermentation temperature.

A third way of adjusting the sweetness is with *arrope*, unfermented grape MUST that has been boiled down to 30% of its normal volume. This may be added either before or after fermentation.

The aged, fortified wines mature in oak COOPERAGE of various sizes arranged into SOLERAS. The Consejo Regulador recognizes 16 types of wine ranging from *Seco* (dry, $\geq$ 4 g/l residual sugar) to Sweet (over 140 g/l RS), and *Dorado* (golden, naturally sweet, with no *arrope*) to *Negro* (black, from at least 15% *arrope*). Depending on style, Málaga may have an ALCOHOLIC STRENGTH of 15–23%. Málaga can also be classified by age:

Pálido: aged up to six months, with no *arrope* addition.
Noble: aged two to three years.
Añejo: aged three to five years.
Trasañejo: aged more than five years.

In addition, *Pajarete* denotes a fortified wine with 45–140 g/l of residual sugar, with no arrope, and aged at least two years. The rare *Lágrima* is produced solely from FREE-RUN juice without any mechanical pressing; *Lacrimae Christi* is a Lágrima aged at least two years.

While many Málaga wines are deep brown, intensely sweet, and raisiny, some tasting slightly burnt through the addition of too much *arrope*, top examples, both dry and sweet, count as some of Andalucía's most compelling and long-lived wines.

For more about the region's dry wines, see SIERRAS DE MÁLAGA. R.J.M. & F.C.

www.vinomalaga.com

Malaga Blanc, dominant grape variety in THAILAND, where it is used mainly as a TABLE GRAPE but also produces relatively soft white wine. Originally from the south of France, where it is named Panse de Provence, the grape is believed to have been introduced to Thailand in 1685 by the first Embassy of the King Louis XIV of France to King Narai the Great of Siam. The grapes' thick skins make them usefully resistant to heavy rain.

Malagousia or sometimes **Malagoussia**, elegant white western Greek grape variety rediscovered by Evangelos Gerovassiliou in the 1980s. It yields full-bodied, perfumed wines in many Greek regions, and total plantings have grown rapidly to reach 802 ha/1,982 acres in 2021.

Malbec, black grape variety once popular in Bordeaux, still the backbone of CAHORS but given a new lease of life by its obvious success in ARGENTINA. It has many synonyms, among them Cot, as it is known in much of western France, including the Loire, where it was once quite widely grown. In the Libournais it is known as Pressac, and in Cahors, suggesting origins in northern Burgundy, it was called Auxerrois until Argentine success encouraged adoption of the name Malbec. It also encouraged enthusiasm for the variety in France where total plantings have continued to increase since their low point in the late 1970s to 8,380 ha/20,707 acres in 2019, some 3,690 ha/9,120 acres in Cahors country. In cooler climates, Malbec has some of the disadvantages of Merlot (sensitivity to COULURE and spring FROST) without as much obvious fruit quality. Indeed it can taste like a rather rustic, even shorter-lived, version of Merlot, although when grown on the least-fertile, high, rugged LIMESTONE vineyards of Cahors it can occasionally remind us why the English used to refer to Cahors as 'the black wine'. Cahors AOC regulations stipulate that Cot must constitute at least 70% of the vineyard. Other appellations of SOUTH WEST FRANCE in which Malbec may play a (smaller) part are Bergerac, Buzet, Côtes de Duras, Fronton, Côtes du Marmandais, Pécharmant, and Côtes du Brulhois. It is also theoretically allowed into the Midi threshold appellations of Cabardès and Malepère but is rarely found this far from Atlantic influence.

DNA PROFILING in 2009 showed that Cot is a natural progeny of Prunelard, an old variety from the Tarn, and Magdeleine Noire des Charentes, the almost extinct mother of Merlot.

Permitted by all major red bordeaux appellations, Malbec was quite popular, especially before the predations of the 1956 frosts, but total plantings fell from 4,900 ha/12,100 acres in 1968 to just over 1,000 ha/2,471 acres in 2011, mainly in Bourg, Blaye, and the Entre-Deux-Mers region. In the last decade, the variety has seen a return to popularity, with plantings up by more than 100% to 2,116 ha. Blended with Cabernet and Gamay, it is also theoretically allowed in a wide range of mid Loire appellations—Anjou, Coteaux du Loir, Touraines of various sorts, and even sparkling Saumur—but has largely been replaced by Cabernets Franc and Sauvignon.

It is in Argentina that Malbec really holds sway, planted on more than 45,657 ha/112,820 acres all over Argentina in 2019, making it the country's most-planted variety by far with more than 20% of the entire vineyard area. Varietal

Argentine Malbecs have some perceptibly Bordelais characteristics, of flavour rather than structure. The wines are generally riper and more velvety than their French counterparts, although they are similarly capable of extended AGEING, and there is now a will to make rather more delicate, fragrant Malbecs. For more detail, see ARGENTINA.

The commercial success and clear appeal to modern wine drinkers of Argentine Malbec has spawned a new fashion for the variety elsewhere, not least in Chile, where varietal bottlings increased considerably in the early 21st century so that total plantings were 2,362 ha/5,837 acres in 2020. Chile's version tends to be more tannic than Argentina's and may be blended with the other Bordeaux grapes which Chile grows in such profusion. Viu, Chile's Malbec specialist, and others blend it with Cabernet Sauvignon.

Australians have so far shown no great respect for their Malbec and had been uprooting it systematically until the early 1990s, although poor CLONAL SELECTION was probably partly to blame. Plantings totalled 562 ha/1,389 acres in 2015, and some Clare Valley producers have made fine wine from it. In New Zealand producers such as Villa Maria value it as an ingredient in BORDEAUX BLENDS, which is also its usual fate in California (see MERITAGE). Malbec was quite significant in California before PROHIBITION, and plantings have steadily increased this century, to 1,582 ha/3,909 acres by 2020.

Many of the small amounts of Malbec, Malbech, or Malbeck planted elsewhere around the world doubtless owe their continued existence to Argentina's success with the variety.

Goldin, C., *The Secrets of Argentine Malbec* (2004).
Robinson, J., et al., *Wine Grapes: A Complete Guide to 1,368 Vine Varieties, Including Their Origins and Flavours* (2012).

Malepère shares many of the wine characteristics of CABARDÈS, another small AOC where the Midi and Aquitaine meet near Carcassonne in the far west of the LANGUEDOC. Climatically, it belongs even more definitively to south-west France than to the Languedoc, from which it is geographically protected by the Hautes Corbières peaks. The vineyards, mainly CLAY and LIMESTONE, are immediately north of LIMOUX. The wines, mainly red and some rosé, are made up of a blend of Bordeaux and Languedoc varieties, but in the case of Malepère, with its wetter, more Atlantic climate, it is the Bordeaux varieties that predominate. Merlot must make up at least half the blend of reds, with CABERNET FRANC and Cot (MALBEC) constituting at least 20%, but Cinsaut, Grenache, Lledoner Pelut, and Cabernet Sauvignon are also allowed as minor ingredients. Rosés are based on Cabernet Franc. Wine production is dominated by CO-OPERATIVES, particularly Les Vignobles de Vendéole.

Malibu Coast, AVA in southern CALIFORNIA approved in 2014 for a 50-mile/80-km stretch of mountainous coast north of Santa Monica encompassing the previously established Malibu-Newton Canyon and Saddle Rock-Malibu AVAs in Los Angeles County. About 50 vineyards originally covered about 81 ha/200 acres, though WILDFIRES have hampered growth.

M.D.K.

malic acid, one of the two principal organic acids of grapes and wines (see also TARTARIC ACID). Its name comes from *malum*, Latin for 'apple', the fruit in which it was first identified by early scientists. Present in nearly all fruits and berries, malic acid is now known to be one of the compounds involved in the complicated cycles of reactions by which plants and animals obtain the energy necessary for life. One of these cycles of reactions is known as the citric acid, Krebs, or tricarboxylic acid cycle, and its elucidation was one of the outstanding triumphs of biochemistry.

Another, which comes into play during the final stages of RIPENING in many fruits, including grapes, causes the decomposition of malic acid. When all of the malic acid has been used up in this latter series of reactions, the fruit becomes overripe, or senescent. The malic acid content of grapes is a very good indication of ripeness because it is specific to each variety and varies according to the climatic conditions of the vintage. The malic acid decomposing reaction is much more rapid in hot summer temperatures, probably because of the more rapid RESPIRATION of malate in the berry. This is, at least in part, one reason for the lower TOTAL ACID concentrations in grapes grown in warmer regions. It accumulates in young grape berries reaching high levels at about VERAISON—sometimes as high as 20 g/l—but, as ripening progresses, the level of malate declines to concentrations of between less than 1 and up to 5 g/l when the grapes are ripe. This large range in ripe grapes is an important source of variation in quality and style.

Tartaric acid, the other main grape acid, does not participate in several of the reaction pathways in which malic acid is an essential component, which is why the hotter the summer, the lower the likely proportion of malic acid in the grapes. Malic acid's different chemical structure allows it to participate in many more of the enzymatic reactions involved in living systems than tartaric acid because it can be pumped across plant membranes serving as a transportable energy source. Because the concentrations of tartaric acid are relatively and desirably stable, attention is given to the tartrate/malate (T/M) ratio, which varies from about 1 to 6 and is characteristic for each grape variety. High malate varieties with a low ratio, such as SYLVANER, COLOMBARD, BARBERA, and CARIGNAN, are desirable for hot districts.

Malic acid is lost not just through the citric acid cycle and other reaction cycles during grape ripening but also in many cases as a result of MALOLACTIC CONVERSION. Temperatures of 18–22 °C/64–72 °F encourage the LACTIC ACID BACTERIA involved in malolactic conversion. The winemaker can exercise some control over this loss of malic acid if necessary, however, since the growth and activity of these organisms can be slowed or inhibited by moderate concentrations of SULFUR DIOXIDE. In addition, since the lactic acid bacteria responsible for malolactic conversion require many micronutrients (vitamins, growth factors, nitrogenous compounds), early and thorough separation of the new wine from its LEES can inhibit bacterial activity and preserve malic acid.

Malic acid is available commercially for use in acidifying foods and beverages and in numerous industrial processes. At one time it was isolated from fruits and other plant tissues but today is more usually synthesized from another organic acid.

B.G.C. & V.L.

Malleco, cool, wet subregion of the Southern region of CHILE 650 km/403 miles from the capital, Santiago. Its reputation as a wine region began only in the 1990s, when Felipe de Solminihac of Aquitania winery in Maipo began planting vines in its clay and granite soils. There is now a small community of winegrowers producing excellent Chardonnay and Pinot Noir.

P.T.

Mallorca, Spanish Balearic island in the north-west Mediterranean which was once the seat of the kings of ARAGÓN. In the 19th century, the island was famous for its sweet MALVASIA wines, which all but disappeared when the vineyards fell victim to PHYLLOXERA. The island has two DOPS: BINISSALEM, Spain's first offshore DOP wine region on the island's central plateau, with good, original reds from the local MANTO NEGRO grape; and PLA I LLEVANT, in the south-east, specializing in reds from the CALLET grape. Wines outside of these DOPs may take the VINO DE LA TIERRA (Vi de la Terra) Mallorca. Vino de la Tierra Serra de Tramuntana-Costa Nord covers wines grown in the high, jagged mountains at the island's northern end.

Malmesbury, ward in the SWARTLAND district of SOUTH AFRICA, and an increasingly important source of good-quality wines from often innovative wine producers, many small-scale.

malmsey, English corruption of the word MALVASIA, derived from the port of Monemvasia which was important in ancient Greece. The word was first used for (probably a wide range of) the unusually sweet, rich wines of Greece and the islands of the eastern Mediterranean, particularly Crete, then called Candia (see GREECE, medieval history). Sweet white wines were prized in the Middle Ages, particularly but not exclusively by northern Europeans, who regarded their own wines as thin and admired the longevity of these liquids, very possibly DRIED-GRAPE WINES, so sturdily high in sugar and alcohol. The acute merchants of GENOA, NAPLES, and VENICE were able profitably to capitalize on this stability in their trading links between east and west.

As European temperatures fell as a result of CLIMATE CHANGE, these richer wines held even more allure. Venetians in particular created a demand for malmsey in 15th-century England. George, duke of Clarence and younger brother of England's King Edward IV, was popularly believed to have been drowned in a BUTT of malmsey in the Tower of London in 1478.

Malvasia vines came to be planted all round the western Mediterranean (even today, Malvasia and MALVOISIE are two of the most commonly used synonyms for various, often quite unrelated, VINE VARIETIES). Malmsey, which originally denoted any strong, sweet wine, was eventually used specifically for the sweetest style of MADEIRA, particularly that made from Malvasia grapes.

Between 2010 and 2012, a number of new PDOs were introduced in Greece for barrel-aged, sweet white wines made from sun-dried grapes, mainly from a mix of varieties, referred to under the group name of Malvasia. Malvasia of Monemvasia in the Peloponnese, Malvasia of Handakas-Candia and Malvasia of Sitia in Crete, and Malvasia of Paros are in essence Greece's modern claim to the legendary style of the Middle Ages.

malolactic conversion, widely known as **malolactic fermentation** and often abbreviated to **MLF** or **malo**, is the conversion of stronger MALIC ACID naturally present in new wine into LACTIC ACID (which has lower ACIDITY) and CARBON DIOXIDE. The term 'conversion' is more accurate because it is not literally a FERMENTATION process, although the release of carbon dioxide may initially give that impression. It is accomplished by LACTIC ACID BACTERIA (LAB), which are naturally present in most established wineries but may have to be cultured and carefully introduced in newer establishments where malolactic conversion is desired. This process is unrelated to and almost never precedes the main, alcoholic fermentation, for which reason it is sometimes called a secondary fermentation. Nevertheless, it is not uncommon for malolactic conversion to be complete by the end of the alcoholic fermentation.

It is written chemically thus:

$$COOH - CHOH - CH_2 - COOH \rightarrow COOH - CHOH - CH_3 + CO_2$$

malic acid→lactic acid + carbon dioxide

Malolactic conversion is conducted for three reasons: to decrease a wine's ACIDITY, to improve wine stability (see STABILIZATION), and to achieve desirable sensory (aroma and flavour) changes. It is desirable in wines which have excessive acidity, particularly red wines produced in cooler climates. It can also add flavour and complexity to both red and white wines, as well as rendering the wine impervious to the danger of malolactic conversion in bottle. Recognition and mastery of malolactic conversion (which would traditionally happen as if by accident when temperatures rose in the spring) was one of the key developments in winemaking in the mid 20th century. By the early 1990s, most fine red wines, many sparkling wines, and a small but increasing proportion of the world's white wine involved full or partial malolactic conversion, thanks either to the lactic acid bacteria present in the winery or to cultured LAB added to the wine. In hotter climates or during warmer years in cooler areas, some winemakers deliberately suppress malolactic conversion in some or all batches of a wine in order to maintain the wine's acidity. Some grape varieties seem to have a greater affinity with malolactic conversion than others. Among white grapes, Chardonnay is a generally successful candidate for the process, while most producers of Riesling and Chenin Blanc deliberately avoid it, despite the high natural acidity in these latter two. Malolactic conversion may reduce unduly the acidity of a wine made from very ripe grapes and already low in acidity, and production of the buttery-smelling DIACETYL during malolactic conversion needs to be managed since excess diacetyl can be unpleasant. Malolactic conversion's effect on decreasing TOTAL ACIDITY is often most marked on those wines which were highest in malic acid before it took place (i.e. the products of particularly cool growing seasons). In some cases, the winemaker may even have to ACIDIFY after malolactic conversion. If all of the malic acid is converted to lactic acid, the total acidity (expressed as tartaric acid) will drop by 0.56 g/l for each g/l of malic acid that was originally present in the wine.

Like most BACTERIA, lactic acid bacteria grow best in very weakly acidic solutions and at temperatures above 20 °C/68 °F. Malolactic conversion is strongly influenced not only by temperature but also by the wine's PH: if it is less than pH 3.1, it is very difficult, though still commonly practised under such conditions in Champagne and Burgundy. Lactic acid bacteria are intolerant of even moderate concentrations of SULFUR DIOXIDE and high concentrations of ETHANOL. Malolactic conversion can therefore be encouraged by adding lactic acid bacteria to the wine soon after alcoholic fermentation has finished. Alternatively, they can be added to the MUST at, or soon after, the start of alcoholic fermentation; this is often referred to as co-inoculation or simultaneous inoculation. At this point conditions are ideal for the lactic acid bacteria—the fermenting wine is warm, its alcohol content is low, the sulfur dioxide added before fermentation has already been volatilized or become bound to other wine constituents, and the dying yeast cells, or LEES, provide the necessary micronutrients. Co-inoculation is becoming increasingly popular, but some oenologists believe it to be detrimental to wine quality because it happens very quickly and at higher temperatures. If malolactic conversion has not been initiated during the alcoholic fermentation (or during post-fermentation MACERATION of reds), the new wine may be transferred to barrels or stainless-steel tanks where the malolactic conversion will take place. Barrels in which malolactic conversion has taken place in a previous vintage may encourage the onset of this process, but it is very important to know what was in the container before so that no form of spoilage is encouraged. Putting fine red wine in barrel prior to the onset of malolactic conversion became fashionable in the early 21st century because it was believed to improve the oak integration and make the wines more approachable when young (particularly useful for EN PRIMEUR tastings), although some winemakers would take the opposite view. The reliability and efficiency of malolactic conversion can also be affected by the yeast strain used for alcoholic fermentation. Some yeast may produce compounds that inhibit lactic acid bacteria, including sulfur dioxide, certain fatty acids, and proteins. Such interactions are an important consideration for the selection of compatible pairings of yeast and lactic acid bacteria starter cultures.

Malolactic conversion may well be regarded as undesirable in some wines, particularly in certain styles of white and sparkling wine. In this case, sulfur dioxide additions and cool temperatures can prevent the activity of lactic acid bacteria. Sterile FILTRATION can insure against the commercial embarrassment of malolactic conversion taking place in bottle. If a bottled still wine starts to fizz, this is the most likely cause, most commonly encouraged by the combination of heat and residual lactic acid bacteria. See FAULTS IN WINE. E.J.B. & P.J.Cos.

AWRI, 'Malolactic fermentation in white and sparkling wines' (2020). www.awri.com.au/wp-content/uploads/2018/03/MLF-in-white-and-sparkling-wine.pdf.

AWRI, 'Malolactic fermentation in red wine' (2020). www.awri.com.au/wp-content/uploads/2020/09/MLF-in-red-wine.pdf.

Bartowsky, E. J., et al., 'Emerging trends in the application of malolactic fermentation', *Australian Journal of Grape and Wine Research*, 21 (2015) 663–9.

Englezos, V., et al., 'Impact of *Saccharomyces cerevisiae* strain selection on malolactic fermentation by *Lactobacillus plantarum* and *Oenococcus oeni*', *American Journal of Enology and Viticulture*, 71/2 (2020), 157–65.

Sumby, K. M., et al., 'Measures to improve wine malolactic fermentation', *Applied Microbiology and Biotechnology*, 103 (2019), 2033–51.

Malta, the central Mediterranean island, has a small wine industry that can trace its history back to Phoenician times, but it was the arrival of the Knights of St John in 1530 that laid the foundations of today's wine industry. Viticulture in Malta flourished until the arrival of the British in 1800, when many vineyards (and olive groves) were uprooted in favour of cotton. By the end of the 19th century, when demand for Maltese cotton had diminished, a replanting programme of sorts was started and, in spite of the outbreak of PHYLLOXERA in 1919, viticulture flourished once again. By the 1950s, 1,000 ha/2,470 acres were under vine, although most were TABLE GRAPE varieties which produced wines so low in sugar and acid that considerable adjustments were needed in wineries rarely equipped for high-quality wine production.

Some 1950s experiments with Muscat and Trebbiano were relatively successful, but it was not until the 1970s that another serious attempt was made with wine grape varieties, this time Cabernet Sauvignon planted by Marsovin at Wardija in the north of the island. TOURISM boomed in the 1980s and demand for wine grew. During the 1990s, with the help of DRIP IRRIGATION and French and Italian expertise, various other VITIS VINIFERA varieties were planted.

By 2022 only about 50 ha/124 acres of the indigenous Ġellewża (red) and 80 ha of Girgentina (white) were left; Gennarua had all but disappeared. INTERNATIONAL VARIETIES make up the rest of the country's 389 ha/961 acres of wine grapes, with Chardonnay and Vermentino providing the island's best white wines and Cabernets Sauvignon and Franc, Merlot, and Syrah dominating the reds.

Only when Malta joined the EU in 2004 were labels required to distinguish between wines made from domestic and imported grapes. In 2007 Malta introduced the wine categories DOK (equivalent to the EU's PDO) and IGT (PGI), GEOGRAPHICAL INDICATIONS with production protocols very similar to Italy's system. There are two DOKs: Malta, for wines produced on the main island, and Gozo, for those from the eponymous island. IGT Maltese Islands encompasses all the wines of the country.

Land holdings tend to be small, and most farmers sell their grapes to large wineries such as Delicata, Marsovin, and Camilleri or to the Vitimalta CO-OPERATIVE. Meridiana, wholly owned by ANTINORI since 2015, is another important winery, with 11 ha of its own vineyards.

Vineyards typically have relatively shallow, poor, LOAMY topsoil on SAND, LIMESTONE, and CLAY with richer and more fertile clayey soils in the north. Some ALLUVIAL soils can be found in the valleys. The climate is MEDITERRANEAN with long, hot, dry summers and cool, rainy winters. The average mean temperatures vary from 12.8 °C/55 °F in January to 27.7 °C/82 °F in August. Strong WIND is common throughout the year, helping to moderate temperatures and keep the vines free of FUNGAL DISEASES; at least one winery, Mar Casar, is practising BIODYNAMIC VITICULTURE. Average rainfall is 575 mm/27 in but is so concentrated in the winter months that IRRIGATION is needed. M.Ta.

Malvar. See LAIRÉN.

Malvasia, name used widely, especially in Iberia and Italy, for at least 20 different grape varieties, often unrelated. Wines produced from them are, typically, deeply coloured whites, but some are reds, usually light.

The word 'Malvasia' itself is thought to be the Italian corruption of 'Monemvasia', the name of a southern Greek port which, in the Middle Ages, was a busy and natural entrepôt for the rich and highly prized dessert wines of the eastern Mediterranean, notably those of Crete, or Candia (see GREECE, history)—although it is not known which grape varieties were responsible for these wines. They may not even have included any of the varieties known today as Malvasia of some sort. But so important was wine from Monemvasia during the time of the Venetian republic that wine shops in VENICE were called *malvasie*.

The French corruption of 'Malvasia' has been used particularly loosely (see MALVOISIE). The word was also corrupted into MALMSEY in English, which was long the name of an important style of MADEIRA, traditionally based on the Malvasia **Cândida** grape (also known as **Malvasia di Lipari**). The Germans call their various though rare forms of Malvasia **Malvasier**.

Italy grows more wine called Malvasia of some form than any other country, with 17 different varieties distinguished in its 2010 vine census, nine white and eight red or pink. In 2015, according to the EU's Eurostat database, most planted, with 6,983 ha/17,255 acres, was **Malvasia Bianca di Candia**, which produces relatively neutral wine in Lazio and throughout central Italy. The variety known as **Malvasia di Candia Aromatico**, quite widely planted in Italy and Greece, is apparently different and closer to **Malvasia di Casorzo**, a red-berried, relatively rare speciality of Piemonte. Italy's second most planted Malvasia is simply called Malvasia Bianca, with total plantings of 2,181 ha/5,389 acres. Third most common was **Malvasia Bianca Lunga**, with 1,135 ha/2,805 acres recorded in 2015 (although that called simply Malvasia Bianca may well be Malvasia Bianca Lunga too). This is the variety, once called Malvasia del Chianti, most common in Tuscany for both dry wines and VIN SANTO and is also grown, as Marăstina, in Croatia (which is probably close to the Croatian variety called MALVAZIJA ISTARSKA, known as Malvasia Istriana when grown in north-east Italy, where it can produce some fine VARIETAL examples).

Total plantings of **Malvasia del Lazio**, a CROSS of MUSCAT OF ALEXANDRIA and SCHIAVA Grossa, had fallen to 676 ha/1,670 acres in 2015. The speciality of BASILICATA, **Malvasia Bianca di Basilicata**, may be related to Malvasia Bianca di Candia. Other, less quantitatively significant, pale-skinned grapes called Malvasia noted in the Italian vine census of 2010 included the widespread Malvasia di Lipari, which is grown on the Italian island of the same name for sweet PASSITO wines; also known as Malvasia di Sardinia (and differentiated on the Italian census) for that island's Malvasias of various sweetnesses; as Greco Bianco di Gerace for the sweet wines of the Calabrian port of Bianco; as Malvasia Cândida to produce malmsey on the island of MADEIRA, where only tiny plantings remain; and as various Malvasias in Cataluña and the Canary Islands.

The Italian vine census also distinguished between a further eight dark- or pink-berried Malvasias, of which **Malvasia Nera di Brindisi** (identical to Malvasia Nera di Lecce and a cross of Malvasia Bianca Lunga and the Puglian red wine grape NEGROAMARO) is the most planted with 1,149 ha/2,839 acres in 2015, making it more common than southern Italy's other red wine Malvasia, **Malvasia Nera di Basilicata**. DNA PROFILING in 2021 showed that the latter is a distinct variety and a natural cross between SUSUMANIELLO (or Somarello), a rare Puglian variety, and Visparola, an old, forgotten, but (genetically speaking) key variety from southern Italy. **Malvasia Nera Lunga** was less quantitatively important than either and was a speciality of Asti in Piemonte. The census also referred to a variety called simply Malvasia Nera, as well as **Malvasia di Schierano**, which makes light, fragrant reds in Piemonte.

The variety more commonly planted to produce malmsey on Madeira today is a much newer variety called **Malvasia Branca de São Jorge**, whose wines are usefully high in both sugar and acidity. Portugal grows several other Malvasias of note. The most important true Malvasia is **Malvasia Fina**, of which there were 2,436 ha/6,019 acres in Portugal in 2020. It goes under many aliases, including the slightly confusing one of BOAL. Most important in the dry whites of DÃO, it is also widely grown in other northern Portuguese regions such as the DOURO. DNA profiling suggested that Malvasia Fina is a natural ALFROCHEIRO × Hebén cross and that dark-berried **Malvasia Preta**, also known as Moreto or Mureto, is a natural Alfrocheiro × CAYETANA BLANCA cross. Malvasia Preta is grown on 733 ha/1,811 acres of vineyard mainly in the Douro for port and red table wines. Pale-skinned **Malvasia de Colares is** the dominant grape of the shrinking COLARES region. **Malvasia Rei** is the Portuguese synonym for PALOMINO FINO.

In Spain, **Malvasía di Sitges** is Malvasia di Lipari, but **Malvasía Volcánica** is a historic speciality of LANZAROTE and can make full-bodied, aromatic whites of real interest. DNA profiling has shown that it is a natural cross of Malvasia di Lipari and the local MARMAJUELO. About half of all Malvasía growing in Spain is on the Canary Islands while most of the rest was Malvasia Castellana, Portugal's SÍRIA, called Cigüente in EXTREMADURA.

The aromatic, thick-skinned variety known simply as Malvasia Bianca in California and grown on 402 ha/994 acres of mainly Central Valley vineyard was brought there from Piemonte and is known strictly as **Malvasia Bianca di Piemonte**. It makes full-bodied, tangy, flirtatious whites there.

So common is the name Malvasia as part of a grape name or synonym that no fewer than 70 are listed in the index of the book *Wine Grapes*. J.V. & J.E.H.

Robinson, J., et al., *Wine Grapes: A Complete Guide to 1,368 Vine Varieties, Including Their Origins and Flavours* (2012).

Malvazija Istarska, characteristic and characterful white wine grape of the Istrian peninsula in northern CROATIA, the country's second most planted variety after Graševina (WELSCHRIESLING) with 1,626 ha/4,018 acres in 2020. Known as **Malvasia Istriana** in north-east Italy, it is genetically close to MALVASIA di Lipari, Malvasia Bianca Lunga, and Malvasia Nera di Brindisi.

malvidin is the PHENOLIC pigment primarily responsible for the colour of red wine. It is found in wine as malvidin 3-glucoside and various acylated derivatives.

Malvoisie is one of France's most confusing vine names, perhaps because, like PINEAU, it was once used widely as a general term for superior wines, notably those whose origins were supposed to be Greek. There is no single variety whose principal name is Malvoisie, but it has been used as a synonym for a wide range of (usually white-berried) grape varieties producing full-bodied, aromatic whites. Despite the etymological similarity, 'Malvoisie' has only rarely been a synonym for MALVASIA. Malvoisie is today found on the labels of some Loire, Savoie, and Aosta wines made from such plantings of PINOT GRIS as remain. **Malvoisie du Valais** is a common synonym for (usually sweet) Pinot Gris in Switzerland. It is also sometimes used for BOURBOULENC in the Languedoc, for CLAIRETTE in Bordeaux, and for SAVAGNIN in the Austrian Tyrol. VERMENTINO is sometimes called Malvoisie in Roussillon and on Corsica.

Malvoisie Rouge d'Italie is an occasional synonym for FRÜHROTER VELTLINER in Savoie and northern Italy.

Robinson, J., et al., *Wine Grapes: A Complete Guide to 1,368 Vine Varieties, Including Their Origins and Flavours* (2012).

Mammolo, heavily perfumed, historic red grape variety producing wines which supposedly smell of violets, or *màmmole*, in central Italy. It seems to have played a significant genetic role in several Tuscan vine varieties. A permitted ingredient in CHIANTI and VINO NOBILE DI MONTEPULCIANO, it was planted on 26 ha/64 acres in 2015. Today it is quantitatively much more important as Corsica's SCIACCARELLU.

Manchuela, DOP of 12,478 ha/30,833 acres in 2021 on the eastern border of CASTILLA-LA MANCHA, straddling Cuenca and Albacete provinces. This is the home of BOBAL, which makes up 41% of vineyards and is mainly used for rosés and unoaked young reds. It is sometimes blended with INTERNATIONAL VARIETIES such as Syrah as well as local varieties TEMPRANILLO, MONASTRELL, GARNACHA, and GARNACHA TINTORERA (Alicante Bouschet). The white MACABEO also produces very drinkable fragrant whites in northern Albacete, while the local Albilla de Manchuela has been rediscovered as a good-quality grape. Overall this high plateau, which reaches an ELEVATION of more than 1,000 m/ 3,280 ft in western Cuenca, shows great potential but has mostly lacked the investment required to develop it. V. de la S. & F.C.

Mandilaria, distinctive speciality of various Greek islands, including CRETE, where it is often blended with the much softer KOTSIFALI, which adds BODY. The grapes have thick skins and therefore the wine produced is deeply coloured and notably high in TANNINS. It can produce harmonious dry reds such as Peza or even sweet reds. Known as Amorgiano on Rhodes. Total plantings had risen to 1,070 ha/2,644 acres in 2021.

manganese, a soil nutrient essential for vine growth but in very low quantities. Manganese deficiency causes leaf yellowing and is found most commonly on soils high in LIMESTONE and other alkaline soils. Acid soils (see SOIL ACIDITY) which are poorly drained and high in manganese can cause toxicity, reducing both vine growth and YIELD. R.E.S. & R.E.W.

manipulation, a slightly pejorative term referring to a range of interventions made by winemakers. Wine is unusual among alcoholic drinks in that, once the grapes have been picked and put into a container, it can more or less make itself. However, winemakers closely monitor the entire process from reception of the grapes to BOTTLING and often intervene in a variety of ways to ensure quality or stylistic goals. These range from traditional techniques such as DESTEMMING, CRUSHING, SAIGNÉE, CHAPTALIZATION, BARREL FERMENTATION, LEES STIRRING, BARREL AGEING, RACKING, CLARIFICATION, and FILTRATION to more modern steps such as optical SORTING, the use of ENZYMES, FLASH DÉTENTE, cold MACERATION, CRYOEXTRACTION, cultured YEASTS, MICRO-OXYGENATION, BARREL ALTERNATIVES, REVERSE OSMOSIS, and SPINNING-CONE COLUMNS—or, more likely, a combination of these methods. Many of these practices are controlled by regulations in most wine-producing countries. In general, those that have been practised for many years (such as chaptalization) are less controversial, even though they may be more interventionist and open to abuse than modern equivalents (such as reverse osmosis). A.O.

Goode, J., *Wine Science: The Application of Science in Wine* (3rd edn, 2021).

mannoproteins are POLYSACCHARIDES released from YEAST cells during FERMENTATION and by AUTOLYSIS during LEES CONTACT. Mannoproteins commercially prepared from yeast lees may also be added during winemaking. Mannoproteins have the potential to protect white and rosé wine from PROTEIN haze and can inhibit the growth of TARTRATE crystals, which promotes tartrate stability. They may also reduce the perception of ASTRINGENCY by interacting with both salivary proteins and TANNINS, disrupting the binding considered necessary for astringency perception. Mannoproteins released during yeast autolysis have also been demonstrated to improve the foaming properties of SPARKLING WINE. R.G.

Lankhorst, P. P., et al., 'Prevention of tartrate crystallization in wine by hydrocolloids: the mechanism studied by dynamic light scattering', *Food Chemistry*, 65/40 (2017), 8923–9.
Núñez, Y. P., et al., 'Isolation and characterization of a thermally extracted yeast cell wall fraction potentially useful for improving the foaming properties of sparkling wines', *Journal of Agricultural and Food Chemistry*, 54/20 (2006), 7898–903.
Ramos-Pineda, A. M., et al., 'Effect of the addition of mannoproteins on the interaction between wine flavonols and salivary proteins', *Food Chemistry*, 264 (2018), 226–32.
Waters, E. J., et al., 'Preventing protein haze in bottled wine', *Australian Journal of Grape and Wine Research*, 11/2 (2005), 215–25.

Manseng Noir, Basque vine variety that DNA PROFILING suggests is identical to the Ferrón of RIBEIRO. It is genetically distinct from the white wine grapes GROS MANSENG and PETIT MANSENG.

Manto Negro, most common grape on MALLORCA, producing scented but light reds which tend to age quickly and are prone to OXIDATION. It may be best blended with a more structured grape such as CALLET.

manzanilla, a *fino* style of SHERRY made in the seaside sherry town of SANLÚCAR DE BARRAMEDA, where the particularly humid maritime air tends to result in a thicker layer of FLOR, a slower maturation process, lower alcohol content, and slightly higher acidity—especially since grapes do not get as ripe in Sanlúcar's coastal vineyards as they do inland. As the wine matures and the flor dies, a Manzanilla may develop into a **Manzanilla Pasada**, which is a Sanlúcar equivalent of a fino on the way to becoming AMONTILLADO. Manzanilla is typically FORTIFIED to 15% alcohol. For more details, see SHERRY. J.B.

Manzoni. See INCROCIO.

Maranges, the southernmost VILLAGE WINE appellation in the Côte de Beaune district of Burgundy, produces medium-bodied red wines of some charm when young. The vineyard stretches across the three villages of Cheilly, Dezize, and Sampigny, each of which takes 'Les Maranges' as a suffix. Formerly the wines were sold either under the village name or, much more frequently, as Côte de Beaune-Villages. Since 1988, such wines may be called Maranges or **Maranges Côte de Beaune**. White wines counted for slightly under 10% of vineyard area in 2018.

See also CÔTE D'OR, and map under BURGUNDY. J.T.C.M.

Maratheftiko, also known as Vamvakada, promising, dark-skinned CYPRUS grape variety gaining ground on the island, with 166 ha/410 acres planted in 2021, producing deeply coloured, fresh, cherry-fruited wines.

marc, the general French term both for grape POMACE and, more widely, for pomace brandy. It is used to distinguish the product from a *fine*, which may be made by distilling local wine. Most traditional wine regions make marc from the pomace, grape skins, and pips left after pressing. This was rarely for financial gain but often because traditional winegrowers hate to see anything they have grown go to waste.

Marche (**Marches** in English), the easternmost region in the central belt of Italy stretching from TUSCANY and UMBRIA to the Adriatic coast (see map under ITALY). It shares a variety of characteristics with these neighbours to the west: a TOPOGRAPHY shaped by land rising from the coastal plains to rolling hills and, westward, to the central spine of the Apennines; and a TEMPERATE climate, though, while it is marked by hot, dry summers, it is not as uniform as its western neighbours. In the north of the region west of Ancona, the climate is more CONTINENTAL, while in the south near Ascoli Piceno it is MEDITERRANEAN. Some viticultural characteristics are shared with Tuscany and Umbria: CALCAREOUS soils from the sea which once covered an important part of central Italy; HILLSIDE VINEYARDS; and large-scale plantings of SANGIOVESE, MONTEPULCIANO, and VERDICCHIO vines. The Marche has been one of the last of the central Italian regions to realize its potential for good-quality wines, however, partly because it is off Italy's main commercial axis of Milan–Bologna–Florence–Rome–Naples, and partly because of the lack of any urban centre more important than Ancona. However, the local white Verdicchio, produced in large volumes by CO-OPERATIVES and large bottlers, is a continuous export success, although it has largely obscured the fact that high-quality wines can and are being made.

The Marche has several wine styles that are now of serious interest, and 40% of its 17,563 ha/18,688 acres of vineyards are dedicated to DOC wines. Of its 15 DOCs and five DOCGS, Verdicchio dei Castelli di Jesi with 2,200 ha of vineyards is Marche's largest. See VERDICCHIO for more information.

For red wines, Montepulciano, with 4,600 ha/11,366 acres, is the second most planted variety after Sangiovese (6,215 ha) and produces its finest expression in Conero DOCG. Rosso Conero DOC is very similar except that higher yields are allowed (13 rather than 9 tonnes/ha) and requires two years of CASK AGEING.

Sangiovese features in no fewer than six of the Marche's 15 DOCs. Traditionally it was blended with Montepulciano in the Rosso Piceno DOC, but the once-obligatory minimum 50% has been reduced to 15%, and VARIETAL Sangioveses are now allowed. Rosso Piceno Superiore indicates a smaller historic zone with marginally lower yields. Styles of both DOCs range from modest stainless steel-fermented, early-drinking versions to fine oak-aged wines. Sangiovese from the Colli Pesaresi near the coast in the north of the region can be particularly elegant. A local speciality are the medium-bodied, fresh, perfumed reds of the growing Lacrima di Moro d'Alba zone near the town of Moro d'Alba in the north-eastern corner of the Verdicchio di Castelli di Jesi zone. Offida white wines, promoted in the early 2010s from DOC to DOCG, can be produced from either PECORINO or PASSERINA grapes, while red Offida must be at least 85% Montepulciano. Offida Pecorino in particular has benefited from the ambitions of a new generation of wine producers determined to unleash its potential by lowering yields. Parallel DOC Terre di Offida is reserved for white wines made of 100% Passerina. W.S.

Merlini, P., and Silvestri, M., *Un Altroviaggio nelle Marche* (2012).
www.imtdoc.it

Marcillac, growing AOC in SOUTH WEST FRANCE whose vigorous red wines are like no other. This is the best-known wine district of the Aveyron *département* (although see also ENTRAYGUES–LE FEL and ESTAING), where growers seek to preserve the area's viticultural tradition on terraced valleys in the Massif Central at ELEVATIONS up to 600 m/2,000 ft.

Its history has been turbulent. Despite the PHYLLOXERA crisis, which was followed by hurried planting of many low-quality HYBRIDS, the vineyard thrived so as to supply wines to the miners at nearby Decazeville. The mines however were closed in 1962, and the planted area fell to a mere 23 ha/57 acres. A handful of growers set about a revival choosing to replant the local FER (here called Mansois) in the region's IRON-impregnated red earth. The vineyard now extends over 200 ha/494 acres. The local CO-OPERATIVE at Valady is an important producer, as is Domaine du Cros, which since 1984 has increased its vineyards from 3 to 34 ha.

Marcillac, usually red and sometimes rosé, must be made of at least 90% Mansois, but few growers add anything else. It is a hard-wooded vine capable of making firm, redcurrant- and raspberry-flavoured wines with excellent structure. BARREL MATURATION has been introduced to temper the acidity of the wines, but often to the detriment of their unique flavour. P.S.

marcottage, French term for the LAYERING method of vine propagation in the vineyard.

Maréchal Foch, red wine grape variety named after a famous French First World War general. This FRENCH HYBRID was bred by Eugène Kuhlmann of Alsace, who cited the VITIS VINIFERA variety Goldriesling as one parent. DNA PROFILING in 2021 identified the hybrid Millardet et Grasset 101 o.p. as the second parent. It has good winter hardiness and ripens very early. It was once widely cultivated in the Loire and is still popular in CANADA and NEW YORK, where it is spelt **Marechal Foch**, is sometimes called simply Foch, and may be vinified using CARBONIC MACERATION. It produces fruity, non-FOXY wines which can stand on their own two feet. J.V.

Maremma, long, loosely defined strip of TUSCAN coastline south of Livorno extending southward through the province of Grosseto. (The Maremma also extends into LAZIO, but this is not a viticultural zone.) Since 1995 it has also been the name of an IGT which was elevated to DOC in 2011 (and legally suffixed 'Toscana' in 2020) but, perversely, without more rigorous production rules. While predominantly dedicated to the production of red wine, the DOC in 2020 owed 28% of its total production to the white grape VERMENTINO.

The DOC area is confined to the province of Grosseto. Within its borders lie no fewer than seven DOCs and two DOCGs, but, although the area is extremely extensive, in 2021 only 2,364 ha/5,841 acres were declared DOC Maremma (up from 1,665 ha in 2012). The Maremma DOC can also be used for declassifying wines from the many DOCs within the region. The Alta Maremma (Upper Maremma) is the highest part of the region, in the north between Massa Marittima and Roccastrada, where vineyards are situated at 150–500 m/490–1,640 ft in ELEVATION, providing a cooler MESOCLIMATE than the warm Maremma plain and resulting in more elegant wines.

In etymological terms, the word 'Maremma' derives from the Latin *mare*, or 'sea', and is related to the French *marais*. Like the MÉDOC in Bordeaux, the low-lying parts of the Maremma were swampy or marshy for much of their history, with chronic problems of malaria.

Production of bottled wine is consequently a recent phenomenon, and quality wine can be said to date from the first bottles of SASSICAIA in the 1970s, although the zone of Morellino di Scansano, high and relatively malaria-free, enjoyed a certain reputation in the past, which it recently has more than confirmed. Thanks to the success of Sassicaia and, later, Ornellaia, the mid 1990s saw an investment boom in the Maremma, its apparent potential for large-scale vineyards on relatively inexpensive land attracting many prestigious producers. Because the warm climate here results in riper grapes, it quickly became a source of blending wine for beefing up other Tuscan DOCs. The history of the region is so recent that eight of Grosseto's 13 DOCs and DOCGs did not exist prior to 1989 (Bolgheri itself having been elevated only in 1983), while several small DOCs owe their status to the success of remarkably few producers, such as Suvereto, which was elevated to DOCG in 2011.

Sassicaia laid the foundation stone for successful Cabernet-based wines, and many estates tried to copy the style while often supplementing their vineyards with plantings of Merlot and Syrah, but the results often lack the elegance and age-worthiness of the prototype. BARRIQUE ageing is still the standard, although large oak CASKS are increasingly used instead. Even if almost every DOC within the Maremma has a provision for INTERNATIONAL VARIETIES, be it as an added percentage or as varietally labelled wines, Sangiovese is still the most common and mandatory ingredient in most of the wines here.

In the Maremma there are three important areas, all promoted to DOCG in 2009. Morellino di Scansano DOCG is Maremma's classic zone for Sangiovese around the town of Scansano. Vineyards rise to 450 m/1,476 ft; Sangiovese (here called Morellino) grown at lower elevations tends to be fuller bodied. Like Chianti Classico, the wines must contain a minimum of 85% Sangiovese, as do those from Montecucco Sangiovese DOCG, further inland than Morellino di Scansano. Unremarkable in the past, it has attracted newcomers unable to afford vineyards in Chianti Classico and Montalcino who have begun to produce high-quality Sangiovese wines. Montecucco DOC is for whites based on Vermentino and reds with up to 60% Sangiovese. Val di Cornia Rosso DOCG on the Tuscan coast south-east of Suvereto, on a spit of land jutting out into the Mediterranean, is for blends of Sangiovese, Merlot, and Cabernet, while the Val di Cornia Bianco DOC is for whites made from Vermentino and Ansonica (the DOC Ansonica Costa dell'Argentario on the coast near the rocky promontory of Argentario is reserved for whites with a minimum of 85% Ansonica, the same variety as Sicily's INZOLIA).

The DOC Monteregio di Massa Marittima, extending over a large area between the coast and the town of Roccastrada, features Sangiovese for reds and Vermentino for whites, complemented by international varieties. Rising to 500 m/1,640 ft, the hills here are virgin vineyard land but the few wines produced here are generally elegant and fresh, suggesting that it has an interesting future.

Bolgheri apart, the Maremma has not turned out to be the promised land it appeared to be in the mid 1990s, although it may eventually produce some excellent wines from the right varieties and CLONES planted in the best sites. W.S.

Margaret River, most important wine region in WESTERN AUSTRALIA, air-conditioned by ocean on three sides. Cabernet Sauvignon and Sauvignon Blanc dominate the region's 5,725 ha/14,147 acres of vineyards, but it is also known for first-class CHARDONNAY. Its wines, together with Margaret River's year-round TEMPERATE CLIMATE, physical beauty, and diverse attractions from surf to woodworks make it a prime centre for wine TOURISM. E.L.L.

margarodes, otherwise known as ground pearls, are a serious insect pest in some vineyards, although they are, fortunately, found only in certain restricted regions. Margarodes weaken and kill vines with a similar action to PHYLLOXERA, and afflicted vines normally die about four years after a decline in VIGOUR is noted.

While many species of margarodes occur on a wide range of host plants worldwide, the most damaging to vines is the *Margarodes vitis* of South America. There are ten species of margarodes in South Africa, five of which infest vine roots, with *Margarodes prieskaensis* being one of the most damaging. The pre-adult insect is a round cyst which attaches itself to the roots and is covered by a hard, waxy covering. The insects are conspicuous by their foul odour.

The mature cysts can remain inactive in the soil for many years. Winged male and female forms mate above the soil surface, and eggs are laid in the vicinity of vine roots in early summer. There are no sources of resistance to margarodes within the VITIS genus which includes vines, so control by grafting on to resistant ROOTSTOCKS seems unlikely. R.E.S.

Wineland, 'Identification, control and management of grapevine margarodes' (2017). www.wineland.co.za/identification-control-management-grapevine-margarodes.

Margaux, potentially the most seductive appellation of the Haut-MÉDOC district of Bordeaux. At their stereotypical best, the wines of Margaux combine the deep ruby colour, structure, and concentration of any top-quality Médoc with a haunting perfume and a silkier texture than is found to the north in ST-JULIEN, PAUILLAC, and ST-ESTÈPHE. Mid 20th century vintages from its two finest properties Ch Margaux (see below) and Ch Palmer certainly demonstrated this and helped to develop this conception of Margaux. Margaux is the most southerly, most isolated, and most extensive of the Médoc's communal appellations (see map under BORDEAUX). Although it is made of several non-contiguous parcels of the best portions of vineyard land (inferior parcels qualifying merely as Haut-Médoc), the appellation takes in not just the substantial village of Margaux but also the neighbouring communities of Cantenac, Soussans, Labarde, and Arsac.

In total almost 1,500 ha/3,750 acres qualified for the Margaux appellation in the mid 2010s, and within its boundaries there are inevitably considerable variations in both topography and soil type. Within the appellation is LIMESTONE, CHALK, CLAY, and SAND, but most of the finest wines should come from gentle outcrops, or *croupes*, where GRAVEL predominates and DRAINAGE is good—although properties here are particularly parcellated and intermingled with one estate often comprising very different, and often distant, plots of land. Ch Margaux, for example, has vineyards in both Cantenac and Soussans.

Margaux has in the past enjoyed enormous *réclame*, and more Margaux properties were included in the 1855 CLASSIFICATION of the Médoc and Graves (more than 20) than from any other appellation. The appellation clearly still has great potential, but in the 1970s, 1980s, and even 1990s a curious number of châteaux failed to keep pace with the substantial improvements in wine quality achieved in the other three major appellations of the Médoc.

Ch Margaux itself, the FIRST GROWTH standard-bearer as well as name-bearer for the appellation, was revived only in 1978 after more than a decade of disappointing vintages (see below for more details). Of the five second growths within the appellation, Chx Rauzan-Ségla, Rauzan-Gassies, Durfort-Vivens, Lascombes, and Brane-Cantenac, the first was seriously revived only when the owners of the couture house Chanel bought it in 1994 (restoring the 'z' in its name), and the second has been one of the most notable under-performers in the whole Médoc. Among the original ten third growths, Desmirail, Ferrière, and Dubignon-Talbot were practically abandoned for years, the last apparently forever. Only Ch Palmer, officially a third growth, could be said to have represented the appellation with any glory and consistency in the second half of the 20th century. Ch Palmer, part owned and managed by the Bordeaux branch of the Sichel family, produced a wine that could without hyperbole be described as legendary in 1961.

Rauzan-Ségla and Rauzan-Gassies were originally one estate and, according to PENNING-ROWSELL, probably the first other than the first growths to establish a reputation abroad. Rausan-Ségla (as it was then spelt), the larger part, or rather many different parts, was long owned by the Cruse family then passed through several corporate hands, the last of which installed effective new winemaking equipment in the mid 1980s before the sale to the Wertheimer family of Chanel.

Ch Lascombes passed from Alexis LICHINE to a British brewer in 1971 and is now run, with considerable RIGHT BANK influence, by an American-led consortium. The large Ch Brane-Cantenac estate, like Durfort-Vivens owned by a LURTON, has been producing lighter wines than its status in the 1855 classification suggests.

Of Margaux's many third growths other than Palmer, Kirwan has yo-yoed rather; Issan was long more famous for its romantic moated château than for its wines; Giscours has experienced a renaissance under new ownership; Cantenac-Brown was only temporarily owned by AXA; Malescot St-Exupéry, originally called St-Exupéry, is slowly taking on more flesh; Boyd-Cantenac is too often dull; while Marquis d'Alesme-Becker, originally called Becker, can be uncomfortably lean.

More care has recently been lavished on Ch Prieuré-Lichine than on Margaux's other fourth growths Chx Pouget and Marquis de Terme, although the latter is much improved since the mid 1980s. Chx Dauzac and du Tertre, Margaux's fifth growths, have seen considerable recent investment.

One of the Médoc's most famous white wines is made here, even though it qualifies only as BORDEAUX AOC (see below). J.R. & J.L.

Brook, S., *The Complete Bordeaux* (4th edn, 2022).
Ginestet, B., *Margaux* (1984).
Penning-Rowsell, E., *The Wines of Bordeaux* (6th edn, 1989).

Margaux, Château, exceptional building and the most important wine estate in the village of MARGAUX in the Bordeaux wine region, and a FIRST GROWTH in the 1855 CLASSIFICATION. There is much potential for confusion since both Ch Margaux and GENERIC wine from the commune of Margaux are colloquially referred to as 'Margaux', but the former is likely to cost many times more than the latter.

With vineyards dating back to the 16th century, Ch Margaux was one of the four New French Clarets captured in the Anglo-French wars at the beginning of the 18th century and sold in the coffee houses of the City of London (see BORDEAUX, history). Thomas JEFFERSON on his visit to Bordeaux in 1787 picked it out as one of the 'four vineyards of first quality'. Sequestered in the French Revolution after the owner's flight to England, it was bought by the Marquis de la Colonilla in 1804 and rebuilt in the First Empire style, by L. Combes, as we know it today—the grandest CHÂTEAU of the Haut-MÉDOC. After passing through several hands, shares were bought by a Bordeaux wine merchant, Fernand Ginestet, in 1925, and the family share was slowly increased to give his son Pierre Ginestet complete ownership in 1949. Also a merchant, he was badly hit by the 'energy crisis' in the early 1970s and had to seek a buyer. The French government refused to allow the American conglomerate National Distillers to buy it, but in 1977 the château was acquired by the French grocery and finance group Félix Potin, headed by the Greek André Mentzelopoulos, domiciled in France and passionate about the property. A great deal of money was spent on restoring the neglected vineyard, *chais*, and mansion, and Émile PEYNAUD was taken on as consultant. André Mentzelopoulos tragically died suddenly in December 1980, and first his wife Laura and then his daughter Corinne took over control, assisted by the late Paul Pontallier, the young director who joined the estate in 1983 (coincidentally one of the property's most successful vintages). Between 1992 and 2003 the Italian Agnelli family of Fiat motor cars became involved in ownership of the estate, but Corinne Mentzelopoulos remained in charge and is now the sole owner with her children Alexandra and Alexis, both involved with the property. A brand-new winery designed by British architect Sir Norman Foster has been in place since 2014 with a research lab, a particular interest of Pontallier's, given pride of place.

The 80 ha/197 acres of red wine grapes are planted with roughly 75% CABERNET SAUVIGNON, 20% MERLOT, and 5% comprising CABERNET FRANC and PETIT VERDOT. Average total red-wine output has been reduced to just over 20,000 from 30,000 cases, of which the resurrected Pavillon Rouge de Ch Margaux is the excellent SECOND WINE. A third wine has been made since 1997 and offered for sale from the 2009 vintage. A hitherto somewhat uninspiring white wine Pavillon Blanc was transformed into an ambitious dry wine. It is made in a separate temperature-controlled cellar, with BARREL FERMENTATION, exclusively from SAUVIGNON BLANC grapes planted on 12 ha/30 ha of separate vineyard. E.P.-R. & J.R.

Faith, N., *Château Margaux* (1980).

marginal climate is one in which it may not be possible to fully ripen grapes every year, typically due to insufficient heat or too little or too much moisture, and where the wines produced are often more marked by vintage variation (see RIPENING). This situation is most often encountered in cool to cold climates. However, a marginal climate for a later-maturing variety such as MOURVÈDRE would be one that is warm enough to ripen earlier-maturing varieties but often has conditions that are too cool or a growing season that is too short to ripen Mourvèdre consistently. Growing grapes in marginal climates presents significant challenges, so VINEYARD SITE SELECTION is particularly important. G.V.J.

Maria Gomes, Bairrada and Vinho Verde synonym for the Portuguese white grape variety FERNÃO PIRES.

Maria Ordoña, Galician synonym for TROUSSEAU.

Marignan and **Marin** are small CRUS close to the southern shore of Lake Geneva whose names may be added to the French appellation SAVOIE. The wine is typically a light, dry white made from the CHASSELAS grape.

Marin, the CALIFORNIA county and wine region most immediately to the north of San Francisco, was planted as early as 1817, though many early growers on its cold, foggy hillsides quickly realized there were more hospitable growing areas further inland and decamped to neighbouring counties. Marin's first modern winery was only bonded in 1979, but this mountainous region continues to slowly attract plantings. More than 71 ha/175 acres of grapes, primarily PINOT NOIR, are now sourced by a number of top wineries, including the modern-day pioneer Sean Thackrey, as well as a few that focus solely on the region, such as Easkoot and Kendric. A.Y.

www.marinwine.org

maritime climate, the opposite of a CONTINENTAL CLIMATE, has a relatively narrow annual range of temperatures. Places with a maritime climate tend to be near or surrounded by oceans (MADEIRA, for example) or other large bodies of water (see LAKE EFFECT). Spring temperatures tend to be lower and autumn temperatures higher than those of nearby inland regions because water masses effectively gain and lose heat more slowly than land masses. During the summer, maritime climates also experience lower DIURNAL TEMPERATURE RANGE than areas that are further inland.

Wine regions with maritime climates tend to have longer yet cooler growing seasons with lower heat accumulation and often experience more precipitation than locations further inland. In the mid latitudes, maritime climates vary according to the ocean temperatures offshore. Many west-coast wine regions are influenced by cold ocean currents, which, combined with warmer inland temperatures, create daily incursions of marine cloud layers or fog in the coastal valleys (e.g. SONOMA and NAPA). Some west-coast wine regions with moderately warmer ocean temperatures offshore, on the other hand, tend to have slightly higher humidity and higher precipitation in the summer (e.g. BORDEAUX). With warmer ocean conditions, east-coast wine regions tend to have the highest humidity levels but also have more of a continental climate due to the westerly winds coming off the continent (e.g. VIRGINIA). See also CLIMATE AND WINE QUALITY.

marl, a CALCAREOUS rock with a significant CLAY content, and the soil derived from it. The composition is somewhere between a fine-grained LIMESTONE and a mudstone, 50–50 in a modern classification though some older schemes use different proportions. Terms such as 'clay marl' and 'limestone marl' loosely indicate greater proportions of clay or limestone. Being very fine-grained, the amounts cannot be discerned without analytical equipment: marl is no more a visible mixture of calcite and clay, as often stated, than grey is a mixture of black and white. Typically, marl is pale-coloured and featureless, sometimes splintery, and with dilute acid fizzes much less vigorously than limestone. Its most famous occurrences are in parts of CHABLIS and the CÔTE D'OR. A.M.

Marlborough, on the north-eastern tip of New Zealand's South Island, where the Polynesians first arrived via canoe more than 700 years ago, is by far the country's biggest wine region, with more than 70% of total vineyard area. There were no commercial vineyards on the island until 1973, when Frank Yukich of Montana planted a panoply of vines in Marlborough's Brancott Valley, including a small amount of Sauvignon Blanc.

Trial and error followed, but it was soon discovered that the region could produce an unprecedented expression of SAUVIGNON BLANC. The inaugural 1985 vintage from CLOUDY BAY electrified the world's wine consumers. Vineyard development has been relentless since, traversing almost 30,000 ha/74,132 acres across the region's two major catchments, the Wairau and Awatere rivers, which flow north-eastwards into the Pacific Ocean. The complex soils can be broadly divided into two categories: fertile ALLUVIUM and low-vigour CLAYS. The industry took some time to discover that the former soil is where Sauvignon Blanc thrives, while the clays host yield-sensitive Pinot Noir and Chardonnay to a far more interesting degree. Vineyards have been replanted accordingly over the past 20 years.

The impressive DIURNAL TEMPERATURE RANGE (11 °C/20 °F in summer), high sunshine hours, and low average annual rainfall (600 mm/24 in) defines the region and the styles across all varieties. Availability of water is increasingly an issue, especially for the drier Awatere Valley and Southern Valleys.

Marlborough's subregional story is still evolving. The Wairau Valley, the Awatere Valley, and the younger viticultural area to the south increasingly referred to as Southern Coast are regarded as three macro-subregions. Within these are smaller subregions. The most well-known is Southern Valleys encompassing five tributaries of the Wairau: the Waihopai, Omaka, Brancott, Ben Morven, and Taylor Pass. Here it is common to find more Pinot Noir and Chardonnay planted to the hillsides on clay, while Sauvignon Blanc and aromatic varieties occupy the gravel and loam on the valley floor.

The coastal Lower Wairau produces the most THIOL-rich expressions of Sauvignon Blanc, while the Awatere's cooler, drier climate is distinctive for its citrus and crushed herb nuances. Further south, vineyards stretch from the intensively planted Blind River to sporadic plantings around Ward and the satellite of Kekerengu.

Wine's importance to Marlborough is apparent in LABOUR statistics, where one in ten workers are directly employed by the industry. Protecting the reputation of Marlborough Sauvignon Blanc is a growing concern among producers, and in 2018 a group of wineries united under the Appellation Marlborough Wine (AMW) trademark to guarantee that basic quality parameters and provenance would be upheld in certified wines. Wines must be 100% Marlborough fruit and bottled in New Zealand.

Marlborough also has the most Pinot Noir planted (2,721 ha/6,724 acres) in New Zealand, followed by an increasing number of Pinot Gris vines (1,221 ha), while Chardonnay (1,109 ha) remains relatively static. A portion of the Pinot Noir and Chardonnay crop goes into making high-quality traditional method SPARKLING WINE. Stylistically Pinot Gris seems to have found a comfortable identity in a Northern Italian-esque mould. Riesling (240 ha) is produced in styles from dry through to lusciously botrytized (see NOBLE ROT), and the region's producers are also experimenting with alternative varieties such as SAUVIGNON GRIS, GRÜNER VELTLINER, ALBARIÑO, and PINOT BLANC. S.P.-T.

Marmajuelo (also known as **Bermejuela**), rare but outstanding white grape variety grown on the CANARY ISLANDS.

Marmandais, Côtes du, Bordeaux satellite AOC in SOUTH WEST FRANCE on either side of the river GARONNE. The town of Marmande, on the Garonne, gave it its name and provided a ready means of transporting the wines to Bordeaux and then to northern Europe, especially the NETHERLANDS, from the Middle Ages until the early 19th century. The arrival of PHYLLOXERA caused many farmers to abandon viticulture, however, and vines are just one of many crops in these gentle Marmandais hills. Geographically the region is simply an extension of eastern GRAVES in the south and ENTRE-DEUX-MERS in the north. Bordeaux grape varieties CABERNET SAUVIGNON, CABERNET FRANC, and MERLOT predominate, and the cooler climate here tends to result in light versions of red, and some rosé, wines. But these varieties may not exceed 85% of a blend, and Côtes du Marmandais's distinction is in the local variety ABOURIOU, which, with FER, Cot (MALBEC), Gamay, and Syrah, must make up the rest. Total vineyard area increased sharply in the 1990s but declined again so that it now hovers around 800 ha/1,976 acres. A very small amount of white wine is made, mainly from Sauvignons Blanc and Gris.

Much of the increasingly sophisticated wine production is in the hands of CO-OPERATIVES, but Elian Da Ros has provided much-needed glamour as an ambitious individual producer.

marque, French for BRAND.

Marqués, occasional name for LOUREIRO.

Marquette, increasingly popular cold-hardy AMERICAN HYBRID bred in Minnesota and grown in Canada and various chilly American states. Makes quite assertive, peppery red wine.

Marsala, town in the province of Trapani in western SICILY and the FORTIFIED WINE produced around it. For over 200 years one of Sicily, and Italy's, most famous products, Marsala has fallen on hard times with declining quality, evaporating markets, and plunging production levels, although there are encouraging signs of revival.

History

Marsala can said to have been born with the arrival in Marsala in 1770 of John Woodhouse, an English merchant and connoisseur of PORT,

SHERRY, and MADEIRA, who noted a striking similarity between the local wines and the fortified wines of Spain and Portugal. These wines were aged in a single-cask SOLERA system but without the addition of spirit (see FORTIFICATION). Woodhouse 'invented' Marsala in 1773 by adding 8 1/2 gal of grape spirit to each of the 400-l/105-gal barrels which he shipped to England. He proceeded to open a warehouse and cellars in the township of Marsala in 1796. The victualling of Nelson's fleet in 1798 doubtlessly assisted in spreading the name of the wine, and Woodhouse was followed by another Englishman, Benjamin Ingham, who founded a Marsala firm in 1812. The largest Marsala house, Florio, whose premises once occupied a full kilometre of seafront, was founded by Vincenzo Florio from CALABRIA in 1833. Marsala's production and marketing has always been dominated by large commercial houses, although there has been little continuity over time. Of the various Italian houses founded in the 19th century, Florio, Rallo, Pellegrino, Curatolo Arini, and Martinez have remained active, while Curatolo Arini, Cantina Intorcia (founded in 1930), and Marco De Bartoli (1979) are the only producers still run by descendants of the founding family.

Winemaking and viticulture

Modern Marsala, as codified in the DOC regulations of 1969, can be fortified only by adding grape spirit. Alcohol levels will also be slightly increased by BLENDING IN *mistella* or *sifone* (see MISTELA), the must of late-picked, overripe grapes, with fermentation blocked by the addition of 20–25% pure alcohol. Modifications to the viticulture of the zone have also had an effect on the wines produced today. The traditional GOBELET vine-training system has been partially replaced by WIRES, and the traditional grapes of the region, GRILLO and INZOLIA, have been partially supplanted by the higher-yielding CATARRATTO. This and enthusiastic IRRIGATION have led to significant increases in yield (the DOC rules allow a generous 10 tons/ha for white varieties, 9 tons/ha for red) and a corresponding drop in the grapes' sugar levels. All these factors have led to poorer base wines, necessitating more routine sweetening and a loss of the intrinsic character of the wine itself.

Furthermore, in the past, the use of ancient and poorly maintained casks for ageing the better categories of wine did little for their quality. Even more damaging, however, has been the proliferation of so-called 'Marsala Speciale', cloying wines flavoured with coffee, chocolate, strawberries, almonds, or eggs, all of which enjoyed a DOC status equal to the real wine from 1969 to 1984, when the use of the name 'Marsala' for these *speciale* forms was banned. The misconception these cooking wines created persists.

Today there are three main styles of Marsala:

Fine denotes a wine made by the addition of alcohol, mistella, and *mosto cotto* to the base wine. It must measure at least 17.5% alcohol and age for at least one year; **I.P.** or Italia Particolare (also called **L.P.**, or London Particolar) is a sweeter style, with a minimum of 17% alcohol and one year of CASK AGEING.

Superiore (or **S.O.M.**, for Superior Old Marsala) allows the addition of only *mistella* to the base wine and must be at least 18% alcohol, with two years of cask ageing. A Superiore Riserva requires at least four years of cask age.

Vergine or 'Soleras' can have only alcohol added to the base wine; it is forbidden to add either *mistella* or *mosto cotto*. Therefore, these wines are always dry. Vergine Marsalas require at least five years of ageing in a SOLERA system; Riserva or *stravecchio* versions require a minimum of 10 years.

Fine and Superiore Marsala also come in a range of sweetness levels, from Secco (a maximum of 40 g/l of RESIDUAL SUGAR) to Semisecco (40–100 g/l) and Dolce (over 100 g/l). Both can also come in three colours: Oro (golden); Ambra (amber: the colour coming from *mosto cotto*—an attempt to create the impression of a cask-aged wine by deepening its colour with concentrate); and Rubino (ruby), made from at least 70% NERO D'AVOLA, PERRICONE, and/or NERELLO MASCALESE grapes.

Although 1,526 ha/3,770 acres of vineyards were registered as DOC in 2020 (down from 1,672 ha in 2012), the production of truly fine wines as the result of long cask ageing is increasing, if at a snail's pace and still in tiny quantities. The Marco de Bartoli estate, the most innovative producer of the zone, may not state the Marsala name on the labels of its Vecchio Samperi, a prototype high-quality Marsala Vergine, as it is made without the required addition of alcohol, although it has the mandatory 18% ABV. The wine is the result of a system called *vino perpetuo*, in which the barrels are regularly TOPPED UP with younger wines, as is Intorcia's *Pre British*, referring to the ancient, and still alive, tradition of making *Alto Grado*, wines with an elevated level of alcohol, while Florio has continued to offer mature and complex Vergine and Superiore wine often sourced from enviably large historic stocks. W.S.

Belfrage, N., *Brunello to Zibibbo—The Wines of Tuscany, Central and Southern Italy* (2nd edn, 2003).

Nesto, B., and Di Savino, F., *The World of Sicilian Wine* (2013).

Marsannay, northernmost appellation of the Côte de Nuits district of the CÔTE D'OR (see map under BURGUNDY). It is unique in Burgundy for having AOC status for red, white, and pink wines. The vineyards of Couchey and Chenove are included with those of Marsannay. Prior to 1987, the wines were sold as generic BOURGOGNE followed by the specification Marsannay or Rosé de Marsannay. The latter style of wine is a speciality of the village pioneered in 1919 by Joseph Clair. The small amount of white wine produced has yet to show particular character. The red wines are attractive and fruity, if lighter than those of neighbouring FIXIN. There were no PREMIER CRU vineyards in 2021, but vineyards such as Clos du Roy and Les Longeroies may yet be elevated. J.T.C.M.

Marsanne, widely dispersed pale-skinned vine variety, making full-bodied, scented white wines. Probably originating in the northern RHÔNE, it has all but taken over here from its traditional blending partner and close relative ROUSSANNE (one naturally gave birth to the other through a CROSS with another as-yet-unknown variety) in such appellations as ST-JOSEPH, ST-PÉRAY (where it is sometimes known as Roussette), CROZES-HERMITAGE, and, to a slightly lesser extent, HERMITAGE itself, where wines such as CHAPOUTIER's Chante Alouette show that the variety can make exceptionally good wines for ageing. The vine's relative productivity has doubtless been a factor in its popularity, and modern winemaking techniques have helped mitigate Marsanne's tendency to flab. It is increasingly planted in the south of France, where, as well as being embraced as an ingredient in most appellations, it is earning itself a reputation as a full-bodied, characterful VARIETAL, or a blending partner for more aromatic, acid varieties such as Roussanne, VIOGNIER, and ROLLE. The wine is particularly deeply coloured, full-bodied, with a heady, if often heavy, aroma of pears, sometimes honeysuckle, verging occasionally on almonds, sometimes bitter in youth. It is not one of the chosen varieties for Châteauneuf-du-Pape, in which GRENACHE BLANC supplies many of Marsanne's characteristics, but France's total plantings had grown to 1,798 ha/4,443 acres by 2019—mainly in the Rhône Valley but supplemented by plantings in the Languedoc and Roussillon. A little is planted in Italy and Switzerland, where as Ermitage it produces both light, dry wines and complex sweet wines in the Valais. Interest was generated in California as part of the RHÔNE RANGERS movement, although total acreage was only 51 ha/126 acres in 2020. Australia has some of the world's oldest Marsanne vineyards, notably in the state of Victoria, and a fine tradition of valuing this Rhône import and the hefty wines it produces, which have sometimes developed relatively fast in bottle. Total plantings had fallen to 137 ha/339 acres by 2022, however.

Marselan, particularly successful CROSS of Cabernet Sauvignon and Grenache Noir made by INRA in 1961. The small-berried variety was developed specifically for the LANGUEDOC, where it copes with both wet and dry growing seasons, is resistant to FUNGAL DISEASES and COULURE, but is very sensitive to TRUNK DISEASES. It can offer respectable levels of both colour and flavour. By 2019 total French plantings had reached 6,426 ha/15,879 acres. It has also spread successfully to Spain, California, Argentina, Brazil, and China, where local WINE CRITICS have suggested that Marselan could become China's signature red variety.

Martial (**Marcus Valerius Martialis**) (*c.*40–103/4 CE), born in Bilbilis, in Spain; he was poor and wrote Latin poetry for a living. In his *Epigrams*, in 15 books, more than 1,500 short poems in all, he writes about the vices he sees around him in ancient ROME, but he prudently uses pseudonyms to disguise the names of those he satirizes: for instance, 'Hesterno fetere mero qui credit Acerram, fallitur in lucem semper Acerra bibit' (1. 28). ('He who thinks that Acerra reeks of yesterday's wine is wrong. Acerra always drinks until daybreak.') Since snobbery and pretentiousness are two of his main targets, he often mentions wine. Misers and the *nouveaux riches* drink OPIMIAN wine (1. 26, 3. 82, 9. 87, 10. 49), and when Martial satirizes the classical cult of old wine (old wine was always preferred to new and was known by its consular year), he invents a wine that has not even got a consular year, because it was laid down before the Republic (13. 111). He generally presumes detailed knowledge about wine on the reader's part, as for instance in 2. 53, 4. 49, 3. 49. The reader needs to know which wines were good and which were not in order to get the point of the epigram. At the end of Book 13 (106–25) is a series of epigrams listing 21 types of wine. Martial expresses his opinions of certain wines tersely, as in the following (13. 122), 'Acetum' (Vinegar):

Amphora Nilliaci non sit tibi vilis aceti
esset cum vinum, vilior illa fuit.

(Don't think an amphora of Egyptian vinegar is mean stuff. When it was wine, it was meaner still.) H.M.W.

Griffin, J., *Latin Literature and Roman Life* (1985).

Marufo, lesser PORT grape variety, also known as Mourisco Roxo, which produces red wines relatively light in colour in northern Portugal. Favoured by a few for light tawny ports, it was grown on 1,766 ha/4,364 acres in 2020.

Marzemino, interesting, late-ripening red grape variety grown in northern Italy, from Lombardy to Friuli but mainly in TRENTINO. DNA PROFILING at SAN MICHELE ALL'ADIGE revealed parent–offspring relationships with both TEROLDEGO and REFOSCO DAL PEDUNCOLO ROSSO, thus anchoring the genetic roots of this variety in northern Italy. Once much more famous than now, it does not have particularly good resistance to FUNGAL DISEASES and is often allowed to over-produce, but it can yield lively wines, some of them lightly sparkling. A big-berried CLONE dominated plantings with just over 785 ha/1,940 acres in Italy in 2015. J.R. & J.V.

mas, southern French term for a domaine.

Masdeu, strong red wine made on and named after an exceptionally well-maintained estate near Perpignan in ROUSSILLON which found a market via London wine merchants and salerooms in the middle of the 19th century as a cheaper alternative to PORT.

Shaw, T. G., *Wine, the Vine and the Cellar* (1864).

Massandra, winery built to extremely high specifications on the outskirts of Yalta in the CRIMEA in the 1890s to supply Livadia, the tsars' summer palace. Miners were imported from GEORGIA to tunnel into the rock and create more than 3 km/1.9 m of cool, damp cellars. Prince Golitsyn (see CRIMEA) was the first winemaker and was succeeded by the first of the Yegorov family, members of which made wine at Massandra for almost a century from 1898. The most successful wines are strong and sweet, many of them VINS DOUX NATURELS as well as FORTIFIED. Many were made to mirror other famous dessert wines such as PORT, SHERRY, MADEIRA, and TOKAJI, using local varieties such as RKATSITELI and SAPERAVI as well as imports such as MUSCAT, PINOT GRIS, and MALBEC and crosses such as Bastardo Magarachsky, a BASTARDO × Saperavi CROSS originated at MAGARACH in 1949. The current buildings at Massandra are used not for winemaking but for AGEING and BOTTLING. Today the produce of nine wineries is sold under the Massandra name.

The **Massandra Collection** was begun by Prince Golitsyn, its oldest member being an 18th-century wine made in the image of SHERRY known as Jerez de la Frontera 1775, but it is today made up substantially of the best Crimean wines. After considerable quantities were poured into the sea before the Nazi invasion, the Collection was evacuated during the German occupation of Yalta 1941–4, some as far as to Georgia, but was back in place in time for the historic Yalta peace conference in 1945. In the early 1990s Sotheby's offered two consignments of strong, very sweet, durable wines from the Massandra Collection at AUCTION in London as part of the auctioneer's trading arrangements with the disintegrating Soviet Union. A further sale was held in 2004. In 2014, under the Russian occupation of Crimea, the winery was nationalized and, in December 2020, put up for auction, whereupon it passed into private hands.

Massic, a white wine which was among the most famous wines of Roman Italy and was much praised by the Roman poets. The type of grape is unknown. The wine was produced on Monte Massico, the line of hills which runs down to the sea on the west coast of Italy between the rivers Garigliano and Volturno. This zone is adjacent to the territory which produced FALERNIAN, and some writers treat Massic as a subtype of that famous wine. The wine was transported to Sinuessa on the coast, where there were numerous kilns producing the AMPHORAE in which the wine was exported. J.J.P.

mass selection, *sélection massale* in French, sometimes translated as 'massal selection', is a viticultural technique used to provide buds for the PROPAGATION of vines. Field vine selection can be either by mass selection, when many vines are selected to provide BUDWOOD, or by CLONAL SELECTION, in which a single mother vine is selected to provide CLONES. In mass selection, the identity of individual vines is not maintained, which is the principal difference between the two approaches.

Mass selection can be either negative or positive. If negative, then undesirable vines in a vineyard are marked so that cuttings are not taken from them. These vines might include those with low yield, poor fruit maturity, virus disease symptoms, higher than average incidence of fungal diseases, or off-types (MUTATIONS). Negative mass selection is also a good opportunity to mark 'rogue vines' (those of another variety) to ensure that mixed plantings do not occur in the future (although see FIELD BLEND). Positive selection identifies the best vines, for example those with good fruit set, larger and looser bunches, and good fruit maturity.

Usually the vineyard assessment is made several times over the season. For example, rogue vines and NEPOVIRUS symptoms are easier to pick out in the spring, whereas differences in grape ripening are obviously best determined just before harvest. Vines are commonly marked by paint on the trunk.

Since there is not the same detailed recording and selection of individual vines, the gains in yield or quality from mass selection are typically less than for clonal selection, but the resultant wine, made from vines with a mixture of different characteristics, may be more interesting than one made from a single clone. The benefits to be had from mass selection will depend on how heterogeneous was the field from which the selection is made. There will be little benefit of mass selection if the vineyard is genetically quite uniform, but if there is a high proportion of rogue vines, off-types, or virus diseases then the grower might expect substantial benefits.

Unfortunately, in many viticultural regions of the world cuttings are taken in winter from vineyards which have not benefited from even the most cursory inspection in the preceding summer. In the winter the dormant vines appear similar, and so mistakes of mixed plantings, off-types, and virus diseases are spread unwittingly from one vineyard to the next generation by propagation. R.E.S.

Dry, P. R., and Coombe, B. G., *Viticulture*, i: *Resources* (2nd edn, 2004).

Masters of Wine, those who have passed the examinations held every year by the **Institute of Masters of Wine (IMW)**, the wine trade's most famous and most demanding professional qualification. The Institute had its origins in the British wine trade in the early 1950s, when a counterpart to the qualifying examinations for other professions was devised by a group of wine merchants in conjunction with the VINTNERS' Company. The first examination was held in London in 1953, and six of the 21 candidates were deemed to have qualified as Masters of Wine. The Institute of Masters of Wine was formed in 1955. The examinations consist of five written papers and three 'practical' (i.e. wine-tasting) papers; since 1999 those who pass all of them must write an approved research paper to qualify as an MW. The examinations are distinguished by the breadth and depth of their scope. University courses (see ACADEME) offer more detailed instruction in the OENOLOGY or VITICULTURE of a particular country or region, while the MW examinations test knowledge of both subjects on a worldwide basis, as well as of such varied subjects as ÉLEVAGE, BOTTLING, transport, QUALITY CONTROL, marketing, commercial aspects of the wine trade, the effects of wine consumption on HEALTH, and general wine knowledge. Each tasting paper requires candidates to describe, assess, and, often, identify up to 12 wines served BLIND. These wines, including SPARKLING and FORTIFIED WINES, may come from anywhere in the world.

Despite a notoriously low pass rate (although it has risen markedly in recent years, and candidates have always been allowed to pass practical and theoretical parts in separate years), by 1978 the number of Masters of Wine had reached 100, including two women. In 1982 the Institute held its first, relatively academic, symposium, at Oxford, but it also lost four of its members and realized that some expansion would be necessary for its survival (it had no executives and no premises until 1987). In 1983 it relaxed its entry requirements and allowed candidates from the fringes of the wine trade, such as WINE WRITERS, to take the examinations. In 1987 the examinations were opened up to those outside the United Kingdom, and the next year the first overseas candidate, an Australian, passed the examinations, at this stage still held in London. Since 1991 examinations have been held, on the same dates, in London, Australia, and North America. By early 2022 there were 419 Masters of Wine (268 men, 151 women) based in 30 countries, and several MWs with no professional connection with wine at all; 209 members live and work outside the UK. Since 1953, 498 people have passed the exams. Numbers of candidates have grown even more rapidly than numbers of Masters of Wine. The examinations are increasingly demanding as the wine world expands, and the standard of preparation offered by the Institute was raised considerably in the mid 1990s and early 2000s. If the aims of the Institute have at times been less clear than the status of its members, and for many years it offered examinations but remarkably little education, this has changed thanks to annual residential courses, regular seminars, tastings, online learning, and a mentoring scheme.

www.mastersofwine.org

Master Sommelier is a qualification a little like MASTER OF WINE except that it is aimed at SOMMELIERS and tests practical wine service skills as well as BLIND TASTING and theoretical knowledge (which tends to involve more rote learning than the MW). Leading up to MS level are certifications: Introductory, Certified, and Advanced. The MS qualification itself became especially celebrated in the US as a result of the 2012 film *Somm* about the trials of several candidates. But in late 2020 a substantial number of cases of sexual harassment of female MS candidates were reported, and as a result seven Master Sommeliers were stripped of their status. There are, rather confusingly, two distinct 'Courts' of Master Sommeliers: that based in the Americas also includes Korea; the other has jurisdiction over Europe, Oceania, and the rest of Asia. In late 2022 there were 269 MSs worldwide, of whom 158 were members of the American Court. In all, four people have passed both MS and MW exams.

Mataro is one of the many synonyms of MOURVÈDRE, used primarily in Australia and by those who do not realize how fashionable Mourvèdre has become.

Mateus. The Palace of Mateus near Vila Real just north of the DOURO Valley in northern Portugal lent its name to **Mateus Rosé**. Bottled in a flask not unlike the BOCKSBEUTEL, this medium-sweet, lightly sparkling rosé blend became one of the world's most famous wine BRANDS. It was created in 1942 by Fernando van Zeller Guedes with the aim of putting wine from this then-neutral country on the world map. Commercial production began towards the end of the Second World War (at very much the same time as that of its rival Lancers). It was originally successful in Brazil; while that market collapsed after the war, the brand proved hugely popular in post-war Britain and then in the US. At its peak in 1978, Mateus, by then supplemented by a white version, accounted for over 40% of Portugal's total table-wine exports with worldwide sales amounting to 3.5 million cases. A small quantity of Mateus Rosé is still made at Vila Real, but most of the wine is now produced by owners SOGRAPE at Anadia in BAIRRADA.

Matrasa, or **Madrasa**, dominant, dark-berried vine of AZERBAIJAN. It is found in other central ASIAN republics and may also be called Kara Shirei and Kara Shirai. Also spelt 'Matrassa'.

Maturana Blanca, recently revived INDIGENOUS white wine grape in RIOJA.

Maturana Tinta, a Spanish synonym for TROUSSEAU. Maturana Tinta de Navarrete, confusingly referred to on some labels in RIOJA as Maturana Tinta *tout court*, is a synonym for the French variety CASTETS.

maturation of wine. See AGEING, BARREL AGEING, and CASK AGEING. The word 'maturation' is sometimes used to refer to grape RIPENING.

mature, tasting term for a fine wine that seems to have enjoyed sufficient AGEING for it to have reached the peak of its potential. In practice it is also used by the most polite, or determinedly optimistic, tasters to describe wines that are past that point. Any hint of orange at the rim of a red wine suggests MATURITY.

maturity, desirable state in a wine when it is consumed. In a sense, the most basic wine designed for early drinking is mature almost as soon as it is bottled, but 'mature' when applied to a wine carries with it the implication that the maturity is the result of a certain amount of AGEING. Such a (red) wine is deemed fully mature when it has dispensed with its uncomfortably harsh TANNINS and acquired maximum complexity of flavour (sometimes described as BOUQUET) without starting to decay. The period of maturity varies considerably with wine type but is probably longer than most wine consumers believe. A wine that has been followed since its youth and begins to taste mature may continue to delight, and possibly evolve for the better, for a decade or more. For more details of the process and of the difference between individual wine types, see AGEING. For maturity in grapes, see RIPENING.

Maule, southern subregion of the Central Valley of CHILE with a rich heritage of OLD VINES, especially CARIGNAN, PAÍS, and MUSCAT.

Maury, both the VIN DOUX NATUREL and Maury SEC, the TABLE WINE, come from an island of black SCHIST around the eponymous village towards the western end of the Agly Valley in France's ROUSSILLON. Summers are hot and dry though slightly cooler in the higher west of the appellation, which extends to the neighbouring villages of Tautavel, St-Paul-de-Fenouillet, and Rasiguères. Maury Sec, recognized as an appellation in 2012, is only red; any white wine is either IGP Côtes Catalanes or Côtes du Roussillon. The principal grape variety is Grenache Noir, which may be blended with Carignan, Mourvèdre, or Syrah. With the decline in popularity of the Vin Doux Naturel, there has been a considerable influx of newcomers and new estates concentrating on *vin sec*.

Maury, the VDN, comes in several varieties. Red versions make up the bulk of the production, either as Grenat or Tuilé. Both must be at least 75% Grenache Noir, with the other colours of Grenache, plus Carignan, Syrah, and Macabeo playing a subsidiary role. Grenat is presented young and fresh, aged a minimum of eight months; Tuilé is an oxidative version aged a minimum of 30 months. (See OXIDATIVE WINEMAKING.)

Blanc and Ambré come from white varieties Grenache Gris and Blanc, Macabeo, Tourbat, and both Muscats. Blanc is the fresh version, while Ambré, like Tuilé, must age at least 30 months.

Hors d'Age entails a minimum of five years oxidative ageing, but the best will spend very much longer in old barrels and maybe also glass BONBONNES exposed to the elements. A wine described as RANCIO will have developed wonderful notes of walnuts and chocolate coffee, the result of ageing for several years in barrels that are never topped up (see TOPPING UP). R.E.G.

Mauzac, or **Mauzac Blanc**, is a declining white grape in SOUTH WEST FRANCE, especially in its birthplace GAILLAC and LIMOUX, where it is the traditional and still principal vine variety. It produces relatively aromatic wines which are usually blended, with Len de l'El around Gaillac and with Chenin and Chardonnay in Limoux. France's total area of Mauzac had fallen to 1,479 ha/3,655 acres by 2019. Thanks to energetic winemakers such as Robert Plageoles, since the late 1980s there has been a revival of interest in Gaillac's Mauzac, which comes in several different hues, sweetness levels, and degrees of fizziness. During the 1970s and 1980s in Limoux, total plantings of Mauzac rose, but they have declined as the appellation, for both still and fizzy wines, has been invaded by Chardonnay.

The vine, whose yields can vary enormously according to site, buds and ripens late, and grapes were traditionally picked well into autumn so that musts fermented slowly and gently in the cool Limoux winters, ready to referment in bottle in the spring. Today Mauzac tends to be picked much earlier, preserving its naturally high acidity but sacrificing much of its particular flavour reminiscent of the skin of shrivelled apples, before being subjected to the usual SPARKLING WINEMAKING techniques. Some gently sparkling Gaillacs are still made by the traditional *méthode gaillacoise*, however, just as a small portion of Limoux's Blanquette is made by the *méthode ancestrale*. Mauzac Noir is much rarer and unrelated.

Mavro means 'black' in Greek and is the common name of the dominant but undistinguished grape on the island of CYPRUS.

Mavrodaphne, dark-skinned grape variety grown particularly round Pátras in the Peloponnese in GREECE, where it is the foundation of Mavrodaphne of Pátras, a FORTIFIED dessert wine which responds well to extended CASK AGEING. This aromatic, powerful variety, also grown to a much more limited extent on the island of Kefalonia, is occasionally vinified dry but only for use in blends. There were 571 ha/ 1,411 acres in Greece in 2021.

Mavrotragano, increasingly appreciated, distinctive red wine grape INDIGENOUS to the Greek island of SANTORINI.

Mavroudi, meaning 'blackish', is a generic name for several Greek red wine grapes.

Mavrud, indigenous Balkan grape variety most closely associated with BULGARIA, capable of producing intense, tannic wine if allowed to ripen fully. Grown on 855 ha/2,113 acres in central southern Bulgaria in 2021 and a speciality of Assenovgrad near Plovdiv, it is small-berried, is low-yielding, and has a long vegetative period. The robust wine produced responds well to OAK AGEING and can age well for up to a decade in bottle.

Mazuelo, official Spanish name for CARIGNAN but used only in RIOJA, where it is sometimes spelt Mazuela and where the variety was historically a not particularly distinguished ingredient. For more details, see CARIÑENA.

MDMP. See METHOXY-DIMETHYLPYRAZINE.

mead, a fermented alcoholic drink, called *hydromel* in France and *Honigwein* or *Met* in Germany, made from honey, which, it is claimed, predates either wine or beer. Monks kept bees for candlewax, and any surplus honey was fermented into mead. The dissolution of the monasteries meant the virtual demise of mead-making in Britain. Since the Second World War, some larger companies have marketed a mixture of wine and honey as mead, but the tradition of genuine mead-making is experiencing a revival. Grape mead is grape juice mixed with honey before fermentation.

mealybugs, small white insects of the family Cicadellidae which suck vine sap. Young mealybugs infect new growth in the spring, typically the undersurface of leaves at the base of the shoot. They also can feed on the fruit, canes, and trunk, and one species, the vine mealybug *Planococcus ficus*, can feed on roots. Mealybugs become mature and reproduce in early summer, and there can be three or more generations a year. Mealybugs prefer a humid environment and so are mostly found in a dense vine CANOPY.

The vine mealybug, first identified in California's Coachella Valley in the early 1990s, is now widespread in the San Joaquin Valley and the Central Coast, where it is regarded as a serious problem. It is spread by infected new plantings and can be controlled by briefly dipping the dormant plants in hot water.

Mealybugs do not cause significant commercial damage by their sap-sucking action alone, but there can be two indirect effects. First, they produce copious quantities of a sugary, sticky liquid called honeydew, which collects over the bunches and foliage and on which fungus grows, often giving it a sooty appearance, sometimes referred to as sooty mould. Grapes affected by this impart a distinctive and undesirable taste to wine, and the fruit may be fit only for DISTILLATION. Mealybugs of the genera *Planococcus* and *Pseudococcus* have been implicated in the spread of LEAFROLL VIRUS, which has serious consequences for the loss of vineyard yield and grape quality. Mealybugs have been confirmed as spreading leafroll virus in South Africa, Israel, the US, Australia, and New Zealand. They are difficult to control because they may live on vine roots and also on other vineyard plants.

Where mealybug infestations are serious, a schedule of preventive sprays is necessary, but the waxy covering of the insect makes such spraying less effective. R.E.S.

Bettiga, L. J., (ed.), *Grape Pest Management* (3rd edn, 2013).

Buchanan, G. A., and Amos, T. G., 'Grape pests', in B. G. Coombe and P. R. Dry (eds.), *Viticulture*, ii: *Practices* (2nd edn, 2006).

University of California Agriculture & Natural Resources, UC IPM Pest Management Guidelines: vine mealybug. www2.ipm.ucanr.edu/agriculture/grape/vine-mealybug.

measles. For how it affects vines, see ESCA.

mechanical harvesting, harvesting by machine in place of the traditional manual HARVEST. Undoubtedly one of the greatest changes from ancient to modern vineyards has been the adoption of machine harvesting, which was first introduced commercially in the 1960s. Whereas manual grape harvesting required literally hordes of pickers to descend on vineyards and complete the harvest, now the vintage may be completed by just one harvester driver, perhaps with a supporting driver and vehicle to receive the harvested grapes. Depending on the YIELD and vineyard TOPOGRAPHY, to harvest a vineyard by hand requires between one and ten person-days per hectare, as opposed to less than five person-hours per hectare by machine.

Mechanical harvesting has been adopted for different reasons in different parts of the world. In some of the earliest developments instigated by Nelson SHAULIS and E. S. Shepardson at CORNELL UNIVERSITY, a major consideration was potential cost savings. In Australia, one of the first countries to embrace the new technology, the scarcity of LABOUR was important. In France, the increasing bureaucracy and costs involved in employing people even temporarily added allure to machine harvesting in the 1980s and 1990s. The net effect was that seasonal workers were more difficult to find, demanded higher wages, and were also perhaps less reliable, all of these factors promoting machines over people at vintage time. Machine harvesting may have been developed in the United States, but the technology was rapidly refined in France.

History

Mechanical harvesting can either increase the efficiency of manual labour or virtually replace it. Very early attempts at mechanization emphasized the first approach, but it has been the second approach which has been the more successful, by developing machines which essentially replace most of the manual operations.

Many forms of integrated machine harvesters have been developed and evaluated. The early New York development was the 'vertical impactor', which used a metal finger to strike the vine cordon; the shock dislodged the berries. However, the most common form of harvesting now is the 'horizontal slapper', which uses fibreglass rods to strike the CANOPY and dislodge the fruit, sometimes as single berries, sometimes as bunches, catching it with horizontal conveyor belts. Recent developments include onboard SORTING and DESTEMMING.

Effect on wine quality

The effect of machine harvesting on wine quality has been the subject of much scientific study, commercial experience, and popular conjecture. The majority of studies have shown that sophisticated mechanical harvesting has no negative effect on wine quality, and some have even argued that there is a positive effect. In New Zealand, for example, it has been shown that machine harvesting of Sauvignon Blanc increases the level of THIOLS in the juice, thereby highlighting the passion fruit and grapefruit flavours that have made this variety so successful.

Certainly most forms of machine harvesting damage some grapes so that parts of berries and bunches are mixed with the juice of broken berries. However, the juice can be protected from OXIDATION by SULFUR DIOXIDE addition, especially if moved quickly in a closed container to the winery. This problem can be minimized by harvesting at night, a practice widely adopted in hotter wine regions where grapes harvested by day can arrive at the winery at over 40 °C/104 °F. Indeed, in these circumstances, machine picking at night is a bonus for wine quality in comparison with hand harvesting by day.

Another disadvantage of machine harvesting is that there can be excessive SKIN CONTACT, which, depending on its duration (usually dictated by transport times), can lead to white wines becoming too high in PHENOLICS. The skin contact involved in transporting mechanically harvested white grapes to a winery can also cause a significant increase in the concentration of PROTEINS in the wine, necessitating higher rates of BENTONITE fining. Long distances between the winery and vineyard may make a mechanical harvest for delicate white wines an impossibility. Machine-harvested grapes can also contain leaves and petioles (see MOG), which may cause taints. Despite much evidence in favour of machine harvesting, some producers will remain with hand harvesting. The gentler nature of hand harvesting (which can also involve some degree of selection, e.g. avoiding unripe bunches or those affected by BUNCH ROT) is preferable for many top-quality wines, especially sparkling wines, for which WHOLE BUNCHES may be pressed without first crushing. However, in Australia, for example, machine harvesting of grapes for sparkling wine is being used in a limited fashion. See also ROBOTS. R.E.S.

Allen, T., et al., 'Influence of grape-harvesting steps on varietal thiol aromas in Sauvignon Blanc wines', *Journal of Agricultural and Food Chemistry*, 59/19 (2011), 10641–50.

Coombe, B. G., and Dry, P. R. (eds.), *Viticulture*, ii: *Practices* (2nd edn, 2006).

mechanical pruning involves using machines for PRUNING vines in winter. Viticulture is a very traditional form of agriculture, and many who tend the vines regard the annual winter pruning as their prime opportunity to interact physically with each vine. Because of this, and because they feel that mechanical pruning cannot offer the precision of manual pruning, many vine-growers oppose mechanical pruning, even at the expense of hours of back-breaking labour in cold and sometimes wet weather.

Early experiments in mechanical pruning were carried out in Australia and New York State in the mid 1970s. The machinery was not as elaborate as that for MECHANICAL HARVESTING, consisting of reciprocating cutters or flails mounted on a tractor. In Australia circular saws were widely used, sometimes mounted on a machine harvester with the picking head removed.

Machine pruning, a form of SPUR PRUNING, is simple in the extreme: a CANE-cutting device intersects the CANOPY, typically in a straight line, so that the vine canes are cut back to near their base. Because not all canes have a common orientation, even in a vertical-shoot-positioned TRAINING SYSTEM, a horizontal cut will produce spurs with a range of bud numbers (two to ten or more). The problem is exacerbated if the existing spurs on the vine are not at the same height, which is common in older vines.

Early commercial experiments followed mechanical pruning with hand pruning to thin out spurs and cut them to a uniform two-bud length, reducing pruning time by half. Encouraged by early experiments in Australia, however, most vines are now left untended after machine pruning. Because of an increase in pruning wounds, some affecting thicker, older wood, such vines are more prone to TRUNK DISEASE.

CANE PRUNING cannot be mechanized in this way, but surplus cane removal after hand-cutting can be, and in New Zealand machines have been developed to strip last season's growth off the trellis wires, offering partial mechanization.

Mechanical pruning is now widespread in Australia, especially in the hotter wine regions, mostly using tractor-mounted circular saws or reciprocating cutter bars, with a single pass cutting through wood of various ages across the top of the vine. Other parts of the world have been slower to embrace mechanical pruning, however, especially those where LABOUR is plentiful and relatively inexpensive. Mechanical pre-pruning is becoming more widespread for the extensive vineyards of southern France. In cooler regions such as northern Europe, mechanical pruning is less useful because machine pruning leaves too many buds, tending to increase yield and slow RIPENING. ROBOTS developed for cane pruning, using 3D vision, were field tested in New Zealand in 2014 following two years' research at the University of Canterbury. Despite this and other research, robotic pruning has not become commonplace.

The 100-plus hours per hectare required for hand pruning can be reduced to less than ten hours per hectare with mechanical pruning. Some of the substantial cost savings associated with this reduction may be lost if extensive hand-pruning follows. A more extreme option is not to prune at all: so-called MINIMAL PRUNING. R.E.S.

Botterill, T., et al., 'A robot system for pruning grape vines', *Journal of Field Robotics*, 34 (2017), 1100–22.

mechanization. Most WINEMAKING operations other than TASTING and overseeing individual barrels can be fully mechanized, but mechanization has been slower to invade the vineyard. Robotic technology is used, for example, in the production of PORT, in the movement of pallets around the winery, and in the preparation of grape samples. For more details of viticultural mechanization, see ROBOTS, MECHANICAL HARVESTING, MECHANICAL PRUNING, TRIAGE, and, most importantly, LABOUR.

medals from wine COMPETITIONS and other JUDGINGS are coveted by many wine producers and used mercilessly as sales aids. There is a certain hierarchy of medals, however. State and national wine shows are important to the wine trade in AUSTRALIA, but a Hobart gold medal may be reckoned less glamorous than a Canberra silver. In France, medals awarded by the fairs in Paris and Mâcon are usually indications of real quality.

medical aspects of wine consumption. See HEALTH.

medical profession. See DOCTORS.

medicine, wine in. From ancient times to the 18th century, wine enjoyed a central role in medicine (see LITERATURE OF WINE). The earliest practitioners of medicine were magicians and priests who used wine for healing as well as religious purposes (see RELIGION). Receipts for wine-based medicines appear in papyri of ancient EGYPT and the tablets of SUMER in about 2200 BCE, making wine humanity's oldest documented medicine.

The beginnings of systematized medicine are commonly attributed to the Greek Hippocrates (*c.*450 BCE), who recommended the use of wine as a disinfectant, a medicine, a vehicle for other drugs, and part of a healthy DIET. He experimented with different wines in order to discover how each might be most appropriately used—whether diluted or not, for example—to cure a specific ailment, from lethargy or diarrhoea to easing difficult childbirth.

The most famous physician of ancient ROME was GALEN (2nd century CE), whose medical experience was shaped by treating injured gladiators in Asia Minor, although Aurelius Cornelius Celsus (25 BCE–37 CE) had already written extensively about the medical uses of various wines from different regions of Greece and Italy. Galen learned (like the Good Samaritan of the BIBLE) that wine was the most effective means of disinfecting wounds, even soaking exposed abdominal contents in wine before returning them to the abdominal cavity in the case of severe stomach wounds. His post as imperial physician involved tasting the emperor's wines in order to select the best and most healthy.

Ancient Jewish civilization prized wine for its medicinal properties. In the Talmud it is stated: 'Wine is the foremost of all medicines: wherever wine is lacking, medicines become necessary.'

The Qur'ān presented Arab doctors with a dilemma. The likes of Avicenna (11th century CE) recognized the importance of wine in healing, but since its consumption was forbidden throughout the world of ISLAM he had to be careful to prescribe it as a dressing only (although he noted boldly that 'wine is also very efficient in causing the products of digestion to become disseminated through the body'). Arabs studied medicine from Greek sources then transmitted it back, slightly amended, to the west. The works of Galen, for example, reached medieval Europe partly via the great medical school of Salerno in Italy, where they were translated from Arabic to Latin, and partly through direct translation from Greek. It was then that the notion of wine as an essential element in a healthy diet gained ground.

The medicinal use of wine continued throughout the Middle Ages, in MONASTERIES, hospitals, and universities. The earliest printed book on wine is by a doctor, one ARNALDUS DE VILLANOVA of the University of MONTPELLIER, who had written at the beginning of the 14th century. Building on the observations of his classical forebears, he offers not only remedies for curing human ailments with appropriate wines but also recipes for curing 'sick' or bad wines too.

A new dimension was added to the role of wine in medicine with the introduction of DISTILLATION in the western world in the 12th century. Hieronymus Brunschwig, the German pharmacologist, wrote in the 15th century that '*Aqua vitae* [the water of life, or ALCOHOL] is commonly called the mistress of all medicines', but warned that 'it is to be drunk by reason and measure'.

Medicinal attitudes towards wine began to change in the latter half of the 19th century—although wine was still being added to sterilize water as late as the 1892 cholera epidemic of Hamburg (vindicated by modern research indicating that wine contains substances which make it a more effective anti-bacterial agent than pure alcohol), and strong, sweet wines such as PORT and BANYULS were still being prescribed as aids to recuperation in the early 20th century. Alcoholism was defined as a disease, and the injurious side-effects of excessive drinking studied. The appearance of temperance societies, sometimes supported by the medical establishment, caused many to re-evaluate the role of wine in DIET and medicine.

One further aspect of the conjunction of wine and medicine is the great influence that DOCTORS have had since ancient times, not just as wine consumers (and producers) but also in promoting or damaging the commercial potential of certain wines. Undoubtedly Roman connoisseurs took note of the recommendations of Galen and others, while in 17th-century France the commercial battle between wine regions reached new heights when Louis XIV's physician prescribed burgundy in preference to champagne. Other examples of vinous prescriptions abound.

For a modern view of the medical effects of wine consumption, see HEALTH. H.B. & P.A.N.

Darby, W. J., 'Wine and medical wisdom through the ages', in *Wine, Health and Society* (1982).
Lucia, S. P., *A History of Wine as Therapy* (1963).
Sigerist, H. E., *The Earliest Printed Book on Wine* (1943) (contains Villanova's *Tractatus de vinis*).

medieval literature. The only medieval successor to the Roman AGRICULTURAL TREATISES is PETRUS DE CRESCENTIIS' *Liber ruralium commodorum* of *c.*1304; otherwise there are few medieval authors who wrote specifically on wine.

One of these is Henri d'Andely, whose *Bataille des vins* dates from just after 1223, and it belongs to the genre of the medieval debate poem. The king of France, Philip Augustus, wants to know which is the best wine: his preference is for whites. Some 70 wines are tasted, and the crown of victory passes all the French wines by, for it goes to the wine of CYPRUS.

Another Old French poem about wine is *La Disputoison de vin et de l'iaue* ('The Debate between Wine and Water'), written sometime between 1305 and 1377, when the papal court was at Avignon. The debate reflects the changing FASHIONS of the time, including those for the wines of BEAUNE, GASCONY, LA ROCHELLE, ST-POURÇAIN-sur-Sioule, and PARIS.

Of the Middle English poets, Chaucer is the one who displays the most knowledge of wine, although he tends to mention different wines only briefly. Chaucer's father and grandfather were among the most important VINTNERS in London and held the office of deputy to the king's butler, who was the person responsible for the collection of taxes on imported wines. Jugs of MALMSEY ('malvasye') and VERNACCIA ('vernage') are, for example, the extravagant presents that the monk in 'The Shipman's Tale' gives his friend the merchant, whom he is about to cuckold.

Wine is just wine in the medieval drinking songs, too. Most of them are in Latin, and they are not in praise of drinking so much as of DRUNKENNESS. The 9th-century poem about

Adam, abbot of Angers, for example, has an address to BACCHUS as its refrain. One of the *Carmina Burana*, 'Potatores exquisiti' (*CB* 179), asks all serious topers to banish moderate drinkers from parties and to drink until speech becomes impaired and walking impossible. Even when one is on one's own, the object of drinking should be inebriation.

H.M.W.

Hanford, J. H., 'The mediaeval debate between wine and water', *Publications of the Modern Language Academy of America*, 28/3 (1913), 315–67.

Raby, F. J. E., *The Oxford Book of Medieval Latin Verse* (1959).

Waddell, H., *Medieval Latin Lyrics* (1933).

Wilson, H., *Wine and Words in Classical Antiquity and the Middle Ages* (2003).

Mediterranean, famous sea, wine-producing climate, diet (see HEALTH), and many other things besides. By classical times, vines were grown for wine in almost all the countries bordering the Mediterranean sea and on many of the islands; from Spain in the west to Byblos in the east, from northern Italy to Egypt, the vine made inexorable progress, with AMPHORAE of wine traversing the sea regularly. Historically the Mediterranean was the focus of viticulture, and most wine was produced in MEDITERRANEAN CLIMATES. In the Middle Ages, particularly when temperatures rose overall (see CLIMATE CHANGE) and when consumers were accustomed to very light, acid wines, viticulture spread much further north than the shores of the Mediterranean (see PARIS, ENGLAND, and GERMAN HISTORY, for example).

Mediterranean climate, a climate type characterized by warm, dry, sunny summers and mostly mild, wet winters. It occurs throughout the Mediterranean basin, on the west coast of the United States, in Chile, in southern and south-western Australia, and on the Cape of South Africa. The autumn and spring seasons range from mostly dry (on the hot, equatorial fringes bordering deserts) to wet at the poleward fringes, where Mediterranean climates merge into those with a more or less uniform rainfall distribution as in central and western Europe.

Mediterranean climates have some distinct advantages for viticulture over uniform- or summer-rainfall climates, provided that IRRIGATION can be given as needed. Sunshine is mostly sufficient, and there is less risk of rainfall in the growing season and of excessive rainfall during ripening and harvest. As a result of these rainfall patterns, the risk of FUNGAL DISEASES is generally lower. And to the extent that many Mediterranean climates can have the disadvantages of high TEMPERATURES during the ripening period, VINEYARD SITE SELECTION can help to minimize these disadvantages, by seeking out cooler coastal or high-ELEVATION sites, for example.

Further favouring Mediterranean climates is the fact that some of the main advances in vineyard management have particular application there. DRIP IRRIGATION in a summer-dry climate, for example, allows a high degree of control over SOIL WATER availability and vine VIGOUR.

J.G. & R.E.S.

Mediterranean fruit fly, *Caratitis capitata*, can be a grape pest in some areas such as parts of Australia and South Africa. Infestations of grapes are often due to a build-up in other soft fruits such as figs, apricots, peaches, nectarines, or citrus. Despite being a major destructive pest for many fruit crops, it is not regarded as serious for vineyards. See also DROSOPHILA.

R.E.S.

Méditerranée, IGP covering the entire Provence-Alpes-Côte-d'Azur region of FRANCE. Of the approximately 9,000 ha/22,000 acres in production in 2020, 60% was devoted to rosé. Grenache, Syrah, and Cinsaut are major blending components, alongside Merlot and CALADOC.

E.A.G.

Médoc, the most famous red-wine district in Bordeaux and possibly the world. The Médoc stretches north-west from the city of Bordeaux along the left bank of the Gironde estuary, a virtually monocultural strip of flat, unremarkable land sandwiched between the *palus*, or coastal marshes, and the pine forests which extend for miles south into the Landes. The vineyard strip is about 5–12 km/3–8 miles wide and runs northwards, with various intermissions for scrub, pasture, polder, and riverbank, more than 70 km/50 miles from the northern suburbs of Bordeaux to the marshes of the lower, more northerly part of the Médoc, the so-called Bas-Médoc (see map under BORDEAUX). Wines produced in the Bas-Médoc use the **Médoc** appellation, while those on the higher ground in the south-eastern section are entitled to the **Haut-Médoc** appellation, although many of them qualify for the smarter individual village, or communal, appellations. From south to north, these are MARGAUX, MOULIS, LISTRAC, ST-JULIEN, PAUILLAC, and ST-ESTÈPHE.

As outlined in BORDEAUX, history, the Médoc is a relatively recent wine region. Before the Dutch diligently applied their drainage technology to the polders of the Médoc in the mid 17th century, the region was salt-marsh, of interest for grazing rather than vine-growing. The ditches were so effective, and Bordeaux merchants so keen to supply vinous rivals to GRAVES and the powerful Portuguese wines that had been shipped in great quantity to the important British market, that New French Clarets were born, and great estates established in the Médoc on the back of their commercial success. In the mid 19th century, the Médoc enjoyed a period of prosperity unparalleled until the 1980s.

The climate on this peninsula is Bordeaux's mildest, moderated both by the estuary and by the Atlantic ocean just over the pines. These forests protect the vineyard strip from strong winds off the ocean and help to moderate summer temperatures, but it is only in the Médoc and the Graves district further south that Bordeaux vignerons are confident of ripening Cabernet Sauvignon grapes with any frequency. The Médoc is also Bordeaux's wettest region, which makes ROT a constant threat and SPRAYING a habit.

A typical estate, or CHÂTEAU, in the greater Médoc district hedges its viticultural bets and grows at least three grape varieties: a majority of Cabernet Sauvignon, supplemented principally by Merlot, together with some Cabernet Franc with, perhaps, a little late-ripening Petit Verdot and occasionally some Malbec. However, Merlot often predominates in the damper, cooler soils of the Bas-Médoc as it is easier to ripen in lesser vintages, and Cabernet Sauvignon comprises only about half of all the vines planted in the district. In 2021, in reaction to concerns posed by CLIMATE CHANGE, the INAO also approved six new varieties for experimental, limited use in AOC Bordeaux wines: red varieties CASTETS, the Portuguese grape TOURIGA NACIONAL, and the French crosses ARINARNOA and MARSELAN; and the white varieties LILIORILA and ALVARINHO.

While the Médoc possesses few distinctive geographical features, many hours have been spent charting the subterranean Médoc. It has long been argued that its great distinction is its soil, in particular its GRAVEL. Many a geological theory has been employed to explain exactly how, and whence, these gravel deposits arrived in the Médoc, and efforts have been made to correlate exact soil and rock types with the quality of wine produced from vines grown on them. Dr Gérard Seguin of the University of BORDEAUX was one of the first to show that the soil's physical attributes are very much more important than its mineral composition and that one of the most important soil attributes is good DRAINAGE (see SOIL AND WINE QUALITY). The gravels of the Médoc are ideal in this respect and are particularly important in such a damp climate—although in hotter vintages mature vines can benefit from the extensive root systems encouraged by the gravel. The gravels of the Médoc are also good at storing valuable heat, thereby promoting RIPENING.

It is traditionally said that the best vines of the Médoc are those which grow within sight of the Gironde, and certainly this is true of all the district's FIRST GROWTHS. Some argue that this is because the gravels deposited here are younger and more effective for vine maturation, others that the MESOCLIMATES of coastal vineyards tend to be slightly warmer, and others still that vines on higher ground have to establish more complex root systems.

About 800 vine-growers farm this land, about one-quarter of which constitutes the CLASSED GROWTHS ranked in the famous 1855 CLASSIFICATION of the Médoc (and Graves).

The Haut-Médoc appellation

The landscape of the Haut-Médoc may not be remarkable, but it is peppered with grandiose château buildings erected and embellished with the money to be made from selling CLASSED GROWTH red bordeaux. Certainly the Haut-Médoc today is nothing if not stratified, thanks largely to the effects of the 1855 CLASSIFICATION of its most famous estates, which recognized 60 of them as first, second, third, fourth, and fifth growths, commercial and social positions from which none but Ch MOUTON ROTHSCHILD has so far been able to escape.

Most of these classed growths are entitled to a village appellation such as Pauillac or Margaux (see map under BORDEAUX), but five of them are in communes without their own appellations and qualify merely as Haut-Médoc. The most highly ranked of these is the third growth Ch La Lagune in Ludon just outside the city, a property which has retained its reputation for robust, concentrated wines. Just north of this well-run property is the fifth growth Ch Cantemerle. The commune of St-Laurent, inland from ST-JULIEN on the main road through the forests of the Médoc, boasts the steady fourth growth Ch La Tour-Carnet and two improving fifth growths, Chx Belgrave and Camensac.

The area classified as Haut-Médoc as opposed to any more specific commune totalled 4,741 ha/11,710 acres in 2020. Many of these vineyards are CRUS BOURGEOIS offering some of the best value to be found in Bordeaux. The top wines share the deep colour, the concentration, the TANNINS, and some of the AGEING potential of the classed growths and are made in a very similar fashion, with the average YIELD hovering around 42 hl/ha, and a leap of faith and selling price is needed to justify the use of new BARRELS. Some other particularly ambitious properties include Chx Agassac, Arnauld, Beaumont, Belle-Vue, Bernadotte, Cambon La Pelouse, Citran, Coufran, Labat, Lamothe-Bergeron, Lanessan, Malescasse, Sénéjac, and Sociando-Mallet.

The Médoc appellation

The total area qualifying for the basic Médoc appellation increased dangerously fast in the 1990s and early 2000s and reached nearly 5,700 ha/14,000 acres by 2004, 1,000 ha more than in 1996 and considerably more than that of the generally finer Haut-Médoc. It was still 5,653 ha in 2020. Growers were encouraged by what they thought would be a steady increase in worldwide demand for red bordeaux. They were wrong, however, and many found themselves in severe financial difficulties by the mid 2000s. Permitted yields are generally the same as for Haut-Médoc, and a high proportion of the wines are dominated by Merlot. Much of the wine produced on these lower, less well-drained, heavier soils is solid if uninspiring CLARET sold in bulk to CO-OPERATIVES or to the BORDEAUX TRADE for blending into GENERIC Médoc, if the growers are lucky. Estates on which an effort is made to produce something more distinctive than this, usually by restricting yields and refining winemaking, include Chx Clos Manou, Les Ormes Sorbet, Poitevin, Potensac, Preuillac, Rollan de By, La Tour de By, Tour Haut-Caussan, and Vieux Robin. Goulée is a Médoc from the owners of Ch Cos d'Estournel of ST-ESTÈPHE. J.R. & J.L.

Brook, S., *The Complete Bordeaux* (4th edn, 2022).
Penning-Rowsell, E., *The Wines of Bordeaux* (6th edn, 1989).
Seguin, G., '"Terroirs" and pedology of wine growing', *Experientia*, 42 (1986), 861–72.

Melnik, firm, even austere, ancient late-ripening BULGARIAN red grape variety grown on 197 ha/487 acres in 2021 exclusively in the Struma Valley around the historic town of Melnik, close to the Greek border, in what was then Thrace. It may therefore have been cultivated here for many centuries (see GREECE, ancient). Many producers have given up making varietal red wine due to the difficulty of getting the grapes ripe enough, but it is proving useful for traditional-method SPARKLING WINE and even rosé thanks to its notable acidity. Its full name is **Shiroka Melnishka Loza**, or 'broad-leaved vine of Melnik', and its berries are notably small with thick, blue skins, though the wines are not usually deep in colour. OAK AGEING and several years in bottle bring out a warmth and style not unlike a NEBBIOLO. Its earlier-ripening offspring **Ranna Melnishka Loza** (Early Melnik or Melnik 55) yields wines with rounder fruit and softer TANNINS.

Melon, or **Melon de Bourgogne**, the most planted grape variety in the Loire Valley, planted on 8,436 ha/20,845 acres in 2019 and famous in only one respect and one region, MUSCADET. As its full name suggests, its origins are Burgundian, and this is one of the many progeny of Pinot and Gouais Blanc (see PINOT). Melon was outlawed from Burgundy just like Gamay at various times during the 16th and 17th centuries. While not as highly regarded as fellow white Burgundian and sibling Chardonnay, several of whose synonyms include the word 'Melon', it does resist cold well and produces quite regularly and generously. It had spread as far as ANJOU in the Middle Ages, according to Bouchard, and so it was natural that the vine-growers of the Muscadet region to the west might try it. It became the dominant vine variety of the Loire-Atlantique in the 17th century, when DUTCH traders encouraged production of high volumes of relatively neutral white wine, in place of the thin reds for which the region had previously been known, as base wines for Holland's enthusiastic distillers.

Melon's importance today rests solely on MUSCADET, although it is also grown to a limited extent in Vézelay in northern Burgundy.

Many of the older cuttings of the variety called PINOT BLANC in California were in fact Melon.

Bouchard, A., 'Notes ampelographiques rétrospectives sur les cépages de la généralité de Dijon', *Bulletin de la Société des Viticulteurs de France* (1899).
Galet, P., *Dictionnaire encyclopédique des cépages* (2nd edn, 2015).

Mencía, increasingly valued red grape variety grown so widely in north-west Spain that in 2020 plantings totalled 8,375 ha/20,695, notably in BIERZO, RIBEIRA SACRA, and VALDEORRAS (see map under SPAIN). DNA PROFILING laid to rest the once-popular theory that Mencía and Cabernet Franc were related but has more recently shown that the variety called JAEN, or Jaen du Dão, in Portugal is Mencía, while Mencia is most likely a natural CROSS between ALFROCHEIRO and the obscure Patorra. In addition, the rediscovery by young winemakers of old, forgotten, low-yielding hillside plots of Mencía on deep SCHISTS has started a PRIORAT-like revolution in the region. The concentration and COMPLEXITY of their wines dispel the notion that this variety necessarily produces light reds. It was the fertile plains on which Mencía was replanted after PHYLLOXERA, with resulting high YIELDS, that gave the variety its reputation for dilution. J.V.

Mendocino County is CALIFORNIA's largest and most northerly wine-producing region. Part of the even larger NORTH COAST AVA, the region is framed by Sonoma County to the south, the Pacific Ocean to the west, and the Mayacamas to the east. Its distance from San Francisco, which is about 100 miles south, kept its 19th-century vineyards small and delayed their impact outside the county. The same isolation kept wine for surreptitious resale there throughout PROHIBITION. Today that distance acts to slow development of the region's oeno-TOURISM and direct-to-consumer sales, though more nimble producers can clear that hurdle.

The vast majority of Mendocino's 7,700 ha/17,470 acres of vineyards are in its southern half. Even so, the meteorological range between the coastal Anderson Valley AVA and the interior appellations is extraordinary. As a result, the county has two distinct viticultural faces: the more famous coastal area, with its sparkling and aromatic whites and Pinot Noirs; and the less known hot interior, planted to broad swaths of inexpensive Cabernet and Chardonnay and peppered with pockets of OLD VINES.

The region includes 12 AVAs. The coverall **Mendocino** AVA includes, from south to north, the sub-AVAs **Yorkville Highlands**, **McDowell Valley**, **Anderson Valley**, **Cole Ranch**, **Pine Mountain-Cloverdale** (shared with SONOMA), **Redwood Valley**, **Potter Valley**, **Eagle Creek**, **Covelo**, and **Dos Rios**. It also includes **Mendocino Ridge**, the only non-contiguous AVA in the US, which applies only to vineyards at 1,200 ft/366 m in ELEVATION or higher. Chardonnay is the region's most planted vine variety, at 4,466 acres/1,807 ha in 2020; Cabernet Sauvignon follows at 3,271 acres, with Pinot Noir just behind. ZINFANDEL, PETITE SIRAH, BARBERA, and CARIGNAN (spelt Carignane here) from third-generation Italian-American growers on the benchlands (see BENCH) can reach great heights in the hands of an artisan winemaker. Fetzer and its sibling Bonterra, which practise ORGANIC VITICULTURE, are the dominant wineries by size; Frey is notable as a producer of ORGANIC WINE, from grape to bottle. See also ANDERSON VALLEY. K.A.W.

Mendoza, the most important wine-producing province in ARGENTINA, with over 70% of the country's vineyards and wine production. In the rain shadow of the Andes Mountain on the western fringe of the country, Mendoza has been the heartland of Argentine wine since the 19th century. The region's 151,233 ha/373,705 acres of vineyards (2020) encompass a wide variety of MESOCLIMATES and soils, with ELEVATION a major factor, as vineyards range up to 2,000 m/6,562 ft.

Provinces, such as Mendoza, are divided into departments, which are subdivided into districts and, in turn, into single vineyards. An IG (Indicación Geográfica, or GEOGRAPHICAL INDICATION) can represent a department, district, or smaller regional zone. The most important wine-producing areas in and around Mendoza are the following:

Luján de Cuyo The heartland of MALBEC, and the country's first CONTROLLED APPELLATION for Malbec, created in 1993, is where most of the traditional and renowned wineries of Mendoza are located—even if most also have vineyards in other areas. Running just south of Mendoza city to the Uco Valley, Luján's wine regions range 690–1,300 m/2,264–4,265 ft in elevation. Average rainfall is about 190 mm/7.2 a year, and the mean annual temperature is 15 °C/37.5 °F. The main districts within Luján de Cuyo are Las Compuertas, Vistalba, Agrelo, Perdriel, Ugarteche, Chacras de Coria, and Mayor Drummond. UNGRAFTED VINES of Malbec and Cabernet Sauvignon, some over 100 years old, are particularly treasured here.

Maipú Just east of Luján, Maipú is slightly warmer because of its lower elevation and renowned for its richer, jammier red wines. The main districts are Cruz de Piedra, Barrancas, Russell, Coquimbito, Lunlunta, Fray Luis Beltrán, and Maipú (as in Luján, there is a department and a district within it with the same name). Together with the department of Luján de Cuyo, they form what the locals call *Primera Zona,* or 'first zone', Mendoza's most traditional high-quality region.

San Rafael and General Alvear The southernmost wine regions of Mendoza balance lower elevation with higher LATITUDE, focusing on classic VARIETAL wines.

Valle de Uco/Uco Valley Arguably the most fashionable wine region in South America Valley de Uco comprises the departments of Tupungato (with its districts El Peral, Anchoris, La Arboleda, Tupungato, and Gualtallary), Tunuyán (Vista Flores, Los Árboles, Los Sauces, Los Chacayes), and San Carlos (Paraje Altamira, La Consulta, Eugenio Bustos, Pampa El Cepillo). Elevations range from 850 m/2,789 ft–1,990 m/6,529 ft. The combination of cool temperatures, very poor soils (many CALCAREOUS), good DRAINAGE, and continuous breezes results in full-bodied wines with high natural ACIDITY. Malbec, Chardonnay, and Cabernet Franc excel.

Eastern and Northern Mendoza Comprising Lavalle, Las Heras, Santa Rosa, La Paz, San Martin, and Rivadavia departments, these vast, mostly low-elevation, warm areas specialize in large volumes and entry-level wines—although some high-quality wines are also made, mostly with TEMPRANILLO and BONARDA. There are some exciting new vineyards in the Andes foothills of Las Heras making fresher, tauter wines from Malbec and Pinot Noir.

Red wines account for almost two-thirds of Mendoza's production, with Malbec accounting for over one-quarter of all plantings—some 38,644 ha/95,491 acres in 2020—followed by Bonarda (CHARBONO) at roughly 10%. Cabernet Sauvignon, Syrah, and Tempranillo are the next most planted varieties, but Cabernet Franc and Pinot Noir are probably the more lionized. In white wines, white Criolla grapes lead in plantings, but it is Chardonnay, Sauvignon Blanc, Torrontés, and Sémillon that lead in quality, especially from the cooler heights of the Uco Valley. Pink-skinned grapes, notably CRIOLLA GRANDE and CEREZA, account for about one-fifth of all Mendoza plantings and are used for inexpensive wine and GRAPE CONCENTRATE. Over 150 grape varieties are planted in Mendoza, and winemakers are ever more adventurous, now making interesting and excellent wines from varieties ranging from MONTEPULCIANO to FIANO. A.B.

Barnes, A., *The South America Wine Guide* (2021).

Menetou-Salon is just west of, and very much smaller than, the much more famous SANCERRE, near the city of Bourges, producing a not dissimilar range of red, white, and rosé wines which can often offer better value—from 602 ha/1,487 acres of vines in 2019, encompassing ten villages. Sauvignon Blanc grown here can make wines every bit as refreshingly aromatic as Sancerre. Soils in the appellation are mainly LIMESTONE from the Upper Jurassic period and can be very similar to those in the more famous zone to the east, although Menetou's vineyards are flatter and less compact, resulting in a less favourable MESOCLIMATE. The best zone is around the village of Morogues, a name used on the labels of producers such as Henry Pellé. The village of Parassy also has a high concentration of vineyards. Sauvignon Blanc represents about 75% of the appellation's total production, while Pinot Noir grapes are responsible for scented, light reds and pinks for early consumption, this lightness owing much to relatively high permitted YIELDS (59 hl/ha for reds and 63 hl/ha for rosés)—yet more evidence of the similarity between Sancerre and Menetou-Salon.

See also LOIRE, including map. J.R. & C.P.

Méntrida, Spanish town and DOP southwest of Madrid in CASTILLA-LA MANCHA (see map under SPAIN) traditionally producing robust red wines from GARNACHA grapes. The producer who first brought international attention to this part of Spain, Marqués de Griñon, grows CABERNET SAUVIGNON, CHARDONNAY, SYRAH, and PETIT VERDOT in his vineyard at Malpica de Tajo, which used to be just outside the denomination but has now been incorporated within it. He spurned the opportunity to jump rank from what was then the lowest to the local DOP and was rewarded in 2002 with his own VINO DE PAGO, Dominio de Valdepusa. Meanwhile, a number of producers in Méntrida proper and in its mountainous northern area, part of the GREDOS region, are turning out delicate Burgundy-style Garnacha and making significant progress with ALBILLO Real grapes as well as with Syrah and Cabernet Sauvignon.
R.J.M., V. de la S. & F.C.

Menu Pineau, an old LOIRE white wine grape sometimes called Arbois Blanc and officially known in France as Orbois, is a progeny of the prolific GOUAIS BLANC. Just 157 ha/388 acres remained in 2019, producing such wines as VALENÇAY, CHEVERNY, and occasionally one labelled TOURAINE. A vigorous vine, its wines are softer than those of CHENIN BLANC.

menzione geografica aggiuntiva. See MGA.

Meranese, or **Meraner** in German, red wines based on SCHIAVA grapes, from around the town of Merano in ALTO ADIGE.

mercaptans, VOLATILE SULFUR COMPOUNDS typically referred to as THIOLS when they contribute positive flavours to a wine. The term mercaptans is generally used in relation to FAULTS IN WINE, for example excessive REDUCTION or when a compound such as methanethiol (asparagus-like) is at a level that dominates the wine and masks its fruit. Such faults typically become worse post-bottling because of the anaerobic environment. V.F.

Blanchard, L., et al., 'Formation of furfurylthiol exhibiting a strong coffee aroma during oak barrel fermentation from furfural released by toasted staves', *Journal of Agricultural and Food Chemistry*, 49/10 (2001), 4833–5.

Ferreira, V. E., et al., 'Elusive chemistry of hydrogen sulfide and mercaptans in wine', *Journal of Agricultural and Food Chemistry*, 66/10 (2018), 2237–46.

merchants are almost as important to the wine world as producers and consumers, and may have been for at least four millennia. Several different types of wine merchant are considered below, but they share a dependence on the vine and the attractions its produce has for the consumer.

Britain

The British wine merchant is, almost necessarily, an importer, or a customer of one. Wine merchants were important in medieval England and Gascony, when they were known as VINTNERS in English. Even today, a wine merchant in Britain enjoys a social standing perceptibly higher than that of, for example, a grocer. This is somewhat ironic since the majority of the wine sold in Britain has been sold by grocers, as opposed to specialists, since at least 1987. This was largely due to the efforts of the licensed supermarkets to improve the range and quality of wines they sell, although it is also simply a function of the fact that so many Britons pass through a supermarket every week. The independent specialist wine merchant, or indie, has to compete with the low margins funded by the sheer quantity of wine a supermarket chain can sell. They do so by offering more personal service, advice, sale-or-return facilities, credit, glass loan, and so on, with the supermarkets and such specialist chains as have survived the onslaught of competition from supermarkets hot on their heels. Hybrids that are a cross between shop and wine bar are increasingly popular.

France

The French term most often translated as merchant is *négociant*, most often a producer/bottler rather than a specialist retailer (known as a *caviste* in French and still a relatively rare phenomenon), since so many wine purchases in France, as in other European wine-producing countries, have been made direct from the producer (*vente directe*) or, increasingly, at the supermarket (*grande surface*). See NÉGOCIANT and BORDEAUX TRADE for more details.

US

As American wine enthusiasts proliferate, so do wine retailers in the US, even though they have to deal with the constraints of the THREE-TIER SYSTEM and, in many states, compete with large supermarket groups. Unlike their British counterparts, the best routinely sell mature FINE WINE by the single bottle rather than by the CASE.

See also E-COMMERCE and wine TRADE.

Mercurey, most important village in the Côte CHALONNAISE district of Burgundy. While most of the production is in red wines made from Pinot Noir, a small quantity of unusually scented white wine from Chardonnay is also made. With 650 ha/1,600 acres under vine, Mercurey produces almost as much wine as the other principal Côte Chalonnaise appellations Givry, Rully, and Montagny combined. The appellation, including the commune of St-Martin-sous-Montaigu, includes 32 PREMIER CRU vineyards making up over 20% of the total.

The red wines tend to be deeper in colour, fuller in body, more capable of AGEING, and half as expensive again as those of the neighbouring villages. Maximum yields for Mercurey are the same as those for VILLAGE WINES in the CÔTE D'OR, unlike the other appellations of the Côte Chalonnaise.

Mercurey is said to have been the favourite wine of Gabrielle d'Estrées, although her lover Henry IV preferred neighbouring Givry. Leading producers include Ch de Chamirey, Faiveley, Michel Juillot, Lorenzon, Raquillet, and de Villaine. J.T.C.M.

Merenzao, relatively rare red grape in VALDEORRAS in north-west Spain, sometimes known as María Ordoña, and a synonym for TROUSSEAU.

meristem culture. See TISSUE CULTURE.

Meritage (rhymes with 'heritage') is a name created by a group of North American winegrowers in 1988 for wines made in the image of a BORDEAUX BLEND, devised to distinguish these wines from VARIETAL wines. This trademarked name is legally available for use on labels only to wineries that belong to the Meritage Alliance and for wines that are made exclusively from two or more of the varieties Cabernet Sauvignon, Cabernet Franc, Merlot, Malbec, and Petit Verdot for red wines (the less widely planted St-Macaire, Gros Verdot, and Carmenère are also allowed) and Sauvignon Blanc, Sémillon, and Muscadelle for whites. In 2022, the Alliance had more than 350 member wineries globally, the majority in CALIFORNIA, NEW YORK, and VIRGINIA.

www.meritagealliance.com

Merlot, or **Merlot Noir**, black grape variety originally associated with the great wines of ST-ÉMILION and POMEROL, but it has become so popular worldwide that by 2010 it was the second most planted variety overall, not far behind CABERNET SAUVIGNON. Its late 20th century increase in popularity may be most readily associated with a short-lived FASHION for it in the United States, but in reality total American Merlot plantings lag behind those of Cabernet Sauvignon by quite a margin, and it is in Bordeaux, and in France overall, that earlier-ripening Merlot is so decisively the most planted red wine grape with a total that had reached 114,785 ha/283,640 acres by 2019 (when Cabernet Sauvignon's total had fallen to 46,971 ha).

It was already documented as a good-quality vine variety in the Libournais in 1784, according to the historian Enjalbert, and in 1868 was noted by A. Petit-Laffitte as the Médoc's premier variety for blending with the much younger grape variety Cabernet Sauvignon. DNA PROFILING has shown it is the progeny of CABERNET FRANC and an obscure western French variety recently named Magdeleine Noire des Charentes. In consequence, Merlot turns out to be the probable half-brother of Cabernet Sauvignon, which helps to explain why Merlot-dominant red bordeaux can taste so like Cabernet-dominant red bordeaux. Merlot the wine is generally plumper, fruitier, and softer than Cabernet, but its flavour is arguably much less emphatic. If any single wine promoted TEXTURE rather than flavour to the front rank of concerns for American winemakers it was Merlot, 'Cabernet without the pain' (cf. ASTRINGENCY).

Throughout Bordeaux and SOUTH WEST FRANCE and, increasingly, much of the rest of the world, Merlot plays the role of constant companion to the more austere, aristocratic, long-living Cabernet Sauvignon, providing a more obvious complement to Cabernet Sauvignon's attributes than the CABERNET FRANC that often makes up the third ingredient in the common BORDEAUX BLEND. It also provides good viticultural insurance in more MARGINAL CLIMATES as it buds, flowers, and ripens at least a week before Cabernet Sauvignon (although this makes Merlot more sensitive to FROST, as was shown dramatically in 1991 when some RIGHT BANK properties hardly produced any wine at all). Its early flowering makes it particularly sensitive to COULURE, which weaker ROOTSTOCKS can help to prevent. Merlot is not quite so vigorous as Cabernet Sauvignon, but its looser bunches of larger, notably thinner-skinned grapes are much more prone to ROT. It is also more sensitive to DOWNY MILDEW. (SPRAYING can be a particularly frequent phenomenon in the vineyards of Bordeaux.) Merlot responds much better than the late-ripening Cabernet Sauvignon to damp, cool soils, such as those of St-Émilion and Pomerol, that retain their moisture well and allow the grapes to reach full size. In very well-drained soils, dry summers can leave the grapes undeveloped. Unlike Cabernet Sauvignon, Merlot is extremely sensitive to the timing of HARVEST, and acid levels can be dangerously low if picking is delayed too long. Merlot arguably reaches its apogee in the finest wines of Pomerol such as PETRUS and LE PIN.

For the vine-grower in anything cooler than a warm or hot climate, Merlot is much easier to ripen than Cabernet Sauvignon and has the further advantage of yielding a little higher. It is not surprising therefore that, in France and northern Italy, total Merlot plantings have long been greatly superior to those of Cabernet Sauvignon.

This is particularly marked in Bordeaux, where Cabernet Sauvignon dominates Merlot only in the famously well-drained soils of the Médoc and Graves—and even here Merlot plantings increased considerably in the late 1990s, typically at the expense of Cabernet Franc. Elsewhere, not just in St-Émilion and Pomerol but also in Bourg, Blaye, Fronsac, and, importantly, those areas qualifying for basic Bordeaux or the rest of the so-called Bordeaux Côtes appellation, Merlot predominates.

Merlot is also more widely planted than either sort of Cabernet in the rest of SOUTH WEST FRANCE. Wherever in this quarter of France the AOC regulations sanction Cabernet Sauvignon (see CABERNET SAUVIGNON for details), they also sanction Merlot, although the latter is favoured in the Dordogne while the Cabernets are preferred in Gascony.

With Syrah, Merlot has been a major beneficiary of the Languedoc's replanting with 'improving' grape varieties. Total plantings in the Languedoc more than doubled between 1988 and 1998 and stood at 27,124 ha/67,025 acres in 2019. Most of this is destined for fruity, easy, early-drinking Pays d'Oc wines, for the only Languedoc appellations to sanction Merlot within their regulations are CABARDÈS and MALEPÈRE.

Merlot has long been grown in Italy, and the country's national total had reached 24,057 ha/59,446 acres by 2015. It is planted particularly in the north-east, often alongside Cabernet Franc, where vast quantities of the wine pronounced 'Merlott' are grown on the plains of both FRIULI GRAVE and PIAVE, even if better, more concentrated wines come in smaller quantities from higher vineyards. In FRIULI, there is even a Strada del Merlot, a tourist route along the Isonzo River. Individual denominations for Merlot abound in FRIULI, VENETO, and TRENTINO-ALTO ADIGE. Merlot is also planted on the Colli BOLOGNESI in Emilia-Romagna. The variety is planted in almost all of Italy's 20 regions. In general, little has been expected from, or delivered by, the sea of light, vaguely fruity Merlot from northern Italy, which makes it all the more remarkable that the variety is being taken seriously by a handful of producers in Tuscany and Umbria and, more recently, in Friuli. Ornellaia in BOLGHERI and the Fattoria di Ama in CHIANTI CLASSICO were some of the first to show that Italy could provide something more in the mould of serious Pomerol, with Masseto and L'Apparita respectively. Many Italian producers still in thrall to INTERNATIONAL VARIETIES prefer Merlot to Cabernet Sauvignon, both for ripening more easily and for being a less dominant blending component with native Italian varieties. In the south of Italy it can be a challenge to give Merlot definition because it ripens too early in the heat.

Merlot is vital to the wine industry of Italian SWITZERLAND and is made at a wide range of quality levels, including some very fine wines indeed.

In eastern and central Europe Merlot plays a very important role. It has also been popular over Italy's north-eastern border in western SLOVENIA and all down the Dalmatian coast in CROATIA, where it can be attractively plummy when yields are restricted. It is also known in HUNGARY, notably around Eger in the north-east and Villány in the south, but (as in AUSTRIA) Cabernet Franc is much more highly regarded. It is also the most widely planted red wine variety in ROMANIA, where total plantings had grown to 11,151 ha/27,555 acres by 2021, and it just behind Cabernet Sauvignon over the border in MOLDOVA and in BULGARIA, particularly the south of the country, where it is often blended with Cabernet Sauvignon.

The fact that it is slightly lower in acidity as well as international *réclame* may have hindered its progress in some warmer climates such as Iberia and most of the eastern Mediterranean, where it is not generally as common as the more structured Cabernet Sauvignon. For example, in 2020, Spain grew 18,651 ha of the latter and less than 11,890 ha of Merlot, most successfully in Penedès.

In the 1990s, and until SIDEWAYS punctured its reputation, Merlot was suddenly regarded as 'the hot varietal' in the Cabernet-soaked state of California, and it demonstrated decisively that it had a particular affinity with the conditions of Washington State and those of Long Island in NEW YORK State.

In 1985, California had a total of hardly 800 ha/2,000 acres of Merlot. This had already risen to about 83,250 ha by 1992 when the faddish American mass market discovered the variety as softer and milder than the state's Cabernet Sauvignons, and demand soared. By 2003 there were 21,000 ha in the ground in California, although the intensity of the FASHION for Merlot led to stretching and over-enthusiastic IRRIGATION for a while. Plantings in all but the coolest regions of the state seem to have settled down, with 15,017 ha/37,107 acres in 2020. See CALIFORNIA for more detail of the wine style.

Merlot has had little success in Oregon's vineyards, where the much cooler climate makes coulure too grave a problem, but in WASHINGTON's sunny inland Columbia Basin Merlot has produced consistently fine, fruity, well-structured reds. Merlot is the state's second most popular black grape variety with 3,671 ha/9,071 acres in 2017, although its susceptibility to WINTER FREEZE can occasionally prove disastrous in this desert climate. Merlot is also grown increasingly in other North American states, notably in NEW YORK's Long Island.

In South America, Merlot has become extremely important to Chile's prolific wine exports. Vines called Merlot have done particularly well in the damper soils of the more southerly wine regions in Chile's Central Valley, although it took some time to distinguish satisfactorily between true Merlot Noir and CARMENÈRE (which almost equalled Merlot's total Chilean plantings of 11,366 ha/28,086 acres by 2020). See CHILE for more detail. Merlot is also planted to a more limited extent in ARGENTINA, URUGUAY (where it can blend well with the local TANNAT), BRAZIL, and BOLIVIA.

Merlot has never really taken off in AUSTRALIA, where plantings in the irrigated interior proliferated in the 1990s to satisfy US demand. From a peak of 10,737 ha/26,532 acres in 2008, the area has been slowly falling, down to 8,115 ha/20,053 acres in 2022, less than one-third as extensive as those of Cabernet Sauvignon.

Merlot clearly has potential in New Zealand, particularly in Hawke's Bay, and plantings were 1,077 ha/2,661 acres in 2022, making it by quite some distance the country's second most planted red wine grape after Pinot Noir and far more popular than the late-ripening Cabernet Sauvignon. South Africa has produced some interesting varietal Merlots and is using it to good effect in various BORDEAUX BLENDS, but it is only the fourth most popular red wine variety after Cabernet Sauvignon, Shiraz, and Pinotage.

Enjalbert, H., *Les Grands Vins de St-Émilion, Pomerol et Fronsac* (1983), translated by H. Coleman as *Great Bordeaux Wines* (1985).

Robinson, J., et al., *Wine Grapes: A Complete Guide to 1,368 Vine Varieties, Including Their Origins and Flavours* (2012).

Merseguera, lacklustre Spanish white grape variety (Esquitxagos in Penedès) widely grown in ALICANTE, JUMILLA, and VALENCIA.

Merwah, or **Merweh**, INDIGENOUS VARIETY of LEBANON traditionally used in the making of arak (local spirit), sacramental wines, and Chateau Musar's white blend. Like OBEIDEH, it is increasingly popular among wine producers, who value its body and acidity. M.R.K.

Meslier St-François is, like MENU PINEAU, a white grape variety that is a local speciality of the Loir-et-Cher *département* in the westward bend of the Loire but has been disappearing at an even faster rate. DNA PROFILING revealed it as a natural cross of GOUAIS BLANC and CHENIN BLANC.

mesoclimate, a term of climatic scale, intermediate between regional climate, or MACROCLIMATE, and the very small-scale MICROCLIMATE. It encompasses the more specific terms TOPOCLIMATE and SITE CLIMATE and has largely replaced both in specialist usage (although the word 'microclimate' is widely and incorrectly used by non-specialists to mean 'mesoclimate'). The usual scale of a mesoclimate is in tens or hundreds of metres, so one speaks correctly of the mesoclimate of a particular vineyard or potential vineyard site.

The full definition of a mesoclimate requires detailed on-the-spot records, but these are seldom available over the long periods (conventionally 30 years or more) needed to iron out short-term climatic fluctuations and, thus, to be fully representative. The process can be considerably shortened if site records can be calibrated continuously against those of a nearby and reasonably comparable older climate-recording station. The differences, once established as consistent over a number of seasons, can be applied to the longer-term records of the latter.

In the absence of any local temperature measurements, it is still possible to make fair estimates by interpolating within known regional trends and then allowing for differences in ELEVATION at the rate of 0.6 °C/1.1 °F per 100 m/330 ft. Following that, individual mesoclimates can be approximated more closely still by allowing for features of TOPOGRAPHY such as slope and ASPECT and even SOIL TYPE. J.G.

Iland, P., et al., 'Climate and the vine', in *The Grapevine: From the Science to the Practice of Growing Vines for Wine* (2011).

Mesopotamia. In ancient Mesopotamia, which lay in the fertile land between the rivers Tigris and Euphrates and is often thought of as the cradle of civilization, the most widely consumed alcoholic drink during all periods was probably beer. However, grape wine is already mentioned in cuneiform texts preserved on clay tablets from Ur dating to approximately 2750 BCE. Vines do not grow so well in the low-lying and humid south of Mesopotamia, and wine seems to have been imported from the more mountainous north. This is probably the origin of the poetic Mesopotamian name for wine, 'beer of the mountains'.

By the first millennium BCE, wine was as widely used as beer, at least in privileged circles. Unfortunately, little information is available about the methods of production. Some wines, such as the so-called 'bitter wine' of Tupliash, an area lying to the east of the river Tigris, seem to have been drunk FLAVOURED with herbs.

From the beginning of the first millennium BCE, however, it appears that wines were more commonly identified by their place of origin than by their type. These are mostly regions in the north or north-west of Mesopotamia (in modern northern Iraq and northern Syria) but also including Suhu (a region in modern Iraq on the middle course of the river Euphrates, downstream from the modern Syrian border). In an inscription detailing offerings made to the god Marduk in his temple at Babylon, King Nebuchadnezzar II (r. 604–563 BCE) mentions 'beer of the mountains', 'clear wine', and the wines of eight different named regions.

A few documents (in the form of clay tablets) survive from the early 8th century BCE from the Assyrian capital Kalhu (modern Nimrud). These are the remnants of a once-vast archive detailing the administration of wine rations to the 6,000-strong palace household, from the king and queen down to assistant cooks and shepherd boys. It has been estimated that the *pithoi* in the Fort Shalmaneser magazine could have held as much as 15,000 litres. The storeroom of the North West Palace was on the same scale, and, combined with other cellars that remain to be discovered, the wine supplies must have been adequate to meet the needs of the palace. The king's wives received the largest daily allotments, perhaps as much as a litre a day. By comparison, six skilled workers or ten ordinary workers had to share the same amount. A harem of women from Arpad, a city of the realm, were given a *sappu* of wine each day, but the number of women and size of the jar are unknown.

Wine and beer were frequently offered, among many other foods and drinks, to deities as part of the cult, and the practice of LIBATION was widespread in temple ritual.

Among the Babylonians and Assyrians, wine was widely used, as was beer, for medicinal purposes (see MEDICINE), especially as a vehicle for various concoctions often of rather dubious, if not frankly revolting, ingredients.

See also ancient SUMER, and see HERODOTUS for details of the earliest recorded mention of the use of BARRELS for transporting wine, down the Euphrates. See also ORIGINS OF VINICULTURE and PALAEOETHNOBOTANY. J.A.B.

Bottéro, J., 'Getränke' ('Drinks'), *Reallexikon der Assyriologie und vorderasiatischen Archäologie* (the standard reference work on the subject, first published in Berlin, 1928, and still being completed).
Kinnier Wilson, J. V., *The Nimrud Wine Lists* (1972).
Powell, M. A., 'Wine and the vine in ancient Mesopotamia', in P. E. McGovern et al. (eds.), *The Origins and Ancient History of Wine* (1995).

metabisulfite, often added to freshly picked grapes to prevent OXIDATION of the must. See SULFUR DIOXIDE.

metals. See MINERALS and LEAD.

metatartaric acid. See TARTRATES.

métayage, French word for a system of sharecropping particularly common in the CÔTE D'OR whereby a vine-grower, or *métayer*, rents a vineyard or, more likely in Burgundy, part of a vineyard and pays rent in the form of wine or grapes.

methanol, another name for **methyl alcohol**, also known as wood alcohol, is the member of the chemical series of common ALCOHOLS with the lowest molecular weight. Methanol is highly toxic. The immediate risk of ingesting any quantity of methanol is blindness, but consumption of 25–100 ml/1–4 fl oz can be fatal. As recently as the mid 1980s, some Italian wines were found to have been contaminated with methanol (see ADULTERATION).

Wines naturally contain very small quantities of methanol: about 0.1 g/l, or less than one-hundredth of the normal concentration of ethanol. Some methanol is naturally present in grapes, and further traces are formed during FERMENTATION, but most is formed by demethylating the pectin materials that are naturally present in the grape (see COLLOID and ENZYMES). Red wines, and particularly those subjected to prolonged MACERATION, are likely to have higher methanol concentrations than average. Brandy in general has rather higher levels of methanol than wine because the DISTILLATION process concentrates it. And wines and brandies made from fruits other than grapes tend to have higher methanol concentrations because grapes have fewer pectins than most other fruits. It would be impossible to ingest a dangerous level of methanol from such drinks, however, without ingesting a fatal amount of ethanol long beforehand.

Methanol is often encountered in everyday life because it is a common solvent for household products as well as being used as fuel for chafing dishes. A.D.W.

méthode ancestrale, sometimes called **méthode artisanale** or **méthode rurale**, very traditional and now FASHIONABLE way of making a lightly sparkling wine. For more details, see SPARKLING WINEMAKING.

méthode champenoise, French term for the intricate traditional method described in detail in SPARKLING WINEMAKING. From 1994 the term was outlawed by EU authorities in favour of one of the following: méthode traditionnelle; méthode classique; or méthode traditionnelle classique. English-language equivalents are 'fermented in this bottle' and TRADITIONAL METHOD.

méthode classique, EU-approved term for the traditional method of SPARKLING WINEMAKING.

méthode dioise ancestrale, SPARKLING WINEMAKING process used for CLAIRETTE DE DIE.

méthode gaillacoise, GAILLAC's version of the MÉTHODE ANCESTRALE. See SPARKLING WINEMAKING.

méthode traditionnelle, méthode classique, and **méthode traditionnelle classique**, alternative EU-approved terms for the traditional method of SPARKLING WINEMAKING.

methoxy-dimethylpyrazine, more properly **2-methoxy-3, 5-dimethylpyrazine**, or MDMP, is a compound identified by aromas of fresh cork or woody and dusty smells. It exists in cork and becomes a TAINT in wine at concentrations above the perception threshold of approximately 2–4 ng/l in red and white wines.

An AWRI study in 2004 isolated this compound and confirmed that it is responsible for a taint described in Australia as 'fungal must'. It has been suggested that this may prove to be second only to TCA as a cause of CORK TAINT in Australian wine, but further research has been hampered by the difficulty involved in measuring the compound.

Simpson, R. F., et al., 'Isolation and identification of 2-methoxy-3,5-dimethylpyrazine, a potent musty compound from wine corks', *Journal of Agricultural and Food Chemistry*, 52/17 (2004), 5425–30.

methoxypyrazines, FLAVOUR COMPOUNDS which result in HERBACEOUSNESS. They contain nitrogen and are secondary products of AMINO ACID metabolism. Three methoxypyrazines have been identified for Cabernet Sauvignon and Sauvignon Blanc grapes: ISOBUTYL-METHOXYPYRAZINE (IBMP), secbutyl-methoxypyrazine (SBMP), and isopropyl-methoxypyrazine (IPMP). Sensory evaluation has confirmed the contribution of IBMP, which has a very low threshold of 215 ng/l in white wine, to the aroma described as characteristic of capsicum or bell pepper and green gooseberries. It is generally the most dominant of the three. IPMP, the most abundant of the three, has a more earthy aroma, characteristic of cooked or canned asparagus (found in some New Zealand Sauvignon Blanc).

Related studies have demonstrated that the levels of IBMP and IPMP compounds in grape berries matches what is known commercially about the herbaceous wine character. First, the berry concentrations of IBMP drop markedly during ripening, as does the herbaceous character, and more so with increased sun exposure. Secondly, concentrations of IBMP are higher for grapes grown in cooler climates; Australian samples have been found to have much lower levels of IBMP than French or New Zealand samples, for example. In wine, methoxypyrazines are particularly stable against OXIDATION. Their sensory impact may be influenced through binding with other wine components. D.D. & R.E.S.

Allen, M. S., et al., 'Contribution of methoxypyrazines to the flavour of Cabernet Sauvignon and Sauvignon Blanc', in P. J. Williams et al. (eds.), *Proceedings of the Seventh Australian Wine Industry Technical Conference* (1990).

Goode, J., *The Science of Sauvignon Blanc* (2012).

Marais, J., 'Effect of grape temperature, oxidation and skin contact on Sauvignon Blanc juice and wine composition and wine quality', *South African Journal of Enology and Viticulture*, 19/1 (1998), 10–16.

Roujou de Boubée, D., et al., 'Location of 2-methoxy-3-isobutylpyrazine in Cabernet Sauvignon grape bunches and its extractability during vinification', *American Journal of Enology and Viticulture*, 53/1 (2002), 1–5.

Methuen Treaty, accord signed between Britain and Portugal in 1703 which gave Portuguese goods preferential treatment in Britain and encouraged the imports of Portuguese wine, at the expense of wine from the rest of Europe, notably France, at a time when PORT was evolving into the strong, sweet drink we know today.

metodo classico, **metodo tradizionale**, and **metodo classico tradizionale,** Italian terms for SPARKLING WINES made by the traditional method.

método tradicional, **método clásico**, and **método tradicional clásico**, Spanish and Portuguese terms for SPARKLING WINES made by the traditional method.

Meunier, how PINOT MEUNIER is known in FRANCE.

Meursault, large and prosperous village in the Côte de Beaune district of Burgundy's CÔTE D'OR producing mostly white wines from the Chardonnay grape (see map under BURGUNDY). Although Meursault contains no GRAND CRU vineyards, the quality of white burgundy from the best of its 19 PREMIERS CRUS is rarely surpassed.

The finest vineyards are Les Perrières, Les Genevrières, and Les Charmes. Between them and the village of Meursault are three more premiers crus: Le Poruzot, Les Bouchères, and Les Gouttes d'Or. Another group by the hamlet of BLAGNY are sold as Meursault-Blagny if white or Blagny premier cru if red, while, at the other end of the village, Les Santenots is sold as Meursault Santenots if white and Volnay Santenots if red, as it usually is. Apart from Les Santenots and the lean but fine red wines of Blagny, the other red wines of Meursault tend to be grown low on the slope and do not feature among the best of the Côte de Beaune.

Les Perrières was cited as a 'tête de cuvée' vineyard in the original CLASSIFICATION of 1861 and might well have been classified as a grand cru. The name derives from medieval quarries, and the vineyard retains a quantity of stones, which reflect the sun back on to the vines. If Les Perrières is regularly the richest wine in Meursault, Les Genevrières comes close in quality, producing particularly elegant wines. Les Charmes is the biggest of the three major vineyards and produces the most forward wines, seductive even in their youth.

Meursault also enjoys a wealth of good wines from other named vineyards such as Chevalières, Tessons, Clos de la Barre, Luchets, Narvaux, and Tillets. These are frequently more interesting than the village wines of PULIGNY-MONTRACHET, where the water table is higher. Furthermore, it is possible to dig cellars significantly deeper in Meursault, which enables many growers to prolong BARREL AGEING through a second winter, which improves the depth, stability, and AGEING potential of the wines. Meursault comprises 283 ha/699 acres of village-appellation vines and 109 ha of premier cru vineyards. A tiny fraction of both is red.

Meursault also hosts one of the three glorious feasts of Burgundy during the third weekend in November (see TROIS GLORIEUSES). On the Monday after the HOSPICES DE BEAUNE sale, some 600 local growers and guests gather at noon for the Paulée de Meursault, an end-of-harvest feast revived in the 1920s by Comte Jules Lafon. Everybody brings their own bottles to share with other tables. The occasion slightly belies the local proverb that he who drinks only Meursault will never be a drunkard. Fine Meursault producers include Ballot-Millot, Boisson-Vadot, Bouzereau, Coche-Dury, Ente, Fichet, various Jobards, Comte Lafon Mikulski, Prieur, Roulot, and others in a village rich with individual domaines. J.T.C.M.

Mexico is the oldest wine-producing country in the Americas. The southernmost point of North America, it has undergone a massive wine renaissance in the past 40 years, with wineries in 15 states taking advantage of the country's long coastlines and mountainous terroir to produce a wide variety of wines.

History

Mexico has been producing wine since 1521, the year Spanish conqueror Hernán Cortés succeeded in subjugating the Mexica state. Travellers and missionaries soon followed, bringing European vines with the intention of producing SACRAMENTAL wine; in 1524, Cortés decreed that all new settlers must plant 1,000 vines for every 100 natives on the lands granted to them. Plantations were established in the territories now occupied by the states of Puebla, Michoacán, Guanajuato, and Querétaro. The movement accelerated in 1531, when King Carlos V of Spain ordered every ship sailing to the New World to bring grapevines. By 1554, New Spain had become a colony formally dedicated to wine production, and vineyards had spread north to San Luis Potosí, Zacatecas, Coahuila, and Sonora.

The industry experienced a setback in 1595, however, when Spain's King Felipe II banned new plantations and ordered the large-scale uprooting of Mexican vines in an effort to protect the Spanish wine industry. Yet some winemakers persevered: Bodegas San Lorenzo, today Casa Madero, became the country's first winery dedicated entirely to the production and commercialization of wine in 1597.

In the 17th and 18th centuries, missionaries continued to spread viticulture as they moved north, with the Jesuit Juan de Ugarte credited for planting the first vineyard in Baja California in the early 1700s. The Franciscan friar Fray Junípero Serra followed, propagating Misión grapes (see MISSION) along the Pacific coast.

Efforts to develop viticulture flourished during the second half of the 19th century. In 1843, the Escuela Nacional de Agricultura opened, teaching the cultivation and management of vines; in 1870, in the town of San Luis de la Paz, Guanajuato, the San Luis Rey winery was founded; and in 1888 the first winery in Baja California was created, taking its name from the mission of Santo Tomás.

Thanks to PHYLLOXERA, Mexico's vineyards covered but a few hundred hectares at the beginning of the 20th century, but locals worked to quickly reestablish production. In 1928 L.A. Cetto was founded, today the country's largest winery with 1,200 ha/3,000 acres of vines; in 1948 15 producers created the Asociación Nacional de Vitivinicultores. The industry received a further boost in 1973 with the launch of a national viticulture programme; by 1979 the Ministry of Agriculture reported 56,295 ha of grapevines.

By the late 1980s the demand for brandy and wine grapes had fallen, and by 1996 only seven wineries were left. However, projects focused on premium wines—such as Monte Xanic, founded in 1987—ploughed ahead, setting the scene for the plethora of new wineries that would blossom in the new millennium. By 2022 Mexico boasted 35,825 ha/88,525 acres of vineyards, 8,633 ha of which were dedicated to the production of TABLE WINES and grape MUST. There were also 400 wineries in 15 states, the majority in Baja California, Coahuila, and Querétaro, followed by Aguascalientes, Baja California Sur, Chihuahua, Durango, Guanajuato, Hidalgo, Jalisco, Nuevo León, Puebla, San Luis Potosí, Sonora, and Zacatecas.

Geography and climate

Winegrowing is focused in the north and central parts of the country, where mountainous terrain and cool Pacific influences temper the abundant sun and warmth.

Baja California, a narrow peninsula sandwiched between the Gulf of California and the Pacific Ocean, is responsible for 70% of Mexico's production. This is where L.A. Cetto, Mexico's largest winery, and Monte Xanic, its first premium winery, are based. Most of its 4,500 ha/11,100 acres of vineyards and 260 winemaking projects are concentrated at its northern end, from Tecate at the US border down through the Guadalupe, Ojos Negros, Santo Tomás, and San Vicente valleys.

The climate is marked by hot days, exceeding 40 °C/104 °F in the summer, and cool nights created by Pacific fog and wind. Annual rainfall does not exceed 300 mm/12 in, so VINE DISEASE pressure is low; the SANDY soils, mixed with small proportions of CALCAREOUS and GRAVELLY soils, keep phylloxera at bay.

Although the region is home to about 40 grape varieties, the local industry is based on Chenin Blanc, Chardonnay, Sauvignon Blanc, Cabernet Sauvignon, Merlot, Syrah, Petite Sirah, Tempranillo, Zinfandel, and Nebbiolo. The latter, also called Nebbiolo de Baja, differs from Piedmontese Nebbiolo in colour, structure, and tannins; in 2018 the University of California at DAVIS Plant Identification Lab associated three samples of Nebbiolo from Valle de Guadalupe with the Italian grape Lambrusca di Alessandria (see LAMBRUSCO). However, there are also many wines produced with certified Nebbiolo clones.

Coahuila is Mexico's second most extensive wine region, with about 900 ha/2,200 acres planted to vines. Far east of Baja California, along the border with Texas, it has a CONTINENTAL CLIMATE, with a DIURNAL TEMPERATURE RANGE of up to 25 °C/77 °F, and poor soils high in calcium carbonate and other MINERALS. The vine thrives in the subregions of Cuatro Ciénegas, San Buenaventura, General Cepeda, Ramos Arizpe, Saltillo, Sierra de Arteaga, Valle de Parras, and Torreón, the plantings concentrated at elevations of 700–2,300 m/2,297–7,546 ft. The dominant grapes are Chardonnay, Chenin Blanc, Cabernet Sauvignon, Malbec, Pinot Noir, and Syrah. Many of Mexico's most well-known wineries are based here, including Casa Madero, America's oldest commercial winery.

Querétaro, Mexico's southernmost wine region, is part of the Mesa del Centro, a large plain at 1,700–2,300 m/5,570–7,546 ft above sea level. The vines are concentrated in San Juan del Río, Tequisquiapan, Ezequiel Montes, Colón, and El Marqués, where hot days, radically cool nights, and abundant summer rains define the climate. Chardonnay, Sauvignon Blanc, MACABEO, and XARELLO grown on the calcareous and clay-loam soils lend themselves well to vibrant whites and traditional-method SPARKLING WINES, styles pioneered by Finca Sala Vivé de Freixenet (HENKELL FREIXENET). Producers also find good results in rosés and reds from MARSELAN, Merlot, Malbec, and Syrah.

In the last decade, the remaining states in the Mesa del Centro have experienced a flourishing of small wineries. The TEMPERATE climate, high elevation, and sandy CLAY and calcareous soils are particularly favourable for white wines from Sauvignon Blanc, Viognier, Macabeo, Riesling, and Grenache Blanc and for reds such as Grenache, Caladoc, Cabernet Franc, Malbec, and Syrah.

Chihuahua, Mexico's largest state, is where the future lies. Bordering the US, it boasts a diverse array of climates, allowing for quality wines to be made from a wide range of grapes, from Gewürztraminer and Malvasia Bianca to Cabernet Sauvignon, Malbec, and Syrah. Investors such as L.A. Cetto, based in Baja California, are betting on Chihuahua for new vineyards, while wineries such as Encinillas, Pinesque, Tres Ríos, Casa Establo, and Santa Clara are already demonstrating the region's potential. C.B.S.

MGA, *menzione geografica aggiuntiva*, meaning 'additional geographical mention', a term used in BAROLO and BARBARESCO to refer to a registered vineyard that may be mentioned on the label, for example Bussia (Barolo Bussia) or Asili (Barbaresco Asili). MGAs are also used in ALTO ADIGE and ROERO. Similar to the French term DÉNOMINATION GÉOGRAPHIQUE COMPLÉMENTAIRE but generally covering a smaller area. See also UGA.

Michigan, Midwestern state in the United States whose boundaries are defined by four of the Great Lakes, the largest freshwater lakes in the world. Ninth in the US for wine production in 2020, it has a well-established wine industry that has jumped from 90 wineries in 2012 to over 150 in 2021, with more on the way as cherry and peach orchards are regularly converted to vineyards.

Geography and climate

Michigan has two parts: the Upper Peninsula, on the north end of Lake Michigan, bordering Wisconsin; and the Lower Peninsula, a large, mitt-shaped land mass surrounded by Lake Michigan to the west, Lake Huron to the east, and INDIANA and OHIO to the south. While wine grapes are grown statewide, the Lower Peninsula holds all of Michigan's five AVAS. The oldest is **Fennville**, the nation's third AVA when it was established in 1981. It nests into **Lake Michigan Shore** in the state's south-west corner. Classified as Region II on the Winkler Index (see CLIMATE CLASSIFICATION), the region benefits from westerly winds off the lake that moderate the temperature year-round. Harvest here often begins one to three weeks earlier than in the northern AVAs.

About 322 km/200 miles north of Fennville, **Leelanau Peninsula** and **Old Mission Peninsula** jut into Grand Traverse Bay, the surrounding waters tempering the Region I climate. Soils are sandy LOAM and GRAVEL, a contrast to the CLAY found further south. Directly east, the emerging **Tip of the Mitt** AVA covers the entire top of the state's Lower Peninsula.

Vine varieties

Of Michigan's 3,375 wine-grape acres in 2020, 2,325 are planted to VITIS VINIFERA. Riesling leads the way in hectarage, producing impressive dry examples in both the north and the south. Pinot Blanc is also well established; PINOT GRIS, AUXERROIS, GEWÜRZTRAMINER, ALBARIÑO, and SAUVIGNON BLANC are on the rise.

In red wines, Pinot Noir, long hoped to be the standard for red wine in northern Michigan, offers a lighter style at its best or, in colder vintages, contributes to excellent dry sparkling wine and rosé. Bordeaux varieties and Syrah ripen more dependably in the south-west, though fine examples of Merlot and Cabernet Franc continue to be produced up north. Increased attention to matching site to grape varieties has winegrowers looking also to GAMAY, GRÜNER VELTLINER, and BLAUFRÄNKISCH. Also notable are the many experimental plantings of varieties such as REFOSCO, TEROLDEGO, LAGREIN, FRIULANO, and TEMPRANILLO, efforts guided in part by Michigan State University's Department of Horticulture.

Viticulture

Research has shown that Michigan's growing season has grown warmer and longer by almost a month in the last 60 years. At the same time, CLIMATE CHANGE bring challenges, such as extreme and persistent WINTER FREEZE that can damage or destroy vines. Rainfall has also increased at the end of the season, although Michigan's dependable Indian summers continue to be a plus. HYBRID grapes are often grown to hedge against humid conditions in the south-west and against cold spells in the north. SUSTAINABLE and innovative farming practices have become a priority for many winegrowers, such as Karma Vista on the Lake Michigan Shore and Mari Vineyards on Old Mission Peninsula. Despite the climatic challenges, the state's industry continues to grow in size as well as reach, with increasing out-of-state distribution. M.T.

michigancraftbeverage.com

Vanderweide, J., Sabbatini, P., and Howell, G. S. (2017), 'Back to the future: A historical viticulture perspective on the Michigan grape industry', *Wine and Vines*, June, 61–4.

Schultze, S. R., and Sabbatini, P., 'Implications of a climate-changed atmosphere on cool-climate viticulture', *Journal of Applied Meteorology and Climatology*, 58 (2019), 1141–53.

microbes, or **microorganisms**, extremely small living beings, a few of which are capable of causing VINE DISEASES and FERMENTATION. Those affecting wines and vines are usually referred to as YEASTS and BACTERIA. **Microbiology** is the study of such microorganisms, which need **micronutrients** as well as nutrients for growth. See also MICROBIAL TERROIR and SOIL BIOTA.

microbial terroir. While there is now greater understanding of the roles played by SOIL, GEOLOGY, CLIMATE, and VITICULTURE in TERROIR and its expression in wine, the study of vineyard microbiology in the soil and on the berries and its influence on wine QUALITY and FLAVOUR is just beginning.

Recent research suggests that fungi and bacteria found on grape skins, including the YEASTS that play a part in SPONTANEOUS FERMENTATION, may also contribute to terroir. In many grape-growing regions, research has shown that region and site—notably MESOCLIMATE and soil—as well as grape variety, ROOTSTOCK, and vineyard management play a role in determining the fungal and bacterial populations found in grapes and MUST. Research by Gayevskiy and Goddard and by Taylor et al. in New Zealand revealed regional differences both in fungal communities on ripe Chardonnay and in indigenous *Saccharomyces cerevisiae* populations found in spontaneous ferments. Subsequent and related research has suggested a link between these regionally distinct yeasts and wine composition. Other recent research by Hall and Wilcox detected non-*Saccharomyces* yeast species and other microbes within healthy, undamaged fruit, raising the possibility that endophytic microbiomes that vary among varieties and locations might also affect wine composition.

ORGANIC MATTER may also play an important intermediary role between vineyard GEOLOGY and what we smell and taste in a wine. Given the at-best indirect relationship between geology and wine flavour, notwithstanding the common use of tasting terms such as MINERAL or 'stony', bacteria and fungi in vineyard soils may bridge the gap between odourless, flavourless ROCKS and the organoleptic distinctiveness of wines from specific origins. For example, as Maltman explains, the smell of wet or warm earth and stones known as petrichor and the earthy odour called GEOSMIN are derived not from the stones themselves but from the release by wetting or warming of volatile organic compounds that form a film on soil and rock surfaces. See also SOIL AND WINE QUALITY and SOIL BIOTA. J.E.H & D.Ca.

Bokulich, N. A., et al., 'Microbial biogeography of wine grapes is conditioned by cultivar, vintage, and climate', *Proceedings of the National Academy of Science*, 111/1 (2014), E139–48.

Burns, K. N., et al., 'Vineyard soil bacterial diversity and composition revealed by 16S rRNA genes: differentiation by vineyard management', *Soil Biology and Biochemistry*, 103/3 (2016) 337–48.

Berlanas, C., et al., 'The fungal and bacterial rhizosphere microbiome associated with grapevine rootstock genotypes in mature and young vineyards', *Frontiers in Microbiology*, 10 (2019) 1142.

Gayevskiy, R., and Goddard, M. R., 'Geographic delineations of yeast communities and populations associated with vines and wines in New Zealand', *ISME Journal*, 6 (2012), 1281–90.

Gobbi, A., et al., 'A global microbiome survey of vineyard soils highlights the microbial dimension of viticultural *terroirs*', *Communications Biology*, 5 (2022).

Hall, M. E., and Wilcox, W. F., 'Identification and frequencies of endophytic microbes within healthy grape berries', *American Journal of Enology and Viticulture*, 70/2 (2019), 212–19.

Maltman, A., 'Minerality in wine: a geological perspective', *Journal of Wine Research*, 24/3 (2013), 169–81.

Taylor, M. W., et al., 'Pyrosequencing reveals regional differences in fruit-associated fungal communities', *Environmental Microbiology*, 16/9 (2014), 2848–58.

microbullage. See MICRO-OXYGENATION.

microclimate, the climate within a defined and usually very restricted space or position. In viticulture, the term typically refers to a small and specific part of the CANOPY.

Common use of the term 'microclimate' to describe the climate of a vineyard site, hillside, or valley is clearly wrong. The correct term for these is usually MESOCLIMATE or possibly 'site climate' or TOPOCLIMATE. Microclimate distances are normally measured in millimetres to a maximum of a few metres; those of mesoclimate from a few to tens or hundreds of metres.

CANOPY MICROCLIMATE is that within and immediately surrounding the vine canopy. There are microclimates on or close to the surfaces of individual leaves, grape bunches, or even berries. Microclimates also exist at various positions or depths within the soil. All these distinctions are important in understanding vine responses to environment.

Microclimate is potentially influenced by management practices such as vine TRELLISING, VINE TRAINING systems, and TRIMMING; vine VIGOUR and the factors affecting it; and SOIL MANAGEMENT and mulching. In this respect it differs in important ways from climatic definitions of greater dimension, such as MACROCLIMATE and mesoclimate, which are wholly or largely uninfluenced by vineyard management. J.G. & R.E.S.

micro-oxygenation, a term that refers generally to the exposure of wine to very small amounts of OXYGEN (the opposite of MACRO-OXYGENATION) but also to a specific vinification technique known in French as *microbullage* that was initiated in 1990 by winemaker Patrick Ducournau in MADIRAN to control the AERATION of wines in tank. The method was authorized by the European Commission in 1996 and is used mainly but not exclusively on red wines. Its guiding principle is that all wines require OXYGEN to a greater or lesser extent, its aim being to enable the winemaker to deliver precise and controlled levels at various stages in the WINEMAKING process. It also addresses the issue of wine storage, effectively transforming large inert storage vessels into selectively permeable containers of infinitely variable dimensions.

Micro-oxygenation can be used during the early stages of alcoholic FERMENTATION to build a healthy YEAST population and help avoid a STUCK FERMENTATION. It also helps to maintain yeast viability, thus minimizing the production of SULFIDES, which may later cause REDUCTION problems. Injections of oxygen during ÉLEVAGE can also help counter the problem of reduction. But, proponents believe, its chief attribute is that it mirrors the effects of oxygen on wines treated to BARREL AGEING: wines in barrel are exposed to oxygen passively and continually, whereas wines stored in tank are exposed to significant amounts of oxygen only during RACKING, with less control. Used in conjunction with OAK CHIPS or INNER STAVES, the technique can provide an efficient, cost-effective alternative to oak barrels. Micro-oxygenation seems to favour POLYMERIZATION of tannins and the retention of PIGMENTED TANNINS resulting respectively in a softer taste and more stable colour. Some Bordeaux producers use micro-oxygenation on new wine during maceration before PRESSING as a way to begin this process while the MUST has all its constituents available. In such instances, a higher dose of oxygen is used. Proponents claim that it is also an effective remedy for GREEN or vegetal characters that are the result of slightly underripe fruit, but research suggests this is due to an uplift in fruity characters that mask the green notes. Too much oxygen, on the other hand, may spoil the fruit aromas. It has been suggested that the introduction of oxygen in this way appears to accelerate the ageing process, but this is contested by those who make the equipment and promote its use. In fact, the effect of micro-oxygenation depends very much on the amount of oxygen, the rate of application, and the period over which it is added.

The micro-oxygenation apparatus consists of a system of two chambers and valves connected to a cylinder of oxygen. The gas is moved into a first chamber that is calibrated to the volume of wine. It then moves into a second chamber and is delivered into the wine, a timer controlling the injection of a predetermined dose. Different devices are used to deliver the oxygen, including a ceramic or stainless-steel diffuser that periodically injects oxygen into the wine as a stream of bubbles or special plastic tubing that allows oxygen to diffuse through the tube wall into the wine in a continuous process. A typical dosage rate is 0.75–3 cc of oxygen per litre of wine per month, and the treatment might take four to eight months. In the absence of good methods to monitor the real-time impact of oxygen addition, the application rate and timing are determined by taste and experience. There are no firm guidelines for how much micro-oxygenation a wine can take, but most winemakers will replicate the oxygen ingress of a barrel (approximately 1–2.5 mg/l/month), adjusted according to grape variety.

The technique was first developed as a response to the fierce TANNINS of Madiran's TANNAT grape and seems particularly well suited to tannic grape varieties. It has also been used on wines high in tannins but relatively low in ANTHOCYANINS—some SANGIOVESE, for example, or PRESS WINES.

Micro-oxygenation does not necessarily preclude barrel ageing. A variation on this technique is used in barrel as a gentler alternative to racking, and one which binds less SULFUR DIOXIDE, for example. This method of adding a measured amount of oxygen into the wine in barrel has been dubbed *cliquage*. The wine is otherwise aged conventionally in barrels, which allow continuous micro-oxygenation due to the structure of the wood and produce big, rich red wines that remain relatively supple. But without racking, the risk of contamination—with BRETTANOMYCES, for example—is much greater. More recently, micro-oxygenation has been used in conjunction with barrel ageing in an effort to shorten the time in barrel. Oxygen rates are typically low (1–2 mg/l/month) and applied for several months depending on perceived wine evolution.

Micro-oxygenation is widely used throughout France, particularly in BORDEAUX, as well as in many other countries. Perhaps its largest take-up, however, was in Chile, where it is particularly appreciated for its ability to moderate the greenness of tannins sometimes found in some Chilean red wines. Results so far suggest the technique is particularly suitable for fashioning wines for short- to medium-term consumption from tannic or potentially reductive grape varieties. V.L. & A.O.

Ma, T., et al., 'Wine aging and artificial simulated wine aging: technologies, applications, challenges, and perspectives', *Food Research International*, 153 (2022).

Parpinello, G. P., et al., 'Effect of micro-oxygenation on sensory characteristics and consumer preference of Cabernet Sauvignon wine', *Journal of the Science of Food and Agriculture*, 92/6 (2012), 1238–44.

Midi, common name for the south of France. Like 'Mezzogiorno' in Italy, it means literally 'midday' and refers to regions where midday is a time of extreme heat and inactivity, at least in summer. The name is often used synonymously with LANGUEDOC and ROUSSILLON, although strictly speaking the Midi encompasses PROVENCE as well.

mildew. See DOWNY MILDEW and POWDERY MILDEW.

Milgranet, rare, recuperated vine speciality of French vineyards north and west of Toulouse producing particularly firm red wine. Probably a GOUAIS BLANC x Négret du Tarn CROSS.

Millau, Côtes de, AOC of just 55 ha/136 acres of vines in the Gorges du Tarn in the far east of Aveyron, SOUTH WEST FRANCE, making reds and some rosés mainly from Gamay and Syrah, and the odd white based on Chenin, sometimes with Mauzac. Pre-PHYLLOXERA, the region's vineyards covered more than 15,000 ha/37,066 acres, an area larger than the whole of present-day BERGERAC. Attempts at revival were thwarted by the First World War. Today there are but half a dozen or so independent growers. The Aguessac CO-OPERATIVE dominates production. The wines are popular within the region but rarely seen outside. P.S.

millerandage, a form of poor FRUIT SET, is a condition of the grape bunch in which there is an excessively high proportion of seedless berries and 'live green ovaries' (LGOs) relative to seeded berries. Poor fruit set in the vine is a consequence of either COULURE or millerandage. Seedless berries are sometimes known as chicken berries (normal seeded berries are the hens). Whereas seedless berries will mature normally, LGOs do not and remain firm and green. They have been known as shot berries in the past, but this nomenclature is inappropriate because they do not fit the definition of a berry. The condition is due either to inclement weather at FLOWERING, which affects some varieties (MERLOT, for example) more than others, or alternatively to BORON deficiency, or FANLEAF DEGENERATION.

Millerandage can cause a major loss of YIELD. Some winemakers believe that millerandage is good for wine quality because of the widely held view that small BERRY SIZE makes better-quality wine. This is based in part on experience with certain CLONES, for example the so-called Mendoza clone of Chardonnay in Australia and New Zealand that typically displays a high proportion of seedless berries. A **Millerandage Index** (MI) was defined for the first time in 2009—the higher the numerical value, the greater the expression of the condition. P.R.D.

Illand, P., et al., 'Flowering and fruit set', in *The Grapevine: From the Science to the Practice of Growing Vines for Wine* (2011).

millésime is French for VINTAGE. A vintage-dated wine is therefore said to be **millésimé**.

minerality, imprecise tasting term and elusive wine characteristic that, along with the descriptor **mineral**, became common currency in the early years of this century. Although descriptors such as 'flinty/gunflint' (*pierre à fusil*), 'stony', and 'chalky' have been in circulation for many years, particularly with reference to white wines such as those from SANCERRE and CHABLIS, the term 'minerality' was adopted much more recently by winemakers, marketers, and WINE WRITERS. If there is little agreement as to its exact meaning, there is even less as to its causes, but it is particularly useful for describing not only an aroma and flavour but sometimes also a TEXTURE that is undeniably present in some wines from a wide range of regions and varieties, especially, but not exclusively, in COOL-CLIMATE whites. It is easier to say what it is not—fruity, vegetal, or animal—than what it is. Other descriptors that are often associated with minerality include 'wet stones', 'smoky', 'oyster shell', 'struck match', 'salty', and 'iodine'. As Parr et al. (2013) point out, the term has also become, for many, an indicator of quality.

Although many TASTING TERMS are metaphorical (there are no blackcurrants in wine made from Cabernet Sauvignon and no brioche in a well-aged champagne), there is a strong temptation to interpret 'mineral' rather more literally, suggesting or presuming that aromas and flavours thus described are derived from the vineyard site and that they are therefore a demonstration of the concept of TERROIR.

However, geologists and soil scientists are clear that there can be no direct connection between the flavour of a wine and the GEOLOGICAL minerals in the rocks that underlie a vineyard or the MINERAL elements in the soil that are nutrients for the vine. In any case, the minerals found in wine are below the threshold of sensory perception. This has not deterred researchers such as Ballester, Parr, and Heymann from trying to elucidate the meaning, reference, and underlying causes of what Ballester describes as 'an ill-defined sensory concept', although there has so far been little progress in identifying compounds in wine that are associated with the perception of minerality.

It has been suggested by both sensory and chemical analysis that the wine components giving rise to the term 'minerality' include high ACIDITY and low PH (possibly due to an alkaline soil such as LIMESTONE or chalk) as well as VOLATILE SULFUR COMPOUNDS. As Heymann et al. point out, the exception to this lack of precision is the identification by Tominaga et al. of the aroma compound benzenemethanethiol (benzyl mercaptan), which is said to give Sauvignon Blanc wines, in particular, a flinty or smoky aroma (see SULFIDES).

Given these suggested connections, it is not possible to determine whether minerality is a TERROIR or a WINEMAKING effect. In any one wine it could easily be either or both. Whereas once New Zealand Sauvignon Blanc wines were typically described and appreciated as FRUIT-DRIVEN and Loire Sauvignons as flinty, the former, almost exclusively sealed under SCREWCAP, are now sometimes considered more sophisticated and complex than they were due to the perception that they are more 'mineral'.

While research has found some common ground among tasters who use this term, there may never be an agreed, precise definition, and further research into the chemical composition of wines perceived as mineral is in progress. Perhaps once we are able to describe and explain the mechanisms that translate vineyard site and viticultural practices into wine characteristics (see, for example, SOIL BIOTA, SOIL AND WINE QUALITY, YEAST), we will also be able to use the word 'minerality' with greater precision.

See also LANGUAGE OF WINE and TASTING-NOTES LANGUAGE.

Ballester, J., et al., 'Exploring minerality of Burgundy Chardonnay wines: a sensory approach with wine experts and trained panellists', *Australian Journal of Grape and Wine Research*, 19 (2013) 140–52.

Green, J., et al., 'Sensory and chemical characterisation of Sauvignon blanc wine: Influence of source of origin', *Food Research International*, 44 (2011) 2788–97.

Heymann, H., et al., 'An exploration of the perception of minerality in white wines by projective mapping and descriptive analysis', *Journal of Sensory Studies*, 29/1 (2013), 1–13.

Maltman, A., 'Minerality in wine: a geological perspective', *Journal of Wine Research*, 24/3 (2013), 169–81.

Tominaga, T., et al., 'Contribution of benzenemethanethiol to smoky aroma of certain Vitis vinifera L. wines', *Journal of Agricultural and Food Chemistry*, 51 (2003), 1373–6.

Parr, W. V., et al., 'The nature of perceived minerality in white wine: preliminary sensory data', *New Zealand Winegrower* (Feb/March 2013), 71–5.

Parr, W. V., et al., 'The evocative notion of minerality in wine: sensorial reality or smart marketing', *Proceedings of the Third Edition of the International Conference Series on Wine Active Compounds* (2014).

minerals in the geological sense are the typically complex, rigid, crystalline compounds (see GEOLOGY) that make rocks and soils, but in the nutrient sense (see VINE NUTRITION) they are the dissolved single elements that the vine requires in order to grow. Wine writings often blur and confuse the two meanings. The term is also used metaphorically in wine tasting (see MINERALITY).

The vine's essential nutrients are often called mineral nutrients or simply minerals because they are fundamentally derived from geological minerals, for example by weathering and CATION EXCHANGE. In practice, though, a vine gets most of its annual nutrients from ORGANIC MATTER, and this is certainly true of NITROGEN, PHOSPHORUS, and SULFUR, which are sparse or absent in rocks. About a dozen other mineral nutrients are essential to vine metabolism.

Vine roots have mechanisms aimed at selecting and balancing their optimal nutrient uptake, but in practice they can be compromised, for example by a low soil PH or interference by some predominant element. Also, there is usually some passive uptake, which can include traces of inert elements not involved in vine metabolism but which might give the grape juice, and possibly the wine, some fingerprint or chemical characteristic of the soil from which it came. Otherwise, in view of differing viticulture and winemaking practices, not to mention possible CONTAMINANTS in the vineyard and winery, the mineral content of a finished wine has no obvious relationship with its vineyard geology. (See also SOIL AND WINE QUALITY.)

Unsurprisingly, analyses of the mineral content of wine are highly varied, though concentrations are always small. POTASSIUM is the exception, with reported values generally between 500 and 1,500 mg/l. The other essential nutrient minerals include CALCIUM and MAGNESIUM, expressed usually in tens of mg/l, and IRON, ZINC, MANGANESE, and COPPER, typically in mg/l or less. A.J.M.

mineral vine nutrition. See VINE NUTRITION.

Minervois, improving western LANGUEDOC appellation for characterful reds, generally suppler than those from CORBIÈRES to the south, together with some rosé and a little white, whose total vineyard area had fallen to 3,245 ha/8,015 acres produced on varied inland terrain in the Aude and eastern Hérault *départements* (see map under LANGUEDOC). The appellation takes its name from the village of Minerve, scene of one of the bloodiest sieges of the Cathar sect in the 13th century. There is considerable archaeological evidence that the Romans practised viticulture here. Cicero records the dispatch of wine to Rome from the *pagus minerbensis*; La Livinière, the first Minervois village to be accorded its own appellation, **Minervois-La Livinière**, is said to take its name from *cella vinaria*, Latin for 'wine cellar'. More recently, the vineyards of Minervois were invaded first by PHYLLOXERA and then by the CARIGNAN vine.

Since 1985, when Minervois was granted AOC status, strenuous efforts have been made to upgrade overall quality, and a number of both CO-OPERATIVES and individual wine producers have made considerable investments both in winery equipment and in planting better vine varieties. Mourvèdre and Syrah must account for at least 20% of the blend, and these two plus Grenache and LLEDONER PELUT must make up a minimum of 60%. Various combinations of Bourboulenc, Rolle (Vermentino), Macabeo, Roussanne, Marsanne, and Grenache Blanc are responsible for the varied quality and character of white Minervois, the first two being best suited to the south-eastern part of the appellation closest to the Mediterranean, while the last two perform best in western, Atlantic-influenced sites. White Minervois is increasingly aromatic and sophisticated.

The appellation can be divided into five climatic zones: Les Côtes Noires in the far north-west on the coolest, most Atlantic-influenced foothills of the Montagne Noire; La Clamoux on ALLUVIAL terraces and flatter land in the south-west towards Carcassonne; La Zone Centrale in the middle of the appellation at an ELEVATION of around 400 m/1,312 ft; La Causse on high land and poor, dry soils in the north-east where yields are lowest; and Les Serres in the warmest, most MEDITERRANEAN south-east.

In the extreme north-east of the region, some of France's rarest and most delicate VIN DOUX NATUREL is produced: MUSCAT DE ST-JEAN-DE-MINERVOIS.

Minho, VINHO REGIONAL in north-west Portugal named after the Minho province, itself named after the river (called Miño in Spain, with which it forms the boundary—see map under PORTUGAL).

Its boundaries are identical to those of VINHO VERDE, but producers may use different grape varieties and make wines with higher alcohol levels than the 11.5% maximum of Vinho Verde. Some producers prefer Minho to Vinho Verde because of the latter's historic reputation for low-quality wines, but this is slowly changing with the rising overall quality of Vinho Verde. S.A.

minimal pruning, a viticultural technique developed by CSIRO in Australia whereby vines are essentially left without any form of PRUNING from one year to the next. The technique has particular application to higher-yielding, low-cost vineyards in warmer areas but was also used in some cooler regions producing high-quality wines, especially where there was a shortage of LABOUR.

The technique was developed and popularized in the late 1970s and 1980s, but its scientific interest can be traced back to a difference of opinion between two eminent viticultural scientists in the late 1960s. When Professor Nelson SHAULIS of CORNELL UNIVERSITY in New York State was visiting CSIRO at Merbein in Victoria, Australia, he debated with Dr Peter May and Allan Antcliff whether an unpruned vine might die. To settle the question a SULTANA (Thompson Seedless) vine was left unpruned; to general surprise, it produced a large crop that ripened satisfactorily. At this time there was interest in MECHANICAL PRUNING, and in many ways minimal pruning is a natural extension of that method. The technique has now been extensively evaluated for vine varieties for both wine production and RAISINS and in both hot and cooler climates.

One might imagine that an unpruned plant would exhaust itself and die if its growth and cropping were not controlled by pruning. Interestingly, the opposite is true. The production of Sultana vines, which have now not been pruned for almost 40 years, has continued to be satisfactory. Although vines are not killed by pruning, it has been shown to have a weakening effect on them. Furthermore, minimal or zero winter pruning is what vines experience in their natural state, and primitive vines survived in the wild for millions of years before they were first cultivated by man and were pruned. A feature of unpruned, or minimally pruned, vines is that there are many short shoots, whereas a pruned vine has fewer shoots which in turn grow more vigorously. A minimally pruned vine typically produces more fruit than one conventionally pruned, especially in the first year or so of minimal pruning. Significantly, a minimally pruned vine establishes a large leaf area earlier in the growing season, which is advantageous for PHOTOSYNTHESIS.

Ripening of this increased crop can be delayed, and if RIPENING is inadequate, due to cool weather for example, then wine quality can be reduced. In hot regions a harvest delay of a week or so is of little consequence, but in cooler climates the delay may be disastrous. Research by Rousseau et al. over a seven-year period in the Languedoc found that minimally pruned vines had higher yields and ripened seven to 25 days later or, for later-ripening varieties such as Mourvèdre, not at all.

Minimally pruned vines look extremely wild and untidy compared with vines pruned by hand. After several years, old wood builds up in the centre of the canopy that is an unpruned vine, and this can exacerbate the threat of pests such as MEALYBUG. During the growing season, however, the vine's appearance may not be too different from that of normally pruned vines. Where minimal pruning is practised in hotter, dry climates, shoots stop growing quite early in the summer, and so the CANOPY can be relatively open with good fruit exposure, a requirement of a good CANOPY MICROCLIMATE. Where the climate is cooler and more humid and the vines are growing in fertile, moist soil, however, shoots may continue to grow, and the bunches of grapes may effectively be buried under several layers of leaves. This shaded canopy may then result in reduced colour and flavour in the grapes and eventual wine. R.E.S.

Clingeleffer, P., and Krake, L., 'Reponses of Cabernet franc grapevines to minimal pruning and virus infection', *American Journal of Enology and Viticulture*, 43/1 (1992), 31–7.

Rousseau, J., et al., 'Incidence of minimal pruning on wine quality', *Acta Horticulturae* (ISHS), 978 (2013), 309–16.

minimum-intervention wine. See NATURAL WINE.

Minnesota, an Upper Plains state in the United States which has benefited from the creation of cool-climate HYBRIDS, many bred at the University of Minnesota. These grapes, such as LaCrescent, Itasca, Frontenac, Marquette, Edelweiss, and many others, are growing in importance both in the northern United States and CANADA. Almost 50 wineries operate in Minnesota. D.F.

Minutolo, very aromatic Puglian white wine grape once known as Fiano Aromatico but unrelated to both FIANO and any Muscat, even though it can taste quite like MUSCAT OF ALEXANDRIA. It was rescued from extinction in the early 21st century.

Miousat, light-berried vine rarity of GASCONY which has been rescued from oblivion there but is still grown in very limited quantities. According to DNA PROFILING, it is HUMAGNE BLANCHE.

Mireval is the large village that gives its name to **Muscat de Mireval**, the sweet, golden VIN DOUX NATUREL appellation that adjoins and is somewhat overshadowed by FRONTIGNAN to the west of it. Production, from about 260 ha/640 acres of MUSCAT BLANC À PETITS GRAINS, has been almost exclusively in the hands of the CO-OPERATIVE, called La Cave de Rabelais in honour of the only well-known writer to have mentioned it. The wine is virtually indistinguishable from Frontignan, and to those who live outside Mireval there seems little justification for Muscat de Mireval's independent existence, although soils here may be a little more CALCAREOUS than those of Frontignan.

mis en bouteille is French for 'bottled', while *la mise en bouteille*, or *la mise*, is French for 'bottling'. A wine that is **mis en bouteille au château** is CHÂTEAU BOTTLED, while **mis en bouteille au domaine** is DOMAINE BOTTLED. Producers may use these terms even if they use a mobile bottling line.

Misket, name for several different perfumed white wine grapes in BULGARIA, including the old, pink-skinned **Misket Cherven**, by far the most important of the Miskets, which makes soft, grapey, dry wines in the south of the country. **Misket Varnenski** is a Dimiat × Riesling CROSS developed for the eastern Varna province, while **Misket Vrachanski** is a more aromatic but even rarer cross.

Mission, California name for the Misin grape of Mexico, PAÍS of Chile, and CRIOLLA CHICA of Argentina, both synonyms for Spain's Listán Prieto, which can still be found on the Canary Islands. Historically very important as a survivor from the earliest VITIS VINIFERA vine varieties to be cultivated in the Americas, this was the original black grape variety planted for sacramental purposes by Franciscan MISSIONARIES in MEXICO, the south-west of the United States, and CALIFORNIA in the 17th and 18th centuries. Mission was an important variety in California until the spread of PHYLLOXERA in the 1880s, and 154 ha/381 acres persist, mainly in the south of the Central Valley. A vineyard planted in 1854 survives in the SHENANDOAH VALLEY, and renewed enthusiasm for the variety has led to new plantings in Sonoma, Napa, and Santa Barbara counties.

Pinney, T., *A History of Wine in America* (1989).

missionaries have doubtless played a role in the establishment of viticulture all over the world and, particularly, in documenting these achievements. Missions and missionaries have had a particularly profound effect, however, on the history of wine production in much of Latin America, in California, in New Zealand, and, to a certain extent, in Japan.

Soon after European colonization of South and Central America, missionaries, particularly Jesuit missionaries, established missions alongside more commercial ventures. Whatever the commercial interest in establishing viticulture, the missionaries grew vines to provide some wine for the EUCHARIST (although see SOUTH AMERICA, history). Both Argentina and Chile date their wine industries from the first successful attempts to cultivate the vine at missions in the foothills on either side of the Andes in the late 16th century; by the 17th century, Peru's viticulture, which probably predated that of both Chile and Argentina, was concentrated around Jesuit missions in coastal valleys. Mexico, however, is the Americas' oldest wine-producing country, and grape seeds were planted almost as soon as Cortés had landed there. Jesuit missionaries are believed to have been the first to cultivate vines for the specific purpose of winemaking in Baja California (northern Mexico) in the 1670s. It was not until the late 18th century that they established their series of missions up the west coast of what is now the American state of CALIFORNIA and brought with them the so-called MISSION grape from Mexico.

Two centuries earlier, in 1545, Portuguese Jesuit missionaries had introduced wine to the feudal lords of southern JAPAN, who developed a taste for wine and continued to import it. Much more recently, it was Jesuit missionaries who sowed the seeds of the modern wine industry in CHINA.

At much the same time or even earlier, in the early 19th century, French Marist missionaries played a significant role in New Zealand's wine history by introducing vine CUTTINGS from Europe, brought expressly to provide sacramental wine. The first Catholic bishop of the South Pacific, from Lyon, arrived with cuttings in 1838, and by 1842 they were reported to be performing well. Mission Estate in Hawke's Bay is still in production, but the Marist seminary has moved to Auckland.

See also RELIGION and MONKS AND MONASTERIES.

Cooper, M., *The Wine and Vineyards of New Zealand* (1984).
Seward, D., *Monks and Wine* (1979).

Mission Haut-Brion, Château La, important GRAVES wine estate now under the same ownership as its long-standing rival Ch HAUT-BRION.

Four wines are now produced here: Ch La Mission Haut-Brion red and white (the latter known as Ch Laville Haut-Brion until 2009), the red SECOND WINE La Chapelle de La Mission Haut-Brion, and a second white produced in common with Ch HAUT-BRION over the road, under the same ownership.

La Mission's winemaking history is as old as its neighbour's. In 1540 Arnaud de Lestonnac, brother-in-law of Jean de Pontac (founding father of Ch Haut-Brion) acquired the first plot of what would become La Mission Haut-Brion. His granddaughter Olive de Lestonnac—also owner of Ch MARGAUX, and the richest woman in Bordeaux at the time—played an important role in the history of the vineyard. She devoted her life and fortune to various philanthropic and religious acts, and the legacy of La Mission Haut-Brion was transferred to the Pères Lazaristes in 1682. Throughout the 18th century, they worked to restore the property to its rightful worth. The property became well known in part thanks to the patronage of the Maréchal de Richelieu. The property was revitalized by the Woltner family, who acquired it in 1919 and in many subsequent vintages managed to make even more concentrated, long-lived wines than their FIRST GROWTH neighbour, typically fermented at much lower temperatures than Ch Haut-Brion. In 1983, however, La Mission was sold to the Dillons, so that both these famous estates, the flagships of the newer PESSAC-LÉOGNAN appellation (although much of La Mission is in fact in the Bordeaux suburb of Talence rather than Pessac), are run by the same team, while still retaining their quite distinct premises and characters. La Mission's red-wine vines are planted on 25.4 ha/62.8 acres of vineyard. White wine grapes are planted on 3.7 ha/9.1 acres, planted with slightly more Sémillon grapes than Sauvignon to produce approximately 600 cases.

Missouri, Midwestern state in the United States which has played an important part in the country's wine history. In the 1860s, Missouri made more wine than CALIFORNIA and NEW YORK combined. Wine production blossomed under a heavy influx of Germans in the Missouri river valley, west of St Louis, and today this area is billed to its many wine TOURISTS as 'the Rhineland of Missouri'.

When the AVA system was initiated in the 1980s, a Missouri area application was rapidly created, and America's first AVA was therefore Augusta, the site of many of Missouri's best vineyards today. Nearby, Hermann AVA, granted a few years later, also reflects the region's historical importance as much as it does any specific climatic or terroir qualities.

Missouri remains one of America's top 20 wine-producing states and enjoys robust support from the state government, with agricultural stations, experimental wineries, and researchers, marketers, and consultants. While in the past fruit and sweet wines dominated their output, many of Missouri's 129 wineries now produce dry and semi-sweet wines from HYBRIDS and AMERICAN VINE SPECIES. Due to the climatic challenges of the CONTINENTAL extremes, VITIS VINIFERA-based wines remain unusual. The most successful VARIETAL Chambourcin, Norton, Seyval Blanc, Traminette, Valvin Muscat, Vidal Blanc, and Vignoles have set a standard for these varieties in other states. D.F.

mistela is the Spanish term, **mistelle** the French, and **mistella** (or *sifone*) the Italian for a mixture of grape juice and alcohol. The FERMENTATION process is arrested by the addition of alcohol, leaving a sweet, stable, alcoholic liquid arguably less complex than an equivalent wine that owes its alcohol content to fermentation. It was the commercially vigorous and adaptable Dutch who developed this sort of drink, so much more stable over long journeys than wine (see DUTCH WINE TRADE). In Spain, such usefully stable sweetening agents are used in blending wines such as SHERRY and MÁLAGA but are also sometimes sold, like France's PINEAU DES CHARENTES, for drinking as an APERITIF. See also VIN DE LIQUEUR, VIN DOUX NATUREL, and Australia's TOPAQUE AND MUSCATS, some of which may comprise or include *mistelle*.

mites, minute insects which feed on leaf surface cells and which can be a significant grapevine pest worldwide. Those that feed on the leaves include grape (or grapeleaf) rust mite (*Calepitrimerus vitis*); Pacific spider mite (*Tetranychus pacificus*), which is the most destructive; two-spotted spider mite, which is only occasionally found on grapes; and Willamette mite (*Eotetranychus willamettei*). Mite feeding slows PHOTOSYNTHESIS and can reduce grape RIPENING.

In Europe, red mite (*Panonychus ulmi*) and two types of yellow mite (*Eotetranychus carpini* and *Tetranychus urticae*) cause the most damage. They feed on green parts of the vine and can affect FRUIT SET and CANE RIPENING, as well as reducing leaf health.

Predatory mites often keep these mites sufficiently under control, so it is important not to destroy them with other sprays. SULFUR sprays applied for erinose or POWDERY MILDEW are effective on some types of mite. White oil applied before BUDBREAK or miticides during summer can control mites. See also ERINOSE MITE. M.J.E.

Mittelburgenland, wine region whose 2,035 ha/5,029 acres of vines in 2022 make up 4.5% of AUSTRIA's total. It runs from just south of the city of Sopron to just north of Koszeg, both in HUNGARY but long pre-eminent urban centres of this German- and Croatian-speaking area that, until the creation of Austrian BURGENLAND in 1921, was known as German West Hungary. Mittelburgenland began styling itself Blaufränkischland even before the potential for this ageworthy red wine grape here and elsewhere in Burgenland emerged in the late 1980s and 1990s; now BLAUFRÄNKISCH represents 52% of Mittelburgenland vines. The varied geological underpinnings of Mittelburgenland's hillsides and plateaus—featuring SCHIST and occasional BASALT, plus LOESS, CLAY, and LIMESTONE—play a role in the diversity and complexity of its Blaufränkisch wines. Especially important wine communes include—in a band along the region's northern edge—Neckenmarkt, Horitschon (with contiguous Raiding), and Deutschkreuz, as well as, in its extreme south, Lutzmannsburg. ZWEIGELT, Merlot, and Cabernet Sauvignon are also common, often blended with Blaufränkisch, and there is some Pinot Noir (Blauburgunder), ST-LAURENT, and a bit of Syrah. Such Blaufränkisch pioneers as Albert Gesellmann and Franz Weninger focused on showcasing top individual vineyards, beginning with Horitschon's Hochäcker. Early in the new millennium, Roland Velich—from a family of growers of sweet and dry white wines in NEUSIEDLERSEE—staked Blaufränkisch claims of avowedly Burgundian stylistic inspiration but combined with multi-site blending modelled on J. L. CHAVE. His Moric wines showcasing OLD VINES in Neckenmarkt and Lutzmannsburg soon achieved internationally coveted status.

Mittelburgenland DAC is the official appellation for Mittelburgenland Blaufränkisch. The KLASSIK and Reserve versions specify successively higher minimum alcohol and a later release date. Ageing in new wood is in principle restricted to Reserve bottlings. QUALITÄTSWEIN that does not qualify for the Mittelburgenland DAC or is not successfully submitted for inclusion can only be labelled for its state of origin, Burgenland. D.S.

Mittelrhein, second-smallest wine region in GERMANY better known to the outside world for its cliffs and castles than its Rieslings, which however can be outstanding. Most of the 468 ha/1,156 acres of vines planted in 2019, 65% of them RIESLING, grow within sight of the river RHINE, often looking down upon it from a considerable height (see map under GERMANY). The first commercial vineyards start just south of Bonn, and none is found on the west bank of the river until Koblenz, 58 km/36 miles upstream. Thereafter they climb both sides of the Rhine gorge, wherever site, MESOCLIMATE, and much hard work make vine-growing a more or less viable exercise. The Mittelrhein also incorporates the remnants of once-flourishing vineyards around Bad Ems and Nassau on the Lahn. There is usually enough rain during the growing season to maintain the health and strength of the vines on their porous, steep, heat-trapping SLATE and QUARTZITE slopes.

The prime Mittelrhein sectors are about 12 km south of Koblenz, around Boppard (the vineyards sharing the name Hamm), and from the far south near the RHEINGAU at Oberwesel and especially Bacharach and adjacent Steeg, whose most notable vineyards are Hahn, Posten, Wolfshöhle, and St Jost. Because of CLIMATE CHANGE, top growers have been relying on vineyards at higher ELEVATIONS or in side valleys such as Oberdiebach to produce dry Rieslings of 12% alcohol or less, thus saving some of the region's dwindling treasure of OLD VINES. Other signs of the times are increasingly impressive SPÄTBURGUNDER and experimental pockets of Syrah. At their best, Mittelrhein Rieslings combine the mineral notes and tension of Mosel wines with the tropical fruit of Nahe Rieslings. While the region's top growers make up in quality for what they lack in numbers, it is TOURISM that sustains the Mittelrhein's part-time vine growers in a wine region that has been shrinking for a century. D.S.

MJT, mean January/July temperature. See CLIMATE CLASSIFICATION.

moelleux, French term meaning literally 'like (bone) marrow', or 'mellow'. Wines described as *moelleux* are usually medium sweet, while very rich BOTRYTIZED wines may be described as LIQUOREUX.

Moët & Chandon, Champagne house producing the single most important champagne BRAND in the world, and part of the vast LVMH group. The Champagne house was founded by Claude Moët, born in 1683 to a family which had settled in the Champagne district during the 14th century. He inherited vineyards and became a wine merchant, establishing his own firm in 1743. He was succeeded by his son Claude-Louis Nicolas and his grandson Jean-Rémy Moët, who used his impressive connections to open up international markets for his wine. Jean-Rémy was a close personal friend of Napoleon Bonaparte and was awarded the cross of the Légion d'Honneur in the final years of the emperor's rule. In 1832, Jean-Rémy handed over the firm to his son Victor and his son-in-law Pierre-Gabriel Chandon. At the same time, the company acquired the Abbey of Hautvillers and its vineyards (see PÉRIGNON, DOM). In 1962, Moët & Chandon's shares were quoted for the first time on the Paris Stock Exchange, leading to a period of considerable expansion. First Moët bought shares in Ruinart Père et Fils, the oldest Champagne house, in 1963. Five years later it acquired a 34% stake in Parfums Christian Dior, increasing this to a 50% stake shortly afterwards. In 1970 Moët took control of Champagne Mercier, a popular brand in France, and capped it all by buying out Dior and merging with the cognac house of Hennessy in 1971 to form the holding company Moët Hennessy. The acquisitions continued unabated, including, in 1981, a stake in the American importers Schieffelin. At one stage the company's American investment also involved the Simi winery in Sonoma, Moët having established Domaine Chandon, the seminal sparkling wine producer, in the Napa Valley in 1973.

This was by no means the company's first venture into the New World. Bodegas Chandon was established in Argentina in 1960, and Provifin, now Chandon do Brasil, followed in 1974, both companies making considerable amounts of wine for the domestic market, much of it sparkling. In Germany, too, a SEKT business was established in the form of Chandon GmbH in 1968. In 1985, the group founded Domaine Chandon in Australia's Yarra Valley and in 1987 established a company in Spain for the production of a CAVA, subsequently sold to HENKELL FREIXENET.

In 1987, Moët Hennessy merged with the Louis Vuitton Group, makers of luxury leather goods and then owners of Champagne houses VEUVE CLICQUOT, Canard-Duchêne, and Henriot, and Givenchy perfumes. The LVMH group's composition continues to evolve, but in 2005 it owned five Champagne houses: Moët & Chandon, Mercier, Ruinart, Veuve Clicquot, and KRUG (having once also owned Pommery, and Lanson briefly while stripping it of its extensive vineyard holdings before selling it on). Of these, Moët & Chandon and Mercier are run most closely in tandem.

Moët, the brand, continues to sell at over twice the rate of its nearest competitors and claims that one in four bottles of Champagne exported comes from the house. It is the leading brand of champagne in most world markets with a share of the champagne market in the United States that can be as high as 50%. By 2020 the non-vintage Brut Impérial had been restyled to be drier with longer AGEING in bottle.

The house prestige cuvée is named after Dom Pérignon, the legendary figure of the Abbey of Hautvillers, and broke new ground in terms of packaging, pricing, and qualitative ambitions when it was launched in 1936. S.E.A.

MOG, or **material other than grapes,** refers to leaves, canes, vines, and other debris picked inadvertently with the grapes at harvest. The amount of MOG is increased by MECHANICAL HARVESTING.

Moldavia. See MOLDOVA.

Moldova, in full the **Republic of Moldova**, may have been one of the smallest states of the former Soviet Union, but it produced more wine than any other, with its biggest winery (Agrovin Bulboaca) the largest wine factory in the USSR. Independent since 1991, it is one of Europe's poorest countries, but wine remains an important part of the economy, and the country still has more grapevines per person than anywhere else in the world, with 122,000 ha/301,469 acres of vineyard in 2020. The country has real potential for wine quality, thanks to its extensive vineyards, temperate CONTINENTAL CLIMATE, and gently undulating landscape. It is effectively landlocked between eastern ROMANIA and UKRAINE, with a short 'coastline' on the river Danube, giving it access to the Black Sea. The Republic of Moldova today has the same borders as its predecessor state, the Moldavian Soviet Socialist Republic, though since 1992 the eastern part of the country has been the breakaway territory of Transnistria. This accounts for around 11% of Moldova's population but is not recognized internationally.

History

Fossil leaves of *Vitis teutonica* dated to the Miocene era confirm that the vine was widely grown in this area around 10 million years ago. The earliest records of domesticated vines occur in Neolithic sites from 6th–5th millennia BCE and on multiple Cucuteni-Trypillia sites in the region from 5200–3500 BCE. Later, there are Iron Age traces of grapes near Etulia, then the Roman province of Dacia left its mark, sharing much of this period of history with today's Romania.

The principality of Moldavia (covering land that is today's eastern Romania and the Republic of Moldova) was founded in 1359, when Bogdan I wrested the territory from Hungarian control. There are several 15th-century records of vineyards and wine from these lands, and wine became significant under the great leader Stefan Cel Mare (1457–1504). In the 16th century, Moldavia became a vassal state to the Ottoman empire, though wine production continued, linked to Christianity and monastic vineyards. Five wars between 1711–1812 with the Russian Empire appears to have slowed down winemaking, until the eastern part beyond the river Prut was annexed to become the Russian province of Bessarabia in 1812.

Russia encouraged vines in the new province, and Tsar Alexander I set up a campaign to repopulate the empty steppe in Southern Bessarabia, requiring colonists (from Germany, Switzerland, and Bulgaria) to be agriculturalists or winemakers in return for exemptions from taxes and military service. Around this time, it became fashionable for Russian aristocrats to own vineyards, often bringing in vines and expertise from France, and in 1842 the School of Viticulture, Gardening, and Viniculture was opened in Stăuceni, possibly the first such school in Europe. The 19th century also saw the founding of several of Moldova's earliest estates, such as Vinaria Purcari in 1827, Romănești winery in 1850, and Castel Mimi in 1893. In 1878, a bottle of Negru de Purcari famously won a gold medal in Paris, bringing it to the attention of the Russian royal family. By 1883, 20% of the Russian Empire's wine came from Bessarabia, with exports to the West also strong as PHYLLOXERA took hold. By the early 20th century 180,000 ha/444,790 of vines had died. In 1940 the country was annexed by the Soviet Union, becoming the Moldovan Soviet Socialist Republic (MSSR) in 1944. By this time, vineyards were typically less than 5 ha and planted either to French varieties or HYBRIDS by poor peasants who couldn't afford expensive GRAFTED VINES. The post-war period saw large-scale collectivization into collective farms called *kolkhoz* and state-owned farms called *sovkhoz*. The policy was to develop the MSSR for agriculture, with a drive to increase wine production, as wine was seen as a prestige product that could be displayed to the world. MECHANIZATION, heavy AGROCHEMICAL use, and modernization of the grape assortment were part of the plan, alongside research into more cold-tolerant vine varieties. Peak vineyard area reached 224,000 ha/553,516 acres between 1971 and 1980, and in 1983 MSSR was the sixth-largest wine producer in the world, producing one-quarter of the USSR's wine.

The arrival of GORBACHEV with his anti-alcohol campaign in 1985 saw uprooting of 75,000 ha, then further losses followed as a consequence of Moldova's complex land reform in the 1990s after independence was declared. It wasn't until well into the 2000s that wineries started to buy up vineyards to improve fruit quality and consistency. Wine reached 9% of total GDP by 2005, but the following year Russia banned all Moldovan wine, causing devastating losses of at least 200 million USD. A further ban followed in 2013, coincidentally around the time Moldova signed free trade agreements with the EU. The sudden need to find other markets required a change of wine style towards dry wines with improved winemaking. Considerable international aid has gone into educating winemakers and modernizing equipment, as well as helping to change legislation to allow the establishment of small independent wineries, quality standards, and PGIS.

Climate and geography

Moldova lies between 46 and 48° N and is low and hilly, averaging 147 m/482 ft above sea level with its highest point reaching just 430 m/1,411 ft. The climate is good for viticulture, with average summer temperatures of around 20 °C/68 °F, and while winters can be extremely cold (−25 °C/ −13 °F), freezing damage is unusual. Moldova has a high proportion of humus-rich black soils, but the relatively dry climate forces vines to root deep into the LIMESTONE bedrock. The country has three PGI wine regions covering 9,600 ha/ 23,722 acres in 2019: **Codru** in the centre of Moldova is bordered by Leova, Cimiștlia, and Tighina, and since 2016 it has included Bălți and vineyards in Transnistria. It has a CONTINENTAL CLIMATE with moderate winters, thanks to the forested hills to the north, and 79% of its vineyards are on slopes. Annual rainfall is 450–550 mm/18–22 in with 2,100–2,200 sunshine hours. It is noted for fresh, floral whites and structured, COOL CLIMATE reds that can age well. **Valul Lui Trajan** in the south-west is Moldova's warmest region, with a more MEDITERRANEAN CLIMATE, low elevation (5–310 m/16–1,017 ft), and well-drained soils with clay and sand that make it best regarded for rich, structured reds. **Ștefan Vodă** in the south-east has a TEMPERATE continental climate, with influence from the Black Sea. Annual rainfall averages 450–550 mm/18–22 in, elevations are just 120 m/394 ft, and annual sunshine hours are 2,200–2,300. Its most famous district is Purcari, noted for long-lived reds.

Moldova also has a national PGI for wine distillates called Divin. There are plans to establish PDOs, but none were in place in 2022.

Viticulture

Moldova is able to grow the great majority of its vines without WINTER PROTECTION. Most vines are CORDON-trained on medium-height TRELLISES. Most vineyard work is done by hand due to low wages, though LABOUR availability is an increasing problem as so many working-age Moldovans work abroad. Privately owned vines tend to be old and may be in poor condition, while wineries have invested in substantial plantings since mid 2000s to ensure consistent fruit quality. Important viticultural concerns include increasing risk of DROUGHT stress, given the dry climate and lack of IRRIGATION, while PHYTOPLASMA is present and DOWNY MILDEW, POWDERY MILDEW, and GREY ROT can be a problem in more humid seasons.

Vine varieties

Of the 74,400 ha/183,846 acres of vines in commercial production in 2020, 55,200 ha are VITIS VINIFERA wine varieties, 7,000 ha are HYBRIDS (notably Isabella), and the rest are TABLE GRAPES. The country's top red wine varieties by volume in 2020 were Cabernet Sauvignon (31%) and Merlot (26%), Pinot Noir (4%), SAPERAVI (4%), and FETEASCĂ Neagra (3%). Top white varieties were Sauvignon Blanc (17%), Chardonnay (16%), Aligoté (8%), Pinot Gris (8%), and Riesling (5%). Local varieties (many shared with Romania) including Fetească (Alba, Regală, and Neagră) and Rara Neagră (BĂBEASCĂ NEAGRĂ) had virtually disappeared in the previous era, but there is increasing interest in replanting them, though total area under local varieties is only an estimated 1,300 ha/3,212 acres. Other local reds that may have quality potential include Codrinschii, Kopchak/Copceac, and Negru de Căușeni (in 2023 the latter two were awaiting approval for planting). SAPERAVI also produces good results in Moldova—it was originally cultivated as part of the Negru de Purcari blend in 1950s but has now spread to the south-west and is appearing in both VARIETAL wines and premium blends. Several wineries are also working with genuinely Moldovan white varieties including Viorica, Alb de Onițcani, Floricica, and Riton. These are varieties developed for cold- and disease-resistance in the Soviet era but capable of producing good-quality wine and expected to play an increasing role as Moldova is making moves towards developing industry-wide SUSTAINABILITY practices. Certified ORGANIC VITICULTURE is limited to a handful of producers.

Wines produced

Modern Moldovan wine styles usually show fresh natural ACIDITY and relatively moderate alcohol levels with good varietal expression. In 2020, white wines led production at 40.2 million litres/10,619,717 gal while reds comprised 36 million litres, rosé 10 million litres, and sweet wines 2.5 million litres. Negru de Purcari may be Moldova's most famous wine. This blend of Cabernet Sauvignon, Saperavi, and Rara Neagră was famously the only wine exported with an English label from Moldova in Soviet times. It was revived as a brand belonging to Vinaria Purcari in 2003, based on historic records, and has inspired several other premium red blends. Moldova continues to make some FORTIFIED WINES, notably Pastoral (previously Cagor), a partially fermented red from heat-treated MUST, often based on Cabernet or Saperavi. There are also a few good ICE WINES from Riesling, Traminer, or Muscat Ottonel. SPARKLING WINE production, both tank- and bottle-fermented, dates to 1950s, with state-owned Cricova the most notable producer.

Modern industry structure

Prior to the first Russian ban in 2006, wine quality across Moldova was often distinctly poor, as old Soviet winemaking technology was commonplace, with little attention paid to HYGIENE or controlling OXIDATION. Today modern equipment is more widespread among key players whose vineyard ownership allows them to control grape quality—and quality can be very high. Bureaucracy has been reduced, and this has encouraged the establishment of small boutique wineries, many of whom have tourism facilities too. By 2021 the country had 226 registered wine producers and 51,000 growers. Wineries are all fully privatized apart from state-owned enterprises Cricova and Mileștii Mici (famous for the largest collection of bottled wine in the world and for the largest network of underground cellars, measuring 200 km/124 miles). In 2020 there were 42 members of the small wineries' association, who must own 1–40 ha/2.5–99 acres to distinguish them from HOME WINEMAKERS.

The wine industry is a strategic and economically important sector for Moldova, creating 16% of the value in the agricultural sector and 3% of total GDP in 2020, and employing around 150,000 people. Production in 2020 was the smallest for 10 years at 0.91 million hl/nearly 20 million gal (although average production has typically been closer to 1.5 million hl). The vast majority is exported, to 63 countries led by Belarus, Georgia, Romania, Russia, Czechia, the UK, and Poland. Inexpensive BULK WINE continues to be the majority by volume of exports, but value in the bottled wine export sector has increased. This has been helped by strong marketing activities and concepts such as the Wine of Moldova country brand launched in 2014. Several aid organizations have been working in Moldova to help restructure and modernize the wine industry. Viticultural research is also underway, and the strategic vision to 2030 includes a move towards a consumer-led, quality-focused industry with sustainability at its heart. C.G.

Gilby, C., *The Wines of Bulgaria, Romania and Moldova* (2018).
www.wineofmoldova.com

Molette is a common white grape variety, yet another progeny of GOUAIS BLANC, used particularly for the sparkling wines of SEYSSEL in SAVOIE. The base wine produced is neutral and much improved by the addition of some ALTESSE.

Molinara, red grape variety grown in 2015 on 605 ha/1,495 acres, mainly in the Veneto region of north-east Italy, particularly for VALPOLICELLA. Its wines tend to be high in acidity, light in colour, and prone to OXIDATION, so the variety is losing ground to CORVINA, RONDINELLA, and INTERNATIONAL VARIETIES in the zone.

Molise, Italy's second smallest and least populated region, is a mountainous area south of ABRUZZO in south-east Italy. Impoverished by a continuous emigration of LABOURERS for almost a century, the region has only 5,374 ha/13,279 acres of vineyards, of which less than one-tenth is devoted to DOC wine production. Production is almost entirely in the hands of CO-OPERATIVE wineries, which sell much of the wine in BULK.

The proximity of Abruzzo—to which the Molise was joined administratively until the 1960s—has left its mark on Molise's viticulture: the two predominant vine varieties are MONTEPULCIANO d'Abruzzo and TREBBIANO d'Abruzzese. There have been attempts to diversify, however, with the planting of grape varieties from southern Italy, especially neighbouring Campania, such as FIANO, GRECO di Tufo, and AGLIANICO. INTERNATIONAL VARIETIES have also been planted. The region has one overarching DOC, Molise, and three other DOCs within it: Biferno, Pentro d'Isernia, and Tintilia del Molise. While this last is based on one of the very few INDIGENOUS VARIETIES of any commercial significance in Molise (and which may only be planted in vineyards of at least 200 m/656 ft ELEVATION), all other DOCs are catch-all denominations based on Trebbiano Toscano and Montepulciano d'Abruzzo and including VARIETAL bottlings, notably of Cabernet Sauvignon and Aglianico.

In the past the region's best wines, produced by the Di Majo Norante winery, were bottled under the IGT in response to the world's lack of interest in Molise's DOCs, but that is changing—evidence that, however slowly, things are moving forwards for Molise. W.S.

Belfrage, N., *Brunello to Zibibbo—The Wines of Tuscany, Central and Southern Italy* (2nd edn, 2003).

Moll, robust but potentially interesting white grape grown on the Spanish island of MALLORCA, also known as Prensal.

Mollar. See NEGRAMOLL.

molybdenum, trace element important for plant growth. A deficiency in vineyard soils is extremely rare but may contribute to poor FRUIT SET and symptoms of NITROGEN deficiency, particularly on acidic soils (see SOIL ACIDITY) and with some varieties, including Merlot. This can be effectively treated with foliar sprays; since such sprays are inexpensive, they often applied as a prophylactic at FLOWERING.

Kaiser, B., et al., 'The role of molybdenum in agricultural plant production', *Annals of Botany*, 96/5 (2005), 745–54.

monasteries. See MONKS AND MONASTERIES.

Monastrell, Spain's fourth most important black grape variety, known in France as MOURVÈDRE, grown on 37,881 ha/93,606 acres in 2020, mainly in Murcia and CASTILLA-LA MANCHA.

The origins of the variety are almost certainly Spanish. Murviedro is a town near Valencia (Mataro, another name for the variety, is another near Barcelona). It is certainly easier to grow in Spain than in the cooler reaches of southern France, for it buds and ripens extremely late, later even than CARIGNAN. Provided the climate is warm, the upright, vigorous Monastrell adapts well to a wide range of soils and recovers well from spring FROST. (It is sensitive to low winter temperatures, however.)

The wine produced from Monastrell's small, sweet, thick-skinned berries tends to be heady stuff, high in alcohol and tannins, with a somewhat gamey, almost animal, flavour when young and well capable of AGEING, provided both OXIDATION and REDUCTION, to which it is particularly prone, is carefully avoided in the winery. It is the principal black grape variety in such DOPS as ALICANTE, ALMANSA, JUMILLA, VALENCIA, and YECLA.

See MOURVÈDRE, its more usual name outside Spain, for more details of where else it is grown.

Monbazillac, serious sweet-white-wine AOC (since 1936) within the BERGERAC district in SOUTH WEST FRANCE. The region's reputation for sweet wines predates the influence of the DUTCH WINE TRADE, going back to the Middle Ages, when Benedictine MONKS farmed the land and discovered the positive aspects of *Botrytis cinerea*. (See NOBLE ROT.)

Like SAUTERNES, Monbazillac is made from Sauvignons Blanc and Gris, Sémillon, and, particularly successful here, MUSCADELLE grapes. These vines grow immediately south of the town of Bergerac on the left bank of the DORDOGNE, close to its confluence with a small tributary, the Gardonette. This environment produces autumn morning mists followed by hot sunshine, a combination that encourages the development of noble rot, particularly on north-facing slopes.

In the past, Monbazillac was too often a sweetened, heavy, often sulfurous wine, but since 1993 there has been a clear distinction between serious sweet Monbazillac and early-picked dry white wine which is sold as Bergerac Sec. In a determined quest for quality, MECHANICAL HARVESTING was banned and at least two TRIES through the vineyard insisted upon. Basic maximum permitted yields here are 40 hl/ha (2.3 tons/acre), as opposed to the 25 hl/ha in Sauternes, but in a good vintage, the average yield in Monbazillac is around 26 hl/ha (as opposed to Sauternes' 22.5 hl/ha). At 2,700 ha/ 6,672 acres planted (out of a potential 3,600 ha), the AOC is considerably larger than Sauternes.

There is also now a further clear division between the basic MOELLEUX wines and those that bear the title SÉLECTION DE GRAINS NOBLES, which are much richer and at their best six to 20 years after the vintage. The top wines (particularly those of Ch Tirecul-la-Gravière) can rival even the finest SAUTERNES. The active CO-OPERATIVE is based in the majestic Ch de Monbazillac on the crest of a hilltop overlooking the Dordogne. P.S.

Monção e Melgaço, inland DOC subregion of VINHO VERDE in north-west Portugal on the left bank of the river MINHO best known for VARIETAL wines made from the ALVARINHO grape which flourishes in its relatively warm, dry, sheltered location. The vineyards rise from the river into the hills on stony alluvial and (predominantly) GRANITIC soils; a leading producer has planted a trial hectare on SCHIST at a dizzying 1,100 m/3,609 ft above sea level. Alvarinho wines here tend to be more muscular and fruity than Albariño from RÍAS BAIXAS across the river, yet they retain impressive freshness because there is no need to lower acidity with MALOLACTIC CONVERSION. Being the speciality, Alvarinho is made every which way, including aged in oak, chestnut, and clay vessels and in sparkling and LATE HARVEST styles. S.A.

Mondavi, important family in the recent history of CALIFORNIA wine, with **Robert Mondavi** (1913–2008) in particular having done more than anyone to raise awareness of the civilizing influence of wine in general and of California as a source of top-quality wine in particular.

Robert's father Cesare came to the US in 1906 from the MARCHE on Italy's east coast. He and his Italian wife Rosa ran a boarding house for miners in Minnesota before moving to LODI in California's San Joaquin Valley in 1922, whence, throughout PROHIBITION, they shipped grapes back east to America's temporarily swollen band of HOME WINEMAKERS. Immediately after Repeal, Cesare turned to winemaking and was joined in the late 1930s by his sons Robert and Peter.

As early as 1936, the Mondavis made their crucial move out of the hot Central Valley (leaving GALLO to build up the world's largest winery there) into the cooler NAPA Valley where they were determined to make TABLE WINES, rather than dessert wines which were then much more popular. The Mondavis acquired the nearby Charles KRUG winery in 1943. Robert Mondavi's obsession with constant fine-tuning of wine quality grew here, inspired by old bottles from the Inglenook winery and guided by oenologist André TCHELISTCHEFF. During the 1950s, he became increasingly fascinated by the CABERNET SAUVIGNON grape, and in 1962 he travelled to BORDEAUX for the first time, a seminal visit which was to convince him of the necessary conjunction between fine wine and gracious living.

This led to disputes with his younger brother Peter which were exacerbated by Cesare's death in 1959. By 1965 Robert was excluded from the Charles Krug winery, where Peter and his descendants remain, and won compensation only after a long and bitter lawsuit. The opening of the Robert Mondavi winery on the Oakville highway in 1966—strikingly Californian, in the mission style, thanks to architect Cliff May—marked the beginning of a new chapter not just for the Mondavis but for California wine. There was restless experimentation with different BARRELS, TOAST, FINING, and FILTRATION regimes; special RESERVE bottlings; comparative tastings with France's most famous wines; wine TOURISM; and cultural events associated with the winery and its wines. In 1979 a groundbreaking JOINT VENTURE was announced between Robert Mondavi and Baron Philippe de ROTHSCHILD: Opus One, with its own lavish winery since 1992. Also in 1979 the company bought a CO-OPERATIVE in Lodi which, producing the high-volume, lower-priced range of Woodbridge wines then known as 'fighting varietals', became its single most profitable venture by far.

During the 1990s, Robert Mondavi extricated himself from day-to-day operations, which then also included joint ventures in Chile and Tuscany, a controlling interest in Ornellaia, an ambitious venture in the Languedoc, and the Byron winery in the Santa Maria Valley.

Although the Robert Mondavi winery had considerable assets in the form of 1,500 acres/ 607 ha of prime Napa Valley vineyard, and though its annual production of Napa Valley wine peaked in the early 1990s at about 500,000 cases (more than any other producer), borrowings, family squabbles, and the prospect of significant inheritance taxes resulted in a public share issue in 1993. In 2004, amid much acrimony, the board voted to sell the company, and it was purchased by CONSTELLATION BRANDS, which disposed of all joint ventures except for Opus One.

Mondavi, R., *Harvests of Joy* (1998).

Mondéjar, DOP in northern CASTILLA-LA MANCHA, Spain, created in 1996 and producing TABLE WINES of modest distinction. TEMPRANILLO is the main variety in the 425 ha/1,050 acres of vineyards.

Mondeuse Blanche is a light-berried vine found in SAVOIE, producing a dry, relatively soft white wine. DNA PROFILING has shown that it is not a white MUTATION of MONDEUSE NOIRE but is, with TRESSOT, one of its progenitors. It is also a parent, with DUREZA from the Ardèche, of the famous SYRAH. J.V.

Mondeuse Noire, one of the oldest and most distinctive red grape varieties of SAVOIE, bringing an Italianate depth of colour and bite to the region in contrast to the softer reds produced by the GAMAY imported only after PHYLLOXERA. The juicy, peppery wines are powerfully flavoured and are some of Savoie's few to respond well to careful OAK AGEING (although, when grown prolifically on Savoie's more fertile, lower sites, Mondeuse can easily be a dull wine too, which may explain why the variety has been underrated).

Total French plantings of Mondeuse Noire fell sharply in the 1970s and were barely 200 ha/500 acres in 2000, but they had reached 302 ha by 2019, showing signs of a renaissance. Most Mondeuse is sold as a VARIETAL Vin de Savoie, sometimes with a CRU name added. It is also grown in the Vin du BUGEY region, and from the 2010s it underwent a small revival in Switzerland, where it was once well respected. It is grown on Etna in Sicily and in California. It was long confused with REFOSCO DAL PEDUNCOLO ROSSO in California, where it is a relative rarity, as it is in Australia. DNA PROFILING suggests that it is a natural progeny of MONDEUSE BLANCHE and TRESSOT. J.V.

Monferrato, extensive DOC in the hills east of Turin in the provinces of Asti and Alesssandria in PIEMONTE. The region is traditionally known for light and often sparkling Barbera del Monferrato, which has gained in quality since the creation of the Barbera del Monferrato Superiore DOCG, for still red wines with a minimum 14 months of ageing and 13% alcohol. While Monferrato serves as an overarching DOC, also for INTERNATIONAL VARIETIES (which, however, cannot be mentioned on labels), the region boasts a handful of interesting smaller denominations dedicated to local varieties. Long considered a workhorse variety, DOLCETTO produces some complex wines in DOCG Ovada, and GRIGNOLINO del Monferrato Casalese DOC is experiencing a renaissance, its pale and tannic reds now proving to be ageworthy as well (and just in time to halt the DOC's demise, as it measured just 270 ha/667 acres in 2020). RUCHÈ di Castagnole Monferrato DOCG is a rare, aromatic red wine with classic Piemontese tannic structure, and Monferrato Casalese is a dry white made from CORTESE and not unlike GAVI, which also lies within Monferrato. Although the region is overshadowed by its more illustrious neighbours, notably the LANGHE, Monferrato's highly original wine styles deserve more attention. W.S.

Monica, basic red grape variety grown in 2020 on 1,203 ha/2,073 acres of SARDINIA, where some varietal Monica di Sardegna is thus labelled. DNA PROFILING recently indicated that it is a natural progeny of Hebén, an old and rare wine and TABLE GRAPE from Spain, suggesting that it was initally brought to the island from Spain when Sardinia was part of the Aragón kingdom. Its wines are generally undistinguished and should be drunk young, although with lower YIELDS the variety could produce a pleasurable, if not always memorable, wine.

monks and monasteries. Wine has always had spiritual and religious significance (see RELIGION AND WINE), and monks and monasteries have long been regarded as playing a crucial part in wine history.

While wine and the vine played a prominent role in most religions of the eastern Mediterranean during prehistory and antiquity, it was in Christian religious symbolism and practice that it achieved particular significance, as an essential element of the EUCHARIST. Such Christian symbolism built on earlier Jewish beliefs in which the vine or vineyard was used in the Old Testament as one of the favourite symbols for the nation of ISRAEL. The adoption of Christianity as the state religion of the Roman Empire during the 4th century CE (see ancient ROME) led to wine attaining the utmost ideological prominence in European society. While monasteries in the eastern Mediterranean and northern Africa continued to make wine in late antiquity, as evidenced in particular by their wine PRESSES, the religious significance of wine is widely regarded as of particular importance at two main periods in its history: first, in ensuring the survival of viticulture following the collapse of the western Roman Empire; and second in the introduction of viticulture and winemaking to the Americas.

It has generally been argued that Christian communities' need for grape-based wine with which to celebrate the Eucharist was one of the main factors enabling viticulture and winemaking to survive in western Europe following the fall of Rome in 476 CE. It is assumed that when transport was difficult, it was easier for isolated Christian communities in northern Europe to cultivate their own vines rather than import wine. Moreover, monks are widely regarded as the only individuals capable of nurturing viticultural and winemaking traditions.

There is, however, little firm evidence for this hypothesis. The Germanic tribes which overran the western Roman Empire were known to be fond of wine, and there is little reason to suppose that they consciously destroyed vast expanses of European vineyards. This is supported by the evidence of surviving elements of the Gallo-Roman aristocracy, who recorded the continued cultivation of vines during the second half of the 5th century in areas of GAUL such as Clermont-Ferrand. Bishops and monks certainly did own vineyards and organized the production of wine throughout the period from the 6th to the 10th century, but in most instances they appear to have been given their vineyards mainly as grants from royalty or the secular nobility. This implies that substantial non-monastic vineyards survived and were developed in the aftermath of the Germanic invasions of the 5th century. The real role of monasteries seems not so much to have been in the preservation of a tradition of viticulture following the collapse of Rome but rather in building up substantial holdings of vineyards and, thus, in being among the most important winemakers of medieval Europe (see also CHARLEMAGNE).

During the Middle Ages, monastic houses came to possess some of the most renowned vineyards of Europe. The Benedictines (who, like the Carthusians, are now popularly associated with a high-quality liqueur based on distilled wine and whose Rule included a daily wine allowance) thus owned extensive vineyards. In BURGUNDY the monks of Cluny owned most of the vines in what is now GEVREY-CHAMBERTIN, while the abbey of St-Vivant owned vineyards in what is now called VOSNE-ROMANÉE. Along the Loire, the Benedictine abbey of St-Nicolas held vineyards in what is now ANJOU, and Benedictine monasteries at BOURGUEIL and La Charité also produced quantities of wine. Further south, the Benedictine abbey at ST-POURÇAIN produced what was one of the most renowned wines in medieval France. In CHAMPAGNE, the Benedictines held six monasteries in the diocese of Reims, while in the RHÔNE they held vineyards at both CORNAS and ST-PÉRAY. In BORDEAUX, they owned such properties as Ch Prieuré in Cantenac (now carrying the suffix of a more recent owner, Alexis LICHINE) and Ch Carbonnieux in GRAVES. In Germany, the abbey at St Maximin in the RUWER was producing about 9,000 l/2,370 gal of wine a year towards the end of the 8th century. Although they also owned many German vineyards, especially in RHEINHESSEN and FRANKEN, the Benedictines' best-known German wine estate was SCHLOSS JOHANNISBERG in the RHEINGAU (see GERMAN HISTORY).

The more ascetic Cistercians, likewise, owned numerous important vineyards throughout Europe. Clairvaux Abbey had extensive vineyards in CHAMPAGNE, and the Cistercians of Pontigny are reputed to have been the first to plant the CHARDONNAY vine in CHABLIS. Their most famous vineyard, however, was the extensive, walled CLOS DE VOUGEOT, and their other holdings in Burgundy included vineyards in MEURSAULT, BEAUNE, and POMMARD. Cistercians also produced fine wines in SANCERRE and PROVENCE. Their most important wine-producing abbey in Germany was KLOSTER EBERBACH in the RHEINGAU, but there were many others, notably at Himmerod and Machern in the MOSEL and Maulbronn in WÜRTTEMBERG. As major landowners throughout Europe, other monastic orders also owned extensive vineyards; the Carthusians, for example, had particular interests in CAHORS, SWITZERLAND, and Trier in the Upper Mosel. (See also PRIORAT.)

The second main viticultural role widely attributed to the monks was their influence on the development of vineyards in the Americas. In the 17th century, the Jesuits were major wine producers on the coastal plain of PERU, and in the 18th century, with the expansion of Spanish interests in CALIFORNIA, the Franciscans, particularly under the leadership of Júnipero Serra, played an important part in introducing viticulture and winemaking to Alta California. Most of the missions established in California during the 1770s and 1780s thus cultivated vines and made wine, with the Mission of San Gabriel becoming particularly famous for its wines, although the majority of mission vineyards nevertheless remained very small.

In the 21st century, monastic winemaking continues, despite the earlier effects of the Reformation in northern Europe. Abbeys and monasteries still producing wine include Göttweig, Heiligenkreuz, and KLOSTERNEUBURG in Austria and Muri-Gries near Bolzano in ALTO ADIGE, while at St Hildegard above Rüdesheim in the German Rheingau almost all the work is actually done by the sisters. Perhaps the most unexpected wine-producing monastery is Cremisan, sandwiched between Israel and PALESTINE.

Quite apart from the general role played by monastic orders in the history of wine, certain individual monks and monasteries enjoy vinous fame on their own account. The classic example of this is the work of Dom PÉRIGNON in improving the quality of the wines of Hautvillers in CHAMPAGNE at the end of the 17th century.

See also MISSIONARIES. P.T.H.U.

Cushner, N. P., *Lords of the Land: Sugar, Wine and Jesuit Estates of Coastal Peru, 1600–1767* (1980).

Goodenough, E. R., *Jewish Symbols in the Greco-Roman Period*, vols. v and vi (1956).

Seward, D., *Monks and Wine* (1979).

Unwin, T., *Wine and the Vine: An Historical Geography of Viticulture and the Wine Trade* (1991).

monopole, Burgundian term for a wholly owned vineyard or CLIMAT.

monopolies. State, province, or national exclusive controls over the sale, and occasionally production, of all alcoholic drinks have a long history. In INDIA, the manufacture of the sort of wine drunk in the immediately pre-Christian era was a state monopoly. In countries such as ALGERIA and (until relatively recently) EGYPT, the state has controlled wine production as well as distribution. The administrators of many ancient civilizations saw the economic and social advantages of exercising a monopoly over the distribution of wine and beer (the only alcoholic drinks known in antiquity). State monopolies on selling alcoholic drinks have been features in many Scandinavian countries, Pennsylvania in the United States, and much of Canada, although some of these monopolies were broken in the 1990s. The disadvantage for consumers can be a restriction of choice and, in many cases, severe restrictions on where and how wine is sold, sometimes with all the safeguards and ignominy associated with the distribution of dangerous drugs. The advantage for producers can be that a sale to a monopoly represents a relatively high-volume order. The two biggest monopolies in terms of volume of wine sold are the Liquor Control Board of Ontario (LCBO) in Canada, which sold about 172 million litres of wine in the twelve months to 31 March 2021, and Systembolaget in Sweden—a fervent advocate of SUSTAINABILITY, especially in packaging—which sold 223 million litres in 2021.

monoterpenes have ten carbon atoms and are members of the group of natural products called TERPENOIDS. Monoterpenes are major contributors to the characteristic flavour properties of MUSCAT grapes and wines and also play a part in the floral aromas of many non-Muscat wines such as RIESLING. Individual monoterpenes that are found in grapes and contribute to the attractive flavour properties of wines include the ALCOHOLS geraniol, nerol, linalool, and citronellol, although more than 40 have now been reported. Monoterpenes were among the first grape and wine FLAVOUR COMPOUNDS to be elucidated and the first to be discovered in glycosylated form (see GLYCOSIDES) as FLAVOUR PRECURSORS. P.J.W.

Strauss, C. R., et al., 'Role of monoterpenes in grape and wine flavor', in *Biogeneration of Aromas*, American Chemical Society (1986).

Montagne de Reims, the 'mountain of Rheims', or the forested high ground between the CHAMPAGNE towns of Rheims and Épernay. Its lower slopes are famed for the quality of PINOT NOIR base wine they produce.

Montagne-St-Émilion, the largest satellite appellation of ST-ÉMILION in Bordeaux with 1,570 ha/3,878 acres in production in 2020. Most soils are some mixture of CLAY and LIMESTONE with GRAVEL and SAND.

Montagnieu, CRU on a steep, south-facing LIMESTONE-scree slope above the Rhône river whose name can be added to the eastern French appellation BUGEY. Montagnieu reds must be from the local MONDEUSE grape. The name may also be used for fine white TRADITIONAL METHOD sparkling wines made principally from ALTESSE, CHARDONNAY, and Mondeuse. The cru name may also be added to AOC ROUSSETTE du Bugey. W.L.

Montagny, the appellation for white burgundy produced in the communes of Montagny-lès-Buxy, Jully-lès-Buxy, Buxy, and St-Vallerin in the Côte CHALONNAISE. The wines have a little more body and more acidity than other whites from this region. Of its 352 ha/870 acres of vineyards, 211 are classified as PREMIER CRU. Much of the production passes through the excellent CO-OPERATIVE founded in 1929 at Buxy, which boasts the motto 'with the good wines of Buxy everyone sings and everyone laughs'. J.T.C.M.

Montalcino, town in TUSCANY in central Italy famous for its long-lived red BRUNELLO DI MONTALCINO. Rosso di Montalcino is also made of 100% Brunello grapes but needs be aged for only one, rather than four, years.

Montecucco, source of promising Sangiovese in the MAREMMA.

Montefalco, small DOC zone in UMBRIA between Assisi and Terni best known for the DOCG Montefalco SAGRANTINO. It is used mainly for the earlier released Montefalco Rosso (60–80% SANGIOVESE, 10–25% Sagrantino); some Montefalco Bianco (a blend with minimum 50% TREBBIANO Spoletino) and varietal GRECHETTO is also made. W.S.

Montenegro, or **Crna Gora**, meaning 'black mountain', is a small country on the Adriatic coast to the south and east of CROATIA, also bordered by BOSNIA AND HERZEGOVINA, SERBIA, KOSOVO, and ALBANIA. Formerly part of YUGOSLAVIA, it became independent in 2006; in 2022 it was a candidate country for EU membership. Its wine culture dates back to pre-Roman times, supported by finds from the city of Budva dated to the 4th century BCE. The industry declined under the Ottomans and PHYLLOXERA, recovering in the early 20th century with the first wine CO-OPERATIVE in 1911.

Wine regions

Montenegro's wine regions lie between latitudes 41.5 and 42.5° N, with ELEVATIONS reaching 600 m/1,970 ft. In the warm MEDITERRANEAN CLIMATE, drought can be a threat, and most commercial vineyards have IRRIGATION. Montenegro had 2,992 ha/7,393 acres of vineyards in 2019 with an average annual production of 103,076 hl/2,722,980 gal of wine.

In 2017, the country was divided into four winegrowing regions: Crnogorski Basen Skadarskog Jezera (Montenegrin basin of Lake Skadar); Crnogorsko-Primorski (Montenegrin coast); Nudo; and Crnogorski Sjever (northern Montenegro). Seven PDOs and two PGIs are in place, though EU registration had not been completed in 2022. The PDOs are Crmnica, Podgorički subregion, Ulcinjski subregion, Boka Kotorska, Nudo, Katunska Nahija, and Bjelopavlići. PGI regions are Crnogorski Basen Skadarskog Jezera, and Crnogorsko Primorje.

The national register records 313 grapegrowers and 88 wine producers, though the country's dominant producer is 13 Jul-Plantaže which makes 96% of Montenegrin wine. It claims Europe's largest single-plot vineyard at 2,310 ha/5,683 acres, the Ćemovsko Polje, in a karst valley close to Lake Skadar.

Red wine grapes account for 72% of vineyards, whites 26%, with the remainder in mixed vineyards. The country grows at least 60 varieties, with the deep-coloured and richly flavoured local VRANAC making up 52% of plantings, while Kratošija (ZINFANDEL) is just 3.6% of plantings. Some research suggests Kratošija may have originated here before it reached Croatia and that it is the male parent of Vranac, along with Duljenga. INTERNATIONAL VARIETIES account for just under 14% of plantings, led by Chardonnay and Cabernet Sauvignon. Of the white INDIGENOUS VARIETIES Krstač is most important. Considerable research is going into rescuing old indigenous varieties from smallholder plots. Extensive work on CLONAL SELECTION is also being carried out, aimed at raising the quality of Vranac. C.G.

Maraš, V., Tello, J., Gazivoda, A., et al., 'Population genetic analysis in old Montenegrin vineyards reveals ancient ways currently active to generate diversity in *Vitis vinifera*'. *Scientific Reports* 10, 15000 (2020).

Montepulciano, name of a vigorous red grape variety planted in much of central Italy, and the name of a Tuscan town at the centre of the zone producing the highly ranked red wine VINO NOBILE DI MONTEPULCIANO (which is not made from this grape variety).

On a 2015 total of 32,724 ha/80,863 acres of vineyard, the grape variety is allowed, alone or as part of a blend, in no less than 3 DOCGs, 36 DOCs, and 88 IGTs, but it is most widely planted in ABRUZZO, where it is responsible for the often excellent-value **Montepulciano d'Abruzzo**, and in the MARCHE, where it is a principal ingredient in such reds as Rosso Conero and Rosso Piceno. It is also grown in MOLISE and PUGLIA. At its best, it produces wines that are deep in colour with ripe, robust TANNINS. Both the colour and the tannins make it a favoured blending ingredient among producers looking to boost their more feeble efforts. Unfortunately, high YIELDS and a tendency to REDUCTION in the wines have ensured that general quality is not as high as it should be. A DOCG for Montepulciano d'Abruzzo Colline Teramane—Montepulciano grown in the hills in the area around Teramo in the northern part of Abruzzo—came into effect with the 2003 vintage and produces some of the region's best wines.

The variety ripens too late to be planted much further north, although Montepulciano has recently shown it can yield dependable quantities of deep-coloured, well-ripened grapes with good levels of alcohol and extract in UMBRIA and the Tuscan MAREMMA. It is sometimes called Cordisco, Morellone, and Uva Abruzzese. DNA PROFILING has suggested a parent–offspring relationship with BOMBINO BIANCO. A tiny amount is grown in Argentina, California, Australia, and New Zealand.

Monterey, one of the major agricultural counties south of San Francisco in CALIFORNIA, with a reputation as 'America's salad bowl'. The coast may be exceptionally picturesque, while the county's inland Salinas Valley is planted with vast stretches of lettuces, broccoli, artichokes, carrots, tomatoes, capsicum/bell peppers, and strawberries which have their own kind of beauty, as described in the novels of John Steinbeck, notably *The Grapes of Wrath*. Chardonnay, Pinot Noir, and some Riesling were the varieties in FASHION in the second decade of the century, although there remained plenty of once-dominant Cabernet Sauvignon in its 18,581 ha/45,915 acres in 2021.

As a wine region, Monterey is not cut from the normal cloth. Rainfall is so low that grapes cannot be grown there without IRRIGATION. Water supply is ample, however, from the underground Salinas River, which defines the large valley so open to the Pacific Ocean that sea fogs and bracing winds cool and darken its northern end, permitting few or no grape varieties to ripen there. Into this contradictory situation came an army of would-be growers who, in 1968–75, took Monterey from one isolated vineyard to the most heavily planted county on the American west coast, with a peak of 14,980 ha/37,000 acres. Plantings have yo-yo'd since, ranging from 8,093 ha to nearly 28,328 ha/70,000 acres between 1975 and 2010 before settling at around 18,600 ha/46,000 acres in 2021.

The first Monterey wine successes came from near the towns of Soledad and Greenfield, and that area—now the AVA of ARROYO SECO—remains near the forefront, although it has since been eclipsed by the Santa Lucia Highlands (see below), a more recent AVA that flanks Arroyo Seco and reaches further north along the western foothills. Monterey County also physically contains the wine regions of CARMEL VALLEY, San Antonio Valley, and most of CHALONE (shared with SAN BENITO County), though all these AVAs remain outside the boundaries of the Monterey AVA itself.

Monterey AVA

The blanket AVA for most of Monterey County, located within the larger CENTRAL COAST AVA, encompasses the AVAs of Arroyo Seco, San Lucas, Hames Valley, Santa Lucia Highlands, and San Bernabe, as well as all other vineyards not included in these more specific regions. The San Lucas AVA was sponsored by the vast Almaden Vineyards when it owned a large amount of land; it has not been actively used on labels since Almaden left the region, although it contains a hefty percentage of Monterey's total acreage in vines. The borders of the AVA are overlapped by the largest contiguous vineyard in the world, San Bernabe's 5,261 ha/13,000 acres owned by Delicato, which also has bases in the Central Valley and Napa Valley and pushed through AVA status for San Bernabe in 2004. Both Hames Valley and San Lucas would be considered hot by the overall standards of Monterey County.

Arroyo Seco AVA

A fairly coherent district within the vastness of Monterey County's Salinas Valley has its anchor point at the scruffy farm town of Greenfield. Most of its vineyards lie to the west of town, on either bank of the dry wash for which it is named in Spanish, but some range east and north to the even scruffier precincts of Soledad. Chardonnay, which has been planted in the region since the 1960s, is the mainstay for most of the wineries who draw upon it, but some cleave resolutely, and less successfully, to Cabernet Sauvignon. Riesling and Rhône varieties have also had some success. Large swaths of the region's vineyards are owned by a few large wine companies such as JACKSON FAMILY WINES, J. Lohr Vineyards and Wines, and Wente Family Estates.

Santa Lucia Highlands AVA

On the western side of the Salinas Valley, Santa Lucia Highlands' Chardonnay, Pinot Noir, and

Syrah vines grow on terraces at up to 365 m/1,200 ft in elevation, looming over the row crops on the valley floor. On well-drained, ALLUVIAL soils of decomposed GRANITE, the region's 2,590 ha/6,400 acres of vineyards experience a remarkable fog-influenced DIURNAL TEMPERATURE RANGE, along with fierce marine WINDS that can turn grape leaves inside-out. Consistently cool-to-moderate weather makes for largely uneventful and rather long growing seasons, with harvest consistently three or more weeks later than other North Coast regions. The wind contributes to berries with thicker skins that are also praised for their tendency to retain high levels of natural ACIDITY. Consequently, the region is arguably Monterey's most celebrated AVA, its grapes, especially Pinot Noir, prized and purchased by wineries throughout California. The best examples of the region's wines strike a balance between ripeness and freshness, with a character that sets them apart from the somewhat generic wines made elsewhere in the county. L.M. & A.Y.

www.montereywines.org
www.santaluciahighlands.com

Monterrei, the smallest DOP in GALICIA, on Spain's border with Portugal, with a history of wine production dating back to Roman times, as suggested by archaeological finds of stone wine presses. Its 500 ha/1,234 acres of vineyard are planted to a bevy of red and white INDIGENOUS VARIETIES. The most planted white grapes are GODELLO and TREIXADURA, which are often blended together; red wines depend mainly on MENCÍA and BASTARDO. 'Superior' designates a wine made with at least 85% any local variety.

Monthelie, village producing red and occasionally white wine in the Côte de Beaune district of Burgundy's CÔTE D'OR (see map under BURGUNDY). It is so dominated by wine production that one local saying has it that a chicken in Monthelie is likely to die of hunger at harvest time.

The wines resemble those of VOLNAY without reaching the same heights of depth and elegance, although they age well and are more powerful than those of AUXEY-DURESSES, the neighbouring appellation to the south with which the PREMIER CRU vineyard Les Duresses is shared. Most other premier cru vineyards of Monthelie (which were expanded considerably in 2006) such as Meix Bataille and Champs Fulliot lie adjacent to Volnay. Increasing amounts of Chardonnay have been planted since the 1980s, for Monthelie also borders the white-wine village of MEURSAULT. La Goulotte, Combe Danay, and the top of Les Duresses are good vineyards for white grapes. J.T.C.M.

Montilla-Moriles, Spanish DOP in ANDALUCÍA, 40 km/25 miles south of Cordoba (see map under SPAIN), producing both FORTIFIED and unfortified wines in the style of SHERRY, usually known simply as **Montilla**. For many years wine from the country around the towns of Montilla and Moriles found its way into sherry SOLERAS. The practice largely ceased in 1945 when the area was awarded its own DOP, although wines made from the PEDRO XIMÉNEZ grape, some of them very fine, are still legally exported to JEREZ and neighbouring MÁLAGA for blending. Since it became a region in its own right, Montilla has had to contend with a popular image as an inferior, cheap alternative to sherry. However, it is remarkable that the region's two most outstanding bodegas, Alvear (founded in 1729) and Pérez Barquero (1905), are at the same level of quality as the three or four best bodegas in the Sherry district.

The soils in the centre of the region associated with lower YIELDS and better wines resemble the chalky ALBARIZA of Jerez, although most of Montilla-Moriles is SANDY and parched. The climate is relatively harsh, with summer temperatures rising to 45 °C/113 °F and short, cold winters. The Pedro Ximénez vine, which accounts for over 95% of the region's 4,655 ha/11,503 acres of vines, seems to thrive in the hot conditions, yielding extremely sweet grapes.

The wines therefore achieve ALCOHOLIC STRENGTHS of 14–16% without FORTIFICATION. Other grape varieties include VERDEJO, Baladí (CAETANA BLANCA), and MUSCAT OF ALEXANDRIA, which tend to produce lighter wines for blending. The PALOMINO vine, which is the basis for most sherry, has not been successful in Montilla.

Winemaking practices in Montilla parallel those for sherry. Pale, dry FINO and AMONTILLADO style wines are made from FREE-RUN juice, while heavier styles similar to OLOROSO are made from the subsequent pressings.

Pale Dry Montilla matures under a film of FLOR, initially in concrete or earthenware TINAJAS, then in a SOLERA similar to those in Jerez. However, in the hot climate of Montilla-Moriles, far removed from the cooling winds of the Atlantic, the flor is usually thinner than in Jerez, and the wines tend to have less finesse as a result (see SHERRY). Heavier oloroso styles are fortified and aged for longer in soleras, where they become dark and pungent. Around half the region's wines are not fortified, which puts them at an advantage in certain markets where duties are levied on alcoholic strength. The region is now most celebrated for its PX wines, which are very sweet but not that strong, and of which some producers make young, vintage-dated examples. V. de la S. & J.B.

Liem, P., and Barquín, J., *Sherry, Manzanilla & Montilla—A Guide to the Traditional Wines of Andalucía* (2012).

Montlouis, or **Montlouis-sur-Loire** as it is officially known, is a dynamic white-wine appellation in the TOURAINE district of the Loire finally out of the shadow of the much larger and more famous VOUVRAY across the river. As in Vouvray, the CHENIN BLANC grape is the sole variety of this historic AOC (1938) which allows wine production in all degrees of sweetness and FIZZINESS according to each VINTAGE's peculiarities. The 450 ha/1,100 acres of vineyards grow on plateaus rolling south-west towards the cooler valley of the Cher. The TUFFEAU is covered by *perruches* (flinty clay), *aubuis* (chalky clay), and Miocene GRAVEL, resulting in a sandier topsoil than in Vouvray. About two-thirds of the region's production is MOUSSEUX, while dry, BARREL AGED, SINGLE-VINEYARD WINES are becoming increasingly popular, a trend started by visionary growers such as François Chidaine and Jacky Blot. In 2020, Montlouis trademarked the term 'Originel' to describe sparkling wines made from a single fermentation in the bottle with no added YEAST nor *liqueur de* TIRAGE. After mandatory DISGORGEMENT, it is topped up with the same wine before the bottle is sealed. The wine may be sold as either *mousseaux* or *pétillant* depending on the pressure in the bottle.

See also LOIRE, including map, and SPARKLING WINEMAKING. P. Le.

Montonico Bianco, ancient light-berried table and wine grape, probably of Greek origin, grown mainly in central Italy. It should not be confused with Mantonico Bianco, another old variety from southern Italy. **Montonico Nero** is a synonym for GAGLIOPPO.

Montpellier, University of. The agricultural component of Montpellier University is known as the Institut Agro, created under the name École d'Agriculture de Montpellier in 1872 in response to the viticultural crises caused by PHYLLOXERA, POWDERY MILDEW, and DOWNY MILDEW in France. The first Professor of Viticulture, Gustave Foëx, established a collection of European (VITIS VINIFERA) and AMERICAN VINE SPECIES (VITIS RIPARIA, VITIS LABRUSCA in particular) and varieties, which remains the world's most comprehensive repository, with more than 7,500 accessions. Pierre Viala was Professor of Viticulture at the end of the 1880s, bringing back from the US phylloxera-tolerant vine species suitable for CALCAREOUS soils. Thanks to his effort, *Vitis berlandieri* was used to obtain rootstocks such as 41 B, which allowed the replanting of the Cognac and the Champagne regions. Viala's successor was Professor Louis Ravaz, who became one of the first vine physiologists in the wine world. During the 20th century, several famous scientists took the position of Professor of Viticulture of the Montpellier school: Jean Branas, Denis Boubals, and Alain Carbonneau, this last being a specialist in CANOPY MANAGEMENT. Since the Foëx period, AMPELOGRAPHY has been a speciality at Montpellier. Until his retirement in 1985, Pierre GALET helped to establish the scientific bases of ampelography. His successor, Jean-Michel Boursiquot, has been one of the major players in the development of molecular ampelography over the last 20 years.

In 2005, the Institut des Hautes Études de la Vigne et du Vin (Institute for Higher Education in Vine and Wine Sciences), or IHEV, was created to organize the education, research, and extension activities of the Institut Agro Montpellier, today led by Professor Laurent Torregrosa. With 40 permanent staff, including 27 professors and associate professors, the institute offers eight training programs (300 students) dedicated to vine management, wine production or wine economics, from Bachelor to PhD, including the renowned Diploma of Oenology. For research in the wine sector, l'Institut Agro Montpellier, INRAE, and Montpellier University are organized into 12 joint research units, with 300 staff, including 25 PhD students. Extension activities are supported by four industrial chairs, three joint technology units, and three experimental estates (Domaine du Chapître, Centre Expérimental INRAE de Pech-Rouge, and Centre de Ressources Biologiques de Vassal).

The main research topics at Montpellier are vine and yeast genetics, fermentation monitoring, ecophysiology, viticulture management, digital viticulture, and VINE BREEDING. Such research aims to address the main challenges of the sector: product innovation, input reduction in vine management and wine production (see SUSTAINABILITY), and adaptation to CLIMATE CHANGE.

Montpeyroux, high-elevation CRU within the LANGUEDOC and strong favourite to be the next Languedoc subregion to receive its own AOC. The region encompasses around 300 ha/740 acres of rocky CLAY and LIMESTONE some 40 km/25 miles north of Montpellier in the foothills of the Larzac mountains, within the AOC TERRASSES DU LARZAC. Wines must be a blend of at least three grape varieties, primarily Syrah, Grenache, and Mourvèdre, with Carignan and Cinsaut in a supporting role. DROUGHT is a common summer problem, and yields on these rocky slopes are notably low, while ELEVATION and WINDS such as the tramontagne help retain freshness in these full-bodied reds. M.S.

Montrachet, or **Le Montrachet**, the most famous GRAND CRU white burgundy, the apogee of the Chardonnay grape produced from a single vineyard in the Côte de Beaune district of the CÔTE D'OR. Claude Arnoux, writing in 1728, could find no words in either French or Latin to describe its qualities, though he noted that it was very expensive and that you needed to reserve the wine a year in advance. Dr Lavalle's view (see BURGUNDY, history), expressed in 1855 and not necessarily valid today, was that whatever the price for a good vintage of Le Montrachet, you would not have paid too much.

Le Montrachet covers just under 8 ha/20 acres straddling the borders of Puligny and Chassagne, two communes which have annexed the famous name to their own (see PULIGNY-MONTRACHET and CHASSAGNE-MONTRACHET). Part of the secret lies in the LIMESTONE, part in its perfect south-east ASPECT, which keeps the sun from dawn till dusk. Curiously, the vines in the Puligny half run in east–west rows, while most in Chassagne run north–south, reflecting the contours of the land.

The principal owners and producers of Le Montrachet are the Marquis de Laguiche, Baron Thénard, DOMAINE DE LA ROMANÉE-CONTI, BOUCHARD PÈRE ET FILS, Domaines Lafon and Prieur in Meursault, and Domaines Ramonet, Colin, and Amiot-Bonfils in Chassagne. Domaines Leflaive and d'Auvenay have also purchased smallholdings. The largest slices belong to the Marquis de Laguiche, whose wine is made by Joseph DROUHIN and Baron Thénard, some of whose wine is distributed by NÉGOCIANTS.

Four more grands crus are associated with Le Montrachet: **Chevalier-Montrachet** (7.48 ha) is situated directly above the Puligny section of Le Montrachet, on thin, stony soil giving wines which are not quite as rich as the latter. Particularly sought after are the wine from Domaine Leflaive; the Chevalier-Montrachet Les Demoiselles from Louis LATOUR and Louis JADOT; and Chevalier-Montrachet La Cabotte from Bouchard Père et Fils.

Bâtard-Montrachet (10.27 ha), on the slope beneath Le Montrachet, also spans the two communes, producing rich and heady wines not quite as elegant as a Chevalier-Montrachet. In the Puligny section of Bâtard is a separate enclave, **Bienvenues-Bâtard-Montrachet** (3.43 ha), while an extension of the Chassagne section is the rarely seen **Criots-Bâtard-Montrachet** (1.57 ha).

See CÔTE D'OR for details of viticulture and winemaking. J.T.C.M.

Arnoux, C., *Dissertation sur la situation de Bourgogne* (1728).

Ginestet, B., *Montrachet* (1988).

Loftus, S., *Puligny-Montrachet* (1992).

Norman, R., *Grand Cru* (2010).

Montravel includes three AOCS in the extreme west of the BERGERAC district in SOUTH WEST FRANCE bordering on Bordeaux's eastern satellites. The appellations **Côtes de Montravel** and **Haut-Montravel** are used for small quantities of sweet wines, with the former generally denoting a MOELLEUX wine and the latter for a sweeter version. Montravel *tout court* is mainly a dry white, although in 2001 the appellation was extended to reds based on Merlot.

For the whites, each of SÉMILLON and the two Sauvignons must make up at least one-quarter of the blend. MUSCADELLE is also approved, as is up to 10% ONDENC. The overall quality of the dry wines increased considerably in the late 1980s, though they remain rarely found outside the area of production. P.S.

Montsant, DOP created in CATALUÑA in 2001 which used to be known as the Falset subregion of the TARRAGONA DOP. Its 1,900 ha/4,700 acres of vineyards were given their own identity in order to highlight their superior quality. It has less of the SCHIST soils of its neighbour PRIORAT, but otherwise its old GARNACHA and CARIÑENA vineyards on steep slopes enable it to produce wines of very similar style and quality at lower prices.

Moon Mountain District, high-ELEVATION California AVA in the Mayacamas foothills famed for structured ZINFANDEL and Cabernet Sauvignon. See SONOMA.

Montù, also known as **Montuni**, late-ripening white grape indigenous to the plains of EMILIA in Italy.

Moravia, Eastern part of CZECHIA whose wine region lies just north of Austria's WEINVIERTEL. Moravia Agria is the name of a grape making refreshing reds in MANCHUELA, while Moravia Dulce is MARUFO.

Morellino di Scansano, particularly successful Sangiovese in Italy's MAREMMA, now suffixed 'Toscana' to increase international brand awareness.

Moreto do Alentejo, undistinguished red grape variety, a natural CROSS of ALFROCHEIRO × CAYETANA BLANCA, that is planted mainly in Portugal's ALENTEJO as well as in BEIRAS.

Morey-St-Denis, important village in the Côte de Nuits district of BURGUNDY producing red wines from Pinot Noir grapes (see map under BURGUNDY). Morey suffers, perhaps unfairly, in comparison with its neighbours CHAMBOLLE-MUSIGNY and GEVREY-CHAMBERTIN because its wines are usually described as being lighter versions of Gevrey or firmer than Chambolle, according to which side of the village they are located. Indeed, in the past, the wines were often sold under those names. Geologically there is no need for Morey-St-Denis to feel inferior as the same stratum of LIMESTONE which runs from the Combe de Lavaux in Gevrey through Morey to the Combe d'Antin in Chambolle.

There are four GRAND CRU vineyards, moving southwards from the border with Gevrey-Chambertin: Clos de la Roche (16.9 ha/42 acres), Clos St-Denis (6.5 ha), Clos des Lambrays (8.7 ha), and Clos de Tart (7 ha), plus a small segment of Bonnes Mares overlapping from Chambolle.

Although Morey chose to append 'St-Denis' to its name in 1927, Clos de la Roche is probably the finest vineyard. The soil is rich in MARL, giving greater depth, body, and AGEING ability than most other vineyards.

Clos St-Denis, sandwiched between Clos de la Roche and the village itself, may be the quintessential wine of Morey-St-Denis—a touch lighter than Clos de la Roche, supple and succulent, the more charming of the two early in life, with a trace of austerity, but the pinnacle of finesse.

Excellent examples of both Clos de la Roche and Clos St-Denis have been made by Domaine Ponsot, Domaine Dujac, and various Ligniers. While Domaine Ponsot was one of the first to bottle their own wines in Burgundy, Domaine Dujac is the comparatively recent creation (in 1968) of Jacques Seysses, an inspirational grower whose example significantly influenced the generation taking over their family domaines in the 1980s.

Clos des Lambrays, all but a monopoly, was promoted from PREMIER CRU to GRAND CRU. Clos de Tart, singled out by Dr Lavalle in 1855 as the only *tête de cuvée* vineyard in Morey, has always been a MONOPOLE: founded by the Cistercian sisters of Notre Dame de Genlis in 1250, it remained in their hands until the French Revolution, when it was auctioned in one piece. In 1932 one of the Marey-Monge family sold it to the Mommessin family, and thence in 2018 to ARTÉMIS DOMAINES.

Successful premier cru vineyards in Morey-St-Denis include Les Ruchots, Clos de la Bussière (monopole of Domaine G Roumier), Les Millandes, Clos des Ormes, and Les Monts Luisants. Domaine Ponsot also produces a rare and curious white wine from the last, based on a plot of ALIGOTÉ planted in 1911.

See also CÔTE D'OR. J.T.C.M.

Morgon, historically the most prominent cru in BEAUJOLAIS, encompassing about 1,100 ha/2,717 acres of vines around the commune of Villié-Morgon. The wines from the ex-VOLCANIC cone known as Côte de Py are the most reputed, although those of Grand Cras and Douby play important, if different, roles. Classic Morgon soil is the degraded 'blue stone' SCHIST found on Py, but other schists and shallow GRANITE sands also appear. The wines can be denser and longer lived than many cru Beaujolais, depending on the parcel, and the appellation has even been used as a verb, as in describing the process by which a young Beaujolais channels a Pinot Noir-dominated red burgundy with age: *il morgonne*. Villié-Morgon has been home to some of the region's well-known provocateurs, including Marcel Lapierre and Guy Breton. J.F.B.

Morillon is an old north-eastern French name for PINOT NOIR and is still a common name for the powerfully aromatic CHARDONNAY of STYRIA in southern Austria. It was a widely used Burgundian vine variety name in the Middle Ages and was, for example, an old name for Chardonnay in CHABLIS country.

Morio-Muskat was once Germany's most popular MUSCAT-like vine variety, particularly with the eager blenders of the PFALZ and RHEINHESSEN in the late 1970s, when its total German area reached 3,000 ha/7,410 acres and demand for LIEBFRAUMILCH was high. Total plantings are falling fast, however, and Germany had only 333 ha by 2020 as this aggressively blowsy cross has undoubtedly had its day. Although Peter Morio's cross was introduced as SILVANER × WEISSBURGUNDER, DNA PROFILING has shown it to be Silvaner × MUSCAT BLANC À PETITS GRAINS, explaining both its name and its grapey flavour.

Moristel, light, loganberry-flavoured speciality of SOMONTANO in northern Spain, also known as Juan Ibáñez. The light red wine produced oxidizes easily (see OXIDATION). It may be better in a blend than as a VARIETAL.

Mornington Peninsula, MARITIME, cool-climate wine region south-east of Melbourne in the Australian state of VICTORIA with 80-odd producers in 2021. Site climate varies widely across this long east–west peninsula, and the differences are notably apparent in the varied styles of its wines, particularly Chardonnay and Pinot Noir.

Morocco, with its high mountains and cooling Atlantic influence, has arguably the greatest potential for producing high-quality wine in North Africa. Viticulture, which existed in the Roman era, was probably introduced by Phoenician settlers. But it was the French colonists who brought large-scale wine production, so that Morocco played a significant part in the world's wine trade in the 1950s and 1960s, although it never produced as much as neighbouring ALGERIA. At independence in 1956, Morocco had 55,000 ha/135,850 acres of carefully husbanded vineyard. With the departing French colonists went winemaking expertise, capital, and a large proportion of domestic consumption. This was compounded in 1967 by new EEC (now EU) quotas which literally decimated Morocco's exports. Frozen out of European markets and faced with stiff competition from other over-producing Mediterranean countries, most producers GRUBBED UP their vineyards and replaced them with cereal crops. Between 1973 and 1984 most vineyards were taken over by the state, which by 1984 had also established a firm grip on the sale of wine, including grape price-fixing regardless of quality.

By the early 1990s, only about 13,000 ha of the nation's 40,000 ha of vines were planted with wine vines, over half of them, many virused, 30 years old or more and therefore economically unproductive. Average yields were well under 30 hl/ha (1.7 tons/acre). The state had a virtual monopoly on the domestic market. The only independent producer to prosper in this post-colonial climate was Brahim Zniber, head of North African wine giant Les Celliers de Meknès and also owner of its main domestic competitor, Thalvin/Domaine Ouled Thaleb. Zniber, who bought his first vineyards from departing French producers in the 1950s and started bottling wines in 1976, encouraged the introduction of a CONTROLLED APPELLATION system and pioneered VARIETAL wines.

In a bid to revive Morocco's rural economy, the late King Hassan II successfully attracted foreign investment in viticulture during the 1990s. Several large Bordeaux groups, including CASTEL, William Pitters, and Taillan, took up the offer of long leases on prime vineyard land from the state holding company SODEA. This policy of seeking inward investment, continued by King Mohammed VI, had a galvanizing effect on the industry from the mid 1990s, and thousands of hectares were replanted with better-quality grape varieties.

Historically CARIGNAN dominated Moroccano's vineyards, but CINSAUT is now the country's most planted variety, with Grenache and Syrah gaining ground. Cabernet Sauvignon and Merlot are also popular. Well over 77% of Moroccan wine is red. Rosé and VIN GRIS account for another 16%. What little white is made tends to be heavy versions of CLAIRETTE and MUSCAT, although there are laudable exceptions, such as the ROUSSANNE of Domaine Val d'Argan, a pioneer in the ORGANIC VITICULTURE movement on the southern coast near Essaouira.

Most vine-growing, however, is concentrated in the north, where the Atlas Mountains and the Atlantic Ocean create cool MESOCLIMATES in a country otherwise largely described as having a semi-arid MEDITERRANEAN CLIMATE. Even so, summer temperatures can reach 35–38 °C/95–100 °F; rainfall between May and October is very low; and DROUGHT cycles and SUNBURN are worsening due to CLIMATE CHANGE. The prevailing WINDS from the Atlantic, which can blow at up to 65 km/40 miles per hour, can also be challenging. Vine TRELLISING and careful row orientation have become more common, and all the major producers now practise DRIP IRRIGATION.

Morocco's appellation system, closely modelled on the French AOC, is called Appellation d'Origine Garantie. AOG rules delimit the geographical area of production and set maximum YIELDS but do not dictate grape varieties. The system, which has yet to achieve any real significance in terms of guaranteeing quality, includes 14 AOG zones, most in the country's cooler, fertile north:

The East: Beni Sadden, Berkane, Angad
Meknès/Fès region: Guerrouane, Beni M'tir, Saiss, Zerhoune
The Northern Plain: Gharb
Rabat/Casablanca region: Chellah, Zemmour, Zaër, Zenata Sahel Sahel
El-Jadida region: Doukkala

Of these regions, Meknès is the centre of Moroccan viticulture. Here in the Middle Atlas, at an ELEVATION of around 600 m/1,968 ft, the vines benefit from moderate rainfall, abundant sunshine, and a mix of SANDY and CLAY and LIMESTONE soils. Domaine de la Zouina, established in 2002 by Bordelais winegrowers Gérard Gribelin and Philippe Gervoson, leads the way.

There are also vast new plantings around Benslimane, outside of Casablanca, and Beni Mellal, north-west of Marrakech, including grapes such as ARINARNOA, MALBEC, MARSELAN, TANNAT, TEMPRANILLO, and VERMENTINO.

Morocco also has three AOCs. **Coteaux de l'Atlas** covers the clay–limestone terroir at the foot of the Atlas Mountains. At 700 m/2,297 ft in elevation, its climate is mild and sunny. Chardonnay is the only variety permitted for white wines; reds can be made from Cabernet Sauvignon, Cabernet Franc, Syrah, and Merlot. **Crémant de L'Atlas** is reserved for TRADITIONAL METHOD sparkling wines from Chardonnay. **Côtes de Rommani** is located south of the Coteaux de l'Atlas, in the Zaër highlands. Domaine la Ferme Rouge is the sole producer, its 300 ha/741 acres of vines growing on sunny hillsides of clay and limestone at an elevation of almost 450 m/1,476 ft. The AOC authorizes the cultivation of 16 grape varieties with an average yield of 60 hcl/ha.

By 2020, Morocco's wine production remained modest, with an annual output of around 600,000 hl, although the local market is buoyed by strong demand from the tourist industry and the country's affluent urban elite, as well as by the high duties on imported wines. Moroccan law prohibits the sale of alcohol to Muslims, but in practice the law is seldom if ever applied. Alcohol is freely available in all the main cities outside the holy month of Ramadan. Not everyone approves of this permissive approach—least of all Morocco's growing ISLAMIST movement, which seeks to ban or limit alcohol consumption.

See also CORKS, of which Morocco is the world's third largest producer, after Portugal and Spain. J.R. & R.Z.

Joy, R., *A Survey of Moroccan Wine* (2003).

morphology. See VINE MORPHOLOGY.

Morrastel is the main French synonym for Rioja's GRACIANO. **Morrastel-Bouschet** is a much lesser CROSS that produced substantial quantities of notably deep red wine in France's LANGUEDOC in the mid 20th century.

Mortágua, confusing western Portuguese red wine grape synonym with multiple meanings: for CAMARATE in Arruda, for TRINCADEIRA in Torres Vedras, and, occasionally in Dão and Setúbal, for TOURIGA NACIONAL.

Moscadello, sometimes **Moscadelleto**, name for the MUSCAT BLANC À PETITS GRAINS grown in and around MONTALCINO in central Italy. Moscadello was the major wine of Montalcino for centuries, being cited by English travellers in the 17th and 18th centuries, long before anyone even noted the presence of important reds. The firm Villa Banfi made an important investment in selling this sweet grapey, fizzy white wine in the 1980s, hoping to repeat the commercial success of LAMBRUSCO, but to little avail.

Moscatel, Spanish and Portuguese for MUSCAT. The term may be applied to both grape varieties and wines. Thus **Moscatel de Grano Menudo** is none other than MUSCAT BLANC À PETITS GRAINS, while **Moscatel de Alejandría**, **Moscatel de Málaga**, and **Moscatel Romano** are MUSCAT OF ALEXANDRIA. **Moscatel Rosado**, on the other hand, may be a South American speciality (see below). Most of the vines known simply as Moscatel in Spanish- and Portuguese-speaking countries are Muscat of Alexandria, although northern Spain has some of the superior small-seeded variety.

Inexpensive wines labelled Moscatel abound in Iberia and are in general sweet and grapey.

See also Moscatel de SETÚBAL.

Moscatel de Alejandría, Spanish name for MUSCAT OF ALEXANDRIA.

Moscatel de Austria, grape variety grown on more than 1,700 ha/4,200 acres in Chile but used mostly in the production of the national aromatic brandy PISCO. Identical to Argentina's TORRONTÉS Sanjuanino.

Moscato, Italian for MUSCAT and the name of a sweetish VARIETAL wine style for which there was a FASHION in certain quarters towards the end of the first decade of the 21st century (see ASTI for details), which resulted in an increase in plantings of Muscat even in California. The Italian vine census of 2010 identified seven different Moscatos. **Moscato Bianco** is the finest Muscat grape variety MUSCAT BLANC À PETITS GRAINS and is that most commonly encountered in Italy, with total plantings of 13,334 ha/32,949 acres in 2015, making it one of the country's most planted white wine grapes, cited in almost 20 DOCS. This is the Moscato responsible for all the light, usually sweet and sparkling wines of Asti and MOSCATO D'ASTI. **Moscato Rosa del Trentino** is a very much rarer red-skinned grape found in TRENTINO and ALTO ADIGE, often called Rosenmuskateller. The golden-berried **Moscato Giallo** (Goldmuskateller) is more widely planted, on 1,108 ha/2,738 acres in 2015, and has a parent–offspring relationship with Moscato Bianco. **Moscato di Terracina** is a recently revived aromatic white grown in Lazio. **Moscato di Scanzo** is a dark-berried speciality of Bergamo which makes small quantities of decadently aromatic, sweet PASSITO reds. Moscato Nero di Acqui is a synonym for MUSCAT OF HAMBURG.

Few of Italy's regions lack their own Moscato-based wines. The majority of these are low in alcohol and at least lightly sweet, ideal accompaniments to fruit and fruit-based desserts. In the south and, especially, the islands, they are typically golden and sweet.

SICILY, and southern Italy more generally, was once renowned for its Moscato wines, many of them made from MUSCAT OF ALEXANDRIA, more commonly known as ZIBIBBO in Italy. The revived popularity of Moscato di PANTELLERIA in the 1980s coincided with, and perhaps influenced, new attempts to achieve a more luscious style of Moscato in Piemonte, and a new category of passito wines, far sweeter than Moscato d'Asti and frequently given BARREL AGEING, began to emerge in the late 1980s. Small quantities of Moscato passito have long been made in the Valle d'AOSTA, principally near the township of Chambave.

Moscato d'Asti, fragrant and lightly sweet, gently fizzy DOCG wine made in the PIEMONTE region of north-west Italy. It is produced from MOSCATO Bianco, Italy's name for MUSCAT BLANC À PETITS GRAINS, whose production in and around the town of ASTI increased enormously in the 20th and early 21st centuries. Canelli, where in 1865 Carlo Gancia produced the first sparkling Moscato and where the historic underground cellars now have UNESCO World Heritage status, is considered the cradle of Moscato in Piemonte. At the end of the 19th century, almost 80% of all Moscato was grown in the CALCAREOUS soils in the triangle formed by Castiglione Tinella, Canelli, and Santo Stefano Belbo, still considered the classic zones for fine Moscato, although expansion of the zone has revealed a real vocation for Moscato on the slopes of Cossano Belbo, Mango, Neviglie, and Trezzo Tinella. Moscato d'Asti is therefore something of a misnomer, since much of the production is not in the province of Asti but in the province of Cuneo (stretching as far as Serralunga Alba in the eastern part of the BAROLO zone), and a significant proportion is in the province of Alessandria.

As a wine, Moscato d'Asti is often lumped together with ASTI, although the two are discernibly different. With a maximum of

2 atmospheres of pressure in the bottle—less than one-third that of Asti—Moscato d'Asti is only slightly frothy, while Asti is fully sparkling. Its ALCOHOLIC STRENGTH is considerably lower (maximum 6.5% as opposed to Asti's 6.5–11%), and Asti can taste sweeter than the more flavourful Moscato d'Asti, even if its RESIDUAL SUGAR is usually slightly lower.

The ripest, and best, MOSCATO grapes are used to produce Moscato d'Asti. The 'wine' is classed as 'partially fermented grape must', for the juice is chilled and filtered immediately after pressing and fermented only when required, ensuring that Moscato's beguiling aromas are not lost. Fermentation is stopped when the wine reaches 5.5% alcohol; the unfermented sugar lends a hedonistic grapey character to the wine and helps to exalt the Moscato's heady perfumes.

Within the Asti DOCG there are two subzones, Santa Maria d'Alba and Strevi, in which only Moscato d'Asti and not Asti Spumante can be produced. Both decree 100% Moscato, lower yields of 9 tons/ha, and 11% minumum potential potential alcohol. (Confusingly, Strevi is also a DOC for a still sweet wine made of LATE HARVEST or dried Moscato grapes).

Moscato d'Asti is not a classic dessert wine, its chief virtues being delicacy, intense aromas, and a sweetness that is as much suggested as forthrightly declared. Moscato d'Asti Vendemmia Tardiva, in contrast, is a full-blown, still, sweet DRIED-GRAPE WINE.

Moscato d'Asti production may have grown enormously but is less than Asti's (33 million bottles compared to 50 million bottles of Asti). It is a classic and unusually refreshing expression of one of the world's most popular grape varieties, even if wines with residual sweetness are considered out of fashion. In an effort to halt Moscato d'Asti's slow decline, a group of young Asti producers specializing in dry Moscato has registered the brand 'EsCamotage' to promote their dry wines. W.S.

www.astidocg.info

Moscato di Sardegna, relatively new (1979) DOC in SARDINIA for sweet, still or sparkling white wines made in the image of MOSCATI D'ASTI.

Moscato di Scanzo, or Scanzo, is a DOCG from the area east of Bergamo in LOMBARDY for an increasingly rare, sweet PASSITO of the dark-berried MOSCATO di Scanzo. The grapes must be dried for at least 21 days or until a minimum of 280g/l of RESIDUAL SUGAR has been obtained. By law the wine must be aged for at least two years. W.S.

Moscato di Strevi. See STREVI.

Moscato Spumante, often the simplest form of light, sparkling Italian white wine made in the style of ASTI but usually with the most basic, industrial ingredients. Not to be confused with the infinitely superior MOSCATO D'ASTI, nor with METODO CLASSICO versions.

Moschofilero, vine variety with deep pink-skinned grapes used to make strongly perfumed, delicate white wine in GREECE, particularly on the high plateau of Mantinia in the Peloponnese, where conditions are sufficiently cool that harvest is often delayed until well into October and alcohol levels are typically low. There are strong flavour similarities with fine MUSCAT, but the origins of this distinct vine variety are as yet obscure. Smaller quantities of fruity light-pink wine are also made from this spicy variety, which is also increasingly used for sparkling wines. So popular has it become that Greece had 1,220 ha/3,015 acres planted by 2021.

Mosel, formerly known as Mosel-Saar-Ruwer, is a major German growing region famed for RIESLING (62% of vine share), the best examples being long-lived, delicate, and dynamic, including some of the world's finest sweet wines. The total area planted, at 8,744 ha/21,607 acres in 2019, has been declining slowly and, except in the best-known vineyards, Riesling grapes command a price that only just covers the costs of farming the generally steep, stony, sheer slopes with their densely planted and often archaically trained vines. (See GERMANY, viticulture.)

As the River Mosel twists from Trier to Koblenz, the vineyards are at their steepest on the outer edge of the curve. Those on the flatter inner edge are frequently planted with varieties other than Riesling. TOPOGRAPHY is all important here, but SOIL, too, is critical. An overwhelming majority of top Mosel, Saar, or Ruwer sites is dominated by Devonian SLATE, which has been used in the region for hundreds of years as a building material and has traditionally been renewed, redistributed, or added to vineyards to promote heat retention. Some of the vineyards between the almost vertical spurs of rock were created in the 16th century with the aid of explosives, a dangerous operation when there was a wine village below. Vineyards have been subjected to the wholesale renovation (known as FLURBEREINIGUNG) later and to a lesser extent than those of most other German regions, the principle obstacle being sheer steepness and difficulty of access to the slopes for earth-moving equipment. Vineyards associated with some of the Mosel's most important villages also proved resistant to the late 19th and early 20th century ravages of PHYLLOXERA, and a few productive stands of vines still date to the 19th century. In those places where phylloxera never penetrated, many vines are UNGRAFTED, and, until the new outbreaks of phylloxera in the early 21st century, could be replanted without grafting, a dwindling but arguably precious legacy.

The Mosel traditionally enjoys a warm summer with an average temperature in July of 18 °C/64 °F, but summer temperatures in the upper 30s °C are no longer a rarity. Today, autumn or winter FROST DAMAGE is rare, but spring frost has become more dangerous due to progressively earlier BUDBREAK. Nights cold enough for EISWEIN production are no longer a given and come increasingly late in the year, while marauding wild boar remain a major impediment to that genre, with a reputation for Christmas or New Year's feasting on any grapes still left hanging.

In the 18th century, many villages produced red wine (see GERMAN HISTORY). By the early 19th century, white wine dominated, and the ELBLING vine was planted on nearly two-thirds of the Mosel vineyard area, but Riesling had become the touchstone of quality. Riesling's prevalence peaked in 1954 with a 90% share of Mosel vineyards before succumbing to the allure of more easily ripened HYBRIDS and, for a decade from the late 1990s, to that of DORNFELDER, in response to increased domestic demand for red wine. None of these non-Rieslings excel, although tiny pockets of SPÄTBURGUNDER (Pinot Noir) and WEISSBURGUNDER (Pinot Blanc) do.

A key to a fine Mosel Riesling is enlivening acidity (especially TARTARIC ACID), which balances any RESIDUAL SUGAR present, along with a frequent if vague impression of wet stone. A low-alcohol Mosel Riesling often tastes merely off-dry even when it has 20–30 g/l residual sugar. TROCKEN wine is increasingly common, representing a return to dryness such as characterized Mosel Riesling when it achieved international acclaim in the late 19th century, albeit in an era with later growing seasons and lower MUST weights than today's. As a result some dry Mosel Rieslings may be 13% or more natural alcohol, but the quintessential Mosel remains for many non-Germans a delicate (7–9% alcohol) Riesling that is fresh and subtly sweet yet invigorating. Only a minority of Mosel growers (notably along the Saar) seriously pursue the goal of non-trocken but far-from-sweet Riesling. (Throughout Germany, most prominent growers have given up on HALBTROCKEN as a concept.) Yet, at levels of residual sugar hardly detectable as such, ravishing dry-tasting Mosel Riesling of 10–12% alcohol is possible.

Processing close to one-fifth of its region's fruit and half of that Riesling makes Moselland CO-OPERATIVE in Bernkastel the world's largest producer of Riesling. Much of the rest—especially from grapes other than Riesling—is bottled by merchant houses. But although the standing of Mosel wine in Germany was debased in the late 20th century by over-production and price warfare, not to mention by the legal adoption of names of famous villages and vineyards to designate GROSSLAGEN, the small upper tier of estate-bottled wine has guaranteed

Mosel Riesling a high profile and devoted following abroad, which has affected the German market as well.

Geography

The **Lower Mosel**, also known as **Terrassen Mosel**, boasts the highest percentage of Riesling vines in the Mosel, if only a minority of its top sites. Curving downstream from Zell to the confluence of the Rhine and Mosel at Koblenz, it incorporates many small, steep vineyards whose terraces often date back centuries and which can be maintained only by hand. Monorails have been installed in many places to ease access. Labour intensity as well as the susceptibility of these sheer rocky slopes to DROUGHT have historically put this subregion at a commercial disadvantage relative to its neighbours upstream. Variations on Devonian slate, frequently rich in QUARTZITE, dominate the soils, though SANDSTONE and occasionally CALCAREOUS rock put in appearances. The precipitous walls of slate outside Koblenz at Winningen—most notably the Uhlen and Röttgen vineyards—are regaining a reputation for high ripeness and excellence that was essentially forgotten for nearly a century, a revival led by the Heymann-Löwenstein estate. Upriver from Winningen, in Kobern, Gondorf, Lehmen, Kattenes, and Hatzenport, several estates are demonstrating Riesling's delicious potential. Numerous villages above and below Cochem still harbour significant Riesling plantings, although their wines are scarcely recognized by name even inside Germany. At Bremm, the terraced Calmont rises 200 m/656 ft from the river. With a 65% incline, it is one of the world's steepest vineyards and, like sites immediately upstream in Neef, St Aldegrund, and Alf, its potential is being demonstrated and its vine presence hanging on for dear life thanks to a few intrepid growers able to access their vineyards using sure, stout feet and hair-raising monorails.

Of perhaps 100 EINZELLAGEN with outstanding potential in the Mosel, over half are in the **Middle Mosel**, which extends upstream from Pünderich with its complex, slatey, crenulated Marienburg, a long, steep wall accessed by boat from the village. A roster of towns and their top sites, nearly all dominated by Devonian slate, includes Enkirch (Batterieberg, Ellergrub, Steffensberg, Zeppwingert), Wolf (Goldgrube), Kröv (a different Steffensberg), and Kinheim (Hubertuslay, Rosenberg). Along the bow of the Mosel between Enkrich and Wolf is the traditionally important merchant base and winegrowing centre of Traben-Trarbach, some of whose once-renowned sites (notably Traben's Gaispfad and Zollturm) cling to the Mosel's right bank. Others (Hühnerberg, Ungsberg, Schlossberg), happily subject to some ambitious recent reclamation, hug the steep, narrow valley of the Kautenbach as it rushes down to meet the Mosel at Trarbach. The red slate of Erden (Treppchen and Prälat) generates some of the Mosel's most celebrated Rieslings, with a prominent citrus and green herb character, and the potential of adjacent Lösnicher Försterlay has recently been demonstrated by prolific winegrower Ernst Loosen (Weingut Dr. Loosen). Neighbouring Ürzig, where virtually all of the top vineyards are united under the name Würzgarten, gives the best Erdeners a run for their money with frequently spicy and strawberry- or kiwi-scented Rieslings from diverse soils prominently including iron-rich, finely eroded Permian sandstone unique in the Mosel.

Below Ürzig the Mosel inscribes one of its periodic tight turns and then enters a straight stretch whose south-facing slopes enjoy international fame—Zeltingen (Himmelreich, Schlossberg, Sonnenuhr), Wehlen (Sonnenuhr), Graach (Himmelreich, Domprobst), and Bernkastel, renowned for its Doctor vineyard—but whose wines from other vineyard sites, including Graben and Lay, are more often labelled for the GROSSLAGE Badstube. Apple, citrus, vanilla, and nut-oil notes typify many of the wines from these sites, as well as, in the case of Bernkastel, a characteristic black-cherry note.

After another twist, the river flows past Lieser (Niederberg Helden) and a side valley at Mühlheim (Sonnenlay) and Veldenz (Elisenberg, Grafschafter Sonnenberg), all three towns getting well-deserved recent exposure in the hands of talented winegrowers. Next comes Brauneberg (Juffer, Juffer Sonnenuhr), whose unusually well-watered walls of south-east–facing slate enjoyed an eminent position in the Mosel pecking order throughout the 19th century. The late 20th century revival of their reputation for stunningly rich yet refined Rieslings (and, indeed, of the reputation of Mosel Riesling as a whole) owes much to the viticultural and promotional labours of Wilhelm Haag (1937– 2013), proprietor of Weingut Fritz Haag and president of the VDP-Mosel from 1984 to 2004. Kesten (Paulinsberg, Paulinshofberg) and Wintrich (Geierslay, Ohligsberg) are also producing impressive Rieslings.

Astride a tight loop in the Mosel hang the amphitheatrical slopes of Piesport, whose Goldtröpfchen site is among the region's best and internationally best-known (although the adjacent Domherr, Grafenberg, Kreuzwingert, and Schubertslay have first-rate potential as well). Tropical and black fruit flavours characterize the best Piesport wines, but this village's name has been tarnished by mass volumes of mediocre wine labelled with the intentionally deceptive GROSSLAGE designation Piesporter Michelsberg. The clay- and iron-rich slate of Dhron, deployed along a tiny, eponymous tributary of the Mosel, is re-establishing a reputation for longevity and distinctive complexity that Riesling labelled Dhroner Hofberger commanded through the mid-20th century. One of the Mosel's narrowest switchbacks and most vertiginous walls of blue slate occurs upstream from Piesport at Trittenheim (Altärchen, Apotheke) and neighbouring Leiwen (Laurentiuslay), wines from the former being characteristically richer and from the latter sleeker and more distinctly mineral. Thanks to a bevy of winegrowing talents, the reputation of these sites is itself now steeply ascendant. Upstream, Thörnich (Ritsch), Detzem (Maximiner Klosterlay), and Pölich (Held) offer in the hands of a few winegrowers glimpses of superb potential. The same is true of vineyards just below Trier at Longuich (Herrenberg, Maximiner Herrenberg), where the abbey of St Maximin, arguably the pre-eminent medieval viticultural institution of the Mosel, established its main press house and planted a forest that has served successfully as a hail shield for five centuries. Some sites just below Longuich at Mehring (Blattenberg, Zellerberg) have potential, although their high CLAY component tends to result in a broader, less dynamic style of Riesling. Numerous historically prestigious sites in Trier are also being revived.

The Mosel tributaries **Saar** and **Ruwer** make up a mere 11% of the official Mosel growing region, but their reputation is out of proportion to their surface area. The higher elevation of their vineyards as well as the Saar's predominance of wind-open side valleys make for generally cooler conditions than in the Middle Mosel, and wine from these subregions traditionally derived its renown from brightness, animation, and clarity, preserved even in rich and BOTRYTIZED sweet wines. The traditional handicap was how often Riesling simply failed to adequately ripen, but there have been at most three vintages since 1987 that could be described in those terms.

The Ruwer vineyards begin at Eitelsbach and Mertesdorf and end barely 8 km/5 miles upstream. A long legacy of high quality combined with MONOPOLE vineyard status has made Eitelsbach's Karthäuserhofberg and Mertesdorf's Maximin Grünhaus (with its famed Abtsberg and Herrenberg vineyards) the Ruwer's best-known estates outside Germany, but Kasel, immediately upstream, boasts excellence and historical renown (from Nies'chen and Kehrnagel), while the potential of higher, cooler sites at Waldrach is being rediscovered. The Ruwer vineyards, dominated by grey and red slate, tend to promote flavours of red fruits, pungent green herbs, and brown spices.

Travelling upstream from the Saar's confluence with the Mosel near Trier comes a hairpin turn with outstanding vineyards along its right bank at Filzen and Kanzem, the latter's Altenberg among the Mosel's finest sites.

Across the river at Wawern, the Herrenberg and Goldberg—perpendicular to the river—are being revived. The Saar straightens to north–south orientation just upstream from Kanzem at Wiltingen, whose Braune Kupp, Gottesfuss, Kupp, and Hölle are all first-rate. But Wiltingen's towering Scharzhofberg—its fame nowadays rightly associated with the superb custodianship of successive Egon Müllers, and for centuries cited as one of the Mosel-area's greatest vineyards—does not lie along the Saar. Rather, with the neighbouring Braunfels, it faces south at the edge of an ancient bed of that river (or perhaps of the Mosel itself), which inscribes a roughly 10-km eastward crescent of important vineyards—some revived since the late 20th century, some still neglected—at Oberemmel (Agritiusberg, Hütte, Raul), Krettnach (Altenberg, Euchariusberg), Niedermennig (Herrenberg, Sonnenberg), and Falkenstein (Hofberg). Upstream from Wiltingen come Ayl (Kupp), Schoden (Herrenberg), and Ockfen (Bockstein). In a side valley, Geisberg—a site long deemed second only to Scharzhofberger and Bockstein—was reclaimed from scrub in 2015–17 by Weingut Van Volxem.

The EINZELLAGE Ayler Kupp is so large and heterogeneous that only recent registration of various cadastral designations has permitted labels to reflect a useful degree of specificity, while steep, elongated, uniquely cobbled, riverside Saarfeilser Marienberg straddles three communes, with consequently diverse labelling. Saarburg's dominant Rausch vineyard is another geological anomaly, for incorporating diabase as well as slate. Furthest upstream of the Saar's vineyards are those of Serrig (Herrenberg, Schloss Saarsteiner, Würtzberg) and, across the River Kastel, the tiny Maximiner Prälat, once among the gems of the medieval St Maximin abbey's necklace of vineyards, condemned in the early 21st century by its steepness and poor access to largely return to scrub.

Parallel to the vineyards along the Saar are those of the **Upper Mosel**, which hug that river's right bank above Trier. Here the Elbling grape dominates (with close to 500 ha/1,236 acres); Riesling is rare; and the soils are calcareous, like those in the adjacent left bank Moselle vineyards of LUXEMBOURG, whose prevalent AUXERROIS, PINOT GRIS, and PINOT BLANC are also planted on these German shores, along with Chardonnay that has recently displayed serious potential. D.S.

Carlberg, L., *Mosel Wine* (2022)

Pigott, S., *Wein Spricht Deutsch: Weine, Winzer, Weinlandschaften* (2007).

Reinhardt, S., *The Finest Wines of Germany* (2012).

Steinberg, E., *Understanding Mosel Wines* (2012).

Moselle, French name for the river known in German as MOSEL which rises in the Vosges Mountains of France, forms the border between LUXEMBOURG (in which it plays a key part in wine production) and Germany, and joins the River Rhine at Koblenz in Germany, 545 km/340 miles later.

In the far north of France, the Moselle AOC, with Côtes de TOUL, constitutes what the French call their *vins de Lorraine*, the last remnants of what was once an important and flourishing Lorraine wine industry. Extensive vineyards around Metz supplied PINOT NOIR grapes to Champagne in the 19th century, and Sparkling Moselle was a popular partner to Sparkling HOCK. After the region became German following the Franco-Prussian war of 1870, it provided base wine for SEKT. PHYLLOXERA did not arrive until 1910, but the poor-quality HYBRIDS chosen for replanting, together with industrialization (see RAILWAYS), the proximity of the First World War battlefields, and the end of the German outlet for the wines, hastened the decline of this wine region. Reduced to 10 ha in 1983, the vineyard is slowly recovering, reaching in 2021 almost 80 ha/198 acres and growing, as CLIMATE CHANGE has brought more warmth to this cool CONTINENTAL region, making it easier to achieve full grape RIPENESS. Today AUXERROIS, PINOT GRIS, and MÜLLER-THURGAU are the most common vine varieties; Pinot Blanc, Gewurztraminer, and Riesling are also permitted. Reds must be made entirely of Pinot Noir; rosés may incorporate GAMAY.

As a result of the success of some German wines in the English-speaking world, Moselle became a GENERIC name for any light, medium-dry, faintly aromatic wine.

Mosel-Saar-Ruwer, from 1971 to 2007 the official name, incorporating the names of two major tributaries, that appeared on all labels of wine from the German growing region now known simply as MOSEL.

mother vine, an identified, preferred individual vine from which CUTTINGS or other vegetative propagation materials are taken. They are normally the consequence of CLONAL SELECTION and VINE improvement programmes. Such vines, including fruiting varieties and ROOTSTOCKS, are certified only if they have been tested for VIRUS DISEASES. The manager of the mother vines must be on guard for changes in mother-vine disease status, due to insect-vectored virus diseases or fungal infection in pruning wounds leading to TRUNK DISEASE, for example. The latter is the common explanation for the continuing spread of trunk diseases by BENCH GRAFTING. R.E.S.

moths, the larval stages of one or several small leafroller (tortricid) moth species, damage grapes in almost all winegrowing regions of the world. Despite the name, most of these species do not 'roll leaves' but mainly feed on flowers and fruit, resulting in yield reductions of up to 10%, often multiplied by secondary infections. In Europe the main species are the **European grapevine moth** (*Lobesia botrana*), also known as eudemis, and the **vine moth** (*Eupoecilia ambiguella*), also known as cochylis, with occasional outbreaks of the **grape tortrix** (*Argyrotaenia ljungiana*) and the **long palped tortrix** (*Sparganothis pilleriana*); in North America the **grape berry moth** (*Paralobesia viteana*), the **orange tortrix moth** (*Argyrotaenia citrana*), and the omnivorous leafroller (*Platynota stultana*), which does form the leaf into a roll, restricting the exposed leaf surface; and in Australia the **light brown apple moth** (*Epiphyas postvittana*) and in New Zealand the **grapevine moth** (*Phalaenoides glycine*). Most of these species can also develop on other (wild) host plants around the vineyard and transfer to the vines.

These species generally have several generations per season, the first generation attacking flowering stages or leaves and later generations the fruit stage. The larval feeding causes little direct damage, but feeding punctures in berries can increase the risk of BOTRYTIS BUNCH ROT or other infections, including several fungi of the genus *Aspergillus* that can produce a mycotoxin (OCHRATOXIN A).

Accidental introductions of several of these species have occurred worldwide, even in the recent past: European grapevine moth to Japan, Chile, Argentina, and California (2009, Napa Valley, eradicated 2014); light brown apple moth to North America (2007), Hawaii, and New Zealand.

A few other species of moths (Tortricidae but also from the Sphingidae, Pyralidae, Zygaenidae, and Noctuidae families) that mainly feed on the leaves or buds can be found in vineyards, but these are generally considered of minor importance.

Leafroller damage is very variable depending on the climate, seasonal weather, surrounding landscape (other vineyards and vegetation), and control by different natural enemies such as parasitic wasps (egg parasitoids and pupal parasitoids) and flies and predatory lacewings, BEETLES, true bugs (hemiptera), spiders, harvestmen (daddy longlegs), bats, etc.

Monitoring of these pests is a key factor for successful INTEGRATED PEST MANAGEMENT. Adults are generally monitored using PHEROMONE or food traps; eggs and larvae can be counted. Long-running area-wide surveillance networks such as in the St-Émilion region of France (www.gdon-libournais.fr) are very successful in monitoring risks, determining observation periods, and improving sustainable management.

Intervention thresholds are very difficult to establish because of the risk of secondary infection (botrytis) and the influence of climatic conditions on both all insect stages and the associated secondary fungal infections.

When population levels are high enough to require control, the measures are mainly based on mating disruption or insecticides (see PESTICIDES). In ORGANIC VITICULTURE, disrupting mating as well as organic pesticides such as BT (*Bacillus thuringiensis*) allow sufficient control if applied at the right developmental stage, between egg-hatching and the caterpillars entering the berries. Attempts at biological control using natural enemies such as egg parasitoids have been largely unsuccessful. The use of the sterile insect technique to eradicate incursions in new areas is being studied, but mass rearing of tortricid is difficult.

See also BEETLES for a European insect which causes leaf rolling. M.v.H.

Bettiga, L. J., (ed.), *Grape Pest Management* (3rd edn, 2013).

Gilligan, T. M., et al., 'Discovery of *Lobesia botrana* ([Denis & Schiffermüller]) in California: an invasive species new to North America (Lepidoptera: Tortricidae)', *Proceedings of the Entomological Society of Washington*, 113/1 (2011), 14–30.

Moueix, important family in the BORDEAUX TRADE, notably, but by no means exclusively, in ST-ÉMILION and POMEROL. The Moueix family came from the Corrèze, a severe district in central France, noted for its hard-headed men. Jean Moueix (1882–1957) bought Ch Fonroque in St-Émilion in 1930, and his son Jean-Pierre (1913–2003) joined him that year, with the purpose of selling only the hitherto somewhat neglected wines, nearly all red, produced on the RIGHT BANK of the Dordogne, from the Côtes de CASTILLON downstream to BLAYE. In 1937, Jean-Pierre formed Établissements Jean-Pierre Moueix on the quay in LIBOURNE. Increasingly successful in the post-war period, it became from 1970 the major NÉGOCIANT there selling the finer châteaux wines, at a time when the traditional merchants were failing.

In 1956, the 70-year-old firm of Duclot in the city of Bordeaux was acquired to deal mainly with the 'left bank' districts (MÉDOC, GRAVES, etc.), as well as selling direct to private customers in France. As Duclot Export it is prominent in the export trade. From 1968 Duclot has been headed by Jean-Pierre's elder son Jean-François (b. 1945), now aided substantially by his son Jean (b. 1987).

In 1970, the younger son, Christian (b. 1946), became a director of J. P. Moueix, with special responsibilities, along with the firm's OENOLOGIST Jean-Claude Berrouet, for the 17 estates owned or farmed by the firm. In 1982 Christian started a JOINT VENTURE in Yountville, NAPA Valley, with two daughters of John Daniel, former owner of Inglenook, before buying them out in 1994. From a 50-ha/124-acre vineyard and an architectural landmark winery opened in 1998, a Bordeaux-style wine named Dominus is produced. He now runs the Libourne négociant with his son Edouard, who lives in what was Ch Belair in St-Émilion and is now Bélair-Monange, incorporating the vines of Magdelaine next door.

In the 1950s, Jean-Pierre Moueix began to acquire châteaux on the right bank: La Fleur-Pétrus (1950 and now much expanded), Trotanoy (1953), Lagrange (1953), La Grave (Trigant de Boisset) (1971), and Certan-Giraud, renamed Hosanna (1999), in Pomerol; and Magdelaine (1952) in St-Émilion.

In the 1970s and 1980s, the firm expanded into FRONSAC, acquiring Canon, Canon de Brem, La Croix-Canon, and Canon-Moueix in the superior Canon-Fronsac appellation and La Dauphine in Fronsac. These properties were sold en masse in 2000.

A number of other properties are farmed on behalf of their owners, including Chx Lafleur-Gazin, farmed since 1976 and purchased in 2021, and Latour-Pomerol in Pomerol. However, much the most important acquisition was a half-share of PETRUS in 1964. Jean-François Moueix and his children now own it all.

Jean-Pierre Moueix, a man of great probity and courtesy, was a notable collector of art and books, and the château in which he lived beside the river Dordogne on the edge of Libourne was once full of the works of such leading modern artists as Picasso and Francis Bacon, some of them fetching record prices at auction after his demise. E.P.-R. & J.R.

mouldy, pejorative tasting term to describe an aroma or flavour that permeates a wine and reduces the fruity, fresh character. The most common source of the mouldy flavour is disease-infected fruit that has not been properly sorted or treated during processing to remove such flavour. See ROT, FUNGAL DISEASES.

Another source of mouldy character is COOPERAGE. When barrels are left empty, it is important to preserve them from mould growth or bacterial spoilage. Generally this is managed by using SULFUR DIOXIDE as an antimicrobial agent, and the barrels must be carefully checked before refilling. See BARREL MAINTENANCE. The word 'mouldy', along with 'musty' or 'mushroomy', is also used to describe a wine that is affected by CORK TAINT. K.C.

Moulin-à-Vent means 'windmill' in French, and the name describes the landmark that denotes one of the most famous BEAUJOLAIS crus. Originally it denoted a small, highly ranked CRU within Romanèche-Thorins, but it has expanded to include 632 ha/1,561 acres in Chénas and Romanèche, as much as anything a reflection of the market power of the name. A vein of MANGANESE running through GRANITE near the two towns' border has often explained the stiffer TANNINS and bite of the wines, as well as their ability to age, but the soils are more varied than usually described, with variations in the granite as well as deep colluvium. The reputation has prompted higher prices for both wine and vines—€100,000 per hectare in 2019, making it the hardest cru in which to acquire land. Nonetheless, long-time properties like Ch des Jacques, owned by Louis JADOT, have been joined by recent arrivals such as Thibaut Liger-Belair and Richard Rottiers. J.F.B.

Moulis, or **Moulis-en-Médoc**, smallest of the six communal appellations of the HAUT-MÉDOC district of Bordeaux (the others being MARGAUX, ST-JULIEN, PAUILLAC, ST-ESTÈPHE, and neighbouring LISTRAC). Although it includes only about 600 ha/1,500 acres of vineyards, Moulis has a considerable diversity of TERROIR, in terms of both topography and soil composition. Countryside that is positively rolling by Médoc standards, and soils that include various GRAVELS, CLAYS, and LIMESTONE, result in wines as varied as the occasionally brilliant Ch Chasse-Spleen, the good-value Ch Maucaillou, and a host of properties whose names include the word 'Poujeaux'. The finest of these is usually long-lived Ch Poujeaux itself. Like Listrac, Moulis is not CLASSED GROWTH country. Perhaps because of this, the best wines can offer good value, being as well structured as any Haut-Médoc, often with some of the perfume of Margaux to the east.

Brook, S., *The Complete Bordeaux* (4th edn, 2022).

Mountain, 19th-century English term for MÁLAGA, which is indeed flanked by mountains. The name is no longer used (except by Spain's roving winemaker Telmo Rodriguez for his sweet golden Málaga) but is commonly found on DECANTER labels produced before PHYLLOXERA devastated the Málaga region in 1876.

Mount Barker, cool subregion of the Great Southern region, WESTERN AUSTRALIA, with a strongly CONTINENTAL climate especially suited to Riesling, Shiraz, and Cabernet Sauvignon. (Also a town in Australia's ADELAIDE HILLS.)

Mount Benson, cool-climate seaside wine region in the Limestone Coast Zone of SOUTH AUSTRALIA awarded its GEOGRAPHICAL INDICATION in 1997, the same year Michel CHAPOUTIER of the Rhône Valley began planting here. The region makes elegant, light- to medium-bodied wines, particularly Shiraz.

Mount Harlan, California wine region and AVA. See SAN BENITO.

Mount Lofty Ranges Zone encompasses the Adelaide Hills, Adelaide Plains, and Clare Valley wine regions in SOUTH AUSTRALIA.

Mount Veeder, California wine region and AVA on the NAPA side of the Mayacamas known for STRUCTURED, long-lived Cabernet Sauvignon.

Moura, DOC subregion of the southern part of Portugal's ALENTEJO with an extreme CONTINENTAL CLIMATE.

Mourisco, or **Mourisco do Minho**, minor dark-skinned Portuguese variety grown in the Beiras and Minho regions, known as Tinta Castañal over the border in Spain's Galicia. **Mourisco Branco** is CAYETANA BLANCA. **Mourisco Roxo** is MARUFO.

Mourvèdre, warm-climate red grape variety whose considerable fortunes in Spain have been declining (see MONASTRELL) while it has become markedly more fashionable elsewhere. Plantings in France, where it is enjoying a resurgence of popularity in the south, had grown to 9,385 ha/23,191 acres by 2019, the second biggest national total after Spain's. It cannot be grown successfully much further north than the southern Rhône, however, since it is so late ripening. It is the characteristic grape variety of BANDOL and is increasingly popular with producers of CHÂTEAUNEUF-DU-PAPE because it ripens at lower sugar levels than GRENACHE. In California and Australia it was often called Mataro but has been enjoying a new lease of life as either VARIETAL Mourvèdre or in a blend with Grenache and Syrah/Shiraz, sometimes called GSM.

Mourvèdre dominated Provence until the arrival of PHYLLOXERA and the search for productive vines to supply the burgeoning market for cheap TABLE WINE. For many decades it marked time in its French enclave Bandol (in 1968 total French plantings were as little as 900 ha) but is now regarded as an extremely modish and desirable 'improving variety' throughout the Languedoc and Roussillon, especially now that CLONES have been selected which no longer display the inconveniently variable YIELDS once resulting from degenerated vine stock.

In southern France, Mourvèdre produces wines considered useful for their STRUCTURE, intense fruit, and, in good years, perfume often redolent of blackberries. The structure in particular can be a useful foil for Grenache in Provence and for Cinsaut further west. In Bandol, it is typically blended with both of these, and the statutory minimum for Mourvèdre is now 50%. Mourvèdre is condoned in a host of AOC regulations all over the south of France from GRIGNAN-LES-ADHÉMAR to COLLIOURE, including CHÂTEAUNEUF-DU-PAPE and environs. It usually plays a useful supporting role, being fleshier than Syrah, tauter than Grenache and Cinsaut, and more charming than Carignan. Somewhat belatedly, Australia realized it had all the wherewithal to produce authentic Rhône blends, despite the loss of precious old-vine Grenache and Mourvèdre in South Australia in the late 1980s (due to an ill-advised VINE-PULL SCHEME). Old-vine Grenache–Shiraz–Mourvèdre (or any combinations thereof) have proliferated since the 1990s as resources have been moved from fortified to table-wine production, although plantings of Mourvèdre, still called Mataro in official statistics, had fallen to 751 ha/1,856 acres by 2015.

Although grown at least since the 1870s, California's unfashionable Mataro was fast disappearing until the RHÔNE RANGERS made the connection with Mourvèdre and pushed up demand for wine from these historic stumps, notably in Contra Costa County between San Francisco and the Central Valley, where there were considerable new plantings in the early 1990s thanks to demand from the likes of Bonny Doon and Cline Cellars. By 2020 the state's total plantings had risen to 483 ha/1,194 acres. Rhône mania spread north to Washington, where there were 165 acres in 2011, but this fell back down to 126 acres in 2017. South Africa had 495 ha/1,223 acres in 2020. It is also grown on Cyprus.

mousse, French term for FIZZINESS.

mousseux, French for 'sparkling'. Some *mousseux* wines are made by the traditional method (see SPARKLING WINEMAKING), while others may be made by the much less painstaking TANK METHOD.

mousy, TASTING TERM commonly associated with a wine FAULT that is extremely difficult to recognize. It cannot be detected aromatically, only when the wine is tasted, and sometimes the flavour of a dirty mouse cage does not develop until after the wine has been swallowed. About one-third of the population are unable to taste the compounds responsible, making it an extremely elusive fault.

The three main chemicals responsible for the fault are 2-acetyltetrahydropyridine (ACTPY), 2-ethyltetrahydropyridine (ETPY), and 2-acetylpyrroline (ACPY). It is difficult to measure in wine, and according to the AWRI the chemicals are present in micrograms per litre.

Research has shown this fault to be microbial in origin and most closely linked with species from the *Lactobacillus* family, responsible for MALOLACTIC CONVERSION. Current studies are also looking at a separate chemical pathway, but this will require further work to fully understand the mechanism.

Although it is not known why some wines are affected and others not, it is clear that those made using winemaking practices that create an environment conducive to microbial activity will be more vulnerable to mousiness. This includes using low levels of SULFUR DIOXIDE or adding SO_2 only after MALOLACTIC CONVERSION, wines with high PH or with high levels of solids after fermentation, and poor control of a wine's exposure to oxygen during ageing. With the increase in low-SO_2 wines and extended LEES CONTACT, it appears that this fault is on the rise. K.C.

Goode, J., *Flawless: Understanding Faults in Wine* (2018).

www.awri.com.au/industry_support/winemaking_resources/sensory_assessment/recognition-of-wine-faults-and-taints/wine_faults/#mousiness

moût de raisins partiellement fermenté issu de raisins passerillés is the cumbersome French name for partially fermented grape must extracted from raisined grapes and is a term used on labels of some French SWEET WINES, since ALSACE, JURANÇON, and GAILLAC have exclusive rights to VENDANGES TARDIVES. According to EU regulations, the must has to have a total sugar content of at least 272 g/l and the finished wine at least 8% alcohol.

mouthfeel, non-specific tasting term, used to refer to tactile attributes such as smoothness but also to heat (see ALCOHOLIC STRENGTH), VISCOSITY, and the sensation of weight in the mouth. For more detail, see diagram and TEXTURE.

Gawel, R., et al., 'A mouth-feel wheel: terminology for communicating the mouth-feel characteristics of red wine', *Australian Journal of Grape and Wine Research*, 6 (2000), 203–7.

Mouton Cadet, the most successful Bordeaux BRAND, began life in 1927, a poor vintage in which Baron Philippe de ROTHSCHILD created what was effectively a SECOND WINE called Carruades de Mouton for Ch MOUTON ROTHSCHILD, but it was not a success. Its successor in 1930 was named Mouton-Cadet, since Philippe was the *cadet*, the youngest, of the family. Eventually, as Mouton Cadet, it developed a prosperous life of its own, and demand was so great that the flexibility of the BORDEAUX AOC appellation was needed.

Today Mouton Cadet is available in red, white, rosé, and organic versions, having been repackaged and reblended in 2004 to rely predominantly on FRUIT-DRIVEN Merlot and Sauvignon Blanc, with tighter control over the 250 growers and seven winemakers involved in its production.

Mouton Rothschild, Château, important wine estate in PAUILLAC in the BORDEAUX wine region and the only one ever to have been promoted within the 1855 CLASSIFICATION, to FIRST GROWTH.

Originally part of the LAFITE estate with which it is intermingled, it became in the middle of the 18th century a separate entity, owned by the de Brane family. In the first half of the following century, Baron Hector de Brane (or Branne) became known as 'the Napoleon of the vines' for his work in developing the Médoc vineyards and, in company with his neighbour Armand d'Armailhacq, in supposedly introducing the

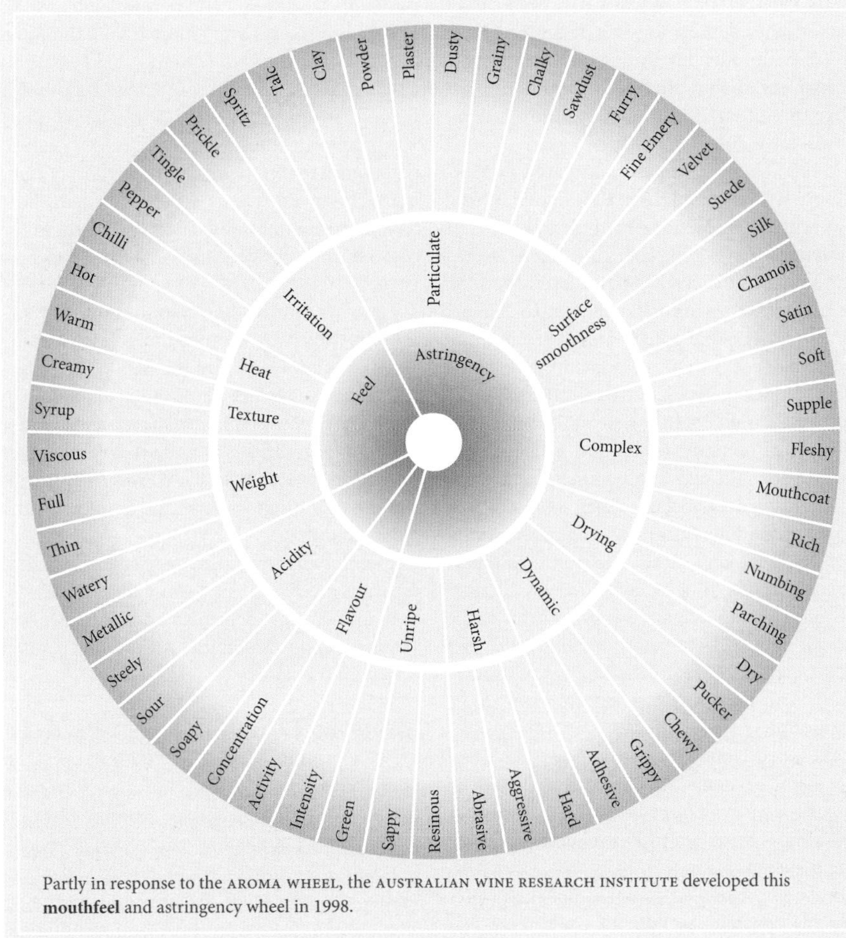

Partly in response to the AROMA WHEEL, the AUSTRALIAN WINE RESEARCH INSTITUTE developed this **mouthfeel** and astringency wheel in 1998.

CABERNET SAUVIGNON vine. In 1830, he sold Mouton to a M. Thuret and retired to his Ch Brane-Cantenac in the commune of MARGAUX. At this time, Mouton had little international repute, and the first entry in a Christie's AUCTION catalogue was in 1834. In 1853, Thuret sold it to Baron Nathaniel de ROTHSCHILD, of the English branch of the family, two years before the 1855 classification which placed Mouton Rothschild at the top of the second growths, a position unsatisfactory to the family but not seriously contested until Baron Philippe de Rothschild took over the running of it from his father in 1922. He startled Bordeaux by employing a poster artist, Carlu, to design an art-deco label, including the Rothschild arrows, for the 1924 vintage and then proposing CHÂTEAU BOTTLING of all the first growths (and Mouton Rothschild). He also instigated what was initially a SECOND WINE, called MOUTON CADET.

On his return in 1945 after the Second World War, Baron Philippe initiated the series of ARTISTS' LABELS, each year designed by a well-known artist, including Cocteau, Braque, Dali, Bacon, and Henry Moore. He also began a campaign to elevate Mouton to first-growth status, which he achieved in 1973. He and his American wife Pauline created a magnificent Musée du Vin, or wine museum, filled with *objets d'art* and open to the public since 1962 on application. In 2013 a new vat room was inaugurated as well as an exhibition space for the artworks which have illustrated the Mouton labels so famously and have been exhibited around the world.

The 80-ha/200-acre vineyard is planted with 80% CABERNET SAUVIGNON grapes, 16% MERLOT (much increased in the late 1990s), 3% CABERNET FRANC, and 1% PETIT VERDOT. Average production is 13,000–16,000 cases. After she succeeded her father Baron Philippe de Rothschild in 1988, Baroness Philippine de Rothschild introduced a second wine, Petit Mouton de Mouton Rothschild, in 1994 and a dry white AOC Bordeaux, Aile d'Argent, in 1991. Since her death in 2014, the estate has been owned by her three children. The wine is famously concentrated and intensely aromatic in good vintages. See ROTHSCHILDS for details of other wine investments and JOINT VENTURES. E.P.-R. & J.R.

Herman, S., and Pascal, J., *Mouton Rothschild, The Museum of Wine in Art* (2003).

movies about wine. See FILMS ABOUT WINE.

Moza Fresca, GALICIAN name for the grape known as SÍRIA in Portugal.

MRL. See RESIDUES and AGROCHEMICALS.

MS. Abbreviation for MASTER SOMMELIER.

Mtsvane, name of two distinct light-skinned, high-quality varieties grown in GEORGIA: the more widely planted **Mtsvane Kakhuri**, meaning 'green from Kakheti', often referred to simply as Mtsvane, and **Goruli Mtsvane**, meaning 'green from Gori', planted in Kartli and Imereti.

Mudgee, inland wine region in NEW SOUTH WALES. The name is an Aboriginal word meaning 'nest in the hills', and indeed the region is perched at about 450 m/1,500 ft up the western slopes of the Great Dividing Range. The cooler temperatures at this ELEVATION and the wide DIURNAL TEMPERATURE RANGE allow for harvests up to four weeks longer than in neighbouring Hunter Valley. The region is most known for generous, bold Cabernet Sauvignon and Shiraz, yet it is also capable of making crisp, ageworthy Riesling. Forward-thinking producers are also focusing on Italian and Mediterranean varieties including Zinfandel, Tempranillo, Graciano, Touriga Nacional, Nebbiolo, Sangiovese, and Barbera. A.R.P.

mulch, materials put on the vineyard soil surface to assist vine growth. Mulch is useful because it keeps soil damp, stops it becoming too hot, and hinders the growth of weeds. Mulches are generally composed of ORGANIC MATTER, providing NUTRIENTS for the vine's growth as the mulch decomposes. Organic mulches have a desirable effect on SOIL HEALTH, by increasing microbial populations and diversity. A common indicator of this is more EARTHWORM activity, related to improved SOIL STRUCTURE and better water infiltration.

Animal manure and straw were common mulches of the past, but in some modern vineyards these have been replaced with thin plastic film. Young vines are planted through the plastic. The response of young vine growth to plastic is often remarkable, especially for vineyards which rely on rainfall rather than IRRIGATION for their water supply. The film controls weed growth, stops water evaporating from the soil surface, and in spring warms the soil, promoting root growth. After a few years the plastic film rips and is blown around the vineyard, possibly presenting disposal problems.

A major disadvantage to straw mulch has been the cost of placing a sufficiently deep mat below each vine. This cost can be reduced by modern techniques of mechanically unrolling bales of hay or, alternatively, by throwing the straw under the vine as the COVER CROP is mown.

Organically farmed vineyards use mulches of living plants as well as dead material. The main disadvantage of living mulches for the young vines is that there may be too much competition for water and nutrients, and so the living mulch may need to be killed off. However, when a thick plant mulch breaks down, then nutrients are released and the soil is improved. Both living and dead organic mulches can cause problems because of INSECTS and FUNGI which can be harboured in the litter around the vine trunk. Generally speaking, however, mulch has more positive than negative effects in the vineyard. R.E.S.

Elmore, C., et al., 'Four weed management systems compared: mulch plus herbicides effectively control vineyard weeds', *California Agriculture*, 51/2 (1997), 14–18.

mulled wine is wine that has been heated with sugar and spices and also, sometimes, slices of fruit and even brandy. This was a particularly common way of serving wine in the Middle Ages, since honey and spices helped to compensate for any shortcomings in wine QUALITY (which were likely to be considerable as the months since the HARVEST wore on, in an age when wine was served directly from the barrel). The verb 'mull' was current at least from the beginning of the 17th century. Recipes vary but red wine is almost invariably used, and cinnamon and cloves are common. It is far less difficult to make good mulled wine than to find DRINKING VESSELS that retain the heat but are not uncomfortably hot to hold.

Müllerrebe, meaning 'miller's grape', is the common, and logical, name for Germany's selection of PINOT MEUNIER, also misleadingly known as Schwarzriesling, grown on 1,807 ha/4,465 acres, mainly in Württemberg, southern Germany, where it is a local speciality.

Müller-Thurgau, waning white grape variety which could fairly be said to have been the bane of German wine production. This cross was developed in 1882 for entirely expedient reasons by a Dr Hermann Müller, born in the Swiss canton of Thurgau but then working at the German viticultural station at GEISENHEIM. His understandable aim was to combine the quality of the great RIESLING grape with the viticultural reliability, particularly the early ripening, of SILVANER. Most of the variety's synonyms (Rivaner in Luxembourg and Slovenia, Riesling-Silvaner in Switzerland, Rizlingszilvani in Hungary) reflect this combination. Late 20th century DNA PROFILING by researchers at Geilweilerhof established that the variety is actually Riesling × Madeleine Royale, a now-extinct TABLE GRAPE of unknown parentage obtained from a cross made in 1845. The variety is all too short on Riesling characteristics, typically smelling vaguely peachy with a fat, flaccid mid PALATE, too often with a slight suspicion of rot, to which its rather large, thin-skinned berries are prone.

The vine certainly ripens early, even earlier than Silvaner. Unlike Riesling, it can be grown anywhere, producing prodigious quantities—sometimes double Riesling's common yield range of 80 to 110 hl/ha (4.6–6.3 tons/acre)—of extremely dull, flabby wine.

Müller-Thurgau was not embraced by Germany's growers until after the Second World War, when the need to rebuild the industry fast presumably gave this productive, easily grown vine allure. In the early 1970s, it even overtook the great Riesling in total area planted (having for some time produced far more wine in total) and remained in that position throughout the 1980s. Typically blended with a little of a more aromatic variety such as MORIO-MUSKAT and with a great deal of SÜSSRESERVE, Müller-Thurgau was transformed into oceans of QUALITÄTSWEIN sugarwater labelled either LIEBFRAUMILCH or one of the internationally recognized names such as Niersteiner, Bernkasteler, or Piesporter (see GROSSLAGEN). But by the late 1990s, Riesling was once again Germany's most planted grape variety—although at more than 11,453 ha/28,301 acres in 2020, total plantings of Müller-Thurgau in Germany are arguably still (too?) significant.

The wood is much softer than Riesling's and can easily be damaged by hard winters. The grapes rot easily (as can be tasted in a number of examples from less successful years), and the vine is susceptible to DOWNY MILDEW, BLACK ROT, and, its own bane, ROTBRENNER, but it will presumably continue to flourish while there is a market for cheap German wine.

Outside Germany it can be much more exciting. In northern Italy's ALTO ADIGE, where extensive acreage of ancient vines testifies to the promotional success by early proponents of Dr Müller's cross, bottlings from easily a score of today's best domaines and grower CO-OPERATIVES testify to the refinement, MINERALITY, COMPLEXITY, and sheer refreshment value that is possible with Müller-Thurgau—just not, it seems, in Germany. Most of the best Alto Adige wines are grown on very steep, stony, high-ELEVATION sites of which Tiefenbrunner's Feldmarschall is one extreme example, but there are others in the VALLE ISARCO. Italy's total area planted in 2015 was 1,296 ha/3,202 acres.

The variety thrives all over central and eastern Europe. It is planted, appropriately enough, in SWITZERLAND, playing an important role in the vineyards of the German-speaking area in the north and east, notably in the canton of Thurgau. In AUSTRIA (where it is sometimes called Rivaner) total area planted had fallen to 1,311 ha/3,240 acres by 2021, mainly in the Weinviertel, where it makes generally light, inconsequential wines. Across Austria's southern border, it is also grown in eastern SLOVENIA (as Rizvanec) and is even more important to the east and north of Austria in CZECHIA and HUNGARY. As Rizlingszilvani, it covers more than a thousand hectares of vineyard around Lake Balaton and produces lakesful of flabby Badacsonyi Rizlingszilvani. In the 1970s Müller-Thurgau was planted enthusiastically by New Zealand grape-growers on the recommendation of visiting German experts as a preferable substitute for the HYBRIDS that were all too prevalent in the country's nascent wine industry, but it has now virtually disappeared.

Elsewhere in the New World, most growers are not driven by the need for early-ripening varieties (and would find the flab in the resultant wine a distinct disadvantage), although some Oregon growers have had success with it (28 ha/69 acres in 2018), and credible examples have been produced in the cooler vineyards of western Washington State, for example in the Puget Sound AVA.

Two of Northern Europe's smallest and coolest wine producers, ENGLAND and LUXEMBOURG, have in their time depended heavily on Müller-Thurgau, and it is still the most widely planted variety in the latter.

Munson, T. V. (1843–1913), Texan credited with putting PHYLLOXERA-resistant roots on French vines and saving Europe's vineyards from devastation. Thomas Volney Munson was a lifelong student of viticulture, especially AMERICAN VINE SPECIES. At Kentucky University he became interested in TEXAS and its grapes and journeyed tens of thousands of miles in 40 states gathering WILD VINE specimens and studying soils and climates. He travelled by horseback and train, hunting from rail cars and jumping off to collect specimens whenever the train stopped. In 1876, Munson settled on the Red River near Denison in Texas, which he described as a 'grape paradise' because of the six or eight species of wild vines there. He developed a vineyard and NURSERY business as well as becoming the authority on the wild grape species of North America. Munson's passion was for VINE BREEDING, and he produced about 300 varieties using local VITIS species *lincecumii*, *champini*, and *candicans*. None, however, became commercially important.

Being aware of phylloxera's predations in Europe, Munson began GRAFTING European vines to American species as ROOTSTOCKS to grant resistance. He passed on the results of his research to Viala, Planchon, and other French experts. In the 1880s and 1890s, French growers accordingly imported huge quantities of American species for use as rootstocks, especially from Texas and Missouri. The French government made Munson a Chevalier du Mérite in 1888, only the second American to have achieved this honour (Thomas Edison having been the first). R.E.S.

Murray Darling, Australia's third largest winegrowing region straddling the Darling River and both sides of the Murray river in VICTORIA and NEW SOUTH WALES. The hot, dry region is dependent on IRRIGATION (the soils have little water-holding capacity, and growing-season rainfall is negligible) and high yields of low-cost grapes, the quality of which has risen as demanded by large companies competing internationally. Chardonnay, Shiraz, and Cabernet Sauvignon are mainstays, but the fraught issue of water availability has prompted interest in recent years in less water-intensive Italian and Mediterranean varieties.

E.N.H.M. & A.R.P.

Muscadel, or **Muskadel**, South African name for MUSCAT BLANC À PETITS GRAINS, used mainly when the variety is made into very sweet but not very modish JEREPIGO.

Muscadelle is the famous also-ran third grape variety responsible, with SÉMILLON and SAUVIGNON BLANC, for the sweet white (and often duller dry white) wines of Bordeaux. By 2019 France's total plantings had fallen to 1,399 ha/3,457 acres, 704 ha of them in the Gironde, where the majority of Muscadelle vines are not in the great sweet white-wine areas of SAUTERNES but in the unfashionable and vast ENTRE-DEUX-MERS, including the fringe sweet-white appellations of PREMIÈRES CÔTES DE BORDEAUX, CADILLAC, LOUPIAC, and STE-CROIX-DU-MONT. Muscadelle is relatively more important to BERGERAC than to Bordeaux, and it is valued as the finest ingredient in some of the best MONBAZILLAC.

Unrelated to any member of the MUSCAT group, the variety shares a vaguely grapey aroma with them but has its relatively ancient origins in SOUTH WEST FRANCE. DNA PROFILING has shown a parent–offspring relationship with the prolific GOUAIS BLANC. The usefully productive Muscadelle leafs late and ripens early and has rarely demonstrated great subtlety in the wines it produces. The occasional VARIETAL French Muscadelle can demonstrate a certain 'green' tang, but its use is almost exclusively in blends, adding the same sort of youthful fruitiness to south-western sweet whites as PINOT MEUNIER does to the north-east sparkling whites called CHAMPAGNE.

The variety known as Sauvignon Vert in California is Muscadelle. In only one corner of the wine world does Muscadelle produce sensational varietal wine: TOPAQUE in Australia. For years Australians thought the grape they called Tokay, which produced these dark, syrupy, wood-matured concentrates for after-dinner drinking, was Hungarian, but the French AMPELOGRAPHER Paul Truel identified it as Muscadelle in 1976. Total national plantings stood at 92 ha/227 acres by 2015, one-third of them in RUTHERGLEN.

Muscadet, one of France's dry white commodity wines currently undergoing revolution while trying to survive. The Muscadet region extends east and south of Nantes near the mouth of the Loire on a shrinking vineyard area of 7,900 ha/19,500 acres in 2020 of gently rolling, Atlantic-dominated countryside that is 95% devoted to one grape variety, MELON de Bourgogne, also nicknamed Muscadet. Known in Burgundy since the 13th century, this vigorous yet subtle variety came to prominence in the Pays Nantais after the terrible 1709 winter revealed its cold hardiness, and the DUTCH WINE TRADE understood its suitability as distilling material for their *brandewijn*. This, doubled by the hastily made, diluted production of the 1980s and 1990s, delayed to recent times the recognition of Melon for TERROIR-driven, long-lived wines.

All Muscadet appellations combined produce the largest quantity of dry white wines in the entire Loire, with **Muscadet Sèvre-et-Maine** representing 75% of the planted surface (6,000 ha/14,800 acres) and of the volume when not depleted by FROST and MILDEW. Named after two small rivers which flow through this, the oldest AOC of the region (1936) is a geological mosaic of metamorphic mica-SCHIST, GNEISS and amphibolite, igneous GRANITE and gabbro, and quaternary SAND and CLAY, leading to a wide spectrum of expressions from crisp and fresh to concentrated and ambitious. To the north-east, **Muscadet Coteaux de la Loire**, also created in 1936, covers 170 ha/420 acres around Ancenis producing a more generous style from steep SLATE slopes, while to the west the 220 ha/540 acres of the flatter and sandier **Muscadet Côtes de Grandlieu** (1994) make briny and vivid wines on the shore of the eponymous lake in the south-west of the region. **Muscadet** is the basic appellation, second in area (1,600 ha/3,960 acres) and volume, producing more generic wines authorized since 2020 to include 10% CHARDONNAY in the blend while forbidding SUR LIE on the label.

Strictly regulated, 'sur lie' requires the wine to be kept on the LEES and bottled between March and November of the year following the harvest, a practice inherited from the tradition of the 'wedding barrel' kept over the winter. The LEES CONTACT helps to balance the high-acid verve of Melon as MALOLACTIC CONVERSION is historically prevented in the large, underground concrete tanks commonly used. Some PRIMEUR wine is also made.

Since the mid 1980s, in reaction to the wine's poor reputation, the most dynamic producers have been experimenting with such techniques as BARREL FERMENTATION, LEES STIRRING, and, more recently, malolactic conversion, vinification in AMPHORA, and SKIN CONTACT. Yet the most substantial evolution of the Muscadet de Sèvre-et-Maine appellation has been the approval of the *crus communaux* in 2011. These geologically identified plots are subject to lower YIELDS (45 hl/ha) and extended ageing (18–24 months minimum depending on the cru, thus prohibiting the use of the 'sur lie' designation). Gorges (where the movement begun), Clisson, and Le Pallet were the first recognized, later joined by Goulaine, Château-Thébaud, Monnières St-Fiacre, and Mouzillon-Tillières, Vallet, La Haye-Fouassière, and Champtoceaux. While these crus represent a tiny minority of the production, they prove the region's potential for unique, long-lived, high-quality Muscadets while remaining great values.

Other wines produced in the Pays Nantais are GROS PLANT, Coteaux d'ANCENIS, and FIEFS VENDÉENS. See also LOIRE, including map. P.Le.

Muscadinia, a section of the botanical genus VITIS, although some botanists have suggested that it should be considered a separate genus rather than a section of *Vitis*. *Muscadinia* includes the two species *Vitis rotundifolia* (including *Vitis rotundifolia* var. *munsonia*) and *Vitis popenoei*, according to recent PHYLOGENIES. *Vitis* contains the true grapevine, also called *Euvitis*, as outlined in BOTANICAL CLASSIFICATION. *Muscadinia* and *Vitis* differ in chromosome number and morphology.

Members of the *Muscadiniae* occur only in the south-eastern United States and Mexico but seem related to *Vitis ludwigii* found as fossil seeds in Tertiary sediments of northern Europe. There is speculation that *Muscadinia* can be regarded as transitional between the temperate genus *Vitis* and *Ampelocissus*, which is adapted to tropical climates. Species of the three genera have similar characteristics.

The **Muscadines**, as they are called, typically have small bunches of large, thick-skinned berries and high yields. The better-known of the two species is *Vitis rotundifolia*, of which only SCUPPERNONG was grown commercially for winemaking until the second half of the 20th century. It has been supplanted by purple-skinned Noble and bronze-skinned Carlos. The very thick skins and musky flavour of Muscadines produce fruit and wine quite different from that of European VITIS VINIFERA vines. The berries have a thick, slippery pulp that is difficult to press, and excessive pressure brings bitterness from the skins. Muscadines are typically low in sugar concentration, usually requiring CHAPTALIZATION, but have medium to high ACIDITY and relatively high levels of antioxidants (see HEALTH).

A few thousand hectares of Muscadine grapes are grown in the cotton belt in the south-eastern United States.

The Muscadines have natural resistance to PIERCE'S DISEASE and can therefore be planted in some areas unsuitable for VITIS species and HYBRIDS of them. They are also usefully resistant to

PHYLLOXERA, NEMATODES, DOWNY MILDEW, and POWDERY MILDEW, which makes Muscadine germplasm valuable in VINE BREEDING. The different chromosome numbers of *Vitis* (2n = 38) and Muscadines (2n = 40) is a barrier to crossing the two sections, since progeny (2n = 39) are typically infertile. However, the development of rare, fertile *Euvitis* × *Muscadinia* interspecific hybrids has made possible their use in VINE IMPROVEMENT programmes.

R.E.S., J.V. & P.C.

Lu, J., et al., 'Interspecific hybridization between Vitis rotundifolia and Vitis vinifera and evaluation of the hybrids', *Acta Horticulturae*, 528 (2000), 479–86.

Hickey, C., et al., 'Muscadine (*Vitis rotundifolia* Michx., syn. *Muscadinia rotundifolia* (Michx.) Small): the resilient, native grape of the Southeastern U.S.', *Agriculture 9/6* (2019), 131.

Wan, Y., et al., 'A phylogenetic analysis of the grape genus (*Vitis* L.) reveals broad reticulation and concurrent diversification during neogene and quaternary climate change', *BMC Evolutionary Biology*, 13 (2013), 141.

Muscardin, red grape variety occasionally making a light, crisp, floral contribution to CHÂTEAUNEUF-DU-PAPE blends.

Muscat, one of the world's great and historic names, of both grapes and wines, that benefited from a FASHION in the early 2010s for wines labelled MOSCATO. Muscat grapes—and many different Muscat varieties, several closely related, in several hues of berry—are some of the very few which produce wines that actually taste of grapes. MUSCAT OF HAMBURG and MUSCAT OF ALEXANDRIA are grown as both wine grapes and TABLE GRAPES (although Hamburg is much better in the second role). MUSCAT BLANC À PETITS GRAINS is the oldest and finest, producing wines of the greatest intensity, while MUSCAT OTTONEL, paler in every way, is a relative parvenu. See also various MOSCATELS and MOSCATOS.

Muscat grapes were probably the first to be distinguished and identified and have grown around the Mediterranean for many, many centuries. With such strongly perfumed grapes (thanks to a particularly high concentration of MONOTERPENES), described in French as MUSQUÉ as though they were actually impregnated with musk, Muscat grapes have always been attractive to bees, and it was almost certainly Muscat grapes that the Greeks described as *anathelicon moschaton* and PLINY the Elder as *uva apiana*, 'grape of the bees'.

Muscat wines, carrying many different labels including Moscato (in Italy) and Moscatel (in Iberia), can vary from the refreshingly low-alcohol, sweet and frothy ASTI Spumante through Muscat d'ALSACE and other bone-dry Muscats, made for example in Roussillon, to sweet wines with alcohol levels of 15–20%, usually by MUTAGE (as in the VINS DOUX NATURELS of southern France and Greece). Since a high proportion of the world's Muscat is dark-berried, and since a wide variety of wood-ageing techniques are used, such wines can vary in colour from palest gold (as in some of the more determinedly modern MUSCATS DE FRONTIGNAN) to deepest brown (as in some of Australia's sweet, fortified Muscats. (See TOPAQUE AND MUSCAT.)

Most Muscat vines need relatively hot climates (although see MUSCAT OTTONEL and GERMAN HISTORY, in which the medieval cultivation of both light- and dark-berried Muscat vines is documented). There are or have been many famous Muscats around the Mediterranean. See MOROCCO, GREECE, SICILY, and SARDINIA.

Robinson, J., et al., *Wine Grapes: A Complete Guide to 1,368 Vine Varieties, Including Their Origins and Flavours* (2012).

Muscat Bailey A, A Japanese HYBRID (Bailey × MUSCAT OF HAMBURG) grape that is becoming a major variety for wine in JAPAN, producing a broad range of wines from rosé to medium-bodied reds. Sudo Wine and Takeda Winery in Yamagata Prefecture have the oldest wine-producing vines, 70–80 years old.

Muscat Blanc à Petits Grains is the cumbersome but descriptive full name of the oldest and most respected variety of Muscat with the greatest concentration of fine grape flavour, hinting at orange-flowers and spice. Its berries and seeds are, as its name suggests, particularly small, and they are round as opposed to the larger, oval berries of MUSCAT OF ALEXANDRIA—another synonym for this superior variety being Muscat à Petits Grains Ronds. But its berries are not, as its principal AMPELOGRAPHICAL name suggests, invariably white. In fact there are pink-, red-, and black-berried versions (although the dark berries are not so deeply pigmented that they can produce a proper red wine), and some vines produce berries whose colour varies considerably from vintage to vintage. Many synonyms for the variety include reference to the yellow or golden (*gallego, giallo, gelber*) colour of its berries. 'Brown Muscat' is one of Australia's names for a Muscat population that is more dark than light, resembling South Africa's Muscadel in that respect (thereby providing more evidence of early viticultural links between these two southern-hemisphere producers). *Wine Grapes* lists no fewer than 60 synonyms of this ancient variety, including Muscat of Frontignan, Frontignac, Muscat Blanc, Muscat d'Alsace, Muskateller, Moscato Bianco, Moscato d'Asti, Moscato di Canelli, Moscatel de Grano Menudo, Moscatel de Frontignan, Moscatel do Douro, Moscatel Galego Branco, Muscatel Branco, White Muscat, Muscat Canelli, and Muscadel. Any Muscat with the words 'Alexandria', 'Gordo', 'Romain', 'Hamburg' or 'Ottonel' in its name is *not* this superior variety.

This particular Muscat may well be the oldest known wine grape variety and the oldest cultivated in France, having been established in Gaul around Narbonne, notably at FRONTIGNAN, by the Romans—and possibly even before then brought to the Marseilles region by the Greeks. DNA PROFILING has found close genetic relationships between this Muscat and several modern Greek and Italian varieties such as MOSCHOFILERO and MALVASIA respectively. Muscat Blanc also seems to be a parent of several other varieties with Muscat in their name, including Muscat of Alexandria. Muscat Blanc has clearly been established for many centuries round the Mediterranean, where its early budding poses few problems. It was certainly already widely esteemed in the vineyards of Roussillon by the 14th century. It is Piemonte's oldest documented variety; is recorded as growing in Germany, as MUSKATELLER, as early as the 12th century; and is the first documented variety grown in Alsace, in the 16th century, suggesting that spring frosts may have been less common then, for the variety has now been replaced by the more accommodating Muscat Ottonel in Alsace.

Muscat Blanc also yields more conservatively than other Muscats and is sensitive to a wide range of diseases, which has naturally limited its cultivation—although it has travelled for so long and so widely that it is particularly widely distributed.

This is the Muscat that predominates in Italy, which has the single biggest area planted with it (see MOSCATO). In France, contrary to most other white grape varieties, this Muscat has been steadily gaining ground over many years but appears to have plateaued, with 7,357 ha/18,180 acres in 2019, plus just under 100 ha of the pink-berried mutation, mainly in the LANGUEDOC and ROUSSILLON, partly because of the development of dry, unfortified Muscat wine there. It has overtaken Muscat of Alexandria to become the most common white wine grape in Roussillon, and it is also important in the Hérault *département*. This is the Muscat solely responsible for France's golden sweet Muscats of BEAUMES-DE-VENISE, FRONTIGNAN, LUNEL, MIREVAL, and ST-JEAN-DE-MINERVOIS. Muscat has also benefited from the development of a virtually CLAIRETTE-free grapey (Tradition) version of the Rhône's fizzy CLAIRETTE DE DIE. This is the predominant Muscat of CORSICA.

As Moscatel de Grano Menudo it is still grown in Spain but to a limited extent; most Spanish wines labelled Moscatel are made from Muscat of Alexandria. In Portugal, there were 859 ha/2,123 acres of Moscatel Galego Branco in the Douro region in 2020. In Eastern Europe, MUSCAT OTTONEL with its shorter growing season is generally more popular, but Muscat Blanc is grown in Slovenia as Rumeni Muškat, in

Hungary as Sárga Muskotály (the third ingredient in TOKAJ), in Romania where it is known as TĂMÂIOASĂ Alba, and in Bulgaria and Russia, where it is called Tamyanka. It was almost certainly this Muscat that was responsible for the famous, long-lived Muscats of CRIMEA.

See MUSKATELLER for more on Muscat in Germany and Austria.

If anywhere could be said to be Muscat's homeland it is GREECE, and its total area of Muscat Blanc à Petits Grains, at 1,692 ha/4,181 acres in 2021, is more than twice as much as that of Muscat of Alexandria (the prime Cypriot Muscat). The small-berried Muscat is accorded the honour of being the only variety allowed in Greece's most rigidly controlled Muscats such as those of Samos, Patras, and Kefalonia. For the moment, Greek Muscat, like its many variations on the MALVASIA theme, is almost invariably sweet, alcoholic, and redolent of history, but drier versions more suited to drinking with food are on the increase. See GREECE for more details.

Outside of Europe, the variety reaches its apogee in Australia, where it has been known as Brown Muscat and Frontignac with all manner of colour of grape skins. Its most glorious incarnation is RUTHERGLEN Muscat. Australian 2022 grape-variety statistics distinguished between a stable total of about 265 ha/655 acres of dark-skinned, small-berried Muscat, also known as Muscat à Petits Grains Rouges, and a total of light-skinned, small-berried Muscat that had increased to 1,057 ha, thanks to plantings in RIVERLAND and RIVERINA, presumably in response to the FASHION for MOSCATO. This was probably also the explanation for the newer plantings in California's SAN JOAQUIN VALLEY, where Muscat of Alexandria has been very much more important than this finer Muscat, which was planted on 1,137 ha/2,810 acres in 2020. In South Africa, the name most often seen on labels is Muscat de Frontignan, although it is also known simply as Muscat Blanc and as MUSCADE. The total area planted in 2020 was 852 ha/2,105 acres, mainly in inland Robertson. This was the Muscat chiefly responsible for the famous 18th-century CONSTANTIA dessert wine.

Robinson, J., et al., *Wine Grapes: A Complete Guide to 1,368 Vine Varieties, Including Their Origins and Flavours* (2012).

Muscat d'Alsace is an Alsace synonym for the vine variety MUSCAT BLANC À PETITS GRAINS. For more details of what to expect of a wine labelled Muscat d'Alsace, see ALSACE.

Muscat de Beaumes-de-Venise is the often delicate VIN DOUX NATUREL from the southern Rhône village of BEAUMES-DE-VENISE, under whose name there are more details.

Muscat de Frontignan is the old name for the once internationally famous wine of FRONTIGNAN. It is also a synonym used in both France and South Africa for the grape variety solely responsible for it, MUSCAT BLANC À PETITS GRAINS.

Muscat de Lunel. See LUNEL for details of this southern Languedoc VIN DOUX NATUREL. It is yet another synonym for the grape variety solely responsible for it, MUSCAT BLANC À PETITS GRAINS.

Muscat de Mireval. See MIREVAL for details of this relatively unimportant southern Languedoc VIN DOUX NATUREL.

Muscat de Rivesaltes is by far the largest MUSCAT appellation of France, covering 90 villages in the Pyrénées Orientales, as well as nine in the Aude—although the drop in plantings, from 4,809 ha/11,883 acres in 2000 to 3,033 ha/7,495 acres in 2020, illustrates the sharp decline in popularity of sweet wines in general and Muscat in particular. The Muscats of 'Perpinyà' and 'Clayrà' (Claira is a neighbouring village of Rivesaltes) were already sought out by 14th-century wine buyers from as far away as Barcelona and Avignon. Today Muscat de Rivesaltes, recognized as an appellation in 1956, is the only Muscat VIN DOUX NATUREL which may be made from MUSCAT OF ALEXANDRIA as well as the finer MUSCAT BLANC À PETITS GRAINS. Average YIELDS of these low-trained vines, often on difficult-to-work dry TERRACES, can be as little as 17 hl/ha (1 ton/acre) (the official upper limit is 30 hl/ha). Since the 1980s, more skilled vinification has helped improve quality, with temperature-controlled fermentations and perhaps some SKIN CONTACT and MUTAGE *sur marc* (on the skins). The skill lies in judging the right moment for mutage, when the wine will be neither too sweet nor too dry. The wines, usually picked with a minimum sugar level of 100 g/l, are bottled at a minimum of 15° alcohol. Generally, Muscat de Rivesaltes is released the spring after the harvest, and Muscat de Noël even earlier, in time for Christmas. It is generally drunk when it is young and fresh, either as an APERITIF or with fruit or creamy desserts, but it can age well. With its decline in popularity, wine producers have turned to Muscat Sec as an alternative dry TABLE WINE, usually sold as IGP Côtes Catalanes, and some have experimented with sweet unfortified Muscat from LATE HARVEST grapes. R.E.G.

Muscat de St-Jean-de-Minervois, a VIN DOUX NATUREL produced in the northern LANGUEDOC. See ST-JEAN-DE-MINERVOIS.

Muscat du Cap Corse, Corsican VIN DOUX NATUREL. See CORSICA.

Muscat of Alexandria is a Muscat almost as ancient as MUSCAT BLANC À PETITS GRAINS and also has dozens of synonyms, but its wine is usually distinctly inferior. In hot climates it can thrive and produce a good yield of extremely ripe grapes, but their chief attribute is sweetness. (In cooler climates, its output can be seriously affected by COULURE, MILLERANDAGE, and a range of FUNGAL DISEASES.) Wines made from this sort of Muscat tend to be strong, sweet, and unsubtle. The aroma is vaguely grapey but can have slightly feline overtones of geranium rather than the more lingering bouquet of Muscat Blanc.

Some indication of its lack of finesse as a wine producer is the fact that a considerable proportion of the Muscat of Alexandria grown today is destined for uses other than wine: Chile, for example, distils most of its thousands of hectares of Muscat of Alexandria to make PISCO; it is even grown under glass in Britain and the Netherlands to provide grapes for the fruit bowl.

Its name suggests origins in Egypt, but genetics suggests Greece and also that it is a progeny of Muscat Blanc à Petits Grains. It was disseminated around the Mediterranean by the Romans, hence its common synonym Muscat Romain. Its southern Italian synonym is ZIBIBBO, under which details of its Italian incarnations can be found.

Today it is most important to wine industries in that old arc of maritime history Iberia, South Africa, and Australia, where it may be known respectively as Moscatel, Hanepoot, and Muscat Gordo Blanco or Lexia, a particularly Australian contraction of the word Alexandria. Spain's total plantings had grown to 10,759 ha/26,586 acres by 2020, more than three times as much as of the other major Muscat, called Moscatel Grano Menudo here. It is not known, however, exactly how much of this serves the wine industry, typically with sweet MOSCATELS of various sticky sorts. Muscat of Alexandria's various Spanish synonyms include Moscatel de Alejandría, Moscatel de Málaga, Moscatel de España, Moscatel Gordo (Blanco), Moscatel Blanco, and Moscatel de Chipiona.

In Portugal its most famous incarnation is Moscatel de SETÚBAL, but Portugal's Muscat of Alexandria grapes, often called Moscatel Graúdo, have also been harnessed to produce aromatic, dry Muscats, much lower in alcohol. This is also the fate of the majority of Australia's relatively static total of 2,210 ha/5,461 acres of Muscat Gordo Blanco, the country's dominant Muscat, once used mainly for FORTIFIED WINES, although from cooler vineyards it can produce sound, unfortified wines that are sweet because they are LATE HARVESTED. Dry wine produced from the Gordo Blanco grown in Australia's irrigated Riverland is typically used for blending with, and often softening, more glamorous grape varieties.

Muscat of Alexandria is the dominant Muscat in South Africa—HANEPOOT is its traditional Afrikaans name—and was the country's fourth most planted white wine variety in the late 1990s, but it is in marked decline; by 2020 there remained 1,560 ha/3,855 acres, mainly in hotter inland regions. For years it provided sticky, raisiny wines for FORTIFICATION, as well as everything from GRAPE CONCENTRATE to RAISINS. Today some drier, lighter wines are also made from it. Muscat of Alexandria is widely grown in California (1,678 ha/4,146 acres) and still grown to a relatively limited extent in Argentina, Peru, Colombia, Ecuador, and even Japan. Although Muscat Blanc is more important in GREECE, Muscat of Alexandria is grown widely there and is the Muscat that predominates in Türkiye, Israel, and Tunisia, although in much of the Near East nowadays these grapes are eaten rather than drunk. In France, total plantings of Muscat d'Alexandrie, or Muscat Romain, have decreased to about 2,166 ha, almost exclusively in Roussillon, where it was introduced for Muscat de Rivesaltes.

Muscat of Frontignan is a common synonym for MUSCAT BLANC À PETITS GRAINS, and this is the Muscat variety that is solely responsible for the VIN DOUX NATUREL of the same name. See also FRONTIGNAN for details of the wine that justifies this synonym.

Muscat of Hamburg is the lowest quality of the wine-producing MUSCATS. DNA PROFILING at CONEGLIANO showed that it is a natural cross of MUSCAT OF ALEXANDRIA and TROLLINGER (also called SCHIAVA Grossa). It comes exclusively in black-berried form and is far more common as a TABLE GRAPE than a wine grape. Its chief attribute is the consistency of its plump and shiny dark-blue grapes, which can well withstand long journeys to reach consumers who like black-skinned Muscat-flavoured grapes. In France it was grown on 3,324 ha/8,214 acres in 2019 and was the most important table grape. It is also relatively important as a table grape in Greece, eastern Europe, and Australia. It was extremely popular as a greenhouse grape in Victorian England, where it occasionally took the name of Snow or Venn, two of its more successful propagators.

In the world of wine production its importance is limited, but it does produce a fair quantity of light, grapey red throughout eastern Europe and some 'Black Muscat' in California; in CHINA, crossed with the indigenous VITIS AMURENSIS, it has spawned a generation of varieties adapted for wine production.

Muscat Ottonel is the palest of all the Muscats, both in terms of the colour of wine produced and in terms of its character. Its aroma is altogether more vapid than the powerful grapey perfumes associated with MUSCAT BLANC À PETITS GRAINS and MUSCAT OF ALEXANDRIA. It was bred in 1839 from CHASSELAS and the no-longer-cultivated Muscat d'Eisenstadt (also called Ingram's Muscat, after its breeder) and released in 1852 in the Loire as a TABLE GRAPE.

Its tendency to ripen earlier than these other two Muscats has made it much easier to cultivate in cooler climates, and nowadays Muscat Ottonel is the dominant Muscat cultivated, on fewer than 200 hectares, in ALSACE. This low-vigour vine, which does best in deep, damp soils, is also grown throughout eastern Europe, notably in AUSTRIA, where it is planted in Burgenland and spelt **Muskat Ottonel**. It may well be that it is at its best as a late-harvest wine, for there are some fine, apparently long-living examples from both HUNGARY and ROMANIA (where the variety is often known, respectively, as Ottonel Muskotály and TĂMÂIOASĂ Ottonel). Romania and Bulgaria, where it is often labelled MISKET, probably have the biggest areas of the variety: 3,100 ha and 5,124 ha respectively.

Muscat Romain, or **Roman Muscat**, is a common name for MUSCAT OF ALEXANDRIA in Roussillon.

Muschelkalk, literally 'shell limestone' in German, is the time-honoured name used in Germany and neighbouring countries for a particular group of CALCAREOUS rocks deposited during a precise geological interval in northern mainland Europe. Muschelkalk consists mainly of LIMESTONE, together with various argillaceous and dolomitic limestones, and MARLS, each with distinctive fossils. Parts of southern PFALZ, RHEINHESSEN, and central FRANKEN in Germany, as well as LEITHABERG in Austria's Burgenland, are sited on Muschelkalk, as are a number of grand cru vineyards in ALSACE.

Classically and internationally, Muschelkalk is the name for the middle division of the three that originally defined the Triassic period of geological time. However, rocks formed at this time away from northern Europe are quite different from those lauded by German producers. See GEOLOGY for more. A.J.M.

mushroom root rot, vine disease. See ARMILLARIA ROOT ROT.

Musigny, Le, great red GRAND CRU in Burgundy's CÔTE D'OR. For more details, see CHAMBOLLE-MUSIGNY.

Muskateller, German for MUSCAT, almost invariably the superior MUSCAT BLANC À PETITS GRAINS or some mutation of it. **Gelber Muskateller**, for example, is the gold-skinned version which is increasingly recognized as superior to MUSCAT OTTONEL in Austria, where 1,480 ha/3,657 acres were planted in 2022 (including the pink-skinned MUTATION **Roter Muskateller**). The variety is popular in STYRIA for light, dry wines and makes both dry and sweet wines in other parts of the country. In Germany, Gelber Muskateller is a distinctly minority interest, but it remains popular in the Pfalz. Roter Muskateller has all but disappeared.

Muskat Ottonel is what German-speaking countries call their MUSCAT OTTONEL.

Muskat-Silvaner, or **Muskat-Sylvaner**, was once, tellingly, the common German-language synonym for SAUVIGNON BLANC used in Germany and Austria.

Muskotály, name used in HUNGARY for Muscat, either **Ottonel Muskotály** (MUSCAT OTTONEL) or **Sárga Muskotály**, the yellow-berried form of MUSCAT BLANC À PETITS GRAINS.

musqué is a French term meaning both 'perfumed', as in musky, and 'muscat-like'. Many vine varieties, including CHARDONNAY, have a Musqué mutation which is particularly aromatic and may add to the variety's own characteristics a grapey scent reminiscent of MUSCAT.

must is the name used by winemakers for a thick liquid that is neither GRAPE JUICE nor WINE but a mixture of grape juice, stem fragments, grape skins, seeds, and pulp that comes from the DESTEMMER-CRUSHER that smashes grapes at the start of the winemaking process, although it is also sometimes used loosely to refer to GRAPE JUICE. The French equivalent is *moût*, the Italian is *mosto*, the Spanish is *pasta*, and the German is *Maische*. Confusingly, Spanish *mosto* refers to the juice once it has been pressed off the skins (see PRESS), and Italian *mosto* can refer to both the juice without the skins and to must. The word 'must' has been used in English for at least a thousand years to refer to fruit being prepared for, or undergoing, FERMENTATION.

must chilling, important WHITE WINEMAKING operation, particularly in WARM CLIMATES, which delays the onset of fermentation until after pressing and helps prevent OXIDATION. See REFRIGERATION and TEMPERATURE. France's first must chiller was installed, by Australians, in the Languedoc in the early 1990s.

must weight, important measure of grape RIPENESS, indicated by the concentration of dissolved compounds in grape juice or must. Since about 90% of all the dissolved solids in grape juice are the fermentable SUGARS (the rest being acids, ions, and a host of other solutes), any measurement of these solids gives a reliable indication of the grapes' ripeness and therefore the POTENTIAL ALCOHOL of wine made from them (see FERMENTATION).

Must weight may be measured approximately in the vineyard before harvest using a REFRACTOMETER or in the winery using a refractometer or a HYDROMETER, calibrated according to one of several different scales used in different parts of the world for measuring the concentration of dissolved solids. This variation is not so surprising when one considers how crucial this statistic is to the winemaking

Baumé (degrees)	Brix/ Balling (degrees)	Oechsle (degrees)	Potential alcohol (% vol)
10	18.0	75	10
11	19.8	84	11
12	21.7	93	12
13	23.5	101	13
14	25.3	110	14
15	27.1	119	15

process and therefore how early in the evolution of each country's wine industry a scale will have been adopted. Each scale merely requires a different calibration of the hydrometer, usually with a reading of zero indicating that the DENSITY of a solution is exactly one, as in pure water.

BAUMÉ is the scale most commonly used in much of Europe, including France, and in Australia. The number of degrees Baumé indicates the concentration of dissolved compounds in a solution calibrated so that it indicates fairly well the potential ALCOHOLIC STRENGTH of a wine made by fermenting the must to dryness, although the figures in the table above are approximate.

In the United States, and increasingly in Australia, ripeness is most commonly measured in degrees BRIX, also sometimes called Balling, both terms borrowed from the sugar-refining industry. The Brix reading simply indicates the percentage of solids (of which about 90% are sugars) by weight.

Winemakers in Germany most commonly use the OECHSLE scale, which simply indicates the density of the juice: a grape juice with a specific gravity of 1.085 is said to be 85 °Oechsle. Austria has its own, similar scale, devised at KLOSTERNEUBURG, which measures ripeness in degrees KMW (or Babo).

Since it takes about 16.5 g/l (0.6 oz/1.76 pt) of sugar to produce 1% alcohol by fermentation (in white wines, closer to 18 g/l in reds, depending on the efficiency of the YEAST strain), it is possible to calculate approximately the potential alcohol using any of these scales. All of these must-weight measurements can be roughly converted among themselves, with Baumé values about five-ninths of Brix/Balling values, and 14.7 °Brix/Balling equalling 60 °Oechsle. Some equivalences are outlined in the table, although, according to published scales, the relationship between the different measurements is not a strict one (as illustrated in Hamilton and Coombe).

A typical dry wine is made from grapes which measure 12–14 °Baumé, 22–25 °Brix or Balling, and 93–110 °Oechsle. Grapes grown in ENGLAND in particularly cool years, however, may reach a natural must weight of around 50 °Oechsle, while some grape varieties in the SAN JOAQUIN VALLEY of California can easily reach 30 °Brix, as they gradually dehydrate under the intense heat. One German wine harvested at Nussdorf in the PFALZ in 1971 was picked at 326 °Oechsle and was still fermenting 22 years later, having reached just 4.5% alcohol; another picked in 2011 in Rheinhessen came in at 338 °Oechsle, but the volume was too small and the sugar too high to ferment. B.G.C.

Hamilton, R. P., and Coombe, B. G., 'Harvesting of winegrapes', in B. G. Coombe and P. R. Dry (eds.), *Viticulture*, ii: *Practices* (2nd edn, 2006).

mutage is the process of stopping GRAPE JUICE or MUST from fermenting, sometimes by adding SULFUR DIOXIDE but usually by adding alcohol, thereby creating an environment in which YEASTS can no longer work. Mutage transforms fermenting must into a **vin muté** such as a VIN DE LIQUEUR or a VIN DOUX NATUREL. The alcohol may be added before or after the grape juice has been separated from the skins (*sur grains* or *sur jus*). Mutage plays a crucial part in making PORT, where the process is known as *fortifição* or occasionally *aguardentação*.

mutation, spontaneous change to genetic material occurring during cell division in organisms such as grapevines. Since so many of today's VINE VARIETIES were selected over the last several centuries, they may have accumulated a substantial load of mutations. WILD VINES are invariably dark-skinned; light-skinned varieties are therefore the result of mutation. Generally mutations are either innocuous or deleterious, but people have had many centuries in which deliberately to select those vines which perform best (a process now formalized as CLONAL SELECTION), so beneficial mutations have been maintained.

Mutation is particularly common among vine varieties with a long history of cultivation such as PINOT NOIR, CARIGNAN, SAVAGNIN, GRENACHE, and TERRET. Although mutation is not always as spectacular as a change in berry colour, most of these varieties have forms called variously Noir (black), Gris (grey), Blanc (white), Rose (pink), Vert (green), Rouge (red), and sometimes more.

Mutations commonly seen in grapevines include leaf, berry, and pulp colour, berry size, seedlessness, compactness of bunches, productivity, flavours, date of ripening, leaf lobation, very large INFLORESCENCES, and absence of inflorescences. Mutation can also cause polyploidy (multiple sets of chromosomes), which leads to 'giant' plants and berries. The two Gamay TEINTURIERS, Gamay Teinturier de Fréaux and Gamay Teinturier de Chaudenay, are thought to be mutations of Gamay de Bouze. A mixture of normal and mutant tissue is known as a chimera, and the varieties Pinot Noir and Pinot Meunier are partners in a so-called periclinal chimera. Such plants are essentially composed of a mutant 'skin' enclosing a 'normal' interior. Pinot Meunier is essentially similar to Pinot Noir, with the exception of white hairs on the shoot tip and young leaves.

Mutation can be induced by chemicals such as colchicine and by ionizing radiation. A form of genetic variation known as somaclonal mutation is induced during TISSUE CULTURE, and it is thought that this will be a useful means of increasing clonal variation among existing varieties. R.E.S. & J.V.

Pelsy, F., 'Molecular and cellular mechanisms of diversity within grapevine varieties', *Heredity*, 104 (2010), 331–40.
Reisch, B. I., et al., 'Grape', in M. L. Badenes and D. H. Byrne (eds.), *Fruit Breeding* (2012).
This, P., et al., 'Historical origins and genetic diversity of wine grapes', *TRENDS in Genetics*, 22/9 (2006), 511–19.

muzzle, the wire which holds a SPARKLING WINE cork in place. Known in French as a **muselet**.

MW, abbreviation for MASTER OF WINE.

Myanmar (formerly Burma), tropical South East Asian nation, bordered by THAILAND, Laos, CHINA, INDIA, and Bangladesh, had two wineries focused on classic VITIS VINIFERA wine styles in 2023. Myanmar Vineyard Estate has 6 ha/17 acres of vineyards at ELEVATIONS of 1,200 m/ 3,937 ft on LIMESTONE slopes on the southern extension of the Himalayan ranges, west of the Shan State capital Taunggyi. Shiraz makes up 65% of the vineyards; the rest is planted to DORNFELDER, TEMPRANILLO, and Sauvignon Blanc. Red Mountain Estate is further south, on the shores of Inle Lake, a popular tourist resort. The 74-ha/185-acre property grows mainly INTERNATIONAL VARIETIES, plus MUSCAT BLANC À PETITS GRAINS for a LATE HARVEST white and CARIGNAN for a rosé. D.G.

mycoderma. See FILM-FORMING YEASTS.

mycoplasma. See PHYTOPLASMA.

mycorrhiza, the symbiotic relationship between vine ROOTS and arbuscular **mycorrhizal fungi** in the soil that increases the surface area of the roots and allows the vine to access and utilize NUTRIENTS in the soil more effectively. The fungi, which thrive in soils high in ORGANIC MATTER, have been shown not only to improve the uptake of nutrients but also to increase resistance to plant pathogens and to improve SOIL STRUCTURE. Enterprising companies are selling mycorrhizal fungi that can be used to inoculate vineyard soils, and there is a growing market for so-called biostimulants that are said to activate indigenous populations of mycorrhizal fungi. See BIOLOGICALS.

Baumgartner, K., 'Encouraging beneficial AM fungi in vineyard soil', *Practical Winery & Vineyard* (Jan/Feb 2003), 57–60.
Trouvelot, S., et al., 'Arbuscular mycorrhiza symbiosis in viticulture: a review', *Agronomy for Sustainable Development*, 35 (2015), 1449–67.

N

Nagyburgundi, occasional Hungarian synonym for BLAUFRÄNKISCH, although Kékfrankos is more common.

Nahe, wine region in GERMANY with 4,202 ha/ 10,383 vine acres in 2019 scattered over a wide area on either side of the river Nahe (see map under GERMANY). The region was defined in its current form as part of the German wine law of 1971, bringing together several geologically and climatically distinct areas.

By turns bucolic and geologically dramatic, the stretch of the river between Monzingen and Bad Münster am Stein features steep and often terraced slopes yielding world-class RIESLING on a geologically complex mix including SANDSTONE, porphyry, and SLATE. A single vineyard, such as the renowned Niederhäuser Hermannshöhle, can incorporate five fundamentally different soil types, and it does not seem to be mere imagination that such geological complexity is mirrored in the flavour of the wines. The general climatic tendency is to warm as the Nahe meanders downstream. Excellent ventilation, low precipitation, and balmy autumnal temperatures, in addition to the steep, southward ASPECT of vineyard slopes, offer ideal circumstances for late-ripening Riesling.

The foremost wine villages (with their most notable vineyards) along this stretch of the Nahe, travelling downstream, are Monzingen (Frühlingsplätzchen, Halenberg), Meddersheim (Rheingrafenberg), Schlossböckelheim (Felsenberg, Kupfergrube), Oberhausen (Brücke, Leistenbreg), Niederhausen (Hermannshöhle, Kerz, Klamm), Norheim (Dellchen, Kirschheck), and Traisen (Bastei, Rotenfels). Wines of pronounced, often pungent spice and mineral inflection with frequent red fruit notes are characteristic for many of the best vineyards in this area. The Rheinland-Pfalz (originally Prussian) viticultural school in Bad Kreuznach and State Domaine of Niederhausen-Schlossböckelheim founded in 1902 (privatized in 1998 and impressively revived in 2009 as Gut Hermannsberg) greatly helped to establish what reputation Nahe Riesling enjoyed prior to the 1980s, while the efforts of Helmut Dönnhoff in Oberhausen and Werner Schönleber at Weingut Emrich-Schönleber have done much to secure the Nahe's current high standing.

On the northern outskirts of Bad Kreuznach, immediately adjacent to the city, the vineyards are substantially LOESS and CLAY, on gentler slopes than those elsewhere along the Nahe, but in certain sites, notably Kahlenberg and Krötenpfuhl, GRAVEL offers excellent drainage and Riesling potential. Immediately west of Bad Kreuznach, Roxheim, dominated by red SANDSTONE, enjoys historical and recently renewed renown for both Pinot Noir and Riesling. Viticulture around Bad Kreuznach, limited by late 20th century urban development, was traditionally dominated by large landholders who also had important holdings in the Middle Nahe, most notably the Anheuser family and the Reichsgraf von Plettenberg.

The Lower Nahe, near its confluence with the Rhine at Bingen, features outstanding steep-slope Riesling from a wide range of soils, notably quartzite-rich SLATE. Top sites include a trio along the Troll-Bach at Dorsheim just west of the Nahe elevated to late 20th century prominence by winegrower and wine journalist Armin Diel (Schlossgut Diel): Burgberg, Goldloch, and Pittermännchen. There are also two standout sites along similar tributary streams at Münster-Sarmsheim, Dautenflänzer and Pittersberg, and another at Bingerbrück—Abtei, a vineyard farmed in the Middle Ages by the Ruppertsberg Abbey.

The aforementioned areas by no means exhaust the historic or current sources of excellent Nahe wine. These include the Alsenz near its confluence with the Nahe at Bad Münster (in particular the Altenbamberger Rotenberg and Ebernburger Schlossberg), as well as a number of villages located several miles north and west of the Nahe, most notably Bockenau, whose towering Felseneck and Stromberg were virtually unknown prior to the 21st-century efforts of Weingut Schäfer-Fröhlich. Sporadic vineyards occur along the Nahe's tributary Glan, from Oberhausen's Leistenberg south to Meisenheim more than 12 km away. Among these, the dramatically terraced Kloster Disibodenberg in Odernheim harbours not only outstanding wine potential but also Germany's oldest known vine vestiges, conceivably dating back within a century or so to the eponymous cloister's most famous resident, sainted Nahe native Hildegard of Bingen.

White wines make up three-quarters of the Nahe's wines, with Riesling dominating in both reputation and plantings, at 29% share of vine surface. MÜLLER-THURGAU comes in number two at 12%, but qualitatively more important is the nearly 16% collective share of WEISSBURGUNDER (Pinot Blanc) and GRAUBURGUNDER (Pinot Gris). SILVANER, dominant in a once flourishing Alsenz Valley, has slipped to 6% Nahe-wide. In red wine varieties, DORNFELDER boasts more acreage, but the Nahe's serious reds are issued from SPÄTBURGUNDER (Pinot Noir). D.S.

Pigott, S., et al., *Wein Spricht Deutsch: Weine, Winzer, Weinlandschaften* (2007).

Reinhardt, S., *The Finest Wines of Germany* (2012).

Namibia in southern AFRICA was first planted to wine grapes in the late 1800s by German colonists. The climate is arid and subtropical, forcing most grape-growing into cooler, higher

ELEVATIONS. By 2022 there were four wineries producing grape wines: Thonningii in the north, in the Otavi Mountains; Kristal Kellerei and Erongo Mountain Winery on the banks of the Omaruru River in west-central Namibia; and Neuras further south, in the Naukluft Mountains.

nanofiltration, a membrane separation technique which is looser than REVERSE OSMOSIS and tighter than ULTRAFILTRATION. It can be used to remove sugars from juice and ultimately results in the ALCOHOL REDUCTION of the final wines. Furthermore, wine CONCENTRATION by nanofiltration can result in a wine with decreased ETHANOL and water content (see ALCOHOL REDUCTION). However, more smaller molecules that contribute to wine flavour can be lost using this technique than with REVERSE OSMOSIS, and it should be used with care.

Wollan, D., 'Membrane and other techniques for the management of wine composition', in A. G. Reynolds (ed.), *Managing Wine Quality 2: Oenology and Wine Quality* (2nd edn, 2021), 183–212.

Naoussa is the most well-known appellation of northern GREECE, on the south-eastern slopes of Mount Vermio at ELEVATIONS of 200–500 m/ 660–1,650 ft, where there is usually no lack of rain and winters are cool by Greek standards. The PDO applies only to red wines made from the XINOMAVRO grape, aged for at least a year in OAK. Traditionally, wine was matured in old wooden CASKS, but there has been considerable experimentation with new, small BARRIQUES. This may be the only appellation in Greece, with the possible exception being Nemea, where producers are working to identify the best subregions, akin to a CRU system in its genesis. SINGLE-VINEYARD bottlings are increasing, from vineyards such as Palaiokalias, Gastra, or Trilofos.

Naoussa reds can age well for several decades, maintaining an ethereal, BAROLO-like personality for a fraction of the price. Naoussa Xinomavro is also used for rosé wines and some impressive BLANC DE BLANC wines, some OAK AGED, but these all are allowed only under the PGI Imathia. PGI wines can contain other varieties as well, such as Merlot and Syrah, which are often used to soften the edges of Xinomavro, resulting in some popular red blends. K.L.

Napa, small city north of San Francisco in CALIFORNIA that gives its name to **Napa County** and, California's most famous wine region and an AVA, the **Napa Valley**. Though Napa Valley's modern history began, arguably, in the 1960s, its wine industry can trace its roots back to the winter of 1838–9 when early settler George C. Yount planted the area's first VITIS VINIFERA vines. Yount, a homesteader, was brought to the region by the Mexican government, which awarded him a land grant in a bid to increase the population of California, which was under its control at the time. Yount's stake was a relatively lonely one until the Gold Rush of 1849 ushered in an era of mass migration to California. This was the mechanism by which many of Napa's first winemakers, generally of European origin, came to settle 'the Valley'.

Napa's wine industry boomed in the wake of the Gold Rush, and by the 1880s there were nearly 150 wineries and over 8,094 ha/20,000 acres of *vinifera* in the ground. Napa achieved a reputation for high quality early on, due to its genial climate, water resources that allow vines to be DRY-FARMED (Napa has a high and independent water table in many places), and the long band of ALLUVIAL fans that stretch along the valley's western foothills. The fact that the region was connected to San Francisco via water routes was also an early advantage; proximity to San Francisco remains a major economic boon still.

In the 1890s PHYLLOXERA devastated Napa's vineyards, and a national recession forestalled reinvestment, leaving many fields vacant. The increasingly vocal temperance movement also made replanting seem unwise, and PROHIBITION was indeed enacted in 1920. A handful of wineries remained in business by selling wine to the clergy, but most operations shuttered. However, the national enthusiasm for HOME WINEMAKING kept many vines in the ground, though the varieties planted shifted to favour the so-called 'shipper varieties'—grapes such as ZINFANDEL, PETITE SIRAH, CARIGNAN, and ALICANTE BOUSCHET that were sturdy enough to survive a cross-country journey via unrefrigerated rail car. Pockets of these gnarled old vines remain in less-fashionable appellations such as Calistoga and Oak Knoll, where now-popular Cabernet Sauvignon has not gained as much traction.

The few Napa wineries that reopened upon Repeal in the 1930s faced many challenges: the Great Depression, a fundamentally altered national palate, and a poor understanding of cellar HYGIENE. It was this last point that sent Beaulieu Vineyards' owner Georges de Latour to France in search of a winemaker with scientific training. He returned in 1938 with André TCHELISTCHEFF, who would do much to elevate the baseline quality of wines at BV and in Napa at large. Tchelistcheff worked closely with many of Napa's winegrowers, including the MONDAVI brothers, who were then at Charles KRUG. In 1966, Robert Mondavi was kicked out of the family winery and started his own eponymous operation; many consider this to mark the birth of Napa's modern history.

Though Napa was slow to recover after Prohibition, the number of new wineries began to pick up speed in the 1960s. This was good news for the wine industry, but environmentalists were concerned that the region's proximity to San Francisco would encourage the kind of unchecked development that turned nearby Marin and Santa Clara counties from agricultural wonderlands into slopes of stacked houses. In 1968 the Agricultural Preserve was enacted. This forward-looking, controversial legislature has helped Napa maintain its agrarian status and preserve its wild lands. The 'Ag Preserve', coupled with restrictions regarding planting on slopes and in proximity to waterways, mean that Napa is effectively 'planted out' at around 18,616 ha/46,000 acres. All together, these vines produce around 4% of California's wine, but its value amounts to more than 25% of the state's wine revenue.

Growth in Napa Valley continued into the 1970s, spurred on by the 1976 JUDGMENT OF PARIS, which attracted a slew of increasingly wealthy investors. Many of these new winery owners were interested in an estate model of operation, where winemaking and grape-growing were farmed out to employees. Because of this, the need for skilled winemakers skyrocketed, and universities such as UC DAVIS began to establish or expand their VITICULTURE and OENOLOGY programmes. As many of Napa's top wineries produce relatively little wine, CONSULTANT winemakers have become more and more common. Today, a small handful of elite winemakers are responsible for a sizable chunk of the area's top brands. This is especially true among the so-called CALIFORNIA CULT producers.

Napa Valley arcs gently to the north-west, with the San Pablo Bay in the south and Mount St Helena, the highest point in Napa County, in the north. Because of this positioning, the southern, bay-side section of Napa Valley is considerably cooler (average summer daytime high of 27 °C/80 °F) than the north (35 °C/95 °F). Nighttime temperatures drop significantly, to a valley-wide average of 12 °C/ 53 °F. This extreme DIURNAL TEMPERATURE RANGE, coupled with the fog that blankets the valley floor every morning during the growing season, help to slow ripening and retain acidity. Overall, the region enjoys a MEDITERRANEAN CLIMATE, with hot, rainless summers and cool, wet winters.

This has allowed many winegrowers to turn to SUSTAINABLE, ORGANIC, or BIODYNAMIC VITICULTURE, even as growers need to contend with pests such as the glassy-winged SHARPSHOOTER, vine and grape MEALYBUGS, and NEMATODES. In the 2000s, the region's main viticultural challenges have been DROUGHT and HEATWAVES, which in turn increase the potential for WILDFIRES.

Napa's magic is derived in no small part from a magnificent diversity of ASPECT, MESOCLIMATE, and soil. The valley itself is around 48 km/30 miles long and 5 miles across at its widest. ELEVATIONS range from sea level to 800 m/ 2,600 ft, and vineyards exist at all ASPECTS to the sun. It is important to note that only the eastern half of the Mayacamas mountain range belongs to Napa; as the county line traces the ridge, the western half resides in SONOMA. Across the valley, the Vaca Mountains are entirely contained within Napa County.

The diverse terrain contains soils from half of the world's 12 recognized soil orders and 33 different series. This variegation has informed the creation of 16 nested AVAs, though Napa's appellation system is still very much a work in progress. In general, they can be divided into two groups: those in middle of the valley (from south to north, Coombsville, Oak Knoll, Yountville, Stags Leap, Oakville, Rutherford, St Helena, and Calistoga); and those on hills and mountains (Wild Horse Valley, Atlas Peak, Chiles Valley, and Howell Mountain in the Vaca Range, and Mount Veeder, Spring Mountain, and Diamond Mountain in the Mayacamas). Some appellations, such as Wild Horse Valley, contain very few vines, while other significant grape-growing areas such as Pritchard Hill, Conn Valley, and the slopes between St Helena and Howell Mountain possess no official designation. One of the biggest controversies of the appellation system is the Napa Valley AVA itself. Due to emphatic lobbying by big producers to allow the inclusion of fruit from far-flung areas such as the Pope and Chiles Valleys, the Napa Valley AVA extends far beyond the limits of what might reasonably be thought of as 'the valley' to include almost the entirety of Napa County. As with the rest of Napa Valley, the majority of the fruit grown here is Cabernet Sauvignon, but Zinfandel and Sauvignon Blanc are also high in quality.

The following are Napa's most significant subappellations.

Atlas Peak AVA
Located in Napa's southern reaches, Atlas Peak is one of its cooler mountain regions. It also boasts one of its taller peaks, cresting at 814 m/2,671 ft above sea level. It is a fairly arid region, and much of the land is tied up in cattle ranches. Viticulturally, it is an appellation of extremes, with massive vineyards such as Antica Gallo's Stagecoach and boutique properties such as Kongsgaard and Au Sommet. Cabernet Sauvignon and Chardonnay are the region's focus.

Calistoga AVA
Napa Valley's northernmost sub-AVA, Calistoga receives little of the cooling fog and winds that come up from the San Pablo Bay, though small cracks in Diamond Mountain allow some ingress. Except for St Helena to the south, the region is almost entirely ringed by mountains, which further act to trap in the heat. Summer temperatures can reach more than 38 °C/100 °F. Napa's volcanic past is on clear display here, both in the IRON-rich soils and the prolific hot springs. Red and black grape varieties dominate: Cabernet Sauvignon, of course, but pockets of OLD VINE Zinfandel, PETITE SIRAH, and CHARBONO also.

Coombsville AVA
Napa's newest AVA has been the backbone of big Napa Cabernet blends for many years, often adding STRUCTURE and freshness. These qualities are directly the result of the climate—being situated in the south-east of Napa Valley, Coombsville lies straight in the path of the daily fog and breezes that come up off the San Pablo Bay. The region is ampitheatre-shaped and carpeted with vines, which stretch from sea level to high up the Vacas, with very few wineries interspersed among the vineyards. Because the region is so relatively cool, it is also well-known for its Chardonnay and, to a lesser extent, Pinot Noir.

Diamond Mountain District AVA
This rugged appellation in the Mayacamas mountain range is only intermittently flat enough to cultivate a vineyard. VOLCANIC soil abounds; though the region is quite warm, the Diamond Creek DRAINAGE allows an influx of cooling Pacific influence to creep downslope. Mainly planted to Cabernets Sauvignon and Franc, the region tends to produce wines that are distinctly 'mountain' in tone, with intense structure and concentration.

Howell Mountain AVA
In the north-east of Napa Valley, Howell Mountain is the most widely cultivated of Napa's mountains (it is something of a plateau, which makes it easier to farm than other craggier mountains) as well as the most populous, being the only one to contain its own town, Angwin. It is arguably the most distinct appellation in that it is drawn entirely by ELEVATION. The AVA starts along the fog line, at 1,400 ft/427 m. Wines produced below the 1,400-ft elevation mark are eligible for the Napa Valley AVA only. Cabernet Sauvignon dominates, but Zinfandel and Merlot can be noteworthy.

Mount Veeder AVA
Mount Veeder, at the south-western end of the valley, just above Carneros, is the coolest of Napa's Mountain AVAs, as well as the least cultivated. It enjoys regular breezes off San Pablo Bay, and its steep hillsides are blanketed in giant redwoods and Douglas fir trees. Winemaking operations here tend to be small and characterful. Unlike the rest of Napa's mountains, very little VOLCANIC soil is found on Mount Veeder. Cabernet Sauvignon, the dominant grape variety, can produce wines with pronounced ageability in this cool mountain terrain.

Oakville AVA
In the centre of the valley, the Oakville appellation varies considerably from east to west. In the east, the AVA boundaries were extended upslope to include Dalla Valle Vineyards, which overlooks the appellation from its sun-kissed, rust-stained perch. Heading west the mountain dissolves into small hills where Rudd, Screaming Eagle, and Plumpjack are located. The centre of the appellation possesses deep, rich soils that turn into ALLUVIAL fans near the Mayacamas foothills. Here such historic vineyards as To Kalon and Martha's are located. The western hillsides are tree-shrouded and steep and contain such impressive properties as Harlan and Futo. This is the heartland for Napa Valley Cabernet Sauvignon, which roundly dominates.

Rutherford AVA
Rutherford is a rectangle-shaped appellation, right in the centre of Napa Valley and at its widest point. It is perhaps most famous for its BENCH—the long, snaky alluvial band that stretches along the valley's west side. Cabernet Sauvignon dominates here, although there is a surprising amount of Sauvignon Blanc, given the heat of the region. Several large landholders own big chunks of Rutherford, including those behind Round Pond, Frog's Leap, and Beckstoffer Vineyards.

Spring Mountain District AVA
Named for the abundant freshwater springs that trickle down or underneath the mountainside towards St Helena below, Spring Mountain District is a craggy, twisted terrain that, despite a few big players like Spring Mountain Vineyards, is home to mostly small family-run operations. Though Cabernet is dominant, less common varieties such as Riesling and Syrah can thrive in the dramatically ranging MESOCLIMATES.

Stags Leap District AVA
This small AVA is the only 'floor' appellation not to stretch across the entire valley. Instead, it is surrounded by Yountville on three sides, with its eastern edge formed by the dramatic bald rock cliffs known as 'the Palisades'. The Palisades not only divide Stags Leap from Atlas Peak to its east but also serve to reflect light and heat down on the vines, making this region warmer than surrounding Yountville. A series of high knolls in the west end of the appellation create a wind tunnel in conjunction with the Palisades that can be so strong that plant STOMATA will close, thereby stalling PHOTOSYNTHESIS. This slows ripening and makes for distinctively TEXTURED Cabernet Sauvignons that tend to be both supple and bright.

Yountville AVA
Yountville occupies the cooler southern end of the valley; because of this, Cabernet Sauvignon can be found next to broad swathes of white

N

wine grapes, including many earmarked for sparkling wine. Although the region is perhaps best known for its culinary scene, anchored by Thomas Keller's French Laundry, it is responsible for some of Napa's most profound and underrated wines. The most viticulturally exciting band of Yountville is the western BENCH, where such luminary vineyards as Dominus's Napanook, Blankiet Estate, and Sleeping Lady are located. These deep, GRAVEL-rich soils are woven through with CLAY, and the gentle climate makes for elegant and understated wines.

See also CARNEROS, an AVA shared with Sonoma, and CALIFORNIA, including map.

K.A.W.

Lapsley, J. T., *Bottled Poetry: Napa Winemaking from Prohibition to the Modern Era* (1996).
Sullivan, C., *Napa Wine: A History from Mission Days to Present* (1994).
Swinchatt, J., and Howell, D. G., *The Winemaker's Dance* (2004).
White, K., *Napa Valley Then and Now* (2015).
www.napavintners.com

Naples, large south Italian port and capital of the CAMPANIA region. The area around Naples had once produced all the greatest wines of ancient ROME, not only FALERNIAN but also CAECUBAN, MASSIC, and SURRENTINE, but in viticultural terms it was never to be that famous again. With the fall of the Roman Empire and the economic decline of Italy, the market for fine wines collapsed.

Its oriental trade, which dates from Naples's medieval period under Byzantine rule, included the strong sweet MALMSEY of Crete, but PUGLIA produced similar wines itself, mostly for consumption in southern Italy. Naples also traded in the VERNACCIA of Liguria, which it sold to Sicily, Majorca, and PARIS. These wines were known collectively as *vini grechi* because, like the wines imported from the Aegean, they were high-quality sweet wines, capable of surviving a long sea voyage. The wines of Campania, which were not in the Greek style but dry, were called *vini latini*. They were considered inferior and were not long-lived enough to be sent overseas to northern Europe. The highest-regarded of the *vini latini* were those of Mount Vesuvius, which were sold to other parts of Italy by the merchants of Naples and Salerno. In addition, Naples sold CALABRIAN wines to Aragón and the Balearic Islands.

All this made Naples the most important Mediterranean wine-trading port in the 14th century, yet, because of its many changes of regime and its severance from Sicily in 1282, Naples never became a political or economic power to match the northern city states. Geographically it was far better placed than VENICE and GENOA to conduct the lucrative trade in Aegean wines and other luxury goods with northern Europe, but by the late 13th century, when Genoa began to send its galleys to Southampton and Bruges, Naples was no longer in a position to compete.

Today the name 'Naples' is more readily associated by American wine lovers with an important charity AUCTION held in the city of the same name in Florida.

H.M.W.

Lopez, R. S., 'The trade of mediaeval Europe: the South', in *The Cambridge Economic History of Europe*, 7 vols., ii: *Trade and Industry in the Middle Ages* (1987).
Melis, F., 'Produzione e commercio dei vini italiani nei secoli XIII–XVIII', *Annales cisalpines d'histoire sociale*, 1/3 (1972), 107–33.

Nascetta, white wine grape recently revived in the LANGHE and increasingly appreciated as a savoury VARIETAL wine.

Nasco, ancient light-berried vine making soft white wines from fewer than 100 ha/247 acres around Cagliari on SARDINIA.

natamycin, an antiobiotic used to control the growth of yeasts and moulds in the food industry but not generally permitted as a wine ADDITIVE except in SOUTH AFRICA.

natural alcohol, defined in EU regulations as the total ALCOHOLIC STRENGTH of a wine before any ENRICHMENT.

natural wine, unregulated term, sometimes abbreviated to **natty wine**, used to describe wines made with ORGANIC grapes and no ADDITIVES other than minimal SULFITE additions.

A 2020 OIV presentation described the natural wine movement as more of a philosophy than a practice, stemming from a desire to have 'minimal intervention to achieve maximum purity'.

General guidelines for these minimalists' wines start with the notion that natural wine is made from one ingredient—hand-picked, organically grown grapes with nothing added: no YEAST, ENZYMES, or LACTIC ACID BACTERIA. The wine should be made with minimal intervention: no ENRICHMENT, ACIDIFICATION, CONCENTRATION, or REVERSE OSMOSIS, no cross-flow or tangential FILTRATION, and no extreme TEMPERATURE CONTROL. Nothing that affects the taste and flavour of the wine is allowed, although some more pragmatic practitioners allow a coarse filtration.

The current natural-wine sector, especially popular with younger wine drinkers, was seen as a response to the increased use of AGROCHEMICALS after the Second World War and the resulting need for AMELIORATION in the winery, such as reliance on cultured yeast, excessive SULFUR DIOXIDE, and sugar and the many other approved additives such as enzymes, BACTERIA, TANNINS, and NUTRIENTS.

Marcel Lapierre of Morgon was a seminal figure in the history of natural wine. In the late 1970s the young Beaujolais vigneron became inspired by a neighbour: vigneron, négociant, and scientist Jules Chauvet (now often referred to as the grandfather of the natural-wine movement). As a scientist, Chauvet conducted studies on FERMENTATIONS with and without sulfite additions. As a vigneron he worked organically and used more traditional winemaking methods, including SPONTANEOUS FERMENTATION, and no additives. Lapierre followed Chauvet's minimalist approach, as did his friends Jean Foillard, Jean-Paul Thévenet, and Guy Breton, forming what is often referred to as the 'gang of four'. Jacques Néauport, who worked with Chauvet, became the pre-eminent CONSULTANT for the blossoming band of natural winemakers.

These new wines found their way to the Paris wine bars in the early 1980s and then influenced winemakers throughout France, most notably in the Loire. By 2015, this wine outlier had become widespread if not mainstream, especially but by no means exclusively in wine bars. Italy, Spain, and Georgia were early hot spots but by the second decade of the 21st century it was a global phenomenon, aided by a proliferation of natural wine fairs.

The movement has inspired both zealous followers and virulent critics. American wine writer Robert PARKER called natural wine advocates 'terroir jihadists'.

The category's existence has led in some quarters to a reconsideration of what had been considered FAULTS, with adherents tolerant of cloudiness and perceptible VOLATILE ACIDITY, for instance. Lower sulfite levels have also led to an increase in MOUSY wines.

The genre has encouraged a return to techniques such as SKIN-FERMENTED white wines and PET-NATS as well as a revival of PIQUETTE. The movement is also in tune with other more general trends such as much wider adoption of organic, BIODYNAMIC, and REGENERATIVE viticulture; lower sulfite and alcohol levels; chillable reds such as those described as GLOU-GLOU; less OAKY wines; and experimentation with materials other than oak for fermentation and ageing such as CONCRETE, CLAY, and glass to decrease the impact of exogenic flavours on the wine.

Being often cloudy and reductive (see REDUCTION), natural wines rarely align with standardized tasting profiles and so have often been rejected in European CONTROLLED APPELLATION tastings with the result that many are now sold with no more geographical specificity than their country of origin. Hence VIN DE FRANCE, and several court cases.

There was an anarchic element to those originally involved in the movement who resisted definitions and regulations, but that is changing as the term has gained marketing power and

N

less purist wines sold as 'natural' have emerged. As an attempt to give the consumer protection, at least one private certification, Vin Méthode Nature, was devised in the Loire in 2020 and is recognized by the INAO.

Nomenclature continues to be problematic. Many conventional winemakers resent the implication that their wines are 'unnatural'. The term 'low intervention' is preferred by some producers. See also ZERO-ZERO wines. A.F.

Feiring, A., *Natural Wine for the People* (2019).
Feiring, A., *Naked Wine* (2011).

nature when applied to a French wine usually means 'still'. Nature, with a capital N, is viewed by wine producers as friend or enemy and everything in between, depending on whether they are, respectively, TRADITIONALISTS or technocrats. See NATURAL WINE.

Naturwein, German term for wine from MUSTS to which neither sugar nor water has been added. Once an important mark of quality, the term was abolished by the 1971 German wine law, which replaced it with the notion of wine with PRÄDIKAT. See GERMAN HISTORY.

Navarra, known in English as **Navarre**, autonomous region in north-east SPAIN which also lends its name to a DOP with 10,000 ha/24,711 acres of vineyard in 2021. The kingdom of Navarra once stretched from BORDEAUX to Barcelona, but today this extensive denomination is overshadowed by RIOJA, a small part of which extends into the province of Navarra (see map under SPAIN). The wines share a common history.

Pilgrims en route to Santiago de Compostela fuelled the demand for wine in the Middle Ages. Later, in the mid 19th century, both Rioja and Navarra benefited greatly from their proximity to France after it was invaded by PHYLLOXERA. Because northern Spain was affected considerably later than south-west France, vineyards here were expanded and large quantities of Navarran wine were sold to producers in France until phylloxera arrived in Navarra itself in 1892. The region recovered fairly quickly, but the area under vine in 1990 was less than one-third of that a century before.

The region splits into five subzones according to climate, from the cooler slopes of the Baja Montaña close to the Pyrenean foothills and the slightly warmer Valdizarbe and Tierra Estella districts in the north of Navarra to Ribera Alta in the centre of the region and Ribera Baja round the city of Tudela in the south. Rainfall totals range between 700 mm/28 in in the north and 400 mm in the south and east, while summer temperatures become correspondingly warmer. With over 30% of Navarra's vineyards, Ribera Baja has traditionally been the most important of the five subzones, although most of the planting in the late 1980s and early 1990s took place in the cooler north.

The GARNACHA grape used to dominate Navarra's vineyards but now makes up just 23% as plantings of TEMPRANILLO have increased since the 1990s, now making up 35% of the vineyards. Examples from Terra Estrella can bear a certain resemblance to those of Rioja, which is directly adjacent. For a long time, Garnacha was mainly relegated to good, dry rosé, which the region continues to make in large quantities, but producers such as Santa Cruz de Artazu, Viña Zorzal, Unsi, and Chivite, working with increased respect for the variety, have since proved Garnacha's ability to produce world-class red wines on its own. Cabernet Sauvignon and Merlot are also widely grown, making up 16% and 14% respectively.

White wines are made principally from CHARDONNAY, which was brought to the region from BURGUNDY in the 1200s, and VIURA. Some distinctive sweet whites are made from Moscatel de Grano Menudo (MUSCAT BLANC À PETITS GRAINS) grown in the south. V. de la S. & F.C.

Barquín, J., Guitiérrez, L., and de la Serna, V., *The Finest Wines of Rioja and Northwest Spain* (2011)
www.navarrawines.com

NDVI. See NORMALIZED DIFFERENCE VEGETATION INDEX.

Néac, small red BORDEAUX appellation to the immediate north-east of POMEROL.

Nebbiolo, great black grape variety responsible for some of the finest and longest-lived wines in the world. It has been known in the PIEMONTE region in the north-west of Italy since at least the 13th century and is that area's most distinctive and distinguished vine. The quality of wines such as BAROLO and BARBARESCO inspires hopeful planting of the variety all over the world.

Nebbiolo in Italy

Documents from the castle of Rivoli dating from 1266, when Conto Umberto de Balma is recorded as obtaining a wine named 'Nibiol', provide early evidence of Nebbiolo's existence. PETRUS DE CRESCENTIIS' *Liber ruralium commodorum* in 1304 made an unambiguous link between the 'Nubiola' grape, which he termed 'delightful', and 'excellent wine'. Some have postulated that the name derives from *nobile*, or 'noble', but a more likely derivation is from *nebbia*, or 'fog', a frequent phenomenon in Piemonte in October when the grape is harvested and also possibly a reference to the thick BLOOM on ripe Nebbiolo berries.

Modern Piemonte has shown its respect for Nebbiolo by restricting its planting to a few areas: of the 2020 total of 6,324 ha/15,627 acres (up from 4,476 ha in 2012), more than 80% were in the province of Cuneo, predominantly in Barolo, Barbaresco, and Roero.

Nebbiolo is always the first variety to bud and the last to ripen, with harvests that regularly last well past the middle of October, and the variety is accordingly granted the most favourable HILLSIDE exposures, generally south to south-west. Perhaps as important as the vineyard site, however, are the soils: Nebbiolo has shown itself to be extremely fussy and, with a few exceptions, notably VALTELLINA and ALTO PIEMONTE, has in the past century given best results only in the CALCAREOUS marls to the north and south of Alba on the right bank of the Tanaro in the DOCG zones of BARBARESCO and BAROLO respectively. Here Nebbiolo-based wines reach their maximum aromatic complexity and express a fullness of flavour which balances the relatively high ACIDITY and substantial TANNINS which are invariably present.

Historically, much more Nebbiolo was planted in Alto Piemonte, under the name SPANNA. Total vineyard area declined rapidly there during Italy's industrial revolution in the 1950s but, thanks to growing international interest in this area's elegant Nebbiolo-based wines, has expanded slowly to 630 ha/1,557 acres in 2019.

NEBBIOLO D'ALBA, an earlier-drinking version of the variety, suggests the heights which it can gain in more choice positions. The ROERO DOCG on the left bank of the Tanaro has predominantly sandy soils which produced better and better wine throughout the 1990s. Roero wines, made from at least 95% Nebbiolo, are notably lighter in style and generally age faster than Barbaresco and Barolo.

Nebbiolo, often called Picutener, also plays the leading role in the postage-stamp-size DOC of CAREMA on the border of the Valle d'Aosta, in the neighbouring and equally Lilliputian DOCs of Donnaz and Arnad-Montjovet in the Valle d'AOSTA itself. In Lombardy's VALTELLINA, Nebbiolo is known as Chiavennasca, with 850 ha/2,100 acres, the only sizeable zone where Nebbiolo is cultivated outside Piemonte. These four areas, subalpine in latitude and definitely cool during the growing season, produce a medium-bodied, fragrant style of Nebbiolo from south-facing vineyards on vertigo-inducing slopes which guarantee enough ripeness to mitigate the grape's tannic asperity and acidic sharpness, helped further by CLIMATE CHANGE. Ripeness can also be achieved by drying the grapes, for example Valtellina's full-bodied, complex dry red wine speciality SFORZATO, or Sfurzat.

These zones apart, Nebbiolo is rarely cultivated elsewhere in Italy, although it is an ingredient in the FRANCIACORTA cocktail. The purported plantings of the variety on the island of Sardinia are in all likelihood DOLCETTO.

Three principal CLONES of Nebbiolo are conventionally identified: Lampia (the most common), Michet, and Bolla. This last is declining because of the pale colour of its wines, while Michet is Lampia afflicted with a virus which causes the vine's canes to fork. Although Michet produces smaller bunches and YIELDS and particularly intense aromas and flavours, it does not adapt itself to all soils and is slowly being replaced by superior clonal material, which can achieve Lampia's intensity but without its viral defects. Quite a few producers continue to cherish virus-affected vines, notably Sandrone, who has propagated material from an unspecified, multi-virus-affected Nebbiolo clone giving 50% more PHENOLICS than Lampia. Most producers prefer to rely on a careful MASS SELECTION in their vineyards rather than staking their future on a single clone. More systematic clonal research in the 1990s confirmed that Nebbiolo has serious problems with VIRUSES, perhaps the result of excessive inbreeding in an ancient variety so concentrated on a relatively small area.

The total area planted with Nebbiolo declined towards the turn of the century but seems to be increasing once more in the Langhe, with 6,324 ha/15,627 acres recorded in Piemonte in 2020. W.S.

Genetic relationships

Through DNA PROFILING, researchers in Anna Schneider's laboratory at Torino and José Vouillamoz at DAVIS found that **Nebbiolo Rosé** is not a clone of Nebbiolo but a distinct variety. Furthermore, Nebbiolo Rosé turned out to have a parent–offspring relationship with Nebbiolo. Several additional parent–offspring relationships were discovered between Nebbiolo and traditional varieties from Piemonte (FREISA, VESPOLINA, and Bubbierasco) and Valtellina (Negrera and Rossola). DNA profiling and sequencing has made it possible to classify 98 Nebbiolo clones into seven main genotypes, which generally coincided with the geographical origin of accessions, pointing to Piemonte (and not Valtellina) as its likely place of origin. It was also possible for the first time to discriminate some Nebbiolo clones from the others. J.V.

Gambino, G., et al., 'Whole-genome sequencing and SNV genotyping of "Nebbiolo" (*Vitis vinifera* L.) clones', *Scientific Reports*, 7/17294 (2017).

Robinson, J., et al., *Wine Grapes: A Complete Guide to 1,368 Vine Varieties, Including Their Origins and Flavours* (2012).

Outside Italy

Vine-growers all over the world are experimenting with Nebbiolo. The results often lack the haunting aromas that characterize the variety, but isolated examples in regions as far apart as Oregon, Washington State, and Australia's King Valley and the Yarra Valley in Victoria suggest the quest may not be fruitless. Nebbiolo has so far somewhat reluctantly accompanied Barbera to both North and South America (including Mexico). In California, Sangiovese has proved generally more successful, but there were just 57 ha/142 acres of Nebbiolo in the ground in 2020 compared with South Africa's 78 ha. High yields have tended to subsume the variety's quality in South America. But as the special charms of Barolo and Barbaresco are increasingly appreciated around the world, it is unlikely that growers will give up hope of making great Nebbiolo outside Italy.

Nebbiolo d'Alba is an Italian DOC red produced from NEBBIOLO grapes grown in 2020 on a growing total of 1,087 ha/2,686 acres of vineyard in 32 communes surrounding the city of ALBA in PIEMONTE. Seven of the communes are partially inside the Barolo DOCG zone, although the areas which can produce Nebbiolo d'Alba—the southern sections of Monforte d'Alba and Novello, the north-eastern tip of La Morra, all but a western slice of Diano d'Alba, the northern parts of Verduno, Grinzano Cavour, and Roddi—have been excluded from the Barolo zone. Most of the vineyard land is on the northern bank of the River Tanaro in the Roero hills (which, absurdly, does not belong under the administration of Alba as it lies outside the LANGHE), on sandier soils that yield wines that are softer, less intense, and faster maturing than a Barolo or a Barbaresco, more generically 'Nebbiolo' and less pointedly characterful. The demarcation of the DOC Nebbiolo d'Alba comprises the whole of the DOCG ROERO and therefore can be used by Roero producers for declassification of their wines, more frequently used than ever since Roero DOCG is much less famous than Nebbiolo d'Alba. W.S.

Nebbiolo delle Langhe, now **Langhe Nebbiolo**, See LANGHE. W.S.

necrosis, a term used to describe death of tissue. For example, necrotic spots of leaf tissue caused by DOWNY MILDEW appear blackish-brown. For many vine foliar diseases and disorders, the yellowing of leaf sections, or CHLOROSIS, precedes necrosis.

négociant, French term for a MERCHANT and one used particularly of wine merchants who buy in grapes, MUST, or wine, blend different lots of wine within an AOC, and bottle the result under their own label. The role of the négociant is particularly worthwhile in BURGUNDY, where the oldest négociants, traditionally concentrated in Beaune, have been joined since the later 20th century by a new breed of smaller operators, often run alongside a grower's own DOMAINE. So many individual growers produce tiny quantities from each of a number of different appellations that it can make sense to make up commercially more significant quantities and bottle them together. Many of the larger Burgundy négociants have significant vineyard holdings of their own. BOUCHARD PÈRE ET FILS and BOISSET, for example, are two of the CÔTE D'OR's most substantial vineyard owners. Louis LATOUR, Louis JADOT, and Joseph DROUHIN are other important Burgundian négociants. The term **négociant-éleveur** implies that the négociant oversees the ÉLEVAGE of the wine it sells (not always the case).

Like all important French wine regions, Bordeaux also has a great concentration of négociants, many of which own CHÂTEAUX (while some of the CLASSED GROWTHS are run alongside a négociant business). For more details, see BORDEAUX TRADE.

Negoska, dark-skinned Greek vine variety producing deeply coloured and relatively tannic wines that are often blended with the more acidic XINOMAVRO, particularly in Goumenissa PDO. An increasing number of successful VARIETAL wines are now also being made.

Negramoll, Iberian dark-skinned grape variety and by far the most commonly planted vine variety on the island of MADEIRA, where it is called TINTA NEGRA. As Negramoll or **Negra Mole** it is grown in the CANARY ISLANDS. DNA PROFILING has shown it to be identical to the Portuguese variety Molar. A distinct variety called Negra Mole in Portugal's ALENTEJO is the same as the Andalucian variety Mollar, or Mollar Cano, of which there were 38 ha/94 acres in 2020.

Negrara, name related to the colour of the berries (*negra* meaning 'black') and corresponding to a group of several distinct grape varieties in northern Italy. **Negrara Trentina** is the most common, and recent DNA PROFILING revealed a parent–offspring relationship with ENANTIO. J.V.

Négrette, black grape variety special to the vineyards north of Toulouse in SOUTH WEST FRANCE. In FRONTON, it must dominate the blend, and it is a more minor component in Vins de Lavilledieu. Wine made from Négrette is more supple, perfumed, and flirtatious than that produced from the more famous south-western black grape variety TANNAT, and it is best drunk young, with its fruit—sometimes described as having a slightly animal, or violet, flavour—unsuppressed by heavy OAK AGEING. The variety is inconveniently prone to POWDERY MILDEW and BOTRYTIS BUNCH ROT and is therefore better suited to the hot, dry climate of Toulouse than to many other wine regions. Total French plantings had fallen slightly to 1,086 ha/2,684 acres by 2019. A little is also planted in California, where it was once known as Pinot St George.

Negroamaro, sometimes written **Negro Amaro**, dark-skinned southern Italian grape variety that fell victim to the EU VINE-PULL SCHEMES with the total area planted falling from 31,000 ha/76,500 acres in 1990 to just 11,431 ha/28,247 acres by 2015. It is particularly associated with the eastern half of the Salento peninsula, in the provinces of Lecce and

Brindisi, where it forms the base, blended with small proportions of Malvasia Nera and (not necessarily legally) the more structured PRIMITIVO, for DOCs such as Salice Salentino, Copertino, Brindisi, Leverano, and Squinzano. It is later ripening than Primitivo, with chunkier tannins. It is also used to produce some lively rosé. For more details, see PUGLIA. The name means 'dark, bitter', but the wines are sometimes a bit soft.

Neheleschol, extremely ancient Middle Eastern light-berried vine with enormous bunches, planted experimentally at Mas de Daumas Gassac in the Languedoc.

Nelson, (Whakatū in Māori) is a GEOGRAPHICAL INDICATION in the north-west of NEW ZEALAND's South Island. North of the Southern Alps, it enjoys mild winters and warm summers. Challenges lie in its vulnerability to north-westerly rain during harvest. Sauvignon Blanc dominates with over 600 ha/1,483 acres, while Pinot Noir, Pinot Gris, and Chardonnay shadow with sub-200 ha each. Nelson's two main subregions lie west of the city: the Waimea Plains has light, alluvial-derived soils, while the Moutere Hills are clay-based. S.P.T.

nematodes, microscopic roundworms generally found in soil which can seriously harm vines and other plants. Some feed on bacteria or fungi and are part of the normal vineyard ECOSYSTEM. Others, however, feed on grapevine roots and thus reduce both the size and efficiency of the root system. Although the vines do not necessarily die, they suffer WATER STRESS and deficiencies in VINE NUTRITION and grow weakly. Some species of nematodes are important because they also transmit VIRUS DISEASES. The viruses spread by nematodes are called NEPOVIRUSES. They can be spread throughout the vineyard from just one infected plant by nematode feeding. Often they show up as a few yellow vines in the vineyard.

The fact that nematodes damage vines was first established in about 1930, in California. Because of characteristic and visually striking root damage, the root-knot nematode, *Meloidogyne* species, was considered most important. However, in 1958 it was discovered that FANLEAF DEGENERATION was spread by nematodes of the species *Xiphenema index*, the so-called dagger nematode. This milestone discovery in plant pathology was made by Hewitt and colleagues of the University of California at DAVIS. It had been established in France as long ago as 1883 that fanleaf degeneration spread through the soil, and some French authorities believed until the 1950s that the aphid-like PHYLLOXERA was responsible for the spread.

Root-knot nematodes occur mainly in SANDY soil. Their presence is visible to the naked eye since the knots (swollen tissue or galls) on the roots formed in response to their feeding resemble a string of beads. One female can lay up to 1,000 eggs, and with up to ten generations a year in warm climates they can spread rapidly. The root-lesion nematode *Pratylenchus* also damages vines by feeding on their roots. Virus particles can survive for many years in root fragments after an infected vineyard is removed. Replanting a new, 'virus-free' vineyard can lead to disappointment, as reinfection with nematode feeding can follow.

At one time vineyards in which nematodes were previously present were subjected to FUMIGATION with injected chemicals before planting, but the nematicides DBCP and methyl bromide have both been banned because of environmental considerations. Fumigation is becoming rare, and in California, for example, INTEGRATED PEST MANAGEMENT is suggested as an important alternative, using PESTICIDES such as spirotetramat. COVER CROPS such as daikon radish and mustard have been found to act as biofumigants that deter some types of nematodes.

Nematode diseases are often spread on infected planting material or by the movement of infected soil on cultivation implements or by irrigation water. Infected nursery plants can be freed of nematodes by HOT-WATER treatment. Biological control using ROOTSTOCKS is possible and generally preferred. Some VITIS species (*V. solonis*, *V. champini*, and *V. doaniana*) show resistance to nematodes. Among the most nematode-resistant rootstocks are Couderc 1613, Ramsey, Schwarzmann, Harmony, and Dog Ridge. New ones have been released in the US but have not been widely adopted; the rootstock breeding programme at CSIRO in Australia is developing rootstocks that are both nematode- and phylloxera-resistant. R.E.S.

Ferris, H., et al., 'Resistance of grape rootstocks to plant-parasitic nematodes', *Journal of Nematology*, 44/4 (2012), 377–86.

University of California Agriculture & Natural Resources, UC IPM Pest Management Guidelines: nematodes. www2.ipm.ucanr.edu/agriculture/grape/nematodes.

Zyl, S., et al., 'Xiphinema index and its relationship to grapevines: a review', *South African Journal of Enology & Viticulture*, 33/1 (2012).

Nepal. Notwithstanding sweet wines produced from imported MUST and a variety of wines made from fruits other than grapes, this mountainous country in ASIA had only one winery producing grape wine commercially from own-grown fruit in 2020. Pataleban, started in 2007 with 500 Japanese vines, has four vineyards east of Kathmandu at ELEVATIONS of 800–1,550 m/2,625–5,085 ft. At these heights, the climate is relatively mild, with winter temperatures averaging 2–8 °C/36–46 °F and summer 24–36 °C/75–97 °F. However, annual rainfall averages 2,812 mm/111 in, most of it falling between June and August. Contending with contracted growing seasons due to these annual monsoon rains, Pataleban has planted 30 grape varieties, of which SOLARIS, CABERNET SAUVIGNON, CHARDONNAY, and PHOENIX have been most productive. T.H.

nepoviruses, group of 13 VIRUS DISEASES which are spread from plant to plant by the feeding of NEMATODES (microscopic worms) on roots. They also have in common a polyhedral structure, hence the name 'nepovirus': 'ne' for nematode and 'po' for polyhedral. Such diseases can be very destructive and almost impossible to control. This is because the virus can survive for years in nematodes and root fragments even after all infected vines have been removed. So, even if a new, supposedly virus-free, vineyard is planted, it will quickly become infected by the nematode feeding. Among the important virus diseases in this group are FANLEAF DEGENERATION, tomato ringspot, and tobacco ringspot. R.E.S.

Bettiga, L. J., (ed.), *Grape Pest Management* (3rd edn, 2013).

Nerello Cappuccio produces wines that are rather softer and earlier-maturing than those made from NERELLO MASCALESE. Recent DNA PROFILING has revealed that 70% of the vines on SICILY referred to as Nerello Cappuccio are in fact CARIGNAN. The remaining 30% were a mixture of other known or unknown varieties, including 125 ha/309 acres of Nerello Cappuccio. J.V.

Branzanti, E., et al., 'Analysis of genetic structure of twelve Sicilian grapevine cultivars', *Acta Horticulturae*, 1046 (2014), 677–80.

Nerello Mascalese. The most important and increasingly respected red grape on ETNA, Sicily, also known as **Nerello Calabrese**, makes fine, firm, pale, but long-lived wines. DNA PROFILING has shown it to be a cross of SANGIOVESE and Mantonico Bianco. Total plantings in 2020 were 3,080 ha/7,611 acres, many of the vines being extremely old. See also NERELLO CAPPUCCIO. J.V.

Nero d'Avola, the characteristic red grape variety of southern SICILY, also known as Calabrese, is a possible progeny of the local Mantonico Bianco, suggesting origins in Calabria on the mainland. It is the island's most planted red wine grape, with 14,749 ha/36,446 acres recorded there in 2020. Producers value the body, deep colour, and sweet-cherry fruit which Nero d'Avola can bring to a blend. VARIETAL Nero d'Avola responds well to BARREL AGEING. Like Syrah, Nero d'Avola requires a good site, warmth, and low VINE TRAINING to succeed. Avola itself is in the southern part of the province of Siracusa, and nearby Pachino, on the extreme south-eastern tip of the island, is particularly reputed for the quality of its Nero d'Avola grapes.

Nero di Troia, fine red wine grape speciality named after a village near Foggia making firm, savoury wines in Castel del Monte in PUGLIA that was recently renamed from Uva di Troia by locals mindful of the success of NERO D'AVOLA. DNA PROFILING has shown that it is a natural offspring of BOMBINO BIANCO and Quagliano from Piemonte. There were 2,512 ha/ 6,220 acres in Italy in 2015.

Netherlands, north European country more often referred to as Holland, whose inhabitants are known as the Dutch. In the 17th century particularly, they played a dominant role in the world's wine and spirit trade (see DUTCH WINE TRADE) and played a key role in draining the MÉDOC lowlands bordering the Gironde.

The country also has its own small wine industry with an impressive history, despite the coolness of the climate. There are records of wine-producing vines growing in Limburg in southern Holland in 1324, and vine-growing around Maastricht ceased only in the early 19th century, discouraged by a series of cold summers and the economic turbulence of the Napoleonic era. It was not until 1967 that the Netherlands became a wine producer once more when Frits Bosch created his Slavante vineyard of just 800 sq m.

Nowadays CLIMATE CHANGE is encouraging more winegrowing and improving wine quality. In 2021 there were about 200 active vine-growers, with an estimated total of 300 ha/740 acres of vines planted.

Vines are spread throughout the country, among 12 PGIS: Drenthe, Flevoland, Friesland, Gelderland, Groningen, Limburg, Noord-Brabant, Noord-Holland, Overijssel, Utrecht, Zeeland, and Zuid-Holland. In 2017 the country introduced its first PDO (called Beschermde Oorsprongsbenaming, or BOB, in Dutch), **Limburg Maasvallei.** This is also the first European cross-border appellation, with vineyards in BELGIUM as well in the Netherlands. Dutch producer Wijngoed Thorn worked closely with Aldeneyck in Belgium to achieve this recognition. By 2021, five more BOBs were registered: **Achterhoek-Winterswijk** along the border with Germany; **Ambt Delden,** in the province of Overijssel; **Mergelland,** in the hills of southern Limburg; **Oolde** in Gelderland; and **Vijlen,** the highest village in the Netherlands at 200 m/ 656 ft in ELEVATION.

The Netherland's best and largest producers tend to be found in the south, in the province of Limburg, where Apostelhoeve, the country's oldest commercial winery, was founded in the 1970s, although Gelderland, the province just north of Limburg, produces the most wine by volume, and Zeeland, in the sunny south-west, is home to one of the best Dutch producers: Kleine Schorre.

Vineyards in the south are planted mainly to VITIS VINIFERA varieties such as Riesling, Müller-Thurgau, Auxerrois, Chardonnay, Pinot Blanc, and Pinot Gris for white wines and Pinot Noir for light reds. In recent years, production of sparkling wines has grown considerably, with the advent of producers such as Wijngaard Raarberg focusing entirely on TRADITIONAL METHOD sparkling wines.

Winegrowing in more northerly and eastern parts of the country, notably Gelderland and Overijssel, depends largely on DISEASE-RESISTANT VARIETIES such as REGENT, RONDO, Pinotin, and Cabernet Cortis for reds and Cabernet Blanc, Johanniter, Merzling, Souvignier Gris, and SOLARIS for white wines. R.d.G.

nets can literally save a grape crop. See BIRDS and HAIL.

Neuburger, sometimes distinguished white grape variety grown almost exclusively on 260 ha/642 acres in AUSTRIA. DNA PROFILING in Austria showed it is a CROSS, possibly accidental, of ROTER VELTLINER × SYLVANER. It makes nutty wine that tastes like an even fuller-bodied WEISSBURGUNDER. It is also encountered in Czechia and Slovakia (as Neuburské), in Slovenia, and in Romania's Transylvania.

Neusiedlersee refers to both the 133-km/ 83-mile-long, notably shallow lake of mysterious origin that plays a critical role in the winegrowing MESOCLIMATES of the northern half of Austrian BURGENLAND and to an official wine region and DAC covering much of that lake's shore, with 6,240 ha/15,419 acres of vines in 2021 making up 14% of Austria's total.

A quick tour of this region highlights its geological, mesoclimatic, and vinous diversity. The villages of Winden and Jois in the region's north-west alternately feature slopes of mica SCHIST and LIMESTONE, and sites such as the Alter Berg and Junger Berg are gradually re-establishing reputations with BLAUFRÄNKISCH and Pinot Noir (Blauburgunder). Among white wines, the Pinot Blanc (WEISSBURGUNDER) in this sector—while not widely planted—also distinguishes itself. At the northern tip of the lake, the low range of hills between the Parndorfer Platte and the lake shore at Weiden and Gols features combinations of GRAVEL, SAND, and CLAY that support all the local red grape varieties—notably Blaufränkisch, ST-LAURENT, Pinot Noir, and ZWEIGELT—as well as Merlot, Cabernet, and even some Syrah. The wealth of white grapes in this sector includes Chardonnay, NEUBURGER, Weissburgunder, and Sauvignon Blanc. Few villages in Austria are more singularly devoted to viticulture nor so crowded with family wineries than Gols, among which Hans 'John' Nittnaus was the pioneer in the 1980s, champion of unblended Blaufränkisch. Josef 'Pepi' Umathum is notable for his rigorous Blaufränkisch vine selection, part of a multifaceted local cultural preservation project. A wide diversity of vine varieties is perpetuated around Mönchhof, Halbturn, and Frauenkirchen further south and east—the so-called Heideboden sector—more dominated by the warmth of the Great Pannonian Plain and less by the lake, a dominance that reaches its Austrian apex at Andau on the Hungarian frontier, known for its rich, powerful Zweigelt.

Along the alternately SANDY and GRAVELLY eastern shore of the Neusiedlersee as it descends towards the Hungarian border and an expanse of reedy swampland east of SOPRON, the villages of Podersdorf, Illmitz, and Apetlon are home—like Rust on the opposite shore—to Austria's most renowned BOTRYTIZED sweet wines, along with occasionally remarkable dry whites. Fog and humidity from Lake Neusiedl and a mosaic of other small lakes engender frequent BOTRYTIS, while sunshine reflected off their surfaces and off the bright white expanses of sand and dried mineral salts serves to project light into the grape clusters and, conjoined with this sector's generally low rainfall, ensures that the rot remains NOBLE. In this so-called Seewinkel sector of the Neusiedlersee, grape varieties include Chardonnay, MUSKATELLER, Sauvignon Blanc, Traminer, Pinot Blanc, and WELSCHRIESLING plus significant amounts of BOUVIER, MUSCAT OTTONEL, Zweigelt, and SCHEUREBE (known locally as SÄMLING 88). Strohwein—STRAW WINE known locally as *Schilfwein*—contrasts with the region's far more prevalent botrytized AUSLESE, BEERENAUSLESE, and TROCKENBEERENAUSLESE wines, while EISWEIN is also made with relative regularity.

In 2011 Neusiedlersee became a DAC associated exclusively with Zweigelt or blends dominated by that grape, with a Reserve category specifying CASK AGEING, higher minimum alcohol, and later release. In 2020 the DAC was extended to encompass sweet wines labelled Spätlese, Auslese, Beerenauslese or Trockenbeerenauslese. D.S.

Neusiedlersee-Hügelland, former name of an Austrian wine region now known as LEITHABERG.

Nevers is the town that gives its name to the central French *département* of Nièvre, most famous in the wine world for the wines of POUILLY-FUMÉ and for its OAK.

New England Australia, inland region in the northern hilltops of NEW SOUTH WALES boasting Australia's highest vineyard at an ELEVATION of 1,320 m/4,330 ft. The elevation coupled with a CONTINENTAL CLIMATE and significant humidity make FROST, HAIL, thunderstorms, and disease pressure significant challenges, but winegrowers are increasingly drawn to the cool climate and TERRA ROSSA soils. Riesling,

N

Chardonnay, and Shiraz dominate, but other varieties including Nebbiolo, Barbera, Sangiovese, Gewürztraminer, and Tempranillo also show promise. A.R.P.

New Jersey, state in the north-east United States with a history of winemaking dating to 1758, when Great Britain's Royal Society offered £100 to any colonist who would produce red or white wine 'of acceptable quality', meaning of the same calibre as that being purchased from France. By 1767, two residents of what is now New Jersey had succeeded, and the region's wine industry had begun.

New Jersey wine flourished in the late 19th and early 20th centuries, with the town of Egg Harbor City even earning the moniker 'Wine City' thanks to the success of the Renault Winery, run by an expat from Champagne. The winery became the largest distributor of 'American champagne' in the US and still sells it under that name thanks to a grandfather clause in federal labelling laws.

PROHIBITION took a toll on industry growth and produced a restrictive state law that allowed only one winery licence for every 1,000,000 state residents. This was repealed in 1981 with the New Jersey Farm Winery Act. By 2022 the state counted over 60 wineries, more than 1,124 ha/3,000 acres of vineyards, and four AVAs: Cape May Peninsula, Warren Hills, Central Delaware Valley (shared with PENNSYLVANIA), and the Outer Coastal Plain.

While the state is the fifth smallest in the nation, it offers a wide variety of MESOCLIMATES thanks to its varied GEOLOGY and the proximity of the Atlantic Ocean, with which it shares 225 km/140 miles of coastline. In the hilly north, soils are mainly CLAY and the climate is temperate, with 2429 growing degree days (GDD; see CLIMATE CLASSIFICATION); the south is warmer (3659 GDD), with mainly SANDY soils. Over 80 grape varieties are grown, with VITIS VINIFERA at 60%, HYBRIDS at 30%, and VITIS LABRUSCA at 10%. Leading white varieties are ALBARIÑO, CHARDONNAY, GRÜNER VELTLINER, PETIT MANSENG, and RIESLING. Leading red varieties include CABERNET FRANC, CABERNET SAUVIGNON, PINOT NOIR, MERLOT, PETIT VERDOT, and BLAUFRÄNKISCH. Major French-American hybrids that flourish in New Jersey include CHAMBOURCIN, VIDAL Blanc, and VIGNOLES.

The state receives on average 64 cm/25 in of rain during the growing season; thus controlling the major fungal diseases POWDERY MILDEW, DOWNY MILDEW, BLACK ROT, and BOTRYTIS is a constant challenge. Still, many winegrowers are making a concerted effort towards SUSTAINABLE VITICULTURE. In the past, WINTER FREEZE was a primary concern, but CLIMATE CHANGE has brought about milder winters. Deer and BIRDS remain a challenge, and control measures for the SPOTTED LANTERNFLY are still being researched.

New Jersey wines now regularly receive critical acclaim in major wine publications and wine competitions. Most wineries are small, selling direct to the consumer at the CELLAR DOOR, though state legislation allows the state's wines to be sold in BYO restaurants, an arrangement that has been very beneficial for wine sales. G.C.P.

New Latitude Wines, term used largely to refer to wines made in the TROPICAL fringes of the global wine map such as CAMBODIA, INDONESIA, MYANMAR, SRI LANKA, THAILAND, and VIETNAM, although it could equally well apply to those grown at high LATITUDE where viticulture has recently been encouraged by CLIMATE CHANGE. See DENMARK, ESTONIA, FINLAND, LATVIA, LITHUANIA, NORWAY, and SWEDEN.

New Mexico, state in south-west United States where VITIS VINIFERA vineyards date to 1629. Spanish Europeans, using water sourced by indigenous Pueblo people near what is now Socorro, New Mexico, planted MISSION grapes to make wine for the EUCHARIST. In 2021, New Mexico had *c.*405 ha/1,000 acres of vineyard and 55 bonded wineries.

Although the territory (New Mexico gained statehood in 1912) produced nearly a million gallons of wine by the early 1900s, the industry was repeatedly wiped out by flooding of the Rio Grande River that bisects the state. PROHIBITION closed down the remaining industry.

The state underwent a renewal in the 1980s, led by European winegrowers, chief among them Paolo D'Andrea, from Friuli, Italy; Herve Lescombes from Algeria by way of France; and the Gruet family from France.

The state's CONTINENTAL CLIMATE is generally categorized as semi-arid and hot. However, New Mexico has 10 USDA climatic zones and a wide range of MESOCLIMATES, and growing DEGREE DAYS vary from 1800 in Taos to 5133 in Las Cruces. ELEVATION plays a crucial role, with vineyards ranging from 1,158 m/3,800 ft in the south to 2,134 m/7,000 ft in the north. Precipitation also varies widely, averaging 75–500 mm/3–20 in annually, with most occurring during July and August, known as the 'monsoon' season. New Mexico vineyards benefit from low humidity that minimizes FUNGAL DISEASE pressure, and the DIURNAL TEMPERATURE RANGE can be as much as 22–28 °C/40–50 °F. Alkaline desert soils are predominant, with a PH range of 6 to 9. (See SOIL ALKALINITY.) Soil SALINITY is problematic in many vineyards given mineral-laden (often sodium) IRRIGATION water, scarce rainfall, and high EVAPORATION rates. Other grape-growing challenges include high WINDS, dust storms, DROUGHT, FROST, and damaging cold events post-harvest before the vine has had time to adapt to local conditions. Elevated temperatures during grape ripening can also result in juice with excessive sugar levels and high pH that must be addressed in the winery (see AMELIORATION and MANIPULATION).

Grapevine acreage is concentrated in the south-west and centre of the state where the climate is milder and there is access to irrigation water from the Rio Grande or wells. The state's three AVAs, Mesilla Valley, Mimbres Valley, and Middle Rio Grande Valley, are in these sections. However, many winegrowers are increasingly setting up wineries further north, closer to popular destinations such as Santa Fe and Taos, to take advantage of the TOURISM potential. Vine-growing can be risky at these higher elevations (especially north of Albuquerque) as vineyards can be regularly killed to the ground by winter cold. Growers there tend to grow UNGRAFTED VINES as this allows them to train a new shoot from the surviving root system rather than replanting.

The state supports an impressively diverse range of grape varieties, from Chardonnay, Pinot Noir, and Pinot Meunier dedicated to the TRADITIONAL METHOD sparkling wines of Gruet, New Mexico's largest producer, to Italian varieties such as Montepulciano, Aglianico, Negroamaro, Refosco, and Teroldego, and Austrian Grüner Veltliner and Zweigelt, not to mention the classic INTERNATIONAL VARIETIES Riesling, Cabernet Franc, Zinfandel, Chenin Blanc, and Malbec. Muscat, often bottled as 'Moscato' in an off-dry to semi-sweet style, pairs especially well with the state's traditionally spicy food.

HYBRIDS, ever popular with New Mexico's growers due to their hardiness, consistent yields, and quality, are gaining more attention due to the constant threat of PIERCE'S DISEASE and PHYLLOXERA in neighbouring states and CLIMATE CHANGE. Chambourcin, Regent, Baco Noir, and Norton are proven reds; in whites, Vidal, Seyval, and Traminette stand out. Frontenac, Marquette, and new releases from the University of Arkansas and CORNELL are also showing potential.

Today, MISSION, New Mexico's original heritage grape, is enjoying a resurgence. Several producers take advantage of its consistent cropping ability and light colour to produce a refreshingly dry rosé. G.G.

New South Wales, Australia's most populous state, situated on the continent's south-east coast, boasts the longest history of grape-growing in Australia.

The original grapevines from the First Fleet were planted at Sydney Cove in 1788, with subsequent vineyards planted around the fertile agricultural lands surrounding Sydney in the early 1800s. In 1833, James BUSBY's collection of vines arrived in Sydney; CUTTINGS from these vines were later taken to other parts of the state and across to Victoria and South Australia, helping to establish viticulture across a great swathe of the country.

Today, New South Wales has eight official wine zones that are further divided into 16 GEOGRAPHICAL INDICATIONS (GIs). Spread over approximately 810,000 square kilometres/ 312,742 square miles, the state features an incredibly diverse range of climates, from warm inland areas reliant on IRRIGATION and cool high-ELEVATION sites perched along the Great Dividing Range to coastal climates marked by significant HUMIDITY. The region is second only to South Australia in terms of volumes produced, contributing 29% of the national crush in 2022.

The state's best-known region is the **Hunter Valley**, 130 km/80 miles north of Sydney. Although the climate is subtropical, with high temperatures, humidity, and regular rainfall making it a less obvious choice for the production of quality wine, the region has become famed for its SÉMILLON, produced in a dry, unoaked style that develops astonishing COMPLEXITY with bottle age. The very best reach their peak at 15–25 years of age, developing toasty, honeyed, nutty, lemon-curd tertiary flavours. The grapes are picked early, resulting in ALCOHOLIC STRENGTH of just 10–11.5%. The region also excels in ripe, generous Chardonnay and has historically been known for a distinctive style of Shiraz with savoury 'sweaty-saddle' overtones, though more recent examples offer a more vibrant red-berry fruit profile.

Lying to the west and south of the Hunter Valley along the western slopes of the Great Dividing Range is the cooler Central Ranges Zone, with three subregions. **Mudgee** is the oldest, with a history of viticulture dating back to 1858; with a temperate CONTINENTAL CLIMATE and VOLCANIC and sandy LOAM soils, it is best known for bold, full-bodied, generous Shiraz and Cabernet Sauvignon, though it is also gaining traction for crisp, ageworthy Riesling. To its south, the cooler, higher ELEVATIONS of **Orange** have gained a reputation for crisp, elegant Chardonnay with bright peach notes, lively Sauvignon Blanc, peppery Shiraz, and mid-weight Cabernet Sauvignon blends. Both Pinot Noir and Riesling show promise, as does the production of TRADITIONAL METHOD sparkling wine. **Cowra** forms the southern end of the zone, a warm, flat, low-lying region producing generous Chardonnay and soft, fruity Shiraz, Cabernet Sauvignon, and Grenache.

The Southern New South Wales zone radiates out north and west from the capital city of Canberra, with four GIs. The **Canberra District** GI encompasses vineyards in both the Australian Capital Territory itself as well as the surrounding hills; with various elevations and a strongly continental climate, it produces everything from Riesling to Shiraz, with noteworthy examples of Chardonnay, Pinot Noir, and Rhône white varieties including Marsanne, Roussanne, and Viognier. To its north-west, the moderately cool-climate **Hilltops** GI, situated on the south-western slopes of the Great Dividing Range, excels with elegant, cool-climate styles of Shiraz and Cabernet Sauvignon. Plantings of Italian and Mediterranean varieties are also on the rise. **Gundagai** sits to its south, its warmer, lower elevations producing ripe Shiraz, Cabernet Sauvignon, and Chardonnay, while **Tumbarumba**, which climbs into the Australian Alps, focuses on cool-climate Chardonnay and Pinot Noir, producing impressive base wines for sparkling wine as well as elegant still wines.

The large catchment area of the Big Rivers Zone comprising the **Murray Darling**, **Perricoota**, **Riverina**, and **Swan Hill** regions is responsible for the vast majority of production in the state. Vineyards are reliant on IRRIGATION, allowing for high yields and substantial production volumes. Much of it is destined for CASK and BULK WINE markets. Many wines produced here end up exported as wines of SOUTH EASTERN AUSTRALIA. Chardonnay is still the most planted variety, although with the rising cost of water required for irrigation, interest is increasing in less water-intensive Italian and Mediterranean varieties.

There are just two GIs north of Hunter: HASTINGS RIVER, up the coast from Sydney, and, further north, meeting the border with Queensland, NEW ENGLAND AUSTRALIA. A.R.P.

www.nswwine.com.au

new varieties, somewhat loose and relative term used to describe VINE VARIETIES that have been specifically and deliberately developed, which effectively means developed since the late 19th century.

There is interest in breeding new varieties which are resistant, for example, to environmental stresses, fungal and bacterial diseases, and nematodes and insects (see VINE BREEDING and DISEASE-RESISTANT VARIETIES). Of these, the major goals are varieties tolerant of the fungal diseases DOWNY MILDEW, POWDERY MILDEW, and BOTRYTIS BUNCH ROT or resistant to PIERCE'S DISEASE. Unfortunately, new varieties, especially HYBRIDS but even some CROSSES, suffer from the stigma of the poor wine quality of the early French hybrids. The uptake of newly developed grape varieties has been further hindered by consumer preference for traditional varieties, especially INDIGENOUS VARIETIES with a long history, and INTERNATIONAL VARIETIES.

The early French hybridizers mentioned in FRENCH HYBRIDS were not the only French vine breeders to have developed new varieties. Louis BOUSCHET and his son Henri used controlled pollination from 1824 to create a range of seedlings which after selection became known as the Bouschet CROSSES, the most important of which was the TEINTURIER variety ALICANTE BOUSCHET—the only one to be officially recommended for planting in France. Another early and successful VITIS VINIFERA vine breeder was Hermann Müller, whose variety MÜLLER-THURGAU was once the most planted in Germany. A succession of new crosses followed, notably from research institutes at Alzey, Freiburg, Geilweilerhof, GEISENHEIM, Weinsburg, and Würzburg. For details of these, see GERMAN CROSSES.

Other newish varieties such as Zweigelt, Blauburger, and Neuburger were bred in Austria, the first two at KLOSTERNEUBURG. The emphasis in RUSSIA has been on breeding varieties with cold tolerance as well as disease tolerance, and there are substantial areas, not just in Russia but in other ex-Soviet republics, planted with varieties such as SAPERAVI Severny, Stepniak, Fioletovy Ranni, and CABERNET SEVERNY. In NEW YORK State and CANADA, the emphasis also has been on developing varieties with cold and disease tolerance, often relying on the French hybrids for resistant genes. Releases such as CAYUGA WHITE (1972), CHARDONEL (1990), and TRAMINETTE (1996), all bred at CORNELL, are being more widely planted. The names of the last two varieties, incorporating those of their respective *vinifera* parents, may make them more acceptable to consumers. There is particular enthusiasm for grapevine breeding in the American Midwest, where new varieties seem to be valued as much by consumers for their local origins as by growers for their cold hardiness and disease resistance (see, for example, LA CROSSE, MARQUETTE, and TRAMINETTE).

New varieties in France, most of them developed in association with the University of MONTPELLIER, have been *vinifera* crosses such as PORTAN, CALADOC, CHASAN, and Arriloba, as well as EGIODOLA and ARINARNOA developed by INRA at Bordeaux.

In France, new varieties must first be registered with the Comité Technique Permanent de la Sélection des Plantes Cultivées (CTPS) as a prelude to their recognition in the EU. Active breeding programmes are underway in many other parts of Europe, notably in CZECHIA and in SLOVAKIA.

Australia has a vine-breeding programme designed to produce varieties suitable for hot climates, and Goyura, TARRANGO, Tullilah, TAMINGA, TYRIAN, and CIENNA have all been released. In California such new varieties as CARNELIAN, RUBY CABERNET, EMERALD RIESLING, SYMPHONY, and FLORA have all enjoyed popularity at some point, while RUBIRED, unlike similarly red-fleshed ROYALTY, is widely planted to add colour to blends.

New varieties of particular interest offer natural disease resistance with much-reduced use of AGROCHEMICALS. These DISEASE-RESISTANT VARIETIES have complex genealogies which may include not just *vinifera* genes but also those of various AMERICAN VINE SPECIES, French hybrids, and even Asian vine species.

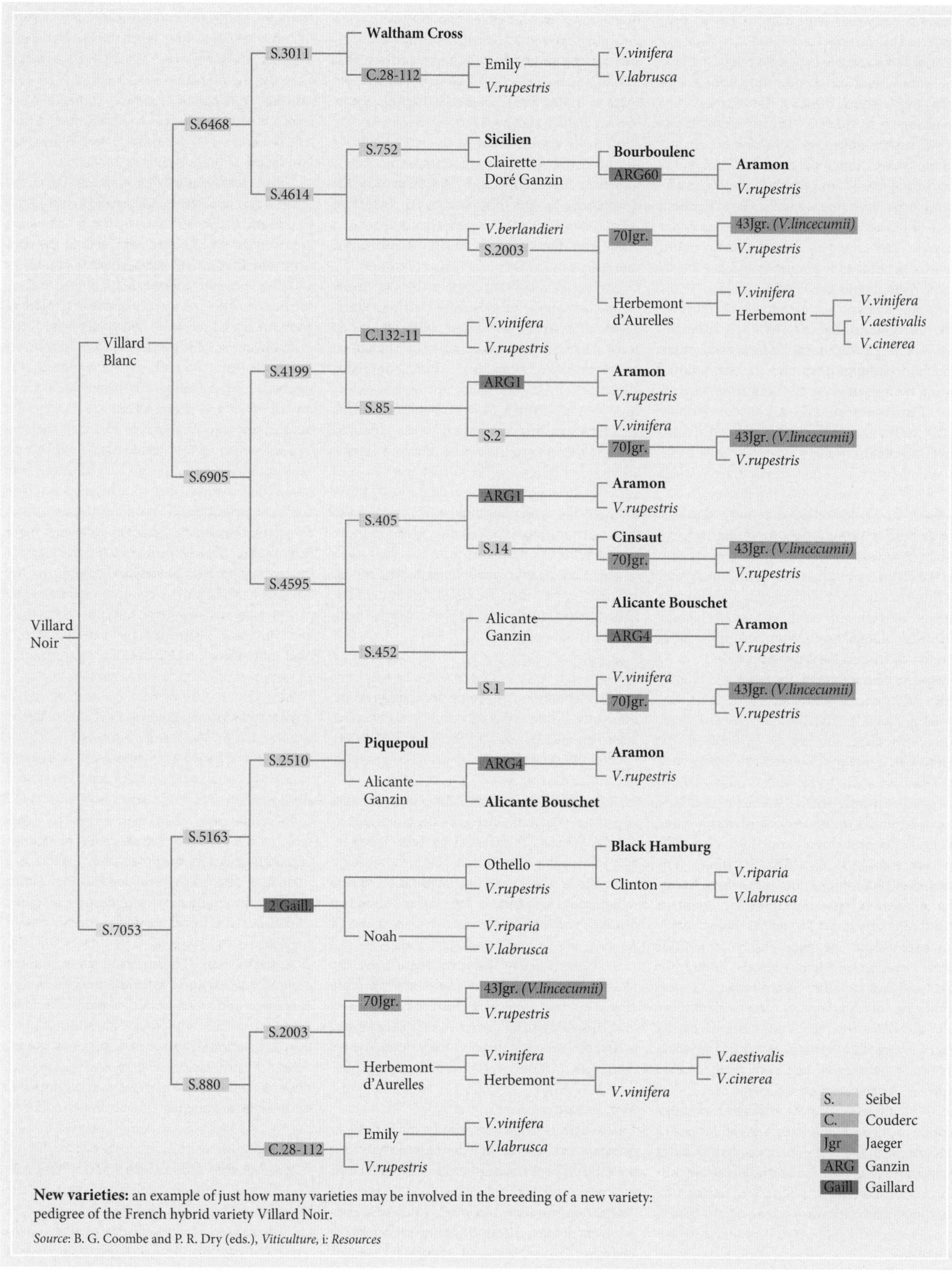

New varieties: an example of just how many varieties may be involved in the breeding of a new variety: pedigree of the French hybrid variety Villard Noir.

Source: B. G. Coombe and P. R. Dry (eds.), *Viticulture*, i: *Resources*

INRAE's ResDur (RÉSistance DURable) programme, for example, released its first four disease-resistant varieties for planting in 2018: the reds Artaban and Vidoc and whites Floréal and Voltis are classified as interspecific hybrids that incorporate genes that confer polygenic resistance to downy and powdery mildew. This has been done by traditional breeding techniques enhanced by the ability to identify genetic markers, not by GENETIC MODIFICATION. They have been included in the French official catalogue of varieties and authorized by the INAO for planting within strict limits as so-called *variétés d'intérêt à fin d'adaptation* (VIFA) in wine regions such as Bordeaux. Further disease-resistant varieties were included in the catalogue in 2021 and 2022: Coliris, Lilaro, Sirano, Selenor, and Opalor.

Such breeding programmes are being carried out in many parts of the world as CLIMATE CHANGE and increasing disease pressure threaten the quality and character of established combinations of variety and vineyard region.

R.E.S. & R.K.C.T.

Covert, C., 'Cold climate grape varieties from eastern U.S. breeding programs', *FPS Grape Program Newsletter* (Oct 2008). iv.ucdavis.edu/files/24502.pdf.

New World, term once much used in the wine world, initially somewhat patronizingly, to distinguish the wine regions established in European colonies from the early 16th to the early 19th centuries, including MEXICO, PERU, CHILE, ARGENTINA, the UNITED STATES, SOUTH AFRICA, AUSTRALIA, and NEW ZEALAND. Colonists needed wine for religious reasons (see EUCHARIST), but vines were also planted on secular estates. In these historical terms, wine's New World contrasts with the OLD WORLD of Europe and the other Mediterranean countries where the vine was widely established by the 4th century. (See individual country entries for these histories.) A more appropriate term for countries with a relatively short history of wine production, for example FINLAND, ESTONIA, or THAILAND, might be 'emerging wine regions'. While the labels Old and New World have precise historical origins, in today's expanding world of wine they are more typically and loosely used to describe different approaches to VITICULTURE and WINEMAKING, as outlined below. What might once have been clear differences between the Old and New Worlds of wine have been steadily eroded by the exchange of ideas and technologies around the globe so that as a way of characterizing wine styles, the terms are little more than short-hand generalizations and far less useful than they once were.

Viticulture

While it is almost impossible to generalize about the viticultural practices of countries as diverse as the United States, Australia, New Zealand, South Africa, Chile, Argentina, and Mexico as opposed to those more usual in Europe, it is possible to outline the approaches and methods typically associated with the phrase 'New World viticulture'.

Planting distances, or VINE DENSITY: there is a particularly marked contrast between the 1 m by 1 m (3 ft by 3 ft) high-density planting of the MÉDOC and the 3.7 m by 2.5 m (12 ft by 8 ft) planting pattern that was long common in California and Australia. But no difference is absolute or constant. In some parts of the Old World, there is a trend towards wider spacings for reasons of economy and MECHANIZATION, while some growers in the New World have been planting more densely, sometimes to an extreme extent, in a search for higher quality.

VINE VARIETIES and ROOTSTOCKS: there is little difference in what is planted in the New and Old Worlds, usually because the New World has concentrated on the INTERNATIONAL VARIETIES made famous in the Old World. New World regions are less likely to have a rich heritage of INDIGENOUS VARIETIES (of VITIS VINIFERA), but some have become specifically associated with certain varieties, for example the PAÍS and CARMENÈRE of Chile, the PINOTAGE and almost extinct PONTAC of South Africa, or the ZINFANDEL of California.

Vineyards and MECHANIZATION: Old World methods are more traditional, and many aspects of modern viticultural technology, especially MECHANIZATION and PRECISION VITICULTURE, have been developed and first used in the New World. MECHANICAL HARVESTING and MECHANICAL PRUNING, for example, were first developed in America, but by the early 1990s there was a high degree of acceptance, of the former at least, in Europe. Technological advance is by no means the sole prerogative of the New World, however. The development and application of new technology in Europe is the equal of anywhere in the world, as evidenced by work there on CLONAL SELECTION, VINE BREEDING, and CANOPY MANAGEMENT. Some vineyard sites in the Old World have been used for viticulture for hundreds of years, but there are probably more potential new vineyard regions to be discovered in the New World (see VINEYARD SITE SELECTION).

R.E.S.

Winemaking

Old World winegrowers are far more likely to be restricted by local regulations governing CONTROLLED APPELLATIONS, whereas both viticulturists and winemakers in the New World are much more willing, and much freer, to experiment and may therefore be more subject to changes of direction and swings of FASHION. The belief in some quarters that the Old World, with its centuries of winemaking tradition, was ruled by Nature, the New World by the application of SCIENCE, has been well and truly turned on its head by the increasingly extreme events brought about by CLIMATE CHANGE. A scientific understanding of Nature and winemaking is now applied throughout the world to adapt to the changing climate and promote SUSTAINABILITY.

New World winemaking was once associated with PROTECTIVE WINEMAKING methods, attempting to shield grapes, juice, MUST, and wine from OXYGEN throughout the winemaking process, especially for white wines and light reds. However, as with so many New/Old World distinctions, this one has become more blurred as research into oxygen management in all parts of the wine world progresses, especially when it comes to BOTTLING and CLOSURES (see, for example, TOTAL PACKAGE OXYGEN and PREMATURE OXIDATION). Obsession with HYGIENE is generally more marked in the New World, with the consequence that WATER use is much higher, although water shortages and the need for water conservation and reuse are now global issues in just about every wine region.

Other winemaking practices that might once have differentiated producers in the New World from those in Old include cooler FERMENTATION temperatures, the use of cultured versus ambient YEASTS, shorter post-fermentation MACERATION time for red wines, and the use of ENZYMES, both for settling and for releasing flavours.

Style

Today 'New World' is just as likely to be used to refer to the style of a wine as to its origin. So-called New World wines are much more likely to be VARIETAL in both how they are described on the label and how they taste, although a growing proportion of these wines are now being made with the clear intention of expressing their geographical provenance (see REGIONALITY and TERROIR). A 'New World' wine is more likely to be immediately appealing on release with less capacity for extended bottle AGEING. FRUIT-DRIVEN was an essentially New World wine description, coined in the 1980s, although today it may be heard and appreciated everywhere.

While the terms 'Old World' and 'New World' have their origin in a historical context, they are perhaps more useful in describing the different approaches to winegrowing and wine styles than in locating a wine in a particular country or continent.

J.E.H.

New York, north-eastern state of the United States between the Atlantic Ocean and the Great Lakes, historically an important source of wine and now third to CALIFORNIA and WASHINGTON in both vineyard hectarage and volume produced. Its inland wine regions share some characteristics with those of ONTARIO across the border in CANADA.

History

Before European colonists arrived in the 17th century, the fertile lands of New York were home to many Native American communities who made ample use of the state's abundant wild grapes. (See AMERICAN VINE SPECIES.) The fruit was used as both food and medicine, fresh and dried. It was the Europeans, however, who attempted to make wine with it, but they found the FOXY flavour of the native VITIS LABRUSCA unpleasant. After several unsuccessful trials with imported VITIS VINIFERA around Manhattan Island, little more was heard of viticulture in New York until the early 19th century. By that time, many of the Lenape people downstate and the Haudenosaunee Confederacy to the north had been forced to flee west by land-hungry settlers and the disease and violence they spread.

Vine-growing slowly developed across the state. While *vinifera* plantings remained challenging, the native vines often hybridized by chance with other *labruscas*, other American vine species such as *Vitis aestivalis*, or even *vinifera* varieties, producing a second generation of native grapes such as CONCORD and ISABELLA. Propagated by vine-growers such as Long Island nurseryman William Robert Prince, who saw the value in their cold hardiness and disease resistance, these vines became the basis for the state's first successful commercial winery, Blooming Grove, founded in 1839 in Washingtonville, about 89 km/55 miles north of New York City, on the Hudson River.

By the 1850s, a fledgling wine industry had started up around the FINGER LAKES of north-central New York, growing to encompass 9,700 ha/24,000 acres of vines by 1890s. Meanwhile, the grape-growing industry that had started in OHIO spread northwards along the Lake Erie shore and into western New York. Some of the region's grapes went into wine, but the temperance movement leading up to PROHIBITION turned vine-growers increasingly towards growing Concord for GRAPE JUICE. This 'grape-belt' would become—and still is—the world's largest Concord grape-growing region, with 6,542 ha/16,166 acres planted in 2021.

Vinifera vines didn't begin to catch on in New York until the 1950s, when viticulturist Dr Konstantin Frank was hired as a consultant at Gold Seal Winery in the Finger Lakes region. Having worked with *vinifera* in his native UKRAINE, he was convinced of their viability in the state's cool climate. Using PHYLLOXERA-resistant ROOTSTOCKS and implementing techniques such as burying the vines for WINTER PROTECTION, he established *vinifera* vineyards fast enough for Gold Seal to release its first commercial *vinifera* wines in 1960. By 1962 Frank was distributing *vinifera* CUTTINGS from his own nursery, where he had 60-some varieties on trial.

Still, winemaking was slow to take off until the Farm Winery Act of 1976, which made it economically feasible for grape-growers to own and operate a small winery by allowing direct sales to consumers. Prior to the act, there were only 20 licensed wineries. By 2019 there were 471, with 14,164 ha/35,000 acres of vineyards. The state continues to have more vinous diversity than any other major wine-producing state, as native American vines, AMERICAN HYBRIDS, and FRENCH HYBRIDS still account for 76% of its vineyards. Most of their produce, however, goes to grape juice, preserves, and TABLE GRAPES; 90% of NY wines are produced from *vinifera* varieties, although CLIMATE CHANGE concerns are inspiring some winegrowers to give hybrids another look.

Pinney, T., *A History of Wine in America, from the Beginnings to Prohibition* (1989).

Geography and climate

New York has 11 American Viticultural Areas (AVAS), with Lake Erie and Niagara Escarpment at the western end; the Finger Lakes (which includes Cayuga and Seneca Lake AVAs) in the centre; Hudson River, Upper Hudson, and Lake Champlain stretching north of New York City, and Long Island (including The Hamptons and North Fork AVAs) at its easternmost point.

As the state extends 705 km/438 miles east to west, from the Atlantic Ocean to Lake Erie, and from latitudes 40.7 to 44.9° N, it's hard to make any generalizations about its climate. While Long Island sits on the same parallel as Sardinia, the region's warm summers are modified by the cold Atlantic; likewise, the state's westernmost vineyards are spared from the harshest effects of the CONTINENTAL CLIMATE due to the moderating influence of Lake Erie (see LAKE EFFECT). An abundance of significant bodies of water (Lakes Ontario, Erie, and Champlain as well as the Finger Lakes and the Niagara and Hudson rivers) and the Catskills and Adirondack Mountain ranges further diversify the topography and range of climates. Average growing degree days (GDD; see CLIMATE CLASSIFICATION) range widely within the state, from 799 C° in northernmost Champlain Valley to 1925 C° in Long Island. Across the state, the greatest viticultural hazards are WINTER FREEZE and rainfall, which can lead to DOWNY MILDEW and ROT.

VINE DENSITY ranges from 1.5×2 m/5×7 ft to sometimes as close as 1×1.5 m/3×5 ft. The most common vine TRAINING SYSTEM for *vinifera* is vertical shoot positioning. In the warmer Long Island region, the open LYRE training system is gaining favour. Where growing seasons are shorter, trellises are managed to maximize SUNLIGHT.

Increasingly extreme weather events are making SUSTAINABILITY a hot topic. Producers have leaned on grape diversity to manage difficult growing seasons and, outside of Long Island, are increasingly embracing HYBRID and INDIGENOUS VARIETIES. The Long Island Sustainable Winegrowing programme was the first of its kind on the east coast, and the New York Wine & Grape Foundation is developing the state's first sustainability certification, scheduled to launch in 2023.

Finger Lakes, also referred to as the FLX, is the state's oldest AVA, with 3,801 ha/9,393 acres of vineyards in 2021 responsible for 90% of the state's wine. The region sits in the middle of the state, defined by 11 narrow, deep lakes carved by Ice Age glaciers that left behind steep SHALE slopes with shallow topsoil. Those significant to the wine industry are Canandaigua, Keuka, Seneca, and Cayuga, which are large enough to temper the cold winters and warm summers while their banks allow for good AIR DRAINAGE and water DRAINAGE. Cayuga and Seneca each have their own AVAs; Seneca,which is the largest lake by volume at 188 m/618 ft deep, creates a 9-mile MESOCLIMATE affectionately referred to as the Banana Belt, where temperatures are 3–8 °C/5–15 °F warmer than its surroundings.

Riesling, the region's widest-planted *vinifera* variety, does exceptionally well here and is made in styles from bone-dry to ICE WINE–sweet, with STRUCTURE and COMPLEXITY that can echo Germany's best. Chardonnay is also popular, lending itself to balanced, often CHABLIS-style wines. Cabernet Franc is the most widely planted red-wine variety and shows up in many forms, from pink PET-NAT to BARREL FERMENTED reds and even APPASSIMENTO styles. Producers are also excited about the potential of SAPERAVI, GAMAY, BLAUFRÄNKISCH, PINOT GRIS, and RKATSITELI. Varieties such as GRÜNER VELTLINER, Pinot Gris, and Cabernet Sauvignon do well in the Banana Belt, while Pinot Noir can make fine reds in exceptional growing seasons; otherwise, it is utilized for rosés and sparkling wines, on its own or in combination with Chardonnay and PINOT MEUNIER.

Hybrid varieties remain important, many bred locally at Cornell AgriTech, the viticultural research arm of CORNELL UNIVERSITY. The most import for FLX wines include Aurora, the Cornell AgriTech-developed CAYUGA WHITE, as well as SEYVAL BLANC and BACO Noir. MARQUETTE and MARÉCHAL FOCH are also showing promise in the region. INDIGENOUS VARIETIES account for the remaining half of plantings and include CONCORD, NIAGARA, and CATAWBA.

A minimalist style in the cellar is trending in the Finger Lakes as winemakers are eager to show a sense of place (see TERROIR) through the wines. Many winegrowers have introduced SINGLE-VINEYARD WINES; some are also focused on increasing texture and complexity in their wines through SKIN CONTACT, LEES CONTACT, and BARREL FERMENTATION and BARREL AGEING in neutral OAK. PET-NATS from *vinifera*, indigenous, and hybrid varieties such as Seyval Blanc, Cayuga White, Catawba, and Delaware are becoming mainstream.

Though most FLX wine is sold locally, the region is the most well-known in the state, its 144 wineries an important draw for TOURISM and its wines featured on restaurant lists from Buffalo to NYC. They also enjoy robust European and Asian Pacific export markets.

Lake Erie is New York's largest AVA, spanning 16,200 ha/40,000 acres along the southern edge of Lake Erie before continuing into PENNSYLVANIA and OHIO. This area averages 1667 F° growing degree days (GDD; see CLIMATE CLASSIFICATION) and benefits from the moderating effect of the lake, which is the smallest, shallowest, and most southerly of the Great Lakes, distanced from the Arctic air masses that prevail over lakes Superior and Huron. In 2022, 7,561 ha/18,684 acres were planted, but the region has only 20 wineries since most of the vineyards are planted to Concord, used for GRAPE JUICE.

Hudson River Region is one of the oldest winemaking regions in the eastern US, its first commercial winery dating to 1837, now called Brotherhood Winery, the oldest continuously operated winery in the US. The region is defined by the Hudson River, framed by steep cliffs that act as a conduit for maritime air and weather generated by the Atlantic Ocean. Glaciers have deposited SHALE, SLATE, SCHIST, and LIMESTONE throughout the region. Growing degree days averaged 1762 from 2010 to 2019, an increase of 9% from the average ten years prior. The short growing season (180–195 days) and cold winters favour cold-hardy varieties such as SEYVAL BLANC. Some VINIFERA varieties, including Chardonnay, Cabernet Franc, Pinot Noir, and Gamay, are also grown. The region's proximity to NYC has led to a robust TOURISM industry supporting 59 wineries in 2022. With only 95 ha/235 acres of vines, many source grapes from other regions.

Upper Hudson is New York's youngest wine region, established in 2019. The AVA covers

N

427,348 ha/1,056,000 acres north and west of Albany, surrounded on three sides by mountains (Adirondack, Taconic, and Catskills), yet just 80 acres/32 ha were under vine in 2022. Humid summers and cold winters favour cold-hardy vines such as La Crescent, MARQUETTE, FRONTENAC, and St Croix. With an average of 1389 F° GDD and only 130–155 days in the growing season, producers focus on early-ripening varieties such as Itasca. Winemakers will often employ MALOLACTIC CONVERSION to lessen acidity.

Champlain Valley of New York is the state's northernmost AVA, averaging only 141 growing-season days and 1439 F° GDD. Established in 2016, the AVA is also referred to as the Adirondack Coast and extends the length of Lake Champlain to the Canadian border. It is home to just seven wineries and 40 ha/100 acres of vineyards planted mainly to hybrids, particularly Marquette.

Long Island extends 190 km/118 miles into the Atlantic at the south-eastern tip of New York State. At only 37 km/23 miles at its widest, the climate is fully MARITIME, with ocean breezes moderating summer's heat and humidity. The region's modern-day history begins with Alex and Louisa Hargrave, who replanted potato fields to vines to start Hargrave Vineyard (now Castello di Borghese), the island's first commercial *vinifera* vineyard, in 1973. The island contains three AVAs: Long Island, the largest, with 826 ha/2,041 acres planted in 2022, comprises the western two-thirds of the island; North Fork of Long Island covers the island's north-eastern peninsula, sandwiched between Long Island Sound and Peconic Bay; while Hamptons Long Island covers the south-eastern peninsula (the 'South Fork'), open to the Atlantic Ocean. The North Fork soils, with less SILT and LOAM than those on the South Fork, require IRRIGATION because of their reduced water-holding capacity. In general, the growing season is at least three weeks longer than in other New York State wine regions, with 215–233 growing days and an average 1925 F° GDD. Only *vinifera* varieties are planted, and dark-skinned varieties thrive. Merlot is considered the region's flagship grape; Cabernets Franc and Sauvignon also excel, presented in VARIETAL or MERITAGE wines. Chardonnay is most widely planted, followed by Sauvignon Blanc and Riesling. Sparkling wines, many produced by the TRADITIONAL METHOD, are also produced. Eastern Long Island, a popular destination for weekend escapes from nearby New York City, enjoys strong sales of its wines to summer visitors.

Niagara Escarpment, in the north-western corner of the state, is defined by a LIMESTONE escarpment which runs some 700 miles from Rochester, NY, through southern Ontario, Canada, and into Michigan. Its 337 ha/883 acres of vines are grown on benchland (see BENCH) between the ridge and Lake Ontario's southern shoreline where air warmed by the lake settles over the vines, protecting them from drastic temperature swings in an otherwise cold climate. The area enjoys a 205-day growing season, the second longest in the state, which allows for *vinifera* such as Riesling, Chardonnay, Sauvignon Blanc, Pinot Noir, Cabernet Sauvignon, and even Syrah to ripen. M.J.D.

Hedricks, U. P., *The Grapes of New York* (1908).
cals.cornell.edu/cornell-cooperative-extension
www.newyorkwines.org

New Zealand, known as Aotearoa in Māori, in the southern Pacific Ocean, may look small on a map next to the nearest land mass, AUSTRALIA, which is 1,600 km/1,000 miles away, but its own land area is greater than that of the United Kingdom. The country has a diverse agricultural economy, with dairy the top contributor, though wine is New Zealand's sixth biggest export and growing, reaching $2.01 billion in export revenue in 2020. Vines were first planted in 1819, but it took more than 150 years for New Zealanders to discover that their country's cool MARITIME CLIMATE was suitable for high-quality wine production. Although production was just 1% of world wine production in 2022, vines cover 41,603 ha/102,803 acres in 19 registered GEOGRAPHICAL INDICATIONS (GIs) spanning 1,200 km/720 miles, almost the full length of the country's North and South islands.

History

New Zealand's first vines were planted in 1819 at Kerikeri in NORTHLAND by the Reverend Samuel Marsden, an English MISSIONARY. Sadly the vines never bore fruit as they were ravaged by goats a few months later. James BUSBY, the first British Resident, produced the first New Zealand wine from his vineyard, planted at nearby Waitangi in 1833. He started selling the wine to British troops in the same year the country's founding document, the Treaty of Waitangi of 1840, was signed.

European settlers from France, Germany, Lebanon, Spain, and Croatia, with their strong traditions of winemaking and consumption, played a pivotal role in New Zealand's early history, though the Dalmatian immigrants who settled West Auckland were arguably the most influential in shaping the modern wine industry. A significant contributing factor was their fortune of settling in rural West Auckland. Land values quite rapidly increased here due to the 1958 opening of the North-Western Motorway and subsequent expansion of Auckland city. This newfound wealth drove the growth of the nascent wine industry.

Yet the early history of New Zealand wine was fraught with difficulties. PHYLLOXERA and POWDERY MILDEW in the late 1800s were major setbacks, while the damaging effects of an emphatic temperance movement threatened nationwide PROHIBITION several times during 1910–34. Rubbing salt in the wound was the post-war economic depression and a 50-year enforcement of six o'clock closing, requiring pubs to close at 6 pm every night, until 1967. Coupled with the working-class taste for beer and the upper-class preference for imported wines, domestic wine sales suffered (per capita consumption of wine was just 2 litres in 1950, while beer was a staggering 100 litres).

In 1960 New Zealand had just 388 ha/959 acres of vineyard, the majority in West Auckland and HAWKE'S BAY. Most of the vines were disease-resistant AMERICAN HYBRIDS, the most prominent being ISABELLA (nicknamed 'Albany Surprise'), and 90% of the wines at this time were FORTIFIED in the style of SHERRY and PORT. A domestic wine renaissance began, catalysed by a progressive government legislating that 'light table wine' could be served in licensed restaurants alongside 'substantial meals'. The duty on wine, beer, and spirits was also raised and imports restricted. Eventually wine-sellers' licences were granted more liberally, though it wasn't until 1990 that supermarkets could sell wine.

The increasing popularity of dry TABLE WINE in the 1970s saw American hybrids giving way to VITIS VINIFERA crossings such as Müller-Thurgau, which were in turn replaced in the late 1970s and early 1980s by Sauvignon Blanc, Chardonnay, Cabernet Sauvignon, and Riesling. A government-sponsored VINE-PULL SCHEME in 1986 resulted in one-quarter of the nation's vines being uprooted, providing a relatively clean slate for the modern era. Much of the planting occurred on a trial-and-error basis; the first commercial Marlborough Sauvignon Blanc was produced in 1979 by Montana, and the first Central Otago Pinot Noir was made in 1987 by Alan Brady for Gibbston Valley Wines. The rest, as they say, is history.

Geography and climate

New Zealand has an incredibly diverse array of local climates, from warm subtropical conditions in the far north to extreme CONTINENTAL CLIMATES in the alpine areas in the south. Most of the country's winegrowing regions lie on its eastern coast, hiding in the rain shadow of the central mountain ranges. This is particularly important on the South Island, as the Southern Alps separate the country's wettest region (as much as 6,000 mm/236 in annually on the West Coast) from its driest (as low as 300 mm in Central Otago). A parallel is sometimes made between the southern LATITUDES of New Zealand's wine regions and those of famous European regions. If New Zealand were in the northern hemisphere, the country would

stretch from North Africa to BEAUNE, but the moderating influence of the Gulf Stream on European vineyards results in hotter growing conditions than in the vineyards of equivalent southern latitudes.

Of the country's ten umbrella GIs (and nine subregional GIs), MARLBOROUGH at the northeastern tip of the South Island looms largest, occupying nearly three-quarters of both total vineyard area and total production volume. Its cool maritime climate, DIURNAL TEMPERATURE RANGE, and diversity of soil types allows it to successfully grow many varieties, but it is almost synonymous with Sauvignon Blanc, which thrives in the rich, ALLUVIAL soils of the Wairau and Awatere Valleys. Sauvignon Blanc also dominates in the adjacent NELSON GI, where a more TEMPERATE but slightly wetter maritime climate exists.

CANTERBURY, including the North Canterbury GI, lies south of Marlborough. Its seaward range protects vineyards from the fierce easterly and southerly winds, and vines are found in either CLAY or LIMESTONE soils.

Further south, along the Waitaki River between the Pacific Coast and the Southern Alps, Waitaki Valley is New Zealand's coolest region, its limestone soils excelling with Pinot Noir. Pinot Noir also dominates in CENTRAL OTAGO, this deep-south region the only one in New Zealand not to benefit from the moderating effect of the Pacific Ocean, some 120 km/75 miles away. The BANNOCKBURN GI in the Cromwell Basin is perhaps its most prestigious subregion, having Felton Road as its calling card. On the North Island, WAIRARAPA is the most southerly GI, an hour's drive north from the capital city, Wellington. Surrounded by ranges that create a rain shadow, Wairarapa and its subregions, including Martinborough, excel with Pinot Noir and smaller amounts of Sauvignon Blanc and Chardonnay.

Further north along the eastern coast lies HAWKE'S BAY, New Zealand's second-largest wine region, though it claims an equivalent of 15% of Marlborough's vineyard area. A multitude of soil types in a maritime setting allows for success with numerous varieties, though the region has a particular penchant for red blends, Syrah, and Chardonnay, with greater acclaim for those from the hallowed Gimblett Gravels subregion.

New Zealand recently lost its claim to the world's most southerly vineyards (to ARGENTINA) but, less significantly, it can still claim the world's most easterly, thanks to an adjacent dateline. This title belongs to GISBORNE, northeast of Hawke's Bay, which also means it is occasionally visited by cyclones from the tropics. Its warm maritime climate sees a preponderance of ripe and lush white wines produced at all quality levels. Further north, the climate continues to become milder and more subtropical. Both AUCKLAND and NORTHLAND are fiercely MARITIME, with fertile soils, frequently of VOLCANIC origin. They each host less than 1% of vineyard area, while the hinterland of Auckland, New Zealand's largest city, is increasingly under pressure from urban sprawl.

New Zealand has not been immune to the effects of CLIMATE CHANGE, and data shows the country saw its seventh-warmest year on record in 2020 and six vintages between 2012 and 2020 among the hottest ever recorded. The depleted ozone here and the little air pollution contribute to the exceptionally high ULTRAVIOLET RADIATION levels, which is an important driver in grape flavour development.

Viticulture

It was only when New Zealand moved away from American hybrids to higher quality *vinifera* varieties in the 1980s and, subsequently, better CLONES in the 1990s that it made sense to invest significantly in higher input and more detailed viticultural practices.

Since then, improved clonal material and more detailed CANOPY MANAGEMENT techniques have led to significant gains in quality. While many different TRAINING SYSTEMS were trialled in the 1990s, today the majority of Sauvignon Blanc in Marlborough is VSP-trained (see VERTICAL TRELLIS) with one or two fruiting wires. VSP with CANE PRUNING is the primary viticultural set-up in New Zealand though there are some CORDON-trained and SPUR-PRUNED vineyards, especially for red Bordeaux varieties.

New Zealanders' pioneering spirit is clear in the viticultural sector with the embrace of increased MECHANIZATION and ROBOTS. Interest in SUSTAINABILITY is also strong, with 96% of all vineyards participating in the certification programme offered by the national wine body New Zealand Winegrowers. The organization also offers members advice on pest, disease, and biosecurity concerns. PHYLLOXERA is a minor threat to New Zealand vineyards as the majority are planted to phylloxera-resistant ROOTSTOCKS. For all regions, POWDERY MILDEW remains a perennial challenge; DOWNY MILDEW is all but absent in Marlborough, and it could in fact be the absence of copper sulfate (see BORDEAUX MIXTURE) in the vineyards that allows Sauvignon Blanc's high THIOL expression. The number of vines succumbing to TRUNK DISEASES has increased. Controlling MEALYBUGS, the vector for LEAFROLL VIRUSES, is a significant challenge, and there is concern about the BROWN MARMORATED STINK BUG and LEAFHOPPERS reaching this remote location.

Vine varieties

SAUVIGNON BLANC, the variety for which New Zealand established an international reputation, is the country's most planted variety (25,326 ha/62,581 acres in 2021) and is responsible for 85% of the country's exports. PINOT NOIR, produced in both still and sparkling form, is a distant second with 5,779 ha/14,280 acres. Chardonnay is in third place with just over 3,000 ha, and Pinot Gris follows closely behind with 2,774 ha. Merlot and Riesling have declined in the 2010s as they fall out of favour with a largely domestic consumer, counting just over 1,000 ha and 600 ha respectively by 2021, while Syrah has been on the rise, claiming 434 ha. Other varieties planted on a total of more than 100 ha are, in declining order, Cabernet Sauvignon, Gewürztraminer (often spelt without the umlaut), Sauvignon Gris, and Malbec. All vine materials are screened for VIRUS DISEASES by a government-run agency.

Winemaking

Because New Zealand's prevalent wine style is fruit-driven Sauvignon Blanc, approximately 95% of its fruit is machine-harvested, then processed quickly to minimize SKIN CONTACT. On delivery, trucks generally tip the grapes straight into a hopper (receival bin) which feeds into the most common fixture in New Zealand wineries, the pneumatic PRESS. TEMPERATURE CONTROL systems are also important, as the MUST of Sauvignon Blanc and other aromatic varieties such as Riesling is typically fermented cool in STAINLESS STEEL tanks with a selected YEAST strain. These wines are released as early as May/June following a March/April harvest. Some producers make an alternative category of Sauvignon Blanc that involves hand-harvesting, WHOLE-BUNCH PRESSING, SPONTANEOUS FERMENTATION in barrel, and LEES CONTACT. Use of technology such as REVERSE OSMOSIS and SPINNING CONES in New Zealand is rare.

New Zealand produces an increasing array of premium red wines from Pinot Noir, Bordeaux varieties, and Syrah, which are typically hand-harvested, while premium Chardonnay is always hand-harvested. Hand-plunging reds in open-top fermenters is a common sight in many wineries, though bigger entities tend to rely on automated punch-down machines (see PUNCHING DOWN). For Bordeaux varieties and some Syrah wines, pump-overs and RACK AND RETURN cap management is used.

While 225- and 228-l OAK barrels still dominate in the maturation of these wines and the fermentation of premium Chardonnay, there has been a trend in the use of larger format barrels such as puncheons (500 l), particularly for white wines. Some producers are experimenting with vessels such as CONCRETE eggs and AMPHORAE.

All winery records are electronic, which makes traceability and auditing transparent.

Industry organization

Of New Zealand's 717 registered wineries, 88% are classified as small (annual sales fewer than 22,000 cases), yet most of the country's wine production is dominated by 20 wineries which sell more than 444,000 cases of wine per year. Several produce many multiples more than this.

Many large players in New Zealand's industry are owned completely or partly by offshore interests. US-based CONSTELLATION BRANDS, owner of the Kim Crawford BRAND, and French-based Pernod Ricard NZ, whose leading brand is Brancott Estate, claim the number one and two spots for New Zealand wine brands globally in volume terms. Australian-owned TREASURY WINE ESTATES own Matua, and US-based E. & J. GALLO moved into the high-volume section of NZ wine in 2020, having secured ownership of Nobilo from Constellation.

Some large wineries remain under New Zealand ownership, most notably Delegats (behind the Oyster Bay brand), the Villa Maria Group, and Yealands Wine Group, which is owned by the regional lines power network, which in turn is held in trust for the local community.

All wineries must legally belong to the national wine body, New Zealand Winegrowers, which is a levy-funded organization founded in 1975.

For details on specific appellations, see AUCKLAND, CANTERBURY, CENTRAL OTAGO, GISBORNE, HAWKE'S BAY, MARLBOROUGH, NELSON, NORTHLAND, WAIRARAPA, and WAITAKI. S.P.-T.

Moran, W., *New Zealand Wine: The Land, the Wines, the People* (2016)
www.nzwine.com

Neyret, **Neret**, or **Neiret**, rare, dark-berried vine, strictly **Neret di Saint-Vincent**, recently rescued from extinction in the Valle d'AOSTA and likely to be related to several transalpine varieties.

NFT, or Non-Fungible Token, is a unique digital file that lives on a BLOCKCHAIN. The file can be in graphic, video or audio format, and its ownership is verifiable, programmable, divisible, and transferrable. NFTs can be coded to provide a stream of royalties to creators when pre-programmed conditions are met and gain value due to their scarcity. The NFT is a digital receipt that verifies the buyer's ownership and the AUTHENTICITY of the bottle. The market for NFTs, mainly digital art tokens, reached $22 billlion in 2021 and continues to grow. In May 2021, auctioneers Acker sold the first-ever NFTs from Burgundy, 2019s from Domaine du Comte Liger-Belair.

However, in line with a sharp drop in more traditional assets caused by the rising interest rate environment, the third quarter of 2022 saw $3.4 billion in NFT sales, down from $8.4 billion in the previous quarter.

Coupling NFTs with the physical twin is an opportunity for the fine-wine industry to create new products where the NFT is unique, and the physical wine has PROVENANCE because the supply chain is based on a blockchain. The NFT allows a wine producer to create new channels for its product, particularly in the fine-wine industry where digital twins can be created that can become as collectible as the physical bottle, due to their scarcity value and authenticity.

The combination of the NFT, together with its physical twin, and the immersive metaverse will offer wine producers the opportunity to create entirely new retail experiences. Just as fashionable sneaker brands are selling NFTs at higher prices than their physical counterparts, we may see NFTs of wine bottles becoming worth as much as their physical twins. M.K.

Niagara, AMERICAN HYBRID grown successfully in NEW YORK State. This VITIS LABRUSCA variety is vigorous, is productive, and withstands low temperatures well. Known as the white answer to CONCORD, one of its parents, it makes wines with a particularly FOXY flavour. It was created in Niagara County, New York, in 1868 and is now also planted widely in Canada and Brazil. For details of the Niagara region, Canada, see ONTARIO.

Nieddera, promising Sardinian red wine grape.

Niederösterreich, or Lower AUSTRIA, is the state in which just over 60% of the country's vineyards are situated. This state's name figures prominently on labels of non-DAC wine grown in any of its eight regions covered by a DAC appellation: CARNUNTUM, KAMPTAL, KREMSTAL,

THERMENREGION, TRAISENTAL, WACHAU, WAGRAM, and WEINVIERTEL. D.S.

Nielluccia, also spelt Nielluccio, Corsica's name for SANGIOVESE, probably brought there by the GENOESE, who ruled the island until the late 18th century. Often blended with SCIACCARELLU (Mammolo), it constitutes an increasing proportion of the island's AOC reds and, particularly, rosés, for which it is especially suitable. It is the principal ingredient in Patrimonio, on whose CLAY and LIMESTONE soils it thrives. It buds early and ripens late and is therefore susceptible to late frosts in spring and rot during the harvest.

nitrogen, mineral element and inert colourless, odourless, tasteless gas that is extremely useful in both grape-growing and winemaking. Nitrogen gas is an inert constituent of the atmosphere, making up 78% by volume. It is also an essential element in AMINO ACIDS, PROTEINS, and ENZYMES, without which life could not exist. In soil, it is an important constituent of ORGANIC MATTER, from which it is released during decomposition in the form of ammonium ions. Although these ions are taken up by plant roots, much of the ammonium is oxidized by specialist soil bacteria to nitrate ions, which are also absorbed by roots. Ammonium and nitrate compounds are important constituents of many FERTILIZERS.

Viticulture

Nitrogen has a major impact on vineyard VIGOUR and potentially on wine quality. It is essential for vine growth and is one of the three major elements, along with POTASSIUM and PHOSPHORUS, needed most for plant growth. It is an important component of proteins and also of chlorophyll. The most common symptoms of nitrogen deficiency, which can be expected on SANDY soils low in organic matter, are reduced vigour and uniformly pale green or yellow leaves. Soil and plant tests can be used as a guide to the use of nitrogen fertilizers.

Much more caution is needed with vines than with most other plants in applying nitrogen fertilizers, or large amounts of manure, or planting in soils naturally rich in nitrogen. The use of COVER CROPS containing clover and other LEGUMES should also be monitored carefully as they might add excessive nitrogen to the vineyard soil.

Whatever the origin, too much nitrogen in a vineyard results in excessive vegetative vine growth, termed 'high vigour'. Such vineyards typically show higher YIELDS than low-vigour vines and reduced quality owing to the SHADE effects. CANOPY MANAGEMENT procedures may be used to overcome some of these effects but will not eliminate them completely. Vineyards with excessive nitrogen supplies are also prone to poor FRUIT SET (COULURE, for example) and are more susceptible to BOTRYTIS BUNCH ROT. Excessive nitrogen is also considered to have a direct and negative effect on red-wine quality, reducing SUGARS, COLOUR, and PHENOLICS and increasing ACIDITY. High nitrogen levels in the soil also lead to increased wine levels of urea, ETHYL CARBAMATES, and HISTAMINES. In some parts of Europe such as Germany, excessive nitrogen fertilization of vineyards in the latter part of the 20th century led to pollution of water supplies with nitrates.

Vineyards producing high fruit quality typically have a restricted supply of nitrogen (although for Sauvignon Blanc, nitrogen is important in the production of THIOL precursors). Along with moderate WATER STRESS, this is one of two important checks on vine growth which result in the vine BALANCE that is essential for premium wine quality. All grass or cereal cover crops can be grown to use up soil-rich supplies of nitrogen and so make it less available to vines.

On the other hand, severe nitrogen deficiency is equally disadvantageous to quality, especially for white wines. Fruit from nitrogen-deficient vineyards can be lower in fermentable SUGARS and may also result in STUCK FERMENTATIONS, with the concomitant risk of forming undesirable SULFIDES. See also ATYPICAL AGEING. R.E.S. & R.E.W.

Winemaking

In combination with phosphorus and potassium, nitrogen can serve as a critical factor in YEAST growth and therefore FERMENTATION. Ammonium ions, primary amino acids, and small peptides, but not the secondary amino acids proline and hydroxyproline, are the principal forms of nitrogen present in grapes that can be used by yeast; these nitrogen components constitute what is often referred to as yeast assimilable nitrogen (YAN). Simple tests have only recently been developed for measuring YAN so that a deficiency of this essential yeast nutrient can now be easily determined. When a deficiency occurs, an ammonium salt, usually DIAMMONIUM PHOSPHATE (DAP), is often added. Nitrogen can also affect wine composition: in high concentrations it is associated with intensified AROMAS, while low concentrations favour the formation of HYDROGEN SULFIDE.

Obtained by fractional distillation of liquid air, nitrogen in both gaseous and liquid forms is a major commercial product used in a wide range of industrial activities. As ammonia, it is the starting material for most fertilizer mixtures. In liquid form, it has myriad uses in REFRIGERATION. In pure gas form, it is used to prevent a wide range of sensitive products from coming into contact with oxygen. Wine is just one of these.

Nitrogen as an INERT GAS is extremely useful to the winemaker in filling the HEAD SPACE in closed stainless-steel tanks and in bottles (see SPARGING and LEFTOVER WINE). Nitrogen is more expensive but more effective than an inert-gas mixture at preserving wine from potential harmful contact with oxygen. M.J.T.

Bell, S.-J., and Henschke, P. A., 'Implications of nitrogen nutrition for grapes, fermentation and wine', *Australian Journal of Grape and Wine Research*, 11 (2005), 242–95.

Peyrot des Gachons, C., et al., 'The influence of water and nitrogen deficit on fruit ripening and aroma potential of *Vitis vinifera* L. cv Sauvignon blanc in field conditions', *Journal of the Science of Food and Agriculture*, 85/1 (2005), 73–85.

Rantz, J. M. (ed.), *Proceedings of the International Symposium on Nitrogen in Grapes and Wine*, Seattle, June 1991, *American Society for Enology and Viticulture* (1991).

Verdenal, T., et al., 'Understanding and managing nitrogen nutrition in grapevine: a review', *OENO One*, 55/1 (2021).

White, R. E., *Understanding Vineyard Soils* (2nd edn, 2015).

Nizza, once one of three Barbara d'Asti subzones, elevated to DOCG status in 2014. See PIEMONTE for more detail.

NMR. See NUCLEAR MAGNETIC RESONANCE.

Noah, seminal figure in the history of wine according to the BIBLE. See also ORIGINS OF VINICULTURE.

Noah is also the name of a relatively undistinguished AMERICAN HYBRID. It is particularly hardy and was once widely grown in France and Eastern Europe. See HONDARRABI.

noble rot, also known as *pourriture noble* in French, *Edelfaüle* in German, *muffa* in Italian, and sometimes simply as botrytis, is the benevolent form of BOTRYTIS BUNCH ROT, in which the *Botrytis cinerea* fungus attacks ripe, undamaged white wine grapes and, given the right weather, can result in extremely sweet grapes which may look disgusting but have undergone such a complex transformation that they are capable of producing probably the world's finest, and certainly the longest-living, sweet wines. Indeed, the defining factor of a great VINTAGE for sweet white wine in areas specializing in its production is the incidence of noble rot. The malevolent form, which results if the grapes are damaged or unripe or if conditions are unfavourable, is known as GREY ROT.

Ideal conditions for the development of noble rot are a TEMPERATE climate in which the humidity associated with early morning mists that favour the development of the fungus is followed by warm, sunny autumn afternoons in which the grapes are dried, the progress of the fungus is restrained, and the development of secondary undesirable fungi and bacteria is impeded. In cloudy conditions in which the humidity is unchecked, the fungus may spread so rapidly that the grape skins split and the grapes succumb to grey rot. If, however, the weather is unremittingly hot and dry, then the fungus will not develop at all, and the grapes will simply accumulate sugar rather than undergoing the chemical transformations associated with noble rot, so the result is less complex SWEET WINE.

In favourable conditions, the botrytis fungus *Botrytis cinerea* spreads unpredictably from grape to grape and bunch to bunch in different parts of the vineyard, penetrating the skins of whole, ripe grapes with filaments which leave minute brown spots on the skin but leave the skin impenetrable by other, harmful micro-organisms. The grapes turn golden, then pink or purple, and then, when they are in a severely dehydrated state, they turn brown, shrivel to a sort of moist raisin, and may seem to be covered with a fine grey powder that looks like ash (to which the word *cinerea* refers). It can take anywhere between five and 15 days to reach this stage, known in French as *pourri rôti*, literally 'roasted rot'. It is almost incredible that such unappetizing-looking grapes can produce such sublime wine, and there have been many instances in which nobly rotten grapes have been discarded, or at least unrecognized, in wine regions unfamiliar with the phenomenon.

These visible changes are an outward sign of the extraordinary changes that occur inside the grape. More than half of the grape's water content is lost due either directly to the action of the fungus or to loss by evaporation as the skins eventually deteriorate. Meanwhile, *Botrytis cinerea* consumes both the SUGAR IN GRAPES and, especially, ACIDS, so that the overall effect is to increase the sugar concentration, or MUST WEIGHT, considerably in an ever-decreasing quantity of juice. The fungus typically reduces a grape's sugar content by one-third or more but reduces the TOTAL ACIDITY by approximately 70%; TARTARIC ACID is generally degraded more than the usually less important MALIC ACID. In BOTRYTIZED wines, most of any balancing acidity is more often due to the concentration of acidity in the shrivelled but non-botrytized berries that are harvested, and then fermented, at the same time.

While it metabolizes these sugars and acids, the fungus forms a wide range of chemical compounds in the grape juice, including GLYCEROL (quite apart from that formed by alcoholic fermentation), ACETIC ACID, gluconic acid, various ENZYMES especially LACCASE and PECTINASE, and the yeast-inhibiting glycoprotein dubbed 'botryticine', which limits yeast growth and increases the production of acetic acid and glycerol during fermentation. The PHENOLICS in the grape skins are also broken down by the fungus so that the TANNIN content of the juice is significantly reduced. In sum, botrytized grape juice is very different from regular grape juice, and not just because of its intense levels of sugar. Masuda et al. identified SOTOLON as a contributor to the aroma of botrytized wines. Blanco-Ulate et al. at DAVIS described for the first time that botrytis infections, during noble rot, act as a developmental trigger in white-skinned berries and promote the biosynthesis in the berry of key botrytized wine flavour and aroma compounds, including the accumulation of ANTHOCYANINS that are normally produced only in red-skinned berries. It is unusual for all grapes on a vine, or even on a single bunch, to be affected in exactly the same way, to exactly the same effect, and at exactly the same speed, which is why the HARVEST of a botrytis-affected vineyard can necessitate several passages, or *tries* (see TRI), during which individual bunches, or parts of them, are picked at optimum infection level, and grapes affected by grey rot may have to be eliminated.

Weather conditions other than alternating early mists and warm afternoons can result in a satisfactory noble-rot infection. In cold, wet weather, noble rot may form at a reasonable rate on fully ripe grapes and grey rot be kept at bay. Wind can help to dehydrate the grapes and concentrate the sugars.

See SAUTERNES for details of common weather patterns there. See BOTRYTIZED wines for details of where and how they are made, as well as their history.

Masuda, M., et al., 'Identification of 4,5-dimethyl-3-hydroxy-2(5H)-furanone (Sotolon) and ethyl 9-hydroxynonanoate in botrytised wine and evaluation of the roles of compounds characteristic of it', *Agricultural and Biological Chemistry*, 48/11 (1984), 2707–10.

Blanco-Ulate, B., et al., 'Developmental and metabolic plasticity of white-skinned grape berries in response to *Botrytis cinerea* during noble rot', *Plant Physiology* 169/4 (2015), 2422–43.

Ribéreau-Gayon, P., et al., *Traité d'Œnologie* 1: *Microbiologie du vin: Vinifications* (7th edn, Paris, 1998), translated by J. Towey, as *Handbook of Enology* 1: *The Microbiology of Wine and Vinifications* (3rd edn, 2021), 255–66.

noble varieties, vague term once used specifically in some regions to refer to what are considered their finest varieties, for example Riesling, Gewurztraminer, Pinot Gris, and Muscat Blanc à Petits Grains in ALSACE, or Sercial, Boal, Verdelho, and Malvasia on MADEIRA. The term has bcome increasingly irrelevant and patronizing given the re-evaluation and rising popularity of lesser-known INDIGENOUS VARIETIES. 'Traditional' might be more congruent in the 21st century.

Nobling is a 1940 CROSS of SILVANER × GUTEDEL (Chasselas) that has declined in importance even in Baden, where all its 47 ha/116 acres grew in 2020. Wines are relatively neutral.

node, the part of a plant's stem at which a leaf is attached. In the grapevine, this zone is swollen and bears the leaf winter BUD and LATERAL SHOOT. TENDRILS or INFLORESCENCES are also borne at nodes on the side opposite to the bud. B.G.C.

Noir, French for 'black' and therefore a common suffix for dark-berried vine varieties.

Noirien is the most common eco-geogroup of related VINE VARIETIES, those found primarily in north-eastern France that are related to or closely associated with Pinot Noir: notably Pinot Gris, Pinot Blanc, Auxerrois, Chardonnay, Melon, and Gamay Noir.

Robinson, J., et al., *Wine Grapes: A Complete Guide to 1,368 Vine Varieties, Including Their Origins and Flavours* (2012).

NoLo, or **NOLO**, a newly popular term for a category of wines with no alcohol (less than 0.5%; see DE-ALCOHOLIZED WINE) or low alcohol (below 1.2%; see LOW-ALCOHOL WINE). They have become more popular thanks to improved quality and increasingly health-conscious (and abstemious) lifestyles.

non-alcoholic wine is a term sometimes used for wine with an ALCOHOLIC STRENGTH of less than 0.5%. For more details, see DE-ALCOHOLIZED WINE.

non-vintage, often abbreviated to NV, a blended wine, particularly champagne or sparkling wine, which may contain the produce of several different VINTAGES, although in champagne-making practice it is usually substantially based on the most recent vintage, to which some additional ingredients from older years, often called 'reserve wines', may be added.

Some mass-market wines are sold without a vintage year and are in practice a blend made throughout the year, so that the first blend of the winter season, typically, may contain a mixture of wine from both the new and last year's vintages.

normalized difference vegetation index (NDVI) is the most widely used indicator of plant biomass in agriculture. In viticulture, NDVI provides a relative measure of the size and density of the CANOPY and therefore correlates with VIGOUR. It is calculated from measures of reflected light at wavebands corresponding to red and infrared light. See also REMOTE SENSING and PLANT CELL DENSITY. R.G.V.B.

Hall, A., et al., 'Optical remote sensing applications in viticulture: a review', *Australian Journal of Grape and Wine Research*, 8/1 (2002), 36–47.

North Carolina, a state on the east coast of the United States with nearly 200 wineries, 931 ha/2,300 acres of wine grapes, and a diversity of wine styles. In 2022 it ranked eighth in the US for wine production (tying with PENNSYLVANIA)—down from number one in 1840, before PROHIBITION effectively destroyed the industry. It remains home to the oldest cultivated grapevine in the US, the Mothervine, which has been producing muscadine grapes since at least the 16th century. (See MUSCADINIA.) This hearty INDIGENOUS VARIETY thrives in the south-central and eastern portions of the state, where the climate is humid subtropical. Moving west and into the Blue Ridge Mountains, temperatures become cooler, with greater DIURNAL TEMPERATURE RANGE and cool breezes. HYBRIDS such as CHAMBOURCIN, CHARDONEL, SEYVAL BLANC, TRAMINETTE, and VIDAL as well as VITIS VINIFERA varieties including Cabernet Sauvignon, Cabernet Franc, Chardonnay, Merlot, and Viognier dominate; there are also pockets of indigenous VITIS LABRUSCA and *Vitis aestivalis* varieties such as CONCORD, NIAGARA, and NORTON (a *vinifera-aestivalis* cross). The state's five AVAS are concentrated in its western end, with **Yadkin** and its subregion **Swan Creek** the largest at 162 ha/400 acres of vines. **Haw River Valley** is the most easterly AVA, between Greensboro and Raleigh. Two AVAs extend into neighbouring states: **Appalachian High Country** crosses into Tennessee and VIRGINIA, and **Upper Hiwassee Highlands** is shared with Georgia. State law specifies that wines labelled North Carolina must contain at least 75% grapes grown within the state; to take an AVA name, at least 85% of the grapes must come from that AVA. B.Y.-I.

www.ncwine.org

North Coast, general CALIFORNIA umbrella region and AVA implying north of San Francisco although it also extends north-east from San Francisco into a portion of Solano County. It includes all vineyards in LAKE, MARIN, MENDOCINO, NAPA, and SONOMA counties. The name appears on some relatively prestigious wines assembled from, especially, Napa and Sonoma and also on some pretty ordinary blends. It is also commonly seen on sparkling-wine labels.

North East Victoria Zone, in the Australian state of VICTORIA, incorporating the wine regions of Alpine Valleys, Beechworth, Glenrowan, King Valley, and Rutherglen.

Northern Rivers Zone, large area on the northern coastal plain of NEW SOUTH WALES in Australia with one GEOGRAPHICAL INDICATION, HASTINGS RIVER.

Northern Slopes Zone, and its GEOGRAPHICAL INDICATION New England Australia is immediately south of Queensland's GRANITE BELT, on the western (inland) side of the Great Dividing Range. While the zone is officially in the state of NEW SOUTH WALES, many Granite Belt producers source grapes from its 77 ha/190 acres of vines which grow in similar conditions, the soils becoming less GRANITIC moving southwards. A.C.

Northland, or Te Tai Tokerau in Māori, is the birthplace of NEW ZEALAND wine. The GEOGRAPHICAL INDICATION (GI), at the very northern tip of the country, has a humid, sunny, warm climate that could be classified as subtropical. From around 70 ha/173 acres of vines in 2021 come rich, tropical expressions of Chardonnay as well as Syrah and Pinot Gris. S.P.-T.

North Macedonia, known since 2019 as the Republic of North Macedonia, is a country in the south-central Balkans, bordered by BULGARIA, SERBIA, KOSOVO, ALBANIA, and GREECE. Archaeological evidence of winemaking goes back to at least the 13th century BCE. The geographical and historical region of Macedonia covers a much larger area, including parts of Greece and south-western Bulgaria. At one time, under the rule of Philip II (359 BCE) and then his son Alexander the Great (323 BCE), it was the most powerful state in the world. By 146 BCE it had become a Roman province, when it was an important grape-growing region. As in much of Balkans, Macedonia came under Ottoman rule for five centuries until 1913. The region was then partitioned between Bulgaria, Greece, and Serbia. After the Second World War, the territory became part of YUGOSLAVIA. It underwent peaceful secession in 1991 and became the Former Yugoslav Republic of Macedonia until disputes over the Greek region of Macedonia were resolved. The country became a candidate for EU membership in 2005, but progress remained stalled in 2022 due to Bulgarian disputes over language.

North Macedonia lies between latitudes 40 and 43° N. It is landlocked and geographically defined by a central valley formed by the Vardar River, while mountains border the country, with 34 peaks over 2,000 m/6,562 ft. There are 53 lakes including the UNESCO-listed Lake Ohrid, believed to be one of the oldest lakes in the world. The country is seismically active, and the climate is transitional from MEDITERRANEAN to CONTINENTAL. Hot, dry summers with 270 sunny days are typical, and annual rainfall ranges from less than 500 mm/20 in in the centre to 1,700 mm/70 in in the mountains, making it the driest region in the Balkans, so IRRIGATION is usual. The grape-growing regions are sufficiently hot that ACIDIFICATION but not ENRICHMENT is allowed.

Wine is the second most important agricultural export in North Macedonia, and vineyards cover 10% of arable land. In the 1980s the region accounted for as much as two-thirds of YUGOSLAVIA's wine production, reaching a peak of 1.8 million hl/47.5 million gal in the early 1990s. By 2020 wine production had fallen to 744,120 hl/16.4 million gal, the smallest harvest for at least a decade.

Today's industry claims 28,213 ha/69,716 acres planted to wine grapes in 2020, with 28 varieties. There were 120 wineries by 2021, though only nine with production capacity over 50,000 hl, including the first winery of the modern era, the Tikveš winery, founded in 1885 and now fully private. There are 16 wine districts within three wine regions: **Pcinja-Osogovo** in the east, **Pelagonija-Polog** in the west, and the most important **Central** or **Vardar River Valley** region, which accounts for 87% of the country's wine grapes. Within it, the Tikveš district is most important, with 43% of the country's vineyards in 2020.

The domestic market for wine remains small, and exports are important at 666,983 hl in 2020. The last few years have seen the industry depend heavily on cheap exports of BULK WINE, especially to Germany, and while this remains notable, producers are working hard to improve quality and shift towards more premium bottled wines. There have been significant investments in updating wineries, and several wineries have recruited foreign CONSULTANTS to modernize winemaking. Another developing trend is identification of better vineyard sites, especially at ELEVATION to mitigate the warm climate. Unusually, it is the larger wineries that are arguably driving quality improvements, including conducting considerable viticultural and winemaking research.

Red-wine varieties predominate, making up 60% of the harvest. Vranec (the usual spelling of VRANAC here), which arrived in 1950s from MONTENEGRO but really suits the warm North Macedonian growing conditions, dominates. The offspring of Kratošija and Duljenga, another Montenegrin grape, Vranec is regarded as the country's flagship variety: it has higher ANTHOCYANIN levels than Cabernet Sauvignon and produces deeply coloured wines, typically over 14% alcohol yet with good acidity (around 6.5 g/l) and relatively low PH, so the resulting wines can be balanced and age well. Other important varieties include SMEDEREVKA, Merlot, Cabernet Sauvignon, Kratošija (the local name for ZINFANDEL), Riesling, Chardonnay, Pinot Noir, RKATSITELI, and PROKUPAC. Stanušina is the only genuinely INDIGENOUS VARIETY so far identified, making light reds and rosé. There are currently three quality categories: regional wines or wines with GEOGRAPHICAL INDICATION (WGI); wines with controlled origin (WCO); and wines with controlled and guaranteed origin (WCGO). C.G.

www.winesofmacedonia.mk

North West Victoria Zone comprises the high-yielding, irrigated vineyards of the

N

Murray Darling and Swan Hill regions falling on the VICTORIA side of the Murray river in Australia.

North Yuba, California wine region and AVA. See SIERRA FOOTHILLS.

Norton, arguably the only variety of AMERICAN VINE SPECIES origin making a premium-quality wine. Little known and little grown outside the eastern and midwestern UNITED STATES, Norton is undoubtedly underrated because of entrenched bias against non-VITIS VINIFERA varieties. In Arkansas and MISSOURI, it was the mainstay of an extremely important wine industry. Leon D. Adams calls Norton 'the best of all native American red-wine grapes' and praises it for its wines' lack of FOXY character.

The origin of this dark-skinned variety is uncertain, but it takes its name from Dr D. Norton of Richmond, Virginia, a pioneer grape-grower. Recent DNA PROFILING has shown that it is a HYBRID which has both *Vitis aestivalis* and *Vitis vinifera* (see VITIS) in its pedigree. It is also known as Cynthiana in Missouri, Arkansas, and Virginia.

Norton is tolerant of BUNCH ROTS and other fungal diseases such as BLACK ROT, ANTHRACNOSE, DOWNY MILDEW, and POWDERY MILDEW, and its roots are tolerant of PHYLLOXERA. The vine is vigorous and requires a long growing season. The grapes are acidic, but the wine is indistinguishable by taste from wine made from *vinifera* grapes. Grapes are very dark coloured and full-flavoured, and Norton reliably produces healthy fruit in places with high summer rainfall even without SPRAYING. Chrysalis of Virginia is the Norton specialist.

Adams, L. D., *The Wines of America* (1985).

Norway is the easternmost country of the Scandinavian peninsula, sharing a long border with SWEDEN and shorter borders with FINLAND and RUSSIA in the north. Wine grapes have been grown here since the 1970s, mainly by hobbyists in the early days. Thanks to CLIMATE CHANGE, which has seen Norwegian winters become considerably milder and shorter, and to the development of hardy and DISEASE-RESISTANT VARIETIES at the University of Minnesota and at GEISENHEIM UNIVERSITY, the country had by 2021 well over 100 members in the Norwegian Grape Growers Association (Foreningen Norske Druedyrkere), 15 of them certified wine producers licensed to sell wine through the Norwegian Wine Monopoly.

With its extensive coastline on the Atlantic Ocean and the Barents Sea, Norway has a mostly MARITIME CLIMATE, with mild lowland temperatures on the coast. Temperatures are colder inland but still milder than other areas in the world on such northerly latitudes (60° N, the same as Alaska) due to the warming influence of the Gulf Stream. Most vineyards are small (1–2 ha, with about 4,000 grapevines per ha) and located in southern and western Norway, although there are some as far north as the Sognefjord (61.1° N), where Slinde Vingard is based.

Though the growing season is short, long SUNLIGHT hours during the summer help greatly in achieving ripeness. In western Norway, the steep slopes of the fjords ensure heat accumulation and good DRAINAGE. Water availability is not an issue, with regular rainfall during the growing season and usually abundant snowfall in winter. The average annual temperature is about 8 °C/46 °F, ranging from 1 °C in February to 16 °C in July. The main viticultural challenge is FROST in spring and autumn.

White wine grapes account for 60% of plantings, dominated by SOLARIS, which ripens consistently and can be used for both still and sparkling wine. Among red wine grapes, RONDO dominates. An increasing number of Norwegian grape-growers are planting VITIS VINIFERA, including Riesling and Pinot Noir.

D.Co.

nose, the most sensitive form of TASTING equipment so far encountered, the sense of TASTE being so inextricably linked with the sense of smell. When the nose is blocked, whether by a cold or by mechanical means, and the taster has to rely on their PALATE, the ability to taste either food or drink is seriously impaired—so much so that cold sufferers have to resort to decongestants if the need for their tasting skills is serious.

'Nose' is also used as a synonym for the smell, AROMA, or BOUQUET of a wine, as in wines having 'a nose of raspberries', 'a raspberry nose', or even 'raspberries on the nose'.

Nosiola, the only remaining white grape variety indigenous to TRENTINO in northern Italy. It is grown principally on the hills around the village of Pressano, where it produces dry wines, and in the Valle dei Laghi to the west of Trento, where it is used to produce Vino Santo (see VIN SANTO). Interest in the variety has been revived in recent years as several producers, notably Foradori, have demonstrated that it can, when made with care, produce whites of real interest, including SKIN-FERMENTED examples. DNA PROFILING at SAN MICHELE ALL'ADIGE revealed a surprising parent–offspring relationship with the Swiss RÈZE.

notch grafting, a method of GRAFTING vines that resembles CLEFT GRAFTING. It differs in that the cut trunk is not split across; instead the SCION pieces are cut to fit a V-shaped notch made on either side of the trunk to a length of about 3 cm/1 in. The scion pieces are often tacked into place. Notch grafts are not as secure as cleft grafts. A related method is the bark graft done later in spring when the bark lifts freely, but again the union is sometimes weak.

B.G.C.

no-till, the increasingly common practice of minimizing soil disturbance between the rows and under the vines. See TILLAGE and ORGANIC VITICULTURE.

nouveau, French for 'new', and a specific style of wine designed to be drunk only weeks rather than months or years after the HARVEST. The most famous and successful nouveau is BEAUJOLAIS Nouveau, which, at its peak in 1988, accounted for more than 800,000 hl/21 million gal, or 60% of all Beaujolais produced. The Beaujolais producers themselves are keen to point out that their Nouveaux are not simply *un phénomène 'marketing'* but that they owe their origins to the 19th century, when the year's wine would complete its FERMENTATION in cask while en route to nearby Lyons, where the new wine provided a direct link with village life in the Beaujolais hills. The phenomenon originated in a group of villages just west of Villefranche whose wines seemed to mature earliest. After the constraints of the Second World War, the Beaujolais producers were gradually allowed to release an increasing proportion of new wine. The original term was PRIMEUR, meaning 'young produce', and from 1951 the Beaujolais producers were allowed to release their primeurs from 15 December. These young, refreshing wines enjoyed great success in the bistros of Paris in the 1950s and 1960s, and by the end of the 1960s the phrase *Le Beaujolais Nouveau est arrivé* had been coined. In the 1970s, the phenomenon spread outside France, thanks to energetic work on the part of producers such as Georges Duboeuf and his agents around the world, as well as Alexis LICHINE in the United States. By the end of 1974, Beaujolais Nouveau had reached Great Britain to such an extent that the first Beaujolais Nouveau race (of bottles of purple ink to London) had been run. Eventually the Nouveau was flown, with inexplicable haste and brouhaha, to markets around the world, the craze reaching Australia in 1982 and Japan and Italy in 1985. Initially the release date was fixed at 15 November, but it was eventually changed to the third Thursday in November, for the convenience of the wine trade and the media, who for much of the late 1970s and 1980s were apparently fascinated by this event.

The immense commercial success of Beaujolais Nouveau inevitably spawned other (much less successful) Nouveaux—infant wines from other regions of France, notably Gamays made in TOURAINE and the ARDÈCHE, a range of wines made in the LANGUEDOC and ROUSSILLON, MUSCADET and many VINS DE PAYS, particularly Côtes de Gascogne.

Italy has produced a range of similar wines, described as **novello**, and Austria's HEURIGE could be said to be a version of the phenomenon. A few southern-hemisphere producers have tried to sell their own early releases as 'Nouveau' because they carry the same year on the label and are available many months before the appearance of Beaujolais Nouveau.

Winemaking techniques have to be adapted to produce wines that are ready to drink so early. The majority of Nouveau wines are red, and many of them are produced, like Beaujolais, by CARBONIC MACERATION or SEMI-CARBONIC MACERATION, which yields particularly fruity, soft, aromatic red wines suitable for drinking young and slightly cool, typically involving a fermentation of only about four days, and fairly brutal STABILIZATION. Those winemakers who do not or cannot practise any form of carbonic maceration may ferment the grapes traditionally but at lower temperatures than usual (in the low 20s °C/*c*.70 °F) and allow only the briefest of MACERATIONS. White grapes, for which carbonic maceration is not suitable, are generally fermented very cool, at 15–20 °C, and boiled candy aromas typically result.

The great attraction of Nouveau wines for producers is that they produce a financial return so quickly. As one taster remarked, their characteristic aroma is the scent of cash flow. Their appeal for the wine drinker is that they are a refreshing and stimulating reminder of the passing of the seasons, a sort of liquid HARVEST TRADITION. Nouveau wines do not deteriorate in bottle substantially more rapidly than non-Nouveau wines, but their lifespan is inevitably shorter.

Nouvelle, vigorous, productive South African mid 20th century CROSS of CROUCHEN and TREBBIANO Toscano which became popular from the mid 1990s for its ability to add obvious METHOXYPYRAZINE aromas to Cape Sauvignon Blanc. By 2020 plantings had reached 411 ha/ 1,016 acres.

Nova Scotia is essentially a peninsula in eastern CANADA surrounded by the Atlantic Ocean, the Bay of Fundy, and the Northumberland Strait. The CONTINENTAL CLIMATE, with obvious MARITIME influences, and relatively short growing season determine the grape varieties that can ripen here: plantings, which totalled 607/ ha/1,500 acres in 2021, include local speciality L'ACADIE as well as Chardonnay and Pinot Noir (for sparkling wine), Riesling, VIDAL, SEYVAL BLANC, and MARÉCHAL FOCH. The province has seven wine regions, with the Annapolis Valley having the greatest concentration of wineries and vineyards. There is one appellation, Tidal Bay, applicable to white wines made from a specified range of varieties, with L'Acadie, Seyval, Vidal, and/or Geisenheim 318 making up its majority, and a maximum permitted alcohol of 11%. The province is increasingly known for TRADITIONAL METHOD sparkling wine and crisp aromatic whites, with several of the 20 wineries also producing FRUIT WINES. J.D.

www.winesofnovascotia.ca

novello, Italian for 'new' or 'young', and a name applied to Italy's NOUVEAU wine.

nuclear magnetic resonance, **NMR**, is a relatively modern analytical technique which is being increasingly used in many sectors of the food industry. It came to prominence in the wine industry in the 1980s thanks to Professor Gérard Martin of Nantes University.

It was hoped that this method would evolve to help solve some of the wine industry's major analytical challenges, for example identification of origin and grape variety (i.e. AUTHENTICATION). The process compares the test samples against an established, verified database, but the establishment of this database is an enormous challenge when all the variables in the world of wine are considered (different grape varieties, blends, possibly vintage, clonal variation, and more). Work is still being undertaken to try to compile such databases, but it is a long and difficult process, and an NMR machine is very expensive.

While the technique has so far proved disappointing as a means of assessing authenticity, it is a useful tool to detect CHAPTALIZATION. The ETHANOL molecule contains six hydrogen atoms, which occupy three distinct sites, and NMR can distinguish between these sites. Deuterium, which is the stable, natural isotope of hydrogen, is distributed differently within the ethanol molecule according to the source of the sugar from which the ethanol is derived. NMR can therefore differentiate between wines which have been enriched with cane sugar, beet sugar or GRAPE CONCENTRATE, particularly if the concentrate is produced in a region that is different from the wine's place of origin since the ratio of hydrogen to deuterium varies slightly according to latitude. G.T.

Nuits, Côte de, named after the principal town of Nuits-St-Georges, is the northern half of the escarpment of the CÔTE D'OR, producing the greatest red wines of Burgundy, from the Pinot Noir grape, and very occasional white wines. The principal villages, from north to south, are GEVREY-CHAMBERTIN, MOREY-ST-DENIS, CHAMBOLLE-MUSIGNY, VOUGEOT, VOSNE-ROMANÉE, Flagey-ÉCHEZEAUX, and NUITS-ST-GEORGES. See also MARSANNAY and FIXIN. The soils on the lower part of the slope tend to be much more fertile than the main parent rock because more immature soil has been incorporated. Wines from Fixin, Brochon, Prémeaux, Comblanchien, and Corgoloin may be sold as **Côte de Nuits-Villages**. These are usually but not exclusively red wines.

See also BEAUNE, CÔTE DE, and the map under BURGUNDY. J.T.C.M.

Nuits-St-Georges, small market town in Burgundy giving its name to the Côte de Nuits, the northern half of the CÔTE D'OR. Nuits-St-Georges has remained fully independent of BEAUNE to the south and Dijon to the north, with numerous NÉGOCIANTS making their headquarters here. The town also boasts its own charity auction, the Hospices de Nuits, held in March, at which time the wines can be more easily judged than those of the HOSPICES DE BEAUNE in November.

The appellation Nuits-St-Georges can be divided into three parts. North of Nuits, abutting Vosne, the wines combine elegance with a rich, heady quality. The heartiest wines, deepest in colour and most tannic, come from the heartland just south of the town, while furthest south, in the commune of Prémeaux, the wines are a little lighter and should not be over-extracted.

Whereas the Intendant Bouchu noted in 1666 a preference for Nuits, 'where the wine is excellent', over Prémeaux, 'where the wine is of good quality', the king of Saxony specifically ordered in 1780 'the wine of Prémeaux, the colour of the stained glass windows of La Sainte Chapelle'.

Nuits boasts 41 PREMIER CRU vineyards but no GRANDS CRUS, perhaps because the town's leading vigneron, Henri Gouges, was too modest when the CLASSIFICATIONS were agreed in the 1930s. However, a dossier has been prepared to promote the eponymous Les St-Georges vineyard, first singled out for its quality as early as the 11th century. Also particularly fine in the southern Nuits-St-Georges sector are Les Cailles and Les Vaucrains, both adjacent to Les St-Georges, while Les Murgers and Les Boudots on the Vosne-Romanée side and Clos St Marc, Clos des Forêts, and Clos de la Maréchale in Prémeaux have good reputations.

Some white wine is also made from the Chardonnay grape, as in the Clos l'Arlot, and from the Pinot Blanc grape in Domaine Gouges' premier cru Les Perrières. The premier cru Les Terres Blanches is clearly better suited to white wine.

Top producers include Henri Gouges, Robert Chevillon, Domaine de l'Arlot, Thibault Liger-Belair, Patrice Rion, and many growers in neighbouring VOSNE-ROMANÉE.

See also CÔTE D'OR and BURGUNDY map.

J.T.C.M.

numbers and wine, a combination that has assumed increasing importance as WINEMAKING has become more scientific and as consumers, faced with a bewildering choice of

N

wines, seek easily appreciated assessments of wine quality such as SCORES. As recently as the 1970s, winemakers had only the vaguest grasp of their wines' vital statistics; and the only numbers of significance to most wine drinkers were those of VINTAGE, PRICE, and, among more sophisticated connoisseurs of bordeaux, the numerical rankings associated with wine CLASSIFICATION.

Numbers are increasingly used for identification, however. Australian wine producers such as PENFOLDS have for decades exhibited a penchant for incorporating BIN numbers into the names of their wines. Individual CLONES of various VINE VARIETIES can be so numerous that they are usually identified by individual numbers, as are CASKS and individual BARRELS in some larger wineries. Some top German wines are identified by barrel (*Fass*) numbers and/or AP NUMBERS.

As the growing of grapes and the making of wine becomes more scientific, numbers as measurements play a key role, as they do in all scientific thinking (see in particular SCORING vineyards).

Consumers, as well as producers, have an interest in measurements taken at all stages of wine production, particularly RESIDUAL SUGAR, and the ALCOHOLIC STRENGTH which appears on most wine labels, even though they cannot be used on their own as a measure of how a wine will taste. J.R.

The meaning of scores

Using a numerical score to denote a wine's quality offers the apparent appeal of brevity, objectivity, and precision. Scores provide an immensely convenient shorthand for the taster, being quick to record and simple to share. They transcend language barriers and are universally understood. With up to 100 values available (if one uses the standard 100-point scale, beginning at 50 but allowing the use of 'plus'), very fine discriminations can be recorded with absolute clarity.

However, while the convenience of wine scoring is not in doubt, such objectivity and precision are somewhat illusory. This is because, despite appearances, scores do not measure an inherent property of wine against an independent scale. They are, rather, rankings of preference, which relate the perceived quality of several wines solely to one another. Although all scoring systems operate on a universal principle—that higher numbers denote higher quality—the choice of which specific numbers to ascribe to a given set of wines is completely arbitrary.

This is a quite separate issue to whether the 5-, 20- or 100-point scale is preferable, as well as to the more fundamental debate concerning objectivity and SUBJECTIVITY in assessing wine quality itself. Even if all the world's tasters were in complete agreement over the quality of every wine and elected to use the same scale, their scores would in all likelihood significantly differ. Nothing other than whim governs where the qualitative boundary between two adjacent scores should lie.

It follows from this that we cannot assume different tasters mean the same thing by identical scores. They might choose a different score to represent an 'average' wine and then distribute their marks either side according to a different method. The same is true for publications: 18 out of 20 in a specialist fine-wine journal does not necessarily refer to the same quality level as the same score in a more mainstream magazine.

An isolated score, therefore, carries no meaning. It can only be understood relative to the taster's overall mark distribution, possibly modulated by the context in which it is published. Furthermore, the averaged scores awarded by a tasting panel cannot be compared with scores awarded by a different panel, since the way each taster allocates points will vary.

The arbitrariness of point allocation undermines the precision as well as the objectivity of scoring. It is very tempting to start subdividing points, since rarely do two wines appear to be identical in quality, and so in the course of a large tasting, awarding quarter-points or plusses and minuses can feel like the honest thing to do. Although of some private value, the wider utility of this practice is doubtful. Tasters are not like machines that can be calibrated before each use; they cannot know for certain that what they mean today by 16 points is not what they meant by 15.5 points last month. The more finely subdivided the points become, the less sure it is that the boundaries between them are in the same place each time. The impression of precision is misleading and, beyond a certain point, conveys no extra information to the reader.

Numbers fully deserve their place in the world of wine, but they deserve also to be understood within the context of their fairly severe limitations. See also wine SCORING and WINE WRITING. A. H.

Peynaud, É., *Le Goût du Vin* (1983), translated by M. Schuster as *The Taste of Wine* (2nd edn, 1996).
Schusterman, R., 'The logic of evaluation', *Philosophical Quarterly*, 30/121 (1980), 327–41.

Nuragus, ancient white Sardinian grape variety grown on 1,008 ha/2,491 acres in 2015, principally to produce the unremarkable varietal Nuragus di Cagliari on the island of SARDINIA.

nursery in viticultural terms is either a place set aside for nurturing young vines or a name for a PROPAGATION and/or a GRAFTING establishment. Open-ground vine nurseries are where CUTTINGS are planted to develop roots and become ROOTLINGS. Cuttings are taken in winter, stored in a cold room, then CALLUSED by burying them in moist sand, often on heated beds, until young roots form at the base (after six to eight weeks). In spring they are planted in rows in the nursery, where the first-year shoots develop. Nursery soils need to be deep, friable, and well drained, free of pathogens and with a good water supply. In the following winter or spring, they are lifted, shoots and roots are trimmed, and the vines planted out in the vineyard. For GRAFTED VINES, the products of BENCH GRAFTING are callused in a humid room before planting in a nursery. B.G.C.

nursery budding and **nursery grafting**, methods for the PROPAGATION of GRAFTED VINES that complement BENCH GRAFTING, used in warm climates where the work can be done in the field. Great flexibility is possible in the type of SCION wood used and in the timing of grafting. Inserted scions are tied tightly with budding tape and, after the inserted bud has started to grow, the ROOTSTOCK foliage is shortened back and later removed. B.G.C.

nutrients. All living things, including vines and yeasts, need NITROGEN, PHOSPHORUS, and POTASSIUM, along with CARBON, hydrogen, OXYGEN, and other MINERALS as nutrients. Lack of nutrients in MUST can lead to STUCK FERMENTATION. For more details of **nutrition** of the vine, see VINE NUTRITION.

NV. See NON-VINTAGE.

NYSAES, New York State Agricultural Experiment Station in Geneva, renamed CORNELL Agritech in 2018.

oak is the main wood used by coopers to make barrels, large wooden vats, and other types of vessels designed for fermentation and ageing of wine. It is also used to make barrel alternatives. It is hard, watertight, easy to machine, and easy to bend to form staves. It can be treated with heat or flames (see barrel making) and has been shown to complement and enhance many types of wine. Thanks to its extractable tannin and aromatic compounds, oak adds tannins, flavour, and aromatic complexity to wine. The tannin compounds in the wood and its oxygen permeability contribute to stabilization and clarification (see barrel ageing).

Oak belongs to the genus quercus, which is extremely widespread throughout the northern hemisphere and comprises approximately 400–500 species. Like other species of forest trees, oaks provide important environmental services such as carbon sequestration, regulating the water cycle, preserving biodiversity, and soil protection, as well as economic services in addition to those related to wine (e.g. carpentry, cabinet-making, veneer).

Botanically speaking, the genus *Quercus* is somewhat ambiguous because there is a main *Quercus* genus and a subgenus with the same name. The subgenus is divided into sections, including *Quercus* (white oaks) and *Lobatae* (red oaks). It is the white oaks that are used in winemaking because they are watertight, unlike red oaks. The species of most interest to coopers are sessile oak (*Quercus petraea*) and pedunculate oak (*Quercus robur*) found mainly in Europe and *Quercus alba* or American white oak.

European oak resources

According to the graph on page 520, which is based on the forest statistics reported by the United Nations Economic Commission for Europe (UNECE) for each European country having a growing stock of over 25 million cubic metres, France is the leading country in Europe, followed by Ukraine and Germany. However, these raw data require a more in-depth analysis because the counting method and the species taken into account can vary from one country to the next. The data for countries with mediterranean climates include high volumes of Mediterranean oaks such as *Quercus ilex* and *Quercus suber* (see corks).

Not all growing stock is available wood for the cooperage sector, which is interested only in those stands containing sessile oak and pedunculate oak. These two fairly similar species are capable of growing in a wide range of soils and climatic conditions. Sessile oak, which covers an area extending from northern Spain to Armenia, prefers regions with an Atlantic climate and is less tolerant of more extreme continental conditions. Pedunculate oak, which stretches over a larger area from northern Portugal to the west of the Ural Mountains in Russia, is more tolerant of the more extreme continental conditions. For the most part, the ranges of the two species overlap. They commonly coexist in forests and can even hybridize.

However, the requirements of these two species differ slightly. Pedunculate oak prefers fairly rich, well-watered soils that facilitate its growth, resulting in larger rings and therefore wider grain. Sessile oak is more tolerant of dry conditions and poorer soils. Its Latin name, *petraea*, means it is the oak that grows on rocks. Therefore, sessile oaks tend to have more moderate annual growth rings and thus a finer grain than pedunculate oaks.

Pedunculate oak is a colonizer and grows more readily in open areas. Sessile oak is a 'social' tree and tolerates closed stands and competition between trees. It gradually colonizes forests consisting of pedunculate oaks, which it completely replaces after a few centuries.

Where both species are found, pedunculate oak is widespread over a large part of its distribution area whereas sessile oak is concentrated in specific regions. Two main areas supply wood for a large part of the cooperage industry in Europe. The first of these stretches from the centre of France to southern Belgium and the west-central part of Germany, with particularly high density in France in the Centre-Val de Loire and Burgundy. According to the French National Forest Service, these regions constitute the world's largest production area for fine-grain oak, as reported by Jarret. This is where the most renowned forests such as Tronçais in the Allier region or Jupille in the Sarthe region are found. The forests in these regions are naturally regenerated, using seeds from the oldest trees to maintain the existing genetic pool.

The second area, which is much more continental, extends from eastern Czechia to Slovakia, Romania, and northern Hungary, with high-intensity zones in northern Hungary, in Slovakia, and in the lower region of the Carpathian Mountains in Romania, as described by Eaton et al.

Oak resources in North America

American white oak is the other species commonly used to make barrels. White oak has a high level of genetic variability and is found in a wide variety of habitats. White oak easily hybridizes with other species of the genus *Quercus* such as swamp oak (*Quercus bicolor*) and bur oak (*Quercus macrocarpa*). As these are sometimes difficult to distinguish, they are typically grouped together under the generic term 'white oak' or 'selected white oak', comprising similar species but dominated by *Quercus alba*.

White oak is found in the eastern United States, from south-western Maine to northern Florida and extending to the Canadian border, although some trees are found in Quebec and Ontario. It extends westward to south-western Minnesota and south to south-western Iowa, eastern Kansas, eastern Oklahoma, and eastern Texas. The best growing conditions are found on the eastern slopes of the Appalachians, in the Ohio Valley, and in the central Mississippi Valley.

The total growing stock is 1,011 million cubic metres. As shown on the graph on page 521, the largest volumes are found in Missouri, Virginia, Tennessee, Arkansas, and Kentucky (USDA Forest Inventory and Analysis, 2020).

White oak is the dominant species in a wide variety of forest habitats and sites. It is found on poor soils, on both glaciated and non-glaciated soils derived from many parent materials, and on SANDY plains, GRAVELLY ridges, rich uplands, coves, and well-drained LOAMY soils. Growth is good on all but the driest, shallowest soils. However, forests need to be managed so that the white oaks are not naturally replaced by other species.

Other oak species

Coopers occasionally use other oak species such as *Quercus mongolica*, commonly called Mongolian oak in Japan, and Pubescent oak, *Quercus pubescens*, which is sometimes used in Italy. The latter, which is a Mediterranean oak, is of particular interest because it is a species more resistant to WATER STRESS. With CLIMATE CHANGE, this species may prove valuable if the current sessile and pedunculate oak forests shrink.

Oak wood

The anatomy of different oaks has implications for BARREL MAKING. A trunk can be thought of as a bundle of tubes or vessels and parenchyma cells running parallel to the trunk with groups of fibres called medullary rays running radially from the outside towards the centre of the trunk. When looking at the end of a stave or cross-section, annual rings can be seen, revealing two types of wood: early wood or spring wood (see GRAIN). The growing conditions of the tree will directly affect the ring width, which is the criterion that coopers have traditionally used to select their wood. Barrels made with tight-grained staves, which come from slow-growing trees, are known to be more aromatic and less tannic than those made with wide-grained staves, originating from slower-growing trees.

The watertightness of oak wood comes mainly from the vessels and the medullary rays. These vessels are like tubes a few hundred microns in diameter. In oak species that are suitable for barrel making, the vessels are filled by a thin layer of cellular membranes, called tyloses, formed when sapwood matures to heartwood. These tiny bags or balloons transform these open tubes into filled tubes, where water cannot circulate. This property gives the wood its longitudinal watertightness. European oaks have a medium rate of tyloses, so that when coopers make a stave they must be careful to follow the grain. Usually, the first step in a stave mill is to split the wood with a wedge, to strictly follow the longitudinal fibres and avoid cutting the vessels. White oak (*Quercus alba*) has a very high rate of tyloses, so it is not necessary to be particularly careful when following the fibres. The wood can be sawn without any risk of leakage. Red oak (*Quercus rubra*) cannot be used in cooperage because it has no tyloses in the vessels and the wood is porous.

On the surface of the barrel, the medullary rays provide watertightness. Liquid cannot go through these structures and has to go around the medullary rays to go through the stave. The liquid progression is stopped quickly when the capillary pressure exceeds the hydrostatic pressure of the liquid in the barrel.

Like other wood, oak is hygroscopic (i.e. it takes up moisture from the surrounding environment). Moisture exchanges between wood and air depend on the relative humidity and temperature of the air and the amount of water in the wood. This has a major influence on the wood's properties and performance. Oak may swell or shrink depending on the moisture content of the wood. It remains stable when the moisture content exceeds its saturation point (31% in mass content of water), but below this value the wood changes dimensions: it swells as it gains moisture and shrinks as it loses moisture. This property is a key factor to be taken into account when making a barrel. It explains why overly dry barrels can leak between the staves but become watertight once the moisture content has increased and the wood swells. Swelling and shrinkage also affect oxygen intake and wood extraction during BARREL AGEING because the moisture content of the barrel is always in balance with the relative humidity and temperature of the cellar.

Lastly, oak wood is rich in TANNINS and aromatic compounds. Tannins are the main reason why oak wood is durable, but the contact between these compounds and wine in a barrel improves the wine by stabilizing its colour, increasing its aromatic complexity, and reducing its ASTRINGENCY (see BARREL AGEING).

While some winemakers have started to use less oak or larger oak or older oak in order to

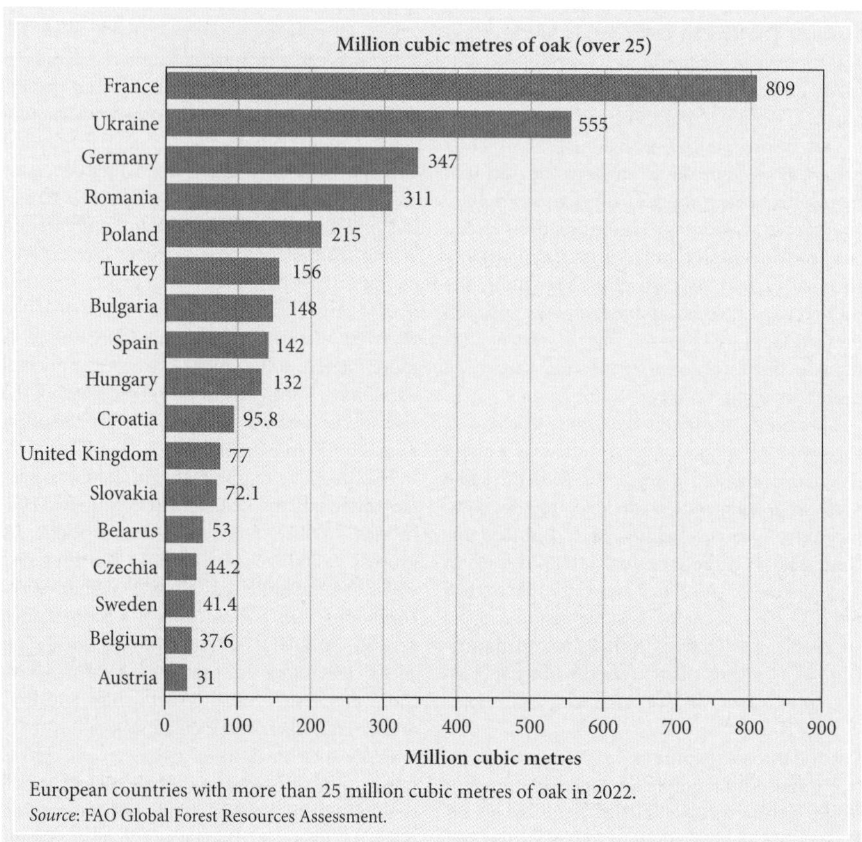

European countries with more than 25 million cubic metres of oak in 2022.
Source: FAO Global Forest Resources Assessment.

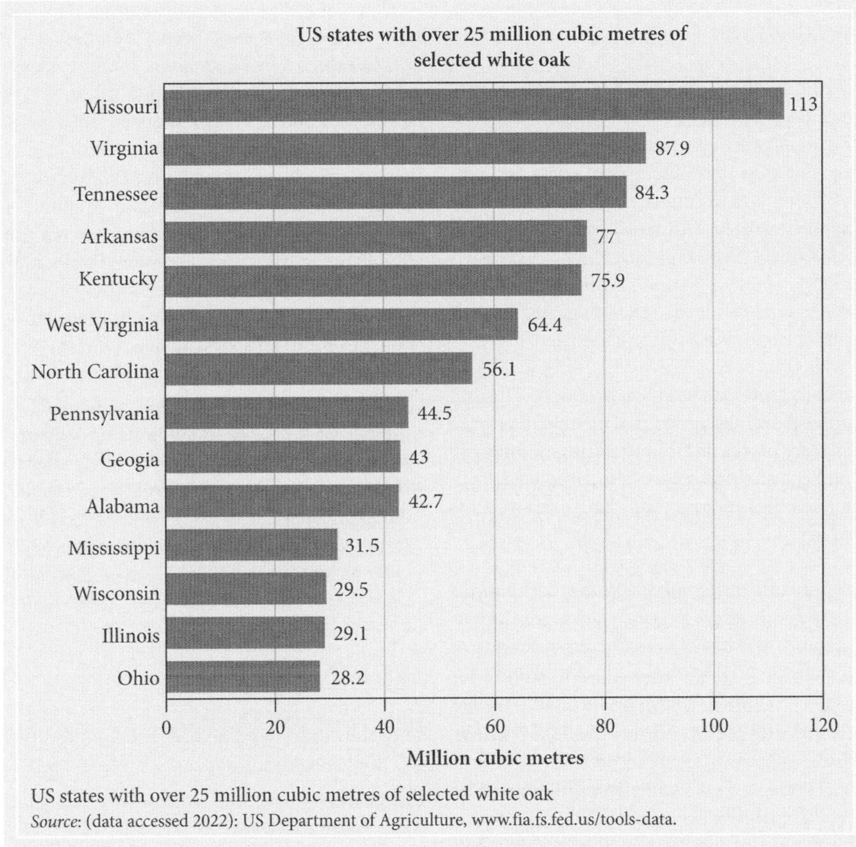

US states with over 25 million cubic metres of selected white oak
Source: (data accessed 2022): US Department of Agriculture, www.fia.fs.fed.us/tools-data.

decrease the oak influence in their wines, it is still of great significance to wine quality and style.

Burns, R. M., and Honkala, B. H. (technical coordinators), 'Silvics of North America', *Agriculture Handbook* 654, USDA Forest Service (1990).

Eaton, E., et al., 'Quercus robur and Quercus petraea in Europe: distribution, habitat, usage and threats', in J. San-Miguel-Ayanz et al. (eds.), *European Atlas of Forest Tree Species* (2016).

Hubert, F., 'Reconstructions phylogénétiques du genre Quercus à partir de séquences du génome nucléaire et chloroplastique', *Biologie végétale*, Université Sciences et Technologies–Bordeaux I (2013).

Jarret, P., *Chênaie atlantique, Guide des Sylvicultures* (2004).

Rogers, R., 'White oak', USDA Forest Service, Southern Research Station. www.srs.fs.usda.gov/pubs/misc/ag_654/volume_2/quercus/alba.htm.

USDA Forest Service, Forest Inventory and Analysis. www.fia.fs.fed.us.

See also OAK FLAVOUR, WOOD INFLUENCE, BARREL, BARREL FERMENTATION, BARREL MAINTENANCE, BARREL AGEING, BARREL RENEWAL, BARREL STORAGE, BARREL TYPES, BARREL INSERTS, INNER STAVES, OAK CHIPS, and OAK ESSENCES. R.T. du C.

oak ageing, the process of ageing a wine in contact with OAK. This typically involves BARREL AGEING, ageing the wine in a relatively small oak container, although the phrase may also be used for CASK AGEING in a larger oak container and can even be used for wines exposed to the influence of OAK CHIPS or INNER STAVES. Wines thus treated may be described as **oak-aged**, **oak-matured**, or **oaked**. (**Oaky** is a tasting term usually applied to wines too heavily influenced by OAK FLAVOUR, which smell and taste more of wood than of the fruit and may be aggressively tannic and dry.) See also BARREL ALTERNATIVES.

oak chips, useful if ersatz winemaking tool, an inexpensive alternative to top-quality BARREL AGEING which imparts OAK FLAVOUR and aroma and which may improve MOUTHFEEL and colour stability, though the resultant wine may be less complex and have poorer AGEING potential.

Oak chips vary considerably both in the provenance of the OAK (from subtle Cher to harsher American oak) and in the size of the chip (from pencil shavings to the more common cashew nut size). Oak chips, just like BARRELS, are also subjected to different degrees of TOAST. The quality of the oak, the method and duration of seasoning, and the degree and duration of toast are far more significant than the shape of the chip or shaving.

Oak chips are used either instead of barrel maturation or to supplement the oak flavour imparted by a used barrel. The average dose of chips is about 1 g/l, or 5 lb per 1,000 gal, typically added at the start of fermentation. Chips offer considerable savings over new cooperage: a sufficient quantity of American oak chips to impart some degree of oak flavour could cost less than one-twentieth of the cost of a new American oak barrel (and an even smaller fraction of the cost of a new French barrel). They are most effective when added during FERMENTATION, when presumably a combination of heat and enzymatic activity combine to generate the most favourable flavour EXTRACTION. Such wines sometimes have such an overpoweringly oaky flavour that they must be blended with unoaked wine. In addition to cost savings, chips have other advantages over barrels: less oak is needed because of the greater surface area in contact with the wine, there is less oak wastage compared with producing barrel staves, the toast is more even, and they take up far less space in the winery.

Research by Wilkinson et al. has shown that the oak character imparted by the chips may intensify after the chips have been removed. This is because the formation of certain oak lactones (see OAK FLAVOUR) takes longer than the period during which the chips are in contact with the wine.

It is possible to buy oak chips impregnated with LACTIC ACID BACTERIA immobilized at the stage immediately prior to exponential growth so that they can be used to encourage MALOLACTIC CONVERSION, but these are not widely used because of the additional costs involved.

Many wine producers are coy about admitting to using oak chips, although, unlike OAK ESSENCE, oak chips may be used perfectly legally in many wine regions. A wine description which mentions 'oak maturation' or 'oak influence' without actually mentioning any form of COOPERAGE is a good clue that chips have been used.

The **oak shavings** which can result from BARREL RENEWAL may similarly be used, and larger **oak cubes** in a perforated bag are sometimes put into older barrels to impart oak flavour.

See also BARREL INSERTS and INNER STAVES.

G.T. & J.E.H.

Wilkinson, K. L., et al., 'Rates of formation of *cis*- and *trans*-oak lactone from 3-methyl-4-hydroxyoctanoic acid', *Journal of Agricultural and Food Chemistry*, 52 (2004), 4213–18.

oak essences, or **oak extract**, are illegal in most wine-producting countries, but some companies are finding creative ways around the regulations. They are an inexpensive means of imparting OAK FLAVOUR and improving wine stability (see STABILIZATION), at least in the short term.

Various powders and liquids are marketed based on extractions from different woods. In some cases, specific TANNINS are targeted and extracted so as to add structure as well as flavour to a wine (see OENOLOGICAL TANNINS).

Doses of powdered oak extracts can vary between 5 and 20 g/hl, but powders are more difficult to use than liquids because of potential problems with CLARIFICATION. The usual dose of a liquid extract is about 0.01% and, since most liquids are based on ETHANOL or brandy, they can be extremely difficult to detect analytically. However, their ability to sustain a wine through bottle AGEING is questionable. G.T.

oak flavour. The wood in which a wine is fermented and/or aged has a profound and often complex effect on its characteristics and flavour (see WOOD INFLUENCE). Certain substances present in wood may also be directly extracted and absorbed into the wine, however. Those extractable substances identified in OAK, the most commonly used wood, are listed below. The flavours of oak-aged wines are the result of compounds extracted from the oak, those derived from the toasting of the wood (see TOAST), and their interaction with compounds in the wine.

Lactones Commonly known as whisky lactones or oak lactones, these compounds, responsible for what is generally called the aroma of oak, or 'oakiness', are derived from LIPIDS in the oak.

Pure lactones, which can easily overpower a wine's inherent AROMA, smell at moderate concentrations of coconut and spice but at lower concentrations can also contribute vanilla sweetness; at higher levels they can smell of green coconut or even vegetal, resinous or mushroom-like. Species and origin of oak affect the concentration, with considerable variation among trees in the same forest, and seasoning and toasting can also develop lactones from precursors in the wood. Higher concentrations are found in American oak. The specific compounds are the cis and trans isomers of β-methyl-γ-octalactone. The former is reported to be more aromatic than the latter.

Doussot, F., et al., 'Extractives content in cooperage oak wood during natural seasoning and toasting; influence of tree species, geographic location, and single-tree effects', *Journal of Agricultural and Food Chemistry*, 50 (2002), 5955–61.

Phenolic aldehydes VANILLIN, a product of lignin degradation, is the best-known member of this group. Toasting increases the level of these (although they decrease at high toast levels). BARREL FERMENTATION reduces their level because yeast metabolism reduces, for example, aromatic vanillin to odourless vanillic alcohol.

Spillman, P. J., et al., 'Accumulation of vanillin during barrel-aging of white, red, and model wines', *Journal of Agricultural and Food Chemistry*, 45/7 (1997), 2584–9.

Volatile phenols These too are the product of lignin degradation, but some of them (eugenol, for example) are also found in untoasted wood. They impart a spice-like roasted character, ranging from clove to smokiness. The main volatile phenol associated with wood is eugenol (clove-like). Others include guaiacol and 4-methylguaiacol (smoky, charred aromas), which may increase at higher levels of toasting, and 4-vinylguaiacol (reminiscent of carnations).

Carbohydrate degradation products This is a large and complex group that includes furfurals, which are produced from toasting wood sugars. Maltol and cyclotene are also produced from the toasting process and have caramel-like flavours.

Tannins and other non-volatile compounds TANNINS and other PHENOLICS act as a reservoir to balance the oxidative/reductive reactions of the wine, protecting it from OXIDATION and lessening the chance of unpleasant sulfur-related reductive aromas (see REDUCTION). Hydrolysable tannins derived from oak lignin are known as ellagitannins. Their concentration decreases with heavy toasting.

Marchal has shown that quercotriterpenosides (QTT), a family of wood compounds, are responsible for increasing sweetness, roundness, and volume in barrel-aged wines. Lignans and coumarines are natural wood compounds involved in bitterness.

Marchal, A., et al., 'Identification of new natural sweet compounds in wine using centrifugal partition chromatography-gustatometry and Fourier transform mass spectrometry', *Analytical Chemistry*, 83/24 (2011), 9629–37.

Compounds arising from wine-oak interaction It is worth noting that wine in the barrel is biologically active. The YEASTS that effect the FERMENTATION of sugars to alcohol also transform some of these directly extracted oak compounds into other compounds with flavours different from the original. The furfurals, for instance, are derived from hemicellulose and are transformed by the yeasts into compounds which have a range of flavours from smoky to coffee. For example, Blanchard has shown that during BARREL FERMENTATION of white wines, furfurylrthiol (FFT) is formed by yeast from the furfural released by toasted staves. Furfural levels increase with the duration of the toasting. Floch has suggested that vanillin could be transformed into vanillylthiol, reminiscent of cloves. Some other compounds such as pyrroles arising from toasting could be converted in odorant thiopyrroles (hazelnut flavours) during fermentation.

Those who cannot afford to extract their oak flavour from new BARRELS may use OAK CHIPS, BARREL INSERTS, INNER STAVES, or even OAK ESSENCE. Although the contribution made by oak barrels cannot be directly compared with that of BARREL ALTERNATIVES, some winemakers believe that the use of chips and inserts gives them better control over the type and amount of oak flavour extracted. Used carefully and in combination with MICRO-OXYGENATION, these products have allowed some wineries to achieve flavour effects in tank that are quite similar to those promoted by barrel ageing, for a fraction of the cost. A.P.

Blanchard, L., et al., 'Formation of furfurylthiol exhibiting a strong coffee aroma during oak barrel fermentation from furfural released by toasted staves', *Journal of Agricultural and Food Chemistry*, 49/10 (2001), 4833–5.

Floch, M., et al., 'Identification and organoleptic contribution of vanillylthiol in wines', *Journal of Agricultural and Food Chemistry*, 64/6 (2016), 1318–25.

oak influence. See WOOD INFLUENCE.

oak root rot, vine disease. See ARMILLARIA ROOT ROT.

Oakville, important source of top-quality NAPA Valley Cabernet.

Obeideh, hardy, vigorous, workmanlike INDIGENOUS VARIETY of LEBANON, high in sugar, low in ACIDITY, used extensively in the making of arak (local spirit), sacramental wines, Chateau Musar's white blend, and now also VARIETAL wines. Obeideh—variously spelt Obaideh, Obeidah, Obeidi, etc.—was once believed to be a strain of Chardonnay, but DNA PROFILING has shown it to be a truly local variety. M.R.K. & J.V.

Óbidos, DOC in LISBOA in western Portugal with a relatively cool Atlantic climate, known particularly for SPARKLING WINES.

ochratoxin A (OTA) is a mycotoxin (i.e. a toxin produced in very small quantities by certain moulds) found in a range of food and beverages such as cereals, beer, coffee, cocoa, and wine. It is closely related to fungal contamination of damaged grapes in the vineyard, most notably but not exclusively by *Aspergillus carbonarius*. (See also BUNCH ROTS and SOUR ROT.)

EU regulations were tightened in 2005, and the limit is currently 2 μg/l for wine and grape juice. The concentration of OTA may be higher in warmer climates but is typically reduced by up to 80% during winemaking, as described by Gil-Serna and colleagues.

Gil-Serna, J., et al., 'Wine contamination with ochratoxins: a review', *Beverages*, 4/1 (2018).

Oechsle, scale of measuring grape sugars, and therefore grape RIPENESS, based on the DENSITY of grape juice. Grape juice with a specific gravity of 1.075 is said to be 75 °Oechsle. This is the system used in Germany, and it has its origins in a system of weighing grape MUST developed first by the Württemberg scientist J. J. Reuss and much refined in the 1830s by the Pforzheim physicist Ferdinand Oechsle (see GERMAN HISTORY).

Like other scales used elsewhere (see BAUMÉ and BRIX), it can be measured with a suitably calibrated REFRACTOMETER or HYDROMETER. A similar scale, devised at KLOSTERNEUBURG, is used in Austria.

Each scale of sugar measurement relates to the others. For example, a grape juice of 14.7 °Brix has a specific gravity of 1.06 and an Oechsle value of (1.06 − 1.0) × 1000 = 60. According to published scales, these relationships are not strict ones (as illustrated in Hamilton and Coombe).

For more details, see MUST WEIGHT. B.G.C.

Hamilton, R. P., and Coombe, B. G., 'Harvesting of winegrapes', in B. G. Coombe and P. R. Dry (eds.), *Viticulture*, ii: *Practices* (2nd edn, 2006).

œil-de-perdrix, French for 'partridge's eye', used as a name and TASTING TERM for pale pink wines made from Pinot Noir, especially in the Neuchâtel canton of SWITZERLAND.

Oeillade Noire, very old, now rare PROVENÇAL dark-skinned grape variety. **Oeillade Blanche** is a synonym for the unrelated PICARDAN.

oenocyanin, a TANNIN product extracted from the skins of black grapes, comprising a mixture of PIGMENTED TANNINS, some ANTHOCYANINS, and other PHENOLICS. Marketed as a food colourant, oenocyanin is a valuable source of natural pigments available from POMACE. Even though it is a tannin derived from grapes and therefore is of a composition more similar to the natural tannins of wine than many OENOLOGICAL TANNINS, regulations in most countries forbid the use of oenocyanin in RED WINEMAKING because it is classed as a colouring agent. P.J.W.

oenological tannins, or **commercial tannins**, are products made by extraction of tannin from oak, chestnut, or birch woods and other suitable plant sources, including grape seeds. These have long been used (and are approved ADDITIVES in many winemaking regulations) with the aim of improving the AGEING characteristics, TEXTURE, depth of colour, and colour stability of red wines and also to inhibit LACCASE activity from *Botrytis cinerea* on red grapes. However, they are most useful for CLARIFICATION.

Versari, A., 'Oenological tannins: a review', *Australian Journal of Grape and Wine Research*, 19/1 (2013), 1–10.

oenologist, or, in the United States and South Africa, **enologist**, one who practises OENOLOGY. CONSULTANT oenologists are likely to concentrate on the activities traditionally considered WINEMAKING but increasingly concern themselves with what happens in the vineyard as well as in the cellar. In general usage, an oenologist is either a scientifically qualified employee or a roving consultant, as opposed to a fully employed practitioner who may or may not have scientific training, the WINEMAKER. In California, certain winemakers are so adept and so modish that their input alone can be enough to double or treble PRICES and transform a wine into a CALIFORNIA CULT wine. Helen Turley was the first. Most famous among them are Philippe Melka and Andy Erickson; others include Heidi Peterson Barrett, Thomas Rivers Brown, Celia Welch, Aaron Pott, Julien Fayard, Graeme MacDonald, and Benoit Touquette.

See also FLYING WINEMAKER.

oenology, or **enology**, the knowledge or study of wine, derived from the Greek *oinos* meaning 'wine'. The term is similar in several other languages: *oenologie* (French), *Önologie* (German), *enología* (Spanish), *enologia* (Italian, Portuguese).

Oenology has been used as a synonym for WINEMAKING, as distinct from VITICULTURE, which is concerned with vines. There is a general tendency towards including the study of viticulture as well as wine production in the term, however, as more people accept that wine is made to a great extent in the vineyard. See also OENOLOGIST.

Oenotria, name given to southern Italy when Greek colonists first arrived in the 8th century BCE or soon after. The Greeks may have found the indigenous inhabitants already producing wine and using STAKES to support the vines, and it is possible that they adopted a word meaning 'stake' (*oinotron*) as a name for the inhabitants. But this word is very rare—a different word (*kharax*) is used in most dialects of classical Greek—so it may be that Oenotria was the name already used by the local population and that the similarity between it and the word meaning 'stake' is purely coincidental.

N.G.W. & H.M.W.

Offida, a DOCG for white and red wines located between the Adriatic coast and the town of Ascoli Piceno in Italy's MARCHE region.

Ohio, US state with approximately 600 ha/1,500 vineyard acres in 2021 and over 360 wineries, is the site of North America's first successful commercial wine venture.

Success as a Cincinnati lawyer and land speculator freed Nicholas Longworth after 1828 to concentrate on horticultural passions. He studied the winegrowing attempts of his predecessors and contemporaries, including the efforts of fellow Swiss settlers brought over by Jean Jacques Dufour at Vevay, Indiana, 75 sinuous miles/121 km downstream along the Ohio River. Having achieved promising results on steep riverside slopes already in the early 1820s, Longworth embarked on an ambitious programme underwriting plantings by tenant farmers (mostly German emigrants) and betting on CATAWBA, a chance AMERICAN HYBRID. Through ambitious promotion, taste for the resulting white wines—dry, high acid, and low alcohol (Longworth disdained CHAPTALIZATION)—grew beyond Cincinnati's German speakers.

An accidental refermentation in the early 1840s convinced Longworth to divert most of his production into sparkling Catawba, which garnered a national following. Cincinnati Catawba drew favourable comparisons at London's Great Exposition of 1851 to Rhenish HOCK, and Longfellow penned a poem, 'In Praise of Catawba Wine'. As 'The Queen City of the West' grew to become the sixth largest in the US, its vine surface nearly tripled to 1,214 ha/3,000 acres between 1846 and 1850. But from the early 1850s, POWDERY MILDEW and BLACK ROT began taking a terrible toll during frequently humid growing seasons, and in the 1860s grape sources for what remained of Longworth's operation moved to Ohio's far north, while his two JURA-born winemakers left for New York's FINGER LAKES.

Vineyards established in the late 1840s on Lake Erie's Bass and Kelley's islands, 16 km/10 miles offshore from Sandusky, Ohio, and 40 miles south of Detroit, MICHIGAN, were soon flourishing with Catawba vines brought from Cincinnati, lake breezes keeping powdery mildew and rot at bay. By 1890, although NEW YORK had long since overtaken Ohio in production, vineyards extended the length of Lake Erie's Ohio shore and—as would continue to be the case, on a much-reduced scale, after PROHIBITION—were responsible for the majority of Ohio wine, most of that from Catawba or from the small share of CONCORD grapes that was not destined for juice and jelly.

By 1960 there were only 47 Ohio wineries (down from 149 in 1940). A late 20th century surge saw that number triple, and by 2021 it had more than doubled again, with five AVAs, four of which are active: Isle St. George, Grand River Valley, Lake Erie (shared with New York and Pennsylvania), and Ohio River Valley (shared with Indiana and Kentucky). Wine-bearing acreage includes both FRENCH HYBRIDS (VIDAL and TRAMINETTE prominent among them) and VITIS VINIFERA (led by Riesling, Chardonnay,

Pinot Gris, and Cabernet Franc). Catawba retains a 4% share. D.S.

oïdium, much-used French name for POWDERY MILDEW, although Anglophones tend to omit the diaeresis.

OIV stands for **Organisation Internationale de la Vigne et du Vin**, the intergovernmental body which represents the interests of vine-growers, and the wine, RAISIN, TABLE GRAPE, and grape-spirit industries of its members, comprising 49 different countries. Most of the major wine-producing and wine-consuming countries are members, although the US, China, and Canada are notable exceptions. Long based in Paris, in 2022 it moved to Dijon.

The OIV was originally formed in 1924 as the Office International du Vin by an agreement between France, Greece, Hungary, Italy, Luxembourg, Portugal, Spain, and Tunisia. Created and based in Europe, its membership expanded after the Second World War to include non-European wine-exporting countries such as Argentina (1953), Australia (1978), the US (1984–2001), and New Zealand (1994). In response to concerns voiced by non-European wine-producing countries, a review of OIV operations was undertaken, and a new international treaty creating the OIV in its present-day form was signed in 2001.

The OIV undertakes a range of activities to promote research, education, and co-operation, provide data and information, and contribute to harmonization within the wine and vine sector, particularly through its recommendations, which influence the regulations of many countries and particularly those of the EU. The OIV publishes a number of important compilations, including the International Code of Oenological Practices, the International Oenological Codex, the Compendium of International Methods of Analysis of Wine and Musts, and the International Standard for Labelling of Wines. Its statistical work forms the basis for much of the available global data on wine. J.P.H.B.

www.oiv.org

Olasz Rizling, or **Olaszrizling**, is the most common name in HUNGARY for the white grape variety known in Austria as WELSCHRIESLING (under which more details appear), planted on 3,417 ha/8,444 acres in 2021, although it was introduced less than a century ago. The Olaszrizling produced around Lake Balaton, Somló, and Eger is particularly prized; in general, the warmer climate imbues Hungarian versions of this variety with more weight than their counterparts in Austria. It is planted in virtually every wine region and made in a wide range of styles.

old vines are reputed to produce grapes which make better-quality wine. The phenomenon is largely anecdotal with few scientific studies having been undertaken (but see VINE AGE). The term is used increasingly on labels as a sign of both quality and scarcity as very old vineyards are rare and often low-yielding. Groups have been established to support and protect old vines globally through marketing and to acknowledge old-vine wines as a distinct category. BOLLINGER was one of the first producers to use the French term *vieilles vignes*, for the produce of UNGRAFTED VINES in one walled vineyard. It is common to see 'old vines' on labels from all parts of the wine world, as well as *vinhas velhas* (Portuguese), *alte Reben* (German), *vecchie vigne* (Italian), and *viñas viejas* (Spanish). Some regions such as the Barossa in Australia are home to very old ungrafted vines that have escaped PHYLLOXERA, some producing continually for well over 150 years.

There are few effective controls on the use of the term, however, and little agreement about exactly how many years it is before a vine can be deemed 'old', although the Barossa Old Vine Charter and South Africa's Old Vine Project have chosen 35 years as the baseline, whereas California's HISTORIC VINEYARD SOCIETY has set the bar at 50 years. D.P.G.

www.barossawine.com/vineyards/old-vine-charter
www.oldvineproject.co.za
www.oldvines.org
www.jancisrobinson.com/files/pdfs/Old_Vines_Register.pdf

old wine. See AGEING and MATURITY.

Old World, term typically used to refer to Europe and the rest of the Mediterranean basin such as the Near East and North Africa. It is used solely in contrast to the New World. However, the historical and geographical distinction is becoming less useful as more and more wine producers travel freely between Old and New Worlds, exchanging ideas and techniques, and as the terms are used as much to describe attitudes, practices, and wine styles as to pinpoint place of origin. For more details of what has characterized the different approaches associated with these widely used but problematic labels, see NEW WORLD. In this book they are used as shorthand, not as precise categories.

olfactory bulb, the most sensitive part of our personal TASTING equipment, at the top of the NOSE.

Olifants River, chiefly BULK WINE-producing region in SOUTH AFRICA among mountains and along the Atlantic western seaboard. Most growers have supplied large local CO-OPERATIVES with wine for DISTILLATION, but an increasing proportion is exported as wine. Vredendal, South Africa's biggest single winery and part of Namaqua, vinifies more than 95,000 tonnes of grapes annually. But there are pockets of vines with serious potential, particularly in Lutzville Valley district and the tiny Bamboes Bay ward.

oloroso, Spanish word with two related meanings in the sherry-making process. Without its initial capital, *oloroso* refers to a strong, rich type of wine that is the counterpoint to the lighter *fino* (see SHERRY). Oloroso with an initial capital refers to one of several commercial styles of sherry. The purest Oloroso is a dry, dark, nutty wine that is essentially bottled *oloroso* and is often labelled Dry Oloroso. Outside of JEREZ, the term 'Oloroso' used to be applied to any commercial sweet, dark blend of basic sherry plus colouring and sweetening wine, but it now must be labelled as Cream or Medium, depending on its sugar content. Oloroso may have an alcoholic strength of 18–22%. See SHERRY for more details.

Oltrepò Pavese, LOMBARDY's most sizeable viticultural area, administratively part of PIEMONTE from 1741 to 1859, extends across the hills of a series of communes in the province of Pavia south of the Po river where the land begins to rise towards the Ligurian Apennines (the name means 'beyond the Po, in the Pavia region'). In 2020, vineyards totalled 13,500 ha/33,359 acres, of which 11,192 ha were registered for DOC wines.

Oltrepò Pavese is also the name of an extensive umbrella DOC encompassing six DOCs and one DOCG for TRADITIONAL METHOD sparkling wines. With 4,000 ha/9,884 acres, CROATINA (confusingly called Bonarda, the name of a quite different, generally inferior grape variety here) is the region's most planted grape variety. However, at more than 3,000 ha, Oltrepò Pavese has the largest area of Pinot Noir in the whole of Italy and at least 150 years of history closely aligned with sparkling-wine production. Carlo Giorgi Vistarino of the eponymous and still existing estate planted the variety in 1865 and began to produce a sparkling wine modelled on champagne a few years later. The region's historic role has been to furnish base wine to the large SPUMANTE houses of Piemonte, which have long relied on this neighbouring zone in Lombardy for varieties not cultivated in their own region, but an increasingly lucrative international market, in combination with deep-pocketed outside investors, has spurred producers on to aim for higher quality. Wines produced in the DOCG, established in 2007, must be made with a minimum of 70% Pinot Noir, with Chardonnay, Pinot Grigio, and/or Pinot Bianco, and age for at least 15 months on the LEES (24 months for VINTAGE-dated wines). Some of the best examples are produced from north-facing vineyards. Cruasé is the collective BRAND name for traditional-method sparkling Pinot Noir rosé, a style in which the region has begun to excel and which faces little competition from other regions.

The majority of the rest of Oltrepò production remains not particularly interesting. Significant amounts of BULK WINE have always been sold in nearby Milan, encouraging abundant production at extremely low prices. CO-OPERATIVES have also tended to reward quantity over quality. Oltrepò Rosso, a blend of BARBERA and Croatina, can yield interesting wines. More interesting are the red wines of the revived Buttafuoco DOC, based on Barbera, Croatina, and UVA RARA grown on CALCAREOUS clay and not unlike those of the LANGHE. The best can easily age a decade or more. The even smaller DOC Sangue di Giuda (blood of Giove) produces red blends using the same varieties.

In a publication dated 1884, the Pavia Chamber of Commerce listed a host of INDIGENOUS VARIETIES, including Moradella, Pissadella, Ughetta di Canneto, Rossara, Barbisino, Pignolo, Besgano, Uva d'Oro, and Sgorbera. The region should seize the opportunity to capitalize on them before they completely disappear. W.S.

Omar Khayyám (d. 1132 CE) was a Persian poet, made famous in the English-speaking world by Edward Fitzgerald's translation (and adaptation) of the *Rubáiyát* ('Quatrains') in 1859 (2nd edn, 1868). In his own life, he was known as a philosopher and a scientist, and he was remembered for a long time, both in the Middle East and Europe, as one of the greatest mathematicians of medieval times. His quatrains would scarcely have been deemed original in his own society (see ARAB POETS). In a time of strict orthodoxy, this genre of occasional verse, which was popular in PERSIA in the 11th and 12th centuries, was the best medium for expressing dangerous personal doubts to a close circle of friends.

Omar Khayyám's own quatrains are the outpourings of a non-conformist intellectual who was opposed to religious fanaticism; they range from a pious outlook to the extremes of scepticism. Wine is an important theme in this poetry. Given the ISLAMIC prohibition against wine, many of the *rubáiyát* may seem heretical; however, the defiant anti-Islamic stance of Bacchism in the 8th and 9th centuries had by the 12th century been transformed in significance by Sufism (Islamic mysticism). Some commentators have, therefore, viewed the *rubáiyát* as a mystical genre, with wine forming part of a sensitive allegory. More recently it has been accepted that wine merely serves to express religious scepticism and provides solace from existential anguish; Omar Khayyám sought to drown the world's sorrows in wine and thus rejected 'the hope of a diviner drink' offered by Islam. Khayyám's was a humanist protest that scorned sectarianism and intolerance: 'If I'm drunk on forbidden wine, so I am! | And if I'm a pagan or idolater, so I am! | Every sect has its own suspicions of me, | I myself am just what I am . . . To be free from belief and unbelief is my religion.'

Although Persian wine poetry was largely influenced by Arabic poetry, the range of Bacchic expression in the *Rubáiyát* is far more limited than what we find in the detailed, sometimes exuberant, descriptions of wine among the earlier Arab poets.

See also PERSIA and ENGLISH LITERATURE, WINE IN. P.K.

Avery, P., and Heath-Stubbs, J. (trans.), *The Ruba'iyat of Omar Khayyam* (1979).

Ondarrabi. See HONDARRABI BELTZA.

Ondenc was once an important vine variety in GAILLAC and all over SOUTH WEST FRANCE but has fallen from favour because it yields poorly and is prone to ROT. During the 19th century it must have been taken to Australia, where it was identified, under the name Irvine's White at Great Western in Victoria, by visiting French AMPELOGRAPHER Paul Truel in 1976. Since then it has all but disappeared from Australian vineyards too.

Ontario produces the majority of CANADA's wine, with more than 180 wineries in 2021 and 7,002 ha/17,300 acres of vines, the majority of which is VITIS VINIFERA. The diverse ethnic ancestry of Ontario's grape-growers is reflected in a range of more than 50 vine varieties, with a primary focus on Chardonnay, Riesling, Pinot Noir, and Cabernet Franc. Gamay also excels, with early plantings dating back to the 1970s. Other varieties include Vidal Blanc, Pinot Gris, Sauvignon Blanc, and Gewurztraminer for whites, along with Merlot, Baco Noir, and Cabernet Sauvignon for reds. Ontario is also the home to the Cool Climate Oenology and Viticulture Institute at BROCK UNIVERSITY.

This COOL-CLIMATE growing region has a CONTINENTAL CLIMATE that is subject to extremes of hot, often humid summers with occasional DROUGHT, as well as winters in which temperatures can fall below −20 °C/−4 °F. However, the degree days (see CLIMATE CLASSIFICATION) during the growing season for the Niagara Peninsula (1500 C°) are greater than for Beaune, France (1315 C°), and Hawke's Bay, New Zealand (1200 C°). Long days and cool nights slow down fruit maturation while retaining ACIDITY.

Ontario has three GEOGRAPHICAL INDICATIONS (GIs) all concentrated in the southern part of the province at latitudes 41–44° N and within influence of two of the Great Lakes, Ontario and Erie, which temper the winter cold and the heat of summer (see LAKE EFFECT).

The **Niagara Peninsula**, Canada's largest wine region (5,989 ha/14,800 acres), has a unique MESOCLIMATE created by its position between Lake Ontario and the Niagara Escarpment, a steep, dolomite-topped ridge that runs from NEW YORK through southern Canada to Wisconsin (dolomitic LIMESTONE is rich in magnesium). This ridge moderates air flow by acting as a passive barrier against continental winds while capturing warm lake air. The resulting extended growing season allows for LATE HARVEST wines, including ICEWINE. Sparkling wines are also made by more than 100 wineries.

Within the Peninsula, there are two regional appellations—**Niagara Escarpment** and **Niagara-on-the-Lake**—and ten subappellations. The vineyards of the Niagara Escarpment face mainly north, the well-drained slopes of CLAY, SILT, and CALCAREOUS clay-LOAM soils sheltered by the escarpment and fed by numerous streams and tributaries. The region is further broken down into the lakeside subappellations **Lincoln Lakeshore** and **Creek Shores** and the benchland subappellations **Beamsville Bench**, **Twenty Mile Bench**, and **Short Hills Bench** (see BENCH). On top of the escarpment, **Vinemount Ridge** has deep clay soils and the Peninsula's only south-facing slopes.

Further east, along the Niagara River, are the vineyards of Niagara-on-the-Lake and its subappellations **Niagara Lakeshore**, **Niagara River**, **Four Mile Creek**, and **St David's Bench**. Compared with those of Niagara Escarpment, temperatures are slightly warmer throughout the growing season and the TOPOGRAPHY is flatter, with long, gentle slopes and generous sunlight exposure. Red-SHALE soils with high silt and clay content are moderate- to well-drained.

Lake Erie North Shore (576 ha/1,400 acres) in south-western Ontario has the province's longest growing season and the highest number of degree days but also the risk of WINTER FREEZE. It comprises a narrow band along Lake Erie's north shore planted mainly to *vinifera* vines. It also includes the South Islands subappellation, applied to a group of nine islands 20 km/12.4 miles offshore, which was previously the distinct Pelee Island appellation.

Prince Edward County, a two-and-a-half-hour drive east of Toronto, is Ontario's smallest GI, with 263 ha/650 acres of vines and over 40 wineries in 2021. A peninsula on Lake Ontario's north shore, the region averages 5 °C/9 °F cooler than Niagara, with short, warm summers and winters cold enough to require WINTER PROTECTION for the vines. Many of the vineyards are situated on stony soils on limestone bedrock, resulting in naturally low yields. Chardonnay and Pinot Noir wines excel here.

Ontario also has several emerging regions, such as Norfolk County, to the north-east of the Lake Erie North Shore appellation. There are growing communities of wineries in the outskirts and to the north and west of Toronto near Georgian Bay and Lake Huron, as well as in the eastern part of the province near Ottawa, Canada's capital.

Wines carrying a viticultural designation must be made exclusively from *vinifera* grapes—except Icewine, which can also be made from VIDAL. The fruit of VITIS LABRUSCA vines, still grown in Ontario, is used primarily for juice and some inexpensive non-VQA sparkling wine.

In 2017 Ontario became the second wine-growing region in the world (after South Africa) to introduce regulations for SKIN-FERMENTED white wines. In order to use the label 'skin fermented white wine', the winery must declare its intent by November of that harvest year, and 100% of the grapes used must be macerated and fermented on the skins for a minimum of ten days. The wine may be still or sparkling. J.D.

www.winecountryontario.ca
www.grapegrowersofontario.com

opening the bottle is an important and potentially difficult operation for bottles sealed with a cork. A wide range of CORKSCREWS is available for opening bottles of still wine. See CLOSURES for details of alternatives to CORK, most of which are much easier to remove and need no special equipment.

If the cork proves too recalcitrant for a corkscrew, the cork should simply be pushed in, if possible, and the wine poured out of the bottle, perhaps into a jug, while the cork is held down with a long, thin instrument. See PORT TONGS for one way of opening bottles with very old corks.

But before the cork can be extracted, any FOIL or wax seal has to be broached. A knife blade or FOIL CUTTER is the simplest way to cut a foil neatly, just below the lip of the bottle, which should be wiped of any residue from the foil, especially if it is an old one and contains LEAD. Some of the increasingly popular wax seals are more difficult to penetrate and call for a sharp knife, or foil cutter, and tolerance of a certain amount of mess. If the wax is soft enough, the corkscrew can simply be inserted through it.

Opening a bottle of SPARKLING WINE is potentially extremely hazardous, as the pressure inside the bottle can expel a cork so fast that it can inflict grave injury. The bottle should be held at 45 degrees (to maximize the wine's surface area) with the cork pointing in the least dangerous direction (and certainly not at anyone, nor at anything precious or fragile). The wire MUZZLE should be untwisted and discarded. While holding the cork in the bottle, usually with the top of the thumb, the bottle should then be very gently rotated off the cork with one hand while the cork is held in place with the other. The cork should be allowed to escape the bottleneck very slowly and the wine poured from the 45-degree angle, perhaps with a thumb in the punt (see BOTTLES). The racing-driver technique of giving champagne a good shake and prising off the cork with two thumbs is about as dangerous as motor racing.

See SERVING WINE for the timing of opening a bottle.

Opimian wine is the wine of the consular year of Lucius Opimius, 121 BCE. It owes its fame to the conjunction of an exceptionally hot summer and a momentous historical event, the assassination of C. Gracchus, which temporarily ended the movement for social reform.

Writing in 46 BCE, Cicero states that the Opimian vintage is already too old to drink (*Brutus* 287), and PLINY the Elder describes it as 'reduced to a kind of bitter honey' but still recognizably wine and exorbitantly expensive (*Natural History* 14. 55–7). Petronius (*Satyricon* 36) and MARTIAL (*Epigrams* 1. 26, 3. 82, 10. 49, etc.) treat Opimian as a literary commonplace rather than a real wine: drinking Opimian in large quantities is what the *nouveaux riches* do to flaunt their wealth, but this is satire, not fact.

To have lasted this long, the wines were almost certainly DRIED-GRAPE WINES. H.M.W.

Oporto, Portugal's second city and the commercial centre, known in Portuguese as Porto, which gave its name to Vinho do Porto, better known as PORT wine. Grapes grown in the arid conditions up river of Oporto in the DOURO Valley would be crushed and vinified before being shipped to port shippers' LODGES on the south side of the River Douro in VILA NOVA DE GAIA. Oporto has long had a substantial population of British merchants, whose meeting place, the FACTORY HOUSE, survives to this day.

The PORTUGIESER red grape is sometimes known as Oporto in Romania.

optical sorting. See GRAPE SORTING.

Optima, also called **Optima 113**, is a 1970 GERMAN CROSS, bred from a cross of SILVANER × RIESLING and MÜLLER-THURGAU. It buds late but ripens very early indeed, sometimes more than ten days before Müller-Thurgau, and can notch up impressive ripeness readings, even if the wines themselves are flabby and undistinguished. Germany's plantings of Optima reached a peak of 420 ha/1,037 acres in 1990 but had declined, unlamented, to 21 ha by 2020. Its offspring ORION has been more successful.

options game, BLIND TASTING game which in practice allows novice tasters almost as great a chance of winning as professionals. Developed by Australian Len EVANS, it requires an informed quiz-master who presents players with a series of increasingly precise options for the identity of the wine. A typical series of options might be: 'Australia, California or Bordeaux?', 'left or right bank?', 'St-Estèphe, Pauillac, St-Julien or Margaux?', '20th or 21st century?', 'first or fifth growth?', 'Latour, Lafite or Mouton?'. Players remain in the game only by choosing the correct successive options.

Orange, coolest of the Central Ranges regions of NEW SOUTH WALES, around the town of Orange. With a CONTINENTAL CLIMATE and ELEVATIONS of 600–1,000 m/1,969–3,281 ft resulting in wide DIURNAL TEMPERATURE RANGE, the region is best known for crisp Chardonnay and also excels with Sauvignon Blanc, Shiraz, and Cabernet Sauvignon. TRADITIONAL METHOD sparkling wines are a speciality. Pinot Noir and Riesling show great promise. A.R.P.

Orange Muscat, also known as Muscat Fleur d'Oranger, white grape variety with MUSCAT characteristics that is a CROSS between CHASSELAS and MUSCAT BLANC À PETITS GRAINS. California plantings of 'Muscat Orange' comprised 316 acres/781 ha in 2020, with a little in Oregon and Australia. There are very limited plantings of this variety in TRENTINO, under the name Moscato Fior d'Arancio, but confusingly the Veneto wine of the same name is made from MOSCATO Giallo.

orange wine, distinctive, dry and tannic white-grape wine style with links to the contemporary NATURAL WINE movement but inspired by antiquity. Known as *vino naranja* in Spanish, *vino bianco macerato* (sometimes *vino orange*) in Italian, *Orangewein* or *maischvergoren* in German. As in RED WINEMAKING, orange wines are made by fermenting the juice of ripe grapes with their skins and pips, occasionally with the stems, usually for between a week and a year, but with white grapes. The prolonged MACERATION of the skins results in wines darker than conventional whites, in the yellow/amber/gold/orange/pink spectrum depending on variety, ripeness, duration of maceration, EXTRACTION methods, and vessel type (CLAY vessels are increasingly popular but not essential). Stylistic differences within the genre are also influenced by, for example, a preference for aromatic varieties or the decision not to clarify the wine (see CLARIFICATION). TANNIN levels are higher than in conventional white wine, which can be useful in gastronomy and for natural-wine adherents who bottle with low to no additions of SULFUR DIOXIDE. The genre was reintroduced west of the Caucasus for high-quality dry wine by neighbours Stanko Radikon and Josko Gravner of Oslavia in FRIULI, the latter having bottled only orange and red wine since 1997, although he prefers the term 'amber' to 'orange'. However, traditional TOKAJI Aszu wines, white PORT, and many wines of GEORGIA were always macerated. The name was coined in 2004 by UK wine merchant David Harvey, then based on ETNA and tasting such wines. Most are currently officially labelled as white wine and often referred to as SKIN-FERMENTED whites, although some jurisdictions—Hungary and Ontario, for example—now include a definition of orange wine in their wine regulations. In 2020 the OIV adopted 'white wine with maceration' into the International Code of Oenological Practices.

J.E.H. & D.A.H.

Orbois. See MENU PINEAU.

order of wines to be served. This can affect how individual wines taste quite considerably. The general convention is a wise one for maximizing pleasure: dry before sweet, ordinary before fine, and, generally, young before old.

A sweet wine can make dry wines taste acidic and unpleasant if they are tasted afterwards, so it makes sense to serve wines in an increasingly sweet sequence (which matches the usual sequence of foods during a meal, although serving the sweet course before cheese can upset things).

Old wines are generally more complex than callow young ones (see COMPLEXITY), and so it generally flatters all wines if the oldest in the sequence are served last. This is not infallible, however. Many young wines are so overwhelmingly robust in comparison to a delicate old wine that they overpower it, and increasing levels of average ALCOHOLIC STRENGTH with each vintage also provides an argument in favour of tasting from (weaker) old to (more powerful) young. For this reason, many tasters approach large tastings of PORT, especially vintage port, from the oldest to the youngest wine. Some wine producers, particularly but not exclusively in newer wine regions, also prefer to show their wines in chronological order of progress, and possibily prowess, from old to young. And those planning particularly generous meals may find that the nuances of the oldest, finest wine they serve last may be lost on some palates already soaked in too many younger wines.

Similar considerations apply to serving wines in an upward sequence of quality.

Oregon, one of the United States known by wine lovers for its PINOTS and with a burgeoning reputation for Chardonnay. Oregon lies between CALIFORNIA and WASHINGTON State; while its southern growing regions can claim climatic kinship with the warm, dry growing regions of these two neighbours, it is the wines from the cooler, wetter, north-west corner of Oregon upon which the state has built its reputation for quality. While Oregonian viticulture can be traced back five generations, the growth of its wine industry has been a more discreet affair than that of California. Inhabited in large part by Californian wine refugees, and historically underfunded, the Oregon wine industry has cultivated an image of rustic charm and natural simplicity. While wineries producing hundreds of thousands of cases do exist, more than 70% of Oregon wineries produce fewer than 5,000 cases a year.

History

VITIS VINIFERA vine varieties arrived in the region in the late 19th century. A census of 1860—a year after statehood was granted—revealed Oregon's wine production was some 2,600 gal/98 hl. Twenty years later, Jackson County alone was producing 15,000 gal and a post-PROHIBITION boom saw 28 wineries making a million gal by 1938, even if much of that was FRUIT WINE. Little progress was made in the next 25 years as California dominated the market.

Oregon's modern era dates from 1961, when HillCrest Vineyard was established near Roseburg (in what is now Umpqua Valley AVA) by Richard Sommer, a refugee from the University of California at DAVIS, where he had been advised that *vinifera* grapes could not be grown in Oregon. Nevertheless, he planted Pinot Noir and other *vinifera* varieties. But it is David Lett of the Eyrie Vineyard who is referred to as 'Papa Pinot', having first planted Pinot Noir in the Willamette Valley in 1965. He was followed by UC Davis classmate Charles Cour, as well as such names as Erath, Ponzi, Sokol Blosser, and Adelsheim, among others. Most pioneers had done time in California before heading north.

Lett brought Oregon into the spotlight in 1979 when his 1975 Eyrie Vineyard Pinot Noir was placed second in a French-sponsored tasting comparing top French wines with their NEW WORLD emulators. Beaune merchant Robert DROUHIN staged a follow-up which served only to confirm the result. Drouhin eloquently endorsed it by purchasing land and building a winery within a stone's throw of Lett's vineyards. Following this, outside interest began to increase.

Between 2000 and 2020, vineyard area in Oregon more than tripled, reaching 15,998 ha/39,531 acres, with more than 900 wineries in production. In vineyard and volume terms, Oregon remains significantly smaller than Washington to its immediate north, but it has achieved a good deal more publicity.

Geography and climate

While almost all Washington State vines are planted in the rain shadow and semi-desert east of the Cascade Mountains, most Oregon vines lie west of the Cascades and are exposed to airflow from the Pacific Ocean through gaps in the Coastal Range. This provides the state with milder winters and cooler summers than Washington.

Southern Oregon has much in common with the warm, arid parts of northern California. In contrast, northern Oregon is notoriously wet and cool, although CLIMATE CHANGE has somewhat adjusted this image: between 2013 and 2020, only 2013 and 2019 featured cool, wet harvests. Since 2012 DROUGHT and WATER STRESS have become more common, with timing of FLOWERING and HARVEST inching ever earlier and warm, dry summers in the middle. The year 2020 was particularly jarring, with a dry summer leading to the worst WILDFIRES in the state's history. Many producers struggled to decide whether to harvest after days of heavy smoke.

Vineyard ELEVATIONS are commonly 110–330 m/250–750 ft, and soils vary by area. The most-referenced soil series in northern Oregon are Jory and Nekia (colluvium with VOLCANIC origins), Willakenzie and Bellpine (marine sedimentary), and Laurelwood (a type of windblown LOESS). These make up a small percentage of a diverse range of soil series throughout the state that are well mapped by the National Resources Conservation Service.

The state boasts 22 AVAS, with the WILLAMETTE VALLEY, the largest AVA by acreage and volume, receiving the most publicity. However, the fastest rate of growth of land under vine is in the Southern Oregon AVA, which stretches south of Eugene to the California border and encompasses the Umpqua Valley AVA (including the AVAs Red Hills Douglas County and Elkton) and Rogue Valley AVA (including Applegate Valley AVA). These southern AVAs are the warmest in Oregon and receive up to 40% less precipitation than the Willamette Valley, with the southernmost region, Rogue Valley, the highest in temperature and elevation in the state.

In the north of Oregon, shared with Washington, are the Columbia Gorge AVA and Columbia Valley AVA (including Walla Walla Valley AVA). Within the Walla Walla AVA, entirely on the Oregon side, lies the Rocks District of Milton-Freewater, known for BASALT cobblestones. In eastern Oregon is Snake River AVA, shared with IDAHO. Its distinctly CONTINENTAL CLIMATE and high elevations (762–914 m/2,500–3,000 ft) with large DIURNAL TEMPERATURE RANGE are attracting attention from young winemakers looking for new frontiers.

Viticulture

When David Lett planted Pinot Noir in the Willamette Valley in 1965, he planted the Wädenswil CLONE on its own roots. Charles Coury and Dick Erath followed with the Pommard clone; they too planted UNGRAFTED VINES. As recently as the early 1990s, most vines were planted on their own roots, leaving them prey to PHYLLOXERA. By the mid 1990s, GRAFTING had become popular, and Dijon clones, known for their ability to ripen early in Oregon's MARGINAL CLIMATE, had been grafted on to phylloxera-resistant ROOTSTOCKS. Producers continue to debate the merits of Dijon, Wädenswil, Pommard, and MASS SELECTION. This is due, in large part, to the array of morphological differences present in Pinot Noir. Other varieties do not see the same debate, although, with a rise in the popularity of Oregon Chardonnay there have been debates over whether Wente or Dijon is the better clone for the area (see HERITAGE CLONES).

Oregon wineries tend towards SUSTAINABLE VITICULTURE. In 2021, 5.5% of Oregon's vineyards were certified for ORGANIC VITICULTURE. Although the state produces only 1% of US wine, it claims 574 ha/1,419 acres or 31.7% of BIODYNAMIC-certified vineyard acreage in the US. LIVE certification (a monitored Low Input Viticulture and Enology programme) is popular as well. DRY-FARMING, once a given, is becoming more challenging with climate change, but a large percentage of vineyards are still dry-farmed. The Deep Roots Coalition in Willamette Valley is working to continue this.

The economies of scale necessary for the production of cheap wine are not a feature of the Oregon wine industry, which is therefore motivated by a need for quality rather than quantity. Crop YIELDS tend to be small, often intentionally in an effort to produce superior, concentrated wines. Vines are mostly CANE PRUNED rather than CORDON-trained and SPUR-pruned, thus demanding more time, care, and skill from the grower. High disease pressure and a tendency towards ORGANIC VITICULTURE means more regular SULFUR spraying and increased LABOUR.

Vine varieties

Pinot Noir accounts for 59% of Oregon's vineyard hectarage and commands a higher average price per ton than any other grape. PINOT GRIS (first planted outside of Europe by David Lett of Eyrie Vineyards) has achieved popularity in a dry style showing more flesh than Pinot Grigio in Italy and more acidity than Alsace versions. CHARDONNAY has been represented since the 1960s but grew in importance after the introduction of Dijon clones in the mid 1990s. If Oregon can be said to have a Chardonnay style, it is taut and fresh while carrying a modest amount of new OAK. RIESLING is commercially viable but declining in plantings, while VIOGNIER plantings have increased in recent years, particularly in southern Oregon.

Among red wine grapes other than Pinot Noir, the Bordeaux varieties MERLOT, CABERNET SAUVIGNON, CABERNET FRANC, and MALBEC are popular in southern Oregon and the Columbia River area. SYRAH and TEMPRANILLO (first produced as a VARIETAL wine in the Americas by Abacela) are also planted sporadically throughout the state, with a heavier concentration in the south. The Willamette Valley has a penchant for GAMAY, with the local Portland market celebrating both fruity NOUVEAU styles as well as more serious examples.

State of the industry

A typical Oregon winery is relatively small, with an annual production of 2,500–20,000 cases. Many use grapes bought from specialist growers in addition to own-grown fruit. ACIDIFICATION is necessary only in the hottest or wettest vintages; and although CHAPTALIZATION is allowed, wines with a natural ALCOHOLIC STRENGTH of at least 12% are easily achieved.

Oregon has the strictest labelling laws in the country, requiring producers who label their wines with the name of an AVA to use 95% fruit from that AVA (compared with the TTB requirement of 85%); wines labelled as Pinot Noir must contain 90% Pinot Noir (rather than the federal standard of 75%, which also applies to other Oregon varieties).

While Oregon's prices generally start well above both Washington and California's bottom tier, they do not reach the ridiculous heights of California's upper echelons. During the American recession following 11 September 2001, many wineries added a lower-priced Pinot Noir to their line-up. Independent NÉGOCIANTS have blossomed, with producers such as A to Z and Union Wine Company cleverly buying over-supplied BULK WINES and blending them into well-priced bargains. The turn of the century also saw the introduction of CO-OPERATIVE and CUSTOM-CRUSH FACILITIES such as The Carlton Winemaker's Studio and 12th & Maple Wine Co. In addition, many wineries rent out space in their own cellars for winemakers to produce their own labels. This has been a godsend for talented winemakers looking to launch a label without outside investment or hefty loans. S.C.-J.

industry.oregonwine.org
www.oregonwine.org
www.oregonwinegrowers.org

organic matter, or **soil organic matter** (SOM), the CARBON-containing matter formed in SOIL as plant, animal, and microbial residues decompose. Carbon comprises 50–58% of SOM.

Normally most organic matter occurs in the top 10–20 cm/4–8 in of the soil, with some deeper as a result of deeply penetrating ROOTS and its redistribution by EARTHWORMS and other burrowing animals. On undisturbed soils, much of the store of readily available SOIL NUTRIENTS is associated with the surface layer and its organic matter, having been extracted from the SUBSOIL over millennia and deposited at the surface in plant litter and the excreta of grazing animals. This applies especially to the less soluble nutrients such as PHOSPHORUS and the mineral nutrients (except BORON), which do not appreciably leach down the profile except in very sandy soils. (See VINE NUTRITION.)

Fresh organic matter reflects the composition of the plant and animal materials from which it was formed. As decomposition proceeds, however, the easily decomposable compounds are assimilated by microorganisms with the release of carbon dioxide and the constituent mineral nutrients. Many of these are retained by the microorganisms, but some will be released (mineralized) to become available to plants. The end point of decomposition is a largely inert organic material called stabilized organic matter or, more colloquially, humus. Although humus has a carbon-to-nitrogen ratio between 10 and 15, which is favourable for NITROGEN mineralization, the production of mineral nitrogen is slow because of the inert nature of humus. Humus helps to give the soil a desirable crumb structure and friability (see SOIL STRUCTURE), which improves the soil's water-holding capacity. Because of its negatively charged surfaces, humus adds to a soil's CATION EXCHANGE CAPACITY.

The total result in undisturbed soils (see NO-TILL) is a constant recycling of nutrients and their steady availability to plants. In well-managed viticulture, the aim is first to build up the amount of soil organic matter and associated MINERAL nutrients, then to maintain them at a level high enough to ensure SOIL HEALTH and a steady supply of nutrients to meet the needs of the vines. On initially infertile soils, this may necessitate a substantial use of FERTILIZERS or, in the case of ORGANIC VITICULTURE and BIODYNAMIC VITICULTURE, the use of plant materials and animal manures. It is also possible to achieve a build-up of soil organic matter through planting COVER CROPS, especially grass species, in the inter-rows. At all stages, the increase in, or maintenance of, soil organic matter demands that TILLAGE, if any, be kept to a minimum.

Viticulture for high-quality winemaking requires that soil organic matter content and fertility be just high enough to ensure a suitable BALANCE between fruiting and moderate vegetative growth. Fertile soils with high organic matter contents can cause excessive vegetative VIGOUR and poor CANOPY MICROCLIMATES. R.E.W.

White, R. E., *Understanding Vineyard Soils* (2nd edn, 2015).

organic viticulture, a system of grape-growing broadly defined as shunning industrially synthesized compounds such as FERTILIZERS, FUNGICIDES, HERBICIDES, and PESTICIDES, as well as anything that has been GENETICALLY MODIFIED. Organic viticulture is a prerequisite for the production of ORGANIC WINE. It contrasts with 'conventional', sometimes even called 'industrialized' or 'chemical' viticulture, in two main ways: by stressing management techniques such as CANOPY MANAGEMENT which seek to prevent rather than cure pests and diseases; and by using naturally occurring substances. The key organic management strategy for perennial crops such as vines, for which no crop rotation is possible, involves stimulating and maintaining healthy populations of a diverse range of soil microorganisms.

The primary route to achieving this in organic vineyards is through the application of organic fertilizer in the form of COMPOST. Unlike soluble fertilizer, this improves the structure and biological properties of the soil, rather than directly feeding the vine itself, and allows the slow release of MINERAL nutrients, by encouraging what in organic-speak is called a 'soil food web' of living organisms such as EARTHWORMS, beneficial bacteria, protozoa, and fungi (see SOIL BIOTA). Synthetic soluble fertilizers provide nutrients but do not promote the intrinsic life in the soil. The principle of feeding the soil and not the plant also means that foliar feed fertilizers—those applied to the leaves of the vine—are prohibited under organic norms.

Growers who switch from conventional to organic soil and FERTILITY management claim that vine shoots need much less frequent TRIMMING as vine VIGOUR is reduced. This makes yields less erratic (organic growers claim to get lower annual YIELDS, but more regular yields overall compared with their conventional counterparts) and reduces the risk of attack by FUNGAL DISEASES. However, the second and especially third years of the three-year conversion period from conventional to organic (or biodynamic) management are critical. This period can produce uneconomically low yields and unsustainably high disease pressure, two not unrelated conditions arising because vines have been unable to begin accessing slow-release nutrients from the soil, its reserves of quick-release soluble fertilizers having been all but exhausted by then.

Therefore to make conversion to organics a success, would-be organic growers must adopt a prevention-rather-than-cure approach by putting in place mechanisms first to create and then to protect both the soil humus and soil microbiology without which vines and soil nutrients would be unable to interact.

This usually means a combination of compost and COVER CROPS. Compost creates the preconditions for soil humification, being rich both in microbiology and in the basic building block of life, CARBON (organic winegrowers aim for finished compost with a carbon–nitrogen or C/N ratio of 15:1). Cover crops then protect this microbiologically rich resource from SOIL EROSION and nutrient leeching.

Humus-rich, cover-cropped soils are more likely to hold vital water and nutrients than impoverished ones, and to promote the growth of MYCORRHIZAL fungi on vine roots, organisms which allow vine roots to penetrate deeper into the soil and facilitate the uptake of micronutrients (see VINE NUTRITION), both of which are said by some to make wines taste more TERROIR-specific and thus more complex.

A small but increasing number of organic and biodynamic winegrowers (see BIODYNAMIC VITICULTURE) have moved to minimal or NO-TILL systems by which inter-rows are almost permanently covered by perennial sward (see COVER CROP). Such minimal tillage preserves topsoil structure; it also means that the vineyard becomes a beneficial carbon-sink rather than the cause of the release of carbon and dust into the atmosphere, both of which may contribute to CLIMATE CHANGE and, in the case of dust, encourage certain vine MITES. Perennial swards can also provide MULCH to prevent weed growth directly under the vines if the inter-row vegetation is cut using the so-called 'mow and throw' technique, in which the mowings are left on the ground.

For disease prevention, organic growers are reliant on naturally occurring substances. For instance, elemental SULFUR and the salt copper sulfate (see BORDEAUX MIXTURE) are used to control POWDERY MILDEW and DOWNY MILDEW respectively. Both these treatments and others commonly used in organic vineyards (e.g. soap, plant oils and teas, seaweed, and powders based on BENTONITE, silicates, milk, and wild herbs) are contact or barrier sprays which, unlike chemically produced systemic sprays, do not enter either the vine's sap or the grape pulp and so are less likely to produce RESIDUES in the wine. Organic growers, especially those in damp, humid climates, are often criticized for relying too heavily on copper-based treatments, leading to COPPER toxicity in the soil. Organic growers argue that copper residues are more easily mobilized where organic management fosters increased levels of soil microbiology, and that organic norms significantly restrict the amount of copper used compared with the amount allowed in conventional vineyards. EU regulations for organic viticulture permit up to 28 kg/ha averaged over a seven-year period, compared with the 30 kg over a five-year period allowed in conventional viticulture. Furthermore, these restrictions have either encouraged organic growers, especially those in marginal European climates, to switch from VITIS VINIFERA to DISEASE-RESISTANT interspecific CROSSES; or have inspired organic growers in both northern and southern hemispheres to find genuinely SUSTAINABLE alternatives to copper and sulfur for mildew control. The most notable of these is aerated compost tea, a low-tech, low-cost, rain-fast way of colonizing vines with beneficial aerobic bacteria, fungi, and other microorganisms that inhibit, consume, or outcompete disease-bearing pathogens. Another increasingly relevant example of this type of approach is the application of strains of the *Trichoderma* fungus to either vine trunks or pruning wounds to protect vines from ESCA. See also BIOLOGICALS.

Other aspects of the organic prophylactic approach to farming in general, and to GREY ROT in particular, include employing canopy management techniques to open up the canopy and reduce the risk of rot. This can result in higher LABOUR costs compared with those of conventional farming. Organic growers who pass these costs on in the price of the wine argue that, from a holistic standpoint, organic viticulture eliminates costs to the wider community such as cleaning up by local authorities of groundwater polluted by anti-rot sprays—an ongoing, sensitive issue. Organic growers also argue that this predisposition towards manual labour provides employment opportunities in communities suffering rural depopulation due in part to increased MECHANIZATION; and that this may account for why organic vineyards in France are now more likely than their non-organic counterparts to be picked by hand, rather than by machine, and to be estate-bottled.

History

The origins of the organic agriculture movement are late 20th century European. Like its predecessors the Enlightenment, the Romantic movement, and Darwinism, organics can be seen as attempting to redefine people's relationship to their natural surroundings. By the end of the 1920s, when the green movement was closely intertwined with reactionary cultural and political phenomena such as National Socialism in Germany and Guild Socialism in Britain, organics had declared itself as opposing the industrialization of agriculture for both social and environmental reasons. Its main target was the mineral 'NPK' FERTILIZER devised in 1836 by Justus von Liebig and mass produced from 1913 using the Haber-Bosch process. These fertilizers transformed the agricultural landscape and economic and social structures. However, two World Wars, austerity, rural depopulation, rapidly rising metropolitan populations, and the ease with which NITROGEN production was switched post-1945 from making munitions to fertilizer meant the infant organic movement provided only a fringe argument against the inexorable industrialization of agriculture. And whereas industrial food conglomerates found GLOBALIZATION both necessary and desirable, organic activists struggled to form international bonds and hence risked accusations of parochialism. The formation in 1972 of the International Federation of Organic Agriculture Movements (IFOAM) to oversee the setting of the majority of the world's organic standards and the certification bodies has helped change this perception.

Nevertheless, although the first organic vineyards were established after the Second World War, it took until the late 1980s for wines produced from organically grown grapes to begin to shake off a reputation for earnest amateurism, inconsistency, and poor value. Critics argue that organic wine's now steadily increasing market share, which began to grow in Europe in the early 1990s, was mainly due to EU subsidies, initially to help growers survive the three-year organic conversion process but now provided to stimulate rural development and optimize the vineyard ECOSYSTEM. However, its advocates see the main selling point for organics in wine as reinforcing the key notion of TERROIR. This 'working with rather than against nature' handily chimed with increased public unease at the effects of industrialized farming on our food rather than in our wine, notably in the UK, where the food scandals of the mid 1990s and early 2000s involving BSE and foot-and-mouth disease provoked widespread public debate. Concern about the perceived threat that GENETIC MODIFICATION might have on food and wine also stimulated greater interest in the alternatives.

More particularly, though, growers themselves began adopting organics in greater numbers because they felt it would preserve and enhance their main equity, terroir, while giving the wines an organoleptic and marketing edge. More effective vineyard machinery for the control of weeds and disease, improved communication regarding which organic techniques work best, and consumer demand have also contributed to the steady growth in organic viticulture worldwide.

Conford, P., *The Origins of the Organic Movement* (2001).

Organic certification and terminology

To be described as 'organic', a vineyard and/or its wine (see ORGANIC WINE) must have third-party certification, usually from a non-governmental organization or 'certifier' accredited by a ministry of agriculture or its equivalent and to criteria which are ISO 17065 compliant. This verifies that the certifier's standards conform to organic global baselines set by IFOAM (see above). Organic certification is granted after a three-year conversion period as wine grapes are a perennial crop (conversion takes two years for annuals such as cereals or carrots). Certification aims to protect both bona fide organic producers and consumers of organic products from anti-competitive activity or fraudulent claims. Certifiers can advise vineyard owners as to why their vineyard does not meet their standards but cannot provide advice on which organic sprays might be best in any particular situation. Agreements in 2012 between the US, Canada, and the EU mean that organic production and labelling finally enjoy a strong degree of transnational if not yet global equivalence (previously an organic French vineyard exporting to the US needed both EU and American certification documents). Winegrowers who impose on themselves stricter standards than those of the organic baseline may join private organic associations such as France's Nature et Progrès or Germany's Ecovin. These bodies require, for example, wider buffer zones between conventional and organic plots, allow fewer FINING agents, and require lower levels of free and total SULFUR DIOXIDE than those permitted for organic wine.

See also BIODYNAMIC VITICULTURE, REGENERATIVE VITICULTURE, SUSTAINABLE VITICULTURE, and NATURAL WINE.

Organic viticulture worldwide

In 1999, 0.5–0.75% of the world vineyard was certified organic or biodynamic or in conversion, the majority of which comprised small, heritage organic estates prioritizing local rather than international markets. As more blue-chip estates in France, notably in the Loire, Alsace, and Burgundy, began converting to organics and biodynamics in the 1990s, conventional wine's potentially negative impact locally and on the wider environment started to be questioned. In California, organic/biodynamic pioneer Jimmy Fetzer's creation of a Mediterranean-style vine garden melding winegrowing with vegetables, olives, fruit, and both fluffy and feathered livestock helped redefine organic wine as a colourfully positive lifestyle choice, finally providing the movement with sex appeal to go with its gravitas.

Organic viticulture's share of the global vineyard (mostly but not exclusively grown for wine) went from under 2% to 6.1% between 2007 and 2018, of which 87% was in Europe. France's organic vineyard area (including the area under conversion) increased fourfold between 2007 and 2018 to 94,000 ha/232,279 acres. Austria's position as one of the world's winegrowing nations with the highest proportion of organic vineyards (15.3% in 2021) is due in large part to its pre-emptive investment in educating potential consumers about organics, thereby creating a ready market for organic food and wine. South Africa's organic vineyard area has been increasing significantly, more than tripling between 2016 and 2017 and growing by 63% in 2018. In 2015 organic vineyards accounted for 3% of global wine production, and the biggest producer of organic wine in 2018 was Italy. According to Agence Bio, global consumption of organic still wines exceeded 5 million hl/132 million gal in 2017, having increased by nearly 50% since 2012, representing 2.75% of global wine consumption, with Germany enjoying almost one-quarter of that total.

See also ORGANIC WINE and BIODYNAMIC VITICULTURE. M.W.

Agence Bio, *Organic Sector in the World* (2020).
FiBL & IFOAM, *The World of Organic Agriculture* (2022).
McGourty, G. T. (ed.), *Organic Winegrowing Manual* (2011).
OIV Focus, *The World Organic Vineyard* (2021).

organic wine, wine made from grapes produced by ORGANIC VITICULTURE and processed (fermented) according to standards for organic winemaking, which, despite increasing harmonization, still vary from country to country, notably regarding the use of SULFUR DIOXIDE. Until 2011 wine produced or sold in the EU from organic grapes had to be labelled 'wine from organically grown grapes'. However, in 2012 new EU rules created the term 'organic wine', referring to that made from organic grapes, giving preference 'to the use of ADDITIVES and PROCESSING AIDS derived from organically farmed raw materials' if they are available, and with restrictions on some oenological practices, including lower maximum levels for added sulfur dioxide: around 15–30% lower than for conventional wines, depending on wine colour, sweetness, and style (for example 100 g/l for red wines and 150 g/l for dry white and rosé wines).

In the US, in contrast, the term 'organic wine', as defined in the National Organic Program (NOP), refers to wine made from organic grapes but with no added sulfites, while 'made with organic grapes' applies to similarly grown wines containing up to 100 mg/l of added sulfites. In Canada, an 'organic wine' must conform to the requirments of the Canadian Organic Regime, for both grape-growing and winemaking: grapes must be certified organic, additives are regulated, and the level of SO_2 depends on the amount of RESIDUAL SUGAR (RS) in the wine (e.g. up to 30 mg/l free SO_2 for wines with less than 50 g/l RS). In both the US and Canada, any other agricultural ingredients that go into organic wine—yeast or yeast nutrients, for example—must be organic if they are available. Paradoxically, all European wines from organic grapes sold in the US must be labelled 'made with organic grapes' rather than 'organic wine', even if they contain no added sulfites because EU rules permit sulfite addition in wines labelled as 'organic wine'. Canada and the EU, however, recognize each other's organic production rules.

Organic winemaking standards worldwide generally permit most other winemaking treatments, including, for example, adding DIAMMONIUM PHOSPHATE as a yeast nutrient (not permitted under the more restrictive NOP) and REVERSE OSMOSIS, because these have also been allowed for organic food (several such processes are pending review in the EU but are allowed because of 'lack of viable alternatives'). Although PVPP and potassium ferrocyanide (see BLUE FINING) are universally proscribed FINING agents for organic wine, most other fining agents are allowed, so that wines labelled in some way as organic may be unsuitable for vegetarians and vegans. (It is a common misconception that organic also equals vegetarian- or vegan-friendly.) Energy-intensive treatments (such as CONCENTRATION, THERMOVINIFICATION, and PASTEURIZATION) are allowed by general organic standards, although members of organic wine producer groups such as Nature et Progrès in France voluntarily agree to shun them. Where possible, naturally derived additives, agents, and aids such as sugar for CHAPTALIZATION, yeast hulls to feed ferments, and egg whites for FINING should be from organic sources. Grape spirit used in organic fortified wines must have been distilled from certified organic grapes/marc/wine.

Organic wines made in the EU must carry the EU organic logo (stars in the shape of a leaf) and the code number of their certifying body.

M.W.

IFOAM, *EU Rules for Organic Wine Production* (2013).

Regulation (EU) 203/2012 of the European Parliament and of the Council.

USDA, *Organic 101: Organic Wine* (2017).

origins of viniculture. The beginning of viniculture, encompassing both VITICULTURE and WINEMAKING, cannot have begun where our species, *Homo sapiens sapiens*, originated in sub-Saharan Africa. While our ancestors might have exploited other high-sugar fruits (e.g. fig and marula) for fermented beverages, the wild Eurasian grapevine (*Vitis vinifera sylvestris*; see WILD VINES) did not grow there. Only when humans came 'out of Africa', 60,000–100,000 years ago, did they encounter the grape. This occurrence, so auspicious for the future cultural and technological history of humanity, probably took place in the area of modern Lebanon, the southernmost point where wild vines grow in the Near East today and probably for the last 100,000 years.

No archaeological evidence of this initial encounter nor of the first wine exists for the Palaeolithic period. Containers which could be chemically analysed have not survived since they were made of perishable materials such as leather or wood. Yet the centrality of FERMENTATION to life on Earth as well as the physiological propensities (sensory, dietary, and mind-altering) of most animals for consuming alcohol imply that humans would soon have discovered how to make wine from wild grapes.

Grapevines that festooned the forests of coastal and mountainous Lebanon would probably have captivated our ancestors, and the colourful fruit, even if it were sour, would almost certainly have been gathered up for food and made into the 'first wine', whether accidentally or by applying traditional African methods. We might imagine the following, according to the 'Palaeolithic Hypothesis' or 'Drunken Monkey Hypothesis': fruit was piled into a primitive container, juice was exuded from grapes near the bottom of the container under the weight of fruit above and, depending on its ripeness, fermentation of this liquid (the ideal, nutritious medium) would be initiated by YEAST on the skins of some of the grapes in a warm climate in several days. Reaching the bottom of the container, our ancestors would have been amazed by the aromatic and mildly intoxicating beverage that was produced. More intentional squeezings and tastings might well have ensued. You had to drink it quickly, since methods for preserving wine were likely poorly developed.

It is also possible that observation led to the discovery of LAYERING, in which some vine woody parts, including STEMS and CANES, would have formed roots when growing along the ground. Once the new vine had sprung up, it might have been trained to grow up a nearby tree or even an artificial support.

A detailed knowledge of PRUNING and VINE TRAINING would have come later, at least by *c.*3000 BCE. By severing a rooted vine part from the parent plant, it could have been transplanted. Controlling the vine's height and shape would have enabled easier care and harvesting. Whoever did this was the world's first vine-grower, and this would have been the world's first vineyard.

For larger-scale, more organized viniculture, we must cast a wider net than the Levant, to include the vast upland region of the eastern Taurus, Caucasus, and Zagros Mountains of north-western Iran. These areas comprise a sort of world centre of the Eurasian grapevine, where its greatest genetic diversity is found and where a wine culture consolidated itself in the Neolithic period, *c.*9500–5000 BCE.

Oldest grape wines

To date, the earliest chemically attested instance of grapes being used in a fermented beverage is at the Neolithic site of Jiahu in the Yellow River in the central plains of ancient China during the seventh millennium BCE. Yet the probable native wild grape was only one of several other fermentable ingredients in this mixed beverage. (With upwards of 30 native wild vine species, China accounts for more than half of the vine species in the world, some of which produce berries containing as much as 19% sugar by weight. No evidence, however, has yet been found to show that any of these species were ever domesticated until recent times.)

For an alcoholic beverage fermented solely from the Eurasian grape, the earliest chemical evidence for grape wine comes from early Neolithic villages of the Shulaveri-Shomutepe culture in present-day Georgia in the South Caucasus region, *c.*6,000–5,800 BCE. This finding is based on the presence of TARTARIC ACID, which is found in large amounts in the Middle East only in grapes, and other scientific evidence (archaeological, archaeobotanical, climatic, etc.).

Previously, the earliest known wine came from another early Neolithic village in the northern Zagros Mountains of Iran: Hajji Firuz Tepe, *c.*5400–5000 BCE. Six jars in a kitchen of an average household would originally have held some 55 l (15 gal) of wine. The intended product was most likely wine and not vinegar or another grape product, because clay stoppers were used to plug the narrow mouths of the jars and a tree resin, probably terebinth with antioxidant properties, was added to the wine as a preservative. Hajji Firuz was among the first year-round settlements based on newly domesticated plants and animals of the Neolithic period. The Eurasian VITIS VINIFERA grapevine might well have been one of those domesticates. The invention of pottery around 6000 BCE gave impetus to the process, since special vessels for preparing, storing, and serving wine could now be made.

The large amount of wine for a single household implies that the Eurasian grape had already been domesticated at Hajji Firuz. In contrast to the wild dioecious plant (with separate male and female vines), the domesticated vine is hermaphroditic (with male stamen and female pistil on flowers of the same plant). It produces much more fruit, since it is not dependent on insects or wind for pollination.

For the vine to have been domesticated, either the sub-macroscopic sexual organs of a hermaphrodite need to be observed (quite unlikely since hermaphrodites comprise only about 6% of the wild population) or, more probably, the would-be Neolithic viniculturalist noted that some vines yielded more fruit than others and proceeded to CLONE them by layering. Transplantation by CUTTINGS, roots, or buds was eventually discovered. Plants could also be selected for special characteristics (e.g. juicier and tastier fruit, different sizes and colour, fewer seeds, etc.) and moved to another place. Cloning could not have been done with the seeds of a desirable plant because they are genetically different to the parent plant. The magnitude of the accomplishment in domesticating *vinifera* vines can be appreciated by considering that of the many other grape species around the world, no evidence yet exists that any of them were domesticated by ancient humans. That distinction belongs solely to the Eurasian grapevine, which produces 99% of the world's wine today.

The Noah Hypothesis

But how early and where was the Eurasian grapevine domesticated? Was it in the South Caucasus or in the northern Zagros Mountains—both areas where the wild vine still grows today—or elsewhere in the Near East? Recent DNA PROFILING of modern wild grape and domesticated VINE VARIETIES in Europe and the Near East (including Türkiye, Armenia, and Georgia but not yet Lebanon or Iran) points to a single Near Eastern domestication event (the so-called NOAH Hypothesis). Specifically, a very close relationship has been shown between wild and domesticated vines from eastern Türkiye and Georgia and important western European cultivars, including Pinot Noir, Nebbiolo, Syrah, and Chasselas. Since the European *Vitis vinifera sylvestris* was far removed from these cultivars, it cannot fully account for their origin.

As the domesticated grapevine was transplanted southwards to Egypt and Shiraz (see PERSIA) and westwards across the Mediterranean and the continent, there was introgression with wild vines in those areas such as Greece, Italy, France, and Spain to yield many more Middle Eastern and European varieties. At a later time, when the grapevine was better understood, independent domestication events may have taken place where the wild grapevine grew—in Spain, for example.

The Noah Hypothesis is plausible for other reasons. Exploitation of wild grapes had been going on since the Natufian period (*c.*11,000–10,000 BCE), as evidenced by the finding of pips at numerous sites along the middle Euphrates in Syria. Several hundred kilometres upstream in the Taurus Mountains of Türkiye, Çayönü on the upper Tigris has yielded wild grape seeds dating back to around 9000 BCE, and many other sites in the region have yielded similar evidence ranging in date as recently as the late Chalcolithic period, *c.*3500 BCE.

To date, only wild Eurasian grape pips, which are generally shorter and broader than their domesticated counterparts (although Pinot is an exception), are reported from the Neolithic sites of the Shulaveri-Shomutepe culture. Once DNA PROFILING methods for extracting and testing ancient grapes have been developed, the wild/domesticated gene can be used to verify the equivocal botanical criteria.

Shulaveris-Gora and nearby Neolithic sites are also notable for having some of the earliest Near Eastern pottery decorated with motifs which may well be grape clusters and vines; these may have served as fermentation and drinking vessels. Chemical analyses were under way in early 2014. Since the later archaeology and history of Georgia was dominated by a wine culture intertwining almost every aspect of life—from everyday meals to special celebrations, religious rites, and the economy as a whole—it may be reasonably hypothesized that the newfound horticultural and technological advances of the Neolithic period laid the basis for what followed and for what continues today.

Recent explorations in the eastern Taurus Mountains are revealing equally extraordinary developments in the Neolithic period there, going back to 9500 BCE. At Göbekli Tepe and Nevali Çori, not far from Çayönü, 'sanctuaries' of three-dimensional monoliths with vivid, realistic portrayals of carved animals, humans, and symbolic motifs were constructed. Pottery had not yet made its appearance, but stone goblets and bowls were made of the highly absorbent clay mineral chlorite, found at many other sites along the upper Tigris extending into Syria. Celebratory scenes are again depicted, possibly fuelled by a fermented beverage. Wine again appears to be a distinct possibility, according to ongoing chemical analyses of copious amounts of ancient organic compounds extracted from the vessels using solvents. But wheat/barley beer cannot be ruled out, since einkorn wheat, one of the Neolithic founder plants, has been traced by DNA to the south-eastern Taurus. A more complex fermented beverage of wine, beer, honey, and other botanicals, underlining the experimental prowess of our Neolithic ancestors, is also possible.

Another startling discovery was announced in 2011 from a cave at Areni in Armenia. In this mountainous area, humans constructed plaster floors for grape PRESSES designed to run the grape juice into underground jars, which constitute the earliest *karas* (in Armenian) or QVEVRI (in Georgian). Grape seeds in the vicinity suggested that the contents of the vessels were wine, and chemical analysis confirmed this. A contemporaneous cemetery within the cave suggests that the wine was used in burial services for the ancestors. This finding bridges the gap from winemaking during the Neolithic period to the recent discovery of a probable wine cellar at Tel Kabri in the Galilee, *c.*1700 BCE, and the enormous Urartian wine cellars of *c.*800–600 BCE, some 2,500 years later. The large-scale production at Areni points to a long gestation period after pottery was invented and large jars for fermentation were developed. But if Areni comes at the end of a long development, we are still left with the question, according to the Noah Hypothesis: where was *Vitis vinifera* first domesticated and wine first made?

Recent DNA analyses of modern wild and domesticated grapevines even suggest that the plant was already domesticated in the Levant as early as *c.*9000 BCE, immediately following the Ice Age during the early Neolithic period. One might question this hypothesis, however, given that Lebanon, as well as large areas of the Middle East, is not represented in the study. It is also doubtful that early Holocene hunter-gatherers would have had the necessary horticultural expertise to transplant and nurture a grapevine until it bore fruit after some 5–7 years. Utilizing, even cultivating, wild grapes for food and drink is one thing, but actually domesticating the Eurasian grapevine is much more difficult. Moreover, dating solely by genetic criteria is problematic. Corroborative archaeological, archaeobotanical, and/or chemical evidence is needed to sustain this hypothesis.

Levantine influence spreads south and west

We do know that viniculture ultimately radiated out from the mountainous Near East to other areas on the western and eastern arms of the Fertile Crescent. It had reached CANAAN by *c.*3500 BCE, to judge from grape seeds, wood, and even whole dried grapes (raisins) recovered from sites in the Jordan Valley. In MESOPOTAMIA, transplantation of the vine and winemaking followed the spine of the Zagros Mountains and had arrived in Shiraz in south-western Iran by at least 2500 BCE.

The southern Levantine industry had matured to such a degree that the tomb of Scorpion I (*c.*3150 BCE), one of the first rulers of a united Egypt, at Abydos was stocked with 4,500 l of wine imported from southern Canaan. The wine was laced with terebinth tree resin, to which fresh fruit (grapes and figs) and various Levantine herbs such as thyme and savory had been added. The grapes might also have been added as raisins. It was essentially a medicinal powerhouse, and the well-documented Egyptian pharmacopoeia of later times clearly drew inspiration, as well as the botanicals themselves, from the Canaanite world. Only the best beverage could serve to usher a pharaoh into the afterlife.

Once the kings and upper classes had been enticed by wine, the next logical step was to transfer viniculture to Egypt itself, so as to tailor the wines to individual tastes and exercise more control. Beginning around 3000 BCE, the Egyptian pharaohs financed the establishment of a royal wine industry in the Nile Delta.

The new Egyptian industry was striking in its level of sophistication from the outset. Of course, the Canaanite specialists had many millennia of tradition behind them when they brought grapevines to the Nile Delta. Even the Egyptian hieroglyph meaning 'grape', 'vineyard' or 'wine' is a telling piece of evidence of viticultural expertise. As the earliest written character referring to the domesticated grapevine and wine from anywhere in the world, the hieroglyph graphically depicts a well-trained vine growing up on to a trellis of vertical poles, forked at their upper ends to hold the vine. The plant is rooted in a container, probably for ease of watering. In short, the best practices of modern vineyard management, including a drip irrigation system, were on display at the inception of the ancient Egyptian industry.

The Canaanite winemakers also had to be creative. Levantine vineyards, generally in hilly terrain with good drainage for winter rains, had a very different TERROIR than the flat, alluvial Nile Delta, where blistering summer heat and much less precipitation meant that crops, especially water-sensitive grapes, had to be irrigated. A trellising system minimized direct exposure of the grapes to intense sunlight. Fortunately the alluvial deposits of the delta, washed down from the upper Nile during the annual flooding, had produced well-drained and fertile soils.

Wine, which was specifically referred to by where it came from in the delta (the ancient equivalent of today's vineyard-specific wines), had achieved canonical status as an essential funerary offering by Dynasty 6, around 2200 BCE. In time, nearly every major religious festival, including the all-important *heb-sed* to guarantee the continued welfare of the pharaoh and the fruitfulness of the land, called for wine offerings and prolific drinking, often lasting for weeks.

With winemaking success in Egypt behind them, the Canaanites ventured further throughout the Mediterranean on their Byblos ships (the telling Egyptian term for a sea-going vessel) made of Cedar of Lebanon. They applied a similar formula wherever they went: import wine and other luxury goods, entice the rulers with wine culture by presenting them with speciality wine sets, and then wait until they were asked to help establish native industries, including viniculture, by transplanting the domesticated Eurasian grapevine.

According to the biomolecular and archaeobotanical evidence, one of the first stops in the island-hopping jaunts of the Canaanites across the Mediterranean was CRETE. Nearly 1,000 kilometres from the port city states of Lebanon and southern Syria, this large island lies on the threshold of the larger Greek world. Although modern scholars are understandably sceptical about the often-contradictory and fantastic tales of classical writers, a recurring theme in many accounts has the Greek wine god DIONYSUS voyaging from PHOENICIA to Crete as a daring seafarer. One beautifully painted drinking-cup (*kylix*) made by the master potter Exekias in the 6th century BCE shows the god single-handedly manning a small sailing boat, its mast festooned with a luxuriant grapevine. Apparently, having been attacked by pirates, Dionysus fought back by miraculously growing the vine and dousing his attackers with wine; they were transformed into frolicking dolphins, who are seen circling around the boat. Could this tale be inspired by an actual voyage that carried the domesticated grapevine to Crete aboard a Byblos ship?

The earliest wine so far identified on Crete was from the late third millennium BCE farming community of Myrtos-Phournou Koryphe, along the southern coast. Numerous large jars (*pithoi*) holding about 90 l were recovered from storerooms and kitchens of ordinary houses throughout the site. The pottery was locally produced, as was presumably the wine. Grape seeds, stems, and skins in some jars suggested fermentation on the lees, minimal filtration, and/or adding fresh grapes for flavour.

Numerous circular vats, often called 'bathtubs', were also found at Myrtos. Such finds, also well attested in ancient Egypt, are most often associated with industrial winemaking. The bathtubs, fitted with spouts for draining the grape juice into large jars, were ideal for FOOT TREADING. As one worker tired, the next would step into the vat and take over. Large-scale production was also marked by a massive funnel, the stock-in-trade of the Near Eastern winemaker, and impressions of grape leaves on the pottery pointed to vineyards in the vicinity.

Much like the royal winemaking industry in Egypt, the Myrtos enterprise appears to have sprung out of nowhere. Did the impetus to make wine at Myrtos come from elsewhere in Greece, or was it brought to this island by the Canaanites? The latter position is better supported. Myrtos lay at the terminus of a well-travelled maritime route for ships coming from Egypt and the Levant, and the distinctly Near Eastern character of its winemaking industry suggests influence from this quarter. The Canaanites were looking to spread their wine culture, and they saw an opportunity in Greece to work with the local Cretan people to advance their interests.

Greek winemaking's debt to the Canaanites, as well as to their Egyptian trading partners, is also reflected in the later signs for 'grape', 'vineyard', and 'wine' in the earliest Greek scripts, including Cretan Hieroglyphic and Linear A. The characters are unquestionably derived from the Egyptian hieroglyph, which shows a well-trained vine growing on a horizontal trellis.

It is also possible that winemaking penetrated Greece from the north, especially from Macedonia, where masses of grape skins and seeds, probably from pressings, have been recovered from Dikili Tash dating to the late fifth millennium BCE, or perhaps came from western Anatolia via the Aegean Islands, where domesticated grape remains and leaf impressions on pottery have been found. A notable finding of domesticated grape pips inside a *pithos* was made at Aghios Kosmas in Attica. The large jar had a hole near its base, just like the Myrtos vessels. This is *prima facie* evidence that winemaking, perhaps along the same scale as that at Myrtos, was known on the mainland at about the same time.

The Canaanites, who became the Phoenicians of the Iron Age, did not stop at Crete. They sailed on to CARTHAGE in Tunisia and other parts of the western Mediterranean. The founders of Carthage, probably in the late 9th century BCE, entered a territory only sparsely occupied by Berber pastoral nomads, who offered little resistance. Unlike more populous regions of the Mediterranean, it allowed the Phoenicians to play the role of true colonialists by forgoing trade agreements and building a settlement completely to their specifications. As Carthage grew in the following centuries, it became the capital of the Punic empire and the breadbasket of the Roman Empire. Its ships plied the waters from Carthage through the Tyrrhenian Sea to the port of ROME at Ostia. Long lines of AMPHORAE spread out on the sea floor at a depth of as much as 1,000 m, representing the cargo lost by foundering ships, mark the approximately 600-km/373-mile route, notably at Skerki Bank about 80 km north-west of SICILY.

Wine was naturally the beverage of choice in Carthage. One of the first AGRICULTURAL TREATISES on viniculture and other forms of agriculture was composed by a 3rd–2nd-century BCE Carthaginian named Mago, who is quoted extensively in later Roman writings (VARRO, COLUMELLA, and PLINY the Elder). Presumably he drew on Phoenician traditions dating from the founding of the colony. To date, however, pips from the 4th century BCE are the earliest excavated evidence for the domesticated grape at Carthage.

Although the wild vine grows in Tunisia, special precautions had to be taken to assure survival of the domesticated grapevine in such a hot climate. Mago advised on how to aerate the soil and plant vineyards (e.g. on north slopes to take advantage of rainfall coming from the Mediterranean) to compensate for the low rainfall. His recipe for raisin-wine involved picking the grapes at peak ripeness, rejecting damaged berries, drying the grapes on reed platforms in the sun for several days (taking care to cover them at night, so that they were not dampened by the dew), resaturating the raisins with fresh juice, and then treading the grapes. A second batch was prepared in the same way, and then the two lots were combined and fermented for about a month, finally being strained into vessels with leather covers. The end result must have been a delicious, luscious elixir, also referred to in the earlier Anatolian texts of HOMER and HESIOD, much like a Tuscan VIN SANTO or Moscato di PANTELLERIA.

The huge Phoenician and Carthaginian shipments of wine, along with other luxury items, conveyed a new, wine-based way of life which gradually permeated the societies, religions, and economies of those they came in contact with. In the wake of the Phoenicians, native fermented beverages, including beers, and mixed fermented beverages of all kinds ('grogs') were marginalized, modified, and displaced.

Wine culture invades Greece, then Italy, then France

Greece, which became a pre-eminent wine culture, was won over from its native 'Greek grog', made from Pramnian wine, honey, and barley, topped with cheese—the so-called *kykeon* of the Homeric epics. Even after the Greeks had become seafaring merchants in their own right and had begun vying with Phoenicia for control of the Mediterranean, their lasting debt to eastern Mediterranean wine culture was demonstrated by their adoption of the Phoenician alphabet, which became the basis of our modern Western and Arabic scripts. The earliest archaic Greek inscription was incised on a wine jug (*oinochoe*) in the 8th century BCE and reads: 'Whoever of all dancers performs most nimbly will win this *oinochoe* as prize.' Later in the same century, a Rhodian wine cup (*kotyle*) from the tomb of a young boy at Pithekoussai, an early Greek colony established on the island of ISCHIA in the Bay of Naples, states in elegant dactylic hexameter poetry, the language of the Homeric epics, that 'Nestor's cup was good to drink from, but anyone who drinks from this cup will soon be struck with desire for fair-crowned Aphrodite.' The Dionysiac interweaving of wine, women, and dance, inspired by Canaanite and Phoenician wine culture, is striking.

During the early first millennium BCE, the Phoenicians ventured ever further into the western Mediterranean, where they founded more bases and colonies along the north coast of Africa, on strategic islands (MALTA, CORSICA, Motya in western SICILY, Lipari, Ibiza, etc.), and along the Spanish coast, even out into the Atlantic at Huelva, near Cádiz.

Greek traders followed suit, establishing colonies on many of the same islands (e.g. eastern Sicily and Corsica), southern Italy (OENOTRIA), northern Africa (e.g. Cyrene), and at Massalia (modern Marseilles) in southern Mediterranean France.

Numerous Iron Age shipwrecks, loaded with amphorae and wine-related paraphernalia, have been located and excavated along the Italian and French coasts. The Phoenician and Greek impact throughout the Mediterranean was so pronounced that one can say that it was mediated by wine culture itself.

The 8th century BCE saw the climax of Phoenician influence on the hearts, minds, and palates of native Mediterranean peoples. The ETRUSCANS of central Italy along the Tyrrhenian Sea illustrates the phenomenon and how it spread. They probably first came in contact with the Phoenicians before the Greeks arrived on their shores, as shown by their 'Orientalizing' industries, which closely reflected Phoenician style, technology, and iconography in metals, pottery, ivory, and glass. Their amphora was modelled after the Phoenician amphora, and where a similarity of form exists, it was likely because it served a similar function: primarily to hold grape wine, which soon began to be supplied by a nascent local industry.

As in other parts of Europe, the Etruscans already had a tradition of making a mixed fermented beverage before the Phoenicians had an impact on their culture. According to the available evidence, this 'grog' probably combined honey, barley, and wheat, even pomegranates, hazelnuts, herbs such as rosemary and thyme, tree resins, wild grapes, and so on. The Phoenician traders lured them into a wine culture by presenting them with cauldrons, kraters (see CRATER), and other drinking vessels. The Etruscans probably first adapted the vessels to their native customs and mixed beverages, similarly to the CELTS further north. After they had adopted the wine culture, they made their own wine vessels in pottery and precious metals, including Phoenician-type gilded drinking bowls.

In turn, the Etruscans became the principal conveyors of wine culture to coastal Mediterranean France by *c.*625–600 BCE. It is not surprising that the GAULS or Celts there should have become equally entranced by the cultural and economic possibilities for wine and began to substitute it for their native beverages.

The Gauls might have had a general knowledge of the Eurasian vine, which grew wild along the northern Mediterranean shore, but any successful exploitation of the domesticated vine to make wine would have required much more horticultural knowledge and technological proficiency, probably provided by the Etruscans. The domesticated grapevine needed to be transplanted and tended. Specialized equipment was needed to transform it into wine, which was preserved by a tree resin additive to stoppered vessels.

Plantings of the domesticated Eurasian grapevine in France were probably transported on Etruscan ships. A Punic shipwreck off the coast of Mallorca at El Sec, dated to the 4th century BCE, illustrates how this might have been accomplished: grapevines were embedded in soil in the ship's cool hull; this would have enabled them to travel safely enough to be replanted.

This supposition has now been corroborated by archaeological, chemical, and botanical findings at the heavily Etruscan-influenced site of Lattes (ancient Lattara), near Montpellier, where numerous Etruscan wine amphorae were imported in the 6th century BCE and stored in harbour storehouses. As analyses have shown, the wine was resinated with pine and laced with botanicals (rosemary, thyme, and/or basil). A century later, local winemaking had begun at the site, as shown by the finding of masses of grape seeds, pedicels, and even fruit (grape skins), commonly associated with treading activity, and what is so far the earliest wine press yet discovered in France.

The Etruscan role in the process was further revealed by a shipwreck (Grand Ribaud F), found just off Hyères east of Marseilles and dated *c.*515–475 BCE. Its hold was filled with grapevines and some 700 to 800 amphorae. All the Etruscan amphorae on board this ship had been carefully stoppered with cork (among the earliest evidence for this technology, and also attested at Lattara) and stacked at least five layers deep in the hull. Significantly, they are of the same pottery type as, and are contemporaneous with, the Etruscan amphorae at Lattara. The ship's final destination may have been Lattara.

The wine culture of Mediterranean France spread inland after the Roman conquest up the Rhône and Rhine rivers to the rest of Europe, where, centuries later, monasteries such as the Cistercian Abbey of Vougeot in Burgundy refined French viniculture so that it became a model for the world. It needs to be stressed, however, that France owes a debt of gratitude to earlier Levantine viniculture.

See also PALAEOETHNOBOTANY. P.E.M.

Barnard, H., 'Chemical evidence for wine production around 4000 BCE in the Late Chalcolithic Near Eastern Highlands', *Journal of Archaeological Science*, 38/5 (2011), 977–84.

Dong, Y., et al., 'Dual domestications and origin of traits in grapevine evolution', *Science*, 379/6635 (2023), 892–901.

McGovern, P. E., *Uncorking the Past: The Quest for Wine, Beer, and Other Alcoholic Beverages* (2009).

McGovern, P. E., 'The beginning of viniculture in France', *The Proceedings of the National Academy of Sciences USA*, 110/25 (2013), 10147–52.

McGovern, P. E., *Ancient Wine: The Search for the Origins of Viniculture* (2nd edn, 2019).

McGovern, P. E., et al., *The Origins and Ancient History of Wine* (1995).

McGovern, P. E., et al., 'Fermented beverages of Pre- and Proto-Historic China', *The Proceedings of the National Academy of Sciences USA*, 101/51 (2004), 17593–8.

McGovern, P. E., et al., 'Early Neolithic wine of Georgia in the South Caucasus', *The Proceedings of the National Academy of Sciences USA* 114/48 (2017), E10309–E10318.

Mirzoian, A., and Hall, G. R., 'Ancient Egyptian herbal wines', *The Proceedings of the National Academy of Sciences USA*, 106/18 (2009), 7361–6.

Robinson, J., et al., *Wine Grapes: A Complete Guide to 1,368 Vine Varieties, Including Their Origins and Flavours* (2012).

Orion, complex, OPTIMA × VILLARD Blanc HYBRID bred at Geilweilerhof in Germany in 1964. This partially DISEASE-RESISTANT VARIETY produces crisp, aromatic white wine, notably in Europe's northernmost wine regions, including England and Denmark. More recent selections such as Calardis Blanc are showing even greater promise. See JULIUS-KÜHN INSTITUT.

Orléans, AOC created in 2006 for wines produced around the city of Orléans where the river Loire turns west. Burgundian influence is evident in the choice of grape varieties, principally Chardonnay and Pinot Meunier. At one time this was an important wine region, but the development of the RAILWAYS changed all that, and today fewer than 100 ha/250 acres of vineyards remain. Only 80 km/50 miles south of Paris, the region's light, pale, fragrant wines have many devotees in the French capital. **Orléans-Cléry** is an even smaller AOC zone south-west of the city on the left bank of the Loire for Cabernet Franc-based reds.

See also LOIRE, including map.

Ormeasco, local name for DOLCETTO on the north-western coast of Italy. For more details, see LIGURIA.

Ortega, a CROSS of MÜLLER-THURGAU and SIEGERREBE that was once popular as an OECHSLE booster in German wines, especially with the blenders of Rheinhessen. It produces extremely full-flavoured wines that often lack ACIDITY but can reach high MUST WEIGHTS, if not quite as high as the equally early-ripening but dwindling

OPTIMA. VARIETAL wines are made, but a little goes a long way, and the vine is susceptible to COULURE and ROT. Germany's total plantings dropped from around 1,200 ha/2,960 acres in the late 1980s to 395 ha in 2020. The variety is also planted to a very limited extent in England, British Columbia, and Sweden.

Ortrugo, white grape grown on 709 ha/1,752 acres in the hills around Piacenza in Emilia, often blended with MALVASIA. Ortrugo dei Colli Piacentini is the DOC for white and sparkling wines made from this grape variety (minimum 90%) in EMILIA-ROMAGNA.

Orvieto, white wine produced near the medieval hill city of the same name, an important artistic centre during the late Middle Ages and Renaissance, is one of Italy's historically renowned white wines and by far the most important DOC in UMBRIA. Within the extensive DOC, partially shared with neighbouring LAZIO, is a historic CLASSICO zone. The vines are grown on TUFA, and wines come in dry (*secco*), medium dry (*abboccato*), medium sweet (*amabile*), LATE HARVEST (*vendemmia tardiva*), and BOTRYTIZED (*muffa nobile*) sweet versions, though the sweet wines are increasingly rare. Owing to the proximity of Lakes Corbara and Bolsano, as well as frequent autumn fogs, Orvieto is one of the very few places in Italy regularly affected by NOBLE ROT. The wine is a blend of Procanico, a local name for TREBBIANO Toscano, and the much more characterful GRECHETTO, VERDELLO, MALVASIA Bianca, and tart DRUPEGGIO. Although Orvieto's reputation was harmed by over-produced wines based on Procanico, today the production rules require a higher proportion of Grechetto than Procanico, and several producers have begun to bottle VARIETAL Grechetto, usefully demonstrating the grape's potential. While yields of up to 11 tonnes/ha are allowed, the actual average yield hovers around a much more reasonable 60 hl/ha, indicating a trend towards quality. Notably, completely dry Orvieto, without any RESIDUAL SUGAR, is rare, a concession to a supposed market taste.

Faced with declining sales and low prices for Orvieto, in 1998 the local CONSORZIO created a red wine DOC Orvietano Rosso based on ALEATICO, Cabernet Sauvignon, and Merlot, as well as MONTEPULCIANO, SANGIOVESE, CILIEGIOLO, and Pinot Noir, blended or as single varieties. Although considerable investments as early as the late 1970s were made in the region, notably by the likes of ANTINORI with its Castello della Sala estate, and a regular influx of consultant OENOLOGISTS, the focus tended to be on INTERNATIONAL VARIETIES and BARRIQUES. More distinctive expressions are expected as local varieties are re-evaluated, but progress has been exceedingly slow. W.S.

www.consorziovinidiorvieto.it

Oseleta, revived red wine grape speciality of VALPOLICELLA, Italy.

Osey, variously spelt **Oseye** and **Osaye**, FORTIFIED WINE from PORTUGAL drunk in England in the 15th century, thought likely to have originated from vineyards near Lisbon, the name being an English corruption of the locality of Azóia north-west of Lisbon. See also CARCAVELOS and SETÚBAL. R.J.M.

Mayson, R., *The Wines of Portugal* (2020).

osmosis. See CONCENTRATION and REVERSE OSMOSIS.

OTR. See OXYGEN TRANSMISSION RATE.

Ottavianello, Puglian name for the French red grape variety CINSAUT.

ouillage, French word meaning both ULLAGE and TOPPING UP. The term **ouillé** is used in the JURA to differentiate white wines made this way from those that are aged OXIDATIVELY or under FILM-FORMING YEASTS.

ovary, the ovule-containing part of the pistil of a FLOWER which, in the grapevine, develops into the grape berry. After FLOWERING, the ovary becomes a berry and the ovules become seeds (see GRAPE). B.G.C.

overcropping, a vine condition which delays grape RIPENING and therefore reduces wine quality. It is associated with low LEAF TO FRUIT RATIOS. Overcropping can be due to PRUNING to many buds with some fruitful varieties or to a loss of leaf area as a result of INSECT PESTS or FUNGAL DISEASES. If climatic conditions are limiting for PHOTOSYNTHESIS, as with low temperatures or very limited SUNLIGHT, then vines may be considered overcropped. The grapes of overcropped vines are typically lower in sugar, colour, and flavour and have an increased PH. Wines made from such fruit are typically described as thin or dilute. Overcropping can be overcome by CROP THINNING.

The term 'overcropping' is also used emotively in arguments against high vineyard yields. Provided that the vine is in BALANCE and good health, even high yields can be properly ripened with good weather and good vineyard management. See also YIELD. R.E.S.

overripeness, a usually undesirable stage in grape maturity whereby grapes start to shrivel (see BERRY SHRIVEL) and acid levels fall to a dangerously low level. Grapes at this stage are sometimes described as exhibiting 'dead fruit' flavours. It may well be the result of extended HANG TIME, once fashionable in CALIFORNIA, for example.

o.w.c. stands for 'original wooden case' and is frequently used as a description in the sale of FINE WINE. See CASE.

own-rooted vine. See UNGRAFTED VINE.

oxidation, the opposite of REDUCTION, is the chemical reaction in which a chemical compound loses electrons. Although controlled and moderate oxidation can be beneficial and is essential for some wine styles (see below), the term usually refers to a wine FAULT resulting from excessive exposure to OXYGEN (as opposed to AERATION, which is deliberate, controlled exposure to oxygen). Wines spoiled by oxidation are said to be **oxidized**. See also OXIDATIVE WINEMAKING.

Oxidation is a threat as soon as the grape is crushed, which is why high-quality grapes are transported to the winery as fast as possible in shallow containers and why field pressing stations sited as close as possible to the vineyard are increasingly common. When the grape is crushed, unless special precautions are taken to exclude oxygen it immediately starts to react with the liberated juice compounds. The most obvious change is the browning of the juice resulting from the oxidation of PHENOLICS catalysed by an ENZYME (polyphenol oxidase) present in grapes and thus referred to as 'enzymatic oxidation' or 'enzymatic browning'. The presence on the grapes of moulds associated with ROT introduces additional oxidative enzymes (LACCASES) which accelerate reactions with oxygen, especially those involved with browning. Small amounts of SULFUR DIOXIDE (5 g/hl) are therefore usually added to the must to inactivate enzymes and counter the oxidation of phenolics. See PROTECTIVE JUICE HANDLING for the techniques involved in minimizing the risk of oxidation.

Some winemakers, however, deliberately encourage a certain amount of pre-fermentation oxidation of grape varieties such as Chardonnay in order to develop a range of flavours other than those associated with primary fruit AROMA. Sometimes known as hyperoxidation, this also enhances enzymatic oxidation of phenolics and their conversion to insoluble polymers, which are then removed by CLARIFICATION treatments. As a result, the wine contains lower amounts of phenolic compounds that may generate brown pigments and haze through non-enzymatic oxidation reactions (see below) and is thus more stable. This technique is usually reserved for non-aromatic grape varieties. See WHITE WINEMAKING for more details.

The last step of FERMENTATION, the REDUCTION of ACETALDEHYDE to ETHANOL, is coupled with the oxidation of the co-enzyme NADH, as shown in this equation:

$$CH_3CHO + NADH + H^+ \rightarrow CH_3CH_2OH + NAD^+$$

Note that no new oxygen is involved in this reaction and that the essence of the reduction is the transfer of electrons from the co-enzyme to the acetaldehyde. Most oxidation–reduction reactions involved in growing grapes and making wine are of this type.

In wine itself, however, exposure to oxygen in the presence of an organism such as ACETOBACTER could result in a reversal of the above reaction, with alcohol being oxidized to acetaldehyde. The NADH produced by oxidizing alcohol is, in turn, oxidized by oxygen from the air. When this happens, the wine loses its fresh, fruity aroma and becomes vapid and flat-smelling. Further exposure to oxygen converts the acetaldehyde to ACETIC ACID, the acidic component of wine VINEGAR, the winemaker's *bête noire.*

Oxygen reacts with the phenolics in both white and red wines through complex chemical oxidation processes that may also promote oxidation of ETHANOL to ACETALDEHYDE. In whites, the COLOUR changes from light yellow to amber and ultimately brown, and at this last stage the quality of a TABLE WINE is usually seriously impaired. In reds, with their greater complement of phenolics (ANTHOCYANINS, TANNINS, and PIGMENTED TANNINS), the colour change is much less apparent, and a red wine can accommodate, and indeed benefit from, considerably greater exposure to oxygen than a white wine. While the natural formation of stable pigmented tannins in a red wine is a process requiring oxidation, other products of the reaction of the wine's phenolics with oxygen bring about highly desirable changes in the sensory properties of the wine. An appropriate level of oxygen exposure is usually accomplished through PUMPING OVER, RACK AND RETURN, RACKING, TOPPING UP, and the usual transfer operations imposed on a red wine. BARREL AGEING also involves regular exposure of the wine to small amounts of oxygen. This has inspired the development of technologies such as MICRO-OXYGENATION and the use of CLOSURES with controlled OXYGEN TRANSFER RATES to control oxygen exposure during ÉLEVAGE and bottle AGEING.

To produce table wines attractive in aroma and colour, and certainly those designed to be drunk young, the winemaker generally restricts the exposure of MUST and wine to oxygen as much as is technically feasible (see PROTECTIVE WINEMAKING for more details).

Some wines, however, such as *oloroso* SHERRY, tawny PORT, MADEIRA, and some traditional white RIOJA, owe their character to deliberate exposure to oxygen. And those who make wines of all sorts are constantly experimenting with various aspects of controlled oxidation, often motivated by the role played by oxygen in AGEING. See WHITE WINEMAKING and RED WINEMAKING.

The term MADERIZATION is sometimes used interchangeably with 'oxidation', although it should theoretically also involve excessive exposure to heat.

See also OXYGEN. V.C.

oxidative winemaking contrasts with PROTECTIVE WINEMAKING and REDUCTIVE WINEMAKING in that the winemaker deliberately exposes the wine to oxygen at various stages in the winemaking process in order to encourage certain reactions and achieve a particular style of wine—*oloroso* SHERRY being an extreme example. See also OXYGEN, AERATION, BARREL AGEING, MICRO-OXYGENATION, and OXIDATION.

oxygen, colourless, odourless, tasteless gas that makes up nearly 21% of the atmosphere. It is essential to all animal life forms and for many other living systems. Unlike NITROGEN, which makes up a much higher proportion of air and is inert, oxygen is highly reactive, being essential for aerobic RESPIRATION in plants, animals, and soils. Oxygen interacts with grape juice, MUST, and wine in good ways (see AERATION) and bad ways (see OXIDATION).

Handling juice

It is important to minimize the amount of oxygen dissolved in the must, especially when it comes to white wine grapes, in order to avoid the oxidation of aromas and PHENOLIC compounds. (See OXIDATION for a very different approach.)

Making wine

Early on in the fermentation (typically on the second day), a small amount of oxygen is required for the multiplication of the YEAST. At this stage, there is no risk of oxidation because the CARBON DIOXIDE given off by the nascent wine prevents exposure to oxygen. However, when fermentation ceases, the wine must be protected from oxygen if it is to remain wine. Early winemakers learnt that, with very few exceptions, wines had to be kept in full containers at all times lest they change into VINEGAR.

Modern winemakers have equipment which allows most steps in making wine to exclude oxygen. One of the most effective has been the STAINLESS STEEL tank. If the tank is not completely full, the ULLAGE space can be filled with INERT GAS to exclude oxygen. Wooden vats, casks, and barrels are not sufficiently impervious for this blanketing technique. Some tanks have lids that can be raised or lowered depending on the volume of liquid in the tank. The oxidation of wine can also be minimized by additions of SULFUR DIOXIDE, which is also used to inhibit microbial activity. ASCORBIC ACID has also been employed to a certain extent as an antioxidant, but it must be used in conjunction with sulfur dioxide (see ERYTHORBIC ACID too). REFRIGERATION of wine in storage slows all reactions, including oxidation, but it has the danger that oxygen solubility increases at low temperatures. For white wines, the aim of PROTECTIVE WINEMAKING is to minimize oxidation, although see WHITE WINEMAKING for alternative approaches.

Oxygen plays a positive role during RED WINEMAKING, when the small doses of oxygen which the wine receives during the inevitable operations of filling, RACKING, and TOPPING UP deepen and stabilize COLOUR, soften and intensify flavour, and assist natural STABILIZATION and CLARIFICATION by encouraging the precipitation of the less stable PHENOLICS.

Bottling

Oxygen management throughout the winemaking process, during FINING, FILTRATION, and BOTTLING, and in relation to wine-bottle CLOSURES (see OXYGEN TRANSMISSION RATE and TOTAL PACKAGE OXYGEN) plays a key role in a wine's AGEING ability, which is why it is currently the subject of increasingly sophisticated research around the world. Academics and producers of SYNTHETIC CLOSURES and AGGLOMERATE CORKS have invested in international research projects that look at all aspects of wine–oxygen interaction and how this highly significant aspect of winemaking may be controlled.

See also OXIDATION, AERATION, MICRO-OXYGENATION, and SERVING WINE. P.J.W. & V.L.

Goode, J., *Wine Science: The Application of Science in Wine* (3rd edn, 2021).

oxygen transmission rate (OTR) is a key property of wine PACKAGING and most commonly discussed with regard to wine-bottle CLOSURES because the interaction between wine and OXYGEN is critical to the way a wine changes post-bottling (see AGEING). Some used to think that CORKS and alternative closures provided an airtight seal that allowed no oxygen into the bottle, except when the closure had failed. But packaging technology companies can measure typical OTR rates for CORKS of about 1 mg/year or lower. While first-generation synthetic corks had OTRs that were too high, resulting in wines that showed signs of oxidation after a fairly short period of time, most manufactured closures, such as synthetic corks or AGGLOMERATE CORKS, now have published OTRs similar to those of CORKS or, particularly in the case of tin-lined SCREWCAPS, much lower. Recent research, much of it funded by closure producers such as Nomacorc, has focused on the effects of different OTRs on wine development, and manufacturers are now able to offer products with engineered levels of OTR in order to give winemakers control over how their wine will develop post-bottling. The trajectory of bottle ageing is affected by OTR and storage temperature, with 'normal' ageing typically defined by the history of BOTTLES sealed with corks and kept in traditional CELLARS.

See also TOTAL PACKAGE OXYGEN. A.L.W.

ozone is a form of OXYGEN having three instead of the usual two oxygen atoms per molecule. It is formed in the upper atmosphere by the action of ULTRAVIOLET RADIATION on normal oxygen; by being opaque to further incoming ultraviolet radiation, it happily prevents most of the potentially very damaging ultraviolet wavelengths from reaching the Earth's surface.

Some synthetic molecules such as the chlorofluorocarbons, once widely used in REFRIGERATION, can, if released into the atmosphere, add to the effects of natural gases from volcanoes and so on to destroy ozone. This happens only at very low temperatures, such as occur over the poles in winter, but is nevertheless a matter of concern.

Some ozone is also released into the lower atmosphere as an industrial pollutant and can cause a recognizable 'stippling' of vine leaves close to industrialized areas. Its significance to viticulture has been studied in California and New York State, but the economic effects remain uncertain.

In a winemaking context, ozone has been advocated as a sanitizing agent for the maintenance of HYGIENE in a winery and for use, for example, on stainless-steel tanks, bottling equipment, and BARRELS, although it is not effective in killing microflora (e.g. BRETTANOMYCES) in material such as OAK because it does not penetrate the oak surface. Ozone is sometimes used in cork manufacture as a preventive measure to retard microbial growth, though, again, its effectiveness is uncertain.

It has also been suggested that fumigating grapes with ozone may reduce the effect of SMOKE TAINT, but this is as yet unproven.

J.G. & P.J.W.

P

Paarl, inland wine district in SOUTH AFRICA home to an increasing number of well-known estates. It reaches north into TULBAGH and WELLINGTON and east towards FRANSCHHOEK, all separate areas of origin. The biggest cellars are KWV's, and the most important branded wine producer is Nederburg, with 21 labels. Much of Paarl's fruit is blended with grapes from districts such as STELLENBOSCH and Wellington to be sold under the more generic regional origin COASTAL REGION.

Pacherenc du Vic-Bilh, defiantly GASCON name for an AOC in the MADIRAN region of SOUTH WEST FRANCE devoted to characterful white wines. Made mainly from a mixture of local grape varieties COURBU, PETIT COURBU, GROS MANSENG, and PETIT MANSENG, sometimes with ARRUFIAC, the deep yellow wine can be either dry or more probably sweet, and the general character is not dissimilar from that of JURANÇON. Some 300 ha/750 acres are dedicated to this keenly priced wine, for which the grapes destined for sweet versions may be picked as late as December. These, made from PASSERILLÉ and not BOTRYTIZED grapes, can last ten years or so in bottle.

P.S.

Perry, D. M., *Madiran and Pacherenc du Vic-Bilh* (2014).

Pacific Northwest, region in the far north-west of the United States encompassing the states of WASHINGTON, OREGON, and IDAHO.

packaging of wine most often involves BOTTLING, but alternative options are proliferating. BOTTLES are still by far the most popular form of wine packaging, not least because GLASS is inert and tasteless so, unlike other packaging materials, has no effect on the wine even over decades. It does have the disadvantages of being very fragile and relatively heavy, as well as using up considerable natural resources during manufacture, TRANSPORT, and recycling. See BOXES, CANS, CARTONS, KEGS, PAPER BOTTLES, PLASTIC BOTTLES, and POUCHES, all of which are made from other materials. See also SUSTAINABILITY and CARBON FOOTPRINT OF WINE.

Padthaway, a significant, moderately cool, primarily grape-growing (rather than winemaking) region in the LIMESTONE COAST ZONE in the south-east of SOUTH AUSTRALIA. While all the mainstream varieties are grown, and while grape quality is, as elsewhere, sensitive to yield, Shiraz is a regional speciality and can produce high-quality, long-lived wine.

Pagadebit, occasionally **Pagadebito** or **Pagadebiti**, is used as a synonym for several different Italian varieties, most notably BOMBINO BIANCO in Puglia. The name refers to the vine's reliable yields which, in theory, should allow growers to pay their debts.

pago, Spanish term for a vineyard, used particularly in JEREZ and CASTILLA Y LEÓN. See also VINO DE PAGO.

Païen, Valais name for SAVAGNIN BLANC.

pairing food and wine. See FOOD-AND-WINE MATCHING.

País, Chilean name for the historic grape variety also known as CRIOLLA CHICA, MISSION, and Listán Prieto. It is most common in Maule and Bío-Bío in southern CHILE and is mainly grown in old, DRY-FARMED plots by elderly farmers, often as FIELD BLENDS. Accurate numbers are elusive, but Chile's official vineyard report for 2020 records 10,443 ha/25,805 acres in total. The variety used to be scorned, but producers throughout Chile have begun making small-volume wines that have also inspired winemakers in California and Spain to reconsider the variety.

Pakistan. According to OIV statistics, the total area of vines in this Asian ISLAMIC republic grew from 3,000 ha/7,400 acres in the late 1980s to 17,534 ha in 2020. They are dedicated to the production of TABLE GRAPES and RAISINS, but VITIS VINIFERA wine may occasionally be made from WILD VINES growing in the high valleys along the Silk Road, where one of the richest resources of ancient, genetically varied plant material may still be found.

Palacios family, a network of talented winemakers in northern Spain. José Palacios Remondo founded Palacios Remondo in Alfaro, RIOJA Oriental, in 1945. He had nine children, of whom four are or were connected with wine: Antonio the second-born, Chelo (Consuelo, a girl) the third, Álvaro the seventh, and Rafa (Rafael) the youngest. Álvaro left in 1989 to play a major part in establishing modern PRIORAT, his most famous wine L'Ermita setting new records for price. Rafa also left to focus on white wine and from 2004 did for VALDEORRAS what his brother had done for Priorat. One of Chelo's sons, Ricardo Perez Palacios, has run Descendientes de J. Palacios in BIERZO since 1999 in conjunction with his uncle Álvaro, who has also taken over and revived Palacios Remondo in Rioja.

palaeoethnobotany and the archaeology of wine. The study of the botanical remains of grapes and wine residues found in archaeological excavations is something of a detective story in which small pieces of evidence are put together to build up a picture of the development of humankind's use and, later, domestication of grapes.

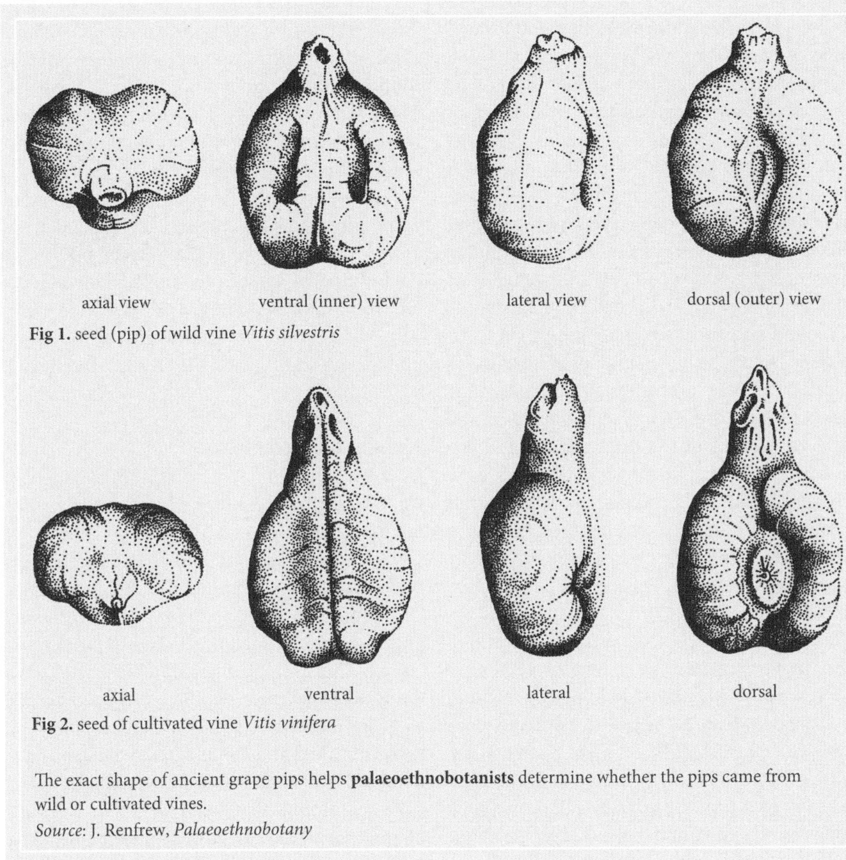

The exact shape of ancient grape pips helps **palaeoethnobotanists** determine whether the pips came from wild or cultivated vines.
Source: J. Renfrew, *Palaeoethnobotany*

The botanical evidence consists of the remains of vine LEAVES, BERRIES, STEMS, and SEEDS (see GRAPE); sometimes even the roots, or the hollows left by them, may subsist too. Their recovery is the result of painstaking examination of archaeological deposits. Usually the finds of grape remains form a very small proportion of the total botanical material recovered, the bulk of which is usually the seeds of annual crops such as cereals, pulses, and oilseeds.

The most common remains of grapes found are grape pips, and they usually subsist because they have become charred at the time of deposition. Once converted to charcoal, they will subsist in recognizable form for many thousands of years buried in the ground. On other archaeological sites they may be preserved in damp or wet soils in a waterlogged condition. Elsewhere, where there is a high concentration of calcium in the groundwater, they may become mineralized or semi-fossilized. Sometimes stray pips were incorporated in handmade clay pots, and when the pots are fired they burn out, leaving a small hole the exact size and shape of the pip.

Occasionally, complete fruits survive in charred form, as when grapes were thrown on to a funeral pyre as part of the ritual (e.g. at Salamis and Athens). Exceptionally, finds of skins of fruits (possibly remains of pressings) survive, for example at early Minoan Myrtos, Crete (see ancient GREECE).

Finds of burnt fruit stalks (PEDICELS) are exceptional but can be taken to indicate the presence of domesticated vines (the stems of bunches of WILD VINES are very strong and robust and do not come away with the fruit in the way that those of cultivated vines do). They have been recovered from the Greek prehistoric sites of Sitagroi and Myrtos.

The Greek prehistoric potters of the early Bronze Age developed the habit of standing their pots on upturned vine leaves to dry in the sun before firing. This resulted in the veins on the underside of these leaves being finely impressed and then baked on the bases of these pots. In some places—the Cyclades, for example—these are the only evidence that grapes were present on these islands at that time. Vine leaves were also used on clay sealings of Bronze Age pots, such as at Menelaion near Sparta. If vine leaves were being used in these ways by the Bronze Age Greeks, they may also have been used for cooking, as they are in Greece today.

The critical question in examining all this palaeoethnobotanical material is how can one tell whether it is derived from wild or cultivated sources. Apart from the fruit stalks, just discussed, it is the size and shape of the pips which give us the clue: the pips of wild grapes are spherical, with a short stalk or beak and a small, round chalazal scar on one side, and two divergent grooves on the other side of the pip. The pips of cultivated grapes are usually larger and pear-shaped. The stalk is usually longer, the chalazal scar larger and often oval in outline, and the grooves on the back of the pip parallel to each other. These features can be seen on the archaeological material, however it is preserved.

The domestication of grapes seems to have first taken place around 6000 BCE in the region between the Black and Caspian seas. The domesticated grapevine provides fresh fruit, raisins, wine, vinegar, grape juice, and a light salad oil obtained by crushing the pips. The most significant product, however, was wine, which was greatly valued. (See ORIGINS OF VINICULTURE for details of a recent study proposing an earlier date for domestication of the grapevine in the Levant.)

Finds of wild grape pips in archaeological contexts go back to the earliest palaeolithic sites in Europe, for example at Terra Amata in the south of France (*c.*350,000 BCE), where the fruits appear to have been eaten. There are a number of sites from the mesolithic period (12th–9th millennium BCE) with finds of wild grape seeds: from Belma Abeurader, France, to Grotte del Uzzo in Sicily, the Frangthi Cave in southern Greece, Çayönü in Türkiye, Tell Abu Heureya in Syria, and Jericho in Jordan. The earliest finds of pips from domesticated grapes come from the neolithic site of Shulaveris-Gora in Georgian Transcaucasia, dated *c.*6000 BCE. From this site too comes a residue of resinated wine in a pot: the earliest find of wine to date. Another site which has yielded traces of neolithic wine is Hajji Firuz Tepe in northern Iran. Here a kitchen was excavated dating to 5400–5000 BCE. In it were six jars set into the floor with their lids nearby. Chemical analysis has shown that they contained wine resinated with resin from the terebinth tree. It is not clear whether this wine was made from wild or cultivated grapes (wild grapes still grow close to the site today). If all these jars had contained wine they would have held around 50 litres, suggesting large-scale wine production at a very early date.

The excavations at the Areni 1 cave complex in ARMENIA have yielded remains of a wine-pressing structure dating to *c.*4000 BCE. It consists of a shallow clay tub, 1 metre wide, with raised edges and a sloping base leading down to the mouth of a large jar. Desiccated grapes, pomace, grape seeds, and grape skins still attached to their pedicels have been found in close proximity to it. Biochemical analyses of the contents of associated pots revealed the presence of malvidin, the pigment responsible for red wine. It is thought that wine pressing here was associated not with regular consumption or feasting but with rituals surrounding the burial of the dead. Remains of both primary and secondary depositions of dismembered and complete human skeletons were found in the inner spaces in the caves.

It is not essential that vines were domesticated before WINEMAKING was invented. What appears to be necessary is having a suitable container in which to store the wine during and after the FERMENTATION process. All the ingredients—the sweet, juicy fruit, and airborne YEAST—are available for wild fruits. Thus, it is possible that the finds from palaeolithic sites (Old Stone Age) in the Mediterranean region of wild grape pips could indicate that winemaking had begun using leather bags even before the beginnings of agriculture.

The finds of grape remains such as pips, stalks, and skins in circumstances suggesting wine production are rare. The finds from House 1 at Dikili Tash in northern Greece of 2,460 grape pips, which have been directly dated to 4,460–4,000 BCE, together with more than 300 empty, pressed grape skins, strongly suggest that they represent winemaking residues. The measurements of the pips suggest that they were morphologically grapes from WILD VINES or from plants in the process of domestication. Another exceptional find comes from Kurban Huyuk in eastern Türkiye, where masses of grape pips and stem and vine fragments were found together with cakes of pressed fruits in a pit dating to the mid to late third millennium BCE. In prehistoric GREECE, they occur associated with spouted vessels on the early Bronze Age sites of Áyios Kosmas, Attica, and Myrtos in Crete. Remains of wine presses also occur occasionally, as at Minoan Vathypetro in Crete, and there are a great number of drinking vessels made from exotic materials from Bronze Age sites suggesting that drinking wine was a special activity.

Analysis of residues found in the bottom of pottery containers has been undertaken by Patrick McGovern of MASCA in the University Museum, Philadelphia, using infrared, liquid chromatography and other chemical techniques to identify traces of tartaric acid, calcium tartrate and terebinth resin indicating the residues of wine. The actual residues in the bases of *pithoi* (see PITHARI) of wine have not been found very often (partly because the analysis of residues found in pottery vessels is still comparatively new in archaeology). Apart from identifying the earliest finds of wine residues, detailed above, these analyses have also given evidence of the earliest trade in wine. This dates back to 3500 BCE at Godin Tepe, IRAN, where a reddish deposit turned out to be formed from TARTRATE crystals (similar to those which form on the bottom of wine corks today). Godin Tepe lies on a well-documented trade route through the Zagros Mountains to lowland Mesopotamia. Even stronger evidence of trade comes from the earliest finds of wine residues in Egypt from the royal tomb of Scorpion I at Abydos dating to 3100 BCE. Here three rooms in the tomb formed a kind of wine cellar filled high with about 700 amphorae arranged in three or four layers, one on top of another. They were stoppered with clay sealings bearing fine seal impressions. Deposits of crusty yellow residues inside the amphorae turned out to be of a resinated wine. In addition, 47 of them contained grape pips, and several had raisins, stalks, skins, pips, and dried pulp intact. Eleven of the jars also contained the remains of sliced sycamore figs which had been strung together and suspended in the wine. Analysis of the clays from which the amphorae were made indicated that they probably came from various regions in the southern Levant. Viticulture was firmly established in the delta region of Egypt and in some of the western oases by the Sixth Dynasty (*c.*2323 BCE). Processes of winemaking are shown in paintings and engravings on the walls of tombs from the Old Kingdom onwards, for example in the tomb chapels at Beni Hasan, especially nos. 15 and 17.

Recent finds in the CANAANITE palace at Tel Kabri in northern Israel, dating to 1700 BCE, have revealed a wine cellar holding the remains of 40 jars that are 91 cm/3 ft tall. Chemical analysis of the residues of their contents, by Andrew Koh of Brandeis University, revealed traces of TARTARIC ACID, as well as flavourings of honey, mint, cinnamon bark, juniper berries, and resins used as preservatives. Of the 40 vessels, 38 contained wine residues all with the same constituents, the equivalent of 3,000 modern bottles of wine. The contents are consistent with winemaking recipes from the ancient texts found at the palace at Mari on the Euphrates in modern SYRIA.

One of the most romantic finds of labelled wine jars must be that from Tutankhamun's tomb. They were sealed with clay and their contents were reduced to dried residues. The 26 wine jars have labels indicating the location of the vineyard, the year of the vintage (the majority belonging to the years 1345 BCE, 1344 BCE, and 1340 BCE), the ownership of the vineyard, and the name of the chief vintner. Most of them came from the western delta, one from the eastern delta, and one from the El Kharga oasis. Two of the vintners had Syrian names; four of the jars were labelled 'sweet wine'.

Analyses have also shown that sometimes wine was mixed with other alcoholic beverages. It appears that this was the case in Minoan Crete, where a number of residue analyses have shown that wine was mixed with barley beer and honey to form what McGovern has called 'Greek grog'. This was also the case in the finds from Midas' tomb at Gordion in Türkiye (*c.*700 BCE), where the funeral feast consisted of a tasty lamb and lentil stew washed down with an intoxicating beverage made from mixing wine, barley beer, and honey mead.

Other early residues of wine are known from 7th century BCE Cyprus and from the contents of AMPHORAE in a Roman shipwreck off the southern coast of France, near Marseilles. There is a Roman glass BOTTLE containing what is claimed to be Roman wine in the museum in Speyer, Germany.

From apparently insignificant remains of grape pips, stalks, pulp, and leaves, and from analyses of dried-up residues in the bottom of pots, found by chance to subsist in sediments on archaeological sites and extracted with painstaking care, it is possible to begin to understand the ORIGINS OF VINICULTURE and its development. J.M.R.

Ancient biomolecules

In 2003, scientists at the Botanical Garden of Geneva, Switzerland, were able to analyse for the first time by DNA PROFILING a tiny amount of DNA from waterlogged and charred grape pips recovered from archaeological sites in France (Iron Age and Greek period, 5th century BCE) and Hungary (Roman times, 2nd to 4th centuries CE). These remains could not be matched to any modern cultivar, but they could be assigned to their most likely geographic origin. More recently, ancient DNA (aDNA) studies have been able to assign archaeological specimens from pre-Roman to medieval times to groups of modern Western European varieties in the Italian peninsula, on Sardinia, and in Armenia. Future studies could help elucidate domestication events, genetic introgression from local wild populations, and the origins and histories of varietal lineages. J.V.

Areshian, G. E., et al., 'Wine and death: the 2010 excavation season at the Areni-1 Cave Complex, Armenia', *Backdirt* (2011), 65–70.

McGovern, P. E., *Ancient Wine: The Search for the Origins of Viniculture* (2nd edn, 2019).

Manen, J.-F., et al., 'Microsatellites from archaeological *Vitis vinifera* seeds allow a tentative assignment of the geographical origin of ancient cultivars', *Journal of Archaeological Science*, 30/6 (2003), 721–9.

Renfrew, J., *Palaeoethnobotany: The Prehistoric Food Plants of the Near East and Europe* (1973).

Sandler, M., and Pinder, R. (eds.), *Wine, A Scientific Exploration* (2003).

Valamoti, S. M., et al., 'Grape pressings from northern Greece: the earliest wine in the Aegean?', *Antiquity*, 81 (2007), 54–61.

Wales, N., et al., 'The limits and potential of paleogenomic techniques for reconstructing grapevine domestication', *Journal of Archaeological Science*, 72 (2016), 57–70.

palate, frequently misspelt term used when describing TASTING as a process and an ability. It is generally used to describe the combined human tasting faculties in the mouth (and, sometimes, NOSE). The impact of a wine on the mouth may be divided chronologically, and somewhat loosely, into its impact on the front, middle, and back palate. The word may also be used more generally as in describing a good taster as 'having a fine palate'. A **pallet** of wine is dozens of CASES. Some may describe a BOUQUET as being composed of a **palette** of FLAVOURS.

Palatinate, originally territory under the jurisdiction of a local authority with sovereign powers, the term came to be used for that part of Germany which today includes both Rheinhessen and the PFALZ wine regions. It is also an alternative English name for the German wine region the Pfalz. See also GERMAN HISTORY.

Palestine, region on the Mediterranean with a viticultural history dating back at least to the third millennium BCE, when CANAANITE winemakers furnished their Egyptian rulers with wine. Winemaking continued, flourishing at times, through eras ruled by Philistines, Hebrews, Assyrians, Babylonians, Greeks, Romans, Byzantines, Arabs, Franks, Ottomans, and others, to the present. Sweet wines from the hinterlands of Gaza and Askalon were prized in Europe through Byzantine times, and, during the Crusades, Palestine was a major source of wines for the merchants of GENOA.

Wine production continued through the ISLAMIC period, albeit in limited ways. Palestinian Christians have always made wine domestically, and MONKS AND MONASTERIES have also played a role, as at Cremisan, founded in 1885 and now Palestine's oldest winery. Contemporary Palestinian wine culture, however, is fraught with challenges, as the land of Palestine is synonymous with the area internationally recognized as the state of ISRAEL and includes the West Bank, a territory currently largely under Israeli rule, and Gaza, internally governed by Hamas, a prohibitionist Islamist government.

Grapes remain a major agricultural crop in Palestine, second only to olives: according to OIV estimates, in 2020, the country's vineyards extended over 3,423 ha/8,458 acres, which include vineyards producing TABLE GRAPES, RAISINS, and products such as grape molasses that are important to the cuisine. A portion of the harvest is also distilled into arak, the national spirit, for local consumption and for export. There is no CONTROLLED APPELLATION system in Palestine, though wine made by Palestinians in the West Bank is labelled with that place name. In Gaza, the government compels winegrowers to work underground, so their wines remain unlabelled. The term 'Palestinian wine' is also sometimes used to describe wine made by self-identified Palestinians within Israel from land that has been in their families from before the founding of the state. The latter includes the hills west of Jerusalem, near the town of Ramleh, and the upper Galilee, by the border with LEBANON, east of Acre. However, as these areas are located within the 1949 armistice lines that serve as Israel's international consensus borders, the wines are labelled 'Made in Israel'. In 2022, there were six Palestinian wineries in the West Bank and another five self-identifying Palestinian winegrowers working within Israel.

Close to 85% of Palestinian vineyards today are in the West Bank, between Bethlehem and Hebron, where the warm MEDITERRANEAN CLIMATE is moderated in parts by ELEVATIONS that reach up to 1,000 m/3,280 ft. Throughout much of the country, well-draining, iron-rich TERRA ROSSA soil dominates, with patches of CLAY and LIMESTONE, especially around Bir Zeit and Beit Jala in the West Bank. Rainfall averages 454 mm/18 in a year. IRRIGATION is used when needed, though DRY-FARMED vineyards are common in parts of the West Bank that experience cooler evening temperatures and HUMIDITY.

Grape-growing in Gaza is largely confined to the lower-elevation (maximum 100 m/330 ft) coastal Gaza Strip, where soils are largely SANDY and CALCAREOUS and the climate is hot and dry, with rainfall averaging just 225 mm/9 in a year in the south, 400 mm in the north, concentrated in the winter months. Irrigation is used when possible, though water SALINITY is a problem.

According to research by Fadi Batarseh (then at the University of Udine, Italy, now winemaker at Cremisan), there are 21 INDIGENOUS VARIETIES in the Holy Land, with up to eight suitable for winemaking. These include the white wine varieties Daabouki/Dabouki (also called Zaini/Zeini), Jandali, and Hamdani (also called Marawe/Marawi); reds include Baladi Asmar, Baluti, Beituni/Bituni, and Shayukhi/Sheukhi. Once mostly subsumed into blends for local consumption or for Christian pilgrims visiting holy sites, these varieties are gaining more attention, though INTERNATIONAL VARIETIES remain more common.

The greatest challenge for Palestinian winegrowers is the Israeli-occupation regime in the West Bank, where they contend with frequent checkpoints, road closures, and work stoppages imposed by the Israeli army; vandalism, land confiscation, and water diversion by colonists; and the rapidly expanding Israeli separation wall which cuts off direct access to many vineyards. Nonetheless, the desire to assert Palestinian identity through indigenous products combined with greater international interest in local wines has sparked the growth of a modern Palestinian wine industry, its wines exported all over the world. J.A.R.

Palette, miniature AOC of just 43 ha/106 acres in PROVENCE in the hills east of Aix-en-Provence. The appellation is relatively old, created in 1948 in recognition of a distinctive LIMESTONE outcrop on the north-facing bank of the river Arc. A single property, Ch Simone, produces most of the wine and for many years was responsible for the most serious wine of the appellation. For seven generations, Ch Simone has been in the Rougier family, who continue to respect the traditional winemaking techniques, involving very OLD VINES, prolonged FERMENTATION, and BARREL MATURATION using very little new wood. FIELD BLENDS of southern vine varieties make extremely dense, long-lived reds, full-bodied rosés, and characterful white wines which belie modern white-winemaking philosophy. The INDIGENOUS VARIETIES permitted are even more numerous than those allowed in CHÂTEAUNEUF-DU-PAPE. E.A.G.

Palhete is a historic Portuguese term for a light-coloured red wine made from a combination of red and white grapes. Following a niche revival of the style, from 2017 the term can only be used to label red wines obtained from the partial MACERATION of red grapes or the maceration of both red and a maximum of 15% white grapes. In the ALENTEJO, light-coloured blends of red and white grapes (very often from TALHA) are traditionally called *petroleiro*. S.A.

Woolf, S. J., and Opaz, R., *Foot Trodden: Portugal and the Wines That Time Forgot* (2021).

pálido, Spanish wine term with more than one meaning: in CONDADO DE HUELVA and RUEDA, it refers to a dry, FORTIFIED wine aged under FLOR in oak for at least three years; in Rueda it must be made from PALOMINO FINO and/or VERDEJO. In MÁLAGA, it describes a sweet, FORTIFIED WINE made from PEDRO XIMÉNEZ and MOSCATEL without the addition of ARROPE. F.C.

Palladius (4th century CE). Next to nothing is known about the life of this agrarian writer of ancient ROME. He is the author of a treatise called, like Varro's earlier work, *De re rustica*, in 15 books. The first book is a general introduction to farming; the last two comprise a guide to veterinary medicine and an account of GRAFTING. The remaining 12 books deal with the tasks to be carried out throughout the agricultural year, one book for each month; Palladius has more to say about the vine than about any other crop. What he says, however, is sound but not original: he relies heavily on earlier authors, especially COLUMELLA (and, to a lesser extent, PLINY and VARRO). Unlike CATO, Varro, and Columella, he was well known in the Middle Ages and in the early Renaissance: he is quoted by Albertus Magnus, Vincent of Beauvais, and PETRUS DE CRESCENTIIS; and an anonymous Middle English translation of his work, connected with Humfrey, duke of Gloucester, survives. There is no direct evidence for his influence on medieval English wine producers, however. H.M.W.

Martin, R., *Recherches sur les agronomes latins* (1971).
White, K. D., *Roman Farming* (1970).

Pallagrello Nero, red wine grape planted on 107 ha/264 acres of CAMPANIA in 2015. Unrelated to the even rarer **Pallagrello Bianco**.

Palmela, DOP on the Setúbal peninsula in southern Portugal. See PENÍNSULA DE SETÚBAL.

palmento, ancient winemaking facility or wine cellar typical of ETNA in Sicily. Especially popular during the 19th century, *palmenti* (plural) were built on the slopes of the volcano to take advantage of gravitational flow to process large quantities of grapes. Palmenti are the direct descendants of the *palmenti rupestri* (*rupestre* means 'what is carved out of rock'), ancient outdoor winemaking facilities cut out of the rock by early Greek settlers on Etna. Many of Etna's monumental palmenti are no longer in use since the EU outlawed them due to alleged health concerns with their sand or dirt floors, which aid in maintaining perfect HUMIDITY levels but cannot be cleaned. Some have been restored, with concrete floors added, in the belief that they are very much part of the TERROIR. W.S.

Palo Cortado, a traditional style of sherry often described as mysterious but in fact simply explained by the fact that nature is greyscale rather than black and white. This is a wine that was originally pre-selected to become a *fino* or *amontillado*, aged under a protective veil of FLOR yeast, as opposed to *olorosos*, which are typically aged in OXIDATIVE fashion from the start. Yet some examples of these more delicate wines do not fully develop the protective veil and end up ageing in an *oloroso* way. As a result, such wines have an intermediate style—the elegance of the Fino/Amontillado with the concentration and body of the Oloroso. This is a rare category of sherry, yet some of the greatest dry sherries are Palos Cortados. For more details, see SHERRY. V. de la S. & J.B.

Palombina, synonym for PIEDIROSSO.

Palomino Fino, white grape variety most closely associated with the making of SHERRY around JEREZ in southern Spain that is generally declining in importance. It is almost certainly of Andalucian origin, supposedly named after one of King Alfonso X's knights, and was introduced to the CANARY ISLANDS, where it is known as Listán Blanco. It is often referred to as simply Palomino.

The vine is relatively susceptible to DOWNY MILDEW and ANTHRACNOSE and responds best in warm, dry soils. Its loose, generous bunches of large grapes make it suitable for TABLE GRAPES as well as wine. Its YIELD is relatively high and regular, about 80 hl/ha (4.5 tons/acre) without IRRIGATION, and the wine produced is, typically, low in both ACIDITY (as low as 3.5 g/l expressed in tartaric acid) and fermentable SUGARS. This suits most sherry producers, who pick Palomino grapes at about 19 °Brix (see MUST WEIGHT) and find Palomino must's tendency to OXIDIZE no inconvenience. However, a handful of Jerez and Canary Island producers have started turning low-yielding, OLD VINE Palomino/Listán Blanco into exciting, complex, unfortified whites.

Spain's official 2020 statistics distinguished between the Canary Islands' 1,580 ha/3,904 acres of Listán Blanco de Canarias, 2,095 ha/5,177 acres of Palomino Fino, and 11,651 ha/28,790 acres of plain Palomino, but according to DNA PROFILING they are genetically identical. The only mainland Spanish regions with sizeable plantings of Palomino other than Andalucía are GALICIA and CASTILLA Y LEÓN, where productive Palomino was planted after PHYLLOXERA but is being replaced by INDIGENOUS VARIETIES. The great majority is in sherry country around Jerez, but as sales of sherry have declined so has the total area of Palomino.

Outside sherry country, in France, for example, it is often known as Listán, or Listán de Jerez, and sometimes just Jerez. In Portugal it is known as Malvasia Rei, planted on 1,394 ha/3,445 acres in 2020, mainly in the north of the country and in Lisboa, where it makes generally bland table wine. However, on the island of Porto Santo, small PARCELS of old vines, under the name Listrão and typically used for local fortified wines, are showing great potential for unfortified wines. CYPRUS imported the Palomino vine because of its dependence on producing inexpensive copies of sherry, but very little remains.

The country with the most Palomino planted outside Europe was at one stage South Africa. Formerly known as Fransdruif in Afrikaans and White French in English, the variety has been losing ground fast. However, its decline is being arrested thanks to the burgeoning interest in fruit from older vineyards as a component in some of the Cape's more avant-garde blends.

California's acreage of the variety, once misidentified as Golden Chasselas, has always been very limited, almost all in the SAN JOAQUIN VALLEY. In Australia, total plantings have shrivelled as dramatically as production of sherry-like wines. New Zealand once also grew a surprising amount of Palomino considering its hardly ideal climate, but the vines have been replaced with more suitable varieties. Argentina has limited planting of the variety but PEDRO GIMÉNEZ predominates.

Pamid, BULGARIA's most widely planted and least interesting INDIGENOUS VARIETY producing rather thin, early-maturing red wines with few distinguishing marks other than a certain sweetness from 1,058 ha/2,614 acres of vines. It does not play a major role in bottles bound for export. It is planted more extensively, on 2,653 ha/6,556 acres in 2021, as Roşioară, in Romania.

Pampanuto, also known as **Pampanino**, synonym for the Puglian white grape variety VERDECA.

Pannobile, a name derived from the Pannonian Plain, refers to a group founded in 1994 of (now) nine growers in Austria's NEUSIEDLERSEE region, all near the north-eastern edge of the eponymous lake, and to a single prestige blended red each of them offers (from some combination of ZWEIGELT, BLAUFRÄNKISCH, and ST-LAURENT grapes) as well as, in some cases, a white (from some combination of CHARDONNAY, PINOT GRIS, PINOT BLANC, and NEUBURGER). D.S.

Pansa Blanca, synonym for the Catalan white grape variety XARELLO.

Pantelleria, VOLCANIC island at the extreme southern limit of Italy and closer in fact to Cape Bon in TUNISIA than to the southern coast of SICILY, to which it belongs administratively. **Moscato di Pantelleria** is one of Italy's finest dessert wines, made from ZIBIBBO (MUSCAT OF ALEXANDRIA). The wine has enjoyed a certain reputation since the 1880s, when the MARSALA house of Rallo began to market it. The viticulture of the island is unusual: vines are GOBELET-trained but buried in a hole (called a *conca* by local growers) and vineyards surrounded by stone walls built from volcanic rock to prevent dehydration by the hot scirocco WINDS that sweep across the island.

Moscato di Pantelleria comes in two versions. The first is the regular Moscato, with at least 11% alcohol and 68 g/l of RESIDUAL SUGAR, although many of the better producers raisin the grapes for 10–12 days to achieve higher levels of total alcohol and residual sugar (see DRIED-GRAPE WINES). The second version, Passito di Pantelleria, is lusher and richer, a true dessert style, with at least 14% alcohol and 100 g/l residual sugar, although many now seek a more decadently sweet style, sun-drying the grapes for up to 30 days and arriving at close to 140 g/l residual sugar. This search for power can come at a cost: the Moscato perfumes tend to be destroyed by the high level of VOLATILE ACIDITY that may result from prolonged sun-drying.

Both the Moscato and the Passito can come with the suffix 'liquoroso', indicating the addition of ETHANOL, which arrests the alcoholic fermentation, leaving a substantial amount of unfermented sugar in the wine. They may be additionally labelled Vino Dolce Naturale, the Italian equivalent of VIN DOUX NATUREL, but these rarely achieve the complexity of the unfortified versions. Changes in the production rules in the early 2010s created a new category of dry white wines labelled as **Pantelleria Bianco** as well as sparkling wines. After a period of neglect, the island's wines are experiencing revived popularity and recognition in Italy, with an undeniable increase in overall quality driven mainly by ambitious small-scale producers, notably Marco de Bartoli and BIODYNAMIC avantgardist Salvatore Ferrandes. Donnafugata's Passito di Pantelleria Ben Ryé, combining high quality with economics of scale, is the wine's international ambassador.

W.S.

Nesto, B., and Di Savino, F., *The World of Sicilian Wine* (2013).
www.consorziopantelleria.it

paper bottles, form of PACKAGING developed by a British company in 2020. Sealed with a SCREWCAP, the paper bottle is five times lighter than a lightweight 345-g glass bottle and has a CARBON FOOTPRINT four times lower than that bottle. The outer framework is made from two layers of recycled paper formed around a plastic inner pouch that uses nearly 70% less plastic than a PLASTIC BOTTLE. The bottle's OXYGEN TRANSMISSION RATE means that the wine should remain in good condition for up to a year after bottling, making it suitable for all but the small percentage of wines intended for bottle AGEING.

Alko, 'Update of wine packaging LCA: final report Alko Oy' (2021). www.alko.fi/INTERSHOP/static/WFS/Alko-OnlineShop-Site/-/Alko-OnlineShop/fi_FI/Tavarantoimittajille/Muut/EN/Alko%20wine%20packaging%20LCA%20update_final%20report.pdf.

Paraguay in SOUTH AMERICA has only a small wine presence due to the tropical conditions. The once-robust vineyards of Colonia Independencia, a colony settled by German winegrowers from BADEN in 1919, had dwindled to less than 200 ha/500 acres by 2021, but there was excitement around a new estate, Bodega Giacometti, 40 ha/99 acres in the Infante Rivarola zone, 700 km/435 miles from Asunción near the Bolivian border. Its first own-grown wines were anticipated to be released in 2023 as sadly their initial plantings were destroyed by ANTS.

E.M.G.

Goldstein, E., *Wines of South America* (2014).

parcel, a defined plot or block of vines, often within a larger vineyard. A parcel, unlike a CLIMAT, typically has one owner. See also SÉLECTION PARCELLAIRE.

Pardillo, once known as Pardilla, is a vine variety planted on 1,418 ha/3,504 acres of LA MANCHA, in Spain, where it makes sturdy whites.

Pardina, light-skinned grape producing rather ordinary wines in EXTREMADURA shown by DNA PROFILING in 2005 to be the same as CAYETANA BLANCA.

Parellada, highly regarded white grape variety originally Aragonese but now grown almost exclusively in CATALUÑA, especially around San Sadurni d'Anoia on just under 9,014 ha/22,274 acres in 2020, where it is widely used, with MACABEO and XARELLO, for the production of CAVA. It is the least planted of these three varieties in PENEDÈS, the region most closely associated with these Spanish sparkling wines. Parellada can produce aromatic, high-quality wine when grown in relatively poor soil and in cooler conditions. It buds early and ripens late. Occasionally made as a VARIETAL still wine.

Paris, capital of FRANCE, once the centre of a thriving wine region and still one of the few capital cities in which vineyards of any size may be found (see also VIENNA). Its several suburban vineyards include 2,000 vines on the slopes of Montmartre, originally densely planted in 1933, whose meagre produce is auctioned for charity. Even smaller plantings (170–400 vines) can be found in various parks across the city. In 2004, 470 vines were planted in the garden of an *hôtel particulier* next to the Bois de Boulogne and now produce a sparkling wine sold onsite for €60 per bottle.

Beyond the inner city, the surrounding Île-de-France region was home to 30,000–45,000 ha/74,132–111,197 acres of vines at the end of the 18th century (more than in Burgundy today). In 2020 it achieved IGP status. Recent plantings include a collaboration in 2021 involving Guillaume d'Angerville of Domaine Marquis d'Angerville and the chef Yannick Alléno, in Conflans-Ste-Honorine.

E.L.

History

Wine was grown around Paris in the 4th century, and its fame as a winegrowing area dates from long after the Roman Empire. Clovis, king of the Franks 481–511, made Paris the capital of his kingdom, and from the 8th century onwards Frisian, Saxon, and English merchants sailed up the river Seine to Paris to buy wine. Under the Merovingians and the Carolingians, Paris was an important centre of trade, and much of the wine sold there would have been produced locally.

A document from the beginning of the 9th century shows that viticulture was a major part of the local economy. The Roll of Irminon, named after the abbot of St-Germain-des-Prés who instigated this survey of his monastery's lands, is the only document of its kind dating back to the time of CHARLEMAGNE. Vineyards at Rambouillet, Dreux, Fontainebleau, Sceaux, and Versailles were cultivated not only by monks but also by laymen, and it is clear from the amounts produced that there must have been a surplus to sell on the open market. Documents from the Abbey of St-Denis, near Paris, show that St-Germain-des-Prés was not unique in this respect. In the 9th century, St-Denis had vineyards in the abbey precincts and possessed winegrowing estates in the Île-de-France, as the Paris basin was known; many smaller monasteries in the area also produced wine for sale (see MONKS AND MONASTERIES).

In the 10th century, Paris was well established as a centre of the wine trade. The main trade route was down the Seine to Rouen and thence overseas. In the late 10th century, merchants from England, Ireland, Flanders, and Picardy visited Rouen, and later Henry II of England gave Rouen the monopoly of transporting wine to England. Later, from the 13th century onwards, the trade route from Paris was down the Seine or up the Oise to Compiègne, where the wine would be loaded on to carts and driven to Flanders. By then the merchants of Paris had managed to acquire for themselves privileges similar to those of their Gascon counterparts (see BORDEAUX). In an edict of 1190, Philip Augustus, king of France, declared that only the merchants of Paris, who were themselves usually wine producers as well (see CLIMATE CHANGE for details of the warmer MACROCLIMATE prevailing then), had the right to sell wine in Paris. They were able to prevent the sale of any wine they wished, thus regulating the import of wines and controlling the quality of the wines sold as 'vins de France'. The wines of AUXERRE, CHABLIS, and Tonnerre had to pass through Paris before they were permitted to be transported further, and wines from other regions were not to be offered for sale before the 'vins de France' had all been sold. The wines of the LOIRE were also put on the market in Paris.

The 'vins de France' included not only the wines of Paris up to Vernon in Normandy but also those of CHAMPAGNE (Reims, Épernay, Châlons-sur-Marne): this usage continued among wine producers until just after the French Revolution. The Capetian kings of France, who reigned 987–1498, were particularly fond of the wines of Paris, but some of what they drank must have been from Champagne, since no distinction was made. In those days the region grew more than it could drink. Some of it was sold to the neighbouring areas of Normandy, Picardy, and Artois; the principal foreign export markets in the Middle Ages were England and Flanders. The 'vins de France' were highly esteemed both at home and abroad: in 1200 they fetched higher prices in London than the wines of ANJOU.

H.M.W.

Dion, R., *Histoire de la vigne et du vin en France* (1959).
Lachiver, M., *Vins, vignes et vignerons* (1988).
Poret, A., *Histoire du grand vigne d'Ile-de-France* (2011).

P

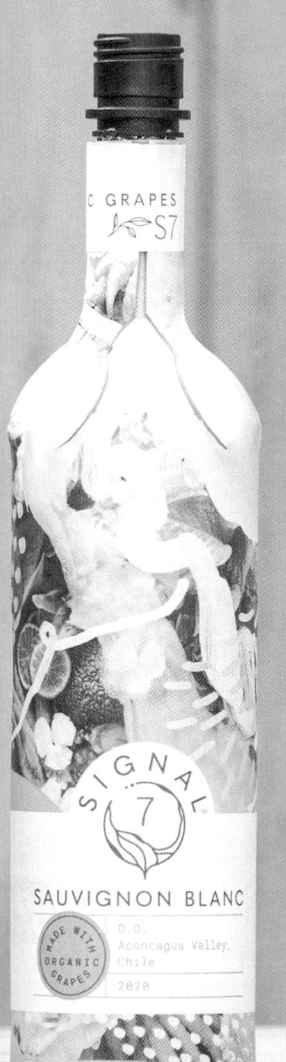
SIGNAL
7
SAUVIGNON BLANC
MADE WITH ORGANIC GRAPES
D.O.
Aconcagua Valley,
Chile
2020

ORGANIC
SIGNAL
7
ROSÉ
MADE WITH ORGANIC GRAPES
Origin:
IGP Mediterranée,
France
2020

SIGNAL
7
SOCIAL RED
MADE WITH ORGANIC GRAPES
Origin:
2020

GRAPES
SIGNAL
7
STASH
MADE WITH ORGANIC GRAPES
Small Batch Series
by Pilar Miranda
D.O. San Antonio Valley
Chile, 2019

3Q
RED WINE
750mL
Product of Italy

Parker, Robert M., Jr (1947–), extremely influential American wine critic whose most obvious contribution to the LITERATURE OF WINE has been the concept of applying NUMBERS to wine. His scores, followed slavishly by some COLLECTORS and even more by INVESTORS, had a demonstrable effect on individual wine PRICES, especially in the 1990s and the early years of the 21st century.

Robert Parker was born in farming country near Baltimore and both trained and worked as a lawyer there. He discovered wine at the age of 20 on his first trip to France. By the mid 1970s, at the height of active consumerism, Parker became frustrated by the lack of truly independent and reliable wine criticism and began to think about launching his own consumer's guide to wine buying.

The first, complimentary, issue of his bi-monthly newsletter the *Wine Advocate* appeared in 1978, and by 1984 he felt confident enough of its success to retire from the legal profession and concentrate on the punishing schedule of tastings and travel on which it was based. By then he had made a name for himself with his enthusiastic, and unusually detailed, endorsement of the 1982 vintage in Bordeaux, and subscriptions grew rapidly alongside the American market for wine FUTURES. By 1998, when a French-language edition was launched, the *Wine Advocate* had more than 45,000 subscribers, mainly in the United States but in more than 35 other countries. There were no advertisements but hundreds of TASTING NOTES and assessments of individual, usually fine, wines. His judgements had a huge effect, not just on market demand and the commercial future of some producers but on wine styles, since he was perceived as favouring concentrated wines relatively high in alcohol, and such wines would be described as **Parkerized**. His power at one stage was so great that it encouraged producers around the world to adapt the style of their wines regardless of their own personal tastes.

Parker's was by no means the first American consumer wine newsletter, but it was the first to use scores—effectively between 85 and 100 for individual wines—quite so obviously. This system was easily and delightedly grasped by Americans familiar with high-school grades, even though Parker himself urged caution, asking readers to use the numerical ratings 'only to enhance and complement the thorough tasting notes, which are my primary means of communicating my judgments to you'. Wine salespeople were less circumspect and used Parker's ratings mercilessly, while the notion of SCORING wine at all came under attack from some other wine authorities, notably Hugh JOHNSON, whose view is that wines themselves vary with time and conditions of tasting and that wine tasting is an intrinsically subjective process. Parker's own view, stated on the cover of every issue of the *Advocate*, was that 'wine is no different from any consumer product. There are specific standards of quality that full-time wine professionals recognize.'

Parker's diligence in recording the impressions of his hard-worked palate provided the ingredients for several lengthy books, including *Wine Buyer's Guides*, essentially *Advocate* compendia. *Bordeaux* first appeared in 1985 and enjoyed considerable success in the United States, in Britain in 1987, and in France in 1989. The fourth edition appeared in 2003. *The Wines of the Rhône Valley and Provence*, which appeared in 1987 and was updated ten years later, reflected Parker's other great passion (he was instrumental in establishing the reputation and ambitious pricing policy of GUIGAL of Côte Rôtie, for example). *Burgundy* (1990), with its complex mosaic of appellations, producers, and vintages, and much subtler wines, succumbed less easily to being 'Parkerized'. Burgundian négociant François Faiveley's 1994 lawsuit was the first of several, subsequent ones involving past associates. By the late 1990s Parker was no longer working alone, and by 2012, when the *Wine Advocate* and associated website were sold to a Singapore former wine merchant for a reported $15 million, he had a substantial, fluctuating team of fellow tasters. Subsequently, in a two-stage deal, the business was sold to Michelin. Parker contributed his last tasting note in 2016 and officially retired in 2019.

Parker was a fervent, if critical, admirer of French wines. He was the first non-Frenchman to write a wine column for *L'Express* magazine and was made a particularly emotional Chevalier de l'Ordre du Mérite National in 1992. The Légion d'Honneur followed in 1999.

The sale, and the emergence of a new, post-Parker generation of American wine enthusiasts with different tastes and idols, resulted in a decline in the *Wine Advocate*'s influence.

Langewiesche, W., 'The million-dollar nose', *The Atlantic Monthly*, 286/6 (2000) 42–62.
McCoy, E., *The Emperor of Wine* (2005).

Parraleta, interesting, fragrant red wine grape rescued from extinction in Spain's SOMONTANO region. It is also grown on Corsica and in Portugal under several aliases including Tinta Caiada.

partially de-alcoholized wine, an EU category for wine that has undergone alcohol reduction but retains a minimum of 0.5% alcohol by volume and does not exceed the legal minimum actual alcoholic strength before de-alcoholization for that category of wine (for still TABLE WINES, 8.5% in the cooler northern regions and 9% in the south). Unlike de-alcoholized wine, partially de-alcoholized wine may be labelled as a PDO or PGI, if permitted by the appellation concerned. Most other countries do not have a formal definition and may use looser terminology such as 'lighter alcohol', 'low alcohol' or 'reduced alcohol'. J.P.H.B.

partial rootzone drying, or **PRD**, Australian IRRIGATION technique designed to control vine VIGOUR and maintain wine quality with minimum interference to YIELD. PRD was developed by scientists Dry and Loveys from the University of ADELAIDE and CSIRO, after observation of basic vine physiology in response to WATER STRESS. Initially using vines with divided root systems, they discovered that when only a portion of a vine's root system was drying, TRANSPIRATION was reduced and shoot growth was slowed as a consequence of the production of the hormone ABSCISIC ACID by drying roots.

Field experiments with Cabernet Sauvignon showed that it was possible to control shoot vigour and reduce the amount of water needed while maintaining yield and quality. This was achieved with two DRIP IRRIGATION lines per row, used alternately for irrigation while the other part of the root system was drying. The results from these studies have been used to interpret some of the known beneficial effects of water stress, especially for red-wine quality. Commercial adoption in vineyards has been limited, but research on grapevines and other crops has clearly shown that PRD can generate a unique physiological response that is distinct from what happens with conventional irrigation, including REGULATED DEFICIT IRRIGATION. R.E.S. & P.R.D.

Iland, P., et al., *The Grapevine: From the Science to the Practice of Growing Vines for Wine* (2011).

Pascale di Cagliari, Sardinian dark grape speciality, posssibly a natural progeny of Gibi (or Hebén) and MONASTRELL from Spain, according to DNA PROFILING.

Paso Robles, very large California wine region and AVA on the inland side of the coastal mountains in SAN LUIS OBISPO County.

An isolated inland plain of gently rolling hills, where the headwaters of the Salinas river congregate, Paso Robles first drew attention for its rich deposits of mercury ore. Mining operations grew quickly during the GOLD RUSH, attracting settlers such as Andrew York, who in 1882 set down the region's first vines of ZINFANDEL and established what would become York Mountain Winery. Despite some early plantings, including notably the Dusi Vineyard's Zinfandel in 1925, Paso remained a sleepy, rural wine region until the 1970s when significant plantings of Cabernet Sauvignon and Chardonnay were shown to be successful. Gary Eberle planted the state's first post-PROHIBITION acres of Syrah in Paso Robles in 1975. The 247,000-ha/612,000-acre region was established

◀ British company Frugalpac pioneered these incredibly light PAPER BOTTLES in 2020. Even with a plastic pouch inside, they have a much lower CARBON FOOTPRINT than lightweight glass BOTTLES and offer a large surface area for BRANDING.

as an AVA in 1983 and divided into 11 sub-AVAs in 2014, largely on the basis of climatological and soil differences. Across Paso Robles the climate varies from relatively cool in its westernmost AVAs to quite warm (Region IV in the eastern highlands according to Winkler's CLIMATE CLASSIFICATION scale). Soils in the western reaches can be quite CALCAREOUS, while alluvial LOESS and even LOAM can be found in the eastern hills. The region's sub-AVAs include the cooler districts of El Pomar, Adelaida, Willow Creek, Santa Margarita Ranch, and Templeton Gap; the warmer alluvial soils of the Creston, Estrella, San Juan Creek, and San Miguel districts; and the hot, windy hillsides of the Paso Robles Highlands and Geneseo districts.

Since its confirmation as an AVA, newcomers in an expanding roster of local wineries have embraced a wide array of grape varieties, with an emphasis on red BORDEAUX and RHÔNE varieties in addition to ZINFANDEL. Chardonnay still makes up 5% of the region's 16,187 ha/ 40,000 acres of vines, though it has been gradually losing ground to the more successful GRENACHE BLANC, MARSANNE, and ROUSSANNE, thanks in no small measure to the winery and vine nursery of Tablas Creek, a 1987 joint venture between the Perrin family of Ch de Beaucastel in CHÂTEAUNEUF-DU-PAPE and their American importer Robert Haas. This partnership firmly anchored Paso Robles specifically, and the Central Coast more broadly, as the epicentre of the RHÔNE RANGER movement in California. A.Y.

Comiskey, P., *American Rhône: How Maverick Winemakers Changed the Way Americans Drink* (2016).

www.pasowine.com

P

passerillé, French word for a grape that has dried, shrivelled, or raisined on the vine in a process known as **passerillage**, concentrating the SUGAR IN GRAPES—an alternative to wines whose sugars have been concentrated by BOTRYTIS. See also CUT CANE.

Passerina, white variety from Italy's Adriatic coast making a wide range of wine styles on 933 ha/2,305 acres of vines in 2015.

Passetoutgrains. See BOURGOGNE PASSETOUTGRAINS.

passing the port. One of the wine trade's most cherished traditions is the rule that PORT, particularly a decanter of vintage port, must be passed round a table from the right hand of diners to the left. No single satisfactory explanation has ever been advanced.

Howkins, B., *Real Men Drink Port . . . and Ladies Do Too!* (2011).

passito, Italian term for DRIED-GRAPE WINE.

Pasteur, Louis (1822–95), scientific genius and gifted scholar, has left a body of work which impinges on physics, chemistry, microbiology, agronomy, and medicine. On the centenary of his birth in 1922, the Institut Pasteur in Paris published a monograph on his principal discoveries listed under the following headings:

1847: Molecular dissymmetry
1857: Fermentations
1862: Supposedly spontaneous generations
1863: Study of wines
1865: Silkworm diseases
1871: Study of beers
1877: Virus diseases
1880: Viral vaccines
1885: Rabies protection

Pasteur's original work on what were supposedly spontaneous generations, or transformations, led him to interpret the process of alcoholic FERMENTATION and to demonstrate that this, far from being spontaneous, was the result of intervention by living cells, YEAST, using sugar for their own nutrition and transforming it into ALCOHOL and CARBON DIOXIDE. 'What causes it? I admit that I have no idea' (*Œuvres de Pasteur*, ii. 77). With something approaching genius, Pasteur understood the phenomenon without being able to provide a precise explanation; contemporary biochemistry was able to explain in detail the different stages of the chemical fermentation mechanism only in the first half of the 20th century.

During his career as a scientist, Pasteur must have devoted only three or four years to the study of wine. Yet in this time he achieved as much as a good specialist researcher would have been delighted to achieve in an entire lifetime. Not only did he apply his theories to fermentation and ensure the mastery of the basics of vinification and conservation of wines, but he also perfected the art of adding TARTARIC ACID, demonstrated the presence of SUCCINIC ACID and GLYCEROL, and made valuable suggestions about the role of OXYGEN in wine AGEING.

But it was above all in the field of microbiological diseases of wine that Pasteur's work has been most valued. One of the early problems assigned to Pasteur was to explain and prevent the vinegar spoilage of red wines shipped in barrel from Burgundy to Britain, as well as to try to explain some of the many FAULTS in French wine which had become apparent at the time. He identified the following transformations in various wine constituents:

mannitic acid: degradation of sugars
tourne: degradation of tartaric acid
bitterness: degradation of glycerol
graisse: production of a polysaccharide

From his discovery of the various microorganisms which caused different wine maladies, such as the ACETOBACTER which turn wine into vinegar, came the whole science of bacteriology. He suggested that the application of heat (now called PASTEURIZATION) would destroy these microorganisms and prevent microbial development, with beneficial effects on the quality of wine. The demonstration of the existence of these BACTERIAL DISEASES was extremely fruitful for the science of OENOLOGY; it resulted in the progressive reduction in VOLATILE ACIDS in wine, which was an important factor in raising quality. Pasteur's research work on wine, and beer, also gave rise to his remarkable studies on the cause and prevention of infectious diseases in humans and animals.

From a drop of faulty wine, characterized by the presence of microorganisms which could be seen with the aid of a microscope and by faults which could be tasted, Pasteur could contaminate a perfectly healthy wine. In 1866 he expressed his thoughts thus: 'When one observes beer and wine experiencing fundamental changes because these liquids have given asylum to microscopic organisms which were introduced invisibly and fortuitously to them, where they since proliferated, how could one not be obsessed by the thought that similar things can and must sometimes happen to humans and animals?'

Whatever the undoubted merits of Pasteur's work, to which we owe the basis of wine microbiology, with all its practical consequences for vinification and wine conservation, it should be noted that he did not understand the positive role that LACTIC ACID BACTERIA could have in degrading MALIC ACID. Because of this it was particularly difficult to grasp the principles of MALOLACTIC CONVERSION, which, in 1930, Jean RIBÉREAU-GAYON elucidated as a bacterial transformation which could be of great benefit to a wide range of wines. It was not until the 1970s that the rest of the wine world was convinced.

For Pasteur, 'yeast make wine, bacteria destroy it'. Pasteur truly created the science of winemaking; if today oenology is a discipline in so many universities throughout the world, it is to Pasteur that we owe this achievement. P.R.-G.

pasteurization, process of heating foods, including wines, to a temperature high enough to kill all microorganisms such as YEAST and BACTERIA. It is named after Louis PASTEUR, the French scientist who discovered that microorganisms were alive and the cause of much wine spoilage.

Heat sterilization techniques have improved greatly since the early versions of pasteurization, which often resulted in burnt or cooked flavours in wines treated, particularly those that had not been subjected to complete CLARIFICATION. Wines are pasteurized by rapid heating to about 85 °C/185 °F for one minute, followed by quick cooling and a return to the storage tank or bottling line. Keeping the wine longer, for up to three days, at about 50 °C/122 °F is used to coagulate heat-unstable proteins and to speed ageing in low-quality red dessert wines. **Flash pasteurization** may also be effected by heating to temperatures as high as 95 °C for a few seconds, followed by rapid cooling. Some wine is **hot bottled** (at about 55 °C) and allowed to cool slowly; for utmost effectiveness, closed bottles of wine are occasionally heated to about 55 °C and cooled to room temperature under a water spray. These techniques are relatively brutal, however, and are used only on ordinary wines which have no potential for improvement after bottle AGEING. See also KOSHER wine. A.D.W.

Patagonia. See ARGENTINA.

Patrimonio. See CORSICA.

Pauillac, small port and communal appellation in the MÉDOC district of BORDEAUX which has the unparalleled distinction of boasting three of the five FIRST GROWTHS ranked in Bordeaux's most famous CLASSIFICATION—Chx LAFITE, LATOUR, and MOUTON ROTHSCHILD—as well as a bevy of other CLASSED GROWTHS rivalling them (and each other) with increasing insistence. For all the importance of its wines, Pauillac gives the impression of being the only settlement in the Haut-Médoc to have an existence independent of wine—an impression reinforced by its size and nearby industrial installations.

This, however, is Cabernet Sauvignon country *par excellence*, and while there is considerable variation between different properties' TERROIRS and winemaking policies and capabilities, certain expressions recur in Pauillac tasting notes: cassis (blackcurrant), cedar, and cigar box (the last two sometimes a reflection of the top-quality French oak COOPERAGE which the selling prices of Pauillac permit). A high proportion of the Médoc's most concentrated wines are produced here.

About 1,200 ha/3,000 acres of vines produce this famous appellation in an almost continuous strip between Pauillac's boundary with ST-JULIEN to the south and ST-ESTÈPHE to the north, separated from the waters of the Gironde estuary by only a few hundred metres of *palus* too marshy for serious viticulture (although very suitable for grazing Pauillac's famous *agneaux présalés*, salt-marsh lamb). This strip of vines, 3 km/2 miles wide and more than 6 km long, dedicated to the production of the world's most famously long-lived red wine, is divided into two by the small river Gaët, whose banks are also unsuitable for vines. As elsewhere in the Médoc, the layers of GRAVEL here provide the key to wine quality, offering excellent DRAINAGE, aided by the almost imperceptibly undulating topography and a series of *jalles* or streams running water off the gravelly plateau and into the Gironde.

The stars of the northern sector of Pauillac are the two ROTHSCHILD properties Chx Lafite and Mouton Rothschild, whose plots of vineyard are intermingled on the plateau of Le Pouyalet, reaching the considerable (for the Médoc) elevation of 30 m/100 ft at its highest point. Clustered around them are their satellite properties, whose wines benefit from the first-class winemaking ability of their owners. Ch Duhart-Milon is Lafite's fourth growth, made in the town of Pauillac. The fifth growths Ch Clerc-Milon and Ch d'Armailhac (the latter called Ch Mouton Baron Philippe and then Ch Mouton Baronne Philippe between 1956 and 1989) are made, to an often very high standard, close to Mouton itself. Other classed growths on this plateau just a stream away from St-Estèphe are the fifth growths Pédesclaux and Chx Pontet-Canet, the latter of which has attracted attention as a result of its espousal of BIODYNAMIC VITICULTURE.

Throughout the 1970s, much was made of the inter-Rothschild rivalry in the northern half of Pauillac, but it was resolved by the next generation. In the mid 1980s and early 1990s, the extreme south of the appellation around the village of St-Lambert was a battleground for wine supremacy, between first growth Ch Latour and, particularly, its near neighbours the two Pichons. All three of these have made considerable investments in their vineyards, *chais*, and more cosmetic aspects of their property, and the Pichons have demonstrated that, just like first growth Latour, they are capable of making sublime wine at the St-Julien end of Pauillac. The Pichon-Longueville estate was originally one, but had already been divided into a smaller 'Baron' portion and a larger Comtesse de Lalande portion by the time the 1855 classification ranked them in the bottom half of the second growths (a very much lower position than they merit today). Pichon-Baron has been lavishly renovated by AXA Millésimes, while ROEDERER, owners of Pichon Lalande, later did the same across the road.

In the hinterland of this southern extreme of Pauillac are neighbouring fifth growths Chx Batailley and Haut-Batailley, whose wines can challenge those of fifth growth Ch Grand-Puy-Lacoste to the immediate north, which can offer some of Pauillac's best value. A dozen of the 18 fifth growths are in Pauillac, and none has been more successful than the Cazes family's flamboyantly styled Ch Lynch-Bages (the name betraying the original Irish connection), whose standing and fame suggest a considerably higher ranking. The biodynamically certified Ch Haut-Bages-Libéral, between Chx Latour and Lynch-Bages, can be great value.

Two of Pauillac's most distinctive products do not feature in the 1855 classification. Les Forts de Latour, the SECOND WINE of Ch Latour, is regularly one of its most successful wines, while the noted co-operative at Pauillac sells some of its dwindling production under the name La Rose Pauillac. J.R. & J.L.

Brook, S., *The Complete Bordeaux* (4th edn, 2022).
Penning-Rowsell, E., *The Wines of Bordeaux* (6th edn, 1989).

Paulée, La. Originally a HARVEST TRADITION, the term was appropriated for a huge BYOB extended lunch in MEURSAULT on the Monday after the annual HOSPICES DE BEAUNE sale and is now used for a series of bibulous events in the United States at which considerable predations are made in COLLECTORS' stocks of TROPHY WINES.

Pays d'Oc, the largest of the six regional IGPS in France, encompasses 120,000 ha/296,526 acres across four *departéments* in the Languedoc and Roussillon, from Gard in the east to the Pyrénées-Orientales in the west (plus a small part of the Lozère *département* north of Gard). Pays d'Oc wines make up around 15% of French wine production, the vast majority being VARIETAL wines made from any of the 58 allowed varieties but particularly Merlot, Cabernet Sauvignon, and Chardonnay. The vast region contains a great many MESOCLIMATES, as demonstrated by the diverse AOCS within it, but generally sunny, dry weather and frequent WINDS allow the region to produce more ORGANIC WINE by volume than anywhere else in France. In 2019, in an effort to combat CLIMATE CHANGE and further reduce the need for AGROCHEMICALS, the region introduced five DISEASE-RESISTANT varieties to the mix: Cabernet Blanc, Cabernet Cortis, Muscaris, Soreli, and Souvignier Gris, which can constitute up to 15% of a blend. More than half the region's production is in red wines; 25% is white; and the rest is rosé (mainly from Grenache, Cinsaut, and Syrah). Sparkling and sweet wines are also made.

PCA, or **2,3,4,5,6-pentachloroanisole**. See TECA.

PCD. See PLANT CELL DENSITY.

PCR, abbreviation for **polymerase chain reaction**, a laboratory method based on DNA analysis used to detect vine pathogens. This technique has helped in determining strains of VIRUS, for example, and the INSECTS responsible for their spread.

Golino, D., et al., 'Laboratory testing for grapevine diseases', in L. J. Bettiga (ed.), *Grape Pest Management* (3rd edn, 2013), 61–8.

PDO, abbreviation for **Protected Designation of Origin**, a superior EU wine category created as part of the 2008 wine reforms. It encompasses all of the EU's CONTROLLED APPELLATION systems such as France's AOC, Spain's DO/DOCA, Italy's DOC/DOCG, and Portugal's DOC.

Translations of PDO (such as AOP in France, DOP in Spain, Italy, and Portugal) are now seen on wine labels. In 2020 PDO wines represented 46% of EU production, although the proportion of PDO wine produced—as well as the quality—can vary dramatically among member states. PDOs enjoy special privileges in the EU wine system, including protection against misuse as well as the right to use TRADITIONAL TERMS and the special EU PDO symbol on the label. Non-EU countries are, in theory, able to register their own GEOGRAPHICAL INDICATIONS (GIs) as PDOs in Europe, but in most cases mutual protection of GIs is agreed with the EU through bilateral wine or free-trade agreements.

The PDO category is regarded as a higher order of geographical designation than the PGI. The quality and characteristics of a PDO are required to be 'essentially or exclusively due to a particular geographical environment with its inherent natural and human factors'—a higher threshold than for the PGI category. The grapes must also be grown entirely in the delimited area. Until recently they had to be sourced exclusively from VITIS, VINIFERA grape varieties, but this has been relaxed to make way for DISEASE-RESISTANT VARIETIES. PDOs generally have more stringent controls than PGIs, covering matters such as maximum yield, vineyard-management techniques, permitted varieties, harvesting, and winemaking. J.P.H.B.

www://ec.europa.eu/info/food-farming-fisheries/food-safety-and-quality/certification/quality-labels/geographical-indications-register

pearls or **pearl glands**, small, spherical nodules that develop on the surface of vine stems, PETIOLES, and the underside of leaves along the large veins. They form under warm humid conditions, such as in a glasshouse, and when the vine's growth is exuberant. They are a multicellular outgrowth of the epidermis, even to the extent of an occasional STOMA, but collapse to a rusty colour and disappear when the humidity drops. B.G.C.

P

Pécharmant, AOC for red wines (400 ha/1,000 acres) within the BERGERAC district in SOUTH WEST FRANCE. The grape varieties are as for Bergerac (Cabernets Franc and Sauvignon with Merlot and sometimes a generous dose of Malbec); their distinctiveness is due to the soil, which contains a good amount of IRON and MANGANESE. The wines are some of Périgord's longest-lived reds, but few escape the region. The best-known producer is Ch de Tiregand, presided over by members of the St-Exupéry family. P.S.

Pecorino, vine speciality of the MARCHE and ABRUZZO on Italy's east coast that has made a VARIETAL comeback because of its firm, dry, minerally white wine that compares well with the local Trebbiano. Total area planted grew from 87 ha in 2000 to 1,628 ha/4,023 acres by 2015. Also a Calabrian synonym for GRECO BIANCO.

pectinase, an ENZYME used to break up grape PECTINS and thus speed up SETTLING. It is also used to promote juice and flavour extraction during SKIN CONTACT.

pectins, carbohydrate polymers made up of galacturonic acid units which have the important function of 'gumming' plant cells together. The group is diverse and includes pectic acid, hemicelluloses, and gums; the associated sugars are galactose, mannose, and arabinose. The pectin content of grapes increases steadily throughout ripening, reaching levels of about 1 g/l. Pectin is an important contributor to COLLOIDS. For the importance of pectin hydrolysing enzymes to winemaking, see ENZYMES. B.G.C.

Pedernã, MINHO synonym for ARINTO.

pedicel, the stalk of an individual flower which, on a bunch of grapes, becomes the short stem bearing each berry. Its length varies with vine variety, from 5 to 15 mm (0.2–0.5 in), and its diameter varies with variety and BERRY SIZE. After FLOWERING, pedicels are liable to develop a separation layer at their base causing the unfertilized flower to drop; the remainder adhere and can develop into berries (as in FRUIT SET). When berries of certain vine varieties ripen, the pedicels may develop a corky abscission at their top, at the junction with the berry. If this does not happen, then pulling off the berry tears the skin and leaves behind a chunk of pulp on the end of the pedicel that is called the BRUSH. B.G.C.

pedogenic limestone. See LIMESTONE.

Pedro Giménez, declining but still quite important white grape variety in ARGENTINA, where, along with the coarse and declining CRIOLLA GRANDE and CEREZA, it is one of the vines underpinning the country's substantial production of everyday wine for domestic consumption. Most of its 9,587 ha/23,690 acres in 2020 were in Mendoza, but it is also found in Chile's PISCO region. It is a spontaneous LISTÁN Prieto (Criolla Chica) × MUSCAT OF ALEXANDRIA (Moscatel) cross and not related to PEDRO XIMÉNEZ.

Pedro Ximénez, white grape variety traditionally associated with ANDALUCÍA in southern Spain, found especially in MONTILLA-MORILES, where it accounts for around 95% of all plantings, and also in CASTILLA-LA MANCHA. By 2020 there were 7,865 ha/19,435 acres of the variety in Spain. Producers in JEREZ and MÁLAGA routinely import the dark, super-sticky wines made from Pedro Ximénez grown in Montilla-Moriles to sweeten blends. Many SHERRY producers sell varietal PX, as it is often called, under their own labels. Traditionally dried in the sun, the thin-skinned grapes are generally lower in acid and alcohol than the sherry grape PALOMINO FINO, which is more productive and less disease-prone than Pedro Ximénez. It is grown as Perrum on about 250 ha/717 acres of Portugal's ALENTEJO.

In Australia, Pedro Ximénez, often breezily called **Pedro**, was once quite widely grown but its total area had fallen to 15 ha/37 acres by 2022. It has been known to shine, most particularly in BOTRYTIZED form to produce the rich, deep golden McWilliam's Pedro Sauterne (*sic*) made in the last century in IRRIGATED vineyards near Griffith in NEW SOUTH WALES. Most of Chile's **Pedro Jiménez** (*sic*) is used for PISCO production, but a VARIETAL dry white is made in the Elqui Valley.

peduncle. See STEM.

Peel, warm coastal region just to the south of Perth in WESTERN AUSTRALIA with CHENIN BLANC and SHIRAZ its best wines.

pé franco, Portuguese for UNGRAFTED.

Pelaverga, pale, rare red grape of Piemonte making slightly fizzy, strawberry-flavoured wines. The even rarer and more admired **Pelaverga Piccolo** is a distinct variety.

Peloursin, obscure red grape variety found in Isère in France's Rhône-Alpes region and known mainly as a parent of PETITE SIRAH.

Pemberton, cool inland region of WESTERN AUSTRALIA with 466 ha/1,152 acres of vines in 2020 and strength in CHARDONNAY.

Penedès in Catalan, **Penedés** in Spanish, is the largest and most important denominated wine zone in CATALUÑA in north-east Spain (see map under SPAIN), producing an innovative range of wines from 24,259 ha/59,945 acres of vineyard in 2021. With its proximity to Barcelona, Penedès has always had a ready outlet for its wines. In the 19th century, it was one of the first regions in Spain to begin mass production, and France, stricken by PHYLLOXERA, became an important market. Phylloxera reached Penedès in 1887, by which time José Raventós had laid the foundations of Cordoníu and the CAVA industry. Vineyards that had once produced strong, semi-FORTIFIED reds were uprooted in favour of white grapes for sparkling wine. Cava has subsequently developed a separate nationally organized DOP.

Penedès underwent a second radical transformation in the 1960s and 1970s largely because of Miguel Torres Carbó and his son Miguel A. Torres (see FAMILIA TORRES), wine (and brandy) producers in the heart of the region at Vilafranca del Penedès. They were among the first in Spain to install TEMPERATURE CONTROL and STAINLESS STEEL tanks. Miguel Torres Jr, who studied OENOLOGY in France, also imported and experimented with such revolutionary vine varieties as Cabernet Sauvignon, Chardonnay, Sauvignon Blanc, Merlot, Pinot Noir, Riesling, and Gewürztraminer, which were planted alongside and blended with INDIGENOUS VARIETIES. Other growers followed in the Torres family footsteps, and Penedès was in the 1980s one of the most dynamic and varied wine regions in Spain. By the late 1990s, however, the region was failing to confirm the high hopes placed in its red wines, which were increasingly overshadowed by those of PRIORAT.

The Penedès DOP allows almost any style of wine or grape variety. The region rises from the Mediterranean like a series of steps and divides into three distinct zones, with ten subzones. Penedès Maritím sits between the sea and the coastal hills, its vineyards planted in LIMESTONE soils at ELEVATIONS of 250 m/825 ft. The warmest part of the region, it traditionally grew MALVASÍA and Moscatel de Alejandría (MUSCAT OF ALEXANDRIA) grapes for sweet FORTIFIED wines, but today still, dry XARELLO and Malvasía de Sitges are more representative wines. Penedès Superior is inland, climbing into the mountains, at 500–800 m (1,640–2,625 ft) in elevation. This is the region's coolest area where some of the best white grapes are grown. The native PARELLADA is its most important variety, but Riesling, Muscat of Alexandria, Gewürztraminer, and Chardonnay are also successful, and Xarello is increasingly positioned as the most TERROIR-expressive wine in the region, with producers bottling high-end 100% VARIETAL examples.

In between is Penedès Central, a plain at 500 m/1,640 ft in elevation. This is the most productive part of the region providing much of the base wine for the sparkling wine industry at Sant Sadurní d'Anoia (see CAVA). MACABEO, Xarello, and PARELLADA are grown for Cava and sparkling wines, together with Chardonnay and red varieties such as TEMPRANILLO (often called here by its Catalan name Ull de Llebre) and Cabernet Sauvignon.

The increased interest in SPARKLING WINE in this century led to the creation of Clàssic Penedès in 2014. Reserved for DOP Penedès sparkling wines made from organically grown grapes (see ORGANIC VITICULTURE), produced using the TRADITIONAL METHOD, and aged at least 15 months before release, the category has drawn some prominent names such as Albet I Noya, AT Roca, and Loxarel away from the DOP Cava. Producers using the MÉTHODE ANCESTRALE can use just DOP Penedès.

In 2021, Vi de Mas classification was introduced in order to highlight top parcels with history and track records for exceptional wines. Vi de Mas wines can come only from officially recognized farm estates (MAS) that predate the phylloxera outbreak of 1900; the parcels themselves must be wholly controlled by the estate, at least ten years old, and organically farmed. Gran Vi de Mas come from vineyards at least 25 years old and have attracted international attention for quality wines for at least a decade. The first five Vi de Mas wines were certified in 2022, with more expected to come.

V. de la S. & F.C.

www.dopenedes.cat

Penfolds, makers of Australia's most famous fine wine **Penfolds Grange**, since 2014 the jewel in TREASURY WINE ESTATES' crown. Penfolds was founded in 1844 at Magill, SOUTH AUSTRALIA, by Dr Christopher Rawson Penfold and his wife Mary. For more than 100 years, Penfolds, in common with most Australian wineries, concentrated on producing FORTIFIED wines and brandy, much of which was exported to the UK. In 1950, Max Schubert, then chief winemaker, visited Europe, primarily to observe the making of SHERRY in Spain, but detoured on the way home to visit Bordeaux, where he was taken in hand by important NÉGOCIANT Christian Cruse. This inspired him to adopt an entirely new approach to fermentation techniques and the use of new oak, the aim being simultaneously to protect the varietal flavour of Shiraz while adding a level of complexity previously unknown in Australia. Schubert's ambition was to create a red that would rival the finest wines of Bordeaux for both quality and the potential to improve with age for up to 50 years. This he achieved with Penfolds Grange, known as Penfolds Grange Hermitage until EU authorities objected to this misappropriation of a French place name. The first vintage of Grange, named after Dr Penfold's cottage in Magill, was 1951; all early vintages were made from Shiraz grapes grown at Magill and Morphett Vale, Adelaide, and the wine was BARREL AGED in new American oak for 12 months. So intense did the first vintages seem that they were rejected as maverick 'dry port'. In 1957 Schubert was ordered to cease production of Grange; instead he took the operation underground, emerging three years later when maturing vintages began to fulfil their promise. The best vintages of Grange improve for up to 30 years and beyond, and the wine became the first NEW WORLD wine to become an internationally acknowledged collectible (see TROPHY WINES). Fruit from Kalimna in the Barossa Valley was introduced in 1961, boosted by grapes from the Clare and Koonunga Hill vineyards. Small amounts of Cabernet Sauvignon are included in most vintages of Grange, and the wood-ageing period has been lengthened to 18–20 months. The wine is not released until five years after the vintage.

A string of award-winning red wines from Penfolds followed, many identified by BIN numbers which originated in the winery stock-keeping system. Of particular note is Bin 707 Cabernet Sauvignon. In 1998 Penfolds released the first vintage of its super-premium Yattarna Chardonnay, now recognized as one of Australia's finest. A stream of 'Special Bin' luxury reds followed in the early 2000s, not least the 2008 Bin 620 Cabernet/Shiraz, priced in line with first-growth bordeaux, and 2010 Bin 170 Kalimna Shiraz, which is even more expensive. If PRICES are a guide, Penfolds had truly arrived on the luxury catwalk by the early 21st century. Penfolds became so famous in CHINA that it was paid the compliment of COUNTERFEITING, with Treasury dreaming up ever more expensive formats of the BRAND. See also RECORKING.

J.H. & H.H.

Caillard, A., *The Rewards of Patience* (8th edn, 2020).

Hooke, H., *Max Schubert, Winemaker* (1994).

Penicillium, one of a group of FUNGI commonly found on rotten grapes. See BUNCH ROTS.

Península de Setúbal, VINHO REGIONAL in southern Portugal (called Terras do Sado until 2009) encompassing the SETÚBAL Peninsula between the Tagus and Sado estuaries and, to the south, the Troia Peninsula and a 60-km/37-mile stretch of the Alentejo Litoral (see PORTUGAL map). The warm MARITIME CLIMATE is particularly well suited to winemaking. In the 19th century, the north-facing slopes around the village of Azeitão were planted with several Moscatel (MUSCAT) varieties for sweet, FORTIFIED Setúbal, but, since this wine's decline in popularity, other varieties have largely taken their place.

Production is heavily concentrated in the hands of one of Portugal's best CO-OPERATIVES, Cooperativa Agrícola de Santo Isidro de Pegões, and three companies—José Maria da Fonseca, Bacalhôa Vinhos de Portugal (previously known as J. P. Vinhos), and Ermelinda Freitas—who have modernized the region's winemaking and vineyards. Accordingly, the Península de Setúbal now produces a wide range of wines, from well-established brands such as Periquita to single-estate wines such as Quinta da Bacalhôa.

Within the region is the Palmela DOC, which has two distinct TERROIRS: the LIMESTONE hills of the Serra da Arrabida, and the SANDY soils of the plain which extends eastwards from the fortress town of Palmela. Here, the widely planted, traditional CASTELÃO grape (which must represent at least two-thirds of any DOC red) can produce distinctive, full-bodied wines which develop savouriness and depth with bottle AGEING. Where the rules are more relaxed, Castelão (here nicknamed Periquita) has become less important, especially where Cabernet Sauvignon, Merlot, and Syrah (and for whites, Chardonnay) have been grown so successfully on the limestone Arrabida Hills. Vine varieties from northern Portugal have taken hold here, too, including

TOURIGA FRANCA, TOURIGA NACIONAL, and, for whites, ALVARINHO, VERDELHO, and ENCRUZADO, which augment local varieties ARINTO and FERNÃO PIRES. To the south (on the Troia Peninsula and in the Alentejo Litoral area) several ambitious estates were established in the early 21st century. The grapes of the ALENTEJO have been most popular, especially ALICANTE BOUSCHET, Aragones (TEMPRANILLO), and TRINCADEIRA—although one producer has made a name for itself with SANGIOVESE. Another is ageing wines under the ocean (see UNDERWATER AGEING). White and red wines here tend to be full-bodied; those benefiting from pronounced Atlantic influence can retain impressive acidity. S.A.

Mayson, R. J., *The Wines of Portugal* (2020).

Peninsulas, The. This wine zone and GEOGRAPHICAL INDICATION on the western edge of SOUTH AUSTRALIA takes in the Southern Eyre Peninsula and the Yorke Peninsula on either side of the Spencer Gulf.

Penning-Rowsell, Edmund (1913–2002), English wine writer with a scholarly interest in the history and wines of BORDEAUX in particular. Educated at Marlborough College and a lifelong socialist, he was a journalist on the *Morning Post* from 1930 until 1935, when he began a career of almost 30 years as a book publisher. He was introduced to the pleasures of wine when his wife's employer at the BBC gave her as a leaving present (only unmarried females were then regarded as suitable employees) some non-vintage MOULIN-À-VENT. Correspondence and eventual friendship with Bristol wine merchant Ronald Avery was another formative influence.

The traditional but non-profit-making ethos of the co-operative buying group the WINE SOCIETY suited him perfectly, and he joined the Society soon after his marriage in 1937. He served as its chairman from 1964 until 1987, a record length of time.

In 1949 he reviewed wine books for the *Times Literary Supplement* and in 1954 wrote his first wine article for the magazine *Country Life*. After 1964, soon after his publishing career came to an end, he became wine correspondent of the *Financial Times*, scrupulously refusing to mention the Wine Society during his chairmanship. His wine primer *Red, White and Rosé* was published in 1967, and a second edition appeared in 1973, but his great gift to the LITERATURE OF WINE is *The Wines of Bordeaux*, which was first published in 1969 and whose sixth edition appeared 20 years later.

Until his sight failed him, he meticulously recorded the facts of his remarkable cellar in a series of cellar books in his characteristic green ink. This unique archive included details of every purchase, every souvenir from his annual round of visits to the wine regions (continued into his ninth decade), and impressions of every bottle sampled.

A perennial figure in Bordeaux at vintage time and at the HOSPICES DE BEAUNE auction, Penning-Rowsell was made a Chevalier de l'Ordre du Mérite Agricole in 1971 and a Chevalier de l'Ordre du Mérite National in 1981.

Loftus, S., 'Purple prose: the wine writers', in *Anatomy of the Wine Trade* (1985).

Pennsylvania, state in the north-east United States ranking sixth nationwide in number of wineries and eighth (tied with NORTH CAROLINA) in volume of wine produced. The state's winemaking history dates to 1683, when William Penn, founder of the colony of Pennsylvania, planted a vineyard with VITIS VINIFERA varieties brought from Bordeaux. They quickly died, but the attempt spurred others, both English hoping to recreate CLARET and Germans homesick for RHENISH wine. Success came in the 1780s with Pierre Legaux, a French immigrant who, with the backing of shareholders including Alexander Hamilton and Aaron Burr, established a commercial winery and nursery with what he believed to be *vinifera* but turned out to be Alexander, a spontaneous *vinifera* × VITIS LABRUSCA hybrid thought to have originated from Penn's original plantings. While Legaux's business ultimately failed, vines from his nursery led to winegrowing ventures all over the east coast and the Midwest.

In 1870 Pennsylvania's industry reached its peak, at 440,971 l/97,000 gal of wine a year. A subsequent shift to growing CONCORD, used mainly for juice and jam, soon followed by PROHIBITION, decimated the industry.

Post-Prohibition, rebound was hampered by the state's Liquor Control Board, which tightly controls the production and distribution of all liquor within the state. It was not until 1968 with the establishment of the Limited Winery License that winemakers were allowed to sell a limited amount of wine directly to customers. From 11 wineries in 1976, there were more than 370 in 2022, with 5,665 ha/14,000 acres of vines.

Concord continues to dominate plantings, grown extensively in the north-western end of the state, in the Lake Erie AVA, shared with NEW YORK and OHIO. More important to the fine-wine industry are the AVAs in the south-east. Lehigh Valley, on a LIMESTONE basin along the east side of the Lehigh river, has well-drained SHALE and limestone soils and a moderate climate supportive of *vinifera* varieties such as RIESLING and CABERNET FRANC, although the local speciality is CHAMBOURCIN. Lancaster, to the south-west, is a continuation of that limestone basin, with richer soils and warmer temperatures.

Winemaking challenges across the state include FROST, humidity, FUNGAL DISEASES, and pests such as the SPOTTED LANTERNFLY and Spotted Wing DROSOPHILA. PennState College of Agricultural Sciences runs a robust research centre focused especially on east-coast vine-growing, including evaluation of disease-resistant and cold-hardy varieties and sustainable winegrowing.

Pinney, T., *A History of Wine in America: From the Beginnings to Prohibition* (1989).
pennsylvaniawine.com

pepper, a tasting term for two very different aromas commonly found in red wines. **Bell peppers**, or **green peppers**, is used characteristically in the US for the aroma of underripe CABERNET SAUVIGNON. A freshly sliced green pepper or capsicum liberates the chemical compound 2-isobutyl-3-methoxypyrazine (see METHOXYPYRAZINES), a vegetable-like or HERBACEOUS aroma to which many tasters have a very low threshold (see FLAVOUR COMPOUNDS).

Young wines made from the SYRAH grape, on the other hand, particularly if it does not reach full maturity, can smell of **black peppercorns**, while GRÜNER VELTLINER sometimes smells of white peppercorns. See ROTUNDONE.

Per'e Palummo. See PIEDIROSSO.

pergola, a form of overhead VINE TRAINING. Where the CANOPY is horizontal, the pergola can alternatively be called TENDONE. Pergola trellises can be either one- or two-armed, depending on whether the vines are trained on one or both sides of the row. If the trellis is joined overhead, it is called a closed pergola.

The pergola is widely used in northern Italy, where the canopies vary but are often inclined rather than horizontal (in Trentino, for example, the slope is 20–30 degrees). *Maggiorina* is an ancient and rare type of pergola found only in ALTO PIEMONTE, for example in BOCA. In Emilia-Romagna the **pergoletta** system is used, while the **pergoletta Capucci** was developed by the eponymous Bologna professor. The **pergoletta a Valenzano** is very similar to the GENEVA DOUBLE CURTAIN. Where the vines have marked VIGOUR, the bunches which hang below the leafy canopy are in SHADE, with predictable negative effects on wine quality. This century there has been a resurgence of interest in pergola systems. It does intercept most if not all SUNLIGHT and so has a high yield potential in marginal climates. The overhead leaf canopy may be an advantage as temperatures increase with CLIMATE CHANGE, and in AOSTA its value in protecting against HAIL has been noted. R.E.S.

pericarp, the 'fruit wall' forming the bulk of a plant's ovary, consisting of sugary flesh and highly coloured skin attractive to animals, especially BIRDS, with the result that the seeds are spread. In the grape berry, the whole fruit except for the seeds (both the skin and the flesh) constitutes the pericarp. See GRAPE for more details.

Pérignon, Dom (1639–1715), Benedictine monk who has gone down in history as 'the man who invented champagne'. The title is the stuff of fairy-tales: the transition from still to sparkling wine was an evolutionary process rather than a dramatic discovery on the part of one man. The life of Dom Pérignon was in fact devoted to improving the still wines of CHAMPAGNE, and he deserves his place in the history books for that reason. Father Pierre Pérignon arrived at the Abbey of Hautvillers, north of Épernay, in 1668. His role was that of bursar, and in the 17th century that included being in charge of the cellars. He collected tithes from surrounding villages in the form of grapes and wine, fermenting and blending until he created wines that sold for twice as much as those of the abbey's rivals. Dom Pérignon introduced many practices that survive in the process of modern wine production, among them severe PRUNING, low YIELDS, and careful harvesting. He also experimented to a great extent with the process and was one of the first to BLEND the produce of many different vineyards. Dom Pérignon produced still white wines, favouring black grapes because a second fermentation was less likely. Ironically, he was often thwarted in his endeavours by the refermentation process (see SECOND FERMENTATION), which produced the style of wine that was eventually to prove so popular. His fame as the 'inventor' of champagne probably spread after his death, embellished by Dom Grossard, the last bursar of the abbey, which closed at the time of the French Revolution. More modern champagne producers have jumped on the bandwagon, promoting the idea of a founder figure. Eugene Mercier registered the brand name Dom Pérignon before MOËT & CHANDON acquired it and used it to launch the first champagne marketed as a PRESTIGE CUVÉE, a 1921 vintage launched in 1936.

See also CHAMPAGNE. S.E.A.

Faith, N., *The Story of Champagne* (1988).
Johnson, H., *The Story of Wine: From Noah to Now* (2020).

Periquita, Portuguese word meaning 'parakeet' that is both a name for CASTELÃO in the PENÍNSULA DE SETÚBAL and a branded red wine from José Maria da FONSECA.

perlant, French term for a wine that is only slightly SPARKLING. **Perlwein** is the German equivalent. See FIZZINESS.

Perle, pink-berried, late-budding, rot-prone GERMAN CROSS of Gewürztraminer and Müller-Thurgau that can still be found in small pockets in Germany, mainly in FRANKEN.

Perlwein, German term for lightly SPARKLING wine, with a pressure inside the bottle of 1–2.5 bar. See FIZZINESS.

Pernand-Vergelesses, village in the Côte de Beaune district of Burgundy's CÔTE D'OR producing red and white wines. The former, made from Pinot Noir, now ripen more successfully than they did in the past. This was never a problem with the finest east-facing vineyard, Ile des Vergelesses, whence Pernand derives its suffix.

The most sought-after wines are the whites on the Pernand side of the hill of Corton (see ALOXE-CORTON). Seventeen of the 58 ha/143 acres entitled to the GRAND CRU appellation Corton-Charlemagne lie within Pernand-Vergelesses. White Pernand wines, made from Chardonnay, have a hard but attractive flinty character which develops well during bottle AGEING. As it ages, BOURGOGNE ALIGOTÉ from this area is said to resemble white Pernand-Vergelesses; and white Pernand to approach the quality of Corton-Charlemagne.

The most famous producer based in Pernand-Vergelesses is Bonneau du Martray, one of the top names in Corton-Charlemagne, while Domaines Dubreuil-Fontaine, Rapet, and Rollin also produce fine ranges of wine.

See also CÔTE D'OR and map under BURGUNDY. J.T.C.M.

peronospora, European name for the very important VINE DISEASE more usually called DOWNY MILDEW.

Perricone, north-west SICILIAN red grape variety whose total area stood at 521 ha/1,287 acres in 2020. Sometimes called by its synonym Pignatello, it has been shown by DNA PROFILING to be an offspring of SANGIOVESE.

Perricoota, riverine region on the northern banks of the Murray river in southern NEW SOUTH WALES.

Perrum. See PEDRO XIMÉNEZ.

Perruno, old, light-skinned Spanish variety from EXTREMADURA and one of the six traditional varieties recently added to those authorized for the production of SHERRY.

Persan, rare but promising SAVOIE red grape which can produce wines worth AGEING. Interest in it is also increasing in neighbouring ISÈRE.

Persia, Near Eastern country officially known as IRAN since 1935, which has known the consumption of wine since ancient times.

Ancient Persia

Much of this area was also known as MESOPOTAMIA in classical times. The earliest chemical evidence for grape wine comes from the Neolithic village of Hajji Firuz Tepe, about 5400–5000 BCE, in the northern Zagros Mountains of north-western Iran. Six jars in a kitchen of an average household would originally have held some 55 l/15 gal of wine, based on the presence of TARTARIC ACID which is found in large amounts in the Middle East only in grapes. The intended product was most likely wine and not vinegar or another grape product, because clay stoppers were used to close the narrow mouths of the jars and a tree resin, probably terebinth with antioxidant properties, was added to the wine as a preservative. Hajji Firuz was among the first year-round settlements based on newly domesticated plants and animals of the Neolithic period. The Eurasian VITIS VINIFERA grapevine might well have been one of those domesticates. The invention of pottery around 6000 BCE gave impetus to the process, since special vessels for preparing, storing, and serving wine could now be made. Similarly, two millennia later, pottery jars, one stored on its side, in rooms at the site of Godin Tepe, further south in the Zagros (dated to about 3500 BCE) in central western Iran, were shown to contain a resinated wine.

More detailed evidence is available from the era of the Achaemenid Dynasty, which ruled ancient Iran from *c.*559 to *c.*331 BCE. Cyrus the Great and Darius extended Persia's power to cover all the lands from the Mediterranean in the west to the river Indus in the east, incorporating the old empires of BABYLONIA and Assyria, which were overwhelmed and extended. Dating from the period just before Persia and Greece became embroiled in the Persian Wars, an enormous archive of documents written on clay tablets in the Elamite language preserves detailed records of the administration of the Achaemenid royal capital Persepolis from 509 to 494 BCE. Here there are records concerning the distribution of large quantities of (grape) wine and *sawur*, another (probably weaker) sort of wine. Sometimes the wine was stored at, or issued from, the ancient city of SHIRAZ, whose name is now associated with so many wines. Wine was normally released in monthly amounts, although in certain cases the issue was daily. One *marrish* (a measure of 10 quarts) of wine was valued at one shekel.

Such 'rations' often amounted to far more than one person could consume: perhaps they would be better described as salaries. Some were given to important women with households of their own to support: these received 30 quarts per month. King Darius writes in one order that 100 sheep and 500 gal of wine should be issued for the royal princess Artystone, no doubt in order for her to give a lavish banquet at her own court. Persian royal ladies were very independent and maintained their own establishments and dependants.

Generally wine was not given to boy and girl workers (who did, however, receive other rations including sometimes beer), except according to one document where some boys received one-third of a quart daily for 156 days. Otherwise the general allowance was 10 or 20 quarts monthly for men and 10 for women. Some labourers received a good deal less.

Presumably in an effort to increase the working-class population available for large-scale labour, special wine rations were provided under the Achaemenid Dynasty as a reward for women labourers who had just given birth to children: women who bore sons received 10 quarts, and those who bore daughters 5 quarts. The issue was sometimes spread out over the entire subsequent year.

Important caravans of diplomatic visitors accompanied by elite guides travelled from as far afield as Kandahar, India, Sardis, and Egypt. Those due to arrive at the capital Persepolis during the cooler months of the year (November to May), when the king and his entourage were in residence, were issued with travel rations to ease their arduous journey at the various stations at which they put up on the Royal Road. The records indicate that these, naturally, included generous amounts of wine.

On occasions wine was issued, along with grain and beer, for the benefit of the royal horses, perhaps when they were used for long journeys. The amounts issued varied from half a pint to 10 pints per animal per month. *Sawur* wine was even made available to the king's camels as an occasional concession.

In the 5th century BCE, HERODOTUS noted that the Achaemenids would make important decisions in a drunken state, then confirm these decisions when sober, and vice versa. The Persian empire was finally split up after the death of Alexander the Great in 323 BCE.

See also ORIGINS OF VINICULTURE and PALAEOETHNOBOTANY. J.A.B. & P.E.M.

Hallock, R. T., *Persepolis Fortification Tablets* (1969).

Shiraz as wine capital

The consumption of wine survived through the Sassanian Period, from the 3rd to the 7th centuries CE, influenced in part by Zoroastrian rite, and continued after the subsequent ISLAMIC conquest of the country.

Shiraz, a city rebuilt 50 km/30 miles from the site of Persepolis by the Arabs in the 8th century and the home town of Hāfiz, Persia's most famous mystic Bacchic poet (see ARAB POETS), had acquired a reputation by the 9th century for producing the finest wines in the Near East.

Thanks principally to the work of Edward Fitzgerald in the 19th century, the medieval polymath and poet OMAR KHAYYÁM has become famous in the west for poetry in which wine plays an important part.

From the diaries of 17th-century English and French travellers and especially the writings of C. J. Wills in the 19th century, we gain a picture of the excellence of some Persian wines. Tavernier (17th century) wrote: 'The wine of Shiraz has by far the greatest foreign as well as native celebrity, being of the quality of an old sherry and constitutes an excellent beverage.' In the same century, Thomas Herbert commented: 'No part of the world has wine better than Shiraz.'

The wine most often described and praised was white, made from thick-skinned, pip-filled grapes grown on terraces round the village of Khoullar, four days' camel ride away from Shiraz (those grown in the immediate vicinity of the city produced watery wine, thanks to excessive IRRIGATION). C. J. Wills describes a 19th-century replication of the traditional Shiraz winemaking process in some detail. The wine, fermented on the skins with regular PUNCHING DOWN, was made either sweet and fruity for long keeping, the stems being removed immediately after fermentation in used jars, or dry and rich in PHENOLICS for drinking in its first year or so. A form of FILTRATION through coarse canvas bags was practised. Wills describes the wine as 'like a light BUCELLAS' when young, to be avoided on account of the headaches it induces. After five years, however, it attains a 'fine aroma and bouquet' and 'nutty flavour'.

See also DRIED-GRAPE WINES, for the Persians were certainly in the habit of drying their grapes. P.K.

Hugh Johnson paints a fascinating and vivid picture of the export of wine from Shiraz to India by European merchants, in 1677 already in BOTTLES 'wrapped in straw and packed in cases... swaying down to the Gulf Coast on mule back. There is scarcely any earlier instance of the regular use of bottles for shipping wine.' Tavernier notes that the 1666 vintage was so bountiful that the Persian king gave permission to export as much wine to the French, English, Dutch, and Portuguese trading companies as was retained by himself and his court. Wine was measured in 'mans', units of weight rather than volume.

For an outline of modern viticulture, see IRAN.

Johnson, H., *The Story of Wine* (1989).
Planhol, X., 'Une rencontre de l'Europe et de l'Iran: le vin de Shiraz', in D. Boidanovic and J. L. Bacque-Grammont (eds.), *Iran* (1972).
Tavernier, J.-B., *Voyages en Perse* (1970).
Wills, C. J., *The Land of the Lion and the Sun* (1891).
Wills, C. J., *Persia As It Is* (1886).

Perth Hills, picturesque, rapidly growing warm region just east of Perth in WESTERN AUSTRALIA.

Peru, the first country in South America to have encouraged systematic viticulture. Under orders from the famous conquistador Francisco Pizarro, the first Peruvian vineyard was planted in about 1547. VINE VARIETIES were imported from Spain's CANARY ISLANDS, particularly Negra Criolla (see NEGRAMOLL), which is used today chiefly for PISCO. By the 1560s Peru is thought to have had 40,000 ha/99,000 acres under vine, producing so much wine that it was exported to other South American countries and even, according to one document, as far as Spain. One of the several ways by which viticulture spread to Argentina was from Peru, with Nuñez de Prado, a 16th-century Spanish conquistador.

The arrival of PHYLLOXERA in 1888 heralded the start of a serious decline in Peruvian viticulture. Only in the 1970s was progress made on establishing suitable planting material, and there are now NURSERIES at Ica, Chincha, Moquegua, and Tacna, as well as a national wine research centre, Centro de Innovación Tecnológica Vitivinícola (CITEVID).

According to OIV statistics, 48,000 ha/118,611 acres of Peru were planted with vines in 2020, yielding mainly TABLE GRAPES. In 2021 Peru had just over 40 wine producers dedicated to still wine production. The main wine producers are Tacama, with 187 ha/462 acres planted, and Queirolo, with 300 ha dedicated to INTERNATIONAL VARIETIES.

Almost all vines have traditionally been grown in Ica province south of Lima, close to the port of Pisco (which gives its name to the national drink). Winter temperatures in this area are so high (6–16 °C/43–60 °F) that full vine DORMANCY cannot be relied on. Summer temperatures are also high, 16–34 °C/60–93 °F in the hottest month, and rainfall is low. Wells have traditionally supplied IRRIGATION water, but levels are falling as DRIP IRRIGATION is being introduced. Yields may reach 12 tonnes/ha (5 tons/acre), but attempts are being made to upgrade techniques and wine quality.

By 2000, projects were also being developed in cooler areas such as Palpa, 100 km/62 miles south of Ica, where Syrah is promising, and Curahuasi, 125 km west of Cusco, where Apu Winery has vineyards planted in LIMESTONE soils at ELEVATIONS as high as 3,300 m/10,827 ft.

There has also been a rediscovery of traditional historical winemaking in areas such as Moquegua, Tacna, and Arequipa, regions in southern Peru that are home to the country's oldest vines, many pre-PHYLLOXERA. Producers are revisiting the CRIOLLAS; some, such as Valle de Caravelí in Arequipa, maintain the tradition of winemaking in clay TINAJAS. Moreover, there are diminutive producers, such as Murga in Pisco Valley and Moquillaza in Cañete and Ica, fully dedicated to vinifying Criolla wines. E.M.G.

Goldstein, E., *Wines of South America* (2014).

pervaporation, a combination of permeation and evaporation, is a two-stage membrane technology used for ALCOHOL REDUCTION that depends on dense silicone membranes which at about 30 °C/86 °F are particularly efficient at separating alcohol from water.

Castro-Muñoz, R., 'Pervaporation-based membrane processes for the production of non-alcoholic beverages', *Journal of Food Science and Technology*, 56 (2019), 2333–44.

Pessac-Léognan, important BORDEAUX appellation created in 1987 for red and dry white wines from the most celebrated part of the GRAVES district immediately south of the city. It takes its somewhat cumbersome name from its two vinously most important communes and includes all of the properties named in the 1959 CLASSIFICATION of Graves and many other fine châteaux too. This is Bordeaux's most urban wine area—indeed, the vineyards of its most famous property Ch HAUT-BRION and its neighbour and stablemate Ch La MISSION-HAUT-BRION are today surrounded by suburban development, including the campus of the University of BORDEAUX, on the boundary of the suburbs of Pessac and Talence. It is hardly surprising that Bordeaux's earliest wine estates were developed here, although the wines of Chx Haut-Brion, La Mission-Haut-Brion, and Pape-Clément justify the properties' existence on grounds far more solid than mere geographical convenience. Further from the city, vineyards are carved out of the pine forests which extend south-west into the Landes. In all, about 1,600 ha/3,952 acres of vineyard within Pessac-Léognan produce red wine, and the total area devoted to white wine grapes hovers around 280 ha/692 acres.

Soils here have particularly good DRAINAGE, being made up of GRAVEL terraces of very different eras. The ENCÉPAGEMENT for red wines is very similar to that of the MÉDOC to the immediate north, being mainly Cabernet Sauvignon grapes with some Merlot and Cabernet Franc, but the wines can be quite different. It is not fanciful to imagine that the best wines of Pessac-Léognan have a distinct aroma that reminds some tasters of minerals, some of smoke, others even of warm bricks. Ch Haut-Brion is the most obvious exponent of this genre. Other current over-achievers include Chx Pape-Clément, Smith Haut-Lafitte, and Haut-Bailly, while Chx de Fieuzal and La Louvière can provide some of Bordeaux's better value.

The region also makes some of the most characterful dry white wines in the world from Sauvignons Blanc and Gris, Sémillon, and Muscadelle grapes grown generally on the lighter, sandier parts of the vineyard, and often produced with considerable recourse to BARREL FERMENTATION and BARREL MATURATION. The most admired (Domaine de Chevalier and Chx Haut-Brion Blanc and La Mission-Haut-Brion Blanc) can develop in bottle over decades. J.R. & J.L.

Brook, S., *The Complete Bordeaux* (4th edn, 2022).
Penning-Rowsell, E., *The Wines of Bordeaux* (6th edn, 1989).

pesticides, substances or mixtures of substances applied to vineyards which are used to prevent, destroy, repel, or reduce the harmful effects of FUNGI, BACTERIA, INSECTS, NEMATODES, or other undesirable organisms regarded as VINE PESTS. Pesticides are made up of AGROCHEMICALS and biocontrols (see BIOLOGICALS) and are usually classified according to their principal use as, for example, fungicides, bactericides, insecticides, nematicides, miticides, etc. Many pesticides have more than one mode of action and may be effective against more than one type of pest. For example, SULFUR is both a fungicide and a miticide in vineyards.

Most pesticides consist of an active chemical constituent in a concentrated form that is suitable for use after mixing with a diluent (water or oil). Less often, pesticides are formulated as dusts, granules, or fumigants and require DUSTING rather than SPRAYING. For reasons of worker safety, there is a move away from these latter formulations. Mixtures of active ingredients may be combined in one product for greater efficacy or versatility: two chemicals may be mixed, for example, to produce a DOWNY MILDEW fungicide with both protectant and eradicant properties. For convenience, two or more pesticides may be combined in a spray mixture. However, problems due to chemical incompatibility may arise when different pesticides are mixed.

Pesticides are, to varying degrees, toxic chemicals, and their potentially harmful effects on humans, other animals, and non-target organisms in the environment must be recognized. Since the 1990s, increasing attention has been paid to the safety of vineyard workers and the environment, with chemicals classified according to toxicity and workers taught safe handling practices. Recycling spray machines are increasingly used to minimize drift on to the environment. See also RESIDUES.

The following factors should be taken into consideration when developing strategies for pesticide use in vineyards: use patterns, rates, the potential development of pesticide resistance, and potential effects on non-target organisms. Use patterns may involve routine application schedules or more flexible strategies that rely on pest warning services and/or the monitoring of pest activity, as in INTEGRATED PEST MANAGEMENT. Such flexible strategies are often adopted to minimize pesticide use.

The continuous use of some pesticides may result in a dramatic increase in the proportion of individuals in a pest population that are able to survive exposure to the pesticide. Chemical resistance is the inherited ability of an organism—be it a disease, weed or insect—to survive doses of an agrochemical that would normally control it. An example has been the development of resistance by the BOTRYTIS fungus to the fungicide Benomyl and also to the dicarboximide group of fungicides. Recognition that increasing the rate or frequency of sprays of some agrochemicals often exacerbates the problem led to the development of resistance management strategies. These include limits to the number of sprays per season of particular agrochemicals, rotation of chemical applications or stipulations that certain chemicals are used only when tank-mixed with other chemicals active against the target pest. These spray programmes have been proven to delay or prevent the development of pest resistance.

See also FUNGICIDES. P.R.D. & M.E.

Emmett, R. W., et al., 'Grape diseases and vineyard protection', in B. G. Coombe and P. R. Dry (eds.), *Viticulture*, ii: *Practices* (2nd edn, 2006).

pests of vineyards. See VINE PESTS.

Petaluma Gap, low spot within California's coastal mountains at the southern boundary of Sonoma County and northern edge of MARIN County that channels cool ocean air and fog into the region; also an AVA. See SONOMA.

pétillant, French term for a lightly sparkling wine, somewhere between PERLANT and MOUSSEUX.

pétillant naturel, lightly sparkling wine which, unlike most other sparkling wines, is the result of a single fermentation that starts in a tank or other FERMENTATION VESSEL, is then interrupted by chilling, and finishes in the bottle, hence the bubbles. They are often relatively low in alcohol and usually dry even if more traditional styles of wine made by the MÉTHODE ANCESTRALE typically contain some RESIDUAL SUGAR. The style has been enthusiastically embraced by producers of NATURAL WINE, who have coined the term PET-NAT for it. A wide range of very varied examples of this increasingly popular style are now made all over the world of wine. See also MONTLOUIS.

petiole, the stalk of a plant's leaf which supports the leaf blade or lamina. Petioles are stem tissue and branch from the main stem of the shoot having similar anatomical features. At both ends of the petiole are swellings that alter the position of the leaf blade according to such stimuli as water stress and low light. Samples of petioles taken at FLOWERING are used as a basis for assessing a vine's status in terms of VINE NUTRITION.

The characteristics of petioles vary with vine variety and growing conditions, being longer on vigorous vines. Between varieties, petiole length varies from 5 to 20 cm/2 to 8 in, petiole colour varies from green to red, and petioles themselves may vary from smooth to hairy. These features help in the identification of varieties (see AMPELOGRAPHY). B.G.C.

petit, 'small' in French and therefore often encountered in wine and grape names.

petit château. See PETITS CHÂTEAUX.

Petit Courbu, ancient, rescued white Basque grape variety capable of adding body, aroma, and quality to the wines of BÉARN, IROULÉGUY, JURANÇON, and PACHERENC DU VIC-BILH as well as those of ST-MONT. Known as Hondarrabi Zuri Zerratia in Spain's Basque country (see TXAKOLI).

Distinct from COURBU.

Petite Arvine. See ARVINE.

Petite Sirah, name common in both North and South America, and first mentioned in California wine literature in the early 1880s, for a related group of black grape varieties. DNA PROFILING techniques suggested in the late 1990s that the name had been applied in California vineyards to no fewer than four different vines: mainly DURIF but also true SYRAH of the Rhône, PELOURSIN (an obscure French vine which turned out to be Durif's parent), and even PINOT NOIR.

Petite Sirah is relatively important in a wide range of warm wine regions, especially in California. It is also grown in Australia (see DURIF) and in Chile, and OLD VINES show its potential in Israel. In California, acreage declined until the mid 1990s then began to climb again, reaching 1,781 ha/4,400 acres by 2003 and then more than doubling to 4,842 ha/11,964 acres by 2020, mostly in Sonoma, Paso Robles, Amador, Mendocino, and Napa. Accurate acreage assessment is difficult because so many of the old Italian vineyards were planted with a mixture of different varieties (see FIELD BLEND).

Historically, Petite Sirah was established in California to bring structure and depth to ZINFANDEL field blends. In the 1990s, its potential for dark, well-balanced, sturdy red wine was revealed in VARIETAL wines. Like Cabernet Sauvignon, it has also been essential as a backbone for some everyday red blends, providing both colour and TANNINS, and producers such as Ridge, Freemark Abbey, and Souvrain have shown it ages impressively well. Some winemakers are now also experimenting with lighter-bodied styles as well as rosé. Petite Sirah grows best in well-drained soils, especially in DRY-FARMED vineyards with HEAD-TRAINED vines. California producers started a promotional push for the grape in 2004 called P.S. I Love You. In MEXICO it is championed by L. A. Cetto.

Petit Manseng, top-quality white grape variety originally from SOUTH WEST FRANCE which is the superior form of MANSENG. Petit Manseng, which is much more suitable for sweet wines than its probable progeny GROS MANSENG, has particularly small, thick-skinned berries which yield very little juice (sometimes less than 15 hl/ha, although up to 40 hl/ha (2.3 tons/acre) is allowed for both JURANÇON and PACHERENC DU VIC-BILH, and even higher for dry wines) but can withstand lingering on the vine until well into autumn, or even December, so that the sugar is concentrated, resulting in shrivelled (i.e. PASSERILLÉ) grapes. The variety is however sensitive to both POWDERY MILDEW and DOWNY MILDEW. By 2019 France's total plantings had grown to 1,484 ha/3,667 acres, although those of Gros Manseng were nearly 4,000 ha. It is known as Iskiriota Zuri Tipia over the border in Spain's Basque country (see TXAKOLI).

The variety, which makes firm, distinctively tangy, often slightly green-hued wines of all SWEETNESS levels, has already been planted to a limited extent in the LANGUEDOC, central Italy, Virginia, California, Georgia, Australia, New Zealand, and Argentina.

Petit Meslier, ancient and almost extinct white variety cultivated in CHAMPAGNE. It used to produce fruity wines, but it has fallen out of favour because of its naturally low yields. DNA PROFILING at DAVIS showed in 2000 that Petit Meslier is a progeny of GOUAIS BLANC and SAVAGNIN. A tiny amount persists in Australia.

Petit Rouge, fine, ancient, dominant, INDIGENOUS VARIETY in the Valle d'AOSTA, making fruity, spicy red wines. Plantings totalled 68 ha/168 acres in 2015.

petits châteaux, a French term meaning literally 'small castles', has a very specific meaning in the BORDEAUX wine region. These thousands of properties are modest both in their extent and in their reputation and price. A CLASSED GROWTH or equivalent is emphatically not a petit château, no matter how few hectares it encompasses, and nor is a CRU BOURGEOIS. The greatest concentration of petits châteaux, invariably family-owned and run, is in the Bordeaux AOC and Côtes de BORDEAUX appellations, although they are found throughout the region. Some of Bordeaux's best wine value is to be found at the most conscientious petits châteaux.

See also CHÂTEAU.

Petit Verdot is one of BORDEAUX's classic black grape varieties. Plantings may be way below those of Cabernet Sauvignon and Merlot, but it is enjoying a revival, in part as a result of CLIMATE CHANGE, and at some estates is starting to replace Cabernet Franc as an influential blending ingredient, particularly on the LEFT BANK. The vine ripens even later than Cabernet Sauvignon and is equally resistant to ROT, sharing Cabernet Sauvignon's thick skins. When it ripens fully, it yields concentrated, tannic, ageworthy wines rich in colour, sometimes rather spicy, but in a cool year it can add a distinctly raw, underripe note to a blend. Its inconveniently late ripening encouraged many producers to abandon it in the 1960s and 1970s so that total French plantings were just over 300 ha/740 acres in 1988, but by 2019 they had increased to more than 1,615 ha/3,991 acres, 1,235 ha of these in the Gironde.

Its qualities are increasingly recognized elsewhere. It is well suited to warm, dry parts of Spain such as CASTILLA-LA MANCHA, where most of the 2020 total of 2,206 ha/5,451 acres are planted. The pioneer was Marqués de Griñon near Toleda. Italy's total plantings also increased in the first decade of the 21st century but were still only 296 ha/731 acres by 2015, while even Portugal, not usually a great fan of INTERNATIONAL VARIETIES, grew 307 ha/759 acres, mainly for blends in the ALENTEJO, by 2020. Outside Europe, it is proving popular in ISRAEL, particularly in high-end blends. It has performed exceptionally well in VARIETAL form in the irrigated inland regions of AUSTRALIA, where by the mid 2000s plantings totalled more than 1,600 ha—although this had fallen to 1,108 ha by 2022. In California, where the state's total plantings were more than 1,403 ha/3,467 acres by 2020, mainly in NAPA and the SAN JOAQUIN VALLEY, it has so far been used mainly as an ingredient in MERITAGE blends. WASHINGTON State has much less and also tends to use it in BORDEAUX BLENDS, while a number of VIRGINIA producers make a speciality of varietal versions. It is also planted on Long Island in NEW YORK and in Canada's British Columbia, but it does need a warm summer. It is therefore well suited to both Argentina and Chile, where 650 ha and 904 ha respectively are grown and varietal versions of 'Verdot' (which may include the inferior GROS VERDOT) abound, and to South Africa where total plantings stood at 734 ha in 2020, concentrated in the prime regions of Paarl and Stellenbosch, where Petit Verdot is welcomed as a seasoning for a Bordeaux blend.

pet-nat, name coined by the NATURAL WINE movement for an amorphous group of very varied lightly sparkling wines, occasionally with some RESIDUAL SUGAR. They may well be cloudy if the wines have not been disgorged (see SPARKLING WINEMAKING). See PÉTILLANT NATUREL.

Petri disease, fungal disease found in young vines (generally younger than five years old) caused by several Ascomycete species, including *Cadophora luteo-olivacea*, *Phaeomoniella chlamydospore*, and *Phaeoacremonium* spp., with *Phaeoacremonium minimum* being the most prevalent. Named after Italian plant pathologist Lionello Petri (1875–1946), who discovered it in 1912. Affected vines appear stunted and weak and show greatly reduced tolerance of stress. Internal symptoms are primarily found in the ROOTSTOCK or at the basal end of the trunk in UNGRAFTED VINES and are characterized by dark brown and/or black streaking of the wood. Though spores of *P. chlamydospora* and *P. minimum* are known to infect pruning wounds in mature vineyards,

P

it has been well documented that infections can originate and spread during the PROPAGATION process in NURSERIES. Vines may be asyptomatic until the fungus becomes virulent under stress conditions. Clean propagation planting material and the avoidance of stress during the first years of vineyard establishment help to minimize the impact of this disease. See also TRUNK DISEASES. J.R.U.-T.

Gubler W. D., et al., 'Esca, Petri, and grapevine leaf stripe disease', in W. F. Wilcox et al. (eds.), *Compendium of Grape Diseases, Disorders, and Pests* (2nd edn, 2015), 52–7.

Petrus, the most famous wine of POMEROL and today the most expensive in BORDEAUX.

In the heart of the small Pomerol plateau, Petrus was bought in stages from 1922, by Mme Loubat, wife of the owner of the Hôtel-Restaurant Loubat in Libourne. By 1949 it consisted of 6.5 ha/16.8 acres planted with 70% MERLOT vines and 30% CABERNET FRANC. In 1969, 5 ha were purchased from the adjoining Ch Gazin. Although it won a gold medal at the Paris International Exhibition in both 1878 and 1889, and although the London-based WINE SOCIETY listed the 1893, Petrus received little international attention until the remarkable, tiny crop of 1945 and the much more widely distributed 1947. Its exceptional concentration of colour, bouquet, and richness of flavour derives from a pocket of CLAY in the middle of the vineyard and the subsoil which affords exceptionally good DRAINAGE.

However, its fame is largely due to M. Jean-Pierre MOUEIX of the Libourne merchants, who started his business before the Second World War. He took over the sole distribution of Petrus in 1952. After Mme Loubat died in 1961, Jean-Pierre Moueix purchased from her nephew in 1964 50% of the shareholding, which Jean-Pierre's elder son Jean-François Moueix inherited in 1969. The other 50% went to Mme Loubat's niece Mme Lily Lacoste, to be acquired by Jean-François in 2001. His son Jean is now in charge of Petrus. Olivier, son of the distinguished OENOLOGIST Jean-Claude Berrouet, manages the property and is in charge of winemaking. The limited size of the property means that all the grapes can be harvested, at optimum ripeness, in a day and a half if necessary.

FERMENTATION VESSELS are neither wood nor stainless steel, but CONCRETE.

There is no official CLASSIFICATION of Pomerol, but Petrus is unofficially recognized as a PREMIER CRU. It tends to fetch a much higher price than any other red bordeaux (although see LE PIN), and at AUCTION it achieves even higher prices relative to the rest. In 2012, a rather grander building superseded Petrus's modest farmhouse.

Petrus de Crescentiis (1230–1310), Italian author whose writings on wine were much read in the Middle Ages (see LITERATURE OF WINE). Petrus de Crescentiis finished his *Liber ruralium commodorum* ('Book on agriculture') *c.*1304. Only part of this work, Book 4, is concerned with wine. He knows and quotes from the classical writers on agriculture (mainly PLINY, COLUMELLA, and VARRO), but he is no mere slavish follower of his authorities, for he has a great deal to say about medieval WINEMAKING practice and his advice is reliable.

The ancients loved old wine, but Petrus knew that medieval wine was a different matter; if wine was kept in a wooden BARREL instead of an impermeable earthenware AMPHORA, it would not last long. Most medieval wine was drunk within a year of the vintage, but sweet or highly alcoholic wines, as some Mediterranean wines were, kept longer. Petrus divides wines into three categories: new (under a year); old (four years); and between new and old. New wine, he says, has no digestive or diuretic properties but inflates the belly. Old wine is bitter and can be off; unless it is mixed with water, it goes to the head. Two-year-old wine is best. Petrus also points out that TOPPING UP casks of wine is essential in order to stop the wine turning into VINEGAR; alternatively, a layer of olive oil can be floated on the surface of the wine. He also explains how to achieve the RACKING of a wine from one cask into another.

Given the soundness of his advice and the clarity of his prose style, it is not surprising that Petrus's book should have been popular. It survives in many manuscripts and early printed editions. By the end of the 15th century, it had been translated into German, French, and Italian. H.M.W.

Marescalchi, A., and Dalmasso, G. (eds.), *Storia della vite e del vino in Italia*, 3 vols. (1933).
Savastano, L. G., *Il contributo allo studio critico degli scrittori agrari italici* (1922).

Peynaud, Émile (1912–2004), Bordeaux oenologist whose work had a profound and worldwide impact on winemaking and wine appreciation in the second half of the 20th century. After the Second World War, Peynaud worked with Jean RIBÉREAU-GAYON before joining him at BORDEAUX University's Institut d'Oenologie, while employed by the house of Calvet. It was here, in the late 1940s, that he began to advise numerous BORDEAUX châteaux on their winemaking. Because this CONSULTANCY work was the activity for which he later became best known, it is perhaps easy to forget his achievements as a taster, scientist, and teacher.

Peynaud wanted to understand the detail of the winemaking process, to eliminate its hitherto haphazard nature, and to produce consistently clean-tasting and healthy wines. Many of the practices that now seem unexceptional in winemaking were by no means axiomatic in the 1950s, and they are rooted in changes resulting from his wide-ranging scientific research. Among these were the complete control of MALOLACTIC CONVERSION, as well as the understanding that quality starts in the vineyard with good-quality grapes, that red grapes should be fully ripe when picked, and that dark grapes' skins (containing the PHENOLICS so crucial to red-wine aromas and textures) should be treated more gently with softer CRUSHING, better-controlled fermentation temperatures, shorter MACERATION, and more moderate PRESSING of the skins for the PRESS WINE. Each technique aimed at improving the flavour and texture of the resulting finished wine.

Taste became the arbiter in winemaking decisions, and it underlay his other cardinal principle: selection. Select only healthy grapes when picking, vinify the produce of plots of vines of markedly different age or quality separately, choose only the best vats to be incorporated in the principal wine, and so on. This was the subject of his first book, *Connaissance et travail du vin*.

Peynaud considered that the ability to taste accurately was as essential to good winemaking as a thorough grasp of OENOLOGY. His second book, *Le Goût du vin*, was as comprehensive and lucid on tasting wine as his first book was on making it.

As with his pupil Michel ROLLAND, critics used to complain that his winemaking methods so marked the wines that they were losing their individuality, but mature bottles tended to show genuine distinction and individuality.

Peynaud would have left his mark on the wine world had his gifts been limited to scientist, technician, and possessor of a refined palate; that his influence has been so widespread is due to his additional great gift as a teacher and communicator. M.W.E.S.

Peynaud, É., *Connaissance et travail du vin* (5th edn, 2021).
Peynaud, É., *Le Goût du vin* (1983), translated by M. Schuster as *The Taste of Wine* (2nd edn, 1996).

Pézenas, small, named CRU in the LANGUEDOC AOC producing red wines mainly from Syrah, Mourvèdre, and Grenache at lower ELEVATIONS than some of the other crus just to its north.

Pfalz, until 1992 known as Rheinpfalz, is the second largest wine region in GERMANY. Its 23,684 ha/58,524 acres of vineyard in 2019 abutt RHEINHESSEN to the north and follow the eastern edge of the Haardt range (a northern extension of ALSACE's Vosges) for about 80 km/50 miles (see map under GERMANY) along the so-called Deutsche Weinstrasse, or German Wine Route, officially established in 1935 to link 40 villages. Relatively sunny and dry, Pfalz has long been a mecca for German TOURISTS but has since the 1980s acquired a national and

P

international reputation as an innovative and exciting winegrowing region buoyed by demand for its red and dry white wines and by the proximity of prosperous metropolitan Mannheim, Ludwigshafen, and Karlsruhe. Of the roughly 10,000 vine-growers in the region, over half deliver their grapes to producers' associations, merchants' cellars, or one of more than 15 CO-OPERATIVES, of which a number boast not only high standards but also significant shares of top vineyards. Not to be underestimated is the continuing influence of Müller-Catoir ex-cellarmaster Hans-Günter Schwarz, whose principles of 'minimalism in the cellar, activism in the vines' have been imparted to two generations of vineyard managers and winemakers who today fill dozens of the most important positions throughout the Pfalz. The Pfalz has also proven fertile 21st-century ground for BIODYNAMIC VITICULTURE: several members of the growers' association respekt-Biodyn are Pfälzer, including long-running VDP president Steffen Christmann and VDP-Pfalz chairman Hansjörg Rebholz.

The vineyards to the north of Neustadt, collectively known as the Mittelhaardt, are the best known in the Pfalz, in large part thanks to wine estates with such historic reputations as Bassermann-Jordan, Bürklin-Wolf, and von Buhl. The top sites of the Mittelhaardt villages largely nestle between the western edge of the villages and the lower slopes of the Haardt, on SANDSTONE, VOLCANIC, and CALCAREOUS marl soils. From south to north, they include: Neustadt (Vogelsang), Haardt (Bürgergarten, Mandelring), Gimmeldingen (Mandelgarten), Königsbach (Idig, Ölberg), Ruppertsberg (Nussbien, Gaisböhl, Hoheburg, Reiterpfad), Deidesheim (Paradiesgarten, Leinhöhle, Hohenmorgen, Kieselberg, Mäushöhle, Grainhübel, Kalkofen), Forst (Ungeheuer, Freundstück, Kirchenstück, Jesuitengarten, Pechstein), Wachenheim (Altenburg, Gerümpel, Goldbächel, Rechbächel), Bad Dürkheim (Michelsberg), Ungstein (Herrenberg, Weilberg), and Kallstadt (Saumagen). While vineyards on the hilly western side of the Weinstrasse north of Kallstadt are relatively little known, those of twin villages Zell and Zellertal are undergoing impressive revival.

The low, rolling calcareous and SANDY hills east of the Weinstrasse—notably at Laumersheim (Kirschgarten, Mandelberg), Grosskarlbach (Burgweg), and Freinsheim—have also demonstrated their ability to generate memorable wines. South of Neustadt, the so-called Südliche Weinstrasse long endured a reputation for high yields of indifferent grape varieties, but—thanks above all to the ambitions of local winegrowers and a boom in dry wines from SPÄTBURGUNDER (Pinot Noir), GRAUBURGUNDER (Pinot Gris), WEISSBURGUNDER (Pinot Blanc) as well as RIESLING—this cooler area has become increasingly fashionable. Top villages (and sites), from south to north, include: Ilbesheim (Kalmit), Birkweiler (Kastanienbusch, Mandelberg), Siebeldingen (Im Sonnenschein), Gleisweiler (Hölle), Burrweiler (Schäwer), and Weyher (Michelsberg). The village of Schweigen, 19 km south of Ilbesheim and adjacent to the small Alsace city of Wissembourg, represents an important anomaly: most of the vineyards with which Schweigen developed its serious late 20th century reputation for Pinot Noir lie within France but are farmed by German estates and authorized to produce German wine.

High YIELDS, MECHANICAL HARVESTING, and a reliance on such CROSSES as MÜLLER-THURGAU, KERNER, and MORIO-MUSKAT were long associated with the Pfalz. But Riesling, always dominant in the prestigious towns of the Mittelhaardt, has staged a comeback and now accounts for one-quarter of vine surface. Red-wine vines gained ground rapidly from the 1990s and now account for just over one-third of Pfalz production. Pinot Noir (Spätburgunder), Weissburgunder, and Grauburgunder now collectively represent just over 20% of Pfalz plantings. SCHEUREBE may be statistically relatively insignificant, but, as with RIESLANER, there are impressive examples as well as signs of a revival, though both have been threatened with removal from Germany's list of authorized varieties. TRAMINER, traditionally associated with the Pfalz, has failed in recent decades to mirror its success in neighbouring Alsace, but the best examples, dry and sweet, can still be excellent.

Across the region, most wine produced is now dry (TROCKEN), as befits both climate and demand. This explains why this region has been a leader in advocating the establishment of GROSSES GEWÄCHS, full-bodied, dry wines (principally Riesling) from the best sites. But the second decade of the 21st century has seen a marked revival of interest in Riesling bottled with some RESIDUAL SUGAR, including KABINETT. Pfalz red wines including Spätburgunder today typically exceed 13% alcohol, and BARREL AGEING is common, although there remains a local market for the traditional, light red as well as pink WEISSHERBST from PORTUGIESER (steadily shrinking and just 5.4% in 2019). DORNFELDER plantings increased five-fold between 1990 and 2015 so that it is now Pfalz's second most planted variety though the resulting wines are generally undistinguished. An increasing amount of Pfalz wine is made sparkling (see SEKT). Standards for sparkling Sekt have been set high, not least by the Sektkellerei Schloss Wachenheim, which specializes in TRADITIONAL METHOD renderings of their own and other growers' generally high-quality base wines, especially from Riesling, Weissburgunder, and Spätburgunder. D.S.

Pigott, S., et al., *Wein Spricht Deutsch: Weine, Winzer, Weinlandschaften* (2007).
Reinhardt, S., *The Finest Wines of Germany* (2012).

PGI, abbreviation for **Protected Geographical Indication**, a wine category created in 2008 as part of the EU wine reform. It encompasses what used to be known as TABLE WINES with a GEOGRAPHICAL INDICATION such as France's VIN DE PAYS, Italy's IGT, Spain's VINO DE LA TIERRA, and Germany's LANDWEIN. In 2020 PGI wines accounted for roughly 20% of total EU wine production. The equivalent abbreviation in many other countries, including France, Spain, Italy, and Portugal, is IGP, although the speed with which the reformed terminology has been adopted varies by country.

The qualifying criteria for a PGI are lower than those for the PDO, or Protected Designation of Origin category. A PGI need only 'possess a specific quality, reputation or other characteristics attributable to [its] geographical origin', in line with the international definition of a geographical indication. A minimum of 85% of the grapes must come from the delimited area, and these may be either VITIS VINIFERA or a CROSS between *vinifera* and other VITIS species. PGIs enjoy special privileges in the EU wine system, including protection against misuse as well as the right to use TRADITIONAL TERMS and the special EU PGI symbol on the label.

Non-EU countries are, in theory, able to register their own geographical indications as PGIs in Europe, although very few choose to go through the registration process because in most cases mutual protection of GIs is agreed with the EU through bilateral wine agreements or free-trade agreements. J.P.H.B.

www.ec.europa.eu/info/food-farming-fisheries/food-safety-and-quality/certification/quality-labels/geographical-indications-register

pH, a scale of measurement of the concentration of the effective, active ACIDITY in a solution and an important statistic, of relevance to how vines grow, how grapes ripen, and how wine tastes, looks, and lasts. Low values of pH indicate high acidity and the tart or sour taste that occurs in lemon juice, for example. Values near 7 are effectively neutral; drinking waters have pH values near 7. Values between 7 and 14 are found in basic or alkaline solutions such as caustic or washing soda. Grape must and wine are acidic, with pHs generally between 3 and 4. pH is the negative logarithm of the hydrogen ion concentration, so a solution with a pH value of 3 has ten times as much hydrogen ion activity as one whose pH is 4.

Soils

Soil pH measures the acidity or alkalinity of a soil. It can be approximately measured in the vineyard using a pH test kit comprising barium sulfate powder and a pH indicator dye, or more accurately in a laboratory in a soil–water suspension or in dilute calcium chloride. Acid soils have a pH less than 7 and alkaline soils a pH greater than 7. Soils formed on acidic parent materials (see SOIL), such as GRANITIC rocks or highly weathered SANDSTONES, generally have acid pH values, whereas those formed on basic parent materials, such as LIMESTONE, BASALT, or dolerite, generally have alkaline pH values. The optimum pH range for grapevines is from 5.5 to 8 (in water) and approximately 0.6–0.8 units lower in calcium chloride solution. Within this range, the possibility of aluminium toxicity (at low pH) or micronutrient deficiency (at high pH) is avoided. However, grapevines are tolerant of soil pH outside this range. There is no evidence of a direct link between soil pH and wine pH. See also SOIL ACIDITY and SOIL ALKALINITY. R.E.W.

White, R. E., *Understanding Vineyard Soils* (2nd edn, 2015).

Grapes

The pH of grapes as well as wines can vary enormously since TEMPERATURE, RAINFALL, SOIL TYPE, viticultural practices, and VINE VARIETIES can all influence the different natural organic acids and minerals of ripe grapes. In general, cool regions produce wines with low pH and hot regions produce wines with high pH. Part of the reason why white wines generally have a lower pH than red wines is that red wines have higher levels of POTASSIUM, which is extracted from the grape skin, where this ion is concentrated, during fermentation. See also GRAPE and ACIDITY.

The pH of grape juice is now well established as a factor affecting wine quality. In particular, high pH values are associated with low acidity, and red wine quality in particular is diminished (see below).

Wines

The pH range of most wines is between 2.9 and 4.2. The perception of acidity or tartness is determined by both the pH and TOTAL ACIDITY. Usually a wine with a higher total acidity will also have a lower pH, but many factors can affect the relationship between the two (soil POTASSIUM, warmth of climate, SHADE during ripening, RIPENESS at harvest, SKIN CONTACT). Wines with a lower pH are less hospitable to harmful BACTERIA, age better, and have a clearer, brighter COLOUR (see below). Wines with higher pH values tend to taste flat, look dull, and be more susceptible to bacterial attack. In the last 20 years, average pH levels have risen considerably as a result of longer HANG TIME and a FASHION for riper wines. While it is possible to manipulate pH values, with grapes and wines it can sometimes be difficult to get both the pH and the total acidity in the desirable range or balance. The pH can be increased or decreased by several methods. (See ACIDIFICATION and DEACIDIFICATION for discussion of the legal and practical aspects of these operations.)

In general terms most YEASTS are tolerant of wine pH, while few bacteria are capable of growing in the strongly acidic environment that wine presents (even fewer with the alcohol levels found in wine).

Keeping wine pH values low is of further importance because the hydrogen ion concentration of the wine influences the effectiveness of SULFUR DIOXIDE. Sulfur dioxide exists in equilibria in multiple forms in wine. It is only the molecular sulfur dioxide form that has antimicrobial effect. The ratio of molecular sulfur dioxide is much higher at low pH; for example, at pH 3, 6% of the sulfur dioxide is in the molecular form, whereas at pH 4, only 0.6% is in that form.

Awareness of pH is also important in winemaking because the PIGMENTED TANNINS that colour red wines exist (like the monomeric ANTHOCYANINS from which they are formed) in several forms of different colours. At low pH values, the high concentration of hydrogen ions forces the pigment molecule into a form with a positive charge and a bright red colour. As pH increases (and hydrogen ion concentration decreases), the pigment molecules tend more and more to change through dull purple to blue and, ultimately, greyish forms. The net result in the several pigments of red wine is a passage from bright to purplish red and finally to a dull brownish red as pH increases. M.J.T.

phenolic ripeness, or **phenological ripeness**. See PHYSIOLOGICAL RIPENESS.

phenolics, very large group of highly reactive chemical compounds of which **phenol** (C_6H_5OH) is the basic building block. These include many natural colour pigments such as the ANTHOCYANINS of fruit and dark-skinned grapes, vegetable TANNINS such as occur in grapes, and many FLAVOUR COMPOUNDS.

The terms **polyphenolics** or **polyphenols** are often used as synonyms of phenolics but should be restricted to plant secondary metabolites featuring more than one phenolic ring and derived from specific metabolic pathways, as Quideau et al. explain.

In grapes

These compounds occur in great profusion in grapes. They are particularly rich in stems, seeds, and skins but also occur in juice and pulp. The concentration of phenolics in grape skins increases if the berries are exposed to sunlight, in particular to ULTRAVIOLET RADIATION, because the phenolic compounds act as a natural sunscreen. Phenolic compounds strongly absorb ultraviolet radiation, a fact used in their laboratory analysis. Manipulating fruit exposure in the vineyard is therefore a way to affect the phenolic content of berries and wine made from them. See CANOPY MANAGEMENT.

Many hundreds of compounds belong to the phenolic category, and they can initially be classified as either non-flavonoid or FLAVONOID. The former include compounds derived from cinnamic and benzoic acids (one of the most abundant in grape juice is caftaric acid, the tartrate ESTER of caffeic acid) and stilbenes such as RESVERATROL. Flavonoids encompass CATECHINS and their polymers, called PROANTHOCYANIDINS or condensed tannins, which are an essential part of the taste and flavour of grapes and other fruits, and pigments, including FLAVONOLS and anthocyanins. With a few exceptions, such as the phenolic amino acid tyrosine that is a constituent of proteins, phenolics belong to the general group known as secondary metabolites, meaning that they are not involved in the primary metabolism of the plant. They are highly water-soluble and are secreted into the berry VACUOLE, many as GLYCOSIDES, and some are FLAVOUR PRECURSORS or precursors of off-flavours. B.G.C. & V.C.

In wines

Phenolic acids (especially cinnamic acids) are the major phenolics in grape pulp and juice and, thus, also in white wines made without SKIN CONTACT. Anthocyanins are localized only in the skins, except in red-fleshed *teinturiers*, so that red winemaking requires a MACERATION phase to extract them into the juice. Flavonols, which are constituents of skins, stems, and leaves, as well as catechins and proanthocyanidins, which are also present in seeds, are simultaneously extracted. Alcohol, produced by FERMENTATION, greatly speeds up this extraction process. Additional phenolics (including gallotannins and ellagitannins as well as flavour compounds such as VANILLIN) may also be present in wine as a result of BARREL AGEING, the use of OAK CHIPS, or the addition of OENOLOGICAL TANNINS. Once extracted into the wine, the hydroxycinnamic acids, anthocyanins, catechins, and tannins are gradually converted to various types of derivatives, including PIGMENTED TANNINS. These reactions are responsible for the colour and taste changes observed during wine AGEING.

Catechins and proanthocyanidin oligomers taste bitter, while larger tannins are responsible for the mouth-puckering ASTRINGENCY in young wines. As the wine ages, tannins and their derivatives form larger and larger particles through aggregation and complexation with other molecules such as PROTEINS and POLYSACCHARIDES. This may result in the development of haze and sediments and other technological problems (e.g. clogging of filtration membranes, adsorption on tank surfaces).

A significant number of flavour precursors as well as FLAVOUR COMPOUNDS also have the phenol structure. Examples of these are vanillin, the key aroma compound of the vanilla bean, and raspberry ketone, the impact compound of raspberries. An ESTER, methyl salicylate, familiar as oil of wintergreen, is also a phenolic compound. These and many others are either grape constituents or are produced as trace components during alcoholic fermentation and by glycoside HYDROLYSIS during the subsequent processing and ageing phases. See also OAK FLAVOUR for details of the part played by the phenolics in new OAK. P.J.W. & V.C.

As a tasting term

The word 'phenolic' is also sometimes used, imprecisely, as a pejorative tasting term, to describe (usually white) wines which display an excess of phenolics by tasting astringent or bitter.

As health benefit

It is in its high phenolics content that red wine is distinguished from white, and it is thought that it may well be the ANTIOXIDATIVE properties of phenolics which reduce the incidence of heart disease among those who consume moderate amounts of red wine. See HEALTH.

Banc, R., et al., 'Benefits of wine polyphenols on human health: a review', *Bulletin of University of Agricultural Sciences and Veterinary Medicine Cluj-Napoca Food Science and Technology*, 71/2 (2014), 79–87.

Frankel, E. N., et al., 'Inhibition of oxidation of human low-density lipoprotein by phenolic substances in red wine', *Lancet*, 341 (1993), 454–7.

Quideau, S., et al., 'Plant polyphenols: chemical properties, biological activities, and synthesis', *Angewandte Chemie International Edition*, 50/3 (2011), 586–621.

P

phenology, the study of the sequence of plant development (see diagram). As applied to vines, it records the timing of specific stages such as BUDBREAK, FLOWERING, VERAISON, and LEAF FALL. Such studies indicate the suitability of VINE VARIETIES to certain climatic zones. See VINE GROWTH CYCLE.

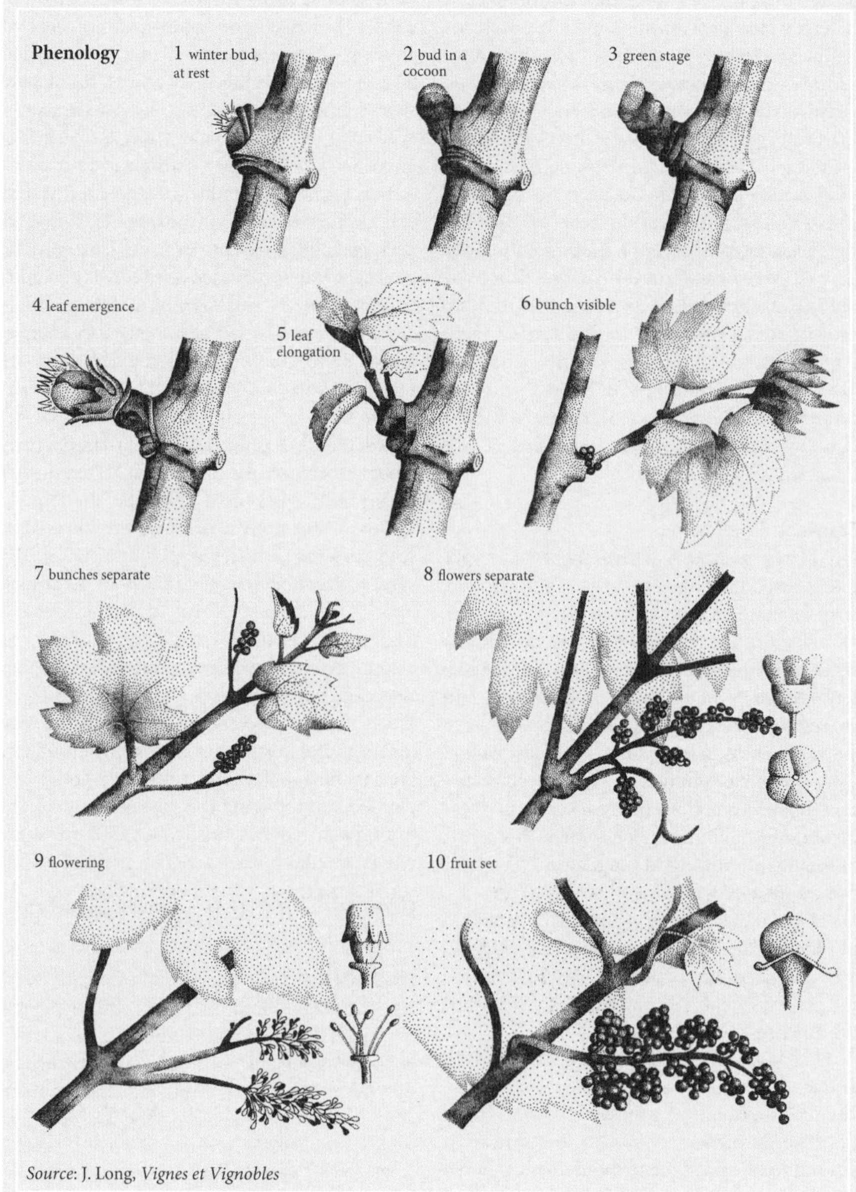

Source: J. Long, *Vignes et Vignobles*

pheromones are, in a viticultural context, synthetic products used in the biological control of vineyard INSECT PESTS. They work by causing sexual confusion (see INTEGRATED PEST MANAGEMENT).

philosophy and wine. Wine first played a part in the history of Western philosophy at the SYMPOSIUM of the early Greek philosophers, where it enlivened and encouraged discussion. Later, during the Enlightenment, David Hume recommended drinking wine with friends as a cure for philosophical melancholy, and Immanuel Kant thought wine softened the harsher sides of men's characters and made their company more convivial. In recent times, philosophers have turned their philosophical attention to wine as an object of perception, assessment, and appreciation. Their enquiries have focused on the relationship between wine and our experience of it, including its intoxicating effect on us (see DRUNKENNESS) and the meaning and value it has for us in our lives (see Scruton 2009).

The issue of objectivity

To know the chemical WINE COMPOSITION and its method of VINIFICATION is not yet to know how it tastes. To know this, one must experience the wine itself by TASTING it. But in tasting a wine, are we discovering properties the wine has or just noting our SUBJECTIVE responses to it? And is every response as good as any other? Here we have a key philosophical question: how subjective are tastes and tasting? In one view, the only objective knowledge we can have of wine is that provided by scientific analysis: the chemist describes the way the wine is, the wine critic describes the way it tastes. The former is objective, the latter merely subjective. But are the two unconnected? Winemakers rely on scientific analysis to achieve the flavours they are aiming for, and experienced wine tasters rely on tasting to identify and describe compounds of flavours or aromas that arise from fermentation. For this to be so, wine tasters must draw objective conclusions about a wine from their subjective responses to it, and wine makers must create conditions they hope will produce a certain taste for the consumer. A revised view would be that, while tasting is a subjective experience of individual tasters, *what* we taste, the TANNINS, or ACIDITY in a wine, are objective properties or characteristics of the wine itself.

Nevertheless, many of the qualities we value in wine such as finesse, BALANCE, COMPLEXITY, HARMONY, and LENGTH can only be confirmed by tasting. And some philosophers would argue that these more complex properties depend on us and should be conceived as some kind of relation between the wines and our responses to them. The problem for this view is whether to treat all such responses as equally good. If we differ in opinion about whether a wine is round or balanced, does this mean there is no fact of the matter about who is right? Is it balanced for me but not for you? On such a subjectivist view, matters of taste are neither right nor wrong: the conclusion is that *de gustibus non est disputandum.*

Tastes and tasting

Philosophers who reject this conclusion argue that taste properties, such as a wine's length or balance, *are* objective features of a wine and that, under the right conditions and with the right experience and training as tasters, they are revealed to us in experience. Tasting a wine involves the taster's subjectivity, but verdicts based on those subjective experiences are not mere matters of opinion and so not subjective in that sense. Certain experiences will be more accurate than others, some people will be better tasters then others, and judgements of a wine can be right or wrong. In this objectivist view, *tastes* are in the wine, not in us, and by improving the skills of *tasting* we can come to know them more accurately (see Smith 2007).

What is meant by 'fine wine'?

A related issue concerns the evaluation of wines and whether there is a clear separation between describing a wine and assessing its QUALITY. Part of this issue is how we should characterize FINE WINE. From the absence of a definition we should not infer there is no category of fine wine, any more than our inability to define 'chair' satisfactorily should lead us to conclude that there are no chairs. Criteria for being a fine wine can be given, as when we can say that a fine wine is one whose complex, individual character rewards the interest and attention paid to it and affords the degree of discrimination we exercise in assessing its qualities and characteristics. But is a fine wine a wine that must be appreciated? Or can experienced wine tasters assess the qualities of a wine without enjoying it? The alternative view is that recognizing a wine's merits depends on the enjoyment, pleasure, or preferences of the individual taster. The dispute here concerns the ultimate nature of wine tasting and wine appreciation. Do we directly perceive the quality of a wine, or do we assess its quality on the basis of what we first perceive? Tasting seems to involve both perception and judgement. But does the perceptual experience of tasting—which relies on the sensations of touch, taste, and smell—already involve a judgement of a wine's quality? Is such judgement a matter of interpretation, and, if so, does assessment require wine knowledge in order to arrive at a correct verdict?

Some philosophers would claim that one cannot assess a wine's quality on the basis of perceptual experience alone and that evaluation goes beyond what one finds in a description of its objective characteristics. According to these thinkers, something else is required to arrive at an assessment of a wine's merits. This may be the pleasure the taster derives from the wine, the valuing of certain characteristics, or the individual preferences of the taster. Is there room in such views for non-subjective judgements of wine quality?

To say that assessments of quality rest on interpretation is to say that one cannot recognize a wine's quality on the basis of perceptual experience alone. And yet according to some philosophers, a novice taster can recognize the merits of wine by taste without the expert knowledge of the wine CRITIC. Moreover, expert knowledge may enable one to recognize a wine as an excellent example of its type, but if that style of wine offers one no pleasure, could one, as a wine critic, still judge it to be (or admire it as) a great wine? Many philosophers would think not, but then on what basis does one judge something to be a great wine, and what could separate experienced and novice tasters in evaluating wines? Do experienced tasters really taste more than novices, or do they simply have a better command of the LANGUAGE OF WINE used by professionals to describe what they taste? Could one appreciate the quality of a wine yet be unable to describe it? Is every taster's opinion equally good, and is the claim that some are better able to appreciate a wine merely snobbery? (See Smith 2013.)

A standard of taste?

Here we address a question raised by David Hume about whether there can be a standard of taste. Hume's solution was to rely on the excellence of JUDGES or critics who: showed delicacy of judgement; were free from prejudice; could draw on a wide range of experience for comparisons; paid due attention; and were unclouded by mood. These may be prerequisites for accurate tasting, but on what basis does such an excellent critic appreciate a truly great wine? An answer to this question can be found in Kant's account of aesthetic judgement (which he did not himself extend to wine). To claim that a wine is great is not just to judge for oneself alone but to judge for all. The judgement is made on the basis of pleasure, but this is not a claim about what one finds personally pleasant or agreeable. It is a judgement about the pleasure the wine affords anyone suitably equipped to taste it. There is no such thing as a wine that is great *for me*. In claiming to recognize a great wine, I am claiming something about *the wine itself*, about how it will (and should) strike others. It is thus a universal claim about the delight all can take in it, and others would be mistaken were they not to judge it so. Kant's solution does not solve all problems of the objectivity of taste, however. Disagreements about a wine's qualities are still disagreements among ourselves, not disagreements settled solely by the properties of the wine itself.

A further problem is created when two (or more) experienced, unprejudiced wine critics differ in their opinions regarding the excellence of a wine. Perhaps they agree in their descriptions of the wine's objective characteristics but diverge in evaluating its merits. If they merely point to divergent qualities, one can argue for pluralism about the qualities and flavours of a wine (see Todd 2010). However, if they genuinely conflict in judgement, but neither has overlooked any aspect of the wine's identifiable properties and both agree in the terms they use to describe and classify wines, we may be tempted to conclude neither is right and neither is wrong. However, subjectivism about standards of taste can be resisted in this case by embracing relativism about matters of taste. According to relativist doctrine, both critics are right: both make true judgements about the wine in question. It is simply that the truth of each judgement is *relative* to a standard of assessment, or set of preferences, not shared by the other. Cultural differences could account for these divergences and there would still be a right answer according to one set of standards or the other. In effect, this is to claim there can be more than one standard of taste and that each critic is right relative to a standard of assessment (see Burnham and Skilleas 2012).

Finally, philosophers have stressed the meaning and value wine has in our lives and our emotional attachment to it, as a celebration of our relationship with our natural surroundings. What a wine expresses is a collaboration between culture and nature that neither entirely controls (see Furrow 2020). The place, culture, and history of a people that falls under the concept of TERROIR are celebrated and acknowledged in drinking a wine that reflects that terroir and the efforts of people to uphold and maintain the traditions with which they transformed soil and vine into grape, grape into wine. The final transformation, according to philosopher Roger Scruton (Smith 2007), occurs when we take wine into ourselves and, through its intoxicating effects, it transforms us and opens us up to one another. B.C.S.

Burnham, D., and Skilleas, O., *The Aesthetics of Wine* (2012).
Furrow, D., *Beauty and the Yeast: A Philosophy of Wine, Life and Love* (2020).
Hume, D., 'Of the standard of taste', *Essays Moral, Political and Literary* (1965), 231–55.
Kant, I., *The Critique of Judgement*, Sections 1–7 (1952).
Scruton, R., *I Drink Therefore I Am* (2009).
Smith, B. C. (ed.), *A Question of Taste: Philosophy and Wine* (2007).
Smith, B. C., 'Wine appreciation: connoisseurship or snobbery?', *World of Fine Wine*, 40 (2013).
Todd, C., *The Philosophy of Wine: A Case of Truth, Beauty and Intoxication* (2010).

phloem, the principal food-conducting tissue of the vine and other vascular plants. Phloem is composed of a mix of CELL types which lie alongside the XYLEM, the water-conducting tissue, and the combination makes up a system of veins or vascular bundles. Despite their proximity, phloem and xylem are entirely different: phloem has thin-walled tubes containing a strongly sugared sap under positive pressure which moves along from areas of strong to weak concentrations, while xylem consists of large, strong-walled tubes through which a dilute mineral solution moves under negative pressure (suction/tension) by forces generated by TRANSPIRATION. During the thickening of woody parts, the CAMBIUM produces cells on the outside that become the new season's phloem; in later years these cells are added to the bark of the vine. Phloem of grapevine wood has the characteristic, unusual among deciduous trees, of reactivation after the next BUDBREAK and can remain functional for three to four years.

The vascular system permeates throughout the plant, but bundles of veins are particularly dense in the LEAF blade, as can be seen by holding it up to the light. This high density facilitates the loading of newly photosynthesized SUCROSE into the phloem tubes for its movement out of the leaf (see TRANSLOCATION).
B.G.C.

Phoenicia, ancient mercantile state of the Iron Age (*c.*1200–539 BCE) and the Persian period until the capture of Tyre by Alexander the Great. The Phoenicians were the successors of the CANAANITES ethnically and culturally and so inherited their aptitude for viniculture. Phoenician territory at its widest extent included modern LEBANON and coastal southern SYRIA and northern ISRAEL. Arwad, Byblos, Beirut, Sidon, and Tyre were among the famous city states of Phoenicia. Vines and olives were grown along the coast and in fertile inland valleys, especially the Beqaá (Bekaa Valley). The Phoenicians were seafaring merchants and colonizers par excellence, spreading the Near Eastern 'wine culture' elsewhere in the Mediterranean. They applied a similar formula wherever they went: import wine and other luxury goods; entice the rulers with the wine culture by presenting them with speciality wine sets; and then wait until they were asked to help in establishing native industries, including viniculture, by transplanting the domesticated Eurasian grapevine. Their greatest colony, CARTHAGE in modern Tunisia, survived until destroyed by the Romans in 146 BCE.

Evidently the Phoenician colonists found in North Africa a fertile region ideal for viticultural development. The Graeco-Roman historian Diodorus Siculus describes the Carthaginian countryside as being (in the 4th century BCE) full of vines, olives, and cattle, especially in the Bagradas Valley and in southern Tunisia. The Carthaginian author Mago left an extensive treatise on agriculture, including instructions on viticulture.

See also ORIGINS OF VINICULTURE and PALAEOETHNOBOTANY.
J.A.B. & P.E.M.

Harden, D., *The Phoenicians* (1962).
McGovern, P. E., *Ancient Wine: The Search for the Origins of Viniculture* (2nd edn, 2019).
McGovern, P. E., *Uncorking the Past: The Quest for Wine, Beer, and Other Alcoholic Beverages* (2009).

Phoenix, a rot-prone DISEASE-RESISTANT VARIETY, a GERMAN cross of BACCHUS and VILLARD Blanc which produces attractive, herbaceous, elderflower-scented wine in England with a minimum of SPRAYING. Despite its parentage, it produces remarkably VITIS VINIFERA-like wine so has been registered as a *vinifera* variety. Consequently, it may be used in the production of PDO wines in the UK. Very little is grown in Germany.

Phomopsis, may refer to either **Phomopsis cane and leaf spot** or **Phomopsis dieback**. Both are caused by the fungus *Diaporthe ampelina*, formerly known as *Phomopsis viticola*, but the symptoms are quite different.

Phomopsis cane and leaf spot, also known as *excoriose* in Europe, occurs in most of the world's viticultural regions, but it is particularly severe in those characterized by a cool and wet spring followed by humid, temperate weather through the growing season. Under these conditions, the disease may cause crop losses of up to 30%. The fungus can infect all green parts of the grapevine, causing black lesions at the base of grape shoots, leaf petioles, and bunch stems; bleached patches on winter canes; the death of affected fruit buds; stunted shoots; small black spots with yellow halos on deformed leaves; and rot on infected berries. Infected wood appears bleached during the dormant season and fruiting structures of the fungi (pycnidia) can be seen embedded in the bark. Although this disease poses the greatest threat in early spring, control measures to protect the fruit may continue into the summer in some regions. Because the fungus colonizes old wood, CANE PRUNING and hand harvesting reduce pressure from this disease. Wine-grape varieties such as Cabernet Sauvignon, Chardonnay, Merlot, and Syrah are less susceptible than some TABLE GRAPES. However, GRENACHE is one of the most susceptible.

Phomopsis dieback is a TRUNK DISEASE that has received less attention than Phomopsis cane and leaf spot. Field studies conducted in California in the mid 2000s found this fungus to be associated with other trunk diseases, especially BOTRYOSPHAERIA DIEBACK. *Diaporthe ampelina* was isolated from perennial cankers in spurs and cordons from grapevines showing a lack of spring growth or reduced shoot growth. Later studies confirmed the presence and severity of *Diaporthe ampelina* as a trunk-disease pathogen causing perennial cankers in Arkansas, Missouri, Texas, and eastern North American vineyards.
J.R.U.-T.

Úrbez-Torres, J. R., et al., 'Phomopsis dieback: a grapevine trunk disease caused by *Phomopsis viticola* in California', *Plant Disease*, 97/12 (2013), 1571–9.
Wilcox, W. F., et al., 'Phomopsis cane and leaf spot', in W. F. Wilcox, et al. (eds.), *Compendium of Grape Diseases, Disorders, and Pests* (2nd edn, 2015), 68–71.

phosphorus is one of the most important MINERAL elements required for vine growth (see VINE NUTRITION), yet the amounts required are sufficiently small that for most vineyards the natural supply from the soil is enough. There is only about 0.6 kg of phosphorus in a tonne of grapes (1.3 lb per ton). Phosphorus in the vine is an essential component of compounds involved in PHOTOSYNTHESIS and sugar–starch transformations as well as the transfer of energy. Phosphorus deficiency in vines is uncommon and found mostly on soils with a large content of iron and aluminium oxides, as in parts of the Yarra and King valleys in VICTORIA, Australia, and the WILLAMETTE VALLEY, Oregon. Its symptoms are a gradual loss of VIGOUR and, sometimes, some red spots on the leaves.
R.E.S. & R.E.W.

photosynthesis, a biochemical reaction which combines water and atmospheric carbon dioxide using the energy of the sun to form SUGARS in plants, including vines. Important in this process are the green chlorophyll pigments in leaves which capture the sun's energy. Photosynthesis is the essential first step in the winemaking process, as the sugars formed in photosynthesis, along with other chemical products derived from sugar, are transported to grape berries (see SUGAR IN GRAPES) and eventually fermented into ETHANOL to produce wine. (According to the neat laws of nature, humans eventually metabolize wine's ethanol back to carbon dioxide and water; see CARBON DIOXIDE.)

Photosynthesis can be summarized by this chemical equation:

$$6CO_2 + 6H_2O + \text{light energy} = C_6H_{12}O_6 + 6O_2$$
$$(\text{carbon dioxide} + \text{water} + \text{sunlight} = \text{sugar} + \text{oxygen})$$

The process of photosynthesis maintains atmospheric supplies of OXYGEN, essential for animal life on Earth. It also takes the carbon dioxide from the atmosphere and is thus increasingly seen as a method of carbon capture by plants in a world becoming concerned with CLIMATE CHANGE. Since these reactions take place inside the leaf, carbon dioxide must be able to diffuse in and oxygen out. This takes place through minute pores called STOMATA on the underside of vine leaves.

The rate of photosynthesis is affected by environmental and plant factors, all of which have an effect on grape RIPENING and hence wine quality. SUNLIGHT, TEMPERATURE, and WATER STRESS are the three most important climatic controls. Photosynthesis is limited by low light levels, as, for example, under overcast conditions or, more commonly, for shaded leaves away from the canopy surface (see CANOPY MICROCLIMATE). Light levels of about 1% of full sunlight are too low for photosynthesis and can occur behind two leaf layers from the canopy surface. Leaves exposed to such very low light levels turn yellow and eventually fall off. Photosynthesis increases almost linearly with light up to about one-third full sunlight; beyond that is said to be light saturated, in that any further increase in sunlight intensity will not increase photosynthesis. So outside leaves on vine canopies are often light saturated in sunny conditions, and some sunlight is effectively wasted.

Photosynthesis is highest with leaf temperatures from about 15–30 °C/59–86 °F, with a slight peak at about 25 °C. Photosynthesis is severely inhibited for temperatures below 15 °C and above 30 °C. During one day in hot DESERT regions, DIURNAL TEMPERATURE RANGE may be so great that vine leaf photosynthesis is inhibited by both low temperatures in the early morning and high temperatures in the afternoon. Low temperatures limit photosynthesis and hence grape ripening in COOL-CLIMATE wine regions such as those of northern Europe. High-quality vintages there are warm, sunny years when photosynthesis is highest.

Dry soil conditions will cause stomata to close, thus interfering with photosynthesis but saving the vine from further desiccation. Such an effect of water stress on photosynthesis and grape ripening can be seen, especially towards HARVEST, in many of the world's wine regions, typically in MEDITERRANEAN CLIMATES. The vine can, however, tolerate mild water stress with no negative effect on wine quality. Indeed, if it occurs before VERAISON, and SHOOT growth is slowed, quality will probably be enhanced. WIND can also cause stomata to close and interfere with grape ripening, as is common in MONTEREY in California, for example.

As a general rule, photosynthesis is enhanced by sunny conditions and mild temperatures. These conditions are known to give maximal sugar concentration in grapes and, conventionally, the best wine quality. R.E.S.

Greer, D., and Weedon, M., 'Modelling photosynthetic responses to temperature of grapevine (*Vitis vinifera* cv. Semillon) leaves on vines grown in a hot climate', *Plant, Cell & Environment*, 35 (2012),1050–64.

Jackson, R., *Wine Science: Principles and Applications* (5th edn, 2020).

Keller, M., 'Photosynthesis and respiration', in *The Science of Grapevines* (3rd edn, 2020).

phylloxera. This small, yellow, aphid-like insect, sometimes referred to as the grape root aphid, has probably had a more damaging impact on wine production than any other VINE PEST or any VINE DISEASE. The grape phylloxera attacks only grapevines and kills vines by attacking their roots. For many years after it first invaded Europe there was no known cure. The effects of phylloxera were first noted in France in 1863, just as the country was recovering from another great scourge of 19th-century European viticulture: oidium, or POWDERY MILDEW, which was first noted in 1847. Like powdery mildew and the other FUNGAL DISEASES yet to arrive (DOWNY MILDEW in 1878 and BLACK ROT in 1885), phylloxera was an unwelcome import from America which devastated European vineyards until appropriate control measures were found. In the history of agriculture, phylloxera rivals the potato blight of Ireland as a plant disease with widespread social effects. In France, for example, almost 2.5 million ha/6.2 million acres of vineyards were destroyed, the pest making no distinction between the vineyards of the most famous châteaux and those of humble peasants. Phylloxera invasion had a major social and economic impact, involving national governments and local committees and requiring international scientific collaboration. For a while the very existence of the French wine industry was threatened. (See BURGUNDY, modern history, for example.)

Phylloxera had many different scientific names between 1855 and 1974, when Louise Russell ended the confusion, proposing *Dactylasphaera vitifoliae* (Fitch) as the correct name for the grape phylloxera, even if the French scientist J.-E. Planchon's *Phylloxera vastatrix* (the devastator) is better known and the

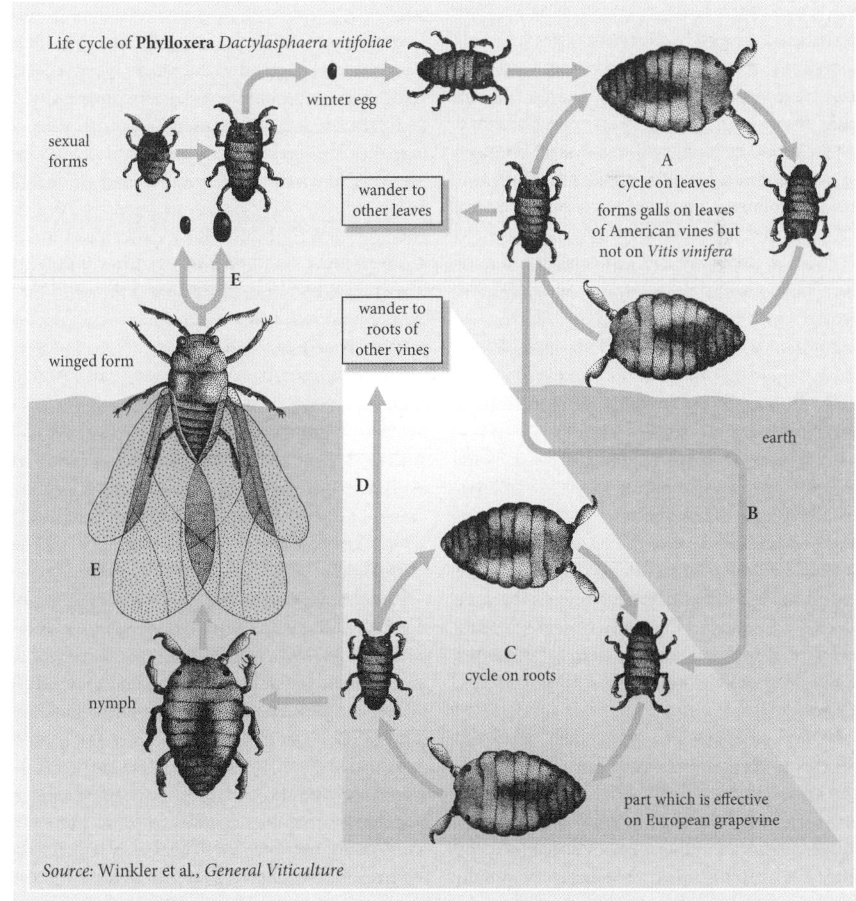

Source: Winkler et al., *General Viticulture*

origin of the common name phylloxera (grape phylloxera is more accurate, since there is also an oak phylloxera, for example).

Biology

The female phylloxera is yellow and about 1 mm/0.039 in long. Typically surrounded by masses of eggs, it is barely visible to the naked eye as it feeds on the roots. There are four to seven generations in the summer, each producing females capable of laying more eggs. As the eggs hatch, so-called 'crawlers' move to other roots of the vine, and some climb the trunk and can spread to other vines, or even vineyards, by the action of wind or machinery dislodging them from the foliage. Phylloxera tends to spread in a circle from the original infected vine. Wind-blown crawlers create secondary infections downwind.

It has a complex life cycle, with both sexual and asexual stages and existing in both root-living and leaf-living forms. It causes damage to vines by injecting saliva to produce galls, by feeding on the sap, and by causing root deformities. In humid regions, there is also an associated life cycle whereby the root-hatched nymph produces a winged form which can travel longer distances and lays male and female eggs. The hatching female in turn lays a winter egg which develops into the stem mother or fundatrix, which lays eggs in a leaf gall (these galls typically being produced only on the leaves of AMERICAN VINES). Nymphs hatching from galls can begin new infections as egg-laying females on roots.

The principal agent for the spread of phylloxera is humans. It is most commonly transported from one vineyard to another on soil and roots of ROOTLINGS. It is also easily moved in the soil that sticks to implements and by IRRIGATION water. Research in New Zealand showed that crawlers present in vine foliage lead to secondary spread over considerable distances; they are moved by machines which brush against foliage, such as foliage trimmers and harvesters, and also by wind.

Phylloxera is native to the east coast of the United States, and so native AMERICAN VINE SPECIES have generally evolved with resistance. Studies have shown that the basis of resistance is the development of cork layers beneath the wound made by phylloxera feeding on the root. This stops the invasion of other microbes (bacteria and especially fungi such as *Fusarium oxysporum*) which eventually rot the root and kill non-resistant vines.

Phylloxera kills vines that do not have this resistance, such as the European VITIS VINIFERA vine species from which most wine is made, by destroying the root system. When first present, the phylloxera numbers build up quickly on roots, galls are formed, and there is initially little apparent root damage. Phylloxera can be diagnosed by the presence on the roots of the bright-yellow females, their eggs, and the characteristic gall symptoms. After a few years, the root rot affects the top growth, shoot growth is stunted, and leaves lose their healthy green colour. Normally a vine dies within several years of the first infection. Vines which are struggling for other reasons are more susceptible to phylloxera and succumb more quickly. Those growing on deep, fertile soil can continue to produce economic crops for many years after phylloxera attack. Phylloxera does not survive well in sandy soil, so vines planted in SAND (such as on the Great Plain of HUNGARY, those planted by Listel on the French Mediterranean coast, or COLARES in Portugal) are immune from attack.

History

Attempts by early European colonists in North America to establish imported *vinifera* vines met with disaster, presumably substantially because of grape phylloxera, to which they had no resistance—although at this time phylloxera had yet to be identified, and other American vine diseases such as PIERCE'S DISEASE in Florida, downy and powdery mildew in all regions, and the very cold winters doubtless played a part in their demise. (See UNITED STATES, history, for more details.)

How did phylloxera come to Europe? In the mid 19th century there was considerable importation of living plants into Europe. This trade was supported by wealthy people who could afford elaborate gardens, greenhouses, and conservatories, encouraged by the Victorians' keen interest in botany. Plants could be imported dormant or kept alive and protected from salt spray by a glass container (the 'Wardian case') built into the ship's deck, like a modern terrarium. In 1865 alone, 460 tons of plants worth 230,000 francs were imported into France, and this trade had grown to 2,000 tons by the 1890s. Jules Planchon, Professor of Pharmacy at MONTPELLIER University, noted that rooted American vines were imported in particularly significant quantities between 1858 and 1862, sent to parts of Europe as far apart as Bordeaux, England, Ireland, Alsace, Germany, and Portugal. No doubt phylloxera was an unsuspected passenger on vine roots at the same time.

The first reporting of phylloxera, like that of the fungal disease powdery mildew, was in England, in 1863, when Professor J. O. Westwood, an entomologist at Oxford University, received insect samples from a greenhouse in the London suburb of Hammersmith. Since the insects were in a leaf gall, the vine species was probably American, and these plants may even have been a source of introduction of the pest to England. In 1863, an unknown vine disease in France was being talked about, with two vineyards in the southern Rhône affected. The first printed report in France was a letter written by a veterinarian in 1867 about a vineyard planted in 1863 at St-Martin-de-Crau (only about 30 km/20 miles north-east of the site of the University of Montpellier's 20th-century phylloxera-free vine collection on the Mediterranean coast, ironically), which developed unhealthy vines in summer 1866, failing to grow the following spring. It is most likely that infection occurred several years beforehand. There were other reports from Narbonne in the Languedoc, from the Gard and Vaucluse *départements* in the southern Rhône in 1867, and from Bordeaux in 1869. (It was usually several years after the initial sighting that the pest's impact had a serious effect; the Médoc, for example, was not commercially compromised until the late 1870s.)

The first of many committees formed to resolve the phylloxera question was a Commission instigated by the Vaucluse Agricultural Society. On 15 July 1868 it began its investigation of affected vineyards in the southern Rhône. One member of the Commission was Jules Planchon, who had good training to work on phylloxera. He had spent a period at Kew Botanical Gardens in England and subsequently became the brother-in-law of J. Lichtenstein, an amateur entomologist. Planchon noticed that dying vines had small yellow insects on their roots and noted the resemblance to *Phylloxera quercus* (the oak phylloxera) living on oak trees. He named the insect believed to be ravaging vineyards *Phylloxera vastatrix*.

The Hérault Commission made its findings public in August 1868, but these caused little interest in any but the local newspapers. There was a marked reluctance to accept that this little yellow insect could be causing such devastation. Other explanations current at the time were OVERCROPPING, winter cold and other bad weather, weakening of the vineyards as a result of continued vegetative reproduction, soil exhaustion, and also God's wrath at contemporary vices. The distinguished entomologist V. Signoret thought phylloxera was an effect, not the cause, and Dr GUYOT thought its presence was due to over-severe PRUNING (the opposite of overcropping)! The debate was ended by the 1869 Commission of the Société des Agriculteurs de France, headed by viticulturist L. Vialla, who gently but firmly debunked all false theories.

Total French wine production fell from a peak of 84.5 million hl/2,200 million gal in 1875 to a mere 23.4 million hl in 1889. But even by June 1873 the French government was sufficiently alarmed by the spread of phylloxera to offer a large prize (300,000 francs) for a remedy, which was to be verified by experimentation carried out by the School of Agriculture at Montpellier. Up to October 1876, 696 suggestions were forwarded to Professors Durand

P

and Jeannenot at Montpellier, and between 1872 and 1876 1,044 treatments were evaluated. Among the deluge of suggestions submitted were those verging on the ridiculous, which included burying a living toad under the vine (to draw the poison) and irrigating the vines with white wine. Entries were received from other countries as diverse as Denmark and Singapore. All of this work, however, produced little benefit, as only two treatments based on the chemical application of various forms of SULFIDE appeared to show much advantage. Surprisingly, carbon bisulfide failed in the evaluation even though it was later used extensively.

Early attempts at commercial control of phylloxera included flooding, which was studied by the Commission in 1873. It was found that flooding in winter for weeks on end controlled the pest, but of course few vineyards were near enough to water supplies or sufficiently flat for this to be a widespread solution (although it is still used in parts of Argentina). Vineyards on sandy soils were noted to be immune, although this offered no control. The insecticidal properties of carbon bisulfide were found in 1854 on grain weevils, and Baron Paul Thénard evaluated it in Bordeaux in 1869. The injection of the liquid carbon bisulfide was to become widespread, so that by 1888 some 68,000 ha/168,000 acres had been treated. The first experiments used too high a dose, severely affecting the vines, but subsequently the practice of injecting it, mixed with water, into the soil, using about 30,000 holes per ha, became common.

By the time of the International Phylloxera Congress at Bordeaux in 1881, two distinct schools of thought had emerged on how the industry might be saved. The chemists considered salvation to lie in carbon bisulfide or related chemicals, or in flooding. In opposition were the 'Americanists', who advocated grafting desired varieties on to American vine species used as ROOTSTOCKS. Gaston Bazille had suggested GRAFTING in 1869, and Leo Laliman of Bordeaux drew early attention to the resistance of these species to phylloxera. Laliman had studied the resistance of American species to powdery mildew in a collection in his vineyards since 1840.

Following successful demonstrations of the ability of American vines to withstand phylloxera, and after the visit of Planchon to America in 1873, where his study was guided by the noted scientist C. V. Riley, state entomologist of Missouri, the use of FIELD GRAFTING began, rising from 2,500 ha/6,178 acres in 1880 to 45,000 ha in 1885. It was Riley who positively identified the unknown French insect as identical to the American one, a critical step in its eventual control; he was one of the first to suggest grafting European varieties to American rootstocks, and his authority and expertise on phylloxera gave weight to the suggestion. Initial American vine imports, cuttings taken from WILD VINES, were from the north-east, growing on acid soils. VITIS LABRUSCA was found to lack phylloxera resistance, but *Vitis aestivalis*, VITIS RUPESTRIS, and VITIS RIPARIA were found to be most effective.

All was not plain sailing, however. Many American species used for rootstocks could not tolerate the CALCAREOUS soils of France (see CHLOROSIS). A second visit to the US by Vialla led to the intervention of Texas nurseryman, breeder, and AMPELOGRAPHER T. V. MUNSON. The two met in 1878, and Munson guided Vialla to species resistant to calcareous soils, *Vitis berlandieri*, *Vitis cordifolia*, and *Vitis cinerea*. Munson was rewarded for his contribution to saving French viticulture by the medal of the French Legion of Honour and a statue in Montpellier.

However, the transition to grafting was not simple. The amount of grafting to be done was almost overwhelming. Rootstock cuttings were planted in the field and in the second year of growth were hand-grafted using SCION buds of the desired variety. There was a concern that the use of these foreign rootstocks (whose own wine is so often reviled for its FOXY flavour) might affect wine quality, and in Burgundy the importation of American vines was prohibited until 1887, although the clandestine activities of growers anxious to save their vineyards forced its repeal.

Eventually rootstock use became the established method for the control of phylloxera, and this has had a dramatic effect on vine NURSERY operations worldwide. There was a period in the late 19th century, however, when it was thought that breeding HYBRIDS of European with American vine varieties might produce vines with sufficient phylloxera resistance not to need grafting, whose wines were not marked by the undesirable FOXY flavour of some American grapes. The class of varieties so created is loosely termed FRENCH HYBRIDS or DIRECT PRODUCERS. These efforts were generally unsuccessful, however, in that the vines had inadequate phylloxera tolerance and produced lower-quality wine, although they became popular with growers because of their high yields and their tolerance of fungal diseases. While hybrids bred in this period were not destined to remain commercially viable, they did form a useful germplasm pool of disease tolerance for highly successful breeding projects in the latter part of the 19th century (see HYBRIDS). Nevertheless, many of the rootstocks used today (see ROOTSTOCKS for a detailed list) were bred by Europeans in the late 19th and early 20th centuries—although hybrids with *vinifera* as one parent have been generally found to have insufficient tolerance to phylloxera (see below).

Geography

Phylloxera is now widespread around the world, having been found in California (1873), Portugal (1871), Türkiye (1871), Austria (1872), Switzerland (1874), Italy (1875), Australia (1877), Spain (1878), Algeria (1885), South Africa (1885), New Zealand (1885), and Greece (1898). There are few parts of the world free from the pest, although these include parts of Australia (on which a strict QUARANTINE is imposed), parts of China, Chile, Argentina, India, Pakistan, and Afghanistan, and some Mediterranean islands such as Crete, Cyprus, and Rhodes.

There are also small sandy vineyards in otherwise affected wine regions (see BOLLINGER and COLARES) which have never been affected by phylloxera either because of isolation or because of the SOIL TEXTURE.

For much of the late 20th century, phylloxera was not regarded as a serious problem, either because it was not present in a region or because of the availability of a wide range of rootstocks suited to different varieties, soil, and climate conditions along with tolerance to other pests such as NEMATODES. About 85% of all the world's vineyards were estimated in 1990 to be grafted on to rootstocks presumed to be resistant to phylloxera.

Late 20th century outbreaks of phylloxera were noted on ungrafted vines in parts of Greece, England, New Zealand, Australia, and Oregon; most dramatically, they were also found on vines grafted on to the AXR1 rootstock (see ROOTSTOCKS for details) in California where the so-called 'biotype B' strain of phylloxera was identified and blamed for the outbreak.

Phylloxera is known to occur naturally as a number of related strains or biotypes. King and Rilling exchanged phylloxera and vine cuttings between New Zealand and Germany, confirming evidence of the biotype differences between the two countries. Interestingly, the AXR1 rootstock was found not to be affected by phylloxera from New Zealand, but it was affected by German phylloxera. New Zealand probably obtained phylloxera from California in 1885, which suggests that the biotype of phylloxera originally in California did not affect AXR1. With the introduction of other biotypes, perhaps on rooted vines imported from eastern American states at a time of nursery shortages in California in the early 1980s, the demise of AXR1 began. It was found to offer insufficient phylloxera tolerance, and a significant proportion of grafted vineyards in Napa and Sonoma valleys succumbed to phylloxera leading to extensive replanting in the 1980s and 1990s.

Better molecular testing of phylloxera strains is now available, and they are referred to as genotypes or as clones or races. The term 'biotype' is now used only to describe strains by reference to their interactions with specific rootstocks, for example by studying and classifying the insects' survival and population growth.

No doubt one of the most important effects of the phylloxera invasion of the world's vineyards was the inadvertent spread of VIRUS DISEASES. As grafting became widespread towards the end of the 19th century, virus diseases were also distributed as a common result of grafting, because virus-infected cuttings were used in grafting. A virus originally present only in the rootstock would spread to the fruiting *vinifera* variety after grafting, and vice versa. Rootstocks do not show virus symptoms, and virology in viticulture was not well understood until the 1950s. With known effects on fruit ripening, perhaps it was virus diseases more than grafting which led to the debate as to the relative merits of 'PRE-PHYLLOXERA' and 'post-phylloxera' wines.

Since the 1980s, BENCH GRAFTING has widely replaced field grafting. This, along with poor sanitary conditions in some nurseries growing rootstock MOTHER VINES, has been associated with the widespread appearance of TRUNK DISEASE fungi in grafted vines. R.E.S.

Gale, G., *Dying on the Vine: How Phylloxera Transformed Wine* (2011).

Granett, J., et al., 'Biology and management of grape phylloxera', *Annual Review of Entomology*, 46 (2001), 387–412.

King, P. D., and Rilling, G., 'Further evidence of phylloxera biotypes: variations in the tolerance of mature grapevine roots related to the geographical origin of the insect', *Vitis*, 30 (1991), 233–44.

Russell, L. M., '*Daktulosphaira vitifoliae* (Fitch), the correct name of the grape phylloxeran (*Hemiptera: Homoptera: Phylloxeridae*)', *Journal of the Washington Academy of Sciences*, 64 (1974), 303–8.

P

phylogeny, or **phylogenesis**, is the chronological reconstruction of the evolutionary history of a given group of organisms. Formerly based on morphological comparisons (see VINE MORPHOLOGY), this field has been revolutionized in the last 30 years by phylogenetics, the DNA analyses of various molecular markers found in the nucleus (inherited from both parents) or in the organelles (e.g. the chloroplasts, maternally inherited in grapevines) and usually represented as a phylogenetic tree. See BOTANICAL CLASSIFICATION for the phylogeny of the GRAPEVINE. J.V.

physiological ripeness, or **physiological maturity**, terms loosely used by some winemakers, especially in CALIFORNIA, to contrast with RIPENESS measured by the typical analytical measures of MUST WEIGHT, ACIDITY, and PH. The terminology is imprecise but typically includes so-called **phenolic ripeness**, or **phenological ripeness**, which refers to changes in colour, TANNINS, and flavour that are important to eventual wine quality. See also GRAPE COMPOSITION AND WINE QUALITY.

The idea of physiological ripening arose when winemakers realized that in many (particularly warmer) wine regions, these chemical measures were not sufficient to predict the optimum HARVEST date for wine quality. A common example is the relatively faster rate of sugar increase in warm to hot climates compared with phenolic development, flavour increase, and acid decrease. The resulting wines tend to be high in alcohol but lacking ripe fruit flavours. In red wines, the TANNINS may be astringent and taste unripe. On the other hand, varietal flavour appears to increase more quickly relative to sugar in cooler climates.

Research into the effects of increased TEMPERATURE on grape composition by Sadras and colleagues in Australia has shown that, in Shiraz and Cabernet Franc, accumulation of ANTHOCYANINS is 'decoupled' from sugar accumulation during ripening. This was due to the delayed onset of anthocyanin accumulation at warmer temperatures. For other recent developments in the prediction of harvest dates, see GRAPE QUALITY ASSESSMENT.

In the late 20th century, there was an increasing tendency to encourage growers to leave grapes longer and longer on the vine. The aim of this prolonged HANG TIME was riper PHENOLICS, especially tannins, but this was often achieved at the cost of excessively high sugar levels. In such circumstances, winemakers may resort to adding WATER to the must, where local regulations allow, or the use of equipment such as the SPINNING CONE to reduce the ALCOHOLIC STRENGTH of the finished wine.

Many wine producers are now trying to find ways to achieve ripeness across all parameters at the same moment as optimal sugar accumulation and acid retention is reached. These include precisely timed IRRIGATION regimes, manipulating crop load, controlling fruit exposure, slowing sugar accumulation by careful reduction of the LEAF TO FRUIT RATIO, and research into YEASTS specifically designed to result in lower alcohol levels. As CLIMATE CHANGE leads to more frequent HARVEST COMPRESSION, there is even greater concern about achieving ripeness across all harvest parameters. J.E.H. & R.E.S.

Sadras, V. O., and Moran, M. A., 'Elevated temperature decouples anthocyanins and sugars in berries of Shiraz and Cabernet Franc', *Australian Journal of Grape and Wine Research*, 18/2 (2012), 115–22.

physiology of the vine. See VINE PHYSIOLOGY.

phytoalexins, anti-microbial compounds produced by plants in response to bacterial or fungal attack. They are not normally present in significant quantities until a plant is invaded by disease. In grapevines, phytoalexins belong to a class of PHENOLICS called stilbenes (see RESVERATROL). G.L.C.

phytoplasma, once known as mycoplasma, small and sometimes microscopic organisms similar to BACTERIA associated with vine diseases of the PHLOEM, transmitted by insects and propagation. The most serious diseases caused, GRAPEVINE YELLOWS, may well continue to have widespread implications for the world's wine industry in the 21st century. The relentless spread of various forms of phytoplasma continues in many European grape-growing regions, France, Germany, Slovenia, and Hungary among others. In recent years, CLIMATE CHANGE has been implicated, as the insect vectors spreading the disease migrate polewards. R.E.S.

Dermastia, M., et al., *Grapevine Yellows Diseases and Their Phytoplasma Agents* (2017).

Piacentini, Colli, diverse DOC zone centred on the hills of Piacenza in Emilia in north-central Italy. See EMILIA-ROMAGNA for more details.

Piave, mainly red wine DOC in the hinterland of Venice in north-east Italy. Like the neighbouring LISON-PRAMAGGIORE, the Piave DOC embraces vineyards in the plain of the Piave river and is demarcated by the pre-alpine Conegliano and Montello hills to the north and the flatlands of the river's Adriatic delta to the south. Even if the vineyard surface in production is only 189 ha/467 acres, the DOC is so extended that it overlaps the DOCGS Conegliano-Valdobbiadene, Asolo, Colli di Conegliano, and Montello, as well as the DOC Lison-Pramaggiore. The wines—mostly VARIETAL reds from Cabernet Franc, Cabernet Sauvignon, Merlot, and RABOSO, or whites from Chardonnay, Manzoni Bianco (INCROCIO), TAI BIANCO, and VERDUZZO—are, at their best, fruity, fresh, and unpretentiously appealing; with permitted yields of up to 90 hl/ha for Merlot and over 80 hl/ha for Cabernet and Tai Bianco, they seem destined to remain that way. The zone doubles as the DOCG **Piave Malanotte**, of which so far only 16 ha/40 acres are in production. A potentially much more interesting red, it is made from Raboso, 15–30% of which must be dried, arguably to counteract the variety's tannic, high-acid character. But in the right hands this variety can produce long-lived, complex red wines, even without the dried-grape component. W.S.

Picapoll Blanco, vine variety making crisp white wine in the far north-east of CATALUÑA which is genetically very similar to CLAIRETTE Blanche but is unrelated to PIQUEPOUL.

picardan, a sweet white wine developed in the LANGUEDOC from CLAIRETTE and PICQUEPOUL grapes by the DUTCH WINE TRADE in the late 17th and 18th centuries. Picardan is also the name of one of the most neutral white grape varieties allowed in CHÂTEAUNEUF-DU-PAPE.

Piceno. See ROSSO PICENO.

picking grapes is seemingly romantic but in practice often back-breaking work. For more details, see HARVEST and LABOUR.

Pico, DOC on the island of the same name which is dominated by Portugal's highest mountain, Ponto do Pico, a volcano. Pico has more vines than other islands in the AZORES because its crust of black BASALT is an inhospitable environment for any other crop. Vines are planted in cracks filled with soil from the neighbouring island of Faial and protected from harsh winds and sea spray by volcanic rock walls (*currais*). In 2004 this unique landscape gained UNESCO World Heritage status, which has spurred investment and innovation in the wine sector. The island tradition is for dry to fully sweet, nutty, honeyed, saltily persistent wines made from overripe and raisined grapes, principally VERDELHO. Its production even exceeded that of MADEIRA during the mid 19th century but has now slowed to a trickle. Contemporary examples are fortified and labelled LICOROSO (with the exception of Czar, the leading exponent, whose wines are labelled 'Not Fortified'). In dry wines, the island's most thrilling are the saline, mineral whites which attained DOC status in 2012. They must comprise a minimum of 85% VERDELHO, ARINTO do Açores, and Terrantez do Pico, varieties said to be Azorean (although Madeira also lays claim to Verdelho). Other dry wines made from a much broader range of white and red grapes (including French and mainland varieties) have enjoyed Vinho Regional Açores status since 2004. Consistent with increased recognition for dry wine, the DOC vineyard area increased from 130 to 712 ha/1,759 acres between 2014 and 2020. S.A.

Ahmed, S., 'Pico, The Azores: Volcanic Wines in the Midst of Waves', *The World of Fine Wine*, 57 (2017) 178–82.

Picolit, also written **Piccolit** and **Piccolito** in the past, fashionable and audaciously priced sweet white VARIETAL wine made in the FRIULI region of north-east Italy, one of the more commercially successful of the DRIED-GRAPE WINES. The grape variety derives its name from the small, or *piccolo*, quantity of grapes it produces, thanks to its exceptionally poor pollination rate in the vineyard. The variety probably originates in Rosazzo in the FRIULI COLLI ORIENTALI.

The wine was already famous in the 18th century but was almost extinct when the Perusini family of the Rocca Bernarda of Ipplis worked to identify and then reproduce hardier CLONES with a reduced failure rate.

Some better estates still make the wine much as it was in the past—Fabio Asquini left copious notes on his working methods—with the bunches, harvested late in mid October, left to dry and raisin on mats before pressing. Other producers have opted for a late-harvest style, with the grapes left even longer in the vineyard, picked with higher MUST WEIGHTS, but not raisined after picking. The use of small oak BARREL AGEING is an innovation introduced in the mid 1980s. Although Picolit is generally considered a dessert wine, it is not luscious and is best considered a VINO DA MEDITAZIONE, a wine to be sipped alone in order to appreciate its delicate floral aromas and its light sweetness, which suggests peaches and apricots.

The wine became the object of a cult enthusiasm in Italy in the late 1960s and 1970s, fetching extremely high prices that non-Italian connoisseurs find difficult to understand or justify; the Picolit boom has also resulted in frequent and illegal blending of the wine with the more neutral VERDUZZO, which has stretched the quantities available but has done no service to the wine's reputation. There were just 121 ha/299 acres of the variety in Italy in 2015. A small amount is grown over the border in western Slovenia.

Picpoul de Pinet, one of the France's few VARIETALLY named AOC wines and arguably the Languedoc's greatest commercial success of the 2010s. Made exclusively from Picpoul Blanc—called PIQUEPOUL outside of the appellation—and awarded its AOC in 2013, the wine comes from about 1,400 ha/3,460 acres of fairly low-lying land between Pézenas and the Bassin de Thau lagoon. A range of hills protects the vines from northern winds, while breezes off the nearby ocean moderate the summer heat. The majority of wines are produced by CO-OPERATIVES and are pale green, crisp, saline, and lemony, although independent producers such as Julie Benau have been working with LEES CONTACT, SKIN CONTACT, and even BARREL AGEING to introduce more texture and complexity. M.S.

Pic-St-Loup, one of the most highly regarded subregions of the LANGUEDOC, elevated to an AOC in 2016. The zone, with mixed but largely CALCAREOUS soils, includes 12 communes around the eponymous and dramatic 658-m/2,159-ft peak north of Montpellier. The CONTINENTAL CLIMATE produces wines with a high degree of freshness, slightly lighter in body than those from many of its AOC Languedoc counterparts and laced with scents of GARRIGUE. Wines are 90% red, the rest rosé, based on Grenache, Mourvèdre, and Syrah, with backup from Cinsaut and Carignan. The zone's white wines are often labelled either as AOC Languedoc or IGP St-Guilhem-le-Désert. M.S.

pièce, size and shape of barrel conventionally used in Burgundy. See BARREL TYPES for more details.

pied de cuve. French term for a fermentation starter made using ambient rather than cultured YEAST. A small volume of grapes is harvested a few days early, crushed, and allowed to start fermenting, thus building a healthy yeast population. The *pied de cuve* is added to the MUST or juice of the main harvest. Using a *pied de cuve* to start a SPONTANEOUS FERMENTATION reduces the risk of sluggish or STUCK FERMENTATION.

Börlin, M., et al., 'The "pied de cuve" as an alternative way to manage indigenous fermentation: impact on the fermentative process and *Saccharomyces cerevisiae* diversity', *OENO One*, 54/3 (2020).

piede franco, Italian for UNGRAFTED VINE.

Piedirosso, one of CAMPANIA's relatively few red wine grapes, very much in second place after AGLIANICO, grown around Naples and on the islands of ISCHIA and Capri. Also known as Per'e Palummo and Palombina, it can make fresh, fruity reds, but total plantings had declined to 593 ha/1,465 acres by 2015.

Piedmont, Anglicized name for PIEMONTE.

pie franco, Spanish for UNGRAFTED VINE.

Piemonte, qualitatively outstanding and highly distinctive wine region in north-west ITALY whose principal city is Turin (see map under ITALY). This subalpine part (its name means 'at the foot of the mountains') of the former kingdom of Savoy was the driving force behind Italian reunification in the 19th century and led the initial phases of Italy's industrial revolution. Its geographical position both isolated and protected it during the period of Habsburg, Bourbon, and papal domination which marked Italian life 1550–1860, while its proximity, both geographical and cultural, to France (the kingdom's court and nobility were Francophone until well into the 19th century) gave it both an openness to the new ideas of the European enlightenment and relative prosperity—in stark contrast to the poverty of much of the rest of the peninsula. In 2020 total annual wine production averaged over 2.7 million hl/59 million gal, with over 80% DOC or DOCG.

In Piemonte vines are planted at ELEVATIONS of 150–400 m/490–1,150 ft and regularly higher for the Alta Langa DOC sparkling wines, with the best, south-facing sites typically devoted to NEBBIOLO, while the coolest positions are planted with DOLCETTO (or MOSCATO in the zones in which it is grown). BARBERA is widely planted in between. Average summer temperatures and rainfall are very similar to those in Bordeaux. Although there are 21 Nebbiolo-based DOCs or

DOCGs, only the world-famous BAROLO and BARBARESCO supply significant amounts of wine. GATTINARA, for example, which is the largest of the Nebbiolo DOCs outside the LANGHE hills, encompassed in 2020 hardly more than 111 ha/274 acres of vineyard. More common is Barbera, planted virtually everywhere in the provinces of ALBA, ASTI, and Alessandria. It was considered Piemonte's workhorse grape until the 1980s, when high-quality and expensive oak-aged Barberas appeared on the market, showing the variety's real potential and radically changing perceptions. While Barbera d'Asti has been a DOCG since 2010, the elevation of its subzone Nizza to DOCG in 2019 is further recognition of Barbera's intrinsic quality. DOLCETTO, almost as ubiquitous as Barbera and similarly considered modest rather than great, delivers most of Piemonte's fruity red wine for early drinking. It ripens even earlier than Barbera and is regularly vinified in less than a week to make sure the fermentation tanks are empty before Barbera and Nebbiolo are harvested.

White grapes, except for the MOSCATO used extensively for various SPUMANTE and FRIZZANTE (most notably ASTI), used to be a virtual afterthought in Piemonte, but the region's production of white wine grew considerably in the late 20th and early 21st centuries. Part of this surge is due to the commercial success of Asti and MOSCATO D'ASTI, but wines based on CORTESE such as GAVI and those from the Colli Tortonesi and Alto Monferrato have become enormously popular since the 1990s. INDIGENOUS VARIETIES such as ARNEIS, a mere curiosity in the early 1980s, is planted on 925 ha/2,286 acres in 2020, producing millions of bottles annually. While the 1980s saw the arrival and a certain acceptance of INTERNATIONAL VARIETIES, they never established a real foothold here, no doubt due to Piemonte's many high-quality indigenous varieties. While the plantings of Chardonnay and Pinot Noir have helped trigger a budding and promising METODO CLASSICO production under the Alta Langa DOC, other white Piemontese varieties, such as ERBALUCE (dry as well as sweet or sparkling), TIMORASSO, and NASCETTA, now with its own subzone Novello under the LANGHE DOC, are beginning to earn deserved recognition.

Piemonte is the only region in Italy that does not allow the production of IGT wine. Instead, an overarching DOC Piemonte, the size of the entire region, was created, encompassing 59 DOCs and DOCGs. The intention was to brand the region's entire production at the highest quality level in order to obtain greater prestige and success in the international market. But the system failed, because the Piemonte DOC's production rules had to be as flexible as those of an IGT to allow both international varieties and higher YIELDS. This weakened the significance of the DOC system as well as the notion of origin in high-quality wines. While the DOC Piemonte is not widely used, several other regions, notably Sicily and Friuli Venezia Giulia, have followed its example. The only radical refinement of the Piemontese DOC system has been the creation of recognized single-vineyard sites, called *menzione geografica aggiuntiva* (MGA), of which especially Barolo and Barbaresco have taken advantage (see BAROLO for more detail).

For more details of individual wines, see ALBA, ARNEIS, ASTI, BARBARESCO, BARBERA, BAROLO, BRACHETTO, CAREMA, CORTESE, DOLCETTO, ERBALUCE, FAVORITA, FREISA, GATTINARA, GAVI, GRIGNOLINO, LANGHE, MOSCATO, NEBBIOLO, ROERO, RUCHÈ, and SPANNA. W.S.

Belfrage, N., *From Barolo to Valpolicella: The Wines of Northern Italy* (2nd edn, 2003).
www.piemonteland.it

Pierce's disease, or **PD**, is one of the vine BACTERIAL DISEASES most feared around the world as it can quickly kill grapevines and a wide range of economically important crops including olives, almonds, and citrus. There is no cure, and it is extremely difficult to control because the bacterium has a wide range of host plants and is spread by insects from several different families.

Along with FLAVESCENCE DORÉE, Pierce's disease is a principal reason for QUARANTINE restrictions on the movement of grape cuttings and other plants between countries. In common with many other economically significant vine diseases, it originates on the American continent and is a principal factor limiting grape-growing in the Gulf Coastal plains of the United States (see TEXAS) and southern CALIFORNIA, but in the last decade it has been found in Europe, first in olive trees but now also in grapevines.

The disease was first described in 1892 in southern California as Anaheim disease, but was later named after the Californian researcher Pierce. By 1906, the disease had destroyed almost all of the more than 16,000 ha/39,500 acres of vines, and there was another epidemic in the 1930s in the Los Angeles basin, which never recovered as a viticultural area. Pierce's disease has continued to cause chronic problems in southern California, in coastal northern California (Napa and Sonoma) in isolated hot spots near riparian vegetation, and in the Central Valley near insect-vector breeding habitats such as pastures and hayfields. The disease is today found across the southern United States and throughout Mexico and Central America. It has also been reported in Venezuela.

The leaves of infected plants develop marginal discoloration that advances to dead tissue. This progressively enlarges until the leaves drop leaving only the PETIOLE attached. The clusters also dehydrate and are left unpicked. Vines die within one to five years after infection, depending on grape variety, vine age, and climate. Originally believed to be a virus, the disease is now known to be caused by a bacterium named *Xylella fastidiosa*. Various strains of the bacterium differ from one another in their ability to multiply within, and cause disease to, certain plant species. For example, grape strains do not multiply in sweet orange, but orange strains (now in South America) cause disease in grapevines. The disease is spread by insects called sharpshooters (see LEAFHOPPERS), which transmit the bacterium from host plants to the vineyards during feeding. In coastal California, vectors originally fed and reproduced in natural vegetation along streams, and the largest numbers of infected vines were therefore typically within 100 m/330 ft of a vineyard edge. Only the spring infections of vines (April–May) establish chronic Pierce's disease; later infections are removed by pruning or killed by winter temperatures.

However, the introduction of the GLASSY-WINGED SHARPSHOOTER into southern California in the 1980s has led to far more widespread damage. This leafhopper also spreads the bacterium, and, significantly for vineyards, it can fly further and more frequently. Vineyards near Temecula, for example, were destroyed by an outbreak spread by this new insect vector. It has moved northwards in the Central Valley, and vigorous QUARANTINE efforts are protecting vulnerable Napa and Sonoma counties for the moment. Since Pierce's disease exists in these counties but the insect vector is limited, a new insect vector could have major implications.

There are no resistant VITIS VINIFERA varieties, and some such as Chardonnay and Pinot Noir are especially susceptible. Varieties developed from MUSCADINE grapes or other wild grape species native to south-eastern USA and Mexico have natural resistance or tolerance and are the only ones to be grown where the disease is endemic. In California, growers are advised to avoid planting near hotspots or use less susceptible varieties. There is no satisfactory chemical control of the bacterium.

However, the discovery of strong single-gene resistance to *Xylella fastidiosa* in forms of *Vitis arizonica* from Texas and northern Mexico led to the possibility of breeding high-quality PD-resistant wine grapes by classical VINE BREEDING. Genetic mapping of this resistance gene enabled the marker-assisted selection of breeding populations, which—coupled with aggressive growing practices to force grapes into a two-year seed-to-seed cycle—has allowed 97% *vinifera* PD-resistant selections to be created over about 12 years at the University of California, DAVIS (see DISEASE-RESISTANT VARIETIES).

In 2013 PD was detected on olive trees in Puglia and has spread northwards killing millions of trees. In 2015–17, several subspecies and strains were detected on around 30

◄ Volcanic Mount PICO, rising to 2,531 m/7,713 ft on the island of the same name dwarfs the Azores Wine Company's brilliantly camouflaged winery in Bandeiras. The lava-rock walls (*currais*) that protect these Arinto dos Açores vines from the WIND and sea spray are essential to the survival of these tenacious vineyards. © Azores Wine Company/ Armando Jorge Mota Ribeiro

different host plants in southern France and Corsica; in 2016 on almonds, grapevines, cherries, and plums in the western Iberian peninsula of Spain, as well as on the Balearic Islands. It has also been found on grapevines in Iran, Türkiye, Taiwan, on Mallorca, and, in 2023, in Portugal. Cold winters appear to limit where the disease occurs in North America and could do the same in northern Europe. The situation in Europe will be worsened by CLIMATE CHANGE, as Godefried et al. report. R.E.S. & M.A.W.

Almeida, R. P. P., 'Can Apulia's olive trees be saved?', *Science*, 353/6297 (2016), 346–8.

Das, M., et al., 'Control of Pierce's Disease by phage', *PLOS ONE* (June 2015).

Dolan, D., 'Pierce's disease resistant vines now a reality after years of research', *Wine Industry Network Advisor* (June 2020).

Godefried, M., et al., 'Xylella fastidiosa: climate suitability of European continent', *Scientific Reports*, 9 (2019), 1–10.

Hoddle, M. S., 'The potential adventive geographic range of glassy-winged sharpshooter, *Homalodisca coagulata*, and the grape pathogen *Xylella fastidiosa*: implications for California and other grape growing regions of the world', *Crop Protection*, 23 (2004), 691–9.

www.cdfa.ca.gov/pdcp/research.html

Pierrevert, AOC in the Alpine foothills of northern Provence, regarded by the INAO as an eastern satellite of the southern RHÔNE. The appellation extends over 300 ha/741 acres east of the LUBERON and includes some of the highest vineyards in France. Wines of all three colours are produced, with rosé the most important. Thanks to the relative harshness of the climate, they are usually marked more by acidity than body. Grenache and Syrah are the dominant grapes. Tourism in the Alpes de Haute-Provence is such that there has been little need to seek export markets.

Pigato, characterful white grape variety producing distinctively flavoured VARIETAL wines in the north-west Italian region of LIGURIA. DNA PROFILING showed that Pigato and VERMENTINO, both long-established in Liguria, and FAVORITA cultivated in Piemonte are all genetically identical.

pigeage, French term for PUNCHING DOWN.

pigmented tannins, also called **polymeric pigments**, are responsible for the colour of red wines, together with ANTHOCYANINS, which are the phenolic red PIGMENTS of dark-skinned grapes. Pigmented tannins comprise a great diversity of molecular species formed by the reactions of anthocyanins with non-pigmented CATECHINS, PROANTHOCYANIDINS (i.e. condensed tannins from grapes), and ellagitannins (i.e. hydrolysable tannins extracted from barrels or added as components of some OENOLOGICAL TANNINS), under the influence of acids and oxygen. Their formation begins in the course of MACERATION and then progresses throughout the AGEING of a red wine, so that the grape anthocyanins as individual molecular species make only a transitory and ever-diminishing contribution to the colour of a red wine.

Although this process has been known for over thirty years, some of the structures postulated for pigmented tannins have only recently been shown to form in wine, owing to progress in the development of analytical techniques, whereas others have not yet been confirmed. Besides, several hitherto unsuspected reaction processes and products have been unravelled in the last few years. Formation of pigmented tannins occurs through both direct addition reactions between anthocyanins and tannins and reactions involving fermentation products such as ACETALDEHYDE and pyruvic acid. The nature and amounts of the resulting products depend on the nature and proportions of the phenolics present and the relative kinetics of the various reactions. Physico-chemical parameters such as PH and temperature and the presence of oxygen, of yeast metabolites, and of co-factors, such as metal ions, also affect the type and/or kinetics of the reactions.

Colour changes, from the purple nuance of young wines towards the red-brown tint of mature wine, are classically ascribed to the conversion of anthocyanins to pigmented tannins. However, pigmented tannins cover a wide range of colours, from orange to purple and blue. Besides, anthocyanin reactions also yield lower molecular weight orange pigments which are not pigmented tannins and various kinds of polymeric pigments (e.g. anthocyanin oligomers, pyranoanthocyanin dimers) which are not derived from tannins. Reactions of tannins under OXIDATIVE conditions also lead to brown-orange pigments that do not derive from anthocyanins. Most of these pigments show increased colour stability with respect to hydration and sulfite bleaching compared with anthocyanins, but this property is neither characteristic of nor specific to pigmented tannins. Known pigments account for only a small proportion of wine colour, meaning that most pigmented tannins are of analytically intractable nature, due to their multiplicity and diversity of structure and the transient nature of individual molecular species as they equilibrate among each other.

There is also conjecture about interactions of pigmented tannins with PROTEINS and POLYSACCHARIDES and the influence of such putative interactions on the properties (particularly taste properties—see below) of the pigmented tannins.

Experience has also shown that the formation of pigmented tannins, as well as conferring stability on the colour of a red wine (for decades, in favourable circumstances), also modulates the ASTRINGENCY of the very high concentration of phenolics of the wine, improving its TEXTURE and other taste properties. The desirable effects of pigmented tannins on mouthfeel are well illustrated by a comparison of the taste properties of a red wine with those of a white wine made, like a red wine, with extensive MACERATION. Such highly tannic white wines (except for the few made deliberately in this way; see ORANGE WINE, QVEVRI, and SKIN-FERMENTED whites for examples) are not just unattractive but crude and coarse on the palate; furthermore, they do not improve with age but remain tannic and undrinkable. In contrast, the pigmented tannins of the red wine make it palatable and soft with good AGEING characteristics, and this despite the fact that their presence increases further the phenolic and tannin polymer content of the red wine relative to that of its macerated white wine counterpart.

Changes in astringency taking place during red-wine ageing are usually attributed to an increase of tannin molecular weight as a result of the formation of co-polymers with anthocyanins since larger polyphenolic species have been claimed to be insoluble and thus non-astringent. However, recent studies have shown that tannin solubility does not decrease with molecular weight and that astringency in fact increases with the tannin size. Besides, tannin reactions in wine do not only yield larger polymers but also lead to lower molecular weight species. The latter reactions may contribute to the decrease of astringency observed during wine ageing. Nevertheless, the taste of pigmented tannins and the effect of incorporating anthocyanin units in a tannin structure on its astringency remain to be investigated. P.J.W. & V.C.

Fulcrand, H., et al., 'The fate of anthocyanins in wine: are there determining factors?', in A. L. Waterhouse and J. A. Kennedy (eds.), *Red Wine Color: Revealing the Mysteries. ACS Symposium Series 886* (2004), 68–88.

pigments, inclusive name for the compounds which impart colour. Colour results from the presence in these compounds of structures or functional groups that absorb light of particular wavelengths. Young red wines get their colour from the ANTHOCYANINS and PIGMENTED TANNINS, with the former decreasing in concentration and the latter reciprocally increasing and making the dominant contribution to colour as the wine ages. In contrast to the broad understanding of the pigments (and their chromophores) responsible for red-wine colour, the yellow to amber colours of white wines are less well understood. PHENOLICS present in the white grapes are evidently involved, and some limited OXIDATION of these is assumed to play a role in desirable white-wine colour development. Brown polymers, resulting from excessive oxidation of white-wine CATECHINS, are known to be responsible for the browning of oxidized wines. See AGEING and COLOUR. P.J.W.

Pignatello, synonym for the Sicilian red grape variety PERRICONE.

Pignola Valtellinese, dark-berried vine almost certainly originating in VALTELLINA. DNA PROFILING revealed a parent–offspring relationship with Rossolino Nero, also of Valtellina. It may be related to NEBBIOLO.

Pignoletto, lively, crisp white grape grown in Umbria and in EMILIA-ROMAGNA in northern Italy on an area totalling about 1,172 ha/2,896 acres in 2015. This ancient variety is also known as GRECHETTO Gentile.

Pignolo, promising red grape variety native to the FRIULI region of north-east Italy, probably first cultivated in the hills of Rosazzo in FRIULI COLLI ORIENTALI. Pignolo is a very shy bearer; it was generally ignored by local growers who preferred other, more productive grape varieties until, like SCHIOPPETTINO, it was given a new lease when in 1978 it was authorized for use in the province of Udine. Plantings in Italy had reached 50 ha/124 acres by 2015.

Little, B., *Pignolo* (2016).

Pineau, a word widely used in France as a synonym for the PINOT group of grape varieties. It seems to have been a portmanteau word for any better-quality vine in medieval France (probably a reference to the pine-cone shape of so many bunches of grapes) but is today a word associated primarily with the Loire. It is the first word of a wide range of vine synonyms, sometimes various forms of Pinot but often CHENIN, most notably as **Pineau de la Loire**.

Pineau d'Aunis, sometimes called Chenin Noir although unrelated to CHENIN BLANC, is a historic Touraine variety making light-red wines once sought by the kings of both France and England, according to Pierre GALET. France's total plantings, 479 ha/1,184 acres in 2019, have remained steady and are concentrated around Tours in the Loire Valley. The variety is one of the many sanctioned for the red and rosé appellations of TOURAINE and ANJOU but is used only to a limited extent, mainly to bring peppery liveliness and fruit to rosés, although in ripe years it can yield a fine red, too, notably in Coteaux du LOIR. See also Coteaux du VENDÔMOIS.

Pineau des Charentes is the VIN DE LIQUEUR of the Cognac region and has enjoyed some *réclame* in France as a strong, sweet APERITIF more likely to be the product of an artisan than of big business. It is made by adding at least year-old cognac straight from cask to must that is just about to ferment, thereby producing what is effectively a mixture of grape juice and brandy. AOC regulations specify that rosé versions must age for at least eight months; reds for 12; and whites for 18, mainly in barrel, though finer examples tend to be aged far longer. Those labelled *vieux* age more than seven years and *extra vieux* more than 12. The final product is bottled at 16–22% alcohol. The style most often encountered outside France is pale gold, decidedly sweet and spirity, but there are many subtler examples, including soft, fruity rosé styles made from the same grapes as red BORDEAUX. See also FLOC DE GASCOGNE.

Pinenc, local name for the FER Servadou red wine grape variety in MADIRAN.

Pinot is the first word of many a French vine variety name and is thought to refer to the shape of Pinot grape bunches, in the form of a pine (*pin*) cone. Pinot is considered one of the most important and ancient grape varieties, possibly a selection from WILD VINES. The variety may well have existed for as long as two millennia. Although Morillon Noir was the common name for early Pinot, a vine called Pinot was already described in records of Burgundy in the 14th century, and its fortunes were inextricably linked with those of the powerful medieval monasteries of eastern France and Germany (see BURGUNDY and GERMAN HISTORY). So long has Pinot existed that an unusual number of CLONES have emerged, more than 1,000 according to the father of modern vine identification Pierre GALET, of which PINOT BLANC, PINOT GRIS, PINOT MEUNIER, and PINOT NOIR are just some of the better known. CHARDONNAY is still occasionally called Pinot Chardonnay. Galet maintained that Chardonnay was not a member of the Pinot family, but DNA PROFILING analysis in 1999 dropped the bombshell that at least 21 distinct varieties are the progenies of Pinot and the obscure and rather ordinary variety GOUAIS BLANC, including ALIGOTÉ, Aubin Vert, AUXERROIS, Bachet Noir, Beaunoir, CHARDONNAY, Franc Noir de la Haute-Saône, Gamay Blanc Gloriod, GAMAY Noir, Knipperlé, MELON, Peurion, ROMORANTIN, Roublot, and SACY. Furthermore, independent DNA analysis in Austria revealed a parent–offspring relationship between Pinot and SAVAGNIN. Other instances of DNA profiling have shown that Pinot is probably a grandparent of TEROLDEGO, MARZEMINO, LAGREIN, and DUREZA, parent of Syrah. A family tree in *Wine Grapes*, with Pinot, Gouais Blanc, and Savagnin at the top (and many blanks for unknown relatives), includes 156 Western European vine varieties, most of them well known. So much for Pinot's genetic importance. As for nomenclature, there are no fewer than 30 entries beginning 'Pinot' in the index of *Wine Grapes*, although they are by no means all distinct.

In German, members of the Pinot group frequently have the word 'Burgunder' in their German names (SPÄTBURGUNDER, WEISSBURGUNDER, and GRAUBURGUNDER) in a reference to Pinot's Burgundian homeland. There was a marked increase in the popularity of these grape varieties throughout the 1980s as tastes changed in favour of drier, fuller German wines. Throughout Eastern Europe, Pinots of various sorts have 'burgund' in their name.

Galet, P., *Dictionnaire encyclopédique des cépages* (2nd edn, 2015).

Robinson, J., et al., *Wine Grapes: A Complete Guide to 1,368 Vine Varieties, Including Their Origins and Flavours* (2012).

Pinotage, a hardy and moderately vigorous red grape variety, is SOUTH AFRICA's most notable contribution to the history of the VITIS VINIFERA vine. In 1924 STELLENBOSCH UNIVERSITY viticulturist A. I. Perold crossed Pinot Noir and Cinsaut, then commonly called Hermitage in South Africa, hence the contraction Pinotage. It took until 1961 for the name to appear on a label, that of a Lanzerac 1959. The grape has been controversial, particularly in earlier decades, when it frequently made reds with a flamboyantly sweetish paint-like pungency (from ISOAMYL ACETATE) and, often, some degree of bitterness. Greater viticultural and winemaking understanding have made such problems increasingly rare, but local and international detractors remain. Many examples are indeed too powerful and jammy, with the excessiveness of a certain type of ambition taking its toll. Nonetheless, some unquestionably good VARIETAL and blended wines are produced, at all levels, from accessibly fruity rosés and lighter reds to fine, deep-coloured, rich, seriously oaked examples, although examples made in the 1960s, long before the era of vinification in BARRIQUE, reveal that Pinotage does not depend on the use of wood to acquire longevity and complexity. Most of the best of them come from mature BUSH VINE vineyards with restricted YIELDS, and some have a perfume recalling the grape's parentage. Fairly simple CO-OPERATIVE winery examples from the 1960s and 1970s that have been drinking well (and rather elegantly) in the second decade of this century, as well as the complex maturation of older wines from the likes of Pinotage specialist Kanonkop in STELLENBOSCH, testify to Pinotage's longevity. So-called 'coffee Pinotage', with mocha notes deliberately derived from artful oaking, became a notorious early 21st century success story in South Africa and in some export markets. Pinotage

P

works well in blends, and attempts continue to establish CAPE BLEND as a generic name for reds with a certain (but disputed) percentage of the grape. Since 1994, plantings of Pinotage, along with other major red varieties, have grown substantially, and by 2020 the total area planted, 6,637 ha/16,400 acres, represented around 6% of all South African vine plantings. Pinotage is also grown, to a much more limited extent, in Australia, New Zealand, Brazil, California, Oregon, Washington, Israel, Zimbabwe, and most vine collections.

May, P. F., *Pinotage: Behind the Legends of South Africa's Own Wine* (2009).

Pinot Beurot, ancient Burgundian synonym for PINOT GRIS.

Pinot Bianco, common Italian name for the white PINOT BLANC grape of French origin and much, much more widely grown than the French original in France. Introduced to north-eastern Italy as Weissburgunder well before the mid 19th century when the region was under Austrian rule, it was once very popular there. By 2000, however, it had been decisively overtaken by Chardonnay and Pinot Grigio, and total plantings in 2015 were just 2,337 ha/5,775 acres.

It is grown particularly in TRENTINO-ALTO ADIGE, the VENETO, FRIULI, and LOMBARDY, although, as in ALSACE, Pinot Grigio enjoys higher esteem in these areas. Pinot Bianco is prized in Alto Adige, however, and has produced some of this region's finest white wines. It was first noted in Piemonte in the early 19th century, and until the mid 1980s the name 'Pinot Bianco' was used to describe Pinot Blanc, Chardonnay, or a blend of the two. Even today there are vineyards in which both varieties grow side by side. Italians often vinify Pinot Blanc as a high-acid, slightly SPRITZIG, non-aromatic white for early consumption, but good Pinot Bianco from low-yielding vineyards in Alto Adige, sometimes fermented and aged in oak barrels, indicate that Pinot Bianco could give much better results in Italy if it were treated with more respect. In Lombardy the high acid and low aroma is useful to the SPUMANTE industry, but CLIMATE CHANGE may make this variety less suitable.

Pinot Blanc, French white vine variety, member of the PINOT group and particularly associated with ALSACE, where most of its French 1,159 ha/2,864 acres in 2019 were to be found. It was first observed in Burgundy at the end of the 19th century, a white mutation of PINOT NOIR. Although its base is Burgundian, today it is found all over central Europe.

For many years no distinction was made between Pinot Blanc and CHARDONNAY since the two varieties can look very similar. No Pinot Blanc is notable for its piercing aroma; its perfume arrives in a cloud. Most wines based on Pinot Blanc are also relatively full-bodied, which has undoubtedly helped reinforce the confusion with Chardonnay, not only in Burgundy but also in north-east Italy, where it is known as PINOT BIANCO. Although Chardonnay dominates white burgundy, Pinot Blanc is technically allowed into wines labelled BOURGOGNE Blanc but is no longer grown in any quantity in Burgundy.

Even in Alsace, Pinot Blanc's French stronghold, it is less important in terms of total area planted than Riesling or even the white AUXERROIS with which it is customarily blended in Alsace, to be sold as 'Pinot Blanc'. In LUXEMBOURG, on the other hand, the higher acidity of Pinot Blanc makes it less highly regarded than Auxerrois.

While in Alsace it is regarded as something of a workhorse (and sometimes called Clevner or Klevner), it has been generally held in much higher esteem in German-speaking wine regions, where it is known as WEISSBURGUNDER. Germany has a much greater area planted than France, up to 5,922 ha/14,634 acres by 2020, making it Germany's fifth most planted white-wine CULTIVAR, with vinous personalities ranging from the full, rich, oaked examples of Baden and the Pfalz to relatively delicate, mineral-inflected variations along the Nahe and Mosel, and with quality aspirations ranging from a workaday norm to occasional brilliance. It is popular with growers seeking food-friendly wines that are softer than Riesling and can show local characters.

As Pinot Bianco it is a popular dry white in Italy and is also grown in Switzerland, but it is in AUSTRIA that, as Weissburgunder, the variety reaches some of its greatest must weights. Also the fifth most planted white wine grape on a total of nearly 1,884 ha/4,655 acres in 2021, it is grown in all regions. As a dry white varietal, Weissburgunder is associated with an almond-like scent, medium to high alcohol, and an ability to age, but it has achieved its greatest glory in Austria in ultra-rich, botrytized TROCKENBEERENAUSLESE form, often blended, typically with WELSCHRIESLING (acting out the respective parts of Sémillon and Sauvignon Blanc in Sauternes).

Pinot Blanc is broadly disseminated over eastern Europe. In Slovenia, Croatia, and Serbia, it is widely grown and may be called Beli (White) Pinot. It is also grown in Czechia and Slovakia and is typically used in Hungary to produce full-bodied, rather anodyne dry whites more suitable for export than INDIGENOUS VARIETIES.

Vine-growers outside Europe recognize that Pinot Blanc has lacked Chardonnay's glamour, but in 2020 there were still 132 ha/326 acres of a variety called Pinot Blanc in California, mainly in Monterey, usually treated to BARREL AGEING and the full range of Chardonnay winemaking tricks, to creditable effect. Older vines bearing this name are almost certainly not Pinot Blanc but the Muscadet grape MELON (now proven to be another member of the extended Pinot group).

Viticulturally, if not necessarily commercially, Pinot Blanc seems particularly well adapted to the Okanagan Valley in British Columbia. Elsewhere in the New World, Pinot Blanc is largely ignored.

Pinot Chardonnay is an old synonym for CHARDONNAY, the classic white grape of Burgundy. It was adopted at a time when Chardonnay was believed to be a white mutation of PINOT NOIR (incorrectly, as it turned out—see PINOT).

Pinot Grigio, during the first decade of the 21st century, took over from Chardonnay as the name of the most popular white wine in the global mass market. It came to signify a vaguely aromatic, dryish, unoaked white. It is also the common Italian name for the French vine variety PINOT GRIS and, as such, is probably the name by which the variety is best known to many wine drinkers. Because of Pinot Grigio's popularity, many producers worldwide choose this name in preference to Pinot Gris. There were about 3,500 ha/8,600 acres of Pinot Grigio vineyard in Italy in 1990 (much less than the area planted with PINOT BIANCO, for example), but so great was demand for Pinot Grigio that its plantings had overtaken those of Pinot Bianco to reach 6,700 ha by 2000 and 18,821 ha/46,507 acres by 2015, almost as much as Chardonnay's 19,769 ha.

The variety is said to have been introduced to Italy via Piemonte in the early 19th century but became a speciality of the north-east. The best and richest wines are produced in FRIULI, with the traditional version called Ramato, SKIN-FERMENTED, resulting in a copper-tinged (*ramato*) wine, while those produced in Alto Adige can be particularly aromatic. But the bulk of Pinot Grigio produced today comes from the VENETO, where large volumes are produced by growers for their local CO-OPERATIVES and then sold to the large bottlers. These Veneto versions tend to be rather neutral and, at their best, inoffensive, the high yields diluting any true Pinot Grigio character. The variety is also grown widely in LOMBARDY although there is less fastidiousness here about distinguishing it from other hues of PINOT, especially when supplying grapes for the sparkling wine industry. Pinot Grigio is planted as far south as EMILIA-ROMAGNA and as far north as ALTO ADIGE.

Pinot Gris is the widely disseminated, fashionable vine variety (see PINOT GRIGIO) that can produce soft, gently perfumed wines with more substance and colour than most whites, which is what one might expect of a variety that is one of the best-known MUTATIONS of PINOT NOIR. If Pinot Noir berries are purplish blue and the berries of the related PINOT BLANC are greenish yellow, Pinot Gris grapes are anything between greyish blue and brownish pink—sometimes on the same bunch. In the vineyard, this vine can easily be taken for Pinot Noir for the leaves are identical and, especially late in a ripe year, the berries can look remarkably similar. At one time, Pinot Gris habitually grew in among the Pinot Noir of many Burgundian vineyards, adding softness and sometimes acidity to its red wine. Even today, as Pinot Beurot, it is sanctioned as an ingredient in most of Burgundy's red-wine appellations, and the occasional vine can still be found in some of the region's famous red-wine vineyards. It was traditionally prized for its ability to soften Pinot Noir, but older CLONES have a tendency to YIELD very irregularly.

Within France, Alsace is where Pinot Gris (once known as Tokay, see GERMAN HISTORY) is most familiar and where by far the majority of the country's 3,139 ha/7,757 acres of the variety grew in 2019. Here it has been gaining ground and is revered as provider of super-rich, usually dry, wines that can be partnered with food without the distraction of too much aroma. For more on the wines, see ALSACE. There also remain small pockets of the variety in the Loire, where it is often known as Malvoisie (in Coteaux d'ANCENIS, 'Malvoisie' is officially allowed as a suffix to the appellation name). It can produce perfumed, substantial wines in a wide range of different sweetness levels. It is also known as Malvoisie in SAVOIE and the Valais in SWITZERLAND, where its wines are also notably full-bodied and richly aromatic—rather different from the neutral mouthwash that is typical mass-market PINOT GRIGIO. The variety is also much admired for its weight and relatively low acidity in LUXEMBOURG, where it represents 15% of the vineyard area.

As with Pinot Blanc, much more Pinot Gris is planted in both Germany (see GRAUBURGUNDER) and Italy (see PINOT GRIGIO) than in France.

The variety, like Pinot Blanc, is widely planted not just in AUSTRIA but throughout eastern Europe, particularly in HUNGARY, where in 2021 it was planted on 1,827 ha/5,415 acres and known as Szürkebarát, although varietal versions may often be exported as the more familiar Pinot Gris or even the more marketable Pinot Grigio, a name it often takes on in MOLDOVA too. Many eastern European synonyms are inspired by the word RULÄNDER, the German name for sweeter styles of Pinot Gris, although the Slovenian name Sivi Pinot is more literal. The variety can make fine wines in both eastern and western SLOVENIA.

With the exception of OREGON, where this mutation of its beloved Pinot Noir has long been the state's leading white-wine grape and was planted on more than 2,104 ha/5,200 acres by 2019, Pinot Gris' impact beyond Europe has been more limited but has been increasing thanks to Pinot Grigio's commercial success. In the late 20th century, there was a dramatic increase in plantings in California, mainly Monterey and Napa, and its 2020 total of 6,649 ha/16,431 acres makes it the state's third most planted white wine grape after Chardonnay and French Colombard, just ahead of Sauvignon Blanc. In Washington State it is third most popular after Chardonnay and Riesling, and it is planted in much of the rest of North America. Pinot Gris has been a fixture in the Argentine vinescape since the LURTON brothers introduced it in the early 1990s, but it is not common in Chile. T'Gallant of the Mornington Peninsula was Australia's Pinot Gris pioneer, using both French and Italian names, and the country's total area had reached 4,935 ha/12,195 acres by 2022. It was improved CLONAL SELECTION and increased interest in AROMATICS that precipitated a renewal of enthusiasm in New Zealand, where Pinot Gris' total 2022 plantings of 2,809 ha/6,941 acres were catching up fast with those of second most planted white wine grape Chardonnay.

Pinot Liébault, unusual and slightly more productive Burgundian selection of PINOT NOIR, first identified in GEVREY by A. Liébault in 1810, according to Galet.

Galet, P., *Dictionnaire encyclopédique des cépages* (2nd edn, 2015).

Pinot Meunier, known as **Meunier** in France, may be France's tenth most planted black grape variety, but it is rarely encountered on a wine label. Most of Pinot Meunier's more than 12,000 ha/29,650 acres are in the CHAMPAGNE region. It is an early, particularly downy, MUTATION of PINOT NOIR and earns its name (*meunier* is French for 'miller') because the underside of its downy leaves can look as though they have been dusted with flour. In Germany it is known as MÜLLERREBE (miller's grape).

The variety is treasured in Champagne, as it was in the once-extensive vineyards of northern France, because it buds later and ripens earlier than the inconveniently early-budding Pinot Noir and is therefore much less prone to COULURE and more dependably productive. Acid levels are slightly higher, although alcohol levels are by no means necessarily lower than those of Champagne's most planted variety, Pinot Noir. Pinot Meunier is therefore the popular choice for Champagne's growers, especially those in cooler north-facing vineyards, in the damp, frost-prone Vallée de la Marne, and in the cold valleys of the Aisne *département*. In fact, so commercially reliable is Meunier for Champagne's powerful vine-growers that until recently it was Champagne's most popular variety by far, but it has now been overtaken by Pinot Noir. Common wisdom has it that, as an ingredient in the traditional three-variety champagne blend, Meunier contributes youthful fruitiness to complement Pinot Noir's weight and Chardonnay's finesse. Few producers boast of their Pinot Meunier, however (with the honourable exception of KRUG), although several Champagne growers make a VARIETAL Pinot Meunier, which is generally lower in PIGMENTS than Pinot Noir.

It has largely disappeared elsewhere in northern France, although it is still technically allowed into the rosés and light reds of Côtes de TOUL, wines of MOSELLE, and, in the Loire, TOURAINE, and ORLÉANS.

See MÜLLERREBE for plantings in Germany. It is also grown to a very limited extent in German-speaking Switzerland. Elsewhere, Meunier tends to be grown by those slavishly following the champagne recipe (as in England and California, for example). But curiously, in Australia Pinot Meunier has a longer documented history as a still red varietal wine (at one time called Miller's Burgundy) than Pinot Noir, notably at Great Western (now called GRAMPIANS) in VICTORIA.

Pinot Nero is Italian for PINOT NOIR, which is grown there chiefly for the SPUMANTE industry (see, for example, FRANCIACORTA and TRENTODOC). There was a total of 5,057 ha/12,496 acres in 2015. The great majority is planted in the province of Pavia in LOMBARDY, where it is increasingly important for both still and sparkling wines in OLTREPÒ PAVESE, but a few producers—Hofstätter, Haas, and Gottardi—are making a name for the variety in Alto Adige.

Pinot Noir is the most important and oldest form of PINOT. It is the grape variety wholly responsible for red BURGUNDY and one that suddenly became the height of FASHION, thanks to the 2004 film SIDEWAYS. It gives its name to the NOIRIEN group of grape varieties. Unlike Cabernet Sauvignon, which can be grown in all but the coolest conditions and can be economically viable as an inexpensive but recognizably Cabernet wine, Pinot Noir demands much of both vine-grower and winemaker. It is a tribute to the unparalleled level of physical excitement generated by tasting one of Burgundy's better reds that such a high proportion of the world's most ambitious wine producers want to try their hand with this capricious and extremely variable vine. Although there is relatively little consistency in its performance in its homeland, Pinot Noir has been transplanted to almost every one of the world's wine regions, except the very hottest, where it can so easily turn from essence to jam.

If Cabernet produces wines to appeal to the head, Pinot's charms are decidedly more sensual and more transparent. The Burgundians themselves refute the allegation that they produce Pinot Noir; they merely use Pinot Noir as the vehicle for communicating local geography, the characteristics of the individual site, the TERROIR on which it was planted. Perhaps the only characteristics that the Pinot Noirs of the world could be said to share would be a certain sweet fruitiness and, in general, lower levels of TANNINS and PIGMENTS than the other 'great' French red varieties Cabernet Sauvignon and Syrah. The wines are decidedly more charming in youth and evolve more rapidly, although the decline of the very best is slow.

No fewer than 50 Pinot Noir CLONES (as opposed to 25 of the much more widely planted Cabernet Sauvignon) are officially recognized within France. According to GALET, the most popular is one of the first generation of virus-free Burgundy clones, 115, followed by the productive Champagne clones 375 and 386. Marsh surveyed top Côte d'Or producers in the early 2000s and found second-generation clone 677 marginally more admired for wine quality than the more widely planted 777 or 828. It is possible to choose a clone of Pinot Noir specially for the quality of its wine, its productivity, its regularity of yield, its resistance to rot, and/or for its likely ripeness (which can vary considerably). A major factor in the lighter colour and extract of so much red burgundy in the 1970s and 1980s was injudicious CLONAL SELECTION, resulting in higher yields but much less character and concentration in the final wine. The most reputable producers of all tend nowadays to have made MASS SELECTIONS from their own vine population. The clone called Pommard is well distributed in the New World, especially in North America, as has been one named after the WÄDENSWIL viticultural station in Switzerland. Often more sought-after now are Burgundian, 'Dijon', or in Australia 'Bernard' clones. In general the most productive clones, which have large-berried bunches, are described as Pinot Droit for the vines' upright growth, while Pinot Fin, Pinot Tordu, or Pinot Classique grows much less regularly but has smaller berries with thicker skin.

Inasmuch as generalizations about a vine variety with so many different forms are possible, Pinot Noir tends to bud early, making it susceptible to spring FROST and COULURE. Damp, cool soils on low-lying land are therefore best avoided. Yields are theoretically low, although too many Burgundians disproved this with productive clones in the 1970s and early 1980s. The vine is also more prone than most to both DOWNY and POWDERY MILDEW, ROT (its grape skins tend to be thinner than most), and viruses, particularly FANLEAF and LEAFROLL. Indeed it was the prevalence of disease in Burgundian vineyards that precipitated the widespread adoption of clonal selection there in the 1970s.

Pinot Noir generally produces the best-quality wine on CALCAREOUS soils and in relatively cool climates where this early-ripening vine will not rush towards maturity, losing aroma and acidity. In Burgundy, for example, where it is typically cultivated alongside the equally early-ripening Chardonnay, Pinot Noir may ripen after Chardonnay in some years, before it in others. There is general agreement, however, that Pinot Noir is very much more difficult to vinify than Chardonnay, needing constant monitoring and fine-tuning of technique according to the demands of each particular vintage.

Pinot Noir is planted throughout eastern France and has been steadily gaining ground so that by 2018 its total area of French vineyard was 36,727 ha/90,754 acres, up from 28,006 ha in 2008, finally overtaking the area planted with Greater Burgundy's other red vine variety, the GAMAY of Beaujolais.

The extension of the CHAMPAGNE region from the 1980s saw Champagne's area planted with the variety—more than 13,000 ha/32,124 acres in 2010 and little changed over the last decade—overtake that of Burgundy, which recorded 10,978 ha in 2019. Pinot Noir is also the principal red wine grape of ALSACE, JURA, SAVOIE, SANCERRE, MENETOU-SALON, and ST-POURÇAIN—and recent global demand for the variety has encouraged some planting in the Languedoc, even if few corners are as suitably cool as LIMOUX. Even in the Greater Burgundy region, Pinot Noir is rarely blended with any other variety, except occasionally with Gamay in a BOURGOGNE PASSETOUTGRAINS and, increasingly, to add class to a MÂCON. See under individual appellation names specified for the CÔTE D'OR and Côte CHALONNAISE for more detail on individual wines. Pinot Noir is the favoured black grape variety in northern Burgundy too, where in 2019 there were 1,048 ha for such wines as IRANCY and particularly northern versions of BOURGOGNE. A tiny amount is cultivated even further north-east for the light reds and VIN GRIS of Lorraine such as Côtes de TOUL and the wines of MOSELLE.

The greatest increase in Pinot plantings in Europe has been in Champagne, where it is used, as it is in the production of a wide range of sparkling wines made around the world in champagne's image, as a still, very pale pink ingredient in the base blend of still wines. The grapes are pressed very gently, and any remaining pigments tend to agglomerate with the dead yeast cells during the champenization process. In such a blend, Pinot Noir is prized for its body and longevity—as well it might be, for that small proportion of champagne made exclusively from Pinot Noir is usually memorably substantial. In Champagne, only a tiny quantity of Pinot Noir is used for still red Coteaux CHAMPENOIS and ROSÉ DES RICEYS, but there is growing interest in the former due to CLIMATE CHANGE.

Pinot Noir has become increasingly well made, and desirable, in all areas where German is or was spoken. In ALSACE, where it has been an important vine since the early 16th century (see GERMAN HISTORY), it is effectively the only black-berried vine variety planted, with a total area of 1,874 ha/4,631 acres in 2019. Climate change means Alsace Pinot Noir has been getting darker and the wines much more substantial. The same phenomenon is even more marked in Germany, where the variety, often but not always called Spätburgunder, was the country's second most planted variety in 2020, just ahead of the waning MÜLLER-THURGAU. See SPÄTBURGUNDER for more details.

So popular is the variety in SWITZERLAND that it is the country's most planted, with more than 3,875 ha in 2020, even more than the area planted with Chasselas, although both are in decline. Graubünden has a particularly strong reputation for its sturdy Pinots. In AUSTRIA, Pinot Noir is also sometimes called Blauburgunder but is not nearly as popular as BLAUFRÄNKISCH and ST-LAURENT.

Pinot Noir is spread widely in the vineyards of eastern Europe, where its name is usually some variant on the local word for Burgundian (although Romania's Burgund Mare is Blaufränkisch). Romania had most (2,039 ha), followed by Moldova (1,271 ha), Hungary (1,171 ha), Croatia (988 ha), and Russia (918 ha), and there are also several hundred hectares in Ukraine. Elsewhere in Europe, the finicky

P

nature of the Pinot Noir vine has set a natural limit on its spread. In Iberia, there has been some successful experimentation in SOMONTANO, and substantial plantings for CAVA in Spanish CATALUÑA, where plantings had gone down slightly to 832 ha in 2020. Portugal's limited plantings are mainly in the north. There have been some noble experiments in some cooler Italian wine regions, notably LOMBARDY, where it is used for sparkling-wine production. See more details under PINOT NERO.

It was wine producers in the New World, however, who turned the full heat of their ambitious attentions on Pinot Noir from the late 1980s and early 1990s. Some even relocated their wineries many hundreds of miles in order to be closer to sources of suitably cool-climate Pinot Noir fruit. OREGON's wine reputation has so far rested heavily on its fine, fruity Pinot Noirs, with a state total of 9,531 ha/23,552 acres in 2020, almost 60% of the total vineyard area. This Pacific Northwestern state, with its cool, wet winters, has long been recognized as producing America's answer to red burgundy. However, as summers have become warmer and wines riper, the differences between Oregon Pinot Noirs and those from CALIFORNIA have narrowed, especially in California's cooler regions such as the Sonoma Coast, Carneros, Chalone, the Gavilan Mountains of San Benito, and Central Coast districts most affected by the Pacific. Both states now produce a range of styles from ripe, fruity, and heavily oaked to leaner earthier examples. California's total acreage remained steady into the 1990s but then took off after the SIDEWAYS effect, so that by 2020 there were 19,378 ha/47,885 acres of Pinot Noir in the state (up from barely 24,000 acres when *Sideways* was made). The variety is also valued as an ingredient in champagne-like sparkling wines, one of Pinot Noir's most important uses outside of Europe. (The variety once called **Pinot St George** in California, now in sharp decline, is NÉGRETTE.)

There are pockets of Pinot Noir, generally accompanied by enthusiasm and ambition, all over the United States, but cool climates such as that of the FINGER LAKES are generally best. And over the Canadian border in ONTARIO and BRITISH COLUMBIA, there are some seriously successful Pinot Noirs. Climate change has helped eastern Canada's Pinot producers considerably.

Much of South America is too hot for successful Pinot Noir production, but newer, Pacific-cooled wine regions are being developed for the variety in CHILE where total planting had reached 4,178 ha/10,324 acres by 2020. Bío-Bío also shows promise. It can be more difficult to find suitably cool terrain in ARGENTINA, but plantings totalled 1,992 ha/4,922 acres in 2020, mainly at the highest ELEVATIONS of Tupungato.

Across the Atlantic in SOUTH AFRICA, on the other hand, at least one producer, Hamilton-Russell, managed to coax convincingly Burgundian flavours from Pinot Noir vines grown in the hinterland of WALKER BAY on the south coast in the 1980s, and this continues to act as a spur to others, with increasingly encouraging results. Total plantings stood at 1,198 ha by 2020—a figure that would have been unthinkable at the turn of the century.

NEW ZEALAND, along with Oregon, is the New World wine producer that has been staking its red wine fortunes on Pinot Noir. By 2022 total plantings had reached 5,807 ha/13,350 acres, making it this small country's second most popular variety by far, with the most impressive results coming from Martinborough, Canterbury, Marlborough, and rapidly growing Central Otago.

Fine Pinot Noir has been more elusive in Australia, and the total area planted is slightly less than New Zealand's, but increasingly interesting examples are being made in cooler spots such as Geelong, Gippsland, Macedon Ranges, Yarra Valley, and Mornington Peninsula, all relatively cool areas around Melbourne in VICTORIA, as well as in TASMANIA. See AUSTRALIA for more details and more potential areas of exciting Pinot Noir production.

Wherever there is a wine producer with a palate, there will be experimentation with Pinot Noir.

Galet, P., *Dictionnaire encyclopédique des cépages* (2nd edn, 2015).

Marsh, S. A., 'The contribution of Pinot Noir clones to the vineyards of the Côte d'Or. An evaluation focusing on clones 114, 115, 667, 777' (MW dissertation, 2004).

Robinson, J., et al., *Wine Grapes: A Complete Guide to 1,368 Vine Varieties, Including Their Origins and Flavours* (2012).

Pinot Noir Précoce, French name for FRÜHBURGUNDER.

Pinot St George, California red grape identified as NÉGRETTE and now difficult to find.

pipe, wine trade term, adapted from the Portuguese *pipa* meaning 'barrel', for a large cask with tapered ends, the traditional measure of PORT as well as of MADEIRA, other Portuguese wines, and MARSALA, although the volume can vary around the country. In the DOURO Valley, where port is produced, the yield of each vineyard is measured in pipes of 550 l/145 gal, while downstream in VILA NOVA DE GAIA, the suburb of Oporto where port is matured, a pipe may vary in size between 580 l and 630 l but is usually taken as 620 l. For shipping purposes, however, a pipe of port is 534.24 l, divided into 21 measures of 25.44 l called *almudes*, while pipes of madeira and Marsala are 418 and 423 l respectively. Gentlemen in Victorian England traditionally laid down a pipe of port for their sons and godsons, but inflation and changing consumption patterns have made this generosity exceptional.

piperitone, a monoterpene recently identified as contributing to the minty character found in some bottle-aged Bordeaux reds. See FLAVOUR COMPOUNDS.

Pons, A., et al., 'Identification and analysis of piperitone in red wines', *Food Chemistry*, 206 (2016), 191–6.

Pipers River, cool, damp wine region in north-east TASMANIA known particularly for sparkling wine.

pips. See GRAPE.

Piquepoul, ancient grape variety from the Vaucluse *département* of southern France that is encountered in Blanc, Noir, and very occasionally Gris versions, with the white being the most planted today, although they have frequently been mixed in the vineyard in their long history in the LANGUEDOC and ROUSSILLON. Piquepoul was cited as a producer of good-quality wine as early as the beginning of the 17th century and, with CLAIRETTE, formed the basis of PICARDAN, exported northwards in vast quantities in the 17th and 18th centuries. Its susceptibility to FUNGAL DISEASES, however, together with its unremarkable yield, reduced its popularity considerably after PHYLLOXERA arrived. In the early 20th century, the variety's good tolerance of sand made it a popular choice for the coastal vineyards that serviced the then-flourishing VERMOUTH industry. Today many of those vineyards are tourist campsites and vermouth is an Italian phenomenon, but PICPOUL DE PINET has been a significant commercial success, and France's total plantings of Piquepoul Blanc continue to increase, reaching 1,829 ha/4,520 acres in 2019, virtually all in the Hérault. A small amount is also grown in California under the name **Picpoul**.

Piquepoul Noir produces alcoholic, richly scented but very pale red that is best drunk young. Although it is allowed as a minor ingredient in CHÂTEAUNEUF-DU-PAPE and LANGUEDOC, it is rarely seen.

piquette, traditionally a thin vinous liquid made by adding water to grape POMACE to extract what has been left behind. From the time of classical GREECE and ROME to the mid 20th century, pomace was given to slaves or low-paid workers for piquette production. (See ancient PRESSES for details of *lorca*, the Roman version.) In the late 20th century, at a time of wine SURPLUS, it was made illegal in the EU except for winegrowers' home consumption. The renaissance of piquette as a commercially available, spritzy, low-alcohol, fermented drink was spearheaded in the US by Wild Arc Farm in New York State in 2017 using an 18th-century French recipe, but there are now pockets of production across North America, Australia, and South Africa. It is particularly popular among proponents of NATURAL WINE. Today's piquette is often made with the addition of sugar, honey or fresh fruit to stimulate fermentation and increase ALCOHOL, or with a small percentage of wine to add BODY. The grape pomace contributes residual grape sugar, as well as colour and TANNINS from prolonged SKIN CONTACT during piquette fermentation. Technically difficult to produce and susceptible to spoilage due to the low-acid, low-alcohol fermentation environment, piquette is nonetheless becoming increasing popular thanks to the FASHION for this style of refreshing drink and the profit margins it gives producers. A.M.R.

Pirque, part of the MAIPO subregion of the Central Valley of CHILE famous for fruity, herbal Cabernet Sauvignon grown at the foot of the Andes.

pisco, aromatic brandy made in Peru, mainly from Quebranta and Negra Criolla (NEGRAMOLL) grapes, and in Chile, mainly from Moscatel (MUSCAT) grapes, rather like Bolivia's *singani*.

pithari (plural **pitharia**), Greek word for a large clay fermentation or storage vessel, also known more traditionally as *pithos*. It is the equivalent of the DOLIUM and bigger than an AMPHORA, although many producers prefer this last term because it is more internationally recognized.

pithos. See PITHARI.

PiWi. See DISEASE-RESISTANT VARIETIES.

Pla de Bages, CATALAN wine region north-west of Barcelona in Spain with just over 550 ha/1,300 acres under vine. Grape varieties are similar to those in neighbouring PENEDÈS, with INTERNATIONAL VARIETIES such as Merlot and Cabernet Sauvignon planted enthusiastically during the 1990s. In the 2000s, a new generation is turning their attentions to INDIGENOUS VARIETIES such as Mandó, SUMOLL, and Picapoll Negre (see PIQUEPOUL). V. de la S. & F.C.

dopladebages.com

Pla i Llevant, literally 'plain and east coast' in Majorcan dialect, is a DOP on the Spanish island of MALLORCA with 440 ha/1,087 acres spread over the plains and into the hills on its east side. Red wines dominate, with Cabernet Sauvignon and Merlot the most planted, followed by the indigeneous variety CALLET.

Planalto Mirandês, easternmost DOC subregion of TRÁS-OS-MONTES in north-east Portugal, with an extreme CONTINENTAL CLIMATE.

Planta Fina, or **Planta Fina de Pedralba**, grown in Valencia, south-east Spain, to make fairly neutral whites. DNA PROFILING has shown that it is not, as has been suggested, identical to VERDEJO but is in fact the Damschino of Sicily and Alicante Branco of Portugal and Madeira.

plant cell density **(PCD)** is a commonly used REMOTELY SENSED indicator of vine VIGOUR or canopy size in Australian viticulture. Like the NORMALIZED DIFFERENCE VEGETATION INDEX (NDVI), it is calculated from measures of reflected light at wavebands corresponding to red and infrared light. R.G.V.B.

Plantet, 5455 SEIBEL, once the Loire's most popular FRENCH HYBRID, has been more successfully eradicated from the French vinescape than some others (see BACO, COUDERC, VILLARD). France had 26,000 ha/63,000 acres planted in 1968 but 764 ha by 2018. Its chief attributes are its productivity and its ability to crop regardless of the severity of the winter and spring frosts (although New York State winters have proved too harsh for it). Varietal versions are occasionally encountered and taste oddly of raspberries.

planting a vineyard ostensibly constitutes that vineyard's birth, but this operation can be undertaken only after other decisions have been taken. The potentially long process of VINEYARD SITE SELECTION is followed by SOIL PREPARATION and the choice of CLONES of both VINE VARIETY and ROOTSTOCK. Decisions must also be made about VINE DENSITY and TRAINING SYSTEM. Following delivery from the NURSERY, the young plants must be properly stored before they are planted.

Planting is normally carried out in winter or spring. It consists of simply digging a small hole sufficient to take the normal dormant ROOTLING, occasionally a CUTTING or, increasingly frequently, a growing plant. The hole can be dug by spade or post-hole auger, but care must be taken, particularly in heavy clay soils, that holes dug by augers do not have such dense sides that form root-growth barriers. Preferably, a high-pressure water jet can create a planting hole and at the same time provide moisture to assist early growth. For large estates, a planting machine adapted from forestry can be mounted behind a tractor to allow workers to put plants into a pre-formed furrow which is then filled in as the machine passes.

A cardinal rule of establishing grapevines, as for other plants, is to press the soil firmly in around the newly planted vine to avoid air pockets and to provide moisture if possible. R.E.S.

planting density. See VINE DENSITY.

planting rights became important when an EU scheme, in force since 1976, restricted the planting of new vineyards in member states. It was part of a group of control measures aimed at reducing the wine SURPLUS within the EU. The 2008 reform of the common market organization for wine (see EU) announced that the scheme would end in 2015 (or, exceptionally, with a transitional period until 2018), raising objections from the majority of wine-producing member states that this would lead to a free-for-all. This opposition led to the creation of a new system of planting authorizations, which is managed by national, sometimes regional, authorities and regulates vineyard plantings not only for PDO and PGI wines but also, more controversially, for WINE WITHOUT GEOGRAPHICAL INDICATION. The annual maximum percentage growth in vineyard area is fixed at 1%.

plastic bottles, form of PACKAGING, usually from the material known to professionals as PET, an abbreviation for polyethylene terephthalate. They have the advantage of being generally much lighter, cheaper, and less breakable than glass BOTTLES, but the disadvantage is that, depending on what they are lined with, they are not inert and may have a high OXYGEN TRANSMISSION RATE. Wine can start to taste of the package itself after only a few months or may become prematurely OXIDIZED. However, a 75-cl plastic bottle typically has a CARBON FOOTPRINT less than half that of a 75-cl glass bottle weighing 420 g. A 21st-century innovation is the space-saving flat bottle made from recycled PET that cuts the cost and CO_2 emissions of transportation and storage.

Alko, 'Update of wine packaging LCA: final report Alko Oy' (2021). www.alko.fi/INTERSHOP/static/WFS/Alko-OnlineShop-Site/-/Alko-OnlineShop/fi_FI/Tavarantoimittajille/Muut/EN/Alko%20wine%20packaging%20LCA%20update_final%20report.pdf.

plastic corks, a widely used but inaccurate term for synthetic closures. See CLOSURES.

plastic sheeting can be used in the vineyard to modify the climate. Studies in Canada and the UK have shown that transparent sheets suspended either side of the fruit zone (cloches) will raise temperatures and advance vine development. They can also protect the vine from wind and rain and reduce the need for FUNGICIDES. Trials in the UK have shown cloches to be an economical way of increasing yield and ripeness. They are also widely used as canopies over TABLE GRAPES to prevent rain damage.

Sheeting has also been used on the ground to avoid rain uptake towards the end of the ripening period, thus allowing grapes to ripen fully but keeping vegetative growth to a minimum. However, such experiments may fall foul of local regulations, as Michel ROLLAND found to his cost in 1999 in FRONSAC. Plastic sheeting or patches can be used to keep weeds down and retain soil moisture around young plants (see MULCH). It can also be used on vines to protect grapes destined for EISWEIN from birds and rain. R.E.S. & J.E.H.

Plavac Mali, grape variety with an interesting genetic history producing dense red wines all along the Dalmatian coast and on many of the Adriatic islands in CROATIA. Mali means 'small', and a white grape variety called simply **Plavac Žuti**, also **Plavec Žuti**, is also known which results in tart, light wines. Both varieties thrive on SANDY soil. Plavac Mali is Croatia's leading red wine grape and produces wines high in TANNINS, alcohol, colour, and ageability. Dingač is the best-known PDO red made from Plavac Mali. DNA PROFILING at DAVIS provided evidence that Plavac Mali, once suspected of being identical to ZINFANDEL, is a natural cross between it and Dobričić, an obscure and ancient southern Croatian red wine grape.

Plavina, grape variety making light reds on the Dalmatian coast in CROATIA which may also be called Brajdica. DNA PROFILING has shown that it is a cross of VERDECA cultivated in Puglia and Croatia's ZINFANDEL.

Pliny (23/4–79 CE). Gaius Plinius Secundus is known in English as 'Pliny the Elder' to distinguish him from his nephew, Pliny the Younger, also a man of letters and Pliny the Elder's adoptive son. Of Pliny the Elder's many works, the only one to survive is the *Natural History*, 37 books dedicated to the Emperor Titus and published posthumously. Book 14 is devoted exclusively to wine, Book 17 provides important information on the techniques of viticulture, and the beginning of Book 23 is devoted to the medicinal properties of wine (see MEDICINE). Although most of the *Natural History* is based on earlier authors rather than on scientific observation, and his information, invaluable as much of it is, must be used with discrimination, the book on wine seems in large part to be the product of independent enquiry. It contains practical advice as well as literary and historical learning. Its most interesting part ranks Italian wines according to quality, and sweet wines seem to be favoured (although see also ATHENAEUS). The best wine used to be CAECUBAN, but in Pliny's day it is FALERNIAN, particularly Falernian of the Faustinian CLOS. Setine is also a wine of the first rank. The next best wines are Alban, SURRENTINE, and MASSIC; Pliny awards third prize to Mamertine, of Messina in Sicily. An early proponent of TERROIR, he concludes that it is the country and the soil that determine quality, not the vine variety; in any case, people's tastes differ. Pliny died during the eruption of Vesuvius when his extraordinary curiosity got the better of his common sense. In his much-quoted writings on wine, he drew on VARRO's *De re rustica*; PALLADIUS' treatise on husbandry is indebted to Pliny. H.M.W. & J.J.P.

André, J., *Pline l'Ancien: histoire naturelle, livre XIV* (1958).

Beagon, M., *Roman Nature: The Thought of Pliny the Elder* (1992).

Pliny the Elder, *Natural History*, translated by H. Rackham (1945).

plonk, vague and derogatory English term for wine of undistinguished quality, is a term of Australian slang that has been naturalized in Britain. During the First World War, the French *vin blanc* with its un-English nasal vowels was adapted in various fantastic ways, from 'von Blink', which sounded like a German officer, to 'plinketty plonk', which suggested the twanging of a banjo. This was shortened to 'plonk', which coincidentally was also British soldiers' slang for 'mud'. By the Second World War this had given rise to 'A/C Plonk' for aircraftman 2nd class, the lowest of the low in the RAF and hence parallel to plonk in the glass.

Despite its etymology, plonk need not be white; and if the word suggests any kind of wine in particular it is cheap red served at a party. For this reason, colour-blind theories have sometimes been proposed, such as that it mimics the sound of a cork being withdrawn from a bottle. But it has no more to do with this sound than with the unceremonious plonking down of glass. L.H.-S.

ploughing. See TILLAGE and LABOUR.

Ploussard. See POULSARD.

Plumpton College in Sussex offers a variety of land-based courses and has been the leading centre of wine ACADEME in the UK since 1988, offering a wide range of degree, school-leaver, and short courses. Plumpton is the only European provider of undergraduate courses in wine production and wine business in English and now also runs the UK's first postgraduate qualification in VITICULTURE and OENOLOGY. With 8 ha/20 acres of its own commercial vineyards as well as a research winery, Plumpton works closely with the local wine industry (see ENGLAND). In 2020 it launched a new national viticulture apprenticeship programme. Its alumni can be found working at and managing vineyards and wineries across the world. J.K.

www.plumpton.ac.uk

podere, Italian for a farm, usually smaller than a FATTORIA and usually a subdivision of one. The word stems from *potere*, meaning 'to be able to' and indicating that the size of the holding was sufficient for one sharecropping family.

points out of 100, common method of SCORING wine promoted notably by American writer Robert PARKER. See also NUMBERS.

Pokdum, Thai name for the dark-skinned Japanese hybrid Black Queen. It was propagated by grower Nong Pok in the Pak Chong area of Nakhon Ratchasima province in the early 1980s. Its future looks uncertain as growers in Thailand continue to switch to white wine grapes such as MALAGA BLANC.

Poland has made wine since the introduction of CHRISTIANITY in 966 CE. The Little Ice Age, increased imports from Hungary, and competition from beer, vodka, and local fruit wines combined to reduce domestic winemaking to near zero by the end of the 15th century. Before the Second World War, pockets of vineyards survived in Podolia (now in UKRAINE) and Warka. After 1945, Poland's border was moved west to include north-west Silesia around Grünberg (renamed Zielona Góra), a major sparkling-wine region in pre-war Germany; this production was eventually discontinued in the 1970s.

Winemaking was resurrected in 1989 by mountaineer Roman Myśliwiec, who planted Ukrainian, Czechoslovak, and Hungarian vine cuttings by his home in Jasło in south-east Poland, later establishing a NURSERY. From 2001 Myśliwiec bottled small batches of grape wine and encouraged growers throughout Poland to plant disease-resistant HYBRIDS such as Hibernal, SEYVAL BLANC, Siberia, Odessa Muscat, LÉON MILLOT, and MARÉCHAL FOCH. A number of commercial wineries followed, and quality grew as new hybrids were trialled including RONDO, REGENT, Cabernet Cortis, Johanniter, SOLARIS, and Souvignier Gris. Five unofficial regions emerged (Lubuskie around Zielona Góra; Lower Silesia around Wrocław; Little Poland around Cracow; Subcarpathia around Jasło; and Małopolski Przełom Wisły around Kazimierz) with their respective growers' associations; local competitions were established, and an annual Polish Vintners' Convention was launched in 2006.

The third wave of Polish wine came in the mid 2010s with the establishment of large commercial wineries, often with outside investment. Winnica Turnau planted 30 ha/74 acres, single-handedly establishing the region of Western Pomerania; wineries such as Srebrna Góra in Cracow, Jaworek, Adoria, and Silesian near Wrocław, and Półtorak in Subcarpathia created a critical mass that reached wider audiences, notably through supermarkets. Meanwhile, smaller estates such as Dom Bliskowice, Dwór Sanna, Jakubów, Kamil Barczentewicz, Kojder, Krojcig, Płochoccy, Skarpa Dobrska, and BIODYNAMIC Wieliczka raised the qualitative bar. While estates catering to local tourists often bottle wines with RESIDUAL SUGAR, the leading estates embrace contemporary styles such as sparkling (both TRADITIONAL METHOD and PET-NAT), lees-aged and oaked white wines, dry rosé, ORANGE, and AMPHORA-aged wines. VITIS VINIFERA varieties such as Riesling, Chardonnay, the Pinots Blanc, Gris, and Noir, ZWEIGELT, and BLAUFRÄNKISCH account for 15% of the national acreage and are growing.

In 2021 the National Support Centre for Agriculture registered 329 wineries and 564 ha/1,394 acres of vines, but an estimated 40% of hectarage is not officially declared because it is either not yet bearing fruit or is not licensed to sell produce. Poland is not currently a member of the OIV but is included in the EU's viticultural zone A. There are currently no IGPs or PDOs. Forecasts suggest a potential 3,000 ha by 2030. W.M.B.

politics and wine. While winemaking and TERROIR affect how wines taste in the glass, politics determines how and which wines make it to consumers. The relations that wine producers have with the state and with each other vary across winemaking and wine-consuming countries. This variation affects the quality, price, export profile, and availability of wine to consumers.

In France, where grapevines predated Roman times, wine and the state have had as cosy a relationship as the vines and the terroir. Indeed, the Church and aristocrats, key political allies of the monarchy, held many vineyards in feudal times, and it was Emperor Napoleon III who commissioned the famous 1855 CLASSIFICATION of the wines of Bordeaux. Crisis struck in the late 19th century as PHYLLOXERA devastated large swathes of vineyards, threatening the voluminous tax receipts from wine and the livelihood of a large number of citizens engaged in its production. The state came to the aid of the growers by organizing a major campaign to pool scientific knowledge and treatments and, eventually, tamed the pest.

With the resolution of the phylloxera blight, some regions developed an addiction to state aid that took decades to break, if it ever was broken. The wine boom that preceded phylloxera, the subsequent bust, and an early 20th century boom so devastated producers of low-end TABLE WINES that they convinced the state to guarantee them a minimum price. But the market fluctuations led to other problems for better-quality producers, notably ADULTERATION AND FRAUD. Underscoring the importance of wine in France, the strong French state delegated the power to set quality standards for superior producers through the formalization of the AOC system in 1935. This system continues to this day with an ever-increasing number of qualifying regions. However, the tight historic relationship between French wine producers and the state appears to be weakening as opposition to wine has emerged under the aegis of public health with strict drink-driving and advertising restrictions. Domestic consumption has declined markedly (see Appendix 2C).

The politics of wine in the United States could not be more different. Despite the best early personal and policy intentions of King James I during the colonial period and of Thomas JEFFERSON during the republic, the land proved inhospitable to vines suitable for winemaking until the mid 19th century in California. Even international recognition of some of California's best wines in the 1890s was not enough to propel the industry to success since wine fell victim to political shifts hostile to the industry.

The temperance movement was consolidating as a political force. So abhorrent was its view of any type of alcohol and so strong were its supporters that the movement succeeded in officially banning alcohol throughout the country for 13 years under PROHIBITION. Although no policy enshrined in the Constitution has ever been so quickly repealed, the damage to the wine industry was severe. During Prohibition, vineyard acreage paradoxically expanded through a loophole that permitted HOME WINEMAKING. Yet the quality of the vines plummeted to such an extent that it took the California wine industry three decades to recover.

An even longer-lasting effect was that, at Repeal in 1933, the states were left to regulate the distribution and sale of alcohol within their boundaries. This has left a patchwork of laws and a system that often prohibits wineries and retailers from selling directly to consumers (online for example), since most states mandate the intervention of a distributor, which can raise prices to consumers and limit choice (see THREE-TIER SYSTEM). Ironically, in a country that prides itself on free markets, the wine industry is arguably even more heavily regulated than that of France.

AUSTRALIA's industry growth and nearly three decades of surging exports (see AUSTRALIAN INFLUENCE) lay in part in overcoming a problem of collective action. With a small domestic market and tremendous productive potential, industry participants realized the importance of export markets. In the 1970s and accelerating in the 1980s, the industry participants and the state coordinated an upgrading of the country's international reputation through setting standards for export and initiating successful marketing campaigns. The relatively low number of producing, or at least exporting, firms made this coordination easier. The Australian example served as a model for other countries, although a reversal of fortunes for Australian wine from the late 2000s has demonstrated limits to this approach.

Changes in the national political regime can revolutionize the wine industry, as the example of SOUTH AFRICA vividly demonstrates. With the collapse of the apartheid regime in 1994, South Africa's international isolation ended as the numerous countries that had trade embargoes in place lifted them. Practically overnight, the number of outlets for South African wines expanded exponentially. Investment flowed in and increasingly high-quality wines flowed out to the rest of the world. A similar political opening has also made for a global market in wines from Central and Eastern Europe, although their export potential has not yet reached the levels of South Africa.

A policy volte face can also lead to significant change: the HONG KONG government slashed import duties from 80% by value to zero in 2008, igniting the local wine trade and propelling Hong Kong to the top spot in the global AUCTION market for wine.

Because wine is an important product in world trade, international politics play a role in structuring the wine. Certainly wine policy is most advanced at the international level within the EU, which now has the final say on many wine regulations and subsidies in the region and often negotiates the laws of the World Trade Organization for European producers. The EU has also been particularly vigilant in protecting its place names, or GEOGRAPHICAL INDICATIONS. And because of its highly symbolic value, wine, particularly French wine but also Australian wine, has been the target of TARIFFS or, at the grassroots level, demonstrations and boycotts.

Future political struggles in the wine world will almost certainly also provide support for the adage 'all politics is local'. As more regions have sought formal delimitation of smaller growing areas, local conflicts over where to draw the lines have ensued. The issues of environmental responsibility, SUSTAINABLE VITICULTURE, and land use have recently appeared on the agendas of winegrowing communities from Napa to Bordeaux and are likely to remain there for the foreseeable future. T.C.

Colman, T., *Wine Politics* (2008).

Pinney, T., *Wine in America*, vols 1 & 2 (2007).

Yoon, S., and Lam, T.-H., 'The alcohol industry lobby and Hong Kong's Zero Wine and Beer Tax Policy', *BMC Public Health*, 12 (2012).

pollen, collective term for pollen grains which carry the male gametes in SEXUAL PROPAGATION for vines as for other plants. Pollen develops within sacs of the ANTHER. Mature grains have a sculptured surface typical for each species. See FLOWERING. See also vineyard ECOSYSTEM. B.G.C.

P

Pollera Nera, ancient dark-berried vine planted in 2015 on 32 ha/79 acres in Liguria and north-west Tuscany.

pollination, the transfer of pollen from the ANTHER to the receptive stigmatic surface. If pollination occurs with the pollen and pistil of the same flower, the process is called self-pollination and the progeny is known as a SELFLING or selfed vine; if it occurs between two different flowers (whether from the same vine or from different vines), the process is called cross-pollination. In cultivated grapevines, flowers are hermaphroditic and most are self-pollinated before the CALYPTRA has fallen (cleistogamy), but cross-pollination may also occur. Fertilization occurs two or three days after pollination depending on the ambient temperature (see FLOWERING). Wild grapes (*Vitis silvestris*) and some primitive cultivars are dioecious (male-only or female-only plants), therefore cross-pollination is essential. B.G.C. & J.V.

See also POLLEN.

Vasconcelos, M. C., et al., 'The flowering process of *Vitis vinifera*: a review', *American Journal of Enology and Viticulture*, 60/4 (2009), 411–34.

pollution. Air pollution arising from industrial gases and particles, AGROCHEMICALS, and fires can damage grapevines in any part of the world. Principal pollutants are sulfur dioxide, OZONE, and SMOKE, as well as, in restricted areas, phenoxy herbicides such as 2,4-D (see AUXINS) applied to nearby crops.

Of greater concern in relation to CLIMATE CHANGE is the generally under-reported atmospheric pollution caused by the release of CARBON DIOXIDE from wineries. See WINERY WASTE. R.E.S.

Boulton, R., et al., *Principles and Practices of Winemaking* (1999).

Pol Roger, Champagne house founded in Épernay in 1849 and still in family hands. The founder's sons changed their surnames to Pol-Roger by deed poll, Pol being a champenois variant of Paul. The wines rank high among the top champagne houses for quality, although it is one of the smaller GRANDES MARQUES. Pol Roger owns 91 ha/225 acres of vineyards on prime sites in the Vallée d'Épernay, on the Côte des Blancs, and (latterly) on the Montagne de Reims. After a near-calamitous cellar collapse in 1900, the cellars saw action in the First World War when the population of Épernay sheltered in them from artillery barrages. Sir Winston Churchill was a devotee of the house, even naming his racehorse Pol Roger. The compliment was repaid after his death, when all non-vintage labels exported to Britain were edged in black for 37 years. The Sir Winston Churchill Cuvée was launched in 1984 as Pol Roger's PRESTIGE CUVÉE. The great-grandsons of the original Pol Roger, Christian Pol-Roger and Christian de Billy, were succeeded by the son of the latter, Hubert de Billy, and now sixth-generation Bastien Collard de Billy. Particularly deep, recently modernized cellars house 11 million bottles, representing five years' supply.

polyethylene is a component in wine packaging such as CARTONS, BOXES, and POUCHES and is used for SCREWCAP liners. Since the 1980s and especially in the last fifteen years it has become increasingly important in the construction of ageing and FERMENTATION VESSELS, particularly for small and medium-sized wineries. Available in many different shapes and sizes, including egg-like ovoids (see CONCRETE), they are easy to clean and move and can be stacked to save space. The OXYGEN TRANSMISSION RATE of those used for ageing is typically similar to that of a second-use oak BARREL, making them useful for winemakers who want oxygenation without OAK FLAVOUR. Heavyweight tanks for fermentation are less permeable. In addition to being light and easy to clean, their great advantage is cost, and the only real limit is the maximum size, which is currently around 35 hl/900 gal.

polymeric pigments. See PIGMENTED TANNINS.

polymerization, the molecular process in which smaller molecules combine to form very large molecules. In all living material, the simple amino acids combine, or **polymerize**, in very large chains to create the PROTEINS, some of which function as ENZYMES. In AGEING wines, simpler PHENOLIC molecules combine to form larger TANNIN **polymers** and PIGMENTED TANNINS which eventually grow so large that they fall from the solution as SEDIMENT. A.D.W.

polyphenols and **polyphenolics**. See PHENOLICS.

polysaccharides, a diverse group of carbohydrates found in all wines and distinguished by their high molecular weight. They can be grouped into three categories according to their origin: from YEAST (MANNOPROTEINS), grape (e.g. PECTINS), and fungi (notably glucans from *Botrytis cinerea*, see BOTRYTIZED wines). Polysaccharides extracted both from yeast LEES and sources other than grapes (e.g. gum arabic) are allowable wine additives in many jurisdictions. Their presence inhibits the formation of undesirable PROTEIN hazes and TARTRATE crystallization. The ability of polysaccharides to form complexes with wine TANNINS and salivary proteins may also influence the perception of ASTRINGENCY and other aspects of MOUTHFEEL in both red and white wine. R.G.

Brandão, E., et al., 'Inhibition mechanisms of wine polysaccharides on salivary protein precipitation', *Journal of Agricultural and Food Chemistry*, 68/10 (2020), 2955–63.

Gawel, R., et al., 'The mouthfeel of white wine', *Critical Reviews in Food Science and Nutrition*, 58/17 (2017), 2939–56.

polyvinylpolypyrrolidone. See PVPP.

pomace, a word used for centuries by English cider-makers (derived from the Latin *pomum* meaning 'apple') for the debris of fruit processing, sometimes referred to as the press cake. In WHITE WINEMAKING, the pomace is the sweet, pale brownish-green mass of grape skins, stems, seeds, and pulp left after PRESSING. In RED WINEMAKING, the pomace is a similar mass of grape debris coloured blackish red left after the FREE-RUN wine has been drained. Because red-wine pomace is what is left after FERMENTATION rather than before, it also includes dead yeast cells and contains traces of alcohol rather than sugar. It typically accounts for 20% of the original grape weight.

In larger wineries, the significant amount of sugar which remains in white grape pomace may be washed out of the solid mixture and fermented to produce material for DISTILLATION into pomace brandy. Similarly, the smaller amounts of alcohol in red grape pomace may in large wineries be recovered by distillation. Pomace of any colour may be used for the newly fashionable PIQUETTE. OENOCYANIN, a food colouring agent, is also recovered from red-wine pomace, particularly in Italy. In some regions the solids from several wineries may be amalgamated for processing to recover TARTRATES and, occasionally, grapeseed oil. Pomace and its by-products have many other possible applications, for example as a fertilizer or in compost, in the food industry, in biofuels, in cosmetics, and sometimes also as stock feed.

Kalli, E., 'Novel application and industrial exploitation of winery by-products', *Bioresources and Bioprocessing*, 5/46 (2018).

Pomerol, small but distinctive wine region in BORDEAUX producing opulent and glamorous red wines dominated by the Merlot grape. Although challenged by their counterparts in its much larger neighbour ST-ÉMILION, Pomerol's most successful wines are some of the world's most sought after, but the glamour attaches to the labels rather than the countryside.

Pomerol is produced from a steady 800 ha/2,000 acres of vineyard on a plateau immediately north-east of LIBOURNE that is as geographically unremarkable as the MÉDOC but without even any buildings or historical landmarks of note. A confusing network of narrow lanes connects about 140 smallholdings, most of which produce only a few thousand cases of wine a year in one of the world's most monocultural landscapes.

Vines were intermittently grown on this inhospitable, unfertile land from Roman times, but viticulture was abandoned during the HUNDRED YEARS WAR and the vineyards not re-established until the 15th and 16th centuries. For hundreds of years afterwards, Pomerol was regarded merely as a satellite district of neighbouring ST-ÉMILION to the east. It was not until the late 19th century that the wines began to be appreciated, and then only in France. In the early 20th century, they became known in northern Europe, notably in BELGIUM, whose wine merchants would import the wines in bulk; Belgian-bottled Pomerols of this period attract high prices at AUCTION. A succession of hard-working intermediaries from the impoverished inland *département* of Corrèze made Libourne their base and developed markets for RIGHT BANK wines in such markets as Paris, Belgium, and Holland, leaving the traditional BORDEAUX TRADE to provide the British market with Médoc, Graves, and Sauternes. Such famous and well-educated British connoisseurs as George SAINTSBURY do not even mention Pomerol. It was not until the 1950s that British merchants Harry WAUGH and Ronald Avery 'discovered' Pomerol and its most famous property, PETRUS.

The most successful of the Libourne merchants is Jean-Pierre MOUEIX, whose fortunes have been interlinked with those of Pomerol. After establishing a reputation for the appellation, the firm acquired a number of properties, as well as contracts to manage other properties, including Petrus, and still sells a significant proportion of the Pomerol made in each vintage.

The success of Petrus in particular, whose wines regularly fetch prices far above those of the Médoc FIRST GROWTHS, is mirrored by worldwide demand far in excess of supply for the wines of similarly minuscule properties such as Chx Lafleur, LE PIN, L'Église-Clinet, and La Fleur de Gay.

Pomerol's finest wines are in general made on the highest parts of the plateau, which is predominantly layers of GRAVEL interleaved with CLAY, becoming SANDIER in the west, where rather lighter wines are made. The subsoil here is distinguished by a local iron-rich clay, the so-called *crasse de fer*, of which Petrus has a stratum particularly close to the surface.

Apparently as important in fashioning wines that are plump, voluptuous, and richly fruity enough to drink at less than five years old and yet which can last for as long as many a great Médoc are VINE AGE and low YIELDS. (At Petrus, for example, the wine produced by vines less than 12 years old is usually excluded from the ASSEMBLAGE.) Yields here are often the lowest for red bordeaux and are zealously restricted at the best properties. The early flowering of the Merlot grape, and the fact that a single vine variety accounts for about 80% of plantings in the appellation, unusual in Bordeaux, means that, as in VINTAGES such as 1984 and 1991, the majority of the crop can be lost to, for example, poor weather at flowering or spring frosts.

Pomerol is also unusual in being Bordeaux's only great wine district to have no official CLASSIFICATION. The properties are in general humble farmhouses, and only Ch de Sales has a building of any pretensions to grandeur, with an extent of more than 40 ha/99 acres. The most sought-after wines, depending on the vintage, include Chx Petrus, Lafleur, Le Pin, La Conseillante, Trotanoy, Certan de May, La Fleur de Gay, La Fleur-Pétrus, L'Église-Clinet, Clinet, L'Évangile, and Vieux Château Certan.

See also LALANDE-DE-POMEROL. J.R. & J.L.

Brook, S., *The Complete Bordeaux* (4th edn, 2022).
Martin, N., *Pomerol* (2012).

Pommard, prosperous village in Burgundy producing the most powerful red wines of the Côte de Beaune district of the CÔTE D'OR, from the usual Pinot Noir grapes. The pendulum of FASHION tends to swing between Pommard and Volnay, until recently favouring the latter. Warm, dry vintages have mitigated the previously rustic TANNINS of Pommard. A fine Pommard will be darker in colour than neighbouring VOLNAY, deeper in flavour, more tannic in structure, less charming when young but capable of developing into a rich, sturdy wine of great power after ten years in bottle. Claude Arnoux noted in 1728 that Pommard lasted longer than Volnay, only in those days he meant 18 months rather than 12.

Pommard stretches from the border of Beaune to the edge of Volnay. On the Beaune side, the finest vineyards are Les Pézerolles and Les Épenots, including the Clos des Épeneaux MONOPOLE of Comte Armand. Towards Volnay, the most impressive PREMIER CRU vineyards include Les Chanlins, Les Jarolières, Les Fremiers, and, in particular, Les Rugiens. The lower section of the latter, Les Rugiens Bas, has the potential to make the richest wines of all in Pommard and is frequently mentioned as being worthy of elevation to GRAND CRU status.

See also CÔTE D'OR and map under BURGUNDY. J.T.C.M.

Arnoux, C., *Dissertation sur la situation de Bourgogne* (1728).
Histoire et chroniques du village de Pommard en Bourgogne (2nd edn, 2014).

Pompeii, a Roman port servicing the rich agricultural region which stretched round the southern bay of Naples from the slopes of Vesuvius across the valley of the river Sarno to the Monti Lattari of the Sorrento peninsula. Archaeology has revealed that the area was intensively occupied by moderate-sized farms, many of which were devoted to viticulture. The decorations in the owners' town houses sometimes reflect the activities on their estates, such as a frieze in the House of the Vettii in which cherubs are working a wine press and presenting wine to be tasted by a prospective buyer. Pompeian wine was 'headache-inducing' according to PLINY (*Natural History* 14.70). Four types of ancient grape were associated with the region: Aminea Gemina Minor, Murgentina, Holconia, and Venucula. It is estimated that the area produced four times the needs of the local population and fuelled an export trade, evidenced by the local AMPHORAE found around the Mediterranean. The remarkable work of Wilhelmina Jashemski from the 1960s onwards has revealed the presence of vineyards within the walls of Pompeii itself, several of which were replanted in the 1990s. Given that many residences had no kitchens, there were numerous eating places and inns serving wine, their walls often painted with lively scenes of inn life. The bar of Euxinus 'At the Sign of the Phoenix', for example, served the wine produced from the tiny vineyard planted behind it. J.J.P.

De Simone, G. F., 'The agricultural economy of Pompeii', in M. Flohr and A. Wilson (eds.), *The Economy of Pompeii* (2016).
Beard, M., *Pompeii: The Life of a Roman Town* (2008).

Pontac, South African name for the distinctive red-fleshed TEINTURIER du Cher grape variety probably imported from SOUTH WEST FRANCE in the late 17th century. Widely planted until PHYLLOXERA devastated the Cape's vineyards from the mid 1880s onwards, Pontac was superseded by higher-yielding and more fashionable varieties, although a vintage port-style wine was made from it as recently as 2008. A campaign to reintroduce the variety has gained some traction, and there are now a few thousand Pontac vines spread across three different viticultural regions. M.F.

Porongurup, subregion of the Great Southern set in the cool elevations of the Porongurup Range in WESTERN AUSTRALIA, notable for floral, taut, long-lived dry RIESLING.

port, a FORTIFIED WINE made by adding brandy to arrest fermenting grape MUST or juice which results in a wine, red or sometimes white, that is both sweet and high in alcohol. Port derives its name from OPORTO (Porto), the second largest city in PORTUGAL, whence the wine has been shipped for over 300 years, notably by English merchants. Port production varies considerably from year to year, partly because of the conditions of each growing season but also reflecting the *benefício*, the amount of wine that may be fortified each year, officially calculated according to stocks and sales. The average annual production during the second decade of the 21st century was 116,000 PIPES (64 million l).

The production of unfortified DOURO wine averaged just over 50 million l between 2011 and 2020.

Fortified wines are made in the image of port in places as far apart as SOUTH AFRICA, AUSTRALIA, and CALIFORNIA, but within Europe EU law restricts the use of the term 'port' to wines from a closely defined area in the DOURO Valley of northern Portugal (one of the first examples of geographical DELIMITATION). See map under PORTUGAL.

History

Port originates from 17th-century trade wars between the English and the French. For a time, imports of French wines into England were prohibited, and then, in 1693, William III imposed punitive levels of TAXATION which drove English wine merchants to Portugal, a country with whom the English had always shared good relations. At first they settled on the northern coast but, finding the wines too thin and astringent (see VINHO VERDE), they travelled inland along the river Douro. Here merchants found wines that were the opposite of those they had left behind on the coast. Fast and furious FERMENTATION at high temperatures produced dark, astringent red wines that quickly earned them the name 'blackstrap' in London. In a determined effort to make sure that these wines arrived in good condition, merchants would add a measure of brandy to stabilize them before shipment.

The English merchants are supposed to have discovered the winemaking technique which results in port in 1678 when a Liverpool wine merchant sent his sons to Portugal in search of wine. At Lamego, a town in the mountains high above the Douro, they found one of the important Cistercian vine-growing monasteries there where brandy was added to the wine during rather than after fermentation, killing off the active yeasts and so producing the sort of sweet, alcoholic red wine that port was to become.

British trade with France ceased altogether in the early 18th century with the outbreak of the War of the Spanish Succession. By this time, a number of port shippers were already well established, and in 1703 England and Portugal signed the METHUEN TREATY, which laid down further tariff advantages for Portuguese wines. By the 1730s, however, the fledgling port industry was blighted by scandal. Sugar was being added and elderberry juice being used to give colour to poor, overstretched wines. Unprincipled over-production brought about a sharp fall in prices and a slump in trade. Prompted by complaints from British wine merchants, the port shippers contacted the Portuguese prime minister of the day, the Marquis of Pombal. Partly to create a lucrative Portuguese monopoly on port production, in 1756 he instituted a series of measures to regulate sales of port. A boundary was drawn around the Douro restricting the production of port to those vineyards within it. Vineyards outside the official wine region, in BAIRRADA for instance, were summarily GRUBBED UP by the authorities.

Geography and climate

Pombal's demarcation, modified a number of times since 1756 (see DOURO), corresponds closely to an area of pre-Cambrian SCHIST surrounded by granite. From the village of Barqueiros about 70 km/40 miles upstream from Oporto, the region fans out either side of the river stretching as far as the frontier with Spain. It is referred to by the port shippers as 'the Douro', or by those in charge of the UNESCO World Heritage sites as Alto Douro Wine Region. The vineyards are shielded from the influence of the Atlantic by the Serra do Marão, a range of mountains rising to an elevation of 1,400 m/4,600 ft. Inland, the climate becomes progressively more extreme. Annual rainfall, which averages 1,200 mm/47 in on the coast, rises to over 1,500 mm on the mountains and then diminishes sharply, falling to as little as 400 mm at Barca d'Alva on the Spanish border. Summer temperatures in the vineyards frequently exceed 35 °C/95 °F. It is hard to imagine a more inhospitable place to grow grapes. The topsoils in this mountainous region of Portugal are shallow, stony, and low in SOIL NUTRIENTS. Over a period of 300 years, however, the land has been worked to great advantage. The valley sides are very steep, but TERRACES hacked from the schist, often with little more than a shovel and crowbar support, give vines a metre or two of soil in which to establish a root system. The bedrock fractures vertically, however, and, once established, vines root deeply in search of water and nutrients.

The Douro region divides into three officially recognized subzones. The Baixo (Lower) Corgo is the most westerly of the three and covers the portion of the region downstream from the river Corgo, which flows into the Douro just above the small city of Régua. This is the coolest and wettest of the three zones and tends to produce the lightest wines suitable for making inexpensive ruby and tawny ports (see Styles of port below). Upstream from the river Corgo, the Cima (Higher) Corgo is the heart of the demarcated region centred on the town of Pinhão. Rainfall is significantly lower here (700 mm as opposed to 900 mm or more west of Régua), and summer temperatures are, on average, a few degrees higher. All the well-known shippers own vineyards or QUINTAS here, and this is where most of the high-quality tawny, Late Bottled Vintage, and vintage port is made. Much of the Douro Superior, the most easterly of the three subregions, is still pioneer country. Although it has long been a part of the demarcated zone, the country is remote and sparsely populated, and in past centuries little headway was made in planting vineyards due to the impossibility of navigating upriver beyond the former rapids of Cachão da Valeira. The Douro Superior is also the most arid part of the region with average temperatures at least 3 °C higher than at Régua 50 km/31 miles downstream. But rising LABOUR costs are forcing producers to consider planting the flatter land close to the Spanish border which is more suitable for MECHANIZATION and has considerable potential for high-quality port and Douro wines.

Viticulture

Viticulture in the Douro has altered radically from the 1970s onwards, more than at any time since PHYLLOXERA swept through the region at the end of the 19th century, leaving many hillsides abandoned. The most noticeable change is the river itself, which was progressively dammed in the 1960s to form a string of narrow lakes.

Methods of cultivation have also changed the Douro landscape. Faced with escalating costs and an acute shortage of labour at the end of the 1960s, growers began to look for alternatives to the tiny, step-like terraces built with high retaining walls in the 19th century. The first bulldozers arrived in the late 1970s to gouge out a new system of terraces called *patamares*. Inclined ramps bound together by seasonal vegetation replaced the costly retaining walls; with wider spacing between the vines (resulting in a VINE DENSITY of 3,500 vines per ha (1,420 per acre) as opposed to 6,000 on some traditional terraces), small caterpillar tractors can circulate in the vineyards.

At much the same time, some growers pioneered a system of planting vines in vertical lines running up and down the natural slope. This 'up and down' planting has been a qualified success, although access and SOIL EROSION are problems where the gradient exceeds 30 degrees. In the 1980s, a flurry of new planting under a World Bank scheme provided farmers with low-interest loans. The traditional, labour-intensive terraces, still impeccably maintained by some growers, now stand alongside newer *patamares* and vine rows planted vertically up the hillside, both of which allow limited MECHANIZATION.

Most of the Douro's vineyards used to be pruned according to the French GUYOT system and were trained on wires supported by stakes hewn from local stone, but now all but the very old vines are SPUR PRUNED and VSP-trained (see VERTICAL TRELLIS) on wires supported by wooden stakes. Most vines used to be GRAFTED *in situ* but now most are bench grafted. IRRIGATION is essential for young vines. July and August are generally dry, and SPRAYING against FUNGAL DISEASES is necessary only in the early summer or in exceptionally wet years. Aside from the usual vineyard PESTS, most of which can be controlled by spraying, wild boar eat grapes and may occasionally damage new vineyards.

The Douro HARVEST usually starts in August in the Douro Superior and continues until early October. The steeply terraced vineyards, eerily quiet for most of the year, come alive as gangs of pickers descend from outlying villages for the duration of the harvest (see also HARVEST TRADITIONS). Yields in the Douro are among the lowest in any wine region in the world, with 500–750 g/17–26 oz per vine from OLD VINES the norm. From younger plantings, those up to 20 years old, 1.5 kg/3.3 lbs is the average production per vine in the best vineyards.

Vine varieties

More than 80 grape varieties are authorized for port production, but until the 1990s few growers had detailed knowledge of the identity of the vines growing in their vineyards. All old vineyards contain a mixture of varieties—often as many as 20 or 30 intermingled in the same plot (see FIELD BLEND). But research conducted in the 1970s (mostly by Cockburn and Ramos Pinto) identified the best varieties, and all new plantings since then have been more orderly. TOURIGA NACIONAL, TINTA BARROCA, TOURIGA FRANCA (often still referred to by its old name, Touriga Francesa), Tinta Roriz (Spain's TEMPRANILLO), and TINTO CÃO are the five most popular black-skinned varieties, although varieties such as SOUSÃO, Tinta Amarela (see TRINCADEIRA), and MOURISCO find favour with certain growers. GOUVEIO, MALVASIA Fina, and VIOSINHO are generally considered among the best varieties for white port.

Port winemaking

Rapid EXTRACTION of COLOUR and TANNINS is the crux of the various vinification methods used to produce red port. Because FERMENTATION is curtailed by fortifying spirit after just two or three days, the grape juice or must spends a much shorter time in contact with the skins than in normal RED WINEMAKING. The MACERATION process should therefore be as vigorous as possible.

Until the early 1960s, all port was vinified in much the same way. Every farm had a winery equipped with LAGARES, low stone troughs, usually built from granite, in which the grapes were trodden and fermented. Some are still in use, mainly at the small, privately owned quintas, and some of the finest ports destined for vintage or aged tawny blends continue to be trodden in *lagares*. The human foot, for all its many unpleasant associations, is ideal for pressing grapes as it breaks up the fruit without crushing the pips that would otherwise release bitter-tasting PHENOLICS.

Lagares would be progressively filled over the course of a day and trodden by the pickers themselves, thigh-high in purple pulp, in the evening. Most *lagares* hold 10–15 PIPES (about 5,500–8,250 l/1,453–2,180 gal), although a number of the larger quintas have *lagares* with a capacity of up to 30 pipes. As a rule of thumb, one or two people per pipe are needed to tread a *lagar*. Fermentation begins as a result of the action of AMBIENT YEASTS on the grapes' sugar. The alcohol produced and the increasing TEMPERATURE of the mass of purple skins, juice, and stems encourages the extraction of the phenolics vital for the character of port. After about two or three hours of hard, methodical treading, the CAP of skins and stalks starts to float to the surface. Regular PUNCHING DOWN of the cap was traditionally performed with long, spiked sticks from planks run across the top of the *lagares* which ideally need some form of cooling.

After 24–36 hours, the level of the grape sugar in the fermenting must declines from 12–13 °BAUMÉ to 6–8 °Baumé. Depending on the intended sweetness of the wine, the wine would be run off the *lagar* into a vat, already about one-fifth full with grape spirit whose ALCOHOLIC STRENGTH is 77%. The spirit kills the yeasts, arresting fermentation. At this stage the must becomes young, sweet, fiery port with an alcohol content of 19–20%.

In the 1960s and 1970s, treading grapes in *lagares* became much less widespread. The Douro Valley and the remote TRÁS-OS-MONTES region, which traditionally supplied labour at harvest time, have suffered from marked emigration, and the port shippers were forced to look for less labour-intensive ways to make wine. Many isolated properties were without electricity then, and shippers set about building central wineries to which grapes from outlying farms could be delivered. Most of these were equipped with AUTOVINIFICATION tanks, which required no external power source and have proved to be a successful alternative to treading in *lagares*. The resulting wine is fortified just like foot-trodden young wines were.

In the late 1990s, however, a new generation of winemakers started to experiment with more novel ways of making port. Two key types have emerged: cap plungers, as introduced by the FLADGATE PARTNERSHIP; and automated treading machines or 'robotic lagares', as designed by the SYMINGTON family. Both systems have become widely used for the making of premium quality ports, although they are too expensive to be used to make the large volumes of standard-quality ports.

All wineries are now equipped with PRESSES, and the mass of grape skins and stems that remains after treading or crushing is forked into a press to extract the last of the juice. This deeply coloured, astringent PRESS WINE is run off and fortified separately. It may be blended back at a later stage or used to bolster a lighter wine.

White port is made in much the same way (see Styles of port below).

The fortifying grape spirit for port used to be distilled from wine made in Portugal, mainly from the Ribatejo (see TEJO) and Estremadura (see LISBOA) regions north of Lisbon, although in recent years most of the spirit has been imported, distilled from the Europe's WINE LAKE. Until 1992, this spirit had to be purchased from the Casa do Douro (see Organization of the industry below), which set a fixed price and controlled distribution. This monopoly was broken by the EU, and producers have since been free to purchase any spirit they choose provided that it complies with the 77% norm of alcoholic strength and is approved by the port industry's regulating authority, the Instituto dos Vinhos do Douro e do Porto (IVDP). Since 2000 there has been a marked improvement in the quality and purity of the fortifying spirit used for premium ports.

See VIN DOUX NATUREL for a comparison of port winemaking techniques with those in the production of French counterparts such as Banyuls.

Organization of the industry

In 2020, 20,000 growers farmed a total of 43,000 ha/106,000 acres of vines in the Douro, mostly in the Cima Corgo where 20,000 ha are under vine. In common with most of the north of Portugal, the region is fragmented into tiny holdings numbering 104,000, although there has been some consolidation in recent years. The average area of vineyard per grower has consequently increased slightly to just over 2 ha/5 acres. The planting of vineyards in the Douro Superior has brought a dramatic reduction in the price of grapes, and there has been a marked reduction in the number of growers, especially in the labour-intensive Baixo Corgo region, over the past decade. Port grapes are supported by the *benefício* (see below), which some argue creates an artificial market.

Vineyards in the Douro are graded according to a complicated points system and classified into nine categories rated A to I. Twelve physical factors including site, ASPECT, EXPOSURE, and gradient are taken into consideration, each of which is allocated a numerical score. In theory, a vineyard could score a maximum of 2,031 points; a property with more than 1,200 points is awarded an A grade. On this basis, the annual *benefício* authorization (the total amount of port that may be made that year) is distributed to individual farmers. This is calculated annually by the IVDP.

Permits are then distributed to farmers detailing the amount of grape must that they may fortify to make port. The amount varies according to the year, but typically A- and B-grade properties may make 550–600 l of port per thousand vines, while properties with a grade of F or below are unlikely to be allowed to make port at all. The surplus is usually made into unfortified wine with its own denomination (see DOURO), but most of this sells for a much lower price than port.

This quality control system, instituted in 1947, served the port industry well for four decades, but pressure for its reform intensified when in 1990 the independence of the Casa do Douro was severely compromised by its purchase of shares in Royal Oporto, then one of the largest port shippers. After a period of instability, in the mid 1990s the Casa do Douro had most of its regulatory powers withdrawn, and these were transferred to an independent interprofessional body representing both growers and shippers, the CIRDD, Commissão Interprofessional da Região Demarcada do Douro. This in turn was absorbed by the IVDP. The Casa do Douro continues to represent the farmers and to hold the register of vineyards as well as holding stocks of wine.

After vinification, the bulk of the new wine traditionally stayed at the QUINTA or farm until the spring after the harvest when it was transported down the river Douro to the shippers' LODGES in VILA NOVA DE GAIA. The cooler climate and markedly high humidity near the coast are thought to be beneficial for slow CASK AGEING, but some shippers now have temperature- and humidity-controlled lodges in the Douro for ageing premium ports, especially aged tawnies. See DOURO BAKE for the traditional effect on port of maturing it upstream in the Douro Valley.

Both growers and shippers have to submit to the authority of the IVDP, a government-run body that ensures that shippers adhere to the so-called *lei do terço* (law of the third), which restricts shippers from selling more than one-third of their stock in any one year. The IVDP is also empowered to analyse and taste a sample from each port shipment before issuing the guarantee seal stuck to the neck of every bottle of port leaving the region.

The market for port has altered dramatically since the Second World War. The so-called 'Englishman's wine' that used to be drunk everywhere from gentlemen's clubs to corner pubs became the Frenchman's wine when France's imports of *le porto* (largely inexpensive wood ports; see Styles of port below) overtook those of the UK in the early 1960s. The British market is still highly coveted by port shippers, however, especially those of British descent, notably the SYMINGTONS, who control shippers such as Cockburn, Dow, Graham, and Warre and the FLADGATE PARTNERSHIP (Croft, Fonseca, and Taylor). In the late 1990s, the US became another important market for vintage port.

Styles of port

There are two broad categories of port, the style shaped by either CASK AGEING or BOTTLE AGEING. Wood-matured ports, often called simply wood ports, are aged either in wooden casks or, sometimes, stainless steel or concrete tanks and are ready to drink straight after FINING, FILTRATION, and BOTTLING. Ports designed to mature in bottle, however, are aged for a short time in wood and are bottled without filtration. It may then take up to 20 or 30 years before such a wine is ready to drink. Within these two general categories there are many different styles of port. The official legislation governing the different categories of port was tightened up considerably in 2002 and has been amended since. The following categories are now permitted.

Ruby is one of the simplest and least expensive styles of port. Aged in bulk for two or three years, it is bottled young while the wine retains a deep ruby colour and a strong, fiery personality. Young wines from more than one vintage are aged in all sorts of vessels (wood, concrete, and stainless steel) before being blended, filtered, and bottled. PASTEURIZATION is sometimes applied to stabilize such wines and can result in 'stewed' flavours, but good ruby with its uncomplicated berry fruit aromas and flavours is often a good, warming drink. When the British FASHION for ruby port and lemonade faded in the 1960s, many shippers dropped the name 'ruby' from the labels of such ports in favour of their own, self-styled brands.

Reserve/Reserva designates a premium ruby, a wine with more colour, character, and depth than a standard ruby. This category has supplanted 'vintage character', a misleading term which was largely used in English-speaking markets.

Tawny is applied to a confusingly wide range of very different styles of port. In theory, tawny implies a wine aged in wood for so much longer than a ruby that it loses colour and the wine takes on an amber-brown or tawny hue. In practice, however, much of the tawny port sold today is no older than the average ruby and may therefore be found at the same price. The difference between a commercial ruby and its counterpart labelled 'tawny' is that, whereas ruby is made from a blend of deep-coloured wines, tawny is often produced from lighter wines grown in the cooler Baixo Corgo vineyards where grapes rarely ripen to give much depth or intensity of fruit. Vinification methods may also be adapted to produce paler-coloured wines, and the colour of the final blend may be adjusted further by adding a proportion of white port so that the wine ends up with a pale pink hue rather than tawny brown. Many bulk tawnies are left upriver for longer than other wines for the heat to speed up the maturation (see DOURO BAKE). The resulting wines often display a slight brown tinge on the rim but tend to lack the freshness and primary fruit character normally associated with young port. The French typically drink inexpensive, light, tawny-style wines as an APERITIF, and supplying this market has become the major commercial activity for many of the larger port shippers.

Aged tawny has been left to age in wooden casks for six or more years, taking on a tawny colour and a soft, silky character as the PHENOLICS are POLYMERIZED (see CASK AGEING). Most of these tawnies are bottled with an indication of age on the label, although *Tawny Reserve* or *Tawny Reserva* may be applied to wines that have spent at least seven years in wood. The terms 10, 20, 30, 40, and 50 Years Old seen on labels are, however, approximations as tawny ports are blended from several years' production. Most aged tawnies are blended according to house style and must be tasted and approved by the IVDP as conforming to the character expected from the age claimed on the label. Made from wines that might have otherwise ended up as vintage port (see below), aged tawnies mature in cask in the cool of the lodges at Gaia until the shipper considers them ready to blend and bottle. Labels on these wines must state that the wine has matured in wood and give the date of bottling, which is important since aged tawny port will not improve in bottle. Once the bottle has been opened, younger aged tawnies may be subject to rapid OXIDATION, losing their delicacy of fruit if left on ULLAGE for more than a few days. (Very old tawnies and colheita ports are usually more robust.) Port shippers themselves often drink aged tawny, chilled in summer, in preference to any other, as its delicate, nutty character suits the climate and temperament of the Douro better than the hefty, spicy character of vintage port, which is better adapted to cooler climes.

Colheita means 'harvest' or 'crop' and therefore by extension 'vintage' in Portuguese, yet colheita ports are in fact very different from vintage ports (below). Colheitas are best understood as tawny ports from a single year, bottled with the date of the harvest on the label. The law states that colheita ports must be aged in wood for at least seven years, although most are aged for considerably longer. The wines take on all the nuances of an aged tawny but should also express the characteristics of a single year. All colheita ports carry the date of bottling, and most wines should be drunk within a year or so of that date. Colheita ports, once the speciality of the Portuguese-owned houses, have in the 21st century been taken up enthusiastically by the British shippers, who sometimes use the words 'Single Harvest' on the label. White ports may also be bottled as colheitas. (MADEIRA may also use the word 'colheita'.)

Vintage port is the most expensive style of port. Vintage port accounts for hardly 1% of all port sold, yet it is the wine which receives the most attention. British shippers, in particular, have built vintage port into a flagship wine, 'declared' in an atmosphere of speculation when the quality of the wine, the quantity available, and the market are judged fit. Wines from a single year, or VINTAGE, are blended and bottled after spending between two and three years in wood. Thereafter, most of the wine is sold and the consumer takes over the nurturing for up to 30 or more years, although an increasing proportion is being drunk much earlier, especially in the US. Vintage port is distinguished from other ports by the quality of the grapes from which the wine is made. Only grapes grown in the best, usually Cima Corgo, vineyards and picked at optimum ripeness following an outstanding summer are made into vintage port. Even then, nothing is certain until at least a year after the harvest when shippers have had time to reflect on the characteristics of the wine and the market. The vintage may be declared only after the IVDP has approved samples and proposed quantities in the second year after the harvest. With the steady improvement in vinification methods since the mid 1980s, some wine of vintage port potential is now made at the best quintas in most years. But a shipper will declare a vintage only if there is sufficient quantity and if it is felt that the market is ready to support another vintage (1931 being a classic example of a qualitatively superb vintage undeclared by most shippers for entirely commercial reasons). Vintage declarations maybe very irregular but very roughly three vintages have been declared in each decade (however, 2016, 2017, 2018, and 2019 were all declared by one or more of the major shippers). Because they should be bottle aged for longer than almost any other style of wine, vintage port bottles are particularly thick, dark, and sturdy. The wines, extremely high in PHENOLICS in their youth, throw a heavy DEPOSIT and need especial care when DECANTING and SERVING.

Single-quinta vintage Just as wine-producing CHÂTEAUX evolved in France in the 18th and 19th centuries, the trend towards the single, winemaking QUINTA has developed in Portugal, and many of the better-known Douro quintas belong to a particular port shipper. Single-quinta ports are made in much the same way as vintage port, aged in wood for two or three years and bottled without filtration so that they throw a sediment (and should therefore be decanted before serving). Although some independent quintas produce a vintage port nearly every year, a number of differences distinguish single-quinta vintages from declared vintage ports. First of all, shippers' single-quinta ports tend to be made in good (but not outstanding) years which are not declared. In years which are declared for vintage port, many of these wines will be the lots that make up the backbone of the vintage blend and are not therefore available for release as wines in their own right. Second, some single-quinta ports are kept back by shippers and sold only when the wine is considered to be ready to drink, perhaps eight or ten years after the harvest. Single quintas or individual vineyards in the Douro were given a fillip in 1986 when the law requiring all port to be exported via Vila Nova de Gaia was relaxed, opening the way for a number of small vineyard owners who previously had been restricted to selling their wines to large firms.

LBV stands for Late Bottled Vintage, a port from a single year, bottled between the fourth and sixth years after the harvest. Three styles of LBV wines have evolved. First there are LBVs bottled without any filtration or treatment so that, like a vintage port, they need to be decanted before serving. These wines, once designated with the word 'traditional', tend to be made in good but undeclared years and are ready to drink sooner than vintage port, four to six years after bottling. Since the revision of the legislation in 2002, unfiltered LBV may also be sold as Envelhecido em Garrafa or 'bottle matured', provided the wine in question has been aged in bottle for a minimum of three years prior to release on the market. Many of the wines in this second style share much of the depth of a true vintage port.

A third style of LBV is the most common. These are wines which have been fined and sometimes filtered and cold stabilized before bottling to prevent the formation of sediment. These wines are made in large volumes and are popular with restaurateurs (as they do not need decanting) but do not have the intensity or depth of an unfiltered LBV.

Crusted port is named for the 'crust' or DEPOSIT that it throws in bottle. In spite of its rather crusty, establishment name, it is the fairly recent creation of British shippers, notably the SYMINGTON group. It is designed to appeal to vintage port enthusiasts, even though crusted ports are not wines from a single year or vintage but blends from a number of years bottled young with little or no filtration. Like vintage port, the wines continue to develop in the bottle, throwing a sediment or crust, so that the wine needs to be decanted before it is served. Rather like traditional LBVs, many crusted or crusting ports offer an excellent alternative to vintage port, providing the port enthusiast with a dark, full-bodied wine at a much lower price. It may be exported from Oporto three years after bottling.

Garrafeira, meaning 'private cellar' or 'reserve', is more commonly associated with Portuguese table wines than with port. Until 2002 it did not form part of the IVDP's officially authorized lexicon but was a style produced by a single shipper, Niepoort. Now a port may be designated as a garrafeira if it comes from a single year and is aged for a minimum of seven years in glass demijohn before bottling (like some MADEIRA). In practice the wines age in 5- or 10-l demijohns for considerably longer than the minimum. After 20, 30 or even 40 years in glass, the wine is decanted off its sediment and rebottled in conventional 75-cl bottles. The wines combine depth of fruit with the delicate, silky texture associated with tawny port. Three dates appear on the label: date of harvest, date of bottling (i.e. when the wine was transferred to demijohn), and date of decanting (i.e. decanted off the sediment that has formed in the demijohn and transferred to a 75-cl bottle).

White port Ernest Cockburn remarked in the early 20th century that 'the first duty of port is to be red'. Nevertheless a significant proportion of white grapes grow in vineyards in the Douro, and all shippers produce a small amount of white port, with some now giving it serious attention. White port is made in much the same way as red except that MACERATION during fermentation is much shorter or even non-existent. Most white ports have a certain amount of RESIDUAL SUGAR, even those labelled 'dry' or 'extra dry'. Intensely sweet wines, made mainly for the domestic market, are labelled *lagrima* (tears) because of their VISCOSITY (see also MÁLAGA). Another, drier style of white port, described as *leve seco* (light dry), are wines with an alcoholic strength of 16.5–17%, rather than the usual 19–20%. There are two distinct styles of white port. Most commercial white ports are aged for no more than 18 months, generally in stainless-steel tanks. These tend to be pale in colour and FRUIT-DRIVEN and are often used to create a long drink with tonic, the so-called 'Portonic'. There is a movement towards wood ageing, which lends character to white port, turning it gold in colour and giving the wine an incisive, dry, nutty tang. Superior white ports may also be bottled with a designation of age: 10, 20, 30, 40, 50 Years Old or Colheita. White ports are also sometimes used by shippers for fine-tuning aged tawnies.

Rosé was initiated by CROFT in 2008 and was initially classified by the IVDP as 'light ruby'. Made from red grapes with minimal SKIN CONTACT, it was subsequently introduced by many shippers, albeit with a huge variation in style and colour, from pale salmon to light ruby. Not without controversy when it was launched, it is said by some to have appealed to a new, younger group of port drinkers. Both rosé and white ports are increasingly used as mixers in cocktails.

Moscatel is occasionally used on its own to make a sweet, fortified VARIETAL white wine with the grape aroma characteristic of MUSCAT. The village of Favaios on the north bank of the Douro makes a speciality of Moscatel.

See also articles on individual port shippers COCKBURN, FERREIRA, FLADGATE PARTNERSHIP, QUINTA DO NOVAL, and SYMINGTONS. R.J.M.

Bradford, S., *The Story of Port* (2nd edn, 1983).
Mayson, R., *The Vineyards of Portugal* (2020).
Mayson, R., *Port and the Douro* (4th edn, 2019).
www.ivdp.pt

Portalegre, northernmost DOC subregion of the ALENTEJO in central-southern Portugal and the most distinctive. On the lower slopes of the predominantly GRANITE Serra de São Mamede, the vineyards, at up to around 800 m/2,625 ft in ELEVATION, are the Alentejo's highest and therefore coolest. This, combined with its unusual (for the Alentejo) mix of old FIELD BLEND vineyards has attracted successive waves of newcomers this century, including a rash of talented winemakers who commandeered grapes that had previously disappeared into the ailing CO-OPERATIVE's melting pot. Sizeable players investing in Portalegre include the Portuguese liqueur company that acquired the co-operative in 2016 and wine producers from both within and without the Alentejo (including luminaries Esporão, Cartuxa, SOGRAPE, and the SYMINGTON family). This together with the successive broadening of permitted grapes to include mainstream Portuguese varieties (and Syrah and Cabernet Sauvignon) has increased its scale of production and profile. S.A.

Portan, like CALADOC and CHASAN, is a CROSS made by French AMPELOGRAPHER Paul Truel at the INRA station at Domaine de Vassal (see INRAE). In this case he crossed GRENACHE NOIR and Portugais Bleu (Blauer PORTUGIESER) to develop a Grenache-like variety that would ripen even in the Midi's cooler zones. Unlike Caladoc, it is waning, planted on just 89 ha/220 acres of Languedoc vineyard in 2019.

Portimão, fishing port and smallest DOC in Portugal's ALGARVE.

Porto, Portugal's second city (OPORTO in English), which has lent its name to PORT wine, Vinho do Porto.

Port Phillip Zone, Australian wine zone surrounding Melbourne, VICTORIA, and encompassing the Geelong, Macedon Ranges, Mornington Peninsula, Sunbury, and Yarra Valley regions.

port tongs, rare instrument for opening a bottle of vintage PORT so old that the cork is likely to crumble under the impact of a CORKSCREW. The specially shaped tongs are heated in a flame and applied to the neck of the bottle, which is then immediately cooled with a cold, damp cloth. The sudden temperature change should result in a clean break. Such tongs can be used on other venerable bottles.

Portugais, or **Portugais Bleu**, French name for Blauer PORTUGIESER. Rare in France today.

Portugal. Among European wine-producing nations, Portugal has been something of a paradox, arguably discussed in the greater world of wine more because of the CORK of which it is by far the dominant producer than for its wines. Sitting on the western flank of the Iberian peninsula, this seafaring nation which discovered so much of the NEW WORLD has long clung firmly to the Old—at least in terms of its tradition of myriad INDIGENOUS VARIETIES. Secluded both geographically and, for much of the 20th century until it joined the EU in 1986, politically as well, Portugal has developed in isolation from other countries, including neighbouring SPAIN. However, the sizeable wine industry that has grown up in this small country owes much to foreign trade. Total area under vine has declined from 385,000 ha/951,000 acres in the late 1980s to 194,000 ha by 2021. This reduction in vineyard area reflects the shift from quantity to quality production as exports have re-oriented away from BULK WINE towards bottled wines. Historically, the Portuguese have rivalled the French and trump the Italians in terms of per capita wine consumption. However, the global financial crisis of 2007/08, which prompted the imposition of austerity measures in 2010, turned Portuguese wine producers' attention firmly to export markets. During the second decade of this century, while exports continued to rise, a surge in domestic consumption driven by tourism propelled Portugal to record the highest wine consumption per capita in 2020.

History

The British have always enjoyed an amicable relationship with the Portuguese. As early as the 12th century, wines were being shipped to England from the MINHO in north-west Portugal. In 1386, the Treaty of Windsor set the seal on a friendship that has persisted, virtually uninterrupted, to the present day. When England went to war with France in the 17th century, Portugal was therefore the natural alternative source for wine. PORT, often called 'the Englishman's wine', originated from this conflict. By the time England and Portugal signed the METHUEN TREATY in 1703, which laid down tariff advantages for Portuguese wines, a thriving community of English and German wine shippers was already well established in OPORTO. Out in the Atlantic, the island of MADEIRA, an important trading post for passing ships, began exporting wine to the newly colonized state and yet-to-be United States of America. Renewed conflict between Britain and France over the French invasion of the Iberian peninsula in 1807 rekindled demand for Portuguese wines. BUCELAS, CARCAVELOS, and a red wine simply called 'Lisbon' were popular in Britain until the 1870s.

In the late 19th century, PHYLLOXERA devastated Portuguese vineyards; some wine regions never really recovered. Many growers resorted to planting high-yielding DIRECT PRODUCERS, which can still be found in the smallholdings of north and central Portugal. For much of the 20th century, Portugal turned its back on the outside world. Following 20 years of political and economic turmoil, the demure son of a DÃO smallholder, Antonio de Oliveira Salazar, became prime minister in 1932. His regime, which lasted for over 40 years, fostered a corporate, one-party state. The Junta Nacional do Vinho (JNV), founded in 1937, initiated a programme of co-operativization. Over 100 winery CO-OPERATIVES were built, mostly in northern Portugal, in less than 20 years. At the time they represented a significant advance, but all too often the system imposed by central government was too inflexible and winemaking standards deteriorated.

It is paradoxical that, against this background of self-imposed seclusion, Portugal should give birth to one of the greatest international wine success stories of modern times: medium-sweet, lightly sparkling rosés called MATEUS and Lancers.

In 1974 Portugal was once again thrown into turmoil by a military-led revolution. But after two years of upheaval the soldier politicians returned to barracks and subsequent democratically elected governments eventually returned Portugal to the European mainstream. Portugal's winemakers have benefited enormously from EU entry in 1986. Monopolistic legislation was overturned and EU money poured in to help update the wine industry, much of which had been hidebound by a lack of investment in modern technology.

During the 1980s and 1990s, the relaxation of state bureaucracy and the availability of grants and low-interest loans resulted in a country-wide wine revolution. It encouraged single estates, or QUINTAS, to cut their links with local co-operatives or PORT shippers and to make and market their own more distinctive wines. Private investors injected a new entrepreneurial spirit into the business of winemaking, establishing state-of-the-art wineries (notably in the ALENTEJO, whose sprawling, flatter landscape offers relative economies of scale). In the second decade of this century, a lively micro-NÉGOCIANT scene has emerged making LOW-INTERVENTION and playful GLOU-GLOU wines. The use of traditional Portuguese techniques, OLD VINE parcels, and lesser-known INDIGENOUS VARIETIES brings a

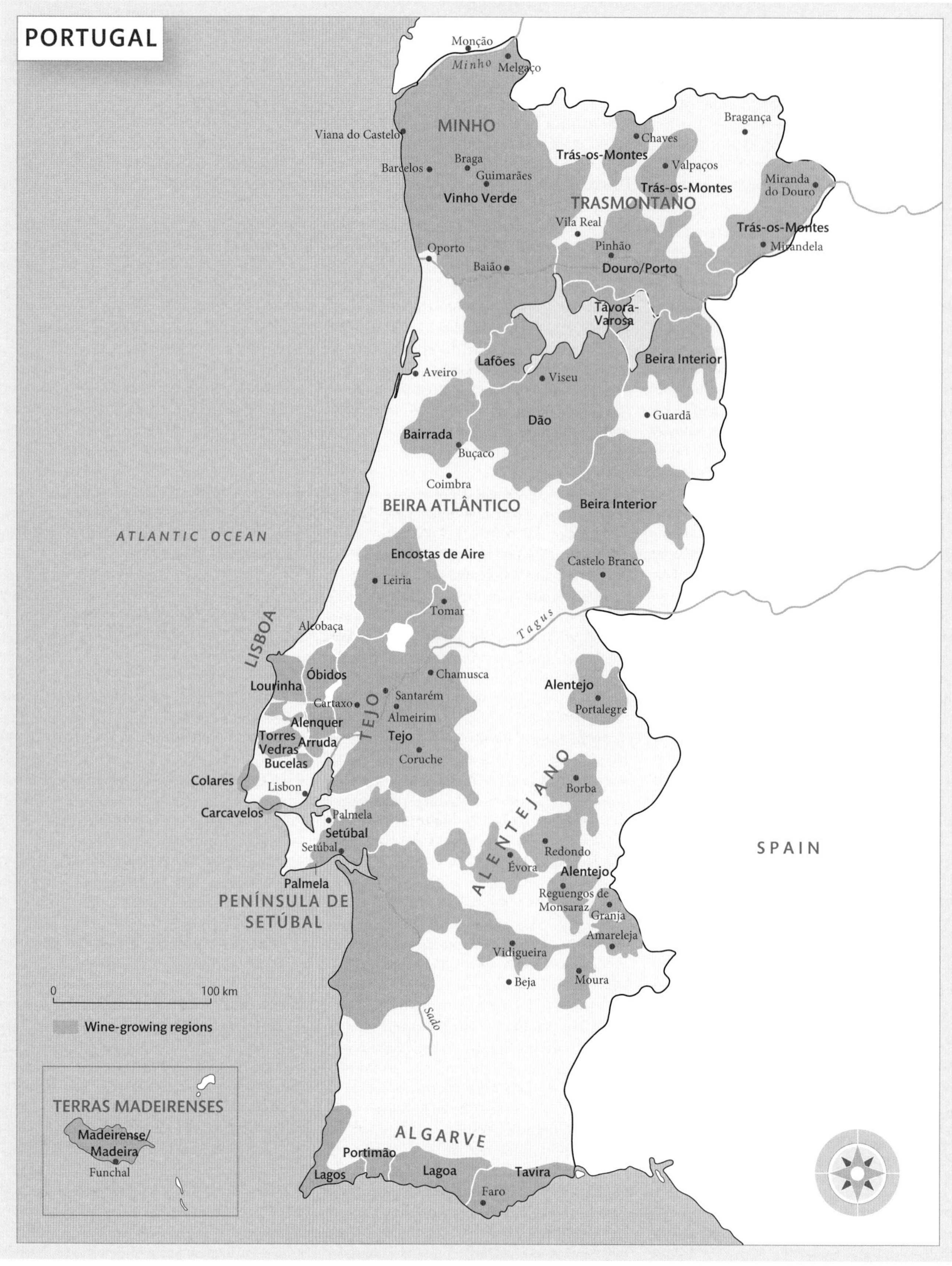
PORTUGAL
Monção
Minho
Melgaço
Viana do Castelo
MINHO
Braga
Barcelos
Guimarães
Vinho Verde
Chaves
Trás-os-Montes
Valpaços
Bragança
Trás-os-Montes
TRASMONTANO
Miranda do Douro
Vila Real
Trás-os-Montes
Mirandela
Oporto
Pinhão
Baião
Douro/Porto
Távora-Varosa
Lafões
Beira Interior
Aveiro
Viseu
Dão
Guardã
Bairrada
Buçaco
Coimbra
BEIRA ATLÂNTICO
Beira Interior
ATLANTIC OCEAN
Encostas de Aire
Leiria
Castelo Branco
Tomar
LISBOA
Alcobaça
Tagus
Óbidos
Chamusca
Lourinha
Santarém
Cartaxo
Alentejo
Portalegre
Almeirim
Alenquer
TEJO
Tejo
Torres Vedras
Arruda
Bucelas
Coruche
Colares
Lisbon
Borba
Carcavelos
Palmela
Setúbal
Setúbal
Redondo
ALENTEJANO
Évora
Alentejo
Palmela
PENÍNSULA DE SETÚBAL
Reguengos de Monsaraz
Granja
Amareleja
SPAIN
Vidigueira
Beja
Moura
0
100 km
Wine-growing regions
Sado
TERRAS MADEIRENSES
Madeirense/ Madeira
Funchal
ALGARVE
Portimão
Lagos
Lagoa
Tavira
Faro

splash of colour to the global wine scene. Forced to adapt, some co-operatives survived (indeed thrived) and others went under. In 2020 there were 74 active co-operatives, producing 36% of Portuguese wine. Inevitably, vineyard transformation was slower, but the benefits of experimentation with non-local and INTERNATIONAL VARIETIES, plus a considerable amount of research into Portugal's unique array of indigenous grapes (see below), have become increasingly apparent, especially in the DOURO, DÃO, and the ALENTEJO, and more recently TEJO and LISBOA.

Geography and climate

For such a small country, Portugal produces a remarkable diversity of wines, perhaps because grapes are grown from tip to toe and on its far-flung islands. Additionally, grape growing represents a high percentage of overall crop production—at 35%, the highest in the world or at least in Europe, according to a study published in 2017 by Adelaide University. Roughly rectangular in shape, it is under 600 km/360 miles long and no more than 200 km wide. The wines produced on the flat coastal littoral are strongly influenced by prevailing Atlantic westerly winds, which buffet the temperate VOLCANIC islands of MADEIRA and the AZORES, lashing the most exposed vineyards with atomized salt. Rainfall, which reaches 2,000 mm/78 in a year on the mountain ranges north of Oporto, diminishes sharply to less than 500 mm in some inland wine areas. The littoral's temperate MARITIME CLIMATE, with warm summers and cool, wet winters, diminishes inland; easternmost areas experience an extreme continental climate. An average annual temperature of around 10 °C/50 °F in the northern hills compares with more than 17.5 °C on the southern plains, where, in summer, temperatures frequently exceed 35 °C/95 °F. Reflecting these contrasting climatic conditions, no two wines could be more dissimilar than VINHO VERDE and PORT, which are produced in adjoining regions.

Vine varieties

Portugal's vineyards have evolved in isolation, leaving Portugal like a viticultural island with a treasure trove of INDIGENOUS VARIETIES, 248 of them according to a 2013 study produced by the Associação Portuguesa para a Diversidade da Videira (PORVID). Since Portugal joined the EU, the most promising have been identified and the overall quality and consistency of wines has commensurately improved. Among whites, LOUREIRO, ALVARINHO, and AVESSO (in Vinho Verde), BICAL and MARIA GOMES (in Bairrada), ENCRUZADO (in Dão), ARINTO (in Bucelas and throughout southern Portugal for blends), ANTÃO VAZ in the Alentejo, and RABIGATO, CÓDEGA DE LARINHO, VIOSINHO, and GOUVEIO (in the Douro) have emerged as leading varieties. Red-wine grapes account for around two-thirds of production. Some of the most celebrated are TOURIGA NACIONAL (originally from Dão and Douro but now prized country-wide), TEMPRANILLO (known as Tinta Roriz in the Douro and Aragonez in the Alentejo), BAGA (in Bairrada), TRINCADEIRA, and the French cross ALICANTE BOUSCHET (in the Alentejo). But as confidence and pride in native varieties and traditional wine styles has grown, more indigenous varieties are being sought out and celebrated. CLIMATE CHANGE concerns have also inspired winegrowers to re-evaluate the tradition of FIELD BLENDS (and/or CO-FERMENTING varieties) and to seek out lesser-known local indigenous varieties well adapted to DROUGHT and heat. INTERNATIONAL VARIETIES have made the most substantial inroads in LISBOA and TEJO, neither of which had a strong heritage of quality wines, unlike BAIRRADA, where the relaxation of DOC rules about varieties has been controversial. Cabernet Sauvignon, Petit Verdot, and Syrah are now not uncommon blend components of wines from the south of Portugal, especially the Alentejo.

Wine laws

Portugal's wine law predates that of most other European countries (although see also TOKAJ in Hungary). In 1756, the then prime minister, the Marquis of Pombal, drew a boundary around the vineyards of the Douro Valley to protect the authenticity of port, one of the wine world's first examples of geographical DELIMITATION. Bucelas, Colares, Carcavelos, Dão, Madeira, Setúbal, and Vinho Verde were all awarded *região demarcada* (demarcated region) status between 1908 and 1929, followed by Bairrada, Algarve, and Douro (for TABLE WINE) in 1979 and 1980. Since Portugal joined the EU, the Regiões Demarcadas or RDs were initially redesignated Denominação de Origem Controlada (DOC), now Denominação de Origem Protegida (DOP). A second tier, Indicação de Proveniencia Regulamentada (IPR), has been replaced by generally larger regions known as VINHO REGIONAL (also called Indicação Geográfica Protegida (IGP), meaning Protected Geographical Indication). Underpinned by the WINE WITHOUT GEOGRAPHICAL INDICATION designation, labelled VINHO if Portuguese, this brings the country's wine laws roughly into line with that of other EU countries.

For details of Portugal's extremely varied wine regions, see also ALENTEJO, ALGARVE, AZORES, BAIRRADA, BUCELAS, CARCAVELOS, COLARES, DÃO, DOURO, LISBOA, MADEIRA, MINHO, PENÍNSULA DE SETÚBAL, TEJO, TRÁS-OS-MONTES, VINHO VERDE, and, most importantly, PORT. R.J.M. & S.A.

Mayson, R. J., *The Wines of Portugal* (2020).
Woolf, S. J., and Opaz, R., *Foot Trodden: Portugal and the Wines That Time Forgot* (2021).
www.winesofportugal.info
www.viniportugal.pt
www.ivv.min-agricultura.pt

Portugieser, or **Blauer Portugieser**, black grape variety that has long been in decline in both Austria and Germany because of its association with overcropping, inexpensive rosé, and pale reds, its name suggesting completely unsubstantiated Portuguese origins. DNA PROFILING has shown it to be a spontaneous SILVANER × Blaue Zimmettraube CROSS, the latter an old dark-skinned variety still found in Germany's Rheinhessen and Hessische Bergstrasse, as well as in Friuli, north-east Italy (as Sbulzìna), and now known to be a parent of BLAUFRÄNKISCH. The birth of Portugieser most likely took place in Lower Styria (today part of Slovenia). The vigorous, precocious vine is extremely prolific and resistant to COULURE, easily producing 120 hl/ha (almost 7 tons/acre) of generally pale, low-acid red.

Blauer Portugieser remains relatively popular with Austrian growers in Pulkautal, Retz, and the Thermenregion although the vineyard area has declined to 1,263 ha/3,121 acres, making it the country's third most planted dark-berried vine. In the right hands it can occasionally yield concentrated wines.

Brought from Austria in the 19th century, Portugieser overtook even SPÄTBURGUNDER (Pinot Noir) in Germany in the 1970s in terms of total plantings, before Dornfelder surpassed it in satisfying German thirst for locally grown if uninspiring red wine. By 2020 Portugieser's total area had fallen to 2,548 ha/6,296 acres (Spätburgunder's was almost 12,000 ha), mainly in Rheinhessen and the PFALZ, where a high proportion is encouraged to produce vast quantities of pink WEISSHERBST.

The variety is so easy to grow that it has spread throughout central Europe and beyond (as PORTUGAIS Bleu it was once grown widely in south-western France). It was ingeniously named Oportó or KÉKOPORTÓ (*kék* meaning 'blue') in Romania and Hungary. It is also grown in northern Croatia as Portugizac Crni, or Portugaljka. J.V. & D.S.

Pošip, impressive southern CROATIAN white wine grape probably originating on the island of Korčula.

post, substantial support for wires and vines common in vineyards with TRELLIS SYSTEMS, usually made from wood, and driven into the ground at intervals down the row. Other materials used include concrete, steel, and plastic. Woods used for such posts are soft woods such as pine, treated to withstand insect and fungus attack, or naturally resistant hardwoods. A common spacing of about 6 m/20 ft between posts is close enough to stop the wire sagging. Smaller-diameter posts placed one beside each vine are called STAKES and are more common on steep or windy HILLSIDE VINEYARDS, for example in the MOSEL and the RHÔNE valleys. R.E.S.

potassium, one of the macronutrients required by the vine for healthy growth, along with NITROGEN and PHOSPHORUS (see VINE NUTRITION). It constitutes about 1–3% of the vine's dry weight and is an important component of grape juice. Potassium deficiencies show up first in older leaves as CHLOROSIS, which may become a marginal burn when severe. Potassium-deficient leaves are often shiny. Severe deficiencies can inhibit growth, YIELD, and sugar content. They can be confirmed easily by analysing for potassium levels in leaves or PETIOLES, and 1–1.5% potassium is the optimal range. Potassium deficiency is more evident during DROUGHT or in cold soils in spring, both of which reduce the roots' uptake of potassium. However, soils containing a significant proportion of mica-type CLAY minerals can supply too much potassium, as occurs in parts of Sunraysia and the Riverland, Australia.

Potassium is widely regarded as the most important element directly affecting wine quality. This is because high potassium levels in grape juice cause high PH, which adversely affects wine quality. Juice potassium levels are influenced by soil potassium levels, although this is not always a straightforward relationship. (Studies in Bordeaux in the 1980s showed positive linear correlations between plant potassium levels and juice potassium, but this was for vines with potassium contents up to and exceeding three times the optimal value.) ROOTSTOCKS also have an important effect on juice potassium, with lower-vigour rootstocks giving lower juice potassium. This effect has been shown both in France and in Australia. In hot climates with low humidity, juice potassium and pH are high, which may be the result of the high TRANSPIRATION rate of vines growing in such an environment.

Studies with Shiraz have shown that SHADE in the canopy causes accumulation of potassium in leaves, stems, and petioles, which is redistributed to the fruit during ripening, causing high juice pH. CANOPY MANAGEMENT techniques which reduce shade can therefore be effective in reducing juice potassium and pH. While skins are only about 10% of the berry weight, they contain 30–40% of grapes' potassium.

R.E.W. & R.E.S.

Smart, R. E., and Robinson, M., *Sunlight into Wine: A Handbook for Winegrape Canopy Management* (1991).

Rogiers, S. Y., et al., 'Potassium in the grape (*Vitis vinifera* L.) berry: transport and function', *Frontiers in Plant Science*, 8 (2017), 1629.

White, R. E., *Soils for Fine Wines* (2003).

potential alcohol, measurement of a wine, juice or MUST which equates to its total ALCOHOLIC STRENGTH if all the sugar were to be fermented out to alcohol. Thus, a SWEET WINE might have an alcoholic strength of 13% but a POTENTIAL ALCOHOL of 20% if all the RESIDUAL SUGAR were fermented into alcohol.

pouches, relatively recent form of wine PACKAGING made from polyethylene and aluminium. They are light (much lighter than a BOX, for example) and the 1.5-l size has a CARBON FOOTPRINT about one-fifth that of a 420-g, 75-cl glass bottle. Small sizes are convenient but may have a much shorter shelf life than the larger size, in which the wine typically stays fresh for up to six months. Plastic taps ensure that wine in an opened pouch keeps reasonably fresh for three or four weeks. Slightly higher levels of free SULFUR DIOXIDE are needed compared with those in a glass bottle, however. See also SUSTAINABILITY.

Alko, 'Update of wine packaging LCA: final report Alko Oy' (2021). www.alko.fi/INTERSHOP/static/WFS/Alko-OnlineShop-Site/-/Alko-OnlineShop/fi_FI/Tavarantoimittajille/Muut/EN/Alko%20wine%20packaging%20LCA%20update_final%20report.pdf.

Pouilly-Fuissé, white-wine appellation which commands the highest prices in the MÂCONNAIS district of Burgundy. The appellation, restricted to the Chardonnay grape, covered 759 ha/1,876 acres in 2018 in the communes of Fuissé, Solutré-Pouilly, Vergisson, and Chaintré (see also MÂCON-VILLAGES). The richest wines are said to come from Fuissé and Pouilly, those of Solutré and Vergisson being fresher and more mineral from vineyards at a higher ELEVATION. From 2020 the best single-vineyard sites have been classified as PREMIER CRU.

As well as in the amphitheatre of Fuissé, grapes are grown in sun traps beneath the two impressive crags of Solutré and Vergisson which mark the end of the LIMESTONE plateau on which all burgundy save Beaujolais is grown. A popular myth is that the soil beneath the crags was enriched by the remains of animals driven from the top of the cliff by Stone Age hunters. The wines are full-bodied and ripe but do not usually attain the elegance of the finer wines from the Côte de Beaune. Normally bottled after a year's BARREL AGEING, they are capable of AGEING well thereafter, particularly those of Domaine Barraud, Ch de Beauregard, Domaine Ferret, Ch de Fuissé, Olivier Merlin, Domaines Saumaize, Saumaize-Michelin, and Guffens-Heynen (the family domaine associated with the NÉGOCIANT Verget). Prices can vary enormously depending on the demands of major export markets in a given year.

The small village of Pouilly also lends its name to two adjacent lesser appellations, POUILLY-VINZELLES and POUILLY-LOCHÉ. J.T.C.M.

Pouilly-Fumé, also known as **Pouilly Blanc Fumé** and **Blanc Fumé de Pouilly**, one of the Loire's most famous wines, perfumed dry whites that epitomize the SAUVIGNON BLANC grape (along with nearby MENETOU-SALON, QUINCY, REUILLY, and, most notably, SANCERRE). All Sauvignon in the AOC is Sauvignon Blanc (no Gris allowed), which totalled 1,342 ha/3,316 acres in 2019. It was often called Blanc Fumé, because wines made from this variety, when grown on the predominantly LIMESTONE soils with some FLINT (*silex*), supposedly exhibit a 'smoky' flavour or a whiff of gunflint (*pierre à fusil*). The wines are certainly perfumed, and it takes extensive local knowledge to distinguish a Sancerre from a Pouilly-Fumé in a blind tasting of both. Pouilly-Fumé is arguably a more homogeneous appellation than Sancerre, which is not surprising since about half as much Pouilly-Fumé is made as white Sancerre, and the appellation is smaller and much flatter. (Some of the finest vineyards are on the slopes of St-Andelain on the right bank of the Loire.) Unlike that of Sancerre, the Pouilly-Fumé appellation applies only to white wines. The best Pouilly-Fumé is both taut and dense and is capable of long ageing. Some producers began experimenting with OAK for both fermentation and maturation in the mid 1980s, and the wines of the region have become more complex. The appellation takes its name from the small town of Pouilly-sur-Loire in the Nièvre *département*.

Pouilly-sur-Loire is also an AOC for wines made from the CHASSELAS grape. Just 27 ha/67 acres remain planted in 2021, typically producing a light and early-drinking wine. See also LOIRE, including map. J.R. & C.P.

Friedrich, J., *Earthly Delights from the Garden of France, Wines of the Loire*, Vol 1: *The Kingdom of Sauvignon Blanc* (2011).

Pouilly-Loché. See POUILLY-VINZELLES.

Pouilly-Vinzelles. Borrowing the prefix from its more famous neighbour in southern Burgundy POUILLY-FUISSÉ, the village of Vinzelles has its own small appellation of 61 ha/151 acres, most of which forms a steep, east-facing slope overlooking the valley of the Saône. The best vineyard is Les Quarts and the leading producer Domaine de la Soufrandière. Otherwise most production is in the hands of the local CO-OPERATIVE, as is the case also for **Pouilly-Loché**, an even smaller appellation of 34 ha.

Poulsard, sometimes called **Ploussard**, is a relatively rare speciality of the JURA, planted on a declining 251 ha/620 acres in 2019. Its long, thin-skinned, almost transluscent grapes make distinctive light tomato-red wines which may be left on the skins for as long as two weeks without colouring the wine too deeply and are sometimes sold as rosé. It does particularly well on MARL in the northern vineyards of the Jura, especially at Pupillin near Arbois, self-proclaimed capital of Ploussard. Its delicate pigment makes it much prized for adding colour to VIN DE PAILLE, and it is also used for rosé CRÉMANT du Jura. Very prone to REDUCTION, Poulsard wines benefit from low or no SULFUR DIOXIDE additions, and in the 21st century they have often been made with semi-CARBONIC MACERATION. Poulsard may also be blended with TROUSSEAU and Pinot Noir. It is also grown to a very limited extent in BUGEY, mainly for the semi-sweet sparkling wines from the CRU of Cerdon.

pourriture, French for ROT. *Pourriture noble* is NOBLE ROT. *Pourriture grise* is GREY ROT, or malevolent BOTRYTIS BUNCH ROT.

Poussard, or Guyot-Poussard, a PRUNING system developed by French viticulturist Eugène Poussard in the early 20th century that maintains the sap flow in the vine. More recently promoted by Italian pruning consultants Simonit & Sirch, it is seen as a way of minimizing pruning wounds, helping to protect vines from TRUNK DISEASES.

Lafon, R., *Modifications à apporter à la taille de la vigne dans les Charentes: Taille Guyot-Poussard mixte et double* (1921).

powdery mildew, sometimes called oidium, the first of the vine FUNGAL DISEASES to be scientifically described, in 1834 in the United States. It is native to North America, where it causes minor damage on native grapes. The fungus was given the name *Oidium tuckerii* after the gardener, a Mr Tucker, who first recognized it in Europe, in Margate, England, in 1845. Today the fungus is more widely known by its scientific name *Erysiphe necator* (formerly *Uncinula necator*). The disease was first noted in France in 1847, where it quickly spread and caused widespread havoc to vineyards and wine quality. Today it is the most widespread fungal disease of cultivated grapevines worldwide, as it proliferates under both wet and dry conditions.

Fruit infected with powdery mildew is universally avoided in winemaking. Wine made from infected bunches loses its fruity aromas, to be replaced by mouldy, wet fur, and earthy characters; wines are described as 'oily' and 'viscous'. The greater the infection, the more obvious the effects.

There is a difference in susceptibility between vine species, with many AMERICAN VINE SPECIES and their HYBRIDS being relatively resistant. Varieties of the European vine VITIS VINIFERA are generally very susceptible, although some variation is noted. For example, Carignan, Colombard, Chardonnay, and Cabernet Sauvignon are extremely susceptible whereas Aramon, Pinot Noir, Malbec, Merlot, and Riesling are more tolerant.

All green parts of the vine are attacked and the infection is very visible. Unlike other fungal vine pathogens, germinated powdery mildew spores penetrate only the outer epidermal cell to feed, then form a fine, translucent, cobweb-like growth that spreads on the surface around this spot. After one to two weeks, grey-white ash-like spores are produced on short, upright stalks. The infection looks powdery, hence the common name. Spores are spread by wind and, with favourable conditions, new infections occur rapidly. The fungus survives over winter within specialized spore bodies on the surface of the vine and also, where temperatures remain mild, within infected buds. If bunches are infected before flowering, then FRUIT SET and YIELD may be considerably reduced. Yield and quality are more commonly reduced when berries are infected during the first weeks of their development, while highly susceptible. Surface cells are killed so that the berries never grow to full size and are susceptible to colonization by spoilage microorganisms. Fruit of darker-skinned varieties also fail to colour properly.

The disease develops and spreads most rapidly in warm weather (20–27 °C/68–80 °F) but is inhibited at temperatures above 32 °C/90 °F. Unlike most fungal diseases, wetness is not required for spores to germinate and cause infection. Exposure to bright sunlight strongly inhibits disease development, due to the negative effects of ULTRAVIOLET RADIATION on the surface-growing fungus and the elevated temperature of irradiated vine tissues. The disease thrives within dense, shaded CANOPIES, and control is greatly aided by CANOPY MANAGEMENT techniques that avoid these and promote sunlight exposure.

Fortunately, control of this disease via applications of SULFUR dust was discovered soon after it appeared in Europe. Sulfur remains the most widely used FUNGICIDE against powdery mildew today, both as dusts in dry climates and as sprayable formulations in higher-rainfall regions. A number of other organic fungicides—including potassium salts, peroxides, oils extracted from plants and distilled from petroleum, and various microbial preparations and by-products (see BIOLOGICALS)—have been developed more recently and used with significant success, based upon their ability to harm the surface-growing fungus on contact. Several different synthetic fungicide families are also very effective and widely used, although the development and spread of resistance to them is an increasing problem. The application of UV radiation in the vineyard at night, using a light carried on a tractor or robotic vehicle, is showing promising results.

Recent developments in vine breeding have produced varieties with natural resistance and acceptable wine quality. These DISEASE-RESISTANT VARIETIES use the natural tolerance of native American species somewhere in their pedigree.
W.W.

Austin, C. N., and Wilcox, W. F., 'Effects of sunlight exposure on grapevine powdery mildew development', *Phytopathology*, 102/9 (2012), 857–66.

Stumner, B. E., et al., 'Powdery mildew and grape and wine quality', *The Australian & New Zealand Grapegrower & Winemaker*, 464 (Sept 2002), 68–74.

Wilcox, W. F., et al., *Compendium of Grape Diseases, Disorders, and Pests* (2nd edn, 2015).

Prädikat

Germany

A Prädikat is a 'distinction' awarded to PDO wines on the basis of increasing grape MUST WEIGHT: either KABINETT, SPÄTLESE, AUSLESE, BEERENAUSLESE, TROCKENBEERENAUSLESE or EISWEIN. Long collectively known as Qualitätswein mit Prädikat (QmP), the wines are now officially known simply as **Prädikatsweine**. Depending on region and grape variety, the minimum must weights in OECHSLE (and equivalent potential alcohol) set by German wine law for each Prädikat range as follows (with the low end applying in each case to the minimum for Riesling in the Mosel):

Kabinett 70–82 °Oe / 9.1–10.9%
Spätlese 76–90 °Oe / 10–12.2%
Auslese 83–100 °Oe / 11.1–13.8%
Beerenauslese and Eiswein 110–128 °Oe / 15.3–18.1%
Trockenbeerenauslese 150–154 °Oe / 21.5–21.9%

In practice, producers set their own estate-specific standards for what counts as Spätlese, Auslese, and so on, with the result that one grower's Spätlese may be another's Auslese. In general, producers opt for far higher must weights than the legal minima, which is unsurprising in this era of CLIMATE CHANGE. The choice of Prädikat is often made on the basis of intended style from among musts of nearly identical sugar content.

Germany's most prestigious growers' association, the VDP, may have 'Prädikatswein' in its name, but it took the lead in eliminating designations of Prädikat from the labels of TROCKEN (dry) wines, including those of their prestige class known as GROSSES GEWÄCHS. The idea is that a Prädikat designation should immediately indicate significant SWEETNESS, typically increasing with must weight. Dry German wines are more likely to be described as QUALITÄTSWEIN.

Austria

Prädikatswein officially excludes Kabinett wine in Austria but includes, in addition to the other Prädikats, Strohwein (or 'straw wine', see VIN DE PAILLE) and AUSBRUCH. As commonly used in Austria, Prädikatswein refers to overtly sweet wines of Auslese or higher must weight. The following minimum KMW must weights (with equivalent Oechsle and potential alcohols) are set for Prädikatswein:

Spätlese 19 °KMW / 94 °Oe / 12.8%
Auslese 21 °KMW / 105 °Oe / 14.5%
Beerenauslese 25 °KMW / 127 °Oe / 18%
Ausbruch 27 °KMW / 139 °Oe / 19.8%
Trockenbeerenauslese 30 °KMW / 156 °Oe / 21.8%
Eiswein 25 °KMW / 127 °Oe / 18%
Strohwein/Schilfwein 25 °KMW / 127 °Oe / 18%

Both German and Austrian laws stipulate certain characteristics that should be met by Prädikatswein over and beyond minimum must weights, such as that Spätlese or Auslese must be harvested from 'fully ripe' grapes; Beerenauslese from BOTRYTIZED grapes; and Trockenbeerenauslese from 'predominantly shriveled botrytis-affected' grapes. But in practice such unquantifiable criteria are virtually assured by the requisite must weight and are not enforced, except for two categories. EISWEIN must be pressed from grapes that have frozen on the vine and not been allowed to thaw. And (in Austria) Strohwein/Schilfwein must be made from grapes suspended on racks or dried on straw or reed mats for at least three months without any use of heaters, fans or dehumidifiers. D.S.

Pramaggiore. See LISON-PRAMAGGIORE.

PRD. See PARTIAL ROOTZONE DRYING.

precipitates, solids which are deposited on the bottom of barrels, casks, tanks, or vats by wine stored in them.

Technically, precipitates are solids which deposit from solutions because of reactions or temperature changes; they differ from SEDIMENTS, which are suspensions of solids which settle from the mixture when agitation ceases. Strictly speaking, therefore, the stem, pulp, and skin fragments and the seeds and dead yeast cells which settle after fermentation as gross LEES are not precipitates, while subsequent deposits of TARTRATES and oxidized PHENOLICS are.

precision viticulture is an approach to wine-grape production which recognizes that the productivity of individual vineyard blocks can show marked spatial variation in relation to variation in the land (SOIL, TOPOGRAPHY) underlying the vineyard. Thus, vineyard management is targeted rather than implemented uniformly over large areas. Research from around the world suggests that grape YIELD, vine VIGOUR, and GRAPE COMPOSITION can vary substantially within a single vineyard under conventional uniform management. In Australia, for example, yield may vary ten-fold (i.e. 2–20 tonnes/ha).

Critical to this approach to grape and wine production is the collection and use of large amounts of data relating to vine performance and the attributes of individual production areas (vineyards, blocks, sub-blocks, zones, etc.) at a high spatial resolution. This approach relies on a number of key enabling technologies including the GLOBAL NAVIGATION SATELLITE SYSTEM (GNSS), GEOGRAPHICAL INFORMATION SYSTEMS (GIS), REMOTE SENSING, PROXIMAL SENSING, and YIELD MONITORS, which, when used in conjunction with the GNSS, enable geo-referenced records of yield to be collected on the go during harvest. Such technologies, and the data derived from them, enable precision viticulture (PV) practitioners to manage vineyards by 'zones' rather than by blocks using targeted management to tailor production according to expectations of vineyard performance and desired goals in terms of both YIELD and/or GRAPE COMPOSITION AND WINE QUALITY. This is feasible given research which has shown that patterns of spatial variation in vineyard performance tend to be constant from one vintage to another, which in turn lends itself to the adoption of ZONAL VITICULTURE and SELECTIVE HARVESTING and the use of data collected in previous years to predict likely performance in subsequent years. Such data also offer hope for improved understanding of TERROIR.

Targeted management may mean the timing and rate of application of water, FERTILIZER, ameliorants such as MULCH or sprays, or the use of machinery and labour for a range of vineyard operations such as pruning or shoot or crop thinning, but selective harvesting is the most widely adopted form of targeted management. See ZONAL VITICULTURE.

Yield monitors and proximal CANOPY sensors are available as 'on the go' sensing technologies for attachment to existing vineyard machinery; methods to simultaneously predict yield and assess grapevine canopy conditions and grape composition are under development. R.G.V.B.

Bramley, R. G. V., 'Precision viticulture: managing vineyard variability for improved quality outcomes', in A. G. Reynolds (ed.), *Managing Wine Quality 1: Viticulture and Wine Quality* (2nd edn, 2021), 541–75.
Bramley, R. G. V., et al., 'Making sense of a sense of place—precision viticulture approaches to the analysis of terroir at different scales', *OENO One* 54 (2020), 903–17. oeno-one.eu/article/view/3858.

premature oxidation, known colloquially as premox, or even pox, is a phenomenon widely seen in white burgundy since the mid 1990s but also evident in many other white wines and occasionally in reds. The first vintage to exhibit the problem clearly was 1996, at about five years old, although it subsequently became clear that 1995 was also implicated.

A white wine which has oxidized naturally over a long period (see OXIDATION and AGEING) is likely to be deep yellow in colour, perhaps browning, with aromas of cooked fruit, sometimes quince, and eventually dank, dead fruit, possibly sherrified and acetic (see ACETALDEHYDE). Typically these negative effects will be immediately apparent on opening and pouring.

A prematurely oxidized white wine will also show some advance in the colour, more in the dull yellow range, and this may happen after the bottle has been open for a minute or two. The first danger sign in terms of aroma is bruised apples or furniture polish, which can strengthen considerably with AERATION. A compound called SOTOLON, characterized by honey or beeswax, is also commonly identified in these wines. Aromas of stewed fruit and prunes are common in prematurely oxidized red wines.

Two specific reasons were identified early on: inadequate CORKS and low SULFUR DIOXIDE levels. This was the worst period for cork quality, with an increase in demand due to growing world wine production but prior to the widespread introduction of SCREWCAPS and alternative CLOSURES. Many producers had also reduced sulfur dioxide levels in the interests of consumer sensitivity.

These problems coincided with a period in which the oxidation potential of white wines has been higher than in the past thanks to CLIMATE CHANGE and the desire for riper styles of wine which may be enjoyed earlier in their life.

Leading Bordeaux researchers Denis DUBOURDIEU and Valérie Lavigne believe that the production of the antioxidant GLUTATHIONE in vineyards is vital to the prevention of premox. Their overall preventive strategy comprises the following steps:

- ensuring adequate supply of NITROGEN to the vine for sufficient and appropriate VIGOUR in order to produce grapes low in PHENOLICS and rich in glutathione and FLAVOUR PRECURSORS
- limiting extraction of phenolic compounds during PRESSING to preserve glutathione
- protecting MUST and wine from oxidation (INERT GAS, sulfur dioxide)
- ensuring a rapid and complete alcoholic fermentation
- reducing the time lag between fermentation and MALOLACTIC CONVERSION (by LEES STIRRING or inoculation with LACTIC ACID BACTERIA)
- ageing the wines in REDUCTIVE conditions (sulfur dioxide, LEES, moderate amounts of new oak)
- limiting the amount of dissolved oxygen when preparing the wine for BOTTLING (see TOTAL PACKAGE OXYGEN)
- choosing a closure that is suited to the wine.

See also RANDOM OXIDATION. J.T.C.M. & V.L.

Lavigne, V., et al., 'Assaying sotolon in wine. Changes in the sotolon content of dry whites wines during barrel and bottle aging', *Journal of Agricultural and Food Chemistry*, 56 (2008), 2688–93.

Morris, J., 'White Burgundy out of the woods?', *World of Fine Wine*, 43 (2014), 100–9.

premier cru, or **premier cru classé**, is a CRU judged of the first rank, usually according to some official CLASSIFICATION. The direct translation of the French term *premier cru*, much used in the context of BORDEAUX, is FIRST GROWTH. A **premier grand cru (classé)** or **premier cru supérieur** may, as in the case of ST-ÉMILION and Ch d'YQUEM, be a rung higher even than this. In Burgundy, scores of vineyards are designated premiers crus, capable of producing wine distinctly superior to VILLAGE WINE but not quite so great as the produce of the GRANDS CRUS. See BURGUNDY in general and each of the villages on the CÔTE D'OR in particular. See also ERSTES GEWÄCHS, ERSTE LAGE, CHAUME, and CHAMPAGNE, geography and climate.

Premières Côtes de Bordeaux, AOC created in 2011 specifically for sweet wine made in the narrow strip extending for 60 km/40 miles along the south-western edge of the ENTRE-DEUX-MERS appellation on the right bank of the GARONNE from Langon almost as far as the city of Bordeaux. It used to apply to the region's red wines too, but from 2011 the reds have been known as CADILLAC CÔTES DE BORDEAUX. In 2020 just 71 ha/175 acres of vineyard were devoted to the production of these blends of Sémillon, Sauvignon Blanc, Sauvignon Gris, and Muscadelle that lack the intensity of great SAUTERNES. Dry whites are sold as BORDEAUX AOC.

premium wine, debased and virtually meaningless term, not unlike RESERVE. See also ICON WINE.

Prensal, also spelt **Premsal**. See MOLL.

pre-phylloxera, term used to differentiate vines, especially European ones, planted before the arrival of phylloxera towards the end of the 19th century from those GRAFTED on to phylloxera-resistant American ROOTSTOCKS which replaced them. In the first half of the 20th century, there was much discussion about the relative merits of wines made from pre- and post-phylloxera vines with, perhaps inevitably, overall agreement that the earlier generation of wines were distinctly superior. As pointed out at the end of PHYLLOXERA, however, it was probably not the grafting itself which resulted in an apparent drop in quality but the effects of the VIRUS DISEASES imported into European vineyards along with all this phylloxera-resistant plant material from across the Atlantic. As OLD VINES are increasingly venerated as the source of distinctive wines, the terms *préphylloxerique* (French), *pre-fillossera* (Italian), and *prefiloxérica* (Spanish) appear more frequently on wine labels.

pre-pruning. See MECHANICAL PRUNING.

preservation systems for wine proliferated in the late 20th and early 21st centuries. Enomatic and similar systems which preserve wine under INERT GAS, usually argon, and dispense the wine from multiple bottles in a temperature-controlled cabinet were designed for retail and hospitality settings. Coravin, invented by a wine-loving medical engineer with a practically teetotal wife, was aimed at the domestic wine drinker, although it is much used by wine professionals for small pours of fine wine. It allows wine to be withdrawn from an unopened bottle via a thin needle through the cork, inert gas being substituted for its volume via rather expensive cartridges. Other systems rely on vacuums or inert gas, while the Eto decanter has a valve designed to halt OXIDATION.

press in a wine context usually means **wine press**, a particularly ancient piece of winemaking equipment, used for the PRESSING operation of separating grape juice or wine from solids. Wine presses or their remains provide some of the longest-surviving evidence of the ORIGINS OF VINICULTURE. In ancient times, the design of presses was varied and ingenious. See ancient EGYPT and GREECE for more details.

Ancient history

CATO (*De agricultura* 18–19) in the 2nd century BCE provided the first detailed description of a press room. He describes a beam or lever press. This would be constructed on an elevated concrete platform with a raised curb, which formed a shallow basin, which sloped gently to a run-off point. On this was constructed the press, consisting of a long, heavy horizontal beam which slotted into an upright at the back and ran between two uprights at the front. The front end of the beam was attached by a rope to a windlass. The grape solids were put under the beam and pressure applied by winding down the end. As the pulp compacted, so wedges were hammered into the slot at the pivot end to lower it. Over time various refinements were introduced. Most notably, according to PLINY (*Natural History* 18. 317), a 'Greek-style' press was introduced during the late republic or early empire in which the windlass was replaced with a vertical screw thread, sometimes with a heavy counterweight. There is ample archaeological evidence from Italy, and elsewhere, for the use of presses. All the Roman AGRICULTURAL TREATISES, apart from the writings of Palladius, assume the use of a press in their descriptions of winemaking. However, the press was an elaborate and comparatively expensive piece of equipment, and its use was far from universal. Some farmsteads have large tanks for treading the grapes in but no evidence of a press. It is not clear whether the must from the treading was always kept separate from that from the pressing. The grape pulp could be subject to a second pressing; but this was carefully kept separate. The pressed grape skins could even be soaked in water to produce *lorca*, a drink to be given to the farm hands (VARRO, *De re rustica* 1. 54), a forerunner of PIQUETTE. J.J.P.

Rossiter, J. J., 'Wine and oil processing at Roman farms in Italy', *Phoenix*, 35 (1981), 345–61.

White, K. D., *Farm Equipment of the Roman World* (1975), 112–15.

Presses today

Wine presses have evolved over the last thousand years or more into the relatively complicated machines used today. The **basket** presses used during the Middle Ages by religious orders were large devices built of wood in which grapes were squeezed by a horizontal wooden disc which just fitted into a cylindrical basket made of wooden staves bound into the cylinder shape by encircling wooden hoops. The juice from the crushed berries escapes through the spaces between the basket staves and flows into a tray below. Some of these traditional presses, usually depending on a giant lever for pressure, still exist and are occasionally used in Burgundy and parts of Italy. Similar, usually smaller versions of the basket press reliant on hand or hydraulic power can be found in many of Europe's less mechanized wineries today, and most producers of CHAMPAGNE and SAUTERNES still rely on variations on this vertical-pressing theme, demanding though they are in terms of time and labour. Modern basket presses, the wooden slats often replaced by stainless steel, are gaining in popularity among producers who wish to work with smaller batches and are willing to tolerate longer set-up and cleaning times in order to treat their fruit as gently as possible. If whole bunches are included, the stems improve drainage.

In modern **horizontal** presses, the basket-press principle has been turned on its side. They can be divided into either batch or continuous presses, the latter almost never used for fine wines. Most batch presses depend upon squeezing a charge of crushed grapes or POMACE against a perforated screen. Pressure may be applied by a moving press head as in the old basket press or, more gently in theory, by using a pneumatic press, in which an airbag or membrane expands to squeeze the pomace against the inner wall of the cylinder. However, more common today are the fully enclosed **tank** presses, which reduce the exposure of the pomace and juice to air. Further protection from oxygen is achieved by flushing the tank with INERT GAS prior to pressing or, in the latest generation of horizontal presses, using NITROGEN during the inflation and deflation of the membrane.

Continuous presses, more common in the 1980s and 1990s, are much harsher and usually worked by either a screw or a belt. With a screw press, the decreasing pitch of an Archimedes screw subjects the pomace to increasing pressure as it is moved along within the perforated cylindrical housing. Belt presses are much rarer and function by pressing intact berries between two perforated moving belts arranged so that the clearance between them decreases. The screw press allows faster throughput and is therefore the cheapest form of press. Both screw and belt presses can also be enclosed. The belt press was really more of an alternative to the crusher since it was still necessary to drain the juice and press the skins further in some other form of press.

Winemakers also use **vertical** presses, which are better suited to pressing reds and FORTIFIED WINES. The pressure is higher than in a pneumatic press but it is impossible to break up the cake, which is why this type of press is rarely used on grapes for white wine.

Many modern presses are controlled by a computer programme designed to optimize the pressing cycle for each grape variety and wine type. The screw press is still found in some large commercial wineries, but tank presses and modern basket presses are increasingly common for fine-wine production. V.L.

Pressac, Bordeaux RIGHT BANK name for the red grape variety Cot or MALBEC.

pressing, winemaking operation whereby pressure is applied, using a PRESS, to grapes, grape clusters or grape POMACE in order to squeeze the liquid out of the solid parts.

For most white wines, pressing takes place prior to FERMENTATION (for exceptions, see ORANGE WINES, QVEVRI, and SKIN-FERMENTED whites, for example). There are various options for extracting juice from grapes: immediate pressing of whole grapes without CRUSHING, immediate pressing of crushed and/or DESTEMMED grapes, or pressing after the crushed and destemmed grapes have undergone a period of SKIN CONTACT.

The most commonly used PRESSES in white winemaking are pneumatic bladder or membrane presses. Using gentle pressure, this type of pressing makes it possible to extract juice containing little PULP. It also results in only a small increase in the level of PHENOLICS in the juice. However, it is necessary to make sure that pressing lasts long enough for the grapes' aromatic qualities to be released into the juice. In certain instances, for example for grapes high in acidity and low in phenolics, skin contact may take place in the press.

Red wines are usually pressed after fermentation (or just before the end) or following extended MACERATION, but see RED WINEMAKING for alternative approaches. The timing and the pressure influences the level of phenolic extraction. The use of vertical presses in red winemaking is increasingly common because the juice filters through the cake to yield particularly clear juice.

See also PRESS, PRESS WINE, and FREE-RUN.

D.D. & V.L.

pressure bomb, or **pressure chamber**, a device for measuring water potential in plants developed by the American plant scientist Per Scholander in the 1960s. It has since been used for studies in grapevine physiology and more recently in California as a guide to the timing of vineyard IRRIGATION. The blade of the leaf is placed in an airtight chamber and pressure is increased until XYLEM fluid exudes from the cut PETIOLE end. However, water potential of the grapevine can vary from hour to hour, depending on sunshine, temperature, humidity, and soil moisture content, so it is difficult to interpret this dynamic value as an irrigation guide.

R.E.S.

Bogart, K., 'Measuring winegrape water status using a pressure chamber'. www.grapes.extension.org/measuring-winegrape-water-status-using-a-pressure-chamber.

Smart, R. E., 'Aspects of water relations of the grapevine (*Vitis vinifera*)', *American Journal of Enology and Viticulture*, 25 (1974), 84–91.

press wine, dark-red wine squeezed from POMACE (grape skins, stem fragments, pulp, dead yeast) in a wine PRESS. Press wine is generally more astringent than FREE-RUN wine, especially when a continuous screw press has been used. A certain proportion of press wine may be usefully incorporated into the free-run wine, adding colour and powerful but not astringent TANNINS, as well as increasing the volume on the mid PALATE. Whether to include press wine in the blend, and how much to include, depends very much on the winemaking process, the desired style of the wine, and the vintage conditions. Otherwise it is used for a lesser bottling.

All white wine except for the free-run juice is effectively press wine, although its quality and characteristics are shaped considerably by how gently the white grapes were pressed and whether there has been any SKIN CONTACT. See also the TAILLE produced in CHAMPAGNE. V.L.

prestige cuvée, one of several names given to a CHAMPAGNE house's highest-quality wine. At one time the houses saw their NON-VINTAGE wine as their greatest expression. Vintage-dated champagne was added to the range and a premium usually charged for it. ROEDERER's Cristal bottling and MOËT & CHANDON's named after Dom PÉRIGNON scaled new heights, however, and today most of the major champagne firms offer one such product, available—at a price and, often, in a specially created bottle—in limited quantity at the top of their range. Also sometimes known as de luxe or luxury cuvées.

price is probably the single most important aspect of a wine to most consumers, just as the price of grapes is one of the most important variables of the viticultural year to most grape-growers. The price of vineyard land is not directly proportional to the price fetched by grapes grown on it, however. See below.

Grape prices

Wine grapes are an important item of commerce throughout the world, and the economic fortunes of many rural communities rise and fall with local wine-grape prices. Although many wine consumers have the impression that most wine grapes are grown on estates which also process them into wine, the majority of the world's wine grapes are sold in the form of fresh fruit, to be vinified quite independently of the grape-grower, whether by commercial wineries or CO-OPERATIVES.

The means to determine prices for wine grapes varies from region to region. Prices are normally fixed annually, taking into account supply and demand as well as individual VINTAGE characteristics. A buoyant wine market bolsters grape prices, whatever the size of the crop, with some wineries attracting fruit away from others by paying higher prices. When the market is depressed it is not unusual to see fruit left on the vine (as in some vintages in Australia, for instance), since the cost of harvesting can be more than the potential income. In many areas, notably Europe and South Africa, SURPLUS grapes have been distilled into alcohol.

Normally grapes are bought and sold according to VINE VARIETY and sugar content. The demand for different varieties is relatively stable, but prices can reflect longer-term changes as varieties move in and out of FASHION. In many European regions, there is some sort of representative body which oversees grape prices. The regional organization in Champagne is the oldest of the French regional associations and has powers and services which extend beyond grape price determination. The Comité Interprofessionnel du Vin de Champagne (CIVC) has in its time determined grape prices by means of a relatively complex series of calculations (see CHAMPAGNE). For many European producers, grape prices are set by co-operatives; although the formulae may not be so rigid as those traditionally employed in Champagne, they must take into account the same factors concerning supply, demand, and intrinsic quality.

Outside Europe the majority of grape-growers sell their produce to private wineries with which they negotiate freely. The US government reports in detail on prices paid after each vintage. The world's record grape prices are probably for Napa Valley Cabernet Sauvignon. Nationwide, however, according to the official report on the 2021 harvest, the average price paid per ton of grapes was just over $8,000, but some producers will pay $20,000 a ton for grapes from the finest sources.

A basic problem in buying and selling wine grapes is that their true value is not known until they are made into wine—and, indeed, until that wine is sold. Region of origin, however, is well recognized as affecting wine style and quality. Concentration of SUGAR IN GRAPES was long regarded as the most important factor in determining wine quality and therefore grape price, but in the era of CLIMATE CHANGE this is giving way to more subtle criteria. Increasingly, progressive wineries are implementing GRAPE QUALITY ASSESSMENT schemes to reward growers for producing high-quality fruit. These schemes may be related to the vineyard site as well as to ROOTSTOCK and CLONE, vineyard management methods, and also perhaps to a detailed chemical ANALYSIS of the fruit. Wineries may keep wine batches from different growers separate and so are able to pay a bonus based on performance. Some enlightened wine producers pay growers per ha/acre and effectively manage grape quality themselves.

Vineyard land prices

Needless to say, those vineyards with a reputation for high wine quality attract high land prices. Perhaps the clearest examples are to be found in the Bordeaux region, where, thanks partly to several important CLASSIFICATIONS of individual châteaux, land prices are also clearly stratified. In 2021, for example, the price of planted vineyard entitled to the basic Bordeaux appellation had fallen to €12,000 per ha (it was about €25,000 per ha in the mid 2000s), while Pauillac, home of three FIRST GROWTHS, commanded €3 million per ha.

Official land transactions in France are overseen by the agency SAFER. According to its statistics for 2021, average land prices in Burgundy (including much less valuable Beaujolais) were by far the highest of any wine region at more than €200,000 per ha, with average Bordeaux land prices overtaking those of Alsace at nearly €120,000. Champagne vineyard land was long considered some of the world's most expensive, but the average prices reported by SAFER fell each year from 2019 to 2021. In the Napa Valley in the early 2020s, an acre of highly sought-after vineyard could sell for as much as $1 million an acre, the equivalent of about €2.37 million per ha.

But there are also extensive tracts of land which have suitable soils and climate to grow quality grapes economically but which are still yet to be 'discovered' and planted to vineyards. As such, they have the value only of their existing land use, which could be low-value grazing.

Wine prices

The price of a wine is a function of the price of the grapes, the price of LABOUR, the price of a winery or the debt outstanding on it, pricing policy on the part of the producer, pricing policy on the part of any merchants involved in selling it, and the cost of TRANSPORT, BOTTLING, LABELLING, and marketing, quite apart from any DUTIES and TAXATION. The interest for the wine producer must be to maximize return on capital without acquiring a reputation for profiteering.

GLOBALIZATION continues to give bigger retailers increasing power to dictate prices and PRICE POINTS, which has had a generally deflationary effect on retail prices, if hardly an inflationary one on absolute value. See also ECONOMICS OF WINE.

The interesting question for the consumer, however, is the extent to which retail wine prices, which can vary more than a thousand-fold, reflect wine quality. The answer is, of course, not very closely. All sorts of factors can depress the price of a wine to make it a bargain relative to the competition. Some national economies offer particularly low production costs (such as SOUTH AFRICA and some of SOUTH AMERICA) when translated into the currencies of many potential importers. Currency movements in general have far more (upward) impact on wine prices than most wine drinkers realize (merchants do not always pass on to consumers the benefit of downward movements). Other political events can also affect wine prices. The fall of communism and the effect of GORBACHEV's anti-alcohol policies on Eastern Europe left SURPLUS PRODUCTION in countries such as BULGARIA, HUNGARY, and ROMANIA, which used to ship enormous quantities to the Soviet Union, and in the 1990s these emerging economies' desire for hard, western currency led them to export goods such as wine at extremely keen prices or as part of barter deals. Specific countries may also benefit, or suffer, as a result of TARIFFS.

Pricing policy in general may be geared to gaining a foothold in a new market, as, for example, South Africa needed to do after the lifting of sanctions in the early 1990s. Or it may have the result of bolstering prices in the belief that high prices automatically buy respect and prestige, a phenomenon associated with some aspirant CALIFORNIA CULT wines.

The above considerations relate to the prices of wine when it is first offered for sale. Serious wine COLLECTORS and those considering investing in wine are interested in what happens to the price of FINE WINE over time. As detailed in INVESTMENT and AUCTIONS, this depends on the precise wine, the era, and period of time, as well as on the rarity value of a given wine, its PROVENANCE and condition, and the general state of the market.

Most ordinary wine drinkers took a certain comfort in the story of what happened to what was then the world's most expensive bottle of wine sold, at Christie's for a record £105,000 in 1985: this particular bottle of Ch Lafite 1787, supposedly once the property of Thomas JEFFERSON, was stood upright on display under warm lights by its owners, the Forbes family, so that, unnoticed, the cork dried out and dropped into the bottle, rendering the wine OXIDIZED and undrinkable. In October 2018 a new record price was set at Sotheby's in New York: $558,000 for a 75-cl bottle of Domaine de la Romanée-Conti 1945 Romanée-Conti, paid by a Chinese buyer.

Not least because of the ASIAN economic boom, the late 1990s saw the prices of the most sought-after fine wines, the so-called TROPHY WINES, draw away from those of other wines, a gap that widened as the Chinese buyers poured into the market for top 2009 and 2010 bordeaux. It is ironic perhaps that, at a time when the difference in quality between wines at the top and bottom ends of the market has never been narrower, the price difference has never been greater. But presumably this reflects the hugely increased number of affluent wine consumers, the finite volumes of wine produced, and the significant position that wine now holds in a number of cultures round the world. Billionaires need billionaires' drinks.

price points, the supposedly particularly significant retail prices, often x.99, that dominate mass-market wine selling. Bigger retailers impose a carefully planned timetable of retail discounts and promotions on their main suppliers, thereby sometimes entailing artificially inflated base price points from which these 'reductions' can be made. In common usage 'price point' is often used instead of 'price'.

Prié, rare but genetically important AOSTA white wine grape that has close relatives in both Switzerland and Spain.

Prieto Picudo, unusual, musky, Spanish medium-red grape grown on 2,871 ha/7,094 acres in 2020, mainly around the city of LEÓN in north-central Spain. These red wines are deeply coloured, often tannic, aromatic, potent, and distinctive.

primeur, French word for 'young produce', which has been adapted to mean 'young wine'. French AOC rules allow all of the following to be released on the third Thursday of November following the harvest: Beaujolais, Côtes du Rhône, Grignan-les-Adhémar, Ventoux, Languedoc, Gamays from Touraine, Anjou, and Gaillac, Coteaux du Lyonnais, Côtes du Roussillon, Mâcon Blanc, Tavel Rosé, Rosé d'Anjou, Cabernet d'Anjou, Saumur Rosé, Bourgogne Blanc, Bourgogne Aligoté, Muscadet, and Gaillac Blanc. For more details of this style of wine, see NOUVEAU.

See also EN PRIMEUR for details of fine wines offered for sale as futures before they are bottled.

Primitivo, Italian name for the originally Croatian ZINFANDEL grape (see also TRIBIDRAG), grown principally in PUGLIA. Once highly prized for blending, in the 1990s it fell victim to the same EU VINE-PULL SCHEME as NEGROAMARO. Plantings fell to under 8,000 ha/19,770 acres by the turn of the century, but the 1994 confirmation by DNA PROFILING that Primitivo was Zinfandel led to commercial success as a VARIETAL (rather than as a blending ingredient) and staunched the loss of vineyards in the 21st century. Since 1999 Italian exporters have been allowed to label their Primitivo as Zinfandel, and by 2015 there were 13,896 ha/34,338 acres planted in Italy. A move to limit the use of the name 'Primitivo' solely to DOC wines was rejected by producers in 2005, to the advantage of the growers, for the success of IGT Primitivo has meant that higher prices are now being paid for the grapes. This in turn has ensured that the variety is being replanted after years in which it was only grubbed up, as the backbreaking work involved in cultivating the BUSH VINES was not remunerative.

It was presumably brought across the Adriatic Sea from Croatia to Puglia in the 18th century. Its Italian name derives from the latter part of the 18th century, when a priest in Gioia del Colle selected vines from promiscuous old vineyards and noted that fruit from these vines matured earlier than those from other vines. As a result, he called the variety *primativo*, from the Latin *primativus*, or 'first to ripen'. In 1799, he planted these cuttings in a vineyard in Liponti, just outside Gioia del Colle.

Historically, it suffered from a poorly conceived DOC in Manduria: a minimum alcohol level of 14% for the regular production and higher alcohol for the *liquoroso* versions (both sweet and dry), which reach a leg-wobbling 18%. Puglians report it is highly prized as a high-strength blending ingredient by many producers of AMARONE.

It is also DOC in its original homeland of Gioia del Colle. As an IGT Salento wine, it has enjoyed a boom since the late 1990s, where careful selection and modern vinification can result in wines of great appeal and value.

Priorat, one of Spain's most inspiring red wines, made in an isolated zone in Catalunya (see CATALUÑA) inland from Tarragona (see map under SPAIN), one of the country's only two to qualify as a DOCA (or DOQ in Catalan). In the 1990s, a true revolution engulfed the region, where production methods for Priorat had barely altered since the 12th century when the Carthusian MONKS first established the priory after which the wine is named.

Priorat is one of the world's few first-class wines to be made from GARNACHA and Mazuelo/Cariñena/CARIGNAN vines. The VINE AGE and concomitantly extremely low YIELDS undoubtedly contribute to the intensity and strength of Priorat.

The landscape is extreme: of the region's 1,900 ha/4,695 acres of vines in 2020, 600 ha are planted on slopes steeper than 35%; 23 ha are dramatically steep, at 90%. Poor, stony soils derived from the underlying SLATE and QUARTZ, called locally *llicorella*, support only the most meagre of crops. MECHANIZATION is almost impossible, and many steeply terraced smallholdings had been abandoned as the rural population left to find work on the coast. The success of new-wave Priorat has been reviving viticulture, however.

The region was long dominated by CO-OPERATIVES, but the 1980s saw an explosion of top-quality independent estates, led by Scala Dei, whose 1975 Priorat was still drinking well in 2022. René Barbier, the scion of the Franco-Spanish winemaking family (whose eponymous firm in Penedès belongs to HENKELL FREIXENET), located some particularly promising vineyard sites, renaming them CLOS. Such French vine varieties as Cabernet Sauvignon, Merlot, and Syrah were planted. Complex blends including small proportions of French varieties, careful winemaking, and ageing in new French oak barrels were the key innovations. The wines of Barbier (Clos Mogador), Costers del Siurana (Clos de l'Obac), Álvaro PALACIOS (Finca Dofí, L'Ermita), Mas Martinet (Clos Martinet), and Clos & Terrasses (Clos Erasmus) had won worldwide acclaim by the late 1990s, with L'Ermita one of Spain's most expensive wines.

By the mid 2000s there were more than 50 bodegas in Priorat; by 2018 there were over 100, many also producing rich, full-bodied white wines from GARNACHA BLANCA, MACABEO, PEDRO XIMÉNEZ, and some VIOGNIER.

In 2019 a new classification system was introduced for both dry red and white wines with the intention of demonstrating Priorat's diverse and special TERROIRS. Wines bottled under the basic DOQ Priorat may come from anywhere within the delimited area. The new designations all require a minimum of 60% Carignan and/or Garnacha for reds, with increased minima for vine age and tighter yield restrictions. In addition, **Vins de Vila** must come solely from one of Priorat's 12 named villages: Bellmunt, Gratallops, El Lloar, La Morera, Porrera, Poboleda, Escaladei, Torroja, La Vilella Alta, La Vilella Baixa, and areas in Masos de Falset and Les Solanes del Molar. **Paratge** wines come from one of 459 single plots recognized by the Consell Regulador (see CONSEJO REGULADOR), and 90% of the vines must also be at least 15 years old. **Vinya Classificada** may be used for specially recognized vineyards with 80% of vines at least 20 years old; **Gran Vinya Classificada** must come from vines planted more than 75 years ago and have a track record of producing exceptional wines. The first three Gran Vinya Clasificada wines to be announced in 2020 were Vall Llach Mas de la Rosa, Mas Doix 1902, and Alvaro Palacios L'Ermita.

Priorat's success has directed increased attention to the surrounding DOP MONTSANT, which can be a source of similar wines at more affordable prices.

Priorat also has a tradition of FORTIFIED WINES, from the nutty, dry or sweet RANCIO wines called Vi Ranci to Vino Dulce Natural, akin to France's VIN DOUX NATUREL. V. de la S. & F.C.

www.doqpriorat.org

proanthocyanidins, oligomers and polymers of flavanols. Proanthocyanidins are PHENOLICS belonging to the FLAVONOID group, also called condensed TANNINS. The term proanthocyanidin refers to the reactivity of these molecules that release red anthocyanidin pigments (i.e. anthocyanin aglycones) when heated in an acidic medium, still commonly used for their analysis.

Several classes can be distinguished by the differing nature of the anthocyanidin released. The most common proanthocyanidins are procyanidins, based on CATECHIN and epicatechin units, which release cyanidin when heated in acidic media. Grape proanthocyanidins also comprise prodelphinidins based on gallocatechin and epigallocatechin units, which release delphinidin when heated in acidic media. Procyanidins are the only proanthocyanidins in grape seeds, whereas tannins of grape skins and stems consist of both procyanidins and prodelphinidins. V.C.

Probus, Marcus Aurelius (232–282 CE), Roman emperor (276–282) who employed troops in the planting of vineyards in GAUL and along the Danube. (See GERMAN HISTORY.) This positive encouragement of viticulture was in marked contrast to the earlier Emperor DOMITIAN.

Procanico, Umbrian name for TREBBIANO Toscano.

processing aids, unlike ADDITIVES, are added to juice, MUST or wine in order to react with and thus remove another component in the wine, so that only trace amounts will remain in the finished product. The purposes of such transient additions include CLARIFICATION, STABILIZATION, FINING, and the removal of off-flavours. However, in some countries the use of certain processing aids, especially those based on animal products such as CASEIN, ISINGLASS, or GELATIN, must be stated on the label for the benefit of VEGETARIANS AND VEGANS or those with ALLERGIES AND INTOLERANCES. See also LABELLING INFORMATION.

procymidone, a systemic FUNGICIDE used to combat BOTRYTIS.

production of a particular vineyard is normally measured as YIELD. The world's production of wine typically totals 260–290 million hl (6,800–7,650 million gal) annually, although 2017 and 2021 fell below that level mainly due to very small crops in parts of Europe, and is considerably in excess of CONSUMPTION, leading to continued surplus, but there is wide variation according to VINTAGE. See WORLD PRODUCTION and, for annual totals, SURPLUS PRODUCTION. The tables in Appendix 2 show the world's significant wine-producing countries and OIV figures for their total area of vineyard, annual wine production, and per-capita consumption.

(See map under WORLD PRODUCTION for the location of different countries' wine regions.)

Prohibition in common parlance most often means a prohibition on the consumption of alcohol (which suggests the importance generally attached to the possibility of intoxication). Prohibition has officially been in force throughout the world of ISLAM for 12 centuries, and elsewhere there have been periods throughout history (usually just after a period of particularly heavy consumption) during which the arguments for Prohibition have seemed convincing. One of these periods was the early 20th century, when Prohibition was enforced in parts of Scandinavia, was put to a referendum in New Zealand, and was enforced most famously in the United States.

Prohibition in the US

'Prohibition' is generally considered the period in the United States, 17 January 1920–5 December 1933, during which, according to the language of the 18th Amendment to the Constitution, the 'manufacture, sale, or transportation of intoxicating liquors' was prohibited throughout the country. The passage of the 18th Amendment crowned a movement going back to the early 19th century.

Beginning with local, voluntary organizations concerned to foster temperance in a hard-drinking country, the movement then undertook to pass restrictive legislation on a local or state basis (Maine went 'dry' in 1851). As the movement increased in vigour and confidence, total prohibition of alcohol consumption rather than temperance became the object. By the last quarter of the 19th century, the aim was to secure a complete national prohibition by means of a constitutional amendment. The work of propaganda to this end was in the hands of organized reformers, especially the Woman's Christian Temperance Union (1874) and the Anti-Saloon League (1895); they had the support of many Protestant churches, especially in the South and Midwest. By the time the 18th Amendment was passed, 33 of the then 48 states were already dry.

The working out of the amendment was provided for by the National Prohibition Act (October 1919), usually called the Volstead Act: it defined 'intoxicating liquor' as anything containing at least 0.5% alcohol, so extinguishing the hope that wine and BEER might escape under a less stern definition. Some uses of wine were, however, allowed under the act: it could be used in religious ceremonies; it could be prescribed as medicine; and it could be used as a food flavouring or in other 'non-beverage' applications. All of these provisions could be and were greatly abused, and the act had to be amended and supplemented as experience showed the problems of enforcement.

The popular conception of Prohibition is that speakeasies abounded, gangsters and bootleggers of all sorts flourished, and every American gladly flouted the law. The reality is harder to determine, but there can be no question that the consequences for the American wine industry were disastrous. A number of American wineries, by obtaining licences to manufacture wine for the permitted uses, managed to continue a restricted operation (the apparent needs of communicants, for example, soared during this period). Effectively, however, the industry was wrecked. In 1919 the official production of wine in the US was 55 million gal/2 million hl; by 1925 it had sunk to just over 3.5 million gal. Winemakers received no compensation. Most wineries simply went out of business and their establishments were broken up.

The Volstead Act permitted the heads of households to manufacture up to 200 gal/7 hl of fruit juice annually; by a benevolent inconsistency, this provision was construed to allow HOME WINEMAKING. In consequence, vineyard acreage in CALIFORNIA shot up to unprecedented size to meet the national demand for fresh grapes: the 300,000 acres/121,000 ha of vineyard in 1919 had nearly doubled by 1926. Most of the new planting was in very inferior grape varieties, however (THOMPSON SEEDLESS and ALICANTE BOUSCHET, for example), and the degradation of the California vineyards thus induced by the conditions of Prohibition had seriously damaging effects on California wine long after Repeal. Nor can the quality of the average home-made wine have done much to enhance national CONNOISSEURSHIP.

The first efforts of the opponents of Prohibition were to achieve 'modification' of the terms of the Volstead Act. They tried for example to alter the definition of 'intoxicating liquor' or to allow individual states to make regulations different from those of the act. These efforts got nowhere; in consequence, the 'Wets' concentrated on achieving Repeal by constitutional amendment. Aided by the economic collapse of 1929 (invalidating the argument that Prohibition was economically sound) and by the adoption of Repeal as a political question (the Democratic party made Repeal a plank in its platform for the 1932 elections), the Repeal movement succeeded: in December 1933 the 21st amendment, repealing the 18th, was ratified. Unfortunately, the amendment left to the separate states the entire regulation of the 'liquor traffic' within their borders, with the result that US liquor laws—including local and state prohibition—remain a crazy quilt of inconsistent and arbitrary rules, another lastingly destructive effect of national prohibition.

The forces that achieved prohibition in the US remain potent and protean. National prohibition in the simple terms of the 18th amendment is not likely to come again; but liquor—wine very much included—continues to be an object of punitive taxation, of moral disapproval in some quarters, and of obstructive legislation in the United States today. See UNITED STATES for more details. T.P.

Asbury, H., *The Great Illusion* (1950).
Krout, J. A., *The Origins of Prohibition* (1925).
Sinclair, A., *Prohibition: The Era of Excess* (1962).

Prokupac, old red grape variety being revived in many regions of SERBIA, where the medium-bodied wines it produces are red-fruited and have the TANNIN structure to suit oak and to age for up to a decade. Its stronghold is Župa south of Belgrade, but elegant versions are now appearing in Šumadija and Tri Morave. It may be blended with INTERNATIONAL VARIETIES or used to produce dark rosé. It is also grown in Kosovo (as Prokupë) and North Macedonia (Prokupec).

proles, three categories of VINE VARIETIES of the VITIS VINIFERA species, grouped according to their geographical origin and, to some extent, their common end use (see BOTANICAL CLASSIFICATION). The classification is the work of Russian ampelographer Negrul in 1946. The differences between these groups may not only be a matter of response to environment but also be partly due to human selection for particular features related to end use, such as berry size for TABLE GRAPES. Detailed observation of vine characteristics can reveal particularly close relationships which indicate that they are likely to have come from the same area. Thus are linked, for example, the CABERNET SAUVIGNON, CABERNET FRANC, MERLOT, PETIT VERDOT, and FER varieties.

Proles occidentalis: varieties native to western Europe, which were selected mostly for winemaking use. Most of the important wine grape varieties are in this group—RIESLING, CHARDONNAY, Cabernet Sauvignon, and so on—and they have common features of small bunches with small, juicy berries.

Proles pontica: the oldest varieties, and those native to the Aegean and Black Seas, which have shoot tips and leaf undersurfaces covered with dense white hairs. Examples of varieties in this group are CLAIRETTE, FURMINT, HÁRSLEVELŰ, and Zante CURRANT.

Proles orientalis: varieties originating in the Middle East, Iran, and Afghanistan. These varieties were selected mainly for TABLE GRAPES and so tend to have large, oval berries in loose, straggly bunches. The berries are often crisp, with less juice and sugar. This group of vines includes most varieties for RAISINS as well as most table grape varieties, such as SULTANA and MUSCAT OF ALEXANDRIA. R.E.S. & J.V.

Negrul, A. M., 'Origin and classification of cultured grape', in A. Baranov et al. (eds.), *The Ampelography of the USSR* (1946), 159–216.

propagation, the reproduction of a plant, whether by sexual or asexual means. Sexual propagation means reproduction by seed and involves the combination of two separate sets of chromosomes, one from the male (POLLEN) and the other from the female (the egg cell inside the ovule); their fusion during fertilization produces an individual with a set of genes different from its two parents. Asexual or vegetative propagation means reproduction without seed, by taking vegetative bits of the parent plant and getting them to form SHOOTS and ROOTS; the progeny are genetically identical to the parent unless MUTATIONS produce distinct CLONES.

For details of micropropagation, see TISSUE CULTURE. For more details of specific propagation methods, see SEXUAL PROPAGATION and VEGETATIVE PROPAGATION. See also LAYERING. B.G.C. & J.V.

Prosecco, extremely popular sparkling wine made in north-east Italy. Italy's largest DOC by far, the Prosecco zone extends from the city of Vicenza in the VENETO to Trieste in FRIULI Venezia Giulia and comprises around 34,000 ha/84,015 acres. Extraordinarily high permitted yields of 18 tonnes/ha produced more than 486 million bottles of light sparkling white wine in 2019 made by the tank method (see SPARKLING WINEMAKING). As suggested by its extent, the DOC was once an IGT. To ensure that no one outside the region was able to jump on the Prosecco bandwagon, the eponymous grape variety on which the wine is based was renamed GLERA in 2009, and Prosecco was registered as a protected denomination of origin (DOC). This was enabled by enlarging the region to include the village of Prosecco in Friuli, which triggered a frenzy of plantings, mostly on plains.

The classic production zone was already considerable, with over 8,446 ha/20,870 acres in the hills between the towns of Conegliano and Valdobbiadene, an area now elevated to DOCG Conegliano-Valdobbiadene. Although most of these DOCG vineyards are on hills and TERRACES at 50–500 m/164–1,640 ft in ELEVATION, the high YIELDS can result in rather neutral wines whose apparent fruitiness owes much to the DOSAGE. Although dry versions exist, more common are Extra Dry (with RESIDUAL SUGAR of 12–17 g/l) and Dry (17–32 g/l). Allowed additions of up to 15% of INTERNATIONAL VARIETIES such as Chardonnay, Pinot Bianco, and Pinot Grigio can help to increase alcohol and flavour. Prosecco Rosato, containing up to 15% Pinot Noir, is allowed as of 2020.

Superior wines are said to come from the CRU of Cartizze, its 107 ha/264 acres on steep hills of San Pietro di Barbozza, Santo Stefano, and Saccol in the commune of Valdobbiadene where yields are not markedly lower but the grapes are generally much riper than most. Most Cartizze wines are Extra Dry.

Ambitiously, the Conegliano-Valdobbiadene DOCG has introduced a system of crus, 43 communes or hamlets (called locally *rive*) whose names may be mentioned on the label if yields are below 12 tonnes/ha, although little expression of origin has so far been evident.

Prosecco col fondo, labeled as *sui lieviti* (on the LEES) now that the Col Fondo name has been trademarked by an industrial-sized producer, can offer more interest. Initially made by small-scale producers—often espousing ORGANIC techniques and, besides Glera, favouring other INDIGENOUS VARIETIES such as Verdiso, Bianchetta, and Pepera in the final blend—these wines are bottle-fermented, left on the lees for at least 90 days, and bottled undisgorged (see PÉTILLANT NATUREL). They are released with the original crowncap and with a sediment at the bottom of the bottle (*col fondo* means 'with sediment'). These wines are bone-dry, somehow mineral in character, and, unlike most Prosecco, worth AGEING for a year or two. Conventional Prosecco producers have begun to experiment with this style, not least because it is more profitable than most Prosecco.

The DOCG **Asolo Prosecco** (previously Colli Asolani Prosecco), from a hilly outcrop on a plain south-east of Treviso, is similar to Conegliano-Valdobbiadene's vineyard area and structure, only its maximum permitted yields of 12 tonnes/ha are markedly lower. W.S.

www.prosecco.it
www.prosecco.wine

Protected Designation of Origin. See PDO.

Protected Geographical Indication. See PGI.

protected viticulture, a form of vine-growing where the vines are protected from climatological excesses to avoid stress. In a conventional agricultural sense, this would involve protection from low temperatures using glass or plastic houses or cloches; such structures are rare in commercial wine grape vineyards because of the prohibitive costs, although they can be seen in the cool climate of ENGLAND or very occasionally in cooler parts of California to protect some Chardonnay vines from poor FRUIT SET. Protected viticulture is more usual for TABLE GRAPES, as in northern Europe, Japan, and New Zealand.

Vines may also be protected from the wind by WINDBREAKS, from frost by various techniques (see FROST PROTECTION), and from drought by IRRIGATION. R.E.S.

protective juice handling, grape- and MUST-processing techniques with the aim of minimizing exposure to OXYGEN and therefore the risk of OXIDATION. This is regarded as especially important for white wines since, once grapes are crushed and juice liberated from the berry, the PHENOLICS react rapidly with oxygen to produce amber to dark-brown polymers (see POLYMERIZATION), which can in turn react with THIOLS and GLUTATHIONE, with a consequent loss of aroma and greater risk of oxidation. Some ordinary wines are made encouraging this oxidation, the brown pigments being removed subsequently by FINING. Most better-quality white wines result from minimal oxygen exposure, saving the phenolics for later contribution to AROMA and BODY. Some ambitious winemakers experimented with deliberate pre-fermentation oxidation of the must in the early 1980s, but this is uncommon today even if some winemakers in Burgundy, for example, choose not to protect their Chardonnay must from oxidation. The introduction of tank PRESSES has aided protective juice handling during the lengthy PRESSING operation enormously, as has the judicious use of SULFUR DIOXIDE in musts and the use of INERT GAS. Grapes for red wines are far less vulnerable to damage from oxygen since they contain much greater concentrations of TANNINS and PIGMENTS.

See also SKIN CONTACT. V.L.

protective winemaking, winemaking philosophy founded on the need to minimize exposure to OXYGEN and concomitant risk of OXIDATION. It is less popular than it was at the end of the 20th century because, while most winemakers understand the need to limit oxidation, they are also aware of the potential risk of REDUCTION in wines that have been made too protectively. Nevertheless, this philosophy is still adhered to for many large-volume commercial white wines. It usually incorporates PROTECTIVE JUICE HANDLING. White wines are then fermented in closed-top tanks to exclude oxygen as much as possible while allowing for the escape of CARBON DIOXIDE from fermentation. All subsequent operations are then conducted as far as possible in closed equipment, and small amounts of SULFUR DIOXIDE are added if exposure to oxygen occurs. Storage and processing at low temperatures favours the retention of some of the carbon dioxide, which has the effect of sweeping out any accidentally dissolved oxygen. Red wines, because of their greater PHENOLIC content, are much less sensitive to exposure to oxygen. Indeed, if they undergo BARREL AGEING, some exposure to oxygen during TOPPING UP contributes to the wine's maturation. V.L.

proteins, very large polymers of the 20 natural AMINO ACIDS. Proteins are essential to all living beings.

In grapes

Proteins may function as ENZYMES, or as structural components of cells. While all functions are important, the enzymatic properties of proteins are the basis of all reactions within living systems.

In wines

Proteins from the grape remain in solution in all white wines, but in some (notably those vinified from MUSCAT, GEWÜRZTRAMINER, SAUVIGNON BLANC, and SÉMILLON grapes) the concentration is often so high that the proteins coagulate to form an unsightly haze or cloud. Such haziness, which can be initiated when the wine is warmed, is irreversible. To avoid this happening after bottling, which renders the wine unstable, the heat-unstable proteins are removed by BENTONITE fining as part of normal winemaking STABILIZATION procedures. Research has shown that the troublesome, heat-unstable proteins of white wines belong to a particular group from the grape known as pathogenesis-related or PR proteins. The unique properties of PR proteins—their stability in acid conditions and resistance to degradation by proteolytic ENZYMES—means that fermentation and the other processes of winemaking selectively eliminate other proteins of the grape leaving the PR proteins as virtually the sole survivors.

The greater concentration of PHENOLICS in red wines means that much of the protein is removed in the LEES as an insoluble tannin–protein complex. See also PRECIPITATES and BOTTLE DEPOSIT. D.D. & V.L.

Waters, E. J., et al., 'Preventing protein haze in bottled wine', *Australian Journal of Grape and Wine Research*, 11/2 (2005), 215–25.

provenance, details of a wine's previous owner(s) and, ideally, storage conditions (see STORING WINE) that have become increasingly important in the FINE WINE market. Gone are the days when 'Property of an English Gentleman' would suffice as an AUCTION catalogue description, effectively implying that the source of the wine in question was beyond reproach. A number of factors have combined to bring provenance centre stage in the buyer's increasing need for a copper-bottomed guarantee of origin.

The growth of the ASIAN market has seen a new kind of collector, both more knowledgeable and more wary than many, keen to ensure as impeccable a source of origin and storage for his or her wines as possible. At the same time, the huge increase in wine PRICES in recent years has generated a parasitic underworld of COUNTERFEITERS, fraudsters, forgers, and confidence tricksters keen to cash in on the bounty that a bottle of expensive fine wine (traded more often than opened) can bring. Budd tries to expose those he encounters from his UK base.

Most auction houses and BROKERS have responded to this growing demand for transparent provenance and optimum storage conditions by sharpening up their inspection and AUTHENTICATION procedures, scrutinizing BOTTLES, CORKS, LABELS, and CAPSULES with greater care and rejecting wines of dubious origin or condition. Some, however, have failed to see the warning signs or, worse, turned a blind eye.

The need for provenance and a history of optimum storage conditions and good-quality transportation goes beyond the auction room and back to the producer. Many now realize that taking measures to ensure traceability and authentication is a key part of protecting their BRAND. Despite this growing awareness, the relevant proofs are often neither required nor given.

RFID (Radio Frequency Identification) temperature sensor technology has been used to monitor wine-shipment temperatures across distribution channels. The RFID chip can be linked to a sequential serial number and a randomly generated number for authentication purposes. It tends to be on the wine case, although some producers have added a temperature sensor to the bottle itself.

One of the upshots of the demand for impeccable provenance has been the growing number of sales direct from a single owner or producer (see AUCTIONS). A.H.L.R.

Budd, Jim, investdrinks-blog.blogspot.co.uk

Tam, S., et al., 'Why wine collectors look for pristine provenance'. www.christies.com/features/Wine-provenance-and-why-it-matters-8592-3.aspx.

Provence, region with considerable potential in the far south-east of France (see map under FRANCE) whose associations with TOURISM and hedonism have perhaps focused too much attention on its relatively expensive rosés.

The precise period during which viticulture was introduced to the region is disputed. Certainly it appears unlikely that the Phocaeans, Greeks from Asia Minor, encountered vines when they founded Massilia (Marseilles) in about 600 BCE. It is likely, however, that the Provincia of ancient GAUL produced its own wines under the influence of classical ROME (although it is not certain that it preceded Narbo, or Narbonne, in the LANGUEDOC as a wine producer). See FRANCE for more details.

The region was much fought over, being under the influence in successive eras of the Saracens, the Carolingians (see CHARLEMAGNE), the Holy Roman Empire, the counts of Toulouse, the Catalans, René of ANJOU, and the House of Savoy. At the end of the 19th century, Provençal viticulture was nearly killed by PHYLLOXERA and struggled into the 1930s, with vineyards near to the coast and RAILWAY recovering more quickly.

As a result of its rich cultural heritage, Provence enjoys a distinctive range of vine varieties which show various historical influences from Italy, notably Sardinia. While Grenache is by far the region's most planted variety, followed by Cinsaut and Syrah, another ten varieties are allowed in Côtes de Provence, including particularly Mourvèdre and TIBOUREN, although the indigenous dark-berried Calitor (known in Provençal as Pécoui Touar) and Barbaroux are being phased out. Historic varieties such as Rousseli, foreign varieties such as XINOMAVRO, ASSYRTIKO, and NIELLUCCIU, and new CROSSES such as Vidoc and Artaban are also being considered to deal with CLIMATE CHANGE.

The climate here is France's most MEDITERRANEAN, with an average of 3,000 hours of sunshine a year and with less than 700 mm/27 in annual RAINFALL, which is concentrated in spring and autumn. Winters are mild but usually allow full vine DORMANCY. The greatest climatological threat is WIND, in particular the famous mistral, a cold wind from the north. Proximity to the sea and careful vineyard siting on south-facing slopes can offer some protection. It has the advantage of minimizing the risk of FUNGAL DISEASES, and Provence is particularly suitable for ORGANIC VITICULTURE.

The magic attached to such names as the Côte d'Azur, St-Tropez, and Provence in general may have increased urban development and pushed up land prices in habitable parts of the region, but it has also attracted outsiders prepared to make significant investments in vine-growing and winemaking, thereby raising standards overall.

Côtes de Provence

At 20,100 ha/51,892 acres of vineyard, this is by far the most significant appellation in Provence, although the sites vary enormously. The AOC applies to a large part of the Var *département* (other than the enclave entitled to the Coteaux VAROIS-EN-PROVENCE appellation) from the sub-Alpine hills above Draguignan, cooled by the influence of the mountains to the north, to the coast at St-Tropez, the epitome of a Mediterranean wine zone. But it also includes pockets of hotter terrain between CASSIS and BANDOL, as well as land immediately south and east of the PALETTE appellation near Aix-en-Provence. The appellation even encompasses a tiny, isolated area of vines at Villars-sur-Var high up in the mountains 50 km/30 miles north of Nice in the Alpes-Maritimes *département*.

About four-fifths of production is of pale pink dry rosé, which seems to find a growing local and export market almost regardless of quality. There is renewed interest in producing 'serious' rosé, however, with a distinctive style combining flavour with a fashionably pale hue (see STABULATION), and many producers even use a limited amount of OAK AGEING. The best really do seem to have a special affinity with the garlic- and oil-based cuisine of Provence, particularly *aïoli*.

Most rosé is based on Cinsaut and Grenache, leaving old-vine Carignan, Syrah, Mourvèdre, and sometimes TIBOUREN for the reds, which now constitute just 10% of production. As Tibouren can add real interest to a blend, the variety is experiencing a revival. White grapes may constitute 20% of rosé blends.

An increasing number of producers, especially in the coastal sector, are paying close attention to white wines, which may be made from various permutations of Clairette, Sémillon, Ugni Blanc, and Vermentino (known locally as Rolle), albeit in much smaller volumes than rosés. Many of the technical innovations brought about by ROSÉ WINEMAKING have been applied to white-wine production as well.

Within the Côtes de Provence appellation, there are subregions called DÉNOMINATIONS GÉOGRAPHIQUES COMPLÉMENTAIRES created to emphasize the regional character of individual zones. In 2022 there were five, applicable to reds and rosés: Fréjus, La Londe, Notre-Dame des Anges, Pierrefeu, and Ste-Victoire. La Londe, a strip of seaside vineyards south-west of the Maures, also allows for VERMENTINO-based white wines.

See also the Provence AOCs of Coteaux d'AIX-EN-PROVENCE, BANDOL, LES BAUX DE PROVENCE, BELLET, CASSIS, PALETTE, and Coteaux VAROIS-EN-PROVENCE. E.A.G.

syndicat-cotesdeprovence.com

proximal sensing is the measurement of attributes of the soil, vine CANOPY, or fruit using sensors mounted on vehicles or vineyard machinery operating in the vineyard (i.e. the sensor is operated close to the target of interest; cf. REMOTE SENSING). Handheld sensors may also be used, especially in support of ZONAL VITICULTURE if zones have already been otherwise established, but are unlikely to be cost-effective if the intention is to collect sufficient data to produce a map.

Proximal soil sensing is a common application in PRECISION VITICULTURE and provides key data input to zonal viticulture. Electromagnetic induction (EMI) is the most common form of proximal soil sensing and is used to identify variation in soil properties which affect the electrical conductivity of the soil (SALINITY, SOIL TEXTURE, SOIL WATER status) or which are correlated with them. Research has shown that patterns of variation in vine performance often closely mimic patterns of variation in these soil attributes. A possible alternative to EMI sensing is to use electrical resistance tomography (ERT) to measure resistivity. Since resistivity is the inverse of conductivity, the information provided by these two types of sensors is essentially the same. However, the requirement for contact with the soil in the case of ERT, coupled with the much larger size of sensor, tends to make them a poor option in established vineyards or where the soil is stony; EMI instruments are generally smaller and do not require contact with the soil.

Proximal canopy sensing is being used increasingly to provide essentially the same PLANT CELL DENSITY and NORMALIZED DIFFERENCE VEGETATION INDEX information as is obtained by remote sensing, but it has the advantage of timeliness, especially when CANOPY changes within the season are of interest, although timeliness is also an attribute of data collected by DRONES. One variation on this theme gaining increasing interest is the use of thermal sensors, which, by sensing canopy temperature, can provide useful input to IRRIGATION scheduling through the detection of WATER STRESS. Another is the use of various forms of digital camera coupled with sophisticated image analysis as tools to improve the accuracy of YIELD estimation, especially early in the season, through the assessment of bunch, berry, and flower number. Such information may promote an accurate yield estimate early enough in the season for it to inform management decisions—whether in the vineyard (e.g. CROP THINNING), at the winery (e.g. installation of additional tanks), or in the marketing or supply-logistics departments.

New proximal sensors for the measurement of fruit attributes related to GRAPE COMPOSITION AND WINE QUALITY are being developed. The ability to use such sensors on the go during harvest is of key interest in precision viticulture, especially to support strategies such as SELECTIVE HARVESTING. R.G.V.B.

Bramley, R. G. V., 'Precision viticulture: managing vineyard variability for improved quality outcomes', in A. G. Reynolds (ed.), *Managing Wine Quality 1: Viticulture and Wine Quality* (2nd edn, 2021), 541–75.

Liu, S., et al., 'A vision-based robust grape berry counting algorithm for fast calibration-free bunch weight estimation in the field', *Computers and Electronics in Agriculture*, 173 (2020), 105360. www.sciencedirect.com/science/article/abs/pii/S0168169919326432

Prugnolo Gentile, synonym for SANGIOVESE in VINO NOBILE DI MONTEPULCIANO.

pruners, devices used for winter PRUNING of grapevines. A pruning hook or knife was used from ancient times until the development of handheld SECATEURS in the mid 19th century, coming into widespread use in the latter half of the century. Secateurs cut with a scissor action, and there are various forms available (including power-assisted versions). Sometimes pruning saws may be needed to remove old CORDONS or ARMS. Vineyard winter pruning is now being mechanized with tractor-mounted machines doing most of the cutting, as described in MECHANICAL PRUNING. R.E.S.

pruning of vines involves cutting off unwanted vegetative parts, typically in the form of CANES in winter. For details of cutting off unwanted vegetative growth in the form of excess SHOOTS in early spring and shoot tips in summer, see SHOOT THINNING and TRIMMING respectively.

Pruning is a vineyard practice developed primarily to produce fewer but larger bunches of riper grapes and is particularly important in cooler climates. More than 85% of a growing season's shoot growth may be removed at winter pruning. There is an important relationship between vine pruning and VINE TRAINING, as the pruning method used depends on the training system employed.

Vines growing in their natural state, as in the WILD VINES of America and the Middle East, are not pruned. At the top of such vines, which are many-branched and often grow up trees, and on other parts of the vine exposed to the sun are many small bunches of grapes. While the vine may have had thousands of buds present in winter which could have produced shoots and fruit, only a small proportion—the highest buds and those near the end of the canes—will burst in spring. This reduced BUDBREAK is the principal means by which unpruned vines in their natural state avoid OVERCROPPING, which may weaken the vine and shorten its life. (See APICAL DOMINANCE.)

History

It is not known when people began to prune vines, but vine pruning was certainly known in ancient EGYPT and was already well established by the beginning of the Roman era, described in detail by such writers as PLINY and VIRGIL. There are also numerous references to vine pruning in the BIBLE. For example, 'a Sabbath of rest unto the land, a Sabbath for the Lord: thou shalt neither sow thy field, nor prune thy vineyard' (Lev. 25. 4). Vine pruning also figures in the description of the Last Days (Mic. 4. 3): 'and they shall beat their swords into ploughshares, and their spears into pruning hooks'.

Aims of pruning

Among the early aims of vine pruning as practised by the ancient Egyptians would have been to increase the size of individual berries and

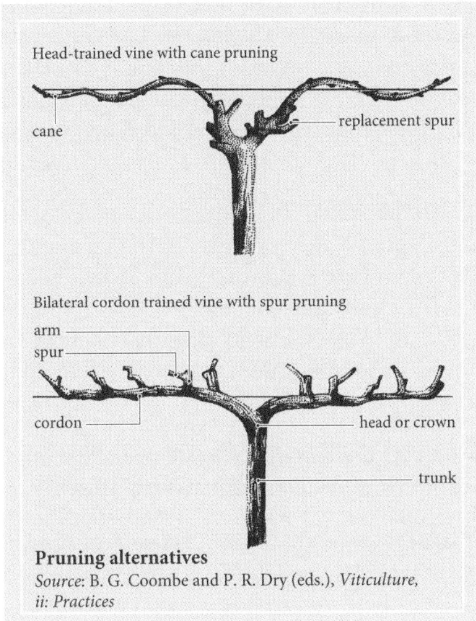

Pruning alternatives
Source: B. G. Coombe and P. R. Dry (eds.), *Viticulture, ii: Practices*

bunches, an important consideration even today in the production of TABLE GRAPES. A vine which is lightly pruned has many buds and will produce numerous shoots and bunches with smaller berries.

Another aim of vine pruning is to establish or maintain the shape of the vine, which makes all other vineyard operations easier. For example, keeping vines pruned back to a more or less constant structure means they can easily be neatly trained and maintained in rows. Otherwise, vines would sprawl and quickly cover the space between rows.

But perhaps the most important aspect of pruning is that it regulates the next season's YIELD by controlling the number of buds which can burst and produce bunches of grapes. The number of buds retained after winter pruning may be influenced by TRADITION, local CONTROLLED APPELLATION regulations, the scientific principles behind BALANCED PRUNING, or chance, as in MECHANICAL PRUNING.

Timing

Pruning is carried out in winter, normally once the first frost causes the leaves to fall, thereby exposing the woody canes. Although the precise timing is not generally critical, it is usually completed by the time of budbreak in spring, ideally before the stage when vines will lose water (see BLEEDING) from pruning wounds (just prior to budbreak). Some early-budding varieties may be pruned very late in an effort to delay budbreak and minimize FROST DAMAGE. As CLIMATE CHANGE brings HARVEST dates forward from the cooler autumn to the hotter conditions of late summer (sometimes referred to as HARVEST COMPRESSION), delayed pruning, sometimes even after budbreak, can help to delay ripening and harvest, but typically by only one or two weeks. (See also DOUBLE PRUNING.) In regions with warm winters, such as tropical and subtropical regions, the vines may not become completely dormant, and vines may have to be pruned when they are covered in leaves. See also TROPICAL VITICULTURE.

Two basic options

The fundamental principles of pruning have changed remarkably little since classical times, although the French viticulturist GUYOT in 1860 introduced firm suggestions as to the length and position of canes, formalizing some of the old ideas.

Along the woody canes—which were green, soft shoots during the previous growing season—are buds which are arranged on alternate sides of the cane about 8 cm/3 in or so apart. Basically there are two types of vine pruning: either to SPURS, or to CANES.

Spur pruning Spurs are cut to retain only two buds, while canes are longer, typically with five to 15 buds. In the spring, each bud on the two-bud spur normally produces one shoot, although up to three is possible. In autumn, these shoots become woody canes. During winter pruning the cane growing from the uppermost bud on the spur is removed, and the cane from the bottom bud is cut back to two buds, creating the new spur. The vine's physiology determines that, when a cane is cut, the last two buds will burst. This is the reason for the common two-bud spur. If spurs were left with three buds, the bottom bud would often not produce a shoot, and so the spur position would move further and further from the cordon or head as the years passed.

Spur pruning is commonly used with free-standing GOBELET-trained vines. The spurs arise from the trunk or from short arms on the trunk, requiring no supporting POSTS or WIRE; spur pruning is therefore among the oldest forms prevailing and was already known to the Roman writers COLUMELLA and PALLADIUS. This method is common in the Languedoc and Roussillon and in the lower-rainfall areas of Spain, Italy, and Portugal, such vineyards being of lower VIGOUR, to which the system is best suited. Some of the older vineyards in California, Australia, and South Africa, for example, also have such vines, often described as head-trained or bush vines.

Another spur-pruned form which is more common with higher-vigour vineyards is cordon training for trellised vines. Here the spurs arise from one or more horizontal arms or CORDONS, which are trained along a wire. Known in France as CORDON DE ROYAT, this pruning method has been used for wine grapes since the end of the 19th century. Of all pruning methods, this one lends itself most readily to MECHANICAL PRUNING since all of the canes to be pruned are more or less in the one plane.

Cane pruning Cane pruning became common after the 1860 studies of the Frenchman Dr Guyot. In traditional French vineyards each vine is typically pruned to one cane with six to eight buds and one spur with two buds. During winter pruning, the cane from the previous year is cut off and a new one laid down, using one of the canes arising from the spur. The number of buds on the cane depends on regional tradition and the small print of the AOC laws. For example, eight buds may be left on Syrah canes in the Côtes du Rhône; eight on all major varieties in Burgundy; in Bordeaux seven buds is the maximum for Sémillon in Sauternes but six for Muscadelle. These small bud numbers per cane (and hence shorter canes) contrast greatly with those used for wine grapes in other regions where vine vigour is higher. For example, in vigorous irrigated vineyards in Australia it is not uncommon to see up to six canes, each with up to 15 buds, left on a single vine after winter pruning. These vines are planted further apart than their Old World counterparts, as discussed in NEW WORLD.

A common observation with cane pruning is that buds in the middle of the cane often do not burst. There are often a few shoots growing near the head of the vine (at the base of the cane), and the last two shoots at the cut end of the cane will invariably grow. See APICAL DOMINANCE. Where the cane was growing in shade the previous year the budburst is invariably poor, as outlined in CANOPY MICROCLIMATE.

In France the colloquial name for canes varies regionally: *courgée* in the Jura, for example, but *aste* in Bordeaux, *baguette* in Burgundy, *archet* or *archelot* in Beaujolais.

Controlling yield

A fundamental question in relation to vine pruning is how many buds to leave on each vine at winter pruning. Does it matter? For some vignerons this first question is never posed, as TRADITION or CONTROLLED APPELLATION laws dictate how the vines are to be pruned, and traditional practices are vigorously defended against any suggestion of change despite scientifically verified alternatives to fixed bud numbers. The winter-pruning period can be a time when the mind is put into neutral and the body is braced to survive long days spent outdoors, often in unpleasant, cold, wet weather.

When vines are pruned to just a few buds, most of them burst successfully, and the emerging shoots will typically grow vigorously. They will be very long, with large leaves, and produce many LATERAL SHOOTS. Early shoot growth is stimulated by the vine's food reserves in the trunk and roots being spread around only a few shoots. As more buds burst per vine, so the amount of food reserves available per shoot decreases. Therefore, a low-vigour vine which has limited reserves of CARBOHYDRATES must be pruned to few buds only compared with one of higher vigour which contains more reserves.

A vine that is very lightly pruned, to scores or even hundreds of buds, will produce many more shoots and bunches of grapes. Individual shoots will be shorter, and the number and size of berries will be reduced. However, the total yield of grapes will typically be greater, and the grapes will take longer to ripen. This may cause no problems in warm and sunny climates but can be disastrous in cooler climates, where it can be a struggle to ripen the grapes anyway before autumn chill and frosts stop the ripening process.

There is therefore more concern about pruning levels in cooler climates than in warmer ones. In Germany, for example, the common rule is to leave about ten buds at winter pruning for each square metre of vineyard land surface. In New York State, Professor Nelson SHAULIS developed balanced-pruning guidelines which rely on the vine's growth as assessed by PRUNING WEIGHT (the weight of annual growth as canes removed at pruning); about 35 buds should be retained per kg of pruning weight. Having weighed a few vines, growers can assess the pruning weight by eye as part of their pruning decisions. For more vigorous vines with higher pruning weights, more buds are retained.

For high-vigour vineyards it may not be sufficient just to prune lightly, as this will lead to crowding of shoots in the vine CANOPY. Recognition of this problem has led to the development of CANOPY MANAGEMENT strategies to avoid dense canopies for vigorous vineyards. Similarly, yield cannot be limited by pruning high-vigour vineyards to just a few buds. The yield will still be considerable, and berries will be large, considered undesirable for wine quality (see BERRY SIZE). Bunches will be tight, increasing the risk of BUNCH ROT, and there will be considerable shoot and leaf growth, which is likely to result in SHADE rather than vine BALANCE.

Mechanization

Winter pruning is one of the most labour-intensive aspects of vine growing, along with hand-harvesting. During the 1960s and 1970s, increases in LABOUR costs and reductions in labour supply in Australia led to experimentation with and eventual development of MECHANICAL PRUNING. This in turn has led to the even more iconoclastic option of MINIMAL PRUNING, or not pruning at all, although the latter is now viewed with increasing disfavour.

By the 21st century, a full spectrum of vine-pruning practice was evident around the world, from the hand-pruning of a lower-vigour vine in a traditional vineyard to less than 10 buds; to one essentially unpruned following the passage of a machine, with hundreds of buds remaining; to mechanical pruning using a tractor-mounted circular saw.

The time taken to prune a vineyard depends on how the vineyard is trained, the VINE DENSITY, and the pruning method. Pruning times can be up to 200 hours or more per ha for high-density cane-pruned vineyards. For wide-row, spur-pruned vineyards trained to cordons, the figure may be as low as 50 hours per ha, and in combination with mechanical pre-pruning this may be reduced even further to less than 10 hours per ha.

Pruning and vine health

TRUNK DISEASES which invade pruning wounds, especially during wet weather, are an increasing concern worldwide. Pruning systems such as cane pruning, which involve fewer wounds per vine than spur pruning and far fewer than mechanical pruning, are preferred, although, since the cane and spur originate in the head, diseases can travel down the trunk and be more destructive. Care must be taken to treat pruning wounds, most commonly with a FUNGICIDE or with natural antifungal products, for example antagonistic fungi such as *Trichoderma*, garlic extract or vanillin. Australian research has led to the widespread use of a range of fungicide products, but in wine regions such as Bordeaux pruning-wound protection is rare, leading to high levels of infection in older vineyards.

Marco Simonit of Italy promotes a modification to the Guyot and other systems which encourages the maintenance of sap flow in the vine, thereby avoiding the potentially damaging effects of pruning wounds and increasing vine longevity. This method, based on studies by Lafon in the Charentes, France, published in 1921 (see POUSSARD), has won fervent admirers around the world despite scepticism in some quarters. R.E.S.

Ayres, M. R., et al., 'Developing pruning wound protection strategies for managing Eutypa dieback', *Australian Journal of Grape and Wine Research*, 23/1 (2016) 103–111.

Cobos, R., et al., 'Effectiveness of natural antifungal compounds in controlling infection by grapevine trunk disease pathogens through pruning wounds', *Applied Environmental Microbiology*, 81/18 (2015), 6474–83.

Galet, P., *General Viticulture* (2000).

Simonit & Sirch, www.simonitesirch.com.

pruning machines. See MECHANICAL PRUNING.

pruning weight, a measure of vine VIGOUR, or, more strictly, capacity, obtained by weighing the canes removed from a vine at winter PRUNING. This is the most useful and common measure of vine growth during the previous growing season. The value may be used, for example, to assess how many buds might be retained at winter pruning to achieve the best vine performance (see BALANCED PRUNING). Similarly, the ratio between the weight of prunings and the fruit produced is a good indication of BALANCE. R.E.S.

Puente Alto, part of the MAIPO subregion of the Central Valley of CHILE, at the foot of the Andes in what is known as Alto Maipo, where ALLUVIAL soils and mountain breezes produce some of Chile's classic Cabernet Sauvignon wines, including Almaviva, Don Melchor, and Viñedo Chadwick. P.T.

Puerto de Santa María, one of the three main towns making and maturing SHERRY.

Puglia, known by English speakers as Apulia, the long (350 km/210 mile) and fertile region on the 'heel' of Italy (see map under ITALY) which has long been of major importance for the production of wine and TABLE GRAPES. A MEDITERRANEAN CLIMATE and a predominance of soils well suited to grape-growing (a CALCAREOUS base from the Cretaceous era overlain by topsoils rich in iron oxide from the Tertiary and Quaternary eras) have created an ideal viticultural environment. Its name derives from the Roman *a-pluvia* or 'lack of rain'.

With 9 million hl/237.75 million gal of wine produced in 2020, Puglia is Italy's second most productive wine region, after Veneto. Many growers have taken subsidies from the EU to grub up their vineyards, but unfortunately many of these were of low-yielding BUSH VINES, while many of the 89,991 ha/222,372 acres of vines remaining in 2020 are high-cropping inferior varieties planted on fertile soils.

While much of Puglia's viticulture is still focused on BULK WINE, the abolition of compulsory DISTILLATION to drain the EU wine lake has forced producers to adopt a more market-oriented approach. Cue INTERNATIONAL VARIETIES, especially Chardonnay and Pinot Grigio, both unremarkable, the first also explicitly allowed in several of Puglia's 32 DOCs and DOCGs, while the majority is sold in bulk to large bottlers in the north to satisfy international supermarket demand.

Puglia's propensity for bulk wine production combined with excessively high YIELDS even at DOC level has tended to overshadow its unique wine styles based on INDIGENOUS VARIETIES. While grape-growers, as opposed to wine producers, are the norm here, with CO-OPERATIVES responsible for most winemaking, many have begun to bottle at least part of their production. Few of these first-timers have knowledge of or formal training in winemaking, which explains what is often very modest quality, although improvements are noticeable.

However, a growing international demand for indigenous varieties provides a commercial impulse; although the region's production of DOC wine is still tiny, a proper framework already exists to accommodate Puglia's most important terroirs and varieties. An overarching IGT Puglia comprises, from north to south, five regional IGTs—Daunia, Murgia, Valle d'Itria, Tarantino, and Salento—each divided into smaller DOCs.

The most important of its 28 DOCSs in 2022 are **Cacc'e e Mmitte di Lucero** for NERO DI TROIA-based red wine in the region of Daunia; **Castel del Monte** for full-bodied reds mainly from Nero di Troia but also AGLIANICO and **Moscato di Trani** for sweet wines in the central plateau of Alta Murgia; **Gioia del Colle** for deep reds with tangy acidity from PRIMITIVO and **Locorotondo** for white wines of VERDECA and Bianco d'Alessano on the lower-lying Bassa Murgia and Valle d'Itria; **Primitivo di Manduria** in Magna Grecia, north-west of Taranto; and **Salice Salentino** and neighbouring **Copertino** in the narrow Salento peninsula, where NEGROAMARO, grown on bush vines within reach of cooling breezes from the Adriatic and Ionian seas, can produce robust, spicy wines of considerable interest.

Unfortunately, because most of its production is either bulk or IGT, Puglia has very few producer associations to help market the higher-quality wines. Puglia's very few CONSORZIOS are practically defunct. What Puglia urgently needs is to ensure the survival of its centenarian bush vines and most interesting indigenous varieties—and, ideally, a viticultural and winemaking institute identical to SAN MICHELE ALL'ADIGE to help shape its future. W.S.

www.winesofpuglia.com

Puisseguin-St-Émilion, satellite appellation of ST-ÉMILION in Bordeaux on about 700 ha/1,750 acres of CLAY and LIMESTONE.

Puligny-Montrachet, village in the Côte de Beaune district of Burgundy's Côte d'Or producing very fine wines from CHARDONNAY and a tiny amount of less-exalted red. Puligny added the name of its most famous vineyard, the GRAND CRU Le Montrachet, in 1879 and has benefited from the association ever since.

Puligny contains two grand cru vineyards in their entirety, Chevalier-Montrachet and Bienvenues-Bâtard-Montrachet, and two which are shared with neighbouring Chassagne: Le Montrachet itself and Bâtard-Montrachet. Below this esteemed level, yet still among the finest of all white wines of Burgundy, are 17 PREMIER CRU vineyards. At the same ELEVATION as Bâtard-Montrachet lie Les Pucelles (made famous by the excellence of Domaine Leflaive's version), Clavoillon, Les Perrières (including the Clos de la Mouchère), Les Referts, and Les Combettes, which produces the plump wines to be expected of a vineyard adjacent to Meursault-Perrières.

A little higher up the slope, at the same elevation as Le Montrachet, lie Les Demoiselles, Le Cailleret, Les Folatières (including Clos de la Garenne), and Champ Canet. Part of Les Demoiselles is classified as grand cru Chevalier-Montrachet, but a very small slice remains as premier cru, being regarded, along with Le Cailleret, as the finest example.

Further up the slope, where the terrain becomes rockier and the soil almost too sparse, are Le Champ Gain, La Truffière, Les Chalumeaux, and the vineyards attached to the hamlet of BLAGNY, which are designated as Puligny-Montrachet premier cru for white wines and Blagny premier cru for reds.

The VILLAGE WINES of Puligny-Montrachet are less impressive, perhaps because the water table is nearer the surface here than in neighbouring MEURSAULT, for example. This phenomenon also means that the deep cellars ideal for AGEING wine are rare in Puligny, and few of the village's growers can prolong BARREL AGEING for more than about a year. Although the Leflaive and Carillon families can both trace their origins as vignerons back to the 16th century, there are surprisingly few domaines in Puligny, and a substantial proportion of its produce is contracted to the NÉGOCIANTS of Beaune.

In centuries past, Puligny, though less noted than Chassagne for its red wines, grew a significant amount of Pinot Noir grapes. They are now almost extinct.

See also MONTRACHET, CÔTE D'OR, and map under BURGUNDY. J.T.C.M.

Loftus, S., *Puligny-Montrachet* (1992).

pulling out. See GRUBBING UP.

pulp, viticulturally, the soft tissue of grape berries inside the skin (also called the flesh or PERICARP) which is the source of the juice of the grape. The word may also be used by winemakers to refer to the solid matter that settles from the juice after must SETTLING. For more detail of grape pulp, see GRAPE. B.G.C.

pumping over, winemaking operation involving the circulation of fermenting red wine through the CAP created by the grape skins and other solids. The French term is *remontage*. This can be carried out with or without AERATION, depending on the fermentation rate and the reducing conditions (see REDUCTION). It prevents drying out of the cap and encourages the EXTRACTION of the skins' valuable colouring matter and TANNINS into the wine. It may be done either in a closed or open-top vat, from one to three times a day depending on the temperature and rate of fermentation. The mechanical systems involved include some adaptation of the AUTOVINIFICATION system, ROTOFERMENTERS, and tanks which incorporate automatic PUNCHING DOWN. However, automation cannot replace the winemaker's decisions about the volume of fermenting wine that needs to be pumped over each day to get the right level of extraction. See also RACK AND RETURN, SUBMERGED CAP, and MACERATION.

pumps, mechanical devices for **pumping**, moving liquids such as wine, grape juice, and suspensions of solids such as MUST from one location to another. Pumps are avoided by some of the most traditional—and some of the most modern (see WINERY DESIGN)—wineries that depend on gravity to move liquid from one level to another for different winemaking processes.

Must from the DESTEMMER-CRUSHER is usually moved to the draining tank or FERMENTATION VESSEL by means of a peristaltic or off-centre helical screw-type pump because this type performs particularly well with solid suspensions. Cloudy juice from the draining tank might well be moved by means of a rotor pump to the fermentation tank, and most of the semi-clear and clear wines being processed are also moved using these types of pump at any step of the winemaking process.

punching down, the winemaking operation of breaking up and submerging the CAP of skins and other solids during red-wine fermentation to stop the cap from drying out, to encourage the EXTRACTION of colour and TANNINS, and to encourage useful AERATION in the making of a deeply coloured red wine. Keeping skins and liquid in contact is relatively simple with small batches of fermenting grapes. In tanks filled to a depth of 1–1.5 m/3–4 ft, a person can physically mix the floating solids into the fermenting grape juice using a wooden punch, stick or paddle or even with their feet. The cap may also be punched down by special metal devices, either by hand or mechanically. It is usually done between one and three times a day depending on the fermentation rate. The French term is *pigeage*. See also MACERATION, RACK AND RETURN, and SUBMERGED CAP.

punt, optional indentation in the bottom of wine BOTTLES, particularly common in bottles of sparkling wine.

pupitre, French name for a rack traditionally used for RIDDLING sparkling wines by hand. For more details, see SPARKLING WINEMAKING.

Puy-de-Dôme, IGP used for white, red, and rosé wines grown in the VOLCANIC soils of the Puy-de-Dôme *département* west of Lyons. As in the AOC Côtes d'AUVERGNE which sits within it, GAMAY and PINOT NOIR predominate. Red wines make up 75% of production, rosés another 15%. What few whites are made tend to be from CHARDONNAY, ALIGOTÉ, and PINOT BLANC.

PVPP, or **polyvinylpolypirrolidone**, a synthetic material used as a FINING agent. Its particular property is the removal of PHENOLIC components from white wine, especially those that are suffering from 'pinking' or 'browning' resulting from mild OXIDATION. D.B.

PX, common abbreviation for the Spanish grape variety PEDRO XIMÉNEZ, particularly for the dark, sticky, ultra-sweet varietal FORTIFIED WINE made from it in Spain. MONTILLA-MORILES is the usual source, and top-quality wines can be almost as dark and viscous as molasses, though are generally lower in alcohol than the SHERRIES of nearby JEREZ.

pyrazines. See METHOXYPYRAZINES.

Pyrenees, hilly, TEMPERATE-climate Australian wine region in the Western Victoria Zone, sandwiched between the Grampians to the west and Bendigo to the east, chiefly known for Cabernet Sauvignon and Shiraz. See VICTORIA.

pyruvic acid, three-carbon compound formed by YEAST at a midway stage in the complex FERMENTATION process. It is converted to ACETALDEHYDE and then to ETHANOL.

P

QbA, or **Qualitätswein bestimmter Anbaugebiete**, see QUALITÄTSWEIN.

QmP, or **Qualitätswein mit Prädikat**, German wine category now officially known as Prädikatswein. See PRÄDIKAT.

Qualitätswein is what PDO wines are called in German. This is Germany's largest wine category and in practice includes all those wines once known as QBA (as opposed to QMP wines which have been renamed Prädikatswein; see PRÄDIKAT). The grapes must originate in one of GERMANY's 13 official wine regions and reach minimum MUST WEIGHTS specified for each region, which may vary by grape variety from 6 to 9% POTENTIAL ALCOHOL. Wines in this category may still be CHAPTALIZED but, thanks to CLIMATE CHANGE and improved viticultural techniques, chaptalization has become much rarer. Increasingly many German producers—including members of the VDP as official policy—bottle dry (TROCKEN and HALBTROCKEN) wines as Qualitätswein, reserving Prädikatswein designations for noticeably sweet wines.

Austria sets a national minimum for Qualitätswein equivalent to 9.7% POTENTIAL ALCOHOL.

quality assurance is a general concept covering the way in which a business is organized so that the quality of the product is assured at all stages. As applied to a wine business, good quality assurance will ensure that the original potential of the grapes and wine is not lost on the way to the bottle. Quality assurance is the totality of all the management actions and procedures that set out to achieve this high standard and therefore incorporates QUALITY CONTROL.

An internationally recognized standard of quality management is ISO 9001:2015. This standard imposes a discipline that demands a uniformity of action throughout the business every time, all of the time.

Another useful though simple tool is Hazard Analysis and Critical Control Points (HACCP). The manufacturing process is divided into its basic stages, then each stage is examined to determine the problems that could occur at each one (hazard identification). Each hazard is then assessed for its potential danger to the process (the hazard analysis). Those that constitute the greatest danger are identified as the critical control points, to which the maximum attention is given. This procedure is now considered so important that it is mandatory throughout the EU for anyone involved in food and beverage handling, and it is gaining worldwide recognition. D.B.

Bird, D., and Quillé, N., *Understanding Wine Technology* (4th edn, 2021).

quality control is a hands-on process of monitoring and controlling all parameters that verify a wine's palatability, STABILITY, compliance with regulations, TYPICALITY, and freedom from FAULTS and CONTAMINANTS. Most large wineries maintain laboratories capable of conducting all but the most difficult of the required ANALYSES, while smaller wine enterprises send samples to an independent commercial laboratory. For complete quality control, a chemical analytical laboratory, a microbiological laboratory, and a statistically controlled tasting panel are required. See also QUALITY ASSURANCE and SAMPLING. D.B.

quality in wine. The concept of quality is regularly used in connection with wine, both for marketing purposes and as a marker of personal evaluation. It is also widely used as an element in JUDGING in wine SHOWS. Nevertheless it is notoriously hard to pin down its precise nature. Even wine professionals comment at times that 'it is a matter of personal taste'. There are many—including Émile PEYNAUD—who argue that the denotation of quality is essentially the subjective enjoyment of pleasure, while others claim that it exists only relative to other factors, such as PRICE or the circumstances of consumption. It is certainly true that our response to wine is in part idiosyncratic, dependent on varying physiological responses and the drinker's cultural background (see PHILOSOPHY AND WINE and TASTING), but that has not precluded a number of ways of trying to define quality. Whether wine quality has a SUBJECTIVE or objective nature is complex, as is the relationship of quality to preference. Arguably it is possible to assess a wine as being of high quality without actually liking it.

Some wine professionals believe that quality can be precisely measured. Certainly there are means such as INFRARED SPECTROSCOPY to evaluate grape quality, but Somers, formerly of the AWRI, argues that, for red wines at least, it is possible to predict a wine's quality by using its ultraviolet absorbance to measure its PHENOLIC concentration. A more marketing-focused perspective is that a high-quality wine is one that is fit for its purpose, but, given the complex motivations for drinking wine, this raises the question of precisely what the purpose is. The American oenologist Maynard AMERINE believed that wine is an aesthetic object and that its evaluation therefore calls for the use of aesthetic criteria.

Some commentators have suggested quality can be measured by such intrinsic indicators as a wine's BALANCE, LENGTH, intensity, harmony, varietal purity, and COMPLEXITY. Such concepts are used in assessing wine throughout the world, although without any consistent application. Other means of grading quality, extrinsic to the drink itself, have also been used. These include the relationship of wine to the price it fetches, as in the best-known CLASSIFICATIONS. This does not however guarantee the actual organoleptic 'quality' of the drink as measured by critical or popular response.

Charters and Pettigrew suggest that drinkers consider wine quality to have a number of dimensions. Some of these are extrinsic to the wine, such as how it has been made; others are intrinsic, including how the wine tastes (involving subdimensions such as concentration, balance, smoothness, drinkability, and interest), its capacity for AGEING, and its TYPICALITY. However, the most important quality dimension for consumers is the amount of pleasure afforded by the wine. Thus one can argue that for most drinkers quality has two components: a series of dimensions which catalyse quality; and a sense of pleasure in the product which is the end result of those catalytic dimensions.

They also suggest a way out of the objective versus subjective quality conundrum. Employing a paradox which mirrors the sociological concept of intersubjectivity, it can be noted that wine drinkers often hold both perspectives simultaneously. Thus quality is partly objective, measured by external criteria which depend on a broad commonality in our response to the components of a wine (such as its balance and intensity) and subject to debate and agreement between drinkers. It is also partly personal and related to the consumer's individual preference. S.J.C

Charters, S., and Pettigrew, S., '"I Like It but How Do I Know If It's Any Good?": Quality and Preference in Wine Consumption', *Journal of Research for Consumers*, 5 (2003).

Charters, S., and Pettigrew, S., 'The dimensions of wine quality', *Food Quality and Preference*, 18/7 (2007), 997–1007.

Somers, C., *The Wine Spectrum: An Approach Towards Objective Definition of Wine Quality* (1998).

Q

quality wine is an expression widely and loosely used for any wine of good quality and was, until 2008, an official wine category throughout the EU and therefore throughout most of Europe. It has been superseded by the PDO and PGI categories. Similarly, everything else, called 'table wine' in its strict pre-2008 EU sense, has been superseded by the cumbersome but clear phrase WINE WITHOUT GEOGRAPHICAL INDICATION.

quarantine of imported plant material plays an important part in international viticulture and can put a (necessary) brake on its spread in new jurisdictions. Like any form of agricultural quarantine, it can annoy travellers but is designed to protect farmers and regional and national economies from the ravages which may be caused by the inadvertent introduction of new pests and diseases from other countries or regions (see the history of DOWNY MILDEW, POWDERY MILDEW, and PHYLLOXERA). Most of the devastating pests and diseases of the European vine species used commonly for wine production, VITIS VINIFERA, have in fact been spread from America, AMERICAN VINE SPECIES having developed a tolerance to these diseases which *vinifera* lacks.

Quarantine systems for viticulture are in place at national borders and also sometimes at regional levels. Most wine-producing countries maintain strict quarantine on vine imports in an attempt to keep out the likes of PIERCE'S DISEASE and FLAVESCENCE DORÉE, both of which could ravage a region's viticulture if they were to spread. Quarantine also works to reduce the spread of other FUNGAL, VIRUS, and BACTERIAL DISEASES as well as insect and nematode VINE PESTS which might not be lethal but may cause significant economic damage. Licences issued for vine importation are typically restricted to a few CUTTINGS per import, which are then subjected to disease testing. The quarantine delays can be up to two or three years, but certification programmes and diagnostic tests such as ELISA developed in the 1980s may reduce this period. Some countries, for example China and Canada, do allow imports of young GRAFTED vines, but these are subject to guarantees about virus status. Nursery plants move freely around the EU with a plant passport to guarantee freedom from virus disease, but they are widely infected with TRUNK DISEASE fungi not currently covered by the passport. Smuggling of vines is not unknown, especially by impatient producers who believe that they are disadvantaged by not having access to better varieties or CLONES and are tempted to resort to what are sometimes referred to as 'suitcase clones'.

Sometimes there are quarantine areas within national boundaries, such as those that exist in South Australia, Tasmania, and Western Australia, in an attempt to avoid the further spread of phylloxera. Some countries and regions are free of major pests or diseases. CHILE, for example, has remained free of phylloxera, even though it is present in Argentina just over the Andes. Increasing international competition in the wine market makes the possibility of sabotage from another region or nation by introduction of a pest or disease less fanciful. The economic health of many of the world's viticultural regions depends on effective vine quarantine being maintained, and continuing vigilance and community support are essential. R.E.S.

Quarts de Chaume, extraordinary yet minuscule enclave within the Coteaux du LAYON appellation producing historically praised sweet white wines from BOTRYTIZED Chenin Blanc grapes. The well-protected, steep slopes of varied carboniferous soils, *poudingues*, and brioverian SCHIST overlooking the right bank of the Layon river is a remarkable TERROIR for high-quality NOBLE ROT development, leading in the best vintages to exceptional natural concentration. Yet as the minimum grape-sugar level in the MUST is extremely high (298 g/l for 85 g/l of RESIDUAL SUGAR at bottling), total annual production can often be as little as a few thousand cases from just over 26 ha/64 acres of planted vineyard, supposedly the finest quarter, or *quart*, of the CHAUME part in Rochefort-sur-Loire (see FRANCE, history, for details). Domaine des Baumard tried to secure permission to use CRYOEXTRACTION, but in 2014 it was decreed that this freeze-concentration technique would be outlawed from 2019. Richer and rarer than those of nearby BONNEZEAUX, and forbidding CHAPTALIZATION, Quarts de Chaume became officially the Loire's first GRAND CRU in 2011. As NOBLE ROT is getting less consistent with CLIMATE CHANGE, more remarkable dry white wines mentioning the main LIEUX-DITS (Rouères, Veau, Zerzille, etc.) are produced under the ANJOU Blanc AOC. P.Le.

quartz, silicon dioxide (silica), a very common rock-forming mineral. It is seen as glassy, colourless grains in rocks such as GRANITE and SANDSTONE, producing sandy soils of low fertility. It also occurs as opaque white veins filling gashes in bedrock, which weathering loosens into fragments that become the milky white stones seen in many vineyard soils. See also GEOLOGY. A.J.M.

quartzite, a metamorphic rock that was originally a quartz-rich sandstone (see GEOLOGY). It is usually pale-coloured or white, with a 'sugary' appearance. It should not be confused with the mineral QUARTZ since it is a rock composed of myriad constituent grains. Once used for any tough quartz-rich rock, in modern usage quartzite refers to a compact, metamorphic fusion of the quartz grains and silica cement of the original SANDSTONE, which makes it robust and resistant to SOIL EROSION.

Quartzite therefore tends to form relatively higher ground with thin, poorly fertile soils, generally not well suited to viticulture, although it does occur in Germany's NAHE and RHEINHESSEN regions, in Spain's CALATAYUD, and in the BAROSSA and CLARE VALLEYS, South Australia. Quartzite is much more commonly seen in vineyards as rock fragments in the soil, including the archetypal GALETS of CHÂTEAUNEUF-DU-PAPE. A.J.M.

Quatourze, an obscure CRU within the LANGUEDOC AOC in southern France for reds based on Grenache, Syrah, and Mourvèdre. Production of appellation wine in this little windswept zone just west of Narbonne is small and dominated by Ch Notre-Dame du Quatourze.

Quebec is the third largest wine region in CANADA. Its modern industry dates to the 1980s, with early plantings at Domaine des Côtes d'Ardoise in 1981. Today there are seven delineated wine regions, with the largest concentration of vineyards to the south and south-east of Montreal close to the United States border. The growing season is relatively short but ranges from warm to hot, while winter temperatures can often dip below −20 °C/−4 °F in some regions, necessitating WINTER PROTECTION for the vines. The Appalachian Foothills region is Quebec's warmest, counting 1171–1348 C° growing degree days (compared with 1315 C° in Burgundy). (See CLIMATE CLASSIFICATION.) Topographical features also create highly localized warm areas that allow vines to survive, if not flourish. In 2021 the province had 163 wineries and 825 ha/2,040 acres of vines, primarily French and Minnesota HYBRIDS, for example VIDAL, MARQUETTE, SEYVAL BLANC, and FRONTENACS Blanc, Gris, and Noir, but with increasing amounts of VITIS VINIFERA varieties such as Chardonnay, Pinot Noir, and Pinot Gris. There are two Protected Geographical Indications (PGIS): Vin du Québec, for still and sparkling wine; and Vin de glace du Québec, for ICEWINE. J.D.

www.quebecwines.com
www.vinsduquebec.com

Queensland, state comprising the north-east quadrant of Australia, its wine regions concentrated in the south-east of the state at the northern end of the Great Dividing Range. The region has supported a wine industry since the 1860s, shortly after Samuel Bassett obtained CUTTINGS from the HUNTER VALLEY and founded Romavilla near the town of Roma. As in other Australian states, wine production waned after the 1890s but was rejuvenated in the 1970s and 1980s. Many of the new wave of pioneers were Italian, such as Angelo Puglisi, who founded Ballandean Estate in 1970. By the 1990s, Queensland wines were seen and talked about in Brisbane, the state capital and a significant population centre.

The early 2000s saw further growth when the Queensland State Government provided assistance with grants and resources and changed the liquor licence laws to allow wineries to open a retail outlet, or CELLAR DOOR, outside of the vineyards and winery. It also allowed a business to be classed as a winery even if it arranged for someone else in Queensland to grow the grapes and make the wine. A plethora of new wine businesses grew as a result—some in wine regions, some in Brisbane, and several in or near the touristic Gold Coast and Sunshine Coast. These developments have been good for dynamism but have made tallying wineries difficult. In 2022 the Queensland Wine Industry Association (QWIA) counted 127 licensed wine producers, while aerial survey data from Wine Australia measured 630 ha/1,557 acres of vineyards in Queensland.

The state has two GEOGRAPHICAL INDICATIONS (GIs). The GRANITE BELT, about three hours south-west of Brisbane, dominates production, the vines planted on the high-ELEVATION tableland of the Great Dividing Range to take advantage of the cooler temperatures and DIURNAL TEMPERATURE RANGE. (Some producers here also take advantage of plantings in the NORTHERN SLOPES ZONE, across the state line in NEW SOUTH WALES.) The smaller, warmer, and hilly SOUTH BURNETT GI sits two-and-a-half hours north-west of Brisbane.

The mainstream varieties Shiraz, Chardonnay, and VERDELHO dominate production volumes, but in recent years there has been a growing interest among both producers and consumers in ALTERNATIVE VARIETIES such as FIANO, VERMENTINO, TEMPRANILLO, TANNAT, and SAPERAVI. A.C.

www.queenslandwine.com.au

quercetin, also spelt **quercitin**, a yellow dyestuff with ANTIOXIDANT properties belonging to the FLAVONOL family, originally extracted from the bark of black oak (QUERCUS), hence the name.

Quercus is the botanical genus to which oak belongs and is therefore the most important family of plants to wine after the vine genus VITIS since it provides both CORK and wine's most classic storage material, OAK. According to the most recent (2017) classification, it is subdivided into two subgenera, *Cerris* and *Quercus*. All oaks used for wine containers and corks belong to the latter. The species most commonly used for BARRELS are the American white oak *Quercus alba* and the European oaks *Quercus robur* and *Quercus petraea*. For more details, see OAK.

The species whose bark is stripped to provide cork is *Quercus suber*.

quercusportal.pierroton.inra.fr/index.php?p=TAXONOMY

Quercy, Coteaux du, a small AOC between Cahors and Gaillac in SOUTH WEST FRANCE devoted to sturdy, rustic reds and some rosés, both made from Cabernet Franc with Cot (MALBEC), Merlot, and TANNAT.

Quincy, rapidly expanding, historic white-wine appellation in the greater Loire region that encompasses just two villages. It produces racy dry wines from Sauvignon Blanc (with up to 10% Sauvignon Gris) grapes from a total area of vines that by 2019 had grown to 317 ha/783 acres of SAND and GRAVEL on the left bank of the Cher tributary. Its long history (it was the second AOC created, after CHÂTEAUNEUF-DU-PAPE, in 1936) and early popularity owe much to its proximity to RIVER transport (especially in comparison with the smaller nearby appellation REUILLY). The wines tend to be a little less delicate than those made in Menetou-Salon and Sancerre to the east.

See also LOIRE, including map. C.P.

quinta, Portuguese word meaning 'farm', which may also refer to a wine-producing estate or vineyard. Single-quinta ports are those made from a single year and from a single estate in the Douro Valley; see PORT.

Quinta do Noval. Founded in 1715, Noval is the name of both the estate and this historic, unusually vineyard-based, PORT shipper. Quinta do Noval was owned by the firm António José da Silva, who in 1973 changed their name to Quinta do Noval-Vinhos, because Noval represented their finest wine (and they also wanted to avoid confusion with all the other da Silva companies in OPORTO). The estate of Quinta do Noval, in the Pinhão Valley, enjoyed a heyday in the mid 20th century when run by Luiz Vasconcellos Porto, before being inherited by the Van Zeller family. Noval's most prestigious, rarest, and expensive wine is Nacional, produced from 2.5 ha/6 acres of UNGRAFTED VINES which, not having American ROOTSTOCKS, are therefore 'national'. The Nacional 1931 VINTAGE (which Noval was virtually alone in declaring) enjoys legendary status.

Quinta do Noval suffered a devastating fire at its lodges in Vila Nova de Gaia in 1981 and has continued to age its wines in air-conditioned lodges in the Douro Valley rather than in Gaia. In 1993 the firm was acquired by the French insurance company AXA; under port-lover Christian Seely, its winery, vineyards, and reputation have since been comprehensively restored with more than three-quarters of the vineyard area having been replanted, mainly with Touriga Nacional, Touriga Franca, and Tinto Cão, innovatively retaining the original vineyard TERRACES while adapting them for modern cultivation wherever possible. A third vintage port, Silval—sometimes produced in a generally declared vintage year alongside Quinta do Noval, sometimes on its own when Quinta do Noval is not declared—was introduced in 1995. Since 2004 Noval has produced a range of DOURO red and white wines under the labels Quinta do Noval and Cedro. The firm's vineyards produce well over 90% of their needs, with the remainder being bought in from other properties in the Douro Valley. Neighbouring Quinta do Passadouro was acquired by Noval in 2019.

quintal, *quintale* in Italian, unit of weight equivalent to 100 kg/220 lbs.

qvevri, uniquely GEORGIAN clay vessel used for FERMENTATION and AGEING of red and white wines for many centuries, especially, but by no means exclusively, in Kakheti in the east. The rounded, wide-mouthed earthenware jars, given their very own PGI in 2021, vary enormously in size, from 50 l/ 13 gal for a family's domestic production to 700–4,000 l for commercial use, the larger ones for ageing rather than fermentation. Unlike Roman AMPHORAE and Spanish TINAJAS, qvevri are buried underground, requiring no TEMPERATURE CONTROL and benefiting from natural SETTLING and CLARIFICATION. Procuring and then cleaning and maintaining these vessels are the main obstacles to their wider use.

The Kakhetian tradition for both red and white wines is to put the lightly crushed whole berries—including skins, pips, and stems, known as *chacha*—into the qvevri. Further west, where the jars are also known as *churi*, less *chacha* is used and MACERATION times are shorter. With red wines, the wine may be moved to a clean qvevri, or even to oak BARRELS, post fermentation. After fermentation and MALOLACTIC CONVERSION, the wide mouth of the qvevri is closed with a slate (occasionally wooden) lid and sealed with clay. Qvevri wines are quintessentially tannic, the best deeply satisfying and flavourful, but the whites are particularly distinctive thanks to their golden colour, tannic structure, and aromas of hay and chamomile, the winemaking sometimes obscuring the grape variety. Qvevri winemaking, recognized as a UNESCO 'intangible heritage' in 2013, is also practised by a few producers in Europe, most notably in Friuli in north-east Italy and western Slovenia. Qvevri is both singular and plural.

Rabigato, grape that adds class and acidity to DOURO white blends and grown particularly in the Douro Superior. Total plantings in the Douro were 1,744 ha/4,310 acres in 2020.

Rabo de Ovelha, white grape variety grown in Portugal, particularly the Alentejo, taking its name from the 'ewe's tail' shape of its bunches. Noted for its freshness and elegant floral and white-fruit notes, it is probably closely related to CAYETANA BLANCA. Total plantings had fallen to 239 ha/591 acres by 2020.

Raboso, name of two closely related but distinct tough red grape varieties grown in the VENETO region of north-east Italy. **Raboso Piave** is more common, on 641 ha/1,584 acres in 2015, as opposed to **Raboso Veronese** grown on 295 ha. Rabosa Piave is characteristic of the flat valley floor of PIAVE, and most is grown in the province of Treviso. Raboso Veronese is sometimes interplanted with Raboso Piave but is also grown in Ferrara and Ravenna in Emilia-Romagna. The name is thought to derive from the Italian *rabbioso*, meaning 'angry', presumably a reference to consumer reaction to the uncompromisingly high ACIDITY and rough TANNINS which characterize the grape and its wine. This is a grape variety which has excellent resistance to disease and ROT but which makes CABERNET SAUVIGNON look rather mellow. Unfortunately Raboso is not high enough in alcohol to compensate for its ASTRINGENCY and can therefore taste extremely austere in youth. Stalwart defenders of the variety insist that, with full ripeness and careful handling in the winery, wines produced can be truly distinguished, the Veneto's answer to the Nebbiolo of Piemonte or the Sangiovese of Tuscany. The reputation and price level of Raboso make it difficult to justify this kind of investment, and vineyard plantings, which continue to decline, reflect this fact.

Raboso Veronese is also planted, to an extremely limited extent, in Argentina, presumably taken there by Italian immigrants.

rachis, the main STEM that runs through a BUNCH of grapes and is joined to the berry by the PEDICEL. See GRAPE.

rack, wine, common horizontal storage for wine bottles, keeping the cork damp and avoiding OXYGEN ingress. See CELLAR.

rack and return, or drain and return, *délestage* in French, is a CAP management procedure which optimizes contact between MUST and solids during fermentation and homogenizes the temperature in the must and the cap. When the cap has risen to the top of the tank, fermenting wine is taken from a bottom valve to a separate receiving vessel. The wine is then gently pumped back over the top of the cap, using a low-pressure pump or sprinkler system. This procedure, usually conducted once or twice during fermentation, is designed to ensure optimum diffusion of TANNINS and PIGMENTS from the fruit into the wine. It is best carried out in the early stages of fermentation when the alcohol is still low to avoid over-EXTRACTION. When the tank is wide rather than tall, MACERATION is more efficient so that rack and return is not as useful. D.D. & V.L.

racking, the winemaking operation of removing clear wine from the settled SEDIMENT or LEES in the bottom of a container. The verb **to rack** has been used thus at least since the 14th century.

Racking is usually achieved by pumping or siphoning the wine away from the sediment into an empty container, but special large **racking tanks** are used by some large wineries. They are equipped with drain lines, the lower ends of which can be adjusted to just clear the sediment layer and permit more rapid and more complete wine removal from the solids.

Racking forms an important part of the annual cycle of cellar work, or ÉLEVAGE, in the production of most fine wines matured in small BARRELS. Racking from barrel to barrel is very LABOUR-intensive, and each racking inevitably involves a barrel that needs thorough cleaning and sulfuring to avoid any risk of BACTERIAL SPOILAGE or BRETTANOMYCES.

According to classical *élevage*, the first racking takes place soon after FERMENTATION and the ensuing MACERATION to separate the new wine from the skins and the gross LEES, with the second one after MALOLACTIC CONVERSION. In cooler regions, another racking typically takes place just after the first FROSTS of winter have precipitated some of the TARTRATES and MICRO-ORGANISMS, while in many cellars there is a fourth in spring and another before the full heat of the summer. Wines may be racked once or twice during a second year in barrel. NEW WORLD winemakers have tended to rack less frequently.

Racking is not only part of the CLARIFICATION process but also provides AERATION, which, in the case of red wines, is essential to the formation of PIGMENTED TANNINS and beneficial to the sensory properties of the wine. Aeration also discourages REDUCTION of any excess SULFUR to malodorous MERCAPTANS.

Raffiac, sometimes **Raffiat**, alternative names for ARRUFIAC.

railways. Until the arrival of a railway in their region, wine producers were almost totally dependent on waterborne means of transport.

Without access to the sea or a navigable RIVER or canal, transport was too difficult and expensive for all but the finest and rarest wines. This gave an overwhelming advantage to regions such as BORDEAUX, which were served by a major port, or CHAMPAGNE, with access to the river system of northern France.

The construction of the railways enabled a number of wines previously unknown outside their region to be exported. In some cases—notably CHIANTI in central Italy and RIOJA in northern Spain—this enabled high-quality wines to achieve their deserved recognition for the first time. The construction of a railway line between the town of JEREZ and the coast in the mid 19th century greatly encouraged exports of SHERRY.

The railways also facilitated the transport of inferior wines. They allowed the late 19th century development of the mass-production vineyards of the LANGUEDOC and ROUSSILLON in the south of France, whose rough wines were transported in vast quantities to northern France and Belgium, thus ruining such marginal northern European vineyards as those around ORLÉANS and, to a lesser extent, those of the French MOSELLE. The railways in ARGENTINA were also crucial in establishing Mendoza as an important wine region far from the capital Buenos Aires. During the 15 years of PROHIBITION in the United States, efficient rail transport of fresh grapes from California to the suddenly numerous HOME WINEMAKERS in the eastern states played a part in maintaining a winemaking tradition in the U.S. N.F.

rainfall, a component of climate which affects grapevines in many and sometimes conflicting ways.

For vines depending directly on rainfall (see DRY-FARMED), there needs to be enough rain, at the right times, to promote adequate growth and to avoid severe WATER STRESS during ripening. On the other hand, more than enough rainfall can lead to excessive vegetation growth and a poor CANOPY MICROCLIMATE. Too much rain during FLOWERING can lead to COULURE, and, in wet regions, soils with poor internal DRAINAGE may become waterlogged. Similarly, rainfall can promote fungal diseases such as DOWNY MILDEW and BOTRYTIS BUNCH ROT by wetting foliage and fruit.

Average annual rainfall in wine regions globally is roughly 700 mm/28 in but ranges from extremely dry, less than 100 mm/4 in (e.g. in Chile's ELIQUI VALLEY), to quite wet, greater than 1,700 m/67 in (e.g. Portugal's VINHO VERDE). Wine regions with 40–60% of their annual rainfall during the growing season (e.g. northern France, eastern US) are less likely to use IRRIGATION, while those in winter-wet, summer-dry seasons (e.g. western US, central Chile), with less than 20% of annual rainfall during the growing season, tend to depend on irrigation. These irrigation needs are supplied by rivers, aquifers, wells, or communal irrigation. The normal unreliability of rainfall means that full wetting of the SOIL PROFILE seldom occurs naturally, and frequent heavy watering is usually needed throughout the growing and ripening season.

No particular upper limit of rainfall is apparent for viticulture, provided that the soils are well drained, leached SOIL NUTRIENTS can be replaced, SUNLIGHT is enough, and HUMIDITY is not so high that FUNGAL DISEASES cannot be controlled. However, heavy rain leading up to harvest is nearly always detrimental to wine quality. The berries often split, resulting in fungal and bacterial infection of the bunches (see BUNCH ROT). At a minimum, the juice and its flavour are diluted. HAIL at this time is especially disastrous. R.E.S. & J.V.G.

Anderson, K., and Nelgen, S., *Which Winegrape Varieties are Grown Where? A Global Empirical Picture* (revised edn, 2020). www.economics.adelaide.edu.au/wine-economics/databases.

Jones, G. V., et al., 'Climate, grapes, and wine: structure and suitability in a variable and changing climate', in P. Dougherty (ed.), *The Geography of Wine: Regions, Terroir, and Techniques* (2012), 109–33.

Jones, G. V., 'The state of the climate', *Proceedings of the 21st GiESCO International Meeting: A Multidisciplinary Vision towards Sustainable Viticulture* (2019), 32–43.

rain-fed. See DRY-FARMED.

raisins, from the French *raisins secs*, are dried grapes, the third most common commercial use for viticulture, after wine and TABLE GRAPES. Terminology varies around the world, but this book uses the word 'raisins' as a catch-all that also includes sultanas and currants.

Drying is a means of preserving grapes for eating (and precedes fermentation in the production of DRIED-GRAPE WINES). Dried grapes are an ancient food supply. The low moisture content of the dried grape (10–15%) and high sugar concentration (70–80%) make the product relatively unsuitable for survival of food-spoilage organisms.

Grapes have been dried since antiquity. Records of grape drying found in EGYPT date back to 3000 BCE, and records of dried grapes are found in biblical times. Aristotle in 360 BCE referred to the seedless character of the Black Corinth grape, today's CURRANT. Legend has it that Hannibal fed his troops with raisins during the crossing of the Alps in 218 BCE.

Three varieties dominate world trade in raisins: SULTANA (also known as Thompson Seedless in America, and Kishmish or Sultanina in Asia and the Near East); Zante Currant (Australia and the US) or Black Corinth (California); and MUSCAT OF ALEXANDRIA (Muscat Gordo Blanco in Australia and White Hanepoot in South Africa). In Australia and California, grapes usually destined for the dried-grape industry have been diverted into wine at times of severe wine-grape shortage.

World production of raisins is gradually increasing, reaching a record of 1.33 million tonnes in 2019/20. The biggest producer of dried grapes is Türkiye (around 23% of global production), followed by the US (17%), China (13%), Iran (12%), and India (11%). Greece is the leading producer within Europe. Climate is a major factor determining where grapes are grown for drying. Temperatures should be high, with plenty of sunshine, while post-harvest humidity and rainfall should be low. In such conditions the evaporation rate is reliably high, and this usually means that the vineyards need IRRIGATION. Rainfall prior to harvest or during drying has catastrophic results, as the fruit can split and rot.

Harvested grapes are placed outside on wooden or paper trays, or concrete or clay slabs. After about 10–14 days, the bunches must be turned over to dry the other side. The grapes may be dipped in solutions containing vegetable oils and potassium carbonate to speed their drying. Drying racks with roofs can help reduce rain damage and allow drying solutions to be sprayed on the fruit. Grapes may also be dried indoors.

Alternative methods of drying fruit on the vines have been developed in Australia and California. The canes supporting the bunches are cut at the base but left on the TRELLIS wires. (See CUT CANE for this method of producing sweet wines in Australia.) The vines may be sprayed with the drying emulsion and then mechanically harvested when dried. Dried grapes should not be packed with more than 13% moisture, and sometimes grapes dried in the field need to be dried further.

Quality factors in raisins are size, hue and uniformity of colour, surface condition, texture of both skin and pulp, and lack of any contamination. The highest-quality raisins are produced from the ripest fruit. R.E.S. & J.E.H.

Whiting, J. R., 'Harvesting and drying of grapes', in B. G. Coombe and P. R. Dry (eds.), *Viticulture*, ii: *Practices* (2nd edn 2006).

Rajinski Rizling and **Rajnai Rizling**, various Eastern European names for the true RIESLING grape of Germany.

Ramandolo. See VERDUZZO.

Ramisco, red grape variety grown exclusively in the shrinking COLARES region of Portugal and therefore probably the only VITIS VINIFERA vine variety never to have been GRAFTED. These rare wines can be tannic in youth but complex and perfumed after AGEING in bottle.

rancio, imprecise tasting term used in many languages for a distinctive style of wine, often FORTIFIED WINE or VIN DOUX NATUREL, achieved by deliberately MADERIZING the wine by exposing it to OXYGEN and/or heat. The wine may be stored in barrels in hot storehouses (as for some of Australia's TOPAQUE AND MUSCAT), or immediately under the rafters in a hot climate (as for some of ROUSSILLON's vins doux naturels), or in glass BONBONNES left out of doors and subjected to the changing temperatures of night and day (as in parts of Spain). The word 'rancio' has the same root as *rancid*, and the wines which result have an additional and powerful smell reminiscent of overripe fruit, nuts, and melted, or even rancid, butter.

Key FLAVOUR COMPOUNDS identified in aged vins doux naturels arise by MAILLARD REACTION of sugars with AMINO ACIDS and by OXIDATION. These compounds are known to be present in, and responsible for, the characteristic flavour of other sweet food products. Thus, for example, furaneol, cyclotene, maltol, and SOTOLON, which are known contributors to the flavour of honey and caramelized sugar products, have been found in these wines along with several lactones that are important to the flavour of dried fruits.

This richness emerges in a complex series of sensations on the nose and palate. 'Rankness, a special character of fullness and richness' was the unflattering description given by Charles Walter Berry, the wine merchant who was Britain's leading cognac connoisseur between the World Wars (rancio can often be found in oak-aged brandies). Tasting descriptors include Roquefort cheese or rich fruit cake with its flavours of candied fruits, apricots, sultanas, almonds, and walnuts. N.F., J.R. & P.J.W.

Cutzach, I., et al., 'Study of the formation mechanisms of some volatile compounds during the aging of sweet fortified wines', *Journal of Agricultural and Food Chemistry*, 47/7 (1999), 2837–46.

random oxidation, also known as sporadic post-bottling oxidation, describes the premature browning that occurs in some white wines some months after BOTTLING. All closures have some variability in their OXYGEN TRANSMISSION RATE (OTR), so some bottles will be exposed to more oxygen than others during bottle AGEING. Wines are protected against oxidation through the addition of SULFUR DIOXIDE at bottling, but if the level of free sulfur dioxide added then is low, some bottles with high OTR will exhibit oxidation when the sulfur dioxide in those bottles is exhausted. The variability in OTR is caused by the closure itself, which is greater for CORKS than for manufactured CLOSURES, but other factors can be as important. These include flaws in bottlenecks or lips where sealing with CORKS or SCREWCAPS occurs, improperly adjusted jaws that crimp corks during bottling, or improper screwcap application. Another proposed cause is poor procedure or intermittent failure on the bottling line, allowing some wines to have much higher levels of dissolved oxygen from the outset (see TOTAL PACKAGE OXYGEN). Random oxidation is mainly a problem with white wines: while oxygen ingress through the closure will certainly damage red wines, they are more resistant to oxidation because of their high PHENOLIC content. Oxidation is also more likely to be noticed in white wines because of the visible browning that accompanies it. See also PREMATURE OXIDATION. A.L.W.

Ranina, Slovenian synonym for the BOUVIER grape.

Rapel, subregion of the Central Valley of CHILE, including Cachapoal and Colchagua.

Rasteau, southern Rhône CRU (promoted from Côtes du Rhône-Villages in 2010) on the east bank of the RHÔNE river. Its 940 ha/2,323 acres of vines are situated on the eastern half of a large hill of MARL and pebbles between the rivers Ouvèze and Aigues; CAIRANNE occupies the western half. Rasteau has an appellation for dry red wines as well as for white, rosé, and red VINS DOUX NATURELS (VDNs). The dry wines are blends based on Grenache with Syrah and/or Mourvèdre; many other minor grapes are also permitted. These are typically concentrated, powerful wines with a sweet ripeness to the fruit flavours, smooth TANNINS, and high alcohol. The VDNs are made in much smaller volumes (just 142 hl/3,751 gal produced in 2020) although the appellation dates to 1944. They also depend on Grenache (Noir, Gris, and Blanc) and come in several styles dependent on grape variety, vinification, and ageing, from the non-OXIDATIVE styles Blanc and Grenat to the oxidative Ambré, Tuilé, and RANCIO. Hors d'Âge indicates a Rasteau aged at least five years. M.C.W.

ratafia is an old, usually domestically produced wine-based APERITIF made in the French countryside by drying grapes to a raisin-like state and then moistening and fermenting them in the spring. Ratafia de Champagne is a mistelle (see MISTELA), made by adding marc (distilled spirit) to unfermented grape juice from Champagne.

ratings, scores applied to individual wines. See NUMBERS AND WINE and SCORING.

Ratti, Renato (1934–88), industrious and dedicated winemaker based at La Morra in BAROLO in the north-west Italian region of Piemonte, now run by his son Pietro. One of a group of so-called modernist Barolo producers seeking a more accessible Barolo (see BAROLO for more details), he was particularly keen to promulgate the notion of TERROIR. In 1979 he became one of the first to draw up a map of the best Barolo vineyards, or CRUS, which, with qualifications, is still valid today. W.S.

Räuschling, historic white grape variety today most commonly planted in German-speaking SWITZERLAND, where it can produce fine, crisp wines. In the Middle Ages it was very widely cultivated in Germany, particularly Baden (see GERMAN HISTORY). DNA PROFILING has shown it is a natural GOUAIS BLANC × SAVAGNIN cross.

Ravat, French vine breeder who gave his name to a number of FRENCH HYBRIDS.

raya, Spanish word meaning 'stripe' or 'streak' and a term for the symbol used to classify SHERRY must. A *raya* is also a coarse style of OLOROSO used in blending medium-dry sherry.

RDI. See REGULATED DEFICIT IRRIGATION.

Rebe, German for 'vine'. **Rebsorten** are vine varieties.

Rebula, Slovenian name for RIBOLLA Gialla.

Recioto, distinctive category of north-east Italian DRIED-GRAPE WINES, a historic speciality of the VENETO. The word derives from the Italian for ear, *orecchio*, because the wine was originally produced only from the ripest grapes in the bunch, from the upper lobes, or ears, although selected whole bunches have long been substituted. The most common forms of Recioto are sweet red Recioto della VALPOLICELLA and the rare sweet white Recioto di SOAVE and Recioto di GAMBELLARA. Even rarer still is Refrontolo, made of dried MARZEMINO grapes, and Torchiato di Fregona, based on GLERA, both in the province of Treviso.

Recioto della Valpolicella, like its dry counterpart AMARONE, is produced from 45–95% CORVINA, the great INDIGENOUS VARIETY of Valpolicella, up to half of which may be replaced by CORVINONE, and 5–30% RONDINELLA, with up to 25% of the INTERNATIONAL VARIETIES authorized in the province of Verona. As for Amarone, these grapes are raisined during the late autumn and winter months after the harvest in special drying rooms equipped with air conditioning and humidity control to avoid the development of BOTRYTIS, which can lead to PREMATURE OXIDATION (although more traditional producers tend to embrace the COMPLEXITY that botrytis under more natural drying conditions can add). Like Amarone it is produced in the Valpolicella DOC zone which has been divided into a CLASSICO subzone and a larger zone whose wines are simply called Recioto. The white Recioto di Soave must be made from at least 70% GARGANEGA and a maximum of 30% TREBBIANO di Soave, Pinot Bianco, and/or Chardonnay (although quality-oriented producers tend to eschew the last two, which are generally included to compensate for lack of flavour and alcohol in grapes from high-yielding vineyards). Recioto di Gambellara must be 100% Garganega.

These wines can represent some of Italy's finest sweet wines, but, owing to sluggish demand and the mediocre quality associated with some dry Soave and Gambellara, the number of producers willing to sacrifice time and LABOUR to produce these wines has been declining, and Valpolicella producers now favour the much more lucrative Amarone. W.S.

récolte, French for HARVEST. A **récoltant** is therefore a GROWER. In CHAMPAGNE, a **récoltant-manipulant** (identified by an 'RM' on the label) is a grower who also makes his or her own champagne, of whom there are more than 1,600 in the region, as opposed to a **récoltant-coopérateur** (RC), who sells champagne made by a CO-OPERATIVE, of whom there are more than 2,000.

recorking, a potentially hazardous exercise conducted by some top wine producers and some fine-wine traders. The aim is to prolong a wine's potential longevity after extended bottle AGEING may have weakened the cork. Estimates of a cork's longevity range from 15 to 30 years, depending on the quality of the cork and the wine's storage conditions. Ch LAFITE used to send its MAÎTRE DE CHAI on recorking tours which doubled as public relations exercises but, having encountered too many bottles of doubtful PROVENANCE and poor condition, they abandoned this practice. Today PENFOLDS is the world's most determined recorker, holding 'clinics' for those who own Penfolds wines of more than 15 years old. Since they began in 1999, Penfolds have certified 130,000 bottles, typically topping them up with wine of a similar age and quality before recorking with advice on when to drink them. The FINE WINE market became suspicious of recorking in any circumstances other than the most public in the late 1980s, as it potentially offers too much possibility for ADULTERATION AND FRAUD.

rectified grape must, or **RGM**, is preserved GRAPE JUICE that has been rectified (i.e. processed to reduce the concentration of solids other than SUGARS). It is generally further treated by removing water to yield **rectified concentrated grape must**, or **RCGM**, which is a common commodity used principally in Europe for ENRICHMENT. The EU authorities were at one time keen to promote its use in place of sugar as a way of helping reduce the European WINE LAKE. Many winemakers who need to use it in northern Europe have a natural antipathy to introducing a product made from what they view as inferior grapes. There are several major producers of RGM in Europe who absorb SURPLUS grape production from areas such as the LANGUEDOC, LA MANCHA, SICILY, and PUGLIA. They submit it to such modern technological processes as ION EXCHANGE and REVERSE OSMOSIS together with super-efficient FILTRATION and evaporators to produce what is in effect a concentrated invert sugar (GLUCOSE and FRUCTOSE) solution from grape juice. See also CONCENTRATION.

red blotch virus. See GRAPEVINE RED BLOTCH VIRUS.

Redding, Cyrus (1785–1870), England's answer to the great wine explorer of France, André JULLIEN. As a young journalist in London, Redding was sent to Paris in 1814, where he was based for five years. There he was introduced to wine regions and a wine-producing culture. Jullien's book was published two years after Redding's arrival in Paris, and his own most important work, *A History and Description of Modern Wines*, written in 1833 when he had returned to England, takes full account of both Jullien and CHAPTAL's previous publications but seems to have been independently inspired by the disparity between the wines then available in Britain (see ADULTERATION) and what he tasted in cellars all over Europe. Like Jullien, he was an intrepid traveller, and his book includes observations not just on European wines but on those of Asia, Africa, and both North and South America. His emphasis on the word 'Modern' owes much to his criticism of earlier writers such as Sir Edward Barry and Alexander HENDERSON (see LITERATURE OF WINE), whose reverence for CLASSICAL WINES he felt was misplaced.

Red Hills, California AVA. See LAKE COUNTY.

Redondo, DOC subregion in central ALENTEJO in southern Portugal whose consistent climate owes much to the sheltering influence of the Serra d'Ossa.

redox potential, or **oxidation–reduction potential**, is in theory a measure of the summation of all of a wine's components' potentials to oxidize. Since wine is made up of components that are either oxidized or reduced (see OXIDATION and REDUCTION), it is a system composed of many joined redox pairs. Oxidation reactions are always coupled to reduction reactions. Electrons made available from an oxidation are taken up by the compound being reduced until an equilibrium is established. The reaction with the most positive value (in which electrons are most easily accepted) will occur at the expense of reactions with lower values. Thus an equilibrium is reached from all the redox pairs and a net redox potential can be determined.

Redox potentials are of only limited value to even the most scientific winemaker, however, since they do not express how rapidly the various reactions will occur. They reveal only the potential situation that will obtain given unlimited time. Redox potentials can also prove to be difficult to measure in practice, and the ability of standard methods to measure the wine's redox chemistry have been disputed. A determination of the concentration of dissolved OXYGEN in a given wine can often prove to be of more value in guiding the winemaker in his or her choice of cellar treatments. A.L.W.

Danilewicz, J. C., et al., 'Wine reduction potentials: are these measured values really reduction potentials?', *Journal of Agricultural Food Chemistry*, 67/15 (2019), 4145–53.

reduced-alcohol wine. See ALCOHOL REDUCTION and LOW-ALCOHOL WINE.

reducing sugars are sugars that can act as very mild reducing agents (see REDOX and REDUCTION). In wine, GLUCOSE and FRUCTOSE are the primary reducing sugars. See also RESIDUAL SUGAR, which shares the same abbreviation but has a different meaning.

reduction, chemical reaction that is in effect the complement of OXIDATION and one in which an element or compound gains electrons. The essential feature of an oxidation is that electrons are transferred from the component being oxidized to the one being **reduced**. The reaction cannot be isolated; to have a reduction, something else must be oxidized. Common reduction reactions are those of iron ore to iron the metal, or the reduction of ACETALDEHYDE to ETHANOL as happens in the final stage of alcoholic FERMENTATION. Wine in a stoppered bottle or other airtight container is said to be in a **reductive** state.

Reducing conditions are desirable towards the end of fermentation so that alcohol is produced along with the carbon dioxide from the acetaldehyde. Reducing conditions are also generally preferable throughout ÉLEVAGE of wine in the cellar, especially for white wines, which can withstand oxidation much less well than reds with their higher content of PHENOLICS.

Wines, especially red wines held in the absence of oxygen, may suffer from excess reduction, resulting in the slow POLYMERIZATION of TANNINS and PIGMENTED TANNINS. **Reduction** and **reductive** are also used as convenient, but rather loose, terms to describe the perception of SULFIDES in wine by a taster (see MINERALITY). The presence of sulfides is usually considered to be a wine FAULT, although sulfur compounds can add complexity at lower levels, depending on the wine style. In some cases, reduction faults can be cured by AERATION, perhaps careful RACKING, an operation which introduces some oxygen, an oxidizing agent strong enough to prevent the reduction of most sulfur compounds.

Reduction has become a much-debated topic in the wine trade since the more widespread adoption of tin-lined SCREWCAPS as closures. While this phenomenon is not caused by screwcaps, the low permeability of screwcaps is less forgiving to wines with residual sulfides at bottling. Very good corks typically show a similar level of permeability to that of screwcaps (see OXYGEN TRANSMISSION RATE). See also REDOX POTENTIAL. V.L. & M.J.T

Goode, J., *Wine Science: The Application of Science in Wine* (3rd edn, 2021).

reductive winemaking, the use of various techniques to minimize the presence of oxygen in GRAPE JUICE and/or wine. Such techniques include the addition of SULFUR DIOXIDE with or without ASCORBIC ACID, blanketing of juice trays and tanks with INERT GAS, and SPARGING with nitrogen during all transfers. This approach, which can enhance the fruitiness of wines, is typically used when the winemaker wants to protect delicate flavours and their FLAVOUR PRECURSORS from OXIDATION. However, it means that PHENOLIC compounds are also protected from oxidation and cannot therefore be removed prior to fermentation so that the final wines can show more bitterness and require more FINING. See REDUCTION for the common but inexact use of 'reductive' as a tasting term. M.J.T.

red winemaking, the production of wines with reddish to purple colours. The great majority of today's red wines depend on CRUSHING and DESTEMMING of the grape clusters as a first step in their production (but see also WHOLE-BUNCH FERMENTATION and CARBONIC MACERATION).

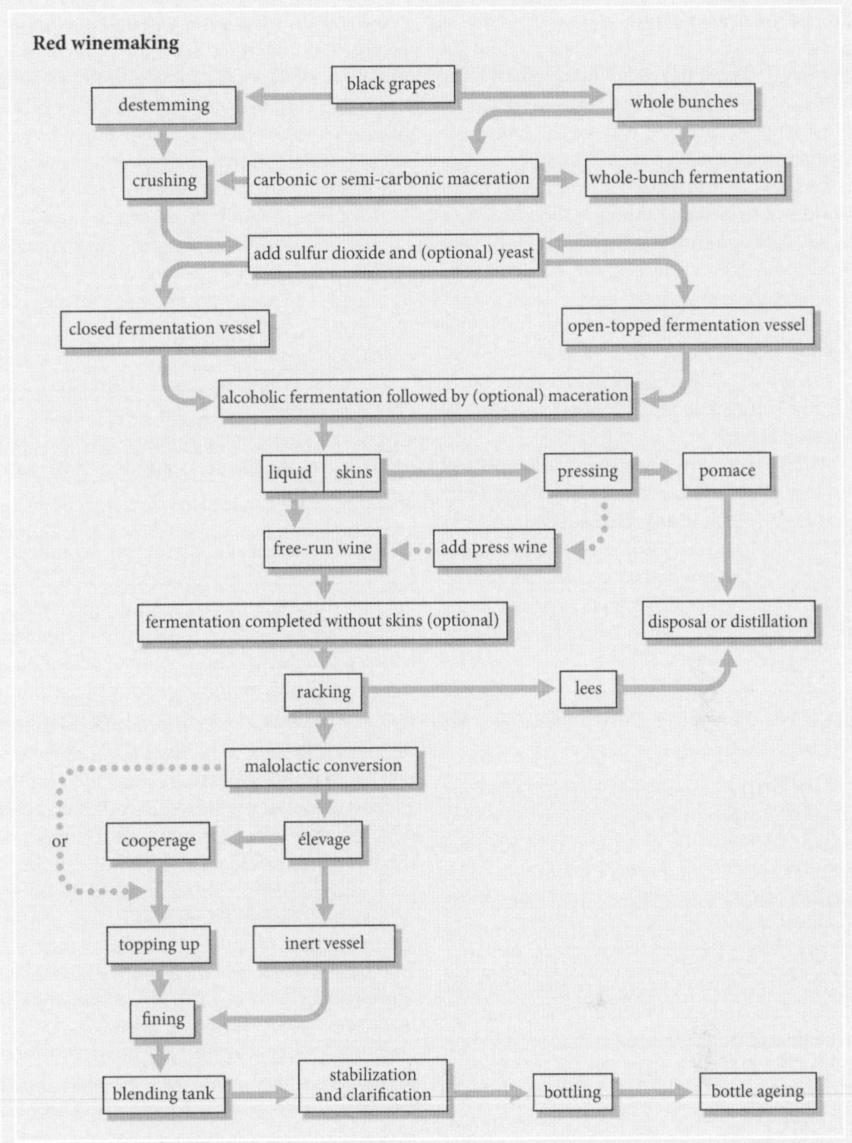

The mixture of skins, seeds, and occasionally some stem fragments, along with the juice, then goes into a FERMENTATION VESSEL, where YEAST converts SUGARS into ALCOHOL. The natural ANTHOCYANIN pigments, which are contained in the skins of black grapes, along with FLAVOUR COMPOUNDS, FLAVOUR PRECURSORS, and large amounts of PHENOLICS (the latter originating from both the skins and the seeds) are extracted into the fermenting wine by the alcohol produced by yeast during FERMENTATION and MACERATION. Without some maceration of juice and skins, wine made from dark-skinned grapes is merely pink (as described in ROSÉ WINEMAKING). Duration of this EXTRACTION process can be anything from a fast two- or three-day fermentation for an everyday wine to a week-long fermentation followed by a further one, two, or even three weeks' maceration for a full-bodied red wine that is designed to age.

Red-wine fermentations are almost always conducted at TEMPERATURES higher than those used for white wines. Red wines fermented at lower temperatures tend to be lighter in colour and body and to display the fruitier range of ESTERS. Some producers deliberately fashion light reds in this style to be consumed chilled.

Red winemaking differs from white winemaking not only in terms of skin–juice contact and temperature but also because some exposure to OXYGEN is more generally desirable than with white wines; BARREL AGEING, or at least CASK AGEING, is also more common for red wines than white. The phenolic compounds extracted from skins, seeds, and stem fragments react more or less slowly with oxygen dissolved in the wine to form PIGMENTED TANNINS, and these, together with the colourless TANNINS that were extracted directly or formed during the maceration, contribute to the TEXTURE of the wine. Another important difference between red and white winemaking is that most red wines undergo MALOLACTIC CONVERSION whereas with whites it is generally a deliberate choice on the part of the winemaker, related to factors such as grape variety, the level of ACIDITY in the grapes, and the intended wine style.

During barrel ageing, when the oxygen supply to the wine is restricted, both the substances produced in the earlier reactions between grape phenolics and oxygen and those derived from extraction of the wood phenolics interact and contribute an entirely new range of flavours (see OAK FLAVOUR).

Further reactions of the grape- and wood-derived phenolic constituents, and augmentation of the grape-derived flavour compounds, all progress during AGEING in bottle. The abundance and great diversity of compounds available in a red wine are the reasons that ageing assumes particular importance for fine red wines. See also WINEMAKING. P.J.W.

red wines actually vary in COLOUR from dark pink to almost black, with an enormous variation in the amount of blue or yellow to be seen at the rim. Their colour depends on the grape varieties used, the vintage characteristics, the health of the grapes, the winemaking methods (in particular the extent of MACERATION and the method of EXTRACTION), the wine's PH, and the amount of time it has spent in tank, barrel, and bottle. A red wine that has suffered OXIDATION or is many decades old may be the same deep tawny colour as a very old white wine.

Red wines are produced in virtually all of the world's wine regions, although the proportion of red wines produced at the cool limit of wine production is low, since it can be difficult to develop sufficient pigmentation of most grapes' skins to produce a proper red wine (although see also TEINTURIERS).

French for red is *rouge*, Italian is *rosso*, Spanish and Portuguese more expressively *tinto*, and German is *rot*.

It has been only since the development of BOTTLES suitable for AGEING wine that red wines have been seen as in any sense superior to white (see ancient GREECE, ROME, medieval ITALY, and FASHION). A general market preoccupation with white wines in the 1970s was overtaken in the 1990s by what was called the **red-wine boom**, encouraged in the US by a TV programme about the FRENCH PARADOX and by a belief in the emerging markets of ASIA that red wine was HEALTHIER.

reflection from soils and in some cases from water is considered by some to influence wine quality. 'Albedo' is the term which describes reflectance of SUNLIGHT. Very white soils, such as the ALBARIZA soils of JEREZ, have high albedo and so can add to the heating of vines growing on them. This is easy to demonstrate by calculation. More difficult to prove or measure is the theory that sunlight reflected from rivers may benefit nearby vineyards, as in the Mosel Valley. While the eye can behold the silvery sheen of water at low sun angles (specular reflection), it is unlikely that this can have any significant warming effect on adjacent vineyards. R.E.S.

Refosco is a group of distinct red varieties cultivated in north-east Italy, Slovenia, and Croatia producing very similar wines. The finest variety is known in Friuli as REFOSCO DAL PEDUNCOLO ROSSO, but others include Refosco d'Istria (also called TERAN, Terrano, and Refošk).

Refosco dal Peduncolo Rosso, named after its red stem, is a member of the REFOSCO group of red grape varieties that makes usefully vigorous wine in the FRIULI region of north-east Italy. It has a long history in the area, apparently praised by PLINY the Elder and reputedly producing the favourite wine of Livia, the second wife of Augustus Caesar, cited in the *Annals of Friuli* of Francesco di Manzano in 1390. DNA PROFILING at SAN MICHELE ALL'ADIGE revealed a parent–offspring relationship with MARZEMINO, another ancient variety of northern Italy.

This vine is cultivated both in HILLSIDE VINEYARDS and in flatter parts of Friuli and gives a deeply coloured wine with plummy flavours and a hint of almonds, a medium to full body, and rather elevated ACIDITY, which can be difficult to control or moderate, the variety being a notoriously late ripener. Refosco has the advantage of good resistance to autumn rains and ROT.

There was a significant return of interest in Friuli's Refosco in the 1980s, and much greater care was taken in its cultivation and vinification in an effort to improve the wine's quality, although total plantings in 2015 were only 1,267 ha/3,131 acres.

The most promising zone for Refosco is FRIULI COLLI ORIENTALI and the Koper district in SLOVENIA. Others include FRIULI GRAVE, LISON-PRAMAGGIORE (in the area outside Friuli), Latisana, and Aquileia.

refractometer, an instrument for measuring a refractive index, which is related to the amount by which the angle of a light wave is changed when passing through the boundary between two media. The amount of refraction is a convenient way to measure solute concentration of a solution and is widely used in viticulture and winemaking to follow the ripeness of grapes (by measuring MUST WEIGHT) and changes during vinification. Refractometers may be precision laboratory instruments or pocket versions that can be used in the vineyard. In either case, TEMPERATURE correction or control is important for accuracy. B.G.C.

refrigeration, cooling process that has had a profound effect on how and where wine is made and how it tastes (see TEMPERATURE), enabling the winemaker to have a much greater degree of control than was possible before mechanical refrigeration became the norm for all but the least sophisticated wineries in the second half of the 20th century. More than any other factor, refrigeration has permitted warm and hot regions to produce wine of internationally acceptable quality.

Making wine

The essence of refrigeration is the transfer of heat from the body being refrigerated to some other place. The most obvious winery application of refrigeration is in the TEMPERATURE CONTROL of FERMENTATION—although refrigeration also allows winemakers to delay the processing of freshly picked grapes or must (see MUST CHILLING) until convenient, even in hot areas, where the use of chilled rooms to cool and store grapes prior to pressing has increased. The energy generated by the conversion of sugar to alcohol, carbon dioxide, and water is only partly used by the YEAST in building cells and by-products. The rest appears as heat, which, above a certain temperature, risks killing the yeast and therefore arresting the fermentation process. The amount of heat generated by fermentation is large: for example, 10 hl/260 gal of grape juice containing 20% sugar will generate about 3.6 million kilocalories, or enough to melt 45 tons of ice.

Not all the heat generated has to be removed by refrigeration, however. Because heat moves naturally by conduction from hotter bodies to cooler ones with which they are in contact, warm fermenting wine loses heat to the walls of the FERMENTATION VESSEL and from the outside of the wall to the atmosphere. Some of the fermentation heat will be removed by radiation from the outside of the fermenting vessel too, provided its temperature is higher than that of the objects in its vicinity. Heat may also be lost by radiation if open-topped fermentation vessels are used or by volatilization of some of the water and alcohol in the wine.

All of these natural heat-removal processes that function independently of refrigeration occur at the surfaces of the fermenting mass. Heat production, on the other hand, occurs throughout the entire volume of the mass. The amount of heat removed from a fermenting mass therefore depends on the surface-to-volume ratio of the fermentation vessel. A 225-l/59-gal BARRIQUE, for example, will probably lose enough generated heat for the temperature to remain within an acceptable range for fermentation. A typical large tank, on the other hand, which might contain several hundred hectolitres, will certainly need active heat removal to keep the temperature of the fermenting mass below danger point.

The development of mechanical refrigeration in the early 20th century made cooling at least a possibility in areas where insufficient naturally cold water was available. Early efforts to control temperature, used in France as recently as the 1970s, included the simple addition of blocks of ice to the fermenting wine (with concomitant dilution). More mechanical early systems of refrigeration cooled the wine by running cold water through metal tubes suspended in the tank. The development of more efficient PUMPS permitted systems which moved wine from the tank through coils immersed in cold water and then back into the tank.

In modern wineries, however, wines are seldom moved for cooling purposes. STAINLESS STEEL tanks with cooling devices, usually coils, inside the tank and cooling jackets incorporated in the external walls are now standard wine equipment. Temperature-sensing probes in tanks signal a computer system which controls the supply of refrigerant to the coils to a level predetermined for each tank by the winemaker.

Refrigeration has become increasingly important in other winemaking processes, however. Some producers, notably in Australia, store grape juice in refrigerated conditions for several months before fermentation. Pre-fermentation cold MACERATION occasionally calls for refrigeration too. In warmer wine regions, some degree of refrigeration may be needed during wine maturation, and refrigerated tanks are routinely used for everyday wines to ensure that TARTRATES are not precipitated in bottle (see STABILIZATION). A.D.W.

Serving wine

Refrigeration plays a part, and all too often a villainous part, in the SERVING of wine. Long before the advent of mechanical refrigeration, and its domestication, wine was deliberately chilled prior to serving (see ancient GREECE, for example). It was fashionable to chill both red and white wines before serving at least from the 16th century. A wide range of wine coolers was used to achieve this until the 20th century, when mechanical refrigeration was domestically available. The modern successors of these large containers for both ice and bottles are the single-bottle wine coolers known as ice buckets and the gel-filled flexible sleeves kept frozen and ready for use.

See also TEMPERATURE.

regenerative viticulture, a system for growing wine grapes that follows the principles of regenerative agriculture, an approach not yet widely defined in regulatory terms and also known as agro-ecology. Advocates of this increasingly discussed approach suggest that it regenerates rather than depletes agricultural land by building soil ORGANIC MATTER to mitigate and undo the adverse consequences of conventional farming and CLIMATE CHANGE. Practices include planting multispecies COVER CROPS in the mid rows to sequester carbon from the atmosphere and put it back into the soil, keeping mid rows and under-vine soil covered by MULCH or sympathetic plants, avoiding soil disturbance (see NO-TILL), increasing biodiversity on the farm, using organic products to promote microbially rich soils (see SOIL BIOTA) with healthy MYCORRHIZAL fungal networks, and carefully grazing cattle and sheep for organic matter and weed management. I.S.-B.

Newton, P., et al., 'What is regenerative agriculture? A review of scholar and practitioner definitions based on processes and outcomes', *Frontiers in Sustainable Food Systems*, 4 (2020), 194.

Regent, particularly successful dark-skinned DISEASE-RESISTANT VARIETY bred at Geilweilerhof in Germany and first registered in 1989. This complex HYBRID of a SILVANER × MÜLLER-THURGAU cross with CHAMBOURCIN reaches full ripeness easily and makes wine with good colour and moderate ACIDITY. It is grown on a total of 1,722 ha/4,255 acres in Germany, particularly in Rheinhessen and the Pfalz, and is also planted in Switzerland, England, Belgium, Scandinavia, and New Mexico.

Reggiano, a DOC in EMILIA-ROMAGNA that used to be called Lambrusco Reggiano until its name was changed to allow the production of still and sparkling reds of up to 60% ANCELLOTTA. (It is notable that total plantings of Ancellotta in Emilia-Romagna in 2017 were 4,300 ha/10,626 acres, almost as much as the 4,635 ha of the most planted LAMBRUSCO, Salamino—presumably a reflection of producers' desire to add colour from the deep-tinted Ancellotta grape to their various Lambrusco grapes.) A wide range of Lambrusco varieties as well as Sangiovese, Cabernet Sauvignon, and Merlot are allowed in DOC Reggiano. YIELDS may be as high as 140 hl/ha. W.S.

Região Demarcada, **(RD)**, Portuguese for 'demarcated region', although the expression is no longer seen on labels. See DOC for more details.

regionality, NEW WORLD term for the concept, now fully accepted there, that the location of a vineyard plays an important part in shaping the character of the wine produced from it. It is less geographically precise and, importantly, less French than the term TERROIR, although the latter is increasingly used worldwide.

More and more wines in, for example, California and Australia, where the word was coined, are labelled and marketed on a geographical as well as VARIETAL basis, even if many producers are wary of the restrictions that would ensue from CONTROLLED APPELLATIONS.

régisseur, French term used particularly to refer to the director or manager of a Bordeaux estate.

Régnié, the most recently created BEAUJOLAIS cru (in 1988), out of land in the neighbouring communes of Régnié-Durette and Lantignié. In a way this was rectifying past oversights: both towns historically had parcels as respected as some in neighbouring CHIROUBLES or BROUILLY. With 391 ha/966 acres under vine, it continues to grow in prominence, its sandy and stony GRANITIC soils both interesting and affordable—especially in the hilly western portion, where ELEVATION and ASPECT conspire to merge its typically fragrant, subtle character with more STRUCTURE. J.F.B.

Reguengos, subregion of the ALENTEJO in southern Portugal, home to a successful CO-OPERATIVE winery and ORGANIC pioneer Herdade do Esporão.

regulated deficit irrigation **(RDI)**, an IRRIGATION scheduling technique which uses mild WATER STRESS at key stages of fruit development to reduce vegetative growth and improve berry RIPENING and thus improve grape quality.

RDI was first applied on peach and pear orchards in Australia in the 1980s. Research showed that it restricted SHOOT growth without significantly affecting YIELD. It is now common practice in many vineyards around the world, especially in those planted to black grape varieties, due to the greater benefits to grape colour.

The main benefits of this strategically managed water stress are less competition between berry ripening and vegetative growth, better water conservation, and reduced BERRY SIZE. Successful application requires careful monitoring of EVAPOTRANSPIRATION and SOIL WATER content and typically results in slightly lower yields. It is most effectively applied through DRIP IRRIGATION, which allows the application of small amounts of water at frequent intervals.

RDI is more stressful to the vine than PARTIAL ROOTZONE DRYING, and its use in hot regions can cause problems if its application is followed by a spell of hot, windy weather with low humidity: vines with limited soil moisture can suffer extremes of water stress, which may, for example, lead to leaf desiccation and even loss of leaves. This situation can be alleviated by carefully monitoring weather forecasts and applying some irrigation.

Water deficit is generally applied from the time berries are pea-sized to a week or so after VERAISON but is generally avoided in the later stages of berry ripening. J.E.H. & R.E.S.

Iland, P., et al., 'Water, soil and the vine', in *The Grapevine: From the Science to the Practice of Growing Vines for Wine* (2011).

Pritchard, T., et al., 'Irrigation Management of Winegrapes with a Limited Water Supply', *UC Drought Management: Winegrapes*. www.ucmanagedrought.ucdavis.edu/Agriculture/Crop_Irrigation_Strategies/Winegrapes.

R

Reichensteiner, white grape variety whose GEISENHEIM creator Heinrich Birk maintained was the first EU CROSS, with French, Italian, and German antecedents. In 1939 he developed this cross of MÜLLER-THURGAU with a cross of the French table grape MADELEINE ANGEVINE and the Italian Calabre. Both wine and vine most closely resemble its undistinguished German parent, but Reichensteiner with its looser bunches is less prone to ROT, and well-pruned plants stand a good chance of reaching Prädikatswein must weights in good years (see PRÄDIKAT). Just 37 ha/91 acres remained in Germany in 2020. Also planted in England and to a limited extent in Switzerland, Japan, and British Columbia. Along with GAMAY, it is a parent of the Swiss crossings GAMARET, GARANOIR, and Mara.

religion and wine. The relationship between religion and wine is as ancient as wine itself.

The earliest archaeological evidence of wine (see ORIGINS OF VINICULTURE) goes back to ancient China, though we know little of the relationship between religion and wine at that time. Our earliest archaeological evidence of religion and wine is found in ancient Egyptian pictorial records (see EGYPT) and Hittite texts and images. These ancient civilizations were profoundly attuned to the spiritual world and used wine in their religious cults, rituals, and celebrations. They offered up wine as LIBATIONS, their priests drank wine, and they placed sealed wine jars in royal and priestly tombs, presumably in preparation for the afterlife.

In the ancient world, agricultural products including wine were seen as gifts from the gods. The Greeks, Etruscans, and Romans even had their own wine gods—Dionysus, Fufluns, and Bacchus, respectively—to whom they offered libations. Various cults developed around the worship of the Greek god of DIONYSUS, often accompanied by religious seasonal festivals and celebrations, and at certain times and places these included ritual dancing, theatrical performance, DRUNKENNESS, and ecstasy. Wine was widely used for medicinal purposes and placed in tombs for the afterlife. Wine was also linked to the pursuit of truth, as the Greek phrase *in vino veritas* suggests. The Greek SYMPOSIUM, however, was a secular affair devoid of religious rituals.

We know little about the Etruscan wine god Fufluns. The Roman god of wine, BACCHUS (Latin from Dionysus), was celebrated in religious rituals, festivals, and processions. Images of Bacchus appear in Roman mosaics, where he is depicted with a lyre player celebrating the kinship between wine and music. Bacchus also adorned Roman tombs and sarcophagi, anticipating and preparing the deceased for the afterlife.

The connection between wine and religion was likewise important in pre-Islamic PERSIA. The mystical poetry of the 14th-century poet Hafez of Shiraz harks back to ancient Persia, and his poetry speaks of ruby red wine in the goblet as a symbol for divine radiance, and the wine shop as an image for the realm of angels.

The most comprehensive understanding of wine and religion can be found in Judaism and Christianity, as recorded in the BIBLE, where wine is described as a blessing from God with the explicit purpose of 'gladdening' people's hearts. They seem to be the only religions practised today that ascribe significant religious import to wine and actively use it in their religious celebrations (the Passover and the EUCHARIST).

Inspired by the Bible and the need for wine in the Eucharist, Christian monks and nuns played a central role in developing viticulture and wine in Europe and beyond. By the 12th century, monasteries were the largest producers of wine in Europe. (See MONKS AND MONASTERIES for further details.)

The theme of wine in the Bible became an inspiration for artists as they carved vines into the stone pillars that upheld some of the great cathedrals of Europe and made stained-glass windows for these cathedrals and churches depicting the spies with a grape cluster returning from the Promised Land (Num. 13. 21–7). In the later Middle Ages, depictions of Christ in the wine PRESS became popular, as did paintings of Jesus celebrating the Lord's Supper with his disciples. Western art history is saturated with biblical imagery, and the theme of wine has a central place in it.

To this day, winemakers such as Aubert de Villaine from DOMAINE DE LA ROMANÉE-CONTI and Tim Mondavi from Continuum take inspiration from the Bible and from the medieval monks and nuns whose passion was to make wine to glorify God—wines that lift attentive drinkers out of the mundane and inspire them towards a sense of wonder, awe, and reverence. G.K.

Hyams, E., *Dionysus: A Social History of the Wine Vine* (1987).
Kreglinger, G., *The Spirituality of Wine* (2016).
Varriano, J., *Wine: A Cultural History* (2010).
Younger, W., *Gods, Men, and Wine* (1966).

remontage, French word for various systems of PUMPING OVER.

The term may also be used in French for soil replacement after erosion in vineyards (see SOIL EROSION).

remote sensing is the detection and/or measurement of features on the Earth's surface using sensors mounted on satellite, aircraft or DRONE platforms. Its application in viticulture is almost entirely confined to the inference of VIGOUR and CANOPY condition. This is achieved by sensing the amount of SUNLIGHT that is reflected from a vineyard in the visible (blue, green, red) and near infrared parts of the electromagnetic spectrum and calculating ratios between them. Commonly used indices in viticulture are PLANT CELL DENSITY (PCD) and the NORMALIZED DIFFERENCE VEGETATION INDEX (NDVI). Research has shown VERAISON to be the optimal time to acquire remotely sensed imagery of vineyards, especially with respect to its use in PRECISION VITICULTURE or ZONAL VITICULTURE to underpin SELECTIVE HARVESTING. However, more frequent acquisition of imagery may be needed when the objective is to assess vine water status to support IRRIGATION management. R.G.V.B.

Gautam, D., and Pagay, V., 'A review of current and potential applications of remote sensing to study the water status of horticultural crops', *Agronomy*, 10/1 (2020), 140.
Hall, A., et al., 'Optical remote sensing applications in viticulture–a review', *Australian Journal of Grape and Wine Research*, 8/1 (2008), 36–47.
Knipper, K. R., et al., 'Evapotranspiration estimates derived using thermal-based satellite remote sensing and data fusion for irrigation management in California vineyards', *Irrigation Science*, 37 (2019), 431–49.

remuage is French for the RIDDLING process. A person or machine that performs **remuage** is a **remueur**.

rendement, French for YIELD, usually expressed in hl/ha.

rendzina, a term, originally Polish, used in some soil classifications for a dark, well-drained soil formed on CALCAREOUS bedrock. Typically, rendzina soils are recently developed, stony, and thin, showing a distinctive natural vegetation. They are common on the LIMESTONES and CHALKS of England and France, as well as in Eastern Europe. A.J.M.

research into grape-growing and wine production is officially and principally in the domain of academe, although some individual viticulturists and winemakers are more prone to experimentation and more subject to the rigour of SCIENCE than others. For a list of important wine research institutions, see ACADEME.

Reserva, term used in both Spain and Portugal to distinguish wines from a supposedly good vintage. In Portugal, a Reserva is a wine from a single vintage with outstanding organoleptic characteristics and an ALCOHOLIC STRENGTH at least 0.5% above the regional minimum. In Spain, a red wine labelled Reserva will have had at least three years' AGEING in cask and bottle, with at least a year of this period in OAK (*barricas* are stipulated for Rioja). Spanish white and rosé wines labelled Reserva must spend a total of at least two years in cask and bottle to qualify, including at least least six months in oak.

See also GRAN RESERVA.

Reserve is a term liberally used by wine producers for various bottlings and one that should indeed be reserved for superior wines. However, unlike RESERVA and RISERVA, the English term 'Reserve' has few controls on its use. Some wineries release several bottlings incorporating the word in their names (Proprietor's Reserve, Estate Reserve, Reserve Selection, Private Reserve, Vintner's Reserve, and the like). The (unregulated) French term is **Réserve** leading to the use of terms such as **Cuvée de Réserve**. In CHAMPAGNE, reserve wines are those held over from a given year for future blending, typically into the NON-VINTAGE cuvée.

residual sugar, occasionally **RS**, the total quantity of SUGARS remaining unfermented in a finished wine. This may include both fermentable sugars, mainly GLUCOSE and FRUCTOSE, which have for some reason (see below) remained unconverted to alcohol during FERMENTATION, and small amounts of those few sugars which are not readily fermented by typical wine YEAST. Some, but by no means all, residual sugar is tasted as SWEETNESS. REDUCING SUGARS, a term used by both the EU and the OIV, refers to all the sugars measured in a finished wine, including residual sugar and any sugars added post fermentation (e.g. in the form of SWEET RESERVE).

Residual sugar in wine is usually measured in grams of total sugars per litre of wine and can vary between about 1 g/l (0.1%) and 150 g/l (15%) or more. Wines with a residual sugar content of less than 2 g/l, such as the great majority of red wines and many white wines that do not taste at all sweet, are generally described as 'dry' (but see SWEETNESS for some more specific definitions). It is rare to find a wine with much less than 1 g/l residual sugar because some sugars are almost invariably impervious to the action of the yeasts. On the other hand, some wines with a residual sugar level even as high as 25 g/l may taste dry because the sweetness is offset by high ACIDITY. Some ordinary wines (usually white) that are naturally high in acids may have sugars (usually the particularly sweet fructose), sweet GRAPE JUICE, or sweet RECTIFIED GRAPE MUST added deliberately to increase their palatability or commercial appeal (see SWEET RESERVE).

Exceptionally sweet wines may be produced either in extraordinarily ripe years or by unusual winemaking techniques such as those involved in freeze CONCENTRATION or in BOTRYTIZED or DRIED-GRAPE WINES. The sweetest form of the unique Hungarian sweet wine TOKAJI, for example, must have a minimum residual sugar of 250 g/l—the 1947 vintage of Tokaji Essencia managed 488 g/l.

Sugar levels in grapes are measured as MUST WEIGHT by various different scales, of which BAUMÉ, BRIX, and OECHSLE are the most common.

One German wine harvested at Nussdorf in the Pfalz in 1971 was picked at 326 °Oechsle, or about 870 g/l sugar, and had reached only 4.5% alcohol in a particularly slow fermentation 20 years later, producing a wine with about 480 g/l residual sugar.

Between 16 and 17 g/l of sugar are required to produce 1% of alcohol in white and rosé wines, and about 18 g/l in reds.

There are many reasons why fermentable sugars may remain unfermented: yeasts vary enormously in their potency, especially their tolerance of higher sugar and higher alcohol concentrations; grape MUSTS vary in their micronutrient and growth-factor content; low TEMPERATURES and chemical additions can also arrest fermentation; and, probably the most influential factor, the expertise of the winemaker plays a deciding role.

Residual sugar presents no great danger in a wine that is yet to be processed in BULK, but in a bottled wine the presence of such sugars may cause FERMENTATION IN BOTTLE. Small amounts of sugar are furthermore readily used by yeast or BACTERIA to produce unwanted ACETIC ACID, off-flavours, and, sometimes, CARBON DIOXIDE gas. The winemaker therefore must ensure either that a wine is effectively free of fermentable sugars (less than 0.2 g/l) for dry wines or that, in the case of most sweet and medium-dry wines, the wine undergoes full STABILIZATION against the risk of further microbiological activity. This can be achieved by FILTRATION. A.D.W.

residues. Residues of AGROCHEMICALS, the commercial preparations used in vineyards for the control of pests, diseases, or weeds, are that portion which is found on the grapes at harvest or in wine. The time between permitted last application and harvest, known as the 'withholding period', commonly results in degradation of the agrochemical. Most of any residue borne on the grapes at harvest is likely to be eliminated with the skins after PRESSING, and more is removed or degraded during juice CLARIFICATION, FERMENTATION, and subsequent FILTRATION.

PESTICIDES may leave deposits or by-products that persist in plant or animal tissues or in soil, water, or air. Some pesticides are rapidly inactivated after application; others (or their by-products) may persist for years. Such residual contamination may affect human or livestock health, limit subsequent crop growth, and pollute the environment. Excessive or illegal pesticide residues in wine may lead to rejection on domestic and/or international markets, perhaps as a result of the use of inappropriate pesticides, incorrect application methods, or application too close to harvest. Residue effects on non-target organisms should also be considered. Useful insects such as bees or natural parasites and predators of insect pests (see ECOSYSTEM) may be affected by pesticide residues.

FUNGICIDE residues may inhibit fermentation by YEAST, as discussed by Caboni and Cabras, but extensive trials have shown that the proper use of fungicides has no adverse effect on the taste or smell of wines, although residues of elemental SULFUR used to prevent FUNGAL DISEASE in the vineyard can be transformed, in REDUCING conditions (see REDUCTION), into foul-smelling HYDROGEN SULFIDE.

Maximum residue limits (MRLs) are established by governments for particular agrochemicals or their metabolites (breakdown products) in particular foodstuffs. MRLs are typically set at levels which are not likely to be exceeded if the chemicals are used in accordance with good agricultural practice and if a dietary-exposure evaluation shows no undue hazard to human health, although some winegrowers and consumers firmly reject the suggestion that even a very low level of residues is safe. Trade in wine internationally can be hindered when markets differ in their MRLs. See also AGROCHEMICALS. R.E.S. & M.E.

Caboni, P., and Cabras, P., 'Pesticides' influence on wine fermentation', *Advances in Food and Nutrition Research*, 59 (2010), 43–62.

resinated wines. Of the earthenware vessels in which the ancient Greeks and Romans kept their wines (see AMPHORAE), only the very best were airtight. Normally they were porous, and it is clear from the Roman writers on agriculture that the insides of jars were therefore coated with resin. It was therefore probably as a purely practical measure that resin was initially used. But soon people must have discovered that the wine would keep even better if they added resin to the wine itself. COLUMELLA deals at length with the different kinds of resin that can be employed in this way (*De re rustica* 13. 20–14), but he emphasizes that the best wines should not have resin put into them. Yet many people came to like the taste of resin and used it not only as a preservative but also as a flavouring agent. PLINY recommends that resin should be added to the fermenting MUST (*Natural History* 14. 124) and discusses which kinds of resin are best: resin from mountainous regions has a more pleasant smell than resin from low-lying areas (16. 60).

The Romans abandoned amphorae in favour of wooden casks in the 3rd century CE because BARRELS were lighter and easier to handle. Wooden casks do not need an inside coating of resin, and this saved the winemaker time and money. Thus the Romans ceased to make resinated wines. Winemakers in Transalpine Gaul, most of whom did not have pine trees nearby, and those of Cisalpine Gaul, Illyria, and the alpine region, where the climate is cooler and wood does not crack so easily, had started using wooden casks in the 1st century CE. Unlike the West, however, Byzantium did not lose its taste for resin when it was no longer needed as a preservative. The pine forests of the eastern part of central Greece and of Euboea still provided the resin to enhance the flavour of some Greek wines after the 7th century.

This was very much not to the taste of one Western visitor to Constantinople. In 968 Liudprand, bishop of Cremona, was sent there to arrange a marriage between the daughter of the late Emperor Romanos and the son of his own patron, Otto I, the Holy Roman Emperor. The mission was not a success. The Emperor Nicephorus treated Liudprand rudely and kept him a virtual prisoner. Liudprand's *De legatione Constantinopolitana* ('The mission to Constantinople') was his revenge. He has not a good word to say for the Byzantines in general and Nicephorus in particular. The work is a masterpiece of invective, and, since Liudprand's purpose is satirical, we should not believe his every word. But his observations on the food and wine he had are interesting. Horrified, he relates how he was given goat stuffed with onions, garlic, and leeks, swimming in fish sauce. Worst of all, and mentioned in his very first chapter, is the wine: undrinkable because it is mixed with resin, pitch, and gypsum. Like the fish sauce, this would not be remarkable in the least to an ancient Roman, but it was not a thing to serve a modern Lombard. Of course, Liudprand may have also encountered perfectly decent, unresinated wine at times during his enforced stay, but it would have spoilt his story to tell us about that.

Still, not all Greek wine was resinated in the Middle Ages. The strong, sweet wines that reached the markets of western Europe were not, but pilgrims travelling to the Holy Land recounted that some local wines were. The account of Pietro Casola, who sailed to Jerusalem in 1494, stopping frequently along the way, is particularly valuable because he takes pains to describe the customs, food, and wines of every region. He often speaks of the excellent sweet wines in Greece, but in Modone, on the southwestern tip of the Peloponnese (near Monemvasia, which gave its name to MALVASIA), he is given a wine that has had resin added to it during fermentation in order, he explains, to preserve it. He objects to its strong unpleasant odour but goes on to describe the fine Malmsey, Muscatel, and Tumney of Modone. Of Cyprus he says that he loves everything about it except the wine, which has resin in it. He must have been unlucky not to have tasted the famous sweet wines that Cyprus exported, but an earlier account by an anonymous French cleric, *Le Voyage de la Saincte Cyte de Hierusalem* of 1480, confirms what he observes about Cyprus and Modone.

See RETSINA for details of modern resinated wine. H.M.W.

Newett, M. M., *Canon Pietro Casola's Pilgrimage to Jerusalem in the Year 1494* (1907).

The Works of Liudprand of Cremona, translated by F. A. Wright (1930).

resins used in winemaking are natural or synthetic materials usually composed of long chains of simpler molecules that are capable of POLYMERIZING. Gum acacia is a natural resin used to stabilize the PIGMENTS in red wine. Another natural resin is Aleppo pine resin, which is used in the preparation of RETSINA.

Synthetic resins, manufactured by polymerization processes, have several uses in winemaking. One of the commonest is epoxy resin, which can be used in the form of a two-part paint for coating the inside of CONCRETE vats, producing an inert and easily cleaned surface. Epoxy-resin compounds are also used for surfacing floors in wineries and bottling halls, being much more resistant than concrete to the acids in wine.

Silicone resins are used in the manufacture of BUNGS for wooden BARRELS; they have the flexibility of rubber but are TAINT-free and non-perishable.

ION EXCHANGE resins can be used in some countries for TARTRATE stabilization and for the manipulation of PH. They are prepared in the form of small beads which are packed into a vertical cylindrical tank known as a column, through which the wine is passed. The particular property of these resins is their ability to exchange the ions which are loosely held on their surface with ions in the liquid phase. D.B.

Bird, D., and Quillé, N., *Understanding Wine Technology* (4th edn, 2011).

OIV, 'Cation-exchange resins', *International Oenological Codex.* www.oiv.int/public/medias/4062/e-coei-1-reseca.pdf.

respiration, biochemical process in animals and plants, including vines, which provides the chemical energy required for other reactions and for growth. Respiration may be considered the opposite of PHOTOSYNTHESIS in that OXYGEN is consumed and CARBON DIOXIDE and energy released, according to the following formula:

$$H_{12}O_6 \text{ sugar} + 6O_2 \rightarrow 6CO_2 + 6H_2O + \text{energy}$$

In addition to SUGARS, other compounds such as STARCH, fats, AMINO ACIDS, organic ACIDS, and more may be broken down to release energy.

In plants, temperature has a major effect on respiration rate. The rate of respiration approximately doubles for each 10 °C/18 °F increase in temperature. Of particular interest to wine drinkers is the respiration of MALIC ACID, which takes place in the grape during RIPENING. This reaction depends on temperature, an important reason acidity levels are higher in wines from cooler climates.

See BERRY CELL DEATH for a condition caused by excessive respiration. R.E.S.

resveratrol. PHENOLIC compound produced by grapevines (and other plants such as blueberry, peanut, and eucalyptus), particularly in response to microbial attack (see PHYTOALEXINS) or artificial agents such as ULTRAVIOLET RADIATION. It is one of a number of compounds (including CATECHIN and QUERCETIN) found in wine thought to contribute to HEALTH aspects of its moderate consumption, though resveratrol is also found in grape juice and raisins. Resveratrol belongs to a class of compounds called stilbenes. In grapevines this also includes its derivatives, piceid, pterostilbene, and polymers of the base resveratrol unit viniferin. Woody parts of the vine normally contain large amounts of stilbenes, principally viniferins, which are thought to protect against wood decay.

In the vineyard, leaves and berry skins produce resveratrol in response to some action, such as fungal attack from DOWNY MILDEW or BOTRYTIS, where its subsequent accumulation at the infection point may slow or stop the infection. Vine species, variety, CLONE, ROOTSTOCK, environment, disease pressure, and vinification methods can affect resveratrol concentration in the finished wine. For example, wines made from MUSCADINIA grapes, from the interspecific HYBRID Castor or from PINOT NOIR tend to have high levels of resveratrol, whereas CABERNET SAUVIGNON has lower levels. Wines produced in cooler regions or areas with greater disease pressure such as Burgundy and New York often have more resveratrol, while wines from hot, dry climates such as Australia and California frequently have less.

The gene for resveratrol synthesis, stilbene synthase, was cloned from VITIS VINIFERA vines and inserted into ROOTSTOCK 41 B. The transgenic plants produced high concentrations of resveratrol and were more resistant to botrytis infection, showing its value as a natural defence agent.

External agents, such as UV radiation or yeast extracts, can induce resveratrol production in vine tissues, which has led to the development of UV trailers that can be towed through the vineyard in an attempt to control diseases.

Red wines have about ten times the resveratrol concentration found in whites. This is not because white grapes make less resveratrol but rather because stilbenes are made in the grape skins, and MACERATION, integral to the production of a red wine, allows EXTRACTION of more of these compounds. Much of the interest in resveratrol comes from its suspected connection to the health benefits of moderate wine consumption. It was reported to be the active component of an Asian medicinal herb made from *Polygonum cuspidatum* root in 1982, but it was not until 1992 that New York researchers Siemann and Creasy made the link between it, wine, and its possible contribution to the FRENCH PARADOX.

Resveratrol has been reported to have many beneficial effects on health, particularly in relation to cardiovascular disease, cholesterol, diabetes, and cancer. However, research has not reached a consensus due to the complexity of running clinical trials and other factors, such as the bioavailability of resveratrol and other phenolic compounds. G.L.C.

Bavaresco, L., et al., 'Wine resveratrol: from the ground up', *Nutrients*, 8/4 (2016).

Berman, A. Y., et al., 'The therapeutic potential of resveratrol: a review of clinical trials', *npj Precision Oncology*, 1/35 (2017).

Goldberg, D. M., et al., 'A global survey of *trans*-resveratrol concentrations in commercial wines', *American Journal of Enology and Viticulture*, 46 (1995), 159–65.
Langcake, P., 'Disease resistance of Vitis spp. and the production of the stress metabolites resveratrol, ε-viniferin, α-viniferin and pterostilbene', *Physiological Plant Pathology*, 18 (1981), 213–26.
Siemann, E. H., and Creasy, L. L., 'Concentration of the phytoalexin resveratrol in wine', *American Journal of Enology and Viticulture*, 43 (1992), 49–52.

retsina, classified in Greece as an *appellation traditionnelle* (one of the EU's TRADITIONAL TERMS), is a term exclusive to dry, RESINATED WINES from Greece. With one South Australian exception, resinated wines are rarely made outside Greece and southern Cyprus.

Modern retsina is made like any other white (or rosé) wine, except that small amounts of resin from the Aleppo pine (*Pinus helepensis*) are added to the juice and left with the wine until the first RACKING or before, the timing determined by taste. The selection of resin is itself an art. Major producing areas are Attica, Evvia, and Viotia, all in southern central Greece close to Athens, but retsina is made all over the country, with 15 areas awarded PGIs for their particular versions. SAVATIANO is usually the principal grape, often enlivened with some RODITIS or occasionally ASSYRTIKO, but a wide range of local varieties are also used, such as ATHIRI on the island of Rhodes and Muscat on Samos.

A profusion of poor-quality retsina damaged Greek wine's image in the 1970s and 1980s, but by the 2000s producers such as Kechris and Gaia were creating exceptional retsinas based on top-quality wine made from Assyrtiko or high-ELEVATION Roditis elegantly flavoured with high-quality, carefully sourced pine resin. Their efforts have inspired a new generation of resinated wines that prove that great retsina is no oxymoron. Top examples can be enjoyed in the same way as a FINO sherry. K.L.

Reuilly. This small but expanding AOC (under 300 ha/740 acres in 2019, up from 30 ha in the early 1990s) sits between the tributaries of the Cher and Arnon in the middle LOIRE. Its LIMESTONE slopes are planted predominantly with Sauvignon Blanc, which makes a fruity, pungent wine. Simple, juicy reds are made from Pinot Noir, and pale rosés from Sauvignon Gris. Denis Jamain is one of the most dedicated producers in the region and one of the few to have converted to ORGANIC VITICULTURE. The wines tend to be earlier-drinking and less complex than those of SANCERRE and MENETOU-SALON. This appellation is not to be confused with that of RULLY in the Côte Chalonnaise.

See also LOIRE, including map. C.P.

Réunion, a French island in the Indian Ocean, its VOLCANIC soils once mainly planted with ISABELLA, now produces small quantities of wines from French varieties such as CHENIN BLANC, GAMAY, PINOT NOIR, and SYRAH at ELEVATIONS of up to 1,300 m/4,625 ft. The CO-OPERATIVE Le Chai de Cilaos, founded in 1992, dominates production.

reverse osmosis is an increasingly popular though rather controversial winemaking intervention or MANIPULATION based on the principle of cross-flow or tangential membrane filtration and osmosis. In standard FILTRATION procedures, the liquid flows perpendicularly to the filter surface, making clogging a major problem. In cross-flow filtration, the liquid flows parallel to the membrane filter so that it helps scour the surface and prevent clogging.

The use of techniques based on cross-flow filtration has become popular for wine STABILIZATION (see ULTRAFILTRATION). Pressure is applied to force small molecules such as water and some salts to pass through the membrane filter (i.e. the permeate) while concentrating the remaining wine compounds (i.e. the retentate).

It is currently used chiefly for two distinct purposes: ALCOHOL REDUCTION and must or juice CONCENTRATION. In the former, a possible alternative to HUMIDIFICATION, a portion of a high-alcohol wine is passed through a reverse-osmosis installation, which removes a colourless permeate that consists almost entirely of water and alcohol and returns the retentate (the rest of the wine) to the tank. The alcohol may then be removed from the permeate by distillation or EVAPORATIVE PERSTRACTION and the water returned to the wine, to produce a wine of reduced alcohol content. This low-alcohol wine can then be used as a blending component to produce a final wine of the desired alcohol level. An advantage of this technique is that only a portion of the wine need be subjected to this potentially intrusive process, typically less than one-quarter.

In the case of must or juice concentration, reverse osmosis is used to remove water from the unfermented grape juice, for example after a rainy harvest, achieving a similar result to that of vacuum evaporation. Controversially, some have seen it as a way of producing more concentrated, denser wines of the sort that appeal to influential critics and the modern marketplace. In countries such as Australia and the United States, the main use of reverse osmosis is on finished wines, where the selective removal of water and alcohol concentrates all other components.

Another important use for reverse osmosis is the reduction of excessive levels of VOLATILE ACIDITY. STUCK FERMENTATIONS are sometimes coupled with high levels of ACETIC ACID, which, because of its low molecular weight (small size), will be removed together with ETHANOL and water.

More recently this technique has been proposed as a way of removing negative flavour compounds (volatile phenols) that result from BRETTANOMYCES spoilage in red wines. J.E.H. & A.O.

Block, D. E., and Miller, K. V., *Unit Operations in Winery, Brewery, and Distillery Design* (2022).
Smith, C., 'The new filtrations', in *Postmodern Winemaking* (2013), 202–18.
Wollan, D., 'Membrane and other techniques for the management of wine composition', in A. G. Reynolds (ed.), *Managing Wine Quality 2: Oenology and Wine Quality* (2nd edn, 2021).

reviews, wine. See TASTING NOTES.

Rèze, very rare Swiss Valais white grape responsible for the sherry-like *vin des glaciers*. In 2005, DNA PROFILING at SAN MICHELE ALL'ADIGE revealed that Rèze has parent–offspring relationships with NOSIOLA and Groppello di Revò in Trentino and Cascarolo in Piemonte. And in 2007, DNA profiling proved its presence in the Alpine Maurienne Valley and in the JURA. Coupled with additional genetic relationships, this makes Rèze one of the main founder varieties of the Alps. In Switzerland, the area of cultivation fell from 400 ha/1,000 acres at the beginning of the 20th century to fewer than 3 ha at the beginning of the 21st century because Rèze and other Valais grapes were superseded by CHASSELAS. J.V.

Vouillamoz, J., & Moriondo, G., *Origine des cépages valaisans et valdôtains* (2011).
Zufferey-Périsset, A.-D. (ed.), *Histoire de la vigne et du vin en Valais: des origines à nos jours* (2009).

Rhein, German name for the river RHINE.

Rheingau, for generations the most economically successful wine region in GERMANY and still one of its most famous abroad. The Church and nobility provided the discipline and organization necessary for a solid business in wine, which survived the unrest and secularization in the early 19th century (see GERMAN HISTORY). The region had 3,185 ha/7,870 acres of vines in 2019, over 90% of which lie on the right bank of the RHINE, between Wiesbaden and the MITTELRHEIN boundary below Lorchhausen (see map under GERMANY). The remainder of the Rheingau vineyards are near Hochheim (the origin of the word HOCK) on the banks of the Main, shortly before its confluence with the Rhine at Mainz.

The region has a favoured MESOCLIMATE. With its primarily southern ASPECT, it is marginally warmer than much of RHEINHESSEN to the south, and its annual RAINFALL of a little over 600 m/23 in means that there is an adequate supply of water for the RIESLING vine to ripen its grapes long into the autumn. Critical to the differences

R

among the Rheingau's diverse cast of Rieslings are SOIL TYPE, proximity to the Rhine, and ELEVATION, with higher, cooler, breezier sites often performing better in recent warmer growing seasons than some of the traditionally most prestigious riverside vineyards, where POTENTIAL ALCOHOLS and the risk of GREY ROT can be excessive.

At GEISENHEIM, the Rheingau has one of the world's leading viticultural institutes, but the region has not been invaded by GERMAN CROSSES to the same extent as other German regions such as Rheinhessen and the PFALZ. Rather, it has stuck by the grapes that brought it fame: Riesling (78% of surface area in 2019) and Pinot Noir (12%, concentrated in Assmannshausen near the region's northern edge).

No German wines have ever achieved higher international standing (or prices) than did the Rieslings of the Rheingau in the late 19th century, and even into the mid 20th century prices were much higher than those of many of Bordeaux's CLASSED GROWTHS. The record of the late 20th century was mixed. Under the stylistic inspiration of the late Bernard Breuer of Rüdesheim and the late proprietor of Schloss Vollrads, Graf Matuschka-Greiffenclau, this region led Germany in a trend towards dry Rieslings, purporting to be closer to a late 19th century model and inherently more adaptable to late 20th century cuisine. The Rheingau CHARTA organization and the local VDP association were early activists in the promotion of low YIELDS, of TROCKEN (dry) Riesling, and of the CLASSIFICATION of top vineyards (see ERSTES GEWÄCHS).

Proximity to the metropolitan markets of Mainz, Wiesbaden, and Frankfurt has further helped Rheingau wines re-establish high reputations, although not enough to secure the continued fortunes of many of the large, formerly noble, estates, many of which have in recent years been sold, closed, or continuing to struggle economically. The Rheingau has also had stiff competition within Germany for both white and red wines from the dynamic, warmer BADEN and Pfalz regions as well as from impressive Rieslings grown in formerly unfashionable sectors of Rheinhessen. And for those craving delicacy in Riesling or wines with a dynamic synergy of fruit, ACIDITY, and RESIDUAL SUGAR, heightened awareness of the NAHE has brought the Rheingau further domestic competition.

The Rheingau's best-known estates (and the state-owned KLOSTER EBERBACH) typically have holdings in multiple, far-flung villages, and many of today's family wineries follow a similar pattern, if usually on a smaller scale. When windows of opportunity become compressed, as has been the case with so many recent vintages, and as mustering crews of pickers becomes increasingly difficult despite the EU's open borders for LABOUR, having such scattered vineyards presents a huge challenge. It is not surprising then that the Rheingau's new elite consists largely of estates with vineyards in just one or two adjacent villages. The Rheingau was traditionally Germany's leader in selective picking of botrytis-affected Riesling (see SCHLOSS JOHANNISBERG) and continues to treasure its AUSLESE, BEERENAUSLESE, and TROCKENBEERENAUSLESE wines even though almost 60% of Rheingau wine today is bottled trocken and a further 27% HALBTROCKEN. In fact, picking out BOTRYTIZED Riesling berries has become essential to ensuring healthy fruit and a suitable potential alcohol level in the dry Riesling made from the remaining grapes.

At Lorchausen and Lorch—the westernmost limit of the Rheingau—the slopes resemble those of the adjacent Mittelrhein. Because Riesling traditionally struggled to ripen here, SILVANER is common and can produce highly distinctive wines, though they are overshadowed by the Rieslings emerging from Lorch's Kapellenberg, Krone, and Schlossberg vineyards. Immediately upstream at Assmannshausen, Pinot Noir dominates, above all in the south-facing Höllenberg. At Rüdesheim, the Rhine begins an east–west orientation, creating the so-called Rüdesheimer Berg, the first of the Rheingau's famous progression of Riesling-dominated south-facing slopes. The steep, stony SLATE- and QUARTZITE-dominated Berg Schlossberg, Berg Roseneck, Berg Rottland, and Berg Kaisersteinfels sites, all directly overlooking the Rhine, can generate Rieslings of peachy richness, spiciness, and depth. Less steep and ostensibly lesser Rüdesheim sites (Bischofsberg, Drachenstein, Kirchenpfad, Klosterlay, Rosengarten) are sometimes also home to impressive Riesling or Pinot Noir. The progression of small villages (and top-class vineyards) continues with Geisenheim (Kläuserweg, Rothenberg), Johannisberg (Goldatzel, Hölle, Mittelhölle, Klaus, Schloss Johannisberg), Winkel (Jesuitengarten, Hasensprung, Schloss Vollrads), Mittelheim (St Nikolaus), and Oestrich (Doosberg, Lenchen, Rosengarten). All are capable of producing Riesling wines of a high order but receive stiff competition from the best Rieslings of Hattenheim (Hassel, Pfaffenberg, Nussbrunnen, Schützenhaus, Wisselbrunnen) and Erbach (Marcobrunn, Siegelsberg, Schlossberg, Steinmorgen). Soils of LOESS, SAND, and MARL alternate in these central Rheingau villages, and sites further from the river are generally later-ripening and more ventilated due to their elevation. The wines of Hallgarten (Hendelberg, Jungfer, Steinberg, Schönhell), Kiedrich (Gräfenberg, Klosterberg, Wasseros, Turmberg), and Rauenthal (Baiken, Gehrn, Nonnenberg, Rothenberg, Wülfen), which lie on higher, stony, phyllite (between SLATE and SCHIST) soils some distance from the Rhine, can yield long-lived, extraordinarily fine wines. At lower elevations near the eastern edge of the Rheingau, Riesling from Eltville (Langenstück, Sonnenberg) and Walluf (Walkenberg), while perhaps never quite rivalling the best Rieslings of the region, can also be memorably complex and long-lived. On the other side of metropolitan Wiesbaden (whose own Neroberg is a serious source of Riesling), Hochheim (Stielweg, Domdechaney, Kirchenstück, Hölle, Königin Viktoriaberg, Herrenberg) boasts gentle slopes with CALCAREOUS underpinnings, generating its own distinctive style of often corpulent but MINERALLY complex Rieslings.

D.S.

Rheinhessen, Germany's largest wine region in 2019 at 26,860 ha/66,373 acres, south and south-west of Mainz. (See map under GERMANY.) For some time it was best known as a source of inexpensive blending wine but that has changed.

The part of the region traditionally most associated with quality is often referred to as the Rheinterrasse, where one-third of the region's RIESLING vines grow. Its most famous vineyards are those in the so-called Roter Hang composed of *Rotliegenden* (Permian red SANDSTONE) at Nierstein (with notable vineyards Hipping, Oelberg, Orbel, and Pettental) and neighbouring Nackenheim (Rothenberg). Aromas of peach and citrus and a smoked-meat pungency characterize wines grown on these red soils.

Immediately south of Nierstein, the communes of Oppenheim, Dienheim, and Ludwigshöhe also boast excellent eastern exposure on the edge of the river RHINE. Most of Rheinhessen is protected from winds and excessive rain by the hills on its western border, which rise to over 600 m/2,000 ft. But the temperature in the vineyards nearest the Rhine is warmer throughout the year than that of the rolling country away from the river, and in severe winters they avoid the worst effects of FROST. LOESS, SAND, and CALCAREOUS soils in most of these villages can also yield distinctive Riesling such as in the underrated Brückchen and Paterberg, while Silvaner—a traditional Rheinhessen stalwart now reduced to 8% of surface area—is resurgent qualitatively in the hands of ambitious producers.

The north of Rheinhessen has its best-known vineyards at Ingelheim (traditionally associated with SPÄTBURGUNDER), at Bingen in the Scharlachberg site, and in the region's highest sector, immediately south-east of Bad Kreuznach, most notably the porphyric Heerkretz and Höllberg of Siefersheim but also sandstone- and melaphyr-based sites in neighbouring Neu-Bamberg and Fürfeld.

But it is the south, the so-called Wonnegau, whose wine villages feature predominantly calcareous vineyards, that has since the 1990s gained international attention for strikingly distinctive Rieslings as well as promising Pinot Noir and a revival of Silvaner. Dittelsheim (Geiersberg, Kloppberg, Leckerberg), Mölsheim (Frauenberg, Am Schwarzen Herrgott), and Hohen-Sülzen (Kirchenstück) but most especially Flörsheim-Dalsheim (Bürgel, Hubacker) and Westhofen (Aulerde, Benn, Brünnenhäuschen, Kirchspiel, Morstein, Steingrube) now loom large in the pantheon of German wine thanks to ambitious winegrowers such as Klaus Peter Keller, Oliver Spanier, and Philipp Wittmann farming sites whose potential had been largely overlooked from the Middle Ages.

Much of Rheinhessen still produces uninspiring wines from GERMAN CROSSES, but once-ubiquitous MÜLLER-THURGAU now takes up only 7.6% of the vineyard area, less than half of its share two decades ago; KERNER only 4%, and DORNFELDER 13%.

The tide has turned in terms of this region's overall reputation, and the notion that it merely divides into Roter Hang and hinterlands has been definitively demolished. A significant number of Germany's pioneers in ORGANIC and BIODYNAMIC VITICULTURE have come from the ranks of Rheinhessen growers, further helping to attract attention to the region. D.S.

Pigott, S., et al., *Wein Spricht Deutsch: Weine, Winzer, Weinlandschaften* (2007).

Reinhardt, S., *The Finest Wines of Germany* (2012).

Rheinpfalz, German wine region. See PFALZ.

Rhein Riesling, or **Rheinriesling**, synonym in German-speaking countries for the great White RIESLING grape variety of Germany.

Rhenish, commonly used term in the Middle Ages to describe wine produced along the Rhine River, in what is now GERMANY and ALSACE.

Rhine, English name for the river known in German as the **Rhein** and in French as the **Rhin** (where it lends its name to the two ALSACE *départements* Haut-Rhin and Bas-Rhin). See also SWITZERLAND and LIECHTENSTEIN.

'Rhine' is sometimes used to indicate German wines not from the MOSEL and has been incorporated into a host of names associated in the English-speaking world with white, usually medium-dry, but not necessarily at all Germanic wines.

Rhine Riesling, synonym once common in Australia for the great WHITE RIESLING grape variety of Germany.

Rhizopus. See BUNCH ROTS.

Rhoditis. See RODITIS.

Rhône, one of the most important wine RIVERS, linking a range of vineyards as dissimilar as those of CHÂTEAUNEUF-DU-PAPE in southern France, sparkling SEYSSEL in Savoie, and Fendant du Valais in SWITZERLAND.

In wine circles, however, the term 'Rhône' usually refers to the wines made in the Rhône Valley in south-east France, which themselves vary so much—north and south of a sparsely planted 50-km/30-mile stretch between approximately Valence and Montélimar—that they are divided into two very distinct zones, the southern Rhône and northern Rhône (although the regional appellation Côtes du Rhône encompasses the less ambitious wines of the north and a much larger area of the south). The Rhône regularly produces more AOC wine than any region other than Bordeaux, with 75% of the 2.7 million hl/71 million gal produced in 2020 being red, 16% rosé, and 9% white.

Of the two zones, the southern Rhône (*Rhône méridional* in French) represents around 94% of production. It is responsible for the overwhelming majority of the approximately 1.6 million hl/42 million gal of wine that qualifies as Côtes du Rhône or Côtes du Rhône-Villages each year.

More prestigious is the northern Rhône (*Rhône septentrional* in French), which includes the appellations of HERMITAGE and CÔTE RÔTIE, representing serious rivals to the great names of Bordeaux and Burgundy in the quality and longevity of their best wines. The northern Rhône is quite different from the southern Rhône in terms of climate, soils, topography, and even vine varieties.

A third district, small but extremely ancient, lies about 40 km/25 miles east of Valence up the Drôme tributary; it comprises the Diois appellations, named after the town of Die, of CHÂTILLON-EN-DIOIS, CLAIRETTE DE DIE, CRÉMANT de Die, and Coteaux de DIE.

And finally there are the outlying appellations that surround the central Côtes du Rhône growing area of the southern Rhône: COSTIÈRES DE NÎMES, CLAIRETTE DE BELLEGARDE, DUCHÉ D'UZÈS, Côtes du VIVARAIS, GRIGNAN-LES-ADHÉMAR, VENTOUX, and LUBERON.

History

Finds of AMPHORAE show that the inhabitants of the Rhône Valley drank wine from Baetica, the eastern province of Roman-occupied SPAIN, in the 1st century BCE. In the 1st century CE, the Romanized elite of the Rhône Valley drank FALERNIAN. From the 1st century BCE onwards, wine was carried up the Rhône: Chalon-sur-Saône was a river port for the GAULS (see Côte CHALONNAISE). In his *Geography*, completed in 7 CE, Strabo emphasized the importance of good RIVER connections for trade in Gaul. From the Mediterranean one can get to the Atlantic Ocean and the Channel by river (*Geography* 4. 1. 2).

Strabo asserted categorically that viticulture was impossible beyond the Cévennes, which was north of the territory of the evergreen oak, *Quercus ilex*, and hence too cold for the vine, which he assumed needed a MEDITERRANEAN CLIMATE. He was proved wrong by the Gauls, who even in Strabo's day had probably discovered that the Côte Rôtie and the hill of Hermitage were superb sites for vineyards. They were certainly making wine by 71 CE, when PLINY said that in Vienne the Allobroges were producing an excellent wine, still unknown to VIRGIL (*Natural History* 14. 18). There were three CRUS, Taburnum, Sotanum, and Helvicum. Pliny's observation that they tasted naturally of resin cannot be correct, for all wine was then stored and transported in earthenware vessels which were lined with resin to make them impermeable, so any wine, and particularly a wine that had come from afar or was old, would have tasted of resin (see RESINATED WINES).

Pliny calls the vine that the growers of Vienne used Allobrogica. It has black grapes and is resistant to cold (*Natural History* 14. 26–7). Given the latter, Allobrogica is unlikely to be SYRAH—unless Pliny, like Strabo, thought that the Rhône Valley's climate was inclement and decided therefore that any vine variety growing there must be able to withstand the cold. The Allobroges are proud of their wines, which fetch a high price (*Natural History* 14. 57). Elsewhere, Pliny remarks that the Gauls have mastered the art of GRAFTING and improved on CATO: the Romans in turn have learned from them (*Natural History* 17. 116). The Allobroges exported their wines not only to Rome but also to Britain.

The people living in the Rhône Valley doubtless carried on making wine after the Romans left, but we have hardly any records at all until the late Middle Ages. Medieval wine merchants eagerly bought and sold the wine of Bordeaux, Gaillac, La Rochelle, the Île-de-France, and the Loire, but there was no trade in Rhône wines until the 14th century. This cannot have been because they were bad wines, for when Pope Clement V moved the papal court to Avignon in 1309 his entourage was quick to discover the local wines (see CHÂTEAUNEUF-DU-PAPE). Some three-quarters of the wines consumed at the papal court came from the Rhône Valley, although the court was fond of Burgundy, too. When Urban V went back to Rome for three years from 1367 to 1370, he had a vine from the Côtes du Rhône planted there.

It was his hatred of political infighting, not his love of French wines, that drove Clement back to Avignon. After his successor Gregory XI returned to Rome for good in 1377, the pope and his Roman household continued to drink the wines of the Rhône.

Châteauneuf-du-Pape owes its name to a new castle built by John XXII, a summer residence in the hills 16 km/10 miles north of Avignon. It was destroyed by German bombers in the Second World War.

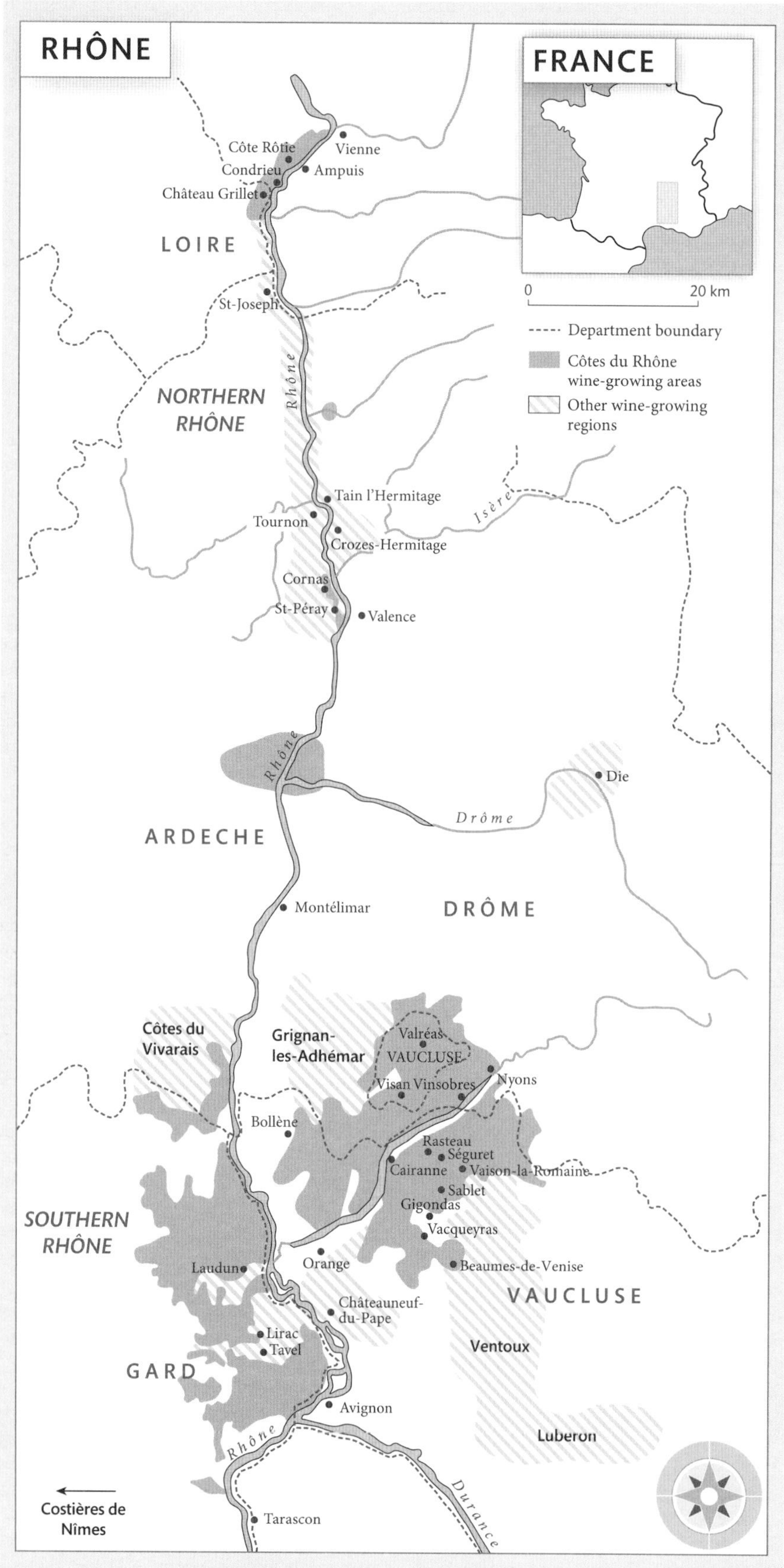

The name Hermitage La Chapelle has its origins in medieval legend. When the Crusader Gaspard de Stérimberg returned from the Holy Land, he gained the permission of Blanche of Castille, queen of France and regent during the minority of her son Louis IX (1226–70), to build a chapel and dedicate it to St Christopher; there he lived as a hermit for 30 years until he died. The white Hermitage Chevalier de Stérimberg from Paul Jaboulet Aîné is named after this knightly recluse on the Hermitage hill.

It was not only the Rhône which benefited from the extravagant habits of the papal court at Avignon: BURGUNDY, too, saw demand for its wines soar. As Burgundy became a major wine-producing region, it realized the dangers of competition from the south, especially because the wines of the Rhône were heavier than its own and hence more likely to survive transport unscathed. The duchy of Burgundy was in a powerful position, for in order to reach the markets of Paris and the north of France the wine of the Rhône had to be carried up the Saône through Burgundian territory. The solution was simple: Burgundy imposed severe restrictions on the entry and transit of all non-Burgundian wines. In 1446 the city of Dijon banned wines from Lyons, Vienne, and Tournon altogether, for the spurious reason that they were 'très petits et povres vins'. These measures remained in force from the 14th to the 16th centuries and were successful. The wines of the Rhône Valley were excluded from the trade with England and the Low Countries, and they were not available in Paris until the 17th century, when transport overland had become less expensive and merchants could afford to carry their wines to the lower reaches of the Loire by ox-drawn cart and then ship them down the Loire. H.M.W.

Dion, R., *Histoire de la vigne et du vin en France* (1959).
Livingstone-Learmonth, J., *The Wines of the Northern Rhône* (2005).

Northern Rhône

The northern Rhône growing area begins just south of Lyon, stretching from Vienne to Valence. It closely follows the Rhône River as it runs north to south along the eastern edge of the Massif Central. Many of the best vineyards are planted on steep terraces that scale this granitic mass, facing south, south-east, and east on the river's right bank. The largest appellation, however, is Crozes-Hermitage on the left bank, representing nearly half of all wine produced in the northern Rhône. The total production of the northern Rhône is around 6% of total Rhône Valley wine.

The northern Rhône is under the influence of a CONTINENTAL CLIMATE, with hard winters and summers whose effect on the grapes can be exaggerated by the region's steep slopes. The north wind, known locally as *la bise*, blows powerfully and often—a mixed blessing, as it helps to reduce disease pressure in the vineyards but also can cause damage, so growing individual vines on stakes known as *échalas* is commonplace. The steep banks of this now heavily industrialized river naturally limited vine cultivation for many centuries, and the best wines are produced on inclines which are expensive to work and help to maximize the effect of the available SUNLIGHT (see TOPOGRAPHY). Since the 1980s, however, when the better wines of the Rhône were recognized as offering some of the best fine-wine value (and winemaking recognized as a potentially noble way of earning a living), there has been considerable expansion, particularly in such appellations as St-Joseph and Crozes-Hermitage but also in, and especially around, more restricted appellations such as Côte Rôtie and Condrieu. Most appellations are based on the right bank of the river, but the left-bank vineyards of Crozes-Hermitage and especially Hermitage are particularly well exposed to afternoon sunshine.

This is the prime territory of the SYRAH grape, which is the only red-wine grape permitted in northern Rhône crus. VIOGNIER is the defining grape variety of the white wines Condrieu and Château-Grillet, while other white northern Rhône wines depend on Marsanne and/or Roussanne, alone or blended.

Most winemaking and vine-growing is in the hands of individuals working small family holdings. About half of all wines are bottled by merchants, of which Paul Jaboulet Aîné, CHAPOUTIER, Delas, and GUIGAL are some of the best known. There are very few CO-OPERATIVES.

For more details, see the specific appellations CHÂTEAU-GRILLET, CONDRIEU, CORNAS, CÔTE-RÔTIE, CROZES-HERMITAGE, HERMITAGE, ST-JOSEPH, and ST-PÉRAY.

Livingstone-Learmonth, J., *The Wines of the Northern Rhône* (2005).

Southern Rhône

The southern Rhône has only the river and a few grape varieties in common with the northern Rhône. The countryside here is flatter and definitively southern, with both houses and vegetation demonstrating the influence of a MEDITERRANEAN CLIMATE. Many other fruits are grown here. One of the chief hazards is the mistral, a cold WIND that can blow down the Rhône valley. Most vines are BUSH-trained, although Syrah vines are usually trained on wires in single GUYOT or CORDON DE ROYAT. If drought persists, some IRRIGATION is permitted during certain periods. Soil types are more diverse than in the northern Rhône, varying from appellation to appellation. The most common are sand and sandstone, limestone, and clay (with greater or lesser quantities of pebbles or larger rounded stones known locally as *galets roulés*).

Most wines are blends rather than made from a single grape variety. Although many growers have experimented with Syrah, much of the southern Rhône is too hot for it to ripen gracefully, and around twice as much GRENACHE is grown. The dominant Grenache can in theory also be supplemented or seasoned by a wide range of other local varieties, but in practice only CARIGNAN, CINSAUT, and MOURVÈDRE are planted to any extent, with Mourvèdre becoming increasingly popular. Of white-wine grapes, the most widely planted for AOC wines are Viognier, Grenache Blanc, Marsanne, Roussanne, and Clairette.

CO-OPERATIVES are very important in the southern Rhône, responsible for about two-thirds of total production. The NÉGOCIANTS of the northern Rhône also have a long tradition of buying wine here for blending and bottling. There is also an ever-increasing number of private estates. Winemaking techniques for red wines are varied. Most choose to destem their crop, but WHOLE-BUNCH vinification is increasing in popularity. CARBONIC MACERATION is rare but increasingly fashionable. Fermentation is typically carried out in concrete tanks, stainless-steel tanks or large wooden *foudres* (see CASK). ÉLEVAGE varies according to grape variety; small barrels and new oak are typically reserved more for Syrah and Mourvèdre than for Grenache.

The southern Rhône is the only part of France other than the LANGUEDOC and ROUSSILLON to have a tradition of making sweet VIN DOUX NATUREL: a Muscat version in BEAUMES-DE-VENISE and varied colours and styles from the Grenache family in RASTEAU.

For more details, see also ARDÈCHE, BEAUMES-DE-VENISE, CAIRANNE, CHÂTEAUNEUF-DU-PAPE, CHÂTILLON-EN-DIOIS, CLAIRETTE DE BELLEGARDE, CLAIRETTE DE DIE, COSTIÈRES DE NÎMES, DUCHÉ D'UZÈS, GIGONDAS, GRIGNAN-LES-ADHÉMAR, LIRAC, RASTEAU, TAVEL, VACQUEYRAS, VENTOUX, VINSOBRES, and VIVARAIS, CÔTES DU.

Côtes du Rhône

is often used colloquially to denote the wines of the Rhône Valley in its broadest sense, but it really refers to the wines of the southern Rhône, in particular those from AOC Côtes du Rhône. This appellation stretches 180 km/112 miles from Vienne in the north to Avignon in the south, but the vast majority is produced south of Montélimar, which is closer to 70 km north to south, and the growing area spans roughly 50 km east to west. It covers 171 communes and nearly 50,000 ha/123,553 acres of vines. Of the 1.3 million hl/34 million gal of AOC Côtes du Rhône produced in 2020, 87% was red, 8% rosé, and 5% white. There is a particularly generous number of permitted secondary grape varieties, but red and rosé wines produced from vineyards south of Montélimar must contain Grenache and either Syrah or Mourvèdre (or both). Principal grape varieties for whites are Bourboulenc, Clairette, Grenache Blanc, Marsanne, Roussanne, and Viognier. Being at the most basic level of the AOC pyramid, the wines, though perfectly enjoyable, are rarely thrilling. There are some exceptions to this rule, however, such as Domaine des Tours, Ch de Fonsalette, and Domaine Gramenon.

Côtes du Rhône-Villages

In theory, AOC Côtes du Rhône-Villages denotes a step up in quality from the more lenient rules of AOC Côtes du Rhône. The appellation covers fewer communes (95 instead of 171); allows the same grape varieties, save for CROSSES; and requires marginally higher minimum alcohol levels and marginally lower maximum YIELDS.

There is a further step up the appellation pyramid with even stricter production criteria, which is AOC Côtes du Rhône-Villages plus a more specific geographical name. This appellation is reserved for the 22 communes or demarcated geographical areas listed below, which are considered to be of particular interest and are allowed to append their name to Côtes du Rhône-Villages—for example AOC Côtes du Rhône-Villages Sablet. All of the following can produce red, rosé, or white wine unless otherwise stated: Chusclan (red and rosé only), Gadagne (red only), Laudun, Massif d'Uchaux (red only), Nyons (red only), Plan de Dieu (red only), Puyméras (red only), Roaix, Rochegude, Rousset-les-Vignes, Sablet, St-Andéol (red only), St-Gervais, St-Maurice, St-Pantaléon-les-Vignes, Sainte-Cécile (red only), Séguret, Signargues (red only), Suze-la-Rousse (red only), Vaison-la-Romaine (red only), Valréas, and Visan. These appellations are a source of some of the best-value wines in the Rhône Valley. M.C.W.

Rhône Rangers, loose affiliation of wine producers in the United States who, in the 1980s, seeking to break free from what they perceived as a 'conventional' domestic wine scene, sought out and planted the grape varieties of France's RHÔNE Valley. Early advocates included Californians Sean Thackrey, Bob Lindquist of Qupé, Randall GRAHM of Bonny Doon, John Buechsenstein of McDowell Valley Vineyards, and Steve Edmunds of Edmunds St John.

Their efforts led to resurgent interest in the US in SYRAH and VIOGNIER, as well as the old-vine GRENACHE and Mataro (MOURVÈDRE) that had languished in California vineyards. Syrah plantings went on to post exponential growth, increasing in California from 80 ha/200 acres in 1990 to over 7,700 ha in 2012. Viognier's rise was almost as dramatic (32 ha/80 acres in 1990; 1,214 ha in 2012).

In 1989 the Perrins of Ch de Beaucastel and US wine importer Robert Haas established Tablas Creek, a winery devoted to Rhône varieties. Based in PASO ROBLES, the partnership has been instrumental in the importation of Rhône varieties—16 in all, including the 13 varieties found in CHÂTEAUNEUF-DU-PAPE. Their effort led to a second planting surge, of such varieties as Grenache Blanc, Picpoul, Vermentino, Clairette, Counoise, Cinsaut, and Terret. Rhône Ranger efforts in California inspired similar endeavours in WASHINGTON, embodied by the likes of Christophe Baron (Cayuse), Charles Smith (K), Greg Harrington (Gramercy Cellars), and Jean-Francois Pellet (Amavi).

The movement created thousands of fans and launched festivals, celebrations, and loose-knit cadres of rootin'-tootin' enthusiasts, who revelled in the category's contrarian exuberance, providing, as it did, welcome alternatives to the usual California diet of VARIETAL Cabernet Sauvignon, Merlot, and Chardonnay. Owing to the Rangers' efforts, Rhône varieties are now planted in nearly every region in the US where VITIS VINIFERA plantings are found. P.C.

Rías Baixas, the leading DOP wine zone in GALICIA, north-west Spain (see map under SPAIN), producing some of the country's most sought-after dry white wines. Between 1987 and 2021 the DOP's vineyard area grew from 237 ha/570 acres to 4,051 ha/100,010 acres with the number of wineries rising from 14 to 161. Named after the flooded coastal valleys, or *rías*, that penetrate up to 30 km/19 miles inland, the zone's reputation is based on the white ALBARIÑO grape. Wines were exported to northern Europe in the 16th and 17th centuries, but after the ravages of PHYLLOXERA many of the traditional vine varieties were abandoned, and by the 1900s the region's vineyards were largely planted with high-yielding HYBRIDS and by Jerez's PALOMINO FINO, producing poor-quality wine. The revival began in the late 1970s, when growers were encouraged to replant INDIGENOUS VARIETIES and producers were given incentives to invest in modern winemaking equipment. The metamorphosis gathered pace with the application of EU funds following Spain's accession to the EU in 1986.

Rías Baixas has five subzones, all within the province of Pontevedra. Many of the purest Albariño wines come from Val do Salnés zone centred on the town of Cambados on the west coast. O Rosal and Condado do Tea are on the northern slopes of the river Miño facing Portugal's VINHO VERDE region. A fourth, small subzone, Soutomaior, was admitted in the late 1990s, to be joined later by Ribeira do Ulla in the far north. All five zones share the same GRANITE-based subsoils and relatively cool, damp MARITIME CLIMATE. The Atlantic influence is strongest in Val do Salnés, where annual RAINFALL averages 1,300 mm/50 in. Vines were traditionally cultivated on pergolas (see TENDONE) to protect grapes from the constant threat of FUNGAL DISEASES, although modern vineyards are planted on a more practical local variant of the GENEVA DOUBLE CURTAIN vine-training system.

Fourteen vine varieties are officially permitted in Rías Baixas, although Albariño accounts for 90% of the vineyard area. Other white grapes which may be blended with Albariño according to local regulations include CAÍÑO BLANCO, as well as TREIXADURA and LOUREIRA, (known locally as Marqués), both of which are found in the VINHO VERDE region. TORRONTÉS and GODELLO are also permitted. On its own, Albariño produces a fragrant, intensely fruity, dry white wine with a natural minimum alcohol often above 12%. YIELDS used to be low, which made the wines expensive, but abusive yield increases began to occur in the 1990s, sometimes aggravated by over-reliance on aroma-enhancing YEASTS. There have been experiments with OAK. Red grapes represent less than 1% of the vineyards, with Sousón (see SOUSÃO) the main variety, yet the wines have gained attention thanks to the work of growers such as Eulogio Pomares (Zárate) and Gerardo Méndez (Forjas del Salnés). V. de la S. & F.C.

Barquín, J., Guitiérrez, L., and de la Serna, V., *The Finest Wines of Rioja and Northwest Spain* (2011).
www.riasbaixaswines.com

Ribatejo, former name of TEJO in Portugal.

Ribbon Ridge, wine region and AVA within the WILLAMETTE VALLEY of Oregon.

Ribeira Sacra, growing Spanish DOP created in 1996. It is the only GALICIAN region specializing in red wines, from the MENCÍA grape, and some less well-known local varieties such as Sousón (SOUSÃO) and Brancellao (ALVARELHÃO). Whites are mainly GODELLO and ALBARIÑO. Most vineyards are situated on hugely impressive terraced SLATE and SCHIST slopes at 400–500 m/1,312–1,640 ft in ELEVATION, their slopes angled at 30–80° and facing south and south-west. The area is divided into five subregions, but only Amandi ('beloved land') appears on labels with any regularity. The other subregions are Chantada, Quiroga-Bibei, Ribeiras do Miño, and Ribeiras do Sil. F.C.

Ribeiro means 'riverbank' or 'riverside' in the Galician language and is the name of a red and white wine DO zone in GALICIA, north-west Spain (see map under SPAIN). Ribeiro spans the valleys of the river Miño and its tributaries and Arnoia downstream from Orense. In the 16th and 17th centuries wines from Ribeiro were exported as far afield as Italy and England, but PHYLLOXERA put paid to the region's prosperity at the end of the 19th century. As in RÍAS BAIXAS, farmers seeking a quick return to profit replanted their holdings with the sherry grape PALOMINO FINO. Over recent years, growers have been encouraged to uproot this productive but unsuitable variety in favour of TREIXADURA, TORRONTÉS, Lado, and other INDIGENOUS VARIETIES that perform well in the damp MARITIME CLIMATE and can be made into the aromatic, crisp white wines that make up 90% of the region's production. The little red wine that is made is dominated by CAÍÑO and other local varieties. There is a very limited production of Tostado, a sweet DRIED-GRAPE WINE. With help from EU funds, wineries have been updated, and the traditional, labour-intensive pergolas (see TENDONE) are being replaced by lower vine-TRAINING SYSTEMS. V. de la S. & F.C.

Ribera del Duero, important wine zone in CASTILLA Y LEÓN in north-central Spain that challenged RIOJA as the leading red wine-producing region in Iberia towards the end of the 20th century when it grew substantially. By 2021 it had a total of 23,500 ha/58,070 acres of vineyard, one-third as much as Rioja. Ribera del Duero spans the upper valley of the River Duero (known as DOURO in Portugal), starting some 30 km/18 miles east of the city of Valladolid (see map under SPAIN). Although Bodegas VEGA SICILIA on the western margin of the denomination has been producing one of Spain's finest wines since the mid 19th century, the region was awarded DOP status only in 1982, when there were just seven wineries. In 2021 there were 310.

At first sight, the Duero Valley is not the most congenial place to grow grapes. At 700–850 m/2,800 ft in ELEVATION, the growing season is relatively short. FROST, commonplace in winter, continues to be a threat well into the spring. Temperatures, which can reach nearly 40 °C/104 °F in the middle of a July day, fall sharply at night, the DIURNAL TEMPERATURE RANGE extending the ripening period to such a degree that the harvest in Ribera del Duero is one of the latest in Europe, sometimes lasting until the end of November.

The region's potential was recognized by the late Alejandro Fernández, who played a key role in the development of the region in the 1980s. Pesquera, his wine vinified from grapes growing around the village of Pesquera del Duero just upstream from Vega Sicilia, was released in the early 1980s to international acclaim. Other growers (many of whom had previously sold their grapes to CO-OPERATIVES) were thereby encouraged to make their own wines and soon challenged Rioja's traditional hegemony inside

Spain. In the 1990s, consumption of top-quality Ribera wines soared within Spain, causing deepening concern in Rioja. Several Ribera producers attained quality levels not much below those of Vega Sicilia and Pesquera. The movement has continued in the 21st century, with wineries such as Dominio de Atauta, Bodegas La Loba, and Antídoto transforming Soria, a cool, high area in the north-west, from a source of cheap rosés to one of top-quality reds.

The region's principal vine variety, the Tinto Fino (also called Tinta del Pais), is a local variant of Rioja's TEMPRANILLO. It seems to have adapted to the Duero's climatic extremes and produces deep-coloured, occasionally astringent, firm red wines without the support of any other grape variety (although Cabernet Sauvignon, Merlot, and Malbec, introduced by Vega Sicilia 130 years ago, are allowed throughout the denomination). Garnacha is used in the production of rosé, and ALBILLO Mayor, allowed in DOP wines since 2019, now produces some promising white wines.

R.J.M., V. de la S. & F.C.

Peñín, J., *Guía Peñín* (annual).
www.riberadelduero.es

Ribera del Guadiana, DOP encompassing about 34,000 ha/84,016 acres of vineyards in Spain's EXTREMADURA region. Its subzones (Cañamero, Matanegra, Montánchez, Ribera Alta, Ribera Baja, Tierra de Barrios) are rarely seen on wine labels. The autonomous Extremadura government is actively encouraging improvements in wine quality, but the results have been slow in coming. V. de la S. & F.C.

Ribera del Júcar, promising Spanish DOP in the Cuenca province of CASTILLA-LA MANCHA whose first vintage was 2003.

Ribéreau-Gayon, dynasty of important OENOLOGISTS closely associated with the history of the Institut d'Oenologie at the University of BORDEAUX.

Ribolla, white grape variety also known as **Ribolla Gialla** to distinguish it from the less interesting **Ribolla Verde**, best known in FRIULI in north-east Italy but also grown, as Rebula, in SLOVENIA. It is distinct from the ROBOLA of the island of Kefalonia in GREECE and is not related to Ribolla Nera. DNA PROFILING found it to be one of the numerous progenies of the prolific GOUAIS BLANC.

Ribolla was first documented in Friuli in 1296, as Rabola. It lost ground steadily in the 19th and 20th centuries, however, in the wake of the PHYLLOXERA epidemic and Friuli's subsequent enthusiasm for French INTERNATIONAL VARIETIES when vineyards were replanted. In the mid 1990s, Ribolla accounted for less than 1% of all the white DOC wines of Friuli, but by 2015 Italy's total plantings were 362 ha/895 acres, and there were champions of the variety on both sides of the Slovenian border. Rosazzo and Oslavia are generally considered Friuli's two classic areas for Ribolla Gialla, but there is even more planted in western Slovenia, in both Brda and Vipava. Extended contact with the variety's particularly yellow skins is increasingly common, and the wine produced can have firm STRUCTURE and, neatly, yellow-fruit flavours. There are very limited plantings in California.

J.V.

Ricasoli, one of the oldest noble families of TUSCANY in central Italy, important landholders between Florence and Siena for over a thousand years. The vast size of their holdings led the medieval republic of Florence to bar them from holding public office lest the combination of territorial dominion and civic position create a threat to republican liberties. Bettino Ricasoli (1809–80), a dominant figure in the political life of his time and the second prime minister of the newly united Italy in 1861, as well as a dedicated agricultural experimenter and reformer, played a fundamental role in the revitalization of the viticulture of his time and invented what came to be the standard varietal formula for the production of CHIANTI. Like all Tuscan landowners of the time, he believed that the sharecroppers should grow the grapes and the large commercial houses—principally controlled by the Tuscan nobility such as ANTINORI and FRESCOBALDI—would age and distribute the finished wines.

He founded the Ricasoli NÉGOCIANT firm, which would assume a position of leadership in Tuscany for the better part of a century.

The 1970s and 1980s were less kind to the fortunes of the house: a partnership with American distillers Seagram in the négociant part of the business in the 1960s, and another with Hardys of Australia, led to huge expansion of production and a general lowering of quality, and the marketing of Ricasoli wines in supermarkets and other mass distribution centres was extremely damaging to their image. In 1993 Francesco Ricasoli repurchased the family business and set about modernizing the estate. By the second decade of this century all the vineyards had been replanted, and Ricasoli was a very substantial producer of Chianti Classico. Very much in the model of a Bordeaux GRAND VIN, they produced a Castello di Brolio Chianti Classico for the first time in 1997. This wine became a GRAN SELEZIONE in the 2011 vintage.

The distinctive character of the neo-Gothic *castello*, combined with the fame of both Brolio and the Ricasoli name, ensures a steady stream of visitors to the CELLAR DOOR tasting room and osteria. D.C.G. & W.S.

rich is a positive tasting term for, generally, a red wine that gives an appealing impression of power and sweetness even though it may have negligible RESIDUAL SUGAR. It may also be found as a label description on bottles of relatively sweet CHAMPAGNE (see DOSAGE).

Richebourg, great red GRAND CRU in Burgundy's CÔTE D'OR. For details, see VOSNE-ROMANÉE.

riddling, an integral stage in the traditional method of making SPARKLING WINES, known as *remuage* in French. It involves dislodging the deposit left in a bottle after a second fermentation has taken place inside it and shaking it into the neck of the inverted bottle. It can be achieved either by hand or, more speedily, by machine (see GYROPALETTE). Modern alternative techniques may eventually render this cumbersome process superfluous, but they have not so far been commercially adopted. A **riddling rack** is English for a PUPITRE. For more details, see SPARKLING WINEMAKING.

Ridge Vineyards, the most internationally admired producer of American Cabernet Sauvignon, from the historic Monte Bello vineyard in the SANTA CRUZ MOUNTAINS. Ridge produces ageworthy, TERROIR-driven, SINGLE-VINEYARD Cabernets and Zinfandels that demonstrate vineyard character and vintage variance over winemaking wizardry and homogeneity. Ridge's Sonoma outpost Ridge Lytton Springs, acquired in 1991 but a source of OLD VINE Zinfandel grapes for a quarter-century before that, is famous for its suave yet durable wines, as is their historic Geyserville vineyard.

Monte Bello was first planted in 1886, and the stone and redwood winery deep in a ravine at 2,600 feet/792 m above Silicon Valley produced its first wine in 1892. The vineyards were abandoned during PROHIBITION (1920–33) but were replanted to Cabernet Sauvignon in the 1940s. In 1959 Dave Bennion and two fellow Stanford Research Institute engineers purchased the winery and vineyard land as a weekend retreat and made a half barrel of such complex Cabernet that it inspired them to rebond the winery in time for the 1962 vintage. During the 1960s the group also made some exceptional Zinfandel from old vineyards both locally and in Sonoma. In 1969 Paul Draper, with winemaking experience from setting up a small winery in the coastal range of CHILE, joined the enterprise and was in charge until 2016 when he turned 80, having identified and secured long-term single-vineyard sources of top-quality grapes. A small amount of Chardonnay has also been made since 1962. Draper, self-taught through tasting fine wines and studying 19th-century techniques, was an outspoken critic of deliberately extended HANG TIME and of what he might call DAVIS dogma in winemaking.

Monte Bello 1971 performed particularly well in both JUDGMENT OF PARIS tastings. In

1987 a decidedly hands-off Japanese wine lover acquired the business, whose export and pricing policies have been admirably and unusually consistent.

Ried, traditional term in AUSTRIA for a vineyard site that is sometimes seen on labels just before the site name.

Rieslaner, increasingly rare, late-ripening SILVANER × RIESLING cross that was grown on a total of 72 ha/178 acres in Franken and the Pfalz in southern Germany in 2020. Provided it reaches full ripeness, it can produce wines with race and curranty fruit.

Riesling has long been arguably the world's most undervalued, often mis-spelt, and most often mispronounced grape. ('Reece-ling' is correct.) Riesling is the great vine variety of Germany and could claim to be the finest white grape variety in the world on the basis of the longevity of its wines and their ability to transmit the characteristics of a vineyard without losing Riesling's own inimitable style; in this sense it is very much more like Cabernet Sauvignon than Chardonnay (although DNA PROFILING in Austria in 1998 revealed a parent–offspring relationship with GOUAIS BLANC, a parent of Chardonnay, Pinot Noir, et al.; see PINOT). Riesling suffered when OAK and heft were considered the height of FASHION because it is no friend of BARRIQUES, and its wines tend to be relatively low in alcohol. In the 1960s and 1970s, the name 'Riesling' was debased by being applied to a wide range of white grape varieties of varied and often doubtful quality, the ultimate backhanded compliment. Rieslings were also associated with SWEETNESS (another black mark in the modern era) and lack the common please-all blandness of, say, Pinot Grigio.

In the late 19th and first half of the 20th centuries, on the other hand, German Riesling wines were prized, and priced, as highly as the great red wines of France. Connoisseurs knew that, thanks to their magical combination of ACIDITY and EXTRACT, these wines could develop for decades in bottle, regardless of ALCOHOLIC STRENGTH and RESIDUAL SUGAR. Riesling is made at all levels of SWEETNESS, and in the second half of the 20th century residual sugar, typically SÜSSRESERVE, was used by producers of basic German wine to compensate for a lack of full ripeness and uncomfortably high acidity. Today, thanks to CLIMATE CHANGE and more widespread determination to increase quality, fine dry Riesling is common in Germany. But while the average residual sugar of Riesling made everywhere has been declining fast, the variety is distinguished for its ability to produce great sweet wines, whether they be the cold-weather speciality EISWEIN or ICE WINE or BOTRYTIZED wines such as BEERENAUSLESE and TROCKENBEERENAUSLESE and their counterparts outside Germany. Riesling's high natural level of TARTARIC ACID provides it with a much more dependable counterbalance to high residual sugar than, for example, the Sémillon grape of Sauternes.

Riesling wine, wherever produced, is also notable for its powerful, rapier-like aroma variously described as flowery, citrus, steely, honeyed, and whichever blend of quasi-mineral elements is conveyed by the individual vineyard site. This distinctive aroma, usually experienced in conjunction with Riesling's natural raciness and tartness, is particularly high in MONOTERPENES, 10 to 50 times higher, for instance, than WELSCHRIESLING, the quite unrelated white grape variety prevalent in central Europe which, much to German fury, borrowed the word 'Riesling' for many of its aliases (RIESLING ITALICO, for example). An important contributor to the bottle-aged bouquet of Riesling wines is the norisoprenoid hydrocarbon 1,1,6-trimethyl-1,2-dihydronaphthalene (see TDN for more detail).

Viticulturally, true Riesling (sometimes called **Weisser**, **White**, **Rhein**, **Rhine**, or **Johannisberg Riesling**) is distinguished by the hardness of its wood, which helps make it particularly cold-hardy, thus a possible choice for relatively cool wine regions, even if it needs the most favoured, sheltered site in order to ripen fully and yield economically. So resistant is it to FROST that winter pruning can begin earlier than with most other varieties. Its growth is vigorous and upright, and it seems able to produce yields of 60 or 70 hl/ha (4 tons/acre) without any necessary diminution of quality. (Maximum yields allowed by the French INAO authorities are higher in Alsace, France's Riesling enclave, for example, than for any other comparable fine wine.) Its compact bunches of small grapes make it relatively prone to BOTRYTIS, and COULURE can be a problem, but its chief distinction in the vineyard is its late budding. Riesling ripens early relative to most INTERNATIONAL VARIETIES but late relative to most other varieties planted in Germany such as the GERMAN CROSSES. In cool vineyards in the northern hemisphere, it is often not picked until mid October or early November (and sometimes even later). Riesling can ripen so early in warmer regions, however, that its wines can taste dull; a long, slow ripening period suits Riesling best and results in maximum flavour and EXTRACT, while maintaining acidity. Thus, many of Germany's (and therefore most of the world's) most admired Rieslings are grown on particularly favoured sites in cooler regions such as the MOSEL, whose crackling, racy, feather-light style of Riesling is unique.

Germany

As outlined in GERMAN HISTORY, Riesling is by no means the oldest documented vine variety grown in Germany (including, as it did for so long, Alsace). ELBLING and SILVANER were widely grown throughout the Middle Ages, while RÄUSCHLING was the speciality of Baden in the south. An invoice dated 1435, from a castle in the extreme south-east of the Rheingau on the river Main, mentions 'riesslingen in die wingarten', presumably Rieslings in the vineyard. Early spellings of words like 'Riesling' have to be treated with care, since the similarly named Räuschling was so much more common then than today, but Riesling seems to have been recognized as a top-quality variety from the late Middle Ages and was planted throughout the Rhine and Mosel from the middle of the 16th century.

Riesling is first mentioned in connection with Alsace as one of its finer products in 1477 by Duke René of Lorraine, even if we have to wait until 1628 for the first documentary evidence of its actually being planted there.

In the 18th century, various prince-bishops and other ecclesiastical authorities did their utmost to encourage Riesling plantings at the expense of other lesser varieties, notably in the Mosel. But the habit of picking grapes earlier than is today customary did the late-ripening Riesling no favours, and by 1930 the proportion of the Rheingau region, supposedly the classic Riesling heartland, planted with Riesling had fallen to 57% (as opposed to 80% by the turn of the century).

This provided a stimulus to Germany's burgeoning viticultural researchers (see GEISENHEIM) to select and develop top-quality CLONES of the variety. Today, partly thanks to the efforts of a special centre for the CLONAL SELECTION of Riesling at Trier, the German vine-grower can choose from more than 60, whereas France has just eight certified clones of Riesling.

Much of the work of these viticultural institutes was also focused on developing the famous GERMAN CROSSES, designed to produce high yields of grapes with high MUST WEIGHTS but without the viticultural inconveniences of Riesling. In the second half of the 20th century, with their country awash in new money and an ocean of high-sugar grape juice, many Germans gave up winegrowing, or at least the steep-slope cultivation of the demanding Riesling vine, trends which sadly continue. In 1980 Riesling represented less than 20% of German vineyard area; even amid signs of a Riesling renaissance among sophisticated wine drinkers, its share of area has barely increased since then, although, after being overtaken by the lacklustre MÜLLER-THURGAU, it has re-established itself as the most planted vine variety with a rising total of 24,150 ha/59,676 acres widely spread throughout the country in 2020.

Undeniably, though, the top winegrowers and sites not just of the Rheingau and the Mosel but also of the Nahe, Mittelrhein,

Rheinhessen, and the Pfalz are largely devoted to Riesling despite—or in fact, precisely because of—its precarious, slow ripening in the face of climatic challenge. In these growing areas, Riesling is selected for the sunniest hillsides, the steepest slopes, the most sheltered rocky crenellations, and pockets of reflected heat. In such spots, Riesling shows dazzling diversity. It can be as delicate as a 7% Saar wine that is somehow satisfyingly complete—or it may be a refreshing, nervy, bone-dry GROSSES GEWÄCHS with 13.5% alcohol, with many of the finest examples grown in Rheinhessen and the Nahe. For more details, see GERMANY.

Elsewhere

For some wine drinkers, Riesling is acceptable only in its French form, a wine from ALSACE, the only part of France where this German vine is officially allowed—a cause of some frustration with the strictures of the INAO. Alsace's plantings of the variety wine producers there view as their most noble have slowly increased, passing the 3,000-ha mark in the late 1980s and standing at 3,441 ha/8,503 acres in 2019. What is needed to produce Alsace Riesling of real class is, as in Germany, a favoured site of real interest such as many of Alsace's famous GRAND CRU vineyards.

The hallmark of Alsace has been dry wines from aromatic grapes such as Riesling, and certainly the great majority of Alsace Rieslings follow the variety's alluring perfume with a taste that is generally full-bodied and dry. The number of authorized clones of Riesling may be a fraction of those available to German growers, but the dry climate of Alsace minimizes the risk of ROT and makes extended ripening a real possibility, however, often resulting in the prized late-harvest wines which qualify as VENDANGES TARDIVES or, even sweeter, SÉLECTION DE GRAINS NOBLES, the richest, most sumptuous ripeness category of Alsace wines. See ALSACE for more detail.

To the north, about 13% of the LUXEMBOURG vineyard is planted with Riesling, which tends to produce dry, relatively full-bodied wines (thanks to CHAPTALIZATION), closer in style to those of Alsace than to those of the Mosel just over the German border.

In AUSTRIA, Riesling is quantitatively not nearly as important as Grüner Veltliner and was planted on 2,040 ha/5,040 acres in 2022, but it is regarded as one of the country's finest wines when made on a favoured site. The most hallowed Austrian Rieslings are dry, full-bodied, concentrated, and aromatic, and a high proportion of them come from terraced vineyards in Lower Austria. Select sites in the Wachau, Kremstal, and Kamptal enjoy an especially high reputation for their aristocratic, whistle-clean Rieslings. Riesling is an important variety in the vineyards of Vienna as well.

Not surprisingly, Riesling works well in the CONTINENTAL CLIMATE of CZECHIA and SLOVAKIA (where Egon Müller of Germany's Saar Valley makes fine Riesling) to the immediate north of Austria's vineyards, where relatively light wines have real crackle and race. Most of Switzerland is too cool to ripen Riesling properly, with the exception of some of the more schistous soils and warmest vineyards of the Valais around Sion.

Although practically unknown in Iberia (*pace* FAMILIA TORRES in Spain's high Penedès), Riesling has infiltrated the far north of Italy, where plantings totalled 1,461 ha/3,610 acres in 2015. It is grown with real enthusiasm in the high vineyards of ALTO ADIGE, where it produces delicate, aromatic wines quite unlike most Italian whites. It is also grown quite successfully in FRIULI, where it is known as **Riesling Renano**; and over the border in Slovenia, delicate **Renski Rizling** is produced in **Podravje**. Riesling, known as **Rajinski Rizling** and variants thereof, is also planted southwards in Croatia.

It is planted throughout the rest of Eastern Europe, with 1,167 ha/2,884 acres of **Rajnai Rizling** in Hungary, 959 ha of **Riesling de Rhin** in Moldova, 255 ha of Rhine Riesling in Bulgaria, and apparently more than 2,000 ha of an unspecified Riesling in Ukraine, although in each of these countries summers can be too warm to coax real excitement from the variety and Welschriesling tends to reign supreme—as it does, for instance, in Romania.

Outside of Europe, true Riesling was for a long time most widely grown in AUSTRALIA, where it was encouraged by the 19th-century influx of Silesians (see POLAND) and remained the most planted white wine grape variety of all until Chardonnay caught up with its nearly 4,000 ha/10,000 acres in 1990. But few new Riesling vines went into the ground, and by 2015 total Australian plantings had fallen to 3,178 ha/7,853 acres in 2022 and become increasingly concentrated on proven hot spots of the Eden and Clare Valleys, Tasmania, and Great Southern, all producing dry Rieslings with a minerally raciness underlying the tangy, lime-accented fruit. A tiny quantity of BOTRYTIZED sweet Riesling is also made. The wines are less phenolic than those of Alsace and less alcoholic than Alsace or Austrian Riesling. They can also richly repay cellaring for up to, or even beyond, 20 years. In the early 21st century, NEW ZEALAND began to produce convincing wines from its total plantings of 619 ha in 2022, mainly in Marlborough and North Canterbury, notably when some producers started making scintillating LATE HARVEST sweet wines, but its production is dwarfed by that of Sauvignon Blanc, Chardonnay, and Pinot Gris.

Riesling (of some sort) is cultivated more widely in South America than one might think wise. Chile has a few hundred hectares, some grown in the far south to good effect, while Argentina had just 74 ha/183 acres in 2020.

But the major change in Riesling's fortunes in the early 21st century was in North America, to the extent that by 2012 the US had the world's second biggest area of Riesling vineyard after Germany. The Riesling revolution began in WASHINGTON State, which claims a special affinity for Riesling, even organizing the world's first truly international conference on the subject (to be followed by similar events in Australia and the Rheingau). By 2017 Washington's total area devoted to Riesling had reached 2,709 ha/6,695 acres, not that far behind Chardonnay plantings. This growth was largely driven by a JOINT VENTURE between the dominant Washington wine producer Château Ste Michelle and Ernst Loosen of the Mosel, with the Eroica BRAND of Riesling a particular success. Washington Riesling is conveniently winter-hardy, and at their best the wines, with varying sweetness levels, benefit from the state's general brightness of fruit. While Oregon's 185 ha/457 acres puts the variety at just over 1% of the state's vineyards, the dedication of a handful of specialist Riesling producers has shown that Oregon can make compelling examples. California's total area of what is occasionally known as **White Riesling** remained at around 1,600 ha/4,000 acres throughout the 1980s; it declined to 750 ha/1,850 acres by 2003 but rose again to more than 3,659 acres by 2020, perhaps encouraged by Riesling's success in Washington. In recent years, the variety has become more popular from small-scale producers making dry and off-dry Rieslings, though it is still made in small volumes across a range of styles, including some very sweet. Riesling is planted all over the state, but it tends to be found at either higher ELEVATION or in coastal areas.

Because of its winter hardiness, Riesling tends to be treasured in the coolest wine regions of North America. In CANADA, Riesling is cultivated with particular success in Ontario, making fine, delicate ICEWINES just over the border from the Finger Lakes region of NEW YORK State, where it is increasingly recognized as the region's most successful variety. Riesling has also emerged as a major VARIETAL in MICHIGAN.

Price, F., *Riesling Renaissance* (2004).

Riesling Italico, or **Riesling Italianski**, white grape variety which Germans would like to see called RIZLING Italico to distinguish it from true RIESLING, known as Riesling Renano in Italy. In Austria it is called WELSCHRIESLING (under which more details can be found); in much of what was YUGOSLAVIA it is called LAŠKI RIZLING, in CZECHIA it is called Ryzlink Vlašský, and in

HUNGARY it is called OLASZ RIZLING. In Romania it is known as Italian Riesling and Graševina. Within Italy, it is most common in LOMBARDY in the north. Provided its tendency to overcrop is curbed, it can produce delicate, crisp, mildly flowery wines. It is grown to a limited extent in ALTO ADIGE, FRIULI and COLLIO.

Riesling-Silvaner is the flattering and misleading name for MÜLLER-THURGAU that is preferred in SWITZERLAND, where the canton of Thurgau is to be found (neighbouring cantons such as Zurich would rather not see Thurgau on their labels). It was also widely used in New Zealand, where it was for some time the most planted variety.

right bank refers to the right side of a river as you face downstream. The expression is much used in BORDEAUX to denote that part of the wine region that is on the right bank, or north, of the GIRONDE and DORDOGNE rivers. It includes, travelling downstream, the Côtes de Bordeaux appellations of FRANCS and CASTILLON, as well as ST-ÉMILION and its satellite appellations, POMEROL and LALANDE-DE-POMEROL, FRONSAC and Canon-Fronsac, and BOURG. The most obvious characteristic shared by these appellations, as distinct from LEFT BANK appellations, is that Merlot and Cabernet Franc dominate rather than Cabernet Sauvignon. The right bank also has more CLAY and less GRAVEL in its soils.

ringing vines. See CINCTURING.

Rioja. La Rioja is the oldest winemaking province in ARGENTINA, but Rioja is probably best known in the wine world as the leading wine region of SPAIN, producing predominantly red wines in the north of the country. Named after the *río* (river) Oja, a tributary of the Ebro, most of the Rioja wine region lies in the autonomous region of La Rioja in north-east Spain, although parts of the zone extend into the neighbouring BASQUE country to the north-west and NAVARRA to the north-east. Centred on the regional capital Logroño, Rioja divides into three zones along the axis of the river Ebro. **Rioja Alta** occupies the part of the Ebro Valley west of Logroño and includes the winemaking town of Haro. **Rioja Alavesa** is the name given to the section of the zone north of the river Ebro which falls in the Basque province of Alava. **Rioja Oriental** extends from the suburbs of Logroño south and east to include the towns of Calahorra and Alfaro. In 2021 Rioja had 65,700 ha/162,348 acres of vines.

History

There is archaeological evidence that the Romans made wine in the upper Ebro Valley (see SPAIN, history). Wine trade was tolerated rather than encouraged under the Moorish occupation of Iberia, but viticulture flourished once more in Rioja after the Christian restoration of the territory at the end of the 15th century. The name 'Rioja' was already in use in one of the statutes written to guarantee the rights of inhabitants of territory recaptured from the Moors. Rioja's wine industry grew around the numerous monasteries (see MONKS AND MONASTERIES) that were founded to serve pilgrims en route to Santiago de Compostela, and the region's first wine laws date from this period.

For centuries Rioja suffered from its physical isolation from major population centres, and the wines found a market outside the region only in the 1700s, when communications improved and Bilbao became an important trading centre. In 1850, Luciano de Murrieta (subsequently the Marqués de Murrieta) established Rioja's first commercial BODEGA in cellars belonging to the Duque de Vitoria and began exporting wines to the Spanish colonies. The Rioja region benefited unexpectedly, but substantially, from the all too obvious arrival of POWDERY MILDEW in French vineyards in the late 1840s. Bordeaux wine merchants crossed the Pyrenees in large numbers, and in 1862 the Provincial Legislature in Alava employed a French adviser to help local vine-growers. Shunned by smallholders who were concerned only with the requirements of the local Basque market, Jean Pineau was finally employed by the Marqués de Riscal, who set about building a bodega at Elciego along French lines. It was finished in 1868, four years before Murrieta built its own similar installation at Ygay.

When PHYLLOXERA began to devastate French vineyards in the late 1860s, yet more merchants came to Spain in search of wine. The inauguration in 1863 of the Tudela–Bilbao railway line, which passed through Haro, encouraged the wine trade between Rioja and France, as did the relaxation of French duties. Rioja enjoyed an unprecedented boom, sometimes exporting as much as 500,000 hl/13.2 million gal of wine a month to France in the late 19th century. New bodegas were established, among them the Compañía Vinícola del Norte de España (CVNE), López de Heredia, La Rioja Alta, and Bodegas Franco-Españolas, all of which were heavily influenced by the French. During this period the 225-l/59-gal oak *barrica*, or BARRIQUE, was introduced from Bordeaux, and these influential maturation containers are still sometimes referred to as *barricas bordelesas* in Rioja (although American OAK was the popular choice).

By the time phylloxera reached Rioja in 1901, Bordeaux had returned to full production with vines grafted on to phylloxera-resistant ROOTSTOCKS. Spain also lost its lucrative colonial markets, and Rioja's wine industry declined rapidly. Several bodegas were established in the period following the First World War, and Spain's first CONSEJO REGULADOR was established in Rioja in 1926, but the Civil War (1936–9) and the Second World War which followed put paid to further expansion. Recovery came in the late 1960s and 1970s, when, encouraged by growing foreign markets and the construction of a motorway connecting Logroño and Bilbao, a number of new bodegas were built in the region, several with the support of multinational companies, which later sold back the wineries to Spanish firms.

By the late 1970s, Rioja had become the calling card for Spanish wines, wooing non-Spanish consumers with its well-aged, vanilla-scented reds. Towards the late 1990s, RIBERA DEL DUERO began to challenge Rioja's hegemony with its darker, richer reds, inspiring many Rioja producers to make richer, riper reds and release them with less age. Two camps emerged: modernists such as Artadi, Roda, and Telmo Rodriguez and staunch traditionalists such as CVNE and R. López de Heredia. By the late 2010s, a third group of producers, such as Badiola, focused on site, with less wood ageing and earlier releases to retain freshness in the wines. This coincides with a trend towards 100% GARNACHA wines, led by producers such as Juan Carlos Sancha.

Climate and geography

Rioja enjoys an enviable position among Spanish wine regions. Sheltered by the Sierra de Cantabria to the north and west, it is well protected from the rain-bearing Atlantic winds that drench the Basque coast immediately to the north. Yet Rioja's wine producers rarely experience the climatic extremes that burden growers in so much of central and southern Spain. It is difficult to make climatic generalizations, however, about a region that stretches about 120 km/75 miles from north-west to south-east. Indeed, Spanish critics argue that within this single DOP there are several entirely different wine-producing regions.

The vineyards range in ELEVATION from 300 m/984 ft above sea level at Alfaro in the east to nearly 800 m on the slopes of the Sierra de Cantabria to the north-west. Average annual RAINFALL increases correspondingly from less than 300 mm/12 in in parts of Rioja Oriental to over 500 mm in the upper zones of Rioja Alta and Rioja Alavesa.

Rioja Alta and Rioja Alavesa share a similar climate and are distinct from each other for mainly administrative reasons, although there are soil differences between the two. Many of the best grapes are grown here on the cooler slopes to the north-west around the towns and villages of Haro, Labastida, San Vicente, Laguardia, Elciego, Fuenmayor, Cenicero, and Briones. These zones share similar CLAY soils based on LIMESTONE. Downstream to the east, the climate becomes gradually warmer, with rainfall decreasing to less than 400 mm/16 in at Logroño. Where the valley broadens, there is a higher incidence of fertile ALLUVIAL soils composed chiefly of SILT. Around Calahorra and Alfaro in Rioja Oriental the climate is more MEDITERRANEAN. In summer DROUGHT is often a problem here, and temperatures frequently reach 30–35 °C/86–95 °F.

In 2017 the Consejo introduced a new classification to bring more attention to Rioja's varied TERROIRS. **Vino de Zona** are made with at least 85% fruit coming from one of the three zones (Alta, Alavesa, or Oriental). **Vino de Municipio** contain at least 85% fruit from a single village, and—much to the chagrin of many producers—the winery must be in that same village. **Viñedo Singular** indicates a wine sourced from a single vineyard at least 35 years old with a maximum yield of 5,000 kg/ha (for reds). These classifications are open to all colours of wine, still and sparkling.

Viticulture and vine varieties

Rioja's vineyards are split among nearly 15,000 growers, most of whom tend their plots as a sideline and have no winemaking facilities of their own. Many growers have an established contract with one of the merchant bodegas, whose numbers rocketed from about 100 in the mid 1990s to more than 500 a decade later. Others belong to one of the 30 CO-OPERATIVES that serve the region and receive around 35% of the grapes.

The number of permitted grape varieties was increased in 2009 to 14 (five red, nine white), and their distribution varies throughout the region. The most widely planted variety is the dark-skinned TEMPRANILLO, which ripens well on the clay and limestone slopes of Rioja Alta and Rioja Alavesa and in 2021 was planted on 51,000 ha/130,000 acres, comprising almost 88% of the total vineyard surface.

Most Riojas are blends of more than one variety, however, and wines made from the GARNACHA vine—which, after phylloxera, superseded native varieties in the Rioja Oriental—are often used to add BODY to Tempranillo. However, 100% Garnacha wines are a promising trend, especially those from around Tudelilla in Rioja Oriental, historically a Garnacha stronghold, and from the old Garnacha vineyards in Nájera in Rioja Alta. In 2021 Garnacha comprised 7.5% of all red grapes in Rioja.

Two further red varieties, Mazuelo (Cariñena or CARIGNAN) and GRACIANO, each make up about 2% of red-grape plantings. Owing to its susceptibility to disease and its low productivity, Graciano fell from favour with Rioja's vinegrowers before a strong revival in the 1990s. VARIETAL versions are no longer oddities.

The fifth red-wine variety, authorized in 2009, was Maturana Tinta. But in a chaotic turn of events, in some places a different variety has actually been planted under that name. When regional viticulturists began recovering old, minority grape varieties around the turn of the 21st century, several red ones showed good potential. Maturana Tinta was one. It was later identified through DNA PROFILING as Galicia's Merenzao, which, in turn, is the Jura's TROUSSEAU—present for centuries, under several names in Spain, Portugal, and the Canary Islands. Another red grape was named Maturana Tinta de Navarrete because it was recovered and reproduced from a few vines in that Rioja village. Although the 'Trousseau' Maturana Tinta was the one registered with the Ministry of Agriculture, the deep-coloured, peppery one from Navarrete was preferred by growers and planted commercially. The Consejo Regulador looked the other way when it was identified as just 'Maturana Tinta' on labels. In 2011 it was shown to be CASTETS, an almost extinct member of the Bordeaux grape family.

Historically, until PHYLLOXERA arrived Rioja's chief white grape variety was called MALVASIA, a synonym for the lowly ALARIJE of west-central Spain. On its own, it produced rich, alcoholic, dry white wines which responded well to OAK AGEING. However, Viura (known elsewhere in Spain as MACABEO) took over as the most planted light-berried variety in the region; from the early 1970s, fresher-tasting, cool-fermented, early-bottled white wines were in FASHION all over Spain. By the 1990s, most white Riojas were made exclusively from Viura, and Malvasía vines were extremely difficult to find, although some of the traditional oak-aged whites and new BARREL FERMENTED wines are blends of Malvasía and Viura.

A third traditional grape, Garnacha Blanca, was legal but rare. In 2009 Verdejo, Sauvignon Blanc, and Chardonnay were also permitted, but there has been very little interest in them. Also legalized then were three recovered local white varieties that have attracted considerably more attention: Tempranillo Blanco, a relatively recent MUTATION of Tempranillo; Maturana Blanca, which is not related to either one of the Maturana Tintas; and Turruntés, a local name for ALBILLO Mayor, which is more common further south, around the Duero/Douro River.

Vineyards in Rioja tend to be small, especially in Rioja Alta and Rioja Alavesa, where vines are often interspersed with other crops. Vines used to be free-standing BUSH VINES trained into low goblet shapes (see GOBELET), but of the thousands of hectares of vineyard which have been planted since the 1970s, most are trained on WIRES. This resulted in a marked and alarming increase in YIELDS in the region in the 1990s, even before IRRIGATION was legalized in the late 1990s. Official DOP limits are 63 hl/ha (3.5 tons/acre) for white wines and 45 hl/ha for reds.

Winemaking

Rioja winemaking is characterized not by fermentation techniques but by BARREL AGEING, so much so that there were an estimated 1,300,000 barrels in Rioja in 2021, most of them the 225-l *barrica bordelesa* introduced by the French in the mid 19th century. The regulations also specify the minimum ageing period for each officially recognized category of wine. In Rioja, red wines labelled CRIANZA and RESERVA must spend at least a year in oak, while a GRAN RESERVA must spend at least two years (plus another two years in bottle). In common with other Spanish wine regions, Rioja favours American OAK, its soft, vanilla flavour now accepted as typical of Rioja, but a similar effect can also be achieved by slow, OXIDATIVE maturation in older barrels. French oak is used increasingly, however. Over 50% of all Rioja falls into one of the three oak-aged categories above (the rest is either white, rosé, or sold as young, unoaked JOVEN red, much of it within Spain), and the larger bodegas therefore need tens of thousands of casks. Most bodegas renew their *barricas* on a regular basis, and the number of traditional producers who pride themselves on the age of their casks is dwindling. Some producers are also spurning the traditional categories and bottling their oak-aged wine with a basic, generic Rioja label so that they can use different-sized barrels or larger oak VATS.

After the widespread adoption of cool-fermentation techniques in the 1970s, the amount of oak-aged white Rioja progressively diminished. López de Heredia, Marqués de Murrieta, and only a few other bodegas upheld the traditional style by ageing their white wines in oak *barricas*. For white and rosé wines labelled Crianza, Reserva, or Gran Reserva, the minimum wood-ageing period is just six months, with a further year, two years, or four years respectively before the wines may be released for sale. By the mid 1990s, however, many producers had switched back to BARREL FERMENTATION.

Espumosa de Calidad de Rioja is the DOCa's sparkling wine category, introduced in 2017 as an alternative to the CAVA label. It allows for white and rosé sparkling wines made from any of the white grape varieties permitted in still Rioja; rosés must contain at least 25% red grapes. All must be made by the TRADITIONAL METHOD, with 15 months' ageing for Crianza wines and 24 and 36 months respectively for those classified as Reserva or Gran Añada.

V. de la S. & F.C.

Barquín, J., Guitiérrez, L., and de la Serna, V., *The Finest Wines of Rioja and Northwest Spain* (2011).
www.gruporioja.es

Ripaille, CRU from a historic vineyard on the southern shore of Lake Geneva whose name may be added to the French appellation SAVOIE for wines from the CHASSELAS grape. Ch de Ripaille is the only producer.

riparia. See VITIS RIPARIA.

ripasso, Italian term meaning literally 're-passed', for the technique of adding extra flavour, BODY, and alcohol to VALPOLICELLA by re-fermenting the young wine on the unpressed skins of AMARONE and/or RECIOTO wines after these DRIED-GRAPE WINES have finished their fermentation in the spring and have been RACKED off. Regularly aged in new BARRIQUES to add a sweet note of vanilla and often with residual sweetness, Valpolicella Ripasso became a roaring success as a cheaper alternative to Amarone, with production rising from 7.5 million bottles in 2007 to more than 30 million bottles in 2020. The marked increase in the volume of Ripasso has been at the expense of straight Valpolicella, which decreased in the same period from 35.9 million bottles to 18.2 million in 2020. W.S.

ripeness, term used to describe that stage of the continuous process of grape RIPENING or development which is chosen by the winemaker and/or grape processor as that desired at HARVEST. What constitutes the ideal chemical and physical composition of grapes at this point is a subjective judgement dependent on wine style, the winemaker's current belief about optimal ripeness, FASHION, and many other factors, so ripeness is a relative term. Grapes considered at perfect ripeness by one winemaker for one purpose may be considered overripe or underripe by different winemakers for other uses. A commercial grower paid by weight may have yet another opinion.

Ripeness is often related to MUST WEIGHT or grape-sugar concentration. Being directly related to POTENTIAL ALCOHOL, the concentration of SUGAR IN GRAPES has a major impact on wine type. The commercial TABLE WINES of the world fall between two extremes. One is represented by very light whites made from grapes harvested early and from cooler regions to give bottled wines that are refreshing, lower in calories, and low in ALCOHOLIC STRENGTH (11–12%). At the other extreme are rich reds such as those of the southern Rhône dominated by alcohol-rich GRENACHE or examples of Cabernet from California's NAPA Valley that have been subjected to extended HANG TIME. These blockbusters may reach 16% alcohol or even more.

Sugar levels are not the only aspect of grape composition to affect what is considered ripeness. Especially in cool climates, ACIDITY levels can be closely monitored to determine the grapes' ripeness. The acidity in grapes declines with ripening and must be below certain values, depending on wine style, so that the resultant wine will not be too tart. In warm to hot regions, it is more common that the acidity is too low and the PH is too high when sugars have reached the desired potential alcohol level.

Measures of sugar, acidity, and pH have been commonly used around the world to define grape ripeness and optimal harvest time, but winegrowers continue to search for better definitions of ripeness to improve wine quality. (See GRAPE QUALITY ASSESSMENT and PHYSIOLOGICAL RIPENESS.) For all grapes, a measure that indicates flavour is so eagerly sought that it may be said to be the grape researcher's holy grail. This is a particularly difficult measurement that can only be done in a laboratory because of the minute concentrations of FLAVOUR COMPOUNDS. INFRARED SPECTROSCOPY is proving to be useful in the ANALYSIS of many different grape and wine components.

It is common for grapes to be tasted in the field, often by the winemakers, in an attempt to assess optimal harvest date. However, the ability to taste PHENOLICS and other compounds in a sugar-rich substrate makes the practice subjective, requiring many years of experience. Flavour is also difficult to assess when it is partly present only as FLAVOUR PRECURSORS.

Individual grapes' physical condition, especially skin thickness and integrity, is also considered as an aspect of grape ripeness relevant to wine quality. The phenomenon of BERRY CELL DEATH in the later stages of ripening and associated with berry shrivel, generally due to heat and WATER STRESS, is a current area of concern.

See also GRAPE COMPOSITION AND WINE QUALITY and GRAPE JUICE COMPOSITION. R.E.S.

ripeness measurement. See MUST WEIGHT, RIPENESS, and RIPENING, GRAPE.

ripening, grape. The important process of grape development which is a prelude to HARVEST. Ripening begins when the berries soften and start to change colour at the stage called VERAISON and is concluded normally by harvest, which can occur at different stages for different wine styles. Ripening can be affected by many plant, pest and disease, and environmental factors, and is in many ways the most important vine process affecting wine quality since it is so critically related to the chemical and physical composition of the harvested fruit.

Following FRUIT SET, grape berries grow in size but are hard, green, and very acidic (see GRAPE). When almost half their final size, veraison occurs. The timing of this will depend on variety and climate, but it is normally 40–60 days after fruit set, longer for cooler climates. The period from veraison to harvest depends on the stage of ripeness required, but for grapes destined for dry TABLE WINE the period varies from about 30 days in hot regions to about 70 days in cooler regions. However, the phenomenon known as HARVEST COMPRESSION is making such estimates less predictable. For early-ripening varieties such as Pinot Noir and Chardonnay, the ripening period is shorter than for a variety such as Cabernet Sauvignon, which ripens relatively late.

Not all bunches on a vine nor berries on a bunch are at the same stage of development; the first flowers to open set the first berries, which in turn go through veraison and ripen first. This means that there can be substantial variation in degree of ripeness, both within and between bunches, and from vine to vine, depending on factors such as CANOPY MICROCLIMATE, PRUNING level, and soil variation. The use of indices of ripeness to determine optimal harvest date is therefore complicated, and SAMPLING requires skill and care. During the latter stages of ripening when the sugar content is above 20 °BRIX or more, depending on variety and the weather, the berry skin may lose some water. So for very ripe grapes the increase in berry-sugar concentration, for example, is due to a loss of water rather than more sugar accumulation in the berry.

It is relevant to consider ripening in terms of the various chemical compounds of most interest to the winemaker. Sugar, or more precisely SUCROSE, is the most important. It is moved from the leaves to the berries by TRANSLOCATION and is broken down to the constituent molecules GLUCOSE and FRUCTOSE by the enzyme INVERTASE. Sucrose typically originates from current PHOTOSYNTHESIS, less likely from stored CARBOHYDRATE reserves in the woody parts of the vine such as its TRUNK, ARMS, and ROOTS. Heavy crop loads relative to active leaf area (see LEAF TO FRUIT RATIO) slow the increase in concentration of SUGAR IN GRAPES, as do factors slowing photosynthesis such as low or high temperatures, WATER STRESS, and low levels of SUNLIGHT. There can also be competition for the products of photosynthesis; if shoot tips are growing actively, for example, then fruit ripening is slowed (see VIGOUR).

The second major indicator of grape ripening is ACIDITY. The concentration of TARTARIC ACID falls during ripening, due to dilution effects associated with berry growth. The concentration of MALIC ACID falls more quickly than that of tartaric during ripening because of temperature-dependent RESPIRATION in addition to dilution. Grapes ripening in COOL CLIMATES therefore tend to have higher acidity as less malic acid is respired. Juice PH rises throughout ripening due to the decreases in free acids and increases in POTASSIUM. In hot regions, high juice pH is a great concern for wine quality, and ACIDIFICATION of the must is usually necessary. Shahood et al.'s proposed analysis of the kinetics of sugar accumulation and malate metabolism (2020) provides better understanding of variations in ripening within a vineyard.

The skin colour of red grapes is due to ANTHOCYANINS; veraison is signalled when they replace the green colour of chlorophyll, the timing of which typically varies even within one bunch. Anthocyanin concentration rises during ripening, and the value at harvest depends on both environmental and plant factors. Temperature and sunlight exposure have major effects; high temperatures and SHADE within the canopy reduce skin coloration in many varieties. Grape TANNINS are distributed between the skins, seeds, and stems. They increase during ripening at a rate comparable to anthocyanins.

The most abundant minerals in the grape are POTASSIUM, CALCIUM, MAGNESIUM, and SODIUM, and they increase in concentration during ripening. Potassium, which is distributed between flesh and skins, is predominant and has a major effect on juice pH. Potassium extracted from skins during fermentation is one reason why red wines have a higher pH than white wines.

FLAVOUR COMPOUNDS are all-important factors in wine quality, even if their measurement is many years away from becoming a common practice. In the early 21st century, analytical techniques (see ANALYSIS) as well as knowledge about their role are still developing sciences.

See also GRAPE COMPOSITION AND WINE QUALITY, FLAVOUR PRECURSORS, and PHYSIOLOGICAL RIPENESS.

R.E.S.

Conde, C., et al., 'Biochemical changes throughout grape berry development and fruit and wine quality', *Food*, 1 (2006).

Ollat, N., et al., 'Grape berry development: a review', *Journal International des Sciences des Vignes et du Vin*, 36/3 (2002), 109–31.

Shahood, R., et al., 'First quantitative assessment of growth, sugar accumulation and malate breakdown in a single ripening berry', *OENO One*, 54/4 (2020), 51077–92.

ripping is a viticultural operation conducted in many parts of the world before PLANTING a vineyard in order to to break up compact soils so that water can penetrate and roots can grow to a greater depth. Normally bulldozers or heavy tractors are used along row lines, which also makes it easier to insert vineyard posts.

Ripping also provides the opportunity to incorporate FERTILIZERS and soil amendments (see SOIL AMELIORATION) such as phosphates, forms of potassium or lime, as they will not readily leach through the soil.

Ripping is a procedure, like IRRIGATION, which can modify some important properties of the soil affecting wine quality; see TERROIR. R.E.S.

Coombe, B. G., and Dry, P. R. (eds.), *Viticulture*, ii: *Practices* (2nd edn, 2006).

ripping out. See GRUBBING UP.

Riserva, nebulous Italian term usually denoting a wine given extended ageing before release, and suggesting a higher quality than the normal version of the same wine. However, only in the rarest of cases do Riservas have stricter production regulations, such as higher minimum ALCOHOLIC STRENGTH (therefore mirroring the SUPERIORE designation) and higher minimum EXTRACT. Chianti Classico, for example, questionably allows CHAPTALIZATION in Riservas to add up to 0.5% alcohol by volume. The ageing requirement for Riservas varies from DOC to DOC but normally is a minimum of one year—and up to 62 months for Barolo Riserva. In many cases this includes a mandatory period of CASK AGEING as well as AGEING in bottle (with the notable exception of Chianti Classico Riserva, which does not require any wood ageing, however common it is in practice). In some cases the prolonged oak ageing accelerates the wine's development, resulting in PREMATURE OXIDATION and stewed fruit flavours, even though the category is meant to denote wines with the inherent capacity for prolonged ageing.

In most cases Riserva does not guarantee higher quality because producers are not required to declare a Riserva before the harvest. This latitude has allowed some producers simply to reclassify their unsold inventory as Riserva in an effort to obtain a higher price, prompting calls for the abolition of the entire category. W.S.

Rivairenc. See ASPIRAN.

Rivaner, another name for MÜLLER-THURGAU, used in Luxembourg, where it is the most planted grape variety, and in Austria.

Riverina, the largest wine-producing region in NEW SOUTH WALES, its 20,113 ha/49,700 acres of vines spread across the flat south-west plains of the state. This is home base for many of Australia's largest wine companies, including Casella of YELLOW TAIL fame. Sunny and warm, with just 229 mm/9 in annual rainfall, the region is reliant on IRRIGATION for its vineyards, planted mainly to Shiraz, Chardonnay, and Cabernet Sauvignon (in that order). Production volume is substantial, with much fruit going into wines labelled SOUTH EASTERN AUSTRALIA. Interest is increasing in less water-intensive Mediterranean varieties. A.R.P.

Riverland, the most productive wine region in Australia, with a sprawl of vineyards irrigated by the Murray river mainly in the state of SOUTH AUSTRALIA. As in neighbouring MURRAY DARLING, CLIMATE CHANGE and water issues have prompted increased interest in warm-climate grape varieties. Petit Verdot is an established speciality, and Italian varieties such as Vermentino, Fiano, Montepulciano, and Nero d'Avola are catching on. SOUTH EASTERN AUSTRALIA is the catch-all description usually found on labels.

rivers have played an important role throughout the history of wine, both as arteries of trade and also through their action in helping to shape valley slopes particularly well suited to the cultivation of the vine. More recently they have provided valuable water for IRRIGATION.

A river is crucial to the earliest detailed account of the wine trade. HERODOTUS, writing in the 5th century BCE, records how in MESOPOTAMIA wine in palm-wood casks was loaded on to boats in the upper reaches of the river Tigris and then sailed down to Babylon, where the boats were broken up because of the impossibility of paddling them upstream against the current.

During the Roman era, rivers continued to play a vital role in the transport of bulky items such as wine. There were two main trade routes in GAUL: a western one from Narbonne to Toulouse and then along the river GARONNE to Bordeaux and the Atlantic; and a northern one up the RHÔNE to Lyons and thence along the Saône, before cutting across country to the MOSEL and the RHINE and eventually reaching the North Sea. These routes witnessed the transport of thousands of AMPHORAE of wine, but they were also a highway along which the idea of vine cultivation and winemaking passed. By the 1st century CE, viticulture was thus well established along the Rhône and the Garonne, and gradually vineyards came to be cultivated along most of the other major river valleys of Gaul such as the LOIRE and the Seine (see PARIS).

By the year 1000, although vineyards were relatively widely established throughout southern Europe, in the north they were found most frequently in river valleys. The main reason for this was the high cost of overland transport, which gave those with easy access to the main fluvial transport routes a distinct competitive advantage. Environmental factors were also important, with the south-facing slopes of such valleys providing ideal sites because of the extra exposure to the sun that they afforded (see VINEYARD SITE SELECTION). This is particularly evident in the development of vineyards in the cool Mosel–Rhine area, where most of those established before 1050 were in close proximity to rivers.

Coastal transport became increasingly important during the later medieval period, but rivers maintained their role as arteries of the wine trade, and, with the opening-up of eastern Europe, rivers such as the Dnestr, the Vistula, and the Danube also came to play as significant a role as did the Garonne, Loire, Seine, Rhône, and Rhine in the west.

In the 19th and 20th centuries, with the development of the RAILWAYS and, subsequently, efficient road transport, it is environmental factors that have been most important in determining the location of vineyards along the slopes of river valleys. Above all, these locations provide additional sunshine, generally alleviate the problems associated with FROST and excess humidity (see HILLSIDE VINEYARDS), and frequently have soils well suited to vine cultivation (see TOPOGRAPHY). Moreover, in some special locations, as in SAUTERNES and along the Rhine, the proximity to water provides the ideal conditions for NOBLE ROT, which can result in some of the world's greatest sweet wines.

In the NEW WORLD, certain rivers have also been important for the development of several wine regions. The Murray river in Australia, for example, is responsible for the existence of that country's extensive RIVERLAND vineyards, California's CENTRAL VALLEY depends on river water, and most of the vineyards in WASHINGTON State depend on water from the Columbia River. P.T.H.U.

Miller, E., et al. (eds.), *The Cambridge Economic History of Europe*, ii: *Trade and Industry in the Middle Ages* (2nd edn, 1987).

Pounds, N. J. G., *An Historical Geography of Europe 450 BC–AD 1330* (1973).

Schenk, W., 'Viticulture in Franconia along the river Main: human and natural influences since AD 700', *Journal of Wine Research*, 3/3 (1992), 185–203.

Rivesaltes, town just north of Perpignan in southern France that gives its name to two of the biggest appellations of ROUSSILLON for VINS DOUX NATURELS, namely Rivesaltes and MUSCAT DE RIVESALTES. Muscat de Rivesaltes, which represents about 70% of France's total fortified Muscat production, can in fact be made throughout Roussillon's recognized wine-producing area, together with the nine villages of the inland part of the appellation of FITOU in the Aude *département* to the north. The Rivesaltes production zone is similarly generous but specifically excludes those vineyards that produce BANYULS. In 2020 a total of 1,533 ha/3,788 acres were dedicated to the production of Rivesaltes.

Rivesaltes comes in four colours: Grenat, Rosé, Tuilé, and Ambré. Grenat, recognized in 2001, is pure Grenache Noir; for the others, Grenaches Blanc and Gris, Macabeo, Malvoisie du Roussillon, MUSCAT OF ALEXANDRIA, and MUSCAT BLANC À PETITS GRAINS also feature. The minimum ageing for Grenat, the youngest style of wine, is eight months, and its essence is fresh red fruit. The base wine for Tuilé concentrates on black grapes that turn a brick colour with age, whereas for Ambré white grapes dominate and the wine turns amber-golden with age. Both are aged in an OXIDATIVE environment for a minimum of 30 months. With five years or more of ageing, the wine is classified as Hors d'Âge. The sugar level must be at least 45 g/l but in practice is usually 60–70 g/l and may be as high as 120. MUTAGE usually takes place *sur grains* (on the skins) rather than *sur jus* (after pressing). After fermentation, often in stainless-steel vats, the wines are usually aged in wooden casks of all ages and sizes and sometimes in a SOLERA. Some wines are made to taste RANCIO, with deliberate exposure of the maturing wine to the punishing heat and light of a Roussillon noon, either outside or alternatively under a cellar roof. A period outside in glass BONBONNES may also be part of the ageing process. Old Rivesaltes features among the vinous treasures of Roussillon, with flavours of raisins, coffee, chocolate, fruits, or nuts, with notes of rancio. The most concentrated can, like Banyuls, be some of the few wines that happily partner chocolate. The colour of the wine is a good guide as to the dessert that will best accompany it. R.E.G.

Riviera di Ponente, or **Riviera Ligure di Ponente**, extensive, overarching Ligurian DOC along the north-western coast of Italy producing wines made of VERMENTINO (called Pigato here), ALICANTE (probably GRENACHE), and ROSSESE di Dolceaqua. For more details, see LIGURIA.

Rizling, term for the white grape variety known variously in central Europe as WELSCHRIESLING, OLASZ RIZLING, LAŠKI RIZLING, RIESLING ITALICO, and Graševina. The Germans disapprove of any name for this inferior grape variety which suggests a relationship with their own noble RIESLING vine but will accept 'Rizling' as a suitably distinctive alternative.

Rkatsiteli, ancient, cold-hardy Georgian white grape variety which was so widely planted in what was the Soviet Union that in 1990 it was estimated to be the world's third most planted overall. Thanks to President GORBACHEV'S VINE-PULL SCHEME, however, it had fallen to fourteenth place by 2000 and to sixteenth by 2016. It is still widely planted in the former Soviet republics, though, being grown in all of its wine-producing independent republics with the exception of TURKMENISTAN. It is, understandably, most important in GEORGIA, particularly in Kakheti, but also widely planted in Ukraine, Bulgaria, MOLDOVA, RUSSIA, and ARMENIA. As Baiyu it reached China and has adapted well to the inland wine regions there with their cold winters. Presumably its cold resistance was what inspired FINGER LAKES grower Konstantin Frank to plant it in New York State, and it is now planted in Virginia and several other American states as well.

Much is demanded of this productive variety, and it achieves much, providing a base for a wide range of wine styles, including FORTIFIED WINES and brandy. The wine is distinguished by a keen level of ACIDITY, easily 9 g/l even when picked as late as October, and by good sugar levels, too.

Roannaise, Côte. Situated only one range of hills west of the BEAUJOLAIS region, this 20-km-long AOC runs just south-west of the N7 as it makes its way to Lyons. It was the direct RIVER and canal links with Paris, however, that gave the region's wines relative fame and popularity in the 19th century, such that annual production was almost 800,000 hl/21.1 million gal at the beginning of the 20th century. Production was down to 4,000 hl by 1994 when AOC status was won; by 2019, just 215 ha of vines were left, planted in GRANITIC soils on slopes at 350–550 m/1,148–1,904 ft in ELEVATION. Lightish reds and some rosés (15% of total production) are made from locally adapted GAMAY grapes, called St-Romain à Jus Blanc here, using Beaujolais cellar techniques, usually CARBONIC or SEMI-CARBONIC MACERATION. White and sparkling wines, mainly Chardonnay and Viognier, must take the IGP Urfé. Wine quality is in the hands of individual winemakers, egged on by the Troisgros family at their famous restaurant near the town of Roanne.

Robe, wine region on the Limestone Coast of SOUTH AUSTRALIA sandwiched between the Southern Ocean and a string of inland lakes that help moderate the cool MARITIME CLIMATE. Soils vary from sandy LOAM to CALCAREOUS sand and TERRA ROSSA. Both white wine grapes (Chardonnay, Sauvignon Blanc) and red (Cabernet Sauvignon, Shiraz) make up the 681 ha/1,683 acres of vineyards.

Robertson, important warm, dry, wine-producing district within the Breede River Valley region in South Africa. Home to many estates and CO-OPERATIVES, it produces some fine whites, including Chardonnays and Sauvignon Blancs, and an increasingly creditable array of reds, most notably Shiraz and Cabernet. Bonnievale is the best-known of the district's wards. Most vineyards fringe the Breede River, which provides the essential IRRIGATION (rainfall is less than 400 mm/16 in annually) and ALLUVIAL soils although CALCIUM-rich outcrops are also found. Most of the INTERNATIONAL VARIETIES perform well here, although Robertson has long enjoyed a reputation for fortified MUSCADELS. Robertson produces more than 15% of the national harvest. Average daily growing-season temperatures are high, though with marked DIURNAL TEMPERATURE RANGE.

roble, Spanish for 'oak', is used on wine labels in SPAIN to indicate red and rosé wines that have been aged at least three months in oak BARRELS. The term is very popular in RIBERA DEL DUERO, the appellation that has taken the most credit for it, although it can be used throughout Spain. F.C.

Robola, wine and grape variety for which the Ionian island of Kefalonia in GREECE is most famous. The distinctively powerful, lemony dry white is made entirely from Robola grapes, which are cultivated almost exclusively on the island. The wine made from these early-ripening grapes is high in both ACIDITY and EXTRACT and is much prized within Greece. DNA PROFILING established that Robola is quite distinct from Rebula (RIBOLLA Gialla). The country's 406 ha/1,003 acres of this variety are mainly limited to the Ionian Islands.

robotic lagar, a computer-operated LAGAR pioneered by the SYMINGTONS for the production of PORT.

robots are an emerging technology in vineyards. They are most commonly designed to replace vineyard operations that are already mechanized using implements carried by a manned tractor, such as TILLAGE or mowing for weed management, or SPRAYING for disease control. Concerns about the use of HERBICIDES for under-vine weed management and the high number of tractor passes required for the mechanical cultivation and mowing alternatives to herbicides (see SOIL COMPACTION) make this the likely first area of adoption. Robots can also be used to carry other sensors to facilitate PRECISION VITICULTURE.

Robots usually navigate a previously mapped area based on high-accuracy satellite positioning, with additional local guidance and safety management by other sensors such as cameras, radar, LiDAR (Light Detection and Ranging), ultrasound, and bump sensors. There is no clear distinction between a robot and an automated TRACTOR. Robots are more likely to be electric and powered by batteries, but some are also driven by diesel combustion engines like conventional tractors or are hybrids.

See also LABOUR and MECHANIZATION. S.N.

Rochelle, La. See LA ROCHELLE.

rock, a rigid, naturally bonded aggregate of geological MINERALS. A mass of SAND or VOLCANIC ash, or a molten lava, would not be regarded as rock although this is the case in some historical texts; neither would concrete. The solid Earth is made chiefly of rock. Its outermost surface is known as bedrock (see GEOLOGY), which is generally overlain by a more or less disintegrated zone of SUBSOIL and then possibly by agricultural SOIL, although in vineyards such divisions are unusually hazy.

A fragment of bedrock is commonly called a rock or a STONE, with more specific names used to indicate its size or smoothness (see GEOLOGY). The stones seen in many vineyard soils may or may not represent the local bedrock (see ALLUVIUM and COLLUVIUM). Vines cannot obtain nutrition directly from bedrock or from stones, except by the action of MYCORRHIZAL fungi. A.J.M.

Rockpile, California AVA nested within Dry Creek Valley AVA. See SONOMA.

Roditis, or **Rhoditis**, slightly pink-skinned grape variety that is Greece's second most common after SAVATIANO, which DNA PROFILING suggests is one of its parents, planted on a total of 9,398 ha/23,223 acres in 2021. Although its name is probably derived from the island of Rhodes, it was traditionally grown, often as a FIELD BLEND with other, differently coloured, varieties called Roditis Something, in the Peloponnese and was even more important in the pre-PHYLLOXERA era. The vine is particularly sensitive to POWDERY MILDEW. It ripens relatively late and keeps its ACIDITY quite well even in such hot climates as that of Ankhialos in Thessaly in central Greece, although it can also ripen well in high-ELEVATION vineyards. It is often blended with the softer Savatiano, particularly for RETSINA. J.V. & J.H.

Roditis Kokkinos, or **Rhoditis Kokkino**, meaning 'red of Rhodes', is a red-skinned Greek grape variety traditionally grown in the Peloponnese that has been shown by DNA PROFILING to be distinct from, even if often planted with, the more common pink-berried RODITIS. Also known as Tourkopoula.

Roederer, Louis, family-owned Champagne house known both for its early links with the Russian court and for its extensive vineyard ownership. The original company was founded by a M. Dubois around 1776; Louis Roederer joined in 1827, becoming owner in 1833. By the second half of the century, RUSSIA had become the major market for Champagne Louis Roederer: 666,386 bottles out of a total company production of 2.5 million were exported there in 1873. In 1876 Louis Roederer was commissioned by Tsar Alexander II to create a special personal cuvée in clear glass crystal bottles that was named Cristal. But in 1917 the Russian Revolution brought the immediate loss of the company's principal export market. Camille Orly-Roederer, widow of the great-nephew of Louis, rebuilt the company after this blow, in particular by strengthening Roederer's vineyard holdings at a time when other houses were selling, a move many later regretted. In 1924, responding to demand for the legendary Cristal, she reintroduced it, bottled in the original design of crystal glass with no PUNT, creating the first PRESTIGE CUVÉE champagne. By the mid 2010s, the company's vineyards extended over 240 ha/593 acres, much of it in the grands and premiers crus villages. By 2022, 115 of the 240 ha were certified organic, and the certification process continues. Both white and rosé Brut Nature and Cristal wines are all farmed BIODYNAMICALLY, followed by vintage Blanc de Blancs from the 2018 vintage. They also have 10 ha of experimental vineyards in which to research their own CLONES, PRUNING, and TRAINING SYSTEMS in order to meet the challenges of CLIMATE CHANGE and have their own vineyard nursery for their MASS SELECTION project.

Mainly thanks to these vineyard holdings, Roederer produces more vintages of Cristal than is usual for a prestige cuvée. The company, unusually for a substantial champagne house, remains independent. Jean-Claude Rouzaud, Camille's grandson, continued in the expansionist vein, buying more vineyards and investing in other wine regions. Roederer Estate in ANDERSON VALLEY, first released in 1988, is one of California's finest sparkling wines. An investment in Jansz in TASMANIA was terminated. The company, now headed by Frédéric Rouzaud, the seventh generation to lead the company, also owns Ramos Pinto in Portugal, Champagne Deutz, Delas Rhône wines, Domaines Ott in Provence, and in Bordeaux Chx de Pez in St-Estèphe and, since 2007, second-growth Ch Pichon Longueville Comtesse de Lalande in Pauillac. In 2019 and 2020 respectively, Merry Edwards and the revered Diamond Creek in California were added.

Roero, increasingly important vineyard area and DOCG on sandy hills on the left bank of the River Tanaro in the PIEMONTE region of north-west Italy which takes its name from the villages of Montaldo Roero, Monteu Roero, and Santo Stefano Roero to the north-west of Alba. Geographically and administratively it is not part of the LANGHE, from which it is separated by the River Tanaro, but it shares its most important red grape variety, NEBBIOLO, although the wines tend to be softer and earlier-maturing than those from BARBARESCO and BAROLO. Despite ongoing marketing efforts, red Roero has proven such a hard sell that most producers resort to the generic Langhe Nebbiolo. Commercially much more significant is Roero Bianco, made from ARNEIS, planted on 832 ha/2,056 acres compared with 184 ha of Nebbiolo. In 2017 the region introduced the MGA system, an official list of 135 single vineyards which may appear on labels. W.S.

www.consorziodelroero.it

Rolland, Michel (1947–), the most famous CONSULTANT oenologist, responsible in several ways for the late 20th century FASHION for overtly ripe, deep-coloured, supple red bordeaux. From 1973 he and his wife Dany ran a laboratory in POMEROL on which many local growers depended for ANALYSIS. They led a team of younger OENOLOGISTS with hundreds of clients all over the world, though especially in Bordeaux. In 2020 the business was transferred to three of the senior staff and renamed Rolland et Associés. In 2013, after separating, Michel and Dany sold Michel's family properties Chx Le Bon Pasteur in Pomerol, Bertineau St-Vincent in LALANDE-DE-POMEROL, and Rolland-Maillet in ST-ÉMILION to Asian investors, but the Rolland team continue to be responsible for their winemaking. They also farm Ch La Grande Clotte in Lussac-St-Émilion, and Dany lives at Ch Fontenil in Fronsac, acquired in 1986. The Bordeaux RIGHT BANK enterprises to which he is consultant are too numerous to list (although they have included L'Angélus, Beau-Séjour Bécot, Clinet, Clos L'Église, La Dominique, La Gaffelière, Grand Mayne, Larmande, Pavie, Pavie-Decesse, and Troplong Mondot). In the MÉDOC and GRAVES they have included many properties managed by NÉGOCIANTS Dourthe as well as Chx Fieuzal, Kirwan, Léoville Poyferré, Malescot St-Exupéry, Pape-Clément, Smith Haut Lafitte, and La Tour Martillac. But it is his consultancies outside France that set him apart from all but a handful of his compatriots in the breadth of his experience. They include, for example, HARLAN in the Napa Valley, Ornellaia in Italy (after TCHELISTCHEFF), and (one of his more novel clients and evidence of his love of travel) Grover in India. The Rollands and their two daughters have also had holdings outside France: Bonne Nouvelle in South Africa (with Remhoogte Estate), Campo Eliseo in Toro (with François LURTON), and Clos de los Siete, Val de Flores, and Mariflor in Argentina. He studied oenology at the University of BORDEAUX during the PEYNAUD era and has continued to declare his philosophy that wine should give maximum pleasure, although he has been criticized for a certain uniformity of style.

Rolle, official alternative southern French name for the increasingly popular VERMENTINO used traditionally in BELLET and parts of the Languedoc and Roussillon. DNA PROFILING has shown it to be distinct from ROLLO.

Rollo, ancient Ligurian white wine grape with several names but distinct from ROLLE, planted on just 15 ha/37 acres in 2015.

Romagna, eastern part of EMILIA-ROMAGNA.

Romagna Albana, white wine made in central Italy from ALBANA grapes and much-maligned despite its long historic presence in the region. Unreasonably high YIELDS of 100 hl/ha and careless winemaking by large CO-OPERATIVES led to Albana's mediocre reputation, which is why its elevation to DOCG in 1986 spurred criticism that the DOC system was flawed.

Only those producers who give Albana their full attention—planting it on suitable sites (rather than simply where SANGIOVESE, Romagna's most important red wine grape, wouldn't ripen), drastically reducing yields, and harvesting it at full ripeness and aromatic development—overcome Albana's supposed neutral and tart character. Some producers are now making SKIN-FERMENTED versions, a style made popular by the NATURAL WINE scene.

With Albana in decline from 7,418 ha/18,330 acres in 1970 to just 818 ha in 2020, local research into Albana CLONES has helped to save the rarest ones from extinction while a greater focus on the selection of suitable sites has led to the production of several SINGLE-VINEYARD WINES, showing that the variety adapts equally well to the CALCAREOUS soils of the township of Bertinoro and the reddish CLAY soils of Faenza. A system of subzones that would bring these differences into focus, analogous to that of ROMAGNA SANGIOVESE, is long overdue.

Albana can come in several versions: *secco* (dry), *amabile* (medium dry), *dolce* (sweet), and PASSITO, reaching its pinnacle in late-picked dry versions as well as BOTRYTIZED dessert wines. W.S.

www.consorziovinidiromagna.it

Romagna Sangiovese, quantitatively and increasingly qualitatively important DOC in EMILIA-ROMAGNA made from SANGIOVESE, the region's most widely cultivated red grape variety, with 6,235 ha/15,407 acres in 2020.

In the recent past the zone's reputation had been sullied by high YIELDS, mediocre wine quality, and the erroneous belief that the CLONES of Sangiovese in Romagna were inferior to those in Tuscany. Sangiovese di Romagna is part of the same Sangiovese Grosso group as, for example, BRUNELLO, but old BUSH VINES around Predappio in Romagna appear to be Sangiovese Lamole, which has a higher PHENOLIC content and produces smaller grapes resulting in higher EXTRACT in the final wines.

The DOC has 16 subzones, which can be broadly grouped into five macro zones. **Faentino**, the vineyard area around Faenza (with the subzones of Serra, Brisighella, Modigliana, Marzeno, and Oriolo), has a diverse array of soils, ranging from IRON-rich red CLAY at 250 m/820 ft in elevation around Marzeno to SANDSTONE in Modigliana, at 500 m on the edge of the Apennine Mountains separating Romagna from Tuscany. The **Forlivese** zone around Forlì (with the subzones Castrocaro-Terra del Sole, Predappio, Bertinoro, and Medola) is mostly at lower elevations with clay soils, except Predappio, an ancient winegrowing area giving some of the region's finest, long-lived Sangiovese from its many old vines and iron- and sandstone-rich soils at up to 450 m. **Cesanese** around Cesena (with the subzones of Cesena, San Vicinio, and Longiano) has hillside vineyards rising to 200 m, CALCAREOUS clay soils, and a more moderate climate thanks to the proximity of the Adriatic coast. The **Riminese** zone includes Verruchio, Coriano, and San Clemente, and **Imolese** includes Imola. Thanks to the work of pioneers such as wine journalist Giorgio Melandri and oenologist Francesco Bordini, whose work in Modigliana has inspired a growing band of TERROIR-centric producers, stylistic differences based on subzones are beginning to become a reality. W.S.

Masnaghetti, A., *Romagna Sangiovese* (2013).
www.consorziovinidiromagna.it

Romagna Trebbiano, DOC in EMILIA-ROMAGNA in central Italy for neutral dry whites made from TREBBIANO Romagnolo grapes. Permitted YIELDS of up to 14 tonnes/ha result in very ordinary wines. Wines of real interest can result if producers aim at quality, but most of its 14,170 ha/35,015 acres are tended by small grape-growers whose produce lands in the undiscerning vats of the huge CO-OPERATIVES here.

Romanée, **Romanée-Conti**, **Romanée-St-Vivant**, great red GRANDS CRUS, for more details of which see VOSNE-ROMANÉE. See also DOMAINE DE LA ROMANÉE-CONTI.

Romania is eastern Europe's quantitatively most important wine producer, fifth in the EU by area under vine and sixth by wine volume. In 2021 there were 180,345 ha/445,642 acres of vineyard, of which 97,043 ha were VITIS VINIFERA, according to data from Romania's National Office for Vine and Wine Products. In 2020 the harvest declined to 3.8 million hl due to difficult climatic conditions but returned to a more typical 4.5 million hl/118,877,427 gal in 2021.

History

The beginning of Romanian viticulture may date to the Cucuteni-Trypillian culture from 5200–3500 BCE, though it's not clear if these people made wine. The region of Dobrogea claims to be the birthplace of the Thracian god DIONYSUS, and the Thracians were well-known wine drinkers. This region, on the Black Sea, was settled in the 7th century BCE by the ancient GREEKS, who may have brought vines of their own, while vineyard tools dating back 2,500 years have been found in Dobrogea and close to Iași. As Rome advanced into the Balkan peninsula, the resident Geto-Dacian tribes came together in opposition under King Burebista (82–44 BCE). It seems that Dacia had a well-established wine culture, but, in an attempt to put an end to repeated invasions, Burebista ordered the destruction of all vineyards. However, after the Roman Emperor Trajan had conquered Dacia (102 CE), coins were minted depicting a woman being offered grapes by two children, proof that not all the vineyards were uprooted.

After the Romans left, the area was overrun by successive waves of migration, leaving few records of wine. It was not until the 11th century that written records of wine reappear. Transylvania appears to have undergone a renaissance of winemaking in the 12th century

with Saxon settlers from the Mosel and the Rhein, and by the 16th century wine was a major source of income in the region. The principalities of Moldavia and Wallachia evolved as part of the Eastern Orthodox world, and in the 16th century they became vassal states paying tribute to the Ottoman Empire, allowing them to avoid mass settlement by Muslims. Catholic-led Transylvania came under the Habsburg crown towards the end of 17th century. By 1812, Moldavia lost Bessarabia, its eastern territory, to Russia. In 1861 Wallachia and Moldavia unified, and in 1877 the newly named Romania declared independence from the Ottomans. Transylvania and Banat did not join Romania until 1918.

There is little detailed evidence of wine in the 19th century as many records were destroyed by the communists, though the arrival of PHYLLOXERA in 1880 seems to have brought formal attention to the wine sector, with NURSERIES and research institutes set up as early as 1893 to restore viticulture with GRAFTED VINES and French grape varieties. However, poor rural growers preferred HYBRIDS over more expensive grafted vines. After the Second World War, the communist government began to confiscate private land, with full-scale collectivization launched in 1949. All wine was processed through state-owned Vinalcool plants, and vineyard area was expanded with an emphasis on MECHANIZATION and heavy use of FERTILIZERS. Vine material was also selected for quantity and FROST resistance rather than for quality. In 1967 the notorious dictator Nicolae Ceauşescu came to power, imposing a brutal and repressive regime until his death by firing squad in the revolution of December 1989. By that time vineyards covered 275,000 ha/679,540 acres.

Privatization after independence was slow and complex. Laws were changed multiple times, and lack of a land register is still causing disputes today. The country ended up with highly fragmented land holdings and dilapidated wineries. Improvements in wine quality remained difficult until the 2000s when a new wave of external investment began. From 2002 onwards, substantial EU funds have had a major impact on replanting and modernizing equipment.

Romania today has a strong domestic market, though official per capita consumption has fallen from a high of 30 l/8 gal in 2008 to 21.2 l/5.6 gal in 2020, not counting black-market homemade wines. White wine accounts for approximately 52.3% of official production, while reds and rosé make up 47.7%, a reflection of tastes moving away from semi-sweet styles towards drier styles and increasing red wine consumption. Romania remains a net wine importer, with imports in 2020 reaching 446,863 hl/9.8 million gal; exports in 2020 totalled 206,658 hl.

Of the country's 404 registered wineries, five producers (Cramele Recaş, Jidvei, Cotnari, Crama Ceptura, and Zarea) dominated the domestic market in 2020, with a 42% share between them. Fragmented land holdings remain a challenge: there were 843,866 registered grape-growers in 2021, with only 460 owning more than 20 ha/49 acres.

Geography and climate

Romania lies between 44 and 48° N and is dominated by mountains, especially the arc of the Carpathian range—half of this range lies in Romania, including the eastern and southern Carpathians (sometimes called the Transylvanian Alps). The Wallachian Plain stretches south to the River Danube and Bulgaria, while the Pannonian Plain lies between the hills and Hungary to the west. Romania's wine regions are widely dispersed throughout the country. Most of the country has a CONTINENTAL CLIMATE except by the Black Sea, which helps to moderate winter temperatures in Dobrogea. Severe winter temperatures below −20 °C/−4 °F occur four to five times per decade, and summer temperatures are increasingly likely to range from hot to very hot (>35 °C/95 °F), causing DROUGHT stress. Most vineyards are not irrigated, and access to IRRIGATION water or boreholes is restricted by the state, so even vine-growers who want to irrigate often cannot do so in practice. Average July temperature is 23.5 °C/74 °F, and average annual rainfall is 400–600 mm/16–21 in.

Viticulture

Vine-TRAINING SYSTEMS used here traditionally were mainly GOBELET, though from the late 1950s collectivization and the drive for quantity saw a switch to neatly wired rows using concrete posts and mainly GUYOT and CORDON training. In older vineyards, VINE DENSITY is typically low. MECHANIZATION of vineyard operations has become common, including MECHANICAL HARVESTING in bigger vineyards, a change forced by difficulties in finding LABOUR. EU funds have subsidized substantial replanting with higher-quality CLONES, especially commercial clones of local grapes such as FETEASCĂ Neagră, with VSP training (see VERTICAL TRELLIS) and much closer spacing (4,000–5,000 vines/ha).

Owing to both increasing extreme weather events resulting from CLIMATE CHANGE and winter cold, most vineyards are planted on gentle slopes (5–25%) and may be in valleys with MESOCLIMATES which offer some protection. Other viticultural hazards include both POWDERY MILDEW and DOWNY MILDEW, as well as GREY ROT, particularly in fragmented vineyards where vines may be left untreated due to the cost of SPRAYING. Another potential problem for grape-growers is theft of fruit, young vine plants, and even metal posts and wires, requiring larger operations to employ full-time security guards and dogs.

Winemaking

Winemaking in Romania has widely been updated to modern international standards with STAINLESS STEEL equipment, TEMPERATURE CONTROL, pneumatic PRESSES, and so on. Some traditional CONCRETE tanks, ROTARY fermenters, and large old Carpathian oak casks still exist, but these are gradually being replaced even if still preferred by some older winemakers. Today's winemaking is generally technically correct, and problems of lack of winery HYGIENE, OXIDATION, and excess VOLATILE ACIDITY have become much less prevalent. The use of OAK has become more sophisticated with premium wines often aged in BARRIQUES and sometimes fermented in oak. French oak is widespread, but Hungarian, American, and some Romanian COOPERAGES are now making high-quality barrels.

Vine varieties

Unusually in this part of Europe, it is INDIGENOUS VARIETIES that dominate Romania's vineyard. The country also has a significant area of HYBRIDS, which should have been uprooted by 2014 under the terms of EU accession agreements, but many of Romania's 800,000 or so vine-growers still grow these hybrids on small plots so there is no political will to change this. Industry data for 2021 showed that the most planted white varieties by far are the two white Feteascăs, Fetească Regală (12,289 ha) and Fetească Albă (12,076 ha), both of which can produce fresh, gently aromatic, dry white wines. Fetească Regală (now thought to be a CROSS of Fetească Albă and Frâncuşă) has more BODY, with perceptible PHENOLICS in its pulp, and can be successfully BARREL FERMENTED, while the more delicate Fetească Albă is more typically vinified without oak and may be used in blends.

The third most planted white-wine variety is Riesling Italico, or WELSCHRIESLING, grown on 7,064 ha/17,456 acres but usually marketed locally simply as 'Riesling'. Note that genuine RIESLING was grown on only 442 ha and is labelled Riesling de Rhin. Sauvignon (5,697 ha), Aligoté (5,205 ha), then Muscat Ottonel (5,156 ha) are next. Other white varieties that have shown significant increases by area include Chardonnay (2,009 ha), Pinot Gris (1,471 ha, usually marketed as Pinot Grigio), and TĂMÂIOASĂ Românească (1,747 ha, the 'frankincense grape', a local CLONE of MUSCAT BLANC À PETITS GRAINS).

Merlot is the most planted red wine variety with 11,152 ha/27,557 acres, followed by Cabernet Sauvignon (5,423 ha). Local grapes Roşioară (Bulgaria's PAMID) planted on 2,653 ha and Băbească Neagră (2,569 ha, with its *gris* (i.e. pink-skinned) variant on a further 297 ha) are both losing ground and typically make light, ordinary reds. Of much greater interest is Fetească Neagră (the 'black maiden grape'), planted on 3,187 ha. This area is increasing rapidly because of its potential as Romania's flagship red grape. Pinot Noir is viewed in certain export markets as Romania's signature grape variety, and the area planted has increased from an estimated 500 ha in 2005 to 2,040 ha in 2021. The variety was imported into Romania around 1900, particularly for sparkling wine production. The variety long known as Burgund Mare ('big Burgundian') is Kékfrankos, or BLAUFRÄNKISCH, grown on 690 ha.

Other specifically Romanian varieties planted to a significant extent include the light-berried 'fat' GRASĂ and crisp Frâncuşă, both grapes of COTNARI. Busuioacă de Bohotin (678 ha/1,675 acres) is a pink-skinned grape traditionally used for aromatic sweet and DEMI-SEC wines but increasingly appearing in quality, dry rosé wines and sparkling wines. It is named after the Romanian word for basil, *busuioc,* for its grapey, floral, red-fruit aromas, and it probably originates around Bohotin in the Moldovan Hills. Some research suggests this is a colour MUTATION of Muscat Blanc à Petits Grains, though this remains unproven. The Galbenă vine of Odobeşti makes light, crisp whites—384 ha are officially registered, with a further 58 ha under its synonym of Zghihară de Huşi—and the white Şarba (307 ha) is also found in this area. Other Romanian varieties planted include Crâmpoşie/Crâmpoşie Selecţionată, Mustoasă de Măderat, Iordană, and Plavaie grown in Odobeşti. There is also some interest in reviving old INDIGENOUS VARIETIES and relatively new local CROSSES such as Negru de Drăgăşani and Novac, both SAPERAVI crosses. Other crosses enthusiastically developed by Romanian viticultural stations include Columna, a Pinot Gris x Grasă CROSS, and the red-wine grape Codană.

Wine laws

Romanian wine law is fully compliant with EU regulations.

DOC (Denumire de Origine Controlată) is the recognized traditional term for PDO wines (i.e. high-quality wines grown and produced within a delimited area). It is supplemented by further classifications according to the grapes' maturity:

DOC-CMD: wines harvested at full maturity bearing a designation of origin
DOC-CT: LATE HARVEST wines
DOC-CIB: late-harvest/BOTRYTIZED sweet wines.

There are currently 33 PDO wines (38 are registered with the EU, some covering multiple wine styles), though they are produced in only seven of the eight major regions.

PGI wines are described as Vin cu Indicaţie Geografică (IG). There are 12 PGIs (Colinele Dobrogei, Dealurile Crişanei, Dealurile Moldovei, Dealurile Munteniei, Dealurile Olteniei, Dealurile Sătmarului, Dealurile Transilvaniei, Dealurile Vrancei, Dealurile Zarandului, Terasele Dunării, Viile Caraşului, Viile Timişului). Each has detailed specifications governing permitted grape varieties, maximum yields, vineyard density, minimum alcohol levels, and permitted winemaking. There has also been a category for VARIETAL wines since 2017. Other protected traditional terms include 'Rezervă', for wine matured for at least six months in oak and six months in bottle, and 'Vin de Vinotecă', for wine matured at least one year in oak and four years in bottle.

Wine regions

Romania's wine regions are divided into eight distinct zones (see map): Podişul Transilvaniei (Transylvanian Plateau); Dealurile Crişanei ai Maramureşului (Hills of Crişana and Maramureş); Dealurile Moldovei (Moldovan Hills) on the eastern slopes of the Carpathians; Dealurile Oltenei si Muntenei (Muntenia and Oltenia), the warm, central region in the southern Carpathians; Dealurile Banatului (Banat) towards the borders with Hungary and Serbia; Colinenele Dobrogei (the low hills of Dobrogea) between the Danube and the Black Sea; and the flatter Terasele Dunarii (Danube Terraces) and Nisipurile din Sudul Tarii (Southern sands), the last being relatively unimportant as a region for good-quality wine.

Transylvania is the high central region producing predominantly white wines, though recently good reds and sweet ice wines have appeared. The most important and oldest Transylvanian delimited wine region is Târnave, with its subregions Jidvei, Blaj, and Mediaş. Other DOC zones include Alba Iulia, Alba, Aiud, and Lechința to the north with Sebeş-Apold in the south-west. These are some of Romania's coolest vineyards at ELEVATIONS up to 500 m/1,800 ft. The mainly white wines typically have appealing fresh acidity and good aromatic expression. Evidence of the medieval immigration of Saxon settlers from the MOSEL Valley is still common in the architecture and in the wine styles. In addition to the common Fetească Regală and Fetească Albă, other varieties grown are Muscat Ottonel, Traminer, Sauvignon Blanc, and recently some successful Pinot Noir, Zweigelt, and Merlot. Apold's Iordană vine makes high-acid, low-alcohol wine used mainly for sparkling wines.

Crişana and Maramureş is slightly warmer than Transylvania though further north. Spring can be mild on the slopes facing south and south-west on the foothills of the Zarand Mountains, so BUDBREAK is usually earlier than in the rest of Romania. Annual rainfall is high, about 650 mm/23 in, and averages 365 mm during the growing season. Soils are typically low in humus but high in IRON, often over VOLCANIC or LIMESTONE bedrock, while vineyards can reach 500 m/1,640 ft in elevation. The region has two DOCs: Miniş in Arad County, influenced by the lake; and Crişana with the sub-denominations of Diosig, Biharia, and Simleu Silvaniei. Permitted white-wine varieties include Fetească Albă and Fetească Regală, Welschriesling, Muscat Ottonel, Traminer, Furmint (Miniş only), Pinot Gris, Sauvignon Blanc, and a traditional local white variety, Mustoasăde Măderat, which makes light, crisp wine. The more MEDITERRANEAN CLIMATE of Miniş gives long, warm autumns, so red wine grapes can ripen well, including Cabernet Franc, Cadarcă (KADARKA), Merlot, Burgund Mare (BLAUFRÄNKISCH), and Pinot Noir. The region was once famous for a sweet red made by the ASZÚ method from Cadarcă, popular with the Habsburg court.

Moldovan Hills, in eastern Romania, is part of the historic principality known as Moldavia (the eastern part is now the republic of MOLDOVA) and is home to possibly the country's oldest, and certainly most famous, wine region, COTNARI, whose golden nectar was at one time almost as sought after as those of TOKAJ and CONSTANTIA. The Moldovan Hills region lies north-east of the Carpathians, beginning at latitude 47° N and stretching southwards for several hundred kilometres. It is Romania's largest viticultural region, accounting for 39% of vineyards and 41% of wine volume in 2020. Vineyards in its north are typically on the slopes of amphitheatres facing south and south-west that protect the vines from the harsh north winds. Elevations vary from 200 to 500 m/656–1,640 ft. The region enjoys more than 2,000 hours of sunshine in an average year, and annual rainfall is only about 500 mm/20 in. Soil types include RENDZINA, chernozem (black, humus-rich soils overlying carbonate bedrock), and podzols (leached, well-drained, acidic soils usually low in fertility). GRASĂ is the variety responsible for most of the best sweet wines, supplemented by TĂMÂIOASĂ, together with Fetească Albă and Frâncuşă, to produce dry and medium-dry lesser wines around Cotnari. Recently a few reds, especially from Fetească Neagră, and rosé from Busuioacă de Bohotin have appeared. DOC regions include Bohotin, Coteşti, Cotnari, Dealu Bujorului, Huşi, Iaşi, Iana, Nicoreşti, Odobeşti, and Panciu. Further south, Fetească Albă is grown, mainly for light, everyday wines, together with Fetească Regală, Welschriesling, Aligoté, and Sauvignon Blanc. A range of red varieties are grown, including Merlot, Cabernet Sauvignon, Fetească Neagră, and BĂBEASCĂ NEAGRĂ. At Bohotin (and increasingly elsewhere in Romania), scented, pink-coloured wine is made from Busuioacă de Bohotin. Local Galbena de Odobeşti and its synonym Zghihară de Huşi both make pleasant if not complex young-drinking whites. Odobeşti is one of the largest and oldest viticultural centres in Romania and may well date from the Roman era. Şarba, a CROSS between Welschriesling and Muscat of Hamburg developed at the Odobeşti research station in 1972, has a grapey aroma and good acidity and is proving popular. The local grape Plavaie is also grown here for light, high-acid, low-alcohol, everyday wines. In Panciu, to the immediate north of Odobeşti, winters are colder, winds stronger, and HAIL more frequent, but some good still white and sparkling wines are made. Coteşti just south of Odobeşti, on the other hand, is distinctly warmer and can produce some deep-coloured reds; it is famous as the location of the 15th-century cellars of prince Ştefan cel Mare. Nicoreşti, east of Panciu, is another red-wine region, particularly well known for its Băbească. This region has seen some new investments but is generally focused on supplying local market demands.

The large area of **Oltenia and Muntenia** in the Carpathian foothills north of the capital Bucharest grows 25% of Romania's vines but produced 38% of the country's wine in 2020. DOC areas include Dealu Mare, Drăgăşani, Pietroasa, Ştefăneşti, Sămbureşti, Banu Mărăcine, Mehedinți, Cernăteşti-Podgoria, and Segarcea. Most famous is the historic and extensive Dealu Mare, meaning 'big hill', best known for its reds and the source of some of Romania's most exciting wines, especially those of the pioneering Davino and SERVE. Vineyards on iron-rich red soils are at ELEVATIONS of 130–550 m/430–1,800 ft, protected from WINTER FREEZE by high hills and forests. Annual rainfall averages around 640 mm/25 in. This is principally a red-wine district with Cabernet Sauvignon, Merlot, some Pinot Noir, recent plantings of Syrah, and considerable focus on Fetească Neagră, both as a VARIETAL wine and in blends. An outcrop of CALCAREOUS soil in the Pietroasa district is known for its lusciously sweet, golden, LATE HARVEST wines, especially Tămâioasă from Pietroasele, which may be BOTRYTIZED. Archaeological finds in Ştefăneşti, an area noted for robust reds, suggest a long history of wine production, possibly dating back to Alexander the Great. Towards the south-west and the River Olt basin lie the historic vineyards of Drăgăşani, which are said to date to the time of Dacian King Burebista, 82–44 BCE. The region stretches over 60 km/36 miles ranging from 200 to 500 m in elevation. Average rainfall is 640 mm, and hail is a frequent hazard. This is a dynamic region of small estates with its own growers' association. Whites show crisp acidity and good aromas, especially Fetească Regală, Tămâioasă (sweet and dry styles), Sauvignon Blanc, and the local Crâmpoşie Selecționată. Local red specialities such as Negru de Drăgăşani and Novac show promise, and there are some good Merlot and Cabernet Sauvignon too. Sâmbureşti is a much smaller wine region specializing in Cabernet Sauvignon. South-west of the university town of Craiova lies the DOC of Banu Mărăcine, with a small vineyard area based

around the viticultural research station. About 20 km/12 miles south of Craiova is the DOC Segarcea, the site of the renovated former royal winery, with much new planting. Mehedinți DOC is the country's warmest zone, with soils of CLAY and LIMESTONE and IRON-rich outcrops. It has five subregions: Severin, Corcova, Golul Drincei, Vânju-Mare, and Oreviţa. This is the sunniest and warmest of the southern Carpathian wine regions and concentrates on red-wine production. In the far south-west, an outcrop of TERRA ROSSA around Oprişor produces some fine reds from Cabernet Sauvignon, Merlot, and Syrah. The climate here is temperate continental with a Mediterranean influence, with rainfall up to 800 mm/31 in per year. Many vineyards here were grubbed up in the 1980s and have only recently been replanted.

Banat grows just 2% of Romania's vines but produces 5% of the country's wine thanks to the presence of Cramele Recaş—in 2020 both the biggest exporter and number one in the domestic market. There are also several smaller boutique estates in the region. Historically it was part of the Transylvanian province of the Austro-Hungarian Empire, and this influence is still clear in the varieties planted: Cadarcă (KADARKA), Italian Riesling (WELSCHRIESLING), Fetească Regală, Burgund (BLAUFRÄNKISCH), and Muscat Ottonel. Today, substantial new vineyards have been planted with selected clones of INTERNATIONAL VARIETIES as well as Fetească Neagră. Banat has a moderate, MEDITERRANEAN-influenced climate, cooler than much of the rest of Romania but warmer than most of Hungary. There are two DOC zones: Banat (with subregions of Moldova Nouă, Dealurile Tirolului, and Silagiu) and Recaş.

The **Dobrogea** region on the Black Sea coast comprised 8% of vineyards in 2020 but just 3% of wine. It is a warm region of low hills, as many as 300 days of sunshine annually and only 150–200 mm/6–8 in rainfall between April and October. There are four DOCs: Murfatlar (with subregions Medgidia and Cernavodă), Babadag, Adamclisi, and Sarica Niculițel (with one subregion, Tulcea). Murfatlar was once best known for whites, including late-harvest wines, but today's emphasis is on richly flavoured reds, especially Merlot, Cabernet Sauvignon, Fetească Neagră, Syrah, and Băbească Neagră. The dry climate allows a few producers to farm ORGANICALLY.

The **Danube Terraces** region stretches along the lower banks of the Danube. Vineyards here are largely devoted to TABLE GRAPES. There are two DOCs: Oltina, on an outcrop of CLAY and LOESS at 200 m/656 ft and known to have been colonized by Romans; and Însurăței, a newer DOC on red soils close to the Danube.

The **Southern Sands** region is a warm area with deep SANDY soils and 18,383 ha/45,425 acres of vines but produces only 2% of Romanian wine, none of notable quality. C.G.

Gilby, C., *The Wines of Bulgaria, Romania and Moldova* (2018).
www.onvpv.ro
www.oniv.ro
www.crameromania.ro

Roman Muscat, synonym for MUSCAT OF ALEXANDRIA.

Rome, classical. '*Vita vinum est*' ('Wine is life'), exclaimed Trimalchio to his dinner guests (Petronius, *Satyricon* 34).

Wine was deeply embedded in Roman culture, as much a staple for the poor as for the wealthy. So the evidence is particularly rich, detailed, and varied—as rich as for any aspect of ancient society. There are the casual, but often illuminating, references in the poets, in letters, and even in the graffiti scratched on inn walls. All the AGRICULTURAL TREATISES, one of the largest bodies of technical literature to survive from antiquity, devote great space to detailed discussion of viticulture (see in particular CATO, *De agri cultura passim*, from the 2nd century BCE; VARRO, *De re rustica*, Book 1, from the end of the 1st century BCE; COLUMELLA, *De re rustica*, particularly Books 3–5, 12, and the separate work 'On trees' from the mid 1st century CE; and his contemporary PLINY, *Natural History*, Books 14, 17, and 23, as well as PALLADIUS from late antiquity). What these reveal is a lively debate about CLIMATE, VINE VARIETIES, PLANTING and PRUNING techniques, technological developments, and the economics of viticulture. A more surprising source of information is Roman law; the sale of wine, particularly wholesale, raised considerable problems for the law of sale, when there was the question of what guarantee of quality the buyer might reasonably expect. The legal texts tell us much about the details of how wine was marketed. Equally interesting material comes from medical writers. Wine played an important role in medical treatment, and much of the information about the colour, quality, and effects of particular wines owes far less to the tasting books of Roman CONNOISSEURS than it does to the notes of the DOCTORS (see MEDICINE). Finally there is ARCHAEOLOGY, of which the most spectacular recent achievement, inspired by the underwater excavation of Roman wrecks, has been the identification of the types of AMPHORAE used to carry the wine and the recognition of the scale and pattern of the wine trade.

Both Pliny (*Natural History* 14. 21–39) and Columella (*De re rustica* 3. 2. 7–28) offer surveys of the main ANCIENT VINE VARIETIES. Columella's classification is the most revealing. His first class consists of the varieties used for the great Italian wines, most notably the types of Aminean. His second class is high-yielding vines, which nevertheless can produce wines which can be aged successfully. The final group is those prolific vine types used largely to produce *vin ordinaire*. This reveals that wine producers were aware of the great diversity in the markets for their wines and chose their vines accordingly.

'Classic wines can only be produced from vines grown on trees', was Pliny's verdict (*Natural History* 17. 199). Although this was disputed by some agricultural writers, the most striking fact about Roman viticulture was that the great wines—CAECUBAN, FALERNIAN, and so on—nearly all came from vineyards in which the vines were trained up trees, usually elms or poplars (see ARBOREAL VITICULTURE). However, all the normal forms of VINE TRAINING were also known and described by agricultural writers, from the low, free-standing BUSH VINE to elaborate TRELLIS SYSTEMS. As in every age, the literature abounds with references to extraordinary YIELDS (for example, over 300 hl/ha (17 tons/acre), high but not unknown in modern terms); but Columella (*De re rustica* 3. 3) considers the economics of a vineyard on the basis of yields ranging from 21 to 63 hl/ha, a range which may look familiar to modern vine-growers concerned with wine quality.

'Be the first to dig the ground . . . but the last to harvest the grapes' was the advice in VIRGIL's poem of the countryside (*Georgics* 2. 410). This is just one of many clues which suggest that the Romans sought to make their white wines—and nearly all the great wines were white—sweet.

The treading of the grapes was usually, but not invariably, followed by their PRESSING. The MUST obtained from the treading was sometimes kept separate, but more frequently it was added to that from the pressing. The grape pulp could be subject to a second pressing—or even, after being soaked for a day, a third—to produce a thin drink for slaves (see PIQUETTE). From the press room the must was run off to ferment in large DOLIA, which were frequently sunk in the ground (like Georgia's QVEVRI). The wine could be racked off into amphorae at any stage from 30 days after being made to various points through the winter and into the next spring. Many white wines of note were probably left SUR LIE, with the possible consequent enhancement of flavour and COMPLEXITY. To those in the post-PASTEUR age of stainless-steel vats, Roman winemaking must seem somewhat slapdash and uncertain. However, the accumulated wisdom and experience conveyed in all the agricultural treatises demonstrate a commitment to care (for example, in stressing the need for cleanliness at all stages) and sophisticated observation (as in the siting of the press room and *dolia* yard with regard to the ambient TEMPERATURE during fermentation).

'We consider the best wine is one that can be aged without any preservative; nothing must be mixed with it which might obscure its natural taste. For the most excellent wine is one which has given pleasure by its own natural qualities.' Columella's statement (*De re rustica* 12. 19) reflected current opinion. However, it is made at the beginning of a long discussion of ADDITIVES for wine. Some of these are less objectionable to modern opinion than others. It was a normal practice to add boiled must to wine either during fermentation or soon after to act both as a sweetener and, so it was thought, a preservative. LEAD-lined vessels were regularly used for the boiling of must because lead acetate is a sweetener. Such a practice is toxic, although ideas that it contributed to the fall of the Roman Empire are highly exaggerated. The addition of quantities of chalk or marble dust may be seen as attempts to modify the acidity of the wine (see DEACIDIFICATION). More surprising is the general advocacy of the addition of seawater or salt during fermentation. This was a distinctive Greek practice, taken over by the Romans. It was supposed both to 'enliven a wine's smoothness' (Pliny, *Natural History* 14. 120) (presumably increasing acidity) and to prevent a mouldy taste (Columella, *De re rustica* 12. 23. 2). RESINATED WINE was common. So were FLAVOURED WINES with all kinds of herbal and plant additives, of which the primary effect was to disguise the inferior nature of the basic wine.

For Roman connoisseurs, the key to a good wine was AGEING. In Roman law the distinction between 'new' wine and 'old' was that the old had been aged for at least one year. Of course, vast quantities of wine were drunk within the first year. However, a higher price could be expected if the producer could hold back even for as short a period as the summer following the vintage. As for the great wines, both white and red, their key characteristic was their capacity to be aged for considerable periods. Falernian was considered drinkable after a decade but at its best between 15 and 20 years; SURRENTINE, another white wine, came into its own after 25 years. It may be that being sealed in an amphora which had an impermeable coating of resin meant that the ageing process was slowed. On the other hand, CATO recommends that air space should be left when amphorae are filled, which must have led to OXIDATION on a level which would be unacceptable now. The frequent mention of the darkening of the colour of the great whites suggests that MADERIZATION was normal and, indeed, desired. The final curiosity of Roman wines was the widespread practice of storing them in lofts over hearths, where they were exposed to smoke and heat. This was seen as a means of accelerating ageing, for which the nearest modern parallel may be the process of heating which MADEIRA is subjected to.

The heyday for Roman viticulture was the 1st century BCE and the first two centuries CE. This was the time for the recognition and development of great wines in central ITALY which could compete successfully with those from the Greek world (see GREECE). It was a period of considerable experimentation and innovation, not least in western areas such as GAUL and SPAIN, which saw the creation of their own vineyards, often by Italian settlers after the areas had become part of Rome's empire. There was clearly a massive increase in the market for wine throughout the empire. Rome itself, with a fluctuating population of a million or more, sucked in imports from Italy and the provinces, while the Romanization of the provinces included the stimulation of new markets for a commodity which was at the heart of Roman culture. The market for wine was a very diverse one, ranging from the elite's desire for great wine to the mass market for wines (for which the thousands of amphorae recovered from sites throughout the empire and beyond are ample testimony).

J.J.P.

Billiard, R., *La Vigne dans l'antiquité* (1913).

Purcell, N., 'Wine and wealth in Ancient Italy', *Journal of Roman Studies*, 75 (1985), 1–25.

Reddy, A., and Braun, C. L., 'Lead and the Romans', *Journal of Chemical Education*, 87/10 (2010), 1052–5.

Tchernia, A., *Le Vin de l'Italie romaine* (1986).

Wilson, H., *Wine and Words in Classical Antiquity and the Middle Ages* (2003).

Romorantin, a white, eastern Loire grape variety that is fast fading from the French *vignoble*. Cour CHEVERNY is an appellation especially created in 1993 for the rather tart Romorantin grown just west of Blois. DNA PROFILING has shown that this is yet another progeny of PINOT and GOUAIS BLANC.

ronco, north-east Italian term derived from the verb *roncare* (meaning 'to clear land', particularly land which is either wooded or overgrown with underbrush); the word has been used for over a century in a wide swathe of northern Italy to indicate a HILLSIDE VINEYARD. The first appearance on a wine label dates from the early 1970s, when it was used by Mario Pasolini in the province of Brescia in LOMBARDY for his Ronco di Mompiano, a legendary VINO DA TAVOLA from MARZEMINO and MERLOT grapes grown within the city walls of Brescia. More or less contemporary examples can also be found from the OLTREPÒ PAVESE, frequently with the diminutive form **ronchetto**. The widest current use is in FRIULI, often in plural as **ronchi**, and where the dialect form is *ronc*. Examples can also be found in ALTO ADIGE and in ROMAGNA.

See also COLLI.

Rondinella, Italian red grape variety grown in the VENETO, especially for Valpolicella. The vine yields profusely and is therefore extremely popular with growers, but its produce is rarely sufficiently flavoursome to please consumers. Rondinella is not as widely planted nor as respected as its parent CORVINA VERONESE, with which it is usually blended.

Rondo, once known as GM 6494–5, red-fleshed DISEASE-RESISTANT VARIETY grown to a limited extent in such northern European countries as DENMARK, ENGLAND, NETHERLANDS, SWEDEN, BELGIUM, and POLAND, where it is treasured for its combination of early ripening and depth of colour. It was bred using some VITIS AMURENSIS genes to withstand cold winters, has small berries, and makes light, fruity wines. It can occasionally suffer from POWDERY MILDEW, however. Despite its parentage, it produces remarkably VITIS VINIFERA-like wine, so it has been registered as a *vinifera* variety. Consequently it may used in the production of PDO wines.

root, one of the three major organs of higher plants, the others being leaves and fruits/seeds. Roots' main functions are anchorage of the plant, storage of reserves of CARBOHYDRATES, absorption of WATER and MINERALS from the soil, and synthesis of specific compounds, such as reduced NITROGEN compounds and such hormones as CYTOKININS and ABSCISIC ACID.

The roots of a commercial vineyard originate from the roots that develop at the base of CUTTINGS, which are more divided than the tap-root style of a SEEDLING's root system. The position and number of the main framework roots, the 'spreaders' which extend out and down, are determined during the first three years.

Although most vine roots occur in the top metre of soil (less if unfavourable soil horizons impede their penetration), there are many examples where roots have penetrated to 6 m/20 ft or more; often these examples are found in dry conditions such as the DOURO Valley. The root framework supports a large number of fibrous roots which, by their continuing growth, explore the soil for MINERALS and water. Root density is highest in friable soil with continuing supplies of minerals, water, and oxygen. MYCORRHIZAL fungi play an important role in increasing the surface area of the roots.

Vine roots are much less dense than those of many other crop plants. Different species of VITIS have different root distribution and habits, a difference that is deliberately used in the breeding of ROOTSTOCKS. B.G.C.

Smart, D. R., et al., 'Grapevine rooting patterns: a comprehensive analysis and a review', *American Journal of Enology and Viticulture*, 57/1 (2006), 89–104.

Van Zyl, J. L., and Hoffman, E., 'Root development and the performance of grapevines in response to natural as well as man-made soil impediments', 21st GiESCO International Meeting (2019). www.ives-openscience.eu/wp-content/uploads/2020/06/VAN-ZYL-and-HOFFMAN.pdf.

root growth, that part of the VINE GROWTH CYCLE which takes place below ground. In most fruit trees, the spring flush of root growth occurs at the same time as BUDBREAK, but for the vine it is delayed. There are two peaks of root growth during the growing season. The first takes place at FLOWERING of the shoots in early summer, and the second coincides with the normal HARVEST period in autumn. There is an important correlation between the size, health, and activity of the vine's root system and the growth of shoots and leaves above ground (see VIGOUR). This is because roots act as storage sites for the vine's crucial reserves of CARBOHYDRATES and NITROGEN compounds, and also as the site for the production of HORMONES such as CYTOKININS, GIBBERELLINS, and ABSCISIC ACID. Vines with restricted or unhealthy roots have low VIGOUR, and this is the basis of the principles of BALANCED PRUNING. Root growth also varies according to VINE AGE. R.E.W. & R.E.S.

root-knot nematode. See NEMATODES.

root-lesion nematode. See NEMATODES.

rootling, a one-year-old vine grown in a NURSERY, the common material used for planting a vineyard. Typically it is a GRAFTED rootling, with the fruiting variety, or SCION, grafted on to a ROOTSTOCK. Most species of the vine genus VITIS, especially VITIS VINIFERA varieties, form roots readily on their CUTTINGS, but some rootstocks such as *Vitis berlandieri* and *Vitis champini* form roots poorly. B.G.C.

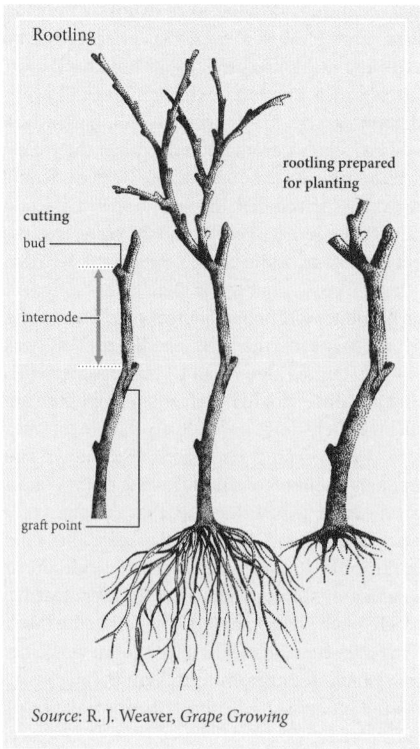

Source: R. J. Weaver, *Grape Growing*

rootstock, the plant forming the ROOT system of a grapevine to which a fruiting variety, or SCION, is grafted. In most vineyards in the world, European wine-producing VITIS VINIFERA vines are grafted on rootstocks which are, with few exceptions, either varieties of one AMERICAN VINE SPECIES or more commonly HYBRIDS of several. See VITIS for details of the different species of this genus. Rootstocks are normally used to overcome soil pests or diseases but may also be used for special soil conditions such as SALINITY.

The use of rootstocks for grapevines became common around 1880 in France in order to combat the devastating root aphid PHYLLOXERA, which attacked the roots of the European grapevine *Vitis vinifera*, and the control of phylloxera remains a major, but by no means the only, reason rootstocks are used.

There are parts of the world where the choice of rootstock is more debated than the choice of the fruiting variety, since the latter might well be regulated by law or tradition. Even in traditional European viticultural regions, the choice of rootstock tends to change with time, helped by long-term experiments and commercial experience. By contrast, in some parts of the NEW WORLD the use of rootstocks is relatively new, or prior use has been restricted to only a few locally available rootstock varieties.

The rootstock AXR1 (alternatively ARG1 or Ganzin 1) had been found so adaptable in California it was described by A. J. WINKLER as 'the nearest approach to an all-purpose rootstock'; it was widely adopted, despite Winkler's qualifying phrase that 'resistance to phylloxera is not high', a viewpoint emphasised by many visiting European viticulturists. In the 1980s, AXR1 succumbed to what was described as a new BIOTYPE of phylloxera, necessitating extensive replantings and causing economic hardship for many. California now uses a wide range of rootstocks.

Sullivan, V., 'New rootstocks stop vineyard pest for now', *California Agriculture* 50/5 (1996), 7–8.

Choice of rootstock

Although at one time it was a common complaint that PRE-PHYLLOXERA wines in Europe were better than those since the invasion (perhaps partly because early rootstocks were not always ideally matched with SOIL TYPES), more recent experiments have shown that little effect on wine quality can be attributed directly to rootstock. Certainly rootstocks can influence VIGOUR, and the high-vigour rootstocks such as Rupestris St George can produce canopies so dense and SHADED that they affect wine quality (see CANOPY MANAGEMENT). Other studies indicate that the high-vigour rootstocks Harmony, Dog Ridge, Freedom, and Ramsey can result in high levels of POTASSIUM and PH in the resultant wine, but again this is very likely an indirect effect mediated through vigour and excessive canopy shade.

Any vigorous rootstock which stimulates vegetative growth late in the season will have a detrimental effect on fruit RIPENING and therefore on wine quality (see VINE PHYSIOLOGY). The use of rootstocks has also led to an increase in vine CHLOROSIS in those regions where LIMESTONE soils are common. Similarly, some rootstocks can induce MAGNESIUM deficiency, which, when severe, can inhibit PHOTOSYNTHESIS and ripening.

One of the earliest and perhaps most significant negative effects of rootstock use has been the impact of GRAFTING on the spread of VIRUS DISEASES, hidden by the fact that rootstock vines often do not show virus symptoms. LEAFROLL VIRUS, for example, delays ripening and can substantially reduce wine quality. Young grafted vines are also commonly infected by TRUNK DISEASE fungi, typically in the rootstock, causing some plants to die early and/or grow irregularly and turning others into a source of infection. Vine improvement has concentrated on avoiding the inadvertent spread of graft-transmitted virus diseases by sourcing virus-free plant material from certified MOTHER VINES of fruiting varieties and rootstocks. However, transmission of trunk-disease fungi in CUTTINGS from infected mother vines is still common.

Rootstocks can have a dramatic effect on YIELD. In the absence of a rootstock, a vine grown on its own roots may not grow at all and die because of root damage from phylloxera or NEMATODES. Grafting on to a rootstock with resistance to soil pests and which is also suitable to LIME conditions or DROUGHT can, on the other hand, increase yield dramatically.

Rootstock selection for any particular vineyard may be guided by known soil pests or diseases (especially nematodes and phylloxera); by suitability to the soil environment (especially lime content, fertility, drought incidence, and waterlogging); or by the effect on the performance of the scion variety that is desired, such as lower vigour or earlier ripening.

Rootstocks also differ in characteristics that are important to nurseries. These include the ability of mother vines to produce plenty of wood, the ease with which cuttings root, and also the ease with which they can be grafted.

Rootstock characteristics

Phylloxera resistance The three most resistant AMERICAN VINE SPECIES are *V. riparia*, *V. rupestris*, and *V. berlandieri*, and the most susceptible species is the European VITIS VINIFERA (see VITIS). Interspecific HYBRIDS containing genes from any of the first three species will therefore have satisfactory resistance, and those hybrids including *V. vinifera* will have suspect resistance. Rootstocks of *V. vinifera* × *V. rupestris* (including AXR1, and Couderc rootstocks 1202 and 93–5) and *V. vinifera* × *V. riparia* parentage should be avoided because they do not have sufficient phylloxera tolerance. Interestingly, *V. vinifera* × *V. berlandieri* rootstocks such as 41 B and 333 EM generally have sufficient resistance. A few examples of rootstocks with high phylloxera resistance are Riparia Gloire, 101–14 Mgt, SO 4, and 5 BB.

Nematode resistance Two principal types of NEMATODES are present in vineyard soils. VITIS species having the most resistance to root-knot nematodes are *V. champini*, *V. longii*, and *V. cinerea*. Those having most resistance to the dagger nematode include *V. candicans*, *V. longii*, and *V. rufotomentosa*. Vines of the MUSCADINIA section of the *Vitis* genus are resistant to both types of nematodes, which explains the interest in this group of vines for rootstock breeding. As for phylloxera, *V. vinifera* is very susceptible to nematodes, so any one rootstock will not have resistance to all nematode species, nor indeed to all nematode races. Rootstocks commonly used for nematode tolerance include Ramsey, Dog Ridge, Harmony, 1613 C, 1616 C, SO 4, and Schwarzmann.

Lime tolerance Both *V. vinifera* and *V. berlandieri* contribute tolerance to the soils high in LIMESTONE common in Burgundy and Champagne. Rootstocks acknowledged to have the highest lime tolerance are 41 B, 333 EM, and the more recently bred Fercal.

Drought tolerance *Berlandieri–rupestris* hybrids are best able to tolerate drought, and these include 110 R and 140 Ru, followed by 1103 P and 99 R. *V. riparia* species and hybrids have low drought tolerance.

Salt tolerance The chloride component of salty soils can be toxic (see SALINITY). The *V. berlandieri* species is considered tolerant, but Australian research has found the *V. champini* rootstock Ramsey to be quite tolerant. *V. vinifera* is also tolerant.

Vigour The species *V. champini*, *V. berlandieri*, and *V. rupestris* and their hybrids give the most vigour, and *V. riparia* the least. Among the most vigorous rootstocks are therefore Ramsey, Dog Ridge, Rupestris St George, 99 R, and 110 R, while Riparia Gloire and 101–14 are among the least vigorous. Vigorous vines tend to delay fruit maturity and can substantially reduce red wine colour.

Some internationally important rootstocks

AXR1, otherwise called **ARG1** in France, Australia, and New Zealand, is a *V. vinifera* × *V. rupestris* hybrid made by Ganzin in 1879. The rootstock was initially popular in France, but at the turn of the century it was found, there and in South Africa, to have insufficient phylloxera resistance. It is popular with growers because the vines are vigorous and yield well, and it is favoured by nurseries because it is easy to graft. It was found satisfactory in California until the 1980s, when it succumbed to phylloxera.

Dog Ridge is a seedling from the species *V. champini* which is suggested for use on light-textured soils with high nematode contents. It is only moderately tolerant of phylloxera. This rootstock is extremely vigorous, so it should not be used in fertile soils, and vines need to be pruned lightly to achieve BALANCE. The rootstock is not suggested for high-quality vineyards.

Fercal was bred at INRA Bordeaux in 1959 and developed especially for high-lime soils. It is a result of crossing Berlandieri-Colombard 2 (itself a *V. berlandieri* × Ugni Blanc hybrid) with 31 Richter. It is resistant to phylloxera and grafts readily. Fercal is of moderate vigour and is more tolerant of chlorosis and drought than 41 B.

Harmony is a hybrid of open-pollinated seedlings selected from *V. champini* and 1613 C. It was selected at Fresno, California, in 1966, and is quite tolerant of root-knot and dagger nematodes. Phylloxera tolerance is, however, low, and vigour moderate to high.

Riparia Gloire de Montpellier is one of the oldest rootstocks used against phylloxera in France, bred in 1880. Of the several *V. riparia* crosses brought in at the time of the phylloxera crisis, this proved the best. It confers excellent phylloxera resistance and is of low vigour, providing for lower yields of improved-quality fruit and early ripening. It is widely used throughout Europe for the production of good-quality wine.

Rupestris St George is sometimes called **Rupestris du Lot** or **Rupestris-monticola**. Bred in 1879, it was another early introduction to France to fight phylloxera, and it is said to be a selection of *V. rupestris* Scheele. This is an extremely vigorous variety with a long growing season. It has excellent resistance to phylloxera, but vines grafted to it can easily overcrop or set poor crops because of extreme vigour. Because of high vigour, it is not used for high-quality vineyards.

Schwarzmann is a *V. riparia* × *V. rupestris* hybrid with high tolerance of phylloxera and nematodes but only moderate vigour. It is suited to deep, moist soils and is not as widely used as it might be.

SO 4, a *V. berlandieri* × *V. riparia* hybrid, is correctly known as **Selection Oppenheim de Teleki No. 4**, from the viticulture school at Oppenheim in Germany. This popular rootstock, used widely in France and Germany, shows excellent phylloxera resistance; it tends to favour FRUIT SET and slightly advanced maturity. Vigour is moderate, as is tolerance to nematodes. SO 4 is not, however, suited to dry conditions, and it is prone to MAGNESIUM deficiency.

5 BB Kober, sometimes called **5 BB Teleki**, is a *V. berlandieri* × *V. riparia* hybrid. The seedling was raised by the Hungarian Sigmund Teleki from seeds produced by a French nurseryman. In 1904 some of the most interesting plants were sent to the Austrian Franz Kober, who selected 5 BB. This is quite a vigorous rootstock which is suited to more humid, clay soils. In many situations vigour is excessive. The rootstock 5 BB is widely used in Europe, especially in Germany and Switzerland.

5 C Teleki is a *V. berlandieri* × *V. riparia* hybrid selected in 1896 by Alexandre Teleki and Heinrich Birk. The rootstock is similar to SO 4 in aptitude and is mostly used in Germany.

41 B is an old rootstock obtained by Alexis Millardet and Charles de Grasset in 1882 at Bordeaux and is a hybrid between Chasselas and *V. berlandieri*. This rootstock has the advantage of being highly tolerant of lime, and so it is widely used in Cognac and Champagne. Its tolerance of phylloxera is sufficient but not absolute. This rootstock is moderately drought-tolerant.

99 Richter is a *V. berlandieri* × *V. rupestris* hybrid created by Franz Richter in 1902. This vigorous rootstock should not be used in cool regions because it can delay ripening. Phylloxera resistance is high and nematode resistance moderate.

101–14 Millardet et de Grasset is a lower-vigour and early-maturing rootstock used in some of the higher-quality vineyards in France. The vine is a *V. riparia* × *V. rupestris* hybrid made by Alexis Millardet and Charles de Grasset. It has high resistance to phylloxera but moderate nematode tolerance. The vine can tolerate only low lime content and has a shallow root system.

110 R, or **110 Richter**, is a relatively old *V. berlandieri* × *V. rupestris* hybrid made by Franz Richter in 1902. This rootstock is noted for its high vigour and thus tends to delay maturity, especially if planted in fertile soils. 110 R has high phylloxera tolerance but low nematode tolerance. It is moderately lime-tolerant and quite drought-tolerant, and so it is widely used in MEDITERRANEAN CLIMATES. Initially it was not used extensively because of poor rooting in the nursery.

140 Ruggeri or 140 Ru is a hybrid produced in 1894 in Sicily by Antonino Ruggeri using *V. berlandieri* and *V. rupestris*. This vigorous rootstock is well suited to dry soils high in lime and to Mediterranean climates. This rootstock should not be planted on fertile, moist soils because of possible excess vigour.

161–49 Couderc is a *V. riparia* × *V. berlandieri* hybrid obtained in 1888 by Georges Couderc. This rootstock has high resistance to phylloxera but is susceptible to nematodes.

333 EM (École de Montpellier) is one of the few rootstocks used (with Fercal and 41 B) which has a *V. vinifera* parent. It was hybridized in 1883 by Gustave Foëx of MONTPELLIER by crossing Cabernet Sauvignon with *V. berlandieri*. Despite initial fears to the contrary, 333 EM has sufficient phylloxera tolerance. This rootstock is slightly more lime-tolerant than 41 B and is also drought-tolerant.

420 A Millardet et de Grasset is one of the oldest rootstocks, obtained in 1887 by Alexis Millardet and his assistant Charles de Grasset. It is a *V. berlandieri* × *V. riparia* hybrid and is highly regarded for good-quality vineyards, being a lower-vigour rootstock which hastens maturity. It is regarded as 'the *V. riparia* for chalky soils'. Phylloxera tolerance is high, but nematode tolerance is low to moderate.

1103 Paulsen was bred in 1896 by Federico Paulsen, the director of an American vine nursery in Sicily, by crossing *V. berlandieri* with *V. rupestris*. It is regarded as a drought-tolerant rootstock with high phylloxera tolerance and moderate nematode resistance. Lime tolerance is intermediate, and vigour moderate to high. It is welcomed by nurseries as being easy to graft and root.

1613 Couderc is a complex hybrid between Solonis (*V. riparia* × *V. rupestris* × *V. candicans*) and Othello (*V. labrusca* × *V. riparia* × *V. vinifera*) bred by Georges Couderc in 1881. Phylloxera resistance is low to moderate, but it finds favour because of moderate to high nematode resistance. It is well suited to fertile, SANDY, LOAM soils and is used mainly in California.

1616 Couderc is a *V. longii* × *V. riparia* cross bred in 1882 to produce a low-vigour rootstock with high nematode and phylloxera tolerance. It is best suited to more humid soils, and it advances maturity.

3309 Couderc is a *V. riparia* × *V. rupestris* cross made in 1881. Georges Couderc planted 18 seeds in a row of the nursery where he had added lime; of the five which did not show chlorosis, 3309 C became the most successful. Phylloxera tolerance is high and lime tolerance medium, and it is better suited to humid than drought-prone soils. Rooting and grafting are easy, and the use of this rootstock is widespread.

R.E.S.

Galet, P., *General Viticulture* (2000).

Institut Français de la Vigne et du Vin, *Catalogue des variétés et clones de vigne cultivés en France* (2nd edn, 2007).

van Leeuwen, C., and Roby, J.-P., 'Choix du porte-greffe', *Vigne et Vin*, 35 (2001), 61–6.

Wine Australia, 'Grapevine rootstock selector tool'. www.grapevinerootstock.com.

Roquebrun. See ST-CHINIAN.

Roriz. See TINTA RORIZ.

rosado is Spanish and Portuguese for ROSÉ; *rosato* is Italian. See also CLARETE.

Rosalia, internationally obscure former Austrian GROSSLAGE situated between LEITHABERG and MITTELBURGENLAND, promoted to DAC in 2018, covering BLAUFRÄNKISCH and ZWEIGELT (including rosé) from a vine surface of just 241 ha/596 acres. D.S.

Rosazzo, subzone of the FRIULI COLLI ORIENTALI DOC in north-east Italy for varietal RIBOLLA Gialla and PIGNOLO wines as well as a DOCG (2011) for a white blend based on FRIULANO, Sauvignon Blanc, and Pinot Bianco.

Rosé de Loire, general appellation created in 1974 for ROSÉ WINE made from any blend of the main dark-skinned grapes of the LOIRE, including Cabernet Franc, Cabernet Sauvignon, PINEAU D'AUNIS, Pinot Noir, Gamay, and Grolleau, with the notable exclusion of Côt (MALBEC). The wine may be produced anywhere within the ANJOU, SAUMUR, and TOURAINE zones and ranges in style from crisp and neutral to flavourful and assertive. Unlike Rosé d'Anjou and Cabernet d'Anjou (see ANJOU), it is always dry. P.Le.

Rosé des Riceys, rare, still, pink wine made in the commune of Riceys in the Aube *département*, the southern end of the CHAMPAGNE region. This dark, rose-coloured wine is made by careful SAIGNÉE of Pinot Noir grapes, by only a handful of producers. It can be one of France's more serious rosés.

Rosenmuskateller, German name for aromatic, pink-berried Moscato Rosa del Trentino, a minor but distinct grape variety particular to ALTO ADIGE and TRENTINO, northern Italy, where it is responsible mainly for rose-perfumed sweet wines. It is also planted to a very limited extent in Austria and Germany.

Rosette, very limited sweetish white-wine AOC just north-west of Bergerac in South West France. It includes some of the PÉCHARMANT zone. Made from Sauvignon, Sémillon, and MUSCADELLE, the wines have a MOELLEUX character that is ideal for APERITIFS, *foie gras*, and mushroom dishes.

Rosette is also the name of an old FRENCH HYBRID, also known as Siebel 1000, which once produced pale red wines in New York State.

rosé winemaking, production of wines whose colour falls somewhere in the spectrum between red and white.

Historically, rosé wines have been made by a number of different processes, but today two methods are in general use: direct PRESSING or short MACERATION. The preferred technique is a short maceration of the juice with the skins (see SKIN CONTACT) of dark-coloured grapes just after CRUSHING, in the PRESS or in a tank, for a period long enough to extract the required amount of colour or ANTHOCYANINS. The juice is then separated from the skins by DRAINING or pressing, and FERMENTATION proceeds as in WHITE WINEMAKING. With the red-skinned GRENACHE grape, traditionally much used for rosés partly because of its relative lack of anthocyanins, a maceration of eight to 12 hours is usually sufficient. Highly pigmented grape varieties may need much less contact time, while very lightly coloured grapes may need a day or two of maceration. See also SAIGNÉE and STABULATION.

Some basic rosés are made by blending a small amount of finished red wine into a finished white wine. While a pinkish colour can be achieved by this process, the hue and flavour of such a wine are quite different from those of a wine made by short-term maceration. CHAMPAGNE is one of the few CONTROLLED APPELLATIONS in which the blending method of rosé winemaking is sanctioned—and in practice rosé champagne is more often made by blending than by maceration.

Pink wines may also be made by using CHARCOAL treatments to remove the colour from red wines which for some reason are not saleable as reds.

A VIN GRIS or BLUSH wine is made as above but with no maceration. Both tend to be even paler than most rosés. For a wine made pink by CO-FERMENTING red and white grapes, see SCHILLERWEIN. A.D.W.

rosé wines, increasingly popular wines in any shade of pink, from hardly perceptible to pale red (see COLOUR). For some reason they are rarely known as pink wines, although the English word BLUSH has been adopted for particularly pale rosés. There was also a FASHION in

California, from the late 1980s, when wine had to be white to be popular, to label pale pink wines made from dark-skinned grapes 'White', as in WHITE ZINFANDEL. Global production of rosé wines tends to fluctuate between approximately 23 and 26 million hl (608–87 million gallons), usually about 8–10% of still-wine production.

In France, which is responsible for 27% of global production, rosés are particularly common in warmer, southern regions where there is local demand for a dry wine refreshing enough to be drunk on a hot summer's day but which still bears some relation to the red wine traditionally revered by the French. PROVENCE is the region most famous for its rosé, although in the greater southern RHÔNE (especially TAVEL), the LANGUEDOC, and ROUSSILLON rosés are at least as common as white wines. Grenache and Cinsaut are two of the grapes commonly used for rosé in the south of France. The Loire Valley also produces a high proportion of rosé wine of extremely varied quality and sweetness levels, particularly around ANJOU, whether lowbrow Rosé d'Anjou or highbrow Cabernet d'Anjou. (See also ROSÉ DE LOIRE.) VIN GRIS and SAIGNÉE are French terms for particular types of rosé. See also ŒIL-DE-PERDRIX.

Spain also takes pink wines seriously—so seriously that it has at least two names for them, depending on the intensity of the colour. A *rosado* is light pink, while darker pink (light red) wines are labelled *clarete*. Portugal's best-known pink wines are exported, for example MATEUS. Pink wines are not especially popular in Italy, where the term used is usually *rosato*, although *chiaretto*, meaning 'claret', is occasionally used for darker rosés. Official German terms for pink wines include WEISSHERBST, ROTLING, and, in WÜRTTEMBERG, SCHILLERWEIN.

The New World was long rather bemused by the concept of rosé, although this changed fast in the early 21st century. Chile was innovative. Australia makes some swashbuckling deep pinks, and South Africa (where red and white wines may be blended to produce a rosé) has a growing market, with Blanc de Noir (*sic*) a legal category for those produced solely from red grapes.

Roseworthy, town north of Adelaide in the state of SOUTH AUSTRALIA, close to the Barossa Valley, known in the wine world for Australia's first agricultural college, established in 1883. It trained a high proportion of winemakers and viticulturists in Australia and New Zealand and contributed greatly to the technical standing of the Australian wine industry (see AUSTRALIAN INFLUENCE) until 1991 when it was relocated to the Waite campus of the University of Adelaide, where the AWRI and CSIRO were already sited. For more details, see ADELAIDE.

Roşioară. See PAMID.

Rossese, name given to at least seven distinct north-west Italian grape varieties, making both red and white wines in Italy, where there were only 5 ha/12 acres of 'Rossese Bianco' (see GRILLO) and 164 ha/405 acres of 'Rossese Nero'. **Rossese di Dolceaqua** is the best known. This esteemed red grape variety produces distinctively perfumed VARIETAL wines in LIGURIA. The variety has a long history in the region, and it has its own DOC in western Liguria. DNA PROFILING has shown it to be the same as Provence's TIBOUREN.

Rossignola, optional, tart ingredient in VALPOLICELLA.

Rosso Conero, Italian red wine DOC based on MONTEPULCIANO grapes whose full potential is yet to be realized. See MARCHE.

Rosso di signifies a red wine from the Italian zone whose name it precedes, often a declassified version of a long-lived, more serious wine such as BRUNELLO DI MONTALCINO or VINO NOBILE DI MONTEPULCIANO.

Rosso Piceno, or **Piceno**, Italian red wine consisting of 35–85% MONTEPULCIANO and a maximum of 50% SANGIOVESE. See MARCHE.

rot, loose term for the decay, with microbial interference, of any part of the vine. Rot is most commonly used as a synonym for BOTRYTIS BUNCH ROT, which is the most important sort of rot for wine quality. Other fruit rots include BLACK ROT, SOUR ROT, and WHITE ROT; rots of other vine parts include ARMILLARIA ROOT ROT and TEXAS ROOT ROT.

rotary drum vacuum filter (or **RDV filter**), form of depth FILTRATION designed to cope with liquids such as LEES that contain a high concentration of solids or particles that would rapidly block other filters.

RDV filtration relies on the constant regeneration of the filter medium, which is achieved by shaving off a fine layer of the filter medium through which the liquid passes. The filter comprises a slowly rotating drum covered in a fine stainless-steel mesh semi-immersed in a trough into which liquid is introduced. An internal vacuum pump draws liquid from the trough through the drum surface. Initially, a slurry of filter media in water is processed to pre-coat the outside of the drum mesh with a filter cake, several centimetres thick. The juice or wine is then sucked through this cake, filtering it in the process. The surface of the cake is slowly shaved by a knife, removing filter cake that has been badly fouled by winemaking solids and exposing fresher filter cake. When the entire cake has been removed in this way, the filter is cleaned and prepared for another batch of juice or wine.

DIATOMACEOUS EARTH (DE) was typically used as the filter medium, but perlite, a processed volcanic rock, is now more common—because it is cheaper and due to safety concerns associated with the inhalation of DE—but it does not resolve issues surrounding the disposal of the filter medium. RDV filters are gradually being replaced by other technologies such as polymeric or ceramic cross-flow filters (see FILTRATION) with wider channels that can handle higher solids than standard wine cross-flow filters, enclosed spinning ceramic disc filters, and decanter CENTRIFUGATION. This transition will take time because this equipment is generally quite expensive, and some of these technologies are still not quite as adept as RDV filters at processing thick lees and not as suitable at handling different types of winery lees. S.N.

Rotbrenner, vine FUNGAL DISEASE found in most of Europe which can cause severe crop losses. Caused by the fungus *Pseudopezicula tracheiphila*, the disease is encouraged by prolonged rainfall and attacks leaves and young bunches. It can be controlled by FUNGICIDES applied early in the growing season. R.E.S.

Roter Traminer, German name for SAVAGNIN ROSE, non-aromatic relative of GEWÜRZTRAMINER.

Roter Veltliner, pink-skinned grape variety formerly widespread in Austria (once planted in California) for the production of TABLE GRAPES and powerful white wine, in 2021 grown on 188 ha/465 acres of Lower Austria. In warm years, if YIELDS are restricted, it can make intensely aromatic, concentrated wines with high EXTRACT, especially in Wagram. DNA PROFILING in Austria revealed in 1998 that Roter Veltliner is a parent of ROTGIPFLER, NEUBURGER, and FRÜHROTER VELTLINER.

Rotgipfler, the marginally less noble of the two white wine grape varieties traditionally associated with the dramatically full-bodied, long-lived, spicy white wine of Austria's THERMENREGION. (The other is ZIERFANDLER.) Plantings have remained fairly steady, at 112 ha/277 acres in 2022. It ripens late, but earlier than Zierfandler, and the wines are particularly high in EXTRACT, ALCOHOL, and BOUQUET. DNA PROFILING in Austria showed in 1998 that Rotgipfler is a natural CROSS of SAVAGNIN and ROTER VELTLINER.

Rothschilds and wine. The Rothschilds first entered the world of wine in 1853 when Baron Nathaniel (1812–70), grandson of Mayer Amschel and a member of the English branch of the family, bought Brane Mouton and renamed it Ch MOUTON ROTHSCHILD. This was common practice among more important CHÂTEAU owners. It was a buyer's market in Bordeaux vineyards then devastated by oidium, or POWDERY MILDEW, and the Rothschild purchase was viewed more as a property transaction than as the acquisition of a distinguished vineyard.

When the important 1855 CLASSIFICATION placed Ch Mouton Rothschild top of the second growths, however, the Rothschilds were particularly exercised by what they regarded as its unfairly low placing.

Nathaniel was succeeded by his son Baron James (1844–81) and then Baron Henri (1872–1947), who was more interested in literature than wine, and James's widow was responsible for Mouton until the arrival of Henri's younger son Philippe (1902–88) in 1922.

Baron Philippe de Rothschild was to prove one of the most influential forces in the wine business of Bordeaux and beyond. Not only did he acquire two neighbouring PAUILLAC fifth growth châteaux—Mouton d'Armailhacq (named at various stages Mouton-Baron-Philippe, Mouton-Baronne-Philippe, and, since the late 1980s, d'Armailhac) in 1933 and Clerc Milon in 1970—but he also established the importance of CHÂTEAU BOTTLING, established MOUTON CADET as one of the world's most successful wine BRANDS and an important NÉGOCIANT business in the MÉDOC, astutely developed the concept (and value) of ARTISTS' LABELS, established the finest collection of wine-related works of art in the world, and in 1979 initiated Opus One, the world's first high-profile JOINT VENTURE, with Robert MONDAVI of California. In 1996 a joint venture with Concha y Toro of CHILE was created to produce the ambitiously priced Cabernet blend Almaviva, and Baron Philippe de Rothschild SA now has a substantial winery in Maipo Valley producing, inter alia, Mapu wines from Maule. Baron Philippe was succeeded at Mouton by his daughter Philippine (1933–2014). Under her leadership, Domaine de Baronarques, a red LIMOUX AOC, was bought with her two sons in 1998. At the same time, Baron Philippe de Rothschild S.A. diversified into VARIETAL wines from the LANGUEDOC.

Just next door to Mouton, Ch LAFITE was bought by Baron James of the French family in 1868 in the face of local competition. He died a few months later but is said to have visited the property briefly in the spring of that year. His son Edmond (1845–1934) was to sow, and indeed provide, the seeds for the establishment of the ISRAELI wine industry by making a vast donation in 1882. James's great-grandson Élie (1917–2007) was the family member who eventually took charge of Lafite, subsequently Lafite-Rothschild, until 1974 when his nephew Eric (1940–) became the château's head, handing over to his daughter Saskia in 2018. In 1962 the fourth growth PAUILLAC Ch Duhart-Milon was acquired. In 1984 the leading SAUTERNES property Ch Rieussec was also purchased along with the Ch Paradis Casseuil in Entre-Deux-Mers, with L'Évangile in POMEROL being added in 1990. Joint ventures were established with Viña Los Vascos (Chile, 1988), Domaine d'Aussières (Languedoc, 1999), Bodegas CARO (Argentina, 1999), and Long Dai, in the Shandong region of China (2008), whose first vintage was 2017.

Since 2021, all of the estates in the Lafite stable, called Domaines Barons de Rothschild or DBR, have started the official path towards ORGANIC certification.

In 1973 Baron Edmond (1926–97), one of the family partners in Lafite but engaged in many other affairs, bought the semi-derelict Ch Clarke of LISTRAC, in 1977–8 building a very large new *cuvier* and CHAI. In 1979 he added Ch Malmaison in the adjoining commune of MOULIS, which was also treated to major renovation, as well as acquiring two more non-classified châteaux in the Médoc. Since 1998, this branch of the Rothschild family have had a joint venture with Anton Rupert of South Africa, Rupert & Rothschild. In 2002 Baron Edmond's son Baron Benjamin created a joint venture with Laurent Dassault in Mendoza, Argentina. In 2003 he bought Ch des Laurets, straddling Puisseguin- and Montagne-St-Émilion. In 2013 two new ventures were developed: one in Marlborough, New Zealand; and a Rioja joint venture, Macán, with VEGA SICILIA. A Central Otago winery, Akarua, was added in 2021.

In 1994 the English financier Lord (Jacob) Rothschild (1936–) opened a wine museum and cellar for the display and sale of Rothschild wines at Waddesdon Manor just north of London. E.P.-R. & J.R.

Littlewood, J., *Milady Vine: The Autobiography of Philippe de Rothschild* (1984).

Rotling, category of German wines made from a mix of red and white grapes or MUST, comprising SCHILLERWEIN from Württemberg, BADEN's Badisch Rotgold, and SACHSEN's Schielerwein.

rotofermenter, or **rotary fermenter**, a horizontal FERMENTATION VESSEL arranged so that the contents can be mixed mechanically, either by rotating the vessel or by rotating an inner shaft fitted with vanes in a stationary vessel. Designed to eliminate the need for PUNCHING DOWN or PUMPING OVER, this equipment speeds the MACERATION phase of RED WINEMAKING. Some European wine producers, for example in Barolo, have invested in them, as have a number of NEW WORLD winemakers. Like most mechanical systems that promote skin–juice contact, they are expensive and require extensive and robust framing structures to mount and hold the horizontal tank. Rotofermenters are usually controlled by computers, with cycles of rotation chosen by the winemaker. P.J.W.

rotundone is a key aroma compound responsible for the distinctive 'spicy', 'peppery' aroma in some red wines, particularly SYRAH/Shiraz from cooler climates. It has also been found in Grüner Veltliner and many other varieties. In red wines it has a very low aroma detection threshold of 16 ng/l, but as many as one in five people cannot smell rotundone, even at very high concentrations. Rotundone is an oxygenated bicyclic sesquiterpenoid compound that was originally discovered in the tubers of *Cyperus rotundus*, a species of sedge. It is also present in black and white peppercorns and a number of herbs and fruits. When rotundone was added at sub-threshold levels to model beverages, it had significant enhancing effects on the overall fruity flavours. In wine, rotundone originates mainly from the GRAPE skins of some varieties and is extracted during alcoholic FERMENTATION. The concentrations of rotundone in Shiraz grapes have been shown to vary significantly between vineyards, between vintages for the same vineyard, and between grapevines within a vineyard, and its presence appears to be associated with variations in soil properties, TOPOGRAPHY, ambient TEMPERATURE, and vine water status (see SOIL WATER). M.H.

Wood, C., et al., 'From wine to pepper: rotundone, an obscure sesquiterpene, is a potent spicy aroma compound', *Journal of Agricultural and Food Chemistry*, 56/10 (2008), 3738–44.

Scarlett, N. J., et al., 'Within-vineyard variation in the "pepper" compound rotundone is spatially structured and related to variation in the land underlying the vineyard', *Australian Journal of Grape and Wine Research*, 20/2 (2014), 214–22.

Nakanishi, A., et al., 'Identification of rotundone as a potent odor-active compound of several kinds of fruits', *Journal of Agricultural and Food Chemistry*, 65/22 (2017), 4464–71.

Geffroy, O., et al., 'May peppery wines be the spice of life? A review of research on the "pepper" aroma and the sesquiterpenoid rotundone', *OENO One* 54/2 (2020), 245–62.

Rouchalin, sometimes **Rouchelin**, occasional name for CHENIN BLANC in south-west France.

Rouchet, Italian red grape variety. See RUCHÈ.

Rouge du Pays, rare Swiss VALAIS red grape used to make deeply coloured red wines. Confusingly renamed Cornalin in 1972. The vine demands a fairly warm climate and restricted YIELDS to produce fresh wines with fine, silky tannins. DNA PROFILING at DAVIS showed that Rouge du Pays is the progeny of PETIT ROUGE and Mayolet, two varieties from the AOSTA Valley, and a parent of true CORNALIN, hence the confusion with the new name. J.V.

Rougeon, also known as Seibel 5898, FRENCH HYBRID red-wine variety grown in the north-eastern UNITED STATES. Very productive and winter-hardy, it produces deeply coloured wines with few hybrid aromas and sometimes has a meaty note, but it needs considerable attention because of its susceptibility to both DOWNY MILDEW and POWDERY MILDEW. D.F.

Roupeiro, the Alentejo name for the common Portuguese white grape variety SÍRIA.

Roussanne, sometimes erroneously spelt **Rousanne**, fashionable white Rhône grape which doubtless owes its name to the russet or *roux* colour of its skin. With MARSANNE, with which it is often blended, it is one of only two grape varieties allowed into the white versions of the northern Rhône's red-wine appellations HERMITAGE, CROZES-HERMITAGE, and ST-JOSEPH and into the exclusively white and often sparkling ST-PÉRAY. In each of these appellations, Marsanne is far more widely grown because the vine tends to be hardier and more productive. Roussanne's irregular YIELDS, tendency to POWDERY MILDEW and ROT, and poor wind resistance all but eradicated it from the northern Rhône until better CLONES were selected, and even today it is preferred there by a minority of producers such as Paul Jaboulet Aîné. Nevertheless, by 2019 French plantings had grown to 2,289 ha/5,656 acres, rather more than Marsanne with which a parent–offspring relationship has been revealed by DNA PROFILING.

Roussanne's chief attribute is its haunting aroma, something akin to a particularly refreshing herb tea, but it does need to reach full maturity in order to express itself elegantly and can OXIDIZE and age relatively easily. In the southern Rhône, Roussanne (but not Marsanne) is one of four grape varieties allowed into white CHÂTEAUNEUF-DU-PAPE, and Ch de Beaucastel here has demonstrated that their particular MASS SELECTION of Roussanne can respond well to OAK AGEING. The variety is also grown in Provence (although the more common pink-berried **Roussanne du Var** or **Rousseli** is a lesser, unrelated variety) and, increasingly, in the Languedoc and Roussillon, where Roussanne's tendency to ripen late is less problematic than in the northern Rhône and where results can be impressive. Although it is usually classified with Marsanne and Vermentino in appellation regulations, it can make a fine blending partner with the fuller-bodied Chardonnay, too. It can suffer in DROUGHT conditions, however.

The variety is also beguilingly fine and aromatic at Chignin in SAVOIE, where it is known as Bergeron, but should not be confused with ROUSSETTE. It is grown to a limited extent in Liguria and Tuscany, where it is a permitted ingredient in Italy's Montecarlo Bianco, and is grown for Clos d'Agon on the Catalan coast in Spain. Indeed, it has so much personality that many producers all around the wine world are experimenting with it on a small scale, both in aromatic, full-bodied white blends and as a VARIETAL. It is also found in Australia, even if Marsanne is much better established. Roussanne is decidedly more popular than Marsanne in California, where there were 330 acres/134 ha in 2020, particularly in the Central Coast.

Roussette, former name for the ALTESSE grape of SAVOIE now used for a number of wines made in eastern France.

Roussette de Savoie is the Savoie appellation for whites made exclusively from Altesse that age well in good vintages. With increasing plantings, this is fast becoming Savoie's most sought-after white-wine appellation. Four CRU names may be suffixed to the appellation: Frangy, Monterminod, Monthoux, and most notably Marestel, a steep south-facing slope in the village of JONGIEUX that yields exceptionally ripe fruit and is probably where the Altesse grape originated. Attractive Frangy wines tend to be drier and more herbal.

In the SEYSSEL appellation, the term 'Roussette de Seyssel' is no longer allowed, although growers have requested that it be reintroduced. In the nearby Ain *département*, **Roussette du Bugey** may be followed by the names of two crus, the rare Virieu-le-Grand and the more notable MONTAGNIEU, from steep vineyards on LIMESTONE scree overlooking the Rhône. W.L.

Roussillon has a distinct identity, both cultural and geographical, from that of the LANGUEDOC, the neighbouring region it was suffixed to until 2016. Its inhabitants are Catalan rather than French or Occitan, with a history rich in Spanish influence, particularly between the 13th and 17th centuries, when it was ruled first from Mallorca and then from Aragón. It became part of France with the Treaty of the Pyrenees in 1659, and the Pyrenees link it rather than separate it from Spanish CATALUÑA. Today Roussillon equates to the *département* of the Pyrénées-Orientales, the eastern section of the mountain range that dominates the landscape, which reaches so high that much of it remains snow-covered throughout the summer. The geology is some of the most varied of any French wine region, with SCHIST, LIMESTONE, GNEISS, CLAY, and GRANITE. The climate is France's sunniest, with an average of 325 days of sunshine a year, often accompanied by strong WINDS—as many as eight different winds. Vines and olives are two of the rare agricultural crops that can thrive in the arid valleys of the Agly, Têt, and Tech, while the lower, flatter land by the coast is today an important source of cherries, plums, peaches, apricots, and nectarines.

Wine-wise, it is one of the rare regions to produce both fortified wine (VIN DOUX NATUREL, or VDN) and TABLE WINE (*vin sec*, as the locals call it).

Viticulture probably came to the region via the Greek establishment of Marseilles in the 7th century BCE and was developed by the Romans. It seems highly likely that the MUSCAT vine was the first to be introduced, in an effort to ape the popular sweet wines of the AEGEAN ISLANDS. In the early 13th century, ARNALDUS DE VILLANOVA is credited with inventing MUTAGE, a process thought to have been applied particularly to the region's whites made from MUSCAT BLANC, Malvoisie, and MACABEO. RIVESALTES had certainly earned an important reputation for its Muscat by the 14th century, which probably predated that of the Languedoc's FRONTIGNAN. Red fortified wines based on Grenache Noir followed so that Roussillon became the world's foremost producer of vins doux naturels, with BANYULS, MAURY, and Rivesaltes among the first appellations in 1936. A good 70 million bottles of Rivesaltes were sold each year in the mid 20th century.

But this specialization was to be its downfall in the second half of the 20th century, when strong, sweet wines became decidedly unfashionable and the many APERITIFS based on these wines, notably the locally produced Byrrh, declined sharply in popularity. At the same time, more attention was paid to the *vins secs*, and two appellations were recognized in 1977: Côtes du Roussillon for all three colours and covering much of the *département*; and Côtes du Roussillon-Villages for red wine only, focused on the Agly Valley, with two named villages CARAMANY and LATOUR-DE-FRANCE. TAUTAVEL followed in 1996, LESQUERDE in 1997, and then Les Aspres in 2017. COLLIOURE Rouge came slightly earlier, in 1971, to be followed by Collioure Rosé and then Collioure Blanc, while Maury Sec was not recognized until 2011. The vineyard area of Roussillon totalled 19,900 ha/49,352 acres in 2019, registering a sharp decline from 38,000 ha in 2000 and 58,000 ha in 1979. Côtes du Roussillon represents 4,451 ha/11,038 acres, and Côtes du Roussillon-Villages, including the five villages, stands at 2,787 ha/6,911 acres. (See map under LANGUEDOC.)

The appellations are based on blends, with at least two, if not three, varieties among Grenache Noir, Carignan, Mourvèdre, and Syrah, with various limitations of precise percentages. Grenache's cousin LLEDONER PELUT is also allowed, while Cinsaut is relatively rare. The most planted varieties in Roussillon are, in descending order, Grenache Noir, Syrah, and Carignan. Next most planted are Muscat Blanc à Petits Grains and Muscat of Alexandria, grown traditionally for MUSCAT DE RIVESALTES but increasingly made as dry IGP wines. The principal grape varieties for the region's white wines are Grenache Blanc, Grenache Gris, and Macabeo, with TOURBAT, known locally as Malvoisie du Roussillon, enjoying a renewal of interest. Varietal wines, especially white wines, and also OLD VINE Carignan are sold either as IGP Côtes Catalanes or even VIN DE FRANCE. The best whites have an astonishing ACIDITY and MINERALITY that quite belies their warm origins.

INTERNATIONAL VARIETIES such as Chardonnay and Merlot are relatively unimportant here and generally not very suited to the growing conditions. These wines are usually labelled 'Pays d'Oc', while 'Côtes Catalanes' is used for the more authentically local varieties. The IGP Côte Vermeille covers the four coastal villages of the appellations of Collioure and Banyuls.

CARBONIC MACERATION has been much employed in the past to counter Carignan's inherent astringency, but more traditional vinification techniques are increasingly used for the 'nobler' varieties. Wine-making has improved enormously, with experience, TEMPERATURE CONTROL, and better use of oak BARRELS; with larger foudres as well as barriques, and even AMPHORAE; and with a search for lower alcohol levels. Viticulture too has evolved with a growing awareness of the problems posed by CLIMATE CHANGE and low rainfall.

CO-OPERATIVES still dominate mass production but are declining in importance as numerous incomers from other French regions and other countries have invested in the potential of this still relatively under-appreciated region. They include an energetic band of producers of NATURAL WINE based on the village of Latour-de-France.

The winegrowers of Roussillon have been some of France's least content with the details of their appellation regulations, which continue to evolve. There can be considerable scepticism about a system devised as far away as Paris and administered from Brussels, especially among those who identify so closely with the inhabitants of Barcelona. It is not unusual to see 'Catalunya Nord' on a label.

See also BANYULS, COLLIOURE, MAURY, MUSCAT DE RIVESALTES, and RIVESALTES. R.E.G.

Ponsich, P., 'Histoire de la vigne et du vin en Roussillon', in Éditions Montalba, *Les Vins du Roussillon* (1980).

row spacing, the space between rows of vines in the vineyard. See VINE DENSITY.

Royalty, also known as **Royalty 1390**, a complex HYBRID red-fleshed TEINTURIER bred in CALIFORNIA principally for its colour. It was released in 1958 along with the similar but much more successful RUBIRED. There is little regal about this particular variety, which is difficult to grow, although a few hundred hectares persist, almost exclusively in the hot SAN JOAQUIN VALLEY.

RS, common abbreviation for RESIDUAL SUGAR.

Rubin, distinctively BULGARIAN cross of Nebbiolo and Syrah developed around 1944. It ripens in mid September and has 50% more ANTHOCYANINS than Cabernet Sauvignon, although interest is waning since the wines seem to age too fast. Confusingly, Rubin is also the name of a Slovakian CROSS and a Romanian HYBRID. C.G. & J.V.

Rubired, California winemaker's secret weapon, a red-fleshed HYBRID released—along with the somewhat similar but much less successful ROYALTY—in 1958 and particularly popular at a time when depth of COLOUR became associated with QUALITY IN WINE. Its productivity and depth of colour made the variety so popular with blenders of wine, juice, and some food products that by 2003 there were more than 5,200 ha/13,000 acres in the state, making it California's sixth most popular red grape. Total acreage was still just over 10,000 acres in 2020. It is grown, without any major viticultural problems, mainly in the hot SAN JOAQUIN VALLEY and is never mentioned on a wine label.

ruby, style of FORTIFIED WINE. See PORT.

Ruby Cabernet, red Carignan × Cabernet Sauvignon CROSS bred in and for CALIFORNIA in 1936 and released in 1948. Dr H. P. Olmo of the University of California at DAVIS (see also EMERALD RIESLING, CARNELIAN) was attempting to combine Cabernet characteristics with Carignan productivity and heat tolerance. The slightly rustic Ruby Cabernet enjoyed a heyday in California in the 1960s and even in 2012 was still grown on more than 2,500 ha/6,000 acres, mainly in the southern SAN JOAQUIN VALLEY (though it is only half as popular as the red-fleshed hybrid RUBIRED). It is even more popular in South Africa, where it was grown in 2020 on a total of 1,943 ha, mainly in hotter inland wine regions, and has also been grown quite extensively in Australia's inland regions, appearing on Australian wine labels during the country's red wine shortage of the late 1990s. There were still 700 ha planted in Australia in 2022.

Ruchè, **Ruché**, **Rouchet**, or occasionally **Roche**, very rare but distinctive red grape variety of the PIEMONTE region in north-west Italy with its own varietal DOC around Castagnole Monferrato. Like NEBBIOLO, the wine is headily scented, and its TANNINS imbue it with an almost bitter aftertaste. There were about about 100 ha/247 acres in Italy in 2015.

Rueda, historic Spanish white-wine DOP named after the unprepossessing town which straddles the main road from Madrid to León in CASTILLA Y LEÓN (see map under SPAIN). In the Middle Ages, vineyards flourished on this bleak Castilian plateau, and cellars were hollowed out of the limestone under the town, but after PHYLLOXERA ravaged the zone Rueda went into rapid decline. The high-yielding PALOMINO FINO grape was used for replanting, a move that in this case was justified since the main local styles were FORTIFIED WINES in the image of SHERRY.

For much of the 20th century, the local VERDEJO grape was Rueda's sleeping beauty. It was awoken in the 1970s, when Bodegas Marqués de Riscal of RIOJA recognized the area's potential for dry white wine and sold a fresh Rueda white alongside its Rioja reds. A high plateau at 700–870 m/2,300–2,800 ft in elevation, Rueda was awarded DO status in 1980, and the local CONSEJO REGULADOR was so successful in relaunching the INDIGENOUS VARIETY that, by the mid 2000s, there was nearly three times as much Verdejo as Palomino. Rueda Dorado, a fortified and OXIDATIVE wine aged for a minimum of two years, and Rueda Pálido, aged under FLOR, are now rare, and modern Rueda is mainly a light, fruity, dry white wine, although there are also richer styles made with BARREL FERMENTATION and LEES CONTACT. It may be made from a blend of Viura (MACABEO) and Verdejo, the latter accounting for at least 50% of the blend, or it may be 100% SAUVIGNON BLANC, a variety introduced by Marqués de Riscal in the early 1980s that overtook Viura in total hectarage by 2017. Rueda Superior must contain at least 85% Verdejo; Gran Vino de Rueda must come from vineyards more than 30 years old and with maximum yields of 6,500 kg/ha. Some sparkling versions are also made.

Red and rosé wines are allowed in the DOP, but only 3% of plantings are in red grapes, mainly TEMPRANILLO. V. de la S. & F.C.

www.dorueda.com

Rufete, late-ripening Portuguese vine variety, also known as Tinta Pinheira, capable of making fruity red wines in BEIRAS and DÃO as well lightish PORT further north. Portugal's plantings had fallen to 2,651 ha/6,551 acres by 2020. In Spain's Castilla-León, 529 ha were recorded in 2020. Grapes need to be fully ripe for their red-fruited wine to succeed.

Ruffiac, **Ruffiat**. See ARRUFIAC.

rugose wood, a complex of four VIRUS DISEASES which comprises Rupestris stem pitting (RSP), Kober stem grooving (grapevine vitivirus A or GVA), CORKY BARK (grapevine vitivirus B or GVB), and LN33 stem grooving (LNSG). Additionally, grapevine vitiviruses C and D have been identified but have not yet been shown to cause disease in grapevines.

Although widespread, this complex of diseases is relatively unknown, as all but corky bark are generally symptomless on VITIS VINIFERA. Rugose wood induces graft incompatibility and can kill the vines, especially in the first years after planting. Typical symptoms are pitting or grooving of the wood. All four diseases can be identified by INDEXING. The effect on wine quality of these diseases is still to be evaluated.

Golino, D., et al., 'Laboratory testing for grapevine diseases', in L. J. Bettiga (ed.), *Grape Pest Management* (3rd edn, 2013), 61–8.

Ruländer is the more traditional German name for PINOT GRIS, which was propagated in the Rheinpfalz in the early years of the 18th century by wine merchant Johann Seger

Ruland. Since the mid 1980s, the name has been reserved for sweeter—and increasingly unfashionable—styles of Pinot Gris, while the increasingly common dry wines are labelled GRAUBURGUNDER.

The name Ruländer is also used in Austria and for some of the Pinot Gris that is widely planted in ROMANIA.

Rully, rambling village in Burgundy's Côte CHALONNAISE providing about 70% white wine from Chardonnay. Grown on light and SANDY soil, the wines are attractive early and rarely age well. Rully is also a good source of sparkling CRÉMANT de Bourgogne. Twenty-three vineyards in the village, one-fifth of the total, are designated PREMIERS CRUS, with Grésigny, Rabourcé, and Cloux being the most frequently seen. J.T.C.M.

rupestris. See VITIS RUPESTRIS.

Russia. Only the most southern parts of the Russian Federation south of the Don River and north of the Caucasus between the Black and Caspian Seas are suitable for viticulture. The principal limiting factors are low temperatures and a short vegetation period.

History

South Dagestan is Russia's most important ancient viticultural area, although WILD VINES growing around the Caspian, Black, and Azov seas and the greater Caucasus were selected and cultivated long ago. There is evidence of viticultural co-operation between the native tribes living on the Black and Azov seas and the ancient Greeks who settled along the north-east coast of the Black Sea from the 5th century BCE.

The next important viticultural period was the time of the medieval Khazar Kaganate (Turks by language but Jews by faith), who may have brought INDIGENOUS VARIETIES from Dagestan to the banks of the Don and then—together with the Magyars—to Pannonia, modern HUNGARY.

After several centuries of viticultural oblivion, the first vineyards in the Novorossiysk zone of the Krasnodar region were established in 1870 and planted to Riesling and Portugieser. By 1914 the Russian vineyard area averaged 50,000 ha/123,500 acres, but this had halved by 1919, due mainly to the effects of the First World War and PROHIBITION. In 1940 vineyards occupied 42,000 ha of Russia. The great development of commercial vineyards came at the end of 1950, and throughout the Soviet era Russia had a highly efficient wine production and, especially, processing and bottling system until President GORBACHEV began an anti-alcoholism campaign in 1985. Just before then, in the mid 1970s, PHYLLOXERA reached the Taman Peninsula just east of the CRIMEA. Vineyards were abandoned or GRUBBED UP. (Only in a few regions, such as the Taman Peninsula, did it prove possible to retain them because the local authorities reported to Moscow that they were used predominantly to craft grape juice, not wine.) Land privatization during the transition to a market economy further shrivelled the Russian wine industry; by 2001, total vineyard area was 69,400 ha, less than half the area cultivated in the late 1980s, and the total grape harvest shrank to less than one-third of its previous level.

Vineyard acreage continued to fall until early 2014, when the annexation of the Crimea, long celebrated for its wines, added at least 25,000 ha to Russia's total vineyard area. It was then that the federal government announced plans to support the Russian wine industry by relaxing regulations and increasing vineyard plantings. As a result, in 2020 the total vineyard area, including Russian-occupied Crimea and Sevastopol, encompassed 94,250 ha, with a total yield of 490,900 tons of both wine and table grapes. On average, about 5,000 ha of new vines are planted annually, but the total vineyard area is reportedly growing by around 1,200 ha as a portion of the new vines replace uprooted plants.

Climate and geography

Most commercial vineyards of pre-2014 Russia (see CRIMEA for separate details) are in the North Caucasus where the climate is moderately CONTINENTAL and winters can be severe; all vines in the northern regions of Rostov Oblast and Stavropol Krai must be buried for WINTER PROTECTION. The most favourable soil and climate conditions are in the Krasnodar region and Dagestan, with active annual temperature summations of 3600–4000 °C (see CLIMATE CLASSIFICATION) and winters warm enough to permit non-protected viticulture thanks to the moderating influence of the Black Sea.

Krasnodar, the most important Russian wine region, is tentatively divided into five zones, of which the Anapa-and-Taman zone stretching along the ancient Kuban estuary is perhaps most promising for wine production, although its fertile soils can encourage excessive VIGOUR and call for disciplined PRUNING. No winter protection is required for vines here (apart from in the eastern zone where grapes are grown for brandy). The Black Sea zone is much more humid, but winters are less severe; thanks to the MARL and CALCAREOUS soils, still, sparkling, and dessert wines are produced here.

Dagestan with its extremely varied climate, some of it semi-desert, is Russia's second most important wine-producing region (and was its principal one in the late 1980s). The flat southern zone along the Caspian Sea between the capital city and AZERBAIJAN, with its strong tradition of viticulture, is one of the most propitious parts of the Russian Federation for wine and brandy production. Grape varieties grown include Pervenets Magaracha, Agadai, White Muscat, Asyl Kara, Red Tersky, Saperavi, Zálagyöngy, Premier, Codreanca, and Moldova.

About 10% of Russian wine is produced in the **Stavropol** region. Winter protection is essential as temperatures fall well below freezing (the median temperature in January is −5 °C/23 °F). Summers are cool and short, with a frost-free period typically lasting just 180–190 days. Precipitation is also low, at 300–500 mm/12–20 in per year. The most common varieties are Levokumsky Ustoichivy (Stable), Sauvignon Blanc, Riesling, Rkatsiteli, and Aligoté.

Even smaller, but by no means less important for wine production, is the **Rostov** region with its dry, hot summers, sub-zero winters that demand winter protection of vines, and a plethora of INDIGENOUS VARIETIES, among them Krasnostop Zolotovsky, Tsimlansky Chorny, Sibirkovy, and Pukhliakovsky (Kecskecsecsű in Hungary). Chechnya now grows only TABLE GRAPES.

A new wine classification put in force in 2015 introduced the terms 'Protected Geographic Indication' (PGI) and 'Protected Appellation of Origin' (PAO). In 2021 the Russian government approved the breakdown of vinelands into vine-growing/winemaking zones (coinciding with the PGIs) and TERROIRS (coinciding with the PAOs). The list includes Dagestan, Don Valley, Terek Valley, Crimea (with Sevastopol), Kuban, North Ossetia–Alania, and Stavropol.

Industry organization

Most Russian vineyards and wineries have now been privatized. Only in Dagestan does the industry remain predominantly state-governed.

SPARKLING WINE comprises a significant proportion of wine consumption in Russia. In 2020, 550 million l/145.3 million gal of still wine and 178 million l of sparkling wine were sold in Russia, with official figures estimating that 55% of the market is domestically made wines and 45% is imported wines. Since 2015, the term 'domestically made' applies only to wines made from Russian-grown grapes instead of imported GRAPE CONCENTRATE and BULK WINE. The fashion for medium-sweet wines of all colours has also been on the wane, making up only 50% of sales by 2021.

A recent trend in Russian wine production has been the development of the so-called GARAGE WINES movement. In 2020 they were already playing a role on the southern Russian gourmet and tourist scene and at international tasting competitions.

Viticulture

Vine-TRAINING SYSTEMS changed enormously during the 20th century. Densely planted vineyards (5,000–10,000 vines per ha) with single-vine supports have given way to TRELLIS SYSTEMS in wider-spaced rows. The many vineyards that need winter protection are either trained with long and medium CANES left in one direction and covered with soil in winter by a vine-laying machine or left to be covered with a high mound of soil. The most widespread training systems for vineyards that do not need winter protection are tall-trunk bilateral CORDON and GUYOT.

In the Soviet era, the trunks of particularly vigorous vines were trained 1.2 m high with row spacing of 3–4 m/10–13 ft, the so-called broad-row training method. Such training systems are still seen in some older vineyards, but more frequently row and vine spacing is generally 2.5–3 m and 1.5–2 m respectively.

Vineyards on non-irrigated lands have medium- and high-TRUNKED forms with row and vine spacing at 2.5–3 m and 0.8–2 m respectively (or tighter for higher-end products.) Three industrial-size NURSERIES located in Krasnodar Krai produce over 4.5 million GRAFTED VINES a year which ensures 80–85% of the demand; the rest are imported, mainly from Italy, Austria, France, and Serbia.

Vine varieties

The varietal assortment of Russia's vineyards is extremely diverse, with over 100 varieties allowed for commercial cultivation. Depending on the region, 70–85% of vineyards are planted to wine grapes, with TABLE GRAPES accounting for 15–30% of the total vineyard area. Among wine grapes cultivated in all viticultural regions of Russia, the most common, comprising almost half of all plantings, are Cabernet Sauvignon and the varieties typically grown for SPARKLING WINES—the Pinots, Chardonnay, Sauvignon Blanc, and Riesling. Also planted are Aligoté, Cebrener Franc, Muscats, Saperavi, and Merlot; the local red wine grapes Krasnostop Zolotovsky and Tsimlansky Chorny (Black); and the Soviet interspecific HYBRIDS Pervenets Magaracha, Dostoiny, and others.

NEW VARIETIES with improved resistance to FUNGAL DISEASES and FROST have been developed by the All-Russia Potapenko Research Institute for Viticulture and Ecology. Most notable among the wine grape varieties are SAPERAVI Severny (Severny means 'northern') and CABERNET SEVERNY. They and other new varieties such as Stepniak and Fioletovy Ranni occupy about 10,000 ha/25,000 acres on various Russian farms. Commercial cultivation of these new, specially bred varieties has allowed considerable expansion of non-protected viticulture.

In the early 1990s, there was a substantial expansion in the total area planted to new, high-yielding wine grape varieties such as Bianca, Pervenets Magaracha, Moldova, and 'all-purpose' varieties suitable for both wine and TABLE GRAPES such as Muscat Derbentsky and Zálagyöngy, as well as to INDIGENOUS VARIETIES such as Sibirkovy, Tsimlansky Chorny, Plechistik, Variushkin, Narma, and Güliabi Dagestansky. V.P.

Саркисян А. Авторский гид Российские вина 2021–2022 (2021).

Пукиш В. Новый Старый Свет. Очерки по истории виноделия Кубани (2015).

Russian River Valley, California AVA that stretches much of the width of Sonoma County along the Russian River. Its 6,070 ha/15,000 vineyard acres are particularly known for Chardonnay and a rich style of Pinot Noir. See SONOMA.

Rust, important wine town in Austria's Burgenland where the LEITHABERG foothills meet the NEUSIEDLERSEE, historically best known for RUSTER AUSBRUCH. Rust is home to the Austrian Wine Academy, the largest wine education centre in mainland Europe.

Ruster Ausbruch, sweet wine from shrivelled grapes grown in quintessentially picturesque RUST, on the western shore of eastern Austria's expansive but curiously shallow Neusiedlersee, which encourages the development of BOTRYTIS. Despite its diminutive size and thanks to the importance of its wine, in 1524 Rust was accorded the right to brand their casks with the initial 'R', and in 1681 it was granted the status of free city under the Hungarian Crown. Methods of production for Ruster Ausbruch evolved contemporaneously with those at the opposite end of the Hungarian Kingdom for TOKAJI Aszú, and with the same dominant grape, FURMINT. (*Ausbruch* and *aszú* are synonymous and signify the 'outbreak' of botrytis.)

While Rust remained an important wine-producing community throughout the 20th century, Furmint all but died out after the First World War (when the town became part of Austrian BURGENLAND), and production of sweet wine was not revived until the 1960s, tentatively and in response to the tastes of German tourists. In the late 1980s, winegrower Robert Wenzel re-introduced Furmint to Rust from Tokaj. In 1991 growers led by Heidi Schröck founded the Cercle Ruster Ausbruch, codifying the production of their community's famous elixir, then made from a wide variety of white (and occasionally black) grapes. In 2020 Ruster Ausbruch acquired the status of DAC, stipulating a minimum MUST WEIGHT of 30 °KMW (146 °Oechsle) and a minimum of 45 g RESIDUAL SUGAR. The grape varieties are restricted to WELSCHRIESLING, WEISSBURGUNDER, CHARDONNAY, MUSKATELLER, and FURMINT. Sweet wines from Rust not meeting the conditions for Ruster Ausbruch are labelled by PRÄDIKAT and for their state of origin, Burgenland, while dry wines may seek approval as LEITHABERG DAC. D.S.

Rutherford, important centre of wine production in California's NAPA Valley.

Rutherglen, historic wine region in NORTH EAST VICTORIA ZONE, famous for its FORTIFIED, sweet TOPAQUE AND MUSCAT from the likes of Morris and Campbell's.

Ruwer, German river, just 40 km/25 miles long but with viticultural significance well beyond its size, which rises in the Hunsrück Mountains and flows into the MOSEL, downstream from Trier. Ruwer wines long bore the designation Mosel-Saar-Ruwer, but since 2007 the region has been subsumed within MOSEL; as of 2019, wines may also specify Ruwer as subregion. Ruwer wines are similar in STRUCTURE to those of the SAAR but have a touch of earthiness to add individuality. See MOSEL.

Saale-Unstrut, small wine region in eastern GERMANY of terraced and sometimes isolated vineyards, starting to recover from the forlorn condition in which they were left by the former East German regime (see map under GERMANY). The main producers in the 798 ha/1,972 acres under vine as of 2019 are the cellars at Naumburg belonging to the state of Sachsen-Anhalt and the co-operative cellar at Freyburg. As in nearby SACHSEN, white wine grapes dominate: Müller-Thurgau (with 15% of vineyard area), Weissburgunder (14%), Riesling (9%), and Silvaner (7%), although both Dornfelder and traditional Portugieser also hold significant shares. Vineyards are predominantly underlain by fossiliferous LIMESTONE. These are continental Europe's northernmost significant vineyards, with a comparatively cool CONTINENTAL CLIMATE and considerable risk of FROSTS. D.S.

Saar, river which rises in the Vosges Mountains and joins the River Mosel at Konz, near Trier. Downstream from Serrig, RIESLING vines grow on SLATE, resulting in wines of long-standing renown. Since 2007, the Saar's vineyards are subsumed under the regional name MOSEL.

Sable de Camargue, IGP in the sand (*sable*) soils along the coast of the eastern Mediterranean best known for wines the colour of the flamingos that gather in the region's many lagoons. Gris and pink wines (94% of production) must be made from at least 70% Cabernets Sauvignon or Franc, Carignans and Grenaches Noir or Gris, Cinsaut, Merlot, or Syrah; red wines switch out the *gris* grapes and Cinsaut for Marselan and Petit Verdot. The high sand content discourages PHYLLOXERA, so many vines remain UNGRAFTED.

Saccharomyces. See YEAST.

Sachsen, Saxony in English, and the third-smallest wine region in GERMANY. Formerly in East Germany, it is also known colloquially as the Elbtal and was home to the first German viticultural training institute (in Meissen) founded 1811–12. The region's 493 ha/1,218 acres of vines in 2018 follow the course of the river Elbe, from Pillnitz on the southern outskirts of Dresden to Diesbar-Seusslitz north of Meissen. Sachsen and SAALE-UNSTRUT are the most northerly wine regions in Germany (see map under GERMANY), featuring relatively cool CONTINENTAL climates and granite- and GNEISS-dominated soils. Yields are low, usually under half the national average, and local demand for an extremely limited supply guarantees prices that should make reviving Saxony's neglected terraces and its reputation for fine wine attractive. It was in Meissen, known for its porcelain factory, that viticulture in Sachsen was first documented in 1161.

White wine grapes that collectively dominate this region's almost entirely dry wines are Müller-Thurgau (14% of vineyard area), Riesling and Weissburgunder (each at 12.%), and Grauburgunder (Pinot Gris, 10%). Nearly 50% of the region's grapes are processed by the regional CO-OPERATIVE and state domaine (Schloss Wackerbarth), but Schloss Proschwitz, founded in 1990 and as such the region's oldest private wine estate, farms 14% of Sachsen vines. D.S.

sack, name for a white FORTIFIED WINE, imported from Spain or the Canary islands, which was much in FASHION in England in the 16th and 17th centuries. Its most famous, fictional, consumer was Sir John Falstaff; in Shakespeare's *The Second Part of King Henry IV*, Act IV, sc. ii, he delivers his classic speech in its praise. The etymology of sack is disputed. The *Oxford English Dictionary* derives the word from the French word *sec* meaning 'dry' but admits that it cannot produce a convincing explanation for the difference in vowels. Moreover, sack was probably sweet. It was matured in wood for up to two years, so it would have been like a cheap OLOROSO. Hence Julian Jeffs proposes another derivation: Spanish *sacar*, 'to draw out', from which *sacas* became exports of wine. Often the place of production was put before the noun, as in Canary sack (see LA PALMA), Malaga sack (see MÁLAGA), Sherris (or Sherry) sack. Sherris is JEREZ, hence the modern word SHERRY. From the end of the 17th century, 'sherry' began to replace 'sack' as the generic term, but 'sack' was still used in the 18th century.

Sack was popular in England, even more so when in 1587 Drake raided the Spanish fleet at Cádiz and captured 2,900 PIPES (not BUTTS at this stage) of sherry intended for the Armada, making drinking sack an act of patriotism. Undoubtedly the English colony did not welcome the second raid on Cádiz in 1595; yet sack continued to be exported to England. With the accession of James I in 1603, tension eased and the merchants flourished once more. Sack appears in the works of many of the major English writers of the 17th century, and, however much the Puritans disapproved of the theatre, they did drink sack: when Cromwell paid an official visit to Bristol he was presented with a pipe of sack. H.M.W.

Jeffs, J., *Sherry* (6th edn, 2019).

sacramental wine, saviour of some CALIFORNIA wineries during PROHIBITION. For more details of the sacramental nature of wine, see EUCHARIST.

Sacramento Valley, northern part of the vast CENTRAL VALLEY of CALIFORNIA from LODI northwards, including University of California at DAVIS, home to California's most famous VITICULTURE and OENOLOGY programme. It also includes the AVAs CLARKSBURG, Dunnigan Hills, and Capay Valley.

Sacy, white grape variety once widely grown in France's Yonne *département*. Its productivity is its chief attribute, its acidity the wine's most noticeable characteristic. This has been used to reasonable effect by the producers of sparkling wines, and the variety, also called Tressallier, is still (just) grown as an ingredient in the white wines of ST-POURÇAIN. See also PINOT.

SAFER stands for Société d'Aménagement Foncier et d'Etablissement Rural, meaning 'land development and rural settlement company'. These non-profit regional companies were set up in France from the 1960s to help restructure farms to be more economically viable and to support young people wanting to set up a rural enterprise. With the key aims of contributing to the sustainable development of rural areas, including viticulture and winegrowing, and to protect natural resources, they buy and allocate land and properties in accordance with the best local interests. See also PRICE, VINEYARD LAND PRICES.

www.safer.fr

Sagrantino, lively, tannic red-grape speciality of Montefalco in UMBRIA. **Montefalco Sagrantino** was elevated to DOCG status in the mid 1990s. Sagrantino has been used as the main ingredient in DRIED-GRAPE WINES but since the 1980s has shown promise as a carefully vinified dry red, as well as in blends with SANGIOVESE for Montefalco Rosso. It was the Arnaldo Caprai winery that created much interest in the variety in the 1990s, but the overall level of viticultural and oenological sophistication in the production zone still needs improvement. A total of 837 ha/2,068 acres were reported in 2020.

saignée, French term meaning 'bled' for a winemaking technique which results in a ROSÉ WINE made by running off, or 'bleeding', a certain amount of FREE-RUN juice from just-crushed dark-skinned grapes after a short, pre-fermentation MACERATION. The aim of this may be primarily to produce a lightly pink wine or to increase the proportion of PHENOLICS and FLAVOUR COMPOUNDS to juice, thereby effecting a form of CONCENTRATION of the red wine which results from fermentation of the rest of the juice with the skins. The second operation was at one time often undertaken by ambitious producers of both red bordeaux and red burgundy but is now rare, unless the weather conditions have resulted in particularly big berries at harvest.

St-Amour, the most northerly of the BEAUJOLAIS crus, technically part of the MÂCONNAIS, and an area with some LIMESTONE, which supports both red wines as well as Beaujolais Blanc from the 315 ha/778 acres of vines. Unsurprisingly, there has often been a sense of conflicted identity here—spurred by diverse soils that also contain chert (a dense sedimentary rock of microcrystalline QUARTZ), SCHIST, and FLINT—and a sense of romance, given the name, which by various accounts comes from a Roman soldier who celebrated a narrow escape from death in Switzerland by converting to Christianity, along with other, earthier creation tales. The wines, in any case, show a delicacy more in line with the best Mâcon reds, without giving up their Beaujolais gusto. J.F.B.

St-Aubin, village in the Côte de Beaune district of Burgundy's CÔTE D'OR tucked out of the limelight between Meursault and Puligny-Montrachet. White wine production increased, justifiably, to 84% of the total by 2019, up from 39% in 1976. Two-thirds of the vineyard area is designated PREMIER CRU, notably Les Charmois, La Chatenière, En Remilly, and Les Murgers Dents de Chien, part of a swathe of mostly south-west–facing vineyards lying between the borders of Chassagne-Montrachet, Puligny-Montrachet, and the hamlet of Gamay, which is included in the St-Aubin appellation. The remaining vineyards have ideal south- and south-easterly ASPECT but are less favourably situated further up the cooler valley.

White St-Aubin is a fresh, energetic wine with some of the character of Puligny-Montrachet, especially in warmer vintages; the reds resemble a suppler version of red Chassagne-Montrachet.

See also CÔTE D'OR and BURGUNDY map. J.T.C.M.

St-Bris was granted full appellation status from the 2001 vintage for its crisp, cool-climate sauvignon (Gris is now allowed as well as Blanc), having been a VDQS since 1974. Total vineyard area in the communes of St-Bris-le-Vineux, Chitry, IRANCY, Quenne, and parts of Vincelottes south of AUXERRE and west of CHABLIS had grown to 161 ha/398 acres by 2018. The wine is too obscure to be made with anything other than artisan passion, but it lacks the breed and concentration of great LOIRE Sauvignon Blanc. Being technically Burgundian but made from a decidedly non-Burgundian grape, it is a curiosity. J.T.C.M.

St-Chinian, good-value, distinctive AOC in the LANGUEDOC in southern France with around 3,000 ha/7,400 acres that extend over spectacular, mountainous terrain in the foothills of the Cévennes between the MINERVOIS and FAUGÈRES appellations (see map under LANGUEDOC). Most wine is characterful red, but some fresh, dry rosé and a small volume of increasingly interesting whites are also made. The small town of St-Chinian itself is in the middle of the zone, which extends north and eastwards to Berlou and Roquebrun which earned their own appellations St-Chinian Berlou and St-Chinian Roquebrun for red wines in 2005. In this northern zone, vines at up to 400 m/1,312 ft in ELEVATION grow on arid SCHISTS and yield low quantities of extremely sharply etched wines with distinct MINERALITY. In the southern zone closer to St-Chinian itself, the (sometimes purple) CLAYS and LIMESTONE, typically at about 100 m, tend to result in fuller, softer wines. Syrah, Mourvèdre, and Grenache and quite frequently its doppelgänger LLEDONER PELUT form the backbone of the red blends, with Carignan and Cinsaut playing more minor roles. Whites are based on Grenache Blanc, with Marsanne, Roussanne, and some Vermentino. Many producers here also grow other varieties with which to make some excellent IGP wines. M.S.

St-Christol, the easternmost red wine CRU within the LANGUEDOC AOC in southern France, named after a village on the eastern boundary of the Hérault *département* with Gard. Production of appellation wine is relatively low here and is chiefly in the hands of the village CO-OPERATIVE.

St-Drézéry, the smallest named red wine CRU within the LANGUEDOC AOC in southern France. Like neighbouring ST-CHRISTOL it is named after a village on the eastern boundary of the Hérault *département* with Gard, and such appellation production as there is is chiefly in the hands of the village CO-OPERATIVE, although Ch Puech-Haut makes fine reds and whites.

Ste-Croix-du-Mont, small 282-ha/697-acre sweet-white-wine appellation on the right bank of the GARONNE river in the Bordeaux region. At their best, especially on the steep, very chalky escarpments leading south down to the river, these mainly SÉMILLON wines can be excellent early-maturing answers to SAUTERNES and, in spite of their higher permitted yield, have a local reputation of being just as generous. Opposite the slope from the Église Ste-Croix-du-Mont, the cool Ciron river meets the warmer Garonne, creating more misty mornings than at LOUPIAC and therefore better BOTRYTIZATION, which, together with raisined grapes, must be hand-picked in several passes. Further inland, apart from a few GRAVEL outcrops, the soil is less noble and the exposures more varied than on the south-facing vineyards: as a result the sweet wines tend to be simpler, vinified and aged in tank rather than barrel, and these inland vineyards produce more dry and red wine. W.J.B.

Ste-Foy Côtes de Bordeaux, about 220 ha/543 acres of vineyards in the extreme east of the BORDEAUX region on the border with, and arguably more properly part of, BERGERAC.

The appellation is named after its principal town, just 22 km/14 miles west of the town of Bergerac. Its red wines are very similar to red Bergerac and BORDEAUX AOC, while its much rarer white wines are often sweet and mostly undistinguished.

St-Émilion, important red-wine district in BORDEAUX producing more wine than any other RIGHT BANK appellation, and home of most of the extravagantly priced GARAGE WINES. A UNESCO World Heritage site, it takes its name from the prettiest town in the Bordeaux region, one of the few to attract tourists to whom wine is of no interest.

The town's historical importance is undisputed. In the 8th century it was a collection of caves hollowed out of the cliff on which a fortified medieval town was to be built. In the Middle Ages its port, Pierrefitte, played an important part in shipping wine down the DORDOGNE river, until it was overtaken by LIBOURNE a few miles downstream. It was on the pilgrim route to Santiago de Compostela, and even today its CONFRÉRIE the **Jurade de St-Émilion** prides itself on maintaining the district's reputation for hospitality. As outlined in BORDEAUX, history, St-Émilion was a wine region long before the MÉDOC on the left bank of the Gironde, even though for most of the 19th century it was less important commercially. In the early 20th century, the wines of St-Émilion were left to the merchants of Libourne to sell in northern France and northern Europe, while the BORDEAUX TRADE concentrated on selling LEFT BANK wines. The reputation of St-Émilion grew steadily throughout the second half of the 20th century, accelerating towards the end of the century, not least because of international interest in some of the *garagistes*. As a result, rivalry between the left and right banks intensified, with St-Émilion and the scores of wine shops lining its narrow cobbled streets being the focus of right-bank wine activity.

Whereas the Médoc is made up of large, grand estates, most of St-Émilion's 600 or so smallholders are essentially farmers, albeit dedicated to a single crop. That crop is dominated by the Merlot and Cabernet Franc (here called Bouchet) vine varieties, Merlot accounting for more than 60% of all vine plantings and imbuing the wines with their characteristic almost dried-fruit sweetness. A little Cabernet Sauvignon is grown, but it can be relied upon to ripen profitably only in favoured spots in the generally cooler soils and MACROCLIMATE of the right bank, and then only if a suitable CLONE has been planted and is grown with care.

In addition, starting with the 2019 vintage, all St-Émilion wines are required to have been farmed under certified SUSTAINABLE VITICULTURE methods, whether HVE, BIODYNAMIC, or ORGANIC VITICULTURE. Those that are not must be bottled under the generic BORDEAUX AOC.

Vine varieties apart, variation is the hallmark of this extensive region. The quality of its wines can range from light, fruity, serviceable CLARETS to fine FIRST GROWTHS capable of AGEING for a century or more. The diversity of soils in the district is such that Bordeaux's most diligent geographer, Henri Enjalbert, devoted his *tour de force* to the region.

Although conventionally the St-Émilion district has been divided into two general soil types—the *côtes* or hillsides below the town and the CLAY-rich CALCAREOUS soil on the LIMESTONE plateau to its east and west—there are myriad soil types (see detailed map in Johnson and Robinson). At its north-western limit is a distinctly GRAVELLY district around Chx Cheval Blanc and Figeac. Much of the appellation zone lies on the plain between the town and plateau and the river Dordogne. Wines made on this lower land, a mixture of gravel, SAND, and ALLUVIAL soils, tend to be lighter and less long lived than the wines produced on the plateau or the hillsides, and most, but not all, of them qualify for the most basic appellation, **St-Émilion**.

But the St-Émilion district also boasts a diversity of appellations and, uniquely in France, has a CLASSIFICATION of individual properties which is regularly updated and depends on tasting. This classification was first drawn up in 1955 and is revised, often controversially, roughly every ten years, the most recent being that drawn up in 2022. Several hundred properties are accorded the misleadingly grand-seeming **St-Émilion Grand Cru** status. In 2020, for example, just 1,058 ha qualified for the simple St-Émilion appellation while 4,196 ha qualified as St-Émilion Grand Cru. But the classification's most significant task is to identify which properties rank as **St-Émilion Grand Cru Classé** and which few qualify as **St-Émilion Premier Grand Cru Classé**. See CLASSIFICATION for details of the 2022 classification, which rated 85 properties Grands Crus Classés, of which 14 are Premiers Grands Crus Classés and two, Chx Pavie and Figeac, have the 'A' status held by Chx CHEVAL BLANC, AUSONE, and ANGÉLUS before they withdrew from the classification. Most of the district's most highly ranked properties are either on the steep, clay-limestone hillsides immediately below the town or on the gravelly section of the plateau 5 km/3 miles west of the town and immediately adjacent to the POMEROL appellation.

Of traditionally famous St-Émilion properties, Ch Figeac—which predated and claims to rival Ch Cheval Blanc—is (unusually for the appellation) attached to Cabernet Sauvignon. Since most other St-Émilions lack this tannic ingredient, the district's wines in general mature much faster than their left-bank counterparts.

This is particularly true of the new wave of small properties which emerged in the 1990s, some of whose wines were offered (though did not necessarily sell) at prices in excess of the famous and established FIRST GROWTHS. See GARAGE WINES.

At the other extreme of value, the St-Émilion CO-OPERATIVE, l'Union des Producteurs de St-Émilion, is one of France's most ambitious, bottling one-quarter of St-Émilion's production. The whole region is characterized by a strong sense of local identity.

The satellite appellations

On the outskirts are the so-called St-Émilion satellites, LUSSAC-ST-ÉMILION, MONTAGNE-ST-ÉMILION, PUISSEGUIN-ST-ÉMILION, and ST-GEORGES-ST-ÉMILION. On this more rolling countryside north of the Barbanne (see LALANDE-DE-POMEROL), the vine is grown alongside other crops, and viticulture accounts for well over half of the total area, or 4,000 ha/9,884 acres. Co-operatives are important here, and Montagne- and Lussac-St-Émilion produce significantly more wine than either Puisseguin or, especially, St-Georges, which was for many years sold as Montagne-St-Émilion. The grape varieties planted are similar to those in St-Émilion proper, but the standard of winemaking is generally more rudimentary. There are, nevertheless, bargains to be sought out. J.R. & J.L.

Brook, S., *The Complete Bordeaux* (4th edn, 2022).
Johnson, H., and Robinson, J., *The World Atlas of Wine* (8th edn, 2019).
Penning-Rowsell, E., *The Wines of Bordeaux* (6th edn, 1989).

The vine variety

St-Émilion is also a synonym for the widely planted white grape variety called UGNI BLANC in France and TREBBIANO Toscano in Italy. The name is used particularly in Cognac in south-west France, where it is widely planted.

S

St-Estèphe, the northernmost of the four important communal appellations in the HAUT-MÉDOC district of BORDEAUX. St-Estèphe is separated from the vineyards of Pauillac's Ch LAFITE only by a stream—indeed, Ch Lafite owns some land in the commune of St-Estèphe itself. To the immediate north of St-Estèphe, across a stretch of polder, lies the Bas-MÉDOC, the lower, lesser portion of this most famous region.

The soils of St-Estèphe contain their fair share of GRAVEL, but often on a CLAY base. Less well drained and cooler than that of their counterparts further south in the Médoc, the soils can delay ripening, leaving St-Estèphe grapes higher in acidity. In Bordeaux's low-rainfall vintages, the water-retaining clays of St-Estèphe have an advantage.

A high proportion of grapes grown on St-Estèphe's area of just over 1,200 ha/2,960 acres of vines used to find their way into the vats of the village's CO-OPERATIVE, which often uses the name Marquis de St-Estèphe. The village may boast fewer famous names and CLASSED GROWTHS than MARGAUX, PAUILLAC, or ST-JULIEN, but its wines have a distinctive style that is deep-coloured, full of extract, perhaps a little austere in youth, but very long lived. This style was perceptibly softened during the 1980s as higher proportions of Merlot grapes blurred the edges of the Cabernet, and winemaking techniques, particularly CONCENTRATION, have been harnessed to make the wines seem softer and fuller.

The stars of St-Estèphe are its two second growths, Chx Montrose and Cos d'Estournel, whose fortunes and reputations have alternated throughout the village's relatively recent history as a fine wine producer. Cos (pronounced 'koss') d'Estournel has the Médoc's most eye-catching architecture, in a façade of pure oriental folly beside the main road through the Médoc's wine villages. Its wines are the commune's most ambitious, styled to age for many decades to come. Ch Montrose produces much more traditionally STRUCTURED, almost Ch LATOUR–like wines, confirming this while implementing an ambitious SUSTAINABILITY programme, including conversion to ORGANIC VITICULTURE.

St-Estèphe's other classed growths are the increasingly dramatic third growth Ch Calon-Ségur, the reliable fourth growth Ch Lafon-Rochet, well sited between Ch Lafite and Cos, and the distinctly modest fifth growth Ch Cos-Labory. Some of the village's most conscientiously made wines, however, are such unclassified estates as the exotic Chx Haut-Marbuzet, Meyney, de Pez, and Haut-Beauséjour (both owned by ROEDERER), Les-Ormes-de-Pez (the latter run in tandem with Pauillac's Ch Lynch-Bages), and Ch Phélan-Ségur.

For more information, see MÉDOC and map of BORDEAUX. J.R. & J.L.

Anson, J., *Inside Bordeaux* (2020).

Duijker, H., and Broadbent, M., *The Bordeaux Atlas* (1997).

Ginestet, B., *St-Estèphe* (1984).

Penning-Rowsell, E., *The Wines of Bordeaux* (6th edn, 1989).

Ste-Victoire, DÉNOMINATION GÉOGRAPHIQUE COMPLÉMENTAIRE within Côtes de PROVENCE.

St-Georges d'Orques, named CRU within the LANGUEDOC AOC just west of Montpellier.

St-Georges-St-Émilion, satellite appellation of ST-ÉMILION in Bordeaux on around 200 ha/500 acres of vines in 2020.

St-Guilhem-le-Désert, small IGP covering vineyards in the foothills of the Cevennes in the north-east of the Hérault *département* of France. The IGP can be used for wines that fall outside of PIC-ST-LOUP and allows a great many grape varieties, including ASSYRTIKO, AGIORGITIKO, and SAPERAVI, among others that might thrive in the region's LIMESTONE soils and MEDITERRANEAN CLIMATE. Two more precise geographic indications may be appended to the IGP: Val de Montferrand, and Cité d'Aniane for wines from the commune made famous by the wines of Mas de Daumas-Gassac.

St-Jean-de-la-Porte, CRU on warm, south-facing slopes east of Chambéry whose name can be added to the eastern French appellation SAVOIE. Use of the name is restricted to wines from the local MONDEUSE grape, from which floral and structured reds are made. W.L.

St-Jean-de-Minervois, small mountain village in the far north-east of the MINERVOIS region that gives its name to the Languedoc's most delicate and refreshing VIN DOUX NATUREL, Muscat de St-Jean-de-Minervois. It is made from MUSCAT BLANC À PETITS GRAINS, to which alcohol is added during fermentation to produce a wine with at least 15% alcohol and 125 g/l RESIDUAL SUGAR. St-Jean's vineyards are hacked out of the stony LIMESTONE and *garrigue* at 250 m/825 ft above sea level. The ELEVATION and cooler CONTINENTAL CLIMATE allows the grapes to ripen a good three to four weeks later than other Muscats grown closer to the Mediterranean, with higher ACIDITY levels and YIELDS that rarely reach the permitted maximum of 30 hl/ha. M.S.

St-Joseph, the second largest AOC in the Northern RHÔNE, producing wine from 1,370 ha/3,385 acres in 2020. A thin sliver of an appellation, stretching 60 km/37 miles from Chavanay in the north to Guilherand-Granges in the south, it is effectively an umbrella appellation that gathers together the succession of dramatic slopes facing south, south-east, and east that have largely been created by tributaries of the Rhône that flow in from the west, cutting through the eastern edge of the Massif Central. When the appellation was created in 1956 it included just six communes, all bunched around its southern pole just across the Rhône River from HERMITAGE: Glun, Mauves, Tournon, Lemps, St-Jean-de-Muzols, and Vion. Another 20 were added in 1969. There is no village of St-Joseph here: the appellation takes its name from an outstanding LIEU-DIT in the commune of Mauves. Most of the appellation is based on GRANITE, with small outcrops of GNEISS in the north, LIMESTONE in the south, and some recent ALLUVIAL deposits and pockets of LOESS throughout.

White wines make up just 13% of production, the full-bodied dry whites based on MARSANNE and/or ROUSSANNE. Red wines depend entirely on SYRAH, those from the southern end of the appellation tending to be slightly more concentrated and STRUCTURED than those from its cooler northern extension. The wines tend to cost less than those from the more prestigious neighbouring appellations of CÔTE RÔTIE, Hermitage, and CORNAS, despite some of the steep, terraced vineyards being just as difficult to work. Wines by producers such as Domaine Jean-Louis Chave, CHAPOUTIER, and Domaine Gonon show, however, that these wines can be exceptionally fine, the reds wines able to age for 20 years or more, but more generally speaking red St-Josephs are best drunk younger, up to eight years. M.C.W.

St-Julien, one of the most homogeneous, reliable, and underrated village appellations in the Haut-Médoc district of Bordeaux. St-Julien may suffer in popular esteem because, unlike PAUILLAC to its immediate north and MARGAUX a few miles to the south, it has no FIRST GROWTH properties. Instead, however, it can boast five superb second growths, two excellent third growths, four well-maintained fourth growths, and, from the 1980s at least, an unrivalled consistency in winemaking skill. St-Julien has been the commune for wine connoisseurs who seek subtlety, balance, and TRADITION in their red bordeaux. The wines may lack the vivid, sometimes almost pastiche, concentration of a Pauillac, the austerity of a classic ST-ESTÈPHE, or the immediate charm of a stereotypical (if all too rare) Margaux, but they embody all the virtues of fine, long-lived blends of Cabernet and Merlot grapes, being deep coloured, dry, digestible, appetizing, persistent, intriguing, and rewarding.

The appellation, the smallest of the Médoc's most famous four, has for years encompassed about 900 ha/2,220 acres of vineyard within the communes of St-Julien and Beychevelle to its immediate south. Both GRAVELLY soils and subsoils with CLAY and LIMESTONE and hardpan here are relatively homogeneous, broken only by a narrow strip of river bank on either side of the *jalle* that bisects the zone and flows into the GIRONDE north of Ch Ducru-Beaucaillou. South of St-Julien is a considerable extent of land classified merely as Haut-Médoc, but to the north the appellation is contiguous with the southern border of Pauillac, and Ch Léoville-Las-Cases in the extreme north of St-Julien shares many characteristics with some fine Pauillac wines, notably Ch LATOUR, which is well within sight.

The Léoville estate, as PENNING-ROWSELL points out, must have been the largest in the entire Médoc in the 18th century, before it was divided into the three second growths known today as the châteaux Léoville-Las-Cases, Léoville-Poyferré, and Léoville-Barton. Léoville-Poyferré, which includes the original château building, enjoyed a heyday in terms of its reputation in the 1920s but also demonstrated something of a return to form in the 1980s. Best value, and perhaps most representative of the appellation, is Léoville-Barton, run from Ch Langoa-Barton, a fine third growth that is, unusually for the Médoc, the home of its owners, the BARTON family. Chx Gruaud-Larose and Ducru-Beaucaillou are the other two St-Julien second growths and produce two of the Médoc's finest wines in most vintages. The third growth Ch Lagrange was much improved in the 1980s by investment from SUNTORY of JAPAN, while fourth growth châteaux St Pierre, Talbot, Branaire-Ducru, and Beychevelle are generally well run. St-Julien's classed growths account for over three-quarters of the appellation's total production, and even such unclassified properties as chx Gloria, Hortevie, and Le Petit Ducru (ex-Lalande-Borie) do not believe in underpricing their admittedly admirable produce.

For more information, see MÉDOC and map of BORDEAUX. J.R. & J.L.

Brook, S., *The Complete Bordeaux* (4th edn, 2022).
Penning-Rowsell, E., *The Wines of Bordeaux* (6th edn, 1989).

St-Laurent, as well as being one of the few villages of any size in the MÉDOC, is the name of a black grape variety today most commonly encountered in AUSTRIA, where it is known as **Sankt Laurent**. DNA PROFILING has confirmed that the variety is a progeny of PINOT. The other parent remains unknown; SAVAGNIN has been suggested but can be ruled out by DNA profiling. It is capable of producing deeply coloured, velvety reds with sufficient concentration—provided yields are limited—to merit ageing in oak and then bottle. Thanks to the German red-wine boom of the 1990s, total German plantings had reached almost 700 ha/1,730 acres by 2012 but had declined to just over 600 ha by 2020, mainly in the Pfalz and Rheinhessen. In Austria its 621 ha in 2021 puts it on an equal footing with the viticulturally more demanding Blauburgunder (PINOT NOIR). Certainly it has had several centuries to adapt itself to conditions in the Thermenregion and Burgenland, where its viticultural disadvantages—dangerously early budding, tendency to drop its flowers, and susceptibility to COULURE and ROT—are less problematic than in Alsace, for example. St-Laurent wine can resemble a powerful Pinot Noir. It is even more important in CZECHIA and SLOVAKIA, where it is once again known respectively as Svatovavřinecké and Svätovavrinecké, having been robbed of its sainthood during the communist regime when it was called simply Vavřinecké. There were 1,012 ha planted in Czechia in 2019, tied with Frankovka (BLAUFRÄNKISCH) as the country's most planted red wine grape. Slovakia had 785 ha planted in 2021, making it the country's second most planted red variety. It is also grown in Slovenia, where it is called Šentlovrenka.

St-Macaire, town in the BORDEAUX region across the river GARONNE from Langon in the GRAVES district. It lends its name to **Côtes de Bordeaux St-Macaire**, an appellation of just 35 ha/86 acres for mostly sweet white wines from SÉMILLON and MUSCADELLE.

St-Mont, AOC in southern GASCONY dominated by the dynamic Plaimont CO-OPERATIVE which has worked hard to identify and revive INDIGENOUS varieties. The 1,200-ha/2,965-acre zone is effectively an extension of the MADIRAN area with much the same grape varieties planted, although yields are generally higher. Reds make up just under 60% of production, and rosé one-quarter, both based on TANNAT, with FER Servadou and Cabernet Sauvignon the usual blending partners. For whites, GROS MANSENG must make up at least 40% of the blend, with ARRUFIAC and PETIT COURBU the preferred other ingredients, thereby differentiating this wine from PACHERENC DU VIC-BILH and JURANÇON to the south. Quality is increasing with every vintage, as is the price differential between it and the local IGP Côtes de Gascogne. P.S.

St-Péray, a small appellation straddling the communes of St-Péray and Toulaud in the far south of the Northern RHÔNE dedicated to white wine made from MARSANNE and/or ROUSSANNE. It was best known for TRADITIONAL METHOD sparkling wines throughout the late 19th and 20th centuries, but now dry still wines are much more common. Comprising just 103 ha/255 acres of vines in 2020, the CRU is suited to white wines thanks to a large outcrop of LIMESTONE rising to nearly 400 m/1,312 ft. The other main soil type is GRANITE. Wines are full-bodied with fairly low acidity. M.C.W.

St-Pourçain, small appellation along the Sioule and Allier rivers in the greater LOIRE region in the cereal- and OAK-producing ALLIER *département* almost precisely in the centre of France. (See map under FRANCE.) It was an important site in Roman times, near RIVER transport and offering suitable HILLSIDE VINEYARDS. White St-Pourçain was one of the most respected wines in France in the Middle Ages (see LOIRE, history, and MEDIEVAL LITERATURE) but is today more of a cool-climate curiosity. Now its 600 ha/1,483 acres of vineyard on soils of CLAY, SAND, LIMESTONE, GRANITE, and GNEISS produce a range of wines, all typically dry, light in BODY, and relatively high in acidity.

The traditional vine variety was SACY, but today the whites must be 50–80% Chardonnay with Sacy the blending partner. Rosés must be GAMAY, which also makes up 40–75% of the region's light red, blended with PINOT NOIR. Sparkling wines are labelled Vin MOUSSEUX de Qualité. The CO-OPERATIVE in the town of St-Pourçain-sur-Sioule itself dominates production.

St-Romain, exquisitely pretty village perched on top of a cliff in the Côte de Beaune district of Burgundy producing red wines from Pinot Noir and white wines from Chardonnay. There are no PREMIERS CRUS in the appellation, which was granted only in 1947 and applies to just 135 ha/334 acres, of which two-thirds produce lively white wine.

The vineyards of St-Romain are situated behind those of AUXEY-DURESSES and at higher ELEVATION, 300–400 m/985–1,310 ft, than is usual in the Côte d'Or. In lesser vintages, the grapes do not ripen as well as elsewhere, but in warmer years the wines can be excellent value. St-Romain is also home to one of the region's best-known COOPERS, François Frères.

See also CÔTE D'OR and map under BURGUNDY. J.T.C.M.

St-Sardos, small wine region on the left bank of the GARONNE near Montauban in SOUTH WEST FRANCE dedicated to red and rosé wines. The main grape variety is Syrah, with some TANNAT and a little Merlot and Cabernet Franc.

St-Saturnin, one of the more exciting red wine CRUS in France's LANGUEDOC, named after the eponymous village. Like Montpeyroux, it falls within the TERRASSES DU LARZAC, in high, rugged country where little other than vines will grow. The St-Saturnin CO-OPERATIVE is particularly dynamic.

Saintsbury, Professor George (1845–1933). Though a distinguished man of letters in his day, Saintsbury is now principally remembered for *Notes on a Cellar-Book*, a seminal work on wine which was an immediate success and has run to many editions.

He was born in Southampton, where his father was superintendent of the docks. The family moved to London in 1850, and Saintsbury attended King's College School, where he acquired his deep love of literature. Aged 17 he won a Postmastership to Merton College, Oxford, but to his everlasting regret he failed to win a Fellowship. For ten years, from the age of 21, he was a schoolmaster, but eventually he settled in London and for a time was assistant editor of the *Saturday Review*.

The actual cellar book was a simple exercise book in which Saintsbury listed the contents of just two cellars, the first in his London house in West Kensington, the second in Edinburgh, where from 1895 to 1915 he held the Regius Chair of Rhetoric and English Literature at Edinburgh University.

In June 1915 he retired from the Chair in Edinburgh, having some ten years previously developed gout, which prevented him from drinking red wine. He eventually retired to Bath, where he published 13 volumes, including *Notes on a Cellar-Book*, which first appeared in July 1920, as well as innumerable articles and pamphlets.

A London DINING club, the **Saintsbury Club**, was founded in his honour in 1931; although nominated as president, the professor, due to ill health, never attended a meeting. The all-male membership, limited to 50, has always comprised men of letters, wine lovers both professional and amateur, and a good sprinkling of DOCTORS and lawyers. The Club meets in Vintners' Hall twice a year, ideally on his birthday 23 October and on his name day 23 April, St George's Day. He also inspired the name of a California winery, in CARNEROS. See also LITERATURE OF WINE. J.M.B.

Saintsbury, G., *Notes on a Cellar-Book* (16th edn, ed. T. Pinney, 2008).

St-Véran, appellation created in 1971 for white wines from the Chardonnay grape in southern Burgundy, between Mâconnais and Beaujolais, to include much of the wine once sold as Beaujolais Blanc. St-Véran encompasses seven communes: Davayé, Solutré-Pouilly, and Prissé on classic LIMESTONE soil adjacent to POUILLY-FUISSÉ and Chânes, Chasselas, Leynes, and St-Vérand, where the sandy red soil of Beaujolais is mixed with limestone. In 2018, 743 ha/1,836 acres were declared under vine. The wines frequently have more body and ageing ability than a typical MÂCON-VILLAGES without rivalling the power and persistence of the wines of Pouilly-Fuissé, which forms an enclave within St-Véran. J.T.C.M.

salary, wine as. The practice of paying workers in wine is an old one (and certainly older than the payments in salt from which the word 'salary' is derived). In ancient PERSIA, for example, wine rations were strictly ordered and were often far in excess of any individual's possible personal consumption.

In the more recent past, but no longer, labourers, and in particular grape-pickers on the bigger BORDEAUX estates would have expected to receive some quantity of wine (rarely of great quality and often lowly PIQUETTE) in addition to wages.

The most notorious, and now outlawed, instance of paying workers with deliberately stupefying quantities of wine was the so-called *dop* system once prevalent in SOUTH AFRICA.

See also LABOUR.

Salice Salentino, DOC for robust red wine made mainly from NEGROAMARO grapes in PUGLIA in south-east Italy. The DOC Salice Salentino Bianco was created for Chardonnay-based whites, although the variety has no history nor much adaptability here. W.S.

salinity, the concentration of salts (mainly sodium chloride) in soils or irrigation water. Grapevines are relatively sensitive to salt injury. Salts in the rootzone affect grapevines in two ways: first, it is harder for the vines to extract water from the soil, and they may suffer from drought; and second, salts can be toxic at high concentrations in the vine's tissues. When vines are irrigated by sprinklers with water containing excessive salt, or are grown on excessively saline soils, leaves may be burnt, and in severe cases this leads to defoliation. Similar effects can occasionally be found in coastal vineyards affected by wind-borne salts. MERLOT vines are particularly susceptible. Saline soils are typically found in hot and dry climates where IRRIGATION has been introduced. For example, salinity is seen as a potential problem for the inland irrigated vineyards of Australia, along the Murray–Darling river systems, and also in PADTHAWAY. The problem is also found in southern France, where there are 10,000 ha/24,700 acres or more of vineyards planted on ancient marine deposits. Salinity in the soil may be monitored by measuring the electrical conductivity of the soil. Rootzone salinity can be overcome by applying slightly more irrigation water than the vines require, so as to leach the salts. Some vine varieties such as COLOMBARD are tolerant of salt, and there are ROOTSTOCKS such as Dog Ridge, Schwarzmann, 140 Ruggeri, and Ramsey which show salt tolerance through salt exclusion in the roots. Grape juice and hence wine may contain elevated sodium and chloride concentrations. The EU limit on sodium and chloride in wine is 394 mg and 606 mg per litre. R.E.S. & R.E.W.

Nicholas, P., *Soil, Irrigation and Nutrition* (2004).
White, R. E., *Understanding Vineyard Soils* (2015).

salt can affect vines. See SALINITY and ROOTSTOCKS. Some, although relatively few, wines may taste slightly salty (see TASTING).

Salvagnin, light red blend of Pinot Noir and Gamay (possibly with some GAMARET and GARANOIR), the first appellation created in SWITZERLAND in 1960. It accounts for about half of all wine produced in the canton of Vaud.

Salvagnin (Noir), sometimes **Savagnin Noir**, is a Jura name for PINOT NOIR, disconcertingly similar to the name of one of the Jura's own vine varieties, SAVAGNIN BLANC.

Sämling 88, common AUSTRIAN synonym for the SCHEUREBE vine variety, of which 307 ha/759 acres were planted in the southern Austrian wine regions of Burgenland and Styria in 2021.

Samos. See GREECE.

sampling, important part of a continuum of wine quality-control procedures which begin in the vineyard and may end when consumers pick a bottle out of a CASE in their CELLAR.

A very small proportion of a vineyard's fruit may be sampled to assess its chemical composition to help predict the HARVEST date, as well as to indicate likely quality and eventual wine style. Grape sampling might simply consist of selecting some berries randomly from the vineyard and expressing juice into a REFRACTOMETER to measure sugar content (see MUST WEIGHT; see also RIPENESS). A more rigorous approach may involve larger samples of either berries or bunches and more elaborate winery laboratory analysis. Even for a uniform vineyard site, berry composition (on a single vine or even within one bunch) will vary greatly due to different times of FRUIT SET and subsequent development. See RIPENESS.

Vineyard sampling has become far more focused since the turn of the century, thanks to PRECISION VITICULTURE and to research into GRAPE COMPOSITION AND WINE QUALITY. Both approaches make it much easier to keep together batches of fruit that have similar quality potential, sometimes referred to as streaming when the fruit is fermented together in large vats. However, some vineyards are harvested without a fruit sample being taken, particularly in more traditional regions where tasting the berries is considered sufficient to judge the time to pick.

Typically the sample is crushed or pressed in the winery to obtain juice, which is then analysed for sugar and typically also ACIDITY and PH. Some modern laboratories use spectrophotometry or near infrared spectroscopy (NIRS) to analyse the concentration of extractable ANTHOCYANINS and the total PHENOLIC compounds in the grapes. See also GRAPE QUALITY ASSESSMENT.

A second sampling is frequently made when a load of grapes is delivered to the winery, particularly if the grapes have been bought by contract, since grape PRICES are often based on grape composition, typically on sugar levels.

During FERMENTATION samples are taken at least daily to verify the regular conversion of sugars to ALCOHOL. Later, during ÉLEVAGE, regular sampling provides the winemaker with valuable guidance. Finally, shortly before BOTTLING, samples are taken for detailed analysis to ensure that the wine meets all regulations and is free of FAULTS and CONTAMINANTS.

An important part of selling wine EN PRIMEUR is the release of **cask samples** drawn from the containers in which the wine is still being matured, typically a BARREL, on which wine merchants and wine writers can base their assessments. Such raw wines, often roughly drawn off into small sample bottles, have not undergone STABILIZATION and can suffer OXIDATION and other faults after only a week or two. The best way to judge a young wine still in cask is sampling in the cellar or winery itself, from a range of different barrels. However, some producers, particularly in Burgundy, are concerned that repeated sampling from a barrel and subsequent TOPPING UP is not likely to benefit the wine. J.H. & R.E.S.

Samsó, Catalan name for CARIGNAN.

Samtrot, German synonym for Pinot Meunier. See MÜLLERREBE.

San Antonio, cool wine valley within the Aconcagua region of CHILE, close to the Pacific Ocean, excelling at white wines and reds of Pinot Noir and Syrah.

San Benito, small CALIFORNIA county 32 km/20 miles inland from MONTEREY Bay that has been continuously planted with grapes since 1849. Geologically distinguished by LIMESTONE-rich soils and fault-driven topography, the region hosted some of the state's earliest plantings of Pinot Noir in what is now the Cienega Valley AVA and, later, some of its most famous plantings of the grape on Mount Harlan AVA, site of the celebrated Calera winery. Wines from the county's two other sub-AVAS, Lime Kiln Valley and Paicines, are rarely seen.

Cienega Valley AVA

Frenchman Theophile Vache began planting vines in the Cienega Valley in 1849 and built a colonial-style adobe building in San Juan Batista that would become known as the Vache Wine Depot to sell his wares. His enterprise would not survive PROHIBITION, but the vines did. Now some of the oldest continuously producing plots in California are owned by the sole producer of note in the region, Eden Rift. The San Andreas fault bisects the AVA, its activity mixing the valley's intensely CALCAREOUS soils with deeper dolomitic and GRANITE-based sandy LOAMS.

Mount Harlan AVA

A one-man, one-vineyard, one-winery AVA established in 1974 by Pinot Noir pioneer Josh Jensen after assisting with the 1970 and 1971 harvests in BURGUNDY and coming away convinced of the virtues of limestone. He located a suitable concentration on Mount Harlan, where he proceeded to establish one of California's iconic wineries, named after the Spanish term for the old lime kiln on the property. Calera's ageworthy single-vineyard Pinot Noirs set a standard for what the grape could do in the late 1970s and early 1980s, when few believed the variety had a future in the state. Calera was sold to Duckhorn Wine Company in 2016. A.Y.

Sancerre, dramatically situated hilltop town on the left bank of the upper LOIRE which lends its name to one of the Loire's most famous wines: racy, pungent, dry white wines made from Sauvignon Blanc. The town's situation on such a navigable RIVER, and the favourable DRAINAGE and TOPOGRAPHY of the rolling countryside around it, assured Sancerre's long history as a wine producer; the suitability of the site for viticulture was obvious from Roman times. Pre-PHYLLOXERA, the region had been largely planted with Pinot Noir. Sancerre's piercing and distinctive Sauvignons, characterized by flavours of gooseberries and nettles, were initially introduced into the bistros of Paris as a sort of white-wine equivalent of BEAUJOLAIS, but, by the late 1970s and early 1980s, Sancerre was regarded as the quintessential white wine for restaurants around the world.

Sauvignon has adapted well to many of the varied TERROIRS around Sancerre, where, in 14 communes, vines are cultivated, particularly on the south-facing slopes of hills that average 200–400 m/655–1,310 ft in ELEVATION. There are three distinct soil types: Kimmeridgian MARL, known as *terres blanches*, found on the westernmost hills, particularly around the hamlets of Chavignol and Amigny, known for powerful, long-lived wines; pebbly LIMESTONE soils, known as *caillottes*, found throughout the appellation, said to produce delicate wines; and FLINTY soils known as *silex* in the eastern part of the appellation, which yield long-living, particularly perfumed wines. Comparisons with POUILLY-FUMÉ, made just a few miles upstream on the opposite bank, are inevitable. The total area given over to the Sancerre appellation, which had declined to about 700 ha/1,730 acres in the 1960s, had reached 3,000 ha/7,413 acres by 2019.

The climate here is distinctly CONTINENTAL, and the vineyards are easily subject to spring FROSTS, but the river to the east and the forests to the west moderate low temperatures. Vines are generally CORDON or single GUYOT trained.

Sancerre's popularity has brought with it the inevitable increase in the proportion of mediocre wine produced (or over-produced) within the zone. In particularly cool years, even the best producers must work hard to avoid excessive VIGOUR, resulting in unpleasantly HERBACEOUS aromas and a lack of fruity substance, but techniques such as grassing, de-budding, and leaf plucking result in healthier grapes and more concentrated wines. TRUNK DISEASES such as ESCA have been a constant presence since 2010, with a 5% loss each year typical in many vineyards.

Many Sancerre *blancs* are ready for drinking almost as soon as they are bottled, but the best certainly keep. Vintages such as 1996, 2002, and 2008 are prized for their flavours of white truffle that emerge with age, and both 2014 and 2017 have produced wines worthy of laying down.

Historically, producers featured the names of villages such as Chavignol more prominently on labels than the appellation itself. And today there is an increasing drive to express the distinctive terroirs found in the appellation. Many growers make SINGLE-VINEYARD WINES such as Les Monts Damnés in Chavignol and Le Chêne Marchand in Bué, with particularly good examples coming from producers such as François Cotat and Vincent Pinard. While there is no official hierarchy, these vineyards command consistently higher prices and offer greater COMPLEXITY and AGEING potential than traditional Sancerre. As in Pouilly-Fumé, some have mastered the art of matching Sauvignon with OAK, which can bring complexity and STRUCTURE to the wines.

Sancerre also exists in light, often beguiling, red and rosé versions, made from Pinot Noir grapes and representing approximately 10% and 6% of total production respectively. These wines enjoy a certain following, mainly in France, but need low YIELDS, very high standards of winemaking, and good weather to imbue them with a good core of fruit. CLIMATE CHANGE is helping, and the reds are becoming far more interesting.

The region is also famous for its goat's-milk cheese, Crottin de Chavignol, which, unsurprisingly, is an excellent match for the region's wines.

See also LOIRE, including map. J.R. & C.P.

Friedrich, J., *Earthly Delights from the Garden of France, Wines of the Loire*, Vol 1: *The Kingdom of Sauvignon Blanc* (2011).

sand, description of sediment or soil which is made up of relatively large particles (bigger than SILT and much bigger than CLAY). See SOIL TEXTURE and GEOLOGY for more details of this particular form of soil classification. Sandy soils can be difficult to cultivate because of their poor ability to store water and nutrients, but they are notable in viticulture for providing a good measure of protection from PHYLLOXERA. Vineyards dominated by sand include those of COLARES in Portugal, the Camargue in the south of France, the Great Plain of HUNGARY, and Maipo Valley in CHILE.

San Diego County, warm area south of Los Angeles, CALIFORNIA, where wine grapes were first planted in 1769 by Franciscan MISSIONARIES. Today most of its vineyards are contained within the South Coast AVA. In 2021, 160 wineries were active, including a number of URBAN WINERIES. Cabernet Sauvignon, Syrah, and Sangiovese dominate the region's 276 ha/682 acres of vines. M.D.K.

sandstone, a sedimentary rock composed of SAND-size particles, most commonly QUARTZ. The grains are held together by natural cement formed by chemical precipitation in the pores. Typically this consists of silica but may be another material such as calcium carbonate, forming a CALCAREOUS sandstone. Most sandstone soils are poorly fertile, slightly acid, and well drained; famously, they offer some resistance to PHYLLOXERA. Sandstone soils are widespread: examples are the Courthézon area of CHÂTEAUNEUF-DU-PAPE, Ballard Canyon (SANTA BARBARA) and the Great Plain of HUNGARY. A.J.M.

San Francisco Bay, commercially expedient, geographically extensive AVA that includes CONTRA COSTA COUNTY, Lamorinda, SANTA CLARA VALLEY, and the much larger LIVERMORE VALLEY. The Bay Area is also home to many an URBAN WINERY, which source grapes from throughout the state.

Sangiovese, qualitatively variable red grape variety that is Italy's most planted wine vine and is particularly common in central Italy. In 1990 almost 10% of all Italian vineyards, or more than 100,000 ha/247,000 acres, were planted with some form of Sangiovese, although this had fallen to 68,428 ha/169,089 acres by 2015. In its various CLONAL variations and names (Brunello, Prugnolo Gentile, Morellino, NIELLUCCIU), Sangiovese is the principal vine variety for fine red wine in TUSCANY, the sole grape permitted for BRUNELLO DI MONTALCINO, and the base of the blend for CHIANTI, VINO NOBILE DI MONTEPULCIANO, and the vast majority of SUPERTUSCANS. It is, in addition, the workhorse red grape of all of central Italy, widely planted in UMBRIA (where it gives its best results in the wines of TORGIANO and Montefalco), in the MARCHE (where it is an important component of Rosso Piceno), and in LAZIO. Sangiovese can be found as far afield as Lombardy and Valpolicella to the north and Campania to the south.

Sangiovese is widely thought to be of ancient origin, as the literal translation of its name ('blood of Jove') suggests, and it has been postulated that it was even known to the ETRUSCANS, although its origins are still debatable.

In 2004 researchers Vouillamoz and Grando at SAN MICHELE ALL'ADIGE proposed the following parents of Sangiovese: the Tuscan 'cherry grape' CILIEGIOLO and Calabrese di Montenuovo, an obscure variety found in Campania though probably originating from Calabria. In 2012 Ciliegiolo and Negrodolce, an old and obscure Puglian variety, were suggested as putative parents of Sangiovese. These two parentages were recently invalidated using another type of DNA marker, showing that Ciliegiolo is in fact the progeny of Sangiovese and Muscat Rouge de Madère (or Moscato Violetto) and that Negrodolce and Calabrese di Montenuovo are also progenies of Sangiovese, whose parents remain unknown. Additional progenies of Sangiovese were also discovered, including numerous varieties from southern Italy such as FRAPPATO, SUSUMANIELLO, GAGLIOPPO, NERELLO MASCALESE, and PERRICONE, showing Sangiovese's significant historical importance in the south. In 1590 Giovanvettorio Soderini mentioned the variety Sangiogheto. This is commonly accepted as the first historical mention of Sangiovese, but there is no evidence that Sangiogheto actually was Sangiovese. Indeed, when Soderini writes about the ways to make a very good wine, he cautions readers to 'beware of the Sangiogheto, who thinks to make wine from it will make vinegar'. This is confirmed in 1738 by Cosimo Trinci, who observed that wines made solely from Sangiovese were somewhat hard and acid, though they were excellent when blended with other varieties, a judgement echoed by Giovanni Cosimo Villifranchi in 1883 Bettino RICASOLI found a way to tame Sangiovese's asperity—a substantial addition of sweetening and softening CANAIOLO—which became the basis of all modern Chianti and of Vino Nobile di Montepulciano (although Ciliegiolo, MAMMOLO, and COLORINO as well as the white grapes Malvasia and, especially, Trebbiano were subsequently added to the authorized blend). The use of small oak barrels, begun in the 1970s, may have softened Sangiovese's tannins but was primarily a response to changing FASHIONS.

Conventional ampelographical descriptions of Sangiovese, based on the pioneering work of G. Molon in 1906, divide the variety into two families: the Sangiovese Grosso, to which Brunello, Prugnolo Gentile, and the Sangiovese di Lamole (of Greve in Chianti) belong, and the Sangiovese Piccolo of other zones of Tuscany, with the implicit identification of a superior quality in the former. Current thinking is that this classification is too simplistic, that there is a large number of clones populating the region's vineyards, and that no specific qualitative judgements can be based on the size of either the berries or the bunches. Significant efforts are at last being made to identify and propagate superior clones; MASS SELECTION in the past sought principally to identify high-yielding clones without any regard for wine quality. The variety adapts well to a wide variety of soils, although the presence of LIMESTONE seems to exalt the elegant and forceful aromas that are perhaps the most attractive quality of the grape.

Sangiovese's principal characteristic in the vineyard is its slow and late ripening—harvests traditionally began after 29 September and even today can easily be protracted until or even beyond mid October—which gives rich, alcoholic, and long-lived wine in hot years and creates problems of high ACIDITY and hard TANNINS in cool years. Over-production tends to accentuate the wine's acidity and lighten its colour, which can OXIDIZE and start to brown at a relatively young age. The grape's rather thin skin creates a certain susceptibility to ROT in cool and damp years, which is a serious disadvantage in a region where rain in October is a frequent occurrence. In the past, Sangiovese was planted with scant attention to ASPECT and ELEVATION in Tuscany, where the vine is often cultivated at up to or even above 500 m/1,640 ft. A good part of late 20th century vinicultural research in Tuscany—which has involved increased VINE DENSITY, lower YIELDS per vine, better clones, more appropriate ROOTSTOCKS, lower vine-TRAINING SYSTEMS, more suitable supplementary varieties for blending, different temperatures and lengths of FERMENTATION, variations in the use of OAK—was dedicated to putting more meat on Sangiovese's bones as well as increasing its international appeal.

Throughout modern Tuscany, Sangiovese has often been blended with a certain proportion of the Bordeaux grape CABERNET SAUVIGNON, whether for Chianti (up to 15% of the total) or Chianti Classico (up to 20%) or a highly priced VINO DA TAVOLA. Even in this commercially successful blend, sanctioned by the DOC authorities in CARMIGNANO, Cabernet can overwhelm the Sangiovese.

In UMBRIA, the variety dominates most of the region's best red wine, as in the Torgiano of the producer Lungarotti. In terms of quantity, Sangiovese is more important in Romagna but is also increasingly significant in terms of quality, as explained in ROMAGNA SANGIOVESE. Two of the best clones currently being used to repopulate Tuscan vineyards, R24 and T19, are from Romagna. Some Sangiovese is grown in the south of Italy, where it is usually used for blending with local grapes, and the success of Supertuscans has inevitably led to a certain amount of experimentation with the variety to the north of Tuscany too.

Outside Italy

Like other Italian grape varieties, particularly red ones, Sangiovese was taken west, to both North and South America, by Italian emigrants. In South America it is best known in Argentina, where there were 1,390 ha/3,435 acres in 2020, mainly in Mendoza province, producing wine that few Tuscan tasters would recognize as Sangiovese.

In California, however, international recognition for the quality of Supertuscans brought a sudden increase in Sangiovese's popularity in the late 1980s and 1990s. By 2003 the area had increased to more than 1,200 ha/3,000 acres, but this had fallen to 587 ha/1,451 acres by 2020, perhaps partly because California Sangiovese, typically more FRUIT-DRIVEN than the prototype, failed to establish a strong identity. ANTINORI, unsurprisingly, persists with the variety at their Antica winery on Atlas Peak above the Napa Valley.

The grape also seems to be losing favour in Washington State where plantings had fallen to below 54 ha/134 acres by 2017. In Australia, however, it has the allure of being classified an ALTERNATIVE VARIETY, and total area was 433 ha/ 1,070 acres by 2022 even if renditions varied considerably in style and quality. It is a minor feature in South Africa and Chile.

Sangiovese di Romagna. See ROMAGNA SANGIOVESE.

sangría, a mixture of red wine, lemonade, sugar, and, sometimes, spirits and fresh fruit, served with particular gusto in Spain's tourist resorts. In 2014 the EU ruled that bottled beverages using the name should be restricted to the produce of Spain and Portugal.

sanitation. See HYGIENE.

San Joaquin Valley, southern half of the vast Central Valley in CALIFORNIA, stretching almost 354 km/220 miles from Stockton to Bakersfield. With 61,000 ha/151,000 acres under vine, it produces 50% of the state's total wine grapes, much going to BULK WINE. It includes the AVAs Madera, Salado Creek, Tracy Hills, River Junction, Diablo Hills, and LODI.

San Juan, wine-producing province in ARGENTINA especially celebrated for Syrah.

Sanlúcar de Barrameda, one of the three main Spanish towns in which SHERRY is made and matured. MANZANILLA is a delicate, pale, dry sherry matured in Sanlúcar.

San Luis Obispo, wine-producing county in the CENTRAL COAST AVA of CALIFORNIA midway between Los Angeles and San Francisco, best understood in terms of its AVAS rather than as a larger whole thanks to stark contrasts among its MESOCLIMATES. Unrelenting summer sun beats down on the high, sheltered plain that is the PASO ROBLES AVA, while only 20 miles/32 km west fogs hang over the narrow, cool coastal shelf of the SLO Coast AVA, which encompasses the AVAs of Edna Valley and Arroyo Grande Valley.

San Luis Obispo (SLO) Coast AVA
Approved in 2022, this 97-km/60-mile-long, 15-mile-wide, 408,585-acre AVA carves out a slice of the county's coast from the redwood forests of Big Sur south to the border with SANTA BARBARA. Its 50 resident wineries grow more than 1,619 ha/4,000 acres of primarily PINOT NOIR and CHARDONNAY, mostly planted within 10 km/6 miles of the ocean, some of which are the coldest vineyard sites in the state.

Edna Valley AVA
Directly south of the coastal town of San Luis Obispo, Edna Valley won quick fame for its Chardonnays, beginning in the mid 1970s. Edna Valley Vineyards, now part of E. & J. GALLO, was the pioneer, and the principal wine company is Niven Family Wine Estates (the Nivens founded Edna Valley Vineyards), producer of Baileyana, Tangent, Zocker, and other labels. The AVA also claims Alban Vineyards, established in 1989 by RHÔNE RANGER John Alban, whose finest Syrahs, Grenaches, and Viogniers are the region's most expensive and are sold strictly via mailing list. Low hills on three sides give the small valley a soup-tureen shape, allowing it to collect moisture-laden air from the Pacific, making FUNGAL DISEASES a frequent threat despite low rainfall. Cool, even temperatures and fog cover result in a very long growing season, often 50% longer than Burgundy. Soils are largely marine SHALES and SAND mixed with richer LOAMS. Planted acreage stood at 1,077 ha/2,661 acres in 2018 but has fallen since as more profitable citrus groves replace vineyards.

Arroyo Grande Valley AVA
A long range of hills sloping towards Pismo Beach at the southern edge of San Luis Obispo County, Arroyo Grande was viticulturally distinguished in the 1980s only by the painstaking decision to plant 350 ha/865 acres of it for Maison Deutz, the California arm of Champagne house Deutz. It was later sold, morphing into Laetitia winery. With 838 acres under vine in 2018, the region continues to produce high-quality CHARDONNAY and PINOT NOIR for Laetitia as well as labels such as Talley Vineyards and Au Bon Climat. While best known for its cool coastal plantings, the sunnier inland hills behind Lake Lopez host 140-year-old ZINFANDEL vines, bottled by Saucelito Canyon, as well as more recent plantings of SYRAH and CABERNET SAUVIGNON.

See also PASO ROBLES. A.Y.

www.slocoastwine.com

San Marino, tiny republic within Italy between EMILIA-ROMAGNA and the MARCHE. Its elusive wines, from 120 ha/296 acres of vineyards, are based on SANGIOVESE for its red, Ribolla di San Marino (which is in fact Umbria's GRECHETTO) and Biancale for its whites.

www.consorziovinisanmarino.com

San Michele all'Adige, Istituto Agrario di, or strictly, since being renamed in 2008, the Edmund Mach Foundation, one of Italy's best-known viti-agricultural schools and centres of ACADEME. It was founded in 1874 in what was then the Austrian South Tyrol and is now the province of Trento in the far north of the country. Its aim is to promote cultural and socioeconomic growth in the agricultural sector and to develop SUSTAINABLE forestry and agriculture. Its first director Edmund Mach set up the institute to include an experimental station and a farm alongside the school. Today a wide range of agricultural and viticultural training and research is undertaken, including the genomics of INDIGENOUS VARIETIES in collaboration with international research institutes, and oenological concerns include the analysis of flavour and PHENOLICS, microbiology, and sensory analysis (see TASTING). The institute hosts the most important AMPELOGRAPHIC collection in Italy, with varieties from Italy and all over the world, and it produces a range of wines under the San Michele all'Adige label.

Santa Barbara, southern CALIFORNIA city and county which gives its name to the southernmost in a string of three heavily planted wine counties on California's CENTRAL COAST (see also MONTEREY and SAN LUIS OBISPO). Though just 160 km/100 miles from Los Angeles, it is home to some of the coolest wine appellations in the state, as the county's northern valleys open directly on to the Pacific Ocean due to the Transverse Ranges that run east to west. The small but cosmopolitan city enjoys a dreamy, dry climate and is awash in Spanish Colonial architecture. Missionaries first planted vines in the late 1700s (see CALIFORNIA, history), and vineyards were common until PROHIBITION. Just offshore, Santa Cruz Island was one of the largest commercial vineyards in California at the turn of the 20th century. Modern commercial winemaking dates back to 1964, with an initial emphasis on CHARDONNAY in the Santa Maria Valley. The planting of Sanford & Benedict Vineyard in 1971 proved that PINOT NOIR could grow in the western reaches of the Santa Ynez Valley, located north of the mountains that frame Santa Barbara's beaches. By 2021 there were more than 6,070 ha/15,000 acres of vines planted. As Chardonnay and Pinot Noir became the region's prized varieties, the latter fueled by the award-winning film SIDEWAYS, winegrowers also created a series of appellations to explore the varying Santa Ynez Valley's many MESOCLIMATES, in which more than 40 grape varieties are grown. From the cooler west to the warmer east, they are the Sta. Rita Hills (focused primarily on BURGUNDY varieties, Ballard Canyon (RHÔNE varieties), Los Olivos District (a mix), and Happy Canyon of Santa Barbara (BORDEAUX varieties). Between the Santa Maria and Santa Ynez valleys near the town of Los Alamos is the Alisos Canyon AVA, created in 2020.

Santa Maria Valley AVA
Located just south of San Luis Obispo County, the west-to-east–oriented Santa Maria Valley opens wide on to the Pacific Ocean, which contributes morning fog and afternoon breezes. Vineyards grow on the flat parts of the floodplain, which is also home to extensive strawberry, broccoli, and other row crops, as well as along the BENCHES and up into the canyons on the north and south sides of the valley. Commercial viticulture started in 1964, with

Chardonnay grown mostly for the North Coast, but local winemakers such as Jim CLENDENEN of Au Bon Climat were successful with Chardonnay and Pinot Noir by the mid 1980s. Cool-climate Syrah is also a star, thanks to Qupé, founded in 1982 by Bob Lindquist. Though about 3,000 acres are planted, only a handful of wineries operate in the appellation, including Cambria (owned by KENDALL-JACKSON), Foxen, Presqu'ile, and Rancho Sisquoc, which released its first wines in 1972. That same year, the Miller family planted Bien Nacido Vineyard, whose nearly 1,000 acres of premium grapes are sold to wineries around the country. The GALLO family owns part of the historic Sierra Madre Vineyard (planted 1971) as well as the newer Rancho Real. Most of the region's grapes are sold to wineries in the greater Santa Barbara area or much further away.

Santa Ynez Valley and sub-AVAs

Due to the east–west orientation of the Transverse Range, the Santa Ynez Valley, which was granted AVA status in 1983, is one of the only valleys on the west coast to open directly on to the Pacific Ocean. That guarantees extremely MARITIME conditions of thick fog and persistent wind on the valley's western side, with much warmer and drier daytime conditions towards the east. The valley's TOPOGRAPHY is also tumultuous, with mountains to the south and east as well as a mix of hills, canyons, and ALLUVIAL fans elsewhere. As such, a diverse range of grape varieties achieve ripeness here, and a series of sub-AVAs have been developed since the early 2000s to explore those MESOCLIMATES.

On the western side, the STA. RITA HILLS AVA is dominated by Chardonnay and Pinot Noir, with growing amounts of Rhône varieties. To the east, the Ballard Canyon AVA (223 ha/550 acres planted) runs between Solvang, Buellton, and Los Olivos and is believed to be the first US appellation dedicated to Rhône varieties; a bottle designed specifically for Syrah, which makes up more than half its plantings, may be used for ESTATE WINES. Further east is Los Olivos District AVA (2016), which covers an alluvial fan that runs from Figueroa Mountain down to the Santa Ynez River and is planted in many varieties. Furthest east is Happy Canyon of Santa Barbara (2009), where warmer weather and VOLCANIC soils shift the focus to Bordeaux varieties. The seventh AVA, Alisos Canyon, is slightly north of Santa Ynez Valley proper and home to primarily Rhône varieties. M.D.K.

sbcountywines.com

Santa Clara Valley, California wine region and AVA south of San Francisco. Its colloquial name, Silicon Valley, derives from its status in the computer high-tech industry. Despite a long vinous history, factories, shopping malls, and homes began to supplant most of its vineyards in the 1950s. By the 1970s the transformation was nearly complete, and the final chapters were being written for once-important winery names such as Almadén and Paul Masson. Mirassou remains today but is now owned by E. & J. GALLO, the wines sourced from throughout California and its vineyards in the Salinas Valley in MONTEREY. A few acres of Santa Clara vines persist to the west in the SANTA CRUZ MOUNTAINS and at its southern end in the Hecker Pass district, but the area's luxury homes for computer programmers make all these vineyards more of a toy than a viable agricultural investment. Twenty small wineries exist, largely for the benefit of TOURISTS. The embedded San Ysidro District AVA east of Gilroy is a single grower, owned by a New York winery. L.M. & A.Y.

Santa Cruz Mountains, diverse 141,700-ha/350,000-acre CALIFORNIA wine region and AVA immediately south of San Francisco explicitly carved out of and separate from the SAN FRANCISCO BAY and CENTRAL COAST AVAs which would otherwise seem to enclose it. This region covers the hillsides and ridgetops of the Coast Range from Highway 92 in San Mateo County in the north down to the town of Interlaken in the south. One of the few AVAs in California defined by ELEVATION rather than watersheds or political boundaries, its western edges begin in the fog-laden foothills facing the Pacific at 122 m/400 ft in elevation, the eastern edges at 240 m, and it rises to nearly 1,000 m/3,280 ft. These mountains are geologically the youngest in the state, having been formed a mere million years ago by tectonic forces still at work along the San Andreas Fault, which runs the length of the region. The crenellated, steep, heavily forested slopes and ridges offer a dizzying array of ASPECTS, MESOCLIMATES, and sedimentary soil types, to the point of preventing generalizations about the region. That said, it is among the coolest of California wine regions, though a warmer pocket on the south-eastern flanks of the mountains, as well as the inland edge of its uppermost summit ridge can ripen BORDEAUX varieties, as RIDGE VINEYARDS has so ably proved with its Monte Bello CABERNET SAUVIGNON.

While Cabernet may be responsible for the region's greatest fame, PINOT NOIR and CHARDONNAY have a longer and arguably more storied history in the region, thanks to BURGUNDIAN émigré Paul Masson, who arrived in 1901 and quickly built a reputation for still and sparkling wines. Masson's protégé, Martin Ray would go on to make some of California's first VARIETAL bottlings of Pinot and Chardonnay, paving the way for later winemaking luminaries such as David Bruce as well as Richard Graf and Merry Edwards at Mount Eden Vineyards (the current name of Masson's original estate). Started in the counterculture woods behind UC Santa Cruz, Bonny Doon and its RHÔNE RANGER founder Randall GRAHM brought more attention to the region in the 1990s, despite sourcing grapes primarily from the CENTRAL COAST. Producers such as Kathryn Kennedy, Bargetto, Storrs, and Thomas Fogarty have joined Ridge, Bruce, and Mount Eden in producing consistently high-quality wines over the years. North Coast producers are increasingly sourcing grapes from the region, albeit in limited quantities. Plantings in the AVA amount to a mere 618 ha/1,526 acres in 2021, with most vineyards 5–25 ha/2–10 acres in size, spread among hundreds of independent growers. The region also has one sub-AVA, the granitic ridge of the Ben Lomond Mountain AVA, which sits north-west of the town of Santa Cruz but rarely appears on labels. Though unofficial, producers often refer to several 'neighbourhoods' of this diverse AVA, including the coolest and most southerly Corralitos, the northernmost Skyline area, the Heart of the Mountains and Summit areas on the ridgeline of the AVA, and the warmer, easterly Saratoga region, sometimes known as Over the Hill. A.Y.

Sullivan, C. L., *Like Modern Edens: Winegrowing in Santa Clara Valley and Santa Cruz Mountains 1798–1981* (1982).

www.winesofthesantacruzmountains.com

Santa Lucia Highlands, California wine region and AVA. See MONTEREY.

Santa Maddalena, known as **St Magdalener** by the many German speakers who make and drink it, was historically the most famous wine of ALTO ADIGE in north-east Italy. (In an Italian government classification of 1941, it was for political purposes ranked after Barolo and Barbaresco as the country's most significant wine, a rating which would be unlikely to be repeated today.) An official subzone, and therefore suffix, of the enormous Alto Adige DOC, it takes its name from the hill of Santa Maddalena north-east of the city of Bolzano (Bozen), long considered particularly suitable for the cultivation of the SCHIAVA (Vernatsch) grape from which the wine is made. Since the late 20th century this light red wine has become so unfashionable that its total vineyard area has shrunk from 456 ha in 1978 to 200 ha/494 acres in 2019, with an average yield of 76.2 hl/ha—much lower than the near 90 hl/ha allowed by law. The production regulations decree a minimum 85% Schiava; about 5% LAGREIN is routinely blended in to deepen its pale colour.

Like other Italian DOCs, when Santa Maddalena sold well its production zone was significantly enlarged from the original nucleus (now called Santa Maddalena CLASSICO) of the communes of Santa Maddalena, Retsch, Justina, Leitach, and St Peter. The zone now stretches to Settequerce (Siebeneich) in the Val d'Adige to the west and to Cornedo (Karneid) in the Val d'Isarco to the east. These latter zones give Schiava of good quality but with less personality than that of Santa Maddalena; fortunately over 85% of current production of Santa Maddalena is Santa Maddalena Classico. The subzone Bozener Leiten partially overlaps with Santa Maddalena but is rarely seen on labels. W.S.

Santa Maria Valley, California wine region and AVA. See SANTA BARBARA.

Sta. Rita Hills. In 1971 Richard Sanford and Michael Benedict turned a former bean farm on the western side of the SANTA YNEZ VALLEY into the Sanford & Benedict Vineyard, proving that PINOT NOIR could thrive in this foggy, windswept region that extends from Lompoc to Buellton. Dozens of vineyards followed, prompting the creation of the Santa Rita Hills AVA in 2001. (The name was later abbreviated per an agreement with Viña Santa Rita in CHILE.) In 2021 about 60 vineyards grow 2,700 acres of mostly Pinot Noir and Chardonnay, with increasing interest in Rhône varieties and other cool-climate grapes. M.D.K.

Santa Ynez Valley, California wine region and AVA. See SANTA BARBARA.

Santenay, somewhat forgotten village and spa in the Côte de Beaune district of Burgundy producing red wines from Pinot Noir and occasional whites. The soils in Santenay are a little richer in MARL than most of the Côte d'Or, producing red wines tending to the rustic. This is largely the fault of a poor selection of Pinot Noir vines whose vigour can fortunately be tamed by the CORDON DE ROYAT training system in place of the usual GUYOT.

Most of the best vineyards—the PREMIERS CRUS La Comme, Clos de Tavannes, and Les Gravières—form an extension from Chassagne-Montrachet. Also reputed are La Maladière, situated behind the main village, and Clos Rousseau on the far border of Santenay, beyond the casino and thermal waters of the higher village.

See also CÔTE D'OR and map under BURGUNDY. J.T.C.M.

Santorini, Cycladic island known in classical times as Thíra, and the most famous wine region in GREECE.

History

The island is a part of the core of an ancient volcano, which erupted *c.*1640–1620 BCE (perhaps a century earlier), destroying the Minoan civilizations of Thíra and, it is thought, neighbouring Crete. A large part of Thíra became submerged and has remained so to this day.

In antiquity the island was not especially famous for its wine, but this was to change in the Middle Ages. It belonged to the Byzantine empire until the Crusaders sacked Constantinople in 1203–4 and Santorini was given to one of the Venetian conquerors, remaining in his family until 1336. It then became part of the duchy of Naxos, but VENICE retained a strong influence; 1479–89 was another period of direct Venetian rule. It was Venetian enterprise that made Santorini an important wine producer. The wine it exported was made from a mixture of grape varieties, chiefly the white ATHIRI and red MANDILARIA, and it was prized for its sweetness and high alcohol which enabled it to withstand the six-month sea voyage, via Venice, to western Europe. Santorini was conquered by the Ottoman Turks in 1579, but the Turks did not discourage the production of the only cash crop that the island's volcanic soil could sustain.

Loanwords from Italian still in use in Santorini today testify to Venice's importance in its winemaking past. For example, the local dialect word for the vintage is *vendemma* from Italian *vendemmia.*

See GREECE. H.M.W.

Santorini today

Modern times have been equally kind to the wines of Santorini. Since at least 2005, Santorini has been the champion of modern Greek wine, at least in terms of visibility, media coverage, and prices commanded, with several producers enjoying superstar status, even in export markets. The fact that Santorini is one of the most beautiful islands in the Mediterranean, with millions of tourists every year, helped popularity but condemned long-term viability via ever increasing real-estate prices.

Santorini is one of the most surreal TERROIRS for viticulture. The WINDS are extreme and the land largely devoid of trees, offering little respite from the fierce gales, so in most places vines have to be trained in a low basket shape (*koloura* or *kladeftiko;* see TRAINING SYSTEMS) for protection. Recent trials with conventional TRELLIS SYSTEMS in some sheltered areas have been successful but highly controversial in the eyes of traditionalists. The island is very sunny and arid, with only morning fog to sustain any form of agriculture. The soils are VOLCANIC and not just free of PHYLLOXERA but immune to it. As a result, vines are UNGRAFTED, that portion below ground being up to 400 years old. YIELDS are seldom more than 15 hl/ha (0.8 tons/acre), which means that Santorini wine may eventually become a thing of the past.

The PDO Santorini allows for dry wines as well as sweet wines made from sun-dried grapes, all based on ASSYRTIKO, with smaller amounts of ATHIRI and AÏDANI. The dry wines are, more often than not, pure Assyrtiko and generally present an outstanding combination of MINERALITY, high alcohol, and high acidity, often resulting in PH levels below 3. Those vinified entirely in stainless steel can be fiercely austere. Nykteri versions, dry but harvested late into the growing season and traditionally at night (*nykta* in Greek), are richer, at least 13.5% alcohol and aged for at least three months in oak barrels. The traditional Nykteri style is for wines made with a short SKIN CONTACT and aged in partly filled old oak casks to initiate deliberate OXIDATION. As strong as 16% alcohol, these are not for the faint-hearted but are some of the world's most impressive and individual white wines, capable of long AGEING.

The Santorini PDO also includes sweet wines called Vinsanto, a term wrongly assumed to be a loanword from the Italian VIN SANTO. However, 'Visanto', the Vino of Santorini, was exported, mainly for religious purposes, to Russia well before Italians initiated the style. Vinsanto is made from sun-dried grapes, mainly Assyrtiko (at least 51%), and oak-aged for several years if not decades. The wines are intensely sweet, with as much as 300 g/l RESIDUAL SUGAR, but are balanced by high acidity, and the best can age for a century or longer.

A small percentage of Santorini's vineyards are planted to red grapes, once popular for use in sweet wines. The MAVROTRAGANO variety is the most esteemed, today used to produce deeply coloured, TANNIC dry reds. The most common is MANDILARIA, used primarily in sun-dried sweet wines. No red wines are (yet) included in the appellation framework. K.L.

Saperavi, ancient and distinctive south-west GEORGIAN grape variety notable for its deep COLOUR (Saperavi means 'dye'), its ACIDITY, firm TANNINS, full BODY, and dark fruit. It is Georgia's signature and most planted red wine grape, representing more than 90% of the vineyard area dedicated to red grapes in Kakheti. As a VARIETAL wine, it is capable, not to say demanding, of long AGEING and finds its finest expression in PDO wines such as Mukuzani, Napareuli, and Kindzmarauli. Its strong personality also makes it very useful in blends. The flesh of this dark-skinned grape is deep pink, and it produces wines that command attention if not always devotion. It ripens late, is relatively productive, and is quite well adapted to cold winters, but not so well that the Russian Potapenko viticultural research institute has been discouraged from producing a **Saperavi Severny**, a hybrid of SEVERNY and Saperavi which was released in 1947 and incorporates not just Saperavi's VITIS VINIFERA genes but also those of the cold-hardy VITIS *amurensis.*

Traditional Saperavi is planted throughout almost all of the wine regions of the former Soviet republics. It is an important variety in RUSSIA, UKRAINE, MOLDOVA, BULGARIA, ARMENIA, and AZERBAIJAN, as well as in its native GEORGIA, although in cooler areas the acidity may be too marked for any purpose other than blending, despite its relatively high sugar levels. It was also used extensively for VINE BREEDING at MAGARACH, the Crimean wine research centre.

Sardinia, Sardegna in Italian, is an island in the middle of the Mediterranean with a history of winegrowing dating back at least 3,000 years according to archaeologists from the University of Caligari, who discovered 15,000 wine-grape seeds at Sa Osa, near Oristano. Because of its strategic geographical position, Sardinia had been ruled by Phoenicians, Carthaginians, Romans, Arabs, Aragon, Genovese, and Pisans before becoming an integral part of ITALY in 1726, when it was ceded to the House of Savoy. Each of these groups left a mark on the island's history, culture, and language as well as its wine industry, which, by the end of the 1900s, boasted 80,000 ha/197,684 acres of vines.

History

In the last 200 years, Sardinia's wine economy has had its ups and downs: PHYLLOXERA arrived in 1883 to decimate the vineyards; they did not recover until after the Second World War, when low-yielding BUSH VINES were widely replaced with high-yielding TENDONE and wire-trained vineyards aided by lavish subsidies from both Rome and the regional government. However, as the subsidies dried up, so did interest in grape-growing. By 2010 only 19,000 ha/47,000 acres remained.

Since then a new generation has taken up winemaking, their efforts boosted by the growing interest in oeno-TOURISM. By 2020 vines covered 27,217 ha/67,255 acres, and wine grew from just 6% to 17% of the agricultural economy, much of which is dedicated to the grazing of animals—sheep in particular—for milk, cheese, and meat.

The focus has moved from quantity to quality as well: in 2020 Sardinia produced 630,000 hl/16,642,839 gal of wine, only a small percentage of which was basic BULK WINE.

Vine varieties

Five grapes represent 70% of the surface under vine: VERMENTINO, Cannonau (GARNACHA), MONICA, NURAGUS, and Carignano (CARIGNAN, also called Bovale Grande in Sardinia). The red variety GRACIANO is also a rising star. It goes by several names here, such as Bovale Sardo, Bovaleddu, and Muristellu, or, in the village of Usini in the north-west, Cagnulari. For whites, there is Semidano, an INDIGENOUS VARIETY that thrives in the VOLCANIC soil of Mogoro in the province of Oristano; TORBATO, which Sella e Mosca has been instrumental in reviving; and Granazza (or Granatza), grown in the village of Mamoiada in the north-east of the island.

Geography and climate

With an area of 24,106 sq km/9,305 sq miles, Sardinia is the second largest island in the Mediterranean. Overall, the climate is hot and dry, with most rain falling in the winter months, although differences in LATITUDE, ELEVATION, and proximity to the sea result in a diversity of MESOCLIMATES. The island boasts one DOCG, 17 DOCS and 15 IGPS.

The DOC production areas of the most popular varieties, Cannonau, Vermentino, Monica, and Moscato (MUSCAT), have been extended to include the entire surface of the island. Three smaller subzones have been created for Cannonau: Capo Ferrato, Oliena, and Jerzu (the smallest). Cannonau CLASSICO must come from the provinces of Nuoro and Ogliastra and be at least 95% Cannonau, compared to 85% in the other subzones.

Vermentino, the island's signature white wine grape, claims Sardinia's only DOCG, Vermentino di Gallura, located in the north of the island. SUPERIORE limits yields to 9 tonnes/ha in contrast to 10 tonnes/ha for the basic DOCG. While most Vermentino wines are picked on the early side to retain refreshing acidity, a rich LATE HARVEST style known as Vendemmia Tardiva has been popularized by producers such as Capichera, Cantina del Vermentino, Cantina Gallura, Depperu, and Tondini. PASSITO and sparkling versions are also made.

Sweet wines are made all over the island, with the most prominent DOCs being Moscato di Sorso Sennori, Nasco di Cagliari, Malvasia di Cagliari, and Girò di Cagliari. There are also sweet sparkling muscats made in Gallura, especially in the high elevations around Mount Limbara, where the wines can be labelled Moscato di Tempio.

Less known but worth seeking out are Vernaccia di Oristano, from Sardinia's western coast, and Malvasia di Bosa, from a tiny DOC within the Oristano province where Cantina Giovanni Battista Columbu is one of the last producers. Both wine styles are aged under FLOR in an oxidized style similar to SHERRY but unfortified.

An occasional good bottle of Nuragus di Cagliari, a white wine from the higher elevations of Cagliari (minimum 500 m/1,640 ft), only underlines the absurdity of the region's high allowed yields (16 tonnes/ha). Some of the island's best reds come from Carignano del Sulcis, a coastal region at the island's south-east end where the SANDY soils allow for UNGRAFTED VINES.

As wine holdings tend to be small across the island (less than a hectare per owner), CO-OPERATIVES play an important part in Sardinia's wine economy. However, the real custodians of Sardinia's original wine styles and cultivation methods are several small producers who, by following ORGANIC or BIODYNAMIC methods while tending to old BUSH VINES, produce wines that truly reflect their origin. Prime examples include Dettori in Sennori, Panevino in Nurri, Sedilesu and Paddeu in Mamoiada, Pusole in Lotzorai, Altea in Serdiana, and Nero Miniera in Carbonia. W.S. & C.O.

Sárga Muskotály, or **Sárgamuskotály**, occasional Hungarian name for the 'yellow Muscat' of TOKAJ (MUSCAT BLANC À PETITS GRAINS).

Sassicaia, trail-blazing Tuscan wine, made largely from CABERNET SAUVIGNON, originally as a house wine by Mario Incisa della Rochetta at the Tenuta San Guido near BOLGHERI. It was one of the first Italian reds made in the image of fine red BORDEAUX and was the first serious wine to emerge from the MAREMMA. The first small commercial quantities were released in the mid 1970s, the wine labelled as a VINO DA TAVOLA. In 1994 Sassicaia was granted its own DOC as an official subzone of Bolgheri (Bolgheri-Sassicaia DOC), the only wine from a single estate in Italy to enjoy this privilege. It is relatively reserved in youth, in contrast to its neighbour Ornellaia (see FRESCOBALDI).

Fini, M., *Sassicaia—The Original Super Tuscan* (2000).

Saumur, town in the LOIRE just upriver from the ANJOU district giving its name to an extensive wine district and several appellations. Lodged between TOURAINE and ANJOU, it shares with the former its geology while it is climatically and politically linked to the latter. Developed first by religious orders and aristocrats—as illustrated by the 'Très Riches Heures du Duc de Berry' painting *c.*1412–16—then by the DUTCH WINE TRADE, Saumur production shifted over time from sweet and dry white wines to sparkling and red, with the PHYLLOXERA crisis as an accelerating factor. The protection of the Mauges hills and the tempering effect of the Thouet and Dive rivers create a favorable MESOCLIMATE for a large diversity of styles, with the exception of heavily BOTRYTIZED wines. Like its direct neighbours CHINON and ANJOU, CHENIN BLANC and CABERNET FRANC are the historic primary grapes, but CHARDONNAY, SAUVIGNON, GAMAY, PINOT NOIR, PINEAU D'AUNIS, CABERNET SAUVIGNON, and GROLLEAU are authorized as minority blending partners. The largest production is white or rosé Saumur MOUSSEUX, whose vineyards extend beyond the limits of the still wine area. TRADITIONAL METHOD sparkling wine has been present in Saumur since the early 19th century when the Ackerman-Laurance house, today still a prominent actor, actively developed it. As the Turonian TUFFEAU was excavated to provide building material for local constructions and royal castles in the Loire and abroad, it left extensive underground, well-tempered cellars perfect for AGEING sparkling wines (and growing button mushrooms, the other major local crop). Based on the high-acid Chenin Blanc, these wines rapidly gained commercial success. The tradition is carried on today by larger houses with superb caves such as Gratien & Meyer, Langlois Chateau (owned by Champagne BOLLINGER), and Bouvet Ladubay, as well as the dominant local CO-OPERATIVE Robert and Marcel in St-Cyr-en-Bourg. CRÉMANT de Loire is also produced, but the criteria are more rigorous: YIELDS of 50 rather than 60 hl/ha, 12 rather than nine months' TIRAGE, and mandatory hand-harvesting.

Historically a famous white-wine area—the strip of vineyards from Saumur to Montsoreau now part of the Saumur-Champigny sector used to be known as the *Côte des blancs*—Saumur Blanc is undergoing a revival after being decades of neglect. SINGLE-VINEYARD WINES from the CHALKY hill of Brézé are leading the pack, confirming the potential of dry white wines whose subtle profiles are sometimes more comparable to BURGUNDY than to the firmer ANJOU Blanc or SAVENNIÈRES from SCHIST.

Saumur Rouge is a much more recent success story, owing its promotion to local mogul Antoine Cristal in the late 19th century, who believed the wines could rival the best BORDEAUX. First vinified as off-dry rosé (under the now-abandoned Cabernet de Saumur AOC), CABERNET FRANC owns its success as a dry red to the **Saumur-Champigny** AOC, where the St-Cyr-en-Bourg co-operative in particular encouraged the planting of Cabernet Franc in the 1970s and 1980s. Created in 1957, the appellation spreads its 1,500 ha/3,700 acres of sandy soils on tuffeau bedrock close to the Loire. Most of its reds are relatively light and fruity, yet the most serious examples can age for decades.

In 2018 another AOC, **Saumur Puy-Notre-Dame,** was made official, with stricter production requirements. Situated in the south-west of the region, its higher ELEVATION, more CONTINENTAL CLIMATE, and Turonian subsoils enriched with IRON, CLAY, and FLINT produce Saumur's most STRUCTURED red wines. A small amount of dry rosé is made under the **Saumur Rosé** AOC (2016), while **Coteaux de Saumur**, a testimony to the sweet-wine history of the area, is made in minute quantities from Chenin Blanc.

See also LOIRE, including map. P.Le.

Saussignac, small (33 ha/72 acres) sweet-white-wine appellation in SOUTH WEST FRANCE. It lies within the BERGERAC district, adjacent to MONBAZILLAC, producing similar but perhaps slightly lighter wines from the same grape varieties. Since the mid 1990s, the appellation has become an enclave of great SWEET WINEMAKING, now led by domaines Richard and Miaudoux. There are 15 or so independent growers (many ORGANIC) and no CO-OPERATIVE. In 2004 appellation laws were strengthened to insist on manual picking and completely natural sweetness, generally due to BOTRYTIS. P.S.

Sauterne, occasionally found on labels of GENERIC sweet white wine. Real SAUTERNES always ends in *s*.

Sauternes. The special distinction of this appellation of 1,930 ha/4,342 acres (including BARSAC), located in the extreme south-east of the Bordeaux region, is that it is dedicated, in a way unmatched by any other large wine region, to the production of sweet white wine. In Germany or Alsace, say, such wines are the exception rather than the rule and are made from vines that more usually produce drier wines.

In Sauternes the situation is quite different: the appellation is entirely reserved for SWEET WINES, and any dry production must be declared as straight Bordeaux. They must come from five communes: Preignac in the lower, flatter reaches, with lighter, more filtering soils; Fargues, Bommes, and of course Sauternes higher up, all planted on hilly terrain of GRAVEL over CLAY; and the fifth, Barsac, on completely different soil, fine red LOAM over LIMESTONE, entitled also to its own appellation. They must all adhere to the INAO regulations stipulating specific vineyard and cellar practices that ensure Sauternes' particular style of sweetness.

The origins of these special wines are shrouded in the mists of time. Sauternes produced red wines ('claret') under the English rule of Aquitaine of the 12th–15th centuries, then dry or semi-sweet white wines under the influence of the DUTCH WINE TRADE in the 15th–17th centuries. During these two periods, there are occasional records of BOTRYTIZED wines, probably produced by accident and only becoming the norm when, in the 1770s, Françoise-Josephine de Lur Saluces of YQUEM mastered the art of harvesting botrytized grapes in successive *tries*, or passes, which were instantly recognized as vastly superior and for which her customers would pay handsomely. Sauternes took off, first in the Paris *salons*, then (following the enthusiasm of Thomas JEFFERSON) in the young United States, then with the Tsar in Russia, finally becoming one of the most coveted wines in all markets.

At the height of this glorious period took place the CLASSIFICATION at the 1855 Universal Paris Fair. Twenty-seven estates were classified, including 15 second growths, 11 firsts, and one 'premier cru exceptionnel' (Yquem), an astounding achievement and a token of Sauternes' extraordinary reputation. Today 48% of the production is controlled by the CRUS CLASSÉS.

Only four grape varieties may be used. SÉMILLON accounts for roughly 80% of plantings because of its susceptibility to NOBLE ROT and its capacity to provide more complex aromas when affected by its onset; SAUVIGNON BLANC attracts noble rot earlier and as a result is currently favoured because of the drier, hotter Septembers of the 21st century (see CLIMATE CHANGE)—and also because it adds freshness of flavour to balance Sémillon's richer, broader style; then come two very aromatic minor grapes, both in decline: MUSCADELLE, because of its fragility, and SAUVIGNON GRIS, providing a more obvious form of Sauvignon aromatics and higher sugar but at the expense of finesse.

Sauternes is the product of a specific MESOCLIMATE located close to the confluence of the cool spring-fed Ciron river with the warmer GARONNE, creating morning mists that envelop the vineyards until the sun burns them away, a perfect medium for the development of *Botrytis cinerea*, or noble rot, a fungus that attacks the already concentrated grapes and causes them to transform their molecular constitution, engendering all the complexity and purity of aromas that make the wines of Sauternes so special. At this stage, if the weather turns from damp to dry (which nowadays it often does in October), the making of great Sauternes becomes possible as the grapes dehydrate and pass from *pourri plein* stage (15–16° POTENTIAL ALCOHOL) to *rôti* stage (upwards of 20°), concentrating not only their sugars but also their aromatic complexity. Until the recent past, when bad weather at this stage often reduced the potential for ultimate concentration, growers strove for as much sweetness as possible—and often didn't get it, then hastily proceeded to harvest what they could save; today, with climate change making sweetness easier to achieve, they often have the luxury of being able to strive for balance, finesse, and harmony rather than for the sheer concentration of sugars that could sometimes make the wines seem heavy, especially if they had been chaptalized (see CHAPTALIZATION), a practice still allowed today in small proportions but hardly ever used, the sugars being naturally so high.

The turning point that pulled Sauternes out of its very difficult period of the 1960s and 1970s was the 1983 vintage. Prices rose, and wise proprietors could at last put money towards long overdue investments, the most important of which was the gradual conversion from tank fermentation (and sometimes ageing too) to BARREL FERMENTATION, allowing for more detailed precision by separating the various 'lots' that could then be progressively and carefully married together during ageing. The trio of 1988, 1989, and 1990 vintages confirmed this very positive trend, culminating in a succession of vintages from 1996 to 2021 when as many as 11 were great, 12 very good, and only two deficient, a series never seen before, even in the mid 1800s.

Today Sauternes is again showing the quality of which it is capable. It combines all the power and voluptuousness of sweetness with a newfound finesse and purity of aroma. It can be enjoyed young or old and can evolve and improve for up to 50 years or more. Given the risks and costs involved in its intricate production, it remains underpriced in relation to the pleasure it brings to those growing numbers of wine lovers who not only pair it with the traditional accompaniments of desserts, blue cheese, and foie gras but are also now finding it an excellent match with Asian and Indian cuisine, seafood, fish, poultry, and more generally anything spicy or salty. W.J.B.

Brook, S., *Sauternes, and Other Sweet Wines of Bordeaux* (1995).
Olney, R., *Yquem* (1986).

S

Sauvignonasse, old Bordeaux white grape hardly encountered there today but also known as Sauvignon Vert and, in Friuli, as FRIULANO (once Tocai Friulano). Recent and as-yet unpublished DNA PROFILING at INRAE suggests that Sauvignonasse gave birth to CHENIN BLANC through a natural cross with SAVAGNIN. It is quite distinct from the more famous SAUVIGNON BLANC, but the two were long confused in Chile, where there are now 469 ha/1,159 acres of Sauvignon Vert. In general the wines produced from Sauvignonasse are much less crisp and aromatic than those of Sauvignon Blanc, and this vine is much more sensitive to DOWNY MILDEW and ROT. According to official statistics, Argentina has a little less of this variety than Chile. In Slovenia the variety is now known as Zeleni Sauvignon.

Sauvignon Blanc is the hugely popular vine variety solely responsible for some of the world's most distinctively aromatic dry white wines: SANCERRE, POUILLY-FUMÉ, and a tidal wave of Sauvignon Blanc and Fumé Blanc from outside France, most notably NEW ZEALAND. The direct, obvious, easy-to-appreciate nature of VARIETAL Sauvignon Blanc seems to answer a need in modern wine consumers who are perhaps more interested in immediate fruit than in subtlety and AGEING ability—which is not to deny that in many great white wines, both dry and sweet, it does also add nerve and zest to its most common blending partner SÉMILLON. It has always shared a certain aromatic similarity with the great red wine grape Cabernet Sauvignon (something approaching HERBACEOUSNESS), and in 1997 Sauvignon Blanc's standing in the world of wine rose when DNA PROFILING established that, with Cabernet Franc, Sauvignon Blanc was a parent of Cabernet Sauvignon, the result of a spontaneous field crossing, probably in the 18th century, in Bordeaux. Further DNA studies have suggested that the variety's origins are probably in the Loire; that it has a parent–offspring relationship with the historic SAVAGNIN BLANC (and is therefore probably its progeny); that it is probably a sibling of the CHENIN BLANC of the Loire; and that it seems genetically close to Sémillon. It is certainly well-connected.

Sauvignon Blanc's most recognizable characteristic is its piercing, instantly recognizable aroma. Descriptions typically include 'grassy, herbaceous, musky, green fruits' (especially gooseberries), 'nettles', and even 'tomcats'. Research into FLAVOUR COMPOUNDS suggests that METHOXYPYRAZINES play an important role in Sauvignon's aroma. Over-productive Sauvignon vines planted on heavy soils can produce wines only vaguely suggestive of this, but Sauvignon cautiously cultivated in the central vineyards of the Loire, unmasked by oak, can reach the dry white apogee of Sauvignon fruit with some of the purest, most refreshingly zesty wines in the world. The best Sancerres and Pouilly-Fumés served as a model for early exponents of New World Sauvignon Blanc, although by the 1980s it was the Loire vignerons, and winemakers all round the world, who were more likely to copy their counterparts in New Zealand in experimenting with fermentation and maturation in oak and picking the grapes at different levels of RIPENESS to add nuance and pungency to the aroma and weight to the palate.

Oak-aged examples usually need an additional year or two to show their best, but almost all dry, unblended Sauvignon is designed to be drunk young, although there are both Loire and Bordeaux examples that can demonstrate durability, if rarely evolution, with up to 15 years in bottle (see POUILLY-FUMÉ and Pavillon Blanc de Ch MARGAUX, for example). As an ingredient in the great sweet white wines of SAUTERNES, on the other hand, Sauvignon plays a minor but important part in one of the world's longest-living wines.

The vine is particularly vigorous, and if the vine's vegetation gets out of hand then the grapes fail to reach full maturity, resulting in wines that are aggressively herbaceous. (And underripe Sémillon can exhibit very similar characteristics—just as underripe Cabernet Sauvignon can smell like Cabernet Franc, which their genetic relatedness may help to explain.) A low-vigour ROOTSTOCK and CANOPY MANAGEMENT can help combat this problem. Sauvignon buds after but flowers before Sémillon, with which it is typically blended in Bordeaux and, increasingly, elsewhere. Until suitable clones such as 297 and 316 were identified, and sprays to combat Sauvignon's susceptibility to POWDERY MILDEW and BLACK ROT were developed, yields were uneconomically irregular and the variety was not popular with growers. In 1968, for example, Sauvignon was France's 13th most planted white grape variety, but within 20 years it had risen to fourth place, and by 2019 its French total of 31,773 ha/78,513 acres put it behind only Ugni Blanc and Chardonnay in France.

In Bordeaux it was not until the late 1980s that Sauvignon overtook Ugni Blanc as second most planted white grape variety after Sémillon, which in 2019 still outnumbered Sauvignon but not by that much—and the newer CLONES of Sauvignon are much more productive than the important but rapidly declining Sémillon. The Gironde's Sauvignon is concentrated in the Entre-Deux-Mers, Graves, and the sweet-wine-producing districts in and around Sauternes. In each of these areas, it is dominated by and usually blended with Sémillon, particularly in Sauternes, where the typical blend incorporates 80% of the more NOBLE ROT–prone Sémillon together with a little Muscadelle, although with the rise and rise of New Zealand Sauvingon Blanc more varietal Sauvignons have appeared in Bordeaux. BORDEAUX Blanc owes much to Entre-Deux-Mers Sauvignon although low YIELDS and, often, expensive OAK AGEING—as in the best dry white PESSAC-LÉOGNAN, GRAVES, and the handful of expensive Médoc whites (sold as BORDEAUX AOC)—are prerequisites for a memorable performance from Sauvignon in Bordeaux.

As with red wines, the satellite areas of SOUTH WEST FRANCE reflect Bordeaux's spread of vine varieties, and Sauvignon is often an easily perceptible ingredient in the dry whites of such areas as BERGERAC, Côtes du MARMANDAIS, and Côtes de DURAS.

It is in the Loire that Sauvignon is encountered in its purest, most unadulterated form. In the often LIMESTONE vineyards of SANCERRE, POUILLY-FUMÉ, and their eastern satellites QUINCY, REUILLY, and MENETOU-SALON, it can demonstrate one of the most eloquent arguments for marrying variety with suitable TERROIR, although CLIMATE CHANGE is making it more difficult to achieve this style. The variety is often called Blanc Fumé here and has happily replaced most of the lesser varieties once common, notably much of the CHASSELAS in Pouilly-sur-Loire. The best examples need a few years in bottle to show their best. From this concentration of vineyards, Sauvignon's influence radiates outwards: north-east towards Chablis in ST-BRIS, south to ST-POURÇAIN-sur-Sioule, and north and west to Coteaux du GIENNOIS and CHEVERNY, as well as to a substantial quantity of well-priced eastern Loire wines, typically labelled TOURAINE. Such Sauvignons tend to be light, racy, and, of course, aromatic. With Chardonnay, it has also been allowed into the vineyards of Anjou, where it is sometimes blended with the indigenous CHENIN BLANC.

Elsewhere in France, Sauvignon Blanc has been an obvious, though not invariably successful, choice for those seeking to make internationally saleable varietal wine. In the Languedoc and Roussillon, its total plantings of 8,785 ha/21,708 acres in 2019 made it the region's second most planted white wine grape, a long way behind Chardonnay, even if yields are often too high to extract quite enough varietal character. Small plantings of Sauvignon can also be found in some of the Provençal appellations.

Across the Alps, Sauvignon's most successful Italian region is the far north-east in FRIULI, with some ALTO ADIGE and COLLIO examples exhibiting particularly fine fruit and purity of flavour. Many of the better bottles from the north-east are made from the extremely pungent and recognizable R3 clone of the Rauscedo vine NURSERY. Attempts to transfer Sauvignon to central Italy have been notably less successful. In the 1980s Italy's plantings of Sauvignon doubled to nearly 3,000 ha/7,410 acres, but by 2010 growth had slowed, leaving a total 3,935 ha in 2019. Overall it is a relatively minor grape in Italy.

The Primorska region across the SLOVENIAN border from here is known as a source of BARREL AGED and site-specific Sauvignon Blanc, with delicate styles more typical of Podravje. In Vipava and Brda districts, both barrel-aged and unoaked styles are produced. The variety conspicuously thrives in Styria in AUSTRIA, where it is capable of expressing the local TERROIR, stylishly combining fruit with aroma, texture, and greater age-worthiness than in many other wine regions. Austria had more than 1,648 ha/4,072 acres of Sauvignon Blanc in 2021, while Germany had a rising total of 1,661 ha in 2020, almost half in the Pfalz and around one-third in Rheinhessen. Parts of SERBIA, especially the Fruška Gora district, and some of CZECHIA, where it is widely planted, clearly have potential for racy Sauvignon. ROMANIA had even more Sauvignon Blanc planted than Cabernet Sauvignon—5,697 ha/14,078 acres in 2021—and neighbouring MOLDOVA also had sizeable plantings of the variety.

Sauvignon Blanc plantings in Spain have increased rapidly this century, reaching 6,933 ha/1,7132 acres in 2020, mainly in Castilla-La Mancha, where varietals can lack definition. It has also been particularly popular with growers in RUEDA. Certainly Portugal and north-western Spain have no shortage of INDIGENOUS VARIETIES (see MINHO and GALICIA) capable of reproducing vaguely similar wine styles. There is a tendency for Sauvignon Blanc to taste oily when reared in too warm a climate, as it sometimes does in Israel and other Mediterranean vineyards where those with an eye to the export market put it through its paces.

This was clearly perceptible in many of Australia's earlier attempts with the variety, although by the early 1990s there was even keener appreciation of the need to reserve it for the country's cooler sites (see AUSTRALIA for more on the wines produced); plantings soared, reaching nearly 7,000 ha by 2012, not least because of the extraordinary popularity of New Zealand examples of the varietal on the Australian market. Several of the best-selling whites in Australia were Marlborough Sauvignons by the start of the second decade of the 21st century—something that would have been unthinkable in the previous century. But plantings had fallen back to just 6,445 ha by 2022 and are outnumbered more than three to one by Chardonnay.

New Zealand has built its wine industry and reputation on the particularly distinctive style of Marlborough Sauvignon Blanc. This is the variety that introduced New Zealand wine to the world, and it did so by developing its own pungent style: intensely perfumed, more obviously fruity than the Loire prototype, with just a hint of both gas and sweetness and, occasionally, gooseberries or asparagus. This style of Sauvignon can now be found in Chile, South Africa, the cooler areas of North America, and virtually all parts of France where Sauvignon is grown. The area planted with Sauvignon Blanc had risen to 26,559 ha/65,629 acres by 2022, representing more than 60% of New Zealand's vines and a far greater area of Sauvignon than anywhere else. The great majority of the country's Sauvignon is grown in the rapidly expanded Marlborough region, although it is also found in all other regions. So popular has Kiwi Sauvignon become that Chardonnay is, unfortunately, relatively ignored in New Zealand.

Chardonnay overtook Sauvignon Blanc in Chile early this century, but the trend has been reversed. According to official statistics, total Chilean plantings of Sauvignon Blanc rose rapidly to 15,224 ha/37,619 acres in 2020 (compared with Chardonnay's 10,920 ha), fuelled especially by the expansion of cooler, often coastal, wine regions from which some remarkably successful examples of true Sauvignon Blanc, in which yields are limited, are emerging. High yields help depress the keynote aromas of Sauvignon Blanc in most other South American wines labelled Sauvignon, although some of the higher-elevation offerings from Argentina, where total plantings of Sauvignon Blanc were 1,489 ha in 2020, are improving.

Thanks to Robert MONDAVI, who renamed it FUMÉ BLANC, Sauvignon Blanc enjoyed enormous success in California in the 1980s, and since the late 1990s a second great wave of popularity for California Sauvignon Blanc has boosted plantings to almost 16,000 acres/6,500 ha by 2020. See CALIFORNIA for more on the wines, which are very occasionally sweet and even BOTRYTIZED, a sort of Sémillon-free Sauternes. There has also been an increase, as elsewhere in the NEW WORLD, in blending in some Sémillon to dry white Sauvignon to add weight and fruit to Sauvignon's aroma and acidity. Like California, WASHINGTON State makes both Sauvignon Blanc and Fumé Blanc, harvesting 8,320 tonnes in 2021, much less than Riesling but slightly more than Pinot Gris. Elsewhere in North America it is not especially notable, although fine white BORDEAUX BLENDS have been made in British Columbia. But perhaps Sauvignon's real success in the New World, New Zealand excepted, has been in SOUTH AFRICA, where local wine drinkers fell upon the Cape's more successful early Sauvignons as a fashionable, internationally recognized wine style. By 1990 there were 3,300 ha of Sauvignon Blanc to South Africa's barely 2,400 ha of Cabernet Sauvignon. By 2020 there were 9,831 ha/24,293 acres and the area was still growing, if more slowly. Cape Sauvignon Blanc, particularly from the cooler vineyards of Cape Point, Elgin, Darling, and Cape Agulhas, shows intense capsicum and peapod flavours and reasonable ageing potential.

Sauvignon Blanc is often simply called **Sauvignon**, especially on wine labels, but it has mutated into variants with darker-coloured berries, notably SAUVIGNON GRIS and Sauvignon Rouge, also grown to a limited extent in the Loire. SAUVIGNON VERT is genetically distinct.

Bowers, J. E., and Meredith, C. P., 'The parentage of a classic wine grape, Cabernet Sauvignon', *Nature Genetics*, 16/1 (1997), 84–7.

Sauvignon Gris, also known as **Sauvignon Rose**, has discernibly pink skins and is a colour mutation of SAUVIGNON BLANC, with which it is sometimes blended. As a VARIETAL, it can produce more substantial wines than many a Sauvignon Blanc, and it is increasingly specified as an authorized grape variety in AOC regulations, notably in Bordeaux and the Loire. It is also planted in Chile, Argentina, Uruguay, and New Zealand. See also FIÉ.

Sauvignon Vert, synonym for SAUVIGNONASSE, except in California, where the variety called Sauvignon Vert is MUSCADELLE.

Savagnin is a very old, genetically important vine variety which has a ramified and fascinating genealogy and whose origins lie in north-east France. Like PINOT, with which it has a parent–offspring relationship, it is so old as to exist in many different mutations, including GEWÜRZTRAMINER, TRAMINER, and HEIDA (Païen), all with the same genetic fingerprint even if they display some clonal variation. DNA PROFILING has further shown that Savagnin is a parent of dozens of varieties, including Chenin Blanc, Grüner Veltiner, Sauvignon Blanc, Silvaner, Trousseau, and Petit Manseng; even more surprisingly, it probably has a parent–offspring relationship with Verdelho.

Robinson, J., et al., *Wine Grapes: A Complete Guide to 1,368 Vine Varieties, Including Their Origins and Flavours* (2012).

Savagnin Blanc is the white-berried, non-aromatic SAVAGNIN best known as the characteristic white wine grape of the JURA in eastern France. Both this pale-skinned clone and a pink-skinned one may be called Traminer, the latter also Roter Traminer, while GEWÜRZTRAMINER is the aromatic, pink-skinned form.

Savagnin Blanc, often called simply Savagnin, is a fine but curious vine variety with a typically light crop of small, round, pale berries. France's vineyard census of 2019 found a grand total of 596 ha/1,473 acres of this variety cultivated almost exclusively in the Jura, where it makes increasingly varied wines alongside the nutty, sherry-like VIN JAUNE, a winemaking oddity. In addition to *vin jaune* and other OXIDATIVE dry white wines, including blends with Chardonnay, there has been a significant rise this

S

century in the number of fresh, unoxidized *ouillé* (TOPPED-UP) Savagnin wines made in unoaked, oaked, and even SKIN-FERMENTED styles. Exuberant floral and citrus aromas are often evident, and, whatever the style, Savagnin is always a firm, long-lasting wine high in EXTRACT and, usually, acidity. The vine is well adapted to the ancient, west-facing MARL slopes of the Jura, but for oxidative styles many believe it is at its finest in the steep vineyards of CHÂTEAU-CHALON.

In Switzerland, Savagnin plantings are growing steadily, and it is now the sixth most planted white variety, with a total vineyard area of 219 ha/541 acres in 2020, 95% of this in the Valais, where it is called Heida or Païen and made in a dry and richly flavoured style.

Official statistics showed that in 2015 Australia had 60 ha/148 acres of Savagnin, virtually all planted in the early years of this century by growers who thought they had been supplied ALBARIÑO by CSIRO, the result of a mis-labelling of cuttings imported from Spain via France. (The 'true' Albariño has since been imported.) Australian Savagnin mostly disappears into blends, but there are some fine fresh examples and a handful of Jura-style oxidative wines. As part of a move to planting 'Alpine' varieties, a little is grown in California. J.H. & W.L.

Savagnin Noir is a Jura name for PINOT NOIR.

Savagnin Rose, the pink-berried SAVAGNIN and non-aromatic version of GEWÜRZTRAMINER, also known in Germany as Clevner and Roter Traminer and in Alsace as KLEVENER DE HEILIGENSTEIN.

Savatiano, sometimes spelt Savvatiano, Greece's most common wine grape, widely planted on 10,263 ha/25,360 acres in 2021 throughout Attica and central Greece. DNA PROFILING has shown it to be a parent of RODITIS. This light-berried vine, with its exceptionally good DROUGHT resistance, is the most common ingredient in RETSINA, although Roditis and ASSYRTIKO are often added to compensate for Savatiano's naturally low acidity. On particularly suitable sites, Savatiano can produce well-balanced, herbal-scented dry white wines.

Savennières, idiosyncratic and celebrated white-wine appellation in the Anjou region, just south-west of the town of Angers on the north bank of the LOIRE. The AOC stretches 6 km/4 miles over five main south-facing, more or less steep hills of SCHIST and VOLCANIC soils that produce CHENIN BLANC with a unique balance of nerve, concentration, and longevity, while the vineyards on the sandier plateaus produce bottlings more giving in their youth. Historically famous as a sweet wine and part of the original zone of ANJOU-Coteaux de la Loire, Savennières fostered the production of dry wines as a way to survive a commercial crisis when it obtained its AOC in 1952. Sweeter versions labelled DEMI-SEC, MOELLEUX, or DOUX are still authorized but rarely seen. The 1980s marked a turning point for the region as winegrowers from LAYON arrived, bringing selective picking techniques to soften the austere style. The revitalization has continued, with plantings rebounding from 46 ha in 1977 to 135 ha/334 acres in 2021. Within the area, two appellations were recognized in 2011: Savennières-Coulée de Serrant, a single estate of just 6 ha/15 acres run by the Joly family on BIODYNAMIC lines, and the 19 ha/47 acres of Savennières-Roche-aux-Moines, bottled by nine estates (as of 2021). Both appellations are bidding to become the Loire's next GRAND CRU after QUARTS DE CHAUME.

See also LOIRE, including map. P. Le.

Savigny-lès-Beaune, small town in BURGUNDY near Beaune, as *lès* (Old French for near) implies, with its own appellation for red wine and a little white. The reds are rival those of BEAUNE itself but lack the depth and character of wines from villages such as Pommard or Volnay more prominently sited on the LIMESTONE escarpment.

The village is divided by the river Rhoin. Those vineyards on the southern side, including PREMIERS CRUS Les Peuillets, Les Narbantons, Les Rouvrettes, and Les Marconnets, are on sandy soil and produce wines similar to those of Beaune, although lighter. Those on the other side, towards Pernand-Vergelesses, including Les Lavières and Les Vergelesses, are on stonier soil.

An engraving dating from 1703 at the Château de Savigny describes the wines as '*nourrissants, théologiques et morbifuges*'— nourishing, theological, and disease-defying. A little white wine is produced from Chardonnay, at its best on the plateau behind and above the village. Domaines Chandon de Briailles and Simon Bize have been the leading producers based here.

See also CÔTE D'OR and map under BURGUNDY. J.T.C.M.

Savoie, eastern French alpine region on the border with both Switzerland and Italy, historically Anglicized to **Savoy**, comprising the two *départements* Savoie and Haute-Savoie together with small parts of neighbouring Ain and Isère. The dramatic countryside is so popular with visitors for both winter sports and summer relaxation that the wines found a ready market, and it was rare for them to leave the region. However, 21st-century interest in lighter wines and INDIGENOUS VARIETIES has encouraged exports.

Savoie became part of France only in 1860 and grows a highly distinctive group of vine varieties that seem to be unrelated even to those of nearby AOSTA. Most Savoie wine is sold under the much-ramified appellation **Vin de Savoie** or increasingly, simply Savoie, although there are individual appellations for ROUSSETTE de Savoie (for wines from ALTESSE), CRÉMANT de Savoie, and SEYSSEL. The Savoie vineyards tend to be clustered on the slopes of the LIMESTONE-based pre-Alpine and Jura foothills at ELEVATIONS of 250–500 m/820–1,640 ft. Owing to the mountainous terrain they are widely dispersed, with varying climate and soil characteristics, justifying the 16 CRUS which can append their names to the Savoie appellation. Some vineyards are high above the banks of the River RHÔNE as it flows from Lake Geneva towards the wine region known as the Rhône Valley. Seyssel is here as well as the CHAUTAGNE and JONGIEUX cru vineyards.

South of here, close to the town of Chambéry that was once famous for its VERMOUTH, is a cluster of CRUS including ABYMES and APREMONT, below the imposing Mont Granier; and ARBIN, CHIGNIN, CRUET, and SAINT-JEAN-DE-LA-PORTE in the Combe de Savoie. These sectors produce two-thirds of Savoie wine.

Further north, in Haute-Savoie, the CHASSELAS grape predominates in a cluster of vineyards on the south-eastern shores of Lake Geneva and makes a range of light, dry, almost appley wines in the crus CRÉPY, MARIGNAN, Marin, and RIPAILLE. Towards Chamonix, the isolated cru of AYSE makes sought-after still and sparkling wine from the obscure GRINGET variety.

Total vineyard area for the Savoie appellation increased from about 1,650 ha/4,075 acres in 1990 to around 2,100 ha/5,190 in 2020. Over two-thirds of production is white: crisp, delicate, lightly scented, and essentially alpine. The most widely planted variety is JACQUÈRE, popular with growers because of its productivity. The finest white varieties are Altesse, with its own appellation ROUSSETTE de Savoie, and ROUSSANNE, known locally as Bergeron, responsible for the cru CHIGNIN-BERGERON. While Chardonnay is declining, rare indigenous varieties such as MONDEUSE BLANCHE are increasing.

Most of Savoie's wines are VARIETAL; among reds, Gamay and Pinot Noir can be perfectly respectable, if relatively light. Most inspiring is the late-ripening MONDEUSE NOIRE (usually labelled simply Mondeuse) with its deep colour, peppery flavour, and occasionally rustic tannins. Arbin has a particular reputation for Mondeuse with notable STRUCTURE and AGEING ability at alcohol levels rarely above 12%. The historic PERSAN variety is enjoying a revival, too, giving plummy, potentially long-lived reds. W.L.

Lorch, W., *Wines of the French Alps: Savoie, Bugey and Beyond* (2019).

scale, types of insects which attack grapevines, comprising at least 13 different species. Scale insects feed by sucking sap, and heavy infestations can weaken vine VIGOUR. Some scale insects excrete honeydew, which can spoil any bunches because a black, sooty mould usually grows on the honeydew. If many bunches are affected, this may taint the resultant wine. Scale insects can spread VIRUS DISEASES. R.E.S.

Schaumwein, German for SPARKLING WINE. *Qualitätsschaumwein* is an alternative term for SEKT.

Scheurebe is the one early 20th century GERMAN CROSS that deserves attention from any connoisseur, and the only one named after the prolific vine breeder Georg Scheu, the original director of the viticultural institute at Alzey in Rheinhessen. Sometimes called simply **Scheu**, it was developed with specific sandy, Rheinhessen soils around Dienheim in mind but has achieved its greatest popularity in the PFALZ. DNA PROFILING in 2012 showed that it is a cross of RIESLING and BUKETTRAUBE, a white-berried SILVANER × SCHIAVA Grossa cross. It is much more than a riper, more productive replica of Riesling. Provided it reaches full maturity (like other such German crosses as BACCHUS and ORTEGA, it is distinctly unappetizing if picked too early), Scheurebe wines have their own exuberant, racy flavours of blackcurrants or even rich grapefruit. It is one of the few varietal parvenus countenanced by quality-conscious German wine producers, not just because it can easily reach high PRÄDIKAT levels of ripeness but because these are so delicately counterbalanced with the nerve of acidity—perhaps not quite so much as in an equivalent Riesling but enough to preserve the wine for many years in bottle. Furthermore, for all its inherent aromatic exuberance, Scheurebe also follows its parent Riesling in reflecting soil and MESOCLIMATE, generating some striking and site-typical variations not just in the Pfalz but in Franken, in rare instances along the Nahe, and around Boppart in the Mittelrhein.

Despite its distinct virtues and distinctive flavours, Scheurebe has been in steady decline in Germany over recent decades, slipping to 1,437 ha/3,551 acres by 2020, of which almost half were in Rheinhessen. This may be because it is associated with sweet wine, which is unfashionable in Germany, but such prejudice seems unwarranted. Estates such as Müller-Catoir, Pfeffingen, and Lingenfelder in the Pfalz and Wirsching in Franken have for many more years vinified impressive, full-bodied dry Scheurebe. (Brüder Dr Becker even makes a respectable sparkling version in Scheurebe's home base in Dienheim.)

The variety is also grown in southern Austria, where it is known as SÄMLING 88 and can make fine sweet wines such as those of Kracher. It is also planted to a very limited extent elsewhere, in Canada and Switzerland, for example.

Schiava, Italian name for several distinct and generally undistinguished dark-skinned grape varieties known as Vernatsch by the German speakers of Alto Adige, or Südtirol as they would call it, and as TROLLINGER in the German region of Württemberg, where they are widely grown. The name Schiava, meaning 'slave', is thought by some to indicate Slavic origins.

The Schiava group is most planted in TRENTINO-ALTO ADIGE in northern Italy, with 204 ha/504 acres in Trentino in 2020 and 635 ha in Alto Adige. The most common is **Schiava Grossa** (Grossvernatsch), which was used to breed many GERMAN CROSSES including KERNER and HELFENSTEINER and has been shown to be a parent of MUSCAT OF HAMBURG. It is extremely productive and until recently has been associated with soft, pale wines without any real character or concentration. However, a renaissance has begun throughout the region with producers around Girlan and from Merano to Bolzano choosing to curb yields and make elegant, complex wines, often from PERGOLA-trained OLD VINES including several different CLONES. Schiava Grossa is also found in Japan and, as the TABLE GRAPE Black Hamburg, in one ancient vine at Hampton Court Palace in England. **Schiava Gentile** (Edelvernatsch) produces better-quality, aromatic soft wines from smaller grapes. The most celebrated and least productive clone is Tschaggele. **Schiava Grigia** and **Schiava Lombarda** are even less important. Light Schiava-based wines have become much less fashionable than in the late 20th century, when they enjoyed much popularity in Switzerland, Austria, and southern Germany. Plantings are in decline as Schiava has been substantially replaced by INTERNATIONAL VARIETIES, although Schiava grapes are still found in most of the non-varietal light red wines of Trentino-Alto Adige.

Schiefer. See SLATE and SCHIST.

Schilcher, rosé wine found mainly in Western Styria in AUSTRIA that is light, acid, fruity, and made from the ancient BLAUER WILDBACHER vine variety.

Schilfwein, literally 'reed wine', name used in Austria's NEUSIEDLERSEE for STRAW WINE, because in this area grapes for such concentrated sweet wines were traditionally dried on mats made from the reeds that grow round the lake.

Schillerwein, pink wine speciality made by CO-FERMENTING red and white grapes or MUST in the WÜRTTEMBERG region in Germany. The term is also used in German SWITZERLAND, but there the grapes must be grown and processed together.

Schioppettino, perfumed red grape variety native to the FRIULI region of north-east Italy often confused with but distinct from Ribolla Nera and a likely offspring of the old, no-longer-cultivated Vulpea. In spite of official attempts to encourage its replanting, Schioppettino was substantially neglected after the PHYLLOXERA epidemic of the late 19th century in favour of the new imports from France: Merlot, Cabernet Franc, and Cabernet Sauvignon. It seemed destined to disappear until an EU decree of 1978 authorized its cultivation in the province of Udine (see also PIGNOLO). The wine is deeply coloured and medium-bodied, with an attractively aromatic richness hinting at violets combined with a certain peppery quality reminiscent of the RHÔNE. Although vine plantings and therefore wine production are still limited, being concentrated in FRIULI COLLI ORIENTALI, the potential is notable. Prepotto close to Slovenia, where, as Pokalca, it has virtually disappeared, is considered its elective home, but quite good quality has also come from the Buttrio-Manzano area. In 2015 total plantings were 87 ha/215 acres.

schist, a metamorphic rock with a distinct planar aspect due chiefly to the parallel alignment of some of its constituent MINERALS, best shown by mica and amphibole (see GEOLOGY). It has developed a coarser grain-size than SLATE, having been subjected to greater burial temperatures and pressures, and as a result splits less cleanly. The transition between slate and schist is therefore gradual, and the distinction rather subjective. The rocks of PRIORAT, for example, are described by some as slate and by others as schist. (To add to the confusion, the German word *Schiefer* is commonly used for both rocks, as is the French word *schiste*, which is also sometimes extended to include SHALE.)

The planes in schist can have any orientation but are commonly close to vertical—ideal for vine roots to penetrate and for rainwater to percolate through. This is probably why in the DOURO vineyards sited on schist perform better than those on the region's massive, relatively impenetrable GRANITE. Schist is also important in parts of the Languedoc—such as BANYULS, FAUGÈRES, parts of ST-CHINIAN, and CORBIÈRES—and in NEW ZEALAND's Central Otago. A.J.M.

Schloss Johannisberg, German wine estate in the RHEINGAU with a history closely interlinked with that of the entire region. First planted by Benedictine monks around 1100, it served in the 18th century under the prince-abbot of Fulda as a model for viticultural success with Riesling. Legend has it that Schloss Johannisberg played an important role in the discovery of BOTRYTIZED wines. Grapes affected by NOBLE ROT were allegedly first harvested at Johannisberg unwittingly, giving rise to the AUSLESE, BEERENAUSLESE, and TROCKENBEERENAUSLESE styles in which, among German growing regions, the Rheingau took the lead. In 1802

Johannisberg became secularized and the property of the prince of Orange. It was won four years later by Napoleon, who presented it to Marshal Kellerman, duke of Valmy, who owned it until 1813. From 1813 to 1815, the property was administered by the allies Russia, Prussia, and Austria; it was then given to the Habsburg Emperor Francis I of Austria at the Vienna Congress. In 1816 he presented it to his chancellor, prince of Metternich Winneburg, whose descendants sold their majority share in the property only in the 1970s. The property today belongs to the Oetker family, whose vast network of businesses includes the sparkling wine producer HENKELL FREIXENET. The historic prestige of the estate resulted in the name Johannisberg Riesling being a synonym for German RIESLING.

See also GERMAN HISTORY. D.S.

Schönburger, pink-berried 1939 GERMAN CROSS with Pinot Noir, Chasselas Rose, and Muscat of Hamburg among its antecedents. It has been more useful to the wine industry of ENGLAND than to its native Germany, where it is hardly grown, although English plantings have been declining. Its wines are white, low in acid, and relatively full-bodied.

Schoonmaker, Frank (1905–76), influential American wine writer and wine merchant. Born in South Dakota, he first became interested in wine when researching travel books in Europe in the late 1920s. Immediately after the Repeal of PROHIBITION, he wrote a series of wine articles for the *New Yorker* which were published as *The Complete Wine Book* in 1934. Soon afterwards he founded an eponymous wine import company and travelled extensively, becoming noted for his abilities as a judge of young wines, his espousal of DOMAINE BOTTLING in Burgundy, and his expertise in German wines. An early advocate of American wines, he was highly critical of the habitual GENERIC naming of them. In the 1940s, he was hired as consultant to the large California producer Almaden, for whom he created the best-selling VARIETAL Grenache Rosé, having been inspired by the French wine TAVEL. Schoonmaker employed Alexis LICHINE, who was to occupy a very similar post immediately before the Second World War, and the two men were to publish the first editions of their respective wine encyclopedias in 1964 and 1967. He published five wine books and numerous shorter works on wine.

Schwarzriesling, a German synonym for Pinot Meunier. See MÜLLERREBE.

Sciaccarellu (sometimes written **Sciaccarello** and **Sciacarellu**) is a speciality of the French island of CORSICA, where plantings totalled 885 ha/2,187 acres in 2015. DNA PROFILING has established that both Sciaccarellu and the Corsican variety known as Malvasia Montanaccio are in fact the genetically important MAMMOLO of Tuscany. The grape variety is capable of producing red fruit-flavoured if not necessarily deep-coloured reds and fine rosés that can smell of the island's herby scrubland. The vine has good disease resistance and thrives particularly successfully on the GRANITIC soils in the south-west around Ajaccio and Sartène. It buds and ripens late and is less important than NIELLUCCIU.

science. It was long maintained that WINEMAKING was an art, but the proportion of the world's wine made by individuals with little appreciation of science, even in the OLD WORLD, has shrunk substantially in the last century. Now most people practising OEONOLOGY and VITICULTURE are scientifically trained, often to a tertiary level. Even by the late 1980s, it had become difficult to discuss wine with many of those who grow and make it without being conversant with a wide range of scientific terms and concepts, including a host of measurements such as PH, TA, RS, GA (GALLIC ACID), and IPT (*indice des polyphénols totaux*). The dramatically improved overall quality of wine since ACADEME took a role in teaching and researching wine-related subjects is eloquent testimony to the beneficial effect of the increasingly scientific approach of all those involved with wine. As in all fields, however, the best scientists are often those who seek to explain rather than dominate; in Old World regions whose wines have been admired for centuries, the best results are often obtained by those who combine scientific knowledge with a respect for TRADITION. For specific applications of science, see, for example, AI, DNA PROFILING, GLOBAL NAVIGATION SATELLITE SYSTEMS, INFRARED SPECTROSCOPY, and PRECISION VITICULTURE.

scion, in viticulture, is the piece of the fruiting vine that is grafted on to the quite separate ROOTSTOCK. When grown, such a plant will have the leaves and desired fruit of one VINE VARIETY (Cabernet Sauvignon, for example) but the roots of the other (rootstock) variety (110 Richter, for example). GRAFTING is very widely used in viticulture since rootstocks are needed to combat soil-borne pests or diseases such as PHYLLOXERA and NEMATODES. B.G.C.

scoring individual wines, and many aspects of their production, became an increasingly popular pursuit with professionals and amateurs alike in the late 20th century.

Scoring vineyards

Vineyards may be scored to assess their suitability for producing good-quality wine grapes. The most famous system is that used in the DOURO Valley of northern Portugal for PORT production. Vineyards are allocated points, from plus 1,680 for the most promising to minus 3,340 for the least favoured, taking into account YIELD, SOIL TYPE, MESOCLIMATE, vineyard maintenance, GRAPE COMPOSITION, ENCÉPAGEMENT, and VINE AGE. Highly classified vineyards are entitled to produce as much wine as they are able each year, while production from lower classifications can be restricted to meet demand. The CHAMPAGNE region of north-east France has a similar, if considerably less precise, system whereby whole COMMUNES are given a percentage rating, between 80 and 100.

Vineyards may also be scored for their adherence to organic growing principles as part of their accreditation (see ORGANIC VITICULTURE). R.E.S.

Smart, R. E., and Robinson, M., *Sunlight into Wine: A Handbook for Winegrape Canopy Management* (1991).

Scoring wines

Wine drinkers are, happily, presented with more choice than ever before. Unhappily, we all seem to have less and less time to make decisions. A score which can be interpreted at a glance is one obvious way of solving both those problems, and it was perhaps understandable that in the late 20th century many wine consumers and, particularly, retailers leaned heavily on scores as a means of buying and selling wine respectively. Some of the various scoring systems and their wider context are discussed in NUMBERS AND WINE. The prototype is that used by the American writer Robert PARKER, who did much to promote the controversial but highly influential practice of awarding points out of 100 between 50 and 100, modelled on the American high-school system. Effectively, wines of interest to readers of his and the many other WINE WRITERS who adopted a similar scoring system were originally those scoring more than 85, but grade inflation has tended to increase this lower limit to 90. Serious COLLECTORS and INVESTORS tend to concentrate on those which score more than 95, so-called TROPHY WINES. Other tasters use other scales, often in Europe points out of 20, but the 100-point scale is more popular with retailers.

These scores have had an extraordinary effect on the wine market. They enable potential INVESTORS, especially wine FUNDS and even FINE WINE traders, to take a position and affect the market without necessarily knowing anything whatsoever about wine. They empower new wine drinkers to make decisions independently of wine traders. And because, unlike TASTING NOTES, they can be understood universally, they can guide potential wine buyers all over the world, thus opening up the wine market in general and the fine-wine market in particular to countries without an established wine culture. Scores undoubtedly played a part in ASIA's dramatic and inflationary entry into the fine-wine market in the mid 1990s, for example, just as they have since encouraged interest from new wine buyers not just in established markets but in expanding markets such as South America and Russia. The implications of extending the market so widely for a commodity as finite as fine wine, especially trophy wines, are obvious, and the price gap between the trophy wines and the rest has continued to widen.

Quite apart from price and demand, however, scoring affected the wines themselves. Because scores are invariably arrived at as a result of a comparative TASTING of many different samples of the same sort of wine, it is inevitable that some of the more subtle wines are overlooked and, particularly with red wines, the deeper-coloured, stronger, more concentrated wines were likely to make a more immediate, and often favourable, impression in Parker's era. Of course this varies with the taster(s), but overall it is undeniable that in the late 20th century wines became more alcoholic, more concentrated, smoother-textured, and less acid—all as an indirect result of comparative tasting in general, and possibly what has become known as 'Parkerization' in particular, although the early 21st century saw a backlash resulting in a FASHION for fresh, much paler reds.

There has been another, more obviously beneficial, effect of the prevalence of scoring individual wines. New wine producers can make a name for themselves and their wines very much faster than has ever been the case. A sample judiciously sent to influential wine CRITICS can ensure immediate commercial success and direct communication with potential consumers. The downside for wine drinkers, of course, is that prices will inevitably rise steeply.

Wine scores, as those who award them try vainly to point out, can never substitute for description, however. Even if in the 1990s the market seemed much more interested in numbers than words, the 21st century has seen—perhaps as a reaction to over-reliance on scores in the US market and as a way for the army of new American recruits to wine drinking to distinguish themselves—an increased reliance on personal TASTE and on the stories behind wines rather than the numbers in front of them.

For more detail of the practicalities and weaknesses of wine scoring, see NUMBERS AND WINE. J.R.

Scotland. While Scotland has a long and proud history of wine importation and wine bottling—the foundation of the Auld Alliance it built with FRANCE—its attempts at viticulture have been less successful. A few small-scale vineyards have tested the water with what one might term 'hardy varieties', but the low average temperatures, high rainfall, and wind exposure have proved too much. In 2021 a 1.5-ha/3.7-acre experimental vineyard was planted overlooking Loch Striven, west of Glasgow, using early-ripening VITIS VINIFERA and modern HYBRIDS, and the results are eagerly awaited. S.S.

Kay, B., and Maclean, C., *Knee Deep in Claret* (1983).

Scott Henry, a vine-TRAINING SYSTEM whereby the CANOPY is divided vertically and the shoots are separated and trained in two curtains, upwards and downwards (see diagram). The canopy is about 2 m/6.5 ft tall, and the shoots and leaves are held in place by foliage wires. The system was developed by an Oregon vine-grower of the same name in the early 1980s when his vines were so vigorous that both yield and quality were reduced. The system was originally developed for CANE PRUNING; a later spur-pruned version has now generally been superseded by the SMART-DYSON system.

The Scott Henry system is suited to moderate-vigour vineyards with row spacing of about 2.5 m or more. It became widely used in many New World countries in the 1990s because of its suitability for MECHANICAL HARVESTING and potential for improving wine quality and yield. A New Zealand company (Delegat) has the world's largest vineyards using this system, around 2,000 ha/4,950 acres in 2021 in Hawke's Bay and Marlborough. R.E.S.

Smart, R. E., and Robinson, M., *Sunlight into Wine: A Handbook for Winegrape Canopy Management* (1991).

screwcaps, sometimes known as ROTEs (roll-on, tamper-evident) and often by the brand name Stelvin, have emerged as a leading competitor to cork in terms of performance and usage. They are cheaper than top-quality corks, and no capsules are needed, but the cost of new bottling equipment and bottles can deter smaller producers.

Screwcaps as an alternative to cork for bottling wine were first used in 1959, when a French company introduced the Stelcap-vin, which had already proved successful for a range of spirits and liqueurs. The rights to manufacture this closure were acquired by Australian Consolidated Industries Ltd (ACI) in 1970, and it was renamed Stelvin® for the Australian market. ACI trials of four closures (three screwcaps with different wadding materials and a cork for comparison) on three red and three white wines, first reported in 1976, concluded that screwcaps were ideal for sealing wine bottles but only if they had the right wadding material and a satisfactory seal between bottle and cap. An industry push towards screwcaps at that time lost momentum, partly through lack of consumer acceptance and partly because awareness of the shortcomings of cork were not very widespread.

As dissatisfaction with cork gradually increased in the 1990s, there were sporadic attempts to introduce screwcaps to the marketplace. In 2000 winemakers in Australia's Clare Valley, famous for its Rieslings, banded together to take a stand on the issue. The Clare winemakers, many of whose wines are made in a style that shows any cork-related faults particularly transparently (see CORK TAINT and PREMATURE OXIDATION), had to overcome a significant logistical obstacle: at the time, no Australian supplier could offer bottles and caps of the required style and quality. As a result, they had to gather together enough

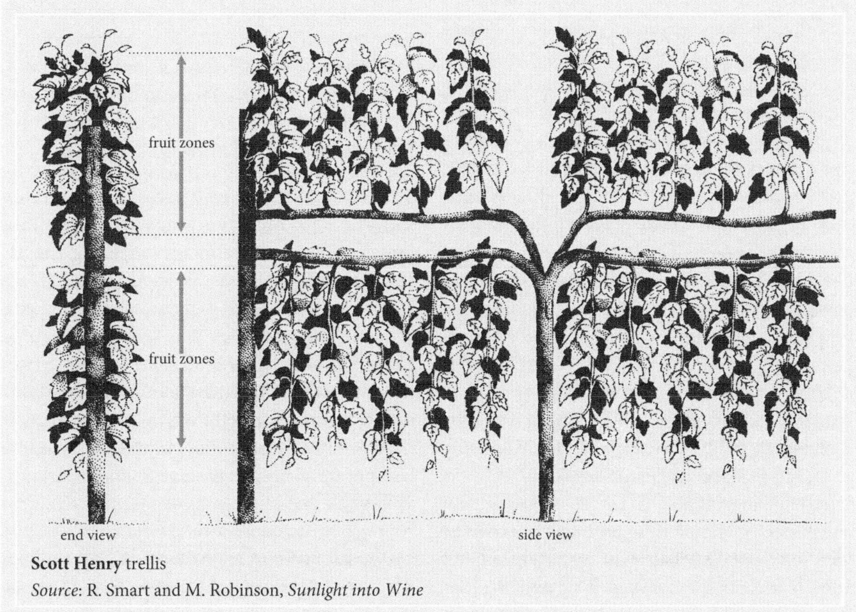

Scott Henry trellis
Source: R. Smart and M. Robinson, *Sunlight into Wine*

like-minded producers willing to adopt screwcaps to generate the threshold order of 250,000 bottles from Pechiney in France. Their effort made the headlines, and momentum increased so that by the 2004 vintage some 200 million wine bottles were sealed with screwcaps in Australia. This Clare initiative prompted New Zealand winemakers to form the New Zealand Screwcap Initiative in 2001. By 2004 an estimated 70% of New Zealand's wines were sealed under screwcap, up from just 1% three years earlier. Ten years later, in 2014, an estimated 95% of New Zealand wines and 80% of Australian wines were screwcap-sealed. Recent (2021) data in the US showed that the proportion of wineries using screwcaps has now exceeded 50%, suggesting a watershed moment in their usage, which had remained at around 40% for a decade.

Screwcaps consist of two components: the aluminium alloy cap, which comes attached to the sleeve; and the liner, which is made of an expanded polyethylene wadding. The liner typically contains a layer that acts as a barrier to gas exchange, overlain by a PVDC (Saranex) film that provides an inert surface in contact with the wine. In production, the screwcap is not screwed on but is held down tight over the end of the bottle, and a set of rollers moulds the sleeve of the cap over the ridges on the outside of the top portion of the neck. This holds the whole closure firmly in place. The cap itself is joined to the sleeve by a series of small metal bridges, which are broken when the cap is twisted. To obtain a tight seal it is especially important that the lip of the bottle be free of defects and that the application be executed correctly. The technology for applying screwcaps is thus much more complex than that required for the insertion of corks or similar closures.

Although they are often considered as a single closure type, not all screwcaps are alike. The most significant difference is in the nature of the liner. In some caps the seal is a tin-foil layer; if applied properly, this closure has a very low OXYGEN TRANSMISSION RATE. This transfer of oxygen into the bottle is much less than natural cork (*c.* 2%) and yields a very different wine after some years of AGEING. Whether this is desirable or not depends on the style of the wine. Careful testing is therefore required before switching from a closure with what might be referred to as a 'normal' OTR (normal being defined by history: a natural cork in a glass bottle at around 13 °C/55 °F). Other liners are designed to mimic the nominal OTR of natural cork. The large OTR discrepancy between screwcap liner types makes it impossible for consumers to know how any one wine sealed with a screwcap is likely to age or whether a wine sealed under screwcap is suitable for long ageing. The same is true of other closure types, which means that, unless a wine is bought for immediate consumption, wine lovers need more information about the OTR of a wine's packaging.

A deluxe version of the screwcap also exists, one in which the thread is not visible on the outside of the sleeve, more closely mimicking a standard CAPSULE and appeasing those who object to screwcaps on aesthetic grounds.

J.A.G., T.M.S. & A.L.W.

Stelzer, T., *Taming the Screw: A Manual for Winemaking with Screw Caps* (2005).
Taber, G., *To Cork or Not to Cork* (2007).

Scuppernong, the best-known of the vine varieties belonging to the *Vitis rotundifolia* species of the MUSCADINIA genus planted in the south-east of the United States and in Mexico. Like other Muscadines, the grapes (in this case bronze-skinned) are very distinctively flavoured. Some well-structured, sweet, dark gold wines are made which taste markedly different from the much more widely known product of VINIFERA varieties. Scuppernong has been substantially replaced in the southern states by Muscadines specially bred for wine production.

sec is French for DRY while **secco** is Italian, **seco** is Spanish and Portuguese, and TROCKEN is German for 'dry'. See SWEETNESS, and DOSAGE for official EU sugar levels.

secateurs, handheld scissors used for winter PRUNING of vines. Two-handled secateurs are used for cutting larger-diameter and older wood of the vine. Pruning can be faster, more effective, and less tiring with pneumatic or electric secateurs (see MECHANICAL PRUNING). R.E.S.

secbutyl-methoxypyrazine (SBMP). See METHOXYPYRAZINES.

sécheresse, French for DROUGHT and occasionally used to refer to WATER STRESS although the latter is more often referred to as *stress hydrique*. When the stress is mild, this is a recognized contributor to wine quality and then the term *déficit hydrique* is preferred.

second crop is one that may form after the main one but on LATERAL SHOOTS. Second-crop bunches are most abundant on strong laterals. In some varieties, a lateral-borne second crop is rare, but on others, such as PINOT NOIR and many MUSCAT varieties, this crop can be large. Usually the existence of a second crop is a negative factor for wine quality since its development runs six to eight weeks behind the main crop and it competes for nutrients, as well as complicating the development and control of VINE PESTS and VINE DISEASES. Worse, it adds a proportion of immature fruit to the HARVEST (especially where MECHANICAL HARVESTERS are used), which usually adversely affects the quality of the resulting wine. A second lateral-borne crop is anatomically different from bunches that develop on so-called 'secondary buds' after the primary BUD has been damaged or killed by FROST, for example. B.G.C. & R.E.S.

Keller, M., *The Science of Grapevines* (3rd edn, 2020).

second fermentation, a fermentation that occurs after the completion of the normal alcoholic FERMENTATION. This may be a requisite step in the process of SPARKLING WINEMAKING or simply a restarting in the winery of an alcoholic fermentation of a wine that still contains fermentable SUGARS. This can happen if, for example, there is a rise in TEMPERATURE or a more powerful YEAST is introduced. The GOVERNO winemaking process associated with TUSCANY in central Italy is another example of deliberate provocation of a second fermentation. MALOLACTIC CONVERSION is sometimes referred to as the second fermentation.

See also FERMENTATION IN BOTTLE.

second growth. See the CLASSIFICATION of Bordeaux.

second wines are wines made from batches of wine or parcels of vines considered not good enough for the principal product, or *grand vin*, made at an estate. The phenomenon was born in BORDEAUX in the 18th century and was revived in the early 20th century at Ch LAFITE, but it was hardly developed commercially until the 1980s, when increased competition forced ever more rigorous selection at the ASSEMBLAGE stage. Some of the more famous second wines are Ch LATOUR's Les Forts de Latour, supplied by vineyards specifically designated for this purpose, and Ch MARGAUX's Pavillon Rouge. So important has the quality and reputation of second wines become that both these first growths also sell a third wine. The branded wine MOUTON CADET began life as the second wine of Ch MOUTON ROTHSCHILD, which much more recently created Le Petit Mouton as its modern second wine. Second wines are likely to contain the produce of young vines together with the least satisfactory lots. In particularly unsuccessful VINTAGES, some properties make no *grand vin* at all so that the second wine, or *second vin*, is the only wine produced that year. In general, a second wine from a poor vintage (when a *grand vin* was also bottled) is rarely an exciting drink, but a second wine from a quality-conscious producer in a good vintage can represent excellent value and typically matures faster than the *grand vin*.

sediment, the solid material which settles to the bottom of any wine container, whether it be a bottle or a vat, tank, cask, or barrel. This sediment is a very heterogeneous mixture which in winemaking consists mainly of dead yeast cells and bacteria (the gross LEES), the insoluble fragments of grape pulp and skin. At subsequent stages it consists also of TARTRATES and, from red wines, PHENOLIC polymers, as well as any insoluble materials added to assist CLARIFICATION or to facilitate FILTRATION.

Sediments in bottled wines are relatively rare and usually signal a fine wine that has already spent some years in bottle. So unaccustomed have modern wine consumers become to sediment that many (erroneously) view it as a fault. Many winemakers therefore take great pains to ensure, through clarification, STABILIZATION, FINING, and filtration that the great majority of wines made today, and virtually all of those designed to be drunk within their first few years, will remain free of sediment for at least a few years. Wines designed for long periods of AGEING, on the other hand, frequently deposit crystals of tartrates, white in white wines and dyed red or black in red wines. Red wines, in addition, deposit some PIGMENTED TANNINS that are the result of phenolic polymerization. The heavy deposits in bottles of vintage port are a particularly dramatic example of this phenomenon. A bottle of wine containing sediment needs special care before SERVING.

Environmentally responsible disposal of sediment from wine production presents a challenge: skins, stems, seeds, and pulp residues can be processed for the recovery of small amounts of sugar, tartaric acid, colouring agents (see OENOCYANIN), and grapeseed oil. Alcohol can also be obtained by a distillery from the skins and stems. However, in most wine regions the costs of recovery greatly exceed the market value of the recovered substances. The solid sediments are frequently returned to the vineyard and worked into the soil instead. See also WINERY WASTE.

See also the quite different phenomenon of BOTTLE DEPOSIT. A.D.W.

seedling, the young plant that develops when a seed germinates. Grape seeds have tiny embryos which develop rapidly as the seed germinates, growing a freely branching tap-root and a shoot. The growth of seedlings is important in VINE BREEDING, though not otherwise in commercial viticulture as vines are propagated from cuttings (see VEGETATIVE PROPAGATION). B.G.C.

seeds. For details of grape seeds, see GRAPE.

For details of the historical evidence provided by finds of ancient grape seeds (and other parts of the grape), see PALAEOETHNOBOTANY.

Ségalin, 1959 INRA cross of Jurançon Noir × PORTUGAIS Bleu which has good colour, structure, and flavour and is authorized in SOUTH WEST FRANCE. (See also CALADOC, CHASAN, and PORTAN.)

Ségurs, important family in the history of the BORDEAUX wine region, originally from the village of PAUILLAC. In 1670 Jacques de Ségur, a notary who was a councillor of the legal Parlement of Bordeaux, became the second husband of Jeanne de Gasq, daughter of another Parlement councillor. As a dowry she brought with her the *seigneurie* of LAFITE, to add to others he had, including Calon in ST-ESTÈPHE, and an estate of about 1,000 ha/2,470 acres to the north of Pauillac. Their son Alexandre de Ségur was born in 1674. His father died in 1691, but in 1695 he married Marie-Thérèse de Clausel, the heiress of LATOUR, which gave him all the southern part of Pauillac and another very large estate. Their son, the future Marquis Nicolas-Alexandre de Ségur, was born in Bordeaux in 1697, and when his father died in 1716 he took over the very large domaine, which then included the farm of MOUTON before it passed in the 1730s to the Marquis de Branne. The marquis, a vice-president of the Bordeaux Parlement, was said to have been called 'le prince des vignes' by Louis XV. He is reputed to have said, 'I make wine at Lafite and Latour, but my heart is at Calon', and on the label of Ch Calon Ségur there is today a large heart. He had four daughters, and their descendants owned Ch Latour until 1962. E.P.-R.

Penning-Rowsell, E., *The Wines of Bordeaux* (6th edn, 1989).

Seibel, common name for many of the FRENCH HYBRID vine varieties bred by Albert Seibel of the Ardèche in the late 19th and early 20th centuries, most of them identified by number and many of them given a more colloquially appealing name. Seibel 5455 is more often called PLANTET, for example, while Seibel 4986 is Rayon d'Or and Seibel 9549 is DE CHAUNAC. The variety once known simply as Seibel in France is Seibel 7053, which is known as CHANCELLOR in New York State.

Sekt, word used in German-speaking countries for SPARKLING WINE. Long governed in Germany by manufacturing rather than wine law, most Sekt there is inexpensive and produced in bulk, often from imported wine. The name Deutscher Sekt designates Sekt from German fruit. A growing minority of German Sekt issues from family wineries, CO-OPERATIVES, and houses specializing in the genre and frequently focused on vineyard-designated BOTTLE FERMENTED wine, especially from RIESLING or SPÄTBURGUNDER (Pinot Noir). In 2020 the VDP introduced the Sekt Statute, making bottle-fermentation obligatory for the VDP Sekt label; the vintage version must age at least 24 months on the LEES, and 36 months for those labelled Prestige.

In AUSTRIA, which has an even longer, stronger Sekt tradition than Germany but a similar dominance of bulk production, federal legislation in 2015 introduced a Sekt Austria PDO. All Sekt bearing the PDO must be made from Austrian grapes; wines labelled Reserve or Grosse Reserve must be bottle fermented and mature for a minimum of 18 or 30 months respectively on the lees. D.S.

selection, increasingly important practice in maximizing wine quality whereby only the finest grapes or lots of wine are allowed in the final blend. See GRAPE SORTING and ASSEMBLAGE. See also SELECTIVE HARVESTING.

Selection was introduced into German wine law in 2000 as a class of hand-harvested, estate bottled, dry-tasting wine subject to the unusual stipulation that the vineyard surface to be utilized had to be declared by 1 May before the harvest, ostensibly to permit greater administrative oversight. To say that this category failed to catch on appears to be an understatement. D.S.

sélection clonale is French for CLONAL SELECTION, while **sélection massale** is French for MASS SELECTION.

Sélection de Grains Nobles, the richest, most sumptuous ripeness category of ALSACE wines, applied to wines made mainly from grapes affected by BOTRYTIS with minimum sugar levels of 276 g/l for RIESLING and MUSCAT, and 306 g/l for GEWÜRZTRAMINER and PINOT GRIS. The term is also used in the Loire AOCs Coteaux de AUBANCE and Coteaux du LAYON for botrytized wines reaching at least 323 g/l sugar, and in MONBAZILLAC in South West France for wines reaching at least 255 g/l.

sélection parcellaire, French term meaning 'parcel selection', generally used to refer to a wine made from a clearly defined and particularly good plot of vines or vineyard PARCEL.

selective harvesting is a key application of PRECISION VITICULTURE and the major management strategy employed in ZONAL VITICULTURE. It involves the separate picking of different parts of a vineyard according to different yield/quality criteria in order to exploit the variation observed within a vineyard and to maximize the uniformity of individual fruit parcels delivered to the winery. These fruit parcels may then be selected for different wines—perhaps for different styles or at different PRICE POINTS. Typically, different parts of the same vineyard block are harvested into separate bins, either during a single operation or at different times. Early adoption of this strategy was predominantly by small-scale producers or by large companies with the equipment to process small lots. However, selective harvesting may also be profitable even when production is geared to large fermentation volumes. For example, a block of Cabernet Sauvignon might be mechanically harvested into either of two bins, depending on location within the block, in order to maximize the volume produced of a high-value VARIETAL wine by allocating fruit from areas producing lower-value material to a lower-value blended wine. Under conventional uniform management, only the latter would have been produced from the block. R.G.V.B.

Bramley, R. G. V., et al., 'Selective harvesting is a feasible and profitable strategy even when grape and wine production is geared towards large fermentation volumes', *Australian Journal of Grape and Wine Research*, 17/3 (2011), 298–305.

Bramley, R. G. V., et al., 'Patterns of within-vineyard spatial variation in the "pepper" compound rotundone are temporally stable from year to year', *Australian Journal of Grape and Wine Research*, 23/1 (2017), 42–7.

Bramley, R. G. V., et al., 'Generating benefits from precision viticulture through selective harvesting', in J. Stafford (ed.), *Proceedings of the 5th European Conference on Precision Agriculture* (2005).

Selektion, term without legal status or specific parameters but often used by growers in AUSTRIA to signify a wine with high quality pretensions or in some way unusual. The term is used, for example, by some growers in the WACHAU to designate wines that fail to qualify for the category SMARAGD because they have too high a level of RESIDUAL SUGAR; and by certain growers in STYRIA to highlight SINGLE-VINEYARD WINES as opposed to lighter KLASSIK bottlings. Not to be confused with SELECTION, a specific category of German wine. D.S.

selfling, or **selfed vine**, a plant created by one VINE VARIETY crossed to itself. This is not a very successful breeding strategy, since most varieties carry deleterious recessive genes, and there is consequently a strong inbreeding depression. This is avoided by crossing unrelated vines, which is a feature of successful VINE BREEDING. See also NEW VARIETIES. R.E.S.

semi-carbonic maceration, red winemaking process which involves a short or partial CARBONIC MACERATION phase followed by a normal alcoholic FERMENTATION. Whole bunches of grapes are placed in a fermentation vessel. The weight of the grapes breaks open those grapes at the bottom of the vessel, and the MUST begins to ferment and produce CARBON DIOXIDE due to the action of AMBIENT YEASTS, derived either from the grapes or from the winemaking equipment or environment. Immediately above this there are whole grapes that are surrounded by juice; above this, whole grapes in an atmosphere of carbon dioxide. This upper layer will undergo true carbonic maceration. The grapes in the middle layer will undergo similar intracellular transformations but at a much slower rate. Thus, alcoholic fermentation and carbonic maceration processes proceed simultaneously. The grapes are then crushed and pressed, and the yeast completes the fermentation off the skins. The great majority of Beaujolais NOUVEAU and most other PRIMEUR wines are made in this fashion. Such wines have a very distinct aroma reminiscent of bananas or kirsch, arising from the distinctive by-products of the intracellular fermentation occurring within the whole berries and without yeast, during the first phase. Variations of the technique include completing the alcoholic fermentation on the skins in order to increase EXTRACTION and AGEING capacity. G.C.

Sémillon, often written plain **Semillon** in non-francophone countries, is a golden grape variety from south-west France and is one of the unsung heroes of white-wine production. Blended with its traditional partner SAUVIGNON BLANC, to which it seems to be vaguely related (underripe Sémillon can taste remarkably like Sauvignon), this golden- or sometimes copper-berried vine variety is the key ingredient in SAUTERNES, arguably the world's longest-living unfortified wine, as it is in most of the great dry whites of Graves (see PESSAC-LÉOGNAN). Unblended, in Australia's Hunter Valley, it is responsible for one of the most idiosyncratic and historic wine types exclusive to the NEW WORLD, but overall it is not fashionable and has been declining in importance.

Outside Sauternes, Sémillon seems destined to play a supplementary role. The wines it produces tend to fatness and, although capable of AGEING, have little aroma in youth. Sauvignon Blanc, with its internationally recognized name, strong aroma, high acidity, but slight lack of substance, fills in all obvious gaps. In the early 1990s, in a world desperate for Chardonnay, Sémillon found itself the passive ingredient in commercially motivated blends—most notably but not exclusively in Australia. Sémillon's weight and high YIELD make it a useful base for commercial blends.

As a vine, Sémillon is easy to cultivate. It is almost as vigorous as Sauvignon Blanc, with particularly deep-green leaves, but flowers slightly later and is not particularly susceptible to COULURE. Nor is it a victim of disease, apart from rot, which, in favourable conditions, is the blessed NOBLE ROT rather than the destructive GREY ROT.

Its greatest concentration is still in Bordeaux, where, although Sauvignon Blanc has been catching up fast particularly for dry white BORDEAUX AOC wines in the Entre-Deux-Mers district, there were still 5,979 ha/14,774 acres in 2020 (down from 9,256 ha in 2000). On the left bank of the Garonne, in the Graves, Sauternes, and its enclave BARSAC, Sémillon still outnumbers Sauvignon in almost exactly the traditional proportions of four to one. Sauvignon and Sémillon fight for dominance in the great, long-lived dry whites of Graves and Pessac-Léognan. In Sauternes, Sémillon's great attribute is its proneness to noble rot, which is the key to wines such as Ch d'YQUEM that may continue to evolve for centuries. Again, oak ageing deepens Sémillon's already relatively deep gold (really ripe grapes may almost look pink). Similar but usually less exciting sweet whites, the most ordinary made simply by stopping fermentation or adding sweet grape MUST, are made in the nearby appellations of CADILLAC CÔTES DE BORDEAUX, CÉRONS, LOUPIAC, and STE-CROIX-DU-MONT.

Like Sauvignon Blanc, Sémillon is allowed in many other appellations for dry and sweet whites of SOUTH WEST FRANCE but is perhaps most notable in qualitative terms in MONBAZILLAC. Thanks to its (declining) importance throughout BERGERAC, Sémillon is the most planted white wine variety in the Dordogne by far, although its 3,528 ha/8,718 acres in 2019 had been overtaken by Merlot. It is technically allowed in most appellations of PROVENCE but has made little impact on the vineyards of the Midi, where acidity is at a premium.

Sémillon's other great sphere of influence has been South America in general and, in particular, Chile, although total plantings there had fallen to 700 ha/1,730 acres by 2020 and Sauvignon is very much more common. Argentina has pockets of prized old-vine Sémillon, but total plantings in 2020, mainly in the Mendoza region, were just 639 ha.

In North America, Sémillon is generally rather scorned, lacking the image of Sauvignon Blanc, although a significant number of producers use the former to add interest to the latter. Total area planted in California stood at 226 ha/559 acres in 2020. A few producers have tried using it to produce BOTRYTIZED wines in the image of Sauternes, and it also adds weight to Sauvignon in white MERITAGE blends. Historically LIVERMORE VALLEY has produced some of the best fruit. Sémillon was once nearly as important in Washington State as Sauvignon Blanc, and the likes of L'Ecole 41 still make a fine dry VARIETAL version, but plantings had fallen to 235 acres by 2017.

It is quite widespread, without being particularly important, throughout eastern Europe, but it is in both SOUTH AFRICA and AUSTRALIA where Sémillon had a particularly glorious past. In 1822, 93% of South Africa's vineyard was planted with this variety, imported from Bordeaux. So common was it then that it was simply called Wyndruif, or 'wine grape'. It was subsequently called Green Grape, a reference to its abnormally green foliage, but has been declining in importance so that in 2020 it was planted on just 990 ha/2,446 acres—although growth in Sauvignon Blanc plantings in South Africa has brought an increase in sophisticated white BORDEAUX BLENDS, often oak aged.

While all the Australian pale grape focus was on the growth of Chardonnay (and the decline of Riesling) from the early 1990s, plantings of Semillon (typically without the accent) stealthily grew from 2,526 ha/6,242 acres in 1990 to 6,310 ha in 2002, although this had fallen to 3,719 ha by 2022. Its role in the Hunter Valley is well known: to produce, from early-picked grapes, low-alcohol (10.5–11%) wines with unmatched cellaring potential. It has also enjoyed success as a wooded style, blended with Sauvignon Blanc, in the Adelaide Hills, and the blend is a popular speciality in Margaret River. See AUSTRALIA for more details.

In New Zealand it has been completely swamped by Sauvignon-mania, and only 28 ha, mainly in Hawke's Bay, remained in 2022.

semi-sparkling wine. See FIZZINESS.

Senegal is home to Domaine du Clos des Baobabs, the only vineyard in West Africa, planted in January 2013. In 2021 it extended over 3 ha/7 acres, mainly Grenache with experimental plantings of Cabernet Sauvignon, Cinsault, Grenache, Sangiovese, and Syrah at a density of 5,000 vines per hectare. The vineyard is in the Petite Côte region, 15 km/9 miles from the sea, where temperatures never drop below 14 °C/57 °F, and there are two distinct seasons: a dry season November–May, requiring vineyard IRRIGATION; and a rainy season June–October. Nearly 2,000 bottles of red wine are produced annually, with the first commercial release in 2019. J.-B.A.

sensitivity, an important factor in TASTING. We all vary in our sensitivities to different compounds, sometimes a thousandfold or more in terms of tasting thresholds. Some of the most obvious examples are dramatic differences between tasters in sensitivities to the effects of BRETTANOMYCES, CORK TAINT, MOUSINESS, and ROTUNDONE.

sequence of wines to be served. See ORDER.

Serbia, officially the **Republic of Serbia** and independent since 2006, is a landlocked nation in the central Balkans and includes the autonomous province of Vojvodina. Archaeological digs at Vinča near Belgrade found grape remains and AMPHORAE dating back to Neolithic times, but it was probably during the ROMAN era that grape-growing became well established in this region. Sirmium, the present-day city of Sremski Mitrovica, was declared one of the four capitals of the Roman Empire in 294, and Emperor Probus is credited with ordering the first vines to be planted on the slopes of Fruška Gora. The Serbian state developed in the Middle Ages during the Nemanjić dynasty, and the wine industry was encouraged by conversion to Christianity. Ottoman rule brought destruction to much of the wine industry, although some Serbians fled north to Srem and Banat taking vines with them. In 1699 the Karlovac Peace Agreement saw Srem and Banat join the Habsburg Empire, which encouraged wine production. As in the rest of the Balkan region, PHYLLOXERA was devastating, and the early 20th century saw the development of growers' CO-OPERATIVES. After the Second World War the industry was collectivized as part of YUGOSLAVIA, and vineyard area rose to 135,000 ha/333,592 acres by 1955. The brutal wars of independence after the break-up of Yugoslavia seriously affected wine production, although the 21st century has seen considerable change. The former state wineries have largely disappeared through bankruptcy, and the number of small to mid-sized, quality-focused estates with vineyards and modern equipment is increasing, undoubtedly helped by significant government subsidies.

Serbia's vineyard register showed 20,501 ha/50,659 acres under vine by 2019, though only 6,827 ha for commercial wine production. An estimated 13% of households own vineyards, though over 90% are smaller than 0.5 ha. There were 353 wineries and 3,997 registered growers by 2019. Wine production averaged 330,000–370,000 hl from 2016 to 2018. The country has been divided into three wine-growing units (Vojvodina, Central Serbia, and KOSOVO), 22 wine regions, and 77 subregions. Most wine is produced without any quality designation, though work is in progress to develop this sector and add further PDO classifications. PGI wines are described as Geografska Indikacija (GI); PDO wines are either Kontrolisano Poreklo i Kvalitet (KPK) or Kontrolisano i Garantovano Poreklo i Kvalitet (KGPK). Serbia imports twice as much wine as it exports (126,000 hl in 2019, largely to Russia and Balkan neighbours).

Vineyards, varieties, and regions

Serbia's largely CONTINENTAL CLIMATE is moderated by mountains such as Fruška Gora and by rivers, especially the Danube, Velika Morava, and Timok. There are as many as 200 varieties grown in the country, with around 30 local grapes. INTERNATIONAL VARIETIES including Cabernet Sauvignon, Merlot, and Pinot Noir arrived with Aleksandar I around the 1920s and can perform well, but more exciting is the rediscovery of PROKUPAC. A century ago, this was the most planted grapevine on Serbian territory. It is naturally vigorous and capable of huge crops, though with low YIELDS, and can make elegant, refined wines. Local varieties such as Morava, Neoplanta, Probus, Seduša, and Začinak are also gaining attention, though there is still a lack of high-quality NURSERY material or CLONAL SELECTION.

The Fruška Gora region, on the hills north of Belgrade, is now Serbia's most dynamic wine region with numerous young winemakers experimenting with NATURAL, BIODYNAMIC, ORGANIC, and AMPHORA wines. The town of Smederevo south of Belgrade gives its name to the white SMEDEREVKA grape (aka Bulgaria's Dimyat). WELSCHRIESLING is important here, often labelled with its historic local name of Grašac. The oldest written mention of Grašac and preserved herbarium specimens dating to the late 18th century have recently been found here.

The northern province of Vojvodina belongs to the Pannonian plain that extends into Hungary and includes the regions of Srem, Šubotica, Bačka, Telečka, Potisje, Banat, and South Banat. The Srem region is close to the Danube on the lower slopes of the Fruška Gora Mountains. The Danube influence moderates winter cold and aids earlier ripening in the summer, while an ELEVATION of around 200–300 m/660–980 ft helps keep freshness in the resulting wines. This is regarded as the heartland of Grašac, while international white-wine grapes including Chardonnay can thrive. Some Gamay and Portugieser (historically grown for vermouth-like Bermet) are present too. The sandy soils of Subotica are of Pannonian origin so it is no surprise there is some overlap with Hungarian varieties such as EZERJÓ, FURMINT, KÖVEDINKA, and KADARKA (including vines dating to 1880), although the area is best known for white wines from Graševina (WELSCHRIESLING) and Riesling. The Banat region lies on the western end of the Carpathians where the hills meet the plain. The rare Serbian white-wine grape KREACA is believed to originate here and is also found over the border in Romania as Creață.

In Central Serbia, there are 13 regions (Beograd, Pocerje-Valjevo, Čačak-Kraljevo, Toplica, Vranje, Niš, Leskovac, Nišava, Knjaževac, Mlava, Negotinska Krajina, Tri Morave, and Šumadija). The most important of these is Tri Morave to the south of Belgrade, especially its subregions Župa and Trstenik. The Župa area, with its mild continental climate moderated by surrounding mountains and rivers, has long been famous for wine production, with records of grape supply to monasteries dating to the 12th century. Today it boasts a group of pioneering new estates and is the heartland of the Prokupac revival. North of Tri Morave, the moderate continental region of Šumadija is arguably the centre of the revival of quality winemaking. It has four subregions—Krnjevo, Oplenac, Rača, and Kragujevac—of which Oplenac includes some of Serbia's best producers. It is also where King Aleksandar built his royal cellar in 1931. It is perhaps most famous for whites made to an old royal recipe, but some of the country's top Cabernet Sauvignon can be found here too. C.G.

www.vinopedia.rs
www.vinoifino.rs

Sercial, Portuguese white grape variety probably originally from BUCELAS, where most is to be found today. It was once quite commonly planted on the island of Madeira, but only about 25 ha/62 acres grew there in 2018. The name came to be used to denote the lightest, most acid, latest-maturing style of MADEIRA rather than the grape variety from which it was made. On the Portuguese mainland it is also known as ESGANA CÃO and is notable for its late ripening and high acidity. It should not be confused with CERCEAL Branco.

Serine, or **Sérine**, old synonym for SYRAH used in the northern Rhône and in the Isère *département* to distinguish a revered and ancient BIOTYPE of this variety that is sometimes mentioned on labels. Variant spellings include **Sereine**, **Sérène**, and **Serinne**.

service of wine. See SERVING WINE and SOMMELIER.

serving wine involves a number of fairly obvious steps, but mastering each of them can maximize the pleasure given by any individual wine. See OPENING THE BOTTLE, BREATHING, DECANTING, GLASSES, FOOD-AND-WINE MATCHING, ORDER OF WINES TO BE SERVED, and LEFTOVER WINE for details of these particular aspects of serving wine.

Perhaps the least obvious requirement of anyone serving wine is that they appear superficially mean, by filling glasses no more than two-thirds, and preferably less than half, full. This allows energetic agitation of the glass if necessary and enables the all-important AROMA to collect in the upper part of the bowl (see TASTING).

The factor which probably has the single greatest effect on how a wine tastes, however, is temperature, and this is one aspect which can be controlled by whoever is serving. Because of the well-known general rule that white (and rosé) wines should be chilled while red wines should be served at something called room temperature (see CHAMBRÉ), and because many refrigerators are set at relatively low temperatures, in practice many white wines are served too cool and many red wines dangerously warm. See TEMPERATURE for some guidance on specific recommended serving temperatures for certain styles of wine. Few wine drinkers have wine thermometers, however, so a certain amount of experimentation with ways of modifying serving temperatures is advisable.

Cooling wine in a refrigerator is much slower than cooling wine in a container holding water and ice (two hours rather than 30 minutes to cool an average bottle from 22 to 10 °C/72 to 50 °F). (Note that a container full of ice cubes but no water is not a very effective cooler as it provides relatively little contact between the bottle and the cooling medium.)

A freezer or ice box would do the job faster but has the serious disadvantage that the bottle will be cooled right down to icebox temperature if left there. This may well freeze the wine and push the cork out. Some refrigerators are, furthermore, set at such low temperatures that wines may emerge simply too cool.

It is a happy coincidence that the ideal cellar temperature, around 13 °C/55 °F, is also ideal for serving a wide range of wines, such as complex dry white wines and light-bodied red wines, and is not so low that it takes impossibly long to warm tannic red wines to a suitable serving temperature.

In cool climates, wine drinkers may have difficulty in warming bottles of red wine to suitably high temperatures for serving, however. Direct heat should not be applied to a bottle, and even contact with a radiator can heat wine to such a dangerously high temperature that some of the more volatile FLAVOUR COMPOUNDS are lost and the ALCOHOL can dominate so that the wine tastes unbalanced.

One of the most effective ways of warming wine, whether intentionally or not, is to pour it out into glasses in a relatively warm environment or, even faster, to pour the wine into a decanter or glasses which previously held hot water. This effect is accentuated if the glasses are cupped in human hands. For this reason, it is usually wise to serve wines slightly cooler than the ideal temperature at which they are best appreciated. Warming wine in microwave ovens can be effective if the oven is big enough and if great care is taken not to overheat the wine—and to remove the FOIL if it is metallic.

Ambient temperature can affect how a wine tastes: crisp, light wines taste either delightfully refreshing or disappointingly meagre when the taster is hot or cold respectively. On the other hand, in tropical climates, where both temperature and HUMIDITY are high, it can be almost impossible to find suitable conditions in which to serve even the finest red wine as, without air conditioning, drinks heat up so rapidly that a red wine has either to be served well chilled or run the risk of being almost MULLED. Light red wines with marked ACIDITY such as BEAUJOLAIS and reds from cooler climates such as the LOIRE, ENGLAND, NEW ZEALAND, TASMANIA, NEW YORK, and CANADA can taste more appetizing in hot climates than CLASSED GROWTH red bordeaux or fine burgundy.

One final aspect of serving wine, about which the Latin poet HORACE wrote extensively, is matching wine to guest and occasion. Part of what might generally be called CONNOISSEURSHIP, this is a pleasure associated with wine which can be almost as great as drinking it.

See also TASTING for the special conditions of serving wine for this particular purpose, a very different one from actually drinking it.

set. See FRUIT SET.

settling, the winemaking operation of holding GRAPE JUICE, MUST, or wine in a vessel for 12–24 hours so that suspended solids sink to the bottom. It is most commonly used to begin the CLARIFICATION of freshly drained and pressed white juice before FERMENTATION and is one of the most important stages in white winemaking. The addition of a small quantity of SULFUR DIOXIDE during this stage reduces the risk of OXIDATION and slows down any activity of yeasts and bacteria. For the same reasons, the juice is often cooled to below 15 °C/60 °F. Settling of particularly viscous grape juice can also be encouraged by the addition of ENZYMES designed to break chains of PECTINS. For white wines, there is another period of settling after fermentation or after BARREL AGEING.

Red wines, whose skins are included in the fermentation vessel, are settled after fermentation and MACERATION. The purpose is to remove not just grape debris but also dead yeast cells and bacteria, or LEES.

Settling is governed by such factors as the size of the solid particles, the difference in their DENSITY from that of the liquid, and the extent to which the liquid moves within the settling vessel. Because must and cloudy grape juice are so much denser than wine, they are much more difficult to settle. Solids as large and dense as seeds and stem fragments settle rapidly. Finely divided pulp debris and dead yeast cells and bacteria which are very small settle more slowly and are easily resuspended by currents within the settling vessel. COLLOIDS, which have dimensions of large molecular size, are very slow to settle because their movement is influenced by the smallest liquid movement within the vessel. The settling of colloids can be greatly assisted by the addition of clarifying or FINING agents such as BENTONITE, albumin (see EGG WHITES), GELATIN or CASEIN, which adsorb them and grow them into complexes large enough to settle. V.L.

Setúbal, port on the Sado estuary south of Lisbon, the capital of PORTUGAL, is also the name of a Portuguese FORTIFIED WINE with its own DOC region (see map under PORTUGAL). It is made predominantly from Moscatel (MUSCAT) grapes, and the region was officially demarcated in 1907 for **Moscatel de Setúbal**. The finest examples grow on LIMESTONE soils on the cool, north-facing slopes of the Arrábida hills. Grapes are also grown on the plain around the town of Palmela. The principal type of Moscatel is MUSCAT OF ALEXANDRIA; a tiny but growing amount (around 50 ha/123.6 acres) of pink-skinned, much earlier-ripening Moscatel Roxo is bottled separately and is generally slightly drier and more complex. Initially Setúbal is made in much the same way as a VIN DOUX

NATUREL. After vinification, however, pungent Muscat grape skins are left to macerate in the wine for five or six months, which imparts a taste of fresh grapes and gives Setúbal its intense aroma and flavour. As for MADEIRA's *canteiro* wines, wood-aged wines are aged above ground in warm to hot conditions to concentrate them. The minimum ageing requirement for Moscatel is 18 months and for Moscatel Roxo, 36 months. Most Setúbal is sold at two to five years of age. Basic examples are unoaked, but those aged in wood—traditionally large oak vats (although other formats are used)—develop an amber-orange colour and spicy candied citrus and raisin flavours. Small quantities are bottled (typically for NON-VINTAGE blends) after 20 years or more in cask, by which time the wine is deep brown and has a rich, grapey intensity and RANCIO character. Leading producer José Maria da FONSECA occasionally bottles and sells stocks dating back to the mid 19th century. Bottles labelled Moscatel Torna-Viagem crossed the equator twice by ship en route to and from the tropics and are considered the finest; multiple experiments by José Maria da Fonseca reportedly bear this out. For details of the unfortified wines made on the Setúbal peninsula, see PENÍNSULA DE SETÚBAL. R.J.M. & S.A.

Mayson, R. J., *The Wines of Portugal* (2020).

Severny, Russian vine variety developed at the All-Russia Potapenko Institute from a Précoce de Malingre seedling with a member of the famously cold-hardy VITIS AMURENSIS vine species native to Mongolia. Severny means 'northern' and is a suffix of several crosses such as SAPERAVI Severny and CABERNET SEVERNY specifically bred for harsh winter climates.

sexual propagation, reproduction by seed involving the union of male and female sex cells (POLLEN and ovule respectively). The important feature of this type of propagation is that the parent plants are genetically different, so the seedling is in turn genetically different from either parent. Throughout the world of nature, this is how genetic diversity is continued, permitting selection of those progeny best suited to survive. In commercial viticulture, this process has been circumvented by propagating selected, desirable individuals and propagating them vegetatively (see VEGETATIVE PROPAGATION). Originally sexual seedlings, all grape varieties have been propagated asexually for many years, decades, or centuries with substantially the same genetic constitution. Sexual propagation is used for VINE BREEDING throughout the world to produce NEW VARIETIES. Success depends on selecting suitable parents, now helped by marker-assisted selection techniques and many years of painstaking evaluation. J.V.

Seyssel, the oldest appellation within the eastern French region of SAVOIE, producing light, dry, and off-dry white still and sparkling wines from vineyards concentrated on the steep slopes of the upper Rhône Valley about 40 km/25 miles downriver of Geneva. Historically, sparkling Seyssel (especially the Royal Seyssel brand) was one of the few Savoie wines to escape the region itself, but it suffered a decline with less than 70 ha/173 acres of vines remaining in the appellation by 2020, about one-quarter used for sparkling wine. ALTESSE (sometimes referred to as Roussette) is the dominant grape variety here, although the local MOLETTE is also grown. Since the CRÉMANT de Savoie AOC was created in 2014, Seyssel sparkling wines are supposed to contain at least 70% Molette, but local growers are fighting to reduce this proportion to allow more Altesse (10% minimum is required). The sparkling wines need to be BOTTLE FERMENTED in the region. They are light and refreshing, and the best can develop in bottle. Still whites (mostly VARIETAL Altesse, while others are Molette) may be floral and crisp, but many are flattened by RESIDUAL SUGAR. W.L.

Seyssuel, commune in the Isère *département*, to the north of CÔTE RÔTIE, on the opposite bank of the RHÔNE. Currently within the IGP Collines Rhodaniennes growing area, Seyssuel was once known for the quality of its wines, but it wasn't replanted after PHYLLOXERA. Three local winegrowers, Pierre Gaillard, François Villard, and Yves Cuilleron, started replanting here in 1996, and they have since been joined by many more as the potential for quality has been confirmed. Neighbouring communes Chasse-sur-Rhône and Vienne have also seen plantings, and local producers hope that these three communes will be collectively promoted to CRU status, likely under the name Seyssuel. The main grapes used are SYRAH for red wine and VIOGNIER for white. M.C.W.

Seyval Blanc, complex, light-skinned FRENCH HYBRID, the most widely planted SEYVE-VILLARD hybrid, number 5276, the result of crossing two SEIBEL hybrids. It is productive, ripens early, and is well suited to relatively cool climates such as that of ENGLAND, where it was the single most planted vine variety in the late 20th century but has been superseded by the popularity of the Champagne grapes and by BACCHUS. It is also popular in NOVA SCOTIA and, to a lesser extent, in the eastern United States, notably in NEW YORK State. Its crisp white wines have no hint of FOXY flavour and can even benefit from BARREL AGEING. In the UK it is mainly used for blending and is particularly successful for sparkling-wine production. As a sparkling wine, it can (somewhat unexpectedly in view of its hybrid origins) be labelled as Quality Sparkling Wine.

Seyve-Villard, series of about 100 FRENCH HYBRIDS developed by hybridizer Bertille Seyve and his partner and father-in-law Victor Villard, much planted in France in the mid 20th century. Perhaps the most famous, however, is SEYVAL BLANC.

Sezão, dark-skinned Portuguese variety of which there were just 23 ha/57 acres in Portugal in 2023, mostly in the Douro Valley. Originally known as SOUSÃO, which is also the Douro synonym for Vinhão, it was renamed in 2012 when DNA PROFILING showed it to be a distinct variety.

Sforzato, or **Sfursat**, a dry red DRIED-GRAPE WINE made in the VALTELLINA zone in the far north of Italy from Nebbiolo, which is known locally as Chiavennasca.

SGN. See SÉLECTION DE GRAINS NOBLES.

shade, the absence of sunlight, for example in a vine CANOPY. This is due to leaves blocking out sunlight, as the transmission of light through one leaf is less than 10% of sunlight. Generally, shade is due to vigorous vines being trained to a restrictive vine-TRAINING SYSTEM.

Sunlight levels in the centre of dense canopies with many leaf layers can be as little as 1% of the levels above the canopy. At this very low level of light, PHOTOSYNTHESIS is zero or negative, and in time the leaves turn yellow and then fall off. Leaves deep in the canopy also experience filtered sunlight with altered spectral composition, in that red light is reduced and far-red light relatively enriched. The ratio of red to far-red light can act as a signal system for the vine and other plants and may play a role in the vine's response to shade. Similarly, ULTRAVIOLET RADIATION (UV) is filtered in the canopy, which can have a significant impact on PHENOLICS. Since the vine evolved in forests, it has tendrils for avoiding shade by climbing towards the sunlight.

Shade can reduce vine YIELD dramatically by reducing bud INITIATION, BUDBREAK, FRUIT SET, and hence berry number, as well as BERRY SIZE. Yields may increase up to threefold where shade has been removed by altering the training system and allowing the sunlight to penetrate.

Shade can also alter grape chemical composition and reduce grape quality. Studies around the world, for a range of vine varieties in a range of climates, have demonstrated that shade decreases levels of SUGARS, ANTHOCYANINS, PHENOLICS, TARTARIC ACID, monoterpene FLAVOUR COMPOUNDS, and apparent varietal character. Other negative effects of shade on wine quality are increases in MALIC ACID, PH, POTASSIUM, and the so-called HERBACEOUS characters. Shaded fruit is also more susceptible to BOTRYTIS BUNCH ROT and POWDERY MILDEW. CANOPY MANAGEMENT can reduce shade in the canopy and, in high-vigour vineyards, will improve yield and quality simultaneously.

With CLIMATE CHANGE and warmer air temperatures, berry SUNBURN has become an issue. It can be addressed by avoiding excessive exposure for bunches facing the mid-afternoon sun. For this reason, east–west row orientation is preferred in hot regions. R.E.S.

Smart, R.E., et al., 'Canopy management to improve grape yield and wine quality: principles and practices', *South African Journal of Enology and Viticulture*, 11/1 (1990), 3–17.

shale, a very fine-grained sedimentary rock, usually dark-coloured, which is weak and easily split because of the way the clayey sediment has settled, so that shale always breaks roughly parallel to the stratification of the sedimentary rock, unlike some metamorphic rocks (see SLATE and, especially, SCHIST). The splintered fragments are flaky and irregular (unlike cleaved slate). Shale weathers easily, to give CLAY-rich soils, often poorly drained. See also GEOLOGY. A.J.M.

shanking. See BUNCHSTEM NECROSIS.

sharpshooters, insects which feed on vine foliage and can carry important vine diseases. See LEAFHOPPERS.

shatter. See FRUIT SET.

Shaulis, Nelson (1913–2000). Born in Pennsylvania, Nelson Shaulis was destined to have a greater impact on world viticultural practice than most of his scientific contemporaries. His eastern US origin was appropriate, as this was the region of his greatest influence, though he began his career at the Agricultural Experiment Station, Geneva (see CORNELL UNIVERSITY), in 1948 and retired as Professor of Viticulture there in 1978.

Shaulis can be considered the father of CANOPY MANAGEMENT, although the term was not coined by him. In his early experiments with CONCORD grapevines, he realized that limits to YIELD and RIPENESS were a consequence of SHADE within the grapevine CANOPY. The solution was simple enough in hindsight but revolutionary for the time. By dividing a dense canopy into two less dense canopies, shade could be reduced, and suddenly yield and ripeness could be dramatically increased. The new TRELLIS design, first published in the mid 1960s, was called the GENEVA DOUBLE CURTAIN. As an important extension to this work, Shaulis and colleagues developed the world's first MECHANICAL HARVESTER of grapes and subsequently undertook important primary research on MECHANICAL PRUNING.

The impact of Shaulis's research has been felt throughout the wine world, but the NEW WORLD, free of yield limits, has benefited most. Shaulis influenced many younger researchers who made canopy management an accepted practice globally, including Carbonneau from Bordeaux (see LYRE), Intrieri and Cargnello from Italy, Kliewer from California, and Smart in Australia and New Zealand. R.E.S.

Shenandoah Valley of California is an AVA in the SIERRA FOOTHILLS. There is also a Shenandoah Valley in VIRGINIA.

sherry, seriously undervalued but slowly reawakening wine from the region around the city of Jerez de la Frontera in ANDALUCÍA, south-west Spain. 'Sherry' was used as a generic term for a wide range of FORTIFIED WINES made from white grapes, but in the mid 1990s the sherry trade successfully campaigned to have the name restricted—at least within the EU—to the produce of the Jerez DOP. (For details of other once-prominent producers of similar wine styles, see CYPRUS, SOUTH AFRICA, and BRITISH WINE.) 'Sherry' is still used as a generic for the traditional and frequently fortified wines of Andalucía, therefore including wines from MONTILLA-MORILES, MÁLAGA, CONDADO DE HUELVA, and other lesser known places; in fact, for the sake of brevity, the word 'sherry' is sometimes used in this book as a synonym for 'traditional wines of Andalucía'.

Despite renewed interest in high-quality sherry, overall production has dropped continuously for a quarter-century and was down to 400,000 hl/10.5 million gal a year by 2021. Apart from Spain, the two most important markets for sherry have been the Netherlands and Great Britain.

'Sherry' is the English corruption of the word 'Jerez', while *Xérès* is its French counterpart and is also the French name for sherry. The words 'Jerez-Xérès-Sherry' appear on all bottles of sherry, on paper seals granted by the CONSEJO REGULADOR to guarantee the origin of the wine.

There are two principal types of sherry: *fino* (or, in Sanlúcar de Barrameda, *manzanilla*), which ages biologically (i.e. under the influence of the film-forming yeast FLOR); and *oloroso*, which ages oxidatively, without the protection of flor. All sherry styles found on labels (Manzanilla, Fino, Amontillado, Oloroso, Pale Cream, Cream, etc., in generally ascending order of BODY) are derived from these two main types. Palo Cortado is a naturally resulting intermediate type between Amontillado and Oloroso. PEDRO XIMÉNEZ is an intensely sweet wine, usually for blending, made from the grape variety of the same name often grown outside the sherry region.

History

Jerez is one of the oldest wine-producing towns in Spain. It may well have been established by the PHOENICIANS who founded the nearby port of Cádiz in 1110 BCE. The Phoenicians were followed by the CARTHAGINIANS, who were in turn succeeded by the ROMANS. Iberian viticulture advanced rapidly under Roman rule, and Jerez has been identified as the Roman city of Ceritium. The local Hispano-Romans lost control around 400 CE, when southern Iberia was overrun by successive kingdoms of Vandals and Visigoths, who were in turn defeated by the Moors after the battle of Guadalete in 711 (see ISLAM). The Moors held sway over different parts of Andalucía for up to seven centuries, and their influence is still evident in the architecture in towns such as Seville, Cordoba, and Granada. Under Moorish domination, Jerez grew in size and stature. The name of the town changed from Ceret to Seris and later to Jerez de la Frontera, when it stood on the frontier of the two warring kingdoms during Christian reconquest in the 13th century.

Viticulture, which continued despite Moorish occupation, was revitalized by the Christians. Exports began and, despite periodic setbacks, trade with England and France was well established by the 1490s, when it was declared that wines shipped abroad would be free from local tax. In 1492 the Jews were expelled from Spain, their vineyards were confiscated, and foreigners, many of them English, took their place as merchants. Certain basic quality controls were established, including the capacity of the sherry cask or BUTT, which has not changed to this day.

At the end of the 15th century, after Christopher Columbus had reached America from his base in Andalucía, the sherry town of Sanlúcar de Barrameda became an important port for the new transatlantic trade, and in the 16th century large quantities of wine were shipped to the Americas from Jerez. In his book *Sherry*, Julian Jeffs speculates that Vino de Jerez (sherry) was almost certainly the first wine to enter North America.

Relations between England and Spain began to deteriorate in the 16th century; although trade continued, the colony of English merchants trading from Sanlúcar began to suffer privations. In 1585, after a number of predatory raids by Sir Francis Drake and his fleet, English merchants were arrested and their possessions seized. Exports ceased. Two years later, in a failed attack on Cádiz, Drake stole '2,900 pipes' of wine. This plunder helped to establish sherry as a popular drink in Elizabethan England.

After the death of Elizabeth I, trade became easier and 'sacke', or SACK, returned to royal circles. The English colony re-established itself and prospered, often by shipping poor-quality wines.

By the 17th century, 'sherris-sack' was well established in England and was drunk by Samuel Pepys, who in 1662 records that he mixed sherry and MÁLAGA. Pepys visited the English colony in Sanlúcar de Barrameda in 1683. At that time, until the construction of a railway in the mid 19th century, most of the sherry bodegas were located on the coast at Sanlúcar and Puerto de Santa María for easy export.

The sherry industry suffered many setbacks at the beginning of the 18th century, when England and Spain became embroiled in a series of conflicts beginning in 1702 with the War of the Spanish Succession. The METHUEN TREATY (1703) diverted trade to Portugal, and a series of restrictive measures imposed by the Gremio or Wine Growers Guild of Jerez sent merchants to Málaga in search of wine. However, the latter half of the century was an era of increasing prosperity stimulated by the arrival of a number of French and British merchants. The firms of Osborne, Duff Gordon, and Garvey date from this period.

The Peninsular Wars (1808–14) devastated Jerez. Andalucía became a battleground, occupied for a time by the French, who pillaged the sherry bodegas and forced a number of families to flee to the relative safety of the Cádiz garrison. With the defeat of the French, merchants set about rebuilding their businesses with spectacular success. Pedro Domecq took over the firm of Juan Haurie in 1822, and Manuel María González Angel, founder of GONZÁLEZ BYASS, began trading in 1835. Sherry exports rose steadily from about 8,000 butts in the early years of the century to over 70,000 butts in 1873, a figure not exceeded again until the 1950s. In the 1850s, the sherry industry was greatly helped by the construction of a RAILWAY linking Jerez and Puerto de Santa María, and a number of merchants left their quayside bodegas. Many new producers took advantage of the sherry boom only to be wiped out by PHYLLOXERA and economic depression a few years later.

By the end of the 19th century, the sherry industry was on the brink of collapse. The boom gave rise to numerous spurious 'sherries' from South Africa, Australia, and France—and from Germany, where a sherry-style potion was made from potato spirit. A spiral of price-cutting began, and sherry was stretched with poor-quality wine imported from other parts of Spain. Demand fell as Victorian society refused sherry, alarmed by scare stories that the wine was detrimental to health. The predations of phylloxera from 1894 helped to stabilize the market, and the shippers who survived the depression held large stocks of unsold wine to tide them through the lean years when all the vineyards were replanted.

In 1910 the leading traders united to form the Sherry Shippers Association, which campaigned vigorously to restore the fortunes of the beleaguered industry. After the First World War exports returned to their late 19th century levels. In 1933 a CONSEJO REGULADOR was formed to protect and control the sherry industry, and in 1935, a year before the outbreak of the Spanish Civil War, Jerez established its own DOP region. The Civil War (1936–9) had little effect on sherry exports, but trade collapsed during the Second World War.

The most dramatic episode in the recent history of sherry began in 1944 when Don Zoilo Ruiz-Mateos y Camacho, mayor of the town of Rota, bought out a small sherry stockholder whose business had suffered badly during the war. In the late 1950s, his son, the now legendary José María Ruiz-Mateos, secured a 99-year contract to supply the important BRAND owners Harveys of Bristol with all their sherry requirements. With help from the banks, he began buying up other bodegas and in 1961 established the Rumasa empire. In the 1970s, Ruiz-Mateos acquired substantial wine interests outside Jerez (see RIOJA), as well as in banking, construction, retailing, tourism, chemicals, and textiles. The group is said to have bought three banks in a single day. Although Ruiz-Mateos contributed greatly to the modernization of the Spanish wine industry, Rumasa initiated a price-cutting spiral which continued to blight the long-term interests of sherry well into the 1990s. Ruiz-Mateos's empire-building abruptly ended in 1983 when, fearing imminent collapse, the government nationalized Rumasa, which at that point controlled about one-third of the sherry industry. Rumasa's component parts were subsequently returned to the private sector.

Since the mid 1980s, the sherry industry has been facing decline. The total vineyard area is less than one-third of what it was at the end of the 1970s. Plots of sunflowers and cereals are now commonplace among the vines. In the early 1990s, with a worldwide market estimated to be around 1.09 million hl/28.7 million gal, stocks were drastically reduced as the sherry industry attempted to bring supply and demand back into balance. By 2012 a new phenomenon surfaced as the supply of grapes from the dramatically smaller vineyard area dropped for the first time below demand. Ruiz-Mateos briefly resurfaced in the early 21st century before his group again went under amid charges of assorted fiscal misdeeds. A few new names have appeared on the Jerez landscape, such as Tradición, Rey Fernando de Castilla, Dios Baco, and El Maestro Sierra. They have typically acquired older soleras from bodegas which either disappeared or were taken over by others.

Another leading actor has been the Estévez group, once led by the idiosyncratic José Estévez, the inventor of a controversial system to remove HISTAMINE from sherries. This group now includes Marqués del Real Tesoro, Tío Mateo, Hijos de Rainera Pérez Marín-La Guita, and Valdespino. Also showing signs of dynamism have been the Sanlúcar de Barrameda bodegas, from the giant Barbadillo to smaller ones such as Hidalgo-La Gitana and Pedro Romero. Equipo Navazos, formed by wine writer and criminologist Jesús Barquín and Estévez group winemaker Eduardo Ojeda, has successfully contributed to the rebirth of interest in sherry worldwide by acquiring exceptional old butts from various bodegas and releasing small bottlings under the brand 'La Bota de . . .'.

Amid calls to rejuvenate the concept of sherry, including the promotion of a larger number of vintage-dated wines (a concept adopted by González Byass for some top-end Olorosos, Amontillados, and Palos Cortados), the Consejo Regulador responded in 2000 by creating two new categories of high-quality sherry: VOS (Very Old Sherry or *Vinum Optimum Signatum*), for wines with an average age surpassing 20 years; and VORS (Very Old and Rare Sherry or *Vinum Optimum Rare Signatum*), for wines over 30; with four subcategories of both, Oloroso, Palo Cortado, Amontillado and Pedro Ximénez. Such methods as carbon dating were introduced to ascertain the age of the wines submitted by bodegas, and demanding blind tastings were instituted to accept or reject samples. This elite category has stirred up fresh interest in sherry, but it is a minor presence on the market as most of the brands release just a few hundred bottles of their prized elixirs every year.

There is also increasing interest in the EN RAMA sherries that are perceived as more authentic and less manipulated than the regular versions.

The most important development, however, may be the return of non-fortified wines produced under flor, as they would have been 200 years ago, a movement pioneered by Equipo Navazos with their wines Navazos Niepoort (since vintage 2008) and Florpower (since vintage 2010). These delicate, lower-alcohol wines are classified either as generic table wine (VINO) or under the IGP Vino de la Tierra de Cádiz (as are the many compelling red wines from the variety TINTILLA DE ROTA). The success of these non-fortified white wines has inspired the Ministry of Agriculture to drop the fortification requirement for sherry, a change that was awaiting approval by the European Commission in 2023.

See also SPAIN, history, and SACK.

Geography and climate

The climate of the Jerez region is strongly influenced by its proximity to the Atlantic. Sea breezes from the gulf of Cádiz alleviate extremes. The oceanic influence is strongest in the coastal towns of Sanlúcar de Barrameda and Puerto de Santa María, where temperatures in July and August may be 10 °C/18 °F lower than in Jerez, 20 km/12 miles inland. Winters are mild and damp with most of the region's annual average rainfall of 650 mm/25 in falling between late autumn and spring. Summer temperatures often reach 30 °C inland, occasionally rising to 40 °C with the levante, a dry, dusty WIND from the south-east.

The vines are sustained during the dry summer months by the porous, white ALBARIZA soils that are at the heart of the Jerez DOP. The roughly triangular demarcated region extends from the town of Chiclana de Frontera in the south-east to the river Guadalquivir in the north-west, tapering inland. However, the best albariza soils cover a stretch of rolling country north of the river Guadalete between Jerez and Sanlúcar de Barrameda. These outcrops of albariza are known collectively as Jerez Superior, and most of these vineyards are within the municipality of Jerez de la Frontera, with secondary pockets around Sanlúcar de Barrameda, Trebujena, Puerto de Santa María, Chiclana, Chipiona, and Rota.

The albariza zone is divided into subdistricts. Those with the deepest, but not necessarily the most CALCAREOUS, albariza soils—like the famous Balbaina, Macharnudo, Carrascal, and Añina districts—produce the most delicate wines for the finest Finos and Manzanillas (see Winemaking below). The most calcareous soils, known as *tajón*, are generally unsatisfactory for viticulture because of potential CHLOROSIS. The finest albarizas include a proportion of SAND and CLAY and tend to vary with depth, with a LIMESTONE content of 25% or more on the surface rising to 60% in the rooting zone 80–100 cm/31–39 in below the surface. In between the hills of albariza, *barro* soils have more clay and would produce fuller, coarser wines and slightly higher yields if they were planted. On the sandy soils known as *arenas*, yields are twice as great as on the albariza, but the quality of the wine is poor. Arena soils were popular with growers at the end of the 19th century as PHYLLOXERA could not survive in it. They are still popular for Moscatel (Muscat of Alexandria). However, viticulture is increasingly concentrated on the albariza soils, and over 80% of the region's vineyards are situated in Jerez Superior.

Viticulture and vine varieties

In the 19th century, many vine varieties were planted around Jerez but, after phylloxera wiped out most of the vineyards in the 1890s, many varieties were never replanted. Only three varieties have been authorized for new vineyards in Jerez: PALOMINO, PEDRO XIMÉNEZ, and MUSCAT OF ALEXANDRIA. Of these, Palomino is the most important and accounts for around 95% of the total vineyard area. There are in fact two types of Palomino: Palomino Basto (also known as the Palomino de Jerez) and Palomino Fino. Palomino Basto has largely been supplanted by Palomino Fino, which provides better YIELDS and is more resistant to disease. Palomino Fino has proved to be a particularly versatile grape and is used for most types of sherry.

Moscatel Gordo Blanco (Muscat of Alexandria) represents about 3% of the Jerez vineyard and is planted principally in the sandy soils on the coast around Chipiona. It is mainly used for sweetening although some producers make VARIETAL Moscatel wines, including one of near-mythical proportions, Valdespino's Toneles.

Pedro Ximénez (known for short as PX) has given ground to Palomino and currently represents less than 100 ha/250 acres of vineyard since Palomino Fino is easier to cultivate. Most sweet wine is now made from Palomino although some smaller producers still maintain small PX SOLERAS which they bottle as a VARIETAL wine.

In late 2022 some of the traditional varieties that almost disappeared after phylloxera, namely Beba, PERRUNO, and Vejeriega, were also authorized. Their presence in the region's vineyards is minimal today, hence we should not expect an explosion of the volume of wine made with these grapes in the foreseeable future.

Since phylloxera swept through Jerez, all vines have been grafted on to American ROOTSTOCKS which are selected according to the soil's LIME content. In the past vines were planted in a hexagonal pattern known as *tresbolillo*, but, with increasing MECHANIZATION, vineyards are planted in orderly rows at a maximum VINE DENSITY of 4,100 vines per ha (1,660 per acre). Yields from the Palomino are high, although the maximum permitted yield for the entire DOP has been set at 80 hl/ha (4.5 tons/acre).

With the onset of mechanization, modern vineyards are trained on WIRES, while the traditional PRUNING method, called *vara y pulgar* and similar to the GUYOT system, is being abandoned. A *vara* (meaning 'stick' or 'branch') with seven or eight BUDS produces the current year's crop. The *pulgar* (meaning 'thumb') is a short SHOOT with one bud which will produce the following year's *vara*.

Winemaking

The HARVEST begins when the Palomino has reached a MUST WEIGHT of at least 11 °BAUMÉ. It was traditionally on 8 September, but in recent decades it tends to start close to mid-August in the inland vineyards. It lasts for about a month.

Grapes are loaded into plastic crates and transported to large, automated wineries, where they are destalked and pressed. Most bodegas use horizontal plate or pneumatic PRESSES to control the EXTRACTION rate, which may not legally exceed 72.5 l/19 gal of juice from 100 kg/220 lb of grapes (16% higher than the extraction rate permitted for CHAMPAGNE, for instance). Others, especially the CO-OPERATIVES, use continuous de-juicers which tend to produce coarser wines with more solids and PHENOLICS. Today acid levels are adjusted with the addition of TARTARIC ACID prior to fermentation, and cold STABILIZATION before bottling is usually essential.

After SETTLING or CENTRIFUGATION, fermentation generally takes place in temperature-controlled, stainless-steel tanks, although a few shippers continue to ferment a small proportion of their wine in butts, mainly to impregnate and season new casks of American oak that are to be used for maturation. (New BARRELS are not valued in Jerez.)

The modernization of the sherry industry which began in the 1960s has removed much of the mysticism that once surrounded the production of sherry. The modern winemaker can predetermine which of the two initial sherry types—*fino* and *oloroso*—each lot of grapes becomes.

The first selection takes place in the vineyard. Wines for the best *finos* are sourced from older vines growing on the best albariza soils, while *olorosos* are made from grapes grown on the heavier clays. Elegance is crucial to *finos*, also made from the best FREE-RUN juice, which has fewer impurities than the slightly coarser and more astringent juices from the press; those are set aside for *olorosos* or inferior *rayas*, particularly coarse *olorosos*. Wine destined for *fino* tends to be fermented at a lower temperature than that made for *oloroso*.

The second selection takes place soon after the end of fermentation. Palomino-based wine has a natural alcohol content of 11–12%. Depending on the style of the wine, sherry may be fortified with grape spirit to 15–17.5% alcohol. The appearance of FLOR, the veil of yeast that forms on the surface of the wine and distinguishes *fino* from other styles of sherry, is determined by the degree of alcohol: growth is inhibited by an ALCOHOLIC STRENGTH much above 16%. Wines destined to develop into *finos* are therefore fortified to 15–15.5%. *Olorosos*, which mature without flor, are fortified to a higher strength.

The sherry bodegas are teeming with the flor YEAST strains. This beneficial FILM-FORMING YEAST grows naturally on the surface of the wine, although some houses now choose to cultivate their own flor culture. Butts used for *fino* are filled only to around five-sixths of their 600-l/160-gal capacity because flor, which both protects the wine from OXIDATION and changes its character, feeds off OXYGEN as well as alcohol, glycerine, and ACETIC ACID.

Flor is also extremely sensitive to heat, and in the warm and dry summer months it tends to die. In Montilla, for example, flor is reduced to a scum-like film in July and August, while it tends to grow more thickly and evenly in the cooler, more humid coastal towns of Sanlúcar de Barrameda and Puerto de Santa María (although this can depend on the architecture, orientation, and management of each building). This accounts for some of the subtle differences in style between *finos* from Jerez and El Puerto and from Manzanilla outlined below.

Left to its own devices, flor would feed on the nutrients in the wine and die before having a profound influence on the wine's character. However, flor is kept alive in casks of *fino* for six years or more by continually topping up the butt with younger wine, which replenishes the yeast nutrients. This is the basis of the SOLERA system, a method of fractional blending which, apart from nurturing flor in *fino*, also maintains a predictable style.

A sherry solera comprises several groups of butts, each of which is known as a criadera. Wine is typically withdrawn from the group containing the oldest wine, which is itself called the solera. This is replenished from the butts that form the first criadera, which is in turn replenished by wine from the second criadera, a process known as 'running the scales'. Simple soleras are fed by three or four criaderas, while more complex systems run to as many as 14. The whole system is fed with new wine from the most recent harvest. Up to 33% of the wine in a solera may be withdrawn in any one year. *Fino* soleras need to be refreshed the most frequently, and by running the scales at regular intervals (usually two or three times a year) flor may be kept alive for eight to ten years, more if the task is carefully done.

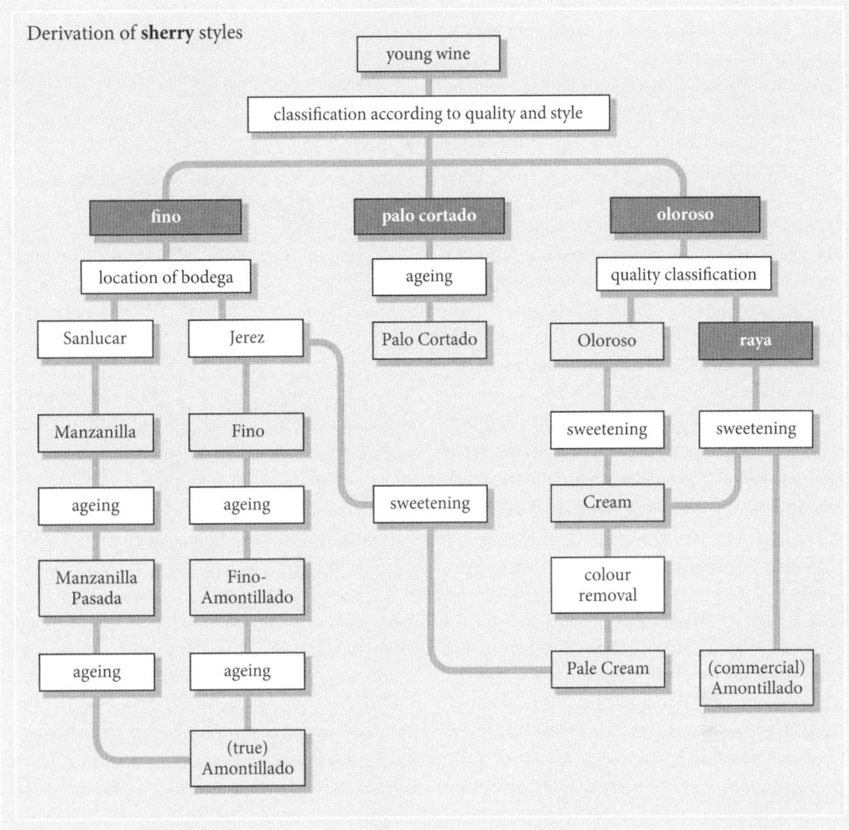

Styles of sherry

The diagram on this page shows how commercial styles of sherry are derived.

The lightest, driest styles are *fino* sherries. These wines are aged under a protective layer of flor and filtered before bottling at a minimum of 15% alcohol. A Manzanilla sherry is a *fino* style aged in SANLÚCAR DE BARRAMEDA, where the flor layer grows thicker; it tends to be lighter, higher in acidity, and lower in alcohol than a *fino*.

Finos which lose their covering of flor become *amontillados*, turning amber in colour and changing in character due to greater contact with the air. *Amontillados* evolve naturally if the flor has exhausted its supply of nutrients, or the style may be induced if the flor is killed off by fortification to 17% alcohol or more. A *fino* beginning to take on the characteristic of an *amontillado* used to be able to be labelled as a *fino amontillado*, but no longer; however, a *fino* from Sanlúcar de Barrameda can be labelled as Manzanilla Pasada. True *amontillados* are completely dry and the finest examples age for many years in their own soleras. (see AMONTILLADO).

Olorosos, on the other hand, are fortified to 18–22% alcohol, inhibiting the development of flor. They age in greater contact with the air, turning brown and gaining in concentration with age. The alcoholic content increases with slow EVAPORATION such that the strength of an old *oloroso* may approach 24%. *Olorosos* are dry, although old wines may taste full and concentrated. *Rayas* (inferior *olorosos* used in blending) may be aged in the open air. Sweet styles may no longer be labelled as OLOROSO; instead they are typically called Cream.

A Palo Cortado is a wine that was chosen to become a *fino* but never developed a full covering of flor and so aged in an oxidative, oloroso way, the final result falling somewhere between the two in delicacy and flavour.

Sweet sherries, most of them styled Cream or Medium, can be made in several ways. Today Palomino grapes are frequently dried to raisins under plastic tunnels, pressed, and fortified before fermentation to make a MISTELA. This is never as sweet or as powerfully concentrated as PX, but the method is widely used for more commercial sherries. Some commercial Cream sherries may be very ordinary blends to which sweetening and colouring wines have been added.

The darkest sherries may be adjusted with ARROPE or *vino de color*, a dark, sweet syrup that has been prepared by boiling down fresh grape must. Pale Cream sherry, typically a blend of *fino* and sweet wine, is normally adjusted with GRAPE CONCENTRATE and fresh, vacuum-concentrated Palomino must. A few bodegas sweeten their wines with fortified Moscatel, but this tends to produce a rather obvious, aromatic, grapey style of sherry.

In the early 2000s, two designations were introduced for particularly old sherries: VOS, Very Old Sherry or *Vinum Optimum Signatum*, for blends at least 20 years old; and VORS, *Vinum Optimum Rare Signatum* or Very Old and Rare Sherry, for blends at least 30 years old. Wines may also be labelled 12, 15, 20, and 30 Years Old.

Organization of the trade

Most properties are small, averaging little over a hectare. Growers typically sell their grapes either directly to a shipper or to one of seven CO-OPERATIVES. Some co-ops maintain their own soleras, but most sell the wine to one of the sherry bodegas.

There is a distinction between types of bodegas that has lost relevance in the last decade: *Bodegas de Crianza y Almacenado* are firms which mature and keep stocks of wine or ALMACENISTAS. They may sell young or aged wines in bulk to the *Bodegas de Crianza y Expedición*, firms which both mature and sell wine for consumption. The Bodegas de Expedición used to be required by law to maintain a significantly higher stock of wine than that of the almacenistas, but that changed in 2013 (now they each have to meet a minimum of 250 hl/6,600 gal., i.e. 50 sherry casks), so it is now a matter of choice by each producer.

Another major change is underway: the disappearance of the historical distinction between *zona de producción* (the entire territory of the DOP) and the *zona de crianza* (the three main towns that form the Sherry triangle). Historically, only wines matured within the towns of JEREZ DE LA FRONTERA, SANLÚCAR DE BARRAMEDA, and PUERTO DE SANTA MARÍA were permitted to use the term 'sherry'. A new regulation published in October 2022 permits the use of the term 'sherry' for wines aged and bottled in any of nine towns in the Sherry DOP.

See also individual articles on sherry shippers CROFT and GONZÁLEZ BYASS; and see specific styles of sherry: FINO, MANZANILLA, AMONTILLADO, OLOROSO, CREAM, PALO CORTADO, and PEDRO XIMÉNEZ.

V. de la S. & J.B.

Gonzalez Gordon, M., *Sherry: The Noble Wine* (1990).

Jeffs, J., *Sherry* (5th edn, 2004).

Liem, P., and Barquín, J., *Sherry, Manzanilla & Montilla: A Guide to the Traditional Wines of Andalucía* (2012).

www.sherry.org

shipping. See TRANSPORT OF WINE.

Shiraz, the Australian name for the SYRAH grape, widely used elsewhere, and therefore a name better known by many consumers than its Rhône original. Because Australian Shiraz was so successful in European markets, the word 'Shiraz' has been used on wine labels for Syrah grown all over the world, notably SOUTH AFRICA, although the word 'Syrah' is also used there to denote a lighter, fresher northern RHÔNE style of wine rather than a typically concentrated, FRUIT-DRIVEN, potent Australian-style Shiraz. The variety was probably taken to Australia, possibly from Montpellier, in 1832 by James BUSBY. It flourished so obviously that it was rapidly adopted by New South Wales and spread from there. From that time onwards, Shiraz (variously called Scyras, Syrah, or Hermitage) was the dominant red variety in Australia and still is, with a total vineyard area of 43,192 ha/106,730 acres in 2022. When the concurrent red-wine and export booms began in the second half of the 1980s, plantings in all regions, very cool to very warm, increased substantially. The result has been a range of styles from elegant, cool-grown Rhône styles (often with a dash of Viognier—see CO-FERMENTATION) through half a dozen important and regionally distinctive richer, riper styles, some traditional (Barossa Valley), some newer (Heathcote). Blends of Shiraz and Cabernet have been an Australian speciality for decades. For more detail, see AUSTRALIA.

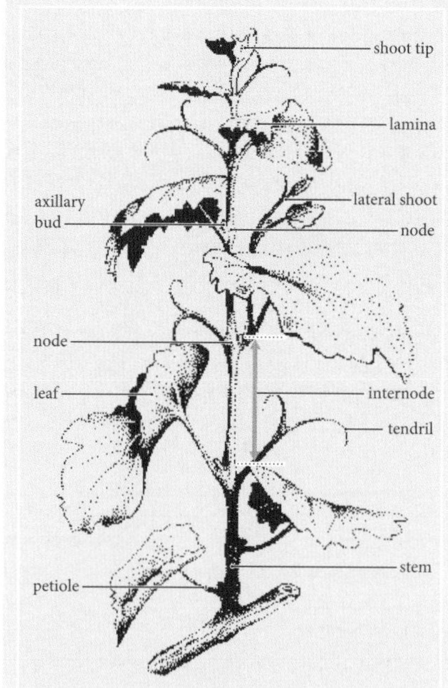

Shoot system: each spring buds burst and produce shoots as shown, which shoots in turn develop (axillary) buds at each node or leaf position along the shoot. If these buds are retained at winter pruning and burst in spring then a new sequence of shoot growth begins. *Source:* J. Long, *Vignes et Vignobles*

The grape variety shares a name, but little else, with the medieval capital of PERSIA, although the (white) wine of Shiraz has been enthusiastically documented.

Shiroka Melnishka Loza. See MELNIK.

Shoalhaven Coast, warm, humid region on the NEW SOUTH WALES coast south of Sydney producing noteworthy SÉMILLON and CHAMBOURCIN, favoured for its MILDEW resistance.

shoestring root rot, vine disease. See ARMILLARIA ROOT ROT.

shoot, new growth in a vine plant that develops from a bud and consists of a stem with leaves and tendrils or INFLORESCENCES; these last become bunches of grapes. Collectively, the shoots and leaves of a vine form its CANOPY. The BUDS of a grapevine burst in spring to begin a new shoot (see BUDBREAK). Shoot growth gradually accelerates to a maximum rate before FLOWERING, then may slow to a stop at about VERAISON, common in unirrigated vineyards in a MEDITERRANEAN CLIMATE. When vines are well-supplied with water, shoots can continue to grow after veraison, which compromises fruit RIPENING; see WATER STRESS.

VIGOUR, which effectively means shoot growth rate, varies hugely between and within vines. A vigorous shoot is evident by its long INTERNODES, large leaves, strong LATERAL SHOOTS, and long tip tendrils well before flowering; weak shoots are the opposite. Despite these differences in growth rate and length at full bloom, shoots, whether weak or vigorous, have 17–20 visible internodes. Later in summer the stem of the shoot changes from green to brown (lignifies) and thus becomes a CANE (see CANE RIPENING).

See also SHOOT TIP and WATER SHOOT.

B.G.C. & R.E.S.

shoot-positioned, general term used to describe some vine-TRAINING SYSTEMS created using a TRELLIS SYSTEM and SHOOT POSITIONING.

shoot positioning, spring and summertime viticultural practice of placing vine SHOOTS in the desired position on a TRELLIS to assist in TRIMMING, LEAF REMOVAL, and HARVEST operations and to facilitate the control of VINE DISEASES and VINE PESTS.

The practice is by no means universal but is more common in wet and humid climates with moderate to high vineyard VIGOUR and a high risk of FUNGAL DISEASES, for example in Germany, Alsace, and New Zealand. Some important examples of non-shoot-positioned CANOPIES are found in drier climates, such as the GOBELET-trained vines of the Mediterranean and also the 'drooping' canopies of vigorous vines in California and Australia.

Typically the shoots are positioned upwards and are held between two pairs of foliage or catch wires, and sometimes the foliage wires themselves are moved to catch the shoots. Generally the operation is carried out manually, but a VINE FOLIAGE LIFTER may also be used. Shoots are then trimmed to resemble a neat hedge so that the shoots do not fall down the sides and cause SHADE. This then facilitates other vineyard operations such as SPRAYING and general cultivation, enabling mechanical operations such as leaf removal. For some training systems, such as GENEVA DOUBLE CURTAIN, shoots are positioned downwards, or upwards and downwards, as in the SCOTT HENRY and SMART-DYSON systems.

R.E.S.

Smart, R. E., and Robinson, M., *Sunlight into Wine: A Handbook for Winegrape Canopy Management* (1991).

shoot thinning, vineyard operation normally carried out by hand in the early spring which consists of breaking off unwanted shoots arising from the vine's HEAD or CORDON. Sometimes these shoots have no bunches and are called WATER SHOOTS. The shoot-thinning operation can be done most quickly when the shoots are 20–40 cm/8–15 in long and the bunches are quite visible, which allows discrimination between fruitful and non-fruitful shoots. The aim of shoot thinning is to reduce the density of the CANOPY and to avoid leaf congestion later in the season. This can help improve wine quality (see CANOPY MANAGEMENT) but is common only in regions with plentiful and relatively inexpensive LABOUR. Shoot thinning by machine is possible but not common. See also DESUCKERING. R.E.S.

shoot tip, the 1 cm/0.4 in of shoot furthest from the vine's original bud, also known as the shoot apex. This small piece of tissue competes very effectively with the grapes for food produced by the mature leaves, and so a vigorously growing vine may slow fruit RIPENING. These nutrients may be temporarily diverted to the grapes by TIPPING the shoots but only until the LATERAL SHOOTS regrow.

The balance between shoot growth and fruit growth has important effects on grape RIPENING and wine quality (see BALANCE, LEAF TO FRUIT RATIO, and VINE PHYSIOLOGY). **Shoot-tip growth** is being increasingly used to monitor vine growth as a guide to vine management. For example, IRRIGATION should be regulated so that shoot growth stops by the time of VERAISON, and Californian, Australian, and French studies have related shoot-tip appearance to measurements of vine WATER STRESS. Also, a vine which is in balance and has been pruned appropriately will not have excessive numbers of shoot tips from the main and lateral shoots. B.G.C. & R.E.S.

short, tasting term for a wine whose impact on the PALATE is not persistent; the opposite of LONG.

shot berry, small, immature, usually seedless berry resulting from insufficient pollination. See MILLERANDAGE.

shows, wine. Now a universal phenomenon, wine shows have occupied a particularly important place in Australia's wine culture, taking place in each AUSTRALIAN state's capital (originally offshoots of general agricultural shows), with some uniquely Australian features. Each class, established by variety and vintage(s), is judged by a panel of three judges, one being panel chair, and three associate judges. To be invited to act as a judge or even an associate judge is regarded as an honour. Judges usually wear white coats, work in silence, and may be expected to evaluate as many as 200 wines a day. If one or more of the judges has given gold-medal points to a wine, it will automatically be retasted and discussed, and the show chair may well be called in. The more experienced judges officiate at up to ten regional and capital city shows a year, know each other well, and have mutual respect for each other. While the discussion—in best Australian fashion—may be robust, it seldom, if ever, becomes ill-tempered. The most important part of the discussion usually turns on style issues.

The trophies and medals awarded to the more successful exhibitors are used extensively in marketing and promotion, being accepted as reliable indicators of quality by retailers and consumers alike. But the greater long-term benefit has been for the winemaker judges, drawn from the leading wineries and schooled by chairs in the tradition of Len EVANS. J.H.

See also JUDGING WINE and COMPETITIONS, WINE.

shutdown, vine. Some growers use this imprecise term for a cessation of the ripening process caused by WATER STRESS and/or temperatures over 35 °C/86 °F, which cause STOMATA to close and PHOTOSYNTHESIS and TRANSPIRATION to stop.

Sicily (known as **Sicilia** in Italian), large and viticulturally important island off the toe of ITALY (see map under ITALY).

Ancient history

Sicily was famed throughout classical antiquity for its agricultural produce, not least its wines. The recent find of a Copper Age (*c.* 3000 BCE) pot with traces of tartaric residue may take the production of wine in Sicily back to prehistory. However, the settlement of colonies of Greeks around the island in the 8th century BCE was an undoubted spur to the growth of viticulture. The local production of western Greek wine AMPHORAE from the 6th century on confirms this development. Flourishing vineyards are testified for the 5th century at the later Greek settlement Akragas (Agrigento). Sicily may have played a key role in the development of viticulture on the Italian peninsula (see ITALY, ancient history). Vines from Morgantina and Tauromenium were transplanted to POMPEII around Vesuvius, the Colli ALBANI, and southern Etruria, where they were well established by the 2nd century BCE (Pliny, *Natural History* 14. 25, 35, and 38). The most notable characteristic of Sicilian wines was their sweetness. The most famous were Mamertine, a sweet, light wine from the north-east of the island around Messina, and a very similar wine from Tauromenium (Taormina); but there is evidence for wine production right down the east coast. Inland there was the Murgentina vine from Morgantina (Serra Orlando). Inscriptions on amphorae testify to a so-called 'Mesopotamian' wine from the south coast near Gela. Sicilian wines were certainly exported (references to Tauromenian, for example, appear on amphorae). J.J.P.

Wilson, R. J. A., *Sicilia under the Roman Empire* (1990).

Medieval history

Throughout the Middle Ages, Sicily's main export product was grain. It also produced olives, citrus fruits, and wine, but wheat has the advantage of being far less capital intensive: whereas olive trees, citrus fruit trees, and vines take years to come into full bearing, wheat can be harvested months after it has been sown. Medieval Sicily owed its wealth to grain.

Under the Normans, who governed Sicily from 1130 to 1194, smallholders owned most of the land, and they made their living mainly by growing wheat or, in the mountainous parts of the island, keeping livestock. They grew vines as well, but the wine made was usually for domestic consumption. In the 14th century, demand for high-quality wine rose, and vineyards spread through Sicily. Many of these vineyards, which produced wine for well-to-do Sicilians or for export, were owned by members of the feudal aristocracy or the local nobility. The principal winemaking towns were strung along the north-eastern and eastern coasts: Cefalù, Patti, Aci, Catania, Augusta, and Syracuse. These not only produced large surpluses of wine but were also able to ship their wine safely to Messina, from where it was taken to Africa and the Levant. From Patti, wine was carried to Constantinople, and Syracuse traded with nearby MALTA. Messina also imported wines from CALABRIA, which it then shipped to northern Italy; Messina and Palermo also carried Sicilian wines to the towns of northern Italy.

Palermo was Sicily's largest and most important city. In the early 14th century, it had 100,000 inhabitants, as did NAPLES; in the whole of Europe only VENICE and Milan, with populations of 200,000, were larger. Because of its size, Palermo and its surrounding countryside could never make enough wine for the city's needs, and so it imported wine from Naples and Calabria, which was cheaper than transporting wine overland from eastern Sicily. This provoked the wrath of the citizens of Catania. Palermo exported wine as well.

From the late 14th century onwards, more and more vineyards around Palermo, Messina, and Catania came to be owned by members of the upper classes; so, after 1400, did taverns. In the 15th century, most of the wine continued to be made in areas near ports: Aci, Catania, Messina, Taormina, and, in the west, Trapani. But further inland, Noto and Randazzo were also important. By far the biggest exporter was Messina, but Francavilla, Patti, Trapani, and Palermo handled a lot of the foreign trade in wine, too.

The wines that Sicily exported were mostly strong, sweet wines capable of surviving the sea voyage, such as VERNACCIA and Muscatello. Other names of wines mentioned in documents are Mantonico (also called Mantonicato), which could be red or white; a white wine named Cuctumini; and finally Mamertino, which shares its name with the classical Mamertinum, which PLINY tells us was grown in Messina (*Natural History* 14. 66). H.M.W.

Epstein, S. R., *An Island for Itself: Economic Development and Social Change in Medieval Sicily* (1992).
Matthew, D., *The Norman Kingdom of Sicily* (1992).

Modern wines and other vine products

While Sicily had been Italy's second most important wine region after the Veneto in 2013, it was in fifth place by 2020, its total vineyard area having fallen to 98,355 ha/243,040 acres (down from 114,290 ha in 2011). Of the 3.6 million hl of wine it produced in 2020, two-thirds were DOC and IGT wines, a clear sign Sicily has firmly set course on quality rather than quantity.

The earlier concentration on quantity over quality, systematically encouraged between 1960 and 1987 by the regional government's subsidies for the transformation of traditional BUSH VINES into more productive WIRE-trained or TENDONE systems, led to a chronic cycle of overproduction, with the EU's compulsory DISTILLATION regime encouraging CO-OPERATIVES to produce wine they knew would be distilled and GRAPE CONCENTRATE used for ENRICHMENT.

Sicily's BULK WINE production has steadily declined since, but it is still used, legally or not, to beef up weaker wines and vintages throughout Italy as well as in France and Germany. Nevertheless, Sicily produces much more white than red wine, notably from the island's 30,227 ha/74,693 acres of white wine grape CATARRATTO; the second most planted variety is the red NERO D'AVOLA, with 14,749 ha/36,446 acres. While Sicily was quick to adapt to demand for INTERNATIONAL VARIETIES such as Syrah, Chardonnay, and Merlot, they play an increasingly shrinking role in the vineyards, while PINOT GRIGIO has increased to 2,749 ha/6,793 acres, up from 1,197 ha in 2010.

In terms of climate and geology Sicily is often, rightfully, considered a continent itself. Its diverse MESOCLIMATES range from distinctly alpine on Mount Etna, where vineyards rise up to 1,000 m/3,280 ft in ELEVATION, to the subtropical on the island of PANTELLERIA, which is closer to Tunisia than it is to the province of Trapani to which it administratively belongs. The island's centre can be hot and dry, although at higher elevations there can be favourable DIURNAL TEMPERATURE RANGE, while many regions are close enough to the coast to benefit from such constant WINDS that FUNGAL DISEASES are a rarity except in the wettest of years.

The drive for quality began at the end of the 1980s when producers such as Planeta and Tasca d'Almerita began producing smartly packaged international varietals that seemed to copy wines from the New World. This drew the attention of large producers from Italy's north, who, attracted by low land PRICES and the virtual absence of a stringent DOC system, created large, fully mechanized estates, typically in the island's centre, which had traditionally been devoted to grain. While capitalizing on the Sicily brand name and image, these wines, unsubjected to practically any quality control and often bottled in Italy's north, did nothing to elevate Sicily's reputation. To curb these unregulated practices, several of Sicily's key producers put their weight behind the creation of a DOC covering the entire island in 2011. YIELD controls and the instigation of mandatory laboratory ANALYSIS and a subsequent panel tasting have had a direct effect on quality. In another effort to eliminate low-quality wines while protecting two of Sicily's most important INDIGENOUS VARIETIES, the white GRILLO and the red NERO D'AVOLA may no longer be mentioned on labels for non-DOC wines.

Several ancient wine regions have been rescued from the brink of extinction. From the island's eastern tip near Messina to Catania and the slopes of Etna, the distinct red NERELLO MASCALESE, in tandem with NERELLO CAPPUCCIO and Nocera, dominate the vineyards. Etna especially has seen an enormous rise in popularity resulting in huge investments and an influx of newcomers. (See ETNA for more detail.) The Faro DOC had been largely abandoned until the 1990s when the Palari estate began producing fine reds from its steep terraces. Between Messina and Milazzo, the DOC Mamertino, a wine region already appreciated by the Romans, declined quickly after the introduction of international varieties and a controversial mandatory addition of Nero d'Avola to the elegant, local, crisp Nocera, but Planeta's investment in the region has triggered a renaissance.

CERASUOLO DI VITTORIA, situated near the town of the same name near Ragusa on the southeastern coast, is Sicily's only DOCG so far. Several producers, notably COS, which ferments some of its wine in AMPHORAE, and Arianna Occhipinti, who espouses BIODYNAMICS, are producing high-quality examples of the classic Nero d'Avola–FRAPPATO blend, while in the southeast the Eloro DOC with the subzone Pachino is Nero d'Avola's place of birth. The success of this accommodating variety is such that it has been planted in every corner of the island, regularly at the cost of other local varieties. The wines used to be made in a commercial straitjacket of rich concentration and oak, completely disguising their origin, but recent examples are fresher and more elegant. Producers Tasca d'Almerita and Centopassi are also beginning to coax out the potential of PERRICONE, an ancient red variety which is as tannic and as fickle to handle as NEBBIOLO.

Sicily's ancient sweet wine traditions can be found on the island of Lipari, where LATE HARVEST or DRIED-GRAPE examples of MALVASIA are turned into Malvasia delle Lipari, while Passito di PANTELLERIA is the greatest expression of ZIBIBBO, or Muscat of Alexandria. Many ALBERELLO vineyards can be found in Sicily's extreme west between Erice and Trapani, but their future seems uncertain now that so many have been GRUBBED UP thanks to EU subsidies. Meanwhile MARSALA, once western Sicily's raison d'être and one of the world's famous FORTIFIED WINES, has long languished on the margins but now is experiencing renewed interest triggered by a handful of stalwarts and a new, energetic generation. W.S.

Belfrage, N., *From Brunello to Zibibbo: The Wines of Southern Italy* (2nd, edn, 2003).
Camuto, R., and Palmento. A., *Sicilian Wine Odyssey* (2010).
Nesto, B., and Di Savino, F., *The World of Sicilian Wine* (2013).
www.consorziodocsicilia.it

Sideritis, Greek pink-skinned vine variety found to a limited extent near Patras in the northern Peloponnese. Originally grown mainly for TABLE GRAPES, it can also make steely, peppery whites.

Sideways, a 2004 film by Alexander Payne of the eponymous book by Rex Pickett about a wine enthusiast's adventures in the CENTRAL COAST. One of its themes was the superiority of Pinot Noir over the then-popular Merlot. It had an immediate effect on demand for varietal Pinot Noir, particularly in the US—to such an extent that it resulted in a global shortage of BULK Pinot. One Languedoc supplier managed to sell GALLO vast quantities of a Grenache blend masquerading as varietal Pinot Noir until being found guilty of ADULTERATION AND FRAUD. An earlier edition of this book figured prominently in the book but not the film. See also FILMS ABOUT WINE.

Siegerrebe, modern GERMAN CROSS grown principally, like certain giant vegetables, by exhibitionists, *Sieger* meaning 'champion'. In Germany it can break, indeed has broken, records for its ripeness levels, but the flabby white wine it produces is so rich and oppressively musky that it is usually a chore to drink. It was bred from SAVAGNIN ROSE and MADELEINE ANGEVINE and has been known to reach *double* the Oechsle reading required for a TROCKENBEERENAUSLESE. Total German plantings had blessedly dwindled by 2020 to 60 ha/148 acres in the Pfalz and Rheinhessen. The variety has also been used to bolster some blends in England, Switzerland, Washington State, and British Columbia.

Sierra de Gredos, mountain range 80 km/50 miles west of Madrid in SPAIN in which are parts of three DOPS in three political regions: Vinos de MADRID, MÉNTRIDA in Castilla-La Mancha, and CEBREROS in Castilla y León. They form a specific viticultural area which one day may have its own appellation. Small vineyards in the mountains are planted with old GARNACHA and

ALBILLO Real vines with some Garnacha Blanca on GRANITE and SLATE soils. A group of young growers began revitalizing the region in the early years of this century. V. de la S. & F.C.

Sierra de Salamanca, VINO DE CALIDAD in the south of Salamanca province in western SPAIN. The Sierra de Francia mountain range has some 300 ha/750 acres of vineyards on acid, GRANITE soils differing from the usual LIMESTONE of Spain's high plateaus. Ten wineries led by the ambitious Viñedos del Cámbrico and La Zorra vinify the mainly TEMPRANILLO and local RUFETE grapes. In 2020 Rufete Serrano Blanco (a variety distinct from Rufete) was authorized as an accepted variety, with promising results. V. de la S. & F.C.

Sierra Foothills, wine region in GOLD RUSH country in CALIFORNIA and an AVA covering the foothills on the western edge of the Sierra Nevada, the snowy mountains which separate California from the rest of the US. Thousands flocked here after 1849 and, miners being notoriously thirsty, the region's vineyards go back almost that far. The Sierra Foothills AVA encompasses the vineyards in El Dorado, Amador, and Calaveras counties while taking in a few others in the flanking Nevada and Mariposa counties. California Shenandoah Valley and Fiddletown are AVAs within Amador County; El Dorado AVA and the sub-AVA Fair Play take in the vineyards in that county. North Yuba AVA is in Yuba County.

El Dorado County and Fair Play AVA

In 1870 El Dorado was California's third most productive region, with 2,000 acres under vine. Despite dwindling to nearly none during PROHIBITION and staying that way until the late 1960s, the county again hosts around 809 ha/2,000 acres of vines and nearly 50 wineries. El Dorado's vineyards are much higher than those of Amador, starting close to 1,500 ft and ranging up above 1,160 m/3,600 ft on wooded hillsides over GRANITIC or VOLCANIC soils. Predictably, conditions are cooler, and the choice of varieties leans towards Cabernet Sauvignon, Merlot, Chardonnay, and Riesling, with Syrah, Petite Sirah, and Zinfandel. El Dorado was one of the few places growing the desired varieties when RHÔNE RANGERS such as Steve Edmunds of Edmunds St. John winery went looking for grapes in the 1980s. His wines prove the possibilities of Syrah in the county's higher ELEVATIONS; Grenache also can be superb.

The subdistrict Fair Play AVA is south of the El Dorado vineyards, which cluster around Placerville (known as Hangtown during the Gold Rush), about halfway to Amador County, but not along the aptly named main road, Highway 49. Thus Fair Play is mildly isolated, but its gaggle of small wineries has a justly deserved reputation for good times and for good-value wines.

Amador County

The heart of the county's wine production is its two AVAs, Fiddletown and California Shenandoah Valley (see below), where pre-PROHIBITION Zinfandel vines thrive and old-school BARBERA has found new life. Modernity also exists here, in Ann Kraemer's Shake Ridge Ranch, near the hamlet of Sutter Creek. Kraemer, an established Napa Valley viticulturist, has applied Napa vineyard expertise to Zinfandel, Syrah, Barbera, Tempranillo, and other varieties now highly sought after by producers looking for authenticity over commercial appeal. Typical ELEVATIONS are 240–360 m/800–1,200 ft.

Fiddletown AVA

Amador County's Fiddletown AVA adjoins the upper, eastern end of California Shenandoah Valley in the foothills east of the town of Plymouth. Amid rolling meadows and patchy pine forest at elevations ranging up to 2,500 feet, Fiddletown grows some of the state's oldest ZINFANDEL in a region now most famous for that grape. Soils are often granitic in origin, somewhat acidic, and well drained. There are few wineries in this AVA, but many elsewhere in Amador County purchase Fiddletown grapes.

California Shenandoah Valley AVA

Not to be confused with the Shenandoah Valley AVA in VIRGINIA, the California version is a mesa between two rivers east of the town of Plymouth. It became famous for hearty Zinfandels before the turn of the century and, after a long slumber, has regained some of its old momentum, again with Zinfandel and also Rhône varieties. More than a score of wineries share a modest acreage that also includes Sauvignon Blanc, Sangiovese, Syrah, and Petite Sirah.

North Yuba AVA

Sitting at the farthest northern extent of the Sierra Foothills AVA, the tiny North Yuba AVA was established in 1985 through the efforts of the only winery in the area, Renaissance Vineyard, which was founded by a controversial religious society known as the Fellowship of Friends. The AVA would not be worth noting but for the efforts of Gideon Bienstock, who made extraordinary wines for Renaissance from 1993 to 2006 and continues to do so at his own winery Clos Saron. L.M. & A.Y.

www.eldoradowines.org
www.amadorwine.com

Sierras de Málaga, Spanish DOP created in the early 21st century as effectively a subappellation of MÁLAGA to include a number of relatively new vineyards producing dry, unfortified wines, some in a subzone known as Serranía de Ronda around the inland town of Ronda. Powerful reds made from Syrah and Petit Verdot, and refreshing dry whites made from MUSCAT, are the region's key wines. The unfortified sweet Muscat wines from Axarquía, a style revitalized by Telmo Rodriguez and Jorge Ordoñez, merit mention, too. F.C.

silica gel and **silica sol**, amorphous forms of silicon dioxide in which there is no crystalline structure, used in white winemaking and rosé winemaking as FINING agents. In white wines it is also used in conjunction with GELATIN, and it may be used after fining with BENTONITE to improve SETTLING. It has also been suggested that its use reduces the risk of overfining.

silt, description of particles of intermediate size between CLAY and SAND. See SOIL TEXTURE and GEOLOGY for more details of this particular form of soil classification. Grains of silt dominate LOESS and are often predominant in ALLUVIAL soils. Silt is a major component of many of the soils in California's NAPA Valley.

Silvaner, called **Grüner Silvaner** in Germany, is an early-budding white grape variety grown mainly in Germany and central Europe (see SYLVANER for an account of it in France). Its very name suggests romantic woodland origins (*silva* means 'forest' in Latin), and certainly it has a long history over much of Eastern Europe, where it may indeed first have been identified growing wild. DNA PROFILING in Austria established that Silvaner is the progeny of SAVAGNIN (Traminer) and Österreichisch Weiss, a variety often mistaken for Silvaner and yet another progeny of GOUAIS BLANC. The cross probably took place in what is now Austria (although hardly any true Silvaner is grown there today), and it certainly came to Germany from the banks of the Danube. A vine known as Silvaner was widely grown throughout the extensive vineyards of medieval Germany. Its arrival from Austria at Castell in FRANKEN in 1659 is well documented, and it is the most planted variety in Franken, where distinctive CLAY and LIMESTONE soils seem to play a defining role in making full-bodied, firm, if aromatically discreet wines. Silvaner enjoyed its greatest popularity in the first half of the 20th century, when it overtook ELBLING to become Germany's most planted vine variety and established a dominant position in Rheinhessen. At 4,581 ha/11,320 acres in 2020, the variety is a distant third among white wine grapes to the even more productive MÜLLER-THURGAU, which rapidly surpassed it in area after the Second World War. GRAUBURGUNDER (Pinot Gris) has been catching up rapidly, however.

This vigorous vine buds a few days before Germany's quintessential RIESLING and can suffer spring FROST DAMAGE. It is not notable for its disease resistance, but it is productive. The chief characteristic of the wine produced is its high natural acid, generally lower than Riesling's in fact but emphasized by Silvaner's lack of BODY and STRUCTURE. Provided YIELDS are not too high, it can offer a suitable neutral canvas on which to display more geographically based flavour characteristics (see TERROIR). Most of Germany's finest Silvaners come from Franken, where Riesling is difficult to ripen and Silvaner has remained popular. Occasional and encouraging examples are made elsewhere, however—such as in certain CALCAREOUS, SANDSTONE, or porphyry sites in RHEINHESSEN—where talented growers have achieved transparency of flavour and distinctively earthy character while avoiding the curse of a coarse, thick mid palate. Silvaner is certainly more than capable of producing versatile, workhorse white wine, and the winegrowers of Rheinhessen, where more Silvaner is grown than anywhere else, have been at pains since the early 1990s to generate consumer awareness and a better image for this grape. It is particularly recommended with white asparagus.

Blauer Silvaner is a local, dark-berried MUTATION that is a speciality of WÜRTTEMBERG.

Outside Germany, Silvaner is relatively important, as Sylvánské Zelené, in CZECHIA, is still grown in SLOVENIA as Zeleni Silvanec, and is grown in Croatia, Ukraine, and Moldova. It is also planted in ALTO ADIGE, where it makes light, piercing wines for youthful consumption. In SWITZERLAND it is the fourth most planted white wine grape. Also called Johannisberg, it can seem positively luscious in comparison with French Switzerland's ubiquitous CHASSELAS. Sylvaner is the second most planted white grape variety in the Valais, where it was once called Rhin, or Gros Rhin (as opposed to Petit Rhin, the local synonym for RIESLING). The variety ripens later than Chasselas and, in villages as warm as Chamoson, Leytron, and Saillon, can result in wines with more body, character, and race.

Despite its useful acidity levels, Silvaner is not widely grown outside of Europe, although California and New Zealand grow it to a strictly limited extent.

Simon, André Louis (1877–1970).

Simon was the charismatic leader of the English wine trade for almost all of the first half of the 20th century and the grand old man of literate CONNOISSEURSHIP for a further 20 years. In 66 years of authorship, he wrote 104 books. For 33 years he was one of London's leading champagne shippers; for another 33 years, the active president of the Wine & Food Society. Although he lived in England from the age of 25, he always remained a French citizen. He was both Officier de la Légion d'Honneur and holder of the Order of the British Empire.

Simon was born in St-Germain-des-Prés, between the Brasserie Lipp and the Deux Magots (the street has since been demolished), the second of five sons of a landscape painter who died (of sunstroke, in Egypt) while they were still young.

From the first his ambition was to be a journalist. At 17 he was sent to Southampton to learn English and met Edith Symons, whose ambition was to live in France. They married in 1902 and remained happy together for 63 years in England. Simon was a man of judgement, single-mindedness, and devotion all his life.

He was also a man of powerful charm, the very model of his own description of the perfect champagne shipper, who 'must be a good mixer rather than a good salesman; neither a teetotaller nor a boozer, but able to drink champagne every day without letting it become a bore or a craving'.

He became a champagne shipper, the London agent of the leading house of Pommery, through his father's friendship with the Polignac family. It gave him a base in the centre of the City's wine trade, at 24 Mark Lane, for 30 years. From it he not only sold champagne; he also soon made his voice heard as journalist, scholar, and teacher.

Within four years of his installation in London he was writing his first book, *The History of the Champagne Trade in England*, in instalments for the *Wine Trade Review*. A. S. Gardiner, its editor, can be credited with forming Simon's English prose style: unmistakably charming, stately, and faintly whimsical at once. He spoke English as he wrote it, with a fondness for imagery, even for little parables—but with an ineradicable French accent that was as much part of his persona as his burly frame and curly hair.

His first *History* was rapidly followed by a remarkable sequel: *The History of the Wine Trade in England from Roman Times to the End of the 17th Century*, in three volumes in 1906, 1907, and 1909—the best and most original of his total of over 100 books. None, let alone a young man working in a language not his own, had read, thought, and written so deeply on the subject before. It singled him out at once as a natural spokesperson for wine, a role he pursued with maximum energy, combining with friends to found (in 1908) the Wine Trade Club, where for six years he organized tastings and gave technical lectures of a kind not heard before; this was the forerunner by 45 years of the Institute of MASTERS OF WINE. In 1919 he published *Bibliotheca vinaria*, a catalogue of the books he had collected for the Club. It ran to 340 pages.

The First World War ended this busy and congenial life, full of dinners, lectures, book-collecting, and amateur theatricals. Before war was declared, Simon was in France as a volunteer, serving the full four years in the French Artillery, where as 'un homme de lettres' he was made regimental postman, before being moved on to liaison with the British in Flanders and on the Somme. It was in Flanders that the irrepressible scribbler wrote his bestseller, *Laurie's Elementary Russian Grammar*, printed in huge numbers by the War Office in the pious hope of teaching Tommy, the British soldier, Russian.

In 1919 Simon bought the two homes he was to occupy for the rest of his life: 6 Evelyn Mansions, near Westminster Cathedral (where he attended mass daily); and Little Hedgecourt, a cottage with 28 acres beside a lake at Felbridge in Surrey. Gardening these acres, making a cricket pitch and an open-air theatre, and enlarging the cottage into a rambling country house for his family of five children were interspersed with travels all over Africa and South America to sell Pommery, until suddenly, in 1933, caught in the violent fluctuations of the franc–pound exchange rate when Britain came off the gold standard, he could no longer pay for his champagne stocks, and Pommery, without compunction, ended their 33-year association.

Simon began a second life at 55: that of spokesperson of wine and food in harmonious association. Already, with friends, he had founded the Saintsbury Club in memory of the crusty old author of *Notes on a Cellar-Book*. With A. J. A. Symons he founded the Wine & Food Society (now INTERNATIONAL WINE & FOOD SOCIETY). Its first (Alsace) lunch at the Café Royal in London in the midst of the Depression (and for 10*s.* 6*d.*) caused a sensation. But its assured success came from the ending of PROHIBITION in America. Sponsored by the French government, Simon travelled repeatedly to the US, founding its first Wine & Food Society branch in Boston in December 1934 and its second in San Francisco in January 1935.

Meanwhile, while working briefly for the advertising agency Mather & Crowther, he conceived the idea of *A Concise Encyclopedia of Gastronomy* to be published in instalments. It sold an unprecedented 100,000 copies. Research, writing, and editing (and finding paper to print) the *Encyclopedia* and the Society's *Quarterly* occupied him throughout the Second World War. His daughter Jeanne and her family moved into Little Hedgecourt for the war and thereafter. His son André was a wine merchant. His two other daughters and a son all retired from the world into religious communities.

Simon was a better teacher than businessman. He was repeatedly helped out of difficulties by adoring friends. Thus the National Magazine Company gave him an office in Grosvenor Gardens in 1941, to be followed by the publisher George Rainbird, still in central

London at Marble Arch. In 1962 his friend Harry Yoxall suggested that, at 85, daily responsibility for the Society and its magazine was too burdensome and bought the title from him for Condé Nast Publications. But in his 90s, Simon was still exceptional company at dinner and gave little picnics for friends beside his woodland lake.

His final book, *In the Twilight*, written in his last winter, 1969, recast the memoirs he had published as *By Request* in 1957. On what would have been his hundredth birthday, 28 February 1977, 400 guests at the Savoy Hotel in London drank to his memory in CLARET he had left for the occasion: Ch LATOUR 1945. H.J.

Singapore makes no grape wine of its own, but the South East Asian island-country is a serious contender for becoming Asia's wine hub in the 2020s, a role played by HONG KONG since 2008. While the DUTY on wine may be considered a deterrent, there are plenty of positives. Located at a crossroads of several key markets, Singapore is the busiest trans-shipment port in the world. The highly affluent population is becoming only more so, a trend that has encouraged a proliferation of wine bars and shops, including a branch of the London wine club 67 Pall Mall, which offers the largest wine collection in South East Asia, including 1,000 wines by the glass. There is also an abundance of secure, competitively priced, temperature-controlled storage facilities, including South East Asia's largest, The Singapore Wine Vault. Singapore also hosts a vast array of food and wine events and trade fairs, including, from 2023, Prowein, the world's largest wine-trade fair, after more than two decades in Hong Kong. A.L.S.

single-vineyard wines, wines made from the produce of one vineyard, and sometimes a single block within a vineyard, are becoming increasingly common throughout the world of wine. Arguably most of the better wines of GERMANY, AUSTRIA, and the Côte d'Or in BURGUNDY were the prototypes. (Many Bordeaux CHÂTEAUX are made up of several non-contiguous plots.)

Sirah is the name by which some PETITE SIRAH is known in South America. It should not be confused with the true SYRAH of the northern Rhône.

Síria, old, light-berried vine variety with many synonyms grown on a declining 4,726 ha/ 11,672 acres all over Portugal, where it was the fourth most planted white wine grape in 2020. Wines are aromatic but often age rapidly. It is known as Crato Branco in the Algarve, Roupeiro and Alva in Alentejo, and Códega in the Douro (distinct from CÓDEGA DE LARINHO). Known in Spain in the 16th century, it was planted on 1,947 ha in 2020, mainly in Castilla y León but also in Galicia. It is often known as Doña Blanca, as Cigüente in Extremadura, and as Malvasía Castellana in Toro.

site climate, the climate of a specified site, for instance a vineyard or part of a vineyard. The scale of definition usually falls within that of MESOCLIMATE.

site selection. See VINEYARD SITE SELECTION.

Sizzano, tiny but slowly growing DOC of 9 ha/ 22 acres in 2019 in the Novara hills in the PIEMONTE region of north-west Italy for seriously ageworthy reds made from SPANNA, the local name for Nebbiolo.

skin, grape. For details of grape skins, see GRAPE.

skin contact, *macération pelliculaire* in French, winemaking operation with the aim of extracting FLAVOUR COMPOUNDS, FLAVOUR PRECURSORS, and ANTHOCYANINS from grape skins into grape juice. In its widest sense it is identical to MACERATION, and some form of skin contact is usually essential to ROSÉ WINEMAKING, but the term is generally used exclusively for the maceration of white grapes before PRESSING and FERMENTATION with the aim of increasing the extraction of constituents that contribute to the aroma of white wines. It typically lasts four to eight hours, but since skin contact tends to reduce must acidity and increase PH the duration depends in part of the evolution of the pH. Destemmed and moderately crushed grapes are put into a vat and covered with INERT GAS and cooled down, if necessary, to a temperature of less than 15 °C/59 °F. At the end of the process, the FREE-RUN juice is collected and the MARC is pressed. Skin contact can also take place directly in airtight pneumatic PRESSES. Skin contact also increases the concentration of AMINO ACIDS, leading to a better rate of fermentation. Vine varieties frequently processed with skin contact are Sémillon, Sauvignon Blanc, Gros Manseng, Muscat, and Riesling. Grapes must be healthy, be fully ripe, and have sufficient acidity and low tannin content. Denis DUBOURDIEU and his team have been responsible for its application to white bordeaux since the late 1980s. It is important to arrest skin contact before excessive amounts of PHENOLICS (which may also darken colour) are extracted. In some vintages and in some regions, especially when the skin is rich in TANNINS due to a hot, dry climate, the technique simply does not work as too much undesirable material is extracted with the minimum amount of additional flavour compounds.

Ribéreau-Gayon, P., et al., *Traité d'Œnologie* 1: *Microbiologie du vin: Vinifications* (7th edn, 1998), translated by J. Towey, as *Handbook of Enology* 1: *The Microbiology of Wine and Vinifications* (3rd edn, 2021).

skin-fermented. All red wines are fermented in contact with the skins of the grapes (see RED WINEMAKING and MACERATION). Many wines are pink because the juice was briefly in contact with the skins of red wine grapes (see ROSÉ WINEMAKING). Most white wines are made by separating the juice from the grape skins before fermentation (see WHITE WINEMAKING). However, a small but increasing proportion of white wines are fermented in contact with grape skins, often described as **fermented on the skins**: *maischevergoren* in German, *vino brisado* in Spanish, *vi brisat* in Catalan, *vini bianchi macerati* in Italian, and *vin blanc de macération* or *vin blanc macéré* in French. 'Skin-fermented white wine', or 'skin-macerated white wine', is therefore a more technically descriptive synonym for ORANGE WINE and is so far regulated only in ONTARIO, South Africa, and Cataluña's Terra Alta DO. Not to be confused with SKIN CONTACT.

Lorteau, S., 'A comparative legal analysis of skin-contact wine definitions in Ontario and South Africa', *Journal of Wine Research*, 29 (2018), 265–77.

slashing, vineyard operation of mowing or cutting a COVER CROP, or cutting vine shoots in summer (see TRIMMING).

slate, a moderately hard, very fine-grained metamorphic rock (see GEOLOGY), the result of the burial of pre-existing rocks such as mudstone, SHALE, and volcanic TUFF, with a marked propensity to cleave into thin sheets. With increased metamorphism, slate becomes SCHIST.

Slate is found, for example, in the Cederberg Mountains, SOUTH AFRICA, and the CLARE VALLEY, South Australia. It is particularly celebrated in Germany's MOSEL and RHINE regions, where it makes famously stony slopes and is thought to hold moisture and heat and radiate warmth at night. A.J.M.

slip-skin. See AMERICAN VINE SPECIES.

SLO Coast, short for San Luis Obispo Coast, a coastal California wine region and AVA. See SAN LUIS OBISPO.

slope, or incline, an important characteristic of any vineyard site that is not completely flat. For more details, see TOPOGRAPHY.

Slovakia is regaining the vibrant wine scene it had before splitting from CZECHIA in 1992. Since then, total vineyard area has fallen from around 25,000 ha/62,000 acres to around 7,000 ha in 2021, and yields are lower than the EU average. This shortfall may be explained by a combination of climatic and political conditions, FROST, poorer VITICULTURE practices, small-scale undeclared private production, and the complexity of legally restoring vineyards post-communism. New wine laws combining the principles of both French and German wine law came into force in 2009, defining six wine-growing regions, authorized grape varieties, and details such as minimum ripeness levels. Since then, interesting wines have been emerging, drier and more TERROIR-focused than 20th-century styles.

Despite a decidedly CONTINENTAL CLIMATE, Slovakia has many MESOCLIMATES suitable for wine-growing. Plantings are predominantly VITIS VINIFERA, although VINE BREEDERS, notably Dorota Pospíšilová, have produced a host of new Slovak CROSSES such as Devín, Dunaj, and Hron, all designed to reach high sugar levels rapidly.

The most resonant wine-growing area is in the west of the country, in the Malé Karpaty (Small Carpathians), where predominantly white wine is made from such grapes as SILVANER, VELTLINER, WELSCHRIESLING, RIESLING, Chardonnay, and various MUSCATS. Another key area is along the southern border, where the warmer climate favours red wine production from the likes of Cabernet Sauvignon and Frankovka (BLAUFRÄNKISCH). Tekov, in the Nitra wine-making region east of the Malé Karpaty, features VOLCANIC soils, remnants of the Sitno volcano, and a tradition of growing FETEASCĂ Regală (called Pesecka Lenka in Slovakia). In the far east, the Slovak portion of the TOKAJ region produces wines much like those across the border in HUNGARY, from FURMINT, MUSCAT BLANC À PETITS GRAINS, HÁRSLEVELŰ, and ZÉTA, their sweetness expressed in *putňový*, although a handful of winemakers are also starting to produce dry-style wines and even sparkling Furmint.

Slovakia consumes virtually all the wine it produces, with the noteworthy exceptions of the fine Rieslings of Kastiel Béla and the production of a growing number of wineries focused on NATURAL WINE such as Strekov 1075 and Slobodné vinárstvo. These winemakers export most of their production to major cities all around the world, helping to confirm Slovakia's potential to produce high-quality wines.

V.K.R.

Slovenia, small and dynamic wine country in Central Europe that typically produces a little over half a million hl of wine annually from 14,900 ha/36,800 acres of vineyard. The country boasts one of the highest per capita wine consumption rates in the world, at about 36 l/7.9 gal a year, which means that little Slovenian wine leaves the country: only around 10% is exported. More than 27,000 winegrowers and 2,500 bottlers are registered, resulting in a highly fragmented vine-growing and winemaking scene. In Maribor, the capital of Štajerska Slovenija, is the 400-year-old *Stara trta* ŽAMETOVKA vine, which is officially the oldest on the planet and still producing grapes.

History

CELTS and Illyrian tribes were making wine here before the ROMANS. In the Middle Ages, wine production was an important economic activity undertaken by MONKS AND MONASTERIES. In 1880, when the country was part of the Austro-Hungarian empire, PHYLLOXERA arrived and literally halved the winegrowing area, extinguishing many INDIGENOUS VARIETIES. By 1935 the region saw its first defined wine zones, including recommended vine varieties, in Drava Banate, a province of what was then YUGOSLAVIA. After the Second World War, production was limited to CO-OPERATIVES, where quantity ruled over quality. However, some outstanding, long-lived whites were produced in those times, especially in the Podravje region, and some are still available from cellar archives. Commercially important private-sector wine businesses started to emerge in the 1970s. In 1967 the PSVVS (Business Association for Viticulture and Wine Production), now Vinska družba, was founded and introduced a seal of approval for Slovenian wines. In 1991 Slovenia established its independence, and in 2004 joined the EU. It was the first of the ex-Yugoslav countries to build a successful wine industry with fully implemented and well-policed wine laws and a thriving private sector.

Geography and climate

Slovenia, laying between latitudes 45 and 47° N, is geographically very diverse, with many MESOCLIMATES. The country is divided into three wine regions, each further divided into nine districts. **Podravje** in the north-east and **Posavje** in the south-east both benefit from a moderate-to-cool CONTINENTAL CLIMATE influenced by the cooling effect of the Alps and warming effect of the Pannonian Plain. To the west, **Primorska** features a moderate-to-warm MEDITERRANEAN CLIMATE.

Annual rainfall averages 800–1,500 mm/31.5–59 in and DRY FARMING is standard. Spring FROST, summer HAIL, and occasional DROUGHT may be experienced in most wine districts.

Primorska With a steady 6,300 ha/15,600 acres of vines, this region has made great progress in quality since early 1990s and is today the most praised Slovenian wine region in certain quarters, having become an epicentre of NATURAL and ORANGE WINE production. Primorska is divided into four districts (PDOs). **Goriška Brda**, bordering Italy's COLLIO DOC and influenced by its Italian neighbours, is currently Slovenia's most esteemed wine district and PGI, having begun the quest for quality as early as the late 1980s. Rebula (RIBOLLA) is the flagship variety. Many of the best wines are oak-aged white and red blends based on Rebula/Chardonnay and Merlot/Cabernet Sauvignon/Cabernet Franc respectively. The dynamic **Vipavska Dolina** (Vipava Valley) district is proud of its native light, aromatic Zelen and flashier Pinela. Merlot and Pinot Noir show some class as well. **Kras** (Carso), a plateau above Trieste, is the home of Teran, a distinctive, highly acidic dark red made from Refošk (REFOSCO) grapes. **Slovenska Istra** on the coast is the warmest district in the country. Refošk and white Malvazija (MALVAZIJA ISTARSKA) prevail. Primorska also boasts some great sweet wines made in PASSITO style; Verduc (VERDUZZO) and Pikolit (PICOLIT) are specialities of Brda. Also grown in Primorska are Rumeni Muškat, Beli Pinot, LAŠKI RIZLING, VITOVSKA Grganja, Klarnica, Glera, Viognier, Barbera, Syrah, Cipro (possibly MAVRO), Pokalca (SCHIOPPETTINO), and Maločrn.

Podravje With 6,100 ha/15,000 acres of vines, this is the second largest wine region in Slovenia and also a PGI, divided into two districts (also PDOs). The extensive **Štajerska Slovenija** (Styrian Slovenia) district with its beautiful rolling hills is slowly regaining its former status, while the rather warmer **Prekmurje** district, a continuation of the Pannonian Plain in the far north-east of the country, is of minor significance. In 1852 Slovenia's first sparkling wine (*penina*) produced by the TRADITIONAL METHOD was made in Gornja Radgona.

White wines dominate in Podravje, making up 92% of production in 2020. The dominant grape variety is LAŠKI RIZLING, usually used for inexpensive blends, but the region's reputation is based on aromatic whites typically produced in STAINLESS STEEL and bottled under SCREWCAPS. The increasingly popular Sauvignon Blanc (which also thrives across the border in STYRIA) has enjoyed some export success, as has Šipon (FURMINT), the traditional grape of the region. Renski Rizling (RIESLING), Chardonnay, Sivi Pinot (PINOT GRIS), Beli Pinot (PINOT BLANC), Dišeči Traminec (GEWÜRZTRAMINER), and Modri Pinot (Pinot Noir) are common for high-quality VARIETAL wines. Most of these varieties were introduced to the region by the Austrian Archduke Johann in 1822. Modri Pinot is the most planted dark-skinned variety, and Modra Frankinja (BLAUFRÄNKISCH) shows much promise.

Podravje and, to a lesser extent, Posavje (see below) are also where the country's best BOTRYTIZED wines are made, mainly from Šipon, Laški Rizling, and Renski Rizling and labelled in German fashion according to sugar level: *pozna trgatev* (SPÄTLESE), *izbor* (AUSLESE), *jagodni izbor* (BEERENAUSLESE), *ledeno vino* (EISWEIN), and *suhi jagodni izbor* (TROCKENBEERENAUSLESE).

Other grape varieties planted in Podravje are the Ranina (BOUVIER), Ranfol, Muškat Ottonel (MUSCAT OTTONEL), Zeleni Silvanec (SYLVANER), Rizvanec (MÜLLER-THURGAU), KERNER, Portugalka (PORTUGIESER), Kraljevina, Rdeča and Bela Žlahtnina (Red and White CHASSELAS), GAMAY, and ZWEIGELT.

Posavje With 2,400 ha/5,900 acres of vines, Posavje is the smallest and historically least important wine region and PGI in Slovenia, producing slightly more reds than whites. Production is widely dispersed and BULK WINE prevails. It has three PDOs: **Bizeljsko Sremič** is known for the indigenous Modra Frankinja (BLAUFRÄNKISCH), sparkling wine (sometimes from the highly acidic local white Rumeni Plavec), and traditional white and red blends called Bizeljčan. **Bela Krajina**, the warmest wine district, can produce some good Modra Frankinja and the best Rumeni Muškat (MUSCAT BLANC À PETITS GRAINS) in the country. It is home to the light red PDO blend Metliška Črnina and white PDO wine Belokranjec. **Dolenjska**, the coolest Slovenian district, has recently developed a strength in sparkling wine, although traditionally it is home to the highly popular Cviček, a light, pale ruby, highly acidic blend of red and white grapes (usually Žametovka and Kraljevina). Other grapes grown here are Sauvignon Blanc, Chardonnay, Beli Pinot, Sivi Pinot, Renski Rizling, Traminec, Šipon, Ranina, NEUBURGER, Modri Pinot, Šentlovrenka (ST-LAURENT), Gamay, Zweigelt, and Rdeča Žlahtnina.

Viticulture and winemaking

Over 60% of Slovenia's vineyards are planted on slopes with more than 15% incline, many of them TERRACED. Handpicking is a norm, though MECHANICAL HARVESTING is on the increase. The high-yield PERGOLA training system *(latnik)* and *casarsa* (similar to GENEVA DOUBLE CURTAIN), once common in Primorska, are being replaced with double or single GUYOT, now the most common training system.

White wines dominate, a fact reflected in the top five grape varieties planted: Welschriesling, Refosco, Chardonnay, Sauvignon Blanc, and Malvasia Istarska. Pinot Gris also excels.

Reds, notably Pinot Noir, have improved considerably since the early 1990s. However, Slovenia is still trying to find its place on the international market with varieties such as Rebula, Šipon, Refošk, and local blends.

Wines were traditionally vinified in large, old wooden casks of Slovenian or Slavonian oak. Modern practice includes the use of stainless steel and BARREL AGEING in Slovenian or French oak of varying sizes. Recently, QVEVRI and CONCRETE eggs have become popular, particularly in Primorska. These are most often connected with SKIN-FERMENTED and so-called ORANGE WINES. MALOLACTIC CONVERSION for whites is common in Primorska but often suppressed in Podravje and Posavje. As in most former Austro-Hungarian Empire countries, the best wines have tended to be VARIETAL, while blends are reserved for entry-level wines and, since the turn of the century, for flagship wines in Primorska. Large, often well-equipped wineries, either CO-OPERATIVES or now privately owned, still represent a significant part of the market, but smaller family estates are in FASHION, their wines often commanding premium prices.

Wine law By law all wines must be analysed, tasted, and scored to determine their quality level before going to market. Zaščitena Označba Porekla (ZOP) is the PDO equivalent, while Zaščitena Geografska Označba (ZGO) corresponds to PGI but is hardly used. Traditional designations still widely in use are: *namizno vino* (table wine); *deželno vino PGO* ('Vins de Pays' coming from a single region); and *kakovostno vino ZGP* (quality wine) and *vrhunsko vino ZGP* (premium quality wine), both of which come from single district.

Priznano Tradicionalno Poimenovanje (PTP) is similar to Austria's DAC. According to the RESIDUAL SUGAR level, all wines in Slovenia are designated as either *suho* (dry), *polsuho* (medium-dry), *polsladko* (medium-sweet), or *sladko* (sweet). R.F.G.

Smaragd, category of white wines made from the ripest grapes in the WACHAU in Austria. Alcohol levels in the unchaptalized Grüner Veltliners and Rieslings that qualify must be more than 12.5% and are commonly 13–14.5%. The category is named after the green lizard that basks in the sun on the Wachau's steep stone terraces above the Danube. See also STEINFEDER and FEDERSPIEL.

Smart-Dyson, vine TRAINING SYSTEM developed in the early 1980s in California and by the end of the 2000s adopted in new plantings in Spain, South Africa, and New Zealand in particular. In South Africa, adoption was encouraged by the experience of companies such as DISTELL, which showed an increase in both yield and quality.

The system was devised by Richard Smart of Australia and John Dyson of New York, and it was initially trialled on Dyson's ranch in Gilroy, California, in 1992 with Merlot vines. It is a vertically divided training system like SCOTT HENRY, but the vine is CORDON-trained and there are upwards- and downwards-pointing SPURS giving rise to the two canopies. It is compatible with MECHANICAL PRUNING, unlike the Scott Henry system, and it can be MECHANICALLY HARVESTED as readily, as can Scott Henry. R.E.S.

Smederevka, white grape variety commonly planted in SERBIA and NORTH MACEDONIA, the name presumably being inspired by the town of Smederevo south of Belgrade. Often blended with other varieties, notably LAŠKI RIZLING, its wine is generally unremarkable. It is the same as Bulgaria's DIMYAT.

smell. The smell of a wine is probably its single most important attribute and may be called its AROMA, BOUQUET, odour or off-odour if it is positively unattractive, or even FLAVOUR.

The sense of smell is the most acute human tasting instrument (a blocked nose robs food and drink of any flavour), but, since it is so closely related to what we call the sense of taste, it is considered in detail under TASTING. Those who lose their sense of smell, either temporarily or permanently, are said to be anosmic.

smoke taint in grapes and wine has become an increasing problem as the incidence and intensity of bushfires or WILDFIRES escalates in many wine regions that are experiencing hotter and drier periods due to CLIMATE CHANGE.

Grape berries can absorb gaseous volatile phenol compounds generated by pyrolysis of woody lignin material in a fire. The uptake of volatile phenols can occur as early as FRUIT SET when the berries are small and green (2–4 mm). Depending on the stage of grapevine development and the level and duration of smoke exposure, smoke-tainted wines can display an array of different sensorial attributes, variously described as 'burnt', 'smoky', 'charry', 'ashtray', 'smoked meat', 'vinyl/plastic', 'disinfectant', 'leather', and 'medicinal/Band-Aid'.

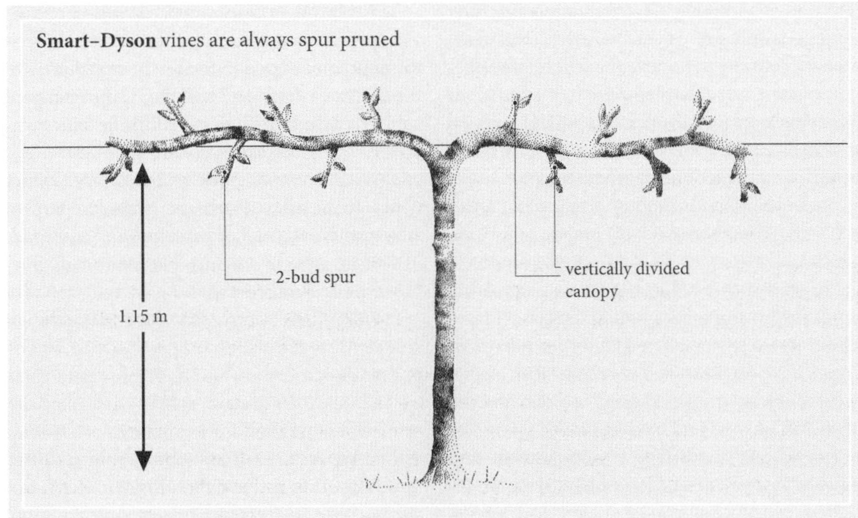

Smart-Dyson vines are always spur pruned

Research since 2003 by the AWRI related the exposure of grapevines to atmospheric smoke to the development of smoke-related flavour and aroma characteristics in the resultant wine. The compounds primarily responsible for the sensory perception of smoke-taint characters include, but are not restricted to, a number of phenols including guaiacols, cresols, and syringols. These phenols can also exist in grapes and wine as GLYCOSIDE FLAVOUR PRECURSORS, which can be broken down during processing, alcoholic FERMENTATION, and MALOLACTIC CONVERSION and through a chemical process during AGEING. Glycoside flavour precursors can also be broken down in the mouth when wine is tasted or consumed, resulting in perceptible smoke characters. These can become more evident during maturation and after bottling. Recent research at Oregon State University suggests that thiophenols (sulphur-containing equivalents of known taint compounds) may also contribute to the sensory attributes of smoke-tainted wine.

All grape varieties are sensitive to smoke taint. The volatile phenol compounds appear to be concentrated near the berry skin, so vineyard and winery practices that reduce skin contact or damage can minimize, but not necessarily remove, the effects of the smoke. Techniques such as hand harvesting, WHOLE-BUNCH PRESSING, lower processing temperatures, less time on skins (before, during, and after fermentation), and separation of press fractions (see PRESS WINE) can reduce the extraction of smoke compounds into wine. The style and STRUCTURE of the wine can also have a significant impact. For example, smoke-taint characters in a full-bodied Shiraz/Syrah may be less obvious than in a lighter-bodied Pinot Noir. The use of certain FINING agents made from activated carbon (see CHARCOAL) has proven to be somewhat effective at removing both the volatile phenol fractions (from wine) and the glycoside precursors (from juice). However, the non-selective nature of activated carbon may also result in the removal of desirable flavour compounds and TEXTURE attributes. REVERSE OSMOSIS has been used successfully to remove the free volatile phenol fraction, but this method is not effective at removing smoke glycosides. Careful leaf removal is also important since leaves may contribute smoke-taint compounds to the ferment.

These compounds can also occur naturally at very low concentrations in grapes and wine which have not been exposed to smoke, especially in varieties such as Shiraz/Syrah, so comparing results with natural background levels is a key to assessing the potential risk prior to harvest if grapes have been exposed to smoke. Risk assessment following smoke exposure includes analysis of volatile phenols and their associated glycosides in grapes and conducting a mini-ferment and sensory assessment of the resultant wine to determine potential effects. M.P.K. & C.A.S.

Krstic, M., et al., 'Review of smoke taint in wine: smoke-derived volatile phenols and their glycosidic metabolites in grapes and vines as biomarkers for smoke exposure and their role in the sensory perception of smoke taint', *Australian Journal of Grape and Wine Research*, 21/51 (2015), 537–53.

Simos, C., et al., 'I can smell smoke—now what?', *Australian & New Zealand Grapegrower & Winemaker*, 672 (2020), 28–31.

Tomasino, E., et al., 'A combination of thiophenols and volatile phenols cause the ashy flavor of smoke taint in wine', *Food Chemistry Advances*, 2 (2023).

smudge pot, small burner, usually fuelled with oil, once popular as a means of FROST PROTECTION and still used in some European vineyards.

snails, vine pests of which at least two types can be of economic significance to wine production: the white Italian snail, *Theba pisana*, and the brown or English snail, *Helix aspersa*. They are mainly a problem in early spring and can strip vines of young foliage if they are in large numbers, which happens particularly in wet conditions. They will contaminate fruit and wine if they are present at HARVEST time. Clean TILLAGE is an important preventive measure, and sprays or baits used early can also control snails. Copper-based FUNGICIDES used on vines also affect snails by repelling and killing them. Ducks and geese feed on snails, and their presence in vineyards will keep numbers down. M.J.E.

Soave, white wine from the VENETO region of north-east Italy, mostly dry but on rare occasions sweet and/or sparkling. Like the neighbouring VALPOLICELLA zone, the Soave zone was expanded enormously with the creation of the Soave DOC in 1968. At the time, both regions were enjoying an export boom, so production flowed off the small hilly zone on to the alluvial plain of the Adige River.

The central CLASSICO zone of HILLSIDE VINEYARDS, first defined and delimited in 1927, is the source of superior Soave. It, together with the north-eastern part of the Colli Scaligero subzone, which includes all hillside vineyards outside the Classico zone, are planted on decomposed VOLCANIC rock and produce steelier wines than those from the western part of Soave, where the higher percentage of LIMESTONE in the soil and the warmer afternoon sun gives fuller, more forward wines.

in 2020 there were 2,800 ha/6,918 acres of vineyards on the plain (compared with 1,500 ha in the Classico zone), and these are responsible for the bulk of ordinary Soave, which has developed a reputation for being insipid. The culprit is excessive YIELDS, sometimes more than 15 tonnes/ha. It was hoped that the introduction of the DOCG in 2002 would correct this situation, but instead of restricting the DOCG to the Classico hills a general Superiore category was created, a half-baked compromise that included most of the produce of the local CO-OPERATIVE. Maximum permitted yields for Soave Superiore DOCG are still high but are reduced to 10 tonnes/ha, and the minimum natural alcohol level is 12%.

In an effort to elevate Soave's reputation, in 2020 the region introduced 33 UGAS (*unità geografica aggiuntive*) which may appear on labels. Regionally referred to as 'crus', these areas (some as large as 1,600 ha) are practically all hillside sites, the majority being in the Classico area, some are unreasonably joined such as Calvarino and Monte Crocetta.

Another potential improvement is the exclusion of TREBBIANO Toscano from DOC and DOCG Soaves. This interloper was introduced to the area in the 1960s, when high yields were the driving force, and it soon displaced the local Trebbiano di Soave (which is, in fact, VERDICCHIO). Today Soave must be at least 70% GARGANEGA and up to 30% Trebbiano di Soave, Chardonnay, Pinot Bianco, and/or the Sauvignon Blanc that has been used to add interest and body to wines from over-productive vines. When yields are controlled, Garganega can give wines of real class. A late-ripening variety, it has a thick skin that helps protect it against the autumn mists rising from the northern part of the Po Valley. Producers such as Pieropan, Gini, Pra, and Ca' Rugate have illustrated the potential not only of Garganega but also of the Soave zone.

Garganega is also the mainstay of the sweet RECIOTO di Soave DOCG, a PASSITO made from raisined Garganega grapes. It can also be sparkling, though examples are rare. W.S.

Lorenzoni, A. (ed.), *Soave Terroir: Le 33 Unità Geografiche Aggiuntive del Soave* (2020).

www.ilsoave.com

social media refers to the use of mobile and web-based technologies for communicating and networking between individuals and organizations. Such networking shares, creates, discusses, and proliferates information in both textual and visual form. Social media have dramatically changed how information about wine is disseminated. Traditional media outlets still share information but have greatly decreased in number, leading to fewer permanent wine columns and paid WINE WRITING positions. Increasingly, wine experts and consumers alike share wine information and opinion via social-media channels such as TikTok, Twitter, Instagram, and Facebook. Although blogs (see INFORMATION TECHNOLOGY) helped create the importance of social media to wine, they waned as mobile applications (apps) proliferated.

Social media were initially differentiated from traditional media as being essentially consumer-generated, whereas traditional media were generated for consumers by experts selected to create such content, but the distinction is becoming increasingly blurred as wine producers and retailers are using social media to establish direct contact with consumers. One of the effects of social media on wine criticism has been a general democratizing of authority, dispersing it broadly across online networks. Consumers increasingly turn to social media for information, thus relying less on expert authority and more on crowd-sourced information. Prior to social media, influential information was concentrated around industrial media sources and established WINE WRITERS. But within social media, specific wine-focused communities have arisen, especially via apps. Nielsen studies have shown that internet users spend significantly more time on social-media sites than anywhere else online.

Social media have also led to a change in both wine publishing and wine marketing. Because of the dynamic nature of social media, the influence of any particular person or media source can change much more rapidly than in the past, and individuals who are charismatic but not necessarily expert can achieve prominence, even influence (see INFLUENCERS). Another consequence of social media is that traditional wine experts can now be in direct contact with their readers, who can publish their reactions to them. Communication is very much a two-way process today.

The impact of traditional marketing approaches such as ad campaigns simply seeking circulation numbers has been eroded, and many wineries implement social-media marketing techniques instead. Such processes can integrate social media with information technology that tracks social media users' mentions of wine in general and specific wines, as well as their wine-based travel. Producers can thereby respond directly to consumers who mention their wines.

The proliferation of information online has also increased general discussion about even small-production and relatively obscure wines among consumers. Thus the democratization of wine information via social media has also encouraged consumers to experiment with a wider range of wines. E.C.B.

sodium, element that is not a required nutrient for vine growth (see VINE NUTRITION). Sodium chloride (common SALT) is, however, a major hazard for vine-growers, particularly in hot, irrigated areas where ground waters are saline or where salty irrigation water is applied to the leaves (see SALINITY). Sodium has an unfavourable effect on soil fertility because it reduces water infiltration due to its tendency to disperse clay particles. This can be overcome by addition of CALCIUM to the soil, normally as gypsum. See also SALINITY. R.E.S.

Sogrape, Portugal's largest wine producer, owned by the Oporto-based Guedes family, whose success is founded on MATEUS Rosé. Since the 1980s, it has invested in new wine regions, acquiring Portuguese winemaking facilities and vineyards in the MINHO, DÃO, BAIRRADA, ALENTEJO, and DOURO (it owns port shippers FERREIRA, SANDEMAN, and Offley, as well as more than 500 ha/1,235 acres of vineyard in the valley). Its Portuguese table-wine brands include Douro icon Casa Ferreirinha's Barca Velha, Legado, Gazela, Quinta de Azevedo, Quinta dos Carvalhais, and Herdade do Peso. Global acquisitions include Finca Flichman (Argentina), Framingham (New Zealand), Los Boldos (Chile), RIOJA-based Bodegas Lan, and UK importer Liberty Wines.

soil, mineral material at the Earth's surface formed by weathering of underlying bedrock (see GEOLOGY), or transported sediments, which form the parent material of the soil. The main distinction between soil and parent material is that a soil is enriched with plant and animal remains that undergo decomposition to form soil ORGANIC MATTER. Because soil formation is an ongoing process, dependent on geology, CLIMATE, vegetation, TOPOGRAPHY, and time, the boundary between a soil and its parent material is usually indistinct. Over very long periods, episodes of erosion and deposition followed by soil formation have led to layered soils, common in old weathered landscapes such as in Australia and southern Africa. However, where soils have formed on one parent material *in situ*, such as in north-west Europe and North America during the 11,000 years since the last Ice Age (see CLIMATE CHANGE, historical and contemporary climate changes), distinctive zones called horizons can form in a vertical array, which is called a SOIL PROFILE. These horizons can be differentiated by their organic matter, colour, thickness, texture, structure, and stoniness. In addition to organic matter, soils are distinguished from rock materials by their structure (see SOIL STRUCTURE), which influences the rate of water infiltration (from RAINFALL or IRRIGATION), resistance to SOIL EROSION, and ease of root penetration. The combined effect of SOIL TEXTURE and structure determines a soil's water-holding capacity, aeration, and DRAINAGE and hence the soil's suitability for healthy ROOT GROWTH and vine performance.

In Australia, where there is a pronounced and relatively abrupt increase in soil clay content between a surface A horizon (topsoil) and a subsoil B horizon, the soil is called duplex. This kind of profile is commonly found in soils referred to as podzolic in many other vineyard regions around the world. Duplex soils may develop impermeable subsoils when the exchangeable sodium content (see CLAY) exceeds a certain threshold. The presence of high magnesium in many Australian subsoils results in this threshold being lower than in North American soils.

See GEOLOGY, STONES AND ROCKS, SUBSOIL, TERROIR, TOPOGRAPHY, and other entries prefaced by SOIL, most importantly SOIL AND WINE QUALITY. R.E.W.

White, R. E., *Understanding Vineyard Soils* (2nd edn, 2015).

soil acidity, or low soil PH, occurs where hydrogen cations (H+) predominate relative to those of the alkali cations CALCIUM, POTASSIUM, SODIUM, and MAGNESIUM adsorbed on the surfaces of CLAY and ORGANIC MATTER. Acidity is found mainly where the alkali mineral elements have been leached out of the SOIL PROFILE under heavy rainfall over extended periods, and their place on the soil's CATION EXCHANGE CAPACITY has been taken by hydrogen ions. Soils developed on coarse-textured sediments (GRAVEL, GRANITE) are prone to be acidic, while soils developed on CALCAREOUS sediments are never acidic.

In soils of less than pH 5, described as highly acid, exchangeable aluminium is released by slow decomposition of the clay and can inhibit grapevine root growth. Such soils are best avoided for viticulture; if this is not possible, then LIME should be applied. The soil acidity of the MÉDOC in Bordeaux, for example, promotes COPPER availability and consequent toxicity, wherever there has been a build-up of copper in the topsoil from spraying vines with BORDEAUX MIXTURE.

In neutral to alkaline soils rich in organic matter, ready decomposition may release mineral NITROGEN, which predisposes to excess VIGOUR, whereas the release of nitrogen in soils of lower pH is limited. Problems of soil acidity are to be expected in most viticultural regions with high rainfall, affecting parts of Europe and some highly weathered soils in south-east Australia and South Africa.

Soil acidity should be contrasted with SOIL ALKALINITY, which is more common in arid areas. It does not follow that soil acidity bears any relation to wine ACIDITY. R.E.S., C.v.L. & R.E.W.

soil alkalinity. A soil is said to be alkaline when the measured PH is above about 7. A pH above about 8.5 usually implies a content of free LIME or CHALK (usually described as CALCAREOUS soil; see also LIMESTONE) or too high a content of soluble salts (including common salt, sodium chloride). In the latter case, such soils are described as SALINE. When these soils are leached, their pH can increase to 9 or more due to the hydrolysis of SODIUM ions (see CATION EXCHANGE) and the ORGANIC MATTER can disperse, forming a black alkali soil. Saline and black alkali soils should definitely be avoided for viticulture. However, some of the best vineyard soils in cool climates are associated with limestone or chalk.

High lime and pH can induce deficiencies of IRON, ZINC, and MANGANESE or BORON in the vines. Lime-induced iron deficiency can cause CHLOROSIS. These deficiencies can usually be controlled by leaf sprays or the selection of particularly well-adapted varieties of ROOTSTOCK.

Soils high in free lime can sometimes create nutritional difficulties through the reduced availability of POTASSIUM. J.G., C.v.L. & R.E.W.

soil amelioration, a viticultural practice for improving soils by the addition of so-called **soil amendments**. These can include FERTILIZERS to overcome mineral nutrient deficiencies (such as superphosphate to add phosphorus); LIME, which will overcome SOIL ACIDITY; and gypsum and ORGANIC MATTER, which will improve SOIL STRUCTURE. These ameliorants are spread on the soil surface and occasionally turned in by TILLAGE. Where there is a need for deep placement, as in liming or the application of rock phosphate (see FERTILIZERS), then RIPPING implements drawn by powerful bulldozers are used before planting. When the lime and gypsum are finely ground, special applicators allow these normally insoluble products to be added through DRIP IRRIGATION systems, but the drippers easily become blocked.

See also BIOCHAR. R.E.S. & R.E.W.

Coombe, B. G., and Dry, P. R. (eds), *Viticulture*, ii: *Practices* (2nd edn, 2006).

soil and wine quality. The SOIL has many attributes that can influence the vine grown in it and thence the composition of grapes and the quality and character of wine. Quite how influential these attributes are remains a matter of debate, with a fairly marked but fast-decreasing divergence between the OLD WORLD and NEW WORLD, if not of opinion then of interpretation.

S

Old World and New World

Opinions in Europe, especially in France, have strongly emphasized soil effects on vines, grapes, and wines at a vineyard level, particularly in relation to vine water status. These are fundamental to the concept of TERROIR which underlies the official French AOC system, although the influence of soil is generally regarded as less significant than that of climate. In Germany, for example, large local differences in climate associated with TOPOGRAPHY are often considered to override soil effects (see MESOCLIMATE and CLIMATE AND WINE QUALITY), although soils are still regarded as an important factor affecting wine quality.

Until a few decades ago, New World opinion tended to minimize the role of soil and instead to stress major differences in regional climate, or MACROCLIMATE. Amerine and Winkler's 1944 CLIMATE CLASSIFICATION of California into five temperature regions epitomized this view. Much of the divergence in approach can be ascribed to differences in historical, geographical, and commercial background. Traditional European vineyards were small, with the identities of their wines often uniquely established over many generations. It was observed that certain sites consistently produced different and/or better wines than others, apparently regardless of VINE MANAGEMENT and WINEMAKING practices and sometimes in the absence of discernible differences in mesoclimate. One general observation, especially marked in Bordeaux, was that the best sites stood out most clearly in poor VINTAGE YEARS. These sites maintained a relative consistency of high quality, whereas others, superficially similar and often very close, suffered greatly diminished quality. The only possible reason seemed to lie in unalterable (and perhaps invisible) properties of the soil.

New World viticulture has generally lacked this experience. Individual vineyards were often much larger, and until fairly recently grapes from individual plots were rarely fermented separately (see SINGLE-VINEYARD WINES). Moreover, the dominant commercial organizations tended to employ extensive BLENDING of wines from different soils and regions, so that any individualities were often masked or lost.

Differences in agricultural history have also influenced the choice of soils for planting vines. In Europe, all the fertile land was needed for cereal production or grazing to provide sufficient food for the people. Since vines would grow almost anywhere, they were often planted on the poorest soils to optimize land use. In the New World, there was generally no shortage of land so that viticulture developed on a wide range of soils, from infertile to fertile, with irrigation a common, and in many cases necessary, practice.

Nevertheless, the absolute need for quality (and, in particular, wine individuality) in a highly competitive world market means that winegrowers in all parts of the wine-growing world have increasingly emphasized the importance of soil as contributing to a site's terroir. This has become especially evident with advances in SOIL MAPPING as part of VINEYARD DESIGN and in PRECISION VITICULTURE, notably in North America and Australia. This approach is now a prerequisite to the design of a new vineyard and particularly any IRRIGATION system. It also makes it possible to identify different plots by soil attributes and to manage and harvest them separately, even in extensive vineyard developments. The results obtained support European experience, as reported by Smart. However, the effect of soil on wine quality is reduced in warmer climates, which is why the influence of terroir is so much more marked in marginal climates such as that of Chablis or England.

Winegrowers and scientists in all parts of the wine world investigate the reasons some soils can give better wines than others. The work of the late Bordeaux researcher Professor Gérard Seguin laid important foundations for such studies and forms a background to the discussion below, which distinguishes between chemical and physical soil attributes.

Physical soil attributes

Scientific opinion now almost universally agrees with Seguin's conclusion that soil's physical characteristics predominate as the main influence over grape and wine quality other than CLIMATE; and, further, that, among the physical characteristics, the most important are those that govern water supply to the vine. These and their relationship to individual soil types are discussed in some detail under TERROIR. See also SOIL WATER, SOIL TEXTURE, DRAINAGE, and VINE PHYSIOLOGY.

Here we may note briefly that the best wines come from soils that are very well drained and furnish a steady, but only moderate, even limiting, water supply to the vines. When combined with appropriate restrictive mineral VINE NUTRITION, this ensures that SHOOT TIP growth is restrained, especially immediately prior to VERAISON. Smaller berries are also usually less liable to congestion and compression within the bunch and are therefore less likely to split or suffer spoilage as a result of FUNGAL DISEASES or BACTERIA. WATER STRESS needs to be just enough to attain these ends and not enough to reduce photosynthesis too much.

Some other physical properties of soils almost certainly influence wine quality and characteristics in subtle ways.

SOIL COLOUR affects soil temperature and that of the air immediately above. Dark-coloured soils absorb and convert much of the sunlight falling on them into heat, and so these are warmer than light-coloured soils and, at night and during daytime cloud cover, radiate more warmth back to the vines and bunches. This can be critical in some cool MARGINAL CLIMATES, allowing fuller RIPENING and thus better wine quality (as in the very dark soils of the Neckar Valley in WÜRTTEMBERG or the Meuse Valley of southern BELGIUM, for example).

The presence of STONES AND ROCKS in the soil or on its surface influences both water and temperature relations. A high proportion of stones or GRAVEL throughout the SOIL PROFILE is commonly associated with very good DRAINAGE but at the same time reduces water-holding capacity and encourages desirably extensive ROOT GROWTH to assure a vine's water supply. In Bordeaux, where the main risk is often excessive water supply to the vines, the most important positive effect on wine quality of stones in the soil is the limitation on water-holding capacity, leading to the level of water deficit that promotes red wine quality. Stony soils, whether sloping or not, usually have the further advantage for wine quality that they are at most only moderately fertile, as discussed below.

Soils containing a large proportion of rocks or stones have the additional advantage of being warm because they hold less water. Water has a high specific calorific capacity and needs a lot of energy to warm it. Wet soils are therefore cold soils. Moderately damp soil beneath surface stones is both a reasonable heat conductor and a good heat storer, because of the high heat-storage capacity of its water content. It is also protected from evaporative cooling. Stony soils also more readily absorb heat and transmit it to depth, because rocks are a comparatively good conductor of heat—much better than dry or loose soil. Such soils are efficient at absorbing and storing warmth and at retransmitting it to the above-ground vine parts during cloud cover and in the evening. See TEMPERATURE VARIABILITY, DIURNAL TEMPERATURE RANGE, and CLIMATE AND WINE QUALITY.

Whatever the mechanisms, there can be little doubt that stony and rocky soils produce many of the world's great wines, provided that water supply to the vine is adequate. Typical are the coarse gravels that characterize the most eminent châteaux of the MÉDOC in Bordeaux; the large stones (GALETS) that completely cover some of the best sites of CHÂTEAUNEUF-DU-PAPE in the southern Rhône; and the coarsely stony gravels that give wines of outstanding quality in the Marlborough region of NEW ZEALAND's South Island and, more recently, in the Gimblett Gravels region of Hawke's Bay in the North Island.

Chemical attributes

The relationship between soil chemistry and wine quality and individuality is in the main poorly understood. The belief that soil influences wine character because the vine takes up flavour compounds direct from the soil is totally unsubstantiated (see, for example, MINERALS and MINERALITY).

Soil NITROGEN is in part an exception to this lack of knowledge. It is clear from Seguin's work, and that of other researchers, that the optimum nitrogen supply to the vine is at most only moderate. The optimum supply for red-wine production is lower than for white wine because nitrogen deficiency increases berry skin PHENOLICS but also limits the build up of FLAVOUR PRECURSORS in white grapes (see Choné et al. and Helwi et al.). Vines receiving much nitrogen, unless severely constrained by other factors, have vigorous and leafy growth. This leads to excessive SHADE within the canopy and thence to poor fruit quality (see CANOPY MICROCLIMATE). The effects of nitrogen, water supply, and various other nutritional and environmental factors can to varying degrees reinforce or counteract each other in this regard. The best combination among them is that giving optimum vine BALANCE. Excessive nitrogen fertilization, leading to excessive vigour, can sometimes be problematic. However, this tendency is countered by the more widespread use of grass or cereal COVER CROPS, which can compete with the vine for nitrogen or even cause a deficiency.

A further complication has arisen from research showing that low nitrogen contents in the berries can be a cause of difficulties in winemaking, leading to STUCK FERMENTATIONS and the presence of HYDROGEN SULFIDE and its malodorous MERCAPTAN derivatives in the wine. This is especially common with grapes grown in warm, sunny climates. While it is known that at least much of the problem can be overcome by adding nitrogen-based YEAST nutrients during fermentation, the problem of combining suitable nitrogen nutrition for vine balance with optimum concentrations of natural nitrogen compounds in the berries remains largely unsolved.

POTASSIUM availability is another soil factor with mixed relationships to wine quality. Deficiencies are common in cool and humid climates, where the efficiency of water use for growth and yield (see HUMIDITY and CLIMATE AND WINE QUALITY) means that potassium and some other elements are diluted in the plant. Potassium-deficient vines are more than usually susceptible to DROUGHT and VINE DISEASES, and the fruit lacks sugar (see SUGAR IN GRAPES) as well as COLOUR and flavour.

Conversely, vines in hot, atmospherically arid climates can accumulate excess potassium in the leaves, stems, and fruit, especially if the soil contains reserves of mica-type clay minerals that release potassium. High potassium levels and PH in grapes, often the result of excessive leaf shading in a poor canopy microclimate, can lead to high wine potassium and pH, with all its attendant quality defects, and improved CANOPY MANAGEMENT can help greatly in assuring more appropriate fruit potassium levels.

The rule for other mineral nutrients appears to be that adequate supplies are needed equally for vine health and for fruit and wine quality, though there is very little evidence concerning the possible role of elements such as magnesium, phosphorus, or iron.

Possible specific roles for the micronutrients (COPPER, ZINC, MANGANESE, IRON, BORON, and MOLYBDENUM) remain obscure but potentially interesting. Their contents in the soil and availability to the plant vary enormously from soil to soil and, in often disparate ways, with SOIL MANAGEMENT. At the moment, however, no micronutrient constituent has been shown to be a decisive factor, either in wine quality or in any particular wine characteristic, and opinions about the effect of micronutrients on grape quality are highly speculative and sometimes exaggerated in non-scientific literature.

SOIL ACIDITY and SOIL ALKALINITY are further possible influences; but again, little firm evidence exists at present. Extremes in either direction, sufficient to upset vine nutrition and health seriously, seem unlikely to improve wine quality. On the other hand, vines can tolerate a fairly wide soil pH range without evident harm, while the potential micronutrient deficiencies that are often encountered at high pH levels can in most cases be readily overcome by foliar sprays or judicious choice of ROOTSTOCKS.

Although little studied by the Bordeaux school, properties related to the SOIL BIOTA can also affect vine growth and fruit quality. In particular, the ORGANIC MATTER in soils for viticulture needs careful evaluation. On the one hand, soils naturally high in organic matter tend to be too fertile, and to supply too much nitrogen, for good wine quality (as explained above). Soils naturally low in organic matter have a reduced nitrogen supply (unless fertilizers are added). On the other hand, many respected TERROIRS that have otherwise favourable characteristics for wine quality are naturally too low in organic matter, or have become so, so that both their physical and biological condition would benefit from its build-up and maintenance (see ORGANIC VITICULTURE). Very sandy soils need organic matter to give them sufficient capacity to store water and nutrients. All soils, and especially clayey soils, benefit from having an adequate organic matter content (1.5–3%) to give them friability (see SOIL STRUCTURE) and to encourage the activity of EARTHWORMS, which help to keep them well aerated and freely draining.

The nature and geological origin of the ROCKS or sediments from which soils are formed (see SOIL and GEOLOGY) are further factors sometimes held to influence wine quality and character. Soils formed from CHALK and LIMESTONE, for example, are highly valued in some cool climates, although not generally in warm regions such as the south of France or inland Australia. Most researchers consider the advantages of chalk and limestone to be related to their free DRAINAGE and the ability of the SUBSOIL to store water. Certain grape varieties, particularly Pinot Noir and Chardonnay, are also regarded by some as having a special requirement for chalk or limestone soils to produce their best wines; but again, this seems to be a largely northern French viewpoint. One universally positive role of chalk and limestone (or deliberately adding LIME) is that the resulting high level of calcium absorption to the soil clay particles helps to maintain a friable and stable SOIL STRUCTURE, thus encouraging aeration and drainage, even at high clay contents.

On the general role of geology, we can conclude that any influence is mostly indirect, via the shaping of TOPOGRAPHY determined by the underlying GEOLOGY, and through effects which are more properly those of the derived soil rather than of the rock or sediment. There can be some direct effects on water supply, however, where vine roots penetrate into the geological stratum underlying the soil or where water stored in the calcareous subsoil can contribute to water supply through capillary movements. Chalk in Champagne, the limestone of St-Émilion, and the Médoc gravel beds of Bordeaux (see SOIL WATER) have been cited in this regard.

Other factors

The great variation of soils over even short distances means that generalizations of any kind are dangerous. In some vineyards, especially those on ALLUVIAL soils, the soil type may change dramatically over a few metres, despite an apparent uniformity at the surface. For the same reason, SOIL MANAGEMENT procedures are seldom equally appropriate across an entire vineyard, let alone between different vineyards.

A second point is that, despite this, management technologies are increasingly available which obviate many of the effects of this variability. This is especially so in the New World. Among the more important is the use of DRIP IRRIGATION, which in climates with a dry summer can go far towards giving the vines a controlled water regime that is little influenced by soil type. Similarly, techniques of soil and (especially) leaf or PETIOLE analysis make possible a more controlled vine nutritional regime, so that differences in nutrient supply by the soil are moderated or even potentially eliminated.

A third point is that most vineyards throughout the world are now grafted to PHYLLOXERA-tolerant ROOTSTOCKS. The various rootstocks differ in their ability to take up mineral elements and water, in their capacity to root to depth, and in their effects on the VIGOUR of the vines grafted on to them. It is therefore possible to compensate for and adapt to particular soils as a means of approaching an optimal combination of vigour, nutrition, and canopy management for vine balance. Rootstocks are particularly effective in modulating water supply to the vines, and drought-resistant rootstocks such as 110 R or 140 Ru should be used in soils with low water-holding capacity in dry climates. Any consideration of soils now has to acknowledge the role of rootstocks.

The growing awareness of soil effects on wine quality and character in the New World has had several repercussions. One is the planting of vineyards on the less fertile hillside soils, as is evident in California and Chile, for example. Another is carrying out detailed SOIL MAPPING before planting as a prerequisite to VINEYARD DESIGN and the installation of irrigation, if used. More recently, ZONAL VITICULTURE, employing GLOBAL NAVIGATION SATELLITE SYSTEM and GEOGRAPHICAL INFORMATION SYSTEM technologies, allows differential management, including harvesting separate zones of a vineyard block to maximize quality. These effects, identified by REMOTE SENSING or PROXIMAL SENSING, are by and large due to soil differences and can be managed by means of PRECISION VITICULTURE techniques.

Conclusions

There can be no doubt that soil characteristics do influence grape quality, yield, and wine individuality, as has been shown by Seguin and by Renouf et al. in GRAND CRU vineyards in Bordeaux. However, in most situations the effects of soil are subsidiary to those of CLIMATE, VINE VARIETY, and VINE MANAGEMENT (see van Leeuwen et al. 2004). Of the influential soil characteristics, the most important are those governing the supply of water to the vine, probably followed by those influencing temperatures in and above the soil. Provided that vine growth is healthy, soil chemistry and vine nutrition do not play a major role, with the notable exception of nitrogen, and in some situations the effect of excess potassium on the pH of must and wine. Nitrogen in undoubtedly the most important nutrient the vine takes up from the soil: it has a major impact on vine vigour, yield, aroma compounds, and tannins (see Choné et al. and Helwi et al.).

Identifying the 'best' soil for winegrowing depends on the objectives of the winegrower and whether the vines are DRY-FARMED or irrigated. If the objective is to produce large yields of grapes for blending and producing lower-priced wines, then deep, well-drained soils that are fertile and either naturally well-watered or irrigated are best. However, if the objective is to produce low to moderate yields of high-quality grapes that can be used for higher-priced wines, and wines that reflect the particular TERROIR of a site, then infertile soils in which the vines are subject to a limiting factor (generally water deficit and/or limited nitrogen) perform best. Water deficit (see WATER STRESS) can be achieved naturally by dry-farming in deep, well-drained soils that have a significant proportion of sand and gravel. In the case of irrigated vines, where usually the soil water content of only the top 10–60 cm is controlled, this deficit can be applied through REGULATED DEFICIT IRRIGATION or PARTIAL ROOTZONE DRYING. In all cases, free drainage is very important. This is usually achieved in sandy, gravelly soils and in heavier textured soils that are well-structured, generally due to a predominance of calcium on the CLAY particles. An organic matter content of 1.5–3% is also important to support a good soil structure, especially of the topsoil, and to sustain an active and diverse SOIL BIOTA. R.E.S., C.v.L. & R.E.W.

Choné, X., et al., 'Terroir influence on water status and nitrogen status of non-irrigated Cabernet Sauvignon (*Vitis vinifera*): vegetative development, must and wine composition', *South African Journal of Enology and Viticulture*, 22/1 (2001), 8–15.

Helwi, P., et al., 'Vine nitrogen status and volatile thiols and their precursors from plot to transcriptome level', *BMC Plant Biology*, 16/173 (2016).

Renouf, V., et al., 'Soils, rootstocks and grapevine varieties in prestigious Bordeaux vineyards and their impact on yield and quality', *Journal International des Sciences de la Vigne et du Vin*, 44/3 (2010), 127–34.

Seguin, G., '"Terroirs" and pedology of wine growing', *Experientia*, 42 (1986), 861–72.

Smart, R., 'Terroir unmasked', *Wine Business Monthly* (June 2004), 34–8.

van Leeuwen, C., et al., 'Influence of climate, soil, and cultivar on terroir', *American Journal of Enology and Viticulture*, 55/3 (2004), 207–17.

van Leeuwen, C., et al., 'Soil related terroir factors, a review', *OENO One*, 52/2 (2018), 173–88.

White, R. E., *Understanding Vineyard Soils* (2nd edn, 2015).

soil biota is the generic term used to describe the population of organisms living in soil. Broadly speaking, these organisms can be divided into the 'reducers' (such as EARTHWORMS, slugs and SNAILS, BEETLES and their larvae, MITES and springtails, Protozoa, and NEMATODES, which feed on leaf litter and animal excreta to break it down into smaller fragments, without achieving much chemical decomposition) and the 'decomposers', which are much smaller organisms that colonize these organic fragments and gradually convert them into humus (see CARBON and ORGANIC MATTER). The decomposers, comprising Archaea, bacteria, actinomycetes, and fungi, are commonly called microorganisms, and the microbial biomass is measured by their collective weight. An active and diverse microbial biomass, interacting with the reducers, creates a soil's microbial ecosystem. Such a properly functioning soil ecosystem is important for the decomposition of ORGANIC MATTER and the turnover of NUTRIENTS in the soil, which is a prerequisite for good SOIL HEALTH. This applies equally well to conventional viticulture as to ORGANIC and BIODYNAMIC VITICULTURE. See also MYCORRHIZA, MICROBIAL TERROIR, and BIOCHAR. R.E.W.

soil colour, a term normally referring to the surface colour of a soil although it may also be applied to various layers or horizons in a SOIL PROFILE. Some viticultural folklore associates red wine with red soils, and white wines with white

S

or grey soils. However, topsoil colour is very heterogeneous, as is the spatial distribution of SOIL TYPES within vineyards potentially planted to a single variety. So any support for such a relationship is at best circumstantial.

Colour can affect soil temperature and that of the air immediately above it. This depends on albedo, the reflectance of SUNLIGHT. Dark-coloured soils or rocks absorb much of the incoming sunlight energy and convert it to heat. Therefore, whereas they reflect less light than light-coloured soils, they radiate more heat at night. This may be especially beneficial in cool climates. Other examples of the exploitation of these thermal characteristics include the vineyards of Deidesheim in the PFALZ region of Germany, where black BASALT rock is mined and spread on the vineyards to help produce grapes with high sugar concentration. Fragmented dark-grey SLATE helps Riesling to ripen in the otherwise cool MOSEL. Dark-coloured SCHIST soils are reportedly the only ones on which grapes can be ripened at the extreme northern limit of viticulture in BELGIUM. At the other extreme, the exceedingly reflective white ALBARIZA soils of JEREZ in southern Spain produce the best (white) grapes for sherry in a very hot climate, which would seem counter-intuitive.

The relationship between soil colour and temperature suitability for vine-growing is far from straightforward, however. Many reddish and brown soils are used for viticulture in hot areas such as the Mediterranean wine regions and also in much of Australia and California. However, such soils predominate in these regions and are not known to offer any advantage to viticulture because of their colour: see CLIMATE AND WINE QUALITY. Differences in soil colour have little effect on sunlight reflected back into the CANOPY which might affect PHOTOSYNTHESIS. French experiments have shown an improvement in grape (and apple) colour from using reflective foil on the soil surface. See further discussion under SUNLIGHT.

Soil colour is in any case a useful indicator of some of a soil's other properties, which probably have more effect on VINE PHYSIOLOGY and therefore on wine quality. For example, black soils may indicate a high content of ORGANIC MATTER. Red or brown are due to the presence of oxidized IRON compounds and normally indicate good DRAINAGE. A pale-grey soil surface, or soil layer, shows that most of the original iron compounds have been reduced as a result of bad drainage and waterlogging and eventually leached downwards, often to be deposited in a heavier-textured SUBSOIL.

The colour of the subsoil is a particularly important indicator of soil suitability for viticulture. Except where it consists largely of decomposing chalk or LIMESTONE, a blue-grey or mottled subsoil shows drainage that is usually too poor for viticulture—or at least, a need for artificial drainage. R.E.S. & R.E.W.

soil compaction in vineyards is due to the passage of machinery, especially if it is heavy and the soil is wet and CLAY-textured. Vineyards are particularly prone to compaction because tractor wheel tracks are confined to narrow strips, often in close proximity to the vine row. The soil is compressed so that the surface absorbs less water and soil pores are destroyed, and the supply of air and water to vine roots is diminished (see SOIL STRUCTURE). Further, soil strength is increased, providing a physical barrier to root growth and EARTHWORM activity. Soil compaction can reduce vine VIGOUR and thus YIELD and, in some instances, wine quality. Soil compaction, which may be the most serious environmental damage done in many vineyards, can be reduced by avoiding the use of heavy machinery on wet soils and by using tracked rather than wheeled vehicles. Traditional horse-drawn equipment is enjoying a (very small) revival, particularly among practitioners of BIODYNAMIC VITICULTURE. R.E.S.

Lagacherie, P., et al., 'Spatial variability of soil compaction over a vineyard region in relation with soils and cultivation operations', *Geoderma*, 134/1-2 (2006), 207–16.

soil depth, a loose term for the depth to the boundary between the SOIL and its parent material; or, alternatively, the depth to which plant ROOT GROWTH is possible before reaching some impermeable barrier. Examples of the latter include the tight and/or poorly drained subsoils of many duplex soils (see SOIL), which occur in south-eastern Australia, South Africa, and the Piedmont region of the eastern US; cemented ironstone, or 'coffee rock', which forms at the base of some iron-rich podzolic soils that have been subject to leaching; or subsoils with poor structure due to exchangeable SODIUM, or excessively high concentrations of salt or acidity, or some other toxic factor which effectively prevents further root penetration.

Soil fertility is a combination of fertility per soil volume unit and the rooting depth, which determines the amount of soil available for each vine. Seguin's work shows that if soil is fertile or moderately fertile per soil volume unit, deep rooting leads to excessive soil fertility (due to the availability of water and nutrients) and thus excessive VIGOUR. As a result, in most cases shallow rooting is a quality factor, because it reduces vigour and yield. Only in soils with very poor fertility per soil volume unit, such as the gravelly soils of the MÉDOC or MARLBOROUGH, New Zealand, is deep rooting an advantage. These soils have such a low water-holding capacity per soil volume unit that, unless the vines are irrigated, deep rooting is necessary to provide a regular supply of water to the vine. Seguin has also shown that deep rooting in these soils where water drains very rapidly prevents the rapid absorption by the root system of rain shortly before harvest, thus helping to prevent ROT.

There is a great deal of evidence, in many other situations, that great wines may be produced on soils where vine rooting is shallow. For example, most great ST-ÉMILIONS are produced on the limestone plateau, where vine rooting rarely exceeds 60 cm/23 in and can be as little as 30 cm (as in parts of the vineyard of Ch AUSONE). The roots do not penetrate the rock, although Duteau et al. have shown that water can move from the bedrock to the roots by capillarity. On the heavy clay soils in PETRUS and Ch CHEVAL BLANC, vine rooting does not exceed 130 cm/50 in because of the clay's physical resistance to root penetration. In the Languedoc, the best wines are produced on shallow soils on the hillsides and simple wines are produced on the plains, where rooting is much deeper.

Shallow soils are therefore of major importance in cool, wet climates, while somewhat deeper soils might be an advantage in very dry climates, especially when IRRIGATION is not allowed or not possible. C.v.L. & R.E.W.

Duteau, J., 'Contribution des réserves hydriques profondes du calcaire à Astéries compact à l'alimentation en eau de la vigne dans le Bordelais', *Agronomie*, 7/10 (1987), 589–865.
Seguin, G., '"Terroirs" and pedology of wine growing', *Experientia*, 42 (1986), 861–72.
van Leeuwen, C., et al., 'Soil-related terroir factors: a review', *OENO One*, 52/2 (2018), 173–188.

soil disinfection. See FUMIGATION.

soil erosion, shifting or removal of soil by wind or running water. Wind erosion is not common in established vineyards, because the vines themselves constitute an effective WINDBREAK, although it can be a problem in young vineyards. Driving sand, in particular, can seriously injure young vines, and there can also be irreparable loss of most valuable topsoil. The danger can be minimized by growing grass COVER CROPS that act as windbreaks as well as directly binding the soil. VINE GUARDS can be used to protect young vines from sandblasting—and from attack by animals such as rabbits and hares.

Erosion by water, on the other hand, is always a potential problem on the sloping sites that normally afford the best MESOCLIMATES for wine quality (see HILLSIDE VINEYARDS). Some steeply sloping sites, such as in the MOSEL region of Germany and the northern RHÔNE, necessitate a constant and laborious replacement of soil from the bottom of the slope to the top. Even in more moderately sloping sites in the Côte d'Or and Champagne, clean TILLAGE of the mid rows may lead to soil erosion during summer storms.

Planting vines across a slope, rather than up and down the slope, provides some measure of erosion control, especially if the vine rows are hilled. Contoured TERRACES are an effective means of erosion control on steeper slopes (between 7 and 15%), as practised in the NAPA Valley, California, and the FRIULI region of north-east Italy. On very steep slopes on stony soils, as in the Vaud region of Switzerland and the DOURO Valley in Portugal, stone terraces have been constructed. However, vineyard cultural operations are easier with rows oriented up and down a slope, in which case other methods must be used to control erosion, such as avoiding unnecessary tillage, spreading MULCHES (including vine prunings) to protect bare soil surfaces, and planting mid-row cover crops. Permanent grass cover crops offer the best protection but are feasible only in those situations where water and NITROGEN supplies are sufficient for both grass and vines. Planting on convex hill slopes helps too, to the extent that there are no external sources of flowing water. Where occasional water flowing on to or across a site cannot be avoided, it can often be made harmless by diversionary banks, directing the flow into drains or permanently grassed waterways which follow the natural flow line.

Other measures to control erosion include maintaining the soil's ORGANIC MATTER content and stable SOIL STRUCTURE (see also SOIL MANAGEMENT). These conditions enable rain to be absorbed readily where it falls. Row orientation and such cultivation as is unavoidable should ideally be directed just a little off the contour, so that any water flow along furrows will be gentle and harmless, able to spill out on to permanently grassed waterways. Cultivation straight up and down slopes predisposes to general erosion, but the practicalities of vineyard design often limit control over the direction and slopes of cultivation. R.E.W.

White, R. E., *Soils for Fine Wines* (2003).

soil fertility, the physical, chemical, and biological characteristics of a soil determining its ability to support vigorous plant growth. A fertile soil is generally understood to be one with a high content of available plant nutrients; moderate to high ORGANIC MATTER content supporting an active and diverse SOIL BIOTA; good SOIL STRUCTURE and DRAINAGE; and typically a LOAMY SOIL TEXTURE that can store large amounts of water. Neither SOIL ACIDITY nor SOIL ALKALINITY will be excessive, so that the mineral nutrients will all be in a favourable balance of availability for plant growth. Research in Australia by Oliver et al. and Riches et al. (see SOIL HEALTH) has identified a minimum set of important biophysical and chemical properties and their optimum ranges for healthy vine growth and yields of quality fruit.

Highly fertile soils, especially those rich in NITROGEN, are undesirable for wine grapes because they encourage excessive vegetation and a shaded CANOPY MICROCLIMATE. This in turn can reduce both YIELD and, especially, the composition of the grapes and their suitability for winemaking. Although vineyard management cannot greatly improve this state of affairs, VIGOUR may be reduced by planting permanent grass COVER CROPS, using low-vigour ROOTSTOCKS, avoiding the use of FERTILIZERS except to correct nutrient deficiencies, and not over-irrigating the vines. On the other hand, the notion that only infertile soils can make good wines is undoubtedly mistaken. CANOPY MANAGEMENT techniques can allow vigorous vines on moderately fertile soils to mimic the canopy microclimates of traditional vineyards on less fertile soils, with resultant improvements in quality. These principles have been elucidated by Carbonneau and Casteran and successfully applied in many situations in the BORDEAUX environment as well as in many NEW WORLD vineyards.

See also SOIL AND WINE QUALITY, CLIMATE AND WINE QUALITY, and BALANCE. R.E.S. & R.E.W.

Carbonneau, A. P., and Casteran, P., 'Interactions "training system × soil × rootstock" with regard to vine ecophysiology, vigour, yield and red wine quality in the Bordeaux area', *Acta Horticulturae*, 206 (1987), 119–40.

Smart, R. E., and Robinson, M., *Sunlight into Wine: A Handbook for Winegrape Canopy Management* (1991).

soil health is, for a soil scientist, synonymous with soil quality, but the term emphasizes the living nature of soil, dependent on the healthy function of SOIL BIOTA. Soil quality may be defined holistically as 'the capacity of a soil to function within ECOSYSTEM boundaries to sustain biological productivity, maintain environmental quality, and promote plant and animal health'. A soil's condition and capability depend on the interaction of many chemical, physical, and biological processes and determine its suitability for the specific aims of a viticulturist or winegrower in a particular location. See also VINEYARD SITE SELECTION. R.E.W.

Doran, J. W., and Parkin, T. B., 'Defining and assessing soil quality', in J. W. Doran, et al. (eds.), *Defining Soil Quality for a Sustainable Environment* (1994).

Oliver, D. P., et al., 'Review: soil physical and chemical properties as indicators of soil quality in Australian viticulture', *Australian Journal of Grape and Wine Research*, 19 (2013), 129–39.

Riches, D., et al., 'Review: soil biological properties as indicators of soil quality in Australian viticulture', *Australian Journal of Grape and Wine Research*, 19 (2013), 311–23.

soil management, the practices of TILLAGE, or NO-TILL, of soils in vineyards, including the use of COVER CROPS, COMPOST, and MULCHES, and other measures to improve the soil's physical, chemical, and biological condition (see SOIL FERTILITY). In the broadest sense, this term can also embrace IRRIGATION, the use of HERBICIDES, and the addition of FERTILIZER.

In the past, soil management has consisted primarily of clean tillage to control WEEDS. The advantages of this approach include the avoidance of herbicides and encouraging roots to go deeper. The disadvantages are increasingly recognized, however. Over time, clean tillage leads to a loss of ORGANIC MATTER, a deterioration in SOIL STRUCTURE, and also a decline in SOIL BIOTA, particularly EARTHWORMS. Modern soil management seeks to conserve and, if necessary, increase the organic matter content; to conserve and improve soil structure and porosity, and thereby improve aeration and free absorption and DRAINAGE of SOIL WATER and resistance to SOIL EROSION; and to maintain a reserve of nutrients in organic and slowly available inorganic forms to provide a steady and balanced supply of SOIL NUTRIENTS matched to the plants' needs.

Aspects of soil management include growing cover crops, with minimal tillage for their establishment; using inorganic fertilizers (as needed) mainly to grow these crops, and thence to supply the vines as far as possible from organic sources; summer mulching with the residues of the cover crop grown *in situ* or with imported vegetable materials or manures, preferably composted; and, when essential, the use of environment-friendly herbicides to control cover crops and weeds. The use of LIME or gypsum may be required for some soils. Avoiding SOIL COMPACTION is also very important. These practices encourage the roots to spread and grow more deeply, improve machine access to the vineyard after rain, help to control vigour, and reduce the use of herbicides.

All these measures serve to improve soil physical conditions for vine ROOT GROWTH, thereby improving vine health, YIELD, and in some instances wine quality. R.E.S. & R.E.W.

McCarthy, M. G., et al., 'Soil and management and frost control', in B. G. Coombe and P. R. Dry (eds.), *Viticulture*, ii: *Practices* (2nd edn, 2006).

White, R. E., and Krstic, M. P., *Healthy Soils for Healthy Vines* (2019).

soil mapping, procedure used before vineyard planting to assist in decisions about IRRIGATION layout, location of VINE VARIETIES and ROOTSTOCKS, application of FERTILIZERS and soil amendments such as LIME and gypsum, and choice of TRAINING SYSTEM. Soil mapping is becoming more common in vineyard developments around the world and represents recognition of the idea that local conditions,

S

especially the soil, have important effects on GRAPE COMPOSITION AND WINE QUALITY. It is also used after a vineyard has been planted, often much later, to help understand vineyard variability.

Ideally, an electromagnetic survey should be carried out (see PROXIMAL SENSING) to identify soil variations within a vineyard block. Accurately located by GLOBAL NAVIGATION SATELLITE SYSTEMS, these data are fed into a GEOGRAPHICAL INFORMATION SYSTEM so that high-resolution maps of the soil's variability can be prepared. Based on these maps, soil pits are dug, usually by a backhoe, at sites covering the full range of variation so that SOIL PROFILES can be described in detail. Where such a preliminary survey has not been carried out, pits may be dug on a grid so that the soil can be sampled and described by a soil specialist, although this is less effective at capturing variability. Soil maps can be used in vineyard design; one of the most useful is that which estimates 'readily available water', or RAW. See TERROIR for a full discussion of the relevant issues; see also SOIL, SOIL AND WINE QUALITY, and PRECISION VITICULTURE. R.E.S. & R.E.W.

Proffitt, T., et al., *Precision Viticulture: A New Era in Vineyard Management and Wine Production* (2006).

soil nutrients, elements (see MINERALS) and ions occurring in the soil which are taken up by plant roots. Soils that are rich in nutrients are often termed 'fertile', but such soils do not always produce good-quality wine (see SOIL FERTILITY). The amounts of nutrients that are available to the vine depend on the soil's mineralogy, the amount and nature of ORGANIC MATTER, and also the soil PH. Soils with a long history of COVER CROPS containing LEGUMES have high levels of topsoil organic matter and are often rich in NITROGEN. However, grass and cereal cover crops compete with vines for nitrogen, in which case nitrogen is not as readily available to the vine. Soils in old vineyards, especially if clean-tilled (see TILLAGE), are often relatively impoverished of organic matter and may have high levels of available COPPER as a result of repeated FUNGICIDE application. Many nutrients including nitrogen and PHOSPHORUS, for example, are less available in acid soils (see SOIL ACIDITY). Others such as IRON, MANGANESE, COPPER, and ZINC are less available in alkaline soils. Nutrient deficiencies are diagnosed by symptoms in the vines, or by plant and soil tests, and can be remedied by applying FERTILIZERS and MANURES. R.E.S. & R.E.W.

Robinson, J. B., 'Grapevine nutrition', in B. G. Coombe and P. R. Dry (eds.), *Viticulture*, ii: *Practices* (2nd edn, 2006).

soil potential, a viticultural term coined in South Africa to describe the ability of a soil to support vigorous vine growth, sometimes referred to as **site potential**. A soil of high potential will be well supplied with water (by rainfall or IRRIGATION), nutrients, and air and will be free-draining, promoting a large and healthy root system. Such a soil will create vines of high VIGOUR, which in turn may require special management. R.E.S.

soil preparation, the treatment of SOIL before PLANTING a vineyard, can be an important viticultural operation. Proper attention at this stage can determine the long-term success or otherwise of a vineyard.

Having selected the best possible site (see VINEYARD SITE SELECTION, TOPOGRAPHY, and TERROIR) and vineyard layout, and having assured suitable DRAINAGE, the potential vine-grower should in most soils, especially in duplex soils (see SOIL) and shallow soils over LIMESTONE and SHALE, undertake deep RIPPING along the paths of the future vine rows. This should be done when the soil is dry enough for compacted layers (see SOIL COMPACTION) and any hard pans (cemented layers) to be shattered by the ripper. Such treatment opens up the SUBSOIL and facilitates penetration by the vine roots.

If a vineyard is replanted, particular care must be taken to remove the roots of the old vines since these can harbour VIRUS DISEASES or FUNGAL DISEASES. Where populations of pathogenic NEMATODES are large, FUMIGATION may be necessary.

If the SOIL ACIDITY is high, with a topsoil pH less than 5.5 in calcium chloride (see PH), adding LIME will be beneficial. SOIL TESTING should be used to identify any nutrient deficiencies or toxicities, to guide the use of lime and other FERTILIZERS, and also to indicate whether gypsum should be applied to improve SOIL STRUCTURE, especially in clayey soils.

Finally, WEEDS need to be controlled. In most climates it is usual to grow an autumn–winter green manure crop to suppress weeds and add ORGANIC MATTER before vine planting in spring. R.E.W.

Boehm, E. W., and Coombe, B. G., 'Vineyard establishment', in B. G. Coombe and P. R. Dry (eds.), *Viticulture*, ii: *Practices* (2nd edn, 2006).

soil profile, the vertical face of a SOIL, exposed by digging, that generally consists of visually and texturally distinct layers (known as horizons) which are more or less parallel to the Earth's surface. During SOIL MAPPING, the soil surveyor describes the properties of each layer (sometimes also sublayers), especially those that will have an impact on vine ROOT GROWTH. See also GEOLOGY and TERROIR. R.E.S.

soil structure describes the physical arrangement of the fundamental mineral particles (as described in SOIL TEXTURE) into larger structures called aggregates. The size, shape, and stability of these aggregates help to determine the friability of the surface soil and its ability to accept rainwater and resist erosion (see SOIL EROSION). The creation of this physical framework also provides a variety of voids or pores that are important for air movement, water DRAINAGE, and ROOT penetration. A stable structure can withstand the effects of TILLAGE and SOIL COMPACTION by vineyard machinery.

To a varying degree in different soil types, soil structure depends on the following factors:

1. The amount and chemical composition of the CLAY. For stable structure, a soil must have a moderate clay content. Montmorillonite clays swell and shrink with wetting and drying, leading to a desirable 'self-mulching' of the soil surface, provided the content of exchangeable CALCIUM is not too high (see SOIL). Calcium ions flocculate clay minerals whereas SODIUM ions cause clay dispersion and the breakdown of aggregates. On the other hand, kaolinitic clays flocculate by edge-to-face attraction at PHS less than 6 and so can form stable aggregates. This effect is enhanced in the presence of iron and aluminium oxides. Illitic and mixed-layer clays are similar in structure to montmorillonite but show much less shrink and swell. In CALCAREOUS soils, calcium carbonate can be an effective bonding agent for aggregation.
2. ORGANIC MATTER content. Well-decomposed organic matter bonds to clay particles and iron and aluminium oxides and so lays the foundation for good structure. Additionally, gums and mucilages secreted by roots and soil microorganisms play an important part in stabilizing soil aggregates, and fine roots can form a mesh holding larger aggregates together.
3. Soil disturbance by tillage. All tillage can be destructive of soil structure, especially in clayey soils when wet. Repeated tillage exposes the organic matter within aggregates to faster decomposition, which weakens soil structure. Tillage is sometimes done to improve the 'tilth' of the surface soil, but this is a temporary effect and does not improve soil structure in the longer term.

Good SOIL MANAGEMENT aims principally to preserve good soil structure or to improve it in soils suffering some degradation. R.E.W.

White, R. E., *Understanding Vineyard Soils* (2nd edn, 2015).

soil testing involves measurements made in the field or laboratory of soil properties that indicate the physical, chemical, and biological condition of the soil (see SOIL FERTILITY). White and Krstic discuss the possible range of indicator properties for which tests can be chosen. Soil testing is a necessary adjunct to SOIL

MAPPING to determine soil PH (see SOIL ACIDITY, SOIL ALKALINITY), the amounts of available NUTRIENTS, and any adverse conditions such as SALINITY or too much SODIUM (see CATION EXCHANGE). Tests can be carried out for biological activity (see SOIL BIOTA) and for the presence of pathogenic organisms (see SOIL PREPARATION). Soil tests done before planting allow the grower to identify any deficiencies of essential elements and consequent FERTILIZER requirements or the existence of possible element toxicities. However, because the grapevine is a perennial plant, tissue analysis of leaf blades or PETIOLES, rather than soil testing, usually gives a better guide to any ongoing fertilizer requirements in established vineyards.

Field inspection to determine SOIL TEXTURE and the soil's natural DRAINAGE to as great a depth as possible is an essential preliminary to any vine planting. See also SOIL AND WINE QUALITY, TERROIR, and VINEYARD SITE SELECTION.

R.E.S. & R.E.W.

Proffitt, T., 'Assessing soil quality and interpreting soil test results' (GWRDC/Wines of Western Australia, 2014). www.winewa.asn.au/wp-content/uploads/2020/04/Assessing_soil_quality_Wine_-grape.pdf.

White, R. E., and Krstic, M. P., *Healthy Soils for Healthy Vines* (2019).

soil texture describes the size distribution of soil particles (those less than 2 mm diameter), simplified to indicate the proportions of clay, silt, and fine and coarse sand (STONES AND ROCKS and ORGANIC MATTER are excluded). The individual constituents are defined below. Soils predominantly of clay are described as heavy-textured. Loams are medium-textured soils, normally containing a fairly even balance of clay, silt, and sand. Sands are light-textured soils, often loose and gritty, with a low clay content. Certain mineral elements, most notably CALCIUM, complement textural differences in helping to determine soil friability (see SOIL STRUCTURE).

Clay is the finest of the size fractions, with particles less than 0.002 mm diameter. When mixed with water, clay particles may remain in colloidal suspension for some time, especially if the proportion of exchangeable SODIUM is greater than 6% of the CATION EXCHANGE CAPACITY. Because their surface areas are so large relative to their volumes, they have by far the greatest capacity for combining with, adsorbing, and holding plant mineral nutrients and water. Fertile soils normally have at least a moderate proportion of clay.

Silt is an intermediate fraction, comprising particles between 0.002 and 0.02–0.05 mm diameter (the upper limit for silt varies according to the particle-size classification used). Silt particles are small enough to be carried large distances by wind and are also carried in suspension by turbulent rivers. Both clay and silt particles are prominent in ALLUVIAL soils deposited by river floods.

Sand particles are divided into fine sand (0.02 to 0.2 mm) and coarse sand (0.2 to 2 mm diameter); again, this size division varies according to the particle-size classification used. Unless mixed with a proportion of clay, sand remains loose under most conditions. In contrast to clay, the surface area of a sand particle is small relative to its volume, so it has little capacity for surface binding and storing of plant nutrients or water.

Soil texture can be measured by a rigorous particle-size analysis in a laboratory or by a soil specialist in the field, who determines texture by feel. Organic matter is destroyed before such a laboratory analysis, but in the field it can make sandy soils feel more silty and clay soils feel less sticky.

Stones and rocks appear to have particular significance for viticulture, through their effects on limiting soil water-holding capacity and, additionally, on TEMPERATURE both within and immediately above the soil. Stony soils are also usually well drained and have a low water-holding capacity, while a surface layer of stones greatly enhances resistance to SOIL EROSION and reduces surface water loss by EVAPORATION.

Commercial viticulture is carried out across a very wide range of soil textures. Clay and clay-loam soils can be suitable provided that they contain ample calcium (as in most LIMESTONE- or CHALK-derived soils) and organic matter to improve their structure. The strongest growth of vines, as with most other plants, is usually on loams and clay-loam soils. Whether or not this is desirable depends on various other management and environmental factors, as described for example under SOIL FERTILITY and VIGOUR. Soils of clay-loam to sandy clay-loam texture can store in the vicinity of 15 mm/0.6 in of available SOIL WATER per 10 cm/4 in of soil depth, in forms that the vine roots can extract.

Soils consisting mostly of sand can pose problems for viticulture because of their lack of storage capacity for both water and nutrients. Typically they will hold 10 mm or less of plant-available water per 10 cm of soil depth. The great depth of some sandy soils can be an offsetting factor, however, as in parts of the BORDEAUX region, because vine roots penetrate many metres if the SUBSOIL texture and DRAINAGE permit and can thus exploit a large enough volume to compensate for the low water-holding capacity per soil volume unit. In soils of low water-holding capacity, the problems of water availability can be overcome by supplying IRRIGATION.

An ideal soil for wine quality, depending on CLIMATE and the rate of evaporation together with the potential for irrigation, will balance texture against root-available depth to give an adequate storage capacity for water and nutrients and to provide the vine with a steady moderate supply of both for BALANCED growth and fruiting. No single soil texture has a monopoly of these characteristics. Seguin notes that in the Bordeaux region the soils giving the best water regimes and producing the best wines range from the dominant deep, stony sands of the MÉDOC, because of their low water-holding capacity, to heavy (but well-structured) clays in POMEROL, because the water is present but not easily available to the vines. Thus in Bordeaux extreme textures are generally better than intermediate textures such as clay-loam soils, which can hold significant supplies of water readily available to the vine.

See also GEOLOGY, SOIL, CLAY, and SOIL WATER.

C.v.L. & R.E.W.

Seguin, G., 'Influence des terroirs viticoles' ('Influence of viticultural terroirs'), *Bulletin de l'OIV*, 56 (1983), 3–18.

van Leeuwen, C., et al., 'Soil-related terroir factors: a review', *OENO One*, 52/2 (2018), 173–88.

White, R. E., *Understanding Vineyard Soils* (2nd edn, 2015).

soil types. Soil types are identified using soil classifications which put soils into groups according to whether they are alike or unlike. Several national classifications are in use, but (with the exception of soil types such as RENDZINA) there is little common terminology. In the world of wine, therefore, terms reflecting the parent rock (e.g. 'granitic') or a soil's texture (e.g. 'sandy', 'gravelly') or its formation (e.g. 'alluvial') are most widely used. For further examples of types of SOIL and ROCK, see individual entries on ALLUVIUM, BASALT, CALCAREOUS, CHALK, CLAY, COLLUVIUM, GNEISS, GRANITE, GRAVEL, LIMESTONE, LOAM, LOESS, MARL, QUARTZITE, RENDZINA, SAND, SANDSTONE, SCHIST, SHALE, SILT, SLATE, TERRA ROSSA, TUFF, TUFFEAU, and VOLCANIC. See also SOIL AND WINE QUALITY and GEOLOGY, however, for evidence of soil's relatively indirect role in shaping wine and wine quality. R.E.W.

soil water, that water held in the pore spaces of the soil within the potential rooting zone for vines. When all the pore space is filled with water, the soil is said to be saturated. Unless the soil is a very heavy clay (see SOIL TEXTURE), it will normally drain within 48 hours to a state called its field capacity (FC), which corresponds to a soil water suction of about 10 kiloPascals (kPa) (see WATER STRESS). With soil EVAPORATION and, most importantly, extraction of water by the vine roots, the soil water content decreases until a point is reached when the vine can no longer extract water fast enough to avoid wilting during the day and non-recovery at night. This condition is called the permanent wilting point (PWP). The amount of water held in the vine rootzone between FC and PWP defines the available water capacity (AWC). The amount of plant-available water (PAW) in a SOIL PROFILE is the product of the AWC and rootzone depth and is sometimes called readily available water (RAW). In poor-draining soils, a lack of OXYGEN quickly kills the vine roots.

Water supply to the vines is the key factor in grape quality. Vines are Mediterranean plants that need very little water: they can easily grow in climates with only 400 mm/15 in of rainfall a year, provided that the soil has at least an average PAW and EVAPOTRANSPIRATION rates are not too high. Some water deficits are essential to growing good-quality grapes, particularly for red winemaking (see WATER STRESS).

Water supply to the vine depends on climatic parameters (RAINFALL, potential evapotranspiration), soil parameters (AWC and soil depth), and plant-related factors (rooting depth, leaf area, crop load). Studies on TERROIR by Morlat and van Leeuwen et al., for example, show that terroir which produces high-quality red wine supplies only moderate amounts of water to the vines, thus inducing water-deficit stress. The gravelly soils of the MÉDOC were intensively studied by the late Gérard Seguin, who used a neutron moisture probe to investigate vine–water relations in these soils as early as 1966. However, the fact that these soils are deep is an exception rather than a general rule and can be explained only by their high gravel content and their low clay content (see SOIL DEPTH). These soils can be subject to temporary waterlogging until flowering, but generally the water table is not within reach of the roots during ripening. If it is, wine quality suffers (van Leeuwen et al. 1994). Mild water stress may become more severe as CLIMATE CHANGE leads to greater evapotranspiration and the need to introduce IRRIGATION to previously unirrigated vineyards in order to maintain quality.

Regular or permanent waterlogging, even if only of the subsoil or the zone immediately overlying it, is a clear counter-indicator for vines, particularly if it occurs during the vine-growing season. The optimum soil-water regime is thus usually found where there is an adequate depth of well-drained soil, with at least moderate contents of CLAY, SILT, and ORGANIC MATTER so that water can be supplied steadily from soil reserves over a long period. The less clay and organic matter, the deeper the soil needs to be to achieve that end. However, too much available soil water can be counterproductive in viticulture if it promotes too much vegetative VIGOUR or helps to prolong vegetative growth into the fruit-ripening period. (See also CLIMATE AND WINE QUALITY, SOIL AND WINE QUALITY.)

Ideally there should be ample available soil water during FLOWERING and FRUIT SET, diminishing so as to create just enough water deficit around VERAISON to inhibit further vegetative growth. Opinions vary as to the optimum water supply between veraison and RIPENING, but most agree that there should be no severe stress through this period; nor should there be so much water available, especially after preceding stress, as to encourage a sudden uptake into the berries or renewed vegetative growth.

The binding capacity of the soil for the water that remains after draining to its FC has its own significance for vine–water relations. Some is so tightly bound to the CLAY that roots cannot extract it at all, and some can only be extracted slowly. This explains why heavy clay soils, such as those of PETRUS in Pomerol which induce early water deficits, can produce very fine red wines (van Leeuwen et al. 1994). The small amount of available water in sandy soils, on the other hand, is readily extracted and therefore easily exhausted. However, in sandy soils, vine rooting is often very deep and the PAW can be too large to grow high-quality fruit (van Leeuwen et al. 1994, 2004).

Even in MEDITERRANEAN CLIMATES with very low summer rainfall, the best soils are not those on the plains with a large PAW but the more shallow, stony soils of the slopes, which have a much lower PAW. However, when the PAW is very small (shallow and very stony soils on hard LIMESTONE bedrock, as in LA CLAPE, near Narbonne), amount and timing of rainfall is critical and water stress might be so severe as to reduce wine quality. In such climates, relatively shallow soils, or sandy/stony soils with limited PAW, combined with supplementary irrigation when needed (and permitted), can have advantages in allowing the best control over water availability to the vines. In hot inland regions, such as the CENTRAL VALLEY, California, and the MURRAY DARLING region in Australia, evapotranspiration rates are so high in summer that, irrespective of soil type, irrigation is essential to grow healthy vines and produce reasonable yields. In the majority of drip-irrigated vineyards in the New World, irrigation may be managed so as to avoid severe water stress but produce a desirable amount of stress at the appropriate time. R.E.S., C.v.L. & R.E.W.

Morlat, R., 'Characterization of viticultural terroirs using a simple field model based on soil depth. I-Validation of the water supply regime, phenology and vine vigour, in the Anjou vineyard (France)', *Plant and Soil*, 281 (2006), 37–54.

van Leeuwen, C., and Seguin, G., 'Incidences de l'alimentation en eau de la vigne, appréciée par l'état hydrique du feuillage, sur le développement de l'appareil végétatif et la maturation du raisin (Vitis vinifera variété Cabernet franc, Saint-Emilion, 1990)', *Journal International des Sciences de la Vigne et du Vin*, 28/2 (1994), 81–110.

van Leeuwen, C., et al., 'Influence of climate, soil, and cultivar on terroir', *American Journal of Enology and Viticulture*, 55/3 (2004), 207–17.

van Leeuwen, C., et al., 'Vine water status is a key factor in grape ripening and vintage quality for red Bordeaux wine. How can it be assessed for management purposes?', *Journal International des Sciences de la Vigne et du Vin*, 43/3 (2009), 121–34.

White, R. E., *Understanding Vineyard Soils* (2nd edn, 2015).

Solaris, increasingly popular, early-ripening, light-skinned, DISEASE-RESISTANT VARIETY bred by Norbert Becker in southern Germany in 1975. The vine's ability to reach high sugar levels in cool climates and produce fruity wines with good acidity has encouraged plantings around the world, for example in Scandinavia, Belgium, Holland, England, and cooler parts of Eastern Europe and Germany.

solera, system of fractional blending used in JEREZ and other wine regions in ANDALUCÍA for maintaining the consistency of a style of SHERRY which takes its name from those barrels closest to the *suelo*, or floor, from which the final blend was customarily drawn. The system was created for commercial reasons in the second half of the 19th century. Previously, sherry was vintage-dated.

The system is effectively a subtler, and much more labour-intensive, version of the BLENDING of TABLE WINES between one vintage and another, although the solera system concerns BARREL-AGED liquids and is made up of several scales. Depending on market demand, a fraction of wine is removed from the oldest scale of the solera, the so-called solera barrels themselves, and replaced (although the barrels are never filled completely) with wine from the next scale of barrels containing wine of the same type but one year younger, the so-called first criadera. They in turn are replenished from the scale two years younger (the second criadera) and so on, the youngest scale being replenished with new wine. This system is particularly useful for FLOR wines because the addition of younger wine provides micronutrients to sustain the flor yeast for several years. It takes several years' operation for a solera to reach an equilibrium average age. Many soleras in Jerez were started decades ago; since no barrel is ever emptied, there is always some of the oldest wine in the final blend. If a product is labelled 'Solera 1880', for example, it should come from a solera established in 1880.

Fewer scales are needed to produce consistent AMONTILLADO or OLOROSO sherries than FINO or MANZANILLA sherries because these fuller, richer wines vary less from year to year.

There is a common belief that the wine is normally bottled from the oldest scale of barrels, but this is not always so. It may well happen that the producer regularly bottles a combination of a few different criaderas, in a proportion that may change every year, so as to keep a sustainable and identifiable style of wine.

The solera system is also used for blending Brandy de Jerez and for many other strong wines such as those in CONDADO DE HUELVA, Alicante (see FONDILLÓN), MÁLAGA, MONTILLA, and MADEIRA in Spain, TOPAQUE AND MUSCAT in Australia, and MARSALA in Italy, as well as in some Roussillon wines in France, in VIN DES GLACIERS in Switzerland, and in the production of top-quality VINEGAR.

For mathematical calculations of the average age of a solera and the time required to reach equilibrium average age, see Baker et al. J.B.

Baker, G. A., et al., 'Theory and application of fractional blending programs', *Hilgardia*, 21 (1952), 383–409.

soluble solids, also called total soluble solids (TSS) and total dissolved solids (TDS), refers to the collective concentration in unfermented grape juice of all solutes (dissolved molecules and ions). The predominant solutes, accounting for about 90% of the total, in the juice of ripe grapes are the reducing sugars GLUCOSE and FRUCTOSE; others are acids (MALIC and TARTARIC), ions (organic and inorganic), and literally hundreds of inorganic and organic molecules that together contribute to the characteristics that make grapes such an adaptable and useful product. Collective concentrations of TSS range from 5 to over 25% and may be expressed in many ways, most usually either as degrees BRIX, BAUMÉ, or OECHSLE. See also MUST WEIGHT. B.G.C.

sommelier, widely used French term for a specialist wine waiter or wine steward, sometimes abbreviated to 'somm' in the US, where an eponymous 2012 FILM was devoted to four sommeliers' efforts to pass the MASTER SOMMELIER exam. The sommelier's job is to ensure that any wine ordered is served correctly and, ideally, to advise on the individual characteristics of every wine on the establishment's wine list and on FOOD-AND-WINE MATCHING. In some establishments, a sommelier, sometimes called a wine director, may also be responsible for compiling the list, buying and storing the wine, and restocking whatever passes for a CELLAR. (All too few restaurants today have their own serious collection of wines, although there are notable exceptions such as, in Paris, the Tour d'Argent, whose cellar is but a few feet from the River Seine, and Taillevent, whose cellar is so important that it has spawned a retail wine business.)

A sommelier should present the wine (or wines) ordered to the person who has selected the wine before opening to ensure that there has been no misunderstanding (and so that the customer can especially check that the vintage corresponds to expectations). This is a good time for the customer to check that the bottle feels at the right SERVING temperature. The bottle should be opened in view of the customer, and, if a wine is to be DECANTED (and that is an option that any decent sommelier should be able to offer), that operation should be performed in public, too.

Some sommeliers offer the cork to the customer to smell, which is well meaning but is no certain guide to whether or not the wine is FAULTY. Some sublime wines come from under some rather unpleasant-smelling corks, and vice versa.

A surer guide to whether a particular bottle happens to be one of the relatively few to exhibit a FAULT (CORK TAINT is the most common) is to examine the small tasting sample usually offered by the sommelier to the customer for this very purpose. A glance will confirm that it is not cloudy, dull, or fizzing when it should not. A swift inhalation should confirm that it smells 'clean'. Few people can then resist actually tasting a mouthful, but it is generally unnecessary as the most common faults are apparent to the eye or nose. Besides, tasting a wine should clearly reveal its all-important TEMPERATURE. This is the moment to ask for an ice bucket (for red wines if necessary) or for a bottle of white wine to be taken out of an ice bucket.

In many countries there are official associations of sommeliers, often with a series of examinations, qualifications, or at least competitions. French, and other, sommeliers compete in these events all over the world; such is the average French person's reverence for the wine knowledge of a sommelier, to win the title Meilleur Sommelier du Monde (Best Sommelier in the World) is henceforth to inhabit another world.

Sommières, fairly large CRU in the eastern LANGUEDOC, located entirely in the Gard *département* 20 km/12 miles from Nîmes. The distinctive red wines are based on GRENACHE, MOURVÈDRE, and SYRAH; CARIGNAN and CINSAUT are also allowed.

Somontano, meaning 'under the mountain', is a DOP in the foothills of the central Pyrenees, in ARAGÓN in north-east Spain (see map under SPAIN), with some 4,000 ha/9,884 acres under vines in 2021. In stark contrast to much of inland Spain, Somontano looks like winemaking country. The heavy winter rains are supplemented by a network of rivers and streams flowing off the mountains. Even in summer, when temperatures can easily reach 35 °C/95 °F, the fields remain green and productive. The main selling point of Somontano in the early 1990s was its dedication to INTERNATIONAL VARIETIES, but by 2010 this had become its main problem, as competing on a varietal basis with Cabernets and Syrahs from all over the world proved an arduous task. The native MORISTEL and PARRALETA varieties represent only 2% of the vineyard surface. TEMPRANILLO, with 10%, is the only significant Spanish variety. The native GARNACHA was on the wane, being mainly used for rosés, until Viñas del Vero discovered and relaunched the impressive old vineyards at Secastilla with a very distinctive single-estate Garnacha red. Some 250 ha of Garnacha are planted. A little over 1,100 ha/ 2,710 acres of vineyard is planted to white wine grapes, mainly Chardonnay and Gewürztraminer, overtaking the traditional MACABEO and almost extinct Alcañón. V. de la S. & F.C.

Sonoma, northern CALIFORNIA town, valley, and one of the state's most important wine counties, with 18 AVAS. The first vines entered Sonoma in the early 1800s, first with Russian colonists who settled at Fort Ross between 1812 and 1841 and then with Spanish missionaries who arrived in the 1820s. By 1920 the region boasted 250 wineries and more than 8,900 ha/ 21,992 acres of vines on land once tended by Sonoma's first peoples, including the Kashia Band of Pomo and Miwok in the coastal areas and the Micewal in the north and into the Napa Valley. The industry contracted significantly during PROHIBITION and the Second World War, not regaining that vine acreage until the 1970s. By 2021 the region boasted more than 25,091 ha/62,000 acres of vines. Historically, ZINFANDEL was the region's most important variety; today Pinot Noir and Chardonnay predominate, and Cabernet Sauvignon and Sauvignon Blanc thrive in warmer inland areas. Of the 50-plus other grape varieties grown, Merlot also plays an important role, and Rhône varieties are increasingly exciting.

Bordered by the cold Pacific Ocean to the west and the Mayacama Mountains to the east, and stretching from San Pablo Bay to just beyond Preston some 97 km/60 miles north, the county's varied TOPOGRAPHY, ELEVATION, and MARITIME influences make growing conditions across the valley diverse, but fog is a commonality even far inland.

As in all of California, Sonoma receives rain only in winter. DROUGHT conditions in the last decade have made viticulture challenging, as parts of the region lose groundwater and reliance on local rivers is restricted. Some businesses have brought in water by truck. Drought also increases the threat of WILDFIRES as dry conditions increase natural kindling, and lack of surface water makes it hard to extinguish flame. Fires that overlap harvest create safety concerns for vineyard teams and the risk of SMOKE TAINT in wines.

The AVAs and subzones follow. See also CARNEROS, an AVA shared between Sonoma and NAPA, and map under CALIFORNIA.

Alexander Valley

The largest and most fully planted of Sonoma County's many vineyard valleys, Alexander Valley takes in the Russian River watershed upstream of Healdsburg north all the way to the Sonoma–MENDOCINO county line north of Cloverdale.

Before PROHIBITION, hops and prunes blanketed the Alexander Valley and remained the major crops, along with some plantings of mixed black grapes for BULK WINE, into the late 1960s and early 1970s. Attention began to turn to more to vines in the late 1970s and increased greatly in the 1990s. Alexander Valley daytime temperatures are among the warmest in Sonoma County, but the DIURNAL TEMPERATURE RANGE is dramatic, meaning that the wines, even when robust, tend to retain good natural acidity. Cabernet Sauvignon is the region's signature variety, with Merlot just behind. In whites, Chardonnay dominates. More recently Malbec has started to gain local interest. Most substantial plantings are on a broad and almost flat valley floor very nearly bisected by the river, although some vineyards climb the slopes surrounding the valley. Significant elevation is found on Alexander Mountain, owned entirely by the JACKSON FAMILY, where vineyards reach as high as 732 m/2,400 ft.

Bennett Valley

An elevated valley surrounded by hills and mountains just south of Santa Rosa, Bennett Valley had 283 ha/700 acres of vines in 2022 farmed primarily by smallholders. Soils are primarily VOLCANIC and CLAY; the climate is moderately cool, tempered by the marine breezes and fog that makes their way inland through the Petaluma Gap. Merlot is its most planted variety, followed closely by Pinot Noir and then Syrah; Chardonnay dominates in white grapes. Chilly spring temperatures make FROST a concern.

Chalk Hill

On the far north-eastern side of the Russian River Valley AVA, Chalk HIll has 603 ha/1,491 acres of vines climbing into the foothills of the Mayacamas. Soils here are primarily a chalky white volcanic ash, thus the name. Chardonnay and Sauvignon Blanc dominate, but Cabernet Sauvignon and Syrah do well in warmer pockets.

Dry Creek Valley

Dry Creek Valley encompasses 3,642 ha/9,000 acres of vines in a strip just 26 km/16 miles long and 2 miles wide heading north and west from Healdsburg, where Dry Creek trickles into the Russian River. The region's well-drained gravelly LOAM and pattern of warm days and cool nights have attracted grape-growers since the 1880s, when Zinfandel and FIELD BLENDS dominated the plantings. Several of these early vineyards are still producing, such as Teldeschi Ranch and Lytton Estate (see RIDGE Vineyards). Zinfandel still rules, sometimes with Petite Sirah and Carignan. Cabernet Sauvignon is next most important, while Rhône varieties such as Grenache, Mourvèdre, and Syrah are gaining attention. Sauvignon Blanc is the region's most lauded white wine grape, grown here since the 1970s, when it gained fame as FUMÉ BLANC; Chardonnay and Italian varieties such as ARNEIS and FIANO are also grown.

Fort Ross-Seaview

Defined by ELEVATION, this AVA sits atop Sonoma's rugged Coastal Mountains at 244–549 m/800–1,800 ft, many vineyards in view of the ocean and often surrounded by canyons or steep drop-offs. Though proximity to the ocean can mean cool temperatures, its exposure above the fog line often brings warmth and ample sun exposure. That said, it is one of the county's rainiest areas. While early plantings in the 1970s and 1980s included Zinfandel, the rainy season demands earlier ripening varieties, and by 2021 Pinot Noir dominated its 225 ha/555 acres of vineyard. Chardonnay and Syrah can also be successful.

Fountaingrove District

Established in 2015 on the far eastern side of Sonoma County, this AVA sits on the steep western slopes of the Mayacamas Mountains. While the appellation extends over 1,538 ha/38,000 acres, only 600 acres were planted in 2020, mainly to Cabernet Sauvignon as well as some Merlot and Syrah. Soils are volcanic and elevation reaches up to 610 m/2,000 ft.

Green Valley of Russian River Valley

On the far western side and fully within the Russian River Valley AVA, Green Valley AVA is the coolest, foggiest stretch of the famous river valley. Pinot Noir and Chardonnay thrive in the climate and the silty-sandy Goldridge soils, lending themselves to both still and sparkling wine.

Knights Valley

One of the more remote growing areas of Sonoma County, Knights Valley hosts only two wineries though 1,010 ha/2,496 acres of vineyard. Though its position as an upland valley on the inland side of the county brings warmer temperatures, afternoon breezes and nightly fog make their way in from the Pacific Ocean to help cool its valley floor, allowing grapes to ripen without losing acidity. Cabernet Sauvignon is the region's most successful variety; Syrah can be exciting, too.

Moon Mountain District

Moon Mountain sits at the south-western foot of the Mayacamas Range, with 607 ha/1,500 vineyard acres in 2020 planted on slopes rising 122–671 m/400–2,200 ft in elevation. Soils are ruddy loam over volcanic rock; the climate is warm, with some of its vineyards above the fog line. The AVA's most famous vineyard, Monte Rosso, was first planted in 1886, and some of its original Zinfandel and Sémillon vines are still productive. Most of the AVA, however, is now planted to Cabernet Sauvignon.

Northern Sonoma

At 133,146 ha/329,000 planted acres, this is the second largest AVA in Sonoma (after Sonoma Coast). It includes all of the county that drains into the Pacific Ocean, including the Alexander, Dry Creek, Green, Knights, and Russian River valleys, leaving out only Sonoma Valley and much of the Petaluma River watershed. It was proposed and is mainly used by E. & J. GALLO.

Petaluma Gap

Recognized in 2017, this is Sonoma County's southernmost AVA, reaching into MARIN County, just north of the Golden Gate Bridge. The 'gap' is a low spot in the coastal mountain range that funnels air inland from the Pacific Ocean, bringing morning fog and afternoon breezes to cool the vines; daily DIURNAL TEMPERATURE RANGE here can be as much as 10 °C/18 °F. Of the region's 1,619 ha/4,000 acres of vines, 75% are Pinot Noir; Chardonnay and Syrah make up most of the rest.

Pine Mountain-Cloverdale Peak

Defined by elevation, this AVA sits within Alexander Valley at its northernmost edge and spills into MENDOCINO county. Situated at 488–914 m/1,600–3,000 ft above sea level, the region's 310 acres of vines sit firmly above the fog line, allowing them many more hours of sunlight per day than lower-elevation sites; simultaneously, stiff winds help keep the vines refreshed. Long HANG TIMES allow for intense Cabernet Sauvignon, which makes up 80% of plantings, alongside other Bordeaux varieties such as Cabernet Franc, Merlot, and Malbec. Sauvignon Blanc dominates in white wine grapes.

Rockpile

When Warm Springs dam created Lake Sonoma in 1983, the reservoir drowned some good patches of Zinfandel, but since 2002 the rocky, shallow-soiled area north-west of the lake has been planted and christened Rockpile AVA, parts of which are within the Dry Creek Valley AVA. At 244–580 m/800–1,900 ft, daytime temperatures are cooler than in the lower elevations of Dry Creek Valley and more even overall. Zinfandel dominates.

Russian River Valley

Most of the Russian River's course is through other AVAs in MENDOCINO and Sonoma counties. Only when the river escapes from Alexander Valley through a narrow gorge in the mountains at Healdsburg then flows on, first south, then west, in its journey to the Pacific does it become the Russian River Valley AVA.

Covering some 6,070 ha/15,000 acres of vines, this AVA includes about one-sixth of all planted vineyards in Sonoma County. Though generally described as cool climate, portions of its eastern and northern stretches are quite warm. The AVA's unifying feature is the cooling nighttime fog that rolls in from the Pacific Ocean. The coolest area is the west, regarded as one of California's high-quality wine areas by the 1970s on the quality of its Zinfandel, although by the 2000s it was more famous for Pinot Noir as well as Chardonnay, its most planted variety. (See also its subappellations Chalk Hill and Green Valley, above.) Its middle zones do well with Sauvignon Blanc and Merlot, while the furthest eastern side is warm enough to ripen even Cabernet Sauvignon.

Sonoma Coast

This AVA stretches all the way from San Pablo Bay to the border with Mendocino county, encompassing coast areas as well as vast inland tracts including parts of the Carneros, Russian River Valley, and Sonoma Valley AVAs. The name created significant controversy when it was established in 1987, as, historically, there were few vineyards directly along the cold Pacific. However, the 2000s saw more plantings and subsequent establishment of the coastal Fort Ross–Seaview AVA (see above) and then the West Sonoma Coast AVA (see below). The AVA's 809 ha/2,000 acres of vineyard include parts of Carneros and Russian River Valley as well as the Petaluma Gap AVA. Pinot Noir and Chardonnay are the most established varieties here, but Syrah and Sauvignon Blanc can be quite exciting.

Sonoma Mountain

Situated on the western slopes of and within the Sonoma Valley AVA (see below), Sonoma Mountain sits on the eastern side of the mountain from which it draws its name, above the towns of Glen Ellen and Kenwood. Federally recognized in 1985, the area is considered the westernmost point in Sonoma County warm enough to consistently ripen Cabernet Sauvignon. It also does well with Chardonnay. Vineyards grow at 122–366 m/400–1,200 ft in gravelly, well-draining soils often surrounded by forest.

Sonoma Valley

For history, especially romantic history, no other AVA in California compares with Sonoma Valley. In addition to being the site of the ragtag 1846 Bear Flag revolt, which eventually secured Alta California for the US rather than Mexico, it had the last of the Franciscan MISSIONARY vineyards, one of the earliest commercial vineyards north of San Francisco (General Mariano Vallejo appropriated the Franciscan plantings), and, courtesy of public relations master Agoston HARASZTHY, the first great winery name of northern California, Buena Vista (now owned by BOISSET). In more modern times, its Hanzell Vineyard started the rush to using French oak BARRELS to age California wines and thereby revolutionized their style, most especially Chardonnay's. The valley runs parallel to the Napa Valley to the east, its southern extremity doubling as the Sonoma portion of CARNEROS. These southernmost areas are the region's coolest thanks to the influence of the San Francisco and San Pablo Bays, and Pinot Noir and Chardonnay dominate. Moving north, away from the bay, the valley tightens, framed by Sonoma Mountain on the west and the Mayacamas on the east, and the temperatures warm significantly. The wide array of soils, aspects, and mesoclimates allows for a broad range of grape varieties, including Gewürztraminer, Pinot Noir, Chardonnay, and Cabernet Sauvignon, although above all else Sonoma Valley is known for its ancient Zinfandel vines, many well over 100 years old (see HISTORIC VINEYARD SOCIETY) and continuing to pump out small yields of intensely flavoured, spicy grapes. Many old vineyards were planted to FIELD BLENDS of Zinfandel, Petite Sirah, Carignan, and other 'mixed blacks', and there is a growing appreciation in the valley for such vineyard-specific blends. See also Bennett Valley and Moon Mountain District (above).

West Sonoma Coast

Recognized in 2022, this AVA is the westernmost slice Sonoma County, encompassing the rugged terrain between the Coastal Range and the Pacific Ocean as far north as Mendocino County and as far south as the Petaluma Gap AVA. Elevation is varied, at 122–549 m/400–1,800 ft, but the steepness of the slopes means that its 405 ha/1,000 acres of vineyards in 2022 are planted almost entirely on the mountaintops, often surrounded by conifer forest. Generally shallow soils and a cool MARITIME CLIMATE tend to mean lower yields and more challenging farming. It is also the rainiest part of the region. Pinot Noir, Chardonnay, and Syrah do especially well. L.M. & E.C.B.

sonomawine.com

sooty mould. See MEALYBUGS and SCALE.

Sopron, wine region and PDO in the extreme north-west of HUNGARY comprising 1,524 ha/3,766 acres. Its climate is much more temperate than that of most of the rest of Hungary, with cooler, wetter summers and milder winters. From the 14th century, when Hungary was recognized as a useful source of fuller, richer wines than those of northern Europe, Sopron was an important centre of the wine trade, dispatching not just its own wines but those of the rest of Hungary to Austria, Poland, and Silesia. Today Sopron produces mainly red wines, the most distinctive coming from grape varieties such as KÉKFRANKOS, Cabernet, Syrah, and Merlot.

sorbic acid (2,4-hexadienoic acid), winemaking additive and preservative discovered in 1940 to inhibit the growth of YEAST and other FUNGI. Sorbic acid, or its salt potassium **sorbate**, is used widely in food and drink production to inhibit the growth of yeast and mould, notably on cheese and meat. It is classified as one of the safest food preservatives. Sorbic acid use has permitted the wide range of everyday commercial wines currently available which contain some RESIDUAL SUGAR but whose ALCOHOLIC STRENGTH alone is not sufficient to inhibit yeast metabolism.

There is a drawback, however. While most people detect about 135 mg/l, a small proportion of humans are sufficiently sensitive to sorbic acid to detect as little as 50 mg/l in wines. It has a particular taste and a rancid odour to some palates, even at levels that are hardly high enough to inhibit yeast. The EU and OIV limit in finished wines is 200 mg/l.

Sorbic acid inhibits the growth of some BACTERIA but not, unfortunately for winemakers, the large group of LACTIC ACID BACTERIA. SULFUR DIOXIDE must be used together with sorbic acid in sweet wines that are low in alcohol in order to prevent the growth of lactic acid bacteria. Some of these lactics metabolize sorbates to produce compounds such as 2-ethoxyhexa-3,5-diene, which has a perception threshold of around 10 mg/l and smells of crushed GERANIUM leaves—definitely a wine FAULT. A.D.W.

sorbitol, one of the sugar ALCOHOLS present in trace amounts in grapes and wines, and closely related to GLUCOSE. It has a mildly sweet taste, is very soluble in water, and, when present in high concentrations, confers a sense of BODY on a liquid.

Since sorbitol can be made easily and cheaply from many agricultural raw materials, this property has been harnessed by a few unscrupulous wine bottlers to increase consumer acceptance of thin, acid, ordinary wines. Sorbitol is not harmful to humans, but its use is prohibited by most wine regulations. A.D.W.

sorì is a PIEMONTESE dialect term used for vineyard sites of the highest quality, particularly for those with an exceptional favourable southern exposure. More subtle variations also exist: a 'morning' sorì (*sorì di mattino*) has a south-eastern exposure; and an 'evening' sorì (*sorì di sera*) has a south-western exposure. The term was first used on a wine label by Angelo GAJA for his Sorì San Lorenzo Barbaresco 1967 and was widely imitated in the subsequent quarter-century.

sorting of grapes. See GRAPE SORTING.

sotolon, compound (3-hydroxy-4,5-dimethylfuran-2(5H)-one) formed from ACETALDEHYDE that is an important component of the spice fenugreek and is found in a wide range of products from BOTRYTIZED wines to roasted tobacco. At a higher level (tens of µg/l), it is responsible for the typical nut and spicy 'curry' aromas that characterize VIN JAUNE from the Jura but also TOKAJI and some fortified wines, including VIN DOUX NATUREL and PORT, especially those that are RANCIO. It forms partially during the ageing process, particularly if this is OXIDATIVE, but in *vins jaunes* it is known to increase after bottling. At a lower level (more than 3µg/l), it is also commonly identified by a honey or beeswax aroma in dry white wines suffering from PREMATURE OXIDATION. Discovered by Japanese scientists in the late 1970s as a flavour compound in raw cane sugar, sotolon has a very low flavour threshold in wine (3 µg/l). W.L. & V.L.

Cutzach, I., et al., 'Role of sotolon in the aroma of sweet fortified wines. Influence of conservation and ageing conditions', *Journal International des Sciences de la Vigne et du Vin*, 32/4 (1999), 223–33.

Kobayashi, A., 'Sotolon: identification, formation, and effect on flavor', in American Chemical Society, *Flavor Chemistry Trends and Developments* (1989).

Lavigne, V., et al., 'Assaying sotolon in wine. Changes in the sotolon content of dry whites wines during barrel and bottle aging', *Journal of Agricultural and Food Chemistry*, 56 (2008), 2688–93.

sour rot, term applied to a decay of injured, mature grapes which take on the smell of vinegar. In much of Europe and cool-climate regions of North America and Oceania, it is caused by the progressive colonization of various non-*Saccharomyces* yeast species and ACETIC ACID BACTERIA, mediated by fruit fly activity (see DROSOPHILA). In California and some similar climates, the term is applied to a breakdown caused by various mould fungi, presumably followed by the secondary colonization of yeast and bacteria. Common entry points for the causal microbes are splits in berry skin caused by tightly compacted clusters or rain as well as mechanical injuries such as bird pecks. The rot is encouraged by warm pre-harvest rain and high humidity. Control relies on avoiding fruit damage, encouraging fruit aeration, reducing cluster compaction, and controlling fruit flies. W.W.

Hall, M. E., et al. 'Grape sour rot: a four-way interaction involving the host, yeast, acetic acid bacteria, and insects', *Phytopathology*, 108/12 (2018) 1429–42.

Wilcox, W. F., et al., *Compendium of Grape Diseases, Disorders, and Pests* (2nd edn, 2015).

Sousão, a dark-skinned grape variety widely planted in northern Portugal, where the wine is notably high in acidity as well as colour and is therefore increasingly valued in PORT blends, including vintage port. In the nearby Minho it is known as Vinhão, its official Portuguese name, and makes particularly lively red VINHO VERDE. Portuguese plantings totalled 4,337 ha/10,717 acres in 2023 and a few hundred hectares in GALICIA, north-west Spain, where, under the name **Sousón**, most goes into blends. Spelt variously **Sousão**, **Souzao**, and all stations in between, it has also been planted by aspirant makers of PORT-style wines in California, South Africa, and Australia, with a certain degree of success.

South Africa, prolific southern-hemisphere wine producer with a lustrous past and now in the midst of a significant renaissance. The famous Muscat-based dessert wines of CONSTANTIA seduced 18th- and 19th-century Europe at a time when names such as LAFITE and Romanée-Conti (see DOMAINE DE LA ROMANÉE-CONTI) were still in the making. The two centuries which followed were, by comparison, a disappointment, with the ordinary being too plentiful and the individual too rare. Only since the early 1990s has the Cape shaken off its political notoriety and vinous obscurity.

With 1.2% of the world's vineyards, South Africa ranked 15th in area under vines in 2021, but its annual output, at around 10.6 million hl/280 million gal, makes it the eighth-largest wine producer in the world. Total area of vineyard for wine grapes has declined from over 100,000 ha in the early 2000s to 90,512 ha/223,660 acres in 2021. The number of cellars has also decreased: by 2021 there were 536, down from almost 600 a decade earlier. The same attrition has seen the number of growers fall from almost 5,000 in 1990 to around 2,613 three decades later.

As in Europe and America, people are drinking less, but better, wine, with average per capita consumption 8.6 l per year in 2021. Meanwhile, to an increasing extent, wine is the beverage of choice of middle-class families in many of the urbanized areas. This shift away from a beer-and-spirits-only consumption pattern has seen the growth of a more sophisticated domestic market. A virtual twenty-fold increase in exports between 1990 and 2019, coupled with compromised profitability at the lowest pricing tier, provides a significant incentive to vine-growers to pursue quality rather than quantity.

This scramble for excellence has confirmed the benefits both of cooler sites and of matching locality to grape varieties. The historic CONSTANTIA area has been rediscovered and replanted. Climatic conditions here and in recently pioneered areas such as ELGIN, WALKER BAY, and CAPE AGULHAS on the eastern seaboard and alongside the cold Benguela current along the west coast differ dramatically from those in the hot hinterland. Many of the country's more adventurous winemakers, working in the warmer SWARTLAND and Olifants River regions, have produced some of the country's most exciting new-generation wines from these appellations.

History

The father of the South African wine industry was a 33-year-old Dutch surgeon sent to establish a market garden to reduce the risks of scurvy on the long sea passage between Europe and the Indies. Jan van Riebeeck, the Cape's first European settler, was a reluctant pioneer, and no viticulturist. But his brief was to set up a supply station for DUTCH EAST INDIA COMPANY sailors on the spice routes; and the Cape's MEDITERRANEAN CLIMATE suggested vines might well flourish.

Seven years after sailing into Table Bay on 6 April 1652, at the head of a ragtag band, he recorded: 'Today, praise be to God, wine was pressed for the first time from Cape grapes.' The cuttings came from 'somewhere in western France' according to viticulturist Professor C. Orffer. Conditions and quality improved when a new governor, Simon van der Stel, established the legendary 750-ha/1,850-acre CONSTANTIA wine estate outside Cape Town in 1685.

Constantia again became the focal point of the wine industry in 1778, when a portion of the now-divided estate was bought by a talented and ambitious grower, Hendrik Cloete. His Constantia dessert wines soon became the toast of European aristocracy. Cape wine exports flourished under British rule, even if mainly of cheap wines. When in 1861 the Gladstone government removed empire-preferential tariffs, French wines had only the Channel to cross to capture the British market, and far-flung Cape colony products became uncompetitive.

PHYLLOXERA struck in 1886, adding a 20-year recuperation period to the trade's already unhealthy fortunes. Making up for lost time, growers rebuilt the industry, planting some 80 million high-yielding vines such as CINSAUT by the early 1900s. A manageable flow swelled into a deluge; unsaleable wine was poured, literally, into local rivers.

The Cape (most South African vineyards are in the hinterland of the Cape of Good Hope) functioned as a vast distillery for much of the 20th century, draining a partly subsidized annual wine lake and guaranteeing a certain quality of life to a politically powerful farming lobby. The growers' body founded in 1918, the KWV (Co-operative Wine Growers' Association), was until 1998 legally empowered to determine production quotas, fix minimum prices, and predetermine production areas and limits—a system which tended to handicap the

private wine producer and favour the bulk grape-grower. Its powers were criticized by free-marketeers and some producers who, even if non-members, were subject by law to KWV regulations. The KWV argued it spared government the embarrassment of direct grower subsidies. Grower benefits, however, were indirect. Wine CO-OPERATIVES and farmers enjoyed Land Bank credit terms well below commercial interest rates, opportunities that were not available to non-whites until the end of the apartheid era. Such was KWV's political influence in pre-democratic South Africa that wine, alone among alcoholic drinks, was exempt from excise duty for many years. Additionally, the 'dop' system, put in place in the 1700s, provided workers with wine, nominally as a portion of their wages. This served to keep them in thrall to their employers and to their employment in the wine industry. This LABOUR system continued long after it was outlawed in 1960 and contributed both to high rates of alcoholism and to poverty among growers.

In the late 1990s, the newly structured KWV was relieved of all the statutory functions previously performed by the 4,600-strong growers' co-operative. Its conversion from co-operative to company was not without controversy. The process was challenged by the Minister of Agriculture, who cited the statutory void which would result from the process and a concern about the real ownership of some of the organization's assets as grounds for his intervention. Resolution was reached through an out-of-court settlement in which the KWV undertook to pay a sum of 369 million rand (equal at the time to $77 million) into the South African Wine Industry Trust to redress inequalities of the past and to assist in the management and promotion of the industry. Financial mismanagement, together with a controversial decision to allow the residue to be used to fund the purchase of 25% of KWV's shares by a black consortium, led to its being wound up after less than ten years.

The export boom which followed South Africa's first democratic elections in 1994 transformed an industry in which as recently as 1990 less than 30% of the harvest reached the market as wine. By 2019, 86% of the grape crop was used to produce wine, with the remainder supplying the domestic brandy and fruit juice industries. While large-scale producers and co-operatives crush a significant percentage of the 1.3-million-ton (2020) crop, most top-quality South African table wine, however, comes from private cellars and a few wholesaler-producers. The biggest wholesaler, DISTELL, still dominates the market in South Africa's vine-related alcohol products, as it has since 1979.

The organizations which are now independent but which were formerly part of KWV still fulfil functions such as research, vine PROPAGATION, advisory services, and administration of the WINE OF ORIGIN system. These include Vinpro, the service organization for the country's primary producers, SAWIS, which collects, processes, and disseminates industry information, and Winetech, which coordinates research, training, and technology transfer.

Burman, J., *Wine of Constantia* (1979).

Fridjhon, M., and Murray, A., *Conspiracy of Giants* (1986).

James, T., *Wines of the New South Africa: Tradition and Revolution* (2013).

Leipoldt, C. L., *Three Hundred Years of Cape Wines* (1952).

Climate and geography

Surrounded on all sides and largely in close proximity to the Atlantic Ocean, South Africa's quality wine regions seem so far to have avoided the worst excesses of CLIMATE CHANGE. The Benguela current makes the Cape cooler than its LATITUDE may suggest, and many new vineyard areas south towards Agulhas as well as on the Cape west coast offer the prospect of a long, slow ripening season.

The winelands are widely dispersed throughout the Western and Northern Cape, some 700 km/420 miles from north to south and 500 km across, strung mainly along the Atlantic, though with newer Cape South Coast vineyards adjacent to the Indian ocean.

Climates and soils vary as dramatically as landscapes: mountains rear out of the sea, unfolding into lush valleys, sere drylands, and a series of inland mountain chains. In the Stellenbosch district alone, just outside Cape Town, there are more than 50 soil types. On the hillsides, decomposing GRANITE prevails. Soils tend to be low in PH (4.5), with a predominance of CLAY (25% and more), but are well drained and moisture retentive.

That portion of the harvest reserved for inexpensive TABLE WINE as well as brandy and fruit juice concentrate comes from hot, irrigated river valleys such as the Orange, Olifants, and Breede, where vineyards yield prodigiously. Around inland Robertson there are some CALCAREOUS lime-rich outcrops akin to the calcareous soil of Burgundy's CÔTE D'OR. But in the cooler coastal areas, the ancient soils depend on substantial LIME additions.

Annual rainfall rises from 250 mm/9.7 in in the near-desert Klein Karoo to 1,500 mm in the lee of the Worcester Mountains, about 100 km inland from Cape Town. Growers, particularly those in the semi-desert areas who depend on IRRIGATION, argue they merely make up the shortfall to reach the 900 mm annual rainfall of a vineyard in the Bordeaux region of France.

Average summer daily temperatures often exceed 23 °C/73 °F during the February and March harvest months, and maximum summer temperatures can rise to nearly 40 °C. However, an increasing proportion of new, cooler vineyard sites are making this caricature of the Cape as a hot-climate viticultural region as questionable a generalization as the old belief that Cape vintage variations are insignificant.

A unique but mixed blessing is the frequent gale-force summer south-easter, the 'Cape Doctor' WIND, that reduces humidity, mildew, and other FUNGAL DISEASES but also sometimes batters vines.

Most wine regions would, according to the WINKLER scale, be classified Region III sites (as in Oakville, Napa Valley) or Region IV (like Sydney and Florence), with some in V (Perth). But several areas experience cooler European (or Winkler II) conditions, especially in high-ELEVATION or sea-cooled vineyards. New appellations such as Walker Bay (on sandy SHALE), Constantia (granite and SANDSTONE), Elgin (shale), and Cape Agulhas have stretched horizons and broadened the Cape's climatological repertoire.

Winegrowing areas

South African wine country is divided into geographical units in which are regions, then districts, and then wards as in this table. For more explanation of their significance, see WINE OF ORIGIN below.

Production Areas Defined in Terms of the Wine of Origin Scheme

GREATER CAPE (overarching geographical unit)
1. WESTERN CAPE (geographical unit)

Overarching Region	Region	Subregion	District	Ward
CAPE COAST	CAPE SOUTH COAST	None	**Cape Agulhas**	Elim
		None	**Elgin**	None
		None	**Lower Duivenhoks River**	None
		None	**Overberg**	Elandskloof/Kaaimansgat Greyton Klein River Theewater
		None	**Plettenberg Bay**	None
		None	**Swellendam**	Buffeljags Malgas Stormsvlei
		None	**Walker Bay**	Bot River Hemel-en-Aarde Ridge Hemel-en-Aarde Valley Sunday's Glen Springfontein Rim Stanford Foothills Upper Hemel-en-Aarde Valley

Continued

Continued

Overarching Region	Region	Subregion	District	Ward
CAPE COAST	CAPE SOUTH COAST	None	None	Herbertsdale Napier Still Bay East
	COASTAL REGION	None	Cape Peninsula (repealed 26 May 2017)	
		None	**Cape Town**	Constantia Durbanville Hout Bay Philadelphia
		CAPE WEST COAST	**Darling**	Groenkloof
		None	**Franschhoek/ Franschhoek Valley**	None
		CAPE WEST COAST	**Lutzville Valley**	Koekenaap
		None	**Paarl**	Agter-Paarl Simonsberg-Paarl Voor-Paardeberg
		None	**Stellenbosch**	Banghoek Bottelary Devon Valley Jonkershoek Valley Papegaaiberg Polkadraai Hills Simonsberg-Stellenbosch Vlottenburg
		None	**Swartland**	Malmesbury Paardeberg/Perdeberg Paardeberg South Piket-Bo-Berg Porseleinberg Riebeekberg Riebeeksrivier
		CAPE WEST COAST	**Swartland**	St Helena Bay
		None	**Tulbagh**	None
			Tygerberg (repealed 26 May 2017)	
		None	**Wellington**	Blouvlei Bovlei Groenberg Limietberg Mid-Berg River
		CAPE WEST COAST	None	Bamboes Bay Lamberts Bay
None	BREEDE RIVER VALLEY	None	**Breedekloof**	Goudini Slanghoek
		None	**Robertson**	Agterkliphoogte Ashton Boesmansrivier Bonnievale Eilandia Goedemoed Goree Goudmyn Hoopsrivier Klaasvoogds Le Chasseur McGregor Vinkrivier Zandrivier

S

Overarching Region	Region	Subregion	District	Ward
None	BREEDE RIVER VALLEY	None	**Worcester**	Hex River Valley Nuy Scherpenheuvel Stettyn
None	KLEIN KAROO	None	**Calitzdorp**	Groenfontein
		None	**Langeberg-Garcia**	None
		None	None	Cango Valley Koo Plateau Montagu Outeniqua Tradouw Tradouw Highlands Upper Langkloof
None	OLIFANTS RIVER	None	**Citrusdal Mountain**	Piekenierskloof
		None	**Citrusdal Valley**	None
		None	None	Spruitdrift Vredendal
None	None	None	**Ceres Plateau**	Ceres
		None	**Prince Albert**	Kweekvallei Prince Albert Valley Swartberg
		None	None	Nieuwoudtville Cederberg Leipoldtville-Sandveld

GREATER CAPE (overarching geographical unit)
2. NORTHERN CAPE (geographical unit)

Overarching Region	Region	Subregion	District	Ward
None	None	None	**Douglas**	None
		None	**Sutherland-Karoo**	None
			Central Orange River	Groblershoop Grootdrink Kakamas Keimoes Upington
		None	None	Hartswater Prieska

GREATER CAPE (overarching geographical unit)
3. EASTERN CAPE (geographical unit)

Overarching Region	Region	Subregion	District	Ward
None	None	None	None	St Francis Bay

NONE (overarching geographical unit)
4. KWAZULU-NATAL (geographical unit)

Overarching Region	Region	Subregion	District	Ward
None	None	None	**Central Drakensberg**	None
		None	**Lions River**	None

NONE (overarching geographical unit)
5. LIMPOPO (geographical unit)

Overarching Region	Region	Subregion	District	Ward
None	None	None	None	None

Continued

Continued

NONE (overarching geographical unit) 6. FREE STATE (geographical unit)				
Overarching Region	**Region**	**Subregion**	**District**	**Ward**
None	None	None	None	Rietrivier FS
NONE (overarching geographical unit) 7. NONE (geographical unit)				
Overarching Region	**Region**	**Subregion**	**District**	**Ward**
None	None	None	None	Lanseria

See separate articles on some of the most frequently encountered geographical names—COASTAL REGION, CONSTANTIA, ELGIN, ELIM, FRANSCHHOEK, GROENEKLOOF, KLEIN KAROO, OLIFANTS RIVER, PAARL, ROBERTSON, STELLENBOSCH, SWARTLAND, TULBAGH, WALKER BAY, WELLINGTON, WESTERN CAPE, and WORCESTER—although new areas are emerging all the time.

Viticulture

The stark contrast between the traditional and the progressive in South African viticulture, often visible on adjoining farms, reflects the disparate objectives of growers. The bulk grape-farmer delivering to one of the less progressive BULK WINE cellars strives for quantity; growers bottling their own crop knows quantity can be the enemy of quality. From the second half of the 20th century, TRELLISING, low VINE DENSITY, and AGROCHEMICAL pest and weed control became common features of the South African viticultural landscape. However, in this century closer planting, greater use of SUSTAINABLE VITICULTURE methods and BIOLOGICALS to control pests and diseases, careful CLONAL SELECTION, painstaking SOIL PREPARATION that can involve additions of over 20 tons of LIME per hectare to achieve higher PH, and PRUNING for lower yields have become the norm on many properties.

Average planting densities are around 3,300 vines per ha/1,300 per acre. Yields in cooler, coastal climates are appreciably lower than the national average: about 49 or 56 hl/ha (2.8 or 3.2 tons/acre) for Cabernet Sauvignon and Chardonnay are considered consistent with quality in Cape conditions. Yields from virus-infected vineyards can drop to below 28 hl/ha (1.6 tons/acre).

Most vineyards are IRRIGATED in summer, with DRIP IRRIGATION having replaced overhead sprays or fixed sprinkler systems on the better estates.

The most common TRELLISING SYSTEM is a simple vertical 'hedge row' developed from a split vine cordon, supported by a wire raised about 750 mm/2.4 ft for ease of pruning. The summer foliage is trained upright in a CANOPY held by one or more wires above the CORDON. Short-SPUR PRUNING is commonly practised (eight to ten spurs, four to five on each cordon, pruned back to two or three buds each).

Most vine diseases and pests found their way from the northern hemisphere long ago. Chemical pesticides are widely used, especially in the higher-yielding vineyards, although farmers are now encouraged by way of the INTEGRATED PRODUCTION OF WINE (IPW) programme to minimize the use of insecticides and to use a more ORGANIC approach. Baboons are also a pest in several areas.

POWDERY MILDEW, locally called 'white rust', is the most serious common disease. DOWNY MILDEW poses a seasonal threat. Both are containable by systemic fungicides. BOTRYTIS is not a serious problem most years and is welcomed by growers specializing in dessert wines.

Cape vineyards were decimated by PHYLLOXERA from 1886, and virtually all vines are grafted on to resistant American ROOTSTOCKS, the most common being Richter 99, 110, 101–14, and Ramsey.

Virus-infected vines, which were once widespread and remain a feature of older and less progressively farmed plantings, shorten the productive lifespans of vineyards. Affected vines succumb to LEAFROLL, CORKY BARK, and FANLEAF, inhibiting PHOTOSYNTHESIS and ripening, diminishing yields but not improving grape quality.

From the mid 1980s, HEAT-TREATED, virus-tested plant material was more freely available, along with a greater selection of imported CLONES of classic varieties. Healthier, earlier-ripening vineyards are the result, and it is now easier to distinguish a significant pattern of regional/varietal characteristics.

Burger, J., and Deist, J., *Viticulture in South Africa* (1981).

Winemaking

Since the advent of democracy in South Africa winemaking has been in a state of flux and experimentation. Younger winemakers who travel extensively, many working vintages in the northern hemisphere, have challenged the orthodoxies of earlier generations and have transformed the face and taste of the Cape's best wines. While many of the more commercial wines reflect an environment where irrigation, higher yields, a warm climate, and low-pH soils are the dominant factors, an increasing number of the better producers offer wines which embody considered viticultural practices, thoughtful vinifications, and ÉLEVAGE which does not depend on new OAK to achieve results.

Controlled MALOLACTIC CONVERSION is widely practised, while reduced dependence on flavour-stripping FILTRATION and STABILIZATION processes has also helped improve the quality of the better wines. New CANOPY MANAGEMENT strategies and increasing VINE DENSITIES also played a role.

Apart from isolated CALCAREOUS outcrops, wines from the Cape's often excessively acid soils tend to require TARTARIC ACID adjustments to MUSTS and wines, as well as severe TARTRATE removal procedures before bottling (see SOIL ACIDITY).

Vine varieties

In South Africa a vine variety is usually known as a cultivar, and South Africa is a cultivar-conscious wine country. Regionality has limited commercial value, with many producers electing to apply the broadest possible appellation in order to maintain flexibility in terms of fruit sourcing. Accordingly, grape variety is still the major factor driving perceptions of quality, style, labelling, and marketing of a wine, although increased VINE AGE and a greater focus on site are changing this. While white varieties used to dominate South African vineyards, the post-1994 transformation of the wine industry has seen premium red varieties reach virtual parity. CHENIN BLANC was long the most planted variety in South Africa and still comprised 18.6% of the national vineyard in 2021. From the 1980s, Sauvignon Blanc and Chardonnay were energetically planted, and by 2021 they comprised 11% and 7.3% of all plantings respectively. Other major white wine grapes include, in decreasing quantity: Colombar(d), Muscat of Alexandria, Sémillon, and Viognier.

Cabernet Sauvignon is South Africa's most planted red grape variety, comprising 11% of the nation's vineyard. Syrah (often called Shiraz in South Africa) has come to rival

Cabernet Sauvignon and in 2021 accounted for 10% of all plantings. Merlot, often blended but popular enough in its own right, occupies slightly more than half the area dedicated to Cabernet. Pinot Noir has improved dramatically as new CLONES have been planted and cooler regions established. PINOTAGE, the Cape's own cross of Pinot Noir and Cinsaut, remains relatively stable at just over 7%. For most of the first half of the last century, high-yielding Cinsaut was the most widely planted red wine grape, but it has declined dramatically in importance and now represents less than 2% of all vineyards. There are yet smaller plantings of Grenache, Mourvèdre, Carignan, Zinfandel, Cabernet Franc, and some PORT varieties—most commonly TINTA BARROCA, often made into a dry red. Italian varieties, notably Nebbiolo and Sangiovese, are beginning to attract attention.

Wine of Origin and labelling

Wine of Origin (WO) legislation introduced in 1973, and variously updated since then, ended decades of a labelling free-for-all in which confused South African wine nomenclature and unverified vintage and grape variety claims baffled the consumer. The following types of wine production zones are now classified: geographical unit (e.g. Western Cape); region (e.g. Coastal), which may represent a merging of several districts; district (e.g. Stellenbosch); and ward (e.g. Bottelary). While the larger units are broadly geographical and/or political, a ward is based on shared soils, climate, and so on (i.e. aspects of TERROIR). 'Estates' are no longer official places of origin, but registered 'estate wines' must be grown, made, and bottled on a single property. Single vineyards may be indicated as such on labels provided they are not larger than 6 ha/ 15 acres, are planted to a single variety, and are registered in accordance with the legal provisions.

A wine may also be 'certified' for vintage provided at least 85% comes from one harvest. For a wine to be labelled as a single VARIETAL, it must contain at least 85% of the variety stated. Varieties in a blend may be indicated on the label providing they are stated in descending percentages and only if they are vinified separately.

A certified wine is identified by a seal which contains a tracking number enabling the authorities to trace every component batch or variety (in the case of a blend) back to the vineyard and the date of harvest. Vineyards are subject to inspection, and wines may be monitored in the cellars. Certification follows an official analysis, tasting, and final label approval. Participation is voluntary, and a little under 50% of the country's wine production is now certified. The process is under the supervision of the government-appointed Wine & Spirit Board. Non-certified wine is liable to spot-check analysis for health requirements.

South Africa meets requirements on prohibition of ADDITIVES and for LABELLING, which must state the ALCOHOLIC STRENGTH (from 1992) to within 0.5%. TRADITIONAL METHOD Cape sparkling wine is labelled Méthode Cap Classique. FLOR-yeast FORTIFIED WINES matured in a SOLERA system are in decline and may no longer be sold as sherry. But wines made in the image of PORT, generally using very similar varieties and the same techniques as in port country, have been very successful.

Although the WO regulations borrow from France and Germany, there are no rulings on crop YIELDS, FERTILIZER quantities, or IRRIGATION levels. CHAPTALIZATION and all other forms of ENRICHMENT are banned, although grape juice concentrate may be added as a sweetener to most wines (see SWEET RESERVE). ACIDIFICATION is permitted. Wines sold as 'dry' on the domestic market may not have a RESIDUAL SUGAR content exceeding 5 g/l (see www.sawis.co.za).

J.P. & M.F.

James, T., *Wines of the New South Africa: Tradition and Revolution* (2013).
Platter, J., *Platter's South African Wine Guide* (annually).
www.wosa.co.za

South America, the world's second most important wine-producing continent, after Europe, with ARGENTINA the most productive of its nations and CHILE right behind, followed by BRAZIL. Other, relatively minor, wine producers are, in descending order of importance, URUGUAY, PERU, BOLIVIA, and PARAGUAY, although see also COLOMBIA, ECUADOR, and VENEZUELA. Spain and, in some parts, Portugal were important influences in the 16th and 17th centuries, although more recently France, Italy, and the United States have helped to shape South America's wine industries. Wine quality has improved extremely rapidly in those countries—Chile, Argentina especially, and Brazil and Uruguay as well.

History

The late 15th century European voyages of discovery, notably to the Americas, were followed by migrations of European settlers there, associated with substantial movement of animals and plants between the two continents. Although INDIGENOUS VARIETIES grew in Central America (see VITIS), there is no evidence that the Aztecs made wine from them. The Spanish conquistadores of the 16th century thus first introduced European VINIFERA vines, their cultivation, and winemaking to MEXICO; as early as 1522 Cortés is recorded as having sent for vine cuttings from Spain. Moreover, by 1524 the planting of vines was a condition of *repartimiento* grants, through which the Spaniards were granted land and labour on the foundation of Mexico City. From Mexico, the spread of viticulture followed swiftly on the heels of Spanish conquests to the south.

Vines were planted in Peru soon after Pizarro's defeat of the Incas between 1531 and 1534, and within 20 years Spanish commentators described vineyards producing a substantial quantity of grapes. Some of the earliest Peruvian vines appear to have been introduced from the CANARY ISLANDS, whereas others seem to have been derived from the seeds of dried grapes brought from Spain. From Peru, viticulture and winemaking then spread south to Chile and Argentina, where vines were cultivated as early as the mid 1550s, although there were even earlier experimental plantings on Argentina's coast. See also MONKS AND MONASTERIES.

The traditional explanation for the rapidity of this spread was that the Spanish conquerors required a ready supply of wine for the EUCHARIST and that monks therefore played a central role in establishing vineyards. There is, however, little evidence to support this view, and many of the early vineyards and attempts to produce wine were on secular estates. Economic factors, such as the cost of importing wine and the difficulties of transporting it overland, meant that the early Spanish conquerors had a very real interest in establishing vineyards if they wished to continue to consume the main alcoholic beverage that they had known in Iberia. In particular, the long sea voyage across the Atlantic, followed by an overland haul across Panama and then a further voyage down the Pacific coast, meant that most wine reaching Peru and Chile from the Iberian peninsula was likely to have deteriorated, even if it had originally been of good quality.

By the end of the 16th century, Spanish restrictions on wine production in 'New Spain', designed to protect the metropolitan wine producers and merchants in Iberia, served to limit further secular development of viticulture in Mexico, but they also appear to have provided an incentive to Peruvian producers, who rapidly became the dominant wine suppliers to the region as a whole. Subsequently, in the 17th century, Jesuit MISSIONS along the coastal valleys of Peru became the most important centres of viticulture in the region.

P.T.H.U.

Dickenson, J., and Unwin, T., *Viticulture in Colonial Latin America: Essays on Alcohol, the Vine and Wine in Spanish America and Brazil* (1992).
Hyams, E., *Dionysus: A Social History of the Wine Vine* (1965).
Tapia, A. M., et al., 'Determining the Spanish origin of representative ancient American grapevine Varieties', *American Journal of Enology and Viticulture*, 18 (2007), 242–51.

South Australia, *the* wine state in AUSTRALIA, responsible for 50% of the annual CRUSH.

S

This share may have fallen from the 75% of the 1940s and 1950s, but the state still dominates the country's wine output. Vine-growing and winemaking are major contributors to South Australia's gross domestic production, yet they occupy only a small percentage of the state's vast land mass. Vine-growing is concentrated in the south-eastern corner, much of it within an hour's drive of the capital Adelaide. The two most significant outposts are the Riverland sprawling along the Murray river and Coonawarra and Padthaway 325 km/200 miles south-east of Adelaide, not far from the border with VICTORIA.

South Australia includes one 'super' zone, Adelaide Zone, which encompasses three subzones (MOUNT LOFTY RANGES ZONE, FLEURIEU ZONE, and BAROSSA ZONE), each of which contain several more specific GEOGRAPHICAL INDICATIONS (GIs). South Australia grapes also are often subsumed in wines labelled with the multi-regional super-zone GI SOUTH EASTERN AUSTRALIA.

Within the Barossa Zone, the BAROSSA VALLEY, an hour north-east of the city of Adelaide, is arguably Australia's best-known wine region, with 11,609 ha/28,686 acres of vineyards spread between warm areas on the valley floor and cooler MESOCLIMATES at higher ELEVATIONS in the surrounding hills. To this day, the Germanic influence of its 19th-century Silesian immigrants is everywhere to be seen—in the town names, the Lutheran churches, the stone buildings, and the names of the leading families. Many of Australia's largest companies have a strong presence here, including PENFOLDS. The valley is also home to the world's oldest continuously producing Shiraz, Grenache, Mataro, Cabernet Sauvignon, and SÉMILLON vines. Substantial plantings of Shiraz date as far back as 1860, the DRY-FARMED and GOBELET-trained vines often yielding as little as 16 hl/ha (1 tonne/acre).

EDEN VALLEY, also within the Barossa Zone, sits 200 m/656 ft higher than the Barossa Valley floor to the east, rising to 450 m/1,480 ft. Overall growing season temperatures are significantly lower than those of the Barossa Valley, hence the final stages of ripening and harvesting take place in much cooler conditions. Riesling, Shiraz, Chardonnay, and Cabernet Sauvignon are the main varieties planted in its 2,169 ha/5,360 acres of vineyards, although increasingly growers are looking to the cooler climate to grow more white varieties. Eden Shiraz is generally spicier and more elegant than Barossa floor examples, with finer tannins and lower alcohol.

CLARE VALLEY headlines the Mount Lofty Ranges Zone. A long, narrow region two hours north of the city of Adelaide, at the gateway to the Flinders Ranges, it has 5,093 ha/12,585 acres of vineyards, some at significant elevation. With a strongly CONTINENTAL CLIMATE, with warm days but cool-to-cold nights in summer, it tends to produce intensely coloured, deeply flavoured Shiraz and Cabernet Sauvignon, often with a patina of EUCALYPT mint. MALBEC also flourishes here, used as a blend component. The region's aromatic, mineral-driven, long-lived Riesling is one of South Australia's most iconic wines.

ADELAIDE HILLS, also part of the Mount Lofty Ranges Zone, is just 15 minutes south-east of the city of Adelaide and incorporates the GIs of Piccadilly Valley and Lenswood, each of which have less than 270 ha/667 acres of vineyards but produce high-quality cool-climate fruit and have been distinguished due to their rare soils and specific mesoclimates. Ripening conditions in Piccadilly Valley are ideally suited to growing Chardonnay and Pinot Noir, and Lenswood is renowned for its Sauvignon Blanc and Merlot. As a whole, Adelaide Hills encompasses 3,957 ha/9,778 acres of vineyards, some at as high as 650 m/2,130 ft. In the 21st century, it has become one of South Australia's most important fine-wine regions, and its proximity to Adelaide lends itself to TOURISM, with over 50 cellar doors operating by 2022. Grapes have been grown here as long as anywhere in the state, but plantings took off in the late 1970s and early 1980s when Petaluma and others recognized the region's potential for growing cool-climate varieties such as Pinot Noir and Chardonnay for both sparking and table wines. The region also excels elegant, cool-climate Shiraz. The Adelaide Plains GI to the north-west has a radically different climate, its flat, hot and fertile soils producing a decidedly warmer style of Shiraz.

The Fleurieu Zone contains the GIs MCLAREN VALE, LANGHORNE CREEK, KANGAROO ISLAND, CURRENCY CREEK, and SOUTHERN FLEURIEU. All are highly MARITIME, with the warmer McLaren Vale, 45 minutes south of the city of Adelaide, making up the bulk of production. Its 7,438 ha/18,380 acres of vineyards connect with the Adelaide Hills in the north and the sandy beaches of the Adelaide coastline in the west. With its MEDITERRANEAN CLIMATE, diverse soils, and a culture of innovation, its 100-plus wineries produce a myriad of wine styles from a multitude of varieties, with a focus on Shiraz, Cabernet Sauvignon, and Grenache and an increasing presence of alterative Mediterranean varieties.

The LIMESTONE COAST ZONE in the far south-east of the state includes the coastal regions of Mount Benson and Robe and the inland regions of Coonawarra, Wrattonbully, Padthaway, and Mount Gambier. Of those regions, COONAWARRA has the largest planted area, at 5,784 ha/14,293 acres of vineyards. Coonawarra experiences a maritime influence due to upwelling of cold ocean currents at certain times of the year and is largely regarded as a cool region. While vines were first planted in Coonawarra in 1890 (by John Riddoch), for all practical purposes it became commercially significant in the early 1960s, celebrated for its TERRA ROSSA soils. It has long been highly regarded for its Cabernet Sauvignon, which accounts for 60% of production, followed by Shiraz and Merlot which collectively make up almost 30%.

WRATTONBULLY, north of Coonawarra, has 2,727 ha/6,739 acres of vineyards. Almost 70% of production is dominated by Cabernet Sauvignon and Shiraz. Nestled in the Narcoorte Ranges, it is characterized by rolling hills and shallow terra rossa soil upon LIMESTONE. The region is home to the World Heritage–listed Naracoorte Caves, many of which were discovered as a result of vineyard development and some of which contained significant ancient fossils and prehistoric remains.

PADTHAWAY sits yet further north, a long, narrow, relatively cool-climate region with 4,160 ha/10,280 acres of vineyards on soils with considerable limestone and an extensive underground water table. Approximately 50% of overall production is equally dominated by Cabernet Sauvignon and Shiraz, and Chardonnay accounts for another 20%.

Mount Gambier, a GI established in 2014, is nestled in the far south-eastern corner of South Australia, pushing up against the Victorian border. Its 327 ha/808 acres of vineyards produce predominantly Sauvignon Blanc, with the balance of the crush dominated by Pinot Noir and Chardonnay.

On the coastal side of the zone, the small GIs of MOUNT BENSON (541 ha/1,337 planted acres) and ROBE (681 ha/1,683 planted acres) are slightly cooler than the inland GIs, with a maritime climate and sand and limestone interspersed. Shiraz predominates, with Sauvignon Blanc steadily increasing and Cabernet Sauvignon making up a significant share of the balance.

Finally, there is the RIVERLAND, with over 1,000 grape-growers and 22,032 ha/54,442 acres of vineyards producing 30% of the nation's crush. About 200 km north-east of the city of Adelaide, stretching along the Murray river from Waikerie to Renmark, the climate here is continental, with long, sunny days and noticeably cooler nights. It built its reputation on Chardonnay, Shiraz, and Cabernet Sauvignon, but there is a new wave of innovative producers exploring alternative varieties and crafting edgy wines. J.H., H.H. & R.J.T.

www.winesa.asn.au

South Burnett, relatively hilly Australian wine region and GEOGRAPHICAL INDICATION (GI) in Queensland about 2.5 hours' drive north-west of Brisbane. It has a subtropical climate with long summers and mild winters. Summer rainfall can be a problem, bringing POWDERY MILDEW. There are excellent examples of SÉMILLON, Chardonnay, Shiraz, and, more lately, VERDELHO, TEMPRANILLO, and ALTERNATIVE VARIETIES. The vineyards, planted in generally fertile red soils, extended 204 ha/504 acres in 2020.

A.C.

South Coast, extensive AVA defining vineyards close to the California coast from Los Angeles County to the Mexican border. The region's most substantial vineyards are in TEMECULA VALLEY in Riverside County. It also includes the AVAs MALIBU COAST and Palos Verdes Peninsula in Los Angeles County and San Pasqual and Ramona Valleys in SAN DIEGO COUNTY.

South Coast Zone, expansive area encompassing all of coastal NEW SOUTH WALES south of Newcastle and east of the Great Dividing Range, stretching to the border with VICTORIA. Includes the Southern Highlands and Shoalhaven Coast regions.

South Eastern Australia, official 'super zone' and GEOGRAPHICAL INDICATION encompassing all relevant wine regions in QUEENSLAND, NEW SOUTH WALES, VICTORIA, and SOUTH AUSTRALIA, used for multi-region, inexpensive blended wines constituting a significant proportion of all wine exported from Australia.

Southern Fleurieu, strongly maritime wine region at the tip of the Fleurieu Peninsula in SOUTH AUSTRALIA.

Southern Flinders Ranges, most northerly wine region of SOUTH AUSTRALIA with 176 ha/435 acres of vines in 2022, mainly Shiraz. The warm, dry climate is moderated by ELEVATIONS of up to 958 m/3,143 ft and broad DIURNAL TEMPERATURE RANGE.

Southern Glazer's is the biggest wine company you've never heard of. The behemoth American distributor stands between wineries and retailers, serving as a licensed wholesaler in 41 US states. *Forbes* estimated the company was the 11th largest private company in the US with revenues of $21 billion in 2021.

The company known as Southern Wine & Spirits was founded in 1968 when Walter Jahn, a drinks executive from New York, bought out a local wine and spirits distributor in Miami. The original financing came from a bank with ties to organized crime, which competitors (but not Southern) frequently mention. The company grew first in Florida and then nationally, with its sales force championing the emergent interest in wine. In 2016 a merger with Dallas-based Glazer's expanded the company's reach to distribute over 150 million cases of wine and spirits every year.

While they have some enormous facilities, such as a streamlined 40,000 sq m/425,000 sq ft warehouse in Nevada, the company has also been known to use sharp elbows in its rise to become the country's largest wine and spirits wholesaler. As with other large distributors, it is a donor to politicians of all stripes and at all levels of POLITICS. The policy goals include maintaining the legally mandated middle-tier in the controversial THREE-TIER SYSTEM or otherwise tilting the playing field in their direction.
T.C.

Emshwiller, J., and Freedman, A., 'Early relationships help shape Southern Wine & Spirits', *Wall Street Journal*, 4 October 1999.

Southern Highlands, Australian wine region in NEW SOUTH WALES located high on the Great Dividing Range, south-west of Sydney. The vineyards, situated at about 700 m/2,297 ft in ELEVATION, endure an erratic climate, with cold winters, humid summers, and often problematic late-season rainfall. Some producers get around this by making TRADITIONAL METHOD sparkling wines, alongside a broad range of table wines produced from varieties such as Chardonnay, Sauvignon Blanc, Pinot Noir, Shiraz, and Cabernet Sauvignon. A.P.

South West Australia Zone comprises the Blackwood Valley, Geographe, Great Southern, Pemberton/Manjimup, and Margaret River wine regions in WESTERN AUSTRALIA.

South West France, generally accepted but unofficially recognized region within FRANCE which incorporates all of the wine districts in the south-western quarter of the country with the exception of BORDEAUX and Cognac.

The vine was cultivated in most of these districts in the Roman era (see FRANCE and GAUL), but winemaking was developed sometimes for the benefit of pilgrims to St-Jacques de Compostelle under the medieval influence of MONKS AND MONASTERIES.

Production has always exceeded the needs of the inhabitants, so producers have had to find ways of establishing markets outside the immediate area. The Adour river was the only means of transport for winemakers to the south of it (the most important being those from Madiran, Jurançon, and Irouléguy), but it was hard to navigate, and there was competition from the growers of other crops. Wines from the areas to the north, in the 'high country' or HAUT-PAYS (mainly Bergerac and its family, Côtes de Duras, Marmande, Buzet, Brulhois, Gascony, Cahors, Fronton, and Gaillac), travelled down the Garonne and its tributaries to Bordeaux, where, however, the authorities imposed severe tolls before allowing the wines to gain access to the open seas.

The HUNDRED YEARS WAR was to have an enduring effect on their trading history, opening the door for the DUTCH WINE TRADE to take the place of once-powerful ENGLAND. It was not until 1776 that the Bordeaux tolls were outlawed.

The climate is heavily influenced by the Atlantic, though few generalizations can be made about such an extensive area. The nearer to Bordeaux, the more Cabernets and Merlot in the vineyards. Further upstream the wines are made from an exciting series of INDIGENOUS VARIETIES such as ABOURIOU, ARRUFIAC, BAROQUE, COURBU, DURAS, FER (Servadou), GROS MANSENG, LEN DE L'EL, MAUZAC, NÉGRETTE, PETIT COURBU, PETIT MANSENG, and TANNAT. The south-west is one of the proudest and greediest regions of France; they need its local wines to drink with *foie gras*, duck, and goose.

For more details, see the individual entries for the wines of AVEYRON, BÉARN, BERGERAC, BRULHOIS, BUZET, CAHORS, CORRÈZE, Côtes de DURAS, Côtes de MILLAU, Côtes du MARMANDAIS, Coteaux du QUERCY, ENTRAYGUES-LE FEL, ESTAING, FRONTON, GAILLAC, IROULÉGUY, JURANÇON, MADIRAN, MARCILLAC, MONBAZILLAC, MONTRAVEL, PACHERENC DU VIC-BILH, PÉCHARMANT, ROSETTE, ST-SARDOS, ST-MONT, SAUSSIGNAC, and TURSAN. P.S.

Soviet Union, the Union of Soviet Socialist Republics, which until the fall of communism included such wine-producing republics as MOLDOVA, UKRAINE, the CRIMEA, UZBEKISTAN, RUSSIA, AZERBAIJAN, GEORGIA and, producing very much less wine, ARMENIA, ESTONIA, KYRGYZSTAN, TAJIKISTAN, KAZAKHSTAN, LATVIA, LITHUANIA, TAJIKISTAN, and TURKMENISTAN. Once a wine-producing behemoth, the USSR lost one-third of its vineyards in the 1980s due to Mikhail GORBACHEV's anti-alcohol measures. In 1990 it accounted for 12% of the world's total vineyard area and 5% of the wine produced. The dissolution of the republic wreaked further havoc on the wine industries of the individual countries as the struggle for economic survival in the new free market economies resulted in a flood of alcohol substitutes, cheap vodkas, brandies, and wines from central and western Europe. By 1996, according to OIV statistics, the former Societ bloc countries accounted for 11% of the world's vineyard but only 3% of the wine produced. By the 21st century, former Soviet bloc countries such as Georgia and Moldova had established robust, respected wine industries while others such as Kyrgystan and Tajikistan continue to struggle.

spacing. See VINE DENSITY.

Spain, country with the most land under vine in the world (964,000 ha/2,382,096 acres in 2021, according to OIV estimates) and yet most years only the world's third most important producer of wine. The dramatic 21st-century increase in irrigated surface and a more controversial insistence on high-yielding CLONES have abundantly offset a 30% reduction in vineyard surface over the past quarter-century, although, after a period of inflated yields that saw Spain's annual average wine production averaging more than 40 million hl/1,060 million gal after 2010, they have returned to early 1990s levels, hitting just 35.3 million hl in 2021.

Spain occupies most of the Iberian peninsula and is the third largest country in Europe, extending from the Pyrenees that form the frontier with France in the north to the strait of Gibraltar just 15 km/9 miles from Africa to

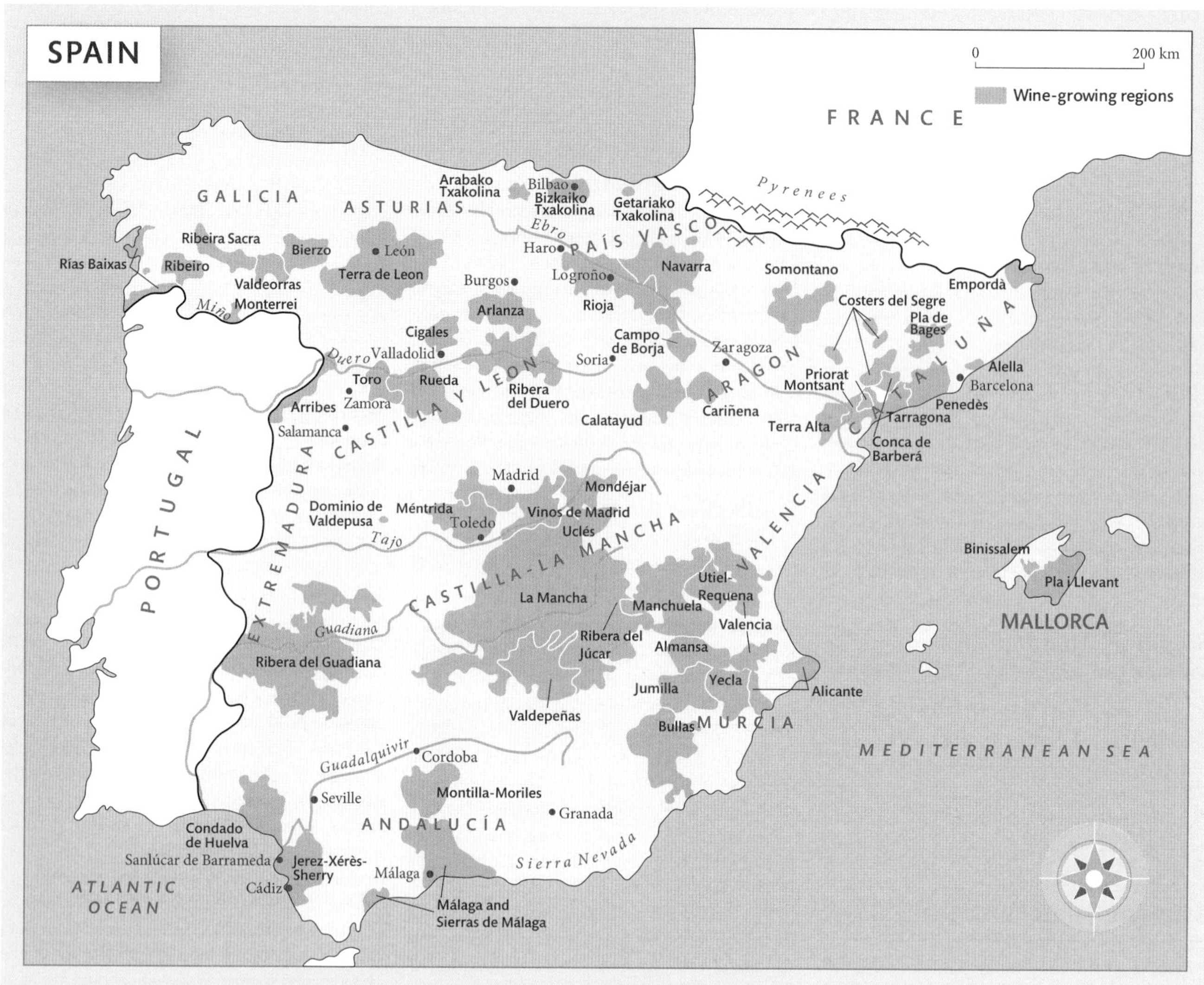

the south. Spain is a diverse country with distinct regional and cultural differences. The principal language spoken throughout Spain is Castilian, although Galician is dominant in GALICIA, Catalan and Spanish are roughly tied in CATALUÑA, and Basque remains a minority language in the BASQUE region.

The country's regional diversity is reflected in its wines, which range from light, dry whites in the cool Atlantic region of Galicia to heavy, alcoholic reds in the Levante and the Mediterranean south. ANDALUCÍA in the south-west is known for the production of fortified and dessert wines, the most famous of which is SHERRY.

Modern production methods were slow to reach Spain but, when they did, typically in the early 1990s, they did so with a vengeance, with modernization sweeping one region after the other, including some (but not all) of the less glamorous ones. A programme of investment which began a decade earlier was further helped by Spain's accession to the EU in 1986. In 1996 vineyard IRRIGATION was legalized throughout the country, radically changing prospects for the drought-stricken central and south-eastern areas.

History to Columbus

Although the winegrowing PHOENICIANS founded Cádiz *c.*1100 BCE on the coast of southern Spain, they did not introduce viticulture to the Iberian peninsula, for the vine had been cultivated in Spain since 4000–3000 BCE. Grapes, found in Spain from the close of the Tertiary era onwards, predate *Homo sapiens* by millions of years.

Cádiz, gateway to the Atlantic, was an important Phoenician trading post. After the Phoenicians came the Carthaginians, themselves inhabitants of a city, Qart Hadasht (see CARTHAGE), founded by Phoenicians. The Carthaginians grew wine in Spain; more importantly, they were a threat to the emerging republic of ancient ROME.

The 2nd century BCE was a time of much unrest under Roman rule in Spain, and no systematic colonization was attempted until Rome finally 'pacified' the whole of the peninsula under Augustus. Political stability furthered trade: as the evidence from AMPHORAE shows, a great deal of wine from Baetica (which approximated to ANDALUCÍA) and Tarraconensis (TARRAGONA) was sold in Rome, and Spanish exports far exceeded exports of Italian wine to Aquitaine and south-eastern GAUL via Bordeaux. Spanish wine reached the Loire valley, Brittany, Normandy, and England, and it was given to the troops guarding the Roman frontier with Germany. Literary evidence confirms the discoveries of archaeology. Strabo says in his *Geography* (completed 9 CE) that, since the fall of Carthage, Baetica has been famous for the beauty of its many vineyards. COLUMELLA, a native of Cádiz in Baetica, sees the wine imports from Baetica and Gaul as symptomatic of the decline of Roman agriculture (1, *Praefatio.* 20).

Most of the Spanish wines, and particularly that of Saguntum, sold in Rome appear to have been PLONK: perfect for getting the porter of one's mistress drunk on, is Ovid's advice (*Ars amatoria* 3. 645–6). Some wines earn praise, however: PLINY says that Tarraconensis is good (*Natural History* 14. 71) and so repeatedly does MARTIAL, himself a native of Spain.

Spain was no mere outpost of empire. It was the birthplace of other Roman authors besides Martial and Columella: Seneca, Lucan, and Quintilian. The emperors Hadrian and Marcus Aurelius came from Spanish families. When the Roman Empire disintegrated, Spain was invaded by barbarians, first by the Suevi and then by the Visigoths. We do not know what happened to viticulture and the wine trade; presumably it continued.

The overthrow of the Visigoths by the Moors in 711 did not mean the end of viticulture, for the ISLAMIC conquerors were enlightened rulers who did not impose their own way of life on their subjects. Better still, many of them liked wine themselves. The Moorish position with regard to wine was ambiguous. Although the Prophet forbade the use of wine, the emirs and caliphs of Spain grew wine; although its sale was illegal, it was subject to excise (see TAXATION). By the time ENGLAND was importing considerable quantities of wine from Spain in the mid 13th century, the Christians had largely succeeded in their reconquest.

Around 1250, wine was regularly shipped from Bilbao to the English ports of Bristol, Southampton, and London. The quality of the wines varied. The best wines were very good indeed: when Edward III fixed maximum prices for wines in 1364, a cask of the best Spanish wine was to cost as much as a cask of the best Gascon, which fetched more than wine from LA ROCHELLE. Spanish wines were popular because being from a hot climate they were high in alcohol and therefore kept better than French or German wines. But some of these wines were just high in alcohol, and that was their only merit. Hence they were often used to ADULTERATE more expensive and weaker wines. Laws forbidding this practice were widely disregarded.

See also SACK, and see also ARNALDUS DE VILLANOVA and EIXIMENIS, two important medieval commentators on aspects of wine who were Catalan by birth. H.M.W.

Blazquez, J. M., 'La economía de la Hispania Romana', in A. Montenegro et al. (eds), *Historia de España: España romana* (1982).

Curchin, L. A., *Roman Spain* (1991).

Jeffs, J., *Sherry* (5th edn, 2004).

Keay, S. J., *Roman Spain* (1988).

Tchernia, A., *Les Vins de l'Italie romaine* (1986).

History from Columbus

Spain emerged as a united Christian country under a single crown in January 1492 following the final defeat of the Moors at Granada. Christopher Columbus reached the West Indies in October of the same year, opening up a whole NEW WORLD to Spanish trade.

The wine regions around Cádiz and MÁLAGA, both important Spanish ports, were the first to attract the attention of foreign traders, and SHERRY, often called SACK, became a popular drink at the English court. Foreign traders in the sherry town of SANLÚCAR DE BARRAMEDA were granted special privileges by the duke of Medina Sidonia in 1517, and an English church was built to encourage more merchants. But relations between England and Spain began to deteriorate in the 1520s and after Henry VIII's divorce from Catherine of Aragón in 1533 brought English merchants into direct conflict with the Spanish. The Anglo-Spanish War lasted 1585–1604, after which trade in wine resumed. But 17th-century trade was sporadic, and trade in Spanish wines was blighted by excessive English import duties. Not surprisingly, the Spanish fostered markets elsewhere in Europe and the New World.

Spanish wine has historically depended on exports to a larger extent than wines from other traditional producing nations in Europe (and this continues to be the case today). During the 17th and 18th centuries, exports to Spain's American colonies surpassed in volume and value those to Britain and northern Europe. Vines had been planted all over the Americas since the very first days of Spanish colonization, and wine was made in MEXICO from the early days of the 16th century. But successive monarchs, particularly Philip III, tried to protect the flourishing export trade by writing edicts curtailing the spread of American vineyards. These were followed very unevenly—the local administration practically ignored them in Chile, but in Argentina they virtually quelled all attempts at developing a national wine industry until independence came in the early 19th century. For more details, see SOUTH AMERICA.

See SHERRY for details of 18th- and 19th-century trade in that important SPANISH WINE.

At the same time, Málaga also enjoyed a spectacular increase in popularity, producing an estimated 35,000 BUTTS of wine in 1829, equivalent to 175,000 hl/4.62 million gal. 'Mountain', as the wine was popularly known in its 19th-century heyday, sat alongside PORT, MADEIRA, and sherry as one of the world's great FORTIFIED WINES.

By all accounts there was little wine of exportable quality from the rest of Spain. Even RIOJA, already Spain's leading table wine at the turn of the 19th century, found few markets other than neighbouring Basque country and South America. The chronicler Richard Ford writing in 1846 notes that Spanish 'wine continues to be made in an unscientific and careless manner'. Cyrus REDDING, writing in the 1851 edition of the *History and Description of Modern Wines*, observes 'the rude treatment of the grape' in Spain. It seems that, outside Jerez and Málaga, little had changed since Roman times. In central and southern Spain, wines continued to be made in crude earthenware TINAJAS, while to the north wooden casks were used. Wine was frequently stored in *cueros*, pigskins lined with pitch or resin, which tainted the wine. Winemaking progressed slowly in Spain.

From the middle of the 19th century, wholesale change was forced on the Spanish wine industry, first by POWDERY MILDEW, which was found in Cataluña in the 1850s, and then by PHYLLOXERA when it arrived in Málaga in 1878. But phylloxera spread relatively late and slowly through Spain, partly because of the long distances between the various Spanish wine regions, and in the 1860s the French, who had also suffered powdery mildew for ten years, had crossed the Pyrenees to compensate for the shortfall in French wine. Rioja and NAVARRA, the closest wine regions to BORDEAUX, benefited most from France's misfortune and the resulting influx of French influence and expertise.

The BARRICA (225-l/59-gal oak cask) which is now used throughout Spain was introduced from Bordeaux, and winemaking was refined along the Bordelais lines (although American OAK continued to be preferred thanks to Spain's flourishing transatlantic trade in the late 18th century, the hardness of American oak—much appreciated in Jerez—and its relatively low cost). Rioja BODEGAS belonging to Marqués de Murrieta, Marqués de Riscal, López de Heredia, and CVNE date back to this period when up to 500,000 hl of wine a month were shipped across the Pyrenees to France.

Phylloxera took hold in Jerez in 1894 and reached Rioja in 1901, by which time the epidemic had been controlled by grafting European vines on to resistant American ROOTSTOCKS. Vineyards were replanted throughout the country, but many INDIGENOUS VARIETIES in such regions as Galicia and Cataluña were rendered virtually extinct. In Cataluña, the post-phylloxera period coincided with the development of the sparkling wine industry which is today one of the largest in the world. Following a visit to the Champagne region, José Raventós introduced the TRADITIONAL METHOD for the production of sparkling wine to the family firm of Codorníu in 1872. The wine, originally christened *champaña*, was a success, and vineyards around the town of San Sadurni de Noya were replanted with the trio of white grapes that now produce over 1.8 million hl of CAVA annually.

The first half of the 20th century was a turbulent era for Spain. Political infighting led to the abdication of Alfonso XIII in 1931 and the proclamation of a republic. However, one of the lasting measures introduced by the monarchist dictator General Primo de Rivera was the DOP system of CONTROLLED APPELLATIONS administered by a CONSEJO REGULADOR, which was first established in Rioja in 1926. Jerez and Málaga followed suit in 1933 and 1937 respectively.

In July 1936, following the election victory of the Popular Front, Spain erupted into civil war. For three years sentiment ran high and Spain tore itself apart, often along regional, separatist lines. Some parts of the country, notably Asturias, Cantabria, Euskadi, Cataluña, and Valencia, were affected more than others, but throughout the country vineyards were neglected and wineries were destroyed. The Nationalist victory in 1939 brought political stability to Spain under the dictatorship of General Franco, but economic recovery was hampered by the Second World War, which effectively closed European markets to Spanish exports.

In the 1950s, the wine industry began to revive, helped by the nationwide construction of large CO-OPERATIVE wineries which had begun some years earlier. This turned Spain, with its vast area of vineyard, into a natural source for inexpensive BULK WINE either sold under proprietary BRAND names or labelled with spurious GENERIC names such as Spanish Chablis or Spanish Sauternes, subsequently outlawed by EU authorities.

The post-war history of the Spanish wine industry was for some time marked by the Rumasa saga, outlined under SHERRY. But Rumasa's horizons ran far beyond Jerez, and by the late 1970s José María Ruiz-Mateos seemed to control Spain. Ruiz-Mateos contributed greatly to the much-needed modernization of the Spanish wine industry, but by the early 1980s there were signs that the empire was in trouble.

The 1960s sherry boom was followed by the international 'discovery' of Rioja, which had reached the top in the domestic market early this century. In the 1970s and 1980s, the family firm of FAMILIA TORRES wrought a single-handed transformation of the wines of PENEDÈS. The death of General Franco in 1975 and the restoration of the monarchy set the foundations for a modern, multi-party democracy in Spain. Greater economic freedom has led to the growth of an urban middle class which has in turn stimulated a new interest in high-quality wine.

Economically deprived rural regions such as La Mancha and Galicia have further benefited from EU finance, which is helping to change the face of the Spanish wine industry. In the 1990s, a fast-paced chain of events brought about more changes than during possibly the previous 90 years. International FLYING WINEMAKERS flocked to Spain; private estates overtook co-operatives in most regions; INTERNATIONAL VARIETIES became commonplace in vineyards from La Mancha to Navarra; irrigation and WIRE-trained vineyards sprouted up everywhere; and wine styles changed radically to the fruitier type favoured on international markets.

Spanish wine law

Spanish wine law is administered through a network of Consejos Reguladores (regulatory councils) representing each delimited region (DOP). The first Consejo was established in Rioja in 1926; the first wine law came in 1932, with the creation of 19 DOPs. The laws have changed many times since then, most notably with a move to align with EU systems in 1996, and again in 2003. Currently, the law recognizes five levels. In ascending order of rank, they are:

Vino de España: allowed only to mention country, grape variety, and vintage, this is the most basic level, although some producers use it for high-end wines, taking advantage of the flexibility it allows.

Vino de la Tierra (VT): equivalent to PGI, these come from legally designated zones that do not qualify as DOPs. There were 42 in 2022.

Vino de Calidad con Indicación Geografica (VC): transitory Spanish denomination between Vino de la Tierra/PGI and DOP (the next step up), of which there were seven in 2022. The EU considers it a PDO level.

Denominación de Origen Protegida (DOP): previously known as (and still often called) DO, and equivalent to PDO, defining the boundaries of the wine region, permitted VINE VARIETIES, maximum YIELDS, minimum alcoholic strength, and any other limitations pertaining to the zone.

Denominación de Origen Calificada (DOCa): a step above DOP, with more stringent rules. In 2022 there were just two: RIOJA and PRIORAT.

Vino de Pago (VP): a PDO launched in 2003 to highlight established vineyards with track records of producing singular wines. Any winery in Spain with singular vineyards may apply to have its own **Denominación de Origen Vino de Pago (DOVP)**. In this way, a Vino de Pago is similar to a Bugundian MONOPOLE or to a single-vineyard appellation such as CHÂTEAU-GRILLET, but a DOVP does not have to be within any tiered system of controlled appellations for that region.

In 2022 there were 101 DOPs (including the 24 Vinos de Pagos, two DOCa, and seven Vinos de Calidad) plus the 42 PGI (Vino de la Tierra).

As each region's Consejo Regulador regulates the growing, making, and marketing of wines within its boundaries, many have also created additional designations and classifications particular to their region's wines.

Geography and climate

Around much of Spain, the land rises steeply from the coast reaching a maximum ELEVATION of 3,482 m/11,420 ft at Mulhacén in the Sierra Nevada just 50 km/30 miles from the Mediterranean. The average elevation countrywide is 600 m/1,969 ft, with a vast plateau taking up much of central Spain. Known as the *meseta*, this undulating table land ranges in elevation from 600 to 1,000 m, tilting slightly towards the west. Four of Iberia's five major rivers (the Duero, Tajo, Guadiana, and Guadalquivir) drain westwards into the Atlantic, while the Ebro flows south-east to the Mediterranean. Other rivers are seasonal, many drying up completely in the summer months.

Great mountain ranges known as *cordilleras* divide Spain into distinct natural regions. The north coast, from Galicia to the Pyrenees, is relatively cool and humid with few extremes. Annual RAINFALL in this part of Spain ranges from 1,000 mm/39 in on the coast to over 2,000 mm on the mountain peaks inland. Galicia, Asturias, and the BASQUE country are intensively cultivated and densely populated.

The Cantabrian cordillera, a westerly spur of the Pyrenees which rises to over 2,600 m in the Picos de Europa, protects the main body of Spain from cool, rain-bearing north westerlies. Rioja in the upper Ebro valley is therefore shielded from the Bay of Biscay so that, although annual rainfall reaches around 1,500 mm on the Basque coast, it declines sharply to the east and is just 450 mm at Haro, the wine-making capital of Rioja, only 100 km inland.

The Spanish climate becomes more extreme towards the centre of the central plateau. Winters are long and cold with temperatures falling well below freezing point (the lowest recorded temperature is −22 °C/−7.6 °F in Albacete). Summers here can be blisteringly hot with daytime temperatures sometimes rising above 40 °C/104 °F. Little rain falls in the summer months, and DROUGHT is a constant problem. Agriculture has adapted to the lack of rainfall, which struggles to reach 300 mm in places. Much of this comes in sudden downpours in spring and autumn, sometimes causing devastating flash floods on the Levantine coast.

South and east from the central plateau the climate is increasingly influenced by proximity to the Mediterranean. The climate on the narrow coastal littoral is equable with long, warm summers giving way to mild winters. These are Spain's holiday Costas, but there are lush market gardens producing rice and citrus fruit around Valencia, and, on the mountain slopes inland, olives, almonds, and TABLE GRAPES are important crops. The hottest part of Spain is the broad Guadalquivir valley in Andalucía, north of the Sierra Nevada, where summer temperatures rise to 45 °C/113 °F. The south-west corner of Andalucía has a climate of its own, strongly influenced by the gulf of Cádiz and the Atlantic (see SHERRY).

Viticulture

The DRIP IRRIGATION that became prevalent in the early years of this century markedly changed the vinous landscape of inland Spain. In most of central and southern Spain, the old BUSH VINES are widely spaced to survive the summer drought with VINE DENSITIES ranging from 900 to 1,600 vines per ha (375–650 per acre) according to the amount of water available (less than one-eighth of the vine density in some MÉDOC or CÔTE D'OR vineyards, for example). Growers have adopted a system of planting known as the *marco real* with 2.5 m between each vine in all directions. Yields from the shrinking proportion of old vines are frequently less than 20 hl/ha (1.1 tons/acre). However, one considerable advantage that accompanies a dry climate is the lack of FUNGAL DISEASES. POWDERY MILDEW, DOWNY MILDEW, and BOTRYTIS BUNCH ROT are virtually unknown in central Spain.

IRRIGATION was one of the most important new developments of the 1990s. The practice had begun to spread unofficially—particularly during the DROUGHTS in south-east Spain of 1994 and 1995—and was formally legalized in 1996. Drip irrigation, pioneered on the Marqués de Griñón Valdepusa estate in Toledo province under the supervision of Australian viticulturist Richard Smart, is the favourite of many growers. Subsurface drip irrigation, which minimizes the losses due to EVAPORATION, became increasingly popular in the early 21st century. Irrigation has been followed by considerably increased YIELDS throughout the country. This, together with a rapid increase in new plantings and productive CLONES, has triggered concerns about wine quality.

Viticultural practices vary sharply from one part of Spain to another. In areas such as Rioja and Penedès, where more systematic replanting is taking place, vines are more densely planted (up to 5,000 vines per ha) and are increasingly trained on wires. In Galicia vines were traditionally trained on pergolas (see TENDONE), both to make maximum use of the limited space in this densely populated part of Spain and to lessen the risk of fungal diseases in the humid climate. Newer vineyards are planted on lower vine-TRAINING SYSTEMS to ease cultivation but have to be regularly sprayed to combat disease. That said, an increasing number of wineries throughout Spain have adopted ORGANIC VITICULTURE: official statistics in 2020 put the total at 12%, but the actual number is thought to be higher as many organic producers do not pursue certification.

In the past, most grapes were harvested by hand and grapes frequently arrived at co-operative wineries already starting to ferment, having been squashed when loaded into large trailers. Quality-conscious bodegas increasingly provide growers with stackable plastic containers to keep the grapes whole during transportation (see HARVEST). Some firms also set out a harvest regime refusing grapes delivered after midday when they have been heated by the sun. Some estates harvest at night. The number of MECHANICAL HARVESTERS is increasing as fast as the acreage of vineyards supported on wires.

Vine varieties

The Spanish have about 250 grape varieties, although 13 varieties make up 83% of the country's vineyards. Since the arrival of phylloxera at the end of the 19th century, farmers tended to favour varieties well adapted to local climatic conditions, but irrigation has changed this tendency considerably. The drought-resistant white AIRÉN is Spain's most planted grape, with 204,699 ha/505,822 acres in 2020, followed by the red grape TEMPRANILLO with 201,502 ha. It travels under such aliases as Cencibel, Ull de Llebre, and Tinto Fino in different parts of the country. GARNACHA is the second most planted red wine grape with 58,764 ha/145,209 acres, and the traditional BOBAL is third with 56,184 ha/138,834 acres. Monastrell (the MOURVÈDRE of France) is fourth with 37,881 ha/93,606 acres. Other white varieties which are also important in Spain are the sherry grapes PALOMINO (planted in Jerez, RUEDA, and parts of Galicia) and PEDRO XIMÉNEZ (Montilla-Moriles and Málaga). The white MACABEO (also called Viura) is widely planted in Rioja and Cataluña, especially Penedès, where, along with Parellada and Xarello, it is grown for Cava sparkling wine. High-quality white varieties which are gaining ground include ALBARIÑO (Galicia) and VERDEJO (Rueda), while other promising grapes which are making a more limited comeback include the white LOUREIRA, TREIXADURA, and GODELLO (all three in Galicia) and the red GRACIANO (Rioja) and MENCÍA (Galicia and Castilla y León).

INTERNATIONAL VARIETIES have made significant inroads in some parts of Spain. Cabernet Sauvignon, Syrah, Merlot, Petit Verdot, Sauvignon Blanc, and Chardonnay have become increasingly important in Cataluña, Somontano, Navarra, Castilla y León, and Castilla-La Mancha. Cabernet Sauvignon, with a total of 18,651 ha/46,807 acres of vineyards, is the most important of these.

Winemaking

Spanish winemaking has changed radically since the 1960s. Stainless steel, once a rarity, is now commonplace, and virtually all bodegas have the means of TEMPERATURE CONTROL for fermentation. These improvements transformed Spanish wines, especially in La Mancha and the Levante, where temperature control is essential to preserving the primary fruit character in both red and white wine. The epoxy-lined CONCRETE tanks still to be found in some co-operative wineries are regaining favour with top producers for red wines, as are oak vats, in a return to traditional fermentation vessels which ensure less temperature variation than stainless-steel tanks.

A vogue for crisp, technically perfect, simple young whites was followed in the 1990s by a resurgence of BARREL-FERMENTED whites.

Spain continues to foster the long-established tradition of ageing red wines in OAK. The use of wooden BARRELS as vessels for fermentation and storage dates back many centuries, but in the second half of the 19th century the French introduced the 225-l BARRIQUE (*barrica*) to Rioja, and its use has subsequently spread throughout the country. Unlike the French, however, traditional Spanish winemakers use at least some American oak, which not only is considerably cheaper than French oak but also can impart a stronger flavour to the wine. The Tempranillo grape in particular seems to produce wine that responds to maturation in new oak. However, French oak has made significant inroads since the early 1990s. Spanish oak-aged reds are usually denoted by the words CRIANZA, RESERVA, or GRAN RESERVA, which are enshrined in local legislation. From the 1970s to the 1990s, the wines often showed a pungent vanilla character, but this was superseded by more FRUIT-DRIVEN aromas and flavours, partly in response to FASHION. After 2000 a return to some TRADITIONS, sometimes including the use of TINAJAS, was apparent among a newer generation of producers keenly attuned to the worldwide trend towards using less technology in high-quality wines.

Most Spanish DOs also stipulate minimum BOTTLE AGE, and traditionally very few Spanish wines were released before they were ready to drink. But some growers, led by the PRIORAT newcomers, started a new habit of renouncing both Crianza and Reserva back labels, selling oak-aged wine without an age classification and often with little bottle age.

For specific wine regions, see ANDALUCÍA, ARAGÓN, BASQUE, CASTILLA-LA MANCHA, CASTILLA Y LEÓN, CATALUÑA, GALICIA, NAVARRA, and RIOJA.

See also SHERRY. V. de la S. & F.C.

de Santa María, F. C. S., et al., *Variedades de vid en España* (2019).
Peñín. J., *Peñín Guide to Spanish Wine* (annually).
www.winesfromspain.com
www.fev.es

Spanna, local name for the NEBBIOLO grape grown in the north of PIEMONTE in north-west Italy, particularly in a historic wine zone in the hills of Biella, Vercelli, and Novara provinces referred to as Alto Piemonte. The exceptions are the Carema and Valli Ossolane DOCS, which use the word 'Nebbiolo'.

Five DOC wines and two DOCGS, Gattinara and Ghemme, are made either wholly or in part from Spanna: three in the Vercelli hills (BRAMATERRA, GATTINARA, LESSONA) and four in the province of Novara (BOCA, FARA, GHEMME, and SIZZANO). Only Gattinara and Ghemme, responsible for some of the longest-lived Spanna wines, are made in any quantity today, but in the 19th century this area had greater plantings and was more famous for its wines than the LANGHE. After the Second World War, the region's wines lost ground to the Langhe's richer Nebbiolo wines, particularly BAROLO and BARBARESCO. The extreme fragmentation of vineyard property and a workforce that moved to the textile factories of nearby Biella accelerated the decline of winemaking in this area, but this group of wine zones is attracting attention once more, not least because of the finesse of its best wines. W.S.

sparging means stripping a wine of a gas by the action of another gas—for example, removing OXYGEN or CARBON DIOXIDE by purging it with fine bubbles of an INERT GAS, usually NITROGEN. The oxygen and carbon dioxide from the wine transfer into the bubbles of inert gas and leave with it out the top of the tank. Sparging can also refer to the removal of HYDROGEN SULFIDE by the action of carbon dioxide produced during fermentation. An alternative to sparging is the use of membrane contactors. Gas passes into or out of the wine without bubbles through a hydrophobic membrane that divides the wine from a gas or vacuum flowing on the other side of the membrane. The membrane is in the form of many thin hollow tubes contained within a cylindrical module. In combination with in-line carbon dioxide and oxygen sensors, they are well suited to automated dissolved gas control and can allow for carbon dioxide to be adjusted up or down to a set level, while oxygen is removed in a single pass. S.N.

Nordestgaard, S., 'Gains in speed, labour and gas consumption for winemakers', *Australian and New Zealand Grapegrower & Winemaker*, 648 (2018), 61–7.

sparkling wine, wine which bubbles when poured into a glass, an important category of wine increasingly seen as an everyday drink rather than one for special occasions. The bubbles form because a certain amount of CARBON DIOXIDE has been held under pressure dissolved in the wine until the bottle is unstoppered (see FIZZINESS). According to the OIV, in 2018 world sparkling wine production (not including carbonated wines) reached 20 million hectolitres for the first time (i.e. 7% of the world's total wine production), with an overall increase of 57% since 2002. Some 70–80% is produced in the EU. IWSR data for 2020 show a global dip in consumption of 4% in volume and 6% in value compared with 2019 but predict growth over the five years to 2025.

Sparkling wine may vary in as many respects as still wine: it can be any wine COLOUR (it is usually white or pink, but sparkling reds such as Australian sparkling Shiraz enjoy a certain following); it can be any degree of SWEETNESS (although a high proportion tastes bone dry and may be labelled BRUT, while Italians specialize in medium-sweet SPUMANTE); it can vary in ALCOHOLIC STRENGTH (although in practice most dry sparkling wines are about 12–12.5%, while the sweeter, lighter *spumante* are 5.5–8%); and it can come from anywhere in the world where wine is produced.

According to EU regulations, the sweetness level of EU wines and those marketed in the EU must be shown on the label. For official EU definitions, see DOSAGE.

Sparkling wines also vary in FIZZINESS, not just in the actual pressure under which the gas is dissolved in the wine but also in the character of the foam. Some sparkling wines seem to froth aggressively in the mouth while others bubble subtly. The average size, consistency, and persistence of the bubbles also vary considerably. Study of foam and foaminess, along with research into YEASTS, are two of the few areas which unite the (sparkling) wine industry with the beer industry.

To the winemaker, however, the most obvious way in which sparkling wines differ is in how the gas came to be trapped in solution in the wine: traditional method, transversage, transfer, tank method, or carbonation, in declining order of cost, complication, and likely quality of sparkling wine, together with the rarer *méthode ancestrale* and *méthode dioise ancestrale*. (See SPARKLING WINEMAKING for details of each method.)

The most famous sparkling wine of all is CHAMPAGNE, the archetypal sparkling wine made in north-eastern France, which represents about 13% of global sparkling wine production. A significant proportion of all sparkling wine is made using the same basic method as is used in Champagne (now called the traditional, rather than the champagne, method), much of it from the same grape varieties—Pinot Noir, Chardonnay, and, to a lesser extent outside Champagne, Pinot Meunier—even though different wine regions often stamp their own style on the resulting sparkling wine. Examples of such wines were made with ever-increasing frequency from the 1980s onwards in CALIFORNIA, AUSTRALIA, and ITALY particularly.

A host of fine, very individual sparkling wines is made using the traditional method but with non-champagne grapes, however. The most prodigious example of this is the popular Spanish CAVA. The LOIRE region of France also produces traditional-method sparkling wine in great quantity, notably in SAUMUR. All of France's CRÉMANTS also use the traditional method. In almost every wine region in the world with aspirations to quality, some traditional-method wine has been made. Wines made by this, the most meticulous method, may be described on the label within Europe as *méthode traditionnelle*, *méthode classique*, or *méthode traditionnelle classique*. Other descriptions include bottle-fermented (although strictly speaking wines made by the transfer method, described below, may be labelled 'bottle-fermented', while only those made by the traditional method can be labelled 'Fermented in this bottle').

Similarly, in almost every wine region in the world, tank-method sparkling wine is made in considerable quantity, often for specific local BRANDS, especially for SEKT in Germany and a host of wines such as PROSECCO, LAMBRUSCO, and ASTI in Italy. RUSSIA has been an enthusiastic market for sparkling wines ever since the imperial court imported such vast quantities of champagne (and base wine to make sparkling) at the end of the 19th century. Today sparkling wine is still made in enormous quantity in both Russia and UKRAINE. Asti and a number of other low-alcohol, sweet Italian, or Italianate, sparkling wines are made using a variation of the tank method.

The transfer method is used for some better-quality branded wines, particularly in Germany, Australia, New Zealand, and the United States.

Some characterful sparkling wines are made eschewing DISGORGEMENT and selling the wine together with the LEES of its second fermentation in bottle. These include dry or lightly sweet PÉTILLANT NATUREL, as well as some of the sweeter styles of wine from GAILLAC, LIMOUX, and CLAIRETTE DE DIE made by specific but similar local methods sometimes called *méthode ancestrale*. In Italy, sparkling wines labelled *sui lieviti*, occasionally *sur lí*, meaning 'on the lees', are always dry. J.R., J.E.H. & E.C.

See also OPENING THE BOTTLE, LABELLING INFORMATION, and DOSAGE.

OIV Focus, *The Global Sparkling Wine Market* (2020).

sparkling winemaking, the process of making SPARKLING WINES, most obviously involves the accumulation of gas under pressure in what was initially a still 'base wine' or, ideally, blend of base wines. The most common methods of achieving this are discussed below, but these are matters of technique rather than substance. Almost all of them depend on initiating a SECOND FERMENTATION, which inevitably produces CARBON DIOXIDE, and most of them incorporate some way of keeping that gas dissolved under pressure in the wine (see FIZZINESS) while separating it from the inconvenient by-product of fermentation, the LEES. What matters most to the quality of a sparkling wine, however, is the quality and character of the blended base wines.

Making and blending the base wine

Wines that are good raw material for the sparkling winemaking process are not usually much fun to drink in their still state. They are typically high in acidity and unobtrusively flavoured. There is a school of thought that the austerity of the still wine of the CHAMPAGNE region, Coteaux CHAMPENOIS, is the most eloquent argument of all in favour of champagne's carbon dioxide content.

It is not just in Champagne, however, that sparkling winemakers argue that BALANCE is the key to assembling a base wine to make sparkling and that the best sparkling wines are therefore

S

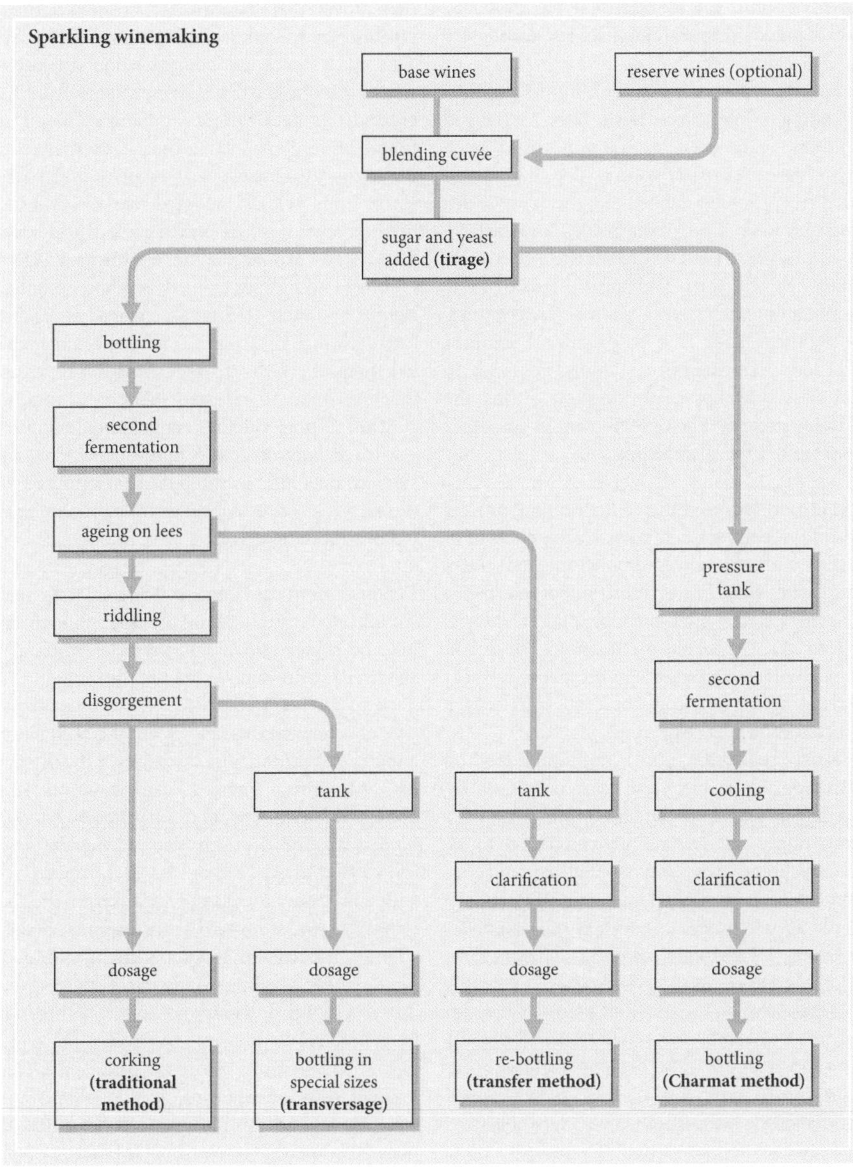

essentially blended wines. Some fine VARIETAL sparkling wines exist (some of the best BLANC DE BLANCS champagnes, for example), but a great sparkling wine never tastes just like the still wine version plus gas; the very nature of sparkling winemaking is to try to make a sum that is greater than the parts (although this may not be achieved, or even attempted, for cheaper wines). Those who aspire to make good sparkling wine are acutely aware that any minor fault in a base wine may be amplified by the sparkling winemaking process.

Accordingly, for better sparkling wines, grapes are invariably hand picked since WHOLE-BUNCH PRESSING is the norm. MECHANICAL HARVESTERS have improved, but there is still a risk of splitting berries and extracting harsh PHENOLICS into the grape juice, which could cause astringent, coarse characteristics which would be magnified by the pressure of bubbles. It is therefore essential to rapidly separate the juice from the skins to reduce phenolic extraction. It is possible that gentler mechanical harvesters will change this, although it is essential to press grapes as soon as possible after picking. Press houses in the vineyards have long been *de rigueur* in Champagne and are increasingly common for other top-quality sparkling wines.

Grapes destined for sparkling wines are usually picked at lower MUST WEIGHTS than the same varieties would be if they were to be sold as a still wine. In very general terms, average YIELDS can be higher for sparkling wines than for still wines (see below), partly because there is no imperative to achieve high sugar levels. In California, for example, HARVEST begins in mid, or sometimes early, August for Pinot Noir and Chardonnay destined for sparkling wines. In Australia, the aim is to pick such varieties just as HERBACEOUS characters have been lost when ripe fruit FLAVOUR COMPOUNDS are beginning to develop (in practice at about 17 to 20 °BRIX in Australia's cooler areas).

PRESSING is an important stage in sparkling winemaking, particularly in Champagne, where black grapes are used, as it is essential that the concentration of phenolics, both ASTRINGENCY and COLOUR, is kept to a minimum. There has been much experimentation with horizontal PRESSES of various types, and modern pneumatic or tank presses can certainly offer a reliably high standard of HYGIENE, but modern technology has found it difficult to improve upon the traditional vertical presses of Champagne, although they are LABOUR intensive. So-called 'thin layer' presses, which minimize pressure, and therefore the extraction of phenolics, by pressing a layer of grapes no more than 70 cm/27 in thick, are used increasingly.

The winemaker can then make the usual still white wine decisions concerning OXIDATIVE versus PROTECTIVE methods of JUICE HANDLING; juice CLARIFICATION; choice of YEAST strain and FERMENTATION rate; protein STABILIZATION; and MALOLACTIC CONVERSION.

The winemaker must also choose the type of vessel to use for the primary fermentation and for maturation of reserve wines (see diagram). STAINLESS STEEL tanks are the most common choice. If oak vessels are used, they will have a more significant influence on the style of the wine, depending on the size, shape, and age of the BARREL or CASK.

Then comes the crucial blending stage, the true art of making sparkling wine and one in which experience is as important as SCIENCE. A large champagne house such as MOËT & CHANDON may be able to use several hundred base wines in order to achieve the house style in its basic expression, that year's NON-VINTAGE blend. A small, independent concern, especially outside Champagne, may have access to only a very limited range of base wines—a disadvantage in a poor vintage, although not necessarily in a good one. And a producer of the most basic carbonated or tank-method wine may simply blend suitable base wines available on the open market.

Traditional method

This method, once known as the champagne method and now known variously as traditional method, classical method, and classical traditional method (or their equivalents in other languages), is the most meticulous way of making wine sparkle; the raw ingredients vary considerably but the basic techniques do not.

Pressing and yield Pressing is the first operation defined in detail by the traditional method, which understandably differentiates rigorously between the fractions of juice from each press load, for the first juice to emerge from the press is highest in sugar and acidity and lowest in phenolics, including pigments. A maximum extraction rate is usually defined in any regulations concerning sparkling wine production (such as those for France's CRÉMANTS). Those who produce traditional-method sparkling wine acknowledge that the first juice to emerge from the press is generally the best, even if there is a certain amount of VINTAGE variation. The extraction of juice is strictly monitored and in the case of champagne is limited to a maximum of 638 litres (169 gal) per 1,000 kg (2,205 lb) of grapes (see CHAMPAGNE for more detail). (This compares with an approximate average extraction rate of 95 l of wine from about 130 kg of grapes for softly pressed still red wines; see YIELD.) Producers of top-quality sparkling wine from other countries tend to follow this guideline but are not as constrained by local regulations and have more flexibility in processing techniques.

Base wines After the making of the base wines (described above), which usually takes place over the winter following the harvest, the final blend is made after extensive tasting, assessment, and ASSEMBLAGE. There is extreme flexibility in blending a non-dated wine, and a high proportion of 'reserve wine' made in previous years may be used. Some producers include up to 45% of reserve wines in their non-vintage blend. (In Champagne, for example, KRUG indulge in the luxury of using base wines from up to ten vintages being held in reserve.) The ingredients in a vintage-dated sparkling wine are more limited, depending on the regulations in the country or region of origin. Many of the base wines made from dark-berried grapes, however lightly pressed, may have a light pink tinge at this stage, although the PIGMENTS are precipitated during *tirage*, the crucial next stage during which the blended wine rests on the lees of a second fermentation in bottle. As soon as the new blend has been made in bulk blending tanks, it usually undergoes cold STABILIZATION in order to prevent subsequent formation of TARTRATES in bottle.

Second fermentation This new blend then has a mixture of sugar and yeast added to it before bottling in particularly strong, dark BOTTLES, usually STOPPERED with a CROWN CAP, so that the carbon dioxide of the second fermentation is captured in the bottle, creating the all-important fizz. Conventionally, an addition or TIRAGE of about 24 g/l of sugar is made. This creates an additional 1.2 to 1.3% ALCOHOLIC STRENGTH and sufficient carbon dioxide to create a pressure inside the bottle of 5–6 atmospheres after disgorgement (see below), which is roughly the FIZZINESS expected of a sparkling wine and one which can safely be contained by a wired champagne cork. During this second fermentation, known as *prise de mousse* in French, the bottles are normally stored horizontally at 12–16 °C/54–61 °F until the fermentation has produced the required pressure and bubbles, usually for four to eight weeks.

Special types of YEAST culture which help sparkling winemakers have been developed (and are much used for still wines too). Such yeasts are particularly good at flocculating and produce a granular deposit that is easy to riddle, or shake, to the neck of the bottle for extraction.

At this stage, RIDDLING agents are increasingly added with the yeast and sugar. Made of some combination of TANNINS, BENTONITES, gelatines, or alginates, they help to produce a uniform skin-like yeast deposit that does not stick to the glass but slips easily down it during the riddling process. The development of smoother glass bottles has also helped.

Ageing on lees Timing of the riddling process after the second fermentation is a key element in quality and style of a traditional-method sparkling wine, the second most important factor affecting quality after blending the base wine. The longer a wine rests on the lees of the second fermentation in bottle, the more chance it has of picking up flavour from the dead yeast cells, a process known as yeast AUTOLYSIS.

Most regulations for traditional-method sparkling wines specify at least nine months' ageing on lees, and the minimum period for non-vintage champagne was increased to 15 months in the early 1990s (vintage champagnes are usually aged for several years). During the bottle-ageing process, the yeast cells autolyse, releasing increasingly complex flavour compounds. The chemistry of autolysis is not fully understood, but it seems that autolysis has significant effects only after about 18 months on the lees and that the most obvious changes occur after five to ten years of lees contact, which inevitably increases production costs considerably. It may be that compulsory periods of lees contact in bottle of only a few months have less effect on quality than has been imagined.

In parallel with the increase in autolytic character over time, the wine is also maturing from the pale and light characteristics of a base wine to a progressively more deeply coloured and richer-flavoured wine. It is this combination that give the complexity and depth to mature sparkling wines.

Riddling The riddling process, known as *remuage* (or shaking) in French, is one of the most cumbersome (and most publicized) parts of the traditional method, but it is undertaken for cosmetic rather than oenological reasons: to remove the deposit that would otherwise make the wine cloudy (as it does in the *méthode ancestrale* described below).

Traditionally, bottles were gradually moved from the horizontal to an inverted vertical by hand, by human *remueurs* or riddlers who would shake them and the deposit every time they moved them towards the inverted vertical position in special *pupitres* or riddling racks. This was a slow and extremely labour-intensive way of moving the deposit from the belly of the bottle to its neck. The CAVA industry based in Cataluña developed an automatic alternative in the 1970s, the *girasol* or GYROPALETTE, which has since been widely adopted for traditional-method sparkling winemaking the world over. The bottles are stacked in large metal crates (300–504 bottles per crate, depending on bottle shape), and their orientation changed at regular intervals (including night-time, unlike the manual method), with accompanying shake, from the horizontal to inverted vertical by remote control. Using riddling agents, well-adapted yeasts, and gyropalettes, bottles may now be riddled in as little as three days, as opposed to the six weeks or more needed for hand *remuage* without riddling agents.

Disgorgement and dosage The final stage in a complicated production process—though it may be shorter than, say, that of a fine oak-aged red—is to remove the deposit now in the neck of an inverted bottle. The conventional way of achieving this is to freeze the bottleneck and deposit by plunging the necks of the inverted bottles into a tray of freezing solution. The bottles are then upended and the crown cap flipped off, and the 2-cm deposit flies out as a solid pellet of ice. Bottles are then topped up with a mixture of wine and sugar syrup, the so-called DOSAGE, stoppered with a proper champagne CORK held on with a wire MUZZLE, and prepared for labelling. Many of the bigger producers employ a technique known as jetting, long familiar to brewers, to protect the wine from OXIDATION: just before the cork is inserted, a small dose of wine, or bisulfite diluted in water, is injected into the neck of the bottle at high pressure; this creates bubbles that rise just to the lip of the bottle, pushing out any oxygen in the head space. Most dry sparkling wine is sweetened so that it contains between 5 and 12 g/l RESIDUAL SUGAR. The higher the natural ACIDITY of the wine, the more dosage is generally required to counterbalance it, although the longer a wine is aged on lees, the less dosage it needs. One of the apparent effects of CLIMATE CHANGE seems to be a noticeable trend towards reducing the amount of sugar added, with grapes being picked riper, with lower acidity.

Alternative methods Riddling and disgorgement are unwieldy processes which contribute nothing to the innate quality of the sparkling wine. It is not surprising therefore that, as LABOUR costs spiralled in the 1980s, there was considerable research into alternative methods of expelling the sediment.

One of the most successful has been the development of encapsulated yeast. Yeast can be trapped in a 'bead' made of calcium alginate.

Such beads are a few millimetres in diameter and are able to hold the yeast trapped in their interior while having large-enough pores to admit sugar and nutrients into the bead so that a full second fermentation can proceed as normal. The great advantage is that the riddling stage takes seconds as the beads simply drop into the neck of the inverted bottle.

Another possible method is to insert a membrane cartridge into the neck of the bottle. Yeast is dispensed into it, and it is then plugged before the bottle is stoppered with the usual crown cap. Like the beads, the cartridge allows ingress of sugar and nutrients for fermentation to take place there, as well as allowing the carbon dioxide gas out. In this case there is no need at all for riddling, and disgorgement simply entails taking off the crown cap and allowing the pressure inside the bottle to expel the cartridge.

Both these alternatives result in a significant amount of non-recyclable packaging, which is apparently the reason the Champenois have not taken them up. However, the market for encapsulated-yeast beads is growing since this method is useful to small wineries—or those taking the first tentative steps towards traditional-method sparkling winemaking—for whom the investment in riddling and disgorgement equipment has been prohibitive. In some cases, the beads are used for a small proportion of a winery's production as it allows the producer to keep stock of wine ready to disgorge and label at short notice. It is particularly suited to LARGE FORMAT bottles. Suppliers of these beads estimate that in the last five years more than one hundred million bottles have been produced using this method.

Transversage

Transversage is an occasional twist on the traditional method whereby, immediately after disgorgement, the contents of bottles of sparkling wine made by the traditional method are transferred into a pressure tank to which the dosage is added before the wine is bottled, typically in another (often small) size of bottle, under pressure. This is how many half-bottles, all airline 'splits' or quarter-bottles, and virtually all BOTTLE SIZES above a jeroboam of champagne are filled.

Transfer method

The transfer method, known as *méthode transfert* in French and Carstens in the United States, also depends on inducing a second fermentation by adding sugar and yeast to a blend of base wines and then bottling the result. It differs from the traditional method, however, in that riddling and disgorgement are dispensed with; after a period of lees contact, the bottles are chilled and their contents transferred to a bulk pressure tank where the sediment is removed by clarification, usually FILTRATION. A suitable dosage is then added and the result is once again bottled, using a counter pressure filler, before being corked and wired. There have been significant improvements in the equipment used for this method, particularly at the filtration stage, reducing the previous loss of wine character. It is popular for the production of large-volume good-quality sparkling wine because it retains the positive attributes of traditional fermentation and maturation on lees while allowing re-blending prior to final bottling in a range of bottle types and sizes.

Continuous method

This process, similar to that used for the tank method but continuous rather than in batches, was developed in the USSR in the 1950s for sparkling wine and was once used to a very limited extent in Portugal for large-volume inexpensive fizz. The main advantages are speed—sparkling wine in a mere three weeks—and cost, though the equipment is necessarily complicated. Base wine, together with sugar and active YEAST culture, is pumped into the first of a series of pressurised tanks, and the second fermentation crucial to virtually all methods of sparkling winemaking begins. This creates CARBON DIOXIDE, which increases the pressure in the tank, but the yeast cannot grow under this pressure and so further yeast has to be added continuously. The second and third tanks are partly filled with some material such as wood shavings, which offer a substantial total surface area on which the dead yeast cells accumulate, and a very limited amount of AUTOLYSIS, or at least reaction between the dead yeast cells and the wine, takes place. In the fourth and fifth tanks there are no yeast cells, and the wine eventually emerges relatively clear, having spent an average of perhaps three or four weeks in the system.

Tank method

This very common method, also called Charmat, *cuve close* (French for sealed tank), bulk method, *granvas* in Spanish, *autoclave* or *metodo Martinotti* in Italian, and *Tankgärung* in German, was invented by the Italian Federico Martinotti a decade before it was improved and patented by Frenchman Eugène Charmat in the early years of the 20th century, even though Charmat gets most of the credit. Its advantages are that it is very much cheaper, faster, and less labour intensive than the above processes, and it is better suited to base wines which lack much capacity for AGEING. A second fermentation is initiated by yeast and sugar added to base wine held in bulk in a pressure tank; after a rapid fermentation, the fermentation is typically arrested by cooling the wine to −5 °C/23 °F when a pressure of about 5 atmospheres has been reached. The result is clarified, a dosage is added, and the resulting sparkling wine is bottled using a counter pressure filler. This style of sparkling wine is the most likely to taste like still wine with bubbles in it, rather than to have any of the additional attributes which can result from fermentation in bottle.

Carbonation

Initially known as the injection, or simply the 'bicycle pump', method, carbonation of wine is achieved in much the same way as carbonation of fizzy soft drinks: carbon dioxide gas is pumped from cylinders into a tank of wine which is then bottled under pressure, or very occasionally it is pumped into bottles. Significant technological improvements allowing carbon dioxide to be introduced immediately prior to bottling via direct injection and membrane systems have resulted in improved (smaller) bubble size and gas retention. However, in general wines produced by this method still tend to have larger bubbles and reduced mousse compared with those produced by a second fermentation. It must have a pressure of at least 3 atmospheres and in EU parlance is referred to as aerated sparkling wine. This is the cheapest, least critical, and least durable way of making wine sparkle and is generally used for perhaps budget and fruity sparkling wines.

Méthode ancestrale or méthode rurale

This method (given new life by the PÉTILLANT NATUREL vogue) results in a lightly sparkling wine, often with some sweetness and sediment, and most closely parallels how wines were originally made sparkling. It involves bottling young wines before all the RESIDUAL SUGAR has been fermented into alcohol. Fermentation continues in bottle and gives off carbon dioxide. Today it is becoming increasingly common in parts of France such as the Loire and the Jura and is spreading throughout the wine world, but variants on this theme are still made in BUGEY, GAILLAC, LIMOUX, and for CLAIRETTE DE DIE *méthode ancestrale* (see below).

The resulting wine, generally stoppered by a CROWN CAP, is less fizzy than a traditional-method sparkling wine. Although no dosage is allowed, the wines may be slightly sweet if the fermentation stops before all the sugar has been consumed by the yeast. The wine may in some cases be decanted off the deposit and rebottled under pressure in a form of transfer method.

Méthode dioise ancestrale

This is an unusual variation on the *méthode ancestrale* above and the transfer method, producing wines similar to ASTI. It is used for the sweet wine Clairette de Die *méthode ancestrale*, most of which is made by the local CO-OPERATIVE. The base wines are fermented in stainless-steel tanks at very low temperatures over several months. The wine is then filtered to remove most but not all of the yeast and is bottled; fermentation continues in bottle until an alcoholic strength of 7–8.5% has been reached. The wine is disgorged six to 12 months after bottling (the minimum time on lees is four months) before being filtered again and immediately transferred to new bottles. The use of liqueur de tirage and liqueur d'éxpedition is both prohibited and unnecessary. E.C.

Spätburgunder is the chief German synonym for PINOT NOIR although 'Blauburgunder' is widely used in Switzerland and Austria. This variety experienced a most dramatic rise in popularity during a red-wine boom in Germany that began in the 1990s and saw total plantings increase from 3,400 ha/8,400 acres in 1980 to more than 11,000 ha by 2003, rising to 11,660 by 2020. There is considerable dispute over the vine's importance in Germany during the Middle Ages, but in modern times it has been cultivated throughout Germany, most notably in parts of the RHEINGAU (especially Assmannshausen), where it owes its toehold to the same 13th-century Cistercian MONKS responsible for its rise to fame in the Côte d'Or, in the southern PFALZ, and in BADEN, WÜRTTEMBERG, and westernmost FRANKEN, as well as along the steep slate slopes of the AHR, where pale, slightly sweet wines have been replaced since the 1980s by dry, full-bodied, deeply coloured ones. Today, impressive Pinot Noir also comes from sites in the NAHE, MOSEL, and RHEINHESSEN. For many years, demand in Germany was so strong that very little Spätburgunder was exported, but examples are attracting increasing attention abroad.

Spätlese, means literally 'late harvest' but, as a so-called PRÄDIKAT, is officially defined by grape sugar at harvest. In Germany, specific minimum MUST WEIGHTS are laid down for each combination of vine variety and region, ranging from 76 to 90 °OECHSLE. In Austria, where the designation is no longer used for dry wines and seldom for sweet, the minimum across the board is 19 °KMW (approximately 94 °Oechsle). The designation 'Spätlese TROCKEN' was widely utilized in the late 20th century, but since the turn of the millennium, increasingly—and within Germany's VDP growers' association, officially—Prädikat terms are being dropped from the names of dry wines. A wine that would once have been labelled 'Spätlese trocken' is likely to be marketed instead as GROSSES GEWÄCHS. D.S.

S

Spätrot, synonym for ZIERFANDLER.

special late harvested, term which should, according to EU labelling law, be applied to wines made in Australia from 'fresh ripe grapes of which a significant proportion have been desiccated under natural conditions in a manner favouring the concentration of sugars in the berries'. In South Africa, the term refers to a lighter style of dessert wine harvested at a minimum of 22 °Balling (see MUST WEIGHT) and with at least 11% alcohol. If the RESIDUAL SUGAR is less than 20 g/l, the label must indicate whether the wine is extra dry, dry, semi-sweet, or sweet.

specific gravity. See DENSITY.

Spergola, synonym for VERNACCIA DI ORISTANO in the Emilia region of Italy, where it makes tart whites.

spiced wines. See FLAVOURED WINES and MULLED WINE.

spinning-cone column, gas–liquid counter-current device for making DE-ALCOHOLIZED WINE or GRAPE CONCENTRATE and for removing SULFUR DIOXIDE from juice, and reducing some wines' ALCOHOLIC STRENGTH, particularly in California. Spinning-cone technology is an advance on the processes operating in a one- or two-stage vacuum evaporator. The device consists of a vertical stainless-steel column containing inverted cones, half of which are fixed to the wall of the column, while the other half spin along a central shaft. The spinning cones continuously and repeatedly spin the wine out in thin liquid films. Simultaneously, vapour that is evaporated from the thin film of liquid (under vacuum at low temperature, and with the aid of an inert stripping gas) flows up the column in the spaces between the successive fixed and rotating cones. Through a process of repeated evaporation and condensation on the cones, the volatiles are enriched in the up-flowing vapour stream. The volatiles, after passing through a condenser, are finally captured in liquid form at the top of the column while the stripped liquid is pumped out the bottom of the column. After the first pass through the column, most of the volatile components of the wine are collected. During the second pass the ETHANOL can be removed. Thus the aroma fraction is recovered separately from the alcohol and can be added back to the wine to restore the flavour profile at a lower alcohol concentration. Spinning-cone technology offers extremely high separation efficiency, with a low pressure drop across the column and low liquid hold-up; hence the juice or wine spends a short time in the column. Accordingly, alcohol and aroma removal are achieved with much less of the product evaporated than in a traditional evaporator. One application of the spinning-cone column is reducing the alcoholic strength of excessively alcoholic wines by 1–3% without loss of FLAVOUR COMPOUNDS to produce a wine with the flavour intensity afforded by fully ripe fruit but without an unacceptable alcohol content. An entire batch of wine can be treated to remove a small amount of alcohol, or a fraction can be treated to remove most of the alcohol and blended back into untreated wine to lower the overall alcohol content.

Advocates of the spinning-cone column claim it can be used to selectively remove unwanted flavours from a finished wine such as those from HYDROGEN SULFIDE, MERCAPTANS, and even excess HERBACEOUS notes. Because of the cost of equipment, this is mainly a service industry since very few producers can afford to buy a spinning cone themselves. An alternative and equally popular technique for reducing alcohol levels in wines is REVERSE OSMOSIS. A.O.

Block, D. E., and Miller, K. V., *Unit Operations in Winery, Brewery, and Distillery Design* (2022).

spitting is an essential practice at professional TASTINGS where several dozen, often more than 100, wines are regularly offered at the same time. Members of the wine TRADE, and WINE WRITERS, rapidly lose any inhibitions about spitting in public. Since there are no taste receptors in the throat, spitting allows the taster to form a full impression of each wine, while minimizing the blunting effects of ALCOHOL. It does not, unfortunately, leave the taster completely unaffected by alcohol. Some ethanol is vaporized and absorbed in the nose and mouth, and, no matter how assiduous the taster, it can also be extremely difficult to prevent any liquid from dribbling down the throat. According to the estimates of this writer, tasting 30 wines can involve ingesting almost a glass of wine, depending on the personal mechanics of TASTING.

Whatever tasters spit into is called a **spittoon**. These can vary from specially designed giant funnels on a stand through wooden CASES filled with sawdust, ice buckets, jugs, or, particularly convenient at a seated tasting and most hygienic and convenient for disposal, personal paper cups. Many professional tasting rooms are equipped with channels or sinks with running water designed to drain away expectorated wine.

spontaneous fermentation refers to alcoholic FERMENTATION that occurs due to AMBIENT YEAST rather than inoculated, cultured yeast. Some producers and marketers prefer the term 'wild ferment'. See YEAST for the terminology used in this book.

spotted lanternfly, an invasive planthopper (*Lycorma delicatula*), native to Asia, first identified in Pennsylvania in 2014 and now found in vineyards in mid-Atlantic states and beyond. It feeds on many plants, including grapevines, cucumbers, and ornamentals, and can cause significant damage that affects the winter hardiness of grapevines. Tree-of-heaven is a favoured host and should be removed around vineyards. The insect lays conspicuous egg masses in and near vineyards; it may be treated by ovicidal and adult insecticide sprays. R.E.S.

www.extension.psu.edu/spotted-lanternfly-management-in-vineyards

spraying, a vineyard practice of applying liquids and powders to control pests, diseases, and weeds. Late last century, vineyard sprayers were often drawn by draught animals and operated with manual pumps; nowadays they are usually mounted on TRACTORS, or drawn by them, and are sometimes mounted on MECHANICAL HARVESTERS in order to spray several rows at once.

The aim of economically and environmentally sound spraying is to achieve maximum coverage of the target (leaves, bunches, or weeds) by applying minimum amounts of the appropriate AGROCHEMICAL (or other products). There should be ideally no spray material lost to the surrounding environment as spray drift. Good coverage depends on having very small droplets, although these are more readily blown off target by wind than large drops. A tractor-mounted tunnel sprayer prevents spray escaping into the environment because the vine canopy beside the tractor is enclosed by a cover or tunnel, usually made of fibreglass, with the spray jets mounted inside the tunnel. Any spray droplets not caught by the vine are caught by the opposite side of the tunnel and can therefore be retrieved and returned to the spray cart. Such units save a lot of spray material, especially early in the growing season when the 'target' is small. Sprayers have also been designed that use LiDAR (Light Detection and Ranging) sensors to detect gaps in the CANOPY and switch the sprays on and off automatically. See also ROBOTS.

Vineyards can also be sprayed from the air using fixed-wing aircraft or HELICOPTERS. Costs can be lower, but coverage is typically not as good as for ground spraying, and low wind conditions are required. Aerial spraying can be used when ground conditions are unsuited for tractors, such as following heavy rain. However, spray drift may endanger the ORGANIC or BIODYNAMIC status of a neighbouring vineyard.

Relatively few vineyards are now sprayed from containers strapped on workers' backs, although this is still done in Portugal's DOURO Valley and on one-person properties. The costs of such spraying operations are very high and generally not sustainable for most commercial vineyards. Agrochemicals in dry powder form are applied by a process known as DUSTING.

See also RESIDUES. R.E.S.

Landers, A., *Effective Vineyard Spraying: A Practical Guide for Growers* (2020).

sprinklers are used for IRRIGATION and (in some vineyards) as a means of FROST PROTECTION. Sprinkler irrigation has largely been replaced by DRIP IRRIGATION, which uses much less water and does not leave wet leaves vulnerable to FUNGAL DISEASES and possible SALINITY damage. Sprinklers have also been used in hot regions of Australia for vineyard cooling, by operating the system intermittently during the hottest part of the day, but this is not economical and wastes WATER. J.G. & R.E.S.

spritzer, common name for a mixture of white wine and sparkling water that is usually drunk as an APERITIF.

spritzig, German term for wines with a slight, attractive prickle of CARBON DIOXIDE. **Spritz** has become an international TASTING TERM, perhaps for onomatopoeic reasons.

spumante, Italian word for sparkling wine from the verb *spumare*, meaning 'to foam or froth', which can appear on labels as *Vino Spumante*, *Vino Spumante di Qualità* or *Vino Spumante di Qualità* followed by a denomination of origin. It is allowed only for wines made sparkling by a second fermentation, either in bottle (*metodo classico*) or by the TANK METHOD and with a minimum pressure of 3.5 bar (see SPARKLING WINEMAKING). By far the most important example in terms of volume is PROSECCO, with more than 400 million bottles of *spumante* produced in 2020.

Second best-known is ASTI made from the MOSCATO Bianco grape cultivated in the provinces of Asti, Cuneo, and Alessandria in PIEMONTE.

Significant quantities of sparkling wines from CHARDONNAY and PINOT NOIR, the classic grapes of CHAMPAGNE, are produced throughout Italy—some using the tank method but most bottle-fermented. The most important, with over 18 million bottles produced in 2020, is Franciacorta, a DOCG solely for sparkling wine and the only Italian fizz to have eliminated the word *spumante* from labels, thus emulating CHAMPAGNE, with which it is often compared. Trento DOC, which produced 9 million bottles in 2020, is reserved for classic-method wine in TRENTINO. OLTREPÒ PAVESE's vast Pinot Noir vineyards supply both base wine for many Piemonte sparkling wines as well as its own Oltrepò Pavese Metodo Classico.

Inspired by the extraordinary commercial success of Prosecco, almost every DOC now has a provision for the production of sparkling wine. While classic-method wines are considered more prestigious, most Italian sparkling wines are tank-method wines and FRIZZANTE rather than *spumante*. W.S.

spur, a viticultural term for a shortened grapevine cane. A spur is a stub formed by pruning the CANE to between one and four NODES, usually two. Spurs are used to provide the next season's fruiting SHOOTS. Of all PRUNING systems SPUR PRUNING is the most severe, since over 90% of the previous year's cane growth is removed. Spurs are also left on cane-pruned vines to provide replacement canes at next pruning. B.G.C.

spur pruning, a form of winter vine PRUNING whereby the canes are cut back to two-bud SPURS (see diagram). Normally the spurs are spaced along a CORDON top and point upwards

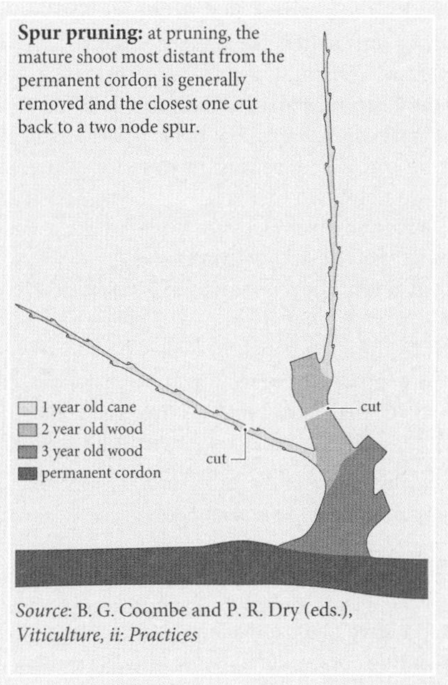

Spur pruning: at pruning, the mature shoot most distant from the permanent cordon is generally removed and the closest one cut back to a two node spur.

Source: B. G. Coombe and P. R. Dry (eds.), *Viticulture, ii: Practices*

(although see SMART-DYSON). There are several advantages to spur pruning: among these are that it takes less time to prune by hand and that the operation can also be mechanized easily (see MECHANICAL PRUNING). Also, setting the spur spacing results in the appropriate shoot spacing in the canopy, which in turn leads to well-exposed leaves and fruit (see CANOPY MICROCLIMATE). Spur pruning is not particularly well suited to very vigorous vineyards, however, as excessive SHADE of the fruit and leaves can lead to the loss of both yield (due to low bud fruitfulness) and quality. The other main form of vine pruning is CANE PRUNING. See also CORDON TRAINING. R.E.S.

Spurrier, Steven (1941–2021), influential and much-loved wine-merchant-turned-wine-writer whose most famous act turned out to be, much to his surprise, organizing the JUDGMENT OF PARIS in 1976, which, almost by chance, opened the door for non-French wines to make their mark. He inherited a fortune which was largely frittered away on projects, usually wine-related, that took his fancy. He could never have been accused of a lack of enthusiasm.

Inspired to work in wine by a glass of Cockburn 1908 given to him by his grandfather when he was 13, he began in the cellars of London wine merchant Christopher's after Rugby school, the London School of Economics, and life as a deb's delight. He went on to set up a wine shop in Paris, Cave de la Madeleine, and then a wine school, l'Académie du Vin, at which the wine flame was lit for countless wine professionals on both sides of the Channel. He worked briefly in the United States and then even more briefly for Harrod's before becoming a wine educator, running Christie's wine school for

Michael BROADBENT, and acting as both wine taster and writer. He was the leading taster as well as columnist for *Decanter* magazine and was instrumental in setting up their lucrative annual wine awards. For all his power and influence, he was unusually modest and generous, always obsessed by his latest scheme, which included most permanently Bride Valley, a vineyard opposite his home in Dorset.

As keen a buyer of art as of wine, he deserved far more honours than he was given, especially from the French, whose wines he adored but who apparently never forgave him for the results of that 1976 blind tasting. The 2008 FILM *Bottleshock* was based on it, with Alan Rickman playing a misleading caricature of Spurrier.

Spurrier, S., *A Life in Wine* (2020).

Sri Lanka, tropical Indian Ocean island nation where fledgling, very small-scale ventures have tried to make wine from established plantings of Cardinal, Black Muscat, and Israel Blue vines originally grown for TABLE GRAPES. In 2022 there is no commercial wine production with locally grown grapes, but there are companies licensed to make wine from imported MUST and GRAPE CONCENTRATE as well as local fruit, including grapes. One is a collaborative venture with an Italian company. D.G.

stabilization, group of wine-processing operations undertaken after CLARIFICATION to ensure that the wine, once bottled, will not form hazes, clouds, or unwanted deposits; become gassy; or undergo rapid deterioration of flavour after BOTTLING. Some deposits and subtle changes in flavour that occur with lengthy AGEING are considered normal in a **stable** wine (see also SEDIMENT).

There are three main causes of instability: unstable PROTEINS and TANNINS; TARTRATES; and microbiological activity.

Many wines contain molecules of proteins and tannins that are not entirely stable and can join together, creating larger molecules that cause a haze to form. This gradually becomes dense enough to form a cloud and, ultimately, a solid deposit. These substances, which are completely harmless and have no effect on the taste of the wine even if they make it appear unpalatable, are most simply dealt with by FINING.

The four basic types of treatment used to stabilize tartrates—refrigeration, additives, ion exchange, and electrical methods—are described in detail under TARTRATES.

Microbiological stability is achieved by ensuring the absence of spoilage microorganisms (such as ACETOBACTER, LACTIC ACID BACTERIA, and YEASTS) at the bottling stage by sterilizing all bottling machinery and submitting the wine to an aseptic FILTRATION. This is easily achieved by the use of a good filtration regime, starting with earth and pad filtration and finishing with a fine membrane filter which will remove all troublesome yeasts and bacteria. The removal of yeasts is especially important for wines that contain residual sugar.

SULFUR DIOXIDE is also valued for its antimicrobial properties. D.B.

Bird, D., and Quillé, N., *Understanding Wine Technology* (4th edn, 2021).

stabulation, winemaking technique used for aromatic whites and rosé wines that increases FLAVOUR PRECURSORS and FLAVOUR COMPOUNDS but does not involve extended MACERATION—ideal if you are trying to make a flavourful but pale rosé or a white with more flavour but without the tannins of a SKIN-FERMENTED wine. After PRESSING, the juice is kept with its LEES (mostly PULP) for 5–15 days before CLARIFICATION, with the lees stirred up once a day by injecting carbon dioxide or adding dry ice. The temperature must be kept low to avoid the onset of fermentation. The technique, first used in Gascony, has also been used in the Loire for Sauvignon Blanc but has become particularly popular for Provence rosé.

Stags Leap District, California wine region and AVA within NAPA Valley known for supple, bright Cabernet Sauvignon.

stainless steel, sometimes referred to as inox (from the French *acier inoxydable*), is widely used for holding wine, especially for FERMENTATION but also during ÉLEVAGE. For wines made PROTECTIVELY it has the great advantage over wood that it is easy to clean and OXYGEN can be completely excluded from it, by the use of INERT GAS to fill the HEAD SPACE if necessary. It has the advantage over CONCRETE that TEMPERATURE CONTROL is even easier, especially with REFRIGERATED jacketing and cooling/warming coils, and any TARTRATES can be hosed out rather than having to be chipped off the concrete walls. For some wines, the exclusion of oxygen can be a disadvantage, however, and there is a risk of REDUCTION. Nor is there any possibility of the gradual, natural CLARIFICATION and STABILIZATION processes that are possible in wooden containers.

stake. The simplest form of vine support is a stake driven into the ground beside the vine. A stake supports an individual vine, whereas POSTS, which are usually thicker than stakes, support several vines from suspended wires. Stakes are a very traditional form of vine support, having been used for centuries. Vines trained to stakes are most common in Europe, although they are not unknown in California. Since vines are climbing plants, they are unable to support themselves unless specially trained with a short trunk which thickens with age, as for GOBELET vines.

Materials used for stakes vary enormously between wine regions, reflecting local availability. Most common is WOOD, which has been used for centuries, although it is only recently that timber has been treated chemically, preventing softwoods from rotting in the ground. However, such treated wood requires special handling for disposal as it is toxic when burnt. Sometimes stakes are made from round timber, as in much of Europe, or from sawn timber, as in California. They can also be made from stone (slaty schist), as in the DOURO Valley of Portugal, or from concrete, as in parts of Italy. R.E.S.

stalk. For information about the stalk of an individual grape or berry, see PEDICEL. For information about the stalk of a bunch of grapes, see STEM.

stamen, pollen-bearing part of a flower that consists generally of an ANTHER borne on a filament. A grapevine flower is small and has five erect stamens that become evident after the CALYPTRA or cap has fallen off at FLOWERING. B.G.C.

standard drinks, unit of measurement used by governments to quantify a normal or regular pour of alcoholic drink by the amount of pure ALCOHOL it contains; also known as a unit of alcohol. Once this has been agreed upon, the theory goes, it is easier for authorities to set safe limits for consumption. There are many stumbling blocks, however, including wide variance among countries with regard to how much alcohol a 'standard drink' contains: 14 g in the US, 13.6 g in Canada, 12 g in France, 10 g in Australia and 8 g in the UK. In addition, both standard servings and the average ALCOHOLIC STRENGTH of wine are greater than when the standards were first set (see HEALTH, Sensible drinking). In some countries it is compulsory to state on wine labels the number of standard drinks each bottle contains. C.S.S.

starch, vine, an insoluble carbohydrate polymer composed of GLUCOSE residues. It is non-osmotic and is the principal storage substance in plants, forming as starch grains. Starch grains occur in the leaf and in cells of storage tissue in stems and roots of the vine. During daylight hours, when SUCROSE levels rise in leaves due to PHOTOSYNTHESIS, starch grains build up. At night they are metabolized to provide the sugar needed for RESPIRATION (this is also their fate in the human gut). Starch, natural storage reserves, are remobilized when buds burst and shoots begin to grow. Unlike many fruits, grape berries do not contain much starch, which is one reason grapes do not ripen after picking (apart from changes associated with dehydration). Starch is the principal CARBOHYDRATE reserve of vines. B.G.C.

state winemaking though less common than it once was, has been important not just in Eastern Europe—during the communist era, when all activity took place under the auspices

S

of the state—but also in TÜRKIYE; in Germany, where the state has owned a number of important vineyards and cellars, including KLOSTER EBERBACH; and, at certain points in their history, in North African countries such as ALGERIA, EGYPT, and MOROCCO.

staves are the shaped wooden planks that are cut and formed into BARRELS. See BARREL MAKING for more details.

Shorter lengths designed to impart OAK FLAVOUR to wines stored in used barrels or in tanks may be called **inner staves** (see BARREL INSERTS and INNER STAVES, respectively).

Steen, name by which CHENIN BLANC used to be known in South Africa.

Steiermark, wine region in AUSTRIA known in English as Styria, comprising the south-east corner of the country and incorporating the official wine regions of SÜDSTEIERMARK, VULKANLAND STEIERMARK, and WESTSTEIERMARK. In the age of Imperial Austria, vineyards in what is now SLOVENIA were also considered part of Steiermark, making a total viticultural area more than twice the size of that remaining in Austria today. In 2006 Slovenia officially renamed a large share of the Podravje region 'Stajerska Slovenija', about which some Austrian neighbours had misgivings. The traditional centre for Styrian viticulture was in fact Maribor in Slovenia (Marburg in German), whence in the early 19th century Archduke John of Austria directed expansion and improvements in winegrowing, including the introduction of most grape varieties found there today. D.S.

Steinfeder, the lightest in terms of MUST WEIGHT and alcohol among the trio of dry white wine categories in AUSTRIA's WACHAU region—specifically for unchaptalized grapes of 73–83 °OECHSLE (15–17 °KMW) which result in wines with no more than 11% alcohol. Consumers will pay much higher prices for the fuller-bodied wines of the categories FEDERSPIEL and SMARAGD, and achieving quality at low levels of POTENTIAL ALCOHOL is increasingly challenging. (See CLIMATE CHANGE.) So Steinfeder wines today, however charming and refreshing, tend to be rendered from relatively few cool sites and solely for local consumption. The name comes from a feathery grass species indigenous to the local vineyard terraces. D.S.

Stellenbosch, important wine district in SOUTH AFRICA, named after the charming university town at its heart 45 km/28 miles east of Cape Town with its Cape Dutch, Cape Georgian, and Victorian buildings shaded by long-established oaks.

Stellenbosch is the Cape's most famous wine district, traditionally associated with the country's most celebrated reds. It has been producing wine since 1679. As well as STELLENBOSCH UNIVERSITY, it is also home to the Wine & Spirit Board and the biggest wine wholesaler DISTELL with its 6,500-barrel maturation cellars. Stellenbosch is surrounded by valleys of vines and the soaring blue-grey mountains of Stellenbosch, Simonsberg, and Helderberg. The district's wards—Banghoek, Bottelary, Devon Valley, Jonkershoek Valley, Papegaaiberg, Polkadraai Hills, Simonsberg-Stellenbosch, and Vlottenburg—all yield wines capable of displaying distinctive differences. Vineyards on the Helderberg (which runs from Stellenbosch to False Bay at Somerset West) enjoy a considerable reputation. Soils and climate vary, from sandy ALLUVIAL loam along the valley floors and river courses to deep, moisture-retaining decomposed GRANITE on the hillsides. The climate is tempered by the Atlantic sweeping into False Bay, a 15-minute drive from the town. The average daily summer temperature is 20 °C/68 °F.

Stellenbosch returns low average YIELDS; it makes less than 9% of the country's wine despite having 17% of the country's vines, as well as South Africa's greatest concentration of leading estates, an extensive wine route network, and scores of restaurants.

Stellenbosch University is the only one in South Africa offering professional degrees in both VITICULTURE and OENOLOGY. Informal teaching in these two subjects started in 1889, but the Department of Viticulture and Oenology was formally opened only in 1917, with Professor A. I. Perold as chair. The university has been an important influence on the Cape wine industry over the decades and continues to produce most of the Cape's leading viticulturists and winemakers. The town is also home to the Agricultural Research Council's ARC Infruitec-Nietvoorbij Institute for Horticulture, Viticulture, and Oenology; and the College for Agriculture and Oenology at nearby Elsenburg. Stellenbosch University is the site of the Institute of Wine Biotechnology.

As elsewhere (see the University of BORDEAUX, DAVIS, and GEISENHEIM, for example), the PHYLLOXERA crisis was a powerful motivation for viticultural research, and from 1890 until about 1920 most of Stellenbosch's work was concentrated on re-establishing the phylloxera-devastated vineyards of the Cape.

During the 1920s, considerable effort was expended on improving the quality of fruit-bearing vine SCIONS, a range that was naturally restricted by strict QUARANTINE regulations. This involved VINE BREEDING which led to NEW VARIETIES, of which PINOTAGE has been the most widely acclaimed. Under the guidance of Stellenbosch oenologists, South Africa was one of the first wine-producing countries to apply widespread TEMPERATURE CONTROL to fermentations. Other globally admired advances have been in plant-material quality, ROOTSTOCKS, root systems, PRUNING, CANOPY MANAGEMENT, vine spacing, vine-row orientation, grape and wine flavour profiles, and optimal ripeness for different wine styles.

Stelvin. See SCREWCAPS.

stem, or **bunchstem**, of a grapevine INFLORESCENCE or bunch of grapes, known by botanists as the peduncle and in French as a *rafle*. The form of the stem, especially the position and length of lateral branches, determines the shape of the BUNCH and is one of many characteristics used to identify vine varieties in the science of AMPELOGRAPHY.

The terms 'stem' and 'stalk' tend to be used somewhat carelessly by winemakers, if not by viticulturists. For information about the stem of an individual berry, see PEDICEL. The practice of **stem inclusion**, using the technique of WHOLE-BUNCH FERMENTATION or occasionally by adding stems to the fermenter, is both traditional and fashionable. It may result in wines described—both approvingly and disapprovingly—as **stemmy**, with vegetal or HERBACEOUS aromas and flavours that typically increase the perception of freshness. See also DESTEMMING.

stemming, paradoxically alternative term for DESTEMMING grapes.

stem pitting, vine virus disease. See RUGOSE WOOD.

stemware. See GLASSES.

sterile bottling or, more correctly, **aseptic bottling**, is the technique of getting wine into a closed bottle without incorporating any micro-organisms that would harm the wine (notably YEAST and BACTERIA). Borrowed from the pharmaceutical packaging industry, this technique does the job of PASTEURIZATION without the use of heat. Aseptic techniques have become the norm for wine bottling because the use of membrane filters (see FILTRATION) has made the task very simple. Many everyday modern wines have small amounts of RESIDUAL SUGAR and therefore require bottling in an aseptic manner, but the degree of care needed depends upon the levels of residual sugar and alcohol.

An aseptic bottling line involves the creation of a clean room, modifying the usual equipment so that it may be sterilized easily. The room is kept under a slight positive pressure of filtered air, and entry is restricted to the few specially trained and clothed personnel required. Micro-organisms are removed from the wine by sterile FILTRATION using membranes, and the corks or other CLOSURES are sterilized by gaseous SULFUR DIOXIDE or other chemical sterilizing agents such as peracetic acid. The bottling and corking machines are usually sterilized by steam, hot water,

S

or chemical sterilants. Frequent sample bottles are removed at random for microbiological analysis, and each bottling run is held in storage until it is certain that no organisms are growing. D.B.

Bird, D., and Quillé, N., *Understanding Wine Technology* (4th edn, 2021).

steward, wine. See SOMMELIER.

stickie, Australian term for sweet, usually fortified, wines. Typical examples are the TOPAQUES AND MUSCATS of RUTHERGLEN and Glenrowan in North East Victoria.

stigma. See FLOWERS, VINE.

stilbene. See RESVERATROL.

stirring, winemaking term which may be used as a synonym for LEES STIRRING or may refer to the important operation of stirring, usually in much larger containers, when blending disparate components in a blend. This is particularly necessary when grape spirit is added to wine, as during FORTIFICATION, since the spirit, with its lower DENSITY, tends to float on top of the wine. Stirring, or dynamizing, also plays an important role in the production of some BIODYNAMIC preparations.

stomata (plural of **stoma**), minute openings on the surface of leaves bordered by two guard cells which open and close, thus regulating the exchange of gases between the atmosphere and the air chambers inside the leaf, especially of water out and carbon dioxide in (see TRANSPIRATION and PHOTOSYNTHESIS). The stomata of the grapevine occur only on the underside of each leaf blade, and there are also limited numbers on berries. B.G.C.

stones and rocks are coarse fragments of bedrock. The two words are practically synonymous, though some may think of rocks as larger or rougher and more angular. Whereas most farmers do their best to get rid of any fieldstone, not least because of potential damage to machinery, in vineyards stony soils are typically revered, probably because many celebrated vineyards around the world are spectacular in their stoniness.

Stones promote good DRAINAGE and restrict SOIL FERTILITY, leading to reduced vine VIGOUR, which in turn influences GRAPE COMPOSITION AND WINE QUALITY. They form an efficient mulch against surface EVAPORATION, protect against SOIL EROSION and force the vine to develop a beneficial extensive ROOT system. The much-repeated claim that stones absorb warmth during the day to re-radiate it at night (see BASALT) is probably overstated, except where the grape bunches are trained close to the ground and where grape ripening is difficult.

Stones exist because they are resisting weathering: they are effectively inert chemically. There is, therefore, no scientific basis for the popular claims that stones imbue wine with certain flavours, such as MINERALITY or 'stoniness'. However, stones exposed to the air rapidly become veneered with bacteria, algae, moulds and the like, and the aromatic compounds derived from them can be tasted by licking the stone and can be smelt when they volatilize, for example on a hot summer day, after a shower of rain, or when wetted at a river's edge. Stones are themselves tasteless and odourless. Only specialized organisms such as lichens and mosses can grow directly on them.

See also SOIL AND WINE QUALITY. A.J.M.

Maltman, A., *Vineyards, Rocks, and Soils: The Wine Lover's Guide to Geology* (2018).

stoppers for wine bottles. See CLOSURES.

storing wine is an important aspect of wine consumption, since wine is relatively sensitive to storage conditions and is one of the very few consumer products that can improve with age (although see AGEING for details of how few, and which, wines this applies to). Until the era of inflation, wine producers and merchants regarded storing and ageing wine as part of their business, but since the 1960s they have steadily relinquished this role. The development of the EN PRIMEUR market and the increase in the number of wine COLLECTORS leaves many wine drinkers with the problem of how to store wine over long periods, often a decade or two.

There are two basic choices: to consign the bottles to professional storage and/or to establish some form of domestic cellar. If wine is put in storage, it is vital to choose a specialist in wine storage since wine is a much more fragile commodity than most things kept in warehouses, and it needs special treatment and conditions. It is important that the wine storage specialist is in sound financial health itself, that it understands the detail of storage conditions needed, and that it provides some facility for marking individual CASES with some identification of their owner. In the case of business failure, this can make the difference between establishing possession and not.

For more details of how to identify and, if necessary, convert part of a home into a suitable place to store wine, see CELLAR.

Ideal storage conditions

Even in ancient GREECE there was some appreciation of the importance of storage conditions on the evolution and health of wine. The key factors are TEMPERATURE, light, HUMIDITY, and security.

If wine is kept too hot or is exposed to strong sunlight, it rapidly deteriorates. If it is kept too cold, it can freeze, expand, and push out the stopper of whatever container it is held in.

For bottles stored for a few weeks, the primary concern is to keep them from strong direct light (white wines in colourless glass are most at risk; see LIGHTSTRIKE) and to ensure that they do not reach temperatures more than about 25 °C/77 °F (although there is some latitude here, depending on the fragility of the wine), at which point the wine may be spoilt and forever afterwards taste cooked.

A fairly wide range of temperatures is suitable for wine storage, although, in general, the lower the storage temperature, the slower the reactions involved in wine maturation and, the theory goes, the more complex the wine eventually. Dramatic temperature swings should be avoided, and an average temperature somewhere in the range of 10–15 °C/50–59 °F is considered suitable (see TEMPERATURE for more details).

Some degree of humidity is beneficial, to ensure that the exposed end of corks don't dry out and allow in oxygen. A level of 75% relative humidity is usually cited, although this, like so many aspects of wine consumption rather than production, suffers from a lack of scientific research. The disadvantage of very damp cellars is that damp labels eventually deteriorate and make identification difficult (and some COLLECTORS prefer pristine labels so any resale value is not prejudiced).

Bottles to be stored for more than a few weeks, however, should be stored so that any cork is kept damp and there is no possibility of its drying out and allowing in the enemy, OXYGEN. This usually entails storing the bottles horizontally, ideally in a wine rack so that individual bottles can easily be extracted, or in a BIN full of wines of the same sort. Many wine producers deliberately mark their CASES ('this way up', for instance) in an effort to keep bottles upside down, and corks damp, during shipment. The increased use of alternative CLOSURES, however, particularly SCREWCAPS, suggests that horizontal storage may no longer be strictly necessary, although horizontal storage tends to save space.

The wine itself in an inverted bottle comes to no harm. Research in the late 1990s suggested that an ideal storage position for wine bottles stoppered with a natural cork is at a slight angle from the horizontal so that the cork is kept damp but the air bubble of ULLAGE just touches the cork rather than lying on top of the middle of the bottle. It has also been suggested by some that champagne ages most gracefully when stored in bottles that are kept upright rather than horizontal, but this was disproven in 1996.

If a maturing wine is agitated, it may disturb the sediment and therefore the AGEING process (although this is an unproven hypothesis). Some cellars are specifically designed with rubber racks for bottles in order to minimize any likely vibration. The need for a secure storage space is obvious, especially since bottles of alcoholic drink seem to be widely regarded as common currency rather than private property.

It is also important that there are no strong, persistent smells in a long-term wine storage area.

See also BULK STORAGE.

Valade, M., 'Extrait de la presentation sur les activités techniques oenologiques en 1995', *Le Vigneron Champenois* (February 1996).

Straccia Cambiale, synonym for the white grape BOMBINO BIANCO.

Strathbogie Ranges, hilly, elevated Australian wine region in the Central Victoria Zone. (See VICTORIA.) Despite its dry, warm-to-hot summers, wide variations in SOIL, ASPECT, and ELEVATION make this a diverse region where Chardonnay and Pinot Noir lead the plantings and Shiraz often comes in a cool-climate guise. E.N.H.M.

straw wines, sweet wines made from grapes dried on straw. See VIN DE PAILLE, ALSACE, AUSTRIA, CZECHIA, LUXEMBOURG, VIN SANTO, and DRIED-GRAPE WINES.

Strevi, independent DOC for a sweet white wine made from late-harvested or dried MOSCATO Bianco grapes in the hills around Strevi in the east of the ASTI zone. As it is usually riper in flavour than most MOSCATO D'ASTI thanks to Strevi's warmer MESOCLIMATE and steep vineyards, it has also been granted subzone status within the Moscato d'Asti DOCG zone. W.S.

Strohwein is German for STRAW WINE, an official category of DRIED-GRAPE WINES in AUSTRIA and SWITZERLAND.

structure, TASTING term that refers not to any FLAVOUR but to the TANNINS, particularly their intensity. It may sometimes incorporate ACIDITY.

Stück, German term for a large wooden BARREL, typically one with a capacity of 1,200 l/317 gal used in the RHINE regions of GERMANY. (In the MOSEL region, the FUDER is more common.) A **Halbstück** contains 600 l and was commonly used for transporting wine in the pre-tanker era, while a **Doppelstück** contains 2,400 l.

stuck fermentation, winemaker's nightmare involving an alcoholic FERMENTATION which ceases before completion. Such fermentations are notoriously difficult to restart, and the wine is at risk of spoilage from OXIDATION and BACTERIAL DISEASE. Before cooling equipment was commonplace, fermentation TEMPERATURES could reach a dangerously high level, often in excess of 35 °C/95 °F. In extreme cases, with temperatures nearing the range at which YEASTS are killed (over 40 °C), the yeast cells release compounds which inhibit future yeast growth, thereby making it difficult or impossible to restart such fermentations even after cooling.

Stuck fermentation has many documented causes, and because there can be several concurrent causes, diagnosis is often difficult. However, one clear cause is the tendency over recent decades to harvest grapes at higher maturity levels (see PHYSIOLOGICAL RIPENESS), which has resulted in grapes with higher sugar levels and wines with a higher alcohol content. Unless fermentation conditions are optimal, various stresses culminate in decreased or, in some cases, complete cessation of fermentation activity before the target sugar content has been reached. One common stress is deficiency of the essential nutrient NITROGEN. Grapes which come from vineyards deficient in nitrogen have a low level of available nitrogen, or yeast-assimilable nitrogen (YAN). This limits the development of yeast cells, and fermentation activity is not sustained after they have become starved of nitrogen. This problem is exacerbated in the fermentation of highly clarified musts (see CLARIFICATION), with which the winemaker is aiming to produce wine low in PHENOLICS. The very low content of suspended grape solids in such musts means that the level of LIPIDS, the compounds that allow yeast to build strong membranes needed to limit the toxic effects of alcohol, is also low. Fermentation at low temperatures (below 15 °C/60 °F) with strict protection from air (oxygen), which prevents yeast from making lipids, greatly increases the risk of stuck fermentation.

There are several ways to reduce the risk of stuck fermentation: adding nitrogen to the juice, either in the form of an ammonium salt (most commonly DIAMMONIUM PHOSPHATE) or a proprietary yeast food which contains significant nitrogen; adding back the 'fluffy' or light fraction of must settlings to increase the level of grape solids (lipids); using a yeast starter culture of a high-alcohol-tolerant strain that has been propagated with excess air; or adding nitrogen and exposing the fermentation to a small amount of air once the yeast is active. These options are usually effective, especially when several are used in combination. The last treatment is most simply achieved by stirring, SPARGING with air or OXYGEN, or PUMPING OVER. Failure of the yeast inoculum to dominate the AMBIENT YEASTS that are invariably present in grape must can result in a stuck fermentation if the ambient yeasts have a lower tolerance to alcohol. Ambient yeasts which produce 'killer toxin' (called zymocidal yeasts; yeast toxin has no effect on human cells) can be especially aggressive by actively eliminating the killer-sensitive wine yeast. Certain LACTIC ACID BACTERIA, which can grow rapidly during the early stages of fermentation when SULFITES have not been added to the must prior to fermentation, can interrupt fermentation. Inhibition of fermentation by ambient yeasts and bacteria can be diminished considerably by using a highly active yeast starter culture, choosing a yeast that is resistant to killer toxin (broad-spectrum resistant strains are not yet available commercially), and by any method that reduces the number of wild micro-organisms present in the must. Should a ferment become stuck despite the use of these procedures, increasing concentrations of the problem stuck wine should be added to a new rescue-yeast starter culture, in the presence of adequate nutrients, including oxygen. P.A.H.

Alexandre, H., and Charpentier, C., 'Biochemical aspects of stuck and sluggish fermentation in grape must', *Journal of Industrial Microbiology and Biotechnology*, 20/1 (1998), 20–7.

Bisson, L. F., and Butzke, C. E., 'Diagnosis and rectification of stuck and sluggish fermentations', *American Journal of Enology and Viticulture*, 51 (2000), 168–77.

Henschke, P. A., 'Stuck fermentation: causes, prevention and cure', in M. Allen, et al. (eds.), *Proceedings of the Australian Society of Viticulture and Oenology: Advances in Juice Clarification and Yeast Inoculation* (1997), 30-8, 41.

Styria, English name for the Austrian wine region STEIERMARK.

subjectivity plays an unavoidable part in wine TASTING. Personal preferences, like SENSITIVITIES, inevitably play some role in wine assessment. For more discussion of this, see PHILOSOPHY AND WINE and QUALITY IN WINE.

submerged cap is a way of keeping the CAP wet and mixed with the fermenting wine to facilitate EXTRACTION. A perforated screen is positioned just under the surface of the liquid to keep the cap submerged, but the pressure of the rising CARBON DIOXIDE tends to force the cap against the screen, making extraction less efficient. A pipe to allow the gas to escape can help to resolve this. It is still quite common to see header boards performing the same function in traditional CONCRETE tanks in the BAROSSA VALLEY. See also PUNCHING DOWN, PUMPING OVER, and MACERATION.

subsoil, the layer of a SOIL PROFILE which underlies the topsoil containing most of the ORGANIC MATTER. It overlies the bedrock (see ROCK) or sediments from which the soil is formed. The subsoil can be heavier-textured in ancient soils and in forest (especially pine forest) regions, due to the progressive downward leaching of the fine CLAY particles.

A fairly heavy-textured subsoil, provided that it drains freely enough, can have advantages for viticulture because it provides a good store of moisture that is well protected against direct EVAPORATION and exploitation by shallow-rooted WEEDS. The usual relative sparseness of vine roots in the subsoil, together with the strength with which clay particles hold water (see SOIL WATER and SOIL TEXTURE), ensures that the stored water can be used only at a limited rate. Seguin cites the clay soils of POMEROL as an example of this. It helps to provide the vine with the consistent regime of water supply that is important for wine quality. See also TERROIR and SOIL AND WINE QUALITY.

On the other hand, many heavy subsoils impede DRAINAGE, particularly those formed from acid rock materials. These can be detrimental to viticulture, unless carefully drained and, possibly, LIMED to overcome SOIL ACIDITY and improve the SOIL STRUCTURE. J.G.

Seguin, G., '"Terroirs" and pedology of wine growing', *Experientia*, 42 (1986), 861–72.

White, R. E., *Understanding Vineyard Soils* (2nd edn, 2015).

subsoiling. See RIPPING.

succinic acid, an acid found to a limited extent in both grapes and wine. Present in low concentrations in ripe grapes, it is a contributor to the fresh or tart taste of the fruit, albeit to a much lesser extent than TARTARIC ACID or MALIC ACID. Like these two principal grape acids, pure succinic acid is a white crystalline solid that is very soluble in water and alcoholic water solutions such as wine.

Succinic-acid concentrations tend to be higher in wine than in grapes because the acid is a by-product of the complex nitrogen metabolic processes involved in YEAST growth during FERMENTATION. Concentrations are generally higher in red wines than in whites. In some wines, a considerable proportion of the succinic acid reacts with one molecule of ETHANOL to form an ESTER, mono-ethyl succinate, which has a very mild, fruity aroma. G.T.

Coulter, A. D., et al., 'Succinic acid: how is it formed, what is its effect on titratable acidity, and what factors influence its concentration in wine?', *Australian and New Zealand Wine Industry Journal*, 19/6 (Nov/Dec 2004), 16–25.

suckering. See DESUCKERING.

sucrose, cane sugar, the most common of the SUGARS, is ubiquitous in plants because it is the preferred compound for PHLOEM translocation of energy and carbon around the plant. Sucrose consists of a GLUCOSE molecule joined to a FRUCTOSE molecule. Breakdown (HYDROLYSIS) of sucrose is achieved readily by the enzyme INVERTASE, which 'inverts' it to these hexoses.

Invertase in the vine occurs in CELL wall spaces but not in those of the leaf, which is why sucrose is confined in vines mainly to leaves and phloem tubes. Invertase is abundant in grape berries both in the cell walls and in the VACUOLES; hence the sugars that accumulate in berries are mainly glucose and fructose. B.G.C.

Südburgenland stretches along AUSTRIA's south-east border with Hungary as far south as SLOVENIA, but the region's 505 ha/1,200 acres of vines in 2021 represent barely more than 1% of the country's total. While fascinating white wines of GRÜNER VELTLINER, WELSCHRIESLING, and WEISSBURGUNDER (Pinot Blanc) are emerging, the region is best known for its profoundly complex and age-worthy BLAUFRÄNKISCH, particularly that grown in Deutsch-Schützen and neighbouring EISENBERG, which gives its name to the DAC that now applies throughout Südburgenland. Non-DAC QUALITÄTSWEIN grown here may only specify BURGENLAND as its place of origin. A curious regional relic of PHYLLOXERA's aftermath is UHUDLER. D.S.

Süd-Oststeiermark, wine region of AUSTRIA, now officially known as VULKANLAND STEIERMARK. D.S.

Südsteiermark, a dramatically hilly Austrian wine region fanning south from Graz, the capital of STEIERMARK, and hugging some 40 km/25 miles of frontier with SLOVENIA. Its reputation and densely planted 2,744 ha/6,781 acres (as of 2021) are disproportionate to its deceptively small outline on a viticultural map. Südsteiermark gained national prominence in the wake of Austria's 1985 wine scandal (see AUSTRIA), when wine lovers sought out small wine estates which had little truck with NÉGOCIANTS and whose vineyards were within walking distance of the point-of-sale. That said, one's shoes and heart need to be stout to tackle the steep terrain of a region whose cool, well-watered growing season and complex mingling of VOLCANIC and sedimentary soils support success with a wide range of white wine grapes, most importantly Sauvignon Blanc, Chardonnay (here generally labelled Morillon), MUSKATELLER, and WELSCHRIESLING but also WEISSBURGUNDER (Pinot Blanc), GRAUBURGUNDER (Pinot Gris), Riesling, and TRAMINER. The few reds are made primarily from Austria's ubiquitous ZWEIGELT, although there is some fine Pinot Noir and BLAUFRÄNKISCH. Varietal diversity was already a feature of greater Steiermark in the early 19th century, but the choice of principal grapes today—and especially the pre-eminence of Sauvignon Blanc—stem from regional dry-wine pioneers of the late 1970s and 1980s, in particular Willhelm Sattler Senior and Manfred Tement.

The Südsteiermark DAC encompasses all eight of the above-mentioned white grapes, as well as BLENDS of these. It recognizes bottlings in the categories regional, communal, and single-vineyard, and it consolidates Südsteiermark's many small wine villages into five official communes (*Gemeinden*)—Eichberg, Ehrenhausen, Gamlitz, Leutschach, and Kitzeck-Sausal—each associated with a more restricted set of 'leading' grape varieties from among Gelber Muskateller, Morillon, Riesling, and Sauvignon Blanc. Other than Welschriesling, no Südsteiermark DAC wine may be marketed before 1 March following its harvest, while the term 'Reserve' may be applied to wines held for 18 or more further months before release.

Since the 1990s, South Styrian wines have typically been marketed in two categories. Steierische KLASSIK refers to tank-aged, early bottled, bracing, dry VARIETALS with 11.5–12.5% alcohol and no MALOLACTIC CONVERSION. Vineyard-designated wines represented a fuller-bodied category, more ambitiously vinified and matured, often featuring pre-fermentative SKIN CONTACT, malolactic conversion, and LEES CONTACT during BARREL AGEING. Both size and age of casks have been increasing in recent years after a period during the 1990s and the early 21st century when new BARRIQUES were FASHIONABLE. There were subsequent signs of these two stylistic categories blurring at some important addresses; meanwhile, the advent of Südsteiermark DAC places the emphasis on place of origin rather than style. A small but strong cadre of contrarian growers espousing NATURAL winemaking techniques, no friends of DAC, has emerged to enliven the 21st-century Südsteiermark scene.

Twelve of the region's most prominent growers, under the name Steierische Terroir & Klassik, have classified their best vineyards as premier or grand cru using the abbreviations '1-STK' and 'G-STK' on price lists and labels. Just as elsewhere in Austria, however, there is not yet a consensus on vineyard CLASSIFICATION, and Austrian wine law recognizes no such classification. D.S.

Südtirol, or **South Tyrol**. See ALTO ADIGE.

sugar addition, winemaking practice more usually called CHAPTALIZATION or, in EU parlance, ENRICHMENT.

sugar concentration in grapes. See MUST WEIGHT.

sugar in grapes, the *raison d'être* of VITICULTURE. The central role of sugar in the utility of grapes for wine, TABLE GRAPES, RAISINS, and other viticultural products cannot be over-emphasized. SUGARS produce SWEETNESS and ferment to produce ETHANOL, both of which are valued by humans. However, of all sugary plant produce, none yields a commodity as highly valued or widely produced as grape wine.

The free sugar that accumulates in grapes, GLUCOSE and FRUCTOSE, is the result of translocation of SUCROSE photosynthesized in leaves and moved via PHLOEM tubes into grape berries during RIPENING, where it is inverted (hydrolysed) by the enzyme INVERTASE. The astonishing feature of grapes is that this accumulation occurs at the same time as water is accumulating in the berry, yet concentration is also increasing; in other words, sugar is increasing proportionately more than water. Other phloem-provided sucrose moves throughout the vine, dispensing energy and the carbon skeletons for all organic molecules. Additionally, sugar is used for carbon storage, as starch in wood, and for the formation of glycosides in the storage of secondary metabolites in vacuoles of cells (see flavour precursors and flavour compounds).

While total sugar content (see must weight) is a key factor in determining optimum ripeness of grapes for wine, sugar–acid balance is equally important; hence the use of sugar–acid ratio as a guide to the date of harvest. See also physiological ripeness and grape quality assessment.

B.G.C.

Keller, M., *The Science of Grapevines* (3rd edn, 2020).

sugars, simpler members of the large group of natural organic chemical compounds called carbohydrates. The sugar of common parlance, sucrose, comes from either sugar cane or sugar-beet plants and is a major international commodity. Sucrose is a molecule made up of one unit of each of glucose and fructose linked together with the elimination of a molecule of water.

Plants produce sucrose by photosynthesis, many of them accumulating sucrose within their cells but others, such as the common wine vine vitis vinifera, breaking this sucrose down into its two simpler constituent parts, glucose and fructose, which are stored in the berries. American vines store small amounts of sucrose in the fruit along with the two simpler forms. Over the millennia during which people have selected grape vines, they have chosen those capable of photosynthesizing high levels of sugars and storing them in berries. For more detail, see sugar in grapes.

Although the amounts of sugars other than glucose and fructose detected in grape must are very small, the process of photosynthesis involves sugars with three, four, five, and seven carbon atoms as well as the six-carbon glucose and fructose.

Sucrose, usually in the form of sugar-beet concentrate or some form of grape concentrate, may be added to some grape musts during fermentation in order to increase the alcoholic strength of the resultant wine (see enrichment).

The total amount of sugars left in a finished wine is called its residual sugar.

Some of the sucrose resulting from photosynthesis, stored in the berries as glucose and fructose before grape harvest, is converted into starch and stored in the vine's trunk and larger arms and roots during winter dormancy; when spring temperatures begin the annual cycle of leaf and fruit production once more, the starch is remobilized to soluble sugars, mainly glucose.

See also must weight. A.D.W.

sui lieviti, Italian for 'on the lees', typically refers to sparkling wines which are not disgorged after the second fermentation has taken place in the bottle. See also sparkling winemaking.

sulfides are the compounds of sulfur with hydrogen or metallic elements in which the sulfur atom exists in its most reduced state (see reduction).

Sulfides occur naturally from yeast metabolism during fermentation. hydrogen sulfide is the most common and can be formed in significant amounts from the reduction of elemental sulfur residues on the grapes from fungicides. It has an intense smell of bad eggs but is fortunately very volatile and can usually be removed by simple aeration.

Sulfide chemistry in wine is complex with multiple equilibria existing between compounds, including the simple hydrogen sulfide, mercaptans, disulfides, and polysulfides. The various concentrations of these depends on how reductive or oxidative the environment is. See reduction.

Sulfides can have unpleasant aromas such as garlic, rotten vegetables or sewers, but they can also confer positive attributes. Benzyl mercaptan, for example, is responsible for the flintiness of some barrel-aged wines, especially whites (see minerality).

Dimethyl sulfide (DMS), which increases with bottle ageing, can contribute a positive aroma of truffle to some white or red wines but is considered a fault at higher concentrations (aromas of cabbage and asparagus).

Winemakers will typically remove problem levels of sulfides through aerobic racking, or judicious additions of tiny amounts of copper (less than 1 ppm).

The removal of disulfides is more complicated because they will not react directly with copper ions. First they must be reduced to the corresponding mercaptan, through the addition of ascorbic acid. The mercaptan will then react with the copper ions.

In a winemaking context, any reference to 'sulfide' or 'sulfides' is usually a criticism. Sulfides should not be confused with sulfites, however. V.L. & M.J.T.

sulfites, a term familiar to wine consumers (most wine labels now state 'Contains sulfites'), winemakers, and regulators. It is an inclusive term for both sulfur dioxide (SO_2) and related compounds formed after the addition of SO_2 to must or wine. For more information, see sulfur dioxide.

sulfur, an element that constitutes about 0.5% of the weight of the Earth's crust and is one of the more important elements for humans. It is extremely important in wine production because of the wide-ranging uses of sulfur dioxide. A pale yellow, brittle, solid substance at room temperature, sulfur was already known to the speakers of ancient Sanskrit as *sulvere*. The book of Genesis in the Bible refers to sulfur as brimstone.

History

Sulfur has been used as a cleansing agent and wine preservative since antiquity. The discovery in the volcanic areas of Mediterranean Europe that sulfur could be used effectively to fumigate rooms led to the Greeks and Romans experimenting with its use to avoid food—and wine—spoilage. Authors such as cato and pliny, for example, mention sulfur among the various substances, such as pitch and resin, used by the Romans to prepare vessels in which wine was stored and to assist in its preservation. In late medieval times, it seems that Dutch and English merchants also used it for similar purposes, and in 1487 a German decree specifically permitted winemakers to burn woodchips soaked in sulfur in barrels before they were filled. By the 18th century, sulfur wicks were being regularly used to sterilize barrels in the best châteaux of Bordeaux (having been introduced by the dutch), and advances in chemistry had also led to the synthesis of derivatives of elemental sulfur, thus enabling inorganic salts containing sulfur to become widely used in winemaking. See sulfur dioxide and sulfide. In the vineyard, sulfur products have been commonly employed for over a century to protect vines against powdery mildew. P.T.H.U.

Johnson, H., *The Story of Wine: From Noah to Now* (2020).

Viticulture

Sulfur is essential for vine nutrition, although sulfur deficiency in vineyards is very rare.

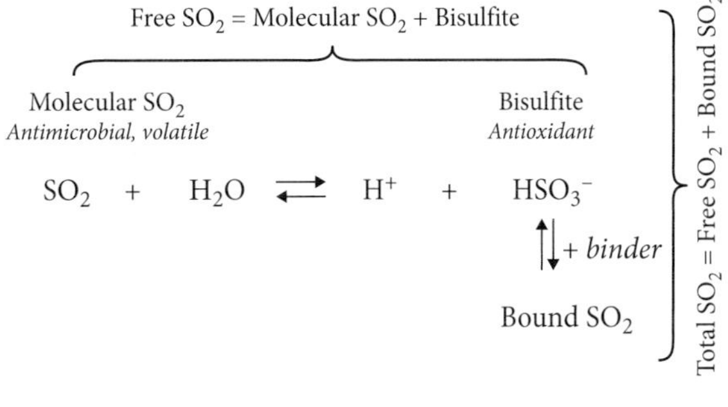

Free SO_2 = Molecular SO_2 + Bisulfite

Molecular SO_2
Antimicrobial, volatile

Bisulfite
Antioxidant

$$SO_2 + H_2O \rightleftarrows H^+ + HSO_3^-$$

$\updownarrow$ + *binder*

Bound SO_2

Total SO_2 = Free SO_2 + Bound SO_2

Vines usually obtain sufficient quantities from soil supplies or from FUNGICIDES. Long-term application of sulfur to vineyards to control POWDERY MILDEW has led to excess SOIL ACIDITY in many European vineyards. Sometimes periodic LIMING may be needed to counter soil acidification. R.E.S.

Winemaking

See SULFUR DIOXIDE, HYDROGEN SULFIDE, and SULFITES.

sulfur dioxide, or **SO_2**, a colourless, pungent gas formed by burning elemental SULFUR, has been used since antiquity as a sanitizing agent and preservative during food production and storage (see SULFUR for more historical detail). Sulfites may be added throughout the winemaking process: to harvested grapes, to pre-fermentation juice or must, to wines post-fermentation, during storage, or prior to packaging.

SULFITES, referring to SO_2 and related compounds, may be added to must or wine, either as SO_2 gas or in the form of a salt (e.g. potassium metabisulfite). Both salt and gas forms of sulfites will rapidly dissolve in water (the main component of grape juice and wine) to yield neutral, volatile molecular SO_2 and negatively charged bisulfite (HSO_{3-}) in equilibrium. The sum of bisulfite and molecular SO_2 is referred to as free SO_2. In wine, free SO_2 exists predominantly (>95%) as bisulfite, with higher proportions of molecular SO_2 with decreasing PH (more acidic conditions).

Bisulfite may also react with other wine components to form bound SO_2. A major SO_2 binder is ACETALDEHYDE (bruised-apple aroma), which can be formed by yeast during fermentation or through OXIDATION of ETHANOL. Other SO_2 binders are weaker and include fermentation products such as PYRUVIC ACID; grape-derived compounds such as ANTHOCYANINS in red wines; and GLUCOSE in sweet wines. Bound SO_2 has negligible preservative activity compared with that of free SO_2. Bound SO_2 has negligible antimicrobial effect on yeasts, but some spoilage bacteria are sensitive to even very low concentrations. However, bound SO_2 and free SO_2 forms are in equilibrium (i.e. they interchange during storage). Total SO_2 or total sulfites refers to the sum of free and bound SO_2, the form regulated in most wine-producing countries (see below).

Sulfites have several important roles in wine production: enzyme inhibition, antimicrobial, and antioxidant.

Free SO_2 (as bisulfite) inhibits enzymatic activity, including polyphenol-oxidase (PPO) enzymes in grapes responsible for browning and oxidation of must following CRUSHING and PRESSING. Uninhibited, these reactions can lead to finished wines with browner hues and lower concentrations of important aroma compounds, including THIOLS, critical to the fruity aromas of Sauvignon Blanc.

Molecular SO_2 is an excellent broad-spectrum antimicrobial. Conveniently, wine YEASTS are relatively more tolerant of molecular SO_2 than many spoilage yeasts. Sulfites are commonly added before fermentation, either to newly harvested grapes or after CRUSHING in order to favour the growth of desired wine yeasts. Post-fermentation additions are used to discourage spoilage yeasts such as BRETTANOMYCES or to stop SWEET WINES refermenting. Molecular SO_2 is particularly effective in preventing bacterial spoilage, including from ACETOBACTER and many strains of LACTIC ACID BACTERIA. Winemakers therefore limit the addition of sulfites to wines intended to undergo MALOLACTIC CONVERSION until after this step is complete.

Finally, free SO_2 (as bisulfite) is an antioxidant which can limit the effects of non-enzymatic OXIDATION during wine AGEING. This antioxidant effect is not due to the direct reaction of sulfites with OXYGEN. Instead, oxygen reacts with wine PHENOLICS to produce oxidized phenolics (called quinones) and hydrogen peroxide, and these oxidation products can have unwanted effects—for example, producing acetaldehyde and other compounds that create oxidized aromas, the loss of some desirable odorants, and generating products that cause wine browning. Free SO_2 acts as an antioxidant by rapidly reacting with both quinones and hydrogen peroxide, preventing further undesirable reactions involving these compounds. Free SO_2 will mostly be converted to sulfate during these reactions, and a portion of free SO_2 will be regenerated from weakly bound SO_2. Free SO_2 is also able to bind acetaldehyde and related oxidized-smelling odorants, as described above, and the resulting bound SO_2 forms are non-volatile and odourless.

Most commercial winemakers aim to have at least 20–40 ppm free SO_2 in stored or packaged wines to limit unwanted oxidation reactions and/or the release of weakly bound oxidized-smelling odorants. Winemakers also typically aim for 0.4–1 ppm molecular SO_2 to prevent microbial spoilage, with the higher end of the range used for sweet wines due to the greater risk of refermentation. Since the proportion of molecular SO_2 increases with decreasing pH, these two targets (molecular, free) must be considered separately.

Winemakers avoid excess addition of sulfites for several reasons. Most consumers perceive the characteristic (and undesirable) burning/irritating sensation of sulfites when the volatile molecular SO_2 form is present at > 2 ppm. Sulfites will also bind and bleach anthocyanins, and high concentrations are therefore undesirable in red wines. Total sulfites are also regulated in most wine-producing countries. Regulatory limits for total sulfites are typically stated in parts per million (ppm) or else the equivalent or near-equivalent units of mg/kg or mg/l. US regulations use the same limit for all wines (350 ppm), but most other wine-producing regions adjust limits based on wine style. In most countries, limits are higher in whites than in reds because whites typically have more SO_2-binding ACETALDEHYDE, and limits are higher in sweet wines than dry wines both because the former have more SO_2-binders such as GLUCOSE and because they are at greater risk of microbial spoilage. For example, in the EU, maximum permitted levels for total sulfites are 150 mg/l in dry red wines, 200 mg/l in dry white, dry rosé, and sweet red wines, 235 mg/l in sparkling wines, and 250 mg/l in sweet white and rosé wines. Certain sweet wines, including SAUTERNES, JURANÇON, BEERENAUSLESE, TROCKENBEERENAUSLESE, and EISWEIN, are permitted to have up to 400 mg/l. EU limits for ORGANIC WINE are lower, with 100 mg/l allowed for dry reds and 150 mg/l for white and rosé. Total sulfite limits in other major wine-producing countries are generally comparable with EU limits (100–400 ppm, depending on style), but in practice most wines contain far lower sulfites than what is permitted. A 2021 survey of international wines commercially available in Korea revealed an average total sulfites content of 100 mg/kg, and only two wines (out of 180) had sulfites over 200 mg/kg.

Total sulfites are regulated for two reasons. First, high levels of total sulfites may indicate unsound winemaking practices such as the use of spoiled fruit or oxidized wine. Second, there are health concerns surrounding sulfites, although consumer concerns about sulfites present below regulatory limits are not supported by existing medical literature. The best-established concern is 'sulfite sensitivity', which may result in adverse, allergy-like responses (e.g. respiratory distress, hives, anaphylaxis) in a small fraction of asthmatics. See ALLERGIES AND INTOLERANCES for more information.

For the majority of the wine-drinking population, sulfites consumed through wine (about 15 mg in a typical glass) are well below the (conservative) acceptable daily intake (ADI) guidelines of a joint committee involving the World Health Organization: *c.* 50 mg/day for a typical 70 kg adult. Even so, research into alternatives to SO_2 is not new, as reported by Lisanti and colleagues, and today there is growing consumer interest in wines produced with minimal or no addition of sulfites (e.g. NATURAL WINES).

With regard to sulfites' antimicrobial function, there are viable alternatives. For example, sulfites can be limited by good winery HYGIENE along with physical techniques such as PASTEURIZATION and sterile FILTRATION, which are effective for preventing microbial growth but may not be suitable for all wines. Chemical additives approved by the EU and the OIV but which may not appeal to non-interventionist winemakers include DMDC (for all microorganisms), the ENZYME lysozyme (for LACTIC ACID BACTERIA), and SORBIC ACID (for YEAST). Additives such as PHENOLICS (e.g. tannins from grape skins or other plants, RESVERATROL from grape skins) and CHITOSAN are approved for other purposes but are reported to have modest antimicrobial activity.

Replacing the antioxidant properties of SO_2 has been less successful, especially for FRUIT-DRIVEN wine styles, because the antioxidant capacity of sulfites is more challenging to replace as free SO_2 is uniquely capable of rapidly scavenging hydrogen peroxide and binding to ACETALDEHYDE and related compounds. Yeast lees can consume oxygen, but storing wine SUR LIE is not appropriate for all wine styles. Other antioxidants such as ASCORBIC ACID and yeast extracts may partially limit the need for SO_2 in these wine styles, as does selecting wine packaging with low OXYGEN TRANSMISSION RATES, but identifying alternatives that are as effective as SO_2 and do not affect the sensory characteristics of the wine remains a challenge. They may be better suited as a complement to reduced SO_2 usage rather than as a replacement.

However effective such alternatives prove to be, producing entirely sulfite-free wines is not feasible, as yeast will convert naturally occurring sulfate into sulfites as part of their AMINO ACID metabolism. Thus, in most wine-producing regions, wine labels are required to bear the phrase 'contains sulfites' (or variations on that theme) only if total sulfites exceed 10 ppm (see LABELLING INFORMATION). G.S.

Cho, Y. S, et al., 'Total SO_2 levels and risk assessment of wine and fruit wine consumed in South Korea', *Food Control*, 127 (2021).

Lisanti, M. T., et al., 'Alternative methods to SO_2 for microbiological stabilization of wine', *Comprehensive Reviews in Food Science and Food Safety*, 18/2 (2019).

Waterhouse, A. L., et al., 'Sulfur dioxide', in A. L. Waterhouse et al., *Understanding Wine Chemistry* (2016).

Wine Australia, 'Know your sulphite limits' (2021). www.wineaustralia.com/news/articles/know-your-sulphite-limits.

sulphate, **sulphide**, **sulphite**, and **sulphur**, the British and non-technical spellings of sulfate, SULFIDE, SULFITE, and SULFUR respectively. This book follows the International Union of Pure and Applied Chemistry (IUPAC) nomenclature recommendations and uses 'sulfate', 'sulfide', 'sulfite', and 'sulfur' throughout since the terms are generally used in a technical context.

Sultana, also known as **Sultaniye**, **Sultanina**, and **Sultanine**. Its origins are thought to be eastern Mediterranean. Even further east it is known by variants on Kismis and in Egypt as Banati. It is the most important white grape variety used to produce the golden RAISINS sometimes called sultanas; in its time it was the single most planted vine variety in the world, covering an estimated 344,000 ha/ 850,000 acres of vineyard, much of it in the Middle East. The fruit of the Sultana vine, called THOMPSON SEEDLESS in California, is remarkable for its versatility. As well as being dried, it can be vinified into a neutral white wine and, especially after treatment with GIBBERELLIN growth regulators to increase BERRY SIZE, is a much sought-after crisp, green, seedless TABLE GRAPE. In widely varying locations, it has provided base material for some (usually undistinguished) wines. In some viticultural regions, such as Australia's RIVERLAND and California's CENTRAL VALLEY, the Sultana harvest has occasionally been diverted to whatever happens to be the most profitable end use, including wine in times of wine-grape shortage.

Sumer. In ancient Sumer (3500–1900 BCE), the earliest literate civilization of southern MESOPOTAMIA, wine and BEER were both widely consumed and are often mentioned as being drunk on the same occasion. 'Wine' almost certainly refers to grape wine in most contexts, although date wine was also prepared by the Sumerians.

At the sacred city of Nippur, just downstream from Babylon, which stood on an important branch of the river Euphrates, the principal quay of the temple was known as the 'Quay of the Vine', although it is not clear if this refers to an original commercial activity or to irrigation or is simply an ornate epithet of the sort beloved of Sumerian poets. In praise poetry addressed to King Shulgi, who was deified in his own lifetime (*c.* 22nd century BCE), the king's martial prowess with the double-edged axe is eulogized with the image of him 'spilling his enemies' blood on the mountain-side like the contents of a smashed wine jug'.

DRUNKENNESS seems to have carried no stigma of disapprobation. In a number of Sumerian literary works, the gods get drunk on wine and beer in circumstances which are not merely amusing but are dramatically important.

See also ORIGINS OF VINICULTURE and PALAEOETHNOBOTANY. J.A.B.

Bottéro, J., 'Getränke', *Reallexikon der Assyriologie und vorderasiatischen Archäologie* (the standard reference work) (1928–).

Kinner Wilson, J. V., *The Nimrud Wine Lists* (1972).

Powell, M. A., 'Wine and the vine in ancient Mesopotamia', in P. E. McGovern, et al. (eds.), *The Origins and Ancient History of Wine* (1995).

Sumoll, minor CATALAN red wine grape usually blended but starting to find favour, particularly in PENEDÈS, where it produces light and refreshing reds. Known as Vijariego Negra on the Canary Islands. The rare Catalan white **Sumoll Blanc**, unrelated to Sumoll, is also promising.

sunburn can damage grapes and is a viticultural term used loosely for a range of conditions. Classical sunburn produces a round halo of burnt skin on the side of the berry facing the sun's position in the western sky, as damage normally occurs in the afternoon. Such sunburn is due to a combination of bright sunshine, high air temperatures, and low winds, and the so-called 'hot spot' can be up to 15 °C/27 °F above air temperature. Berries which were previously shaded from the sun are most sensitive, as their skins have not been conditioned by exposure to sunlight. Sunburn sensitivity is higher for vineyards suffering WATER STRESS because the leaves droop, leading to greater sun exposure.

The condition in which grapes develop pigmentation in response to the ULTRAVIOLET component of sun exposure is also loosely called sunburn, although this is a change in skin colour rather than damage. This is particularly obvious with some white varieties, and the skin can develop deep yellow or even brown colours. Whether such exposure is harmful to the berry is arguable, and exposure to sun encourages the production of a range of PHENOLIC compounds, including QUERCETIN (see FLAVONOLS), which are generally associated with wine quality, especially for red varieties. R.E.S.

Smart, R. E., and Sinclair, T. R., 'Solar heating of grape berries and other spherical fruits', *Agricultural Meteorology*, 17/4 (1976), 241–59.

Sunbury, historic Australian wine region in VICTORIA close to Melbourne's northern suburbs, principally known for Shiraz, that enjoys the cooling influence of the Macedon Ranges to the north and the ocean to the south.

sunlight, the ultimate energy source of all life and of wine itself. Through a process known as PHOTOSYNTHESIS, part of sunlight's energy is used by plants such as grapevines to combine CARBON DIOXIDE from the air with WATER taken up from the soil, to form SUGAR IN GRAPES. This is the building block for other plant products, as well as being the immediate source of energy for all of a plant's biochemical processes, via its RESPIRATION back to carbon dioxide and water.

In climatology the traditional measurement of sunlight was as hours of bright sunlight, but it is now generally measured in terms of total energy using electronic sensors. This is more pertinent in viticulture since photosynthesis of individual grapevine leaves is 'light-saturated' at around one-third full sunlight, although a

CANOPY of leaves will photosynthesize at higher rates with increased sunlight. Photosynthesis is reduced at very low light levels in a shaded canopy. It is also reduced by high (> 35 °C/95 °F) or low (< 15 °C/59 °F) temperatures and by WATER STRESS.

The amount of sunlight received at the Earth's surface depends primarily on factors related to location and cloudiness. LATITUDE, time of day, and time of year determine the potential sunlight at any one place—higher at lower latitudes, at midday, and in summer. Clouds have two important characteristics: they absorb and scatter sunlight. So at the Earth's surface, the proportions of direct and diffuse sunlight depend on cloudiness. This in turn depends on atmospheric conditions and location, typically higher in maritime than in interior regions. The latter are generally more arid and have fewer clouds, receiving more sunlight and therefore being hotter. They are more common in, for example, North and South America, Australia, and South Africa, while much of Europe is more cloudy.

Cloudiness may have more implications for viticulture and wine quality than have been reported. With cloudless skies, around 85% of sunlight is in the direct solar beam, so there are shadows of low sunlight intensity behind a single leaf layer (see CANOPY MICROCLIMATE), and either shadows or sunlit portions occur within the canopy. However, when the sky is cloudy, the solar beam is diffused and comes from all over the sky; there are no distinct shadows, and light penetrates deeper into the canopy, so that a higher proportion of the leaves and berries are sunlit, although they receive lower sunlight levels and will be cooler. A cloudy climate may therefore affect GRAPE COMPOSITION AND WINE QUALITY in ways that have not been widely researched.

Another important role of sunlight in viticulture is that of heating the vines and the soil. Grape berries for example may be heated up to 15 °C/27 °F above air temperature for black berries exposed to bright sunlight in low wind conditions. Leaves are heated less when exposed to sunlight, as they are evaporatively cooled by the process of TRANSPIRATION. Berry temperatures are of considerable importance in affecting the chemical make-up of the grapes. Similarly, leaf temperatures have important effects on photosynthesis and RESPIRATION, and this also directly affects GRAPE COMPOSITION AND WINE QUALITY. Soil temperature depends on the reflectivity to sunlight of the soil surface; thus dark soils absorb more sunlight and are warmer than white or light-coloured soils (see SOIL COLOUR). The total amount of sunlight energy over all of the spectrum is important in heating vines and soils.

The intensity of sunlight is not its only characteristic of importance to grapevines. Another is spectral quality or the proportion of sunlight at different wavelengths. This does not vary greatly from region to region or under full sunlight versus cloud; but it does vary enormously within the vine canopy.

The total spectrum of solar radiation comprises ULTRAVIOLET RADIATIONS, visible light, and infrared (heat) radiations, in order of increasing electromagnetic wavelengths. Visible light is in the wavelength range 400–760 nanometres (nm) (1 nm is one-millionth of a millimetre). Within that range, in order of increasing wavelength, are the component colours of the visible light spectrum: violet, indigo, blue, green, yellow, orange, and red.

Most of the wavelengths between 400 and 700 nm are absorbed by leaves and are used to varying degrees for photosynthesis. Those absorbed and used most efficiently are in the blue and (especially) red parts of the spectrum, centred around 440 and 660 nm respectively. It is the partial reflection of the intermediate wavelengths, by the photosynthetically active pigment chlorophyll, that gives plant leaves their characteristic green colour. Thus shade light, as well as being much less intense than full sunlight, is still more impoverished of its photosynthetically useful wavelengths. If overall light intensity is reduced eight- or tenfold, that of red light around 660 nm can be reduced a hundredfold in deep canopy shade.

Also important physiologically are the barely visible far-red wavelengths, between 700 and 760 nm. These and the adjacent infrared wavelengths are hardly absorbed at all, being either reflected or transmitted through the leaves. Canopy shade light is therefore relatively rich in them. The ratio of normal red to far-red wavelengths (measured as 10-nm-width bands centred around 660 and 730 nm, and known as the R : FR ratio) is between 1.0 and 1.2 in the open, whereas in deep canopy shade it can be 0.1 or less.

It is the R : FR ratio, rather than light intensity as such, that appears to govern many plant reactions to shading within the canopy, probably through the action of a wavelength-sensitive pigment known as phytochrome. A low R : FR ratio, characteristic of deep canopy shade, promotes rapid spindly stem growth (trying to reach the light); sparse leaves and light-green colour; sparse lateral branching; and poor bud FRUITFULNESS. Conversely, a high R : FR ratio, as in normal external light, promotes stocky growth, with strong lateral branching; deep green leaf colour; and good bud fruitfulness. Direct exposure of the bunches to such light also promotes the formation of ANTHOCYANIN pigments in the berry skins of red wine grape varieties and appears to be associated with superior flavour and potential wine quality.

Smart reviews general aspects of light-quality effects on grapevine growth and fruit composition and deals comprehensively with sunlight relations in the context of vine canopy microclimate, canopy management, and wine quality.

See also VINE PHYSIOLOGY. J.G. & R.E.S.

Smart, R. E., 'Principles of grapevine canopy microclimate manipulation with implications for yield and quality. A review', *American Journal of Enology and Viticulture*, 36 (1985), 230–9.

Smart, R. E., and Robinson, M., *Sunlight into Wine: A Handbook for Winegrape Canopy Management* (1991).

Suntory, traditional Japanese food and alcoholic drinks company that has discreetly become a significant player in the world's wine business. Founded in 1899, the company was selling a sweet red wine in 1907 and by 1936 was developing its vineyards in the Tomi no Oka region of Yamanashi prefecture. It has since invested considerably in developing viticultural and oenological prowess in JAPAN and is one of the country's most important wine producers.

Its first foreign acquisition was Ch Lagrange in ST-JULIEN in 1983 when Suntory became the first non-Western company to own a Bordeaux CLASSED GROWTH. Five years later they acquired Weingut Robert Weil, one of the best-run estates in the RHEINGAU, still run by Wilhelm Weil. Both properties have benefited from considerable investment. In 2010, when the Chinese wine market was booming, they acquired ASC, one of China's most successful importers, together with its Hong Kong and Macau operations. In Bordeaux, Suntory first participated with CASTEL in Grands Millésimes de France in 1989, and the company now operates both Chx Beychevelle and Beaumont as well as the négociant Barrière Frères.

Jancis Robinson, 'A yen for quality' (June 2013). www.jancisrobinson.com/articles/a-yen-for-quality.

Supérieur, **Supérieure**, or **Supérieures**, French term appended to the name of some AOC wines (see BORDEAUX AOC and GRAVES) or to the term PREMIER CRU, generally signifying a more ambitious level.

Superiore, Italian term applied to DOC wines which are deemed superior because of their higher minimum ALCOHOLIC STRENGTH, usually by 0.5 or 1%, a longer period of AGEING before commercial release, a lower maximum permitted YIELD or all three. Among the more significant wines which fall into this category are the three BARBERA DOCs or DOCGS of PIEMONTE (Alba, Asti, Monferrato), BARDOLINO, CALDARO, FRIULI GRAVE, VALPOLICELLA, and VALTELLINA. Triggered by the EU reforms of 2008, the Superiore versions of several DOCs such as FRASCATI have been elevated to DOCG status while, confusingly, the normal DOC continues to co-exist. Promotions like this are often petty compromises, born out of resistance to elevating the often much smaller historic CLASSICO heartland of a zone to DOCG status. W.S.

super second, a specialist term in the FINE WINE market for CLASSED GROWTH wines from BORDEAUX to denote the best-performing wines that are not actually FIRST GROWTHS. There is no absolute agreement about which properties qualify as super seconds, and reputations are constantly changing, but in the MÉDOC and GRAVES Chx Pichon-Lalande, Pichon-Baron, Pontet Canet, and Lynch Bages in PAUILLAC, Cos and Montrose in ST-ESTÈPHE, all three Léovilles and Ducru-Beaucaillou in ST-JULIEN, Ch Palmer in MARGAUX, and Ch La MISSION HAUT-BRION in PESSAC-LÉOGNAN have all been nominated at one time or another.

Supertuscan, term which emerged in the 1970s to describe the wines labelled as VINO DA TAVOLA made in the central Italian region of Tuscany. Prototype Supertuscans were Tignanello and SASSICAIA, both initially marketed by ANTINORI. The Vino da Tavola denomination was replaced by IGT in 1992, while 'Supertuscan' continues to be used for Bordeaux blends aged in BARRIQUE. For more details, see TUSCANY.

sur lie, French term meaning 'on the lees', customarily applied to white wines whose principal deviation from everyday WHITE WINEMAKING techniques was some form of LEES CONTACT. The term has been used most commonly for the French dry white MUSCADET to differentiate those wines which remained on their lees after fermentation, usually in tank, in an effort to increase flavour and texture. The practice, and term, has since spread south to the LANGUEDOC and outside France and has proved a useful way of adding flavour and value to the produce of relatively neutral grape varieties. See also STABULATION.

surmaturité, French for OVERRIPENESS.

surplus production was for years the single greatest problem facing the world's wine industry, aggravated by improved efficiency in the vineyard and falling consumption in Europe's important wine markets. The most palatable effect of this surplus for wine consumers has been its dampening impact on PRICES at the bottom end of the wine market.

Even in the late 1950s, relatively soon after the shortages of the Second World War, the world produced almost 15% more wine than it consumed, but wine consumption was rising rapidly, and it was assumed that demand would catch up. By the late 1970s, average YIELDS began to increase substantially. This was largely the result of increased viticultural proficiency but also reflected the availability of particularly productive CLONES of established vine varieties, as well as FERTILIZERS and the more widespread use of AGROCHEMICALS to combat VINE DISEASES. Just at this point, consumption began to decline, especially markedly in the principal wine-producing countries (which had been the principal wine markets): France, Italy, USSR, Spain, and Argentina.

The exceptionally large European harvests of 1979 and 1980 plunged what is now the EU into crisis and forced measures which included compulsory DISTILLATION of about one-fifth of total production (only of the lowest-quality wine), a VINE-PULL SCHEME, and a somewhat fruitless attempt to control yields, which continued to rise by an average of about 0.5% a year. By the late 1980s, the world was producing 19% more than it could consume (see table), with particularly marked surpluses in France, Italy, and Spain as well as a surplus of industrial alcohol as a result of compulsory distillation.

World totals in million hl of wine

	Production	Consumption	Surplus	% Surplus
1976–80	326.0	285.7	40.3	12
1981–5	333.6	280.7	52.8	16
1986–90	292.8	237.0	55.8	19
1991–5	261.3	222.7	38.6	15
1996	272.5	223.2	49.3	18
1997	264.4	223.5	40.9	15
1998	262.1	227.8	34.4	13
1999	281.2	225.1	56.1	20
2000	280.0	226.6	53.4	19
2001	266.6	226.9	39.7	15
2002	257.8	228.6	29.2	11
2003	266.7	234.7	32.0	12
2004	296.4	237.6	58.8	20
2005	278.0	236.9	41.1	15
2006	282.6	244.7	37.9	13
2007	267.8	252.4	15.4	6
2008	268.7	248.7	20.0	7
2009	272.2	240.9	31.3	11
2010	264.3	240.3	24.0	9
2011	267.4	241.2	26.2	10
2012	254.7	241.2	13.5	5
2013	278.6	238.7	39.9	14
2014	270	238	32	12
2015	273	239	34	12
2016	270	244	26	10
2017	248	246	2	1
2018	294	244	50	17
2019	258	241	17	7
2020	260	234	26	10
2021	260	236	24	9
2022	258	232	26	10

Note: These figures are based on OIV official statistics.

The breakup of the Soviet Union, long a net wine importer, and the introduction of free-market economies within the former Soviet republics in the early 1990s deprived many Eastern European wine producers of their traditional and none too fastidious market, creating fresh pressure on the world's wine suppliers.

Surpluses on a smaller scale, sometimes simply of the wrong type of wine, have resulted in national vine-pull schemes such as those enacted in NEW ZEALAND and ARGENTINA in the late 1980s and early 1990s respectively.

By the early and mid 1990s, there was overproduction in all continents except the Americas, most especially in Europe and particularly of poor-quality TABLE WINE. This did nothing to alleviate severe shortages in the mid to late 1990s of red wines suitable for export in many countries, however, most notably in South Africa and Australia, where there was a shortage of commercially desirable wine grapes of both colours. Substantial plantings of Chardonnay vines in the mid 1990s in Australia and California resulted in a surplus of that grape variety.

In the late 2000s, the EU, concerned about the size of its WINE LAKE, embarked on a rigorous programme of draining it with a vine-pull scheme and limitations on new plantings. The result was a dramatic decrease in total EU vineyard area, and total vineyard area shrank

throughout the ex-Soviet republics, but this was partly outweighed by extraordinary vineyard expansion in China.

However, this has been offset to a large extent by increased vineyard productivity and vineyard expansion outside Europe—especially in China. Overall, the total annual volume of wine produced since 2000 has see-sawed within a range of 250–290 million hectolitres according to the vagaries of weather, government policies, and global events. At the same time, global wine consumption has fluctuated within a range of 230–250 million hectolitres. The gap between production and consumption is narrowing, but for the time being the global wine surplus remains a stubborn fact of life.

Surrentine wine from vineyards on the slopes of the Sorrento peninsula in southern Italy achieved prominence from the latter half of the reign of Augustus in the first decade of the 1st century CE. It ranked high in Classical ROME, but behind CAECUBAN and FALERNIAN, in PLINY's assessment. It was produced from the vine known as the Aminea Gemina Minor, which, unusually for one of the classic wines, was trellised rather than grown up trees. The wine itself was a rather thin white wine, which nevertheless could be described as 'strong'. It may well have had high acidity. There are recommendations to age it for 20 to 25 years. It never won universal approval—'a high-class vinegar' was the opinion of both the emperors Tiberius and Caligula, and there are some signs that its MEDICINAL properties were among its most important selling points. J.J.P.

Pliny the Elder, *Natural History*, translated by H. Rackham (1945), Book 14.

sur souches, French expression meaning 'on the stumps' or, in the context of a purchase of a future vintage of wine, 'on the vine'. The BORDEAUX TRADE has, at times of particularly buoyant sales, occasionally bought futures in a crop even before it was harvested.

Süss, literally 'sweet' in German. Used on labels in AUSTRIA to designate wines with more than 45 g/l RESIDUAL SUGAR.

Süssreserve, German term for SWEET RESERVE, the unfermented or part-fermented MUST much used in the 1970s and 1980s to sweeten all but the finest or driest German wines. Its use has drastically declined because GERMANY is making an increasing proportion of dry wines (see TROCKEN and HALBTROCKEN) and because better producers of sweeter wines prefer to stop the fermentation while there is still some RESIDUAL SUGAR in the wine rather than add unfermented juice.

sustainability has become an increasing concern for wine producers, shippers, merchants, and consumers. In an era of CLIMATE CHANGE, environmental concerns have been uppermost, but considerations of economic and social sustainability are becoming increasingly common too. Santiago-Brown defines sustainability as 'the continuous pursuit of equilibrium between economic, social, and environmental variables and their trade-offs over time'.

For producers, and certainly for vine-growers, SUSTAINABLE VITICULTURE is the most obvious first step, but an increasing number are considering their entire CARBON FOOTPRINT, including thorough consideration of all vehicles, equipment, and products used in the vineyard, winery, cellar, packaging, and even shipping. Some producers market themselves on their sustainable credentials, planting trees and practising REGENERATIVE VITICULTURE to act as carbon sinks, insulating their buildings, recycling with a vengeance, and switching to low-input (such as electric) vehicles and alternative energy sources. Many of these decisions result in increased costs, however, demanding a reconciliation of environmentally sound choices with economically feasible ones—and all of these decisions have to be made with potential wine QUALITY in mind. For example, temperature-controlled shipping containers can increase carbon use, but many producers and retailers of fine wine would argue that they are necessary to avoid heat damage. On the other hand, a producer of more basic wine may well decide that shipping to export markets in BULK is more sustainable than BOTTLING at source. Others may decide to reduce the amount of energy needed for packaging and shipping by choosing ALTERNATIVE PACKAGING for their wine.

Within the winery, some of the most important considerations are water and energy usage and what happens to the wide range of WINERY WASTE. Winery waste-water recycling is becoming more widespread worldwide, often through legislative pressure, with waste water typically recycled for non-potable purposes such as IRRIGATION and cooling systems. But temperature control can use enormous amounts of energy. Sustainability-aware producers are increasingly locating or relocating temperature-sensitive operations (i.e. most of them) to hillsides or underground where temperatures are naturally low. Sustainability concerns are becoming increasingly important in WINERY DESIGN. Outside pressure, including generous tariffs for adopters (notably in Germany and California), is also encouraging the use of renewable energy, often helped by dramatic reductions in the price of alternative energy sources such as solar-powered cells.

The final stage of production, BOTTLING, is the heaviest consumer of energy via glass BOTTLE production. Wineries may select lighter glass and recycled glass bottles to reduce energy consumption.

Around the globe, many regions have developed sustainability schemes to encourage producers to improve their practices. Oregon, California (especially the Napa Valley), New Zealand, and South Africa were quicker off the mark than most. The social and economic elements of long-term sustainability depend fundamentally on the overall health of the LABOUR force, a business's compliance with local laws, the financial stability of the business, and the local ECONOMY.

For many consumers, recycling wine bottles is one of their most obvious contributions to sustainability of any sort. In some parts of the world it is possible to recycle other aspects of wine packaging, including CLOSURES. There has also been a discernible increase in selling wine in bulk to environmentally aware consumers with their own recycled bottles, a throwback to traditional practice in some of Europe's wine-producing areas.

Forbes, S. L., et al. (eds.), *Social Sustainability in the Global Wine Industry: Concepts and Cases* (2020).
Sachs, J., 'The next frontier', *The Economist* (21 Sep 2013). www.economist.com/finance-and-economics/2013/09/19/the-next-frontier.
Santiago-Brown, I., 'Sustainability assessment in wine grape growing' (2014). digital.library.adelaide.edu.au/dspace/handle/2440/85988.

sustainable viticulture, a systemic approach to growing wine grapes that pursues the goal of a socially equitable, environmentally sound, and economically feasible vineyard and takes into account the particular context of the wine region where the grapes are grown. Its objective is to promote a vineyard that will provide economically for the winegrower while maintaining its ability to consistently produce and improve grape quality over time. Because of the unpredictable nature of agriculture, there may be trade-offs over the medium term. For example, in a wetter growing season with higher disease pressure, money may be spent on extra fungal sprays and not on improving an irrigation system; in the event of FROST or fire damage, financial resources might not be sufficient to invest in new machinery at the same time.

Conventional, ORGANIC, BIODYNAMIC, and REGENERATIVE farming systems are all pathways to achieving sustainability in wine-grape growing provided all pillars of sustainability—environmental, social, and economic—are embraced and the grower is committed to following sustainability principles and best practices in viticulture. Different sustainability programmes use different methodologies to assess vineyards, and to date there is no consensus on the minimum targets or the best methods to assess them.

Environmentally sound vineyards aim to carefully manage external on-farm inputs (e.g.

◀ Inkwell Wines' ORGANICALLY certified SHIRAZ vineyard in the South Australia's MCLAREN VALE is farmed according to the principles of SUSTAINABLE and REGENERATIVE VITICULTURE. The meadow-flower insectary in the foreground dramatically decreases PEST and VINE DISEASE pressure. Mid-row COVER CROPS promote soil life and CARBON sequestration while promoting water conservation and a healthy CANOPY. © Dr Irina Santiago-Brown

water, chemicals, fuel) and reduce the use of synthetic chemicals. Socially equitable vineyards employ staff ethically and without bias and support the communities to which they belong. Economically feasible vineyards endure as businesses over time.

Sustainability assessments were developed in order to collect data, educate growers, and respond quickly to a world in constant change. Climate change, race, gender, and social-equity awareness movements as well as scientific discoveries are key factors in the evolution of programmes in viticulture. In response to such factors, many have been reshaped to improve decision-making, make claims of sustainability more measurable, and give consumers the ability to see beyond marketing-speak. Such assessment programmes include California Sustainable Winegrowing Alliance (CSWA), Sustainable Winegrowing New Zealand (SWNZ), Sustainable Wine South Africa (SWSA), and HVE, among others.

See also LUTTE RAISONNÉE and SUSTAINABILITY.

I.S.-B.

Gerling, C. (ed.), *Environmentally Sustainable Viticulture: Practices and Practicality* (2015).

Santiago-Brown, I., 'Sustainability assessment in wine grape growing' (2014). [digital.library.adelaide.edu.au/dspace/handle/2440/85988].

Susumaniello, lively, deep-coloured PUGLIAN red wine grape. One of SANGIOVESE's many offspring.

Svatovavřinecké, Czech name for ST-LAURENT.

Swan District, Australia's second oldest wine region, established in 1829, in WESTERN AUSTRALIA. FORTIFIED WINES, long a specialty in the hot climate, remain the state's best when produced by the likes of Talijancich, Faber, and John Kosovich. These days, however, more attention is paid to dry wines, especially CHENIN BLANC (the district provides nearly 60% of the state's Chenin production) as well as SHIRAZ and GRENACHE from 890 ha/2,199 acres of vines in 2020.

E.L.L.

Swan Hill, hot Australian wine region immediately south-east of the Murray Darling region, straddling the Murray river, partly in VICTORIA and partly in NEW SOUTH WALES.

sward. See COVER CROP.

Swartland, fashionable wine-producing district in SOUTH AFRICA which, since the late 1990s, has attracted some of the country's most adventurous and least interventionist winemakers. This focus is partly explained by the relatively high percentage of older vineyards planted with varieties well suited to DRY FARMING. For red wines these are mainly Rhône varieties, while the whites are typically blends based on low-yielding old CHENIN BLANC vineyards. There is a strong community spirit here and an energetic local association of Swartland Independent Producers.

Sweden has a fringe climate for winegrowing, though CLIMATE CHANGE is increasing its potential. Though there is evidence of grape-growing for winemaking that dates to the Stone Age, modern Swedish wine production started in the 1990s and is centred around the southernmost municipality Skåne. Other winegrowing areas include the Baltic islands Gotland and Öland, Halland on the west coast, and Blaxta outside Stockholm. By 2020 Sweden had an estimated 150 ha/371 acres under vine. Key challenges include RIPENESS and ROT. SOLARIS is by far the dominant vine variety; RONDO, Siramé, Cabernet Cortis, Muscat, Johanniter, FRÜHBURGUNDER, LÉON MILLOT, and REGENT are also favoured, as is VIDAL for ICE WINES. Some ambitious producers grow Chardonny, Merlot, and Pinot Noir. Sweden does not have to apply for EU PLANTING RIGHTS and does not have CONTROLLED APPELLATIONS. The potential for SPARKLING WINE production has inspired the Swedish Sparkling Wine Association to create rules to ensure even quality, including a minimum requirement of 85% Solaris, which keeps notable ACIDITY and generous fruit aromas.

Only one-eighth of Sweden's 200-plus wine growers are commercial operations. The Swedish MONOPOLY bans cellar-door sales, which forces wineries to rely simply on wine TOURISM.

E.L.-L.

svensktvin.se

sweetness, one of the primary tastes involved in TASTING and a fundamental component of wine. It varies considerably and is sensed by taste buds principally on the tongue. Wines taste sweet mainly because of the amount of RESIDUAL SUGAR they contain (although the impact of this on the PALATE is greatly influenced by factors such as the levels of ACIDITY, TANNINS, and CARBON DIOXIDE in the wine as well as by the serving TEMPERATURE). ETHANOL, or alcohol, can also taste sweet, as can GLYCEROL and a high level of PECTINS. Any wine with less than 2 g/l residual sugar is considered bone dry, but a dry wine with residual sugar of less than 2 g/l that is relatively high in alcohol (such as many a Chardonnay, for example) can taste quite sweet. A sweet VOUVRAY, on the other hand, made in a cool region from the naturally acidic grape variety CHENIN BLANC, may contain well over 30 g/l residual sugar, but in youth it can taste dry.

A wide variety of different terms in different languages are used to describe sweetness, although they invariably relate strictly to the residual sugar rather than to the taste impression. The table below gives the official EU classification of sweetness levels. Producers are not generally obliged to put this information on the label of a still wine (although see ALSACE), though it is mandatory for sparkling wines. See DOSAGE for specific terminology.

Some wine drinkers have been conditioned to be suspicious of any sweetness in a wine, perhaps because neophytes generally prefer some residual sugar (which is why it is not uncommon for wine BRANDS to contain some, up to 20 g/l even in red wines), and sweetness is therefore associated with a lack of sophistication. Some of the greatest wines of the world are sweet, however. So long as there is sufficient ACIDITY to balance the sweetness, a sweet wine is by no means cloying. Indeed, a comparative tasting of great young sweet wines is more likely to leave the taster with the impression of excess acidity than excess sugar.

See SWEET WINES and SWEET WINEMAKING for more details of sweeter wines.

sweetness codes are becoming more common on back labels and in sales literature. This is particularly true of RIESLINGS and ALSACE whites because they can vary so widely in how sweet they taste. They may take the form of a scale or numerical rating.

sweet reserve, preserved GRAPE JUICE held for BLENDING purposes, to sweeten wines. The unfermented grape SUGARS counterbalance the sometimes overly high ACIDITY of wines produced in cool regions (it was once widely used in parts of GERMANY, where such juice is known as *Süssreserve*) or from grapes naturally high in acidity such as RIESLING, UGNI BLANC, and COLOMBARD. The alternative, stopping the fermentation and leaving some RESIDUAL SUGAR, is harder to manage accurately.

Historically grape juice was preserved simply by adding offensively high doses of SULFUR DIOXIDE.

Modern REFRIGERATION and near-sterile FILTRATION enable the production of sweet reserve that does not reek of sulfur dioxide. The sweet juice usually undergoes CLARIFICATION and refrigeration to eliminate yeast growth and can be stored at very low temperatures for up to 12 months.

In many wine regions, sweet reserve is being replaced by GRAPE CONCENTRATE or RECTIFIED GRAPE MUST. Grape concentrate is cheaper to store because it is much richer in sugar, which also prevents the growth of microorganisms so that it can be stored without recourse to expensive refrigeration. Rectified grape must is preferred simply because it more closely resembles a solution of sugar and water than does preserved juice.

sweet winemaking, the production of wines with noticeable amounts of RESIDUAL

RS g/l	English	French	German	Italian	Spanish
up to 4 (or not exceeding 9 provided that the total acidity expressed as grams of tartaric acid per litre is not more than 2 grams below the RS content)	dry	sec	trocken	secco or asciutto	seco
more than 4 and not exceeding 12 (or not exceeding 18 provided that the total acidity expressed as grams of tartaric acid per litre is not more than 10 grams below the RS content)	medium dry	demi-sec	halbtrocken	abboccato	semiseco
more than 12 and not exceeding 45	medium (or medium sweet)	moelleux	lieblich	amabile	semidulce
at least 45	sweet	doux	süss	dolce	dulce

SUGAR and which may vary considerably in ALCOHOLIC STRENGTH and production techniques. Local regulations differ significantly but, with a few exceptions, non-grape sugar may be added only (and rarely) for the purposes of CHAPTALIZATION, to increase the final alcoholic strength, and not to add sweetness after fermentation. The most common method of sweetening basic wine is the addition of some form of sweet grape juice, followed by STABILIZATION (for any wine containing sugar is theoretically susceptible to a SECOND FERMENTATION).

The finest sweet wines are made by concentrating the SUGAR IN GRAPES, however, and the combined effect of the alcohol produced and the residual sugar tends to inhibit further YEAST activity. The four common ways of doing this are by the benevolent NOBLE ROT effect of the botrytis fungus on the vine as it nears maturity in perfect conditions (see BOTRYTIZED wines); by processing frozen grape clusters (see ICE WINE and CRYOEXTRACTION); or by drying mature grapes either on the vine or after picking (see DRIED-GRAPE WINES). Many sweet wines are made by simply leaving the grapes on the vine for as long as possible in order to concentrate the grape sugars (see LATE HARVEST). If BOTRYTIS BUNCH ROT fails to materialize, the grapes simply start to raisin or shrivel, a condition known in French as *passerillé*. Such wines (sweet JURANÇON, for example), described as *moelleux* in French, can be extremely rich and satisfying but are typically less complex and less long-lived than those made from grapes transformed by the action of noble rot.

Some everyday sweet wines are made simply by fermenting the wine out to dryness and subsequently adding SWEET RESERVE, GRAPE CONCENTRATE or RECTIFIED GRAPE MUST just before a sterilizing membrane FILTRATION and STERILE BOTTLING. These wines owe their stability not to their composition but to the fact that all microorganisms have been filtered out. They are best drunk within a year of bottling and within a day or two of opening the bottle. LIEBFRAUMILCH is an example of this type of wine, and the sweetening agent is called SÜSSRESERVE in German.

Another technique, sometimes employed for inexpensive sweet white wines, is to ferment a must relatively high in sugars, between 200 and 250 g/l, until the alcohol level has reached about 11 or 12%, and then chill the wine and add a substantial dose of SULFUR DIOXIDE.

One quite different way of transforming grapes into a liquid that is both sweet and stable is to add spirit to grape juice either before fermentation (see MISTELA) or during it (see VIN DOUX NATUREL). Such liquids are usually more than 15% alcohol, much stronger than most table wines.

Many FORTIFIED WINES are sweet. See also LATE HARVEST, BOTRYTIZED wines, DRIED-GRAPE WINES, and ICE WINE for details of how these particularly fine sweet wines are made.

sweet wines are widely under-appreciated, especially in view of how difficult some of them are to make (see SWEET WINEMAKING). Sweet wines have been popular for various periods since ancient times; indeed, most of the most admired wines of classical ROME were sweet and white, many of them DRIED-GRAPE WINES made by deliberate raisining to concentrate the sugars. In the Middle Ages the great city states of Italy such as VENICE and GENOA profited from the popularity of wines made so much sweeter than northern European wines by the effects of the MEDITERRANEAN CLIMATE. By the late 17th century, the DUTCH WINE TRADE was energetically profiting from the sweet wines of western France. And subsequently the sweet wines of CONSTANTIA and TOKAJ in particular were considered the height of FASHION.

For specific modern sweet wines, see AUSLESE, BANYULS, BARSAC, BEERENAUSLESE, BONNEZEAUX, BOTRYTIZED wines, CÉRONS, CLAIRETTE DE DIE, EISWEIN, ICE WINE, JURANÇON, LAYON, LOUPIAC, MAURY, MOELLEUX, MONBAZILLAC, MONTLOUIS, various MOSCATELS, MOSCATO, MUSCAT, PICOLIT, PREMIÈRES CÔTES DE BORDEAUX, PX, QUARTS DE CHAUME, RASTEAU, RECIOTO, RIVESALTES, STE-CROIX-DU-MONT, SAUTERNES, SÉLECTION DE GRAINS NOBLES, SPECIAL LATE HARVESTED, TROCKENBEERENAUSLESE, VENDANGES TARDIVES, VIN DE PAILLE, VIN SANTO, and VOUVRAY.

See SWEETNESS for details of sweet-wine descriptions in various languages and what they entail.

Switzerland, small Alpine country in central Europe beginning to look outwards into the greater world of wine. Annual wine production is steady at slightly less than a million hl/26.4 million gal from about 15,000 ha/37,050 acres of often spectacular vineyards. The majority of these are in the western, French-speaking part of the country, Suisse romande. There are also extensive vineyards all over eastern, German-speaking Switzerland (or Ostschweiz) and many vineyards in Ticino, the Italian-speaking south of Switzerland (or Svizzera italiana). The country is divided into 26 cantons, of which all produce some wine (see map). For many years, Swiss wine labelling lacked the discipline applied to the north in Germany or the controls imposed to the west in France, but from the early 1990s a CONTROLLED APPELLATIONS system was applied with increasing rigour, initially in French-speaking Switzerland. Since controls on wine imports were relaxed in the mid 1990s (and disappeared altogether in 2006), the Swiss wine industry has been forced to up its game, replacing much of the light, white, and relatively neutral wine that was once the norm with serious offerings of both colours. The principal white grape variety is CHASSELAS, and, when well vinified, it can express well the country's diversity of soils and climates. The Valais has a clutch of interesting INDIGENOUS VARIETIES, and some increasingly sophisticated red wines are made in all Swiss wine regions, particularly Ticino and Graubünden. Switzerland is able to supply only 35% of domestic consumption; 65%, mainly red wine, is imported.

History

Seeds from WILD VINES of the Neolithic Age, 3000–1800 BCE, have been found at St-Blaise in Neuchâtel, and recent findings of a significant amount of VITIS pollen in deposits below a lake near Sion in the Valais, as well as grape pips and PEDICELS at the Iron Age archaeological site of Gamsen near Brig in the Haut-Valais, suggest that winemaking already existed *c.* 800–600 BCE, before the ROMAN era. In the Middle Ages, vine-growing spread under monastic influence, notably that of the Cistercians (see MONKS AND MONASTERIES), who planted the original Dézaley vines

TERRACED vineyards shaped by dry-stone walls—up to 23 m/75 ft high in some places—make viticulture possible and reduce SOIL EROSION in these HILLSIDE VINEYARDS in Sion above the Rhône Valley in SWITZERLAND's Valais region. Slopes are typically 50%, making MECHANIZATION in these small PARCELS virtually impossible. © Dr José Vouillamoz

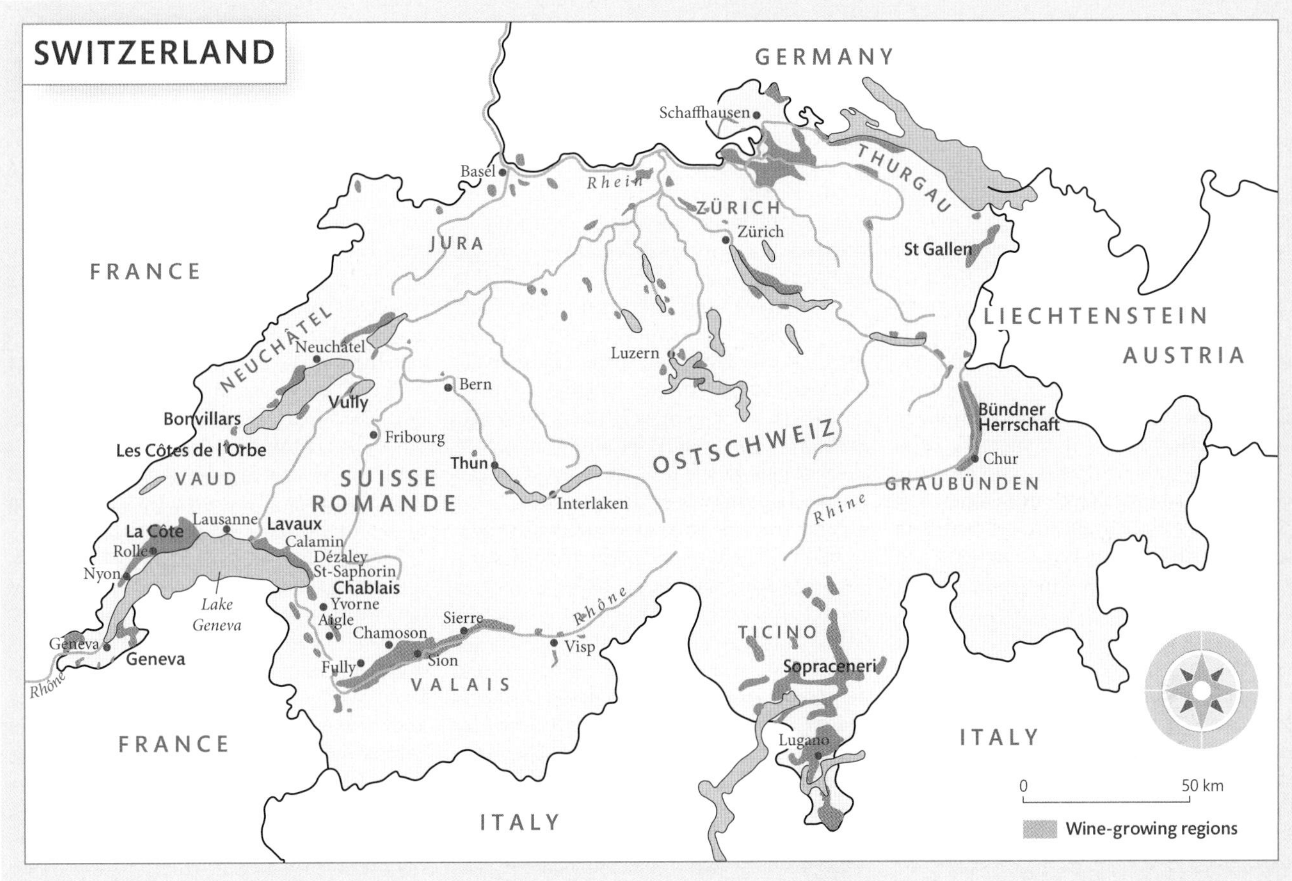

in Vaud. As elsewhere, medieval wines were thin, acidic, and often helped by the addition of honey and other flavourings. In the 17th century, Swiss vignerons were already feeling the effects of wine imports from warmer climes, notably from further down the RHÔNE Valley.

Switzerland was far more seriously affected by the viticultural catastrophes of the late 19th century (see DOWNY MILDEW, PHYLLOXERA, and POWDERY MILDEW) than most other wine-producing countries. Between 1877 and 1957 the total Swiss vineyard declined by 60%, from 33,000 ha to 12,500 ha/30,890 acres, a decrease encouraged by competition from cheaper imported wines, increasing industrialization, and development of the all-important lakesides. In the mid 20th century, CLONAL SELECTION and FERTILIZERS were harnessed with particular enthusiasm in attempts to increase productivity from Switzerland's relatively inconvenient, expensive-to-work vineyards. More recent developments in both vineyard and cellar are concerned with quality.

Climate

Although Switzerland is on a particularly suitable latitude for wine production (45–47° N), a large proportion of the country is simply too high in ELEVATION. However, the country's lakes and the föhn, a local WIND which warms up sizeable portions of the south of the country, particularly Graubünden in the upper Rhine Valley, enable full grape ripening to take place in many valleys and on lakesides. And in the Valais in the south-west, sunshine is so dependable (an average of more than 2,000 hours a year, rising sometimes to over 2,500 hours) that vineyards can be up to 750 m/2,460 ft; some, such as Visperterminen, reach as high as 1,090 m above sea level. The Valais is sheltered by the Alps and, like south-east Switzerland, benefits particularly from the föhn, but it can be dry, and IRRIGATION with mountain water is sometimes necessary. Most Swiss wine regions have an annual rainfall of 500–1,800 mm/19.5–70 in a year, the wettest region being Ticino, which suffers violent but short (HAIL) storms and is also the warmest, with average July temperatures of more than 21 °C/70 °F. Elsewhere, average July temperatures are 17.5–20 °C with wide DIURNAL TEMPERATURE RANGE, and winter temperatures in the vineyards rarely fall below danger level for vines. The Valais is most at risk.

Viticulture

Slopes as steep as 90% in places and (in some regions) rainfall make SOIL EROSION a prime concern for many Swiss vine-growers. TERRACES are common in Switzerland's steep vineyards, and COVER CROPS are increasingly common. Sophisticated MECHANIZATION is possible only on some of the flatter vineyards on the plain or on some of the terraces of eastern Switzerland. A wide variety of TRAINING SYSTEMS are used, including CORDON, GOBELET, GUYOT, TENDONE (in Ticino), and the Swiss German speciality *taille à l'onglet* designed to protect the vines against spring FROST danger there. Elaborate monorail systems and sometimes even helicopters may be used to transport equipment and, at harvest, grapes.

Many vine-growers sell their grapes direct to NÉGOCIANTS or CO-OPERATIVES. YIELDS are nationally restricted, according to Switzerland's somewhat microscopic unit of measurement, to 1.4 kg/sq m for Chasselas grapes and 1.2 kg/sq m for red and superior white grapes, quite generous allowances, although some cantons, such as those of eastern Switzerland and Geneva, Neuchâtel, and the Valais, apply their own stricter limits, and national average yields are about the same as in France.

The most common viticultural problems are downy mildew, powdery mildew, BOTRYTIS BUNCH ROT, soil erosion, and occasional spring frost in the east of the country.

Switzerland's most important viticultural research station is at Changins (see AGROSCOPE) near Nyon in Suisse romande.

Winemaking

The essential stylistic difference between Swiss wine and that of neighbouring Germany and Austria is that ACIDITY is sometimes seen as an evil rather than a virtue; MALOLACTIC CONVERSION (MLF) is occasionally practised, particularly in the Vaud. However, many indigenous varieties, such as Arvine, Completer, and Rèze, have high acidity and do not undergo MLF. The resulting softness can be emphasized by the additional alcohol provided by CHAPTALIZATION. This pre-fermentation sugar addition had been common for many Swiss wines, although the practice is unnecessary in much of the Valais and the Rhine Valley and is eschewed by most of Switzerland's best artisan winemakers. Ordinary wines may have their alcohol content increased by up to 3%, although Swiss consumers are increasingly favouring lighter, drier wines.

Swiss PRESSES, made by Bucher and Sutter, are known throughout the winemaking world and are put to particularly effective work in their native land, where the aim is to extract as much juice as possible from the country's precious grapes with only the gentlest of pressure from an inflatable membrane.

DESTEMMING is the norm, and some form of CARBONIC MACERATION is often employed for German-speaking eastern Switzerland's red wines. As elsewhere, BARREL MATURATION has become increasingly popular for Swiss reds in general.

Switzerland has several pink wine specialities such as the Valais' Dôle Blanche, a blend of Pinot Noir and GAMAY grapes, and Œil-de-Perdrix ('partridge eye'), made only from Pinot Noir, originally in Neuchâtel. Federweisser (sometimes Federweiss) or WEISSHERBST are respectively white or rosé wine made from dark-skinned grapes in German Switzerland, where SCHILLERWEIN is a local rosé made from both red and white grapes grown and processed together, like GEMISCHTER SATZ in Austria.

Before the practice was banned in 2005, Swiss wine merchants depended on imported wines, particularly deeply coloured red ones, to add bulk to many of their wines. Although Switzerland remains outside the EU, its CONTROLLED APPELLATIONS are in some instances stricter than those of the EU.

Vine varieties

Switzerland's most planted grape variety is Pinot Noir, or Blauburgunder as it is known by Swiss German speakers, planted on 29% of the country's vineyard land. CHASSELAS, or Gutedel in German, is the most planted white variety, with 27%. In the Valais it is called Fendant, a name used until the late 19th century in Vaud, where wines have since then been sold under their geographical appellations. Dorin in Vaud and Perlan in Geneva are brand names introduced in the late 20th century with mitigated success.

The conveniently early ripening MÜLLER-THURGAU, in Dr Müller's native land erroneously still known as Riesling-Silvaner or Riesling-Sylvaner, is the most common white grape variety in German Switzerland, having substantially replaced the historic RÄUSCHLING vine, particularly around Zurich just south of the German border.

Other white grape varieties include, in decreasing order of importance, CHARDONNAY, which can be elegant in the cantons of Neuchâtel and Geneva, richer in Vaud and the Valais; SILVANER, whose wines, fuller bodied than Chasselas, are sold as Johannisberg in the Valais; PINOT GRIS, called Malvoisie in the Valais; Arvine, the Valais' most revered indigenous variety; SAVAGNIN BLANC, known as Heida in the Valais, especially high up at Visperterminen, and its aromatic pink variant GEWURZTRAMINER; and SAUVIGNON BLANC, notably in Geneva canton.

Other red wine grapes include MERLOT, Switzerland's second most widely planted dark-skinned variety, reigning in Ticino to such an extent that it accounts for 80% of production; GAMAY, which is widely planted in Vaud, the Valais, and Geneva; GAMARET and GARANOIR, the most successful CROSS obtained at Changins; and SYRAH, which can produce respectably ripe wine in sheltered parts of the Valais. The northern Ticino speciality Bondola has largely been replaced by Merlot. In addition to Gamaret and Garanoir, a number of popular crosses have been developed since 1965 at Changins as suitable for Switzerland's very particular growing conditions: Charmont and Doral (both Chasselas × Chardonnay); a Valais speciality, Diolinoir (Robin Noir × Pinot Noir); Mara, a full sibling of Gamaret and Garanoir; and Divico and Divona, two recent PiWis (see DISEASE-RESISTANT VARIETIES)

But of most interest to students of AMPELOGRAPHY is the Valais' rich collection of 14 ancient INDIGENOUS VARIETIES, each with substantial body, ageing potential, and its own whiff of history: the dry or sweet AMIGNE, mainly in Vétroz; the powerfully scented and complex ARVINE; the elegant HUMAGNE BLANCHE; the almost extinct RÈZE; the local rarities of the Haut-Valais LAFNETSCHA and Himbertscha; and, among dark-skinned varieties, the noble and historical Rouge du Pays, today more usually known as CORNALIN, and the powerful HUMAGNE ROUGE, both initially originating from the neighbouring AOSTA VALLEY in Italy; Rouge de Fully (or Durize) and Eyholzer Roter are even rarer; COMPLETER is Graubünden's indigenous white wine grape.

The wine regions

Swiss wine country is divided into six main regions: in decreasing order of importance, Valais, Vaud, German-speaking Switzerland, Geneva, Ticino, and Trois-Lacs (Neuchâtel). The country's emerging controlled appellation system is applied by each canton individually.

Valais The 4,766 ha/11,777 acres (2020) of productive vineyards of this south-western canton produce 40% of every Swiss vintage. Concentrated on the south-facing slopes of the sunny upper Rhône Valley, the region is known as 'the California of Switzerland'. Many of these beautiful vineyards are terraced with historic dry-stone walls into *tablars*, horizontal slices of vineyard cut into the mountainside, farmed as a part-time activity by 22,000 smallholders. Typical of what they produce is the ubiquitous FENDANT (made from the Chasselas grapes which cover one-quarter of the *vignoble*) and medium-weight reds labelled either Pinot Noir or Dôle, a blend in which Pinot Noir must dominate the Gamay element, while up to 15% of other varieties may be included. (Dôle Blanche is a pale rosé made from a blend of Pinot Noir and Gamay grapes, with the permitted inclusion of up to 10% white wine in the final blend.)

Some of the most concentrated Silvaners, sold here as JOHANNISBERG, come from particularly well-favoured sites at Chamoson. ARVINE is accorded the greatest respect, however, for its exotic intensity; while Cornalin (or Rouge du Pays), Syrah, and Humagne Rouge (confusingly known as Cornalin in Aosta) make some of Switzerland's most characterful reds. Fine, sweet, late-harvest wines, made from Amigne, Ermitage (Marsanne), Malvoisie (Pinot Gris), and Arvine picked in November and December, can easily reach 20% POTENTIAL ALCOHOL. They may be described as FLÉTRI, or withered, a reference to partial raisining on the vine. In 1996 a few dozen of the best producers introduced a strict quality charter, Grain Noble ConfidenCiel. Wines made from such indigenous varieties as Rouge de Fully (Durize), Lafnetscha, Himbertscha, and Rèze are curiosities, the last featuring historically in the VIN DES GLACIERS from the Val d'Anniviers above Sierre.

Vaud Switzerland's second most important wine canton is also in French Switzerland, round the northern shore of Lake Geneva, or Lac Léman (almost everything has at least two names in Switzerland). The canton's six wine regions are La Côte, Lavaux, and Chablais on the north shore of Lake Geneva, Les Côtes de l'Orbe on the plain between lakes Geneva and Neuchâtel, Bonvillars on Lake Neuchâtel, and Vully on Lake Morat. The canton's eight appellations encompass the six regions as well as two GRANDS CRUS: Dézaley in the commune of Puidoux and Calamin in the commune of Epesses. Chasselas accounts for 70% of the production from about 3,800 ha/9,390 acres, although, under the influence of the Vaud's varied soils, its character can vary from almost insultingly innocuous to an almost POUILLY-FUMÉ-like steeliness. In La Côte, the aromatic floral notes of the variety itself tend to dominate the wines. In Yvorne, Aigle, Bonvillars, and Calamin the mineral character of individual soils can easily dominate the fruit, while Dézaley and St-Saphorin often manage to demonstrate both fruit and MINERALITY.

A little Chardonnay and Pinot Gris are also grown here. Red wines, especially Gamay, are a speciality of La Côte, although Plant Robert, an old BIOTYPE of Gamay, is a speciality of Lavaux. Salvagnin, a designation accorded by a special tasting panel, approximates to a Vaud version of the Valais' Dôle, although it can be made from Pinot Noir or Gamay or both. Similarly, Terravin is a Chasselas whose quality has a local seal of approval. Many of Switzerland's largest NÉGOCIANTS are based here.

In 2002 some of the best producers, including Domaine La Colombe, Pierre-Luc Leyvraz, and Blaise Duboux, created the association Arte Vitis to promote Vaud's TERROIRS.

Geneva The 1,400 ha/3,460 acres of vineyards around the city at the south-western end of the lake are much flatter than those of the Valais and Vaud and benefit from good sunlight, those next to the lake often escaping spring frost danger. Chasselas dominates white wine production, and Riesling-Sylvaner (Müller-Thurgau) is on the wane, while all manner of newcomers, including Chardonnay, Aligoté, Sauvignon, Sémillon, and Kerner, have become popular. In reds, Gamay clearly dominates and is particularly successful here, whether as a well-STRUCTURED red, a PRIMEUR or a rosé. Pinot comes second, closely followed by GAMARET, planted extensively in recent years (120 ha/297 acres by 2020). GARANOIR, Merlot, and even Cabernet Sauvignon are increasingly popular with growers and consumers alike. This was the birthplace of Switzerland's burgeoning controlled appellations.

Neuchâtel Only 600 ha/1,480 acres of the ancient CALCAREOUS soils, on the well-situated south-facing slopes above Lake Neuchâtel, grow vines, but with characterful results. Pinot Noir and Chasselas feature as usual. The pale pink Pinot Œil-de-Perdrix is a Neuchâtel invention, as is the Chasselas *non filtré* (unfiltered) released on the third Wednesday in January following the harvest. This was the first canton to restrict yields.

Eastern cantons In Switzerland's 17 German-speaking cantons are 2,600 ha/6,425 acres of vines, ranging from 0.2 ha in Nidwald to more than 600 ha in the canton of Zürich. Schaffhausen, effectively an outcrop into south BADEN in Germany, has nearly 500 ha/1,483 acres of vines. Here in eastern Switzerland nearly 80% of production is red wine, particularly the rot-resistant Mariafeld and 2–45 clones of Blauburgunder (Pinot Noir) and, to a lesser extent, the crosses Gamaret and Garanoir developed locally at the Changins viticultural research station. Räuschling is once again gaining ground in Limmatal and on the shores of the lake south of Zürich, where Blauburgunder is often labelled Clevner. Riesling–Sylvaner (Müller-Thurgau) is the dominant white grape variety of eastern Switzerland, while Completer is a local speciality of Bündner Herrschaft near the border with Austria and Liechtenstein in Graubünden, where a small quantity of sweet Freisamer and serious red wine, mainly Blauburgunder, is also produced.

Italian-speaking Switzerland There are just over 1,100 ha/2,718 acres of vineyard in the southern canton of Ticino, with barely 30 ha over the border with Graubünden in the Italian-speaking Mesolcina Valley. This makes Ticino Switzerland's fourth most important wine canton, and 80% of its production is of the Bordeaux red variety Merlot, imported in 1906. Here, vineyards lower than 450 m/1,475 ft are sunny enough to ripen this variety; higher vineyards may have to concentrate on Pinot Noir. Merlot del Ticino can be relatively light or, from well-sited vineyards and carefully vinified, often using new oak, can be a serious challenge for fine red bordeaux. The pale yellow Merlot Bianco, made from gently pressed black-berried Merlot, has become quite popular. Sopraceneri, north of Monte Ceneri, is an important wine region of which the local red grape variety Bondola is a speciality. It tends to be included in the rustic local version of 'house wine' called Nostrano, or 'ours', as opposed to Americano, which may include the HYBRIDS and AMERICAN VINES still representing 7% of total production here.

Other cantons The German-speaking but central canton of Bern has more than 200 ha/495 acres of vines, mainly on the north shore of Lake Bienne, although there are some vines on the Thunersee west of Interlaken. On the southern shores of Lake Neuchâtel are 100 ha of mainly Chasselas and Pinot Noir in the canton of Fribourg, most of them on the north shore of Lake Morat. The Swiss canton of Jura also has a few hectares of vines. J.R. & J.V.

Vouillamoz, J. F., *Swiss Grapes: History and Origin* (2020).

Wallace, E., *Vineglorious! Switzerland's Wondrous World of Wines* (2014).

Swiss Wine Guide (2010).

www.swisswine.ch

Sylvaner is the French name for the Eastern European variety known in German as SILVANER (under which name details of all non-French plantings appear). In France it is practically unknown outside ALSACE, where it was the most planted vine in the lower, flatter, more fertile vineyards of the Bas-Rhin until Riesling overtook it in the 1990s. Total plantings had fallen to 891 ha/2,202 acres by 2019.

Sylvaner may be an old vine and, at one time, an extremely important one in Germany at least, but in Alsace many of the wines are dull, even if quite full-bodied with good acidity (unlike many Pinot Blancs). Only specific TERROIRS such as the Grand Cru Zotzenberg and old vines manage to imbue Alsace Sylvaner with as exciting a character as the best FRANKEN Silvaners.

Sylvoz, a vine-TRAINING SYSTEM developed by the Italian grower Carlo Sylvoz in which canes of up to, say, ten BUDS in length are tied to a wire below a high CORDON. The vines can be trained with a high cordon, about 2 m/6.5 ft, or a mid-height cordon at about 1 m. Depending on the number of buds retained, the system can be very high yielding. A variation of the Sylvoz is the Casarsa system common in northern Italy, where the canes are not tied below the cordon but fall downward as a result of their own weight when bearing leaves and fruit. The Sylvoz system is suited to vines of high vigour, where high YIELDS are acceptable and where it is necessary to minimize pruning LABOUR. R.E.S.

Eynard, I., and Dalmasso, G., *Viticoltura moderna: manuale pratico* (1990).

Symingtons, leading family of PORT wine shippers for five generations whose group of port companies includes Graham, Dow, Warre (the oldest British port company, founded in Oporto in 1670), Quinta do Vesúvio, Smith Woodhouse, and COCKBURN. The founder of the family firm was Andrew James Symington, who arrived in Oporto from Glasgow in 1882 at the age of 19 and afterwards married the Anglo-Portuguese Beatriz Leitão de Carvalhosa Atkinson, whose ancestors had been in port since the 17th century. (Many of the Symingtons are now dual nationals.) Andrew became a partner in Warre in 1908. At the time George Warre was senior partner in Dow, and in 1912 a swap took place whereby Symington took a share in Dow while Warre regained a part of the firm that his family had founded. The Symingtons ran production and the vineyards for the two firms while the Warres ran sales and marketing in London. The Warre family sold their remaining shareholding to the Symingtons in 1961. W. & J. Graham & Co. was purchased from the Graham family in 1970 along with the smaller sister company of Smith Woodhouse. The family owns Quinta do Bomfim near Pinhão, which provides the fruit for Dow (along with Quinta da Senhorada Ribeira, acquired in 1998, having originally been sold by the family in 1954 when the fortunes of port were at a particularly low ebb). It also owns Warre, Quinta da Cavadinha in the Pinhão Valley, and Graham, Quinta dos Malvedos at Tua. The group was instrumental in reviving interest in single-quinta ports in the late 1980s (see PORT, styles). In 1989 the

Symingtons acquired Quinta do Vesúvio, a 326-ha/806-acre estate widely regarded as one of the finest vineyards in the Douro (see FERREIRA). From 1991 Quinta do Vesúvio has been a brand in its own right. The family personally own substantial additional vineyards whose fruit is sold to their various port companies. In 1996 a new winery, Quinta do Sol near Regua, was opened. The Symingtons operate another six small wineries on individual vineyards throughout the Douro, some of them equipped with the ROBOTIC LAGARES that the family pioneered in 1998. Between 2006 and 2010 the Symingtons bought COCKBURN, but each of these many companies has its own separate stocks, and the family maintains a full range of vintage and wood ports for each company.

In 1988 the BLANDY family offered the Symingtons a partnership in their MADEIRA business, hoping to reverse a general decline in sales of madeira. The Symingtons acquired a controlling interest in the Madeira Wine Company and ran it until 2011, when the Blandy family regained control, with the Symingtons remaining shareholders. The Symingtons have established their own wine distribution companies in Portugal, Britain, and the US.

The Symingtons have become firm believers in DOURO table wines. Their flagship wine Chryseia is made jointly with Bruno Prats, past owner of Ch Cos d'Estournel of ST-ESTÈPHE. In 2009 the two families acquired Quinta de Roriz, where Chryseia is now made. The Douro TABLE WINES Quinta do Vesúvio, Quinta do Ataíde, and the Altano range are grown on the family's Douro vineyards.

In 2017 the Symingtons acquired the 206-ha Quinta da Fonte Souto in the Alentejo with 42 ha/104 acres of vineyard situated at 490 m/1,608 ft in ELEVATION near Portalegre. Symington Family Estates is a B Corp, one of a group of companies independently audited for social and environmental standards, and is a member of IWCA (International Wineries for Climate Action).

S

Symphony, white-berried vine cross of red-skinned GRENACHE and light-skinned MUSCAT OF ALEXANDRIA developed in CALIFORNIA at DAVIS by Dr H. P. Olmo. It has lived the tenuous existence of all crosses, especially ones that make powerfully aromatic wines. A small vogue as an off-dry white wine in the 1990s led to a flurry of new plantings, but the state total is again in decline, standing at 596 ha/1,472 acres in 2020.

symposium, meaning 'drinking together', was one of the most important social forms in the world of ancient Greece—a considerably less cerebral affair, then, than its 20th-century counterpart. From Greece it spread to Etruria and the rest of Italy and flourished until the end of antiquity. Symposia were usually intimate gatherings: the room normally held seven or 11 couches, on each of which two men reclined on their left side, a custom adopted from oriental feasting; respectable women did not take part, and the servants and entertainers were mostly handsome slaves, both male and female. As part of the lifestyle of the leisured class, symposia were lavish affairs: in the richest households, the vessels for the mixing and drinking of wine would have been of gold or silver, although most will have been content with fine painted pottery. Both the shapes and the decoration of Greek pottery bear witness to the strong influence of the symposium.

The drinking of wine at the symposium followed the meal and was distinct from it, although a dessert of nuts, fruit, cakes, and the like often accompanied the wine. The end of the meal proper was marked by the drinking of a small amount of neat wine in honour of the 'Good Daemon' as a 'demonstration of the power of the good god', after which the tables were removed and the guests washed their hands and were offered garlands and perfumes. The wine was then mixed with water in a *krater* (mixing bowl; see CRATER) according to one of the numerous possible ratios (as detailed under ancient GREECE). From each bowl, a LIBATION was first offered together with a prayer (the god or gods invoked seem to have varied), and the Paean, a hymn of praise to Apollo, was also sung at the beginning of the proceedings by the whole company. A standard *krater* had a capacity of 14 l/3.7 gal, and various ancient writers indicate that three *kraters* would be emptied at a temperate symposium, so, although the alcoholic strength of the mixture was not high, the amount consumed must have been considerable (42 l for 14 or 22 people, apparently). The ratio for the dilution of the wine was determined by a *symposiarch* or master of ceremonies, chosen from the company, who also regulated the progress of the drinking: he could propose toasts and order any member of the company to drink more, the aim being to maintain a level of pleasurable but controlled intoxication. However, since the drinking involved an element of competition and the proceedings might last all night, the outcome was often outright DRUNKENNESS, as vase paintings and literary evidence make clear.

The most basic forms of entertainment arose out of the drinking itself: there were various drinking challenges with forfeits, and the heeltaps of wine were used to play the game of *kottabos*, in which each drinker would shoot the last drops of wine from his cup with a flick of the wrist at the target, which was usually a light bronze disc, balanced on top of a stand or tripod; when hit, it would fall into the basin beneath with a satisfying clatter.

Music and poetry played an important part in the entertainment: most, if not all, of the LYRIC POETRY of archaic Greece is now thought to have had its origins in the symposium, with its preoccupations of warfare and politics, wine and feasting, and love. Some extemporized poetry was no doubt sung at classical symposia, but it was more normal to perform existing poems, which often celebrated great men and deeds of the past: the collection of Athenian songs of this type (*skolia*) preserved in ATHENAEUS' *Deipnosophistae* (694–96 BCE) offers a sample of the traditional songs of one city.

Like the drinking, the singing was both communal and competitive: a branch of myrtle was passed round, and each man as he received it had to sing, sometimes picking up the song from the last singer, although good singers might be called on for a 'party piece'. Singers often accompanied themselves on the lyre, but slave girls were also hired to play the flute to entertain the company, to accompany singers, and to provide music for dancing; professional dancers, acrobats, and mimes might also perform. Flute players would also be expected to provide sexual services at the end of the evening if required (hence the assumption that any women present at a symposium were not respectable).

Urbane and cultured conversation was also an essential feature; at times this might be structured, and given a competitive aspect, by the posing of riddles or the exchange of witty (and often abusive) comparisons applied to fellow guests. This too might be stimulated by professional help: the career of the parasite who pays for his dinner with his jokes and clowning can be traced back to HOMER. The genre of the literary symposium, a gathering of learned figures conversing on literary or philosophic issues, as in Plato's *Symposium* (whence the modern use of 'symposium'), may give a misleadingly high-minded impression of the average Greek symposium, but such discussion clearly had its place, albeit at a less rarefied level.

Finally, those revellers still awake might go out into the street as a *komos*, a mobile party with wine and music, calling on other symposia or making rowdy attempts to rouse those now asleep. R.B.

Bibliographical note: the most recent detailed studies are Hobden, F., *The Symposion in Ancient Greek Society and Thought* (2013), and Węcowski, M., *The Rise of the Greek Aristocratic Banquet* (2014), especially Part I; Murray, O., 'The culture of the symposion', in K. A. Raaflaub and H. van Wees (eds.), *A Companion to Archaic Greece* (2009), 508–23, is an excellent overview.

Athenaeus' *Deipnosophistae* collects many stories of symposia, while XENOPHON's *Symposium* gives the flavour of a classical symposium better than the more famous one of Plato; both are accessible in translation in the Loeb Classical Library.

synthetic closures, also known rather imprecisely as 'plastic corks'. See CLOSURES.

Syrah, one of the noblest and most fashionable red wine grapes, if nobility is bestowed by an ability to produce serious red wines capable of AGEING majestically for decades and if fashionability is measured by the extent to which new CUTTINGS have been going into the ground all over the world, despite the depredations of SYRAH DECLINE. So valued was the durability of France's HERMITAGE, arguably Syrah's finest manifestation, that many red BORDEAUX were in the 18th and 19th centuries *hermitagé* (see ADULTERATION AND FRAUD). And so popular is the variety that in 2016 it was the world's sixth most planted wine grape of either colour, with a global total of 185,568 ha/458,353 acres.

Syrah's origins have been the subject of much debate and hypothesis, involving Syracuse in SICILY, ancient PERSIA (SHIRAZ being its most common synonym, especially in Australia), the vine family *Vitis allobrogica* recognized as producing fine wine in the Rhône since Roman times (see RHÔNE, history). However, DNA PROFILING at DAVIS and MONTPELLIER in 1998 established that Syrah is in fact the progeny of two vines from south-east France, MONDEUSE BLANCHE and DUREZA. DNA probability analysis strongly suggests that PINOT is a great-grandparent of Syrah, and both Viognier and Mondeuse Noire seem to be closely related to Syrah too.

The vine is relatively productive and disease resistant, sensitive to COULURE but conveniently late budding and not too late ripening. Care has to be taken with ROOTSTOCKS because it is sensitive to CHLOROSIS. Its distinctively savoury qualities are much reduced once the YIELD is allowed to rise, and it has a tendency to lose aroma and ACIDITY rapidly if left too long on the vine.

Many vignerons in the northern Rhône, Syrah's homeland, distinguish between a small-berried, superior version of Syrah, which they call Petite Syrah (not to be mistaken for the variety known in North and South America as PETITE SIRAH), and the larger-berried Grosse Syrah, which produces wines with a lower concentration of PHENOLICS. However, AMPELOGRAPHERS reject this distinction; Grosse Syrah is a synonym of MONDEUSE NOIRE. On the other hand, the BIOTYPE that goes by the name of SERINE is worth distinguishing. The total ANTHOCYANINS in Syrah can be up to 40% higher than those in the tough, dark Carignan, which makes it, typically, a wine for the long term that responds well to OAK maturation, even new oak when the grapes are really ripe.

The most famous prototype French Syrahs—Hermitage and CÔTE RÔTIE—are distinguished by their longevity or, in the case of newer producers, ambition. Only ST-JOSEPH and that paler shadow CROZES-HERMITAGE can sensibly be broached within their first five years. Syrah that has not reached full maturation can be simply mean and ASTRINGENT, with more than a whiff of black pepper or burnt rubber. When planted on the fringes of the Rhône such as in the ARDÈCHE, Syrah may avoid this fate only in riper vintages, which are becoming increasingly common.

Until the 1970s, French Syrah plantings were almost exclusively in and around the very limited vineyards of the northern Rhône Valley and were dwarfed in area by total Syrah plantings in the vine's other major colony, AUSTRALIA, where it is known as Shiraz and has been that country's major black grape variety for decades. For more details, see SHIRAZ.

Since then, however, Syrah has enjoyed an extraordinary surge in popularity throughout southern France so that total French plantings rose from 2,700 ha/6,670 acres in 1968 to exactly ten times that 20 years later; it had reached 67,040 ha by 2019, making it the country's third most planted red grape after Merlot and Grenache. The increases were noticeable throughout the southern Rhône, particularly in Châteauneuf-du-Pape country, where there was a FASHION for planting Syrah (although Mourvèdre is increasingly regarded as a more suitable blending partner for Grenache this far south). And in the Languedoc and Roussillon, Syrah has been so enthusiastically adopted as an officially approved 'improving variety' that adds STRUCTURE and savour to blends as well as yielding exciting VARIETAL wines that its 39,206 ha in 2019 made it the region's most planted variety, just ahead of Grenache. Yields very much in excess of the low yields that characterize the arid hill of Hermitage have tended to dilute its northern Rhône characteristics in many cases, producing a much more supple, more obviously fruity, if still savoury style of Syrah, often distinguished by a particularly polished TEXTURE. In the northern Rhône it is rarely blended, except perhaps with a little Viognier (the original CO-FERMENTATION recipe), while in the south it is typically blended with Grenache, Mourvèdre, Carignan, and/or Cinsaut. In Provence, the very Australian blend of Syrah and Cabernet Sauvignon is relatively common, and Syrah is one of the most successful vine imports to Corsica, where there were 509 ha/1,258 acres.

Another unexpectedly successful site for mature, concentrated Syrah is the Valais in Switzerland, particularly around the suntrap village of Chamoson on the upper reaches of the Rhône Valley. Here classic northern Rhône techniques are employed, sometimes to great effect. Although keener on Bordeaux grapes, Italians have been planting Syrah, whose total area in 2015 was 7,693 ha/19,010 acres, most successfully so far around Cortona in southern Tuscany. The variety was initially introduced to Piemonte from MONTPELLIER in 1899. Spanish growers have embraced the variety with even more enthusiasm with 2020 plantings of 17,617 ha/43,533 acres, more than half of them in CASTILLA-LA MANCHA. Spanish Syrah tends to be plumper than most, but pioneer Marqués de Griñon has made convincingly fine examples. In Portugal there were 6,133 ha/15,155 acres in 2020, mostly in the Alentejo and Lisboa regions. Syrah is planted to a limited extent in most warmer wine regions of Europe and the eastern Mediterranean, but only Türkiye has more than a few hundred hectares planted. To ripen fully, Syrah demands a warm climate, but if temperatures are too high its telltale fragrance is lost. This has acted as a brake on Syrah's success in the US. Perhaps partly thanks to the RHÔNE RANGERS, California growers rushed to plant the variety in the late 20th century; there were still barely 400 acres of it in the state in 1992, but by 2003 there were 6,800 ha/17,000 acres. But many of these plantings were opportunistic, Syrah the wine had no clear identity, the SIDEWAYS effect suggested Pinot Noir was more fashionable, and the variety may have been damaged by the low-quality image of cheap Australian SHIRAZ (see YELLOW TAIL, for instance). In 2020 total plantings were back down to 6,035 ha/14,912 acres, with a much more significant proportion of them in suitable areas and vinified by a sensitive hand. For more details, see CALIFORNIA.

Promising results from such vineyards as Red Willow, Cayuse, and various Red Mountain vineyards suggest that WASHINGTON State may have considerable potential for fine, bright Syrah wines. In 1999 only a handful of Washington Syrahs were produced, but by 2011 total plantings exceeded 1,850 ha/4,572 acres, surpassed only by Cabernet and Merlot. It is much less important in Oregon but is planted to a limited extent in many other US states warm enough to ripen the variety. Syrah, sometimes labelled Shiraz (the choice generally reflecting the style of the wine), has been hugely popular in SOUTH AFRICA, so that its 2020 total plantings of 9,151 ha/22,613 acres make it the country's second most planted red wine grape after Cabernet Sauvignon. It is planted in all but the very coolest spots and makes wines in a wide range of styles. The introduction of virus-free CLONES has improved wine quality, but the variety is so susceptible to South Africa's own, fatal vine virus that can be transmitted via GRAFTS that it is known as Shiraz disease.

Much of New Zealand is too cool for Syrah, but plantings have increased to 444 ha/1,097 acres, chiefly in HAWKE'S BAY.

The variety has been hugely successful in CHILE, on the other hand, where total plantings grew from under 700 ha in 1998 to 7,400 ha/18,286 acres by 2020. The wines are generally relatively rich and dense although the range of styles has been widening as cooler areas are developed, resulting in more elegant, Rhône-like styles of Syrah. Argentina, where Malbec rather than Syrah is an obvious alternative to the Bordeaux grapes, nevertheless has even more land planted with Syrah, nearly 11,796 ha/29,149 acres by 2020, making it the country's sixth most planted variety of any colour. San Juan province seems particularly well suited to the variety, which is also grown in Bolivia, Peru, and Uruguay.

Syrah decline, mysterious fatal phenomenon affecting SYRAH exclusively, known as *dépérissement* in French, whereby a part of the trunk swells and becomes bulbous, generally around the graft (see GRAFTING), forming splits in the wood. The vine may continue to function normally for a few years, but eventually the leaves redden prematurely during summer, VIGOUR rapidly declines, and within a year or two the vine is dead. It was first noticed in the Languedoc in the 1990s and has affected Syrah virtually wherever it is grown, apart from Australia. The most susceptible Syrah clones are 73, 99, 100, 174, 300, 381, 382, 383, 525, 585, and 877; the least susceptible are 470, 471, 524, and 747. Syrah decline appears to be attributable to physiological incompatibility between certain SCION clones and ROOTSTOCKS rather than to a VIRUS or other biotic agent. W.W.

Syria, country in the Middle East with—almost incredibly, considering its recent history (see WAR, EFFECTS ON WINE)—at least one first-class wine producer. Domaine Bargylus was founded in 2005 by the Saade family (also owners of Ch Marsyas in LEBANON) in the mountains above the port city of Latakia. Working with 12 ha/30 acres of vines planted in CLAY and LIMESTONE soils at 900 m/2,953 ft in ELEVATION, they produce a fine red blend of SYRAH, CABERNET SAUVIGNON, and MERLOT and a Bordeaux-style white blend.

Syria has a particularly long history of wine production (see ORIGINS OF VINICULTURE and MESOPOTAMIA).

Szamarodni, term used in Tokaj to denote a wine made from a mix of both ASZÚ and healthy berries. See TOKAJ for more detail.

Szekszárd, wine region and PDO in southern HUNGARY with a special LOESS soil as deep as 10–15 m/35–50 ft in places. The varied landscape allows different MESOCLIMATES to shape the wines. The steep slopes of the Szekszárd Hill are dissected by erosional valleys and ravines with the eastern and southern slopes generally providing the best wines. The KADARKA grape, once the chief component of BIKAVÉR, made Szekszárd's viticulture famous in the 18th and 19th centuries, and its attractively scented, relatively soft wine can once again be found fairly easily, either as a varietal Kadarka or in blends including BIKAVÉR. G.R. & G.M.

Szepsy, István, The most respected winemaker in Hungary. Records of his winemaking forebears date from at least the 16th century. He currently owns about 107 ha/264 acres of the best vineyard land in the TOKAJ villages of Mád, Bodrogkeresztúr, Tarcal, Tállya, Mezőzombor, and Rátka, of which 54 ha/133 acres are planted. He created the new style of Tokaji dry wines by perfecting the selection of old Furmint CLONES and concluded that the best-quality wine can only be achieved by making dry wines or Tokaji Aszú from old vines from the first-growth PARCELS and in the best vintages such as 2017.

Szürkebarát, Hungarian name for PINOT GRIS.

TA. See TOTAL ACIDITY.

table grapes, the common term for those grapes specially grown to be eaten as fresh fruit. Of the grapes grown worldwide, table grapes represent the second most frequent use, following wine. Nearly 27 million tonnes were grown in 2016, and the trend is upwards. The most important producing country is China, followed at quite some distance by India, Türkiye, Egypt, and the US. The fruit is consumed primarily within the producing country because it is relatively low in value and perishable. However, with refrigeration the opportunities for export are increasing; Chile, for example, has developed a substantial export trade in table grapes over the last four decades. Table grapes are used widely by the emerging wine industries of ASIA.

The varieties of grapes for fresh consumption are usually specialized and different from those for wine and drying. They should taste good and have a reasonably consistent BERRY SIZE, bright colour, firm flesh texture, not too many seeds, and skins tough enough to withstand storage and transport. Recently developed seedless varieties are increasingly popular. Some important table grape varieties are Barlinka, Calmeria, CARDINAL, CHASSELAS, Dattier, Emperor, Flame Seedless, Gros Vert, Italia, MUSCAT OF ALEXANDRIA, MUSCAT OF HAMBURG, Perlette, Ruby Seedless, Alphonse Lavallée (Ribier), and SULTANA (or Thompson Seedless).

Table grapes are typically grown in warm to hot regions to encourage early maturity and freedom from any ROT brought on by rain. Low night temperatures assist the colour development of some varieties, while both very high and very low daytime temperatures may inhibit colour development. Many of the table grape regions of the world are inland DESERT areas.

There are some important differences between table grape and wine grape vineyard management. For table grapes, the aim is generally to produce maximum berry size, and so IRRIGATION and FERTILIZERS are used more liberally than for wine grapes. Sloping and overhead TRELLIS SYSTEMS such as the pergola and TENDONE are common, where the shoots and leaves form a canopy over the fruit, avoiding excessive and direct sun exposure (see SUNBURN).

Because they are worth more than most wine grapes (although see Ch d'YQUEM, MONTRACHET, and DOMAINE DE LA ROMANÉE-CONTI), table grapes typically require more manual vineyard work. This can include SHOOT THINNING, CROP THINNING, and sometimes berry thinning. These practices lead to larger berries which ripen early. GROWTH REGULATORS are also commonly used to thin flowers, but more particularly to increase berry size of seedless varieties such as Sultana. CINCTURING or girdling can also be used to hasten ripening.

Table grapes are harvested earlier than wine grapes, as a lower sugar level and higher acidity make them taste more refreshing, in the range of 15 to 18 °BRIX (whereas wine grapes would preferably be harvested for dry wines at about 22 °Brix).

Some table grape varieties can be kept in cool stores for up to 20 weeks, although 8–12 weeks is more common. Long storage life is promoted by low temperatures such as −1 °C (at which the sugar content stops them freezing), a relative humidity of about 96%, and SULFUR DIOXIDE fumigation for mould control.

R.E.S. & J.E.H.

FAO-OIV Focus, *Table and Dried Grapes* (2016).

table wine, term used internationally to distinguish wines of average ALCOHOLIC STRENGTH from FORTIFIED WINES, which have been strengthened by the addition of alcohol. In this context, 'table wines' rely solely on FERMENTATION for their alcoholic strength, which tends to be between 9 and 15%, occasionally even higher.

Within the EU, the term 'table wine' had until the reforms of 2008 a specific meaning and was applied to the vast but declining quantity of wine produced within it that did not qualify as superior so-called QUALITY WINE. Within Italy the situation was rather different, as explained in VINO DA TAVOLA.

In the US, the term 'table wine' denotes wine with less than 14% alcohol, while wines with between 14 and 24% alcohol are officially 'dessert wines', whether fortified or not, and attract a higher tax rate.

Tacoronte-Acentejo, DOP wine region of 1,014 ha/2,506 acres of vines on the west-facing slopes up to 800 m/2,625 ft in the north-east of the volcanic island of Tenerife in the CANARY ISLANDS. Tacoronte-Acentejo produces red wines made predominantly from the dark-berried LISTÁN NEGRO and NEGRAMOLL grapes. The fertile VOLCANIC soil imparts a peculiar character to these wines. V. de la S. & F.C.

Tahiti in French Polynesia has about 6 ha/15 acres of CARIGNAN, Italia, and MUSCAT OF HAMBURG on the island of Rangiroa on the Tuamotu archipelago which supplies Domaine Ampélidacées with two harvests a year using TROPICAL VITICULTURE techniques.

Tai Bianco, north-east Italian synonym for SAUVIGNONASSE that has replaced the name Tocai Bianco, to which Hungarians objected.

taille, French term for PRUNING. The name is also used in CHAMPAGNE and sometimes elsewhere for the coarser, later juice which flows

TALHA BRANCO
450 LT
XXI
TALHA BRANCO
XXII
TB

from the PRESS in the traditional method of SPARKLING WINEMAKING.

taint is the term used to refer to the effect of an external CONTAMINANT once its presence can be tasted in a wine. See, for example, CORK TAINT, LADYBUG TAINT, and SMOKE TAINT. An off-flavour, on the other hand, is generally the result of a chemical or microbial action within the MUST or wine.

Tai Rosso, north-east Italian synonym for GRENACHE.

Tairov. See UKRAINE.

Taiwan, otherwise known as the Republic of China, island off, and independent of, CHINA with about 3,128 ha/7,729 acres of vines in 2020 but fewer than 100 ha devoted to wine grapes. Prior to the dismantling of the government alcohol MONOPOLY following Taiwan's accession to the World Trade Organization in 2002, winemaking was prohibited. Today there are only a handful of wineries. Grape-growers favour HYBRIDS such as Black Queen for red wines and Golden Muscat for whites to deal with the heat, humidity, and rain, which averages over 2,500 mm/98 in annually, much of it falling during typhoon season. D.G.

Tajikistan, mountainous, former Soviet, central Asian republic between UZBEKISTAN and CHINA with 36,281 ha/89,652 acres of vineyards in 2020 according to the OIV, most of it for TABLE GRAPES and RAISINS.

Viticulture and winemaking were developed in Tajikistan even before the military campaigns of Alexander the Great in the 4th century BCE. Ancient documents testify to the cultivation of numerous VINE VARIETIES in the country, which were made into wine, vinegar, and *bekmes* (GRAPE CONCENTRATE), as well as being traded as table grapes and raisins. Viticulture was highly developed in Osrushan in Ura-Tyube, Fergana, and the Zeravshan Valley.

In the north, the adoption of ISLAM inspired growers to replace wine varieties with table and raisin varieties. Central, south, and south-eastern parts of the country were less affected by this trend. In the Soviet era, grape production was ramped up such that the country was putting out 600,000 liters/158,503 gal of wine annually. Production nosedived after Mikhail GORBACHEV's anti-alcohol campaign in 1985, with massive uprooting of vineyards across the country; further economic and political stress has taken a toll such that fewer than five wineries remained in the 2010s.

talha, AMPHORA-like vessel traditionally used in the ALENTEJO in southern Portugal to ferment wine on skins (see SKIN-FERMENTED). The Roman ruins at São Cucufate evidence a long history of winemaking around Vila de Frades in VIDIGUEIRA, the epicentre of talha winemaking. The name is thought to derive from the Latin *tinalia*, meaning 'large pot'. Typically hand-made of local clay (although moulded concrete examples also exist), talhas come in different shapes and sizes. They are usually coated inside with *pez*, a mix of beeswax and pine resin, to reduce wine seepage and oxygen ingress through the clay. Seals of cloth, clay, wood, or olive oil protect wines from OXIDATION. A hole about 30 cm/12 in from the bottom is stoppered with a cork, or *batoque*, which is replaced with a spout for decanting the finished wine. The rise of Alentejo's CO-OPERATIVES in the 1950s and 1960s dealt a blow to this artisanal production method, but some local *tascas* (taverns) and families maintained the faith. With growing interest in clay-fermented and ORANGE WINE this century, talha winemaking has undergone a revival. In 2010 VINHO DE TALHA DOC was introduced to preserve the traditions for contemporary (bottled) examples, which can be sophisticated. In 2021 Portugal's most expensive wine was a single-talha red. S.A.

White, P. J., *Talha Tales: Portugal's Ancient Answer to Amphora Wine* (2022).
Woolf, S. J., and Opaz, R., *Foot Trodden: Portugal and the Wines That Time Forgot* (2021).
www.vinhodetalha.vinhosdoalentejo.pt

Tália, occasionally written **Thalia**, Portuguese name for the ubiquitous white grape variety known in France as UGNI BLANC and in Italy as TREBBIANO Toscano.

Tămâioasă, name for MUSCAT grape or wine in ROMANIA. Most widely seen as **Tămâioasă Românească**, a name which has been used both for MUSCAT BLANC À PETITS GRAINS and for a different variety that has been given the name **Tămâioasă Bucureşti** to avoid confusion. **Tămâioasă Roză** is the pink-skinned MUTATION of the former.

Popescu, C. F., et al., 'Identification and characterization of Romanian grapevine genetic resources', *Vitis*, 56/4 (2017), 173–80.

Tamarez, old but relatively uninspiring white grape grown in the ALENTEJO.

Tamar Valley, the largest winegrowing area of TASMANIA, stretching from Relbia, just south of Launceston, following the Tamar River/kanamaluka north to Rowella. Its diverse MESOCLIMATES and sheltered slopes support many grape varieties and wine styles.

Taminga, white grape variety bred specifically for hot AUSTRALIAN conditions by A. J. Antcliff, with TRAMINER as one of its parents. Taminga is not widely planted but is capable of producing fresh, aromatic white wine of fair quality in a variety of different sites with an average yield of 90 hl/ha (5 tons/acre). It seems well suited to making BOTRYTIZED sweet wines.

Tamyanka, Bulgarian, Russian, and Serbian name for MUSCAT BLANC À PETITS GRAINS.

tank method, a bulk sparkling-winemaking process which involves provoking a second fermentation in wine stored in a pressure tank. See SPARKLING WINEMAKING for more details and alternative names.

tanks. See CONTAINERS.

Tannat, distinctive, tannic, deep-black-berried vine variety most famous as the principal ingredient in MADIRAN, where its inherent ASTRINGENCY is mitigated by blending with Cabernet Franc, some Cabernet Sauvignon, and FER and wood ageing for at least 20 months. If Madiran is Tannat's noblest manifestation, slightly more approachable (if sometimes more rustic) wines are made to much the same recipe for ST-MONT, as well as for the distinctively firm reds and rosés of IROULÉGUY and the rare reds and pinks labelled TURSAN and BÉARN.

Overall plantings in France have remained fairly static and were 2,790 ha/6,894 acres in 2019. Although it may owe its French name to its high tannin content, the vine may well be Basque in origin and, like MANSENG, was taken to URUGUAY by Basque settlers in the 19th century, where it is by far the most important vine variety; rather like MALBEC in ARGENTINA, it seems to thrive better in the warmer climate of its new home in South America than in SOUTH WEST FRANCE. In Uruguay, where it has been called Harriague after its original promulgator, there were 1,575 ha/3,892 acres in 2022. Strategies for softening the grapes' tannins include blending with such grapes as Pinot Noir and Merlot as well as all the usual winemaking techniques (see MACERATION and MICRO-OXYGENATION, the latter having been developed for Tannat in Madiran in particular). PORT and BEAUJOLAIS styles have also been made from it. From Uruguay it spread to other wine-producing countries in South America, and there were 257 ha/636 acres in California in 2020. The variety is seen as a minor but intriguing challenge by winemakers all over the world.

tannins, diverse and complex group of chemical compounds that occur in the bark of many trees and in fruits, including the grape. Strictly speaking, a tannin is a compound that is capable of interacting with PROTEINS and precipitating them; this is the basis of the process of tanning animal hides (hence the name tannin) and is also a process that is believed to be responsible for the sensation of ASTRINGENCY. Tannins in wine come predominantly from the grapes and, to a much lesser extent, from

◀ An 18th-century clay TALHA in the XXVI Talhas winery in Vila Alva in the south of Portugal's ALENTEJO region. Around 1.6 m/5.25 ft tall, 1 m wide, and holding around 600 l/158 gal, it is relined every 6–8 years with a mixture of dearomatized resin and beeswax to reduce OXYGEN ingress. © Julia Harding MW

the WOOD in which the wine is aged. See also OAK FLAVOURS.

The natural tannins of grapes, or condensed tannins, also called PROANTHOCYANIDINS since they release red anthocyanidin pigments when heated in acidic media, are FLAVONOIDS consisting of oligomers and polymers of CATECHINS. Formation of proanthocyanidins occurs under the control of ENZYMES as part of the metabolism of the grape, but they may rearrange to longer or shorter molecules in the acidic wine medium. Other catechin polymers can be formed in wine as a result of enzymatic or chemical oxidation reactions. These polymeric flavonoids that can range from colourless through light yellow to amber, as well as PIGMENTED TANNINS resulting from reactions of anthocyanins with catechins and tannins, may also be regarded as tannins. Wine may also contain hydrolysable tannins, deriving from gallic acid and ellagic acid, extracted from oak COOPERAGE in the course of BARREL AGEING, from OAK CHIPS, or added as OENOLOGICAL TANNINS.

Tannins play an important role in the ageing of wine, particularly red wines, where pigmented tannins are crucial to the colour and sensory properties. Handling tannins during RED WINEMAKING is one of the most critical steps in optimizing the quality and character of a red wine, yet the process is based almost totally on experience and intuition because our understanding of the principles involved is still incomplete.

The tannins in grapes are predominantly in the skins and seeds of each berry and also the STEMS, the amount of tannins in grape pulp being much lower. Thus, the more skins, seeds, and stems are involved in the winemaking process, the higher the possible resultant level of tannins. Tannin levels in white and rosé wines, which are made largely by excluding or minimizing these grape components, are therefore lower than in reds. Although white wines contain structures similar to the pigmented tannins of a red wine, the absence of ANTHOCYANINS condensed into the tannins of white wines accounts for how different they look.

Tannins are most often encountered by the human palate in over-steeped tea, and by wine drinkers in young reds designed for a long life in bottle and in whites made with prolonged or excessive SKIN CONTACT. They produce the taste sensation of bitterness and the physical tactile 'drying' sensation of astringency. Catechins and small tannins are said to be responsible for bitterness, while larger ones elicit the astringency sensation, presumably by interaction with the proteins of the mouth but also by the adherence of the tannins to the oral mucous membranes (see below).

Traditional methods for measuring tannins report them as if they were all gallic acid, and such analyses, including the widely used Folin Ciocalteu method, are popular because of their analytical convenience. Alternative methods for measuring the phenolic compounds of grape tannins more directly and as other than gallic acid are time consuming and require considerable analytical expertise. Gallic acid or GA-equivalent concentration averages about 300 mg/l in white wines but 1,800 mg/l in reds. The tannin types and their extraction rates vary considerably with VINE VARIETY and WINEMAKING methods. Varieties notably high in tannins include CABERNET SAUVIGNON, NEBBIOLO, SYRAH, and TANNAT.

Since the late 1980s, much research into red winemaking has been aimed at minimizing the bitter and astringent impression made by tannins on the palate while enhancing the TEXTURE and AGEING properties which they confer on a wine. These studies have involved, among other variations, ever more refinement of MACERATION techniques and deliberately controlled exposure to OXYGEN at various points during the winemaking process (see MICRO-OXYGENATION, for example). It is also widely recognized that the influence of such viticultural factors as grape RIPENESS and grape composition on the properties of tannins is not yet understood.

Different WOOD TYPES contain different sorts of tannins, but these have the most effect on wine when the cooperage is new. The tannins of the various species and varieties of OAK, the most common wood used in winemaking, vary among themselves and according to how the oak was seasoned (see BARREL MAKING). Oak tannins differ in significant ways from grape tannins, although the consequences of such differences on the stability of wine colour and on the sensory properties (including mouthfeel) of barrel-matured red wines in particular are yet to be scientifically rationalized. For more details, see OAK FLAVOUR. Wine consumers may experience a certain amount of wood oak flavour in a wide range of wines, including some relatively immature wines, both red and white, whether the result of genuine BARREL AGEING or the use of OAK CHIPS. They are therefore often exposed to the effects of tannin on the palate, which can be considerably mitigated by the right choice of accompanying food (see DIET).

Winemakers can adjust excessively high tannin levels by FINING with casein, gelatin, or albumin, which selectively precipitate large-sized astringent tannins. Formation of soluble complexes with macromolecules such as proteins may also prevent tannins from interacting with salivary proteins and eliciting astringency. Given sufficient time, tannins are removed naturally, however, during wine ageing. The tannins POLYMERIZE and form aggregates that eventually precipitate as SEDIMENT so that they no longer have any bitter or astringent effect on the palate. Depending on the wine composition and PH, reactions of tannins can also yield smaller tannins and pigmented tannins, thus resulting in lower astringency.

See also OENOLOGICAL TANNINS, which may be deliberately added in the course of winemaking to increase a wine's tannin level.

P.J.W. & V.C.

Cheynier, V., 'Flavonoids in wine', in O. M. Andersen and K. R. Markham (eds.), *Flavonoids: Chemistry, Biochemistry and Applications* (2006).

Tasting tannins

Tannins cannot be smelt or tasted; they cause tactile sensations. A significant development of the 1990s was a keener appreciation of the different sorts of sensory impact of tannins on the palate (see TEXTURE). In Australia, this led in particular to the development of a MOUTHFEEL wheel rather like the AROMA WHEEL. Tannins may be variously described as hard, bitter (if accompanied by BITTERNESS), green, ripe (if perceptible but only after the impact of fruit that has reached PHYSIOLOGICAL RIPENESS has been felt on the palate), coarse, grainy, wood (if obviously the effect of CASK AGEING), long chain (an American expression for POLYMERIZED), short chain, and polymerized. Research in the US by Revelette et al. has shown that it is not just the quantity of tannins in a wine that determines its astringency but also the quality of those tannins, specifically their tendency to 'stick' to another surface such as the mucous membranes.

Canon, F., et al., 'Wine taste and mouthfeel', in A. G. Reynolds (ed.), *Managing Wine Quality 2: Oenology and Wine Quality* (2nd edn, 2021).

Noble, A. C., 'Astringency and bitterness of flavonoid phenols', in P. Given and D. Paredes (eds.), *Chemistry of Taste: Mechanisms, Behaviors, and Mimics* (2002), 192–201.

Revelette, M., et al. 'High-performance liquid chromatography determination of red wine tannin stickiness', *Journal of Agricultural and Food Chemistry*, 62/28 (2014), 6626–31.

Soares, S., et al., 'Sensorial properties of red wine polyphenols: astringency and bitterness', *Critical Reviews in Food Science and Nutrition*, 57/5 (2017), 937–48.

Tanzania is the second largest wine producer in sub-Saharan Africa. VITIS VINIFERA vines were brought by European missionaries as early as the 1930s; since the 1970s the country has been producing wine on a commercial basis. Most vinegrowing is focused in the Dodoma region, a plateau at about 1,150 m/3,773 ft in ELEVATION. In the warm, arid climate, vinegrowers harvest twice a year (see TROPICAL VITICULTURE). Most farms are very small, and growers sell to the CO-OPERATIVE or larger wineries. Italian varieties such as MARZEMINO, TEROLDEGO, and AGLIANICO are popular, as is CHENIN BLANC for white wines. In 2020 the Tanzania Agricultural Research Institute began the process of importing 13 new grape varieties from SOUTH AFRICA in a bid to increase wine-grape production.

tariffs applied to imports (as opposed to a country's TAXATION policy) can have a considerable effect on the structure of the world's wine trade. In late 2020, for example, China imposed punitive tariffs on imports from Australia, including wine, which had the effect of virtually robbing Australian wine producers of their most lucrative market overnight. In 2019, as part of a dispute about subsidies for aircraft manufacturers, President Trump imposed a 25% import tariff on wines from a variety of European countries, including France. The dispute was settled in 2021 but not before it had a direct effect on the fortunes of many French vignerons and the range offered by some American retailers.

Tarragona, Mediterranean port in Spanish CATALUÑA which has played an important part in a flourishing wine industry since Roman times (see SPAIN, history, and map). Until the 1960s, wines called Tarragona were predominantly sweet, red, FORTIFIED, and drunk as a cheap alternative to PORT. Awarded DOP status in 1976, Tarragona continues to ship communion wine all over the Christian world (see EUCHARIST). Over 70% of Tarragona's wine production today is white, however, a large proportion of which is sold to the CAVA houses in PENEDÈS. The MONTSANT DOP created in 2001 was carved out of the original Tarragona zone.

Tarrango, red wine grape variety developed at Merbein in AUSTRALIA in 1965. The aim of this TOURIGA × SULTANA cross was to provide a slow-ripening variety suitable for the production of light-bodied wines with low TANNINS and relatively high ACIDITY. As a result, some Australian wines have been fashioned in the image of BEAUJOLAIS, but the variety will ripen satisfactorily only in the hot irrigated wine regions of Australia such as the RIVERLAND. Brown Brothers of Milawa have been particularly persistent with this variety.

tartaric acid, the most important of the ACIDS found in grapes and wine. Of all the natural organic acids found in plants, this is one of the rarer. The grape is the only fruit of significance that is a tartrate accumulator, and yet it is of critical importance to the winemaker because of the major part it plays in the taste of the wine. Tartaric acid exists in wine in equilibria, as the acid form, the tartrate, and bitartrate ion forms. It is the principal component of the mixture of acids and salts that constitutes wine's all-important buffer system (see BUFFERING CAPACITY) and maintains the stability of its ACIDITY and COLOUR.

Tartaric acid is of further interest because its potassium acid salt (potassium tartrate or cream of tartar), while being moderately soluble in grape juice, is less soluble in alcoholic solutions such as wine. Most winemakers therefore try to ensure that no excess tartrates remain in the wine when it is bottled lest these crystals frighten less sophisticated consumers by their resemblance to glass shards. See TARTRATES for more on this important by-product of the winemaking process.

Grapes and the resultant wines vary considerably in their concentrations of tartaric acid. Among the thousands of cultivated VINE VARIETIES, some are noted for their high concentrations of tartaric acid, while others have very low levels. In general, wine grapes have higher concentrations of acids than do TABLE GRAPES. Among wine grape varieties, however, there is considerable variation in concentrations of the two principal acids: tartaric acid and MALIC ACID. For example, Palomino, the sherry grape, is particularly high in tartaric acid, while Pinot Noir and Malbec, or Côt, are relatively low in tartaric.

The relative amounts of these two acids that are present in grapes, which varies with VINTAGE, do not necessarily govern the relative amounts in wines, however. Precipitation of potassium acid tartrate, as outlined above, reduces tartaric-acid concentration, while malic acid is frequently decomposed by MALOLACTIC CONVERSION. Wines that have not undergone this conversion generally have slightly more tartaric acid than malic acid.

Weather and soil, as well as grape variety, affect the amounts of different acids in the grape and wine. Cooler climates in general favour higher concentrations of acids and lower levels of POTASSIUM in the grape skins. Malic acid is much more effectively metabolized in warm conditions during the grape ripening period than is tartaric acid. Soils deficient in potassium may result in grapes of low PH because potassium ions are exchanged with hydrogen ions during the ripening process. Another curious difference is that tartrate levels are very high in grape flowers. Tartaric acid is not respired during ripening, meaning that its amount per berry stays relatively constant during berry RIPENING. More than half of the tartrate in ripe berries can be present as a salt. The proportion of free to salt form varies with variety and the concentration of metal cations in the juice; potassium is by far the most abundant. B.G.C. & M.J.T.

tartrates, the general term used by winemakers to describe the harmless crystalline deposits that separate from wines during FERMENTATION and AGEING. In French the substances are called *tartres*, in German *Weinsteine* (literally, 'wine stones'), *tartrati* in Italian, and *tartratos* in Spanish. The principal component of this deposit is potassium bitartrate, the potassium salt of TARTARIC ACID, which has therefore given rise to the name. Small amounts of pulp debris, dead yeast cells, precipitated phenolic materials such as TANNINS and PIGMENTED TANNINS, and traces of other materials make up the impurities contaminating the potassium bitartrate (see SEDIMENT).

The LEES that sink to the bottom of the FERMENTATION VESSEL during the later stages of fermentation contain lower concentrations of tartrates than do the crystalline deposits that form on the walls of the vessel, making the latter the preferred source for commercial tartrates.

The main forms of tartrates used commercially are pure crystalline tartaric acid used as an acidulant in non-alcoholic drinks and foods, cream of tartar (pure potassium bitartrate) used in baking, and Rochelle salt (potassium sodium tartrate) used mainly in electroplating solutions. The wine industry is the only source of tartrates available to commerce and the crystalline encrustations left inside fermentation vessels are therefore regularly scraped off and purified for eventual commercial use.

Tartrates separate from new wines because potassium bitartrate is less soluble in solutions of alcohol and water such as wine than it is in plain water or in grape juice. The exact figures for wines vary slightly according to grape variety and region, but experience shows that about half of the tartrate soluble in grape juice is insoluble in wine. The problem is that the tartrate may remain in a supersaturated state in the complex wine mixture only to crystallize at some unpredictable later time (during storage or in bottle).

Although tartrates precipitated in red wines usually take on some red or brown colouring from adsorbed wine pigments and are commonly regarded as mere sediment, in white wines they can look alarmingly like shards of glass, or sugar, to the uninitiated. The modern wine industry has in the main decided that tartrate STABILIZATION is preferable to consumer education.

There are four basic types of treatment used to stabilize tartrates: REFRIGERATION, ADDITIVES, ION EXCHANGE, and electrical methods.

The historic method is to cool the wine to just above its freezing point (−8 °C/17.6 °F) and hold it at that temperature for a period of around a week. The crystals fall to the bottom of the vat, and the stabilized wine is racked off and filtered. However, this is a rather drastic treatment, risking a reduction in the quality of the wine, and has been superseded by the contact process. In this method the wine is seeded with finely divided potassium bitartrate crystals that act as seed crystals. It works at a higher temperature and, with vigorous stirring, takes two hours or less, causing little damage to the wine. The risk of these methods is the higher levels of dissolved oxygen in the wine.

The oldest treatment is to add metatartaric acid prior to bottling. Unfortunately, this protection is not permanent because the metatartaric acid gradually decomposes into tartaric acid, adding to the tartaric-acid concentration, and its protection is temperature dependent: at 25 °C/77 °F it will generally work for around six months, whereas at 10 °C/50 °F it will last for 18 months. MANNOPROTEINS derived from decomposing yeast cells are entirely natural and have several useful properties in that they not only inhibit the crystallization of tartrates but also protect against PROTEIN haze in white and rosé wines and increase the foaming properties of SPARKLING WINE. The greatest advantage of mannoproteins is that their properties are long-lasting. A similar additive is carboxymethylcellulose (CMC), otherwise known as cellulose gum and chemically similar to wallpaper glue; it is used especially for white wines but is not allowed in the production of ORGANIC wines. A new additive with similar properties, potassium polyaspartate, was approved by the OIV in 2016.

Using ION EXCHANGE, the wine is passed through a column of polymerized resin where the potassium ions in the wine are exchanged for sodium ions from the resin. The resultant wine contains sodium bitartrate, which is much more soluble than potassium bitartrate. When the resin becomes saturated with potassium ions it can be regenerated by passing a solution of sodium chloride (common salt) through it, which is identical to the process of using ion exchange resins to soften hard water.

The principal electrical method is known as ELECTRODIALYSIS and is suitable only for large wineries because the equipment is expensive, but the treatment is very successful. It involves passing the wine through specially designed membranes under the influence of an electric charge where the potassium, calcium, and tartrate ions are attracted through the pores of the membrane thus reducing the concentration of the potassium bitartrate in the wine.

Tartrates are most commonly encountered in untreated wines from relatively cool regions because they have the greatest concentration of tartaric acid. In white wines, colourless, perfectly shaped crystals of potassium acid tartrate are found. In red wines, there are usually sufficient adsorbed tannins and PIGMENTED TANNINS to colour the crystals reddish brown and to ensure that they are small and irregular in shape.

Although much is made of potassium bitartrate, calcium tartrate can also cause problems. It cannot be removed by any form of refrigeration because its solubility does not decrease with temperature. It forms much smaller crystals than the potassium version, and these can be avoided only by using ion exchange or electrodialysis. D.B.

Bird, D., and Quillé, N., *Understanding Wine Technology* (4th edn, 2021).

OIV, 'International Code of Oenological Practices'. www.oiv.int/en/technical-standards-and-documents/oenological-practices/international-code-of-oenological-practices.

Tasmania, or **lutruwita** in palawa kani, the revived language of Tasmanian Aborigines, is a cool, small island-state to the south of Victoria in mainland AUSTRALIA. The country's coolest region overall, it has increasingly attracted winemaking interest, growing from 20-odd winemakers in the early 1990s to almost 200 farming 2,000 ha/4,942 acres of vines in 2022.

The island has a single GEOGRAPHICAL INDICATION but a complex geography with diverse soil types and varied levels of rainfall. There are seven unofficial but generally recognized growing areas, all concentrated at the eastern end of the island, which is far drier than the western end. **Tamar Valley** is the oldest and largest, producing 39% of Tasmania's crush in 2022. A sheltered river valley, it follows the Tamar River/kanamaluka from Relbia, just south of Launceston, north to Rowella near the coast. Average temperatures are similar to those in mainland southern VICTORIA, although the wide array of MESOCLIMATES and soils (GRAVEL, CLAY, BASALT, sandy LOAM, and LIMESTONE) supports many grape varieties, from CHARDONNAY and PINOT NOIR destined for sparkling wines to CABERNET SAUVIGNON and MERLOT for richer reds.

To the Tamar Valley's west is the small but growing **North West/Cradle Coast** region (2% of crush), and to the east is **Pipers River** (14.3%). Cool and wet thanks to the cooling influence of the Bass Strait, the marked DIURNAL TEMPERATURE RANGE, and the surrounding mountains, the area has become particularly known as a source for Chardonnay and Pinot Noir for sparkling wines.

Almost one-quarter of Tasmania's crush comes from the **Coal River Valley** on Tasmania's south coast, just east of Hobart/nipaluna. One of the warmest and driest locations in Tasmania due to the rain shadow of Mount Wellington/kunanyi, the region was pioneered by Swiss entrepreneur Peter Althaus, who established the Bordeaux-centric Domaine A (now owned by Moorilla Estate) in 1973. Long-lived, full-bodied red blends and oaked Sauvignon Blanc can be found here.

The climate is similar in **Derwent Valley**, just west of Hobart, where Moorilla Estate, Tasmania's oldest winery, began planting vines in 1958. **Huon Valley** and d'Entrecasteaux Channel, south of Hobart, are cooler locations with a capacity for FROST in spring but boast some of the highest levels of ULTRAVIOLET RADIATION in the state. Finally, the **East Coast**, a spectacularly scenic stretch of land between Bicheno and Dunalley along the coast of the Tasman Sea, is growing in importance, producing 12.8% of crush in 2022.

PINOT NOIR makes up nearly 50% of vineyard plantings, and CHARDONNAY another one-quarter, much of both destined for sparkling wine, which makes up 37.4% of all wine produced. A small amount of PINOT MEUNIER is also grown.

In still wines, white wines prevail, with aromatic white varieties such as SAUVIGNON BLANC (8.6%), PINOT GRIS (8%), and RIESLING (6.3%) following Chardonnay. Meanwhile, SYRAH, at 1.2%, has overtaken CABERNET SAUVIGNON and MERLOT to be Tasmania's third most planted red grape variety.

PHYLLOXERA has never infected Tasmania, and many vines remain UNGRAFTED, while others are grafted as a precautionary measure. Nearly half the island's vineyards are managed under VinØ (Vin Zero), a non-accredited SUSTAINABLE VITICULTURE initiative established by governing body Wine Tasmania that looks at soil health, biodiversity, environmentally responsible pest management and water usage, and the acknowledgement and respect of the aboriginal people of Tasmania/lutruwita who have long been custodians of the land. C.H.-C.

www.winetasmania.com.au
www.tacinc.com.au

taste. What we call the sense of taste is to a very great extent the sense of SMELL. See TASTING for more details. As for our own personal taste in wine, it is overall SUBJECTIVE, even if subject to our own personal SENSITIVITIES. There are no rights and wrongs in wine preferences. See also QUALITY IN WINE and PHILOSOPHY AND WINE

tastevins, or **wine tasters**, as they are known by collectors of wine antiques, are shallow, often dimpled, saucers used for TASTING by professionals (and occasional self-conscious amateurs). Because they were usually used in a cellar or on purchasing journeys where robust construction was essential, they were almost invariably made of silver. The earliest English references to tasters date from the 14th century, but only a single extant example predates 1600. British tasters mostly copy the BORDEAUX model, being 65–110 mm (2.5–4.5 in) in diameter with sloping sides and a domed base and lacking a handle. Extremely rare tasters were made of glass or porcelain, usually Worcester.

Tastevins are far more plentiful in France than elsewhere. Most have a single handle and a slightly domed base. Many are decorated with a different pattern on either side of the handle. Late-19th- and 20th-century examples are often plated. R.N.H.B.

Some BURGUNDY producers still use tastevins in their own cellars, where they can be useful to demonstrate hue and clarity even in a dim light. For actual tasting, GLASSES are more efficacious, even if less easily portable. Contemporary manufacture of tastevins is sustained by many CONFRÉRIES, most obviously the Burgundian Chevaliers du Tastevin.

Butler, R., *Great British Wine Accessories 1550–1900* (2009).

Mazenot, R., *Le Tastevin à travers les siècles* (1973).

tasting, the act of consciously assessing a wine's quality, character, or identity (see BLIND TASTING). It is certainly not synonymous with, nor necessarily contemporaneous with nor accompanied by, the act of drinking it. The ideal conditions for the act of tasting, and the organization and classification of formal wine tastings, is outlined under TASTINGS. This article is concerned with the activities and mechanisms involved in consciously receiving the sensory impressions a wine can stimulate.

How we taste

Most of what is commonly called the sense of taste is in fact the sense of SMELL, whether applied to wine or to any food or drink, since by chewing we transform our food into liquid which gives off smellable vapour. To verify this it is enough to eat or drink something with the nose pinched shut or to consider the extent to which we 'lose our appetite' when we have a head cold which blocks the nose. The human brain senses what we call flavours and aromas in the olfactory bulb, which, as Buck and Axel so elegantly demonstrated in their Nobel prize-winning work, is reached via a thousand different olfactory receptor cells, each expressing a single odorant receptor gene, these genes representing about 3% of an individual's genetic make-up. Unexpectedly, each olfactory receptor cell is sensitive to a very small group of related aromas. From the olfactory bulb these messages are sent to other parts of the brain and processed, combining them and forming a pattern. Most aromas are composed of many different molecules, each of which activates several of these olfactory receptors, making odorant patterns, so that humans are able to recognize and, particularly, memorize up to 10,000 different aromas. The olfactory bulb is reached mainly by the nostrils and to a lesser extent by a channel at the back of the mouth called the retronasal passage (which is why most healthy people can still perceive some flavour even if they do not consciously smell what they consume). The human olfactory sense is extremely acute and possibly as acute as that of most mammals. Concentrations of some compounds of one part per trillion (see Bushdid et al.) can be sensed, recognized, and remembered by the average person. A single whiff can transport us immediately to something experienced many years before.

The tasting capacity of the mouth is much more limited. In the mouth, our tactile sense can register FIZZINESS, TEMPERATURE, VISCOSITY, EXTRACT, the apparent heat generated on the palate by excessive ALCOHOL, and the sensation induced by TANNINS of drying out the insides of the cheeks.

The tongue also has certain taste receptors located in taste buds, which can sense the five 'primary tastes' of SWEETNESS, ACIDITY, BITTERNESS, saltiness, and (more recently recognized) UMAMI. There is considerable genetic variation in how many taste buds we have, with roughly one-quarter of the population considered extremely sensitive 'supertasters'. To supertasters the substance PROP (6-n-propylthiouracil) tastes extremely bitter and taste sensations in general are intensified and exaggerated. To so-called 'non-tasters', PROP is virtually tasteless, while about half of us are 'medium tasters', find PROP mildly bitter, and experience taste sensations without distorting extremes. It was thought that different parts of the tongue were particularly sensitive to one of these primary tastes, but Bartohuk et al. showed that in fact we have taste receptors for all the primary tastes in each taste bud.

With the exception of some wines matured near the sea such as MANZANILLA or some produced from vineyards with a serious SALINITY problem, very few wines taste salty, and in even fewer can umami be detected. Sweetness and acidity, on the other hand, are two of the most important measurements of a wine, although it is important to recognize that the apparent sweetness of a wine is not necessarily the same as its RESIDUAL SUGAR. High acidity can easily make a wine taste much drier than it actually is, for example.

It is clear that the mouth's tasting ability, apart from being usefully linked to the olfactory bulb by the retronasal passage, is in *measuring* the wine, assessing its dimensions of sweetness, acidity, bitterness, fizziness, viscosity, potency, and ASTRINGENCY. The mouth is capable of making an overall assessment of a wine's TEXTURE and STRUCTURE, while the nose senses what we call its flavour. Just as what is commonly called the sense of taste is really the sense of smell, so what is commonly called flavour is really AROMA or, in older wines, BOUQUET. (See FLAVOUR, however, for a proposal that the word be used to incorporate all the measurements sensed by the mouth.)

The essential character and most complex distinguishing marks of any wine are in its smell, which is made up of hundreds, probably thousands, of different FLAVOUR COMPOUNDS, present in widely varying permutations and concentrations in different wines.

What is commonly called tasting therefore involves persuading as many of these flavour compounds as possible to reach the olfactory bulb, while ensuring that contact is made between the wine and all of the inside of the mouth for the purposes of assessing a wine's dimensions and texture.

How to taste

The operation of tasting is generally divided into three stages involving sequentially the eye, the nose, and the mouth (although, as outlined above, this is not the same as the simple sequential application of the senses of sight, smell, and taste).

Eye The job of the eye in wine tasting is mainly to assess clarity and colour, as well as to monitor the presence of CARBON DIOXIDE and ALCOHOL (the former indicated by bubbles, the latter possibly by any TEARS of the wine that may form on the inside of the glass when it is rotated).

The clarity of a wine is an indication, hardly surprisingly, of the extent to which CLARIFICATION has been carried out and also of the wine's condition. Many wine FAULTS result in a haze of some sort. In the late 1990s, anti-FILTRATION sentiment was so strong in California that some highly priced Chardonnays looked positively cloudy, a common characteristic in many NATURAL WINES. A wine with particles floating in it, however, may simply be an innocent casualty of poor SERVING technique in which a wine has not been properly separated from its entirely harmless SEDIMENT. Experienced tasters can sometimes discern quality simply by looking at a wine's luminescent clarity and subtle range of hues.

The colour of a wine, both its intensity and its hue, is one of the potentially most valuable clues to any BLIND TASTER. Intensity of colour is best judged by looking straight through a glass of wine from directly above (preferably against a plain white background). Different grape varieties tend to make deeper or lighter coloured wines (Cabernet Sauvignon, Syrah, Tannat, Malbec, and TEINTURIER varieties make particularly deep red wines; Gewürztraminer and Pinot Gris are examples of varieties which make particularly deep white wines, because the grape skins are deep pink). A deep colour also indicates youth, long MACERATION (possibly over-EXTRACTION), and thick-skinned grapes in a red wine; sometimes age, SKIN-FERMENTATION, some OXIDATION, and BARREL AGEING, although not if preceded by BARREL FERMENTATION, in white wines.

The actual hue can also provide clues and can be best assessed by tilting the glass away at an angle so that the different shadings of colour at the rim can be seen, again preferably against a plain white background. A bluish tinge in a red wine indicates youth, while orange/yellow indicates AGE (or OXIDATION). Very pale green in a white wine may indicate Riesling, while a pink tinge suggests that the wine was made from pink-skinned grapes such as Gewürztraminer and Pinot Gris. For more information, see COLOUR.

This stage in tasting for any purpose other than identification is usually very short and, if tasters are SCORING various aspects of a wine, many wines gain maximum points for appearance.

Nose As demonstrated above, this is the single most important stage in wine tasting. The trick is to persuade as many flavour compounds as possible to vaporize and come into contact with the olfactory bulb (although what we smell is in fact an AZEOTROPIC mixture of many, rather than isolated individual, flavour compounds). It is then necessary, of course, to be in a suitable frame of mind to interpret the messages received by the olfactory bulb, which is why the act of tasting requires concentration.

The simplest way to maximize the evaporation of a wine's volatile elements is by the judicious use of TEMPERATURE and agitation. Higher temperatures encourage any sort of evaporation, so ideal tasting temperatures tend to be slightly higher than ideal SERVING temperatures. It is unwise to taste wines so hot that the alcohol starts to evaporate at such a rate that it dominates the flavour, however, so an ideal tasting temperature for wines, red or white, is somewhere between 15 and 20 °C/59–68 °F. At these relatively elevated temperatures, faults as well as attributes should be perfectly apparent. What is lost is the refreshment factor, but then the point of tasting rather than drinking is analysis rather than pleasure. Sparkling wines tend to be tasted slightly cooler to retain the carbon dioxide.

Many professional tasters first smell, or 'nose', a wine without agitating it to see how powerful its aroma is without this encouragement, then deliberately increase the number of molecules liberated by a wine by agitating the wine and increasing its surface area, preferably rotating it in a bowl-shaped glass with a stem (see GLASSES) so that no wine is lost.

As soon as the wine has been agitated, the aroma collects in the bowl of the partly filled glass above the wine and can be transmitted to the olfactory bulb up the nostrils with one thoughtful inhalation.

The taster monitors first whether the wine smells fresh and clean or whether any off-odours indicate the presence of a wine FAULT. The next basic measurement might well be of the intensity of the aroma (if it is an attractive smell, then intensity is preferable). And then comes the complex part of the operation, which is much more difficult to describe: the sensation and attempt at description of the individual components that make up the aroma, or 'bouquet' as it is sometimes called if it has taken on the complexities associated with AGEING. For a discussion of this, see TASTING TERMS.

Quite apart from those components which result from the grapes themselves, the aroma can provide certain overall hints about viticulture and winemaking techniques. Leaf aldehydes suggest that the grapes were less than fully ripe. Oak ageing may be betrayed by a certain amount of OAK FLAVOUR; scents of spices and toast can be the result of the degree of TOAST which the barrels received. Tropical fruit aromas suggest that the fermentation was particularly long and cool. DIACETYL, which can smell like butter and other dairy products, is a particularly obvious sign of MALOLACTIC CONVERSION. The subject is too complex for more than the most cursory treatment here, but the books cited below provide more detail.

As a wine undergoes gentle AERATION in the glass, it may well begin to give off other compounds with time. World-famous taster Michael BROADBENT, for example, kept a series of records of how a single glass of wine tasted, marked according to how long after pouring each note was made. Most good wines seem to get better with time and then to start to deteriorate. In blind tasting, however, a taster's first impressions are usually the most accurate, and insights are rarely provided by constant repetition of the 'nosing' process.

Mouth In terms of aroma—'flavour' in its narrow sense—the mouth, or palate as it is sometimes called, usually merely confirms the impressions already apparent to the nose when some vapour escapes the mouth and reaches the olfactory bulb via the retronasal passage. Many tasters take in a certain amount of air over their mouthful of wine to encourage this process (and are often mocked for the accompanying noise).

The main function of the mouth in the tasting process is to assess the texture and measure the dimensions rather than the character of a wine by assessing sweetness, acidity, bitterness, saltiness, umami if any, viscosity, and tannin level. Monitoring the combination of sweetness, viscosity, and any sensation of 'heat' gives a good indication of the likely alcohol content of any individual wine, ETHANOL tending to leave a burning sensation in the mouth. The insides of the mouth may also register the TEXTURE, analysing the impact of the TANNINS. For this reason, it is a good idea to rinse the mouth thoroughly with wine so that all possible touch receptors may come into contact with it—another reason why wine tasting looks both ridiculous and disgusting to outsiders.

After rinsing a wine around their mouths and noting the impressions given by the vapour rising up the retronasal passage, most professional tasters then demonstrate their devotion to duty rather than alcohol by SPITTING. The taster then notes how LONG the impressions given by the wine seem to persist after spitting or swallowing.

Conclusions Perhaps the most important stage, however, is a fourth stage of analysis, in which all previous impressions are evaluated. This includes most particularly considering whether the measurements taken by the mouth suggest that the wine is in BALANCE and monitoring the LENGTH of the aftertaste, these last two factors being important indicators of quality. A fine wine should continue to make favourable sensory impressions throughout the entire tasting process.

Experience is necessary to judge balance. A significant, if decreasing, proportion of young red wines designed for long-term evolution, for example, are not by any objective criterion in balance. Their tannins may still be very marked and make the wine an unpleasantly astringent drink, even if they suggest that the wine will keep well. (Making red wines with less obvious tannins so that they can be both aged and drunk in their youth has been one of the prime recent preoccupations of winemakers.) Similarly, the acidity in a young German wine may be aggressively dominant, but experience shows that it is essential to preserve a top-quality Riesling, for example, for the ten or 20 years' bottle ageing it may deserve.

Professional tasting usually involves making TASTING NOTES, often under the four headings noted above. It may also involve SCORING by allotting NUMBERS to different elements according to a carefully predetermined scale, especially if wine JUDGING is involved. Tasting notes can be set out in many different ways, and experienced tasters tend to devise their own abbreviations and symbols.

Tasting for pleasure, which is what most wine drinkers do every time they open a bottle, requires nothing more complicated than a moment's concentration and an open mind.

Factors affecting taste

We cannot know what other tasters experience, for the tasting mechanism is far from public. Furthermore, individuals vary in their SENSITIVITY to different compounds and dimensions of wine. But even as individuals, the way our brains process information sent from sensory receptors changes all the time so that the same wine will have a different effect on us depending on the state of our PALATES. The most obvious example of this is how different something tastes before and just after we have had a mouthful of red-hot chilli or brushed our teeth with a mint toothpaste. But even something as apparently innocuous as a particularly hot drink or salty solution can affect the way we taste. An acid wine will seem less acid if tasted immediately after a very acid one, which is why the ORDER of serving and tasting is crucial but extremely difficult to get right until every wine has been tasted. See also FOOD-AND-WINE MATCHING.

Our overall physical well-being affects how we taste. If we are run down, we tend to produce less saliva and, because saliva contains compounds which have a buffering effect on many aspects of taste, both foods and drinks can taste quite different (this is quite apart from the fact that good HEALTH is needed to tackle a succession of alcoholic liquids).

How we taste can be quite markedly affected by our mood and of course by the physical environment in which we taste (see TASTINGS). Tasting in a very humid atmosphere is markedly more difficult than when the atmospheric pressure is high, flavour compounds are readily volatilized, and taste impressions seem crystal clear. J.R. & Hg.H.

Bartoshuk, L. M., et al., 'The biological basis of food perception and acceptance', *Food Quality and Preference*, 4/1–2 (1993), 21–32.
Broadbent, M., *Wine Tasting* (9th edn, 2003).
Buck, L., and Axel, R., 'A novel multigene family may encode odorant receptors: a molecular basis for odor recognition', *Cell*, 65/1 (1991), 175–87.
Bushdid, C., et al., 'Humans can discriminate more than 1 trillion olfactory stimuli', *Science*, 343 (2014), 1370–2.
Peynaud, É., *Le Goût du Vin* (1983), translated by M. Schuster as *The Taste of Wine* (2nd edn, 1996).
Robinson, J., *How to Taste (Wine)* (rev. edn, 2008).
Schuster, M., *Essential Winetasting* (2000).

tasting notes are the usual record of professional or serious wine TASTINGS. They are conventionally divided into notes (sometimes together with SCORES or NUMBERS) for what is sensed by the eye, the nose, and the mouth, together with overall conclusions (see TASTING). The thoughtful organizer of a tasting prepares a **tasting sheet** which provides as a minimum a list of complete names of all the wines served, in the relevant ORDER of serving, with sufficient space to write full tasting notes. Sometimes these are carefully divided into sections—Appearance, Aroma/Bouquet, Taste, and Conclusions, for example—but this is an optional extra as tasters vary according to how much they want to write on each aspect. Most experienced tasters develop their own shorthand and habits, both good and bad. The number of words in a personal average tasting note can vary between one and 100 or more, in the case of a particularly complex wine which evolves in the glass. Tasting notes, especially of wines worth AGEING, are all the more valuable if they are dated. Most tasting notes remain of personal use only, but the late Michael BROADBENT produced two important books based entirely on his, and the majority of Robert PARKER's output was made up of his. Comparison of the two authors provides a reasonable guide to the different styles of British and American tasting notes respectively. Many tasting notes contain a long list of flavours (subject to considerable SUBJECTIVITY and variation in SENSITIVITY), but assessment of a wine's vital statistics—SWEETNESS, ACIDITY, TANNINS, and ALCOHOLIC STRENGTH, as well as MATURITY—is also useful.

The advent of sophisticated INFORMATION TECHNOLOGY has introduced the possibility of entering tasting notes directly into a database, and many wine websites are made up principally of tasting notes, although any nearby liquid poses a threat to a keyboard (which can become unpleasantly sticky during a tasting of sweet wines). This method of record-keeping should, in theory at least, lessen the usual problem of declining legibility of tasting notes towards the end of a tasting.

tasting-notes language. The language we use to write or speak about wine may vary according to our intended audience—is the aim to sell to a potential customer, to inform an enthusiast, or to display academic rigour in an exam or a BLIND-TASTING competition? The language of wine can be descriptive (what is this wine like?) or evaluative (how good a wine is this?).

Using language to convey sense impressions, as we do when we describe a wine's properties, is inherently problematic. The brain receives so many data through the senses of smell, taste, vision, and touch that it has to select in order to prevent it from being overwhelmed. Thus the brain does not measure the world around us but models it by constant filtering (known as higher-order processing), and there is no one-to-one correspondence between sense data and conscious perception. Hence a TASTING NOTE cannot be an exact representation of a wine: it conveys the taster's interaction with the wine.

A further problem is that an individual's experience shapes their later perceptions, giving people not only different prototypes of sense impressions (i.e. different notions of what a typical X should be) but also different grids with which to make sense of the raw data received by the brain: a taster who has never encountered a gooseberry cannot detect the smell of gooseberries in a wine. In other words, what is selected in the brain's higher-order processing is determined by a taster's personal history and culture and, if he or she is part of a tasting-group, for example, other tasters' comments.

Finally, due to physiological and genetic factors, individuals vary in their perceptual acuity, especially in their sensitivity to the thousands of possible AROMAS. It follows that no two people will describe a wine in identical terms. Ann C. Noble's AROMA WHEEL, for example, is an excellent teaching aid in that it can be used to broaden tasters' vocabularies and sharpen their perceptions, but its range of aromas can be neither exhaustive nor definitive.

This is not to say that everything we say about a wine is subjective: some components of wine, such as ACIDITY, RESIDUAL SUGAR, TANNIN level, and ALCOHOLIC STRENGTH, are measurable, so it is possible for a taster to be right or wrong about these. However, human tasters are not calibrated scientific instruments, and perception of one component may influence that of another: high acidity can make residual sugar less noticeable, and, conversely, low acidity can make a sweet wine appear cloying. Hence a good tasting note will not just list observations about appearance, NOSE, PALATE, and FINISH but must attempt a holistic description by considering how a wine's components balance each other. BALANCE and LENGTH being criteria for quality assessment, a holistic tasting note must inevitably be evaluative as well as descriptive.

Although tasters who resort to florid use of metaphor and simile are often mocked as pretentious, we cannot analyse a wine without using figurative language. Some descriptive terms are literal—adjectives denoting colour, for instance—but to describe the TEXTURE of a wine a taster will need figurative language such as 'silky', 'grainy', or 'chewy'. Some descriptions of the nose will be literal because they are grounded in fact; others are analogies. Yet a taster who describes a Gewürztraminer as smelling of roses without knowing that one of the variety's constituents is damascenone (rose oil) would regard their choice of language as figurative. Dullness is not a virtue: a dry list of the component parts of a wine may fail to communicate the beauty and complexity of a high-grade wine; on the other hand, excessive inventiveness is liable to be counterproductive. A tasting note should be not only precise but also comprehensible, and this means that competent tasters must draw, to a greater or lesser extent, on a shared vocabulary which needs to be taught.

An agreed vocabulary, such as the systematic approach that is mandatory for the WSET diploma, represents a learnt culture of wine. The discipline of putting sense impressions into words is indispensable if the taster is to analyse and remember a wine and, later, to recognize and identify examples of the same wine style. Competence develops with experience, and this means knowing not only what to look for but also how to describe it.

See also LANGUAGE OF WINE and PHILOSOPHY AND WINE. H.M.W.

Allhoff, F. (ed.), *Wine and Philosophy: A Symposium on Thinking and Drinking* (2007).
Lehrer, A., *Wine and Conversation* (2nd edn, 2009).
Smith, B. C. (ed.), *Questions of Taste: The Philosophy of Wine* (2007).
Todd, C., *The Philosophy of Wine: A Case of Truth, Beauty and Intoxication* (2010).

tastings, events at which wines are tasted. Informal tastings take place every time a bottle of wine is opened by a wine enthusiast. More formal ones take place when wine producers

T

show their wines to potential buyers or commentators. The most common sort of formal tasting is one held for the purposes of wine assessment, typically by wine MERCHANTS keen to sell their wares, sometimes by a generic body keen to promote wines of a particular style or provenance. Formal tastings are also held by wine clubs and societies for less commercial purposes: EDUCATION or simple pleasure perhaps.

A **horizontal tasting** is one in which a number of different wines of the same VINTAGE are compared, while a **vertical tasting** is a comparison of different vintages of the same wine, most commonly the same Bordeaux CHÂTEAU. George SAINTSBURY is credited with the first recorded use of these expressions.

A BLIND TASTING is one whose purpose is that the taster assesses unknown wines as objectively as possible, in some contexts also identifying them as closely as possible.

A **comparative tasting** is one in which various different examples of the same sort or style of wine—CLASSED GROWTHS of the same vintage, or wines from the same appellation, or a single VARIETAL, for example—are tasted and compared. Such tastings form the basis of much modern WINE WRITING and should be conducted blind for a true, unprejudiced assessment.

Equipment

The only essential equipment for a wine tasting, apart from the wine, is suitable GLASSES and, if bottles are stoppered with a cork, a CORKSCREW, but it is almost impossible to hold a tasting without a substantial area of flat surface on which to put bottles and glasses safely, usually in the form of a table to which there is good access. The next most useful objects are undoubtedly spittoons (see SPITTING) and something in which to pour away LEFTOVER WINE from a tasting sample (bottles plus funnels are customary, although spittoons can also be used for this purpose). The thoughtful organizer ensures that there is some plain white surface against which to hold a glass of wine (see TASTING). This typically involves lining up bottles on a table with a white surface (to see a wine's colour and clarity most easily) or a covering such as a tablecloth or sheet. A truly assiduous host provides tasters with a tasting sheet on which is a full and accurate list of wines to be tasted, in the correct order, with appropriate space for tasting notes. Water for rinsing of glasses and palates and some neutral-tasting food for 'cleaning the palate' can be helpful too. Cheese is usually too strong (see FOOD-AND-WINE MATCHING); bread or dry, savoury crackers are generally preferred by professionals.

Conditions

Ideal conditions include a strong natural light, ambient temperature between 15 and 18 °C/59–64 °F, and an absence of any extraneous smells. (It is clear therefore that tasting in most cellars, even those of the finest winemakers, is far from ideal.) In practice, a tasting that involves many people inevitably generates its own heat and smell, so it is wise to begin at a lower ambient temperature and not to be too exercised about a whiff of aftershave or polish, which is soon absorbed into the ambient atmosphere.

Organization

One glass per taster usually suffices, and between one-fifteenth and one-twentieth of a bottle is enough for a decent tasting sample. Ensuring that tasters are served rather than serving themselves can limit wine consumption.

The number of different wines suitable to be shown at a single tasting is a controversial topic. Some tasters claim to be able to assess up to 200 wines in a day at JUDGING sessions such as the Australian wine SHOWS, while the most experienced professionals in CHAMPAGNE deliberately limit themselves to fewer than a dozen wines at a time. A novice taster should probably start with no more than four wines, while a professional might feel a tasting which offered only 15 was hardly worth the detour.

What is clear is that it is difficult to *enjoy* more than a dozen wines at a time and that the ORDER in which any selection is served is vital to the impression they give.

tasting terms

tasting terms, the myriad and oft-mocked words used by tasters in an often vain attempt to describe sensory impressions received during TASTING.

The difference between a taster and a social drinker is this need to describe, to attempt the difficult task of applying words to individual, invisible sensations, particularly the aromas sensed by the OLFACTORY BULB.

The sense of smell is an exceptionally private one, for which there is no common public domain which can be codified. The best we can do is describe aromas by other aromas of which they remind us. Hence 'blackcurrant' or CASSIS, frequently for Cabernet Sauvignon; 'strawberry' or 'raspberry' perhaps for Pinot Noir; 'vanilla' for OAK; and so on. Science is starting to correlate the FLAVOUR COMPOUNDS found in different GRAPE VARIETIES (if not yet different TERROIRS) with those found in the objects used as taste descriptors.

There is as yet no official wine-tasting LANGUAGE, or even TASTING-NOTES LANGUAGE, although there have been many valiant attempts at establishing one and, particularly as research on flavour compounds and FLAVOUR PRECURSORS continues apace, this is becoming an increasingly attainable goal. The Scottish doctor Alexander HENDERSON was one of the first to attempt it in the English language in *The History of Ancient and Modern Wines* in 1824, CHAPTAL having applied about 60 French terms in his *L'Art de faire le vin* in 1807. These early tasting vocabularies tended to concentrate on the dimensions of a wine rather than its flavour or aroma, using words such as 'acidic', 'sweet', 'bitter', and 'light'.

Terms used for mouth sensations

The most straightforward of these 'dimensional terms', which describe what is sensed in the mouth (and the even more public and obvious visual impressions), are still in use today; since for the most part they describe what is measurable, they are useful, indisputable, and not affected by SUBJECTIVITY or SENSITIVITY. Inevitably, some jargon has evolved, of which the following are the most obvious examples.

Body—a noun; see BODY.
Big—high in alcohol.
Concentrated—having intense (though possibly subtle) flavours.
Crisp—attractively high in ACIDITY.
Fat—full-bodied and viscous.
Finish—a noun for aftertaste; see FINISH.
Flabby—lacking in ACIDITY.
Full—of BODY.
Green—too acid, made of unripe fruit; see GREEN.
Hard—too much TANNIN and too little fruit.
Heavy—too alcoholic; too much EXTRACT.
Hot—too alcoholic.
Light—agreeably light in BODY.
Long—impressively persistent aftertaste; see LONG.
Short—opposite of LONG.
Smooth—imprecise term for pleasing TEXTURE.
Soft—low in tannins.
Well balanced—having good BALANCE.

Terms used for aroma

It is in their attempts to find 'character terms' to apply to these more subtle, more private olfactory sensations that wine tasters can seem so foolish.

Some 'idioterms' are just plain fanciful, descriptions obviously applied in sheer desperation at the apparent impossibility of the task. In this category come the 'fading but well-mannered old lady', and who can forget James Thurber's 'naive domestic burgundy but I think you'll be amused by its presumption'? A more recent example is 'sexy', an increasingly common, but delightfully imprecise, tasting term.

Other sorts of terms, 'simile terms', are applied in a serious attempt to recall palpable objects which give rise to similar aromas: the fruits, flowers, vegetable, and mineral descriptors, for example.

Particularly common terms used to describe aroma, or flavour, include:

Buttery—see DIACETYL.
Fruity—intense impact of fruit flavours, sometimes a euphemism for 'slightly sweet'.
Grapey—mixture of intensely aromatic and the aromas associated with MUSCAT grapes.
Oaky—pejorative term for a wine excessively marked by OAK.
Toasty—see TOAST.

There are also 'derivative terms', which must once have been coined by an authority and continue to be widely used even though they are literally inaccurate. So many wine tasters have been taught to describe the powerful and characteristic smell of GEWÜRZTRAMINER as 'spicy', for example (perhaps because *Gewürz* is German for 'spice'), that this is the most common tasting term for the aroma, even though it does not smell like any particular spice at all (much more like lychees or rose petals, in fact).

It will be of the 'simile terms' that a common tasting vocabulary is finally composed—although there is the obstacle of many different languages, cultures, and national conventions to be overcome first. Max Leglise, a researcher in Burgundy, has attempted to concoct essences of each of his approved terms so that there is an objective standard for them. (Unfortunately, synthetic flavourings deteriorate.) Professor Ann C. Noble at DAVIS, clearly frustrated by the looseness with which tasting terms are applied, has done sterling work with her AROMA WHEEL. This corresponds sufficiently closely with the tasting terms suggested by Professor Émile PEYNAUD, Bordeaux's tasting guru, as to give us all hope that an international tasting language that is no more ambiguous than any other will one day be available to the world's wine tasters.

Brochet and DUBOURDIEU established in 2001 that each expert taster has his or her own set of tasting terms which typically correspond to a personal set of prototypes, 'ideal' wines, rather than detailed analytical description. In a separate study involving white wines coloured red, they also demonstrated that many tasting terms are colour-specific and that if tasters see red wine they will assign tasting terms associated with objects of that colour.

See also AROMA WHEEL and LANGUAGE OF WINE.

Broadbent, M., *Wine Tasting* (9th edn, 2003).
Brochet, F., and Dubourdieu, D., 'Wine descriptive language supports cognitive specificity of chemical senses', *Brain and Language*, 77/2 (2001), 187–96.
Morrot, G., et al., 'The color of odors', *Brain and Language*, 79/2 (2001), 309–20.
Peynaud, É., *Le Goût du Vin* (1983), translated by M. Schuster as *The Taste of Wine* (2nd edn, 1996).

Taurasi, full-bodied reds from CAMPANIA produced from the distinctive AGLIANICO grape grown on 1,153 ha/2,849 acres of vineyards in a zone north-east of the city of Avellino. Taurasi is regularly referred to as 'the BAROLO of the south' due to its high levels of ACIDITY and TANNINS which demand AGEING. DOCG regulations require three years of ageing, one of which must be in wood; RISERVA bottlings must be aged for four years.

By 2020 there were 60 producers of Taurasi—up from just ten in the 1980s—and more than 200 grape-growers. Mastroberardino was until the early 1990s the only label on the export market, absorbing most of the grapes produced by farmers. This dynamic changed when grape-growers began bottling their own produce with the help of consulting OENOLOGISTS. The downside of this is that many wines tend to taste similar, but several producers are experimenting with ORGANIC VITICULTURE, AMBIENT YEAST fermentations, and ageing in large CASKS rather than BARRIQUES, resulting in muscular, concentrated, and complex wines which develop notes of red berries, tobacco, tamarind, and iron with age.

The Taurasi DOCG comprises 17 villages on both sides of the river Calore in the province of Irpinia. The valley can be divided roughly into four sections:

The north-west section is the lowest part, at 300 m/984 ft in elevation, and the warmest, with full southern ASPECT and ALLUVIAL and CALCAREOUS clay soils, producing earlier-drinking Taurasi reds.

The north-east section is higher, with CLAY and calcareous soils, and gives more compact, lower-alcohol wines.

The south-east section, with vineyards on the slopes of the Picentini Mountains rising well over 700 m, includes diverse soil types, including calcareous clay, TUFF, SANDSTONE, and VOLCANIC soils. Here the grapes ripen slowly and retain high levels of acidity, creating wines that require extensive ageing.

The south-west part, which partially overlaps the Fiano di Avellino DOC (see CAMPANIA), produces a wide range of styles from mainly calcareous clay and sandstone soils.

In the absence of academic research into Taurasi's geology and terroir, Feudi di San Gregorio has been mapping the region in detail while producing a range of wines specific to different parts of the region, resulting in a range of publications which are bound to become fundamental for the study and recognition of the various Taurasi styles. W.S.

De Cristofaro, P., *Feudistudi: Irpinia's Vineyards and Wines Almanac 2021/2022* (2022).
www.campaniastories.com

Tautavel, communal appellation of Côtes du ROUSSILLON-Villages which applies to the relatively low-ELEVATION clay-LIMESTONE vineyards of the communes Tautavel and Vingrau. The opulent reds are not unlike nearby FITOU. Syrah and Mourvèdre must account for 30% of the blend, with Grenache Noir and/or Lladoner Pelut at least 20%, and there should be no more than 60% Carignan. R.E.G.

Tavel is one of France's few appellations to produce exclusively rosé wine. Situated on the west bank of the RHÔNE to the south of LIRAC, it was one of the first six *appellations d'origine contrôlées* (see AOC) to be established in France in 1936. Its wines have fallen out of fashion in recent years due to their dark hue, which is stipulated in the appellation rules. Soils are mixed, with outcrops of SAND and a bed of the round stones called *galets roulés* towards the eastern part of the appellation nearest the river, while the Malaven Valley in the western part is littered with white LIMESTONE scree known locally as *lauses*. Wines must be a blend of Grenache with other permitted varieties, of which Cinsaut is particularly notable, making up nearly 20% of plantings. Once picked, grapes are cold-macerated (see MACERATION) for 12–48 hours before PRESSING. The wine is always dry and can be unusually long-lived for a rosé, up to ten years for top examples from estates such as Ch d'Aqueria and Domaine de la Mordorée. Tavel is also home to Eric Pfifferling of Domaine l'Anglore, whose wines are inspiring a renaissance of Tavel wines. M.C.W.

Tavira, fishing port and easternmost DOC in the ALGARVE in southern Portugal.

Távora-Varosa, DOP named after two Douro tributaries immediately south of the DOURO in central-northern Portugal. The surrounding mountains insulate the region from humid Atlantic westerlies and harsh continental influence from the east. With GRANITIC soils and a TEMPERATE climate, the mainstay of production is sparkling wines—the region was Portugal's first to attain classification for *espumante* (TRADITIONAL METHOD) sparkling wines in 1989 (which are made from Portuguese and French varieties). S.A.

tawny, style of FORTIFIED WINES usually associated with extended CASK AGEING. See PORT, for example.

taxation. Wine has attracted the attention of the taxman since ancient times. Its production, sale, and distribution have been so closely regulated by the authorities for one simple reason, whatever their attitude to alcohol: revenue. The civilizations of the ancient Middle East (see ancient EGYPT and MESOPOTAMIA) were the first to recognize this useful attribute. It was carefully regulated in parts of ancient GREECE, but it was the Romans who, in this as in many other aspects of wine history, helped realize its potential.

In ancient ROME tax was paid from the moment the grape appeared on the vine (Roman vine-growers paid a vineyard tax calculated on the quality of the land) to when it was consumed. It was paid either in kind or in cash and represented a huge proportion of state income. Some areas in the empire, CALABRIA, for example, paid its entire tax to Rome in wine, which was then sold or distributed free to the urban masses.

Medieval kings found wine taxation fabulously lucrative. During England's occupation of western France, for example, the crown benefited doubly by receiving DUTIES paid on wine exported from BORDEAUX and then again on the same wine as customs when it entered London. During the early part of the 14th century, when this trade was at its peak, wine duties collected in Bordeaux surpassed the king's total tax revenue in England.

Not surprisingly, taxes on wine have been perceived as a fast, easy way of raising cash, and the state has shown no scruples in doubling or tripling them at times of emergency—often to pay for wars such as the HUNDRED YEARS WAR, the English Civil War, and the Napoleonic Wars.

Although they may complain, in certain circumstances wine merchants have been happy to pay tax because it legitimizes their business. Wine merchants within the Islamic empire of the caliphs (usually Jewish or Christians) viewed their payments as a kind of insurance policy; the state would not outlaw their activities, despite the Qur'ānic ban on alcohol, because the income was so useful (see ISLAM).

Wine taxation has uses beyond mere revenue. Different levels can be used to reward or punish trading partners. For example, throughout the 18th century, French wines attracted twice as much DUTY as Portuguese wines (see METHUEN TREATY). Not surprisingly, trade in French wines suffered and port became the staple English wine (see WAR).

Differential taxation has also been used to manipulate consumer tastes for reasons of health or morality. Gladstone's Act of 1860 reduced the duty on light, less alcoholic wines in an attempt to switch the British palate away from the heavy, FORTIFIED WINES and spirits that earlier taxation had favoured.

Taxation has at times had indirect consequences. During the 18th century, when duties were high and complicated (French wines were subject to 15 separate duties), ADULTERATION AND FRAUD and smuggling increased in England. Grievances against excessive taxation of wines entering Paris have been recognized as one of the sparks that lit the fire of revolution in 1789.

It was inevitable that, as soon as wine was taxed, certain parties should be exempt. Traditionally these have included the crown, the Church, and sections of the nobility; such exemptions go back at least as far as ancient EGYPT. This privilege has been extended in modern times (so far as customs duties go) to travellers via the system of duty-free allowances.

See also TARIFFS. H.B.

Briggs, A., *Wine for Sale: Victoria Wine and the Liquor Trade 1860–1984* (1985).

Francis, A. D., *The Wine Trade* (1972).

Hyams, E., *Dionysus: A Social History of the Wine Vine* (2nd edn, 1987).

Taylor's, important independent PORT shipper and a key part of the FLADGATE PARTNERSHIP. The original firm of port shippers was established in 1692 by Job Bearsley, and his son Bartholomew bought Casa dos Alambiques at Salgueiral near Régua, the first known British port shipper's property in the DOURO Valley. Between then and 1844 there were no fewer than 21 name changes. However, with the arrival of Joseph Taylor in 1816, John (later Baron) Fladgate in 1837, and Morgan Yeatman in 1844, the company assumed the name **Taylor, Fladgate & Yeatman**, or Taylor's for short. See the FLADGATE PARTNERSHIP for more details.

Foulkes, C. (ed.), *A Celebration of Taylor's Port* (1992).

Tazzelenghe, relatively obscure 'tongue-cutting' red grape of Italy's Colli Orientali in FRIULI.

TBA, understandably common abbreviation for TROCKENBEERENAUSLESE. Also for **2,4,6-tribromoanisole**, a musty- or dusty-smelling compound which may affect wine produced in a contaminated winery. The cause so far identified is the microbial degradation by fungi in the winery of tribromophenol (TBP) used in wood preservatives or as a flame retardant in paints and plastics. It is therefore only indirectly related to cork, which can act as a 'carrier' of the taint. The perception threshold in red and white wines is approximately 3–4 ng/l, down to 2 ng/l in sparkling wine. Further research is needed to assess the frequency of this fault. It has not so far been possible to distinguish TBA from TCA by tasting. J.H. & A.L.W.

T-budding, a BUDDING method used extensively in woody horticultural plants, including the grapevine, normally for field GRAFTING on to a ROOTSTOCK. The method entails making a T-shaped cut in the bark of the rootstock, when the bark is slipping, then lifting back the flaps to permit insertion of a shield-shaped piece cut from the SCION with a bud on it. After insertion, the bud is wrapped tightly with budding tape to ensure close contact of the tissues and high humidity around the cuts. T-budding can be done when the bark of the stock lifts freely, during two to three months over midsummer. Scion buds may be taken from stored winter cuttings or green current shoots. As with CHIP BUDDING, T-budding may be used for TOP GRAFTING. B.G.C.

TCA, or **2,4,6-trichloroanisole**, is a potent TAINT compound associated with musty odours and flavours in a range of food and beverages. It is the principal unpleasant-smelling compound most commonly considered responsible for CORK TAINT and is therefore generally encountered by consumers only when a specific cork-sealed bottle is contaminated. The formation of TCA is described under HALOANISOLES.

TCA is extremely potent, with an aroma threshold in wine of 2–5 ng/l in red and white wines but only 1–1.5 ng/l in sparkling wine because the CARBON DIOXIDE volatilizes taint compounds. Some winemakers now demand TCA testing of all barrels they purchase, as any wood or oak product can and is occasionally contaminated, and winery designers now eschew wood in production areas. See CORK for cork producers' strategies to reduce or eliminate TCA. J.E.H. & A.L.W.

Tchelistcheff, André (1901–94), consultant oenologist and founding father of the modern California wine industry. Tchelistcheff was born in Moscow, the sickly son of a Russian professor of law. After a brush with death in the army, he trained as an engineer-agronomist in Czechoslovakia then, at the age of 36, decided to study VITICULTURE and OENOLOGY in more detail, in Paris. While working on a farm near Versailles, he became a graduate assistant to the director of the department of viticulture at the National Institute of Agronomy as well as taking a course in wine microbiology at the Institut PASTEUR. An obviously talented student who combined intellectual rigour with a philosophical bent, he worked briefly at MOËT & CHANDON and had already been offered jobs in Chile and China before being introduced to his future employer. Georges de Latour was a Frenchman who had established himself as a highly successful businessman and owner of Beaulieu Vineyard in the Napa Valley, but he was anxious to import a French-trained winemaker for the post-PROHIBITION era.

During his 35-year career at Beaulieu, Tchelistcheff introduced the principles of winery HYGIENE as well as pioneering TEMPERATURE-CONTROLLED fermentation, mastery of MALOLACTIC CONVERSION, and FROST DAMAGE prevention techniques such as the orchard heaters and WIND MACHINES which dominated the Napa Valley for so long. He also made considerable progress in the prevention of various VINE DISEASES and established a reputation as both wine and vineyard CONSULTANT.

From his first years in California, Tchelistcheff established an identity independent of Beaulieu, with his own small laboratory in St Helena advising other Napa and Sonoma wineries and training a younger generation of winemakers such as the young MONDAVI brothers. He was a consultant to Buena Vista winery, for example (see HARASZTHY), from 1948, and in 1967 he began a long association with Ch Ste Michelle in WASHINGTON State. He was also one of the first to recognize the viticultural potential of the CARNEROS district of northern California. Although he retired from Beaulieu in 1973, four years after it was sold to the Heublein corporation, he continued to be an active consultant to a host of California wineries as well as to Ornellaia of BOLGHERI in Italy (where his son Dimitri subsequently advised). In 1991, however, he was wooed back to Beaulieu by the multinational corporation which by then owned it.

Tchelistcheff was a charter member of the American Society of Enologists and was made a Chevalier de l'Ordre du Mérite Agricole by the French government in 1954, being promoted to Officier in 1979. Tchelistcheff was unique in the wine world for the geographical breadth and historical depth of his singularly acute views on the contemporary wine scene.

TCP. See HALOANISOLES.

TDN, the FLAVOUR COMPOUND norisoprenoid hydrocarbon 1,1,6-trimethyl-1,2-dihydronaphthalene found particularly in RIESLING. TDN formation responds to fruit MICROCLIMATE and is increased by high temperatures and solar radiation. Low-PH wines seem to be more prone to TDN formation, which is also affected by YEAST strain and by the choice of Riesling CLONE and ROOTSTOCKS. At or just above the detection threshold, it adds to the complexity of a bottle-aged wine but at relatively high concentrations, particularly in wines that have been in bottle for two or more years, and in excess TDN can impart an undesirably pronounced kerosene/petrol-like flavour. H.S.

Ziegler, M., et al., 'Impact of rootstock, clonal selection, and berry size of *Vitis vinifera* sp. Riesling on the formation of TDN, vitispiranes, and other volatile compounds', *Journal of Agricultural and Food Chemistry*, 68/12 (2020), 3834–49.

tears (to rhyme with 'ears'), term used to describe the behaviour of the liquid climbing and falling in a glass of relatively strong wine. The wine wets the inside of a clean glass and climbs up a few millimetres or even centimetres. At the upper edge of the thin layer on the inside wall, patches of the film thicken, become more drop-like, and eventually roll back down the inside wall to the liquid surface. These traces of what look like particularly viscous droplets are also sometimes called 'legs' and may give some indication of a wine's ALCOHOLIC STRENGTH. (But note that some of the finest German wines may have only 7 or 8% alcohol but still form very obvious tears.)

James Thomson, a British physicist and engineer, observed in 1855 what he called 'tears of strong wine' and related the phenomenon to surface tension. Unfortunately his work was overlooked, and this relation to surface tension is usually credited to Italian physicist Carlo Marangoni, who published it in 1871. However, the exact physical explanation of the phenomenon was not obtained until 2009.

A few physical relationships are involved in producing tears. The attractive forces between molecules in the liquid–air interface give rise to surface tension forces. A similar type of force also acts between a liquid molecule and the molecules of a solid surface, and yet another intermolecular force acts between the solid and the air molecules. These are called interfacial tensions.

If the interfacial tension between the solid glass and the air is higher than the interfacial tension between the solid and the liquid, then molecules of liquid will adhere to the glass and wet areas higher and higher above the liquid surface. A point is reached at which the weight of the liquid clinging to the wall just balances the force trying to lift more liquid up the wall surface.

Wine is mainly a solution of alcohol and water. While the thin film of wine climbs up the inner wall of the glass, another physical action occurs: the alcohol evaporates faster than the water from the film surface. This changes the composition of the film, increasing its concentration of water and thereby increasing both its air–liquid and solid–liquid surface tensions. This increase in surface tensions, and especially in the solid–liquid surface tension, causes perpetual tears: the tears keep going down and the wine keeps going up. Eventually the drop becomes so heavy that interfacial tension can no longer hold it to the glass surface. It then runs down the wall, forming a tear or leg.

Dubious readers can convince themselves of this somewhat complicated explanation of an apparently simple phenomenon by observing the lack of tears in glasses of pure water. That evaporation is necessary can be demonstrated by simply covering a glass that previously demonstrated **tearing**. Tearing ceases, though it will resume upon removal of the cover.

It is often thought that tears are the result of GLYCEROL, but in fact entirely unrelated phenomena are responsible. Tears are *not* a measure of viscosity.

Tears occur in many multicomponent liquid mixtures but not in all. For example, it is most obvious in wines above about 12% alcoholic strength, but at lower concentrations the effect is either small or completely non-existent because the surface tension of the air–solid is no longer higher than that of the liquid–solid.

Tadmor, R., 'Marangoni flow revisited', *Journal of Colloid and Interface Science*, 332 (2009), 451–4.

TeCA, or **tetrachloroanisole**, more properly **2,3,4,6-tetrachloroanisole**, is a musty- or dusty-smelling compound that can taint wine if the concentration is above the perception threshold of around 20 ng/l in red or white wine and 4 ng/l in water. The formation of TeCA is described under HALOANISOLES. PCA or 2,3,4,5,6-pentachloroanisole has a much higher perception threshold, at around 5,000 ng/l, but is nearly always present with TeCA.

teinturier literally means 'dyer' in French, which is the function for which these vines with their red-fleshed grapes were initially grown, notably in the Midi, to add at least apparent depth to the pale wines of the dominant ARAMON in the early years of the 20th century.

The original variety called **Teinturier**, or sometimes **Teinturier du Cher**, was probably extremely ancient and was first noted around Orléans in the 17th and 18th centuries, where it imbued the pale-pink wines of the region with valuable colour. DNA PROFILING strongly suggests a parent–offspring relationship with SAVAGNIN.

As long ago as 1824, the Frenchman Louis BOUSCHET decided to try to breed vines with coloured flesh, and the 1828 cross of Aramon × Teinturier du Cher resulted in the popular Petit Bouschet. Henri Bouschet, Louis's son, crossed Petit Bouschet with Grenache to produce the very popular ALICANTE BOUSCHET, a deeply coloured *teinturier*, known as Garnacha Tintorera in Spain, *tintorera* being Spanish for *teinturier*. Other red-fleshed varieties bred by the Bouschet family and used for their 'dyeing' properties at one time include Morrastel Bouschet, Carignan Bouschet, and GRAND NOIR DE LA CALMETTE.

Red-fleshed versions of the lightly coloured GAMAY grape have been widely grown, not just in the Loire but outside France. The Gamay *teinturiers* include Gamay Fréaux, Gamay de Bouze, and Gamay de Chaudenay. Gamay Fréaux and Gamay de Chaudenay are said to be mutations of Gamay de Bouze. Colobel (Seibel 8357) is a *teinturier* FRENCH HYBRID which was the only such variety to be authorized in France.

Germany's useful red-fleshed varieties include Carmina, Deckrot, DUNKELFELDER, Kolor, and Sulmer. ROYALTY 1390, Salvador, and the popular RUBIRED are all California creations, while the important Georgian *teinturier* is SAPERAVI, which is, if not red fleshed, then certainly deep-pink fleshed.

Galet, P., *Dictionnaire encyclopédique des cépages* (2nd edn, 2015).

Robinson, J., et al., *Wine Grapes: A Complete Guide to 1,368 Vine Varieties, Including Their Origins and Flavours* (2012).

Tejo, DOC and VINHO REGIONAL (called Ribatejo until 2009) in central-southern Portugal. It corresponds to the province of the same name on both sides of the river Tagus (Tejo) inland from the capital Lisbon (see map under PORTUGAL). This new name reflects a desire to distance it from its historic reputation for vast quantities of indifferent wine produced by its CO-OPERATIVES from ultra-high yielding vines grown on the river's fertile floodplains, as does the abolition of six DOC subregions (Almeirim, Cartaxo, Chamusca, Coruche, Santarém, and Tomar) heavily associated with the co-operatives. Today the DOC and Vinho Regional share the same borders; soils, not subregions, tend to define the region's best wines. Large, family-owned agricultural estates, which started to make wine themselves in the 1990s rather than selling to the co-operatives, led the charge in GRUBBING UP vineyards on the fertile alluvial riverbank soils (*campo*), instead concentrating production on less fertile, well-drained sandy soils (*charneca*), calcareous CLAY (*bairro*), and SANDSTONE, with pockets of LIMESTONE and SCHIST in the north. Old-vine CASTELÃO and FERNÃO PIRES from *charneca* soils are among the region's best; with renewed interest, they are being positioned as Tejo's signature varietal wines. Old-vine ALICANTE BOUSCHET, a dark horse, can be very good too, and TOURIGA NACIONAL from northern Portugal and such INTERNATIONAL VARIETIES as Syrah, Cabernet Sauvignon, Sauvigon Blanc, Chardonnay, and Viognier have helped raise Tejo's profile with bargain-hunters abroad. In 2021 three co-operatives still accounted for almost half the region's production (60:40 white/red), but, having almost halved the vineyard area this century, the direction of travel is upwards with a growing number of boutique labels. S.A.

Mayson, R. J., *The Wines of Portugal* (2020).
www.cvrtejo.com

Temecula Valley, CALIFORNIA high DESERT wine region in Riverside County and AVA inland of the coastal mountain range 56 km/35 miles north of San Diego. Temecula is the viticultural aspect of a large 1960s development called Rancho California, which used vineyards to attract urban escapees from Los Angeles, Orange, and San Diego counties. The warm, dry region credits the Rainbow Gap, a narrow opening in the coastal ridge, for funneling cool marine air into the area. The Cilurzo family created the first commercial winery in 1968, followed by Callaway Winery in 1974 and, six years later, Hart Winery. Steady growth was devastated by PIERCE'S DISEASE in the late 1990s. That disaster inspired a renaissance of viticulture and wine TOURISM, prompting the development of nearly 50 wineries working with 1,012 ha/2,500 acres by 2021. Cabernet Sauvignon, Syrah and Petite Sirah dominate. M.D.K.

temperate climates are generally defined as environments with moderate rainfall spread across the year or over a portion of the year, with sporadic DROUGHT, mild to warm summers, and cool to cold winters. There are two types of temperate climate: MARITIME and CONTINENTAL. G.V.J

temperature is critically important to VITICULTURE, WINEMAKING, wine MATURATION, and wine SERVICE, each in very different ways.

Climate, viticulture, and temperature

Temperature is widely considered the most important climatological factor affecting grapevines, although others such as SUNLIGHT, RAINFALL, HUMIDITY, and WIND are also important. Gladstones comprehensively reviews the role of temperature in viticulture. Temperature records are available from climate recording stations, and modern statistical procedures allow the calculation of temperatures between station locations that may be more representative of actual vineyard sites (see TOPOGRAPHY, MESOCLIMATE, and CLIMATE CHANGE).

Temperatures at particular stages of vine growth or during ripening can have specific effects. During the winter, the risk of killing dormant vines is one basis for defining climatic suitability for viticulture (see WINTER FREEZE). This is the main limiting factor in cool climates with marked CONTINENTALITY. Most fully dormant VITIS VINIFERA vines with well-matured canes can withstand air temperatures down to about −15 °C/5 °F. Native AMERICAN VINE SPECIES are in general hardier, and AMERICAN HYBRIDS intermediate. However, there is considerable variation among VINE VARIETIES.

The winter hardiness of RIESLING, for instance, is almost certainly one of the reasons for its historical success in Germany. The chance of winter killing of vines in Europe increases from south-west to north-east (see RUSSIA, for example). Extensive commercial viticulture without WINTER PROTECTION reaches its limit where the average mean temperature of the coldest month falls below about −1 °C/30 °F.

Air TEMPERATURE VARIABILITY largely determines the risk of FROST DAMAGE after BUDBREAK with temperatures below 0 °C/32 °F adversely affecting the growth of the vegetative parts of the plant and hard freezes (< −2.2 °C/< 28°F) reducing yields significantly. Temperatures around FLOWERING contribute to differences in FRUIT SET (by influencing COULURE, most notably) and to the FRUITFULNESS of the developing new buds which form shoots and bunches the following year. Both fruit set and bud fruitfulness are favoured by moderately high temperatures. Nearing maturation, early frost or freezes can lead to the splitting of the grapes, which influences disease development and can result in a significant loss of yield. Finally, both average temperature and temperature variability during ripening can have a direct influence on fruit and wine qualities, as discussed under CLIMATE AND WINE QUALITY.

Vines in cool climates start growing in the spring at about the time when the mean air temperature reaches 10 °C/50 °F. The rate of vine growth and development then increases to a maximum at a mean temperature of about 22–25 °C/72–7 °F. Temperature is often discussed in viticulture as mean temperature for the full growing season and for the warmest month, which are often used as a reasonable basis for broad comparisons (see CLIMATE CLASSIFICATION and COOL-CLIMATE VITICULTURE). In the traditional heat-accumulation methods for viticultural climate classification, values are based on excesses of daily or monthly average mean temperatures over 10 °C. Such classifications can at best only approximate the temperatures experienced by the vines. Hourly or shorter time intervals give better results.

Air temperature is not the only kind governing vine growth and fruiting, however. Vines and soils are warmed by sunlight, which has major effects on grape berry temperature, leaf temperature, grape composition, and, subsequently, wine quality. Some evidence now confirms the old belief that soil temperature is also important. This control appears to be mediated by the root-produced hormone CYTOKININ, although soil temperature can also affect vine temperature, especially at night. The composition of the soil, its colour, drainage, and the duration and angle of exposure to the sun are all important factors in this respect. See SOIL COLOUR, STONES AND ROCKS, TOPOGRAPHY, and MESOCLIMATE. G.V.J.

Gladstones, J., *Viticulture and Environment* (1992).

Winemaking and temperature

Temperature and TEMPERATURE CONTROL are of critical importance in making good-quality wine (although great wine may have been made fortuitously, long before the theory of temperature control was understood and temperature was deliberately manipulated). Temperature has direct effects on the rates of the biochemical reactions involved in FERMENTATION and on the slower reactions involved in CLARIFICATION and STABILIZATION of wine. REFRIGERATION slows down the reactions of harmful microorganisms, as well as the reactions involved in AGEING.

In warm regions, therefore, care should be taken to ensure that grapes arrive at the winery in a cool, and relatively undamaged, condition. The harmful effects of microorganisms such as ACETOBACTER and enzymatic OXIDATION are encouraged by high temperatures. Low temperatures are vital if there is any interval between HARVEST and CRUSHING; the potential quality of white wines in particular can be lost through carelessness at this early phase of winemaking. During DESTEMMING and crushing, when the PHENOLICS in grape juice are in direct contact with oxygen, OXIDATION begins at a rate proportional to the temperature. To slow browning of white grape juice, therefore, care is usually taken to keep temperatures as low as possible (see MUST CHILLING). SULFUR DIOXIDE may also be added to the must. Oxidation of red must is less of a problem because its higher phenolic content, including the red colour compounds, can conceal small amounts of amber or brown, although lower temperatures during pre-fermentation processes (around 15 °C/59 °F) allow better control of the fermentation temperature.

If temperature control is desirable prior to fermentation, it is critical during it. At temperatures below 10 °C/50 °F, most yeasts will act very slowly or not at all, while at temperatures above 32 °C/90 °F they are damaged and finally killed. Secondly, higher fermentation temperatures speed up some reactions so that undesirable flavour compounds become apparent. Thirdly, at higher temperatures, there is a risk that some of the desirable FLAVOUR COMPOUNDS are volatilized in the rapidly evolving stream of carbon dioxide, resulting in a less fruity wine. In the extreme case of temperatures nearing the range at which yeasts are killed, the yeast metabolism produces more VOLATILE ACIDITY and yeast cells secrete compounds which inhibit future yeast growth, thereby making it difficult or impossible to restart this STUCK FERMENTATION even after cooling.

There are yeast strains which grow and ferment very slowly at very low temperatures, only just above freezing. Such strains are particularly useful in cool wine regions such as Switzerland and parts of Germany and also for the production of wines such as CLAIRETTE DE DIE.

White wines are in general fermented at lower temperatures than red, partly in order to conserve the primary grape AROMAS, partly because there is no MACERATION, for which heat may be useful in encouraging the extraction of phenolics and other flavour compounds from the grape skins. Temperatures of 12–17 °C/50–63 °F are common when the aim is to make fruity, well-balanced, light-coloured wines (although see also BARREL FERMENTATION). Grape varieties such as Sauvignon Blanc, Riesling, and Muscat tend to be fermented at higher temperatures than more neutral varieties to encourage the accumulation of secondary fermentation aromas. Old World white wine fermentation temperatures are likely to be 18–20 °C/64–68 °F. The techniques of barrel fermentation and LEES CONTACT, such as are often applied to Chardonnay grapes, often involve slightly higher fermentation temperatures too, although the small size of the barrel (in comparison with the normal stainless-steel tank) helps to control temperature.

Temperature control is also extremely important during RED WINEMAKING. The main concern here is the extraction of sufficient TANNINS, ANTHOCYANINS, and flavour compounds from the grape skins. Temperature is one of the factors governing this extraction, agitation and time being the others. Fermentation temperatures of 25–27 °C/77–81 °F in the must, and therefore 30 °C in the CAP, generally produce the best flavour and EXTRACTION in red wines, provided other conditions are optimal (and grape variety, agitation, and time all play a part interlinked to temperature in the maceration process). Temperatures higher than this threaten the yeast activity, while temperatures below it limit extraction and favour the production of secondary aromas.

Temperature continues to be an important factor in wine production long after the fermentation phase. Oxidation and loss of fruitiness in white wines can be discouraged by low temperatures, while the bacterial activity that stimulates MALOLACTIC CONVERSION can be positively encouraged by storing the newly fermented wine at 18–20 °C/64–68 °F until this conversion is completed.

Fermentation temperatures govern the types of ESTERS that are formed and accumulate in the wine. Lower temperatures (10–15 °C/50–59 °F) favour both the production and retention of the fruity esters, which have lower molecular weights. Among these are nearly all of those possible by reactions between ACETIC, propionic, isobutyric, and isovaleric acids with ETHANOL, propyl, isobutyl, and FUSEL OIL. These are the esters which give fruits their characteristic flavours (ISOAMYL ACETATE, for example, is the flavour material of ripe bananas). Higher fermentation temperatures (20–25 °C/68–77 °F) result in the production of lower amounts of esters. V.L.

Storage temperature

In the same way that it affects the reactions involved in winemaking, temperature becomes the governing factor in the much slower reactions in bottle that constitute wine AGEING. Interactions among the thousands of natural organic chemicals in the wine during this important phase of its maturation are directly affected by temperature. If the storage temperature is very high, say 30 °C/86 °F, a wine would mature extremely quickly and probably taste cooked or jammy. At a CELLAR temperature of 10 °C/50 °F, a wine would age very slowly, and if a wine is kept at 0 °C/32 °F there would be extremely high deposits of TARTRATES and PHENOLICS. In practice, a reasonable cellar temperature for ageing wines to be drunk within one's own lifetime is somewhere between 10 and 15 °C/50–59 °F. (The cellars of the Swedish state MONOPOLY were so cold that any fine, old wine bought in Sweden would taste markedly different from the same wine aged in the more temperate climate of France, for example.)

Even lower down the temperature scale, wine freezes at a temperature below 0 °C that is roughly half its ALCOHOLIC STRENGTH, so usually somewhere between −5 and −8 °C/23–18 °F. For this reason, in cool climates, care should be taken to insulate wine stored in places such as garden sheds or garages where winter temperatures are not maintained at a level acceptable to humans.

Serving temperature

The temperature at which a wine is served has a profound effect on how it smells and tastes. Different styles of wine deserve to be served at different temperatures to enhance their good points and try to mask any faults or imbalances. The following are some general observations, with suggested guidelines in italics.

The higher the temperature, the more easily the volatile FLAVOUR COMPOUNDS evaporate from the surface of wine in a glass. So, to maximize the impact of a wine's AROMA or BOUQUET, it is sensible to serve it relatively warm, say 16–18 °C/61–64 °F (at temperatures over 20 °C/68 °F the ALCOHOL can begin to evaporate so markedly that it unbalances the wine). *Serve complex and mature wines relatively warm.*

Conversely, the lower the temperature, the fewer volatiles will evaporate; at a serving temperature of about 8 °C/46 °F, all but the most aromatic wines appear to have no smell whatsoever. *The gustatory faults of a low-quality wine can be masked by serving it very cool.*

The higher the temperature, the more sensitive is the PALATE to sweetness, so it makes sense to serve sweet wines which may not have quite enough ACIDITY to counterbalance the sweetness quite cool, say at about 12 °C/54 °F. For the same reason, medium-dry wines served with savoury food will probably taste dry if served well chilled. *In general, chill sweet wines.*

The lower the temperature, the more sensitive the palate to TANNINS and BITTERNESS. Peynaud points out that the same red wine will taste 'hot and thin at 22 °C/72 °F, supple and fluid at 18 °C/64 °F, full and astringent at 10 °C/50 °F'. *Tannic or bitter wines such as many Italian red wines and any young red designed for ageing should be served relatively warm.*

The effect of temperature on apparent acidity is more widely disputed by scientists, but it is generally observable that flabby wines can seem more refreshing if they are served cold, say at 10 °C/50 °F. (This may be related to the effect of temperature on sweetness described above.) *To increase the refreshment factor of a wine, serve it cool.*

Temperature also has an observable effect on wines containing CARBON DIOXIDE. The higher the temperature, the more gas is released, which means that fizzy wines can be unpleasantly frothy at about 18 °C/64 °F. *Sparkling and lightly sparkling wines are generally best served well chilled.* Since very few wines with a complex bouquet ever have any perceptible gas, this is no great limitation (those who make Australia's extraordinary sparkling Shiraz claim it is best served at room temperature, but these sparkling wines are not particularly fizzy).

General rules are therefore:

Serve tannic red wines relatively warm, 15–18 °C/59–64 °F.
Serve complex dry white wines relatively warm, 12–16 °C/54–61 °F.
Serve soft, lighter red wines for refreshment at 10–12 °C/50–55 °F.
Cool sweet, sparkling, flabby white, and rosé wines, and those with any off-odour, at 6–10 °C/43–50 °F.

Of course wine tends to warm up to match the ambient temperature, so initial serving temperatures at the bottom end of these brackets—or even cooler—are no bad thing, especially in warmer environments. For more details of how to cool and warm bottles, see SERVING WINE.

See also TASTING (as opposed to drinking) for its different requirements of wine temperature.

Peynaud, E., *The Taste of Wine* (2nd edn, 1996).

temperature control during WINEMAKING is crucially important, as outlined in TEMPERATURE. Although it has been widely and systematically practised only since the 1960s and 1970s, its efficacy was appreciated as long ago as Roman times (see DIE). See REFRIGERATION for details of how wine may be cooled at various points in its life. In cool wine regions or during particularly cool years, a FERMENTATION VESSEL may need to be heated to encourage alcoholic FERMENTATION, most easily by circulating warm water in equipment also designed to carry cooling cold water or, in smaller cellars, simply by closing doors and installing a heater or two. Some form of heating may also be required to encourage MALOLACTIC CONVERSION.

temperature variability, a characteristic of climates referring to the short-term variability of temperature from day to day and week to week. Temperature variability plays an important role in determining the risks of FROST DAMAGE to dormant vines in spring and autumn, as well as those of HEAT STRESS and direct heat damage to the vines and fruit in summer. Such variability is driven by shifts in the circulation of the atmosphere that bring air masses with widely different temperature characteristics to wine regions. Stable temperatures on these time scales are best for grapevine physiology, whereas wide swings in temperatures have distinct viticultural and oenological implications (see TEMPERATURE and CONTINENTAL CLIMATE). This is especially important with extreme heat events (> 40 °C/104 °F) when grapevines will shut down to conserve water and energy, ultimately taking time to recover and return to optimum photosynthetic activity. In cool regions, low temperature variability is important for improved wine quality since it may influence consistent growth characteristics in the vines and the formation of PIGMENT, AROMA, and FLAVOUR in the ripening berries. Under such circumstances, these processes are favoured relative to the mere accumulation of SUGAR IN GRAPES. See also DIURNAL TEMPERATURE RANGE. G.J.V.

Jones, G.V., et al., 'Climate, grapes, and wine: structure and suitability in a variable and changing climate', in P. Dougherty (ed.), *The Geography of Wine: Regions, Terrior and Techniques* (2012).

Tempranillo has been planted so enthusiastically in Spain that it was the world's third most popular wine grape variety in 2016. In some ways it is Spain's answer to Cabernet Sauvignon, the vine variety that puts the spine into a high proportion of Spain's most respected red wines, and is increasingly planted elsewhere. Its grapes are thick-skinned and capable of making deep-coloured, long-lasting wines that are, unusually for Spain, not notably high in alcohol. Often replacing GARNACHA, BOBAL, or MONASTRELL, it became the most popular red wine grape in Spain in the early 21st century and by 2021 was planted on a total of 202,917 ha/501,419 acres in virtually all regions except for those in the far south and north-west, overtaking AIRÉN as the country's most planted variety of either colour.

Temprano means 'early' in Spanish, and Tempranillo probably earns its name from its propensity to ripen early, certainly up to two weeks before the GARNACHA with which it is still regularly blended to make RIOJA. This relatively short growing cycle enables it to thrive in the often harsh climate of Rioja's higher, more Atlantic-influenced zones Rioja Alta and Rioja Alavesa, where it constitutes by far the majority of all vines planted. Tempranillo has traditionally been grown in widely spaced bushes here, but this relatively vigorous, upright vine has also responded well to training on WIRES.

Wine made from Tempranillo grown in relatively cool conditions, where its tendency to produce MUSTS slightly low in acidity is a positive advantage, can last well, but the variety does not have a particularly strong flavour identity. Some find strawberries, others spice, leather, and tobacco leaves, but yields and winemaking skill are critical in determining its style.

In Rioja it is traditionally blended with Garnacha, plus a bit of Mazuelo (Carignan), Graciano, and Viura. In PENEDÈS it is known as Ull de Llebre; in VALDEPEÑAS as Cencibel. The variety is ideally suited to the cool conditions of RIBERA DEL DUERO, where, as Tinto Fino, it is by far the principal grape variety, but the seasoning of varieties imported from Bordeaux is a minor but signficant ingredient in that high plateau's most famous wine, VEGA SICILIA. Indeed, throughout Spain, blends of Tempranillo with Cabernet Sauvignon and/or Merlot are common, notably in Navarra and Castilla-La Mancha.

Its Spanish synonyms also include Tinta Madrid, Tinta del País, and Tinta de Toro, where its particularly concentrated form has played a major part in the style and popularity of TORO wines.

Tempranillo is one of relatively few Spanish varieties to have been adopted to a great extent in Portugal, where it is known both as Aragonez and (Tinta) Roriz and, after a dramatic increase in popularity, was the country's single most planted variety. For more, see TINTA RORIZ.

As Tempranillo or **Tempranilla** and making rather light, possibly over-irrigated reds, it has been important in Argentina's wine industry but lost ground to more marketable varieties in the late 1980s. Plantings stood at 5,430 ha/13,418 acres in 2020, mainly in Mendoza.

There were 359 ha/887 acres in southern France in 2019, most notably in the Aude and used for blending. Thanks to mildly increased interest in the variety and all things Spanish, in 2020 California grew 370 ha/914 acres of Tempranillo, once known there as Valdepeñas. Abacela pioneered fine Tempranillo in southern Oregon, where there were 142 ha/352 acres in 2019, and there has been small-scale enthusiasm for the variety in Washington State.

As vine-growers the world over search for new, recognizably high-quality ALTERNATIVE VARIETIES, Tempranillo is spreading around the globe, notably in Australia, where plantings had reached 844 ha/2,086 acres by 2022.

Italy grows a tiny amount of vines called Tempranillo, but DNA PROFILING unexpectedly showed that some Tempranillo has been grown in Tuscany and Basilicata under the widely applied name Malvasia Nera.

DNA profiling has shown that Tempranillo is a spontaneous cross between the old Spanish light-skinned grape ALBILLO Mayor and the obscure, no longer cultivated, Benedicto from Aragón.

Tempranillo Blanco, a pale-berried MUTATION, has been identified in Rioja, where VARIETAL versions have been made.

tendone, the Italian name for the overhead vine-TRAINING SYSTEM widely used in southern Italy, especially in ABRUZZO. It is also common in South America, where it is used for both TABLE GRAPES and wine grapes and is called *parral* (Argentina) or *parron* (Chile). English terms used include both 'arbour' and 'pergola', although the system is little used in English-speaking countries.

The vines are normally trained with trunks about 2 m/6.5 ft high, and a system of wooden frames and cross wires supports the foliage and fruit. Typically in Abruzzo the vines are planted in a 2.5 × 2.5 m square (up to 3 × 3 m for TREBBIANO), and from each staked vine four shoots are trained in different directions along the wires.

Arbours are normally high enough from the ground to allow tractors and implements to pass underneath, but not so high as to make hand work difficult. The vines are pruned to either canes or spurs (see PRUNING). Because all of the sunlight is captured, the system can be very productive: 30 to 70 tonnes of grapes per hectare (12–28 tons/acre) when water supply is plentiful.

Such training systems are limited in use because of the expense of their construction and the high cost of LABOUR required to manage them. Worker productivity is lower because of fatigue, and, where the vines are vigorous, the leaves form a very dense CANOPY so that the fruit and lower leaves are heavily SHADED. This reduces both YIELD and quality and increases the risk of POWDERY MILDEW.

Furthermore, the ventilation under such canopies is very restricted, and the build-up of humidity favours BOTRYTIS BUNCH ROT. The arbour system is used for table grapes in many parts of the world and has the advantage that the fruit hangs freely and makes access easy. Inclined overhead trellis systems which do not completely cover the ground are often used for table grapes, as in South Africa (where it may be called the verandah system), and occasionally for wine grapes around the borders of fields in the VINHO VERDE region of Portugal. R.E.S.

tendril, coiling, clasping organ that enables the stems of plants to climb (see WILD VINES). In many plants, these organs are modifications of stems, leaves, or leaflets, but in the grapevine they are modified INFLORESCENCES, developing at two of every three consecutive NODES. Tendrils are sensitive to touch (thigmotropic); when sufficiently elongated, they react to pressure on their surface by coiling around the touched object, be it a wire, a part of the vine, or any other adjacent material. Once coiled, the tendrils become lignified, very tough, and difficult to remove. B.G.C.

tent, medieval term for strong red wine from Iberia, mainly Spain (notably deeper in colour that the CLAIRET then still associated with Bordeaux). It is an Anglicized version of the word TINTO, Spanish and Portuguese for 'red'.

tenuta, Italian word for an agricultural holding, estate, or farm, usually larger than, for example, a PODERE.

Teran, **Terrano**, names for Refosco d'Istria, a member of the REFOSCO group, used, respectively, in CROATIA, the Kras district of SLOVENIA, and the CARSO DOC in the extreme east of Friuli. The Slovenians registered Teran as a geographical entity so that Croatian producers must now specify Hrvatska Istra on the label to make it clear that Teran is the variety not the appellation. Often confused with the distinct REFOSCO DAL PEDUNCOLO ROSSO.

Terlano, or **Terlaner** in German, long-lived white wines from around the town of Terlano in ALTO ADIGE. It is also the name of a large subzone of the Alto Adige DOC.

Termeno Aromatico. See GEWÜRZTRAMINER.

termites can be pests in older vineyards, where they tunnel into old wood and can weaken it so much that the vine may partially collapse. Very occasionally newly planted cuttings are attacked where growing conditions are poor. M.J.E.

Teroldego, old, well-connected grape variety which makes deep-coloured, seriously lively, fruity wines named Teroldego Rotaliano because they are made almost exclusively in the Campo Rotaliano in TRENTINO, north-east Italy, with suitable tannins for relatively early drinking. Wine made from this variety is rather prone to REDUCTION. From the mid 1980s, Elisabetta Foradori initiated a qualitative revolution, and her wines have become the benchmark for classic, ageworthy Teroldego. The variety was known in the Campo Rotaliano as early as the 15th century, and DNA PROFILING at SAN MICHELE ALL'ADIGE has shown a parent–offspring relationship with LAGREIN from Alto Adige and that the variety is quite closely related, through DUREZA, to Syrah. Total plantings in Italy in 2015 were 730 ha/1,804 acres. Also found in Brazil. See also MARZEMINO.

Robinson, J., et al., *Wine Grapes: A Complete Guide to 1,368 Vine Varieties, Including Their Origins and Flavours* (2012).

terpenes, distinctive FLAVOUR COMPOUNDS associated with the floral and citrus aromas found in wines made from such varieties as Muscat, Gewürztraminer, and Riesling.

terpenoids, an important group of plant chemicals including many essential oils, CAROTENOIDS, plant HORMONES, sterols, and rubber. They contribute much to the unique qualities of the vine. Chemically they are multiples of branched, five-carbon (isoprene) units yielding a variety of compounds with diverse properties: the C10 monoterpenes make an important contribution to floral aromas (see FLAVOUR COMPOUNDS); the C15 sesquiterpenoids include the hormone ABSCISIC ACID; and the C20 diterpenes include the GIBBERELLIN hormones. Carotenoids, with 40 carbon atoms, contribute to the skin colour of so-called white grapes and are metabolized to norisoprenoid flavour compounds that contribute to non-floral aroma of grapes. B.G.C. & P.J.W.

Terra Alta, Spanish for 'high land' and a DOP in Spanish CATALUÑA (see map under SPAIN), with 5,820 ha/14,382 acres of vineyards in 2020 at an average ELEVATION of 480 m/1,575 ft. Its development parallels that of neighbouring TARRAGONA, in that growers are following the lead of PRIORAT, notably recovering and relaunching their formerly despised GARNACHA grapes and making some impressive wines. One-third of total worldwide production of GARNACHA BLANCA comes from Terra Alta, and in 2011 the local CONSEJO REGULADOR introduced a special seal for high-quality wines made solely from the grape. Red wines, which make up 70% of production, rely especially on Garnacha Tinta, locally called Vernatxa. F.C.

terraces make work in vineyards planted across sloping land considerably easier and can also help combat SOIL EROSION. Terraces more or less follow the contours of the land, and so row spacing may be irregular. Terraces are created when the hillside is re-formed into a series of horizontal steps between the rows. The world's most famous vineyard terraces are those of the PORT wine region of the DOURO Valley in northern Portugal, where there has been considerable experimentation with different designs, although they are also common in much of SWITZERLAND, the northern RHÔNE, and elsewhere.

In centuries past, such terraces were laboriously constructed by hand and supported by stone walls. For modern vineyards, the cost of laying stones by hand can be prohibitive and skilled craftspeople hard to find. Most modern terraces are formed by bulldozers. Terraces are expensive to create and are therefore justified only for expensive wines.

An alternative to creating terraces is to plant vines up and down the hillsides, as in Germany and other parts of northern Europe. This practice avoids the expense of forming terraces but can lead to soil erosion and worker fatigue, and some slopes are too steep for tractors. See also HILLSIDE VINEYARDS. R.E.S.

Terrano. See TERAN.

Terrantez, Portuguese white wine grape that is practically extinct on the island of MADEIRA but can occasionally be encountered in historic bottles. It is not, as some have suggested, a synonym for GOUVEIO.

terra rossa, strikingly red soil usually associated with the dissolution of LIMESTONE in a MEDITERRANEAN CLIMATE. The colour is due

T

principally to the insoluble residue of CLAYS stained with inert iron oxide and hydroxide minerals such as hematite and goethite. The soils are characterized by a low water-holding capacity, good drainage and aeration, and adequate vine nutrients (see VINE NUTRITION), but their eye-catching colour does not bestow any special benefits on the vine. Examples are found in Coonawarra (SOUTH AUSTRALIA), Istria (CROATIA), LA MANCHA (Spain), and LEBANON's Bekaa Valley. A.J.M.

Terrasses du Larzac, the rising star of the LANGUEDOC which was elevated very rapidly from Languedoc CRU to AOC in 2014. A large and fairly disparate appellation, it is characterized by its myriad soil types and wide DIURNAL TEMPERATURE RANGE—as much as 20 °C/36 °F—due to the Larzac plateau, which rises to almost 1,000 m/3,281 ft to the north. The wines are full-bodied yet crisp reds based on Grenache Noir, Syrah, and Mourvèdre, with small amounts of Cinsaut and Carignan allowed; the iron-rich CLAYS known as *ruffes* can give them a brimstone edge. The appellation is home to some of the Languedoc's biggest and most famous names, though not all label their wines under the AOC as some contain Cabernet Sauvignon, a variety not permitted under this designation. M.S.

Terret is one of the Languedoc's oldest vine varieties and, like PINOT, has had plenty of time to mutate into different shades of grape (see MUTATION), which may even be found on the same plant. **Terret Gris** was once by far the most planted white wine variety in the Languedoc, even if it was concentrated in the Hérault *département*. Terret Gris and **Terret Blanc**, both in decline, can be made into a relatively full-bodied but naturally crisp VARIETAL white. The French vineyard survey of 2019 notes 842 ha/2,081 acres of Terret Blanc, only 40 ha of Terret Gris. Some varietal versions are made, and both are allowed into the white wines of Minervois, Corbières, and the Languedoc.

Terret Noir is the even rarer dark-berried version, one of the permitted varieties in red CHÂTEAUNEUF-DU-PAPE, to which it can add useful STRUCTURE and interest. All Terrets bud usefully late and keep their ACIDITY well.

terroir, much-discussed term for the total natural environment of any viticultural site, sometimes used to refer to the effect of that natural environment on wine quality and TYPICALITY. No precise English equivalent exists for this quintessentially French term and concept. The phrase 'a sense of place' has become popular because terroir links the sensory attributes of a wine to the location in which it was produced. The OIV's 2010 definition of terroir also incorporates the cultural dimension: 'a concept which refers to an area in which collective knowledge of the interactions between the identifiable physical and biological environment and applied vitivinicultural practices develops, providing distinctive characteristics for the products originating from this area'.

Major components of terroir are SOIL (as the word suggests, *terra* being Latin for 'earth' or 'land') and local TOPOGRAPHY, together with their interactions with each other and with MACROCLIMATE, which in turn affects MESOCLIMATE and vine MICROCLIMATE. In each particular location, soil and climate provide a set of resources specific to the place where the vines grow (temperature, light, water, CO_2, nutrients) which influences vine PHENOLOGY, VINE PHYSIOLOGY, and grape RIPENING. Hence, the place where the vines grow influences GRAPE COMPOSITION, which results in specific sensory attributes, as discussed by van Leeuwen et al. (2018).

Major regional CLASSIFICATIONS of European vineyards have been largely founded on the concept of terroir, although these may be based on climate rather than soil. A few decades ago OLD WORLD and NEW WORLD viticulturists, winemakers, and researchers may have argued about the importance of terroir in final wine quality. More recently their views have been converging, and both New World and Old World countries have organized international terroir congresses in the last ten years. However, some authors such as Matthews still consider terroir to be a myth.

It can certainly be argued that modern improvements in vineyard and winery technology have, by raising and unifying standards of wine quality, to some extent obscured differences in both style and quality of wines that in the past were (sometimes wrongly) attributed to terroir in its true sense. But, paradoxically, the same improvements can serve to unmask genuine terroir-related differences. By eliminating extraneous odours and tastes derived from FAULTS IN WINES, they allow a fuller expression of intrinsic grape characteristics which can be related to the vineyard site.

The wines of Burgundy are most often cited as evidence of the reality of the terroir effect. Many growers have different plots which they cultivate in the same way. They then vinify the grapes from these plots in a similar way, yet the wines produced differ significantly in quality and style. GUIGAL's single-vineyard bottlings in Côte Rôtie are one famous example of this approach to terroir, which is increasingly being followed by producers all around the world who espouse REGIONALITY. Heitz Wine Cellars in the Napa Valley, for example, released its first vineyard-designate wine, Martha's Vineyard, in 1966, and today many other New World producers release single-vineyard wines, for example Catena's Adrianna Vineyard Mundus Bacillus Terrae from Mendoza or Henschke's Hill of Grace in the Eden Valley, Australia. 'Single vineyard' is today a proud statement on many wine labels from all parts of the wine world, even if the vineyard in question may extend over hundreds of hectares.

Both the OIV and Moran argue that terroir also includes human input in the vineyard and winery. Winegrowers choose their plant material (ROOTSTOCK and VINE VARIETY) and adapt their management choices (vineyard floor, TRAINING SYSTEMS, CANOPY MANAGEMENT) to optimize wine quality in each particular environment, which could be described as 'managing terroir' (van Leeuwen et al., 2018).

Many authors have studied specific terroir factors without taking into account the vine, focusing instead on geology (Wilson), geomorphology (Fanet), soil microbiology (Bourguignon), and climate (Tonietto and Carbonneau). The limitation of these approaches is that they remain highly descriptive and do not explain how these factors influence wine quality.

Dr Gérard Seguin, of the University of BORDEAUX, was the first author to conduct multidisciplinary terroir studies, including soil, climate, and the impact of each on vine physiology and grape ripening. He showed that a wide range of soil types are able to produce high-quality wines in Bordeaux. These soils have in common moderate fertility and well-regulated, moderately sufficient water supply to the vines. DRAINAGE was always excellent, so that both waterlogging and sudden increases in water supply to the vines were avoided no matter the amount of rainfall, hence buffering the vintage effect. Renouf et al. established a relationship between soil type and wine quality in hundreds of PARCELS across five vintages at famous Bordeaux wine estates. The highest-quality wine was produced significantly more frequently on specific soil types (in particular GRAVEL and CLAY), while on others (soils with waterlogging, deep COLLUVIAL soils) the wine produced was more often blended into the second or third wine of the estate. GEOGRAPHICAL INFORMATION SYSTEMS (GIS) and geostatistics have made possible data-driven terroir zoning (see PRECISION VITICULTURE). This approach was successfully implemented by Bramley et al., but the zoning produced needs subsequent validation through sensory analyses.

Van Leeuwen et al. (2004) found that the effect of soil is secondary to that of climate. However, both the climate and the soil effects are mediated through their influence on water supply to the vine (see WATER STRESS). The respective effect of soil and climate may vary: the latter is more likely to dominate on a regional scale, the latter on a smaller scale, as explained by Bramley and Gardiner.

Studies of terroir in Burgundy, cited and illustrated by Johnson and Robinson, show that the best wines are from stony clay-LOAM soils, formed on the middle slopes from MARL (a clay and soft limestone mixture) mixed with SILT and rubble from outcropping hard LIMESTONE further up. These soils combine good drainage with just the right capacity to store and supply water to the vines.

Extensive studies by Carbonneau and colleagues in the Bordeaux region and by Smart and colleagues in Australia and New Zealand have revealed a further common feature of vineyards producing the best wines. All have a high degree of leaf and bunch exposure to direct sunlight, with little complete shading of internal and lower leaves (see further discussion under SUNLIGHT, CANOPY MICROCLIMATE, and CANOPY MANAGEMENT). Variation in this respect is explained by differences in vegetative VIGOUR and vine BALANCE. Best quality is associated with only moderate vigour, which typically results from a somewhat restricted water supply, limited NITROGEN, and (in some cases) appropriate TRAINING SYSTEMS and CANOPY MANAGEMENT. These studies suggest that soil effects on wine quality are indirect (i.e. soil conditions regulating water and nitrogen supply to the vine affect vine vigour, which in turn affects fruit and leaf exposure to sunlight, which in turn affects wine quality). While exposure to sunlight is amenable to management control on soils that are not too fertile, vine supply of water, in the absence of IRRIGATION, is very largely not. It is therefore a prime contributor, together with local TOPOGRAPHY, to the immutable influence of terroir.

An implication is that GEOLOGY, often cited as a basis of terroir, has in general no more than an indirect role. To varying degrees, parent ROCK materials do contribute to the natures of the soils derived from them; they also shape local topography and therefore MESOCLIMATE. Occasionally the parent materials contribute directly because vine roots can penetrate fissures in them, as in the cases of CHALK subsoils and the SCHISTS of the Douro Valley, contributing to the regulation of water supply. In the broad sense, however, it remains the soil itself and its water relations that play the decisive role.

The effect of terroir on wine quality is now quite well understood: it is mainly mediated through vine water supply by the soil and the climate, although mineral supply (and especially nitrogen supply) can also play a role. This effect of terroir can partly be obtained by good canopy and irrigation management in dry climates. However, the effect of terroir on wine style is just starting to be unravelled. The high quality of Ch AUSONE (limestone), Ch CHEVAL BLANC (gravel and clay), and PETRUS (heavy clay) can be explained by the natural regulation of water supply to the vines. But why do they taste different, and why do they each have their own style, despite very similar viticultural and oenological practices? This aspect of terroir is extremely interesting, because top wines are not only very good but also unique, with their own style. Research into aroma compounds in grapes and wine, reviewed by van Leeuwen et al. (2020), is providing more evidence of the way terroir can shape aromas and TYPICALITY.

Another aspect of terroir is that its clearest expression occurs when grape ripening is relatively slow and therefore late in the season (van Leeuwen and Seguin, 2006). This occurs in cool climates or in warmer climates when varieties are sufficiently late ripening. In all quality wine regions in Europe, growers have chosen varieties that just achieve ripeness under the local climatic conditions. When grapes ripen in August in the northern hemisphere (e.g. Central Valley, California) or in February in the southern hemisphere (e.g. the Murray river basin, Australia), it is difficult to produce wines with refined aromatic expression. Terroir can only be understood when soil, climate, and vine are taken into account simultaneously. When early-ripening varieties are planted in warm climates, wines are heavy, lacking freshness and aromatic expression (except for aromas produced by winemaking practices). This is the case with warm-climate Chardonnay, for instance. A much better expression is obtained in cool climates (Chardonnay in Chablis, Sauvignon Blanc in New Zealand). Growers in the New World are becoming more aware of this and seeking out cooler regions—for example, Sonoma Coast instead of the Napa Valley for Pinot Noir and Chardonnay, or New Zealand, Tasmania, or high-ELEVATION vineyards in Mendoza, Argentina.

The hierarchy of terroir factors

In the relatively flat topography of Bordeaux, soil and its water relations are major drivers of terroir expression. The situation is clearly different in areas such as Germany's MOSEL region at what was once the cold limit of commercial viticulture (see CLIMATE CHANGE). The topographic differences between individual sites decide whether grapes, particularly varieties such as RIESLING, will ripen fully at all. At high latitudes, topography and mesoclimate are inescapably major components of terroir.

It has also been argued that mesoclimatic differences may not merely govern the degree of ripeness attained but could also affect the more subtle grape and wine qualities commonly attributed to terroir; see CLIMATE AND WINE QUALITY, TEMPERATURE VARIABILITY, and DIURNAL TEMPERATURE RANGE. This is evidenced by Urvieta et al. (2020), who show terroir influence (largely driven by mesoclimatic differences) on phenolic compounds in Mendoza, Argentina. Soil might similarly influence grape and wine qualities through its effect on MICROCLIMATE; see STONES AND ROCKS, SOIL COLOUR, and SOIL AND WINE QUALITY.

All these effects serve to underline terroir as a real concept, not something expressed merely through the relationships between vine vigour, balance, and the vine canopy. The distinction is critical because, to the extent that the latter is true, other approaches might achieve the same end. Two stand out in importance.

1. The use of larger or more complex vine-training systems, such as Carbonneau's LYRE trellis, making it possible to maintain good leaf and fruit exposure on larger and more productive vines. This in turn allows the exploitation of more moist, and possibly more fertile, soils, giving higher yields without any necessary loss of fruit and wine quality.

2. In regions with dry summers, the use of controlled IRRIGATION, especially that made possible by DRIP IRRIGATION. This allows vegetative vigour to be held at appropriate levels for vine balance but also water to be supplied during ripening as needed. It is an important advance in regions of MEDITERRANEAN CLIMATE as long as water is sustainably available.

It seems inconceivable, however, that these developments will ever totally eliminate the regional and local differences in wine qualities that have been traditionally ascribed to terroir. Differences in MACROCLIMATE, MESOCLIMATE, and soil MICROCLIMATE remain, while there are many conceivable avenues by which differences in soil chemistry—for instance, in trace element balances—might have small effects on wine flavours and aromas which are nevertheless detectable by the sense of TASTE. To the extent that terroirs remain unique (and poorly understood), one can therefore hope that they will continue to help mould the infinite variety and individuality of the best wines, giving the special nuances of character that make wine such a fascinating study for winemaker and consumer alike.

In this book we have chosen to focus on the natural environment as the key determinant of terroir, but the term can also be used to give economic and cultural value to a wine. Charters et al. explore terroir in the wider context of the humanities and social sciences.

See also MICROBIAL TERROIR. R.E.S. & C.v.L.

Bourguignon, C. and L., *Le Sol, la Terre et les Champs* (2008).

Bramley, R. G. V., et al., 'Making sense of a sense of place: precision viticulture approaches to the analysis of terroir at different scales', *OENO One*, 54/4 (2020), 903–17.

Bramley, R. G. V., and Gardiner, P. S., 'Underpinning terroir with data: a quantitative analysis of biophysical variation in the Margaret River region of Western Australia', *Australian Journal of Grape and Wine Research*, 27/4 (2021), 420–30.

T

Charters, S., et al. (eds.), *The Routledge Handbook of Wine and Culture* (2022).
Fanet, J., *Les Terroirs du Vin* (2001).
Goode, J., *Wine Science: The Application of Science in Wine* (3rd edn, 2021).
Johnson, H., and Robinson, J., *The World Atlas of Wine* (8th edn, 2019).
Matthews, M. A., *Terroir and Other Myths of Winegrowing* (2016).
Moran, W., 'Terroir: the human factor', *Australia and New Zealand Wine Industry Journal*, 16/2 (2001), 32–51.
OIV, 'Definition of vitivinicultural terroir' (2010). www.oiv.int/public/medias/379/viti-2010-1-en.pdf.
Patterson, T., and Buechsenstein, J., *Wine and Place: A Terroir Reader* (2018).
Renouf, V., et al., 'Soils, rootstocks and grapevine varieties in prestigious Bordeaux vineyards and their impact on yield and quality', *Journal International des Sciences de la Vigne et du Vin*, 44/3 (2010), 127–34.
Seguin, G., ' "Terroirs" and pedology of wine growing', *Experientia*, 42 (1986), 861–73.
Smart, R. E., 'Vineyard design to improve wine quality the Orlando way', *Australian and New Zealand Wine Industry Journal*, 11 (1996), 335–6.
Tonietto, J., and Carbonneau, A., 'A multicriteria climatic classification system for grape-growing regions worldwide', *Agricultural and Forest Meteorology*, 124/1–2 (2004), 81–97.
Urvieta, R., et al., 'Terroir and vintage discrimination of Malbec wines based on phenolic composition across multiple sites in Mendoza, Argentina', *Scientific Reports*, 11/2863 (2021).
van Leeuwen, C., and Seguin, G., 'The concept of terroir in viticulture', *Journal of Wine Research*, 17/1 (2006), 1–10.
van Leeuwen, C., et al., 'Influence of climate, soil, and cultivar on terroir', *American Journal of Enology and Viticulture*, 55/3 (2004), 207–17.
van Leeuwen, C., et al., 'Soil-related terroir factors: a review', *OENO One*, 52/2 (2018), 173–88.
van Leeuwen, C., et al., 'Recent advancements in understanding the terroir effect on aromas in grapes and wines'. *OENO One*, 54/4 (2020), 985–1006.
Wilson, J. E., *Terroir: The Role of Geology, Climate and Culture in the Making of French Wines* (1998).

tête de cuvée, French term occasionally used for selected top bottlings.

tetrachloroanisole. See TECA.

Texas, south-western state in the United States, currently the country's fifth largest wine-producing state after California, Washington, Oregon, and New York, with about 2,031 ha/5,020 acres planted mainly with VITIS VINIFERA vines in production in 2019. The first vineyard was planted by the Spanish missionaries near what is now El Paso in the mid 1600s. Wine production built to more than 200,000 gal/7,570 hl by 1853. In the 1880s, the famous VITIS taxonomist T. V. MUNSON, from Denison, Texas, shipped native Texas vine species to France and saved the European wine community from devastation by PHYLLOXERA. In the early 20th century, the Texas wine industry was almost eliminated by PROHIBITION. Dr Clint McPherson and Robert Reed of Texas Tech University revived the modern wine industry in 1976 with the creation of Llano Estacado Winery in Lubbock, experimenting with multiple grape varieties and spurring others to do the same. The industry has grown steadily since. While determining producing wineries in Texas is difficult because the official count of winery permits includes non-producing locations, there were over 500 permits as of 2021, with 300–400 of these belonging to wineries producing wines from Texas grapes.

Texas vines have to combat not just DROUGHT and PIERCE'S DISEASE but also WINTER FREEZE, HAIL, WIND, BLACK ROT, TEXAS ROOT ROT, black berry MOTHS, and CROWN GALL. Texas wineries compensated for these adversities by importing grapes from other states until increased plantings and an industry initiative to improve quality resulted in legislation mandating that wines labelled with vineyard, AVA, or county designations respectively must contain 95%, 85%, and 75% grapes from the designated area, and the remainder must be from 100% Texas grapes.

Like many modern US winegrowers, Texans first planted and vinified the traditional French varieties Cabernet Sauvignon, Merlot, and Chardonnay, often with disappointing results. In recent years, winegrowers have achieved success with Mediterranean grape varieties such as Tempranillo, Sangiovese, Roussanne, Viognier, and Vermentino.

The state had a total of eight AVAs in 2022, spread throughout five main regions.

The Texas High Plains region is located in the north-west portion of the state extending north into the Texas panhandle. The **Texas High Plains AVA** is the state's second largest AVA at over 3 million ha/8 million acres, although only 1,240 ha/3,000 acres were planted in 2019. The AVA sits atop the Caprock Escarpment, the boundary of which demarcates the Texas High Plains from the lower plains of the Central Texas region to the east. High ELEVATION with fertile red soils, hot days, cool nights, and frigid winters allows full vine DORMANCY. Vineyards are planted at elevations of 915–1,220 m/3,000–4,000 ft, affording plenty of daytime sunshine for ripening and relatively cool night temperatures for acid retention. Drought is the main challenge here. Depending upon vintage, the AVA supplies 75–85% of Texas wine grapes, though the majority are transported to the Texas Hill Country for fermentation and bottling. The region was initially known for Cabernet Sauvignon and Chardonnay, more recently for Tempranillo, Syrah, Sangiovese, Vermentino, and Roussanne.

The West Texas region is of historical more than commercial significance. It is home to the oldest winery in Texas, Val Verde, which has operated continuously for over a century and is known mainly for sweet FORTIFIED WINES. This arid region encompasses three AVAs: **Mesilla Valley**, which extends from New Mexico into Texas; **Texas Davis Mountains**, which produces good Cabernet Sauvignon and a small quantity of Sauvignon Blanc; and the tiny (129 sq km/50 sq mile) **Escondido Valley**.

To the east is **Texas Hill Country AVA**, the largest AVA in Texas and the second largest in the US, encompassing 3,884,982 ha/9,600,000 acres but only approximately 1,000 acres of vineyards. Soils vary, with LIMESTONE bedrock found throughout the region. The majority of the state's wineries are located here, with grapes imported from the Texas High Plains AVA to fulfil production needs. Fine *vinifera* wines are produced, mainly in vibrant white and focused red styles. The AVAs of **Bell Mountain** and **Fredericksburg** are within the larger Texas Hill Country AVA, with the town of Fredericksburg one of the largest wine-tourism destinations in the US.

The North Texas region is north of Texas Hill Country and east of the High Plains. Humidity makes it difficult to grow *vinifera*, though there has been increased investment in plantings and wineries in recent years due to tourism from nearby Dallas and Fort Worth. The city of Grapevine, which lies between the two, has fashioned itself as a major wine destination. Just under 100 miles north, the **Texoma AVA** is being developed as another wine tourism destination.

The South-Eastern or Gulf Coast region is located in the south-eastern quadrant of the state, centred on Houston. At 123 ha/305 acres of bearing vines in 2017, the region suffers from both humidity and Pierce's disease. The warm, humid pine forests in its far north-eastern reaches are suitable for HYBRID and non-*vinifera* grapes such as Pierce's disease-resistant Lenoir (Black Spanish), Cynthiana (NORTON), and Blanc du Bois. One of the state's most respected wines, a Madeira-style FORTIFIED wine made with Blanc du Bois by Haak Vineyards & Winery, is produced here. J.T.

Dupuy, J., *The Wines of the Southwest USA* (2020).
www.txwines.org

Texas root rot, caused by the fungus *Phymatotrichopsis omnivora*, which lives in the soil. This vine FUNGAL DISEASE can prevent grape-growing on CALCAREOUS soil in parts of the south-western United States. A circular patch of vines can suddenly die in summer. The disease is avoided by planting disease-free material in non-infested soil. The vigorous ROOTSTOCK Dog Ridge can be planted where the fungus is suspected. R.E.S.

texture, the dimension of TASTING that draws together attributes such as smoothness and ASTRINGENCY that produce tactile rather than flavour sensations in the mouth. These sensations are often referred to collectively as MOUTHFEEL. In practice, the sensory perception of texture, experienced through the sense of touch and arising from the trigeminal nerve, is closely intertwined with the senses of taste and smell. Astringency, BODY, VISCOSITY, BITTERNESS, and ACIDITY are among the interrelated factors influencing texture. Because of the complexity of the interactions among the many wine constituents that may be involved, formal sensory studies relating wine composition to texture are limited. Nevertheless, evidence to date indicates that wine TANNINS, PIGMENTED TANNINS, ETHANOL, and POLYSACCHARIDES are all involved with this sensation. TASTING NOTES sometimes try to describe the texture of a wine by comparing it to a type of material such as silk or velvet or by likening it to the texture of a foodstuff (e.g. grainy or chewy). A mouthfeel wheel was developed in Adelaide in Australia in answer to Davis's AROMA WHEEL (illustrated under MOUTHFEEL). Its purpose was to establish a vocabulary for describing the sensations of texture in red wines. More recent research by Gawel et al. has focused on texture and mouthfeel in white wines. P.J.W. & J.E.H.

AWRI, 'Factors affecting wine texture, taste, clarity, stability and production efficiency' (2017). www.wineaustralia.com/getmedia/76591f5c-fef2-4bcb-9880-6e85c508990f/Final-Report-3-1-4.

Gawel, R., et al., 'A "mouth-feel wheel": terminology for communicating the mouth-feel characteristics of red wine', *Australian Journal of Grape and Wine Research*, 6 (2000), 203–7.

Gawel, R., et al., 'The mouthfeel of white wine', *Critical Reviews in Food Science and Nutrition*, 58/17 (2017), 2939–56.

Thailand, South East Asian country where viticulture began in the 1960s on the low plain around the capital Bangkok and has flourished, despite the challenges involved in TROPICAL VITICULTURE. Although the early vineyards were developed to produce TABLE GRAPES, the main varieties planted were VITIS VINIFERA, including MALAGA BLANC, MUSCAT OF HAMBURG, Perlette, CARDINAL, and POKDUM. In the mid 1980s, grapes from the so-called 'floating vineyards' in the Chao Phraya delta became the raw material for Spy, a popular wine cooler produced by Siam Winery, a venture established by the man who devised the energy drink Red Bull. The winery remains Thailand's largest, with an upscale label, Monsoon Valley, sourced primarily from vineyards in the hinterland of Hua Hin, south-west of Bangkok, growing predominantly COLOMBARD, CHENIN BLANC, and SYRAH. It also has vineyards in Chang Mai and in the highlands around the Khao Yai National Park north of Bangkok. Situated at 350m/1,148 ft in ELEVATION, Khao Yai has since become home to several wineries, including pioneers PB Valley Khao Yai Winery, started in the mid 1990s by the Boon Rawd Corporation, brewer of Singha beer, and GranMonte Estate, founded in 1999. Chenin Blanc and Syrah are the region's core varieties; GranMonte also grows VIOGNIER, VERDELHO, and DURIF.

The Thai Wine Association has been a cohesive force in setting and maintaining standards for the industry. Some producers in Asia supplement locally grown grapes with imported grapes, GRAPE CONCENTRATE or BULK WINE, but the association requires that its members declare any imported component above 10% clearly on their labels. It also helped launch Thailand's first regional GEOGRAPHICAL INDICATION, for the Khao Yai region, recognized by the Thai government and awaiting EU approval in 2022. D.G.

Theophrastus (370–288 BCE), philosopher and botanist from Lesbos who discusses viticulture in his 'plant researches'.

thermal amplitude. See DIURNAL TEMPERATURE RANGE.

Thermenregion, Austrian wine-growing region named for its thermal springs, also unofficially known as the Südbahn for the historical railway south from VIENNA that forms its backbone. In 2021 it encompassed 1,901 ha/4,697 acres of vines or 4.2% of national vine surface. Thermenregion DAC was created in 2023. The northern Thermenregion, especially around GUMPOLDSKIRCHEN, features two white INDIGENOUS VARIETIES seldom encountered anywhere else: ROTGIPFLER produces wines with a striking combination of body and brightness, while ZIERFANDLER (sometimes called Spätrot) recalls CHENIN BLANC in its juxtaposition of opulence with brightness with spiced quince and citrus notes. Weingut Stadlmann's bottling from the Mandel-Höh vineyard demonstrates how profound, seductive, and long-lived Zierfandler can be. But nearly every significant white grape of NIEDERÖSTERREICH shows some success in this same sector.

Red wines from the southern Thermenregion, centred around Baden, once had a major presence in foreign as well as domestic markets as blends of Blauer PORTUGIESER, Pinot Noir (Blauburgunder), and BLAUFRÄNKISCH. Today the overwhelming emphasis is on varietal bottlings of Pinot Noir and ST-LAURENT. D.S.

thermotherapy, a technique to eliminate VIRUS DISEASES from grapevines by growing infected plants at high temperatures (about 38 °C/100 °F) and then propagating from SHOOT TIPS. These shoot tips can produce plants free of virus diseases, but some diseases such as FANLEAF DEGENERATION virus are eliminated much more easily than others—LEAFROLL, for example. Each tip produced must be checked to see whether it is virus-free and then can become registered as a new CLONE. New techniques of TISSUE CULTURE have generally been found more effective at virus elimination. Thermotherapy should not be confused with HOT-WATER TREATMENT. R.E.S.

thermovinification, process sometimes used in RED WINEMAKING, whereby heat is applied to grapes or MUST before FERMENTATION to increase the speed/extent of extraction of colour from grape skins, treat mouldy grapes, and remove GREEN aromas. Sometimes the term is used specifically to refer to a process that was quite widely adopted in the 1970s, particularly in France, involving one hour or less of heat treatment at around 70 °C/160 °F that liberates coloured must, which is then cooled, pressed, clarified, and fermented much as in traditional WHITE WINEMAKING. However, the term is also used more broadly to refer to a range of techniques entailing the heating of red grapes. Some involve much longer periods of hot skin contact (sometimes referred to as MPC or MACÉRATION PRÉFERMENTAIRE *à chaud*), skin contact for part of the fermentation, and/or coupling heat treatment with other processes such as exposure to a vacuum (see FLASH DÉTENTE). Most of these variations try to address criticisms of some wines made by thermovinification, particularly poor colour stability due to insufficient TANNIN extraction and standardized fruity ESTER flavours that can occur when highly clarified red juices are fermented at lower temperatures. Thermovinification techniques are most commonly used to make everyday wines from grapes low in ANTHOCYANINS or from grapes that are not fully ripe. Used with grapes affected by rot such as BOTRYTIS, the enzyme LACCASE is denatured, thus avoiding OXIDATION of the juice and depletion of red wine colour. Heat treatment also volatilizes ISOBUTYL-METHOXYPYRAZINE and other compounds associated with green aromas. The heating is performed using various types of heat exchangers or immersion systems. Thermovinification is rarely used in making fine wines, however, which almost invariably rely on traditional maceration to extract colour and flavour from the grape skins. S.N.

Nordestgaard, S., 'Pre-fermentation heating of red grapes: a useful tool to manage compressed vintages?', *Australian and New Zealand Grapegrower & Winemaker*, 637 (2017), 54–61.

thiamine. See VITAMINS.

Thiniatiko, red grape occasionally found on the Greek island of Kefalonia making rich

wines. According to DNA PROFILING, it is identical to MAVRODAPHNE.

thinning vines. See CROP THINNING and SHOOT THINNING.

thiols, or **volatile thiols**, are VOLATILE SULFUR COMPOUNDS produced by YEAST during FERMENTATION. They are generally derived from FLAVOUR PRECURSORS in the grapes and are therefore at their maximum levels immediately after fermentation. Although the terms 'thiol' and MERCAPTAN are synonymous, the former is typically used in a positive context when discussing varietal character, for example in SAUVIGNON BLANC wines, the latter in the negative context of FAULTS IN WINE. They have a particularly low perception threshold (ng/l).

Volatile thiols, also known as **polyfunctional thiols**, for example those described in FLAVOUR COMPOUNDS that bring aromas likened to grapefruit and passion fruit to white wines such as Sauvignon Blanc, are essential for the perception of freshness but can also be responsible for black-fruit flavours in red wines.

So-called age-related thiols such as 2-furfurylthiol (coffee-like) and benzylmercaptan (gunflint, smoky) are powerful aroma molecules formed by the reaction of HYDROGEN SULFIDE with certain compounds in OAK or grapes. Even at extremely low levels (a few parts per trillion), these compounds contribute to the empyreumatic (charry, smoky) notes in some aged wines. Benzylmercaptan can cause off-odours if present at too high a level. V.F.

Blanchard, L., et al., 'Formation of furfurylthiol exhibiting a strong coffee aroma during oak barrel fermentation from furfural released by toasted staves', *Journal of Agricultural and Food Chemistry*, 49/10 (2001), 4833–5.

Ferreira, V. E., et al., 'Elusive chemistry of hydrogen sulfide and mercaptans in wine', *Journal of Agricultural and Food Chemistry*, 66/10 (2018), 2237–46.

Tominaga, T., et al., 'Contribution of benzenemethanethiol to smoky aroma of certain *Vitis vinifera* L. wines', *Journal of Agricultural and Food Chemistry*, 51/5 (2003), 1373–6.

third growth. See the CLASSIFICATION of Bordeaux.

Thompson Seedless is the common California name for the seedless white grape variety SULTANA. It acquired this name from an early grower of the variety near Yuba City, one William Thompson. Thompson Seedless is California's most planted grape variety. Almost all of the vines are planted in the hot, dry SAN JOAQUIN VALLEY, with three-quarters in Fresno County, the powerhouse of California RAISIN production. In 1960 almost 70% of all grapes crushed for white wine were Thompson Seedless, clearly indicating what made up the 49% of 'other grapes' then allowed in wines labelled as VARIETALS. In the 1970s, Thompson Seedless was particularly useful to the California wine industry in helping to bulk out inexpensive white JUG WINE blends at a time when demand far outstripped supply of premium white wine grape varieties. Today, however, it is used mainly for raisins, as material for DISTILLATION or for GRAPE CONCENTRATE to sweeten bottled waters or cold tea drinks.

Thongue, Côtes de, IGP in the Hérault between Béziers and Pézenas named for the river that runs through it. Both Bordeaux and Mediterranean varieties make up the IGP's 10,000 ha/24,711 acres of vines.

Thrapsathiri, Cretan vine variety making rich, full-bodied whites. Probably identical to the Cyclades' Begleri and recently identified in Italy, thanks to DNA PROFILING, under the name Malvasia di Rimini. J.V.

three-tier system. With the repeal of PROHIBITION, most US states promulgated regulations that made vertical integration of the industry illegal, mandating that it be separated into three 'tiers': producer (or supplier, in the case of imports), wholesaler, and retailer (or restaurant). As a result of the legal protection of the middle tier and the rapid consolidation of wholesalers, notably SOUTHERN GLAZER's, many producers, retailers, and consumers chafe at the lack of a full liberalization of the US wine market. For more, see UNITED STATES, regulation, and DIRECT SHIPPING. T.C.

thrips, tiny (1–2 mm long) winged insects which readily feed on grapevine flowers and developing bunches, causing scarring and disfigurement of grapes by eating away at the small berries. While thrips are sometimes thought to be the cause of poor FRUIT SET, there is little evidence to support this. M.J.E. & R.E.S.

Tibouren could almost be said to be *the* Provençal grape variety, but DNA PROFILING has shown it to be identical to ROSSESE di Dolceacqua. It has a long history in south-east France and the ability to produce such quintessentially Provençal wines as earthy rosés with a genuine scent of the GARRIGUE (its wine is not naturally deep in colour). In 2019 total French plantings were a static 451 ha/1,114 acres, almost all in the Var. Tibouren is cultivated by a number of the more quality- and history-conscious producers of Provence, and some of them bottle it as a VARIETAL rosé. Particularly early-budding, it is sensitive to COULURE and therefore yields irregularly. Its original sphere of influence was around St-Tropez, where it is thought by some to have been imported as recently as the end of the 18th century by a naval captain, Antiboul, after whom it was named.

Tierra del Vino de Zamora, DOP just west of TORO with 648 ha/1,601 acres and just nine wineries in 2020. TEMPRANILLO dominates terrain similar to that of its better-known neighbour.

tight spacing, American colloquial expression for closely planted vineyards; see VINE DENSITY.

tillage, the vineyard process of ploughing the soil, normally to kill weeds, also referred to as cultivation. The type of tillage and its frequency vary from region to region around the world. In medieval times, before vines were planted in rows, tillage was by handheld hoes. Animals were subsequently used to pull ploughs. For modern vineyards, tractor-mounted discs or tines disturb the topsoil and kill weeds between the rows. Tillage within the vine row requires a special plough that will avoid trunks. Initially these were manually operated to dodge in and out; later, touch or electronic sensors were used to activate a hydraulic mechanism. Because of root and trunk damage, this practice was replaced from the 1960s onwards by the use of undervine HERBICIDES. However, since the last two decades of the 20th century, growers wishing to avoid the use of AGROCHEMICALS have returned to undervine tillage. This has been assisted by the development of hoes which are more efficient and have more sensitive and accurate 'tripping' mechanisms, thus reducing damage to the vines. Some producers, including those as notable as Ch LATOUR and Leflaive of Puligny-Montrachet, have gone back to using HORSES, which often seem to appear when WINE WRITERS are nearby.

A fastidiously tilled vineyard is still regarded as a sign of good husbandry in some regions, but there is a growing recognition for many vineyards that tillage damages SOIL STRUCTURE and can lead, for example, to problems of water infiltration, SOIL COMPACTION, and SOIL EROSION. The planting of COVER CROPS or allowing volunteer plants to grow is becoming more common. R.E.S.

time and wine. See AGEING.

Timorasso, relatively rare Piemontese vine variety enjoying a renaissance for its aromatic, durable white VARIETALS. There were 123 ha/304 acres reported in Italy in 2015.

tinaja, large earthenware vessel, probably developed from the Roman AMPHORAE, occasionally still used to ferment and store wine in central and southern SPAIN and southern CHILE. Tinajas are used by some producers in LA MANCHA, VALDEPEÑAS, and MONTILLA-MORILES, although modern versions are mostly made from reinforced concrete. They are relatively cheap but have the disadvantages that they are

T

◀ GranMonte's Chenin Blanc vineyard in the Asoke Valley, Khao Yai, is harvested once a year at the end of THAILAND's winter in February or March. Harvesting at night reduces the amount of energy needed to cool the grapes, minimizes OXIDATION and provides better working conditions for the pickers. © GranMonte

not very efficient in terms of space, are difficult to clean (especially if the neck is narrow), and offer relatively poor TEMPERATURE CONTROL unless they are buried underground like QVEVRI. Increased interest in amphorae in winemaking has led to a certain reprise, however.

tinta, the Spanish and Portuguese feminine adjective for 'red', is therefore the first word of many unrelated Spanish and Portuguese names and synonyms for dark-skinned vine varieties, for example TINTA RORIZ.

Tinta Amarela. See TRINCADEIRA.

Tinta Barroca, common, relatively thick-skinned grape variety planted in Portugal's DOURO Valley, mainly for PORT, and grown on a total of 3,501 ha/8,651 acres in Portugal in 2020, significantly down on 2012's 5,444 ha. It is favoured by growers for yielding large quantities of grapes with exceptionally high levels of sugar and is typically planted on higher or north-facing slopes. However, Barroca is prone to both DOWNY and POWDERY MILDEW, is easily damaged by extreme heat, and has berries which have a tendency to shrivel on the vine. By no means as highly prized as the other leading port grapes—TOURIGA NACIONAL, Touriga Franca, and Tinta Roriz—Barroca produces reasonably well-structured but slightly jammy, rustic wines which can be useful in a blend. In Portugal Tinta Barroca is rarely used on its own but full-throttle, unfortified, dry, VARIETAL Tinta Barroca (sometimes misspelt and referred to as Tinta Barocca or Tinta das Baroccas) is a speciality in South Africa, where there were 155 ha/383 acres in 2020 and where it is also used in FORTIFIED port-like wines.

Tinta Caiada. See PARRALETA.

Tinta de Toro. See TEMPRANILLO and TORO.

Tinta Francisca, lesser red grape variety used in the production of PORT in Portugal's DOURO Valley. The wine produced can be notably sweet but is not particularly concentrated. Some see similarities with Pinot Noir. It has been planted to a very limited extent in South Africa.

Tinta Miúda, 'small red one', Portuguese wine grape grown traditionally around Lisbon and in the LISBOA region. The vine is low-yielding but can produce seductive and powerful wines. Identical to the GRACIANO of Rioja and MORRASTEL of the Languedoc, it ripens late and is therefore susceptible to ROT in the Atlantic-influenced west of the country, though it is valued by winemakers for the colour and acidity it contributes to a blend. There were 326 ha/806 acres in Portugal in 2017.

Tinta Negra, previously **Tinta Negra Mole**, name for NEGRAMOLL on the island of MADEIRA, where it is by far the most commonly planted variety. DNA PROFILING has shown it to be identical to the Portuguese variety Molar. It is therefore indubitably a VITIS VINIFERA variety, unlike many of the vines that replaced the so-called tradtional varieties SERCIAL, VERDELHO, BUAL, and MALVASIA on Madeira after the ravages of POWDERY MILDEW and PHYLLOXERA in the 19th century. It yields relatively high quantities of sweet, pale red wine which turns amber with the madeira production process and then yellow-green with age. Only in the last decade has it been permitted to name the variety on the label.

Tinta Pinheira, former name for the Portuguese grape variety RUFETE.

Tinta Roriz, official name for the Spanish vine variety TEMPRANILLO in northern Portugal. Thanks to recent popularity, it has become Portugal's most planted variety by quite a margin, with total plantings of 20,161 ha/49,819 acres by 2020. It is particularly important in the DOURO Valley, where it vies with TOURIGA FRANCA as the most planted variety in some areas, particularly in the Cima Corgo and Douro Superior. It is relatively easy to grow in the Douro but has a tendency to over-produce and performs best in those years when yields are inherently low. VARIETAL wines are also made in Dão, where it is gaining ground. In the Alentejo, under the name ARAGONEZ, it is often blended with the local TRINCADEIRA.

Tintilla de Rota, Andalucian name for a variety shown by DNA PROFILING to be GRACIANO. Here it can make rather charming sweet FORTIFIED reds.

tinto, Spanish and Portuguese for 'red', so that *vino* (*vinho* in Portuguese) *tinto* is red wine (as opposed to the lighter red CLARETE produced in Spain). This is the origin of the name of the red wine once known in England as TENT.

Like TINTA, 'Tinto' is also the first word of many Spanish and Portuguese names and synonyms for black grape varieties. TEMPRANILLO, for example, is known as Tinto Fino in Ribero del Duero.

Tinto Cão, meaning 'red dog', top-quality black grape variety for the production of PORT. Having almost disappeared from the vineyards of the DOURO Valley in northern Portugal (despite its long history there), it is being planted with greater enthusiasm since it was identified as one of the five finest port varieties, although it is not one of the deepest coloured nor especially productive. It is also grown for TABLE WINES in the DÃO region and has been planted experimentally at DAVIS in California and in Australia.

Tinto del País, synonym for TEMPRANILLO, as is **Tinto Fino**, in RIBERA DEL DUERO.

tipping, the viticultural practice of cutting off SHOOT TIPS at flowering. Normally about 10–20 cm (4–8 in) of shoot tip are removed. This can help reduce the problem of COULURE, or poor FRUIT SET, for some susceptible varieties.

tirage, French for that part of the SPARKLING WINEMAKING process during which sugar and yeast (known in French as the *liqueur de tirage*) are added to the blended base wines in order to provoke a second fermentation, thereby creating CARBON DIOXIDE gas. It is sometimes used to refer to the entire period during which the sparkling wine matures on the LEES of this second fermentation.

tissue culture, the culturing of excised cells, tissues, and organs using artificial media of salts and nutrients, used especially in PROPAGATION and GENETIC MODIFICATION. The techniques can be used to develop vines with particularly useful properties much faster than by conventional PROPAGATION. Usually a CALLUS develops first, then roots and buds develop within the callus, leading to a new vine that can flower and set seed. The formation of roots or buds is achieved by subtle changes in the ingredients of the culture solution, especially in the relative amounts of the hormones AUXIN and CYTOKININ. Aseptic conditions are essential. Meristem culture, or the culture of the terminal 1 mm of vine shoot, especially after its fragmentation, has permitted the production of large numbers of plantlets in tubes that are free of some VIRUSES and CROWN GALL disease. Large numbers of vine plantlets can be 'micro-propagated' by these methods, which can rapidly build up healthy populations of scarce VINE VARIETIES. See diagram overleaf. B.G.C.

titratable acidity. See TOTAL ACIDITY.

toast (*chauffe* in French), given to a barrel towards the end of the process of forming it over a heat source, is one of the processes in BARREL MAKING that most obviously affect eventual wine flavour. The heat source also inevitably toasts the inside of the barrel to a degree that varies according to the heat of the fire and the length of time the barrel is held over it. This heating process dramatically alters the wood's physical and chemical composition. The toasted wood provides a buffer between the ALCOHOL in wine and the TANNINS in wood. In general, the less a barrel is toasted, the more tannins and other wood characteristics will be leached into the wine by the alcohol. Wine matured in lightly toasted barrels therefore tends to taste 'oaky', 'woody', or even 'vegetal', while wine matured in heavily toasted barrels is more likely to taste 'toasty' or 'spicy'. See also OAK FLAVOUR.

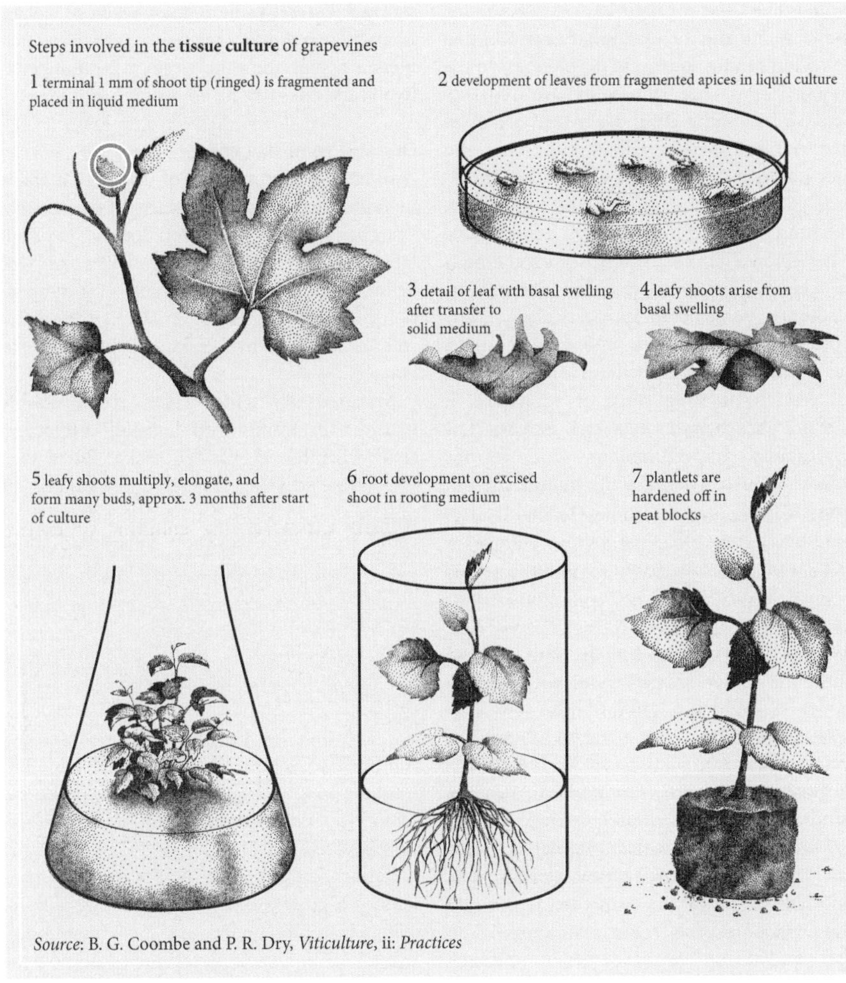

Source: B. G. Coombe and P. R. Dry, *Viticulture*, ii: *Practices*

Burgundy BARRELS are in general more heavily toasted than Bordeaux BARRIQUES, partly because a heavy toast is better suited to the flavours of Pinot Noir and Chardonnay grapes than to those of Cabernet Sauvignon, Merlot, Sauvignon Blanc, and Sémillon but also because in Burgundy producers tend to put must for white wines or very young red wines into barrel with more LEES, which remove many of the compounds that result from toasting. The following terms are used, although they are imprecise and cannot really be compared between coopers.

White toast: extremely light toast, sufficient to make the barrel stable, achieved by low temperature or by wetting the barrel to decrease the production of compounds during toasting.

Light toast: there is little colour change in the wood. Wines aged in these barrels are usually quite fruity but can be somewhat tannic.

Medium toast: the wood is browner. Wines aged in such barrels are said to smell of vanilla and coffee. They will normally be less tannic than those aged in light-toast barrels and are often described as rounder, smoother, and more persistent.

Heavy toast: the wood is very dark. Wines aged in these barrels are usually marked by aromas of roasted coffee beans, toasted bread, ginger, nutmeg, cloves, and smoked meats. The above flavour descriptions apply to wine aged in French oak barrels.

The word 'char' is usually associated with American whiskey barrels, which are made over steam or natural gas but then set on fire and burned (charred). Traditionally American oak wine barrels were simply un-charred bourbon barrels, but American cooperages now toast to the customer's specifications.

The higher the toast, the greater the risk of blisters inside the staves. Coopers have recently developed new toast levels using different combinations of temperature and duration.

In addition to the origin of the wood and the way it was seasoned, toast is a crucial factor when ordering a barrel. M.C.K. & A.P.

Tocai, or **Tocai Friulano**, old Friulan name for SAUVIGNONASSE, now replaced by FRIULANO.

California has limited plantings of the variety they still call Tocai Friulano, which is also produced by Millbrook in the Hudson Valley, NEW YORK.

Tai Rosso is used as a synonym for GRENACHE NOIR in the VENETO.

Togo is a wine hub in West Africa, behind only SOUTH AFRICA in volumes of wine traded. Currently any wine produced in Togo is made from imported juice, but at the end of 2020 the country's first VITIS VINIFERA vineyard was planted, about 1,500 vines of Chardonnay and PINOTAGE rooted into SCHIST and GNEISS soils in the Plateaux region, 150 km/93 m north of the capital, Lomé. This is a private venture with support from Springfontein Wine Estate in South Africa. The vineyard sits at the end of a steep, craggy hiking trail at ELEVATIONS of 720–760 m/2,362–2,493 ft, where the MESOCLIMATE is cooler than the country's otherwise tropical conditions: temperatures range from 10–32 °C / 50–90 °F, winds are brisk, and annual rainfall is 1,700 mm/67 in.

Tokaj, town, PDO (*Oltalom alatt álló eredet megjelöléssel* or OEM in Hungarian), and the most famous wine region in HUNGARY. Mount Tokaj is the prominent VOLCANIC cone at the southernmost tip of the region, which includes the foothills of the entire Zemplén Mountains (which, in turn, form the southern range of the Tokaj-Eperjes Mountains). Hungarians often use the name Tokaj to mean the whole region, but locals refer to themselves as being from the Hegyalja, to emphasize their separateness from the residents of the town of Tokaj itself. However, even they prefer to call their wine **Tokaji** (the –i suffix indicating place of origin, as with the –er in New Yorker) regardless of any more precise location within the region.

History

The first known occurrence of the name, in the form 'Tokay', is in a 13th-century genealogy and history entitled *Gesta Hungarorum*. The *Gesta*, and many sources after it, refer to the emblematic hill of the region not as Tokaj but as Tarcal, today the name of a village at the western foot of the hill. Remarkably, Tarcal was also the name of the hill in Syrmia far to the south, today known as Fruška Gora in SERBIA, which yielded the most famous wine of medieval Hungary. Records enumerating the administrative units have existed since 1641, but these early sources are rife with gaps and contradictions. Hungarian wine legislation of the time lists 27 communities with a right to label their wines as Tokaj. The vineyards around most of these communities were first CLASSIFIED in the 18th century, in a manner that was rigorous at the time but is not entirely useful today. By the 18th century, this extraordinary wine had been introduced to the French court (see HUNGARY, history) and was subsequently introduced to the Russian imperial court by the Habsburgs. Only CONSTANTIA from the Cape of Good Hope, and to a lesser extent Moldavian COTNARI, rivalled the reputation of this wine, with Tokaji Esszencia regarded as an all-purpose restorative.

During most of the 20th century, Tokaj languished. Its recovery from PHYLLOXERA was slow, and its reputation suffered with the dissolution of the Austro-Hungarian Empire in 1918. Under Soviet domination, quantity rather than quality was encouraged, although a number of individual growers and winemakers continued to uphold traditions and some exceptional wines were made. It potentially encompasses 11,149 ha/27,549 acres, but only 5,946 ha/14,692 acres are planted today. A small portion of the region extends into SLOVAKIA, where wines of a similar style are made.

Geography

Located in north-eastern Hungary, the Zemplén Mountains have a cool climate, as does the entire Tokaj-Eperjes range within the Carpathian volcanic chain. The mean temperature in the foothills is 9–10 °C/48–50 °F annually, 21 °C in July, and −3 °C in January. The favourable south-south-eastern aspect of the foothills contributes to the excellent MESOCLIMATES found on the slopes. The best vineyard sites occupy the southern slopes, where they are sheltered from northern and north-westerly winds by relatively high, forested peaks. Of these, the top sites are open to the east or the west to promote air circulation and to discourage FROSTS. High levels of humidity, due to the location of the vineyards above the confluence of the Bodrog and Tisza rivers, encourage special fungoid flora, including the all-important BOTRYTIS.

The volcanic activity which began 15 million years ago and dominated geological processes here for six million years created a great TOPOGRAPHICAL diversity in the Tokaj-Eperjes range. The spectrum of VOLCANIC rocks that can be found in the area includes rhyolite, rhyodacite, dacite, andesite, and zeolite. These various rock types occur as lavas and differ mainly in terms of silica content. In addition, pyroclastic rocks, most significantly TUFFS, are also found. During and after the principal eruptions, a variety of post-volcanic alterations left their stamp on Tokaj. Volcanic rocks tend to weather faster than other igneous types, and the process is accelerated here by the flow of post-volcanic groundwater and hot springs, which deliver to the surface large quantities of potassium and trace elements, enriching the volcanic detritus.

The major centres of post-volcanic changes are around Mád (sites such as Szent Tamás, Úrágya, Betsek, and Urbán), Erdőbénye, Tolcsva, and Sárospatak. The southern fringes of the range were overlain by LOESS at a much later stage, during the Quaternary period when the region's main soils were developed. On the steeper slopes, the thin soils are typically mixed with weathered andesite and are quite hard to till. In the low valleys, loess, clay, and glacial deposits evolved. Easily weathered volcanic glass still mingles with the soils today, enriching them in NUTRIENTS that are available to the vines. The most widespread soil type is the clayey *nyirok*, a red soil created by weathering volcanic rocks, particularly stony andesite. When too wet, *nyirok* is so sticky that it adheres to the spade; if it dries out, it will yield to nothing short of a pickaxe. It does not absorb water very well and has low permeability. Its red colour, from ferrous hydroxide, turns darker as its humus content increases (see ORGANIC MATTER). Slightly less common is the soil type known as yellow earth, which forms from LOESS and clayey loess, as well as sandy loess on the Kopaszhegy near Tokaj and the hills north of Olaszliszka. Loess has good drainage and here has a low LIME content. Szarvas near Tarcal is a famous example of a vineyard with loess soil. Loess is not found in the interior of the Tokaj-Eperjes chain nor in the valleys, but on the south-eastern slope of Mount Tokaj it can be found at ELEVATIONS as high as 405 m/1,330 ft.

A further soil type is the crumbly rock flour that forms from the mechanical weathering of white rhyolite, pumice, and perlite. It does not retain water and has a low heat capacity, so vines planted in it may easily dry out during a DROUGHT or freeze in extreme cold. Rock flour is common in Peres-hegy at Erdőbénye, the Tolcsvai-hegy, and the Oremus vineyard at Sátoraljaújhely.

Nomenclature

The two leading vine varieties, FURMINT and its offspring HÁRSLEVELŰ, have their genetic origin in Tokaj. Both varieties tend to produce dry wines worth AGEING based on ACIDITY, tension, BODY, and BALANCE.

For centuries, the two main categories of Tokaji were *szűrt bor* (filtered wine) and *csinált bor* (made wine). The former were made much the same way as most wine is made today, by simply PRESSING the grapes and fermenting the MUST. The latter were wines produced by the more complicated Aszú process (see below under Sweet wines). Clearly distinct from this noble sweet category was the typically dry *ordinarium*. Even in the old days, a distinction was made between free-run juice and press juice, although they were not necessarily handled separately. *Főbor* (principal wine) was the old name of Szamorodni-style wine, at least insofar as it was made by pressing the harvested fruit as is, without separating BOTRYTIZED berries from grapes unaffected by NOBLE ROT. From 1707 onward, Eszencia, the highest grade of Tokaji, was also increasingly referred to as *legfőbb bor*, meaning 'supreme wine' (*legfőbb* is the superlative of the adjective *fő*).

Dry and semi-dry wines

An increasing proportion of dry wine is made in Tokaj. These are wines matured only briefly. They are typically fermented dry but may contain some RESIDUAL SUGAR (even if at a level well below semi-sweet wines). With a few exceptions, they are fermented in stainless steel and will last three to five years, depending on the vintage.

Matured dry wines These are invariably matured in wood, with a small proportion also fermented in wooden casks, and have a very long cellaring potential. As botrytis is undesirable in these wines, the grapes must come from high-elevation vineyards (about 250 m/820 ft) designed specifically for this purpose. These are mostly SINGLE-VINEYARD and expensive wines.

Szamorodni Made from both botrytized and non-botrytized berries, these wines have a ripeness level comparable to that of BEERENAUSLESE, but they are fermented dry (*száraz*) and subjected to subtle maturation under a FILM-FORMING YEAST. These wines are very like the Jura's VIN JAUNE. More common is a sweet version (see below).

Főbor An old style now extremely rare, Főbor are close to Szamorodni in style without being matured under OXIDATIVE conditions. Főbor can be dry or sweet, depending on the natural proportion of overripe fruit and shrivelled, possibly botrytized, berries.

Sweet wines

Szamorodni Szamorodni wines are typically made in the sweet style (*édes*), when the sugar content of the grapes is so high that the must will not ferment fully dry. Although the minimum RESIDUAL SUGAR is 45 g/l, the average is 80–120 g/l, and some reach 180–200 g/l, taking on a fresh, fruity character and smooth texture that brings them very close to a young Aszú wine in style. This barrel-aged selected botrytized wine is matured for at least six months in oak (and more usually one to two years). It is not necessarily OXIDIZED.

Late Harvest/Cuvée These are mostly sweet wines made in the same way as natural sweet wines in other regions, by a single fermentation of selected bunches, and are ready for release 12–16 months after harvest. This style emerged in the early 21st century in reaction to the substantial time and capital investment required to mature Aszú wines in compliance with regulations. Often marked by a mineral character (see MINERALITY), they may contain 50–180 g/l residual sugar and (optionally) a proportion of botrytized berries similar to that

Style	Residual sugar (g/l)	Dry extract (g/l)
Aszú	120	35
Eszencia	450	50

for Aszú wines. Cuvée wines are generally made from botrytized grapes, but barrel ageing is optional.

Aszú

This is the classic sweet Tokaji, made from hand-selected, shrivelled, botrytized grapes and usually the sweetest wine of any producer. The table shows minimum RESIDUAL SUGAR and EXTRACT required for these designations.

Before pressing, the botrytized grapes are soaked for 16–36 hours in fresh must, *murci* (fermenting wine), or new wine that has completed fermentation. The wine is then matured under oxidative conditions without any FORTIFICATION, including at least one and a half years in barrel (and more likely two to three years). The unique second fermentation gives a special, deeper character to the wines.

The sweetness of Tokaji Aszú wines was classified by *puttonyos* until 2014, from 3 puttonyos (60–90 g/l residual sugar) to 6 puttonyos (150–180 g/l). Now all Tokaji Aszú must have at least 120 g/l residual sugar (although most growers agree that the highest-quality wines have around 180–230 g/l), a minimum of 19% potential alcohol, and a finished alcohol of at least 9%. The maximum yield per hectare for aszú parcels is 10 tonnes (counted in green grapes) and a kilo of aszú berries can produce no more than 2.2 litres of wine.

The following categories of sweet Tokaji are relatively rare:

Eszencia The free-run juice of hand-picked botrytized berries. Residual sugar should be at least 450 g/l; but levels of 800 g/l or more are not unheard of. Eszencia takes years to achieve a modest alcohol level of 4–5%. It is rarely sold commercially, and smaller wineries will not handle it separately. It is typically used for blending to improve the concentration of Aszú wines.

Fordítás Made by refermenting wine or must poured on Tokaji Aszú 'paste' (marc) left after pressing sweet wines, typically with more than 60 g/l sugar (minimum 45 g/l).

Máslás Rarity made by refermenting new wine or must poured on Tokaji Aszú LEES. These are sweet wines, typically with 50–90 g/l sugar, but no longer an official category.

The Mádi Kör, the local wine authority, has drawn up a rather Burgundian vineyard CLASSIFICATION which means in practice that the member wineries are obliged to follow stricter regulations in vine-growing and winemaking than are required by general Hungarian rules.

G.R & G.M.

Alkonyi, L., *Tokaj* (2000).
Alkonyi, L., *Tokaj: the Myth of Terroir* (2004).
Balassa, I., *Tokaj-Hegyalja Szőleje és Bora* (1991).
Tokaj-Hegyalja Vineyard and Wine, English summary.
Mészáros, G., et al., *Terra benedicta* (2019).
Tokaj-Hegyaljai Album (1867).

Tokay was the name under which TOKAJ used to travel. It was also the original name of the Australian STICKIE made from raisined Muscadelle grapes that has been renamed TOPAQUE.

Tokay d'Alsace, or simply **Tokay**, was long the Alsace name for PINOT GRIS, but the term was officially outlawed from 2007.

tonneau, traditional Bordeaux measure of wine volume, once a large wooden cask holding 900 l, or 252 imperial wine gallons, the equivalent of four BARRIQUES. A PARIS tonneau was 800 l, but, because of the prominence of GASCON merchants in London and English merchants in Bordeaux, the Bordeaux measure became the standard. By the end of the 18th century, tonneaux had been replaced by the easier-to-transport smaller barrique, yet the tonneau, the exact equivalent of 100 CASES of wine, is still the measure in which the Bordeaux wine trade deals.

Such was the importance of wine to medieval trade in general (see BORDEAUX and DUTCH WINE TRADE) that a tonneau, or ton in English, evolved from being the space occupied by a tun of wine to become the unit of measurement for the carrying capacity of any ship, whatever its load.

Topaque and Muscat, extremely sweet FORTIFIED WINES that used to be called Liqueur Tokay and Liqueur Muscat. They taste something like a cross between MADEIRA and traditional dark MÁLAGA, and they are two of AUSTRALIA's great gifts to the world made from, respectively, MUSCADELLE, traditionally known as Tokay in Australia (although the term was officially phased out in 2020), and a very dark-skinned strain of MUSCAT BLANC À PETITS GRAINS, called here Brown Muscat or Muscat à Petits Grains Rouge. The centre of production is a hot north-eastern corner of the state of Victoria around the towns of Rutherglen and Glenrowan. Grapes are semi-raisined on the vine, partially fermented, and then fortified with grape spirit before being subjected to an unusual wood-ageing programme that resembles a cross between a sherry SOLERA and, under many a hot tin roof, a Madeira ESTUFAGEM. The results can be uncannily fine quality, are bottled when they are ready to drink, and do not change with BOTTLE AGE. These wines are quite sweet enough to serve with virtually any dessert. In the late 1990s, the winemakers of Rutherglen joined forces to create a four-tier nomenclature for Muscat (and, by extension, Topaque). At the bottom is Rutherglen Muscat, next is Classic, then Grand, and finally Rare. It is a voluntary, self-regulated system but a very real guarantee of style, which becomes progressively richer and more complex with each tier. Rare is released in tiny quantities each year, limited by the maintenance of a very old Solera base.

top grafting, or **top working**, the viticultural operation of changing the fruiting VINE VARIETY of a mature vineyard by inserting a BUD of the selected variety in each vine but retaining the established root system. An array of approaches is available—CLEFT GRAFTING, NOTCH GRAFTING, CHIP BUDDING, or T-BUDDING—usually applied high on the original trunk just below the HEAD. If the operation is done well, only one season's crop is lost. The main risk is that of systemic disease spread from the original planting, especially VIRUS DISEASES to which different varieties and ROOTSTOCKS have different tolerances. B.G.C.

topoclimate, a local climate as determined by TOPOGRAPHY, for instance that of a particular hill, valley or slope. It is commonly subsumed under the broader term MESOCLIMATE.

topography, a term describing the land surface features of any area, which can have considerable implications for local climate (see MESOCLIMATE) and therefore for viticulture. The classic reference work by Geiger gives the most comprehensive general account of topographic effects on local climate. Topographic elements having the most influence on the climate are local ELEVATION; slope; the relative isolation of hills; aspect; and proximity to water masses such as oceans, lakes, and rivers.

Local elevation Other things being equal, temperature falls by about 0.6 °C/1.1 °F per 100 m/330 ft greater elevation. This is known as the lapse rate.

Slope At night, air is chilled by direct contact with a land surface which is rapidly losing heat by radiation. The chilled air, being denser, flows down slopes to the flat land or valleys below and is replaced by warmer air from above the land surface. The turbulent surface air over slopes at moderate elevations is therefore usually warmer at night and in the early morning than that settled over the adjacent flats and valley floors. This band on a hill slope is known as its

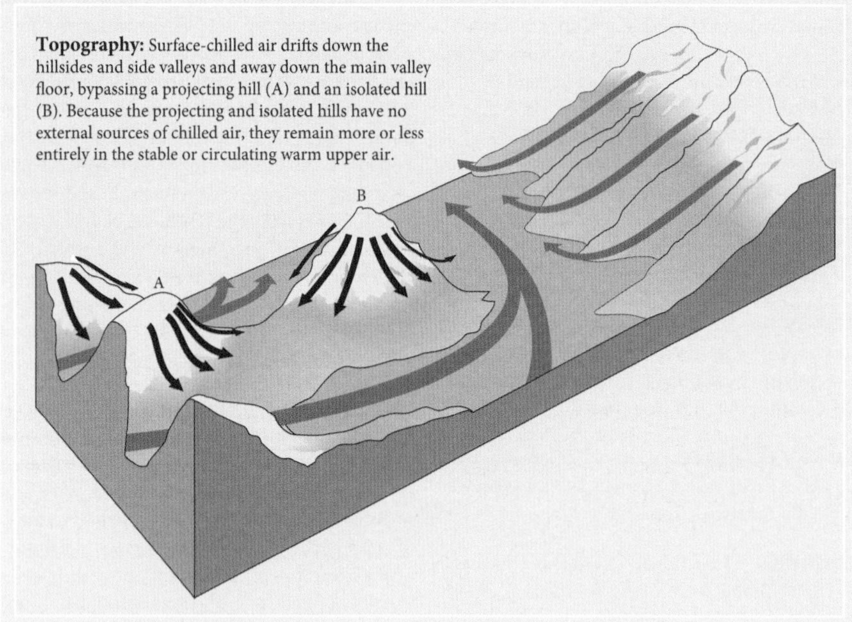

Topography: Surface-chilled air drifts down the hillsides and side valleys and away down the main valley floor, bypassing a projecting hill (A) and an isolated hill (B). Because the projecting and isolated hills have no external sources of chilled air, they remain more or less entirely in the stable or circulating warm upper air.

'thermal zone', and especially in cool climates it is valued for viticulture because of its enhanced ripening potential and length of frost-free period. The steeper the slope, the more pronounced is its thermal zone. See also HILLSIDE VINEYARDS.

Relative isolation of hills Thermal zones are strongest on isolated and projecting hills or mountains, because these have little or no external source of surface-chilled air. Cooled air from their own surfaces that slips away can be replaced only by totally unchilled air from above. The implications of this are discussed under CLIMATE AND WINE QUALITY; see also TERROIR. Examples of viticulturally famous isolated hills include the hill of Corton at ALOXE-CORTON in Burgundy; the Kaiserstuhl in BADEN; and, on a larger scale, the Montagne de Reims in CHAMPAGNE.

Aspect Slopes which face the sun through much of the day (southerly aspects in the northern hemisphere, northerly aspects in the southern hemisphere) are the warmest, and those facing away from the sun are the coolest. The influence of aspect is modified by other climate parameters. For example, the degree of daytime warming is increased by more sunshine and by protection from wind. Differences in soil temperature are important not only for nutrition of the vine but also for growth and fruiting through export of the growth substance CYTOKININ to the vine tops.

The climatic contrasts among aspects are greatest at high latitudes and in cooler vineyard regions, as well as early and late in the vine-growing season. The steeper the slope, the more aspect will affect its climate.

Easterly aspects of slopes facing the equator have the advantage that they are warmed earliest in the day, when soil and air temperatures are lowest. Notable examples of this are found in the CÔTE D'OR of Burgundy and in the RHINE Valley of Germany and Alsace. West-facing slopes can, however, induce higher daytime air temperatures because absorption of sunlight and warmer air temperatures are complementary. This is important in very cool climates.

Proximity to oceans, lakes, and rivers Water absorbs and stores large quantities of heat, with relatively little change in temperature because of the depth to which the heat penetrates, together with the high specific heat of water compared with rocks or dry soil. Its resulting temperature inertia greatly modifies the temperature regimes of adjacent land. Cool air from over the water is drawn to replace heated air rising over the land in the afternoons, while at night a reverse convection results from chilled air descending from the cold land surface and rising over the now relatively warm water. In some vineyard areas, these breezes may, in fact, be very strong winds if they are funnelled by mountains, as in the Salinas Valley in MONTEREY, California. This daily alternating pattern of air circulation makes the climate adjacent to water bodies significantly more constant than it would otherwise be, in terms of both temperature and humidity. Both factors are important in CLIMATE AND WINE QUALITY. There is also a reduced incidence of spring FROSTS and WINTER FREEZE injury in regions liable to these. Examples of this LAKE EFFECT are found in NEW YORK State, in the vineyards of Ontario in CANADA, and around RUSSIA's Black Sea coast.

The effects of rivers and lakes are normally confined to their immediate valleys, but MARITIME influences can extend considerable distances inland from coasts in the form of land and sea breezes. Notable examples of the latter occur in the BORDEAUX region of France; the NAPA Valley and SONOMA and other near-coastal regions of California; and the HUNTER VALLEY and Swan Valley of Australia's east and west coasts respectively. J.G. & R.E.S.

Geiger, R., *Das Klima der bodennahen Luftschicht* (4th edn, 1961), translated as *The Climate near the Ground* (1966).

topping. See TRIMMING.

topping up, the operation of refilling any sort of wooden container to replace wine lost through EVAPORATION. The container should be kept full or nearly full lest the ubiquitous ACETOBACTER use OXYGEN from the HEAD SPACE to start the process of transforming wine into VINEGAR.

Winemakers differ in what they view as the ideal topping-up regime for various different wines, but modern practice is to top up at least monthly, using wine of the same provenance.

Depending on the amount of evaporation, which is affected by fluctuations in temperature and humidity in the cellar, and the spare time available to the winery staff, topping up is done anything from twice a week during the first months of BARREL AGEING to once every six weeks. The ideal cellar temperature should be about 10–15 °C/50–60 °F: not so cold as to hinder development but not so warm as to encourage bacterial growth. New barrels may also need more frequent topping up since the new oak absorbs up to 5 l of wine. In Bordeaux the BUNG is usually left at the top of the barrel for the first six months, after which some producers roll red-wine barrels to one side so that the bung is in the so-called bung-over position, in which case regular racking provides the opportunity for topping up. However, it is impossible to check levels of SULFUR DIOXIDE or VOLATILE ACIDITY unless the bung is at the top.

See also ULLAGE. D.D. & V.L.

Torbato, mid- to late-ripening vine variety today most obviously associated with SARDINIA, where VARIETAL dry whites are produced from a grand total of under 10 ha/25 acres, with particular success around Alghero.

It was once quite widely cultivated in ROUSSILLON, where it is known as TOURBAT, or Malvoisie du Roussillon, but was almost abandoned before new and healthier plant material was imported from Sardinia in the 1980s. DNA PROFILING has indicated that it is a natural progeny of Hebén, an old and rare wine and TABLE GRAPE from Spain, suggesting that it was initally brought to the island when Sardinia was part of the Aragón kingdom. J.V.

Torgiano, small hillside DOC zone between Perugia and Assisi in the central Italian region of UMBRIA. It was considered Umbria's finest red wine in the 1960s and 1970s when the production of bottled wine was almost entirely in the hands of the Lungarotti family, who demonstrated that the SANGIOVESE vine could yield excellent wine outside TUSCANY. Production rules have regrettably been changed to allow VARIETALS based on INTERNATIONAL VARIETIES with no history in the zone such as Pinot Grigio, Chardonnay, and Pinot Noir. Rosso di Torgiano, originally a Sangiovese-based wine, now allows up to 50% Merlot and/or Cabernet Sauvignon. At least 70% Sangiovese is required in DOCG Torgiano Rosso Riserva, but overall the current spirit of Torgiano appears to be marketing-oriented.

torna viagem literally means 'round trip' in Portuguese and is occasionally found on labels of ancient SETÚBAL which have been subjected to lengthy sea voyages for ageing purposes. This is the equivalent of the *vinho da roda* of MADEIRA. José Maria da Fonseca have been experimenting with the genre since 2000.

Toro, revolutionized Spanish red-wine zone in CASTILLA Y LEÓN (see map under SPAIN) whose wines were famous within Spain in medieval times. This wild and remote zone spans the Duero Valley east of Zamora. At an ELEVATION of 600–825 m/2,000–2,800 ft, growing conditions are severe, with cold winters, hot summers, and just 350–400 mm/13–15 in of annual rainfall. The region's principal grape variety, Tinta de Toro, is a local variant of TEMPRANILLO which has adapted to the region's climatic extremes. Left to their own devices, the vines will easily ripen their grapes to a POTENTIAL ALCOHOL level of 16%; with care, the wines average 14.5–15% in ALCOHOLIC STRENGTH. In the late 1990s a number of producers began to move away from the region's traditional heavy, bulk reds, a move which gained notable momentum when some of top names in Ribera del Duero, Rioja, and even Bordeaux were awakened to the region's potential and launched their own estates, including Vega Sicilia's Pintia, Mauro's San Román, Sierra Cantabria's Numanthia-Termes (subsequently acquired by LVMH), Michel Rolland's Campo Elíseo, and Telmo Rodríguez's Pago La Jara. By 2020 Toro boasted 62 bodegas (up from five in 1987, when it was accorded DO status) and 5,900 ha/14,579 acres of vineyard, including 120 ha of vines more than 110 years old, thanks to the sandy soils that escaped PHYLLOXERA. Since 2021 GARNACHA can be used for a VARIETAL wine, and white wines may include Moscatel (MUSCAT BLANC À PETITS GRAINS) and ALBILLO Real in addition to the previously allowed VERDEJO and Malvasia Castellana (SÍRIA). V. de la S. & F.C.

www.dotoro.com

Torontel, Chilean white wine grape, also called Moscatel Amarilla, that DNA PROFILING has shown to be one of the numerous natural progenies of Listán Prieto (see PAÍS) and MUSCAT OF ALEXANDRIA. There were still 638 ha/1,577 acres in 2019, mainly BUSH VINES in MAULE. J.V.

Torres. See FAMILIA TORRES.

Torres Vedras, DOC subregion of LISBOA in western Portugal.

Torrontés, name of many distinct white grape varieties grown in Argentina and Spain, not always named with precision.

Argentina grows at least three different varieties with 'Torrontés' in their name. The most common, planted on 7,659 ha/18,926 acres in 2020, is **Torrontés Riojano**, a natural cross of MUSCAT OF ALEXANDRIA and CRIOLLA CHICA (California's MISSION grape), as shown by DNA PROFILING in 2003. It is the most planted white wine grape after the undistinguished Pedro Giménez and is regarded as Argentina's most distinctive white wine grape. See also TORONTEL. **Torrontés Sanjuanino**, a distinct speciality of San Juan province and another natural cross of Muscat of Alexandria and Criolla Chica, was planted on just 1,628 ha (and, as Moscatel de Austria, 108 ha of Chile), while plantings of **Torrontés Mendocino** were 563 ha. This third variety is also the result of a natural CROSS of Muscat of Alexandria, but the other parent is so far unknown.

The fragrant Torrontés Riojana is often seen as the Argentine white wine variety with the greatest potential, although some wines can be over-alcoholic and bitter. Carefully grown and vinified, Torrontés Riojana can produce wines that are high in acidity and intriguingly aromatic in a way reminiscent of but not identical to MUSCAT, although much is also used for blending. Grown all over the country and to a limited extent in Uruguay, the variety seems particularly well adapted to the arid growing conditions of Argentina, particularly the high, sandy vineyards of Cafayate where at ELEVATIONS of over 1,600 m/5,250 ft its high natural acidity and assertive flavour are particularly distinguished.

Torrontés Sanjuanino is less aromatic and has bigger berries and more compact clusters. Torrontés Mendocino, also planted mostly in San Juan, lacks Muscat aroma.

DNA PROFILING has shown that the name Torrontés is applied to at least four varieties in Spain: one in Montilla-Moriles, one in Navarra, one in Ribeiro in Galicia (which may be identical to either FERNÃO PIRES or BICAL), and one in Extramadura, where it is a synonym for ALARIJE. Torrontes is also a common synonym for several different varieties in Portugal. Altogether, Torrontes represents an identification minefield on the Iberian peninsula. The situation is much clearer in Argentina, even if the varieties' parents are not the most noble.

Toscana, central Italian region known in English as TUSCANY.

total acidity (TA), measure of the total ACIDITY, both FIXED ACIDS and VOLATILE ACIDS, present in grape juice or wine. With ALCOHOLIC STRENGTH and RESIDUAL SUGAR, total acidity is one of the most common wine measurements involved in any wine ANALYSIS.

It is obtained by a laboratory process called titration (which is why it is also referred to as titratable acidity, although technically they are not exactly the same, according to Boulton), in which very small additions of an alkali of known strength are made to a measured quantity of the grape juice or wine until the amount of added alkali just equals the amount of acids in the sample. The value of these total acids can be calculated and expressed as grams of any number of different acids per litre of juice or wine. By tradition, different wine regions have chosen to express total acidity variously as TARTARIC ACID or sulfuric acid, or milliequivalents.

France and a few other European countries tend to express total acidity as sulfuric, even though the amount of this compound in grapes and wine is minuscule, but most major producers and exporters report acidity as tartaric. A further complication arises with what is termed the end point of the titration, with some countries using pH 7 and others pH 8.2. For many years both the OIV and EU methods of analysis have specified a pH 7 end point, but some countries are slow to change, resulting in confusion in the international wine market.

The total acidity of wines expressed as tartaric acid normally varies between about 4 g/l and 9 g/l and primarily depends on the grape variety and the climate. Warmer-climate wines generally have lower acid levels; some of the highest levels can be found in bottle-fermented SPARKLING WINES and in cool-climate late-harvest wines. The total acidity of ripe grape juice or must should ideally be in the general range of 7 to 10 g/l expressed as tartaric acid, although it may in practice be between 3 and 16 g/l. (Some acid is usually lost during winemaking, as a result of MALOLACTIC CONVERSION and cold STABILIZATION, so one may need to start with a higher acidity than the final level desired.) G.T.

Boulton, R., 'The relationship between total acidity, titratable acidity and pH in wine', *American Journal of Enology and Viticulture*, 31/1 (1980), 76–80.

total dry extract, or **TDE**. See EXTRACT.

total package oxygen (TPO) is the awkward but efficient neologism used to refer to the total amount of OXYGEN that can and does influence the development, quality, and longevity of a wine once it has been bottled. It includes oxygen that passes through the CLOSURE (see OXYGEN TRANSMISSION RATE), oxygen that diffuses out of the closure itself, oxygen in the HEAD SPACE, and dissolved oxygen in the wine. New methods based on luminescence have enabled the accurate measurement of TPO without opening the bottle. It is clear that if the pick-up of oxygen at BOTTLING is not controlled there can be a dramatic effect on the wine even after just six months in bottle, so there is little point in stoppering the bottle with closures that are highly engineered to control oxygen transmission rate. A.L.W.

Dimkou, E., et al., 'Impact of dissolved oxygen at bottling on sulfur dioxide and sensory properties of a Riesling wine', *American Journal of Enology and Viticulture*, 64/3 (2013), 325–32.

Toul, Côtes de, small AOC (100 ha/247 acres) in the far north-east of France which remains, with the even more northerly French wine region on the MOSELLE, as a reminder of what was once a flourishing Lorraine wine industry. It was subsequently marginalized by industrialization, injudicious replanting after PHYLLOXERA, the First World War, and the delimitation of the nearby CHAMPAGNE region which had once drawn wine from here. Gamay with some Pinot Noir is responsible for the local pale pink speciality VIN GRIS. Pinot Noir is the only ingredient in Toul's relatively light reds. AUXERROIS is the most successful variety for dry whites.

Touraine, a vast, important LOIRE region centred on the town of Tours, second in production to ANJOU. This is 'the garden of France' and Loire château country *par excellence*, enjoyed by France's pre-revolutionary aristocrats and now a UNESCO World Heritage Site. The local TUFFEAU was quarried extensively to build these and more distant châteaux, leaving caves ideal for winemaking and wine maturation.

Touraine's most famous wines are the still red wines from BOURGUEIL, CHINON, and St-Nicolas-de-Bourgueil to the west and its still and sparkling, dry to sweet CHENIN BLANC from VOUVRAY and MONTLOUIS to the east. Wines labelled simply Touraine come from a much larger zone, incorporating about 4,331 ha/10,702 acres of vineyard extending from SAUMUR in the west as far as the city of Blois in the east. The AOC encompasses very varied soils which may include tuffeau, CLAY, SAND, FLINT, and GRAVEL. Viticulture is concentrated on the steep banks of the Loire and its tributaries the Vienne, the Indre, and the Cher. Cereals predominate on the cooler soils of the plateaus between river valleys. The climate of the region is considerably varied, with the most eastern vineyards being distinctly CONTINENTAL and affected by seriously cold winters, while vineyards at the western extreme are tempered by the influence of the Atlantic.

This soil and climate diversity explains the broad range of grape varieties planted. White Touraine, the most important colour, must be made from SAUVIGNON BLANC with only up to 20% Sauvignon Gris allowed as a blending partner. Vinified to be quaffable, the best of these can provide a less expensive alternative to SANCERRE and POUILLY-FUMÉ. Touraine Rouge should be based on Côt (MALBEC) or CABERNET FRANC depending on the location of the vineyard, with the latter favoured in the warmest sector west of Tours. Varietal GAMAY is also allowed within the Touraine appellation, especially for PRIMEUR wines. Rosés have to be blends from among the ten dark-skinned grapes grown in the region.

The Chenin-based Touraine MOUSSEUX production is limited, representing respectively one-quarter and one-tenth of the volume of the more popular SAUMUR Mousseux and CRÉMANT de loire.

Five communes may attach their name to Touraine. **Touraine-Amboise**, which encompasses 90 ha/222 acres of vines on both banks of the Loire close to the famous château of Amboise, produces mainly red wines based solely on Côt since 2021 after wineries such as La Grange Tiphaine proved the variety's affinity for the region's flinty LIMESTONE soil. Touraine-Amboise rosé is made with Côt and/or Gamay, while its white wines, dry to MOELLEUX (rarely seen) depending on the year, are made exclusively from the long-lived Chenin Blanc.

Touraine-Azay-le-Rideau comprises just 37 ha/91 acres of vineyard on both banks of the Indre, south of the Loire between Tours and Chinon on flinty, chalky soil. It produces twice as much briny white wine from Chenin Blanc as it does sprightly rosés (mainly from Grolleau). The 83 ha of **Touraine-Mesland** are dedicated mostly to Gamay-based red and rosé grown on a sandy limestone plateau immediately above the right bank of the Loire between Vouvray and Blois. A little Chenin in all sweetness levels is also made. In the Cher Valley towards the Sologne, **Touraine-Chenonceaux** (168 ha) and **Touraine-Oisly** (29 ha) are in Sauvignon Blanc country, the latter for whites only. The Chenonceaux reds depend on Côt with Cabernet Franc.

Touraine-Noble Joué is its own 30-ha appellation just south of Tours for VIN GRIS, a blend made from at least 40% PINOT MEUNIER with Pinots Gris and Noir.

See also LOIRE, including map. P. Le.

Tourbat is the ROUSSILLON name for Sardinia's white grape variety TORBATO. It is alternatively known as Malvoisie du Roussillon and is one of the many varieties allowed into the several VINS DOUX NATURELS of the region and Côtes du Roussillon whites.

Touriga is used as a synonym for TOURIGA NACIONAL, particularly in Australia.

Touriga Franca (formerly known as **Touriga Francesa**) is the most widely planted grape variety in the DOURO Valley and the second most widely planted variety in Portugal after TINTA RORIZ, with a total of 14,656 ha/36,216 acres in 2020. Despite the name, it has no connection with France and has been shown by DNA PROFILING to be the relatively recent progeny of the Douro varieties TOURIGA NACIONAL and MARUFO. On warmer south-facing slopes it is valued for both PORT and Douro wines and is classified as one of the best port varieties. Although it is more susceptible to ROT and the wine it produces is not as concentrated as that of Touriga Nacional, in hot, dry years it can outperform the latter. Favoured by growers for its consistent yields, it is respected by winemakers for its wines' perfume and persistent fruit. It is also widely planted in TRÁS-OS-MONTES and is spreading to other Portuguese regions such as BEIRAS, TEJO, and the ALENTEJO.

Touriga Nacional, the most famous vine variety for PORT and, increasingly, for fine dry reds, and not just in PORTUGAL. It produces small quantities of very small berries in the DOURO Valley and the Portuguese DÃO region (where it probably originated) which result in deeply coloured, very tannic, concentrated wines, often with a floral aroma in youth. The vine is vigorous and robust but is prone to COULURE and may produce just 300 g/10 oz of fruit per vine, making it unpopular with growers. This almost led to its extinction in the mid 20th century, but considerable work has been done on CLONAL SELECTION so that newer plantings are slightly more productive and average sugar levels even higher. Touriga Nacional has become more important in the Douro than in its native Dão, where it can make fine VARIETAL reds, although the variety is regarded by many as better in a blend. Touriga Nacional plantings have been increasing considerably, not least because it has migrated south into most other Portuguese wine regions. Its total area had reached 13,301 ha/32,867 acres by 2020, making it the country's third most planted variety. Touriga Nacional has also been travelling extensively outside Portugal—notably to Australia in its capacity as an ALTERNATIVE VARIETY (71 ha/175 acres in 2022), California (121 ha/299 acres in 2020), and South Africa (101 ha/250 acres in 2020). The proliferation of varietal versions from Portugal and its success elsewhere are likely to encourage its worldwide spread. In 2020 it was added to the varieties permitted in Bordeaux AOC, within certain limits, because of its ability to withstand the heat (see VIFA).

tourism. Wine-related tourism continues to be increasingly important to both producers and consumers. For many centuries, not even wine merchants travelled, but today many members of the general public deliberately make forays to explore a wine region or regions. This is partly a reflection of the increased interest in both wine and foreign travel generally but also because most wine regions and many producers' premises are attractive places. VINEYARDS tend to be aesthetically pleasing in any case, and the sort of climate in which wine is generally produced is agreeable at least during the growing season and very possibly for most of the year. Getting to grips with this specialist form of agriculture combines urban dwellers' need to commune with nature with acquiring privileged, and generally admired, specialist knowledge. And then there is the possibility of TASTING and of buying wines direct from the source, which may involve keen prices and/or acquiring rarities. For producers, CELLAR DOOR sales, unmediated by distributors, wholesalers or other retailers, are the most profitable of all.

Wine tourism is certainly not new to Germany. The RHINE has long welcomed tourists, who are encouraged to travel by steamer and stop at wine villages en route, and the MOSEL Valley is surely one of the most photographed in the world. German tourists, on the other hand, have long plundered the Weinstuben of ALSACE and represent an important market for the region's wines.

In France, wine tourism was often accidental. Northern Europeans heading for the sun for decades travelled straight through BURGUNDY and the northern RHÔNE and could hardly fail to notice vineyards and the odd invitation 'Dégustation–Vente' (tasting–sale). (And it is true that a tasting almost invariably leads to a sale.) Wine producers in the LOIRE have long profited from their location in the midst of châteaux country and within an easy Friday night's drive of Paris.

BORDEAUX was one of the last important French wine regions to realize its potential for wine tourism, although the city itself has determinedly made up for lost time. The village of ST-ÉMILION has had scores of wine shops and restaurants for decades, but it was not until the late 1980s that the MÉDOC, the most famous cluster of wine properties in the world, had a hotel and more than one restaurant suitable for international visitors. Alexis LICHINE was mocked for being virtually the only CLASSED GROWTH proprietor openly to welcome visitors, but there are now others, albeit fewer than one would expect.

Much of southern Europe is simply too hot and too far from suitable resorts to make wine tourism comfortable and feasible, but AGRITURISMO has played an extremely important part in the viticultural economy of Italy.

In various NEW WORLD wine regions, tourism has also become an important aspect of business. The most obvious example is the NAPA Valley, whose main roads in summer are as busy as any rush-hour thoroughfare. Other popular examples, when travel has been allowed, have been SOUTH AFRICAN vineyards within easy reach of Cape Town and offering summer weather with no time difference to visitors from northern European winters; HUNTER VALLEY for visitors to and residents of Sydney; parts of NEW YORK State; and the vineyards of ENGLAND, whose owners depend heavily on income from 'farmgate' sales. There has also been considerable investment in wine tourism facilities in Argentina, China, and New Zealand, but this is one of the growth areas virtually throughout the wine world.

Some tour operators and travel agents specialize in wine tourism, and the number of wine regions without their own special wine route or winery trail is decreasing rapidly. The first annual wine tourism conference was held in 2011.

www.greatwinecapitals.com

tourne, wine fault caused by the metabolism of TARTARIC ACID by LACTIC ACID BACTERIA, which affects a wine's colour and flavour.

trade wars. See TARIFFS.

tractor, the most common vineyard machine. Tractor dimensions have had a significant impact on VINEYARD DESIGN. In many parts of Europe where tractors replaced horses, tractor designers obliged by creating either narrow, or row-straddling, tractors (known in France as *tracteurs enjambeurs*). The narrowest vineyard tractors are not much wider than their drivers, about 80 cm/31 in. In the NEW WORLD, however, vineyards were changed to accommodate the tractors, with row spacings of 3–4 m (10–13 ft). Modern ones are much narrower and can fit down rows less than 2 m apart.

The introduction of tractors and other forms of MECHANIZATION to viticulture has had profound economic and sociological effects. Less LABOUR was required, encouraging the population drift to the cities. However, tractors and associated machinery are the major cause of SOIL COMPACTION, and environmentally aware manufacturers and growers prefer tractors with tracks to those with wheels. The most advanced tractors and those that have gone furthest to limit their environmental impact and reduce soil compaction are electric and either driver-operated or autonomous, using both ROBOTICS and ARTIFICIAL INTELLIGENCE. Such vehicles have been pioneered by Monarch in California.

At the opposite end of the spectrum, but with similar motivation, a very few growers have returned to HORSE-drawn ploughs, especially popular among those practising BIODYNAMIC VITICULTURE. R.E.S. & J.E.H.

trade, wine. The world of wine is better known for its sociability than its profitability. What is needed to make a small fortune in the wine business is said to be a large fortune. The wine trade is considerably more appealing, however, than many others. It routinely involves immersion in an often delicious product and travel to some of the more beautiful corners of the world (TOURISM), typically with a MEDITERRANEAN CLIMATE, as well as providing widely admired expertise.

One of the attractions of the wine trade is the people. It has long attracted a wide range of individualists who, if they were not interesting and amusing before they or their visitors have tasted their wares, seem so afterwards. Producers and merchants alike tend to be generous and to appreciate the fact that it is difficult to sell or buy wine without first tasting and sharing it.

Apprenticeship is probably the easiest route into the wine trade, although some form of specialist EDUCATIONAL qualification such as those offered by the WSET can help too. The general areas in which full-time employment may be found include vineyard management, winemaking and quality control, sales and marketing, wholesaling, retailing, and (the job with potentially the most power and perks) buying. There are also the overcrowded fields of WINE WRITING, consulting (in some form), and INVESTMENT. See also wine MERCHANTS.

traditional method, official EU term for the most painstaking way of making wine sparkle, once known as the champagne method. See SPARKLING WINEMAKING for how it works.

Skelton, S., *The Knight Who Invented Champagne* (2021).

traditional terms are words or phrases used on wine labels that enjoy special protection within the EU. They can be phrases such as *appellation d'origine contrôlée* or *vin de pays* which are alternatives to PDO or PGI. They can also be 'the description of a product characteristic' referring to production method (e.g. RANCIO, PASSITO, EISWEIN), ageing method (e.g. SUR LIE, RISERVA, GARRAFEIRA), colour (e.g. *chiaretto*), place of production (e.g. *château*), or, rather more obscurely, 'a particular event linked to the history of a PDO or PGI wine' (e.g. Liebfraumilch). Terms such as *château*, *sur lie*, vintage, CLASSIC, and so on have been the source of some controversy, as non-EU producers have protested that the EU should not limit the rights

MONARCH

of all producers to use words that are purely descriptive or in the public domain. J.P.H.B.

www.ec.europa.eu/info/food-farming-fisheries/food-safety-and-quality/certification/quality-labels/geographical-indications-register/tdt

traditionelle Flaschengärung, **klassiche Flaschengärung**, and **traditionelle klassiche Flaschengärung**, German terms for SPARKLING WINES made by the traditional method.

Traditionsweingüter Österreich, 'traditional wineries of Austria' in English, is a promotional organization in Austria representing the CARNUNTUM, KAMPTAL, KREMSTAL, THERMENREGION, TRAISENTAL, WAGRAM, and WIEN wine regions. The organization, with 77 winery members in 2022, has developed a CLASSIFICATION of selected vineyard sites (95 as of 2022) under the rubric ERSTE LAGE, pledging not to market wines dedicated to those sites prior to September of the year following their harvest—a restraint that was rare in 1992 when the Traditionsweingüter were organized. In attempting to set an example of model vineyard classification, the Traditionsweingüter invites growers from outside its group to submit candidates for its intensive BLIND TASTINGS, so that in theory all the best sites in the regions it represents will receive their due. An upgrading of selected sites to the status of GROSSE LAGE was in its initial stages in 2022. D.S.

training systems, methods of VINE TRAINING, which vary considerably around the world. Since the grapevine is a true VINE and is not self-supporting like a tree, innumerable training systems for vines have been devised over the millennia of cultivation. Confusion between the terms 'training systems', TRELLIS SYSTEMS, and PRUNING is widespread. In fact they are three distinct, if closely related, entities. A trellis is a physical structure, consisting normally of POSTS, generally made of wood, and WIRES. The word training describes the actions of pruning in winter and TRIMMING in summer, as well as SHOOT and CANE placement, so that the vine's TRUNK, ARMS, and CORDONS and BUDS are appropriately located on the trellis system. Those training systems which involve trellises are often named after the trellis.

The viticulturist's choice of training system will be affected by the cost of the system, the availability of any materials required, the availability of the skilled LABOUR required to install and manage it, CLIMATE, TOPOGRAPHY, vine VIGOUR, VINE VARIETY, MECHANIZATION requirements, and, in many instances, knowledge of alternative systems. In many places in the world, especially in Europe, little thought is given to using any but the region's traditional system. Outside Europe, more consideration is given to the choice of training system, because research into CANOPY MANAGEMENT has shown substantial benefits in terms of YIELD, wine quality, and disease reduction by adopting newer designs. Training systems may be dictated by requirements for MECHANICAL HARVESTING and MECHANICAL PRUNING.

A basic difference in training systems about which the casual observer may wonder is why some vineyards have trellis systems with wires and others not. While self-supporting GOBELET vines are common in southern Europe, in many countries such vineyards are considered old-fashioned, and WIRES to suspend foliage are used instead. A particular disadvantage of gobelet training is that the yield has to be limited when the vines are young while the trunk and arms grow sufficient girth and strength to be self-supporting. The yield of older gobelet vineyards is reduced by limited SUNLIGHT interception. The control of vine vigour and VINE DISEASES are the principal reasons for adopting more elaborate systems. Lifting the foliage up and containing it between wires allows trimming and LEAF REMOVAL for better fruit exposure. Both tractor access to the vineyard and airflow within it are also improved by shoot positioning.

The vine is pruned in winter as a means of training the framework to ensure that canes with buds are appropriately positioned to be supported by the trellis system.

A vine-training system should aim to maximize yield and quality and to facilitate cultural operations such as SPRAYING, TILLAGE, HARVESTING, and pruning. In truth, many are designed to minimize the cost of installation or the annual costs of VINEYARD MANAGEMENT. As the degree of mechanization increases, so does the need for the vineyard to be uniform and orderly. For example, mechanical leaf removal and harvesting are made easier by locating the bunches of grapes in a single zone. Similarly, mechanization of trimming and pruning is made easier if the vine shoots and canes all point in the same direction; commonly vertically upwards. The vine framework should ideally be at a convenient waist height for any hand operations.

There are many vine-training systems, ranging from the densely planted (10,000 vines per ha or 4,000 per acre), neatly trimmed vertical hedges of the vineyards of the Médoc to the less common vineyards of a few hundred vines per hectare trained up trees around agricultural fields in the Vinho Verde region of Portugal or vines growing up trees in southern Bolivia (see ARBOREAL VITICULTURE).

Vine-training systems can be classified in a number of ways. In France it is common to classify vines as low-trained (*vignes basses*) or high-trained (*vignes hautes*). For low vines, the trunk is up to 50 cm/20 in high, sometimes shorter. Such training systems are suited to lower-vigour vineyards. Grape RIPENING may benefit from the fruit being closer to the ground, but both harvest and pruning are much less comfortable manual operations, and vines may also be more disease prone. The many examples of low-trained vines in France include the extensive southern areas of gobelet, the CORDON DE ROYAT vines of Burgundy and Champagne, and the double GUYOT of Bordeaux.

High vines are less common in modern France but were certainly known by Roman authors (see AGRICULTURAL TREATISES). Interest in high vines was more recently rekindled by

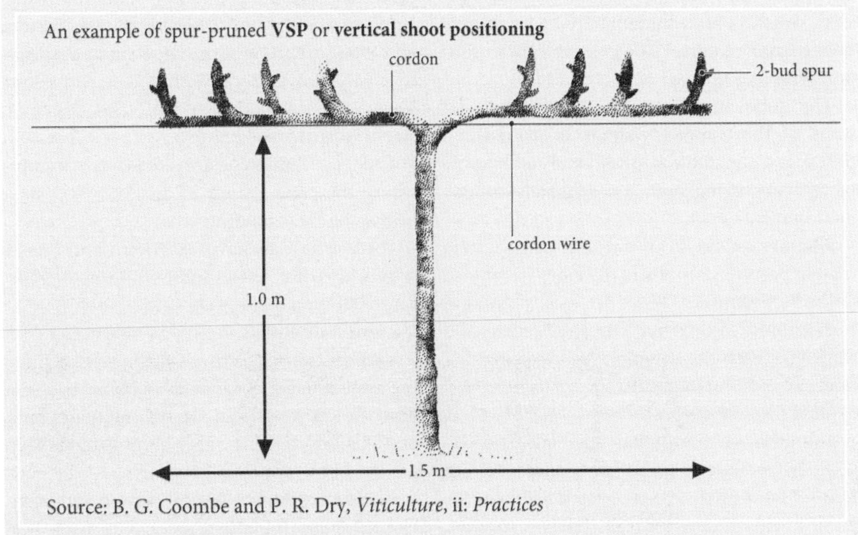

Source: B. G. Coombe and P. R. Dry, *Viticulture*, ii: *Practices*

◀ The Monarch electric, driver-optional TRACTOR, designed and built in LIVERMORE, California, and launched in 2021, saves LABOUR and reduces SOIL COMPACTION and the overall CARBON FOOTPRINT OF WINE. Here it is being used ROBOTICALLY with a flail mower to cut winter COVER CROPS. One of the four company founders is VITICULTURIST Carlo MONDAVI. © Erik Castro

T

the 1950 publication by the Austrian viticulturist LENZ MOSER. He recommended low-density vineyards with wide rows by trunks about 1.25 m/4 ft high. Higher training does reduce FROST risk but requires thicker and more expensive supports, although vineyard work is made easier. 'High-culture' vines can be trained either cordon or Guyot. Vineyards of the New World have typically used high vine-training systems. Overhead trellises such as Italy's TENDONE are special examples of high vines.

There are other possible ways of classifying vine-training systems, however. The cordons may be classed as short, for example 0.5 m in a closely spaced cordon de Royat, or may be many metres in length as for the Portuguese cruzeta (see below). An alternative classification takes account of whether the foliage is free, as for example in the gobelet vines of the Midi, or SHOOT-POSITIONED or constrained into a plane, such as the vertical systems common in Alsace and Germany in which the foliage is held in place by WIRES and maintained by trimming (or occasionally with the shoots woven into the canopy).

The vine canopies can also be classified by their plane: arbours or tendone-trained vines have horizontal canopies about 2 m above the ground, and most shoot-positioned canopies are vertical. Some canopies have shoots all growing upwards, as in the LYRE trellis, while the GENEVA DOUBLE CURTAIN (GDC) has shoots which are trained downwards, and the SCOTT HENRY and SMART-DYSON systems have shoots trained both upwards and downwards. Vines may have a DIVIDED CANOPY in either the horizontal plane, such as the GDC or lyre trellis, or vertically, as in the Scott Henry or Smart-Dyson. Training systems can be simple, like the free-standing gobelet vines of Rioja, or elaborate, like the Ruakura twin two tier (RT2T) developed for research purposes in New Zealand, which is both horizontally and vertically divided and requires 20 wires per row to support fruit and foliage.

The following list gives brief details of some of the training systems in use around the world, including traditional and some newer ones being used for deliberate canopy management.

alberate, an old form of vine-training system used in parts of Italy where the vines are trained on or between trees. There are local variations, such as those in Bologna, Tuscany, Veneto, and Romagna, with the common feature being that trees are used for support.

alberello, see GOBELET.

aplotaria, a traditional method used on wind-blown Greek Cyclades islands such as Paros. UNGRAFTED VINES sprawl across the ground without any form of trellis or support. The vine is protected from the wind and the berries from the sun. A similar method, known in Spanish as *rasteras*, is used in some old vineyards in the south of Chile, on Spain's La Palma, and in COLARES, Portugal, for example.

arbour, see TENDONE.

arched cane, a variation on many different forms of training systems where canes are arched rather than being tied horizontally; see GUYOT. Alternative names include bow-trained, *arcure* in French, *capovolto*, or Guyot *ad archetto* in Italy. This practice is claimed to lead to better BUDBREAK in the centre of the canes, where buds do not normally burst well (see APICAL DOMINANCE). It can be considered a variation of Guyot training.

ballerina, a form of Smart-Dyson developed in King Valley, VICTORIA, Australia. One vertical and two transverse curtains are created from one or two cordons trained to spurs pointing upwards. Many bilateral cordon training systems can easily be converted to ballerina.

barra, used for monoculture in Vinho Verde whereby vines are trained in one direction along a single wire at shoulder height.

basket training, known as *kouloura* or its taller-trunked variant *kladeftiko* on the Greek island of SANTORINI, often used for free-standing vines where canes are wound one around the other for mutual support. Common for some BUSH VINE systems which are pruned. Typically they are of low vigour.

bush vines, see BUSH VINES and GOBELET.

Casarsa, or Casarsa Friuli, an Italian training system like the SYLVOZ, except the canes are not tied down after pruning.

cassone padavano, a horizontally divided Italian system, pruned like the Sylvoz.

Cazenave, an Italian vine-training system which uses a modified form of Guyot pruning where short arms containing spurs and canes (five to six buds) are arranged along a horizontal CORDON. The canes are tied about vertically to a wire above. Because the pruner is able to leave so many buds per vine, this system is suited to fertile soils.

Château Thierry, a form of GUYOT training where the cane is tied in an arch to a stake beside the free-standing vine.

cordon de Cazenave, an Italian and French system used for fertile soils, with one or more canes left on a CORDON DE ROYAT.

cordon de Royat, see CORDON DE ROYAT.

cordon-trained, term to distinguish a training system using cordons as opposed to a vine head and canes. These are typically horizontal and bilateral but may also be unilateral. They are used in warm to hot regions.

cordon vertical, a vertical cordon with alternating spurs to either side. Not used very commonly as growth tends to be mainly from the top buds.

cruzeta, a system used in the VINHO VERDE area of Portugal where vines are trained to a wide cross arm about 2 m/6 ft off the ground. More sophisticated than *latada* but less so than *barra*.

double header, a system developed by Terry Bennett, a grower in Tasmania, to allow CANE-pruned vines in his COOL-CLIMATE vineyard to achieve BALANCE by pruning to more buds but avoiding shoot crowding. This was achieved by removing each second vine in the row.

duplex, a system developed in California in the 1960s with flexible cross arms to allow for machine harvesting. While the fruiting wires are horizontally divided by 1 m/3 ft, the foliage was not shoot-positioned to create two separate curtains as for the GENEVA DOUBLE CURTAIN. As a consequence, it is not nearly as beneficial in terms of yield, quality, and disease avoidance and is now little used.

espalier, see ESPALIER.

éventail, French for 'fan', system with multiple arms, each giving rise to a spur or short cane. Originally the form used in Chablis, with the arms lying on the ground, this has been modified to the *taille de Semur* system, where each arm is tied to a lower wire in the one plane.

factory roof system, commonly used for TABLE GRAPES, in South Africa and Israel, for example, where the CANOPY is trained up at an angle to meet in a gable near the row centre. This may also be called a closed, one-arm PERGOLA and provides excellent access to the fruit for any hand work required.

fan-shaped, a training system distantly related to *éventail* that is used in central Europe, particularly Russia, where the vine trunks are spread out in the shape of a fan, which makes it easier to bury vines for WINTER PROTECTION. The Italian version is called *ventagli*.

Flachbogen, the German name for a training system like the Guyot whereby one cane is laid horizontally either side of the head and shoots are trained vertically between foliage wires. The shoots are trimmed at the top. See VERTICAL TRELLIS.

Geneva double curtain (GDC), see GENEVA DOUBLE CURTAIN.

gobelet, see GOBELET.

Guyot, see GUYOT.

Halbbogen, a German training system whereby the vine is pruned to one cane of about 15 buds' length and is arched in the middle over a wire about 25 cm/10 in above the base and end of the cane. Shoots are trained each year vertically between foliage wires and are trimmed at the top. See APICAL DOMINANCE.

head-trained, common term for a vine trained so that spurs and canes arise in one zone, called the head. Such vines may be cane- or spur-pruned.

Hudson River umbrella, a system used in the eastern US whereby canes are arched downwards from a high head.

Isère, a training system much like Château Thierry (see above).

latada, traditional 3-m-high trellis used on Madeira for vines grown around fields of other crops, equivalent to VINHO VERDE's *ramada*.

Lenz Moser, see LENZ MOSER.

lyre, see LYRE.

MPCT, or minimal-pruned cordon-trained, describes the system developed and extensively used in Australia, mainly for BULK WINE production. Young vines are trained to a form of CORDON at about 1.5 m height and, apart from wrapping early cane growth on the wire, receive minimal hand work, including pruning. See MINIMAL PRUNING.

palmette, an Italian training system, with one vine trained to four horizontal canes, one pair above the other.

parral, see TENDONE.

parron, see TENDONE.

Pendelbogen, the German name for the arched-cane training system described above. There is a 50-cm height difference between the end of the cane and the highest point, which is thought to improve BUDBREAK in the middle of the cane. Most of the shoots are trained vertically upright between foliage wires and normally require trimming at the top. Pendelbogen means 'pendulum bow', and there are related training forms: not just Halbbogen ('half bow') but also Rundbogen ('round bow') and Doppelbogen ('double bow'). The name has also been applied to a mid-height Sylvoz system in New Zealand.

pergola, see PERGOLA.

Perold, a South African term for vertical trellis, named after A. I. Perold, the breeder of PINOTAGE.

pyramid, an Italian training system where vine shoots are trained over a group of stakes tied together at the top, forming a pyramid.

ramada, VINHO VERDE name for *latada* above.

raggi Belussi, an Italian overhead training system suspended from above and with two vines planted together and trained in four directions. Pruned like the Sylvoz.

raggiera or **raggi**, an Italian training system where vines are trained overhead on wires like the spokes of a wheel. One vine may be trained up a central stake or tree and divided into cordons, or several vines may be at the one position with each trained along a different radius.

Scott Henry, see SCOTT HENRY.

shelf, or *tana*, local name for overhead trellis in Japan.

slanting trellis, a system in which the canopy is trained along an inclined support. This trellis can be used for both table- and wine-grape production.

Smart-Dyson trellis, see SMART-DYSON.

Sylvoz, see SYLVOZ.

Te Kauwhata two tier (TK2T), developed at the Te Kauwhata Research Station in New Zealand, a system which is vertically divided, with shoots trained vertically upwards. Limited commercial use in California and New Zealand.

tendone, see TENDONE.

three-wire trellis, another California trellis system with a pair of fixed foliage wires above the cordon. Shoots are not positioned and fall across these wires under their own weight.

traverse trellis, European name for the T trellis.

T trellis, common in Australia, where the vine is trained to two horizontal cordons about 0.5 m apart. It takes its name from the appearance of the vine trunk and cordons. Shoots are not positioned, and so the canopy is not divided. Can be machine pruned and harvested and is widely used in bulk wine-producing areas.

tunnel, an alternative name for a form of overhead vine training where the vines are planted in two rows and trained overhead.

two-wire vertical trellis, common terminology in California, where one wire is occupied by the cordon and the second is a fixed foliage wire. Shoots grow up and over this wire and fall under their own weight to form a bell-shaped canopy. When the vines are vigorous, the canopy is very shaded.

U, an alternative name for the LYRE trellis.

umbrella kniffin, a system used in eastern America, where canes from a mid-height head are trained over a top wire and tied below.

V, a vine-training system in the shape of the letter where shoots are trained upwards into two curtains. This form does not work as well as the LYRE or U system, where the cordons are separated at the base.

vertical cordon, a rare training system as top buds tend to burst first, making it difficult to manage.

vertical trellis, see VERTICAL TRELLIS.

VSP, or vertical shoot positioning, describes a system used throughout the world where annual shoot growth is trained vertically upwards and held in place by foliage wires (typically two pairs). See VERTICAL TRELLIS.

Y, a vine-training system in the shape of the letter and equivalent to the V system except that the trunk of the vine forms the vertical part of the letter.

The above cannot pretend to be a comprehensive list of the multitude of training systems used worldwide, nor of all their local names, nor how patterns of usage are changing, especially in the New World; but it does give some indication of the extraordinary variation in vine-training systems. The greatest complexity of training systems in the world is to be found in Italy, while those used in France tend to be determinedly regional. R.E.S.

Carbonneau, A., et al., *Traité de la Vigne: Physiologie, Terroir, Culture* (3rd edn, 2020).

Galet, P., *General Viticulture* (2000).

Smart, R. E., and Robinson, M., *Sunlight into Wine: A Handbook for Winegrape Canopy Management* (1991).

Traisental, wine region in AUSTRIA astride a roughly 12 km/7 mile stretch of the Traisen river just before it empties into the right bank of the Danube below KREMS. Inaugurated in 1995, it comprises 851 ha/2,103 vine acres (1.9% of Austria's total) and benefits from a DIURNAL TEMPERATURE RANGE similar to that of the WACHAU as well as from distinctive and unusual active LIME-rich conglomerate soils (see GEOLOGY) whose efficacy grower Ludwig Neumayer of Inzersdorf demonstrated from the late 1980s with GRÜNER VELTLINER, RIESLING, WEISSBURGUNDER, Sauvignon Blanc, and wine based on an old GEMISCHTER SATZ. Traisental DAC (since 2006) applies to Grüner Veltliner and Riesling, with a DAC Reserve designation stipulating higher minimum alcohol and later release. D.S.

Trajadura, white grape variety used to add body and a certain citrus character to Portugal's VINHO VERDE if it is picked sufficiently early. It was planted on 1,794 ha/4,433 acres of Portugal in 2020, more than the area devoted to TREIXADURA as it is known across the Spanish border in Galicia. It is often blended with LOUREIRO and sometimes with ALVARINHO.

Traminer, name applied to both white-berried and pink-berried non-aromatic BIOTYPES of SAVAGNIN. The more famous, distinctly aromatic, pink-skinned version is known as GEWÜRZTRAMINER or Traminer Aromatico. **Traminer Rose**, **Roter Traminer**, and variations on that theme are sometimes used more specifically for the pink-berried form. Traminer was first noted in the village of Tramin or Termeno in what is now the Italian Tyrol (see ALTO ADIGE) in the 13th century. These CLONES are known in various parts of the world, particularly in central and eastern Europe, by names which are derivations of the word Traminer.

Traminette, relatively recent, complex AMERICAN HYBRID showing promise in cooler

American states. Its heady whites hint strongly at its GEWÜRZTRAMINER genes.

transfer method, SPARKLING WINEMAKING process, now less common than it was, that involves provoking a second fermentation in bottle and then transferring its contents into a tank, where the wine is separated from the deposit.

translocation, plant physiological process whereby soluble materials such as dissolved salts, organic materials, and growth substances are moved around the vine in the PHLOEM. (The phloem tissue is in the outer part of the trunk or stems, and so it can be disrupted by CINCTURING.) Sucrose is the principal form in which CARBOHYDRATES are moved, and the phloem sap also contains amino acids and organic acids, inorganic nutrients, plant hormones, and alkaloids. Examples of translocation are the movement of inorganic nutrients absorbed by roots from the soil to other parts of the vine, for example POTASSIUM going into the fruit, which may prejudice wine quality. Translocation also includes the important movement of SUCROSE formed by PHOTOSYNTHESIS away from the leaves to the fruit, which will eventually become ALCOHOL in wine. From the point of view of wine, the translocation of sucrose, MALIC ACID, TARTARIC ACID, elements, and compounds containing NITROGEN during RIPENING are crucial to the chemical composition of grapes and thus to eventual wine quality.

Movement of foodstuffs is invariably towards points of need, such as growing shoot tips for the early part of the season, flowers, then developing berries, and also towards the permanent vine parts such as trunks and roots for the accumulation of reserves later in the season. HORMONES such as auxins, cytokinins, and gibberellins play an important role in regulating translocation. The vine is capable of translocating products over long distances and so, even though the shoot supporting a bunch may be shaded, the grapes will still ripen depending on materials imported from other parts of the vine.

R.E.S.

Carbonneau, A., et al., *Traité de la Vigne: Physiologie, Terroir, Culture* (3rd edn, 2020).

Keller, M., *The Science of Grapevines* (3rd edn, 2020).

Transmontano, large, mountainous VINHO REGIONAL in north-east Portugal with the same borders as TRÁS-OS-MONTES but which allows a broader range of grape varieties.

transpiration, physiological process whereby water taken up from a vine's roots is evaporated through the leaves, important in preventing the vine from overheating in warm and sunny weather. Water and dissolved elements move in the so-called transpiration stream through the woody part of the vine in tissue called the XYLEM. The xylem fluid also contains relatively large amounts of AMINO ACIDS (especially glutamine), organic acids (especially malic), and small amounts of sugars. Total water loss from a vineyard is called EVAPOTRANSPIRATION, and this includes transpiration from the vines and also any weeds or COVER CROP present, plus EVAPORATION from the soil surface.

Transpiration is an energy-driven process due to leaves absorbing SUNLIGHT. Water vapour passes from the leaf to the atmosphere via small pores on the underside called STOMATA. Energy is required to provide the latent heat of evaporation for the phase change from liquid (water) to gas (water vapour), which takes place in the cavity below the stomata. The cell walls of the substomatal cavity are wet owing to a long column of water extending from the roots. Provided the vine is well supplied with water, leaves facing the sun will be only 2–3 °C/3–5 °F warmer than the air, while if water supply is limited then this figure can exceed 10 °C/18 °F and the vine will suffer both HEAT STRESS and WATER STRESS.

Transpiration is controlled by both atmospheric and plant factors. High transpiration rates are due to low humidity, high sunshine, high temperature, and high wind speed. Typically during the day, as temperature rises humidity falls, and so transpiration is fastest in the early afternoon. As soils dry, the risk of water stress increases, and so by partially closing stomata the vine is able to regulate its water status to some extent. However, as stomata close then PHOTOSYNTHESIS stops, as carbon dioxide entry into the leaf is inhibited.

Rates of transpiration vary with the weather and growth stage of the vineyard. For a vineyard in full leaf in the middle of the season, daily evapotranspiration rates may be as high as 40,000 l/ha for a hot, dry, and sunny climate. For a vineyard planted with 2,000 vines per ha, this rate is equivalent to 20 l (4.4 gal) per vine per day. The amount of water transpired is very high relative to both the vine's growth overall and the fruit produced.

Research has shown that, contrary to earlier assumptions, vines transpire at night as well as during the day. This transpiration is driven by a vapour pressure gradient of water, from wet cell walls in the sub-stomatal cavity to the drier atmosphere outside. A study by Rogiers et al. investigated the fact that SÉMILLON is more prone to water stress than many other varieties because its stomata are more open, both day and night, and are slow to shut under water stress.

R.E.S.

Keller, M., *The Science of Grapevines* (3rd edn, 2020).

Rogiers, S. Y., et al., 'Does night-time transpiration contribute to anisohydric behaviour in a *Vitis vinifera* cultivar?', *Journal of Experimental Botany*, 60/13 (2009), 3751–63.

transport of wine has changed considerably over the ages, but a wide variety of different methods, from tanker to a lone bottle sent by mail, are still used.

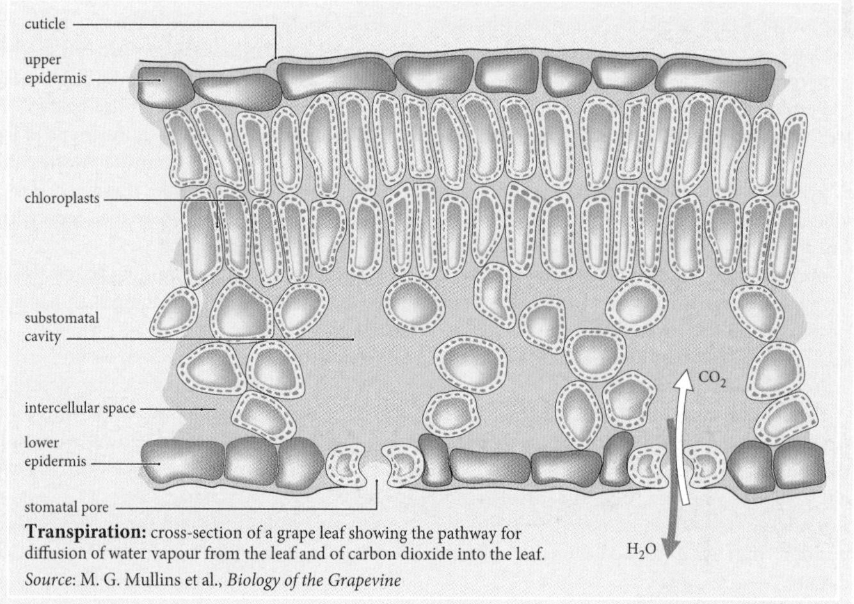

Transpiration: cross-section of a grape leaf showing the pathway for diffusion of water vapour from the leaf and of carbon dioxide into the leaf.
Source: M. G. Mullins et al., *Biology of the Grapevine*

The Avontuur, a centenarian 44-metre/144-foot sailing vessel, docking in Shoreham, southern England, having carried wines from the island of PICO in the Azores, thereby ▶ reducing the CARBON FOOTPRINT of transportation, which is particularly high for wine GLASS BOTTLES. © Raymond Reynolds

AVONTUUR

Ancient history

Wine was transported in bulk in antiquity in a variety of ways: in huge wineskins or barrels loaded on the backs of two- or four-wheeled carts, but also via waterborne transport, which had a great advantage because of the inefficiency of the harnesses used on animals. For most of the Mediterranean area, wine was carried in large AMPHORAE, which were loaded in the holds of ships. The pottery jars required considerable packing (heather, straw, etc.) to cushion them against breakages. They could be transferred to smaller vessels for transport up inland waterways. A recent discovery has been of wrecks carrying DOLIA, a kind of tanker for the bulk transport of wine. Barrels were widely used in northern Europe (see CELTS) and later in the Mediterranean, although the amphora tradition died out completely only in the medieval period. J.J.P.

Moulin, M. M., 'Le Transport du raisin ou du vin par la route à l'époque romaine en Gaule et dans les provinces voisines', in R. Chevallier et al., *Archéologie de la vigne et du vin* (1990).

Peacock, D. P. S., and Williams, D. F., *Amphorae and the Roman Economy* (1986).

Modern transport

In the Middle Ages, RIVERS played an important role in transporting wine, and only those wine regions with access to good water transport (by sea and/or river) were likely to develop much trade. In the 19th and early 20th centuries, the advent of a RAILWAY system transformed wine regions as dissimilar as the LANGUEDOC, ROUSSILLON, RIOJA, CHIANTI, and MENDOZA. Today wine is generally transported by road and sea, although some wine is shipped by rail in the US, and a shocking number of special bottles are air-freighted from Europe to billionaires in Asia and the US. Recently, however, several enterprising companies have revived the practice of transporting wine by sailing boat in an effort to lower the CARBON FOOTPRINT of shipping.

For centuries the transport of wine meant BULK TRANSPORT, and the most common container used for transporting wine was the barrel. SHERRY, for example, was still shipped to British bottlers in its special casks, or BUTTS, until well into the 20th century (when the empty butts were used for Scotch whisky maturation). In the latter half of the 20th century, however, container shipment in bulk tankers became the norm, although an increasing proportion of wine is bottled not just in its country or region of origin but actually at the winery (see BOTTLING). However, for both financial and SUSTAINABILITY reasons, the proportion of wine (particularly wine at the lower end of the market) shipped in bulk has risen dramatically this century, and the technology of bulk transport has improved considerably. Unlike wine in bulk, bottles are breakable and can easily be pilfered.

From the consumer's point of view, the most important aspect of the transport of wine is TEMPERATURE. If wine is exposed to high temperatures, it may well deterioriate considerably, even if it has been subject to effective STABILIZATION. Spikes of temperature can also lead to spoilage due to OXIDATION. Conscientious producers try to avoid shipping wine in high summer, while scrupulous wholesalers insist that insulated containers sometimes called reefers are used for shipments in hot weather and/or through the TROPICS, although they are more expensive. Some shippers of fine wines include temperature sensors in the shipment. Stowing wine below sea level on ships minimizes the temperature variation.

Exposure to light can also be a problem: research indicates that exposure to UV radiation at any point in the distribution chain may damage wine quality (see LIGHTSTRIKE). The risk is reduced by the use of brown rather than clear bottles.

In the US the DIRECT SHIPPING of bottled wine between certain states has been heavily restricted by law.

transversage. See SPARKLING WINEMAKING.

Trás-os-Montes, meaning 'behind the mountains', is a large DOC in north-east Portugal bounded by high mountains on one side and the Spanish frontier on the other (see map of PORTUGAL). The mountains cast a rain shadow over the region, although it becomes progressively more arid towards Spain. With vineyard ELEVATIONS of 350–800 m/1,148–2,625 ft (and another at 1,070 m/3,510 ft, claiming to be Portugal's highest) plus varied mesoclimates and soil types (mostly GRANITE, but also SCHIST and CALCAREOUS soils), Trás-os-Montes has three DOC subregions, from west to east: Chaves, Valpaços, and Planalto Mirandês. Higher vineyards in Planalto Mirandês supply wine for MATEUS Rosé and several imitative brands. Old FIELD BLEND parcels growing in TERROIR similar to neighbouring ARRIBES in Spain are being sought out by winemakers for fresh, characterful, minimal-intervention wines. See also TRANSMONTANO. S.A.

cvrtm.pt

Trbljan, relatively important light-berried vine variety grown particularly on the coast of CROATIA just north of Zadar. Several hundred hectares are planted. The grape is also sometimes called Kuč.

Treasury Wine Estates, one of the world's biggest wine companies. It was grown out of the first Australo-American wine group and in 2022 had access to more than 12,700 ha/31,382 acres of vineyard around the world. Its brands include PENFOLDS, Wolf Blass, 19 Crimes, Lindeman's, Squealing Pig, Seppelt, Pepperjack, Beaulieu Vineyard, and Stags' Leap Winery. At the heart of the business is TWE's global, multi-regional sourcing model, which includes what they call 'production assets' in the Barossa Valley, the Napa Valley, Marlborough, Bordeaux, and Tuscany. The group also makes a CHAMPAGNE with Thiénot. Winemaker Peter Gago is Treasury's peripatetic public face.

In 2013 the company wrote off US$35 million worth of wine in response to sluggish sales in the US. Exports to the once-dominant Chinese market slumped in 2021 thanks to punitive TARIFFS.

Trebbiano. At least six distinct varieties grown in Italy are known principally as Trebbiano, including **Trebbiano Toscano**, whose national total of 35,441 ha/87,577 acres in 2015 made it one of the most planted white wine grapes in Italy. Next most planted, largely in Emilia-Romagna, on 19,1059 ha was the remarkably similar **Trebbiano Romagnolo**. **Trebbiano Giallo** is found on 2,275 ha, particularly in Lazio, and **Trebbiano Spoletino** is an Umbrian speciality grown on 121 ha. **Trebbiano Modenese** is grown on 287 ha and is associated with production of the local vinegar, while **Trebbiano Abruzzese** (also known as **Trebbiano d'Abruzzo** although this is actually the name of the wine) is quite unrelated to any other Trebbiano (see ABRUZZO). Meanwhile, many an Italian synonym incorporates the word Trebbiano, most notably Trebbiano di Soave, Trebbiano di Lugana, and Trebbiano Valtenesi, which are all the Marche grape VERDICCHIO. There are almost as many possible histories of Trebbiano as there are different varieties called Trebbiano (the index of *Wine Grapes* has no fewer than 28 entries for grape names beginning with Trebbiano). The Bolognese agronomist PETRUS DE CRESCENTIIS certainly described a vine called Tribiano as early as 1303, but which one? Today, Trebbiano is planted all over Italy (with the exception of the cool far north), to the extent that it is likely that the great majority of basic *vino bianco* will contain at least some of the variety, if only to add acidity and volume.

The stronghold of Trebbiano Toscano, shown by DNA PROFILING to have a parent–offspring relationship with the GARGANEGA of Soave, is central Italy. It is known as UGNI BLANC and St-Émilion in France, or Tália in

Portugal, and is widely planted around the world. Any grape called simply Trebbiano is likely to be Trebbiano Toscano.

See under its most common French name UGNI BLANC for details of Trebbiano in France.

This gold-, even amber-berried grape variety is so productive and is so much planted in both France and Italy (the world's two major wine-producing countries) that it may well still produce more wine than any other vine variety in the world—even though the total area it was planted on appears to have slipped from fifth to ninth place between 1990 and 2016. It is cited in more DOC regulations than any other single variety (about 80) and may well account for more than one-third of Italy's entire DOC white-wine production. Trebbiano Toscano the wine is typically light, crisp, and wet.

Some idea of Trebbiano Toscano's ubiquity is given by listing just some of the wines in which it is an ingredient: VERDICCHIO, ORVIETO, and FRASCATI, together with SOAVE (Trebbiano Toscano was planted in place of Trebbiano di Soave in the 1960s and 1970s, when yield was a more important consideration than quality, but has now been outlawed). The variety has after all had many centuries to adapt itself to local conditions. Between Tuscany and Rome, in UMBRIA, the variety can be known as Procanico, which some agronomists believe is a superior, smaller-berried Trebbiano. Only the fiercely varietal-conscious north-eastern corner of Italy is virtually free of this bland ballast.

Trebbiano's malign influence was most noticeable in central TUSCANY in much of the 20th century, however, where Trebbiano was so well entrenched that CHIANTI and therefore VINO NOBILE DI MONTEPULCIANO laws sanctioned its inclusion in this red wine, thereby diluting its quality as well as its colour and damaging its reputation. Trebbiano is now very much an optional ingredient, however, increasingly spurned by quality-conscious producers. Once Trebbiano fell out of favour with Chianti producers, an attempt was made to transform it into innocuous dry whites. Fortunately the market for these wines has dwindled, and in the 2000s much Trebbiano in Tuscany was GRUBBED UP or used in VIN SANTO.

Trebbiano Toscano has also managed to infiltrate Portugal's fiercely nationalistic vineyards, as Tália or Thalia, and is widely planted in Bulgaria and in parts of Croatia as well as in Greece. As well as being used for Mexico's important brandy production, Trebbiano is well entrenched in the southern hemisphere, where its high yields and high acidity are valued. There were still nearly 1,288 ha/3,183 acres of 'Ugni Blanc' in Argentina in 2020 as well as plantings in Brazil and Uruguay.

South Africa also calls its relatively limited plantings Ugni Blanc but relies more on COLOMBARD for brandy production and cheap, tart, blending material, as does California, whose remaining 42 ha/103 acres of the vine, there called 'St. Emilion', are exclusively in the Central Valley, although interesting VARIETAL versions called Trebbiano are not entirely unknown. Australia, where Colombard is also more important, has limited plantings of Trebbiano, mainly in the irrigated areas, where it provides a usefully tart ingredient in basic blended whites and is also sometimes used by distillers.

The influence of Trebbiano/Ugni Blanc will surely continue to decline as wine drinkers seek flavour with increasing determination.

Trebbiano Romagnolo, along with its almost amber-berried clone Trebbiano della Fiamma, dominates white-wine production in EMILIA-ROMAGNA and results in generally remarkably undistinguished dry whites. The variety is cultivated across a wide swathe of ROMAGNA in the provinces of Bologna, Forlì, and Ravenna, and only about one-fifth is registered for the production of DOC wines. It is permitted on its own or as a blending component in no fewer than ten Emilia-Romagna DOCs. Permitted yields of almost 100 hl/ha (5.7 tons/acre) do little to assist a grape not known for its striking personality, and most Trebbiano di Romagna is, at best, suitable for a picnic.

Perhaps Italy's most exciting Trebbiano, **Trebbiano d'Abruzzese** (see ABRUZZO) is not a Trebbiano at all but the BOMBINO BIANCO of Puglia, but this has yet to be proved by DNA PROFILING, which has suggested the variety is related to Trebbiano Spoletino. Trebbiano Spoletino was rescued from extinction by Giampaolo Tabarrini and Paolo Bea, followed by Cantina Novelli in Umbria at the beginning of this century, and has clearly gained ground, with 121 ha in 2015. Trebbiano Giallo and Trebbiano Modenese are, perhaps appropriately, closely associated with vinegar production.

Robinson, J., et al., *Wine Grapes: A Complete Guide to 1,368 Vine Varieties, Including Their Origins and Flavours* (2012).

Treixadura, Galician name for Portugal's scented, delicate white TRAJADURA and treated in much the same way. This is the main grape of Ribeiro and may be blended with Galician Torrontés and Lado. It is also grown in the Rías Baixas region, where it is often blended with ALBARIÑO, LOUREIRA, and/or GODELLO. Total Spanish plantings had grown to almost 1,006 ha/2,486 acres by 2020.

trellis systems, support structures for the vine framework required for a given TRAINING SYSTEM. Normally these are constructed, although vines are still very occasionally trained to trees (see ARBOREAL VITICULTURE). The simplest trellis system consists of a STAKE driven beside a vine to which the vine trunk or shoots are tied. Nowadays WIRES are used to support vines and foliage, as POSTS are installed at intervals along the row.

There are several designs of end assemblies, but they are all firmly anchored in the ground so as to support the strain in the wire due to the weight of the crop, the vines, and any WIND stresses. At intervals along the row are intermediate posts, usually made from wood, which also help carry the vine weight. In a well-constructed trellis system, the wires should be strained so tight that the wire does not sag, and this in turn facilitates MECHANIZATION. Details of some common trellis systems and end assemblies are given by Smart and Robinson.

The majority of the world's vineyards, however, have very simple trellis systems. For some, the vines are free-standing (see GOBELET), where the major support for the weight of the vine and crop is from the vine trunk.

For more information on the wide range of trellis systems used in various regions, see TRAINING SYSTEMS. R.E.S.

Smart, R. E., and Robinson, M., *Sunlight into Wine: A Handbook for Winegrape Canopy Management* (1991).

Trentino, the southern and principally Italian-speaking half of Italy's central alpine region of TRENTINO-ALTO ADIGE. Trento is the regional capital. Viticulture is centred in the valley of the Adige and the hills immediately to the east and west of the river and in side valleys such as the Valle dei Laghi and the Val di Cembra. The terrain further east and west into the Dolomites is too rugged and mountainous for viticulture, although CLIMATE CHANGE is an incentive for reviving abandoned plots once considered too marginal for growing grapes. Although the region is on latitude 46° N, the climate is not uniformly cool, as the Dolomites offer protection from cold northern winds and nearby Lake Garda has a moderating effect, so viticulture is by no means confined to early-ripening vine varieties.

Of Trentino's 10,210 ha/25,229 acres in 2020, more than 15% of the vineyards rise over 500 m/1,640 ft in ELEVATION. Three-quarters of Trentino's total wine production is white and geared towards volume, with almost 3,000 ha of PINOT GRIGIO, more than 2,600 ha of Chardonnay, and 900 ha of MÜLLER-THURGAU. Of the region's total output, 90% is controlled by 15 CO-OPERATIVES and 14 NÉGOCIANTS. This commercial model has led to overproduction of Chardonnay and Pinot Grigio, although the creation of the DELLE VENEZIE DOC, reserved exclusively for Pinot Grigio, has seen volumes shrink and prices rise. Pinot Noir is gaining in interest, in part because the region's high-altitude vineyards are handling the effects of climate change better than BURGUNDY. Riesling might follow.

The region's DOC system has been designed with large-scale production of INTERNATIONAL VARIETIES in mind: the overarching Trentino DOC permits yields up to 15 tonnes/ha as well as innumerable grape varieties. It is, however, subdivided into five subzones with some local focus: Trentino Isera and Trentino Ziresi for MARZEMINO grapes, Trentino Castel Beseno for MOSCATO, Val di Cembra for Müller-Thurgau, and Trentino Sorni for NOSIOLA and SCHIAVA. (Sorni is also home to the local centre of viti-agricultural ACADEME, SAN MICHELE ALL'ADIGE.) The DOC Valdadige covers the same area and varieties as the Trentino DOC and extends into ALTO ADIGE and north-western VENETO.

Trento DOC (for marketing reasons written as TrentoDOC) designates the entire region for production of METODO CLASSICO sparkling wine based on Chardonnay and Pinot Noir. The base wine requires high levels of acidity, guaranteed in grapes coming from elevations of 400–700 m/1,310–2,300 ft. Wines must be aged at least 18 months on the LEES, although Ferrari, the undisputed leader, ages its non-vintage wine for 24 months or longer.

The Teroldego Rotaliano DOC, limited to TEROLDEGO grown on the gravelly Campo Rotaliano, has only a handful of producers, notably Elisabetta Foradori, who has successfully proved that with low yields TEROLDEGO can produce serious wines. Yet because yields can be as high as 17 tonnes/ha, and most production is in the hands of the local co-operative, most quality-conscious producers prefer to label their wines under the more anonymous but less tarnished IGT Vigneti delle Dolomiti. Two other DOCs, Casteller and Lago di Caldaro (the latter shared with ALTO ADIGE to the north), are devoted almost exclusively to light, pale, Schiava-based reds, although Schiava claims only 204 ha/504 acres in Trentino and is declining fast. W.S.

www.vinideltrentino.com

Trentino-Alto Adige, autonomous, alpine northern Italian region through which flows the Adige river (called Etsch by the region's many German speakers). It is made up of ALTO ADIGE, or the South Tyrol, in the north and TRENTINO in the south (see map under ITALY).

TrentoDOC, TRADITIONAL METHOD sparkling wines from TRENTINO, written thus for marketing reasons.

Trepat, increasingly fashionable indigenous red-skinned wine grape of north-east Spain, particularly in Conca de Barberá and Tarragona. Total plantings were 1,265 ha/3,126 acres in 2020, producing both still and sparkling rosés as well as aromatic light reds.

Tressallier, ST-POURÇAIN synonym for SACY.

Tressot, ancient red grape variety of Burgundy, already described in the 14th century along with PINOT NOIR. Tressot is exclusively cultivated in the Yonne (CHABLIS country), but CLIMATE CHANGE is encouraging Burgundians to re-evaluate its potential. DNA PROFILING has suggested that Tressot is a natural CROSS between DURAS and PETIT VERDOT and that it most likely begat MONDEUSE NOIRE via a natural cross with MONDEUSE BLANCHE. Confusingly, it is also a Burgundian name for the Jura's (unrelated) TROUSSEAU vine. J.V.

tri, French for a sorting process, notably postal, but in a winemaking context it means the selection of suitable grapes. This usually takes the form of a *triage* (see GRAPE SORTING) on reception of the grapes at the winery or cellar, using a sorting table or *table de tri*. However, in the production of BOTRYTIZED wines, a *trie* (note the feminine form), or several *tries*, is made in the vineyard whereby the pickers proceed along the rows selecting only those clusters (and occasionally only those berries) that have been successfully attacked by NOBLE ROT.

tri, table de, French for 'sorting table'. See GRAPE SORTING.

triage, French for GRAPE SORTING.

Tribidrag, earliest known name for ZINFANDEL in its Croatian birthplace.

tribromoanisole. See TBA.

Tricastin, Coteaux du, old name for GRIGNAN-LES-ADHÉMAR.

trichloroanisole. See TCA.

Trimbach, family-run wine producer based at Ribeauvillé in ALSACE. The company was established in 1626. Its wines are characterized by very fine fruit and high, ripe acidity. Riesling constitutes half of production, and even its most basic offering can stand many years' AGEING. Two of its most famous bottlings are Rieslings: the very fine, rare, and long-lived Clos Ste-Hune (in fact from the Alsace Grand Cru Rosacker); and Cuvée Frédéric Émile, named after the 19th-century Trimbach who expanded the business to become an important merchant house as well as vine-grower. The family, including three members of the 13th generation, works 63 ha/156 acres of vineyards in ten different villages around Ribeauvillé, famous for the diversity of its soils. Recent additions include 2 ha of Alsace Grand Cru Brand from vintage 2018.

trimming, the vineyard operation of removing unwanted SHOOT growth which can cause SHADING and hinder SPRAYING. Although it is usually done with a trimming machine mounted on a tractor, it may also be carried out with a handheld machete or similar device. The operation normally removes the SHOOT TIP and a few leaves below it, or about 30 cm/12 in of growth, thus leaving the shoots trimmed to about 15–25 NODES, or 70–150 cm/31–58 in. Trimming is essential in vineyards with high VINE DENSITY to stop shoots from adjacent rows from growing together. Regrowth may be such as to demand up to six trimmings a year, particularly in vineyards well supplied with water (by rainfall or IRRIGATION) and NITROGEN. If shoots are trimmed too short then there may be insufficient leaf area to ripen the crop properly (see LEAF TO FRUIT RATIO). Resulting wines will be lower in alcohol and of lighter body and colour. Sometimes vineyards are trimmed so neatly on the top and sides that vine rows can look like a recently trimmed hedge, hence the alternative term 'hedging'. R.E.S.

Trincadeira, sometimes called **Trincadeira Preta**, or black Trincadeira, is a productive red grape highly valued by winemakers in southern PORTUGAL, in 2020 grown on a total of 7,546 ha/18,647 acres of vineyard all over the country. Known in the DOURO as Tinta Amarela, it is very susceptible to ROT and therefore performs well only in the driest of climates, with better results in the Douro Superior, where it can yield fine, attractively scented wines, than in Baixo Corgo, the coolest and wettest of the Douro's three subregions. Trincadeira is therefore ideally suited to the ALENTEJO, where it can produce deep-coloured, spicy wines in the right conditions but tends to herbaceousness if not picked at the right time. R.J.M.

Trincadeira das Pratas, traditional, minor, but potentially high-quality Portuguese white grape originally known as Tamarez in the Alentejo but not the same as the Tamarez of the Tejo. A likely ALFROCHEIRO × Hebén spontaneous CROSS, it can, but does not always, produce delicate, perfumed dry whites.

Triomphe (d'Alsace), HYBRID bred by Kuhlmann in Alsace from Knipperlé and a *riparia-rupestris* AMERICAN VINE. It has good resistance to POWDERY MILDEW, but the wine produced, however deeply coloured, tastes FOXY. The vine is responsible for some English reds.

trocken German for 'dry', a legally defined term when applied to the wines of AUSTRIA and GERMANY. The term can be applied to a still wine with a maximum of 4 g/l RESIDUAL SUGAR, or up to 9 g/l if the TOTAL ACIDITY is less than the residual sugar by no more than 2 g/l (9 g/l residual sugar and total acidity not less than 7 g/l). Given Riesling's high acidity, the upper limit effectively applies to many Austrian and most German wines from that grape. This legal definition of dryness should not be confused with an organoleptic impression that most tasters would describe as dry, which often applies to Riesling HALBTROCKEN. Confusingly, trocken when applied to SEKT (Austrian or German sparkling wine) designates a decidedly sweet wine containing 17–32 grams of residual sugar, as it corresponds to the similarly sweet category of *sec* in CHAMPAGNE. See also DOSAGE

See also FEINHERB and SWEETNESS. J.R. & D.S.

Trockenbeerenauslese, commonly referred to as **TBA**, the PRÄDIKAT with the highest MUST WEIGHT defined by Austrian and German wine law. *Trockenbeeren* refers to grapes (*Beeren*) that have shrivelled on the vine, typically under the influence of NOBLE ROT. Other than in Austria's NEUSIEDLERSEE region, TBA was traditionally confined to rare vintages, but rigorous selection and sorting of fruit (with prestige and high prices as incentives) as well as warmer weather (see CLIMATE CHANGE) have made for considerably increased frequency, especially of tiny lots fermented in glass demijohns. Musts in the upper 200s of OECHSLE, no longer freakishly uncommon, can sometimes take a year or more to ferment to the 5.5% alcohol requisite for wine. A significant share of any TBA is lost to the filter pads in the process of bottling it in stable condition. J.R. & D.S.

Trois Glorieuses, annual weekend devoted to wine and food in and around Beaune. See HOSPICES DE BEAUNE and PAULÉE for more details.

Trollinger, or **Blauer Trollinger**, is the most common German name for the distinctly ordinary black grape variety known as SCHIAVA Grossa in Italy, VERNATSCH in the Tyrol, and Black Hamburg by many who grow and buy TABLE GRAPES. It almost certainly originated in what is now the Italian Tyrol (see ALTO ADIGE), and its German name is a corruption of Tirolinger. In Germany it is associated exclusively with WÜRTTEMBERG, where it has been cultivated since the 14th century (see GERMAN HISTORY). Total plantings of 2,051 ha/5,068 acres sufficed to sustain the variety's position as Germany's fourth most planted red-wine vine in 2020, a rather astonishing statistic when one considers that virtually all of the resultant pale red is drunk by thirsty Württembergers.

Tronçais is a sort of French OAK named after a forest near NEVERS.

trophy wines, small group of wines more expensive than any others and becoming more so under sustained attack from the world's best-heeled COLLECTORS, INVESTORS, and drinkers. A Bordeaux FIRST GROWTH, PETRUS or LE PIN from a fine VINTAGE is a trophy wine. The wines of DOMAINE DE LA ROMANÉE-CONTI and Domaines LEROY, Rousseau, and Roumier count, as do the single-vineyard bottlings of GUIGAL, most PRESTIGE CUVÉES from Champagne, VEGA SICILIA, and the rare red-label wines of Bruno Giacosa and Giacomo Conterno Monfortino.

New World trophy wines include PENFOLDS Grange and all the CALIFORNIA CULT wines. The key to identifying trophy wines is their international fame (often determined by a particularly high SCORE) and, especially, PRICE. Their prices rose markedly from the late 1990s because of the dramatic increase, particularly in ASIA, in the number of potential buyers of these 'limited-edition' wines prepared to acquire them at any price—billionaires need billionaires' wines.

tropical viticulture. Although the grapevine is regarded by many as a strictly temperate plant, it is now increasingly grown in the tropics, defined approximately as the region bordered by the tropics of Cancer and Capricorn. Countries in which grapes are cultivated in tropical conditions include AUSTRALIA, BOLIVIA, BRAZIL, CAMBODIA, COLOMBIA, CUBA, ECUADOR, INDIA, INDONESIA, KENYA, Laos, MADAGASCAR, MEXICO, MYANMAR, NAMIBIA, Nigeria, PARAGUAY, the Philippines, SRI LANKA, TAHITI, TANZANIA, THAILAND, TOGO, VENEZUELA, and VIETNAM. About 90% of this tropical vineyard area of around 175,000 ha/432,435 acres produces TABLE GRAPES, but increasing amounts are dried for RAISINS, especially in India, or fermented into wine.

Within the tropics there are many different climates, modified by differences in ELEVATION and RAINFALL. Only those areas with pronounced wet and dry seasons, and those which are virtually arid, are suitable for commercial tropical viticulture. In the lowland areas, grapevines adopt an evergreen growth habit but can be manipulated into cropping two to three times per year, mainly by PRUNING and removal of all remaining leaves at the point chosen as the end of season, and by the application of chemicals such as hydrogen cyanide solution which induce dormant buds to burst uniformly within one week of application. Other chemicals which retard growth and induce flower buds to form are used mainly for table grapes (see GROWTH REGULATORS).

In areas with pronounced wet (at least 1,800 mm/70 in) and dry seasons, fully ripe wine grapes can be produced only in the dry season. In the Indian 'two season, one crop' system, which has now been adopted in most Asian wine-producing countries, vines are pruned long to produce grapes in the dry season then pruned short (one bud) for only vegetative growth in the rainy season. If IRRIGATION is available in arid regions, then 'two seasons, two crops' is possible.

In some tropical countries, in the interests of both quality and availability, grapes can be ripening as temperatures are rising (35–40 °C/95–104 °F), contrary to most TEMPERATE areas, where ripening proceeds as temperatures fall.

Highland tropical areas with elevations in excess of 1,000 m/3,280 ft to 1,400 m/4,590 ft, depending on the distance from the equator, can have climates that are almost temperate and allow grapevines to follow a climate-controlled growth cycle, including natural LEAF FALL, as for non-tropical areas.

Irrigated grapevines can be very productive in the tropics, giving YIELDS of fresh fruit of 140–280 hl/ha, or 8–16 tons/acre per season, so tropical viticulture can yield relatively inexpensive wine, as in north-east Brazil. In Asian countries, on the other hand, producers are increasingly encouraging vines to produce a single higher-quality crop every 12 months despite the extra costs.

Depending on the climate, tropical grapes can be programmed to reach maturity at times of the year when other fresh fruit is not available or when international prices are very high. For example, north-east Brazil and Maharashtra, India, export table grapes in April/May. W.W.S.

www.tropical-viticulture.com

Trousseau, well-connected and well-travelled red wine grape indigenous to the JURA, where it makes distinctively perfumed, powerful wines that age well and are much more deeply coloured than POULSARD provided yields are controlled. Research in the early 21st century pinpointing the best (warmer) vineyard sites for the variety led to increased plantings: 182 ha/450 acres by 2019. It buds early and may be affected by spring FROSTS, and it is an irregular yielder. In the mid 19th century, the French AMPELOGRAPHER Comte A. Odart maintained that Trousseau was the same as Portugal's BASTARDO, as DNA PROFILING has confirmed. Under the names Bastardo, Maturana Tinta, Merenzao, and Verdejo Tinto, it has been grown in Iberia for at least two centuries, although its journey from eastern France remains a mystery. DNA PROFILING strongly suggests that the variety is a sibling of both CHENIN BLANC and SAUVIGNON BLANC and probably has a parent–offspring relationship with that other Jura variety SAVAGNIN. Grapes called Bastardo are grown in Oregon, Crimea, and Moldova.

Trousseau Gris is a colour mutation that was once known as Gray Riesling in California and is enjoying a small renaissance there.

trunk, the main stem of a tree, from the ground to the first branches or, in the case of a grapevine, to the CORDONS or HEAD. Newly formed vine trunks are pliable and need support (see VINE TRAINING). The height of the trunk of a grapevine is variable, typically from 10 cm/4 in (in BUSH VINES) to more than 10 m/30 ft (in vines growing up trees; see ARBOREAL VITICULTURE), and is determined by the specifications set for each TRAINING SYSTEM and TRELLIS. The trunk height determines the position of the CANOPY relative to the ground. Vine trunks are woody and form part of the bulk needed for storage reserves, especially of CARBOHYDRATES and NITROGEN compounds. In climates with freezing winters, multiple trunks are used to facilitate replacement after winter killing, and in extremely cold climates trunks are buried during the winter (see WINTER PROTECTION).

The trunk of any plant (including the OAK tree, used for COOPERAGE and CORKS) contains a sleeve of conducting tissue with the CAMBIUM in its centre, bark (with PHLOEM) on the outside, and wood (with XYLEM) on the inside. Through these tissues, xylem sap moves upward, carrying water, minerals, and compounds from the roots to the leaves, and phloem sap moves multi-directionally carrying sugars and elaborated molecules from the leaves to the rest of the vine. The downward passage of phloem sap in vines can be interrupted by trunk CINCTURING or girdling. See also TRUNK DISEASES. B.G.C.

trunk diseases, group of FUNGAL DISEASES that infect the wood of the vine and other economically important perennial woody crops such as fruit and nut trees. They are caused by a wide range of Ascomycota and Basidiomycota fungi. Spores from most of these fungi infect grapes through PRUNING wounds, colonizing the vascular system, resulting in symptoms such as wood necrosis, cankers, and/or wood rot. Vascular flow is interrupted over time, causing a progressive death of SPURS, CANES, CORDONS, and TRUNK, leading to the eventual death of the vine. Trunk diseases affect both young and mature vineyards, occur wherever grapes are grown, and are one of the most important biotic factors reducing YIELD, limiting vineyards' lifespan, and increasing production costs.

In young vineyards, BLACK FOOT and PETRI DISEASE are the most prevalent of these diseases, constituting what is known as the young-vine decline complex. Symptoms and negative effects on vine growth can be observed as early as a few months after planting. Though spread of these diseases can occur in the vineyard, it has been well-demonstrated that vine propagation in NURSERIES using infected MOTHER VINES is one of the main sources of infection.

Trunk diseases affecting mature vineyards include ESCA and the canker diseases BOTRYOSPHAERIA DIEBACK, EUTYPA DIEBACK, and PHOMOPSIS dieback. These diseases are caused by airborne spores (conidia or ascospores) under favourable environmental conditions. Studies have also shown that some of the fungi responsible for trunk diseases can remain latent until the vine is exposed to abiotic and/or biotic stress conditions. Symptoms are characterized by dieback and death of spurs, canes, cordons, and trunks and eventual vine death due to canker formation in the vascular tissue.

Since establishing and maintaining a vineyard is very costly, a long lifespan for vines is essential for economic success, as well as for the widely reported relationship between VINE AGE and wine quality. The decline and death of young and mature vines can cause substantial economic loss to grape-growers. It is therefore imperative that management strategies such as sanitation and pruning-wound protection are implemented from the year of planting. See also TRUNK RENEWAL.

The International Council of Grapevine Trunk Diseases, formed in 1998, meets biannually to coordinate research into tackling these increasing threats (www.ucanr.edu/sites/ICGTD). J.R.U.-T.

Gramaje, D., et al., 'Managing grapevine trunk diseases with respect to etiology and epidemiology: current strategies and future prospects', *Plant Disease*, 102 (2018), 12–39.

Hrycan, J., et al., 'Grapevine trunk disease fungi: their role as latent pathogens and stress factors that may favor disease development in grapevines', *Phytopathologia Mediterranea*, 59 (2020), 395–424.

trunk renewal, management technique to replace vine TRUNKS injured by WINTER FREEZE or by TRUNK DISEASE. It originated in the north-east of the US and involves removing a disabled trunk and vine framework by cutting below the injury and replacing it by taking a sucker from below the cut and training it upwards. This procedure is one of rejuvenation, as the new trunk and vine are healthy tissue. R.E.S.

Smart, R., 'Timely trunk renewal to overcome trunk disease', *Practical Winery & Vineyard* (October 2015), 64–70.

Tsaoussi, white grape speciality of the Greek island of Kefalonia, where it may be blended with the more distinctive ROBOLA.

Tsimlyansky Cherny, vine speciality of Rostov in RUSSIA making tannic, characterful reds.

Tsolikouri, relatively important white wine grape of GEORGIA, although only about one-tenth as widely planted there as the popular RKATSITELI. It makes full-bodied semi-sweet and dry wines with moderate acidity and is also used to make sparkling wines.

TTB, acronym for the Alcohol and Tobacco Tax and Trade Bureau, the US regulatory body responsible for AVA approvals, federal taxation, label approvals, and winemaking protocols (although states are permitted to enact more stringent rules than those applied nationally). The TTB is an offshoot of the Bureau of Alcohol, Tobacco, and Firearms (ATF).

Tualatin Hills, northernmost wine region and AVA of the WILLAMETTE VALLEY of Oregon.

tufa, a rock formed by the localized precipitation of calcium carbonate, typically in association with springs, caves, riverbeds, and lake edges. It should not be confused with the marine LIMESTONE of the Loire region known in French as TUFFEAU, nor with the widespread non-calcareous VOLCANIC deposit called TUFF that is much more relevant to viticulture. A.J.M.

tuff is a fine-grained VOLCANIC rock created when fine, ashy material ejected during a volcanic eruption settles, accumulates, and through time becomes progressively hardened. Tuffs vary in composition and colour, depending on the chemistry of the parent volcano, but all comprise several silicate minerals (see GEOLOGY) and so have plenty of potential nutrients for the vine. Geologically, young tuffs can still be relatively soft and easily weathered. **Tuffaceous** soils, such as those found in parts of southern Italy and SICILY, can therefore be deep and fertile. The relative softness of young tuff is exploited in places such as TOKAJ, EGER, and Bükk in Hungary for excavating extensive wine cellars. Confusingly, some wine literature refers to tuff as TUFA, which is geologically quite different. In Italy, *tufo* is sometimes used rather inexactly to refer to certain LIMESTONE soils as well as to those of volcanic origin. A.J.M.

tuffeau, a common rock type in the central LOIRE. *Tuffeau blanc* is CALCAREOUS and provides much better DRAINAGE than most LIMESTONES.

This is the rock used to build many of the châteaux of the Loire, and remaining hollows in the rock have been adapted for winemaking and storage. The overlying *tuffeau jaune* is more sandy and is particularly suitable for the Cabernet Franc vine, underlying some of the best vineyards in CHINON and SAUMUR-Champigny. It is distinct from both TUFA and TUFF. A.J.M.

Tulbagh, inland wine district in SOUTH AFRICA just east of SWARTLAND that is best-known for its whites but produces some fine reds too.

Tumbarumba, high-ELEVATION, cool Australian wine region in southern NEW SOUTH WALES specializing in Chardonnay and Pinot Noir for sparkling wine and gaining attention for elegant, cool-climate, still Chardonnay wines. Spring FROST is a major threat on these GRANITE-and-BASALT slopes, requiring careful site selection. A.R.P.

Tunisia, North African country with a long heritage of winemaking, likely since the Phoenicians established the city of CARTHAGE on the coast over 2,500 years ago. Phoenician agronomist MAGO is, in fact, considered to be one of the first authors on viticulture.

Muslim rule curbed wine production from the 7th century until the French occupation in the 1880s. Under the French, Tunisia's vineyard area greatly expanded, and the country became a major exporter of wine and grapes following France's PHYLLOXERA crisis. Its peak winegrowing period was the 1930s when it had 50,000 ha/123,553 acres under vine. Since Tunisia's independence in 1956, vineyard area has fallen dramatically, reaching just 21,702 ha in 2016, just over 9,600 ha of which are for wine production, in the hands of barely a dozen wineries. Annual wine production ranges between 200,000 and 220,000 hl/5,283,441–5,811,785 gal.

Most wine is produced in the region of Cape Bon, on a peninsula about 100 km/62 miles north-east of Tunis. Its MEDITERRANEAN CLIMATE is similar to that of Sicily, with average annual rainfall of 350 mm/13.7 in and an average temperature of 20 °C/68 °F. Red Mediterranean varieties are dominant, with CARIGNAN accounting for over half the vineyard area and Cinsault and Syrah following its lead. Production is focused on full-bodied rosés and rich red wines, although recent improvements in winemaking mean that white wines from Chardonnay, Muscat of Alexandria, Verdejo, and Viognier also sate the growing domestic market. Most Tunisian wines are consumed locally, with a small but growing wine route in Cape Bon and wine clubs in Tunis. A.B.

Türkiye, widely known as Turkey until 2022, has the fifth largest vineyard area in the world, although it is shrinking rapidly. Since 1990, the surface under vines has decreased from 580,000 ha to 419,000 ha/1,035,372 acres in 2021. Only 3% of the 4.2 million tonnes of grapes harvested in 2020 were used for Türkiye's total wine production of 847,000 hl/22.4 million gal. The rest is used in equal amounts for making molasses (an integral part of Turkish cuisine), for TABLE GRAPES, and for RAISINS, of which Türkiye is the world's leading producer.

Wine has long been overlooked by Turks who have developed a drinking culture over the national aniseed-flavoured spirit rakı. It has been gaining popularity among young people since the early 2000s, and the overall quality has improved along with the wine culture. Despite this, domestic per capita consumption is less than a litre, inspiring producers to target exports in order to survive. However, only 2.9% of the annual production is exported.

According to the market regulator Tobacco and Alcohol Department (TADAB) in 2021, there are 185 registered wineries of which 50 have commercial significance. The majority are urban enterprises rather than businesses established by grape-growers.

History

Anatolia, the peninsula where the Asian part of Türkiye is located today, has played an important role in the ORIGINS OF VINICULTURE. South-eastern Anatolia is most likely where the grapevine was first domesticated. Traces of a wine culture in archaeological sites have been traced back to the Neolithic period in the form of wine-related vessels. Anatolia's position as a bridge between Asia and Europe initiated the further spread of viniculture to the rest of the grape-growing world, an argument supported by linguistics, grape genetics, and archaeology.

The ancient civilizations that inhabited Anatolia, from Assyrians and Hittites to the Phrygian Kingdom, Urartians, and Lydians, had cultivated grapes and made wine with their relevant customs, ceremonies, and festivities, continuing through the Classical and Byzantine periods. Alongside its religious attributes, wine was a commodity traded in volume along major river routes and through ports. Between 1650 and 1200 BCE, when the Hittites ruled most of Anatolia, there were laws safeguarding viticultural practices and trade routes, identifying the different types of wine consumed. Hittites used the word *wiyana* for wine, influencing the words used in many modern languages. Numerous artefacts depicting grapes and wine-related rituals in the Museum of Anatolian Civilizations in Ankara reveal the rich heritage of these civilizations.

When Turks settled in ANATOLIA late in the 11th century they had already converted to ISLAM. As their dominance over the region strengthened, they transformed the largely Greek-speaking region into a Turkish-Muslim one. Although alcohol consumption was prohibited for the Muslim population, non-Muslim communities were given concessions to manufacture and trade it. Its consumption was tolerated in order to preserve the multicultural social structure of the empire and to provide a balance between the Islamic influence and pre-Islamic drinking rituals that included even many iron-fisted sultans. The economic return of the alcohol trade was also too great to ignore. In 1904, 340 million litres of wine were produced, a large portion of which was exported to PHYLLOXERA-hit European markets.

In the aftermath of the First World War and the Turkish War of Independence, the forced migration of Armenian and Greek settlers, who had been responsible for most of the wine production and trade, left Turkish viniculture unattended. Vast vineyards were left unclaimed, and centuries-old knowledge and traditions were lost in an instant. During this period, Türkiye's total wine production decreased to only 2 million litres.

Modern history

After the foundation of the republic in 1923, constructive steps were taken to revive viticulture and winemaking. As a first step, private enterprises were allowed to produce wine alongside the state monopoly. Vine-growers were given technical know-how through agriculture faculties, subsidies for modern winery equipment were provided, and CONSULTANTS were invited from France to determine suitable viticulture areas and vine varieties.

While the earliest established wineries were acquisitions from Greeks, Kemal Atatürk, the founder of the republic, initiated AOÇ Wine Factory in 1925 in the new capital Ankara. At the end of the 1920s, large-scale private sector wineries were initiated by Doluca in Thrace and Kavaklıdere in Ankara. Competition from the state monopoly Tekel and some regional growers encouraged the industry to focus on marketing and sales rather than wine quality and diversity well into the last decade of the 20th century.

A new chapter began in the mid 1990s when Sarafin and Gülor, early boutique wineries in southern Thrace, planted their vineyards with INTERNATIONAL VARIETIES and produced VARIETAL wines. Their success spurred many new producers, equipped with modern technology and often supported by foreign consultant winemakers. Despite protective tax policies, the liberalization of wine imports in 2003 fuelled further interest in wine culture and mediated the improvement of Turkish wine quality, especially under the leadership of female winemakers educated abroad.

Türkiye's restricted local market and the long-serving, Islamist-leaning government's

2013 law banning all forms of alcohol promotion, including on company websites, forced producers to search for new markets. Attempts to promote Turkish wine through tasting events and competitions revealed a need to focus on local grape varieties and winemaking styles in order to find a place in export markets. By 2021 more than 60 INDIGENOUS VARIETIES were in use, helping preserve the country's legacy of old BUSH VINES.

Geography, climate, and grape varieties

Owing to prolonged administrative neglect, the winegrowing regions of Türkiye are not officially designated. Geographically, the country is divided into seven regions with a wide variety of climatic conditions. Türkiye's relatively low latitudes are compensated by the high ELEVATION of most viticulture areas.

More than half of the vineyards dedicated to wine and a large proportion of the registered wineries are in the **Aegean** region. The port city of Izmir is the epicentre of the wine industry and home to Bornova Misketi, a variety related to MUSCAT BLANC À PETITS GRAINS and used for dry, semi-sweet, and DRIED-GRAPE WINES. Dark-skinned local varieties Foça Karası and Urla Karası are being replanted by a group of passionate producers. Cabernet Sauvignon, Merlot, Syrah, and Petit Verdot produce richly structured wines while the fruit of generally older Alicante Bouschet and Carignan vines is used mostly for blending. Chardonnay and Sauvignon Blanc can make fine wines when grown at high elevations, as proven by Sevilen, the region's leading producer. The popular wine route in the Urla district has provided a good model for similar collaborations of regional producers.

The prevailing MEDITERRANEAN CLIMATE of the Aegean coast influences the mountainous interior thanks to the east–west orientation of the mountain ranges. The seedless Sultaniye (SULTANA), Türkiye's most widely cultivated grape, is typically used for drying, and its use in winemaking is gradually decreasing. Inland in Manisa, Kavaklıdere's Pendore vineyards focus mainly on black varieties under the consultancy of Stéphane DERENONCOURT. The high plateau further inland, around Güney in Denizli, has a semi-arid CONTINENTAL CLIMATE with hot, dry summers and cold, snowy winters. At ELEVATIONS reaching up to 900 m/2,950 ft, a wide variety of domestic and INTERNATIONAL VARIETIES are grown, serving many producers in Türkiye. Attention is focused on Syrah and Cabernet Franc, while the local Çalkarası grape is largely used for rosé wines. Pamukkale and Küp are the region's leading producers, having the experience of more than 60 vintages.

The windy northern Aegean island of Bozcaada is home to some of Türkiye's oldest wineries and vineyards and grows mainly local varieties such as the dark Kuntra and Karalahna and pale Çavuş and Vasilaki, mostly as BUSH VINES. Despite this traditional wine culture, the island was put on the wine map thanks to the efforts of the visionary winery Corvus.

More than 40% of all registered producers in Türkiye are based in the **Marmara** region in the hinterland of Istanbul. Most of the winemaking activities are in Eastern Thrace, the European territory of Türkiye, surrounded by the Black Sea to the north, the Sea of Marmara to the south, and the Aegean Sea to the west.

In the southern part of **Thrace** around Tekirdağ, the climate is typically Mediterranean. Planted mainly with international varieties, the vineyards enjoy southern exposure along the lower, sandy-clay slopes of the Ganos range facing the Sea of Marmara. Kayra, now part of DIAGEO, won instant recognition for creativity and dynamism after taking over the former state monopoly Tekel in 2005. Further southwest, the Gallipoli peninsula has a mild climate mediated by the surrounding seas and winds that regulate the otherwise humid conditions. CLAY soils yield deep, concentrated reds from Merlot and both Cabernets in the hands of Doluca, long the region's leading winery, and newer estates such as Suvla and Vinero. To the east, in the hilly area across the Dardanelles strait, the Paşaeli winery has revived old plantings of dark Karasakız (Kuntra of Bozcaada) and the white Sıdalan. Adakarası, an aromatic variety grown on the island of Avşa in the Sea of Marmara, is often used for rosé.

The province of Kırklareli in the foothills of Strandja Mountains is close to the Black Sea, which allows for a mild continental climate. Soils are particularly varied and include GRANITE, LIMESTONE, TERRA ROSSA clay, and QUARTZ gravels. The region's late-ripening Papaskarası yields smooth, spicy reds with bright acidity. Some of Türkiye's notable new producers, led by energetic grower Chamlija, are found in this relatively cool climate.

The vineyards in **Central Anatolia** follow the course of the Kızılırmak, Türkiye's longest river. Kalecik district, north-east of Ankara, is home to the black grape Kalecik Karası, which was saved from extinction in the 1970s. The soft, fragrant examples made in the 1990s by Kavaklıdere encouraged significant plantings. The region's vineyards are at elevations of 650 m/2,132 ft on LOAM and GRAVEL soils. The river and the surrounding mountains moderate what is otherwise a severe continental climate.

Upriver in the south-east, Cappadocia has an elevation of over 1,000 m/3,280 ft, its sandy, VOLCANIC soils planted with bush vines, often UNGRAFTED. The climate is continental and arid, with annual rainfall as low as 350 mm/13.8 in. Winters are very cold and mostly snowy, while summers are hot and dry. Winter and spring FROST can pose problems. For white wines, Emir is the region's most promising grape variety, used in dry and sparkling wines; Narince, Sauvignon Blanc, and Chardonnay have also performed well. Turasan and Kocabağ are the region's oldest producers, while Gelveri makes AMPHORA wines from local varieties grown in old vineyards at the foot of Hasan Mountain in Güzelyurt, near Aksaray.

The climate of Tokat shows Central Anatolian character, though it is geographically part of the damp **Black Sea** region, which is known mostly for growing tea and hazelnuts. The native grape Narince yields full-bodied, perfumed whites, often oak-aged. Most vineyards lie at an average of 400 m/1,310 ft elevation and follow the course of the Yeşilırmak River. Established in 1958, Diren is the region's only winery.

The dry, hot summers and mild, wet winters of the **Mediterranean** region's southern shores are not ideal for viticulture, so most vineyards and wineries are nestled on a high plateau in the Taurus Mountains. Likya winery near Antalya has been leading efforts to revive local varieties.

Most of the mountainous **Eastern Anatolia** region lies above 1,000 m. In this markedly continental climate, DIURNAL TEMPERATURE RANGE is wide and annual rainfall can be less than 400 mm/16 in. Vineyards along the Euphrates River in the provinces of Elazığ and Malatya benefit from the moderating influence of the river and the gigantic dams built on its course. The local variety Öküzgözü, which produces fruity reds, has become so popular that its cultivation has increased significantly throughout Türkiye. Among the few wineries operating in this region, Kayra's facility in Elazığ is the most significant.

South-eastern Anatolia is a major grape-growing region, but most of the produce is used for purposes other than wine. Boğazkere, named after its harsh TANNINS, is its principal grape, harvested from dry-farmed bush vines along the banks of the Tigris river north-west of Diyarbakır. As the climate is extremely hot, the best fruit comes from high-elevation sites around the villages of Çüngüş and Çermik. The local classic blend with Öküzgözü gives balanced reds to match the region's meat dishes. Although long-standing political unrest has made the area unfavourable for wineries, Shiluh winery in Mardin carries the flag of the Syriac Christian community's archaic winemaking traditions. U.C.

www.tarimorman.gov.tr/TADB
www.tuik.gov.tr

Turkmenistan, central Asian republic and former state of the Soviet Union that sprawls between the Caspian Sea, UZBEKISTAN, AFGHANISTAN, and IRAN. Evidence of vine-growing in the country dates back to the 3rd century BCE. Greek and Roman writers report that grapes were cultivated in Marghian (the Murghab

Valley) and in Aria (the Tejen Valley). The Kopetdag ravines still have a great diversity of WILD VINES that have served as a basis for many INDIGENOUS VARIETIES. Different wine vessels depicting grape bunches found during excavations of the village of Baghir near the capital Ashkhabad testify to the fact that Turkmenistan has a long history of winemaking.

By 2020, however, most of the country's approximately 19,673 ha/48,613 acres of vineyards were TABLE GRAPES and RAISINS. Vineyards are mainly in the Ashkhabad region with some in Mary and Chardzhou regions. Only a limited selection of wine grapes are grown including Terbash, Tara Uzüm Ashkhabadski, Riesling, Saperavi, Kizil Sapak, and Bayanshira. The vast Karakumy Desert occupies a large part of this hot, dry country. Almost all vineyards need IRRIGATION, but only the north part of the Tashauz region needs WINTER PROTECTION.

Tursan, 320-ha/790-acre AOC in the Landes in SOUTH WEST FRANCE producing wine in all three colours, mainly red and rosé made from CABERNET FRANC and TANNAT grapes with FER and Cabernet Sauvignon. Most wines come from the Geaune CO-OPERATIVE and are sold locally. The white version, a blend focused on the local variety BAROQUE and GROS MANSENG, is more interesting; three-star chef Michel Guérard of Eugénie-lès-Bains sells his oaked version under the name Baron de Bachen. P.S.

Tuscany, the most important region in central ITALY (see map under ITALY), where it is known as Toscana. Today Tuscany is at the centre neither of Italy's economic life nor of its political life, but it is the region which formed Italy's language, its literature, and its art, and thus it has assumed a central place in the country's culture and self-image. The landscape, immortalized in the work of artists from Giotto to Michelangelo and part of every European's cultural baggage, has remained largely unchanged to this day: a succession of hills and valleys covered with cypresses, umbrella pines, and olive groves—and vineyards.

Ancient history

In the ancient world, Tuscany, and at certain points of its history a much larger area, was known as Etruria. See ETRUSCANS for the ancient history of Tuscany.

Medieval history

If we know more about the wines of medieval Tuscany than we do about the wines of other regions of medieval Italy, it is not because they were better or there were more of them: the reason is the region's, and particularly Florence's, economic and political importance.

Viticulture flourished despite the frequent, small-scale civil wars. The region produced more or less equal amounts of oil and wine, but by far the largest crop was wheat. Smallholders were rare in this part of Italy, since the land was mostly owned by monasteries, the local aristocracy, and (increasingly) merchants in the cities. The system of agriculture was often that known as *mezzadria*, sharecropping whereby the landowner would provide the working capital and the land in return for half (*mezzo*, hence the name) the crop. In 1132, for instance, the Badia (Abbey) di Passignano (whose wine is now made and sold by the merchants ANTINORI) leased some of its land to a wealthy cobbler for half his crop of olive oil and wine.

The regional centre for selling wine was the Mercato Vecchio in Florence. The earliest reference to wine retailers in the city dates from 1079, and in 1282 the wine sellers formed a guild, the Arte dei Vinattieri. Giovanni di Piero Antinori, a member of the noble family that continues to make and sell wine in Tuscany today, joined it in 1385. To uphold the profession's reputation, the guild imposed a strict code of practice. The statutes insisted on cleanliness and exact measures; the shop was not to be situated within 100 yards of a church, and it was not to serve children under 15. No cooked food could be sold, and shops were not to shelter ruffians, thieves, or prostitutes. The wine trade was vital to the Florentine economy. Tax records show that more than 300,000 hl/7.9 million gal of wine entered the city every year in the 14th century. The Florentine historian Villani, writing in 1338, estimated that weekly consumption of wine was a gallon a head. Given that Florence had approximately 90,000 inhabitants, this meant that well over 90% was sold elsewhere, to the surrounding country or other Tuscan cities, some overseas via the port of Pisa, mainly to Flanders, PARIS, and Marseilles.

By no means would all this wine have been Tuscan: a lot came from CRETE (Candia), CORSICA, or NAPLES. Tuscany itself produced red wine, which was usually called simply *vino vermihlio*, but occasionally names appear. The reds of MONTEPULCIANO and Cortona were heavy, those of Casentino lighter. In the late 14th century, we find Montalcino referred to as BRUNELLO. The most important of Tuscany's white wines were called 'Vernaccia' and 'Trebbiano', probably named after their respective grape varieties VERNACCIA and TREBBIANO, but neither was an exclusively Tuscan wine. Of the two, Vernaccia was the more highly reputed. In its sweet form it was associated primarily with LIGURIA, although sweet Vernaccia was also made in Tuscany. The dry style of Vernaccia, made in San Gimignano (but also elsewhere) and not found before the 14th century, was not exported overseas, because only the sweet version could survive the long sea voyage to France, Flanders, or England. Trebbiano, too, could be dry or sweet. The first recorded mention of CHIANTI is in the correspondence of the Tuscan merchant Francesco di Marco Datini in 1398, and it is a *white* wine. Datini was fond of it: in 1404 Amadeo Gherardini of Vignamaggio, which is still a well-known estate, wrote to Datini and sent him half a barrel of his personal stock. Another of Datini's favourites was (red) CARMIGNANO.

Datini's letters give us an idea of what a rich merchant bought for his own consumption. He had MALMSEY sent to him from Venice and Genoa, and, more exotically, the equally strong, sweet wine of Tyre from Venice. These foreign wines were luxury items. Another expensive wine from outside Tuscany that Datini loved was Greco. It was grown in PUGLIA, and so highly prized was it that in the 14th century the commune of San Gimignano abandoned its tradition of giving distinguished visitors a few ounces of saffron and instead made them a present of the precious Greco.

Dante and Boccaccio both mention Vernaccia, a byword for luxury. No Tuscan author wrote exclusively about the wines of the region until Francesco Redi. His *Bacco in Toscana* ('Bacchus in Toscana'), published in 1685, is subtitled *ditirambo*, the Greek dithyramb being a choral lyric in praise of DIONYSUS. Redi's poem, however, has little to do with the classical genre and is no more than an excuse for showing off his learning to fellow members of the Accademia della Crusca: he provides 228 pages of unhelpful and pretentious notes to deluge 980 lines of verse. Neither the poem nor the notes contains anything interesting or new about Tuscan wine and viticulture, and the notes Leigh Hunt wrote to his translation (1825) of *Bacco in Toscana* are a good deal more amusing (although of more use to the historian of language than to the historian of wine). The only wines Redi mentions, and praises, are VERNACCIA, CHIANTI, CARMIGNANO, and, finally, MONTEPULCIANO, which he regards as the king of all wines. H.M.W.

Flower, R., *Chianti: The Land, the People and the Wine* (1979).

Melis, F., 'Produzione e commercio dei vini italiani nei secoli XIII–XVIII', *Annales cisalpines d'histoire sociale*, 1/3 (1972), 107–33.

Modern history

Tuscan viticulture was dominated historically by large estates owned by wealthy local families, most of them of noble origin, and tilled by a workforce of sharecroppers. The demise of this system in the 1950s and 1960s led to a hiatus in investment or even ordinary maintenance, plummeting wine quality, and eventual sale of the properties to new owners. A wave of winegrowers from Milan, Rome, and Genoa—joined in the 1980s by a sizeable contingent of foreigners—has shown both a commendable commitment to quality and an equally commendable openness to new and more cosmopolitan ideas. See also ANTINORI, FRESCOBALDI, and RICASOLI, local noble families with considerable wine interests.

Geography and vine varieties

Tuscany produces wines in a wide variety of ELEVATIONS, ASPECTS, and SOILS. Vineyards spread from the plains of the MAREMMA on the Tuscan coast and steep hillsides as high as 550 m/1,800 ft above sea level in Gaiole-in-Chianti and Lamole in Greve-in-Chianti. A mere 8% of the land is flat, and HILLSIDE VINEYARDS, at elevations of 150–600 m/500–1,968 ft, supply the vast majority of the better-quality wines. The SANGIOVESE vine, the backbone of the region's production, seems to require the concentration of SUNLIGHT that slopes can provide to ripen well in these latitudes, as well as the less fertile soils on the hills. Growers also value the significant DIURNAL TEMPERATURE RANGE as an important factor in developing its aromatic qualities.

Sangiovese, covering more than 36,000 ha/ 88,957 acres in 2020, is by far Tuscany's most planted grape variety. The second most planted, with 2,400 ha, is the insipid white TREBBIANO Toscano, though it has been rapidly losing ground to VERMENTINO (1,741 ha) since it lost its once mandatory role as ingredient in many of the region's Sangiovese-based wines. In the past enormous yields were demanded from both varieties, and the DOCs that were generously demarcated in the 1960s encouraged large-scale plantings of high-yielding CLONES with scant attention to site suitability, giving Sangiovese an undeserved reputation as a mediocre grape variety. As the DOC laws did nothing to encourage the production of good-quality wines, many producers enthusiastically embraced INTERNATIONAL VARIETIES, especially Merlot and Cabernet Sauvignon, which they aged in French BARRIQUES and sold at high prices. Except for the most famous wines, the popularity of these SUPERTUSCANS is now in decline. Several iconic producers persevered with Sangiovese, devoting their best sites to it and drastically lowering YIELDS. As they refused to blend Trebbiano Toscano with Sangiovese, they also had to resort to the lowly VINO DA TAVOLA category. The situation has since been redressed, especially in CHIANTI CLASSICO where at the end of the 1980s intensive research in clonal material, rootstocks, and site specifics led to a noticeable increase in quality, while the creation of the IGT Toscana brought the Supertuscan rebels back into the fold of a slightly higher denomination. Merlot is still regularly a blending partner (up to 20% varieties other than Sangiovese is allowed), but the trend is for varietal Sangiovese wines, regularly from single vineyards. Many ferment with AMBIENT YEAST and age their wines in traditional large oak CASKS rather than small French BARRELS.

BRUNELLO DI MONTALCINO, a 100% Sangiovese wine by law, and despite the lapse in credibility caused by a blending scandal in 2008, has long shown that Sangiovese can produce world-class, long-lived wines. Its neighbour VINO NOBILE DI MONTEPULCIANO has been more reluctant to embrace Sangiovese fully; since 2010 the production rules allow for 30% international varieties. This has been partially redressed by the introduction of an official system of subzones, which may appear on labels only if the wine is 85% Sangiovese with the balance indigenous varieties only.

BOLGHERI has been Tuscany's hotspot for Bordeaux varieties (see SASSICAIA) although many of the wines contain a portion of Sangiovese to add acidity to Cabernet and Merlot, which can be too ripe when grown on the hot Maremma plains. Further inland and higher up in the hills where a cooler climate prevails, the DOC Montecucco has attracted newcomers who regularly produce wines on a par with the best from Chianti Classico. DOC Monteregio di Massa Marittima seems equally promising for fine wine, especially when vineyards are planted on elevations above 300 m/984 ft. Neighbouring Montalcino, Orcia DOC might compete with Monteregio di Massa Marittima if newcomers persist with Sangiovese rather than international varieties. Valdarno di Sopra, near Arezzo, is set to become Italy's first DOC to be 100% organic as per its legally binding production rules.

Not all the myriad DOCs and DOCGs in Tuscany (63 in total in 2022) are either significant or particularly different from the supposedly lower IGT category. Producers therefore often prefer to label their wines with the more widely recognized IGT Toscana. Of Tuscany's 60,000 ha, 99% are registered for the production of DOC and DOCG wine, with stricter production rules than for basic table wine. While the Chianti DOCG continues to supply the mass market with distinctly modest wines, most of Tuscany's wine regions are now focused on high quality. While the trend for indigenous varieties seems unstoppable, international varieties remain dominant in several areas, notably in CARMIGNANO, Bolgheri, Suvereto, and, for Syrah, Cortona. Most of Tuscany seems too warm to produce truly great white wines (although an increasing number of *rosato*, or rosé, wines compensates). VERMENTINO, a relative newcomer in central Tuscany, seems to be the most credible indigenous answer, while the minerally and elegant VERNACCIA DI SAN GIMIGNANO deserves a comeback.

For more details of specific Tuscan wines, see BOLGHERI, BRUNELLO DI MONTALCINO, CARMIGNANO, CHIANTI, CHIANTI CLASSICO, CHIANTI RUFINA, ELBA, GALESTRO, VERNACCIA, VINO DA TAVOLA, VINO NOBILE DI MONTEPULCIANO, and VIN SANTO. W.S.

Belfrage, N., *Brunello to Zibibbo: The Wines of Tuscany, Central and Southern Italy* (2nd edn, 2003).

Txakoli, usually white wine made in Spain's BASQUE country, known as **Chacolí** in Castilian. Like VINHO VERDE it is strongly Atlantic-influenced and is usually sold young, very slightly sparkling, and low in alcohol. A century ago over 1,000 ha/2,471 acres of vines stretched from Bayonne to Bilbao, but after PHYLLOXERA ravaged the region few vineyards were replanted. With cool summers and annual RAINFALL of 1,500 mm/58 in, this is challenging grape-growing country. DOWNY MILDEW can be a problem.

The high-trained HONDARRABI Zuri and Hondarrabi Zuri Zerratia (PETIT COURBU) white grape varieties account for 85% of Txakoli. Mune Mahatsa (FOLLE BLANCHE), RIESLING, Iskiriota Zuri Handia (GROS MANSENG), and Iskiriota Zuri Tipia (PETIT MANSENG) play minor parts. The 2% of Txacoli wines that are not white are light reds from Hondarrabi Beltza.

There are three DOPs for Txacoli. **Getariako Txakolina**, extending in 2021 to 433 ha/1,070 acres around San Sebastian in the province of Guipuzcoa (see map under SPAIN), is the appellation responsible for the classic low-alcohol, herbal, spritzy style of Txacoli.

A richer, fuller style comes from **Bizkaiko Txakolina** DOP, which covers 428 ha/1,058 acres of vineyards in the Vizcaya province, whose capital is Bilbao. DOP **Arabako Txakolina**, or Txacoli de Álava, covers 100 ha in the Álava province and produces wines similar to those from Bizkaiko Txakolina.

In both DOPs, the embrace of LEES CONTACT to increase depth and texture in the wines creates a richer style reminiscent of the wines of Galicia. In November 2021, three designations were introduced: **Txacoli Bereziak**, indicating a wine that has been aged at least five months in barrel and on lees; **Apardunak**, for sparkling wines produced by the MÉTHODE ANCESTRALE; and **Apartak**, meaning 'singular' and indicating a wine made using non-traditional methods such as SKIN CONTACT or AMPHORA ageing. F.C.

typicality, English word dating back to the 17th century though now often replaced by the neologism **typicity** to translate the French wine-tasting term *typicité* (and Italian *tipicità*), coined in the late 1970s and promoted by agronomist Jean Salette as a way to accentuate the importance of CONTROLLED APPELLATIONS and counter the international competition that French wines were increasingly facing. The term refers to a wine's quality of being typical of its type, geographical provenance, and even its VINTAGE YEAR, and it is perhaps because typicality is a SUBJECTIVE notion, rather than a physical attribute that can be measured by ANALYSIS, that it is so much discussed and that individual tasters are likely to differ as to what they consider typical of a particular wine.

Typicality may be of less concern to most wine drinkers than how good a wine tastes, but it becomes important in wine JUDGING if the wine has been entered into a particular class. It is also important to professional wine buyers, particularly when choosing wines to represent a GENERIC style. The notion of typicality may also be a source of contention when producers submit their wines to the tasting panel of a controlled appellation in order to obtain the *agrément*, permission to put the name of the appellation on the label. For example, a producer in Alsace who is making a high-quality skin-fermented Pinot Gris may fall foul of the tasting panel if they consider the wine too tannic or oxidative and therefore atypical.

Typicality demands a specific set of characteristics for every wine type. For example, a deep white wine of modest ACIDITY and relatively high ALCOHOLIC STRENGTH, smelling strongly of ALDEHYDES, would be extremely atypical of Chablis but would display the typicality of a FINO style of SHERRY. Similarly, a very young red wine smelling strongly of CARBONIC MACERATION would be typical of many a young BEAUJOLAIS but very unlike a young BORDEAUX.

As winemakers increasingly travel between wine regions, absorbing and applying different techniques, some distinctions between wine 'archetypes' are being eroded, and there is more disagreement than ever as to what constitutes typicality. See also REGIONALITY.

Baudouin, P., 'AOC: originalité ou typicité?', *Revue des Œnologues*, 102 (2003).

typicity. See TYPICALITY.

Tyrian. Australian NEW VARIETY, a cross of SUMOLL and CABERNET SAUVIGNON. See CIENNA.

Tyrol. Hardly any wine is made in this western part of Austria, but considerable quantities are made in that part of the Tyrol ceded to Italy after the First World War, now known as the South Tyrol, Südtirol in German, or ALTO ADIGE in Italian.

Uclés, promising Spanish DOP in the Cuenca province of CASTILLA-LA MANCHA.

UGA, *unità geografica aggiuntiva*, meaning 'additional geographical unit', the term used for any one of the 11 named COMMUNES within CHIANTI CLASSICO that may appear on the label as a suffix to the DOC name (e.g. Chianti Classico Radda). It is also used to refer to the 33 named single vineyards within the SOAVE DOC. In VINO NOBILE DI MONTEPULCIANO, UGAs are 12 vineyard areas identified on the basis of geological research. Since these largely and fortunately coincide with the historic boundaries of 12 parishes already registered in the 18th century, they are known as *pievi* (plural of *pieve*, or 'parish'). See also the slightly different MGA, as well as France's DÉNOMINATION GÉOGRAPHIQUE COMPLÉMENTAIRE.

Uganda, East African country that has a small wine industry pioneered by the Mukaira Foundation, which started growing wine grapes in 2006 and bottles under the Valley Wines label. Most vineyards are in the south-west of the country.

Ugni Blanc (which is in fact Italy's ubiquitous TREBBIANO Toscano) is France's most planted white grape variety by far, with more than twice as much French vineyard devoted to it than to Chardonnay, and yet it is rarely seen on a wine label. Just as AIRÉN, Spain's most planted white variety, supplies that country's voracious brandy stills, so the copious, thin, acid wine of Ugni Blanc washes through armagnac and, especially, cognac stills. In Charentes it is often known as St-Émilion.

But despite EU encouragement to pull up poorer-quality vines, as well as a distinctly sluggish market for brandy, France's total plantings of Ugni Blanc fell by little more than 10% between the late 1980s and 2019, to 92,514 ha/228,607 acres, and actually went up in the last decade.

Ugni Blanc supplanted the FOLLE BLANCHE that was pre-PHYLLOXERA the main ingredient in French brandy production because of its good resistance to POWDERY MILDEW and GREY ROT. It was probably imported from Italy during the 14th century when the papal court was established at Avignon. Other Italian varieties were presumably similarly transported, but Trebbiano Toscano's extraordinarily high YIELDS and high ACIDITY may have helped establish it in southern France, where it is still grown widely today. It is still grown in Provence, the southern Rhône, and in and around Bordeaux, but the great majority of plantings are in the Charentes. It is, like most copiously produced wines, low in EXTRACT and character, relatively low in alcohol, but usefully high in acidity. This exceptionally vigorous vine buds late, thereby avoiding most spring FROST damage, which makes it popular with growers. Yields can easily reach 150 hl/ha (8.5 tons/acre). Because it ripens relatively late, there is a natural geographical limit on its cultivation, but in areas such as Charentes it is simply picked before it is fully ripe.

For more details of this variety, see TREBBIANO Toscano (although it is usually known throughout South America, where it is widely planted, as Ugni Blanc).

Uhudler, wine speciality of SÜDBURGENLAND in Austria—usually pink, sometimes white—made from the several AMERICAN HYBRIDS introduced post-PHYLLOXERA to this region (as to so many others in Europe, though very seldom with such lasting influence). Long legally contentious and maligned for its dependence on American hybrids, it was eventually banned; it did not regain recognition until 1992. D.S.

Ukraine is the second largest country in Europe, its southern borders washed by the waters of the Black and Azov seas. The history of winemaking on its shores dates to the 4th century BCE, when ancient Greeks settled the area. The roots of the modern-day industry date to the 11th and 12th centuries, when MONKS AND MONASTERIES introduced viticulture to northern Ukraine.

Wine production has since waxed and waned as this part of the world has suffered much political upheaval. In 1913 its total vineyard area was 54,000 ha/133,000 acres, but owing to the effects of the First World War and PHYLLOXERA it had shrunk to 13,000 ha/32,124 acres by 1919. Holdings then mushroomed to 103,000 ha by 1940, only to be decimated by the Second World War, when total plantings dropped to 68,000 ha.

In the post-war Soviet period, state farms specializing in viticulture were established and were subsequently amalgamated into specialized trusts and large companies. Nurseries were also established to meet the need for PROPAGATION material. By the time the CRIMEA was ceded to Ukraine by the Soviet Union in 1954, the national total vineyard area was boosted to an estimated 400,000 ha/988,421 acres.

Since then there has been a steady and significant decline, exacerbated by Russia's annexation of Crimea in early 2014. By 2020 vineyards covered 39,100 ha/96,618 acres, supplying 134 licensed wineries. Of these, 80% are large wineries, but there is a growing interest in smaller artisan productions, and tastes are changing from sweet to dry-style wines. In 2022 Ukraine was again under attack from Russia, which mounted a full-scale invasion in February of that year. While the Transcarpathian wine region appeared to be stable, wineries in and around Kyiv, Kherson, Chernihiv, Mykolaiv, and Odesa have suffered, with some under occupation and other parts under constant enemy fire. The future fate of wineries in the occupied territories, such as Prince Trubetsky, Tavria, and Bilozerka, is unknown. Several wineries have been bombed, and the Gostomel glass factory in Kyiv, which supplied bottles for many local producers, was destroyed. However, Ukrainian winemakers who can continue to make wine are persevering, producing wine with a focus on exports while the domestic market is in decline.

Geography and climate

Ukraine's landscape is diverse, from plains and steppes in the south to hilly areas in the centre to the Carpathian Mountains in the west. The climate is predominantly CONTINENTAL, favourable for viticulture in most regions, although the north-east can get quite cool, requiring WINTER PROTECTION for the vines. Since most vineyards are located in dry zones, IRRIGATION plays a major part, with DRIP IRRIGATION employed for some higher-quality wines.

The vast majority of vineyards are concentrated in the Odesa region (23,700 ha/58,564 acres), where three out of four of the country's proposed CONTROLLED APPELLATIONS are located: PDO Yalpuh, PDO Chabag, and PGI Prydunaiska Bessarabia. The other, PGI Zakarpattia, is in Transcarpathia, near the borders with Hungary, Slovakia, and Romania.

Vine varieties

Vineyards are planted mostly to VITIS VINIFERA varieties grafted on to phylloxera-resistant ROOTSTOCKS. The most planted grape variety was long RKATSITELI, which has accounted for as much as 40% of all plantings in some regions, but INTERNATIONAL VARIETIES such as Chardonnay, Pinot Noir, Cabernet Sauvignon, Merlot, and others have taken over some of its share. The 61 recognized varieties listed in the Ukrainian State Register in 2021 also include Eastern European varieties such as FURMINT, KÉKFRANKOS, and SAPERAVI as well as INDIGENOUS VARIETIES such as Cevat Kara, Kefessyia, and Telti Kuruk.

For much of the 20th century, viticultural and oenological research in Ukraine was carried out by the famous centre of wine ACADEME in the former Soviet Union, the Institute for Vine and Wine MAGARACH, founded in 1828 in Yalta in the Crimea. Today its importance has been usurped by the Tairov Institute for Viticulture and Oenology, which has bred 150 varieties since its founding in Odesa in 1905. O.P.-T.

ullage, which derives from the French *ouillage*, has had a variety of meanings and uses in the English-speaking wine trade. It can mean the process of EVAPORATION of wine held in wooden containers such as a BARREL. The HEAD SPACE left in the container is also called the ullage, or ullage space, and the wine in that state is said to be **on ullage**. The word 'ullage' is also used for any space in a stoppered wine bottle not occupied by wine (see FILL LEVEL). And a bottle or barrel not entirely full is said to be **ullaged**. The ullage space in a barrel is not empty but contains water and alcohol vapours together with some CARBON DIOXIDE previously dissolved in the wine. See TOPPING UP for the measures undertaken to avoid the risks of ullage.

Ull de Llebre, meaning 'hare's eye', is the Catalan name for TEMPRANILLO.

ultrafiltration, a form of cross-flow FILTRATION which can be used for ALCOHOL REDUCTION and, more controversially, for TANNIN removal or for CONCENTRATION. It is looser than REVERSE OSMOSIS but tighter than sterile filtration. It can also be used to separate COLLOIDS from their solution and is used as an alternative to FINING. Proponents suggest it is also useful for removal of browning and for reducing tannins in PRESS WINES, but it is subject to strict regulation.

Smith, C., 'The new filtrations', in *Postmodern Winemaking* (2013), 202–18.

Wollan, D., 'Membrane and other techniques for the management of wine composition', in A. G. Reynolds (ed.), *Managing Wine Quality 2: Oenology and Wine Quality* (2nd edn, 2021), 183–212.

ultraviolet radiation, or **UV radiation**, radiation of shorter wavelength (< 400 nm) than so-called visible SUNLIGHT, which is very damaging to all life because of its mutation-inducing properties. PHENOLIC compounds absorb ultraviolet radiation, and levels of QUERCETIN in grape berries are related to ultraviolet exposure. It is proven that ultraviolet exposure increases levels of phenolics and therefore COLOUR in red wines, which can be an advantage of vineyards at high ELEVATION and of those closer to the 'ozone hole' over the Antarctic. It also increases RESVERATROL levels.

See also CANOPY MANAGEMENT and POWDERY MILDEW. R.E.S.

Jug, T., and Rusjan, D., 'Advantages and disadvantages of UV-B radiations on grapevine (*Vitis* sp.)', *Emirates Journal of Food and Agriculture*, 24/6 (2012), 576–85.

Smart, R. E., et al., 'Canopy management to improve grape yield and wine quality: principles and practices', *South African Journal of Enology and Viticulture*, 11/1 (1990), 3–25.

umami, Japanese term derived from two words meaning 'delicious' and 'essence' and used to refer to what some consider to be the fifth primary taste (see TASTING). More a quality than a specific flavour, it is variously described as 'savoury' or 'meaty' and is found in high levels in foods such as soy sauce, Parmesan, fresh tomato juice, tuna, and seaweed. Umami levels in other foods are increased by the addition of monosodium glutamate (MSG).

Eastern thinking has for many centuries recognized five primary tastes, but it was not until 1907 that Professor Ikeda of Tokyo Imperial University identified and isolated the AMINO ACID glutamate, or glutamic acid, as the source of the flavour he named 'umami'. He subsequently developed the seasoning monosodium glutamate so that umami levels in other foods might be increased. Recent research identifying the receptors on the tongue that detect amino acids gives further credibility to the existence of this fifth taste.

The level of amino acids in wine is thought to be affected by the RIPENESS of the grapes and the process of FERMENTATION. However, it is extremely difficult to isolate the taste of umami in wine because of the way it interacts with the other four primary tastes.

Proponents of umami suggest that its presence brings a 'completeness' to the flavour of a wine but warn that it may increase the BITTERNESS and ASTRINGENCY of some tannic reds.

Umbria, fourth smallest of ITALY's 20 regions, in terms of both physical size and population, and one of the country's very few landlocked regions (see map under ITALY). It shares many geological and climatic similarities with neighbouring TUSCANY, which produced six times as much wine in 2020. Umbria's DOCS seem repetitive at best, obstructive of the distinction of different TERROIRS at worst. Most of its 13 DOCs are similar in terms of GRAPE VARIETIES, YIELDS, and minimum ALCOHOLIC STRENGTH, with a strong bias towards INTERNATIONAL VARIETIES. SANGIOVESE, with a total of 2,204 ha/5,446 acres planted in 2020, is Umbria's most important red wine grape, followed by Merlot (1,158 ha), the indigenous SAGRANTINO (837 ha), and Cabernet Sauvignon (560 ha). Of white wine grapes, the lacklustre Tuscan import TREBBIANO Toscano (also called Procanico in Umbria) comes first with 2,041 ha, followed by the superior GRECHETTO (1,444 ha) and Chardonnay (447 ha). Almost all of these varieties are either allowed or an obligatory component in every DOC's production regulations, regardless of their suitability for the local conditions.

Regrettably, Trebbiano Toscano dominates in Umbria's most important white DOC, ORVIETO. The blend must include at least 60% Trebbiano and/or Grechetto. Orvieto's terroir is very suitable for the production of high-quality whites, and in the 1980s the region attracted Tuscan wine producers and CONSULTANTS keen to broaden their portfolio with a white from a nearby location. But instead of working with local varieties, they planted Chardonnay and Sauvignon Blanc, which may have promised a

higher return but have done little to increase Orvieto's reputation. Although quality has undoubtedly improved, currently most Orvieto wines are made with one or more international white varieties and contain RESIDUAL SUGAR. Spoleto, Umbria's other all-white DOC, relies on the more characterful Trebbiano Spoletino, requiring at least 50% in the Bianco and 85% in VARIETAL bottlings. The Montefalco DOC also requires at least 50% Trebbiano Spoletino in its Bianco; Montefalco Grechetto must include a minimum of 85% Grechetto.

In Umbrian red wines, Sangiovese gives pleasant, if not memorable, wines in the Colli Altotiberini, Colli Amerini, Colli Martani, Colli Perugini, and Colli del Trasimeno DOCs, often blended with Merlot and Cabernet Sauvignon. The best Umbrian Sangioveses have been produced by Lungarotti (see TORGIANO). It is also the basis for Rosso di Montefalco, made in the HILLSIDE VINEYARDS of the Montefalco DOC zone between Assisi and Terni. Here it is blended with a small percentage of the local Sagrantino, a grape that comes into its own in the DOCG Montefalco Sagrantino. Already documented in the 16th century, this ancient variety was almost extinct by the 1960s. Thanks to a flowering of interest in it in the 1990s, total plantings in the DOC were 837 ha/2,068 acres in 2020. Traditionally used for PASSITO sweet wines, it is now more often made into full-bodied, OAK AGED, concentrated dry reds which, by law, must be aged for at least 33 months. Regularly compared with BRUNELLO in its aromatics and with BAROLO in its tannic grip, Montefalco Sagrantino quenched international thirst for high-octane wines at the time, although some are simply too oaky and alcoholic. Research into sites that can provide an extended ripening season and into the best CLONES should help. W.S.

Belfrage, N., *Brunello to Zibibbo: The Wines of Tuscany, Central and Southern Italy* (2nd edn, 2003).

underwater ageing. Inspired by the quest for the perfect environment for AGEING wines and by the example of champagne preserved for nearly two centuries on the floor of the Baltic Sea, in the last two decades wine producers have been experimenting with underwater ageing of their wines, both still and sparkling, generally in bottle but occasionally in cask or AMPHORA, mostly under the sea, at a range of depths, but also in water-filled tanks in the winery. One producer on the south-west coast of France is even fermenting wines underwater in specially devised CONCRETE tanks: a submarine winery.

Several factors may affect the way a wine ages underwater, depending on the type of wine, the location, and the water depth. These include temperature, darkness, pressure, salinity, movement of the tides, and, for bottled wines, reduced oxygen ingress. This last could well be the most influential factor, since esterification of alcohols and acids is unchanged (see ESTERS) and other reactions that are normally triggered by OXYGEN are slowed so that the wine remains in a REDUCTIVE state. If a bottled sparkling wine is submerged with its LEES, then pressure and tides may have a significant impact because of the greater interaction between the lees and the wine. The influence of underwater pressure is unclear (at −40 m under the sea, the pressure is typically 4.5 bar compared with 6 bar in a bottle of fully sparkling wine; at −60 m, it is 7 bar), although trials have shown not only very little oxygen ingress but also no escape of CARBON DIOXIDE.

While these experiments have been well publicized, often accompanied by photos of barnacled bottles, much of the evidence remains anecdotal, with producers and tasters generally agreeing that the wines do taste different from their exact counterparts aged in a cellar, often fresher and more youthful in both colour and aroma. However, one four-year experiment conducted by Gaia Wines at −20 m off the coast of SANTORINI showed distinct differences between pairs of wines in terms of the number and concentration of aromatic compounds, suggesting that it is the reduced-oxygen environment that has the greatest impact on still wines in particular. Analysis at DIJON of still and sparkling wines aged for a year off the western tip of Brittany has shown that wines age more slowly, that the level of SULFUR DIOXIDE remains constant, and that red wines retain their red colour.

ungrafted vine, also known as an own-rooted or self-rooted vine, is a vine which has not been grafted to a ROOTSTOCK (see GRAFTING). Ungrafted vines grow perfectly well, although some varieties (e.g. SÉMILLON) are known to produce weak root systems, while SYRAH, for example, produces strong ones. The terms *pie franco, pe franco, piede franco, franc de pied,* and *würzelecht* are occasionally used on labels in Spain, Portugal, Italy, France, and Germany respectively. See also PHYLLOXERA. R.E.S.

unicorn wine, a wine that is so rare it is almost mythical. The term was originally coined in the 2010s by FASHION-conscious American SOMMELIERS boasting of their drinking exploits on SOCIAL MEDIA.

unità geografica aggiuntiva. See UGA.

United Kingdom. See Great BRITAIN for general matters, and see ENGLAND and WALES for wine produced there.

United States of America has become a juggernaut in the wine world in a relatively short time. Since its first and mostly doomed attempts at winemaking in the 1600s, the country has become not only the largest wine consumer in the world, averaging over 32 million hl/845 million gallons of wine per year by 2021 according to OIV estimates, but also the globe's fourth-largest producer of wine.

Vines now cover some 400,000 ha/988,422 acres, making the country sixth in vineyard surface area globally. Some of this goes into the production of RAISINS, an important crop in California, but the majority is used by the more than 11,300 wineries coast to coast.

The country is a major exporter, shipping 338.4 million l/89.4 million gal of wine in 2021, and has become a significant importer as well, behind only Germany in terms of volume and number one in terms of value according to OIV data, at €6.2 billion in 2021.

CALIFORNIA is by far the most important wine-producing state in both volume and prestige, contributing 81% of the country's total production of 24.1 million hl/637 million gal of wine in 2021, followed by WASHINGTON, OREGON, and NEW YORK, but all 50 states in the Union now produce wine, most of them from locally grown grapes.

wineamerica.org/impact/

History

European settlement in what is now the US goes back to the late 16th century (see also VÍNLAND) but it was two centuries later that wine was first successfully produced there. The long delay was not for lack of trying. The abundant native AMERICAN VINE SPECIES immediately drew the attention of the first settlers; winemaking was an official aim of the VIRGINIA and Carolina colonies, and it was encouraged and repeatedly tried in all of the American colonies.

However, the colonists found wine made from the INDIGENOUS VARIETIES unpalatable, and began to import cuttings of VITIS VINIFERA vines from Europe to Virginia. The experiment was frequently repeated over the whole length of the Atlantic seaboard with vines from every great European wine region, but the result was uniform failure. The vines were destroyed by extremes of climate, by native PESTS, and by previously unknown VINE DISEASES. The facts were not clearly understood for more than two centuries, since the trials were isolated and uncoordinated, and no adequate knowledge of plant pathology existed. The cycle of hopeful experiment followed by complete failure went on in profitless repetition (see Thomas JEFFERSON, for example).

All Europe took part in the effort. French VIGNERONS were imported along with French vines by the Virginia Company in 1619, and French expertise continued to be sought thereafter: Huguenot exiles were employed in Carolina in 1680, in Virginia in 1700, and in Pennsylvania in 1683. Germans attempted winegrowing at Germantown in Pennsylvania;

◀ These bottles of Champagne Drappier's Brut Nature spent 646 days, post-DISGORGEMENT, in protective cages at a depth of 31 m/102 ft and a TEMPERATURE of 8–13 °C/46–55°F in the Bay of Lannion off the coast of BRITTANY. UNDERWATER AGEING conditions have been shown to have a significant effect on the AGEING of wine. © Champagne Drappier

U

in Florida a colony of Greeks, Italians, Frenchmen, and Spaniards tried vine-growing in 1767. All of these, and innumerable other efforts, were based on *vinifera* varieties and failed (see PHYLLOXERA and FUNGAL DISEASES).

A new direction was taken through the discovery of a chance HYBRID—the combination of a native VITIS LABRUSCA and an unknown *vinifera*—called the Alexander grape, in PENNSYLVANIA, not far from where William Penn had planted *vinifera* in 1683. Its hybrid character was unrecognized for many years, but it in fact showed the way in which vine-growing in the eastern United States would be developed. The variety became the basis for the first successful commercial wine production in the US—that of Jean Jacques Dufour in what is now INDIANA around 1806.

Thereafter, many new AMERICAN HYBRIDS of American vine species—either with each other or with a European *vinifera* variety, and formed almost invariably by chance—were introduced and contributed to the possibilities of winemaking in the US. The most important were CATAWBA, DELAWARE, ISABELLA, and NORTON, all introduced in the first half of the 19th century. With the exception of Norton, most were better adapted to white-wine production than to red, and most had more or less of the so-called FOXY aroma.

Dufour's efforts—and his 1826 book *The American Vinedresser's Guide*, the first book on vine-growing published in the US—inspired Nicholas Longworth to try his hand at winegrowing in OHIO, where his international success with Catawba inspired wine industries in neighbouring NEW YORK and MICHIGAN. Other winemaking centres sprung up wherever European wine-drinking emigrants landed: around Hermann, MISSOURI; Altus, ARKANSAS; along the Delaware River in NEW JERSEY; and further afield.

In the south, before the Civil War broke out in the 1860s, scattered vineyards growing American native or hybrid vines and small wineries could be found throughout the Carolinas and Georgia and extended to the frontiers of TEXAS and Kansas. The federal government supported vine-growing through plant exploration, the distribution of plants, and experimental work in the analysis of grapes and wines. In the decade before the Civil War, interest in vine-growing burgeoned and many new hybrid varieties were introduced, some of them now the outcome of controlled rather than accidental hybridizing.

The most important single result of this activity was CONCORD, a vine with good resistance to pests and diseases, well adapted to the extreme growing conditions of the area that then constituted the United States, but whose extremely FOXY grapes were largely unsuitable for wine (or at least wine as most wine drinkers know it). The ubiquity of Concord has had a large part in establishing a taste for GRAPE JUICE among Americans.

Meanwhile, although the fact was quite unknown in the US, *vinifera* grapes were successfully grown and wine made in the Spanish settlements on the Rio Grande in New Mexico (beginning around 1629) and Texas (mid 1600s) and in the Franciscan missions of California (beginning around 1779). The Mexican–American War of 1846–8, followed by the GOLD RUSH of 1849, brought the *vinifera*-growing regions of the south-west into the US. At the time, the vine was already grown on a small but commercial scale in Los Angeles. Plantings thereafter spread over the state, and production grew rapidly from a few hundred thousand gallons in 1860 to more than 30 million gal/1.1 million hl by the end of the century.

The first *vinifera* variety grown in New Mexico and California was MISSION. Importations and trials of many other *vinifera* varieties quickly began. Among the most interesting is ZINFANDEL, long associated specifically with California, where it is still widely grown.

On the east coast, vine-growing continued to develop, such that New York became the second-largest wine producer in the US by 1890, surpassing Ohio, Illinois, and Pennsylvania. In 1919, the last year before national PROHIBITION was enforced, the US produced 55 million gal of wine. During the Prohibition years, some commercial wine production was allowed, for SACRAMENTAL and 'medicinal' purposes, and HOME WINEMAKING became more popular than ever before, resulting in an increase in total vine acreage thanks to demand for GRAPE CONCENTRATE, but the industry was largely destroyed.

Upon Repeal (from 1934), the US industry had to reconstitute itself. Some of the old firms reappeared, and many new firms were founded. But it took time to put things right: the country was in the lowest depths of economic depression, and wine was an unfamiliar luxury. High-alcohol sweet wines became the mainstay of the trade and remained so for the next generation. The federal government failed to re-establish its research programmes for wine, but important OENOLOGICAL and VITICULTURAL research was carried out by the state universities of California at DAVIS and CORNELL UNIVERSITY in New York. Promotional work was largely in the hands of the Wine Institute of California, founded in 1934.

The Second World War, by cutting off European supplies, brought new prosperity to US industry but new instability as well. Large distilling companies bought up established wineries in order to have a product to sell. A seller's market prevailed until, after the war, the artificially stimulated demand collapsed. The distillers departed from the wine trade, which fell into somnolence. Little effort was made to develop new markets; wineries typically sold their wines in BULK to wholesalers who often bottled wines under GENERIC names such as Burgundy, Chablis, Sherry, and Champagne, from a severely limited range of grape varieties.

In the east, especially, the decline was marked; in Ohio, for example, the 149 wineries of 1940 had dwindled to 47 by 1960. One valuable new development was the introduction, by Philip WAGNER, of hybrid grape varieties developed in France (see FRENCH HYBRIDS) such as SEYVAL, SEIBEL, and BACO into the eastern vineyards; these gave larger yields and made more attractive and interesting wines than did the old American hybrids. Another innovation was the effective introduction of VARIETAL labelling by the American merchant Frank SCHOONMAKER, a practice that was to become standard.

Beginning around 1970, wine production in the US took on a new energy and glamour. New wineries, large and small, were started in California: there were 240 wineries in 1970, 770 in 1989, almost 1,700 in 2004, and 4,807 by 2022, comprising 43% of the total number of wineries in the country. New vineyards were planted, and winegrowers made unprecedented efforts to find the best matches between grape variety and location, aspiring to new levels of quality and complexity. Innovation in technology was eagerly sought, at the same time as traditional European methods were introduced and adapted. Large-scale foreign investment from Japanese, British, French, Spanish, Swiss, and German companies was attracted to the American wine industry, notably a number of French CHAMPAGNE firms who invested, some of them briefly, in California sparkling wine production in the 1980s.

The explosion of new activity in the industry was matched by consumer developments: wine classes, wine societies, wine publications, and, eventually, internet sales and websites proliferated to exploit the interest and anxieties of a public long ignorant and indifferent but now eager to learn. Consumption of wine—now dominated by TABLE WINE—rose from 10 million hl/267 million gal in 1970 to 33 million hl in 2021.

Outside California the boom in wine was, proportionately, even greater. The old regions—New York and Ohio especially—began to sprout new enterprises after a long quiescence. The vineyards were transformed by the introduction not only of hybrids developed in France, such as Seyval and Seibel, but of *vinifera* varieties—now, thanks to modern understanding of plant pathology and the availability of PESTICIDES and FUNGICIDES, at last able to be grown successfully in the eastern US after more than three centuries of failure. States such as Maryland, New Jersey, Pennsylvania, and Virginia which had once supported viticulture on only a modest scale now saw the growth of a renewed and expanded industry. Centres of wine research and education such as Cornell University in NY, BROCK UNIVERSITY just across the NY border in ONTARIO, and VIRGINIA TECH helped develop better understanding of COOL-CLIMATE VITICULTURE. By the late 2010s, the east coast, from the Great Lakes to the Atlantic coast, had the fastest winery growth in the US and accounted for 25% of the total number of wineries by 2021. New York, Pennsylvania, and Virginia claimed more than one-third of that number, but even cold Maine boasted 38 wineries and Rhode Island, the smallest state in the Union, another 18.

TEXAS and NEW MEXICO, sites of very old but very small-scale *vinifera* winemaking, now boasted large viticultural developments. ARIZONA developed a robust wine industry with a specialty in sparkling wine. The wine industry in WASHINGTON grew to become the third largest by volume in the US (just after California and New York), and OREGON was right behind. Michigan embraced Riesling and other aromatic varieties suited to its cold winters, and Minnesota, Wisconsin, and the Midwest cultivated an industry with cold-climate HYBRIDS such as La Crescent, Frontenac, and Marquette developed by the University of Minnesota. Mid-South states such as Arkansas and Missouri look to the University of Arkansas for new hybrids that can withstand the region's cold winters and humid summers; the University of Florida has created varieties such as Blanc du Bois that are resistant to PIERCE'S DISEASE, a serious issue in the deep south.

Many obstacles to the production and sale of wine still exist, however, some of them natural, such as climate, and some of them political, such as the complex web of taxes and restrictions imposed by the different states. The spirit of Prohibition is still vigorous in some states, whether it takes the old form of moral disapproval or the protectionism of alcohol beverage MONOPOLIES. Since 1989 the federal government has required warning labels on all bottles of wine sold in the US (see LABELLING INFORMATION). And in the late 1990s, further, sometimes severe restrictions were placed on the shipment of wine between states, making it even more difficult for consumers to buy wine direct from wineries (see Regulations, below).

But, on any view, the US wine industry in the latter half of the 20th century underwent a remarkable development from the ruins left after Prohibition, renewing old activities, spreading into new regions, expanding production, developing new methods in viticulture and winemaking, and reaching new levels of quality.

T.P., J.R. & L.M.

Adams, L., *The Wines of America* (4th edn, 1990).

Lapsley, J. T., *Bottled Poetry: Napa Winemaking from Prohibition to the Modern Era* (1996).

Pinney, T., *A History of Wine in America: From the Beginnings to Prohibition* (1989).

Pinney, T., *A History of Wine in America: From Prohibition to the Present* (2005).

Robinson, J., and Murphy, L., *American Wine* (2013).

Regulations

Following repeal of Prohibition in 1933, each of the 48 (now 50) states was allowed to set its own regulations governing the sale and distribution of alcoholic beverages. As a result, an arcane, confusing regulatory environment involving in effect 50 separate countries has evolved. (Within some of them there still exist 'dry' counties which prohibit the sale of any alcohol.) The prevailing THREE-TIER SYSTEM is, however, under increasing economic and legal pressures. The consistent theme throughout the rules is that no enterprise can act as supplier, wholesaler (distributor), and retailer. A chief exception to this rule is California, where wineries can circumvent this structure. In many states, boutique (farm) wineries can sell their wines directly to consumers, but most sell them to wholesalers, which then sell to retailers and restaurateurs. After a series of aggressive acquisitions, the number of wholesalers dramatically shrunk between 1985 and 2005, each enjoying what is effectively a state-sanctioned monopoly on alcohol sales and profits. An actual state MONOPOLY operates in Pennsylvania and New Hampshire.

A 2005 US Supreme Court ruling gave all states a choice: either allow inside-the-state and into-the-state shipping by wineries or prohibit both. Such shipments would enable consumers interested in DIRECT SHIPPING to bypass the three-tier system. The effects were gradual, but by 2022, 47 states had opened up to winery-direct shipping, although most states require wineries to obtain a shipping licence and impose a limit on the number of cases that can be shipped per person or per address per year. The same freedom does not apply to retailers, however: only 13 states allow shipments from out-of-state retailers. But the three-tier system has not disintegrated, because all but the smallest producers need wholesalers to display and to distribute their wares across the immense continent and to keep restaurants supplied with their bottles. Seeking to protect their privileges, wholesalers have amassed clout in state legislatures nationwide by giving sizeable contributions to officeholders' fundraising campaigns.

For details on regulations governing wine labelling, see AVA, the US version of a CONTROLLED APPELLATION system. Label approval, AVAs, and federal taxation are overseen by the TTB.

D.F. & T.C.

Viticulture and winemaking

US wine law specifies only geographical boundaries for its AVAs. It sets no limitations on what sorts of vine varieties may be used or how they are farmed. It also does not prescribe how a wine is made, save to require that any ADDITIVES be 'GRAS' or 'generally recognized as safe' as determined by the FDA (Food and Drug Administration), and it sets maximum limits on these additives.

Lacking any historical ties between grape variety and place, the US has long led the movement towards VARIETAL wines, focusing on variety instead of place. The vast majority of these wines are made from INTERNATIONAL VARIETIES, with Chardonnay and Cabernet Sauvignon leading the way and Pinot Noir, Merlot, Pinot Grigio, and Sauvignon Blanc following. However, their grip on the market is loosening. Widespread concern about CLIMATE CHANGE and water availability in warm-climate regions has instigated increased interest in Mediterranean varieties such as SYRAH, GRENACHE, and TEMPRANILLO and redirected attention to old DRY-FARMED vineyards planted to varieties such as MATARO, PETITE SIRAH, and CARIGNAN. (See HISTORIC VINEYARD SOCIETY.) Meanwhile winegrowers in MARGINAL CLIMATES are increasingly looking towards cold-hardy, DISEASE-RESISTANT hybrid varieties that will allow for less use of AGROCHEMICALS in the vineyard. There are more than 350 wine-grape varieties grown in the US today, and consumers are encouraging exploration with their increased openness to and desire for unique local wines.

That said, BRANDS are big business in the US. Just 50 companies supply 90% of US wine, most of them based in California but also including CONSTELLATION BRANDS (based in New York) and Ste Michelle Wine Estates and Precept Brands (located in Washington State). Economies of scale dictate that most wines sold in the US come from conventionally farmed, IRRIGATED vineyards that rely on some degree of MECHANIZATION for vine maintenance and harvesting. This has gained the US a reputation for the sorts of wines often referred to as NEW WORLD style: clean, robust flavours focused on fruit, often created by scrupulously clean, technical winemaking.

In the 1990s and 2000s, this often meant big, rich, high-alcohol wines, as winegrowers strove for ever more RIPENESS, more EXTRACTION, and more flavour, often using a robust battery of tools to reach those ends, including additives such OENOLOGICAL TANNINS and ACIDS, cultured YEASTS and yeast NUTRIENTS, GRAPE CONCENTRATE, OAK CHIPS, and many other tricks of the trade. As alcohols rose, so did the practice of HUMIDIFICATION or removing alcohol using REVERSE OSMOSIS or SPINNING CONES.

These and many other technological tricks are still widely deployed, but there has since been a backlash, fuelled in part by WINE WRITERS who have publicized the amount of MANIPULATION and AMELIORATION that can happen in winemaking and have championed LOW INTERVENTION WINES and in part by ever more savvy consumers with greater access to a wider variety of wine than ever before, along with a deeper interest in how wine is made and where it comes from.

Winemakers, for their part, responding not only to the market but also to rising temperatures, water shortages, WILDFIRES, and concerns for the SUSTAINABILITY of their land and community, have increasingly been looking towards ORGANIC, BIODYNAMIC, and REGENERATIVE VITICULTURE and LOW-INPUT VITICULTURE. This century has also seen a marked increase in attention to matching variety to place in pursuit of making wines with a sense of TERROIR. So while the US remains dominated by clean, fruity, reliable wines made in the cellar, there are also plenty of wines with ample personality, from PET-NATS to PIQUETTES and ORANGE WINES that employ SPONTANEOUS FERMENTATION and extended SKIN CONTACT sometimes even in AMPHORAE. The vagueness of the US AVA system can also be its advantage: it allows for endless experimentation.

See also AVA, CORNELL UNIVERSITY, DAVIS, VIRGINIA TECH, and specific entries on ALASKA, ARKANSAS, ARIZONA, CALIFORNIA, HAWAII, IDAHO, MICHIGAN, MISSOURI, NEW YORK, NORTH CAROLINA, OHIO, OREGON, TEXAS, WASHINGTON, and VIRGINIA.

Acitelli, T., *American Wine: A Coming-of-Age Story* (2015).
Adams, L., *The Wines of America* (4th edn, 1990).
Lukacs, P., *American Vintage: The Rise of American Wine* (2000).
Penn, C. (ed.), 'Review of the Industry', *Wine Business Monthly* (Feb 2022).
Robinson, J., and Murphy, L., *American Wine* (2013).
www.wineamerica.org

Upper Goulburn, hilly, cool, high-ELEVATION wine region in Australia's Central Victoria Zone, between the snowfields of Mt Buller on one extremity and Strathbogie Ranges on the other. Chardonnay is the foremost variety. See VICTORIA.

U

urban wineries, a 21st-century phenomenon that introduced city-dwellers from London to Hong Kong to WINEMAKING. Wine was long made in unglamorous warehouses on the outskirts of American cities, and much of the wine produced in the Soviet era was finished in urban processing plants close to centres of consumption. But the first of this new era of self-consciously artisanal urban wineries was probably Edmunds St John, established in the San Francisco Bay Area in 1985, vinifying grapes grown in nearby California wine country. The Bay Area still has one of the greatest concentrations of the several hundred urban wineries located in North American cities, including New York, with the advantage of having thousands of potential customers on their doorstep. Some urban wineries fulfil an educational role, and an increasing number offer hospitality in some form.

Urgestein, literally 'primordial rock', amorphous term used in AUSTRIA and sometimes in GERMANY to refer to especially ancient VOLCANIC or metamorphic rocks of crystalline structure underlying a vineyard. The term has no standing among geologists (see GEOLOGY).

D.S.

Uruguay is South America's fourth most important wine-producing country with an area under vines of just under 6,000 ha/14,826 acres, of which more than 95% is for wine production. In a good year, Uruguay produces over a million litres (264,172 gal) of wine, although it can fall to almost half that in a poorer vintage.

The history of winemaking in the country is linked to its independence, officially starting in the 19th century although there are reports of Jesuit MISSIONARIES bringing vines more than a century before. Vineyards were largely planted by immigrants, mainly Basque and Italian families. This tradition of family smallholdings continues, with the average vineyard being no more than 5 ha/12 acres. In all there are over 1,200 growers but fewer than 160 wineries, and only about one-quarter of those focus on higher quality and export. Wine was initially produced for local consumption and, with one-third of the population of the country living in the capital Montevideo, four-fifths of the vineyards are in the immediately neighbouring *departmentos*, especially in Canelones. Most other vineyards are in the west, close to the Río de la Plata (River Plate), which forms the border with Argentina, or further east in the coastal region of Maldonado near to Brazil. Domestic wine consumption is high, standing at 20 l/4 gal per person per year in 2021.

With the formation of Mercosur, announced at the end of the 1980s, the Uruguayans realized that they would have to protect their wine industry from Chilean and Argentine wine, which benefited from lower production costs. To achieve this, the Uruguayan National Institute for Vitiviniculture (INAVI) embarked on a three-pronged campaign. Firstly, encouragement was given to growers to plant VITIS VINIFERA varieties, rather than the AMERICAN VINES and HYBRIDS that then dominated. Secondly, the Uruguayans were urged to be proud of their own wines, with stress being laid on their purity and SUSTAINABILITY. (In an American report published at the 2004 World Economic Forum, Uruguay was ranked as the third most environmentally sustainable country in the world after Finland and Norway.) Finally efforts were made to conquer export markets despite limited promotional resources. BRAZIL, because of a shortage of domestic red wine, is the most important export market, accounting for two-thirds of the total, but Uruguay exports to some 51 countries today.

Wines are divided into two classes, VCP (*Vino de calidad preferente*) and VC (*Vino Común*). VCP wines must be made from *vinifera* grapes and be sold in 75 cl, or smaller, bottles. VC wine, which is sold widely in demi-johns and tetrapacks (see CARTONS), is predominantly rosé based on MUSCAT OF HAMBURG grapes, although this variety is in sharp decline thanks to increasing demand for *vinifera* wines.

For better-quality wines the dominant grape variety is TANNAT, introduced to Uruguay by Basque settlers and made with increasing enthusiasm and expertise. It accounts for over one-quarter of all plantings of wine grapes and over 1,600 ha/3,954 acres. Other important red wine grapes are Merlot, Cabernet Sauvignon, and Cabernet Franc. White wines (around one-quarter of total production) tend to be made from Sauvignon Blanc and Chardonnay, although Albariño is on the rise.

Most of the vineyards lie on deep CLAY soils on gently rolling hills to the north of Montevideo, but those in the Cerro Chapeu region on the Brazilian border and in El Carmen in the centre of the country are on sandier soils; Sierra de Mahoma has poor SCHIST soils; and vines in Colonia are planted on river GRAVELS. The most explosive growth has been in Maldonado, on the eastern coast, where over 400 ha/988 acres are grown on mainly GRANITE soils; the region has become notable for crisp white wines and focused reds.

The climate in Uruguay is influenced by the Atlantic and often compared with that of Bordeaux or Galicia, averaging over 1,000 mm/39 in of rain each year. Humidity can be excessive even though the climate seems to be getting warmer and drier, so the ESPALIER training system is popular, gradually replacing the once-widespread LYRE. Vintages are variable in Uruguay, with drier, warmer vintages such as 2018 seen as the best.

International interest in Uruguayan wine is seen not only in its growing market but also in significant new investments taking place within the country. Cerro del Toro is a new Japanese investment; Viña Edén is owned by a Brazilian investor; and Argentine billionaire Alejandro Bulgheroni's Garzón Winery remains one of the biggest 21st-century wine investments in South America. Uruguayan families are also pushing new boundaries. Familia Deicas continues to invest in ever-more-extreme vineyards; the Bouza family have moved beyond traditional Canelones to pioneer wine regions around Maldonado; and there are a clutch of new Uruguayan wineries including Bodega

Oceánica José Ignacio just inland from the popular José Ignacio beach town. A.B.

Barnes A., *The South America Wine Guide: The Definitive Guide to Wine in Argentina, Chile, Uruguay, Brazil, Bolivia & Peru* (2021).
Dominé, A., and Herrera, M., *The Unique Wines of Uruguay* (2013).
Goldstein, E., *South American Wines* (2014).
uruguay.wine

US. See UNITED STATES of America.

USSR. See SOVIET UNION.

Utiel-Requena, Spanish DOP with some 34,000 ha/84,016 acres of vines producing sturdy reds and mostly rosés, in the hills inland from VALENCIA in south-east Spain (see map under SPAIN). At about 700 m/2,300 ft in ELEVATION, Utiel-Requena is the coolest of Valencia's three DOPs and was once famous for its heavy DOBLE PASTA reds. Consequently the region is dominated by the sweet, dark BOBAL grape variety, although the TEMPRANILLO vine has become important this century. White grapes MACABEO, MERSEGUERA, and Tardana are also grown for still and sparkling wines. F.C.

Uva Abruzzese, occasional name for the red MONTEPULCIANO grape.

Uva di Troia, old name for NERO DI TROIA.

Uva Rara, red wine grape variety too widely grown in north-west Italy to justify its Italian name, whose literal translation is 'rare grape'. In the Novara hills it is often used to soften the SPANNA grapes grown here in a range of scented red wines.

Uzbekistan, independent central Asian republic with Tashkent as its capital. The most prolific grower of grapes among the former Soviet republics, it is a major supplier of TABLE GRAPES and has since the mid 2000s embarked on an effort to reinvigorate its wine industry. By 2020 the country had 112,298 ha/277,494 acres of vineyard according to OIV figures.

History

The grapes and wines of Uzbekistan have long been famous beyond its own frontiers. Between the 6th and 2nd centuries BCE, people in the Fergana Valley grew wheat, barley, and grapes using IRRIGATION, and Fergana grapes were prized in CHINA to the east.

It is thought that some central Asian VINE VARIETIES originated as the wild subspecies VITIS *silvestris* C.C. Gmel as a result of long-term selection. Some varieties were brought to Uzbekistan from IRAN between the 6th and 4th centuries BCE; others were brought by Greeks and Arabs in the 7th and 8th centuries CE.

Viticulture and winemaking flourished in Uzbekistan until the end of the 7th century, when, as a result of the Arab conquest of central Asia, wine grape varieties gave way to TABLE GRAPE and RAISIN varieties (see ISLAM).

After central Asia was annexed to RUSSIA in the second half of the 19th century, demand for table grape varieties rose, and European wine varieties from MOLDOVA, CRIMEA, and other regions were also imported into Uzbekistan. In 1917 Uzbekistan had 37,000 ha/91,000 acres of vineyards, mainly owned by individual smallholders. The first specialized Soviet state farms were established in the 1920s. Prior to the widespread GRUBBING UP of vineyards due to the anti-alcohol measures of Mikhail GORBACHEV in the mid 1980s, Uzbekistan was producing 13.6 million decaliters of wine annually.

Modern viticulture

Uzbekistan, in the very heart of central Asia, is on the same latitude as Italy. The country's relief varies considerably, with the Tian-Shan and the Pamir and Alai spines in the east, and mountains account for about 30% of the total area of the country. The climate of Uzbekistan is very CONTINENTAL. The average January temperature ranges from 3 to −3 °C/37–22 °F and that of July is 26–32 °C/79–89 °F. Late spring and early autumn FROSTS are commonplace. The active temperature summation (see CLIMATE CLASSIFICATION) is 4000–4500 °C. The annual rainfall is 100 mm/4 in in the lowlands, with 1,000 mm in the mountains.

The leading viticultural zones, accounting for about 75% of vines, are the Samarkand, Surkandaria, Namandan, Tashkent, Bukhara, and Kashkadaria regions. About 90% of vines need WINTER PROTECTION. Only the mountain vineyards at ELEVATIONS of at least 800 m/2,600 ft do not require IRRIGATION.

The country's assortment of vines, all UNGRAFTED, still has features typical of the viticulture of central Asia. Table-grape varieties predominate; wine-grape varieties include those brought in during Soviet times such as SAPERAVI, RKATSITELI, Tavkveri, Bayanshira, Khindogni, MUSCAT, and ALEATICO, as well as INDIGENOUS VARIETIES such as Soyaki and INTERNATIONAL VARIETIES such as CABERNET SAUVIGNON, MERLOT, PINOT NOIR, and RIESLING. Sparkling wines are especially popular, and there is a long history of sweet and semi-sweet reds.

The Scientific Research Institute of Horticulture, Viticulture, and Winemaking, named after academician Makhmud Mirzaev, is Uzbekistan's centre of wine ACADEME and sole vine NURSERY.

V

Vaccarèse, rare, relatively light red grape variety permitted in CHÂTEAUNEUF-DU-PAPE producing wines similar to CINSAUT. Also known as Brun Argenté and Camarèse.

Vacqueyras, after GIGONDAS, the second of the Côtes du Rhône villages (see RHÔNE) to be awarded its own appellation, in 1990. Although it is next to Gigondas, much of the TERROIR is very different. The body of the appellation consists of a large deposit of old ALLUVIUM from the Ouvèze river since overlaid with CLAY and LIMESTONE, situated to the south-west of the Dentelles de Montmirail. Called the Garrigues Plateau, it is flat, sits at around 100 m/328 ft in ELEVATION, and is open to the sun and the mistral. Further north, a small section of the appellation near the village of Vacqueyras climbs into the foothills of the Dentelles. There are also significant outcrops of SAND that skirt around the western, eastern, and southern edges of the Garrigues.

In 2020 Vacqueyras was produced from 1,452 ha/3,588 acres of vineyards, and 94% of this was red. The style is typically highly concentrated and STRUCTURED, and TANNINS are prone to rusticity in hot, dry years. Reds must be majority Grenache and include some Syrah and/or Mourvèdre; they may include small amounts of several minor varieties. Whites must be a blend of two or more of the permitted varieties (Bourboulenc, Clairette, Grenache Blanc, Marsanne, Roussanne, and Viognier). Whites made up 5% of total volume in 2020, but plantings of white varieties are on the increase. Rosé makes up just 1%. Vacqueyras is the only CRU on the east bank of the Rhône permitted to make red, white, and rosé wines. M.C.W.

vacuole, the central compartment of plant CELLS, separated from cytoplasm by a membrane. In grape berries, vacuoles within flesh cells contain the solution that forms GRAPE JUICE. B.G.C.

vacuum evaporation. See CONCENTRATION.

Valdadige, or Etschtaler in German, basic DOC of the Adige (Etsch) Valley that, unusually, extends across three regions, though is used principally by producers in TRENTINO and also by some in north-western VENETO. Vineyards in ALTO ADIGE theoretically qualify, but the Alto Adige DOC is usually used instead.

Val de Loire, one of six massive regional IGPS in France, sprawling across 14 *départements*, from the Atlantic coast inland to Puy-de-Dôme. White wines dominate, particularly from SAUVIGNON BLANC; reds and rosés are made from a range of varieties, from GAMAY and CABERNET FRANC to PINEAU D'AUNIS.

Valdeorras, easternmost DOP in GALICIA in north-west Spain (see map under SPAIN). Steeply terraced vineyards are planted predominantly with inappropriate but productive vine varieties such as Garnacha Tintorera (ALICANTE BOUSCHET) and the white PALOMINO. The indigenous white GODELLO, which had all but disappeared from Galicia in the wake of PHYLLOXERA, is being aggressively replanted. This moderately productive variety is susceptible to disease, but Valdeorras is protected from the Atlantic by mountains immediately to the west. If carefully vinified, it can produce an aromatic wine with an ALCOHOLIC STRENGTH of 12–13% and a glycerine content that gives it a particularly creamy and umami-rich aspect. In the late 1990s, some of Spain's most acclaimed BARREL-FERMENTED whites were Godello wines from Valdeorras made by the Guitián family, who pioneered this style. The MENCÍA grape, which makes fruity reds, is similarly respected by a new wave of producers in Valdeorras.

Valdepeñas, wine region in CASTILLA-LA MANCHA in south-central Spain producing soft, ripe red wines. The sea of rolling vineyards that is Valdepeñas is really an extension of LA MANCHA (see map under SPAIN), but Valdepeñas has developed a reputation for quality over and above its larger neighbour and has consequently earned a separate DOP. Physical conditions in Valdepeñas are similar to those in La Mancha. The Sierra Morena dividing CASTILE from ANDALUCÍA immediately to the south is a barrier to the moderating influence of the Mediterranean. At an ELEVATION of 700 m/2,300 ft, Valdepeñas shares the arid CONTINENTAL conditions that prevail through much of central Spain.

As in La Mancha, the white, DROUGHT-resistant AIRÉN is the dominant grape variety, but the red Cencibel, as the TEMPRANILLO of Rioja is known here, has been gaining ground in Valdepeñas' 22,000 ha/54,363 acres of vineyard. Much of the 'red' wine made in the region is a blend of red and white grapes somewhat lacking in colour and BODY. The best red wines, however, are made of Cencibel, which has the capacity to age well in OAK, and increasingly they include Cabernet Sauvignon, Merlot, Syrah, and even Petit Verdot. The best wines have the soft, smooth, vanilla character, although not the price tag nor the COMPLEXITY, of a well-aged RIOJA. V. de la S. & F.S.

Val di Cornia. See MAREMMA.

Valdiguié, sometimes called Gros Auxerrois, enjoyed its finest hour in late 19th-century France, when, as a dark-berried grape variety from the Lot, it was valued for its productivity and its resistance to POWDERY MILDEW. In the early 20th century, it was known as 'the ARAMON of the south-west' for its emphasis on quantity at the expense of quality. It has now been all but eradicated from France, where just 88 ha/217 acres remained in 2018, mainly in the Tarn *département*.

In 1980 French ampelographer Pierre GALET visited the US and identified the variety then sold rather successfully as Napa Gamay as none other than this undistinguished vine from south-west France, of which there were then 1,600 ha/4,000 acres planted in California. By 2020 the area had shrunk to 232 acres, but it occasionally turns up on the label of a fruity VARIETAL wine.

Galet, P., *Dictionnaire encyclopédique des cépages* (2nd edn, 2015).

Valdobbiadene. See CONEGLIANO-VALDOBBIADENE.

Valençay, small, cool AOC region on the south bank of the Cher tributary of the LOIRE in northern France with about 155 ha/383 acres in production by 2019. LIMESTONE, FLINT, and SILT are planted with a wide range of LOIRE grape varieties. Reds make up slightly more than half the production, relying predominantly on Gamay, with Pinot Noir, Côt, and Cabernets Franc and Sauvignon allowed in the blend. The few rosés produced use the same grape varieties with the possibility of up to 30% PINEAU D'AUNIS. The crisp, citrusy whites must be at least 70% Sauvignon Blanc (Valençay is only about 20 miles/30 km from QUINCY and REUILLY) and can incorporate MENU PINEAU, SAUVIGNON GRIS, and/or more rarely Chardonnay.

Valencia, Spain's biggest port and third-largest city, also lends its name to an autonomous region and one of three wine denominations (see DOP) in the Comunidad Valenciana region (see map under SPAIN). It includes four VINO DE PAGO (Chozas Carrascal, El Terrerazo, Los Balagueses, and Vera de Estenas) and the promising IGP Castelló, with some interesting red wines from the MONASTRELL grape.

The vineyards of the appellation are well away from the city, inland from the fertile market gardens and paddy fields bordering the Mediterranean. Production of white wine exceeds red. There are four subzones: Alto Turia in the north-west, where MERSEGUERA and MACABEO dominate on slopes at 700–1,100 m/2,297–3,609 ft in ELEVATION; Valentino in the centre (growing, among others, Merseguera, MALVASIA, PEDRO XIMÉNEZ, GARNACHA, and TEMPRANILLO); and Claraiano in the south, where white varieties dominate near the sea and red varieties including MONASTRELL and INTERNATIONAL VARIETIES Cabernet Sauvignon and Merlot take over inland. The Moscatel de Valencia subregion is nested within the Valentino subzone and is devoted entirely to MISTELAS made from Moscatel Romano (MUSCAT OF ALEXANDRIA). F.C.

Valle d'Aosta. See AOSTA.

Valle de Güimar, DOP with 635 ha/1,569 acres of vineyard in 2020 at up to 1,400 m/4,593 ft in ELEVATION occupying a valley in the dry south-eastern part of Tenerife in the Spanish CANARY ISLANDS. A few tiny wineries, improved technically with EU subsidies, make distinguished wines from the white LISTÁN Blanco grape.

Valle de la Orotava, DOP with just 216 ha/534 acres of vines registered in 2021 on the lush northern flanks of Mt Teide on Tenerife in the Spanish CANARY ISLANDS. LISTÁN Blanco and LISTÁN NEGRO dominate plantings on these high VOLCANIC slopes, much of it UNGRAFTED and trained in *cordon trenzado* ('braided cordon'), a unique, traditional TRELLIS SYSTEM. V. de la S.

Vallée du Paradis, IGP for still red, rosé, and white wines, and VIN GRIS in the AUDE *département* and in the commune of Rivesaltes in the Pyrénées-Orientales *département* of southern France. The designation is often used for wines falling outside the regulations for CORBIÈRES or FITOU and for varietally labelled wines from Mediterranean and INTERNATIONAL VARIETIES. The name references a legend about an epidemic that decimated the region's cattle save for those in this valley.

Valle Isarco, or Eisacktaler in German, source of pure, dry white wines from the upper reaches of ALTO ADIGE.

Valles de Benavente, VINO DE CALIDAD in Castilla y León in Spain, just south of LEÓN and producing wines of similar style. PRIETO PICUDO is the main grape variety. F.C.

Valpaços, DOC subregion of TRÁS-OS-MONTES in north-east Portugal.

Valpolicella, lively red wine from the VENETO region in north-east Italy. Vines are grown in three distinct zones formed by a series of adjacent valleys descending from the pre-alpine Lissini Mountains north of Verona down to the plains in the south. The Fumane, Marano, and Negrar valleys, with vineyards on hillsides rising to 400 m/1,312 ft, form the historic nucleus and have their own DOC, Valpolicella Classico, with 3,500 ha/8,648 acres of vines. Between the Classico zone and the plains to the east lie the 433 ha of Valpantena vineyards on both hillsides and plains. The total area of vineyard given over to regular DOC Valpolicella in the valleys of Illasi, Tramigna, and Mezzane is 4,500 ha. Valpolicella, like a number of other historic areas of Italy, saw its production zone greatly enlarged when it achieved DOC status in 1968. It was extended eastward as far as the boundary of the SOAVE white-wine zone, as well as south on to the fertile plains on the northern edge of the Po Valley. Although the total Valpolicella zone is large and varied, in general soils are more CALCAREOUS and temperatures lower in the north and on the HILLSIDES, in the Classico area, while soils on the plains are distinctly heavier and deeper and temperatures higher. Most quality-conscious producers' vineyards are to be found on hillsides only.

The name Valpolicella is derived from a mixture of Latin and Greek, meaning 'the valley of many cellars'. CORVINA has historically been regarded as the best grape of Valpolicella, being used to produce a wide range of styles, all from the same hills. The youthful wines resemble a good BEAUJOLAIS in that they can be enjoyed chilled and have, at their best, a delicious sour-cherry character. The fuller wines come from better sites on the hills, as do the RECIOTO and AMARONE wines made from dried grapes.

By the late 1960s, when the DOC regulations were drawn up, any pretence of quality wine production seemed to have been abandoned. Lesser grape varieties MOLINARA and RONDINELLA were allowed as part of the blend, and excessive YIELDS were permitted. As a result, quality fell almost as quickly as the prices paid to growers for their grapes. By the late 1980s, many of the vineyards on the hills in the Classico zone were abandoned as viticulture there became less and less profitable. Only those growers on the plains, where yields were several times higher than those from the hills, were able to make money. Consequently, the grapes from these prolific vineyards made most Valpolicella, and these were the wines that shaped—one might say tarnished—the image of the wine.

Hillside viticulture was salvaged by Amarone, a wine once considered a 'faulty' Recioto that had fermented to complete dryness and only commercially produced since the 1960s. As described in the AMARONE entry, there has been an explosion in total production this century. As the price paid for Amarone grapes is about three times that paid for regular Valpolicella grapes, the denomination's total surface area increased by 30% in the decade preceeding 2020 to almost 8,500 ha/21,000 acres. To prevent overproduction of Amarone, the total amount of grapes coming from a single estate that may be dried has been reduced from 70% to 50%, and further plantings have been blocked until at least 2023.

The commercial success of Amarone reduced average annual production of regular Valpolicella from 41 to 18 million bottles between 2005 and 2020. Meanwhile the production of Valpolicella RIPASSO, a normal Valpolicella run over Amarone skins, adding alcohol and EXTRACT to the wine, has soared from 7 million bottles in 2007 to more than 30 million bottles in 2020. Ripasso's rapid growth is a direct result of Amarone's popularity: the volume of Ripasso obtained by this method may be double the volume of the Amarone that has been racked off before (see RACKING), while 10–15% of Amarone must be added to improve its quality as well as diminish the total volume of Amarone. With falling prices for Amarone and the Ripasso marketed as a cheaper alternative, this policy may prove toxic in the long run.

Faced with the continuous threat of overproduction, not least due to the enormous size of CO-OPERATIVES here, and the embarrassment that the wine the denomination is named after has been reduced to mere supermarket fodder over the last decades, the CONSORZIO has launched a campaign to encourage producers to increase the production of Valpolicella Superiore without resorting to Ripasso or dried grapes, in the hope that more wines with a clear expression of origin will emerge. W.S.

Masnaghetti, A., *Valpolicella, Amarone: The Vineyards* (2013) (map).
www.consorziovalpolicella.it

Valtellina, Italy's northernmost wine zone, is a narrow valley formed by the river Adda as it flows west into Lake Como in the alpine far north of LOMBARDY where the NEBBIOLO grape (here called Chiavennasca) is cultivated. Despite its 46° N latitude, the valley—protected to the north by the Alpi Retiche and to the south by the Alpi Orbie—has a relatively privileged MESOCLIMATE (not unlike the warmer wine regions across the border in SWITZERLAND) with a high percentage of sunny days and moderate rains evenly spread throughout the year. The steep, terraced vineyards optimize solar radiation for grape RIPENING as daytime heat is stored by the stone walls of the TERRACES and the very rocky soils of the vineyards and released during the cooler hours of the evening and night. All of this helps compensate for lower median temperatures than in Nebbiolo's classic areas in PIEMONTE to the south-west and contributes to the sleek, perfumed, long-lived wines produced in the area.

Although Nebbiolo is well adapted to Valtellina, it arrived relatively recently: the detailed works of Francesco Saverio Quadrio in the 17th century make no mention of the grape. Its cultivation in Valtellina appears to date from the early 19th century, when more than 6,000 ha/15,000 acres of vineyards were registered here, more than one-third planted with Nebbiolo. In 2020 the region had just 890 ha/2,200 acres of vineyards planted on a thin 45-km/28-mile strip of terraces on the right bank of the Adda, with 814 ha planted to Nebbiolo. This isolated zone has been classified as DOC Valtellina Rosso, whose maximum yield of 10 tonnes/ha is unlikely to be achieved in practice. A step up is Valtellina Superiore DOCG (215 ha), from separate demarcated areas where yields are restricted to 8 tonnes/ha and the wine must be aged for at least 24 months (36 for Riserva). At the pinnacle of quality are five subzones within the Superiore area, each with a distinct style of Nebbiolo: delicate Maroggio (25 ha); elegant and mineral Sassella (114 ha); harmoniously precocious Grumello (78 ha); earthy and powerful Inferno (55 ha); and fresh and FRUIT-DRIVEN Valgella (137 ha). All these DOCs must contain at least 90% Nebbiolo. The handful of INTERNATIONAL VARIETIES planted here, among them Pinot Noir and Sauvignon Blanc, may be sold as IGT Alpi Retiche. The zone's only other DOCG is reserved for the SFORZATO di Valtellina (or Sfurzat in local dialect), a full-bodied, dry red made from Nebbiolo grapes that have been dried for three months and which must be aged for at least 20 months, including 12 months in BARREL.

Until recently the vineyard area had declined significantly because of the increasing cost of working the narrow TERRACES which are impossible to mechanize. The region's vineyards are extremely fragmented with many small smallholders; their produce was traditionally bought and bottled by NÉGOCIANTS, who, together with the four local CO-OPERATIVES, were long the dominant economic force in the zone. However, today négociants play a more active role in grape-growing, and more producers are bottling their own wines, often from single vineyards. Ar.Pe.Pe, founded in 1984, has achieved virtual cult status, while other notable producers include Rainoldi, Fay, the négociant Nino Negri, and Mamete Prevostini, and it is becoming difficult to find a mediocre bottle of wine from Valtellina. W.S.

Masnaghetti, A., *I Cru di Enogea: Valtellina* (2012) (map).
Benetti, D., *I Luoghi del Vino di Valtellina* (2018).
www.vinidivaltellina.it

Valtiendas, VINO DE CALIDAD in CASTILLA Y LEÓN in Spain producing TEMPRANILLO-based red wines similar in style to those of neighbouring RIBERA DEL DUERO but lighter thanks to ELEVATIONS of 900 m/2,953 ft and CALCAREOUS soils. Established in 2007, the region had seven wineries and 170 ha/420 acres of vines in 2021. F.C.

vandalism has long affected wine production, but as wine prices have risen so has the cost of wine vandalism, which can now be publicized easily. Disgruntled ex-employees, commercial rivals, and pranksters are the usual culprits. Perhaps the most famous instance was the loss of six vintages of BRUNELLO DI MONTALCINO in the cellars of its most famous producer, Gianfranco Soldera of Case Basse in 2012. A former employee went to jail for opening the taps on every cask. The year before the cellars of lauded PRIORAT producer Terroir Al Limit were broken into and tank taps opened, with bleach added to contaminate various casks. Foreign ownership may have been a factor here, as at Domaine Jones in FITOU, where wine was destroyed in early 2013. Moana Park in Hawke's Bay, NEW ZEALAND, was the next victim.

Vineyards are generally more public but much more accessible. In 2010 someone threatened to poison the venerable vines of DOMAINE DE LA ROMANÉE-CONTI unless a substantial ransom was paid. In the same year, protesters against GENETIC MODIFICATION vandalized a trial planting of GM vines in Alsace.

Van Duzer Corridor, wine region and AVA within the WILLAMETTE VALLEY of Oregon defined by regular and strong ocean breezes funnelled through a break in the Coast Range.

vanillin, a phenolic ALDEHYDE that is a component of the lignin structure of OAK wood and is responsible for the vanilla note in wines. It is especially extracted from barrel wood. If new oak casks are used for wine maturation, this vanillin adds complexity to the flavour (see OAK FLAVOUR). Vanillin levels tend to be higher in American than in French oak.

Var, *département* and large IGP in PROVENCE reaching from the Mediterranean Sea north to the Alpes de Haute-Provence. While the IGP allows for still and sparkling wines of all colours, since the 2000s it has specialized in rosé wines, encouraged by the Centre du Rosé, a research institute founded in 1999 in Vidauban. Nearly three-quarters of IGP wines are rosé, made mainly from GRENACHE, CINSAUT, CARIGNAN, SYRAH, and MOURVÈDRE. White wines are mainly Rolle (VERMENTINO), Viognier, and Chardonnay. Three subregions may appear on labels: Argens, Coteaux du Verdon, and Ste-Baume.

varietal, adjective used to describe a wine named after the dominant grape variety from which it is made. The word is also used casually as a noun as shorthand for 'varietal wine', but it is increasingly misused as a noun in place of VINE VARIETY. A varietal wine is distinct from a wine named after its own geographical provenance (as the great majority of European wines are) and a GENERIC wine, one named after a supposed style, often haphazardly borrowed from European geography, such as 'Chablis' and 'Burgundy'. Varietal wines are most closely associated with the NEW WORLD, where they constitute the great majority of wines produced. The concept was nurtured by Maynard AMERINE at the University of California at DAVIS in the wake of PROHIBITION as a means of encouraging growers to plant worthy vine varieties. It was advocated with particular enthusiasm by Frank SCHOONMAKER in the 1950s and 1960s and was embraced during the CALIFORNIA wine boom of the 1970s to distinguish the more ambitious wines, often made from Cabernet Sauvignon and, increasingly, Chardonnay, from the lack-lustre generics of old. Varietal labelling was also adopted, for a similar purpose, in AUSTRALIA, SOUTH AFRICA, NEW ZEALAND, and elsewhere.

Originally, when the United States' acreage of classic vine varieties was relatively limited, a varietal needed only 51% of that variety in the blend to be so labelled. In 1973 this requirement was increased to 75% (although some particularly strongly flavoured NEW YORK State vine varieties were exempted from this increased requirement; see FOXY). See also LABELLING INFORMATION.

The French INAO authorities are not proponents of varietal labelling, understanding that they have nothing to gain and much to lose by entering into this commonwealth of nomenclature. Within France, varietal wines (typically IGP) are called *vins de cépage* and are often regarded as of lower rank than AOC wines.

Italian authorities, in their attempts to reformulate the DOC system and wine-quality categories in the 1990s, were equally keen to emphasize uniqueness and place over grape variety whenever possible. Such attitudes are understandable and, in the long term, may pay dividends, but there is little doubt that an important factor in the success of many New World wines has been the ease with which consumers can grasp the concept of varietal labelling. In the 1980s, Chardonnay and Cabernet Sauvignon became the most recognizable names in the world of wine.

Varietal blends made from two or even three different varieties—and with those varieties clearly stated on the label—have become increasingly common. Popular varietal blends include Sauvignon/Sémillon among white wines and Cabernet/Merlot, Cabernet/Shiraz, and Grenache/Shiraz/Mourvèdre (GSM) among reds. It is usual to list the varieties on the label in declining order of importance in the blend.

Thanks to changes in EU rules, WINES WITHOUT GEOGRAPHICAL INDICATION may now also state the variety and vintage on the label, although this is sometimes constrained at a national level. In theory this should help consumers and enable such wines to compete with varietal wines from New World.

variety of vine or grape. See VINE VARIETIES.

Varois-en-Provence, Coteaux, enclave within the Côtes de PROVENCE appellation which takes its name from the Var *département*. More than 90% of the wines from its 2,900 ha/7,166 acres of vines are rosé. The wooded hills around Brignoles are based on LIMESTONE and are so buffered from warming MARITIME influence by the hills of Ste-Baume that vines will not ripen their fruit at all reliably at ELEVATIONS of more than about 350 m/1,100 ft.

Reds and rosés may incorporate a wide array of grape varieties: Grenache and Cinsaut primarily but also Syrah and Mourvèdre (which will ripen only in the warmest sites), while Cabernet Sauvignon, Carignan, and the Provençal speciality TIBOUREN are allowed a minor role. For white wines, Grenache Blanc is added to those varieties permitted for Côtes de Provence Blanc (see PROVENCE), although Vermentino is increasingly appreciated.

Varro, Marcus Terentius (116–27 BCE), was a prolific Roman writer who wrote on subjects as diverse as grammar, geography, history, law, science, philosophy, and education; the rhetorician Quintilian called him 'the most learned man among the Romans' (*Institutio oratoria* 10. 1. 95). Yet the only one of his works to survive in its entirety is his manual of agriculture, *De re rustica*. Varro started it in his 80th year and addressed it to his wife, who had bought a farm. Varro was a man of letters; unlike CATO's treatise, from which he borrows occasionally, his own is a literary exercise, written in a highly wrought style. *De re rustica* is full of antiquarian learning as well as practical advice, and Varro often looks back to the time when the inhabitants of Italy were all hard-working honest farmers, with none of the decadence that prevails among the city dwellers of his day. The treatise is divided into three books, each of which is a dialogue; most of the material on wine comes in the first book. He defines old wine as at least a year old; some wine goes off before that, but some, like FALERNIAN, becomes the more valuable the longer it is kept. Varro's work was used by later writers such as VIRGIL, PLINY, COLUMELLA, and PALLADIUS. Varro's own chief authority, by his own admission, is Mago of CARTHAGE, about whom nothing is known and of whose work nothing survives. Among the many Greek authors he mentions as his sources are Aristotle, Xenophon, and Theophrastus. H.M.W.

Martin, R., *Recherches sur les agronomes latins* (1971).
Skydsgaard, J. E., *Varro the Scholar* (1968).
White, K. D., *Roman Farming* (1970).

vat, large CONTAINER for STORING wine and/or ÉLEVAGE. A vat may also be used as a FERMENTATION VESSEL. In English-speaking countries, they may also be known as tanks; in France they are called CUVES.

For many centuries WOOD was the most common material, but in the mid to late 20th century inert materials such as CONCRETE, enamel, epoxy resin, and STAINLESS STEEL replaced wood except in particularly traditional or traditionalist areas. At the start of the 21st century, wooden fermentation vats once again became more fashionable though they are very expensive.

For details of wine maturation in wooden vats, see CASK AGEING.

vat size varies enormously. FERMENTATION VESSELS in large commercial wineries contain, typically, between 50 and 300 hl (1,320–8,000 gal), although smaller enterprises may use much smaller wooden or CONCRETE vats. The ratio of height to width has implications for red winemaking in determining the area of the CAP. Blending tanks in large commercial wineries usually hold around 3,500 hl (92,000 gal) and may contain up to 10,000 hl. Grupo Peñaflor, Argentina's largest wine company, boasts the largest wine vat in the world, made from concrete and with a capacity of about 53,000 hl—large enough to hold a dinner party for several hundred inside—and still used for wine storage.

Vaucluse, *département* in inland PROVENCE between the Drôme and Bouches-du-Rhône. The IGP covers a vast area, including ALLUVIAL plains as well as slopes in the Luberon mountains, and allows more than 200 grape varieties, although most wines are made from traditional southern French varieties such as SYRAH and GRENACHE or from INTERNATIONAL VARIETIES. 'Aigues' may be appended to wines made in any of 59 villages in the Luberon. 'Principauté d'Orange' may be used for wines from around Orange, an area that includes AOCS such as CHÂTEAUNEUF-DU-PAPE and RASTEAU.

VDN, abbreviation for VIN DOUX NATUREL.

VDP, or the **Verband Deutscher Prädikatsweingüter**, officially registered as the Verband Deutscher Prädikatsweingüter but marketing itself under the title VDP.Die Prädikatsweingüter, German growers' association, in 2001 incorporating 200 wine estates in GERMANY whose influence and prestige far exceeds the less than 4% share of German vineyard surface controlled by its members. In 1910, just two years after consolidating the top MOSEL estates into the GROSSER RING, the mayor of Trier persuaded like-minded organizations in the RHEINGAU and PFALZ to band together to form a national association for the purpose of selling its members' wines at AUCTION. Over the years, other regional groups joined what was until 1972 known as the Verband Deutscher Naturweinversteigerer to signify its auctioning (*Versteigerung*) of wine from unchaptalized (see CHAPTALIZATION), undiluted MUSTS (NATURWEIN). By the late 1990s its membership included estates in all of Germany's 13 winegrowing regions.

In their effort at promoting and preserving German wine culture, the national and regional branches of the VDP still maintain their tradition of wine auctions, although today bottles rather than casks of wine are on offer, and prices, prestige notwithstanding, have little bearing on market prices. The VDP's contribution to the image of fine and rare German wines is based on its members' disciplined dedication to standards going far beyond those mandated by law as regards maximum YIELDS, minimum MUST WEIGHTS, environmental SUSTAINABILITY, and commitment to varieties traditionally associated with each region. Both the release of individual wines and membership in the VDP are subject to regular internal inspection. Members' labels and capsules carry the VDP name and logo, an eagle and grape cluster. The VDP's efforts at vineyard classification and QUALITY CONTROL as well as its LABELLING practices have been influential beyond its membership, most notably on a 2001 German wine law.

See also GROSSES GEWÄCHS and GERMANY, labelling. D.S.

VDQS, or **Vin Délimité de Qualité Supérieure**, was France's minuscule interim wine quality designation between VIN DE PAYS and AOC, which accounted for less than 1% of the nation's wine production. The VDQS category was scrapped after the 2010 vintage, and most have been promoted to AOC.

Vega Sicilia, concentrated and notably long-lived red wine that is Spain's undisputed equivalent of a FIRST GROWTH, made on a single property now incorporated into the RIBERA DEL DUERO denomination. This 1,000-ha/2,500-acre farm either side of the main road east of Valladolid has been making wine in its present form since 1864, when Eloy Lecanda planted vines from Bordeaux alongside Tinto Fino, also known as Tinta del País (a local strain of TEMPRANILLO). Until 1927 it was the only wine estate in what is now Ribera del Duero. The current style was defined around 1910, when the winery was leased by Cosme Palacio, a Rioja grower. A succession of different owners has since managed to maintain the quality and reputation of Vega Sicilia as Spain's finest red wine. However, Vega Sicilia fell on lean times at several junctures and was able to make a substantial leap in quality and, more importantly, in consistency after being bought by the Álvarez family in 1982.

The more than 200 ha/500 acres of vineyard on varied soils but mainly marl with some gypsum overlooking the river Duero are planted mainly with Tinto Fino, supplemented by varying, small proportions of Cabernet Sauvignon.

Bodegas Vega Sicilia produces three wines, all red and aged in American and French oak coopered on the estate. Valbuena is released at five years old while the most famous wine, Unico, made only in the best VINTAGES, is generally released after spending about ten years in a combination of wooden tanks; small, new BARRIQUES; large, old barrels; and bottles. The rare Reserva Especial is a blend of three vintages of Unico and can last for decades.

In 1991 Bodegas Vega Sicilia acquired the nearby Liceo winery and created the immediately acclaimed Bodegas Alión, which makes much more modern reds from 150 ha of 100% Tempranillo grapes, aged in 90% French oak.

Vega Sicilia established Oremus in TOKAJ in 1993; and in 2001 Pintia, Vega Sicilia's bodega in the TORO region, produced its first vintage. Then, in a JOINT VENTURE with Benjamin de ROTHSCHILD, Vega Sicilia created the Macán estate in Rioja, first vintage 2009. A new winery in Rías Baixas, Deiva, was scheduled to produce its first vintage in 2023. The entire portfolio has been branded Tempos.

As Vega Sicilia celebrated its 150th anniversary in 2014, tensions between different members of the Álvarez family were widely publicized. V. de la S. & J.R.

Peñín, J., *Vega Sicilia: Journey to the Heart of a Legend* (2002).

vegetarian and vegan wines are increasingly popular. The main area of concern is the use of animal-based products for FINING and STABILIZING wine (although some producers are now using plant-based fining agents). Of the most common agents, only BENTONITE is suitable for vegans as well as vegetarians; CASEIN and albumin (see EGG WHITES) are acceptable to most vegetarians; ISINGLASS and GELATIN would be unacceptable to most vegetarians and vegans. Although such materials are PROCESSING AIDS rather than ADDITIVES, it is impossible to guarantee that there is absolutely no residue in the wine, and some wine drinkers may object to the use of an animal-derived product at any stage—even the use of HORSES in vineyards. An increasing number of wine producers and retailers make this information available on the bottle or at the point of sale. See also LABELLING INFORMATION and INGREDIENT LABELLING.

vegetative propagation, reproduction of a plant by asexual means. In viticulture, CUTTINGS on which both roots and shoots will grow are used. In those limited locations where PHYLLOXERA and other root pests are not present and ROOTSTOCKS are not used, LAYERING can be used to replace missing vines. Micropropagation (see TISSUE CULTURE) is a modern application in which small amounts of a MOTHER VINE may be propagated in large numbers rapidly. Unlike SEXUAL PROPAGATION, the progeny of vegetative propagation is genetically identical, unless MUTATION intervenes. B.G.C.

vein banding, vine disease. See FANLEAF DEGENERATION.

Veltliner, **Valtlin Zelene**, **Veltlinske Zelené**, **Veltini**, common Eastern European names for the four distinct Austrian grape varieties mistakenly thought to originate from VALTELLINA in Lombardy (northern Italy): GRÜNER VELTLINER, ROTER VELTLINER, FRÜHROTER VELTLINER, and occasionally Brauner Veltliner. J.V.

vendange, French word for HARVEST. A *vendangeur* is a grape-picker, and a temporary lodging for grape-pickers may be called a *vendangeoir*.

Vendanges Tardives means literally 'late harvests' and in France is restricted to ALSACE, JURANÇON, and GAILLAC. Strict regulations cover its production. Although all Alsace Vendanges Tardives wines are made from ripe grapes and without the aid of CHAPTALIZATION, the wines themselves vary considerably in how sweet they are, with some of them tasting rich but almost bone dry. Beginning with the 2021 vintage, all Alsace wine labels must indicate the wine's sweetness level using a standardized scale—a helpful guide when it comes to FOOD-AND-WINE MATCHING. SÉLECTION DE GRAINS NOBLES is Alsace's even riper category. See also AUSLESE and BEERENAUSLESE, their counterparts in Germany, and LUXEMBOURG.

vendange verte. See CROP THINNING.

vendemmia, Italian for VINTAGE YEAR or HARVEST. **Vendimia** is Spanish for 'harvest'.

Vendômois, Coteaux du, AOC of 120 ha/297 acres in 2019 producing a wide range of light wines between the Coteaux du LOIR and the city of Vendôme in the northern LOIRE Valley. The wines are necessarily crisp in this cool, often damp climate (annual rainfall averages 680 mm/27 in), but a pale pink VIN GRIS from the PINEAU D'AUNIS grape can be an attractive local speciality. Pineau d'Aunis must also constitute at least half of any blend for the reds, the make-up being Cabernet Franc, Pinot Noir, and/or Gamay. The few white wines that are made rely on Chenin Blanc, often aided by up to 20% Chardonnay.

See also LOIRE, including map.

Veneto, Italy's most productive wine region, encompassing 80,000 ha/197,684 acres of vines in the north-east (see map under ITALY). It stretches westward to Lake Garda and northward to the Alps and the Austrian border from the Terraferma behind the lagoons and city of VENICE, an important power in the wine trade of the Middle Ages whose legacy has shaped some wines in the Veneto and along the Adriatic. In the mid 1990s the volume of wine produced in the Veneto overtook that of PUGLIA and SICILY; and in 2020 it was more than 11 million hl/241 million gal. Initially much of this growth was due to the runaway success of PINOT GRIGIO, now overtaken by that of PROSECCO.

In theory, a significant proportion of Veneto wine is of good quality, with 29 DOCs and 14 DOCGs representing well over half the total. The reality is somewhat different. This proportion has been artificially inflated both by drastic enlargements of the DOC zones (to plains which were cereal-growing areas prior to the Second World War) and/or by sanctioning extremely generous YIELDS. The resulting wines, although nominally of DOC level, are too frequently characterless or leaning too heavily on Bordeaux varieties. Good bottles of BARDOLINO, VALPOLICELLA, SOAVE, and CONEGLIANO-VALDOBBIADENE Prosecco are not difficult to find, however; and the CORVINA vine variety, which forms the basis of Valpolicella and Bardolino, and GARGANEGA, the basis of Soave, are capable of making seriously interesting wines if grown in the right place (i.e. the hills on the LATITUDE 45.30° N which run eastward from Lake Garda to the north of the fertile Adige river plain). Other HILLSIDE zones of real potential include the Colli Berici to the south, especially for Tai Rosso (GRENACHE) and CARMENÈRE; Breganze to the north of Vicenza, especially for both Cabernets; the Colli Euganei south-west of Padua for BORDEAUX BLENDS and Serprino, akin to Prosecco FRIZZANTE; and the hillside part of the Piave DOC zone for the high-acid RABOSO, which used to freshen up many an AMARONE. Native varieties such as Friulano, Garganega, and Verduzzo are cultivated in these zones, as are imports such as Merlot and Cabernet, mainly Franc (brought to the area in the wake of the Napoleonic invasion in the early 19th century). The Garganega-based Bianco di Custoza and Gambellara, two country cousins of Soave, the sparkling Prosecco of Conegliano, and the Fior d'Arancio of the Colli Euganei (a fuller-bodied answer to MOSCATO D'ASTI) round out the regional picture, one characterized by large quantities of pleasant, easy-drinking wines. Producers throughout the region provide exceptions, especially those who show an interest in TERROIR rather than volume. The small Lessini DOC, producing TRADITIONAL METHOD sparkling wine from the Durella grape, and the revived Custoza DOC are two bright spots.

Veneto's centre of ACADEME is the experimental viticultural institute at CONEGLIANO.

For details of notable specific wines, see AMARONE, BARDOLINO, BREGANZE, CUSTOZA, GAMBELLARA, LISON-PRAMAGGIORE, PIAVE, PROSECCO, RECIOTO, SOAVE, and VALPOLICELLA. W.S.

Belfrage, N., *Barolo to Valpolicella: The Wines of Northern Italy* (2nd edn, 2003).
www.uvive.it

Venezuela is a minor South American wine producer, and consumer, but TROPICAL VITICULTURE has been practised here since the arrival of European immigrants at the end of the 19th century—although there is evidence that Jesuit MISSIONARIES first planted vines at Cumana in the 16th century and that vine-growers emigrated here from BADEN, Germany, in the early 19th century. Situated between latitudes 9° and 11° N, the country has an average temperature of 27 °C/81 °F, making vine DORMANCY impossible, and the rainy seasons dictate the two harvests per year. ELEVATION varies from 30 to 643 m/100–2,110 ft, with the best vineyards at the higher end of that range.

Many producers use GRAPE CONCENTRATE or import BULK WINE to make products that range from LAMBRUSCO-like blends to base wines for SANGRÍA. But by 2021 Venezuela had around 450 ha/1,112 acres planted to wine grapes, mainly Tempranillo, Syrah, Petit Verdot, Chenin Blanc, Macabeo, and Malvazíja Istarska. Seventy per cent of the plantations are in Zulia, north-western Venezuela; the rest, including Bodegas Pomar, the country's leading producer, are mainly in Lara, east of and adjacent to Zulia, in the arid, hilly Segovia Highlands. E.M.G.

Goldstein, E., *Wines of South America* (2014).

Venice, overarching DOC created in the early 2010s stretching from the hills of CONEGLIANO-VALDOBBIADENE to the Venetian lagoon in an attempt to capitalize on the name of this world-famous city which was the cultural and, once, commercial centre of north-east Italy.

In its time Venice exerted considerable and sometimes lasting influence on the wines of the world. Medieval Venice had no agriculture or viticulture and obtained its wine and grain from LOMBARDY to the west; Venice's importance was in its trade. In 840 a treaty, known as the Pactum Lotharii, between CHARLEMAGNE's grandson Lothair and the doge of Venice protected Venice's neutrality and guaranteed its security from the mainland. This treaty made Venice independent from the west and from Byzantium. Thus Venice became the most important of the Italo-Byzantine ports, and its position was strengthened when the Byzantines discovered that Venice's rivals Amalfi, NAPLES, and Gaeta had been collaborating with the Saracens. Initially Venice owed its wealth to its trade, acquiring possession of Crete, Modon, and Coron in the Aegean and being granted exemptions from the TAXATION in Constantinople that was to ruin the Byzantine economy (see GREECE, medieval history). The Crusades only strengthened Venice's position at the frontier between northern Europe and the eastern Mediterranean.

With its eastern expansion came the trade in sweet wines, so much more esteemed by northern Europeans than their own thinner ferments. Most of these were from CRETE, known then as Candia. Many of them carried the name of the Greek port from which they were shipped, Monemvasia (hence MALVASIA di Candia and MALMSEY). Some of these wines were sold in Constantinople; others were taken to Venice for redistribution, either overland to Florence (via Ferrara) or by sea to Paris, England, and Flanders. In addition to buying and selling Aegean wines, Venice also dealt in Italian wines, from Trevi, the northern Adriatic, and the MARCHE, and in the even richer wines of Tyre (in modern LEBANON), which was owned by the Venetians for most of the 13th century.

However, in trade with Syria and Palestine, Venice came second to GENOA, and the rivalry extended to trade with northern Europe: Genoa led the way there, and Venice, which was less well placed, did not start shipping wine to northern Europe until the early 14th century. By that time Genoa had already won the battle: at the end of the 13th century, Venice had ceased to be the richest and most important port in Italy, but not before it had imported the Greek techniques of increasing sugar and alcohol content by deliberately making DRIED-GRAPE WINES. Johnson suggests a direct link between such practices, employed on the islands along the Dalmatian coast, and those subsequently (indeed currently) used by some in the VENETO hinterland of Venice to make RECIOTO versions of VALPOLICELLA and SOAVE.

Venice was also to become the centre of GLASS production and therefore played an important, if indirect, role in the history of wine.

See also ITALY. H.M.W.

Johnson, H., *The Story of Wine: From Noah to Now* (new edn, 2020).
Lopez, R. S., 'The trade of mediaeval Europe: the south', in *The Cambridge Economic History of Europe*, 7 vols., ii: *Trade and Industry in the Middle Ages* (1987).
Melis, F., 'Produzione e commercio dei vini italiani nei secoli XIII–XVIII', *Annales cisalpines d'histoire sociale*, 1/3 (1972), 107–33.
Nicol, D. M., *Byzantium and Venice* (1989).

Ventoux, one of the largest appellations in France, covers some 5,675 ha/14,023 acres of vineyards on the south-eastern fringes of the southern RHÔNE between GRIGNAN-LES-ADHÉMAR and the LUBERON. It takes its name from Mont Ventoux, a peak rising 1,912 m/6,273 ft high that dominates the region. The communes entitled to the appellation are on its western and southern flanks and some of the surrounding flat land. Much of the best TERROIR is found in the foothills of the western flank. Historically Ventoux has produced TABLE GRAPES along with other tree fruits such as cherries, and until the 1970s wine production was dominated by CO-OPERATIVES. In the 1990s, the establishment of domaines producing significantly superior wines such as Ch Pesquié and Domaine de Fondrèche generated more interest in the area. By 2020 it was one of the most dynamic appellations in the Rhône Valley, with more than 130 estates. Reds and rosés make up the bulk of production, blended from a wide variety of southern Rhône grapes. Clairette, Bourboulenc, and Grenache Blanc are the principal varieties for the little white produced. M.C.W.

veraison, word used in viticulture for that intermediate stage of grape-berry development which marks the beginning of RIPENING. It is derived from the French term *véraison*. At the beginning of veraison, the berries are hard, green, and about half their final size. During veraison, the berries change skin colour and soften, SUGARS and volume increase, and ACIDITY decreases. The colour of the grape before veraison is due to green chlorophyll, and at veraison berry skins change colour to red-black (see ANTHOCYANINS) or yellow-green (see CAROTENOIDS), depending on the variety.

The inception of veraison is rapid and dramatic, but not all berries on a vine, nor indeed in a bunch, show veraison simultaneously. This is because of variation in time of FLOWERING. About six days after colour change, the berries soften, begin to accumulate GLUCOSE and FRUCTOSE, and start to enlarge. The first to soften are those which are exposed and in warmer MICROCLIMATES (on the west-facing part of exposed bunches or near a POST, for example); the last berries to undergo veraison are those in the CANOPY shade and on short shoots. It is difficult therefore to be precise about the single date of veraison; more commonly a date is recorded when, say, 50% of the berries on a vine show veraison. At about the same time as veraison occurs, CANE RIPENING begins.

The onset of veraison (and cane ripening) is controlled by both plant and environmental factors. Exposed grapes on vines which have a high LEAF TO FRUIT RATIO and which are experiencing mild WATER STRESS (and hence no active shoot growth) undergo veraison first. By contrast, veraison is delayed in vines with large crops, in those with many actively growing shoot tips, and for shaded fruit (see SHADE). Veraison is observably early in vineyards producing high-quality fruit, with both veraison and cane ripening developing quickly. Environmental factors associated with the early onset of veraison are warm, sunny, and dry weather.

R.E.S.

Keller, M., 'Phenology and growth cycle', in *The Science of Grapevines* (3rd edn, 2020).

Verdea, ancient Tuscan light-berried vine now a speciality of the Colli Piacentini in north-central Italy.

Verdeca, Puglia's most popular light-berried vine producing neutral wine suitable for the VERMOUTH industry and declining in popularity, with 912 ha/2,254 acres remaining in 2015. DNA PROFILING has shown that it is a parent, with TRIBIDRAG (Zinfandel), of the widespread Dalmatian variety PLAVINA, indicating an ancient viticultural bridge across the Adriatic Sea. More recently, Verdeca has been shown to be identical to the much more highly regarded Greek variety LAGORTHI and to have a parent–offspring relationship with MALVASIA Bianca Lunga.

J.V.

Verdejo, characterful grape so FASHIONABLE in Spain that its total plantings increased more than fourfold between 2004 and 2020 to 25,504 ha/63,022 acres. With its distinctive blue-green BLOOM, which presumably inspired its name, the variety is RUEDA's pride and joy (and helped stave off a challenge for primacy from imported SAUVIGNON BLANC, with which it is often blended). The variety ripens relatively early but is very susceptible to POWDERY MILDEW. DNA PROFILING has shown that Verdejo and GODELLO (under its Portuguese name Gouveio) are siblings and that Verdejo is a natural SAVAGNIN × Castellana Blanca cross, the latter an old variety from Huesca in northern Aragón. Wines produced are aromatic, HERBACEOUS (somewhat reminiscent of laurel), but with great substance and EXTRACT, capable of AGEING well into an almost nutty character.

J.V.

Verdelho, name once given to several Portuguese white grape varieties and most closely associated with the island of MADEIRA, where the Verdelho vine became increasingly rare in the post-PHYLLOXERA era, but the name was long used to denote a medium-dry style of wine somewhere between SERCIAL and BUAL levels of richness. Of the original four VITIS VINIFERA varieties that were traditionally grown on Madeira, Verdelho is the most planted today, with 58 ha/143 acres in 2018. A further 452 ha of Verdelho was recorded on the Portuguese mainland in 2020, mainly in the ALENTEJO. Musts have moderate levels of sugar and notably high ACIDITY. The Verdelho found on Madeira is the same as that found growing in the AZORES, and this Verdelho, CUTTINGS of which were presumably picked up on one of these Atlantic islands en route to the Antipodes, was extremely important in 19th-century Australia. Planted on 1,061 ha/2,622 acres in 2022, it has had notable success in vibrant, tangy, full-bodied TABLE WINES in more recent times, particularly in the Hunter Valley of New South Wales, Victoria, and some of the hotter regions of Western Australia. See AUSTRALIA for more details. Verdelho has been planted to a very limited extent in SAVENNIÈRES in the Loire for just as long and makes some interesting varietal wine there. It is also grown in New Zealand, California, and Argentina.

A quite distinct variety once called Verdelho or Verdelho do Dão in Portugal is now officially known as Gouveio and has been identified as Spain's GODELLO.

Verdelho Roxo is a red-berried colour MUTATION of Verdelho (while the now virtually extinct Verdelho Tinto of the MINHO is unrelated).

Verdello, white Umbrian grape variety once prized for its ACIDITY. Just 179 ha/442 acres remained in 2015.

Verdesse, revived white grape of SAVOIE and ISÈRE in eastern France whose wine can be powerful and highly aromatic.

Verdicchio, one of central Italy's classic and potentially finest white wines, produced since at least the 14th century. It is made from the Verdicchio grape (see below) in two DOC zones of its home territory of the MARCHE: Verdicchio dei Castelli di Jesi, to the west of Ancona and a mere 30 km/20 miles from the Adriatic Sea; and the Verdicchio di Matelica zone, considerably further inland and at higher ELEVATIONS, close to the border with UMBRIA.

At 2,000 ha/4,942 acres, Castelli di Jesi is Marche's largest DOC and one which makes no distinction between vineyards on plains and those on the hills, with the exception of the much smaller historic Classico zone in the hills near the town of Cupramontana. Here several small producers make complex wines, often from single vineyards. Under their initiative a start was made in the early 2010s to identify subzones based on ASPECT, ELEVATION, and SOIL TYPES.

An overwhelming majority of the production of the Castelli di Jesi DOC is controlled by CO-OPERATIVES and NÉGOCIANT houses. The wine's fame was largely due to the efforts of Fazi-Battaglia, a large négociant firm which introduced the amphora-shaped bottle and scroll-shaped label, initially a positive factor in gaining recognition for the wine but later responsible for the image of kitsch and frivolity with which Verdicchio has been saddled. It did not help that, in its heyday in the 1970s, the wine was flash-pasteurised (see PASTEURIZATION) to make it stable for travel, negatively impacting quality.

While most Verdicchio is made in a modern style, without SKIN CONTACT and with TEMPERATURE CONTROLLED fermentations, quite a few herald a return to traditional methods, using SKIN FERMENTATION to give the wines a certain fullness and authority. The best wines are cool with mandarin fruit, lifted lemony acidity, MINERALITY, and a slight chew on the finish. The finest can age ten or more years.

Verdicchio di Matelica, a much smaller zone of 200 ha/494 acres with marginally lower yields and better exposed HILLSIDE VINEYARDS, was long supposed to produce fuller, more characterful wine, but this is no longer a given, since many quality-oriented producers in Castelli di Jesi have voluntarily decreased yields.

Two DOCGS were created in 2011: Castelli di Jesi Verdicchio Riserva and Verdicchio di Matelica Riserva, for wines aged for at least 18 months before release.

Perhaps partly because of its high natural acidity, Verdicchio can also produce fine PASSITO wines. It was also one of the first Italian SPUMANTES, with a tradition which can be traced back to the middle of the 19th century and which remains an integral part of DOC production.

Verdicchio, the grape

The Verdicchio grape has been in the Marche for centuries. but DNA PROFILING has recently established that it is identical to TREBBIANO di Soave, Trebbiano di Lugana, and Trebbiano Valtenesi. In SOAVE it can add perfume to the steely GARGANEGA, while further west, on its own in a warmer zone, it gives full-bodied LUGANA of real interest.

Most of Italy's Verdicchio, some 2,762 ha/6,825 acres, is planted in the Marche. W.S.

Robinson, J., et al., *Wine Grapes: A Complete Guide to 1,368 Vine Varieties, Including Their Origins and Flavours* (2012).

Verdiso, revived grape speciality in Conegliano in the VENETO region of north-east Italy making lively, varied whites.

Verdot. See PETIT VERDOT and GROS VERDOT.

Verduzzo, wine made from VERDUZZO FRIULANO and/or VERDUZZO TREVIGIANO, principally in FRIULI and in the PIAVE DOC in the bordering province of Treviso in the Veneto in seven DOC zones, although only Friuli Grave and Friuli Colli Orientali produce significant quantities and the latter is qualitatively far superior due to its HILLSIDE VINEYARDS. The wine exists in a dry, occasionally sparkling, and regularly sweet version, although the last, obtained either by LATE HARVESTING or by raisining the grapes (see DRIED-GRAPE WINES), can frequently be more medium dry than lusciously sweet. Sweet Verduzzo, less common than dry Verduzzo, is the more interesting wine, golden in colour, and often with delightful density and honeyed aromas, even if it lacks the COMPLEXITY of an outstanding dessert wine. The grapes' TANNINS can impart a certain astringency, which is more noticeable when it has been fermented dry.

Ramandolo, to the north of Udine, is considered the classic zone for fine sweet Verduzzo, but the Friuli Colli Orientali DOC, when first established, permitted the use of the name Ramandolo for any sweet Verduzzo in the production zone, converting, as it were, a place name into a generic name. This anomaly has been corrected with the establishment of a Ramandolo DOCG for generally sweet wines, with maximum yields of 8 tonnes/ha (as opposed to 11 tonnes/ha permitted for Colli Orientali Verduzzo) from two villages, Nimis and Tarcento. W.S.

Verduzzo Friulano, also known as **Verduzzo di Ramandolo**, white grape variety recorded as early as 1409 in north-east Italy. Total plantings of 687 ha/1,698 acres were recorded in 2015.

Verduzzo Trevigiano makes much duller wine than the distinct VERDUZZO FRIULANO. It was planted on around 531 ha/1,312 acres in 2015, mainly in the provinces of Treviso and Venezia.

verjus, or **verjuice**, the tart, apple-flavoured juice of unripe grapes, has many variations and many culinary uses, especially in dressings and sauces. It adds ACIDITY to a dish but unlike VINEGAR does not clash with wine. Traditional in many countries of the world, it is made from underripe grapes cut during CROP THINNING or from second-crop berries that are unripe at harvest. One method is to press the grapes then preserve the partially fermented but highly VOLATILE juice with salt. Alternatively, the grapes may be boiled before PRESSING to kill the YEAST and prevent fermentation but must then be used immediately or frozen. Most commercial producers gently press the grapes, cold settle, and filter the juice before packaging, in which case STERILE BOTTLING is essential to prevent the verjus from fermenting.

Vermeille, Côte, IGP for wines falling outside the regulations of BANYULS or COLLIOURE in the foothills of the Pyrenees in southern France. Red wines dominate, although still wines of all colours are allowed, as are sweet and RANCIO styles.

Vermentino, attractive, aromatic white grape variety widely grown in north-western Italy, on Sardinia, to a limited extent on Corsica (as Vermentinu), and in southern France. DNA PROFILING has shown it to be identical to the Ligurian PIGATO and the Piemonte variety FAVORITA. However, Ligurians have distinguished between their Pigato and their Vermentino, and the two may well be different CLONES of the same variety. Vermentino has long been considered identical to the ROLLE of Provence, the synonym which an EU regulation of 2019 obliges French producers to use on their labels because Vermentino forms part of several Italian DOC/DOCG names.

France has the world's greatest area planted with Vermentino/Rolle: 7,023 ha/17,354 acres in 2019, considerably boosted by recent plantings in the Languedoc, fuelled by varietal FASHION. The Var *département* grows about 2,203 ha/5,444 acres, about the same as the entire Languedoc and Roussillon, and it is both the southern Rhône's and Corsica's most planted white grape variety, dominating the island's white AOC wines. The wines vary from floral to citrus but are almost always refreshing.

There were 6,703 ha/16,563 acres of Vermentino Bianco in Italy in 2015. On Sardinia, Vermentino is the most planted white wine grape and is often picked deliberately early to retain acid levels but still manages to produce lively wines of character, although examples of a richer, fuller style are increasing, especially in the **Vermentino di Gallura** DOCG. The interest in white INDIGENOUS VARIETIES has been a boon for those growers along the Tuscan coast who had either the foresight or good fortune to plant Vermentino, which is the fastest-growing variety in the MAREMMA, reaching 914 ha/2,259 acres in 2022.

Some Vermentino is also grown on Malta, in California, in Texas, and in North Carolina, but of the non-European wine producers the land of ALTERNATIVE VARIETIES, Australia, has been quickest to embrace this popular variety with plantings in many different regions.

Vermentino Nero is a minor, unrelated Tuscan red wine grape once almost extinct.

Vermont, state in the north-east United States, bordering Canada, distinguished by the Green Mountains running its length from north to south. Attempts at vine cultivation date to the earliest colonial settlers, but not until the 1990s did a craft-scale commercial wine industry take root.

The central mountains are bounded by the Lake Champlain Valley to the west and the Connecticut River Valley to the east. A longitudinally oriented, complex LIMESTONE bedrock contributes to regional SOIL FERTILITY. Fossils from Earth's oldest coral reef, estimated at 450 million years of age, line the north-western border, and the eastern rift valley is eroded VOLCANIC material. The mixed surficial GEOLOGY shows the impact of repeated glaciation: both eastern and western valleys were massive glacial lakes in the last ice age, adding rich CLAY deposits to upper strata.

Warm, humid summers, late spring FROSTS, and short growing seasons with extreme winter temperatures make Vermont inhospitable to VITIS VINIFERA, while HYBRIDS bred to resist both disease and extreme cold thrive. Early vineyards employed FRENCH HYBRIDS including SEYVAL BLANC and LÉON MILLOT; they have been joined by hardier AMERICAN HYBRIDS such as MARQUETTE, LA CRESCENT, FRONTENAC (Noir, Gris, and Blanc), and multiple selections from private breeders.

By 2021 there were 60 ha/200 acres under vine and two dozen commercial wineries producing still and sparkling wines (both TRADITIONAL METHOD and MÉTHODE ANCESTRALE) at artisanal scales. The Lake Champlain basin hosts most vineyards, but numerous regional MESOCLIMATES can support vines. Vermont has gained notoriety for its engagement with REGENERATIVE VITICULTURE practices and LOW-INTERVENTION approaches in the wineries, as well as for its distinctive wines, with some having gained international acclaim. T.T.

vermouth, herb-flavoured FORTIFIED WINE available in many styles and qualities. The

practice of adding flavouring to wines dates as far back as Neolithic times (see FLAVOURED WINES, history), though modern vermouth owes more to the styles popular in 18th-century Europe, flavoured in particular with wormwood (*wermut* or *vermut*) or *artemesia absinthum*, which was thought to have curative powers for gastric ills. These aromatized wines enjoyed a certain success in French royal circles and subsequently became known as *vermutwein* and, in Anglicized form, vermouth. Modern large-scale vermouth production dates from 18th-century PIEMONTE, close to the Alps which could supply the necessary herbs. By the 19th century, BRANDS such as Cinzano, Martini, and the French Noilly Prat threw off any pretence of curative powers and became extremely popular during the cocktail age as mixers.

After the Second World War, vermouth had become a wan, lacklustre drink made in industrial quantities, often flavoured by the addition of a concentrate designed for consistency. There was little interest in the category until the cocktail renaissance of the 1990s. By the 2000s, a rash of small-production vermouths, often made from high-quality wine and flavoured with intensely local ingredients, gave vermouth back some of the respect it had lost. Today, so many herbs and spices are used to flavour fortified wines that the definition of vermouth is necessarily elastic. Wines can be almost dry, with the strong aroma of wormwood and other bitter alpine herbs, or sweet, red, and more vaguely herbal. French styles tend to be the most delicately alpine, such as those from Chambéry, which once boasted an AOC; Italian versions are bolder and traditionally red; Italy also has the only geographically protected vermouth designation, IGT Vermouth di Torino. Spain has its own unique tradition, including SOLERA-aged examples, but there are vermouths coming from nearly every wine-producing country. In the best cases, the new vermouths are another window into a region's TERROIR, flavoured with local ingredients and to local tastes.

Wondrich, D. (ed), *The Oxford Companion to Spirits and Cocktails* (2022).

Vernaccia, name used for several, unrelated Italian grape varieties, mainly white but sometimes red, *vernaculus* meaning 'native' or 'indigenous' in Latin. These vary from the extreme north of the country (VERNATSCH being merely a Germanic version of Vernaccia) to the fizzy red **Vernaccia di Serrapetrona** of the MARCHE made from the vine variety known locally and in Umbria as **Vernaccia Nera** (a central-Italian synonym for GRENACHE), Vernaccia di Pergola (a southern-Italian synonym for ALEATICO), and VERNACCIA DI ORISTANO, a unique variety famous on the island of SARDINIA. The most highly regarded form is the dry white Tuscan varietal VERNACCIA DI SAN GIMIGNANO. Wines called Vernaccia, or sometimes **vernage**, are often cited in the records of London wine merchants in the Middle Ages, but the term could have been used for virtually any sort of wine, Latin being the common language then. Vernaccia was a particularly common product of LIGURIA in north-west Italy and Tuscany. For more details of medieval trade in Vernaccia, see GENOA, ITALY, and TUSCANY.

Vernaccia di Oristano, distinct variety (see VERNACCIA) grown almost exclusively on 232 ha/573 acres of western SARDINIA in 2015, making a wide range of white wines with varying SWEETNESS levels and sometimes fortified and SHERRY-like.

Vernaccia di San Gimignano, potentially distinctive dry white wine made from the historic local vine variety of the same name, probably unrelated to any other Vernaccia, cultivated in the sandstone-based soils around the famous towers of San Gimignano in the province of Siena in TUSCANY in central Italy. There are references to Vernaccia in the archives of San Gimignano as early as 1276. The wine was the first ever awarded DOC status, in 1966, and was elevated to DOCG status in 1993 in recognition of its unquestioned superiority over the standard bland Tuscan white blend of Trebbiano Toscano and Malvasia.

In the late 20th century, Vernaccia di San Gimignano enjoyed some export success and producers were encouraged to make crisp, refreshing wines. Demand for them has since declined, despite attempts to create COMPLEXITY via small BARREL MATURATION. Since the beginning of this century the CONSORZIO has promoted SUSTAINABLE VITICULTURE, and some producers have adopted ORGANIC VITICULTURE. Some are also experimenting with SKIN-FERMENTED Vernaccia in AMPHORAE. The best examples have a 'minerally', salty impact on the palate and gain both complexity and notes of ripe yellow fruit and beeswax with age.

By 2010 total plantings of Vernaccia had declined to 500 ha/1,236 acres, perhaps because of sales success with red wines based on SANGIOVESE (which has always been grown around San Gimignano) and because it was usurped by an influx of INTERNATIONAL VARIETIES. However, by 2020 the tide had been stemmed, with 730 ha registered for the production of Vernaccia.

W.S.

www.vernaccia.it

Vernatsch, German name for the generally undistinguished light-red grape variety SCHIAVA.

Veronelli, Luigi (1926–2004), Italy's most influential food and wine critic from 1956, when he founded the magazine *Il Gastronomo* and began to collaborate with Italy's major daily newspapers, news weeklies, and the national television network RAI-TV, until his death. Born into an affluent cosmopolitan Milanese family, Veronelli was an unabashed Francophile and a frank admirer of the French AOC system, in particular of its designated CRUS, a CLASSIFICATION which he attempted to apply to Italian vineyards and their products in his many books on his country's wines. Polemical in character and a romantic anarchist in his political convictions, Veronelli long championed the cause of the small peasant proprietor and was a particularly bitter opponent of Italy's DOC systems, which he considered rigged in favour of the country's large commercial wineries. A trip to California in the early 1980s turned him into a promulgator of the BARRIQUE, then almost unknown in Italy, and his writing was extremely influential in spreading the use of small oak barrels in Italy. He can be credited with the discovery and identification of many of the country's better producers in the late 20th century, a role which won him a group of devoted friends and an equally large group of sworn enemies.

Belfrage, N., *Life beyond Lambrusco* (1984).

vers de la grappe, insect pest and an important cause of BOTRYTIS BUNCH ROT. This French term is generally used to refer to the European grapevine moth and the vine moth (see MOTHS).

vertical trellis, a vine-TRAINING SYSTEM widely used throughout the world in which the shoots are trained vertically upwards in summer. The system is commonly called **vertical shoot positioning**, or **VSP**. The shoots are held in place by foliage wires which, in turn, are attached to vineyard POSTS. In many vineyards there are two pairs of foliage wires, and commonly the vines are subjected to TRIMMING at the top and sides to maintain a neat, hedge-like appearance. Both SPUR PRUNING and CANE PRUNING are possible. This trellis system is widely used in Alsace, Germany, eastern Europe, the United States, South America, Australia, and New Zealand, with high vines (TRUNKS of about 1 m/3 ft) and relatively low-density plantings. The vineyards of Bordeaux, Burgundy, and Champagne are also vertically shoot-positioned, although the vines are planted closer together and the trunks are much shorter.

R.E.S.

verticillium wilt, FUNGAL DISEASE which causes apparently healthy vines to collapse suddenly. The fungus *Verticillium dahliae* lives in the soil and can attack new vineyards. Young vines are usually affected, and often the vine recovers. There is no control apart from avoiding planting on sites where the fungus exists. Fortunately it is uncommon.

R.E.S.

Vespaiola, white wine grape speciality of Vicenza in the VENETO region of north-east

Italy, said to take its name from the wasps (*vespe*) attracted by the sugar levels of its ripe grapes. Its most famous product is the Torcolato sweet wine of BREGANZE. As a dry white wine, Vespaiolo (*sic*) is typically acidic and neutral if the grapes are not fully ripe, but a number of more complex examples are now appearing. Total plantings were just 9 ha/222 acres in 2015. It may have a parent–offspring relationship with VERNACCIA DI ORISTANO.

Vespolina, low-yielding red grape variety known almost exclusively in, and probably native to, the area around GATTINARA in the PIEMONTE region of north-west Italy. Commonly blended with its close relative NEBBIOLO, it was planted on just 88 ha/217 acres in 2015, occasionally in the OLTREPÒ PAVESE zone across the border in LOMBARDY, where it is known as Ughetta.

Veuve Clicquot, Champagne house as famous for its eponymous leader, the great champagne widow (*veuve* in French), as for its wines. Nicole Barbe Ponsardin (1777–1866) married François Clicquot, the son of the house's founder, in 1798. After the premature death of her husband in 1805, the 27-year-old widow took over the reins of the company, which she renamed Veuve Clicquot Ponsardin. Despite her youth, she steered the house carefully through the turbulent years of the First and Second Empires, defying Napoleon's blockades to ship the wine to Russia and finding an export market in virtually every European court. 'La grande dame de la Champagne' is credited with inventing the RIDDLING process and adapting a piece of her own furniture into the first riddling table for that purpose. In 1818 she was first to elaborate a rosé champagne by addition of red wine from Bouzy. On her death, the company passed to her former chief partner, another shrewd operator, Édouard Werlé, who introduced the famous yellow label, still used for the NON-VINTAGE wine, and the house remained in the hands of the Werlé family until in 1987 it became part of the Moët Hennessy-Louis Vuitton group (see LVMH). The house style is based on Pinot Noir grapes and, in particular, those grown at Bouzy, where the house has large holdings. La Grande Dame is Clicquot's PRESTIGE CUVÉE, named, of course, after the widow. In 1990, the Champagne house purchased a majority stake in the WESTERN AUSTRALIAN winery Cape Mentelle and its New Zealand subsidiary CLOUDY BAY, completing the purchase in 2000.

Crestin-Billet, F., *Veuve Clicquot: La grande dame de la Champagne* (1992).

Vézelay, recently promoted (2017) Burgundy AOC near Avallon, south-west of Auxerre and CHABLIS, for white wines made from Chardonnay. The also attractive Pinot Noir vineyards remain as BOURGOGNE. J.T.C.M.

Victoria, third most important wine state in Australia in terms of volume of wine produced. From its nadir in the mid 1950s, when there were fewer than 30 wineries in operation, Victoria has recovered to the point where its viticultural map once again resembles that of the 19th century, populated by some 800 wine producers, more than any other state. A swing among local tastemakers towards subtler, lighter wines than was the Australian stereotype—with Chardonnay and Pinot Noir especially in FASHION—has thrust Victoria and its cooler regions into the spotlight in recent decades. But even these cooler spots are on notice, with CLIMATE CHANGE prompting a widespread rethink of suitable sites and VINE VARIETIES.

Hubert de Castella came to Victoria in 1854 from his native Switzerland and was a leading figure in the golden age of Victorian viticulture up to 1890 (when it produced half the wine made in Australia). He wrote several books, the most famous entitled *John Bull's Vineyard*, a eulogy suggesting Victoria could supply England with all the wine it might ever need. Instead, a combination of PHYLLOXERA, changing land use, changing consumption patterns, the removal of inter-state duties, and the First World War saw the end of the hundreds of vineyards and wineries spread across the very cool southern half of the state.

What is now the North East Victoria Zone, with **Rutherglen** as its epicentre, became the focus of winemaking, producing a range of FORTIFIED WINES and red TABLE WINES, some of the latter almost indistinguishable from some of the former. Foremost among the former are the super-sweet TOPAQUES AND MUSCATS, fortified wines of unique style and extraordinary concentration of flavour. Rutherglen and **Glenrowan** to its south also produce rich, full-bodied dry reds (from mainly SHIRAZ and DURIF), as well as a range of other, less convincing, table wines, but with their very warm summer and autumn days (and cold nights) they are best suited to fortified wines.

The North East Victoria Zone also includes King Valley, Alpine Valleys, and Beechworth. **Alpine Valleys** and **Beechworth** provide a total contrast to Rutherglen and Glenrowan. Their ELEVATION (the highest King Valley vines are above 800 m/2,625 ft) creates a significantly cooler climate eminently suited to table wines, albeit with a wide spectrum of varieties. **King Valley** is the state's largest grape-growing region outside the Murray Darling/Swan Hill area and is an incubator for VARIETAL wines of every hue: Prosecco (GLERA), ARNEIS, VERDUZZO, GRACIANO, MARZEMINO, MONDEUSE, PETIT MANSENG, SAGRANTINO, SANGIOVESE, and TANNAT.

The Port Phillip Zone has five regions clustered around Melbourne: **Yarra Valley**, **Mornington Peninsula**, **Geelong**, **Sunbury**, and **Macedon Ranges**. Well over 300 wineries here enjoy a range of climatic conditions all cooler than those of BORDEAUX, variously cooled by ELEVATION or MARITIME influences. Pinot Noir and Chardonnay are the dominant varieties, capable of producing wines of world class, with the Yarra Valley, Mornington Peninsula, Geelong, and the southern part of Gippsland leading the way.

Shiraz is sometimes seen as a newcomer in these parts, but in fact Craiglee (at Sunbury) has long made superb examples, evidenced by a cache of 1872 discovered almost 100 years later buried in the then defunct winery. Yarra Yering has been producing its No. 2 Dry Red for over 50 years, quietly using a little VIOGNIER—a move widely mimicked in recent decades, notably in Geelong and the Yarra Valley. In keeping with local drinking trends, a cooler articulation of Shiraz (often styled SYRAH to signal an elegant, medium-weight rendition) is on the rise in parts of the Port Phillip Zone. Both Cabernet Sauvignon and Merlot can be superb, too, especially with warmer vintages and appropriate VINEYARD SITE SELECTION. Pinot Gris remains extremely significant in many Victorian wine regions.

Heathcote is the darling of the Central Victoria Zone. The TEMPERATE climate and 500-million-year-old Cambrian soils—decompressed igneous greenstone which has become a vivid red-brown with age—produces some of Australia's most striking Shiraz, deeply coloured and velvety rich. Here, too, alcohol levels have become more moderate and Heathcote has seen a diversifying of its vineyard towards Mediterranean varieties including SANGIOVESE and TEMPRANILLO. **Bendigo**, which once included Heathcote, is likewise red-wine country, with Cabernet Sauvignon also excellent.

Goulburn Valley is the oldest Victorian region with a continuous history of viticulture thanks to Tahbilk, which still makes an iconic Shiraz exclusively from vines planted in 1860. Marsanne grows alongside Shiraz, Cabernet Sauvignon, and, of course, the ever-present Chardonnay. The newcomers, planted in 1990, are ROUSSANNE and VIOGNIER.

Upper Goulburn and **Strathbogie Ranges** are the cooler customers of Central Victoria on account of elevations rising to some 700 m/2,297 ft, although it is not enough to inhibit generous flavours and MOUTHFEEL in the Pinot Noir, Shiraz, and Cabernet Sauvignon of the Strathbogie Ranges. Riesling, Gewürztraminer, Pinot Gris, Chardonnay, and Viognier are the dominant white varieties.

The red-wine dominance continues into the Western Victoria Zone. The Pyrenees on the eastern side can provide Shiraz and Cabernet

Sauvignon as sumptuous as that of Heathcote or Bendigo, but as you move west into the Grampians (with Great Western registered as a subregion in 2007), the subtly cooler climate yields more elegant wines with pepper, spice, and EUCALYPT flavours alongside vibrant red fruit.

Sparsely populated **Henty** in the far southwest is dramatically cooler; indeed on some criteria it is the coolest region on the Australian mainland. That's why grapes for sparkling wines initially made a home here, latterly joined by ultra-fine and intense Riesling, Semillon, Sauvignon Blanc, Chardonnays, and microquantities of Pinot Noir.

The North West Victoria Zone takes in the **Murray Darling** and **Swan Hill** regions on the Murray river as it meanders for 500 km/305 miles marking the border between New South Wales and Victoria before moving through South Australia's Riverland. The story is no different: modified hydroponics in desert sand with historically unlimited WATER provide sky-high YIELDS of at times surprisingly good-quality grapes. But recent DROUGHTS and increasing SALINITY have encouraged both more effective water usage and an increase in Mediterranean vine varieties suitable for dry climates.

J.H. & E.N.H.M.

www.winevictoria.org.au

Vidal, white grape variety and a FRENCH HYBRID more properly known as **Vidal Blanc** or **Vidal 256** and widely grown in CANADA, where it is particularly valued for its winter hardiness. Grown to a limited extent in the Midwest and eastern UNITED STATES, particularly NEW YORK State, it is a hybrid of UGNI BLANC and one of the Seibel parents of SEYVAL BLANC. The wine produced, like Seyval's, has no obviously FOXY character and can smell attractively of currant bushes or leaves. Its slow, steady ripening and thick skins make it particularly suitable for sweet, LATE HARVEST (non-BOTRYTIZED) wines and ICE WINE, for which it, with RIESLING, is famous in Canada. Vidal-based wines do not have the longevity of fine Rieslings, however.

Vidiano, Greek light-skinned variety enjoying a revival on its homeland of CRETE, where it was grown on 195 ha/482 acres in 2021. Wines are richly fruited and fresh, sometimes blended with a more aromatic variety such as Muscat or Sauvignon Blanc. More concentrated examples are amenable to BARREL FERMENTATION.

Vidigueira, DOC subregion of the ALENTEJO in southern Portugal which marks the border between the upper and lower (hotter) parts of the region. However, Vidigueira's relative proximity to the coast and cold air descending from the Serra de Portel escarpment tempers the heat, hence the region's tradition of making white wine from ANTÃO VAZ. White wines (and old FIELD BLENDS of varieties such as Perrum, Diagalves, and Mateúdo) have received strong impetus from the revival of TALHA wines, of which Vidigueira is the heartland. They offer the spicy, textural appeal of ORANGE WINES, with mellow honeyed fruit. Modern red wines are well-structured; standout varieties include ALICANTE BOUSCHET and Tinta Grossa from Portugal's few remaining hectares. S.A.

vieilles vignes, French for OLD VINES.

Vien de Nus, red grape variety grown on 9 ha/22 acres in 2015, and mainly blended, around the town of Nus in Italy's Valle d'AOSTA.

Vienna, capital city of Austria and, unusually, a wine region in its own right. See WIEN.

Vietnam, South East Asian country with a history of viticulture dating from French colonial times. Recent attempts to revive viticultural traditions and make wine have had mixed results. The most suitable locations for conventional viticulture in this hot, humid country are in the highlands—on the slopes of Ba Vi Mountain west of Hanoi, for example, where VITIS VINIFERA vines were grown by French colonists about a century ago, or on the upper slopes of the central highlands. Contrarily, however, Vietnam's first commercial grape winemaking venture, the Thien Thai Winery, was established on the steamy southern coastal plain at Phan Rang, in Ninh Thuan province, 350 km/210 miles north-east of Ho Chi Minh City. The attraction was the existence of established vineyards producing substantial quantities of TABLE GRAPES, mostly from red-berried CARDINAL vines grown on PERGOLAS. The first wines, both still and sparkling, were released in 1995, but the winery was mothballed in 2002. Subsequently, two of Vietnam's largest food and beverage companies began drawing on grapes grown in Ninh Thuan for still and sparkling grape wines. Hanoi-based Thang Long Liquor uses primarily Cardinal, Shiraz, and Sauvignon Blanc for its grape wines; Lam Dong Foodstuffs, through its beverage subsidiary Vang Đàlạt and upmarket Chateau Dalat label, also grows Cabernet Sauvignon, Merlot, and Chardonnay. While many domestic wine labels rely on imported BULK WINE bottled locally, there are now a number of small-scale operations in Ninh Thuan committed to local grape wines. Under natural conditions, the southern vines bear almost continuously (see TROPICAL VITICULTURE). Systematic PRUNING has been adopted in some wine-grape vineyards, however, to induce three output peaks ('vintages'). D.G.

VIFA stands for **variété d'intérêt à fin d'adaptation**, literally 'variety of interest for adaptation' (i.e. grape varieties that might be suitable for a changing climate and environment). This term was introduced by the INAO in 2021 to allow the regulatory body of a PDO in France to apply for permission to plant, on an experimental basis for at least 10 years and within specific limits, up to 20 varieties (10 red and 10 white) that they believe might be suitable to overcome specific viticultural problems such as increased incidence of FUNGAL DISEASES, high temperatures, or DROUGHT. These may include both VITIS VINIFERA and authorized HYBRIDS. See also NEW VARIETIES and DISEASE-RESISTANT VARIETIES.

vigna is Italian for VINEYARD, while a **vignaiolo** is a vine-grower.

vigne is French for a VINE, and sometimes VINEYARD. **Vigneron** is French for a vine-grower, or for someone who is both grower and winemaker, whereas a **viticulteur** merely grows vines. The term **vigneron** is now used widely outside France for a wide range of people engaged in wine production.

A **vignoble** is French for a vineyard, although the term *vignoble* can be used more broadly, as in 'the entire French *vignoble*'.

Vignoles, also known as Ravat 51, late-budding, early-ripening FRENCH HYBRID popular in cooler wine regions in the Midwest and eastern UNITED STATES. It can make fresh, delicate white wine and is particularly well suited to sweet-wine production.

vigour in a viticultural sense is the amount of vegetative growth, an important aspect of any vine. This may seem of unlikely interest to wine drinkers, but it has significant effect on wine quality. Very low-vigour vines do not always have sufficient leaf area to ripen grapes properly, while high-vigour vines typically produce thin, pale wines, sometimes low in alcohol, wrongly thought to result from OVERCROPPING. Vigour changes through a vine's lifetime, as discussed in VINE AGE.

High-vigour vines show a lack of BALANCE between shoot and fruit growth. Vigorous vineyards show rapid shoot growth in the spring, and shoots continue to grow late into the growing season. Shoots on vigorous vines have long INTERNODES, thick stems, large leaves, and many, usually long, LATERAL SHOOTS. Vigorous vineyards are generally, but not necessarily, associated with high YIELDS. Rank vegetative growth may produce so much SHADE that FRUITFULNESS declines, leading to even more vegetative growth and a loss of varietal character, colour, body, and general wine quality.

Vine vigour is easy to quantify using PRUNING WEIGHTS and other vine measurements as outlined by Smart and Robinson, and these approaches, along with SCORING, can be used as a form of quality control. For an alternative approach to the assessment of vine vigour using

REMOTE SENSING, see NORMALIZED DIFFERENCE VEGETATION INDEX.

The vigour of a vineyard is essentially dependent on two features: the size and health of the root system; and the pruning level. First, what grows above ground is some sort of mirror of what grows below. A vine with a large and healthy root system will have the substantial reserves of CARBOHYDRATES and balance of HORMONES to support considerable vigorous shoot growth. On the other hand, a vine with a small and/or unhealthy root system, be it due to shallow soil, DROUGHT, root pests such as PHYLLOXERA, or diseases such as TRUNK DISEASE or ARMILLARIA ROOT ROT, will support only low-vigour growth.

Vines should be pruned to bud numbers relative to the amount of early shoot growth they can support. This is the concept of BALANCED PRUNING, and one criterion used is to retain at winter PRUNING about 25–30 buds per kg of pruning weight. Use of this sort of rule means that the subsequent shoot growth will be in balance with the vine's carbohydrate reserves, ensuring balance between shoot and fruit growth, as well as moderate vigour.

High vigour is a common problem of modern vineyards, for many and varied reasons. The vines may be planted in a region with a benign climate on too deep a soil, which is well supplied with water (from rainfall and/or IRRIGATION) and nutrients, especially NITROGEN (from natural fertility or FERTILIZERS or added COMPOST). Such soils are said to have high SOIL POTENTIAL in that they promote excessive vine vigour. Modern control methods can also keep vines free of stress associated with weeds, pests, and diseases. CANOPY MANAGEMENT techniques are used to maintain yield and wine quality in such situations.

An alternative approach is to devigorate the vines, most commonly by controlling the water supply, which is of course easier to do when irrigating in an arid climate than when vineyards are supplied by rainfall alone. COVER CROPS that compete for the available water are another useful tool. Other techniques include nutrient stressing, increasing crop load by leaving more buds at winter pruning or by growing shoots downwards as in the GENEVA DOUBLE CURTAIN training system. R.E.S.

Smart, R. E., and Robinson, M., *Sunlight into Wine: A Handbook for Winegrape Canopy Management* (1991).

Vijariego (also known as **Bujariego** and **Vijiriega**), white grape variety from the CANARY ISLANDS which produces distinctive dry wines there on vineyards totalling 167 ha/413 acres in 2020. A little is also planted in Andalucía.

Vilana, white grape variety that is native to and the most widely grown on the island of CRETE, with total Greek plantings of 546 ha/1,349 acres in 2021. It is solely responsible for the delicate spicy dry white Peza PDO, and is blended with THRAPSATHIRI for Sitia PDO.

Vila Nova de Gaia, or Gaia New Town, a city on the south side of the DOURO estuary from the Portuguese city of OPORTO where PORT is traditionally aged. Rising from the waterfront, long, single-storey buildings called LODGES line the narrow, cobbled streets. Under the clay-tiled roofs, shippers mature their stocks of port, as well as TASTING, BLENDING, BOTTLING, and selling it. Until 1986 the law required that all port destined for export had to be shipped from within the strictly defined area of the Gaia entrepôt. Port may now be shipped from anywhere within the demarcated Douro region so that export markets are open to small firms, QUINTAS, and CO-OPERATIVES without premises in Vila Nova de Gaia. R.J.M.

Villages, common suffix of an AOC name for a French wine. Generally speaking, an X-Villages wine must be made from one or several of a selection of communes whose produce is known to be superior to that of the rest of the X zone. See, for example, BEAUJOLAIS, MÂCON, and Côtes du RHÔNE.

village wine is a term used particularly in BURGUNDY for a wine which qualifies for an AOC that coincides with the name of the village or commune in which the wine is made. It contrasts with a lesser GENERIC wine, which takes the name of a region, and wines from PREMIER CRU and GRAND CRU vineyards.

Villány, wine region and PDO in HUNGARY extending over 2,390 ha/5,906 acres on the terraced southern and eastern slopes of the Villány Mountains. These mountains protect the vineyards from cold northern influences resulting in a special sub-MEDITERRANEAN CLIMATE. The soils consist of CALCAREOUS rocks deposited in the marine basins of the Mesozoic. Dolomite, MARL, and LIMESTONE are covered with sandy LOESS. This layer is sometimes mixed with limestone debris, having a higher concentration of CALCIUM. This is the cropland of more acidic wines, while the purely loess soil produces softer wines. Villány is mostly known for its red BORDEAUX BLENDS, sometimes rather heavy and tannic but with good AGEING potential. Cabernet Franc grows well here, with the top VARIETAL examples labeled Villányi Franc. The everyday drinking wine is the softer PORTUGIESER, and KÉKFRANKOS is often used in blends. Some white wines are also made, mostly from Olaszrizling (WELSCHRIESLING), Chardonnay, and HÁRSLEVELŰ. G.M.

Villard is the common French name for a great French viticultural secret, their most widely planted HYBRIDS. Most are members of the vast SEYVE-VILLARD group.

In France, **Villard Noir** is Seyve-Villard 18.315 while **Villard Blanc** is Seyve-Villard 12.375. Villard Noir was planted all over France, from the northern Rhône to Bordeaux, and was treasured for its resistance to DOWNY MILDEW and ROT. Villard Blanc made slightly more palatable wine (though the must can be difficult to process). Both varieties yield prodigiously and for that attribute were so beloved by growers that in 1968 there were 30,375 ha/75,058 acres of Villard Noir and 21,397 ha of Villard Blanc in France (making them the fifth and third most planted black and white grape varieties respectively).

To the great credit of the authorities, and thanks to not inconsiderable bribes for GRUBBING UP, by 1998 these respective totals had been shaved to 3,245 ha and 1,129 ha, mainly in the Tarn and the Ardèche. In 2019 Villard Noir plantings were down to 986 ha, while Villard Blanc, now planted to a very limited extent in several American states, is grown on only 133 ha in France.

vin, French for 'wine' and therefore a much-used term (see below). **Vin blanc** is white wine, **vin rosé** is pink, **vin rouge** is red wine, **vin mousseux** is sparkling wine, and so on. For **vin ordinaire**, see VIN DE FRANCE. For **vin biologique**, see ORGANIC WINE. For **vin blanc cassis**, see KIR.

viña, viñedo, Spanish word for VINEYARD.

Vin de France, category created in 2009 for the most basic French wine, formerly called *vin de table*, known in the EU as WINE WITHOUT GEOGRAPHICAL INDICATION and in France as VSIG. Unlike the old *vin de table*, a Vin de France may be labelled with a vintage and/or vine variety, a change designed to make it more competitive with inexpensive VARIETAL wine produced outside Europe. On average this category accounts for less than 8% of all French wine, but it includes an increasing number of superior-quality wines made outside the tighter strictures of AOC/AOP and IGP regulations. See also FRANCE.

vin de liqueur, strong, sweet drink made by adding neutral grape spirit or eau de vie to GRAPE JUICE or MUST, so-called MUTAGE, either before or during FERMENTATION. The resulting liquids have an ALCOHOLIC STRENGTH of 16–22% but no secondary products of fermentation such as GLYCEROL or SUCCINIC ACID. Confusingly, the term is also used by the EU to refer to all FORTIFIED WINES. See LIQUEUR WINE.

The principal members of this special category of French specialities, known as *mistelles* (see MISTELA) if the fortification takes place before fermentation has started, are the PINEAU DES CHARENTES of Cognac country, its Armagnac counterpart FLOC DE GASCOGNE, MACVIN DU JURA (made from local MARC added to grape juice and tasting strongly of the former), and CLAIRETTE DU LANGUEDOC. Most vins de liqueur are pale gold, but soft, fruity rosé versions of both Pineau and Floc can be found in the regions of production. Vin de liqueur differs from VIN DOUX NATUREL in that the alcohol is generally added earlier, and the resulting drinks therefore tend to be, and taste, more spirit-dominated. Some MUSCAT DE FRONTIGNAN may also qualify. Many wine regions have their own versions of this easy-to-make strong, sweet APERITIF: Champagne has its Ratafia, while the Languedoc has Cartagène. Where there are no regulations governing their production, they are sometimes made further along the scale towards vins doux naturels. Like vins doux naturels, these sweet wines can be enhanced by serving them cool, and the wine in an opened bottle should retain its appeal for well over a week.

vin de paille is French for 'straw wine' (STROHWEIN in German), a small group of necessarily expensive but often quite delicious, long-lived, sweet white wines. These are essentially a subgroup of DRIED-GRAPE WINES made from grapes traditionally dried on straw. Cyrus REDDING's catalogue of wines produced in the early 19th century makes it clear that *vins de paille* were much more common then and, although he was most enthusiastic about 'Ermitage-paille' (from HERMITAGE vines), he found *vins de paille* in the JURA, ALSACE, and Corrèze. At about the same time some producers in RUST in Austria were also using the technique.

For much of the 20th century, no *vin de paille* was made in Hermitage, but Gérard Chave revived the practice with healthy, not late-picked, MARSANNE grapes in 1974, dried on straw in the attic, and has since been followed by CHAPOUTIER, Jaboulet, and others.

Average yields are minuscule once the grapes have been raisined, but the results, invariably sold in half-bottles, can be luscious in the extreme.

Less than 1% of Jura's wine production is of *vin de paille* from ARBOIS, L'ÉTOILE, and Côtes du JURA made mainly from SAVAGNIN, POULSARD, and/or Chardonnay grapes picked relatively early and typically dried in boxes in a ventilated loft for at least six weeks. The minimum POTENTIAL ALCOHOL allowed is 19% (14% in Hermitage). Jura producers must age their *vins de paille* for at least three years, including a minimum of 18 months in cask. The wines must have a natural ALCOHOLIC STRENGTH of at least 14% and tend to be less intensely sweet than in the Rhône, where the minimum alcohol level is just 12.5%. Some have an oxidative note (see OXIDATION) and all are capable of long AGEING. Many Jura producers avoid these appellation rules, making a lower-alcohol version or one with less OAK AGEING and labelled VIN DE FRANCE.

See also ALSACE and LUXEMBOURG.

Livingstone-Learmonth, J., *The Wines of the Northern Rhône* (2005).
Lorch, W., *Jura Wine* (2014).

Vin de Pays, French expression meaning 'country wine' which was adopted for an intermediate category of wines created in France in 1973, and formalized in 1979, to recognize and encourage the production of wines between VIN DE TABLE and AOC in quality. This category has been superseded by IGP wines.

vin de presse, French for PRESS WINE.

Vin de Savoie. See SAVOIE.

Vin des Glaciers, also known as **Vin du Glacier**, or **Gletscherwein** in German, 'glacier wine', is a local speciality in the Val d'Anniviers near Sierre in the Valais in Switzerland. The white wine, traditionally made of the now obscure RÈZE vine, comes from communally cultivated vines and is stored at high ELEVATIONS in casks refilled just once a year in a SOLERA system. The resultant product is deliberately MADERIZED and valued for its rarity.

vin de table, the old name for France's most basic level of wine, which, having been a copious embarrassment, has dwindled to a relative trickle. It has been replaced by VIN DE FRANCE.

vin doux naturel translates directly from French as 'a wine that is naturally sweet' but is a term used to describe a French wine speciality that might well be considered *un*naturally sweet. Nature's sweetest wines contain so much grape sugar that the yeasts eventually give up the FERMENTATION process of converting sugar into alcohol, leaving a residue of natural sugars in a stable wine of normal alcoholic strength (see SWEET WINEMAKING). Vins doux naturels, on the other hand, are made by MUTAGE, by artificially arresting the conversion of grape sugar to alcohol by adding spirit before fermentation is complete, thereby incapacitating yeasts with alcohol and making a particularly strong, sweet half-wine in which grape flavours dominate wine flavours. They are normally made of the grape varieties MUSCAT and GRENACHE and should have an ALCOHOLIC STRENGTH of 15–18% and a POTENTIAL ALCOHOL of at least 21.5%. The minimum RESIDUAL SUGAR level varies from 45 g/l for Rasteau and Banyuls to 100 g/l for the various Muscat de Somethings.

The Greeks, happily ignorant of DISTILLATION, already knew how to make a sweet wine by adding concentrated MUST. Almost as soon as the techniques of distillation were introduced into western Europe, it was discovered that distilled wine, or alcoholic spirit, had the power to stop fermentation, thereby reliably retaining the sweetness so prized by our forebears. The Catalan alchemist ARNALDUS DE VILLANOVA (Arnaud de Villeneuve) of Montpellier University's then flourishing medical school perfected the process and in 1299 was granted a patent from the king of Majorca, then ruler of ROUSSILLON, which was to become the world's centre of vin doux naturel production.

This is essentially how PORT as we know it, created nearly 400 years later, is made strong and sweet, and the technique is also used in the production of MADEIRA and MÁLAGA. In each case, spirit is added when the fermenting must has reached about 6% alcohol, except that whereas the added spirit constitutes 5–10% of the final volume of a vin doux naturel, typically resulting in an alcoholic strength of just over 15%, the added spirit usually represents 20% of the final volume of port, whose alcoholic strength is closer to 20%. The spirit added to vins doux naturels is considerably stronger than that added to port, however: about 95% alcohol as opposed to the traditional 77% used in port FORTIFICATION. Nowadays, however, the spirit may well come from exactly the same source, one of France's larger distilleries.

A young vin doux naturel therefore, like young port, tastes relatively simply of grapes, sugar, and alcohol (although, since some fermentation has usually taken place, it may contain a more interesting array of fermentation products than most VINS DE LIQUEUR, which are made by adding spirit before fermentation or just as fermentation is starting). Naturally aromatic MUSCAT BLANC À PETITS GRAINS grapes are therefore particularly well suited to the production of vins doux naturels designed to be drunk young (and, usually, chilled to offset the sugar and alcohol). The best known of these golden sweet liquids made from this Muscat vine variety was historically MUSCAT DE FRONTIGNAN. The Languedoc has three other AOC vins doux naturels, however: Muscats de LUNEL, MIREVAL, and ST-JEAN-DE-MINERVOIS; and CORSICA has its Muscat du Cap Corse. The Muscat vin doux naturel made in the Côtes du Rhône village of BEAUMES-DE-VENISE is probably easier for non-locals to appreciate than the southern Rhône's other vin doux naturel appellation of RASTEAU, whose Grenache-based heady red and tawny sweet wines, some of them deliberately made RANCIO, have more in common with the vins doux naturels of Roussillon. The best of these tend to come from BANYULS and, like the best ports, owe their complex flavours to ageing, whether in cask, BONBONNE, or, occasionally, bottle. MAURY is a smaller appellation in the mountains with enormous (and occasionally realized) potential, although most wine made there now is dry TABLE WINE, while the extensive coastal RIVESALTES and Muscat de Rivesaltes appellations are much more varied. Grand Roussillon is a largely theoretical vin doux naturel appellation designed as a lesser Rivesaltes.

Non-vintage-dated vins doux naturels are common, particularly among the Languedoc Muscats into which a little of the previous year's output may be blended so as to smooth out vintage differences. In Roussillon, however, it is common to find indications of age and vintage dates, although most vins doux naturels are ready to drink as soon as they are sold. Many, particularly the Muscats, benefit from being served young and chilled, but the alcohol preserves the freshness of wine in an opened bottle for at least a week.

vine, the plant, often known as the grapevine, whose fruit is transformed into wine.

A vine in its broadest sense is any plant with a weak stem which supports itself by climbing on neighbouring plants, walls, or other supports. Of this group of plants, the grapevine is the most famous and the most commercially important. (In this book the word 'vine' is used to mean the grapevine.) There are various forms of climbing vines which rely on different mechanisms for attachment. The so-called ramblers rest on each other, and some, as for roses, have spines to help adhesion. The grapevine is one of the so-called tendril climbers with TENDRILS on the stem; the garden pea has leaf tendrils.

Because the vine is unable to support itself, it is generally grown on TRELLIS SYSTEMS. Some TRAINING SYSTEMS still use trees for support, for example the *alberate* of Italy (see also ARBOREAL VITICULTURE). However, most vineyards of the world are trained to some combination of POSTS and wires. Vines can be trained so that they are free-standing, but this requires special PRUNING and TRAINING to keep the trunk short, otherwise the vine will fall over. The GOBELET of the Mediterranean region is the most widespread of the free-standing forms.

Most of the world's wine is made from VITIS VINIFERA, the *vinifera* species of the *Vitis* genus (see BOTANICAL CLASSIFICATION for a more detailed explanation of where the vine fits into the world of plants).

Grapevines are the world's most important fruit crop, with about 7.3 million ha/18.04 million acres of vineyards producing around 258 million hl/6,816 million gal of wine in 2022, as well as GRAPE JUICE, TABLE GRAPES, RAISINS, GRAPE CONCENTRATE, RECTIFIED GRAPE MUST, and limited industrial products. Wine production accounts for 70% of all vineyard output.

The grapevine is grown on all continents except Antarctica, but most of the world's vineyards are in Europe. Spain had nearly 1 million ha/2.4 million acres of vineyards in 2022, France just over 0.8 million ha, and Italy more than 0.7 million; between them these three countries produced more than half of the world's wine in 2022, Italy more than 19%, and France 17.7%. China has nearly 11% of the world vineyard area but produced only 1.6% of world wine in 2022.

Vinifera cannot tolerate extreme winter cold. Requiring warm summers for fruit maturation, the vine is grown approximately between the 10 and 20 °C isotherm in both hemispheres, or about between latitudes 30° N and 50° N, and 30–40° S, although CLIMATE CHANGE has seen the vine planted ever closer to the poles (see map of WORLD PRODUCTION, page 842). Principally in order to minimize the damage associated with FUNGAL DISEASES, the grapevine has traditionally been grown in MEDITERRANEAN CLIMATES with warm, dry summers and mild, wet winters. The ready availability of AGROCHEMICALS, and to a lesser extent disease-tolerant varieties, has allowed this range to be extended, especially since the Second World War. Winter DORMANCY is essential for vine longevity, and the hot and humid climates nearer the equator are not conducive to either grape production or wine quality (although see TROPICAL VITICULTURE).

Most of the world's vineyards are planted with traditional VINE VARIETIES, which have been perpetuated for centuries by vegetative PROPAGATION. Different CLONES of these varieties may also be distinguished.

Many viticultural practices are very traditional, especially in Europe, where in many cases they are prescribed by law. Cultural operations and the reasoning behind them are introduced under VITICULTURE, VINE PHYSIOLOGY, VINE DISEASES, and VINE PESTS. The effects of climate and soils are also discussed in, respectively, CLIMATE AND WINE QUALITY and SOIL AND WINE QUALITY.

See VINE MORPHOLOGY for discussion of the parts of the vine and VINE PHYSIOLOGY for details of how the vine functions. See also VINE GROWTH CYCLE and, for a historical perspective, ORIGINS OF VINICULTURE. R.E.S. & J.E.H.

Iland, P., et al., *The Grapevine: From the Science to the Practice of Growing Vines for Wine* (2011).

Keller, M., *The Science of Grapevines* (3rd edn, 2020).

vine age, often observable by the size of a vine or the girth of its TRUNK. Vine age is widely considered a factor that can affect wine quality; many believe that, in general, older vines make better wine. Although there is no agreement and no legislation as to what constitutes 'old', vines more than 50 years old could justifiably be described as such. AOC legislation in many cases specifically excludes the produce of vines less than two or three years old, although this probably represents a bias against the fruit of very young vines rather than an affirmation of the qualities of older ones, and it is unusual for vines to crop before their third year. Some French producers deliberately exclude wine from vines under a certain age from their top bottlings and put it into SECOND WINES. The concept that older vines make better wine is much used in marketing wine in Europe (see OLD VINES) and has more recently been adopted by producers in regions as diverse as California, Chile, South Africa, and Australia, where the BAROSSA wine region is home to UNGRAFTED VINES which remain alive and producing, some after more than a century and a half. Conversely, some winemakers observe that young vineyards produce their highest-quality wine when relatively young. For example, in the world-famous JUDGMENT OF PARIS blind tasting in 1976, which first pitted California Cabernets and Chardonnays against top-quality red bordeaux and white burgundies, Stag's Leap Wine Cellars S.L.V. Cabernet Sauvignon 1973 came out on top, scoring more highly than Ch MOUTON ROTHSCHILD 1970 and Ch HAUT-BRION 1970, even though this was the first vintage of this Napa Valley red and the vines were only three years old. Both of these apparently opposed viewpoints may be correct, as will be discussed below.

After planting, conventional VINE TRAINING takes two to three years to form the vine framework. Bunches formed in these early years are often discarded in favour of vegetative growth. Once a vine is allowed to produce fruit and is about three to six years of age, it usually fills its allotted growing space above ground, then the YIELD and annual shoot growth normally stabilize, changing only with a major alteration to management or growing conditions. Vineyards which are protected from stresses, pests, and diseases; in a hospitable soil; and free from an excess or deficit of water (see WATER STRESS) or mineral nutrients (see VINE NUTRITION) can be very long-lived. An outstanding example is the famous vine at Hampton Court Palace near London, which is still producing large crops of MUSCAT grapes (under glass) despite having been planted in 1768. Another example is a vine reported to be over 400 years of age in the town of Maribor, SLOVENIA, which is still producing an annual crop of grapes that are vinified in celebration.

The VIGOUR and yield of many commercial vineyards may begin to decline after 20–30 years, and by 50 years many vineyards are yielding at such a low level as to be considered uneconomic, sooner if the wood is diseased (see TRUNK DISEASES) or has suffered physical damage from aggressive PRUNING or rough MECHANIZATION resulting in missing vines.

Below ground, however, the picture can be different. Champagnol defines three stages of ROOT GROWTH. During the first stage, the root system colonizes available space, and this takes until the seventh to tenth years, taking longer in poor soils and with low VINE DENSITY. In the so-called adult stage, there is little change in the volume of soil exploited, but in the final, senescent stage there is a supposed reduction in root activity. This can be from the effects of DROUGHT, from SOIL COMPACTION by machinery and TILLAGE or from lack of oxygen at depth. It has also been noted that root pests and diseases may weaken the root system, especially in the case of UNGRAFTED VINES infested with PHYLLOXERA. Long-term application of some fertilizers and spray materials can increase SOIL ACIDITY while application of poor-quality IRRIGATION water can load the soil with salts, reducing root, soil, and vine health.

Grapevines are climbing plants that usually require external support. In cultivation, this is in the form of a TRELLIS SYSTEM, which may be complex, with numerous posts and wires, or simple, like the BUSH VINES which are the mainstay of many old vineyards. The above-ground framework of the vine may weaken with age due to the increased size and weight of the branches or via pathogen attack or mechanical damage. Annual winter PRUNING may weaken vines over time; the increasing number of pruning wounds can accumulate over years, allowing wood-rotting pathogens to invade (see TRUNK DISEASES) or restricting sap flow via dessication. While some pathogens can kill a vine within a few years, many are ever-present in vineyards and can be slow to cause obvious visible symptoms. Other less common pathogens that may cause rapid vine decline, preventing old age, are often under quarantine control or regional treatment to limit their spread, for example phylloxera, *Xylella fastidiosa* (see PIERCE'S DISEASE) or FLAVESCENCE DORÉE. The large amount of living wood and stored CARBOHYDRATES above and below ground in the structure of many old vines is thought to increase resilience to stress. Dead wood that is the result of pruning cuts or vine age can be decomposed by TERMITES or microbes, weakening the permanent structure of the vine.

The conventional explanation for improved quality with vine age is because of reduction in yield, and indeed for many celebrated vineyards the two go hand in hand. However, since older vines are often lower in vegetative vigour and physically large in size, there may be more balanced growth resulting in a more desirable MICROCLIMATE. This may in turn offer an indirect but plausible explanation for the effect of increasing vine age on wine quality.

This BALANCE between vegetative growth and fruit can also explain the apparent paradox that some vineyards seem to produce their best quality when very young, often with the first few crops. Such vines have very open CANOPIES and so in the first fruiting year there is a favourable LEAF TO FRUIT RATIO. Commonly the vine is more vigorous in subsequent years, the shoots grow longer, and quality may be reduced because of increasing SHADE. Such vineyards can produce premium quality for the first few crops, then quality may decline until the vine is older and vigour is reduced. However, appropriate CANOPY MANAGEMENT can improve wine quality in these in-between years. R.E.S. & D.P.G.

Champagnol, F., *Éléments de physiologie de la vigne et de viticulture générale* (1984).

Grigg, D., 'An investigation into the effect of grapevine age on vine performance, grape and wine composition, sensory evaluation and epigenetic characterization' (2017). digital.library.adelaide.edu.au/dspace/bitstream/2440/113314/1/01front.pdf.

Vinea Wachau, full title **Vinea Wachau Nobilis Districtus**, is an organization representing most wine estates (nearly 200) in Austria's WACHAU region, called into existence in 1983 by a quartet including the late Josef Jamek, who helped define the styles of dry, unchaptalized wine (see CHAPTALIZATION) that came to characterize this region and eventually the wines of NIEDERÖSTERREICH as a whole. The Vinea Wachau established three stylistic tiers—STEINFEDER, FEDERSPIEL, and SMARAGD—imposing them on the region in the aftermath of Austria's 1985 wine scandal. In the 1990s, a Vinea Wachau executive board that featured Toni Bodenstein of Weingut Prager, Franz Hirtzberger, Emmerich Knoll, and F. X. Pichler was instrumental in achieving prestige for Austrian wine on export markets. In 2006 the Vinea Wachau strengthened its founding principles by publishing a **Wachau Codex**, unusual for the number of cellar procedures—including any form of must CONCENTRATION or separation (such as DEALCOHOLIZATION)—that it proscribes, as well as for its explicit rejection of any new WOOD flavours. D.S.

vine breeding, the crossing of one vine variety or species with another to produce a new variety. Grapevines are highly heterozygous outcrossers and do not breed true from seed, which is the reason for their universal VEGETATIVE PROPAGATION. If both parent varieties belong to the same species (in practice, usually the European VITIS VINIFERA) of the VITIS genus, then the result is commonly called a CROSS (occasionally crossing), while the results of crossing varieties from more than one species (typically, a *vinifera* variety and a member of an AMERICAN VINE SPECIES) are commonly called HYBRIDS.

These NEW VARIETIES are traditionally created by dusting POLLEN from the male parent on to the receptive stigma of the female parent (see FLOWERS, VINE) and then germinating the seed from the berry which subsequently grows (although see GENETIC MODIFICATION for more recent techniques). There is a relatively low probability that any one seedling will become a useful variety, and extensive testing, probably over more than ten years, for viticultural and winemaking suitability is required before any new variety is released.

The convention is to express the female parent first, thus KERNER is a Schiava Grossa × Riesling cross, while BACO 22A is a Folle Blanche × Noah hybrid (Noah itself being an AMERICAN HYBRID).

Vine breeding was particularly important in the early 20th century, notably in France, Germany, and Romania, as a European response to controlling the spread of the PHYLLOXERA pest (see HYBRIDS and FRENCH HYBRIDS). Breeding of new varieties which combine high yields with good wine quality and resistance to pests and diseases has been an important activity in such German centres as Geilweilerhof and GEISENHEIM.

A main emphasis of grape breeding has been to combine the pest and disease resistance that exists in wild grape species with the high-quality fruit from *vinifera* varieties. For instance, VITIS AMURENSIS and VITIS RIPARIA contain genes for winter hardiness, and *vinifera* and *Vitis berlandieri* for lime soil tolerance (see CHLOROSIS). Among various *Vitis* species can be found genetic resistance to the fungal diseases DOWNY MILDEW, POWDERY MILDEW, and BOTRYTIS BUNCH ROT; the bacterial diseases of CROWN GALL and PIERCE'S DISEASE; and the soil pests of PHYLLOXERA and NEMATODES. A desire to minimize the use of AGROCHEMICALS has encouraged breeding DISEASE-RESISTANT VARIETIES to combine these natural resistances, notably in Germany and the United States.

Because of increasing emphasis on a few familiar VINE VARIETIES and also the lingering suspicion of hybrids caused by the poor wine performance of the early French hybrids, some consumers view the results of breeding programmes with suspicion. Yet such programmes can offer the opportunity of an improved range of flavours and styles produced from vineyards which do not require any other means of pest and disease protection.

See also NEW VARIETIES and INTERNATIONAL GRAPE GENOME PROGRAM. R.E.S. & M.A.W.

Burger, P., et al., 'Grape breeding', in S. M. Jain and P. M. Priyadarshan (eds.), *Breeding Planation Tree Crops: Tropical Species* (2014).

Cantu, D., and Walker, M.A. (eds.), *The Grape Genome* (2019).

Heinitz, C. C., et al., 'Crop wild relatives of grape (*Vitis vinifera* L.) throughout North America', in S. L. Greene et al. (eds.), *North American Crop Wild Relatives*, vol. 2 (2019), 329–51.

vine density is a measure of how closely spaced vines are in the vineyard, both within the row and between rows. The choice of vine spacing is one of the most fundamental decisions in PLANTING a vineyard, and between, even within, the world's wine regions there is enormous variation in spacing. The traditional vineyards of France's Bordeaux, Burgundy, and Champagne regions have about 10,000 plants per ha (4,050 per acre) and sometimes more, with vines spaced typically 1 m apart both within and between the rows. In many NEW WORLD vineyards, on the other hand, a spacing of 2.5 m/8 ft between vines along the row and 3.7 m/12 ft between rows, or 1,080 vines per ha, is quite common. Probably the most widely spaced vineyards of the world are those of the Vinho Verde region in Portugal, La Mancha in Spain, and some parts of Chile, Japan, and Italy (see TENDONE), with spacings as wide as 4 m by 4 m, or just 625 vines per ha.

Some argue that high vine densities lead to improved wine quality. It is true that many of the world's most famous vineyards, almost invariably in Europe, have very narrow spacings, and therefore high densities, but it is difficult to argue that this is a prerequisite for quality production. Narrow spacings are indeed appropriate to vineyards of moderate VIGOUR, which is a feature of the low SOIL POTENTIAL of these vineyards (see TERROIR and SOIL AND WINE QUALITY). Some New World winegrowers have been encouraged to plant high-density vineyards on fertile vineyard soils in expectation of matching the quality of famous European vineyards. The theory is that such dense planting will cause root competition and substantial devigoration, but this has infrequently, if ever, been demonstrated, and the result is often a high-vigour vineyard which is very difficult to manage and where SHADE reduces both quality and quantity. The outcome of this endeavour depends ultimately on SOIL WATER available to the vine. If well-supplied with water, high-density plantings do not lead to devigoration.

The belief that 'tight spacing' encourages wine quality was widely promulgated in the 1980s and 1990s in California. Despite many commercial experiments, it remains to be demonstrated that wine quality is automatically increased, while the costs of establishing and running such a high-density vineyard certainly are. Research and commercial experience in Europe indicate that close row and vine spacings are suited only to vineyards of low soil potential. In high-vigour situations, some New World vine-growers have responded by removing one vine in two down the row, and sometimes two in three. This has been found to restore vine BALANCE, and yield and quality have subsequently improved.

High-density vineyards are the traditional form of viticulture in many parts of the world, as spacing need only be sufficient to allow the workers unhindered access. Some very early vineyards were not even planted in rows but were haphazardly arranged. Before PHYLLOXERA invaded Europe, unhealthy plants could be replaced by LAYERING a cane from an adjacent vine. These considerations, and the fact that vines then were generally less vigorous, encouraged high-density vineyards, and densities were as high as 40,000 plants per ha, or just one-quarter of a square metre per plant. Once GRAFTING to ROOTSTOCKS developed as a response to phylloxera, however, then the additional cost of each plant encouraged lower vine densities. The introduction of first draught animals and then TRACTORS led to the planting of vineyards in rows with a further reduction in vine density.

Many New World vineyards were planted after the introduction of tractors, necessitating row spacings of about 3 m/10 ft or more for early and wide tractors, although over the last few decades tractor width has decreased to less than 2 m/6.5 ft. Over this period vine vigour has also increased, but this has not necessarily affected vine density since the modern tendency is to train shoots vertically upwards on a VERTICAL TRELLIS rather than allow them to sprawl into the row. By contrast, most European vine-growers have chosen to persist with narrow rows and to develop either narrow tractors or over-row tractors, known in France as *tracteurs enjambeurs.*

Vineyard density is a major consideration affecting the vineyard's yield, quality, cost of establishment and maintenance, and therefore profitability. Planting costs are proportional to the number of plants used; costs for TRELLIS SYSTEMS and DRIP IRRIGATION are higher with narrower row spacings. The time taken to till and spray is also greater when rows are closer together.

Under most circumstances, the YIELD of densely planted vineyards is higher, especially in the first years of the vineyard's life and with vines planted on low soil potential. R.E.S.

Galet, P., *General Viticulture* (2000).

vine diseases. Diseases caused by microbes can limit the distribution of vines and affect both yield and quality. See BACTERIAL DISEASES, FUNGAL DISEASES, TRUNK DISEASES, VIRUS DISEASES, PHYTOPLASMA diseases, and the names of individual diseases. See also CLIMATE EFFECTS ON VINE DISEASES.

vine foliage lifter, machine which lifts vine foliage in the growing season. Once the foliage is vertical, it can be secured by WIRES and is then well placed for TRIMMING to maintain a constant CANOPY outline. This is a particular aid to CANOPY MANAGEMENT. See also SHOOT POSITIONING.

vinegar, sour liquid condiment that depends etymologically, and often materially, on wine. The French word for it, composed of *vin* (wine) and *aigre* (sour), is a direct descendant of its Latin equivalent. Not just wine but any solution containing a low concentration (less than 15%) of ETHANOL will turn to vinegar if exposed to OXYGEN. The ethanol is oxidized first into an ALDEHYDE and then to ACETIC ACID by the oxygen in the atmosphere. Winemakers over the centuries have learnt to shelter wine from the action of atmospheric oxygen, and nowadays they will do all they can to prevent their wines turning to vinegar, 'vinegary' being a tasting term of great disapprobation (while 'winey' is quite a compliment when applied to a vinegar). Once the VOLATILE ACIDS in a wine have reached a certain point, however, it can have a future only as wine vinegar.

The OXIDATION of any dilute aqueous alcohol solution is greatly hastened by the action of a group of bacteria known as ACETOBACTER from the environment. These bacteria also hasten the reaction of some of the alcohol with some of the newly produced acetic acid to form the ESTER known as ETHYL ACETATE. This compound, when added to the tart taste of acetic acid, gives the complex character to a good wine vinegar.

The everyday vinegar of the marketplace varies geographically. In southern Europe wine vinegar is the norm, for example, while in northern Europe malt, cider, and distilled vinegars predominate, and in the Far East rice vinegar is most usual.

Today a wide range of vinegars are produced, many flavoured with herbs and fruits, some, such as Italian balsamic vinegar, given BARREL AGEING according to rules as strict as those governing AOC wine production. The most powerful vinegars are so strong in ethyl acetate that their flavour can overpower that of a subtle wine. In foods served with subtle wines, wine itself can be used as a condiment, contributing the same sort of ACIDITY as a vinegar would have done. See also VERJUS.

A domestic vinegar SOLERA is one solution for LEFTOVER WINE. A.D.W.

vinegar fly. See DROSOPHILA.

vine growth cycle, the annual march of the vine's development, which begins at budbreak in the spring and concludes at leaf fall in the autumn. There are distinct developmental stages along the way (see PHENOLOGY), the principal ones being BUDBREAK, FLOWERING, FRUIT SET, VERAISON, RIPENING, HARVEST when the grapes are mature, and LEAF FALL. The pace of development between these phenological stages varies greatly with vine variety. Very early varieties, such as MADELEINE ANGEVINE, go through the stages up to ripeness in a short time and can therefore ripen in regions with a short growing season and relatively cool temperatures. In late varieties, such as MOURVÈDRE, CARIGNAN, and CLAIRETTE, all stages are prolonged, and much more heat and time are needed to bring them to maturity.

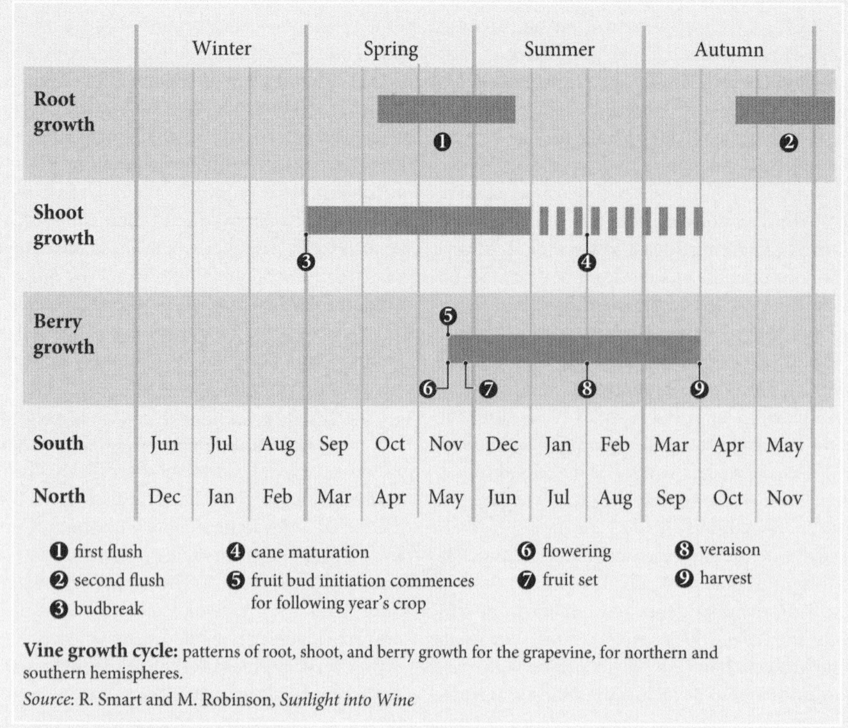

Vine growth cycle: patterns of root, shoot, and berry growth for the grapevine, for northern and southern hemispheres.
Source: R. Smart and M. Robinson, *Sunlight into Wine*

The length of the growth cycle also depends on climate, especially temperature. In hot regions, the period from budbreak to harvest may be as short as 130 days for early varieties, but in cooler regions this period can be over 200 days.

The vine often begins to grow later in the spring than most other deciduous plants, when the average air temperature is normally about 10 °C/50 °F in cool climates. The first sign of impending growth is vines bleeding as the soil warms, then the buds swell, and eventually the first tinges of green are seen in the vineyards as the shoot tips burst from the buds. The young shoots grow very slowly at first, producing small leaves on each side of the shoot. This early shoot growth depends on the reserves of carbohydrates stored in the vine, but soon the leaves are old enough for photosynthesis and to produce the carbohydrates which become the tissue of further shoot growth.

After about four weeks in warm climates, the principal period of most rapid shoot growth begins. Shoots may grow more than 3 cm/1 in a day, and differences in shoot length can be observed from day to day. Shoot growth slackens at flowering, 40–80 days after budbreak depending on temperature, but can continue to the end of the season under conditions of mild temperatures and over-generous supplies of water and nitrogen. More commonly, especially for dry-farmed vines, water stress reduces shoot growth between flowering and veraison, and it may cease altogether later in the season. The shoot tips are sometimes trimmed but will often grow again from lateral buds.

Small flower clusters are apparent on the young shoots as buttons, and in the few weeks before flowering the stems and the individual flowers are obvious. Flowering takes place when the average daily temperatures are about 15–20 °C/59–68 °F and is followed by the so-called fruit-set process.

The next significant stage is that of veraison, about 40–50 days after fruit set, when the green, hard berries, which have grown to about half their final size and contain low concentrations of sugars but are high in organic acids, soften and change colour to either red-black or yellow-green, depending on the variety. The berries begin rapidly to build up sugar and accumulate carbohydrate reserves in the roots, trunk, and arms. (See ripening.)

The most appropriate date of harvest depends on the desired stage of ripeness for winemaking. It is earliest for sparkling wines, intermediate for table wines, and delayed for dessert wines and fortified wines. Harvest date may also be influenced by weather conditions and by disease levels (see bunch rots). Fruit ripening normally proceeds quickly in hot areas, with rapid increases in sugars and ph and a decline in acidity, especially malic acid. In cooler regions the rate of ripening is slower, and the fruit typically has lower sugars and higher acidity. Rainfall near harvest can cause problems due to berry splitting, botrytis, and other bunch-rotting fungi (see rot). After rain, there is normally a rush to harvest grapes while they are still sound.

Leaf fall, the least precisely marked of all the developmental stages, indicates the end of the season. Some leaves may fall off during the growing season, especially if the vine comes under stress, for example from drought, disease, or shade. A significant proportion of the leaves may also be removed by mechanical harvesting. With continued warm and sunny weather following harvest, the leaves remain healthy and are photosynthetically active in replacing carbohydrate reserves in the vine trunk and roots. Once these levels are built up, the vines often lose their green chlorophyll colour and turn yellow. The first frost or the low temperatures of the winter season usually cause leaf fall, and the vines are then in a dormant state. After pruning in winter, the vines are ready for the growth cycle to begin again.

See also vineyard annual cycle. R.E.S.

Galet, P., *General Viticulture* (2000).
Keller, M., 'Phenology and growth cycle', in *The Science of Grapevines* (3rd edn, 2020).

vine guards, plastic tubes which became popular internationally in the 1980s and 1990s to protect young vines. As well as protecting vines from wind, they also protect from herbicides and vineyard pests, especially rabbits, and reduce vine-training costs, although in warmer wine regions they can create an excessively hot microclimate around the young plant. The guards are normally in place for one year, sometimes two. Wine tourists now witness coloured vine guards as the most obvious feature of new plantings. R.E.S.

vine identification. See ampelography and dna profiling for details of these two very different methods of identifying different vine varieties.

vine improvement, a group of practices designed to improve vine planting material for the benefit of vineyard yield and the quality of the fruit and wine produced. This is currently focused on eliminating harmful virus diseases and also on genetic improvement by clonal selection. Some virus diseases such as leafroll can have dramatic effects on yield and wine quality and are transmitted by infected planting material. More recently there has been concern about fungal trunk disease infections, also spread by propagation. Clonal selection is a technique which, by identifying and selecting high-performance vines for propagation, can achieve both elimination of disease and genetic improvement. See also vine breeding.

Although virus diseases had affected European vines since the end of the 19th century, it took some time for preventive action to be taken on a national scale. The first attempt at controlling the quality of planting material in

France was made in 1944, when the Section de Contrôle des Bois et Plantes de Vigne was formed (its functions now subsumed within FranceAgriMer, the intermediary body between the French ministry of agriculture and the grape and wine sectors), charged with avoiding the spread of virus diseases and also with ensuring that all rootstocks used had sufficient resistance to PHYLLOXERA. Previously, NURSERIES had been free to propagate whichever vines they chose, with sometimes disastrous effects for their clients; instead they were encouraged to take healthy CUTTINGS from specially planted and disease-free MOTHER VINES.

In Germany there has been a high regard for the health of buds and ROOTSTOCK for GRAFTING, and rigorous clonal selection programmes and registration of CLONES has ensured high-quality planting material. Similar schemes operate in other European countries.

In non-European countries there has also been an awareness of the importance of quality control of propagation material. After the Second World War, the California wine industry created a model system for improving the quality of planting material. Research at the University of California at DAVIS had demonstrated the importance of virus diseases and had shown how they might be detected. A so-called 'clean rootstock program' was developed which aimed to distribute only virus-free cuttings to nurseries, using THERMOTHERAPY and INDEXING in particular to produce virus-free plants. This has subsequently become known as FOUNDATION PLANT SERVICES (FPS) and has distributed high-health vines, now produced by TISSUE CULTURE and improved virus testing, all around the world. Vine improvement began in Australia in the 1970s and in New Zealand in the 1980s, with such schemes becoming less centralized over time. In New Zealand, the Bragato Research Institute in Marlborough has adopted this role. R.E.S.

Galet, P., *General Viticulture* (2000).

Nicholas, P. R., 'Grapevine planting material', in P. R. Dry and B. G. Coombe (eds.), *Viticulture*, i: *Resources* (2nd edn, 2004).

vine management, a term embracing all management practices in the vineyard, including especially SOIL PREPARATION and DRAINAGE; PRUNING and CANOPY MANAGEMENT; use of FERTILIZERS, MULCHES, and COVER CROPS; TILLAGE and WEED CONTROL; use of FUNGICIDES and PESTICIDES; IRRIGATION; vine TRIMMING and LEAF REMOVAL; CROP THINNING to control YIELD; and HARVEST methods. See also VINEYARD MANAGEMENT COMPANY.

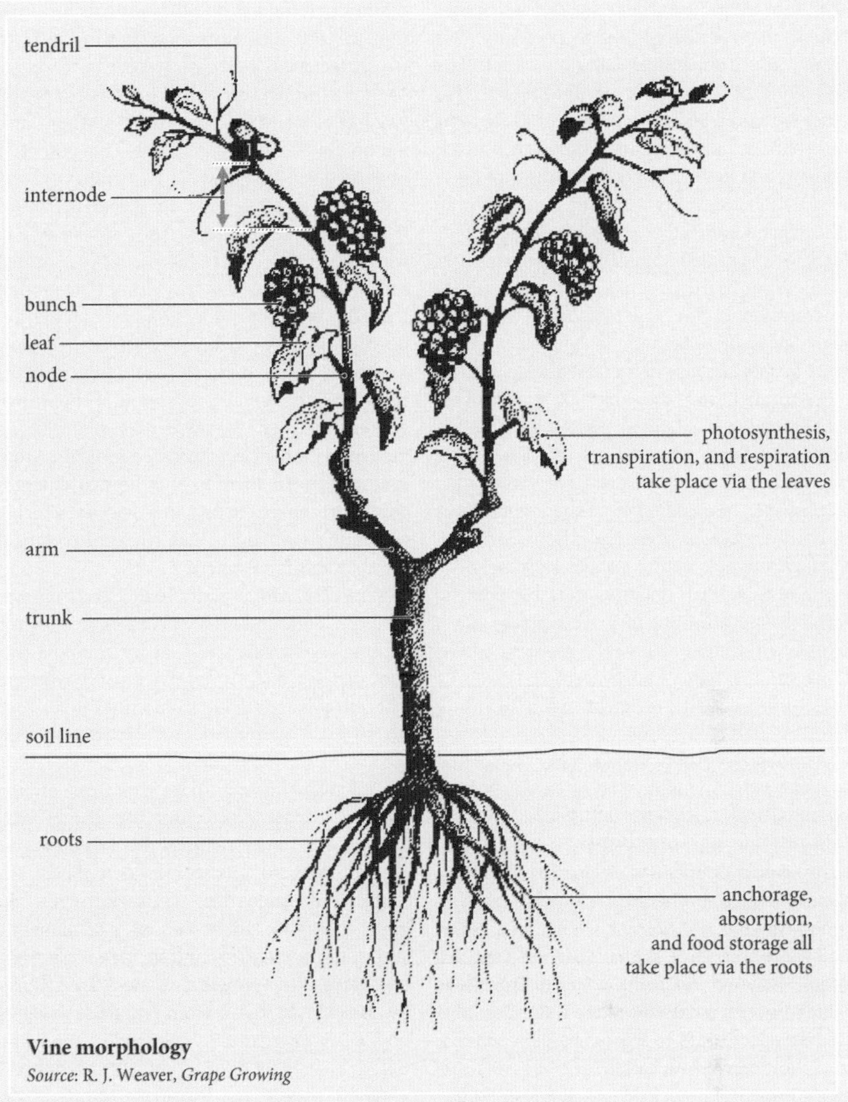

Vine morphology
Source: R. J. Weaver, *Grape Growing*

vine morphology is the study of the form and structure of the vine plant, as distinct from VINE PHYSIOLOGY, which is the study of its function. See ANTHER, ARM, BEARER, BERRY, BRUSH, BUD, BUNCH, CALYPTRA, CAMBIUM, CANE, CELL, CORDON, FLOWERS, GRAPE, HEAD, INFLORESCENCE, INTERNODE, LATERAL SHOOT, LEAF, NODE, OVARY, PEDICEL, PERICARP, PETIOLE, PHLOEM, POLLEN, PULP, ROOT, SHOOT, SPUR, STAMEN, STEM, STOMATA, TENDRIL, TRUNK, VINE, WATER SHOOT, and XYLEM. B.G.C.

vine nutrition, the supply of inorganic nutrients (also called mineral nutrients or nutrient elements) to the vine. Vines, like other plants, require the essential macronutrients NITROGEN, PHOSPHORUS, POTASSIUM, SULFUR, CALCIUM, MAGNESIUM, and chlorine (at concentrations greater than 1,000 ppm in their tissues), as well as the micronutrients MANGANESE, IRON, ZINC, COPPER, MOLYBDENUM, and BORON (at concentrations less than 1,000 ppm in their tissues). See MINERALS.

Among horticultural plants, the vine is regarded as having low nutrition requirements. A common but conservative recommendation for vineyards, depending on the soil and the grower's objectives for the wine to be made, would be 0–50 kg/ha nitrogen, 0–25 kg/ha phosphorus, and 0 to 100 kg/ha potassium. These low requirements reflect the low levels of nutrients that are removed from the vineyard each year by the grape HARVEST. (See SOIL NUTRIENTS.)

Measurements have been made in many countries of the amounts of elements contained in the grapes picked and also in the leaf litter and winter prunings. These values vary with region, variety, and yield but are in the range of 12–24 kg/ha of nitrogen, 3–6 kg/ha of phosphorus, and 25–40 kg/ha of potassium for a 10 t/ha crop. A general recommendation therefore would be to apply this amount of fertilizer if there were any doubt that the vineyard soil would be able to supply it. In general, SOIL TESTING before PLANTING can indicate any likely deficiencies. In mature vineyards, the standard procedure is to test either the leaves or the leaf stalks (PETIOLES) for their nutrient content and apply fertilizers only as the need is indicated. Grapevine leaves can show distinctive

symptoms of some nutrient deficiencies, but for others an experienced eye is necessary. For many crops, an annual addition of fertilizer will do little harm if it is not needed. For vines, however, such an addition is likely to be unnecessary and even wasteful since their needs are low, and there is always the danger of over-fertilization, especially with nitrogen, which can directly and indirectly reduce wine quality. Furthermore, repeated applications of nitrogen as ammonium-based or urea fertilizers leads to acidification of the soil over time. Similarly, high levels of potassium in soils can reduce wine quality because of increased wine PH.

Continued use of the same PARCEL of land for viticulture over extended periods of time reduces the levels of nutrients. Studies of old vineyard soils in Bordeaux have shown that fertility can be restored by heavy applications of ORGANIC MATTER, LIME, phosphorus, and potassium. Organic matter such as MULCHES, COMPOST, and animal manures can be used to fertilize vineyards, but they are typically lower in nutrient content and may be more expensive. However, they often improve SOIL STRUCTURE by their organic-matter content. Such forms of fertilizer are favoured for ORGANIC VITICULTURE.

Although research shows little connection between nutrition of the vine and a wine's quality or specific character, other than through influences on vine VIGOUR, there is a perception that soil directly affects wine character by giving wines a special chemical signature that is unique to the site. Recent studies in Canada and elsewhere have shown that the vineyard origin may be determined by analysis of a wine's trace elements, but there is not necessarily any relationship to wine character. See MINERALS for more explanation; see also SOIL AND WINE QUALITY and TERROIR. R.E.S. & R.E.W.

Danzer, K., et al., 'Classification of wine samples according to origin and grape varieties on the basis of inorganic and organic trace analyses', *American Laboratory* (Oct 1999), 26–34.

White, R. E., *Understanding Vineyard Soils* (2nd edn, 2015).

vine pests can make viticulture uneconomic and can have drastic effects on wine quality unless controlled. They include ANIMALS, INSECTS, and NEMATODES (while VINE DISEASES include the microorganisms BACTERIA, FUNGI, PHYTOPLASMA, VIROIDS, and VIRUSES).

The principal commercial wine grape VITIS VINIFERA is indigenous to Eurasia, while the majority of severe vine pests and diseases come principally from east and south-east North America. Their accidental introduction to Europe from the 1850s onwards had dramatic consequences for local viticulture. The fungal disease POWDERY MILDEW was bad enough, but fortunately a control was soon at hand; the insect pest PHYLLOXERA was not so easy to control, and for a period following its introduction in 1863 the entire French wine industry was threatened. Fortunately it was solved by GRAFTING *vinifera* vines on to ROOTSTOCKS derived from AMERICAN VINE SPECIES, which have natural resistance to phylloxera. This practice is now used worldwide.

In general, vine pests are easier to control than diseases, although the AGROCHEMICALS used to control insects (PESTICIDES) are among the most potent used in viticulture. The modern tendency is to depend less on pesticides and to develop strategies such as INTEGRATED PEST MANAGEMENT (see also BIOLOGICALS). Phylloxera is a threat to only a small proportion of the world's vineyards, as an overwhelming majority are grafted to rootstocks considered resistant. However, at present there is only limited chemical control of the insect pest MARGARODES, which is currently confined to a few vineyard regions of the southern hemisphere.

Vine pests can have dramatic effects on wine quality. At one end of the spectrum are the pests causing severe vine stress, as for example with root damage due to NEMATODES or phylloxera. This effect is frequently transient as it is a prelude to death and/or vine removal (see GRUBBING UP).

The following are some examples of how some pests can affect vines and reduce wine quality. Leaf area removal by ANTS, BEETLES, deer, kangaroos, LOCUSTS, MOTHS, rabbits, and SNAILS can jeopardize PHOTOSYNTHESIS and grape RIPENING. Leaves can also be damaged and photosynthesis reduced by LEAFHOPPERS and MITES. Vine growth and yield are reduced by attacks on roots from gophers, badgers, phylloxera, margarodes, nematodes, and squirrels, as well as by destruction of the trunk and arms by BORERS and TERMITES. Monkeys can cause significant damage to shoots, leaves, and fruit in JAPAN, as can elephants in Thailand. Damage to the grapes themselves by insects and BIRDS can lead to BUNCH ROTS, which can be spread by FRUIT FLY. Some pests can taint grapes, as for example the LADYBUG, or the honeydew of MEALYBUGS and SCALE. Last but not least is the very important role of pests in carrying (vectoring) diseases. The dreaded and lethal bacterial PIERCE'S DISEASE is spread by leafhoppers, as is the phytoplasma disease FLAVESCENCE DORÉE. Important VIRUS DISEASES that can substantially reduce wine quality and yield are spread by nematodes and mealybugs.

For more detail, see major entries under ANIMALS, BEETLES, BIRDS, DROSOPHILA, INSECT PESTS, MITES, NEMATODES, and PHYLLOXERA; other entries are to be found under the pests' common names. R.E.S.

vine physiological status, term often used to describe the condition of the vine. How the vine is responding to its environment is a most important consideration for the production of premium-quality wine, especially during the fruit RIPENING period, but its status during the preceding year may also affect YIELD. R.E.S.

vine physiology, the science of the function of the VINE, including the growth and development of the vine shoot and root systems, its fruiting, and the major physiological processes such as PHOTOSYNTHESIS, TRANSLOCATION, and TRANSPIRATION. Physiology is also concerned with controls on plant growth and development, including both environmental and internal control by HORMONES. Both VINE NUTRITION and degree of WATER STRESS are affected by the vineyard soil, and TEMPERATURE and SUNLIGHT are the most important climate influences.

The vine's physiology can be manipulated by vineyard management techniques to alter growth, yield, and quality. For example, decisions on TRAINING SYSTEMS and PRUNING levels will alter the light incident on leaves, thus affecting photosynthesis and sugar supply to the grapes during RIPENING. IRRIGATION is another important form of manipulation. The term VINE PHYSIOLOGICAL STATUS is often used to describe the condition of the vine, as for example the degree of water stress it is experiencing. Manipulating such conditions is the aim of the vineyard manager intent on maximizing yield and/or wine quality. R.E.S.

Carbonneau, A., et al., *Traité de la Vigne: Physiologie, Terroir, Culture* (3rd edn, 2020).

Keller, M., 'Phenology and growth cycle', in *The Science of Grapevines* (3rd edn, 2020).

vine products, the range of products produced from the vine. The GRAPEVINE is the world's most important fruit crop, and WINE and its brandy distillates are by far the most important of its products. Other products include RAISINS, TABLE GRAPES, GRAPE JUICE, GRAPE CONCENTRATE, VINEGAR, VERJUS, grapeseed oil, and RECTIFIED GRAPE MUST. There are other minor products: grapevine cuttings can be used for PROPAGATION or even occasionally for barbecue firewood; vine leaves are used in Middle Eastern and Greek cuisine and for wrapping certain cheeses; cosmetics based on grapevine products have been developed; and pharmaceutical companies have even started selling grape-derived RESVERATROL tablets with supposed HEALTH benefits. R.E.S. & J.E.H.

vine-pull schemes have been instituted in various parts of the world at different times, generally in response to a perceived wine SURPLUS.

In the late 1980s and early 1990s, smallholders in the south of France and Italy in particular took advantage of substantial financial inducements to abandon viticulture on all or part of their land in an effort to drain the European WINE LAKE. About 300,000 ha/741,000 acres of French vineyard and about 400,000 ha of Italian vineyard were ripped out between the late 1970s and 1991. France's total vineyard was reduced by a further 80,000 ha and Italy's by about 150,000 ha between 1991 and 1996, while a further 284,000 ha were ripped out in Spain and 126,000 ha in Portugal. In the following decade, the uptake was greatly reduced, with just 30,000 ha grubbed up, mainly in France.

As a result of the EU reforms of 2008, there were further financial incentives to grub up vines in much of Europe, but this time farmers were able to apply directly to the EU. As a consequence, 161,164 ha/398,244 acres of vines were grubbed up between 2008 and 2011, equivalent to 10% of the European vineyard area. During the same period, 111,364 ha/275,186 acres were grubbed up without the inducement of a subsidy. However, this has not necessarily resulted in a reduction in wine production. In SPAIN, for example, vineyard restructuring has increased yields despite the ripping out of 150,000 ha of vines.

Such schemes are not exclusive to the EU. An even more comprehensive vine-pull scheme was enacted within a single country, the Soviet Union, as part of GORBACHEV's attempts to curb alcohol consumption. Between 1985 and 1990, the total area under vine in the old USSR fell from more than 1.3 million ha/3.21 million acres to 880,000 ha/2.2 million acres.

Other national vine-pull schemes may be directed at particular types of vine in an effort to reduce production of certain wine types—in recent history usually wine of the most basic sort. Such schemes were applied in both ARGENTINA and NEW ZEALAND in the late 1980s, for example.

For details of the mechanics of pulling out vines and why a grower might do so, see GRUBBING UP.

vine removal. See GRUBBING UP.

vine spacing. See VINE DENSITY.

vine training, the process of establishing a vine framework in the required shape. It may begin in summer by tying down and TRIMMING growing shoots, followed by suitable winter PRUNING. Normally vines are trained to a supporting structure which may be as simple as a STAKE in the ground or a more complex TRELLIS SYSTEM made from wire and wood, metal, or concrete posts. Training is normally complete within the first two or three years of a vine's life and is well established before grape production begins. It will, however, take longer where vines are planted at wide distances apart and with complex trellis systems such as the TENDONE. Training normally consists of forming the TRUNK, the CORDONS or HEAD, and any ARMS required.

See under TRAINING SYSTEMS for more details of individual forms. R.E.S.

vine-training systems. See TRAINING SYSTEMS.

vine varieties, distinct types of vine within one species of the vine genus VITIS (see also BOTANICAL CLASSIFICATION). Different vine varieties produce different varieties of grape, so that the terms 'vine variety' and 'grape variety' are used almost interchangeably. Each variety of vine, or grape, may produce distinct and identifiable styles and flavours of wine. 'Vine variety' is *cépage* in French, *cepa* in Spanish, *Rebsorte* in German, *vitigno* in Italian, and *casta* in Portuguese. Professional botanists favour the term grapevine CULTIVARS.

All of the vine varieties we know today initially originated from WILD VINES. Domestication was made possible by propagating the best vines (see ORIGINS OF VINICULTURE) either by CUTTINGS or LAYERING (see PROPAGATION), thus producing genetically identical new plants. Afterwards, new vine varieties could originate from natural CROSSES between the vine varieties that had been selected, or between vine varieties and wild vines, or by selecting other wild vines.

Most important vine varieties used to produce wine are of the European vine species VITIS VINIFERA. A number of varieties of AMERICAN VINE SPECIES and their AMERICAN HYBRIDS have also been used to make wine, however, although many suffer a bad reputation because of the resultant wines' FOXY character (the dark-skinned NORTON is a notable exception). American species are also used as ROOTSTOCKS. Wine has also been made from a range of Asian vine varieties and from the FRENCH HYBRIDS.

It is clear that specific vine varieties were recognized in ancient GREECE and ROME, since some are already described in CLASSICAL TEXTS such as those of Pliny and Columella (see ANCIENT VINE VARIETIES). The extent to which the vine varieties of Europe originate from wild vines or were introduced is not known. Also, with the fall of the Roman Empire, cultivated vineyards were abandoned, and such varieties as were deliberately cultivated presumably interbred with local wild vines and native *vinifera*. The result of this intermixing over time is that many European regions have developed their own INDIGENOUS VARIETIES.

There are between 5,000 and 10,000 known varieties of *vinifera*. Ampelographers Pierre Viala and Victor Vermorel listed about 5,000 different varieties in their great seven-volume AMPELOGRAPHY published between 1901 and 1910. Many of these were synonyms, and Robinson, Harding, and Vouillamoz proposed a total of 1,368 varieties cultivated around the world for commercial wine production in 2012, although another 200 or so could now be added to that total. Thousands of other varieties exist in grape germplasm collections, but they are not cultivated for commercial bottling and sale. VINE IDENTIFICATION and the study of individual varieties' characteristics and aptitudes is a scientific activity known as ampelography, recently supplemented by DNA PROFILING.

Vine varieties are often named for the colour of their berries, with many French varieties, for example, coming in *noir* (black), *rouge* (red), *violet*, *rose* (pink), *gris* (grey-pink), *jaune* (yellow), *vert* (green), and *blanc* (white) hues. This book uses the convention of adopting a capital letter for each word in a vine variety's name (except prepositions), without quotation marks, even though 'Pinot Noir' would be botanically more correct for a cultivar name. Examples of MUTATIONS are Pinot Blanc and Pinot Gris, while Sauvignon Vert is a quite different variety from Sauvignon Blanc. See individual variety names for more details.

Varieties were classified and grouped into families by Levadoux, but DNA profiling is now shedding light on the true origin for many varieties and being harnessed to yield the pedigrees of both traditional and modern vine varieties. Varieties can be broadly grouped into three major botanical categories called PROLES, which are related to their geographical origins and to some extent their end use. Varieties can also be classified in more detail by their country or region of origin, although as some varieties have been planted widely throughout the world (see INTERNATIONAL VARIETIES) this distinction is becoming unclear.

Another classification is by end-product use, and so vine varieties may be described as being for wine, TABLE GRAPES, RAISINS, GRAPE JUICE, or ROOTSTOCKS (although some varieties, such as SULTANA, are in practice used for several of these). Among wine vine varieties, some are particularly well suited to different styles of wine: sparkling, fortified, sweet, or dry still wine, for example. Within each group there are varieties more likely to make notable, ageworthy wines and those suitable only for lower-value products.

Varieties themselves are often subdivided into various CLONES. While particular clones of many varieties have been selected through performance evaluation by CLONAL SELECTION, in many cases they cannot be separated by appearance.

See also NEW VARIETIES.

Most widely planted varieties

Of all vine varieties, remarkably few have achieved an international reputation, and most of these are French. Obvious examples of these international varieties include Cabernet Sauvignon, Pinot Noir, Syrah/Shiraz, Merlot, Chardonnay, Sauvignon Blanc, and Riesling.

Variety	Global area 1990		Global area 2000		Global area 2010		Global area 2016	
	ha	rank	ha	rank	ha	rank	ha	rank
Cabernet Sauvignon R	127,678	8	223,074	2	290,083	1	310,671	1
Merlot R	154,752	7	213,368	4	267,888	2	266,440	2
Tempranillo R	47,429	24	93,370	10	232,988	4	219,379	3
Airen W	476,396	1	387,978	1	252,364	3	203,801	4
Chardonnay W	69,282	13	145,543	5	199,743	5	201,649	5
Syrah R	35,086	36	102,490	8	185,117	6	181,185	6
Grenache R (Garnacha, Cannonau)	282,997	2	216,349	3	181,553	7	150,096	7
Sauvignon Blanc W	44,677	25	65,190	15	111,552	9	124,700	8
Trebbiano Toscano W	207,442	5	137,201	6	111,290	8	120,343	9
Pinot Noir R	41,539	30	68,810	16	98,623	10	105,480	10
Sangiovese R	98,946	11	68,877	13	78,030	13	73,464	11
Bobal R	106,149	10	100,128	9	80,120	12	59,189	12
Riesling W	52,164	21	43,316	23	50,014	18	54,106	13
Côt (Malbec)	17,263	54	26,285	37	38,158	23	52,233	14
Monastrell R (Mourvèdre)	108,213	9	76,304	12	69,742	14	51,930	15
Rkatsiteli W	280,569	3	67,354	14	58,641	16	51,374	16
Cabernet Franc R	39,619	32	48,595	19	53,008	17	49,309	17
Pinot Gris W	6,509	78	18,893	44	43,773	19	48,570	18
Carignan R (Mazuelo)	202,869	6	127,692	7	75,716	11	47,312	19
Macabeo W (Viura)	43,504	26	48,128	21	40,864	20	38,625	20

Source: Anderson, K., and Nelgen, S., *Which Winegrape Varieties are Grown Where? A Global Empirical Picture* (revised edn, 2020), updated January 2022.

As an increasing proportion of all wine is labelled VARIETALLY, there has been an increasing correlation between these most famous varieties and those which cover the greatest total area of vineyard land. Nevertheless an OIV report in 2017 shows that more of the Earth's surface is devoted to the TABLE GRAPE Kyoho than to any well-known wine grape.

The table shows the changing fortunes of the 20 most planted wine grape varieties in the world over a 20-year period, based on Kym Anderson's 2020 research.

Choice of variety

Vine-growers are rarely free to choose which vine variety to plant in a given vineyard. They may have acquired a planted vineyard in full production and cannot afford the crop loss involved in changing variety either by GRUBBING UP established vines or by FIELD GRAFTING a new variety on to the trunk and root system of the old one. Different varieties need different conditions of soil and climate. Cabernet Sauvignon simply will not ripen regularly in cool regions, for example.

In much of Europe, the varieties permitted are likely to be regulated. In France, for example, some of these restrictions can be traced back to the Middle Ages (see PINOT NOIR), but formalization took place from 1935 with the AOC laws which authorize only specified varieties for each CONTROLLED APPELLATION, distinguishing between principal and secondary varieties (see Appendix 1 for details). Similarly, some varieties were completely banned. For the production of more basic VIN DE TABLE, l'Institut des Vins de Consommation Courante decreed in 1953 for each viticultural region three classifications of varieties: recommended, authorized, and tolerated until eventual removal. These laws and those in other European countries have subsequently been overtaken by EU laws with the similar intent of allowing only specified varieties in regions or appellations. For discussion of these restrictions, see VINE VARIETIES, EFFECT ON WINE.

In the NEW WORLD, the choice of vine variety or varieties is often in practice determined by the style of wine that is eventually desired, many of them involving just one vine variety, typically sold as a VARIETAL wine. Mono-varietal PDO wines within Europe such as Beaujolais (Gamay), Sancerre (Sauvignon Blanc), and Barolo (Nebbiolo) are much less likely to state the variety on the label. Two or more complementary varieties are often blended, such as the productive and full-bodied Marsanne mixed with the lighter, rarer Roussanne for white HERMITAGE, or Sémillon, Sauvignon Blanc, and Muscadelle in SAUTERNES, and Pinot Noir, Chardonnay, and Pinot Meunier in CHAMPAGNE. Even more complex blends of varieties are common in CHÂTEAUNEUF-DU-PAPE. However, blends are also widely produced in many other wine regions but without the constraints of regulation and with more freedom to experiment.

J.R., J.E.H. & J.V.

Anderson, K., and Nelgen, S., *Which Wine Grape Varieties Are Grown Where?* www.adelaide.edu.au/wine-econ/databases/winegrapes-front-1213.pdf.

Galet, P., *Dictionnaire encyclopédique des cépages* (2nd edn, 2015).

Mullins, M. G., et al., *Biology of the Grapevine* (1992).

OIV, 'Distribution of the world's grapevine varieties' (2017). www.oiv.int/public/medias/5888/en-distribution-of-the-worlds-grapevine-varieties.pdf.

Robinson, J., et al., *Wine Grapes: A Complete Guide to 1,368 Vine Varieties, including Their Origins and Flavours* (2012).

van Leeuwen, C., 'Choix du cépage en fonction du terroir dans le Bordelais', in *Un raisin de qualité: de la vigne à la cuve*, n° Hors Série du *Journal International des Sciences de la Vigne et du Vin* (2001), 97–102.

vine varieties, effect on wine. Of all the factors such as SOIL, CLIMATE, VITICULTURE, and detailed WINEMAKING techniques which have an effect on wine quality, vine variety is probably the easiest to detect in a BLIND TASTING. The colour of the grapes' skin determines what COLOUR of wine can be produced: red wine can be produced only from dark-skinned grapes. Only grape varieties which ripen readily and/or are prone to NOBLE ROT are likely to produce good SWEET WINES, while only those with high levels of natural ACIDITY are likely to produce good SPARKLING WINES. But, even more important for blind tasting, individual grape varieties tend to produce wines with identifiably different flavours. In very general terms, it is a mark of quality in a vine variety that it is capable of producing wines with distinguished and distinctive flavours, even if those flavours are heavily influenced by weather, TERROIR, vineyard practices, and winemaking. Lesser vine varieties tend to produce wines that are neutral and undistinguished, however promising the vineyard site. However, some more neutral varieties are better able to reveal other influences such as their place of origin or TERROIR or aspects of WINEMAKING (e.g. LEES AGEING), or they may be distinguished by their TEXTURE or STRUCTURE.

When more than one vine variety is used to produce a single wine, it is important that the wines produced by those varieties are complementary. Cabernet Sauvignon tends to blend well with wines that have more luscious fruit such as Merlot or warm-climate Syrah/Shiraz, for example, while the weight of Sémillon is a good foil for the aroma and acidity of Sauvignon Blanc. Another French example widely copied elsewhere is Grenache with Syrah and, possibly, Mourvèdre.

Wine quality is maximized if the vine variety or vine varieties are well suited to the site, in terms of climate, soil, ROOTSTOCK, VINE DENSITY, TRAINING SYSTEM, PRUNING regime, and other viticultural methods. When a new vineyard is planted in a region where the choice of variety is not regulated by local wine laws, the variety is often selected on the basis of climatic similarity with an existing wine region (see HOMOCLIMES), taking soil and TOPOGRAPHY into consideration, although combinations such as Coonawarra for Cabernet Sauvignon or Oregon for Pinot Noir are now well established. In parts of Europe, on the other hand, the matching of vine variety to site, or even whole regions, is so entrenched (see VINE VARIETIES above) as to be restrictive, particularly at a time when CLIMATE CHANGE may well require the planting of more heat- and drought-tolerant varieties.

In BORDEAUX, for example, where Merlot and Cabernet Sauvignon have long dominated, permission was granted by the INAO in late 2020 to plant six new varieties predicted to be more resilient to the challenges of climate change: two white varieties, ALVARINHO and LILIORILA; and four reds, ARINARNOA, CASTETS, MARSELAN, and TOURIGA NACIONAL. These recommendations follow ten years of trials with 52 varieties from seven countries, and there are strict limits on their use. (See VIFA for more detail.)

Varieties vary in the range of environments they can tolerate. Chardonnay, for example, is extremely versatile and can produce good wine in climates which vary from the coolness of Chablis to the hot interior valleys of California. Varieties such as Pinot Noir and Nebbiolo, on the other hand, appear to be extremely fastidious. See also CLIMATE AND WINE QUALITY.

European regulations for CONTROLLED APPELLATIONS, which typically disapprove of citing vine varieties on the label, are predicated on the belief that for every appellation there is an ideal vine variety or blend of varieties, or that the character of the appellation is stronger than that of any vine variety. While this is an attractive proposition (and it is certainly true that, for example, the appellation of a red bordeaux or a white Alsace wine is often more strongly identifiable than any single vine variety), it seems questionable for most wine regions. R.E.S. & J.E.H.

Galet, P., *General Viticulture* (2000).

Robinson, J., et al., *Wine Grapes: A Complete Guide to 1,368 Vine Varieties, Including Their Origins and Flavours* (2012).

vineyard, name given to the agricultural field where grapevines are grown.

The contrast in connotations between the words 'vineyard' and 'field' illustrates something of the special nature of vines as a crop. This may be partly connected with the symbolism of, and pleasures associated with, wine, but it is also a function of the aesthetic appeal of vineyards in all seasons, whether the increasingly luxuriant green CANOPY of spring and summer, the flame-coloured leaves of autumn (even if these invariably indicate the presence of VIRUS DISEASE or some other stress), or the rows of poignant black stumps in winter. The beauty of vineyards and vines plays an important part in wine TOURISM; it is difficult to imagine substantial numbers of people making a pilgrimage to a region famous for any other agricultural crop.

In most parts of the world, the vineyard is a well-defined entity, generally demarcated by the borders of the straight rows. *Vignoble* is a common French term for a vineyard at all quality levels. In Bordeaux, and elsewhere, CRU may be used synonymously with a top-quality, often classified, vineyard, while in Burgundy the terms CLIMAT or, in the case of a walled vineyard, CLOS are more common. In Italy the terms cru, VIGNA, SORÌ, and RONCO are all used. Recognition of single vineyards is less developed in Spain although VINO DE PAGO is a classification for single-estate wines.

In an agricultural sense, vineyards are typically monocultures, with vines the only plants growing apart from COVER CROPS and WEEDS. Less frequently, however, vineyards are grown intermingled with other crops, the so-called *coltura promiscua* that was once the norm in much of central Italy. In the VINHO VERDE region of northern Portugal, vines are still occasionally grown as borders around other fields which may contain field crops or orchards. Originally trained to wires attached to bordering trees, the vines of Vinho Verde are nowadays more commonly trained on wooden or metal supports, known as *ramada*, although they may still surround fields in which other crops are grown. There is growing interest worldwide in finding ways to increase vineyard biodiversity and protect wildlife. In addition to cover crops, trees and hedges may be planted around, occasionally within, vineyards, an approach sometimes referred to as agroforestry. Trees may provide a crop; they may help protect vines from heat or FROST; and they can contribute significantly to the vineyard ECOSYSTEM. See also ARBOREAL VITICULTURE.

Any one vineyard may be made up of smaller units, PARCELS, or blocks, which may contain different vine varieties, CLONES, ROOTSTOCKS, or vines of different ages. Sometimes fields are separated by headlands, hedges or drainage ditches, for example, or they may be contiguous. Even relatively small vineyards are rarely homogeneous in terms of SOIL and TOPOGRAPHY. Soils in particular may vary considerably within one single vineyard (see VOUGEOT or MONTRACHET, for example).

Vineyards vary in size, depending on many factors. Owing to fragmentation of vineyards by inheritance, some vineyard owners in BURGUNDY may lay claim to only a few rows often indistinguishable to outsiders from the adjacent vines. At the other end of the scale in the NEW WORLD, there are often large corporate vineyards. One of the world's largest vineyards is the 2,800-ha/6,920-acre San Bernabe ranch in the Salinas Valley of MONTEREY in California. While relatively rare, such extensive vineyards are also found in Europe, for example Plantaze's 2,300-ha/5,700-acre vineyard in MONTENEGRO.

Some vineyards are particularly famous for their wine because of their specific combination of VINE VARIETY, clone, rootstock, and climate conditions, which can be distinguished at the various levels of MACROCLIMATE, MESOCLIMATE, and MICROCLIMATE. Of particular importance are the soil conditions, which, together with TOPOGRAPHY, mesoclimate, and CANOPY MICROCLIMATE, constitute what the French (and others) call TERROIR. See under each of these entries for a discussion of their relative contribution. For example, a feature of the famous Bordeaux PREMIERS CRUS is that, as well as producing great wine in good years, they are able to do well in acknowledged low-quality years because the terroir allows the vine to ripen the fruit adequately when other, less exalted vineyards cannot.

See also HILLSIDE VINEYARDS, PLANTING, VINEYARD ANNUAL CYCLE, and VINEYARD SITE SELECTION. J.E.H. & R.E.S.

vineyard annual cycle. The march of the seasons through the year dictates the work to be done in vineyards (see VINE GROWTH CYCLE). Spring is the time of BUDBREAK, and early TILLAGE and SPRAYING must be done. Early spring is also the common time for PLANTING vineyards, once the danger of FROST is past. As the temperatures rise, the vine shoots grow more rapidly, and FLOWERING takes place in early summer. This can be a busy period, as often FUNGICIDE sprays are to be applied and the first SHOOT POSITIONING is carried out. Soon after FRUIT SET is the time for the second shoot positioning. In those vineyards of the world where IRRIGATION is practised, the first applications of water are often made around this time and may continue up to the time of harvest. About this period the NURSERIES are busy BENCH GRAFTING, and it is also the time for FIELD GRAFTING. As the summer progresses, TRIMMING is carried out, typically before VERAISON. Many vine-growers are involved with further spraying of AGROCHEMICALS and often continued tillage and mowing (see COVER CROPS). Depending on the vine variety and region, the HARVEST may be in early, mid, or late summer or sometimes in the autumn. Whenever it occurs, it is one of the busiest periods in the vineyard, often involving SAMPLING to test grape RIPENESS before the harvest itself. Depending on the spread of varieties, the harvest may be brief or protracted, but few other jobs are attended to in the vineyard at this time. The period immediately following harvest is busy in the wineries but not so in the vineyards, and vineyard workers and viticulturists often take their annual leave then. This is also the common time for soil RIPPING and for maintenance of machinery and TRELLIS SYSTEMS. Once the leaves fall, the serious business of PRUNING begins; depending on the scale of operations, this may continue right up until budbreak. This is also the time when CUTTINGS are taken for PROPAGATION. R.E.S.

vineyard design, important component of vineyard planning before vineyard planting (except in traditional European wine regions where VINE SPACING, VINE VARIETY, and ROOTSTOCK may well be prescribed). In a new vineyard, normally the first step is a topographic survey, followed by a soil survey and SOIL MAPPING, today in some instances using GLOBAL NAVIGATION SATELLITE SYSTEM technology. Based on this important information, block layout and IRRIGATION design proceeds, and finally on a block-by-block basis decisions are made about variety, CLONE, rootstock, row and vine spacing, and TRAINING SYSTEM. In this way, the vineyard will optimize use of local resources and the potential of the site. R.E.S.

vineyard management company, a business which executes all viticultural operations, from land development and VINE MANAGEMENT to fruit sales, and which can provide all necessary equipment, machinery, and LABOUR. What would become the first such company began in the Napa Valley in 1945 as a general agricultural management company for orchards. Since then, vineyard management companies have become specialized and often employ trained viticulturists to implement up-to-date best practices for pest and disease management, nutrient applications (see VINE NUTRITION), IRRIGATION solutions, and CANOPY MANAGEMENT. These companies are particularly important in the US, especially where people outside of the wine trade invest in vineyard land. Examples of this increasingly important business structure can also be found in both Australia and New Zealand. S.C.-J.

vineyard site selection can be the single most important aspect of grape production, even if it is not always appreciated as such. If, for example, the new vineyard is in a cool region, then the TOPOGRAPHY of the site may be a critical factor in avoiding FROST DAMAGE, and the ASPECT chosen may be vital to ensure adequate warmth for RIPENING (see HILLSIDE VINEYARDS). In those parts of Europe where vineyards have been in existence for centuries, another important consideration may be whether or not it qualifies for a certain CONTROLLED APPELLATION.

Vineyard site selection embraces more than just choosing the vineyard location, as the decision will affect the vineyard's YIELD, the quality of the wine produced, and therefore the vineyard's long-term profitability. The site's regional climate, or MACROCLIMATE, for example, determines by virtue primarily of temperature and sunshine hours which VINE VARIETIES should be grown and the resulting likely wine style and quality. For example, lower temperatures produce more delicately flavoured wines, and hot climates produce wines relatively high in alcohol. (Such effects are discussed under CLIMATE AND WINE QUALITY.) Vineyards are often planted at higher ELEVATIONS to take advantage of lower temperatures, increasingly so in regions affected by CLIMATE CHANGE. The site selection process might include evaluating climatic data from distinguished wine regions either locally or internationally in an attempt to locate similar climates, or HOMOCLIMES, as has been done with considerable success in Australia. With its enormous range of LATITUDE and elevation, Chile has a greater opportunity than most countries to match climates.

Modern science is creating new methods of vineyard site selection, especially based on GEOGRAPHICAL INFORMATION SYSTEMS (GIS) and digitized databases. Researchers at VIRGINIA TECH in the US, for example, identified sites with the greatest potential by overlaying maps of the same area according to different selection criteria such as elevation and land use, slope and aspect, and WINTER FREEZE risk. Such approaches provide a useful alternative to the more expensive trial-and-error method more usually employed.

Similarly, rainfall and humidity affect the likelihood of many VINE DISEASES, especially important fungal diseases such as POWDERY MILDEW, DOWNY MILDEW, and BOTRYTIS BUNCH ROT. The likelihood of these diseases can be estimated by reference to climate records. In addition, the threat of NEMATODES may be evaluated by knowledge of indigenous types or of the previous crops grown on the site. It may even be possible to avoid the introduction of PHYLLOXERA and other pests and diseases by creating a local QUARANTINE. If phylloxera and nematodes are considered a likely problem, the appropriate ROOTSTOCKS can be used.

The site climate, or MESOCLIMATE, affects, for example, the extent to which cold air drains away and the likelihood of spring and autumn FROST. A site's proximity to bodies of water such as lakes (see LAKE EFFECT) can be important in providing protection from injury due to particularly low temperatures, as in NEW YORK State and SWITZERLAND. These attributes depend on local TOPOGRAPHY.

The balance between RAINFALL and EVAPORATION indicates the likelihood of DROUGHT and, for some regions at least, whether IRRIGATION is desirable and the amount of water required. In many parts of the world, availability of high-quality water for irrigation is an essential factor in site selection. This may involve locating vineyards near streams or rivers; with access to underground (artesian) water; or on sites with opportunities to build dams or reservoirs.

SOIL conditions present at the site will determine vineyard VIGOUR, with deep, fertile soils, for example, leading to vigorous growth, the possibility of high YIELDS, and the concomitant need to manage the problems this creates (see CANOPY MANAGEMENT). Premium-quality vineyards are typically found on soils with low water-holding capacity and low SOIL FERTILITY. Site selection normally involves a process of SOIL MAPPING and physical and chemical analysis of soil samples. This allows potential problems such as poor DRAINAGE or SOIL ACIDITY to be treated appropriately before the vineyard is planted. Knowledge of soil depth indicates likely vine vigour.

Vegetation growing at the site (and the productivity and quality of other agricultural crops grown in the region) can be used as an indicator of the vineyard performance. The types of trees present give guidance as to the soil properties, and their size for their age indicates soil fertility and water supply.

Not all the important features of potential vineyard sites are natural ones. Frontage to busy roads is essential if retail sales are expected from the vineyard site. Good communications with markets and proximity to a supply of LABOUR can also be significant. The performance and reputation of other vineyards in the area are also commercially important. R.E.S.

Smart, R. E., and Dry, P. R., 'Vineyard site selection', in Dry, P. R., and Coombe, B. G. (eds), *Viticulture*, i: *Resources* (2nd edn, 2004).
www.grapes.extension.org/vineyard-site-selection/

vineyard weather stations contain a number of electronic instruments to measure the climate within a vineyard. Normally they comprise sensors for sunshine, air and soil temperatures, wind speed and direction, humidity, rainfall, leaf wetness, and occasionally EVAPORATION. Data are stored in a data logger which may be downloaded to a laptop or phone or remotely interrogated by a computer via the internet. Such weather stations are used primarily for disease prediction, especially for fungal diseases such as DOWNY MILDEW and POWDERY MILDEW, and also for predicting vine PHENOLOGY. R.E.S.

vin gris is not, happily, a grey wine but a pink wine that is usually decidedly paler than most ROSÉ, made exactly as a white wine from dark-skinned grapes and therefore without any MACERATION. No rules govern the term *vin gris*, but a wine labelled **gris de gris** must be made from lightly tinted grape varieties described as *gris* such as GRENACHE GRIS or Grolleau Gris.

In France, where it is a speciality of the Côtes de TOUL in the north-east and in certain parts of the LOIRE, *vin gris* is usually made from PRESSING, but not macerating, dark-skinned grapes, often Gamay, which rarely ripen sufficiently to produce a deeply coloured red. It is also made in the Midi, notably by Castel beside the saltpans of the Camargue, where care is needed to tint rather than dye the resultant wine. The term is also occasionally encountered outside Europe—although BLUSH wines are extremely similar to, if almost invariably sweeter than, *gris* wines. See also SCHILLERWEIN and other German light pinks.

The style is particularly popular in Morocco, which produces gris with an orangey-pink hue, mainly from traditional varieties such as Cinsaut and Grenache Gris but also from Merlot and Cabernet Sauvignon. Moroccan Gris de Boulaouane is one of CASTEL's French supermarket staples.

Vinhão, official Portuguese and local MINHO name of the dark-skinned grape SOUSÃO.

vinho, Portuguese for 'wine', **vinho** is how Portugal's WINE WITHOUT GEOGRAPHICAL INDICATION is described on the label.

Vinho de Talha, introduced in 2010 for new-wave bottled wines from the ALENTEJO made in TALHA, fermentation vessels typically made of clay, sometimes CONCRETE. Grapes must be destemmed and wines must remain in talha on skins until at least 11 November (St Martin's Day in the year of harvest, when talhas were traditionally first tapped). Grapes must be sourced from (and permitted by) Alentejo's eight DOC subregions. In 2020 Vinho de Talha DOC wines represented 0.1% of Alentejo's production. S.A.

White, P.J., *Talha Tales: Portugal's Ancient Answer to Amphora Wines* (2022).
vinhodetalha.vinhosdoalentejo.pt

Vinho Regional, second tier of designated wine regions in Portugal. Although the new term Indicação Geográfica Protegida (IGP), sometimes shortened to Indicação Geográfica (IG), meaning Protected Geographical Indication (PGI), has been introduced since the EU wine market reforms of 2008, most Portuguese regions have chosen to keep the old denomination Vinho Regional (VR).

These large regions covering entire provinces—MINHO, TRANSMONTANO, DURIENSE, Beira Atlântico, Terras da Beira (see BEIRAS), Terras do DÃO, TEJO, LISBOA, Alentejano for ALENTEJO, PENÍNSULA DE SETÚBAL, ALGARVE, and Terras Madeirenses for MADEIRA—allow greater flexibility in terms of permitted grape varieties, YIELDS, and ageing requirements. The Vinho Regional denomination is therefore popular with innovative winemakers wishing to bottle relatively young wines or blend Portuguese and INTERNATIONAL VARIETIES. In the centre and south of the country (Lisboa, Tejo, Península de Setúbal, and the Alentejo), producers are largely ignoring the DOCs in favour of Vinho Regional. S.A.

Vinho Verde, large DOC in north-west PORTUGAL known for its distinctively light, fresh wines and some gastronomic top-tier whites. Vinho Verde originated as a rough-and-ready local wine on a domestic scale. Following fermentation in open stone LAGARES, the wine would be run off into CASK where the secondary MALOLACTIC CONVERSION produced carbon dioxide. This was retained in the wine, giving it a slight sparkle. Huge-volume BRANDS are typically widely sourced, slightly sweet, spritzy (carbonated), NON-VINTAGE blends for early consumption (*vinho verde* means 'green wine', a reference to the youthful state in which wines were customarily sold). However, since the 1980s a shift towards better viticultural practices and more PROTECTIVE WINEMAKING has challenged the old stereotype, resulting in a middle tier of fruitier wines and a top tier of dry, complex wines (the latter typically subregional VARIETAL wines). The region's verdant coastal strip (known as the Costa Verde or Green Coast) extends from Vale da Cambra south of the river DOURO to the river Minho that forms the frontier with Spain over 130 km/80 miles to the north (see PORTUGAL map). The big brands represent most of production where rain-bearing westerly winds from the Atlantic support intensive cultivation on its GRANITIC soils. These fertile soils extend inland, along the rivers which criss-cross the region and act as conduits for tempering ocean winds.

In 2019/20, 16,000 growers (including 600 bottling their own wines) cultivated 16,232 ha/40,100 acres under vine for DOC production totalling 787,948 hl/20,815,384 gal (83% white, 12% red, 5% rosé). Some growers' plots are little bigger than a suburban back garden. To make the most of these small plots, vines were traditionally grown high above the ground around stakes or trees (known as *uveira* or *vinha de enforcado*) or on PERGOLAS (known as *ramadas* or *latadas*) built on stout granite posts up to 4 m/13 ft high, leaving space for other crops underneath. Similarly, farmers trained vines on pergolas around the perimeters of fields planted to corn (once the region's biggest crop). These high-trained vines also helped to reduce the risk of GREY ROT, which is endemic during the warm, damp growing season; average annual RAINFALL is as high as 1,500 mm/59 in. However, this tradition of polyculture, which remained embedded well into the last century, was conducive neither to MECHANIZATION nor to quality, both of which had become critical to making economically viable wine once the Portuguese wine industry entered a more competitive phase following the country's accession to the EU. Vineyards planted (or restructured) since the 1990s are on lower TRAINING SYSTEMS, resulting in riper, healthier grapes. At the same time, with ruthless CANOPY MANAGEMENT and grape selection a handful of young guns are making interesting small-batch wines from vines trained the old-fashioned way. Increased professionalism in the vineyard has been mirrored in winemaking. Since the 1980s, the average ALCOHOLIC STRENGTH has increased from 9–10% to 11–12% without sacrificing the region's signature freshness.

The Vinho Verde DOC is officially divided into nine subregions: Amarante, Ave, Baião, Basto, Cávado, LIMA, MONÇÃO E MELGAÇO, Paiva, and Sousa. Monção e Melgaço on the Spanish border produces one of the best but least typical Vinhos Verdes from the ALVARINHO grape, the wines up to 13% alcohol. Further south along the river Lima around the towns of Braga, Barcelos, and Guimarães, the dominant grape varieties are LOUREIRO (which thrives in the LIMA subregion), TRAJADURA, and Pedernã (ARINTO). Inland, in Amarante, AZAL shows promise, while in the Baião subregion bordering the Douro AVESSO is gaining ground, producing a slightly fuller style of wine in a warmer, drier climate.

Basic Vinhos Verdes must be 8–11.5% alcohol so more potent basic wines are sold as VINHO REGIONAL MINHO. Vinho Verde labelled with a single variety, subregion, or quality level (Escolha, Grande Escolha, Superior, Colheita Selecionada) have different (generally higher) minimum alcohol levels and are subject only to a maximum POTENTIAL ALCOHOL of 14%. Since 1999 the DOC includes sparkling wines (labelled ESPUMANTE) made by the TRADITIONAL METHOD and bottled-aged for at least nine months.

Until the 1980s, Vinho Verde was predominantly red, made in a naturally fizzy, acidic, bone-dry style from red grapes such as Vinhão, Alvarelhão, and Espadeiro. Examples still exist and are prized locally, but little leaves northern Portugal. Ambitious estates have pushed the boundaries with Vinhão, making deeper-fruited, still reds, sometimes OAK-AGED or even blended with Alvarinho to tame the TANNINS. Rosés (on the increase) and modish GLOU-GLOU styles made from a wider range of grape varieties seem a better fit for the TERROIR.

See also MINHO. S.A.

de Castro, R., 'The viticulture of Vinho Verde: the early days and from the turn of the century to the present', in Fundação Francisco Girão, *Francisco Girão: An Innovator in Viticulture in the North of Portugal* (vol. II, 2011).

Mayson, R. J., *The Wines of Portugal* (2020).

Woolf, S. J., and Opaz, R., *Foot Trodden: Portugal and the Wines That Time Forgot* (2021).

www.vinhoverde.pt

viniculture. While some use this term interchangeably with VITICULTURE, this book uses it to denote both vine-growing and a culture of wine drinking.

vinifera. See VITIS VINIFERA.

vinification, the practical art of transforming grapes into wine. In its widest sense, it is synonymous with WINEMAKING, but strictly speaking it encompasses only those processes which take place in the winery up to the point at which the ÉLEVAGE of the new wine begins. See also OENOLOGY.

vin jaune, meaning literally 'yellow wine' in French (not to be confused with ORANGE WINE), extraordinary style of wine made in France, mainly in the JURA region, using a technique similar to that used for SHERRY but without FORTIFICATION.

All Jura areas make a *vin jaune*, but the most famous is CHÂTEAU-CHALON. The wine must be made from the signature local white grape variety SAVAGNIN, grown ideally on grey MARL. The grapes are picked well ripened, ideally at not more than 13.5% POTENTIAL ALCOHOL, to allow for an increase during the ageing process, and are fermented as normal. The wine is then put into old 228-l/60-gal casks usually not quite filled so that the local benevolent FILM-FORMING YEAST, called here the *voile* or veil, can develop on the surface. It is similar to the FLOR which is responsible for FINO sherries but can develop at a lower ALCOHOLIC STRENGTH, and a much thinner layer, coloured grey, is considered the best. The ageing 'cellars' (which may be above or below ground) are ventilated deliberately to allow temperature fluctuations during which the activity of the *voile* will change. The presence of the veil prevents severe OXIDATION, but the important factor in making *vin jaune* is that the wine is left in cask for at least five years, untouched other than to allow regular sampling to check the amount of ETHANAL (a crucial compound for the taste of *vin jaune*) and for a dangerous rise in VOLATILE ACIDS. It may not be bottled for a full six years and three months after the harvest. Inoculation or seeding of yeasts to form the *voile* for Savagnin wines was introduced in the 1970s, and today this is used by some producers but is disapproved of by purists who believe that natural methods produce a better wine and are reliable if 'cellar' conditions are right and barrels have previously held wine aged under the *voile*.

The finest *vin jaune* from the best vintages will last for 50 years or more in its distinctive 62-cl *clavelin* bottle (the amount of wine left after keeping a litre in a cask for six years, supposedly). Research in the 1990s showed that the compound SOTOLON develops in bottle, providing the distinct spicy, fenugreek or light 'curry' flavours in *vin jaune*. The wine should be served at cellar temperature or warmer, and the bottle should be opened well in advance. The wine may be drunk with all sorts of savoury dishes, particularly chicken cooked in the wine itself, a classic dish, and the local Comté cheese.

A similar wine, called *vin de voile*, is made by at least one producer in GAILLAC. Other isolated French producers are also experimenting, as are some Australian producers growing Savagnin. W.L.

Vínland. Driven westward by overpopulation in the second half of the 9th century, the Scandinavians colonized Iceland, then Greenland, then finally, a century later as some sources tell us, Vínland, 'Wine Land', which must have been on the east coast of America.

Two sagas—Grenlinga Saga, the 'Saga of the Greenlanders', composed in the late 12th century, and Eirik's Saga, dated mid 13th century—give accounts of the discovery of Vínland, where wild vines, wheat, grassland, and game are found.

Scholars do not agree on the precise location of Vínland. The sagas do not give clues, and, although archaeologists have found what appear to be traces of Norse settlements on the east coast of America, the evidence is inconclusive. Besides, the climate was warmer around 1000 CE than now (hence the colonization of Greenland; see CLIMATE CHANGE) so that vines could survive further north.

The sagas were written from oral accounts many generations after the actual events. Even though the stories told in the sagas differ in some respects, they are not fantasy. An earlier and unrelated source supports the existence of Vínland. Around 1075 Adam of Bremen wrote a history of the archbishopric of Bremen and Hamburg, which until 1104 included the Scandinavian countries. Adam travelled to the royal court of Denmark, where King Svein Ulfsson, nephew of King Canute, tells him that Vínland has wild vines, which make excellent wine. So were the first winemakers in America Norse colonists? If they were, the wine must have been made not from the European VITIS VINIFERA but from native AMERICAN VINE SPECIES, almost certainly VITIS LABRUSCA, which grows wild on the eastern coast of the United States. H.M.W.

Jones, G., *The Norse Atlantic Saga: Being the Norse Voyages of Discovery and Settlement to Iceland, Greenland, America* (1964).

Magnusson, M., and Pálsson, H., *The Vínland Sagas* (1965).

Sigurdsson, G., 'The quest for Vinland in saga scholarship', in W. F. Fitzhugh and E. I. Ward (eds.), *Vikings: The North Atlantic Saga* (2000), 232–7.

vin muté, wine that has undergone MUTAGE.

vino, Italian and Spanish for 'wine' and, colloquially and unfairly, an English name for basic quaffing wine, or PLONK. In Italy and Spain, the term has replaced VINO DA TAVOLA and VINO DE MESA respectively as the most basic level of wine, WINE WITHOUT GEOGRAPHICAL INDICATION.

vino da meditazione, unofficial Italian category of wines considered too complex (see COMPLEXITY) but often simply too alcoholic and/or sweet to drink with food. Such wines, many of them extra strong and/or sweet because they are DRIED-GRAPE WINES, are probably best sipped meditatively after a meal.

vino da tavola, Italian for TABLE WINE, was the official EU category denoting the lowest of the vinous low until 2009 when it was replaced with VINO. It also played a key role in the transformation of Italian wines in the late 20th century. Historically the great majority of each Italian wine harvest qualified as basic Vino da Tavola, but the designation was for a period worn as a badge of honour by some of the finest, and most expensive, wines produced in Italy but that did not conform to the DOC laws of the time.

These new **vini da tavola** were born in the early 1970s with the commercial debut of Tignanello and SASSICAIA, both marketed by the Florentine house of ANTINORI. Although the wines were produced in different geographical zones (CHIANTI CLASSICO and BOLGHERI respectively) and from different grape varieties (a predominance of Sangiovese and Cabernet Sauvignon respectively), they shared four significant characteristics that were to mark the evolution of this category of wines. They both represented an attempt to give more BODY, intensity, and longevity to Tuscan red wines.

Unlike the prevailing Tuscan red-wine norm, these blends excluded white grapes. Non-traditional, non-Italian varieties were used in both blends (from 1975 when Tignanello substituted Cabernet Sauvignon for the native CANAIOLO). And, in a move that was to delight French COOPERS, small oak barrels, principally of French origin, were used for the BARREL AGEING of both wines. This latter innovation was a radical break with the traditional practice of using large casks of Slavonian oak and marked a general movement towards an international style. The move was not welcomed by all in the domestic market and forced Antinori to seek a wider international public for the wines.

The *vini da tavola* were born out of frustration with the DOC laws that came into practice in the late 1960s. These laws enshrined the practices of low quality and high quantity that prevailed in Italy in the post-war years, so producers trying to pursue a quality route found their way blocked by absurd regulations. In Chianti, for instance, producers were compelled by DOC laws to add at least 10% white grapes to their blend. Any producer wishing to produce a superior red wine had to ignore this stipulation. Rather than do battle, they stepped outside the legal framework at the urging of Italian wine journalist Luigi VERONELLI, a vehement opponent of the mediocrity of the DOC laws.

INTERNATIONAL VARIETIES were enthusiastically planted, and other Cabernet Sauvignon-based wines began to appear in the image of Sassicaia, particularly after the mid 1980s. The native Sangiovese grape was hardly neglected, however, and a substantial number of BARRIQUE-aged, 100% Sangiovese wines were also launched, as *vini da tavola*, in the 1980s, following in the path of Montevertine's Le Pergole Torte, whose first vintage was 1977.

Experiments with earlier-maturing varieties SYRAH and, with notable success, MERLOT became increasingly common in the late 1980s, both for blending with Sangiovese and for VARIETAL wines. Some non-traditional white varieties were also planted, notably CHARDONNAY and SAUVIGNON BLANC, and various OAK treatments essayed with variable success.

Sassicaia was a pioneering wine, not only in its use of Cabernet but also in its revaluation of a zone never known for producing fine or even commercial wine. When first offered commercially, Sassicaia had to be sold as a *vino da tavola*, not because, as with Tignanello, it eschewed the legal constraints of the area but because there was no DOC for BOLGHERI reds at the time. Its example was rapidly followed by other peripheral areas of Tuscany. Such wines, with their ambitious price tags, came to be known as SUPERTUSCANS.

Inspired by these highly priced Tuscan 'outlaws', ambitious producers in other regions were quick to launch their own *vini da tavola*, in some instances even when they could have qualified as DOC wines. Some of these wines returned to the DOC fold in the 1990s, partly as a result of the greater prestige and credibility now accorded to the wines of their zones and regions. In 1992 Giovanni Goria, the then Minister of Agriculture, introduced the IGT designation to allow producers to add more information to their wine labels, but some important wines are still deliberately sold simply as VINO.

See also SUPERTUSCAN.

vino de aguja, Spanish for a wine that is PÉTILLANT. In Catalan, *vi d'agulla*.

Vino de Calidad (con indicación geográfica), transitory Spanish denomination between VINO DE LA TIERRA and DOP, of which there were seven in 2022. It identified wines 'produced and vinified in a specific area or place, with grapes of the same origin' with some degree of recognition and quality. Eventually this denomination is to be merged, with DO, into DOP.

Vino de la Tierra, wines from legally designated zones in Spain which have not qualified for DOP status. With changes to EU denominations (see PGI), this category is now known as *Indicación Geográfica Protegida* (IGP), a term which can also be found on Spanish labels and which may eventually replace it. Of the 42 Vinos de la Tierra in 2022, Cádiz, Valdejalón, Bajo Aragón, Castilla, Castilla y León, Extremadura, Ibiza, Valles del Sadacia, 3 Riberas, and Castelló are regions to watch. F.C.

Vino de Mesa, old Spanish term for TABLE WINE, the most basic category of wine now known in EU terms as WINE WITHOUT GEOGRAPHICAL INDICATION. See VINO.

Vino de Pago, special Spanish category of supposedly exceptionally high-quality, single-estate wines, granted their own appellation. In 2022 there were 24, 12 of them in CASTILLA-LA MANCHA, where Dominio de Valdepusa was the first to be created. See also PAGO.

Vino de Tea, a traditional specialty of LA PALMA in Spain's Canary Islands, is a blend of mainly NEGRAMOLL aged in barrels made from the Canary pine (*Pinus canariensis*) to take on a resinous flavour. F.C.

Vino Nobile di Montepulciano, potentially important red wine based on SANGIOVESE, known locally as Prugnolo Gentile, made exclusively in the township of Montepulciano 120 km/75 miles south-east of Florence in the hills of TUSCANY in central Italy. Vino Nobile has an illustrious history, having been lauded as a 'perfect wine' by the cellarmaster of Pope Paul III in 1549 and 'the king of wines' by Francesco Redi in his 'Bacchus in Toscana' of 1685, while the first record of the name dates from 1787 when it was listed in the expense accounts of Giovan Filippo Neri for a trip to Siena. After the introduction of the DOC in 1966, the total vineyard area rose from fewer than 150 ha/370 acres in 1970 to 1,377 ha in 2020.

Vino Nobile di Montepulciano was one of the first four DOCGS conferred in 1980. Traditionally producers would have blended in Canaiolo, Mammolo, and Trebbiano, but since the mid 1980s Sangiovese has come to the fore as the principal variety. Since 1999 DOCG regulations require at least 70% Sangiovese in the blend; in 2009 the production regulations were changed to allow up to 30% of varieties such as Cabernet Sauvignon, Merlot, and Syrah, reflecting an already common practice. This amendment was criticized widely as the 'internationalization' of a historic Tuscan wine.

Vines are planted on east- to south-east-facing slopes at ELEVATIONS of 250–600 m/2,000 ft; vineyards on the plain do not qualify as Vino Nobile. Soils are generally higher in CLAY than in either Montalcino or Chianti Classico. The region consists of two distinct zones: the hills around the township of Montepulciano and, about 10 km west and separated by the Val di Chiana plain, the hills around the township of Valiano, the latter dominated by extensive holdings. It is further divided into 20 subzones, but these are practically obsolete since the creation in 2020 of the *unità geografica aggiuntiva* (UGA), here called a *pieve*, or parish. Twelve *pievi* (plural for *pieve*) have been identified on the basis of geological research, which also largely coincided with the boundaries of 12 parishes registered in the 18th century. The *pieve* name may appear on labels from 2024, with the obligatory addition of the word 'Toscana' to distinguish the wines from Montepulciano d'Abruzzo.

Vino Nobile must be aged for two years, at least one of them in BARREL; Riservas require three years of ageing, with 12 months in barrel. The DOC Rosso di Montepulciano, which allows the wines to be released in March following the vintage, was created for earlier-maturing wines but, because it is much less profitable than Vino Nobile, is used for smaller volumes of wine.

Stylistically Vino Nobile sits between CHIANTI CLASSICO and BRUNELLO DI MONTALCINO, combining the elegance of the first with the firm STRUCTURE of the second. The wines tend to fall into two camps: a traditional style using Sangiovese either on its own or blended with CANAIOLO and aged in large casks of Slavonian oak and generally requiring prolonged ageing; or a more modern approach in which Sangiovese is blended with INTERNATIONAL VARIETIES and aged in new French oak. This modern style, although still dominant, has been losing ground because it results in wines that are less recognizably Vino Nobile. W.S.

www.consorziovinonobile.it

Vino Santo. See VIN SANTO.

Vin Santo, 'holy wine', TUSCANY's classic amber-coloured dessert wine, is produced throughout this central Italian region. It is made traditionally from the local white grape varieties TREBBIANO Toscano and MALVASIA (although the red SANGIOVESE is also used to produce a wine called Occhio di Pernice, or 'eye of the partridge') which have been dried on straw mats under the rafters, in the hottest and best-ventilated part of the peasant home (see DRIED-GRAPE WINES). The grapes were normally crushed between the end of November and the end of March, depending on the desired RESIDUAL SUGAR level in the wine (the longer the drying process, the greater the evaporation and the sweeter the MUST), and then aged in small barrels (50–300 l/13–79 gal). These barrels, often bought second-hand from the south of Italy, were frequently made of chestnut, but the 1980s saw a decisive turn towards OAK. The barrels themselves are sealed and never TOPPED UP, resulting in ULLAGE and OXIDATION, which gives the wine a RANCIO-like aroma and its characteristic amber colour. Some producers believe in using a *madre*, or starter culture, comprised of yeast cells from previous batches of Vin Santo, in order to help the fermentation and to add COMPLEXITY to the blend. Others, in true Tuscan fashion, view the *madre* as a throwback to the time when all Vin Santo was marred by FAULTS and refuse to countenance its use.

The wine can range from ultra-sweet to a bone-dry version which more closely resembles a dry FINO sherry than a dessert wine. The practice of keeping the barrels under the roof in a space called the *vinsantaia* encouraged refermentation each year when warm weather arrived and tended to exhaust the unfermented sugars that had remained in the wine. Today, most producers keep their Vin Santo in a cellar with a more constant temperature to retain a degree of freshness in the finished wines.

Pre-1990s, most Vin Santo was sold as a VINO DA TAVOLA, simply because the authorities had struggled to codify the bewildering array of styles contained within the many localized traditions. The DOCs under which Vin Santo is now produced include Chianti, Chianti Classico, Chianti Rufina, Carmignano, Montepulciano, Colli dell'Etruria Centrale, and Val d'Arbia.

The quality of the wine itself varies wildly, not only as a result of variation in grape composition, RESIDUAL SUGAR, and winemaking competence but because the land is divided between so many smallholders, all of whom seem to feel obliged to produce Vin Santo as an obeisance to the tradition of offering this wine to guests as a gesture of esteem. Although some delicious Vin Santo is made, a considerable proportion have serious wine faults, particularly an excess of VOLATILITY, usually a direct consequence of lengthy BARREL AGEING. DOC rules insist the wine is matured for at least three years, and the better producers rarely release their Vin Santo before five years. Cask maturation, without RACKING, may last for up to ten years for the most traditionally made wines.

Vin Santo is also made in Gambellara in the VENETO, and TRENTINO produces a version called **Vino Santo**, made from the NOSIOLA grape and a decisively sweet DRIED-GRAPE WINE.

D.C.G. & W.S.

Vinsanto is the official term for the sweet wines of SANTORINI.

Tachis, G., *Il libro del Vin Santo* (1988).

Vinsobres, the most northerly of the nine CRUS of the southern RHÔNE, dedicated to red wines from 531 ha/1,312 acres of vineyards in 2020. Grenache must dominate a blend with Syrah and/or Mourvèdre (it may also contain a further 17 varieties). The commune is situated on a south-east-facing slope of a large hill. Soils are mixed: largely CLAY and SAND north-east of the village, clay and pebbles north-west of the village, and clay, sand, pebbles, and LIMESTONE directly south of the village. Relatively high-ELEVATION vineyards (up to 450 m/1,476 ft) and a northerly situation make for a cooler climate than most other southern Rhône crus, as does the pontias, a cool easterly air current that follows the Aigues, a tributary of the Rhône that skirts around the foot of the hill. The style is concentrated but fresh, with a bold tannic structure. M.C.W.

vintage can either mean the physical process of grape-picking and winemaking, for which see HARVEST, or it can mean the year or growing season which produced a particular wine, for which see VINTAGE YEAR. A vintage wine is one made from the produce of a single year.

vintage assessment is important enough to have an immediate effect on PRICE but is also notoriously difficult because quality and character can vary so much between producers and properties. A vintage is often assessed at the most difficult stage in its life, its infancy, for reasons of commerce and curiosity. Wine MERCHANTS and WINE WRITERS habitually taste wines from the most recent vintage in a wine region important for INVESTMENT when they are just a few months old and are still in cask (see EN PRIMEUR). Quite apart from the fact that the wines are at this stage still being made (see ÉLEVAGE), samples may give a misleading impression because they have been specially chosen and groomed to show particularly well at this early stage, or because too long has elapsed since they were drawn from cask (OXIDATION is a common problem), or, if they are tasted directly from cask, because they are undergoing a distorting treatment such as FINING. Furthermore, this sort of vintage assessment may be before the ASSEMBLAGE process and provides only a snapshot of embryonic wine from a small proportion of the total number of barrels produced.

This sort of comparative tasting can usually give some indication as to which are the most and least successful wines of a given vintage, but it can be difficult to stand back from the individual samples, accurately remember exactly how the same wines from previous vintages tasted at the same stage, and make any reliable assessment of the likely characteristics and potential of the young vintage as a whole. Vintages of which the collective assessment at this young stage was subsequently agreed to have been too enthusiastic include 1975 in Bordeaux and 1983 and 1996 in Burgundy, but other examples abound. (Wine merchants have proved themselves much less likely to err on the side of caution, although 2001 Bordeaux and 2011 Burgundy are generally agreed to have been underestimated.)

The assessment of a mature vintage is a much less hazardous process that is usually undertaken in the form of a horizontal TASTING, although of course SUBJECTIVITY plays its part as it does in all tasting.

Broadbent, M., *Great Vintage Wine Book II* (1991).
Broadbent, M., *Wine Vintages* (1998).

vintage charts are both useful and notoriously fallible, partly because young VINTAGE ASSESSMENT is so fraught with difficulty and partly because of the difficulty of generalizing about a district in which there may be hundreds of different producers, each with a different vineyard regime, winemaking policy, and style of wine.

The most useful vintage charts are the most detailed but also those that are regularly updated on the basis of continuous and relevant tasting. The INTERNATIONAL WINE & FOOD SOCIETY was one of the first to issue a vintage chart, in 1935. The Society has since then published one annually, updated by a committee expressly charged with this task.

vintage port. See PORT.

vintage year, the year in which a wine was produced. Most, but not all, of a vintage's characteristics result from the particular WEATHER conditions experienced in that year, which makes CLIMATE CHANGE so significant for the style and quality of many wine regions. In the southern hemisphere, a **vintage-dated** wine invariably carries the year in which the grapes were picked, even though much of the VINE GROWTH CYCLE was actually in the previous year. In the northern hemisphere, vintage-dated wines carry the year in which both the vine growth occurred and the grapes were picked (with the exception of those rare examples of EISWEIN picked in early January, which are dated with the year whose vine growth produced the wine). The expression 'vintage year' is also sometimes used of a year producing particularly high-quality wines.

In a literal sense, all newly fermented wine is vintage wine, being from a single year. Only at the BLENDING stage may wine of a recent year, or vintage, be mixed with older wines into an undated blend. Many everyday wines—such as the JUG WINES of the US and CASK WINE in Australia—are not vintage dated. Some top-quality CHAMPAGNE, most SHERRY, and many other FORTIFIED WINES are NON-VINTAGE too. In most other circumstances, however, a non-vintage wine is inferior to a vintage-dated one. For wines designated within the EU as WINE WITHOUT GEOGRAPHICAL INDICATION, stating the vintage date on the label is now optional (having previously been prohibited), depending on local wine regulations.

The vintage year printed on a wine label can help the consumer decide when to open a particular bottle, being especially relevant to wine meant for AGEING (others, the great majority of wines, should simply be drunk as young as possible). Since the capacity of a wine to improve with age is one obvious test of its quality, a vintage's status is only fully established in retrospect (whatever those charged with selling it may say; see VINTAGE ASSESSMENT).

The concept of vintage year has a long history. OPIMIAN wine, made in the consular year of Lucius Opimius, 121 BCE, was celebrated for decades afterwards as a particularly fine vintage. The celebrated RHINE Steinwein of 1540 CE, last drunk in 1961, was made in a freak year so hot and dry that the Rhine dried up and people could walk across its bed.

Vintage years did not become a normal commercial consideration until the end of the 17th century, when BOTTLES and CORKS replaced BARRELS for long-term wine storage. Vintages became particularly important towards the end of the 18th century, when the modern bottle shape evolved, allowing bottles to be stored on their sides. The better red wines of Bordeaux came to be 'laid down' for many years, and it was then that what is now regarded as the traditional Bordeaux style of winemaking for prolonged AGEING in bottle became established.

Broadbent gives details of some of the more famous Bordeaux vintages. The celebrated 1784 clarets, sought out and imported by America's wine-loving President Thomas JEFFERSON, were from one of the many fine vintages spanning the late 18th century and first years of the 19th century, culminating in the reputedly outstanding 'comet' year of 1811. Other runs of predominantly good Bordeaux vintages followed in the 1840s and again in the 1860s and the first half of the 1870s, a period long remembered as the crowning glory of the PRE-PHYLLOXERA era. The limited climatic records available suggest that these were predominantly warm periods.

Vintage years in contemporary Bordeaux and throughout central and western Europe tend still to be those of ample sunshine (especially in spring, and again in late July and August) and average or higher TEMPERATURES leading to a normal or early HARVEST date. Bad vintage years have almost invariably been cool and/or wet, with below-average sunshine.

In hot and reliably sunny viticultural climates, on the other hand, the best years for table wines are usually average or cooler than average. This generalization does not apply to sweet FORTIFIED WINES, which need more or less unlimited warmth and sunshine. Nor does it necessarily apply to all TABLE WINES or to all hot areas. For instance, wet, cloudy, and relatively cool summers in the very warm Hunter Valley of NEW SOUTH WALES are usually inferior for red table wines, although they may still produce good-quality white table wines. However, the perturbations of CLIMATE CHANGE have made such generalizations less dependable.

The reactions of vines and grapes to seasonal conditions or weather events can also differ widely according to SOIL TYPE within an area. As demonstrated by the extensive studies of Seguin in Bordeaux, vines on well-drained, deep soils may be less affected by variations in RAINFALL, whereas those on shallow and poorly drained soils will alternate between DROUGHT stress and waterlogging under the same rainfall. For this reason, the best vineyards for wine quality, with favourable TERROIR, are the least subject to vintage variation and can maintain consistently high quality.

In addition, VINE VARIETIES can react quite differently to the weather conditions depending on their individual timings of BUDBREAK, FLOWERING, and RIPENESS and the relative sensitivities of their berries to rain, diseases or damaging heat. PINOT NOIR, like most other early-maturing red grape varieties, is very sensitive to heat, which affects wine style and quality. ZINFANDEL, with its tightly packed bunches, is notoriously sensitive to any rain towards harvest time. The least rain and water uptake causes berry splitting and subsequent total BUNCH ROT. This is probably the main reason its extensive use is confined to California and Puglia, where the ripening season is typically free of rain. CHENIN BLANC is similarly susceptible, at least in climates such as those of California and South Africa, where the preceding weather is mostly hot and dry. By contrast, CABERNET SAUVIGNON, with its looser bunches, is relatively tolerant of both heat and rain and is therefore generally less affected by vintage differences, so long as the weather has been warm enough to ripen it.

A final point is that critical weather events, particularly heavy rainfall and HAIL, are not necessarily uniform within a given district and year. Even if they were, vineyard management decisions can lead to quite different results—depending, for instance, on the extent to which SPRAYING has been practised or whether grapes are picked before, during, or after rains at harvest time.

Nor is weather the only possible external influence on the characteristics of a particular vintage year. Market conditions may dictate how or whether certain viticultural practices such as PRUNING and CROP THINNING are carried out so as to influence crop quality or YIELD. Social history may also dictate some characteristics of a vintage year, as in some of the vintages ripened in European vineyards during the Second World War. There have also been very rare instances of CONTAMINANTS from a new pesticide, for example, which have affected particular vintages of certain wines, sometimes on a less than localized scale, as in the use of Orthene in Germany in 1983.

For all these reasons, vintages are seldom uniformly good, medium, or bad, even within a small area (see VINTAGE ASSESSMENT). A generally recognized 'vintage' year can have its failures, often for reasons totally beyond the competence of winegrowers and winemakers. Equally, 'poor' vintages can usually still produce good wines from particular locations and grape varieties, whether because of the characteristics of the TERROIR, thanks to more prescient vineyard management, or both.

See AUCTIONS and INVESTMENT IN WINE. See also LABELLING INFORMATION. R.E.S. & J.R.

Broadbent, M., *Vintage Wine* (2002).

vintner, late Middle English word for wine MERCHANT, which superseded **vinter**. Mainly because of England's links with BORDEAUX, vintners were some of the most important people in the City of London in the 14th and early 15th centuries (four mayors of London were vintners in Edward II's reign). The **Vintners' Company** evolved from the 'Mistery of Vintners', a group of London and Gascon merchants who enjoyed a practical monopoly on London's important wine trade with Gascony from at least 1364. It was formally incorporated in 1437 and was recognized by Henry VIII as one of the '12 great' livery companies. It is still based at **Vintners' Hall** by the Thames in London, in a section of the City known as Vintry ward, where for centuries wine would be unloaded from ship for sale throughout southern England. Independently of UK licensing restrictions, the Vintners' Company may grant Free Vintner status to members, allowing them to sell wine under certain conditions. Both the WSET and the Institute of MASTERS OF WINE are the result of initiatives of the Vintners' Company.

The word has also come to be used for a wine producer as well as a wine merchant, particularly in North America. KENDALL-JACKSON's Vintner's Reserve Chardonnay is one of the most successful BRANDS in the US.

Simon, A., *History of the Wine Trade in England*, ii (1964).

vin viné is a traditional term for a wine made strong and sweet by the addition of alcohol to grape juice or must at some point before fermentation is complete. A VIN DOUX NATUREL and a VIN DE LIQUEUR are both therefore *vins vinés*. See also MUTAGE.

Viognier became one of the world's most fashionable white grape varieties in the early 1990s, mainly because its most famous wine, CONDRIEU, is distinctive, was associated with the modish RHÔNE, and was then relatively scarce. By the mid 2000s, it was planted all over the Languedoc and had spread to the great majority of the world's wine regions, and in Australia it had become a common blending partner with various red grapes, especially SYRAH, for CO-FERMENTATION, copying traditional practice in CÔTE RÔTIE. CHÂTEAU-GRILLET is the only other all-Viognier French appellation. DNA PROFILING has shown a parent–offspring relationship with MONDEUSE BLANCHE and therefore, not unexpectedly, a close one with SYRAH. It also suggests a close genetic relationship with FREISA from Piemonte, a likely progeny of NEBBIOLO, making Viognier a cousin of Nebbiolo—something of a surprise.

The vines need a relatively warm climate and can withstand drought well but are prone to POWDERY MILDEW. The grapes are a deep yellow, and the resulting wine is high in colour, alcohol, and a very particular perfume redolent of apricots, peaches, and blossom, sometimes with a deeply savoury undertow. Condrieu is one of the few highly priced white wines that should probably be drunk young, while this perfume is at its most heady before the wine's slightly low ACIDITY fades.

The vine was at one time a common crop on the farmland south of Lyons and has been grown on the infertile terraces of the northern Rhône for centuries, but its extremely low productivity, often due to COULURE, saw it decline to an official total of just 14 ha/35 acres in the French agricultural census of 1968—mostly in the three northern Rhône appellations in which it is allowed: Condrieu, Château-Grillet, and, to an even lesser extent, Côte Rôtie, in which it may be included as a stabilizing agent up to 20% but usually closer to 5% of the Syrah-dominated total.

French NURSERIES saw an increase in demand for Viognier CUTTINGS from the mid 1980s, however (when the red wines of the Rhône enjoyed a renaissance of popularity), and by 1988 were selling half a million a year. By 1997 more than 100 ha/250 acres of Viognier qualified for the Condrieu appellation, and by the turn of the century Viognier plantings throughout the LANGUEDOC and ROUSSILLON had reached 1,540 ha (from 139 ha in 1993). By 2019 this total had reached 4,446 ha/10,986 acres. Considerable further plantings in the northern and southern Rhône, many of them outside appellation boundaries, took the total French area of Viognier up to 6,894 ha by 2019—quite a contrast to 50 years earlier. French Viognier is often sold as a relatively inexpensive VARIETAL, although here and elsewhere the variety has shown itself a willing and able blending partner, not just with other Rhône varieties such as ROUSSANNE, MARSANNE, GRENACHE BLANC, and VERMENTINO/ROLLE but also, usefully, with Chardonnay. This latter blend has had some success in Italy, where total plantings had grown to 1,827 ha/739 acres by 2015. Graf Hardegg makes some fine varietal Viognier in Austria, and it has its champions, such as Gerovassiliou of Greece, in many European wine regions, but it is rarely planted to any great extent.

California has the world's second biggest area of Viognier planted: just over 6,315 ha/2,555 acres in 2020, much of it in the Central Coast. Many examples are notably high in alcohol when ripened under the reliable California sun—and Viognier has to be fully ripe before it reveals its trademark heady aromas. So seductive is it that there has been considerable experimentation with it all over North America, particularly in VIRGINIA, which has adopted it as its signature white wine, and also in Washington, Oregon, Texas, and British Columbia. By 2020 Argentina had 723 ha/1,787 acres and Chile had 761 ha/1,880 acres, both of them having made some convincing examples of this popular variety, which is also planted in Brazil and, with notable success, in Uruguay. Australian producers, led by Yalumba, have welcomed it with particular enthusiasm, using it both as a varietal white wine and as a 5–10% blend with Shiraz. Total plantings stood at 692 ha/1,710 acres in 2022. In New Zealand it is generally slightly less expressive but was planted on 65 ha/161 acres by 2022. South Africa has been catching up fast and had 730 ha/1,804 acres widely spread around the country by 2020. Today the consumer can choose from a range of recognizably perfumed, if slightly light, southern French varietal Viogniers, some of them produced from vines FIELD GRAFTED over to Viognier from less fashionable varieties, some of them perhaps perfumed by other aromas including a dollop of Muscat. The California way with Viognier is a notably alcoholic one, but when it works these monsters can be magnificent.

Viosinho, distinctive white variety producing some fine, TEXTURED, aromatic white wines, especially at higher ELEVATIONS, in the DOURO and Trás-os-Montes. Traditionally a constituent of white PORT, Viosinho is now also used to make unfortified wines and, partly because of its low yields and tendency to oxidize (see OXIDATION), it is generally blended with RABIGATO and GOUVEIO. Total plantings had risen to 1,223 ha/3,022 acres by 2020.

Viré-Clessé, white-wine appellation created in 1998 by separating out two of the top Mâcon-Villages, noted not just for their quality but also for the rich style of their wines. Bizarrely, the appellation initially banned wines with RESIDUAL SUGAR such as those made by Jean Thévenet of Domaine de la Bon Gran, but common sense subsequently prevailed. Although most wines are vinified dry, Viré-Clessé tends to produce heady, full-bodied whites of a sunny disposition. J.T.C.M.

Virgil (Publius Vergilius Maro) (70–19 BCE), Latin poet and good, if unoriginal, source of information on viticulture in ancient ROME. Like HORACE, Virgil benefited from the patronage of the Emperor Augustus, and much of his poetry was written in praise of Roman and Italian virtues. The rural virtues are expounded in the *Georgics*, a didactic poem about agriculture, published in 37 BCE. The second of the four books is devoted mainly to vine-growing. Although it is of little use as a practical manual, it does give a lively and colourful picture of the life and problems of the vine-grower. Like HESIOD, Virgil's purpose was moral, and his main concern is to describe the farmer's virtues of austerity, integrity, and hard work, which made Rome great. Although Virgil is from a literary point of view a more interesting writer than his chief source VARRO, he is not an independent authority, and it is to his predecessors CATO and Varro, and to the later COLUMELLA and PLINY, that we must turn for first-hand information about Roman viticulture. H.M.W. & H.H.A.

Griffin, J., *Latin Literature and Roman Life* (1985).
Johnston, P. A., *Vergil's Agricultural Golden Age: A Study of the Georgics* (2nd edn, 1988).

Virginia, mid-Atlantic state in the eastern United States increasingly known for quality and diversity in its wines. BORDEAUX-style reds, especially made from Cabernet Franc and Petit Verdot, sometimes bolstered with Tannat, can achieve a sophistication combining American ripeness and European elegance. This often leads to the observation that Virginia is, oenologically as well as physically, about halfway between California and France. Viognier established Virginia's reputation for white wines, but PETIT MANSENG is the current rage, beloved for its effusive tropical fruit flavours combining high acidity and sweetness. Albariño, Sauvignon Blanc, and Italian white varieties also do well, and a few producers make outstanding Chardonnay. Pinot Noir can succeed in select sites at high ELEVATIONS.

Virginia traces its winemaking history to its earliest colonial days and counts Thomas

JEFFERSON as its most famous oenophile. Virginia's modern wine history begins in the 1970s, when Italy's Zonin family bought land north of Charlottesville and established Barboursville Vineyards. It took off in the 1990s when Dennis Horton, a restless experimenter with grape varieties, introduced his Viognier and topped some of California's best in a blind tasting. Early expansion in this phase included plantings on farms and vacation properties not ideally suited to grapevines and was hindered by disease-ridden vine stock purchased from west coast NURSERIES. Better vine stock and increased professionalism fuelled a rise in quality in the early 21st century, aided by forward-thinking regulatory and financial support from the state government and oenology and viticulture assistance from VIRGINIA TECH. Virginia's wineries also benefit from the state's booming TOURISM, which features colonial and Civil War history as well as the scenic Skyline Drive in the Blue Ridge Mountains.

By 2021 Virginia boasted nearly 300 wineries. The state's viticultural backbone stretches along the eastern foothills of the Blue Ridge Mountains, from south of Charlottesville northward to Loudoun County in the exurbs of Washington D.C., and includes eight AVAs: Eastern Shore, Northern Neck George Washington Birthplace, Peninsula, Middleburg, Monticello, North Fork of Roanoke, Rocky Knob, and Shenandoah Valley (shared with West Virginia and not to be confused with Shenandoah Valley in California's SIERRA FOOTHILLS).

FUNGAL DISEASES such as DOWNY MILDEW are perpetual enemies in Virginia's humid climate. Late-spring FROSTS can devastate YIELDS, and Atlantic tropical storms can complicate harvest. So, despite success in growing VITIS VINIFERA varieties, there is increasing interest in French-American HYBRIDS for their disease resistance and lesser need for chemical inputs. Younger winemakers are dabbling in NATURAL WINES and PET-NAT, finding an enthusiastic audience in urban consumers who have embraced a 'drink local' mindset. Most Virginia wines are sold at the winery or over the internet and can be difficult to find through traditional retail distribution. D.M.

Virginia Tech (VT) in Blacksburg, VIRGINIA, is home to thriving research, teaching, and extension programmes in OENOLOGY, VITICULTURE, and FERMENTATION science. Oenology research in the Department of Food Science and Technology, established by B. W. Zoecklein in 1986, aims to improve wine AROMA and flavour through advances in grape chemistry achieved in the vineyard and through the application of targeted fermentation management practices in the cellar. Oenology extension supports the growing Virginia wine industry through collaborative applied research, workshops, and analytical services.

Virginia Tech's viticulture research and extension programmes are conducted through the Alson H. Smith Agricultural Research and Extension Center near Winchester in the northern Shenandoah Valley. Grape research has focused on aspects of cold stress physiology; vine and vineyard management to optimize YIELD; evaluation of wine QUALITY, VINE VARIETIES, and CLONES; and VINE PEST management. Technical information is disseminated through industry meetings, web-based resources, and a Wine Grape Production Guide (ecommons.cornell.edu/handle/1813/67189). Viticulture, oenology, brewing, and fermentation courses are offered at undergraduate and graduate level. A.C.S.

viroids, particles smaller than VIRUSES which are thought capable of producing virus-like disease effects in the grapevine. Viroids can be found in nominally virus-free vines following THERMOTHERAPY and are known to cause significant diseases for other crops. They are transmitted by VEGETATIVE PROPAGATION as for viruses, but viroid-free grapevines can be produced by TISSUE CULTURE. No viroids have so far been identified with commercially important grapevine diseases. The viroid Yellow Speckle is widespread in Australia but is not known to harm the vines. R.E.S.

virus diseases, group of VINE DISEASES caused by very small and simple organisms, consisting of ribonucleic acid (RNA) wrapped in a protein sheath. Some virus diseases can seriously affect grapevine yield and wine quality, and, since they are mainly spread by PROPAGATION in CUTTINGS, there has been an emphasis on VINE IMPROVEMENT and CLONAL SELECTION to prevent their spread. Virus diseases began to affect European vines probably from about 1890, when GRAFTING on to ROOTSTOCKS was used in France to control PHYLLOXERA. Grafting doubles the risk of virus spread and, unlike many fruiting varieties, rootstocks infrequently show virus symptoms.

Virus diseases are mostly spread by taking cuttings from infected plants, although some are spread by NEMATODES and insects. They are mostly detected by inoculating sensitive plants (see INDEXING) and more recently by serological techniques based on immunological reactions (see ELISA) and RNA analysis. Often viruses do not kill the vine but each year may reduce both growth and yield. For example, rootstocks infected with LEAFROLL VIRUS show no symptoms, but the virus can greatly reduce wine quality as it delays fruit RIPENING. It is probably the most important vine virus disease in many parts of the world. Considerable viticultural effort has been expended in vine improvement and in developing virus-free vines. However, the increased use of NURSERY-propagated cuttings repeatedly taken from virus-free MOTHER VINES, especially rootstocks, has inadvertently led to the spread of TRUNK DISEASES, potentially causing greater harm than the virus diseases they were meant to control.

Common virus diseases are CORKY BARK, FANLEAF DEGENERATION, LEAFROLL VIRUS, RUGOSE WOOD, and NEPOVIRUSES. See also BACTERIAL DISEASES, FUNGAL DISEASES, and PHYTOPLASMA diseases.

New virus diseases continue to be discovered. Grapevine Pinot Gris virus (GPGV), for example, first discovered in Italy in 2012, is now reported worldwide, including in other varieties which may be symptomless. Little is known of effects on growth, yield, and quality, but the virus causes spring-time leaf mottling and deformation on Pinot Gris. R.E.S.

Bettiga, L. J., (ed.), *Grape Pest Management* (3rd edn, 2013).

CABI, Grapevine Pinot gris virus, Invasive Species Compendium. www.cabi.org/isc/datasheet/120353.

viscosity, the quality of being **viscous**, the extent to which a solution resists flow or movement. Honey is more viscous than sugar syrup, for example, which is considerably more viscous than water. Viscosity, which approximates to what wine tasters call BODY, can be sensed by the human palate in the form of resistance as the solution is rinsed around the mouth.

A very sweet wine is more viscous than a dry one, even if they have the same ALCOHOLIC STRENGTH. Alcohol itself is more viscous than water, and higher-strength wines are therefore more viscous than lower-strength wines. An increase of 1% in alcoholic strength increases viscosity relative to water by about 0.04 units, while an increase of 10 g/l in RESIDUAL SUGAR increases viscosity by about 0.03 units. The most viscous wines of all, therefore, are those that are both sweet and strong.

It has been thought that the viscosity and the (quite unrelated) GLYCEROL content of a wine were the main factors in the formation of 'tears' on the inside of a wine glass. While they may be minor factors, the explanation is very different. See TEARS. A.D.W.

Vitaceae, the family in the plant kingdom which includes the genus VITIS containing the grapevine. There are 13–17 genera (taxonomists often disagree) altogether with about 900 species, which are spread through tropical and temperate zones around the world. The plants in the family are characteristically climbers with leaves opposite tendrils. See also BOTANICAL CLASSIFICATION. R.E.S. & J.V.

Vital, low-acid white grape grown in central Portugal, mainly in the Lisboa region, known as MALVASIA Corada in the Douro. Total Portuguese plantings of this vigorous, productive vine were 457 ha/1,129 acres in 2020. It can make fine, minerally wines (see MINERALITY) if planted in cool-enough terrain.

Vitales, the order in the plant kingdom which includes the family Vitaceae, including the genus VITIS, the grapevine. See BOTANICAL CLASSIFICATION.

vitamins, a group of organic compounds that are essential dietary components, deficiencies causing a variety of well-known disorders in humans. The levels of vitamins in grapes increase during RIPENING, but the final values are relatively low compared with those of many other fruits. The most abundant is ASCORBIC ACID (vitamin C), the levels of which vary considerably—15–150 mg/l, which is only 10% of that in oranges (although ascorbic acid is often added during winemaking). Average values for the concentrations of other vitamins are about 1–10 parts per million (ppm) for niacin, pyridoxine, and pantothenic acid; 0.1–1 ppm for thiamine and riboflavin; and 0.001–0.01 ppm for biotin and folic acid. These levels in grapes are too low to be considered as a serious dietary source and are further reduced in wine by the use of SULFUR DIOXIDE and by YEAST growth (although AUTOLYSIS can add others). Wine also contains low concentrations of vitamin B_{12} (cobalamine).

The 'bioflavonoids', or vitamin P, a complex that includes D-catechin and many other FLAVONOIDS, occur in GRAPE JUICE in large amounts, especially in dark-skinned berries, and may play a part in warding off heart disease (see HEALTH).

B.G.C. & A.D.W.

viticulteur, French term for a vine-grower.

viticulture, the science and practice of grape culture. Viticulture is practised consciously by VITICULTURISTS, often instinctively by grape-growers or vine-growers. Practices vary enormously around the world; some of these differences are highlighted under NEW WORLD.

Grapes can be grown, over a wide range of LATITUDES, in CLIMATES ranging from very hot (southern California, inland Australia) to very cool (England, Luxembourg, Denmark). Viticulture is practised in very wet climates (parts of England and New Zealand) to very dry ones (Atacama in Chile, Central Valley in California). The TOPOGRAPHY can be very steep, as in the Mosel Valley of Germany or the Douro Valley of Portugal, or very flat plains, as in many regions of Australia and Argentina. VINE DENSITY can vary enormously: from vineyards planted with large numbers of very small vines, as is common in Champagne and Bordeaux (10,000 vines per ha/4,050 per acre), to few, large vines as in the traditional Vinho Verde vineyards of Portugal (600 vines per ha). Some vineyards may be tended entirely by manual LABOUR, while others are MECHANIZED. Vineyards may rely on IRRIGATION for their survival where they are grown in deserts, while in others, such as parts of France, irrigation is severely restricted.

The following entries follow the sequence of vineyard development from initial planning through to picking: VINEYARD SITE SELECTION; choice of ROOTSTOCK, VINE VARIETY, and CLONE; SOIL TESTING and SOIL PREPARATION; choice of VINE DENSITY and TRELLIS SYSTEM; vine PLANTING, VINE TRAINING, and PRUNING; control of VINE PESTS, VINE DISEASES, and WEEDS; and fruit SAMPLING and HARVEST. See also VINEYARD ANNUAL CYCLE.

Effects on wine quality

For still wines, the VITICULTURIST may well have a greater impact on wine quality than the WINEMAKER since so many of the factors affecting quality are determined in the vineyard. The belief that 'wine is made in the vineyard not the cellar' became increasingly widespread during the 1990s and is now probably more widely quoted than ever.

Quite apart from the decisions involved in vineyard site selection, there are obvious ways in which viticulture can influence wine quality—selection of vine variety, rootstock, clone—and some where the effects are more difficult to identify.

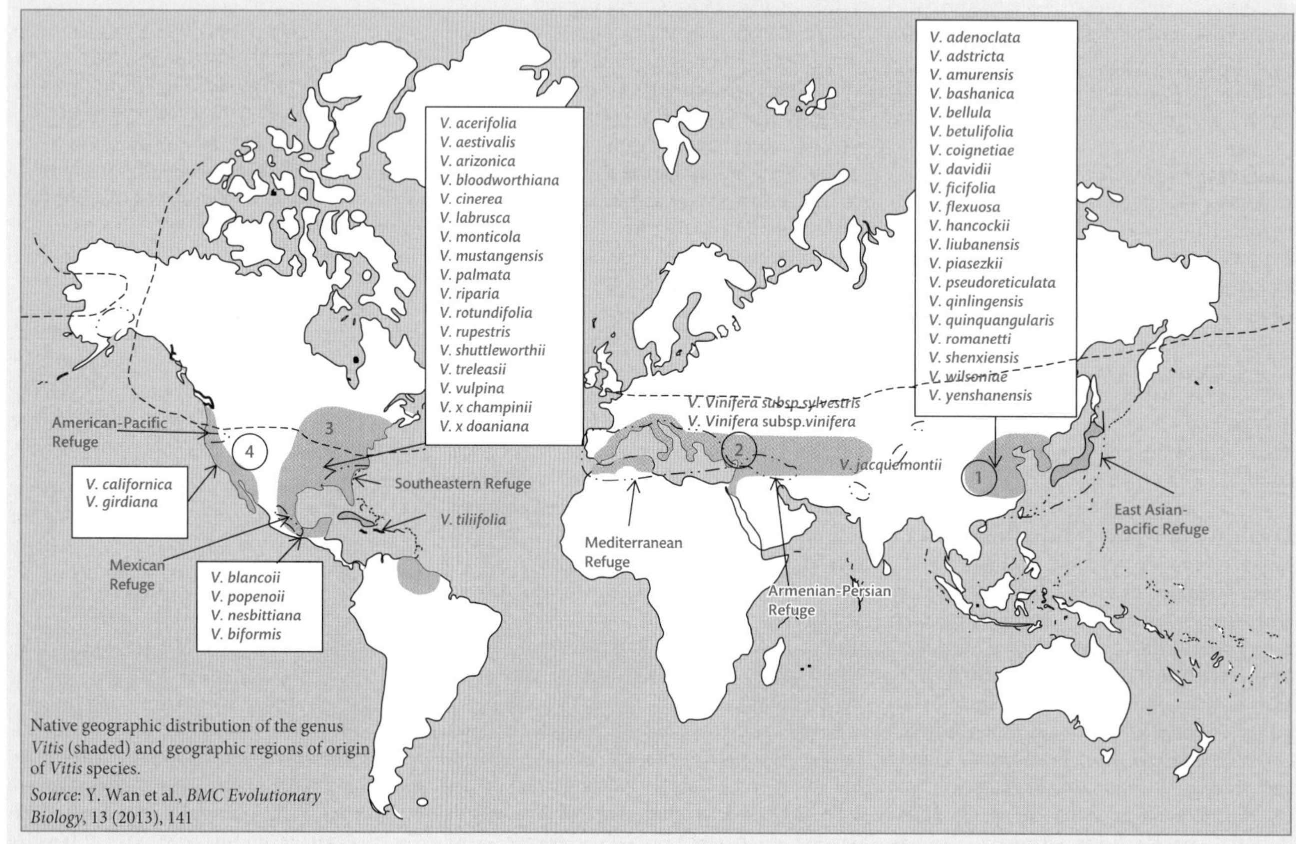

Native geographic distribution of the genus *Vitis* (shaded) and geographic regions of origin of *Vitis* species.

Source: Y. Wan et al., *BMC Evolutionary Biology*, 13 (2013), 141

Usually premium-quality wines come from vineyards planted to soils with good DRAINAGE and of low SOIL FERTILITY (see also TERROIR). However, inappropriate vineyard management can destroy the potential for wine quality. For example, over-enthusiastic applications of nitrogen FERTILIZERS will result in excess vineyard VIGOUR which may delay RIPENING and encourage FUNGAL DISEASES. The SPRAYING regime adopted by the vine-grower can determine whether the grapes are affected by BUNCH ROT or not.

The choice of vine-TRAINING SYSTEM and associated trellis system can have fundamental effects on wine quality, for example by reducing excessive SHADE. Limits on YIELD are also imposed by appellation laws in some regions. Where vines are pruned lightly to many buds and develop too low a LEAF TO FRUIT RATIO, the fruit will not ripen properly, and wine quality will be reduced.

Vineyards may require judicious IRRIGATION to prevent excessive WATER STRESS (although the practice is banned or restricted in many European regions), but excessive irrigation (like excessive RAINFALL) can cause delayed ripening and a loss of wine quality. Vineyards should be subject to grape sampling programmes so that harvest takes place when the fruit has reached the level of maturity appropriate for the wine style. More broadly, lack of concern for the vineyard SOILS and ECOSYSTEM will not make the most of the vineyard site, nor promote its SUSTAINABILITY. R.E.S.

Dry, P. R., and Coombe, B. G. (eds.), *Viticulture*, i: *Resources* (2nd edn, 2004).
Galet, P., *General Viticulture* (2000).

viticulturist, someone who practises VITICULTURE. In many countries the grape-grower is termed simply 'grower' rather than 'viticulturist', the latter being more often used for professionals who typically have some formal tertiary training in viticulture. Grape-growers or vine-growers may also be termed 'winegrowers' if they are also involved in winemaking. R.E.S.

Vitis, the genus of the plant kingdom which includes the VINE (see BOTANICAL CLASSIFICATION). *Vitis* is one of 13–17 genera in the family VITACEAE and contains in turn about 60 species. Centres of *Vitis* diversity are equally divided between the east and south-east of North America and Asia, mainly in the TEMPERATE zones of the northern hemisphere, with a few in the tropics. The most important species for wine production is the single European species (strictly speaking, Eurasian) VITIS VINIFERA, often written *V. vinifera* or simply *vinifera*.

As shown on the map, there are many different AMERICAN VINE SPECIES. They became the subject of attention by early European settlers as *vinifera* failed to cope with indigenous diseases in the early colonies on the east coast. However, they proved generally unsatisfactory for wine because of their strongly flavoured berries (see FOXY). These indigenous American species have since been crossed with *vinifera* to form new varieties (see AMERICAN HYBRIDS) and among themselves to produce the ROOTSTOCKS used in modern viticulture.

Among Asian species, VITIS AMURENSIS is the world's most northerly vine species and has been used to introduce cold hardiness into VINE BREEDING programmes. Varieties of *amurensis* and *Vitis coignetiae* (see YAMABUDO) are grown in JAPAN.

Note that the systematic botanical classification of species within the *Vitis* genus has been a subject of confusion for more than a century. Hedrick documents this early confusion, especially that concerning *Vitis vulpina*, which has often been wrongly confused with VITIS RIPARIA, the great taxonomist Linnaeus being the origin of the confusion. GALET clarified the taxonomy in 1967, but there is still some doubt about the taxonomy of Asian species. The French taxonomist Planchon proposed that *Vitis* species be divided into two so-called sections. The first, *Vitis* (originally called *Euvitis*), contains the great majority of species including the 'European' wine grape species *Vitis vinifera*; the second, MUSCADINIA, contains only two species indigenous to North America. These two sections differ in chromosome number and many morphological features. The species of the section *Vitis* have proven to be closely enough related to interbreed easily when this has been attempted, but CROSSES between members of the two sections typically produces sterile hybrids. *Muscadinia* is sometimes considered a separate genus, but recent DNA PHYLOGENIES do not support this distinction.

For *Vitis silvestris*, see WILD VINES. See also VINE, VITIS VINIFERA, AMERICAN VINE SPECIES, VINE VARIETIES, PROLES, CLONE, HYBRIDS, and CROSS. R.E.S. & J.V.

Antcliff, A. J., 'Taxonomy: the grapevine as a member of the plant kingdom', in P. R. Dry and B. G. Coombe (eds.), *Viticulture*, i: *Resources* (2nd edn, 2004).
Galet, P., *General Viticulture* (2000).
Hedrick, U., *The Grapes of New York* (1908).
Soejima, A., and Wen, J., 'Phylogenetic analysis of the grape family (Vitaceae) based on three chloroplast markers', *American Journal of Botany*, 93/2 (2006), 278–87.
Wan, Y., et al., 'A phylogenetic analysis of the grape genus (*Vitis* L.) reveals broad reticulation and concurrent diversification during neogene and quaternary climate change', *BMC Evolutionary Biology*, 13 (2013), 141.

Vitis amurensis, often written *V. amurensis* or just *amurensis*, an Asian vine species of the VITIS genus which takes its name from the Amur Valley of northern China. The exceptionally cold climate in which it originates makes it useful to vine breeders seeking to introduce genes for cold hardiness. Professor Helmut BECKER in particular developed HYBRIDS which included both RIESLING and *amurensis* in their complex pedigrees (e.g. SOLARIS). See also CABERNET SEVERNY.

Vitis labrusca, often written *V. labrusca* or just *labrusca*, species of the VITIS genus native to North America. The juice of its grapes and the wine made from them usually have a pronounced flavour described as FOXY.

Vitis riparia, often written *V. riparia* or just *riparia*, species of the VITIS genus native to North America much used in developing suitably resistant ROOTSTOCKS and HYBRIDS.

Vitis rupestris, species of the *Vitis* genus native to North America much used in developing suitably resistant ROOTSTOCKS and HYBRIDS. For more details, see VITIS.

Vitis vinifera, often written *V. vinifera* or *vinifera*, the species of vine from which most of the world's wine is made and to which all the most familiar VINE VARIETIES belong. *Vinifera* is not a classical Latin word but one made up by Linnaeus (see BOTANICAL CLASSIFICATION) to denote 'wine-grape bearing'.

Vinifera is one of about 60 species of the *Vitis* genus, the majority of which originate in North America or Asia. The relationship of *vinifera* to other species of the *Vitis* genus is described under VITIS. The relationship of *Vitis vinifera* to other members of the plant kingdom is discussed under BOTANICAL CLASSIFICATION. *Vinifera* grapes are used principally for winemaking, TABLE GRAPES, and RAISINS. (See VINE for more details.) There are some 5,000 to 10,000 *vinifera* VINE VARIETIES, grouped into three PROLES.

The species is thought to originate in south-eastern Anatolia or in Transcaucasia (see ORIGINS OF VINICULTURE) and was spread through the Mediterranean and Europe by the Phoenicians and Greeks and later by the Romans. *Vinifera* was spread through the NEW WORLD, initially by Cortés in SOUTH AMERICA and subsequently into western North America. The Dutch took *vinifera* grapevines to the Cape of Good Hope in 1616 (see SOUTH AFRICA), and the English to Australia, then New Zealand, beginning in 1788.

Vinifera is distinguished from other *Vitis* species by a range of general botanical features, including vigorous shoots mostly free of hair, prominent NODES and BUDS, regularly intermittent TENDRILS or BUNCHES, leaves generally orbicular and more or less deeply lobed, PETIOLAR sinus often in a U or lyre shape, and conspicuous dentation (so-called teeth) around the edge of the leaf. *Vinifera* flowers are typically hermaphroditic (both male and female), and there are differences in seeds, too (see GRAPE). Because *vinifera* vines are selected for their fruit characters, the seeds typically represent a small proportion of the berry weight, 10% compared with 80% for *Vitis berlandieri*.

Further details about *vinifera* can be found under the following entries, which describe more fully aspects of the commercial culture of this species, emphasizing its use in winemaking: VINE VARIETIES, VINE GROWTH CYCLE, VINE BREEDING, VINE DISEASES, VINE PESTS, VINE PRODUCTS, VINE TRAINING, and VITICULTURE.

R.E.S. & J.V.

Robinson, J., et al., *Wine Grapes: A Complete Guide to 1,368 Vine Varieties, Including Their Origins and Flavours* (2012).

Vitovska, high-quality but rare white wine grape from the Karst region of south-west Slovenia and north-east Italy rescued from near-extinction in the 1980s. A CROSS between MALVASIA Bianca Lunga and GLERA, it produces distinctively fresh and firmly STRUCTURED wines, especially when SKIN-FERMENTED.

Viura is the RIOJA synonym for the MACABEO grape.

Vivarais, Côtes du, AOC on the right bank of the RHÔNE immediately opposite GRIGNAN-LES-ADHÉMAR largely in the Ardèche. The region's 225 ha/556 acres in 2020 are widely dispersed on mainly LIMESTONE soils in a cooler, wetter climate than the rest of the southern Rhône. Red and rosé wine dominates. A small amount of white is made, mainly from Grenache Blanc.

M.C.W.

Vizetelly, Henry (1820–94), prolific English wine writer whose detailed accounts of the history of port and champagne are particularly celebrated. Vizetelly came from a family of printers, and so it is particularly appropriate that today his influence is perhaps most marked in the continued, and increasingly imprecise, reproduction of the engravings which distinguished his many and various books about wine. He was introduced to wine in 1869 when he was sent to Paris to report on the French vintage for the *Pall Mall Gazette*, narrowly escaping execution during the Franco-Prussian War the next year. He spent much of the 1870s visiting the vineyards of France and Germany and in 1877 visited Portugal, Madeira, and the Canary Islands. Whereas JULLIEN and REDDING provided global wine surveys for the specialist reader, Vizetelly managed both to delve more deeply into specific wine regions and to produce books which appealed to a wider market. On his eventual return to England, he became a publisher; as Zola's English publisher, he was imprisoned and financially ruined.

Gabler, J. M., *Wine into Words: A History and Bibliography of Wine Books in the English Language* (1985).

vocabulary, tasting. See LANGUAGE OF WINE, TASTING-NOTES LANGUAGE, and TASTING TERMS.

voile. See FILM-FORMING YEAST.

Vojvodina, autonomous region within SERBIA.

volatile. All wines are volatile in that they contain volatile FLAVOUR COMPOUNDS and some level of VOLATILE ACIDS, but 'volatile' is used as a pejorative tasting term for a wine in which the level of ACETIC ACID has risen unacceptably high.

volatile acidity (or **VA**) is a measure of the volatile acids in wine, those that can be distilled. ACETIC ACID is the most prevalent, which is why it is used as the routine measure of VA. Acids such as carbonic, sulfurous, and LACTIC may also be present in trace amounts. It is not the acetic acid itself that causes changes in the aroma of a wine but the ESTER known as ETHYL ACETATE, the reaction product of acetic acid and ETHANOL.

VA in wine is usually considered to be a FAULT but at low levels—below the detection threshold of about 0.7 g/l—the VA may seem to LIFT the aroma. Higher levels result in loss of fruity aromas, less precision, and, at worst, aromas and flavours of VINEGAR and nail-polish remover, but this will depend on the wine style (sweet wines have higher VA levels) as well as the sensitivity of the taster. A few fine red wines are rich enough in BODY, TANNINS, and ALCOHOL to bear quite high concentrations of acetic acid, although they would surely be even better without it. The legal limits for VA in wine in the EU are 1.07 g/l for white and rosé wines and 1.2 g/l for red wines.

There are two sources of VA in wine. YEAST naturally produce small amounts of VA during FERMENTATION (usually up to 0.5 g/l). Its production is influenced by yeast strain, fermentation temperature, and, for white and rosé wines, juice turbidity. SPONTANEOUS FERMENTATIONS or those that are sluggish will often have elevated levels of VA, which may result in a STUCK FERMENTATION.

The second source of VA is acetic acid bacteria from either the vineyard or the winery. These bacteria are always present, but it is only when they are provided with ideal growing conditions that they form acetic acid. The two main genera in this family are GLUCONOBACTER, which breaks down grape sugars to produce acetic acid, and ACETOBACTER, which will convert ETHANOL to acetic acid in the presence of oxygen. Diseased fruit in the vineyard will have elevated levels of these bacteria. Post fermentation, acetobacter may start growing again if there are low levels of SO_2 or high levels of oxygen. Good cellar hygiene and regular analysis of SO_2 and VA levels will prevent this from happening.

K.C. & V.L.

volatile sulfur compounds, or **VSCs**, group of powerful and conspicuous FLAVOUR COMPOUNDS which play a significant role in wine flavour. Some typically contribute positive fruity flavours; others are considered FAULTS IN WINE. Whether they are seen positively or negatively depends on their concentration, on the style of wine, and on the taste preferences of the wine drinker, although HYDROGEN SULFIDE is always a fault. For more details, see THIOLS, SULFIDES, and REDUCTION.

V.F.

volatility, property of having excessive VOLATILE ACIDS.

volcanic describes the processes and products of volcanic eruptions. The products include ejected fragments which settle to produce rocks such as TUFF and lava solidified to give BASALT. Volcanic materials are very varied, but all involve several silicate minerals (see GEOLOGY) and are therefore rich in potential SOIL NUTRIENTS. The rapid weathering of recently produced volcanic rocks in the tropics, for example, yields some of the most fertile soils on Earth.

So-called volcanic soils were not themselves involved in volcanism but are derived from parent rocks which in most cases erupted tens or hundreds of million years previously. They are typically slightly acid, well-drained, and dark-coloured. The silicate minerals and the nutrients they yield are identical to those in non-volcanic rocks, but some commentators claim that vines grown on volcanic soils have something in common, for example a salty flavour or a specific TEXTURE.

The numerous wine-producing areas with volcanic rocks include SANTORINI and the CANARY ISLANDS; Italy's SOAVE, ETNA, and Monte Vulture in BASILICATA; TOKAJ in Hungary, IDAHO, WASHINGTON, and OREGON in the US; and the Kaiserstuhl-Tuniberg region of BADEN in Germany. See BASALT and TUFF for further examples.

A.J.M.

Volnay, attractive small village in the Côte de Beaune district of Burgundy's Côte d'Or producing elegant red wines from Pinot Noir. The wines of Volnay were celebrated under the *ancien régime* for their delicacy: Claude Arnoux describes them as partridge-eye pink in colour and the finest of all the wines of the Côte de Beaune, although they had to be drunk very young. Since then they have alternated in fame with those of neighbouring POMMARD depending on whether FASHION dictated wines of breed or of power.

More than half Volnay's vineyards are of PREMIER CRU status, stretching in a broad swathe from Pommard to MEURSAULT, continuing into the latter village. Because Meursault is renowned for its white wines, its single really fine red-wine vineyard of Les Santenots is sold as **Volnay Santenots**, which has its own appellation. The best part of this vineyard is Les Santenots-du-Milieu, although it is not as typical of Volnay as Le Cailleret, which it abuts. First-class wines are also made in such vineyards as Champans, Clos des Chênes, Taillepieds, and various MONOPOLES: Clos des Ducs (Marquis d'Angerville), Clos du Château des Ducs (Domaine Michel Lafarge), and Clos de la Bousse d'Or and Clos Verseuil (Clerget).

See also CÔTE D'OR and map under BURGUNDY. J.T.C.M.

Arnoux, C., *Dissertation sur la situation de Bourgogne* (1728).

VORS and VOS, classifications for age-dated SHERRY.

Vosges OAK comes from the mountains to the immediate west of ALSACE.

Vosne-Romanée, village in the Côte de Nuits district of Burgundy's CÔTE D'OR producing arguably the finest red wines made anywhere from Pinot Noir grapes (see map under BURGUNDY). As well as excellent wines at VILLAGE and PREMIER CRU level, there are six GRAND CRU vineyards, three of which share the name Romanée, the suffix to which Vosne was hyphenated in 1866.

The grands crus are Romanée-Conti, La Romanée, La Tâche, Richebourg, Romanée-St-Vivant, and La Grande Rue. Between them they produce, with Musigny and Chambertin, the greatest wines of the Côte de Nuits. They have more finesse than any other, but to this is allied as much power and stuffing as their nearest rivals.

A vineyard formerly known as Le Cloux was rechristened La Romanée in 1651, presumably on account of Roman remains being discovered nearby. In 1760 the property was bought by the Prince de Conti, subsequently becoming known as Romanée-Conti. Just above this vineyard, whose wines can be the most expensive in the world, is La Romanée. Romanée-Conti has brown, CALCAREOUS soil about 60 cm/23 in deep with 45–49% CLAY and liable to serious SOIL EROSION in the upper, steeper part. La Romanée also has a notably steep slope with less clay and more RENDZINA in the make-up of the soil. The former is the MONOPOLE of the DOMAINE DE LA ROMANÉE-CONTI (DRC), the latter of Comte Liger-Belair. About 300 cases are made each year from the tiny 0.84 ha/2 acres of La Romanée, double that is produced from the 1.8 ha of Romanée-Conti.

Another monopoly of DRC, and regarded as nearly as fine as the vineyard from which it takes its name, is La Tâche, whose 6 ha (including much of the vineyard of Les Gaudichots, which used to be separate but is considered to be of the same quality) produce a wine which is explosively seductive even when young, whereas Romanée-Conti takes longer to show its astonishing completeness. La Tâche seems to thrive even in lesser years, being judged the only wine worthy of bottling by the Domaine de la Romanée-Conti in 1950 and 1951.

The next most sought-after Vosne-Romanée wine is Richebourg, whose 8 ha are shared between ten growers, notably Domaine de la Romanée-Conti, Domaine LEROY, Grivot, branches of the Gros family, and Domaine Méo-Camuzet. As the name suggests, this is one of the most voluptuous wines of Burgundy and can equal La Tâche in some years.

Romanée-St-Vivant, taking its name from the monastery of St-Vivant founded at Vergy *c.* 900 and subsequent owner of the vineyard, can also make very fine wine, but it is usually lighter and less powerful than its neighbours, being further down the slope and having deeper soil. There are half a dozen owners, of which the largest is Domaine de la Romanée-Conti (5.3 ha out of 9.43). Domaine Leroy and Louis LATOUR's Domaine de Corton Grancey are the next largest owners.

Between La Tâche to the south and La Romanée-Conti to the north lie the 1.4 ha of La Grande Rue, originally classified as PREMIER CRU but promoted, as its location suggests is only right, to grand cru. The vineyard is a monopoly of Domaine Lamarche. Among the best of Vosne-Romanée's premier cru vineyards are Les Malconsorts on the Nuits-St-Georges side, Cros Parantoux made famous by Henry Jayer, above the grands crus, and Les Beauxmonts and Les Suchots abutting Flagey-Échezeaux. Part of Les Beauxmonts is actually in the latter commune, although it is sold as Vosne-Romanée, as is the village wine of Flagey.

While the renown of the Domaine de la Romanée-Conti dominates Vosne-Romanée, it should not overshadow other significant influences: Henri Jayer, for his unparalleled winemaking skills; René Engel, for his patriarchal influence and local historical research and publications; and Lalou Bize-LEROY, who bought and transformed the former Domaine Nöellat. Other particularly fine domaines are those owned by the various members of the Gros family, Domaine Jean Grivot, and Sylvain Cathiard. J.T.C.M.

Crum, G., *Domaine de la Romanée-Conti* (2018).
Meadows, A., *The Pearl of the Côte* (2010).
Norman, R., *Grand Cru* (2010).
Olney, R., *Romanée-Conti* (1991).

Vougeot, small village in the Côte de NUITS district of Burgundy producing red wines from the Pinot Noir grape. The name is derived from the diminutive of Vouge, a small stream rising nearby. There are only 2.3 ha/6 acres of vineyards producing VILLAGE WINE and 13 ha designated PREMIER CRU; the village's fame rests squarely with the 50-ha GRAND CRU, Clos de Vougeot.

The fame of Clos de Vougeot is historical since it was the flagship vineyard of the Cistercians (see MONKS AND MONASTERIES), who planted and enclosed what is significantly the largest grand cru vineyard of the Côte de Nuits. Geologically, this is not a homogeneous site: the top, abutting Musigny and Grands Échezeaux, has a light CALCAREOUS and GRAVELLY soil on oolitic LIMESTONE which drains beautifully and gives the wines of greatest distinction; the middle section is on softer limestone with CLAY and some gravel, with moderate drainage on a very gentle slope. The bottom section, almost flat, stretching down to the main D974 road, consists of poorly drained ALLUVIAL clay.

When the wines could be blended by the monks to produce a complete wine from differing constituent parts, Clos de Vougeot doubtless deserved its reputation. Now that the vineyard is fragmented between 80 or more owners, its grand cru status is less easy to defend, especially as the wines do not shine in their infancy. Classic Clos de Vougeot is likely to be dense and ungiving when young, robust rather than elegant. However, after a decade it opens out into one of the most complete wines of the Côte d'Or with deep, rich flavours reminiscent of truffles and undergrowth.

Of the premier cru vineyards, Le Clos Blanc, the monopoly of Domaine de la Vougeraie in succession to Héritiers Guyot, has produced white wine since first planted by the monks in 1110. The other premier crus are Les Cras, Les Petits Vougeots, and Clos de la Perrière, a MONOPOLE of Domaine Bertagna.

Reliable producers of Clos de Vougeot include Ch de la Tour (the largest owners), Méo-Camuzet, Anne Gros, and Domaine d'Eugénie.

See also CLOS DE VOUGEOT, CÔTE D'OR, and map under BURGUNDY. J.T.C.M.

Vouvray, the most important white-wine appellation in the TOURAINE district just east of the city Tours on the right bank of the LOIRE. Vouvray is CHENIN BLANC (although up to 5% MENU PINEAU grapes are theoretically allowed). No other wine made only from this long-lived Loire grape variety, often called Pineau de la Loire, is made in such quantity, from more than 2,200 ha/5,430 acres of vineyard. Vouvray wines vary enormously in quality, thereby offering a true representation of the grape's finicky behavior.

Vouvray itself is a small, pretty town whose wines owe much to the MONKS AND MONASTERIES who refined local viticulture from the Middle Ages. But it was not until the creation of the AOC in 1936 that Vouvray established an identity of its own; before then most of it was shipped out for blending by the energetic DUTCH WINE TRADE, and much of the wine sold as Vouvray came from anywhere in Touraine.

The region's best TERROIR has historically been the flat, stony plateau that overlays the TUFFEAU cliffs overlooking the Loire from Rochecorbon to Vernou-sur-Brenne. Small rivers dissected this plateau, creating perpendicular valleys with sheltered slopes further from the Loire (in Parçay-Meslay, Reugny, Chançay, and Noizay). Three main topoils cover the LIMESTONE bedrock: a mix of FLINTY-clay or *perruches* (known for wines with great AGEING potential), a CHALKY-clay called *aubuis* (known for wines of concentration), and younger sandy GRAVELS (more suited to sparkling wines). Wine style is also influenced by the weather, as the locals claim that this is where the Atlantic climate meets the CONTINENTAL CLIMATE, inducing much VINTAGE variation. In the least generous years, dry and sparkling wines make up the bulk of production, but top vintages yield styles from bone-dry SEC wines to golden MOELLEUX and LIQUOREUX wines that can age a century or more.

Making top-quality Vouvray Moulleux or Liquoreux wines is as hazardous as making any top-quality sweet white wine which owes its sweetness to NOBLE ROT or extreme RIPENESS because the vine-grower is at the mercy of the weather, which can be changeable in autumn. Thanks to CLIMATE CHANGE, winegrowers increasingly rely on passerillage (see PASSERILLÉ) more than on botrytis to acheive natural sweetness.

Great dry wine (with less than 8 g/l of RESIDUAL SUGAR) is slowly on the rise as a small but increasing number of producers lower yields and hand-harvest their grapes to produce expressive wines. Historically, still Vouvray wines are vinified in neutral vessels such as old oak casks or stainless-steel tanks and bottled by the spring, the wine's naturally high acidity preserved as MALOLACTIC CONVERSION rarely occurs. Yet recently some producers are experimenting with longer ageing for special cuvées. Many demi-sec (medium-dry) wines are also made.

Sparkling wines remain an important style of Vouvray, representing nearly 60% of production in 2021. MOUSSEUX and PÉTILLANT versions are vinified by the TRADITIONAL METHOD and aged on the LEES for at least 12 months. The majority is sold in France as entry-level sparkling wine, with few growers realizing the remarkable potential of the style. Commercial still Vouvray also exists, a medium-sweet, reasonably acidic wine that has little capacity for development. The thousands of members of the Confrérie de la Chantepleure, a wine fraternity founded in 1937, actively promote Vouvray wines. P.Le.

See also LOIRE, including map.

VQA, Vintners Quality Alliance, the similar but separate CONTROLLED APPELLATION systems that operate in the provinces of ONTARIO and BRITISH COLUMBIA. VQA wines must be made entirely from grapes grown in CANADA. Although certification is voluntary, the provincially regulated VQA standards are legally enforceable by Vintners Quality Alliance Ontario and the British Columbia Wine Authority respectively. J.D.

www.vqaontario.ca
www.bcvqa.ca

Vranac, very promising indigenous Balkan red grape variety grown in southern CROATIA, Herzegovina (see BOSNIA), Kosovo, Montenegro, NORTH MACEDONIA (where it is known as **Vranec**), and SERBIA. The wines produced are deeply coloured and can be rich in EXTRACT, responding unusually well to BARREL AGEING. There is an element of refreshing bitterness on the finish of these wines. DNA PROFILING has shown Vranac to be the offspring of Duljenga, an old Montenegrin variety, and Kratošija (see TRIBIDRAG).

VSIG stands for Vin Sans Indication Géographique, the French equivalent of a WINE WITHOUT GEOGRAPHICAL INDICATION and the official EU category for wines sold as VIN DE FRANCE.

VSP, **vertical shoot positioning**. See TRAINING SYSTEMS and VERTICAL TRELLIS

VT. See VENDANGES TARDIVES.

Vulkanland Steiermark, wine region of Austria, known prior to 2016 as Südoststeiermark and accorded DAC status in 2018. It covers a vast area and harbours 1,671 ha/4,129 acres of vines, or 3.7% of Austria's vineyard. Top growers stake claims for the distinctiveness of their individual sectors and villages, of which the best-known are Kapfenstein, Straden, Klöch, and Bad Radkersburg. Generally warmer than the rest of STEIERMARK (and warmer as one goes south), this region has a long-standing reputation for both dry and off-dry TRAMINER. Authorized grape varieties for the DAC are WELSCHRIESLING, Morillon (Chardonnay), Riesling, Gelber MUSKATELLER, GRAUBURGUNDER (Pinot Gris), WEISSBURGUNDER (Pinot Blanc), Sauvignon Blanc, and TRAMINER as well as BLENDS from these; but further limitations apply to village-level and SINGLE-VINEYARD WINES. D.S.

Wachau, important wine region in Austria comprising (in 2021) 1,291 ha/3,190 acres of spectacular, typically south-facing vineyards upstream of KREMS on the Danube. 'Wachau' was long used to refer collectively to the vast array of vineyards within a radius of roughly 16 km/10 miles around Krems, then regarded as its capital. But in the aftermath of Austria's 1985 wine scandal, the recently formed growers' association VINEA WACHAU lobbied successfully for a more restricted delimitation. Today the Wachau constitutes just under 3% of Austria's vine surface and, owing to relatively low yields, represents an even smaller proportion of total wine production, but it has since the 1990s arguably become Austria's most prestigious wine region.

The region and its growers' association are best known for the stylistic division of dry, unchaptalized wines (see CHAPTALIZATION) into the weight classes STEINFEDER, FEDERSPIEL, and SMARAGD, each defined by a distinct range of MUST WEIGHT and ALCOHOLIC STRENGTH. These remained unchanged when the three-tiered Wachau DAC, which stipulates hand harvesting, was created in 2020. The Gebietswein (regional wine) category permits all 17 locally significant grape varieties: Grüner Veltliner, Riesling, Chardonnay, Pinot Blanc (Weissburgunder), Pinot Gris, Sauvignon Blanc, Neuburger, Muskateller, Roter Veltliner, and Zweigelt, as well as blends. Wines labelled for commune (village) are restricted to nine varieties, while SINGLE-VINEYARD WINES must be either Grüner Veltliner or Riesling.

Much of the Wachau is dramatically terraced and defined by ancient rocks of VOLCANIC origin—along with their metamorphic and decomposed variants. GRAVEL and ALLUVIUM characterize some level stretches near the Danube, and LOESS—the ancient glacial dust that dominates many vineyards east of Krems—has settled among rocky slopes in certain places. The role of fast-draining, nutrient-poor soils based on rocks of crystalline structure is far from understood, but local growers as well as many consumers with a penchant for Wachau wine are confident of their ability to distinguish this region's wines according to their vineyards or at least their basic SOIL TYPES. The Wachau's TERRACES accumulate heat and drain moisture so quickly that vine SHUTDOWN is a hazard in years characterized by heat or DROUGHT. This circumstance prompted the installation of IRRIGATION lines, an initiative not without controversy but one that seems to have been instrumental in the more than three decades during which Wachau wines have achieved consistently higher must weights, more harmonious ACIDITY, and greater prestige than at any time since the Middle Ages. A further effect of selective irrigation was to extend the Wachau's already characteristically late harvests into November and sometimes December, though, in the face of climatic warming (see CLIMATE CHANGE) and the gradual increase in alcohol levels, a trend towards earlier harvest is recently in evidence. The Wachau also experiences some of the wine world's most extreme DIURNAL TEMPERATURE RANGES, thanks to a dependable daily pattern by which warm air is sucked upstream along the Danube from the Pannonian-Hungarian Plain, then displaced by cold moving in the opposite direction from the pre-Alps and forests that dominate the west and north of the region.

The Wachau's best-known villages, travelling upstream from east to west, with some of their most famous vineyards, are:

Unterloiben (Kreutles, Steinertal)
Oberloiben (Loibenberg, Schütt)
Dürnstein (Hollerin, Kaiserberg, Kellerberg)
Weissenkirchen (Achleiten, Klaus, Steinriegel, Weitenberg)
Joching (Kollmitz, Pichl Point)
Wösendorf (Hochrain, Kollmütz, Kirchweg)
Spitz (Axpoint, Hochrain, Setzberg, Singerriedel, Tausendeimerberg aka Burgberg)

The Spitzerbach, with its associated village of Viessling and its vineyards Brück and Schön, extends west into high hills from Spitz and away from the Danube, offering favourable conditions in an era of climate change. While the Wachau's right-bank vineyards generally generate little excitement, there are recent pockets of interest, and those of former Roman garrison Mautern—immediately opposite the Danube from Stein, which is part of the official KREMSTAL—are of contemporary as well as historical importance, thanks primarily to the Nikolaihof estate, associated with viticulture since at least the 5th century. Average holdings in the Wachau have largely resisted the national trend towards consolidation, partly due to the continuing success of the Domäne Wachau (formerly Freie Weingärtner Wachau) CO-OPERATIVE, whose nearly 200 members collectively own almost one-third of the Wachau's vineyard area. D.S.

Wädenswil, viticultural research station on Lake Zurich in German-speaking Switzerland established in the late 19th century and now part of AGROSCOPE.

Wagga, abbreviation for the School of Agricultural and Wine Sciences, Wagga Wagga, now part of CHARLES STURT UNIVERSITY.

Wagner, Philip (1904–96), Baltimore newspaper editor, VITICULTURIST, WINEMAKER, and author of books on vines and wine. Beginning as a HOME WINEMAKER during PROHIBITION, Wagner published *American Wines and How to*

Make Them (1933). Interested in improving the basis of eastern American winemaking, Wagner began to import and test FRENCH HYBRID vines in 1939 and to distribute them from the NURSERY and vineyard he founded, Boordy Vineyard, in Maryland. His *A Wine-Grower's Guide* (1945) was the first work to publicize French hybrids in the US; in the same year he produced, at Boordy, the first French hybrid wine on record in the US. Wagner's success with his wines, his activity in supplying French hybrids from his nursery, and the persuasiveness of his writing in favour of a better selection of VINE VARIETIES entitle him to be regarded as the man who changed the course of winemaking in the eastern US. T.P.

Wagram is a 2,439-ha/6,027-acre wine region of Austria (5.4% of its vineyards) on the largely LOESS and broadly terraced left bank of the Danube between KREMSTAL and VIENNA. Until 2007 it was part of a region known as 'Donauland', including today's TRAISENTAL as well as the right-bank vineyards of KLOSTERNEUBURG. After years of heated discussion, a Wagram DAC was announced in February 2022 that includes Klosterneuburg and its right-bank neighbourhood and recognizes 27 villages (three times as many as in the similarly sized and better-known Kremstal). The only significant limitations are that village-designated wines are restricted to seven of the region's 13 widely planted grape varieties and SINGLE-VINEYARD WINES to Grüner Veltliner, Roter Veltliner, and Riesling.

GRÜNER VELTLINER dominates plantings, at 54% of all vines in 2021. ROTER VELTLINER (no relation of Grüner Veltliner), while representing little more than 4% of Wagram vine hectarage, yields piquant, distinctive wines. Like RIESLING (with its 5.4% regional share), Roter Veltliner tolerates the dry conditions associated with those Wagram vineyards that are underlain by GRAVEL. Most other grapes familiar from parts of NIEDERÖSTERREICH west of Vienna are at home in the Wagram (ZWEIGELT being second most planted by far at 12.5%), which also boasts some impressive recently revived remnants of GEMISCHTER SATZ. D.S.

Wairarapa, GEOGRAPHICAL INDICATION (GI) at the southern end of New Zealand's North Island about one hour's drive from the nation's capital, Wellington. The dry, cool climate is ideal for PINOT NOIR, which occupies half the region's 1,039-ha/2,567-acre vineyard area and is naturally low yielding due to habitually cool weather at FLOWERING. The region comprises several subregions, of which Martinborough (GI) is the most southerly and largest, with 42 wineries, including the famed Ata Rangi and Dry River. Vineyards rest on free-draining alluvial GRAVELS and CLAY terraces. Gladstone (GI) is centrally located while Masterton lies to the north, with ten producers between them. Most wineries are small, family-run affairs with CELLAR DOORS that benefit from weekend traffic from city dwellers. Nearly one-third of the total vineyard area is Sauvignon Blanc, while Chardonnay and Pinot Gris cover less than 100 ha/247 acres each. S.P.-T.

Waitaki, GEOGRAPHICAL INDICATION in North Otago, is the coolest viticultural region in New Zealand, with 59 ha/146 acres of vines planted on LIMESTONE soils. The climate and soils show particular promise for PINOT NOIR, though excellent Pinot Gris, Riesling, and Chardonnay are also produced. S.P.-T.

waiter, wine. See SOMMELIER.

Wales had 35 vineyards covering 58 ha/143 acres in 2021. CLIMATE CHANGE has benefited well-sheltered sites, and better YIELDS coupled with more interest in local wines has made viticulture more financially viable than it was in the past. Wine quality is still behind that of neighbouring ENGLAND, although a 2018 Blauer FRÜHBURGUNDER from a Welsh vineyard won a gold medal in a major UK wine COMPETITION (Decanter World Wine Awards).

Wales has the same CONTROLLED APPELLATION system as England, allowing producers to make Welsh Quality Wine and Welsh Regional Wine in both still and sparkling. S.S.

Walker Bay, southerly, relatively cool MARITIME wine district in South Africa. Its most important wards are Hemel-en-Aarde Valley, Upper Hemel-en-Aarde Valley, and Hemel-en-Aarde Ridge. Walker Bay's vineyards produce many of South Africa's most promising wines made from Chardonnay and Pinot Noir.

Wälschriesling. See WELSCHRIESLING.

war, effects on wine. Wine is a way of life literally rooted in the soil. It is also capital- and LABOUR-intensive and reliant on a complex distribution network, which make it highly vulnerable during times of war.

The most visible effect of war is the destruction of vineyards. Just as it was customary for warring ancient Greeks to cut down or burn the vines of their enemies, so the BARBARIAN invaders of Roman Europe signalled victory in the same way.

Planting on newly captured territory likewise symbolized success. When the Christians drove the Moors from medieval SPAIN, they planted vines behind them, as did the Crusaders who briefly held parts of the Holy Land. It is difficult to imagine a clearer expression of a battle won and determination to stay than the planting of such a long-term crop as vines.

Certain regions have suffered ruin disproportionately because of their strategic geographical position. The location of the CHAMPAGNE region at the crossroads of northern Europe has ensured the destruction of its vineyards dozens of times, most famously when they were bisected by the trenches of the First World War.

The short-term effects of war have sometimes had permanent consequences. The Thirty Years War (1618–48), which ravaged 17th-century Europe, was so destructive that many northern German vineyard areas were never replanted (see GERMAN HISTORY). Recovery was hampered by the sheer scale of the devastation, by lack of a labour force due to depopulation, and by destruction of capital equipment.

Plundering of existing wine stocks is another common feature of European war, with Champagne, once again, an obvious example. When Russian soldiers occupied the region in 1814 they were not slow to help themselves. In this case the Champagne houses did at least have the subsequent consolation that the Russians became their wines' most loyal peacetime consumers until 1917. In general, however, terrible hardship resulted from forced requisitioning and outright plunder. Civil conflicts, such as the French Wars of Religion in the 16th century, were at least as destructive.

The sale and distribution of wine is a complex operation which is inevitably dislocated by war. TRANSPORT becomes hazardous. During the HUNDRED YEARS WAR (1337–1453), ships carrying wine between Bordeaux and England were attacked so often that convoys were arranged for safety.

Wars also frequently led to a ban on trade with the enemy. When Britain and France were at war in the early 18th century, French wine imports into Britain were prohibited. Smuggling was one answer to the problem; switching to wine produced by the ally Portugal was another. Thus war altered trading and consumption patterns, and PORT became the staple wine of Georgian England.

Wars do not bring uniform misfortune. The demand for wine to provision troops in some cases provided a stimulus to wine regions not directly involved in the fighting. The Roman army needed huge supplies to send it into battle. Records show that, when Edward I embarked on his Scottish campaign in 1300, he first bought in vast quantities of wine from Bordeaux.

It is also probable that the influx of American forces into Second World War Europe and its aftermath was an important factor in building the wine market in the UNITED STATES.

Historically the effects of war on wine, as on so many other commercial activities, have been mixed, and in some cases one grower's suffering made another's fortune.

See also SYRIA, LEBANON, GEORGIA, AZERBAIJAN, and UKRAINE. H.B.

Bonal, F., *Le Livre d'or de Champagne* (1984).
Johnson, H., *The Story of Wine: From Noah to Now* (2020).
Kladstrup, D. and P., *Wine and War: The French, the Nazis, and the Battle for France's Greatest Treasure* (2001).

warm-climate viticulture is characterized by growing seasons long and warm enough for regular ripening of mid-season grape varieties (such as CABERNET FRANC, MERLOT, SYRAH (or Shiraz), and SANGIOVESE) and late-mid-season varieties (such as CABERNET SAUVIGNON and NEBBIOLO) to make mainly medium- to full-bodied red TABLE WINES. CLIMATE CLASSIFICATION indices indicate that warm-climate viticulture is typically practised in Winkler Regions III and IV, Huglin Index warm-temperate and warm classes, and within 17–19 °C/62.6–66.2 °F on the growing-season average-temperature index.

Typical regions are BORDEAUX and the northern RHÔNE Valley in France; the RIOJA Alta in Spain; much of northern ITALY and TUSCANY; the intermediate and warmer coastal valleys of California, such as NAPA and SONOMA; the north and east coasts of the North Island of NEW ZEALAND; Margaret River and the south coast of WESTERN AUSTRALIA; the Barossa Valley and Coonawarra in SOUTH AUSTRALIA; and much of central and northern VICTORIA.

Warm viticultural climates, if sunny enough, will ripen early and mid-season grape varieties to high sugar levels and make the best sweet, FORTIFIED WINES. They will also ripen late-maturing grape varieties such as MOURVÈDRE (Mataro), CARIGNAN, GRENACHE, TREBBIANO, and CLAIRETTE for making table wines. Examples are the south of France, the DOURO Valley of Portugal and the island of MADEIRA, the Adelaide district and McLaren Vale in South Australia, the MURRAY DARLING regions of South Australia and Victoria, and the Hunter Valley and Mudgee in NEW SOUTH WALES in Australia.

Typical hot-climate viticultural regions are those producing TABLE GRAPES and RAISINS in GREECE and TÜRKIYE and in the SAN JOAQUIN VALLEY of California. Growing-season average mean temperatures are mostly 21–22 °C/69.8–71.6 °F or higher. Subtropical and TROPICAL VITICULTURE for table grapes and wine, using mainly non-VITIS VINIFERA grape varieties, also falls into this temperature category. G.V.J.

Warre, important PORT shipper. See SYMINGTONS.

Washington, state in the Pacific Northwest that ranks second in wine-grape production in the US, with 24,281 ha/60,000 acres of wine grapes in 2021 and an average annual wine production of 181,843,600 l/40 million gal (about 5% of the national total). Over 99% of Washington's wine grapes are produced in the eastern part of the state, from irrigated vineyards in the arid to semi-arid lowlands of the Columbia Basin. Washington boasts 20 AVAS and over 1,000 wineries, with 90% producing fewer than 5,000 cases annually.

History

Italian and German immigrants planted Washington's first documented wine-grape vineyards in the Walla Walla and Yakima valleys during the latter half of the 19th century. By the 1870s Walla Walla was home to grapevine NURSERIES and was annually producing thousands of gallons of wine. Devastating WINTER FREEZE events in eastern Washington in the 1880s led many growers to doubt the long-term viability of their vineyards, stalling the early growth of the wine industry. Wine production was revitalized in the early 1900s by W. H. Bridgman, who successfully established vineyards with multiple VITIS VINIFERA varieties on Snipes Mountain in the Yakima Valley. Following the end of PROHIBITION in 1933 and until the early 1960s, the Washington wine industry was dominated by sweet FORTIFIED WINES produced from blends of *vinifera* and HYBRID grapes. Pioneering viticultural research in the Yakima Valley by Dr Walter Clore confirmed the viability of multiple European cultivars, and under his guidance wine-grape plantings continually expanded: during the 1970s, plantings of European varieties expanded from 162 ha/400 acres to 1,207 ha/3,000 acres, and Washington wines produced by Chateau Ste Michelle and Associated Vintners began to be marketed throughout the US. By the end of the 1970s there were 16 wineries in Washington producing 1 million gallons of wine. Critical acclaim for Washington Riesling in the 1970s and for Cabernet Sauvignon- and Merlot-based wines in the 1980s spurred the expansion of Washington's vineyards and wineries, such that by 1990 over 7 million gallons of wine were produced by 92 wineries. The Yakima Valley became Washington's first federally sanctioned AVA in 1983, followed the next year by the Columbia Valley and Walla Walla Valley AVAs. The number of wineries and vineyard hectarage have continued to increase at a rapid rate into the 21st century.

Geography

Washington's most dramatic landscape feature is the Cascades, a range of mountains oriented north–south and punctuated by VOLCANIC peaks, some recently or potentially active, that include Mt Rainier, which rises over 4,267 m/14,000 ft. West of the Cascades, wine-grape vineyards have been planted on the coastal lowlands surrounding Puget Sound (Puget Sound AVA) and further south in the lowlands between the Cascades and Willapa Hills. Most of Washington's vineyards lie east of the Cascades in the Columbia Basin, a large low-ELEVATION plain traversed by the Columbia River, the fourth-largest river in the US. The viticultural areas east of the Cascades are predominantly situated at elevations below 610 m/2,000 ft, within the 11.25-million-acre Columbia Valley AVA, which includes 15 sub-AVAs whose boundaries are based on local variations in GEOLOGY, SOIL TYPE, and geomorphology. The vineyards in many sub-AVAs, including the Horse Heaven Hills, Red Mountain, Candy Mountain, Snipes Mountain, Rattlesnake Hills, Royal Slope, and Wahluke Slope AVAs, are situated on the south-facing slopes of ridgelines that traverse the Columbia Basin.

Washington's winegrowing regions are situated at latitudes 46–48° N, which corresponds to the area of France between Bordeaux and Burgundy. At these latitudes, throughout most of the growing season the sun is above the horizon for longer each day than in the wine regions of California.

Geology and soils

East of the Cascades, vineyards within the Columbia Basin are underlain almost everywhere by BASALT bedrock. In most vineyards, the bedrock is beyond the reach of vine roots as it is locally covered by the deposits of ancient rivers and lakes and, at most elevations below 366 m/1,200 ft, by SILT, SAND, and GRAVEL deposited by ice-age floods. The Missoula floods, which are the most recent of the flood events and have the most impact, were derived from the repeated failure of glacial ice dams in northern IDAHO between 13,000 and 16,000 years ago. The surficial sediments of the Columbia Basin, which comprise most vineyard soils, consist predominantly of wind-deposited silt and sand derived from the deposits of the Missoula floods. Since the flood sediments were largely sourced from the glacial erosion of GRANITIC rocks outside the Columbia Basin, the soils are chemically distinct from the underlying basalt bedrock.

The Lake Chelan and Rocky Reach AVAs on the western side of the Columbia Basin have granitic bedrock overlain by sediments deposited by glaciers, meltwater streams, and outburst floods. Further south along the Columbia Basin's western edge, the Naches Heights, Rattlesnake Hills, and Columbia Gorge AVAs contain regions underlain by bedrock derived from lavas and ash erupted from Cascade volcanoes.

The vineyard soils of eastern Washington are mostly deep and well-drained with very little CLAY and ORGANIC MATTER. Owing to the arid climate of eastern Washington, they often contain horizons of calcium carbonate (caliche; see GEOLOGY) with elevated PH values. A unique feature of many Columbia Basin vineyards are granite boulders (erratics) that were floated into place within icebergs that were entrained in the Missoula floods.

Since the vineyard soils in Washington west of the Cascades were mostly transported and deposited by streams and glaciers, they vary substantially in texture and overlie a large variety of bedrock types. Their thickness generally precludes interactions between vine roots and the underlying bedrock. They are generally much richer in clay and organic matter than the soils of the Columbia Basin.

Climate

The major influences on Washington's climate are the Pacific Ocean and the Cascades. West of the Cascades, the climate is heavily influenced by the cool (13 °C/55 °F) waters of the Pacific Ocean, which moderate temperatures. The climate of the Columbia Basin, east of the Cascades, is much more CONTINENTAL. Precipitation throughout Washington is highly seasonal, derived from Pacific storm systems that are most common October–April.

The Cascades deprive the Columbia Basin of eastern Washington of most of the moisture from Pacific storm systems. The moist Pacific air masses expend the bulk of their moisture in the Cascades, then the air is warmed by compression as it descends the eastern slopes of the Cascades, further reducing humidity and inhibiting cloud formation. These processes combine to create a dramatic rain shadow, so that much of eastern Washington's grape-growing areas receive less than 254 mm/10 in of annual precipitation. Sunny skies are the norm in eastern Washington from June to September, and during this time it is common for parts of the Columbia Basin to receive no measurable rainfall for 60–80 days. The AVAs on the mountainous fringes of the Columbia Basin, such as the Columbia Gorge and Walla Walla Valley, receive substantially more precipitation than AVAs nearer the basin's centre, such as Red Mountain and Yakima Valley.

The relatively cloud-free skies and dry air of the Columbia Basin allows temperatures to drop rapidly after sunset and warm quickly at daybreak. These conditions commonly produce wide DIURNAL TEMPERATURE RANGES, especially in the late summer and fall. The FROST-free period in the Columbia Basin generally occurs between mid April and mid October, yielding a growing season of 180–200 days. Growing degree days (see CLIMATE CLASSIFICATION) typically range from 2800 in cooler sites to 3600 in the warmest locations. Throughout the year, colder air often becomes ponded in the valleys that lie between the ridgelines of the Columbia Basin. This creates inversions where the coldest daily low temperatures are experienced at the lowest elevations on the valley floors. Every seven years on average, eastern Washington vineyards experience potentially damaging WINTER FREEZE events associated with Arctic air masses that push westward over the Rocky Mountains and into the Columbia Basin. During these events, temperatures often drop below −18 °C/0 °F.

In western Washington, summer is typically very dry, but a persistent layer of cool Pacific air often promotes the formation of fog and low clouds except in late summer. Western Washington's Olympic Mountains and the western slopes of the Cascades record the highest annual precipitation (2,540 mm/100 in or more) in the continental US. The lowland areas that host western Washington's vineyards receive more moderate annual precipitation (35–45 in). Due to the climate-moderating effects of the nearby Pacific Ocean and the topographic barrier of the Cascades, Western Washington generally has a longer frost-free growing season and less susceptibility to hard winter freeze events compared with the Columbia Basin. However, western Washington vineyards accumulate far fewer growing degree days (1500–2000) and receive far less solar radiation relative to their Columbia Basin counterparts due to the strong marine influence.

Viticulture

IRRIGATION is a necessity for most of Washington's vineyards. Water is sourced primarily from the Columbia and Yakima Rivers and from aquifers within the basalt bedrock. Vines can only be DRY-FARMED west of the Cascades, in the western part of the Columbia Gorge AVA, and in the eastern part of the Walla Walla Valley AVA. Most vineyards in the Columbia Basin are planted above valley floors on south-facing slopes, in a thermal belt that lies at elevations of 244–457 m/800–1,500 ft. Many vineyards have installed WIND MACHINES to mitigate damage from late-spring and early-fall freeze events. To protect vines from damage from winter incursions of Arctic air, viticulturists commonly bury canes or the lower parts of vine trunks after harvest. (See WINTER PROTECTION.)

The most common vine-TRAINING SYSTEM is vertical shoot positioning (VSP; see VERTICAL TRELLIS) in rows oriented north–south, but growers are beginning to implement other training methods as new areas less suited to traditional trellising are planted. The silt-based soils of Columbia Basin vineyards require COVER CROPS as they are highly susceptible to SOIL EROSION. Many growers regularly apply COMPOST between the rows to build ORGANIC CONTENT and promote biological activity in the desert soils.

Most of Washington's vines are own-rooted since it was long thought that the Columbia Basin's cold winters and clay-poor soil would thwart the infiltration of PHYLLOXERA. Unfortunately, phylloxera has recently been discovered to be spreading, albeit very slowly, in Columbia Basin vineyards. Many viticulturists have thus begun a programme of replanting on ROOTSTOCK. The arid, sunny, and often windy climate of the Columbia Basin discourages the growth of fungi, so the incidence of fungal diseases such as POWDERY MILDEW is low compared with most viticultural regions.

Varieties and styles

Washington's diverse topography and climate and the availability of irrigation water enables the cultivation of many grape varieties. At least 80 wine-grape varieties are currently planted. Of the 200,000 tons annually harvested, 60% are red varieties and 40% are white. Of the red varieties, the most commonly planted are Cabernet Sauvignon (50%), followed by Merlot (20%) and Syrah (17%). The most common white varieties are Chardonnay (40%), Riesling (35%), Pinot Gris (10%), and Sauvignon Blanc (10%). Washington's Chateau Ste Michelle Winery is the world's largest single producer of Riesling, with a half-million cases distributed annually. In the vineyards within the Puget Sound area, COOL-CLIMATE white grapes such as Müller-Thurgau, Madeleine Angevine, and Siegerrebe dominate. Pinot Noir is also cultivated in some of the warmer regions west of the Cascades, and plantings of this grape will likely expand there as the climate warms. (See CLIMATE CHANGE.)

Washington's ripening season is cooler than that of California, which helps to preserve ACIDITY and maintain the balance between phenolic ripeness and sugar content (see RIPENING). Critics often describe Washington wines as possessing TYPICALITY and bright fruit flavours and as bridging OLD WORLD and NEW WORLD styles.

K.R.P.

www.washingtonwine.org

water is the most important constituent of wine (see WINE COMPOSITION) and access to reliable supplies of good-quality water, particularly for IRRIGATION, is a pressing problem for an increasing number of wine producers, particularly in inland Australia and much of California—not least because of CLIMATE CHANGE, DROUGHT, and problems associated with SALINITY.

SOIL WATER, the product of RAINFALL and/or irrigation, is a prerequisite for vine growth and survival. PHOTOSYNTHESIS, without which grapes would never ripen, depends on water being available (which is why RIPENING stops if WATER STRESS is too severe). Water in the form of well-timed rain can also be useful in dusting off grapes immediately prior to HARVEST.

Water is also vital in the winery: HYGIENE's best friend is the hosepipe, and many systems of TEMPERATURE CONTROL depend on copious supplies of water. In warmer regions, the operation known euphemistically as HUMIDIFICATION is sometimes undertaken for ALCOHOL REDUCTION.

And then there is water as a drink. For centuries wine was always diluted with water; indeed, drinking undiluted wine was the mark of a barbarian in ancient GREECE and ancient ROME. Wine was a safer drink than most available water until the 17th century in major cities and much later than that elsewhere. In the late 1960s, this book's founding editor was offered unlimited wine as part of her board when working in a smart Italian hotel but had to pay for bottled water, the only reliable drinking water.

Modern wine drinkers rarely choose to dilute their wine (other than to make the occasional SPRITZER), but for HEALTH reasons they are well advised to drink at least as much water alongside every glass of wine. Despite its incontrovertible appeal, wine is a poor quencher of thirst.

water addition. See HUMIDIFICATION.

waterberry, an alternative name, current in California, for BUNCHSTEM NECROSIS, the physiological disorder of grape berry stems, drying and shrivelling grapes as they approach RIPENESS.

water deficit. See WATER STRESS.

water shoot, a shoot that arises from the wood of the vine, not from buds left at PRUNING. In fact they mostly arise from BASAL BUDS embedded in the wood and are generally not FRUITFUL. Suckers are a type of water shoot which arise at the base of the TRUNK at or below soil level. B.G.C.

water stress is the physiological state of plants, including vines, suffering from a shortage of water. Water stress during the later stages of the viticultural growing season is common, since a considerable proportion of the world's vines are grown in MEDITERRANEAN CLIMATES, where rain falls principally in the winter months and irrigation is restricted or not used. By the time of ripening, after mid summer, the amount of SOIL WATER may well be limiting. It is commonly held that mild water stress, often referred to as **water deficit**, is desirable for optimum wine quality, especially for red wines, but there is little agreement about exactly how much. There is, however, almost universal agreement that water deficit should be sufficient before VERAISON to stop SHOOT TIPS actively growing. Otherwise the shoot tips attract assimilates, the products of PHOTOSYNTHESIS, away from the ripening fruit, to the detriment of wine quality.

Water deficit is essential for growing good-quality dark-skinned grapes. It not only reduces shoot growth but also limits berry size and increases the PHENOLICS in the skins. However, these beneficial effects require a CANOPY free from SHADE and, generally, low YIELDS. A combination of high yields and water stress leads to poor ripening due to insufficient photosynthesis. This explains why great wines may be produced in very dry climatic conditions in southern France or Spain, for example, but only when yields are kept to 30 hl/ha or less. Peyrot des Gachons et al. have shown that water stress is not generally favourable for the quality of white wines, causing them to be less aromatic.

IRRIGATION can be used to overcome water stress. Although the practice is outlawed or severely restricted in some European countries, CLIMATE CHANGE is provoking reconsideration of this approach. Water stress results in restriction of growth and loss of yield. Unirrigated or DRY-FARMED vineyards in hot climates may yield only 2–5 tonnes/ha, for instance. PARTIAL ROOTZONE DRYING is an irrigation method which aims to stimulate the vines' perception of water stress while minimizing any drop in yield. Another irrigation strategy designed to induce water stress is REGULATED DEFICIT IRRIGATION. However, this technique is more likely to reduce yield and can induce excessive water stress in hot weather if not applied judiciously. Both techniques are successfully used in California and Australia to control water stress in vines at critical times to achieve better fruit and wine quality.

Water stress depends on two components: the available water content in the rootzone of the vine (see SOIL WATER); and the evaporative demand of the atmosphere, which shows signs of increasing as a result of climate change. The latter depends on factors affecting the rate of EVAPORATION, which is high on sunny, hot, windy days with low humidity. On days with extremely high evaporation, even well-watered vines can show temporary wilting. On the other hand, vines growing in dry soils but in overcast, cool, and humid climates do not show as much water stress. The combination of climate, soil, and vine architecture (consisting of VINE DENSITY, TRELLIS and TRAINING SYSTEMS, and PRUNING) which results in maximum vine stress is high evaporation, low soil water content, and large exposed leaf area (per unit of soil surface); minimum stress results from low evaporation, wet soils, and small leaf area.

Water stress is measured by vine physiologists as water potential in the plant but is more easily understood in terms of the effect on the vine. One of the first signs of impending water stress is the drooping, or wilting, of TENDRILS near the shoot tip, followed by wilting of the young, then the mature, leaves. With severe stress, the leaves exhibit yellowing, then NECROSIS, and may eventually fall off. Berries start to shrivel. As water stress develops in the vine, the plant responds by endeavouring to reduce water loss. In NEW WORLD countries in particular, where irrigation is more common, water stress is sometimes indicated by measurements of SOIL WATER content or suction, with irrigation decisions based on this information.

The direct measurement of water stress as experienced by the vine has been made possible by the commercial availability in the last decade of the 20th century of equipment such as PRESSURE BOMBS, which measure leaf or stem water potential. *In situ* tensiometers to measure water potential in the vine trunk have also been developed. Although time-consuming, such measurements can indicate day-to-day fluctuations in vine water status and are widely used in California and in other irrigated wine regions. They can be used to monitor irrigation, although such data are not always easy to interpret because the readings are affected by ambient weather conditions (temperature, sunshine, and humidity), which vary according to the time of day (discussed by Smart).

A very promising technique to measure the water deficit experienced by vines is to analyse carbon isotope discrimination by measuring the ratio of ^{13}C to ^{12}C in the sugar content of fully ripe grapes. In the process of photosynthesis, plants incorporate preferentially ^{12}C and thus 'discriminate' against ^{13}C, but in water-stress conditions isotope discrimination is less effective so that the $^{13}C/^{12}C$ ratio is lower. This ratio can therefore be used as a measurement of average water uptake conditions from veraison through to ripeness, as described in van Leeuwen et al. (2009). The measurement can be outsourced to specialized laboratories and requires no other field work than grape SAMPLING. Possible applications are the assessment of vine water status in TERROIR studies and validation of irrigation strategies at the end of the season.

A well-watered vine opens the pores called STOMATA on the underside of the leaf in response to the first light of dawn, and they remain open all day, allowing the free exchange of water vapour (the air humidity) and CARBON DIOXIDE between the leaf interior and the atmosphere. Water stress causes the vine leaf partially to close stomata during the day, and the hormone ABSCISIC ACID regulates this response. Initially this may be in the middle of the day, but subsequently, as the stress worsens, they are shut for most of the day. While this action is sufficient to reduce further water loss, photosynthesis is reduced because of the lack of carbon dioxide. Further, because the cooling benefit of transpiration is lost, leaves exposed to direct sunlight show a temperature increase of around 5 °C/40 °F or more. Using modern thermal imaging techniques, these elevated temperatures can be detected by PROXIMAL or REMOTE SENSING, as described by Matese et al. Recent studies have shown that stomata may stay open during the night, so that night-time water losses may occur (referred to as 'night-time transpiration') but with no benefit for photosynthesis since this occurs only in daylight conditions.

Water stress also affects a range of other vine functions. It can substitute for winter cold in promoting DORMANCY in TROPICAL VITICULTURE. During the growing season, DROUGHT causes shoot growth to slow and then stop as the leaf tip loses activity. Leaves are smaller and paler in colour, and the growth of LATERAL SHOOTS is also inhibited. Severe stress early in the season can reduce FRUIT SET, and later stress reduces BERRY SIZE.

The effect of water stress on wine quality is not straightforward. There is no doubt that severe water stress interrupts grape RIPENING and reduces wine quality (especially when yields are high). It is not clear whether water stress leads to higher SUGARS and better wine in dry viticultural areas such as the LANGUEDOC and ROUSSILLON in southern France. In humid MARITIME CLIMATES, such as that of BORDEAUX, however, there has been ample demonstration that mild water stress during ripening is favourable to wine quality. For example, the Bordeaux growing seasons of 1989, 1990, 1995, 1998, 2000, 2005, 2009, and 2010, all superior VINTAGES, were all relatively dry. Van Leuwen et al. (2009) show that all the driest vintages produced good quality while all the wettest vintages were relatively poor. R.E.S., C.v.L. & R.E.W.

Matese, A., et al., 'Estimation of water stress in grapevines using proximal and remote sensing methods', *Remote Sensing*, 10/1 (2018), 114.

Peyrot des Gachons, C., et al., 'The influence of water and nitrogen deficit on fruit ripening and aroma potential of *Vitis vinifera* L. cv Sauvignon blanc in field conditions', *Journal of the Science of Food and Agriculture*, 85/1 (2005), 73–85.

van Leeuwen, C., et al., 'Vine water status is a key factor in grape ripening and vintage quality for red Bordeaux wine. How can it be assessed for vineyard management purposes?', *Journal International des Sciences de la Vigne et du Vin*, 43/3 (2009), 121–34.

White, R. E., *Understanding Vineyard Soils* (2nd edn, 2015).

Waugh, Harry (1904–2001), English wine merchant famous for his longevity, courtesy, and open mind. He did not enter the wine trade until he was 30, joining as a clerk in a long-established City of London business associated with the fashionable West End company of Block, Grey & Block, where he went to work and first displayed his ability in selecting and selling fine wines. At that time, few British wine merchants visited the sources of their wines, and most relied on agents or their principals, who paid regular visits to Britain. In this way, Waugh met such well-known Bordeaux merchants as Christian Cruse, Jean Calvet, and Ronald BARTON.

During the Second World War, Waugh served in the Welsh Guards; at the beginning of 1946 he joined the London office of Harveys of Bristol. With wine in very short supply after six years of war, there was great demand for red bordeaux, the favoured table wine among regular wine drinkers. On holiday in Bordeaux, he was introduced by Édouard Cruse to the wines of POMEROL, then almost unknown in Britain. In 1950 he acquired and imported in cask the distinguished 1949 vintage of the then obscure PETRUS; by coincidence, so did that other Bristol wine merchant Ronald Avery. He also visited other French wine regions, including Beaujolais, then imported as a somewhat anonymous quaffing blend, but he introduced Harveys' customers to individual CRU Beaujolais.

After the devastating FROSTS of February 1956, Waugh, by then a director of Harveys, went with a colleague to Bordeaux and, through broker Jean-Paul Gardère, bought large quantities of the fine 1955 vintage, thereby bypassing the BORDEAUX TRADE, for which he was long remembered. He was a regular visitor for his firm to Oxford and Cambridge colleges, and in 1953 he instituted an annual Oxbridge undergraduate wine-tasting competition, sponsored until 1990 by Harveys (and subsequently by POL ROGER).

In 1962 the families who owned Ch LATOUR decided to sell and offered this famous Bordeaux FIRST GROWTH to Harveys. Although Waugh and his chairman were in favour, the majority of the board was against, so that Pearson, publishers of the *Financial Times*, acquired a 51% stake, while Harveys were allotted only 25%. Waugh became one of two Harvey representatives on the board, on which he remained through two changes of ownership. He introduced as joint managers Jean-Paul Gardère and his friend Henri Martin, proprietor of Ch Gloria (see ST-JULIEN). In 1966 when Harveys was bought by Showerings, producers of Babycham, a popular perry, Waugh, then 62, retired. (Seven years later his first children, twins, were born, both of whom went on to work in the UK wine trade.)

Then began Waugh's close association with wine amateurs in the United States. For many years he made regular lecture tours and achieved a reputation in the US unequalled by any other British wine professional. Several volumes of *Harry Waugh's Wine Diary* were published as a record of his punishing itineraries. He did much to publicize Ch Latour and Bordeaux in general. He also introduced California wines to British (and east-coast American) wine connoisseurs in the early 1970s when they were little known. For his services to French wines, he received the French Mérite Agricole in 1984, and in 1988 he was made a Chevalier de l'Ordre du Mérite National. In 1989 he was made an honorary member of the Institute of MASTERS OF WINE. He will always be remembered for his reply to someone who asked whether he had ever mistaken claret for burgundy: 'not since lunch'. E.P.-R.

Waugh, H., *Harry Waugh's Wine Diaries*, vols. i–ix (vols. i–v were individually entitled) (1966–81).

weather, probably the single most exasperatingly unpredictable variable in the viticultural equation, as in most other farming activities. For details of overall weather patterns, see CLIMATE, MACROCLIMATE, and CLIMATE CLASSIFICATION. For accounts of specific climatological phenomena with implications for wine production, see DEW, DROUGHT, FLOODING, FROST, HAIL, RAINFALL, SUNLIGHT, TEMPERATURE, and WIND. The weather in a specific growing season is the most important influence on the characteristics of a particular VINTAGE YEAR.

weed control, a range of viticultural practices to avoid WEEDS competing with vines—particularly young vines—for water and NUTRIENTS. The practices vary from region to region and with VINE AGE, with the common options being TILLAGE (ploughing) or HERBICIDES.

Mechanical control of weeds involves cultivating down the row alley using discs or tines. Tilling directly under the row is more difficult, as the weeding device needs to avoid the TRUNKS. A number of appropriate cultivators have been developed, with the swing-back action achieved manually in early models but now controlled automatically by touch-sensing the trunk. Even so, such tilling disturbs the ground under the vine row where the majority of roots are, and many machines can cause some vine damage. Hand hoeing of weeds is still found in some vineyards, although often this is restricted to the control of particularly difficult weeds in young vineyards. The alternative is to use herbicides, and spraying an undervine strip is common.

Mowing between the rows is common in summer rainfall areas or where there is plentiful IRRIGATION, otherwise the weeds growing there cause excessive WATER STRESS and sometimes NITROGEN deficiency, leading to incomplete fermentations. Other methods of weed control include using MULCH or cereal straw, for example, placed as a mat under the rows. This has the added advantage of increasing ORGANIC MATTER, EARTHWORM populations, and water infiltration. During the vines' early years, weeds may also be controlled by planting through a strip of plastic. R.E.S.

University of California Agriculture & Natural Resources, 'Integrated weed management', www.ipm.ucdavis.edu/PMG/r302700111.html.

weeder, implement used in vineyards for removing WEEDS, typically from the vine row. These machines, usually mounted on a tractor, have fallen from favour owing to the damage to some vines and the introduction of certain diseases because of vine injury, although modern machines cause less damage. In many parts of the world, undervine weeders has been replaced by HERBICIDES or the use of undervine MULCH.

R.E.S.

weeds. A weed is defined as a plant out of place. Although vine-growers have traditionally regarded a weedy vineyard as a sign of poor management, attitudes changed in the late 20th century, and the sight of a 'weedy' vineyard is now commonplace. Weeds, now sometimes referred to more kindly as volunteer COVER CROPS, are considered environmentally desirable as part of the vineyard ECOSYSTEM. Alternatively, some vineyards are frequently tilled to keep them free of weeds, to the detriment of SOIL STRUCTURE. HERBICIDES are also used, perhaps in combination with less frequent TILLAGE.

There is no doubt that weed growth can inhibit the growth of vines, especially when they are young. When the vine root system is small and shallow, weeds compete for water and nutrients, especially NITROGEN, but with older vines the competition can be less as the vine root system is larger and deeper. Some plant species seem to have a further effect in inhibiting others, a phenomenon known as allelopathy. In very weedy vineyards, the weeds may also compete with the vines for light.

Weeds can cause inconvenience and discomfort to vineyard workers and can also harbour VINE PESTS and VINE DISEASES, although they can also usefully shelter predators of insect vine pests. Weeds play an important part in the spread of the disease FLAVESCENCE DORÉE. In some vineyards, other plants may be deliberately encouraged to grow between the rows as a COVER CROP.

Weeds which occur in vineyards obviously vary from region to region and are representative of the local flora. Those present depend on prior land use, soil preparation, seed reserves in the soil, and the extent to which seeds arrive in the vineyard, by wind or on implements, for example. Weeds which are difficult to control and can be found in many vineyards worldwide include field bindweed (*Convolvulus arvensis*), Johnson grass (*Holcus halepensis*), and Bermuda or couch grass (*Cynadon dactylon*).

R.E.S.

Bettiga, L. J. (ed.), *Grape Pest Management* (3rd edn, 2013).

weighing of grapes is an important operation at any centre where grapes are received from a number of different growers who are paid by weight. This applies to most wine CO-OPERATIVES and many individual wineries, even if the more progressive take other factors such as grape quality and health into account before determining PRICE. Weighing is normally done with large platform scales on which the lorry is weighed full and empty.

It is also important to weigh grapes before PRESSING in order to measure the volume of juice extracted in relation to the fruit weight. See, for example, CHAMPAGNE for the regulations concerning pressing and yield.

Wein (pronounced 'vine') means 'wine' in GERMAN and is therefore how a WINE WITHOUT GEOGRAPHICAL INDICATION would be described in Germany and Austria. It is also the first syllable of a host of important German wine names such as **Weinbau** ('vine-growing'), **Weinbrand** ('basic brandy'), and **Weingut** ('wine estate') as distinct from a **Weinkellerei**, which buys in grapes, must, or wine but probably owns vineyards only if it describes itself as the all-purpose **Weingut-Weinkellerei**. A **Weinprobe** is a wine tasting; **Weinsäure** is TARTARIC ACID, some of which may eventually be precipitated as crystal TARTRATES, or **Weinsteine**. A wine made by blending ingredients from more than one EU country is a **Wein aus der europäischen Gemeinschaft**.

Weinviertel, a vast arc of viticulture in AUSTRIA north of the Danube, extending along the border of CZECHIA, then east and south along the River March and Austria's frontier with SLOVAKIA, its western edge abutting the KAMPTAL and WAGRAM, and its southern fringes abutting the urban vineyards of VIENNA. With 14,001 ha/34,597 acres of vines (2021), the Weinviertel is Austria's largest official wine region, generating roughly one-third of Austrian wine. Volume has gone hand in hand with modest prices and relative lack of cachet, but it has also made the Weinviertel an indispensable feature of Austria's passionate wine-drinking culture, and an increasing number of quality-conscious growers are carving a niche for themselves and this region among their country's many wine sophisticates.

By 2021 half of the Weinviertel's vineyard area was planted with GRÜNER VELTLINER, but that dominance came about only after the middle of the last century. In a region this large and diverse geologically, climatically, and culturally, it is not surprising that growers have scored striking successes with many grape varieties, notably MUSKATELLER, Pinot Blanc (Weissburgunder), Riesling, and TRAMINER. Among the more important wine communities of the Weinviertel are Maissau, Retz, and Röschitz; Falkenstein, Poysdorf, and Wolkersdorf in the north-east (prominent for SEKT base wine but capable of far greater distinction); along with west-centrally located Ebenthal and Hohenruppertsberg. An important cluster of tiny villages abuts Vienna, especially in the Bisamberg sector adjacent to Vienna's 21st District, of which the best known is Stetten, being home to the Weinviertel's most prominent pioneer of ambitious quality, Roman Pfaffl.

Weinviertel DAC was the first Austrian DAC appellation and applies only to wines made from Grüner Veltliner. A DAC Reserve category stipulates marginally higher minimum alcohol and a later release date. Other than slight differences in the adjectives used to characterize their styles, criteria for Weinviertel DAC are not materially different from those governing Grüner Veltliner in the KAMPTAL, KREMSTAL, or TRAISENTAL DACs. Since its inception in 2002, many growers have chosen to submit only one or two of their Grüner Veltliner bottlings for DAC approval, and several prominent producers now submit none. Any QUALITÄTSWEIN grown in the Weinviertel that does not meet DAC requirements or that is not submitted for approval gets labelled for its state of origin, NIEDERÖSTERREICH.

D.S.

Weissburgunder, or **Weisser Burgunder**, is the synonym for PINOT BLANC used in German-speaking wine regions. The Germans have a much greater area planted, up to 5,922 ha/14,634 acres by 2020, than the French (although less in total than they have of the Pinot Gris they call GRAUBURGUNDER). It is now Germany's fourth most planted white wine variety, with vinous personalities ranging from the full, rich, oaked examples of Baden and the Pfalz to relatively delicate, mineral-inflected variations along the Nahe and Mosel, and with quality aspirations ranging from a workaday norm to occasional brilliance. It is popular with growers seeking food-friendly wines that are softer than Riesling and can reflect local TERROIR.

Weissburgunder is the fifth most planted white wine grape in Austria, accounting for nearly 1,884 ha/4,655 acres and 4.2% of the total vineyard area. As a dry white VARIETAL, Weissburgunder is associated with scents of almond and apple, inherent textural creaminess, and an ability to age. It has also received attention in Austria for rich, BOTRYTIZED wines, either solo or in a blend.

weisser, meaning 'white', is a common prefix in German for pale-skinned grape varieties (e.g. **Weissburgunder** or **Weisser Burgunder** is PINOT BLANC in German-speaking wine lands).

Weisser Riesling, common synonym for the great White RIESLING grape variety of Germany.

Weissherbst is by German law a rosé wine at least 95% of which is made by direct pressing of a single red wine grape variety named on the label (SPÄTBURGUNDER and PORTUGIESER are especially common). In practice, the 5% red wine permitted to achieve a desired colour is rarely added since consumers expect Weissherbst to be very pale. The term is also used in

German-speaking SWITZERLAND for very much the same style of wine. See also SCHILLERWEIN.

Wellington, warm inland wine district in SOUTH AFRICA just north of PAARL, which produces full-bodied wines, mainly reds.

Welschriesling, or **Wälschriesling**, important white grape variety which, as Germans are keen to point out, is completely unrelated to the great RIESLING grape of Germany. Indeed it rankles with many Germans that the noble word is even allowed as a suffix in the name of this inferior variety, preferring the word 'Rizling', as used in synonyms such as **Welsch Rizling** or **Welschrizling**. Welsch simply means 'foreign' in Germanic languages, which provides few clues but suggests that the variety may well have originated in a non-German-speaking country. *Wine Grapes* lists five reasons why its country of origin is most likely to be CROATIA, where it is by far the single most planted vine variety, and why its official name should be Graševina, its historical Croatian name. It is also widely planted in much of the rest of central and eastern Europe.

Welschriesling may be the variety's most common name in AUSTRIA, but it is known in Hungary as OLASZ RIZLING (under which more details of its importance in Hungary are to be found), in Slovenia and Serbia it is LAŠKI RIZLING (as well as the historical name Grašac in Serbia), and in CZECHIA and SLOVAKIA it is the very similar Rizling Vlašský. The Italians call it RIESLING ITALICO (as opposed to Riesling Renano, which is the Riesling of Germany), and variants of this are used all over Eastern Europe. In ROMANIA, Riesling Italico is the third most planted white variety but is known locally simply as 'Riesling'. Welschriesling is also planted in CHINA.

It does best in dry climates and warmer soils and has a tendency to produce excessively acid wines in cool climates. Like German Riesling, it is a relatively late-ripening vine whose grapes keep their ACIDITY well and produce light-bodied, relatively aromatic wines. Welschriesling can easily be persuaded to yield even more productively than Riesling, however, and indeed this and its useful acidity probably explain why it is so widely planted throughout eastern Europe and, partly, why so much of the wine it produces is undistinguished (although poor-quality viticulture and winemaking equipment may also have played a part).

As a wine, Welschriesling reaches its apogee in AUSTRIA, where, despite long-standing decline, it remains the country's second most planted white grape after Grüner Veltliner. While the bulk of Austrian Welschriesling goes into lightweight wines intended for casual and immediate consumption or into Austrian SEKT, it figures both solo and blended (especially with Chardonnay) in impressively rich yet lively late-harvest BOTRYTIZED wines made on the shores of the Neusiedlersee in Burgenland, where one-third of Austria's 2,942 ha/7,270 acres of the variety is planted. TROCKENBEERENAUSLESE bottlings can boast impressive longevity, albeit not that of a corresponding German Riesling. Increasingly, prominent winegrowers, especially in SÜDSTEIERMARK and SÜDBURGENLAND, are crafting serious dry Welschriesling from OLD VINES, the wines often benefiting from long LEES CONTACT. All of these more ambitious efforts capitalize on the grape's stubborn acid retention—which, like its DROUGHT-tolerance, could become increasingly valuable in the face of CLIMATE CHANGE—without being handicapped by its inherently unassuming aromatics.

Croatia's 4,525 ha/11,181 acres of Graševina are planted all over the country, but the finest wines are produced in Slavonia in the east. It is second only to Grüner Veltliner in Czechia with 1,182 ha planted, and in Slovakia it is the second most planted variety after Müller-Thurgau, with 1,685 ha in 2021.

Robinson, J., et al., *Wine Grapes: A Complete Guide to 1,368 Vine Varieties, Including Their Origins and Flavours* (2012).

Wente. See HERITAGE CLONES.

Western Australia, or **WA**, is Australia's biggest state, home to the country's second-oldest wine region (after the Hunter Valley, in NEW SOUTH WALES). The Swan River Colony was founded by British settlers in 1829, on the traditional lands of the Whajuk Noongar people. As a part of the Land Acquisition system established by the Colonial Office, the land was divided into lots, which were given to settlers under condition of improving the land. Houghton was originally known as Swan Location 11 and was named 'Houghton' in November 1836, after the most senior ranking officer in its original ownership syndicate (Houghton, Yule and Lowis). It later rose to prominence as a premium grape-growing company under the leadership of Dr John Ferguson (1859). Viticulture—for wine, TABLE GRAPES, and RAISINS—was developed in the Swan due to the suitable soils and, perhaps more pertinently, its proximity to the growing Perth colony. The Swan Valley (as it is now called) was at the centre of WA's viticulture for the next century (specializing in FORTIFIED WINE, VERDELHO, CHENIN BLANC, and SHIRAZ). The 1960s and 1970s were dynamic times in WA's viticultural history, when Margaret River and the Great Southern emerged as commercially significant and premium regions. Tony Smith at Denbarker and John Roche at Frankland can be credited with the beginnings of the commercial eras in the Great Southern. The catalyst for Margaret River's development was a vigorously researched report in 1966 from renowned agronomist Dr John Gladstones that highlighted the potential of Margaret River as a viticultural region. State Viticulturist Bill Jamieson and Dorham Mann at the Department of Agriculture supported the research and assisted with regional certification, vine CUTTINGS, viticulture advice, and winemaker training. Without their work, it is unlikely that the tenacious Dr Tom Cullity would have planted the vines at what is now Vasse Felix in 1967 which marked the beginning of Margaret River's modern commercial era.

Geography and climate

WA comprises nine wine regions, stretching from just north of Perth down to the southwest tip of Australia and continuing east for some 400 km/249 miles to the eastern boundary around Boxwood Hill. From north to south, these are the zones and GEOGRAPHICAL INDICATIONS (GIs):

Greater Perth Zone, including the **Swan District** GI, 25 km/16 miles north-east from Perth, on the traditional land of the Whajuk Noongar people, has a warm MEDITERRANEAN CLIMATE. Olive Farm released the region's first commercial wine in the early 1830s. Fortified wines have long been a specialty, although a new generation of winemakers are revitalizing the wine landscape with dry versions of Chenin Blanc, the region's dominant variety, as well as Shiraz and Grenache. The GPZ represents 8.76% of total WA crush in 2021, from 890 ha/2,200 acres of vines.

Perth Hills is a small GI (less than 1% of total crush in 2021) that runs 32 km/20 miles east from Perth to Bickley Valley. Whajuk Noongar *boodja* (land). The specialty is warm-climate Shiraz, and VIOGNIER can be exceptional.

Peel, in Pinjarup country, 59 km/37 miles south of Perth, had little more than 50 ha/124 acres of vines—mostly Chardonnay, Cabernet, and Shiraz—and a handful of wineries in 2021.

Geographe has a varied climate as one moves inland from the Indian Ocean coast. Pinjarup and Kaniyang *boodja*. Picturesque rolling hills on the Darling Scarp support a range of crops and dairy cows; in the vineyards Shiraz leads, followed by Chardonnay, Sauvignon Blanc, and SÉMILLON. The region is developing a reputation for TEMPRANILLO, MALBEC, and ZINFANDEL, with pockets of brilliant GRENACHE. The GI was responsible for 6.16% of total crush in 2021.

Margaret River is WA's most premium GI, responsible for 47% of the state's total crush in 2021. Wardandi *boodja*. The region sits 270 km/162 miles south of Perth, a cape framed by two oceans on three sides. The significantly MARITIME CLIMATE contributes to some of Australia's finest Chardonnay and Cabernet Sauvignon. The Gingin clone (see HERITAGE CLONES) dominates plantings and produces powerful, voluminous, long-lived, high-acid iterations. The South Australian Cabernet CLONES SA125 and SA126 account for most plantings in WA, however the Houghton clone now leads in Margaret River, favoured for its superior flavour, STRUCTURE, and ability to express the regional DNA of Margaret River—the best examples stand out for their red-berry, liquorice, and iodine COMPLEXITY and ferrous MINERALITY. Sauvignon Blanc and Sémillon—often blended together—are also star performers here, making up almost 12,000 tonnes in 2021 between them. Margaret River has no legally defined subregions, but many winegrowers recognize distinct growing areas such as Karridale (southern area, cooler, wetter), Yallingup (in the north, warmer), Wilyabrup (halfway between Margaret River town and the northern cape, noted for Cabernet Sauvignon), and the Wallcliffe/Boodjidup area (just south of the township, cooler although not as cool as Karridale).

Blackwood Valley, a landlocked region well inland from Margaret River (on Bibbulmun *boodja*) first planted to grapes in 1978. The diversity of varieties grown within the GI speaks as much to its ability to foster a wide range of vines as it does to the lack of certainty of the region's strengths. Broad-acre farming dominates the landscape, with Sauvignon Blanc, Sémillon, Shiraz, and Cabernet Sauvignon the main varieties.

Pemberton/Manjimup, colloquially referred to as Southern Forests, are two cool, inland GIs, both Bibbulmun *boodja*. **Manjimup** is directly south of Blackwood; **Pemberton** is further south. Although the data for these regions are bundled as one, much of the total can be attributed to Pemberton. Sauvignon Blanc leads by a factor of two here followed by Chardonnay and Pinot Noir (speaking to the region's dominance in WA as a resource for SPARKLING WINE). The areas, particularly Pemberton, are blanketed by towering Karri trees, which form the basis of the region's history as timber towns. Pemberton/Manjimup accounted for 5.8% of total crush in 2021.

Great Southern, Australia's largest GI by land size, stretching 200 km/124 miles east to west and 100 km north to south, accounting for 28.4% of total crush in 2021. Minang and Kaniyang *boodja*. Its five subregions each have distinct strengths. **Frankland River**—generally cool, with wide DIURNAL TEMPERATURE RANGE in summer—excels at structured, long-lived Cabernet Sauvignon and Shiraz, and austere Riesling. Further inland, **Mount Barker** offers fleshier, powerful Riesling as well as Cabernet Sauvignon and Shiraz. **Porongurup,** a cool, elevated extrusion of rock, is best known for floral, long-lived Riesling and Pinot Noir. **Denmark,** under the maritime influence of the Southern Ocean, counts Chardonnay, Pinot Noir, Shiraz, and Sauvignon Blanc as lead varieties. Further west, **Albany** wraps around the coast's numerous coves and bays. Although Riesling is fifth in crush volume in 2021, it is one of the Great Southern's most consistent varieties. E.L.L.

www.winewa.asn.au

Western Cape, the most important of the five geographical units making up South Africa's production areas defined by the country's WINE OF ORIGIN scheme and accounting for well over 90% of the nation's vineyards and wineries. (Even the extensive COASTAL REGION is a region within it.) On wine labels it generally indicates a multiregional BLEND.

western grapeleaf skeletonizer, a vine pest and native insect of Mexico and the states of Arizona, New Mexico, and Texas, first found in California in 1941 in San Diego County and sighted in the Napa Valley in 2022. The young larvae feed on the soft leaf tissue, leaving a skeleton framework. Left unchecked this insect will completely defoliate a vine, seriously affecting RIPENING, and may then feed on the berries. Chemical control is possible, but timing is critical. The granulosis virus, if introduced to the vineyard, reduces populations effectively, as do insect parasites.

University of California Agriculture & Natural Resources, 'Western grapeleaf skeletonizer'. www.ipm.ucanr.edu/PMG/r302301011.html.

Western Victoria Zone comprises Grampians, Henty, and Pyrenees regions in the Australian state of VICTORIA.

Weststeiermark, the least known of the three subdivisions of STEIERMARK (Styria) in Austria and a DAC since 2018. Its significant total expanse harbours a mere 550 ha/1,350 acres of vines, dominated by the local speciality, SCHILCHER, made from Blauer Wildbacher grapes and most often as rosé. Weststeiermark DAC, however, allows for eight additional grape varieties as well as BLENDS and encompasses bottlings at regional, communal, and SINGLE-VINEYARD levels. D.S.

whip graft, the form used in GRAFTING which simply involves an angled slice across the SCION stem and a similarly angled cut of the stock, with the two cuts then matched and the graft tied tightly with grafting tape. **Whip-and-tongue** is the same except that another cut is made to raise 'tongues' of stem tissue that dovetail with each other and improve the strength of the graft. B.G.C.

Whispering Angel, the world's best-selling BRAND of rosé that ignited the pink-wine revolution from its base in PROVENCE. In 2006 Sacha, son of Alexis LICHINE, sold his father's château in Margaux and moved to Ch d'Esclans in the hills above Fréjus. The next year he launched the notably pale Whispering Angel, which grew to become the height of FASHION and Americans' favourite imported French wine. LVMH acquired a majority stake in the brand and Ch d'Esclans in 2019. A total of 9 million bottles of Whispering Angel were sold in 2021.

white has a special meaning when applied both to grapes and wine. Any light-skinned grape may be called a white grape, even though the grape skin is not white but anything from pale green through gold to pink. In a similar fashion, white wines are not white but vary in colour from almost colourless to deep gold. See COLOUR.

White Riesling, common synonym for the great white RIESLING grape variety of Germany.

white rot, FUNGAL DISEASE affecting vines that occurs in those parts of Europe most prone to HAIL, also known as hail disease. Crop losses can be as high as 80%. The fruit is attacked after a hailstorm and, because the berry skin is lifted from the flesh, the berries appear white, hence the name. High summer rainfall, high humidity, and high temperatures also favour the disease. The fungus responsible is *Coniella diplodiella*, which is controlled by a range of chemical sprays. R.E.S.

white winemaking, the production of wines with almost imperceptible to golden COLOUR. If the juice is separated from the grape skins gently and soon enough (as in the production of CHAMPAGNE), white wines can be made from black-skinned grapes, but the great majority of white wines are made from grapes with yellow or green skins. White wines can be made from grapes of all hues, so long as there is no SKIN CONTACT or MACERATION with dark-skinned grapes. The only exception to this is the red-fleshed TEINTURIERS. White wines are distinguished from their red counterparts by their absence of ANTHOCYANINS and PIGMENTED TANNINS. As with any WINEMAKING operation, the production of white wines generally entails CRUSHING and DESTEMMING the grape clusters on arrival at the winery, although occasionally white grapes may be crushed beforehand at a field pressing station (and see also WHOLE-BUNCH PRESSING and STABULATION). After crushing and destemming, the sweet MUST requires draining and PRESSING to separate the liquid from the solids. The timing of the separation of juice

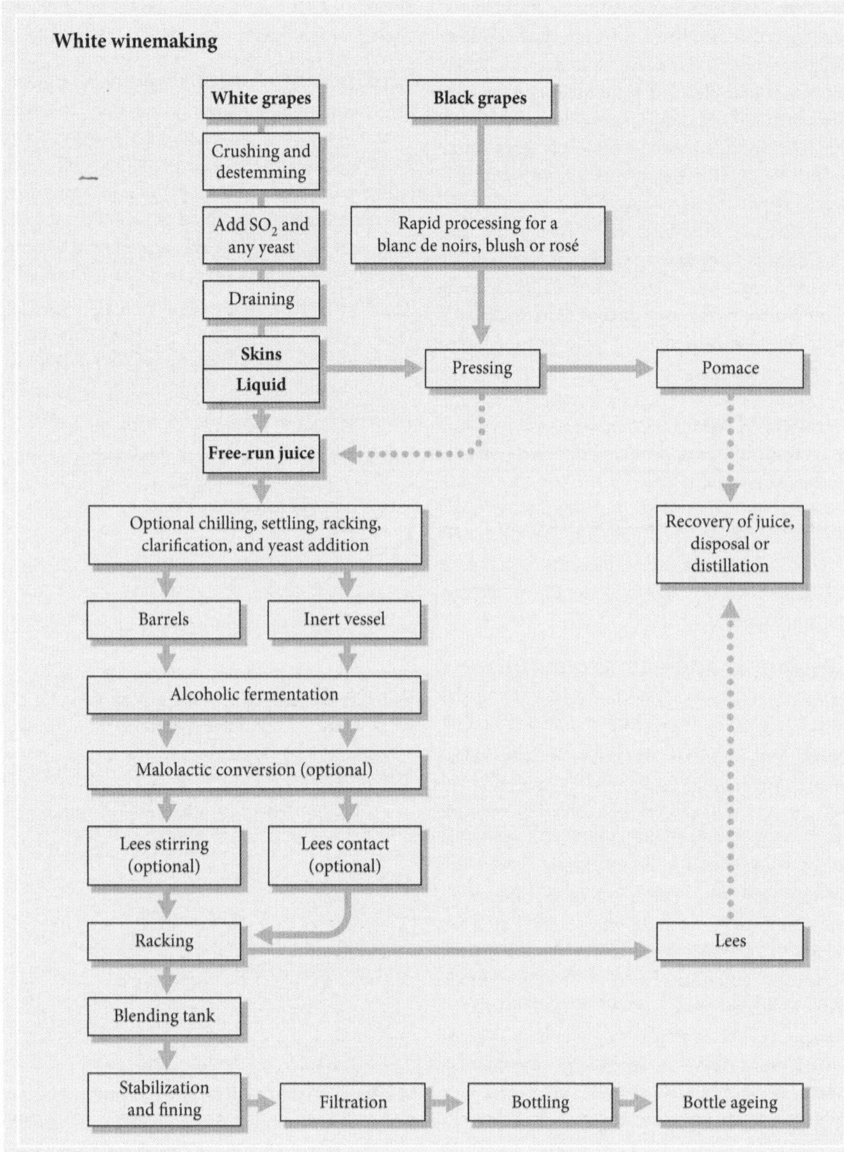

from solids constitutes the major difference between red and white winemaking: before FERMENTATION for whites and afterwards for reds.

Prolonged contact between juice and grape skins (see SKIN CONTACT and MACERATION) encourages the transfer of soluble materials, including PHENOLICS, FLAVOUR COMPOUNDS, and FLAVOUR PRECURSORS, from the skins to the juice. The extracted phenolics, which are essential to a red wine, providing both colour and TANNIN, are generally undesirable in a white wine, for they promote OXIDATION and can lead to ASTRINGENCY. The skin phenolics also lead to the development of amber to brown colours deemed inappropriate for most white wines (but see ORANGE WINES and other SKIN-FERMENTED whites). The challenge for the white winemaker is therefore to find the balance, through suitable juice-handling techniques, between appropriate transfer of the flavour compounds and minimal phenolic extraction. Because of their light colour and delicate flavours, white wines show the unappetizing effects of oxidation much faster than red wines, and so white winemaking is in general a more delicate operation than RED WINEMAKING. Small amounts of ACETALDEHYDE are produced by the reaction of oxygen with alcohol, and this compound can easily spoil the AROMA of a fresh, fruity young wine. There are two possible solutions to this inconvenience. Exposure to oxygen may be minimized during extraction, winemaking, ÉLEVAGE, and right up to and including BOTTLING (see PROTECTIVE WINEMAKING, for example). Alternatively, a policy of unprotected handling is adopted whereby the juice is deliberately, and sometimes in the case of everyday wines violently, aerated so that its susceptible phenolics oxidize, these brown compounds being removed during CLARIFICATION. This technique is sometimes referred to as hyperoxidation (see OXIDATION). The disadvantage of this pre-fermentation oxidation is that it removes some of the compounds that would have contributed to AROMA.

White wines are usually fermented at cooler temperatures than reds, now much easier to control than in the past thanks to REFRIGERATION. However, BARREL FERMENTATION followed by BARREL AGEING is a common phenomenon for more ambitious white wines, particularly for wines made from the CHARDONNAY grape. Among these barrel-fermented white wines, LEES STIRRING is also popular (though less so than in the past), as is MALOLACTIC CONVERSION.

P.J.W.

white wines, made with much less SKIN CONTACT, are much lower in PHENOLICS than red wines (see WHITE WINEMAKING). This does not necessarily mean, however, that they are inherently less interesting or shorter lived (see AGEING). They vary enormously in colour from virtually colourless to deep gold or ORANGE—even, in extreme age, deep tawny (not unlike the colour of some very old red wines). They are made in virtually all wine regions, although in hot regions ACIDIFICATION and some form of REFRIGERATION are usually needed to produce white wines suitable for modern tastes. White wines are typically much more versatile when it comes to FOOD-AND-WINE MATCHING.

French for 'white' is *blanc*, Italian is *bianco*, Spanish is *blanco*, Portuguese is *branco*, and German is *weiss*, while in most eastern European languages the word for 'white' is some variant of *byeli*.

White Zinfandel was California's great commercial success story of the 1980s. Although Bob Trinchero of Sutter Home was not the first to vinify California's heritage ZINFANDEL grapes as a white, and therefore BLUSH, wine, he launched 'White' Zinfandel down the commercial slipway in 1972, and it gained traction after he bottled the 1975 vintage with a little RESIDUAL SUGAR left in the wine. The semi-sweet pale pink sent Trinchero's own sales rocketing from 25,000 cases in 1981 to 1.5 million cases six years later, and other producers followed. The wine evolved as a way of making California's vast hectarage of Zinfandel acceptable to the predominantly white-wine-drinking American public, and its popularity saved many OLD VINE Zin vineyards from being GRUBBED UP. While the style began to fall out of favour in the 2000s as US consumers increasingly gravitated to drier rosés, it has seen a renaissance in the 2010s as respected producers such as Turley and Broc Cellars interpret it as a bone-dry rosé.

whole-bunch fermentation, ultra-traditional method of red-wine FERMENTATION

in which grape berries are not subjected to DESTEMMING. This was the default position before the introduction of the DESTEMMER-CRUSHER. Aside from the influence of the STEMS themselves, the process generally involves an element of CARBONIC MACERATION at the start of the ferment. The possible disadvantages are that, unless the stems are very ripe (i.e. well LIGNIFIED) and the MUST is handled very gently, the stems may impart harsh TANNINS and GREEN flavours to the wine. The technique also involves a greater total capacity of FERMENTATION VESSELS, which are often open-topped to allow PUNCHING DOWN of the CAP. The practical advantages are that the stems can ease the drainage of the juice through the cap, aerate the ferment so that it is slightly cooler, and encourage healthy oxygenation by increasing the cap's interface with the atmosphere during MACERATION. Stems may also absorb a very small amount of alcohol, which may be a benefit in warmer vintages with higher-alcohol wines. On the other hand, the level of POTASSIUM in the juice is increased slightly, resulting in lower ACIDITY in the wine.

Whole-bunch fermentation is most common in BURGUNDY and now more generally with Pinot Noir. An increasing number of winemakers in both hemispheres are experimenting with the inclusion of stems, varying the percentage of whole bunches according to the vintage conditions, the overall character of the fruit, the ripeness of the stems, and the desired wine style. There are many variations: some winemakers layer whole bunches with destemmed fruit, while some prefer to put the whole bunches at the bottom of the tank. A few crush the whole bunches to avoid the flavours of carbonic maceration. Proponents suggest that whole-bunch fermentation imparts organoleptic benefits such as firmer TANNINS and increased aroma, freshness, elegance, COMPLEXITY, and apparent sweetness. Opponents—most famously the late Henri Jayer of Burgundy—point to the potential loss of colour (absorbed by the stems), tougher tannins, and increased herbal or green characters in the wine.

A more labour-intensive and therefore expensive technique that is said to result in all the benefits of whole-bunch fermentation, such as freshness and fruit purity, and none of the possible disadvantages involves cutting the individual berries off the STEM and retaining the PEDICEL, thereby keeping the berries intact at the start of fermentation. It might be more accurately described as whole-berry fermentation.

Wimalasiri, P. M., et al., 'Whole bunch fermentation and the use of grape stems: effect on phenolic and volatile aroma composition of *Vitis vinifera* cv. Pinot Noir wine', *Australian Journal of Grape and Wine Research* (2021).

whole-bunch pressing, WHITE WINEMAKING technique whereby the grapes are not subjected to DESTEMMING and bunches of ripe grapes are pressed whole, with the stems used as conduits for what can often be particularly viscous juice. This works best for very ripe grapes and would not be suitable if a period of SKIN CONTACT precedes PRESSING since excess TANNINS could be leached into the must from the STEMS. This technique is almost universal in the production of top-quality SPARKLING WINES and most other white wines from dark-skinned grapes and in the direct pressing of BOTRYTIS-affected clusters of super-ripe grapes as in SAUTERNES. It is also increasingly popular with some quality-conscious producers of white wines in some wine regions since the juice that results tends to be low in PHENOLICS and PROTEINS.

whole-cluster fermentation. See WHOLE-BUNCH FERMENTATION.

whole-grape fermentation. Alternative name for CARBONIC MACERATION.

Wien is how the natives of Vienna refer to the Austrian capital and also identifies the official 580-ha/1,433-acre winegrowing region it comprises. Vienna serves as an axis between Danubian growing regions, nowadays dominated by GRÜNER VELTLINER but also starring RIESLING (11.5% of Viennese vine surface), and those regions more strongly influenced by the warmth of the Pannonian-Hungarian Plain and significantly planted with diverse red wine grapes (16% of Vienna's total), notably in two important viticultural neighbourhoods on the city's southern fringe, Oberlaa and Mauer. Although traditional FIELD BLENDS shrank in the early 21st century to less than 15% of the city's vineyard area, they represent a distinctive contribution to its winegrowing and drinking culture and in 2013 were made the basis for Wiener Gemischter Satz DAC, whose regulations (see below) make it theoretically possible to produce a volume of DAC wine much larger than what could be rendered solely from Vienna's surface of field blends, which are mostly dominated by or consist exclusively of white wine grapes, with older vineyards generally incorporating significant shares of Grüner Veltliner as well as Chardonnay, Pinot Blanc (WEISSBURGUNDER), Pinot Gris, and NEUBURGER. Riesling, ROTGIPFLER, SILVANER, TRAMINER, WELSCHRIESLING, ZIERFANDLER, and unidentified vines are also common.

The Kahlenberg and Nussberg vineyards, along with sites in the nearby suburbs of Grinzing, Sievering, and Neustift—all in Vienna's 19th District—offer a stunning panorama of the city thanks to the ELEVATION. The sunny exposure, attendant breezes, and soils typically rich in fossils and LIMESTONE also commend them as high-quality sites. MUSTS seldom dip below 12.5% POTENTIAL ALCOHOL. On the Danube's left bank, important vineyards extend north and west from the suburbs of Stammersdorf and Strebersdorf to the edges of the Bisamberg and the WEINVIERTEL, some of whose growers also have holdings in Wien. Each wine district has managed to keep the look of a wine village, even within the borders of a large city. Their often-bucolic wine taverns are a refuge for thirsty urbanites and an emblematic part of Austria's HEURIGER culture of grower-dispensed new wine. No account, however brief, of modern Viennese wine history would be complete without mention of the role played by Fritz Wieninger as a model winegrower and international ambassador for his vine-rich native city.

Wiener Gemischter Satz DAC is the official Austrian appellation of origin designed to showcase Vienna's mixed-vine plantings. As officially defined, these wines must include at least three white grape varieties, though these may be planted in dedicated blocks as opposed to truly intermingled, provided those blocks are contiguous. No single variety may constitute more than half of a wine's volume, and if it consists of just three varieties then none may constitute less than 10% of the total volume. Wines from grapes grown in Vienna but vinified and bottled in another region—and there are many producers just outside the city limits in the neighbouring WEINVIERTEL or THERMENREGION as well as in KLOSTERNEUBURG—may apply for a dispensation to allow their Viennese wines that meet all other DAC requirements to be bottled as Wiener Gemischter Satz DAC. Wines of this DAC that are bottled without vineyard designation may not (with the usual half-percentage labelling tolerance) exceed 12.5% alcohol, whereas those labelled as SINGLE-VINEYARD WINES must reach a minimum 12.5%, which nowadays happens as a matter of course. It seems possible that the creation of this DAC will encourage Viennese growers to plant more vineyards with GEMISCHTER SATZ. Since Wien is the name of an Austrian state as well as of an official wine region, Viennese wines that do not qualify for the Wiener Gemischter Satz DAC may be labelled Wien (see other DAC regulations). D.S.

WIETA, or **Wine and Agricultural Ethical Trade Association**, is an organization dedicated to improving social and employment conditions in the wine industry of SOUTH AFRICA. Members include grape-growers, wine producers, trades unions, retailers, agents, importers, and exporters of South African wine. Its code of conduct includes a prohibition on child and enforced LABOUR and obliges members to provide a safe and healthy working environment with freedom of association, the right to collective bargaining, a living wage, reasonable

working hours, regular employment, security of tenure, and protection against unfair discrimination. Members are subject to regular audits and, when compliant, are accredited by WIETA. WIETA compliance is incorporated in a single seal issued by the Wine & Spirit Board and covering not merely compliance in terms of the WINE OF ORIGIN scheme but also environmental SUSTAINABILITY (see INTEGRATED PRODUCTION OF WINE) and ethical responsibility. M.F.

Wildbacher. See BLAUER WILDBACHER.

wild ferment. See SPONTANEOUS FERMENTATION.

wildfires have become an increasingly severe consequence of CLIMATE CHANGE affecting several wine regions around the world, especially CALIFORNIA and AUSTRALIA, where SMOKE TAINT has had a significant impact on production. A.Y.

wild vines, plants of the genus VITIS growing in their natural state without any cultivation by people. Such vines are lianas and are often found climbing trees (see ARBOREAL VITICULTURE) but may also grow as shrubs. They are widespread in the Americas, especially in the east and south-east, in Asia, and up until the late 1800s in Europe. Indigenous wild grapevines can sometimes be confused with feral or naturalized vines derived from plants once cultivated. Examples of feral vines are the wild vines of the Pays BASQUE and the AMERICAN VINE SPECIES *Vitis riparia* and *Vitis rupestris* along the Rhône and Garonne rivers after importation as ROOTSTOCKS. Wild vines are typically spread by BIRDS eating the berries and passing the seeds. Where wild vines of different species grow together, it is common for natural HYBRIDS to develop, as for example in the east of America (see AMERICAN HYBRIDS). Such hybrids can also develop from natural pollen interchange with cultivated grapes.

Perhaps the most famous of all wild vines are those described in the legend about the discovery of VÍNLAND. The early settlers and explorers in the Americas and the Caribbean found profuse growth of wild vines in the woods. Such vines had tolerance to the harsh winter climate, to indigenous pests such as PHYLLOXERA, to FUNGAL DISEASES such as DOWNY MILDEW and POWDERY MILDEW, and to PIERCE'S DISEASE, and so they could grow without check, while the VITIS VINIFERA vines imported from Europe perished in cultivation.

Wild vines of the wine-producing *vinifera* species were once widespread in Europe and western Asia, although they have disappeared from large areas of Europe since the introduction of the American pests and diseases noted above and because humans have taken over so many of their natural habitats. Sometimes such wild vines are called *Vitis vinifera* subsp. *silvestris*, while cultivated vines are called *Vitis vinifera* subsp. *vinifera* (sometimes *sativa*). The main difference between the two forms lies in the sexes of the flowers: the subspecies *silvestris* is dioecious, with flowers that are either male-only or female-only on the same plant, while the subspecies *vinifera* is hermaphroditic, with flowers containing functional male and female parts. This feature of subspecies *vinifera* results in better FRUIT SET and has been the basis of selection from the wild by humans.

Wild vines are important to modern viticulture as they are the source of many resistance genes that can used in breeding NEW VARIETIES. The genetic diversity of wild *Vitis* varieties has not yet been extensively explored, and the possibilities for improving modern varieties' resistance to pathogens and environmental stresses such as DROUGHT are endless. See also GENETIC MODIFICATION. R.E.S. & J.V.

Arrigo, N., and Arnold, C., 'Naturalised *Vitis* rootstocks in Europe and consequences to native wild grapevine', PLOS ONE, 2/6 (2007).

Grassi, F., et al., 'Phylogeographical structure and conservation genetics of wild grapevine', *Conservation Genetics*, 7/6 (2006), 837–45.

Myles, S., et al., 'Genetic structure and domestication history of the grape', *Proceedings of the National Academy of Sciences of the United States of America*, 108/9 (2011), 3530–5.

wild yeast. See YEAST.

Willamette Valley, named for the Willamette River running through it, is OREGON's most famous wine region and oldest AVA, established in 1983. Starting just north of Portland, sandwiched between the Cascade Range to the east and Coastal Range to the west, the region spans 241 km/150 miles north to south and 97 km/60 miles at its widest point. However, the planted area is less than 0.1% and is further divided among 11 sub-AVAs. Most specify an ELEVATION of at least 61 m/200 ft to distinguish themselves from the more fertile valley floor. PINOT NOIR dominates plantings in all Willamette AVAs, with PINOT GRIS and CHARDONNAY in attendance.

Tualatin Hills, the northernmost sub-AVA, was officially established in 2020 though it has one of the oldest histories. The site of David Hill Vineyard and Winery was planted in 1965 by Charles Coury, the second person to root VITIS VINIFERA in the Willamette Valley. The soils here are predominantly Laurelwood, a mix of weathered BASALT and LOESS.

Yamhill-Carlton District, named for two towns, lies in the rain shadow of the Coast Range, on the hillsides of a south-facing bowl. The free-draining coarse-grained marine sedimentary soil series known as Willakenzie stops vegetative growth earlier in the season and encourages more complete RIPENING. The AVA's first commercial vineyard was established in 1974 by the Campbells of Elk Cove Vineyards. Ken Wright, another early advocate for this area, authored the proposal for its AVA status.

Chehalem Mountains was established in 2006 with a proposal authored by David Adelsheim, Paul Hart (Rex Hill Vineyard), and Richard Ponzi. It contains the AVAs of Ribbon Ridge and Laurelwood District. The planted areas feature all three of the Willamette Valley's predominant soil types: VOLCANIC, marine sedimentary, and loess.

Laurelwood District, located within the Chehalem Mountains AVA, was established in 2020 and named for the Laurelwood community, though the name also references the Laurelwood soils, which differ from those of the Tualatin Hills AVA only in their greater homogeneity.

Ribbon Ridge was named in 1865 for its twisting spine but did not receive recognition as an AVA until 2005. It is geographically isolated from the surrounding Chehalem Mountains AVA by creek valleys on all sides. The area is east-facing and features marine sedimentary soils that are younger and finer-textured than those of the Yamhill-Carlton AVA.

Dundee Hills, often referred to as 'the Red Hills of Dundee', is unique for its ruddy-coloured volcanic clay soils known as Jory. This AVA was home to the first *vinifera* plantings in the Willamette Valley, planted by David Lett of The Eyrie Vineyards in 1965. Pioneers Erath and Sokol-Blosser also contributed to the region's fame.

McMinnville, named for the city, was granted its AVA in 2005 based on the Nestucca formation, a bedrock foundation consisting of marine SANDSTONE, mudstone, and basalt, with shallow topsoils.

Eola-Amity Hills stands out for shallow basalt soils that have a lower water-holding capacity than the similarly volcanic Jory soils of the Dundee Hills. Respected for Pinot Noir, the region also has more land devoted to Chardonnay than any other AVA (just over 8%).

Van Duzer Corridor is distinguished from its neighbouring AVAs by having the lowest number of growing degree days (see CLIMATE CLASSIFICATION), highest WINDS, and lowest elevation. The soils are quick-draining sedimentary and volcanic, with shallow ALLUVIAL overlay. The high winds dry the vine CANOPIES, leading to thicker grape skins and lower FUNGAL DISEASE pressure, which some growers use as an advantage to implement ORGANIC farming or BIODYNAMIC VITICULTURE.

Mount Pisgah, Polk County, Oregon, established in 2022, encompasses a small mountain to the west of the city of Salem. Elevation ranges up to 255 m/835 ft, and producers here cite lower average temperatures, lower average wind speeds, and silty clay-LOAM topsoils as their points of differentiation. Only three producers are located within this AVA: Illahe, Open Claim, and Amalie Robert.

Lower Long Tom, established 2021, is the southernmost sub-AVA, consisting of a series of north-to-south hills bisected by streams that feed the Long Tom River, which runs on the AVA's eastern boundary. Soils are predominantly Bellpine with some Bellpine/Jory complex (see OREGON, Geography and climate). While Pinot Noir dominates, the region's generally warmer temperatures support a range of varieties, particularly Chardonnay, Riesling, Pinot Gris, and Sauvignon Blanc. S.C.-J.

wind, or strong air movement, is a problem on many coastal and otherwise exposed viticultural sites. Major valleys can also be windy, acting as funnels and having their own distinctive systems of wind force and directions. The mistral of the southern Rhône is one of the more notorious examples of this, as is the Salinas Valley in MONTEREY. The detrimental effects of wind on vines are described under WIND STRESS; installing WINDBREAKS can provide a solution.

Hot, dry winds in summer are a particular hazard of viticultural regions bordering deserts. The sirocco of North Africa afflicts the vineyards of southern Europe, occasionally reaching France, for example. The hot, very dry, strong zonda winds of ARGENTINA can cause major problems for vineyards.

The effects of wind are by no means all detrimental, however. The normally regular afternoon sea breezes of coastal regions with otherwise summer-dry climates, such as those of Portugal, California, and much of southern Australia, have a useful moderating effect on viticultural climate and are thought to contribute significantly to the quality of their wines (see CLIMATE AND WINE QUALITY). In all environments, some air movement is needed to prevent excessive build-up of HUMIDITY within the vineyard and to encourage drying of wet foliage and bunches, thereby reducing the risk of FUNGAL DISEASES. Night winds (or WIND MACHINES) largely prevent radiation FROSTS, while during sunlight hours the moderate movement of leaves encourages a more uniform spread of intermittent sunlight exposure among them, thus promoting a more efficient use of SUNLIGHT. Some degree of windiness is also often an unavoidable concomitant of the TOPOGRAPHIES that are viticulturally the best in other respects, for example in Waipara in NEW ZEALAND.

In summary, winds cannot be entirely avoided; nor are they wholly undesirable. The selection of sheltered sites, where possible, is important in windy regions. Beyond that, the answers to wind problems lie mainly in suitable vineyard strategies of TRELLISING and where necessary in the use of windbreaks. J.G.

windbreak, a barrier of vegetation or other materials to break the force of WINDS and avoid WIND STRESS. The benefits of windbreaks go beyond reducing physical vine damage. A combination of reduced wind force and (in dry atmospheres) the maintenance of higher HUMIDITIES among the vines reduces closure of the leaf pores (STOMATA) and therefore enhances potential PHOTOSYNTHESIS. Quite substantial YIELD increases are commonly recorded in the lee of effective windbreaks, amply exceeding any losses that might be incurred through any reduced area of vineyard or SHADING by the windbreaks.

The best natural windbreaks are fast-growing trees or tall shrubs whose roots do not extend too far laterally. Tall winter COVER CROPS such as cereal rye, planted between the vine rows, can also afford useful protection to young vineyards in early spring. VINE GUARDS can also protect young vines from wind. J.G. & R.E.S.

Veste, M., et al., 'Windbreaks as part of climate-smart landscapes reduce evapotranspiration in vineyards, Western Cape Province, South Africa', *Plant, Soil and Environment*, 66 (2020), 119–27.

wind machine, a strong fan for stirring up and mixing cold, dense air settled on the land surface with warmer air from above, thereby preventing FROSTS on still spring nights when there is no WIND to do the job. Such machines, introducing an aeronautical look to vineyards, have been used on valley floors that are prone to radiation frosts, such as in the NAPA Valley of California. HELICOPTERS can be used to the same effect. J.G.

wind stress can reduce vine YIELD and RIPENING in some exposed vineyards. Severe gusts of wind can have dramatic effects on vineyards, breaking SHOOTS and removing leaves. However, even lower-velocity wind can also cause vine problems which are apparent only to the trained eye. Wind cools plants by removing the warming effects of the sun's rays, as well as other more substantial effects on physiology. For some plants, including vines, wind can have a major effect on growth. Shoot length, leaf area, and fruit growth can all be substantially reduced. The problem is particularly acute for young vines, as in older vineyards the CANOPY can usually offer some degree of self-protection. FLOWERING, FRUIT SET, and VERAISON may be delayed.

Some vines respond negatively to movement of shoots and leaves, probably a response involving plant HORMONES. A major effect of wind is that of closing STOMATA. Freeman and colleagues of the University of California showed that wind speeds of 3 m/10 ft per second in the Salinas Valley caused stomata to close partially, which has the effect of reducing both PHOTOSYNTHESIS and TRANSPIRATION. Vines ripening in windy places will show reduced ripening and higher PH. R.E.S.

Freeman, B. M., et al., 'Influence of windbreaks and climatic region on diurnal fluctuation of leaf water potential, stomatal conductance, and leaf temperature of grapevines', *American Journal of Enology and Viticulture*, 33 (1982), 233–6.

wine, alcoholic drink made by fermenting the juice of fruits or berries (see FRUIT WINES). By extension, this most general definition can also include products of the FERMENTATION of sugar solutions flavoured with flowers or herbs, but it normally excludes those of hydrolysed barley starches involved in brewing and the products of the fermentation of sugar-containing liquids destined for DISTILLATION. There are also certain drinks, such as mead, cider, and perry, which depend on sugar fermentations for their alcohol content but for historical reasons merit their own names.

The narrower definition, relevant to this book and accepted throughout Europe, is that wine is 'the alcoholic beverage obtained from the fermentation of the juice of freshly gathered grapes, the fermentation taking place in the district of origin according to local tradition and practice'. This is to distinguish 'proper' wine from alcoholic drinks made from imported grape concentrate, which are known in Europe as MADE-WINE. These include BRITISH WINE and a significant proportion of the liquid produced by HOME WINEMAKING. New World definitions of wine are very similar except that the last phrase is omitted and wine may be made from a mixture of grapes grown many hundreds of miles apart.

Etymology

The modern English *wine* comes from Old English *wīn*, pronounced like modern 'wean'; that indeed was how Chaucer pronounced his *wyn*, but Shakespeare's pronunciation was closer to our own. The Old English form was in turn descended from the Latin *vīnum*, or as the Romans wrote it *vinvm*, by way of a loanword represented in all Germanic languages (e.g. German *Wein*, Icelandic *vín*). A similar loan into Celtic has yielded Welsh *gwin* and Irish *fíon*. The explanation is that the Germans and CELTS, whose native beverage was beer, learnt to drink wine from the Romans; with it came the Latin word, borrowed while Latin *v* was still pronounced [w]. From Germanic territory drink and name passed in turn to the Slavs (e.g. Russian *vinó*) and Balts (Lithuanian *vȳnas*, Latvian *vīns*).

Within Latin itself, from *vīnum* comes the noun *vīnea* 'vineyard'; this word, reinterpreted of a single vine (classically *vītis*, whence 'viticulture'), yielded French *vigne*, which was naturally brought over to England by the Normans. However, once the native English began to learn their masters' language, they adjusted it to suit their own speech habits. Since English then as now lacked the palatal sound of French *gn*, it was simplified to *n*, so that *vigne* became *vine*. This was adopted into English and subjected to the normal sound-changes of the late medieval and early modern period: the final *-e* ceased to be pronounced and the long *i* became a diphthong. The French word was also substituted in the term for the place where vines were grown, originally *wīngeard*, now 'vineyard', with the vowel shortened as often in compounds (e.g. 'shepherd' vs 'sheep').

Whereas *vitis* can be related to an Indo-European verb-root meaning to 'wind' or 'twine', as in English *withy*, the ultimate origins of *vinum* and *vinea* are less clear. Similar words are found in many Mediterranean languages, even those belonging to different language-families, but few interrelations can be established. For instance, although Latin *ī* often comes from *ei*, since the change did not take place till the late 2nd century BCE it cannot have occurred in *vinum*, for which forms with *vin-* are found in the kindred languages of ancient Italy. This rules out a direct link with the term current in ancient GREECE, according to dialect *woinos* (*ϝοῖνος*) or *oînos* (*οἶνος*), as in OENOLOGY, akin to the **woiniyo-* (*denotes a reconstructed form) underlying Armenian *gini* and sometimes associated with Sanskrit *veṇi* or *veṇī* 'braid'. The form *wiyana* and *wayana* are quoted from the ancient ANATOLIAN languages Hittite and Luvian: outside Indo-European, a Semitic noun **wayn*, 'grape, vine, wine', which yields Hebrew *yayin* and Ethiopic *wäyn* besides an Arabic *wayn* 'black grape' found in an ancient lexicon, has sometimes been considered the source of the Greek word and sometimes a derivative. Even Georgian *γvino* has been proposed: no theory is convincing, except after a few glasses. L.H.-S.

Editorial note:
See WINE COMPOSITION, WINEMAKING, WINE TYPES, and the other entries which immediately follow. The word 'wine' appears in only these titles. Otherwise, for instance, for wine press see PRESS, for wine and religion see RELIGION AND WINE, for wine trade see TRADE, and so on. For details of specific wines, see under their names or their provenance.

Wine & Spirit Education Trust. See WSET.

wine composition differs quite considerably from GRAPE COMPOSITION, partly because parts of the grape are discarded during WINEMAKING and partly because the processes involved effect a complicated series of transformations. Alcoholic FERMENTATION, for example, transforms sugars into alcohol, while MALOLACTIC CONVERSION reduces the level of malic acid in favour of lactic acid. The precise composition of a wine varies with WINE TYPE, HARVEST conditions and timing, VINTAGE characteristics, and the age of the wine (see AGEING for details of how wine composition may change with age). Nevertheless, the table gives some guidance as to the likely range of concentrations of the essential constituents of the approximately 1,000 so far identified.

Navarre, C., and Langlade, F., *L'Oenologie* (7th edn, 2010).

wine grape, a term used to describe grapes used for winemaking, as opposed to TABLE GRAPES for eating and RAISINS for use by the dried-fruit industry. For discussion about the plant which bears wine grapes, see VINE; for more detail of the fruit itself, see GRAPE.

Wine Group, The, Based in Livermore, California, The Wine Group (TWG) is the second largest wine producer by volume in the US, behind E. & J. GALLO. Privately owned and relatively secretive about its financial affairs, it boasts among its brands the Sonoma biodynamic pioneer Benziger, the Lodi Zinfandel-led 7 Deadly portfolio, and Concannon, established in 1883 in Livermore by Irish immigrant James Concannon and the first to bottle Petite Sirah as a stand-alone VARIETAL in the US. TWG's considerable market clout, however, comes from the BOXED wine juggernauts Franzia and Almaden; the moderately priced Cupcake bottled line; and the slightly more expensive Chloe Wine Collection.

winegrowing, collective term for VITICULTURE and WINEMAKING.

wine lake, term coined for Europe's wine SURPLUS. With the introduction of compulsory DISTILLATION in 1982, it was rapidly transformed into an ALCOHOL lake. See EU for the various reforms that have been introduced to try to balance supply and demand.

winemaker, one who makes WINE. In its broadest sense, the term includes those who

Wine composition

Component	Proportions per l	Comments
Dissolved gases		
CARBON DIOXIDE	0–50 cc	
SULFUR DIOXIDE		
Total	80–200 mg	More in some sweet wines
Free	10–50 mg	More in some unstable wines
Volatile substances		
WATER	700–900 g	
ETHANOL (alcohol)	8.5–15% by vol	More in fortified, less in low-alcohol wines
HIGHER ALCOHOLS	0.15–0.5 g	
ACETALDEHYDE	0.005–0.5 g	Higher amounts in sherry and similar wines
ESTERS	0.1–0.3 g	
ACETIC ACID	0.35–0.6 g	
Fixed substances		
RESIDUAL SUGAR	0.8–180 g	According to type of wine; more in sweet and botrytized wines
GLYCEROL	5–12 g	
PHENOLICS	0.2–0.5 g; 1.5–4.0 g	Lower range for white wines, higher range for reds
Organic acids		
TARTARIC ACID	3–10 g	Depending on grape origin
MALIC ACID	0–4 g	According to climate and extent of malolactic conversion
LACTIC ACID	0–1 g	
SUCCINIC ACID	0.2–1.5 g	
CITRIC ACID	0–1 g	Found in wines where additions have been made
Mineral salts		
Sulfates	0.1–0.4 g	Expressed as potassium salts
Chlorides	0.25–0.85 g	
Phosphates	0.08–0.5 g	
Mineral elements		
POTASSIUM	0.7–1.5 g	
CALCIUM	0.06–0.9 g	
IRON	0.002–0.006 g	

Based on Navarre, C., and Langlade, F., *L'Oenologie* (7th edn, 2010)

engage in HOME WINEMAKING as a hobby, although in a professional sense a winemaker is someone employed (sometimes by themselves) to produce wine. An increasing proportion of such people recognize that wine production includes every aspect of vineyard management, and there are wine producers all over the world whose production is so small that they personally conduct, or at least oversee, every stage from planting to marketing.

A wine production unit of any size, however, will employ both a VITICULTURIST, or vineyard manager, and a winemaker, whose active responsibilities begin with receiving grapes from the vineyard and continue with their SAMPLING, CRUSHING, PRESSING, FERMENTATION, ÉLEVAGE, BOTTLING, and storage—all those operations outlined in WINEMAKING. Larger wine producers may even employ a team of winemakers, each with different responsibilities.

Curiously, there is no obvious synonym for the word 'winemaker' in any of the major European languages, perhaps because historically wine was thought to make itself. The most common candidates have very different literal translations into English: *maître de chai* in Bordeaux; *Kellermeister* in Germany; *enologo* in Italy; *œnologue* in some French wineries. While most (though not all) modern winemakers have studied OENOLOGY and will certainly consider themselves oenologists, the term OENOLOGIST is in Europe more usually applied to an outside CONSULTANT than to a full-time employee. The most temporary winemakers of all are the breed known colloquially as FLYING WINEMAKERS or, if lower down the pecking order, CELLAR RATS.

During the early 1980s, some winemakers enjoyed a brief period of near-cult status, most notably in the NEW WORLD, until VITICULTURISTS re-established their status to become the wine gurus of the 1990s and early 2000s. Today there are ever-closer links between those responsible for vineyard and cellar, and in an increasing number of cases they are the same person.

Most successful winemakers understand that making fine wine depends not only on a respectful understanding of the complicated biochemistry involved but also, perhaps more importantly, on an appreciation of the greatest potential within each lot of grapes and then the skill and patience to reveal that potential in the finished wine.

winemaking, the practical art of producing WINE. In its most general sense it encompasses all operations in both vineyard and cellar, but for the purposes of this entry winemaking excludes vine-growing, or VITICULTURE.

Winemaking, while a sophisticated practical art for several millennia, became an applied SCIENCE only towards the end of the 19th century after Louis PASTEUR's discovery of the existence and activities of BACTERIA and YEAST. Since then, knowledge of the detailed chemical and biochemical reactions involved in their metabolic processes has steadily increased, as has the sophistication of the CONTAINERS and equipment used in the professional cellar.

Winemaking in brief is a series of simple operations, the first of which is CRUSHING or smashing the fruit to liberate the SUGAR in the juice for FERMENTATION, which is the second step and occurs naturally when YEAST cells come into contact with sugar solutions. The new wine must then be subjected to numerous treatments to ensure CLARIFICATION and STABILIZATION and various other cellar operations which are collectively called ÉLEVAGE before the final step, BOTTLING.

Details in this sequence of operations vary considerably with WINE TYPE and its origin. General (as opposed to local) differences of technique dictated by different sorts of wine are outlined in WHITE WINEMAKING, RED WINEMAKING, ROSÉ WINEMAKING, SWEET WINEMAKING, and SPARKLING WINEMAKING and under the names of various FORTIFIED WINES.

Halliday, J., and Johnson, H., *The Art and Science of Wine* (1992).

Rankine, B., *Making Good Wine: A Manual of Winemaking Practice for Australia and New Zealand* (rev. edn, 2004).

Wine of Origin, area-of-origin designation scheme described in detail in SOUTH AFRICA. Established in 1973, it is the oldest and arguably the most extensive and rigorous in the NEW WORLD.

wine press. See PRESS for details of the equipment used during PRESSING. For the interface between wine and the press, see WINE WRITERS.

winery, modern, essentially NEW WORLD term for the premises on which wine is made. Its first recorded use was in the United States in 1882. It may refer to either the entire enterprise or to the specific building(s) used for WINEMAKING. The nearest French equivalent is CAVE (but see also CHAI and CUVE). WINERY DESIGN is a specialist art most dramatically practised in RIOJA, BORDEAUX, and northern CALIFORNIA, where, neatly, the FASHION is for caves: winemaking facilities burrowed into hillsides, the cost of maintaining suitable temperatures and humidity in such subterranean tunnels being minimal. However, there are spectacular examples all over the wine world today, with increasing emphasis on SUSTAINABILITY.

winery design is a specialist branch of building design. Although WINEMAKING can take place almost anywhere, modern wineries are much more than mere processing facilities. Nowadays wineries should be efficient in energy and resource consumption, suit the individual styles of wine and winemaking, and, of equal importance, support the BRAND image, often through architectural appearance, public display of winemaking processes, specialized hospitality and CELLAR DOOR facilities, and other amenities designed to engage the TOURIST and customer.

To ensure functionality and efficient workflow, a winery layout is based on a thorough understanding of the logistics of the specific winemaking practices and processes from grape receipt through production, bottling, storage, and shipping. Other issues include winery offices, laboratory, tasting bench, equipment sizes and types, and finish materials. The impacts of site conditions, environmental concerns, health and safety matters, and maintenance are also considered. Finally architectural requirements in terms of style and functionality of the winery and associated facilities, including cellar-door sales, amenities, access, and infrastructure, are incorporated.

Building a winery to make an architectural statement is not new—the 19th-century CHÂTEAUX of Bordeaux, like the imposing Ch MARGAUX or the whimsical Ch Cos d'Estournel in ST-ESTÈPHE, or Andrea Palladio's 16th-century Villa di Maser in the VENETO make that clear. There are also 21st-century icons created by the world's greatest architects. Ysios by Santiago Calatrava and Marques de Riscal by Frank Gehry are two examples, both in RIOJA; Clos Pegase of NAPA Valley by Michael Graves, Craggy Range in NEW ZEALAND by John Blair, and Graham Beck Coastal Cellar in SOUTH AFRICA by Johan Wessels are three examples outside of Europe.

Other wineries find beauty in their simplicity and clarity. Many top producers aim for quick, cool, and gentle processing, which means GRAVITY flow instead of PUMPS wherever possible, as at Ridge in the SANTA CRUZ MOUNTAINS. If the site permits, as many as seven different levels may be achieved, where grapes are received at the highest level and shipping takes place from the lowest, as at Calera in MONTEREY. If the winery can be part-buried into a hillside, it aids natural TEMPERATURE and HUMIDITY control. Otherwise, creating cellars deeply dug from ancient LIMESTONE deposits is a possibility, as in Champagne or on the South Downs in England. Perhaps the most ambitious winery project thus far has been realized in the Loisium Wine Centre in Langenlois, Austria, by Stephen Holl with clients Karl and Brigitte Steininger. The entire medieval wine-village with its subterranean cellars has been transformed to include hotel, spa, and restaurant set amid the vineyards.

A well-planned winery development can conserve resources, manage WINERY WASTE and noise pollution, and be easy to maintain. A winery can offer high potential environmental

SUSTAINABILITY, utilizing techniques such as renewable construction materials, solar panels for energy, and recycling winery waste water for IRRIGATION. P.K.C.S.

Dethler, J. (ed.), *Chateaux Bordeaux* (1989).
Hebert, H. S., *The New Architecture of Wine: 25 Spectacular California Wineries* (2019).
Richards, P., *Wineries with Style* (2004).
Stanwick, S., and Fowlow, L., *Wine by Design* (2010).
Zoecklin, B. (ed.), *Winery Planning and Design* (17th edn, digital).

winery waste comprises the liquid, solid, and gaseous waste that results from the process of turning fruit into wine. Globally the wine industry has been working to establish SUSTAINABLE systems to deal with these waste streams so as to maintain the beautiful rural environments in which wine is typically made. In many wine regions, there are now stringent local and sometimes national guidelines, policies, and legislation covering this area.

Water is a by-product of the HYGIENE or sanitation required to make wine, for example washing tanks, fermenters, and barrels. Roughly two volumes (litres/gallons) of water is used in the production of one volume of wine, though the exact amount depends on winemaking processes, winery equipment, and winery practices. Over a year, about 70% of the total volume of waste water generated is during the VINTAGE period, so sustainable waste-water systems need to be designed to handle these loads at this time.

Liquid winery waste tends to have a high oxygen requirement or BOD (organic acids, sugars, alcohol, etc.), low levels of nitrogen and phosphorus relative to carbon, and high solids content; it is generally acidic (low PH) due to organic acids, moderately saline (from sodium-based cleaning chemicals); and there may be imbalances in sodium, calcium, and magnesium.

This kind of waste water stored for a period of time releases malodours and degrades any land/vegetation that it continually comes into contact with. There are winery waste-water treatment systems all over the world that are now able to turn this liquid waste stream into a reusable resource via solids removal, pH adjustment, anaerobic digestion and/or aeration, clarification, and final polishing. Treated water is often then reused to irrigate golf courses, vineyards, or winery gardens or be used back in the winery. These treatment systems can further capture and reuse the biogas generated (primarily methane) as a fuel for electricity and heat generation in combined heat and power systems.

What are collectively known as cleaner production procedures can help minimize water use in the winemaking process and thereby reduce treatment costs and reliance on potable water. These procedures include waste-stream segregation, for example keeping stormwater out of the waste system and diverting heavily polluted waste water (from CRUSHING or FERMENTATION areas, for example) away from less polluted; improved operating practices, for example screening solids from the waste system, using high-pressure hoses, and sweeping floors rather than hosing them down with water; personnel practices, including management initiatives, employee training, and incentives; and procedural measures, including documentation, material handling and storage, material tracking, and inventory control.

Winery solid wastes include STEMS, MARC, LEES (tartrates, grape solids, and dead yeast cells), spent DIATOMACEOUS EARTH used in FILTRATION, and sludge, which is a by-product of waste-water treatment.

Stems and marc are produced only during the vintage period. Approximately two units of marc are generated for every ten units of grapes processed. Marc can be distilled to recover alcohol, cream of tartar for TARTARIC ACID production, colour extract, and tannin extract. Marc can also be co-composted for under-vine application or used as a stock feed. Lees can be collected and sent to the still for alcohol recovery. Stems can be used to improve the organic levels of soils if they are thinly spread and worked into the soil. Many garden COMPOSTS use grape stems and sludge as an ingredient.

Spent diatomaceous earth can be processed by third parties to produce tartaric acid. Spent earth also has agronomic benefits and can be worked into most soil types to improve the SOIL STRUCTURE. However, many filtration processes now use cross-flow membrane technology instead of diatomaceous earth, thereby reducing waste.

More recently, some wineries are turning their attention to gaseous waste. Chx Smith Haut Laffite and Montrose in Bordeaux and Domaine Dujac in Burgundy, for example, have implemented a system to capture the CARBON DIOXIDE produced during fermentation and recycle it to produce sodium bicarbonate. Heat capture and reuse onsite can further aid in minimizing energy demands and improving sustainable operations.

When the correct resources, management initiatives, and support are allocated to ensuring winery waste is treated in an environmentally sustainable manner, wineries will continue to exist in harmony with their surroundings. S.J.G. & K.H.

GWRDC, 'Winery wastewater online resource kit' (2011). www.gwrdc.com.au/tools-resources/winery-wastewater-management-recycling.
Kumar, A., et al., 'Winery wastewater generation, treatment and disposal: a survey of Australian practice' (2009). www.wineaustralia.com/getmedia/a4fa7c36-71d2-403f-9e59-13762b464a66/Winery-wastewater-survey-report.pdf.

Wine Society, The, seminal British member-owned wine club-cum-merchant. The International Exhibition Co-operative Wine Society (IECWS), generally known as The Wine Society, was founded in 1874 by an architect, an eye surgeon, and a prominent Customs and Excise official following a food and wine exhibition in London's Royal Albert Hall that year. The objects and rules included a membership holding of one share only, no dividends to be paid on these until extinction on the member's death, and the introduction of unfamiliar wines as well as those in general use—all to be bought 'for ready money only' at the lowest possible price. The Society remained small for many years, attaining its 5,000th member only in 1922, but grew substantially between the two World Wars. The number of active shares exceeded 180,000 by 2022.

The Society is governed by a Committee of Members. Edmund PENNING-ROWSELL was the Society's longest-serving chairman, from 1964 until 1987.

The Society's cellars were under the London Palladium theatre and London Bridge railway station (where the London AUCTIONEERS subsequently stored their wine) until the Society moved out of London to purpose-built and regularly extended premises in Stevenage in 1965. The Wine Society is one of the two biggest independent retail wine merchants in Britain (the other being its mail-order direct rival LAITHWAITE's) with a turnover exceeding £130 million in 2021. The policy of cash-with-order is retained. The Society is distinguished by its fair prices, perceptive buying, the efficiency of its bureaucracy, and the quality of wine STORAGE offered to members.

wine tasters. The animate sort are humans, often of widely varying abilities, experiences, SENSITIVITIES, preferences, and prejudices, engaged in the pursuit of wine TASTING. The inanimate sort are shallow, usually silver, saucers for tasting young wines, known in French and often in English as TASTEVINS.

wine types may be classified in several ways, the most usual being by alcohol level. Those whose ALCOHOLIC STRENGTH is entirely due to FERMENTATION, and usually in the range of 9 to 15%, are what we tend to call simply 'wine' or sometimes 'table wine' (although TABLE WINE used to have a specific meaning within the EU). Such wines may be further classified by COLOUR into RED WINES, WHITE WINES, ROSÉ WINES, and, more recently, ORANGE WINES. Or they may be classified according to their concentration of dissolved carbon dioxide as SPARKLING WINES, still wines, and a host of terms in between such as PERLANT and FRIZZANTE. Wines may also be classified according to SWEETNESS.

Wines with higher concentrations of alcohol, between 15 and just over 20%, are called FORTIFIED WINES in this book since (with the exception of some DRIED-GRAPE WINES) they owe some of their alcoholic strength to the process of FORTIFICATION (i.e. the addition of spirit). PORT and SHERRY are the best known of these wines, officially called *vins de liqueur* in EU terminology. This higher-strength category also includes sweet alcoholic drinks made by adding grape spirit to grape juice or partly fermented grape juice at various points, for details of which see VIN DOUX NATUREL, VIN DE LIQUEUR, and MISTELA.

Wines which have been deliberately manipulated so that their alcohol levels are particularly low, say below 5.5%, are sometimes called LOW-ALCOHOL wines. However, some regular wines such as MOSCATO D'ASTI and lighter SAAR wines may have a NATURAL ALCOHOL of between 5 and 9%. See also DE-ALCOHOLIZED WINE.

Wine types may also be loosely, and somewhat subjectively, classified according to when they are drunk, for example APERITIF wines (or 'appetizer wines'), 'food wines' or 'dinner wines', and SWEET WINES or DESSERT WINES. See also VINO DA MEDITAZIONE.

Although geographical classifications are of wines not wine types, once-popular GENERIC wines represent an attempt at a geographical classification of wine types.

wine without geographical indication is the EU term adopted since 2008 to designate those wines, previously categorized as TABLE WINES, that have neither a PDO (Protected Designation of Origin) nor a PGI (Protected Geographical Indication). Such wines must be labelled with the word 'wine', in the appropriate language(s), and the country of origin must also appear somewhere on the label. Examples include **Vin de France** in France, **Vino** in Italy and Spain, **Vinho** in Portugal, and **Deutscher Wein** in Germany. They are also permitted to specify on the label VINTAGE YEAR and/or grape variety (varieties), though some countries have not implemented this in their local wine law.

wine writers, imprecise term to include all those who communicate via today's burgeoning media (see SOCIAL MEDIA) on the subject of wine. Some of them style themselves wine CRITICS (notably the consumerist Robert PARKER), while such literary stylists as Hugh JOHNSON and Gerald Asher are or were undoubtedly wine writers. One sort of commentator hardly ever writes at all but occupies regular slots on radio or television, often reaching a much wider audience than most authors could hope to.

Such was the increase in wine-writing opportunities in the late 20th century that by the early 1980s, for probably the first and only time ever, it was possible, with luck and hard work, to make a living as a wine writer with no other source of income. But it would be unreasonable to expect an activity as pleasurable as wine writing to be lavishly rewarded financially, and many wine writers also rely either on a private income or on income from dangerously closely related activities such as trading in wine or undertaking specific commissions for wine companies. Wine-writer ethics became a hot topic after several well-publicized cases of unseemly activity. As detailed in the LITERATURE OF WINE, Britain had a long tradition of wine merchants who wrote, who sometimes became wine writers who used to trade. Kermit Lynch is an American example of this phenomenon, Michael Fridjhon a South African one, while John Platter and James Halliday are examples of wine producers turned wine writers in South Africa and Australia respectively.

Wine writers in continental Europe such as France's Michel Bettane, Spain's Jose Peñín, and Italy's phalanx of specialists tend to concentrate on the wines of their own countries.

Britain may have the greatest concentration of full-time wine writers in the world, perhaps partly because it is a centre of wine book publishing—and possibly because the British wine market is so diverse that British consumers need more advice than most. It certainly has the highest proportion of women among the country's wine writers; in the United States and most European countries wine writing has been dominated by men, although this is at last changing.

Changes in wine writing have wrought changes in wine writers. Given the 1990s preponderance of buyer's guides, TASTING NOTES, and SCORING in place of writing, there was a time when it would have been quite possible to be a highly successful wine writer without ever visiting a vineyard or cellar. A sound palate and a good database (see INFORMATION TECHNOLOGY) would in theory be quite sufficient, if a poor substitute for the excitement of exploring the world of wine.

See also WINE WRITING.

wine writing, a parasitical activity undertaken by WINE WRITERS, enabled by vine-growing and winemaking but more usually associated with wine TASTING, and even with wine drinking, than with either of the former. For an analysis of wine books through the ages, see LITERATURE OF WINE; for a discussion of words used to describe wine, see LANGUAGE OF WINE.

The proliferation of information and comment available free online and on SOCIAL MEDIA, together with the paucity of advertising of wine, led in the early years of the century to a sharp decline in regular columns, newsletters, and books devoted to wine.

Virtually all countries of any interest to wine exporters have at least one specialist wine consumer magazine (and major wine-producing and wine-trading countries tend to have specialist trade publications too), but they have increasingly looked to expand into other, more profitable activities such as events and COMPETITIONS. The world's best-selling wine magazine is the glossy, New York–based *Wine Spectator*. Its American consumer rival is *Wine Enthusiast*, but there are several lively wine-trade publications. Britain fields *Decanter* (of which there is also a Chinese edition) and *The World of Fine Wine*. Europe's three major wine-producing countries offer much less consumer wine coverage than might be imagined. Few print publications are without an online version and associated app(s).

In the world of books, food outweighs wine very substantially; indeed many bookstores locate such wine titles as they do stock in an obscure corner of their cookery section. New wine titles continue to appear, perhaps sometimes the result of publishers' famous fondness for the fruits of the vine, but only a handful of authors can generate the sort of sales the increasingly agglomerated book trade now seeks worldwide, and self-publishing is increasingly common.

Buyer's guides, typically annual, proliferate, and for a while more and more of the words written about wine resembled shopping lists with SCORES rather than literature. But specialist wine books, some of them stunningly good, have been striking back.

Winiarski, Warren (1928–), Napa Valley winegrower whose debut vintage, 1973, of Stag's Leap Cabernet Sauvignon took first place in the orginal 1976 JUDGMENT OF PARIS. The prospect of a life making wine in the Napa Valley lured him with his young family from a lectureship in Chicago in 1964. After apprenticing briefly with Lee Stewart at Souverain and then with Robert MONDAVI, he put down the roots of Stag's Leap Wine Cellars, with partners, in 1972. A more cerebral winemaker than many of his neighbours, Winiarski played an important part in creating and retaining Napa Valley's official status as an agricultural preserve. In 2007 he sold Stag's Leap Wine Cellars to Chateau Ste Michelle of WASHINGTON State with ANTINORI holding a minority advisory stake. In 2018 he made a major donation to the Shields Library at the University of California at DAVIS to enable it to establish the world's most comprehensive collection of wine writers' archives. This was followed in 2021 with a further donation enabling an update, in view of CLIMATE CHANGE, of the famous WINKLER climate classification of California.

Winkler, Albert Julius (1894–1989), scientist at the University of California at DAVIS whose name (and that of Maynard AMERINE) is commonly associated with a method of CLIMATE CLASSIFICATION involving heat summation whereby California was divided into five viticultural regions, Regions I (the coolest) to V (the warmest). He edited *General Viticulture*, published in 1962 and revised in 1974, which was long considered the most comprehensive book on VITICULTURE in the English language.

winter freeze, a climatic stress which can be lethal to parts or all of the vine. In areas of high LATITUDE and high ELEVATION, the risk of very cold winter weather is substantial, particularly in CONTINENTAL CLIMATES away from the moderating effects of oceans (although even in MARITIME CLIMATES winter freeze can kill thousands of vines in exceptionally cold winters such as that of 1956 in ST-ÉMILION and POMEROL). Such continental climates typically show colder temperatures but also greater TEMPERATURE VARIABILITY.

Cold-hardy varieties, such as the American vine CONCORD, can be grown in the midwestern United States in sites with annual minimum temperatures of −29 °C/−20 °F occurring once in three years. European VITIS VINIFERA varieties sensitive to cold require relatively warmer sites, however, where annual minimum temperatures of −20 °C/−4 °F are recorded no more than once in a decade. CROWN GALL disease commonly develops on vines injured by winter freeze, killing tissue and causing trunk splitting.

An essential first step towards avoiding winter freeze injury is wise VINEYARD SITE SELECTION. Sites which export cold air, such as those offering AIR DRAINAGE on free-standing hills, can avoid winter injury by being up to 5 °C/9 °F warmer than sites which import cold air, such as those on valley floors. Vineyard sites within a few kilometres of large bodies of water (such as the MÉDOC, which suffered far less from the great winter freeze of 1956 than the inland vineyards of St-Émilion and Pomerol, for example) are also preferred because of the moderating effects on temperature (and see LAKE EFFECT in North America).

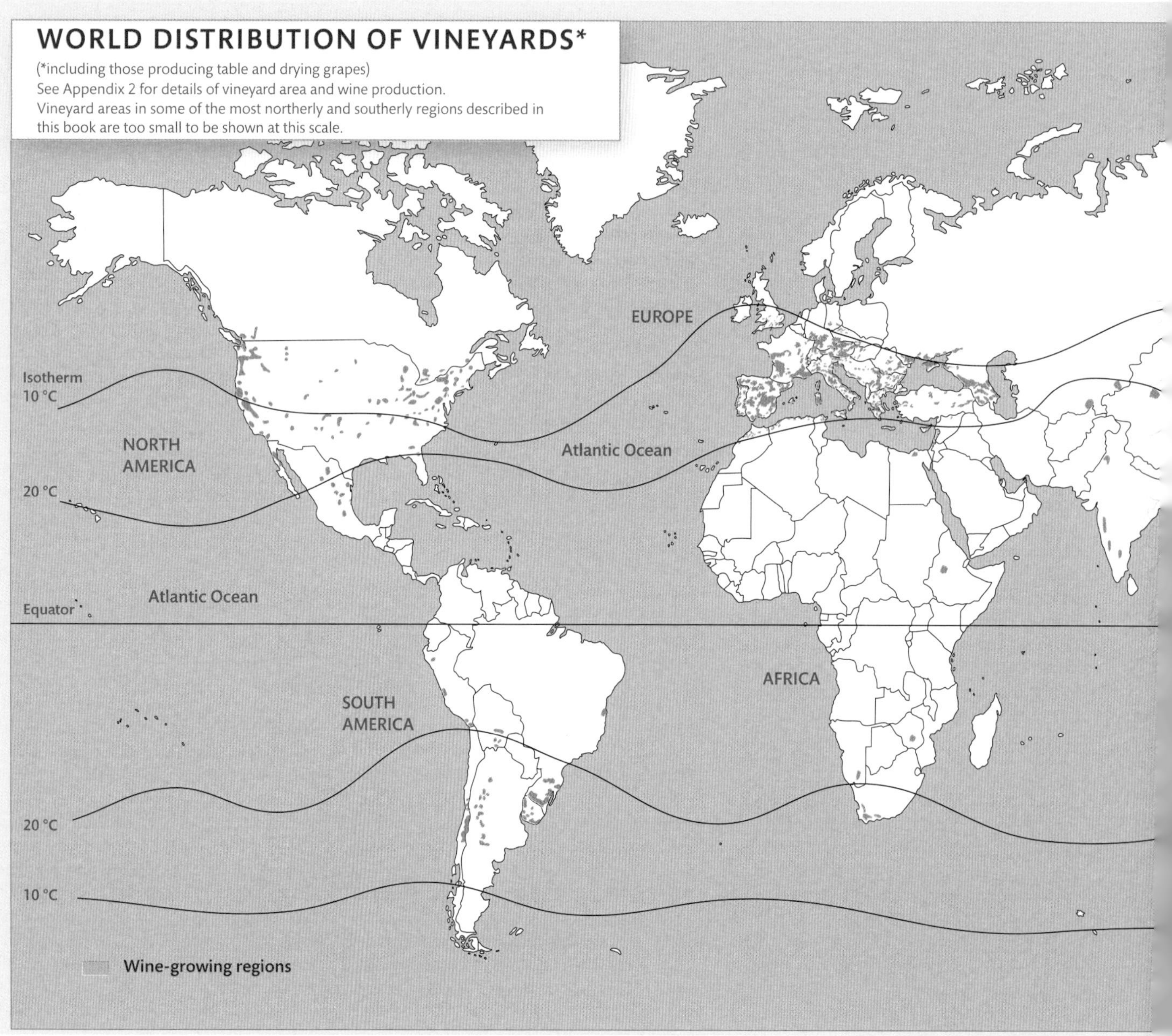
WORLD DISTRIBUTION OF VINEYARDS*
(*including those producing table and drying grapes)
See Appendix 2 for details of vineyard area and wine production.
Vineyard areas in some of the most northerly and southerly regions described in this book are too small to be shown at this scale.
EUROPE
Isotherm 10 °C
NORTH AMERICA
Atlantic Ocean
20 °C
Atlantic Ocean
Equator
AFRICA
SOUTH AMERICA
20 °C
10 °C
Wine-growing regions

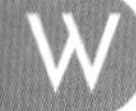

Selecting varieties with noted winter hardiness is also important. Varieties such as CABERNET FRANC and RIESLING are more winter-hardy than Pinot Noir, Chasselas, and Cabernet Sauvignon. In turn, *vinifera* varieties are less hardy than some interspecific HYBRIDS such as SEYVAL or TRAMINETTE, which in turn are less winter-hardy than such American varieties as DELAWARE and CONCORD. VINE BREEDERS have used VITIS AMURENSIS as a parent to produce winter-hardy varieties such as CABERNET SEVERNY and VITIS RIPARIA to breed complex winter-hardy hybrids such as MARQUETTE. Choice of ROOTSTOCKS which avoid stress is also critical for vine survival.

The vine's reserves of CARBOHYDRATES act like a biological antifreeze. The aim of vine management to avoid winter stress is to achieve maximum carbohydrate reserves at the end of the growing season. This entails choice of suitable TRAINING SYSTEM, appropriately severe PRUNING level, and SHOOT THINNING and CROP THINNING so as to restrict YIELD, which, when excessive, can act to reduce levels of vine carbohydrates.

An alternative strategy to avoid winter kill is to bury the vines in autumn (see WINTER PROTECTION). TRUNK RENEWAL is an established practice in upstate New York to recover vines affected by freeze injury. R.E.S.

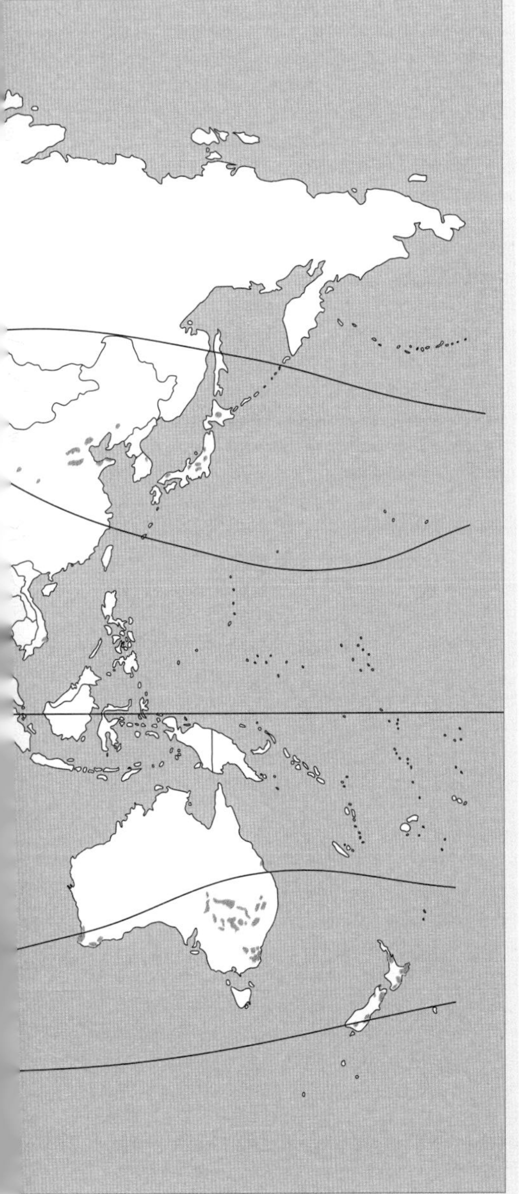

winter protection, cumbersome viticultural techniques aimed at protecting vines in cold, CONTINENTAL CLIMATES against the effects of WINTER FREEZE. Most commonly, vines are buried in autumn to benefit from the fact that winter temperatures below the soil surface are never more than a few degrees Celsius below freezing point, whereas the air temperature can be more than 20 °C/36 °F colder. Burying vines is, however, LABOUR-intensive and expensive. This was traditionally practised in central Europe and North America but is uncommon now because of the cost. Only in the vineyards of RUSSIA, parts of UKRAINE, some of the central Asian republics, and CHINA is it still considered an acceptable price to pay for viticulture, although some severe winters in upper NEW YORK State in the early 21st century have engendered some reconsideration. The procedure has been modified so that just those few CANES to be used for fruiting the following year are buried. Vines are also trained to have several TRUNKS, so-called 'spare-parts viticulture', so that those killed in winter can easily be replaced. Growers in ONTARIO, Canada, have widely adopted wind machines to combat winter freeze, and more recently GEOTEXTILES. It is possible that TRUNK DISEASE may contribute to winter-freeze injury, and their symptoms may be confused. J.R. & R.E.S.

Willwerth, J., et al., 'Best management practices for reducing winter injury in grapevines' (2014). www.brocku.ca/webfm/Best_Practices_Manual__Winter_Injury_Sept_14_(5).pdf.

Winzer, which is the German equivalent of the French VIGNERON, is a common prefix in Germany for a CO-OPERATIVE wine cellar, as in **Winzergenossenschaft**, **Winzerverein**, and **Winzervereinigung**.

wire, used to form vine TRELLIS SYSTEMS, along with POSTS. Wine consumers might never credit something as mundane as wire in vineyards with their enjoyment, yet it is difficult to conceive of how wine could be so widely produced without it. The widespread use of wire revolutionized trellising of vines, making it possible to train vines to forms which maximize their production and MECHANIZATION. High-tensile wire can support very heavy loads without breaking. Normally, thicker wire is used to support the weight of grapes in a trellis, and thinner wires to support foliage. See TRELLIS SYSTEMS and TRAINING SYSTEMS. R.E.S.

WO. See WINE OF ORIGIN.

wood has been the most popular material for wine CONTAINERS both for TRANSPORT and STORAGE for centuries, and even today trees are almost as important to some wines as vines. Merchants in ancient ARMENIA shipped wine down the Tigris in palm-wood casks seven centuries BCE, according to HERODOTUS. Wooden BARRELS eventually succeeded AMPHORAE as containers for both transport and storage in the 3rd century CE.

It was not until the mid 20th century, however, that wood was irrevocably replaced by the bottle and tanker for transport and widely replaced by inert materials such as CONCRETE and STAINLESS STEEL for storage and FERMENTATION.

For fine wines, wood is still valued as the prime material for maturing (see BARREL AGEING and CASK AGEING) and for fermenting certain types of white wine, for some handmade red wines (see BARREL FERMENTATION), and for some larger fermentation vats.

The chemistry of wine's maturation in wood is still not fully understood, but experience shows that wood (unlike sealed tanks made of inert materials) exposes the wine to a certain amount of OXYGEN and actively aids CLARIFICATION and STABILIZATION of the wine matured in it—quite apart from the wide range of flavours and characteristics which may be added and transformed as a result of exposure to that particular wood, either directly as OAK FLAVOUR or indirectly as WOOD INFLUENCE.

See also WOOD TYPES.

Wood also plays a part in viticulture, not just because the vine's own wood is important (see CANE and TRUNK) but also because wood is a common material for POSTS and STAKES in the vineyard.

For more detail of wood structure, see CAMBIUM and XYLEM.

Guimberteau, G. (ed.), *Le Bois et la qualité des vins et eaux-de-vie* (1992).

wood alcohol. Alternative name for harmful METHANOL.

wood influence. If a wine is fermented or matured in a wooden container, many different aspects of that container may shape its character and flavour, quite apart from those compounds that may be directly extracted from the oak wood and absorbed into the wine as wood flavour (see OAK FLAVOUR). The most obvious advantage of holding a wine in wood (see BARREL AGEING and CASK AGEING) rather than in an inert material is that wood encourages

natural CLARIFICATION and STABILIZATION. The precise influence of a wooden container on any wine held in it is a function of the way that wine was made as well as of the following aspects.

Wood type

Historically, barrels and tanks have been made from many different WOOD TYPES although OAK is now the most common. The type of wood, even the type of oak, can have a powerful effect on flavour and STRUCTURE. There can be large differences between oak species. For example, the compounds extracted from white oak or from European oaks such as sessile and pedunculate oak are very different.

Origin of the wood

In addition to the species—and a barrel may be made from more than one—the origin of the oak can also have an effect on the wine in the barrel. This is influenced by genetic lineage, forest management, growth conditions, and climate.

For example, white oak from Missouri will not have exactly the same aromatic profile as white oak from other US states. Sessile oak from the Loire Valley will be different in terms of aromatic aldehydes and eugenol compared with sessile oak from the Carpathians. However, scientific studies tend to show a high degree of variability between trees in one forest or between forests, so the way coopers buy and select their wood is critical.

Manufacturing techniques

Several aspects of BARREL MAKING can have a marked impact on wine flavour, for example whether the STAVES are sawn or split (see OAK) or how the staves are graded (by GRAIN or by chemical composition). If the grain is not respected, the watertightness and aromatic profile of the wood may be affected.

The method of drying the wood, from seasoning in the open air to kiln drying, can also affect the character of the wine, as does the local climate, the ways the staves are stacked, and whether they are sprinkled with water.

Lastly, the degree to which the staves are heated while being bent and the level of barrel TOAST also have an obvious and profound effect on flavour (see BARREL MAKING).

Size of container

The larger the container, the smaller the ratio of surface area to volume and the greater the contact between the wine and the oak, so the barrel must be chosen in relation to the richness and style of the wine. Barrels holding less than 190 l/50 gal can overwhelm wine with OAK FLAVOURS. Containers holding more than 570 l/150 gal will provide little wood oak flavour, particularly after their first use. (See BARREL TYPES for detail of barrel sizes most commonly used.)

The use of large wooden VATS or tanks as FERMENTATION VESSELS fell out of favour after the advent of STAINLESS STEEL and other inert materials because the latter are much easier to clean than wood and because TEMPERATURE is harder to control in large-volume wooden containers, but there is currently a resurgence of interest in them (and in CONCRETE). Fermenting in a wooden vat is particularly suitable for high-quality wines with a firm tannic structure. It allows better integration of the wood and offers many of the advantages of barrel ageing.

Many of Italy's and some of the southern Rhône's, Germany's, and Alsace's most revered wines are the product of cask ageing in large, old wooden casks. Proponents of such wooden vats note that some of the greatest wines in the world are made in them and suggest that ageing in large wooden tanks provides gentle oxygenation of the wine and, hence, a desirable form of pre-bottling maturation.

Age of container

Barrels may be valued simply because they are containers made from a material that clarifies and stabilizes wine naturally, offers wine some mild but useful oxygenation, and can actually add OAK FLAVOUR to wine. The newer the barrel, the more wood flavour it is capable of imparting, and in most wine regions new barrels command a premium, with one-year-old barrels selling for approximately 70%, two-year-old barrels selling for less than 50%, and five-year-old barrels selling for just 10% of the cost of a new barrel.

However, some winemakers deliberately minimize oak flavour by using only a small proportion of new barrels or by 'breaking in' new barrels on lesser wines. Within a given type and style of wine, the richest wines will absorb the most oak with positive effects. A wine needs to have sufficient structure and aroma to balance those brought by the oak, and wines matured in 100% new oak are becoming much less common.

Older barrels are important for wines where the winemaker seeks slow oxygenation of the wine but no perceptible oak flavour, such as in making PORT, SHERRY, and, in many cases, RIOJA. Some champagne producers ferment or age their base wines in older oak.

When new oak was the height of FASHION at the end of the 20th century, some winemakers boasted of using '200% new oak', meaning that wines were first put into one new barrel and then into another. Very few wines can withstand such an onslaught.

Time

Time remains the winemaker's greatest tool. A wine's character is also influenced by how long it remains in wood, which can vary from about two months for relatively light white wines to two or even three years for certain red wines. More traditionally minded producers in Spain, Italy, and Portugal may keep wines in old wooden cooperage for even longer. The most practical approach is to age the wine in barrels for 12 months, because the barrels are never empty (see BARREL MAINTENANCE) and you don't need two sets of barrels, but the decision typically depends on the winemaker's preference and the capacity of the wine to support the oak. Wines with exceptional tannin structure can undergo the longest ageing; lighter wines will be quickly OXIDIZED and overwhelmed by the flavours and TANNINS from the oak. In general, the length of time a wine spends in barrel has reduced as grapes are picked riper and tannins are less ASTRINGENT.

Vintage

The character of individual VINTAGE YEARS also affects the influence of any wood on a wine's flavour. Wines, especially red wines, vary so much from vintage to vintage that it is impossible to specify the perfect barrel for a given wine. For this reason, some winemakers order a range of different WOOD TYPES with variation in TOAST in anticipation of each harvest.

Wine-making techniques

Just as important as the direct flavour effects from the wood are the indirect or secondary flavour effects that are more the result of the environment of the wooden tank or barrel. For more details, see CASK AGEING and BARREL AGEING respectively. White wines fermented in barrel may change enormously in character. For more details, see BARREL FERMENTATION.

Storage conditions

Exact temperatures and humidity levels, even draughts, can affect the character of a wine held in a wooden container. For more details, see BARREL STORAGE. M.C.K. & R.T. du C.

Prida, A., and Puech, J.-L., 'Influence of geographical origin and botanical species on the content of extractives in American, French, and East European oak woods', *Journal of Agricultural and Food Chemistry*, 54/21 (2006), 8115–26.

wood types. Over the years, many different kinds of wood have been used to make small BARRELS and larger VATS and CASKS. Acacia, cypress, chestnut, ash, redwood, pine, eucalyptus, and poplar are just a few of the woods that have been used.

Chestnut has long been popular for large oval casks in the Rhône, Beaujolais, and parts of Italy and Portugal, but as this wood offers strong TANNINS and is also relatively porous, chestnut barrels and tanks are often coated with paraffin or silicone to neutralize the wood. Wines made in unlined new chestnut barrels can be so tannic as to be undrinkable.

In other countries, pine and eucalyptus have been used for casks, but these woods produce wines with flavours that strike many consumers as odd unless the wood is very well seasoned (see BARREL MAKING) or coated on the inside. Acacia is used successfully, notably in Austria and Istria (see CROATIA), although some coopers say it is very porous. In Chile, the local evergreen beech, or *rauli*, wood was once common. Redwood was used for large upright tanks in America for many years, although very few have been built since the early 1970s. Redwood is rarely made into barrels because the wood is difficult to bend and the flavours are aggressive. Since the advent of neutral STAINLESS STEEL and enamel-lined tanks, wooden COOPERAGE must offer something extra to the wine to be worth the premium.

By far the most popular wood type in use in winemaking today is OAK, which has none of the disadvantages outlined above and whose particular aspects of WOOD INFLUENCE and OAK FLAVOUR have come to be appreciated by both winemakers and wine drinkers. M.C.K.

Worcester, warm inland wine district within the Breede River Valley region in South Africa. This extensive fertile district beyond the Du Toitskloof Mountains and within the Breede River Valley region produces about 12% of the national wine crop. Generally warm and reliant on IRRIGATION, the region used to be heavily dependent on Colombard and Chenin Blanc, but Chardonnay, Sauvignon Blanc, Viognier, and Shiraz have all become relatively important too.

world production of wine is concentrated in two bands of generally TEMPERATE to MEDITERRANEAN CLIMATE in each hemisphere, as shown on the map on page 842. TROPICAL VITICULTURE is becoming increasingly common but so far on a small scale relative to the established wine-producing countries. The limits of viticulture are also shifting polewards, particularly in the northern hemisphere, as a result of CLIMATE CHANGE. (See LATVIA, for example.)

Total production of wine is affected by each year's weather (particularly by FROST, poor FRUIT SET, or HAIL, especially but not exclusively within Europe) and by the effects of VINE-PULL SCHEMES, offset by those of new plantings. The underlying trend is downwards, largely because of determined efforts by the EU to reduce its wine SURPLUS.

See also PRODUCTION, CONSUMPTION, and, for precise figures, SURPLUS of wine as well as Appendices 2A, 2B, and 2C.

World Wine Trade Group (**WWTG**) is a group of government and industry representatives from the following non-EU wine countries: Argentina, Australia, Canada, Chile, Georgia, New Zealand, South Africa, the United States, and Uruguay. It was founded in 1998 as a counterweight to the hegemony of the EU and its wine regulatory model in international affairs. It aims to facilitate international trade in wine through information sharing, discussion of regulatory issues, and joint actions to address trade barriers. While little known, it is highly influential. Members have signed two treaty-level agreements on mutual recognition of winemaking practices and requirements for labelling (see LABELLING INFORMATION), and the principles of these agreements have been included in other international free-trade agreements involving Pacific Rim countries. The WWTG is active in working with other Asia-Pacific economies on wine issues and has also established important guidance on matters such as SUSTAINABILITY, regulatory principles, and certification. J.P.H.B.

www.wwtg-gmcv.org

Wrattonbully, now substantial wine region just north of Coonawarra in SOUTH AUSTRALIA with a strongly LIMESTONE-based soil. Cabernet Sauvignon is the most planted grape variety.

WSET. The Wine & Spirit Education Trust is the world's leading provider of wine, spirits, and sake EDUCATION. Based in London, it offers classroom and online courses and qualifications for both industry professionals and consumers at four different levels, culminating in the WSET Diploma, which is the usual prerequisite for studying to become a MASTER OF WINE. These qualifications are offered through a network of over 800 course providers across more than 70 countries in more than 15 languages. Since its inception as an educational charity in 1969, WSET has awarded over 1 million people a WSET qualification.

Württemberg, wine region in southern Germany (in the State of Baden-Württemberg) with 11,394 ha/28,155 acres of vineyard in 2019 which loosely follow the River Neckar and its tributaries (see map under GERMANY) and whose soils are dominated by MARL and fossil-rich LIMESTONE. Much of the region lies between Stuttgart (including several suburbs) and Heilbronn with vineyards to the north segueing into those of BADEN's Kraichgau. In these sectors, steep, DROUGHT-sensitive, and demanding terraced slopes look down on the Neckar. The climate varies from south to north but is at its most CONTINENTAL along the Kocher, Jagst, and Tauber, three tributaries at the north-eastern edge of the region. Nearly 19% of Württemberg's vineyards are planted in RIESLING, while other white wine varieties are in decline and collectively amount to little more than 10% of the vineyard surface. Just over two-thirds of the region is planted to dark-skinned grapes, notably TROLLINGER with 18%, LEMBERGER with 16%, Schwarzriesling/Müllerrebe (PINOT MEUNIER) with 12%, and SPÄTBURGUNDER (Pinot Noir) with 12%.

Württemberg's Swabian populace is known for its thirst and the local wines for being drunk before leaving the region, but an increasing number of producers have begun garnering attention abroad. While Swabians are also notorious for thrift, their wines sell for prices well above German averages. Some 70% of Württemberg's production represents smallholders who sell to 32 CO-OPERATIVES which process their fruit at a single huge central cellar (see ZENTRALKELLEREI). The viticultural institute at Weinsberg (affiliated with a state winery) perpetuates a 150-year reputation for research and teaching. D.S.

würzelecht, German for UNGRAFTED.

Würzer is a Gewürztraminer × Müller-Thurgau CROSS made at the German viticultural station of Alzey in 1932 and only planted in any significant quantity in the 1980s, peaking in 1995 at 121 ha/300 acres, mainly in Rheinhessen. Planted on only 50 ha/124 acres in 2020, it is overpoweringly heady and yields well, but a little goes a very long way indeed.

X

Xarello, or **Xarel-lo**, fine white grape variety planted on an increasing total of 10,445 ha/25,810 acres of CATALUÑA in 2020, producing powerful, ageworthy still and sparkling wines. Under the name Pansa Blanca, it is particularly important in ALELLA. It is most commonly found in PENEDÈS, however, where, with Parellada and Macabeo, it makes up most CAVA blends. It needs careful pruning, and the wine it produces can be very strongly flavoured. It is the rather vegetal smell of Xarello that often distinguishes so many Cavas from other TRADITIONAL METHOD sparkling wines. Xarello was recently authorized in France.

Xenophon, writer in ancient GREECE in the late 5th century BCE famous for his *Anabasis*. In the *Economics*, a dialogue between a farmer, Ischomachos, and the famous philosopher Socrates, the planting and care of vines is discussed: vines should be planted in well-dug earth, at an angle, and the earth should be trodden down around the vine. H.H.A.

Xérès, French name for both JEREZ and SHERRY.

Xinomavro, black grape variety grown on 2,185 ha/5,399 acres (in 2021) all over northern GREECE as far south as the foothills of Mount Olympus, where Rapsani is produced, but most famous as the grape of NAOUSSA. Its name means 'acid black', and the wines can indeed seem harsh in youth, but they age well, losing their colour relatively quickly and becoming much more perfumed and complex. One of the few Greek vine varieties which may not reach full ripeness in some years, it is blended with a small proportion of the local NEGOSKA to produce Goumenissa and is also used as a base for sparkling wine on the exceptionally cool, high vineyards of AMYNDEO. The wines tend to be well-structured by both TANNINS and ACIDITY and have an attractive bite. It has also been planted in Gansu in CHINA at a JOINT VENTURE project by Mihalis Boutaris of Kir-Yianni in Naoussa.

xylem, the principal water-conducting tissue in vascular plants. In woody stem tissues, the secondary xylem forms the wood. The CAMBIUM differentiates xylem tissue on its inside. A single ring of xylem is produced each year with the first-formed vessels (in spring) being larger than those of late wood. This is how the annual rings which help to assess the age of a plant are formed. In the grapevine, the vessels are large and porous so that its wood is very water conductive, a feature of vines generally. In autumn, however, vessels may become blocked by structures which plug the tubes, called tyloses, formed by the 'ballooning' of adjacent cell material into the vessel through pits in the walls; some vessels remain functional for up to seven years, but most become blocked by tyloses in their second or third year. The secondary xylem of QUERCUS forms the wood from which oak barrels are made. (See also PHLOEM.) B.G.C.

Xynisteri, the most common white grape variety grown on Cyprus, more than 2,085 ha/5,152 acres in 2020, more than one-quarter of the island's vineyard. It is preferred to the dark-skinned MAVRO for the rich fortified wine COMMANDARIA, the island's most distinctive wine, and also makes dry whites of varying quality.

Yamabudo, meaning 'mountain vine' in Japanese and also known as crimson glory vine, is the common name for the Asian vine species *Vitis coignetiae,* which grows wild in Japan. The vine has small berries and high acidity and is showing promise for a range of red wines, from fresh and lively to rich.

Yamhill-Carlton District, wine region and AVA in the WILLAMETTE VALLEY of Oregon.

YAN. See NITROGEN.

Yarra Valley, historic, cool-climate Australian wine region just north-east of Melbourne, VICTORIA. Its 120-plus producers (2021) make internationally recognized Chardonnay, Pinot Noir and Cabernet blends, and, increasingly, Shiraz. In some quarters, CLIMATE CHANGE and the presence of PHYLLOXERA have prompted replanting, GRAFTING, exploitation of cooler exposures, and the emergence of later-ripening varieties such as GRENACHE. Iconic heritage producers such as Mount Mary, Yarra Yering, and Yeringberg rub shoulders with dynamic experimentalists in a creative melting pot that is a popular and growing centre for wine TOURISM.
E.N.H.M.

Ycoden-Daute-Isora, complicated name from the Guanche pre-Hispanic times for the most ancient geographically DELIMITED wine region in the CANARY ISLANDS. It is centred on the town of Icod de los Vinos, where wine has been made since the Spanish conquest in the 15th century. It now produces some of the best dry whites in the islands, from LISTÁN Blanco (PALOMINO FINO) and, increasingly, from the more distinctive VIJARIEGO and MARMAJUELO. In the 1990s, coastal vineyards were consistently uprooted and vines were planted inland at much higher ELEVATIONS on the verdant VOLCANIC slopes. By 2021 there were 1,600 ha/ 3,954 acres under vine. V. de la S. & F.C.

yeast, microscopic, single-celled fungi, having round to oval cells which reproduce by forming buds, are vital to the alcoholic FERMENTATION process, which, starved of oxygen, transforms grape juice to wine. SUGARS are used as an energy source by yeast, with ETHANOL and CARBON DIOXIDE as major by-products of the reactions.

The word 'yeast' (which may be singular or plural unless it encompasses yeasts from more than one species) is an old one whose meaning has changed significantly with the flowering of microbiological science. It originally derived from an ancient word meaning 'to boil', 'to seethe' or 'to be troubled'. In 16th-century English, it referred to the froth on the top of a brewing tank and to the semi-solid material that could be collected both from that froth and from the bottom of the tank. From the mid 17th century, the meaning of the word 'yeast' changed to that of a single-celled plant, a *thallophyte* and one of the lowest members of the plant kingdom along with algae, lichens, and fungi.

In common with other fungi, yeasts are differentiated from plant cells by absence of chloroplasts, which contain the plant cell's chlorophyll. The modern fermentative yeasts have evolved from an ancestral yeast by a process of genome duplication, rearrangements, and deletions estimated to have occurred over the past 100 million years, most likely in response to the high availability of sugar as flowering plants evolved. The genetic, and hence phenotypic, diversity of the pre-eminent fermentation yeast, *Saccharomyces cerevisiae*, is now immense.

Nomenclature

The nomenclature of various yeasts is far from straightforward and is in the process of being revised. Taxonomists—scientists who classify and name plants and animals—have traditionally had difficulty with the various microorganisms, both because early microscopes revealed little detail and because the appearance of an organism depended on the conditions of its growth, isolation, and preparation for observation. The result has been that names have changed over time as laboratory equipment improved and as new techniques were perfected. In particular, the development of methods to study the genetic information contained in chromosomal DNA has provided more reliable ways to characterize and classify yeasts. Indeed, a *Saccharomyces cerevisiae* yeast was the first higher organism to have its whole genome sequenced, by 1996. Genome analysis has revealed that some yeasts which were thought to be closely related were in fact only distantly related, and vice versa. Furthermore, some characteristics of yeasts that were used to differentiate species, such as the pattern of sugars that can be fermented, were found to represent natural variation within that species and consequently did not represent different species. For this reason, many yeast names in common usage several decades ago are no longer accepted.

Saccharomyces cerevisiae is the name now most frequently used for the yeast involved in making wine and beer and in leavening bread. *Saccharomyces*, the genus name, means 'sugar fungus', and *cerevisiae* derives from the same root as 'cereals'. Older literature frequently called this yeast *Saccharomyces ellipsoideus* because the cells associated with fruit juices appeared more elliptical than the often-circular bakers' yeast. Within this yeast species are several hundred different strains or selections, each with real or fancied minor differences. Some strain differences relate to fermentation vigour, lack of off-flavour formation, ESTER production, and enhancement of a wine's VARIETAL character, such as fruity notes in Sauvignon Blanc. Many strains are being DNA-sequenced to reveal the genetic basis of their important winemaking characteristics, which will ultimately facilitate the breeding of strains with enhanced fermentation characteristics (see GENETIC MODIFICATION). Another species within the same genus, *Saccharomyces uvarum*, is often used in the distilling and brewing industries. It can grow at lower temperatures than *S. cerevisiae* and is often the dominant yeast fermenting musts located in cool-climate viticultural regions of countries including New Zealand, France, and Italy. It and other closely related species, *Saccharomyces kudriazvevii* and *Saccharomyces paradoxus*, as well as their hybrids made by breeding with *Saccharomyces cerevisiae*, are showing potential for increasing the diversity of wine aromas and flavours. Several of the non-*Saccharomyces* yeast species which are commonly associated with grapes and fermentation (see below), such as *Candida zemplinina* (previously called *stellata*), *Lachancea* (previously *Kluyveromyces*) *thermotolerans*, *Metschnikowia pulcherrima*, and *Torulaspora delbrueckii*, are now being used in combination with *Saccharomyces cerevisiae* to introduce new and diverse flavour profiles in wine.

Editorial note:
In this article and throughout the book we use the term **ambient yeasts** to refer to yeasts of any genus that are present in the vineyard or winery (i.e. the opposite of inoculated yeasts); some writers refer to non-inoculated yeasts as 'native' or 'indigenous' yeasts. We use **wild yeasts** to refer to non-*Saccharomyces* yeasts, although 'wild yeasts' is used by many writers to refer to non-inoculated yeasts of any genus.

Cultured versus ambient yeasts

Ecology studies have shown that intact grape berries harbour a number of other yeast and yeast-like genera in significant populations. Spread around wineries and vineyards by insects, particularly fruit flies (DROSOPHILA), and possibly air currents, the most common genera are *Aureobasidium*, *Klöckera/Hanseniaspora*, and *Candida*, with *Pichia*, *Lachancea* (formerly *Kluyveromyces*), *Metschnikowia*, *Zygosaccharomyces*, and *Torulaspora* usually representing a low proportion. *Saccharomyces* species are rarely isolated from grape berries unless they are damaged by, for example, disease, birds, insects, or hail. More sensitive to SULFUR DIOXIDE and generally intolerant of an ALCOHOLIC STRENGTH above 5%, these wild yeasts are generally active during the early stages of non-inoculated or spontaneous fermentations, especially those occurring when insufficient or no sulfur dioxide is added to the MUST or GRAPE JUICE. Fortunately, there are usually enough *Saccharomyces cerevisiae* cells present on the surfaces of harvesting, transportation, and winery processing equipment that enter the must or grape juice, so that these latter yeasts continue the fermentation above the unstable alcoholic strength of 5%, depleting the supply of sugar and producing a stable wine. Inoculation with *Saccharomyces* yeast does not totally suppress wild yeasts which are naturally present in musts and juices during the early stages of fermentation. Therefore, wine is commonly the result of a mixed microflora, although the impact of wild yeasts on the wine is usually very much restricted by the inoculated yeast.

Ambient yeast, generally a mixture of yeast genera and species, have in the past been much more commonly used than cultured yeast in the traditional wine regions of Europe. (See also PIED DE CUVE.) The concept of 'château' or resident/indigenous populations of ambient yeast which promote the particular character of an estate wine is controversial among wine scientists. (See also MICROBIAL TERROIR.)

The advantage of a well-adapted population of ambient yeast is that they are generally composed of more than one strain and, because of their different abilities and aptitudes, they may be capable of producing a wine with a more balanced, wider range of flavours and characteristics. In an attempt to verify such a view, current research is working systematically with mixed-culture fermentations in combination with chemical analysis of FLAVOUR COMPOUNDS (referred to as 'metabolic footprinting') and sensory evaluation of wines to compare inoculated with uninoculated ferments. Given the more unpredictable nature of ambient-yeast fermentations, it is likely that even more sophisticated blended yeast cultures, which better simulate the apparent characteristics of spontaneous ferments, will be developed in the future.

Increasing numbers of OLD WORLD producers and the majority of NEW WORLD winemakers use cultured yeast (sometimes called pure culture, selected yeast or inoculated yeast). The advantage of cultured yeast is that it has been specifically selected and extensively characterized, so that its behaviour across a defined range of grape-juice parameters is robust and predictable. Among the many genera of yeasts, there are astounding variations in terms of alcohol production and tolerance, aroma and flavour, rate of fermentation, temperature tolerance, flocculation characteristics, sulfur-dioxide tolerance, REDUCING potential, and micronutrient requirements. Most wild yeasts cannot tolerate alcohol concentrations above 5%. However, a tolerance of up to 13 or 15% is required for yeasts used in the production of dry wine. Accordingly, strains of *S. cerevisiae* have historically been preferred as cultured strains, although non-*Saccharomyces* yeasts are increasingly being developed as co-inoculants (either simultaneously or sequentially) with commercial *S. cerevisiae* strains.

Strains have been selected and exploited by OENOLOGISTS and winemakers for characteristics such as fermentation vigour, high-alcohol and sulfur-dioxide tolerance, tolerance to temperature extremes, ability to referment wine to make sparkling wine, freedom from ACETIC ACID (VOLATILE ACIDITY) and sulfidic off-flavours, film or FLOR formation needed for SHERRY production, enhancement of wine varietal character, fruity-ester profile and intensity, increased MOUTHFEEL, lower alcohol production, low-foaming, sedimentation (flocculant) property, yeasticidal properties, improved red wine colour, better tolerance to nutrient deficiencies, lower potential to form sulfur dioxide, and compatibility with LACTIC ACID BACTERIA. Yeast with a high alcohol production and tolerance may be chosen for FORTIFIED WINES or dry red wine made from overripe grapes with very high sugar content in some New World wine regions. Yeast which flocculate particularly well, such as that called Épernay, may be used for SPARKLING WINEMAKING; FILM-FORMING YEAST are used to make sherry; while a yeast with good tolerance of sulfur dioxide may be useful in certain examples of SWEET WINEMAKING. Strains with well-defined flavour characteristics are becoming popular and can offer better colour and tannin structure, improved fruity/ESTERY notes or greater enhancement of varietal flavour; strains which emphasize, for example, the tropical/passion-fruit aroma in Sauvignon Blanc are now widely available.

Because the selection and characterization of new yeast isolates is a laborious and time-consuming process, a variety of conventional breeding techniques are increasingly being used. These include selecting natural variants from a population or using a mutagen such as ULTRAVIOLET RADIATION to increase genetic variability; culturing yeast under specific stressful conditions (often referred to as adaptive or directed evolution); and hybridization or rare-mating, which exploits the sexual cycle in yeast. See also GENETIC MODIFICATION.

Cultured yeast production

Yeast are cultured in large sterile tanks with vigorous aeration under conditions which encourage biomass but discourage alcohol formation. They are then filtered, washed, dried, and packed in sterile containers, often under vacuum, for transfer to the winery (or brewery or bakery). Well over one hundred different strains are now produced worldwide as active dried wine yeast preparations. Active dried yeast is quickly and simply reactivated with warm water or diluted grape juice at 40 °C/104 °F for 15 minutes. Some wineries culture their favoured yeast in grape juice with or

without vigorous aeration and add about 2–4% by volume to the juice or must to initiate fermentation. Following use in winemaking, the yeast and grape debris are freed of as much wine as possible and usually discarded. A minor proportion may be processed to recover alcohol, TARTRATES, and occasionally grapeseed oil. P.A.H. & A.B.

How yeast works

Yeast, like most living organisms, need a good supply of carbon and NITROGEN; a source of SULFUR, PHOSPHORUS, and OXYGEN; and various MINERALS and micronutrients (e.g. trace elements, and several VITAMINS) for growth and reproduction. The usual carbon sources are the six-carbon sugars, GLUCOSE and FRUCTOSE. Wine yeast can also use SUCROSE, which may be added to the juice of underripe grapes (CHAPTALIZATION) and is used in SPARKLING WINEMAKING to induce the second fermentation. Grape AMINO ACIDS and ammonium compounds most often supply the nitrogen; most fruit juices, including grape juice, provide the other components necessary for growth. Nutrient supplements, based on nitrogen or vitamins, may be added to encourage yeast activity at the beginning of fermentation. This is especially important in the case of underripe grapes, ROT, grapes from low SOIL POTENTIAL vineyards, or grape- and must-processing conditions that deliberately or unwittingly lead to nutrient depletion, such as harvesting and transport under hot conditions that permit extensive microbial growth, or excessive CLARIFICATION. Grape solids provide a source of LIPIDS, which, in the absence of oxygen, are used to build stronger cell membranes that confer better tolerance to fermentation stresses, such as extremes of alcohol and temperature. Oxygen is an especially important nutrient, which is supplied in large quantity during production of the yeast starter culture. Small amounts of oxygen may also be supplied during the early or middle stage of fermentation to improve yeast survival and fermentation activity later in fermentation, especially in anaerobic, high-sugar, highly clarified grape juice at low temperatures (see STUCK FERMENTATION).

All cells require energy to exist, grow, and reproduce. Yeast can release a small amount of the energy stored in glucose and fructose of grape juice by a series of complex biochemical reactions known as glycolysis. This nearly universal biological process is so complex and involves so many steps that it has taken scientists years of research to understand it. Through a series of ENZYME reactions, the yeast cell splits the six-carbon sugar molecule into two molecules of the three-carbon compound PYRUVATE. The final two steps, known collectively as fermentation, convert the pyruvate to ETHYL ALCOHOL and carbon dioxide. In this fermentative decomposition of pyruvate, the first step is removal of the terminal carbon dioxide from pyruvate, leaving the two-carbon fragment ACETALDEHYDE. Acetaldehyde is then reduced to ethyl alcohol. A small amount of acetaldehyde is also converted to ACETIC ACID, which is required for cell processes (e.g. biosynthesis of lipids, needed to make cell membranes); some acetic acid escapes from the cell and contributes to wine volatile acidity.

When all of the sugar is fermented to alcohol and carbon dioxide, and a small amount of oxygen is present, yeast can reconvert some of the ethyl alcohol back to acetaldehyde. Further oxidative decomposition occurs, by a complex series of reactions, to carbon dioxide and water. This process, which takes place in the mitochondria within the cell and which releases most of the energy originally stored in sugar, is known as RESPIRATION. The exposure of wine to oxygen is, however, rigorously prevented except in some circumstances, such as in the making of FLOR wines such as FINO sherry. Normally wine is protected from air during fermentation by the blanket of carbon dioxide produced.

During fermentation of grape juice, yeast produce small amounts of other compounds as by-products of glycolysis and the metabolism of amino acids and other nutrients. Some of these compounds are volatile and contribute fermentation-derived characteristics to the AROMA of wine. The most important compounds are esters, aldehydes, and ketones, fatty acids, higher alcohols, and volatile sulfur compounds (HYDROGEN SULFIDE and MERCAPTANS). Recent research has shown that some of these volatile compounds play a much greater role in the distinctive aroma profile of certain grape varieties than previously believed. Furthermore, advances in the understanding of how yeast control the formation of these aroma compounds is leading to the development of new yeast strains which can alter the emphasis of various aroma notes in wine. GLYCEROL, acetic acid, and SUCCINIC ACID, which contribute to the taste of wine, are the most important non-volatile compounds produced by yeast.

In addition to yeast-derived compounds, there are also complex metabolic/enzymatic interactions that exist between yeast and various grape-derived compounds, many of which contribute to the characteristic aroma and flavour of specific grape varieties. For example, a certain class of enzymes termed glycosidases are released by yeasts and are capable of hydrolysing various FLAVOUR PRECURSORS, notably sugar conjugates of MONOTERPENES, norisoprenoids, aliphatics, PHENOLS, and benzene derivatives. Monoterpenes are important to the aroma of wines made from floral grape varieties such as MUSCAT, RIESLING, and TRAMINER, while β-damascenone, which is responsible for stewed-apple, rose, and honey aromas in young wine, is an example of an important norisoprenoid. See FLAVOUR COMPOUNDS.

Cysteine- or GLUTATHIONE-linked compounds represent another important class of grape-derived flavour precursors that generate polyfunctional volatile THIOLS with fruity aromas when hydrolysed by enzymes present in some strains of yeast. These compounds, which contribute box tree, passion-fruit, grapefruit, guava, and gooseberry aromas, are important in Sauvignon Blanc wines and have also been identified in wines made from Colombard, Riesling, Sémillon, Merlot, and Cabernet Sauvignon.

Some yeasts also have the ability to degrade phenolic acids to volatile vinyl phenols (e.g. 4-vinylphenol and 4-vinylgaiacol), which contribute to phenolic off-flavour. BRETTANOMYCES yeasts are able to convert these unstable vinylphenols to the stable ethylphenols (e.g. 4-ethylphenol and 4-ethylgaiacol), responsible for phenolic, medicinal, and barnyard aromas in wine. Yeast also produce carbonyl compounds, which, under some circumstances, can enhance red-wine colour. For example, acetaldehyde and pyruvic acid can react with anthocyanins to form more stable pigmented pyranoanthocyanins that can contribute to the stable colour of aged red wines. On the other hand, most aldehydes are ultimately converted to the corresponding alcohol (just as acetaldehyde becomes ethyl alcohol), such that the oak-derived aldehyde vanillin is reduced to vanillic alcohol, thereby lowering flavour intensity.

After the yeast have converted all of the sugar, they slowly die, flocculate, and fall to the bottom of the vessel, forming a sediment known as gross LEES. In bottle-fermented sparkling wines, the interaction between this sediment and the wine in the bottle is an important element in sparkling winemaking (see AUTOLYSIS). The traditional STIRRING of wine on yeast lees in barrel and in tank is now becoming widely practised as a means to improve palate weight and texture.

P.A.H. & A.B.

Boulton, R. B., et al., *Principles and Practices of Winemaking* (1998).

König, H., et al. (eds.), *Biology of Microorganisms on Grapes, in Musts and in Wine* (2009).

Swiegers, J. H., et al., 'Yeast and bacterial modulation of wine aroma and flavour', *Australian Journal of Grape and Wine Research*, 11 (2005), 139–73.

Ugliano, M., and Henschke, P. A., 'Yeasts and wine flavour', in M. V. Moreno-Arribas and C. Polo (eds.), *Wine Chemistry and Biochemistry* (2009), 313–92.

Varela, C., et al., 'Discovering a chemical basis for differentiating wines made by fermentation with "wild" indigenous and inoculated yeasts: role of yeast volatile compounds', *Australian Journal of Grape and Wine Research*, 15/3 (2009), 238–48.

Yecla, DOP in Murcia in south-east Spain, sandwiched between JUMILLA, ALICANTE, and ALMANSA (see map under SPAIN) and dominated by La Purísima, a large CO-OPERATIVE. The red MONASTRELL represents the majority of the 6,420 ha/15,864 acres of grapes grown in the region.

yellow mosaic, vine disease. See FANLEAF DEGENERATION.

yellows. See GRAPEVINE YELLOWS.

Yellow Tail, Australian wine BRAND whose growth in the US, from a standing start in 2001, set records in the history of branding and gave birth to the infamous 'critters' (small animals on labels) wine category. The CASELLA FAMILY had just 16 ha/40 acres of vines in RIVERINA and supplied BULK WINE until John Casella with an aggressive, export-orientated manager planned an assault on the embryonic US market for Australian wines in the late 1990s. A first attempt failed, but new branding involving a yellow kangaroo image and the irritating but eye-catching logo [yellow tail] (*sic*), together with particularly fruity, not to say sweet, wines and a bold profit-sharing scheme with their US importer W. J. Deutsch & Sons, paid off. Annual US sales rose from 200,000 cases in the launch year to 7.5 million in 2004, by which time Yellow Tail was the top imported wine brand in the US. But the brand is often blamed for ruining, or at least cheapening, the image of Australian wine there.

yema bud, alternative name for CHIP BUDDING.

yield, how much a vineyard produces, is an important statistic in wine production and has been a subject of intense interest from at least the time of classical ROME, not least because of alleged effects on wine quality.

Factors affecting yield

Vineyard yield depends on many factors, which will be briefly described here. For a more complete discussion, see the individual factors listed.

Yield may be measured as either a weight of grapes or a volume of wine (see below) and is usually considered per unit area of vineyard, since this is what matters in agricultural terms. Those who believe that increasing VINE DENSITY is associated with improved wine quality argue that yield per vine is a more important consideration. Disciples of CANOPY MANAGEMENT, on the other hand, argue that the amount of sunlit leaf area per unit of land is more important than yield per vine or per hectare.

Yield per vine depends on the number of bunches per vine and the average bunch weight. The number of bunches per vine depends on the winter PRUNING policy, the BUDBREAK, and the number of bunches per shoot, or FRUITFULNESS. Bunch weight depends on the number of FLOWERS per bunch and the success of FRUIT SET in forming berries, then on the weight of individual berries.

Yield per vine also depends on VINE AGE (very old vines often produce very little), on the way the vines have been managed, and on the WEATHER over at least the last two years, together with other factors such as VINE PESTS and VINE DISEASES.

After VIGOUR and pruning, the weather is one of the most important factors affecting vineyard yield. Cold winters may promote budbreak, but FROSTS in spring can kill young shoots and bunches. Warm, sunny weather promotes FLOWERING and POLLINATION, but cold, wet, and windy weather can cause poor fruit set. Some varieties are more prone than others to poor set. DROUGHT conditions commonly reduce berry size—to less than half that of vines well supplied with water in extreme cases. Rain will generally increase yield as it causes berries to swell, but too much rain near harvest causes BOTRYTIS BUNCH ROT and potentially a considerable loss in yield.

Perhaps surprisingly, the weather the preceding season can also have an effect on yield. It has been shown that warm, sunny weather during flowering encourages bunch INITIATION in the buds that are forming to produce shoots and bunches for the next growing season. So this weather pattern can prepare the vine for a high potential yield the following year.

How yield is measured

Conventional units of yield are the weight of fresh grapes per unit land area, such as tonnes/ha or tons/acre. (One ton/acre is about 2.5 tonnes/ha.) This is the standard measurement in most NEW WORLD wine regions.

Although many Italians and Swiss measure yield in weight of grapes, in most other European countries production is measured in volumes of wine per unit area, normally expressed as hectolitres per hectare, or hl/ha. In many cases, this measurement is an extremely important one, often limited to a maximum (depending on the VINTAGE) specified by local regulation (see AOC, DOC, etc. and the note below).

The two measurements interrelate, although the volume of wine produced by a given weight of grapes can vary considerably according to vine variety, individual vintage conditions, winery equipment, winemaking policy, and, most importantly, wine type. To make 100 litres of red wine, which is fermented in the presence of grape skins that can be pressed rather harder than white grape skins, about 130 kg (0.13 tonnes) of grapes are needed. To make 100 litres of white wine, about 150 kg are needed (more like 160 kg for top-quality SPARKLING WINEMAKING). Assuming an average of 140 kg of grapes per 100 litres of wine, 1 tonne/ha is about 7 hl/ha, while 1 ton/acre is about 17.5 hl/ha (typically slightly less for whites, slightly more for reds).

Despite its importance in measuring yield, there is no uniform approach in determining the area of a vineyard. Excluding the essential and normally cultivated areas along the ends (called headlands) and at the sides, which are indubitably part of the productive unit, effectively reduces the size of many vineyards by 10% or so, and the figure may be higher for small vineyards.

Yields and wine quality

A necessary connection between low yields and high-quality wine has been assumed at least since Roman times when *Bacchus amat colles* encapsulated the prevailing belief that low-yielding HILLSIDE VINEYARDS produced the best wine. Wine law in many European countries is predicated on the same belief, and the much-imitated AOC laws of France specify maximum permitted yields for each appellation (even if an additional allowance is often permitted; see below).

There is little doubt that heavily cropped vines with a low LEAF TO FRUIT RATIO ripen more slowly, so that in cooler climates the fruit may not reach full RIPENESS and wine quality suffers. It is less widely understood that undercropping can also adversely affect wine quality. A high leaf to fruit ratio will certainly ripen grapes, but the resultant shaded CANOPY MICROCLIMATE will produce grapes high in POTASSIUM and PH and low in PHENOLICS and flavour.

It should also be noted that, within a given wine region (Bordeaux is a notable example), there is no correlation between size of the crop and quality of the wine. Some of the finest red bordeaux VINTAGE YEARS of the 1980s, for example, were also those in which yields were relatively high; while the lowest crop levels of the decade were recorded in lesser vintages such as 1984 and 1980.

There are countless commercial examples of high vineyard yields associated with low quality, however. Very high yields are common to vineyards of high VIGOUR, which in turn is typically due to planting on very fertile soil, well supplied with water and nutrients, but the negative effects are more likely to be the result of excessive shoot and leaf growth and canopy SHADE. High-yielding vineyards are also often in hot climates, where the climate reduces the potential for wine quality anyway.

Very low yields may be the deliberate result of careful pruning, SHOOT THINNING, or even CROP THINNING, but they may also be associated with excessive vine stress. This can be due, for example, to weeds, pests, or disease or to very shallow soils and WATER STRESS (as in many traditionally dry-grown vineyards of Mediterranean Europe), and a vine that is too severely stressed will not function properly and will not produce premium wine.

The yield which a vineyard can ripen properly will depend on the VINE VARIETY, the region, vine management practices (particularly pruning and vine-TRAINING SYSTEMS), and climate as well as weather. For example, a yield of 8 tonnes/ha, or 56 hl/ha, might be considered excessive in a very cool climate, but a yield four times this figure might be easily ripened to a similar or higher sugar level in a warmer climate. Some varieties seem more prone than others to crop-level effects on wine quality, and in general red wine varieties are more affected than white. PINOT NOIR is an outstanding example, as the inverse relationship between yield and quality in red burgundy demonstrates. Both Pinot Noir and MERLOT show less colour in the skins and wine, whereas yield effects are much less evident in deeply pigmented varieties such as Syrah.

Some specific examples

Vineyard yields vary enormously around the world and (in some regions with less dependable climates) from year to year. Among the highest reported yields are about 100 tonnes/ha for TABLE GRAPES grown on complex trellises in Israel (if their juice were made into wine, this would convert into about 1,750 hl/ha!). The Argentine vine-breeder Angel Gargiulo was in the 1970s and 1980s encouraged to breed new wine grape varieties specifically designed for the Argentine environment which can yield up to 500 hl/ha (but were commercially planted only to a very limited extent). Commercial, well-managed vineyards in irrigated DESERT regions in California, Australia, and Argentina can routinely produce 15 tons/acre, almost 38 tonnes/ha (260 hl/ha). At the other end of the spectrum, pests, disease, drought, or bunch rot can all reduce yields to less than 1 tonne/ha, or 7 hl/ha. See Ch d'YQUEM as well as Domaine LEROY and CHAPOUTIER for some examples of particularly low yields, encouraged for the sake of wine quality.

Some attempt at calculating national average yields may be made using OIV statistics, although these are more reliable for some countries than for others, and they include vineyards dedicated to TABLE GRAPES or RAISINS as well as to wine grapes, which makes comparisons difficult. According to figures for 2020, South Africa has the highest national average yield, at 85 hl/ha. See EU for a discussion of yields in Europe.

Certain wine types (most red wines, for example) are apparently more sensitive to yield, perhaps because wines from higher-yielding vineyards are often lighter in colour, but this is more likely the result of a vine vigour producing a shaded canopy, which is known to depress PHENOLIC synthesis. Vineyards dedicated to sparkling wines, or base wines for brandy, are in general allowed to yield rather more than those dedicated to still wine production. In Champagne, for example, permitted yields of 12 tonnes/ha (5 tons/acre) or over 80 hl/ha are common.

From a financial point of view, high yields are attractive to vine-growers, who have traditionally been paid on the simple basis of weight (although quality factors such as MUST WEIGHT are also taken into account; see PRICE of grapes). Vine-growers whose aim is to produce good-quality wine may, however, deliberately restrict yields by such measures as pruning, crop thinning, and shoot thinning, although the evidence for a direct yield–quality equation is lacking. One of the most important economic issues facing modern viticulture is whether high-vigour and high-yielding vineyards can produce high-quality wine using vineyard management techniques such as CANOPY MANAGEMENT.

The fact that yields are officially limited by regulation in the two most important wine-producing countries of France and Italy has undoubtedly encouraged worldwide respect for low yields—and perhaps some inertia in those countries for researching ways of increasing both quality and quantity. Alternatively, such restrictions could be seen as a device to avoid production surplus. It should be noted, however, that the official maxima cited in wine regulations were almost routinely increased in France by a device called the *plafond limite de classement*, or PLC, which allowed a certain increase (often 20%) on the base yield according to the conditions of the year. Average yields for the top appellations of the MÉDOC in 1989, 1990, and 1996, for example, were between 55 and 60 hl/ha when the theoretical maximum yield is 45 hl/ha.

Although the PLC has been abolished and the wording has changed, the practice has not. Leeway still exists thanks to the so-called *rendement butoir*, which is higher than the basic maximum. Derogations are also made when yields are severely reduced by severe weather such as HAIL. Another mechanism, the so-called *volume complémentaire individual* (VCI), helps producers balance their stocks when a vintage is expected to face challenges in terms of either quantity or quality, but it applies to wine and not to grapes.

See also PRUNING. R.E.S. & J.R.

Galet, P., *General Viticulture* (2000).

Gargiulo, A. A., 'Quality and quantity: are they compatible?', *Journal of Wine Research*, 2/3 (1991), 161–81.

Keller, M., *The Science of Grapevines* (3rd edn, 2020).

yield monitors, sensors fitted to mechanical grape harvesters which assess and record the amount of fruit being harvested in real time. When used in conjunction with a differential GLOBAL NAVIGATION SATELLITE system, they allow maps of yield to be produced. Such maps are a tool in the implementation of PRECISION VITICULTURE and ZONAL VITICULTURE. R.G.V.B.

Yquem, Château d', the greatest wine of SAUTERNES and, according to the famous 1855 CLASSIFICATION, of the entire BORDEAUX region. It is sweet, golden, and apparently almost immortal.

It had been in the Lur Saluces family since 1785 when Françoise-Joséphine, descendant of original owners the de Sauvage family, married Louis-Amédée de Lur Saluces, in whose family it remained until 1999 when it was sold, after a bitter family struggle, to LVMH. The Lur Saluces generations initiated the system of progressively harvesting only botrytized grapes, a system that quickly spread to neighbouring estates and caught the eye of the Parisian salons, of Thomas JEFFERSON, of the Russian tsars, and finally of all major markets. In the 20th century, the estate was dominated by the Marquis Bertrand de Lur Saluces and, from 1968, by his nephew Comte Alexandre de Lur Saluces, both of whom were totally dedicated to the continued supremacy of Yquem.

The château, dating from the 15th century (the vineyard is considerably older), stands on the crest of an imposing hill overlooking all of the Sauternes FIRST GROWTHS. The vineyard on all sides extends to 100 ha/247 acres in production, of which 80% of vines are Sémillon, the rest Sauvignon Blanc. Production is intentionally restricted to around 96,000 bottles, a fraction of the typical output of a top red-wine property in the MÉDOC. The secret of Yquem's renown is its strict and ever-changing selection from its varied soils, aspects, and MESOCLIMATES according to vintage. The estate's owners have always been determined to run risks and sacrifice quantity for painstakingly upheld quality. Each year, all necessary passes through the vineyard are meticulously performed so that only the best BOTRYTIS-affected grapes are picked. The YIELD is generally just 8–9 hl/ha (the Sauternes appellation permits up to 25). The first pressing is undertaken gently in a horizontal bladder PRESS and accounts for a good 75% of the final volume; the rest is from subsequent pressings in a traditional vertical press made from modern stainless steel. The selected juice is run off into new barrels for BARREL FERMENTATION and then maturation, previously for three years but in the LVMH era closer to 30 months, with the different lots kept separate until they are progressively blended into the final wine.

Since 1959, a dry white wine, Y, or Ygrec, has been intermittently produced. Initially it was a unique wine that smelled strongly of Sauternes but tasted dry or medium-dry. From 2004 it has become a much fresher dry white Bordeaux, with a higher proportion of Sauvignon Blanc in the blend, the acidity balanced by a point of sweetness. W.J.B.

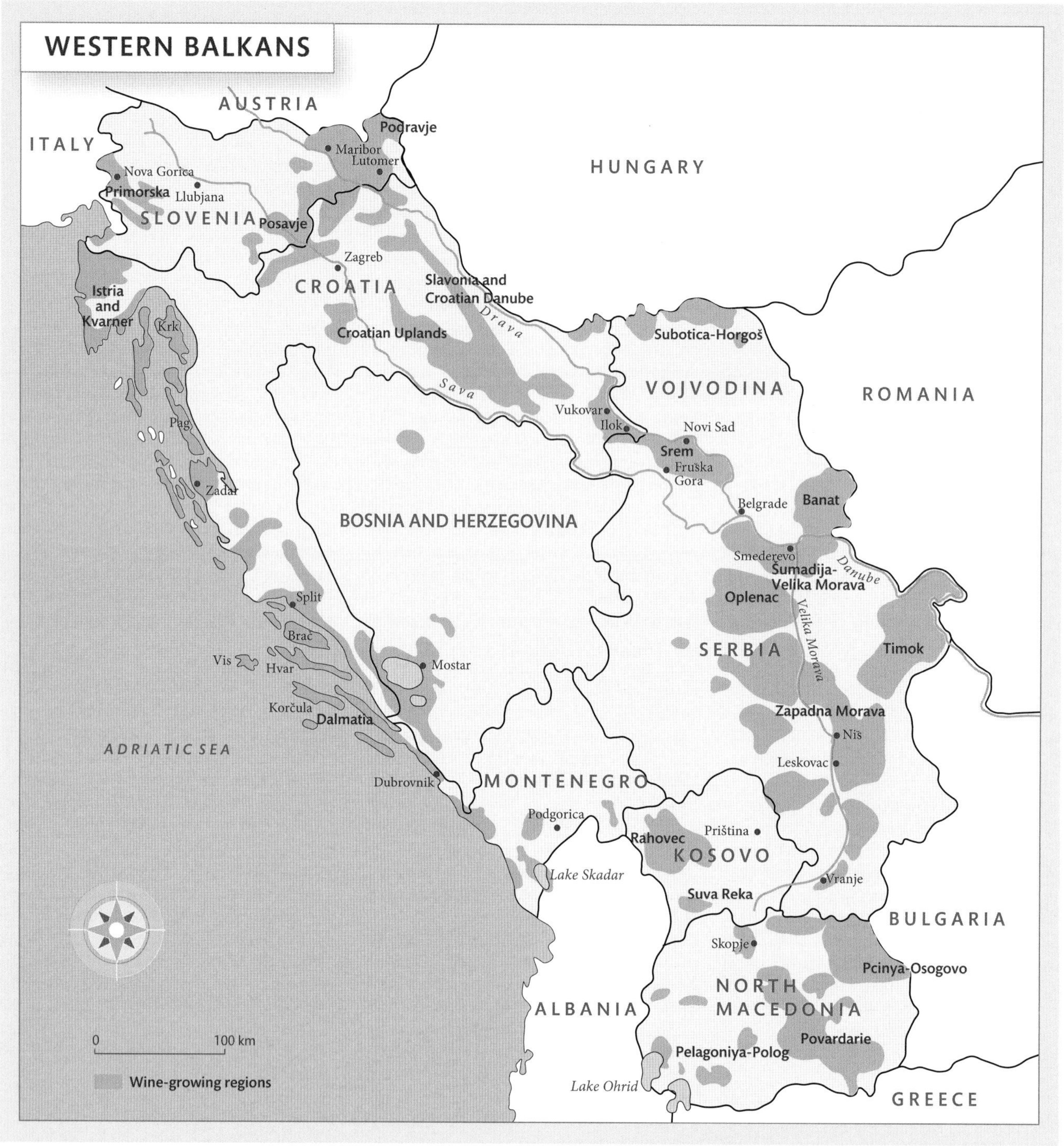

Olney, R., *Yquem* (1985, 1986).

Yonne, a river and a *département* in north-west BURGUNDY as well as an IGP often used for wines falling outside the regulations for AOCS such as CHABLIS, ST-BRIS, and IRANCY. The region is also an important source of OAK for wine barrels. See CHABLIS for more information.

Yugoslavia, eastern European union of peoples that existed for barely 60 years before breaking up amid bloodshed, privation, and extreme ethnic tension at the beginning of the post-communist era in the early 1990s.

Viticulture in this region dates back at least to Roman times and almost certainly earlier, to the Illyrians in the 4th–5th centuries BCE. In the socialist era, production of volume at low prices was the priority in large state-controlled CO-OPERATIVES. At its peak in the 1970s, the former Yugoslavia was one of the world's top ten wine producers, making around 6 million hl/158 million gal a year, and was famous for wines such as Lutomer Laški Rizling, once the UK's best-selling white wine. Marshal Tito's regime was less hardline than those running other Eastern Bloc countries, and some degree of private land ownership, and even private wine production, was permitted. Some family producers were able to start bottling their wine as early as the 1970s. The first private producer, industry hero Stanko Čurin, and (Tito's favourite) Movia of SLOVENIA kept producing throughout this era. This meant that some connection between land and vine growing was retained and provided a strong foundation for the emergence of today's private wine producers. Yugoslavia has since been split into (roughly from north to south) SLOVENIA, CROATIA, SERBIA, KOSOVO, MONTENEGRO, BOSNIA AND HERZEGOVINA, and NORTH MACEDONIA. C.G.

Z

Zalagyöngye, Muscat-like TABLE GRAPE cross of a variety bred in EGER and Pearl of Csaba that is planted on 605 ha/1,495 acres in Hungary, where some undistinguished wine is also made from it, mainly in Kunság. It is also grown in Italy, Croatia, Romania, and Israel for table grapes and is usually called by a local translation of the expression 'Queen of the Vineyards'.

Zalema, Spanish white grape variety still making light, neutral whites from 3,952 ha/ 9,766 acres of Andalucía in 2020, particularly in the southern CONDADO DE HUELVA zone, where its MUSTS and wine can oxidize easily. It is being replaced by higher-quality varieties such as PALOMINO.

Žametovka, Slovenian dark-skinned grape variety most famous for a single plant (see SLOVENIA). Wine made from this variety from the Dolenjska wine region in Posavje in the south of the country is typically an ingredient in the pale, tart, local Čvicek wine.

Zefír, early-ripening 1951 Hungarian CROSS, said to be LEÁNYKA × HÁRSLEVELŰ, producing soft, spicy white wine.

Zelen, old, south-west SLOVENIAN vine variety making crisp, aromatic dry whites in Vipavska Dolina.

Zenit, 1951 Hungarian CROSS of EZERJÓ and BOUVIER which ripens usefully early on 697 ha/ 1,722 acres (as of 2020) to produce crisp, fruity, but not particularly aromatic white wines.

Zentralkellerei, a vast central co-operative wine cellar peculiar to GERMANY. See CO-OPERATIVES.

zero-zero, term for wine to which no ADDITIVES, especially SULFITES, have been added and nothing subtracted by, for example, FINING or FILTRATION. See also NATURAL WINE.

Zéta, Hungarian vine CROSS of FURMINT and BOUVIER, formerly known as Orémus, which, with Furmint, Hárslevelű, and Sárga Muskotály, is permitted in TOKAJ, where there were 116 ha/ 287 acres in 2020. The Bouvier character can dominate unless it is very ripe.

Zibibbo, Sicilian name for the MUSCAT OF ALEXANDRIA white grape variety, sometimes made into wine, notably Moscato and Passito di PANTELLERIA, although more usually sold as TABLE GRAPES. It is very much less common in Italy than Moscato Bianco (MUSCAT BLANC À PETITS GRAINS). In 2020 there were 2,686 ha/ 6,637 acres planted on Sicily. The rich, sweet, orange-gold Moscato di Pantelleria is geographically closer to Tunisia than to Sicily, which administers it. In fact this is the only wine with even a modicum of international renown that is made remotely near the city after which the variety is named.

Zierfandler, the finer of the two white wine grape varieties traditionally associated with Gumpoldskirchen, the dramatically full-bodied, long-lived spicy white wine of the THERMENREGION district of Austria. (The other is ROTGIPFLER.) Plantings had fallen to just 62 ha/153 acres by 2020. It ripens late, as its synonym Spätrot suggests, but keeps its acidity better than Rotgipfler. Unblended, Zierfandler has sufficient nerve to make LATE HARVEST wines with the ability to evolve over years in bottle, but many Zierfandler grapes are blended, and sometimes vinified, with Rotgipfler. The variety, as Cirfandli, is also known in Hungary. DNA parentage analysis suggests it may be a natural cross of ROTER VELTLINER and a relative of SAVAGNIN (Traminer).

Žilavka, the most famous grape variety in Herzegovina (see BOSNIA AND HERZEGOVINA). This characterful variety makes distinctive whites that manage to combine high alcohol with high acidity and a certain nuttiness of flavour. The Žilavka made around the inland town of Mostar is particularly prized. It is not, however, necessarily made exclusively from Žilavka grapes. Žilavka is also found in North Macedonia and to a limited extent in Serbia.

Zimbabwe, southern AFRICAN country with a chequered history of very small-scale wine production since the 1960s. Production peaked at over 6 million l/1.3 million gal in the mid 1990s; however, land redistribution policies and economic instability reduced vineyard area from over 650 ha/1,606 acres to under 40 ha by 2019.

Historically, wine was made by two CO-OPERATIVES, Cairns Holdings (owner of Mukuyu wine estate) and African Distillers, with around 16 growers supplying them with grapes. By 2019 there were only three active vineyards left, and both co-operatives were importing wine from SOUTH AFRICA in tankers, diluting, sweetening, and bottling it under their own brands. Apart from Bushman Rock, Zimbabwe's only surviving boutique wine producer with just 10 ha/25 acres, most of the domestic harvest was destined for DISTILLATION or turned into wine-based products.

Recent changes in land-tenure policies and economic factors have renewed interest and investment in wine production. Mukuyu, which lost all its vineyards, started a replanting programme with 19 ha/47 acres in 2021.

Existing vineyards are in the eastern part of the country, south-east of the capital, Harare, in the provinces of East Mashonaland and Manicaland. The TEMPERATE climate averages eight hours of daily sunshine, and mean annual temperatures are just under 19 °C/66 °F. Summer rain falls from November to April, but DROUGHT is a constant threat. Uneven budding and ROT are annual hazards in the long, hot, humid summers, and the grapes can be affected by dilution and HAIL. The better vineyard areas lie at an ELEVATION of about 1,500 m/4,920 ft. Wines are frequently adjusted by ACIDIFICATION and ENRICHMENT (Zimbabwe has no official wine regulations). Chenin Blanc, Colombard, Sauvignon Blanc, Chardonnay, Semillon, Viognier, and Hanepoot (MUSCAT OF ALEXANDRIA) vines produce dry and off-dry whites; Shiraz, Merlot, Cabernet Sauvignon, Cabernet Franc, and Alicante Bouschet produce reds. T.D.C.

zinc, essential element for healthy vine growth. A deficiency of zinc affects the plant's ability to synthesize the hormones AUXINS, deficiency in which results in a failure of the SHOOTS to grow normally. The principal symptoms are CHLOROSIS between the veins of young and old leaves, their small size, and a widened leaf sinus where the PETIOLE attaches. FRUIT SET can also be poor. Zinc deficiency commonly occurs in vineyards on SANDY soils and on some high-PH soils; it is treated by daubing pruning wounds with pastes containing zinc or by applying a zinc spray to the leaves in summer. R.E.S. & R.E.W.

Zinfandel is the best-known California name of the black grape variety known in its native CROATIA as both TRIBIDRAG and CRLJENAK KAŠTELANSKI and in Puglia as PRIMITIVO. California grows far more of the variety than anywhere else: nearly 16,017 ha/39,578 acres in 2020.

For much of the 20th century, the viticultural 'pioneer' Agoston HARASZTHY was credited with introducing this important variety to California from his native Hungary, but a more worthy Zinfandel hero is the California historian Charles L. Sullivan, who unearthed the truth, or at least part of it, about Zinfandel's route to California. It was he who pointed out that there was no mention of Zinfandel in Haraszthy's copious promotional literature in the early 1860s and that the variety was well known on the American east coast long before Haraszthy arrived in California in 1849.

The vine was imported, possibly unnamed, to the US from the Austrian imperial nursery in Vienna by George Gibbs of Long Island, probably in 1829. He took it to Boston, and by the early 1830s it had acquired such names as 'Zenfendel' and 'Zinfindal' among New England growers, many of whom added it to the range of VITIS VINIFERA vines they grew under glass as a TABLE GRAPE.

Many of those who participated in the California GOLD RUSH of 1849 turned to agriculture, often dependent on shipments of plant material from the east coast. 'Zinfindal' was included in a particularly important consignment which arrived in 1852, and by 1859 the variety was grown in both Napa and Sonoma. In 1862 the secretary of the Sonoma Horticultural Society gave some wine made from these grapes to a French winemaker working in California who reported that it tasted like 'a good French claret'.

Because Zinfandel has no French connection, it had escaped the detailed scrutiny of the world's AMPELOGRAPHIC centre in MONTPELLIER, and its European origins rested on local hypothesis until the application of DNA PROFILING to vines in the early 1990s. Only then was it irrefutably demonstrated that, as had been suspected, Zinfandel and the variety known as PRIMITIVO in Puglia are one and the same. Subsequent DNA profiling at DAVIS established that the Croatian variety PLAVAC MALI is in fact a cross between Zinfandel and Dobričić, an obscure and ancient Croatian variety found on the island of Šolta near Split. This suggested a probable Dalmatian origin for Zinfandel too, and Croatian researchers Pejic and Maletic collaborating with Carole Meredith at Davis searched the coastal vineyards for Zinfandel until in 2001 they discovered an ancient and almost extinct variety in the region of Kaštela near Split called Crljenak Kaštelanski (literally 'red grape of Kaštela') that was established as Zinfandel by DNA profiling. Analysis of this variety's DNA showed an exact match with that of a 90-year-old herbarium specimen of an ancient Croatian vine known locally as Tribidrag. Montenegrin growers strongly contest this Croatian origin.

Zinfandel took firm hold on the California wine business in the 1880s, when its ability to produce in quantity was prized above all else. Many was the miner or other beneficiary of California's gold rush whose customary drink was Zinfandel. By the turn of the century, Zinfandel was regarded as California's own CLARET and occupied some of the choicest North Coast vineyard. During PROHIBITION it was the choice of many a HOME WINEMAKER, but since then its viticultural popularity has become its undoing.

In 20th-century California, Zinfandel occupied much the same place as SHIRAZ (Syrah) did in Australia and for many decades suffered the same lack of respect simply because it was the most common black grape variety, often planted in unsuitably hot sites and expected to yield more than was good for it. Zinfandel may not be quite such a potentially high-quality grape variety as Syrah, but it is certainly capable of producing fine wine, especially from older, HEAD-TRAINED vines, as Ridge Vineyards and others have proved. And the fact that so many of California's oldest vines are Zinfandel means that the best wines that bear its name (which are sometimes FIELD BLENDS) are exceptionally complex (see VINE AGE) and ageworthy.

Zinfandel's viticultural disadvantages are uneven ripening and thin-skinned berries in compact clusters. Bunches sometimes have harsh, green berries on the same cluster as those that have reached full maturity, and once grapes reach full ripeness (in direct contrast to its great California rival Cabernet Sauvignon, for example) they will soon turn to raisins if not picked quite rapidly. Zinfandel performs best in warm but not hot conditions and prefers well-drained soils that naturally reduce VIGOUR and excess moisture.

Although Zinfandel has been required over the years to transform itself into virtually every style and colour of wine that exists, it is best suited to dry, sturdy, vigorous reds. Dry Creek Valley in Sonoma, the Sierra Foothills, and Lodi has demonstrated a particular aptitude for this underestimated variety. See CALIFORNIA for more details of Zinfandel the wine, both red and white.

In the late 1980s, thanks to the enormous popularity of WHITE ZINFANDEL, Zinfandel plantings, which had been declining, increased by up to 1,215 ha/3,000 acres a year, mostly in the Central Valley, so that they totalled 34,000 acres/13,760 ha in 1992, just ahead of California's total acreage of Cabernet Sauvignon at the time. The resurgence of Zinfandel continued in the late 1990s as red Zinfandel began to enjoy mildly cult-like status (with many examples commanding prices over $30), driving total plantings to 50,000 acres/20,000 ha in 2003, only slightly less than Merlot and two-thirds as much as California's most important black variety Cabernet Sauvignon. By 2020 Zinfandel was California's third most planted black variety, just ahead of Merlot but some way behind Pinot Noir.

Zinfandel is also grown to a much more limited extent in warmer sites in other western states in the US as well as in Mexico. Because of its prominence in California, Zinfandel is grown in many of the world's wine regions, albeit to a very limited extent—quite apart from Puglia, where it is known as Primitivo, and NORTH MACEDONIA and MONTENEGRO on the other side of the Adriatic, where it is known as Kratošija. There is some 'Zinfandel' in the Languedoc, South Africa, and Australia, where there were 86 ha/213 acres in 2015, and Cape Mentelle in Western Australia has been particularly successful with it.

Robinson, J., et al., *Wine Grapes: A Complete Guide to 1,368 Vine Varieties, Including Their Origins and Flavours* (2012).

zonal viticulture, form of PRECISION VITICULTURE in which vineyards are divided into zones of characteristic performance in terms of YIELD and/or grape composition. These are then managed as separate units with respect to SELECTIVE HARVESTING and/or particular inputs.

Typically, zones are identified on the basis of visual inspection, imagery acquired by REMOTE SENSING or PROXIMAL SENSING, yield maps, and/or maps of other vineyard attributes, simple classification of such data or the use of statistically based clustering algorithms.

This approach has been adopted in several locations in Australia, Chile, Spain, and the US.

R.G.V.B.

Zweigelt, or **Blauer Zweigelt**, is Austria's most popular dark-berried grape variety, covering 6,130 ha/15,148 acres by 2022. It is a BLAUFRÄNKISCH × ST-LAURENT cross, bred by Dr Fritz Zweigelt at the KLOSTERNEUBURG research station in 1922, which combines the brightness of the first with the fruitiness of the second if it is not overcropped or picked too late. It is popular with growers because it ripens earlier than Blaufränkisch and is vigorous, productive, not picky about site, and expressive even when unoaked and bottled early. Grown throughout all Austrian wine regions, its wines range from exuberantly fruity reds and rosés to highly extracted, oak-influenced versions, particularly in BURGENLAND's DAC. So successful has it been in Austria that the variety is also popular over the border in Czechia and Slovakia as well as in western Hungary. It has also been planted in Canada, across the US, and, surprisingly widely, on Hokkaido in JAPAN. Recognizing the influential Dr Zweigelt's collaboration with Austria's 1938–45 Nazi government, there is growing pressure to revert to a synonym devised in the 1980s for his most successful crossing: Rotburger.

zymase, group of ENZYMES which encourage the conversion of GLUCOSE and FRUCTOSE into ETHYL ALCOHOL during fermentation.

zymurgy, the study or practice of FERMENTATION. It is a word more useful in Scrabble than in everyday life.

Z

APPENDIX 1

CONTROLLED APPELLATIONS AND THEIR PERMITTED GRAPE VARIETIES

It is still impossible to tell from the labels of many geographically named wines which grape varieties were used to make them. The following is a unique guide to the varieties officially allowed into the world's CONTROLLED APPELLATIONS (therefore by no means all known wine names), grouped by country or, where appropriate, by region. Within the groups the appellations are listed alphabetically using local names.

For each appellation, varieties are listed alphabetically, not in order of importance. Italics denote minor grape varieties. Regulations sometimes use local synonyms or spellings for grape varieties and occasionally give alternative names in brackets. We have followed that usage rather than trying to impose consistency.

R, W, P, and S denote red, white, pink, and sparkling wines respectively. Where both white and rosé sparkling wines may be produced using a different mix of varieties, these are abbreviated WS and PS. In some instances, appellation regulations allow the inclusion of a stated percentage of other (unnamed) red or white varieties, which generally refers to those that are locally authorized for PDO wines within that appellation or region, indicated below by *OR*, *OW*, and *OR&W*.

VARIETAL appellations and appellations that permit a very wide range of varieties are not included in this list because they are so numerous and because the region of origin and the grape variety are, in most cases, clearly stated on the label.

AUSTRIA

Carnuntum (R) Blaufränkisch, Zweigelt, *OR* (W) Chardonnay, Grüner Veltliner, Weissburgunder, *OW*
Leithaberg (W) Chardonnay, Grüner Veltliner, Neuburger, Weissburgunder
Neusiedlersee (W) any local white varieties
Rosalia (P) any local red varieties
Ruster Ausbruch (W) any local white varieties
Südsteiermark (W) Gelber Muskateller, Grauburgunder, Morillon, Riesling, Sauvignon Blanc, Traminer, Weissburgunder, Welschriesling
Vulkanland Steiermark (W) Gelber Muskateller, Grauburgunder, Morillon, Riesling, Sauvignon Blanc, Traminer, Weissburgunder, Welschriesling
Wachau (R) Pinot Noir, St Laurent, Zweigelt (W) Chardonnay, Frühroter Veltliner, Gemischter Satz, Grauburgunder, Grüner Veltliner, Müller-Thurgau, Muskat Ottonel, Muskateller, Neuburger, Riesling, Roter Veltliner, Sauvignon Blanc, Traminer, Weissburgunder
Wagram (R) Blauburgunder, St Laurent, Zweigelt (W) Chardonnay, Frühroter Veltliner, Gelber Muskateller, Grauburgunder, Grüner Veltliner, Riesling, Roter Veltliner, Sauvignon Blanc, Traminer, Weissburgunder
Weststeiermark (W) Gelber Muskateller, Grauburgunder, Morillon, Riesling, Sauvignon Blanc, Traminer, Weissburgunder, Welschriesling (P) Blauer Wildbacher
Wiener Gemischter Satz (W) at least three white varieties out of a possible 40

CROATIA

Dingač (R) Plavac Mali
Ponikve (R, P) Plavac Mali Crni (W) Posip Bijeli, Rukatac

CYPRUS

Commandaria (R, W) Mavro, Xynisteri

FRANCE

In 2021 the INAO introduced a category for experimental varieties (see VIFA). These are included below for the appellations that have taken up this option so far (see Bordeaux, for example).

Alsace and North-East

Crémant d'Alsace (S) Auxerrois, Chardonnay, Pinot Blanc, Pinot Gris, Pinot Noir, Riesling

Vin d'Alsace Edelzwicker (W) Auxerrois, Chasselas, Gewürztraminer, Muscat Blanc à Petits Grains, Muscat Ottonel, Pinot Blanc, Pinot Gris, Pinot Noir, Riesling, Savagnin Rose, Sylvaner

Côtes de Toul (R) Pinot Noir (W) Aubin, Auxerrois (P) Gamay, Pinot Noir, *Aubin, Auxerrois, Pinot Meunier*

Moselle (R) Pinot Noir (W) Auxerrois, Müller-Thurgau, Pinot Gris, *Gewurztraminer, Pinot Blanc, Riesling* (P) Pinot Noir, *Gamay*

Bordeaux

Blaye (R) Cabernet Franc, Cabernet Sauvignon, Merlot, *Carmenère, Cot, Petit Verdot*

Bordeaux, Bordeaux Supérieur (R) Cabernet Franc, Cabernet Sauvignon, Carmenère, Cot, Merlot, Petit Verdot, plus, experimentally, *Arinarnoa, Castets, Marselan, Touriga Nacional* (W) Muscadelle, Sauvignon Blanc, Sauvignon Gris, Sémillon, *Colombard, Merlot Blanc, Ugni Blanc*, plus, experimentally, *Alvarinho, Liliorila* (*Alvarinho* only for Bordeaux)

Bordeaux Clairet (P) Cabernet Franc, Cabernet Sauvignon, Carmenère, Cot, Merlot, Petit Verdot, plus, experimentally, *Arinarnoa, Castets, Marselan, Touriga Nacional*

Bordeaux Rosé (P) Cabernet Franc, Cabernet Sauvignon, Carmenère, Cot, Merlot, Petit Verdot, *Sauvignon Blanc, Sauvignon Gris, Sémillon*, plus, experimentally, *Arinarnoa, Castets, Marselan, Touriga Nacional, Alvarinho, Liliorila*

Bordeaux Haut-Benauge (W) Muscadelle, Sauvignon Blanc, Sauvignon Gris, Sémillon

Bourg, Côtes de Bourg, Bourgeais (R) Cabernet Franc, Cabernet Sauvignon, Cot, Merlot (W) Colombard, Muscadelle, Sauvignon Blanc, Sauvignon Gris, Sémillon

Côtes de Blaye (W) Colombard, Ugni Blanc, *Muscadelle, Sauvignon Blanc, Sauvignon Gris, Sémillon*

Côtes de Bordeaux (R) Cabernet Franc, Cabernet Sauvignon, Cot, Merlot, *Carmenère, Petit Verdot* (W) Muscadelle, Sauvignon Blanc, Sauvignon Gris, Sémillon, *Colombard, Ugni Blanc*

Crémant de Bordeaux (WS) Cabernet Franc, Cabernet Sauvignon, Carmenère, Cot, Merlot, Muscadelle, Petit Verdot, Sauvignon Blanc, Sauvignon Gris, Sémillon, *Colombard, Merlot Blanc, Ugni Blanc* (PS) Cabernet Franc, Cabernet Sauvignon, Carmenère, Cot, Merlot, Petit Verdot, Sauvignon Blanc, Sauvignon Gris, Sémillon

Entre-Deux-Mers, Entre-Deux-Mers Haut-Benauge (W) Muscadelle, Sauvignon Blanc, Sauvignon Gris, Sémillon, *Colombard, Mauzac, Merlot Blanc, Ugni Blanc* (R) Cabernet Franc, Cabernet Sauvignon, Carmenère, Cot, Merlot, Petit Verdot

Fronsac, Canon Fronsac (R) Cabernet Franc, Cabernet Sauvignon, Merlot, *Carmenère, Cot, Petit Verdot*

Graves, Graves Supérieures (R) Cabernet Franc, Cabernet Sauvignon, Carmenère, Cot, Merlot, Petit Verdot (W) Muscadelle, Sauvignon Blanc, Sauvignon Gris, Sémillon

Graves de Vayres (R) Cabernet Franc, Cabernet Sauvignon, Carmenère, Cot, Merlot, Petit Verdot (W) Muscadelle, Sauvignon Blanc, Sauvignon Gris, Sémillon, *Merlot Blanc*

Haut-Médoc, Listrac-Médoc, Margaux, Médoc, Moulis, Pauillac, St-Estèphe, St-Julien (R) Cabernet Franc, Cabernet Sauvignon, Carmenère, Cot, Merlot, Petit Verdot

Lalande-de-Pomerol, Lussac-St-Émilion, Montagne-St-Émilion, Puisseguin-St-Émilion, St-Georges-St-Émilion (R) Cabernet Franc, Cabernet Sauvignon, Cot, Merlot, *Carmenère, Petit Verdot*

Pessac-Léognan (R) Cabernet Franc, Cabernet Sauvignon, Carmenère, Cot, Merlot, Petit Verdot (W) Muscadelle, Sauvignon Blanc, Sauvignon Gris, Sémillon

Pomerol (R) Cabernet Franc, Cabernet Sauvignon, Cot, Merlot, Petit Verdot

St-Émilion (R) Cabernet Franc, Cabernet Sauvignon, Carmenère, Malbec, Merlot, *Petit Verdot*

Sauternes, Barsac, Ste-Croix-du-Mont, Loupiac, Cadillac, Cérons, Premières Côtes de Bordeaux, Côtes de Bordeaux St-Macaire (W) Muscadelle, Sauvignon Blanc, Sauvignon Gris, Sémillon

Burgundy

Regional appellations

Bourgogne, Bourgogne La Chapelle Notre-Dame, Bourgogne Le Chapitre, Bourgogne Chitry, Bourgogne Côtes d'Auxerre, Bourgogne Côte Chalonnaise, Bourgogne Côte St-Jacques, Bourgogne Coulanges-la-Vineuse, Bourgogne Hautes-Côtes de Beaune, Bourgogne Hautes-Côtes de Nuits, Bourgogne Montrecul or **Montre-Cul** or **En Montre-Cul** (R) Pinot Noir, *César* (Yonne only), *Chardonnay, Pinot Blanc, Pinot Gris* (W) Chardonnay, Pinot Blanc, *Pinot Gris* (P) Pinot Gris, Pinot Noir, *César* (Yonne only), *Chardonnay, Pinot Blanc*

Bourgogne Aligoté, Bouzeron (W) Aligoté

Bourgogne Clairet (P) Pinot Gris, Pinot Noir, *Chardonnay, Pinot Blanc, César* (Yonne only)

Bourgogne Côte d'Or (R) Pinot Noir, *Chardonnay, Pinot Blanc, Pinot Gris, César* (Yonne only) (W) Chardonnay, Pinot Blanc, *Pinot Gris*

Bourgogne Côtes du Couchois (R) Pinot Noir, *Chardonnay, Pinot Blanc, Pinot Gris*

Bourgogne Epineuil (R) Pinot Noir, *César, Chardonnay, Pinot Blanc, Pinot Gris* (P) Pinot Gris, Pinot Noir, *Chardonnay, Pinot Blanc*

Bourgogne Mousseux (S) César (Yonne only), Gamay, Pinot Noir, *Aligoté, Chardonnay, Gamay de Bouze, Gamay de Chaudenay, Melon, Pinot Blanc, Pinot Gris*

Bourgogne Passe-tout-grains (R, P) Gamay, Pinot Noir, *Chardonnay, Pinot Blanc, Pinot Gris*

Bourgogne Tonnerre (W) Chardonnay, Pinot Blanc, *Pinot Gris*

Coteaux Bourguignons (R) Gamay, Pinot Noir, César (Yonne only), *Aligoté, Chardonnay, Gamay de Bouze, Gamay de Chaudenay, Melon, Pinot Blanc, Pinot Gris* (W) Aligoté, Chardonnay, Melon, Pinot Blanc, Pinot Gris (P) Gamay, Pinot Gris, Pinot Noir, César (Yonne only), *Aligoté, Chardonnay, Melon, Pinot Blanc*

Crémant de Bourgogne (S) Aligoté, Chardonnay, Gamay, Melon, Pinot Blanc, Pinot Gris, Pinot Noir, Sacy

Beaujolais

Beaujolais, Beaujolais-Villages (R, P) Gamay, *Aligoté, Chardonnay, Gamay de Bouze, Gamay de Chaudenay, Melon, Pinot Gris, Pinot Noir* (W) Chardonnay

Beaujolais Supérieur (R) Gamay, *Aligoté, Chardonnay, Gamay de Bouze, Gamay de Chaudenay, Melon, Pinot Gris, Pinot Noir*

Brouilly, Chénas, Chiroubles, Côte de Brouilly Fleurie, Juliénas, Morgon, Moulin-à-Vent, Régnié, St-Amour (R) Gamay, *Aligoté, Chardonnay, Melon*

Chablis region

Irancy (R) Pinot Noir, *César, Pinot Gris*

Petit Chablis, Chablis, Chablis Premier Cru, Chablis Grand Cru (W) Chardonnay

St-Bris (W) Sauvignon Blanc, Sauvignon Gris

Vézelay (W) Chardonnay

Côte Chalonnaise

Note: The communes indicated with an asterisk contain PREMIER CRU vineyards.

Givry* (R) Pinot Noir, *Chardonnay, Pinot Gris* (W) Chardonnay, *Pinot Blanc, Pinot Gris*

Mercurey*, Rully* (R) Pinot Noir, *Chardonnay, Pinot Gris* (W) Chardonnay, *Pinot Gris*

Montagny* (W) Chardonnay

Côte d'Or

Note: The communes indicated with an asterisk contain PREMIER CRU vineyards.

Aloxe-Corton* (R) Pinot Noir, *Chardonnay, Pinot Blanc, Pinot Gris* (W) Chardonnay, *Pinot Blanc*

Auxey-Duresses*, Chassagne-Montrachet*, Chorey-lès-Beaune, Côte de Nuits-Villages, Fixin*, Meursault*, Monthelie, Morey-St-Denis*, Nuits-St-Georges*, Puligny-Montrachet*, St-Aubin*, St-Romain, Santenay*, Savigny-lès-Beaune*, Vougeot* (R) Pinot Noir, *Chardonnay, Pinot Blanc, Pinot Gris* (W) Chardonnay, Pinot Blanc (plus *Aligoté* for the premier cru Monts Luisants in Morey-St-Denis)

Blagny*, Côte de Beaune-Villages (R) Pinot Noir, *Chardonnay, Pinot Blanc, Pinot Gris*

Chambolle-Musigny*, Gevrey-Chambertin*, Pommard*, Volnay*, Vosne-Romanée* (R) Pinot Noir, *Chardonnay, Pinot Blanc, Pinot Gris*

Côte de Beaune, Beaune*, Ladoix*, Pernand-Vergelesses* (R) Pinot Noir, *Chardonnay, Pinot Blanc, Pinot Gris* (W) Chardonnay, Pinot Blanc, *Pinot Gris*

Maranges* (R) Pinot Noir, *Chardonnay, Pinot Blanc, Pinot Gris* (W) Chardonnay

Marsannay (R) Pinot Noir, *Chardonnay, Pinot Blanc, Pinot Gris* (W) Chardonnay, Pinot Blanc, *Pinot Gris* (P) Pinot Gris, Pinot Noir, *Chardonnay, Pinot Blanc*

Côte d'Or—Grands Crus

Bonnes-Mares, Chambertin, Chambertin-Clos de Bèze, Chapelle-Chambertin, Charmes-Chambertin, Griotte-Chambertin, Latricières-Chambertin, Mazis-Chambertin, Mazoyères-Chambertin, Ruchottes-Chambertin, Clos des Lambrays, Clos de la Roche, Clos St-Denis, Clos de Tart, Clos de Vougeot, Échezeaux, La Grande Rue, Grands Échezeaux, Richebourg, Romanée-Conti, Romanée-St-Vivant, La Romanée, La Tâche (R) Pinot Noir, *Chardonnay, Pinot Blanc, Pinot Gris*

Charlemagne, Corton-Charlemagne (W) Chardonnay, *Pinot Blanc*

Corton (R) Pinot Noir, *Chardonnay, Pinot Blanc, Pinot Gris* (W) Chardonnay, *Pinot Blanc*

Montrachet, Bâtard-Montrachet, Bienvenues-Bâtard-Montrachet, Chevalier-Montrachet, Criots-Bâtard-Montrachet (W) Chardonnay

Musigny (R) Pinot Noir, *Chardonnay, Pinot Blanc, Pinot Gris* (W) Chardonnay

Mâconnais

Note: The communes indicated with an asterisk contain PREMIER CRU vineyards.

Mâcon-Villages (W) Chardonnay

Mâcon (R, P) Gamay, Pinot Noir (W) Chardonnay

Mâcon followed by a commune name (R, P) Gamay (W) Chardonnay

Pouilly-Fuissé*, Pouilly-Vinzelles, Pouilly-Loché, St-Véran, Viré-Clessé (W) Chardonnay

Champagne

Champagne (S) Arbane, Chardonnay, Meunier, Petit Meslier, Pinot Blanc, Pinot Gris, Pinot Noir

Coteaux Champenois (R, P, W) Arbane, Chardonnay, Meunier, Petit Meslier, Pinot Blanc, Pinot Gris, Pinot Noir

Rosé de Riceys (P) Pinot Noir

Corsica

Ajaccio (R, P) Barbaroux (Barbarossa), Nielluccio, Rolle (Vermentinu), Sciacarello, *Aleatico, Carcajolo, Carignan, Cinsaut, Grenache, Morrastel (Minustello)* (W) Rolle, *Biancu Gentile, Codivarta, Genovese, Ugni Blanc (Rossola)*

Patrimonio (R, P) Nielluccio, *Grenache, Rolle (Vermentinu), Sciacarello,* (W) Rolle

Vin de Corse, Coteaux du Cap Corse (R, P) Grenache, Nielluccio, Sciacarello, *Aléatico, Barbaroux, Carcajolo, Carignan, Cinsaut, Morrastel (Minustello), Mourvèdre, Rolle (Vermentinu), Syrah* (W) Rolle, *Biancu Gentile, Codivarta, Genovèse, Ugni Blanc (Rossola)*

Jura

Arbois, Arbois Pupillin (R, P) Pinot Noir, Poulsard, Trousseau, *Chardonnay, Savagnin* (W) Chardonnay, Savagnin Blanc, *Pinot Noir, Poulsard, Trousseau* (Pinot Noir is not permitted for the production of *vin de paille*)

Arbois Vin Jaune, Château-Chalon, Côtes du Jura Vin Jaune, L'Étoile Vin Jaune (W) Savagnin Blanc

Côtes du Jura (R, P) Pinot Noir, Poulsard, Trousseau, *Chardonnay, Savagnin Blanc* (W) Chardonnay, Savagnin Blanc, *Pinot Noir, Poulsard, Trousseau* (Pinot Noir is not permitted for the production of *vin de paille*)

Crémant du Jura (S) Chardonnay, Pinot Gris, Pinot Noir, Poulsard, Savagnin, Trousseau

L'Étoile (W) Chardonnay, Savagnin Blanc, *Poulsard*

Languedoc and Roussillon

Cabardès (R, P) Cabernet Franc, Cabernet Sauvignon, Grenache, Merlot, Syrah, *Cinsaut, Cot, Fer*

Collioure (R) Carignan, Grenache, Mourvèdre, Syrah, *Cinsaut, Counoise* (W) Grenache Blanc, Grenache Gris, Macabeu, Marsanne, Rolle, Roussanne, Tourbat, *Carignan Blanc, Muscat Blanc à Petits Grains, Muscat d'Alexandrie* (P) Carignan, Grenache, Grenache Gris, Mourvèdre, Syrah, *Cinsaut, Counoise*

Corbières (R) Carignan, Grenache, Lledoner Pelut, Mourvèdre, Syrah, *Cinsaut, Grenache Gris, Piquepoul Noir, Terret Noir*, plus, experimentally, *Marselan* (W) Bourboulenc, Grenache Blanc, Macabeu, Marsanne, Rolle, Roussanne, *Carignan Blanc, Clairette, Muscat Blanc à Petits Grains, Piquepoul Blanc, Terret Blanc, Viognier* (P) Carignan, Cinsaut, Grenache, Lledoner Pelut, Mourvèdre, Syrah, *Bourboulenc, Carignan Blanc, Clairette, Grenache Blanc, Grenache Gris, Macabeu, Marsanne, Piquepoul Blanc, Piquepoul Noir, Rolle, Roussanne, Terret Blanc, Terret Noir, Viognier*

Corbières Boutenac (R) Carignan, Grenache, Mourvèdre, Syrah

Costières de Nîmes (R, P) Grenache, Mourvèdre, Syrah, *Carignan, Cinsaut, Marselan* (W) Grenache Blanc, Marsanne, Roussanne, *Bourboulenc, Clairette, Maccabeu, Rolle, Viognier*

Côtes du Roussillon (R) Carignan, Grenache, Mourvèdre, Syrah, *Cinsaut, Lledoner Pelut* (W) Grenache Blanc, Grenache Gris, Macabeu, Marsanne, Rolle, Roussanne, Tourbat, *Carignan Blanc, Viognier* (P) Grenache, Grenache Gris, Syrah, *Carignan, Cinsaut, Lledoner Pelut, Macabeu, Mourvèdre*

Côtes du Roussillon-Villages, Côtes du Roussillon-Villages Latour-de-France, Côtes du Roussillon-Villages Tautavel (R) Carignan, Grenache, Mourvèdre, Syrah, *Lledoner Pelut*

Côtes du Roussillon-Villages Caramany, Côtes du Roussillon-Villages Lesquerde (R) Carignan, Grenache, Syrah, *Lledoner Pelut*

Côtes du Roussillon-Villages Les Aspres (R) Grenache, Mourvèdre, Syrah, *Carignan*

Crémant de Limoux (W, R) Chardonnay, Chenin Blanc, Mauzac, Pinot Noir

Faugères (R, P) Grenache, Lledoner Pelut, Mourvèdre, Syrah, *Carignan, Cinsaut* (W) Grenache Blanc, Marsanne, Rolle, Roussanne, *Clairette, Viognier*

Fitou (R) Carignan, Grenache, *Mourvèdre, Syrah*

Grand Roussillon (R, P, W) Grenache, Grenache Blanc, Grenache Gris, Macabeu, Tourbat, *Muscat Blanc à Petits Grains, Muscat d'Alexandrie*

La Clape (R) Grenache, Mourvèdre, Syrah, *Carignan, Cinsaut* (W) Bourboulenc, Clairette, Grenache Blanc, Marsanne, Rolle, Roussanne, Piquepoul Blanc, *Macabeu, Terret, Viognier*

Languedoc (R) Grenache, Lledoner Pelut, Mourvèdre, Syrah, *Carignan, Cinsaut, Counoise, Grenache Gris, Morrastel, Piquepoul Noir, Rivairenc, Terret Noir*, plus, experimentally, *Agiorgitiko, Calabrese, Marselan, Montepulciano, Oeillade* (W) Bourboulenc, Clairette, Grenache Blanc, Marsanne, Piquepoul Blanc, Rolle, Roussanne, Tourbat, *Carignan Blanc, Grenache Gris, Macabeu, Muscat à Petits Grains, Terret Blanc, Viognier*, plus, experimentally, *Assyrtiko, Carignan Gris, Clairette Rose, Piquepoul Gris, Rivairenc Blanc, Rivairenc Gris, Terret Gris* (P) Grenache, Lledoner Pelut, Mourvèdre, Syrah, *Bourboulenc, Carignan Blanc, Carignan, Cinsaut, Clairette, Counoise, Grenache Blanc, Grenache Gris, Macabeu, Marsanne, Morrastel, Piquepoul Blanc, Piquepoul Noir, Rivairenc, Rolle, Roussanne, Terret Blanc, Terret Noir, Tourbat, Viognier*, plus, experimentally, *Carignan Gris, Clairette Rose, Marselan, Oeillade, Piquepoul Gris, Rivairenc Blanc, Rivairenc Gris, Terret Gris*

Note: For the varieties permitted in specific DÉNOMINATIONS GÉOGRAPHIQUES COMPLÉMENTAIRES within the Languedoc AOC (e.g. Grés de Montpellier), see the detailed regulations on www.inao.gouv.fr or www.vitis.org.

Limoux (R) Cot, Merlot, Syrah, Grenache, *Cabernet Franc, Cabernet Sauvignon* (W) Chardonnay, Chenin Blanc, Mauzac

Limoux, Blanquette de Limoux (S) Mauzac, *Chardonnay, Chenin Blanc*

Limoux Méthode Ancestrale (S) Mauzac

Malepère (R) Merlot, *Cabernet Franc, Cabernet Sauvignon, Cinsaut, Cot, Grenache, Lledoner Pelut* (P) Cabernet Franc, *Cabernet Sauvignon, Cinsaut, Cot, Grenache, Merlot*

Maury (R) Grenache, *Carignan, Lledoner Pelut, Mourvèdre, Syrah*

Maury Ambré, Maury Blanc (W) Grenache Blanc, Grenache Gris, Macabeu, Tourbat, *Muscat Blanc à Petits Grains, Muscat d'Alexandrie*

Maury Grenat, Maury Tuilé (R) Grenache, Grenache Blanc, Grenache Gris, *Carignan, Macabeu, Syrah*

Minervois (R) Grenache, Lledoner Pelut, Mourvèdre, Syrah, *Carignan, Cinsaut, Piquepoul Noir, Rivairenc, Terret Noir* (W) Bourboulenc, Grenache Blanc, Maccabeu, Marsanne, Rolle, Roussanne, *Clairette, Grenache Gris, Muscat Blanc à Petits Grains, Piquepoul Blanc, Terret Blanc, Viognier* (P) Grenache, Lledoner Pelut, Mourvèdre, Syrah, *Bourboulenc, Carignan, Cinsaut, Clairette, Grenache Blanc, Grenache Gris, Maccabeu, Marsanne, Piquepoul Blanc, Piquepoul Noir, Rivairenc, Rolle, Roussanne, Terret Blanc, Terret Noir*

Minervois-La Livinière (R) Grenache, Lledoner Pelut, Mourvèdre, Syrah *Carignan, Cinsaut, Piquepoul Noir, Rivairenc, Terret Noir*

Pic St-Loup (R) Grenache, Mourvèdre, Syrah, *Carignan, Cinsaut, Counoise, Morrastel* (P) Grenache, Mourvèdre, Syrah, *Cinsaut, Counoise, Grenache Gris, Morrastel*

Picpoul de Pinet (W) Piquepoul Blanc

Rivesaltes Ambré, Rivesaltes Rosé, Rivesaltes Tuilé Grenache Blanc, Grenache Gris, Grenache, Macabeu, Tourbat, *Muscat Blanc à Petits Grains, Muscat d'Alexandrie*

Rivesaltes Grenat (R) Grenache

St-Chinian (R, P) Grenache, Lledoner Pelut, Mourvèdre, Syrah, *Carignan, Cinsaut* (W) Grenache Blanc, Marsanne, Rolle, Roussanne, *Carignan Blanc, Clairette, Viognier*

Terrasses du Larzac (R) Carignan, Grenache, Mourvèdre, Syrah, *Cinsaut, Counoise, Lledoner Pelut, Morrastel, Terret Noir*

Loire and Central France

Anjou (R) Cabernet Franc, Cabernet Sauvignon, *Grolleau, Pineau d'Aunis* (W) Chenin Blanc, *Chardonnay, Sauvignon Blanc* (WS) Chenin Blanc, *Cabernet Franc, Cabernet Sauvignon, Chardonnay, Gamay, Grolleau, Grolleau Gris, Pineau d'Aunis* (PS) Cabernet Franc, Cabernet Sauvignon, Gamay, Grolleau, Grolleau Gris, Pineau d'Aunis

Anjou Coteaux de la Loire (W) Chenin Blanc

Anjou-Villages, Anjou Brissac (R) Cabernet Franc, Cabernet Sauvignon

Bourgueil, St-Nicolas-de-Bourgueil (R, P) Cabernet Franc, *Cabernet Sauvignon*

Bonnezeaux (W) Chenin Blanc

Cabernet d'Anjou (P) Cabernet Franc, Cabernet Sauvignon

Châteaumeillant (R) Gamay, *Pinot Noir* (Gris) Gamay, *Pinot Gris, Pinot Noir*

Cheverny (R, P) Pinot Noir, *Côt, Gamay* (W) Sauvignon Blanc, Sauvignon Gris, *Chardonnay, Chenin Blanc, Orbois*

Chinon (W) Chenin Blanc (R, P) Cabernet Franc, *Cabernet Sauvignon*

Coteaux d'Ancenis (W) Pinot Gris (R, P) Gamay, *Cabernet Franc*

Coteaux de l'Aubance (W) Chenin Blanc

Coteaux de Saumur (W) Chenin Blanc

Coteaux du Giennois (R, P) Gamay, Pinot Noir (W) Sauvignon Blanc

Coteaux du Layon, Coteaux du Layon Chaume, Quarts de Chaume (W) Chenin Blanc

Coteaux du Loir (R) Pineau d'Aunis, *Cabernet Franc, Cot, Gamay* (W) Chenin Blanc (P) Pineau d'Aunis, *Cot, Gamay, Grolleau*

Coteaux du Vendômois (R) Cabernet Franc, Pinot Noir, Pineau d'Aunis, *Gamay* (W) Chenin Blanc, *Chardonnay* (Gris) Pineau d'Aunis

Côtes d'Auvergne (R, P) Gamay, *Pinot Noir* (W) Chardonnay

Coulée de Serrant (W) Chenin Blanc

Cour-Cheverny (W) Romorantin

Crémant de Loire (S) Cabernet Franc, Cabernet Sauvignon, Chardonnay, Chenin Blanc, Grolleau Gris, Grolleau Noir, Orbois, Pineau d'Aunis, Pinot Noir

Fiefs Vendéens Brem (R) Pinot Noir, Négrette, *Cabernet Franc, Cabernet Sauvignon, Gamay* (W) Chenin Blanc, Chardonnay, *Grolleau Gris* (P) Pinot Noir, Gamay, *Cabernet Franc, Cabernet Sauvignon, Grolleau Gris, Négrette*

Fiefs Vendéens Chantonnay, Fiefs Vendéens Mareuil (R) Cabernet Franc, Négrette, *Cabernet Sauvignon, Gamay, Pinot Noir* (W) Chenin Blanc, Chardonnay (P) Gamay, Pinot Noir, *Cabernet Franc, Cabernet Sauvignon, Négrette*

Fiefs Vendéens Pissotes (R) Pinot Noir, Négrette, *Cabernet Franc, Cabernet Sauvignon, Gamay* (W) Chenin Blanc, Chardonnay (P) Gamay, Pinot Noir, *Cabernet Franc, Cabernet Sauvignon, Négrette*

Fiefs Vendéens Vix (R) Cabernet Franc, Négrette, *Cabernet Sauvignon, Gamay, Pinot Noir* (W) Chenin Blanc, Chardonnay, *Sauvignon Blanc* (P) Gamay, *Cabernet Franc, Cabernet Sauvignon, Négrette, Pinot Noir*

Gros Plant du Pays Nantais (W) Folle Blanche, *Colombard, Montils*

Haut-Poitou (R) Cabernet Franc, *Gamay, Gamay de Bouze, Gamay de Chaudenay, Merlot, Pinot Noir* (W) Sauvignon Blanc, Sauvignon Gris (P) Cabernet Franc, Gamay, Pinot Noir

Jasnières (W) Chenin Blanc

Menetou-Salon (R, P) Pinot Noir (W) Sauvignon Blanc

Montlouis-sur-Loire (W) Chenin Blanc

Muscadet (W) Melon, *Chardonnay*

Muscadet-Côtes de Grandlieu, Muscadet-Coteaux de la Loire, Muscadet-Sèvre et Maine (W) Melon

Orléans (R) Pinot Meunier, Pinot Noir (W) Chardonnay, *Pinot Gris* (P) Pinot Meunier, *Pinot Gris, Pinot Noir*
Orléans-Cléry (R) Cabernet Franc
Pouilly-Fumé, Blanc Fumé de Pouilly (W) Sauvignon Blanc
Pouilly-sur-Loire (W) Chasselas
Quincy (W) Sauvignon Blanc, *Sauvignon Gris*
Reuilly (R) Pinot Noir (W) Sauvignon Blanc (P) Pinot Gris, Pinot Noir
Rosé d'Anjou (P) Cabernet Franc, Cabernet Sauvignon, Cot, Gamay, Grolleau, Grolleau Gris, Pineau d'Aunis
Rosé de Loire (P) Cabernet Franc, Cabernet Sauvignon, Gamay, Grolleau, Grolleau Gris, Pineau d'Aunis, Pinot Noir
St-Pourçain (R) Gamay, Pinot Noir (W) Chardonnay, Sacy, *Sauvignon Blanc* (P) Gamay
Sancerre (R, P) Pinot Noir (W) Sauvignon Blanc
Saumur (R) Cabernet Franc, *Cabernet Sauvignon, Pineau d'Aunis* (W) Chenin Blanc (P) Cabernet Franc, Cabernet Sauvignon (S) Chenin Blanc, Chardonnay, Cabernet Franc, Cabernet Sauvignon, Gamay, Grolleau, Grolleau Gris, Pineau d'Aunis, Pinot Noir, Sauvignon Blanc
Saumur-Champigny (R) Cabernet Franc, *Cabernet Sauvignon, Pineau d'Aunis*
Saumur Puy-Notre-Dame (R) Cabernet Franc, *Cabernet Sauvignon*
Savennières, Savennières Roche aux Moines (W) Chenin Blanc
Touraine (R) Cabernet Franc, Cot, *Cabernet Sauvignon, Gamay, Pinot Noir* (W) Sauvignon Blanc, *Sauvignon Gris* (P, SP) Cabernet Franc, Cabernet Sauvignon, Cot, Gamay, Grolleau, Grolleau Gris, Meunier, Pineau d'Aunis, Pinot Gris, Pinot Noir (WS) Chardonnay, Chenin Blanc, Cabernet Franc. Grolleau, Grolleau Gris, Orbois, Pineau d'Aunis, Pinot Noir
Note: There is some variation for Touraine reds depending on the exact location of the vineyards.
Touraine Amboise (R) Cot (W) Chenin Blanc (P) Cot, *Gamay*
Touraine Azay-le-Rideau (W) Chenin Blanc (P) Grolleau, *Cabernet Franc, Cabernet Sauvignon, Cot, Gamay*
Touraine Chenonceaux (R) Cabernet Franc, Cot (W) Sauvignon Blanc
Touraine Mesland (R) Gamay, Cabernet Franc, Cot (W) Chenin Blanc, *Chardonnay, Sauvignon Blanc* (P) Gamay, *Cabernet Franc, Cot*
Touraine Noble Joué (P) Pinot Meunier, Pinot Gris, Pinot Noir
Touraine Oisly (W) Sauvignon Blanc
Valençay (R) Cot, Gamay, Pinot Noir, *Cabernet Franc* (W) Sauvignon Blanc, *Chardonnay, Orbois, Sauvignon Gris* (P) Cot, Gamay, Pinot Noir, *Cabernet Franc, Pineau d'Aunis*
Vouvray (W) Chenin Blanc, *Orbois*

Loire fringes

Côte Roannaise, Côtes du Forez (R, P) Gamay

Provence

Bandol (R) Cinsaut, Grenache, Mourvèdre, *Carignan, Syrah* (W) Bourboulenc, Clairette, Ugni Blanc, *Marsanne, Sauvignon Blanc, Sémillon, Rolle* (P) Cinsaut, Grenache, Mourvèdre, *Bourboulenc, Carignan, Clairette, Syrah, Ugni Blanc*
Bellet, Vin de Bellet (R) Braquet, Fuella Nera, *Cinsaut, Grenache* (W) Rolle, *Blanqueiron, Bourboulenc, Chardonnay, Clairette, Mayorquin, Muscat Blanc à Petit Grains, Ugni Blanc (Roussan)* (P) Braquet, Fuella Nera, *Blanqueiron, Bourboulenc, Cinsaut, Clairette, Grenache, Mayorquin, Rolle, Ugni Blanc (Roussan)*
Cassis (R) Cinsaut, Grenache, Mourvèdre, *Barbaroux, Carignan, Terret Noir* (W) Clairette, Marsanne, *Bourboulenc (Doucillon), Pascal Blanc, Sauvignon Blanc, Terret Blanc, Ugni Blanc* (P) Cinsaut, Grenache, Mourvèdre, *Barbaroux, Bourboulenc (Doucillon), Carignan, Clairette, Marsanne, Pascal Blanc, Sauvignon Blanc, Terret Noir, Ugni Blanc*
Coteaux d'Aix-en-Provence (R, P) Cinsaut, Counoise, Grenache, Mourvèdre, Syrah, *Cabernet Sauvignon, Caladoc, Carignan* (W) Rolle, Clairette, Grenache Blanc, Sauvignon Blanc, Ugni Blanc, *Bourboulenc, Sémillon*
Coteaux Varois-en-Provence (R, P) Cinsaut, Grenache, Mourvèdre, Syrah, *Cabernet Sauvignon, Carignan, Tibouren* (W) Clairette, Grenache Blanc, Rolle, Sémillon, Ugni Blanc
Côtes de Provence (R, P) Cinsaut, Grenache, Mourvèdre, Syrah, Tibouren, *Barbaroux, Cabernet Sauvignon, Carignan, Clairette, Rolle, Sémillon, Ugni Blanc,* plus, experimentally, *Agiorgitiko, Calabrese, Moschofilero, Verdejo, Xinomavro* (W) Clairette, Sémillon, Ugni Blanc, Rolle, plus, experimentally, *Verdejo*
Note: Barbaroux and Calitor authorized only for vineyards planted before 1994.
Côtes de Provence Fréjus (R) Grenache, Mourvèdre, Syrah (P) Grenache, Mourvèdre, Syrah, Tibouren, *Cinsaut*
Côtes de Provence La Londe (R) Grenache, Mourvèdre, Syrah, *Cabernet Sauvignon, Carignan* (W) Rolle, *Clairette, Sémillon, Ugni Blanc* (P) Cinsaut, Grenache, *Carignan, Clairette, Mourvèdre, Rolle, Sémillon, Syrah, Tibouren, Ugni Blanc*
Côtes de Provence Notre-Dame des Anges (R, P) Cinsaut, Grenache, Syrah, *Cabernet Sauvignon, Carignan, Clairette, Mourvèdre, Rolle, Sémillon, Tibouren, Ugni Blanc*
Côtes de Provence Pierrefeu (R) Grenache, Mourvèdre, Syrah, *Cabernet Sauvignon, Carignan* (P) Cinsaut, Grenache, Syrah, *Clairette, Mourvèdre, Rolle, Sémillon, Tibouren, Ugni Blanc*
Côtes de Provence Ste-Victoire (R, P) Cinsaut, Grenache, Syrah, *Cabernet Sauvignon, Carignan, Clairette, Mourvèdre, Rolle, Sémillon, Ugni Blanc*
Les Baux-de-Provence (R) Grenache, Mourvèdre, Syrah, *Cabernet Sauvignon, Carignan, Cinsaut, Counoise* (W) Clairette, Grenache Blanc, Rolle, *Bourboulenc, Marsanne, Roussanne, Ugni Blanc* (P) Cinsaut, Grenache, Syrah, *Cabernet Sauvignon, Carignan, Counoise, Mourvèdre*
Palette (R, P) Cinsaut, Grenache, Mourvèdre, *Brun Fourca, Cabernet Sauvignon, Carignan, Castets, Durif, Muscat Blanc à Petits Grains, Muscat de Hamburg, Syrah, Téoulier, Terret Gris, Tibouren* (W) Araignan (Picardan), Bourboulenc, Clairette, Clairette Rose, *Colombard, Furmint, Grenache Blanc, Muscat Blanc à Petits Grains, Muscat d'Alexandrie, Pascal, Piquepoul Blanc, Terret Gris (Terret Bourret), Ugni Blanc*
Pierrevert (R) Grenache, Syrah, *Carignan, Cinsaut, Clairette, Grenache Blanc, Marsanne, Mourvèdre, Piquepoul Blanc, Rolle, Roussanne, Téoulier (Manosquin), Ugni Blanc, Viognier* (W) Clairette, Grenache Blanc, Marsanne, Piquepoul, Rolle, Roussanne, Ugni Blanc, Viognier (P) Cinsaut, Grenache, Syrah, *Carignan, Clairette, Grenache Blanc, Marsanne, Mourvèdre, Piquepoul Blanc, Rolle, Roussanne, Téoulier (Manosquin), Ugni Blanc, Viognier*

Rhône

Beaumes de Venise (R) Grenache, Syrah, Mourvèdre, *Bourboulenc, Brun Argenté (Camarèse/Vaccarèse), Carignan, Cinsaut, Clairette, Clairette Rose, Counoise, Grenache Blanc, Grenache Gris, Marsanne, Muscardin, Piquepoul Blanc, Piquepoul Noir, Roussanne, Terret Noir, Ugni Blanc, Viognier*
Cairanne (R) Grenache, Mourvèdre, Syrah, *Bourboulenc, Brun Argenté (Camarèse/Vaccarèse), Carignan, Cinsaut, Clairette, Clairette Rose, Counoise, Grenache Blanc, Grenache Gris, Marsanne, Muscardin, Piquepoul Blanc, Piquepoul Noir, Roussanne, Terret Noir, Viognier* (W) Clairette, Grenache Blanc, Roussanne, *Bourboulenc, Marsanne, Piquepoul Blanc, Viognier*
Châteauneuf-du-Pape (R, W) Bourboulenc, Brun Argenté (Vaccarèse), Cinsaut, Clairette, Clairette Rose, Counoise, Grenache, Grenache

Blanc, Grenache Gris, Mourvèdre, Muscardin, Picardan, Piquepoul Blanc, Piquepoul Gris, Piquepoul Noir, Roussanne, Syrah, Terret Noir

Châtillon-en-Diois (R, P) Gamay, *Pinot Noir, Syrah* (W) Aligoté, Chardonnay

Condrieu, Château-Grillet (W) Viognier

Cornas (R) Syrah

Coteaux de Die (W) Clairette

Côte Rôtie (R) Syrah, *Viognier*

Côtes du Rhône (R, P) Grenache, Mourvèdre, Syrah, *Bourboulenc, Brun Argenté (Vaccarèse/Camarèse), Caladoc, Carignan, Cinsaut, Clairette, Clairette Rose, Counoise, Couston, Grenache Blanc, Grenache Gris, Marsanne, Marselan, Muscardin, Piquepoul Blanc, Piquepoul Noir, Roussanne, Terret Noir, Ugni Blanc, Viognier* (W) Bourboulenc, Clairette, Grenache Blanc, Marsanne, Roussanne, Viognier, *Piquepoul, Ugni Blanc*

Côtes du Rhône-Villages (R, P) Grenache, Mourvèdre, Syrah, *Bourboulenc, Brun Argenté (Vaccarèse, Camarèse), Carignan, Cinsaut, Clairette, Clairette Rose, Counoise, Grenache Blanc, Grenache Gris, Marsanne, Muscardin, Piquepoul Blanc, Picquepoul Noir, Roussanne, Terret Noir, Ugni Blanc, Viognier* (W) Bourboulenc, Clairette, Grenache Blanc, Marsanne, Roussanne, Viognier, *Piquepoul Blanc, Ugni Blanc*

Côtes du Vivarais (R, P) Grenache, Syrah, *Cinsaut, Marselan* (W) Clairette, Grenache Blanc, Marsanne, *Roussanne, Viognier*

Crémant de Die (S) Clairette, *Aligoté, Muscat Blanc à Petits Grains*

Duché d'Uzès (R, P) Grenache, Syrah, *Carignan, Cinsaut, Mourvèdre* (W) Grenache Blanc, Marsanne, Rolle, Roussanne, Viognier, *Clairette, Ugni Blanc*

Gigondas (R, P) Grenache, Mourvèdre, Syrah, *Bourboulenc, Brun Argenté (Camarèse/Vaccarèse), Cinsaut, Clairette, Clairette Rose, Counoise, Grenache Blanc, Grenache Gris, Marsanne, Muscardin, Piquepoul Blanc, Piquepoul Noir, Roussanne, Terret Noir, Ugni Blanc, Viognier*

Grignan-les-Adhémar (R, P) Grenache, Syrah, *Bourboulenc, Carignan, Cinsaut, Clairette, Grenache Blanc, Marsanne, Marselan, Mourvèdre, Roussanne, Viognier* (W) Bourboulenc, Clairette, Grenache Blanc, Marsanne, Roussanne, Viognier

Hermitage, Crozes-Hermitage, St-Joseph (R) Syrah, *Marsanne, Roussanne* (W) Marsanne, Roussanne

Lirac (R, P) Cinsaut, Grenache, Mourvèdre, Syrah, *Carignan, Clairette Rose, Counoise, Grenache Gris, Marsanne, Piquepoul Blanc, Piquepoul Noir, Roussanne, Ugni Blanc, Viognier* (W) Bourboulenc, Clairette, Grenache Blanc, Roussanne, *Marsanne, Piquepoul Blanc, Ugni Blanc, Viognier*

Luberon (R, P) Grenache, Mourvèdre, Syrah, *Bourboulenc, Carignan, Cinsaut, Clairette, Grenache Blanc, Marsanne, Marselan, Rolle, Roussanne, Ugni Blanc, Viognier* (W) Bourboulenc, Clairette, Grenache Blanc, Marsanne, Rolle, Roussanne, *Ugni Blanc, Viognier*

Rasteau (R) Grenache, Mourvèdre, Syrah, *Bourboulenc, Brun Argenté (Camarèse, Vaccarèse), Carignan, Cinsaut, Clairette, Clairette Rose, Counoise, Grenache Blanc, Grenache Gris, Marsanne, Muscardin, Piquepoul Blanc, Piquepoul Noir, Roussanne, Terret Noir, Ugni Blanc, Viognier*

Rasteau Vin Doux Naturel Grenache, Grenache Blanc, Grenache Gris, *Bourboulenc, Brun Argenté (Camarèse, Vaccarèse), Carignan, Cinsaut, Clairette, Clairette Rose, Counoise, Marsanne, Mourvèdre, Muscardin, Piquepoul Blanc, Piquepoul Noir, Roussanne, Syrah, Terret Noir, Ugni Blanc, Viognier*

Note: Grenache is not allowed in Ambré, Grenat, Rosé, and Tuilé versions of Rasteau Vin Doux Naturel.

St-Péray (W, S) Marsanne, Roussanne

Tavel (P) Bourboulenc, Cinsaut, Clairette, Clairette Rose, Grenache, Grenache Blanc, Grenache Gris, Mourvèdre, Piquepoul, Piquepoul Gris, Piquepoul Noir, Syrah, *Calitor, Carignan Blanc, Carignan*

Vacqueyras (R) Grenache, Mourvèdre, Syrah, *Bourboulenc, Brun Argenté (Camarèse/Vaccarèse), Carignan, Cinsaut, Clairette Rose, Counoise, Grenache Blanc, Grenache Gris, Marsanne, Muscardin, Piquepoul Noir, Roussanne, Terret Noir, Viognier* (W) Bourboulenc, Clairette, Grenache Blanc, Marsanne, Roussanne, Viognier (P) Cinsaut, Grenache, Mourvèdre, Syrah, *Brun Argenté (Camarèse/Vaccarèse), Carignan, Clairette, Clairette Rose, Counoise, Grenache Blanc, Grenache Gris, Marsanne, Muscardin, Piquepoul Noir, Roussanne, Terret Noir, Viognier*

Ventoux (R, P) Carignan, Cinsaut, Grenache, Mourvèdre, Syrah, *Bourboulenc, Clairette, Counoise, Grenache Blanc, Marsanne, Marselan, Piquepoul Noir, Rolle, Roussanne, Viognier* (W) Bourboulenc, Clairette, Grenache Blanc, Roussanne, *Marsanne, Rolle, Viognier*

Vinsobres (R) Grenache, Mourvèdre, Syrah, *Bourboulenc, Brun Argenté (Camarèse, Vaccarèse), Carignan, Cinsaut, Clairette, Clairette Rose, Counoise, Grenache Blanc, Grenache Gris, Marsanne, Muscardin, Piquepoul Blanc, Piquepoul Noir, Roussanne, Terret Noir, Ugni Blanc, Viognier*

Rhône fringes

Coteaux du Lyonnais (R, P) Gamay, *Gamay de Bouze, Gamay de Chaudenay* (W) Aligoté, Chardonnay, *Pinot Blanc*

Savoie and Bugey

Note: Varietal labelling is used for all the Bugey appellations where a wine is made exclusively from one variety.

Bugey, Bugey followed by a commune name (R) Gamay, Mondeuse Noire, Pinot Noir (W) Chardonnay, *Aligoté, Altesse, Jacquère, Mondeuse Blanche, Pinot Gris* (P) Gamay, Pinot Noir, *Mondeuse Blanche, Pinot Gris, Poulsard*

Bugey Manicle (R) Pinot Noir (W) Chardonnay

Bugey Montagnieu (R) Mondeuse Noire (S) Altesse, Chardonnay, Mondeuse, *Gamay, Jacquère, Molette, Pinot Noir*

Bugey Mousseux, Bugey Pétillant (WS) Chardonnay, Jacquère, Molette, *Aligoté, Altesse, Gamay, Mondeuse Blanche, Mondeuse Noir, Pinot Gris, Pinot Noir, Poulsard* (PS) Gamay, Pinot Noir, *Mondeuse Noir, Pinot Gris, Poulsard*

Bugey Cerdon (PS) Gamay, Poulsard

Crémant de Savoie (S) Aligoté, Altesse, Chardonnay, Gamay, Jacquère, Mondeuse, Mondeuse Blanche, Pinot Noir; for the *département* of the Haute-Savoie only: Chasselas, Molette; plus, experimentally, *Bia, Corbeau, Dousset, Hibou Noir, Mondeuse Grise, Pinot Gris, Petite Ste-Marie*

Roussette de Bugey, Roussette de Bugey followed by a commune name (W) Altesse

Roussette de Savoie, Roussette de Savoie followed by a cru name (W) Roussette

Seyssel (W) Altesse (S) Altesse, Chasselas, Molette

Vin de Savoie, Savoie (P, R) Gamay, Mondeuse, Pinot Noir; for the *département* of Savoie, Cabernet Franc, Cabernet Sauvignon, Persan; for the *département* of Isère, Étraire de la Dui, Joubertin, Persan, Servanin; plus, experimentally, *Corbeau, Dousset, Hibou Noir, Mondeuse Grise* (W) Aligoté, Altesse, Chardonnay, Jacquère, Mondeuse Blanche, Velteliner Rouge Précoce; for the *département* of Haute-Savoie, Chasselas, Gringet, Roussette d'Ayze; for the *département* of Isère, Marsanne, Verdesse; plus, experimentally, *Bia, Mondeuse Grise, Petite Ste-Marie, Pinot Gris* (S) Aligoté, Altesse, Chardonnay, Gamay, Jacquère, Mondeuse, Mondeuse Blanche, Pinot Noir, Velteliner Rouge Précoce, Chasselas

(Haute-Savoie only), plus, experimentally, *Bia, Corbeau, Dousset, Hibou Noir, Mondeuse Grise, Petite Ste-Marie, Pinot Gris*

Vin de Savoie Abymes (W) Jacquère, *Aligoté, Altesse, Chardonnay, Marsanne* (Isère only), *Mondeuse, Velteliner Rouge Précoce, Verdesse* (Isère only), plus, experimentally, *Bia, Mondeuse Grise, Petite Ste-Marie, Pinot Gris*

Vin de Savoie followed by Apremont, Cruet, Montmélian, St-Jeoire-Prieuré (W) Jacquère, *Aligoté, Altesse, Chardonnay, Marsanne, Mondeuse Blanche, Velteliner Rouge Précoce, Verdesse*, plus, experimentally, *Bia, Mondeuse Grise, Petite Ste-Marie, Pinot Gris*

Vin de Savoie followed by Arbin, St-Jean-de-la-Porte (R) Mondeuse

Vin de Savoie Ayze (W, S) Gringet, *Altesse, Roussette d'Ayze*

Vin de Savoie followed by Chautagne, Chignin, Jongieux (R) Gamay, Mondeuse, Pinot Noir, *Cabernet Franc, Cabernet Sauvignon, Persan*, plus, experimentally, *Corbeau, Dousset, Hibou Noir* (W) Jacquère, *Aligoté, Altesse, Chardonnay, Marsanne, Mondeuse Blanche, Velteliner Rouge Précoce, Verdesse*, plus, experimentally, *Bia, Mondeuse Grise, Petite Ste-Marie, Pinot Gris*

Vin de Savoie Chignin-Bergeron (W) Roussanne

Vin de Savoie followed by Crépy, Marignan, Marin, Ripaille (W) Chasselas, *Aligoté, Altesse, Chardonnay, Gringet, Mondeuse Blanche, Roussette d'Ayze, Velteliner Rouge Précoce*, plus experimentally, *Bia, Mondeuse Grise, Petite Ste-Marie, Pinot Gris*

South West France

Béarn (R, P) Cabernet Franc, Cabernet Sauvignon, Tannat, *Courbu Noir, Fer, Manseng* (W) Gros Manseng, Petit Manseng, Raffiat de Moncade, *Camaralet de Lasseube, Courbu, Lauzet, Petit Courbu, Sauvignon Blanc*

Bergerac (R) Cabernet Franc, Cabernet Sauvignon, Cot, Merlot, *Fer Servadou, Mérille* (W) Muscadelle, Sauvignon Blanc, Sauvignon Gris, Sémillon, Ugni Blanc, *Chenin Blanc, Ondenc* (P) Cabernet Franc, Cabernet Sauvignon, Cot, Merlot, *Fer Servadou, Mérille, Muscadelle, Sauvignon Blanc, Sauvignon Gris*

Brulhois (R, P) Cabernet Franc, Cabernet Sauvignon, Cot, Fer Servadou, Merlot, Tannat, *Abouriou*

Buzet (R, P) Cabernet Franc, Cabernet Sauvignon, Cot, Merlot, *Abouriou, Petit Verdot* (W) Muscadelle, Sauvignon Blanc, Sauvignon Gris, Sémillon, *Colombard, Gros Manseng, Petit Manseng*

Cahors (R) Cot (Malbec), *Merlot, Tannat*

Corrèze (R) Cabernet Franc, *Cabernet Sauvignon, Merlot*

Corrèze Coteaux de la Vézère (R) Cabernet Franc (W) Chenin Blanc

Corrèze Vin de Paille Cabernet Franc, Cabernet Sauvignon, Chardonnay, Merlot, Sauvignon Blanc

Coteaux du Quercy (R, P) Cabernet Franc, Cot, Merlot, Tannat, *Gamay*

Côtes de Bergerac (R) Cabernet Franc, Cabernet Sauvignon, Cot, Merlot (W) Muscadelle, Sauvignon Blanc, Sauvignon Gris, Sémillon, Ugni Blanc, *Chenin Blanc, Ondenc*

Côtes de Duras (R) Cabernet Franc, Cabernet Sauvignon, Cot, Merlot (W) Chenin Blanc, Mauzac, Muscadelle, Ondenc, Sauvignon Blanc, Sauvignon Gris, Sémillon, Ondenc, *Colombard, Ugni Blanc* (P) Cabernet Franc, Cabernet Sauvignon, Cot, Merlot, *Muscadelle, Sauvignon Blanc, Sauvignon Gris, Sémillon*

Côtes de Millau (R) Gamay, Syrah, *Cabernet Sauvignon, Duras, Fer* (W) Chenin Blanc, *Mauzac* (P) Gamay, *Cabernet Sauvignon, Duras, Fer, Syrah*

Côtes du Marmandais (R, P) Cabernet Franc, Cabernet Sauvignon, Merlot, *Abouriou, Cot, Fer, Gamay, Syrah* (W) Sauvignon Blanc, Sauvignon Gris, *Muscadelle, Sémillon*

Côtes de Montravel, Haut-Montravel (W) Muscadelle, Sauvignon Blanc, Sauvignon Gris, Sémillon, *Ondenc*

Entraygues-Le Fel (R, P) Cabernet Franc, Cabernet Sauvignon, Fer, *Mouyssaguès, Négret de Banhars* (W) Chenin Blanc, *Mauzac, St-Côme*

Estaing (R, P) Cabernet Franc, Cabernet Sauvignon, Fer, Gamay, *Abouriou (Gamay St-Laurent), Castet, Duras, Merlot, Mouyssaguès, Négret de Banhars, Pinot Noir* (W) Chenin Blanc, Mauzac, *St-Côme (Rousselou)*

Fronton (R, P) Négrette, *Cabernet Franc, Cabernet Sauvignon, Cinsaut, Cot, Fer, Gamay, Mérille, Syrah*

Gaillac (R, P) Duras, Fer, Prunelard, Syrah, *Cabernet Franc, Cabernet Sauvignon, Gamay, Merlot* (W, S) Len de l'El, Mauzac, Mauzac Rose, Muscadelle, *Ondenc, Sauvignon Blanc*

Gaillac Méthode Ancestrale (S) Mauzac, Mauzac Rosé

Gaillac Premières Côtes (W) Len de l'El, Mauzac, Mauzac Rosé, Muscadelle, *Ondenc, Sauvignon Blanc*

Gaillac Primeur (R) Gamay

Gaillac Vendanges Tardives (W) Len de l'El, Ondenc, *Mauzac, Mauzac Rose, Muscadelle*

Irouléguy (R) Cabernet Franc, Tannat, *Cabernet Sauvignon* (W) Courbu, Gros Manseng, Petit Courbu, Petit Manseng (P) Cabernet Franc, Cabernet Sauvignon, Tannat, *Courbu, Gros Manseng, Petit Courbu, Petit Manseng*

Jurançon (W) Gros Manseng, Petit Manseng, *Camaralet de Lasseube, Courbu, Lauzet, Petit Courbu*

Jurançon Vendanges Tardives (W) Gros Manseng, Petit Manseng

Madiran (R) Tannat, *Cabernet Franc, Cabernet Sauvignon, Fer*

Marcillac (R, P) Fer, *Cabernet Sauvignon, Merlot, Prunelard*

Monbazillac (W) Muscadelle, Sauvignon Blanc, Sauvignon Gris, Sémillon, *Chenin Blanc, Ondenc, Ugni Blanc*

Montravel (R) Merlot, Cabernet Franc, Cabernet Sauvignon, Cot (W) Muscadelle, Sauvignon Blanc, Sauvignon Gris, Sémillon, *Ondenc*

Pacherenc du Vic-Bilh (W) Courbu, Gros Manseng, Petit Courbu, Petit Manseng, *Arrufiac, Sauvignon Blanc*

Pécharmant (R) Cabernet Franc, Cabernet Sauvignon, Cot, Merlot

Rosette (W) Muscadelle, Sauvignon Blanc, Sauvignon Gris, Sémillon

Saussignac (W) Muscadelle, Sauvignon Blanc, Sauvignon Gris, Sémillon, *Chenin Blanc, Ondenc, Ugni Blanc*

St-Mont (R) Tannat, Cabernet Sauvignon, Fer, *Cabernet Franc, Merlot* (W) Arrufiac, Gros Manseng, Petit Courbu, *Courbu, Petit Manseng* (P) Tannat, Cabernet Sauvignon, Fer, *Arrufiac, Cabernet Franc, Courbu, Gros Manseng, Merlot, Petit Courbu, Petit Manseng*, plus, experimentally, *Manseng Noir, Tardif*

St-Sardos (R, P) Syrah, Tannat, *Cabernet Franc, Merlot*

Tursan (R, P) Cabernet Franc, Tannat, *Cabernet Sauvignon, Fer, Merlot* (W) Baroque, Gros Manseng, *Chenin Blanc, Claverie, Petit Manseng, Raffiat de Moncade, Sauvignon Blanc, Sauvignon Gris*

GREECE

Amyndeo (R, P, S) Xinomavro

Ankhialos (W) Roditis, *Savatiano*

Archanes (R) Kotsifali, Mandilaria

Handakas-Candia (R) Kotsifali, Mandilaria (W) Vilana, *Assyrtiko, Athiri, Vidiano, Thrapsathiri*

Dafnes (R) Liatiko

Goumenissa (R) Xinomavro, *Negoska*

Lemnos (R) Limnio, Muscat of Alexandria (W) Muscat of Alexandria

Mantinia (W) Moschofilero, Asproudes

Malvasia-Sitia (W) Assyrtiko, Athiri, Liatico, Malvasia di Candia Aromatica, Muscat Blanc à Petits Grains, Thrapsathiri

Malvasia-Candia (W) Assyrtiko, Athiri, Liatico, Malvasia di Candia Aromatica, Muscat Blanc à Petits Grains, Thrapsathiri, Vidiano

Messenikola (R) Messenikola, *Carignan*, *Syrah*
Monemvasia-Malvasia (W) Monemvasia, Assyrtiko, Asproudes, Kydonitsa
Naoussa (R) Xinomavro
Nemea (R) Agiorgitiko
Paros (R) Mandilaria, Monemvassia (W) Monemvassia
Patras (W) Roditis
Peza (R) Kotsifali, Mandilaria (W) Vilana
Rapsani (R) Krassato, Stavroto, Xinomavro
Rhodes (R) Mandilaria, Mavrothiriko (W) Athiri, Assyrtiko, Malagousia (P) Mandilaria, Mavrothiriko
Samos (W) Muscat Blanc à Petits Grains
Santorini, Santorini Vinsanto (W) Assyrtiko, *Aïdani*, *Athiri*
Sitia (R) Liatiko, *Mandilaria* (W) Vilana, *Thrapsathiri*
Slopes of Meliton (R) Cabernet Franc, Cabernet Sauvignon, Limnio (W) Assyrtiko, Athiri, Roditis
Zitsa (W, S) Debina

HUNGARY

In most Hungarian PDOs, any grape varieties authorized within the region may be used, with the following exceptions.

Csopak (W) Olaszrizling, *Furmint*
Egri Bikavér (Bulls Blood of Eger) (R) Kékfrankos, *OR*
Etyeki Pezsgő (W) Chardonnay, Pinot Noir, Pinot Gris, Pinot Blanc
Kőszeg (R) Blauburger, Cabernet Franc, Cabernet Sauvignon, Kékfrankos, Merlot, Pinot Noir, Zweigelt (R Superior) Blauburger, Kékfrankos, *Cabernet Franc*, *Cabernet Sauvignon*, *Merlot*, *Pinot Noir*, *Zweigelt* (R Grand Superior) Blauburger, Kékfrankos (W) Chardonnay, Cserszegi Fűszeres, Furmint, Olaszrizling, Pinot Blanc, Rajnai Rizling, Sauvignon, Zenit
Nivegy Völgy (W) Olaszrizling
Soltvadkerti (W) Ezerjó
Sümeg (R) Cabernet Franc, Kékfrankos, Merlot, Pinot Noir, Syrah, Zweigelt (R Penta) Kékfrankos, *Merlot*, *Zweigelt* (W) Chardonnay, Furmint, Hárslevelű, Juhfark, Kéknyelű, Olaszrizling, Sárfehér (W Penta) Furmint, Olaszrizling, *Chardonnay*, *Hárslevelű*, *Juhfark*, *Kéknyelű*, *Sárfehér* (P Penta) Kékfrankos, Zweigelt, *Cabernet Franc*, *Furmint*, *Merlot*, *Pinot Noir* (WS) Chardonnay, Furmint, Hárslevelű, Kékfrankos, Kéknyelű, Olaszrizling, Pinot Noir, Sárfehér (PS) Cabernet Franc, Kékfrankos, Merlot, Pinot Noir, Syrah, Zweigelt
Szekszárdi Bikavér (Bulls Blood of Szekszárd) (R) Kékfrankos, Kadarka, *OR*
Villányi Franc (R) Cabernet Franc

ITALY

Most Italian DOCs and DOCGs allow a percentage (anywhere between 5% and 50% is common) of other varieties authorized for DOC wines within the region, either red (OR) or white (OW), sometimes both (OR&W). In some instances aromatic varieties are excluded. Only those varieties specifically named in the regulations, as compulsory or optional, are listed below. The *disciplinare* for each appellation can be found on the Italian Ministry of Agriculture's website (www.politicheagricole.it/flex/cm/pages/ServeBLOB.php/L/IT/IDPagina/4625), but the information is not updated as often as on the Lavinium website (www.lavinium.it/doc-e-docg).

Abruzzo

Abruzzo (R) Montepulciano, *OR* (W) Trebbiano Abruzzese, Trebbiano Toscano (W passito) Malvasia, Moscato, Passerina, Pecorino, Riesling, Sauvignon Blanc, Traminer, *OW* (WS) Chardonnay, Cococciola, Montonico, Passerina, Pecorino, Pinot Nero (PS) Montepulciano, Pinot Nero, *OR&W*
Cerasuolo d'Abruzzo (R) Montepulciano, *OR*
Controguerra (R, P) Montepulciano, *OR* (W) Trebbiano Abruzzese, Trebbiano Toscano, *Malvasia*, *Passerina* (Malvasia only in passito) (WS) Trebbiano Abruzzese, Trebbiano Toscano, Chardonnay, Verdicchio, Pecorino
Ortona (R) Montepulciano (W) Trebbiano Abruzzese, Trebbiano Toscano, *OW*
Terre Tollesi or **Tullum DOCG** (R) Montepulciano, *OR*
Villamagna (R) Montepulciano

Basilicata

Grottino di Roccanova (R, P) Sangiovese, *Cabernet Sauvignon*, *Malvasia Nera di Basilicata*, *Montepulciano* (W) Malvasia Bianca di Basilicata
Matera (R) Sangiovese, Primitivo (W, WS) Malvasia Bianca di Basilicata, *OW* (P, PS) Primitivo, *OW*
Matera Moro (R) Cabernet Sauvignon, Merlot, Primitivo
Terre dell'Alta Val d'Agri (R) Cabernet Sauvignon, Merlot, *OR* (P) Cabernet Sauvignon, Malvasia di Basilicata, Merlot, *OR&W*

Calabria

Bivongi (R, P) Gaglioppo, Greco Nero, *Castiglione*, *Nero d'Avola*, *Nocera* (W) Greco Bianco, Guardavalle, Montonico Bianca, *Ansonica*, *Malvasia Bianca*
Cirò (R, P) Gaglioppo (W) Greco Bianco
Lamezia (R, P) Gaglioppo, Greco Nero, Magliocco, Marsigliana (W) Greco Bianco, *OW* (WS) Greco Bianco, Mantonico (PS) Greco Bianco, Magliocco, Mantonico
Melissa (R) Gaglioppo, *Greco Bianco*, *Greco Nero*, *Malvasia Bianca*, *Trebbiano Toscano* (W) Greco Bianco, *Malvasia Bianca*, *Trebbiano Toscano*
S. Anna di Isola Capo Rizzuto (R, P) Gaglioppo, Greco Bianco, Nerello Cappuccio, Nerello Mascalese, Nocera, Malvasia Bianca, Malvasia Nera
Savuto (R, P) Aglianico, Gaglioppo, *Greco Nero*, *Nerello Cappuccio* (W) Chardonnay, Greco Bianco, Montonico, *Malvasia Bianca*, *OW*
Scavigna (W) Chardonnay, Traminer, *Pinot Bianco*, *Riesling Italico*, *OW* (P, R) Aglianico, Magliocco, Marsigliana, *OR*
Terre di Cosenza (R) Magliocco, *OR* (W) Greco, Guarnaccia Bianca, Montonico, Pecorello (P) Greco Nero, Magliocco, Gaglioppo, Aglianico, Calabrese, *OR&W* (WS) Mantonico, *OW* (PS) Mantonico, *Greco Nero*, *Magliocco*, *Gaglioppo*, *Aglianico*, *Calabrese*
Terra di Cosenza Colline del Crati, Terra di Cosenza Esaro (R) Magliocco, *OR* (W) Greco Bianco, Guarnaccia Bianca, Montonico Bianco, Pecorello, *OW* (P) Greco Nero, Magliocco, Gaglioppo, Aglianico, Calabrese, *OR&W*
Terre di Cosenza Condoleo (R) Greco Nero, *OR* (W) Greco, Guarnaccia Bianca, Montonico Bianco, Pecorello, *OW* (P) Greco Nero, Magliocco, Gaglioppo, Aglianico, Calabrese, *OR*
Terre di Cosenza Donnici (R, P) Magliocco, Greco Nero, *Malvasia Bianca*, *Greco Bianco*, *Mantonico Bianco*, *Pecorello Bianco* (W) Montonico Bianco, *Greco Bianco*, *Malvasia Bianca*, *Pecorello Bianco*
Terre di Cosenza Pollino (R) Magliocco, Gaglioppo, *OR* (W) Greco Bianca, Guarnaccia Bianca, Montonico Bianco, Pecorello, *OW* (P) Greco Nero, Magliocco, Gaglioppo, Aglianico, Calabrese, *OR*
Terra di Cosenza San Vito di Luzzi (R) Magliocco, Gaglioppo, *OR* (W) Malvasia Bianca, Greco Bianco, Guarnaccia Bianca, *OW* (P) Magliocco, Gaglioppo, Malvasia, Greco Nero, Sangiovese, *OR*
Terra di Cosenza Verbicaro (R, P) Magliocco (Guarnaccia Nera), Greco Nero, Malvasia Bianca, Guarnaccia Bianca, Greco Bianco, *OW* (W) Greco, Guarnaccia Bianca, Malvasia Bianca, *OW*

Campania
Aversa (W, S) Asprinio
Campi Flegrei (R) Aglianico, Piedirosso, *OR* (W) Falanghina, *OW*
Capri (R) Piedirosso, *OR* (W) Falanghina, Greco, *Biancolella*
Castel San Lorenzo (R, P) Barbera, Sangiovese (W) Malvasia Bianca, Trebbiano Toscano
Cilento (R) Aglianico, Piedirosso, Primitivo, *OR* (W) Fiano, Trebbiano Toscano, *Greco Bianco*, *Malvasia Bianca*, *OW* (P) Sangiovese, *Aglianico*, *Piedirosso*, *Primitivo*, *OR*
Costa d'Amalfi (R, P) Aglianico, Piedirosso, Sciascinoso (W, S) Biancolella, Falanghina
Costa d'Amalfi Furore (W) Biancolella, Falanghina, *Fenile*, *Ginestra*, *Pepella*, *Ripoli*
Costa d'Amalfi Tramonti (R, P) Aglianico, Piedirosso, Sciascinoso, *Tintore*
Falerno del Massico (R) Aglianico, Piedirosso (W) Falanghina
Galluccio (R, P) Aglianico, *OR* (W) Falanghina, *OW*
Irpinia (R, P, RS) Aglianico, *OR* (W, WS) Fiano, Greco, *OW*
Ischia (R) Guarnaccia, Piedirosso (Per'e Palumno), *OR* (W, S) Biancolella, Forastera, *OW*
Penisola Sorrentina (R, RS) Aglianico, Piedirosso (Per'e Palumno), Sciascinoso, *OR* (W) Biancolella, Falanghina, Greco Bianco, *OW*
Sannio (R, P) Sangiovese, *OR* (W) Malvasia Bianca di Candia, Trebbiano Toscano, *OW* (S) Aglianico, Falanghina, *OR&W*
Taurasi DOCG (R) Aglianico
Vesuvio, Vesuvio Lacryma Christi (W) Caprettone, Verdeca, *Falanghina*, *Greco* (R, P) Piedirosso, Sciascinoso, *Aglianico*

Emilia-Romagna
Bosco Eliceo (W) Trebbiano Romagnolo, *Malvasia di Candia*, *Sauvignon Blanc*
Colli di Faenza (R) Ancellotta, Cabernet Sauvignon, Ciliegiolo, Merlot, Sangiovese (W) Chardonnay, Grechetto Gentile, Pinot Bianco, Sauvignon Blanc, Trebbiano Romagnolo
Colli di Parma (R) Barbera, Bonarda, Croatina (S) Chardonnay, Pinot Bianco, Pinot Nero
Colli di Rimini (R) Cabernet Franc, Cabernet Sauvignon, Merlot, Sangiovese, Syrah, *Alicante*, *Montepulciano*, *Petit Verdot*, *Rebo* (W) Bombino Bianco, Sangiovese, Trebbiano Romagnolo
Colli di Rimini Rebola (W) Grechetto Gentile
Colli di Scandiano e Canossa (R) Marzemino, *Cabernet Sauvignon*, *Malbo Gentile* (W, S) Spergola, *Malvasia di Candia*, *Pinot Bianco*, *Pinot Grigio*, *Trebbiano Romagnolo*
Colli d'Imola (R) one or more non-aromatic local red varieties (W) one or more non-aromatic local white varieties
Colli Piacentini Monterosso Val d'Arda (W) Malvasia di Candia Aromatica, Moscato Bianco, Ortrugo, Trebbiano Romagnolo, *Beverdino*, *Sauvignon Blanc*
Colli Piacentini Novello (R) Barbera, Croatina, Pinot Nero, *OR*
Colli Piacentini Trebbianino Val Trebbia (W) Malvasia di Candia Aromatica, Moscato Bianco, Ortrugo, Sauvignon Blanc, Trebbiano Romagnolo
Colli Piacentini Valnure (W) Malvasia di Candia, Ortrugo, Trebbiano Romagnolo
Colli Piacentini Vin Santo (W) Malvasia di Candia Aromatica, Marsanne, Ortrugo, Sauvignon Blanc, Trebbiano Romagnolo
Colli Piacentini Vin Santo di Vigoleno (W) Santa Maria, Melara, Bervedino, Ortrugo, Trebbiano Romagnolo
Colli Romagna Centrale (R) Barbera, Cabernet Sauvignon, Merlot, Montepulciano, Sangiovese (W) Bombino, Chardonnay, Pinot Bianco, Sauvignon Blanc, Trebbiano
Gutturnio (R) Barbera, Croatina
Modena (RS, PS) Lambrusco, *Ancellotta*, *Fortana* (WS) Montuni, Trebbiano
Reggiano (R) Ancellotta, Cabernet Sauvignon, Fogarina, Lambrusco, Malbo Gentile, Marzemino, Merlot, Sangiovese (WS) Lambrusco, Malbo Gentile
Reno (W, S) Albana, Trebbiano Romagnolo, *OW*
Romagna (PS) Sangiovese, *Albana*, *Bombino Bianco*, *Chardonnay*, *Famoso*, *Garganega*, *Grechetto Gentile*, *Pinot Bianco*, *Pinot Grigio*, *Riesling*, *Manzoni Bianco*, *Merlot*, *Uva Longanesi* (WS) Trebbiano Romagnolo, *Albana*, *Bombino Bianco*, *Chardonnay*, *Famoso*, *Garganega*, *Grechetto Gentile*, *Manzoni Bianco*, *Pinot Bianco*, *Pinot Grigio*, *Riesling*, *Sangiovese*
Romagna Cagnina (R) *Terrano*
Romagna Pagadebit (W) *Bombino Bianco*

Friuli-Venezia Giulia
Carso or **Carso-Kras** (R) Terrano, *OR*
Collio Goriziano or **Collio** (R) Cabernet Franc, Cabernet Sauvignon, Merlot, Pinot Nero (W) Chardonnay, Friulano, Malvasia, Picolit, Pinot Bianco, Pinot Grigio, Ribolla Gialla, Riesling, Riesling Italico, Sauvignon Blanc, *Müller-Thurgau*, *Traminer Aromatico*
Friuli (R) Cabernet Franc, Cabernet Sauvignon, Carmenère, Merlot, Pinot Nero, Refosco dal Peduncolo Rosso (W) Chardonnay, Friulano, Malvasia Istriana, Pinot Bianco, Pinot Grigio, Ribolla Gialla, Riesling, Sauvignon, Traminer Aromatico, Verduzzo Friulano (S) Chardonnay, Pinot Bianco, Pinot Grigio, Pinot Nero
Friuli-Annia (W) Chardonnay, Friulano, Traminer Aromatico, Malvasia Istriana, Pinot Bianco, Pinot Grigio, Sauvignon Blanc, Verduzzo Friulano (R, P) Cabernet Franc, Cabernet Sauvignon, Merlot, Refosco dal Peduncolo Rosso (S) Chardonnay, Pinot Bianco
Friuli Aquileia (R) Refosco dal Peduncolo Rosso, *OR* (P) Cabernet Franc, Cabernet Sauvignon, Merlot, Refosco dal Peduncolo Rosso (W) Friulano, *OW* with the exception of Müller-Thurgau, Traminer Aromatic (S) Chardonnay
Friuli Colli Orientali (R) Cabernet Franc, Cabernet Sauvignon, Carmenère, Merlot, Pignolo, Pinot Nero, Refosco dal Peduncolo Rosso, Refosco Nostrano, Schioppettino, Tazzelenghe (W) Chardonnay, Friulano, Malvasia Istriana, Picolit, Pinot Bianco, Pinot Grigio, Ribolla Gialla, Riesling, Sauvignon Blanc, Verduzzo Friulano
Friuli Colli Orientali Cialla (R) Refosco dal Peduncolo Rosso, Schioppettino (W) Picolit, Ribolla Gialla, Verduzzo Friulano
Friuli Grave (R, P) Cabernet Franc, Cabernet Sauvignon, Carmenère, Merlot, Pinot Nero, Refosco dal Peduncolo Rosso (W) Chardonnay, Friulano, Pinot Bianco, Pinot Grigio, Riesling, Sauvignon Blanc, Verduzzo Friulano (S) Chardonnay, Pinot Bianco, Pinot Nero
Friuli Isonzo (R, P) Cabernet Franc, Cabernet Sauvignon, Franconia, Merlot, Pignolo, Pinot Nero, Refosco dal Peduncolo Rosso, Schioppettino (W) Chardonnay, Friulano, Gewürztraminer, Malvasia, Pinot Bianco, Pinot Grigio, Riesling, Riesling Italico, Sauvignon Blanc, Verduzzo Friulano
Friuli Latisana (R, P) Merlot, *Cabernet Franc*, *Cabernet Sauvignon*, *Carmenère* (W, S) Friulano, *Chardonnay*, *Pinot Bianco*
Ramandolo DOCG (W) Verduzzo Friulano
Rosazzo DOCG (W) Friulano, *Chardonnay*, *Pinot Bianco*, *Sauvignon Blanc*, *Ribolla Gialla*

Lazio
Aprilia (R, P) Sangiovese, *Cabernet Sauvignon*, *Merlot* (W) Trebbiano Toscano, *Chardonnay*
Atina (R) Cabernet Sauvignon, *Cabernet Franc*, *Merlot*, *Syrah*
Bianco Capena (W) Malvasia del Lazio, Malvasia di Toscana, Malvasia di Candia, *Trebbiano Giallo*, *Trebbiano Toscano*, *Bellone*, *Bombino* (*Uva di Spagna*)

Cannellino di Frascati DOCG (W) Malvasia Bianca di Candia, Malvasia del Lazio, *Bellone, Bombino Bianco, Greco Biano, Trebbiano Giallo, Trebbiano Toscano*

Castelli Romani (R) Cesanese, Merlot, Montepulciano, Nero Buono, Sangiovese (P) any of the varieties permitted in the DOC (W) Malvasia Bianca di Candia, Malvasia Puntinata, Trebbiano di Soave, Trebbiano Giallo, Trebbiano Toscano, Trebbiano Verde

Cerveteri (W) Trebbiano Toscano, *Malvasia di Candia, OW* (R, P) Montepulciano, Sangiovese, *Merlot, OR*

Circeo (W, WS) Trebbiano Toscano, *Chardonnay, Malvasia del Lazio* (R, P, PS) Merlot, *Cabernet Sauvignon, Sangiovese*

Colli Albani (W, S) Malvasia Bianca di Candia, *Malvasia del Lazio, Trebbiano di Soave, Trebbiano Giallo, Trebbiano Toscano*

Colli della Sabina (R, P) Sangiovese, *Montepulciano, OR* (W) Malvasia del Lazio, *Trebbiano Giallo, Trebbiano Toscano*

Colli Etruschi Viterbesi or **Tuscia** (R) Sangiovese, *Montepulciano, OR* (W) Trebbiano Toscano, *Malvasia del Lazio, Malvasia Toscana*

Colli Lanuvini (W, S) Malvasia Bianca di Candia, Malvasia Puntinata, *Trebbiano Giallo, Trebbiano Toscano, Trebbiano Verde* (R) Merlot, *Montepulciano, Sangiovese*

Cori (R) Nero Buono, *Cesanese di Affile, Montepulciano* (W) Bellone, *Greco Bianco, Malvasia del Lazio*

Est! Est!! Est!!! di Montefiascone (W, S) Trebbiano Toscano (Procanico), *Malvasia Bianca Lunga, Malvasia del Lazio, Trebbiano Giallo*

Frascati DOC (W, S), **Frascati Superiore DOCG** (W) Malvasia Bianca di Candia, Malvasia del Lazio, *Bellone, Bombino Bianco, Greco Bianco, Trebbiano Giallo, Trebbiano Toscano*

Genazzano (R) Ciliegiolo, *OR* (W) Malvasia di Candia, *OW*

Marino (W, S) Malvasia Bianca di Candia, *OW*

Montecompatri-Colonna (W) Malvasia Bianca di Candia, Malvasia Puntinata, Trebbiano, *Bellone, Bonvino*

Nettuno (R) Merlot, Sangiovese, *OR* (W) Bellone (Cacchione), Trebbiano Toscano, *OW* (P) Sangiovese, Trebbiano Toscano, *OR&W*

Roma (R, P) Montepulciano, *Cabernet Franc, Cabernet Sauvignon, Cesanese Comune, Cesanese di Affile, Sangiovese, Syrah* (W, S) Malvasia del Lazio, *Bellone, Bombino Bianco, Greco Bianco, Trebbiano Giallo, Trebbiano Verde*

Tarquinia (R, P) Montepulciano, Sangiovese, *Cesanese Comune, OR* (W) Trebbiano Giallo, Trebbiano Toscano, *Malvasia del Lazio, Malvasia di Candia, OW*

Velletri (R) Montepulciano, Sangiovese, *Cesanese Comune, Cesanese di Affile, OR* (W) Malvasia Bianca di Candia, Malvasia Puntinata, Trebbiano Giallo, Trebbiano Toscano, Trebbiano Verde, *OW*

Vignanello (R) Ciliegiolo, Sangiovese (W) Trebbiano Giallo, Trebbiano Toscano, *Malvasia Bianca di Candia, Malvasia del Chianti, OW*

Zagarolo (W) Malvasia Bianca di Candia, Malvasia Puntinata, Trebbiano Giallo, Trebbiano Toscano, Trebbiano Verde, *Bellone, Bombino*

Liguria

Cinque Terre (and subzones) (W) Albarola, Bosco, Vermentino, *OW*

Colli di Luni (R) Sangiovese, *OR* (W) Trebbiano Toscano, Vermentino, *OW*

Colline di Levanto (R) Ciliegiolo, Sangiovese (W) Vermentino, *Albarola, Bosco*

Golfo del Tigullio-Portofino (R, P) Ciliegiolo, Dolcetto, *OR* (W, S) Bianchetta Genovese, Vermentino, *OW*

Pornassio or **Ormeasco di Pornassio** (R, P) Dolcetto (Ormeasc)

Val Polcèvera (R, P) Ciliegiolo, Dolcetto, Sangiovese, *OR* (W, S) Albarola, Bianchetta Genovese, Vermentino, *OW*

Lombardy

Botticino (R) Barbera, Marzemino, *Sangiovese, Schiava Gentile*

Buttafuoco dell'Oltrepò Pavese (R) Barbera, Croatina, Ughetta (Vespolina), Uva Rara

Capriano del Colle (R) Marzemino, Merlot, Sangiovese, *OR* (W) Trebbiano di Lugana, Trebbiano di Soave, Trebbiano Toscano, *OW*

Casteggio (R) Barbera, *Croatina, Pinot Nero, Ughetta (Vespolina), Uva Rara*

Cellatica (R) Barbera, Marzemino, *Incrocio Terzi No. 1, Schiava Gentile*

Curtefranca (R) Cabernet Franc, Cabernet Sauvignon, Carmenère, Merlot (W) Chardonnay, Pinot Bianco, Pinot Nero

Franciacorta DOCG (WS, PS) Chardonnay, Pinot Bianco, Pinot Nero, *Erbamat*

Franciacorta DOCG Satèn (WS) Chardonnay, Pinot Bianco

Garda Classico (R, P, PS) Groppello Gentile, Groppello Mocasina, Groppello S. Stefano, *Barbera, Marzemino, Sangiovese, OR* (W) Riesling, Riesling Italico, *OW*

Garda Colli Mantovani (R, P) Merlot, Rondinella, *Cabernet Sauvignon, Molinara, Negrara Trentina, Sangiovese* (W) Chardonnay, Garganega, Riesling, Riesling Italico, Sauvignon Blanc, Trebbiano di Soave, Trebbiano Giallo, Trebbiano Toscano

Lugana (W) Trebbiano di Lugana (Turbiana)

Oltrepò Pavese (R, P, PS) Barbera, Croatina, Pinot Nero, Ughetta (Vespolina), Uva Rara, *OR* (W) Riesling, Riesling Italico, Pinot Nero, *OW*

Oltrepò Pavese Metodo Classico DOCG (SW, SP) Pinot Nero, *Chardonnay, Pinot Blanco, Pinot Grigio*

Riviera del Garda Classico (R, P) Barbera, Groppello Gentile, Groppello di Mocasina, Gropello S. Stefano, Marzemino, Sangiovese (W) Riesling Italico, Riesling Renano

Riviera del Garda Classico Valtènesi (R, P) Barbera, Groppello Gentile, Groppello di Mocasina, Gropello S. Stefano, Marzemino, Sangiovese

San Colombano al Lambro (R) Barbera, Croatina, *Uva Rara* (W) Chardonnay, Pinot Nero

San Martino della Battaglia (W) Friulano, *OW*

Sangue di Giuda dell'Oltrepò Pavese (S) Barbera, Croatina, Pinot Nero, Uva Rara, Ughetta (Vespolina)

Scanzo or **Moscato di Scanzo DOCG** (R) Moscato di Scanzo

Sforzato di Valtellina or **Sfursat di Valtellina DOCG** (R) Nebbiolo (Chiavennasca)

Terre del Colleoni or **Colleoni** (S) Chardonnay, Incrocio Manzoni, Pinot Bianco, Pinot Nero, Pinot Grigio

Valcalepio (R) Cabernet Sauvignon, Merlot (W) Chardonnay, Pinot Bianco, Pinot Grigio

Valtellina Rosso DOC, Valtellina Superiore DOCG (R) Nebbiolo (Chiavennasca)

Marche

Colli Maceratesi (R) Sangiovese, *Cabernet Franc, Cabernet Sauvignon, Ciliegiolo, Lacrima, Merlot, Montepulciano, Vernaccia Nera, OR* (W, S) Maceratino, *Chardonnay, Grechetto, Incrocio Bruni 54, Malvasia Bianca Lunga, Pecorino, Sauvignon Blanc, Trebbiano Toscano, Verdicchio, OW*

Colli Pesaresi (R, P) Sangiovese, *OR* (W, S) Biancame, Chardonnay, Pinot Bianco, Pinot Grigio, Pinot Nero, Riesling Italico, Sauvignon Blanc, Trebbiano Toscano (Albanella), Verdicchio, *OW*

Colli Pesaresi Focara (R) Cabernet Franc, Cabernet Sauvignon, Merlot, Pinot Nero, *OR*

Colli Pesaresi Roncaglia (W) Chardonnay, Pinot Bianco, Pinot Grigio, Pinot Nero, Sauvignon Blanc, Trebbiano Toscano (Albanella)

Esino (R) Montepulciano, Sangiovese, *OR* (W) Verdicchio, *OW*

Falerio (W) Trebbiano Toscano, *Passerina, Pecorino, OW*

I Terreni di Sanseverino (R) Vernaccia Nera, *OR*

I Terreni di Sanseverino Moro (R) Montepulciano, *OR*

Offida DOCG (R) Montepulciano, *OR*

Pergola (R, P, S) Aleatico, *OR*

Rosso Cònero (R) Montepulciano, *OR*

Rosso Piceno or **Piceno** (R) Montepulciano, Sangiovese, *OR*

San Ginesio (R) Sangiovese, *Cabernet Franc, Cabernet Sauvignon, Ciliegiolo, Merlot, Vernaccia Nera, OR* (S) Vernaccia Nera

Serrapetrona (R) Vernaccia Nera, *OR*

Terre di Offida (W, S) Passerina, *OW*

Molise

Biferno (R, P) Montepulciano, *Aglianico, OR* (W) Trebbiano Toscano, *OW*

Molise (R, P) Montepulciano, *OR* (S) Chardonnay, Moscato, Pinot Bianco, *OW*

Pentro di Isernia or **Pentro** (R, P) Montepulciano, *Tintilia, OR* (W) Falanghina, *Trebbiano Toscano, OW*

Piemonte

Alba (R) Nebbiolo, *Barbera, OR*

Albugnano (R, P) Nebbiolo, *Freisa, Barbera, Bonarda*

Alta Langa DOCG (S) Chardonnay, Pinot Nero, *OR&W*

Asti DOCG (S) Moscato Bianco

Barbaresco DOCG (R) Nebbiolo

Barolo DOCG (R) Nebbiolo

Boca (R) Nebbiolo (Spanna), *Uva Rara (Bonarda Novarese), Vespolina*

Bramaterra (R) Nebbiolo (Spanna), *Croatina, Uva Rara (Bonarda Novarese), Vespolina*

Calosso (R) Gamba Rossa, *OR*

Canavese (R, P, PS) Barbera, Bonarda, Freisa, Nebbiolo, Neretto, Uva Rara (Bonarda di Cavaglià), *OR* (W, WS) Erbaluce

Carema (R) Nebbiolo, *OR*

Cisterna d'Asti (R, S) Croatina, *OR*

Colli Tortonesi (R, P, S) Aleatico, Barbera, Bonarda Piemontese, Cabernet Franc, Cabernet Sauvignon, Croatina, Dolcetto, Freisa, Grignolino, Lambrusca di Alessandria, Merlot, Nebbiolo, Pinot Nero, Sangiovese (W) Barbera Bianca, Chardonnay, Cortese, Favorita, Müller-Thurgau, Pinot Bianco, Pinot Grigio, Riesling Italico, Riesling Renano, Sauvignon Blanc, Sylvaner Verde, Timorasso

Colli Tortonesi Monleale (R) Barbera, *OR*

Colli Tortonesi Terre di Libarna (R) Barbera, *OR* (W, S) Timorasso, *OW*

Collina Torinese (R) Barbera, Freisa, *OR*

Colline Novaresi (R, P) Nebbiolo (Spanna), *OR* (W) Erbaluce

Colline Saluzzesi (R) Barbera, Chatus, Nebbiolo, Pelaverga, *OR*

Coste della Sesia (R, P) Nebbiolo (Spanna), *OR* (W) Erbaluce

Dogliani DOCG (R) Dolcetto

Fara (R) Nebbiolo (Spanna), *Uva Rara (Bonarda Novarese), Vespolina, OR*

Gabiano (R) Barbera, *Freisa, Grignolino*

Gattinara DOCG (R) Nebbiolo (Spanna), *Uva Rara (Bonarda di Gattinara), Vespolina*

Gavi or **Cortese di Gavi DOCG** (W) Cortese

Ghemme DOCG (R) Nebbiolo (Spanna), *Uva Rara (Bonarda di Novarese), Vespolina*

Langhe (R) any locally authorized red varieties (R passito) Barbera, Dolcetto, Nebbiolo, *OR* (W) any locally authorized white varieties (W passito) Arneis, Chardonnay, Nascetta, Riesling, *OW* (P) Barbera, Dolcetto, Nebbiolo, *OR*

Lessona (R) Nebbiolo (Spanna), *Uva Rara (Bonarda Novarese), Vespolina*

Loazzolo (W) Moscato Bianco

Monferrato (R) any locally authorized red varieties (W) any locally authorized white varieties (P) Barbera, Bonarda, Cabernet Franc, Cabernet Sauvignon, Dolcetto, Freisa, Grignolino, Nebbiolo, Pinot Nero, *OR*

Piemonte (R, P) Barbera, Croatina, Dolcetto, Freisa, Nebbiolo, *OR* with the exception of Brachetto, Malvasia Nera Lunga, Malvasia di Schierano, Malvasia di Casorzo (W) Chardonnay, Cortese, Erbaluce, Favorita, *OW* (S) Chardonnay, Cortese, Erbaluce, Favorita, Pinot Bianco, Pinot Grigio, Pinot Nero, *OW* with the exception of Moscato Bianco

Pinerolese (R, P) Barbera, Bonarda, Chatus, Nebbiolo, *OR*

Roero DOCG (R) Nebbiolo, *OR* (W, S) Arneis, *OW*

Rubino di Cantavenna (R) Barbera, *Freisa, Grignolino*

Sizzano (R) Nebbiolo (Spanna), *Uva Rara (Bonarda Novarese), Vespolina, OR*

Valli Ossolane (R) Croatina, Merlot, Nebbiolo, *OR* (W) Chardonnay, *OW*

Valsusa (R) Avanà, Barbera, Becuet, Dolcetto, Neretta, *OR*

Verduno or **Verduno Pelaverga** (R) Pelaverga Piccolo, *OR*

Puglia

Alezio (R, P) Negroamaro, *Malvasia Nera di Lecce, Montepulciano, Sangiovese*

Barletta (R, P) Uva di Troia, *OR* (W) Malvasia Bianca, *OW*

Brindisi (R, P, PS) Negroamaro, *Malvasia Nera di Brindisi, Montepulciano, Sangiovese, Susumaniello, OW* (W) Chardonnay, Malvasia Bianca, *OW*

Cacc'e Mmitte di Lucera (R) Uva di Troia (Sumarello), *Bombino Bianco, Malvasia Bianca, Malvasia Bianca Lunga, Malvasia Nera di Brindisi, Montepulciano, Sangiovese, Trebbiano Toscano*

Castel del Monte (R) Aglianico, Montepulciano, Uva di Troia, *OR* (W, SW) Bombino Bianco, Chardonnay, Pampanuto (Pampanino), *OW* (P, PS) Aglianico, Bombino Nero, Uva di Troia, *OR*

Castel del Monte Riserva DOCG (R) Nero di Troia, *OR*

Colline Joniche Tarantine (R, P) Cabernet Sauvignon, *OR* (W, S) Chardonnay, *OW*

Copertino (R, P) Negroamaro, *Malvasia Nera di Brindisi, Malvasia Nera di Lecce, Montepulciano, Sangiovese*

Galatina (R, P) Negroamaro, *OR* (W) Chardonnay, *OW*

Gioia del Colle (R, P) Montepulciano, Negroamaro, Primitivo, Sangiovese, *Malvasia Nera* (W) Trebbiano Toscano, *OW*

Gravina (P, R) Montepulciano, Primitivo, *Aglianico, Cabernet Sauvignon, Merlot, Uva di Troia* (W, S) Greco, Malvasia Bianca, Malvasia Bianca Lunga, *Bianco d'Alessano, Chardonnay, Fiano, Verdeca*

Leverano (P, R) Malvasia Nera di Lecce, Montepulciano, Negroamaro, Sangiovese, *OR* (W) Malvasia Bianca, Vermentino

Lizzano (R, P) Bombino Nero, Montepulciano, Negroamaro, Pinot Nero, Sangiovese, Malvasia Nera di Brindisi, Malvasia Nera di Lecce (W) Chardonnay, Pinot Bianco, Trebbiano Toscano, *Bianco d'Alessano, Malvasia Bianca Lunga, Sauvignon Blanc*

Locorotondo (W, S) Bianco d'Alessano, Verdeca, *OW*

Martina or **Martina Franca** (W, S) Bianco d'Alessano, Verdeca, *Bombino Bianco, Fiano, Malvasia Bianca*

Matino (R, P) Negroamaro, *Malvasia Nera, Sangiovese*

Nardò (R, P) Negroamaro, *Malvasia Nera di Brindisi, Malvasia Nera di Lecce, Montepulciano*

Orta Nova (R, P) Lambrusco Maestri, Montepulciano, Sangiovese, Trebbiano Toscano, Uva di Troia

Ostuni (W) Francavilla, Impigno, *Bianco d'Alessano, Verdeca*

Rosso di Cerignola (R) Negroamaro, Uva di Troia, *Barbera, Malbec, Montepulciano, Sangiovese, Trebbiano Toscano*

Salice Salentino (R, P, PS) Negroamaro, *OR* (W, WS) Chardonnay, *OW*

San Severo (R, P) Montepulciano, Sangiovese, *Merlot, Malvasia Nera, Uva di Troia, OR* (W, S) Bombino Bianco, Trebbiano Bianco, *OW*

Squinzano (R, P, PS) Negroamaro, *Malvasia Nera di Brindisi, Malvasia Nera di Lecce, Sangiovese, OR* (W, WS) Chardonnay, Malvasia Bianca, *OW* with the exception of *Moscato*

Tavoliere delle Puglie or **Tavoliere** (R, P) Nero di Troia, *OR*

Terra d'Otranto (R, P) Malvasia Nera, Malvasia Nera di Basilicata, Malvasia Nera di Brindisi, Malvasia Nera di Lecce, Negroamaro, Primitivo, *OR* (W, WS) Chardonnay, *OW* (PS) Negroamaro, *OR*

Sardinia

Alghero (R, P, PS) any locally authorized non-aromatic red variety (W, WS) any locally authorized non-aromatic white variety

Campidano di Terralba or **Terralba** (R) Bovale (Bovaleddu), Bovale Grande (Bovale di Spagna), *OR*

Mandrolisai (R, P) Bovale Sardo, Cannonau, Monica, *OR*

Sicily

Alcamo (R) Calabrese (Nero d'Avola), *Cabernet Sauvignon, Frappato, Merlot, Perricone, Sangiovese, Syrah* (W, WS) Catarratto Bianco, *Ansonica (Inzolia), Chardonnay, Grecanico, Grillo, Müller-Thurgau, Sauvignon Blanc, OW* (P, PS) Cabernet Sauvignon, Calabrese (Nero d'Avola), Frappato, Merlot, Nerello Mascalese, Perricone, Sangiovese, Syrah

Cerasuolo di Vittoria DOCG (R) Frappato, Nero d'Avola

Contea di Sclafani or **Valledolmo-Contea di Sclafani** (R) Nero d'Avola, Perricone (W) Catarratto

Contessa Entellina (R, P) Nero d'Avola (Calabrese), Syrah, *OR* (W) Ansonica (Inzolia), *OW*

Delia Nivolelli (R) Cabernet Sauvignon, Merlot, Nero d'Avola, Perricone, Pignatello, Sangiovese, Syrah, *OR* (W) Grecanico, Grillo, Inzolia, *OW* (S) Chardonnay, Damaschino, Grecanico, Grillo, Inzolia

Eloro (R, P) Frappato, Nero d'Avola, Pignatello

Erice (R) Calabrese (Nero d'Avola) *OR* (W) Catarratto, *OW* (S dolce) Moscato di Alessandria (Zibibbo) (S brut) Chardonnay, *OR&W*

Etna (R, P) Nerello Mascalese, *Nerello Mantellato (Nerello Cappuccio), OR* (W) Carricante, Catarratto Bianco Comune, Catarratto Bianco Lucido, *OW* (S) Nerello Mascalese, *OR*

Faro (R) Nerello Mascalese, Nerello Cappuccio, Nocera, *Calabrese (Nero d'Avola), Gaglioppo (Montonico Nero), Sangiovese*

Mamertino di Milazzo or **Mamertino** (R) Calabrese (Nero d'Avola), Nocera, *OR* (W) Catarratto, Grillo, Ansonica (Inzolia), *OW*

Marsala Oro, Marsala Ambra Ansonica (Inzolia), Catarratto, Damaschino, Grillo

Marsala Rubino Calabrese (Nero d'Avola), Nerello Mascalese, Perricone (Pignatello), *Ansonica (Inzolia), Catarratto, Damaschino, Grillo*

Menfi (R, P) Alicante, Alicante Bouschet, Cabernet Sauvignon, Merlot, Nerello Mascalese, Nero d'Avola, Perricone, Syrah, *OR* (W) Catarratto, Chardonnay, Grecanico, Grillo, Inzolia, *OW* (WS) Catarratto, Chardonnay, Grecanico, Grillo, Inzolia, *OR&W* (PS) Frappato, Nerello Mascalese, Nero d'Avola, Pinot Nero, *OR*

Monreale (R) Calabrese (Nero d'Avola), Perricone, *OR* (W) Catarratto, Ansonica (Inzolia), *Trebbiano Toscano, OW* (P) Nerello Mascalese, Perricone, Sangiovese, *OR*

Noto (R) Nero d'Avola, *OR*

Pantelleria (W, S) Zibibbo (Moscato di Alessandria), *OW*

Riesi (R) Cabernet Sauvignon, Calabrese (Nero d'Avola), *OR* (W, S) Chardonnay, Ansonica (Inzolia), *OW* (P) Cabernet Sauvignon, Calabrese (Nero d'Avola), Nerello Mascalese, *OR&W*

Riesi Superiore (R) Calabrese (Nero d'Avola), *OR*

Salaparuta (R) Nero d'Avola, *OR* (W) Catarratto, *OW* with the exception of Trebbiano Toscano

Sambuca di Sicilia (R, P) Nero d'Avola (Calabrese), *OR* (W) Ansonica (Inzolia), *OW* (W passito) Ansonica (Inzolia), Grillo, Sauvignon Blanc

Santa Margherita di Belice (R) Cabernet Sauvignon, Nero d'Avola, Sangiovese, *OR* (W) Ansonica, Catarratto Bianco Lucido, Grecanico, *OW*

Sciacca (R) Cabernet Sauvignon, Merlot, Nero d'Avola, Sangiovese, *OR* (W) Catarratto Bianco Lucido, Chardonnay, Grecanico, Inzolia, *OW* (P) the varieties specified for red and white

Sicilia (R, P) Frappato, Nerello Mascalese, Nero d'Avola, Perricone, *OR* (W) Catarratto, Grecanico, Grillo, Inzolia, *OW* (WS) Carricante, Catarratto, Chardonnay, Grecanico, Grillo, Inzolia, Moscato Bianco, Pinot Nero, Zibibbo, *OW* (PS) Frappato, Nerello Mascalese, Nero d'Avola, Pinot Nero, *OR*

Siracusa (R) Nero d'Avola, *OR* (W) Moscato Bianco (Moscato Giallo), *OW*

Vittoria (R) Calabrese (Nero d'Avola), Frappato

Tuscany

Barco Reale di Carmignano (R, P) Sangiovese, *Cabernet Franc, Cabernet Sauvignon, Canaiolo Nero, Canaiolo Bianco, Malvasia, Trebbiano Toscano*

Bianco dell'Empolese (W) Trebbiano Toscano, *OW*

Bianco di Pitigliano (W, S) Trebbiano Toscano, *Ansonica, Chardonnay, Grechetto, Greco, Malvasia Bianca Lunga, Pinot Bianco, Riesling Italico, Sauvignon Blanc, Verdello, OW*

Bolgheri (R, P) Cabernet Franc, Cabernet Sauvignon, Merlot, *Sangiovese, Syrah, OR* (W) Sauvignon Blanc, Trebbiano Toscano, Vermentino, *OW*

Bolgheri Sassicaia (R) Cabernet Sauvignon, *OR*

Brunello di Montalcino DOCG (R) Sangiovese

Candia dei Colli Apuani (R, P) Sangiovese, *Merlot, OR* (W, S) Vermentino, *OW*

Capalbio (R, P) Sangiovese, *OR* with the exception of Aleatico (W) Trebbiano Toscano, *OW* with the exception of Moscato Bianco

Carmignano DOCG (R) Sangiovese, *Cabernet Franc, Cabernet Sauvignon, Canaiolo Bianco, Canaiolo Nero, Malvasia del Chianti, Trebbiano Toscano*

Chianti DOCG (R) Sangiovese, *OR&W* (*OW* not allowed in **Chianti Colli Sensesi**)

Chianti Classico (R) Sangiovese, *OR*

Colli dell'Etruria Centrale (R, P) Sangiovese, *OR&W* (W) Trebbiano Toscano, *OR&W*

Colline Lucchesi (R) Canaiolo, Ciliegiolo, Merlot, Sangiovese, Syrah, *OR* (W) Chardonnay, Grechetto, Greco, Malvasia, Sauvignon Blanc, Trebbiano Toscano, Vermentino, *OW*

Cortona (R) Syrah, *Merlot, OR*

Cortona Vinsanto (W) Grechetto, Malvasia Bianca, Trebbiano Toscano, *Sangiovese*

Cortona Vinsanto Occhio di Pernice (R) Malvasia Nera, Sangiovese

Elba (R) Sangiovese, *OR* (W, S) Ansonica, Trebbiano Toscano, Vermentino, *OW* (P) Sangiovese, *OR&W*

Grance Senesi (R) Sangiovese, *OR* (W) Malvasia Bianca Lunga, Trebbiano, *OW*

Maremma Toscana (R, P, PS) Cabernet Sauvignon, Cabernet Franc, Merlot, Sangiovese, Syrah, Ciliegiolo, *OR* (W, WS) Trebbiano Toscano, Vermentino, Vigonier, *OW*

Montecarlo (R) Sangiovese, *Cabernet Franc, Cabernet Sauvignon, Canaiolo Nero, Ciliegiolo, Colorino, Malvasia Nera di Lecce, Merlot, Syrah, OR* (W) Pinot Grigio, Pinot Bianco, Roussanne, Sauvignon Blanc, Sémillon, Trebbiano Toscano, Vermentino, *OW* with the exception of Moscato Bianco, Traminer Aromatico

Montecucco (R) Sangiovese, *OR* with the exception of Aleatico, Malvasia Nera, Malvasia Nera di Brindisi (P) Ciliegiolo, Sangiovese, *OR* with the exception of Aleatico, Malvasia Nera, Malvasia Nera di Brindisi (W) Trebbiano Toscano, Vermentino, *OW*

Monteregio di Massa Marittima (R, P) Sangiovese, *OR* with the exception of Aleatico (W) Trebbiano Toscano, Vermentino, *OW* with the exception of Moscato

Montescudaio (R) Sangiovese, *OR* (W) Trebbiano Toscano, *OW*

Morellino di Scansano DOCG (R) Sangiovese (Morellino), *OR*

Orcia (R, P) Sangiovese, *OR&W* (W) Trebbiano Toscano, *OW*

Parrina (R, P) Sangiovese, *OR* with the exception of Aleatico (W) Ansonica, Chardonnay, Sauvignon Blanc, Trebbiano Toscano, Vermentino

Pomino (R) Merlot, Pinot Nero, Sangiovese, *OR* (W) Chardonnay, Pinot Bianco, Pinot Grigio, *OW* (S) Chardonnay, Pinot Bianco, Pinot Nero, *OW* (vinsanto) Chardonnay, Pinot Bianco, Pinot Grigio, Trebbiano Toscano, *OW*

Rosso della Val di Cornia or **Val di Cornia Rosso DOCG** (R) Cabernet Sauvignon, Merlot, Sangiovese, *OR* with the exception of Aleatico

Rosso di Montalcino (R) Sangiovese

Rosso di Montepulciano (R) Sangiovese, *OR*

San Gimignano (R, P) Sangiovese, *Cabernet Sauvignon*, *Merlot*, *Pinot Nero*, *Syrah*, *OR*

Sant'Antimo (R) any locally authorized red varieties (W) any locally authorized white varieties

San Torpè (W) Trebbiano Toscano, *OW* (P) Sangiovese, *OR* with the exception of Aleatico

Sovana (R, P) Sangiovese, *OR*

Suvereto DOCG (R) Cabernet Sauvignon, Merlot, *OR*

Terratico di Bibbona (R, P) Merlot, Sangiovese, *OR* (W) Vermentino, *OW*

Terre di Casole (R) Sangiovese, *OR* (W) Chardonnay, *OW*

Terre di Pisa (R) Cabernet Sauvignon, Merlot, Sangiovese, Syrah, *OR*

Val d'Arbia (W) Trebbiano Toscano, Malvasia Bianca Lunga, *OW* (P) Sangiovese, *OR&W*

Val d'Arno di Sopra or **Valdarno di Sopra** (P, PS) Merlot, *Cabernet Sauvignon*, *Syrah*, *OR* (W, WS) Chardonnay, *Malvasia Bianca Lunga*, *Trebbiano Toscano*, *OW* (passito) Malvasia Bianca Lunga, *Chardonnay*, *OW*

Val d'Arno di Sopra Pietraviva, Val d'Arno di Sopra Pratomagno (R) Sangiovese, *Cabernet Sauvignon*, *Merlot*, *OR* (W) Sauvignon Blanc, *Chardonnay*, *OW*

Valdichiana Toscana (R, P) Cabernet Franc, Cabernet Sauvignon, Merlot, Sangiovese, Syrah, *OR* (W, S) Chardonnay, Grechetto, Pinot Bianco, Pinot Grigio, Trebbiano Toscano, *OW*

Val di Cornia (R, P) Cabernet Sauvignon, Merlot, Sangiovese, *OR* (W) Ansonica, Malvasia Bianca Lunga, Trebbiano, Vermentino, Viognier, *OW*

Valdinievole (R) Canaiolo Nero, Sangiovese, *OR&W* (W) Trebbiano Toscano, *OW*

Vino Nobile di Montepulciano DOCG (R) Sangiovese (Prugnolo Gentile), *OR&W*

Vin Santo del Chianti, Vin Santo del Chianti Classico, Vin Santo di Carmignano (W) Malvasia Bianca Lunga, Trebbiano Toscano, *OR&W*

Vin Santo del Chianti Occhio di Pernice, Vin Santo del Chianti Classico Occhio di Pernice, Vin Santo di Carmignano Occhio di Pernice (P) Sangiovese, *OR*

Vin Santo di Montepulciano (W) Grechetto Bianco (Pulcinculo), Malvasia Bianca, Trebbiano Toscano, *OW*

Vin Santo di Montepulciano Occhio di Pernice (P) Sangiovese (Prugnolo Gentile), *OR&W*

Trentino-Alto Adige

Alto Adige (Südtirol) (W) Chardonnay, Pinot Bianco, Pinot Grigio, *Kerner*, *Müller-Thurgau*, *Riesling*, *Sauvignon Blanc*, *Sylvaner*, *Traminer Aromatico* (S) Chardonnay, Pinot Bianco, Pinot Nero

Alto Adige Colli di Bolzano (Südtirol Bozner Leiten), Alto Adige Meranese (Südtirol Meraner Hügel), Alto Adige Santa Maddalena (Südtirol St Magdalener) (R) Schiava Gentile, Schiava Grigia, Schiava Grossa, *OR*

Alto Adige Terlano (Südtirol Terlaner) (W) Chardonnay, Pinot Bianco, Müller-Thurgau, Pinot Grigio, Riesling, Riesling Italico, Sauvignon Blanc, Sylvaner, *OW*

Alto Adige Valle Isarco (Südtirol Eisacktal) Klausner Laitacher (R) Lagrein, Pinot Nero, Portoghese, Schiava

Caldaro or **Lago di Caldaro** (R) Schiava Gentile, Schiava Grigia, Schiava Grossa, *OR*

Casteller (R) Lagrein, Lambrusco a Foglia Frastagliata (Enantio), Merlot, Schiava Gentile, Schiava Grossa, Teroldego

Trentino (R) Cabernet Franc, Cabernet Sauvignon, Carmenère, Merlot (W) Chardonnay, Pinot Bianco, *Manzoni Bianco*, *Müller-Thurgau*, *Sauvignon Blanc* (P) Enantio, Lagrein, Schiava, Teroldego

Trentino Sorni (R) Lagrein, Schiava Gentile, Schiava Grigia, Schiava Grossa, Teroldego (W) Chardonnay, Müller-Thurgau, Nosiola, Pinot Bianco, Pinot Grigio, Sylvaner Verde

Trentino Castel Beseno Superiore (W) Moscato Giallo, *OR*

Trento (S) Chardonnay, Pinot Bianco, Pinot Meunier, Pinot Nero

Valdadige or **Etschtaler** (R, P) Enantio (Lambrusco a Foglia Frastagliata), Schiava Gentile, Schiava Grigia, Schiava Grossa, *Cabernet Franc*, *Cabernet Sauvignon*, *Lagrein*, *Merlot*, *Pinot Nero*, *Teroldego* (W) Chardonnay, Garganega, Müller-Thurgau, Nosiola, Pinot Bianco, Pinot Grigio, Riesling Italico, Sauvignon Blanc, Trebbiano Toscano

Umbria

Amelia (R, P) Sangiovese, *OR* (W) Trebbiano Toscano, *OW*

Assisi (R, P) Merlot, Sangiovese (W) Trebbiano, *Grechetto*, *OW*

Colli Altotiberini (R, P) Sangiovese, *OR* (W) Trebbiano Toscano, *OW* (S) Chardonnay, Grechetto, Pinot Bianco, Pinot Grigio, Pinot Nero, *OW*

Colli del Trasimeno (R, P) Cabernet Sauvignon, Ciliegiolo, Gamay, Merlot, Sangiovese (W) Chardonnay, Grechetto, Pinot Bianco, Pinot Grigio, Trebbiano Toscano, *OW* (WS) Chardonnay, Grechetto, Pinot Bianco, Pinot Grigio, Pinot Nero, *OW* (PS) Pinot Nero, *Chardonnay*, *Pinot Bianco*

Colli Martani (R) Sangiovese, *OR* (W) Trebbiano Toscano, *OW* (S) Chardonnay, Grechetto, Pinot Nero, *OW*

Colli Perugini (R, P) Sangiovese, *OR* (W) Trebbiano Toscano, *OW* (S) Chardonnay, Grechetto, Pinot Bianco, Pinot Grigio, Pinot Nero, *OW*

Lago di Corbara (R) Cabernet Sauvignon, Merlot, Pinot Nero, Sangiovese, *OR* (W) Grechetto, Sauvignon Blanc, *OW*

Montefalco (W) Trebbiano Spoletino, *OW* (R) Sangiovese, *Sagrantino*, *OR*

Orvieto (W) Grechetto, Trebbiano Toscano (Procanico), *OW*

Rosso Orvietano (R) Aleatico, Cabernet Franc, Cabernet Sauvignon, Canaiolo, Ciliegiolo, Merlot, Montepulciano, Pinot Nero, Sangiovese, *OR*

Spoleto (W, S) Trebbiano Spoletino, *OW*

Todi (R) Sangiovese, *OR* (W) Grechetto, *OW*

Torgiano (W) Trebbiano Toscano, *OW* (R, P) Sangiovese, *OR* (WS) Chardonnay, Grechetto, Pinot Grigio, Pinot Nero, Vermentino, *OW* (PS) Sangiovese, *OR&W*

Torgiano Rosso Riserva DOCG (R) Sangiovese, *OR*

Valle d'Aosta

Valle d'Aosta or **Vallée d'Aoste** (R, P) any locally authorized red varieties (W) any locally authorized white varieties

Valle d'Aosta Arnad-Montjovet, Valle d'Aosta Donnas (R) Nebbiolo, *OR*

Valle d'Aosta Blanc de Morgex et de La Salle (W) Prié Blanc

Valle d'Aosta Chambave, Valle d'Aosta Enfer d'Arvier, Valle d'Aosta Torrette (R) Petit Rouge, *OR*

Valle d'Aosta Nus (R) Petit Rouge, Vien de Nus, *OR*

Veneto

Amarone della Valpolicella DOCG (R) Corvina Veronese (Cruina), Corvinone, *Rondinella, OR*

Arcole (R, P) Merlot, *OR* (W, S) Garganega, *OW*

Asolo Montello or **Montello Asolo** (R) Cabernet Franc, Cabernet Sauvignon, Carmenère, Merlot, *OR* (W) Bianchetta, Chardonnay, Glera, Manzoni Bianco, Pinot Bianco, *OW*

Asolo Prosecco DOCG (W) Glera, *Bianchetta Trevigiana, Perera, Verdiso* (S) Glera, *Bianchetta Trevigiana, Glera Lunga, Perera, Verdiso*; plus *Chardonnay, Pinot Bianco, Pinot Grigio, Pinot Nero* with some restrictions

Bagnoli Friularo or **Friularo di Bagnoli DOCG** (R) Raboso Piave, *OR*

Bagnoli di Sopra or **Bagnoli** (R) Cabernet Franc, Cabernet Sauvignon, Carmenère, Merlot, *Raboso Piave, Raboso Veronese* (P) Merlot, Raboso Piave, Raboso Veronese, *OR* (W) Chardonnay, Friulano, Sauvignon Blanc, *Raboso Piave, Raboso Veronese, OW* (S) Raboso Piave, *OR&W*

Bardolino DOC, Bardolino Superiore DOCG (R) Corvina Veronese (Cruina), Rondinella, *Corvinone, Molinara, OR*

Bianco di Custoza or **Custoza** (W, S) Bianca Fernanda (Cortese), Friulano, Garganega, Trebbiano Toscano, *Chardonnay, Incrocio Manzoni 6.013, Malvasia, Pinot Bianco, Riesling Italico, Riesling Renano*

Breganze (R) Merlot, *Cabernet Franc, Cabernet Sauvignon, Carmenère, Marzemino, Pinot Nero* (W) Tai, *Chardonnay, Pinot Bianco, Pinot Grigio, Sauvignon Blanc, Vespaiolo*

Breganze Torcolato (W passito) Vespaiola

Colli Berici (R) Merlot, Tai Rosso, *Cabernet Franc, Cabernet Sauvignon, Carmenère, Pinot Nero, OR* (W, S) Garganega, Sauvignon Blanc, *OW* (S metodo classico) Chardonnay, Pinot Bianco, Pinot Nero

Colli Berici Barbarano (R, S) Tai Rosso

Colli di Conegliano DOCG (R) Cabernet Franc, Cabernet Sauvignon, Marzemino, Merlot, *Incrocio Manzoni 2.15, Refosco dal Peduncolo Rosso* (W) Chardonnay, Manzoni Bianco (Incrocio Manzoni 6.0.13), Pinot Bianco, *Riesling Renano, Sauvignon Blanc*

Colli di Conegliano Refrontolo (R) Marzemino

Colli di Conegliano Torchiato di Fregona (W) Boschera, Glera, Verdiso, *OW*

Colli Euganei (R) Cabernet Franc, Cabernet Sauvignon, Carmenère, Merlot, *Raboso Piave, Raboso Veronese* (W, S) Garganega, Sauvignon Blanc, Tai, *Moscato Bianco, Moscato Giallo, OW*

Colli Euganei Fior d'Arancio or **Fior d'Arancio DOCG** (W, S) Moscato Giallo

Conegliano Valdobbiadene Prosecco DOCG (W, S) Glera, *Bianchetta Trevigiana, Glera Lunga, Perera, Verdiso* (S) Glera, *Bianchetta Trevigiana, Chardonnay, Perera, Pinot Bianco, Pinot Grigio, Pinot Nero, Verdiso*

Corti Benedettine del Padovana (R, P) Merlot, *Cabernet Franc, Cabernet Sauvignon, Carmenère, Raboso Piave, Raboso Veronese, Refosco* (W) Chardonnay, Friulano, Pinot Bianco, Pinot Grigio, Sauvignon Blanc

Delle Venezie (W) Chardonnay, Garganega, Müller-Thurgau, Pinot Bianco, Friulano, Verduzzo Friulano, Verduzzo Trevigiano, *OW*

Gambellara (W, S) Garganega, *Chardonnay, Pinot Bianco, Trebbiano di Soave*

Garda Classico (R, P, PS) Groppello Gentile, Groppello Mocasina, Groppello S. Stefano, *Barbera, Marzemino, Sangiovese, OR* (W) Riesling, Riesling Italico, *OW*

Lessini Durello or **Durello Lessini** (S) Durella, *Chardonnay, Garganega, Pinot Bianco, Pinot Nero*

Lison DOCG (W) Tai, *OW*

Lison-Pramaggiore (R) Merlot, *Cabernet Franc, Cabernet Sauvignon, Carmenère, Malbec, Refosco dal Peduncolo Rosso* (W) Tai (Friulano), *Chardonnay, Pinot Grigio, Sauvignon Blanc, Verduzzo Friulano, Verduzzo Trevigiano* (S) Chardonnay, Pinot Bianco, Pinot Nero

Merlara (R) Merlot, *Cabernet Franc, Cabernet Sauvignon, Carmenère, Marzemino, Raboso, Refosco dal Peduncolo Rosso* (W) Tai (Friulano), *Chardonnay, Malvasia, Pinot Bianco, Pinot Grigio, Riesling, Riesling Italico*

Montello or **Montello Rosso DOCG** (R) Cabernet Franc, Cabernet Sauvignon, Carmenère, Merlot, *OR*

Monti Lessini (W) Chardonnay, *Durella, Garganega, Pinot Bianco, Pinot Grigio, Pinot Nero, Sauvignon Blanc*

Piave (R) Merlot, *Cabernet Franc, Cabernet Sauvignon, Carmenère, Raboso*

Piave Malanotte or **Malanotte del Piave DOCG** (R) Raboso Piave, *Raboso Veronese, OR*

Prosecco (W, WS) Glera, *Bianchetta Trevigiana, Chardonnay, Glera Lunga, Perera, Pinot Bianco, Pinot Grigio, Pinot Nero, Verdiso* (PS) Glera, *Pinot Nero*

Recioto della Valpolicella DOCG (R, S) Corvina Veronese (Cruina), Corvinone, Rondinella, *OR*

Recioto di Gambellara DOCG (W, S) Garganega

Recioto di Soave DOCG (W, S) Garganega, Trebbiano di Soave, *OW*

Riviera del Brenta (R, P) Cabernet Franc, Cabernet Sauvignon, Carmenère, Merlot, Raboso Piave, Raboso Veronese, Refosco (W) Chardonnay, Friulano, Pinot Bianco, Pinot Grigio (S) Chardonnay, *Friulano, Pinot Bianco, Pinot Grigio*

Soave DOC, Soave Superiore DOCG (W) Garganega, *Chardonnay, Trebbiano di Soave*

Valpolicella, Valpolicella Ripasso, Valpolicella Valpantena (R) Corvina Veronese (Cruina), Corvinone, Rondinella, *OR*

Venezia (R) Merlot, *OR* (W, WS) Glera, Friulano, Verduzzo Friulano, Verduzzo Trevigiano, *Pinot Nero, OW* with the exception of Moscato (P, PS) Raboso Piave, Raboso Veronese, *OR*

Vicenza (R, P) Merlot, *OR* (W, S) Garganega, *OW*

Vigneti della Serenissima or **Serenissima** (WS, PS) Chardonnay, Pinot Bianco, Pinot Nero

PORTUGAL

Alenquer (R) Aragonez (Tinta Roriz), Castelão, Tinta Miúda, Touriga Nacional, Trincadeira (Tinta Amarela), *Alicante Bouschet, Amostrinha, Baga, Cabernet Sauvignon, Caladoc* (max 15%), *Camarate, Jaen, Preto Martinho, Syrah, Tinta Barroca, Touriga Franca* (W) Arinto (Pedernã), Fernão Pires (Maria Gomes), Rabo de Ovelha, Seara Nova, Vital, *Alicante Branco, Alvarinho, Chardonnay, Jampal, Malvasia Rei, Ratinho, Sauvignon Blanc, Viosinho*

Alentejo, including the subregions of **Portalegre**, **Borba**, **Redondo**, **Évora**, **Reguengos**, **Moura**, **Granja-Amareleja**, and **Vidigueira** (R, P) Alfrocheiro (Tinta Bastardinha), Alicante Bouschet, Aragonez (Tinta Roriz, Tempranillo), Cabernet Sauvignon, Castelão, Grand Noir, Moreto, Syrah (Shiraz), Tinta Caiada (Pau Ferro, Tinta Lameira), Tinta Grossa (Carrega Tinto), Touriga Nacional, Trincadeira (Tinta

Amarela, Trincadeira Preta), *Baga, Caladoc, Carignan, Cinsault, Corropio, Durif (Petite Syrah), Grenache, Manteúdo Preto, Merlot, Nero d'Avola, Petit Verdot, Pinot Noir, Sangiovese, Tannat, Tinta Barroca, Tinta Carvalha, Tinta Miúda, Tinto Cão, Touriga Franca, Zinfandel, Gewürztraminer, Pinot Gris (Pinot Grigio)* (W) Antão Vaz, Arinto (Pedernã), Fernão Pires (Maria Gomes), Manteúdo, Perrum, Rabo de Ovelha, Síria (Roupeiro, Códega), Tamarez (Molinha), Trincadeira das Pratas, *Alicante Branco, Alvarinho, Bical (Borrado das Moscas), Chardonnay, Chasselas, Diagalves, Encruzado, Gouveio, Larião, Malvasia Fina, Malvasia Rei, Marsanne, Moscatel Graúdo, Mourisco Branco, Petit Manseng, Riesling, Roussanne, Sauvignon Blanc, Sémillon, Sercial (Esgana Cão), Tália (Ugni Blanc, Trebbiano Toscano), Verdelho, Vermentino, Viognier, Viosinho*

Arruda (R) Aragonez (Tinta Roriz), Castelão, Tinta Miúda, Touriga Nacional, Trincadeira (Tinta Amarela), *Caladoc* (max 15%), *Alicante Bouschet, Cabernet Sauvignon, Camarate, Jaen, Syrah, Tinta Barroca, Touriga Franca* (W) Arinto (Pedernã), Fernão Pires (Maria Gomes), Rabo de Ovelha, Seara Nova, Vital, *Alicante Branco, Chardonnay, Jampal, Malvasia Rei, Sauvignon Blanc, Viosinho*

Bairrada (R, P) Alfrocheiro (Tinta Bastardinha), Aragonez (Tinta Roriz, Tempranillo), Baga (min 50% of this last), Bastardo, Cabernet Sauvignon, Camarate, Castelão, Jaen (Mencia), Merlot, Petit Verdot, Pinot Noir, Rufete (Tinta Pinheira), Syrah (Shiraz), Tinta Barroca, Tinto Cão, Touriga Franca, Touriga Nacional (W) Arinto (Pedernã), Bical (Borrado das Moscas), Cercial (Cercial da Bairrada), Chardonnay, Fernão Pires (Maria Gomes), Pinot Blanc, Rabo de Ovelha, Sauvignon Blanc, Sercialinho, Verdelho, Viognier

Beira Interior (R, P) Alfrocheiro (Tinta Bastardinha), Alicante Bouschet, Aragonez (Tinta Roriz, Tempranillo), Baga, Bastardo (Graciosa), Cabernet Sauvignon, Caladoc, Camarate, Castelão, Grand Noir, Jaen (Mencia), Marufo (Mourisco Roxo), Merlot, Mourisco, Nebbiolo, Petit Bouschet, Petit Verdot, Pinot Noir, Rufete (Tinta Pinheira), Sangiovese, Syrah (Shiraz), Tinta Barroca, Tinta Carvalha, Tinta Francisca, Tinta Negra (Molar, Saborinho), Tinto Cão, Touriga Franca, Touriga Nacional, Trincadeira (Tinta Amarela, Trincadeira Preta), Vinhão (Sousão) (W) Alicante Branco, Alvarinho, Arinto (Pedernã), Arinto do Interior, Azal, Batoca (Alvaraça), Bical (Borrado das Moscas), Cercial, Chardonnay, Chasselas, Códega do Larinho, Encruzado, Fernão Pires (Maria Gomes), Folgasão, Folha de Figueira (Dona Branca), Fonte Cal, Gouveio, Malvasia Fina, Malvasia Rei, Moscatel Galego Branco (Muscat à Petits Grains), Rabigato, Rabo de Ovelha, Riesling, Sauvignon Blanc, Sémillon, Síria (Roupeiro, Códega), Tamarez (Molinha), Verdejo, Verdelho, Viognier, Viosinho

Biscoitos (W) Terrantez da Terceira, Terrantez do Pico, *Arinto (Pedernã), Chardonnay, Fernão Pires (Maria Gomes), Galego Dourado, Generosa, Gouveio, Malvasia, Malvasia Fina (Boal), Branco, Moscatel Galego, Moscatel Graúdo, Rio Grande, Seara Nova, Sercial (Esgana Cão), Viosinho*

Bucelas (W) Arinto (Pedernã), *Sercial (Esgana Cão), Rabo de Ovelha*

Carcavelos (R) Castelão, Preto Martinho (W) Galego Dourado, Ratinho, Arinto (Pedernã)

Colares (R) Ramisco (W) Malvasia

Dão (R, P) Alfrocheiro (Tinta Bastardinha), Alicante Bouschet, Alvarelhão (Brancelho), Aragonez (Tinta Roriz, Tempranillo), Baga, Bastardo (Graciosa), Camarate, Castelão, Cornifesto, Jaen (Mencia), Monvedro, Moreto, Mourisco, Pilongo, Rufete (Tinta Pinheira), Tinta Carvalha, Tinto Cão, Touriga Fêmea, Touriga Nacional, Trincadeira (Tinta Amarela, Trincadeira Preta) (W) Alicante Branco, Arinto (Pedernã), Arinto do Interior, Barcelo, Bical (Borrado das Moscas), Branda, Cerceal Branco, Douradinha, Encruzado, Fernão Pires (Maria Gomes), Gouveio, Luzidio, Malvasia Fina, Malvasia Rei, Moscatel Galego Branco (Muscat Blanc à Petits Grains), Rabo de Ovelha, Sémillon, Síria (Roupeiro, Códega), Tamarez (Molinha), Terrantez, Uva Cão, Verdelho, Verdial Branco

Douro (R, P) Alfrocheiro (Tinta Bastardinha), Alicante Bouschet, Alvarelhão (Brancelho), Alvarelhão Ceitão, Aramon, Baga, Barreto, Bastardo, Carignan, Casculho, Castelã, Castelão, Cidadelhe, Cinsault, Concieira, Cornifesto, Donzelinho Tinto, Engomada, Espadeiro, Goncalo Pires, Grand Noir, Grangeal, Jaen (Mencia), Lourela, Malandra, Malvasia Preta, Marufo, Melra, Mondet, Moreto, Mourisco de Semente, Nevoeira, Patorra, Petit Bouschet, Português Azul (Blauer Portugieser), Preto Martinho, Roseira, Rufete (Tinta Pinheira), Santareno, Sevilhão, Sousão (Vinhão), Tinta Aguiar, Tinta Amarela (Trincadeira, Trincadeira Preta), Tinta Barroca, Tinta Caiada (Pau Ferro, Tinta Lameira), Tinta Carvalha, Tinta da Barca, Tinta Fontes, Tinta Francisca, Tinta Grossa (Carrega Tinto), Tinta Martins, Tinta Mesquita, Tinta Penajoia, Tinta Pereira, Tinta Pomar, Tinta Roriz (Aragonez, Tempranillo), Tinta Tabuaço, Tinto Cão, Tinto Sem Nome, Touriga Fêmea, Touriga Franca, Touriga Nacional, Valdosa, Varejoa (W) Arinto (Pedernã), Arinto do Douro (Dorinto), Avesso, Batoca (Alvaraça), Bical (Borrado das Moscas), Branco Especial, Branco Gouvães (Alvarelhão Branco), Branco Guimarães, Branco Valente, Caramela, Carrega Branco, Cercial, Chasselas, Códega (Roupeiro, Síria), Códega do Larinho, Diagalves, Donzelinho Branco, Estreito Macio, Fernão Pires (Maria Gomes), Folgasão, Dona Branca (Folha de Figueira), Gouveio, Gouveio Estimado, Gouveio Real, Jampal, Malvasia Fina, Malvasia Parda (Farinheira), Malvasia Rei, Moscadet, Moscatel Galego Branco, Mourisco Branco, Pé Comprido, Praça, Rabigato, Rabigato Moreno, Rabo de Ovelha, Ratinho, Samarrinho (Budelho), Sarigo, Sémillon, Sercial (Esgana Cão), Tamarez (Molinha), Verdelho, Verdial Branco, Viosinho, Vital (Malvasia Corada)

Encostas d'Aire, Encostas d'Aire Alcobaça (R, P) Alfrocheiro, Alicante Bouschet, Amostrinha, Aragonez (Tinta Roriz), Baga, Bastardo, Castelão, Rufete, Tinta Miúda, Touriga Franca, Touriga Nacional, Trincadeira (Tinta Amarela), *Cabernet Sauvignon, Caladoc, Grand Noir, Syrah* (W) Alicante Branco, Arinto (Pedernã), Bical (Borrado das Moscas), Boal Branco, Cercial, Diagalves, Fernão Pires (Maria Gomes), Jampal, Malvasia Fina, Rabo de Ovelha, Ratinho, Seara Nova, Tamarez, Trincadeira Branca, Vital, *Chardonnay*

Encostas d'Aire Ourém (R) Trincadeira (Tinta Amarela), (W) Fernão Pires (Maria Gomes)

Graciosa (W) Terrantez da Terceira, Terrantez do Pico, *Arinto (Pedernã), Chardonnay, Fernão Pires (Maria Gomes), Galego Dourado, Generosa, Gouveio, Malvasia, Malvasia Fina (Boal), Branco, Moscatel Galego, Moscatel Graúdo, Rio Grande, Seara Nova, Sercial (Esgana Cão), Viosinho*

Lafões (R) Amaral, Jaen, Pilongo (W) Arinto (Pedernã), Cercial, *Dona Branca, Sercial (Esgana Cão), Rabo de Ovelha*

Lagoa (R) Negra Mole, Trincadeira (Tinta Amarela), *Alicante Bouschet, Aragonez (Tinta Roriz), Cabernet Sauvignon, Castelão, Monvedro, Moreto, Syrah, Touriga Franca, Touriga Nacional* (W) Arinto (Pedernã), Síria (Roupeiro), *Manteúdo, Moscatel Graúdo, Perrum, Rabo de Ovelha, Sauvignon Blanc*

Lagos (R) Castelão, Negra Mole, Trincadeira (Tinta Amarela), *Alicante Bouschet, Aragonez (Tinta Roriz), Bastardo, Cabernet Sauvignon, Monvedro, Touriga Nacional* (W) Arinto (Pedernã), Malvasia Fina, Síria (Roupeiro), *Manteúdo, Moscatel Graúdo, Perrum*

Lourinhã (R) Cabinda (W) Alicante Branco, Alvadurão, Boal Espinho, Malvasia Rei, Marquinhas, Tália

Madeira (R) Bastardo (Graciosa), Listrão, Malvasia Cândida-Roxa, Tinta, Tinta Negra (Molar, Saborinho), Verdelho Tinto, *Complexa*, *Deliciosa*, *Triunfo* (W) Folgasão (Terrantez), Malvasia Cândida, Malvasia de São Jorge (Malvasia, Malvazia), Malvasia Fina (Boal, Bual), Moscatel Graúdo, Sercial (Esgana-Cão), *Verdelho*, *Caracol*, *Rio Grande*, *Valveirinho*

Madeirense (R, P) Aragonez (Tinta Roriz, Tempranillo), Bastardo, Cabernet Sauvignon, Complexa, Deliciosa, Listrão, Malvasia Cândida Roxa, Merlot, Pinot Noir, Syrah (Shiraz), Tinta Barroca, Tinta Negra (Molar, Saborinho), Touriga Franca, Touriga Nacional, Triunfo (W) Alvarinho Lilás, Arinto (Pedernã), Arnsburger, Caracol, Chardonnay, Chenin Blanc, Folgasão, Malvasia Bianca, Malvasia Cândida, Malvasia de São Jorge, Malvasia Fina, Malvasia Rei, Moscatel Graúdo, Rio Grande, Sauvignon Blanc, Sercial (Esgana Cão), Tália (Ugni Blanc, Trebbiano Toscano), Verdelho

Óbidos (R) Alicante Bouschet, Amostrinha, Aragonez (Tinta Roriz), Baga, Cabernet Sauvignon, Caladoc, Camarate, Carignan, Castelão, Jaen, Merlot, Pinot Noir, Preto Martinho, Syrah, Tinta Barroca, Tinta Miúda, Touriga Franca, Touriga Nacional, Trincadeira (Tinta Amarela) (W) Alicante Branco, Alvarinho, Antão Vaz, Arinto (Pedernã), Chardonnay, Encruzado, Fernão Pires (Maria Gomes), Jampal, Loureiro, Malvasia Rei, Moscatel Graúdo, Rabo de Ovelha, Ratinho, Riesling, Sauvignon, Seara Nova, Verdelho, Viognier, Viosinho, Vital

Palmela (R, P) Alicante Bouschet, Aragonez (Tinta Roriz), Bastardo, Cabernet Sauvignon, Castelão (Periquita), Merlot, Petit Verdot, Syrah, Tannat, Tinta Miúda, Tinto Cão, Touriga Franca, Touriga Nacional, Trincadeira (Tinta Amarela), Moscatel Galego Roxo (Moscatel Roxo) (W) Alvarinho, Antão Vaz, Arinto (Pedernã) Chardonnay, Fernão Pires (Maria Gomes), Loureiro, Malvasia Fina, Moscatel Galego Branco, Moscatel Graúdo (Moscatel de Setúbal), Pinot Blanc, Rabo de Ovelha, Roupeiro Branco, Sauvignon, Sémillon, Verdelho, Viosinho

Pico (W) Terrantez da Terceira, Terrantez do Pico, *Arinto* (*Pedernã*), *Chardonnay*, *Fernão Pires* (*Maria Gomes*), *Galego Dourado*, *Generosa*, *Gouveio*, *Malvasia*, *Malvasia Fina* (*Boal*), *Branco*, *Moscatel Galego*, *Moscatel Graúdo*, *Rio Grande*, *Seara Nova*, *Sercial* (*Esgana Cão*), *Viosinho*

Portimão (R) Castelão, Negra Mole, Trincadeira (Tinta Amarela), *Alicante Bouschet*, *Aragonez* (*Tinta Roriz*), *Cabernet Sauvignon*, *Monvedro*, *Syrah*, *Touriga Nacional* (W) Arinto (Pedernã), Síria (Roupeiro), *Manteúdo*, *Moscatel Graúdo*, *Perrum*, *Rabo de Ovelha*

Port (R) Alfrocheiro (Tinta Bastardinha), Alicante Bouschet, Alvarelhão (Brancelho), Alvarelhão Ceitão, Aramon, Baga, Barreto, Bastardo, Carignan, Casculho, Castelã, Castelão, Cidadelhe, Cinsault, Concieira, Cornifesto, Donzelinho Tinto, Engomada, Espadeiro, Goncalo Pires, Grand Noir, Grangeal, Jaen (Mencia), Lourela, Malandra, Malvasia Preta, Marufo, Melra, Mondet, Moreto, Mourisco de Semente, Nevoeira, Patorra, Petit Bouschet, Português Azul (Blauer Portugieser), Preto Martinho, Roseira, Rufete (Tinta Pinheira), Santareno, Sevilhão, Sousão (Vinhão), Tinta Aguiar, Tinta Amarela (Trincadeira, Trincadeira Preta), Tinta Barroca, Tinta Caiada (Pau Ferro, Tinta Lameira), Tinta Carvalha, Tinta da Barca, Tinta Fontes, Tinta Francisca, Tinta Grossa (Carrega Tinto), Tinta Martins, Tinta Mesquita, Tinta Penajoia, Tinta Pereira, Tinta Pomar, Tinta Roriz (Aragonez, Tempranillo), Tinta Tabuaço, Tinto Cão, Tinto Sem Nome, Touriga Fêmea, Touriga Franca, Touriga Nacional, Valdosa, Varejoa (W) Arinto (Pedernã), Arinto do Douro (Dorinto), Avesso, Batoca (Alvaraça), Bical (Borrado das Moscas), Branco Especial, Branco Gouvães (Alvarelhão Branco), Branco Guimarães, Branco Valente, Caramela, Carrega Branco, Cercial, Chasselas, Códega (Roupeiro, Síria), Códega do Larinho, Diagalves, Donzelinho Branco, Estreito Macio, Fernão Pires (Maria Gomes), Folgasão, Dona Branca (Folha de Figueira), Gouveio, Gouveio Estimado, Gouveio Real, Jampal, Malvasia Fina, Malvasia Parda (Farinheira), Malvasia Rei, Moscadet, Moscatel Galego Branco, Mourisco Branco, Pé Comprido, Praça, Rabigato, Rabigato Moreno, Rabo de Ovelha, Ratinho, Samarrinho (Budelho), Sarigo, Sémillon, Sercial (Esgana Cão), Tamarez (Molinha), Verdelho, Verdial Branco, Viosinho, Vital (Malvasia Corada)

Setúbal (R) Aragonez (Tinta Roriz, Tempranillo), Bastardo (Graciosa), Castelão, Touriga Franca, Touriga Nacional, Trincadeira (Tinta Amarela, Trincadeira Preta), Moscatel Galego Roxo (W) Antão Vaz, Arinto (Pedernã), Fernão Pires (Maria Gomes), Malvasia Fina, Moscatel Galego Branco (Muscat Blanc à Petits Grains), Moscatel Graúdo (Moscatel de Setúbal), Rabo de Ovelha, Roupeiro Branco, Verdelho, Viosinho

Tavira (R) Castelão, Negra Mole, Trincadeira (Tinta Amarela), *Alicante Bouschet*, *Aragonez* (*Tinta Roriz*), *Cabernet Sauvignon*, *Syrah*, *Touriga Nacional* (W) Arinto (Pedernã), Síria (Roupeiro), *Diagalves*, *Manteúdo*, *Moscatel Graúdo*, *Tamarez*

Távora-Varosa (R) Alvarelhão, Aragonez (Tinta Roriz), Baga, Bastardo, Cabernet Sauvignon, Grand Noir, Jaen, Malvasia Preta, Marufo, Pinot Noir, Rufete, Syrah, Sousão, Tinta Barroca, Touriga Franca, Touriga Nacional, Trincadeira, Vinhão, Gewürztraminer, Pinot Gris (W) Arinto, Bical, Cercial, Chardonnay, Códega do Larinho, Dona Branca, Fernão Pires, Folgasão, Gouveio, Malvasia Fina, Malvasia Rei, Pinot Blanc, Rabo de Ovelha, Riesling, Sauvignon Blanc, Síria (Roupeiro), Tália, Verdelho

Tejo (R, P) Alfrocheiro, Alicante Bouschet, Amostrinha, Aragonez (Tinta Roriz), Baga, Bastardo, Bonvedro, Cabernet Franc, Cabernet Sauvignon, Cabinda, Caladoc, Camarate, Carignan, Castelão, Cinsault, Grand Noir, Grenache, Grossa, Jaen, Merlot, Molar, Monvedro, Moreto, Negra Mole, Parreira Matias, Petit Verdot, Pinot Noir, Preto Cardana, Preto Martinho, Ramisco, Rufete, Sousão, Syrah, Tannat, Tinta Barroca, Tinta Caiada, Tinta Carvalha, Tinta Miúda, Tinta Pomar, Tintinha, Tinto Cão, Touriga Franca, Touriga Nacional, Trincadeira (Tinta Amarela), Valbom, Fernão Pires Rosado, Gewürztraminer, Pinot Gris (W) Alicante Branco, Almafra, Alvadurão, Alvarinho, Antão Vaz, Arinto (Pedernã), Bical (Borrado das Moscas), Boal Branco, Boal Espinho, Cerceal Branco, Cercial, Chardonnay, Chenin, Códega do Larinho, Diagalves, Encruzado, Fernão Pires (Maria Gomes), Galego Dourado, Gouveio, Jampal, Loureiro, Malvasia, Malvasia Fina, Malvasia Rei, Marquinhas, Moscatel Galego Branco, Moscatel Graúdo, Pinot Blanc, Rabo de Ovelha, Ratinho, Riesling, Sauvignon, Seara Nova, Semillon, Sercial (Esgana Cão), Síria (Roupeiro), Tália, Tamarez, Trincadeira Branca, Trincadeira das Pratas, Verdelho, Viognier, Viosinho, Vital

Torres Vedras (R) Aragonez (Tinta Roriz), Castelão, Tinta Miúda, Touriga Nacional, Trincadeira (Tinta Amarela), *Alicante Bouschet*, *Cabernet Sauvignon*, *Caladoc* (max 15%), *Camarate*, *Jaen*, *Syrah*, *Tinta Barroca*, *Touriga Franca* (W) Arinto (Pedernã), Fernão Pires (Maria Gomes), Rabo de Ovelha, Seara Nova, Vital, *Alicante Branco*, *Alvarinho*, *Antão Vaz*, *Chardonnay*, *Malvasia Rei*, *Sauvignon*, *Viosinho*

Trás-os-Montes (R, P) Alicante Bouschet, Aragonez (Tinta Roriz), Baga, Bastardo, Castelão, Cornifesto, Gorda, Malvasia Preta, Marufo, Rufete, Sousão, Tinta Barroca, Tinta Carvalha, Tinto Cão, Touriga Franca, Touriga Nacional, Trincadeira (Tinta Amarela), Moscatel Galego Roxo (Moscatel Roxo) (W) Alvarinho, Arinto (Pedernã), Bical, Boal Branco, Carrega Branco, Códega do Larinho, Donzelinho Branco, Fernão Pires (Maria Gomes), Gouveio, Malvasia Fina, Moscatel Galego Branco, Rabigato, Samarinho, Siria (Roupeiro), Viosinho

Trás-os-Montes Chaves (R, P) Alicante Bouschet, Aragonez (Tinta Roriz), Baga, Bastardo, Castelão, Cornifesto, Malvasia Preta, Marufo,

Tinta Barroca, Tinta Carvalha, Tinto-Cão, Touriga Franca, Touriga Nacional, Trincadeira (Tinta Amarela), Moscatel Galego Roxo (Moscatel Roxo) (W) Alvarinho, Arinto (Pedernã), Bical, Boal Branco, Códega do Larinho, Fernão Pires (Maria Gomes), Gouveio, Malvasia Fina, Moscatel Galego Branco, Rabigato, Siria (Roupeiro), Viosinho

Trás-os-Montes Planalto Mirandês (R, P) Alicante Bouschet, Aragonez (Tinta Roriz), Bastardo, Cornifesto, Gorda, Marufo, Rufete, Tinta Barroca, Touriga Franca, Touriga Nacional, Trincadeira (Tinta Amarela) (W) Bical, Boal Branco, Carrega Branco, Códega do Larinho, Donzelinho Branco, Fernão Pires (Maria Gomes), Gouveio, Malvasia Fina, Moscatel Galego Branco, Rabigato, Samarinho, Siria (Roupeiro), Viosinho

Trás-os-Montes Valpaços (R, P) Aragonez (Tinta Roriz), Bastardo, Cornifesto, Marufo, Tinta Barroca, Tinta Carvalha, Tinto Cão, Touriga Franca, Touriga Nacional, Trincadeira (Tinta Amarela) (W) Arinto (Pedernã), Bical, Boal Branco, Códega do Larinho, Donzelinho Branco, Fernão Pires (Maria Gomes), Gouveio, Malvasia Fina, Moscatel Galego Branco, Rabigato, Siria (Roupeiro), Viosinho

Vinho Verde (R, P) Alicante Bouschet, Alvarelhão (Brancelho), Amaral, Baga, Borraçal, Doçal, Doce, Espadeiro, Espadeiro Mole, Grand Noir, Labrusco, Mourisco, Padeiro, Pedral, Pical (Piquepoul Noir), Rabo de Anho, Sezão, Touriga Nacional, Trincadeira (Tinta Amarela, Trincadeira Preta), Verdelho Tinto, Verdial Tinto, Vinhão (Sousão) (W) Alvarinho, Arinto (Pedernã), Avesso, Azal, Batoca (Alvaraça), Cainho, Cascal, Diagalves, Esganinho, Esganoso, Fernão Pires (Maria Gomes), Folgasão, Gouveio, Lameiro, Loureiro, Malvasia Fina, Malvasia Rei, Pintosa, São Mamede, Sémillon, Sercial (Esgana Cão), Tália (Ugni Blanc, Trebbiano Toscano), Trajadura (Treixadura)

Vinho Verde Amarante (R, P) Amaral, Borraçal, Espadeiro, Vinhão (Sousão) (W) Arinto (Pedernã), Avesso, Azal, Trajadura (Treixadura)

Vinho Verde Ave (R, P) Amaral, Borraçal, Espadeiro, Padeiro, Vinhão (Sousão) (W) Arinto (Pedernã), Loureiro, Trajadura (Treixadura)

Vinho Verde Baião (R, P) Alvarelhão (Brancelho), Amaral, Borraçal, Vinhão (Sousão) (W) Arinto (Pedernã), Avesso, Azal

Vinho Verde Basto (R, P) Amaral, Borraçal, Espadeiro, Padeiro, Rabo de Anho, Vinhão (Sousão) (W) Arinto (Pedernã), Azal, Batoca (Alvaraça), Trajadura (Treixadura)

Vinho Verde Cávado (R, P) Amaral, Borraçal, Espadeiro, Padeiro and Vinhão (Sousão) (W) Arinto (Pedernã), Loureiro, Trajadura (Treixadura)

Vinho Verde Lima (R, P) Borraçal, Espadeiro, Vinhão (Sousão) (W) Arinto (Pedernã), Loureiro and Trajadura (Treixadura)

Vinho Verde Monção e Melgaço (R, P) Alvarelhão (Brancelho), Borraçal, Pedral, Vinhão (Sousão) (W) Alvarinho, Loureiro, Trajadura (Treixadura)

Vinho Verde Paiva (R, P) Amaral, Borraçal, Pedral and Vinhão (Sousão) (W) Arinto (Pedernã), Avesso, Loureiro, Trajadura (Treixadura)

Vinho Verde Sousa (R, P) Amaral, Borraçal, Espadeiro, Vinhão (Sousão) (W) Arinto (Pedernã), Avesso, Azal, Loureiro, Trajadura (Treixadura)

SPAIN

Note: The Spanish regulations, or *pliegos de condiciones*, for each DOP specify which red and white varieties are allowed, usually distinguishing between 'recommended' and 'authorized' (the latter shown here in italics). Many DOPs also produce rosado, sparkling, and other styles of wines. For details of varieties allowed in these wines, see the individual *pliegos*, most of which are on the government website: www.mapa.gob.es/es/alimentacion/temas/calidad-diferenciada/dop-igp. Single-estate DOPs, known as VINOS DO PAGO (e.g. Dominio de Valdepusa or Pago Guijoso), are not listed below.

Abona (R) Castellana Negra, Listán Negro (Almuñeco), Malvasía Rosada, Negramoll, Tintilla, *Bastardo Negro* (*Baboso Negro*), *Cabernet Sauvignon, Listán Prieto, Merlot, Moscatel Negro, Pinot Noir, Ruby Cabernet, Syrah, Tempranillo, Vijariego Negro* (W) Albillo Criollo, Bermejuela (Marmajuelo), Doradilla, Forastera Blanca, Gual, Malvasía Aromática, Malvasía Volcánica, Moscatel de Alejandría, Sabro, Verdello, Vijariego Blanco (Diego), *Bastardo Blanco* (*Baboso Blanco*), *Listán Blanco de Canarias, Pedro Ximénez, Torrontés*

Alella (R) Garnacha Tinta, Syrah, *Cabernet Sauvignon, Garnacha Peluda, Mazuela, Merlot, Monastrell, Sumoll Tinto, Tempranillo* (W) Xarello, *Chardonnay, Chenin Blanc, Garnacha Blanca, Macabeo, Malvasía Aromatica, Moscatel de Grano Menudo, Parellada, Picapoll Blanco, Sauvignon Blanc*

Alicante (R) Monastrell, Bobal, Garnacha Tinta (Gironet, Giró), Garnacha Tintorera (Alicante Bouschet), *Cabernet Sauvignon, Cabernet Franc, Merlot, Petit Verdot, Pinot Noir, Syrah, Tempranillo* (W) Moscatel de Alejandría, Alarije (Subirat Parent), Merseguera (Verdosilla), Verdil, *Airén, Chardonnay, Macabeo, Planta Fina de Pedralba, Sauvignon Blanc*

Almansa (R) Garnacha Tintorera, Monastrell, *Cabernet Sauvignon, Cabernet Franc, Garnacha Tinta, Merlot, Petit Verdot, Pinot Noir, Syrah, Tempranillo* (W) Verdejo, *Chardonnay, Macabeo, Sauvignon Blanc, Moscatel de Grano Menudo*

Arabako Txakolina or **Chacolí de Álava** or **Txakoli de Álava** (R, P) Ondarribi Beltza (W) Ondarribi Zuri, *Chardonnay, Izkiriota* (*Gros Manseng*), *Izkiriota Ttippia* (*Petit Manseng*), *Ondarribi Zuri Zerratia* (*Petit Courbu*), *Riesling, Sauvignon Blanc*

Arlanza (R) Tinta del País, *Cabernet Sauvignon, Garnacha Tinta, Mencía, Merlot, Petit Verdot* (W) Albillo Mayor, Viura

Arribes (R) Juan García (Mouraton), Rufete, Tempranillo (Cencibel, Tinto de Toro), *Bruñal* (*Albarin Tinto*), *Garnacha Tinta, Mencía* (W) Doña Branca (Cigüente), *Albillo Mayor, Albillo Real, Verdejo*

Bierzo (R) Mencía, *Garnacha Tintorera* (W) Doña Blanca (Cigüente), Godello, *Alarije* (*Subirat Parent, Malvasía Riojana*), *Palomino*

Binissalem Mallorca (R) Manto Negro, *Cabernet Sauvignon, Callet, Gorgollasa, Merlot, Monastrell, Syrah, Tempranillo* (W) Moscatel de Grano Menudo, Moscatel de Alejandria, Moll (Prensal Blanca), *Chardonnay, Giro Ros, Macabeo, Parellada*

Bizkaiko Txakolina or **Chacolí de Vizcaya** or **Txakoli de Bizkaia** (R, P) Ondarrabi Beltza (W) Ondarrabi Zuri, *Chardonnay, Izkiriota* (*Gros Manseng*), *Izkiriota Ttippia* (*Petit Manseng*), *Mune Mahatsa* (*Folle Blanche*), *Ondarrabi Zuri Zerratia* (*Petit Courbu*), *Riesling, Sauvignon Blanc*

Bullas (R) Monastrell, *Cabernet Sauvignon, Garnacha Tinta, Garnacha Tintorera, Merlot, Petit Verdot, Syrah, Tempranillo* (W) Macabeo, *Airén, Chardonnay, Malvasía, Moscatel de Alexandría, Moscatel de Grano Menudo, Sauvignon Blanc*

Calatayud (R) Garnacha Tinta, Tempranillo, Syrah, *Bobal, Cabernet Sauvignon, Mazuela, Merlot, Monastrell* (W) Chardonnay, Garnacha Blanca, Macabeo, *Gewürztraminer, Malvasía Riojana, Moscatel de Alexandría, Sauvignon Blanc*

Campo de Borja (R) Garnacha Tinta, Garnacha Tintorera, Mazuelo, Syrah, Tempranillo, *Cabernet Sauvignon, Caladoc, Marselan, Merlot* (W) Chardonnay, Garnacha Blanca, Macabeo, Moscatel de Alejandría, Moscatel de Grano Menudo, Verdejo, *Sauvignon Blanc, Viognier*

Cariñena (R) Cabernet Sauvignon, Cariñena (Mazuela), Garnacha Tinta, Merlot, Syrah, Tempranillo, *Juan Ibáñez* (*Moristel*), *Monastrell, Vidadillo* (W) Chardonnay, Macabeo, *Garnacha Blanca, Moscatel de Alejandría, Parellada*

Cataluña or **Catalunya** (R) Cabernet Franc, Cabernet Sauvignon, Garnacha Peluda, Garnacha Tinta (Lladoner Tinto), Merlot, Monastrell (Garrut), Pinot Noir, Samsó (Mazuela), Syrah, Trepat, Ull de Llebre

(Tempranillo), *Garnacha Roja, Garnacha Tintorera, Marselan, Petit Verdot, Picapoll Tinto, Sumoll Tinto* (W) Chardonnay, Garnatxa Blanca (Garnacha Blanca, Lladoner Blanc), Macabeo (Viura), Moscatel de Alejandría, Parellada (Montonec, Montonega), Picapoll Blanco, Riesling, Sauvignon Blanc, Xarello, *Albariño, Chenin Blanc, Gewürztraminer, Malvasia de Sitges (Malvasia Aromatica), Moscatel de Grano Menudo, Pedro Ximénez, Subirat Parent, Sumoll Blanco, Vinyater, Viognier*

Cava (S) Chardonnay, Garnacha Tinta, Macabeo (Viura), Parellada, Pinot Noir, Trepat, Xarello, *Malvasia (Subirat Parent), Monastrell*

Cigales (R) Garnacha Gris, Garnacha Tinta, Tinta del País (Tempranillo), *Cabernet Sauvignon, Merlot, Syrah* (W) Verdejo, *Albillo Mayor, Sauvignon Blanc, Viura*

Conca de Barbera (R) Ull de Llebre (Tempranillo), Trepat, *Cabernet Franc, Cabernet Sauvignon, Garnacha Tinta, Samsó (Mazuelo), Merlot, Monastrell, Sumoll Negre, Pinot Noir, Syrah* (W) Macabeo, *Chardonnay, Chenin Blanc, Garnacha Blanca, Moscatel de Alejandría, Moscatel de Grano Menudo, Parellada, Sauvignon Blanc*

Condado de Huelva (R) Cabernet Franc, Cabernet Sauvignon, Merlot, Syrah, Tempranillo (W) Chardonnay, Colombard, Garrido Fino, Listán del Condado, Moscatel de Alejandría, Moscatel de Grano Menudo, Palomino Fino, Pedro Ximénez, Sauvignon Blanc, Verdejo, Zalema

Costers del Segre (R) Cabernet Franc, Cabernet Sauvignon, Garnacha Peluda, Garnacha Tinta, Garnacha Tintorera, Gonfaus, Malbec, Merlot, Monastrell, Petit Verdot, Pinot Noir, Samsó (Mazuela), Sumoll Tinto, Syrah, Tempranillo, Trepat (W) Alarije (Subirat Parent), Albariño, Chardonnay, Chenin Blanc, Garnacha Blanca, Gewürztraminer, Godello, Macabeo, Malvasía Riojana, Moscatel de Alejandría, Moscatel de Grano Menudo, Parellada, Riesling, Sauvignon Blanc, Verdejo, Viognier, Xarello

El Hierro (R) Listán Negro, Negramoll, Tintilla, *Baboso (Bastardo) Negro, Moscatel Negro, Vijariego Negro* (W) Bermejuela, Güal, Malvasía Aromática, Malvasía Volcánica, Moscatel de Alejandría, Vijariego Blanco, *Albillo, Breval, Baboso (Bastardo) Blanco, Burrablanca, Forastera Blanca, Listán Blanco de Canarias, Malvasía Rosada, Pedro Ximénez, Torrontes, Verdello*

Empordà (R) Samsó (Cariñena), Garnacha Tinta, *Cabernet Franc, Cabernet Sauvignon, Garnacha Peluda, Merlot, Monastrell, Syrah, Ull de Llebre* (W) Garnacha Blanca, Garnacha Roja, Macabeo (Viura), Moscatel de Alejandría, *Chardonnay, Gewurztraminer, Malvasía Aromática, Moscatel de Grano Pequeño, Picapoll Blanco, Sauvignon Blanc, Xarello*

Getariako Txakoli or **Chacolí de Guetaria** or **Txakoli de Getaria** (R) Ondarrabi Beltza, (W) Ondarrabi Zuri, *Chardonnay, Izkiriota (Gros Manseng), Ondarrabi Zuri Zerratia (Petit Courbu), Riesling*

Gran Canaria (R) Castellana Negra, Listán Negro (Almuñeco), Malvasía Rosada, Negramoll, Tintilla, *Bastardo (Baboso) Negro, Listán Prieto, Moscatel Negro, Vijariego Negro* (W) Albillo, Bermejuela (Marmajuelo), Doradilla, Forastera Blanca, Gual, Malvasía Aromática, Malvasía Volcánica, Moscatel de Alejandría, Sabro, Verdello, Vijariego Blanco (Diego), *Bastardo (Baboso) Blanco, Breval, Burrablanca, Listán Blanco de Canarias, Pedro Ximénez, Torrontés*

Jerez-Xérès-Sherry (W) Moscatel de Grano Menuda, Palomino Fino, Pedro Ximénez, *Beba, Cañocazo, Mantúo Castellano, Mantúo de Pilas, Perruno, Vigiriega*

Jumilla (R) Monastrell, *Cabernet Sauvignon, Cencibel (Tempranillo), Garnacha Tinta, Garnacha Tintorera, Merlot, Petit Verdot, Syrah* (W) Airén, Chardonnay, Macabeo, Malvasía Aromática, Moscatel de Grano Menudo, Pedro Ximénez, Sauvignon Blanc, Verdejo

La Gomera (R) Castellana Negra, Listán Negro (Almuñeco), Malvasía Rosada, Negramoll, Tintilla, *Baboso (Bastardo) Negro, Cabernet Sauvignon, Listán Prieto, Merlot, Moscatel Negro, Pinot Noir, Ruby Cabernet, Syrah, Tempranillo, Vijariego Negro* (W) Albillo, Bermejuela (Marmajuelo), Doradilla, Forastera Blanca, Gual, Malvasía Aromática, Malvasía Volcánica, Moscatel de Alejandría, Sabro, Verdello, Vijariego Blanco (Diego), *Breval, Listán Blanco de Canarias, Pedro Ximénez, Torrontés*

La Mancha (R) Bobal, Cencibel (Tempranillo), Cabernet Sauvignon, Garnacha Tinta, Syrah, *Cabernet Franc, Graciano, Malbec, Mencía, Merlot, Monastrell, Moravia Dulce (Crujidera), Merlot, Petit Verdot, Pinot Noir* (W) Airén, Macabeo (Viura), Verdejo, *Chardonnay, Gewürztraminer, Moscatel de Grano Menudo, Parellada, Pedro Ximénez, Riesling, Sauvignon Blanc, Torrontés, Viognier*

La Palma (R) Castellana Negra, Listán Negro (Almuñeco), Malvasía Rosada, Negramoll, Tintilla, *Bastardo (Baboso) Negro, Listán Prieto, Moscatel Negro, Vijariego Negro, Xarello Rosat* (W) Albillo Criollo, Bermejuela (Marmajuelo), Forastera Blanca, Doradilla, Gual, Malvasía Aromática, Malvasía Volcánica, Moscatel de Alejandría, Sabro, Verdello, Vijariego Blanco (Diego), *Bastardo (Baboso) Blanco, Burrablanca, Listán Blanco de Canarias, Pedro Ximénez, Torrontés*

Lanzarote (R) Listán Negro (Almuñeco), Negramoll (Mulata), Malvasía Rosada, Tintilla, *Bastardo (Baboso) Negro, Cabernet Sauvignon, Merlot, Moscatel Negro, Pinot Noir, Ruby Cabernet, Syrah, Tempranillo, Vijariego Negro* (W) Albillo, Gual, Malvasía Volcánica, Moscatel de Alejandría, Vijariego Blanco (Diego), Verdello, *Burrablanca, Breval, Listán Blanco de Canarias, Pedro Ximénez, Torrontés*

León (R) Mencía, Prieto Picudo, *Garnacha Tinta, Tempranillo* (W) Albarín Blanco, Godello, Verdejo

Málaga (R) Romé (W) Moscatel de Málaga (Moscatel de Alejandría), Moscatel Morisco (Moscatel de Grano Menudo), Pero Ximén (Pedro Ximénez), *Doradilla, Lairén*

Manchuela (R) Bobal, Cabernet Sauvignon, Cencibel (Tempranillo), Garnacha Tinta, Garnacha Tintorera, Mazuela, Merlot, Monastrell, Syrah, *Cabernet Franc, Frasco (Tinto Velasco), Graciano, Malbec, Moravia Agria, Petit Verdot, Pinot Noir, Rojal Tinta, Touriga Nacional* (W) Chardonnay, Macabeo (Viura), *Albillo Real, Garnacha Blanca, Moscatel de Alejandría, Moscatel de Grano Menudo, Pardillo, Sauvignon Blanc, Tardana (Planta Nova), Verdejo, Viognier*

Manzanilla-Sanlúcar de Barrameda (W) Moscatel, Palomino Fino, Pedro Ximénez

Méntrida (R) Garnacha Tinta, *Cabernet Franc, Cabernet Sauvignon, Graciano, Merlot, Petit Verdot, Syrah, Tempranillo* (W) Albillo Real, Chardonnay, Macabeo, Moscatel de Grano Menudo, Sauvignon Blanc, Verdejo

Mondéjar (W) Malvar, Torrontés, *Macabeo, Moscatel de Grano Menudo, Sauvignon Blanc, Verdejo* (R) Cabernet Sauvignon, Syrah, Tempranillo, *Garnacha Tinta, Merlot*

Monterrei (R) Mencía, Merenzao (Bastardo), *Caíño Tinto, Sousón, Tempranillo (Araúxa)* (W) Doña Blanca, Godello, Treixadura, *Albariño, Blanca de Monterrei, Caíño Blanco, Loureira*

Montilla-Moriles (W) Moscatel de Alejandría, Moscatel de Grano Menudo, Pedro Ximénez, *Baladí, Chardonnay, Layren (Airen), Macabeo, Torrontés, Sauvignon Blanc, Verdejo*

Montsant (R) Garnacha Tinta, Mazuela (Samsó, Cariñena), Ull de Llebre (Tempranillo), *Cabernet Sauvignon, Garnacha Peluda, Merlot, Monastrell, Picapoll Negro, Syrah* (W) Garnacha Blanca, Macabeo, *Chardonnay, Moscatel de Grano Menudo, Parellada, Picapoll Blanco, Pansal*

Navarra (R) Garnacha Tinta, Graciano, Mazuelo, Tempranillo, *Cabernet Sauvignon, Merlot, Pinot Noir, Syrah* (W) Garnacha Blanca, Moscatel de Grano Menuda, Subirat Parent (Malvasía Riojana), Viura, *Chardonnay, Sauvignon Blanc*

Penedès (R) Garnacha Negra, Monastrell, Samsó, Sumoi, Ull de Llebre (Tempranillo), *Cabernet Franc, Cabernet Sauvignon, Merlot, Petit Verdot, Pinot Noir, Syrah, Moneu* (W) Macabeu, Parellada, Xarello, *Chardonnay, Chenin, Garnacha Blanca, Gewürztraminer, Muscat of Alexandría, Muscat de Frontignan, Malvasía de Sitges, Sauvignon Blanc, Subirat Parent, Riesling, Sumoi Blanc, Viognier, Forcada*

Pla de Bages (R) Cabernet Sauvignon, Garnacha Negre, Merlot, Samsó (Cariñena), Sumoll, Ull de Llebre (Tempranillo), *Cabernet Franc, Garró (Mandó), Picapoll Negro, Syrah* (W) Chardonnay, Parellada, Picapoll Blanco, Macabeo, *Gewürztraminer, Malvasía Aromática (Malvasía de Sitges), Sauvignon Blanc*

Pla i Llevant (R) Callet, Fogoneu, Manto Negro, Gorgollassa, *Cabernet Sauvignon, Merlot, Monastrell, Pinot Noir, Syrah, Tempranillo* (W) Prensal, Giró Ros, Chardonnay, Macabeu, Moscatel de Grano Menudo, Moscatel de Alejandría, Parellada, Riesling, Viognier

Priorato (R) Garnacha Tinta, Samsó, *Cabernet Franc, Cabernet Sauvignon, Garnacha Peluda, Merlot, Picapoll Tinto, Pinot Noir, Syrah, Ull de Lliebre (Tempranillo)* (W) Chenin Blanc, Garnacha Blanca, Macabeo, Moscatel de Alejandría, Moscatel de Grano Menudo, Pansal (Xarello), Pedro Ximénez, Picapoll Blanco, Viognier

Rías Baixas (R) *Brancellao, Caíño Tinto, Castañal, Espadeiro, Loureiro Tinto, Mencía, Pedral, Sousón* (W) Albariño, Loureira, Treixadura, *Caíño Blanco, Godello, Torrontés*

Ribeira Sacra (R) Brancellao, Caiño Bravo, Caiño Longo, Caíño Tinto, Mencía, Merenzao, Sousón, *Garnacha Tintorera, Gran Negro, Mouratón, Tempranillo* (W) Albariño, Albarín Blanco (Branco Lexitimo), Caiño Blanco, Doña Blanca (Doña Branca), Godello, Loureira (Loureiro Blanco), Torrontés, Treixadura

Ribeiro (R) Brancellao, Caiño Bravo, Caíño Longo, Caíño Tinto, Ferrón, Mencía, Sousón, *Garnacha, Tempranillo* (W) Albariño, Caíño Blanco, Godello, Lado, Loureira, Torrontés, Treixadura, *Albillo, Palomino*

Ribera del Duero (R) Tempranillo (Tinto Fino, Tinta del País), *Cabernet Sauvignon, Garnacha Tinta, *Garnacha Tintorera, Malbec, Merlot, *Monastrell, *Pirulé (Jaén), *Valenciana (Bobal)* (W) Albillo Mayor, **Alarije (Pirués), *Chasselas Doré, Cayetana Blanca* (*these varieties authorized only if part of a field blend planted before 1982)

Ribera del Guadiana (R) Bobal, Cabernet Sauvignon, Garnacha Tinta, Garnacha Tintorera, Graciano, Jaén Tinto, Mazuela, Merlot, Monastrell, Petit Verdot, Pinot Noir, Syrah, Tempranillo (Cencibel, Tinto Fino), *Castelão, Malbec, Touriga Nacional, Trincadeira* (W) Alarije, Borba, Cayetana Blanca, Chardonnay, Chelva (Montúa), Cigüente, Eva (Beba de los Santos), Malvar, Moscatel de Alejandría, Moscatel de Grano Menudo, Pardina, Parellada, Pedro Ximénez, Perruno, Sauvignon Blanc, Verdejo, Viura (Macabeo), *Antão Vaz, Arinto, Colombard, Fernão Pires, Xarello*

Ribera del Júcar (R) Bobal, Cabernet Sauvignon, Syrah, Tempranillo, *Cabernet Franc, Garnacha Tinta, Garnacha Tintorera, Merlot, Monastrell, Petit Verdot* (W) Airén, Macabeo, Verdejo, *Moscatel de Grano Menudo, Chardonnay, Pardillo (Marisancho), Sauvignon Blanc*

Rioja (R) Garnacha Tinta, Graciano, Maturana Tinta, Mazuelo, Tempranillo (W) Alarije (Malvasía Riojana), Albillo Mayor (Turruntés), Chardonnay, Garnacha Blanca, Malvasía Riojana, Maturana Blanca, Sauvignon Blanc, Tempranillo Blanco, Verdejo, Viura

Rueda (R) Tempranillo, *Cabernet Sauvignon, Garnacha Tinta, Merlot, Syrah* (W) Sauvignon Blanc, Verdejo, *Chardonnay, Palomino Fino, Viognier, Viura*

Sierras de Málaga (R) Blaufränkisch, Cabernet Franc, Cabernet Sauvignon, Garnacha Tinta, Graciano, Jaén Tinto, Malbec, Merlot, Monastrell, Moscatel Negro, Petit Verdot, Pinot Noir, Romé, Syrah, Tempranillo, Tintilla de Rota, Tinto Velasco (W) Chardonnay, Colombard, Doradilla, Garnacha Blanca, Gewürztraminer, Macabeo, Malvasía Aromática, Montúa, Moscatel de Alejandría, Moscatel de Grano Menudo, Pardina (Jaén Blanco), Pedro Ximénez, Perruno, Riesling, Sauvignon Blanc, Verdejo, Vermentino, Vijariego Blanco, Viognier

Somontano (R) Cabernet Sauvignon, Garnacha Tinta, Merlot, Moristel, Parraleta, Pinot Noir, Syrah, Tempranillo (W) Chardonnay, Garnacha Blanca, Gewürztraminer, Macabeo, Riesling, Sauvignon Blanc, *Alcañón*

Tacoronte-Acentejo (R) Listán Negro (Almuñeco), Negramoll, Tintilla, Vijariego Negro, *Bastardo (Baboso) Negro, Cabernet Sauvignon, Castellana Negra, Listán Prieto, Malvasía Rosada, Merlot, Moscatel Negro, Pinot Noir, Ruby Cabernet, Syrah, Tempranillo* (W) Gual, Listán Blanco de Canarias, Malvasía Aromática, Moscatel de Alejandría, Pedro Ximénez, Verdello, *Albillo Criollo, Bastardo (Baboso) Blanco, Bermejuela (Marmajuelo), Breval, Burrablanca, Doradilla, Forastera Blanca, Malvasía Volcánica, Sabro, Torrontés, Vijariego Blanco (Diego)*

Tarragona (R) Tempranillo (Ull de Lliebre), *Cabernet Sauvignon, Garnacha Tinta, Merlot, Monastrell (Garrut), Pinot Noir, Samsó (Carignane), Sumoll Tinto, Syrah, Trepat* (W) Macabeo, *Chardonnay, Garnacha Blanca, Malvasía de Sitges (Malvasia Grossa), Moscatel de Alejandría, Moscatel de Grano Menudo, Parellada (Montonenc, Montonega), Sauvignon Blanc, Subirat Parent (Malvasia), Sumoll Blanc, Vinyater, Xarello (Cartoixà), Xarello Vermell*

Terra Alta (R) Garnacha Peluda, Garnacha Tinta, Samsó, *Cabernet Franc, Cabernet Sauvignon, Garnacha Tintorera, Merlot, Syrah, Ull de Lliebre* (W) Garnacha Blanca, Macabeo, Parellada, *Chardonnay, Chenin Blanc, Moscatel de Grano Grande (Moscatel de Alejandría), Moscatel de Grano Menudo, Pedro Ximénez, Sauvignon Blanc, Viognier*

Tierra del Vino de Zamora (R) Tempranillo, *Cabernet Sauvignon, Garnacha Tinta* (W) Malvasía, Moscatel de Grano Menudo, Verdejo, *Albillo, Godello, Palomino*

Toro (R) Tinta de Toro (Tempranillo), *Garnacha Tinta* (W) Malvasía Castellana (Doña Blanca), Verdejo, *Albillo Real, Moscatel de Grano Menudo*

Uclés (R) Cabernet Sauvignon, Cencibel (Tempranillo), Syrah, *Garnacha Tinta, Merlot* (W) Macabeo, Verdejo, *Airen, Chardonnay, Moscatel de Grano Menudo, Sauvignon Blanc*

Utiel-Requena (R) Bobal, Cabernet Sauvignon, Garnacha Tinta, Merlot, Syrah, Tempranillo, *Cabernet Franc, Garnacha Tintorera, Petit Verdot, Pinot Noir* (W) Chardonnay, Macabeo, Merseguera, Planta Nova (Tardana), Sauvignon Blanc, *Moscatel de Grano Menudo, Parellada (Montonega), Verdejo*

Valdeorras (R) Brancellao, Caíño Tinto, Espadeiro, Ferrón, Mencía, Merenzao, Sousón, Tempranillo, *Garnacha Tintorera, Gran Negro, Mouratón* (W) Albariño, Dona Branca, Godello, Lado, Loureira, Torrontés, Treixadura, *Palomino*

Valdepeñas (R) Cabernet Sauvignon, Syrah, Cencibel (Tempranillo), *Garnacha Tinta, Merlot, Petit Verdot* (W) Airén, Macabeo (Viura), Verdejo, *Chardonnay, Moscatel de Grano Menudo, Sauvignon Blanc*

Valencia (R) Garnacha Tintorera, Monastrell, *Bobal, Bonicaire, Cabernet Franc, Cabernet Sauvignon, Garnacha Tinta, Graciano, Forcallat Tinta, Malbec, Mando, Marselan, Mazuela, Mencía, Merlot, Miguel Arco, Petit Verdot, Pinot Noir, Syrah, Tempranillo* (W) Macabeo, Merseguera, Moscatel de Alejandría, Verdil, *Albariño, Chardonnay, Garnacha Blanca, Gewürztraminer, Moscatel de Grano Menudo, Planta Fina de Pedralba, Planta Nova, Pedro Ximénez, Riesling, Sauvignon Blanc, Sémillon, Subirat Parent (Malvasía Riojana), Tortosí, Verdejo, Viognier*

Valle de Güímar (R) Castellana Negra, Listán Negro (Almuñeco), Malvasía Rosada, Negramoll, Tintilla, *Bastardo (Baboso) Negro, Cabernet Sauvignon, Listán Prieto, Merlot, Moscatel Negro, Pinot Noir, Ruby Cabernet, Syrah, Tempranillo, Vijariego Negro* (W) Albillo Criollo, Bermejuela (Marmajuelo), Forastera Blanca, Doradilla, Gual, Malvasía

Aromática, Malvasía Volcánica, Moscatel de Alejandría, Sabro, Verdello, Vijariego Blanco (Diego), *Burrablanca, Listán Blanco de Canarias, Pedro Ximénez, Torrontés*

Valle de la Orotava (R) Listán Negro, Malvasía Rosada, Negramoll, *Bastardo Negro, Moscatel Negra, Tintilla, Vijariego Negro* (W) Albillo Criollo, Bermejuela (Marmajuelo), Forastera Blanca, Doradilla, Gual, Malvasía Aromática, Malvasía Volcánica, Moscatel de Alejandría, Sabro, Verdello, Vijariego Blanco (Diego), *Bastardo (Baboso) Blanco, Breval, Burrablanca, Listán Blanco de Canarias, Pedro Ximénez, Torrontés*

Vinos de Madrid (R) Garnacha Tinta, Tinto Fino (Tempranillo), *Cabernet Sauvignon, Graciano, Merlot, Negral (Garnacha Tintorera), Petit Verdot, Syrah* (W) Albillo Real, Malvar, *Airén, Macabeo (Viura), Moscatel de Grano Menudo, Parellada, Sauvignon Blanc, Torrontés*

Ycoden-Daute-Isora (R) Castellana Negra, Listán Negro (Almuñeco), Malvasía Rosada, Negramoll (Mulata), Tintilla, *Bastardo (Baboso) Negro, Moscatel Negra, Vijariego Negro* (W) Albillo, Bermejuela (Marmajuelo), Forastera Blanca (Doradilla), Gual, Malvasía, Moscatel de Alexandría, Sabró, Verdello, Vijariego (Diego), *Bastardo (Baboso) Blanco, Listán Blanco, Pedro Ximénez, Torrontés*

Yecla (R) Monastrell, *Cabernet Sauvignon, Garnacha Tinta, Garnacha Tintorera, Merlot, Syrah, Tempranillo, Petit Verdot* (W) Airén, Chardonnay, Macabeo, Malvasía, Moscatel de Grano Menudo, Merseguera, Sauvignon Blanc, Verdejo

SWITZERLAND

Dôle (R) Gamay, Pinot Noir, *OR*

Dôle Blanche (P) Pinot Noir, *Gamay* (optionally blended with up to 10% Valais AOC white wine)

Dorin (W) Chasselas

Ermitage du Valais/Hermitage du Valais (W) Marsanne

Goron (R, P) any varieties as long as the grapes are picked and vinified in the Valais

Johannisberg du Valais (W) Silvaner

Malvoisie du Valais (W) Pinot Gris

L'Œil-de-Perdrix (Valais) (P) Pinot Noir, *Pinot Blanc, Pinot Gris*

L'Œil-de-Perdrix de Neuchâtel (P) Pinot Noir, *Pinot Gris*

Perdrix Blanche (W) Pinot Noir

APPENDIX 2A

TOTAL VINEYARD AREA BY COUNTRY

These 2010 and 2020 OIV figures include vineyards dedicated to TABLE GRAPES and RAISINS. OIV figures are given in hectares so the equivalent figures in acres have been rounded.

	2010 (000 ha)	2010 (000 acres)	2020 (000 ha)	2020 (000 acres)
Spain	1,036.59	2,561.41	961.10	2,374.92
France	804.01	1,986.71	798.64	1,973.48
China (mainland)	551.66	1,363.15	782.60	1,933.84
Italy	738.91	1,825.84	718.72	1,776.00
Türkiye	513.62	1,269.16	431.07	1,065.20
US	432.73	1,069.28	402.41	994.37
Argentina	217.75	538.06	214.80	530.78
Chile	204.25	504.70	207.49	512.71
Portugal	236.02	583.19	194.64	480.97
Romania	191.21	472.49	190.18	469.93
Iran	221.08	546.28	169.63	419.16
India	114.38	282.63	161.25	398.46
Australia	170.70	421.80	146.24	361.38
Moldova	146.00	360.77	140.00	345.95
South Africa	132.00	326.17	128.18	316.74
Uzbekistan	115.13	284.49	113.68	280.90
Greece	112.27	277.42	112.03	276.82
Germany	102.17	252.46	103.18	254.96
Afghanistan	65.72	162.39	99.53	245.94
Russia	62.20	153.70	96.75	239.07
Egypt	68.84	170.10	84.63	209.12
Brazil	92.07	227.50	80.44	198.77
Algeria	74.41	183.87	74.52	184.14

	2010 (000 ha)	2010 (000 acres)	2020 (000 ha)	2020 (000 acres)
Bulgaria	79.49	196.42	65.87	162.77
Hungary	71.75	177.30	65.23	161.19
Georgia	48.81	120.60	49.45	122.19
Austria	45.95	113.54	48.06	118.76
Syria	56.13	138.71	47.76	118.01
Morocco	47.43	117.19	42.36	104.67
Ukraine	87.00	214.98	41.80	103.29
Peru	18.00	44.48	40.75	100.69
New Zealand	37.44	92.52	40.68	100.53
Mexico	27.68	68.41	39.24	96.97
Tajikistan	39.92	98.64	36.24	89.54
Turkmenistan	18.28	45.16	26.72	66.03
Republic of North Macedonia	21.54	53.21	25.77	63.69
Croatia	35.16	86.89	23.06	56.99
Tunisia	25.33	62.58	22.88	56.53
Serbia	50.92	125.82	20.47	50.57
Czechia	17.31	42.76	17.93	44.29
Japan	19.35	47.81	17.74	43.83
Pakistan	16.42	40.57	16.94	41.85
Armenia	17.40	43.00	16.07	39.71
Azerbaijan	15.40	38.05	16.03	39.61
Kazakhstan	10.21	25.24	15.64	38.64
Slovenia	16.00	39.54	15.14	37.40
Slovakia	19.63	48.52	15.08	37.26
Switzerland	14.98	37.01	14.70	36.31
Korea	18.89	46.68	14.17	35.02
Canada	11.65	28.78	13.17	32.54
Yemen	14.67	36.24	12.88	31.83
Albania	9.71	24.00	11.24	27.77
Belarus	3.23	7.97	8.79	21.73
Israel	7.20	17.79	8.76	21.65
Libya	9.14	22.58	8.75	21.63
Namibia	5.91	14.61	8.22	20.30
Cyprus	9.78	24.17	7.77	19.21
Lebanon	13.98	34.53	7.53	18.60
Uruguay	8.60	21.26	6.44	15.91
Iraq	11.01	27.21	6.31	15.59
Kyrgystan	6.47	15.98	5.24	12.94
Thailand	4.76	11.76	5.05	12.49
Bosnia and Herzegovina	5.73	14.16	4.76	11.76
Palestine	2.30	5.69	4.19	10.36
Saudi Arabia	13.31	32.89	4.03	9.95
Bolivia	4.44	10.97	3.61	8.92
Jordan	3.44	8.50	3.31	8.19
Montenegro	2.56	6.33	3.04	7.52
Guatemala	2.53	6.25	2.85	7.04
Madagascar	2.74	6.76	2.73	6.75
Colombia	2.77	6.84	2.69	6.64
China—Taiwan	3.37	8.33	2.66	6.57

	2010 (000 ha)	2010 (000 acres)	2020 (000 ha)	2020 (000 acres)
Ethiopia	1.85	4.58	2.52	6.23
Cuba	1.83	4.52	1.69	4.18
Vietnam	0.86	2.13	1.29	3.20
Venezuela	1.09	2.70	1.28	3.15
Luxembourg	1.22	3.01	1.22	3.02
Tanzania	3.76	9.30	1.12	2.76
Belgium	0.00	0.00	0.53	1.30
UK	0.64	1.57	0.49	1.21
Zimbabwe	0.42	1.04	0.45	1.12
Malta	1.83	4.52	0.41	1.01
Philippines	0.41	1.00	0.40	0.98
Paraguay	0.38	0.93	0.37	0.92
Sweden	0.00	0.00	0.11	0.26
Ecuador	0.08	0.20	0.08	0.21
Bahrain	0.05	0.13	0.05	0.13
Reunion	0.03	0.08	0.04	0.10
Honduras	0.04	0.09	0.04	0.10
Kuwait	0.01	0.02	0.02	0.06
UAE	0.02	0.05	0.02	0.04
World total	7,453.92	18,418.63	7,363.61	18,195.84

APPENDIX 2B

WINE PRODUCTION BY COUNTRY

These 2010 and 2020 OIV figures include vineyards dedicated to TABLE GRAPES and RAISINS. OIV figures are given in hectolitres so the equivalent figures in gallons have been rounded.

	2010 (000 hl)	2010 (000 gal)	2020 (000 hl)	2020 (000 gal)
Italy	48,525	1,281,885	49,066	1,296,186
France	44,381	1,172,413	46,673	1,232,970
Spain	35,353	933,920	40,949	1,081,758
USA	20,887	551,772	22,750	601,001
Australia	11,420	301,682	10,900	287,947
Argentina	16,250	429,276	10,796	285,200
South Africa	9,327	246,391	10,385	274,345
Chile	8,844	233,632	10,337	273,075
Germany	6,906	182,436	8,405	222,037
China (mainland)	13,000	343,421	6,587	173,997
Portugal	7,148	188,829	6,418	169,546
Russia	6,756	178,473	4,433	117,107
Romania	3,287	86,833	3,829	101,151
New Zealand	1,900	50,192	3,290	86,913
Hungary	1,646	43,482	2,913	76,953
Austria	1,737	45,886	2,398	63,348
Greece	2,950	77,930	2,283	60,310
Brazil	2,459	64,959	2,257	59,624
Georgia	1,034	27,315	1,800	47,551
Republic of North Macedonia	772	20,394	936	24,724
Moldova	840	22,190	920	24,304
Switzerland	1,030	27,210	834	22,032
Bulgaria	1,030	27,210	823	21,741

	2010 (000 hl)	2010 (000 gal)	2020 (000 hl)	2020 (000 gal)
Peru	520	13,737	810	21,398
Japan	750	19,813	805	21,263
Croatia	1,433	37,856	800	21,134
Slovenia	570	15,058	743	19,628
Serbia	1,200	31,700	705	18,624
Uruguay	769	20,315	695	18,360
Ukraine	3,002	79,304	660	17,435
Canada	507	13,393	656	17,332
Türkiye	601	15,877	623	16,445
Czechia	564	14,899	603	15,930
Turkmenistan	390	10,303	498	13,156
Kazakhstan	172	4,544	438	11,571
Morocco	333	8,797	409	10,805
Mexico	346	9,140	398	10,514
Slovakia	190	5,019	353	9,325
Tunisia	222	5,865	350	9,246
Belarus	251	6,631	304	8,020
Albania	300	7,925	275	7,265
Uzbekistan	213	5,627	218	5,759
Israel	245	6,472	200	5,283
Algeria	475	12,548	193	5,086
India	160	4,227	180	4,755
Cuba	108	2,853	144	3,804
Armenia	59	1,559	110	2,906
Estonia	28	740	110	2,906
Lebanon	65	1,717	100	2,642
Luxembourg	110	2,906	97	2,562
Azerbaijan	117	3,091	90	2,378
Cyprus	114	3,012	89	2,351
Bolivia	74	1,955	84	2,219
Madagascar	83	2,193	79	2,074
Montenegro	180	4,755	70	1,849
Bosnia and Herzegovina	45	1,189	69	1,825
UK	28	740	65	1,717
Egypt	44	1,162	53	1,400
Lithuania	72	1,902	32	856
Latvia	20	528	20	533
Belgium	5	132	19	489
Paraguay	13	343	17	449
Kyrgystan	16	423	14	362
Zimbabwe	18	476	14	362
Malta	15	396	12	317
Ethiopia	13	343	8	221
Netherlands	0	0	8	211
Poland	0	0	5	132
Tajikistan	2	53	2	58
Panama	2	53	1	21
Denmark	0	0	1	14
Syria	1	26	1	13
Sweden	0	0	0	3
World total	261,927	6,919,326	262,209	6,926,829

APPENDIX 2C

PER CAPITA CONSUMPTION BY COUNTRY

These 2010 and 2020 figures are based on official OIV statistics, which use the UN's World Population Prospects database of those aged 15+. OIV figures are given in litres, so the equivalent figures in gallons are rounded.

	2010 (litres)	2010 (gal)	2020 (litres)	2020 (gal)
Portugal	52.4	13.9	49.1	13.0
Luxembourg	64.8	17.1	48.1	12.7
Italy	46.1	12.2	46.7	12.3
France	57.1	15.1	43.6	11.5
Slovenia	43.4	11.5	43.0	11.4
Georgia	27.7	7.3	36.6	9.7
Switzerland	44.3	11.7	34.1	9.0
Denmark	41.5	11.0	31.5	8.3
Austria	33.5	8.8	30.2	8.0
Australia	30.0	7.9	28.5	7.5
Germany	28.9	7.6	27.6	7.3
Belgium	30.4	8.0	27.6	7.3
Argentina	32.2	8.5	27.4	7.2
Croatia	41.8	11.0	27.1	7.2
Uruguay	27.2	7.2	25.2	6.6
Sweden	28.4	7.5	25.0	6.6
Estonia	13.8	3.6	24.9	6.6
Netherlands	25.4	6.7	24.8	6.6
São Tomé Príncipe	30.4	8.0	24.6	6.5
Greece	35.1	9.3	24.6	6.5
Hungary	27.7	7.3	24.2	6.4
Namibia	5.2	1.4	24.1	6.4
UK	24.6	6.5	23.9	6.3

	2010 (litres)	2010 (gal)	2020 (litres)	2020 (gal)
Norway	18.4	4.9	23.6	6.2
Czechia	22.1	5.8	23.3	6.2
Ireland	20.1	5.3	23.3	6.1
New Zealand	26.5	7.0	23.2	6.1
Spain	27.3	7.2	22.7	6.0
Seychelles	15.6	4.1	21.0	5.5
Antigua and Barbuda	9.0	2.4	20.0	5.3
New Caledonia	34.6	9.1	19.9	5.3
Iceland	18.5	4.9	16.8	4.4
Cape Verde	15.0	4.0	16.0	4.2
Romania	29.4	7.8	15.7	4.1
St Lucia	8.2	2.2	15.1	4.0
Republic of North Macedonia	8.8	2.3	14.9	3.9
Cyprus	17.2	4.5	14.9	3.9
Slovakia	13.8	3.7	14.0	3.7
Lithuania	9.9	2.6	13.9	3.7
Canada	16.0	4.2	13.9	3.7
Moldova	11.7	3.1	13.3	3.5
Serbia	25.5	6.7	12.7	3.4
Albania	9.0	2.4	12.6	3.3
Belarus	8.5	2.3	12.3	3.2
USA	11.1	2.9	12.0	3.2
Chile	23.3	6.2	11.6	3.1
Turkmenistan	11.1	2.9	11.6	3.1
Malta	18.5	4.9	10.7	2.8
Montenegro	26.6	7.0	10.1	2.7
Russia	8.8	2.3	8.6	2.3
Guinea-Bissau	6.1	1.6	8.4	2.2
Bulgaria	9.3	2.4	8.3	2.2
South Africa	9.6	2.5	7.5	2.0
China—Macao	11.3	3.0	6.2	1.6
Latvia	1.0	0.3	5.7	1.5
Maldives	4.4	1.2	5.5	1.5
Paraguay	9.5	2.5	5.3	1.4
Finland	12.9	3.4	5.0	1.3
China—Hong Kong	4.2	1.1	4.7	1.2
Belize	1.9	0.5	4.6	1.2
Armenia	2.0	0.5	4.4	1.2
Grenada	3.7	1.0	4.3	1.1
Kazakhstan	2.1	0.6	4.1	1.1
Bosnia and Herzegovina	3.7	1.0	4.0	1.1
Poland	2.7	0.7	3.9	1.0
Tunisia	2.2	0.6	3.9	1.0
Gabon	9.7	2.6	3.7	1.0
Peru	2.9	0.8	3.7	1.0
St Vincent	3.7	1.0	3.7	1.0
Vanuatu	3.4	0.9	3.2	0.8
Japan	2.3	0.6	3.2	0.8
Singapore	2.7	0.7	3.0	0.8
Ukraine	6.3	1.7	2.8	0.7
Botswana	4.4	1.2	2.7	0.7

	2010 (litres)	2010 (gal)	2020 (litres)	2020 (gal)
Costa Rica	2.7	0.7	2.6	0.7
Eswatini	0.5	0.1	2.6	0.7
Ivory Coast	2.6	0.7	2.6	0.7
Brazil	2.5	0.7	2.4	0.6
Morocco	1.5	0.4	2.4	0.6
Lebanon	1.6	0.4	2.1	0.6
Suriname	1.1	0.3	2.0	0.5
Jamaica	1.1	0.3	2.0	0.5
Fiji Islands	1.5	0.4	2.0	0.5
Angola	7.0	1.9	1.7	0.5
Cuba	1.7	0.5	1.7	0.4
Algeria	1.1	0.3	1.6	0.4
Mauritius	1.9	0.5	1.5	0.4
Tonga	1.5	0.4	1.5	0.4
Bahrain	2.5	0.7	1.3	0.3
Mexico	0.8	0.2	1.2	0.3
Türkiye	1.1	0.3	1.1	0.3
Bolivia	1.2	0.3	1.1	0.3
Republic of Korea	0.6	0.1	1.1	0.3
China (mainland)	1.4	0.4	1.1	0.3
Dominican Republic	1.3	0.3	1.0	0.3
Lesotho	0.1	0.0	1.0	0.3
French Guiana	0.0	0.0	1.0	0.3
Burkina Faso	0.5	0.1	1.0	0.3
Kyrgystan	0.7	0.2	0.9	0.3
China—Taiwan	0.7	0.2	0.9	0.2
Trinidad and Tobago	0.9	0.2	0.9	0.2
Cameroon	0.8	0.2	0.9	0.2
Ecuador	0.6	0.2	0.8	0.2
Azerbaijan	1.2	0.3	0.7	0.2
Republic of Congo	1.9	0.5	0.7	0.2
Comoros	0.3	0.1	0.6	0.2
Israel	1.1	0.3	0.6	0.2
Uzbekistan	0.6	0.2	0.6	0.2
Colombia	0.4	0.1	0.6	0.2
Senegal	1.1	0.3	0.6	0.1
El Salvador	0.5	0.1	0.6	0.1
Guyana	0.0	0.0	0.5	0.1
Madagascar	0.8	0.2	0.5	0.1
Papua New Guinea	0.1	0.0	0.4	0.1
Guatemala	0.3	0.1	0.4	0.1
Ghana	0.6	0.1	0.3	0.1
Laos	0.3	0.1	0.3	0.1
Benin	1.1	0.3	0.3	0.1
Philippines	0.2	0.1	0.3	0.1
Malaysia	0.2	0.1	0.2	0.1
Nigeria	0.2	0.1	0.2	0.1
Kenya	0.2	0.1	0.2	0.1
Vietnam	0.2	0.0	0.1	0.0
Egypt	0.1	0.0	0.1	0.0

PICTURE ACKNOWLEDGEMENTS

© Sebastian Basco	v
© Jon Wyand	vii
© Jon Wyand	ix
© Philippe Martineau / Le Pictorium / Alamy Stock Photo	xxi
© Jon Wyand	xxiii
© Robert Herbst	xxv
© Jon Wyand	xxvii
© Victor Barros Ferreira	xxix

Alpha openers courtesy of Királyudvar, Tokaj, Hungary

Figure SPM.1 from IPCC, 2021, with adapted captions, from: Summary for Policymakers. In: *Climate Change 2021: The Physical Science Basis. Contribution of Working Group I to the Sixth Assessment Report of the Intergovernmental Panel on Climate Change* [Masson-Delmotte, V., Zhai, P., et al. (eds.)]. Cambridge University Press, Cambridge, United Kingdom and New York, NY, USA, pp. 3–32, doi:10.1017/9781009157896.001. 187